GUIDE TO

REFERENCE

BOOKS

EIGHTH EDITION

GUIDE TO REFERENCE BOOKS

CONSTANCE M. WINCHELL

Reference Librarian, Retired

Columbia University

AMERICAN LIBRARY ASSOCIATION

Chicago, 1967

Library of Congress Catalog Card Number 66-29240

Copyright © 1967 by the American Library Association

Third Impression, August 1968

Manufactured in the United States of America

PREFACE

HISTORY

❧ The *Guide to Reference Books* has had a long and notable history. Begun in 1902, when the American Library Association published the *Guide to the Study and Use of Reference Books* by Alice Bertha Kroeger, this pioneer work achieved an immediate success and was soon adopted as a textbook in library schools and training classes. Annual supplements for 1903 to 1907 were printed in the *Library Journal,* and in the fall of 1908, a second edition, revised and considerably enlarged, was issued. Miss Kroeger, who for many years had taught reference work in the Drexel Institute Library School in Philadelphia, died in 1909.

In 1910 the Publishing Board of the American Library Association asked Isadore Gilbert Mudge to continue the *Guide.* Thus began a connection which lasted for almost thirty years, and included the third to the sixth editions, of 1917, 1923, 1929, and 1936, with intervening supplements. Miss Mudge became the outstanding authority on reference books, and her *Guide* was known and consulted in libraries throughout the world. She was particularly well fitted for the work by her long experience both as a teacher and as a reference librarian: at the University of Illinois, at Bryn Mawr College, at Simmons College, and finally at Columbia University, where she was Reference Librarian from 1911 to 1941 and Associate Professor in the School of Library Service from 1926 to 1938. Her thorough familiarity with reference books and reference techniques, her clear thinking, her wide knowledge and remarkable memory, her deep interest in the subject and in the student and research worker, all combined to impress her influence on succeeding generations of students, faculty, and all those who used her book. Probably no other one person contributed so much to raising the standards of reference collections and reference service in the libraries of this and other countries.

Miss Mudge prepared the first supplement to the sixth edition, *Reference Books of 1935–37*. After her retirement in 1941, the Editorial Committee of the American Library Association asked the present writer to prepare the succeeding supplements, covering 1938–1940, 1941–1943, and 1944–1946, and then to compile the seventh edition of 1951. Since then four three-year supplements have been issued: 1950–1952, 1953–1955, 1956–1958, 1959–June 1962.

To make plans and establish policies for an eighth edition, the Editorial Committee of the American Library Association appointed the following librarians to serve as an Advisory Committee: Mary Neill Barton, Former Head, General Reference Department, Enoch Pratt Library; Frances Neel Cheney, Associate Director, Peabody Library School; Frances Briggs Jenkins, Professor, Library School, University of Illinois; and David Roy Watkins, Head, Reference Department, Yale University Library. The suggestions and counsel of this committee have in large measure determined the general composition of this edition.

PURPOSE

The fundamental principles of reference work remain more or less constant through the years, but the rapid expansion of the publication of reference books in all fields makes essential a careful selection to fit the needs of each library. The purpose of this volume is to list reference books basic to research—general and special—and thus to serve as: (1) a reference manual for the library assistant, research worker, or other user of library resources; (2) a selection aid for the librarian; and (3) a textbook for the student, who, either in library school, training class, or college course in bibliography, is pursuing a systematic study of reference books.

The needs of these types of users have influenced the organization and make-up of this volume, in that the requirements of the first two groups have made the manual more comprehensive than it might have been if intended for a textbook only, while the introductions to sections and many of the annotations have been provided particularly for the library school student.

SCOPE

This eighth edition, although definitely based on earlier editions and incorporating much of the same material and many of the same titles, is completely revised, reorganized, and enlarged. Because of the large numbers of reference books now being published, the number of titles has been increased from some 5500 to about 7500.

As in the seventh edition, the books listed are those which might be included in a large general reference collection or with which general reference librarians should be familiar. These include many scholarly works in English and in foreign languages. Since a work of this kind cannot be all-inclusive, each section includes a selection of basic reference materials in that particular field. For additional titles and more specialized works, it will be necessary to consult the manuals, guides, and bibliographies devoted to subject fields.

CLOSING DATE

The year 1964 was the closing date for listing new works and new editions except in a few instances where

new titles were received early in 1965. Occasionally it seemed essential to list a new edition published in 1965—notably the third edition of the *Union List of Serials*—in order to make the record of such works comprehensive and up to date. For the most part, however, titles issued in 1965 have not been included.

ARRANGEMENT

Following the advice of the Advisory Committee and also the answers to questionnaires sent to representative librarians, the overall arrangement of this edition differs radically from that in previous editions, which, in general, followed the Dewey Decimal Classification order. This eighth edition has been arranged to be more in keeping with the subject organization of many libraries and with the content of courses in library schools, i.e., Part A, General Reference Works; Part B, The Humanities; Part C, Social Sciences; Part D, History and Area Studies; Part E, Pure and Applied Sciences.

While types of reference books vary in different subject fields and not all types are available for all subjects, the same categories do recur in many of the subject divisions and subdivisions of this *Guide*. With some slight variations and with additions or omissions as seemed advisable under each subject, the categories are listed in the following order: (1) Guides and manuals; (2) Bibliographies; (3) Indexes and abstract journals; (4) Encyclopedias; (5) Dictionaries of special terms; (6) Handbooks; (7) Annuals and directories; (8) Histories; (9) Biographical works; (10) Atlases; (11) Serial publications.

Whenever subdivisions by countries are used, the United States is listed first, with other countries following in alphabetical order. Entries listed under Russia may at times also contain some information relative to the Union of Soviet Socialist Republics, and vice versa. Users of the *Guide* would do well to refer to both headings for information on either of these areas.

SERIAL ENTRIES

Annuals and other serials are listed with open entries. In many cases the date of the last volume received up to 1964 is indicated in parentheses.

For works published in parts, an attempt has been made to list all parts received through 1964, followed by the notation "(In progress)."

REPRINTS

Many older reference works are now being issued in reprints of various kinds. Insofar as information on these was easily available, the reprint publisher has been included in the imprint. However, as it was not possible to check every title for this information, such listings will be incomplete. Recent reprint catalogs should be checked for further information.

CROSS REFERENCES

Under subjects, a moderate number of cross references call attention to closely allied headings and to individual works listed under other subjects. Cross references by code number are used for titles to which references are made. The detailed author, title, and subject Index should be an aid in locating specific books or particular types of material.

CODE NUMBERS

To facilitate the finding of titles, each entry has been assigned a code number. The code numbers were formed by giving a letter to each of the five main sections, such as A, B, C, with an additional letter for subsections: AA, AB, BA, BB, etc. Items were then numbered consecutively in each subsection. When, in the revision of the manuscript, titles were omitted or added, the code numbers were omitted or altered, i.e., in some cases numbers have been canceled, and in others, small letters—a, b, c, etc.—have been added to the numbers in order to insert additional titles. The code numbers are intended solely as an aid in finding titles and have no other significance.

ACKNOWLEDGMENTS

Once again it comes time to express my appreciation to all those who have made this enterprise possible. Without the cooperation and help of the many who have given so generously of their time and specialized knowledge, a compilation such as this could not have been accomplished. My thanks go especially to the members of the Advisory Committee for their cooperation and understanding in establishing general policies and for reading some sections of the manuscript; to Robert F. Beach, Librarian, Union Theological Seminary; Janet Bogardus, Librarian, Federal Reserve Bank of New York; Shirley Dakin, First Assistant, Economics Division, New York Public Library; Theodore C. Hines, Assistant Professor, School of Library Service, Columbia University; James Humphrey III, Librarian, Metropolitan Museum of Art, New York City; Gerald D. McDonald, Chief, American History Division, New York Public Library; the late Catherine K. Miller, Music Division, New York Public Library; Elisabeth H. Nebehay, Chief, Acquisitions Department, United Nations Library; Russell Shank, Associate Professor, School of Library Service, Columbia University; Maurice F. Tauber, Melvil Dewey Professor, School of Library Service, Columbia University; and to the following members of the staff of the University of Wisconsin Libraries, who, under the leadership of James van Luik of the Library School, made preliminary suggestions in the fields of the pure and applied sciences: Doris A. Bennett, Geography and Geology Librarian; Frances Christison, Physics and Mathematics Librarian; Helen Crawford, Medical Librarian; Catherine Crocker, Biology Librarian; Edith Flather, Astronomy Librarian; Dolores Nemec, Pharmacy Librarian; Emory M. Pittenger, Agricultural Librarian; Janet Zupko, Chemistry Librarian; Leroy Zweifel, Engineering Librarian.

Among the members of the Columbia University Libraries staff who deserve especial mention are: *Art and Architecture:* the late Mary W. Chamberlin, Librarian, Fine Arts Library; Adolf K. Placzek, Avery Library; *Binding Department:* Marianne Von Dobeneck, Head; *Business and Economics:* Ben C. Driver, Librarian; Frank Gibson, Acquisitions Department, Business and Economics Library; *Chemistry:* Marianne Cooper, Librarian, Chemistry Library; *East Asia:* Miwa Kai, As-

sistant Librarian, East Asian Library; *Education:* Katherine W. Kridl, Supervising Librarian; Florence B. Wilkinson, Assistant Librarian, Reference Department, Teachers College Library; *Engineering, Mathematics, and Physical Sciences:* H. Ellis Mount, Science and Engineering Librarian; Jacqueline K. Johnson, Assistant Engineering Librarian; Hermine W. Waterson, Librarian, Mathematics Library; Marcia Weiss, Physics Library; *Law:* Ludwig Neuberger, Reference Librarian, Law Library; Dorothy E. Chamberlain, Head, Law Section, Cataloging Department; *Library Service:* Thompson M. Little, Librarian, School of Library Service; *Medicine and Natural Sciences:* Thomas P. Fleming, Librarian, Medical and Natural Sciences Libraries; Cecile E. Kramer, Assistant Librarian, Medical Library; Sophie Gerlach, Reference Librarian, Medical Library; Samuel J. Waddell, Head, Medical Reference Section; Judy R. Slick, Librarian, Biological Sciences; Robert McAfee, Jr., Librarian, Geology Library; Harold A. Scroonian, Librarian, Geology Library; *Music:* Thomas T. Watkins, Librarian; John D. Bush, Assistant Librarian, Music Library; *Psychology:* Kathryn H. Speert, Librarian, Psychology Library.

Particular thanks should go to the editorial staff of the American Library Association: Pauline J. Love, Director, Publishing Department; Marion Dittman, Editor of Publications; and Pauline Cianciolo, Assistant to the Director, for their continued patience, cooperation, and understanding; to Eleanor Buist, Slavic bibliographer, Columbia University Libraries, for her help with the Russian materials; to Suzanne Wemple, Instructor in History, Barnard College, for assistance with Hungarian titles; to John Kobasa, Cataloging Department, Columbia University Libraries, who checked for accuracy many titles in Polish and other East European languages; to Bertha M. Frick, Associate Professor, retired, School of Library Service, for her contribution to the section on Medieval and Renaissance Manuscripts; to John Neal Waddell, School of Library Service, Columbia, who read many sections of the manuscript, made valuable suggestions, and was always available for consultation; to Eugene P. Sheehy, Head, Reference Department, Columbia University Libraries, for help in checking queries, continuing advice, and constant encouragement; to the various members of the Reference staff, who through the years have given unbounded assistance; and to many other librarians, desk assistants, and pages in the libraries where we have worked.

To my personal staff during the years of preparation goes my very special gratitude for their loyalty and devotion beyond what I had any right to expect: to Edna Gordon, who worked so closely with me in all processes and at all points, examining materials, preparing copy for several sections—e.g., Economics, Statistics, Law, and Music—and reading, revising, and checking the manuscript and proof; to Jean McK. Murphy, former Head, Art and Music Division, Queensborough Public Library, who not only did most of the work on the Fine Arts section, but also spent many hours checking the manuscript and index; to Martha Page, who typed the entire manuscript; to Lela C. M. Cox, who copied large numbers of index slips; and to my nephew, Paul Winchell, who cut and pasted on cards all entries from the seventh edition. Without all of these this work could never have been completed.

C. M. WINCHELL

New York City

CONTENTS

❧ *This table of contents lists only a few of the subdivisions of some sections.*
To locate specific subjects see Index.

A

GENERAL REFERENCE WORKS

B

THE HUMANITIES

C

SOCIAL SCIENCES

D

HISTORY AND AREA STUDIES

E

PURE AND APPLIED SCIENCES

REFERENCE WORK

AND

REFERENCE BOOKS

ISADORE GILBERT MUDGE

❧ The following introduction is reprinted from the sixth edition
of GUIDE TO REFERENCE BOOKS *for it still expresses adequately, although*
briefly, the essential points every student and reference worker
should know about reference work and the study of reference books.

REFERENCE DEPARTMENT

❧ The Reference Department of a library is that part of the system which is charged especially with the task of aiding readers in their use of the library, particularly in their use of the resources and books within the library walls as distinguished from the withdrawal of books for home reading. In a large library such a department will have its own staff, often of considerable size, with a chief reference librarian; several reference assistants, often with specialized work; minor desk attendants; pages; etc. In a somewhat smaller library one trained reference assistant may handle the whole work, while in the still smaller library all reference work may have to be done by the librarian or a general assistant. Whatever the size of the library, it will have questions of one sort or another brought to it by its readers, and these must be

answered in so far as the resources of the library permit. Much of the reputation of the library in its community will depend upon the success with which it handles its reference questions.

Reference work is often spoken of as if it consisted only of the actual use of reference books in answering questions for readers. In its widest and best development, however, the work of a reference department covers everything necessary to help the reader in his inquiries, including the selection of an adequate and suitable collection of reference books; the arrangement and maintenance of the collection in such a way that it can be used easily and conveniently; the making of such files, indexes, and clipping collections as are needed to supplement the library catalog and the book collection; the training of a capable staff of reference assistants and their supervision in such a way as to insure skillful and pleasant service and good teamwork; the provision of posted signs, printed directions, lists, and bulletins to help the reader who can profit by such guides; expert aid in the use of the catalog and other records; suggestions as to books to be used for special purposes; instruction of individuals, groups, or classes in the use of reference books and reference methods; and constant work in answering individual questions, in helping individual readers to find some elusive fact, or in correcting some wrong method of research on the part of an inexperienced reader. While a large part of this work will be administrative and advisory, with the purpose of helping the reader to help himself, there will always be included, also, a considerable amount of actual research work in looking up questions, both those that come in by mail or telephone, and those which readers, even with some advice and assistance, have found too difficult. A live reference department is not limited to work within its own walls, but through interlibrary loan, telephone reference work, knowledge of outside specialists—either individuals, institutions or learned societies, government or public service bureaus, etc.—from whom help can be obtained, can often open up many profitable sources of information to its readers and investigators. In libraries connected with educational institutions, either colleges and universities or secondary schools, the work of the reference department will often include a regular course of lectures and classwork on the use of books and libraries. Such a course, especially if it is a required course for freshmen or other beginning students, not merely an elective course for advanced students, can be of great assistance in increasing the intelligent and effective use of library resources.

REFERENCE BOOKS

However varied the work of a reference department may be, the reference book is the basis of its work. The most important element in the equipment of such a department is an adequate and live collection of reference books, and the most important asset of a reference assistant is a knowledge of reference books and experience in using the right book at the right time and in the right way. The possession of the right books and the knowledge of how to use them are two things essential to the success of a reference department, and the latter is no less important than the former. The ignorant assistant can render comparatively useless the finest collection of reference books, while the skilled assistant, who knows how to get from each book all the varied kinds of information that it is planned to give, can show astonishing results even when limited to only a few basic books.

From the point of view of use, books may be divided into two groups: those which are meant to be read through for either information or enjoyment, and those which are meant to be consulted or referred to for some definite piece of information. Books of this second class are called *reference* books, and are usually comprehensive in scope, condensed in treatment, and arranged on some special plan to facilitate the ready and accurate finding of information. This special arrangement may be alphabetical, as in the case of most dictionaries or encyclopedias; chronological, as in historical outlines and similar compends; tabular, as in the case of statistical abstracts; regional, as in atlases; classified or systematic as in the case of some bibliographies, technical hand-

books, etc. As such books are used for the finding of single definite facts, some alphabetical approach to the fact is usually needed, and if the book is not itself arranged alphabetically, it is usually provided with a detailed alphabetical index. Works which follow any of these indicated arrangements are reference books, pure and simple, and are not used for consecutive reading. There are other books, however, which, while intended primarily to be read through for either information or pleasure, are so comprehensive and accurate in their treatment and so well provided with indexes that they serve also as reference books. Examples of such books are the *Cambridge History of American Literature,* anthologies such as Stevenson's *Home Book of Verse,* standard histories such as the *Cambridge Modern History,* and many of the textbooks and treatises used in college work. The reference department of a large library will necessarily contain both formal reference books and these "borderland" books as well, but the student of reference books will naturally devote most of his attention to the formal reference books, both because they are fundamental and because they need careful study before all their uses can be learned. Later, however, in doing actual reference work, he should realize that the formal reference books constitute only a part, though a very important one, of his collection of reference material and that the treatment of some reference questions will involve first the use of some standard reference book in the reference collection, then reference from that to some book in the stack to which the formal reference book has furnished a clue, or even to some source of information outside the library.

HOW TO STUDY
REFERENCE BOOKS

Only constant and practical use of a reference book will make a student thoroughly familiar with its character and use, but the following suggestions will help him in his preliminary examination of the book.

1. Examine title page carefully for information as to
   a) scope of work as indicated in title
   b) author's name
   c) author's previous record (often indicated by list of degrees, positions, titles of earlier works, etc.)
   d) publisher
   e) date of publication. Check date of publication by reference to copyright date and date of Preface; while these dates offer no absolute guarantee of the date of information in the book, they sometimes help in determining this, especially in cases where they are considerably earlier than the imprint date.

2. Read Preface or Introduction for
   a) further information as to scope of work
   b) special features claimed
   c) limitations, if any
   d) comparison with other books on same subject.

3. Examine book itself for
   a) arrangement
   b) kind of entry
   c) cross references, i.e., extent to which included, whether given in main work or in separate list, etc.

d) supplementary lists, noting number and kind and how connected with main work

e) indexes, noting fullness and exactness of reference

f) quality and kind of articles, noting whether they are popular or scientific, signed or unsigned, impartial or biased, and especially whether they are equipped with satisfactory bibliographical references in the form of either appended bibliographies, references throughout the text, or bibliographical footnotes. Several articles should be read carefully, compared with similar articles in other books. The student should, if possible, look up some subjects upon which he has either some special knowledge or means of securing accurate information. However important the form and convenience of arrangement of a reference book may be, the trustworthiness of its information is of still greater importance, and a knowledge of its comparative accuracy or inaccuracy is fundamental to any real knowledge of the book.

4. In examining both Preface and articles, note any evidence of lack of impartiality; e.g., if the book deals with a controversial subject, religious, political, etc., does it represent only one side; or, in the case of a biographical work, are the selection of names, kind and length of article, etc., determined in any way by the desire to secure subscribers.

5. In studying the arrangement of a book, note the possibility of variation in books which follow the same general arrangement; e.g., in a work arranged alphabetically, note what rules for alphabetizing have been followed. Among encyclopedias, for ex-

ample, the *Britannica*[1] and the *Americana* follow different rules, and the student who does not observe that fact may miss the article for which he is looking. The alphabetizing of words containing an umlauted vowel is a possible source of confusion in many books, and in foreign reference books, in general, one should always remember points in which the foreign alphabetizing differs from the English. A fuller discussion of some of these points will be found on page 86 of this *Guide*.

6. If the work in question purports to be a new edition, note carefully the extent of revision claimed for it and check this by comparison with earlier editions. New or revised editions often present very special difficulties, and the examination should be extended enough to determine whether the revision is

a) so complete and thorough that it supersedes the earlier work

b) thorough, but with the omission of some material included in the earlier work which is still useful, in which case the two editions may have to be used together, or

c) so insufficient and superficial that the earlier edition is still to be preferred.

A reference worker needs such information about a book for two purposes:

a) to decide whether or not the book should be purchased

b) to be able to explain to readers who ask for a so-called new edition why its purchase was considered advisable.

---

[1] In the sixth edition the *New international* encyclopedia was cited.

REFERENCE MATERIALS

FOR

SPECIAL SUBJECTS

❧ A working reference collection, large or small, will include reference books in specialized subject fields as well as comprehensive works such as general bibliographies, encyclopedias, dictionaries, and indexes. For special subjects there are certain recognized types of reference materials. The principal ones are: (1) Guides and manuals; (2) Bibliographies; (3) Indexes and abstracts; (4) Encyclopedias; (5) Handbooks; (6) Dictionaries of special terms; (7) Annuals and directories; (8) Histories; (9) Biographical works; (10) Atlases and collections of plates or illustrations; (11) Serial publications.

1. GUIDES AND MANUALS. Guides and manuals to the literature of the subject are usually prepared for students or research workers as aids to finding bibliographies and other reference materials in the field, e.g., Parke, *Guide to the Literature of Mathematics and Physics* (EF1) and

Chamberlin, *Guide to art reference books* (BE1).

2. BIBLIOGRAPHIES. Of fundamental importance, bibliographies of the subject are usually of two kinds: (a) basic bibliography, comprehensive up to a fixed date; (b) current bibliography, recording the literature of a given period, frequently one year at a time. In some cases a current bibliography connects exactly with the basic work and gives a comprehensive record for the whole field, e.g., Nickles, *Geologic Literature on North America* (EE23) which covers publications to 1918, and is continued from 1919 by current bibliographies cumulating decennially. Together these furnish a full record of the literature of the subject.

Reference bibliographies are useful for: (a) verification of incorrect or incomplete titles; (b) finding of what material exists on a given topic; (c) an estimate of the value of a book or article, which may be given by an annotation or by reference to a critical review; (d) an abstract or digest of a particular book or article or note of its contents or plot; (e) information on the fundamental or best books on a subject; (f) a statement of the various forms or editions in which a work has appeared, or historical or bibliographical data about a famous or rare book or edition; (g) biographical data about an author.

Not all bibliographies will furnish information on all of these points; therefore, different types are needed in the reference collection. For most reference purposes, the comprehensive bibliography, which records books, periodical articles, and other analytical material, is the most useful. Within its stated limits it should give full and definite information about each item included, and should be so arranged and indexed that works can be found quickly by author, or by broad or specific subject. If the bibliography is to serve as a critical guide to the literature, annotations or other indications of standing should be given. Frequently this type of information is best found in the selective bibliography which lists outstanding books and articles for a given subject.

3. INDEXES AND ABSTRACTS. Indexes and abstracts may be of periodicals, publications of learned societies, book reviews, or composite books including essays, poetry, plays, short stories, etc. To the reference worker, the importance of a good index, whether it be to an individual book, to a separate periodical, or to a group of periodicals or books, cannot be overestimated. Indexes of various kinds are required in all reference collections. *See* pages 525–26 for a brief discussion on the place of the abstract journal in reference work.

4. ENCYCLOPEDIAS. The *Encyclopaedia of the Social Sciences* (CA27) is an outstanding example of an encyclopedia of a subject or group of related subjects. In a well-made work of this kind, the editors and contributors will be specialists, and their special knowledge will be evident in the choice of subjects, length and authority of articles, fullness and selection of bibliographies, etc.

5. HANDBOOKS. Handbooks are compilations of miscellaneous information which, in some fields, are particularly important as reference aids, e.g., in branches of engineering there are handbooks which, although prepared primarily for the practicing engineer, are useful for answering reference questions in a library. Literary, historical, and statistical handbooks are needed in libraries of all sizes.

6. DICTIONARIES OF SPECIAL TERMS. Dictionaries of special terms are of two types: (a) The dictionary of terms in one language supplements the general dictionaries of the language by more specific definitions and differentiations of terms and by many special and tech-

nical terms omitted from the general dictionary, e.g., *Dorland's Illustrated Medical Dictionary* (EJ47). Its main purpose is exact definitions, but it may supply some encyclopedic information, illustrations, and bibliographical references. (b) The bilingual or polyglot dictionary of foreign terms, such as De Vries, *French-English Science Dictionary* (EA107) or Elsevier's *Dictionary of electronics . . . in six languages* (EI102), supplements the general bilingual dictionary with the technical terminology of a particular field. Its main use is as an aid in translations, in the reading of technical articles in a foreign language, and in correspondence involving the use of technical terms.

7. ANNUALS AND DIRECTORIES. Annuals and directories vary considerably in different subject fields. They may be mainly (a) records of current developments in the subject; (b) statistical compilations; (c) directories of persons, institutions, firms, or official bodies; or (d) a combination of any or all of these.

8. HISTORIES. Histories of a subject give the main facts and names in its development, often contain biographical and bibliographical information, and, if provided with detailed indexes, may serve to some extent as encyclopedias of the subject. Good examples are Garrison, *Introduction to the History of Medicine* (EJ81) and Sarton, *Introduction to the History of Science* (EA181).

9. BIOGRAPHICAL WORKS. Biographical works, both retrospective and current, supplement the general biographical dictionaries with information about persons connected with a particular subject, e.g., Baker, *Biographical Dictionary of Musicians* (BH43), *American Men of Science* (EA183), and Thieme-Becker, *Allgemeines Lexikon der bildenden Künstler* (BE71).

10. ATLASES AND COLLECTIONS OF PLATES OR ILLUSTRATIONS. Special atlases and collections of illustrations are useful when maps and illustrations are needed for graphic representation of a subject. Examples are Wright and Filson, *Westminster Historical Atlas to the Bible* (BB144), Goode and Shannon, *Atlas of English Literature* (BD343), and Parmentier, *Album Historique* (DA49), or the volumes of plates in the *Cambridge Ancient History* (DA95).

11. SERIAL PUBLICATIONS. Much of the important work in subject fields is reported in the specialized journals of the subject. In some cases these journals will be indexed in the general or special periodical indexes or abstracts, but the reference assistant should always be aware of the possibility of unindexed journals. Periodicals as such are not included in this *Guide,* but they will be needed frequently in reference work to supplement the more formal reference materials.

ABBREVIATIONS

🌑 *The following list includes only the principal bibliographical abbreviations used in this book for which some explanation or translation seems needed. Shortened forms of publishers' names and some other abbreviations which are practically self-explanatory, e.g., Assoc., Inst., Soc., etc., have not been included here.*

aarg. (Swed.) aargang: *annual volume*
Abt. (Ger.) Abteilung: *part*
Afd. (Dan.) Afdeling: *part*
afl. (Dutch) aflevering: *part*
A.L.A.: *American Library Association*
ampl. (It.) ampliata: *enlarged*
Aufl. (Ger.) Auflage: *edition*
augm. (Fr.) augmenté: *enlarged*
aum. (Sp.) aumentado: *enlarged*
Ausg. (Ger.) Ausgabe: *printing, edition*
avd. (Nor.) avdeling: *part, volume*

Bd. (Dan.) Bind, (Ger.) Band: *volume*
bd. (Nor.) bind, (Swed.) band: *volume*
bearb. (Ger.) bearbeitet: *compiled, edited*
begr. (Ger.) begründet: *established*
Bull.: *Bulletin*
Burt. (Lettish) Burtricā: *part*

c.: *copyright*
ca.: *circa*
cm.: *centimeters*
col.: *columns, colored*
comp.: *compiled*
compl.: *completed, completely*
Cong.: *Congress*
corr. (Fr.) corrigé, (Sp.) corregido: *corrected*

d. (Ger.) der: *the*
deel (Dutch): *volume, part*
doc.: *document*
dopl. (Czech) doplněné: *enlarged*
druk (Dutch): *printing, copy, edition*

ea.: *each*
ed.: *edition, editor*
éd. (Fr.) édition: *edition*
ed. (It.) edizione, (Sp.) edición: *edition*
Eng.: *English*
erw. (Ger.) erweiterte: *enlarged*
estab. tip. (Sp.) establecimiento tipografico: *publishing company*

f. (Ger.) für: *for*
facsim.: *facsimile*
fasc. (Fr.) fascicule: *part, number*

gänzl. (Ger.) gänzlich: *entire, complete*
Gos., Gosudarst. (Russ.) Gosudarstvo: *state*
Govt. Prt. Off.: *Government Printing Office*

Hft. (Dan.) Hefte, (Ger.) Heft: *part, number*
hft. (Nor.) hefte: *part, number*
Hlbbd. (Ger.) Halbband: *half binding*

hrsg. (Ger.) herausgegeben: *published, edited*

il.: *illustrated, illustrations*
impr. (Fr.) imprimé, imprimerie, imprimeur: *printed, printing, printing firm, printer*
impr. (Sp.) imprenta, impresión: *printing office, impression, edition*
Impr. Nat. (Fr.): *Imprimerie Nationale*
incompl.: *incomplete*
Internat.: *International*
Introd.: *Introduction*
Izd., Izdat. (Russ.) izdatel': *publisher*

jaarg. (Dutch) jaargang: *annual volume*
Jahrg. (Ger.) Jahrgang: *annual publication*

l.: *leaves*
Lfg. (Ger.) Lieferung: *number, part*
Lib.: *Library*
livr. (Fr.) livraison: *part, issue*

n. (It.) numero: *number*
Nachtr. (Ger.) Nachtrag: *appendix, supplement*
Nákl. (Czech) náklad, nakladatel: *edition, publisher*
Nakl. (Polish) nakład: *edition, publisher*
n.d.: *no date*
neubearb. (Ger.) neubearbeitet: *revised*
n.F. (Ger.) neue Folge: *new series*
nouv. (Fr.) nouveau, nouvelle: *new*
n.p.: *no publisher, no place*
Nr. (Dan., Ger.) Nummer: *number*
nr. (Nor.) nummer: *number*
n.s.: *new series*
núm. (Sp.) número: *number*
numb.: *numbered*
N.Y.: *New York*

o.a. (Swed.) och andra: *and others*
omarb. (Swed.) omarbetad: *revised*

p.: *page*
pa.: *paper*
Pr.: *Press*
Pref.: *Preface*
prel.: *preliminary*
přepr. (Czech) přepracované: *rewritten*
priv. pr.: *privately printed*
priv. pub.: *privately published*
pt. (Fr.) partie: *part*
Pub.: *Publishers, published*
pub. (Fr.) publié: *published, publication*
publ.: *publication*

réd. (Fr.) rédigé: *edited, compiled*

redig. (Swed.) redigerad: *edited*
ref. (Fr.) refondue: *reorganized*
repr.: *reprinted*
rev. (Sp.) revisado: *revised*
revid. (Swed.) reviderad: *revised*
rif. (It.) rifatta: *restored, repaired*
riv. (It.) riveduto: *revised*

sec. (Sp.) sección: *section*
sér. (Fr.) série: *series*
sess.: *session*
Sost. (Russ.) sostavitel': *compiler*
Stat. Off.: *His Majesty's Stationery Office*
subs.: *subscription*
suppl. (Fr.) supplément: *supplement*

t. (Fr.) tome, (Sp.) tomo: *volume*
T., Th. (Ger.) Teil, Theil: *part*
tidskr. (Swed.) tidskrift: *periodical*
tip. (It.) tipografia: *printing firm*
tr.: *translated, translator*
tr. (Fr.) traduit: *translated*
tr. (Swed.) tryckt: *printed*
trad. (Sp.) traducido: *translated*

u. (Ger.) und: *and*

u.A. (Ger.) und Andere: *and others*
übers. (Ger.) übersetzt: *translated*
udarb. (Dan.) udarbeidet: *prepared*
Udg. (Dan.) Udgave: *edition*
uit. (Dutch) uitgaaf: *publication*
uitg. (Dutch) uitgegeven: *published*
ung. (Ger.) ungarische: *Hungarian*
umgearb. (Ger.) umgearbeitete: *revised*
Univ.: *University*
Univ.-Buchdr. (Ger.) Universitäts-Buchdrukerei: *university press*
uppl. (Swed.) upplaga: *edition*
utarb. (Nor.) utarbeidet: *prepared*
utg. (Nor.) utgave: *edition*

v. (It.) volume: *volume*
v. (Ger.) von: *from*
veränd. (Ger.) verändert: *revised*
verb. (Dutch, Ger.) verbesserte: *improved*
verm. (Ger.) vermehrte: *enlarged*
vollst. (Ger.) vollständig: *completely*
v.p.: *various paging*
vyd. (Czech) vydání: *edition*

Wash.: *Washington, D.C.*
wesentl. (Ger.) wesentlich: *essential, main*

GUIDE TO

REFERENCE

BOOKS

A

GENERAL

REFERENCE

WORKS

In Part A are grouped those reference works which are not devoted to special subjects: the universal and national bibliographies, directories of societies, encyclopedias, language dictionaries, periodicals, newspapers, government publications, and dissertations. With these have been included sections on librarianship and library resources, biography, and genealogy. Each section has an introductory note which should be consulted for further information about the types of works included.

Representative works in all of these fields will be in most libraries, the number being dependent on the size and type of library. This *Guide* will serve as an aid in the selection of such materials, but should be supplemented by such works as the *Subscription books bulletin* (AA309) and the guides to reference books published in other countries as listed on p.27–29.

Bibliography

Bibliographies, general and special, are basic materials in a reference collection. In this section of the *Guide* the more general works are treated; subject bibliographies are listed with their subjects where, with few exceptions, they are noted first whether or not the subhead "Bibliography" appears.

General bibliographies fall into several major categories, viz.:

1. Bibliographies of bibliographies, of which outstanding examples are Besterman (AA13) and the *Bibliographic index* (AA14).

2. Library catalogs, particularly those of national libraries, e.g., the Library of Congress (AA63–AA66), the British Museum (AA67), and the Bibliothèque Nationale in Paris (AA72). These serve not only as comprehensive bibliographies of works in many languages but also, to a large extent, as national bibliographies of their own countries.

3. Specialized bibliographies in the manuscript and rare book fields, of which perhaps the most needed in the general library would be De Ricci's *Census of medieval and Renaissance manuscripts in the United States and Canada* (AA144) and Goff's *Incunabula in American libraries; a third census* (AA168).

4. Selective bibliographies, designed to aid librarians and others in the task of book selection, e.g., *The reader's adviser* (AA269); the *Standard catalog for public libraries* (AA272); the *Standard catalog for high school libraries* (AA293); and the *Children's catalog* (AA289); as well as such book selection periodicals as *The booklist and Subscription books bulletin* (AA273) and *Choice: books for college libraries* (AA285).

5. National bibliographies. These are of prime importance in any but the smallest library, and an extensive collection will be needed in large and academic libraries. American libraries will need the *United States catalog* and the *Cumulative book index* (AA342–AA343); the *Publishers' trade list annual* (AA347) and its complements, *Books in print* (AA348) and *Subject guide to Books in print* (AA349); the *American book publishing record* (AA344); the *Publishers' weekly* (AA350) and its supplements. Large libraries will, of course, also need the preceding works of Evans (AA333) and Sabin (AA334) and will wish to add the *British national bibliography* (AA507) and whatever other foreign lists are appropriate.

GENERAL WORKS

Guides and manuals

Bowers, Fredson. Principles of bibliographical description. Princeton, N.J., Princeton Univ. Pr., 1949. 505p. il. **AA1**

A full, detailed treatment of analytical bibliography as applied to the description of books. Covers the principles of describing incunabula, and English and American books from the 16th to the 20th centuries. Most of the principles would be applicable to printing in other countries. Complements McKerrow's *Introduction to bibliography* (AA4).

Esdaile, Arundell. A student's manual of bibliography. [3d ed.] rev. by Roy Stokes. London, Allen & Unwin and the Lib. Assoc., [1954]. 392p. il. (The Library Assoc. series of library manuals. I) **AA2**

1st ed. 1931.

This edition has been revised and the bibliographies brought up to date. A manual, treating the nature of bibliography, the history and make-up of the book, illustration, binding, the collation and description of books; with a discussion of some basic bibliographies.

Kinney, Mary Ramon. Bibliographical style manuals: a guide to their use in documentation and research. Chicago, Assoc. of College and Reference Libraries, 1953. 21p. (ACRL monographs no.8, June 1953) **AA3**

Discusses style manuals used in the humanities, the social sciences, the sciences, and bibliography and library science.

McKerrow, Ronald B. An introduction to bibliography for literary students. Oxford, Clarendon Pr., 1927. 359p. il. (Repr. 1951) **AA4**

A survey of the mechanical side of book production which is of particular interest to students of the literature of the 15th and 16th centuries. Covers the making of the printed book; the early printing press; paper and decoration; bibliographical technique; formats of books; meaning of "edition," "impression," etc.; evidence as to edition; dating editions; variations in copies; cancels, etc. The appendix includes notes on early printing presses, types, abbreviations, etc.

Malclès, Louise-Noëlle. Manuel de bibliographie. Paris, Presses Universitaires de France, 1963. 328p. **AA5**

A new work, not merely a new edition of the author's *Cours de bibliographie à l'intention des étudiants* . . . (Genève, Droz, 1954. 350p.). The content is of the same general character but considerably rearranged and brought up to date. It lists bibliographies and other reference materials in all fields and thus serves as an abridgment of the author's *Les sources du travail bibliographique* (AA301) for those not needing the larger set.

International in scope with emphasis on French materials.

Masanov, IUrii Ivanovich. Teoriia i praktika bibliografii; ukazatel' literatury, 1917–1958. Pod red. . . . E. I. Shamurina. Moskva, Izd-vo Vsesoiuznoi Knizhnoi Palaty, 1960. 479p. **AA6**

A comprehensive guide to the literature in Russian published 1917–58 on the theory and practice of bibliography, including history of the book, publishing, library practice, classification and cataloging, and types of bibliographies. An appendix lists reviews of bibliographies.

Mez'er, Avgusta Vladimirovna. Slovarnyi ukazatel' po knigovedeniiu. Moskva, Sotsekgiz, 1931–34. 3v. **AA7**

1st ed. 1924.

A bibliographical manual and index to the literature, covering such subjects as archive and manuscript lists, bibliographies, dictionaries, reference books, library science, etc. Supplements the 1924 edition. Serves as subject index to many articles related to Russian cultural history.

Schneider, Georg. Handbuch der Bibliographie. 4. gänzl. veränd. u. stark verm. Aufl. Leipzig, Hiersemann, 1930. 674p. **AA8**

A guide to general bibliography, national bibliography, bibliographies of incunabula, newspapers, society publications, etc.; lists of biographical dictionaries. Includes comment and annotations. A basic work, though now out of date.

The first three editions (1923–26) contained an introductory theoretical-historical treatment of bibliography, which has been omitted in the 4th edition. An English translation of this portion of the 3d edition is available under the title *Theory and history of bibliography,* tr. by R. R. Shaw. N.Y., Columbia Univ. Pr., 1934. 306p.

Stein, Henri. Manuel de bibliographie générale; bibliotheca bibliographica nova. Paris, Picard, 1897. 895p. **AA9**

Includes universal bibliographies, national and regional bibliographies, subject bibliographies. Appendixes contain: (1) alphabetical list of places having printing presses before the 19th century, arranged by the modern name, with indication of the Latin name of each place, the date of establishment of its press, and references to sources of information; (2) indexes of periodicals; (3) printed catalogs of libraries.

The main list and appendixes 2 and 3 were continued by the lists of new bibliographies, indexes, and catalogs given in each number of *Le bibliographe moderne,* 1897–1931, edited by Henri Stein.

Totok, Wilhelm and **Weitzel, Rolf.** Handbuch der bibliographischen Nachschlagewerke. 2. stark erw., völlig neubearb. Aufl. Frankfurt am Main, Klostermann, 1959. 335p. **AA10**

1st ed. 1954.

A selective bibliography of bibliographies, less extensive than Malclès' *Les sources du travail bibliographique* (AA301) and intended mainly for students' use. Emphasis is placed on European and American works.

Bibliography of bibliography

Arnim, Max. Internationale Personalbibliographie, 1800–1943. 2. verb. und stark verm. Aufl. Leipzig, Hiersemann, 1944–52. 2v. **AA11**

A revised edition of a useful bibliography which was first published in 1936, covering the years 1850–1935. This edition has been extended to cover the first half of the 19th century as well as more recent years. It indexes bibliographies contained in books, periodicals, biographical dictionaries, academic annuals, *Festschriften*, etc. In many cases the references lead to biographical as well as to bibliographical information. International in scope with the emphasis on German names, but the first edition should be consulted for many names which were dropped from the second for political reasons. Identification in this edition is simplified by the addition of occupations and, frequently, the date of death.

—— —— Bd.III, 1944–1959 und Nachträge, von Gerhard Bock und Franz Hodes. Stuttgart, Hiersemann, 1961–63. 659p.

Baer, Eleanora A. Titles in series: a handbook for librarians and students. 2d ed. N.Y., Scarecrow, 1964. 2v. **AA12**

1st ed. 1954–60.

This edition revised and cumulated to include some 40,000 book titles published in series in America and foreign countries prior to Jan. 1963.

v.1, arranged by series; v.2, index to titles in v.1, by author and title.

Omits publishers' series, government publications, yearbooks, and reprints.

Besterman, Theodore. A world bibliography of bibliographies and of bibliographical catalogues, calendars, abstracts, digests, indexes, and the like. 3d and final ed., rev. and greatly enl. throughout. Genève, Societas Bibliographica, 1955–56. 4v. **AA13**

1st ed. 1939–40; 2d ed. 1947–49.

v.1–3, A–Z; v.4, Index.

A classified bibliography of almost 85,000 separately published bibliographies of books, manuscripts, and patent abridgments. International in scope.

The index volume lists in one alphabet: (1) Authors, editors, translators, etc.; (2) Titles of serial and anonymous works; (3) Libraries and archives, etc.; (4) Patents (under Patents, lists subjects covered by British patent specifications).

"Bibliographies which would appear in the index under the same heading as in the text are excluded, unless they appear in the text under more than one heading."—*Pref.*

Despite the word "final" in the listing above, it is reported that the author is now compiling materials for a 4th edition (*see* note in *Wilson library bulletin* 37:528. March 1963).

Bibliographic index; a cumulative bibliography of bibliographies, 1937– . N.Y., Wilson, 1938– . **AA14**

Published in three forms: (1) permanent cumulated volumes, coverage varying; (2) annual volumes to supplement the permanent volumes; (3) current issues published quarterly 1938–June 1951. Beginning Dec. 1951, issued semiannually in June and Dec., the latter issue being the annual cumulation.

An alphabetical subject arrangement of separately published bibliographies, and bibliographies included in books

and periodicals. 1000–1500 periodicals, including many in foreign languages, are examined regularly. An extensive and useful list.

Bibliographische Berichte, im Auftrag des Deutschen Bibliographischen Kuratoriums; bearb. von Erich Zimmerman. Jahrg.1, Hft.1, 1959– . Frankfurt a. M., Klostermann, 1959– . Quarterly. **AA15**

v.4– , title also in English: *Bibliographical bulletin.*

"Neue Folge der *Bibliographischen Beihefte* zur *Zeitschrift für Bibliothekswesen und Bibliographie.*"

A classified listing of recent bibliographies, those found in periodicals and books as well as those separately published. Coverage is international with, naturally, a high percentage of German titles; approximately 450 items listed in each issue. Annual subject (no author) index.

Bibliographical services throughout the world, 1950–59, by Robert L. Collison. Paris, UNESCO, 1961. 228p. **AA16**

A cumulative report covering materials derived from the volumes published 1951–59. In two main parts: pt.1, Bibliographical activities in various countries and territories, arranged alphabetically by country and indicating whether or not there is a National Committee of Bibliography, and listing national bibliographies, periodical indexes, current bibliographies of special subjects, etc.; pt.2, Bibliographical activities of international organizations.

Bohatta, Hanns and **Hodes, Franz.** Internationale Bibliographie der Bibliographien; ein Nachschlagewerk, unter Mitwirkung von Walter Funke. Frankfurt am Main, Klostermann, 1950. T.1, 652p. **AA17**

Issued in 7 pts., 1939–50.

A classified bibliography of bibliographies. T.1 covers general and national bibliography and subject bibliography with author and subject indexes. T.2 was to cover Personalbibliographie.

Collison, Robert Lewis. Bibliographies, subject and national; a guide to their contents, arrangement and use. 2d ed., rev. and enl. London, Crosby Lockwood; N.Y., Hafner, 1962. 185p. **AA18**

A handbook containing 300–400 carefully selected and annotated references to bibliographies.

Pt.1 covers subject bibliographies arranged in Dewey Classification order, and pt.2, universal and national bibliographies.

Index bibliographicus. 4th ed. La Haye, Federation Internationale de Documentation, 1959–64. v.1–2. (In progress) **AA19**

Contents: v.1, Science and technology; v.2, Social sciences.

1st ed., Geneva, 1925; 2d ed., Berlin, 1931; 3d ed., Paris, 1951–52. 2v.

The 4th edition is a completely revised listing of currently published abstracting and bibliographic services arranged by the Universal Decimal Classification. Indication is given of title, publisher, address, year of first issue, frequency, coverage (approximate number of abstracts, reviews, etc.), arrangement, indexes, etc. v.2 includes descriptive annotations, usually in French.

In preparation: v.3, Humanities; v.4, General bibliographies.

Internationale Bibliographie des Buch- und Bibliothekswesens, mit besonderer Berücksichtigung der Bibliographie, 1904–12, 1922–39. Leipzig, Harrassowitz, 1905–40. 13v. and n.F. 1–14. **AA20**

First series, 1904–12, 1922–25, had title *Bibliographie des Bibliotheks- und Buchwesens* and appeared as *Beihefte* to the *Zentralblatt für Bibliothekswesen,* 29, 31–32, 34, 36–37, 39–40, 42, 51, 54, 56, 58. None issued for 1913–21. The new series covers 1926–39.

A comprehensive record of books and periodical articles

in different languages on various aspects of bibliography, library science, and library history.

Krieg, Michael O. Mehr nicht erschienen; ein Verzeichnis unvollendet gebliebener Druckwerke. Bad Bocklet, Wien, Walter Krieg Verlag, 1954–58. 2v. (Bibliotheca bibliographica, Bd.II, 1.–2. Teil) **AA21**

A bibliography of works supposed to have been published in several volumes which have never been completed. In the main, the listings are for European publications from the beginning of printing to the early 1930's with emphasis on German works, but some American works are included. In many cases, gives references to bibliographies where the titles are listed.

Northup, Clark Sutherland. Register of bibliographies of the English language and literature, with contributions by Joseph Quincy Adams and Andrew Keogh. New Haven, Conn., Yale Univ. Pr., 1925. 507p. (Cornell studies in English, 9) (Repr.: N.Y., Hafner, 1962) **AA22**

Not so limited as its title indicates; includes also many related bibliographies of other subjects and so serves, to a certain extent, as a general bibliography of bibliography.

United States

Stillwell, Margaret Bingham. Americana: selected bibliographies and bibliographical monographs. (In her Incunabula and Americana, p. 341–440 [AA159]) **AA23**

An important list of more than 600 bibliographies of Americana before 1800. For full description *see* AA159.

Australia

Canberra. National Library of Australia. Australian bibliography and bibliographical services. Canberra, Australian Advisory Council on Bibliographical Services, 1960. 219p. **AA24**

Subject arrangement with author index. Lists "catalogues and bibliographies in the usual sense, indexes, abstracts, digests, union lists and catalogues, booksellers' lists, calendars of archives and manuscripts, and services designed for bibliographical ends."—*Pref.* Indicates location of copies in Australian libraries.

Brazil

Simões dos Reis, Antonio. Bibliografia das bibliografias brasileiras. Rio de Janeiro, 1942. 186p. il. (Ministério da Educação e Saude. Inst. Nacional do Livro. Coleção B. I. Bibliografia I) **AA25**

Lists 712 bibliographies of Brazil arranged chronologically, 1741–1941.

Canada

Tanghe, Raymond. Bibliography of Canadian bibliographies. Toronto, pub. in assoc. with the Bibliographical Soc. of Canada by Univ. of Toronto Pr., 1960. 206p. **AA26**

Added title page in French.

Annotations are in English or French according to the language of the title.

Nearly 1700 separately published items, classified under 29 headings, "wholly or principally Canadian." Indexes of compilers, subjects, and authors as subjects.

—— —— Supplement, 1960 & 1961; 1962 & 1963. Toronto, Bibliographical Soc. of Canada, 1962–64. 24p.; 27p.

Chile

Laval, Ramón Arminio. Bibliografía de bibliografías chilenas. (In Santiago de Chile. Bibliografía general de Chile. 1915. v.1, p.i–lxix) **AA27**

—— —— Suplemento y adiciones, por Herminia Elgueta de Ochsenius. Santiago de Chile, Impr. Cervantes, 1930. 71p.

Lists bibliographies on Chile published either as separates or in periodicals.

Colombia

Giraldo Jaramillo, Gabriel. Bibliografía de bibliografías colombianas. 2. ed. corr. y puesta al día por Rubén Pérez Ortiz. Bogotá, Inst. Caro y Cuervo, 1960. 204p. (Inst. Caro y Cuervo. Publicaciones. Serie bibliográfica, I) **AA28**

Lists bibliographies in books and periodicals in classified arrangement with author index.

Cuba

Peraza Sarausa, Fermin. Bibliografías cubanas. Wash., [Govt. Prt. Off.], 1945. 58p. (U.S. Library of Congress. [Latin Amer. ser., no.7]) **AA29**

At head of title: The Library of Congress. Hispanic Foundation.

Introduction in Spanish and English. Annotations in Spanish.

A classed bibliography of Cuban bibliographies.

Denmark

Møller, Arne J. Dansk Bibliografier, udvalg af Danske bibliografiske Arbejder. København, Levin og Munksgaards, 1929. 28p. **AA30**

Dominican Republic

Floren Lozano, Luis. Bibliografía de la bibliografía dominicana. Trujillo, Roques Roman, 1948. 66p. **AA31**

A bibliography of bibliographies in all subjects, both those separately published and those included in books and periodicals.

Europe, East

Die Bibliographie in den europäischen Ländern der Volksdemokratie; Entwicklung und gegenwärtiger Stand, von Tudor Borov [et al.]. Leipzig, Verlag für Buch- und Bibliothekswesen, 1960. 165p. (Bibliothekswissenschaftliche Arbeiten aus der Sowjetunion und den Ländern der Volksdemokratie in deutscher Übersetzung. Reihe B. Bd.3) **AA32**

A guide to the bibliography of Albania, Bulgaria, Poland, Rumania, Czechoslovakia, and Hungary.

Germany

Leipzig. Deutsche Bücherei. Bibliographie der versteckten Bibliographien aus deutschsprachigen Büchern und Zeitschriften der Jahre 1930–1953. Leipzig, Verlag für Buch- und Bibliothekswesen, 1956. 371p. (Sonderbibliographien der Deutschen Bücherei, 3) **AA33**

Lists bibliographies published 1930–53, as parts of books or in periodicals. Aims to be comprehensive in listing bibliographies consisting of 60 titles or more. Arrangement is

alphabetical by subject, with a classified index of subject headings.
Continued by:

Bibliographie der deutschen Bibliographien; Jahresverzeichnis der selbständig erschienenen und der in deutschsprachigen Büchern und Zeitschriften enthaltenen versteckten Bibliographien. Bearb. von der Deutschen Bücherei. Jahrg.1, 1954– . Leipzig, Verlag für Buch- und Bibliothekswesen, 1957– . v.1– . Annual. **AA34**

An annual listing which includes separately published bibliographies as well as those in periodicals and books.

Widmann, Hans. Bibliographien zum deutschen Schrifttum der Jahre 1939–1950. Tübingen, Niemeyer, 1951. 284p. **AA35**

Because of the breakdown of the well-organized bibliographical system of Germany due to war, this bibliography attempts to list bibliographies of the period dealing with German publications and includes: international bibliographies; bibliographies of books published in Germany; bibliographies of translations into German; regional and personal bibliographies; and bibliographies arranged by subject field.

Greece, Modern

Phousaras, G. I. Bibliographia tōn hellēnikōn bibliographiōn, 1791–1947. Athéna, Bibliopōleion tes "Hestias," 1961. 284p. **AA36**

A classified listing of modern Greek bibliographies—1614 numbered entries. Indexes by name, subject, date, and place.

Hungary

A magyar bibliográfiák bibliográfiája, 1956/57– . Budapest, Országos Széchényi Könyvtár, 1960– . Irregular. **AA37**

Added title page in Latin: Bibliographia bibliographiarum hungaricarum.

"Összeállította Bélley Pál és Ferenczyné Wendelin Lidia."

A detailed listing of bibliographies published in Hungary, including those in books, periodicals, yearbooks, etc. as well as separately published ones. Arranged by Universal Decimal Classification with index of names and subjects.

Ireland

Eager, Alan R. A guide to Irish bibliographical material; being a bibliography of Irish bibliographies and some sources of information. London, Lib. Assoc., 1964. 392p. **AA38**

A bibliography of bibliographies (including periodical articles and parts of books as well as separately published works) which "aims to serve as a quick reference guide to all who are interested in Irish studies and research work."—*Introd.* Classed arrangement with author and subject indexes.

Italy

Ottino, Giuseppe and **Fumagalli, Giuseppe.** Bibliotheca bibliographica italica. Catalogo degli scritti di bibliologia, bibliografia e biblioteconomia pub. in Italia e di quelli risguardanti l'Italia pub. all'Estero. Roma, Pasqualucci, 1889; Torino, Clausen, 1895–1902. 2v. and 4 suppl. **AA39**

Basic volumes, 6450 entries; supplements—for 1895, 1896, 1896–99, 1900—entry no. 6451–8259.

Supplements 1 and 2 by Ottino; supplements 3 and 4 by Emilio Calvi.

The basic bibliography of Italian bibliographies, in clas-sified order covering: history of the book and printing; general, regional, local, personal bibliography; bibliographies of subjects; libraries and library economy. Continued by:

Fumagalli, Giuseppe. La bibliografia. Roma, Fondazione Leonardo, 1923. lxxxixp., 169p. (Guide bibliografiche) **AA40**

P.1–lxxxix contain a survey of Italian bibliography and bibliographers. The rest of the work is a classified bibliography of bibliographies in all fields with an author index. It includes a selection of titles from the Ottino *Bibliotheca* (AA39) and additional works published from 1901 to 1923.

Istituto Nazionale per le Relazioni Culturali con l'Estero. La bibliografia italiana, a cura di Giannetto Avanzi. 2. ed. interamente rifatta, con tre appendice e una aggiunta. Roma, 1946. 570p. (On cover: Bibliografie italiane) **AA41**

Half title: Guida sistematica e analitica degli scritti principali di bibliologia, bibliografia, biblioteconomia pubblicati in Italia dal 1921 al 1946.

The 2d edition of one of the volumes listed in the series below.

A work of first importance for the record of Italian bibliography. Covers: history of the book; general, national, regional, and personal bibliography; libraries; graphic arts, etc.

—— Bibliografie del ventennio. Roma, 1941. 14v. **AA42**

A series of separately published bibliographies listing works published in Italy, 1922–41. Volumes cover: Archeologia, arti figurative, musica. 498p.; La bibliografia italiana. 248p. (*see* AA41 for revised edition); Filologia classica e romanza. 152p.; Geografia e viaggi. 194p.; Letteratura italiana. 238p.; Letterature straniere. 455p.; Medicina. 165p.; Mussolini e il fascismo. 81p.; Scienze economiche e sociali. 167p.; Scienzi fisiche, matematiche ed agrarie. 211p.; Scienze naturali. 101p.; Scienzi religiose, filosofia, pedagogia. 173p.; Studi storici militari, etnografia popolare. 214p.; Il pensiero giuridico italiano. 5v.

Italia bibliographica 1952– . . . 2da ed. migliorata . . . Firenze, Sansoni, 1953– . (Amor di libro) Annual. **AA43**

Ed.: 1952–55, Giuseppe Sergio Martini.

An annual bibliography of bibliographies published in Italy. The first part lists monographs alphabetically by author; the second part lists, by subject, bibliographies appearing in books and periodicals.

Quinquennial indexes: 1952–56, 1957–61. These include indexes by subject and by author.

Latin America

Jones, Cecil Knight. A bibliography of Latin American bibliographies. 2d ed. rev. and enl. by the author with the assistance of James A. Granier. . . . Wash., Govt. Prt. Off., 1942. 311p. (U.S. Library of Congress. Latin Amer. ser., no.2) **AA44**

At head of title: The Library of Congress, Hispanic Foundation.

1st edition published in 1922 under title *Hispanic American bibliographies.*

Includes bibliographies, collective biographies, histories of literature, some general and miscellaneous works useful for reference purposes, encyclopedias, *anuarios, almanaques,* etc.

Mexico

Millares Carlo, Augustin and **Mantecón, José Ignacio.** Ensayo de una bibliografía de bibliografías mexicanas. (La imprenta, el libro, las bibliotecas, etc.) México, Biblioteca de la II Feria del Libro y Exposición Nacional del Periodismo, 1943. 224p. **AA45**

At head of title: Departamento del Distrito Federal. Dirección de Acción Social. Oficina de Bibliotecas.

Arranged by class. 1777 entries.

Includes general bibliographies relating to America that have references to Mexico, and bibliographies relating to Mexico, including general, individual, regional, subject, periodicals, etc.

Netherlands

U.S. Library of Congress. General Reference and Bibliographical Division. A guide to Dutch bibliographies, prep. by Bertus H. Wabeke. Wash., 1951. 193p.   **AA46**

Contents: pt.1, Comprehensive bibliographies: general, Netherlands, overseas territories; pt.2, Subject bibliographies; pt.3, Other bibliographies: academic dissertations, government publications, pamphlets, periodical press, personal bibliographies.

Lists more than 750 bibliographies. If copies are not available in the Library of Congress, an effort has been made to locate at least one copy of every item in a library in the United States.

Norway

Sommerfeldt, Wilhelm Preuss. Norsk bibliografisk litteratur, 1919–1944. 3. med tillegg 1944–1946. Oslo, Damm, 1944–46. 47p. (Norsk bibliografisk bibliotek, bd.3, hft.1)   **AA47**

A classified list of Norwegian bibliographies that appeared in books and periodicals published 1919–44.

Poland

Bibliografia bibliografii i nauki o książce. Bibliographia Poloniae bibliographica. 1945/1946–   . Warszawa, Biblioteka Narodowa, Inst. Bibliograficzny, 1947–   . Annual (Irregular).   **AA48**

A classified bibliography of current Polish bibliographies in the fields of bookmaking, librarianship, documentation, etc., including monographs and periodical articles.

Published irregularly as follows: 1945–46 (1955); 1947 (1947–49. 4 pts.); 1948 (1952); 1949 (1954); 1950–51 (1956); 1952–53 (1957); 1954 (1956); 1955 (1956); 1956 (1958); 1957 (1959); 1958 (1961); 1959 (1961); 1960 (1962).

Hahn, Wiktor. Bibliografia bibliografij polskich. Wyd. 2., znacznie rozsz. Wrocław, Zakład im. Ossolińskich, 1956. 645p.   **AA48a**

A greatly expanded 2d edition of the author's bibliography of Polish bibliography published in 1921. Classified arrangement, with author and title indexes.

Portugal

Anselmo, António Joaquim. Bibliografia das bibliografias portuguesas. Lisboa, Biblioteca Nacional, 1923. 158p. (Publicações da Biblioteca Nacional. Biblioteca do bibliotecário e do arquivista, 3)   **AA49**

Contents: (1) Bibliografias gerais; (2) Bibliografias especiais e monografias bibliográficas; (3) Publicações periodicas de bibliografia. Author and subject index.

Spain

Foulché-Delbosc, Raymond and **Barrau-Dihigo, Louis.** Manuel de l'hispanisant. N.Y., Putnam, 1920; Hispanic Soc. of America, 1925. 2v.   **AA50**

v.1, Répertoires; v.2, Collections.

A useful manual of Spanish bibliography including material on Portugal as well as on Spain. v.1 lists bibliographies: national, regional, special; biographical works; bibliographies of special subjects; descriptions of public and private archives, libraries, and museums. v.2 gives contents of printed collections and series, published 1579–1923.

Union of Soviet Socialist Republics

Bibliografiia sovetskoi bibliografii. 1939, 1946–   . Moskva, 1941–   . Annual.   **AA51**

Issued by Vsesoiuznaia Knizhnaia Palata.

Suspended 1940–45. The section of the Soviet national bibliography that is a classified annual index to bibliographies published separately or as parts of books or articles.

Informatsionnyi ukazatel' bibliograficheskikh spiskov i kartotek, sostavlennykh bibliotekami Sovetskogo Soiuza. Moscow, 1957–   . Semimonthly.   **AA52**

Continues *Vazhneishie bibliograficheskie raboty bibliotek,* issued 1943–48.

Currently published classified lists of bibliographies and card indexes in various fields.

Kirpicheva, Iraida Konstantinova. Bibliografiia v pomoshch' nauchnoi rabote; metodicheskoe i spravochnoe posobie. Pod red. P. N. Berkova. Leningrad, 1958. 480p.   **AA53**

A guide and manual to Russian bibliographies, including a section on bibliographical technique followed by sections on general and subject bibliography.

Translated into German as:

—— Handbuch der russischen und sowjetischen Bibliographien: die Allgemeinebibliographien, Fachbibliographien und Nachschlagewerke Russlands und der Sowjetunion. [Tr. from the Russian] Leipzig, Verlag für Buch- und Bibliothekswesen, 1962. 225p. (Bibliothekswissenschaftliche Arbeiten aus den Ländern der Volksdemokratie in deutscher Übersetzung. Reihe B, Bd.5)   **AA54**

Moscow. Publichnaia Biblioteka. Svodnyi ukazatel' bibliograficheskikh spiskov i kartotek, sostavlennykh bibliotekami Sovetskogo Soiuza. Obshchestvennye nauki; khudozhestvennaia literatura. Iskusstvo. 1960–   . Moskva, 1961–   . Annual.   **AA55**

Sokurova, M. V. Obshchie bibliografii russkikh knig grazhdanskoi pechati, 1708–1955; annotirovannyi ukazatel'. Izd. 2. Leningrad, 1956. 283p. (Bibliografiia russkoi bibliografii)   **AA56**

At head of title: Gosudarstvennaia Publichnaia Biblioteka im. Saltykova-Shchedrina.

1st ed. 1944.

A definitive guide to general bibliographies of Russian books. Gives full description, notes on authors and editors, and citations to pertinent literature and critical reviews. Includes an extensive list of sources, a name index, and chronological chart. The introductory essay on bibliography is by the general editor, P. N. Berkov.

Yugoslavia

Bibliografija jugoslovenskih bibliografija, 1945–55. Beograd, Bibliografski Inst. FNRJ, 1958. 270p.   **AA57**

At head of title: Savez društava bibliotekara FNRJ. Sekcija za bibliografiju.

Bibliographies on all subjects published in Yugoslavia between 1945 and 1955, in classified arrangement with author and subject indexes. Entries are in Latin characters, with the indication "čiril" if the work cited is in the Cyrillic alphabet.

UNIVERSAL

Bibliography

Brunet, Jacques Charles. Manuel du libraire et de l'amateur de livres. 5. éd. originale entièrement refondue et augm. d'un tiers. Paris, Didot, 1860–80. 9v. il.   **AA58**

Facsimile reprint: Berlin, Altmann, 1921–22. 6v.; Paris, Dorbon-Aîní, 1928. 6v.

v.1–5, Author and title list, A–Z; v.6, Subject index; v.7–8, Supplement, by P. Deschamps and G. Brunet, Author and title list, with subject index in v.8; v.9, Dictionnaire de géographie ancienne et moderne à l'usage du libraire et de l'amateur de livres, par P. Deschamps. 1870.

Brunet's *Manuel* is a general bibliography of rare, important, or noteworthy books not limited to those of any one period or language but especially strong for French and Latin titles and for publications before the 19th century. For each book listed it gives author, full title, place, publisher, date, size, number of volumes, but not generally paging, and, in the case of rare books, bibliographical and critical notes with mention of copies and prices at famous sales, and occasional facsimiles of title pages, printers' marks, etc. The arrangement of the main work (v.1–5) is alphabetical by author and title, and there are two subject indexes: one in v.6 to the main work and one in v.8 to the supplement. Footnotes throughout v.1–5 refer to titles omitted from the main author list but included in the subject volume (v.6).

Covers much the same ground as Grässe's *Trésor de livres* (AA60) but is generally said to contain a larger portion of French books while Grässe lists more German titles. The two books must often be used together as each lists titles not given in the other.

Georgi, Gottlieb. Allgemeines europäisches Bücher-Lexicon. Vor dem Anfange des XVI. seculi bis [1757]. Leipzig, Georgi, 1742–58. 5 pts. and 3 suppl. in 2v.   **AA59**

Pt.1–4, A–Z; pt.5, French works, A–Z; Suppl. 1–3, 1739–47, 1747–54, 1753–57.

Arranged alphabetically by author, giving, for each work, author, short title, place, publisher, date, price.

Grässe, Johann Georg Theodor. Trésor de livres rares et précieux. Dresden, Kuntze, 1859–69. 7v.   **AA60**

v.1–6, A–Z; v.7, Supplement.

Facsimile reprints: Paris, Welter, 1900–1901. 8v.; Berlin, Altmann, 1922. 7v.

Based on Brunet (AA58) but contains more entries of German books. Sales prices of books are given.

Peddie, Robert Alexander. Subject index of books published before 1880. London, Grafton, 1933–48. 4v.   **AA61**

1st ser., 1933, 745p.; 2d ser., 1935, 857p.; 3d ser., 1939, 945p.; new ser., 1948, 872p.

Each series furnishes an alphabetical subject list of some 50,000 books in various languages published before 1880 (1881), the date from which the British Museum subject indexes (AA68) continue the record. Includes many small and specific subject entries, e.g., place names, excluding, however, personal names.

The third series includes in its alphabetical arrangement every subject heading used in the three series, with cross references to the first and second series. This record is not continued in the "new series."

Watt, Robert. Bibliotheca britannica; or, A general index to British and foreign literature. Edinburgh, Constable, 1824. 4v.   **AA62**

For full description *see* AA493.

Library catalogs

Printed catalogs of libraries are useful reference aids to catalogers, reference librarians, and research workers because they supply verification of titles; information about authorship; description of books; editions, contents, or occasional notes which throw light on a reference search; and they often contain analytical or other added entries not given in the library's own catalog. They indicate, of course, the location of at least one copy of each title listed. Dictionary and subject catalogs are also useful as subject bibliographies.

The catalogs of the great national libraries, such as the Library of Congress, the British Museum, and the Bibliothèque Nationale, are of particular importance because these libraries are entitled by law to receive copies of all books copyrighted in their respective countries. These catalogs, therefore, are the most comprehensive single records of publications in these countries. National libraries also contain material in many other languages, and their catalogs are often extremely usable records of foreign-language materials.

Many printed catalogs of smaller libraries have been issued, only a few of which are listed here. While most of these are old, they may still be useful for bibliographical information and even for locational purposes. A somewhat longer list of American library catalogs is given in Winchell, *Locating books for interlibrary loan,* p.49–55 (AB149).

National libraries

The author catalogs of the Library of Congress—National Union Catalog series represented in the entries AA63–AA65 vary in title, form, and coverage as indicated in the combined annotation. These are complemented by the subject catalog, AA66.

U.S. Library of Congress. A catalog of books represented by Library of Congress printed cards, issued to July 31, 1942. Ann Arbor, Mich., Edwards, 1942–46. 167v. (Repr.: N.Y., Rowman & Littlefield)   **AA63**

—— —— Supplement: cards issued Aug. 1, 1942–Dec. 31, 1947. Ann Arbor, Mich., Edwards, 1948. 42v. (Repr.: N.Y., Rowman & Littlefield)

Library of Congress author catalog: a cumulative list of works represented by Library of Congress printed cards, 1948–1952. Ann Arbor, Mich., Edwards, 1953. 24v. (Repr.: N.Y., Rowman & Littlefield)   **AA64**

Contents: v.1–23, Authors; v.24, Films.

National union catalog: a cumulative author list representing Library of Congress printed cards and titles reported by other American libraries, 1953–1957. Ann Arbor, Mich., Edwards, 1958. 28v.   **AA65**

Contents: v.1–26, Authors; v.27, Music and phonorecords; v.28, Motion pictures and filmstrips.

—— 1958–1962. N.Y., Rowman & Littlefield, 1963. 54v.

Contents: v.1–50, Authors; v.51–52, Music and phonorecords; v.53–54, Motion pictures and filmstrips.

—— 1952–1955 imprints: an author list representing Library of Congress printed cards and titles reported by other American libraries. Ann Arbor, Mich., Edwards, 1961. 30v.

Compiled by the Library of Congress under the auspices of the Committee on Resources of American Libraries of the American Library Association.

National union catalog: a cumulative author list. Wash., Lib. of Congress, Card Division. Monthly, with quarterly and annual cumulations.

Because of the immensity of the collections, the excellence

of the cataloging, and the full bibliographical descriptions, the *Catalog* of the Library of Congress has been for many years an invaluable work in any library and indispensable in those where research is done. Of first importance in cataloging, acquisition, and reference work, and for the bibliographer and research worker, it is valuable for author bibliography, verification of titles, bibliographical information, historical notes, location of copies, etc.

History: Until 1942, the catalog was produced only on cards, and to make the information available outside of Washington, "depository sets" were placed in various large libraries in different sections of the country. These sets consisted of main entry cards only and were kept up to date by the addition of new cards as printed. To make the catalog even more generally accessible, the Association of Research Libraries, in 1942, sponsored the photographic reproduction of a depository catalog and its publication in book form. The cards were photographed and printed in reduced size. The main catalog includes all cards printed from 1898 to July 31, 1942; the supplement, those issued Aug. 1, 1942—Dec. 31, 1947.

Scope: It is an author and main entry catalog (with cross references but not added entries) of books and other materials for which Library of Congress printed cards were available in: (1) the Library of Congress (as cards had not been printed for all the Library's books, the catalog is not a complete record of the Library's holdings, but does represent a large percentage); (2) many government department libraries; and (3) various libraries throughout the country, as a result of the cooperative cataloging program.

Information given is detailed and represents a high degree of accuracy, usually including, as pertinent: full name of author, dates of birth and death; full title; place, publisher, and date; collation (paging, illustrations, maps, tables, size, etc.); series; edition; notes on contents, history, etc.; tracing for subject headings and added entries; L.C. class number, sometimes Dewey class number, and L.C. card number. Frequently a considerable amount of analysis is noted for composite books, sets, periodicals, etc.

1942–1947: It should be noted that the *Supplement* and later cumulations contain cards issued during the periods covered regardless of the imprint date of the book recorded, and revised cards are treated in the same manner as new ones. The *Supplement* also includes some 26,000 title entries for anonymous and pseudonymous works for which the Library of Congress had supplied the authors, the so-called "bracketed authors." The title entries were made by crossing out the author's name; the card was then filed under title. For those cards which were printed before Aug. 1942, the author card will be in the main set; for cards printed Aug. 1942–1947, in the *Supplement*.

1948–1952: Coverage and form differ somewhat from series to series. From 1948 on, catalogs are issued quinquennially and are printed from the type prepared for the printed cards and not photographed. Furthermore, the principles and rules of cataloging by the Library of Congress were changed during 1947, and these changes are incorporated in the catalog beginning in 1948. As a consequence, cataloging is less full and information given less extensive, e.g., author's birth and death dates are given only to distinguish between persons of the same name, collation is somewhat abbreviated, and descriptive notes are less full.

In this and the following series, besides main entries and cross references for books, pamphlets, maps, music scores, periodicals, and other serials, essential added entries are included. Motion pictures and filmstrips are grouped in v.24.

1953–1957: The great innovation in this period was the move toward a *National union catalog,* by the inclusion of monographs not represented by L.C. printed cards, reported by some 500 other North American libraries, together with the indication of location of titles by the symbols of libraries. Includes printed cards in all languages written in the Roman, Cyrillic, Greek, Gaelic, or Hebraic alphabets and contains entries for books, pamphlets, maps and atlases, periodicals, and other serials. *Motion pictures and filmstrips* and *Music*

and phonorecords are now published separately (*see* BG68, BH38). All serials represented by L.C. printed cards are included, but holdings of serials not cataloged by the Library of Congress are omitted and listed in *New serial titles* (AF99).

1958–1962: Coverage was expanded to include cards in the Arabic and Indic alphabets and in Chinese, Japanese, and Korean characters. The number of libraries reporting holdings increased to about 750.

National union catalog, 1952–1955: This series, supplementary to the regular set, and not included in its chronological sequence, lists titles previously included in earlier catalogs with additional locations, as well as newly reported titles, many not represented by L.C. printed cards. The catalog is not fully edited so that there may be some duplication under variant forms of entry, but cross references are given whenever possible.

Current: The current catalog is printed in nine monthly issues: Jan., Feb., April, May, July, Aug., Oct., Nov., and Dec.; three quarterly cumulations: Jan.–March, April–June, July–Sept.; and an annual cumulation. As there is no quarterly cumulation for Oct.–Dec., the monthly issues must be used until the arrival of the annual, usually as much as nine or ten months later.

The monthly issues contain the cards prepared for works published during the current and past two years; the quarterly and annual cumulations contain all cards printed during the period regardless of imprint date. The annuals cumulate into the quinquennial sets.

Library of Congress catalog. Books: subjects, 1950–1954. A cumulative list of works represented by Library of Congress printed cards. Ann Arbor, Mich., Edwards, 1955. 20v.   **AA66**

—— —— 1955–1959. Paterson, N.J., Pageant Books, 1960. 22v. (Available from Rowman & Littlefield, N.Y.)

Quinquennial cumulations, arranged alphabetically by subject, of entries for publications printed 1945 or later which have been cataloged or recataloged, during the periods covered, by the Library of Congress and libraries participating in the cooperative cataloging program, and which are represented by L.C. printed cards. Included are the types of material in the languages indicated for the *National union catalog* (AA65). From 1950 to 1952, maps, motion pictures, and music scores were also included, but from 1953 on, these were issued separately. (*Maps and atlases,* issued separately 1953–55, was discontinued, and these entries are included in the 1955–1959 cumulation.)

Continued by quarterly and annual supplements. Quarterly issues exclude entries for belles-lettres and imprints earlier than the current and two preceding years. Annual cumulations include entries for publications with imprint dates of 1945 or later which have been currently cataloged (*see* Introd.).

British Museum. Dept. of Printed Books. General catalogue of printed books. London, Trustees, 1931– . v.1– .   **AA67**

Previous ed. (entitled *Catalogue of printed books*), 1881–1900. 95v.; Supplement, 1900–1905. 13v. (Photographic reprint. Ann Arbor, Mich., Edwards Bros., 1946–50)

v.1–51, A–Dezw, of the new catalog were published between 1931 and 1954, but mounting costs caused its discontinuance. These volumes included entries cataloged up to the time of the publication of each volume and included much recataloging and revision of the previous catalog.

In 1959, the Trustees began to issue, by photo-offset lithography, the Working Catalogue of the Reading Room, covering books cataloged through 1955, without further editing but with the manuscript amendments which were contained in the volumes. This catalog begins with v.52 and will continue through the alphabet, after which v.1–51 will be brought up to 1955 to conform to the rest of the set, and will be reproduced in the same manner. It is hoped that the entire catalog, in some 300 volumes, will be delivered by 1966.

At this time it will be a complete record of the printed books in the Library of the British Museum, which have appeared from the 15th century to the end of 1955, in all languages except the Oriental.

The Library of the British Museum is particularly important because of the extent and richness of its collections in all fields and in all languages, and also because its possession of the copyright privilege helps make it the most comprehensive collection of British publications in existence. Its catalog, therefore, is an indispensable bibliographical source for the scholar and librarian. In the main, it is an author catalog only, with catchword title entries, cross references for anonymous books, etc. Subject entries are included to a limited extent, principally for the following: (1) under personal names, biographical works are included; (2) under countries, e.g., England, France, etc., are entered official publications, some works about the country, and many titles in which the name of the country occurs; (3) under names of sacred books, e.g., Bible, Kur'an, etc., are entered both texts and works about them. Two important reference features are: (1) the large amount of analytical material included (analysis of series, etc.), and (2) the many cross references from names of editors, translators, or other personal names.

The amount of bibliographical information varies; titles taken from the 19th-century catalog usually include only author, title, editor, place, and date, whereas more recent cataloging adds publisher, paging, and size. Some cataloging for early printed books is fairly full.

Special sections to be noted include: Bible (2v.); England (4v. and index); Liturgies; London (3v.); Periodical publications (3v.). These serve as comprehensive bibliographies of these areas. For Academies *see* AC2.

—— —— Additions, 1963– . London, 1964– . Annual.

v.1–4, A–Z.

"The first in a proposed series of annual volumes showing the entries added each year to the *General catalogue . . .* "— *Pref.*

Annual volumes will not be issued for 1956–62 since it is hoped that a decennial supplement covering 1956 to 1965 will be published.

—— Subject index of the modern works added to the library, 1881–1900, ed. by G. K. Fortescue. London, 1902–3. 3v. **AA68**

Supersedes earlier indexes published for this period. Continued by 5-year supplements as follows:

—— —— 1901–05, 1906–10, 1911–15, 1916–20, 1921–25, 1926–30, 1931–35 (2v.), 1936–40 (2v.), 1941–45, 1946–50 (4v.). London, 1906–61. v.1–10.

Title varies slightly.

An alphabetical subject catalog of the modern works added to the library since 1881. Contains entries for well over 750,000 titles, but is sometimes difficult to use. Subjects are often general rather than specific, with many subheadings, and there is no table of headings used, although there are many cross references. Arrangement under headings is neither alphabetical nor chronological. Bibliographical information usually includes author, brief title, paging, place, and date. Personal names are not included as these are covered in the *General catalogue*.

For *Subject index of books published before 1880, see* Peddie (AA61).

Deutscher Gesamtkatalog, hrsg. von der Preussischen Staatsbibliothek. . . . Berlin, Preussische Druckerei– u. Verlags Aktiengesellschaft, 1931–39. v.1–14. **AA69**

v.1–14, A–Beethordnung. No more published.

v.1–8 had title *Gesamtkatalog der preussischen Bibliotheken* and listed books contained in about 18 important libraries. With v.9, 1936, beginning the letter B, the scope was changed to include the contents of some 100 German and Austrian libraries—an ambitious undertaking, unfortunately

suspended because of the war. The few volumes published show that, for the letters covered, the work is (1) indispensable for catalogers, reference workers, and bibliographical investigation generally, in the matter of German publications, and (2) useful for non-German subjects, also, as it contains much foreign material in many languages, including English works not listed in the British Museum catalog (AA67) and French works not listed in the catalog of the Bibliothèque Nationale (AA72).

Arranged alphabetically by author and anonymous title; includes books published up to 1930. The cataloging is detailed and exact, and for this reason the volumes issued are still useful.

Deutscher Gesamtkatalog. Neue Titel. Berlin, Staatsbibliothek, 1893–1944. **AA70**

Issued weekly (frequency varies slightly), with quarterly and annual cumulations which supplement the *Deutscher Gesamtkatalog* (AA69).

Title varies. 1910–37 had title *Berliner Titeldrucke.*

Partially cumulated in to:

Berlin. Preussische Staatsbibliothek. Berliner Titeldrucke; fünfjahrs Katalog, 1930/34–1935/39. Berlin, Staatsbibliothek, 1935–40. **AA71**

Both issued in 8v. A–Z, paged continuously.

No more published.

Title varies: 1935/39 called *Deutscher Gesamtkatalog. Neue Titel.*

Lists works published 1930–39 cataloged in more than 100 German libraries, thus supplementing the *Deutscher Gesamtkatalog.*

Paris. Bibliothèque Nationale. Catalogue général des livres imprimés: Auteurs. Paris, Impr. Nationale, 1900–1963. v.1–189. (In progress) **AA72**

v.1–189, A-Tissonière.

An important modern catalog, the value of which cannot be overestimated. An alphabetical author catalog, including only entries under names of personal authors, with the necessary cross references; does not include title entries for anonymous books or entries for anonymous classics, periodicals or society transactions or government or corporate authors. The cataloging is excellent; the information given includes author's full name whenever possible, title, place, publisher, date, edition, paging or volumes, format, and occasional notes of contents, original publication in case of reprints from periodicals, etc. An important reference feature, in the case of authors whose works are voluminous, is the detailed alphabetical title index under the author's name, which indicates in what volumes or editions a given work may be found, and also indicates alternative and changed titles.

Each volume includes titles acquired up to the date of publication of the particular volume, so that there is a wide spread in the coverage between the first volumes published in 1900 and those issued half a century later.

It has now been announced that the present catalog will be continued to the end of the alphabet, but beginning with v.189 will include no entries after 1959. Quinquennial supplements will be published beginning with 1960–64. These will include anonymous works and joint authors—types of entries omitted from the main catalog.

Nonnational libraries

United States

Astor Library, New York. Catalogue. N.Y., Craighead Pr., 1857–66; Cambridge, Mass., Riverside Pr., 1886–88. 9v. **AA73**

1st catalog, known as the Cogswell catalog from its compiler, J. G. Cogswell, 1857–66. 5v.: v.1–4, A–Z; v.5, Supplementary author list, A–Z; Subject index. 2d catalog, comp. by C. A. Nelson and known as the Nelson catalog, 1886–88. 4v. Authors: A–Z.

The books listed in these two catalogs are now part of the New York Public Library.

Boston Athenaeum. Catalogue, 1807–71. Boston, 1874–82. 5v. **AA74**

Dictionary catalog, including some analysis; comp. by C. A. Cutter.

Peabody Institute, Baltimore. Catalogue of the library. Baltimore, 1883–1905. 13v. **AA75**

1st catalog, 1882–92. 5v.; 2d catalog, including additions since 1882, 1896–1905. 8v.

A well-made dictionary catalog, with the following special features: (1) full contents of voluminous sets, arranged alphabetically; and (2) full author and subject analysis of composite books and some periodicals; this analysis makes the work almost as much an index as a catalog.

Princeton. University. Library. Alphabetical finding list. Princeton, N.J., Univ. Lib., 1921. 5v. **AA76**

—— Classed list. 1920. 6v.

A title-a-line catalog.

Great Britain

[Crawford, James Ludovic Lindsay, *26th Earl of*]. Bibliotheca Lindesiana . . . Catalogue of the printed books preserved at Haigh Hall, Wigan, co. pal. Lancast. . . . Aberdeen, Univ. Pr., 1910. 4v. **AA77**

The library of a rich general collection which includes many rarities and incunabula.

Additional volumes published with continuing volume numbers: v.5–6, A bibliography of royal proclamations of the Tudor and Stuart sovereigns and of others published under authority 1485–1714. Oxford, Clarendon Pr., 1910. 2v.; v.7, *A bibliography . . . of philately.* Aberdeen, Univ. Pr., 1911. 924col. (*see* BF70).

Edinburgh. University. Library. Catalogue of the printed books. Edinburgh, Univ. Pr., 1918–23. 3v. **AA78**

John Rylands Library, Manchester. Catalogue of the printed books and manuscripts. Manchester, Cornish, 1899. 3v. **AA79**

London Library. Catalogue, by C. T. Hagberg Wright and C. J. Purnell. London, 1913–14. 2v. **AA80**

An author catalog of a library of more than 250,000 volumes. This edition incorporates the material of the 1st edition, 1903, and the 8 annual supplements to that edition.

—— —— Supplement, 1913–20, 1920–28, 1928–50. London, 1920–53. 3v.

The 3d supplement adds some 150,000 titles.

—— Subject index of the London Library . . . by C. T. Hagberg Wright. London, 1909–55. v.1–4.

v.1, Main subject list; v.2, Additions, 1909–22, by C. T. Hagberg Wright and C. J. Purnell; v.3, Additions, 1923–38; v.4, Additions, 1938–1953.

Oxford. University. Bodleian Library. Catalogus librorum impressorum Bibliothecae Bodleianae in Academia Oxoniensi. . . . Oxford, e Typographeo Academico, 1843–51. 4v. **AA81**

Reproductions

Guide to microforms in print, 1961– . Albert James Diaz, ed. Wash., Microcard Eds., 1961– . Annual. **AA82**

"A comprehensive guide, in alphabetic order, to materials which are available on microfilm and other microforms from United States publishers. Theses and dissertations are not listed . . . *not* a union list . . . essentially a listing of microform publications offered for sale on a regular basis."— [*Prelim. note*].

Subject guide to microforms in print, 1962/63– . Albert James Diaz, ed. Wash., Microcard Eds., 1962– . Annual. **AA83**

A companion to the preceding entry, listing materials under subject classification.

Modern Language Association of America. Reproductions of manuscripts and rare printed books. Short title list. (In Modern Language Assoc. of America. Publs. 65:289–338. April 1950) **AA84**

"Complete to January 1, 1950."

"Rotographs or microfilms of the . . . materials listed . . . are now on deposit in the Library of Congress."

These are available for interlibrary loan, or microfilm copies may usually be purchased.

Tilton, Eva Maude. A union list of publications in opaque microforms. 2d ed. N.Y., Scarecrow, 1964. 744p. **AA85**

1st ed. 1959.

Not a union list in the usual sense (i.e., library locations are not provided), but a compilation of publishers' lists in one alphabet by main entry. Includes listings from European as well as from American publishers. Contains the record of many master's and doctor's theses.

Union Library Catalogue of the Philadelphia Metropolitan Area. Committee on Microphotography. Union list of microfilms. Rev., enl., and cumulated ed. Ann Arbor, Mich., J. W. Edwards, 1951. 1961col. **AA86**

Supersedes the 1942 edition and its 5 supplements. Lists some 25,000 titles held on microfilm by 197 institutions, reported through June 1949. Includes materials of all kinds, the fullness of information depending on what was furnished by the individual library. Arrangement is alphabetical, and each entry gives Library of Congress subject classification, bibliographical information, and the location of negative and positive microfilms and of the originals when available. Newspapers are listed by title, with full information on the years covered and the location of negatives and positives, except when the newspaper is included in *Newspapers on microfilm* (AG12), in which case reference is given to the latter.

—— —— 1949–1959. Ann Arbor, 1961. 2v.

A supplement to the basic list, including more than 52,000 entries of all types of materials, reported by 215 libraries during the period July 1, 1949—July 31, 1959.

Lists all serials except newspapers, which are now listed in *Newspapers on microfilm* (AG12).

Omits dissertations which are covered by *Dissertation abstracts* (AI11) and various other materials listed in existing bibliographies (*see* Introd.).

No more published.

U.S. Library of Congress. Processing Dept. British manuscripts project; a checklist of the microfilms prep. in England and Wales for the American Council of Learned Societies, 1941–1945, comp. by Lester K. Born. Wash., 1955. 179p. **AA87**

Lists the contents of 2652 reels of microfilm containing reproductions of manuscripts and some rare printed materials found in libraries in England and Wales. The period covered is from medieval times to the 18th century. Copies of the films may be purchased from the Photoduplication Service of the Library of Congress.

Translations

See also Pure and Applied Sciences, p.528.

Bibliographie der Übersetzungen deutschsprachiger Werke. Verzeichnis der in der Deutschen Bücherei eingegangenen Schriften, bearb. und hrsg. von der Deutschen Bücherei. Leipzig, Verlag für Buch- und Bibliothekswesen, 1954– . Jahrg.1– . Quarterly. **AA88**

Subtitle varies.

A quarterly bibliography listing translations from German into other languages, published since 1951. Arranged by language, each subdivided by large class groups, with indexes: classified, author, and publisher. Bibliographic information is detailed; the translated title is followed by the original German title in brackets; and prices are included. A volume covering 1945–50 is planned.

Delavenay, Émile and **Delavenay, Katherine M.** Bibliographie de la traduction automatique. Bibliography of mechanical translation. 's-Gravenhage, Mouton, 1960. 69p. (Janua linguarum. Studia memoriae Nicolai van Wijk dedicata. Nr.11) **AA89**

Classified listing of books and articles. Author index.

Fromm, Hans. Bibliographie deutscher Übersetzungen aus dem Französischen, 1700–1948 . . . Baden-Baden, Verlag für Kunst und Wissenschaft, 1950–53. 6v. **AA90**

Title pages and introductory matter in German, French, and English. The main list records books and some periodical articles under author and French title, followed by full bibliographical information of German translations.

v.1–6: Verzeichnis A, Alphabetical list of authors and titles of translations from French, A–Z; Verzeichnis B, Translations of French texts by German authors; Verzeichnis C, Alphabetical list of German collections, series, miscellanies, anthologies, etc., containing only translations from French. Index A, Alphabetical index of translators; Index B, Alphabetical index of German titles arranged in List A under the French titles.

Index translationum. Répertoire international des traductions. International bibliography of translations. Paris, Internat. Inst. of Intellectual Cooperation, 1932–40. no.1–31; n.s. v.1, 1948– . Paris, UNESCO, 1949– . Annual. **AA91**

The first series was quarterly; the new series is annual. Entries are arranged by country, and under these by the 10 major headings of the Universal Decimal Classification. Complete bibliographical information, including the original language and title, are given when available. Both series include indexes of authors, publishers, and translators. The last issue of the first series, published in Jan. 1940, covered 12 countries including the USSR. The new series began with a coverage of 26 countries, which was increased to 75 in 1961.

Kaiser, Frances E. Translators and translations: services and sources. A project of the Georgia Chapter, Special Libraries Association. N.Y., Special Libraries Assoc., 1959. 60p. **AA92**

Includes lists of translation services, pools of translations, and bibliographies of translations. Geographical, subject, and language indexes.

U.S. Dept. of State. Office of International Information. Livres américains traduits en français et livres français sur les États-Unis d'Amérique (Répertoire d'ouvrages disponibles en librairie au Iᵉʳ mai 1951). 2. éd. Paris, Services Américains d'Information, 1952. 123p. **AA93**

Title also in English: *American books in French translation and French books about the United States of America.*

Anonyms and pseudonyms

☙ Many reference books have been published on the authorship of anonymous and pseudonymous works. They differ considerably in use and authority, their value depending upon their comprehensiveness within their given field, the quality of research that has gone into their making, and particularly upon whether or not they give the authority for their attribution of authorship. The last point is of special importance, as the question of authorship is often a matter of dispute and difficult to establish; hence, it is frequently important to be able to check as many sources as possible in order to come to a decision. For a discussion of a selected list of such reference books, *see* the following bibliography:

Bibliography

Taylor, Archer and **Mosher, Fredric J.** The bibliographical history of anonyma and pseudonyma. Chicago, Univ. of Chicago Pr. for the Newberry Library, 1951. 289p. il. **AA94**

Bibliography, p.207–79.

Preliminary chapters discuss homonyms, Latinized names, pseudepigrapha, anonyma and pseudonyma, confusing titles; and fictitious facts of publication. A classified guide to dictionaries and lists of anonyma and pseudonyma, and an index to the historical chapters are included.

United States and England

Cushing, William. Anonyms; a dictionary of revealed authorship. Cambridge, [Mass.], Cushing, 1889. 829p. **AA95**

Includes both English and American works. In two alphabets: (1) anonymous titles followed by name of author; (2) index of authors found only in the *Anonyms.* Does not give authorities.

—— Initials and pseudonyms; a dictionary of literary disguises. N.Y., Crowell, [c1885–88]. 2v. **AA96**

In two series, together including about 18,500 initials and pseudonyms, principally English and American, with a few well-known Continental names. Each series is in two parts: (1) initials followed by real name; (2) real name followed by pseudonym or initials, with short biographical notices. Does not give authorities.

Gaines, Pierce Welch. Political works of concealed authorship during the administrations of Washington, Adams and Jefferson, 1789–1809, with attributions. New Haven, Conn., Yale Univ. Lib., 1959. 148p. **AA97**

450 items, chronologically arranged. Gives sources of the attributions.

Halkett, Samuel and **Laing, John.** Dictionary of anonymous and pseudonymous English literature. New and enl. ed. by James Kennedy, W. A. Smith and A. F. Johnson. Edinburgh, Oliver and Boyd, 1926–62. 9v. **AA98**

1st ed., Edinburgh, Paterson, 1882–88. 4v.

v.1–6, A–Z. Supplement, v.6, p.273–449; v.7, Index and 2d suppl.; v.8, 1900–1950; v.9 (see below).

v.8–9 by Dennis E. Rhodes and Anna E. C. Simoni.

A comprehensive list, arranged alphabetically by first word of title not an article, giving for each item listed: title (sometimes shortened), size, paging, place, date, author's name, and (in some cases) the authority for attribution of authorship. The best list for English works, although as most of the authorities cited are general in character, the work is not final authority in cases of disputed authorship.

v.8 aims to give the authorship of as many anonymous and pseudonymous works as possible, published in the English language between 1900 and 1949 inclusive.

From 1950 on, the same kind of information may usually be found in the *British national bibliography* (AA507), for books published in Great Britain, and in the *National union catalog* (AA65).

v.9, originally planned to "consist entirely of additions and corrections to the period before 1900" (*Pref.*), now includes also as many additional items for the 1900–1950 period as possible.

Argentina

Cutolo, Vicente Osvaldo. Diccionario de alfónimos y seudónimos de la Argentina (1800–1930). Buenos Aires, Ed. Elche, 1962. 160p. **AA99**

Belgium

Delecourt, Jules Victor. Bibliographie nationale. Dictionnaire des anonymes et pseudonymes, XVᵉ siècle–1900. Mis en ordre et enrichi par G. Delecourt. Bruxelles, Academie Royale, 1960– . v.1– .   **AA100**
v.1, 1281p.
A reworking and updating of the author's *Essai d'un dictionnaire des ouvrages anonymes et pseudonymes publiés en Belgique au XIVᵉ siècle et principalement depuis 1830.* Bruxelles, 1863. 548p.

De La Montagne, Victor Alexis. Vlaamsche pseudoniemen. Bibliographische opzoekingen. Roeselare, De-Seyn-Verhougstraete, 1884. 132p.   **AA101**

Brazil

Barros Paiva, Tancredo de. Achêgas a um diccionario de pseudonymos, iniciaes, abreviaturas e obras anonymas de auctores brasileiros e de estrangeiros, sobre o Brasil ou no mesmo impressas. Rio de Janeiro, J. Leite, 1929. 248p.   **AA102**

Canada

Audet, François Joseph and **Malchelosse, Gerard.** Pseudonymes canadiens. Montreal, G. Ducharme, 1936. 189p.   **AA103**
Pt.1 lists by pseudonym with real name and brief annotation; pt.2, by real name, referring to the pseudonyms. French-Canadian writers only.

Colombia

Pérez Ortiz, Rubén. Seudónimos colombianos. Bogotá, 1961. 276p. (Publicaciones del Inst. Caro y Cuervo. Ser. bibliográfica, 2)   **AA104**
In two parts: the first is a list by pseudonym, giving real name; the second is a list of Colombian authors indicating any pseudonyms which they have used.

Cuba

Figarola-Caneda, Domingo. Diccionario cubano de seudónimos. Habana, Impr. "El siglo XX," 1922. 182p.   **AA105**

Czechoslovakia

Dolenský, Antonín. Slovník pseudonymů a kryptonymů v československé literatuře. . . . 3. přepracované vydání. Praha, [Tiskem M. Knappa v Karlíně], 1934. 155p.   **AA106**

Ormis, Ján Vladimir. Slovník slovenských pseudonymov. [Turč. Sv. Martine], Slovenská Národná Knižnica, 1944. 366p. (Knihy slovenskej národnej knižnice v Turčianskom Svätom Martine. Sväzok I)   **AA107**

Dominican Republic

Rodriguez Demorizi, Emilio. Seudónimos dominicanos. Ciudad Trujillo, Ed. Montalvo, 1956. 280p.   **AA108**

England

See United States and England, p.11.

France

Quérard, Joseph Marie. Les supercheries littéraires dévoilées. . . . 2. éd. Paris, Daffis, 1869–[79]. 7v. (v.1–3, repr.: Paris, Maisonneuve & Larose, 1964)   **AA109**
Subtitle: Galerie des écrivains français de toute l'Europe qui se sont déguisés sous des anagrammes, des astéronymes, des cryptonymes, des initialismes, des noms littéraires, des pseudonymes facétieux ou bizarres, etc. 2. éd., considérablement augm., pub. par Gustave Brunet et Pierre Jannet. Suivie 1ᵉ, Du Dictionnaire des ouvrages anonymes, par Ant.-Alex. Barbier. 3. éd., rev. et augm. par Olivier Barbier. . . . 2ᵉ, D'une table générale des noms réels des écrivains anonymes et pseudonymes cités dans les deux ouvrages.
v.1–3, J. M. Quérard. Les supercheries littéraires dévoilées, 2. éd., A–Z; v.4–7, A. A. Barbier. Dictionnaire des ouvrages anonymes. 3. éd., A–Z. Anonymes Latins.
The same edition of Barbier was also issued separately (Paris, Féchoz, 4v. Repr.: Hildesheim, Olms, 1963. 4v.). The *Table générale des noms réels* was never issued.
Gives notes about the books and editions listed, but in general does not give authority for identification of authors. Supplemented by the following:

Brunet, Gustave. Dictionnaire des ouvrages anonymes [de Barbier], suivi des Supercheries littéraires dévoilées [de Quérard]: supplément à la dernière édition de ces deux ouvrages (Edition Daffis). Paris, Féchoz, 1889. 310col., cixp. 122col., xivp. (Repr.: Paris, Maisonneuve & Larose, 1964)   **AA110**
Contents: Dictionnaires des ouvrages anonymes (Supplément); Essai sur les bibliothèques imaginaires; Les devises des vieux poètes: étude littéraire et bibliographique, par M. Gustave Mouravit; Appel aux bibliophiles, aux érudits et aux curieux ["Désiderata," i.e., une liste d'anonymes et de pseudonymes dont le mystère n'a pas été découvert]; Les supercheries littéraires dévoilées (Supplément); Varia: Pseudonymes étrangers. Traductions supposées. Supercheries typographiques.

Germany

Berlin. Preussische Staatsbibliothek. Namenschlüssel die Verweisungen der Berliner Titeldrucke zu Pseudonymen, Doppelnamen und Namensabwandlungen, 1892–1935. [2. ed.] Berlin, Staatsbibliothek, 1936. 780p.   **AA111**
The *Berliner Titeldrucke* (*Deutscher Gesamtkatalog. Neue Titel, see* AA71) is the accessions list of books added during 1892–1935 to the Staatsbibliothek and to the libraries of the Prussian universities and *Hochschule.* This *Namenschlüssel* is an alphabetical index to forms of authors' names which differ from the author entry chosen for the *Titeldrucke,* and includes pseudonyms, parts of compound names not used as entries, varying spellings of transliterated names, early and medieval names for which the correct entry is not obvious, etc. For each of such unused forms a reference is given to a volume of the *Titeldrucke* where the full entry for the book may be found under the author entry chosen by the Staatsbibliothek.

Holzmann, Michael and **Bohatta, Hans.** Deutsches Anonymen-Lexikon, 1501–1910. Weimar, Gesellschaft der Bibliophilen, 1902–28. 7v. (Repr.: Hildesheim, Olms, 1961)   **AA112**
v.1–4, 1501–1850; v.5, supplement, 1851–1908; v.6, 1501–1910, additions and corrections; v.7, 1501–1926, additions and corrections.
Includes, in the four lists, some 83,000 entries. Arranged alphabetically by title, with author's name supplied for each and the authority for the information indicated.

—— Deutsches Pseudonymen-Lexikon. Wien, Akademie Verlag, 1906. 323p. (Repr.: Hildesheim, Olms, 1961)   **AA113**

Gives pseudonym, followed by real name, and indicates the authority for the information.

Hungary

Gulyás, Pál. Magyar írói álnév lexikon; a magyarországi írók álnevei és egyéb jegyei. Függelék: Néhány száz névtelen munka jegyzéke. Budapest, Akadémiai Kiadó, 1956. 706p.   **AA114**

Added title page in Latin: Lexicon pseudonymorum hungaricum: pseudonyma et alia signa scriptorum regni hungariae.

An alphabetical list of pseudonyms and initials with the author's name supplied for each, and authorities indicated. Includes also a list of anonymous works whose authors were identified.

Italy

Melzi, Gaetano, *Conte.* Dizionario di opere anonime e pseudonime de scrittori italiani, o come che sia aventi relazione all'Italia. Milano, Coi Torchi di L. di Giacomo Pirole, 1848–59. 3v. (Repr.: N.Y., Burt Franklin, 1960)   **AA115**

—— —— Supplemento, comp. da Giambattista Passano. Ancona, Morelli, 1887. 517p.

Covers the 16th to the 19th centuries.

—— —— Supplemento al Melzi e al Passano di Emmanuele Rocco. Napoli, Chiurazzi, 1888. 16p.

Luxembourg

Hury, Carlo. Dictionnaire de pseudonymes d'auteurs luxembourgeois. Luxembourg, Impr. P. Linden, 1960. 17p. (Bibliographia luxemburgensis, 2)   **AA116**

Mexico

Manrique de Lara, Juana and **Monroy, Guadalupe.** Seudónimos, anagramas, iniciales, etc., de autores mexicanos y extranjeros. México, Secretaría de Educación Pública, 1943. 78p.   **AA117**

Netherlands

Doorninck, Jan Izaac van. Vermomde en naamlooze schrijvers, opgespoord op het gebied der Nederlandsche en Vlaamsche letteren. 2. uitg. der "Bibliotheek van anonymen en pseudonymen." Leiden, Brill, 1883–85. 2 pts. in 1v.   **AA118**

v.1, Pseudonyms and initials. 671col.; v.2, Anonyms. 681 col.

Kempenaer, A. de. Vermomde Nederlandsche en Vlaamsche schrijvers, vervolg op J. I. van Doorninck's Vermomde en naamlooze schrijvers, opgespoord op het gebied der Nederlandsche en Vlaamsche letteren. Leiden, Sijthoff, [1928]. 690col.   **AA119**

Poland

Bar, Adam. Słownik pseudonimów i kryptonimów pisarzy polskich oraz Polski dotyczących, opracował Adam Bar . . . i Tad. Godłowskiego . . . Kraków, [Nakł. Krakowskiego koła Związku Bibljotekarzy Polskich], 1936–38. 3v. (Prace bibljoteczne Krakowskiego koła Związku Bibljotekarzy Polskich. VII–IX)   **AA120**

v.1–2, Alphabetical list of pseudonyms, initials, etc., with full name, title, and source of attribution; v.3, Real name followed by pseudonym.

Portugal

Fonseca, Martinho Augusto da. Subsidios para um diccionario de pseudonymos, iniciaes e obras anonymas de escriptores portuguezes contribuição para o estudo da litteratura portugueza. Lisboa, Academia Real das Sciencias, 1896. 298p.   **AA121**

Russia

Masanov, Ivan Filippovich. Slovar' psevdonimov russkikh pisatelei, uchenykh i obshchestvennykh deiatelei. V chetyrekh tomakh. Podgotovil k pechati IU. I. Masanov. Redaktor B. P. Koz'min. Moskva, 1956–60. 4v.   **AA122**

An enlarged edition of Masanov's dictionary of Russian pseudonyms (Moskva, 1941). v.3 completes the Russian alphabet and lists Latin and Greek pseudonyms and other symbols used by Russian authors. v.4 contains a name index, and additions to v.1–3.

Scandinavia

Bygden, Anders Leonard. Svenskt anonym- och pseudonym-lexikon. Bibliografisk förteckning öfver uppdagade anonymer och pseudonymer i den svenska litteraturen. Upsala, Berling, 1898–1915. 2v.   **AA123**

Collin, Edvard. Anonymer og Pseudonymer i den danske, norske og islandske Literatur samt i fremmede Literaturer, forsaavidt disse omhandle nordiske Forholde, fra de aeldste Tider indtil Aaret 1860. Kiøbenhavn, Lund, 1869. 209p.   **AA124**

Ehrencron-Müller, Holger. Anonym- og Pseudonym-Lexikon for Danmark og Island til 1920 og Norge til 1814. København, Hagerup, 1940. 391p.   **AA125**

Pettersen, Hjalmar Marius. Norsk anonym- og pseudonym-lexikon. Kristiana, Steen, 1924. 690col., [34]p.   **AA126**

1st edition, 1890, had title *Anonymer og pseudonymer i den norske literatur* 1678–1890.

—— —— Tilføielser og rettelser. (In Nordisk tidskrift för bok- och biblioteksväsen 12:118–26. 1925)

Spain

Ponce de León Freyre, Eduardo and **Zamora Lucas, Florentino.** 1500 seudónimos modernos de la literatura española (1900–1942). Madrid, Inst. Nacional del Libro Español, 1942. 126p.   **AA127**

Rodergas i Calmell, Josep. Els pseudònims usats a Catalunya. (Recull de 3.800) Barcelona, Ed. Millà, 1951. 408p.   **AA128**

Spanish America

Medina, José Toribio. Diccionario de anónimos y seudónimos hispanoamericanos. Buenos Aires, Impr. de la Univ., 1925. 2v. in 1. (Buenos Aires. Univ. Nacional. Inst. de Investigaciones Históricas. Publ. 26–27) **AA129**

Victorica, Ricardo. Errores y omisiones del Diccionario de anónimos y seudónimos hispano-americanos de José Toribio Medina. Buenos Aires, Viau & Zona, 1928. 338p.   **AA130**

—— Verdades que levantan roncha. Belitres enfurecidos. Gaceta del foro, ano 15, 11 abril 1930, p.273–78.

Has about 16 columns of *"Nuevas adiciones al 'Diccionario' de Medina,"* p.274–78, in alphabetical order.

—— Nueva epanortosis al Diccionario de anónimos y seudónimos de J. T. Medina. Buenos Aires, Rosso, 1929. 207p. **AA131**

Feliú Cruz, Guillermo. Advertencias saludables a un criticastro de mala ley. Buenos Aires, Impr. de la Univ., 1929. 56p. **AA132**

Repr. from *Boletín del Inst. de Investigaciones Históricas* 8:254–59; 9:237–80. abril–junio, oct.–dic. 1929.

A criticism of Ricardo Victorica's *Errores y omisiones del Diccionario de anónimos y seudónimos hispanoamericanos de José Toribio Medina* (AA130).

Uruguay

Scarone, Arturo. Diccionario de seudónimos del Uruguay . . . Montevideo, Garcia & Cia., 1942. 632p. **AA133**

"Segunda ed. con un Apéndice" of the 3d edition which was first published under this title in 1941. The first two editions have title *Apuntes para un diccionario de seudónimos y de publicaciones anónimas.*

Yiddish

Chajes, Saul. Thesaurus pseudonymorum quae in litteratura hebraica et judaeo-germanica inveniuntur. Pseudonymen-Lexikon der hebräischen und jiddischen Literatur. Wien, Glanz, 1933. 335p., 66p. **AA134**

Added title page in Yiddish.
In Yiddish, with index in romanized form of name.

Fictitious imprints

Brunet, Gustave. Imprimeurs imaginaires et libraires supposés, étude bibliographique suivie de recherches sur quelques ouvrages imprimés avec des indications fictives de lieux ou avec des dates singulières. Paris, Tross, 1866. 290p. (Repr.: N.Y., Burt Franklin, 1963) **AA135**

Parenti, Marino. Dizionario dei luoghi di stampa falsi, inventati o supposti in opere di autori e traduttori italiani, con un'appendice sulla data "Italia," e un saggio sui falsi luoghi italiani usati all'estero, o in Italia, da autori stranieri. Firenze, Sansoni, 1951. 311p. il. (Biblioteca bibliografica italica . . . 1) **AA136**

Arranged alphabetically by place, and then chronologically, with an index of actual and pseudonymous authors. Many facsimiles.

Weller, Emil. Die falschen und fingirten Druckorte. Repertorium der seit erfindung der Buchdruckerkunst unter falscher Firma erschienenen deutschen, lateinischen und französischen Schriften. 2. verm. und verb. Aufl. Leipzig, W. Engelmann, 1864. 2v. **AA137**

v.1, German and Latin works, 1510–1862; v.2, French works, 1530–1863.

ANCIENT, MEDIEVAL, AND RENAISSANCE MANUSCRIPTS

❧ The field of manuscripts is a very specialized one, rich in guides, bibliographies, and catalogs. Only a few of these dealing with the ancient, medieval, and Renaissance periods are listed here. It should be remembered that one of the main sources for descriptions of manuscripts is the exhibition catalog. Such catalogs, usually richly illustrated and with detailed descriptions, are issued by libraries and museums (e.g., the Morgan Library, the Walters Art Gallery in Baltimore, the Huntington Library) to describe particular exhibits. These should be acquired and preserved by libraries as needed.

For American manuscripts in special subject fields, *see* that subject, e.g., History—United States.

Bibliography

Scriptorium; revue internationale des études relatives aux manuscrits. t.1 (1946/47)– . Anvers, Standaard Boekhandel, [1947–]. plates, facsims. Semiannual. **AA138**

Subtitle also in English. Contributions in English, French, German, and Spanish.

Includes current bibliographies of manuscript studies and facsimile editions.

Catalogs

Lowe, Elias Avery. Codices latini antiquiores; a palaeographical guide to Latin manuscripts prior to the ninth century. Oxford, Clarendon Pr., 1934–63. v.1–10. facsims. (In progress: to be complete in 11v.) **AA139**

"Edited under the auspices of the Union Académique Internationale for the American Council of Learned Societies and the Carnegie Institution of Washington."

"A succinct description based upon actual examination of the originals of all known Latin literary manuscripts on papyrus, parchment, or vellum which may be regarded as older than the ninth century, accompanied by a specimen, unreduced, of the script and supplemented by a selected bibliography" [at the end of each volume].

Arranged by present location of manuscripts.

Contents: pt.I, Vatican City; pt.II, Great Britain, Ireland; pt.III–IV, Italy; pt.V, Paris; pt.VI, France; pt.VII, Switzerland; pt.VIII–IX, Germany; pt.X, Austria, Belgium, Czechoslovakia, Denmark, Egypt, and Holland.

The eleventh and final part "will include items from Hungary, Luxembourg, Poland, Spain, Sweden, U.S.S.R., U.S.A., and Yugoslavia, together with addenda, corrigenda and an index to the whole work."

Within date and language limits, this is the most comprehensive and detailed catalog of manuscripts ever published. It is far more than a "palaeographical guide" as it includes notes about decoration, content, and history of the manuscripts. Prefaces point out items of particular paleographic or textual importance and discuss characteristics of significant book centers in various regions. The extensive references serve also as a general bibliography of manuscripts.

Bibliography

British Museum. Dept. of Manuscripts. The catalogues of the manuscript collections [by T. C. Skeat]. Rev. ed. [London], Trustees of the British Museum, 1962. 45p. **AA140**

First issued in *Journal of documentation* 7:18–60. 1951.

Annotated list of 176 printed and handwritten catalogs of the Museum's various collections of Western manuscripts.

Supplements Kristeller (AA141).

Kristeller, Paul Oskar. Latin manuscript books before 1600; a list of the printed catalogues and unpublished inventories of extant collections. New ed. rev. N.Y., Fordham Univ. Pr., [1960]. 234p. **AA141**

"First published in *Traditio: studies in ancient and medieval history, thought and religion* 6:227–317, 1948 and 9:393–418, 1953."

A valuable guide to public collections in Europe and the United States. Indicates the number of manuscripts included in a list, and analyzes lists covering more than one collection. Excludes archives and most private collections. Includes some lists of Greek and vernacular manuscripts since most collections are not divided according to language. Gives cross references but no index.

Contents: A, Bibliography and statistics of libraries and their collections of manuscripts; B, Works describing manuscripts of more than one city; C, Printed catalogues and handwritten inventories of individual libraries, by cities.

Paris. Bibliothèque Nationale. Les catalogues imprimés de la Bibliothèque Nationale. Liste établié en 1943 suivie d'un supplément (1944–1952). Paris, 1953. 204p., xxviip. **AA142**

Catalogs of manuscripts: p.4–57, iii–v. Lists some 250 catalogs of manuscripts in various languages, subjects, and collections.

Supplements Kristeller (AA141).

Richard, Marcel. Répertoire des bibliothèques et des catalogues de manuscrits grecs. 2. éd. Paris, Centre Nationale de la Recherche Scientifique, 1958. 276p. (Inst. de Recherche et d'Histoire des Textes. Publ. 1) **AA143**

1st ed. 1948.

Includes lists of manuscripts in periodicals as well as those published separately. Covers collections in Europe, the Middle East, Egypt, and North and South America, indicating size and character. Detailed index.

Contents: 1, Bibliographie; 2, Catalogues spécialisés; 3, Catalogues régionaux; 4, Villes.

"Revues et Actes académiques cités," p.253–60.

Union lists

Ricci, Seymour de. Census of medieval and Renaissance manuscripts in the United States and Canada, . . . with the assistance of W. J. Wilson. N.Y., Wilson, 1935–40. 3v. (Repr.: N.Y., Kraus, 1961) **AA144**

"Published under the auspices of the American Council of Learned Societies."

Arranged alphabetically by states, cities, and libraries, including private collections.

Brief descriptions include: Probable date and place of origin, material on which written, size, number of leaves, kind of binding, former owners, and references to printed descriptions.

Contents: v.1, Alabama–Massachusetts; v.2, Michigan–Canada. Errata and addenda; v.3, Indices: [1], General index of names, titles and headings; [2], Scribes, illuminators and cartographers; [3], *Incipits;* [4], Gregory numbers for Greek New Testament manuscripts; [5], Present owners; [6], Previous owners.

—— —— Supplement, originated by C. U. Faye, continued and ed. by W. H. Bond. N.Y., Bibliographical Soc. of America, 1962. 626p.

Gives cross references to the *Census* when additional or corrected information is supplied and for manuscripts whose ownership has changed.

Proposes to have an annual listing in the *Publications* of the Bibliographical Society of America.

Facsimiles

Palaeographical Society, London. Facsimiles of [ancient] manuscripts and inscriptions. 1st–2d ser. London, 1873–1894. 5v. 465pl. (facsims.) **AA145**

Cover title: Facsimiles of ancient manuscripts . . .

Eds.: E. A. Bond, E. M. Thompson, G. F. Warner.

Each plate with page of corresponding letterpress giving transcription and description.

Issued in parts. 1st ser.: 13 pts. (260pl.); 2d ser.: 10 pts. (205pl.).

Contents: *1st ser.:* v.1, Introduction. Phoenician. Greek. Gothic; v.2, Oscan. Latin and modern languages; v.3, Latin and modern languages. *2d ser.:* v.1, Introduction. Egyptian. Semitic. Greek. Latin and modern languages; v.2, Latin and modern languages. Lists of manuscripts, etc. in the two series are arranged topographically.

—— —— Indices to ser. I and II. London, 1901. 63p.

Contents: Chronological; Authors and subjects; Country of origin; Character of handwriting; Ornamentation; Scribes and artists; Materials other than vellum; Present owners; Former owners.

—— Facsimiles of ancient manuscripts, etc. 1st–2d ser. London, 1903–1930. 4v. 452pl. (facsims.)

At head of title: New Palaeographical Society.

Eds.: E. M. Thompson, G. F. Warner, F. G. Kenyon, J. P. Gilson, J. A. Herbert, and H. I. Bell.

Each plate with page of corresponding letterpress giving transcription and description.

Issued in parts. 1st ser.: 10 pts. (250pl.); 2d ser.: 13 pts. (202pl.).

Contents: *1st ser.:* v.1, Introduction. Greek. Latin and modern languages; v.2, Latin and modern languages; *2d ser.:* v.1, Introduction. Greek. Latin and modern languages; v.2, Latin and modern languages.

—— Indices to 1st ser. London, 1914. 50p.

—— Indices to 2d ser. London, 1932. 43p.

Comp. by F. Wormald.

Contents of both indexes follow the same lines as those in the original series (*see* above).

One of the most comprehensive and useful of the many paleographical sets. Full-page reproductions, with some manuscripts allotted more than one plate. Descriptions include data about the entire volume represented with information as to its text, history, and miniatures (if any), some of which are also included in the reproductions. References sometimes given.

Société Française de Reproductions de Manuscrits à Peintures. Bulletin. année 1–21. Paris, 1911–1938. 21v. plates. (facsims.) **AA146**

Reproductions and descriptions of important illuminated manuscripts, of both Western and Eastern origin, in the libraries of various countries. Usually, each volume is devoted to manuscripts in a particular library. Descriptions by recognized scholars include bibliographic details, notes on script, provenance, authorship, and text as well as the illumination.

Bibliography

Paris. Bibliothèque Nationale. Dépt. des Manuscrits. Listes des recueils de fac-similés et des reproductions de manuscrits conservés à la Bibliothèque Nationale, pub. par M. Omont. 3. éd. par Ph. Lauer. [Paris], 1935. 226p. **AA147**

Full entry for each item including analysis of sets. Cross references and comprehensive index.

Contents: I, Recueils de fac-similés classés par ordre alphabétique d'auteurs ou de matières [483 entries]; II, Reproductions de manuscrits: (1) Collections de Leyde, du Vatican, de Paris, de Bruxelles et de Copenhague [90 entries], and (2) Manuscrits classés par ordre alphabétique d'auteurs ou de matières [573 entries]; III, Série orientale, classement par recueils [7 entries] et par ordre alphabétique de langues [17 languages including Mexican. 128 entries].

This comprehensive list (almost 1300 entries) is an invaluable aid to manuscript study in many areas. Can be supplemented by the lists published in *Scriptorium* (AA138).

Handbooks and scripts

Cappelli, Adriano. Lexicon abbreviaturarum. Dizionario di abbreviature latine ed italiane, usate nelle carte e codice specialmente del medio-evo . . . 6. ed. (anastatica) corr. con 9 tavole fuori testo. Milano, Hoepli, 1961. lxxiiip., 531p. facsims. **AA148**

An anastatic reprint of the 3d edition, published in 1929.
Main part is an alphabetical list of abbreviations given both in manuscript facsimile and in printed letters followed by the words for which they stand. Supplemental lists include: 1, Conventional signs; 2, Epigraphical abbreviations; 3, Ancient roman and arabic numerals; 4, Signs indicating money, weights, and measures.
Bibliography of works on abbreviations, p.517–31.
Supplemented by:

Pelzer, Auguste. Abréviations latines médiévales. Supplément au Dizionario di abbreviature latine ed italiane de Adriano Cappelli. Louvain, Publ. Universitaires; Paris, Béatrice-Nauwelaerts, 1964. 86p. **AA149**

Chassant, Alphonse Antoine Louis. Dictionnaire des abréviations latines et françaises usitées dans les inscriptions lapidaires et métalliques, les manuscrits et les chartes du Moyen Âge. 5. éd. Paris, J. Martin, 1884. liip., 172p. facsims. **AA150**

1st ed. Evreux, 1846.
"Abréviations latines," p.1–121; "Abréviations françaises," p.123–43.
Gives manuscript form of abbreviations followed by printed words for which they stand. Supplemental lists include: Abbreviations of numerical expressions, conjoined letters or monograms, numbers, dates, and Roman signs used in Christian epitaphs before the 7th century.

Johnston, Harold Whetstone. Latin manuscripts; an elementary introduction to the use of critical editions for high school and college classes. Chicago, Scott, Foresman, 1897. 135p. facsims. (Inter-collegiate Latin ser.) **AA151**

Contents: 1, The history of the manuscripts; 2, The science of paleography; 3, The science of criticism.

Martin, Charles Trice. The record interpreter: a collection of abbreviations, Latin words and names used in English historical manuscripts and records. 2d ed. London, Stevens, 1910. 464p. **AA152**

Contents: (1) Abbreviations of Latin words used in English records; (2) Abbreviations of French words used in English records; (3) Glossary of Latin words found in records and other English manuscripts, but not occurring in classical authors; (4) Latin names of places in Great Britain and Ireland; (5) Latin names of bishoprics in England; (6) Latin names of bishoprics in Scotland; (7) Latin names of bishoprics in Ireland; (8) Latin forms of English surnames; (9) Latin Christian names with their English equivalents.
Compiler was assistant keeper of the public records. The 1st edition, published in 1892, was an amplification of his appendix to Andrew Wright's *Court-hand restored* (9th ed. 1879).

Thompson, *Sir* **Edward Maunde.** An introduction to Greek and Latin palaeography. Oxford, Clarendon Pr., 1912. 600p. 250facsims. (Repr.: N.Y., Burt Franklin, 1964) **AA153**

Gives transcription of each facsimile.
Includes chapters on the history of Greek and Roman alphabets, materials and writing implements, forms of books, abbreviations, contractions, and numerals.
Bibliography, p.571–83, includes lists of published facsimiles.

Ullman, Berthold Louis. Ancient writing and its influence. N.Y., Longmans, 1932. 234p. 48facsims. on XVIpl. (Our debt to Greece and Rome) **AA154**

Gives transcription of each facsimile.

Devotes three chapters to the origin and development of the Greek alphabet and script, but the major part is given to the Latin scripts of the Middle Ages, including the national hands, Carolingian and Gothic scripts, and the writing of the Italian Renaissance. Includes chapters on abbreviations, ligatures, and numerals.
Bibliography, p.231–34.

—— The origin and development of humanistic script. Roma, Ed. di Storia e Letteratura, 1960. 146p. 70facsims. **AA155**

Bibliographical footnotes.
Index of manuscripts, p.142–44.
Thorough study of the script on which printed roman letters are based.

Illumination

See Chamberlin, *Guide to art reference books* (BE1).

Scribes and artists

Aeschlimann, Erardo and **Ancona, Paolo d'.** Dictionnaire des miniaturistes du Moyen Âge et de la Renaissance dans les différentes contrées de l'Europe . . . 2. éd. rev. et augm. Milan, Hoepli, 1949. 239p. 155pl. (part col.) **AA156**

For full information *see* BE158.

Bradley, John William. A dictionary of miniaturists, illuminators, calligraphers, and copyists, with references to their works, and notices of their patrons, from the establishment of Christianity to the eighteenth century . . . London, Quaritch, 1887–89. 3v. (Repr.: N.Y., Burt Franklin, [1958]) **AA157**

For full information *see* BE159.
In addition to these two dictionaries (AA156, AA157), *see* the lists of scribes and artists in the *Indices* of the Palaeographical Society series (AA145) and the *Indices* of the De Ricci *Census* and *Supplement* (AA144).

EARLY AND RARE BOOKS

Incunabula and early printed books

❧ The books listed below are the principal general bibliographies and catalogs of incunabula that should be known by the general librarian. Various important bibliographies of the incunabula of special countries, and catalogs of incunabula in individual libraries, will also be needed for special work. For lists of these *see* Stillwell, *Incunabula and Americana*, p.251–329 (AA159); the list of sources in the *Gesamtkatalog der Wiegendrucke* (AA169); and Goff, *Incunabula in American libraries* (AA168).

For dictionaries of place-names associated with early printing presses, *see* Gazetteers—Ancient and Medieval, p.445.

Guides

Haebler, Konrad. Handbuch der Inkunabelkunde. Leipzig, Hiersemann, 1925. 187p. **AA158**

A handbook on the literature, history, physical make-up, and printing of incunabula.

Stillwell, Margaret Bingham. Incunabula and Americana, 1450–1800. A key to bibliographical study. N.Y., Columbia Univ. Pr., 1931. (Repr.: N.Y., Cooper Square Pub., 1961) 483p. facsims. **AA159**

Contents: *Incunabula:* 1, Printed books of the 15th century; 2, Identification and collation; 3, Bibliographical reference material; *Americana:* 1, Preliminary survey of sources and methods; 2, Century of maritime discovery; 3, Two centuries of colonial growth, 1500–1700; 4, Later Americana and the Revolutionary periods; 5, Early printing in America; *Reference sections:* 1, Notes and definitions; 2, Foreign bibliographical terms: French, German, Italian, and Spanish; 3, Latin contractions and abbreviations; 4, Place names of 15th century printing towns; 5, Incunabula: selected bibliographies and monographs (600 items); 6, 15th century woodcuts: selected monographs; 7, Americana: selected bibliographies and monographs (more than 600 items).

An indispensable reference work and guide for the collector or librarian. Important both for the text and for the extensive annotated bibliographies.

Bibliography

Hain, Ludwig Friedrich Theodor. Repertorium bibliographicum, in quo libri omnes ab arte typographica inventa usque ad annum MD.... Stuttgart, Cotta, 1826–38. 2v. in 4. (Repr.: Berlin, Altmann, 1925) **AA160**

A basic list arranged alphabetically, the items numbered serially throughout. The "Hain number" is referred to in many later bibliographies of incunabula.

Copinger, Walter Arthur. Supplement to Hain's Repertorium bibliographicum; or, Collections towards a new edition of that work. London, Sotheran, 1895–1902. 2v. in 3. (Repr.: Leipzig, Lorentz, 1926) **AA161**

Pt.1, nearly 7000 corrections of and additions to the collation of works described in Hain; pt.2, list of nearly 6000 volumes not in Hain: v.1, A–O; v.2, P–Z. v.2 also includes "The printers and publishers of the XV century with lists of their works," by Konrad Burger (p.319–670), which is an index to the *Supplement to Hain's Repertorium,* and to the works of Campbell, Pellechet, and Proctor.

Reichling, Dietrich. Appendices ad Hainii-Copingeri Repertorivm bibliographicvm; additiones et emendationes. Monachii, Rosenthal, 1905–11. 7v. **AA162**

Pts.1–6 in two sections each: I, Additions; II, Emendations; pt.[7], Indices fascivlorvm I–VI.

—— —— Svpplementvm (maximam partem e bibliothecis Helvetiae collectvm) cvm indice vrbivm et typographorvm. Accedit index avctorvm generalis totivs operis. Monasterii Gvestphalorvm, Theissingianis, 1914. 109p., cxxxvp.

Burger, Konrad. Supplement zu Hain und Panzer. Beiträge zur Inkunabelbibliographie, Nummernconcordanz von Panzers lateinischen u. deutschen Annalen u. Ludwig Hain's Repertorium bibliographicum. Leipzig, Hiersemann, 1908. 440p. **AA163**

—— Ludwig Hain's Repertorium bibliographicum. Register. Die Drucker des XV. Jahrhunderts. Leipzig, Harrassowitz, 1891. 428p. (Centralblatt für Bibliothekswesen. Beihefte, Bd.2, Hft.8) **AA164**

Panzer, Georg Wolfgang Franz. Annales typographici ab artis inventae origine ad annum 1500. Norimbergae, Zeh, 1793–97. 5v. **AA165**

Arranged by places, and under each chronologically.

—— —— ab anno 1501 ad annum 1586. Norimbergae, 1798–1803. 6v.

Numbered v.6–11. v.10–11, Indici.

Proctor, Robert. Index to the early printed books in the British Museum; with notes of those in the Bodleian Library. London, K. Paul, 1898–1938. Pts.1–2 in 6v. **AA166**

Pt.1, To 1500: v.1, Germany; v.2, Italy; v.3, Switzerland to Montenegro, including France, Netherlands, Austria-Hun-

gary, Spain, England, Scandinavia, Portugal; v.4, Register. 1898–99. 4v.

A chronological list under each country by names of presses. The index volume contains an alphabetical list of towns, printers, and publishers; a list of books mentioned in Hain and of those not in Hain; authors of books printed in the Low Countries; and books printed in England.

Pt.2, 1501–1520: sec. 1, Germany, 1903; sec. 2, Italy; sec. 3, Switzerland and Eastern Europe, by Frank Isaac. London, Quaritch, 1938.

—— —— Supplements 1898–1902. London, 1900–1903. 5 pts.

Pts.1–4, Supplements; pt.5, Register.

British Museum. Dept. of Printed Books. Catalogue of books printed in the XVth century now in the British Museum. London, 1908–62. Pts.1–9. facsims. **AA167**

Work supervised by A. W. Pollard.

Pts.1–2, Germany; pt.3, Germany, German-speaking Switzerland and Austria-Hungary; pts.4–7, Italy; pt.8, France, French-speaking Switzerland; pt.9, Holland, Belgium.

Arranged under places by printers' names. Gives historical notes about printers, and full title, description, collation, and date of purchase of each book. Pt.3 contains also an introduction by A. W. Pollard, a typographical map, facsimiles, and indexes to pts.1–3 by (1) Hain's numbers, (2) concordance of Proctor's numbers, (3) printers and towns. Covers the same ground as the first part of Proctor's *Index to the early printed books* (AA166) but with much fuller descriptions.

Union lists

Goff, Frederick Richmond. Incunabula in American libraries; a third census of fifteenth century books recorded in North American collections. N.Y., Bibliographical Soc. of America, 1964. 798p. **AA168**

First census by the Bibliographical Society, 1919; *Second census* by Margaret Bingham Stillwell, 1940.

A much enlarged edition recording 47,188 copies of 12,599 titles held by 760 owners. Roughly 90 percent of the total registered are held by institutions. The method of listing follows closely that of the *Second census,* and the style is virtually the same. The entries have been renumbered, but the Stillwell number is indicated in a subsidiary position.

Authors are listed alphabetically, in general conforming to Hain, or to the form used in the British Museum *Catalogue of books printed in the XVth century* (AA167) or in the *Gesamtkatalog der Wiegendrucke* (AA169). (Works in Hebrew are listed in a separate section under "Hebraica.") Information under each entry usually includes author (with variant spellings), short title, place, printer, date, size, references to descriptions in printed catalogs, and location of copies.

Additional sections include: Variant author-forms and entries; Index of printers and publishers; Concordances to the numbers used in the *Gesamtkatalog,* Hain, Proctor's *Index,* and the *Second census* if the sequence of numbers has been changed; Deletions from the *Second census;* Addenda.

Gesamtkatalog der Wiegendrucke, hrsg. von der Kommission für der Gesamtkatalog der Wiegendrucke. Leipzig, Hiersemann, 1925–40. v.1–8¹. **AA169**

v.1–8¹, A–Federicis. No more published.

As far as published, the most comprehensive record of incunabula yet made, based on information collected during more than twenty years' work by the Kommission. The sections issued record nearly half again as many editions as Hain (AA160), and the information given for each is much fuller, including: (1) author entry, title, date, etc.; (2) collation, types, capitals, and illustrations; (3) transcripts of title, colophon, and other extracts; (4) references to descriptions in Hain and other bibliographies; and (5) location of copies, which includes a complete record of all copies if not more than 10 are known and, for commoner books, a selection of copies in representative libraries in different countries, both European and American. Indispensable in both cataloging and reference work in the scholarly library.

Accurti, Thomas. Editiones saeculi XV pleraeque bibliographis ignotae. Annotationes ad opus quod inscribitur "Gesamtkatalog der Wiegendrucke" voll.I–IV. Florentiae, 1930. 170p. **AA170**

—— Aliae editiones saeculi XV pleraeque nondum descriptae. Annotationes ad opus cui titulus "Gesamtkatalog der Wiegendrucke," voll.I–VI. Florentiae, Ex "Tipografia Giuntina," 1936. 130p. **AA170a**

Guarnaschelli, Teresa Maria and **Valenziani, E.** Indice generale degli incunaboli delle biblioteche d'Italia, a cura del Centro Nazionale d'Informazioni Bibliografiche. . . . Roma, Libreria dello Stato, 1943–54. v.1–3. facsims. (In progress) **AA171**

v.1, A–B; v.2, C–F; v.3, G–L.
Added title page: Ministero dell' educazione nazionale. Indici e cataloghi. Nuova serie, 1.

Pellechet, Marie Léontine Catherine. Catalogue général des incunables des bibliothèques publiques de France. Paris, Picard, 1897–1909. v.1–3. **AA172**

v.1–3, A–Gregorius Magnus.
No more published.

—— —— Unpublished manuscript by Louis Polain continuing the work from Gregorius to Z. v.4–14 on 11 reels.

Microfilm copy from the original manuscript in the possession of the French government.

Polain, Louis. Catalogue des livres imprimés au quinzième siècle des bibliothèques de Belgique. Bruxelles, Soc. des Bibliophiles, 1932. 4v. facsims. **AA173**

v.1–3, A–S; v.4, T–Z; Supplément (no.4070–4109). Additions. Tables: A, Facsimilés; B, Concordance des numéros avec ceux de Campbell, *Gesamtkatalog,* Hain, Pellechet, Voullième; C, Imprimeurs; E, Gravures; F, Table générale alphabétique des matières; (D, Table des bibliothèques, annoncé dans l'introduction, p.xxi, was not published).

History

Bühler, Curt Ferdinand. The fifteenth-century book: the scribes, the printers, the decorators. Philadelphia, Univ. of Pa. Pr., 1960. 195p. il. **AA174**

Gives an excellent survey of the development of the 15th-century book. Includes bibliographical notes and an index.

Book collecting

Guides and manuals

Benjamin, Mary A. Autographs: a key to collecting. N.Y., W. R. Benjamin Autographs, 1963. 313p. 35pl. **AA175**

First pub. 1946.
This edition has been corrected and revised with a new preface and a selected list of reference works.

Gives information on terminology, evaluation, facsimiles, reproductions and manuscript copies, care and preservation. Emphasis is on American historical materials. Includes author and subject index.

Bradley, Van Allen. More gold in your attic. N.Y., Fleet, [1961]. 415p. il. **AA176**

A useful handbook on book collecting written in a popular style. An enlargement of its companion volume *Gold in your attic* (1958), but omits the chapters "Dictionary for book

hunters" and "Library for book hunters (an annotated bibliography)."

Includes a "Price index and guide to valuable books and pamphlets of the New World," p.227–415.

Carter, John. ABC for book-collectors. [3d ed. rev.] London, Hart-Davis, 1961. 208p. **AA177**

1st ed. 1952.
An alphabetical dictionary of bibliographic and booksellers' terms with definitions as used in Great Britain and the United States, often spicy and reflecting the personal "prejudices" of the author.

Hamilton, Charles. Collecting autographs and manuscripts. Norman, Univ. of Okla. Pr., [1961]. 269p. il. **AA178**

Contains information on building a collection, forgeries, evaluation, care and preservation, etc. Includes more than 800 facsimiles of autographs and other reproductions from all countries and periods; a brief, annotated bibliography; and an index of authors, subjects, and titles.

Bibliography

Bennett, Whitman. A practical guide to American book collecting (1663–1940); with all items arranged in sequence as a chronological panorama of American authorship and with each subject considered from bibliographical, biographical and analytical aspects. N.Y., Bennett Book Studios, 1941. 254p. **AA179**

Lists about 1000 outstanding American books, with annotations giving bibliographical information about first printing.

Brussel, Isidore Rosenbaum. Anglo-American first editions. . . . London, Constable; N.Y., Bowker, 1935–36. 2v. (Half title: Bibliographia, studies in book history . . . no.9–10) **AA180**

Pt.1: East to West, 1826–1900 . . . English authors whose books were published in America before their publication in England. 1935. 170p; pt.2: West to East, 1786–1930 . . . American authors whose books were published in England before their publication in America. 1936. 131p.

Gives detailed bibliographical information with descriptive annotations.

Carteret, Léopold. Le trésor du bibliophile romantique et moderne, 1801–75. Paris, Carteret, 1924–28. 3v. index. il., facsims. **AA181**

v.1–2, Éditions originales, A–Z; v.3, Livres illustrés du XIXᵉ siècle; Index volume, Tables générales, ouvrages cités, illustrateurs et graveurs. 207p.

—— Le trésor du bibliophile; livres illustrés modernes 1875 à 1945, et Souvenirs d'un demi-siècle de bibliophile de 1887 à 1945. Paris, Carteret, 1946–48. 5v. il., facsims. **AA181a**

Title varies.

Heard, Joseph Norman. Bookman's guide to Americana. 2d ed. N.Y., Scarecrow, 1960. 407p. **AA182**

1st ed. 1953–56. 2v.
A listing of more than 8000 out-of-print titles, mostly from current dealers' catalogs. Most items range in price from $4 to $10.

Howes, Wright. U.S.iana, 1650–1950; a selective bibliography in which are described 11,620 uncommon and significant books relating to the continental portion of the United States. Rev. and enl. [i.e., 2d] ed. N.Y., Bowker, for the Newberry Library, 1962. 652p. **AA183**

This list of uncommon books relating to the continental United States, compiled primarily for the use of the average collector, indicates their relative sales value in five categories from $10 to more than $1000. For the rarer items indication is frequently given of the location of one or more perfect copies in American libraries.

Johnson, Merle De Vore. American first editions. 4th ed., rev. and enl. by Jacob Blanck. N.Y., Bowker, 1942. 553p. (Repr.: Cambridge, Mass., Research Classics, 1962) **AA184**

1st edition, 1929, planned as a continuation of Patrick K. Foley, *American authors, 1795–1895* (Boston, 1897).

This edition lists the first editions of more than 200 American authors having "collector interest."

Parenti, Marino. Prime edizioni italiane; manuale di bibliografia practica ad uso dei bibliofili e dei librai. 2. ed. riv. e ampl. Milano, Libri d'Arte e di Filologia, 1948. 526p. **AA185**

1st ed. 1935.

An alphabetical list of Italian authors from the 16th to the 19th centuries, with dates of their first editions.

—— Rarità bibliografiche dell' ottocento; materiali e pretesti per una storia della tipografia italiana nel secolo decimonono. 3. ed. rif. e di molto ampl. Firenze, Sansoni, 1953–62. v.1–7. il., facsims. (Contributi alla biblioteca bibliografica italica 3, 13, 16, 19, 22, 24, 25) **AA186**

Detailed bibliographical information, with descriptive notes and references to sources of rare 19th-century Italian books.

Private press books, ed. by Roderick Cave and Thomas Rae, 1959– . London, Private Libraries Assoc., 1960– . v.1– . Annual. **AA187**

Publisher varies.

"Attempts to include the work of all private presses printing in English, and the more important of those printing in other languages."—*Note* (v.5, 1963). Alphabetical by name of press, with the titles published during the year covered. Each year has an index by author, title, and press.

Ricci, Seymour de. The book collector's guide; a practical handbook of British and American bibliography. Philadelphia, Rosenbach Co., 1921. 649p. **AA188**

A guide for the collector and book buyer, covering the period from Chaucer to Swinburne and listing books which, because of rarity, market value, etc., were most sought after by collectors, including first editions, illustrated books, 17th- and 18th-century drama, and standard works. Arranged alphabetically by author, giving bibliographical description, prices at sales, notes, etc.

Vatican. Biblioteca Vaticana. The books published by the Vatican library, 1885–1947; an illustrated analytic catalogue. Vatican City, Apostolic Vatican Lib., 1947. livp., 183p. il. **AA189**

English version of *I libri editi dalla Biblioteca vaticana.* 1947.

Gives detailed descriptions of the books published by the Vatican. Excellent illustrations.

Historical children's books

Darton, Frederick Joseph Harvey. Children's books in England: five centuries of social life. [2d ed.] with introd. by Kathleen Lines. Cambridge, Univ. Pr., 1958. 367p. facsims. **AA190**

1st ed. 1932.

A scholarly survey covering the literature from the fables of the Middle Ages to the early 20th century. Devoted to printed works "produced ostensibly to give children spontaneous pleasure, not primarily to teach them . . . ." Thus schoolbooks are omitted.

This edition has corrected a few details in the text and added titles to the chapter bibliographies.

Muir, Percival Horace. English children's books 1600 to 1900. London, Batsford; N.Y., Praeger, [1954]. 256p. il. **AA191**

Supplements Darton's *Children's books in England.* Includes a much broader selection, but treatment is briefer. Excellent bibliographies, with notes and often annotations, accompany each chapter. Profusely illustrated with many reproductions of title pages. Includes index to authors, titles, and illustrations.

Gumuchian et Cie., *booksellers, Paris.* Les livres de l'enfance du XV° au XIX° siècle, préface de Paul Gavault. Paris, Gumuchian, [1931?]. 2v. il. **AA192**

v.1, Text, i.e., Bibliography of 6251 items, with full bibliographical description of each; v.2, 338 plates, containing a total of 1080 facsimiles of illustrations from books described in v.1, beautifully reproduced, many of them hand-colored.

Important both for the careful description of rare books and for the wealth of illustration. May be supplemented by two simpler lists issued by the same firm (Catalogues 15 and 18): (1) *100 noteworthy firsts in juvenile literature* (1932. 30p.), and (2) *500 early juveniles* (1933. 39p.).

Rosenbach, Abraham S. Wolf. Early American children's books. With bibliographical descriptions of the books in his private collection. Portland, Me., Southworth Pr., 1933. lixp., 354p. il. **AA193**

Includes Foreword by A. Edward Newton; Introduction; Early American children's books, p.3–287; Index of authors and titles; Index of printers and publishers; List of printers, publishers, and booksellers; Bibliography.

Printers' marks

Delalain, Paul Adolphe. Inventaire des marques d'imprimeurs et de libraires de la collection du Cercle de la Librairie. 2. éd. rev. et augm. Paris, Cercle de la Librairie, 1892. 355p. il. (Bibliothèque technique de la Cercle de la Librairie) **AA194**

Gives names, dates, and addresses of printers with descriptions of the marks and devices used by them in the various countries of Europe.

McKerrow, Ronald B. Printers' and publishers' devices in England and Scotland, 1485–1640. London, Bibliographical Soc., 1913. 216p. 65 double pl. **AA195**

Contains description and facsimiles of 428 devices, a dictionary of certain printers' names with information about transfers of devices, and five indexes of devices and compartments by: (1) sizes, (2) printers and booksellers, (3) mottoes, (4) initials of designers and engravers, (5) subjects.

Polain, Louis. Marques des imprimeurs et libraires en France au XV° siècle. Paris, Droz, 1926. 207p. il. (Documents typographiques du XV° siècle, t.1) **AA196**

Renouard, Philippe. Les marques typographiques parisiennes des XV° et XVI° siècles. Paris, Champion, 1926–28. 381p. il. (Revue des bibliothèques, suppl. 14–15) **AA197**

Illustrations and descriptions of the marks of Parisian printers.

Roberts, William. Printers' marks; a chapter in the history of typography. London, N.Y., Geo. Bell, 1893. 261p. il. **AA198**

A chronological account describing the marks of the early and important printers of Europe. Includes some modern examples, mostly from England. Contains more than 200 illustrations.

Silvestre, Louis Catherine. Marques typographiques. . . . Paris, Jannet, successeur de L. C. Silvestre, 1853; Impr. Renou, 1867. 2v. facsims. **AA199**

Subtitle: Recueil des monogrammes, chiffres, enseignes, emblèmes, devises, rébus et fleurons des libraires et imprimeurs qui ont exercé en France, depuis l'introduction de l'imprimerie, en 1470, jusqu'à la fin du seizième siècle: à ces marques sont jointes celles des libraires et imprimeurs qui pendant la même période ont publié, hors de France, des livres en langue française.

Watermarks

Briquet, Charles Moïse. Les filigranes. Dictionnaire historique des marques du papier dès leur apparition vers 1282 jusqu'en 1600, avec 39 figures dans le texte et 16,112 facsimilés. Paris, Picard, 1907. 4v. facsim. **AA200**
2. ed. Leipzig, Hiersemann, 1923. 4v.

The Briquet album; a miscellany on watermarks, supplementing Dr. Briquet's Les filigranes, by various paper scholars. Hilversum, Holland, Paper Publications Soc., 1952. 158p. il. (Monumenta chartae papyraceae historiam illustrantia, 2) **AA201**
"Indexes to Briquet's *Les filigranes* in German, English and Italian," p.125–54.

Auction records

American book-prices current, a record of literary properties sold at auction in the United States and in London, England . . . 1894/95– . N.Y., Amer. Book-Prices Current, 1895– . v.1– . Annual. **AA202**
Publisher varies.
Subtitle varies. Before v.64, 1958, included only records of sales held in the United States.
Contents: pt.1, Books, serials, etc.; pt.2, Autographs and manuscripts; pt.3, Broadsides; pt.4, Maps.
Arrangement and information given vary somewhat but usually include author, title, edition, place and date of publication, size, binding, condition, where sold, date of sale, catalog number of lot, and price. Includes materials of all periods and languages.

—— Indexes. 1916–22; 1923–32; 1933–40; 1941–45– . Quinquennial.

Book-auction records, a priced and annotated annual record of London [and other] book-auctions, June 1902– . London, N.Y., Henry Stevens, 1903– . v.1– . Quarterly, 1920–40; annual, 1941/42– . **AA203**
Publisher varies.
Subtitle varies. From v.12, Edinburgh, Glasgow, and Dublin sometimes included. From 1939/40, also includes principal New York auctions.
Entries are "exact reproductions, abbreviated, of the auctioneers' catalogue-descriptions," and include date of sale, number of lot, price, and name of buyer.
When issued quarterly, each number was arranged alphabetically by author, with an index in each volume. Annual volumes arranged alphabetically by author.

—— General index, 1902–12, 1912–23, 1924–33, 1934–43, 1944–48, 1948–58. London, Stevens, 1924–62. 6v.
Subtitle: Giving instant clues to the contents . . . and, incidentally, to anonymous authors, autographs, bibliophiles, binders, bindings, distinguished owners, editors, fore-edge paintings, holograph manuscripts, illustrators, notable presses, pseudonyms, translators, etc.

Book-prices current, Dec. 1886– . London, Sergeants Pr., 1888– . v.1– . Annual (Irregular). **AA204**
Publisher varies.
Subtitle: A record of the prices at which books have been sold at auction.
v.1–27, 1886–1913, arranged by date of sale; v.28– , 1914– , arranged alphabetically by author and some titles. Useful both as a record of market prices of secondhand books, and as a supplement to the various general and national bibliographies for titles and editions not noted in such bibliographies.

—— Index, 1887–96, 1897–1906, 1907–16. London, Stock, 1901–20. 3v.

McKay, George Leslie. American book auction catalogues, 1713–1934; a union list . . . with introd. by Clarence S. Brigham. N.Y., N.Y. Pub. Lib., 1937. 540p. facsims. **AA205**
A "list of some 10,000 auction catalogues . . . issued in what is now the United States, that list books, pamphlets, broadsides, newspapers, manuscripts, autographs and bookplates."—*Pref.* Arranged chronologically. Locates copies.

—— —— Supplement no.1–2. 1946–48. (Repr. from New York Public Library. Bull. 50:177–84. 1946; 52: 401–12. 1948)

PRINTING AND PUBLISHING
General works
Bibliography

Bigmore, Edward Clements and **Wyman, Charles William Henry.** A bibliography of printing, with notes and illustrations. London, Quaritch, 1880–86. 3v. il. (Repr. photo-offset: N.Y., P. C. Duschnes, 1945. 2v.) **AA206**
Arranged alphabetically by author, with some subject references and form headings. Biographical, historical, and descriptive annotations.

Lehmann-Haupt, Hellmut. One hundred books about bookmaking; a guide to the study and appreciation of printing. N.Y., Columbia Univ. Pr., 1949. 87p. **AA207**
Revised and enlarged edition of the author's *Fifty books about bookmaking* and *Seventy books about bookmaking*.
The titles are largely in English. Classified and annotated.

McMurtrie, Douglas Crawford. The invention of printing; a bibliography. Prep. as an activity of the Work Projects Administration (Illinois). Chicago Public Library Omnibus Project . . . section on printing bibliography, co-sponsored by the Chicago Club of Printing House Craftsmen. Chicago, Chicago Club of Printing House Craftsmen, 1942. 413p. **AA208**
Lists 3228 titles, of which 2026 are of separate publications, books or pamphlets. Copies are located in American and European libraries.
Includes a section of commemorative writings of more than 1000 items.

Periodicals

Ulrich, Carolyn Farquhar and **Küp, Karl.** Books and printing; a selected list of periodicals, 1800–1942. Woodstock, Vt., Wm. E. Rudge, 1943. 244p. **AA209**
An annotated and selected bibliography of periodicals classed under such headings as history of printing, printing types, design, layout and typography, illustration, paper, binding, publishing, book trade, collecting, bibliography, libraries, directories, societies, etc.

Directories

Adressbuch des deutschsprachigen Buchhandels, 1954– . Frankfurt am Main, Buchhändler-Vereinigung GMBH, 1954– . Annual (Irregular). **AA210**
Contents: Buchhandels-Adressbuch für die Bundesrepublik Deutschland und West-Berlin; Adressbuch des österreichi-

schen Buch- , Kunst- , Musikalien- und Zeitschriftenhandels; Schweizer Buchhandel Adressbuch; Verzeichnis des Buchhandels anderer Länder.

An extensive directory of book dealers in Germany, Austria, and Switzerland with less coverage for other nations.

American book trade directory; lists of publishers, booksellers, periodicals, trade organizations, wholesalers, etc. N.Y., Bowker, 1915– . Biennial (formerly triennial). **AA211**

Title varies: *American book trade manual,* 1915, 1919, 1922; *American book trade directory,* 1925– .

Coverage varies. 1963 includes: (1) Publishers in the United States (current and former); (2) Booksellers in the United States, Puerto Rico, and regions administered by the United States; (3) Book-trade information (organizations, trade periodicals and reference books, greeting-card publishers); (4) Book trade in Great Britain, the Republic of Ireland, and Canada; (5) International book trade.

American Library Association. Resources and Technical Services Division. International subscription agents. Chicago, Assoc., 1963. 84p. **AA212**

Compiled by a joint committee of the Serials and Acquisitions sections.

An alphabetical list of 187 foreign agents, giving address and description of service for each. Geographical index included.

Cassell's Directory of publishing in Great Britain, the Commonwealth and Ireland, 1960–61. London, Cassell, 1960. 395p. **AA213**

Gives information for the Commonwealth similar to that provided for the United States in the *Literary market place* (AA217), i.e., lists of publishers, agents, literary services, book clubs, prizes, etc.

Directory of dealers in secondhand and antiquarian books in the British Isles. [5th ed.] 1960–62. London, Sheppard Pr., [1961]. 224p. il. **AA214**

[1st ed.], 1951/52, pub. 1951.

Contains an alphabetical list of dealers, geographical index, specialty index, and permanent want-list index. Includes dealers in Australia, New Zealand, Southern and Western Africa, and Hong Kong.

Gorokhoff, Boris I. Publishing in the U.S.S.R. [Bloomington, Ind., 1959]. 306p. (Indiana University publs. Slavic and East European ser., v.19) (Distr. by Indiana Univ. Pr.) **AA215**

Surveys the Soviet publishing network for books, magazines, and newspapers, including documentation services and matters of copyright and censorship. Emphasizes science and technology. Extensive statistical appendix.

For companion volume on Soviet libraries *see* AB70.

Guía de editores y de libreros de España, 1961. Madrid, Inst. Nacional del Libro Español, 1961. 744p. **AA216**

Publishers and bookstores are separately listed.

Literary market place, 1940– . The business directory of American book publishing. N.Y., Bowker, 1940– . Annual. (1964–65) **AA217**

Subtitle varies.

A useful and usable directory of organizations, periodicals, publishers, etc., which might be helpful in the placing, promotion, and advertising of literary property. Lists officers and key personnel. Classified under such headings as: agents, artists and art services, associations, book clubs, book publishers, book reviewers, columnists and commentators, editorial services, employment agencies, literary prizes and awards, magazines, newspapers and news services, radio and television, and many others.

—— The book industry telephone directory: names and numbers, 1952– . Supplement to the Literary market place, 1952– . Annual. **AA218**

Title varies: *Book industry register,* 1952/53–1959/60.

An alphabetical listing of the names found in the matching annual volume of *LMP.* Gives name, firm, address, telephone number, and code number of the section of *LMP* in which the name is listed.

Publishers' international year book: world directory of book publishers. 1960/1961– . London, Alexander P. Wales, 1960– . v.1– . **AA219**

In two sections: (1) publishers, and (2) booksellers, each arranged alphabetically by country. In the 2d edition, 1962, pt.1, Publishers, covers 69 countries; pt.2, Booksellers, 62 countries.

Répertoire des éditeurs et liste des collections. Paris, Cercle de la Librairie, 1963. 294p. Loose-leaf. **AA220**

Pub. irregularly.

Extensive lists of: French publishers and noncommercial organizations which publish; book dealers; foreign publishers who distribute in France; publishers' union committees, etc.

The *Liste des collections* is an index to some 3000 series titles, with indication of the issuing publisher.

Sijthoff's Adresboek voor den Nederlandse Boekhandel en aanverwante vakken. Tevens bevattend een opgave van de in Nederland verschijnende nieuwsbladen en tijdschriften. Leiden, Sijthoff, 1855– . v.1– . Annual. **AA221**

Title and publisher vary.

Suspended 1944–46.

Dictionaries and encyclopedias

Lexikon des gesamten Buchwesens, hrsg. von Karl Löffler u. Joachim Kirchner unter Mitwirkung von Wilhelm Olbrich. Leipzig, Hiersemann, 1935–37. 3v. **AA222**

An encyclopedia of concise articles, many with bibliographical references, on a great variety of subjects connected with books and the book arts, e.g., printers and printing, publishing, illustration, places of printing, organizations and societies, manuscripts, etc. Contains many biographies.

Lexikon des Buchwesens, hrsg. von Joachim Kirchner. Stuttgart, Hiersemann, 1952–56. 4v. il. **AA223**

Based on the preceding entry, but in somewhat briefer form.

v.1–2 include encyclopedic articles on subjects connected with the book, with many biographies. v.3–4 contain plates showing illustrations, facsimiles of title pages, examples of book binding, printing presses, libraries, etc.

Nordisk Leksikon for Bogvaesen, redg. af Esli Dansten, Lauritz Nielsen, og Palle Birkelund. København, Nyt Nordisk Forlag Arnold Busck; Oslo, Dreyers Forlag; Stockholm, Förlaget Biblioteksböcker, 1949–57. v.1–2(7–12). (In progress) **AA224**

v.1, A–Kogebøger (pub. in parts, Hft.1–6); v.2 (incompl.), L–Sohlman (Hft.7–12).

Signed articles, some of fair length, with bibliographies, on all phases of the book industry: bookmaking, bibliography, illustration, etc. Includes many biographies.

Terms

Allen, Edward Monington. Harper's Dictionary of the graphic arts. [1st ed.] N.Y., Harper, 1963. 295p. **AA225**

More than 6500 basic terms used in the graphic arts industries with definitions and explanations, including descriptions of methods and processes, uses and purposes of tools, etc.

American Paper and Pulp Association. The dictionary of paper, including pulps, boards, paper properties and related papermaking terms. 2d ed. N.Y., Assoc., 1951. 393p. **AA226**

1st ed. 1940.

Definitions, given in nontechnical language, are full and definite.

Bookman's glossary. 4th ed., rev. and enl. by Mary C. Turner. N.Y., Bowker, 1961. 212p. **AA227**

1st ed. 1925.

Basically American but including some common British variations. Includes an alphabetical listing of words and terms used in the production and distribution of books, new and old; names of persons, such as famous book designers, binders, papermakers, etc. Appendixes give: Foreign book-trade terms; Proofreaders' marks; Selected reading list.

Collins, Frederick Howard. Authors' and printers' dictionary. 10th ed. rev. London, Oxford Univ. Pr., 1956. 442p. **AA228**

Subtitle: A guide for authors, editors, printers, correctors of the press, compositors and typists.

A dictionary of proper names, abbreviations, foreign words and phrases, and common words frequently misspelled or misused with definitions and indication of correct or preferred usage, etc.

Glaister, Geoffrey Ashall. Glossary of the book: terms used in paper-making, printing, bookbinding and publishing, with notes on illuminated manuscripts, bibliophiles, private presses, and printing societies. Including illustrations and translated extracts from Grafisk uppslagsbok (Esselte, Stockholm). London, Allen & Unwin, 1960. 484p. il. **AA229**

Pub. in U.S. by World (Cleveland, Ohio) as *An encyclopedia of the book*. 1960. 484p. il.

An encyclopedic dictionary written primarily from the British point of view but international in coverage. Authoritative, well edited, and well illustrated.

Hertzberger, Menno. Dictionnaire à l'usage de la librairie ancienne pour les langues française, anglaise, allemande, suédoise, danoise, italienne, espagnole, hollandaise. Paris, Internat. League of Antiquarian Booksellers, 1956. 190p. **AA230**

Title also in English: *Dictionary for the antiquarian book-trade*.

Keyed to the French word, with indexes in each of the other languages.

Kenneison, W. C. and **Spilman, A. J. B.** Dictionary of printing, papermaking and bookbinding. London, Newnes, 1963. 215p. il. **AA231**

Explanatory definitions of terms.

Labarre, E. J. Dictionary and encyclopaedia of paper and paper-making, with equivalents of the technical terms in French, German, Dutch, Italian, Spanish and Swedish. 2d ed. rev. and enl. London, Oxford Univ. Pr., 1952. 488p. il. **AA232**

1st ed. 1937.

A detailed dictionary of technical terms with, in many cases, encyclopedic articles and descriptions, and with foreign-language equivalents. Indexes in each language.

✔ **Orne, Jerrold.** The language of the foreign book trade; abbreviations, terms, phrases. 2d ed. Chicago, Amer. Lib. Assoc., 1962. 213p. **AA233**

1st ed. 1949. The new edition has been expanded to include 16,000 definitions from 11 languages, arranged by language with English equivalent supplied for each, compared with 6000 definitions from 8 languages in the earlier work.

Schlemminger, Johann. Fachwörterbuch des Buchwesens, deutsch, englisch, französisch; . . . aus Buchhandel, Verlag, Buchgewerbe, Graphik und dem Gesamtgebiet des Buchwesens. 2. wesentlich erw. Aufl. Darmstadt, Stoytscheff, 1954. 367p. **AA234**

1st edition, 1946, had title *Buch-Fachwörterbuch; deutsch, englisch, französisch*.

✔ **Thompson, Anthony.** Vocabularium bibliothecarii. 2d ed. English, French, German, Spanish, Russian. Collaborator for Russian, E. I. Shamurin; collaborator for Spanish, Domingo Buonocore. Paris, UNESCO, 1962 [i.e., 1963?]. 627p. **AA235**

Classified arrangement with index in English language. Gives equivalents only.

For full information *see* AB24.

Handbooks

Melcher, Daniel and **Larrick, Nancy.** Printing and promotion handbook; how to plan, produce, and use printing, advertising, and direct mail. 2d ed. N.Y., McGraw-Hill, 1956. 438p. il. **AA236**

An alphabetically arranged handbook for persons, including beginners, who buy printing and direct-mail services, plan advertising, etc.

History

Binns, Norman E. An introduction to historical bibliography. 2d ed. rev. and enl. . . . London, Assoc. of Assist. Librarians, 1962. 387p. il. **AA237**

1st ed. 1953.

A history of bookmaking, from the manuscript book to the printed word, in various countries, with additional chapters on publishing and bookselling, copyright, and development of book-trade bibliography. Bibliographies at the end of each chapter; index.

Fumagalli, Giuseppe. Lexicon typographicum Italiae. Dictionnaire géographique d'Italie pour servir à l'histoire de l'imprimerie dans ce pays. . . . Florence, Olschki, 1905. 587p. il. **AA238**

Subtitle: Contenant 1e l'indication de toutes les localités d'Italie géographique et politique, où l'imprimerie a été introduite jusqu'à nos jours, avec la synonymie latine, française, etc., et celle des lieux supposés d'impression; 2e des notices bibliographiques sur les éditions principes de chaque ville, bourg, chateau, etc., et sur les faits les plus remarquables se rapportant à l'histoire de l'art typographique dans ces localités; 3e des notices biographiques sur les plus célèbres imprimeurs italiens; 4e des notices statistiques sur l'état présent de l'imprimerie en Italie; 5e des renseignements historiques sur les arts auxiliaires de l'imprimerie; lithographie, gravure, papeterie, fabrication des encres, des presses, des caractères, etc.

—— —— Giunte e correzioni. Additions et corrections. Florence, Olschki, 1939. 84p.

Hunter, Dard. Papermaking; the history and technique of an ancient craft. 2d ed. rev. and enl. N.Y., Knopf, 1947. 611p. **AA239**

1st ed. 1943.

Chronology of papermaking, paper, and the use of paper. 2700 B.C.–A.D. 1945, p.463–584; Bibliography, p.585–602.

Lehmann-Haupt, Hellmut [and others]. The book in America; a history of the making and selling of books in the United States. 2d [rev. and enl. American] ed. N.Y., Bowker, 1951. 493p. (Repr. 1964) **AA240**

1st American ed. 1939. Originally published in Leipzig as: *Das amerikanische Buchwesen*. 1937.

Bibliography, p.422–66.

A survey history of book production and distribution in the United States from 1638 to mid-twentieth century.

McMurtrie, Douglas Crawford. The book; the story of printing and bookmaking. [3d rev. ed.] N.Y., Oxford Univ. Pr., 1943. 676p. il.   **AA241**

The history of bookmaking, printing, and illustration from early to modern times. Bibliography, p.603–46.

Updike, Daniel Berkeley. Printing types, their history, forms, and use; a study in survivals. [3d ed.] Cambridge, Mass., Belknap Pr., 1962. 2v. il., facsims.   **AA242**

1st ed. 1922; 2d ed. 1937.

A richly illustrated historical survey with bibliographical references.

Wroth, Lawrence Counselman. A history of the printed book, being the third number of the Dolphin. N.Y., Limited Eds. Club, 1938. 507p. il.   **AA243**

A well-illustrated history with references at the ends of chapters.

Biography

Ascarelli, Fernanda. La tipografia cinquecentina italiana. Firenze, Sansoni Antiquariato, 1953. 259p. il. (Contributi alla Biblioteca bibliografica italica. 1)   **AA244**

Intended to cover all printers active in Italy up to and including 1600. Arrangement is geographical by region, then alphabetical by city, and chronological by printer. Adequate indexes.

Bibliographical Society, London. [Dictionaries of printers and booksellers in England, Scotland and Ireland]. London, Soc., 1905–32. 5v.   **AA245**

Century of the English book trade . . . 1457–1557, by E. Gordon Duff. 1905. 200p.; *Dictionary of printers and booksellers in England, Scotland and Ireland and of foreign printers of English books, 1557–1640*, by R. B. McKerrow. 1910. 346p.; *Dictionary of the printers who were at work in England, Scotland and Ireland, from 1641 to 1667*, by H. R. Plomer. 1907. 199p.; *Dictionary of the printers and booksellers who were at work in England, Scotland and Ireland from 1668 to 1725*, by H. R. Plomer. 1922. 342p.; *Dictionary of the printers and booksellers who were at work in England, Scotland and Ireland from 1726 to 1775;* those in England by H. R. Plomer, Scotland by G. H. Bushnell, Ireland by E. R. McC. Dix. 1932. 432p.

Good, short biographies, with bibliographies. The different volumes in the series contain indexes as follows: **1457–1557,** Index of Christian names, Index of London signs, Chronological index of foreign places, printers and stationers; **1557–1640,** Indexes of (1) London signs, (2) London addresses, (3) Places other than London; **1668–1725,** Index of printers and places to the two volumes, 1641–67 and 1668–1725; **1726–75,** Indexes of (1) Places in England, Wales other than London, (2) Places in Scotland other than Edinburgh, (3) Places in Ireland, (4) Places abroad; Circulating libraries in England and Scotland arranged in order of date.

Lepreux, Georges. Gallia typographica; ou, Répertoire biographique et chronologique de tous les imprimeurs de France depuis les origines de l'imprimerie jusqu'à la Révolution. Paris, Champion, 1909–14. 5v. (Revue des bibliothèques. Suppl.)   **AA246**

As originally planned, to consist of 20v. and a general index.

In two series: (1) Série parisienne, and (2) Série départmentale.

Contents: Série parisienne, t.1, Livre d'or des imprimeurs du roi; Série départmentale: t.1, Flandre, Artois, Picardie; t.2, Champagne et Barrois; t.3, Normandie (in 2v.); t.4, Bretagne.

A monumental work, containing full biographies with detailed bibliographical references. Each volume is in two parts: (1) biographies, and (2) documents.

Renouard, Philippe. Imprimeurs parisiens, libraires, fondeurs de caractères et correcteurs d'imprimerie, depuis l'introduction de l'imprimerie à Paris (1470) jusqu'à la fin du XVIe siècle. Leurs adresses, marques, enseignes, dates d'exercice. Notes sur leurs familles, leurs alliances et leur descendance. Paris, Claudin, 1898. 480p. il.   **AA247**

Contents: Libraires, imprimeurs, correcteurs et fondeurs de caractères; Auteurs qui vendaient eux-mêmes leurs ouvrages; Table des adresses classées par rues; Table des enseignes; Liste chronologique; Table des noms de personnes.

A new edition, with considerable additional material and new references to sources of information, was published in the *Revue des bibliothèques*, v.32–44. 1922–34.

Who's who in graphic art; an illustrated book of reference to the world's leading graphic designers, illustrators, typographers and cartoonists. Ed. by Walter Amstutz. 1st ed. Zurich, Amstutz & Herdeg Graphis Pr., 1962. 586p., lxviip. il.   **AA248**

Text in English, French, and German.

Contains material about 414 artists from 37 countries, arranged by country with an introductory essay for each country. Each artist is allotted a full page, giving his photograph, signature, address, and a brief biographical sketch, the fields in which he specializes, bibliography, and approximately 10 illustrations of his work. Indexes of artists arranged alphabetically, by country, and by special field.

Copyright

Nicholson, Margaret. A manual of copyright practice for writers, publishers, and agents. 2d ed. N.Y., Oxford Univ. Pr., 1956. 273p.   **AA249**

1st ed. 1945.

A handbook for the layman on various phases of copyright practice. Includes such topics as how to copyright literary property, author's rights, duration of copyright, renewals, fees, etc. The appendix gives the text of the Universal Copyright Convention, as well as the Copyright Law of the United States and the Berne Convention.

United Nations Educational, Scientific and Cultural Organization. Copyright laws and treaties of the world. Wash., UNESCO and the Bureau of Nat. Affairs, 1956– . Loose-leaf.   **AA250**

Kept current by yearly supplements.

Presents, either in the original English text or in specially prepared English translations, the laws and regulations of some 119 states and territories.

In four parts: I, States and multilateral copyright conventions, arranged alphabetically. For each state gives: (1) Information primarily domestic in scope; (2) Information primarily international in scope. II, Territories. III, Multilateral conventions, giving for each convention: the text of the Convention; the status of adherences to the Convention; and the states among which the Convention or portions thereof are applicable. IV, Rome Convention rights in two sections: (1) States, giving an index to national legislation; (2) Multilateral conventions, giving the Rome Convention and regional conventions.

Copy preparation

See also Von Ostermann, *Manual of foreign languages,* BC2.

Chicago. University. Press. A manual of style containing typographical and other rules for authors, printers, and publishers, recommended by the University of Chicago Press, together with specimens of type. [11th ed.] Chicago, Univ. of Chicago Pr., 1949. 497p.   **AA251**

A clearly written and much used manual. Frequently reprinted.

Lasky, Joseph. Proofreading and copy-preparation; a textbook for the graphic arts industry. [Latest revision] N.Y., Mentor Pr., 1954. 656p. il. **AA252**

1st ed. 1941.

A useful, detailed handbook containing, besides chapters on the practical work of proofreading and preparation of copy, lists of compounds, abbreviations, proper syllabication of words, including Latin, Spanish, and French words, etc.

U.S. Government Printing Office. Style manual. Rev. ed. Wash., Govt. Prt. Off., 1959. 496p. **AA253**

A useful and extensive manual giving the practices of the Government Printing Office on copy preparation, with rules for capitalization, punctuation, abbreviations, etc., and, on p.375–476, information on foreign languages, including alphabets, with pronunciation, special rules, lists of numbers, etc.

——— ——— Word division; supplement to Government Printing Office style manual. 6th ed. 1962. 190p. **AA254**

This edition includes many new words, particularly scientific and technical words. Gives rules of word division and lists the syllabication of several thousand words.

Words into type, new rev. ed. based on studies by Marjorie E. Skillin, Robert M. Gay, and other authorities. N.Y., Appleton, 1964. 596p. **AA255**

1st ed. 1948.

A guide in the preparation of manuscripts for writers, editors, proofreaders, and printers.

Includes sections on preparation of the manuscript; techniques for copy and proof; typography and illustration; printing style; grammar; and use of words.

Bookbinding

Banister, Manly Miles. Pictorial manual of bookbinding. N.Y., Ronald, 1958. 40p. il. **AA256**

A practical manual showing techniques and processes by drawings and photographs.

Clough, Eric A. Bookbinding for librarians. London, Assoc. of Assist. Librarians, 1957. 204p. **AA257**

A handbook on bookbinding with a glossary and a select bibliography.

Cockerell, Douglas. Bookbinding, and the care of books: a text-book for bookbinders and librarians; with drawings by Noel Rooke and other illustrations. 5th ed. London, Pitman, 1953. 345p. il. **AA258**

1st ed. 1902; 3d ed. 1911; 4th ed. 1948.

Diehl, Edith. Bookbinding, its background and technique. N.Y., Rinehart, 1946. 2v. il. **AA259**

v.1 gives the history from the Middle Ages to modern times; discusses national styles and specialties, e.g., decoration of book edges, book covers and girdle books, etc.; and includes a bibliography, p.205–19; a glossary, p.223–34; and a section of 91 plates of illustrations of historical bindings. v.2 is devoted to techniques, illustrated with line drawings.

A standard work in its field.

Feipel, Louis Nicholas and **Browning, Earl W.** Library binding manual, prep. under the direction of the Joint Committee of the A.L.A. and L.B.I. Chicago, Amer. Lib. Assoc., 1951. 74p. il. **AA260**

An elementary manual on the binding and preservation of printed materials in libraries. Glossary, p.62–72; Sources and authorities, p.73–74.

Johnson, Pauline. Creative bookbinding. Seattle, Univ. of Wash. Pr., 1963. 263p. il. **AA261**

A practical introduction to bookbinding, including chapters on book design; the parts of a book; materials, tools, and equipment; working procedures; simple constructions and binding procedures; decorated papers; leather; book repair; supply sources; bibliography. Well illustrated.

Library Binding Institute. Library binding handbook. Boston, 1963. 49p. il. **AA262**

A brief manual of recommendations and practices and the text of the "Library Binding Institute Standard for Library Binding."

Lydenberg, Harry M. and **Archer, John.** The care and repair of books. Rev. by John Alden. N.Y., Bowker, 1960. 122p. **AA263**

"4th rev. ed."

Bibliography, p.101–13.

A practical handbook.

Book illustration

Bolton, Theodore. American book illustrators; bibliographic check lists of 123 artists. N.Y., Bowker, 1938. 290p. **AA264**

Lists, under the name of the illustrator, the books illustrated by him, and attempts also to note the magazine appearance of the illustrations whenever possible. "Planned as a companion volume to Merle Johnson's *American first editions*" (AA184).

SELECTION OF BOOKS

❧ Book selection in a library must be geared to the interests and needs of the community it serves, whether it be a small town, rural area, industrial center, school, college, university, or business concern. Demands are as varied as the interests of people, and many types of book selection aids are needed.

In special fields, many of the cyclopedias, histories, bibliographies, and manuals contain material of first importance for the right choice of books, either for purchase or for special use. *Living with books,* by Helen E. Haines (2d ed. N.Y., Columbia Univ. Pr., 1950), discusses principles and practices of book selection by libraries and comments on many guides to selection.

The following list is a selection of general guides which, in purpose of selection, annotation, technical excellence in cataloging and classification, or special indexing, have reference as well as advisory value.

Guides

A.L.A. catalog, 1926; an annotated basic list of 10,000 books; ed. by Isabella M. Cooper. Chicago, Amer. Lib. Assoc., 1926. 1295p. **AA265**

History: 1st *A.L.A. catalog,* 1893; 2d, 1904; Supplements, 1904–11, ed. by Elva L. Bascom, and 1912–21, ed. by May Massee.

A classed list, arranged in the main by Dewey Decimal Classification, giving, for each book, usual bibliographical information, Library of Congress card number, and an annotation to indicate its scope and value. Separate lists for biography and fiction and a list of children's books.

——— 1926–1931; 1932–1936; 1937–1941, ed. by Marion Horton; 1942–1949, ed. by Florence Boochever, assisted by Minna H. Breuer. Chicago, Amer. Lib. Assoc., 1933–52. 4v.

Supplements to the basic list, the first listing approximately

3000 titles; the second and third, 4000 titles each; the fourth, 4500 titles.

Dickinson, Asa Don. The world's best books, Homer to Hemingway; 3000 books of 3000 years, 1050 B.C. to 1950 A.D. selected on the basis of a consensus of expert opinion. N.Y., Wilson, 1953. 484p.   **AA266**

An alphabetical list which is "a unification, a condensation and a revision of, as well as an addition to, its four predecessors." Contains notes about each author and brief description or evaluation of each book. Includes a chronological list and a list classified by subject or literary form.

Earlier works were: *1000 best books; Best books of our time; Best books of the decade 1926–35; Best books of the decade 1936–45.*

Hackett, Alice Payne. 60 years of best sellers, 1895–1955. N.Y., Bowker, 1956. 260p.   **AA267**

Earlier edition, 1945, called *Fifty years of best sellers, 1895–1945.*

Includes discussions of best sellers, and of best sellers in various subject fields, with lists of best sellers arranged by number of copies sold, by subject, and by year.

Have you read 100 great books? N.Y., Jasper Lee Co., 1950. 144p.   **AA268**

1st ed. 1946.

Lists of great books compiled by well-known persons, libraries, and schools, with a cumulated alphabetical list of 1500 great books. Also included are some excerpts from well-known works and a variety of miscellaneous quotations from and about books.

Hoffman, Hester Rosalyn. The reader's adviser: an annotated guide to the best in print in literature, biographies, dictionaries, encyclopedias, Bibles, classics, drama, poetry, fiction, science, philosophy, travel, history. 10th ed. rev. and enl. N.Y., Bowker, 1964. 1292p.   **AA269**

1st ed. 1921; 9th ed. 1960.

Title varies: 1921–41, *Bookman's manual;* 1948–58, *Bessie Graham's Bookman's manual;* 1960, *Reader's adviser and bookman's manual.*

Designed primarily for the bookseller and the librarian. This new edition continues to cover general works and emphasize the humanities but has enlarged the sections on natural and social sciences. The chapter on Bibles has been greatly expanded, and a new section on religions of mankind has been added.

An up-to-date, standard work useful in any library.

Regis, *Sister.* The Catholic bookman's guide; a critical evaluation of Catholic literature. Contributors: Vernon J. Burke [and others]. 1st ed. N.Y., Hawthorn, 1962. 638p.   **AA270**

An annotated, classified bibliography covering: Sources and evaluation; Religion; Philosophy and psychology; Literature; Social sciences.

Sonnenschein, William Swan. Best books; a readers' guide and literary reference book, being a contribution towards systematic bibliography. 3d ed. (entirely rewritten). London, Routledge, 1910–35. 6v. paged continuously, 3760p.   **AA271**

1st ed. 1887; 2d ed. 1891; supplement to 2d ed. entitled *Reader's guide,* 1895.

A very comprehensive list, no longer current.

Pt.1: classes A, Theology; B, Mythology and folklore; C, Philosophy. Pt.2: classes D, Society; E, Geography. Pt.3: classes F, History and historical biography; G, Archaeology and historical collaterals. Pt.4: classes H, Natural science, H*, Medicine and surgery; I, Arts and trades. Pt.5: class K, Literature and philology. Pt.6: Authors, titles, and subjects index; a synopsis of classification; list of British publishers, learned societies, etc.

Standard catalog for public libraries. 4th ed. 1958; a classified and annotated list of 7610 non-fiction books recommended for public and college libraries, with a full analytical index. Comp. by Dorothy Herbert West and Estelle A. Fidell. N.Y., Wilson, 1959. 1349p.   **AA272**

[1st] ed. 1934; [2d] ed. 1940; [3d] ed. 1949.

The present edition is a more highly selective catalog, listing 7610 books as compared with 12,300 titles in the 1949 edition. Arranged in three parts: pt.1, classified catalog, arranged by the Dewey Decimal Classification; pt.2, author, title, subject, and analytical index; pt.3, directory of publishers. Recommended titles are starred. A carefully selected list with well-chosen annotations, quoting source. The most useful guide to selection for medium-sized public libraries.

——— 1959–63. N.Y., Wilson, 1964. 526p.

A cumulative supplement, adding 2820 books.

Kept up to date by annual supplements.

Current

The booklist and Subscription books bulletin. 1905– . Chicago, Amer. Lib. Assoc., 1905– . v.1– . Semimonthly (monthly in August).   **AA273**

The booklist and the *Subscription books bulletin* were combined with v.53, no.1, Sept.1, 1956.

The Booklist section is a selected, annotated list of recent publications recommended especially for small and medium-sized libraries. Arranged by broad classes, fiction, books for young adults, children's books, new editions and series, U.S. government publications, pamphlets and paperbacks. Complete bibliographical information is given for each entry, including price. Annotations describe, evaluate, and indicate the kind of library for which the book is recommended.

The reviews of the Subscription Books Committee precede the Booklist section but are not paged separately. The annual index lists the subscription book titles in a preliminary section.

For cumulations *see Subscription books bulletin reviews* (AA309a).

British book news; a guide to book selection. London, British Council, 1940– . Monthly.   **AA274**

A useful, selective, annotated list of "best books" arranged according to the Dewey Decimal Classification. Each number has an index, and there is a separate cumulation of author and title indexes for the year. Annual issues, 1940–50.

Title varies: no.1–14, *A selection of recent books published in Great Britain;* no.15– , *British book news.*

Bulletin critique du livre français. Paris, Assoc. pour la Diffusion de la Pensée Française, 1945– . v.1– . Monthly.   **AA275**

Publisher varies.

A selected list of books in all subject fields published in France, with descriptive annotations. Also lists the contents of issues of leading periodicals. The index of authors cumulates annually.

Frankfurt am Main. Deutsche Bibliothek. Deutsche Bibliographie; das deutsche Buch; Auswahl wichtiger Neuerscheinungen. 1950– . Frankfurt/M., Buchhändler-Vereinigung, 1950– . Bimonthly.   **AA276**

Title varies: 1950–54, no.5, *Das deutsche Buch; Neuerscheinungen der deutschen Verlage.*

Edited by the Deutsche Bibliothek. A selective, classified list, with author index, of new German publications, including annotations.

Índice cultural español. Index culturel espagnol. Madrid, Directeur Générale des Relations Culturelles, 1946– . Monthly.   **AA277**

Also published in English: *Spanish cultural index.*

Contains reviews of selected books and periodical articles and gives contents of some important journals published in Spain. Covers all subject fields.

Libri e riviste d'Italia; rassegna bibliografica mensile. Roma, Centro di Documentazione, 1950– . Monthly.

AA278

Title and publisher vary.

A selected list of current Italian publications covering all subject fields, with fairly long reviews. Indexes of subjects and authors cumulate annually.

Also published in English, French, German, Italian, and Spanish. English edition: *Italian books and periodicals*.

Books for college students

Bertalan, Frank J. Books for junior colleges; a list of 4000 books, periodicals, films, and filmstrips. Chicago, Amer. Lib. Assoc., 1954. 321p. **AA279**

Compiled from lists submitted by junior college librarians on a basis of frequency of nomination. Classified arrangement, with an index (p.244–321) by author and subject. No annotations.

Clapp, Jane. College textbooks. N.Y., Scarecrow, 1960. 1096p. **AA280**

Subtitle: A classified listing of 16,000 textbooks used in 60 colleges, coded to show most frequently used texts and texts used in general courses, and in several departments of instruction.

Committee on College Reading. Good reading, ed. by J. Sherwood Weber. 19th ed. N.Y., New Amer. Lib., [1964]. 285p. (Mentor books) **AA281**

1st ed. 1933.

Sponsored by the College English Association; endorsed by the Adult Education Association of the U.S.A., the American Library Association, and the National Council of Teachers of English.

An annotated list of about 2000 titles arranged by subject areas. Gives author, title, editions, and price. A very useful, up-to-date compilation moderately priced. Revised about every four years.

Grace, *Sister* **Melania** and **Peterson, Gilbert C.** Books for Catholic colleges; a supplement to Shaw's List of books for college libraries; comp. under the auspices of the Catholic Library Association. Chicago, Amer. Lib. Assoc., 1948. 134p. **AA282**

—— —— Supplement 1948–1949, 1950–1952, 1953–1955. Chicago, Amer. Lib. Assoc., 1950–56. 3v.

A supplement to Charles B. Shaw's *List of books for college libraries* (Chicago, Amer. Lib. Assoc., 1931); Supplement, 1931–38 (1940). The Shaw list is now much out of date, but a new edition is in preparation.

Harvard University. Library. Lamont Library. Catalogue, prep. by Philip J. McNiff. Cambridge, Harvard Univ. Pr., 1953. 562p. **AA283**

"The Lamont Library, opened in January 1949, contains a live, working collection of books selected to serve the required and recommended course reading needs of Harvard undergraduates, in addition to a good general collection of books that it makes readily available."—*Introd.*

The *Catalogue* contains more than 39,000 entries arranged by a classification scheme, the table of contents serving as a synopsis of the scheme. It is a finding list, giving only very brief bibliographical information. Author index.

Trinkner, Charles L. Basic books for junior college libraries: 20,000 vital titles . . . Northport, Ala., Colonial Pr., [1963]. 783p. **AA284**

A list of in-print books, prepared by 225 librarian coordinators and 2600 subject specialists. Arranged in four parts: pt.1, basic nonfictional works arranged by subject (p.16–689); pt.2, recommended literary works for junior colleges (p.690–709); pt.3, basic reference collection of 500 titles (p.710–20); pt.4, list of 150 recommended periodicals (p.721–25).

Appendix includes list of coordinating librarians, Dewey Classification index, and a directory of publishers.

Entries are brief, giving only author, short title, date, price, and publisher. No annotations and no author index. May be useful as an acquisitions tool but limited as a guide to selection.

Current

Choice: books for college libraries. A publication of the Association of College and Research Libraries, a division of the American Library Association. Middletown, Conn., Olin Lib., Wesleyan Univ., 1964– . v.1– . Monthly (except bimonthly, July-Aug.) **AA285**

A book review journal planned to assist college libraries in the selection of current books. Annotations are written (but not signed) by a large panel of consultants.

Books for children and young people

American Library Association. A basic book collection for elementary grades. 7th ed., comp. by Miriam Snow Mathes [and others]. Chicago, Assoc., 1960. 136p.

AA286

1st ed. 1922.

A classified and annotated list of books and magazines for a small elementary school library. Each title graded, kindergarten through eighth grade, and priced.

—— A basic book collection for junior high schools. 3d ed., ed. by Margaret V. Spengler [and others]. Chicago, Assoc., 1960. 136p. **AA287**

1st ed. 1950.

A classified and annotated list of books and magazines recommended as first purchases in small and medium-sized junior high school libraries.

Includes author, title, and subject index.

—— A basic book collection for high schools. 7th ed., comp. by Eileen F. Noonan [and others]. Chicago, Assoc., 1963. 184p. **AA288**

1st ed. 1924.

Classified and annotated list of about 1400 books and 70 periodicals, selected as a buying guide for high schools and public libraries. Includes author, title, and subject index.

Children's catalog; a catalog of 3310 selected books for public and school libraries . . . ed. by Dorothy Herbert West and Rachel Shor. 10th ed. N.Y., Wilson, 1961. 915p. **AA289**

1st ed. 1909; 2d ed. 1916–17; 9th ed. 1956.

The most comprehensive bibliography in its field. Arranged in four parts: pt.1, classified catalog, arranged by Dewey Decimal Classification, giving full bibliographic information and annotations; pt.2, author, title, subject, and analytical index; pt.3, list by grades; pt.4, directory of publishers. Titles especially recommended are starred.

Kept up to date by annual supplements.

Eakin, Mary K. and **Merritt, Eleanor.** Subject index to books for primary grades. 2d ed. Chicago, Amer. Lib. Assoc., 1961. 167p. **AA289a**

1st ed., 1943, by Eloise Rue.

This completely revised edition indexes nearly 1000 in-print books geared to today's curriculum.

Eakin, Mary K. Subject index to books for intermediate grades. 3d ed. Chicago, Amer. Lib. Assoc., 1963. 308p.

AA290

2d ed., 1950, by Eloise Rue.

1800 text and trade books commonly used throughout the country are analyzed under approximately 4000 subject headings. Each entry is graded and gives complete source information, so that it is easy to locate quickly specific materials at specific grade levels. Practical also for setting up units of study.

Larrick, Nancy. A parent's guide to children's reading. Rev. ed. Garden City, N.Y., Doubleday, [1964]. 312p. il. **AA291**

1st ed. 1958.

Contains information on reading guidance; using the public and school library; buying books for children. Includes list of book selection aids and an annotated list by subject of books and magazines for children, p.211–93. An excellent guide available in hard cover and paperback.

National Council of Teachers of English. Committee on Senior High School Book List. Books for you; a reading list for senior high school students. N.Y., Washington Square, [1964]. 344p. il. **AA291a**

1st ed. 1945.

This new edition, comprising more than 2000 titles, has retained about half of the titles from the 1959 edition and the 1961 supplement, and added about 900 new ones.

Arranged in 45 categories; gives author, title, publisher, and date. Titles starred represent books "mature in content," and those marked with dagger books of "marked literary quality."

Contains author and title indexes.

Smith, Irene. A history of the Newbery and Caldecott medals. N.Y., Viking, [1957]. 140p. il. **AA292**

A narrative account including lists of medal winners and of runners-up.

Standard catalog for high school libraries. 8th ed. A selected catalog of 4,212 books, . . . ed. by Dorothy Herbert West, Estelle A. Fidell and Rachel Shor. N.Y., Wilson, 1962. 1257p. (Standard catalog ser.) **AA293**

1st ed. 1926–28; 2d ed. 1932; revised every 5 years.

In three parts: pt.1, classified catalog, arranged according to the Dewey Decimal Classification number with full bibliographical information, suggested subject headings, and annotation; pt.2, author, title, subject, and analytical index, arranged in one alphabet; pt.3, directory of publishers. Titles are starred for first purchase.

Planned especially for school libraries but useful also as a guide to selection of books for smaller public libraries.

Kept up to date by annual supplements.

A committee of the Catholic Library Association prepares annual Catholic supplements which may be acquired separately or bound with the *Standard catalog.*

Strang, Ruth, Gilbert, Christine B. and **Scoggin, Margaret C.** Gateways to readable books; an annotated graded list of books in many fields for adolescents who find reading difficult. 3d ed. N.Y., Wilson, 1958. 181p. **AA294**

1st ed. 1944.

Includes more than 1000 titles.

Reference books

❧ The present edition of this *Guide to reference books* should give aid on many points in the selection of reference books for different types of libraries. Earlier editions, particularly the seventh, should be consulted for works omitted here. Other lists, prepared in other countries or from different points of view, will contain some titles not included in this book and will help in selection where additional titles are wanted.

Enoch Pratt Free Library, Baltimore. Reference books; a brief guide for students and other users of the library, comp. by Mary Neill Barton. 5th ed. Baltimore, Lib., 1962. 135p. il. **AA295**

The 1st edition (1947), containing 147 titles, has been expanded to 663 titles in the present 5th edition.

A simple, clear explanation of how to use reference books, with lists of general reference books and outstanding titles in the main subject fields. Intended for use in connection with courses in the use of the library and as a selection aid in small and medium-sized libraries. Well selected, with very good annotations.

Fleischhack, Curt, Rückert, Ernst and **Reichardt, Günther.** Grundriss der Bibliographie. Leipzig, Harrassowitz, 1957. 263p. (Lehrbücher für den Nachwuchs an wissenschaftlichen Bibliotheken, II) **AA296**

An annotated guide to bibliographies, both general and in special subject fields.

Includes also general encyclopedias and biographical dictionaries. International in scope. Not as extensive as Totok and Weitzel (AA10) or Malclès (AA301) but a useful brief survey of the areas covered.

Garde, P. K. Directory of reference works published in Asia. Répertoire des ouvrages de référence publiés en Asie. Paris, UNESCO, 1956. 139p. (UNESCO bibliographical handbooks. 5) **AA297**

Arranged by Universal Decimal Classification and then by country. Lists "ready-reference" books, such as atlases, bibliographies, biographical dictionaries, linguistic and subject dictionaries, directories and yearbooks, general and subject encyclopedias, gazetteers, etc. The area covered includes India; Pakistan and Afghanistan; the countries of east and southeast Asia; Indonesia and the Philippines.

Harris, John. Guide to New Zealand reference material and other sources of information. 2d ed. [Dunedin], New Zealand Lib. Assoc., 1950. 114p. **AA298**

———— Supplement no. 1–2, June 1951–Aug. 1956, comp. by A. G. Bagnall. 1951–57. v.1–2.

1st ed. 1947.

A listing in classified arrangement of books, periodicals, and official documents.

McColvin, Lionel Roy. Reference library stock; an informal guide. London, Grafton, 1952. 312p. **AA299**

"The lists of books have been compiled largely by Mr. R. L. W. Collison . . . "—*Pref.*

A selective listing of the more important reference books for a general reference library, arranged by subject, with introductory chapters on reference work in general. Titles are annotated, and there is an index by subject, but none by author or title. Although emphasis is placed on British works, the book is an excellent introduction to the subject for librarians anywhere.

Maichel, Karol. Guide to Russian reference books, ed. by J. S. G. Simmons. Stanford, Calif., Hoover Inst., 1962–64. v.1–2. (Hoover Inst. Bibliographical ser. 10 and 18) (In progress) **AA300**

Contents: v.1, General bibliographies and reference books. 1962. 92p.; v.2, History, auxiliary historical sciences, ethnography, and geography. 1964. 297p.

The first 2v. of a projected 6v. series expected to list more than 3500 titles of reference works pertaining to all phases of Russian life.

These are classified, annotated guides to materials in Russian and other languages with broad chronological coverage. Author, title, and subject indexes in each volume, with a cumulated index projected for v.6.

Other volumes will be devoted to the social sciences, religion, and philosophy; the humanities; and science, technology, and medicine.

Malclès, Louise-Noëlle. Les sources du travail bibliographique. Genève, E. Droz; Lille, Giard, 1950–58. 3v. in 4. **AA301**

A notable contribution to bibliographical manuals, designed to serve as textbook and guide, with introductions and discussions in each chapter. Not limited to bibliographies; also includes dictionaries, encyclopedias, atlases, texts, important periodicals, collections, and other types of reference and source materials. While basic works of earlier dates are included, emphasis has been put upon publications of the last twenty-five years, and particularly 1940–1950. International in scope, with natural emphasis on French and European works.

Contents: t.1, General bibliographical survey; bibliographies of bibliographies; universal bibliographies; the book of the 15th and 16th centuries; printed catalogs of libraries; union catalogs; national bibliographies; encyclopedias; biography; periodicals; society publications; periodical indexes; a special section on Slavic and Balkan countries; a section on encyclopedias of the book, and a list of technical dictionaries of publishing and library terms.

t.2, pt.1–2, Bibliographies spécialisées (Sciences humaines), covering prehistory, anthropology, ethnography, sociology; linguistics; history; languages and literatures; religions; geography; archaeology and art; music; political and social sciences; philosophy; and special sections on the language, literature, and history of Slavic and Balkan countries and the Near, Middle, and Far East.

t.3, Bibliographies spécialisées (Sciences exactes et techniques), lists bibliographies, dictionaries, treatises, manuals, yearbooks, periodicals, etc., in the history of science and in the various sciences, including medicine and pharmacy but excluding agriculture.

A full index by author, subject, and title is included in v.1; in v.2, pt.2; and in v.3.

Musiker, Reuben. Guide to South African reference books. 3d rev. ed. Grahamstown, Rhodes Univ. Lib., 1963. 161p.   **AA302**

1st ed. 1955.

A guide to some 500 works used for reference purposes published, with few exceptions, in South Africa. Arranged by subject in Dewey Decimal Classification order with author, title, and brief subject index.

Neiswender, Rosemary. Guide to Russian reference and language aids. N.Y., Special Libraries Assoc., 1962. 92p. (S.L.A. bibliography, no.4)   **AA303**

A listing of 221 titles with evaluative annotations, covering textbooks and readers, dictionaries, encyclopedias, geographical reference works, bibliographies, indexes, translation digests, current biographical sources, etc. Appendixes include a comparative table of seven transliteration systems, a glossary of Russian bibliographic and book-trade terminology, etc.

Nihon no Sankō Tosho Henshú Iinkai. Nihon no sankō tosho. Tokyo, 1962. 353p.   **AA304**

A guide to basic Japanese reference works designed for the general reader, containing approximately 2900 entries of books and serials published up to Oct. 1961.

Each entry consists of author, title, imprint, collation, and, in most instances, a brief annotation. Prices are included for titles published in 1955 or later.

The work is divided into four sections: Generalia, Humanities, Social Sciences, and Science and Technology. Each section is broken down into specific subjects; within each subject, titles are listed according to the following general pattern: bibliographies, dictionaries and encyclopedias, handbooks, chronological tables, biographical dictionaries and directories, pictorial works, yearbooks, statistical works, and documents.

Included is an alphabetical index to authors, titles, and general subject headings.

Entirely in Japanese.

Roberts, Arthur Denis. Introduction to reference books. 3d ed. London, Lib. Assoc., 1956. 237p.   **AA305**

1st ed. 1948.

A textbook prepared primarily for students in the School of Librarianship at University College, London, and devoted to descriptions of the various kinds of reference books, with citations of some titles as examples but not attempting to list works in special subject fields. A useful introduction written from the British point of view.

Sabor, Josefa Emilia. Manual de fuentes de información. Obras de referencia: enciclopedias, dicionários, bibliografías, biografías, etc. Buenos Aires, Ed. Kapelusz, 1957. 335p. (Contribuciones bibliotecológicas. 2)   **AA306**

A manual and guide designed particularly as a textbook for students but useful in other countries, especially for its information on Latin-American materials. It limits its scope to special types of reference works. A general introduction on the theory of reference work and the bibliographies pertaining thereto is followed by chapters on encyclopedias, dictionaries, national bibliographies, bibliographies of periodicals and government documents, biographical dictionaries, statistical annuals, and works of general information. Although there is some variation, most sections deal with the works of Spain, Latin America, France, Italy, Great Britain, Germany, Portugal, and the United States. An appendix lists reference works dealing with 10 Latin-American countries. The selection is of basic works, the annotations are descriptive and critical, and the whole is a well-planned manual, the first such work in the Spanish language.

Shores, Louis. Basic reference sources: an introduction to materials and methods. Chicago, Amer. Lib. Assoc., 1954. 378p.   **AA307**

A revision and expansion of the author's *Basic reference books;* prepared as a text for a general reference course, with emphasis on the principles of reference practice.

The first chapter treats "The practice of reference"; the remaining chapters are devoted to types of general and special reference materials with discussion of some 554 basic titles.

Southern Association of Colleges and Secondary Schools. Commission on Colleges and Universities. The classified list of reference books and periodicals for college libraries. W. Stanley Hoole, ed. . . . 3d ed. Atlanta, Ga., 1955. 227p.   **AA308**

1st ed. 1940; 2d ed. 1947.

In five major groupings: (1) general, (2) biological sciences, (3) humanities, (4) physical sciences, (5) social sciences.

This edition revised and in some respects rearranged. Periodicals now follow books under each subject grouping, and there is a single combined index.

Not annotated.

Subscription books bulletin. Chicago, Amer. Lib. Assoc., 1930–1956. 27v. Quarterly.   **AA309**

Gives unbiased, critical reviews of encyclopedias, dictionaries, biographical works, atlases, collections, etc. Prepared by a voluntary committee of librarians to help librarians and others in the selection of reference works. The reviews are based on careful examination of the books, and indication is given as to whether or not the work is recommended. A valuable aid in any library.

Continued in *The booklist and Subscription books bulletin* (AA273), Sept. 1, 1956– ; reviews cumulated in:

Subscription books bulletin reviews, prep. by the American Library Association, Subscription Books Committee. Chicago, Amer. Lib. Assoc., 1961– . [v.1–] **AA309a**

[v.1–3], 1956–1960, 1960–1962, 1962–1964, contain reprints of the reviews published in *The booklist and Subscription books bulletin,* Sept. 1, 1956–July 15, 1964. Each issue is arranged alphabetically by the titles of the works reviewed.

Têng, Ssǔ-yü and **Biggerstaff, Knight.** An annotated bibliography of selected Chinese reference works. Rev. ed. Cambridge, Harvard Univ. Pr., 1950. 326p. (Harvard-Yenching Inst. studies, v.2)   **AA310**

1st ed. 1936.

Describes, in English, general and subject bibliographies, encyclopedias, dictionaries, geographical works, biographical works, tables, and yearbooks.

Walford, Albert John. Guide to reference material, ed. by A. J. Walford, with the assistance of L. M. Payne. London, Lib. Assoc., 1959. (Distr. in U.S. by Bowker, N.Y.) 543p.   **AA311**

"The aim is to provide a guide to reference books and bibliographies, with emphasis on current material and on material published in Britain."—*Introd.* A well-edited list of 3000 principal titles, classified and annotated, with many additional titles mentioned in the notes. Strong British emphasis.

————— Supplement. London, Lib. Assoc., 1963. 370p.

Adds some 1500 titles, with 500 others in notes, published mainly between 1957 and 1961, with some titles of earlier periods omitted from the main work.

Zischka, Gert A. Index lexicorum; Bibliographie der lexikalischen Nachschlagewerke. Wien, Brüder Hollinek, 1959. 290p.   **AA312**

A bibliography of "encyclopedia-like reference books" rather than a bibliography of dictionaries. International in scope, particularly strong in German works; lists some 7000 titles grouped in 21 sections, general encyclopedias followed by reference works in various subject fields. No language dictionaries, but in the subject sections are listed such works as specialized dictionaries and encyclopedias, glossaries, handbooks, biographical dictionaries, yearbooks, gazetteers, etc. No subject bibliographies. Annotations limited. Index of personal authors and subject headings but no title listings, even for anonymous or composite works.

Book review indexes

Bibliographie der Rezensionen, 1900–43. Gautzsch b. Leipzig, Dietrich, 1901–44. v.1–77. (Internationale Bibliographie der Zeitschriftenliteratur, Abt. C)   **AA313**

Ceased publication.

1901–10 inclusive, 1v. per year, indexes reviews of books printed in some 3000 German periodicals; 1911–14, 2v. per year: the first volume of each year indexes reviews in German periodicals, the second volume indexes reviews in about 2000 periodicals in languages other than German; 1915 has 2v. for German reviews and 1v. for non-German; volumes for 1916–24 index only German reviews except that v.33 covers non-German for 1917–19; 1925–43 are annual volumes alternating German and *fremdsprachigen*. A very comprehensive list, especially useful in American and English research libraries as it indexes many American and English sets not included in the *Book review digest*. Does not give digests or quotations from the reviews listed. The volumes which index reviews in German periodicals cover the same list as the *Bibliographie der deutschen Zeitschriftenliteratur* (AF148) and supplement that work; the volumes indexing non-German periodicals do the same thing for the *Bibliographie der fremdsprachigen Zeitschriftenliteratur* (AF117).

Book review digest, 1905– . N.Y., Wilson, 1905– . v.1– .   **AA314**

A digest and index of selected book reviews in more than 75 English and American periodicals, principally general in character. Arranged alphabetically by author of book reviewed, with subject and title index. For each book entered, gives a brief descriptive note, quotations from selected reviews with exact reference to periodical in which review appeared, and references only—without quotation—to other reviews. Indicates length of review in number of words. From the public library point of view, the reviews indexed being taken principally from the general journals and not to any great extent from the special ones. Monthly, with a semi-annual cumulation in August, and an annual cumulation of the main list in February which forms an annual volume; the subject, title, and pseudonym index cumulates monthly,

the index in a current number referring to all previous issues of the current volume since the last cumulation.

Cumulated subject and title indexes for the previous 5-year period are included in the annual volumes for 1921, 1926, 1931, 1936, 1941, 1946, 1951, 1956, and 1961.

Book review index, v.1, no. 1, Jan. 1965– . Detroit, Gale Research, 1965– . v.1– . Monthly, with quarterly cumulations.   **AA314a**

Intends to index all reviews appearing in more than 200 publications.

Periodicals indexed are primarily in the fields of general fiction and nonfiction, humanities, social sciences, librarianship and bibliography, and juvenile and young adult books.

✓**Index to book reviews in the humanities.** v.1, no.1, March 31, 1960– . Detroit, Mich., Phillip Thomson, 1960– . Annual.   **AA315**

"Humanities" is broadly interpreted here to include social sciences as well. Indexes almost 700 periodicals (all in English), and several thousand book titles are now included in each issue. v.1 has no cumulative index; in v.2–3, 1961–62, the quarterly issues are cumulated into an annual volume; from 1963– , published annually.

SELECTION OF PERIODICALS

❧ Periodicals form an important part of the reference collections of a library. Current periodicals in many fields are needed to provide up-to-date articles on subjects of contemporary interest, and back files, especially those which are indexed in one or another of the general periodical indexes, are extremely valuable for reference work. However, the acquisition, maintenance, and binding of periodicals becomes an ever expanding item in the library budget, and careful consideration must be given to the selection of titles to be acquired and preserved. Selected and specialized lists will be found in the periodical indexes; e.g., the list in the *Abridged readers' guide* (AF123), which indexes some 25 periodicals, would be useful in the small public or school library, whereas the lists of periodicals indexed in the *Readers' guide* (AF122) and the *Social sciences and humanities index* (AF124) would be valuable aids to selection in a larger library; the lists in the subject indexes, e.g., the *Art index* (BE125) and the *Education index* (CB127), would be guides in these fields. It is well to remember that an indexed periodical has far more reference value than one that is not indexed. Some of the book selection guides (*see* p.24) include periodicals. For other lists of periodicals, *see* Periodicals, p.132.

Farber, Evan Ira. Classified list of periodicals for the college library. 4th ed., rev. and enl. to July 1957. Boston, Faxon, 1957. 146p. (Useful reference ser., no.86)   **AA316**

1st ed. 1934.

An annotated, classified list with alphabetical title index. Information given usually includes: title, date of first volume, frequency, place of publication, price, Library of Congress card number, sponsoring body if there is one, indexes in which it is indexed, and annotation giving brief description. Titles recommended for first purchase are starred.

AUDIO-VISUAL MATERIALS

American Library Association. Audio-Visual Committee. Films for libraries, selected by a subcommittee of the

American Library Association, Audio-Visual Committee. Chicago, Assoc., 1962. 81p.   **AA317**

"Intended to be an authoritative guide to the best [16mm] films currently available for library collections."—*Pref.*

Arranged by title with excellent annotations. Includes subject index.

Brings up to date *Films for public libraries,* 1955 and its *Supplement,* 1957.

Audio-visual equipment directory. 1953–   . Fairfax, Va., Nat. Audio-Visual Assoc., 1953–   . il. Annual.   **AA318**

1st ed. 1953; 2d ed. 1955; annual since 1958.

Subtitle: A guide to current models of audio-visual equipment.

AV index. 1961–   . Detroit, Audio-Visual Research Inst., 1961–   . Annual.   **AA319**

A selected list of materials, published during the 1950's, containing about 1800 articles with annotations for 623. Pt.1, information on A-V tools, materials, and procedures and reference guide; pt.2, A-V information, arranged by broad subject.

A very useful guide to sources of information on how to use A-V tools as aids in teaching.

"Entries in one edition will not be repeated in later editions."—*Foreword.*

Educational Media Council. Educational media index . . . N.Y., McGraw-Hill, [1964]. 14v.   **AA320**

Contents: v.1, Pre-school and primary, grades K–3; v.2, Intermediate, grades 4–6; v.3, Art and music; v.4, Business education and training; v.5, English language; v.6, Foreign language; v.7, Guidance, psychology, and teacher education; v.8, Health-safety and home economics; v.9, Industrial and agricultural education; v.10, Mathematics; v.11, Science and engineering; v.12, Geography and history; v.13, Economics and political science; v.14, Master title index.

"Guide to the source, content, and cost of non-book materials . . . films, kinescopes and filmstrips . . . slides and transparencies . . . maps, charts, and graphs . . . flat pictures . . . videotapes and phonotapes . . . phonodiscs . . . programmed instructional materials . . . models and mockups . . . cross-media sets."—*Pref.*

Contains bibliographies.

Supersedes: *Educational film guide.* N.Y., Wilson, 1936–62. Annual; *Filmstrip guide.* N.Y., Wilson, 1948–62. Irregular.

For critical review *see Subscription books bulletin* 61: 1033–38. July 15, 1965.

Educators grade guide to free teaching aids. 1955–   . Randolph, Wis., Educators Progress Service, 1955–   . Annual.   **AA321**

Annotated list of free maps, bulletins, pamphlets, exhibits, charts, and books. Arranged by broad subject. Includes title, subject and source indexes.

Educators guide . . . Randolph, Wis., Educators Progress Service.   **AA322**

This service issues: *Educators guide to free films.* 1941–   . Annual; *Educators guide to free filmstrips.* 1949–   . Annual; *Educators guide to free tapes, scripts, and transparencies.* 1955–   . Annual.

Annotated lists giving source, availability, terms of loan, etc., arranged by subject with subject and title indexes.

Also provides an annual series of guides to free materials on special subjects, including: *Free guidance materials.* 1962–   ; *Free science materials.* 1960–   ; *Free social studies materials.* 1961–   .

McClusky, Frederick Dean. The A-V bibliography. [2d ed.] Dubuque, Iowa, Wm. C. Brown Co., 1955. 218p.   **AA323**

A comprehensive bibliography of the literature on audio-visual instruction, with broad classifications.

The 2d edition contains about 2000 new items and drops a number that were included in the 1st edition; therefore,

both editions need to be used. A new section lists doctoral dissertations in the audio-visual field from 1921 through 1954.

Moldstad, John A. Sources of information on educational media. Prep. in cooperation with the U.S. Dept. of Health, Education, and Welfare, Office of Education. Wash., Govt. Prt. Off., 1963. 29p. il.   **AA324**

Contents: Published lists of new educational media; Information about equipment; Bibliographies; Organizations; Graduate programs; Locations to visit. Gives full bibliographic information and annotations. A very useful guide.

Reid, Seerley and **Carpenter, Anita.** A directory of 3660 16mm film libraries. Wash., Govt. Prt. Off., 1958. 236p. (U.S. Office of Education. Bull. 1959. no.4)   **AA325**

A listing of companies, institutions, and organizations which lend or rent films, arranged by state and then by city. Gives number and type of films owned by each.

Rufsvold, Margaret Irene and **Guss, Carolyn.** Guides to newer educational media: films, filmstrips, phonorecords, radio, slides, television. Chicago, Amer. Lib. Assoc., 1961. 74p.   **AA326**

Bibliography, p.50–64.

U.S. Office of Education. Educational AM and FM radio, and educational television stations, by state and city. Wash., Govt. Prt. Off., 1948–   . Irregular.   **AA327**

Title varies: 1948–   , *List of standard and FM educational radio broadcasts by state and city.*

In tabular form; gives call letters, frequency power, licensee, and general manager and/or program director.

NATIONAL AND TRADE

Bibliography

See also Bibliography of Bibliography, p.3.

Courtney, William Prideaux. A register of national bibliography; with a selection of the chief bibliographical books and articles printed in other countries. London, Constable, 1905–12. 3v.   **AA328**

v.1–2 list the bibliographies published before 1905; v.3 is a supplement containing about 10,000 additional references principally to bibliographies published 1905–12.

An old but useful handbook to bibliographies on all subjects, international in scope though mainly British in origin. Arranged alphabetically by the subjects of the bibliographies listed; refers not only to bibliographies in book form, but also to lists in periodicals and to other analytical material.

Larsen, Knud. National bibliographical services, their creation and operation . . . Paris, UNESCO, 1953. 142p. il. (Unesco bibliographical handbooks, 1)   **AA329**

A guide to the establishment of national bibliographies, union catalogs, and information services, with information on techniques, administration, etc. and some comment on existing services.

Bibliography, p.124–36; index.

Pinto, Olga. Le bibliografie nazionali. 2. ed. riv., corr. ed aggiorn. Firenze, Olschki, 1951. 94p. (Biblioteca di bibliografia italiana, 20)   **AA330**

1st ed. 1935.

This edition covers more than 70 countries; arrangement is alphabetical by country, and then chronological. Titles are annotated.

Schneider, Georg. Allgemeine nationale Bibliographien. (In his Handbuch der Bibliographie, 4. Aufl. 1930, p.159–368 [AA8])   **AA330a**

An extensive listing of national bibliographies, including bibliographies of literature.

U.S. Library of Congress. General Reference and Bibliography Division. Current national bibliographies, comp. by Helen F. Conover. Wash., 1955. 132p.　　**AA331**

An annotated listing of the current records of the book trade in 67 countries. In addition, lists periodical indexes, government publications, and directories of periodicals and newspapers.

United States

U.S. Library of Congress. A catalog of books represented by Library of Congress printed cards. Ann Arbor, Mich., Edwards, 1942–　.　　**AA332**

This catalog and its successors (*see* AA63–AA66) present an outstanding collection of American imprints, due in part to the possession of the copyright privilege by the Library of Congress, and thus they serve as a valuable addition to the national bibliographies.

Early

Evans, Charles. American bibliography; a chronological dictionary of all books, pamphlets and periodical publications printed in the United States of America from the genesis of printing in 1639 down to and including the year 1800; with bibliographical and biographical notes. Chicago, pr. for the author, 1903–59. 14v. **AA333**

Publisher varies: v.13–14 published by the American Antiquarian Society, Worcester, Mass.

The most important general list of early American publications, indispensable in the large reference or special library. Includes books, pamphlets, and periodicals, arranged chronologically by dates of publication; gives for each book author's full name with dates of birth and death, full title, place, date, publisher or printer, paging, size, and, whenever possible, location of copies in American libraries. Each volume has three indexes: (1) authors, (2) classified subjects, (3) printers and publishers.

Although Mr. Evans had originally hoped to continue to 1820, as indicated on the title pages of v.1–12, 1639–1799 (pub. 1903–34), he finally decided to stop with 1800 and, in fact, carried through the letter M of 1799. v.13 (pub. 1955) starts with the letter N for 1799 and continues through 1800 with author and subject indexes. In this volume, compiled by Clifford K. Shipton, the system used by Evans has been modified somewhat, e.g., titles have been shortened, and cross references are given from the title when anonymous works are listed under author.

v.14 (pub. 1959), edited by Roger Pattrell Bristol, is a cumulated author-title index to the whole work, including pseudonyms, attributed authors, other names appearing on the title page, governmental bodies, etc. Newspapers and almanacs are grouped under these respective headings and are not listed under specific title.

Evans' American bibliography. Supplement (checking ed.) by Roger P. Bristol. Charlottesville, Bibliographical Soc. of the Univ. of Virginia, 1962–　.　　**AA333a**

Issued in parts. Arranged chronologically. A preliminary checking edition of a supplement to include titles not found in Evans.

Bristol, Roger Pattrell. Index of printers, publishers and booksellers indicated by Charles Evans in his American bibliography. Charlottesville, Bibliographical Soc. of the Univ. of Virginia, 1961. 172p.　　**AA333b**

Under each name indicates—chronologically and then by item number—references to be found in Evans.

Henry E. Huntington Library and Art Gallery, San Marino, Calif. American imprints, 1648–1797, in the Huntington Library, supplementing Evans' American bibliography; comp. by Willard O. Waters. (Repr. from:

Huntington Library Bull. no.3, Feb. 1933, p.1–95)　　**AA333c**

Arranged chronologically, with author index. Lists 736 "titles of books, pamphlets, broadsides, maps, etc., supplementary to the Evans' bibliography. It comprises, besides items apparently not listed in that work, a number appearing there but with titles or imprints varying from the copies here described."—[*Prelim. note*].

New York. Public Library. Rare Book Division. Checklist of additions to Evans' American bibliography in the Rare Book Division of the New York Public Library, comp. by Lewis M. Stark and Maud D. Cole. N.Y., Lib., 1960. 110p.　　**AA333d**

1289 entries. Lists originals, photostats, and facsimiles, for the latter frequently indicating the location of the original.

Sabin, Joseph. Dictionary of books relating to America, from its discovery to the present time. Begun by Joseph Sabin, and continued by Wilberforce Eames for the Bibliographical Society of America. N.Y., Sabin, 1868–92; Bibliographical Soc. of America, 1928–36. 29v. (Repr.: Amsterdam, N. Israel, 1961–62)　　**AA334**

Half title: *Bibliotheca Americana,* by which title it is sometimes known.

An important bibliography of Americana, including books, pamphlets, and periodicals printed in the Western Hemisphere, and works about the region printed elsewhere. Comprises 106,413 numbered entries, but the actual number of titles recorded is much greater, as that total does not count the added editions and titles mentioned in the various notes. The arrangement is by author, with some title entries for anonymous works and many entries under names of places. Information given includes full title, place, publisher, date, format, paging, often contents and bibliographical notes with reference to a description or review in some other work, and, in many cases, names of libraries possessing copies.

A list of "Library Location Symbols" is given in v.29, p.299–305, which is more extensive than the partial list given in v.1.

Wing, Donald Goddard. Short-title catalogue of books printed in England, Scotland, Ireland, Wales, and British America . . . 1641–1700. N.Y., Columbia Univ. Pr., 1945–51. 3v.　　**AA335**

For full information *see* AA504.

Includes books printed in the American colonies during this period.

19th century

Shaw, Ralph Robert and **Shoemaker, Richard H.** American bibliography: a preliminary checklist. N.Y., Scarecrow, 1958–65. v.1–19, and Addenda. (In progress)　　**AA336**

Contents: v.1–19, 1801–1819. Addenda; list of sources; library symbols.

A preliminary checklist "gathered entirely from secondary sources," designed as a first step in filling the gap in American national bibliography between 1800, when Evans stops, and 1820, when Roorbach starts. The Preface explains purpose and procedure. Each volume covers one year. Author and title indexes are planned. Locations of copies are given when they were included in the original citations.

The Addenda volume lists 1768 items, 1801–19.

Shoemaker, Richard H. Checklist of American imprints, 1820–　. N.Y., Scarecrow, 1964–　. v.1–　. (In progress)　　**AA337**

Planned as a continuation of Shaw above to give more complete listings than those in Roorbach (AA338). Is expected to list more than eight times as many titles as Roorbach for this year, with more complete information and with location of copies.

Roorbach, Orville Augustus. Bibliotheca americana, 1820–61. N.Y., Roorbach, 1852–61. 4v. (Repr.: N.Y., Peter Smith, 1939)   **AA338**

v.1, 1820–52, with a list of periodicals published in the United States; v.2, Supplement, Oct. 1852–May 1855; v.3, Addenda, May 1855–March 1858; v.4, March 1858–Jan. 1861.

A trade catalog of American publications, including reprints, arranged alphabetically by author and title, giving publisher, size, price, and, in some cases, date.

Kelly, James. American catalogue of books (original and reprints), published in the United States from Jan. 1861 to Jan. 1871, with date of publication, size, price, and publisher's name. N.Y., Wiley, 1866–71. 2v. (Repr.: N.Y., Peter Smith, 1938. 2v.)   **AA339**

Continues the record of American bibliography from Roorbach's last volume, giving about the same kind of information. Each volume contains a list of societies and their publications. v.1 also contains a list of pamphlets, sermons, and addresses on the Civil War, 1861–66.

Both Roorbach and Kelly are unsatisfactory, as they are far from complete and often inaccurate, but they must be used as they are the most general lists for the period 1820–70.

Stevens, Henry. Catalogue of the American books in the library of the British Museum at Christmas MDCCCLVI. London, H. Stevens, 1866. 4 pts. in 1v.   **AA340**

Contents: (1) American books printed in the United States. 628p.; (2) Catalogue of the Canadian and other British North American books. 14p.; (3) Catalogue of the Mexican and other Spanish American and West Indian books. 62p.; (4) Catalogue of the American maps. 17p.

Includes some works not included in Roorbach and gives fuller titles for others that are included there.

American catalogue of books, 1876–1910. N.Y., Publishers' Weekly, 1876–1910. 9v. in 13. (Repr.: N.Y., Peter Smith, 1941)   **AA341**

Cumulates the *Annual American catalogue,* 1886–1910.

The basic work—1876, Author and title entries of books in print, July 1, 1876; Subject entries. 2v.—is supplemented by volumes covering various periods (e.g., three, five, or eight years) usually with author/title and subject volumes.

The standard American list for the period covered; comprehensive and generally reliable although information given is based upon reports from publishers and not, in most cases, on actual examination of the books themselves.

Aims to include, with certain exceptions, all books published in the United States which were for sale to the general public.

20th century

United States catalog; books in print. Jan. 1, 1928. 4th ed. N.Y., Wilson, 1928. 3164p.   **AA342**

1st ed. 1899. v.1, Author list; v.2, Title index.
2d ed. 1902.
3d ed. Jan. 1, 1912.

Supplements (entitled *Cumulative book index*) for intervening years were published as follows: [cumulation], 1902/05; annual supplements, 1906–10; [cumulations], 1912/17, 1918/June 1921, June 1921/June 1924; annual supplements, July 1924–Dec. 1927.

Cumulative book index, a world list of books in the English language, 1928/32– . N.Y., Wilson, 1933– .   **AA343**

Often referred to as *C.B.I.*

Published periodically since 1898 with cumulations to form supplements to the *United States catalog.* Frequency varies. Now published monthly, except July and Aug. (*see* AA345), cumulating at intervals. Semiannual volumes are eventually superseded by the permanent cumulations.

Cumulations needed to supplement the 4th edition of the *United States catalog* are: 1928/32 (pub. 1933); 1933/37 (pub. 1938); 1938/42 (pub. 1945); 1943/48 (pub. 1950); 1949/52 (pub. 1953); 1953/56 (pub. 1959); biennial since 1957.

The *United States catalog* and the *C.B.I.* constitute a comprehensive record of American publications from 1898 to date that is indispensable for reference work in its field. The most frequently used parts will be the 4th edition (1928) and its supplements, but the earlier volumes must be used for: (1) books out-of-print by 1928; (2) fuller information, e.g., paging, date, etc., on some titles still in print.

Each volume is a dictionary catalog with entries under author, title, and subject.

The 4th edition of the *United States catalog* includes publications in the regular book trade; privately printed books; regular importations of American publishers; Canadian books (in English) not also published in the United States; publications of universities, societies, and scientific institutions, e.g., Smithsonian Institution; and a selected list of publications of the national and state governments. For each book, gives: author, short title, edition, publisher, price, and, generally but not always, date, paging, and illustration; gives also Library of Congress card numbers, and, for a book entered in the *Book review digest,* its Dewey Decimal Classification number and a tracing of the subject headings used for it in the *United States catalog.*

The volumes (1928/32–) have a wider scope and include a comprehensive listing of books and pamphlets, in English, issued in the United States and Canada and a selection of publications from other parts of the English-speaking world: Australia, Great Britain, New Zealand, South Africa, etc. Omitted are government documents, maps, sheet music, paperbound editions, and ephemeral material. In proportion to the size of the catalog there are very few inaccuracies, although, as some of the entries have had to be made without examination of the books and are based on publishers' descriptions and lists, the work is not a final authority on bibliographical detail. As a first aid, it is indispensable: (1) in order department work; (2) as an adjunct to the library's own catalog; and (3) as a reference tool for many purposes: verification of titles, authors' names and dates, authorship when only the title or subject of a book is known, lists of books on a given subject, etc. Subject lists of fiction, e.g., ghost stories, sea stories, etc., and the use of the subhead Fiction under many subjects make it useful for certain types of questions about fiction.

Each volume includes a list of publishers with addresses.

Current

American book publishing record, v.1, Feb. 1, 1960– . N.Y., Bowker, 1960– . Monthly.   **AA344**

At head of title, BPR.

Includes the same information as that given in the weekly lists in *Publishers' weekly* (AA350), cumulated monthly and rearranged by subject according to Dewey Decimal numbers. Indexed by author and title.

—— Annual index, v.3, 1962– . N.Y., Bowker, 1963– .

Eds.: 1962– , Lynn Miller and Margaret McFarland.

In two sections: (1) title index, and (2) author index, with references to the issue and to the Dewey Decimal Classification in the monthly issues.

Cumulative book index. N.Y., Wilson, 1898– . Monthly.   **AA345**

Often referred to as *C.B.I.*

Subtitle, 1930– , A world list of books in the English language.

Compiled on the same principles as the cumulated supplements listed in AA343, including, in dictionary catalog form, a record of books published not only in the United States but also in the English language in other parts of the world.

See AA343 for further information.

Paperbound books in print. N.Y., Bowker, 1955– . Monthly. **AA346**

Frequency varies. Aug. 1963– , monthly, with cumulative issues three times a year—in Oct., Feb., and June—which list available paperbacks in three sections: (1) subject, (2) author, and (3) title.

The monthly issues, called *The month ahead,* present previews of forthcoming books under general subject groupings with an author/editor index.

Publishers' trade list annual, 1873– . N.Y., Bowker, 1873– . Annual. **AA347**

A collection of publishers' catalogs, arranged alphabetically by publishers' names, and bound up in one, two, or three large volumes per year. As the catalogs are not compiled on any uniform system, the amount of information given about books varies greatly, ranging from full information and occasional notes in some lists to only short title and price in others; in general, dates of publication are omitted. Lists only books in print. An alphabetical list of the publishers included is given in the first volume.

Except for brief indexes in 1902–4, no indexes were issued until 1948 when *Books in print* (AA348) began publication, followed in 1957 by the *Subject guide to Books in print* (AA349).

Books in print: an author-title-series index to the Publishers' trade list annual, 1948– . N.Y., Bowker, 1948– . Annual. **AA348**

Each volume includes an author index and a title index, in each case giving publisher and price. Fuller information may then be found by referring to the pertinent publisher's catalog in the *Publishers' trade list annual.*

A very valuable addition for both acquisition and reference work in a library.

Useful for finding the publisher and price of a book; for finding the author's name if only the title is known; and as an index to the vast amount of material in the *Publishers' trade list annual.*

Subject guide to Books in print: an index to the Publishers' trade list annual 1957– . N.Y., Bowker, 1957– . Annual. **AA349**

A companion volume to *Books in print,* listing under subject the books to be found there. Conforms to the subject headings and cross references set up by the Library of Congress. Works to which the Library of Congress does not assign subject headings (e.g., fiction, poetry, drama, and Bibles) are not indexed.

Publishers' weekly, the book industry journal, 1872– . N.Y., Bowker, 1872– . v.1– . Weekly. **AA350**

Subtitle varies; publisher varies.

The standard American book-trade journal, containing lists of new publications, lists of books announced for publication, news notes, editorials and articles, advertisements of books wanted, etc. The principal bibliographical list is the weekly list of new publications, for which the amount of information, promptness of listing, and indexing have differed through the years. It is now an author list with full title, imprint, collation, Dewey Decimal number, Library of Congress card number and subject headings, and occasional descriptive notes.

Lists books of all publishers on all subjects, but omits federal and state government publications, subscription books, dissertations, periodicals, etc.

Special numbers issued during the year vary but usually include: Spring announcement number in January; Summer announcement number in April; Fall children's book number in July; Fall announcement number in August.

—— Interim index to forthcoming books: a supplement

that expands and up-dates Publishers' weekly announcement numbers, v.1– , March 1964– . N.Y., 1964– . Quarterly. **AA351**

Published some two months after the announcement numbers; revises and updates the information given therein, providing a quick index to books about to be published. In two parts: author index and title index.

Textbooks in print, including teaching materials, 1956– . N.Y., Bowker, 1956– . Annual. **AA352**

Issued 1872–1926 as a number in *Publishers' weekly* under various titles; 1927–55, as the *American educational catalog.*

Subtitle 1964: An author and title index to elementary, junior and senior high school books, comp. from data furnished by the publishers and classified by subject with supplementary readers and pedagogical books.

U.S. Copyright Office. Catalog of copyright entries, 1891–1946. Wash., Govt. Prt. Off., 1891–1947. **AA353**

Title varies. Before 1906 issued by the Treasury Dept.; 1906–46, issued by the Copyright Office as *New series.*

Contents: Arrangement differs slightly. Pt.1, *Books,* 1909–27 issued in two groups; 1928–46 in three groups as follows: group 1, v.25–43, *Books* proper, frequency varies, annual index; group 2, v.25–43, *Pamphlets,* etc., including lectures, sermons, maps, etc., monthly, with annual index; group 3, v.1–19, *Dramatic compositions,* motion pictures (before 1920, motion pictures were included in pt.4), monthly, with annual index. Pt.2, v.1–41, *Periodicals and newspapers,* quarterly, with annual index. Pt.3, v.1–41, *Musical compositions,* monthly, with annual index (for full information *see* BH37). Pt.4, v.1–41, *Works of art,* photographs, etc., quarterly, with annual index.

For 1946 each part was issued as an annual.

—— —— Ser. 3– . Wash., Govt. Prt. Off., 1947– .

With the third series the arrangement and the format have been changed to make the contents of the set more easily available. The *Catalog* is now subdivided into separate parts following the classification as given in the Copyright Act: pt.1, *Books and pamphlets,* including serials and contributions to periodicals (1947–Jan./June 1953, issued in two sections, pt.1A and pt.1B, which were combined to form the new pt.1 with v.7, no.2, July/Dec. 1953); pt.2, *Periodicals;* pt.3–4, *Dramas* and works prepared for oral delivery; pt.5, *Music* (1947–1956, issued in two sections: pt.5A, Published music, and pt.5B, Unpublished music. From 1957, these are combined into pt.5 [*see* BH37a]); pt.6, *Maps and atlases;* pt.7–11A, *Works of art,* reproductions, scientific and technical drawings, photographic works, prints, and pictorial illustrations; pt.11B, *Commercial prints and labels;* pts.12–13, *Motion pictures and filmstrips.*

Each part is published semiannually (but appears about a year late) and lists the works copyrighted during the period. The *Books* section includes books published in the United States, and, when copyrighted in this country, books in foreign languages published outside the United States, and books in the English language first published abroad.

All types of books are included: literature, fiction, nonfiction, business reports and yearbooks, trade catalogs and directories, manuals, instruction books, research studies in many fields, etc.

Orton, Robert Merritt. Catalog of reprints in series, 1940– . N.Y., Wilson, 1940– . Annual (slightly irregular). **AA354**

In two parts: (1) An author and title list giving the reprint edition or editions in which a work has appeared with date and price of reprint, and (2) List of reprint publishers and series.

Vertical file index: subject and title index to selected pamphlet material. N.Y., Wilson, 1935– . Monthly (except Aug.), with annual cumulations. **AA355**

Title varies: v.1–23, 1935–54, *Vertical file service catalog.*

A list of free and inexpensive pamphlets, booklets, leaflets, and mimeographed material considered to be of interest to general libraries. Subjects range from those suitable for school libraries to specialized technical reports.

Arranged alphabetically by subject (deemed suitable for vertical file use) with title index.

Regional

🐝 The various general publications listed above (AA333–AA355) are reasonably comprehensive for works issued at the main publishing centers, but are less complete for material printed by local presses, especially before 1875. For local publications, regional bibliographies must often be consulted. A good list of such works is given in Stillwell, *Incunabula and Americana,* p.382–408, 423–27 (AA159).

A slightly more recent listing is:

McMurtrie, Douglas Crawford. Locating the printed source materials for United States history; with a bibliography of lists of regional imprints. (In Mississippi Valley historical review 31:369–406. Dec. 1944) **AA356**

Lists of regional imprints, arranged alphabetically by state, p.379–403; American imprints check list, p.403–6.

Historical Records Survey. Bibliography of research projects reports; check-list of Historical Records Survey publications. Rev. April 1943. Wash., Federal Works Agency, W.P.A., 1943. 110p. (W.P.A. Technical ser. Research and records bibliography, no.7)   **AA357**

A final record of publications superseding all earlier listings.

Lists inventories of federal archives in the states; inventories of county archives; inventories of municipal and town archives; transcriptions of public archives; vital statistics; church archives publications; manuscript publications; American imprints inventory; American portrait inventory; guides to civilian organizations; miscellaneous publications; microfilm records; depositories of unpublished material, etc.

Because of this record, the volumes published in these various series are not listed here, with the exception of the American imprints inventory listed below.

—— American imprints inventory, prep. by the Historical Records Survey, Division of Women's and Professional Projects. Works Progress Administration. Wash., Historical Records Survey, 1937–42. no.1–20, 23–26, 31–32, 36, 38–42, 44–45, 52.   **AA358**

no.21, 22, 27–30, 33–35, 37, 43, 46–51 had not been published when the work of the *American imprints inventory* ceased.

no.1, A preliminary check list of *Missouri* imprints, 1808–1850. 1937. 225p.; no.2, M. R. Martin, Check list of *Minnesota* imprints, 1849–1865. 1938. 219p.; no.3, A check list of *Arizona* imprints, 1860–1890. 1938. 81p.; no.4, Check list of *Chicago* ante-fire imprints, 1851–1871. 1938. 727p.; no.5, D. C. McMurtrie, Check list of *Kentucky* imprints, 1787–1810. 1939. 205p.; no.6, D. C. McMurtrie and A. H. Allen, Check list of *Kentucky* imprints, 1811–1820, with notes in supplement to the Check list of 1787–1810 imprints. 1939. 235p.; no.7, A check list of *Nevada* imprints, 1859–1890. 1939. 127p.; no.8, Check list of *Alabama* imprints, 1807–1840. 1939. 159p.; no.9, Lucile M. Morsch, Check list of *New Jersey* imprints, 1784–1800. 1939. 189p.; no.10, Check list of *Kansas* imprints, 1854–1876. 1939. 773p.; no.11, Chicago Historical Society Library, A check list of the Kellogg collection of "patent inside" newspapers of 1876. 1939. 99p.; no.12, D. C. McMurtrie, A check list of the imprints of *Sag Harbor, L.I.,* 1791–1820. 1939. 61p.; no.13, A check list of *Idaho* imprints, 1839–1890. 1940. 74p.; no.14, A check list of *West Virginia* imprints, 1791–1830. 1940. 62p.;

no.15, A check list of *Iowa* imprints, 1838–1860, in supplement to those recorded by Alexander Moffit in the *Iowa journal of history and politics* for Jan. 1938. 1940. 84 (i.e., 85)p.; no.16, List of *Tennessee* imprints, 1793–1840, in Tennessee libraries. 1941. 97p.; no.17, A check list of *Ohio* imprints 1796–1820. 1941. 202p.; no.18, A check list of *Wyoming* imprints, 1866–1890. 1941. 69 (i.e., 70)p.; no.19, Lucy B. Foote, Bibliography of the official publications of *Louisiana,* 1803–1934. 1942. 579p.; no.20, Check list of *Tennessee* imprints, 1841–1850. 1941. 138p.; no.23–24, 41–42, A check list of *Wisconsin* imprints, 1833–1849, 1850–1854, 1855–1858, 1859–1863. 1942. 4v.; no.25, Check list of *New Mexico* imprints and publications, 1784–1876: imprints, 1834–1876; publications, 1784–1876. 1942. 115p.; no.26, A check list of *Nebraska* non-documentary imprints, 1847–1876. 1942. 132p.;

no.31, A check list of *California* non-documentary imprints, 1833–1855. 1942. 109p.; no.32, A check list of *Tennessee* imprints, 1793–1840. 1942. 285p.; no.36, A check list of *Utica,* N.Y., imprints, 1799–1830. 1942. 179p.; no.38 (misnumbered 25), Supplemental check list of *Kentucky* imprints, 1788–1820, including the original printing of the original Kentucky copyright ledger, 1800–1854, and the first account of the run of Baptist minutes in the collection of Mr. Henry S. Robinson, ed. by John Wilson Townsend. 1942. 241p.; no.39, A check list of *Arkansas* imprints, 1821–1876. 1942. 139p.; no.40 and 45, A check list of *Massachusetts* imprints, 1801–1802. 1942. 2v.; no.41–42, *see* no.23–24; no.44, A check list of *Washington* imprints, 1853–1876. 1942. 89p.; no.45, *see* no.40; no.52, Preliminary check list of *Michigan* imprints, 1796–1850. 1942. 224p.

Albania

Legrand, Émile. Bibliographie albanaise; description raisonnée des ouvrages pub. en albanais ou relatifs à l'Albanie du 15. siècle à l'année 1900. Oeuvre posthume, compl. et pub. par Henri Gûys. Paris, Welter, 1912. 228p.   **AA359**

Lists books in Albanian and other languages, published in or relating to Albania, 1474–1900. Chronological with author and subject indexes.

Continued by:

Gûys, Henri. Bibliographie albanaise; description raisonnée des ouvrages en albanais ou relatifs à l'Albanie de 1900 à 1910. Tirana, 1938.   **AA360**

Bibliografi shqipe, 29.XI.1944–31.XII.1958. [Ed. by] Jup Kastrati. Tiranë, N. Sh. Botimeve "Naim Frashëri," 1959. 498p.   **AA361**

Classified listing of Albanian publications of the period. Author index.

Argentina

See also Latin America, p.53.

Anuario bibliográfico de la República Arjentina. año [1]–9. 1879–87. Buenos Aires, 1880–88. 9v.   **AA362**

Ed. by Alberto Navarro Viola.

A selected, critical annual list, classified by subject with author index.

Gutiérrez, Juan María. Bibliografía de la primera imprenta de Buenos Aires desde su fundación hasta el año 1810 inclusive. . . . Buenos Aires, Impr. de Mayo, 1866. 43p., 34p., 246p. (Readex microprint)   **AA363**

Pt.1, Celebridades argentinas del siglo XVIII; pt.2, Orijenes del arte de imprimir en la America Española; pt.3, Bibliografía de la primera imprenta de Buenos Aires [215 imprints].

Pts.2–3, repr. from the *Revista de Buenos Aires,* June 1865–Aug. 1866.

Current

Bibliografía argentina de artes y letras. Buenos Aires, Fondo Nacional de las Artes, 1959– . no.1– . Quarterly. **AA364**

A selective, classified bibliography, including periodical articles as well as books. Author index in each issue with annual cumulated indexes of names and anonymous titles. Many issues include special bibliographic studies.

Boletín bibliográfico nacional . . . 1937– . no.1– . Publicación oficial. Buenos Aires, 1937– . Annual. **AA365**

Title varies: 1937–49, *Boletín bibliográfico argentino.*
Publishing body varies. 1953/54– by the Biblioteca Nacional.

Lists books in the original and translation; translations of foreign books published in Argentina; and foreign books that deal with Argentina. Classified with author index.

Australia

Canberra, Australia. National Library. Annual catalogue of Australian publications, no.1–25. 1936–60. Canberra, 1937–61. **AA366**

no.1 does not include official publications; no.2–25 generally include books published in Australia with supplements to previous issues; books of Australian interest published overseas; official publications of the Commonwealth and territories; selected list of Australian periodicals, annuals, and serial publications; and a directory of Australian publishers. Official publications omitted 1941–44.
Superseded by *Australian national bibliography* (AA369).

Ferguson, John Alexander. Bibliography of Australia. 1784–1900. Sydney, Angus & Robertson, 1941–63. 5v. **AA367**

For complete record see DF1.

Foxcroft, A. B. Australian catalogue; a reference index to the books and periodicals published and still current in the Commonwealth of Australia. . . . Melbourne, Whitecombe and Tombs, 1911. 118p., 72p. **AA368**

An author and catchword title index to books in print. Includes a *List of public documents,* Jan. 1911.

Current

Australian national bibliography, Jan. 1961– . Canberra, National Lib. of Australia, 1961– . Monthly, with annual cumulations. **AA369**

This new title supersedes the former *Annual catalogue of Australian publications* (AA366), its monthly supplement *Books published in Australia* . . . , and the *Monthly list of Australian government publications.*

Lists books and pamphlets published in Australia and those published overseas dealing with Australia. Includes government publications, and the first issue of new periodicals, newspapers, etc.

Arrangement is alphabetical by main entry, with comprehensive bibliographic data for each item. Includes prices and Dewey Decimal numbers. Subject and title index.

Canberra, Australia. National Library. Books of general interest. Canberra, 1911– . Monthly. **AA370**

Title varies: 1911–36, *Books added;* 1937–July 1951, *Select list of books added;* Aug. 1951– , *Books of general interest.*

A monthly classified list of selected books and pamphlets acquired by legal deposit. Arrangement and coverage vary. No cumulations.

Austria

See also Germany, p.43.

Langer, Eduard. Bibliographie der österreichischen Drucke des XV. und XVI. Jahrhunderts. Bd.1, Hft.1, Trient-Wien-Schrattenthal, bearb. von Walther Dolch. Wien, Gilhofer & Ranschburg, 1913. 171p. **AA371**

No more published.

Current

Oesterreichische Bibliographie; Verzeichnis der österreichischen Neuerscheinungen. Bearb. von der Österreichischen Nationalbibliothek. Wien, 1946– . v.2– . **AA372**

Frequency varies: 1946, quarterly; 1947–48, monthly; 1949– , semimonthly, with quarterly indexes and annual cumulated indexes.

A listing of trade publications which also includes university and official publications, newspapers, periodicals, and music scores. Classified, with author and subject index. v.1 announced for later publication.

—— Register 1946–50. Wien, 1951–52. 348p.

—— Verfasser- und Stichwortregister . . . *See* AA490.

Belgium

Bibliographie nationale. Dictionnaire des écrivains belges et catalogue de leurs publications, 1830–80. Bruxelles, Weissenbruch, 1886–1910. 4v. **AA373**

Aims to furnish a comprehensive record, for the period 1830–80, of works by Belgian authors (either citizens or residents of the country), published either in Belgium or abroad, with record also of earlier works by the same authors and of periodicals with which they were associated as either editors or regular contributors. Includes books, pamphlets, official publications, many reprints from periodicals and newspapers, theses. Information given for each work includes author's name (frequently with brief biographical data), title, place, publisher, date, size, paging, illustrations, price. Contents and other notes are frequently included, especially notes of reprints from periodicals.

Bibliotheca belgica. Bibliographie générale des Pays-Bas, fondée par Ferdinand van der Haeghen. Re-éditée sous la direction de Marie-Thérèse Lenger. Bruxelles, Culture et Civilisation, 1964– . v.1–5. (In progress) **AA374**

Issued in 5v. (A–Z); v.6 to be an index. Originally published in irregular order, in 230 *livraisons,* 1880–1964, now reassembled and published in quarto volumes in alphabetical sequence.

Includes works of the 15th and 16th centuries (with some inclusion of important later works) printed in Belgium and Holland, and books by Belgian and Dutch authors printed elsewhere, giving for each work listed: full title, imprint and collation, location of copies, and often full bibliographical and historical notes with biographical notes about authors and references to sources.

This new edition will make this valuable material easily available for the first time.

Coopman, Theophiel and **Broeckaert, Jan.** Bibliographie van den Vlaamschen taalstrijd. Gent, Siffer, 1904–14. 10v. (K. Vlaamsche Academie voor Taal- en Letterkunde) **AA375**

v.1–10, 1787–1886.
Bibliography of Flemish-language materials.

Foppens, Jean François. Bibliotheca belgica, sive Virorum in Belgio vitâ, scriptisque illustrium catalogus, librorumque nomenclatura; continens scriptores à clariss. viris

Valerio Andrea, Auberto Miraeo, Francisco Sweertio, aliisque, recensitos, usque ad annum MDCLXXX. Bruxellis, P. Foppens, 1738. 2v.   **AA376**

Includes writers of the various Low Countries, arranged alphabetically by Latin form of the name, giving brief biographical notices and lists of their writings. Covers from earliest printing to 1680. Indexes by place and by religious order.

Vlaamsche bibliographie. Lijst der boeken, vlug- en tijdschriften, muziekwerken, kaarten, platen en tabellen, in België van 1830 tot 1890 verschenen. Uitg. op last der Koninklijke Vlaamsche Academie voor Taal- en Letterkunde, door Fr. de Potter. Gent, Siffer, 1893–[1902]. 894p.   **AA377**

Lists the Flemish books published in Belgium. Classified, with author index.

Incorporates the material included in the various editions of the *Vlaamsche bibliographie,* by F. A. Snellaert (1851–88).

Current

Bibliographie de Belgique, 1. partie: Liste mensuelle des publications belges ou relatives à la Belgique, acquises par la Bibliothèque Royale, 1.– . année, 1875– . Bruxelles, Bibliothèque Royale, 1875– . v.1– . Monthly.   **AA378**

Title and headings also in Dutch.

This bibliography has undergone many changes in title, scope, plan, editor, and publisher. For the history of these, and for a collation by volumes of the set to 1931, *see* "Histoire des transformations de la Bibliographie de Belgique" by Fernand Remy, in *Bibliographie de Belgique* 57:356–98, 1931. As at present organized, aims to cover books, pamphlets, etc. issued in Belgium; books by Belgian authors published abroad; and books by foreigners relating to Belgium. Since 1959 these latter have been listed in a *Fascicule spécial,* "Liste annuelle des publications d'auteurs belges à l'étranger et des publications étrangères relatives à la Belgique . . ." with separate indexes.

A classified list with two alphabetical indexes: (1) authors, anonymous titles, etc.; and (2) rubrics in both languages for each number and for each annual volume. Information given for each entry is in full catalog form and includes author's name, full title, place, publisher, date, size, illustrations, and usually price.

La librairie belge: ouvrages d'expression française édités en Belgique, 1945/55– . Bruxelles, Cercle Belge de la Librairie, [1959?–].   **AA379**

A listing in one alphabet by author, title, and catchword, with full bibliographic information under main entry. Further volumes to cover 5-year periods are planned.

Bolivia

Gutiérrez, José Rosendo. Datos para la bibliografía boliviana. 1. sección. La Paz, Arzadum, 1875. 255p. **AA380**

Lists 2203 items.

—— —— 2. suplemento; últimas adiciones y correcciones á la primera sección. La Paz, Impr. de la Union Americana, 1880. 24p., 126p.

no.2204–3089.
No more published.

René-Moreno, Gabriel. Biblioteca boliviana; catálogo de la sección de libros i folletos. Santiago de Chile, Impr. Gutenberg, 1879. 880p. (Readex microprint)   **AA381**

Arranged alphabetically by title with index of authors,

translators, etc. 3529 entries. Full bibliographical information with annotations.

—— —— 1. suplemento . . . Epítome de un Catálogo de libros y folletos, 1879–99. Santiago de Chile, Impr. Barcelona, 1900. 349p.

no.3530–5176.

—— —— 2. suplemento, 1900–1908. Santiago de Chile, Impr. Univ., 1908. 349p.

no.5177–6815.
The most important Bolivian bibliography.

Abecía, Valentín. Adiciones a la Biblioteca boliviana de Gabriel René-Moreno, con un apéndice del editor, 1602–1879. Santiago de Chile, Impr. Barcelona, 1899. 440p.   **AA382**

Current

Bibliografía boliviana. 1962– . [Ed. by] Werner Guttentag Tichauer. Cochabamba, Los Amigos del Libro, 1963– . Annual.   **AA383**

An alphabetical listing of books and pamphlets published in Bolivia, with title and subject indexes and a list of publishers.

Brazil

Bibliografia brasileira, 1938/39–1955. Rio de Janeiro, 1941–59. (Irregular)   **AA384**

Published by Ministério da Educação e Cultura. Instituto Nacional do Livro (form of name varies).

Ceased publication.

1938/39, pub. 1941; 1940, pub. 1954; 1941, pub. 1952; 1942/45, pub. 1953. 2v.; 1946, pub. 1947; 1947/52, pub. 1957; 1953, pub. 1954; 1954, pub. 1956; 1955, pub. 1959.

A comprehensive dictionary catalog, arranged by author, title, and subject in one alphabet. Includes trade books only. A list of publishers at the back of each volume.

Sacramento Blake, Augusto Victorino Alves do. Diccionario bibliographico brazileiro. Rio de Janeiro, Typ. Nacional, 1883–1902. 7v. (Readex microprint)   **AA385**

Arranged alphabetically by *first* names.

—— —— Indice alphabetico, comp. pelo Jango Fischer. Rio de Janeiro, Impr. Nacional, 1937. 127p. (Readex microprint)

Current

Boletim bibliográfico brasileiro, v.1, no.1– . Nov.–Dez. 1952/Jan.–Fev. 1953– . Rio de Janeiro, 1953– . Bimonthly.   **AA386**

Published under the auspices of the Sindicato Nacional das Emprêsas Editoras de Livros e Publicações Culturais.

A classified list based on the legal deposit, claiming to include all Brazilian publications for the period covered and giving full bibliographical information and prices. Does not include serials. Title index in each issue.

Rio de Janeiro. Biblioteca Nacional. Boletim bibliográfico. Rio de Janeiro, 1951– . Semiannual.   **AA387**

A new series, much more comprehensive than the old which began in 1918 and was published irregularly to 1938. Based on legal deposit, it lists Brazilian publications by a simplified Decimal Classification scheme and includes books, pamphlets, music, official publications, etc. Full bibliographical details are given and, in many cases, prices. Name index including authors and subjects of biographies. The second part of each year includes a classified list of periodicals and a directory of publishers.

Bulgaria

Pogorelov, Valerij. Opis na starite pechatani Bulgarski knigi, 1802–1877. Sofija, Narodna Biblioteka, 1923. 795p.   **AA388**

Chronological arrangement with author index.

Supplements and corrections were published by N. Načov, 1923; St. Stanimirov (1926); N. S. Deržavin (1934).

Sofia. Narodna Biblioteka "Vasil Kolarov." Bulgarska vuzrozhdenska knizhnina; analitichen repertoar na Bulgarskite knigi i periodichni izdaniia, 1806–1878. Sustavil Man'o Stoianov. Sofia, Nauka i Izkustvo, 1957– . v.1–   **AA389**

Alphabetical listing of 8900 books and periodical articles with various indexes: chronological, subject, etc.

Téodorov-Balan, Aleksandar. Bulgarski knigopis za sto godini, 1806–1905. Sofia, Drzhavna Pechatnitsa, 1909. 1667p.   **AA390**

A century of Bulgarian bibliography.

Current

Bulgarski knigopis; mesechen bibliografski biuletin za depoziranite v Instituta Knigi i Novi Periodichni Izdaniia. Sofia, 1897– . Annual, 1897–1944; quarterly, 1945–48; monthly, 1949– .   **AA391**

Title varies; publisher varies. From 1897 to 1952, issued by the National Library; since 1953, by the Bulgarian Bibliographical Institute (Bulgarski Bibliografski Institut Elin Pelin) which is now the legal depository.

Lists books and new periodicals. Classified arrangement with annual author indexes.

Canada

Canada. Public Archives. Catalogue of pamphlets in the Public Archives of Canada, with index, prep. by Magdalen Casey. Ottawa, Acland, 1931–32. 2v. (Publ. of the Public Archives of Canada, no.13)   **AA392**

v.1, 1493–1877; v.2, 1878–1931.

1st ed. 1903; 2d ed., covering period 1611–1867, 1911; 3d ed. 1916. The new edition lists a total of 10,072 items, arranged chronologically, with author and subject indexes in each volume. Includes material published in Canada and pamphlets about Canada published elsewhere.

Canadian catalogue of books published in Canada, about Canada, as well as those written by Canadians, with imprint 1921–1949 (consolidated English language reprint edition), with cumulated author index. Toronto, Toronto Public Libraries, 1959. 2v.   **AA393**

v.1, 1921–1939; v.2, 1940–1949.

Reprints of the English-language sections of the annual lists issued during this period, with a cumulative author index in each of the two volumes.

From 1921 to 1943, included books, pamphlets, and selected government documents; from 1944 to 1949, federal government publications were omitted. Usually each annual number was in two sections: (1) books in English, and (2) books in French. The reprint edition is of the English sections only.

Dionne, Narcisse Eutrope. Inventaire chronologique. . . . Québec, 1905–12. 4v. and suppl. (76p.).   **AA394**

Published by the Royal Society of Canada. Also issued in the Society's *Proceedings and transactions,* 2d ser., v.10–12, 14. 1904–6, 1908; 3d ser., v.5. 1911.

[v.1, pt.1], Inventaire chronologique des livres, brochures, journaux et revues publiés en langue française dans la province de Québec, depuis l'établissement de l'imprimerie au Canada jusqu'à nos jours, 1764–1905; [v.1, pt.2], Tables des noms et des matières; v.2, Québec et Nouvelle France, bibliographie; Inventaire chronologique des ouvrages publiés a l'étranger en diverses langues . . . 1534–1906; v.3, Inventaire chronologique des livres, brochures, journaux et revues publiés en langue anglaise dans la province de Québec . . . 1764–1906; v.4, Inventaire chronologique des cartes, plans, atlas, relatifs à la Nouvelle-France et à la province de Québec, 1508–1908; Inventaire chronologique des livres, brochures, journaux et revues . . . 1. suppl., 1904–12.

Gagnon, Philéas. Essai de bibliographie canadienne 1895–1913. Québec, 1895–1913. 2v.   **AA395**

For full information *see* DB84.

Haight, Willet Ricketson. Canadian catalogue of books, 1791–1897. Toronto, Haight, 1896–1904. 3v. (Facsimile repr.: Vancouver, Devlin; London, Pordes, 1958)   **AA396**

Basic volume, 1791–1895, pt.1 of a projected list for that period, 1896. 130p.; Supplements 1–2, 1896–97, Annual Canadian catalogue, 2v. 1898. 48p.; 1904. 57p.

No more published.

Martin, Gérard. Bibliographie sommaire du Canada français, 1854–1954. Québec, Secrétariat de la Province de Québec, 1954. 104p.   **AA397**

For full information *see* DB87.

Morgan, Henry James. Bibliotheca canadensis: or, A manual of Canadian literature. Ottawa, G. E. Desbarats, 1867. 411p.   **AA398**

An alphabetical list of the authors of works, pamphlets, and contributions to the periodical press, with brief biographical notices and lists of their works.

The biographical sketches are occasionally of some length and include, in addition to authors whose books are listed, sketches of Canadian journalists for whom no separate publications are listed.

Tod, Dorothea D. and **Cordingley, Audrey.** A check list of Canadian imprints, 1900–1925. Catalogue d'ouvrages imprimés au Canada. Prelim. checking ed. Ottawa, Canadian Bibliographic Centre. Public Archives of Canada, 1950. 370 l.   **AA399**

Prepared to fill the gap in Canadian national bibliography.

An alphabetically arranged checklist of books and pamphlets (of more than 50 pages). Government documents and serial publications are not included.

Tremaine, Marie. A bibliography of Canadian imprints, 1751–1800. Toronto, Univ. of Toronto Pr., 1952. 705p.   **AA400**

A full record of what is known of the first fifty years of the Provincial press. Books, magazines, pamphlets, newspapers, broadsides, and handbills are included, both those actually issued and those known to have been projected. Full bibliographical information is given for each item, and copies are located in Canadian, American, and foreign libraries. Good descriptive notes make this a guide to the society and thought of the period. A section on printing offices and a good general index to the volume.

Turek, Victor. Polonica Canadiana: a bibliographical list of the Canadian Polish imprints, 1848–1957. Toronto, Polish Alliance Pr., 1958. 138p. (Canadian Polish Congress. Polish Research Inst. in Canada. Studies, 2)   **AA401**

Nearly 800 items, most of them annotated.

Current

Canadiana, 1950– . Ottawa, Nat. Lib. of Canada, 1951– . Monthly, with annual cumulations.   **AA402**

Succeeds the *Canadian catalogue of books,* 1921–1949 (AA393). 1950/1951 (pub. 1962). Coverage varies somewhat. Recent volumes are in three parts: pt.1, a classified arrangement of "publications of Canadian origin and interest," listing books, pamphlets, periodicals, yearbooks, etc., with index to authors, titles, added entries, subjects of biographies, place-names in titles, etc.; pt.2, publications of the Government of Canada, in two sections, English and French; pt.3, publications of the Provincial governments of Canada. Beginning in 1964, pts.2 and 3 have a combined index of personal authors and distinctive titles. The annual volumes cumulate, with minor revisions, the monthly issues with complete indexes.

From June 1964– , pt.4 has been added, listing moving pictures produced in Canada in two sections, English and French.

Société des Écrivains Canadiens. Bulletin bibliographique. v.1– . Montréal, Société, 1937– . Annual.
AA403

Lists Canadian works published in French, and French or foreign works published or reprinted in Canada, with author and title indexes.

Caribbean

Bibliografía de Centroamérica y del Caribe, 1956– . Comp. bajo los auspicios de la Unesco por la Agrupación bibliográfica cubana José Toribio Medina y realizada por la Dirección General de Archivos y Bibliotecas de España. Habana-Madrid, Agrupación, 1958– . Annual.
AA404

Director Técnico: Fermín Peraza Sarausa.

Covers: Costa Rica, Cuba, El Salvador, Guatemala, Haiti, Honduras, Nicaragua, Panama, Puerto Rico, Republica Dominicana.

Current Caribbean bibliography. Port-of-Spain, Trinidad, Caribbean Commission, Central Secretariat, 1951– 57. v.1–7.
AA405

Subtitle: An alphabetical list of publications issued in the Caribbean territories of France, Great Britain, the Netherlands, and the United States (subtitle varies).

Ceased publication.

v.7 includes: "A bibliography of West Indian literature, 1900–1957," comp. by E. Berthe Canton, p.1–56. This includes the titles classified as Belles-lettres, published in the areas noted above.

Florida. University, Gainesville. Libraries. Catalog Dept. Caribbean acquisitions; materials acquired by the University of Florida, 1957/58– . Gainesville, [Univ. of Florida], 1959– . Annual.
AA406

Lists books, pamphlets, periodicals, newspapers, and microforms "published in or about the Caribbean area, as well as books by authors from the area." Covers the West Indies and Bermuda; Colombia, Venezuela, and the Guianas; Central America and Mexico. Titles in the humanities and social sciences predominate.

Classified arangement with author index. A retrospective volume is planned to cover the years 1947–56.

Ceylon

Ceylon. Office of the Registrar of Books and Newspapers. Catalogue of books (books printed in Ceylon and registered under the Printers and Publishers Ordinance) . . . Nuwara Eliya, Ceylon, Govt. Pr., 1951– . Quarterly (issued as pt.V of the Ceylon Government Gazette).
AA407

Lists books, pamphlets, government publications, and periodicals. The book section is classified without author index.

Preceded by the Office's *Register of books printed in Ceylon,* 1889– .

Ceylon national bibliography, v.1, no.1, Jan. 1963– . Nugegoda, Ceylon, Nat. Bibliography Branch, Dept. of

the Govt. Archivist, 1964– . v.1– . Monthly (?).
AA408

In Sinhalese, Tamil, and English.

A current record of material deposited with the Registrar of Books and Newspapers. Each language division is in two parts (varies slightly): (1) Alphabetical author, title, and subject index; (2) Classified by the Dewey Decimal Classification.

Two preliminary numbers were issued in English, no.1–2, Nov. and Dec. 1962, but apparently are not counted in the new voluming.

Chile

Briseño, Ramón. Estadística bibliográfica de la literatura chilena. Obra compuesta, en virtud de encargo especial del consejo de la Universidad de Chile. Santiago de Chile, Impr. Chilena, 1862–79. 2v.
AA409

t.1, 1812–1859. Impresos chilenos. Obras sobre Chile. Escritores chilenos; t.2, 1860–1876. Prólogo. Prensa chilena por órden alfabético. Prensa chilena por órden cronolójico. Prensa periodística chilena. Bibliografía chilena en el país, desde 1812 hasta 1859. Bibliografía chilena en el extranjero, desde 1860 hasta 1876. Curiosidades bibliográfico-chilenas.

Medina, José Toribio. Bibliografía de la imprenta en Santiago de Chile desde sus orígenes hasta febrero de 1817. Santiago de Chile, Autor, 1891. 179p. (Readex microprint)
AA410

—— —— Adiciones y ampliaciones. Santiago de Chile, Univ. de Chile, 1939. 140p. il.

—— Biblioteca hispano-chilena (1523–1817). Santiago de Chile, Autor, 1897–99. 3v.
AA411

Includes no books printed in Chile, only books printed in Europe or America by Chileans or by Spaniards who wrote in Chile.

Lists 876 titles chronologically, with critical and bibliographical notes and references to authorities. Locates copies.

Montt, Luis. Bibliografía chilena. Santiago de Chile, Impr. Univ., 1904–21. 3v.
AA412

v.1, 1780–1811 (1918); v.2, 1812–1817 (1904); v.3, 1817–1818 (1921).

Of v.1, 264 pages were printed which the author intended to revise; of v.3, 160 pages were printed; sheets of both of these were destroyed, but in 1918 and 1921, reprints of the pages as originally printed were issued.

Revista de bibliografía chilena. Pub. por la Biblioteca Nacional, enero 1913–oct. 1918, 1927–29. Santiago de Chile, Impr. Univ., 1913–29. 9v.
AA413

Quarterly, 1927–29 (1913–18, monthly); 1913–18, have title *Revista de bibliografía chilena y extranjera.* None issued Nov. 1918–1926.

No more published.

A valuable contemporary bibliography, which included special bibliographies in addition to the current record.

Santiago de Chile. Biblioteca Nacional. Bibliografía general de Chile. Por Emilio Vaïsse. Santiago de Chile, Impr. Univ., 1915–[18]. v.1–2.
AA414

Repr. from *Revista de bibliografía chilena y extranjera.*

1. pt. Diccionario de autores y obras (bio-bibliografía y bibliografía): t.1, Bibliografía de bibliografiás chilenas, por R. A. Laval. Diccionario: A–Barros Arana; t.2, Barros B –Bustos.

—— —— Suplemento y adiciones a la Bibliografía de bibliografías, por H. Elgueta de Ochsenius. Santiago de Chile, Impr. Cervantes, 1930. 71p.

A bio-bibliographical dictionary, listing writings of Chilean authors.

No more published.

—— Anuario de la prensa chilena, pub. por la Biblioteca Nacional. 1886–1916. Santiago de Chile, 1887–1927. 31v. **AA415**

Catalog of books deposited in the library under the law of 1872; and from 1891, books by Chilean authors, or relating to Chile, published in other countries.

From 1892, each volume, except 1895, contains an appendix of *publicaciones omitidas* from previous volumes. Musical compositions are entered in volumes for 1896–1900.

Current

Servicio bibliográfico chileno. Chilean bibliographic news service, 1940– . Santiago de Chile, Zamorano y Caperan, 1940– . Monthly; Quarterly (varies). **AA416**

A record of publications which includes prices in both Chilean and United States currency.

Subtitle varies: no.111/112– , Todos los libros publicados en Chile (All the books published in Chile).

China

Cordier, Henri. L'imprimerie sino-européenne en Chine. Bibliographie des ouvrages publiés en Chine par les Européens au XVIIe et au XVIIIe siècles. Paris, Leroux, 1901. 73p. il. (Publ. de l'École des Langues Orientales Vivantes. 5. sér., t.3) **AA417**

Lists mainly works written in the Chinese language or translated into Chinese by missionaries.

First published in 1883 as "Essai d'une bibliographie des ouvrages publiés en Chine par les Européens au XVIIe et au XVIIIe siècles" in *Mélanges orientaux* (Publ. de l'École des Langues Orientales Vivantes. 2. sér., t.9).

Quarterly bulletin of Chinese bibliography, v.1–4, 1934–37; n.s. v.1–7, 1940–47. Peiping, Nat. Lib. of Peiping, 1934–47. Irregular. **AA418**

Includes general articles, book reviews, notes and news, and an annotated, selected list of new books published in China, divided into three sections: (1) Books in Chinese; (2) Books in foreign languages; (3) Government publications. Scope of contents varies.

Colombia

Laverde Amaya, Isidoro. Bibliografía colombiana. Bogotá, M. Rivas, 1895. v.1. 296p. **AA419**

v.1, A–O; no more published.

Bio-bibliography; includes mainly 19-century publications, with a few of earlier date.

Medina, José Toribio. La imprenta en Bogotá (1739–1821). Notas bibliográficas. Santiago de Chile, Impr. Elzeviriana, 1904. 101p. (Readex microprint) **AA420**

—— La imprenta en Cartagena de las Indias (1809–1820). Notas bibliográficas. Santiago de Chile, Impr. Elzeviriana, 1904. 70p. (Readex microprint) **AA421**

Posada, Eduardo. Bibliografía bogotana. Bogotá, Impr. Nacional, 1917–25. 2v. facsim. (Biblioteca de historia nacional, v.16, 36) **AA422**

Arranged chronologically, 1738–1831, with author and subject indexes both alphabetical and by date.

Current

Anuario bibliográfico colombiano, 1951– . Bogotá, Inst. Caro y Cuervo, Dept. de Bibliografía, 1952– . Annual. **AA423**

Publisher varies.

Books, pamphlets, and periodicals published in Colombia, and foreign publications dealing with Colombia. Arrangement is alphabetical, books and periodicals in separate lists, and there are indexes by publishers, authors, and titles.

1951/56– , comp. by Ruben Perez Ortiz.

Costa Rica

Dobles Segreda, Luis. Índice bibliográfico de Costa Rica. San José, Lehmann, 1927–36. v.1–9. **AA424**

t.1: sec. 1, Agricultura y veterinaria; sec. 2, Ciencias físicas y naturales; t.2: sec. 3, Filologiá y gramática; sec. 4, Geografía y geología, Lista de mapas de Costa Rica; t.3: sec. 5, Matemáticas, ingeniería y finanzas; sec. 6, Psicología, filosofía y religión; t.4: sec. 7, Novela, cuento y artículo literario; sec. 8, Teatro; t.5, sec. 9, Historia hasta 1900; t.6, sec. 10, Historia desde 1900 hasta 1933; t.7, sec. 11, and t.8, sec. 11 (cont.), Política y derecho desde 1831 hasta 1935; t.8, sec. 12, Milicia; t.9, sec. 13, Hígiene y Medicina.

Other volumes were projected to cover *educación, sociología y demografía, poesía, Índice alfabético de autores* (*biográfico y bibliográfico*), but have not been published.

Lines, Jorge A. Libros y folletos publicados en Costa Rica durante los años 1830–1849. San José, Univ. de Costa Rica, Facultad de Letras y Filosofía, 1944. 151p. il. **AA425**

Lists 103 titles arranged chronologically with author index.

Current

San José, Costa Rica. Biblioteca Nacional. Boletín bibliográfico; publicaciones nacionales correspondientes al año 1935/38–55. San José, Impr. Nacional, 1939–56. Annual. **AA426**

Ceased publication.

Superseded by:

Anuario bibliográfico costarricense, 1956– . San José, Impr. Nacional, 1958– . Annual. **AA427**

At head of title: Asociación costarricense de bibliotecarios. Comité nacional de bibliografía "Adolfo Blen."

Lists titles in two alphabets: one by author, the second classified by subject. An index of specific subjects and of names not appearing as main entries.

Cuba

Bachiller y Morales, Antonio. Catálogo de libros y folletos publicados en Cuba desde la introducción de la imprenta hasta 1840. (In his Apuntes para la historia de las letras y de la instrucción publica de la Isla de Cuba. Habana, P. Massana, 1861. v.3, p.121–241. Reprinted in his Apuntes . . . Habana, Cultural, 1936–37. v.3, p.243–457) **AA428**

Arranged chronologically. No index.

—— —— Suplementos y adiciones. (Revista de Cuba 7:354–64, 491–98; 8:71–78, 124–35. abril, mayo, julio, agosto 1880)

Medina, José Toribio. La imprenta en La Habana (1707–1810): notas bibliográficas. Santiago de Chile, Impr. Elzeviriana, 1904. 199p. (Readex microprint) **AA429**

Trelles y Govín, Carlos Manuel. Ensayo de bibliografía cubana de los siglos XVII y XVIII. Seguido de unos apuntes para la bibliografía dominicana y portorriqueña. Matanzas, "El Escritorio," 1907–8. 228p., and suppl., 76p. (Readex microprint) **AA430**

—— Bibliografía cubana del siglo XIX. Matanzas, Quirós y Estrada, 1911–15. 8v. (Readex microprint) **AA431**

t.1, 1800–1825; t.2, 1826–1840. Seguido de una Relación de periódicos publicados en Cuba en el siglo XX, por F. Llaca, y unas Noticias curiosas referentes á escritores de los siglos XVII y XVIII, por M. Perez Beato; t.3–8, 1841–1899. Ensayo de biblioteca cubana del siglo XIX; Indice.

—— Bibliografía cubana del siglo XX (1900–1916). Matanzas, Quirós y Estrada, 1916–17. 2v. (Readex microprint) **AA432**

—— Biblioteca científica cubana. Matanzas, J. F. Oliver, 1918–20. v.1–2. il. (Readex microprint) **AA433**
Lists 9500 titles of books and periodical articles.

—— Biblioteca geográfica cubana. Matanzas, J. F. Oliver, 1920–25. 340p., and suppl., 64p. (Readex microprint) **AA434**
Main work and supplement list 3900 titles of books and periodical articles.

—— Biblioteca histórica cubana. Matanzas, J. F. Oliver, 1922–26. 3v. (Readex microprint) **AA435**
Lists 17,000 titles of books and periodical articles.

Current

Anuario bibliográfico cubano: 1937– . Gainesville, Fla., Anuario Bibliográfico Cubano, 1938– . v.1– . Annual. **AA436**
Through 1959 (pub. 1960) published in Havana.
Ed., Fermín Peraza Sarausa.
Arrangement varies from year to year, but each issue gives an excellent coverage.
Supplemented by the quarterly bibliographies which appeared in the *Boletín del Anuario bibliográfico cubano* 1938–June 1962, and now appearing as separate *Trimestre bibliográfico*, v.1, no.1– , July/Sept. 1962– , also issued in Gainesville.

Czechoslovakia

Bibliografický katalog, 1922–28. Red. Lad. J. Živný. Praha, 1923–28. (Publikace Československého Ústavu Bibliografického v Praze, sv. 2–16) Weekly. **AA437**
Half title in German and French.
Classified, with annual author index. Published by the Institut Bibliographique Tchécoslovaque à Prague.

Bibliografický katalog Československé Republiky; literární tvorba z roku, 1929–46. V Praze, Nákl. Ministerstva Školství a Národní Osvěty, 1930–47. 18v. in 21. Annual. **AA438**
A classified, annual catalog of books and pamphlets with indexes of authors and subjects. Does not include periodicals.

Knihopis českých a slovenských tisků od doby nejstarší až do konce XVIII století. Praha, Nákl. Československé Akademie. Věd., 1925–63. v.1–2, pts.1–8. (In progress) **AA439**
v.1 (to 1500), A–Z, and atlas of facsim.; v.2, Tisky z let, 1501–1800, pts.1–8(incompl.), A–Švancar.
Title varies: v.1–2, sešit 18, *Knihopis československých tisků.*
Publisher varies.
Bibliography of Czech and Slovakian imprints from early times to the end of the 18th century.

Kunc, Jaroslav. Knižní novinky, 1935–1947; seznam původních i přeložených českých knih Ústřední knihovny hl. m. Prahy. Praha, 1948. 2v. **AA440**

Mišianik, Ján. Bibliografia slovenského písomníctva do konca XIX. stor. (Doplnky k Risnerovej bibliografii) Bratislava, Slovenská Akadémia vied a umení, 1946. 300p. (Práce z vedeckých ústavov Slovenskej Akadémie vied a umení. Rad. A. Sv.5) **AA441**
Supplement to Rizner (AA443).

Nosovský, Karel and **Pražák, Vilém.** Soupis československé literatury za léta 1901–1925. . . . V Praze, Nákl. Svazu Knihkupců a Nakladatelů, 1931–38. 2v. in 3. **AA442**
v.1–2, author list, A–Z; v.3, classified subject index.

Rizner, L'udovít Vladimir. Bibliografia písomníctva slovenského na spôsob slovníka od najstarších čias do konca r. 1900. S pripojenou bibliografiou archeologickou, historickou . . . vydáva matičná sprava. V Turcianskom Sv. Martine, Nákl. Matice Slovenskej, 1929–34. 6v. **AA443**
An alphabetical catalog of Slovakian literature to 1900. Often gives brief biographical notices of authors.

Current

Bibliografický katalog Československé Republiky. . . . Ročník 1, 1933– . V Praze, 1933– . Weekly. **AA444**
From 1933 to 1947, published concurrently with the yearly bibliography of the same name (AA438), of which 1946 is the last volume received.
Since 1946 the weekly has been issued in three parts, the titles of which have varied; since Jan. 1951 they have appeared as: *České knihy* (weekly); *Slovenská kniha* (approximately 15 issues per year); *České a slovenské hudebniny* (approximately 10 issues per year). The first and third of these (Czech books, and Czech and Slovak music) are published by the National Library in Prague, the Slovak books by the Slovak University in Bratislava; both are legal repositories.
Arrangement is classified; indexes have been issued annually by author and subject for most years.

Denmark

Early

Nielsen, Lauritz. Dansk Bibliografi, 1482–1550, 1551–1600, med saerligt hensyn til dansk bogtrykkerkunsts Historie. København, Gyldendal, 1919–35. 2v. and *Registre* (126p.). il. **AA445**
1482–1550, Author and title list, A–Z, no.1–298. 1919. 247p.; 1551–1600, Author and title list, A–AE, no.299–1672. 1931–33. 677p.; *Registre:* alphabetical author index, alphabetical title index, chronological index, subject index.
Two companion works listing together 1672 items and giving for each item: title, detailed collation, bibliographical references, and location of copies. Indexes of places and of printers and publishers in each work.

Bruun, Christian Walther. Bibliotheca danica. Systematisk Fortegnelse over den danske Literatur fra 1482 til 1830, efter Samlingerne i det Store Kongelige Bibliothek i Kjøbenhavn. Kjøbenhavn, Gyldendal, 1877–1931. 4v., suppl., and index. **AA446**
A classified bibliography of Danish materials from 1482 to 1830.
v.4 includes a *Supplement* (1914) and a *Register* (1927–31) by Lauritz Nielsen.
The index is in three parts: (1) Authors; (2) Anonymous works; (3) Subjects.

—— —— Reprint: København, Rosenkilde og Bagger, 1961–63. 5v.
v.5 consists of the original supplement, published in 1914, and an additional supplement covering 1914–62, by Eric Dal; and the original indexes with an additional index to the new supplement.

—— —— Supplement 1831–1840 til Bibliotheca danica og Dansk Bogfortegnelse, udarb. af H. Ehrencron-Müller. København, Gads, 1943–48. Hft.1–4. **AA447**

Hft.1, Alfabetisk Fortegnelse, 1943, 422col.; Hft. 2, Systematisk Fortegnelse, 1944, col.425–860; Hft.3–4, Supplement til Bibliotheca danica . . . Bibliotheca slesvico-holsatica til 1840; Alfabetisk Fortegnelse, 1945, col.863–1184; Systematisk Fortegnelse, 1948, col.1187–1564.

Hft.1–2 are designed to fill the gap in Danish bibliography between the Bruun *Bibliotheca danica* (AA446), which covers the period to 1830, and the *Dansk Bogfortegnelse* (AA448), which starts with 1841. Hft.3–4 form a catalog of Schleswig-Holstein literature from the earliest times to 1840.

19th and 20th centuries

Dansk Bogfortegnelse (The Danish national bibliography), 1841/58–1945/49. København, Gads, 1861–1953.
AA448
19th-century cumulations vary in number of years covered. Quinquennial since 1915.
From 1915/19 to 1930/34 includes *Islandsk Bogfortegnelse*.
Covers all material entered for copyright. Alphabetical author and title list, followed by classified list, with a subject index to the latter.

Ehrencron-Müller, Holger. Stikordsregister til den danske Skønlitteratur indtil 1840. . . . København, Gads, 1941. 29p.
AA449
————— 1841–1908. København, Gads, 1918. 81p.
————— 1909–1940. København, Gads, 1941. 128p.

Dania polyglotta; répertoire bibliographique des ouvrages, études, articles, etc., en langues étrangères parus en Danemark de 1901 à 1944. Copenhague, Bibliothèque Royale, 1947–51. v.1–3.
AA450
Publié par l'Institut Danois des Échanges Internationaux de Publications Scientifiques et Littéraires sous la rédaction de son directeur K. Schmidt-Phiseldeck avec la collaboration de Henning Einersen.
Contents: v.1, Ouvrages; v.2, Périodiques, études et articles; v.3, Addenda, musique, index.
Includes books and articles published in Denmark in foreign languages by native and foreign scholars.
Works in each volume are grouped under language and then arranged by class, with a general author index.
Continued by the annual *Dania polyglotta*, 1. Année, 1945– . Copenhague, Bibliothèque Royale, 1946– .

Current

Dansk Bogfortegnelse, 1851– . København, Gads, 1851– . Annual.
AA451
Annual cumulation of the current list of the same title forming an annual supplement to the 5-year *Dansk Bogfortegnelse* (AA448).
The current list is published weekly in *Det danske Bogmarked*, cumulating at intervals. The annual cumulation forms the permanent volume for the year. An author and title list, followed by a classified index.
A separately paged supplement *Islandsk Bogfortegnelse* was included irregularly, 1899–1920; see AA544.
1851–55, called *Maanedlig dansk Bogfortegnelse*.

Dominican Republic

Anuario bibliográfico dominicano. 1946–47. Ciudad Trujillo, 1947–48. 2v.
AA452
At head of title: Oficina de Canje y Difusion Cultural.
Supersedes the *Boletín bibliográfico dominicano* of which only two numbers were published: no.1, July–Aug. 1945, which covered 1944, and no.2, Sept.–Dec. 1945, which covered 1945.

Ecuador

Espinosa Cordero, Nicolás. Bibliografía ecuatoriana, 1534–1809. Cuenca, Impr. del Colegio Nacional "Benigno Malo," 1934. 171p. (Pt.4 of his Estudios literarios y bibliográficos, p.93–256)
AA453
Includes brief biographical notes.

Medina, José Toribio. La imprenta en el Quito (1760–1818): notas bibliográficas. Santiago de Chile, Impr. Elzeviriana, 1904. 86p. (Readex microprint)
AA454

England

See Great Britain, p.45.

Finland

Suomalainen kirjallisuus 1544–1939/43. Aakkosellinen ja aineenmukainen luettelo. La littérature finnoise 1544–1939/43. Catalogue alphabétique et systématique. Helsingissä, 1878–1905; Helsinki, 1912–52. (Added title page: Suomalaisen Kirjallisuuden Seuran. Toimituksia. 57osa; 1–16 lisävihko)
AA455
The set consists of: (1) a basic volume, 1544–1877, by Valfrid Vasenius; (2) five supplements to this, covering 1878–79, 1880–85, 1886–91, 1892–95, 1896–1900; and (3) continuation volumes: quinquennial, 1901/05–1916/20; triennial, 1921/23–1936/38; quinquennial, 1939/43.
Alphabetical by author and title, with classed indexes.
Continued by:

Suomen kirjallisuus. Finlands literatur. The Finnish national bibliography, 1944/48– . Helsinki, Helsingen Yliopiston Kirjasto, [1954–]. Quinquennial, 1944/48; triennial, 1949/51– .
AA456
Volumes published in irregular order, some not yet complete.

Katalog öfver den svenska literaturen i Finland samt arbeten på främmande språk. 1886–[1900]. Helsingfors, 1892–1924. 6v. (Skrifter utgifna af Svenska Literatursällskapet i Finland. 21, 53, 54, 166: 1 and 2)
AA457
Title varies slightly.
Lists all works in Swedish published in Finland; all works in Swedish written by Finnish authors but published abroad; and all works in foreign languages published in Finland.

Pipping, Fredrik Wilhelm. Luettelo suomeksi präntätyistä kirjoista, kuin myös muutamista muista teoksista, joissa löytyy joku kirjoitus suomen, kielellä, tahi joku johdatus sitä tuntemaan. Helsingfors, Finska Litteratursällsks Tryck, 1856–57. 756p. (Suomalaisen Kirjallisuuden Seuran. Toimituksia. 20)
AA458
Lists Finnish imprints in chronological order from 1542 to 1856. Author index.

Current

Suomessa ilmestyneen kirjallisuuden luettelo. Katalog över i Finland utkommen litteratur, 1945– . Helsinki, Kirjallisuuden Seuran Kirjapainon Oy, 1950– . Annual.
AA459
Quarterly 1945–48; annual since 1949.
Lists new Finnish and Swedish books alphabetically in two sections with subject indexes, also divided by language. Books and periodical articles in foreign languages published in Finland are listed as pt.3, but have no subject index.

France

Paris. Bibliothèque Nationale. Catalogue général des livres imprimés. Auteurs. Paris, Impr. Nationale, 1900– . v.1– . **AA460**

v.1– , A– .

The Bibliothèque Nationale has received copies of all books published in France since the establishment, by law, of the *dépôt légal* in the reign of Henri II. It has the largest collection of French books in existence, and its printed *Catalogue* is the most important general bibliography of French publications. For full description *see* AA72.

Répertoire de bibliographie française; contenant tous les ouvrages imprimés en France et aux colonies et les ouvrages français publiés à l'étranger, 1501–1930. . . . Paris, Letouzey, 1937–41. Fasc.1–10. **AA461**

v.1 (fasc. 1–6), A–Angélique; v.2 (fasc. 7–10), Angelis–Arthaud.

An attempt at a comprehensive record of French bibliography, 1501–1930, including, in general, books published in France and books in French published in French colonies and abroad with certain omissions. Unfortunately, no more published.

Early

✓ **British Museum. Dept. of Printed Books.** Short-title catalogue of books printed in France and of French books printed in other countries from 1470 to 1600 now in the British Museum. London, Trustees, 1924. 491p. **AA462**

Books printed in France, p.1–450; Books in French printed elsewhere, p. 451–91.

An important record of about 12,000 editions, including many items not found in the printed catalog of the Bibliothèque Nationale. Information given includes: author, brief title, editor, translator, etc., place, publisher, date, size.

Brunet, Jacques Charles. Manuel du libraire et de l'amateur de livres. 5. éd. augm. Paris, Didot, 1860–80. 9v. **AA463**

For full description *see* AA58.

Harvard University. Harvard College Library. Dept. of Printing and Graphic Arts. Catalogue of books and manuscripts. Pt.1: French 16th century books. Comp. by Ruth Mortimer under the supervision of Philip Hofer and William A. Jackson. Cambridge, Belknap Pr. of Harvard Univ. Pr., 1964. 2v. il., facsims. **AA464**

An extensive illustrated bibliography, with detailed descriptions and references to other sources.

La Croix du Maine, François Grudé and **Du Verdier, Antoine.** Les bibliothèques françoises de La Croix du Maine et de Du Verdier. Nouv. éd. rev., corr., et augm. . . . par Rigoley de Juvigny. Paris, Saillant & Nyon, 1772–73. 6v. **AA465**

The original edition of La Croix du Maine published Paris, 1584; of Du Verdier, Lyons, 1585. The two works complement each other and form a bio-bibliographical catalog of French publications to about the end of the 16th century. A valuable record although it includes many inaccuracies.

Le Petit, Jules. Bibliographie des principales éditions originales d'écrivains français du XV° aux XVIII° siècle. Paris, Quantin, 1888. 583p. il., facsims. (Photographic repr.: Paris, Jeanne et Brulon, 1927) **AA466**

Facsimiles of title pages with long, detailed descriptions of original editions.

Tchemerzine, Avenir. Bibliographie d'éditions originales et rares d'auteurs français des XV°, XVI°, XVII° et XVIII° siècles contenant environ 6000 fac-similés de titres et de gravures. Paris, Plée, 1927–34. 10v. il. **AA467**

Gives detailed bibliographical descriptions, line-by-line transcriptions, and many reproductions of title pages and engravings.

18th century

Quérard, Joseph Marie. La France littéraire, ou Dictionnaire bibliographique des savants, historiens et gens de lettres de la France, ainsi que des littérateurs étrangers qui ont écrit en français, plus particulièrement pendant les XVIII° et XIX° siècles. Paris, Didot, 1827–64. 12v. (Repr.: Paris, Maisonneuve, 1964. 12v.) **AA468**

v.1–10, A–Z; v.11–12, supplements containing: Corrections, additions; Auteurs, pseudonymes et anonymes; v.11, A–Razy; v.12, Re–Roguet. Emphasis is on the humanities and pure science.

v.11–12 (pub. 1854–64) list by real name the authors of pseudonymous and anonymous works, giving the pseudonyms under which each has written, with brief biographical information, titles of works, etc. They serve as an index to Quérard's *Supercheries littéraires dévoilées* (AA109).

19th and 20th centuries

Quérard, Joseph Marie [and others]. La littérature française contemporaine, 1827–49 . . . Dictionnaire bibliographique . . . accompagné de biographies et de notes historiques et littéraires. Paris, Daguin, 1842–57. 6v. **AA469**

A continuation of Quérard's *La France littéraire* (AA468), on the same general plan.

Title varies.

✓ **Catalogue général de la librairie française,** 1840–1925. Paris, Lorenz, 1867–1945. v.1–34. **AA470**

Publisher varies.

Usually cited as *Lorenz.*

v.1–11, edited by Otto Lorenz; v.12–28, pt.2, by D. Jordell; v.28, pt.3–v.32, by Henri Stein; v.33–34, by the Service Bibliographique Hachette.

The standard French list for the 19th and early 20th centuries. Covers French publications by periods ranging from 3 years to 25 years, the volumes for each period consisting of: (1) a main author and title list containing full information, i.e., author's full name, full title of book, edition, place (if other than Paris), date, publisher, paging, size, price, and occasional brief notes; and (2) a subject list arranged by broad subjects, with briefer information. Includes books, pamphlets, some theses and annuals, but not periodicals, and lists some Belgian and Swiss publications. Special features are: (1) the inclusion of brief biographical notes about the authors whose works are listed; (2) the linking together of all entries for the same author by cross references from the later volumes to the earlier ones; (3) occasional brief notes which tell whether a book has been crowned by the French Academy; which refer, in case of reissues or later editions, to date of first edition; and which give, in case of books or pamphlets reprinted from periodicals, reference to volume or date of the periodical, etc. The information about original publication in periodicals is often very useful.

Vicaire, Georges. Manuel de l'amateur de livres du XIX° siècle, 1801–1893. Paris, Rouquette, 1894–1920. 8v. **AA471**

v.1–7, A–Z, 1801–1893; v.8, Table des ouvrages cités. Crowned by the French Academy.

An attempt to do for 19th-century French literature what Brunet's *Manuel* (AA58) does for general literature of an earlier period. Covers some of the same period as Lorenz (AA470), but with a selection of material, listing fewer titles than Lorenz but giving fuller information and annotations for those listed. Gives full titles and bibliographical notes, original price, and, often, prices realized at various auction sales.

Current

✓"**Biblio,**" catalogue des ouvrages parus en langue française dans le monde entier, oct. 1933– . Paris, Service Bibliographique des Messageries Hachette, 1933– . v.1– . Monthly (10 issues a year with annual cumulations). **AA472**

Subtitle varies.

The most easily used trade bibliography covering books published in France and French books published in Belgium, Switzerland, Canada, etc. A dictionary catalog, published monthly with annual cumulation, entering each book under author, subject, and title with many cross references. Full information—given under author entry—includes author's name, full title, date, place (if other than Paris), publisher, paging, size, illustrations, series, price.

The monthly issues contain bio-bibliographical sketches, frequently of some length, brief book reviews, etc., which are not carried over into the annual volumes. As these sketches are indexed in the *Biography index* (AJ2), libraries may wish to retain them.

✓**Bibliographie de la France;** journal général de l'imprimerie et de la librairie. Paris, Cercle de la Librairie, 1811– . v.1– . Weekly. **AA473**

Arrangement and parts issued vary.

The standard weekly list, recording material received through the *dépôt légal,* including books, pamphlets, official publications, music, prints, and, in addition, a monthly record of gifts to the Bibliothèque Nationale. At present, each number consists of three main parts: (1) *Bibliographie officielle,* (2) *Chronique,* and (3) *Annonces.*

1. pt.: The *Bibliographie officielle* contains *Livres,* a classed list of books, pamphlets, etc., recorded with full cataloging information which includes author, full title, place, publisher, date, size, paging, price (if information about price is supplied by publisher), and pressmark of the book in the Bibliothèque Nationale. The following supplements are published at irregular intervals and began at different dates: A, Périodiques; B, Gravures, estampes et photographies; C, Musique; D, Thèses; E, Atlas, cartes et plans; F, Publications officielles gouvernementales et administratives; G, Catalogues des ventes publiques. Special supplements are also issued from time to time. At the end of the year there is a general author and title index to the record of books and gifts, an alphabetical list of new periodicals, an index to musical works, and a table of illustrators. Coverage of these indexes varies somewhat from year to year.

2. pt.: The *Chronique* contains publishing news, postal and copyright information, legal and government notes, occasional historical articles, obituaries, lists of literary prizes, etc.

3. pt.: The *Annonces* section consists of advertising pages with indexes as follows:

Les livres de la semaine, a classified list, which cumulates into *Les livres du mois,* also classified with indexes of authors and of titles. This cumulates into the quarterly and semi-annual indexes, *Les livres du trimestre* and *Les livres du semestre,* which are author and title lists rather than classified.

Les livres de l'année (AA474a), which cumulates these indexes, is in three parts: (1) classified, (2) titles, and (3) authors. It includes not only all the works listed in the *Annonces,* but also books listed in the *Bibliographie officielle* which did not appear in the *Annonces.*

Livres et matériel d'enseignement, consisting of publishers' announcements with annual indexes by author and by title under classification headings.

For full description of the *Bibliographie* and all its parts *see* Malclès, *Les sources du travail bibliographique* 1:122–26 (AA301).

Librairie française, catalogue général des ouvrages en vente. 1. jan. 1930. Paris, Cercle de la Librairie, 1930. 3v. **AA474**

Continued by compilations in the same form covering 1930–33, 1933–45, 1946–55.

v.1–2, Répertoire par auteurs; v.3, Répertoire par titres.

Compiled from the annual volumes of the *Les livres de l'année* of the *Bibliographie de la France* (AA473). Lists books, new periodicals, publications of corporate bodies, and some documents.

Gives for each book listed: author, title, paging, date, publisher, binding, illustration, format, price.

——— Les livres de l'année, 1933–1938, 1946/48– . Annual. **AA474a**

Not pub. 1939–45?.

Cumulates the listings in the *Bibliographie de la France* (AA473) and is itself cumulated into the *Librairie française.*

Each volume is in three parts: pt.1, Classified by the main divisions of the Decimal Classification; pt.2, Titles; pt.3, Alphabetical lists of authors, illustrators, publishers, booksellers, etc.

Regional

❧ Many regional bibliographies, for provinces, departments, towns, etc., must often be used for local publications not included in the general bibliographies listed above. Local bibliographies are listed freely in the *Répertoire bibliographique de l'histoire de France* (DC65). For lists of older publications *see* Stein's *Manuel,* p.501–7 (AA9), and the article *"Bibliographie"* in *La grande encyclopédie* 6:637–38 (AD27).

Germany

Early

Borchling, Conrad and **Claussen, Bruno.** Niederdeutsche Bibliographie; Gesamtverzeichnis der niederdeutschen Drucke bis zum Jahre 1800. . . . Neumünster, Karl Wachholst, 1931–36. 2v. **AA475**

v.1, 1473–1600; v.2, 1601–1800; Nachträge, 1481–1800; Ergänzungen u. Verbesserungen, col.1871–91; Indexes (of places, printers, names, first lines, catchwords, etc.), col.1893–2018; Letzte Nachträge u. Verbesserungen, col. 2019–20.

Arranged chronologically; lists more than 4700 items, described in detail with line-by-line transcription and with some location of copies.

British Museum. Dept. of Printed Books. Short-title catalogue of books printed in the German-speaking countries and German books printed in other countries from 1455 to 1600 now in the British Museum. London, 1962. 1224p. **AA476**

One of a series of short-title catalogues, similar in scope and arrangement. Arranged alphabetically by author and anonymous title, with some collective headings, as used in the Museum's *General catalogue of printed books* (AA67), followed by an index of publishers, with titles listed chronologically under publisher.

Panzer, Georg Wolfgang Franz. Annalen der ältern deutschen Litteratur. . . . Nürnberg, Grattenauer, 1788–1805. 2v. **AA477**

v.1, to 1520; v.2, 1521–26.

Zusatze. . . . Leipzig, Hempel, 1802. 198p. Suppl. to v.1.

Supplemented by Joseph Heller in *Serapeum,* 4. Jahrg. (1843), p.299–303, 6. Jahrg. (1845), p.312–20, 327–33; and by E. O. Weller's *Repertorium typographicum. Die deutsche Literatur in ersten Viertel des sechzehnten Jahrhunderts.* . . . Nördlingen, 1864 (added title page: Georg Wolfgang Panzers, Annalen der älteren deutschen Literatur (MD–MDXXVI. 3. Th.).

Now largely superseded by later compilations of incunabula, e.g., British Museum. *Catalogue of books printed in the XVth century* . . . v.2–3 (AA167).

18th and 19th centuries

❧ The 18th and 19th centuries are well covered by series of catalogs published by three German bookdealers: Heinsius, beginning with 1700; Kayser with 1750; and Hinrichs with 1850, thus overlapping each other but together providing a continuous record from 1700 to 1910, when the *Deutsches Bücherverzeichnis* superseded and carried on Kayser and Hinrichs, following the general bibliographical practices of Kayser.

There are subject indexes to Kayser covering 1750–1832 and 1891–1910, and Georg (AA482) provides a subject approach from 1883 to 1912, but there are no cumulated subject indexes for 1700–50, or 1833–82.

Heinsius, Wilhelm. Allgemeines Bücher-Lexikon, oder vollständiges alphabetisches Verzeichnis aller von 1700 bis zu Ende 1892 erschienenen Bücher. Leipzig, Brockhaus, 1812–94. 19v. (Repr.: Graz, Akademische Druck, 1963) **AA478**

No more published. Publisher varies.

Lists books, pamphlets, and periodicals alphabetically by author or catchword title in chronological periods: 1700–1810 in 4v.; thereafter to 1892 in volumes, usually but not always quinquennial. Gives author, title, paging, place, publisher, date, and price. Through 1867, prices are given in thalers and neugroschen, after 1867 in marks and pfennigs.

Supplementary lists: 1700–1827, Romane, Schauspiele; 1868–92, Karten und Pläne.

Kayser, Christian Gottlob. Vollständiges Bücher-Lexikon, 1750–1910. Leipzig, Tauchnitz, 1834–1911. 36v. (Repr.: Graz, Akademische Druck, 1961–62) **AA479**

No more published. Publisher varies.

1750–1832, in 6v. Continued to 1910 by volumes published at irregular intervals.

Lists books, pamphlets, periodicals, etc. in an author list with some title entries, giving, for each book listed, author, title, place, publisher, date, volumes, paging, series, prices of different editions, etc. Entry is generally under the author's name, but works having such titles as Wörterbuch, Lexikon, Jahresverzeichnis, etc. are entered under title rather than compiler, and under that entry are alphabetized by main subject word in title, the alphabetizing word being indicated by a different type or spacing. Before 1870, prices were given in thalers and neugroschen, after that date in marks and pfennigs. Includes some Austrian and Swiss publications.

—— —— Sachregister. Leipzig, Schumann, 1838. 511p.
Indexes v.1–6, 1750–1832.

—— —— Sach- und Schlagwortregister, 1891–1910. Leipzig, Tauchnitz, 1896–1912. 5v.

Each index covers two volumes of the main work, as follows: v.27–28, 1891–94; v.29–30, 1895–98; v.31–32, 1899–1902; v.33–34, 1903–6; v.35–36, 1907–10.

Hinrichs, J. C. Fünfjahrs-Katalog der im deutschen Buchhandel erschienenen Bücher, Zeitschriften, Landkarten, etc.; Titelverzeichnis und Sachregister, 1851–1912. Leipzig, Hinrichs, 1857–1913. 13v. **AA480**

Title varies.

Five-year cumulations of *Hinrichs' Halbjahrs–Katalog,* with additions and corrections. No more published.

Thelert, Gustav. Supplement zu Heinsius', Hinrichs' und Kaysers Bücher-Lexikon. . . . Grossenhain, Baumert, 1893. 405p. **AA481**

Subtitle: Verzeichniss einer Anzahl Schriften, welche seit der Mitte des neunzehnten Jahrhunderts in Deutschland erschienen, in den genannten Katalogen aber garnicht oder fehlerhaft aufgeführt sind; mit bibliographischen Bemerkungen.

Georg, Karl [and others]. Schlagwort-Katalog; Verzeichnis der Bücher und Landkarten in sachlicher Anordnung. 1883–1912. Hannover, 1889–1913. 7v. **AA482**

Subtitle varies; publisher varies.

v.1, 1883–87; v.2, 1888–92; v.3, 1893–97; v.4, 1898–1902; v.5, 1903–7; v.6, 1908–10; v.7, 1910–12.

Lists, under subject and form headings, works published during these periods.

20th century

❧ Since World War II there have been two bibliographic centers in Germany: the *Deutsche Bücherei* in Leipzig, in East Germany; and the *Deutsche Bibliothek* in Frankfurt am Main, in West Germany. Each publishes a series of bibliographies which follow much the same patterns, i.e., a weekly, a semiannual (or annual), and a quinquennial cumulation. Each attempts to list all books published in both parts of Germany, and German books published elsewhere. There is, thus, much duplication, but some entries will be found listed in one work and not in the other.

The *Deutsches Bücherverzeichnis* (AA486), published in Leipzig, continues in the same form the earlier series of the same title which was a continuation of Kayser (AA479).

Leipzig

Deutsche Nationalbibliographie und Bibliographie des im Ausland erschienenen deutschsprachigen Schrifttums. Reihe A, Reihe B. Leipzig, Verlag für Buch- und Bibliothekswesen, 1931– . **AA483**

Subtitle varies.

Continues, with changed title and scope, the *Wöchentliches Verzeichnis,* 1842–1930.

Reihe A, *Neuerscheinungen des Buchhandels* (books in the book trade), weekly; Reihe B, *Neuerscheinungen ausserhalb des Buchhandels* (books outside the book trade, e.g., dissertations, society publications), semimonthly.

Both sections are classified under 24 large groupings with author and catchword title indexes in each issue. Separate quarterly indexes (*Vierteljahrsregister*) by author and catchword title for each Reihe.

Includes books, periodicals, maps, but not music.

Halbjahresverzeichnis der Neuerscheinungen des deutschen Buchhandels mit Voranzeigen, Verlags- und Preisänderungen, Stich- und Schlagwortregister, 1797–1944. Leipzig, Börsenverein der Deutschen Buchhändler, 1798–1944. v.1–292. 1. Hlbjh. **AA484**

Title varies. Until 1915 was *Hinrichs' Halbjahrs-Katalog.* Ceased publication. Continued by:

Jahresverzeichnis des deutschen Schrifttums, 1945/46– . bearb. und hrsg. von der Deutschen Bücherei und dem Börsenverein der Deutschen Buchhändler zu Leipzig. Leipzig, Börsenverein, 1948– . v.1– . Annual. **AA485**

Cumulates Reihe A and B of the *Deutsche Nationalbibliographie* (AA483).

Each year in two sections: I, *Titelverzeichnis,* listing works by author or catchword title; II, *Stich- und Schlagwortregister,* listing works under catchword title and subject.

Cumulated into the *Deutsches Bücherverzeichnis* (AA486).

Deutsches Bücherverzeichnis; Verzeichnis der in Deutschland, Österreich, der Schweiz und im übrigen Ausland herausgegebenen deutschsprachigen Verlagsschriften sowie der wichtigsten Veröffentlichungen ausserhalb des Buchhandels, 1911– . Leipzig, Verlag für Buch- und Bibliothekswesen, 1915– . v.1– . **AA486**

Subtitle varies; publisher varies.

Five-year cumulations, claiming to include all titles listed in the *Halbjahresverzeichnis* and the *Jahresverzeichnis*. Each period is in two sections: (1) *Titelverzeichnis* (listing works by author and anonymous title); (2) *Stich- und Schlagwortregister* (the subject index). The period 1941–50 is covered in one listing and includes works previously omitted because of Nazi proscription or war conditions.

A continuation of Heinrichs and Kayser, compiled on the same general plan as Kayser. Lists German-language publications of the book trade in Germany, Austria, and Switzerland; some works outside the book trade (but not theses or musical texts as these have bibliographies of their own); the more important official publications; and books in other languages published in Germany. Includes books, periodicals, and maps.

Frankfurt am Main

Deutsche Bibliographie; wöchentliches Verzeichnis. Frankfurt a. M., Buchhändler-Vereinigung GMBH, 1947– . Weekly. **AA487**

Comp. by the Deutsche Bibliothek, Frankfurt a. M. From 1947 to 1952 was entitled *Bibliographie der deutschen Bibliothek*.

Attempts to include a record of all books published in the German language either in Germany or in other countries. Includes prices. Classified under 26 large groupings, with weekly author and catchword title indexes. Indexed monthly in the *Verfasser- und Stichwortregister* (AA490).

Cumulated into:

Deutsche Bibliographie; Halbjahres-Verzeichnis. Frankfurt a. M., Buchhändler-Vereinigung GMBH, 1951– . Semiannual. **AA488**

1951–52, had title *Bibliographie der deutschen Bibliothek; Halbjahres Verzeichnis.*

The semiannual cumulation of the *Wöchentliches Verzeichnis* is in two parts: pt.1, Titelverzeichnis; pt.2, Stich- und Schlagwortregister.

Deutsche Bibliographie, 1945/50– . Bücher und Karten. Frankfurt a. M., Buchhändler-Vereinigung GMBH, 1952– . Quinquennial. **AA489**

Five-year cumulation of the *Deutsche Bibliographie* issued by the Deutsche Bibliothek. Attempts to list all publications for Germany; German-language books of the book trade in Austria and Switzerland; and German-language publications of other countries. Periodicals, dissertations, and music are omitted.

For periodicals *see Deutsche Bibliographie: Zeitschriften* (AF38).

Each chronological period is in two parts: T.1, Alphabetisches Titelverzeichnis (alphabetical listing by author and anonymous title); T.2, Stich- und Schlagwortregister (the subject listing).

Verfasser- und Stichwortregister zu Deutsche Bibliographie, wöchentliches Verzeichnis; Österreichische Bibliographie; Das schweizer Buch, Ausg. A, Januar 1953– . Frankfurt a. M., Buchhändler-Vereinigung GMBH, 1953– . Monthly. **AA490**

Comp. by the Deutsche Bibliothek, Frankfurt a. M.

From 1953 to June 1960 had title *Verfasser- und Sachregister.*

A current author and catchword title index to three current national bibliographies: German, Austrian, and Swiss.

Entries are arranged in a single alphabet, with symbols to indicate the Austrian and Swiss items. No cumulations of the monthly issues.

Great Britain

British Museum. Dept. of Printed Books. General catalogue of printed books. London, 1931– . v.1– . **AA491**

The possession of the copyright privilege helps to make this the most comprehensive collection of British materials in existence, and therefore it serves as an extensive national bibliography. For full information *see AA67.*

Lowndes, William Thomas. Bibliographer's manual of English literature. New ed. rev., corr., and enl. by H. G. Bohn. London, Bell, 1858–64. 6v. in 11. **AA492**

Contents: v.1–5 (in 10 pts.), A–Z; v.6, Appendix containing lists of publications of societies and printing clubs, books issued by private presses, lists of series, etc.

Arranged alphabetically by author, with many title and catchword entries. Lists about 50,000 works, giving for each: author, title, place, date, size, with occasional notes as to rarity, value, editions, reprints, etc., and often records of prices at various 19th-century sales. Now much out of date for prices, and sometimes inaccurate, but still useful for other information.

Watt, Robert. Bibliotheca britannica; or, A general index to British and foreign literature. Edinburgh, Constable, 1824. 4v. *not accurate* **AA493**

v.1–2, Author list, arranged alphabetically, with author's full name and dates, very brief biographical data, and for each book brief information which generally includes title, date, size, number of volumes; v.3–4, An alphabetical subject list, serving as an index to the author volumes, giving for each book its date and brief title, and referring to the section of the author list (indicated by number and letter) where somewhat fuller information can be found. Anonymous titles are listed in this section.

Often useful for material not given in more modern catalogs, but sometimes inaccurate and so must be used with some caution.

Corns, Albert Reginald and **Sparke, Archibald.** A bibliography of unfinished books in the English language, with annotations. London, Quaritch, 1915. 255p. **AA493a**

An alphabetical list of works which began publication but were never finished.

Before 1640

Bibliographical Society, London. Hand-lists of books printed by London printers, 1501–1556, by E. G. Duff, W. W. Greg [and others]. London, Soc., 1913. 4 pts. in 1v. il. **AA494**

Sold only to members of the Society.

Lists of the books printed by 89 printers up to the grant of a charter to the Stationers' Company in 1557. Publication in parts began in 1895 and sections have no continuous paging, thus allowing the complete work to be bound either alphabetically by printers' names or chronologically by their dates. Prepared as a basis for further work in the English bibliography of the period.

British Museum. Dept. of Printed Books. Catalogue of books in the library of the British Museum printed in England, Scotland, and Ireland, and of books in English printed abroad to the year 1640. London, Museum, 1884. 3v. **AA495**

Alphabetically arranged, with index by title, subject, and form, e.g., plays, poems, etc., and an index of printers, booksellers, and stationers.

Cambridge. University. Library. Early English printed books in the University Library, 1475–1640. Cambridge, Univ. Pr., 1900–1907. 4v. **AA496**

v.1, 1475–1500, Caxton to F. Kingston; v.2, 1501–1640,

E. Mattes to R. Marriot and English provincial presses; v.3, Scottish, Irish and foreign presses, with addenda; v.4, Indexes.

Includes 8083 titles, arranged by presses, with full indexes of authors and titles, printers and stationers, engravers and painters, towns, portraits, music.

London. Stationers' Company. Transcript of the registers of the Company of Stationers of London, 1554–1640, ed. by Edward Arber. London, priv. pr., 1875–77; Birmingham, 1894. 5v.   **AA497**

In chronological order with no indexes, these are transcripts of the manuscript registers. Difficult to use and sometimes inaccurate. For the most part superseded by Pollard and Redgrave, *Short-title catalogue* (AA498).

Pollard, Alfred William and **Redgrave, G. R.** A short-title catalogue of books printed in England, Scotland and Ireland, and of English books printed abroad, 1475–1640; comp. . . . with the help of G. F. Barwick . . . and others. London, Bibliographical Soc., 1926. 609p. (Photographic repr.: Oxford, Univ. Pr., 1946)   **AA498**

Frequently cited as *S.T.C.*

The most comprehensive record of English books for this period including about 26,500 editions (26,143 numbers, with several hundred items inserted with subnumbers). Arranged alphabetically by author and other main entries; gives, for each item, author, brief title, size, printer, date, reference to entry of the book in the Stationers' registers, and indication of libraries possessing copies. This last important feature aims to record all known copies of very rare items and, in the case of commoner books, a selection in representative British and American libraries and collections. The total number of libraries referred to is 148 (133 British, 15 American).

Bishop, William Warner. A checklist of American copies of "Short-title catalogue" books. 2d ed. Ann Arbor, Univ. of Michigan Pr., 1950. 203p.   **AA498a**

Compiled as a convenient guide to the location of *S.T.C.* titles in American libraries, this is a record of *S.T.C.* numbers indicating holdings in some 110 libraries and collections. The 2d edition includes corrections and additions to the list in the 1st edition, published 1944, and records the holdings of about 10 more libraries.

Henry E. Huntington Library and Art Gallery, San Marino, Calif. Huntington Library supplement to the record of its books in the Short title catalogue . . . comp. by C. K. Edmonds. Cambridge, Harvard Univ. Pr., 1933. 152p. (Huntington Library Bull. Oct. 1933, p.1–152)   **AA498b**

Contains two lists: (1) short-title list of books included in the *S.T.C.* of which the Huntington copies are either unrecorded or recorded incorrectly, and (2) list, with full cataloging information, of books or editions within the period not recorded in the *S.T.C.*

Morrison, Paul G. Index of printers, publishers, and booksellers in A. W. Pollard and G. R. Redgrave, A Short-title catalogue. . . . Charlottesville, Bibliographical Soc. of the Univ. of Virginia, 1950. 82p.   **AA498c**

Newberry Library, Chicago. English books and books printed in England before 1641 in the Newberry Library; a supplement to the record in the Short title catalogue, comp. by Gertrude L. Woodward. Chicago, 1939. 118p.   **AA498d**

Ramage, David. A finding-list of English books to 1640 in libraries in the British Isles (excluding the national libraries and the libraries of Oxford and Cambridge). Based on the numbers in Pollard and Redgrave's Short-title catalogue . . . Durham, Eng., Council of the Durham Colleges, 1958. 101p.   **AA498e**

"A project of the Standing Conference of National and University Libraries."

Gives additional locations for some 14,000 *S.T.C.* items,

arranged by *S.T.C.* number, plus a supplementary list of titles not in *S.T.C.*

17th and 18th centuries

Arber, Edward. Term catalogues, 1668–1709 A.D. with a number for Easter term, 1711 A.D. London, Arber; N.Y., Dodd, 1903–6. 3v.   **AA499**

Subtitle: A contemporary bibliography of English literature in the reigns of Charles II, James II, William and Mary, and Anne; edited from the very rare quarterly lists of new books . . . issued by the booksellers of London.

Copies of contemporary records arranged chronologically, with indexes by titles, names, and subjects in each volume.

Bibliotheca annua: or, The annual catalogue for the year, 1699–[March 25, 1704]. London, J. Nutt, 1700–1703. no.1–4. (Repub.: London, Gregg Pr., 1964)   **AA500**

Subtitle [varies slightly]: Being an exact catalogue of all English and Latin books, printed in England from January, $169\frac{8}{9}$, to [March 25, 1704]. To which is added the titles of French books imported within the said time; as also most of the prizes [sic] that they are generally sold for.

Classified annual catalogs, with indexes for some years. For these years this work would be easier to use than the *Term catalogues* (AA499). Titles are quite full, and include edition, publisher, and price.

British Museum. Dept. of Printed Books. Thomason Collection. Catalogue of the pamphlets, books, newspapers, and manuscripts relating to the Civil War, the Commonwealth, and Restoration, collected by George Thomason, 1640–1661. London, Trustees, 1908. 2v.   **AA501**

Running title: The Thomason tracts.

A very rich collection for this period, arranged chronologically with author, anonymous title, and subject index. Newspapers, 1641–43, listed in v.2, p.371–440.

London catalogue of books. . . .   **AA502**

Bibliographies with this title, published first by Bent and later by Hodgson, were issued covering, with considerable duplication of years, books published in Great Britain from 1700 to 1855. The 19th-century volumes formed one of the sources from which the 1801–36 and 1835–63 volumes of the *English catalogue* (AA505) were compiled and for ordinary purposes are therefore not often needed; but a library having the 18th-century volumes will still use them for material not included in Watt (AA493) or Lowndes (AA492).

For record of editions published *see* Adolf Growoll, *Three centuries of English booktrade bibliography*. N.Y., Dibdin Club, 1903. 195p.

London. Stationers' Company. Transcript of the registers of the Worshipful Company of Stationers; from 1640–1708 A.D. London, priv. pr., 1913–14. 3v.   **AA503**

Ed. by G. E. Briscoe Eyre. Entries transcribed by H. R. Plomer.

Wing, Donald Goddard. Short-title catalogue of books printed in England, Scotland, Ireland, Wales, and British America and of English books printed in other countries, 1641–1700. N.Y., pr. for the Index Society by the Columbia Univ. Pr., 1945–51. 3v.   **AA504**

Published as a continuation of Pollard and Redgrave's *Short-title catalogue . . . 1475–1640* (AA498). Items are located in more than 200 libraries; relatively common books are given five locations in Great Britain and five in the United States in as varied geographical areas as possible in order to provide convenient locations for scholars in various parts of the country. It is not a census of copies, and "it is only when less than five copies are located in either British or American libraries that any deduction can be drawn that copies mentioned are all that the editor has found." Location symbols are not those used by the *S.T.C.* (AA498) or the *National union catalog* (AA65), but follow a system devised by Wing.

The scope and method of selection and entry are described in the preface, which should be carefully read before the book is used in order not to misinterpret or misunderstand the information given.

Hiscock, Walter George. The Christ Church holdings in Wing's Short-title catalogue, 1641–1700, of books of which less than 5 copies are recorded in the United Kingdom. [Oxford], Christ Church, 1956. 165p. **AA504a**

—— The Christ Church supplement to Wing's Short-title catalogue, 1641–1700. Oxford, pr. for Christ Church at the Holywell Pr., 1956. 47p. **AA504b**

A list of works in Christ Church not listed by Wing, with a section of errata in Wing.

Morrison, Paul G. Index of printers, publishers and booksellers in Donald Wing's Short-title catalogue . . . Charlottesville, Univ. of Virginia Pr. for the Bibliographical Society of the Univ. of Virginia, 1955. 217p. **AA504c**

Similar to the compiler's index to Pollard and Redgrave.

Philadelphia. Library Company. A check-list of the books in the Library Company of Philadelphia in and supplementary to Wing's Short-title catalogue, 1641–1700, by Edwin Wolf. Philadelphia, 1959. 106p. **AA504d**

Nearly 4000 titles, listed by Wing number.

19th and 20th centuries

English catalogue of books . . . issued . . . in Great Britain and Ireland . . . 1801– . London, S. Low, 1864–1901; Publishers' Circular, 1906– . **AA505**

Volume covering 1801–36, published in 1914 and unnumbered, includes authors and catchword titles in one alphabet. [v.1] covers 1835–63. Later 19th-century volumes were published at irregular intervals: 1901–35 volumes cover 5-year periods; 1936–41; 1942–47; 1948–52; 1952–55; 1956–59; 1960–62.

The standard English trade list, reasonably comprehensive for books and pamphlets issued at the main publishing centers but less complete for the provincial presses. Arrangement is alphabetical by author with title and catchword subject entries, except that from 1837 to 1889 the subject entries are in separate index volumes (*see* below). Information given varies but usually includes author, title, publisher, date, size, and price.

With the 1960–62 volume, arrangement is changed: (1) paperback section, authors and titles in one alphabet; (2) author section, giving the full bibliographical information; (3) title section, including inverted titles; (4) maps and atlases; (5) list of publishers.

Cumulates the annual *English catalogue of books,* 1835– .

—— Index to the English catalogue of books, 1837–1889. London, S. Low, 1858–93. 4v.

Forms a subject index to v.1–4 of the author catalog. No more published, as from v.5 on, the *English catalogue* includes authors and catchword subjects in one alphabet.

Current

British books, incorporating the Publishers' circular and booksellers' record, no.4847, v.173, May, 1959– . London, Publishers' Circular, 1959– . Monthly. **AA506**

A new title and new format for the former *Publishers' circular* . . . (1837–1959), with issue and volume numbering continued from the old series. Now a monthly instead of a weekly, but continues to include articles, announcements, etc. with the listings of new books which serve as the basis for compilation of the *English catalogue* (AA505).

British national bibliography, 1950– . London, Council of the British Nat. Bibliography, British Museum, 1950– . **AA507**

Pub. weekly with four cumulations a year: Jan.–March, Jan.–June, Jan.–Sept., and annual volume (5-year cumulations; *see* below).

An excellently planned and executed national bibliography, prepared at the British Museum and based upon the books deposited at the Copyright Office. It aims to list and describe every new work published in Great Britain with certain specific exceptions: periodicals (except the first issue of a new periodical or a periodical under a new title); music; maps; certain government publications; cheap novelettes, etc.

The main section in each issue is classified by the Dewey Decimal Classification. Each weekly issue has an author and title index, and the last issue for each month has a cumulated author, title, and subject index for the month. Each cumulation has an alphabetical index under author, title, editor, translator, series, and subject.

Full cataloging detail is given in the classified section including: author, title, place, publisher, date, paging, illustrations, centimeter size, series, and price. The alphabetical section provides briefer information, adequate for many purposes, giving author, title, publisher, price, and classification number. The latter serves as an index number for finding the more detailed information in the classified section.

—— Cumulated subject catalogue, 1951–54, 1955–59. London, 1958–63. (In progress)

1951–54, 2v.; 1955–59, 3v.

Cumulations of the material appearing in the classified sections of the annual volumes, made by cutting and arranging the entries in classified sequence and reproducing by photo-offset printing. Information, therefore, is that current at the time of the annual volumes. (Material from the 1950 volume was omitted due to the different format.)

—— Cumulated index, 1950–54, 1955–59. London, 1955–61. 1150p., 1578p. (In progress)

Each 5-year volume is a cumulation in one alphabetical sequence of the author, title, and subject sections of the annual volumes. These indexes serve as keys to the *Cumulated subject catalogue* and thus together they provide a comprehensive record of British publications for the period, superseding the annual volumes.

Whitaker's Cumulative book list, 1939/43– ; the complete list of all books published in the United Kingdom, . . . giving details as to author, title, sub-title, size, number of pages, price, date, classification and publisher of every book. London, Whitaker, 1945– . v.1– . (In progress) **AA508**

1939/43, author and title in one alphabet; 1944/47, 1948/52– , in two sections: (1) author list, and (2) title list; 1953/57, 1958/62 each in one alphabet: author, title, and some subjects.

—— . . . 1924– . London, Whitaker, 1924– . v.1– . **AA509**

Subtitle varies.

Issued quarterly, cumulating throughout the year; since 1939, cumulating into larger volumes as listed above (AA 508).

Each issue consists of a classified list of recent publications, cumulated from the weekly lists in *The bookseller* (AA510), with a detailed author and title index.

The bookseller: The organ of the booktrade, 1858– . London, Whitaker, 1858– . **AA510**

Monthly, 1858–1908; weekly, 1909– .

Includes weekly alphabetical lists with monthly cumulations in last issue of month, which cumulate into *Whitaker's Cumulative book list.*

Current literature. London, Whitaker, 1858– . Monthly. **AA511**

Title varies.

Includes a classified "Publications of the month" which cumulates to form the classified section of *Whitaker's Cumulative book list.*

✓ **Reference catalogue of current literature** . . . 1874– . London, Whitaker, 1874– . Irregular.   **AA512**

v.1, Author index; v.2, Title index.

Subtitle, 1961: A national inclusive book-reference index of books in print and on sale in the United Kingdom, with details as to author, title, editor, translator, reviser, year of publication or year of latest edition, number of edition, size, number of pages, illustrations and illustrator, series, binding —where not cloth—price, whether net or non-net, and publisher's name, containing 350,000 entries and giving 2,000,000 details concerning books published and for sale.

1874–1932, a collection of publishers' catalogs bound together alphabetically by name of firm, with a detailed alphabetical index in a separate volume. Published about every fourth year. Since then, published at irregular intervals and consolidated into two lists, author and title, including information as given in subtitle.

Paperbacks in print: a reference catalogue of . . . paperbacks in print and on sale in Great Britain. London, Whitaker, 1960– . Semiannual.   **AA513**

Title and subtitle vary.

Each issue in three sections: (1) classified, where the most complete information is given; (2) author index; (3) title index.

Privately printed

Dobell, Bertram. Catalogue of books printed for private circulation, collected by Bertram Dobell and now described and annotated by him. London, Dobell, 1906. 238p.   **AA514**

An author list, with full descriptions, including author's name, title, size, paging, date, price, size of edition when known, and bibliographical and historical notes with occasional quotations from the books themselves. Includes some, but not all, of the books listed by Martin (AA515).

Some 939 titles from this list are now in the Library of Congress, having been acquired in the Dobell collection of privately printed books purchased in 1914.

Martin, John. Bibliographical catalogue of privately printed books. 2d ed. London, pub. for the author by J. Van Voort, 1854. 593p. il.   **AA515**

The 1st edition, 1834, was in two parts: (1) List of books, omitting pamphlets, arranged chronologically 1672–1833, giving author's name, title, place and printer when known, date, size and paging, with many bibliographical and historical notes and occasional references to authorities and copies; (2) List of books printed at private presses and for distribution among members of literary clubs, arranged by presses. General index of authors and titles. The list by presses contains some material not found in the appendix volume of Lowndes (AA492). The 2d edition is a revision of the first part only, correcting some errors, adding previously omitted titles, and extending the list to 1853, but omitting the section of private presses.

Regional

❧ The general works listed above are reasonably comprehensive for books issued at the main publishing centers, but are less inclusive for material of local interest issued by provincial printers. For works of this latter type, local bibliographies of towns and counties must be consulted. A list of some of these was given in the *Guide to reference books,* 7th ed., p.38–39, and is not repeated here. They vary greatly in character but, taken as a whole, they serve three main purposes: (1) as lists of local

imprints; (2) as bibliographies of local history; (3) as regional biographical dictionaries, since some of them include biographical sketches of local writers, etc. As they sometimes include considerable analysis of material in periodicals, and even newspapers, they supplement, to that extent, the indexes to periodicals.

Greece

Gkinēs, Dēmētrios and **Mexas, Balerios G.** Hellēnikē bibliographia, 1800–1863. Anagraphē tōn kata tēn chronikēn tautēn periodon hopou dēpote Hellēnisti ekdothentōn bibliōn kai entypōn en genei. . . . Brabeutheisa hypo tēs Akadēmias Athēnōn. En Athēnais, Grapheion Dēmosieumatōn Akadēmias Athēnōn, 1939–57. 3v. (Pragmateiai tēs Akadēmias Athēnōn, Tomos II)   **AA516**

Contents: T.I, 1800–1839; T.II, 1839–1855; T.III, 1856–1863, and supplement, 1800–1855.

Ladas, Georgios G. and **Chatzedemos, Athanasios D.** Hellēnikē bibliographia; symbolē sto dekato ogdoo aiōna. Athēna, 1964. 282p. il. (Prostēkes, diorthoseis kai symplērōseis stēn Hellēnikē bibliographia tōn Émile Legrand, Louis Petit kai Hubert Pernot)   **AA517**

18th century.

Legrand, Émile. Bibliographie hellénique, ou, Description raisonnée des ouvrages publiés en grec par des Grecs aux XVᵉ et XVIᵉ siècles. Paris, Leroux, 1885–1906. 4v. il. (Repr.: Paris, Maisonneuve, 1963. 4v.)   **AA518**

Publisher varies. Title varies.

v.1–4, 1476–1600.

v.1–2, Works published in Greek by the Greeks, 1476–1599; v.3, Works published in Latin by the Greeks, 1469–1550; v.4, Works published in Greek and other languages, 1551–1600.

—— Bibliographie hellénique, ou, Description raisonnée des ouvrages publiés par des Grecs au dix-septième siècle. Paris, Picard, 1894–96; Maisonneuve, 1903. 5v.   **AA519**

v.1–3, 1601–1700; v.3–5 include *"Notices biographiques."*

Broader in scope than the author's volumes for the 15th and 16th centuries, including *tout ouvrage ayant un Grec pour auteur ou éditeur, tout ouvrage auquel le nom d'un Grec est attaché d'une façon quelconque.*

—— Bibliographie hellénique, ou, Description raisonnée des ouvrages publiés par des Grecs au dix-huitième siècle, oeuvre posthume, complétée et pub. par Louis Petit et Hubert Pernot. Paris, Garnier, 1918–28. 2v. il.   **AA520**

v.1–2, 1701–1790.

—— Bibliographie ionienne; description raisonnée des ouvrages publiés par les Grecs des Sept-Îles ou concernant ces îles du 15. siècle à l'année 1900. Oeuvre posthume complétée et pub. par Hubert Pernot. Paris, Leroux, 1910. 2v.   **AA521**

v.1, 1494–1854; v.2, 1855–1900.

Politēs, Nicolaos G. Hellēnikē bibliographia: katalogos tōn en Helladi ē upo Hellēnōn allachou ekdothentōn bibliōn apo tou etous. v.p. 1907–32. 3v.   **AA522**

Imprint varies: v.1–2, Athens, P. D. Sakellarios; v.3, pt.1, Athens, Spendone; v.3, pt.2, Thessalonika, M. Triantspullos.

v.1–2 repr. from *Athens, Ethnikon kai kapodistriakon panepistēmion. Epistemonike epeterus* 3:393–540. 1906–7 (pub. 1909); 6:139–612. 1909–10 (pub. 1911); v.3, issued in 2 pts., 1927–32.

v.1–2 cover years 1907–10; v.3, 1911–20. Includes books published in Greece and books by Greeks published elsewhere.

Current

Bulletin analytique de bibliographie hellénique, 1945– .
Athènes, Inst. Français d'Athènes, 1947– . Annual.
AA523

1945 (v.6), fasc.1, was published in 1947; 1946 (v.7) appeared in 3 fasc. in 1947; 1947 was published in 1948 in three issues (fasc.1/2, 3/4, and 5); 1948– , annual. The earlier volumes (v.1–5 for 1940–44, and v.6, fasc.2–3) are not yet published.

In two sections: (1) books and pamphlets; (2) periodicals. Classified arrangement with author index. Full bibliographical detail, followed by abstracts or reviews.

Greek bibliography. Athens, Nat. Prt. Off., 1960– . v.1, no.1– . Quarterly.
AA524

At head of title: Ministry to the Prime Minister's Office. General Direction of Press, Research and Cultural Relations Division.

A preliminary issue, designated no.1, was issued in Feb. 1959. The publication is an English-language edition of a new Greek national bibliography, *Deltion hellēnikēs bibliographias,* same date, same numbering. Arrangement is classified, with indexes scheduled for the fourth quarterly issue of each year. An edition in French is also published simultaneously.

Guatemala

Bibliografía guatemalteca. Obras editadas. Collección bibliográfica del tercer centenario de la fundación de la primera imprenta en Centro América. Guatemala, Tipografía Nacional, 1960–63. v.1–8. (In progress) **AA525**

An attempt to provide a record of printing in Guatemala from 1660 to the present by combining older works covering the early periods with new compilations for more recent times.

Contents: v.1, Juan Enrique O'Ryan. Bibliografía guatemalteca de los siglos XVII y XVIII. 2. ed. [1660–1800]. (Text is a reprint of *Bibliografía de la imprenta en Guatemala en los siglos XVII y XVIII.* Santiago de Chile, 1897.)

v.2, José Toribio Medina. La imprenta en Guatemala, 1660–1821. 2. ed. 1960. 2v. (Originally published in Santiago de Chile. 1910.) Includes two supplements of *Algunas adiciones,* one by Gilberto Valenzuela, v.2, p.637–72, published originally in *La imprenta en Guatemala* (1933. 72p.) and the other by Arturo Taracena Flores, v.2, p.673–92.

v.3–5, Gilberto Valenzuela. Bibliografía guatemalteca, y catálogo general de libros, folletos, periodicos, revistas, etc.

v.3, 1821–1830, 2. ed. (1. ed. 1933); v.4, 1831–1840; v.5, 1841–1860.

v.6–8, Gilberto Valenzuela Reyna. v.6, 1861–1900; v.7, 1901–1930; v.8, 1931–1940.

These volumes give detailed bibliographical information with annotations about books, pamphlets, etc., and in many cases the texts of decrees, official notices, etc.

Guatemala. Tipografía Nacional. Catálogo general de libros, folletos y revistas editados en la Tipografía Nacional de Guatemala desde 1892 hasta 1943. Guatemala, Tipografía Nacional, 1944. 352p.
AA526

Alphabetical by year, no index.

Villacorta Calderon, José Antonio. Bibliografía guatemalteca; exposiciones abiertas en el Salón de historia y bellas artes del Museo Nacional, en los meses de noviembre de 1939, 40, 41 y 42. Guatemala, Tipografía Nacional, 1944. 638p. il.
AA527

Based on the exhibit on the history of printing in Guatemala held at the Museo Nacional. Covers the period from the introduction of printing in 1660 to 1942, with extensive bibliographies, location of copies, facsimiles of title pages, etc.

Current

Índice bibliográfico guatemalteco, 1958– . Gonzálo Dardon Córdova, ed. Guatemala, Inst. Guatemalteco-Americano, 1959– . Annual.
AA528

At head of title: Cooperación interbibliotecaria.

A catalog by author and subject of books, periodical articles, and pamphlets published in Guatemala, and others about Guatemala published abroad.

Haiti

Bissainthe, Max. Dictionnaire de bibliographie haïtienne. Wash., Scarecrow, 1951. 1052p.
AA529

Includes three main bibliographic lists, each arranged alphabetically and covering: (1) works published in Haiti, or by Haitians abroad, Jan. 1804–Dec. 1949; (2) works published in Hispaniola and Santo Domingo, or concerning them, from the beginning to 1949; (3) newspapers and periodicals from Santo Domingo and Haiti, 1764–1949, and an index of journalists working on them. Title and subject indexes. Many entries have brief annotations—both bio- and bibliographical —and library locations are given. Complements Duvivier (AA530).

Duvivier, Ulrick. Bibliographie générale et méthodique d'Haïti. . . . Port-au-Prince, Haïti, Impr. de l'État, 1941. 2v.
AA530

Covers material published in Haiti from the earliest period to date of publication. Classed arrangement; no index.

Hawaii

Current Hawaiiana. . . . v.1, no.1, June 1944– . Honolulu, 1944– . Quarterly.
AA531

"Issued by Hawaiiana Section, Hawaii Library Association, through the cooperation of the University of Hawaii."

Lists monographs and serials dealing with or published in Hawaii, and periodical articles published elsewhere. Bibliographical information is usually complete, except for prices.

No cumulated indexes.

Honduras

Durón, Jorge Fidel. Índice de la bibliografía hondureña. Tegucigalpa, Impr. Calderon, 1946. 211p.
AA532

Attempts to list all works published in Honduras (alphabetized by first letter only). For these it largely supersedes the *Repertorio* listed below (*see* AA533). However, the *Repertorio* includes some lists not included in the *Índice.*

Instituto Hondureño de Cultura Interamericana. Repertorio bibliográfico hondureño, por Jorge Fidel Durón. Tegucigalpa, 1943. 68p.
AA533

1st tentative edition of a national bibliography covering all periods. First three sections are books exhibited at the Primera Exposición y Feria del Libro Hondureño y Americano: (1) Repertorio bibliográfico hondureño; (2) Libros de autores norteamericanos; (3) Libros de autores chilenos.

Sec. 4 is a list of books published in Honduras, and sec. 5, an "Índice de nombres." All sections and index are alphabetized by first letter only. Index is a list of names only, does not give page references.

Hungary

Szabó, Károly. Régi magyar könyvtár. Budapest, A. Magyar Tudományos Akadémia Könyvkiadó Hivatala, 1879–98. 3v. in 4.
AA534

v.1, Books in Hungarian, 1531–1711; v.2, Non-Hungarian

books published in Hungary, 1473–1711; v.3, Hungarian authors, non-Hungarian books published outside Hungary: pt.1, 1480–1670;. pt.2, suppl. 1671–1711 and author index.
Continued by:

Sztripszky, Hiador. Appendix ad I–II tomos. Additiones et emendationes, 1472–1711. Adalékok Szabó Károly "Régi magyar könyvtár" cimü munkájának 1–2 kötetéhez. Pótlások és igazitások. Budapest, 1912. 710p.
AA535

Petrik, Géza. Bibliographia hungarica. Magyar könyvészet [1712–1910]. Budapest, Magyar Könyvkereskedök Egyesülete, 1885–1942. 11v. **AA536**
Title varies.
[Ser. 1], 1712–1860. 4v.; [ser. 2], 1860–75. 467p.; [ser. 3], 1876–85. 556p. by Sándor Kiszlingstein; [ser. 4], 1886–1900, 1107p.; [ser. 5], 1901–10, 2v.; [ser. 6], 1911–20. 2v. by Sándor Kozocsa.
Arranged alphabetically by author and anonymous title.

Magyar könyvészet, 1921–23, az 1921–23 években megjelent magyar könyvek betürendes jegyzéke és tárgymutatója. Budapest, Magyar Könyvkiadók és Könyvkereskedök, Zenemükiadók és Zenemükereskedök Egyesülete, 1924–26. 491p. **AA537**
Pub. in 6 pts., A–Z.
No more published.

—— A magyarországi nyomdák és egyéb sokszorositóvállalatok 1936–1941 évi kötelespéldányszolgáltatása és nyomtatványaik (könyvek, hirlapok, folyóiratok, térképek, zenemüvek) 1936–41. Budapest, Országos Széchényi Könyvtár, 1939–44. 6v. (Magyarország évi könyvészete, 1–6) Annual. **AA538**
Not published for 1942–1960. Resumed publication with 1961/62 as:

—— A magyarországi könyvek, zenemüvek és térképek cimjegyzéke. 1961/62– . Budapest, Országos Széchényi Könyvtár, 1963– . **AA539**
Annual cumulation of *Magyar nemzeti bibliográfia* (AA 540) with an author index.

Current

Magyar nemzeti bibliográfia; bibliographia hungarica. Kiadja az Országos Széchényi Könyvtar. 1 füzet, január-március 1946– . Budapest, 1946– . Monthly. **AA540**
A classed listing with headings in Hungarian, Russian, English, and French. 1946, quarterly; 1947 to date, monthly. Monthly and annual indexes until 1960. Since 1961/62, only monthly indexes, as it is cumulated in *Magyar könyvészet* (AA539).

Iceland

Cornell University. Library. Catalogue of the Icelandic collection bequeathed by Willard Fiske. Comp. by Halldór Hermannsson. Ithaca, N.Y., 1914. 755p. **AA541**
"When this catalogue went to press the collection numbered about 10,200 volumes. . . . The catalogue, however, does not comprise all of these, since the Runic portion, containing some 500 volumes, and a few other books, have not been recorded . . . some few titles are included which are to be found in the University library outside of the collection."
—*Pref.*

—— —— Additions, 1913–26, comp. by Halldór Hermannsson. Ithaca, N.Y.; London, Milford, 1927. 284p.

—— —— Additions, 1927–42, comp. by Halldór Hermannsson. Ithaca, N.Y., Cornell Univ. Pr., 1943. 295p.
Some 5000 items are included in this supplement, making a total in the collection of 21,830. This supplement also includes various titles to be found in the library outside the collection.

—— Catalogue of Runic literature, forming a part of the Icelandic collection bequeathed by Willard Fiske. Comp. by Halldór Hermannsson. London, N.Y., Oxford Univ. Pr., 1918. 105p. **AA542**

Islandica; an annual relating to Iceland and the Fiske Icelandic collection in Cornell University Library. Ithaca, N.Y., Cornell Univ. Lib., 1908– . **AA543**
The bibliographical volumes of this set by Halldór Hermannsson include: v.1, Bibliography of the Icelandic sagas and minor tales. 1908. 126p. (*see also* v.24); v.2, The Northmen in America. 1909. 94p.; v.3, Bibliography of the sagas of the kings of Norway and related sagas and tales. 1910. 75p. (*see also* v.26); v.4, The ancient laws of Norway and Iceland. 1911. 83p.; v.5, Bibliography of the mythical-heroic sagas. 1912. 73p. (*see also* v.26); v.6, Icelandic authors of today, with an appendix giving a list of works dealing with modern Icelandic literature. 1913. 63p.; v.9, Icelandic books of the 16th century (1534–1600). 1916. 72p. (*see also* v.29); v.11, The periodical literature of Iceland down to the year 1874; an historic sketch. 1918. 100p.; v.13, Bibliography of the Eddas. 1920. 95p. (*see also* v.37); v.14, Icelandic books of the 17th century (1601–1700). 1922. 121p. (*see also* v.29); v.19, Icelandic manuscripts. 1929. 80p.; v.23, Old Icelandic literature; a bibliographical essay. 1933. 50p.; v.24, The sagas of Icelanders; a supplement [to v.1]. 1935. 113p.; v.26, The sagas of the kings and the mythical-heroic sagas; two bibliographical supplements [to v.3 and v.5]. 1937. 84p.; v.29, Bibliographical notes [including] Additions to the bibliographies of Icelandic books of the 16th and 17th centuries [v.9 and v.14]. 1942. 91p.; v.37, Jóhann S. Hannesson. Bibliography of the Eddas. A supplement to v.13. 1955; v.38, Jóhann S. Hannesson. The sagas of Icelanders (Íslendinga sögur). 1957.

Islandsk Bogfortegnelse, 1899–1910, 1912–1920, af Bogi T. J. Melsted. København, 1899–1922. Annual (Irregular). **AA544**
Supplement to *Dansk Bogfortegnelse* (AA451) and bound with it as follows: 1899–1910 with volume for 1899–1910; 1912 with 1914; 1913–14 with 1915; 1915 with 1917; 1916–18 with 1918; 1919 with 1921; 1920 with 1922.

—— 1915/19–1930/34. [In Dansk Bogfortegnelse, 1915/19–1930/34 (AA448)] **AA545**
5-year cumulations.

Kiel. Universität. Bibliothek. Islandkatalog der Universitätsbibliothek Kiel und der Universitäts- und Stadtbibliothek Köln, bearb. von Olaf Klose. Kiel, Universitätsbibliothek, 1931. 423p. (Kataloge der Universitätsbibliothek Kiel, hrsg. von Christoph Weber, 1) **AA546**
Lists more than 7900 titles, in classified arrangement with author and title index.

Current

Reykjavik. Landsbókasafn. Árbók. [1]–18 ar; 1944– . Reykjavik, 1945– . il. Annual. **AA547**
Contains an annual list of Icelandic publications, "Íslenzk rit."

India

National bibliography of Indian literature, 1901–1933. Gen. eds.: B. S. Kesavan and V. Y. Kulkarni. New Delhi, Sahitya Akademi, 1962– . v.1– . (In progress) **AA548**
Contents: v.1, Assamese, Bengali, English, Gujarati.
Covering 1901 through 1953, this work aims to include "books of literary merit, and important and significant books"

in the following categories: general works, philosophy and religion, social sciences, linguistics, arts, literature, history, biography and travel, and miscellaneous.

In Roman script with annotations in English.

Index translationum indicarum: a cumulation of entries for India in "Index translationum," UNESCO, Paris, v.2–11. Cumulation by D. L. Banerjee. Calcutta, Nat. Lib., 1963. 450p.   **AA549**

A cumulation of some 2800 translations published in India, 1947–58, and listed in *Index translationum* (AA91). Arranged by Indian language and then alphabetically by author. Gives author of original, title of translation, name of translator, place, publisher, date, pages, illustrations, price, and language and title of the original.

Current

Impex reference catalogue of Indian books. New Delhi, Indian Book Export and Import Co., 1960–   . v.1–   . Irregular (?).   **AA550**

Subtitle: The list of all important Indian books (in English) in print, giving in one alphabetical list details as to author, title, sub-title, number of pages, price, year of publication, classification and publisher of every book under author, title and catchword title, as well as a special classified list giving details of each book under author in each separate subject grouping.

—— Impex supplement, 1960–62; an alphabetical list of all important new books, new editions and reissues of old publications . . . 1962. 215p., 219p.

Indian national bibliography. General ed., B. S. Kesavan. Calcutta, Central Reference Lib., 1958–   . v.1–   . Quarterly, with annual cumulation, 1958–63; monthly, with annual cumulation, 1964–   .   **AA551**

A national bibliography which attempts to list all new publications appearing in the 15 major languages of the country, including first issues of new periodicals but excluding musical scores, maps, and several categories of ephemera.

Vernacular scripts have been transliterated into the Roman alphabet, and the text is in English. Each issue is in two parts: pt.1, General publications; and pt.2, Government publications. In each section the entries are classified by Dewey Decimal Classification with a detailed index of authors, titles, and subjects.

Indonesia

Ockeloen, G. Catalogus van boeken en tijdschriften uitg. in Ned. Oost-Indië van 1870–1937. Batavia, Kolff, 1940. 2v.   **AA552**

Contents: [v.1], Nederlandsche taal; [v.2], Inheemsche talen.

Arranged alphabetically by author or anonymous title.

—— Catalogus van in Ned.-Indie verschenen boeken in de jaren 1938–1941 en enkele aanvullingen op de gestencilde catalogus verschenen in 1939. Batavia, Kolff, 1942–   . v.1–   .   **AA553**

Contents: v.1, Nederlandsche uitgaven.

For v.2, covering books published in Indonesian, *see:*

—— Catalogus dari buku-buku jang diterbitkan di Indonesia. 1945/49–1954. Bandung, G. Kolff & Co., 1950–55. 4v.   **AA554**

v.1 consists of two parts: the first lists books published in Indonesia 1945–49 in Indonesian and Western languages; the second replaces the 1937–41 bibliography, originally published in 1942 and subsequently destroyed by war action, now compiled again from the original cards. The gap between the two parts is accounted for by the fact that few books were issued during the war years, and that almost no bibliographical data on them exist.

Current

Berita bibliografi, 1955–   . Djakarta, Gunung Agung, 1955–   . Monthly, with annual cumulations.   **AA555**

A 5-year cumulation, 1955–59, is announced, also a 10-year retrospective volume, 1945–54.

Lists books, pamphlets, periodicals, and newspapers published in Indonesia, as well as Indonesian books published overseas. In dictionary arrangement: author, title, and subject in one alphabet.

Indonesia. Kantor Bibliografi Nasional. Bibliografi nasional indonesia. no.1, Th.XI, Djanuari-Maret, 1963–   . Quarterly.   **AA556**

A continuation of the Office's *Berita bulanan,* v.1–10, 1953–1962. Monthly.

Produced by the Office of National Bibliography, and the official list, but because it depends on the deposit of books, it is not so comprehensive as the commercial list noted above (AA555).

Iran

Ketābhā-ye Īrān. v.1, 1333–   sh., [1954/55–   ]. Tehrān, Anjoman-e Ketàb, 1334–   sh., 1955–   . Annual. **AA557**

Title varies.

In Persian.

No.3–7 have added title page in English: Bibliography of Persia. National bibliography. Tehran, pub. by the Book Society of Persia.

Ireland

Dix, Ernest Reginald McClintock. Catalogue of early Dublin-printed books, 1601 to 1700, with an historical introduction and bibliographical notes by C. Winston Dugan. Dublin, [O'Donoghue; London, Dobell], 1898–1905. 4v. and suppl., all paged continuously, 386p.   **AA558**

—— —— Supplement of additions to pts.I–IV. Dublin, 1912. p.325–86.

Dublin. National Library of Ireland. List of publications deposited under the terms of the Industrial and Commercial Property (Protection) Act, 1927. no.1–5, Aug. 1927/ Dec. 1929—1935/36. Dublin, Stat. Off., [1930–37]. Annual.   **AA559**

Contents: (1) Books and pamphlets; (2) Annuals; (3) Periodicals and publications of societies; (4) Official publications, issued by the Stationery Office; (5) Newspapers; (6) Music; (7) Maps.

Israel

Bar-David, Jacob. Katalog Bar-David, 1957–   . Tel-Aviv, Bar-David Literary Agency, 1957–   . Annual.   **AA560**

Added title page in English: Bar-David's Israel book catalog listing titles published. v.1 had title *Katalog ha-sefer ha-Yiśrĕ'ēlī.*

Introductory notes in Hebrew and English.

A collection of publishers' catalogs listing books published in Israel. Some publishers list all books published by them; others list only books in print.

Italy

British Museum. Dept. of Printed Books. Short-title catalogue of books printed in Italy and of Italian books printed in other countries from 1465 to 1600 now in the British Museum. London, Trustees, 1958. 992p. **AA561**

An author catalog, giving shortened title, place, publisher, date, and size, similar in scope and arrangement to the Museum's other catalogs in this series. Appended is a lengthy list of printers and publishers, with titles printed by each, arranged chronologically.

Bibliografia italiana; bollettino delle pubblicazioni italiane ricevute per diritto di stampa dalla Biblioteca Nazionale Centrale di Firenze. Anno 1–67, 1867–1933. Milano, etc., 1868–1933. Monthly (varies slightly).　　　**AA562**

From 1886 to 1900 the *Bibliografia,* being compiled at the Biblioteca Nazionale Centrale di Firenze, was also issued by the library under title *Bollettino delle pubblicazioni italiane ricevute per diritto di stampa* (AA562a).

Published in two parts, 1867–69: I, Bibliografia; II, Avvisi. Published in three parts, 1870–87: 1, Catalogo delle pubblicazioni italiane; 2, Cronaca; 3, Avvisi. Beginning with 1888, the *Cronaca* and *Avvisi* were discontinued in that form, being superseded by the *Giornale della libreria* (AA566).

✓**Florence. Biblioteca Nazionale Centrale.** Bollettino delle pubblicazioni italiane ricevute per diritto di stampa, 1866– 1957. Firenze, Biblioteca, 1886–1957. 72v. Monthly.　　　**AA562a**

Classified with annual indexes. During its span, the most complete current record of Italian publications, based on copyright deposit.

Ceased publication.

Continued by *Bibliografia nazionale italiana* (AA565).

✓**Pagliaini, Attilio.** Catalogo generale della libreria italiana, 1847–99. Milano, Assoc. Tip.-Libr. Ital., 1901–22. 6v.　　　**AA563**

Author and title list, 3v., 1901–5; Subject index, 3v., 1910–22.

—— —— 1.–4. supplemento. Milano, Assoc. Tip.-Libr. Ital., 1912–58. 11v. (In progress)

1st suppl., 1900–10, Authors and titles. 2v. 1912–14; 2d suppl., 1911–20, Authors and titles. 2v. 1925–28; Subject index to 1st–2d suppl., 1900–20. 4v. 1933–40; 3d suppl., 1921– 30, Authors and titles. 2v. 1932–38; 4th suppl., 1931–40, Authors and titles. 2v. 1956–58.

Subject indexes have not yet been published for the 3d and 4th supplements.

The standard Italian list, covering a period of 53 years in its basic volume and continued by decennial supplements. The 1847–99 volumes include more than 200,000 titles, comprising the principal books and pamphlets of the period but omitting minor pamphlets, periodicals, separates, and government and society publications. Consists of: (1) Main author and title list, giving fairly full information, i.e., author's name, title (somewhat abridged), place, publisher, date, paging, size, illustrations, original price when obtainable; (2) Subject index to the author list. Based upon the catalogs of the large Italian libraries, catalogs of book dealers and publishers, and about 200 Italian bibliographies.

The supplements follow the arrangement, coverage, and format of the original.

Current

Associazione Italiana Editori. Catalogo collettivo della libreria italiana, . . . Milano, Soc. Anonima per Pubblicazioni Bibliografico-Editorali, 1948– .　　　**AA564**

An Italian *Books in print,* being a collection of publishers' catalogs with an alphabetical index. Editions have appeared in 1949, 1955, and 1959.

Earlier lists of a similar nature were the *Catalogo collettivo della libreria italiana* (1891. 2v.) and the *Catalogo dei cataloghi del libro italiano* (1922, 1923, and 1926 with supplements 1928, 1930, and 1932).

Bibliografia nazionale italiana; nuova serie del Bollettino delle pubblicazioni italiane ricevute per diritto di stampa. Gennaio, 1958– . Firenze, 1958– . Anno 1– . Monthly.　　　**AA565**

—— Catalogo alfabetico annuale, 1958– . Firenze, Biblioteca Nazionale Centrale, 1961– . v.1– . Annual.

At head of title of each series: Centro Nazionale per il Catalogo Unico delle Biblioteche Italiane e per le Informazioni Bibliografiche.

A new national bibliography in two forms. The monthly series is a successor to the *Bollettino* (AA562a), being a current record of books and pamphlets received by legal deposit. Entries are reproduced in catalog card form; arrangement is by Dewey Decimal Classification; bibliographical information is complete, usually including prices; and tracings for subject and added entries are indicated. Author-title index in each issue but no cumulated index.

This series is complemented, but not superseded, by the annual volume into which these entries are cumulated into one alphabetical main entry catalog, including all information from the monthly listing except the tracings and the classification numbers. Without the latter it cannot be said to serve as an author index to the monthly classified sections, but it does include an index of subjects and one of secondary names. v.1, 1958, also contains separate alphabets for: musical scores; serials and *numeri unici;* and maps.

Giornale della libreria; pubblicazione settimanale, 1888 – . Milano, Assoc. Italiana Editori, 1888– . v.1– . Semimonthly, with quarterly cumulations.　　　**AA566**

Publisher and frequency vary.

Superseded the *Cronaca* and *Avvisi,* published until 1887 as pts.2 and 3 of the *Bibliografia italiana* (AA562).

Contains classified lists of recent publications and announcements of forthcoming publications. As it appears more promptly than the *Bibliografia nazionale italiana,* it is useful for current information.

Italy. Ufficio della Proprietà Letteraria, Artistica e Scientifica. Bollettino. n.s. v.1– . Roma, 1945– . Monthly (Irregular).　　　**AA567**

Issued by the Presidenza del Consiglio dei Ministri, Servizi Informazione e Proprietà Intellettuale (varies slightly).

Like the *Bollettino* of the Biblioteca Nazionale Centrale in Florence (AA562a) and the *Bibliografia nazionale italiana* (AA565), this is a copyright depository listing; its book section, however, arranged by subject areas and with cumulated annual author indexes, is said to be not so complete as the Florence listings.

Also includes lists of phonograph records and moving pictures.

Libri e riviste; rassegna bibliografica mensile. Anno 1, no.1, Marzo 1950– . Roma, Capriotti, 1950– . Monthly.　　　**AA568**

"Edito sotto gli auspicii del Centro di documentazione della Presidenza del Consiglio dei Ministri . . ."

Subtitle varies.

Each issue in three sections: (1) "Libri del mese" consists of reviews of new books, listed by class; (2) "Le riviste del mese" gives annotated contents of journals, arranged alphabetically by titles of the journals under broad classifications; (3) "Rassegna bibliografica," a classified listing of new titles published in Italy, giving complete bibliographical information, including price.

Japan

Samura, Hachirô. Kokusho Kaidai, zôtei. Tokyo, Rikugôkan, 1926. 2v.　　　**AA569**

An annotated bibliography of 27,000 Japanese books published up to 1867.

Tokyo. National Diet Library. Kokuritsu Kokkai Toshokan zôsho mokuroku. 1948–1958. Tokyo, 1960–62. v.1– 3. (In progress)　　　**AA570**

English title: National Diet Library. Catalog. A catalog of publications acquired, 1948–58.

Contents: ser. 1, General works, philosophy and religion, history and geography; ser. 2, Social sciences; ser. 3, Science, technology, industry.

A subject catalog with author indexes.

Current

Shuppan nenkan, [1951]– . Tokyo, Shuppan Nyûsusha, 1951– . Annual. **AA571**

Includes information on publishing for the previous year; a classified listing of books published; new periodicals; lists of publishers, organizations, etc.; and laws and ordinances governing publication.

This title supersedes *Nihon shuppan nenkan*, which appeared in 2v. (1943–44/46, and 1947/48; no volume was issued for 1949), and was preceded by *Shuppan nenkan* (1930–41) and *Shoseki nenkan* (1942). A separate annual dealing with periodicals, *Zasshi nenkan*, was published from 1939 to 1942, when it merged with *Nihon shuppan nenkan*.

Shuppan nyûsu [Publications—News and reviews], Nov. 11, 1946– . Tokyo, Shuppan Nyûsusha, 1946– . 3 times a month. **AA572**

Contains reviews and articles; lists new publications and gives information on forthcoming books.

Original title *Shuppan kôhô*, beginning [Oct. (?)], 1944. Title changed with Nov. 11, 1946 issue.

Tokyo. National Diet Library. Zen-Nihon shuppan-butsu sô-mokuroku [Japanese national bibliography]. 1948– . Tokyo, Kokuritsu Kokkai Toshokan, 1951– . Annual. **AA573**

A subject listing, including books, periodicals, newspapers, films, records, maps, etc.; government publications are under issuing agency. Title index.

With v.12, 1959, issued in two parts: pt.1, Government publications; pt.2, Non-governmental publications.

Latin America

British Museum. Dept. of Printed Books. Short-title catalogues of Portuguese books and of Spanish-American books printed before 1601, now in the British Museum, by H. Thomas. London, Quaritch, 1926. 55p. **AA574**

The Portuguese section was issued in an enlarged edition (AA649), but as no significant additions had been made to the Spanish-American section up to 1940, this was not revised.

Historia y bibliografía de las primeras imprentas rioplatenses, 1700–1850; misiones del Paraguay, Argentina, Uruguay, por Guillermo Fúrlong [and others]. Buenos Aires, Ed. Guaranía, 1953–59. v.1–3. il. (In progress) **AA575**

Contents: t.1, La imprenta en las reducciones del Paraguay, 1700–27. La imprenta en Córdoba, 1765–67. La imprenta en Buenos Aires, 1780–84; t.2, La imprenta en Buenos Aires, 1785–1807; t.3, La imprenta en Buenos Aires, 1808–1810. La imprenta en Montevideo, 1807–1810.

Aims to furnish a complete record of printing in Argentina, Paraguay, and Uruguay from 1700 to 1850. A history of early printing in the area is followed by the bibliography. Information about each item is detailed, including transcript of title page or colophon, collation, location, contents, description of type, etc. Biographical notes on author and printer are often given, and references to other bibliographical sources.

Medina, José Toribio. Biblioteca hispano-americana (1493–1810). Santiago de Chile, Impreso y Grabado en Casa del Autor, 1898–1907. 7v. il. (Repr.: Amsterdam, N. Israel, 1958–62. 7v. Also Readex microprint) **AA576**

Treats books published by Americans or Spaniards who lived in America and who wrote on matters pertaining to America; and books written in Spanish or Latin and printed in Spain or elsewhere by Spaniards or Americans; and books

published on the Peninsula by individuals whatever their nationality or language.

8481 titles, transcribed line for line; with bio-bibliographical notes, and frequent references to authorities and to libraries containing copies of the works described.

t.1–5, 1493–1810; t.6, Prólogo. Sin fecha determinada, siglo XVII–XIX. Adiciones. Ampliaciones. Dudosos. Manuscritos; t.7, Algo más de Léon Pinelo. Nuevas adiciones. Sin fecha determinada. Ultimas adiciones. Ampliaciones. Notas biográficas. Índice alfabético.

—— Historia y bibliografía de la imprenta en el antiguo vireinato del Río de la Plata. La Plata, Taller de Publicaciones del Museo, 1892. 4 pts. in 1v. il. (Historia y bibliografía de la imprenta en la América Española . . . [pt.2]) **AA577**

Added half title: Anales del Museo de la Plata. Materiales para la historia física y moral del continente sud-americano. Publicados bajo la dirección de Francisco P. Moreno . . . Sección de historia americana. III.

Contents: pt.1, Historia y bibliografía de la imprenta en el Paraguay (1705–1727); pt.2, En Córdoba del Tucumán (1766); pt.3, En Buenos Aires (1780–1810); pt. 4, En Montevideo (1807–1810). Índice alfabético.

—— Notas bibliográficas referentes á las primeras producciones de la imprenta en algunas ciudades de la América Española (Ambato, Angostura, Curazao, Quayaquil, Maracaibo, Nueva Orleans, Nueva Valencia, Panamá, Popayán, Puerto España, Puerto Rico, Querétaro, Santa Marta, Santiago de Cuba, Santo Domingo, Tunja y otros lugares). (1754–1823) Santiago de Chile, Impr. Elzeviriana, 1904. 116p. **AA578**

Pan American bookshelf. Wash., Pan Amer. Union, Columbus Memorial Lib., 1938–1948. 11v. Monthly.**AA579**

A very useful monthly bibliography with annual author index. Listed books currently received in the Columbus Memorial Library—usually, but not always, recent material.

Ceased publication with the Dec. 1948 issue.

Succeeded by:

LEA: Librarians, editors, authors; libros, editores, autores. . . . Wash., Union Panamericana, 1949–50. no. 1–12. **AA580**

Ceased publication with no.12, Feb. 1950. Superseded by *Revista interamericana de bibliografía* (AA585).

Sanz, Carlos. Bibliotheca americana vetustissima; últimas adiciones. Madrid, Librería General V. Suárez, 1960. 2v. il. **AA581**

—— —— Comentario crítico e índice general cronológico. Madrid, Librería General V. Suárez, 1960. 79p.

The first two of these volumes are "final" supplements to the Harrisse bibliography of the same title (DB4); the third is an index to the Harrisse volumes, the two new volumes, and two other works by Sanz, *Henry Harrisse* . . . 1958, and *El gran secreto de la carta de Colón*, 1959. In 1958 the same publishers reprinted the original Harrisse volumes, issuing all these titles under the series title, "Bibliotheca americana vetustissima."

Current

Fichero bibliográfico hispanoamericano: catálogo trimestral de toda clase de libros en español publicados en las Américas. N.Y., Bowker, 1961– . v.1– . Quarterly; monthly, Sept. 1964– **AA582**

This comprehensive bibliography hopes to list all new books published in the Americas in the Spanish language in all subjects and by all publishers. Arranged by Dewey Decimal Classification with an index by authors and titles, followed by a list of publishers and a table of conversion for the moneys of the various countries.

Libros en venta en Hispanoamérica y España. Un servicio

informativo prep. bajo la dirección de Mary C. Turner. N.Y., Bowker, 1964– . v.1– . **AA583**

A new *Books in print* for books in the Spanish languages, listing more than 87,000 titles published in Spain, the United States, and the Latin-American countries: Argentina, Bolivia, Colombia, Costa Rica, Cuba, Chile, Dominican Republic, Ecuador, El Salvador, Guatemala, Honduras, Mexico, Nicaragua, Panama, Paraguay, Peru, Puerto Rico, Uruguay, and Venezuela.

In three main sections: (1) authors, (2) titles, and (3) classified by Dewey Decimal Classification, with a subject index to the last.

Pan American Union. Columbus Memorial Library. List of books accessioned and periodical articles indexed for the month of Sept., 1950– . Wash., 1950– . Monthly. **AA584**

Title varies.

From Sept. 1950 through Jan. 1951 only monographic publications were included; beginning with Feb. 1951 each issue is divided into two parts, the second consisting of periodical articles. Some issues include articles on libraries or reports of conferences. Material dealing with Latin America, but published elsewhere, is included.

Revista interamericana de bibliografía; Review of inter-American bibliography. v.1– . Wash., Dept. of Cultural Affairs, Pan Amer. Union, 1951– . il. Quarterly (Frequency varies). **AA585**

Supersedes *LEA* (AA580).

Lists of recent books, bibliographies, reviews, and articles on bibliographical topics are included. Annual index.

Luxembourg

Bibliographie luxembourgeoise, 1944/45– par Pierre Frieden. Luxembourg, Bibliothèque Nationale, 1946– . Annual. **AA586**

The first issue covered Sept. 10, 1944–Dec. 31, 1945; subsequent issues cover the calendar year.

The national bibliography, listing all materials published in Luxembourg, including official publications, new periodicals, and newspapers. Coverage varies. Since 1958 includes outstanding articles in periodicals. Arrangement is classified and since 1958 has author and subject indexes.

Mexico

Andrade, Vicente de Paula. Ensayo bibliográfico mexicano del siglo XVII. 2. ed. México, Impr. del Museo Nacional, 1899 [1900]. 803p. (Readex microprint) **AA587**

Reprinted, in part, from the *Memorias de la Sociedad Científica Antonio Alzate.* 1894.

Lists 1228 titles, transcribed line for line. Arranged chronologically and followed by alphabetical indexes of (1) authors, (2) anonymous works.

Beristain de Souza, José Mariano. Biblioteca hispano americana septentrional; o, Catálogo y noticias de los literatos que o nacidos o educados, o florecientes en la América Septentrional Española, han dado a luz algún escrito, o lo han dejado prep. para la prensa, 1521–1850. [3. ed.] México, Ed. Fuente Cultural, 1947. 5v. in 2. il., facsims. **AA588**

1st ed. 1816–21; 2d ed. 1883. 3v.

v.1–5, A–Z. Also includes *Suplemento especial* to v.5 (called v.6?) and lists of anonyms, bio-bibliographical notes, and indexes. Based upon the 2d edition, this is a reissue, with additions and corrections. Arrangement is confusing and must be studied with care.

–––––– Suplemento especial II–III. México, Ed. Fuente Cultural, 1951. 2v. il., facsims.

Also numbered as v.7–8 of main work.

Berroa, Josefina. México bibliográfico, 1957–1960; catálogo general de libros impresos en México. México, J. Berroa, 1961. (Distr. in U.S. by Bowker, N.Y.) 189p. **AA589**

An author list of approximately 4000 titles, followed by a subject index.

Gives full cataloging with prices.

García Icazbalceta, Joaquín. Bibliografía mexicana del siglo XVI. Catálogo razonado de libros impresos en México de 1539–1600, con biografías de autores y otras ilustraciones . . . Nueva edición por Augustín Millares Carlo. México, Fondo de Cultura Económica, 1954. 581p. il., facsims. (Biblioteca americana, proyectada por Pedro Henríquez Ureña y publicada en memoria suya; Serie de literatura moderna: historia y biografía [27]) **AA590**

1st ed. 1886. "Primera edición en la Biblioteca Americana, 1954."

This edition uses the text of the original which listed 116 titles, transcribed line for line, without change of wording, but with additions and emendations resulting from later investigation. Additional titles are included, with an appendix, and an analytical index. Quotations, and very full bibliographical and historical notes are given, with references to sources and, in many cases, location of copies.

–––––– –––––– Índice alfabético, formado por Catarina A. Janvier, trad. y arreglo de Manuel Toussaint y Justino Fernández. México, Porrúa, 1938. 19p.

The index was originally printed in English in New York in 1889. This is a Spanish translation.

González de Cossío, Francisco. La imprenta en México, 1594–1820. Cien adiciones a la obra de Don José Toribio Medina. México, Antigua Librería Robredo, 1947. 205p. facsims. **AA591**

–––––– La imprenta en México, 1553–1820. 510 adiciones a la obra de José Toribio Medina en homenaje al primer centenario de su nacimiento. México, Univ. Nacional de México, 1952. 354p. facsims.

The second work continues the first and does not duplicate the entries given there. Both volumes include full bibliographical information and line-by-line transcription.

León, Nicholás. Bibliografía mexicana del siglo XVIII. México, Francisco Diaz de Leon, 1902–1908. v.1^{1-6a}. facsims. **AA592**

Publication first begun in *Anales del Museo Michoacano,* 1890. Planned to be issued in two parallel sections: one purely bibliographical (including reprints in whole or in part of the rarer works); the other biographical, historical, and critical. Line-by-line transcription. Each part A–Z (pt.6a, incomplete, A–N).

v.1$^{2,4-5}$ are numbered 4, 8, 10 of *Boletín* del Instituto Bibliográfico Mexicano.

–––––– –––––– Índice[s] . . . arreglado por Roberto Valles. México, Ed. Vargas Rea, 1945–46. 3v. (Biblioteca Aportación Histórica)

Índice de nombres, 1945. 61p.; Índice de impresos, 1946. 29p.; Índice de anónimos, 1946. 44p.

Medina, José Toribio. La imprenta en México (1539–1821). Santiago de Chile, Autor, 1908–1912. [v.1, 1912] 8v. il. (Readex microprint) **AA593**

12,412 entries.

–––––– La imprenta en Guadalajara de México (1793–1821): notas bibliográficas. Santiago de Chile, Impr. Elzeviriana, 1904. 104p. **AA594**

–––––– La imprenta en la Puebla de Los Angeles (1640–1821). Santiago de Chile, Cervantes, 1908. 823p. il. **AA595**

—— La imprenta en Mérida de Yucatán (1813–21): notas bibliográficas. Santiago de Chile, Impr. Elzeviriana, 1904. 32p. (Readex microprint) (Ed. commemorativa del centenario de nacimiento del autor, con un prólogo y dos apéndices por Victor M. Suárez. Mérida, Ed. Suárez, 1956. 102p.) **AA596**

—— La imprenta en Oaxaca (1720–1820): notas bibliográficas. Santiago de Chile, Impr. Elzeviriana, 1904. 29p. **AA597**

—— La imprenta en Veracruz (1794–1821): notas bibliográficas. Santiago de Chile, Impr. Elzeviriana, 1904. 34p. **AA598**

Valton, Emilio. Impresos mexicanos del siglo XVI (incunables americanos) en la Biblioteca Nacional de México, el Museo Nacional y el Archivo General de la Nación. Estudio bibliográfico precedido de una introducción sobre los orígenes de la imprenta en América. México, Impr. Universitaria, 1935. 244p. il., facsims. **AA599**

Detailed bibliographical descriptions of 16th-century Mexican imprints.

Anuario bibliográfico mexicano, 1931–33. Compilación de Felipe Teixidor. México, Secretaría de Relaciones Exteriores, 1932–34. v.1–3. **AA600**

Based upon the copyright accessions of the National Library.
1934–39 not published.
Continued by:

Anuario bibliográfico mexicano de 1940–1941/42; comp. por Julian Amo. México, Secretaría de Relaciones Exteriores, Dept. de Información para el Extranjero, 1942–44. v.1–2. Annual. (Serie bibliografías mexicanas) **AA601**

A classed list, with combined author index for 1941–42. No more published.

Current

Boletín bibliográfico mexicano; reseña bimestral de libros y folletos, impresos en los E. U. Mexicanos. Oct. 1939– . México, 1939– . Monthly to 1947; bimonthly 1947– . **AA602**

Subtitle varies.
Classified with author indexes.

Recent books in Mexico. Bulletin of the Centro Mexicano de Escritores. Mexico, 1955– . v.1– . Bimonthly. **AA603**

A small bulletin in English including articles on Mexican literature, book reviews, and classified lists of selected new publications. Annual alphabetical index of all authors noted in reviews and lists. (Not a complete national bibliography but, in the absence of one, may help.)

Netherlands

Early

Nijhoff, Wouter and **Kronenberg, M. E.** Nederlandsche bibliographie van 1500 tot 1540. 'sGravenhage, Nijhoff, 1923. 1002p. **AA604**

A comprehensive record of the imprints of this period, giving full titles and collation, with bibliographical references and location of copies.

—— —— 1.-4. aanvulling. 1925–34. 328p.

—— —— 2. deel, door M. E. Kronenberg. 1936–40. 1158p.

Titles numbered in continuation of basic work.

—— —— Inleiding tot een derde deel. Winst en verlies. 1942. 175p.

—— —— 3. deel, door M. E. Kronenberg. 1951–61. 3v.

v.3 of this 3d series includes various indexes: of printers, names, etc.

17th–19th centuries

Abkoude, Johannes van. Naamregister van de bekendste en meest in gebruik zynde Nederduitsche boeken, welke sedert het jaar 1600 tot het jaar 1761 zyn uitgekomen. . . . Nu overzien, verb. en tot het jaar 1787 verm. door Reinier Arrenberg. 2. druk. Rotterdam, Arrenberg, 1788. 598p. **AA605**

First pub. 1743–56. Rev. and reissued by Arrenberg, 1773.

—— Alphabetische naamlijst van boeken, welke . . . 1790–1832, in Noord-Nederland zijn uitgekomen. 'sGravenhage, van Cleef, 1835. 755p. 159p. **AA606**

Continued by: C. L. Brinkman, Alphabetische naamlijst . . . 1833–1849 (AA608).

—— Alphabetische naamlijst van fonds-artikelen, voorkomende in het naamregister van Nederlandsche boeken, alsmede in de Alphabetische naamlijst van boeken, achtervolgens uitg. bij R. Arrenberg en de Gebroeders van Cleef, en waarvan het regt van eigendom aan anderen is overgegaan. 'sGravenhage, van Cleef, 1839. 122p. **AA607**

Brinkman, C. L. Alphabetische naamlijst van boeken, plaat- en kaartwerken die 1833–1849 in Nederland uitg. of herdrukt zijn. Amsterdam, Brinkman, 1858. 792p. **AA608**

—— —— Wetenschappelijk register . . . 1850–1875. Met alphabetische opgave der onderwerpen. Bewerkt door R. van der Meulen. Amsterdam, Brinkman, 1878. 464p.

Pamphlets

Hague. Koninklijke Bibliotheek. Catalogus van de pamfletten-verzameling berustende in de Koninklijke Bibliotheek. Bewerkt, met aanteekeningen en een register der schrijvers voorzien, door W. P. C. Knuttel. 'sGravenhage, Algemeene Landsdrukkerij, 1889–1920. 9v. **AA609**

v.1–7, Chronological, 1486–1853; v.8, Supplement; v.9, Alphabetical subject index, 1486–1795.

Tiele, Pieter Anton. Bibliotheek van Nederlandsche pamfletten. Amsterdam, Frederik Muller, 1858–61. 3v. **AA610**

Chronological list, 1482–1702 (9668 entries).

19th and 20th centuries

Brinkman's Catalogus van boeken, plaat- en kaartwerken die gedurende de jaren 1850– in Nederland zijn uitg. of herdrukt. . . . Amsterdam, Brinkman, 1883–93; Leiden, Sijthoff, 1903– . **AA611**

Title varies slightly.
1850–82, 1437p.; 1882–91, 2v.; 1891–1900, 2v.; 1901–10, 2v.; 1911–15– , published in 5-year cumulations, each in several divisions with separate title pages.

Each issue, except that for 1850–82 which has only the *Catalogus,* is in two main parts, separately paged: (1) *Catalogus,* or main author and title list, giving full information including author, title, editor or translator (if any), illustration, size, paging, publisher, date, price; (2) *Repertorium,* or subject index to the *Catalogus,* giving brief information only and referring to the word under which full information is found in the *Catalogus.* From 1891–1900 on, each *Repertorium* contains a *Titel-catalogus,* supplementary to *Brink-*

man's *Titel-catalogus* (AA612). In the issue for 1926–30, the scope of the work was enlarged to include: (1) separate lists of periodicals and (2) Dutch works published in Belgium. (In this volume this is a separate list; in later volumes these titles are incorporated in the main alphabet.)

Brinkman's Titel-catalogus van de sedert het begin dezer eeuw tot 1888 in Nederland verschenen werken op het gebied der nieuwe letterkunde (romans, novellen, gedichten, tooneelstukken en kinder-boeken) . . . Bewerkt onder toezicht en met voorbericht van R. van der Meulen. . . . Amsterdam, Brinkman, [1888–89]. 232p.   **AA612**

A title index—for works of fiction, poetry, drama, music, juvenile literature, etc.—to *Brinkman's Catalogus* (AA611). Gives brief title, date, and author's names, the latter supplying the cross reference to the fuller description in *Brinkman's Catalogus*. Continued by supplements included in *Brinkman's Catalogus*.

Bibliotheca belgica. Bibliographie générale des Pays-Bas. Bruxelles, 1964–   .   **AA613**

For full record *see* AA374.

Current

Brinkman's Cumulatieve catalogus van boeken, . . . in Nederland en Vlaanderen zijn uitg. of herdrukt, benevens aanvullingen over voorafgaande jaren in een alfabet gerangschikt volgens auteur, titel en onderwerp. Leiden, Sijthoff, 1846–   . v.1–   . Monthly, with annual cumulations.   **AA614**

Publisher varies; before 1881, Amsterdam, Brinkman. Title varies; before 1930 had title *Brinkman's Alphabetische lijst*.

Before 1930, an annual list on the same plan as the main author list in *Brinkman's Catalogus* (AA611) with brief subject index to the author list. From 1930 on, published at varying intervals with cumulations, the last number of the year covering 12 months and forming an annual volume.

Superseded by the quinquennial volumes.

Netherlands East Indies

See Indonesia, p.51.

New Zealand

Johnstone, A. H. Canterbury books, 1847–1955: a bibliography. Christchurch, N.Z., Whitcomb and Tombs, 1956. 195p.   **AA615**

Attempts to be "as comprehensive a list as possible of books, pamphlets, newspapers, etc., published in Canterbury, about Canterbury, or by authors associated with Canterbury."—*Introd.*

Current

Current national bibliography of New Zealand books and pamphlets published in 1950–   . (In Index to New Zealand periodicals, 1950–   , AF158)   **AA616**

An alphabetical author, title, and subject list of all books and pamphlets published in New Zealand, and those published elsewhere by New Zealanders or having reference to New Zealand. Does not include prices.

New Zealand. General Assembly. Library. Copyright publications, 1933/34–   . Wellington, Gov't Printer, [193?]–   .   **AA617**

An annual list, supplemented by monthly lists in mimeographed form, of material received under the provisions of the Copyright Act. Full bibliographical information is given, including prices. There are sections listing government publications, overseas publications deposited, maps, music, new periodicals, and periodicals that have ceased publication.

Nicaragua

Managua. Biblioteca Americana de Nicaragua. Bibliografía de libros y folletos publicados en Nicaragua (en 1942, o antes según fecha de publicación), que se encuentran en algunas bibliotecas particulares de Nicaragua. A bibliography of books and pamphlets published in Nicaragua (with 1942 or earlier as date of publication) to be found in certain private libraries of Nicaragua. Managua, Ed. Nuevos Horizontes, [1945]. 157p. (Its Serie bibliográfica, no.4, pt.1, enero 1945)   **AA618**

Continued by:

—— Bibliografía de trabajos publicados en Nicaragua . . . A bibliography of works published in Nicaragua. 1943–45/47. [Managua, Ed. Nuevos Horizontes], 1944–48. v.1–3. (Its Serie bibliográfica, no.1, 6, 7–9, julio 1944, mayo 1945, mayo 1948)   **AA619**

Ed., 1943–44, Graciela González.
Spanish and English.
Ceased publication (?).

Nigeria

Nigerian publications; current national bibliography, 1950/52–   . Ibadan, Ibadan Univ. Pr., 1953–   . Annual.   **AA620**

Early volumes carried subtitle: A list of works received under the Publications Ordinance by the Library. University College, Ibadan.

Lists books and pamphlets published in Nigeria, or about Nigeria or by Nigerians published abroad. Includes official publications and first issues of periodicals.

Norway

Early

Pettersen, Hjalmar. Bibliotheca norvegica. Christiania, Cammeyer, 1899–1924. 4v. in 5.   **AA621**

Each volume has added title page in English.

Contents: v.1, Norsk boglexikon, 1643–1813 (English title page: Descriptive catalogue of books printed in Norway, 1643–1813). 1899–1908. 621p.; v.2, Norge og nordmaend i udlandets literatur (Norway and the Norwegians in foreign literature; descriptive catalogue of books and papers relating to Norway). 1908–17. 3v. 843p.; v.3, Norske forfattere før 1814 (Norwegian authors before 1814; descriptive catalogue of their works). 1911–18. 595p.; v.4, Norske forfattere efter 1814. 1. samling med suppl. til Bibliotheca norvegica I–III (Norwegian authors; descriptive catalogue of their works printed in foreign countries). 1913–24. 798p.

19th and 20th centuries

Hauff, Nils Selmer. Stikords-katalog over norsk literatur, 1883–1907. Kristiania, Cappelen, [1908–9]. 93p. **AA622**

A catchword-title index to Norwegian materials for this period.

Norsk bokfortegnelse, 1814/47–1951/55. Kristiania, 1848–1921; Oslo, Norske Bokhandlerforening, 1928–62. (In progress)   **AA623**

Title varies.

Now compiled by the University Library as the *Norwegian national bibliography*.

19th-century cumulations vary in number of years covered. Decennial, 1891–1920; quinquennial, 1921–   .

Includes books, pamphlets, periodicals, official publications, theses, and maps. Arranged alphabetically by author and title, giving full bibliographical description, followed by a classified section.

Current

Norsk bokfortegnelse. The Norwegian national bibliography. Årskatalog 1952– . Utarb. ved Universitetsbiblioteket i Oslo, Norske Avdeling. Oslo, Norske Bokhandlerforening, 1953– . Annual. **AA624**

Supersedes the *Aarskatalog over norsk litteratur* 1893–1951. Quarterly issues cumulate into annual volumes, then into the quinquennial.

Arrangement is alphabetical by author and title; there are also series entries with contents. Maps are listed separately, and there is a classified index.

Norsk bokhandlertidende. v.1– . Oslo, Grøndahl, 1880– . Weekly. **AA625**

Panama

Panama (City). Biblioteca Nacional. Bibliografía panameña. Panama, 1953. 66p. **AA626**

At head of title: Ministerio de Educación, Comité Nacional Pro-bibliotecas, Biblioteca Nacional.

An alphabetical listing, in preliminary form, of books, pamphlets, and documents printed in Panama in the 20th century, with a few titles on Panama published elsewhere.

Paraguay

See also Latin America, p.53.

Paraguay. Biblioteca Nacional. Bibliografía paraguaya: catálogo de la Biblioteca Paraguaya "Solano López." Asunción, Talleres Nacionales de H. Kraus, 1906. 984p. **AA627**

Rich in the early history of Paraguay.

Peru

Biblioteca peruana. Apuntos para un catálogo de impresos. Santiago de Chile, Biblioteca del Inst. Nacional, 1896. 2v. **AA628**

Ed. by Gabriel René-Moreno.

A fully annotated work. Basic.

Contents: v.1, pts.1–2, Libros y folletos peruanos de la Biblioteca del Instituto Nacional; v.2, pts.1–2, Libros y folletos peruanos de la Biblioteca Nacional y Notas bibliográficas.

Medina, José Toribio. La imprenta en Lima (1584–1824). Santiago de Chile, Autor, 1904–7. 4v. (Readex microprint) **AA629**

—— La imprenta en Arequipa, el Cuzco, Trujillo y otros pueblos del Perú durante las campañas de la independencia (1820–1825); notas bibliográficas. Santiago de Chile, Impr. Elzeviriana, 1904. 71p. (Readex microprint) **AA629a**

Vargas Ugarte, Rubén. Impresos peruanos. Lima, [Ed. San Marcos], 1949–57. 7v. in 6 (His Biblioteca peruana, t.6–12) **AA630**

Contents: v.1, Impresos peruanos publicados en el extranjero 1546–1825; v.2–7, Impresos peruanos 1584–1825.

Aims to include all books and pamphlets published in Peru; arranged chronologically, with author index in each volume. Line-by-line transcription with detailed bibliographical description. Locates copies.

Current

Anuario bibliográfico peruano. 1943– . Lima, 1945– . v.1– . Annual. (Ediciones de la Biblioteca Nacional, 1–) **AA631**

Ed.: 1943–54, Alberto Tauro; 1955– , Cristobal de Losada y Puga.

An annual bibliography which attempts to record books, pamphlets, and all other publications printed in Peru; and works of Peruvian authors and works relating to Peru printed abroad.

Classified, with indexes of periodicals, authors, printers, etc.

Each volume includes a section of periodicals and newspapers and a separate bio-bibliographical section of Peruvian authors who died during the years covered. These bibliographies are extensive and are indexed separately.

Lima. Universidad Mayor de San Marcos. Biblioteca. Boletín bibliográfico. v.1, 1923– . Lima, 1923– . Quarterly. **AA632**

Suspended 1930–Oct. 1934.

Usually, each year includes a list of books and pamphlets published in Peru, with full bibliographical information, and a list of articles from Peruvian periodicals.

Philippines

Medina, José Toribio. Bibliografía española de las Islas Filipinas (1523–1810). Santiago de Chile, Impr. Cervantes, 1897–98. 556p. **AA633**

Reprinted from *Anales* de la Universidad de Chile, 1897–98.

A list of 667 titles arranged chronologically, with author index.

—— La imprenta en Manila desde sus orígenes hasta 1810. Santiago de Chile, Autor, 1896. 280p. facsim. **AA634**

—— —— Adiciones y ampliaciones. Santiago de Chile, Autor, 1904. 203p.

Pérez, Angel and Güemes, Cecilio. Adiciones y continuación de "La imprenta en Manila" de d. J. T. Medina; ó rarezas y curiosidades bibliográficas filipinas de las bibliotecas de esta capital. Manila, Santos y Bernal, 1904. 620p. (Readex microprint) **AA635**

Retana y Gamboa, Wenceslao Emilio. La imprenta en Filipinas; adiciones y observaciones á la Imprenta en Manila de d. J. T. Medina. Madrid, Minuesa de los Ríos, 1897. 276cols. (Readex microprint) **AA636**

—— Aparato bibliográfico de la historia general de Filipinas. Madrid, Minuesa de los Ríos, 1906. 3v. **AA637**

v.1, 1524–1800; v.2, 1801–86; v.3, 1887–1905.

Includes: (1) Philippine imprints regardless of subject; (2) Books about the Philippines regardless of what language written in or where published; (3) Publications of Filipinos wherever printed.

Arranged by years with the following indexes in v.1: (1) Anónimos y principales materias, refundidos; (2) Publicaciones periódicas; (3) Biblioteca idiomática oriental; (4) Lugares geográficos; (5) Nombres propios de personas.

—— Tablas cronológica y alfabética de imprentas e impresores de Filipinas (1593–1898). Madrid, Victoriano Suárez, 1908. 114p. (Readex microprint) **AA638**

Poland

Wierzbowski, Teodor. Bibliographia polonica XV ac XVI ss. . . . Varsoviae, Kowalewski, 1889–94. 3v. **AA639**

v.1 contains titles of works in the Warsaw University Library (destroyed by fire); v.2–3, works found in other libraries, Polish and foreign, with indication of location. Arranged chronologically with indexes of authors, subjects, persons, and places.

Estreicher, Karol. Bibliografia polska. Kraków, Czcionkami Drukarni Universytetu Jagiellońskiego, 1870–1939; 1951. v.1–34. (In progress) **AA640**

In three series: ser. 1, an alphabetical list for the 19th century. 7v. (v.1–5, A–Z; v.6–7, Supplement, A–Z); ser. 2, chronological lists, 1455–1880. 4v. (v.8–9, 1455–1799; v.10, 1800–1870; v.11, 1871–1889); ser. 3, alphabetical list, 15th–18th centuries, v.1–23 (whole no. v.12–34), A–Zal.

The exhaustive bibliography of Polish imprints from 1455 to 1880.

Continued to 1900 by:

—— Bibliografia polska 19. stulecia, lata 1881–1900. Kraków, Spółka Księgarzy Polsk., 1906–16. 4v. **AA641**

—— Bibliografia polska 19. stulecia. Wyd. 2. Kraków, [Państwowe Wydawn. Naukowe, Oddziat w Krakowie], 1959– . v.1– . (Polska Akademia Nauk. Bibliografia polska Karola Estreichera, cz.1, t.1–) **AA641a**

Added title page in French.

v.1, A– .

The beginning of a 2d edition of the 19th-century bibliography.

20th century

Dąbrowska, Wanda, Czarnecka, J. and **Słomczewska, J.** 555 książek wydanych w okresie powojennym. Warszawa, Ludówy Inst. Oświaty i Kultury, 1946. 80p. **AA642**

Lists 555 books published in Poland, July 1944—May 1, 1946. Classified, with author and title index and subject index.

Przewodnik bibliograficzny. ser. 1, v.1–37, no.6, 1878–June 1914; ser. 2, v.1–9, 1920–28; ser. 3, v.1–5, 1929–33. Kraków, Základ Narodowy Imienia Ossolinskich, 1878–1933. **AA643**

1914–19 replaced by *Bibliografia polska,* v.1–6.

Zabielska, Janina. Bibliography of books in Polish or relating to Poland published outside Poland since Sept. 1st, 1939. London, Polish Lib. (5 Princes Gardens, S.W. 7), 1954–59. v.1–2. **AA644**

Contents: v.1, 1939–1951 (no.1–5625); v.2, 1952–1957 and supplements to 1939–1951 (no.1–4175).

First published in 1953 by the Polish University College Library, which was closed and taken over by the Polish Library.

Each volume arranged chronologically.

Current

Przewodnik bibliograficzny; urzędowy wykaz druków wydanych w Rzeczypospolitej Polskiej. . . . R.2 (14), nr.1/3– . Warszawa, Biblioteka Narodowa, 1946– . Weekly (Frequency varies). **AA645**

Superseded *Urzędowy wykaz druków, 1928–39,* and continues its numbering in parentheses. v.1 of the new title is planned as a retrospective volume for 1939–45. Includes Polish imprints, books, pamphlets, new periodicals, and many government publications, and also foreign publications dealing with Poland which are in the National Library. Arrangement is classified, with an annual alphabetical index. Some volumes also have subject indexes.

Portugal

Early

Academia das Sciencias de Lisboa. Bibliografia geral portuguesa. Lisboa, Impr. Nacional, 1941–42. v.1–2. il. **AA646**

Date on cover of v.2, 1944.

Contents: v.1–2, Século XV.

Detailed bibliographical descriptions with introduction and notes, facsimiles, and the following indexes in each volume:

Matérias, Gravuras, Impressores, Bibliotecas e arquivos, Toponímico, and Geral.

Anselmo, António Joaquim. Bibliografia das obras impressas em Portugal no século XVI. Lisboa, Oficinas Gráficas da Biblioteca Nacional, 1926. 367p. il. (Publicações da Biblioteca Nacional) **AA647**

Reprinted from *Anais das bibliotecas e arquivos,* sér. 2, v.2–6, 1921–25.

Detailed bibliographical descriptions.

Barbosa Machado, Diogo. Bibliotheca lusitana historica, critica, e cronologica. Na qual se comprehende a noticia dos authores portuguezes, e das obras, que compuzerão desde o tempo da promulgaçaõ da ley da graça até o tempo prezente. Lisboa, 1741–59. 4v. (Repr.: Readex microprint) **AA648**

A bio-bibliographical work arranged by given names, providing much information not available in later works. Covers from early times to mid-18th century.

An abridgment by B. J. de Sousa-Farinha, entitled *Summario da Bibliotheca lusitana,* was published in Lisbon, 1786–87. 3v.

British Museum. Dept. of Printed Books. Short-title catalogue of Portuguese books printed before 1601, now in the British Museum, by Henry Thomas. London, Trustees, 1940. 43p. **AA649**

A revised and enlarged edition of the Portuguese section of their earlier catalogue (AA574).

Manuel II, King of Portugal. Livros antigos portuguezes, 1489–1600, da bibliotheca de Sua Majestade Fidelissima, descriptos por S. M. el-rei D. Manuel. . . . Cambridge, Univ. Pr., 1929–35. 3v. il. **AA650**

v.1, 1489–1539; v.2, 1540–1569; v.3, 1570–1600 e Supplemento 1500–1597.

General

Coimbra, Carlos. Dicionário de bibliografia portuguesa . . . Edição de A. de Gusmão Navarro. Lisboa, Torres, 1933–37. v.1– . **AA651**

No more published.

Loose-leaf. Issued in parts.

A–Barros (with a few sheets giving entries for various other parts of the alphabet). A new attempt to list Portuguese books of all periods.

Silva, Innocencio Francisco da. Diccionario bibliográphico portuguez. Estudos applicaveis a Portugal e ao Brasil. Lisboa, Impr. Nacional, 1858–1923. v.1–22. il. **AA652**

v.10–21 continuados e ampliados por Brito Aranha. v.1–7, A–Z; v.8–22 (supplement v.1–15), A–Z, A–Au.

Bio-bibliography arranged alphabetically by *first* names of authors. Includes books published from the 15th to the 19th centuries.

—— Índice alfabético, [por] José Soares de Souza. [São Paulo?], Dept. de Cultura, Divisião de Bibliotécas, 1938. 264p.

Current

Boletim de bibliografia portuguesa. v.1, 1935– . Lisboa, Biblioteca Nacional, 1937– . Annual, 1935–1951; monthly, 1955– . **AA653**

Not published, 1940–42; 1952–54.

The national bibliography of Portugal, listing books, pamphlets, some periodical articles, and government publications.

The annual volumes were arranged alphabetically by author. Beginning in 1955, published monthly and arranged by Universal Decimal Classification. Annual indexes were planned but have not been received. Announcement was also made of a supplementary fascicule listing Portuguese periodical publications; this also has not been received.

Livros de Portugal; mensario bibliográfico, no.60– . Maio 1952– . Lisboa, Grémio Nacional dos Editores e Livreiros, 1952– . Monthly. **AA654**

Began publication in Nov. 1940: no.1–58, 1940–46. Suspended publication. Resumed with no.60, maio 1952.

Contains notes, advertisements, etc., and a list of recent books. Gives prices.

Puerto Rico

Anuario bibliográfico puertorriqueño; índice alfabético de libros, folletos, revistas y periódicos publicados en Puerto Rico durante 1948– , comp. por Gonzálo Velazquez. Río Piedras, Estado Libre Asociado de Puerto Rico, Dept. de Instrucción Pública, 1950– . v.1– . Annual. **AA655**

Publisher varies.

An author, subject, and title listing of books, pamphlets, and periodicals. An excellent catalog, but slow in appearing (1957/58 pub. 1964).

Rumania

Adamescu, Gheorghe. Contribuţiune la bibliografia românească. Bucureşti, Cartea Românească, 1921–1928. 3 pts. **AA656**

For annotation *see* BD882.

Bianu, Ioan, Hodos, Nerva and **Simonescu, Dan.** Bibliografia românească veche 1508–1830. Ed. Academiei Române. Bucureşti, Atelierele Socec & Co., 1903–43. 4v. il. **AA657**

Issued in parts: v.1, 1508–1716; v.2, 1716–1808; v.3, 1809–1830; v.4, Additions et corrections (1943) by Ioan Bianu and Dan Simonescu.

An exhaustive bibliography, arranged chronologically, with index of names and titles.

Veress, Endre. Bibliografia română-ungară. Bucureşti, Cartea Românească, 1931–35. 3v. il. **AA658**

v.1, Românii in literatura ungară şi Ungurii in literatura română (1473–1780); v.2, (1781–1838); v.3, (1839–1878).

Records some 2377 titles in chronological order with full description and location of copies. Each volume has added title page and preface in French.

Current

Bucharest. Biblioteca Centrală de Stat. Anuarul cărţii din Republica Populară Romīnă, 1952/54– . Bucureşti, Ed. Stiinţifică, 1957– . **AA659**

Classified arrangement, with alphabetic index of authors and titles.

Rumania. Ministerul Culturii. Buletinul bibliografic al cărţii. Bucureşti, Camera Cărţii din R.P.R., 1952– . Semimonthly. **AA660**

Lists books, maps, and some government publications in classified order, with author and title indexes which cumulate quarterly.

Russia
(including the Ukraine)

16th and 17th centuries

Zernova, Antonina S. Knigi kirillovskoi pechati, izdannye v Moskve v XVI–XVII vekakh; svodnyi katalog. Pod red. N. P. Kiseleva. Moskva, 1958. 150p. **AA661**

At head of title: Ministerstvo kultura RSFSR. Gosudarstvennaia ordena Lenina Biblioteka SSSR im. V. I. Lenina. Otdel redkikh knig.

A union catalog of 16th- and 17th-century Moscow imprints in *kirillitsa* printing type, the alphabet for Russian prior to reform under Peter I and continued for ecclesiastical printing. Describes copies in six of the largest libraries of Moscow and Leningrad.

18th century

Akademiia Nauk URSR, Kiev. Biblioteka. Knigi grazhdanskoi pechati XVIII veka; katalog knig, khraniashchiksia v Gosudarstvennoi Publichnoi Biblioteke Ukrainskoi SSR. Sost.: S. O. Petrov. Kiev, 1956. 300p. **AA662**

Catalog of the books and journals, printed between 1708 and 1800 in Russian, which are preserved in the State Library in Kiev. Arrangement is by author, or title of anonymous work, with indexes for translators, places of publication and publishers' names, and broad subject fields.

Leningrad. Publichnaia Biblioteka. Opisanie izdanii grazhdanskoi pechati. 1708–ianvar' 1725g. Sost.: T. A. Bykova i M. M. Gurevich. Red. i vstup. stat'ia P. N. Berkova. Moskva, Izd-vo Akademii Nauk SSSR, 1955. 625p. il. (Its Opisanie izdanii, napechatannykh pri Petre I; svodnyi katalog) **AA663**

Descriptive bibliography with extensive annotations of works published in the Russian "civic" type introduced under Peter I. Locational symbols for libraries in Moscow and Leningrad. Appendixes include books in foreign languages published in Russia.

—— Opisanie izdanii napechatannykh kirillitsei 1689–ianvar' 1725g. Sost.: T. A. Bykova i M. M. Gurevich. Red. i vstup. stat'ia P. N. Berkova. Moskva, Izd-vo Akademii Nauk SSSR, 1958. 402p. il. (Its Opisanie izdanii napechatannykh pri Petre I; svodnyi katalog) **AA664**

A detailed, descriptive bibliography of Russian books printed in the prereform alphabet, *kirillitsa*, between 1689 and 1725; appendixes include foreign books pertaining to Russia.

These two volumes of the Russian union catalog are continued, chronologically, by *Svodnyi katalog russkoi knigi . . . XVIII veka, 1725–1800* (AA666).

Sopikov, Vasilii Stephanovich. Opyt rossiiskoi bibliografii. [Izd. 2] Red., V. N. Rogozhin. St. Petersburg, 1904–6. 5v. **AA665**

Originally published 1813–21.

v.1 is a classed arrangement of books under the heading "Church Slavic." v.2–5 list other books in Russian to 1813.

Subject index in P.O. Morozov. *Alfavitnyi ukazatel' imen.* 1876. 47p.; various indexes in V. N. Rogozhin. *Ukazatel' . . .* 1908. 253p.

Although largely replaced by more recent bibliographies for the 18th century, the Sopikov number is often cited as part of the bibliographic description.

Svodnyi katalog russkoi knigi grazhdanskoi pechati XVIII veka, 1725–1800. Red. kollegia: I. P. Kondakov i dr. Moskva, Izdanie Gos. Biblioteki SSSR im. Lenina, 1962–64. (In progress) **AA666**

v.1–2, A–P.

A chronological section of the union catalog of Russian books from 1708 to the present, now in progress. Includes works of 5 pages or more published in Russia or abroad. Entries are annotated, refer to entry numbers in earlier standard bibliographies, and give locational symbols for copies in the major libraries of Leningrad and Moscow.

For first quarter of 18th century, *see* AA663 and AA664.

U.S. Library of Congress. Eighteenth century Russian publications in the Library of Congress; a catalog. Prep. by Tatiana Fessenko. Wash., Slavic and Central European Division, Reference Dept., Lib. of Congress, 1961. 157p.   **AA667**

More than 1300 fully cataloged works with identification "in almost 100 instances . . . [of] the foreign authors of Russian translations which up to now have been listed as anonymous in Russian bibliographies."—*Pref.* Appendixes for other tentative identifications and for itemized holdings of incomplete works, and title index.

19th century

Akademiia Nauk URSR, Kiev. Biblioteka. Knigi pervoi chetverti XIX veka; katalog knig, khraniashchikhsia v Gosudarstvennoi Publichnoi Biblioteke Ukrainskoi SSR. Sost.: S. O. Petrov. Kiev, 1961. 398p.   **AA668**

Continues the Library's catalog of 18th-century books (AA662) with 2800 works published in the first quarter of the 19th century, primarily St. Petersburg and Moscow imprints. Arranged by author or anonymous title, with indexes for translators and editors, cities and publishers, and broad subject. Annotations include references to 19th-century bibliographic listings.

U.S. Library of Congress. Cyrillic union catalog. N.Y., Readex Microprint Corp., 1963. 1244 cards in 7 boxes. (Micro-opaque)   **AA669**

Contents: pt.I, Authors and added entries; pt.II, Titles, with complete listing of library locations; pt.III, Subjects.

A union catalog of more than 700,000 cards, representing 178,226 titles in Russian, Belorussian, Bulgarian, Serbian, and Ukrainian. Substantially complete for monographic holdings of the Library of Congress as of March 1956. Reported holdings of 185 other American libraries are also included, with the most complete information on locations in pt.II. "The title catalog is a useful finding aid for the reader who knows the title of a given book but not its author. It is also useful to the reader unversed in the intricate rules of cataloging corporate authors."—*Introd.* Library of Congress card numbers, where available, appear in parentheses following title. English translations of titles, other than belles-lettres, are given for all post-1917 publications. Subject catalog contains form headings for fiction, drama, poetry. *See also:* Readex Microprint Corporation. *Cyrillic union catalog of the Library of Congress: description and guide to the Microprint edition.* N.Y., 1964. 12p.

U.S. Library of Congress. Reference Dept. Russia: a check list preliminary to a basic bibliography of materials in the Russian language. Wash., 1944–46. Pts.1–10.   **AA670**

Contents: pt.1, Belles lettres. 1944. 99p.; pt.2, Economic conditions and social history prior to 1918. 1944. 74p.; pt.3, Fine arts. 1944. 38p.; pt.4, Law and institutions prior to 1918. 1944. 62p.; pt.5, Folklore, linguistics and literary forms. 1944. 21p.; pt.6, Church and education prior to 1918. 1944. 33p.; pt.7, History, including auxiliary sciences, prior to 1918. 1945. 123p.; pt.8, Theatre and music prior to 1918. 1945. 23p.; pt.9, Soviet Union. 1945. 86p.; pt.10, Reference books. 1946. 227p.

Each section is arranged alphabetically. Titles are given in transliteration according to Library of Congress rules.

Pt.10 includes, in Addenda, a list of reference books in languages other than Russian, and a list of bibliographical and bibliothecal periodicals.

See also U.S. Library of Congress, *Cyrillic union catalog* (AA669).

Current

Ezhegodnik knigi SSSR; systematicheskii ukazatel'. 1941– . Moskva, Izd-vo Vsesoiuznoi Knizhnoi Palaty, 1946– . Annual.   **AA671**

Continues *Ezhegodnik knigi* issued by RSFSR, Gosudarstvennaia Tsentral'naia Knizhnaia Palata, annually for the years 1925–29 (Moskva, 1927–31); and *Ezhegodnik knigi,* 1935 (Moskva, 1936). Semiannual 1946–56. Issued in 2 v., 1959– , of which v.1 covers social sciences and humanities and v.2, science and technology.

The book annual of Soviet national bibliography cumulating, in classified arrangement, a selection from the weekly *Knizhnaia letopis'* (AA672). Indexes for names, titles, languages other than Russian, translations from foreign languages, and subjects.

Knizhnaia letopis' . . . v.1– . 1907– . Moskva, 1907– . Weekly.   **AA672**

Issued by Vsesoiuznaia Knizhnaia Palata.

1907– , available on microfilm from Library of Congress. Reprint: N.Y., Kraus, 1965.

For a detailed history of the title with a list of indexes and bibliography, *see* Sokurova, *Obshchie bibliografii russkikh knig grazhdanskoi pechati, 1708–1955,* p.179–222 (AA56).

As the principal organ of Soviet national bibliography, this work currently lists, in Russian, books and pamphlets published in the USSR in all languages. Each issue contains a language index to non-Russian publications.

Arranged in 31 classes. Each entry includes a classification number based on a variant of the Universal Decimal Classification. Quarterly indexes: name, geographical, and subject; *Ukazatel' seriinykh izdanii* is an annual index to publishers' series. An annual cumulation of a selection of titles from the weekly appears as *Ezhegodnik knigi SSSR* (AA671).

For monthly supplement, *see:*

—— dopolnitel'nyi vypusk, 1961– . Moskva, 1961– . Monthly.   **AA672a**

Issued by Vsesoiuznaia Knizhnaia Palata.

A monthly supplement to the main organ of Soviet national bibliography, *Knizhnaia letopis'* (AA672), which continues with reduced coverage. Includes certain types of publications formerly registered in the weekly, but categories transferred have varied. In general, lists small editions if printed in 101 copies or more and over 5 pages in length, and unpriced materials not intended for the book trade. List of dissertations, included in 1961, was omitted in 1962 and 1963, and resumed in 1964. Quarterly indexes (name, subject, and geographical) and annual index to publishers' series.

U.S. Library of Congress. Monthly index of Russian accessions. v.1, April 1948– . Wash., Govt. Prt. Off., 1948– . v.1– . Monthly.   **AA673**

Title varies: 1948–57, *Monthly list of Russian accessions.*

A union list of Russian-language monographs and periodicals issued in and outside the Soviet Union, received by the Library of Congress and a group of cooperating libraries. Whenever possible, publications printed in other languages in the Soviet Union are also included. Each issue is in three parts: pt.A, Monographs; pt.B, Periodicals, with their tables of contents translated into English; pt.C, Alphabetical subject index to A and B under English subject headings. Pts.A and B are classified in 17 main subject groups.

All titles are given first in English followed by the Russian in transliteration.

Beginning with v.5, an author index to monographs and a periodical location index are included annually as appendixes to the first two issues of the following volume (varies slightly). These are preceded by a cumulative index to v.1–3, April 1948–March 1951, issued in one volume (1953), and a cumulative index to v.4, April 1951–March 1952 (1957).

Pt.C includes in each issue a list of Russian periodicals available in English translation from cover to cover.

An "Introductory note" in each issue explains arrangement and coverage, which differ somewhat from volume to volume.

Scotland

See also Great Britain, p.45.

Aldis, Harry Gidney. List of books printed in Scotland before 1700, including those printed furth of the realm for Scottish booksellers, with brief notes on the printers and stationers. Edinburgh, Edinburgh Bibliographical Soc., 1904. 153p. **AA674**

A preliminary hand list of 3919 titles, arranged chronologically with an alphabetical index, and an index of printers, booksellers, and stationers.

Maclean, Donald. Typographia Scoto-Gadelica; or, Books printed in the Gaelic of Scotland from the year 1567 to the year 1914, with bibliographical and biographical notes. Edinburgh, Grant, 1915. 372p. **AA675**

Alphabetically arranged with full bibliographical information.

Slavic and Eastern Europe

U.S. Library of Congress. Processing Dept. East European accessions index. v.1–10. Wash., Govt. Prt. Off., 1951–61. Monthly. **AA676**

v.1, no.1–14, covers Sept./Oct. 1951—Dec. 1952.
Title varies; v.1–6, *East European accessions list.*
Ceased publication.
Similar in form to the *Monthly index of Russian accessions* (AA673) and the quarterly accessions list *Southern Asia* (DE28); covers monographs published since 1944, and periodicals since 1950, currently received by the Library of Congress and some other American libraries, published in 10 East European countries (except Russia) or elsewhere in their languages. The countries are arranged alphabetically, with separate listings under each by subject for monographs and for serials; English translations or explanations are given for all titles, and contents notes for periodicals. Beginning with v.2, there is a subject guide (pt.B) to all the material listed in each issue, and a cumulative list of periodicals covered in the volume.

Neuerscheinungen wissenschaftlicher Literatur aus den Ländern der Volksdemokratie: Albanien, Bulgarien, Polen, Rumänien, Tschechoslowakische Republik, Ungarn und der Volksrepublik China. Jahrg.1, Nr.1–Jahrg.4, Okt. 1951–Juni 1955. Berlin, Zentralstelle für Wissenschaftliche Literatur, 1951–55. 7v. Semimonthly. **AA677**

Title varies slightly. Ceased publication.
Covers social sciences, science, and technology, arranged by subject. Entries include author, title, German equivalent of title, place, publisher, date, pages, price, and language of original. Supplements, listing periodicals, are issued irregularly. No index.

South Africa

Nienaber, Petrus Johannes. Bibliografie van Afrikaanse boeke. Johannesburg, Voortrekkerpers Bpk., 1943–54. v.1–3. **AA678**

Contents: Deel 1, 6 April 1861—6 April 1943. 841p.; Deel 2, April 1943–Okt. 1948. 352p.; Deel 3, Nov. 1948–Okt. 1953. 359p.
A comprehensive bibliography. Each volume in three main sections: (1) Author list; (2) Title list; (3) Classified list.

S.A. Katalogus/Catalogue; 5th complete ed., 1900–1954, and list of publishers in South Africa. Johannesburg, Technical Books & Careers, 1956. v.1, A–K. **AA679**

Suid-Afrikaanse katalogus.
Earlier editions had title *South African catalogue of books.* 4th ed. 1900–1950.
An author-title listing of books published in South Africa since 1900. The cumulated editions do not always include all previously listed titles, and therefore earlier editions should be preserved.

Current

Africana nova. Sept. 1958– . Capetown, South African Public Lib., 1958– . Quarterly. **AA680**

Subtitle: A quarterly bibliography of books currently published in and about the Republic of South Africa. Based on the accessions to the Africana Department, South African Public Library, including material received by Legal Deposit.

In English and Afrikaans.
Arranged by Dewey Decimal Classification, with author index in each issue, and annual index. Preceded by lists of current publications published in the *Quarterly bulletin* of the South African Public Library, Sept. 1946–June 1958.

SANB: Suid-Afrikaanse nasionale bibliografie. South African national bibliography, 1959– . Pretoria, State Lib., 1960– . Quarterly, with annual cumulation. **AA681**

Replaces the monthly copyright list issued since 1938 in mimeographed form, unclassified and noncumulating. The new series, based on legal deposit, is arranged by Dewey Decimal Classification with a name and title index.

Spain
General

Aguiló y Fustér, Mariano. Catálogo de obras en lengua catalana impresas desde 1474 hasta 1860. Madrid, Rivadeneyra, 1923. 1077p. il. **AA682**

A classified catalog of books in the Catalan language, with a general index and an index of printers.

Boston. Public Library. Ticknor Collection. Catalogue of the Spanish library and of the Portuguese books bequeathed by George Ticknor. Boston, 1879. 476p. **AA683**

Includes also the collection of Spanish and Portuguese literature in the general library.
A dictionary catalog of an important 19th-century collection.

California. University. Library. Spain and Spanish America in the libraries of the University of California; a catalogue of books. Berkeley, 1928–30. 2v. **AA684**

v.1, General and departmental libraries; v.2, The Bancroft Library.
A catalog of very rich collections. Each volume is arranged alphabetically with a subject index.

Heredia y Livermore, Ricardo, *Conde de Benahavis.* Catalogue de la bibliothèque de M. Ricardo Heredia. Paris, E. Paul, 1891–94. 4v. il. **AA685**

A sales catalog of this famous collection of Spanish and other rare works. For index *see* AA687.

Hidalgo, Dionisio. Diccionario general de bibliografía española. Madrid, Impr. de las Escuelas Pias, 1862–81. 7v. **AA686**

A general list of works published in Spain, arranged alphabetically by title, with author and classed indexes.

Molina Navarro, Gabriel. Índice para facilitar el manejo y consulta de los catálogos de Salvá y Heredia. Madrid, Molina, 1913. 162p. **AA687**

A combined index to the catalogs of Salvá (AA690) and Heredia (AA685).

Palau y Dulcet, Antonio. Manual del librero hispanoamericano; bibliografía general española e hispano-americana desde la invención de la imprenta hasta nuestros tiempos con el valor comercial de los impresos descritos. 2. ed. corr. y aum. por el autor. Barcelona, Librería Palau, 1948–61. v.1–13. (In progress) **AA688**

v.1–13, A–Por.
1st ed. 1923–27. 7v.
A very useful, comprehensive, alphabetical record, listing material under author, or under title for anonymous works. Covers material published in Spain and Spanish America from the beginning of printing to mid-20th century.

Ribelles Comín, José. Bibliografía de la lengua valenciana. . . . Madrid, "Rev. de Arch., Bibl. y Museos," 1915–31. 3v. facsim.   **AA689**

Subtitle: O sea catálogo razonada por orden alfabético de autores de los libros, folletos, obras dramáticas, periódicos, coloquios, coplas, chistes, discursos, romances, alocuciones, cantares, gozos, etc., que escritos en lengua valenciana y bilingüe, han visto la luz pública desde el establecimiento de la imprenta en España hasta nuestros días.

v.1, siglo XV (i.e., descriptions and notes of printed editions to 1918 of works in the Valencian dialect composed before the end of the 15th century); v.2, siglo XVI; v.3, siglo XVII.

No more published.

Salvá y Pérez, Vicente. Catálogo de la biblioteca de Salvá, escrito por Pedro Salvá y Mallen, y enriquecido con la descripción de otras muchas obras, de sus ediciones, etc. Valencia, Impr. de Ferrer de Orga, 1872. 2v. il. (Repr.: Barcelona, Porter-Libros, 1963)   **AA690**

A classified catalog with indexes giving detailed descriptions of works published from the 16th to the mid-19th centuries. For index see AA687.

Vaganay, Hugues. Bibliographie hispanique extra-péninsulaire; 16ᵉ et 17ᵉ siècles. (In Revue hispanique 42:1–304. 1918)   **AA691**

A listing of 1198 works of authors from the Hispanic peninsula, which were printed outside of Spain from 1502 to 1700. Arranged chronologically.

Early

Antonio, Nicolás. Bibliotheca hispana vetus; sive, Hispani scriptores qui ab Octaviani Augusti aevo ad annum Christi MD. floruerunt. Matriti, J. Ibarra, 1788. 2v.   **AA692**

——— Bibliotheca hispana nova; sive, Hispanorum scriptorum qui ab anno MD. ad MDCLXXXIV, floruere notitia. Matriti, J. de Ibarra, 1783–88. 2v.   **AA693**

The date 1783 on the title page of v.1 of AA693 is a misprint for 1788.

2d ed., edited by T. A. Sánchez, J. A. Pellicer, and R. Casalbón; 1st ed., pub. 1672 as *Bibliotheca hispana.*

An excellent and indispensable work, dealing with the writings of persons born in the Spanish peninsula regardless of the language in which they wrote. AA692, covering to 1500, is in narrative form; AA693, 1500–1684, is a bibliographical dictionary.

British Museum. Dept. of Printed Books. Short-title catalogue of books printed in Spain and of Spanish books printed elsewhere in Europe before 1601 now in the British Museum, by Henry Thomas. London, 1921. 101p.   **AA694**

Haebler, Konrad. Bibliografía ibérica del siglo XV. Enumeración de todos los libros impresos en España y Portugal hasta el año de 1500 con notas críticas. La Haye, Nijhoff; Leipzig, Hiersemann, 1903–17. 2v.   **AA695**

Each volume alphabetically arranged with detailed bibliographical information and annotations. Indexes of printers, etc.

Hispanic Society of America. Library. List of books printed before 1601 in the Library of the Hispanic Society of America, by Clara Louise Penney. Offset reissue, with additions. N.Y., Soc., 1955. 305p. (Hispanic notes and monographs. Catalogue ser.)   **AA696**

First printed 1929. Additions, p.275–305.

——— List of books printed 1601–1700, in the Library, by C. L. Penney. N.Y., Trustees, 1938. 972p. (Hispanic notes and monographs. Catalogue ser.)   **AA697**

With two appendixes: (1) 15th–16th century books not included in *List of books printed before 1601;* (2) Check list of printing sites and printers of Hispanic books 1468?–1700.

Vindel, Francisco. Manual gráfico-descriptivo del bibliófilo hispano-americano (1475–1850), con un prólogo de Pedro Sáinz Rodríguez. Madrid, [Impr. Góngora], 1930–34. 12v. in 13. il. (incl. facsim.)   **AA698**

v.1–10, A–Z; v.11, Tasación e índices; v.12, Suplemento, siglo XV.

An author list of 3442 books, mainly early. Information for each includes: author's name, title, place, publisher or printer, date, size, generally paging. A special feature is that for each item a reproduction of some page of the work, usually title page or colophon, is given.

20th century

Catálogo general de la librería española e hispanoamericana, 1901–30. Autores. Madrid, Inst. Nacional del Libro Español, 1932–51. 5v.   **AA699**

v.1–5, A–Z.

Publisher varies.

A comprehensive list giving full name of author, title, edition, place, publisher, date, paging, size, price.

Catálogo general de la librería española, 1931–1950. Madrid, Inst. Nacional del Libro Español, 1957–63. v.1–3 (In progress)   **AA700**

v.1–3, A–Q.

This series follows the same plan as the earlier one but does not include Spanish-American imprints.

Bibliografía española; revista general de la imprenta, de la librería y de las industrias que concurren á la fabricación del libro. Madrid, Asociación de la Librería, 1901–22. 22v. Monthly.   **AA701**

Continued by:

Bibliografía general española e hispano-americana, 1923–marzo/abril 1942. Madrid-Barcelona, 1923–42. 16v.   **AA702**

Monthly, 1923–36; bimonthly, 1941–42. Publication suspended July 1936–Jan. 1941. 1923–36 in three parts: (1) *Bibliografía,* a list of new publications, giving for each item author's name, title, place, date, publisher, paging, size, and price; (2) *Crónica;* (3) *Anuncios.* v.1–9 have a general author index to the books listed in the monthly *Bibliografía;* v.10 has, instead, a cumulated author list of the entries in v.9–10.

Continued by:

Bibliografía hispánica, año 1–16. mayo/junio 1942–dic. 1957. Madrid, Inst. Nacional de Libro Español, 1942–57. Monthly.   **AA703**

Ceased publication.

Each monthly issue in two sections: (1) articles on the book trade, bibliographies, book reviews, etc.; (2) *Repertorio bibliográfico,* which is a classed list of books published, with an annual index of authors and titles. This section is usually paged separately and continuously, with a special title page, so that it may be bound separately. Variations are: v.1, 1942, *Repertorio* paged separately in each issue but not continuously; v.2–3, 1943, *Repertorio* not separately paged; v.8, 1948, *Bibliografía* published three times per year, *Repertorio* published separately monthly; v.9, 1949–57, monthly issues containing both sections, paged separately.

Continued by *El libro español* (AA707).

Current

Anuario español e hispanoamericano del libro y de las artes gráficas con el Catálogo mundial del libro impreso en lengua española dirigido por Javier Lasso de la Vega Jimenez-Placer. Madrid, Ed. del Anuario Maritimo Español, 1945– . v.1– . Biennial. (Early volumes irregular)   **AA704**

v.1–2 had title *Catálogo de los libros publicados en España en 1944 [en 1945].* (1945–46).

Some volumes have cumulated indexes.

Arranged by decimal classification with author indexes. v.5 and 9 include *Relación de las tesis doctorales manuscritas existentes en la biblioteca de la Universidad de Madrid;* v.10 includes *Las tesis doctorales leídas en la Universidad de Chile.*

Bibliografía española. v.1– . 1958– . Madrid, Ministerio de Educación Nacional. Dirección General de Archivos y Bibliotecas, Servicio Nacional de Información Bibliográfica, 1959– . Annual.   **AA705**

A new national bibliography based on copyright receipts in the national library. Arranged by Universal Decimal Classification, with index of authors, titles, and subjects, and with supplementary lists of publishers, series, and periodicals.

Bibliotheca hispana; revista de información y orientación bibliográficas. v.1– . Madrid, Consejo Superior de Investigaciones Científicas, Inst. Nicolás Antonio, 1943– . il. Quarterly.   **AA706**

Since v.13, issued in two sections, each of which has four issues per year and its own annual index. The sections contain the following subject materials: Sec. 1, Letras: Obras generales, bibliografía, religión, filosofía, pedagogía, estadística y demografía, sociología y política, economía, derecho, filología, literatura, geografía, historia, arte, juegos y deportes. Sec. 2, Ciencias: Ciencia en general, matemáticas, astronomía, física, química, ciencias naturales, medicina, ingeniería y construcción, ciencia y arte militares, agricultura y ganadería, industria, comercio, economía doméstica.

Entries are annotated, and periodical articles are also included.

El libro español; revista mensual . . . t.1, núm.1– . Enero, 1958– . Madrid, Inst. Nacional del Libro Español, 1958– . Monthly; biweekly.   **AA707**

The merger of the Institute's two former titles: *Bibliografía hispánica* and the more popular *Novedades editoriales españolas* with its supplement *Libros del mes.* The new title is much like the former *Bibliografía* . . . : the first half consisting of articles of interest to the book trade, bibliographic studies, etc.; the latter being the monthly (biweekly since 1964) list of new books, the *Repertorio bibliográfico clasificado por materias.*

Annual author, title, and subject indexes are issued for the *Repertorio.*

Sweden

Early

Sveriges bibliografi intill år 1600, av Isak Collijn. Uppsala, Svenska Litteratursällskapet, 1927–38. 3v. il. (Svenska litteratursällskapet. Skrifter)   **AA708**

Bd.1, 1478–1530 (pub. 1934–38); bd.2, 1530–82 (pub. 1927–31); bd.3, 1583–99 (pub. 1932–33); Alfabetiskt register till bd.1, bd.2–3; Typografiska tabeller, 1483–1525, 1526–99.

v.1 is a revision of *Sveriges bibliografi,* 1481–1600, by G. E. Klemming and Aksel Anderson. Uppsala, 1927. 216p.

Arranged chronologically, with alphabetical indexes. Gives full descriptions, with bibliographical references and location of copies. Continued by:

—— 1600–talet. Bidrag till en bibliografisk förteckning, av Isak Collijn. Uppsala, Almqvist, 1942–46. 2v. (Svenska litteratursällskapet. Skrifter)   **AA709**

Arranged alphabetically with no chronological approach. Gives brief biographical facts of authors, full description, and location of copies. Covers 17th century.

19th and 20th centuries

Linnström, Hjalmar. Svenskt boklexikon, 1830–65. Stockholm, Linnström, 1883–84. 2v.   **AA710**

Alphabetical arrangement.

Svensk bok-katalog, 1866/75–1951/55. Stockholm, Tidningsaktiebolaget Svensk Bokhandel, 1878–1962. (In progress)   **AA711**

Publisher varies.

Beginning with the volumes for 1941/50, is issued by the Bibliographical Institute of the Royal Library in Stockholm, and is called *The Swedish national bibliography.*

1866/75, 1876/85, 1886/95, published as 10-year volumes. Thereafter, volumes have been published as 5-year cumulations except for 1941/50.

Includes books, pamphlets, periodicals, government publications, and theses. Each cumulation is in two parts: (1) alphabetical author and title list; (2) classed list.

Current

Svensk bokförteckning. . . . The Swedish national bibliography, ed. by the Bibliographical Institute of the Royal Library, Stockholm. Jan. 1953– . Stockholm, 1953– .   **AA712**

Beginning with Jan. 1953, the bibliography is compiled by the Bibliographical Institute and is printed in monthly, quarterly, semiannual, and annual cumulations from weekly entries in *Svensk bokhandel* (AA713).

Supersedes an earlier monthly publication with the same title, issued 1913–52, and *Aarskatalog för svenska bokhandeln,* 1861–1952.

Cumulates into the *Svensk bok-katalog* (AA711).

Svensk bokhandel. Svenska bokförläggareföreningens och Svenska bokhandlareföreningens officiella organ. Stockholm, 1952– . v.1– .   **AA713**

Formerly entitled *Svensk bokhandels-tidning,* 1863–1951. A weekly alphabetical list of new publications.

Switzerland

Bern. Schweizerische Landesbibliothek. Katalog . . . Alphabetisches Verzeichnis der bis 1900 erschienenen Druckschriften. Bern, Francke, 1910.   **AA714**

Added title page in French.

Contents: Abt. A: Geschichte, Geographie und Landeskunde. 2v. No more published.

—— Katalog . . . Systematisches Verzeichnis der schweizerischen oder die Schweiz betreffenden Veröffentlichungen, 1901–20, 1921–30, 1931–40, 1941–47. Bern, Huber, [1927]–54. (In progress)   **AA715**

Added title page: *Catalogue de la Bibliothèque Nationale Suisse. Répertoire méthodique des publications suisses ou relatives à la Suisse.* Contents and preface in German and French.

The catalog for each period is in two volumes: v.1, Classed list, arranged by the Decimal Classification; v.2, Biographical and topographical catalog, each arranged alphabetically.

A subject list which serves both as a short-title catalog of the works listed and as an index to the fuller descriptions in the *Bibliographisches Bulletin* (*Bulletin bibliographique*) (AA723) for the same years. Gives author, brief title, date of publication, and also the year of the *Bulletin,* if that differs from publication date, in which full description is given.

Ceased publication. Continued by:

—— Schweizer Bücherverzeichnis. Répertoire du livre suisse. Elenco del libro svizzero. Katalog der schweizerischen Landesbibliothek. 1948/50– . Zürich, Schweizerischer Buchhändler- und Verlegerverein, 1951– . Quinquennial (since 1951).   **AA716**

This cumulates the titles listed in *Das schweizer Buch* (*Le livre suisse*), ser. A and B (AA723), and supersedes the *Systematisches Verzeichnis.* Beginning with 1951/55, forms pt.1 of the *Schweizerische Nationalbibliographie.*

In two parts: (1) Author catalog (including anonymous titles) with index of catchwords, editors, translators, etc.; (2)

Subject catalog in German with an index from the French forms.

Lonchamp, Frédéric Charles. Bibliographie générale des ouvrages publiés ou illustrés en Suisse et à l'étranger de 1475 à 1914 par des écrivains et des artistes suisses. . . . Paris et Lausanne, Librairie des Bibliophiles, 1922. 500p. il. **AA717**

A list of 3376 items giving for each: author, title, date, printer or publisher, size, paging, and note of illustrations, with name of artist. Indexes of (1) titles, and (2) artists.

Das schweizerische Buch: Le livre en Suisse. 1896–1914. Bern, Kollektivausstellung Schweizer, 1914. 287p. **AA718**

Classed arrangement with author index.
Continued by:

Schweizerischer Buchhändlerverein. Das schweizerischer Buch, 1914–1930. Zürich, Orell Füssli, 1931. 282p. **AA719**

—— Livres suisses; Das Buch der Schweiz, 1931–1938. Zürich, Schweizerische Landesausstellung, 1939. 232p. **AA720**

Société des Libraires et Éditeurs de la Suisse Romande, Geneva. Catalogue des éditions de la Suisse romande, rédigé par Alex. Jullien. . . . Genève, Jullien, 1902–12; Société, 1929. 3v. and suppl. **AA721**

A record of books published in French Switzerland.
Basic volume, listing books in print in 1900. 1902. 280p.; Supplements, 1901–1909. 1912. 181p.; 1910–1927. 1929. 404p.; Supplément, corrections . . . comprenant en particulier les éditions Edwin Frankfurter à Lausanne. 1929. 16p.

—— Catalogue des ouvrages de langue française publiés en Suisse, 1928–1945, red. par Alexandre Jullien. Neuchâtel, Impr. Delachaux et Niestle, 1948. 377p. **AA722**

Current

Das schweizer Buch; Bibliographisches Bulletin der schweizerischen Landesbibliothek. Le livre suisse . . . Il libro svizzero. 1.– ; 11 März 1901– . Bern-Bümpliz, Benteli, 1901– . v.1– . **AA723**

Frequency varies. Title varies; 1901–42, *Bibliographisches Bulletin der Schweiz.*
Beginning with v.43, 1943, issued in two series: Série A, semimonthly, listing publications in the book trade; Série B, bimonthly, listing publications outside the book trade, e.g., theses, institutional publications, etc.
Each issue is in classified arrangement with author and subject index. The indexes for Séries A and B cumulate together semiannually and annually.
These, in turn, are cumulated into the 5-year *Schweizer Bücherverzeichnis* (AA716).

—— Série A . . . Verfasser- und Stichwortregister. *See* AA490.

Turkey

Türkiye bibliyoğrafyasï, 1928/1938, 1939/1948. Istanbul, Devlet Basïmevi, 1939; 1957– . (Türkiye cümhuriyeti maarif vekilliği [1939/48–maarif vekâleti]. Basma yazi ve resimleri derleme müdürlügü) (In progress) **AA724**

Serve as cumulative decennial volumes, superseding the annuals (AA725).
1928/1938 in 2v.; v.1, Official publications; v.2, Non-official publications, arranged by Universal Decimal Classification.
1939/1948, in 3v.: v.1, Arranged by Universal Decimal Classification, covering general, philosophy, religion, social

sciences, and philology. 1957; v.2, Abstract science, applied science, literature, history, geography, and biography. 1962; v.3, Alphabetical index. 1964.

Current

Türkiye bibliyoğrafyasï . . . 1934– . Istanbul, Devlet Basïmevi, 1935– . **AA725**

Annual, 1934; semiannual, 1935–38; quarterly, 1939–43; monthly, 1944–48; quarterly, 1949– .
A classified catalog with author and title indexes in each issue 1934–43; annual indexes 1944– .
Records books, pamphlets, and government publications in Turkish and other languages. Includes a separate section of new periodicals and newspapers.

Yeni yayïnlar; aylïk bibliyografya dergisi. Cilt:1– . Tem. 1956– . Ankara, 1956– . Monthly. **AA726**

Includes a classified list of recent publications.

Union of Soviet Socialist Republics

See Russia, p.59.

Uruguay

See also Latin America, p.53.

Estrada, Dardo. Historia y bibliografía de la imprenta en Montevideo, 1810–1865. Montevideo, Librería Cervantes, 1912. 318p. (Readex microprint) **AA727**

Chronological. Supplemented by:

Arredondo, Horacio. Bibliografía uruguaya. (In Revista del Inst. Histórico y Geográfico del Uruguay, Montevideo 6:433–610. 1929) (Readex microprint) **AA728**

Arranged chronologically, 1559–1865. Line-by-line transcription. Locates copies.

Current

Anuario bibliográfico uruguayo, 1946–49. Montevideo, Biblioteca Nacional, 1947–51. v.1–3. Annual. **AA729**

Ceased publication.
The 1946 issue includes a *Bibliografía de bibliografías uruguayas.*
Lists books and pamphlets.

Bibliografía uruguaya. Montevideo, Biblioteca del Poder Legislativo, 1962– . v.1, Jan./April, 1962– . 3 times a year. **AA730**

The last issue of the year, Sept./Dec., cumulates listings for the year. In 1962, published in 2v.: v.1, *Noticias bibliográficas,* arranged alphabetically and listing books, pamphlets, and documents with indexes of titles, publishers, and names, and an index by Dewey Decimal Classification; v.2, *Bio-bibliografías,* with an index of pseudonyms and a list of literary prizes.

Venezuela

Medina, José Toribio. La imprenta en Caracas (1808–1821); notas bibliográficas. Santiago de Chile, Impr. Elzeviriana, 1904. 29p. (Readex microprint) **AA731**

Current

Anuario bibliográfico venezolano, 1942– . Caracas, Tipografía Americana, 1944– . v.1– . Irregular. **AA732**

At head of title: República de Venezuela. Biblioteca Nacional, Caracas.

Preceded by volume called *Año 1, 1916.*

Pub. irregularly: 1942–45, annual; 1947/48 (pub. 1950); 1949/54 (pub. 1960). 2v.

Lists books, pamphlets, government publications, etc., and periodical articles.

1949/54 in 2v.: v.1, titles published in Venezuela; v.2, material about Venezuela published abroad.

A well-arranged, classed list with author, subject, and title index, and an index of printers.

Wales

See also Great Britain, p.45.

Bibliotheca celtica, a register of publications relating to Wales and the Celtic peoples and languages for the years 1909–1927/28. Aberystwyth, Nat. Lib. of Wales, 1910–34. 9v. **AA733**

Includes works written in one of the Celtic languages or relating to any of the Celtic people, and works written in English on non-Celtic subjects by Welshmen.

—— n.s. (1939–62) v.1–4. (In progress)

Contents: v.1, 1929/33 (pub. 1939); v.2, 1934/38 (pub. 1952); v.3, 1939/43 (pub. 1961); v.4, 1944/48 (pub. 1962).

This series follows the same general plan as the first series, but omits works written by Welshmen in English on non-Celtic subjects. Two more volumes are planned to cover 1949–52.

—— 3d ser. v.1, 1953– . (1954–) Annual.

This annual series continues the earlier set and increases its coverage by adding periodical articles on Celtic subjects.

Cardiff, Wales. Free Libraries. Catalogue of printed literature in the Welsh Department, by John Ballinger and J. I. Jones. Cardiff, Free Lib. Committee; London, Sotheran, 1898. 559p. **AA734**

An author and subject catalog, in one alphabet, of Welsh materials.

Rowlands, William. Cambrian bibliography: containing an account of the books printed in the Welsh language, or relating to Wales, from the year 1546 to the end of the eighteenth century; with biographical notices. Ed. and enl. by D. Silvan Evans. Llanidloes, J. Pryse, 1869. 762p. **AA735**

Annotations, etc. in Welsh. English preface.

Yugoslavia

Kukuljević-Sakcinski, Ivan. Bibliografia hrvatska. I. Tiskane Knjige. Zagreb, Brzotiskom, D. Albrechta, 1860. 233p. **AA736**

Added title page: Bibliografia jugoslavenska. Kn. I.

—— —— Dodatak k prvomu dielu. Tiskane knije. Zagreb, 1863. 31p.

No more published.

Lists Croatian books from early times to 1860.

Novaković, Stojan. Srpska biblijografija za noviju književnost. Beogradu, Drzhavnoj Shtampariji, 1869. 644p. **AA737**

Covers period 1741–1867.

Arranged chronologically with author and subject indexes.

Current

Bibliografija jugoslavije: knjige, brošure i muzikalije, Jan. 1950– . Beograd, Bibliografski Inst. FNRJ, 1950– . Monthly, 1950–52; semimonthly, 1953– . **AA738**

Caption title also in Serbian, English, and French.

Lists books, pamphlets, sheet music, and government pub-

lications in Serbian, Croatian, and other languages. Classified by Universal Decimal Classification with author/title and subject indexes.

Slovenska bibliografija, 1945/1947– . Časopisje in knjige, članki in leposlovni prispevki v časopisju in zbornikih izdala in založila narodna in univerzitetna knjiznica v Ljubljani. Ljubljana, Državna Založba Slovenije, 1948– . Annual. **AA739**

Classified by Universal Decimal System with author indexes.

Simonič, Franc. Slovenska bibliografija. I. del.: Knjige. 1550–1900. Ljubljana, Slovenska Matica, 1903–5. 627p. **AA740**

Alphabetical arrangement.

A B

Librarianship and Library Resources

❦ Reference materials pertaining to libraries include works used primarily by librarians as well as those needed by readers. The former concern library techniques and methodology; the latter are mainly directories of libraries: libraries of specific countries, special libraries, or collections in particular fields. Many of these directories, both of the United States and of other countries, will help scholars to locate libraries which house special collections or which are strong in specified subjects. In some cases specialties are described in some detail; in others a mere listing of outstanding collections is given.

Readers may occasionally wish to consult the library's manuals and codes, such as the list of subject headings or the classification scheme, and the librarian should, if possible, make these available to persons interested.

GENERAL WORKS

Bibliography

Cannons, Harry George Turner. Bibliography of library economy. A classified index to the professional periodical literature in the English language relating to library economy, printing, methods of publishing, copyright, bibliography, etc. from 1876 to 1920. Chicago, Amer. Lib. Assoc., 1927. 680p. **AB1**

1st ed. 1910.

Includes an alphabetical subject index to the classified lists, but no author index.

Continued by *Library literature* (AB6).

Gropp, Arthur E. Bibliografía sobre las bibliotecas nacionales de los países latinoamericanos y sus publicaciones. Wash., Pan Amer. Union, 1960. 58p. (Pan American Union. Columbus Memorial Library. Bibliographic ser., no.50) **AB2**

A total of nearly 1200 items (books and articles) on national libraries and library systems in Latin America. Arrangement is by country, with an author index.

Linares, Emma. Bibliografía bibliotecológica. Wash., Pan Amer. Union, 1960. 233p. (Pan American Union. Columbus Memorial Library. Bibliographic ser., no.49)
AB3

A classified list of 3000 items on library organization and operation. Includes books, parts of books, articles, and documents, mostly in Spanish or English. Author index.

U.S. Library of Congress. African Section. African libraries, book production, and archives; a list of references, comp. by Helen F. Conover. Wash., Reference Dept., Lib. of Congress, 1962. 64p. **AB4**

Annotated list of periodicals, articles, reports, and some books, arranged by subject with author index.

Current

Internationale Bibliographie des Buch- u. Bibliothekswesens, 1904–12, 1922–39. Leipzig, Harrassowitz, 1905–40. 13v. and n.F. 1–14. **AB5**

Each issue contains a section giving material about libraries.

For full description *see* AA20.

Library literature, 1921/32– . N.Y., Wilson, 1934– . Quarterly, with annual and triennial cumulations.
AB6

Subtitle and publisher vary.

An index to current books, pamphlets, periodical literature, and theses relating to librarianship, arranged alphabetically by author and subject. Some 160 journals are covered. Includes foreign material. Abstracts and digests, appearing in earlier issues, have been discontinued since 1958.

Library science abstracts. v.1, no.1, 1950– . London, Lib. Assoc., 1950– . Quarterly. **AB7**

Classified abstracts taken from some 200 periodicals, books, pamphlets, reports, etc. Annual indexes by author and by name and subject. International in scope.

Year's work in librarianship, 1928–50. London, Lib. Assoc., 1929–54. v.1–17. **AB8**

v.1–11 (1929–38); v.12 (1939–45); v.13–17 (1946–50). Ceased publication.

Running comment, each chapter by a special writer, on the principal publications of the year in various fields of librarianship and bibliography. Gives full bibliographical references in footnotes, and includes both books and periodical articles.

Five years' work in librarianship, 1951/55– . London, Lib. Assoc., Chaucer House, 1958– . Quinquennial.
AB9

Supersedes *Year's work in librarianship* (AB8) and follows the same plan.

"Primarily a report and assessment of developments in Britain . . . of international bodies and significant developments in other countries particularly in the Commonwealth." —*Introd.*

Dissertations

Cohen, Nathan M. [and others]. Library science dissertations, 1925–60. Wash., Govt. Prt. Off., 1963. 120p. (U.S. Office of Education. Bull. 1963. no.38) **AB10**

Subtitle: An annotated bibliography of doctoral studies.

". . . attempts to provide summaries of all dissertations relating to library science completed between 1925–60."— *Foreword.* Includes all dissertations accepted by library schools in the United States, as well as dissertations written in other university departments which treated a facet of librarianship.

Arranged by broad subject in chronological order. Includes an author and subject index.

Periodicals

International Federation for Documentation. Library and documentation journals. 2d rev. ed. The Hague, 1961. 30p. (Its Publ. 336) **AB11**

1st edition had title *Library and documentation periodicals.* 1956. (FID publ. 295).

Lists about 400 journals giving title, former title (if any), editor, publisher, dates, etc., with indication of abstracting journal. Arranged according to: (1) journals issued by international organizations; (2) journals issued by national organizations; and (3) journals dealing occasionally with library science and documentation.

Includes an index of countries and of titles.

Handbooks of usage

Cook, Margaret Gerry. The new library key. 2d ed. N.Y., Wilson, 1963. 184p. **AB12**

1st ed. 1956. Based on Zaidee Brown's *The library key.* 7th ed. rev. N. Y., Wilson, 1949.

A revised and rewritten edition primarily for college students and adults. Discusses the preparation of a term paper; the make-up and use of a book; the card catalog; periodicals and periodical indexes; and general and special reference books.

Douglas, Mary Peacock. The teacher-librarian's handbook. 2d ed. Chicago, Amer. Lib. Assoc., 1949. 166p.
AB13

Covers such topics as organization of the book collection, classification and cataloging, book selection and ordering, nonbook materials, instruction in the use of books and libraries, care of library, publicity, etc.

Encyclopedias and dictionaries

Handbuch der Bibliothekswissenschaft. Begründet von Fritz Milkau. 2. verm. und verb. Aufl. hrsg. von Georg Leyh. Wiesbaden, Harrassowitz, 1950–60. v.1–3. il. (In progress) **AB14**

1st ed. 1931–42 (3v. and index).

To be completed in 4v., issued in *Lieferungen* of about six signatures each.

Contents: v.1, Schrift und Buch. 1952; v.2, Bibliotheksverwaltung. 1958–60; v.3, Geschichte der Bibliotheken. 1955–57. 2 Hälfte.

A scholarly work on the history of books, libraries, and librarianship with emphasis on German and Western European aspects of the subject. Long, signed articles with many bibliographical footnotes.

Landau, Thomas. Encyclopaedia of librarianship. 2d rev. ed. London, Bowes; N.Y., Hafner, 1961. 397p. **AB15**

An alphabetical work "covering all aspects of librarianship," with entries varying in length from a few words to signed articles of several pages. Usage covered is almost entirely British. Some articles include bibliographies.

The state of the library art, ed. by Ralph R. Shaw. New Brunswick, N.J., Graduate School of Lib. Service, Rutgers Univ., 1960–61. 5 v. **AB16**

Contents: v.1, pts.1–2, in 1v.: Cataloging and classification, by Maurice F. Tauber. Subject headings, by Carlyle J. Frarey; pts.3–5, in 1v.: Classification systems, by Maurice F. Tauber and Edith Wise. Gifts, by Donald E. Thompson. Exchanges, by Donald E. Thompson; v.2, pts.1–2, in 1v.: Training laymen in use of the library, by George S. Bonn. Bibliographies, abstracts, and indexes, by Margaret S. Bryant; pt.3, Charging systems, by Leila H. Kirkwood; v.3, pts.1–3, in 1v.: Library buildings, by Ralph E. Ellsworth. Shelving, by Louis Kaplan. Storage warehouses, by Jerrold Orne; v.4, pts.1–5, in 1v.: Notched cards, by Felix Reichmann. Feature cards (Peek-a-boo cards), by Lawrence S. Thompson. Punched cards, by Ralph Blasingame, Jr. Electronic searching, by Gerald Jahoda. Coding in yes-no form, by Doralyn J. Hickey; v.5, pt.1, Production and use of micro-forms, by Reginald R. Hawkins; pt.2, Reading devices for micro-images, by Jean Stewart and others; pt.3, Full-size photocopying, by William R. Hawken.

A series of handbooks with articles by specialists, reviewing and summarizing the literature. Each part includes an extensive bibliography.

Terms

American Library Association. Committee on Library Terminology. A.L.A. glossary of library terms, with a selection of terms in related fields, prep. by Elizabeth H. Thompson. Chicago, Assoc., 1943. 159p.   **AB17**

Includes terms used in American libraries, bibliography, printing, and publishing.

Foreign terms usually have been omitted.

Gross, Otti. Library terms . . . Englisch-deutsch und deutsch-englisch. Hamburg, Eberhard Stichnote, 1952. 163p.   **AB18**

Preface and title page in English and German.

Lists some 3500 terms in each language. Includes also English and German abbreviations and a list of symbols used in library practice.

Harrod, Leonard Montague. The librarian's glossary. [2d rev. ed.] London, Grafton, 1959. 332p.   **AB19**

Subtitle: Terms used in librarianship and the book crafts.

Contains about 1200 entries, usually defined according to British usage. Includes some foreign terms.

Mamiya, Fujio. A complete dictionary of library terms; technical terms used in libraries, bibliographies and by printing and binding trades in English, German, French, Chinese and Japanese languages . . . rev. and enl. ed. Tokyo, Japan Lib. Bureau, 1952. 614p. il.   **AB20**

Added title page in Japanese.

Terms in all five languages are arranged in one alphabet, with equivalents in English, Japanese, and sometimes one or more of the other languages. Words in Chinese and Japanese are transliterated for use as main entries.

Massa Gil, Beatriz, Trautman, Ray and **Goy, Peter.** Diccionario técnico de biblioteconomía. Technical dictionary of librarianship. México, F. Trillas, S.A. 1964. 387p. il.   **AB21**

Definitions of more than 3000 terms used in librarianship and related fields of book production, preservation, and use. In two parts: pt.1, Spanish-English; pt.2, English-Spanish. In each part terms are arranged alphabetically, followed by the equivalent term in the other language, then the definition in the first language. Definitions are concise, but several meanings are often given for a term.

Pipics, Zoltán. A könyvtáros gyakorlati szótára. Dictionarium bibliothecarii practicum. 20 nyelvű szakszótár a könyvtári feldolgozó munkához magyar és nemzetközi használatra. (Ad usum internationalem in XX linguis) [Budapest, Akademia Nyomda, 1963(?)] 317p.   **AB22**

Library terms in 20 languages.

Special Libraries Association, New York. Contributions toward a special library glossary, prepared for the A.L.A. Committee on Library Terminology by Linda H. Morley [and others]. 2d ed. N.Y., Assoc., 1950. 22p.   **AB23**

1st ed. 1948.

Definitions of some 100 terms that have special, additional, or changed meanings in the special library field. Collected in connection with the *A.L.A. glossary* (AB17) but often with fuller explanation than in the complete *Glossary*.

Thompson, Anthony. Vocabularium bibliothecarii. 2d ed. English, French, German, Spanish, Russian. Paris, UNESCO, 1962. 627p.   **AB24**

1st ed. 1953; supplement 1958.

About 2800 terms are included; definitions are given only where a word has two meanings, or where there is no equivalent in one of the languages.

As in the 1st edition, terms are arranged in columns by Universal Decimal Classification number, and translation is from English into the other languages, with indexes by each language to classification number.

Russian and Spanish have been added in this edition.

Wieckowska, Helena and **Pliszczyńska, Hanna.** Podręczny słownik bibliotekarza. Warszawa, Panstwowe Wydawnictwo Naukowe, 1955. 309p.   **AB25**

Librarian's glossary; Vocabulaire du bibliothécaire; Lexikon des Bibliothekars; Slovar' bibliotekaria.

A dictionary of about 3000 Polish library terms with definitions in Polish and equivalents in English, French, German, and Russian. Separate glossaries for each of these languages give, for each foreign term, its Polish equivalent.

Directories

International

Esdaile, Arundell. National libraries of the world: their history, administration and public services. 2d ed. compl. rev. by F. J. Hill. London, Lib. Assoc., 1957. 413p.   **AB26**

1st ed. 1934.

Describes the national libraries of 32 countries. Each library is treated in a separate chapter giving history, description of buildings, catalogs, departments, staff, finances, etc., and a brief bibliography.

International library directory. 1st ed. London, A. P. Wales Organization, Pub. Division, 1963. 1083p.   **AB27**

Subtitle: A world directory of libraries.

An alphabetical list of libraries in some 150 countries, arranged by country and town, or by country, state or province, and town. Gives name, address, name of librarian, and number of volumes. A rather elaborate system of abbreviations refers to a key, giving further information as to type of library and subjects included in the collections.

United Nations Educational, Scientific and Cultural Organization. Guide to national bibliographical information centers. 2d ed. Paris, 1962. 74p.   **AB28**

1st ed. 1953.

Gives the national bibliographical centers for 77 countries, arranged alphabetically by country. Includes name, address, character and aims, specialization, resources, terms of consultation, reproduction services, and publications issued by the organization.

For material relating to the international exchange of publications *see* the following:

—— Handbook on the international exchange of publications. 3d ed., ed. and rev. by Gisela von Busse. Paris, 1964. 767p.   **AB29**

Text in English, French, Spanish, and Russian.

1st ed. 1950. Pt.1 covers forms, methods, conventions, and agreements of exchange of publications; pt.2 lists under country: exchange centers, bibliographical information centers, lists of national bibliographies, directories, etc.; and under place-name, the organizations and institutions with whom exchange relations may be established, usually noting the publications of the organization.

United States

American Library Association. A.L.A. membership directory . . . with lists of national, state, provincial, and

local library associations, agencies, supervisors, periodicals. 1949– . Chicago, Assoc., 1950– . Annual.
AB30

None published for 1950.
Supersedes in part the *A.L.A. handbook*.

American library directory. 24th ed., a classified list of libraries in the United States and Canada with personnel and statistical data, plus a selected list of libraries around the world, comp. by Eleanor F. Steiner-Prag. N.Y., Bowker, 1964. 1282p. Biennial.   **AB31**

1st ed. 1923. Frequency varies.

Libraries are arranged alphabetically by state and then by city. Gives name; librarian, and usually names of department heads; number of volumes; circulation; income; budget; special collections. For large libraries information is more detailed. Additional lists include: (1) public library extension agencies, school library agencies, library schools and training courses, U.S. Armed Forces libraries overseas, U.S. information centers, international library directory; (2) index to educational institutions, regional libraries, and memorial names; (3) index to special libraries, armed forces libraries, and memorial names.

American school library directory. [rev. 1958] N.Y., Bowker, [1958–]. v.1–3. Loose-leaf (In progress)
AB32

Subtitle: A geographical list of school libraries with statistical data.

1st ed. 1952–57. 4v.

Contents: pt.1, Southern states, 1959; pt.2, Western and southwestern states, 1961; pt.3, Mid-western states, 1963; pt.4, North-eastern states, revision in preparation.

Arranged by state and then alphabetically by city. Gives name, address, and data on enrollment, number of volumes, annual library book budget. Names and addresses are given for library supervisors but not for school librarians.

Kruzas, Anthony T. Directory of special libraries and information centers. 1st ed. Detroit, Gale Research, [1963]. 767p.   **AB33**

A directory of some 10,000 special libraries, arranged in two parts: pt.1, United States; pt.2, Canada. Alphabetical arrangement by name of company, organization, government, etc. operating the library. Gives address, founding date, staff, subjects covered, publications, number of holdings. Includes subject index.

Medical Library Association. Directory. 2d ed. Hamden, Conn., Shoe String, 1959. 274p.   **AB34**

1st ed. 1950.

A directory of the 552 medical libraries which are members of the Association, giving name, address, date of founding, source of support, staff, budget, size, annual circulation, policies on interlibrary loan and photographing, etc.

A list of personal members with addresses, and an index of libraries and special collections, complete the volume.

Special Libraries Association. Directory of members as of October 15, 1962. N.Y., Assoc., 1962. 139p. Irregular.   **AB35**

Title varies. 1st ed. (1937), List of members.

Australia

Library Association of Australia. Special Libraries Section. Directory of special libraries in Australia. Sydney, Assoc., 1961. 122p.   **AB36**

1st ed. 1954.

A listing of 505 libraries giving address, subject fields, and lending policy of each.

Library Association of Australia. Public Libraries Section. Directory of public, reference and lending libraries in Australia, comp. from official sources and ed. by Ken-

neth J. Ling . . . Sydney, Assoc., [1961]. 1v. unpaged.
AB36a

A listing of 262 libraries, arranged by state, with information as to history, services, staff, collections, etc.

Austria

Handbuch österreichischer Bibliotheken. [2. ed.] Wien, Österreichische Nationalbibliothek, 1961–63. 3v.   **AB37**

[1. ed.] in *Biblos-Schriften*, Bd.1, 14. 1953–57 (title varies).

[2. ed.] in three parts: pt.1, Bibliotheksverzeichnis; pt.2, Statistik und Personalverzeichnis; pt.3, Rechtsvorschriften und Erlasse zum österreichischen Bibliothekswesen (*Biblos-Schriften*, Bd.30, 31, 34).

Pt.1 lists some 1000 Austrian libraries by city, giving address, number of volumes, special subjects, hours, name of librarian; pt.2, statistics and Who's who; pt.3, laws and regulations of Austrian libraries.

Belgium

Hove, Julien van. Répertoire des organismes de documentation en Belgique: centres de documentation, bibliothèques, dépots d'archives, musées, etc. Bruxelles, Éd. de la Librairie Encyclopédique, 1947. 333p.   **AB38**

Gives address, name of person in charge, hours, lending conditions, description of collections.

Brazil

Rio de Janeiro. Instituto Brasileiro de Bibliografia e Documentação. Bibliotecas especializadas brasileiras; guia para intercâmbio bibliográfico. Rio de Janeiro, Conselho Nacional de Pesquisas, 1962. 375p. il.   **AB39**

A directory of some 470 libraries with special collections, giving location, name of director, details of organization, resources, and publications. Includes public, university, research, museum, government, and business libraries, arranged by subject of specialization, with name index.

Rio de Janeiro. Instituto Nacional do Livro. Guia das bibliotecas brasileiras. Registadas até 31 março de 1942. 2. ed. Rio de Janeiro, Impr. Nacional, 1944. 475p. map. (Its Coleção B2. Biblioteconomia, II)   **AB40**

Includes a total of 1328 libraries, 463 being public or semi-public and 865 private. Describes organization and resources of each.

——— ——— Suplementos . . . (Bibliotecas registadas entre 1 de abril de 1942 e 31 de março de 1945). Rio de Janeiro, Ministerio de Educação e Saúde, 1946. 329p. (Its Coleção B2. Biblioteconomia, II)

Cuba

Peraza Sarausa, Fermín. Directorio de bibliotecas de Cuba, 1943– . La Habana, Anuario Bibliográfico Cubano, 1943– . (Biblioteca del bibliotecario, 2) Irregular.
AB41

1963 ed. available. Address orders to: Dr. Fermín Peraza, Publisher, Box 12, 572 University Station, Gainesville, Fla.

Denmark

Einersen, Henning and **Iversen, Mogens.** Dansk Biblioteksfører, udg. af Fællesrepræsentationen for den danske Bibliotekarstand. 3. udg. København, Dansk Bibliografisk Kontor, 1955. 137p.   **AB42**

1st ed. 1915.

A directory of scholarly, technical, and public libraries. Includes indexes by name of library and by subject.

Finland

Nivanka, Eino. Suomen tieteellisten kirjastojen opas. Kolmas, uusittu ja täydennetty painos. Helsinki, 1962. 146p. (Tieteellisten kirjastojen lautakunta) **AB43**

Title also in English: Guide to the research libraries of Finland. 3d rev. and enl. ed. (Council of Research Libraries in Finland)

Introductory matter in Finnish, Swedish, and English.

Lists 279 libraries by subject with description of administration, resources, etc. Includes name index in Finnish, Swedish, and English, also Finnish-Swedish-English word list.

—— Directory of Finnish research libraries. Abridged ed. tr. by Leena Salminen. Helsinki, Council of Research Libraries in Finland, 1962. 52p. **AB43a**

A condensed English-language edition, giving information on 54 important Finnish research libraries.

France

France. Direction des Bibliothèques de France. Répertoire des bibliothèques d'étude et organismes de documentation. Paris, Bibliothèque Nationale, 1963. 1233p. 3v. in 1. **AB44**

Contents: I, Paris, Seine et Seine-et-Oise; II, Départements; III, Supplément et index.

Supersedes the *Répertoire des bibliothèques de France* (1950–51), issued by UNESCO.

A directory and survey of 2383 numbered libraries and documentation centers of France. Gives name, address, library personnel, regulations of use, catalogs, resources, history, publications, etc. Includes name and subject index.

Leroy, Émile. Guide pratique des bibliothèques de Paris. Paris, Éd. des Bibliothèques Nationales, 1937. 283p. **AB45**

Directory information including history of the libraries in Paris: university, scientific, learned society, government, and foreign. Detailed description of the Bibliothèques Nationales and their catalogs, p.17–107. Includes bibliographies.

Serrurier, Cornelia. Bibliothèques de France; description de leurs fonds et historique de leur formation. La Haye, Nijhoff, 1946. 346p. **AB46**

Describes about 70 important French libraries, mainly municipal, giving for each a historical sketch, indication of content, brief listing of important holdings, and bibliographical references.

Germany

Jahrbuch der deutschen Bibliotheken, hrsg. vom Verein deutscher Bibliothekare. Leipzig, Harrassowitz, 1902– . v.1– . Annual (Irregular). **AB47**

Principal contents of v.40, 1963: (1) List of libraries arranged alphabetically by towns; (2) List of librarians with brief biographical data; (3) Statistics.

Minerva-Handbücher. Ergänzungen zu "Minerva," Jahrbuch der gelehrten Welt, hrsg. von Hans Praesent. Berlin, de Gruyter, 1929–34. Abt. 1, Bd.1–3. **AB48**

. 1. Abt. *Die Bibliotheken:* Bd.1, Deutsches Reich; Bd.2, Österreich; Bd.3, Schweiz.

For full information *see* AC13.

For *Minerva see* CB62.

Germany, East

Jahrbuch der Bibliotheken, Archive und Dokumentationsstellen der Deutschen Demokratischen Republik. Jahrg. 1– . 1959– . Berlin, 1961– . **AB49**

"Im Auftrage des Staatssekretariats für das Hoch- und Fachschulwesen hrsg. von der Deutschen Staatsbibliothek Berlin."

A directory of libraries, archives, and documentation centers, giving detailed information including statistics. Contains a list of library schools, associations, and a who's who of persons employed.

Great Britain

ASLIB directory: a guide to sources of information in Great Britain and Ireland, ed. by Miriam Alman. London, ASLIB [Assoc. of Special Libraries and Information Bureaux], 1957. 2v. **AB50**

Contents: v.1, Indexes and appendixes. 179p.; v.2, Directory of libraries and information services. Regional index. 1018p.

"A completely new version of *The Aslib Directory* 1928."

v.1 contains a classified index by the Universal Decimal Classification, showing which libraries specialize in certain subjects, with a subject index to the classification; and a name index to organizations, institutions, societies, libraries, special collections, etc.

v.2, arranged alphabetically by city, gives for each library: name, date of founding, address, hours, lending regulations, scope, size, classification used, catalogs, publications, etc.

Burkett, J. Special library and information services in the United Kingdom. London, Lib. Assoc., 1961. 200p. il. **AB51**

A survey, rather than a directory, of particular types of special library services covering: Government libraries; British central scientific libraries; Public authorities (coal, gas, and electricity; the U.K. Atomic Energy Authority; the British Broadcasting Corporation); Industrial libraries (metal, engineering and electrical, chemical and other industries); Municipal contribution to special librarianship; Appendix—the libraries of international organizations.

Each chapter written by a specialist.

Gt.Brit. Treasury. Organisation and Methods Division. A guide to government libraries. 2d ed. London, Stat. Off., 1958. 139p. **AB52**

1st ed. 1952.

This edition "has been prepared chiefly for the benefit of users outside government departments." Gives directory information for about 80 libraries, including brief history, facilities available, catalogs, special collections, etc.

Irwin, Raymond. The libraries of London. 2d ed. rev. London, Lib. Assoc., 1961. 332p. **AB53**

1st ed. 1949.

Based on a series of lectures by specialists; describes in some detail the history, purpose, collections, etc. of the great national libraries, the libraries of the University of London, libraries of various learned societies, and a selected group of special libraries. References throughout the text.

Libraries, museums and art galleries year book, 1954/55. Advisory ed., L. R. McColvin. London, Clark, 1955. 648p. **AB54**

1st ed. 1897; 10th ed. 1937; 1948 and 1954/55 eds. unnumbered.

Partial contents: library, bibliographical, and museum associations; libraries, museums, galleries: (1) in Great Britain and Northern Ireland, with index; (2) overseas, arranged by countries, giving address and some brief information.

Library Association. Year book, [189?]– . London, Assoc., [189?]– . Annual. (1964) **AB55**

None published 1896–98, 1906, 1908, 1910–13.

Includes officers and council, committees, royal charter and by-laws, syllabus of examinations, facilities for study and training, suggested text and reference books, examination papers set, publications of the Association, list of members, etc.

Library Association. Medical Section. Directory of medical libraries in the British Isles. London, Assoc., 1957. 91p. **AB56**

Lists medical, dental, pharmaceutical, and veterinary libraries, giving address, date of founding, description of collections, hours, etc. Includes general index and index of personnel.

Munby, Alan Noel Latimer. Cambridge college libraries; aids for research students. 2d ed. Cambridge, Eng., W. Heffer, 1962. 56p. **AB57**

1st ed. 1960.

Descriptions of the research facilities of 22 college libraries plus the Fitzwilliam Museum and the University Archives. Devotes itself to the rare and early collections, not the "working libraries."

India

Indian Association of Special Libraries and Information Centres. Directory of special and research libraries in India. Calcutta, Oxford Book & Stationery Co., 1962. 282p. **AB58**

Lists 123 libraries, including academic and public with special research collections. In columnar form gives information as to size, administration, personnel, resources, etc. Arranged alphabetically by name of library with indexes to name, place, subject, and nature of management.

Indian library directory. 3d ed. Delhi, Indian Lib. Assoc., 1951. 117p. **AB59**

1st ed. 1938; 2d ed. 1944.

363 libraries are listed, with much useful information (in tabulated form) on stock, personnel, expenditures, etc. Further chapters list libraries by geographical location and by type of library; schools of library service, with detailed information; library literature published in India. Chapter 7 (p.112–17) is a who's who of librarians.

Italy

Italy. Direzione Generale delle Accademie e Biblioteche. Annuario delle bibliotheche italiane. 2. ed. Roma, Palombi, 1956–59. 3v. il. (160pl.). Irregular. **AB60**

1st ed. 1949/51 in 3v. Aggiornamento, 1954.

Pt.1, A–M; pt.2, N–Z; pt.3, Roma, Vaticano, S. Marino. University, public, and other libraries, arranged under towns, A–Z, described with considerable detail, including historical information. Contains bibliographic references.

Japan

Special Libraries Association, Japan. Directory of research libraries. [no place, no pub.] 1956. 375p., 76p. **AB61**

Primarily in Japanese, but with information in English interspersed and indexes in English.

Mexico

México. Departamento de Bibliotecas. Directorio de bibliotecas de la República Mexicana. [México], Secretaría de Educación Pública, 1962. 154p. **AB62**

Arranged by state, then by city; gives address, name of director, number of volumes, and date of founding. Includes all types of libraries, many small as well as large.

Parsons, Mary D. and **Gordillo, Roberto A.** Directory of Mexico City libraries. Mexico, Mexico City College Pr., 1958. 95p. il. **AB63**

Title page and text in Spanish and English.

More than 100 libraries are listed with address, date of founding, size, personnel, hours, and brief description of contents.

Middle East

Dagher, Joseph A. Répertoire des bibliothèques du Proche et du Moyen-Orient. Paris, UNESCO, 1951. 182p. **AB64**

A directory of the libraries of the Near and Middle East giving date of founding, authority, catalog, specialties, conditions of use, etc.

Netherlands

Bibliotheek- en documentatiegids voor Nederland, samengesteld onder auspiciën van de Centrale Vereniging voor Openbare Leezalen en Bibliotheken, Nederlandse Vereniging van Bibliothecarissen en het Nederlands Instituut voor Documentatie en Registratuur. 'sGravenhage, 1957. 246p. **AB65**

A directory of 1125 libraries and documentation centers, arranged by town, giving name of library, address, hours of opening, size of collections, etc. Includes name and subject index. Revises data in two earlier works: *Nederlandse bibliotheekgids* (4th ed. 1949) and *N.I.D.E.R. documentatiegids voor Nederland* (1937).

Pakistan

Pakistan Bibliographical Working Group. A guide to Pakistan libraries, learned and scientific societies and educational institutions, including museums and art galleries. Karachi, 1957. 132p. (Its Publ. no.3) **AB66**

Contents: sec. 1, Libraries, p.1–43; sec. 2, Educational institutions, p.45–103; sec. 3, Museums and art galleries, p.106–8; sec. 4, Learned and scientific societies and institutions, p.110–20.

Spain

Spain. Dirección General de Archivos y Bibliotecas. Guía de las bibliotecas de Madrid. Madrid, Servicio de Publicaciones del Ministerio de Educación Nacional, 1953. 556p. (Its Guías de archivos y bibliotecas) **AB67**

Publicaciones de educación nacional, obra no.8.

Covers the national library and the university, college, research, scientific, government, and special libraries in Madrid. Gives history, description of collections, publications, information as to administration, regulations of use, etc.

Sweden

Ottervik, Gösta [and others]. Libraries and archives in Sweden, from the Swedish manuscript by Richard Cox. Stockholm, Swedish Inst., 1954. 216p. il. **AB68**

Covers (1) university, research, and public libraries, and (2) national, regional, royal, and private archives. Gives detailed descriptions with excellent illustrations.

Includes appendix listing national bibliographies, and name and subject index.

Switzerland

Schweizerische Vereinigung für Dokumentation. Archive, Bibliotheken und Dokumentationsstellen der Schweiz . . . 3. Aufl. des "Führer durch die schweizerische Dokumentation." Bern, Sekretariat der . . . Vereinigung für Dokumentation, 1958. 144p. **AB69**

Title also in French and Italian. 3. éd. du "Guide de la documentation en Suisse."

Arranged geographically; lists and describes the libraries and documentation centers of Switzerland. Indexes of institutions, of catchwords and personal names, and of subject specialties.

Union of Soviet Socialist Republics

Horecky, Paul L. Libraries and bibliographic centers in the Soviet Union. [Bloomington, Ind., 1959] 287p. (Indiana University publ. Slavic and East European ser., v.16) (Distr. by Indiana Univ. Pr.) **AB70**

Surveys library networks and collections, catalogs and cataloging, buildings and equipment, and the library profession. Bibliography, p.259–75.

For companion volume on Soviet publishing *see* AA215.

Biography

Frati, Carlo. Dizionario bio-bibliografico dei bibliotecari e bibliofili italiani dal sec. XIV al XIX. Firenze, Obschki, 1933. 705p. il. **AB71**

—— —— Aggiunte de Marino Parenti. Firenze, Sansoni Antiquariato, 1952–60. 3v.

A biographical dictionary of Italian librarians and bibliophiles with detailed lists of works by and about each of them. Includes index by place of libraries mentioned and author index to works cited.

New York State Library School Association. New York State library school register, 1887–1926. James I. Wyer memorial ed. [i.e., 6th ed.]. N.Y., Assoc., 1959. 175p. il. **AB72**

A biographical register of the faculty and graduates of the New York State Library School during the period of its existence. Important because so many outstanding members of the library profession graduated from this famous school.

Ruiz Cabriada, Agustín. Bio-bibliografía del Cuerpo Facultativo de Archiveros, Bibliotecarios y Arqueólogos, 1858–1958. Madrid, Junta Técnica de Archivos, Bibliotecas y Museos, 1958. 1342p. (Junta Técnica de Archivos, Bibliotecas y Museos. Ediciones conmemorativas del centenario del Cuerpo Facultativo, 1858–1958. no.7) **AB73**

Alphabetical by author; an extensive listing of the publications in a variety of fields of several hundred scholars connected with the Cuerpo. A brief biographical sketch precedes the listings for each. Combined index of authors, titles, subjects.

Who's who in librarianship, ed. by Thomas Landau. Cambridge, Eng., Bowes and Bowes, 1954. 269p. **AB74**

The first of its kind for British librarians. Includes some 3000 sketches with supplementary classified lists.

Who's who in library service. 3d ed. A biographical directory of professional librarians of the United States and Canada. Dorothy Ethlyn Cole, ed. N.Y., Grolier Soc., 1955. 546p. **AB75**

1st ed. 1933; 2d ed. 1943.

Includes more than 11,000 names of professional librarians and persons active in related fields.

LIBRARY RESOURCES

International

Brummel, Leendert and **Egger, E.** Guide to union catalogues and international loan centers. Pub. under the auspices of the International Federation of Library Associations (IFLA). The Hague, Nijhoff, 1961. 89p. **AB76**

Added title page in French.

Text in English and French.

A listing of some 200 union catalogs with information for each on scope, size, area covered, etc. Lists also printed union catalogs and international loan centers.

Fraenkel, Josef. Guide to the Jewish libraries of the world. London, Cultural Dept. of the World Jewish Congress, 1959. 64p. **AB77**

Arranged by continent, then by country. Describes the collections and services.

United States

Ash, Lee. Subject collections: a guide to special book collections and subject emphases as reported by university, college, public, and special libraries in the United States and Canada. 2d ed. rev. and enl. N.Y., Bowker, 1961. 651p. **AB78**

1st ed. 1958.

The 2d edition contains about 20,000 entries under some 1300 subjects, including about 300 collections of the Library of Congress omitted from the 1st edition. Excluded are special collections of local history and local genealogy.

Information was drawn from questionnaires, resulting in some unevenness.

Downs, Robert Bingham. American library resources; a bibliographical guide. Chicago, Amer. Lib. Assoc., 1951. 428p. **AB79**

A bibliography of bibliographies rather than a description of resources, since it indicates holdings of libraries only insofar as there are bibliographies listing them. Bibliographies, union lists, surveys, checklists, and catalogs of particular libraries and special collections from all parts of the country are included, whether published in periodicals or separately as books or pamphlets. In a few cases unpublished bibliographies are also listed. In general, the arrangement follows the Dewey Decimal Classification. A full index by author, subject, and library helps in locating individual titles as well as special collections on particular subjects. However, it must be borne in mind that other libraries may have collections of equal or greater importance for which no lists are available.

—— —— Supplement 1950–1961. 1962. 226p.

—— Resources of New York City libraries, a survey of facilities for advanced study and research. Sponsored by the A.L.A. Board on Resources of American Libraries. Chicago, Amer. Lib. Assoc., 1942. 442p. **AB80**

Surveys the collections of some 400 libraries, general and special (excluding private libraries), in the five boroughs of greater New York. Arranged by broad subjects with subdivisions listing the collections in order of importance. Detailed index. Directory of libraries, p.299–307. Bibliography, p.309–403, includes 819 numbered items which locate copies in New York libraries.

—— Resources of southern libraries; a survey of facilities for research. Chicago, Amer. Lib. Assoc., 1938. 370p. **AB81**

Research collections of 316 libraries in 13 southern states are described in essay form by a committee of librarians and subject specialists. Arranged by broad subject. Detailed index. Includes bibliography, p.312–30.

Hilton, Ronald. Handbook of Hispanic source materials and research organizations in the United States. 2d ed. Stanford, Calif., Stanford Univ. Pr., 1956. 448p. **AB82**

1st ed. 1942.

Covers libraries, museums, art galleries, etc. having collections or doing research in the Hispanic field. Deals mainly with the fine arts, humanities, and the social sciences, with some exceptional collections in the natural sciences. Arranged by state, city, and library, with descriptions of collections; in some cases lists rare items.

"Hispanic" comprises Spain, Portugal, and Hispanic America of the pre- and post-Columbian periods, Florida, Texas, the Southwest, and California until annexation by the United States.

Johnston, William Dawson and **Mudge, I. G.** Special collections in libraries in the United States. Wash., Govt. Prt. Off., 1912. 140p. (U.S. Bureau of Education. Bull. 1912, no.23)   **AB83**

A classed subject list, with alphabetical index of subjects, names of libraries, collectors, donors, etc. Gives statistics and brief descriptions of collections, with references to printed catalogs or detailed descriptions. A supplement was printed in the *Library journal* 38:331–33. June 1913.

An old but still valuable list for some historical information.

New York. Public Library. A guide to the reference collections of the New York Public Library, comp. by Karl Brown. N.Y., Lib., 1941. 416p.   **AB84**

Reprinted with revisions from the *Bulletin* of the New York Public Library, May 1935–Feb. 1941.

Arranged according to the general classification scheme used by the New York Public Library. Usually includes, under classes, statement of extent and character, strength or weakness, related subjects and class marks, special collections, special catalogs, indexes, files of clippings and pamphlets, lists of reference lists on the subject in *Bulletin,* etc. Useful, detailed index.

Ruggles, Melville J. and **Mostecky, Vaclav.** Russian and East European publications in the libraries of the United States. N.Y., Columbia Univ. Pr., 1960. 396p. (Columbia University studies in library service, no.11)   **AB85**

Surveys problems of selection, acquisition, finance, cataloging, and bibliographic control, and provides extensive quantitative data on existing collections.

Special Libraries Association. Special library resources. N.Y., Assoc., 1941–47. 4v.   **AB86**

Contents: v.1, United States and Canada; v.2, Alabama–Montana; v.3, Nebraska–Wyoming, Canada; v.4, Indexes. v.1–2, ed. by Rose L. Vormelker; v.3–4, by Isabel L. Towner.

Covers research library collections in the special library field and in public and university libraries. Arranged alphabetically by state, city, and library. Usually gives name, address, staff, and number of books, pamphlets, periodicals, vertical file drawers, etc. Gives information about interlibrary loan and reproducing facilities.

For the most part v.2–3 include additional libraries to those in v.1. v.4 includes an organization index and a subject index.

Williams, Edwin Everitt. Farmington Plan handbook. Rev. to 1961 and abridged. Ithaca, N.Y., Office of the Executive Secretary, Assoc. of Research Libraries, 1961. 141p.   **AB87**

Original edition, 1953, contains background information not repeated here. Principal value of the present edition is its list, by library, of allocations of acquisition responsibility for foreign research materials; a second list arranged by Library of Congress classification symbol; and a detailed index by subject. Includes supplementary lists of recent Farmington Plan bibliography, statistics of accessions, and foreign agents.

❦ Directories of special library associations are also available, e.g., the Music Library Association, Medical Library Association, American Association of Law Libraries, etc., and various local directories of libraries, e.g., *Directory of special libraries in Boston, vicinity and member libraries in New England* (6th ed. 1961); *Directory of libraries and informational services in Philadelphia and vicinity* (11th ed. 1964); *Special libraries directory of Greater New York* (10th ed. 1963); *Library*

and reference facilities in the area of the District of Columbia (6th ed. 1959).

Great Britain

British Museum. The British Museum, a guide to its public services. London, Trustees, 1962. (Distr. by British Information Services, N.Y.) 72p. il.   **AB88**

Esdaile, Arundell. The British Museum Library, a short history and survey. London, Allen and Unwin, 1946. 388p.   **AB89**

Pt.1, Historical survey; pt.2, The collections and their catalogues.

Ker, Neil Ripley. Medieval libraries of Great Britain; a list of surviving books. 2d ed. London, Offices of the Royal Historical Soc., 1964. 424p. (Its Guides and handbooks, no.3)   **AB90**

"Intended as a guide to medieval books and book-catalogues and to the modern catalogues in which they are described."—*Pref.*

Philip, Alex. J. An index to the special collections in libraries, museums and art galleries (public, private and official) in Great Britain and Ireland. London, F. G. Brown, 1949. 190p.   **AB91**

Attempts to bring to light unique and often hidden collections in small, and sometimes large, libraries, dealing with special subjects. Arranged by subject, giving location and brief description.

Statistics

See also Annuals, following.

Jackson, William Vernon. A handbook of American library resources. 2d ed. Champaign, Ill., Illini Union Bookstore, 1962. 88p. il.   **AB92**

1st ed. 1955.

Statistics of American scholarly and research libraries.

Annuals

The Bowker annual of library and book trade information, ed. 1– , 1956– . Sponsored by the Council of National Library Associations. N.Y., Bowker, 1956– . Annual.   **AB93**

Title varies: 1956–58, *American library annual* [new series]; 1959–60, *American library and book trade annual.*

A compendium of miscellaneous information in two parts: pt.1, Library statistics, book trade statistics, general library and book trade information, guide to national bibliographical centers; pt.2, Associations, joint committees, etc., library buying guide, index.

LIBRARY SCIENCE

Handbooks

American Library Association. Federal Relations Committee. Federal services to libraries, prep. by Phillips Temple. Chicago, Assoc., 1954. 227p.   **AB94**

Describes the services of the federal government which are available to libraries.

Ashworth, Wilfred. Handbook of special librarianship and information work. 2d ed. London, ASLIB, 1962. 508p.   **AB95**

1st ed. 1955.

A manual dealing with the organization and administration

of special libraries. Reflects English practice. Includes bibliographies.

Jackson, Ellen. A manual for the administration of the federal documents collection in libraries. Prep. for the A.L.A. Committee on Public Documents. Chicago, Amer. Lib. Assoc., 1955. 108p. **AB96**

Includes annotated bibliography, p. 83–103.

Osborn, Andrew D. Serial publications: their place and treatment in libraries. Chicago, Amer. Lib. Assoc., 1955. 309p. il. **AB97**

Describes the principles of serials organization, their selection, acquisition, checking, cataloging, housing, reference use and circulation, binding, reprints, abstracting and indexing, union lists, etc.; has a special chapter on the publications of the League of Nations, United Nations, and Organization of the American States.

Medical Library Association. Handbook of medical library practice, with a bibliography of the reference works and histories in medicine and the allied sciences. 2d ed. rev. and enl. Janet Doe [and] Mary Louise Marshall, eds. Chicago, Amer. Lib. Assoc., 1956. 601p. **AB98**

1st ed. 1943. For full information *see* EJ1.

Schellenberg, Theodore R. Modern archives, principles and techniques. Chicago, Univ. of Chicago Pr., 1956. 247p. il. **AB99**

First pub. by F. W. Cheshire, Melbourne, Australia.

A text on the administration, organization, and use of archival materials.

Strauss, Lucille Jackson, Strieby, Irene M. and **Brown, Alberta L.** Scientific and technical libraries: their organization and administration. N.Y., Interscience, [1964]. 398p. il. **AB100**

Brings up to date *Technical libraries; their organization and management,* ed. by Lucille Jackson, 1951.

A practical manual with references at the end of each chapter. An appendix (p.305–88) lists basic reference works, periodicals, etc. and bibliographies for some subject fields. An author and a subject index.

Tauber, Maurice F. and **associates.** Technical services in libraries: acquisitions, cataloging, classification, binding, photographic reproduction and circulation operations. N.Y., Columbia Univ. Pr., 1954. 487p. (Columbia University studies in library service, no.7) **AB101**

A thorough survey of policies and practices. Designed as a textbook for the student and as a manual for administrators and other librarians concerned. Particular attention is given to problems of the research library.

Wilson, Louis Round and **Tauber, Maurice F.** The university library: the organization, administration, and functions of academic libraries. 2d ed. N.Y., Columbia Univ. Pr., 1956. 641p. (Columbia University studies in library service, no.8) **AB102**

1st ed. 1944.

This edition, substantially revised, aims to reevaluate the service of academic libraries in terms of books, personnel, and quarters, and to formulate policies as to their organization, function, and administration. Each chapter is concluded by a bibliography.

Cataloging

Manuals

Mann, Margaret. Introduction to cataloging and the classification of books. 2d ed. Chicago, Amer. Lib. Assoc., 1943. 276p. il. **AB103**

The standard text.

Shera, Jesse Hauk and **Egan, Margaret Elizabeth.** The

classified catalog: basic principles and practices. With a code for the construction and maintenance of the classified catalog by Jeannette M. Lynn and Zola Hilton. Chicago, Amer. Lib. Assoc., 1956. 130p. il. **AB104**

Includes bibliography, p.122–27.

Codes

United States

American Library Association. Division of Cataloging and Classification. A.L.A. cataloging rules for author and title entries. 2d ed., ed. by Clara Beetle. Chicago, Assoc., 1949. 265p. **AB105**

An expansion and revision of the 1908 edition of *Catalog rules, author and title entries.*

U.S. Library of Congress. Descriptive Cataloging Division. Rules for descriptive cataloging in the Library of Congress (adopted by the American Library Association). Wash., Govt. Prt. Off., 1949. 141p. **AB106**

—— —— Supplement. 1949–51. Wash., Govt. Prt. Off., 1952. 19p.

Includes additions and changes in the rules, and memoranda on policy and procedure.

The Descriptive Cataloging Division also issues special sections of its code: e.g., Manuscripts. Preliminary ed., 1954. 10p.; Motion pictures and filmstrips. 2d preliminary ed., 1953. 18p.; Phonorecords. 2d preliminary ed., 1964. 11p.; Pictures, designs, and other two-dimensional representations. Preliminary ed., 1959. 16p.

Cataloging rules of the American Library Association and the Library of Congress. Additions and changes, 1949–1958. Wash., Lib. of Congress, 1959. 76p. **AB107**

Includes all changes in the *A.L.A. cataloging rules for author and title entries* and the *Rules for descriptive cataloging in the Library of Congress.* Except for music, microprint materials, and one rule dealing with entry for motion pictures, it does not include rules or changes in rules for nonbook materials.—*Foreword.*

France

Association Française de Normalisation. Direction des Bibliothèques. Code de catalogage des imprimés communs. Dictionnaire des cas. Paris, 1945. 256p. (Annexes, 125p.) **AB108**

Paris. Bibliothèque Nationale. Département des Imprimés. Usages suivis dans la rédaction du Catalogue général des livres imprimés de la Bibliothèque Nationale, recueillis et coordonnés par E. G. Ledos. Nouvelle éd. entièrement refondue par Amand Rastoul. Paris, Bibliothèque Nationale, 1940. 70p. **AB109**

Germany

Instruktionen für die alphabetischen Kataloge der preuszischen Bibliotheken vom 10. Mai 1899. 2. Ausg. in der Fassung vom 10. August 1908. Berlin, Behrend, 1909. 179p. (Repr. 1944) **AB110**

—— The Prussian instructions; rules for the alphabetical catalogs of the Prussian libraries, tr. from the 2d ed., authorized Aug. 10, 1908, with an introd. and notes, by Andrew D. Osborn. Ann Arbor, Univ. of Michigan Pr., 1938. 192p. (Univ. of Michigan general library publ. no.4)

Fuchs, Hermann. Kommentar zu den Instruktionen für die alphabetischen Kataloge der preussischen Bibliotheken. 3. erneut durchgesehene Aufl. Wiesbaden, O. Harrassowitz, 1962. 302p. il. **AB111**

1st ed. 1955.

Great Britain

British Museum. Dept. of Printed Books. Rules for compiling the catalogues of printed books, maps and music in the British Museum. Rev. ed. London, Trustees, 1936. 67p. **AB112**

Vatican

Vatican. Biblioteca Vaticana. Norme per il catalogo degli stampati. 3. ed. Città del Vaticano, Biblioteca, 1949. 396p. **AB113**

1st ed. 1931; 2d ed. 1939.

—— Rules for the Catalog of printed books, tr. from the 2d Italian ed. by Thomas J. Shanahan [and others]; ed. by Wyllis E. Wright. Chicago, Amer. Lib. Assoc., 1948. 426p.

One of the most comprehensive codes. Spanish translation published as *Normas para catalogación de impresos.* Edición española. Ciudad del Vaticano, Biblioteca Apostólica Vaticana, 1940. 472p.

French translation published as *Règles pour le catalogue des imprimés.* Éd. française. Cité du Vatican, Bibliothèque Apostolique Vaticane, 1950. 402p.

Special subjects

See also the special sections of the code of the Descriptive Cataloging Division of the Library of Congress (AB106).

Boggs, Samuel Whittemore and **Lewis, Dorothy Cornwell.** The classification and cataloging of maps and atlases. N.Y., Special Libraries Assoc., 1945. 175p. il. **AB114**

A manual of practice, intended primarily for separate map collections.

Joint Committee on Music Cataloging. Code for cataloging music and phonorecords. Chicago, Amer. Lib. Assoc., 1958. 88p. **AB115**

Prepared by a joint committee of the Music Library Association and the American Library Association, Division of Cataloging and Classification.

A revision of the preliminary edition of the Music Library Association's *Code for cataloging music* (1941–42).

National League of Nursing Education. Committee on the Revision of the Library Handbook for Schools of Nursing. A library handbook for schools of nursing. 2d ed. N.Y., Nat. League for Nursing, 1953. 265p. **AB116**

1st ed. 1936.

Contents: pt.1, Organization and administration of a nursing school library, p.1–72; pt.2, List of subject headings, p.73–205; pt.3, Classification outline and index, p.206–263; general index, p.264–65.

Classification

Manuals

Merrill, William Stetson. Code for classifiers; principles governing the consistent placing of books in a system of classification. 2d ed. Chicago, Amer. Lib. Assoc., 1939. 177p. **AB117**

1st ed. 1928.

Bibliography

Special Libraries Association. Classification Committee. Classification schemes and subject headings lists. Loan collection of Special Libraries Association, comp. by Bertha Barden and Barbara Denison. 5th ed. N.Y., Assoc., 1961. 97p. **AB118**

An annotated list of 788 schemes and lists arranged by subject.

Schedules

U.S. Library of Congress. Subject Cataloging Division. Classification: Classes A–Z. Wash., Govt. Prt. Off., 1917–64. **AB119**

Contents: *Outline of the Library of Congress classification.* Rev. and enl. ed. 1942. Repr. 1962. 21p.; Class A: *General works: Polygraphy.* 3d ed. 1947, repr. with suppl. pages, 1963. 47p., 7p.; Class B: *Philosophy and religion:* pt.1, B–BJ: *Philosophy.* 2d ed. 1950, repr. with suppl. pages, 1960. 166p., 45p.; Class B, pt.2, BL–BX: *Religion.* 2d ed. 1962. 639p.; Class C: *History: Auxiliary sciences of history.* 2d ed. 1948, repr. with suppl. pages, 1961. 167p., 11p.; Class D: *History: General and Old World.* 2d ed. 1959. 747p.; Class E–F: *History: America.* 3d ed. 1958. 607p.; Class G: *Geography, anthropology, folklore, manners and customs, recreation.* 3d ed. 1954. 502p.; Class H: *Social sciences.* new ed. in prep.; Class J: *Political science.* 2d ed. 1924, repr. with suppl. pages, 1961. 434p., 137p.; Class L: *Education.* 3d ed. 1951, repr. with suppl. pages, 1960. 200p., 43p.; Class M: *Music and books on music.* 2d ed. 1917, repr. with suppl. pages, 1963. 157p., 101p.;

Class N: *Fine arts.* 3d ed. 1922, repr. with suppl. pages, 1962. 165p., 77p.; Class P: *Philology and literature:* P–PA: *Philology, linguistics, classical philology, classical literature.* 1928, repr. with suppl. pages, 1964. 447p., 35p.; PA: Supplement. *Byzantine and modern Greek literature, medieval and modern Latin literature.* 1942. 24p. new ed. in prep.; PB–PH: *Modern European languages.* 1933, repr. with suppl. pages, 1957. 226p., 27p.; PG (in part): *Russian literature.* 1948, repr. with suppl. pages, 1955. 256p., 7p. new ed. in prep.; PJ–PM: *Languages and literatures of Asia, Africa, Oceania, America, mixed languages, artificial languages.* 1935. 246p. Suppl. 1936. 3p. new ed. in prep.; P–PM: Supplement. *Index to languages and dialects.* 2d ed. 1957. 71p.; PN, PR, PS, PZ: *Literature (general), English and American literatures, fiction in English, juvenile literature,* with suppl. pages, 1956. 272p., 235p. new ed. in prep.; PQ, pt.1: *French literature.* 1936, repr. with suppl. pages, 1957. 185p., 11p.; PQ, pt.2: *Italian, Spanish, and Portuguese literatures.* 1937, repr. with suppl. pages, 1955. 223p., 9p. new ed. in prep.; PT, pt.1: *German literature.* 1938, repr. with suppl. pages, 1957. 312p., 11p.; PT, pt.2: *Dutch and Scandinavian literatures.* 1942, repr. with suppl. pages, 1955. 102p., 15p. new ed. in prep.;

Class Q: *Science.* 5th ed. 1950, repr. with suppl. pages, 1963. 215p., 65p.; Class R: *Medicine.* 3d ed. 1952, repr. with suppl. pages, 1960. 240p., 25p.; Class S: *Agriculture, plant and animal industry, fish culture and fisheries, hunting sports.* 3d ed. 1948, repr. with suppl. pages, 1959. 101p., 37p.; Class T: *Technology.* 4th ed. 1948, repr. 1964. 325p.; Class U: *Military science.* 3d ed. 1952, repr. with suppl. pages, 1960. 86p., 15p.; Class V: *Naval science.* 2d ed. 1953. 115p.; Class Z: *Bibliography and library science.* 4th ed. 1959. 226p. new ed. in prep.

Grout, Catherine W. An explanation of the tables used in the schedules of the Library of Congress classification, accompanied by an historical and explanatory introduction. N.Y., Columbia Univ., School of Lib. Service, 1940. 108p. **AB120**

Describes the geographical, chronological, special subject, and form divisions used to subdivide subjects in the Library of Congress classification.

Dewey, Melvil. Dewey Decimal Classification and relative index. 16th ed. Lake Placid Club, N.Y., Forest Pr., [1958]. 2v. **AB121**

Contents: v.1, Tables; v.2, Index.

First published anonymously in 1876 under title *A classi-*

fication and subject index; 2d–14th editions published under title *Decimal classification and relativ index.*

A complete revision "designed for use in classification . . . in general libraries, regardless of size, except (1) those libraries which prefer to use an abridged edition and (2) those with special collections which prefer to use close classification. . . . Responsibility for editorial policy rests with the Decimal Classification Editorial Policy Committee, a joint committee of the Lake Placid Club Education Foundation, the American Library Association, and the Library of Congress."—*Foreword.*

———— 8th abridged ed. Lake Placid Club, N.Y., Forest Pr., [1959]. 405p.

Lake Placid Club Education Foundation. Guide to the use of Dewey Decimal Classification, based on the practice of the Decimal Classification Office at the Library of Congress. Lake Placid Club, N.Y., Forest Pr., 1962. 133p.   **AB122**

A practical guide designed to help the classifier by providing instructions and directions for the use of the Decimal Classification schedules.

Bliss, Henry Evelyn. A bibliographic classification, extended by systematic auxiliary schedules for composite specification and notation. N.Y., Wilson, 1940–53. 4v. in 3.   **AB123**

For description of this classification, *see* M. F. Tauber, "Classification systems," in *The state of the library art,* v.1, pt.3 (AB16).

International Federation for Documentation, Brussels. Classification décimale universelle. Tables de classification pour les bibliographies, bibliothèques, archives, administrations, publications, brevets, musées et ensembles d'objets pour toutes les espèces de documentation en général et pour les collections de toute nature. Édition complète, publiée avec le concours de la Commission Internationale de la Classification Décimale et du Nederlandsch Instituut voor Documentatie en Registratuur (La Haye). . . . [Bruxelles], 1927–33. 4v. and index. il. (Its Publ. 151)   **AB124**

———— 5. éd. internationale. Bruxelles, 1939–42. Pts. 1–6. (In progress) (Its Publ. no.204, 205, 207, 249, 251, 252)

Contents: Généralités; Religion, Théologie; Sciences sociales; Médecine; Sciences appliquées, Art de l'ingénieur; Affaires et entreprises.

———— Universal Decimal Classification. Complete English ed., 4th international ed. London, British Standards Inst., 1943–64. (In progress)   **AB124a**

Contents: Generalities; Pure sciences, Physical sciences; Applied sciences.

———— Abridged English ed. 3d ed. rev. London, British Standards Inst., 1961. 254p. (Its Publ. no.289 rev.)

Application may be made to International Federation for Documentation, 7 Hofweg, The Hague, Netherlands, for information concerning the availability of full and abridged editions in various languages.

British Standards Institution. Guide to the Universal Decimal Classification (UDC). London, [1963]. 128p. (FID publ. no.345)   **AB125**

Ranganathan, Shiyali R. Colon classification; basic classification. [6th ed., repr. with amendments] Bombay, N.Y., Asia Pub. House, [1963]. 3 pts. in 1v. (Madras Library Association. Publ. ser. 26)   **AB126**

Contents: pt.1, Rules; pt.2, Schedules of classification; pt.3, Schedules of classics and sacred books with special names.

For description of this classification *see* M. F. Tauber, "Classification systems," in *The state of the library art.* v.1, pt.3 (AB16).

U.S. National Library of Medicine. Classification. [2d ed.] Wash., Govt. Prt. Off., 1956. 314p.   **AB127**

Subtitle: A scheme for the shelf arrangement of books in the field of medicine and its related sciences.

1st edition entitled *Classification: medicine.* 1951.

The notation was developed from the block of letters, QS–QZ and W, unused by the Library of Congress and assigned to the National Library of Medicine.—Cf. L. J. Strauss, *Scientific and technical libraries,* p.151 (AB100).

Harvard University. Graduate School of Business Administration. Baker Library. A classification of business literature. [Rev. ed.] Hamden, Conn., Shoe String, 1960 [c1937, 1961]. 256p.   **AB128**

1st ed. 1937.

Substantially a reissue of the 1st edition with major changes only in the B schedule for *Business and economic theory,* and minor changes to reflect new techniques and concepts. Designed primarily to serve a large collection of business materials.

Subject headings

Manuals

Haykin, David Judson. Subject headings; a practical guide. Wash., Govt. Prt. Off., 1951. 140p.   **AB129**

A manual of rules and practices used in the choice and use of subject headings, with examples. Based mainly on the procedure followed at the Library of Congress.

Schedules

Ball, Miriam Ogden. Subject headings for the information file. 8th ed. N.Y., Wilson, 1956. 179p.   **AB130**

1st ed. 1917.

Designed for use by public libraries; this edition has been revised to include additional scientific and technical terms. Based on headings in use in the Public Library of Newark, N.J.

Columbia University. Libraries. Law Library. Subject headings in Anglo-American and international law used in the dictionary catalog of the Columbia University Law Library, comp. under the direction of Miles O. Price. [3d ed.] N.Y., School of Lib. Service, Columbia Univ., 1957. 182p.   **AB131**

Earlier eds. 1939 and 1949.

Ellinger, Werner Bruno. Subject headings for the literature of law and international law. South Hackensack, N.J., pub. for the American Association of Law Libraries by F. B. Rothman, 1963. 380p. (AALL publ. ser., no.6)
                                                                   AB132

Based on the *Subject headings . . . of the Library of Congress.* 6th ed. 1957 and its supplements (AB137).

Frick, Bertha Margaret. Sears List of subject headings, with suggestions for the beginner in subject heading work. 8th ed. N.Y., Wilson, 1959. 610p.   **AB133**

1st ed. 1923. 1st–3d eds. by Minnie Earl Sears; 4th–5th eds. by Isabel S. Monro; 6th–8th eds. by Bertha Margaret Frick. 1st–5th editions had title *List of subject headings for small libraries.*

"Follows the Library of Congress form of headings, abridged and simplified to meet the needs of smaller libraries."—*Pref.*

Kapsner, Oliver Leonard. Catholic subject headings. 4th ed., with an appendix on names of saints. Collegeville, Minn., St. John's Abbey Pr., 1958. 418p.   **AB134**

Subtitle: A list designed for use with Library of Congress

Subject headings or the Sears List of subject headings, ed. . . . under the auspices of the Catholic Library Association.
1st ed. 1942.

Pettee, Julia. List of theological subject headings and corporate church names based upon the headings in the catalogue of the Library of Union Theological Seminary, New York City. 2d ed. Chicago, Amer. Lib. Assoc., 1947. 653p. **AB135**

Incorporates the Library of Congress subject headings in theology. Appendix gives historical and descriptive information on all the church bodies in the list.

U.S. Library of Congress. Subject Cataloging Division. Music subject headings used on printed catalog cards of the Library of Congress. Wash., 1952. 133p. **AB136**

—— Subject headings used in the dictionary catalogs of the Library of Congress [from 1897 through Dec. 1955]. 6th ed., ed. by Marguerite V. Quattlebaum. Wash., 1957. 1357p. **AB137**

Supplemented by monthly and cumulative supplements.
A very comprehensive list, though including only those headings used in the Library of Congress catalog.

Documentation, information storage and retrieval

Bourne, Charles P. Bibliography of the mechanization of information retrieval. Menlo Park, Calif., Stanford Research Inst., 1958. 22 l. **AB138**

Annual supplements 1–4, 1959–62.
Continued in *American documentation. Literature notes.* v.14, no.2 (April 1963)– . Quarterly.

An annotated list of books, articles, reports, and technical papers treating documentation and information retrieval techniques.

—— Methods of information handling. N.Y., Wiley, [1963]. 241p. il. **AB139**

Describes tools, equipment, and techniques used in information processing—storage and retrieval. Beginning with the basics of file organization, continues into methods of coding, notation, punched cards, and computer systems.
Many references throughout text and at end of each chapter.

Casey, Robert S. Punched cards; their applications to science and industry. 2d ed. N.Y., Reinhold, [1958]. 697p. il. **AB140**

An instruction manual for the use of punched cards, including a discussion of principles and procedures in the design of punched-card systems. Each chapter written by a specialist.
Contains an annotated bibliography, p.638–72. Includes author and subject index.

International Federation for Documentation. Manuel pratique de reproduction documentaire et de sélection. Paris, Gauthier-Villars, 1964. 343p. il. (Publ. FID, no. 353) **AB141**

A manual on the methods and techniques of document reproduction and selection, with short articles on each special type of reproduction. Bibliographical references throughout the text. Includes index.

Spangler, Marshall. General bibliography on information storage and retrieval. [Schenectady, N.Y.?], General Electric, Computer Dept., 1962. 390p. **AB142**

Intended to be "a comprehensive list of contemporary documentation on information storage and retrieval." Covers material appearing since 1949, with a few articles as early as 1917.
The format of the bibliography is designed to be compat-

ible with punched-card compilation and computer-oriented reproduction.—cf. *Introd.*
Arranged alphabetically by author.
Includes source index, chronological index, and significant word index.

Filing and indexing

American Library Association. A.L.A. rules for filing catalog cards, prep. by a special committee, Sophie K. Hiss, chairman. Chicago, Assoc., 1942. 109p. **AB143**

Collison, Robert Lewis. Indexes and indexing: a guide to the indexing of books, and collections of books, periodicals, music, gramophone records, films and other material, with a reference section and suggestions for further reading. N.Y., J. de Graff, [1959]. 200p. il. **AB144**

Includes an annotated bibliography.

Engineering Societies Library, New York. Bibliography on filing, classification, and indexing systems for engineering offices and libraries. N.Y., [1960]. 33p. (Its Bibliography, no.14) **AB145**

An annotated bibliography of 155 numbered articles, books, and pamphlets, arranged in three parts. A subject index refers to the numbered items.

U.S. Library of Congress. Processing Dept. Filing rules for the dictionary catalogs of the Library of Congress. Wash., Govt. Prt. Off., 1956. 187p. **AB146**

Rev. ed. of the 1945 *Filing manual.*

Wheeler, Martha Thorne. Indexing; principles, rules and examples. 5th ed. Albany, Univ. of the State of New York, 1957. 78p. (Its Bull. no.1445 . . . Jan. 1957) **AB147**

1st ed. 1905.
An excellent manual.

Interlibrary loan

American Library Association. Association of College and Research Libraries. General interlibrary loan code, enl. and rev., 1952. Prep. by the Committee on Interlibrary Loans . . . [Chicago, 1952]. (Repr. from: College and research libraries v.13, no.4, Oct. 1952) **AB148**

1st ed. 1940.
A manual of accepted policies and standard procedures approved by the American Library Association, to be followed in handling interlibrary loans.

Winchell, Constance Mabel. Locating books for interlibrary loan, with a bibliography of printed aids which show location of books in American libraries. N.Y., Wilson, 1930. 170p. **AB149**

Pt. 1, Locating books for interlibrary loan, a discussion of the standards to be met and the reference methods to be followed in finding books not in the home library; pt.2, Some 800 printed aids which show location of books in American libraries.

Microreproduction

Ballou, Hubbard Walter. Guide to microreproduction equipment. 2d ed. Annapolis, Md., National Microfilm Assoc., 1962. 519p. il. **AB150**

1st ed. 1959.
A revised directory of models and manufacturers of various types of microreproduction equipment, including cameras, readers, handviewers, processors, contact printers, enlargers, accessories, etc. Gives detailed information and illustrations of the equipment available in this country and some foreign countries.
Kept up to date by frequent supplements.

——— ——— Supplement A. . . . 1963. 87p.; Supplement B. . . . 1964. 136p.

Combined index of supplements A and B contained in Supplement B.

Lewis, Chester M. and **Offenhauser, William H.** Microrecording, industrial and library applications. N.Y., Interscience, 1956. 456p. il.   **AB151**

A handbook with bibliographies.

Reference work

Chicago. University. The reference function of the library; papers presented before the Library Institute at the University of Chicago, June 29 to July 10, 1942, ed. by Pierce Butler. Chicago, Univ. of Chicago Pr., 1943. 366p.   **AB152**

Surveys the reference field and covers the reference function in the large public library, the small and medium-sized public library, the school library, the college library, the university and research library; special problems in art and music, maps, social sciences, science and technology, rare books, etc.; and administrative and personnel problems.

Each chapter by a specialist.

Hutchins, Margaret. Introduction to reference work. Chicago, Amer. Lib. Assoc., 1944. 214p.   **AB153**

A good general introduction to reference work, including sections on: (1) The scope of reference work; (2) Reference questions; (3) Selection of reference materials; (4) Organization of reference materials; (5) Organization and administration of reference service; (6) The less common functions of a reference librarian; and (7) Evaluating and reporting reference work.

Surveys

Erickson, Ernst Walfred. College and university library surveys, 1938–1952. Chicago, Amer. Lib. Assoc., 1961. 115p. (ACRL monograph, no.25)   **AB154**

A study of 12 college and university library surveys, describing methods employed, recommendations, and results. Includes bibliography.

Based on the author's doctoral dissertation, completed at the University of Illinois in 1958.

Jonikas, Peter. Bibliography of public library surveys. Chicago, Office for Adult Education, Amer. Lib. Assoc., 1958. 21 l.   **AB155**

A listing of 280 surveys held by the libraries of the University of Chicago and the American Library Association headquarters, acquired before May 1, 1957. Includes indexes by region, state, and place and by population group served.

Supplemented and brought up to date by Charles A. Bunge. "Statewide public library surveys and plans, 1944–1964, a bibliography," *ALA Bull.* 59, no.5: 364–74. May 1965.

A C

Societies

❧ Information is frequently requested in libraries on the organization, officers, publications, addresses, and history of various associations and societies, and for such purposes the directories listed in this section may be useful. The *Encyclopedia of associations* (AC28) is the most comprehensive list for the United States, giving details about associations in many fields. Lists of international associations are also much in demand, and the larger library will need directories for countries other than the United States.

For society directories in particular subject fields, *see* subhead "Directories" under the subject, e.g., Social sciences—Directories.

INTERNATIONAL

Annuaire de la vie internationale: unions, associations, instituts, commissions, bureaux, offices, conférences, congrès, expositions, publications; publié pour l'Union des Associations Internationales avec le concours de la Fondation Carnegie pour la Paix Internationale et de l'Institut International de la Paix, 1908/09–1910/11. Bruxelles, Off. Central des Inst. Internat., [1909–12]. 2v.   **AC1**

Contains a great deal of information about the history, organization, membership, purposes, meetings, etc. of all types of international organizations, governmental and private, but not so much about their publications. Each volume includes: (1) Public (i.e., governmental) unions, conferences, etc., arranged by subject according to the Universal Decimal Classification; (2) Private organizations, same arrangement; (3) Chronological list of international meetings, giving name, date, and place; and (4) Index of persons, Index of subjects. While the second volume contains the later information, it does not entirely displace the first but refers to it for earlier material.

British Museum. Library. Catalogue of printed books: Academies. London, Clowes, 1885. 1018col., 100col.   **AC2**

Included in alphabetical order under "Academies" in v.1 of the Edwards reprint of the British Museum *Catalogue of printed books* (AA67).

A useful historical record. In two parts: (1) Catalogue of the publications of societies, arranged alphabetically by place with subarrangement by name of society; (2) Alphabetical index of names of societies.

The listings for academies in the new British Museum *Catalogue* (AA67) are scattered throughout rather than being collected in a single volume.

Buchanan, Mary Elizabeth (Torrance). World directory of women's organisations. London, Directory, [1953]. 222p, xxxiip.   **AC3**

Arranged alphabetically by country, with an introductory section in international organizations (p.13–28). For each organization are given address, foundation date, membership, officers, objects and activities, affiliation. 136 countries are covered. An index by country and organization, arranged in the order of the text, but no general alphabetical or subject indexes.

Buttress, F. A. World list of abbreviations of scientific, technological and commercial organizations. 2d ed. London, Leonard Hill; N.Y., Hafner, 1960. 300p.   **AC4**

1st ed. 1954.

A listing of more than 2500 abbreviations followed by the full name and address of the organization. For non-English entries, an English translation follows the title. Due to transliteration difficulties, Russian abbreviations are omitted.

Directory of non-governmental organisations offering assistance in the developing countries. Rome, Centre for Labour and Social Studies, 1964– .   **AC5**

Arranged alphabetically by western European country, listing and describing the various educational and research associations which give aid to other countries.

Gt.Brit. Central Office of Information. Reference Division. Guide to international organizations. London, 1953– . Loose-leaf.   **AC6**

Pt.1, Governmental organizations; pt.2, Nongovernmental organizations.

Information for each organization usually includes: headquarters, membership, creation and purpose, organization and activities, etc.

Index generalis; general yearbook of universities and of higher educational institutions, academies, . . . scientific institutes, . . . learned societies . . . Paris, Dunod, 1920– 39; 1953–55. Annual.   **AC7**

For description *see* CB59.

International congress calendar, 1960/61– . Brussels, Union of Internat. Assoc., 1961– . Annual.   **AC8**

Title also in French: *Calendrier des congrès internationaux.* Introductory notes in English and French.

Lists projected meetings of international congresses, for about five years. Includes a classified index of organizations, a geographical index, and a subject key-word index.

International Institute of Differing Civilizations. Répertoire international des centres d'étude des civilisations et de leurs publications. International guide to study centers on civilizations and their publications. Bruxelles, 1955. 156p.   **AC9**

Gives name of institution, address, director, object, periodical publications, nonperiodic publications, etc.

International organisations. Amsterdam, J. H. de Bussy, 1960. 99p.   **AC10**

Gives fairly detailed information about some 75 economic, social, and scientific organizations of special importance to western Europe.

Ljunggren, Florence and **Geddes, Charles L.** An international directory of institutes and societies interested in the Middle East. Amsterdam, Djambatan, 1962. 159p.   **AC11**

A listing with descriptive information, by country, of some 350 societies, institutes, university departments, etc. from all parts of the world which are interested in research, or in advanced instruction in any subject pertaining to the Middle East.

Minerva. Jahrbuch der gelehrten Welt, 1891/92–1913/ 14, 1920–38, 1952–56. Strassburg, Trübner, 1891–1914; Berlin, de Gruyter, 1920–38; 1952–56.   **AC12**

Includes concise information about learned societies, museums, etc. throughout the world. For full description *see* CB62.

Minerva-Handbücher. Ergänzungen zu "Minerva," Jahrbuch der gelehrten Welt. Berlin, de Gruyter, 1927– .   **AC13**

Contents: 1. Abt. *Die Bibliotheken:* Bd.1, Deutsches Reich. 1929; Bd.2, Österreich. 1932; Bd.3, Schweiz. 1934.

2. Abt. *Die Archive:* Bd.1, Deutsches Reich, Dänemark, Estland, Finnland, Lettland, Litauen, Luxemburg, Niederlande, Norwegen, Österreich, Schweden, Schweiz. 1932.

3. Abt. *Die deutschen Museen:* Bd.1, Die Museen in Bayern. 1939; Bd.2, Die Museen in Nordwest-Deutschland. 1942.

4. Abt. *Die gelehrten Gesellschaften:* Bd.1, Die deutschen Kommissionen und Vereine für Geschichte und Altertumskunde. 1940.

National Council of Women of the United States. International directory of women's organizations. N.Y., Research and Action Associates, 1963. [v.p.] il.   **AC14**

Gives information on international and American women's organizations, including name, purpose, date of founding, officers, address, membership, affiliations, etc. In six groupings; no index.

Pan American Union. Division of General Information. Pan American associations in the United States: a directory with supplementary lists of other associations, inter-American and general. 4th ed. rev. Wash., 1962. 52p. il.   **AC15**

1st ed. 1955.

Title varies: 1st–2d ed., *Pan American societies in the United States.*

Union of International Associations. Les congrès internationaux de 1681 à 1899, liste complète. International congresses, 1681 to 1899, full list. Bruxelles, 1960. 76p. (Documents, no.8; Publ. no.164)   **AC16**

Chronological arrangement of more than 1400 congresses giving name, place of meeting, and dates, with key-word indexes in French and in English.

—— Les congrès internationaux de 1900 à 1919, liste complète. International congresses 1900 to 1919, full list. Bruxelles, 1964. 143p. (Publ. no.188)   **AC17**

Treats 2528 international congresses. Includes cumulative subject index in English and French, for both volumes.

—— International initialese; guide to initials in current international use. Enl. 2d ed. Sigles internationaux; répertoire alphabétique des abréviations d'usage courant. Bruxelles, 1963. 48p. (Publ. no.182)   **AC18**

Initials used by international organizations now in existence or having ceased operations only recently.

—— The 1,978 international organizations founded since the Congress of Vienna: chronological list, with an introduction by G. P. Speeckart. Brussels, 1957. 204p. (Documents, no.7, 1957)   **AC19**

A chronological list 1815–1956 (with two earlier listings for 1693 and 1783).

United Nations Educational, Scientific and Cultural Organization. Directory of cultural relations services. Répertoire des services de relations culturelles. Repertorio de los servicios de relaciones culturales. Paris, 1959– . Loose-leaf.   **AC20**

Provides information on the structure and activities of national and regional cultural relations services. In three parts: (1) governmental services; (2) intergovernmental services; and (3) international nongovernmental services.

White, Lyman Cromwell. International nongovernmental organizations; their purposes, methods, and accomplishments . . . assisted by Marie Ragonetti Zocca. New Brunswick, N.J., Rutgers Univ. Pr., 1951. 325p.   **AC21**

Covers the period from the middle of the 19th century . . . to the beginning of World War II.

Each chapter covers a type of organization (e.g., communications, transport, and travel; the arts and sciences; religion; social welfare; sports; etc.), and there is an index by names of individual organizations.

Notes and references, p.279–304.

World list of future international meetings . . . June 1959– , prep. by the International Organizations Section. Wash., Reference Dept., Lib. of Congress, 1959– . Monthly, and quarterly. **AC22**

Pt.1, Science, technology, agriculture, medicine; pt.2, Social, cultural, commercial, humanistic.

Lists future meetings which are "internationally organized, financed, and/or sponsored."

Through June 1962, each issue covered projected meetings for three years; thereafter, only the quarterly issues (Sept., Dec., March, June) contain a record of all meetings for the three-year span, and the interim monthly issues include only the new meetings and changes in previously listed meetings.

Indexed by subject, by sponsor, and by place of meeting.

World of learning, 1947– . London, Europa Publs., 1947– . **AC23**

For complete entry *see* CB69.

UNITED STATES

Bibliography

Metropolitan Research Company. Association index: a source-list of directories and other publications listing associations. Los Angeles 55, Calif., Box 5345 Metropolitan Station, 1958. 122p. **AC24**

Lists alphabetically 1083 directories which list associations in all subject fields, with an index giving subject, association names and abbreviations, publication titles, and authors.

Directories

Asia Society, Inc. American institutions and organizations interested in Asia: a reference directory. 2d ed. Ed., Ward Morehouse; asst. ed., Edith Ehrman. N.Y., Taplinger, 1961. 581p. **AC25**

1st ed. 1957.

Gives descriptions of almost 1000 Asian programs (with full information on their organization, activities, publications, etc.) in universities, religious and educational organizations, foundations, museums, libraries, scientific and professional groups, etc.

Bowker, Richard Rogers. Publications of societies; a provisional list of the publications of American scientific, literary, and other societies from their organization. N.Y., Publishers' Weekly, 1899. 181p. **AC26**

Gives name of society, institution, or college, with date of founding, address, and lists of publications. Still occasionally useful for historical information about 19th-century organizations.

Directory of university research bureaus and institutes. 1st ed. Detroit, Gale Research, 1960. 199p. **AC27**

Subtitle: A guide to college and university sponsored bureaus, institutes, experiment stations, laboratories and other research organizations established on a permanent basis and carrying on a continuing research program: agriculture, business, conservation, education, engineering, government and public affairs, labor, law, life sciences, mathematics, science and technology, social sciences.

Classified, with indexes by sponsoring institution and by geographic location.

Encyclopedia of associations. 4th ed. Detroit, Gale Research, 1964. 2v. **AC28**

1st ed. 1956.

Contents: v.1, National organizations of the United States; v.2, Geographic and executive index.

A classified listing with descriptions of more than 12,500 associations including: trade and business; agricultural; governmental; scientific, engineering, and technical; educational and cultural; social welfare; health and medical; public affairs; fraternal, nationality and ethnic; religious; patriotic; athletics and sports; labor unions; chambers of commerce; Greek letter societies, etc.

Alphabetical and key-word index. v.2 includes a geographic index arranged by state and city, and an executive index listing alphabetically the chief executives of the organizations recorded in v.1.

—— v.3, New associations. no.1, Dec. 1964– . Looseleaf.

To be published periodically to supplement the 1964 edition by listing new associations and older associations not previously listed.

Foundation directory. Ed.1– . N.Y., Russell Sage Foundation, 1960– . **AC29**

For full information *see* CA35.

Griffin, Appleton Prentiss Clark. Bibliography of American historical societies (the United States and the Dominion of Canada). 2d ed. rev. and enl. Wash., 1907. (In Amer. Historical Assoc. Annual report, 1905. v.2) **AC30**

A very important list, useful both for information about the societies included and as an index to the contents of their publications.

For full description *see* DB15.

AUSTRIA

Jahrbuch der österreichischen Wissenschaft, 1947/48– . Wien, Österreichischer Bundesverlag für Unterricht, Wissenschaft und Kunst, 1948– . Biennial. **AC31**

At head of title: Österreichische Akademie der Wissenschaft.

Lists academies, universities, libraries, museums, societies, etc., with their officers, address, history, and general information; there is also a classed listing of learned journals, giving addresses but no bibliographical data.

BELGIUM

Belgium. Service Belge des Échanges Internationaux. Liste des sociétés savantes et littéraires de Belgique. Bruxelles, 1960. 141p. [Its Publ. no.9] **AC32**

Gives information on officers, membership, publications, purposes, etc.

BULGARIA

Bulgarska Akademiia na Naukite. Tsentralna Biblioteka. Opis na izdaniiata na Bulgarskata Akademiia na Naukite. 1869–1953. Sofiia, 1956. 535p. **AC33**

Added title page in French: Bibliographie des publications de l'Académie des Sciences de Bulgarie, 1869–1953.

FRANCE

Caron, Pierre and **Jaryc, Marc.** Répertoire des sociétés françaises de sciences philosophiques, historiques, philologiques et juridiques. Publié par la Fédération des

Sociétés Françaises de Sciences Philosophiques, Historiques, Philologiques et Juridiques. Paris, Maison du Livre Français, 1938. 280p.   **AC34**

Gives name, date of founding, address, officers, number of members, publications, etc. Arranged geographically with indexes of persons, places, etc.

Lasteyrie du Saillant, Robert Charles, *Comte de.* Bibliographie générale des travaux historiques et archéologiques publiés par les sociétés savantes de la France, dressée sous les auspices du Ministère de l'Instruction Publique. Paris, Impr. Nationale, 1888–1918. 6v. **AC35**

Publication of the Comité des Travaux Historiques et Scientifiques. Issued in parts, 1885–1918.

v.1–4 cover the literature published to the year 1885; v.5–6, 1886–1900.

A monumental undertaking, the most important work on French societies. Arranged alphabetically first by *département,* then by town, and under each by society. For each society gives: brief history, changes of name, suspensions, mergers, etc.; full titles, dates, etc. of all of its publications; full contents of each volume. An index of societies (arranged by *département*) at the end of v.6 links together references to the same society in the main part and the supplement. Includes also societies in the French colonies and French societies abroad. Most useful at present for the historical matter about the societies and for the titles, collation, and contents of the sets of their publications, but cannot be used rapidly for the analytical material. An alphabetical author and subject index was projected but never published. Continued on the same plan and scale by the following:

Bibliographie annuelle des travaux historiques et archéologiques publiés par les sociétés savantes de la France . . . 1901/02–1909/10. Paris, Impr. Nationale, 1906–14. v.1–3 in 9 pts.   **AC36**

Each volume consists of three annual issues.

Contents: v.1, 1901/02–1903/04; v.2, 1904/05–1906/07; v.3, 1907/08–1909/10.

An annual continuation of the above, listing in the nine annuals 42,612 analyticals. Indexes to be noted: v.3, no.3, 1909/10, has general index of societies (but not of analyticals) in v.1–3; v.1, no.1, 1901/02, has both an author and a subject index to the analytical material in that issue. Continued by:

Bibliographie générale des travaux historiques et archéologiques, publiés par les sociétés savantes de la France; dressée sous les auspices du Ministère de l'Éducation Nationale par René Gandilhon . . . Période 1910–1940. Paris, Impr. Nationale, 1944–61. 5v.   **AC37**

Follows the plan of the original work with slightly increased coverage, adding to history and archaeology such related materials as geography, folklore, prehistoric studies, obituaries, etc.

GERMANY

Domay, Friedrich. Handbuch der deutschen wissenschaftlichen Gesellschaften; einschliesslich zahlreicher Forschungsinstitute und Arbeitsgemeinschaften in der Bundesrepublik Deutschland. Wiesbaden, Franz Steiner Verlag, 1964. 751p.   **AC38**

Detailed information about German scientific and learned societies covering: natural sciences, technology, economics, commerce, building, social sciences, law, medicine, and other learned societies.

Gives name, address, officers, foundation, aims, organization, periodicals, membership, bibliographical references, etc.

Müller, Johannes. Die wissenschaftlichen Vereine und Gesellschaften Deutschlands im neunzehnten Jahrhundert; Bibliographie ihrer Veröffentlichungen seit ihrer Begründung bis auf die Gegenwart. Berlin, Asher, 1883–87; Behrend, 1917. v.1–2.   **AC39**

A useful record of 19th-century societies and their publications.

Contents: v.1, to about 1882; v.2, 1882–1914.

Contents of each volume: (1) Short classified list of societies; (2) Main list arranged alphabetically by place and under place by society, giving for each society a list of its publications with record of what constitutes a complete set for the period covered, note of indexes, names of editors, etc., and, for the monographic sets, contents by author and title; (3) Alphabetical index of titles of periodicals, names of societies, editors, and authors.

Stifterverband für die deutsche Wissenschaft. Vademecum deutscher Forschungsstätten. . . . unter Beratung der deutschen Forschungsgemeinschaft. Bonn, Scheur und Kroth, 1954. 458p.   **AC40**

Lists German research institutes and learned societies in various fields, arranged by class, giving name, address, chief officer, subject area, etc. Indexes by place and subject.

GREAT BRITAIN

Handley-Taylor, Geoffrey. Literary, debating and dialect societies of Great Britain, Ireland and France, comprising a directory of existing and dissolved societies with an index to the histories and archives in the Library of the Taylor Education Institution of Colorado. Hull, Lotus Pr., 1951–54. 5 pts.   **AC41**

Information restricted mainly to date of foundation, officers, and address, with no indication of activities. Societies whose history or archives have been presented to the Taylor Educational Institution are marked with a dagger.

Keeling, Guy Willing. Trusts and foundations; a select guide to organizations and grant-making bodies operating in Great Britain and the Commonwealth, ed. by Thomas Landau. Cambridge, Bowes and Bowes, 1953. 194p.   **AC42**

Gives information about some 1000 foundations and trusts, including, when possible: name, address, trustees, history, purpose, activities, conditions, grants, capital, publications, etc.

The main list is alphabetical. Indexes: (1) Classified (by Dewey Decimal Classification); (2) Alphabetical subject. Appendix 1, Government grants to voluntary agencies; Appendix 2, Bibliography.

Scientific and learned societies of Great Britain: a handbook compiled from official sources. London, Allen & Unwin, 1884– . v.1– . Annual.   **AC43**

Title varies. Publisher varies.

For full information *see* EA158.

Trade associations and professional bodies of the United Kingdom; a directory and classified index. 1962– . Comp. by Patricia Millard. London, C.B.D. Research, 1962– .   **AC44**

In two sections: (1) alphabetical, and (2) classified. Gives name, address, and telephone number only.

ITALY

Maylender, Michele. Storia delle accademie d'Italia, con prefazione di Luigi Rava. Bologna, Cappelli, 1926–30. 5v.   **AC45**

A dictionary of Italian academies of all periods and kinds, arranged alphabetically by the significant word in the academy's name. Fuller for historical than for bibliographical information; useful particularly for material about old or obscure organizations.

—————— "Repertorio alfabetico e bibliografico" by Giuseppe Gabrieli. (In Accademie e biblioteche d'Italia 10:71–99. marzo/aprile 1936).

JAPAN

Japan. National Commission for UNESCO. Handbook of scientific societies in Japan. [Tokyo], 1954. 49p. **AC46**

Covers science, engineering, agriculture, medicine, and comprehensive learned societies.

For each society gives name, address, staff, history, purpose, publications, membership, meetings, and library.

—— Culture sciences. 1956. 36p.   **AC46a**

Covers literature, philosophy, history, law, and economics.

MEXICO

Salas Ortega, Guadalupe. Directorio de asociaciones e institutos científicos y culturales de la República Mexicana. México, Dirección General de Publicaciones, 1959. 242p.   **AC47**

At head of title: Universidad Nacional Autónoma de México. Departamento de Psicopedagogía.

A directory of cultural and scientific associations, universities, institutions, etc. in alphabetical arrangement, with a geographical index and supplementary lists of libraries and museums.

POLAND

Informator nauki polskiej. 1958– . Warszawa, Państowowe Wydawnictwo Naukowe, 1958– . Annual. **AC48**

A directory of Poland's learned societies, universities, scientific institutes, museums, and archives, giving addresses, names of directors and other personnel, and title and periodicity of serial publications. The name index, with addresses, is a substantial directory of Polish scientists. Recent volumes also include an index to names of institutions.

An English edition is entitled *Polish research guide.*

Polska Akademia Nauk. Directory. [Warsaw], Ossolineum, [1957]. 128p.   **AC49**

A directory in English of the Polish Academy of Sciences and its subdivisions and allied societies as established in 1952, with a list of serial and periodical publications and name index.

Wepsiec, Jan. Polish institutions of higher learning. N.Y., Polish Inst. of Arts and Sciences in America, 1959. 110p.   **AC50**

Includes directory-type information on universities and colleges, learned societies, observatories and botanical gardens, museums, libraries and bibliographical centers in Poland, as well as similar institutions maintained by Poles abroad.

PORTUGAL

Centro de Documentação Científica, Lisbon. Instituições científicas, literárias e artísticas portuguesas. Lisboa, Inst. de Alte Cultura, 1954–58. 2v. (Its Publ. no.55)   **AC51**

Contents: Série A (completa). 4. ed. 1958. 237p.; Série B (seleccionada). 1954. 54p.

UNION OF SOVIET SOCIALIST REPUBLICS

Akademiia Nauk SSSR. Biblioteka. Bibliografiia Izdanii Akademii Nauk SSSR; ezhegodnik. v.1– . 1956– . Moskva, 1957– . Annual.   **AC52**

Added title page in English *Bibliography of publications of the Academy of Sciences of the USSR: a yearbook.*

All publications of the USSR Academy of Sciences for a given year are recorded under departments and institutes of the Union Academy and its affiliates. Publications of republic academies are not included. Articles in symposia and irregular serials (transactions, learned papers, etc.) are analyzed by author and title. The name index includes authors of articles in regularly appearing journals, with abbreviation of periodical title and number.

A D

Encyclopedias

❧ A good encyclopedia, or collection of encyclopedias, forms the backbone of much of the reference work in any library. Such books should be selected with care and used intelligently, with full understanding on the part of reference assistants of the relative merits and defects of the different works. The making of an authoritative encyclopedia is a very expensive undertaking, calling for heavy outlay for experienced writers, good editorial planning and oversight, and accurate printing and proofreading. Such work cannot be done cheaply, and reputable publishers recognize this fact and spend what is necessary to produce an authoritative, well-edited work. However, as the immediate profits from cheap work are large and as many buyers do not discriminate between good and poor encyclopedias, unscrupulous publishers will sometimes utilize cheap hack writers, or reprint, with only slight changes, out-of-date material. Such encyclopedias are made only to sell, and, from the point of view of any real authority, are nearly worthless though perhaps costing almost as much as the really good works.

Continuous revision. Most of the good, general encyclopedias, including the juvenile encyclopedias, are now following the "continuous revision" policy, which means that instead of publishing thoroughly revised numbered editions at spaced intervals, editorial staffs are kept constantly at work surveying subjects and planning revision, so that with each annual printing changes are made to bring some articles up to date. Many of the encyclopedias try to revise all articles in a given subject field at the same time, but in some cases topics may be changed in one part of the work and left unchanged in others. Even with careful editing this method results in inconsistencies and some unevenness, as the editors themselves admit. A large portion of the material is stable and may be left untouched for several years; other parts are revised as deemed necessary, frequently in rotation over a period of years. Some subjects are changed with almost every printing, dates and statistics are altered frequently, and new facts and developments added. Sometimes whole articles are entirely rewritten, either by the original contributor or by someone else; material may be cut from one part of an article to make room to insert something new in another part; and in some cases short articles may be omitted entirely. In some years a greater amount of revision may be made than in others.

Purchasing an encyclopedia. An encyclopedia should never be purchased without a full knowledge of its character and an examination of the work itself. If the librarian does not have the requisite knowledge or the opportunity to make a careful comparison, purchase should be deferred until the book has been examined and reviewed by experts. The reviews in *Subscription books bulletin reviews* (AA309a) will often be helpful. For encyclopedias using continuous revision, librarians will need to develop a buying policy and to decide on how often sets should be replaced. It is frequently better to depend on current publications and yearbooks for recent events and information and to use encyclopedias for the articles of basic and lasting importance.

If a library cannot afford the latest edition of a good expensive encyclopedia, it is better to buy a secondhand copy of a recent printing of a thoroughly good work than a cheap new encyclopedia of the hack-work or commercial type. An encyclopedia that was once good is never entirely superseded, and this fact should be taken into account if the publisher of a new work or a new edition offers a discount on the new edition for the return of the old. The small library may be justified in giving up its old edition, but the large library which does much reference work should keep one copy each of such older works. These are useful in supplying: (1) information as to the condition or view of a given subject, art, or science at the date when the book was compiled, and (2) minor biographical and other articles omitted from the later edition to make space for new material.

Testing an encyclopedia. Read the preface carefully to ascertain the purpose and scope of the encyclopedia. What do the editors intend to do? For whom is the work prepared? For advanced scholars? For popular use? For schools? For children? If designed for schools or colleges, are the contents geared to curriculum needs and to the indicated age levels? What is the scope? How were the topics to be treated chosen? How much revision is noted?

Having read the preface, check the volumes to see how well the promises have been carried out. If the set is a new work, compare it with other works of the same general size and type. If it is a revised edition, compare it with the preceding edition and sometimes with even earlier editions to test the amount and kind of revision. Check certain sections in each, comparing articles for changes in wording, dates, omissions, additions, etc. Is the article signed by the same writer as in previous editions or has it been written by another? Have the bibliographies been revised and new titles added? Read articles on subjects with which you are familiar and check them for accuracy, adequacy, and up-to-dateness.

In general, test the work for authority, bibliographies, arrangement, and physical make-up as follows:

I. Authority
  A. Editor—is he capable and experienced and has he really edited the book himself or merely allowed the use of his name?
  B. Contributors—are the articles signed? Are the writers outstanding in their fields?
  C. Publisher—is he well known, reputable, and experienced?
  D. Plan—is there a definite plan followed consistently throughout and showing editorial supervision?
    1. Are articles full and adequate or too brief?
    2. Do the articles show balance in selection and treatment? Longer articles for important subjects, briefer ones for less important?
    3. Does the work maintain a high standard throughout?
  E. Accuracy and up-to-dateness
    1. Is it an entirely new work?
    2. Is it based on an earlier work?
      a) Has it been completely revised and reset?
      b) Does it use the continuous revision policy?
      c) Have old plates been used with only slight alterations?
      d) Has revision been made consistently throughout?
    3. Are articles dated?
      a) Is information dated for such frequently changing figures as population, statistics, election figures, crop reports, wages, etc?
      b) Are maps dated?
  F. Viewpoint—does it show signs of national, political, religious, or other point of view which influences the slant or shows bias or prejudice?

II. Bibliographies
  A. Purpose
    1. Are they to serve as sources for the authority of the article and for additional information?
    2. Are they reading lists on given subjects?
  B. Arrangement
    1. Are they appended to the articles?
    2. Are they grouped together in a single volume?
  C. Adequacy
    1. Is the bibliographical information adequate and given in good form? (Minimum requirements: author's name, with initials, title, place, date.)
    2. Are titles of recent date included?
    3. If it is a revised work, have the bibliographies been revised and new works added?
    4. Are they arranged so as to be easily usable?
    5. Are books in foreign languages included?

III. Arrangement
  A. Alphabetical
    1. Are there long articles covering large fields or many short articles on small subjects?
    2. Is the arrangement "letter by letter" or "word by word"?
    3. Is there a comprehensive index which leads to small subjects within larger articles?
  B. Topical
    1. Are there tables of contents showing the arrangement?
    2. Is there an alphabetical index?

IV. Format and physical make-up
  A. General appearance
    1. Paper, typography

a) Is the paper of good quality? Will it withstand heavy usage?

b) Is the typography clear, of good size, and well spaced?

c) Are the headings clear, simple, and easy to use?

2. Illustrations, plates, diagrams, maps, etc.

a) Are these of good quality and well reproduced?

b) Do they amplify and explain points in the articles they accompany or are they merely used to add to the general attractiveness of the book? Are they adjacent to the text they illustrate?

c) Is the authority noted for the maps, giving date, scale, source, etc.?

3. Binding

a) Is it substantial and suited for hard wear?

b) Are the volumes numbered clearly on the spines?

c) If arrangement is alphabetical, is there clear indication of coverage on the spines, i.e., are there sufficient letters given so that it is obvious where one volume ends and the next begins?

d) If arrangement is topical, are contents noted on spines?

B. Special features

1. Does the set include supplementary lists or appendixes?

2. Are there errata lists?

3. Does it include special lists of abbreviations used?

4. Does it indicate pronunciation?

5. How are cross references given?

a) In the body of the work?

b) In the index?

c) Are they accurate and usable or are there "blind" references?

V. Method of keeping the work up to date

A. Supplements

1. If there are supplements, how often are they issued?

2. Are they arranged in the same manner as the basic set?

3. Are articles in the basic set brought up to date in the supplement?

4. Are there cross references to the main work?

5. Do the new articles maintain the standard of the original?

B. Annuals

1. Is the standard of authority maintained? Are articles signed?

2. Is there any connection maintained with the basic work, by means of cross references or other device?

3. How promptly are volumes issued?

4. Does the date given in the title refer to the year covered or the year published?

5. Is there any cumulated index to preceding volumes?

AMERICAN AND ENGLISH

(In these listings, encyclopedias using the "continuous revision" policy are entered without dates.)

Encyclopedia Americana. N.Y., Chicago, Encyclopedia Americana. 30v. il. **AD1**

History: 1st ed. 1903–4, 16v. unpaged; several partial revisions, especially an edition in 22v., published 1912 under the title *The Americana,* which included some new articles and changes in others. The 1918–20 edition was a complete revision, reset throughout with much new material, and is the basis of succeeding editions. Now uses the continuous revision policy (*see* p.81).

A good, comprehensive encyclopedia for general use.

Important articles are signed with full name and title of the contributor. Some have bibliographies, though often not brought up to date. Illustrations are numerous, maps are included with articles, and references to them are included in the index. Alphabeting is word by word. Pronunciation is frequently indicated. For the most part, articles are short, and on small subjects, but many articles of some length are included.

The *Americana* has always been particularly strong in its information about American towns and cities. Other special features are the evaluations of particular books, operas, musical compositions, works of art, etc.

Since 1943 the index volume (v.30) has been an alphabetical index arranged in dictionary form, instead of the classed index of previous editions. It is kept to date with each printing and should always be consulted in order that pertinent material treated in various parts of the work will not be overlooked.

Encyclopaedia Britannica. A new survey of universal knowledge. Chicago, Encyclopaedia Britannica. 24v. il. **AD2**

v.1–23, A–Z; v.24, Atlas and index.

History: 1st ed. 1768–71. 3v.; 9th ed. 1875–89. 25v.; 10th ed., a supplement to the 9th ed., with a combined index to the main work and the supplement, 1902–3. 10v.; 11th ed. 1911. 29v.; 12th ed. 1922. 3v. and 13th ed. 1926. 3v., not revisions of the whole work but supplements to the 11th ed.; 14th ed. 1929. Now uses the continuous revision policy (*see* p.81), and does not number editions.

The most famous encyclopedia in English, and for some purposes the best. Until modified in the 20th-century editions, it differed from most European and American encyclopedias in its fundamental plan, which called for a collection of important monographs on large subjects by specialists, often very scholarly and important, with good bibliographies, excellent illustrations, but no separate treatment of small subjects and no biographical sketches of living persons. Small subjects were treated only as parts of larger subjects and could be found only through the index. This plan, which was seen most typically in the 9th edition, was modified somewhat in the supplementary 10th edition and still more, to meet modern demands, in the 11th edition. With the 14th edition the traditional monographic policy was largely abandoned in favor of shorter articles under more specific headings.

Although the library fortunate enough to have sets of all editions of the Britannica will still make occasional use of the early editions for older subjects or points of view, biographies, etc., the 1st–8th editions are now mainly of only historical interest. The 9th and 11th editions and their supplements, however, must still be used. The 9th edition, under the able editorship of William Robertson Smith, was the high watermark of the *Britannica,* and its scholarly articles may be used profitably for subjects where recent information is not essential. The 11th edition, although more popular in style than the great 9th edition, is scholarly and carefully edited, and should still keep its place on the shelves of the reference room.

Recent editions: The 14th edition, first published in 1929, was revised, reset, and reorganized to include short articles on small subjects as well as many long articles. Some of the latter have been carried over from the 9th and 11th editions, sometimes revised and abridged but still carrying the signature of the original author. Although now essentially an American work, the set still reflects traces of its British origins, e.g., in spelling, in some headings, and in the relative length of treatment of many British topics. As noted above, since 1929 the continuous revision policy (*see* p.81) has been used, and editions are no longer numbered.

A useful and generally well-made encyclopedia, with long, detailed articles on many subjects. Articles are signed with initials, the list of contributors being given in the index volume. Alphabeting is letter by letter; pronunciation is not indicated. Maps are included in the index volume, with a separate index. Bibliographies appended to some articles include titles in various languages, and give place of publication and date. Frequently, even if the article has been rewritten, the bibliographies have not been brought up to date. In recent years the tendency has been to shorten the bibliographies and to omit scholarly works in favor of those easily available.

v.24 includes a comprehensive, detailed index which must always be used in order that all pertinent material may be found.

—— 10 eventful years; a record of events of the years preceding, including and following World War II, 1937 through 1946; prep. under the editorial direction of Walter Yust, ed. of Encyclopaedia Britannica. Chicago, Encyclopaedia Britannica, 1947. 4v. il.

An alphabetically arranged encyclopedia covering events, personalities, and developments in science, technology, literature, etc. of a crucial 10 years. Does not supersede the annual *Britannica book of the year* (AD9) for the period, as many articles in the annuals are not included, but it cumulates, summarizes, and surveys the events of the period. Includes useful chronologies, tables, and summaries. Many articles are signed, bibliographies are included, and illustrations are clear, as is the typography. Comprehensive index.

Chambers's Encyclopaedia. New ed. London, N.Y., Oxford Univ. Pr., 1959. 15v. il.   **AD3**

History: 1st ed., ed. by Dr. Andrew Findlater, 1850–68; new ed., recast by David Patrick, 1888–92; 1923–27 rev. and reset; new ed. 1950.

A completely new edition of this well-known British encyclopedia with a new format, new selection of articles, and a reapportionment of space was published in 1950. Later editions are revisions of this. It "addresses itself to the educated layman who has some general grounding in a variety of subjects from which he can proceed to more exact and detailed information in a special field."

As in previous editions, many short articles on small subjects appear. Most articles are signed with initials. Contributors include outstanding scholars, primarily British. Population figures are dated, illustrations are good but not distinguished, pronunciation is not indicated.

Not all articles have bibliographies, but when given they usually include the standard works on the topic as well as recent publications.

v.15, Maps and indexes, includes: maps by John Bartholomew and Sons, with a section of historical maps; an index to the maps which gives very brief gazetteer information; a list of contributors with titles of principal articles contributed by each; a classified list of articles; and a general subject index to the whole work with many cross references.

Collier's Encyclopedia. N.Y., Collier. 24v. il., maps.
                                                                         AD4

1st ed. 1949–51. 20v.
v.24, Bibliography and index.
Uses the continuous revision policy (*see* p.81).

A usable, readable encyclopedia for the student and layman. Aimed at the college level; is more advanced than the juvenile encyclopedias in its treatment and choice of subjects, but its coverage is not so great and information is not usually so detailed as in the *Britannica* (AD2) or the *Americana* (AD1). The style is popular, clear, and concise. Many articles are long and well developed, others are short under small subjects. In recent printings all articles are signed with full names. Alphabeting is letter by letter. Pronunciation is indicated by the international phonetic alphabet. Illustrations, both in color and in black and white, are pertinent and well reproduced; maps are prepared by Rand McNally.

Bibliographies are not given at the ends of articles but are grouped together in the last volume, where they serve as reading lists in the various subject fields. Arranged under broad subjects with subdivisions. Insofar as possible, within each subdivision, general and elementary subjects are treated first, followed by more advanced and specialized works. Titles, starting at high school level and progressing through college level and beyond, were selected with a view to their availability, and therefore most are of a recent date; all are in the English language.

The consolidated index indexes text, illustrations, maps, and bibliography.

Columbia encyclopedia in one volume. 3d ed., ed. by William Bridgwater and Seymour Kurtz. N.Y., Columbia Univ. Pr., 1963. 2388p. il., maps.   **AD5**

1st ed. 1935; 2d ed. 1950.

A compact work, with concise articles planned especially for home and office use and for library use when exhaustive articles by specialists are not needed. Particularly well adapted for quick reference. The 3d edition is thoroughly revised, every article has been reviewed, many have been rewritten, and new ones have been added. Scientific, technical, and economic articles have been brought up to date and new developments included. Particular attention has been given to Africa and Asia. The work is strong in place-names and in biography, including sketches of living persons. Pronunciation is marked. By means of special type, cross references are given to headings where additional information can be found. Brief selected bibliographies, usually consisting of two or three titles of works in English, are appended to many articles. 20 outline maps have been added, as well as 42 pages of drawings, each devoted to a single subject.

Lincoln library of essential information. Buffalo, N.Y., Frontier Pr. 2v. il.   **AD6**

1st ed. 1924.

A serviceable encyclopedia, now revised with every printing. Nonalphabetical. Material is grouped by subject field in compact form, often using graphs, charts, and tables. Alphabetical index.

Useful in home, school, or library.

Encyclopedia annuals

Appleton's Annual cyclopaedia and register of important events . . . v.[1]–15, 1861–75; v.16–35 (n.s., v.1–20), 1876–95; v.36–42 (3d ser., v.1–7), 1896–1902. N.Y., Appleton, 1862–1903. 42v. il.   **AD7**

Index for 1861–75 (v.1–15), 1876. 442p.; Index for 1876–87 (v.16–28; n.s., v.1–12), 1888. 144p. Other indexes included in the set are: Index to n.s. v.1–20, 1876–95, in n.s. v.20, p.769–866; Index to 3d ser. v.1–7, 1896–1902, in 3d ser. v.7, p.845–66.

Published as an annual supplement to the *American cyclopaedia*. Of little use now as a supplement, but still useful for: (1) record of the events of a given year, especially the political, governmental, economic, and military events, which are given with greater detail in this year-by-year record than in later general accounts; volumes covering the Civil War and Reconstruction periods are useful to students of American history; (2) many minor articles, particularly obituaries and biographies, which are either omitted from later encyclopedias or given briefer treatment than in the annual volume for the year when the person was of especial interest.

Americana annual, an encyclopedia of events, 1923– . N.Y., Americana Corp., 1923– . v.1– . il.   **AD8**

The date in the title is the date of publication; the record of events is for the previous year. Serves both as an annual supplement to the *Encyclopedia Americana* (AD1) and as an annual record of progress and events. Contains many biographies and has a necrology list at the end of each volume (position varies). Survey articles are signed with full names and titles of contributors.

Britannica book of the year, 1938– . Chicago, Encyclopaedia Britannica, 1938– . il. Annual. **AD9**

Annual volumes to serve as annual surveys and as supplements to the *Encyclopaedia Britannica* (AD2). The date in the title is the date of publication; the record of events is for the previous year. Includes many signed survey articles as well as short articles under specific headings. Some biography is included. A necrology list is included under Obituaries.

Chambers's Encyclopaedia. World survey. London, Newnes, 1952– . il. Annual. **AD10**

A general survey of world affairs. The main part of the book deals with: international, political, economic, and cultural subjects arranged by subject field; national and local affairs arranged by country; and a short section of biographies and obituaries.

Collier's Yearbook, 1939– , covering the events of 1938– . N.Y., Collier, 1939– . Annual. **AD11**

Title varies: 1938–1940, was called *National yearbook.*

Designed to serve both as a supplement to *Collier's Encyclopedia* (AD4) and as an annual survey. Alphabetically arranged.

New international year book, a compendium of the world's affairs, 1907– . N.Y., Dodd, 1908–31; Funk & Wagnalls, 1932– . v.1– . il. **AD12**

An annual encyclopedia, up to date and authoritative, designed as a supplement to the *New international encyclopaedia* and as an annual record of the progress and events in any subject. Plan and arrangement vary. Recent volumes include signed survey articles and brief biographical sketches. An obituary list is at the back of each volume. The date of the volume is the date of publication; the record of events is for the previous year.

Juvenile

Britannica junior, prep. under the supervision of the editors of the Encyclopaedia Britannica. . . . Chicago, Encyclopaedia Britannica. 15v. il. **AD13**

"Published with the editorial advice of the faculties of the University of Chicago and the University Laboratory School."

Planned for elementary and junior high school levels. First published in 1934 as a reissue, with some alterations, of *Weedon's Modern encyclopedia.* Has since been much revised and now uses the continuous revision policy (*see* p.81).

Articles are written as simply as possible on the subjects in which children are interested. They are not signed, but a list of contributors is given in v.1, with the titles of articles for which they are responsible. Alphabeting is letter by letter. Pronunciation is indicated. Type face is large and clear; illustrations, in color and in black and white, are good but not distinguished. v.1 is a ready-reference index; v.15 includes an atlas section with its own index.

Compton's Pictured encyclopedia and fact-index. Chicago, Compton. 15v. il. **AD14**

Issued annually. Uses the continuous revision policy (*see* p.81).

Subtitle: To inspire ambition, to stimulate the imagination, to provide the inquiring mind with accurate information told in an interesting style, and thus lead into broader fields of knowledge, such is the purpose of this work.

A good juvenile encyclopedia, one of the leading American works in this field. Planned especially for upper elementary and high school use; attempts to keep in close touch with school needs, but is useful also for the adult who needs a somewhat simpler article than that given in the standard encyclopedias for adults.

General policy is to use long articles on large subjects, with smaller subjects analyzed or treated in the Fact-index.

Has a clear, direct style and pays especial attention to illustration, graphic charts, and maps. Indicates pronunciation of unusual words. Alphabeting is letter by letter. Not all articles include bibliographies, but for some, reference outlines for organized study are given, and some include brief bibliographies, sometimes divided into books for younger readers and books for advanced students and teachers.

Instead of a general index volume, a Fact-index at the end of each volume serves as a guide to all volumes for subjects beginning with the letter or letters covered in the volume. The Fact-index is not only an analytical index to all text and illustrative material in the main work, but also includes dictionary-type information, brief biographical sketches, etc. on subjects not treated elsewhere.

Supplemented by the *Compton yearbook: an illustrated factual record of outstanding events.*

Encyclopedia international. 1st ed. N.Y., Grolier, 1963–64. 20v. (v.20, index) **AD15**

A new encyclopedia, contemporary in tone and make-up, designed primarily for the high school student and for family use. The style is clear and concise. Articles are usually short, on small subjects, but some longer survey articles are included; those of more than 150 words are usually signed with full name. Alphabeting is letter by letter. Pronunciation of difficult words is indicated by a simplified phonetic system. Cross references are plentiful. Only a small proportion of the articles include bibliographies. These are usually titles of easily available recent adult works, although earlier standard titles are occasionally noted. Study guides for the major articles give outlines of the subject covered with references to related articles. Illustrations, including color plates, are plentiful, and there are many graphs and charts. The political, historical, physical, and economic maps, prepared by C. S. Hammond, Jeppesen, and others, vary in quality of reproduction.

The index is comprehensive and well organized and should always be used in order to find full information.

World book encyclopedia. . . . Chicago, Field Enterprises Educ. Corp. 20v. il. **AD16**

Issued annually. Uses the continuous revision policy (*see* p.81).

A good juvenile encyclopedia, one of the leading American works in the field; approximates the form and treatment of the standard works for adults and so is especially good for the older child who is nearly ready to use adult material.

Alphabeted word by word. For the most part has short articles on small topics, although some long articles are also included. Articles are signed. There are many cross references to related subjects. Pronunciation is indicated for unusual names and words. Bibliographies are brief but well chosen, sometimes with short annotations. Illustrations and graphs, in color and in black and white, are clear and pertinent.

A separately issued *Reading and study guide* serves as a classified index to the set. It is divided into 44 subject fields with many subdivisions indicating the headings used in the main work.

Supplemented by the *World book year book, an annual supplement.*

FOREIGN LANGUAGE

☙ While a good encyclopedia in English must always be the basis of encyclopedia reference work in a library used by English-speaking readers, foreign encyclopedias offer much that cannot be found in English works—the *Enciclopedia italiana* (AD48), for example, far surpasses any other encyclopedia in the quality and number of its illustrations and contains some articles superior to anything found elsewhere; *Enciclopedia universal (Espasa)* (AD68) is rich in Spanish and Spanish-American subjects, especially biography; *La grande encyclopédie* (AD27) contains articles on topics in European history and literature not available in the same quality in other encyclopedias, while the various editions of *Larousse* (AD28–

AD31) have a wealth of articles on small topics–minor biography, individual works of literature, plays, theaters, and songs–not easily found in other encyclopedias.

In general, library use of such works will be for three main types of questions: (1) to find an article in a foreign language for a reader who does not use English readily; (2) to find a foreign article that is better than the corresponding article in English; or (3) to find something on topics omitted altogether in English encyclopedias–usually topics in biography, topography, history, or literature of the country of origin of the encyclopedia. It is for this third type of question that the foreign encyclopedia is most frequently used in American libraries.

Thus, the user of reference books will often need to make use of the great foreign encyclopedias, but to use them adequately requires a somewhat different technique from that required to use an encyclopedia in English. Theoretically the library assistant should know the language of the encyclopedia, but much can be done with a very slight knowledge of the language if the user has an intelligent "dictionary habit" and will keep certain basic points in mind. Often he does not need to read the article, but merely to find it for a reader who will use it. Without the correct technique, however, he may actually miss an article, even though it is in its proper alphabetical place. Two of the points which the library assistant, with a limited knowledge of foreign languages, needs to keep in mind are: (1) the alphabet of the language he is using, and (2) variations in the forms of names: proper, personal, geographical, etc. The alphabet must be kept in mind because even languages using the Latin alphabet have variations in letters which *must be known* if an article is to be found in its correct alphabetical place. In Spanish, for example, there are two-letter sounds not found in English, Ch and Ll, and a word or name beginning Ch follows Cz; in Norwegian the letter Æ comes after Z; Czech has 41 letters; and other languages show other variations.

Variations in form of proper names must also be kept in mind, especially when the initial letter is affected. The reference assistant looking for an Italian article on Hannibal, for example, will find it under Anibale; if he is looking for articles on St. Stephen, he must look under Étienne in a French encyclopedia, Esteban in a Spanish, Stefano in an Italian. If he is looking for an Italian article on John Adams, he must be prepared to recognize Giovanni Adams; if he is looking for a medieval personage named John, he must search under John, Jean, Jehan, Johann, Johannes, Jan, Giovanni, or other variations according to the language of the reference work he uses. Surnames do not show so great a variation, but their alphabetizing must be watched, e.g., in a Swedish encyclopedia the biography of the German writer Görres will alphabetize at the end of the letter G, many pages after Gy, instead of with Go, as it does in German and English. Geographical names, of course, vary in form also: an Italian article on Florence must be looked for under the Italian Firenze; a Norwegian article on Egypt will be found under Ægypten at the end of the alphabet. Keeping in mind these points about alphabets and forms of names will help even an inexperienced reference assistant to use foreign encyclopedias intelligently.

The *general* encyclopedias in foreign languages are entered below. For encyclopedias *about* a particular country, *see* that country under History and Area Studies (p. 472 ff.).

Brazilian

Encyclopedia e diccionario internacional, organizado e redigido com a collaboração de distinctos homens de sciencia e de lettras brasileiros e portuguezes. W. M. Jackson, ed. Lisboa, Rio de Janeiro, [1919]. 20v. il.   **AD17**

A good popular encyclopedia in Portuguese, general in scope but with special emphasis upon Brazilian names and topics. Contains a large amount of Brazilian biography.

Bulgarian

Bulgarska Akademiia na Naukite. Bulgarska entsiklopediia. Kratka bulgarska entsiklopediia. Sophiia, Izd-vo na Bulgarskata Akademiia na Naukite, 1963– . v.1– . il. (In progress)   **AD18**
v.1, A–Gera.

Czech

Masarykův slovník naučný; lidová encyklopedie všeobecných vědomostí. . . . V Praze, Nákl. "Československého Kompasu," 1925–33. 7v. il.   **AD19**

Contains little bibliography but has many biographies, including those of persons still living.

Ottův slovník naučný. Illustrovaná encyklopædie obecných vědomostí. V Praze, Otto, 1888–1909. 28v. **AD20**
v.1–27, A–Z; v.28, Supplement.

—— Nové doby. Dodatky k velikému Ottovu slovníku naučnému. Redakci vede B. Němec. V Praze, "Novina," 1930–43. v.1–6². il. (In progress?)
v.1–6², A–Užok.
Publisher varies.
The standard Czech encyclopedia. Signed articles, many biographies, some bibliography including works in many languages.
Maps, many folded; town plans; illustrations include plates and line drawings in text.

Danish

Salmonsens Konversationsleksikon. 2. Udg. København, Schultz, 1915–30. 26v. il.   **AD21**

1st edition had title *Salmonsens Store illustrerede Konversationsleksikon.* 1893–1911. 19v.
v.1–25, A–Ø; v.26, Supplement.
The standard Danish encyclopedia, with signed articles, bibliographies, maps, town plans, and illustrations. Marks pronunciation of proper names.
Supplemented by the *Salmonsen Leksikon Tidsskrift.* København, Schultz, 1941–57. Aarg. 1–15. Monthly with biennial indexes. (No index for 1956–57; 10-year index, 1941–1950, pub. 1951)

Hagerups Illustrerede Konversations Leksikon. 4. gennemsete og forøgede Udg. redigeret af P. Engelstoft. København, Hagerup, 1948–53. 10v. il.   **AD22**

1st ed. 1892–1900; 3d ed. 1921–25.
A general encyclopedia with short articles, most of them signed. Little or no bibliography.

Dutch

Winkler Prins Encyclopaedie. 6. geheel nieuwe druk. Amsterdam, Elsevier, 1947–54. 18v. il.   **AD23**

1st ed. 1870–82; 5th edition, 1932–38, had title *Winkler Prins' Algemeene encyclopaedie.*
A standard Dutch work, originally based on Brockhaus, with well-balanced articles, some of them signed; some in-

clude brief bibliographies listing works in various languages. Illustrations and maps are good. Includes town plans. Biographies include living persons. The 6th edition has been completely revised and reset.

—— Supplement- en register. 1955. 496p.

This detailed index supersedes the previous indexes covering v.1–12.

—— Supplement, 1960. 1960. 800p.

P.11–54, International statistical survey; p.55–80, Necrology. The rest of the volume is an alphabetically arranged encyclopedia covering the political, economic, scientific, and social developments of the world from 1950 to 1960. Includes biography.

Eerste Nederlandse systematisch ingerichte encyclopaedie . . . Samengesteld onder leiding van H. J. Pos, J. M. Romem [and others]. Amsterdam, E.N.S.I.E., 1946–60. 12v. il. **AD24**

A classed encyclopedia, each article written by a specialist. Includes bibliographies.

v.10, Lexicon en register; v.11, Supplement; v.12, Lexicon en register, beknopt overzicht der wereldgeschiedenis in synchronistische tabellen.

v.10 includes, in the same alphabet with the index, much encyclopedic information not covered in the main set: e.g., biographical sketches, gazetteer information about places, definitions of historical terms; v.12 is an index to v.11 (the supplement) and also a lexicon adding new entries and bringing up to date material in the lexicon in v.10. Includes much gazetteer information.

Finnish

Otavan iso tietosanakirja; encyclopaedia fennica. Helsinki, Kustannusosakeyhtiö Otava, 1960–63. v.1–6. il. (In progress) **AD25**

1st ed. 1931–39. 15v.

v.1–6, A–Pyra.

A general encyclopedia in Finnish, with many short articles, often signed; many illustrations in text; plates and maps. Often indicates pronunciation of foreign names. Includes biographical articles of people of many nations, including living persons.

Otavan yksiosainen tietosanakirja. Päätoimittaja Kalle Vaarnas toimitussihteeri Anja Hurme. Helsinki, Otava, 1960. 4266col. il. **AD26**

Brief articles; small, clear illustrations.

French

La grande encyclopédie, inventaire raisonné des sciences, des lettres et des arts, par une société de savants et de gens de lettres; sous la direction de Berthelot, Derenbourg, [etc.]. Paris, Lamirault, 1886–1902. 31v. il. **AD27**

Secrétaire général: v.1–18, F. Camille Dreyfus; v.19–31, André Berthelot.

v.23–31 published by Société Anonyme de La Grande Encyclopédie.

The most important 19th-century French encyclopedia with authoritative signed articles, excellent bibliographies, and many entries under small subjects. Out of date now for sciences, etc., but an excellent authority in other fields, especially for medieval and Renaissance subjects, and for literature, history, etc. of continental Europe. Very good for French and other continental biographical and gazetteer information. The bibliographies are especially important. Has fewer illustrations and plates than recent English or American encyclopedias.

Larousse, Pierre. Grand dictionnaire universel du XIXᵉ siècle français. Paris, Larousse, [1865–90?]. 17v. **AD28**

v.1–15, A–Z; v.16, suppl. A–Z; v.17, suppl. A–Z.

A famous encyclopedia, well edited and well written—one of first importance and still useful in many cases. Combines the features of dictionary and encyclopedia, and as an encyclopedia is an extreme example of entry under small subject, including many articles on individual works of literature— e.g., poems, plays, novels, romances, newspapers, periodicals, songs, etc., entered under their titles—and a very large amount of minor biography not included in other general encyclopedias. Gives words and music (melody only) of about 600 songs. Good for questions of European literature, biography, and history.

—— Larousse mensuel illustré, revue encyclopédique universelle, pub. sous la direction de Claude Augé et Paul Augé, 1907–57. Paris, Larousse, 1907–57. v.1–14 and index to v.1–7. il. **AD30**

v.1, 1907–10; v.2–12, 3 years to a volume; v.13, 1952–55; v.14, 1956–57 (v.11, 1938–mai 1940 and v.11, no.400, 1938–47). Ceased publication.

An excellent monthly encyclopedia designed as a supplement to the *Nouveau Larousse illustré* (1898–1907. 8v.). Each monthly number is alphabetical, with a final alphabetical index for each volume; and for v.1–7 (1907–28), a cumulated index in a separate volume. A good source for contemporary French biography, obituaries, portraits, etc. Contains many reviews of plays, novels, and other literary works. The issues for 1914–18 include many articles on World War I; and no.400, 1938–47, entitled *La seconde guerre mondiale* (522p.), includes a chronology and its own index.

Grand Larousse encyclopédique en dix volumes. Paris, Librairie Larousse, 1960–64. 10v. **AD31**

Essentially a new work although based on the series of earlier Larousse encyclopedias. The general plan remains the same, i.e., a dictionary as well as an encyclopedia, articles are brief, and entries specific. Some articles are based on those in older sets, but many are new or rewritten, information is brought up to date, and there are new illustrations and plates, which in general are superior to those previously used. Bibliographies, arranged by encyclopedia entry, are grouped at the back of each volume with *see* references at the ends of the appropriate articles. Titles are almost entirely in French and seem well up to date.

Largely supersedes the earlier *Nouveau Larousse illustrè*. 1898–1907. 8v. and the *Larousse du XXᵉ siècle*. 1958. 6v.

Encyclopédie française. . . . Paris, Comité de l'Encyclopédie Française, c1935–64. v.1–20. il. Loose-leaf. (In progress) **AD32**

v.1, L'outillage mental: pensée, langage, mathématique. 1937. Nouv. éd. 1957; v.2, La physique, 1955; v.3, Le ciel et la terre. 1956; v.4, La vie. 1937. Nouv. éd. 1960; v.5, Les êtres vivants. 1937; v.6, L'être humain. 1936–54; v.7, L'espèce humaine. 1936; v.8, La vie mentale. 1938–56; v.9, L'universe économique et social. 1960; v.10, L'état moderne. 1938–56. Nouv. éd. 1964; v.11, La vie internationale: divisions et unité du monde actuel. 1957; v.12, Chimie: science et industries. 1958; v.13, Industrie, agriculture. 1962; v.14, La civilisation quotidienne. 1954; v.15, Éducation et instruction. 1939; v.16–17, Arts et littératures, 1935–36; v.18, La civilisation écrite. 1939; v.19, Philosophie, religion. 1957; v.20, Le monde en devenir (Histoire, évolution, prospective). 1959.

A nonalphabetical encyclopedia containing monographic articles grouped by large classes, and with alphabetical index to each volume to serve until the general alphabetical index to the whole set appears. The announced plan of the publication calls for a volume of bibliography and proper names index, and a subject index volume. Until the index volumes have been published, it is impossible to judge what the use or the value of the set as a practical general reference encyclopedia will be. In the volumes issued so far, the illustrations, though good, are not numerous, and there is comparatively little bibliography.

In recent years some of the first volumes to be published have been replaced by new editions, which are, in reality, wholly new volumes, in some cases written from a different viewpoint, e.g., v.10, the 1st edition, *L'état moderne,* was written in the day of fascism, nazism, etc. The new edition presents quite a different concept. It is recommended that, as long as justified, both volumes be kept.

Encyclopédie, ou Dictionnaire raisonné des sciences, des arts et des métiers, par une société des gens de lettres. Mis en ordre et publié par D. Diderot; et quant à la partie mathématique, par J. d'Alembert. Lausanne & Berne, Sociétés Typographiques, 1780–82. 36v.   **AD33**

—— Recueil de planches. 1780–82. 3v.
> Published in various editions.
> Often cited as *Diderot.*
> A famous work by the 18th-century French encyclopedists with emphasis on the arts, sciences, and mechanical trades, reflecting the philosophical concepts of the time.

German

Brockhaus' Konversations-Lexikon. Der grosse Brockhaus. 16. völlig neubearb. Aufl. Wiesbaden, Brockhaus, 1952–60. 12v.; Ergänzungsbd., 2v.; Atlas.   **AD34**
> 1st ed. 1796–1808; frequently revised; 15th ed. 1928–35. 21v. Earlier editions called *Brockhaus' Konversations-Lexikon.*
> The most recent edition of a standard German encyclopedia, earlier editions of which influenced encyclopedia-making in many countries.
> This edition is a revision and complete resetting; and is more condensed, with 12 volumes instead of 21. Characterized by short articles, on small subjects, with profuse illustration, including many small illustrations in text. Articles are unsigned, many with bibliographies, sometimes quite extensive; illustrations include good maps, black-and-white and colored plates, many portraits, coats of arms of cities, etc. Includes biographies of living persons.

—— Ergänzungsband. Wiesbaden, Brockhaus, 1958. 3 pts. in 1v. il., maps.
> Contents: T.1, Neue Artikel und aktuelle Ergänzungen; T.2, Welt und Mensch der Jahrhundertmitte; T.3, Karten Verzeichnis (Index to the maps in v.1–13).

—— II. Ergänzungsband. A–Z. Wiesbaden, Brockhaus, 1963. 792p. il.
> Alphabetically arranged, with new articles and supplementary material to articles in the main alphabet.
> Includes a section of plans of 19 German cities.

—— Atlas; Erdkunde, Wirtschaft, Geschichte. Wiesbaden, Brockhaus, 1960. 664p. plates, maps.
> For annotation *see* CK214.

Brockhaus' kleines Konversations-Lexikon. Der kleine Brockhaus. Völlig umgestalltete Neuausgabe. Wiesbaden, Brockhaus, 1962. 2v. il.   **AD35**
> Subtitle: 80,000 Stichwörter, 5000 bunte und einfarbige Bilder, Karten, Übersichten, Zeittafeln.

—— Der neue Brockhaus. Allbuch in 5 Bänden und einem Atlas. 3. völlig neubearb. Aufl. Wiesbaden, 1958–60. 5v. and atlas. il.   **AD36**

Der grosse Herder, Nachschlagewerk für Wissen und Leben. 5. neubearb. Aufl. von Herders Konversationslexikon. Freiburg, Herder, 1953–56. 10v.   **AD37**
> 1st ed. 1854–57; 4th ed. 1931–35. 12v.
> v.1–9, A–Z; v.10, Der Mensch in seiner Welt.
> A well-illustrated, well-made general encyclopedia with short articles and little bibliography, written from the Catholic viewpoint.

—— Ergänzungsband. 1962. 2v.
> Each of these two volumes includes material supplementary to the main work, and has additional sections on *Die*

Welt in unserer Zeit: T.1, Natur und Technik; T.2, Geist und Kultur.

Meyers neues Lexikon in acht Bänden. Leipzig, VEB Bibliographisches Inst., 1961–64. v.1–7. il. (In progress)   **AD38**
> 1st ed. 1840–55.
> Contents: v.1–7, A–Tema.
> Although not so numbered, this is the 9th edition of a long line of encyclopedias, bearing the name of Meyer, published in Leipzig since 1840. The firm was liquidated in 1945. The incomplete 8th edition of 1936–42 (v.1–9) was influenced by Nazi ideology; this edition strongly reflects the current political orientation of the East German government. Includes numerous short articles with little or no bibliography. Biographies include living persons. Many illustrations, including maps, plates (black and white and colored), plans of cities, coats of arms, etc. Except for some recent technical articles, the 6th and 7th editions will still prove to be more useful for general library purposes, because of the longer articles and the more scholarly, unbiased approach.

Bertelsmann Lexikon. Gütersloh, C. Bertelsmann Verlag, 1959. 4v.   **AD39**
> Jubiläumsausgabe.
> Contains some 100,000 entries with 316 plates, numerous maps, and an index.
> The basic four volumes will be supplemented by general works on world history of art, German history, technology, zoology, and hygiene. Also an atlas volume. For atlas *see* CK213.

💐 Of the older German encyclopedias, these two are outstanding and, in the research library, are frequently useful for topics not treated in the modern encyclopedias:

Allgemeine Encyclopädie der Wissenschaften und Künste von genannten Schriftstellern bearb. und hrsg. von J. S. Ersch und J. G. Gruber. Leipzig, Brockhaus, 1818–50. 167v. il.   **AD40**
> Contents: 1st sec., A–G. 99v.; 2d sec., H–Lig. 43v.; 3d sec., O–Phyx. 25v.
> Unfinished. Editors vary, but set is usually referred to as *Ersch und Gruber Encyclopädie.*
> A scholarly work particularly useful for biography, bibliography, and geographical information.

Zedler, Johann Heinrich. Grosses vollständiges universal Lexikon aller Wissenschaften und Künste. . . . Halle, Zedler, 1732–50. 64v. portraits.   **AD41**

—— —— Nöthige Supplemente. . . . Leipzig, 1751–54. v.1–4.
> v.1–4, A–Caq.
> No more of the supplement published.
> One of the great encyclopedias. Particularly useful for biography and bibliography of the 16th and 17th centuries.

Greek

Megalē hellēnikē enkyklopaideia. Ekdosis 2., enēmerōmenē dia symplērōmatōn. Athēnai, Ekdotikos Organismos "Ho Phoinix," 1959–60. 24v. and suppl. v.1–4.   **AD42**
> Ed. by Paulos Drandakēs.
> 1st ed. 1926–34. 24v.
> A general encyclopedia in modern Greek. Many articles are of some length and have bibliographies. Illustrations are poor.

Neōteron enkyklopaidikon lexikon; methodikē kai systēmatikē sympyknōsis kai eklaikeysis holōn tōn andrōpinōn gnōseōn. [2d ed.] Athēnai, Ekdosis tēs Enkyklopaidikēs Epitheorēseōs "Hēlios," [1957–59]. 18v. il.   **AD43**
> A general encyclopedia in modern Greek, including many

long articles as well as short ones. Some of them signed. Includes very little bibliography. The poor quality of the paper results in poor reproduction of illustrations.

Hebrew

Encyclopaedia hebraica. Tel-Aviv, Encyclopaedia Pub., 1948–63. v.1–14, 16. il. (In progress) **AD44**

Text in Hebrew. A general encyclopedia with articles contributed and signed by some 500 outstanding Jewish and non-Jewish scholars. Bibliographies include titles in many languages. Illustrated in black and white with occasional plates in color.

Hungarian

Révai nagy lexikona az ismeretek enciklopédiája. Budapest, Révai Testvérek. 1911–27. 20v.; v.21, 1935. il. **AD45**

Unsigned articles, the longer ones with bibliographies of some length. Includes biographies of living persons. Illustrations in black and white with some good colored plates; maps. v.19, p.769–863, and v.20–21 are supplements.

Uj magyar lexikon. [Szerkesztette az Akadémiai Kiadó lexikonszerkesztösége. Szerkesztö bizottság: Berei Andor et al.] Budapest, Akadémiai Kiadó, 1959–62. 6v. **AD46**

A new work, in dictionary arrangement, with generally brief articles. Strong in geographical and personal names, the latter including contemporaries. Point of view is stated in the preface as Marxist-Leninist. No bibliographies included. Useful for current information but does not replace older works.

Indonesian

Ensiklopaedia Indonesia. Bandung, 's-Gravenhage, N. V. Penerbitan, W. Van Hoeve, 1954–[56]. 3v. **AD47**

A general encyclopedia with emphasis on Asiatic affairs, characterized by brief articles, little or no bibliography. Attractive format with good typography, illustrations, and maps.

Italian

Enciclopedia italiana di scienze, lettere ed arti. Roma, Istit. della Enciclopedia Italiana, fondata da Giovanni Treccani, 1929–37. 35v. il. **AD48**

An important encyclopedia with excellent long articles, many bibliographies, and a wealth of illustrations of all types, i.e., excellent maps and colored plates, dark sepia plates of unusual beauty, and innumerable text illustrations, some of which are almost equal to plates. Some articles have a Fascist viewpoint. All articles, even very short ones, are signed. Includes many biographical articles, genealogical articles containing additional biographies, and biographies of living persons. While all subjects are illustrated, the illustrations for travel and particularly for art subjects are most notable. Many portraits.

—— v.36, Indici. 1939.

A detailed index to the set, including Appendice I.

—— Appendice I. 1938. 1147p. il.

Includes new articles, and additions and corrections to the main set. Four parts of an Appendice were published 1934–36, covering the letters A–Pavia. Material in these is not entirely taken over in *Appendice I,* and therefore the earlier parts should be preserved by libraries that received them.

—— Appendice II, 1938–1948. 1948–49. 2v. il.; Appendice III, 1949–1960. 1961. 2v. il.

10-year supplements on the same basic plan as the main work, i.e., an alphabetical arrangement of articles signed by authorities, with bibliographies. Well illustrated, though the illustrations are not so plentiful or so beautifully reproduced as in the main work. Cross references are used liberally when additions and corrections are made to articles in previous volumes. The second volume in each set includes an analytical index to both volumes.

Dizionario enciclopedico italiano. Roma, Istit. della Enciclopedia Italiana, 1955–61. 12v. il. **AD49**

An encyclopedic dictionary, giving meanings of words with etymologies and examples of usage, and concise encyclopedic articles. These are not signed and have no bibliographies, but include a large number of biographies, characters of fiction, titles of individual works of literature, gazetteer information, detailed discrimination of word meanings, etc. Includes abbreviations. Illustrations are excellent, some in color, and more numerous than in many encyclopedias. Excellent maps.

Enciclopedia Hoepli. Milan, Hoepli, 1955–62. v.1–5. il. (In progress) **AD50**

Contents: v.1–5, A–Q.

A general encyclopedia, with short unsigned articles. Little or no bibliography.

Japanese

Dai-hyakka jiten [Great encyclopedia]. Tokyo, Heibonsha, 1931–35, 1939. 28v. and suppl. **AD51**

Entirely in Japanese.

Korean

Korean encyclopedia. Seoul, Hakwon Pub. Co., 1958–60. 6v. il. **AD52**

A general encyclopedia in Korean. The headings for articles on Western subjects are given in Korean followed by English translation. Contains considerable biography, including living persons. " . . . valuable as the single, most reliable source of information about Korea."—*Journal of Asian studies* 20:238. Feb. 1961.

Lithuanian

Lietuvių enciklopedija. [Boston], Lietuvių Enciklopedijos Leidykla, 1953–65. v.1–32. il. (In progress) **AD53**

v.1–32, A–Val.

A general encyclopedia in Lithuanian, with natural emphasis on Lithuania.

Articles vary in length: some quite long, with many short ones on small subjects. Some are signed. Brief bibliographies. Includes living persons.

Mexican

Diccionario enciclopédico U.T.E.H.A. México, Union Tipográfica Editorial Hispano Americana, 1950–52. 10v. il. **AD54**

A Mexican encyclopedia, general in scope but stressing Mexico and Latin America.

—— Appendice. 1964. 2v.

Norwegian

Aschehougs konversasjons leksikon. 4. utg. Redaksjon: Arthur Holmesland, Alf Sommerfelt [og] Leif Størmer. Redaksjonssekretaer: John Dahl. Oslo, H. Aschehoug, 1954–1961. 18v. il. **AD55**

1st ed. published as *Illustreret norsk konversations-leksikon,* 1907–13. 6v.

Short, popular, signed articles; good illustrations, maps; little bibliography; many biographies, including persons still living. Particularly good for contemporary Norwegian biography.

Norsk allkunnebok. Redaktør: A. Sudmann [and others]. Oslo, Fonna, 1948–1960. 10v. and atlas. il. **AD56**

The first encyclopedia to be written entirely in the *nyorsk* (*landsmål*) language. Short articles, usually signed.

Polish

Ilustrowana encyklopedja Trzaski, Everta i Michalskiego. Opracowana pod red. dra Stanisława Lama. Warszawa, Trzaska, Evert i Michalski, 1927–28. 5v. il. **AD57**

—— Trzaski, Everta i Michalskiego encyklopedja XX wieku. Lwów, Trzaska, Evert i Michalski, 1938. 2120col. il.

A general encyclopedia with very short articles, little or no bibliography. Biographies include living persons. The supplementary volume treats the 20th century.

Orgelbrand, Samuel. S. Orgelbranda Encyklopedja powszechna z ilustracjami i mapami. Warszawa, Orgelbrand, 1898–1912. 18v. il. **AD58**

v.1–16, A–Z (supplement in v.16); v.17–18, Supplement. Short popular articles, many biographies.

Russian

Bol'shaia sovetskaia entsiklopediia; redaktsiei N. I. Bukharina, V. V. Kuibysheva [and others]. Moskva, "Sovetskaia Entsiklopediia," 1927–47. 65v. **AD59**

The most extensive of the Russian encyclopedias, soviet in treatment, international in scope. Volumes published irregularly. Signed articles. Extensive bibliographies.

—— Soiuz sovetskikh sotsialisticheskikh respublik. 1947. 1946p., lxxxp.

A historical supplement on the USSR. Classed arrangement, with no index and therefore very difficult to use. Does not include government and politics. Chronology, p.i–xl; bibliography, p.xli–lxxx.

Translated into German as *Enzyklopädie der Union der Sozialistischen Sowjetrepubliken,* hrsg. von S. I. Wawilor [u.A.]. (Berlin, Verlag Kultur und Fortschritt, 1950. 2v. il.) This includes a personal name index.

—— Vtoroe izdanie. Moskva, 1949–58. 51v. il. **AD60**

A new edition of the Soviet encyclopedia, revised and reset with most of the articles new or rewritten; articles in the 1st edition are signed, in the 2d they are not; etymological derivations are given much more freely in the 1st edition; bibliographies are quite extensive and have been compiled to include works published as recently as 1951 and 1952. For the most part bibliographies contain only Russian titles, although for articles on foreign subjects some titles in other languages are occasionally included. Illustrations and maps are more numerous and of better quality in the new work, and the general make-up of the volume is more attractive.

The main alphabet ends with v.49; v.50 is devoted to the USSR, corresponding to the supplement to the 1st edition; v.51 supplements the 2d edition as a whole with some 950 articles, many of which are biographical, and contains tables of weights and measures, currencies, and foreign words and phrases.

v.50, translated into German as *Die UdSSR; Enzyklopädie der Union der Sozialistischen Sowjetrepubliken.* Hrsg.: W. Fickenscher unter Mitwirkung von H. Becker [et al.]. Leipzig, Verlag Enzyklopädie, 1959. 1104p. il.

—— —— Alfavitnyi ukazatel' ko vtoromu izdaniiu. [Leningrad, 1960] 2v.

An alphabetical index to subjects and authors.

Malaia sovetskaia entsiklopediia. Glav. red. B. A. Vveden-

skii. Izd. 3. [Moskva], Gos. Nauch. Izd-vo "Bol'shaia Sovetskaia Entsiklopediia," [1958–60]. 10v. il. **AD61**

A 3d edition of the shorter Soviet encyclopedia, containing some 50,000 articles as compared with 31,000 in the 2d edition of 11v. A general encyclopedia with some emphasis on terms of non-Russian origin.

—— [Index] Alfavitnyi predmetno-imennoi ukazatel' k. 3. izd. 1961.

Brockhaus' Konversations-Lexikon. Novyi entsiklopedicheskii slovar'. Izdateli F. A. Brokgauz (Leiptsig), I. A. Efron (S.-Petersburg). S.-Petersburg, Brokgauz-Efron, [1912–17?]. v.1–29. il. **AD62**

v.1–29, A–Otto. No more published.

A revised edition, showing considerable change, of the great Russian *Brockhaus* (pub. 1890–1907 in 41v. and 2 suppl.).

Valuable for historical subjects.

Entsiklopedicheskii slovar' t-va "Br. A.i.I. Granat i Ko." Moskva, [1911?–34?]. v.1–33, 35, 37–40, 41²⁻⁸, 43–45¹⁻³, 46, 48, 50. il. **AD63**

v.1–33, A–P; v.35, Rab–Rast; v.37–40, Riut–Sots; v.41²–41⁸, Soius–Tors; v.43–46, Faler–chet; v.48, Chet–Chulkov; v.50, Shkol–Evol.

Uneven in treatment but occasionally useful for material not included in the other encyclopedias.

Annual

Bol'shaia sovetskaia entsiklopediia. Ezhegodnik. 1957– . Moskva, 1957– . il. Annual. **AD64**

Records events, chiefly of the preceding year, by country (the USSR and constituent republics, and other countries of the world) and under such headings as international organizations, science and technology, and international cultural events. Each volume contains a biographical directory of persons of various nationalities. A detailed table of contents, but no index.

Bibliography

Kaufman, Isaak Mikhailovich. Russkie entsiklopedii. Moskva, 1960– . v.1– . (In progress) **AD65**

At head of title: Ministerstvo kul'tury RSFSR. Gosudarstvennaia ordena Lenina Biblioteka SSSR im. V. I. Lenina.

Contents: v.1, Obshchie entsiklopedii, bibliografiia i kratkie ocherki.

Provides detailed bibliographic descriptions, with notes and commentary, for Russian encyclopedias. v.1 describes 22 general encyclopedias of the pre-Revolutionary and Soviet periods, indicating a publishing date for each volume of each edition.

Serbo-Croatian

Enciklopedija Leksikografskog Zavoda. [Redaktori: Marko Kostrenčić, Miroslav Krleža] Zagreb, Izd. Leksikografskog Zavoda FNRJ, 1955–61. v.1–5. il. (In progress) **AD66**

A well-made general encyclopedia with many short articles and some long ones, unsigned; little or no bibliography. Biographies include living persons. Illustrations and maps are good, and plentiful.

Slovakian

Slovenský náucný slovník; príručná encyklopedia vedomostí v troch dieloch, redakčné práce viedol Pavel Bujnák . . . Bratislava, "Litevna," 1932. 3v. il. **AD67**

A general encyclopedia with very brief articles, unsigned

and with no bibliography, but with a long article on the *Československá Republika,* v.1, p.167–288, including statistics, maps, illustrations, etc. Biographies include living persons.

Spanish

Enciclopedia universal ilustrada europeo-americana. Barcelona, Espasa, 1905–33. 80v. in 81. il. **AD68**

v.1–70 in 71, A–Z; Apéndice, v.1–10, A–Z.

Often cited as *Espasa.*

A useful encyclopedia for the large reference or special library. It has long articles, bibliographies, good illustrations and maps, and includes short articles on small subjects; especially strong in biography and in gazetteer information. Special features are the many maps: geographical, geological, historical, and statistical; the numerous plans of even small cities; colored plates of uniforms, flags, coins, etc. of each country; and the reproductions of paintings and other works of art given usually under title and sometimes under the artist's name. Useful for its large amount of Spanish and Spanish-American biography.

Etymologies are included, and equivalents of words are given in French, Italian, English, German, Portuguese, Catalan, and Esperanto.

—— Suplemento anual, 1934– . Barcelona, Espasa-Calpe, 1935– .

Arrangement of supplementary volumes is different from that of the basic work, i.e., instead of a straight alphabetical arrangement of all material, they are arranged alphabetically by large classes, e.g., Agricultura, Biografía, Geografía, Química, etc., with small topics in an alphabetical arrangement under some of these large classes, and a general alphabetical index to all classes and topics at the end of the volume.

Volumes cover 1934, 1935, 1936–39 (2v.), 1940–41, 1942–44, 1945–48, 1949–52, 1953–54, 1955–56, 1957–58.

Diccionario enciclopédico abreviado; versiones de la mayoría de las voces en francés, inglés, italiano y alemán y sus etimologías. 6. ed. Madrid, Espasa-Calpe, 1954–55. 7v. il. **AD69**

1st ed. 1940.

A general encyclopedia with, for the most part, brief articles and no bibliography. For many words gives equivalents in French, English, Italian, and German, with etymologies.

Illustrations not clearly reproduced.

Diccionario enciclopédico Salvat. 9. ed. Barcelona, Salvat Editores, 1960. 12v. il. **AD70**

1st ed. pub. under title *Diccionario Salvat.*

A medium-sized, general encyclopedia. Articles are usually brief, but some long; are unsigned; and include little or no bibliography. Illustrations and maps are good.

Swedish

Svensk uppslagsbok. 2. omarb. och utvidg. upplagen. Malmö, Förlagshuset Norden, 1947–55. 32v. il. **AD71**

1st ed. 1929–37. 30v. and suppl.

An excellent modern encyclopedia edited by a board of specialists; well printed and beautifully bound. Many articles are signed. Bibliographies are scant. Profusely illustrated with pertinent maps, city plans, portraits, and many fine photographs. Contains numerous biographical sketches including living persons.

Bonniers Folklexikon. Stockholm, Ab Nordiska Uppslagsböcker, 1951–55. 5v. il. **AD72**

Short, unsigned articles with some bibliographical notes. Includes small, generally clear illustrations with some colored plates and maps. Strong in biographical and gazetteer information.

A small, handy encyclopedia for the library which does not need the more expensive *Svensk uppslagsbok* (AD71).

Focus, uppslagsbok; Almqvist & Wiksells stora illustrerade bildnings- och uppslagsverk. Stockholm, Almqvist & Wiksell, 1958–60. 5v. il. **AD73**

A general encyclopedia with many short articles and small illustrations. v.5 is an index with a section of synonyms and one of tables of statistics and miscellaneous information.

Swiss

Schweizer Lexikon. Zurich, Encyclios-Verlag, 1945–48. 7v. il. **AD74**

A general encyclopedia with short articles, usually with brief bibliographies. Illustrations are clear and well chosen.

Turkish

Türk ansiklopedisi. Ankara, Millî Eğitim Basimevi, 1946–64. v.1–12. (In progress) **AD75**

v.1–4 had title *Inönü ansiklopedisi.* Title changed with *fasikül* 34.

Published under the auspices of the Turkish government; is international and general in scope with emphasis on Turkish and Islamic materials. Contains a large amount of biography, including living persons. Articles are usually short, unsigned, and without much bibliography. Illustrations and maps are plentiful.

Ukrainian

Ukrains'ka radians'ka entsyklopediia. Kiev, Akademiia Nauk Ukr.R.S.R., 1959–64. v.1–16. il. (In progress) **AD76**

A general encyclopedia in the Ukrainian language. v.16 completes the alphabet. v.17 will be a special volume on the Ukrainian Soviet Socialist Republic.

Union of Soviet Socialist Republics

See Russian, p.90.

A E

Language Dictionaries

❧ For a general survey of the whole field of language dictionaries consult the article "Dictionary" in the *Encyclopaedia Britannica,* 11th edition. This is valuable for its historical information and includes an extensive bibliography of dictionaries in many languages, though many of these now, of course, are considerably out of date.

Dictionaries are the main sources for information about words: their spelling, pronunciation, meaning, derivation, etc. Theoretically the dictionary is concerned only with the word, not with the thing represented by the word, differing in this respect from the encyclopedia which gives information primarily about the thing. Practically, however, the large modern dictionary is very often encyclopedic and gives information about the thing as well as the word, thus combining the features of the two types of reference books. As the large English dictionary is the most familiar "family reference book," this encyclopedic feature has been continually strengthened by the addition of many special lists and excellent illustrations, until the best modern works of this sort can now be used for many more purposes than information about words. Dictionaries which contain many illustrative quotations can often be used to find or identify a quotation, thus supplementing the special dictionaries of quotations. The student of reference books should familiarize himself with the special features and supplementary lists of each of the great dictionaries if he wishes to make each of these books serve all the purposes that it can be made to serve.

Dictionaries should be purchased cautiously. Because they are expensive undertakings, unscrupulous publishers sometimes employ incompetent editors or insufficient help or offer a reprint of an old work with little or no revision. Furthermore, devious means are employed to hide such practices. The prospective purchaser, therefore, should use the same care in examining a dictionary before purchase as is recommended in the case of encyclopedias.

In studying a dictionary the student should follow the general directions for examining reference books and, keeping in mind the purpose the dictionary is intended to serve, should also note carefully the following points:

1. Period of the language covered
2. Vocabulary
   a) Extent and how counted—is the count by main words only or does it include all derived and compound forms, etc.?
   b) Special elements included, e.g., slang, dialect, obsolete forms, scientific or technical terms, etc.
3. Treatment of each word, with reference to:
   a) Spelling, including plurals, verb tenses, participles
   b) Syllabication and hyphenization
   c) Pronunciation—how marked; is the system accurate and intelligible?
   d) Etymology
   e) History—are changes in meaning, usage, etc., marked and *dated?*
   f) Definition—is it clear, correct, adequate?
   g) Illustrative quotations—are they given freely, with exact reference, and in chronological order and dated so that the history can be traced?
   h) Standard and usage—is a word indicated as obsolete, colloquial, etc.?
   i) Encyclopedic information
   j) Synonyms and antonyms
4. Illustrations
5. Abbreviations—to what extent included, and how, i.e., in separate list or in main alphabet?
6. Special types of words included in addition to the ordinary vocabulary, i.e., Christian names, foreign phrases, biographical lists, geographical names, etc. To what extent are these included, and where: in main alphabet or in appended lists?
7. Special features

ENGLISH LANGUAGE

💥 Dictionaries of the English language have been divided rather arbitrarily, according to their place of compilation and publication, into American and English dictionaries. Of course, both types cover the same field—the English language as a whole—and conform, in the main, to the same standards, but there are certain minor differences. In cases where there are known differences in spelling, pronunciation, meaning, etc., each dictionary will generally give both usages, but the English work will prefer the English usage or form, while the American work will prefer the American. An American dictionary generally includes more Americanisms; an English dictionary, more local English terms, colonial words, etc.

Bibliography

Mathews, Mitford McLeod. A survey of English dictionaries. Oxford, Univ. Pr.; London, Milford, 1933. 123p. il.   **AE1**

A historical survey of English dictionaries from earliest times to the 19th century. Also includes chapters on "The historical principle in lexicography," "Review of lexicographic methods," and "Chief features of some modern dictionaries."

Murray, *Sir* **James A. H.** Evolution of English lexicography. Oxford, Univ. Pr., 1900. 51p.   **AE2**

An interesting and authoritative survey of the history and development of the English dictionary.

Starnes, DeWitt Talmage and **Noyes, Gertrude Elizabeth.** The English dictionary from Cawdrey to Johnson, 1604–1755. Chapel Hill, Univ. of North Carolina Pr., 1946. 299p. il.   **AE3**

Includes a bibliography and census of copies in American libraries of all known editions, p.228–41.

American

Century dictionary and cyclopedia with a new atlas of the world. [Rev. and enl. ed.] N.Y., Century, [c1911]. 12v. il.   **AE4**

1st ed. 1889–91, 6v., with two supplementary volumes, *Cyclopedia of names,* 1894, and *Atlas,* 1897; partially revised from time to time and plates altered, but never entirely revised and reset. Revisions to note especially are: (1) 1901 edition, 10v., v.1–8, Dictionary, v.9, Names, v.10, Atlas; (2) two supplementary volumes published 1909, numbered v.11–12 to continue the 1901 edition and containing about 100,000 new words, senses, and phrases and a 92p. supplement to the *Cyclopedia of names;* (3) the 1911 edition, 12v.

v.1–10, Dictionary; v.11, Cyclopedia of names; v.12, Atlas.

Printed from the same plates as the earlier editions, but with alterations in the plates to include a considerable amount of new material. In addition, there is bound at the end of each volume the corresponding portion of the alphabet from the two supplementary volumes published 1909, making two alphabets in each volume linked together by cross references.

The most comprehensive and detailed American dictionary and the best example of the encyclopedia type, including detailed etymologies and thousands of illustrative quotations, with exact reference to source. Now out of date for current usage but still useful for many types of questions.

v.11, *Cyclopedia of names,* includes personal and geographical names, famous works of literature and art, monuments, etc. Pronunciation is indicated. To a large extent, but not entirely, superseded by the *New Century cyclopedia of names* (AJ19).

New Century dictionary of the English language, based on matter selected from the original Century dictionary and entirely rewritten, with the addition of a great amount of new material. . . . ed. by H. G. Emery and K. G. Brewster. N.Y., Appleton, 1948. 2v. (2790p.).   **AE5**

Supplements: Synonyms and antonyms, Abbreviations, Business terms, Foreign words and phrases, Proper names exclusive of biography and geography, Biographical names, Geographical names.

Not a revision of the *Century dictionary* (AE4), but a much smaller work including a smaller vocabulary selected from the *Century* with new definitions and a different selection of quotations. More than 160,000 entries with more than 12,000 illustrative quotations.

Funk & Wagnalls new standard dictionary of the English language, prep. by more than 380 specialists and other scholars under the supervision of I. K. Funk, Calvin Thomas, F. H. Vizetelly. N.Y., Funk & Wagnalls, 1964. 2816p. il.   **AE6**

1st edition, 1893, had title *Standard dictionary;* the *New Standard,* first published in 1913, is a thorough revision of the 1893 edition, reset and printed from new plates throughout. Later issues or reprints of this edition show changes in the plates, insertion of new words, etc.; e.g., the issues published since World War II include some new words inserted in their proper alphabetical place by cutting out or compressing old material, and late editions include a supplement of new words.

Contents: (1) Dictionary, including in one alphabet all ordinary dictionary words and also the various proper names, i.e., biographical, geographical, mythological, Biblical, etc.; Supplement of new words and additional meanings, p.xxxvi–lxix; (2) Appendix: Disputed pronunciations, Rules for simplified spelling, Foreign words and phrases, Statistics of population.

A serviceable one-volume work. Its special feature is emphasis upon current information, i.e., present-day meaning, pronunciation, spelling, and the subordination of the historical. Full vocabulary—about 450,000 words including 65,000 proper names—aims to include all live words of the language in standard speech and literature of the day and terms commonly used dialectically by large numbers of people in different parts of the English-speaking world. Prefers simpler spelling; when several forms are used by authorities, indicates those used by the American Philological Association, American Spelling Reform Association, and Simplified Spelling Board. Marks syllabication and hyphenated words plainly, using single hyphen for the first and double hyphen for the second; indicates pronunciation by two respellings: (1) by the revised scientific alphabet, N.E.A., and (2) by the ordinary respelling used in textbooks. Gives antonyms as well as synonyms. Includes illustrative phrases and quotations, and contains considerable encyclopedic information, many illustrations, and good colored plates.

Webster's New international dictionary of the English language. 2d ed., unabridged . . . a Merriam-Webster. William Allan Neilson, ed. in chief; Thomas A. Knott, gen. ed.; Paul W. Carhart, managing ed. Springfield, Mass., Merriam, 1961. cxxxvip, 3194p. il.   **AE7**

1st ed. of *Webster's Dictionary,* 1828; the *New international,* 1909; 2d ed. of *New international,* 1934, revised throughout and reset. Later printings show some changes and corrections in plates, mainly in spelling, punctuation, or pronunciation, but in some cases adding new information or revising the treatment. In 1939 a "New words" section was added at the front of the book, p.xcvii–civ; in 1961, this section was called "Addenda section," p.xcvii–cxxxv. It includes several thousand new words or words used with new or different meanings, including scientific and technical terms, slang, abbreviations, etc.

Contents: (1) Dictionary, including in the same list both the usual dictionary words and also foreign phrases, abbreviations, proverbs, noted names of fiction, and all proper names except those in the biographical and geographical lists; (2) Appendix: (a) Abbreviations, (b) Arbitrary signs and symbols, (c) Forms of address, (d) Pronouncing gazetteer, (e) Pronouncing biographical dictionary. In addition to the foregoing, the "Reference history" edition contains a separately paged supplement "Reference history of the world" by A. B. Hart, c1934.

The oldest and most famous American dictionary, well rounded, with no marked specialization or bias, ably edited, reliable, and noted particularly for the clearness of its definitions. For many years the most used and, for general purposes, the most useful of the one-volume dictionaries. A special feature introduced in the 1909 edition and continued in the 2d edition (1934) is the divided page, containing in the upper part the main words of the language and in the lower part, in finer print, various minor words, e.g., different kinds of cross references, reformed spellings, such Biblical proper names as are entered only to show pronunciation, a few obsolete words and a few extremely rare words, and foreign-language quotations, proverbs, and longer phrases. Other special points to remember in using the work are: definitions given in historical sequence; pronunciation indicated by Webster phonetic alphabet (not by the International phonetic); hyphenization indicated by single hyphen, division of syllables by either accent or centered period. Vocabulary claimed is "600,000 vocabulary entries."

Webster's Third new international dictionary of the English language, unabridged. A Merriam-Webster. Ed. in chief: Philip Babcock Gove and the Merriam-Webster editorial staff. Springfield, Mass., Merriam, 1961. 2662p. il.   **AE8**

" . . . a completely new work, redesigned, restyled and reset."—*Pref.* Not only new, but vastly different from the 2d edition (AE7); it has become the most controversial reference book of the generation, both attacked and defended in the newspaper and periodical press. Because of its departures from accepted Webster practices, thorough familiarity with the introduction is essential to efficient use of the text. A few of the major points to be observed are:

Usage: This edition presents the language as it is now *used,* with a new concept of acceptability of usage, construction, pronunciation, etc.; therefore, much is included, often without qualification, which may be regarded by many as colloquial, vulgar, or incorrect.

Scope: Some 100,000 new entries appear, with new scientific and technical terms especially well represented, but the total has been reduced from 600,000 to 450,000, meaning that many obsolete and rare words have been dropped; the divided page system has been abandoned; abbreviations are included in the main alphabet; the gazetteer and the biographical dictionary have been dropped; all proper nouns have been excluded, although proper adjectives remain, all in lower case.

Treatment of words: Individual definitions, in the Webster tradition, are generally clear and to the point; meanings are given as before, chronologically, with early usage first; etymologies have been expanded; pronunciations are given as used in "general cultivated conversational usage as well as in formal platform speech"; regional pronunciations are also frequently shown; indication of pronunciation is given by a newly devised system with the key only in the introduction, not on each page; the devices to indicate word division, stress, and hyphenization have been revised and are explained and illustrated in the introduction; punctuation and indentation are at a minimum.

Quotations: Illustrative quotations are abundant, undated, and almost exclusively from recent sources, many of them popular. Citations are to author only.

Regardless of varying opinions of editorial judgment, this edition will be wanted in most American libraries, though the 2d edition will be wisely retained as well.

Desk dictionaries

☙ Good desk dictionaries are needed both in libraries and in homes, and librarians should know the main features and merits of the various works available. Those listed below are planned for much the same kind of use and include comparable vocabularies. All have been issued in recent editions and include new words and meanings; all are authoritative; all give clear, concise definitions, etymologies, synonyms, antonyms, etc.; and all have small line drawings.

General arrangement in each differs, as does the arrangement under individual entry, and systems of indicating pronunciation vary. Some of the particular features and special points of each are noted below. Fuller discussion will be found in *Subscription books bulletin reviews* (AA309a).

The publishers also issue other editions and/or abridgments of these dictionaries; *see* publishers' catalogs for their announcements.

American college dictionary. Clarence L. Barnhart, ed. in chief; Jess Stein, managing ed.; assisted and advised by 355 authorities and specialists. N.Y., Random, 1962. 1444p. il. **AE9**

1st ed. 1947.

A modern, desk-size dictionary designed to provide an accurate guide to current usage. All entries are in one alphabet, including proper names of persons and places, abbreviations, foreign phrases, inflected forms of words in which the stem is changed, etc. Pronunciation is indicated by the "traditional textbook key," given on the endpapers and in abbreviated form at the bottom of every other page. Definitions are given in reverse chronological order, modern usage first. Etymologies follow.

The typography is particularly good.

Funk & Wagnalls standard college dictionary. Text ed. N.Y., Harcourt, 1963. 1606p. il. **AE10**

1st ed. 1922; Em′-pha-type ed. 1947.

This edition completely revised and reset. More than 150,000 terms in one alphabet, including proper names, geographical names, abbreviations, foreign phrases, etc. Pronunciation is indicated by diacritical marks, shown on front endpaper and at bottom of every other page.

Slang and colloquialisms are so marked. Order of definitions usually follows frequency of use, rather than semantic evolution. Etymologies are given at the end of the entry.

Appendixes: Colleges and universities in the United States and Canada; Common signs and symbols; Vocabulary building; Punctuation; Guide to reference works; Preparing a manuscript for publication and proof-readers' marks.

Thorndike-Barnhart comprehensive desk dictionary, ed. by Clarence L. Barnhart. Garden City, N.Y., Doubleday, 1962. 896p. il. **AE10a**

First pub. 1951.

A vocabulary of more than 80,000 words, selection based on the Thorndike-Lorge word counts. Gives examples of usage, word origins, abbreviations, idioms, synonyms, and antonyms. Biographical and geographical names are included in the same alphabet.

Webster's New world dictionary of the American language. College ed. Cleveland, World, 1962. 1724p. **AE11**

First pub. 1953.

A new work, not based on existing dictionaries, including more than 142,000 entries, all in one alphabet: proper names, place-names, abbreviations, foreign phrases, etc. Pronunciation is given by a phonetic system, with key on inside of front cover and at the bottom of every other page.

Etymologies are given first. Definitions follow in chronological order, earliest meanings first. Typography is good.

Appendixes: Colleges and universities of the United States; Forms of address; Tables of weights and measures; Special signs and symbols.

Webster's Seventh new collegiate dictionary. A Merriam-Webster. Based on Webster's Third new international dictionary. Springfield, Mass., Merriam, 1963. 1221p. il. **AE12**

1st ed. 1898; 6th ed. 1949.

This 7th edition, including some 130,000 entries, has been entirely revised and reset, and includes some 20,000 new words and meanings.

Based on *Webster's Third* (AE8), it reflects the new concepts and policies of that dictionary. Emphasis is on "standard language," with only a small selection of slang and colloquial terms and meanings; colloquial terms usually are not so designated.

Pronunciation is indicated by a diacritical system, the key to which is given in full on the front and back endpapers and in abbreviated form at the bottom of every other page.

Etymologies are full and given at the beginning of the entry; definitions follow in chronological order, the modern meaning coming last. Synonyms are given but not antonyms.

Appendixes include: Abbreviations; Arbitrary signs and symbols; Biographical names (more than 5000 names with pronunciation, dates, and identifying phrase); Pronouncing gazetteer containing more than 10,000 names of places; Forms of address; Pronouncing vocabulary of common English given names; Vocabulary rhymes; Spelling, punctuation, etc.; Colleges and universities in the United States and Canada.

Juvenile dictionaries

❦ In recent years a number of dictionaries have been published especially adapted to the use of school children of various age levels. For the most part, these are based on the recorded usage of words found in the textbooks and other reading materials in use in the schools. The *Subscription books bulletin reviews* (AA309a) should be consulted for more detailed reviews of these dictionaries. The *Children's catalog* (AA289) and the *Standard catalog for high school libraries* (AA293) will also be helpful in their selection.

Thorndike-Barnhart beginning dictionary. Rev. and enl. by E. L. Thorndike and Clarence L. Barnhart. Garden City, N.Y., Doubleday, 1962. 720p. il. **AE13**

First pub. 1959.

Based on the *Thorndike Century beginning dictionary*, and designed for elementary school children. Includes almost 15,000 entries with simple definitions.

Thorndike-Barnhart junior dictionary, by E. L. Thorndike and Clarence L. Barnhart. Rev. ed. Garden City, N.Y., Doubleday, 1962. 784p. il. **AE14**

A revision of the *Thorndike Century junior dictionary*. First pub. 1959.

Thorndike-Barnhart advanced junior dictionary, ed. by E. L. Thorndike and Clarence L. Barnhart. 2d ed. Garden City, N.Y., Doubleday, 1962. 946p. **AE15**

First pub. 1957.

Designed for junior high schools. Contains more than 65,000 entries. Vocabulary based on curriculum needs. All entries in one alphabet, including biographical and geographical names.

Thorndike-Barnhart high school dictionary, by E. L. Thorndike and Clarence L. Barnhart. 3d ed. Garden City, N.Y., Doubleday, 1962. 1096p. il. **AE16**

A revision of the *Thorndike Century senior dictionary*. First pub. 1941.

Contains a larger vocabulary than the previously listed dictionaries, with more advanced definitions.

Webster's Elementary dictionary. A Merriam-Webster. Springfield, Mass., Merriam, 1961. 579p. il. **AE17**

First pub. 1956.

Written specifically for children in the 4th, 5th, and 6th grades. Based on recorded usage of words found in books and magazines used at these ages. 18,000 vocabulary entries. Simple definitions; no examples of usage.

Webster's New secondary school dictionary. A Merriam-Webster. Springfield, Mass., Merriam, 1961. 921p. il.
AE18

First pub. 1959 by the American Book Co.

Planned especially for junior high school pupils. Contains more than 44,000 vocabulary entries, based on texts used in junior high schools.

World book encyclopedia dictionary. Clarence L. Barnhart, ed. in chief. A Thorndike-Barnhart dictionary. Chicago, Field Enterprises, 1963. 2v. il. **AE19**

Prepared specifically to complement and supplement the *World book encyclopedia* (AD16) and therefore does not include biographical and geographical entries and other encyclopedic information.

All entries—words, phrases, abbreviations, proper names, foreign words—are in a single alphabet. Includes some 180,000 words. Pronunciation is by an adapted International Phonetic Alphabet. Gives definitions, etymologies, synonyms, antonyms, and examples of usage. Indicates slang, informal, and substandard speech.

Designed for high school and home use; more advanced than the graded dictionaries but less comprehensive than the unabridged dictionaries.

English

Murray, *Sir* **James Augustus Henry.** New English dictionary on historical principles; founded mainly on the materials collected by the Philological Society. Oxford, Clarendon Pr., 1888–1933. 10v. and suppl. **AE20**

v.1–10, A–Z; Supplementary volume: Historical introduction, p.vii–xxvi; Supplement A–K, 542p.; L–Z, 325p.; List of spurious words, p.327–30; Bibliography, i.e., list of books most commonly quoted in the Dictionary, 91p.

Known variously as *Murray's Dictionary,* the *New English dictionary,* and the *Oxford dictionary.* Often cited as *N.E.D.,* or *O.E.D.* For history of the work *see* its Supplementary volume, p.vii–xxvi.

The great dictionary of the language, compiled on a different plan from any of the other standard English dictionaries and serving a different purpose. It is based upon the application of the historical method to the life and use of words, and its purpose is to show the history of every word included from the date of its introduction into the language, giving differences in meaning, spelling, pronunciation, usage, etc. at different periods of the last 800 years, and supporting such information by numerous quotations from the works of more than 5000 authors of all periods, including all writers before the 16th century and as many as possible of the important writers since then. The vocabulary is very full, and is intended to include all words now in use or known to have been in use since 1150, excluding only words which had become obsolete by 1150. Within these chronological limits, aims to include: (1) all common words of speech and literature, and all words that approach these in character, the limits being extended further into science and philosophy than into slang and cant; (2) in scientific and technical terminology, all words English in form except those of which an explanation would be intelligible only to a specialist, and such words not English in form as are in general use or belong to the more familiar language of science; and (3) dialectal words before 1500, omitting dialectal words after that date except when they continue the history of a word once in general use, illustrate the history of a literary word, or have a literary currency.

Words included are classified as: (1) main words, (2) subordinate words, and (3) combinations; information for all main words is entered under the current modern or most usual spelling, or, if obsolete, under most typical later spelling, with cross references from all other forms. Information given about each main word is very full and includes: (1) identification, with (a) usual or typical spelling, (b) pronunciation, indicated by respelling in an amplified alphabet or, in case of obsolete words, by marking of stress only, (c)

grammatical designation, (d) specification, e.g., musical term, etc., (e) status, if peculiar, e.g., obsolete, archaic, etc., (f) earlier spelling, (g) inflexions; (2) morphology, including derivation, subsequent form history, etc.; (3) signification, arranged in groups and historically, with marking of obsolete senses, erroneous uses, etc.; (4) quotations, arranged chronologically to illustrate each sense of a word, about one quotation for each century, given with exact reference. The complete work has a total vocabulary of 414,825 words and includes 1,827,306 quotations.

The most important use of this dictionary is for historical information about a word, but it has many other secondary uses, e.g., while not intentionally encyclopedic, it has a good deal of encyclopedic information including some not given in other dictionaries, and while not specializing in slang, it does include many colloquial and slang words, Americanisms, etc. Where such words are included, the information is often better than in the special slang dictionaries.

The supplementary volume is a partial, not a complete, supplement, in that it does not comprise all supplementary material collected since the publication of the first parts of the original work but is limited in the main to new words and senses of the past 50 years, with inclusion also of: (1) other items of modern origin and currency omitted in the main work; (2) earlier evidence of American uses; and (3) some correction or amplification of previous definitions to bring the work into line with recent research. Recent words added include scientific and technical terms, colloquialisms, and slang —American, British, and colonial—and a larger proportion of proper names than in the original work.

The *New English dictionary,* large and comprehensive though it is, is necessarily selective, and could not include all words for the whole period covered or even all material collected during the compilation of the work. Since the completion of the dictionary in 1928, four period and regional dictionaries, on the same extensive plan, either have been published or are in course of publication to supplement the *New English dictionary* by including words, uses, illustrations, etc. which could not be included in that dictionary. These are:

Middle English dictionary, begun under the editorship of Prof. Clark S. Northup at Cornell University, continued under Prof. Samuel Moore and Dr. Thomas A. Knott at the University of Michigan, and now being edited there by Prof. Hans Kurath and Sherman M. Kuhn (AE99).

Dictionary of American English, under the editorship of Sir William Alexander Craigie and James R. Hulbert (Univ. of Chicago Pr., 1936–44. 4v.) (AE80).

Dictionary of the older Scottish tongue, begun under the editorship of Sir William Alexander Craigie and now being edited by A. J. Aitken (AE91).

Scottish national dictionary, under the editorship of William Grant and David Murison (AE95).

—— **Oxford English dictionary,** being a corrected reissue, with an introduction, supplement and bibliography, of A New English dictionary on historical principles; founded mainly on the materials collected by the Philological Society and ed. by James A. H. Murray, Henry Bradley, W. A. Craigie, C. T. Onions. Oxford, Clarendon Pr., 1933. 12v. and suppl. **AE21**

A reprint, on thinner paper and with somewhat smaller margins, from the plates of the original edition with the correction of such typographical errors as had been discovered.

In 1895 "a new name for the Dictionary was introduced, though no change was made on the title-page. On the cover of the section containing *Deceit* to *Deject* . . . above the title, appeared for the first time the designation 'The Oxford English Dictionary,' which was repeated on every section and part issued after 1 July of that year. The new name, being more distinctive than the old, has steadily come more and more into use, and the abbreviation O.E.D. tends to supplant N.E.D., although the latter is still frequently employed." —*Historical introd.,* p.xx.

—— **Shorter Oxford English dictionary** on historical

principles; prep. by W. Little, H. W. Fowler, J. Coulson . . . rev. and ed. by C. T. Onions. 3d ed. Oxford, Clarendon Pr., 1962. 2v.   **AE22**

1st ed. 1933; 3d ed. 1944, repr. with rev. addenda, 1955, and corrections, 1962.

Also published in 1v. as the *Oxford universal dictionary.* 1955. 2515p.

An authorized abridgment of the *New English dictionary,* which, while in the main an abridgment, also includes some additional material, especially new words too recent to have been included in the original work, or older words omitted there, with some later illustrative quotations. Important, therefore, in the library which already has the larger work, as well as in the small library which has not been able to afford the complete *Oxford English dictionary.*

"The aim of this Dictionary is to present in miniature all the features of the principal work. It is designed to embrace not only the literary and colloquial English of the present day together with such technical and scientific terms as are most frequently met with . . . but also a considerable proportion of obsolete, archaic and dialectal words and uses."—*Pref.*

Desk dictionaries

Cassell's English dictionary; including words and phrases current among English-speaking peoples of the world, together with many technical and scientific terms in common use. Compl. rev. and enl. by Arthur L. Hayward and John J. Sparkes. London, Cassell, 1962. 1347p.   **AE23**

First pub. 1891.

Revised at intervals, the present edition is said to be the most thorough revision in its long history. Now contains some 130,000 words and phrases, including technical and scientific terms in common use in the English-speaking countries of Great Britain, North America, Africa, Australia, and New Zealand. Includes new words such as "beat generation," "beatnik," "brinkmanship," etc.

Fowler, Henry Watson and **Fowler, F. G.** Concise Oxford dictionary of current English, based on the Oxford dictionary. 5th ed. rev. by E. McIntosh. Etymologies rev. by G. W. S. Friedrichsen. Oxford, Clarendon Pr., 1964. 1558p.   **AE24**

1st ed. 1911; 4th ed. 1960.

Sometimes cited as *C.O.D.*

An excellent, small desk dictionary based upon the work done for the *New English dictionary* (AE 20). Aim is to include words in current speech, scientific and technical terms, many colloquial and slang expressions, etc.

The 4th edition was completely revised and reset. In the 5th edition the etymologies (given at the ends of the entries) have been thoroughly revised.

Appendixes: General abbreviations; Pronunciation of non-English words; Tables of weights and measures.

Pocket Oxford dictionaries are also issued in both English and American editions.

Oxford illustrated dictionary. Text ed. by J. Coulson [and others]. Illustrations ed. by Helen Mary Petter. Oxford, Clarendon Pr., 1962. 974p. il.   **AE25**

An illustrated dictionary including much encyclopedic material in addition to the usual dictionary information, and various explanatory illustrations usually in the form of line drawings.

Vocabulary is "based on that of the *Concise Oxford dictionary,* and the definitions retain its historical ordering," but there is less full treatment of the more familiar words in order to give a wider scope to the treatment of things, often by means of illustration. All terms are in one alphabet, including proper nouns, abbreviations, foreign phrases, etc. As far as possible, pronunciation is shown without respelling, by placing symbols over the letters; when respelling is necessary, a phonetic system is used. Little or no etymology.

A useful dictionary, from the English viewpoint.

Abbreviations

❧ Lists of abbreviations are important in most libraries. Some of the separately compiled lists follow. Abbreviations are also included freely in the *Century dictionary* (AE4), *Funk and Wagnalls new standard* (AE6), and *Webster's Third new international* (AE8). The desk dictionaries also usually include abbreviations. The lists in *Who's who* (AJ155) and *Who's who in America* (AJ45) are useful for the abbreviations of societies, academies, degrees, etc.

Allen, Edward Frank. Allen's Dictionary of abbreviations and symbols; over 6000 abbreviations and symbols commonly used in literature, science, art, education, business, politics, religion, engineering, industry, war. N.Y., Coward-McCann, 1946. 189p.   **AE26**

Particularly strong in the business field.

De Sola, Ralph. Abbreviations dictionary: abbreviations, acronyms, contractions, signs and symbols defined. [1st rev. ed.] N.Y., Duell, 1964. 227p.   **AE27**

1st ed. 1958.

Subtitle: Including civil and military time systems, Greek alphabet, international civil aircraft markings, numbered abbreviations, proof-reader's marks, punctuation and diacritical marks, radio alphabet, Roman numerals, ship's bell time signals, signs and symbols.

Fawcett, F. Dubrez. Cyclopedia of initials and abbreviations. London, Business Publ., 1963. 185p.   **AE28**

A comprehensive listing of abbreviations in many fields, international in scope, British in viewpoint. A supplement, p.167–85, gives expanded information on some entries.

Gale Research Company. Acronyms dictionary. 1st ed. Detroit, Gale Research, 1960. 211p.   **AE29**

Subtitle: A guide to alphabetic designations, contractions and initialisms: association, aerospace, business, electronic, governmental, international, labor, military, public affairs, scientific, societies, technical, transportation, United Nations.

Matthews, Cecily C. A dictionary of abbreviations; comprising all standard forms in commercial, social, legal, political, naval and military, and general use. London, Routledge, 1947. 232p.   **AE30**

In one alphabetical list with appendixes of scientific symbols. From the British viewpoint.

Schwartz, Robert J. The complete dictionary of abbreviations. N.Y., Crowell, 1955. 211p.   **AE31**

Lists more than 25,000 abbreviations, general and specialized, including societies, institutions, government agencies, members of the New York Stock Exchange, degrees, etc., as well as scientific and technical abbreviations.

Shankle, George Earlie. Current abbreviations. N.Y., Wilson, 1945. 207p.   **AE32**

A comprehensive compilation, all in one alphabetical arrangement except that Greek-letter fraternities are alphabetized at the end of the appropriate English letter according to the English spelling of the Greek initial.

Wilkes, Ian. British initials and abbreviations. London, Leonard Hill Books, 1963. 111p., index (unpaged).**AE33**

Abbreviations for British and international organizations and institutions. An unusual feature is the index by subject category.

Basic English

Ogden, Charles Kay. The general Basic English dictionary, giving more than 40,000 senses of over 20,000 words, in Basic English. . . . N.Y., Norton, 1942. 441p. il. **AE34**

Originally published in London, Evans Bros., 1940 (repr.

1964). The American edition adds, p.439–41, lists of Basic English words by form, such as Operations, 100; Things: 400 General, 200 Pictorial; Qualities: 100 General, 50 Opposites.

"For the use of learners of English. . . . Using only the 850 words of Basic . . . and fifty international words, which go with them, it gives a knowledge of over 20,000 English words, covering at least 40,000 separate senses and special word-groups. . . . Great care has been given to idioms."—*Note.*

Etymology

❦ For the etymology of the English language the best authority is Murray's *New English dictionary* (AE20). Smaller works include:

Partridge, Eric. Name into word: proper names that have become common property. A discursive dictionary. London, Secker & Warburg, 1949. 644p. **AE35**

Common words derived from personal, geographical, and other names, with "discursive" explanations.

—— Origins: a short etymological dictionary of modern English. [2d ed. with some corrections and additions] London, Routledge & Paul, 1959. 970p. **AE36**

An etymological dictionary of the 12,000 most common words in modern English. Omits dialect and slang, except in a few instances, and does not include many scientific and technical terms. Includes lists of prefixes, suffixes, and word elements.

Schröer, Michael Martin Arnold. Englisches Handwörterbuch in genetischer Darstellung auf Grund der Etymologien und Bedeutungsentwicklungen, mit phonetischer Aussprachebezeichnung und Berücksichtigung des Amerikanischen und der Eigennamen, mitbearbeitet und hrsg. von P. L. Jaeger. Heidelberg, Carl Winter, 1937–64. Lfg. 1–21. (In progress) **AE37**

Lfg. 1–21, A–sweat.

A scholarly dictionary in German on the etymology of English words, with many examples of usage, etc.

Skeat, Walter William. An etymological dictionary of the English language. New ed., rev. and enl. [4th ed.] Oxford, Clarendon Pr., 1910. 780p. **AE38**

The standard scholarly work giving full histories of more than 14,000 words, with references to sources.

Contents: (1) Dictionary; (2) Appendix: Lists of Prefixes, Suffixes, Homonyms, Doublets, Indogermanic roots; Distribution of words according to languages from which they are derived.

—— A concise etymological dictionary of the English language. New and corr. imp. Oxford, Clarendon Pr., 1911. 663p. (Repr. 1958) **AE39**

Explanations, etymologies, histories, and quotations are much abbreviated.

Weekley, Ernest. Etymological dictionary of modern English. London, Murray; N.Y., Dutton, 1921. 1659col. **AE40**

Popular work, for the general reader rather than for the specialist, giving the histories of the literary and colloquial vocabulary, omitting most scientific terms.

—— A concise etymological dictionary of modern English. . . . Rev. ed. London, Secker & Warburg; N.Y., Dutton, 1952. 480p. **AE41**

An abridged version of the above, which it does not supersede. References to "remote languages" and illustrative quotations are omitted; some new words are added and others dropped.

Idioms and usage

Bryant, Margaret M. Current American usage. N.Y., Funk & Wagnalls, [1962]. 290p. **AE42**

A handbook which "attempts to bring together the most recent information about frequently debated points of usage in English speech and writing."—*Introd.* Debated points in current usage are discussed with citations to dictionaries, linguistic treatments, and articles in current periodicals, as well as to special investigations made especially for use in this book.

Evans, Bergen and **Evans, Cornelia.** A dictionary of contemporary American usage. N.Y., Random, 1957. 567p. **AE43**

An informally written, scholarly, and sometimes witty dictionary of contemporary American usage, reflecting the personal opinions of the authors. Arranged alphabetically, with explanations of grammar and rhetoric, word usage, literary concepts, clichés, phrases, idioms, figures of speech, etc. Informative and provocative.

Fowler, Henry Watson. Dictionary of modern English usage. 2d ed., rev. by Sir Ernest Gowers. Oxford, Clarendon Pr., 1965. 725p. **AE44**

1st ed. 1926.

Alphabetically arranged; definitions of terms—sometimes with disputed spellings and spelling of plurals, pronunciation, etc.—are interspersed with brief essays on the use and misuse of words and expressions, parts of speech, etc. Reflects the author's personal opinions, and comments are often astringent and witty. The revision by Sir Ernest Gowers aims to bring the work up to date without sacrificing the "Fowleresque flavour." It adds a classified guide to enable the reader to find items given by Fowler under enigmatic titles.

Gowers, *Sir* **Ernest Arthur.** Plain words: their ABC. [1st Amer. ed.] N.Y., Knopf, 1962. 298p. **AE45**

This is the American title of the work published in London by the Stationery Office, 1954, with the title *The complete plain words.* It is a reconstruction of the author's *Plain words* and *ABC of plain words.*

Not a manual in the usual sense but an aid to correct usage, written in a discursive style. Intended especially for those writing "official English" in correspondence, reports, etc.

Horwill, Herbert William. Dictionary of modern American usage. 2d ed. Oxford, Clarendon Pr., 1944. 360p. **AE46**

1st ed. 1935.

Not a dictionary of standard American usage, but a handbook, by an English writer, intended primarily to assist English visitors in America or English readers of American books and magazines by explaining words or phrases which have a meaning or use in the United States different from that in England. Includes about 1300 main words.

Nicholson, Margaret. A dictionary of American-English usage, based on Fowler's Modern English usage. N.Y., Oxford Univ. Pr., 1957. 671p. **AE47**

For Fowler's *Dictionary of modern English usage, see* AE44.

" . . . an adaptation of MEU, not a replacement. AEU is a simplified MEU, with American variations, retaining as much of the original as space allowed."—*Pref.* Some of the articles were shortened, some omitted, and new entries and illustrations added. Fowler's own mannerisms have been retained.

Standard handbook of prepositions, conjunctions, relative pronouns and adverbs. By the Funk and Wagnalls Editorial Staff. N.Y., Funk & Wagnalls, 1953. 116p. **AE48**

A handbook of usage showing derivation; current usage; differentiation in use of prepositions, conjunctions, etc. Includes a list of prepositional idioms.

Wood, Frederick T. Current English usage; a concise dictionary. London, Macmillan; N.Y., St. Martin's, 1962. 273p. **AE49**

A concise handbook indicating the correct and incorrect use of words and expressions. British viewpoint.

Obsolete

☙ Smaller dictionaries of unusual, obsolete, and provincial words are often useful for additional instances and quotations and for incidental information about local customs, observances, etc., even though most or all of the words in such dictionaries are now included in the large works of Murray (AE20) and Wright (AE86). The following are the best-known dictionaries of this type.

Halliwell-Philips, James Orchard. Dictionary of archaic and provincial words, obsolete phrases, proverbs, and ancient customs from the 14th century. 13th ed. London, Routledge, 1889. 2v.   **AE50**

1st ed. 1847. Frequently reprinted without change.

———— ———— Supplementary English glossary by T. Lewis O. Davies. London, Bell, 1881. 736p.

Defines archaic and provincial words and gives many illustrative quotations showing their use.

Nares, Robert. Glossary of words, phrases, names, and allusions in the works of English authors, particularly of Shakespeare and his contemporaries. New ed., with considerable additions both of words and examples, by J. O. Halliwell and Thomas Wright. London, Routledge, 1905. 981p.   **AE51**

1st ed. 1822; 1st Halliwell and Wright ed. 1857. Frequently reprinted.

Rich in quotations.

Skeat, Walter William. Glossary of Tudor and Stuart words, especially from the dramatists. Ed., with additions, by A. L. Mayhew. Oxford, Clarendon Pr., 1914. 461p.   **AE52**

Pronunciation

Greet, William Cabell. World words, recommended pronunciations. 2d ed. rev. and enl. N.Y., Columbia Univ. Pr., 1948. 608p.   **AE53**

A revised and much enlarged revision of *War words,* published in 1943, and of *World words,* published 1944. Gives pronunciation of some 25,000 names and words including battlefields, places made familiar by the war, names of persons in the news, and difficult words. Pronunciation is given "by a simplified Websterian alphabet . . . and by a phonetic respelling." Compiled especially for radio broadcasters of the Columbia Broadcasting System. Includes the pronunciation of many names not easily found elsewhere.

Jones, Daniel. Everyman's English pronouncing dictionary, containing 58,000 words in international phonetic transcription. 11th ed. compl. rev., enl., brought up to date, and reset, and with a glossary of phonetic terms. N.Y., Dutton, 1956. 538p.   **AE54**

Earlier editions had title *An English pronouncing dictionary.*

Words, including some proper names, are listed, followed by pronunciation in the phonetic alphabet. No definitions.

Kenyon, John Samuel and **Knott, Thomas Albert.** A pronouncing dictionary of American English. [2d ed.] Springfield, Mass., Merriam, 1949. 484p. il.   **AE55**

1st ed. 1944.

A dictionary giving the pronunciation, by the phonetic alphabet, of the colloquial speech of cultivated Americans, recording the variant pronunciations in different parts of the country, as East, West, South, North. Besides the common words, includes proper names, especially for America; some British personal and place-names; a few foreign names of general interest; and names in literature and history likely to be encountered by college students in their reading. No definitions.

NBC handbook of pronunciation. 3d ed. Originally comp. by James F. Bender for the National Broadcasting Company; rev. by Thomas Lee Crowell, Jr. N.Y., Crowell, 1964. 418p.   **AE56**

1st ed. 1943.

A guide to the pronunciation of proper names, common words often mispronounced, and "perennially difficult names from history and the arts." The pronunciation is indicated by respelling and phonetically; reflects "General American" usage; and is intended to be that spoken by the professional broadcaster.

Includes more than 20,000 entries. A new feature is the "Names in the News" section.

Punctuation

Partridge, Eric. You have a point there; a guide to punctuation and its allies. With a chapter on American practice by John W. Clark. London, Hamish Hamilton, 1953. 230p.   **AE57**

Shaw, Harry. Punctuate it right! N.Y., Barnes & Noble, [1963]. 176p.   **AE58**

A useful, well-arranged handbook explaining current practices of American punctuation. Includes many examples.

Rhymes

Holofcener, Lawrence. A practical dictionary of rhymes, based on new principles for songwriters and other versifiers. N.Y., Crown, 1960. 211p.   **AE59**

A lengthy introduction on some of the techniques of song writing precedes the list of rhymes.

Johnson, Burges. New rhyming dictionary and poets' handbook. Rev. ed. N.Y., Harper, 1957. 464p.   **AE60**

1st ed. 1931.

Contents: Forms of English versification with examples; Rhyming dictionary, one-syllable rhymes, two-syllable rhymes, three-syllable rhymes.

[Lathrop, Lorin Andrews]. Rhymers' lexicon, comp. and ed. by Andrew Loring, [pseud.] . . . introd. by George Saintsbury. 2d ed. rev. London, Routledge; N.Y., Dutton, 1905. 879p.   **AE61**

Pt.1, monosyllables and words accented on the last syllable; pt.2, words accented on the penult; pt.3, words accented on the antepenult.

Wood, Clement. Wood's Unabridged rhyming dictionary, introd. by Ted Robinson. . . . Cleveland, N.Y., World, 1943. 1040p.   **AE62**

Gives rhyming sounds for single, double, and triple rhymes grouped according to consonantal opening. Rhymes are based on sound, not spelling, and pronunciation is given.

Also includes sections on: The vocabulary of poetry, Complete formbook for poets, Fixed forms, Mechanics of rhyme, Versification self-taught, and Advanced versification.

Slang

Burke, William Jeremiah. The literature of slang . . . with an introductory note by Eric Partridge. N.Y., N.Y. Pub. Lib., 1939. 180p. (Repr. from the New York Public Library. Bull. 1936–38)   **AE63**

An annotated, classified bibliography of books, articles, and miscellanea, with author index. Covers the literature of various types of cant, jargon, and slang.

Barrère, Albert and **Leland, C. G.** Dictionary of slang, jargon and cant; embracing English, American and Anglo-Indian slang, pidgin English, gypsies' jargon and other irregular phraseology. London, Bell, 1897. 2v.   **AE64**

Berrey, Lester V. and **Van den Bark, Melvin.** American thesaurus of slang. 2d ed. A complete reference book of colloquial speech. N.Y., Crowell, 1953. 1272p. **AE65**

1st ed. 1942.

Arranged in two parts: (1) general slang and colloquialisms subdivided into categories arranged according to dominant idea; and (2) special slang of particular classes and occupations including such sections as underworld, trades and occupations, sports, military, western, etc. Includes an alphabetical word index. In the 2d edition new words have been added and outmoded terms omitted, so that the new edition does not entirely supersede the earlier one.

Farmer, John Stephen and **Henley, W. E.** Slang and its analogues, past and present; a dictionary, historical and comparative, of the heterodox speech of all classes of society for more than three hundred years, with synonyms in English, French, German, Italian, etc. London, Routledge, 1890–1904. 7v. (Repr.: N.Y., Kraus, 1965. 7v. in 4) **AE66**

An older and still useful slang dictionary, listing about 100,000 words. Gives explanation, derivation, kind of usage, illustrative quotations with references to sources, and synonyms in French, German, Italian, and Spanish.

An abridged edition was published 1905. 533p.

Partridge, Eric. Dictionary of slang and unconventional English: colloquialisms and catch-phrases, solecisms and catachreses, nicknames, vulgarisms, and such Americanisms as have been naturalized. [5th ed. with much enl. suppl.] London, Routledge & Paul, 1961. 2v. (1362p.) **AE67**

v.1, The Dictionary, is a reprint of the original edition of 1937; v.2, The Supplement, incorporates into one alphabet the *Addenda* of the 2d, 3d, and 4th editions (with some revisions) and new material running to some 100,000 words. These additions consist mainly of new words and phrases with the emphasis on slang, particularly of World War II.

The author's *Smaller slang dictionary* (London, Routledge & Paul, 1961. 204p.) is an abridgment of the larger work, "omitting absolutely all matter that could offend against propriety or even delicacy."—*Foreword.*

—— A dictionary of Forces' slang, 1939–1945. London, Secker & Warburg; N.Y., Saunders, 1948. 212p. **AE68**

Naval slang by Wilfred Granville; Army slang by Frank Roberts; Air Force slang by Eric Partridge.

All in one alphabet.

—— Dictionary of the underworld, British and American. London, Routledge; N.Y., Macmillan, 1949, [i.e., 1950]. 804p. **AE69**

Subtitle: Being the vocabularies of crooks, criminals, racketeers, beggars and tramps, convicts, the commercial underworld, the drug traffic, the white slave traffic, spivs.

—— Slang, today and yesterday, with a short historical sketch and vocabularies of English, American and Australian slang. London, Routledge, 1933. 476p. **AE70**

A history and discussion with glossaries of words.

Weingarten, Joseph Abraham. An American dictionary of slang and colloquial speech. N.Y., [priv. pr.], 1954. 390p. **AE71**

Attempts to give the earliest date for each word and phrase with reference to authority.

Wentworth, Harold and **Flexner, Stuart Berg.** Dictionary of American slang. N.Y., Crowell, 1960. 669p. **AE72**

A very full listing, including many taboo expressions, with considerable explanation of usage, and a high percentage of references to source and date. The appendix includes various classified lists and an extensive bibliography.

Synonyms and antonyms

Allen, Frederic Sturges. Allen's Synonyms and antonyms. Rev. and enl. ed., ed. by T. H. Vail Motter. N.Y., London, Harper, 1938. 427p. **AE73**

First pub. 1921.

Alphabetical arrangement, giving for each word a list of its synonyms and antonyms, but no definitions. Gives sense discriminations; examples of cant, slang, and colloquialisms; and many British equivalents of American terms. These last are usually listed only under the American word.

Crabb, George. Crabb's English synonyms. Rev. and enl. by the addition of modern terms and definitions arranged alphabetically, with complete cross references throughout, with introd. by John H. Finley. N.Y., Harper, 1945. 717p. **AE74**

1st ed. 1817; several times revised or reprinted. A spot check of the 1945 printing shows no change from the 1917 centennial edition.

An alphabetical list, arranged by the first word of a group of synonymous words, with explanation and differentiation of the use and meaning of the words in the group; cross references from each of the words.

Fernald, James Champlin. Funk & Wagnalls standard handbook of synonyms, antonyms, and prepositions. Compl. rev. ed. by the Funk and Wagnalls Editorial Staff. N.Y., Funk & Wagnalls, 1947. 515p. **AE75**

Previously pub. 1914 under title *English synonyms and antonyms.* This edition revised and reset. Arranged by key words, listing synonyms and antonyms and giving a discussion on the discrimination among the words. Alphabetical index.

March, Francis Andrew and **March, Francis A., Jr.** March's Thesaurus-dictionary. Issued under the editorial supervision of Norman Cousins. New supplement by R. A. Goodwin. Garden City, N.Y., Hanover, 1958. 1240p. **AE76**

1st edition, 1902, entitled *A thesaurus dictionary of the English language.*

A standard work, giving for each word a definition and cross references to key words under which will be found groups of words of related significance.

The new Supplement, p.1191–1240, "lists and defines some 1800 words and phrases that have come into general use since the turn of the century." The treatment and arrangement are the same as those used in the basic work, and by means of symbols and cross references the supplementary material is integrated with the original.

Roget's International thesaurus. 3d ed. N.Y., Crowell, 1962. 1258p. **AE77**

A complete revision and resetting of the new edition of 1946. First published in 1911 under title *The standard thesaurus of English words and phrases classified and arranged so as to facilitate the expression of ideas and assist in literary composition.*

Arranged by categories classified according to the idea or signification of a word, with an alphabetical word index referring to the category.

Soule, Richard. A dictionary of English synonyms and synonymous expressions, designed as a guide to apt and varied diction. New ed. rev. and enl. by Alfred Dwight Sheffield. Boston, Little, 1938. 614p. **AE78**

1st ed. 1871. Many times reprinted with various revisions. This edition called "3rd edition."

Alphabetical listing followed by synonyms. No definitions or discussion.

Webster's Dictionary of synonyms. 1st ed. A Merriam-Webster. A dictionary of discriminated synonyms, with antonyms and analogous and contrasted words. Springfield, Mass., Merriam, 1951. 907p. **AE79**

First printed 1942.

A comprehensive dictionary of synonyms, including also antonyms and lists of analogous words and their opposites. Words of like meaning are distinguished from one another by careful discrimination and illustrations from classical and contemporary writers. Includes an introduction on the history of English synonymy.

For many purposes the most useful of the dictionaries of synonyms.

Regional and dialect

American

☙ There are now three important dictionaries of American English: Craigie's *Dictionary of American English on historical principles* (AE80), Mathews' *Dictionary of Americanisms on historical principles* (AE81), and Thornton's *American glossary* (AE84), which together give a fairly comprehensive coverage. Mencken's *American language* (AE82), while not technically a dictionary, is useful for its historical treatment and the large number of words included. Additional lists and articles on special, historical, and current usage may be found in *American speech*, 1925–　; *Dialect notes*, published by the American Dialect Society, 1890–1939; and the Society's monographic *Publications*, 1944–　.

While the above are the most generally useful dictionaries, some older works are still occasionally helpful for historical purposes, e.g., J. R. Bartlett, *Dictionary of Americanisms* (1877); Sylva Clapin, *New Dictionary of Americanisms* (1902); James Maitland, *American slang dictionary* (1891). Some of the more recent slang dictionaries should be used for contemporary speech.

✓ **Craigie,** *Sir* **William Alexander** and **Hulbert, James R.** Dictionary of American English on historical principles. Chicago, Univ. of Chicago Pr.; Oxford, Univ. Pr., 1936–44. 4v.　　**AE80**

v.4, p.2529–52, Bibliography, giving "a record of the bulk of the reading done for the Dictionary . . . and expanding into completeness the short-title references used in citations."

Compiled on historical principles, with explanations of meaning or use dated when period is clearly determined, and with illustrative quotations dated and arranged chronologically. Symbols indicate: a word or sense found in English before 1600; a word or sense originating within the present limits of the United States; a term or sense known only from the passage cited.

Does not attempt to present a complete historical dictionary of every word which has been current since the settlement of the first English colonists but, instead, to show "those features by which the English of the American colonies and the United States is distinguished from that of England and the rest of the English-speaking world," including for that purpose "not only words or phrases which are clearly or apparently of American origin, or have greater currency here than elsewhere, but also every word denoting something which has a real connection with the development of the country and the history of its people."—Cf. *Pref.*, p.v.

The period covered is to the end of the 19th century, with later information for some words established before that date. Types of words included are: names of plants, trees, and animals; names of natural or artificial products; and special terms, e.g., topographical, medical, legal, military, naval, business, educational, etc. Colloquialisms are included, but slang and dialect words are restricted to those of early date or special prominence.

✓ **Mathews, Mitford McLeod.** A dictionary of Americanisms on historical principles. Chicago, Univ. of Chicago Pr., [1951]. 2v. (1946p.)　　**AE81**

Bibliography, p.1913–46.

More limited in scope than Craigie's *Dictionary of American English* (AE80); deals with *Americanisms,* meaning "a word or expression that originated in the United States," including (1) outright coinages; (2) foreign words which first became English in the United States; and (3) words used in senses first given them in American usage (cf. *Pref.*). Compiled from sources up to time of publication, excluding manuscript material. Many of the quotations are the same as in Craigie, although the bibliographies vary widely. Definitions and illustrative quotations are given chronologically; usually only one pronunciation is indicated. Some variant spellings are given.

Mencken, Henry Louis. The American language; an inquiry into the development of English in the United States. 4th ed., corr., enl., and rewritten. N.Y., Knopf, 1936. 769p.　　**AE82**

————　Supplements, 1–2. 1945–48.

————　Abridged edition. N.Y., Knopf, 1963. 777p., cxxivp.　　**AE83**

For full information *see* BC24.

Thornton, Richard H. An American glossary, being an attempt to illustrate certain Americanisms upon historical principles. London, Francis; Philadelphia, Lippincott, 1912; New Haven, Conn., Amer. Dialect Soc., 1931–39. 3v. (v.3, in Dialect notes, 1931–39) (Repr.: With an introduction by Margaret M. Bryant. N.Y., Ungar, 1962. 3v.)　　**AE84**

v.1–2, A–Z; v.3, Supplement A–Z.

Includes: (1) forms of speech now obsolete or provincial in England which survive in the United States; (2) words and phrases of American origin; (3) nouns indicating quadrupeds, birds, trees, etc. that are distinctly American; (4) names of persons, of classes of people, and of places; (5) words that have assumed a new meaning; (6) words and phrases of which there are earlier examples in American than in English writers.

The list of words is largely historical and includes little modern slang. For each word a definition and explanation are given as well as illustrative quotations with exact references to sources, chronologically arranged. These quotations are numerous, some 14,000 in the first two volumes, and are taken from books, pamphlets, newspapers, and periodicals published in various parts of the country.

The Supplement, edited by Louise Hanley, is based on material collected by Thornton after the publication of his *Glossary* and later turned over by him to the American Dialect Society. Examples and illustrative quotations are from a wide general reading, but especially full for the *Congressional globe* and *Congressional record*, 1860–1900, with indication, for words taken from this source, of both the name of the speaker and the part of the country from which he came. This third volume, though first published in *Dialect notes,* is separately paged and has its own title page, so that it can be bound to stand with v.1–2.

Wentworth, Harold. American dialect dictionary. N.Y., Crowell, 1944. 747p.　　**AE85**

"American printed sources quoted," p.737–47.

Includes more than 10,000 terms with 60,000 quotations showing usage. "Deals mainly with dialect in the sense of localisms, regionalisms, and provincialisms; folk speech, urban as well as rustic New England and Southern United States dialects viewed in their deviations from General Northern or Western. . . ."—*Pref.*

British

✓ **Wright, Joseph.** English dialect dictionary; being the complete vocabulary of all dialect words still in use, or known to have been in use during the last 200 years; founded on the publications of the English Dialect Society. London, Frowde, 1898–1905. 6v. **AE86**

Contents: v.1–6, A–Z; Supplement, Bibliography, Grammar.

Aims to cover the complete vocabulary of all English dialect words still in use, or known to have been in use from 1700 on, in England, Ireland, Scotland, and Wales, including words occurring in both the literary language and the spoken dialect. Gives for each word: (1) exact geographical area over which it extends; (2) pronunciation; and (3) etymology. Includes American and colonial words still in use in Great Britain or contained in early books and glossaries. Gives many illustrative quotations and, incidentally, considerable information about popular games, customs and superstitions, with bibliographical references to sources of fuller information.

Colonial

Baker, Sidney John. New Zealand slang; a dictionary of colloquialisms, the first comprehensive survey yet made of indigenous English speech in this country—from the argot of whaling days to children's slang in the twentieth century. Christchurch, N.Z., Whitcombe and Tombs, [1941]. 114p. **AE87**

Morris, Edward Ellis. Austral English; a dictionary of Australasian words, phrases, and usages, with those aboriginal-Australian and Maori words which have become incorporated in the language, and the commoner scientific words that have had their origin in Australasia. London, Macmillan, 1898. 525p. **AE88**

Pettman, Charles. Africanderisms; a glossary of South African colloquial words and phrases, and of place and other names. London, N.Y., Longmans, 1913. 579p. **AE89**

Good definitions. Illustrative quotations are given with date and exact page reference.

Yule, *Sir* **Henry** and **Burnell, A. C.** Hobson-Jobson; a glossary of colloquial Anglo-Indian words and phrases, and of kindred terms, etymological, historical, geographical and discursive. New ed., by William Crooke. London, Murray, 1903. 1021p. **AE90**

A standard work still not superseded.

Scottish

Craigie, *Sir* **William Alexander.** Dictionary of the older Scottish tongue from the 12th century to the end of the 17th. Chicago, Univ. of Chicago Pr.; Oxford, Univ. Pr., 1931–64. Pts.1–21. (In progress) **AE91**

Pts.1–21, A–Lyue.

Beginning with pt.17, ed. by A. J. Aitken.

"Intended to exhibit the whole range of the Older Scottish vocabulary, as preserved in literature and documentary records, and to continue the history of the language to 1700, so far as it does not coincide with the ordinary English usage of that century."—*Pref. note.*

Jamieson, John. Etymological dictionary of the Scottish language . . . to which is prefixed a dissertation on the origin of the Scottish language. New ed., carefully rev. and collated, with the entire supplement incorporated, by John Longmuir and David Donaldson. Paisley, Gardner, 1879–82. 4v. and suppl., 1887. **AE92**

1st ed., 2v., 1808; suppl. by Jamieson, 2 v., 1827; an edition incorporating the words of the supplement but omitting its quotations, ed. by J. Johnstone, 1840–41; the rev. ed. by Longmuir and Donaldson, as above.

A comprehensive work, now out of date for etymologies, but still useful for the number of words included, the definitions, and the large amount of incidental information on local usages, customs, etc.

—— Jamieson's Dictionary of the Scottish language, abridged by J. Johnstone and rev. and enl. by Dr. Longmuir, with suppl. . . . by W. M. Metcalfe. Paisley, Gardner, 1910. 2v. in 1. **AE93**

1st ed. of the Johnstone abridgment of Jamieson, 1840; ed. rev. by Longmuir, 2v., 1867.

v.1, The Johnstone-Longmuir abridgement. 635p.; v.2, Supplementary dictionary, by W. M. Metcalfe. 263p.

Jarvie, James Nicol. Lallans; a selection of Scots words arranged as an English-Scottish dictionary, with pronunciation and examples. London, Wren Books, 1947. 159p. **AE94**

English-Scottish. Includes Scots proverbs and quotations.

Scottish national dictionary, designed partly on regional lines and partly on historical principles, and containing all the Scottish words known to be in use or to have been in use since *c.* 1700; ed. by William Grant and David Murison. Edinburgh, Scottish Nat. Dictionary Assoc., 1931–64. v.1–6, pt.3. (In progress, to be completed in about 10v.) **AE95**

v.1–6 [3], A-Naither.

Scope: "*The Scottish National Dictionary* deals with (1) Scottish words in existence since *c.* 1700: (a) in Scottish literature, (b) in public records, (c) in glossaries and in dictionaries, (d) in private collections, (e) in special dialect treatises, and (2) Scottish words gathered from the mouth of dialect speakers by competent observers. The general vocabulary will include (1) Scottish words that do not occur in Standard English except as acknowledged loan words; (2) Scottish words the cognates of which occur in St. Eng.; (3) words which have the same form in Scots and St. Eng. but have a different meaning in Sc., *i.e.*, so-called Scotticisms; (4) legal, theological or ecclesiastical terms which within our period have been current in Scottish speech . . . (5) words borrowed since *c.* 1700 (from other dialects or languages) which have become current in General Scots, or in any of its dialects, especially Gaelic words in counties on or near the Sc. Western limit and Gypsy words in the Border counties."—*Introd.,* p.xlv.

Treatment: For each word gives variant spellings, grammatical function, status (e.g., obsolete, colloquial, etc.), pronunciation, illustrative quotations with exact references to sources, and origin of word, if known.

Anglo-Saxon

Bessinger, Jess Balsor. A short dictionary of Anglo-Saxon poetry, in a normalized early West-Saxon orthography. Toronto, Univ. of Toronto Pr., 1960. 87p. **AE96**

"A gloss to the crucial 40 per cent of the poetic vocabulary—some 3000 parent words."—*Pref.*

Bosworth, Joseph. Anglo-Saxon dictionary based on the manuscript collections of the late Joseph Bosworth, ed. and enl. by T. Northcote Toller. Oxford, Clarendon Pr., 1882–98. 1302p. **AE97**

—— —— Supplement, by T. Northcote Toller. Oxford, Clarendon Pr., 1908–21. 768p.

1st ed. 1838.

Still the standard work with many illustrative quotations and exact references to sources. The letters A–G are extensively revised and enlarged in the Supplement.

Hall, John Richard Clark. Concise Anglo-Saxon dictionary. 4th ed., with a supplement by Herbert D. Meritt. Cambridge, Univ. Pr., 1960. 432p., [20p.]. **AE98**

1st ed. 1894; 3d ed., rev. and enl., 1931.

References are given to the headings in the *New English dictionary* (AE20) under which quotations are cited from the Anglo-Saxon texts, thus making it serve as an index to the large amount of valuable information on Old English words included in the *New English dictionary* but often overlooked because it is found under the headings of words now obsolete.

Middle English

Kurath, Hans and **Kuhn, Sherman M.** Middle English dictionary. Ann Arbor, Univ. of Michigan Pr., 1952–64.
v.1– . (In progress) **AE99**

v.1, A–B; v.2, C–D; v.3, pt.1, E–F; v.3, pt.2, G–Grith (fasc.1–3).

This important dictionary, a research project of the University of Michigan, is based on a large collection of Middle English quotations, which includes all those assembled for the *New English dictionary* (AE20), both published and unpublished, in addition to hundreds of thousands gathered for this work. It is to be completed in some 65 parts and will include about 10,000 pages. The bibliography and a full description of the editing plan appeared as a separate part in 1954 (105p.).

To cover the language from 1100 to 1475; gives the histories of words with many illustrative quotations arranged chronologically. Many cross references.

Stratmann, Francis Henry. Middle-English dictionary, containing words used by English writers from the 12th to the 15th century; new ed. rearranged, rev., and enl. by Henry Bradley. Oxford, Clarendon Pr., 1891. 708p.
AE100

This standard work will still be useful until Kurath (AE99) is completed. Gives etymologies and references to sources.

FOREIGN LANGUAGES

☙ Foreign-language dictionaries are important in any library, though their use will vary greatly according to the size and type of the library and the character of the library clientele. The needs of the small library used by English-speaking readers may be met by a modest equipment of French, German, Spanish, Italian, and Latin dictionaries, while the small or branch library in a locality which has a considerable foreign population will need also the dictionaries of the languages represented. Large public libraries, and especially university libraries, need the best dictionaries of all principal languages and many minor languages.

Two main types of dictionaries are represented in the following list: (1) the standard monolingual dictionary, such as Grimm (AE262), and (2) the bilingual dictionary, such as the various French-English and German-English dictionaries. The first type is the more complete and must be consulted when the fullest vocabulary or detailed and historical information is needed, but it can be used only by someone fairly familiar with the language and is not generally needed in the smaller library. The second type, which is the kind most used in the average library, is planned for people who are learning a language, is much less complete in vocabulary, and usually contains no historical information, as its main purpose is not detailed definition but the explanation of a foreign word by its equivalent in another language. Emphasis in this listing has naturally been placed on the foreign-language-into-English dictionary, although in some cases others are included, e.g., Greek-German.

The ordinary bilingual dictionary is generally satisfactory for most words of the literary language but is often weak in scientific terms and technical expressions. For these, scientific and technical dictionaries should be consulted.

Bilingual dictionaries also differ according to the users for whom they are compiled. In a French-English dictionary, prepared for the use of English-speaking students

learning French, the French-English section is the more important, and this will be developed carefully, while the English-French section may be given briefer treatment. The reverse is true of a dictionary prepared for French students learning English. A library which can afford to have several dictionaries of a language should take this difference into account and represent both points of view.

As so large a proportion of the use of foreign dictionaries in an American library is for the purpose of finding the English meaning of a foreign word, the many other possible uses of such books are sometimes overlooked. The larger dictionaries frequently contain some encyclopedic information; those that include many quotations may often be used to supplement the dictionaries of foreign quotations; and the larger historical or dialectal dictionaries which include obsolete words, local usages, etc. may be used for information on small points of local history, manners and customs, folklore, etc.

See name of subject for scientific, technical, and other special dictionaries, e.g., Chemistry—Dictionaries, etc.

For more extensive lists of dictionaries, consult the bibliographies, AE104–AE108.

Bibliography

Collison, Robert Lewis. Dictionaries of foreign languages; a bibliographical guide to the general and technical dictionaries of the chief foreign languages, with historical and explanatory notes and references. N.Y., Hafner, 1955. 210p. **AE104**

Gives historical and critical notes on the general, special, and bilingual dictionaries of the languages of Europe, Asia, and Africa. Includes special lists of French, German, Italian, Spanish, Russian, and Scandinavian dialect dictionaries; an appendix gives technical dictionaries in various languages arranged by subject.

Lewanski, Richard C. A bibliography of Slavic dictionaries. N.Y., N.Y. Pub. Lib., 1959–63. 3v. **AE105**

Contents: [v.1], Polish; v.2, Belorussian, Bulgarian, Czech, Kashabian, Lusatian, Old Church Slavic, Macedonian, Polabian, Serbocroatian, Slovak, Slovenian, Ukrainian; v.3, Russian.

v.1 issued in 1959 as *A bibliography of Polish dictionaries.*

A comprehensive bibliography of Slavic dictionaries and glossaries with subject, author, and language indexes. The volume of Russian dictionaries lists the numerous bilingual dictionaries of the Soviet Union, as well as many types of monolingual dictionaries, with the exception of the biographical and bio-bibliographical dictionaries, comprehensively covered by Kaufman (AE493).

U.S. Library of Congress. General Reference and Bibliography Division. Foreign language–English dictionaries. Wash., 1955. 2v. **AE106**

Contents: v.1, Special subject dictionaries, 1524 items, with emphasis on science and technology; v.2, General language dictionaries, 1465 items.

A revised edition of U.S. Library of Congress. Division of Bibliography. *Foreign language–English dictionaries,* comp. by Grace Hadley Fuller. 1942–44.

Walford, Albert John. A guide to foreign language grammars and dictionaries. London, Lib. Assoc., 1964. 132p.
AE107

Includes French, Italian, Spanish, Portuguese, German, Scandinavian languages, and Russian.

A selective list with critical and evaluative notes.

Zaunmüller, Wolfram. Bibliographisches Handbuch der Sprachwörterbücher: ein internationales Verzeichnis von

5600 Wörterbüchern der Jahre 1460–1958 für mehr als 500 Sprachen und Dialekte. Stuttgart, Hiersemann, 1958. (Distr. in U.S. by Hafner, N.Y.) 496col. **AE108**

A very useful, annotated bibliography of language dictionaries attempting to be complete for those published during the last 100 years with a selection of those published between 1460 and 1850. The first and the last editions are noted. The most important items are starred. Arranged alphabetically under language names with subdivisions for the large language groups. These subdivisions usually include as pertinent: (1) General (monolingual) dictionaries since 1850; (2) Bilingual or polylingual dictionaries; (3) Orthography, pronunciation, dictionaries of names; (4) Synonyms, style, usage, rhymes, etc.; (5) Slang, foreign words; (6) Dialect dictionaries; (7) Etymological dictionaries; (8) Dictionaries of old speech; (9) General dictionaries before 1850. Includes an index of names and one of the languages under each continent.

Contains more languages than Collison (AE104).

Afrikaans

Bosman, Daniel Brink and **Merwe, I. W. v. d.** Tweetalige woordeboek. 4. hers. Kaapstad, Nasionale Pers, Beperk, 1962. 2v. **AE109**

v.1, Afrikaans-Engels; v.2, Engels-Afrikaans.

Kritzinger, Matthys Stefanus Benjamin. Groot woordeboek: Afrikaans-Engels, Engels-Afrikaans. 8. verb. uitg. Pretoria, Van Schaik, 1959. 1300p. **AE110**

Terblanche, Hendrik Josephus. Nuwe praktiese woordeboek. New practical dictionary. 4. intgebreide uitg. [Johannesburg], Afrikaanse Pers-Boekhandel, 1959. (Distr. in U.S. by W. S. Heinman, N.Y.) 1119p. **AE111**

1st ed. 1949.

English-Afrikaans; Afrikaans-English.

Intended to represent the spoken and written language of everyday life, with emphasis on current idiom and general practice.

Woordeboek van die Afrikaanse taal. Pretoria, Die Staatsdrukker, 1950–61. v.1–4. il. (In progress) **AE112**

v.1–4, A–I.

Planned as the standard Afrikaans dictionary and sponsored by the government, the Suid-Afrikaanse Akademie vir Wetenskap en Kuns, and the University of Stellenbosch; the work of scholars from all over the Union. No etymologies or historical developments are given; pronunciation is indicated only in doubtful cases.

Albanian

Drizari, Nelo. Albanian-English and English-Albanian dictionary. 2d enl. ed., with a suppl. of new words. N.Y., Ungar, 1957. 320p. **AE113**

1st edition, 1934, had title *Fjalór Shqip-Inglisht dhe Inglisht-Shqip.*

Mann, Stuart Edward. An historical Albanian-English dictionary. London, Longmans, 1948. 601p. **AE114**

A standard work concerned primarily with linguistics but useful as a bilingual dictionary.

—— An English-Albanian dictionary. Cambridge, Univ. Pr., 1957. 434p. **AE115**

" . . . in some degree the counterpart of my *Historical Albanian-English dictionary* . . . It is an attempt to express the essential vocabulary of the English literary language in modern literary Albanian."—*Pref.*

Amharic

Armbruster, Carl Hubert. Initia amharica; an introduction to spoken Amharic. Cambridge, Univ. Pr., 1908–20. v.1–3¹. **AE116**

No more published.

Contents: pt.1, Grammar; pt.2, English-Amharic vocabulary with phrases; pt.3, Amharic-English vocabulary with phrases. v.1 (incompl.).

Baeteman, Joseph. Dictionnaire amarigna-français, suivi d'un vocabulaire français-amarigna. Dire-Daoua (Ethiopie), Impr. Saint Lazare, 1929. 1262col., 426col. **AE117**

Annamese

See Vietnamese, p.132.

Arabic

Badger, George Percy. English-Arabic lexicon, in which the equivalents for English words and idiomatic sentences are rendered into literary and colloquial Arabic. London, Paul, 1881. 1244p. **AE118**

A famous 19th-century work.

Blachère, Regis, Chouémi, Moustafa and **Denizeau, Claude.** Dictionnaire arabe-français-anglais. (Langue classique et moderne) Arab/French/English dictionary. Paris, Maisonneuve et Larose, 1964– . v.1, fasc.1– . **AE119**

Intends "to comprise all the vocabulary that constitutes . . . 'literary' Arabic."—*Foreword.* Meanings are given in French, then English.

Elias, Elias Antoon and **Elias, Edward E.** Elias' Modern dictionary, English-Arabic. 12th ed. with several additions and alterations. Cairo, Elias, 1961. 806p. il. **AE120**

"Containing about 68,000 words."

Frequently reprinted.

—— Elias' Modern dictionary, Arabic-English. 9th ed. with several additions and alterations. Cairo, Elias, 1962. 870p. il. **AE121**

"Containing about 64,500 words."

Hava, J. G. Arabic-English dictionary for the use of students. New ed. Beirut, Catholic Pr., 1951. 915p. **AE122**

Excellent medium-sized dictionary.

Appendix: List of Arabic words derived from foreign languages, p.906–15.

Khalil Saad, *Bey.* Centennial English-Arabic dictionary of the American Press. Paul Erdmann, managing ed.; Asa'ad Kheirallah, Arabic ed. Beirut, Amer. Pr., [pref. 1926]. 1058p. **AE123**

Arabic as used in the Levant.

Lane, Edward William. Arabic-English lexicon, derived from the best and the most copious eastern sources. In two books: the first containing all the classical words and significations commonly known to the learned among the Arabs; the second, those that are of rare occurrence and not commonly known. Book I. London, Williams and Norgate, 1863–93. 1v. in 8 pts., paged continuously. (Repr.: N.Y., Ungar, 1955–56. 3064p.) **AE124**

Book II never published.

Includes references to the literature.

Spiro, Socrates, *Bey.* Arabic-English and English-Arabic vocabulary of the modern and colloquial Arabic of Egypt. 2d–3d ed. rev. Cairo, Elias, 1923–29. 2v. **AE126**

Arabic-English. 2d. ed. 1923. 516p.; English-Arabic. 3d ed. 1929. 325p.

The colloquial Arabic of Egypt.

Theodory, Constantine. A dictionary of modern technical terms. Arabic-English. Beirut, Dar-Al-Kutub Press, 1959. 464p. **AE127**

1st ed.

Added title page in Arabic.

Includes much more than scientific and technical terms, e.g., proverbs and aphoristic phrases, literary expressions, political and diplomatic phrases, military terms and expressions, psychological and educational terms, etc.

Grouped into chapters by general topic.

Wehr, Hans. A dictionary of modern written Arabic, ed. by J. Milton Cowan. Ithaca, N.Y., Cornell Univ. Pr., 1961. 1110p. **AE128**

A translated, edited, and enlarged version of the author's *Arabisches Wörterbuch für die Schriftsprache der Gegenwart.* Leipzig, Harrassowitz, 1952. 2v. Supplement, 1958. The *Journal of Near Eastern studies* (13:208. 1954) called the German edition "doubtless the best dictionary of modern written Arabic now available."

The English edition integrates the contents of the *Supplement.*

Wortabet, John and **Porter, Harvey.** English-Arabic and Arabic-English dictionary; with a supplement of modern words and new meanings by John L. Mish. [enl. ed.] N.Y., Ungar, 1954. 455p., 423p. **AE129**

The reprint of a basic dictionary long out of print, with a supplement containing modern words and expressions.

Wörterbuch der klassischen arabischen Sprache . . . hrsg. durch die Deutsche Morgenländische Gesellschaft. Wiesbaden, Harrassowitz, 1957–64. Lfg. 1–6. **AE130**

"Auf Grund der Sammlungen von August Fischer, Theodor Nöldeke, Hermann Reckendorf, und anderer Quellen."—*Title page.*

A scholarly work of classical Arabic with extensive references to the literature. The main words are translated into both German and English.

Aramaic

See Hebrew, p.116.

Armenian

Aukerian, Haroutiun and **Brand, John.** Dictionary, English and Armenian. Venice, Armenian Academy of St. Lazarus, 1821–25. 2v. **AE131**

Froundjian, Dirair. Armenisch-deutsches Wörterbuch. München, R. Oldenbourg, 1952. 505p. **AE132**

Added title page in Armenian.

A useful dictionary of current Armenian, including many technical terms.

Kouyoumdjian, Mesrob G. A comprehensive dictionary, Armenian-English. Cairo, Sahag-Mesrob Press, [1950]. 1158p. **AE133**

A useful dictionary of modern Armenian, giving equivalents in English.

Aryan

Buck, Carl Darling. A dictionary of selected synonyms in the principal Indo-European languages; a contribution to the history of ideas. Chicago, Univ. of Chicago Pr., 1949. 1515p. **AE134**

Arranged by semantic groupings. Under each term the equivalent word is given in about 30 of the major Indo-European languages, followed by a description of its etymology and semantic history.

Carnoy, Albert Joseph. Dictionnaire étymologique du proto-indo-européen. Louvain, Publications Universitaires, 1955. 223p. (Bibliothèque du Muséon. v.39) **AE135**

At head of title: Université de Louvain. Institut Orientaliste.

Pokorny, Julius. Indogermanisches etymologisches Wörterbuch. Berne, A. Francke, 1949–59. 1183p. **AE136**

A standard etymological dictionary of the various Indogermanic languages. More than a revision of the Walde-Pokorny *Vergleichendes Wörterbuch der indogermanischen Sprachen* (Berlin, de Gruyter, 1927–32), which was based on materials published only through 1923. This uses sources through 1947, and is arranged according to the European, rather than the Indian, alphabet.

Turner, *Sir* **Ralph Lilley.** A comparative dictionary of the Indo-Aryan languages. London, Oxford Univ. Pr., 1962–65. Fasc.1–5. **AE137**

A comparative dictionary of more than 50 of the related languages of India, descended from that of the Aryan invaders, with English translations. Frequently gives references to the literature. Words are given in transliteration into the roman alphabet.

Announced to be in 9 or 10 parts, with indexes by language of all words cited.

Assyro-Babylonian

Bezold, Carl. Babylonisch-assyrisches Glossar; nach dem Tode des Verfassers unter Mitwirkung von Adele Bezold zum Druck gebracht von Albrecht Götze. Heidelberg, Winter, 1926. 343p. **AE138**

Chicago. University. Oriental Institute. The Assyrian dictionary. Editorial Board: Ignace J. Gelb [and others]. Chicago, Oriental Inst., 1956– . (In progress) **AE139**

Cited as CAD, i.e., *Chicago Assyrian dictionary.*

Contents: v.1¹, A–Alz, 1964; v.3, D, 1959; v.4, E, 1958; v.5, G, 1956; v.6, H, 1956; v.7, I–J, 1960; v.16, S, 1962; v.21, Z, 1961.

A scholarly Assyrian-English dictionary, giving meanings in English with examples and citations to literature. Of first importance.

Deimel, Anton. Šumerisches Lexikon. Rome, Sumptibus Pontificii Inst. Biblici, 1927–50. 4v. (Scripta Pontificii Inst. Biblici) **AE140**

Contents: T.1, Lautwerte der Keilschriftzeichen in šumerischen, akkadischen und hethitischen Texten; T.2, Vollständige Ideogram-Sammlung. 4v.; T.3, Bd.1, Sumerisch-akkadisches Glossar. Bd.2, Akkadisch-šumerisches Glossar; T.4, Bd.1, Pantheon babylonicum. Bd.2, Planetarium babylonicum, von P. Gössman.

Muss-Arnolt, William. Concise dictionary of the Assyrian language. Berlin, Reuther; N.Y., Lemcke, 1905. 1202p. **AE141**

Assyrian, English, and German.

Soden, Wolfram von. Akkadisches Handwörterbuch, unter Benutzung des lexikalischen Nachlasses von Bruno Meissner (1868–1947). Wiesbaden, Harrassowitz, 1959–63. Lfg. 1–5. (In progress) **AE142**

Lfg. 1–5, a–katamu.

A scholarly work, somewhat less comprehensive than the *Assyrian dictionary* (AE139). Detailed review in *Bibliotheca orientalis,* 17:166–68. 1960.

Basque

Lhande, Pierre. Dictionnaire basque-français et français-basque (dialectes labourdin, bas-navarrais et souletin) d'après le Dictionnaire basque-espagnol-français de l'abbé R. M. de Askué [i.e., Azkué] et les dictionnaires manuscrits des abbés M. Harriet, M. Hiribarren et Pierre Foix. Paris, G. Beauchesne, 1926–38. v.1– . **AE143**

v.1, Basque–français. 1117p. (Pub. in 9 pts.)

The standard work.

Bengali

Dev, Ashu Tosh. Students' favourite dictionary: English-to-Bengali & English. 18th ed. Calcutta, S. C. Mazumder, 1962. 1609p. il. maps.   **AE144**

Subtitle: Etymological, explanatory, with pronunciation, compound words, phrases, current technical terms, . . . foreign words and phrases, historical, mythological and classical allusions, proverbs, etc.

Bohemian

See Czech, p.106.

Brazilian

See Portuguese, p.124.

Breton

Ernault, Émile. Dictionnaire étymologique du breton moyen. (In his Le mystère de Sainte Barbe. Nantes, Soc. des Bibliophiles Bretons, 1885–87. p.189–400)   **AE145**

An etymological dictionary of medieval Breton.

—— Glossaire moyen-breton. 2. éd. corr. et augm. Paris, Bouillon, 1895–96. 833p.   **AE146**

Supplement to the above.

Forms v.2 of Henry d' Arbois de Jubainville and Émile Ernault. *Études grammaticales sur les langues celtiques.* Paris, 1881–96.

Includes words found in manuscripts and texts of the 12th to the 16th centuries inclusive, together with an etymological treatment of some modern terms.

Hemon, Roparz. Dictionnaire breton-français. 2. éd. rev. et corr. La Baule, Éd. de Bretagne, 1948. 445p.   **AE147**

Vallée, François. Grand dictionnaire français-breton, avec le concours de É. Ernault et R. Le Roux. Rennes, Éd. de l'Impr. Commerciale de Bretagne, 1931–[33]. 814p.

—— —— Supplément. La Baule, Skridou Breizh, 1948. 176p.   **AE148**

Bulgarian

Chakalov, G. Anglo-bulgarski rechnik. English-Bulgarian dictionary. Sophia, IUni, 1948. 1229p.   **AE149**

Mladenov, Stefan and **Balan, Alexsandar Teodorov.** Bulgarski tulkoven rechnik. Sofia, "Decho Stefanov," 1951– . v.1– .   **AE150**

Contents: t.1, A–K. 1126p.

A scholarly dictionary, still unfinished.

Stephanove, Constantine. Complete Bulgarian-English [and English-Bulgarian] dictionary (including a lexicon of geographical, historical, proper, etc., names, a list of the English irregular verbs, weights and measures, etc.) Sofia, Nickoloff, 1914; Haemus, 1929. 2v.   **AE151**

Bulgarian-English. Nickoloff, 1914. 902p.; English-Bulgarian. 2d ed. rev. and enl. Haemus, 1929. 1063p.

Abbreviations

U.S. Library of Congress. Slavic and Central European Division. Bulgarian abbreviations: a selective list, prep. by Konstantin Z. Furness. Wash., Govt. Print. Off., 1961. 326p.   **AE152**

A listing of abbreviations culled from current Bulgarian texts with the emphasis on governmental and other organiza-

tional titles, and some general terms. Each entry gives the Bulgarian abbreviation with its transliteration, and the expansion in Bulgarian and in English translation.

Burmese

Burmese-English dictionary, comp. by J. A. Stewart and C. W. Dunn. London, Luzac and Co., 1940–63. Pts.1–4. (In progress)   **AE153**

Published under the auspices of the University of Rangoon. Imprint varies.

Vocabulary is drawn from Burmese literature from its beginning in the 15th century A.D. to the present; comprehensive bibliographies of sources are included. Although not strictly an etymological dictionary, etymological notes are given. An important, scholarly work which will probably supersede Judson (AE154).

Judson, Adoniram. The Judson Burmese-English dictionary. Rev. and enl. by Robert C. Stevenson; ed. by F. H. Eveleth. Rangoon, Amer. Baptist Mission Pr., 1921. 1123p. (Repr.: Rangoon, Baptist Board of Publ., 1953)   **AE154**

—— English and Burmese dictionary. 8th ed. Rangoon, Amer. Baptist Mission Pr., 1922. 928p.   **AE154a**

Also published in London by Kegan Paul.

Catalan

Aguiló y Fúster, Mariano. "Diccionari Aguiló"; materials lexicogràfics aplegats. Rev. i publ. sota la cura de Pompeu Fabra i Manuel de Montoliu. Barcelona, Inst. d'Estudis Catalans, 1914–34. 8v. (Biblioteca filològica de l'Inst. de la Llengua Catalana, III, VIII)   **AE155**

A scholarly work with illustrative quotations and references to the literature.

Alcover Sureda, Antonio Maria. Diccionari català-valencià-balear; inventari lexical y etimòlogich de la llengua que parlen Catalunya espanyola y Catalunya francesa, el regne de València, les illes Balears y la ciutat d'Alguér de Sardenya, en totes ses formes literàries y dialectals, antigues y modernes. Palma de Mallorca, Alcover, 1930–59. v.1–9.   **AE156**

v.1–9, A–Som.

A dictionary of the literary and spoken language as found in the various parts of Spain and the islands where Catalan is used. Gives etymologies and regional variations.

Diccionari enciclopèdic de la llengua catalana, amb la correspondència castellana. Nova ed., redactada segons les normes de l' "Institut d'Estudis Catalans," la qual conté tots els vocables, modismes i aforismes, mots tècnics de ciències, arts i indústries, biografies de personatges cèlebres, antics i moderns, nom i descripció de poblacions, rius i muntanyes de les comarques on és parlat et català en qualsevol de les seves variants. Barcelona, Salvat, 1930–35. 4v. il.   **AE157**

Previously published under title *Diccionari de la llengua catalana ab la correspondència castellana.* 1888–89. 2v.

Fabra, Pompeu. Diccionari general de la llengua catalana. [2. ed.] Barcelona, A. Lopez Llausas, 1954. 1761p.   **AE158**

Celtic

Holder, Alfred. Alt-celtischer Sprachschatz. Leipzig, Teubner, 1896–1913. 3v.   **AE159**

v.3 includes a *Nachträge* to v.1. (Incomplete; no more published.)

Chinese

Shu, Hsin-ch'ěng [and others.] Tz'ǔ hai [Chinese encyclopedic dictionary]. Shanghai, Commercial Pr., 1915. 2v.
AE160

—— —— Supplement. Shanghai, Commercial Pr., 1931. unpaged.

Comes in five editions, Edition A, B, C, D, and E, all having the same text but differing in size of page, kind of paper, etc.

Wieger, Leon. Chinese characters, their origin, etymology, history, classification and signification. Tr. into English by Leo Darrout. 2d ed., enl. and rev. according to the 4th French ed. N.Y., Paragon Book Repr. Corp., 1965. 820p. il.
AE161

"Unabridged and unaltered republication of the 2d ed. . . . 1927."

Bilingual

Cheng, I-li and **Tsao, Cheng-shiu.** A new English-Chinese dictionary, with index in Chinese, by Cheng Yi-li and Tsao Cheng-shiu. [Peking], Sheng Huo, Tu Shu, [etc.], 1953. 2143p.
AE162

Fenn, Courtenay Hughes. The five thousand dictionary, a Chinese-English pocket dictionary and index to the character cards of the College of Chinese Studies, California College in China, originally comp. by Courtenay H. Fenn . . . with the assistance of Mr. Chin Hsien Tseng. 5th ed. with add. and rev. by George D. Wilder . . . and Mr. Chin Hsien Tseng. . . . Peking, 1940. 697p. **AE163**

"Numerical list of radicals" attached to lining paper.
Repr. as: Rev. Amer. ed. Cambridge, Harvard Univ. Pr., 1942. 694p.

Giles, Herbert Allen. Chinese-English dictionary. 2d ed. rev. and enl. Shanghai, Kelly; London, Quaritch, [1909]–12. 3v.
AE164

Goodrich, Chauncey. A pocket dictionary. Chinese-English, and Pekingese syllabary. N.Y., Columbia Univ. Pr., 1944. 308p.
AE165

1st ed. 1891.
"Reproduced by offset lithography from the edition printed in Shanghai in 1918 by the American Presbyterian Mission Press."

Mathews, Robert Henry. Mathews' Chinese-English dictionary. Rev. Amer. ed., pub. for the Harvard-Yenching Institute. Cambridge, Harvard Univ. Pr., 1943. 1226p.
AE166

Originally published in 1931.
"Within the necessary limitations of a photographic edition, and as far as interstices of the original edition allow, errors have been corrected, pronunciations and definitions revised, and new entries inserted—in all amounting to some 15,000 items. A whole introduction on pronunciation has been added, and a list of the syllabic headings is included for quick reference. . . . An additional feature of the new edition is that all cases of the neutral, i.e., unstressed, tone are indicated."—*Foreword* to American edition.

—— A Chinese-English dictionary, comp. for the China Inland Mission. Rev. English index. Pub. for the Harvard-Yenching Institute. Cambridge, Harvard Univ. Pr., 1944. 186p.

Williams, Samuel Wells. A syllabic dictionary of the Chinese language; arranged according to the Wu-Fang Yuen Yin, with the pronunciation of the characters as heard in Peking, Canton, Amoy and Shanghai. Shanghai, Amer. Presbyterian Mission Pr., 1903. 1254p.
AE167

A reprint of the 1874 edition, with four pages of "Errata and corrections."

Coptic

Crum, Walter Ewing. Coptic dictionary. Oxford, Clarendon Pr., 1939. 953p.
AE168

Coptic-English.
Issued in 6 pts., 1929–39.
Includes illustrative quotations with references to sources. Indexes in English, Greek, and Arabic.

Cornish

Nance, Robert Morton. An English-Cornish dictionary. Marazion, pr. for the Federation of Old Cornwall Societies by Worden, 1952. 200p.
AE169

1st ed., 1934, by R. M. Nance and A. S. D. Smith.

—— A new Cornish-English dictionary. St. Ives, pr. for the Federation of Old Cornwall Societies by James Lanham, 1938. 209p.
AE170

Williams, Robert. Lexicon Cornu-Britannicum; a dictionary of the ancient Celtic language of Cornwall, in which the words are elucidated by copious examples from the Cornish works now remaining; with translations in English. Llandovery, Roderic, 1865. 400p.
AE171

"The synonyms are also given in the cognate dialects of Welsh, Armoric, Irish, Gaelic, and Manx."—*Title page*.

—— —— **Loth, Joseph.** Remarques et corrections au Lexicon Cornu-Britannicum de Williams. Paris, Bouillon, 1902. 70p.
AE171a

Croatian

See Serbo-Croatian, p.127.

Czech

Příruční slovník jazyka ceského. Vydává Československá Akademie Věd. V Praze, Státní Pedagogické Nakl., 1935–57. 8v. in 9.
AE172

The authoritative dictionary of the Czech language, with illustrative examples from standard authors. Issued by the Czech Academy.

Slovník spisovného jazyka ceského. Praha, Nakl. Československé Akademie Věd, 1958–64. Fasc.1–25. (In progress)
AE173

At head of title: Československá Akademie Věd. Sekce Jazyka a Literatury. Ustav pro jazyk český.
v.1, A–M, completed with fasc.14; v.2 (fasc.15–25), N–ryb.
A smaller work based on the preceding. Includes more up-to-date words.

Trávníček, František. Slovník jazyka ceského. 4. přepr. a dopl. vyd. Praha, Slovanské Nakl., 1952. 1081p.
AE174

Earlier editions were by Pavel Vása and F. Trávníček. *Slovník jazyka ceského.* Prague, Borový, 1935–36; 3d ed. 1946.
A standard work.

Bilingual

Jonáš, Karel. A complete pronouncing dictionary of the English and Bohemian languages for general use. Úplný slovník anglicko-český pro obecnou potřebu. S dokonalou anglickou výslovností. [Berwyn, Ill., Pancner, 1949] 723p.
AE175

5th edition.
Frequently reprinted. Editions show little change from one to another.
A useful small dictionary.

—— Slovník česko-anglický s úplnou anglickou výslovností. A Bohemian and English dictionary. Vydání se všeobecným doplňkem. 6th ed. Berwyn, Ill., Pancner, 1951. 621p. **AE176**

Procházka, Jindřich. Slovník anglicko-český a českoanglický . . . English-Czech and Czech-English dictionary. 16th rev. and enl. ed. Prague, Orbis, 1959. 423p., 589p. **AE177**

Subtitle: Giving pronunciation of all English words, with special regard to idiomatic phrases and phraseology of commercial correspondence.

Frequently reprinted with various editors.

Abbreviations

U.S. Library of Congress. Slavic and Central European Division. Czech and Slovak abbreviations: a selective list, ed. by Paul L. Horecky. Wash., 1956. 164p. **AE178**

"Entries for the most part denote governmental, political, economic, cultural, and social bodies," with some general terms that are commonly abbreviated.

Etymology

Holub, Josef and **Kopečny, František.** Etymologický slovník jazyka českého. V Praeze, Státní Nakl. Učebnic, 1952. 575p. **AE179**

3. přepracované vydání.

Danish and Norwegian

Norsk riksmålordbok, utarb. av Trygve Knudsen og Alf Sommerfelt. Oslo, Aschehoug, 1930–57. 2v. in 3. **AE180**

Issued in parts, 1930–57.

The standard Norwegian dictionary of the "literary" language—the language of the educated class—with many illustrative quotations showing usage, primarily since 1870.

Ordbog over det danske Sprog, grundlagt af Verner Dahlerup; med Understøttelse af Undervisningsministeriet og Carlsbergfondet udg. af det Danske Sprog- og Litteraturselskab. København, Gyldendal, 1919–1954. 27v. **AE181**

—— Liste over Forkortelser med en Lydskrifttavle og en Efterskrift. København, 1956. 113p.

The scholarly dictionary of the Danish language since 1700, giving etymologies, illustrative quotations, etc.

Bilingual

Bjerke, Lucie and **Søraas, Haakon.** English-Norwegian dictionary. London, Harrap, 1964. 562p. **AE182**

"First published in Norway 1963 by H. Aschehoug & Co. (W. Nygaard) Oslo."—*Verso of title page.*

Brynildsen, John. Dictionary of the English and Dano-Norwegian languages. Danisms supervised by Johannes Magnussen, English pronunciation by Otto Jespersen. Copenhagen, Gyldendal, 1902–7. 2v. **AE183**

Added title page: Engelsk-dansk-norsk Ordbog.

Still one of the best English-Dano-Norwegian dictionaries.

—— Norsk-engelsk ordbog. 3. omarb. utg. Oslo, Aschehoug, 1927. 1228p. **AE184**

Gleditsch, Th. [and others]. English-Norwegian dictionary. London, Allen & Unwin, [1950]. 855p. **AE185**

From the 2d Norwegian edition (Oslo, 1948).

A dictionary of modern written and spoken English for the general reader.

Jorgenson, Theodore and **Galdal, Peter.** Norwegian-En-glish school dictionary. [Northfield, Minn.], St. Olaf College Pr., 1955. 448p. **AE186**

1st ed. 1943.

Uses the new orthography made obligatory by the language reform of 1938, but also gives many parallel forms and may be used in reading older literature. Shows articles, plural endings, principal parts, forms of the adjectives, etc.

Magnussen, Johannes Julius Claudi [and others]. Danish-English [and English-Danish] dictionary. Copenhagen, Gyldendal; London, Allen & Unwin,1944–54. 2v. **AE187**

v.1, 5th ed., by Hermann Vinterberg and Knud Herløv. 412p.; v.2, 6th ed., by Hermann Vinterberg and Bodil Ladgaard. 476p.

Vinterberg, Hermann and **Bodelsen, Carl Adolf.** Dansk-engelsk Ordbog . . . København, Gyldendal, Nordisk Forlag, 1954–56. 2v. **AE188**

Etymology

Falk, Hjalmar Sejersted and **Torp, Alf.** Norwegisch-dä-nisches etymologisches Wörterbuch. Auf Grund der Übersetzung von H. Davidsen neu bearb. deutsche Ausg., mit Literaturnachweisen strittiger Etymologien sowie deutschem und altnordischem Wörterverzeichnis. Heidelberg, Winter, 1910–11. 2v. **AE189**

Translated from *Etymologisk ordbog over det norske og det danske sprog.* Kristiania, 1903–6.

Kalkar, Otto. Ordbog til det aeldre danske Sprog. 1300–1700. København, Thiele, 1881–1907. 4v.

—— —— Nachträge, 1908–1918.

—— —— Kilde-fortegnelse og Forkortelses-liste til 1.–5. bd. 1925. xxviiip. **AE190**

The standard work for Old Danish, preceding in time that covered by the *Ordbog over det danske Sprog* (AE181).

Torp, Alf. Nynorsk etymologisk ordbog. Christiania, Aschehoug, 1919. 886p. **AE191**

Treats Nynorsk or Landsmål, the language of the "country people."

Dravidian

Burrow, Thomas and **Emeneau, Murray Barnson.** A Dravidian etymological dictionary. Oxford, Clarendon Pr., 1961. 609p. **AE192**

The Dravidian languages are spoken in southeastern India and northern Ceylon. This dictionary gives etymologies of all known Dravidian languages with English equivalents. Treats the four major literary languages and many nonliterary. Selective bibliography, p.xxiii–xxvii.

Dutch

Dale, Johan Hendrik van. Van Dale's Nieuw groot woordenboek der Nederlandse taal. Bewerkt door C. Kruyskamp en F. de Tollenaere. 8. druk. 'sGravenhage, Nijhoff, 1958. 2379p. **AE193**

Appeared in 15 pts.

An excellent, well-established dictionary. This edition includes a supplement containing: proper names in Greek and Roman mythology; foreign phrases; Biblical names; errata.

—— Van Dale's Handwoordenboek der Nederlandse taal. 5. geheel nieuwe uitg. 'sGravenhage, Nijhoff, 1948. 1034p. **AE194**

A concise edition of the preceding.

Verschueren, Joseph. Modern woordenboek. 6. herziene druk, met medewerking van W. Pée en A. Seeldraeyers. Turnhout, Brepols, [1956]. 2v. il. **AE195**

Subtitle: Geheel in de nieuwe spelling steeds bijgewerkt in het kumulatief bijvoegsel.

An encyclopedic dictionary somewhat on the style of the *Petit Larousse,* including both dictionary information and encyclopedic articles on persons, places, and subjects.

Woordenboek der Nederlandsche taal. 'sGravenhage, Nijhoff, 1882–1964. v.1–21. (In progress)   **AE196**

Ed. by M. de Vries and others.

v.1–11, 13–16, 18, compl.; v.12, pt.1 (fasc.1–20), P–Plets; pt.2 (fasc.21–39), Pletten–Quar; pt.3 (fasc.1–19), R–Renvooi; v.17 (fasc.1–25), Tiend–Trommel; v.19 (fasc.1–3), Ver–Verbarmen; v.21 (fasc.1–12), Ves–Vlas.

—— Supplement, 1942–56. v.1.

—— Bronnenlijst, bewerkt door C. H. A. Kruyskamp. 1943. 144p.

—— —— 1. Aanrulling (1954). 19p.

The standard dictionary compiled on historical principles, with etymologies, references to sources, synonyms, etc.

Early

Verdam, Jacob, Middelnederlandsch handwoordenboek. 2. uitg. 'sGravenhage, Nijhoff, 1932. 812p. (Repr. 1956)   **AE197**

Enlarged from the 1st edition, 1911, with revision of section Sterne–Z by C. H. Ebbinge Wubben.

Verwijs, Eelco and **Verdam, Jacob.** Middelnederlandsch woordenboek. 'sGravenhage, Nijhoff, 1885–1952. deel 1–10 ¹⁻², 11.   **AE198**

Contents: deel 1–9, A–Z; deel 10¹, Tekstcritiek van J. Verdam, en Bouwstoffen, eerste gedeelte (A–F) door Willem de Vreese; deel 10², Bouwstoffen, tweede gedeelte (G–Z) door G. I. Lieftinck; deel 11, afl. 1–5, Aanvullingen en verbeteringen op het gebied van dijk- en waterschapsrecht, bodem en water, aardrijkskunde, enz. door A. A. Beekman (A–Z).

A comprehensive dictionary of the older language. v.10 includes an extensive bibliography of sources; v.11, additions and corrections in the fields of water rights, geography, etc.

Bilingual

Bruggencate, Karel ten. Engels woordenboek. 15. verb. en verm. uitg., door P. J. H. O. Schut en R. W. Zandvoort. Groningen, Wolters, 1956–59. 2v.   **AE199**

v.1, English-Dutch; v.2, Dutch-English.

A practical desk-sized dictionary, reflecting current usage.

Jansonius, H. Groot Nederlands-Engels woordenboek voor studie en practijk. Leiden, Nederlandsche Uitgeversmaatschappij N.V., 1950. 2v.   **AE200**

A comprehensive Dutch-English dictionary.

—— —— Supplement. 1959. 428p.

Kramers, Jacob. Cassell's English-Dutch, Dutch-English dictionary; comp. by F. P. H. Prick van Wely. London, Cassell, 1951. 1376p.   **AE201**

Prick van Wely, F. P. H. Engels handwoordenboek. 7. verb. druk, bewerkt door F. Prick van Wely. Den Haag, van Goor, 1955. 2v.   **AE202**

Contents: 1. deel, Engels-Nederlands; 2. deel, Nederlands-Engels.

Uses the new spelling.

Etymology

Franck, Johannes. Franck's Etymologisch woordenboek der Nederlandsche taal. 2. druk door Dr. N. van Wijk. Met registers der Nieuwhoogduitsche woorden, enz. 'sGravenhage, Nijhoff, 1912. 897p.   **AE203**

—— —— Supplement door C. B. van Haeringen. 'sGravenhage, Nijhoff, 1936. 235p. (Repr. with Suppl. Nijhoff, 1949)

Dialect

Bibliography

Meertens, Pieter Jacobus and **Wander, B.** Bibliografie der dialecten van Nederland, 1800–1950. In opdracht van de Dialectencommissie der Koninklijke Nederlandse Akademie van Wetenschappen. Amsterdam, Noord-Hollandsche Uitgeversmaatschappij, 1958. 400p.   **AE204**

An extensive bibliography arranged by province and then by city, preceded by a section of general materials.

Egyptian

Budge, Ernest Alfred Thompson Wallis. An Egyptian hieroglyphic dictionary. With an index of English words, king list and geographical list, with indexes, list of hieroglyphic characters, Coptic and Semitic alphabets, etc. London, Murray, 1920. 1356p.   **AE205**

Erman, Adolf and **Grapow, Hermann.** Wörterbuch der aegyptischen Sprache; im Auftrage der Deutschen Akademien. Leipzig, Hinrichs, 1926–50. 6v.   **AE206**

v.6, Deutsch-aegyptisches Wörterverzeichnis, in alphabetischer und sachlicher Ordnung nebst Verzeichnissen der koptischen, semitischen und griechischen Wörter.

—— —— Die Belegstellen, bearb. von H. Grapow u. W. Erichsen. Leipzig, Hinrichs, 1935–53. v.1–5.

An authoritative work in German, covering both the hieratic and the hieroglyphic vocabularies.

Faulkner, Raymond O. A concise dictionary of Middle Egyptian. Oxford, Univ. Pr. for the Griffith Inst., 1962. 327p.   **AE207**

Estonian

Nurm, E., Raiet, E. and **Kindlam, M.** Õigekeelsuse sõnaraamat. Tallinn, Eesti Riiklik Kirjastus, 1960. 871p.   **AE208**

At head of title: Eesti NSV Teaduste Akadeemia, Keele ja Kirjanduse Instituut.

Saareste, Andrus Kustas. Eesti keele mõisteline sõnaraamat. Dictionnaire analogique de la langue estonienne. Avec un index pourvu des traductions en français. Stockholm, Vaba Eesti, 1958–63. v.1–2, 3 ¹⁻⁶. il. (Eesti Teaduslik Selts Rootsis. Väljaane 3)   **AE209**

To be in 4v.

Contents: v.1–3⁶, A–toimesaam.

An analogical dictionary of the Estonian language containing "the entire subject matter of Wiedemann's Dictionary [AE212]; new words now commonly used . . . ; dialectal words . . .; examples to make clear all nuances of meaning and style, taken from colloquial or standard Estonian; proverbs; and pictures of objects which cannot be described adequately or which are comparatively rare. At the end of the Dictionary there will be an alphabetical index in Estonian and French of all words to be found in it."—[*Descriptive statement*].

Bilingual

Pöhl, Hans. Inglise-eesti sõnaraamat. Tallinn, Pihlakas, 1927. 732p.   **AE210**

Added title page in English: English-Estonian dictionary.

Vrangel', M. Dictionnaire estonien-français. Revu par

Joh. Aavik et Oskar Peters. Tallinn, Société d'Édit. "Istandik", 1932. 350p.   **AE211**

Wiedemann, Ferdinand Johann. Eesti-saksa sõnaraamat . . . Estnisch-deutsches Wörterbuch. 3. unveränderter Druck . . . von Jakob Hurt redigierten Aufl. Mit einer Einleitung versehen von Albert Saareste. Dorpat, Estnische Literaturgesellschaft, 1923. Tartu, Eesti Kirjanduse Seltsi Kirjastus, 1923. 1406col., cixp. map.   **AE212**
1st ed., St. Petersburg, 1869.
The Estonian and German titles are printed side by side. Introduction in Estonian and German.

Ethiopian

Dillman, August C. F. Lexicon linguae aethiopicae cum indice latino. Lipsiae, T. O. Weigel, 1862–65. 1522col. (3v.) (Repr.: N.Y., 1955)   **AE213**
────── Supplément au Lexicon linguae aethiopicae . . . (1865) et édition du lexique de Juste d'Urbin (1850–1855) par Sylvain Grébaut. Paris, Impr. Nationale, 1952. 520p.
────── **Aklilu, Amsalu.** Etymologischer Beitrag zu Dillmanns Lexicon . . . 1962. (Thesis, Tübingen. 74p.)

Fijian

Capell, Arthur. A new Fijian dictionary. Glasgow, Wilson Guthrie & Co., 1957. 464p.   **AE214**
Obtainable from the Government Printer, Suva, Fiji, and the Crown Agents for Oversea Governments and Administrations, 4 Millbank, London.
"First published 1941. 2d ed. 1957."
Fijian-English, p.1–342; English-Fijian, p.345–464.

Finnish

Suomalaisen Kirjallisuuden Seura, Helsingfors. Nykysuomen sanakirja. Päätoimittaja: Matti Sadeniemi. 2. painos. Porvoo, Söderström, 1957–62. 6v.   **AE215**
An authoritative dictionary of contemporary Finnish.

Bilingual

Alanne, Vieno Severi. Suomalais-englantilainen sanakirja. Helsinki, Werner Söderström, 1956. 1111p.   **AE216**
Finnish-English dictionary.
1st ed. 1919.

Tuomikoski, Aune and **Slöör, Anna.** Englantilais-suomalainen sanakirja. 3. painos. Helsinki, Suomalaisen Kirjallisuuden Seura, 1957. 1100p. (Suomalaisen Kirjallisuuden Seuran Toimituksia 212. osa)   **AE217**
English-Finnish. Definitions given with examples and variant meanings.

Vuolle, Aino. Finnish-English dictionary. 8th ed. Helsinki, Söderström, 1962. 526p.   **AE218**
1st ed. 1940.
────── Englantilais-suomalainen sanakirja. Porvoo, Helsinki, Söderström, 1961. 535p.
Useful concise dictionaries, frequently reprinted.

Finno–Ugric

Etymology

Collinder, Bjorn. Fenno-Ugric vocabulary; an etymological dictionary of the Uralic languages. Stockholm, Almqvist & Wiksell, 1955. 211p.   **AE219**

French

Académie Française, Paris. Dictionnaire de l'Académie Française. 8. éd. Paris, Hachette, 1931–35. 2v.   **AE220**
1st ed. 1694.
The standard conservative dictionary of the French language for spelling and usage. Does not include etymologies or show historical development. Primarily for the literary language; includes very few scientific and technical terms.

Hatzfeld, Adolphe and **Darmesteter, Arsène.** Dictionnaire général de la langue française du commencement du XVIIᵉ siècle jusqu'à nos jours. 9. éd. Paris, Delagrave, 1932. 2v.   **AE221**
1st ed., 1890–95, pub. in fascicules.
Gives etymologies, examples showing first usage, changes in meaning, etc.

Larousse, Pierre. Nouveau Larousse classique: dictionnaire encyclopédique. Paris, Larousse, 1957. 1284p. il. maps.   **AE222**
Designed for students, the vocabulary of this desk-size dictionary has been adapted to their needs, including such technical and scientific words as they will find in the course of their work. Includes personal and geographical names, and gives other encyclopedic information.

────── Petit Larousse: dictionnaire encyclopédique pour tous. Paris, Larousse, 1959. 1795p. il.   **AE223**
A considerably revised edition of this popular desk dictionary previously entitled *Nouveau petit Larousse illustré*, with many newly listed words, new definitions, and a much-improved format.
Pt.1 gives definitions of words with examples of usage, followed by a brief section of foreign phrases. Pt.2 is an alphabetical encyclopedia of proper names—biographical, geographical, and historical—with brief information. Profusely illustrated.

Littré, Émile. Dictionnaire de la langue française. Éd. intégrale. Paris, Jean-Jacques Pauvert, 1956–58. 7v.   **AE224**
Éd. intégrale: la seule complète des étymologies et des différents suppléments et additifs reclassés dans le texte selon les intentions de l'auteur.
A reprint of the famous Littré (1873–78. 4v. and suppl.) in modern format, in which the material in the supplement of the early work has been incorporated into the main alphabet. An older work still important for the history, etymology, and grammar of the French language. Includes many quotations from literature with exact references to sources.
An abridgment was published as:
────── Dictionnaire de la langue française. Abrégé du dictionnaire de É. Littré par A. Beaujean. 12. éd. conforme pour l'orthographe à la dernière éd. du Dictionnaire de l'Académie Française. Paris, Hachette, 1914. 1295p., 123p. (Repr.: Paris, Éds. Universitaires, 1950. 1294p.)

Quillet Flammarion. Dictionnaire usuel Quillet Flammarion par le texte et par l'image, rédigé sous la direction de Pierre Gioan. Paris, Quillet-Flammarion, [1956]; N.Y., Dutton, 1960. 1458p. il., maps.   **AE225**
A dictionary including in one alphabet: words, with definitions; personal and place names; etc. Very brief information.

Robert, Paul. Dictionnaire alphabétique et analogique de la langue française; les mots et les associations d'idées. . . . Paris, Société du Nouveau Littré, 1951–64. Fasc. 1–54. (In progress)   **AE226**
Fasc.1–54, A–Troquer.
A historical dictionary of the French language, giving for each entry: etymology, definitions, synonyms, antonyms, and cross references to words with related meaning, with extensive quotations from French writers, selected to clarify usage and trace historical changes in meaning. The dictionary is sponsored by the Académie Française.

Bilingual

Chevalley, Abel [and others]. Concise Oxford French dictionary. Oxford, Clarendon Pr., 1934–40. 2v. il.   **AE227**

Frequently reprinted.

French-English, comp. by A. Chevalley and M. Chevalley. 1934. 895p.; English-French, comp. by G. W. F. R. Goodridge. 1940. 295p.

"In accordance with our wish to emulate in the French-English field the work of the brothers Fowler on current English, the principles governing the selection of vocabulary in the *Concise Oxford dictionary* [AE24] have been adopted." —*Pref.*

Deak, Étienne. Grand dictionnaire d'américanismes, contenant les principaux termes américains avec leur équivalent exact en français. 3. éd. augm. Paris, Éd. du Dauphin, [1962]. 700p.   **AE228**

Translations into French of American slang, popular phrases, new terms, some botanical terms, etc.

Guiraud, Jules. Dictionnaire anglais-français [et français-anglais] à l'usage des professeurs, des littérateurs, des traducteurs, des commerçants, des industriels, des élèves, des facultés, des grandes écoles et des classes supérieures des lycées et collèges. 3. éd. Paris, Belin, 1947. 2v. **AE229**

Anglais-français, 2187p.; Français-anglais, 1127p.

Includes general, literary, and scientific terms, proper names, etc. Indicates differences in meanings and is rich in examples showing usage.

Harrap's Standard French and English dictionary, ed. by J. E. Mansion. London, Harrap, 1947–48. 2v.   **AE230**

Pt.1, French-English, repr. with corrections. 1948. 912p.; pt.2, English-French, repr. with corrections. 1947. 1488p. Frequently reprinted.

1st ed. 1934–39.

American edition has title *Heath's Standard French and English dictionary.* N.Y., Heath. 2v.

—— Supplement. 3d ed. Comp. by R. P. L. Ledésert, with the assistance of P. H. Collin. London, Harrap, 1961. 2 pts. Pt.1, French-English. 85p.; pt.2, English-French. 51p.

A superior dictionary with emphasis on the language of the 20th century; gives many examples of usage. Strong in scientific and technical terms. The supplement adds many new words.

Harrap's Shorter French and English dictionary. London, Harrap, 1940–44. 2v.   **AE231**

Abridgment of the entry above.

Pt.1, French-English. 1940; pt.2, English-French. 1944.

Larousse modern French-English [English-French] dictionary by Marguerite-Marie Dubois [and others]. N.Y., McGraw-Hill, 1960. 2v. in 1. (768p., 752p.) il. **AE232**

A desk-size dictionary, the work of several French, British, and American collaborators. Colloquial and slang expressions are included.

New Cassell's French dictionary: French-English, English-French. Compl. rev. by Denis Girard [and others]. N.Y., Funk & Wagnalls, 1962. 762p., 655p.   **AE233**

A familiar and useful desk dictionary which has gone through five editions and many reprintings. This is a thoroughly revised work by different editors: many new words have been added, as well as new meanings; obsolete terms have been omitted; and errors have been rectified. Includes translations of phrases and expressions. Gives pronunciation.

Sachs, Karl and **Villatte, Césaire.** Encyklopädisches französisch-deutsches und deutsch-französisches Wörterbuch. 4. Bearb. von Karl Moser; durch einen Nachtrag ergänzt. [33 Aufl., mit Nachtrag] Berlin-Schöneberg, Langenscheidt, 1952. 2v.   **AE234**

v.1, Französisch-deutsch, by K. Moser; v.2, Deutsch-französisch, by A. Biel [and others].

1st ed. 1869–79.

Added title page in French.

A comprehensive, scholarly French-German dictionary. Pronunciation is indicated by the Toussaint Langenscheidt phonetic method.

—— —— Nachträge, bearb. von Karl Knauer. 1956. 2v.

v.1, Französisch-deutsch. 80p.; v.2, Deutsch-französisch. 76p.

Abbreviations

Baudry, Hubert. "D.A." Dictionnaire d'abréviations françaises et étrangères, techniques et usuelles, anciennes et nouvelles. La Chapelle-Montligeon (Orne), Éd. de Montligeon, 1951. 157p.   **AE235**

8000 abbreviations in all fields, including science, technology, the arts, etc. Arrangement is alphabetical, with supplementary listings of banking, postal, and telegraphic terms, technical and chemical symbols, etc.

Etymology

Bloch, Oscar and **Wartburg, W. von.** Dictionnaire étymologique de la langue française. 4. éd. rev. et augm. par W. von Wartburg. Paris, Presses Universitaires de France, 1964. 682p.   **AE236**

1. éd. 1932.

An etymological dictionary of contemporary French, giving date of earliest appearance, derivatives, etc.

Dauzat, Albert. Dictionnaire étymologique de la langue française. [10. éd. rev.] Paris, Larousse, 1960. 824p.   **AE237**

1st ed. 1938.

Designed for the general reader; gives etymologies, with date of first usage, definitions, derivatives, etc.

Gamillscheg, Ernst. Etymologisches Wörterbuch der französischen Sprache . . . mit einem Wort- und Sachverzeichnis von Heinrich Kuen. Heidelberg, Winter, 1928. 1136p. (Sammlung romanischer Elementar- und Handbücher hrsg. von Wilhelm Meyer-Lübke. 3.Reihe, Wörterbücher 5)   **AE238**

A scholarly dictionary in German with references to sources. Not as comprehensive as Wartburg (AE239), but a useful 1v. work.

Wartburg, Walther von. Französisches etymologisches Wörterbuch; eine Darstellung des galloromanischen Sprachschatzes. Bonn, Klopp; Basel, Helbing und Lichtenhahn, 1928–64. v.1–5, 7–11, 14, 16. (In progress) (Repr.: Tübingen, J. C. B. Mohr, 1948–)   **AE239**

Imprint varies.

The great German dictionary of French etymology, giving the historical development of the meanings of the words with dates. Includes dialectal forms.

Volumes are being published simultaneously in *Lieferungen* numbered consecutively as issued, forming parts of different volumes. Now completed are: v.1–5, A–L; v.7–11, N–Si; v.14, U–Z; v.16, Germanische Elemente.

—— —— Beiheft: Ortsnamenregister. Literaturverzeichnis. Übersichtskarte. 2. Aufl. Bonn, Klopp, 1950. 135p. 2 maps.

—— —— Supplement zur 2. Aufl. des Bibliographischen Beiheftes, red. von Margarete Hoffert. 1957. 54p.

Slang

Sandry, Géo and **Carrère, Marcel.** Dictionnaire de l'argot moderne. 3. éd. rev. et augm. Paris, Éd. du Dauphin, 1956. 254p.   **AE240**

A general section is followed by special lists in various categories; e.g., business, racing, prison, etc., which are not duplicated in the main list.

Synonyms

Bailly, René and **Toro, M. de.** Dictionnaire des synonymes de la langue française. Paris, Larousse, 1946. 626p.
AE241

A convenient, usable, alphabetically arranged dictionary giving definitions, discriminations in meanings, and examples of usage.

Bénac, Henri. Dictionnaire des synonymes, conforme au Dictionnaire de l'Académie Française. Paris, Hachette, 1956. 1026p. **AE242**

A dictionary of synonyms with explanations and examples showing discriminations in meaning.

Lafaye, Pierre Benjamin. Dictionnaire des synonymes de la langue française, avec une introduction sur la théorie des synonymes. 8. éd. suivie d'un supplément. Paris, Hachette, 1903. 1106p., 336p. **AE243**

1st ed. 1858; 3d ed., 1865–69, was the first edition to include the supplement.

A standard older work giving definitions, explanations, and examples.

Old–17th century

Cayrou, Gaston. Le français classique: lexique de la langue du dix-septième siècle expliquant d'après les dictionnaires du temps et les remarques des grammariens, le sens et l'usage des mots aujourd'hui vieillis ou différemment employés. 6. éd. Paris, Didier, 1948. 884p. il.
AE244

1st ed. 1923.

A dictionary of 17th-century French, with many quotations from the literature and exact references to sources. Includes some 2200 words.

Dubois, J. and **Lagane, René.** Dictionnaire de la langue française classique. Paris, Librairie Classique Eugène Belin, 1960. 507p. **AE245**

Attempts to define those 17th-century words no longer in general use, and words with changed meanings. Includes more words (about 5200) and quotations from more authors than Cayrou (AE244), and often the quotations are different.

Godefroy, Frédéric Eugène. Dictionnaire de l'ancienne langue française et de tous ses dialectes, du IXe au XVe siècle, composé d'après le dépouillement de tous les plus importants documents, manuscrits ou imprimés, qui se trouvent dans les grandes bibliothèques de la France et de l'Europe, et dans les principales archives départementales, municipales, hospitalières ou privées. Pub. sous les auspices du Ministère de l'Instruction Publique. Paris, Bouillon, 1891–1902. 10v. (Repr.: N.Y., Kraus Reprint Corp., 1961) **AE246**

v.1–7, A–Traioir; v.8, Traire–Z; Complément, A–Carrefour; v.9–10, Complément, Carrel–Z.

The standard dictionary of old French, with a wealth of illustrative quotations.

—— Lexique de l'ancien français, pub. par les soins de J. Bonnard et Am. Salmon. Paris, Welter, 1901. 544p.
AE247

An abridgment of the larger work, omitting the quotations and many of the words, and including some additional words.

Grandsaignes d'Hauterive, Robert. Dictionnaire d'ancien français. Moyen Âge et Renaissance. Paris, Larousse, 1947. 592p. **AE248**

Gives spelling variations, meaning, modern approximation, etymology, time when current, etc.

Huguet, Edmond. Dictionnaire de la langue française du seizième siècle. Paris, Champion; Didier, 1925–62. v.1–6¹. (In progress) **AE249**

v.1–6¹, A–pres. (Appearing in fasicules, 1–51/52)

A scholarly dictionary of 16th-century French including words no longer in use and those whose meanings have changed. Rich in illustrative examples, with exact references to source.

Tobler, Adolf. Tobler-Lommatzsch, Altfranzösisches Wörterbuch; Adolf Toblers Nachgelassene Materialien bearb. und hrsg. von Erhard Lommatzsch ... Wiesbaden, Steiner, 1925–65. v.1–6^{1–8}. (In progress) **AE250**

"Von der 25. Lieferung an mit Unterstützung der Akademie der Wissenschaften und der Literatur (Mainz)."—*Title page.*

An outstanding German work, which attempts to include all words of the 12th to the 14th centuries, being particularly strong in the literary language. Gives etymologies of each word with examples of usage and references to other treatments.

Vandaele, Hilaire. Petit dictionnaire de l'ancien français. Paris, Garnier, [1940]. 536p. **AE251**

Compiled to furnish students with a compact, convenient dictionary to Old French. Not a substitute for Godefroy (AE246), but useful as a small dictionary.

Bibliography

Levy, Raphael. Répertoire des lexiques du vieux français. N.Y., Modern Language Assoc. of America, 1937. 64p.
AE252

Gives the titles of all printed alphabetical lists of words of Old French, with various indexes. The period studied covers from the 11th through the 15th centuries.

Regional and dialect

Bibliography

See also Collison (AE104); Zaunmüller (AE108); *Guide to reference books*, 7th ed., p.234–35.

Wartburg, Walther von. Bibliographie des dictionnaires patois. Paris, Droz, 1934. 146p. map. (Société de Publications Romanes et Françaises, v.8) **AE253**

A comprehensive listing of regional and dialect dictionaries from all parts of France, and from other French-speaking countries. A review, with some additions and corrections by Raphael Levy, appeared in *Modern language notes* 50:128. 1935.

Location of copies of the dictionaries listed is indicated in George S. C. Adams, *Census of French and Provençal dialect dictionaries in American libraries* (Lancaster, Pa., Lancaster Pr., 1937. [Linguistic Soc. of America special publ.]), which also indicates some additional titles.

—— —— Supplément, publié par Hans-Erich Keller, avec la collaboration de Jean Renson. Genève, Droz; Lille, Giard, 1955. 56p. (Société de Publications Romanes et Françaises, sous la direction de Mario Roques. [Publ.] 52)

The supplement lists dictionaries published from 1934–55, and in some cases corrects errors found in the main volume.

Friesian

Dijkstra, Waling [and others]. Friesch woordenboek (Lexicon frisicum), met medewerking van anderen, benevens lijst van Friesche eigennamen, bewerkt door Johan Winkler. Uitg. ingevolge besluit der Staten van Friesland,

onder toezicht van de door Gedeputeerde Staten Benoem-
de Commissie. Leeuwarden, Meijer, [1896–1911]. 4v.
AE254

v.4 has title: Friesche naamlijst (Onomasticon frisicum)
door Johan Winkler (1898). This includes both personal and
geographical names.

Frysk wurdboek: Frysk-Nederlânsk, Nederlânsk-Frysk.
Utjefte fan de Fryske Akademy. Bolswert, A. J. Osinga,
1952–56. 2v. [v.1, 1956] **AE255**

v.1, Frysk-Nederlânsk; v.2, Nederlânsk-Frysk.
v.1 replaces the earlier *Lyts Frysk wirdboek,* 1944.

Gaelic

Dwelly, Edward. The illustrated Gaelic-English dictionary, containing every Gaelic word and meaning given
in all previously published dictionaries, and a great number never in print before. To which is prefixed a concise
Gaelic grammar. [4th ed.] Glasgow, MacLaren, [1941].
1034p. 675 il. **AE256**

1st ed. 1901–11.
"The first edition . . . appeared in parts under the title of
Faclair gàidhlig le dealbahn, and the nom-de-plume of 'Ewen
MacDonald.' "—*Pref.*
Appendix: Proper names, and persons and places men-
tioned in old Gaelic folktales and poetry from Armstrong's
Gaelic dictionary.

Maclennan, Malcolm. Pronouncing and etymological dictionary of the Gaelic language: Gaelic-English, English-
Gaelic. Edinburgh, Grant, 1925. 613p. **AE257**

MacLeod, Norman and **Dewar, Daniel.** Dictionary of the
Gaelic language: Gaelic and English, English and Gaelic.
Edinburgh, Grant, 1909. 1005p. **AE258**

Georgian

Cherkesi, E. Georgian-English dictionary. [Oxford], pr.
for the Trustees of the Marjory Wardrop Fund, Univ. of
Oxford, 1950. 257p. **AE259**

An excellent dictionary, based on a textual comparison of
the English and Georgian versions of the books of the Old
and New Testaments and other sources. The *Russian-
Georgian dictionary* of D. Chubinashvili (1886) and the
works of early Georgian scholars were used as reference.
Ancient as well as modern Georgian terms are included.

Čhikobava, Arnol'd Stepanovich [and others]. Khartuli
enis ganmartebithi lekhsikoni. Tiflis, 1950–55. v.1–4. (In
progress) **AE260**

Added title page in Russian: Tolkovyi slovar' gruzinskogo
iazyka.
Text in Georgian.

Gvardzhaladze, Tamara and **Gvardzhaladze, Isidore.** En-
glish-Georgian dictionary by Thamar and Isidore Gvarja-
ladze. 2d ed. Tbilissi, State Pub. House, 1955. 450p.
AE261

Added title page in Georgian.

German

Grimm, Jacob and **Grimm, Wilhelm.** Deutsches Wörter-
buch. Im Auftrage des Deutschen Reiches und Preussens
mit Unterstützung des Reichsministeriums des Innern, des
Preussischen Ministeriums für Wissenschaft, Kunst und
Volksbildung, und der Notgemeinschaft der deutschen
Wissenschaft hrsg. von der Preussischen Akademie der
Wissenschaften. Leipzig, Hirzel, 1854–60. 16v. **AE262**

The great dictionary of the German language completed
in 1960 after more than 100 years in preparation. Since it was
issued in *Lieferungen,* not in alphabetical sequence, but in

various parts of the alphabet simultaneously, the volumes
show wide divergence in dates of publication, as well as in
scope and method of presentation.
Compiled on historical principles. The design of the
Brothers Grimm "was to give an exhaustive account of the
words of the literary language (New High German) from
about the end of the 15th century, including their earlier
etymological and later history, with references to important
dialectal words and forms; and to illustrate their use and history abundantly by quotations. . . . "—*Encyclopaedia Britannica,* 11th ed. 8:189.
As the dictionary throughout uses small letters instead of
capitals for common nouns, it is the main German authority
for the noncapitalization of nouns in German.

Karg-Gasterstädt, Elisabeth and **Frings, Theodor.** Alt-
hochdeutsches Wörterbuch, auf Grund der von Elias v.
Steinmeyer hinterlassenen Sammlungen im Auftrag der
Sächsischen Akademie der Wissenschaften zu Leipzig.
Berlin, Akademie-Verlag, 1952–64. Lfg. 1–16. (In prog-
ress) **AE263**

Lfg. 1–16, A–Blo.
A scholarly dictionary of Old High German, with many
examples and exact references to the literature.

Klappenbach, Ruth and **Steinitz, Wolfgang.** Wörterbuch
der deutschen Gegenwartssprache. Bearbeiter: R. Klappenbach und H. Malige-Klappenbach. Berlin, Akademie-
Verlag, 1961– . Lfg. 1–11. (In progress) **AE264**

Contents: Lfg. 1–11, A–Durchfallen.
At head of title: Akademie der Wissenschaften zu Berlin.
Institut für deutsche Sprache und Literatur.
A dictionary of the present-day language, with examples
from and references to modern writers.

Lexer, Matthias von. Matthias Lexers Mittelhochdeutsches Taschenwörterbuch. 29. Aufl. (mit Nachtrag).
Stuttgart, S. Hirzel Verlag, 1959. 343p., 67p. **AE265**

1st ed. 1879; 28th ed. 1956.
A standard small dictionary of Middle High German. A
larger work is the author's *Mittelhochdeutsches Handwörterbuch.* Leipzig, 1872–78. 3v. and Nachträge.
The first section is a reprint of earlier editions. The *Nachträge* section of 67 pages was prepared by Ulrich Pretzel, assisted by Wolfgang Bachofer and Rena Leppin.

Paul, Hermann. Deutsches Wörterbuch. 5. völlig neubearb. und erw. Aufl. von Werner Betz. Tübingen, Max
Niemeyer, 1957–63. Lfg. 1–9. (In progress) **AE266**

1st ed. 1897.
In 1956–57 the same publishing firm (in Halle) issued an
earlier 5th edition, edited by Alfred Schirmer. The present set,
also called 5th edition, edited by another scholar, now appears with no explanation for the resulting confusion, except
that the editor states that he began the work in 1940. There
are some variations in the text of the definitions, but much of
it is verbatim repetition of the Schirmer edition.
A new edition of a standard work, strong in the historical
development of words and particularly good for the 18th
century.

Schulz, Hans. Deutsches Fremdwörterbuch. Strassburg,
Trübner; Berlin, de Gruyter, 1913–42. 2v. **AE267**

v.2 in the series "Wörterbücher der Deutschen Akademie."
An authoritative work dealing with words of foreign origin,
with examples and dated references to sources.

Der Sprach-Brockhaus. Deutsches Bildwörterbuch für
Jedermann. 6. verb. Aufl. Wiesbaden, Brockhaus, 1954.
799p. il. **AE268**

1st ed. 1935.
A practical desk-sized dictionary, which includes geographical names, technical terms, colloquialisms, etc. Small
line drawings are used to illustrate the text.

Trübners deutsches Wörterbuch; im Auftrag der Arbeitsgemeinschaft für deutsche Wortforschung, hrsg. von Alfred Götze. Berlin, de Gruyter, 1936–57. 8v. **AE269**

An excellent dictionary strong in etymologies and word histories, with many references to sources.

Bilingual

Flügel, Johann Gottfried. Allgemeines englisch-deutsches und deutsch-englisches Wörterbuch von Felix Flügel. 3. verb. u. verm. Abdruck der 4. gänzlich umgearb. Aufl. von J. G. Flügel's Vollständigem Wörterbuch. . . . Braunschweig, Westermann, 1908–12. 2v. in 3. **AE270**

Added title page in English: A universal English-German and German-English dictionary.

T.1, Bd.1–2, Englisch-deutsch; T.2, Deutsch-englisch.

An older dictionary rich in quotations with exact references to sources.

Harrap's Standard German and English dictionary. Ed. by Trevor Jones. London, Harrap, 1963– . v.1– . (In progress) **AE271**

Pt.1, German-English, A–E.

A scholarly dictionary intended for general use. Each word is treated separately instead of under groupings. Scientific terms are included. Gives examples of usage.

Langenscheidt's Concise German dictionary. N.Y., Barnes & Noble, 1964. 744p., 672p. **AE272**

2v. in 1: v.1, English-German. 2d ed., ed. by Heinz Messinger and Werner Rudenberg; v.2, German-English. 4th ed., ed. by Heinz Messinger. (Each part available separately.)

A good desk dictionary. Gives both American and British usages and spellings.

Langenscheidt's New Muret-Sanders encyclopedic dictionary of the English and German languages. Compl. rev. 1962. Ed. by Otto Springer. London, Methuen; N.Y., Barnes & Noble, 1962–64. Pt.1, 2v. (In progress) **AE273**

Contents: pt.1, English-German. 2v.

The *Muret-Sanders Enzyklopädisches englisch-deutsches und deutsch-englisches Wörterbuch* (Grosse Ausg. Berlin-Schöneberg, Langenscheidt, 1908. 2v. in 4) has long been an outstanding bilingual dictionary.

The 1962 edition is, in effect, a new work although based on the old. Printed in Roman type, each word has received new treatment, and thousands of new words have been added to make the work representative of 20th-century usage. "In pronunciation, spelling, and vocabulary, American English is treated with the same degree of completeness and accuracy as British English . . . " (*Pref.*), but some reviewers feel that American usage has been emphasized. Includes scientific and technical terms; for biological terms, the Latin names are given following the German equivalent. Pronunciation is indicated; idiomatic phrases and colloquialisms are given.

New Cassell's German dictionary: German-English, English-German, based on the editions by Karl Breul, compl. rev. and reedited by Harold T. Betteridge. N.Y., Funk & Wagnalls, 1958. 629p., 619p. **AE274**

An almost completely rewritten edition of the work edited for many years by Karl Breul, and in new format, using Latin typography rather than Fraktur as in earlier editions. Attempts to be an "all-purpose" dictionary: modernized to reflect current usage, omitting out-of-date material, and adding words in science, economics, technology, etc. A very useful bilingual dictionary.

Pattermann, Wilhelm. Deutsch-englisches Wörter- und Phrasenbuch, mit Berücksichtigung des amerikanischen Englisch. Anhang: Aussprachwörterbuch. Wien, Alexa-Verlag, 1949–52. 2v. **AE275**

Lists up-to-date English and American equivalents of German words and expressions, under key German word, placing emphasis on the shade of meaning implied by use in a particular context. No etymologies.

Sachs, Karl and **Villatte, Césaire.** Encyclopädisches französisch-deutsches und deutsch-französisches Wörterbuch. Berlin-Schöneberg, Langenscheidt, 1952. 2v. **AE276**

For complete entry *see* AE234.

Spalding, Keith. An historical dictionary of German figurative usage. Oxford, Blackwell, 1952–64. Fasc. 1–16. (In progress) **AE277**

Fasc.1–16, A–Fen.

Records figurative expressions, proverbs, quotations, and other established phrases appearing in German literature since approximately 1750, with explanations in English; the annotations illustrating use and change of meaning are often drawn from sources preceding this date. Equivalent English phrases or expressions are given for each entry. A complete list of sources is planned for the conclusion of the work.

Wildhagen, Karl. English-German, German-English dictionary . . . London, Allen & Unwin; Wiesbaden, Brandstetter-Verlag, 1962. 2v. **AE278**

Subtitle: A comprehensive and strictly scientific representation of the vocabulary of the modern and present-day languages, with special regard to syntax, style, and idiomatic usage.

Added title page in German.

v.1, English-German, is the "third, revised and enlarged edition." 822p. 1st ed. 1938; v.2, pts. 1–2, German-English. 1347p. 1st ed. 1953/54.

v.2 by Karl Wildhagen and Will Héraucourt.

A well-edited desk-size dictionary. Both volumes include lists of abbreviations. v.1 has a list of proper names indicating pronunciation in the phonetic alphabet; v.2 has a list of geographical names, one of proper names, tables of weights and measures, and a section on German grammar.

Abbreviations

Greiser, Josef. Lexikon der Abkürzungen . . . mit Anhang: Abkürzungen aus dem Finanz- und Steuerrecht. 2. Aufl. ergänzt und erw. nach dem neuen Stande vom 1. Januar 1955. Osnabrück, A. Fromm, 1955. 271p. **AE279**

A dictionary of modern German abbreviations, including many for international organizations.

Etymology

Kluge, Friedrich. Etymologisches Wörterbuch der deutschen Sprache. 19. Aufl. . . . bearb. von Walther Mitzka. Berlin, de Gruyter, 1963. 917p. **AE280**

A standard work frequently reprinted with varying amounts of revision. This edition has been printed in roman type.

Especially strong in word development with dated examples of usage. Includes a *Sachverzeichnis* of words grouped into categories, and a bibliography of sources, p.xi–xvi.

Orthography and usage

Duden, Konrad. Der grosse Duden, bearb. von Otto Basler unter Mitwirkung der Fachschriftleitung des Bibliographischen Instituts. Leipzig, Bibliographisches Inst., 1957–63. v.1–7. il. **AE281**

Contents: Bd.1, Rechtschreibung der deutschen Sprache und der Fremdwörter. 14. Aufl. [1957]; Bd.2, Stilwörterbuch der deutschen Sprache. 5. Aufl. [1963]; Bd.3, Bildwörterbuch der deutschen Sprache. [c1958]; Bd.4, Grammatik der deutschen Sprache. [1959]; Bd.5, Fremdwörterbuch. [c1960]; Bd.6, Aussprachewörterbuch. [c1962]; Bd.7, Etymologie. [1963].

v.1–2 frequently republished.

Mackensen, Lutz. Neues deutsches Wörterbuch: Rechtschreibung, Grammatik, Stil, Worterklärung, Fremdwörterbuch. Laupheim (Wttbg.), Pfahl-Verlag, 1953 [i.e., 1952]. 837p. **AE282**

A modern dictionary of some 128,000 words, indicating correct usage.

Viëtor, Wilhelm. Deutsches Aussprachewörterbuch. 4/5 durchgesehene Aufl. besorgt von Ernst A. Meyer. Leipzig, Reisland, 1931. 469p. **AE283**

First pub. 1908–12, in 8 pts.

Indicates pronunciation by the International phonetic system.

Slang

Küpper, Heinz. Wörterbuch der deutschen Umgangssprache. 3. neubearb. und erw. Aufl. Hamburg, Claassen Verlag, 1963– . Bd.1– . **AE284**

1st ed. 1955.

A dictionary of German slang and colloquial expressions.

Wolf, Siegmund A. Wörterbuch des Rotwelschen; Deutsche Gaunersprache. Mannheim, Bibliographisches Inst., 1956. 430p. **AE285**

A historical dictionary of underworld slang, with dated references to the literature.

Synonyms

Dornseiff, Franz. Der deutsche Wortschatz nach Sachgruppen. 5. Aufl. mit alphabetischem Generalregister. Berlin, de Gruyter, 1959. 166p., 922p. **AE286**

1st ed. 1933–34.

This edition considerably expanded, especially in supplementary material and index.

The main part is arranged as a thesaurus in 20 main categories with many subdivisions. A detailed index refers to the appropriate sections.

Eberhard, Johann August. Synonymisches Handwörterbuch der deutschen Sprache. 17. Aufl. durchgängig umbearb., verm. und verb. von Otto Lyon. Mit Übersetzung der Wörter in die englische, französische, italienische, und russische Sprache. Leipzig, Grieben, 1910. 1201p. **AE287**

A treatment of some 1600 German words giving synonyms and showing discrimination in meanings. Equivalents are given in English, French, Italian, and Russian.

Farrell, Ralph Barstow. Dictionary of German synonyms. Cambridge, Univ. Pr., 1953. 428p. **AE288**

Arranged by English word with German equivalents and definitions, and discussion and examples of differences in meaning.

Wehrle, Hugo and **Eggers, Hans.** Deutscher Wortschatz: ein Wegweiser zum treffenden Ausdruck. 12. Aufl. Stuttgart, Ernst Klett, 1961. 821p. **AE289**

12th ed. of Anton Schlessing's *Deutscher Wortschatz* (1st ed. 1880–81), an outstanding work for many years.

This edition has been much enlarged, completely revised, and rearranged. The first part is arranged systematically by idea, in much the manner of Roget's *Thesaurus* (AE77). The second part is an alphabetical list of words referring to the paragraph sections of the first part.

Regional and dialect

For regional and dialect dictionaries *see* Collison (AE104); Zaunmüller (AE108); *Guide to reference books,* 7th ed., p.237–38.

Greek

Estienne, Henri. Thesaurus graecae linguae, ab Henrico Stephano constructus. Post editionem anglicam novis ad-

ditamentis auctum, ordineque alphabetico digestum tertio ediderunt Carolus Benedictus Hase . . . Guilielmus Dindorfius et Ludovicus Dindorfius. Paris, Didot, 1831–65. 8v. in 9. **AE290**

1st ed. 1572.

An authoritative dictionary from its first publication, reedited by outstanding scholars in the 19th century. Still of first importance.

Snell, Bruno and **Fleischer, Ulrich.** Lexikon des frühgriechischen Epos. Mit Unterstützung der UNESCO, der Deutschen Forschungsgemeinschaft und der Joachim-Jungius-Gesellschaft, Hamburg, vorbereitet und hrsg. vom Thesaurus Linguae Graecae . . . Göttingen, Vandenhoeck und Ruprecht, 1955–65. Lfg. 1–4. **AE291**

Lfg. 1–4, α–ἄυ.

A new *Thesaurus linguae graecae,* attempting to list all words in the texts of the earliest literary works up to, but not including, the works of Antimachos; covers Homer, Hesiod, and others. As planned, the Greek *Thesaurus* will consist of a series of dictionaries, each covering a different literary period.

Bilingual

Edwards, Gerald Maclean. English-Greek lexicon. 2d ed. Cambridge, Univ. Pr., 1915. 338p. **AE292**

A good small dictionary, frequently reprinted.

Liddell, Henry George and **Scott, Robert.** Greek-English lexicon. . . . A new ed. rev. and augm. throughout by Henry Stuart Jones . . . with the assistance of Roderick McKenzie . . . and with the cooperation of many scholars. . . . [9th ed.] Oxford, Clarendon Pr., 1925–40. 2111p. **AE293**

1st ed. 1843. This new 9th edition is revised throughout and enlarged by the addition of many words including scientific and technical terms.

Issued in 10 pts., 1925–40. Frequently reprinted. Preliminary leaves include: List of authors and works, p.xvi–xli; Epigraphical publications, p.xli–xliii; Papyrological publications, p.xliii–xlv; Periodicals, p.xlv–xlvi; General list of abbreviations, p.xlvi–xlviii. Addenda and corrigenda, p.2043–2111.

The standard Greek and English lexicon, covering the language to about 600 A.D., omitting Patristic and Byzantine Greek. Omits place-names for which Passow's dictionary (AE294) must be used.

—— —— Abridged. 26th ed. rev. and enl. Chicago, Follett, 1941. 835p.

Passow, Franz. Handwörterbuch der griechischen Sprache. Neubearb. und zeitgemäss umgestaltet von Val. Chr. Fr. Rost und Friedrich Palm. Des ursprunglichen Werkes 5. Aufl. Leipzig, Vogel, 1841–57. 2v. in 4. **AE294**

The standard Greek and German lexicon, useful to the English reader also because it includes geographical names omitted in Liddell and Scott (AE293). A new, much-enlarged edition, by Wilhelm Crönert, was started, but only pts.1–3 (A–An) were issued (Göttingen, Vanderhoeck, 1912–13).

Preisigke, Friedrich. Wörterbuch der griechischen Papyrusurkunden mit Einschluss der griechischen Inschriften, Aufschriften, Ostraka, Mumienschilder usw. aus Ägypten, . . . hrsg. von Emil Kiessling. Heidelberg, Selbstverlag des Erben, 1924–58. v.1–4¹⁻². (In progress) **AE295**

Contents: Bd.1–2, A–Ω; Bd.3, Besondere Wörterliste; Bd.4, Lfg. 1–2, A–δεν.

Greek-German.

A dictionary of words found in the papyrus documents, inscriptions, etc.

Woodhouse, Sidney Chawner. English-Greek dictionary; a vocabulary of the Attic language. London, Routledge, 1910. 1029p. (Repr. 1950) **AE296**

Yonge, Charles Duke. English-Greek lexicon; ed. by Henry Drisler. N.Y., Amer. Book Co., 1890 [c.1870]. 663p., cxvp. **AE297**

Includes *Greek synonyms from the French of Alex. Pillon,* edited with notes by T. K. Arnold (cxvp.); and an appendix of Greek proper names.

Now largely superseded, except for dialect words, by Woodhouse (AE296) and Edwards (AE292).

Etymology

Boisacq, Émile. Dictionnaire étymologique de la langue grecque, étudiée dans ses rapports avec les autres langues indo-européennes. 4. éd., augm. d'un index par Helmut Rix. Heidelberg, Winter, 1950. 1256p. **AE298**

1st ed. 1907–16.

This edition includes a useful index which lists the words in all languages cited in the text.

Frisk, Hjalmar. Griechisches etymologisches Wörterbuch. Heidelberg, Winter, 1954–63. v.1–2$^{1-4}$. (Indogermanische Bibliothek. II.Reihe-Wörterbücher) (In progress) **AE299**

Lfg. 1–2$^{1-4}$, A–ὄμβρος.

An authoritative work tracing the etymologies of classical Greek with references to sources, etc.

Hofmann, Johann Baptist. Etymologisches Wörterbuch des Griechischen. Munich, Oldenbourg, 1949–50. 433p. **AE300**

A small dependable work, more up to date than Boisacq (AE298).

Christian and medieval

Bauer, Walter. A Greek-English lexicon of the New Testament and other early Christian literature; a translation and adaptation of Walter Bauer's Griechisch-deutsches Wörterbuch zu den Schriften des Neuen Testaments und der übrigen urchristlichen Literatur. 4th rev. and augm. ed., 1952, by William F. Arndt and F. Wilbur Gingrich. Chicago, Univ. of Chicago Pr.; Cambridge, Univ. Pr., 1957. 909p. **AE301**

A translation and adaptation from the German. Bauer's work has now appeared in a 5th edition revised (Berlin, Töpelmann. 1958. 1780col.).

Du Cange, Charles Du Fresne. Glossarium ad scriptores mediae et infimae graecitas . . . réimp. du Collège de France. Paris, Geuthner, 1943. 1250p. (Repr.: Graz, 1958) **AE302**

1st ed. 1688.

In spite of its age, still the authoritative dictionary of medieval Greek, including many quotations with exact reference to sources.

Lampe, Geoffrey William Hugo. A patristic Greek lexicon. Oxford, Clarendon Pr., 1961–64. v.1–3. (In progress) **AE303**

Greek-English.

"The object of this work is primarily to interpret the theological and ecclesiastical vocabulary of the Greek Christian authors from Clement of Rome to Theodore of Studium."— *Pref.* It is complementary to Liddell-Scott-Jones in that common meanings of words noted there are not repeated in the Lampe work, though unusual usages may be. Biblical words and usages to be found in the Septuagint and the New Testament are also omitted.

List of authors and works, p.xi–xlv.

Moulton, James Hope and **Milligan, George.** Vocabulary of the Greek Testament, illustrated from the papyri and other non-literary sources. London, Hodder, 1914–29 [pref. 1929]. 705p. **AE304**

Sophocles, Evangelinus Apostolides. Greek lexicon of the Roman and Byzantine periods (from B.C. 146 to A.D. 1100). Memorial ed., ed. by J. H. Thayer. N.Y., Scribner, 1887. 1188p. (Repr.: N.Y., Ungar, 1957. 2v.) **AE305**

1st ed. 1870.

Various reprintings.

A dictionary of the later classical Greek of the Roman and Byzantine periods. Useful for the Church Fathers.

Modern Greek

Akadēmia Athēnōn, Athens. Lexikon tēs hellēnikēs glōssēs. Historikon lexikon tēs neas hellēnikēs tēs te koinōs homiloumenēs kai tōn idiōmatōn. Athēnai, Typographeion "Hestia," 1933–53. v.1–4^1. (In progress) **AE306**

v.1–4^1, a–gaz.

Dēmētrakos, Dēmētrios B. Mega lexikon tēs hellēnikēs glōssēs. Athens, Dēmētrakou, 1936–50. 9v. **AE307**

Ed. by Iōannēs S. Zerbos.

Covers all periods from ancient times to mid-20th century.

Kykkōtēs, Hierotheos. English-Greek and Greek-English dictionary including English and Greek grammar, geographical and proper names and abbreviations. [2d ed.] London, Humphries, 1947. 766p. **AE308**

2d ed. repr. 1954.

1st ed. 1942.

A useful small dictionary with appendixes of abbreviations, proper names, grammatical rules, etc.

Kyriakidēs, A. Modern Greek-English dictionary with a Cypriote vocabulary. 2d ed. (rev. throughout). Athens, Constantinides, 1909. 908p. **AE309**

1st ed. 1892.

A standard dictionary of modern Greek, giving examples of usage, etc.

Mega anglo-hellēnikon lexikon; syntachthen hypo epiteleiou epistēmonōn, technikōn kai logotechnōn. Athēnai, Ekdoseis "Odysseus," [1962?]. 4v. **AE310**

An English-Modern Greek dictionary, giving many examples of usage, colloquial phrases, etc. Pronunciation of English words is shown by the phonetic alphabet.

Swanson, Donald Carl Eugene. Vocabulary of modern spoken Greek (English-Greek and Greek-English) . . . with the assistance of Sophia P. Djaferis. Minneapolis, Univ. of Minn. Pr., 1959. 408p. **AE311**

Hawaiian

Judd, Henry, Pukui, Mary Kawena and **Stokes, John F. G.** Introduction to the Hawaiian language (an English-Hawaiian vocabulary) . . . with a complementary Hawaiian-English vocabulary. Honolulu, Tongg Pub. Co., 1945. 314p. **AE312**

Subtitle: Comprising five thousand of the commonest and most useful English words and their equivalents, in modern Hawaiian speech, correctly pronounced.

Pukui, Mary Kawena and **Elbert, Samuel H.** Hawaiian-English dictionary. Honolulu, Univ. of Hawaii Pr., 1957. 362p. **AE313**

A larger and more up-to-date Hawaiian-English dictionary than any previously published. Based to some extent on the Lorrin Andrews, *Dictionary of the Hawaiian language,* rev. by Henry H. Parker (Honolulu, 1922. 674p.), this has been thoroughly revised, the vocabulary increased from some 14,000 to 25,000 entries, and the definitions rewritten, etc. Includes a chapter on grammar and a bibliography.

—— English-Hawaiian dictionary. Honolulu, Univ. of Hawaii Pr., 1964. 187p. **AE313a**

Hebrew

Ben-Yehudah, Eliezer. Thesaurus totius Hebraitatis et veteris et recentioris, auctore Elieser Ben Iehuda. Berlin-Schöneberg, Langenscheidt; Jerusalem, Ben-Yehudah Hozaa-la'Or, [1908]–59. 16v. **AE314**

Added title pages in Hebrew, German, French, and English. Equivalents given in these languages, but all explanations are in Hebrew. v.8–16 edited by Morris [i.e., Moses] Hirsch Segal.

English title: *A complete dictionary of ancient and modern Hebrew.*

Grasowsky, Judah. Millōn 'ivri. 9th ed. [Tel Aviv], [1957]. 1113p. **AE315**

Includes both Biblical and modern Hebrew.

Bilingual

Alcalay, Reuben. The complete English-Hebrew dictionary. Tel Aviv, Massadah Pub. Co., 1959–61. 4v. **AE316**

Reissued: N.Y., Taplinger, 1963. 2150p.

Title page and inroduction in Hebrew. Added title page in English. Vocabulary is extensive; gives equivalents only.

Gesenius, Wilhelm. Hebräisches und aramäisches Handwörterbuch über das Alte Testament . . . 17th ed. 1921. Leipzig, Vogel, 1921. 1013p. **AE317**

Hebrew-German with German-Hebrew index.

Gives etymologies and references to sources.

—— Hebrew and English lexicon of the Old Testament, with an appendix containing the Biblical Aramaic. . . . Boston, Houghton, 1906. 1127p. (Corr. impression. Oxford, Clarendon Pr., 1952. 1126p.) **AE318**

Subtitle: Based on the lexicon of William Gesenius as translated by Edward Robinson. Edited, with constant reference to the Thesaurus of Gesenius as completed by E. Rödiger, and with authorized use of the latest German editions of Gesenius' Handwörterbuch über das Alte Testament, by Francis Brown with the coöperation of S. R. Driver and Charles A. Briggs.

The best Hebrew-English dictionary of Biblical Hebrew.

Goldberg, Nathan. New functional Hebrew-English, English-Hebrew dictionary, with illustrative sentences and derivative words and expressions. N.Y., Ktav Pub. House, 1958. 355p. **AE319**

Grossman, Reuben and **Sachs, H.** Compendious Hebrew-English dictionary comprising a complete vocabulary of Biblical, Mishnaïc, medieval and modern Hebrew. Rev. and ed. by Moses H. Segal. 10th ed. Tel-Aviv, Dvir, 1953. 423p. (Repr. 1956) **AE320**

Added title page in Hebrew.

Jastrow, Marcus. Dictionary of the Targumim, the Talmud Babli and Yerushalmi, and the Midrashic literature. With an index of Scriptural quotations. London, Luzac; N.Y., Putnam, 1903. 2v. **AE321**

A photographic reprint, less expensive, was issued by Shapiro, Vallentine (London, 1926).

A standard English dictionary of Talmudic Hebrew.

Kaufman, Judah. English-Hebrew dictionary by Israel Efros, Judah Ibn-Shmuel Kaufman, Benjamin Silk, ed. by Judah Kaufman. Tel Aviv, Dvir, [1929]. 751p. **AE322**

Frequently reprinted.

Koehler, Ludwig Hugo and **Baumgartner, Walter.** Lexicon in Veteris Testamenti libros. Wörterbuch zum hebräischen Alten Testament in deutscher und englischer Sprache. A dictionary of the Hebrew Old Testament in English and German, ed. by Ludwig Koehler; Wörterbuch zum aramäischen Teil des Alten Testaments in deutscher und englischer Sprache. A dictionary of the Aramaic parts of the Old Testament in English and German, ed. by Walter Baumgartner. Leiden, Brill, 1948–53. 1138p. **AE323**

Preface and introduction in German and English. Equivalents of terms also given in German and English. Includes quotations with exact references to sources.

—— —— Supplementum. Leiden, Brill, 1958. 227p.

Includes tables of scripts and transcriptions; abbreviations and signs; a German word list with Hebrew and Aramaic equivalents; additions and corrections.

Segal, Moses Hirsch. A concise Hebrew-English dictionary comprising the Hebrew of all ages. Tel Aviv, Dvir, 1955. 260p. **AE324**

Bound with *A concise English-Hebrew dictionary with the English pronunciation in Hebrew transliteration.* 4th ed. by H. Danby and M. H. Segal. Tel Aviv, 1947. 461p.

Shilo dictionary: English-Hebrew. Contains over 13,000 words and phrases translated into modern idiomatic Hebrew. N.Y., Shilo Pub. House, 1962. 284p. **AE325**

Ed. by Zevi Scharfstein.

Hindi, Hindustani, Punjabi, Urdu

(These Indian languages have very close affiliations.)

Craven, Thomas. New royal dictionary; English into Hindustani and Hindustani into English, comp. originally by Rev. Thomas Craven . . . and in subsequent editions rev. and enl.; 1932 ed. rev. by Bishop J. R. Chitambar. Lucknow, Methodist Pub. House, 1932. 328p., 372p. **AE326**

Pt.1, English-Hindustani; pt.2, Hindustani-English.

Printed in the Latin alphabet.

Fallon, S. W. New Hindustani-English dictionary, with illustrations from Hindustani literature and folk-lore. Banāras, Medical Hall Pr.; London, Trübner, 1879. 1216p. **AE327**

—— New English-Hindustani dictionary, with illustrations from English literature and colloquial English, tr. into Hindustani. . . . Lahore, Gulab Singh, [1905]. 703p. il. (Repr. 1941) **AE328**

Māyā Simba. The Panjábí dictionary. Lahore, Singh, 1895. 1221p. **AE329**

Panjabi-English.

Pathak, Ram Chandra. Bhargava's Standard illustrated dictionary of the Hindi language. Hindi-English, Anglo-Hindi. Benares, Shree Ganga Pustakalaya, [1946?]–1951. 2v. **AE330**

[v.1], Hindi-English. 5th ed. rev. and enl. [v.2], Anglo-Hindi. 9th ed. ("incorporating about 5000 new words in the main body of the Dictionary").

Raghu, Vira. A comprehensive English-Hindi dictionary of governmental and educational words and phrases. Nagpur, Internat. Academy of Indian Culture, 1955. 189p., 1579p. il. (Sarasvati-Vihara ser. v.35) **AE331**

" . . . the most comprehensive dictionary of the modern Hindi language yet published."—J. A. Mish, N.Y. Pub. Lib., in *Library journal* 81:2694. Nov. 15, 1956.

Particularly strong in all aspects of governmental administration, law and political science, and the sciences.

Ferozsons English-Urdu dictionary. English words with their equivalents in Urdu. 4th ed. Comp. by a Board of Eds. Lahore, Ferozsons, 1961. 910p. **AE332**

Ferozons Urdu-English dictionary; Urdu words, phrases and idioms with English meanings and synonyms. [1st ed.] Lahore, Ferozsons, 1960. 831p. **AE332a**

Platts, John Thompson. Dictionary of Urdu, classical

Hindi and English. London, Oxford Univ. Pr., 1960. 1259p. **AE333**

"Reprinted . . . from sheets of the 5th (1930) impression." First pub. 1884.

Hungarian

Magyar Tudományos Akadémia, Budapest. Nyelvtudományi Intézet. A magyar nyelv értelmezö szótára. Budapest, 1959–62. 7v. **AE334**

A thorough and carefully edited dictionary of standard, modern Hungarian. Usage is illustrated by copious quotations, with sources indicated.

Szarvas, Gábor and **Simonyi, Zsigmond.** Lexicon linguae hungaricae aevi antiquioris, auspiciis Academiae Scienciarum Hungaricae. Budapestini, Sumptibus et Typis Victoris Hornyánszky, 1890–93. 3v. **AE335**

Added title page in Hungarian.

A dictionary of the early Hungarian language compiled on historical principles.

Bilingual

Halász, Elöd. Német-magyar szótár. 6. kiadás. Budapest, Akadémiai Kiadó, 1952. 368p. **AE336**

Added title page: Deutsch-ungarisches Wörterbuch.

—— Magyar-német szótár. 6. kiadás. Budapest, Akadémiai Kiadó, 1960. 480p. **AE336a**

Added title page: Ungarisch-deutsches Handwörterbuch.

Országh, László. Angol-magyar szótár. English-Hungarian dictionary. Budapest, Akadémiai Kiadó, 1960. 2333p. **AE337**

—— Magyar-angol szótár. Hungarian-English dictionary. 2d ed. compl. rev. and enl. Budapest, Akadémiai Kiadó, 1963. 2144p. **AE337a**

An up-to-date Hungarian dictionary which emphasizes terms of modern speech and includes many new technical words.

—— Angol-magyar kéziszótár. A concise English-Hungarian dictionary. 3d rev. ed. Budapest, Akadémiai Kiadó, 1957. 1080p. **AE338**

—— Magyar-angol kéziszótár. A concise Hungarian-English dictionary. 2d enl. ed. Budapest, Akadémiai Kiadó, 1959. 1167p. **AE339**

Abbreviations

U.S. Library of Congress. Slavic and Central European Division. Hungarian abbreviations: a selective list, comp. by Elemer Bako. Wash., Govt. Prt. Off., 1961. 146p. **AE340**

Approximately 2500 abbreviations, followed by the full word or words in Hungarian and the English equivalent. Emphasis is on governmental and other organizational names; but terms frequently found in Hungarian publications are also included.

Etymology

Bárczi, Géza. Magyar szófejtö szótár. Budapest, Egyetemi Nyomda, 1941. 348p. **AE341**

Bibliography, p.xix–xxiii.

Gombocz, Zoltán and **Melich, János.** Magyar etymologiai szótár. Lexicon critico-etymologicum linguae hungaricae. A Magyar Tudományos Akadémia megbizásából . . . Budapest, Magyar Tudományos Akadémia, 1914/30–44. Pt.1–17. **AE342**

Pt.1–10, A–érdëm. 1599col.; pt.11–17, erdö–gaz. 1160col. No more published.

Icelandic

Blöndal, Sigfús. Islandsk-dansk ordbog. Hovedmedarbejdere: Björg Thorláksson Blöndal, Jon Ófeigsson, Holger Wiehe. Reykjavík, Thorláksson, 1920–24. 1052p. **AE343**

Old Icelandic, including dialect and colloquial words.

Bödvarsson, Árni. Íslenzk ordabók, handa skólum og almenningi. Reykjavík, Bókaútgáfa Menningarsjöds, 1963. 852p. **AE344**

Cleasby, Richard. An Icelandic-English dictionary, initiated by Richard Cleasby. Subsequently rev., enl., and compl. by Gudbrand Vigfusson. 2d ed. with a suppl. by Sir William A. Craigie containing many additional words and references. Oxford, Clarendon Pr., 1957. 833p. **AE345**

The original edition, first published in 1874, was started by Cleasby and completed by Vigfusson. This is a lithographic reprint with the addition of a 52p. supplement. The introduction and biographical sketch of Cleasby included in the first edition are omitted, but the section on grammar is reprinted.

Fritzner, Johan. Ordbog over det gamle norsk sprog. Omar., forøget og forbedret udg. Christiania, Norske Forlagsforenina; Chicago, Relling, 1886–96. 3v. (Repr.: Oslo, Møller, 1954–55. 3v.) **AE346**

—— —— Tillegg . . . ved Didrik Arup Seip og Trygve Knudsen. Oslo, Møller, 1955. 155p.

Includes many references, quotations, variations in meanings, etc.

Zoëga, Geir Tómasson. Icelandic-English and English-Icelandic dictionary. 2d–3d ed. Reykjavík, Kristjánsson, 1922–32. 2v. **AE347**

Added title page in Icelandic.

Icelandic-English, 1922. 631p.; English-Icelandic, 1932. 712p.

The best dictionaries of modern Icelandic and English. Frequently reprinted.

Etymology

Jóhannesson, Alexander. Isländisches etymologisches Wörterbuch. Bern, A. Francke, 1951–56. 1406p. **AE348**

Contains some 20,000 words, including so-called poetic words and mythological names but omitting personal and place-names. Arrangement is by Indo-germanic roots, with an index of Icelandic words. Linguistic literature through 1950 has been drawn upon.

Vries, Jan de. Altnordisches etymologisches Wörterbuch. Leiden, Brill, 1957–61. 689p. **AE349**

Issued in 9 pts.

Old Icelandic and Old Norwegian. Gives equivalents in other Scandinavian languages, references to sources, etc.

Indo-European

See Aryan, p.104.

Indonesian

Echols, John M. and **Shadily, Hassan.** An Indonesian-English dictionary. 2d ed. Ithaca, N.Y., Cornell Univ. Pr., [1963]. 431p. **AE350**

1st ed. 1961.

Indonesian-English only. "Intended to be a practical, comprehensive dictionary of modern Indonesian . . . A large number of technical terms have been included, but no attempt has been made to be exhaustive."—*Pref.*

Includes illustrative phrases and sentences.

Kramer, A. L. N. Kamus Indonesia; Nederlands-Indonesisch en Indonesisch-Nederlands. 4. druk. Den Haag, G. B. van Goor, 1959. 600p. **AE351**

Added title page in Indonesian.

—— Van Goor's Concise Indonesian dictionary; English-Indonesian, Indonesian-English. Hague, Van Goor, 1952. 359p. **AE352**

Title page also in Indonesian.

A concise dictionary prepared primarily for schools and elementary usage.

Irish

Royal Irish Academy, Dublin. Contributions to a Dictionary of the Irish language. . . . Dublin, Academy, [1939]–1964. (In progress) **AE353**

Parts published irregularly as completed.

A, fasc.1, arr. by Anne O'Sullivan and E. G. Quin. 1964. 288col.

degra–duus, arr. by Mary E. Byrne and Maud Joynt. 1959–60. 2 fasc. (460col.)

G, arr. by Mary E. Byrne. 1955. 178col.

I, arr. by Máirín O Daly and Anne O'Sullivan. 1952. 2 fasc. (234col.)

M, arr. by Maud Joynt. [1939] 208col.

N–O–P, arr. by Maud Joynt. [1940] 212col.

R, arr. by Maud Joynt. 1944. 124col.

S, arr. by Máirín O Daly, Anne O'Sullivan and E. G. Quin. 1953. 434col.

T, arr. by David Greene and E. G. Quin. 1943–48. 2 fasc. (394col.)

U, arr. by Teresa Condon. 1942. 98col.

"The object of the present publication is to make immediately available . . . the mass of collected material . . . in the Royal Irish Academy pending publication of the . . . Dictionary as planned. This and the following fasciculi are then to be regarded merely as 'Contributions' towards a dictionary, not as installments of the final work."—*Note* in fasc.M.

—— Dictionary of the Irish language based mainly on Old and Middle Irish materials: general ed., Osborn Bergin. Dublin, Academy, 1913–57. Fasc.1–4. **AE354**

Fasc.1, D–Degóir, ed. by Carl J. S. Marstrander. 1913; fasc.2, E–Extais, ed. by Maud Joynt and Eleanor Knott. 1932; fasc.3, F–fochraic, ed. by Maud Joynt and Eleanor Knott. 1950; fasc.4, fochratae–futhu, ed. by Maud Joynt and Eleanor Knott. 1957.

The authoritative dictionary of the Irish language, based on materials collected for many years by the Academy from printed books, manuscripts, and the spoken language. Arranged on historical principles, with many quotations illustrating the development both of meanings of words and of their grammatical inflections. Begins with the letter D, leaving A–C to be published last, because the letters A–Dn were covered in Kuno Meyer's *Contributions to Irish lexicography* (Halle, Niemeyer; London, Nutt, 1906. 670p.), of which the Academy's dictionary is a continuation.

Bilingual

De Bhaldraithe, Tomás. English-Irish dictionary. Baile Átha Cliath, Oifig an tSoláthair, 1959. 864p. **AE355**

"Made and printed for the Stationery Office by Hely's Ltd., Printers, Dublin."

"The aim of this dictionary is the practical one of providing Irish equivalents for English words and phrases in common use. It is not then to be regarded as an exhaustive word-store of modern literary Irish or of the current spoken language."—*Pref.*

Dinneen, Patrick Stephen. Irish-English dictionary; being a thesaurus of the words, phrases and idioms of the modern Irish language. New ed. rev. and greatly enl. Dublin, Pub. for the Irish Texts Society by the Educ. Co. of Ireland, 1927. 1340p. **AE356**

1st ed. 1904.

McKenna, Lambert A. J. English-Irish dictionary. Dublin, Govt. Publs., 1935. 1546p. **AE357**

Title also in Irish. Planned as a complement to Dinneen above.

O'Reilly, Edward. Irish-English dictionary, with copious quotations from the most esteemed ancient and modern writers . . . and numerous comparisons of Irish words with those of similar orthography, sense, or sound in the Welsh and Hebrew languages. A new edition, carefully rev. and cor. With a suppl. . . . by John O'Donovan. Dublin, Duffy, 1864. 724p. **AE358**

Etymology

Vendryes, Joseph. Lexique étymologique de l'irlandais ancien. Dublin, Dublin Inst. for Advanced Studies; Paris, Centre National de la Recherche Scientifique, 1959–60. [Fasc.1–] **AE359**

[Fasc.1], A; fasc.2, M, N, O, P.

Following each Irish word is a brief equivalent in French. The etymology is then presented in detail with exact references to sources.

Italian

Accademia della Crusca, Florence. Vocabolario degli Accademici della Crusca. 5. impressione. Firenze, Tip. Galileiana di M. Cellini ecc., 1863–1923. v.1–11. **AE360**

1st ed. 1612.

v.1–11, A–O.

The great dictionary of the Academy, published in various editions. The 5th edition was never completed; it was planned to replace it by:

Accademia d'Italia. Vocabolario della lingua italiana. Milano, Soc. Anonima per la Pubblicazione del Vocabolario. 1941– . v.1– . **AE361**

v.1, A–C.

A scholarly work with quotations showing usage.

Battaglia, Salvatore. Grande dizionario della lingua italiana. Torino, Unione Tipografico-Editrice Torinese. 1961–64. v.1–3. (In progress) **AE362**

—— —— Indice degli autori citati nei volumi 1–3. 1964. 80p.

Contents: v.1–3, A–Dag.

Designed to replace, as a new work not a revision, the century-old standard *Dizionario della lingua italiana* of Niccolò Tommaseo and Bernardo Bellini. Torino, Unione Tip.-Ed., 1861–79. 4v. in 8.

A scholarly work, with the collaboration of many specialists; planned on historical principles, with full definitions and examples of meanings and usages in chronological order. Numerous citations to sources both early and modern, which are listed in the separate *Indice*.

Melzi, Gian Battista. Il novissimo Melzi: dizionario enciclopedico italiano. 35. ed. ampliamente aggiornata. Milano, Antonio Vallardi, 1959. 2v. il. **AE363**

Contents: I, Parte linguistica. 1446p.; II, Parte scientifica. 1424p.

A useful small dictionary and encyclopedia of the *Petit Larousse* (AE223) type. v.1 is a dictionary; v.2, a small encyclopedia.

Palazzi, Fernando. Novissimo dizionario della lingua italiana: etimologico, fraseologico, grammaticale, ideologico, nomenclatore e dei sinonimi. 2. ed. rev., agg., e corr. Milano, Casa Ed. Ceschina, 1939 (repr. 1959). 1404p. il. **AE364**

Contains approximately 64,000 words.

Panzini, Alfredo. Dizionario moderno delle parole che non si trovano nei dizionari comuni. 9. ed. . . . con un proemio di A. Schiaffini e con un'appendice di ottamila voci nuovamente compilata da B. Migliorini. Milano, Hoepli, 1950. 997p. **AE365**

7th ed. 1935.

A dictionary reflecting the opinions of the author who attempted to list and define words in many categories—political, scientific, and general—not found in the standard dictionaries.

—— —— Parole nuove: appendice di dodicimila voci al "Dizionario moderno" di Alfredo Panzini [par] Bruno Migliorini. Milano, Hoepli, 1963. 327p.

An enlarged appendix of new words.

Bilingual

Cassell's Italian-English, English-Italian dictionary, comp. by Piero Rebora, with the assistance of Francis M. Guercio and Arthur L. Hayward. London, Cassell, 1958. 1079p. **AE366**

"First published 1958."

A general dictionary of the Italian language as written and spoken today. "So far as any such work can claim to be new, this is a new lexicon."—*Pref.*

Hazon, Mario. Garzanti comprehensive Italian-English, English-Italian dictionary. N.Y., McGraw-Hill, 1963. 2090p. **AE367**

Published in 1961 under title *Dizionario inglese-italiano, italiano-inglese.*

A well-edited and useful new work. Coverage is excellent, including many technical and colloquial words. Includes proper names: personal and geographical.

Hoare, Alfred. Italian dictionary. 2d ed. Cambridge, Univ. Pr., 1925. 906p. **AE368**

1st ed. 1915.

For many years considered the best Italian-English dictionary, and still one of the most useful.

—— Short Italian dictionary, abridged from the author's larger dictionary. Cambridge, Univ. Pr., 1923–26. 2v. **AE369**

v.1, Italian-English, 2d ed.; v.2, English-Italian, new and enl. ed.

Frequently reprinted.

Lysle, A. de R. and **Gualtieri, Lora Lamia.** Nuovo dizionario moderno delle lingue italiana e inglese. Ed. riv. e aggiornata, con aggiunta di un supplemento commerciale. Torino, Casanova, 1951. 2v. **AE370**

Contents: v.1, Inglese-italiano; v.2, Italiano-inglese.

A modern dictionary including words in common use, colloquial and slang expressions, scientific and technical words, etc.

Earlier editions published under title *Nuovo dizionario moderno-razionale-pratico inglese-italiano.*

Reynolds, Barbara. The Cambridge Italian dictionary. Cambridge, Univ. Pr., 1962– . v.1– . (In progress) **AE371**

Contents: v.1, Italian-English. 899p.

"First, and underlying all its criteria, is the fact that [the *Dictionary*] has been compiled, selected, and arranged from the point of view of the English-speaking user."—*Introd.*

Emphasis is on inclusiveness and elucidation of vocabulary for both the literary scholar and the student of the spoken language. Thus, many little-used and obsolete words are included, together with numerous terms from specialized vocabularies; the editors have relied on subject specialists for the selection of these terms and for their definitions. Etymological derivation is not usually given, but etymologically related words are often grouped together, with cross references from the alphabetical listings of the individual terms.

Although Hoare's *Italian dictionary* (AE368) is an acknowledged predecessor, the present work is not to be considered a mere revision of that work.

Spinelli, Nicola. Dizionario italiano-inglese, inglese-italiano. 3. ed. interamente rifatta. Torino, Società Ed. Internazionale, 1955. 2v. **AE372**

A modern, well-edited dictionary, with good word discriminations and definitions.

Etymology

Battisti, Carlo and **Alessio, Giovanni.** Dizionario etimologico italiano. Firenze, G. Barbèra, 1950–57. 5v. **AE373**

Sponsored by the Istituto di Glottologia of the Università di Firenze.

The first extensive etymological dictionary in Italian, giving derivations, similar words in other languages, definitions, etc. Coverage is comprehensive including archaic and modern terms, scientific and technical words, and some dialectal forms.

Orthography and usage

Gabrielli, Aldo. Dizionario linguistico moderno; guida pratica per scrivere e parlar bene. [1. ed.] Milano, Ed. Scholastiche Mondadori, 1956. 1113p. **AE374**

A practical manual of modern Italian for writers and speakers. In two parts: pt.1 is an alphabetically arranged dictionary of usage giving grammatical and stylistic rules, with examples of idiomatic construction, foreign words and phrases, etc.; pt.2 is an alphabetical list of words giving gender, transitive and intransitive verbs, some proper nouns, etc.

Synonyms

Cinti, Decio. Dizionario dei sinonimi e dei contrari. 7. ed. riv. e amp. Milano, Sormani, 1955. 631p. **AE375**

A small, useful dictionary of synonyms and antonyms.

Tommaseo, Niccolò. Dizionario dei sinonimi della lingua italiana. Compl. riv. e aum. da Giuseppe Rigutini. Milano, Vallardi, 1944. 1000p. **AE376**

A thesaurus arranged by category, with definitions showing discrimination of meaning.

Japanese

Daijiten [Great dictionary]. Comp. by Heibonsha. Tokyo, Heibonsha, 1934–36. 26v. **AE377**

Otsuki, Fumihiko. Dai-genkai. Tokyo, Fuzambo, 1932–35. 4v. and index. **AE378**

Entirely in Japanese.

Compiled along Western lines by an author educated in western countries. Said by a Japanese authority to be especially important for inclusion of the etymology of words—something not done by other Japanese lexicographers.

Daniels, Otome. Dictionary of Japanese (sōsho) writing forms. London, Lund, Humphries, 1944. 309p., 48p. **AE379**

Ueda, Mannen. Ueda's Daijiten; a Japanese dictionary of Chinese characters and compounds. Amer. ed. Cambridge, Harvard Univ. Pr., 1942. [2918p.] il. **AE380**

Entirely in Japanese.

Various pagings.

Table on lining papers.

"Published under the sponsorship of the Department of Far Eastern Languages of Harvard University, with the financial aid of the Rockefeller Institute."—*Foreword.*

—— and **Matsui, K.** Dai-nihon kokugo jiten. Tokyo, Fuzambo, 1928–29. 4v. and index.   **AE381**

1st ed. 1921.

Bilingual

Brinkley's Japanese-English dictionary. With an introd. by Eric B. Ceadel. Cambridge, Heffer, 1963. 2v.   **AE382**

Originally published in 1896 with title *An unabridged Japanese-English dictionary.*

Frequently includes synonyms as well as examples of usage in sentences, the latter given in roman letters, Japanese characters, and English translation.

Hepburn, James Curtis. A Japanese-English and English-Japanese dictionary. 7th ed. Tokyo, Maruya; London, Trübner, 1903. 962p.   **AE383**

One of the first Japanese-English dictionaries. Still useful.

Hyōjun Rōmaji Kai. All-Romanized English-Japanese dictionary. Tokyo, Author, 1961. 732p.   **AE384**

A pocket dictionary designed to aid the traveler and the student to determine Japanese words and expressions for English terms.

Kenkyusha's New English-Japanese dictionary on bilingual principles. Tamihei Iwasaki and Jujiro Kawamura, gen. eds. A new ed. rev. and enl. Tokyo, Kenkyusha, 1960. 2204p.   **AE385**

Kenkyusha's New Japanese-English dictionary. Senkichiro Katsumata, gen. ed. An entirely new ed. Tokyo, Kenkyusha, 1954. 2136p.   **AE386**

A new edition of a standard dictionary.

Nelson, Andrew Nathaniel. The modern reader's Japanese-English character dictionary. Tokyo, Tuttle, 1962. 1048p.   **AE387**

Designed primarily for current usage, this dictionary contains more than 5000 basic characters and almost 70,000 compounds, with brief definitions in English.

Rose-Innes, Arthur. Beginners' dictionary of Chinese-Japanese characters, with common abbreviations, variants and numerous compounds. Technically arr. and rev. by W. Kos. New 4th ed. 2d reprint. Tokyo, Meiseisha Pub. Co., 1960. 507p.   **AE388**

Tables on endpapers.

A dictionary of some 5000 characters, with explanations for beginners as to how to find characters, how to determine the radical, etc.

Korean

Gale, James Scarth. Unabridged Korean-English dictionary. 3d ed., ed. by Alexander A. Pieters. Seoul, Christian Literature Soc., 1931. 1781p.   **AE389**

First published in 1897 as *A Korean-English dictionary.*

Contains some 82,000 definitions; includes names of persons and places.

New English-Korean dictionary. Kwang Man Kauh, ed. adviser; Sung Shik Cho [and others], gen. eds. Seoul, Omungak Pub. Co., 1964. 2276p.   **AE390**

Underwood, Horace Grant. A concise dictionary of the Korean language in two parts, Korean-English & English-Korean. Yokahama, Kelly & Walsh, 1890. 196p., 292p.   **AE391**

Underwood, Joan V. Concise English-Korean dictionary, romanized. Rutland, Vt., Tokyo, Charles E. Tuttle Co., 1954. 320p.   **AE392**

Subtitle: The 8000 most useful English words and phrases with Korean equivalents in both Roman and Korean letters.

Small pocket dictionary.

Yu, Hyŏng-ki. New Life Korean-English dictionary. Hyungki J. Lew, ed. Amer. ed. Wash., Educ. Services, 1952. 866p.   **AE393**

Lappish

Nielsen, Konrad. Lappisk ordbok, grunnet på dialektene i Polmak, Karasjok og Kautokeino. Oslo, Aschehoug; Cambridge, Harvard Univ. Pr.; London, Williams, 1932–56. 4v. (Inst. for Sammenlignende Kulturforskning. [Publikasjoner], ser. B: Skrifter. 17)   **AE394**

English title: Lapp dictionary, based on the dialects of Polmak, Karasjok and Kautokeino.

Lappish, English, and Norwegian; preliminary matter in Norwegian and English in parallel columns.

v.1–3, 1932–38.

v.4, The vocabulary classified according to the meanings of the words, with many illustrations of Lappish life and customs. 1956. il.

Latin

Thesaurus linguae latinae, editus auctoritate et consilio academiarum quinque germanicarum Berolinensis, Gottingensis, Lipsiensis, Monacensis, Vindobonensis. Lipsiae, Teubner, 1900–63. (In progress)   **AE395**

v.1–5, A–E, and v.6$^{1-3}$, F–H, compl.; v.7^1, fasc.1–7, I–Iocus; v.8, fasc.1–10, M–Multitudo.

The great dictionary of the language, in Latin; indispensable in the university or large reference library. Plans to record, with representative quotations from each author, every word in the text of each Latin author down to the Antonines, with a selection of important passages from the works of all writers to the 7th century. In the section A–B, proper names are included in the main alphabet, but from C on they are given in the following supplement:

—— Supplementum: Nomina propria [Onomasticon]. Lipsiae, Teubner, 1907–23. v.2–3$^{1-2}$.

v.2–3$^{1-2}$, C–Don.

—— Index librorum scriptorum inscriptionum ex quibus exempla adferuntur. *Lipsiae,* Teubner, 1904. 109p.

—— —— Supplementum. 1958. 13p.

Bacci, Antonio. . . . Lexicon eorum vocabulorum quae difficilius latine redduntur. Ed. 4. Rome, Soc. Libraria "Studium," [1963]. 846p. (v.1 of his Varia latinitatis scripta)   **AE396**

A dictionary giving Latin translations for the Italian forms of modern words and terms, such as atom bomb, diploma, countess, hypodermic injection, professional, and for geographic divisions, e.g., Korea, Colombia, etc.

Bilingual

Benoist, Eugène and **Goelzer, Henri.** Nouveau dictionnaire latin-français . . . 11. éd. rev. corr. Paris, Garnier, [1934]. 1682p.   **AE397**

Cassell's New Latin-English, English-Latin dictionary, by D. P. Simpson. London, Cassell, [1959]. 883p.   **AE398**

U.S. edition has title *Cassell's New Latin dictionary. Latin-English, English-Latin.* N.Y., Funk & Wagnalls, 1960. 883p.

A thoroughly new edition of this long-popular desk dictionary.

Gaffiot, Felix. Dictionnaire illustré latin-français. [Nouv. éd.] Paris, Hachette, 1963. 1719p. il., maps.   **AE399**

Ed. by René Durand.

1st ed. 1934.

A modern Latin-French dictionary.

Harpers' Latin dictionary. A new Latin dictionary founded on the translation of Freund's Latin-German lexicon, ed. by E. A. Andrews. Rev., enl., and in great part rewritten by Charlton T. Lewis and Charles Short. N.Y., Cincinnati, Amer. Book Co., 1907. 2019p. (Repr.: Oxford, Clarendon Pr., 1955) **AE400**

1st ed. 1879.

Frequently reprinted. The most generally useful of Latin-English dictionaries.

Lewis, Charlton T. Latin dictionary for schools. N.Y., Cincinnati, Amer. Book Co., 1916. 1191p. **AE401**

Not a complete Latin dictionary but a work designed to include and explain "every word or phrase in Latin books commonly read in schools." A very usable dictionary for the student.

Smith, *Sir* **William** and **Hall, Theophilus D.** Copious and critical English-Latin dictionary. N.Y., Amer. Book Co., 1871. 754p. **AE402**

Includes a dictionary of proper names.

Smith, *Sir* **William.** Smaller Latin-English dictionary [3d ed.] rev. by J. F. Lockwood. London, Murray, 1933. 823p. (Repr.: N.Y., Barnes & Noble, 1960) **AE403**

1st ed. 1855; 2d ed. 1881. Frequently reprinted.

Includes tables of the Roman calendar, measures, weights, and money.

Etymology

Ernout, Alfred and **Meillet, Antoine.** Dictionnaire étymologique de la langue latine, histoire des mots. 4. éd. rev. et corr. et augm. d'un index. Paris, Klincksieck, 1959–60. 820p. **AE404**

Ouvrage publié avec le concours du Centre National de la Recherche Scientifique.

1st ed. 1932; 3d ed. 1951.

One of the best of the modern etymological dictionaries.

Walde, Alois. Lateinisches etymologisches Wörterbuch. 3. neubearb. Aufl. von J. B. Hofmann. Heidelberg, Winter, 1930–54. 2v. (Indogermanische Bibliothek. II. Reihe, Wörterbücher) **AE405**

————— Register zusammengestellt von Elsbeth Berger. 1956. 287p.

A scholarly etymological dictionary which indicates the first appearance of each Latin word with references to documents and usage.

Christian Era

Blaise, Albert. Dictionnaire latin-français des auteurs chrétiens. Revu spécialement pour le vocabulaire théologique par Henri Chirat. Strasbourg, "Le Latin Chrétien," 1954. 865p. **AE406**

Covers from Tertullian to the end of the Merovingian period, i.e., from the end of the 1st to the 7th century, and includes new terms and classical terms with new meanings. Many quotations with exact reference to sources. Bibliography of works cited is given on p.9–29.

Souter, Alexander. Glossary of later Latin to 600 A.D. Oxford, Clarendon Pr., 1949. 454p. **AE407**

Covers the Christian literature from 180 A.D. to 600 A.D., and thus is planned to supplement the proposed *Oxford Latin dictionary* which will omit Christian Latin authors.

Medieval Latin

Arnaldi, Francisco. Latinitatis italicae medii aevi inde ab a. CDLXXVI usque ad a. MXXII lexicon imperfectum

cura et studio. . . . Bruxelles, 1936–61. Fasc.1–3. (Bulletin Du Cange archivum latinitatis medii aevi. v.10, 12, 20–29, 31) **AE408**

Fasc.1–3, A–Systema.

Published in the *Bulletin Du Cange* without separate paging.

Baxter, James Houston and **Johnson, Charles.** Medieval Latin word-list from British and Irish sources prep. . . . with the assistance of Phyllis Abrahams under the direction of a committee appointed by the British Academy. Oxford, Univ. Pr., 1934. 466p. **AE409**

A word list rather than a formal dictionary—a first step in the task of making a comprehensive dictionary of medieval British Latin. Gives brief information, i.e., Latin word, date, and equivalent English word or phrase.

Du Cange, Charles Du Fresne, *Sieur.* Glossarium mediae et infimae latinitatis conditum a Carolo Du Fresne, domino Du Cange; auctum a monachis Ordinis S. Benedicti, cum supplementis integris D. P. Carpentarii, Adelungii, aliorum, suisque digessit G. A. L. Henschel; sequuntur Glossarium gallicum, Tabulae, Indices auctorum et rerum, Dissertationes. Ed. nova, aucta pluribus verbis aliorum scriptorum a Léopold Favre. Niort, L. Favre, 1883–87. 10v. il. (Repr.: Paris, Librarie des Sciences et des Arts, 1937–38; Graz, Akademische Druck- & Verlagsanstalt, 1954. 5v.) **AE410**

v.1–8, A–Z; v.9, Glossaire français; v.10, Indices.

The great dictionary of medieval Latin, originally published 1678 and several times revised. This is the latest edition but is very little changed from the edition of 1840–57, 8v., which is still usable and as good for general purposes as the later edition.

————— ————— Petit supplément au Dictionaire de Du Cange par Charles Schmidt. Strasbourg, Heitz, 1906. 71p.

Maigne d'Arnis, W. H. Lexicon manuale ad scriptores mediae et infimae latinitatis, ex glossariis Caroli Dufresne, D. Ducangii, D. P. Carpentarii, Adelungii et aliorum, in compendium accuratissime redactum; ou, Recueil de mots de la basse latinité. Paris, Migne, 1866. 2336col. **AE411**

Gives definitions in Latin and in French.

Mittellateinisches Wörterbuch bis zum Ausgehenden 13. Jahrhundert. . . . München, C. H. Beck, 1959–64. Bd.1, Lfg. 1–7, Abkürzungs- und Quellenverzeichnisse. (In progress) **AE412**

In Gemeinschaft mit den Akademien der Wissenschaften zu Göttingen, Heidelberg, Leipzig, Mainz, Wien, und der Schweizerischen Geisteswissenschaftlichen Gesellschaft, hrsg. von der Bayerischen Akademie der Wissenschaften und der Deutschen Akademie der Wissenschaften zu Berlin.

Contents: Abkürzungs- und Quellenverzeichnisse. 94p.; Bd.1, Lfg. 1–7, a–aszelon.

A number of German-speaking Latinists are collaborating to produce another scholarly dictionary of medieval Latin. Designed to extend the scope of the standard *Thesaurus,* i.e., to cover the centuries from the decline of classical Latin to the end of the 13th century, it follows generally the plan of the *Thesaurus* in its treatment of individual words. Among many sources drawn upon for vocabulary, the extensive series *Monumenta germaniae historica* is particularly heavily utilized.

Niermeyer, Jan Frederik. Mediae latinitatis lexicon minus. Leiden, Brill, 1954–63. Fasc.1–10. (In progress) **AE413**

Subtitle: Lexique Latin médiéval-français/anglais. A medieval Latin-French/English dictionary.

Fasc.1–10, Ab–sequipeda.

A new scholarly dictionary designed to be less bulky than Du Cange but more extensive than the word lists. Explanations of meanings are given both in French and in English, and there are numerous quotations showing the history and usage of words. The majority of the quotations come from sources between A.D. 550 and 1150.

Novum glossarium mediae latinitatis ab anno DCCC usque ad annum MCC; edendum curavit Consilium Academiarum Consociatarum. [Copenhagen], Ejnar Munksgaard, 1957– . (In progress) **AE414**

Contents: Letter L, ed. by Franz Blatt. 1957; M–mozytia by Franz Blatt. 1959–63.

—— Index scriptorum mediae latinitatis ab anno DCCC usque ad annum MCC qui afferuntur in Novo glossario ab Academiis Consociatis iuris publici facto. [Copenhagen], Ejnar Munksgaard, 1957. 194p. Fasc. unnumbered. **AE414a**

Designed to cover the "general" language of authors from the 9th to the 13th centuries. Word treatment is primarily lexicographic rather than historical or encyclopedic. Supplements but does not replace Du Cange. The *Index scriptorum* constitutes a useful bibliography of the major Latin authors of the period.

Sleumer, Albert. Kirchenlateinisches Wörterbuch . . . 2. sehr verm. Aufl. des "Liturgischen Lexikons" unter umfassendster Mitarbeit von . . . Joseph Schmid, hrsg. von . . . Albert Sleumer. . . . Limburg a.d. Lahn, Steffen, 1926. 840p. **AE415**

Subtitle: Ausführliches Wörterverzeichnis zum Römischen Missale, Breviarium, Rituale, Graduale, Pontificale, Caeremoniale, Martyrologium, sowie zur Vulgata und zum Codex juris canonici; desgleichen zu den Proprien der Bistümer Deutschlands, Österreichs, Ungarns, Luxemburgs, der Schweiz und zahlreicher kirchlicher Orden und Kongregationen.

Bibliography

Starnes, DeWitt Talmage. Renaissance dictionaries, English-Latin and Latin-English. Austin, Univ. of Texas Pr., 1954. 427p. il. **AE416**

A history of English-Latin and Latin-English lexicography down to the 18th century, particularly of the period 1500–1660. Includes a bibliography of references pertaining to the history of Latin-English lexicography, p.393–94, and a short-title list of Latin-English and English-Latin dictionaries (1500–*ca.* 1800) in American libraries with location of copies.

Lettish

Anglu-latviešu vārdnīca: sastādījis autoru kolektivs M. Stradinas redakcijā. Riga, Latvijas Valsts Izdevniecība, 1957. 916p. **AE417**

More comprehensive, with more meanings and phrases, than the dictionary by Dravnieks (AE418). Gives pronunciation of English words by phonetic alphabet.

Dravnieks, Jēkabs. English-Latvian dictionary (Angliski-latviska vārdnīca). [N.Y.], Grāmatu Draugs, [195–?]. 606p. **AE418**

1st ed., Riga, 1933.

Mühlenbach, K. Mülenbacha Latviešu valodas vārdnīca. Redigējis, papildinājis, turpinājis J. Endzelīns . . . Mühlenbachs Lettisch-deutsches Wörterbuch. Red., ergänzt und fortgesetzt von J. Endzelin. Riga, hrsg. vom Lettischen Bildungsministerium, 1923–32. 4v. **AE419**

Lettish-German.

A scholarly work, including etymologies.

—— —— Papildinājumi un labojumi. Ergänzungen und Berichtigungen [von] J. Endzelin und E. Hausenberg. 2. unv. Aufl. Chicago, Der Gruppe der Lettischen Baltologen in Chicago, 1956. 2v.

A supplement covering A–Z, published as v.5–6 of main set.

Turkina, Eiženijà. Latviešu-anglu vārdnīca; M. Andersones redakcijā. Pārstradats un papildanāts 2. izd. Ap 31,000 vārdu. Riga, Latvijas Valsts Izdevniecība, 1962. 775p. **AE420**

Added title page in English: Latvian-English dictionary, ed. by M. Andersone. 2d ed. rev. and enl. Approx. 31,000 entries.

Lithuanian

Dabartinės lietuvių kalbos žodynas. Redakcine kolegija: J. Balčikonis, K. Korsakas [et al.]. Vilnius, Valstybinė Politinės ir Mokslinės Literatūros Leidykla, 1954. 990p. **AE421**

At head of title: Lietuvos TSR Mokslų Akademija. Lietuvių Kalbos ir Literatūros Institutas.

A dictionary of present-day Lithuanian.

Bilingual

Baravykas, Vaclovas. Anglų-lietuvių kalbų žodynas. Apie 30,000 žodžių ir posakių. Redagavo A. Laučka ir A. Dantaitė. [Chicago?], JAV, 1959. 583p. **AE422**

English-Lithuanian.

Lalis, Anthony. Dictionary of the Lithuanian and English languages. 3d rev. and enl. ed. Chicago, "Lietuvos," 1910–15. 2pts. **AE423**

Pt.1, Lithuanian-English, 1910. 439p.; pt.2, English-Lithuanian, 1915. 835p.

Niedermann, Max, Senn, Alfred and **Salys, Anton.** Wörterbuch der litauischen Schriftsprache: litauisch-deutsch. Heidelberg, Carl Winter Universitätsverlag, 1932–63. v.1–3, 4$^{1–41}$. (Indogermanische Bibliothek. II. Reihe, Wörterbücher) (In progress) **AE424**

Editors vary.

v.1–4^{41}, a–tvótinti.

A dictionary of the modern literary language giving examples of usage.

Péteraitis, Vilius. Lietuviškai angliškas žodynas; Lithuanian-English dictionary. 2. laida. Chicago, Letuviškos Knygos Klubas, 1960. 586p. **AE425**

1st ed. 1948.

Prepared for the use of Lithuanians in English-speaking countries.

Etymology

Fraenkel, Ernst. Litauisches etymologisches Wörterbuch. Heidelberg, Carl Winter Universitätsverlag, 1962–64. Lfg. 1–17. (Indogermanische Bibliothek. II. Reihe, Wörterbücher) (In progress) **AE426**

Bd.1, A–prive (appeared in 8 Lfg. 1955–58). New title page and preliminary matter issued in 1962.

Bd.2 (Lfg. 9–17), privy–z. 1959–64.

An extensive etymological dictionary.

Malay

Wilkinson, Richard James. Malay-English dictionary (romanised). Mitylene, Greece, Salavopoulos and Kinderlis; Singapore, Kelly and Walsh, 1932. 2v. (Repr. 1956) **AE427**

—— An abridged Malay-English dictionary. 7th ed. (romanised), rev. by A. E. Coope. N.Y., Macmillan, 1948. 269p.

Winstedt, *Sir* Richard Olof. An unabridged Malay-English dictionary. 3d ed., with a new appendix 1959. Singapore, Marican, [1960?]. 375p. **AE428**

—— A practical modern English-Malay [Malay-English] dictionary. Singapore, Kelly and Walsh, 1952. 2v. **AE429**
English-Malay. 388p.; Malay-English. 204p.

Mongolian

Boberg, Folke. Mongolian-English dictionary. Copenhagen, Munksgaard, 1954–55. 3v. **AE430**
v.1–2, Mongolian-English, A–Vivangkhirit; v.3, English-Mongolian, A–Zodiac and Index to v.1–2.
First Mongolian dictionary "published to a Western language since 1849."

Lessing, Ferdinand D. Mongolian-English dictionary, comp. by Mattai Haltod, John Gombojab Hangin, Serge Kassatkin and Ferdinand D. Lessing. Berkeley, Univ. of Calif. Pr., 1960. 1217p. **AE431**
"Excluding the strictly archaic language, the dictionary contains the vocabulary of all periods from 1940 on, including the modern terminology developed since sovietization . . . strictly technical Buddhist terms and expressions are presented in a special Supplement."—*Introd*.
Selected bibliography of dictionaries and grammars, p.xiv.

Norse, Old

See Icelandic, p.117.

Norwegian

See Danish and Norwegian, p.107.

Pali

Buddhadatta, A. P. English-Pali dictionary. Colombo, Pali Text Society, [1955]. 588p. **AE432**

—— Concise Pali-English dictionary. Colombo, Colombo Apothecaries Co., 1949. 281p. **AE432a**

Pali Text Society, London. Pali-English dictionary, ed. by Thomas W. Rhys Davids and William Stede. Chipstead (Surrey), Soc., 1921–25. 4v. (Repr.: London, Luzac, 1949) **AE433**
Issued in 8pts.
A standard dictionary with reference to sources.

Trenckner, Vilhelm. Critical Pali dictionary. Begun by V. Trenckner, rev., cont. and ed. by Dines Andersen, Helmer Smith, and Hans Hendriksen. Copenhagen, Royal Danish Academy of Sciences and Letters, 1924/48–62. v.1–2$^{1-2}$. (In progress) **AE434**
A scholarly critical dictionary with English definitions and many references to sources.
v.1, A–asota.
Epilegomena to v.1 by Helmer Smith. 1948. 97p.
Contents: Abbreviations, bibliography, concordances, devices of transliteration.
v.2, fasc.1–2, a–appatik (1960–62).
Publication resumed in 1960, again from the beginning of the alphabet, but not duplicating the work already published.

Persian

Dehkhodā, Ali Akbar. Lughat nāmah. Téhéran, Chāpkhāna Majlis, 1946–53. v.1– . **AE435**
In Persian.
Contents: A (incompl.); P (incompl.); Ṣ (Th) (compl.); Ḥ (incompl.); Ẓ (Dh) (compl.); Zh (compl.); Ẓ (Ḍ) (compl.); Ẓ (compl.); L (incompl.).

Bilingual

Arīyān-pūr, 'Abbas. The new unabridged English-Persian dictionary, by Abbas Aryanpur (Kashani), with the collaboration of Jahan Shah Saleh and numerous consultants, translators, etc. [Tehran, Amir-Kabir Pub. & Prt. Inst., 1963–64] v.1–4 (4771p.). il. (In progress) **AE436**
Contents: v.1–4, A–R.

Hayyīm, Sulaimān. The larger English-Persian dictionary, designed to give the Persian meanings of 80,000 words, idioms, phrases and proverbs in the English language, as well as the transliteration of difficult Persian words. Téhéran, Bēroukhim, 1941–43. 2v. **AE437**
Added title page in Persian.
Each volume has Addenda, including some words omitted from the text, important proper names, foreign words and phrases, a few colloquial and slang expressions, abbreviations used in English literature, and Persian abbreviations.

—— New Persian-English dictionary, complete and modern, designed to give the English meanings of over 50,000 words, terms, idioms, and proverbs in the Persian language as well as the transliteration of the words in English characters. Together with a sufficient treatment of all the grammatical features of the Persian language. Téhéran, Bēroukhim, 1960–62. 2v. **AE438**
First pub. 1934–36.

—— The shorter Persian-English dictionary treating 30,000 words and idioms used in modern Persian. 2d ed. rev. and enl. Téhéran, Bēroukhim, 1958. 814p. **AE439**
1st ed. 1954.

Palmer, Edward H. Concise dictionary of the Persian language. English-Persian; Persian-English. London, Routledge & Paul, 1949. 726col. **AE440**

Razi, F. D. The modern Persian dictionary (Persian-Urdu-English), comp. by F. D. Razi, assisted by M. Rasheed Ahmed. Lahore, Ripon Printing Pr., 1952. 240p. **AE441**

Wollaston, *Sir* Arthur Naylor. Complete English-Persian dictionary, comp. from original sources. London, Murray, 1904. 1491p. **AE442**
1st impression: London, Low, 1894.

Pidgin English

Mihalic, Francis. Grammar and dictionary of Neo-Melanesian. Techny, Ill., Mission Pr., [c.1957]. 60p., 318p. **AE443**
Contents: Grammar, p.2–60. Dictionary: Neo-Melanesian to English, p.3–165; English to neo-Melanesian, p.168–286; word groups, p.287–318.

Polish

Karlowicz, Jan, Kryński, Adam [and others]. Słownik języka polskiego. Warszawa, Wydawnictwo Kasy im. Mianowskiego, Inst. Popierania Nauka, 1900–35. 8v. **AE444**
Imprint varies. Editors vary.
A standard dictionary.

Polska Akademia Nauk. Słownik języka polskiego. Redaktor naczelny Witold Doroszewski. Warszawa, Wiedza Powszechna, 1958–64. v.1–6. (In progress) **AE445**
v.1–6, A–Pre.
A major scholarly dictionary of the Polish language, with many references to the literature.

Słownik staropolski. [Komitet redakcyjny: Kazimierz Nitsch, przewodniczący] Warszawa, 1953–64. v.1$^{1-5}$, 2$^{1,5-7}$, 3$^{1-6}$, 4$^{1-4}$. (In progress) **AE446**

At head of title: Polska Akademia Nauk.
Contents: A–Czeluść, Da–Dobrowoly, I–Jen, Kotowist–Królewski, Lndaki–Modlitwa.
A scholarly dictionary of Old Polish.

Bilingual

Kierst, W. Słownik angielsko-polski i polsko-angielski. Warszawa, Trzaska, Evert i Michalski, 1926–28. 2v.
AE447

v.1, English-Polish; v.2, Polish-English.
A useful Polish–English dictionary, frequently reprinted. (A recent photographic reprint is *Słownik podręczny . . . Concise dictionary.* Warszawa, Wiedza Powszechna, 1957. 2v. in 1)

Kościuszko Foundation dictionary: English-Polish, Polish-English, by K. Bulas, L. L. Thomas and F. J. Whitfield. The Hague, Mouton, 1959–61. 2v. (Poland's Millennium ser. of the Kościuszko Foundation) (Also distr. by the Kosciuszko Foundation, 15 E. 65th St., New York 21, N.Y.)
AE448

v.1, English-Polish. 1037p.; v.2, Polish-English. 772p.
The second volume emphasizes "twentieth century standard Polish"; the first volume includes some English dialect and slang. Includes examples of usage. A substantial bilingual dictionary.

Lilien, Ernest. Lilien's Dictionary . . . pt.1, English-Polish. Stevens Point, Wis., Wydawnictwa Słownika Liliena, 1944–52. 960p. il.
AE449

Pt.1, English-Polish, fasc. 1–19, A–hellbent.
Ceased publication.
An extensive and well-executed dictionary of current Polish, including many technical and scientific terms. Unfortunately unfinished.

Stanisławski, Jan. Wielki słownik angielsko-polski. Red. naukowy, Wiktor Jassem. Warszawa, Wiedza Powszechna, 1964. 1175p.
AE450

Added title page: The great English–Polish dictionary.
"Comprises over 100,000 words, phrases and expressions commonly used in the English language of the 19th and 20th centuries."—*Pref.* Includes also terms in technology, medicine and science, colloquialisms, Americanisms, etc.

Abbreviations

U.S. Library of Congress. Slavic and Central European Division. Polish abbreviations: a selective list, comp. by Janina Wojcicka. 2d ed. rev. and enl. Wash., 1957. 164p.
AE451

1st ed. 1955.
Lists some 2600 abbreviations which have gained currency in Poland since 1945—particularly names of government agencies, societies, companies, and institutions—but with some general abbreviations as well.

Etymology

Brückner, Alexander. Słownik etymologiczny języka polskiego. [2. wyd.] Warszawa, Wiedza Powszechna, 1957. 805p.
AE452

Reprint, with new introduction, of work published: Kraków, Nakład i Własność Krakowskiej Spółki Wydawniczej, 1927.

Sławski, Franciszek. Słownik etymologiczny języka polskiego. Kraków, Nakl. Tow. Milosnikov Jezika Polskiego, 1952–64. v.1–2$^{1-4}$. (In progress)
AE453

v.1–2$^{1-4}$, A–Kooperacja.
Redaktorzy: Kazimierz Nitsch i Andrzej Siudut.

Bibliography

Lewanski, Richard C. A bibliography of Polish dictionaries with a supplement of Lusatian and Polabian dictionaries. N.Y., New York Pub. Lib., 1959. 63p.
AE454

Grouped as monolingual, bilingual, and polyglot. Lists dictionaries of many types: language, e.g., general, dialect, etymology, orthography, slang, synonyms, etc.; geography; biography; pseudonyms; abbreviations; and technical and scientific dictionaries in various fields. Includes author and subject indexes and a list of principal sources.

Polyglot

Britannica world language dictionary. (Pt. II & III of Funk & Wagnalls New practical standard dictionary of the English language. N.Y., 1954. p.1539–1944) **AE455**

Pt.II gives, in parallel columns, the most common English words and their translations into six other languages; pt.III is in six sections: French, German, Italian, Spanish, Swedish, and Yiddish. Each section contains the most common words of that language, with pronunciation and English equivalent. Also included are brief grammatical rules, useful expressions, etc.

Dony, Yvonne P. de. Léxico del lenguaje figurado, comparado, en cuatro idiomas: castellano, français, English, deutsch. Buenos Aires, Ed. Desclée, De Brouwer, 1951. 804p.
AE456

"27,846 locuciones distribuídas en 4071 grupos."
A dictionary of expressions, proverbs, idioms, etc., arranged in groups under the main Spanish word with equivalents in French, English, and German. Indexes in each of these languages.

Duden pictorial encyclopedia, in five languages: English, French, German, Italian, Spanish. Containing 30,000 words explained by pictures. . . . N.Y., pub. by the Murray Print. Co. for Frederick Ungar Pub. Co., [c1943]. [2588p.]. il.
AE457

"Based on the widely used Duden picture vocabularies, which originally were produced in Germany, in the late 1930's."—*Pref.*
Covers science and arts, state and community, man, family and home, trades and vocations, trade and transport, physical culture and recreation, etc. with pictorial drawings, keyed to expressions in the various languages.

Pei, Mario A. and **Gaynor, Frank.** Liberal arts dictionary in English, French, German, Spanish. N.Y., Philosophical Lib., 1952. 307p.
AE458

Intended to supplement the desk-size English dictionary for the ordinary reader, and to give translations for specific terms in the artistic, literary, and philosophical fields. Definitions are given under the English form of words, followed by equivalents in French, German, and Spanish, with an index for each of these three languages.

Portuguese
(including Brazilian Portuguese)

Dicionário geral luso-brasileiro da língua portuguesa. Lisboa, Rio de Janeiro, Editorial Enciclopédia, [1963]– . v.1– . (In progress) **AE459**

Contents: v.1, A–Apel. 956p.
To be in four parts: (1) Dicionário geral de vocábulos comuns; (2) Dicionário onomástico; (3) Dicionário de vocábulos e locuções estrangeiras; (4) Dicionário de abreviaturas.

Figueiredo, Cândido de. Dicionário da língua portuguesa. 10. ed. actualizada segundo as regras do Acordo Ortográfico . . . e em perfeita harmonia com o "Vocabulário resumido" de 1947 da Academia das Ciências. Lisbon, Bertrand, 1949–50. 2v. **AE460**

Includes etymologies.

Freire, Laudelino de Oliveira. Grande e novíssimo dicionário da língua portuguesa . . . com a colaboração técnica do J. L. de Campos. Rio de Janeiro, Noite, 1939–44. 5v. **AE461**

A large dictionary including some 208,000 entries giving etymologies, some examples of usage, etc.

Lima, Hildebrando de and **Barroso, Gustavo.** Pequeno dicionário brasileiro da língua portuguêsa. 10. ed. supervisionada e consideràvelmente aumentada por Aurelio Buarque de Hollanda Ferreira com a assistência de José Baptista da Luz e revista e aumentada por inúmeros especialistas. Rio de Janeiro, Civilização Brasileira, 1961. 1287p. **AE462**

1st edition edited by Hildebrando de Lima and revised by various editors through the years.

A standard and practical dictionary of Brazilian Portuguese.

Magne, Augusto. Dicionário da língua portuguesa, especialmente dos períodos medieval e clássico. Rio de Janeiro, 1950–54. v.1–2. (Brazil. Ministério da Educação e Saúde. Inst. Nacional do Livro) (In progress?) **AE463**

v.1–2, A–Al.

This promised to be a vast new dictionary, tracing the development of the Portuguese language from its beginning to the present day. Emphasis is on early forms, but modern scientific terms are also included. A considerable list of philological sources is given.

Mesquita de Carvalho, José. Dicionário prático da língua nacional. 3. ed. Rio de Janeiro, Ed. Globo, 1953. 1185p. **AE464**

1st ed. 1945.
Brazilian Portuguese.
Gives derivations, cognates, etc.

Moraes Silva, António de. Grande dicionário da língua portuguesa. 10. ed. rev., corrigida muito aumentada e actualizada segundo as regras do Acordo Ortográfico Luso-Brasileiro de 10 agosto de 1945, por Augusto Moreno, Cardoso Júnior e José Pedro Machado. Lisboa, Ed. Confluência, 1949–59. 12v. **AE465**

v.1–11, A–Z; v.12 consists of a number of special sections: an epitome of Portuguese grammar; a statement of the Acordo Ortografia and its decisions; and various word lists: foreign words and phrases, place-names, irregular verbs, root words, abbreviations, etc.

A new edition of this famous dictionary, first published in 1789. Of first importance, generally considered to be the best Portuguese dictionary. Includes quotations from the literature in chronological order showing usage.

This edition takes into account the Portuguese-Brazilian *Acordo Ortográfico* of 1945, which aimed at instituting a uniform system of orthography for the Portuguese language.

Soares, António Joaquim de Macedo. Dicionário brasileiro da língua portuguêsa. Elucidário etimológico crítico das palavras e frases que, originárias do Brasil, ou aqui populares, se não encontram nos dicionários da língua portuguêsa, ou nêles vêm com forma ou significação diferente (1875–1888). Coligido, revisto e completado por . . . Julião Rangel de Macedo Soares. Rio de Janeiro, 1954–55. 2v. **AE466**

At head of title: Ministério da Educação e Cultura. Instituto Nacional do Livro.

Bilingual

Ferreira, Júlio Albino. Dicionário inglês-português, [português-inglês], nova edição revista e melhorada pelo Armando de Morais. Porto, Barreira, 1952–54. (Pt.1, 1954) 886p., 896p. **AE467**

One of the better bilingual dictionaries.

Houaiss, Antônio and **Avery, Catherine B.** The new Appleton dictionary of the English and Portuguese languages. N.Y., Appleton, 1964. 636p., 665p. **AE468**

Added title page in Portuguese.
Pt.1, English-Portuguese; pt.2, Portuguese-English.

Each part contains approximately 60,000 words and expressions. Particular emphasis is on Portuguese as it is spoken and written in Brazil. Equivalents are given or, when necessary, explanations or definitions. Includes a large general vocabulary as well as a wide selection of words from specialized fields. Pronunciation is indicated by the phonetic system.

Novo Michaelis dicionário ilustrado; baseado em material selecionado do antigo dicionário Michaelis e inteiramente remodelado, revisto e aumentado pela Seção Lexicográfica das Edições Melhoramentos, sob a orientação de Fritz Pietzschke. São Paulo, Ed. Melhoramentos; Wiesbaden, Brockhaus, 1958–61. 2v. il. **AE469**

Added title page in English.
On spine: Brockhaus picture dictionary.
v.1, English-Portuguese; v.2, Portuguese-English.

English subtitle: Comprehensive modern vocabulary; idiomatic phrases, pronunciation key, numerous plates with more than 4000 conceptions, based on matter selected from the original Michaelis dictionary and completely reorganized, revised, and enlarged.

A new work based on Henriette Michaelis. *Novo dicionário da língua portugueza e ingleza.* [8. ed.] (Leipzig, Brockhaus, 1945). Frequently reprinted. Long a standard work of current Portuguese, including technical terms used in commerce and industry, the arts and sciences, etc.

Taylor, James Lumpkin. A Portuguese-English dictionary. Stanford, Calif., Stanford Univ. Pr., 1958. 655p. **AE470**

A completely new Portuguese-English dictionary (including Brazilian Portuguese) containing some 60,000 entries. Planned "to provide an everyday working tool for as large a number of persons as possible." Gives not only English equivalents, but often one or more synonyms and, in some cases, examples of usage. Includes many technical and scientific terms, particularly the names of Brazilian fauna and flora.

Etymology

Nascentes, Antenor. Dicionário etimológico da língua portuguesa. Rio de Janeiro, Alves, 1932–52. 2v. **AE471**
v.2, Proper names. 389p.

Silva Bastos, J. T. da. Diccionário etymológico, prosódico e orthográphico da lingua portugueza. 2. ed. Lisboa, Parceria António Maria Pereira, 1928. 1434p. **AE472**

Synonyms

Costa, Agenor. Dicionário geral de sinónimos e locuções da língua portuguêsa; reunindo a sinonimia e as locuções de dezessete dicionários com seus significados nas ordens direta e inversa. [2. ed., cuidadosamente rev. e aum.] Rio de Janeiro, Biblioteca Luso-Brasileira, 1960. 2v. **AE473**

Nascentes, Antenor. Dicionário de sinónimos. Coimbra, Livraria Atlântida, 1957. 343p. (Colecção brasileira de filología portuguesa) **AE474**

Punjabi

See Hindi, Hindustani, Punjabi, Urdu, p.116.

Romansh

Dicziunari rumantsch grischun, publichà da la Società Retorumantsha cul agüd de la Confederaziun e dal Chantum grischun. Fundà da Robert de Planta, Florian Melcher, Chasper Pult. Redacziun: Andrea Schorta, Alexi Decurtins. Cuoira, Bischofberger, 1938–64. Fasc. 1–47. il. (In progress)   **AE475**

Fasc.1–47 comprise v.1–3, 4¹⁻².

A scholarly work giving etymologies, references to sources, and explanations in German.

Velleman, Antoine. Dicziunari scurznieu de la lingua ladina . . . Ladinisches Notwörterbuch mit deutscher, französischer und englischer Übersetzung. . . . Abridged dictionary of the Ladin (or Romansh) language, with German, French and English translation and numerous indications referring to topography and population. Samaden, Engadin Pr., 1929. 928p.   **AE476**

Romansh-German-French-English dictionary.

Rumanian

Academia Română, Bukharest. Dicţionarul limbii române, intocmit şi publicat după îndemnul si cu cheltuiala Maiestăţii Sale Regelui Carol I. Bucureşti, Impr. Naţională, 1913–40. v.1, pt.1, pt.2, fasc.1–8; v.2, pt.1, pt.2, fasc.1–2.   **AE477**

v.1, pt.1, A–B; pt.2, fasc.1–8, C–Cojoáica; v.2, pt.1, F–I; pt.2, fasc.1–2, J–Lepăda.

A scholarly dictionary compiled on historical principles, including literary, obsolete, and regional terms; etymologies; and examples of usage.

Definitions and explanations are in Rumanian, but an equivalent word in French is also given.

Academia Republicii Populare Romîne. Institutul de Lingvistică din Bucureşti. Dicţionarul limbii romîne moderne. [Bucureşti], Ed. Academiei Republicii Populare Romîne, 1958. 961p. il.   **AE478**

Based on the *Dicţionarul limbii romîne literare contemparane,* also published by the Academia, 1955–?.

An abridged dictionary, not attempting the full treatment found in the prewar *Dicţionarul* of the Academia Română.

Bilingual

Axelrad, Philip. Complete Roumanian-English dictionary. N.Y., Biblioteca Româna, 1918. 532p. (Repr.: Philadelphia, McKay, 1942)   **AE479**

Schönkron, Marcel. Rumanian-English and English-Rumanian dictionary. With supplement of new words, English-Rumanian. N.Y., Ungar, 1952. 235p., 482p., 19p.   **AE480**

A reprint of the original 2v. edition, *Dicţionar englez-român* (Craiova, 19?) and *Dicţionar român-englez* (Craiova, 1930?), with the addition of 19p. of new words, translated by Simone Mavrodineanu.

Russian

Akademiia Nauk SSSR. Institut IAzykoznaniia. Slovar' russkogo iazyka v chetyrekh tomakh. Moskva, Gos. Izdvo Inostrannykh i Natsional'nykh Slovarei, 1957–61. 4v.   **AE481**

A general dictionary of the Russian language. Emphasis is on current usage with examples quoted from Russian literature of the 19th and 20th centuries. Intended for more general use than the larger, specialized lexicon *Slovar' sovremennogo russkogo literaturnogo iazyka* (AE482).

Akademiia Nauk SSSR. Institut russkogo iazyka. Slovar'

sovremennogo russkogo literaturnogo iazyka. Moskva, 1950–64. v.1–16. (In progress)   **AE482**

Contents: v.1–16, A–F.

Issuing body varies.

The major dictionary for modern literary Russian, based on the vocabulary used in literary, artistic, social, political, and general scientific works of the 19th and 20th centuries. Entries include the field in which the word is used, variant meanings, some variant forms, derivations, references to other dictionaries, and—in most cases—extensive illustrative quotations with their sources. Loan words from other languages are numerous.

Dal', Vladimir Ivanovich. Tolkovyi slovar' zhivogo velikorusskago iazyka. 4. izd. St. Peterburg, Izdanie M. O. Vol'fa, 1912–14. 4v. (Repr.: 2d ed., Moscow, 1935, 1955; 4th ed., Tokyo, 1934; Paris, 1954)   **AE483**

The standard pre-Revolutionary dictionary for Russian and dialect vocabulary, including slang. The 3d and 4th editions include revisions made by J. Baudouin de Courtenay.

Ozhegov, S. I. Slovar' russkogo iazyka. Izd. 4. Moskva, Gos. Izd-vo Inostrannykh i Natsional'nykh Slovarei, 1960. 900p.   **AE484**

A 1v. dictionary, with approximately 53,000 words.

Tolkovyi slovar' russkogo iazyka. Pod. red. D. N. Ushakova. Moskva, Gos. Izd-vo Inostrannykh i Natsional'nykh Slovarei, 1935–40. 4v. (Repr.: Moscow, 1948; Ann Arbor, 1948)   **AE485**

This general dictionary, published earlier than the Academy's 4v. dictionary (AE481), retains value for the inclusion of words and definitions of contemporary political significance.

Bilingual

Langenscheidt's Russian-English, English-Russian dictionary; with special emphasis on American English. 1st ed. Berlin, Langenscheidt; London, Methuen, 1964. 505p.   **AE486**

Pt.I by E. Wedel; pt.II by A. Romanov.

General vocabulary has approximately 35,000 entries, with references to declension and conjugation tables for Russian. Americanisms are "followed by their respective British semantic (or orthographic) equivalents."—*Pref.*

Miuller (Müller), Vladimir Karlovich. English-Russian dictionary. 6th ed. N.Y., Dutton, 1959. 699p.   **AE487**

Added title page in Russian.

The English–Russian part of the earlier Müller dictionaries, reedited by the Moscow State Pedagogical Institute of Foreign Languages. A general dictionary of 60,000 words.

For the Russian-English volume *see* Smirnitskii (AE488).

Smirnitskii, Aleksandr Ivanovich. Russian-English dictionary. 3d ed. rev. and enl. under the editorship of O. S. Akhmanova. N.Y., Dutton, 1959. 951p.   **AE488**

An American printing of the 3d Russian edition, first published in 1952. Although certain features favor the Russian-speaking user, this is a useful up-to-date general dictionary.

For the English-Russian volume *see* Miuller (AE487).

Abbreviations

Koritskii, B. F. Slovar' sokrashchenii russkogo iazyka; 12,500 sokrashchenii. Moskva, Gos. Izd-vo Inostrannykh i Natsional'nykh Slovarei, 1963. 486p.   **AE489**

In addition to full expansion of the term, shows pronunciation, stress, and, for those abbreviations and acronyms used substantively, grammatical gender. The more important journals are included, as well as Russian forms of abbreviations for international and foreign organizations.

U.S. Library of Congress. Reference Dept. Russian ab-

breviations: a selective list, comp. by Alexander Rosenberg. 2d rev. and expanded ed. Wash., 1957. 513p.
AE490

Based on Soviet publications 1930–56. The Russian is followed by an English translation. An appendix lists some Soviet trademarks in agriculture, aviation, motor vehicles, photography, radio, and television.

Etymology

Preobrazhenskii, Aleksander Grigor'evich. Etymological dictionary of the Russian language. N.Y., Columbia Univ. Pr., 1951. 674p., 416p., 144p. (Columbia Slavic studies)
AE491

The republication, in 1v., of a dictionary of value for the study of the history of the Russian language, literature, and civilization and of Indo-European comparative linguistics. v.1–2 (A–Suleia) appeared first, 1910–16; v.3 was published in 1949. The reprint follows the original except for alteration to modern orthography.

Vasmer, Max. Russisches etymologisches Wörterbuch. Heidelberg, Winter, Universitätsverlag, [1950–58]. 3v. (Indogermanische Bibliothek. II. Reihe, Wörterbücher)
AE492

Publ. in 27 Lfg.
Bibliography of sources, v.1, p.xi–xliii.
A dictionary of importance for the etymology of the Russian language, its dialects, and foreign words used in Russian.

Bibliography

Kaufman, Isaak Mikhailovich. Terminologicheskie slovari; bibliografiia. Moskva, Izd-vo "Sovetskaia Rossiia," 1961. 419p.
AE493

An annotated bibliography of glossaries and subject dictionaries, primarily Russian, published from the 18th century through 1961. Classified arrangement, with alphabetical indexes for authors and titles, and subjects. The 1755 entries include lists of specialized terminology in periodical literature, as well as separately published dictionaries.

Sanskrit

Apte, Vaman Shivaram. The practical Sanskrit-English dictionary. Eds.-in-chief: P. K. Gode and C. G. Karve. Rev. and enl. ed. Poona, Prasad Prakashan, 1957–59. 3v.
AE494

1st ed. 1890.
A revision of the earlier text with the addition of new words, changes of meaning, and more quotations.

Böhtlingk, Otto von and **Roth, Rudolph.** Sanskrit-Wörterbuch hrsg. von der Akademie der Wissenschaften. St. Petersburg, Akademie der Wissenschaften, 1855–75. 7v.
AE495

"Verbesserungen und Nachträge zu Theil 1–5," Bd.5, col. 941–1678; "Verbesserungen und Nachträge zum ganzen Werke," Bd.7, col.1685–1822.

Böhtlingk, Otto von. Sanskrit-Wörterbuch in kürzerer Fassung. St. Petersburg, Akademie der Wissenschaften, 1878–89. 7v. in 4.
AE496

—— —— Nachträge . . . bearb. von Richard Schmidt. Leipzig, Harrassowitz, 1928. 398p. (Repr.: Graz, Akademische Druk- u. Verlagsanstalt, 1959. 7v. in 3)

Mayrhofer, Manfred. Kurzgefasstes etymologisches Wörterbuch des Altindischen. A concise etymological Sanskrit dictionary. Heidelberg, Winter, 1953–64. Lfg. 1–18. (Indogermanische Bibliothek. II. Reihe, Wörterbücher) (In progress)
AE497

Contents: Bd.1, (Lfg. 1–8); Bd.2, (Lfg. 9–17); Bd.3 (Lfg. 18).

A Sanskrit-German etymological dictionary. The basic language is German, but all Sanskrit catchwords are translated also into English, the substance of the introduction is summarized in English, and the list of abbreviations is in German and English.

Monier-Williams, *Sir* **Monier.** A dictionary, English and Sanskrit. Lucknow, Akhila Bharatiya Sanskrit Parishad, 1957. 859p.
AE498

"1st ed. 1851; reprinted lithographically in India from sheets of the 1st ed. by Bureau of Agricultural Information, Uttar Pradesh, Lucknow 1957."

—— A Sanskrit-English dictionary etymologically and philologically arranged with special reference to cognate Indo-European languages. New ed., greatly enl. and improved, with the collaboration of E. Leumann, C. Cappeller, and other scholars. Oxford, Clarendon Pr., 1899. 1333p.
AE499

Sanskrit-English, with etymologies and references to the literature.

Serbo-Croatian

Rječnik hrvatskoga ili srpskoga jezika, na svijet izdaje Jugoslavenska Akademija Znanosti i Umjetnosti. U. Zagrebu, U Knížarnici L. Hartmana na Prodaju, 1880–1959. v.1–17[1].
AE500

v.1–17[1], A–Svezati.
The standard dictionary of the Yugoslavian Academy.

Bilingual

Bogadek, Francis A. New English-Croatian and Croatian-English dictionary. 3d ed. enl. and corr. N.Y., Stechert, 1949. 2v. in 1. (Repr. 1959)
AE501

Drvodelić, Milan. Englesko-hrvatsko-srpski rječnik. Zagreb, Školska Knjiga, 1962. 1104p.
AE502

Added title page in English: English-Croato-Serbian dictionary.

—— Hrvatsko-engleski rječnik. Zagreb, Školska Knjiga, 1953. 940p.
AE503

Added title page in English: Dictionary of the Croatian and English languages.

Petrović, Ilija M. A practical dictionary of the English and Serbian languages. 2d ed. Beograd, Prosveta, 1951. 770p.
AE504

Subtitle: Designed to give the pronunciation and accent of English words, containing also an appendix of personal and geographical names.
Added title page in Serbian.

Ristić, Svetomir and **Simić, Zivojin.** An English-Serbocroatian dictionary. Beograd, Prosveta, 1959. 867p.
AE505

Added title page in Serbo-Croatian.

Abbreviations

U.S. Library of Congress. Slavic and Central European Division. Yugoslav abbreviations; a selective list. 2d enl. ed. prep. by Ilija P. Plamenatz. Wash., 1962. 198p.
AE506

"Intended . . . to include the more common abbreviations which have come into use since World War II, especially names of government institutions and official bodies, industrial and trade establishments and the more important newspapers and periodicals . . ."—*Introd.*
The main list contains nearly 3000 abbreviations; the 2d

edition adds some 200 newly identified abbreviations in an appendix.

Slovak

Slovenská Akadémia Vied. Ústav Slovenského Jazyka, Slovník slovenského jazyka. [Vedecký redaktor: Štefan Peciar] Bratislava, Vydavateľstvo Slovenskej Akadémie Vied, 1959–64. v.1–4.   **AE507**
v.1–4, A–U.
The new Slovakian dictionary compiled by the Academy.

Jánošik, Anton and **Jóna, E.** Slovník spisovného jazyka slovenského. Turčiánsky, Svätý Martin, 1946–49. Pts. 1–58. (In progress)   **AE508**
Contents: Sošit 1–58, A–intrigán.

Bilingual

Slovensko-anglický slovník. [Autori: Júlia Vilikovská, Ján Vilikovský, Ján Šimko. 1. vyd.] Bratislava, Slovenské Pedagogické Nakl., 1959. 477p.   **AE509**
Added title page: Slovak-English dictionary.

Vilikovský, Ján. Anglicko-slovenský slovník. Bratislava, Vydavateľský Odbor YMCA, 1946. 654p.   **AE510**

Slovene

Slovenska Akademija Znanosti in Umetnosti, Ljubljana, Yugoslavia. Slovenski pravopis. [Uredniški odbor Anton Bajec et al. Nova izdaja] Ljubljana, Državna Založba Slovenije, 1962. 1054p.   **AE511**
The standard Slovenian dictionary, superseding the 1950 edition. Contains some 100,000 words, two thirds more than in the earlier work.

Bilingual

Kern, Frank Jauh. A pronouncing English-Slovene dictionary for general use. Angleško-slovenski besednjak z angleško izgovarjavo. [Cleveland, Amer. Home Pub. Co., 1944] 273p.   **AE512**
Cover title: English-Slovene dictionary . . . 2d ed.
First published 1919 under title *A complete pronouncing dictionary of the English and Slovene languages.*

Kotnik, Janko. Slovene-English dictionary. 4th (rev. and enl.) ed. Ljubljana, Državna Založba Slovenije, 1959. 762p.   **AE513**
1st ed. 1945.
Added title page in Slovenian.

Škerlj, Ružena. Angleško-slovenski slovar. 5. izpopoljena izdaja [English-Slovene dictionary. 5th enl. and rev. ed.]. Ljubljana, Državna Založba Slovenije, 1960. 812p.   **AE514**
Added title page in English.

Spanish

Academia Española, Madrid. Diccionario de la lengua española. 18. ed. Madrid, Ed. Espasa-Calpe, 1956. 1370p.   **AE515**
1st ed. 1726–39.
A standard work; the 18th edition incorporates into one alphabet the new words found in the supplement to the 1947 edition, as well as additional new words, particularly in the fields of science and technology. Etymologies have also been revised.

—— Diccionario histórico de la lengua española. Seminario de Lexicografía: Director, Julio Casares . . . Madrid, 1960–61. [pts. 1]–2. (In progress)   **AE516**
Pts. 1–2, A–abundar.
A new attempt at a major historical dictionary of the language to replace the earlier unfinished work with the same title (Madrid, Hernando, 1933–36. v.1–2, A–Cevilla).
Each word is treated in scholarly detail, with variations in meaning illustrated by numerous quotations, chronologically listed. Citations are given to exact source.
An extensive list of works consulted.

—— Diccionario manual e ilustrado de la lengua española. [2. ed.] Madrid, Ed. Espasa-Calpe, 1950. 1572p. il.   **AE517**

Alonso Pedraz, Martin. Enciclopedia del idioma; diccionario histórico y moderno de la lengua española (siglos xii al xx), etimológico, tecnológico, regional e hispanoamericano. Madrid, Aguilar, 1958. 3v.   **AE518**
A new work intended to be more comprehensive in number of words listed but less detailed in treatment of individual words than the Academia Española's *Diccionario histórico* (AE516). For many words, treatment is full, giving etymology, morphology, definitions with citations of usage, examples of phrasal combinations, and dates of appearances in early dictionaries. For other words for which there are no new or specialized meanings, the standard definitions from the Academia's *Diccionario* are often used almost verbatim.

Larousse, Pierre. Nuevo pequeño Larousse ilustrado; diccionario enciclopédico pub. bajo la dirección de Claude y Paul Augé; adaptación española de Miguel de Toro y Gisbert. [18. ed.] Paris, Larousse, 1954. 1520p. il.   **AE519**
Diccionario, A–Z, p.1–1015; Locuciones latinas y extranjeras, p.1017–48; Historia y geografía, p.1049–1520.
A *Petit Larousse* in Spanish. Frequently reprinted.

Vox; diccionario general ilustrado de la lengua española. Prólogo de d. Ramón Menéndez Pidal. 2. ed. corr. y notablemente ampl. por d. Samuel Gili Gaya. Barcelona, Spes, 1953. 1815p. il.   **AE520**
1st ed. 1945.
A good general dictionary which includes etymologies, synonyms, etc.

Bilingual

Cassell's Spanish-English, English-Spanish dictionary, ed. by Edgar Allison Peers, and others. London, Cassell, 1959; N.Y., Funk & Wagnalls, 1960. 1477p.   **AE521**
A new work, similar in scope and arrangement to other bilingual desk dictionaries of the same publisher.

Castillo, Carlos and **Bond, Otto F.** The University of Chicago Spanish dictionary; a new concise Spanish-English and English-Spanish dictionary of words and phrases basic to the written and spoken languages of today. Chicago, Univ. of Chicago Pr., 1948. 226p., 252p.   **AE522**
Added title page in Spanish.
"Compiled for the general use of the American learner of Spanish and the Spanish learner of English, with special reference in either case to New World usages as found in the United States and in Latin America."—*Foreword.*
Includes about 30,000 words most commonly used. Introductory material to each section deals with pronunciation, parts of speech, suffixes, lists of irregular verbs, etc.

Crowell's Spanish-English and English-Spanish dictionary by Gerd A. Gillhoff. N.Y., Crowell, 1963. 1261p. il.   **AE523**

Strong in words and expressions used in Spanish-American countries, which are prefixed by abbreviations of the countries in which they are used. Includes commercial, scientific, and technical terms, as well as colloquial and idiomatic expressions with examples of usage.

Cuyas, Arturo. Appleton's Revised English-Spanish and Spanish-English dictionary, containing more than one hundred and twenty thousand principal and subsidiary terms, with idioms and technical usages; new pronouncing keys and the fundamental forms of the irregular verbs; rev. and enl. by Lewis E. Brett (part I) and Helen S. Eaton, with the assistance of Walter Beveraggi-Allende (part II). 4th ed. N.Y., Appleton, 1961. 697p., 575p. **AE524**

Title page also in Spanish.

Martínez Amador, Emilio M. Standard English-Spanish and Spanish-English dictionary . . . 3. ed. Boston, Heath; Barcelona, Ed. Ramón Sopena, 1958. 2130p. **AE525**

Added title page in Spanish.

1st ed. 1946.

Subtitle: Each part contains over 60,000 entries including thousands of modern colloquialisms, idioms, Americanisms, and technical terms; full lists of geographical terms, proper names, common abbreviations, and tables of weights and measures in both languages, together with introductions on pronunciation for both English and Spanish.

Raventós, Margaret H. A modern Spanish dictionary. London, English Universities Pr., 1953. 1230p. **AE526**

Includes many new terms, such as pressure-cooker, nylon stockings, etc.; does not generally include Latin-American variations of words. Special lists of geographical names with different spellings in the two languages, proper names, abbreviations, weights and measures, and currency.

A good modern dictionary for students and for the general reader.

American edition has title *McKay's Modern Spanish-English, English-Spanish dictionary.* N.Y., McKay, 1954.

Velázquez de la Cadena, Mariano [and others]. New revised Velázquez Spanish and English dictionary. Newly revised by Ida Navarro Hinojosa. Chicago, Follett, 1959. 698p., 778p. **AE527**

Pt.1, Spanish-English. 698p.; pt.2, English-Spanish. 778p.

First published 1852; frequently reprinted with various revisions. One of the most useful and authoritative Spanish-English dictionaries for general purposes.

This edition has been thoroughly revised and includes in the main alphabet "thousands of new terms and idiomatic expressions of general use, replacing expressions no longer in common usage . . ."—*Pref.* The supplementary lists of geographical names, proper names, and weights and measures have also been revised.

Etymology

Corominas, Juan. Diccionario crítico etimológico de la lengua castellana. Bern, Ed. Francke, 1954–57. 4v. **AE528**

A comprehensive etymological dictionary giving dates of origin of words, with quotations showing usages and derivations. Covers the languages of both Spain and Spanish America and includes the ancient languages, such as pre-Roman Iberian and vulgar Arabic, as well as dialects and Latin-American influences.

v.4 includes *Adiciones y rectificaciones,* p.897–1092, and various *Índices,* p.1093–1224.

García de Diego, Vicente. Diccionario etimológico español e hispánico. Madrid, Ed. S.A.E.T.A., [1954]. 1069p. **AE529**

Synonyms

Benot y Rodriguez, Eduardo. Diccionario de ideas afines y elementos de tecnología. Buenos Aires, Ed. Anaconda, 1940. 1515p. **AE530**

A classified dictionary of synonyms modeled on Roget's *Thesaurus* (AE77).

Casares y Sanchez, Julio. Diccionario ideológico de la lengua española. 2. ed. Barcelona, Ed. Gustavo Gili, 1963. lxxip., 482p., 887p. **AE531**

First pub. 1942. Frequently reprinted.

Contents: pt.1, Parte sinóptica; pt.2, Parte analógica; pt.3, Parte alfabética.

Pt.2 consists of lists of words grouped by association of ideas; pt.3 is an alphabetical dictionary defining these words.

Medieval–18th century

Boggs, Ralph Steele [and others]. Tentative dictionary of medieval Spanish. Chapel Hill, N.C., 1946. 2v.(537p.). **AE532**

A preliminary work, issued in multigraph form, sponsored by the Old Spanish Group of the Modern Language Association. Useful until a complete dictionary for this period is published.

Gili y Gaya, Samuel. Tesoro lexicográfico (1492–1726). Madrid, 1947–[57]. Fasc.1–4. (In progress) **AE533**

Fasc.1–4, A–E.

The combined entries, 55,000 in number, of all available dictionaries of the Spanish language, both published and in manuscript, which appeared between 1492 and 1726. All definitions and translations for each word are listed chronologically by first appearance. When completed, this will be a valuable work, making available to scholars information often difficult to obtain from original sources.

Indexes

Romera-Navarro, Miguel. Registro de lexicografía hispánica. Madrid, Consejo Superior de Investigaciones Científicas, 1951. 1013p. **AE534**

Supplement to *Revista de filología española* (Anejo LIV).

An alphabetical index of 50,000 Spanish words, with 80,000 references to etymologies, linguistic studies, etc. in monographs, treatises, and scholarly journals.

Regional

For regional dictionaries consult Collison (AE104); *Guide to reference books,* 7th ed., p.249–50.

Sumerian

See Assyro-Babylonian, p.104.

Swahili

Inter-Territorial Language (Swahili) Committee of the East African Dependencies. A standard English-Swahili [Swahili-English] dictionary (founded on Madan's English-Swahili dictionary), [prep.] under the direction of the late Frederick Johnson. London, Oxford Univ. Pr., H. Milford, 1939. 2v. (Repr. 1955) **AE535**

Swedish

Ordbok öfver svenska språket, utg. af Svenska Akademien. Lund, Lindstedt, 1898–1964. v.1–24[1]. (In progress) **AE536**

v.1–24[1], A–Samordig.

The great Academy dictionary of modern Swedish, giving etymologies, references to the literature with dates, etc.

Östergren, Olof. Nusvensk ordbok. Stockholm, Wahlström & Widstrand, 1918–64. v.1–9[1–2]. (In progress) **AE537**

Bd.1–9[1–2], A–Uppskräda.

An important dictionary of modern Swedish.

Söderwall, Knut Fredrik. Ordbok öfver svenska medeltids-språket. Lund, Berlingska Boktryckeri, 1884–1918. 2v. in 3. (Samlingar utgifna af Svenska Fornskrift-Sällskapet) **AE538**

Issued in 24 pts.

—— —— Supplement. 1925–64. Hft.1–29. (In progress)

A dictionary of the Swedish of medieval times.

Illustrerad svensk ordbok. Redaktor: Bertil Molde. Stockholm, Natur och Kultur, 1955. 1917p. il. **AE539**

A modern Swedish dictionary with line drawings based on the *Thorndike junior dictionary* (AE14) and the *American college dictionary* (AE9).

Bilingual

Freudenthal, Fritiof. Engelsk-svenskt lexikon, utg. . . . under medverkan av Uno Cronwall [och] Rudolf Löfgren. 2. revid. uppl. [Stockholm], Natur och Kultur, 1953. 348p. (Natur och Kulturs lexikon) **AE540**

Also published as *English-Swedish dictionary*. London, Allen and Unwin, 1956.

1st ed. 1943.

Harlock, Walter Ernest. Svensk-engelsk ordbok, skolupplaga, under medverkan av Arvid Gabrielson, John Holmberg och Margareta Angström. 2. översedda uppl. Stockholm, Svenska Bokförlaget, 1947. 1048p. **AE541**

1st ed. 1944. Earlier editions by Oscar E. Wenström and Walter E. Harlock.

A practical dictionary with good discrimination in meanings.

Nöjd, Ruben, Tornberg, Astrid and **Ångström, Margareta.** McKay's Modern English-Swedish and Swedish-English dictionary. N.Y., McKay, 1954. 248p., 220p. **AE542**

"First pub. 1954."

v.1, comp. by Ruben Nöjd; v.2, by Astrid Tornberg and Margareta Ångström.

Stockholm edition (Svenska Bokförlaget, [1949?]) has title *Engelsk-svensk ordbok*.

Etymology

Hellquist, Elof. Svensk etymologisk ordbok. Ny omarb. ach utv. uppl. Lund, Gleerup, 1935–39. 2v. **AE543**

1st ed. 1920–22.

A standard work including place- and personal names, with etymologies and cognate words in various western European languages.

Synonyms

Dalin, Anders Fredrik. Svenska språkets synonymer. 4. (rev.) uppl. granskad och red. av N. G. Bergman. Stockholm, Beckman, 1941. 407p. **AE544**

Words are arranged in groups by association, with definitions showing discrimination in meanings.

Wessén, Elias. Våra ord, deras uttal och ursprung. Kortfattad etymologisk ordbok. Stockholm, Svenska Bokförlaget, Norstedts, 1961. 502p. (Nämnden för svensk språkvåd) **AE545**

A revised and enlarged edition of Lars Levander and E. Wessen. *Våra ord*. Stockholm, Bonnier, 1932.

An alphabetically arranged dictionary of synonyms.

Syriac

Brockelmann, Carl. Lexicon Syriacum. Ed. 2, aucta et emendata. Halis Saxonum, Niemeyer, 1928. 930p. **AE546**

Oraham, Alexander Joseph. Oraham's Dictionary of the stabilized and enriched Assyrian language and English. Chicago, Consolidated Pr. (Assyrian Pr. of America), 1943. 576p. **AE547**

Not a dictionary of classical Assyrian but of that language sometimes called by scholars "Nestorian Syriac"; includes "the ancient, medieval and the modern literary phases of this language."—*Foreword*.

Payne Smith, Robert. Thesaurus syriacus, collegerunt Stephanus M. Quatremere, Georgius Henricus Bernstein [et alii]. Oxford, e Typ. Clarendoniano, 1879–1901. 2v. **AE548**

—— —— Supplement . . . collected and arranged by his daughter, J. P. Margoliouth. Oxford, Clarendon Pr., 1927.

—— Compendious Syriac dictionary, founded upon the Thesaurus syriacus of R. Payne Smith, ed. by J. Payne Smith (Mrs. Margoliouth). Oxford, Clarendon Pr., 1903. 626p. **AE549**

Syriac-English.

An abridgment of the *Thesaurus* above.

Tamil

English-Tamil dictionary. Chief ed.: A. Chidambaranatha Chettiar. With a foreword by A. Lakshmanaswami Mudaliar. [Madras], Univ. of Madras, 1963– . v.1– . (In progress) **AE550**

v.1, A–F.

Gnana Prakasar, S. An etymological and comparative lexicon of the Tamil language . . . with indexes of words quoted from Indo-European languages. [Ceylon], Thirumakal Pr., 1938–44. v.1[1–5]. **AE551**

Tamil-English-Tamil.

Etymological and philological treatment of Tamil and other Dravidian dialects.

Madras. University. Tamil lexicon. Madras, Univ. of Madras, 1924–36. 6v. **AE552**

Gives transliterations and English translations for more than 100,000 Tamil words. All previous dictionaries in the language were drawn upon, and many outstanding scholars collaborated in the compilation. Terminology of special fields —e.g., law, architecture, medicine—is included. The outstanding dictionary of the language. Does not include etymologies.

—— —— Supplement. 1938–39.

Thai

Haas, Mary R. Thai-English student's dictionary. Stanford, Calif., Stanford Univ. Pr., 1964. 638p. **AE553**

Jumsai Manich, *Mom Luang.* (Advanced) English-Thai

dictionary. 5th unabridged ed. London, Macmillan, 1955. 2v. 1568p. il. **AE554**

McFarland, George Bradley. Thai-English dictionary. . . . Stanford, Calif., Stanford Univ. Pr.; London, Milford, Oxford Univ. Pr., 1944. 1019p., 39p. **AE555**

"A photolithographic reprint of the first edition" originally published in Bangkok in 1941.

Bibliography, p.xx–xxi.

Based on earlier dictionaries, this is a new work reflecting modern usage. Gives Thai script, transliteration, and definition in English. Includes scientific terms. In the addenda the scientific Latin names of flora, birds, fishes, shells, and snakes are translated into Thai.

Phloyphrom, Plang and **Golden, Robert Dorne.** Pru's Standard Thai-English dictionary . . . with the cooperation of Brother Urbain-Gabriel. Bangkok, Pricha Co., 1955. 1774p. **AE556**

Gives Thai script, transliteration, and equivalent word in English.

Sethaputra, So. New model English-Thai dictionary. 2d ed. Library ed. Bangkok, 1952. 2v. **AE557**

1st ed. 1940.

"It is the aim of this dictionary . . . to illustrate rather than define" (*Pref.*), by giving illustrative phrases and sentences rather than equivalents and definitions.

Tibetan

Bell, *Sir* Charles Alfred. English-Tibetan colloquial dictionary. 2d ed. Calcutta, Bengal Secretariat Book Depot, 1920. 562p. **AE558**

Tibetan words in Tibetan, also in romanized type.

Dās, Sarat Chandra. Tibetan-English dictionary with Sanskrit synonyms. Rev. and ed. under the orders of the government of Bengal, by Graham Sandberg and A. William Heyde. Calcutta, Bengal Secretariat Book Depot, 1902. 1353p. (Repr.: Calcutta, 1951) **AE559**

Gould, *Sir* Basil John and **Richardson, Hugh Edward.** Tibetan word book. . . . London, N.Y., and Bombay, Milford, Oxford Univ. Pr., 1943. 447p. **AE560**

Jaschke, Heinrich August. Tibetan-English dictionary, with special reference to the prevailing dialects, to which is added an English-Tibetan vocabulary. Prep. and pub. at the charge of the Secretary of State for India in Council. London, Kegan Paul, 1949. 671p. **AE561**

First printed 1881. Several times reprinted.

Turkish

Ağakay, Mehmet Ali [and others]. Türkçe sözlük. 2. baski (düzeltilip genişletilerek yeníden yazílmístír). Ankara, Yeni Matbaa, 1955. 828p. **AE562**

Bilingual

Alderson, A. D. The concise Oxford Turkish dictionary, ed. by A. D. Alderson and Fahir Íz. Oxford, Clarendon Pr., 1959. 807p. **AE563**

Abridged edition of *A Turkish-English dictionary* by H. C. Hony (AE565) and *An English-Turkish dictionary* by F. Íz (AE566). Suitable for student use.

"Reduces the original to about one-third of their length. Omits close synonyms, geographical and scientific terms easily recognizable and those Arabic & Persian forms now commonly replaced by Turkish ones."

Fahrettin, Iskender. English-Turkish dictionary. N.Y., Ungar, 1954. 694p. **AE564**

Includes supplement of new words by John L. Mish.

Small dictionary which gives equivalents only. A companion volume to Thomson (AE570).

Hony, H. C. A Turkish-English dictionary . . . with the advice of Fahir Íz. 2d ed. Oxford, Clarendon Pr., 1957. 419p. **AE565**

A modern Turkish-English dictionary prepared primarily for the English student studying Turkish. The 2d edition is revised and enlarged, with the emphasis on the "inclusion of common phrases and idioms . . . rather than the inclusion of large numbers of comparatively rare words."

Íz, Fahir and **Hony, H. C.** An English-Turkish dictionary. Oxford, Clarendon Pr., 1952. 510p. **AE566**

Companion volume to Hony's *Turkish-English dictionary* above, and intended to be used in conjunction with it. "Compiled mainly with a view to the needs of Turkish students."— *Pref.*

Moran, Ahmet Vahit. Türkçe-İngilizce sözlük. A Turkish-English dictionary. A. Vahit Moran. İstanbul, Kâgît ve Basím İşleri, 1945. 1462p. **AE567**

Published by the Turkish Ministry of Public Instruction.

Attempts to include new words and technical terms, as well as those used in the older Turkish literature. Gives Turkish proverbs and sayings with English translation and, when possible, the corresponding English phrases. An appendix lists new words used in the new Turkish Constitution.

Redhouse, *Sir* James William. Turkish and English lexicon, showing in English the significations of the Turkish terms. Constantinople, pr. for the Amer. Mission by A. H. Boyajian, 1890. 2224p. (Repr.: Constantinople, H. Matteosian, 1921) **AE568**

—— Yeni Redhouse lûgatí, ingilizce-türkçe. Revised Redhouse dictionary, English-Turkish. [Eds.: J. K. Birge and others] İstanbul, Amerikan Bord Neşriyat-Dairesi, 1950. 1196p. **AE569**

"The general plan has been to include all words which appear in both the Oxford concise dictionary and Webster student dictionary, although selection not limited to such words. Contains a total of 60 to 70,000 definitions."

Thomson, H. M. Turkish-English dictionary. N.Y., Ungar, 1954. 573p. **AE570**

1st ed., İstanbul, Kanaat Kütüphanesi, 1932.

Includes supplement of new words by John L. Mish.

A companion volume to Fahrettin (AE564).

Etymology

Kadri, Hüseyin Kâzim. Türk lûgatí: Türk dillerinin iştikakî ve edebi lûgatlar. İstanbul, Maarif Matbaasi, 1927–45. 4v. **AE571**

An etymological dictionary with many quotations from the literature.

Ukrainian

Akademiia Nauk URSR, Kiev. Instytut movoznavstva. Ukrainsko-russkii slovar'. Glav. redaktor I. M. Kyrychenko. Kiev, Izd-vo Akademii Nauk Ukr. SSR, 1953–63. 6v. **AE572**

Added title page in Ukrainian.

A major Ukrainian-Russian dictionary, giving examples of usage in Ukrainian from literary and other sources.

Andrusyshen, C. H. and **Krett, J. N.** Ukrains'ko-anhliis'kyi slovnyk. Ukrainian-English dictionary. Toronto, pub. for the Univ. of Saskatchewan by Univ. of Toronto Pr., 1957. 1163p. **AE573**

Approximately "95,000 words with full definitions plus about 35,000 . . . phrases." The orthography, based on a system of 1928, "does not differ radically" from the system accepted officially in the Ukrainian SSR in 1946.

Urdu

See Hindi, Hindustani, Punjabi, Urdu, p.116.

Vietnamese

Le Van Hung, *Mrs.* and **Le Van Hung,** *Dr.* Vietnamese-English dictionary, with the international phonetic system and more than 30,000 words and idiomatic expressions. Paris, Éd. Europe-Asie, 1955. 820p. **AE574**

Nguyẽn-dinh-Hòa. Vietnamese-English dictionary. Saigon, Binh-Minh, 1959. 568p. **AE575**

U.S. Armed Forces Security Agency School. Language Branch. Vietnamese-English etymological glossary. Wash., 1952. 367p. **AE576**

"The contents are confined especially to political and military terminology . . . therefore the glossary does not pretend to be an exhaustive or even a comprehensive dictionary."— *Introd.*

Welsh

Evans, Daniel Silvan. Dictionary of the Welsh language. Carmarthen, Spurrell, 1887–1906. Pts.1–5. **AE577**

Pts.1–5, A–Eiddig. 1892p.
Welsh-English. Includes many quotations, with references to sources.
No more published.

Geiriadur prifysgol cymru; a dictionary of the Welsh language. Caerdydd, Gwasg Prifysgol Cymru, 1950–65. Pts.1–19. (In progress) **AE578**

Pts.1–19, A–Enil.
A scholarly historical Welsh-English dictionary which follows the same general pattern as the *Oxford English dictionary* (AE21). Each entry gives etymology, definition in Welsh, English equivalent, and date of earliest use of the word. Most entries also give illustrative quotations drawn from an extensive bibliography of sources.

Lloyd-Jones, J. Geirfa barddoniaeth gynnar Gymraeg. Caerdydd, Gwasg Prifysgol Cymru; Oxford, Univ. Pr., 1931–63. v.1–2. (In progress) **AE579**

v.1–2, A–Heilic (pub. in 8 pts.).
A scholarly dictionary in Welsh, with references to sources, etc.

Bilingual

Jones, Thomas Gwynn and **ap Gwynn, Arthur.** Geiriadur cymraeg-saesneg a saesneg-cymraeg. Caerdydd, Hughes a'i Fab; Educ. Pub. Co., 1950. 205p. **AE580**

Welsh-English, English-Welsh.

Spurrell, William. Geiriadur saesneg a chymraeg; Spurrell's English-Welsh dictionary, ed. by J. Bodvan Anwyl, aided by the late Sir Edward Anwyl. Foreword by the Right Hon. David Lloyd George . . . 11th ed. rev. and enl. Carmarthen, W. Spurrell, 1937. 2v. in 1. **AE581**

In two parts: pt.1, English-Welsh; pt.2, Welsh-English.
v.2 has special title page: Geiriadur cymraeg a saesneg. Spurrell's Welsh-English dictionary . . . 13th ed. thoroughly rev.

Yiddish

Joffe, Judah A. and **Mark, Yudel.** Great dictionary of the Yiddish language. N.Y., Yiddish Dictionary Committee, 1961– . v.1– . il. (In progress) **AE582**

Main title page and text in Yiddish.
To be in 10v.
A scholarly all-inclusive Yiddish-Yiddish dictionary covering the language from the earliest extant records to the living Yiddish of today and in all countries where Yiddish was or is spoken. Includes scholarly and dialectic words and slang.

Abelson, Paul. English-Yiddish encyclopedic dictionary: a complete lexicon and work of reference in all departments of knowledge. N.Y., Jewish Pr. Pub. Co., 1915. 1749p. il. **AE583**

Added title page in Yiddish.

Harkavy, Alexander. English-Yiddish [Yiddish-English] dictionary. 22d ed. rev. and enl. N.Y., Hebrew Pub. Co., [195?]. 2v. in 1. **AE584**

Frequently reprinted.

Yugoslavian

See Serbo-Croatian, p.127.

Zulu

Doke, Clement Martyn, Malcolm, D. McK. and **Sikakana, J. M. A.** English-Zulu dictionary. Johannesburg, Witwatersrand Univ. Pr., 1958. 572p. **AE585**

Emphasis is on current usage, with considerable inclusion of slang, colloquialisms, and idioms.

Doke, Clement Martyn and **Vilakazi, Benedict Wallet.** Zulu-English dictionary. 2d ed. rev. with addendum. Johannesburg, Witwatersrand Univ. Pr., 1958. 918p. **AE586**

A companion volume to the entry above.
2d ed. (rev.) 1953, reprinted 1958.
Based on earlier works, this is a dictionary of current usage, including idiomatic forms, some scientific and technical words, etc.

Doke, Clement Martyn. Zulu-English vocabulary. Johannesburg, Witwatersrand Univ. Pr., 1958. 342p. **AE587**

An abridgment of the dictionary by Doke and Vilakazi (AE586), made by deleting derivative forms, etymologies, illustrative phrases and sentences, rarer words and meanings, etc.

A F

Periodicals

❦ Periodicals form a very important element in reference work in any library, supplementing the book collections in several important ways. They are especially useful for supplying:

1. Latest information available in print (particularly important in the sciences, in technology, and in political, economic, and industrial questions of current interest).

2. Information on which the library has no book or about

which no books are written (as in the case of very new, small, or obscure subjects, or subjects of purely local or temporary interest).

3. Contemporary opinion on a given subject, person, book, etc. (Periodicals, newspapers, and contemporary memoirs are the three main sources for such information, and, of these three, periodical files are the most easily used and the most serviceable in the average library.)

4. Current bibliographies (particularly annual or periodic bibliographies in a given subject field).

To make the best use of periodical literature and to answer the ordinary questions about periodicals, the reference worker needs, in addition to the catalog of his own library, three types of reference aids. These are:

1. The *bibliography* or *catalog* of periodicals, which is a list of the periodicals themselves (but not an index to the contents), and furnishes information about the periodicals listed, their correct titles, history, character, editors, prices, publishers, etc.

2. The *union list* of periodicals, which supplies information as to where sets of the periodicals included in the list may be found. Such lists are usually national, regional, or local. They may be general, e.g., the *Union list of serials in libraries of the United States and Canada* (AF98), or by subject field, e.g., *Union list of technical periodicals in two hundred libraries of the Science-Technology Group* of the Special Libraries Association (EA52).

3. The *index* to periodicals, which furnishes a guide to the contents of files of periodicals, serving the same purpose for articles in periodicals that the library catalog does for books in the library.

BIBLIOGRAPHY

British Museum. Dept. of Printed Books. Catalogue of printed books; periodical publications. 2d ed. London, Museum, 1899–1900. 2v. 1716col., 508col. **AF1**

Repr. as v.41 of the Edwards reprint of the British Museum *Catalogue of printed books* (AA67).

Arranged alphabetically by place of publication with an index of titles. Gives brief information about each title, i.e., title, dates, place, and note of changed titles. For the verification of titles this is one of the most important of the general lists for the period before 1900 because of (1) the great number of periodicals included, and (2) the convenient double arrangement by place and by title.

—— General catalogue of printed books. Photolithographic ed. to 1955. London, 1963. v.184–86 (Periodical publications).

Arranged alphabetically by place of publication. v.185 is devoted to London. No title index.

This new catalog includes 20th-century publications, but it loses some of its value because of the lack of the title index.

Deutsche Forschungsgemeinschaft. Verzeichnis ausgewählter wissenschaftlicher Zeitschriften des Auslandes, VAZ. Wiesbaden, Franz Steiner Verlag, 1957. 2v. (Its Veröffentlichungen) **AF2**

—— —— Register. Wiesbaden, 1957. 333p. (Its Veröffentlichungen)

An attempt to present a critical selection of the most important titles of the world's periodical literature. Those considered fundamental for a given field are designated "A," those serving more specialized research purposes "B." Classed arrangement with alphabetical index by title.

Handbuch der deutschsprachigen Presse ausserhalb Deutschlands, hrsg. im Auftrage des "Göttinger Arbeitskreises" von Karl O. Kurth. Würzburg, Holzner-Verlag, 1956. 399p. **AF3**

A geographically arranged list of current German-language newspapers and periodicals published outside of Germany and concerned primarily with trade and manufacturing, although some publications dealing with political science, economics, and the humanities are also listed. Gives detailed information about each title.

International guide: world little magazines—literature and art trends. Los Angeles, London, Villiers, 1959– . v.1– . Annual. **AF4**

Subtitle varies.

"An annual reference to world literary movements, little magazines, literary and art quarterlies and smaller art presses."

New titles, changes of address, notices of suspension, etc. appear in the "Chronicle" section of *Trace*. London, Villiers, 1952– . Quarterly.

Union of International Associations. Directory of periodicals published by international organizations. 2d ed. Bruxelles, [1959]. 241p. (Its Publ. no.162. FID Publ. no.318) **AF5**

1st ed. 1953.

"Pub. with the assistance of Unesco."

Lists current periodicals of intergovernmental as well as nongovernmental organizations. A classified list with title index in English and French.

Births, deaths and magazine notes: a record of new titles, changed titles, and deaths in the periodical world. (In *Bulletin of bibliography,* April 1900–) **AF6**

This list has been a regular feature in each issue since April 1900. Edited by different people with varying title.

Abbreviations

For abbreviations of scientific and technical periodical titles, *see* p.530.

Rust, Werner. Verzeichnis von unklaren Titelkürzungen deutscher und ausländischer Zeitschriften. Leipzig, Harrassowitz, 1927. 142p. **AF7**

A world list of initial abbreviations, arranged alphabetically. Gives full name of periodical and alternative abbreviation.

United States

Bibliography and history

American periodicals, 18th century–1800/1850; a consolidated index to the microfilm series of 18th century periodicals and to the first 10 years of the 1800–1850 series. Ann Arbor, Mich., Univ. Microfilms, 1956. 19p. **AF8**

American periodical series, ser. 2, 1800–1850. [List of contents] Year 11– . Ann Arbor, Mich., Univ. Microfilms, 1957– . Annual. **AF9**

v.1–10 superseded by a consolidated index (AF8).

A listing of the titles included in the project for microfilming early-19th-century American periodicals. Arrangement is by reel number, the numbering being alphabetical by title for each year's microfilming.

Goldwater, Walter. Radical periodicals in America, 1890–1950; a bibliography with brief notes. With a genealogical chart and a concise lexicon of the parties and groups which issued them. New Haven, Conn., Yale Univ. Lib., 1964. 51p. **AF10**

A list of 321 titles with information on volumes and dates, and with brief annotations.

Hoffman, Frederick J., Allen, Charles and **Ulrich, Caroline F.** The little magazine; a history and a bibliography. Princeton, N.J., Princeton Univ. Pr., 1946. 440p. il. **AF11**

"A little magazine is a magazine designed to print artistic work which for reasons of commercial expediency is not acceptable to the money-minded periodicals or presses."— *Introd.*

In two sections: (1) History, p.1–230; (2) Bibliography, p.233–398, followed by a detailed index to titles, change of titles, editors, contributors, etc. The history gives a general survey of little magazines from about 1910, with discussion of the more important ones, many of which included the first works of writers who later achieved prominence, and thus have a definite place in the literary history of the period. The annotated bibliography gives, in chronological order, detailed information about a long, selected list of these little magazines which will be of particular use to libraries in determining titles, number of issues published, outstanding contributors, etc.

Mott, Frank Luther. A history of American magazines. . . . Cambridge, Harvard Univ. Pr., 1930–57. 4v. il. **AF12**

v.1, 1741–1850. 848p.; v.2, 1850–1865. 608p.; v.3, 1865–1885. 649p.; v.4, 1885–1905. 858p.

A comprehensive history with many bibliographical footnotes throughout and a chronological list of magazines at the end of v.1–3. Because of these and the detailed indexes, the publication is of great value in reference work.

Current

Ayer, *firm, Philadelphia.* N. W. Ayer and Son's Directory of newspapers and periodicals. . . . Philadelphia, Ayer, 1880– . v.1– . maps. Annual. **AF13**

Subtitle, 1964: A guide to publications printed in the United States and its Territories, the Dominion of Canada, Bermuda, the Republics of Panama and the Philippines; descriptions of the states, provinces, cities and towns in which they are published; classified lists; 70 maps.

Title varies.

Absorbed Rowell's *American newspaper directory* (1869–1908. 40v.) in 1910.

Partial contents, 1964: (1) Statistical tables; (2) Population of cities of 2500 and over; (3) Catalog of American newspapers, dailies, weeklies and monthlies, as follows: (a) United States, arranged by states and cities, (b) Canada, arranged by provinces and cities, (c) Bermuda, (d) Republic of Panama, (e) Republic of the Philippines; (4) List of daily newspapers with indication of whether morning or evening, and special Sunday, weekly, semiweekly editions and circulation; (5) Agricultural publications; (6) College publications; (7) Publications in foreign languages arranged by language; (8) Negro publications; (9) Religious publications arranged by states with indication of denomination; (10) Fraternal publications; (11) Magazines of general circulation, classified; (12) Trade, technical and class publications, by subject; (13) Labor publications; (14) Alphabetical index (omitting daily and weekly papers).

The standard American list; comprehensive, listing newspapers and periodicals, but not claiming completeness, as it intentionally omits certain classes of papers, e.g., publications of schools and smaller colleges, local church papers, and most house organs issued merely to exploit goods of their firms. The main list, no.3, covers more than 1200 pages and gives: (1) some descriptive and statistical matter about each state; a list of its counties, marking those which have no newspapers;

and considerable gazetteer information about each city, i.e., its distance and direction from some important place, its railroads, leading manufactures, products, and institutions, and (2) detailed information about each paper or periodical listed including its name, frequency, character or politics, date of foundation, size of column and page, subscription price, circulation figures, names of editors and publishers. Has many good maps, at least one for each state, and a standard time map.

Editor and publisher. International yearbook number for 1920– . N.Y., Editor and Publisher, 1920– . Annual. (1964) **AF14**

Issued annually by the weekly *Editor and publisher.* Contains a large amount of useful statistical and directory information in the field of American and foreign journalism.

Intends to be a complete listing of all daily newspapers, with circulation, rates, executive personnel, departmental managers, and editors; weekly newspapers; printing equipment and its suppliers; syndicates and wire services; advertising agencies; newspaper representatives; schools of journalism; foreign correspondents, etc.; as well as a listing of "every daily newspaper in every country of the world."

Gebbie Press house magazine directory: a public relations and free lance guide to the nation's leading house magazines. N.Y., Gebbie Pr., 1952– . il. Triennial. **AF15**

Title varies: *The nation's leading house magazines.*

Gives editors' names, company names, magazine titles, circulation figures, frequency of issue, type of readership, special interests, size and format, type of printing, and illustrations for many of the covers. Arranged alphabetically with title index and geographical breakdown.

Special Libraries Association. New York Chapter. Advertising Group. Guide to special issues and indexes of periodicals, ed. by Doris B. Katz, Charlotte Madison and Mary Margaret Regan. N.Y., Assoc., 1962. 125p. **AF16**

An alphabetical listing of nearly 800 trade and technical journals, indicating for each whether it has (1) an advertisers index; (2) an editorial index; and (3) any of various special sections or annual issues. Subject index.

Standard periodical directory. Ed.1– . 1964/65– . N.Y., Oxbridge, 1964– . Annual. **AF17**

Subtitle: The complete guide to more than 20,000 United States & Canadian periodicals: industrial, business, medical, farm, scientific, scholarly, technical, legal, general interest, arts & humanities, trade, government, social sciences, newsletters, financial services, literary, house organs, directories, political, annuals, engineering.

Alphabetical subject arrangement with author index and subject guide. Information given includes name and address of publisher, editorial content and scope, year founded, frequency, subscription rate, total circulation, advertising rate, etc.

Ulrich's Periodicals directory; a classified guide to a selected list of current periodicals, foreign and domestic. 10th ed., ed. by Eileen C. Graves. N.Y., Bowker, 1963. 667p. **AF18**

1st ed. 1932. Now issued triennially.

A very useful classified list of almost 20,000 periodicals from many countries. Coverage has varied in the different editions. Titles are grouped in subject classifications arranged alphabetically. Entries usually include, as pertinent: title, subtitle, sponsoring group, date of origin, frequency, price, editors, publisher, place of publication, annual and cumulative indexes. Also gives information on: bibliographies, book reviews, film reviews, music and record reviews, illustrations, maps, charts, advertisements, statistics, circulation, etc.

An especially useful feature is the notation of the indexing and abstracting services (38 titles) in which titles are indexed or abstracted.

"Bibliographies are included under specific subjects depending on scope of material covered and also under the headings 'General bibliography' and 'Books and book trade.'"
—*Pref.*

Index by titles and by subjects. The work concludes with a list of periodicals which have ceased publication since the 1959 ed., p.663–67.

Earlier issues may be useful, both for the listing of periodicals no longer published and for special lists included, e.g.: *A list of clandestine periodicals of World War II,* by Adrienne Florence Muzzy, in the 5th ed. 1947.

Working press of the nation. Ed. and publisher Tom Farrell. N.Y., Farrell Pub., 1947– . v.1– . Biennial; annual since 1959. **AF19**

First issue was entitled *Working press of New York City.*

Contents, 1964: v.1, *Newspaper and allied services directory:* a directory and guide to daily newspapers, news services, feature syndicates, newsreels, photo services, weekly newspapers, foreign newspapers, special interest newspapers; v.2, *Magazine and editorial directory:* a directory and guide to service, trade, professional, industrial, farm, agricultural, consumer, news publications; v.3, *Radio and television directory:* a directory and guide to radio stations, television stations, networks, radio programs, television programs, sports directors, film buyers, newscasters, program personnel.

Includes detailed information on mass media communications, newspapers, periodicals, radio, and television, with names of personnel.

Africa

Ruth Sloan Associates, Washington, D.C. The press in Africa, ed. by Helen Kitchen. Wash., 1956. 96p. **AF20**

Lists the periodicals and newspapers published in each country of Africa, usually giving title, place, frequency, language, circulation, editor, publisher, orientation, and influence.

Australia

Press directory of Australia and New Zealand, 1914– . Sydney, N.S.W., Country Pr., 1914– . v.1– . Irregular. (15th ed. 1961) **AF21**

A listing of newspapers and periodicals arranged geographically. Gives directory information including considerable gazetteer information about places. Alphabetical index.

Austria

Handbuch österreichs Presse, Werbung, Graphik. Wien, Verband Österreichischer Zeitungsherausgeber, 1953– . Annual. **AF22**

Statistical and directory information on Austrian newspapers and periodicals. Classified with title index.

Belgium

Hove, Julien van. Répertoire des périodiques paraissant en Belgique. Bruxelles, Librairie Encyclopédique, 1951. 358p. **AF23**

Added title page: Repertorium van de in België verschijnende tijdschriften.

Alphabetical listing of more than 2000 periodicals currently appearing in Belgium, with full bibliographical data. Indexes by subject, editorial bodies, and place of publication.

—— —— Supplément 1–2. 1955–60. 304p., 215p.

The supplements list new periodicals published during the periods covered, as well as omissions and changes in title from the previous volumes.

Brazil

Periódicos brasileiros de cultura. Edição preliminar. Rio de Janeiro, 1956. 182p. (Inst. Brasileiro de Bibliografia e Documentação) **AF24**

Arranged by Universal Decimal Classification, with subject and title indexes; gives publication data for current periodicals and often indicates the general indexes in which a periodical is indexed.

Canada

Ayer, *firm, Philadelphia.* N. W. Ayer and Son's Directory of newspapers and periodicals . . . Philadelphia, Ayer, 1880– . **AF25**

For full information *see* AF13.

Probably the most convenient list of Canadian newspapers and periodicals since *McKim's Directory of Canadian publications* (1892–1942) ceased publication. The latter gave full particulars of newspapers and periodicals as well as gazetteer information on places of publication.

Colombia

Bogotá. Biblioteca Nacional. Catálogo de todos los periódicos que existen desde su fundación hasta el año de 1935, inclusive. Ed. oficial. Bogotá, El Gráfico, 1936. 2v. **AF26**

Contents: t.1, Periódicos nacionales, A–P; t.2, Periódicos nacionales, R–Z. Periódicos extranjeros, A–Z.

A listing of the issues of periodicals in the National Library. Does not give bibliographical information beyond title, name, and numbers and dates of issues held.

Congo

Berlage, Jean. Répertoire de la presse du Congo Belge (1884–1954) et du Ruanda-Urundi (1920–1954) . . . Bruxelles, Commission Belge de Bibliographie, 1955. 64p. (Bibliographia belgica 10) **AF27**

Title also in Flemish.

365 titles in alphabetical arrangement with four indexes: (1) chronological, (2) place-name, (3) broad classification, and (4) publisher (persons and organizations).

Cuba

Directorio de revistas y periódicos de Cuba. 1942– . La Habana, Anuario Bibliográfico Cubano, 1942–53; Gainesville, Fla., 1963– . v.1– . Annual. (Biblioteca del bibliotecaria) **AF28**

Ed., Fermín Peraza y Sarausa.

Publication suspended, 1954–62.

The 1963 edition, issued in Florida, lists more than 100 titles of periodicals published in Cuba, with a special section of 22 titles of Cuban periodicals published outside of Cuba.

Czechoslovakia

Malec, Karel. Soupis bibliografií novin a časopisů, vydávaných na území Československé Republiky. Praha, Orbis, 1959. 216p. **AF29**

Bibliography of bibliographies of Czechoslovak periodicals and newspapers from the 18th century through 1958.

East Europe

U.S. Library of Congress. Slavic and Central European Division. East and East Central Europe; periodicals in

English and other west European languages. Comp. by Paul L. Horecky, with the assistance of Janina Wojcicka. Wash., 1958. 126p. **AF30**

Lists serials dealing with the countries and peoples of the area—published in Western languages either outside or in the area—and serials devoted to publishing translations or abstracts.

France

Arbour, Roméo. Les revues littéraires éphémères paraissant à Paris entre 1900 et 1914. Répertoire descriptif. Paris, Librairie José Corti, 1956. 93p. **AF31**

Lists 154 "little magazines" published in Paris which lived less than four years, with locations in Parisian libraries. Gives full bibliographical description, with names of editors, etc., as well as the names of the principal contributors. Index of personal names and an appendix of 31 titles not found in the libraries of Paris.

Caron, Pierre and **Jaryc, Marc.** Répertoire des périodiques de langue française, philosophiques, historiques, philologiques et juridiques. Publié par la Féderation des Sociétés Françaises de Sciences Philosophiques, Historiques, Philologiques et Juridiques. Paris, Maison du Livre Français, 1935. 351p. **AF32**

Alphabetical list, p.1–278, no.1–1421; Supplément, p.279–92, no.1421 bis–1476; IIᵉ supplément, no.1477–1496.

—— —— 1. supplément, no.1477–1686. 1937. 68p.

Incorporates, in regular alphabetical order and numbering, the titles (no.1477–1496) of the original IIᵉ supplément.

—— —— 2. supplément, no.1687–1900. 1939. 62p.

An important list of French periodicals existing in the 1930's, giving exact title, date of founding, names and addresses of chief editors, periodicity, average number of pages per volume, size, price, etc. Indexes of persons, places, and subjects.

Hatin, Louis Eugène. Bibliographie historique et critique de la presse périodique française. . . . Paris, Firmin-Didot, 1866. cxviip., 660p. il. **AF33**

Subtitle: Catalogue systématique et raisonné de tous les écrits périodiques de quelque valeur publiés ou ayant circulé en France depuis l'origine du journal jusqu'à nos jours, avec extraits, notes historiques, critiques, et morales, indication des prix que les principaux journaux ont atteints dans les ventes publiques, etc.

A bibliography of the retrospective, not of the current, type, with detailed bibliographical and historical notes about each periodical listed. Covers 1631–1865. Useful for historical information, though never complete.

Paris. Bibliothèque Nationale. Catalogue des périodiques clandestins diffusés en France de 1939 à 1945, suivi d'un catalogue des périodiques clandestins diffusés à l'étranger. Paris, Bibliothèque Nationale, 1954. 282p. **AF34**

Preparé et redigé successivement par Renée Roux-Fouillet et Paul Roux-Fouillet.

Lists clandestine periodicals to be found in the Bibliothèque Nationale, either in the original or in photostat copies. In three sections: (1) Periodicals distributed in France (about 1015 titles); (2) Periodicals distributed in other countries (about 71 titles); (3) Supplement. Index.

Paris. Bibliothèque Nationale. Département des Périodiques. Bibliographie de la presse française politique et d'information générale, 1865–1944. Paris, Bibliothèque Nationale, 1964– . (In progress) **AF35**

Chronologically, a successor to Hatin (AF33). Limited to journals (mainly dailies and weeklies) of political or general news nature. 89 fascicules, each covering a *département* (and numbered alphabetically by name thereof), are being issued

as they are completed; the finished work will comprise 4v., with a general preface and a title index. Each fascicule includes a preface or historical note, an alphabetical listing with bibliographical details of the periodicals, and a chronological table of titles.

—— Répertoire de la presse et des publications périodiques françaises. 1960, par H. F. Raux. Paris, Éditions de la Documentation Française, 1961. 1161p. **AF36**

1st ed. 1957 (pub. 1958).

A comprehensive classified list of current French periodicals giving full bibliographical information about each title. Includes indexes by names cited and by societies, and an alphabetical index of titles which not only indexes the present volume but also includes titles from the first edition that have ceased or suspended publication, and titles that began and ceased during the period between editions. It also contains the titles of various categories of periodicals not included in the classified section, e.g., alumni association bulletins, school papers, parish bulletins, etc., and for these the place of publication and address are given. In all, the index lists some 21,000 titles.

Current

Annuaire de la presse française et étrangère et du monde politique; Annuaire international de la presse. 1880– . Paris, Administration et Rédaction, 1880– . v.1– . il. Annual. **AF37**

Title varies. Continues E. Mermet's *La publicité en France,* 1878–80.

An important and useful bibliography and annual, containing not only full information about French journals and the French press but also a considerable amount of the statistical, gazetteer, political, and governmental information needed by French journalists. Contains many portraits. Scope and contents of volumes before 1914 differ somewhat from the volumes issued since 1914.

Principal contents, 1963: Names of French officials; Lists of members of the Senate and Chamber of Deputies; Press associations with names of officers and members; Critics; Pseudonyms; Advertising agencies; Lists of papers and periodicals published in (1) Paris, arranged alphabetically by classes, (2) *Départements,* arranged alphabetically by *départements* and towns, (3) Colonies, and (4) Abroad.

Index of French newspapers and periodicals; index of foreign newspapers; indexes of names, advertising agencies, etc.

Germany

Deutsche Bibliographie: Zeitschriften Verzeichnis, 1945–1952, 1953–1957. Bibliographie der in Deutschland erscheinenden periodischen Veröffentlichungen sowie der deutschsprachigen Periodica Österreichs, der Schweiz und anderer Länder. Bearb. von der Deutschen Bibliothek, Frankfurt a. M. Frankfurt a. M., GMBH, 1954–63. v.1–2⁴. (In progress) **AF38**

Title varies slightly.

A comprehensive list of German-language publications appearing in Germany and other countries. For each title usually gives: editor, publisher, size, price, frequency, irregularities in publication, and changes in title.

Each period in two parts: (1) a classified section, and (2) an index section. The latter includes indexes by title, editor, publisher, society or sponsoring organization, and subject.

Diesch, Carl. Bibliographie der germanistischen Zeitschriften. Leipzig, Hiersemann, 1927. 441p. (Modern Language Assoc. of America. Germanic Sec. Bibliographical publ. v.1) **AF39**

A chronological, classed arrangement covering from the 18th to the 20th centuries. Lists more than 4600 titles with information on full title, editor, volumes and years published, place, publisher, etc. Title and name indexes.

Kirchner, Joachim. Die Grundlagen des deutschen Zeitschriftenwesens mit einer Gesamtbibliographie der deutschen Zeitschriften bis zum Jahre 1790. Leipzig, Hiersemann, 1928–31. 2v.   **AF40**

Contents: T.1, Bibliographische und buchhandelsgeschichtliche Untersuchungen; T.2, Die Bibliographie der deutschen Zeitschriften bis zur französischen Revolution. Statistische Ergebnisse. Register der Zeitschriften. Namenregister.

Current

Die deutsche Presse; Zeitungen und Zeitschriften. Hrsg.: Inst. für Publizistik der Freien Universität Berlin. Berlin, Duncker und Humblot, 1954– .   **AF41**

Succeeds the *Handbuch deutsche Presse*, 1951. An introductory section is devoted to essays and statistical data. The major parts are Sec. II, a directory of newspapers with a separate list for the Soviet Zone, and Sec. III, a classified list of periodicals for both zones. Indexes by titles, persons, and presses.

Der Leitfaden für Presse und Werbung. 1947– . Essen-Stadtwald, Stamm–Verlag GMBH, 1947– . Annual.   **AF42**

Introductory and explanatory material in German, English, and French. Lists: (1) German newspapers in alphabetical and in geographical order; (2) periodicals, alphabetically and classified; (3) German newspapers and periodicals published in non-German–speaking countries; and (4) sections on advertising, cinema, and posters.

Great Britain

Before 1800

Couper, William James. The Edinburgh periodical press; being a bibliographical account of the newspapers, journals, and magazines issued in Edinburgh from the earliest times to 1800. Stirling, Mackay, 1908. 2v. facsim. **AF43**
v.1, 1642–1711; v.2, 1711–1800.
Full bibliographical information with historical sketches.

Crane, R. S. and **Kaye, F. B.** Census of British newspapers and periodicals, 1620–1800. Chapel Hill, Univ. of North Carolina Pr., 1927. 205p.   **AF44**

Lists 970 papers and periodicals, with indication of the holdings in 62 American libraries.
Contents: (1) British periodicals, 1620–1800, accessible in American libraries; (2) British periodicals, 1620–1800, not found in American libraries; (3) Chronological index; (4) Geographical index of periodicals published outside of London.

Henry E. Huntington Library and Art Gallery, San Marino, Calif. Check list of English newspapers and periodicals before 1801 in the Huntington Library; comp. by Anthony J. Gabler. (In Huntington Library Bull. Cambridge, Mass., Harvard Univ. Pr., 1931. no.2, p.1–66)   **AF45**

Arranged alphabetically with chronological index.

Oxford University. Bodleian Library. Catalogue of English newspapers and periodicals in the Bodleian Library, 1622–1800. By R. T. Milford and D. M. Sutherland. Oxford, Bibliographical Soc., 1936. p.167–346. (Oxford Bibliographical Soc. Proceedings and papers, v.4, pt.2)   **AF46**

Alphabetical title catalog, p.171–344; index to editors, authors, and contributors, p.345–46.

Bibliography

Weed, Katherine Kirtley and **Bond, Richmond Pugh.** Studies of British newspapers and periodicals from their beginning to 1800; a bibliography. Chapel Hill, Univ. of North Carolina Pr., 1946. 233p. (Studies in philology, extra ser., no.2)   **AF47**

Contents: Bibliographies and bibliographical studies; Beginnings of the newspaper; General studies; Individual newspapers and periodicals; Editors, authors, and publishers; Towns and counties; Special subjects; Newspapers and periodicals in Europe and in America.

Lists some 2100 books and periodical articles printed mainly 1800–1940, under subject with author index.

Current

Newspaper press directory; and advertisers' guide. . . . London, Benn Bros., 1846– . v.1– . il. Annual. **AF48**
Publication suspended 1941–44.
Publisher varies.
Contains particulars of newspapers, magazines, reviews, and periodicals published in Great Britain and Northern Ireland, Ireland, the British Commonwealth, and the principal countries of the world.
For British and Commonwealth countries information is detailed, giving title, political affiliation if any, beginning date, circulation, address, publishers, advertising rates, time published, etc.

Toase, Mary. Guide to current British periodicals. London, Lib. Assoc., 1962. 256p.   **AF49**

Gives detailed descriptions of 3800 current British periodicals, including England, Wales, Scotland, Northern Ireland, and the Channel Islands. Classified arrangement with combined title and subject index. Appendix I is a list of abstract journals.

Willing's Press guide, 1874– . London, Willing, 1874– . v.1– . Annual.   **AF50**

A useful inexpensive list.
Principal contents, 1964: Alphabetical list of newspapers and periodicals issued in the United Kingdom, with year of establishment, when published, price, publisher's name and address; Classified list; London suburban papers; London addresses of provincial publications; Provincial publications arranged under counties; Provincial publications arranged under towns; Titular changes and amalgamations; Dominion and Commonwealth publications; Reporting and news agencies.

Hungary

Dezsényi, Béla. A magyar hirlapirodalom elsö százada (1705–1805). Budapest, Magyar Nemzeti Múzeum Országos Széchényi Könyvtára, 1941. 66p. (Magyarország idöszaki sajtójának könyvészete, 1)   **AF51**

Lists, with location, periodicals and newspapers published in Hungary from 1705 to 1805.

Kemény, György. Magyarország idöszaki sajtója, 1911–töl 1920–ig. Budapest, Magyar Nemzeti Múzeum Országos Széchényi Könyvtára, 1942. (Magyarország idöszaki sajtójának könyvészete, 4)   **AF52**

An alphabetical list of periodicals and newspapers published in Hungary from 1911 to 1920.

Budapest. Országos Széchényi Könyvtár. A magyar sajtó bibliográfiája, 1945–1954. Dezsényi Béla, Falvy Zoltán [és] Fejér Judit. Budapest, "Müvelt Nép," 1956. 159p. (Az Országos Széchényi Könyvtár kiadványai. 36)   **AF53**

Alphabetical listing of periodicals and newspapers published in Hungary between 1945 and 1954.

India

Nifor guide to Indian periodicals, 1955/1956– . Poona, Nat. Information Service, 1955– . **AF55**

The first directory of its kind in India; gives a classified listing of 2127 Indian periodicals and newspapers, and a separate alphabetical list of 1526 additional unclassified titles.

The classified section is in four main sequences—language, subject, periodicity, and geographical—followed by 12 statistical tables. The language section (under 23 languages and dialects) gives the main information about each periodical including title, date of establishment, size, frequency, cost, editors, and publishers, with references to subject classifications.

Indonesia

Anderson, Benedict R. Bibliography of Indonesian publications: newspapers, non-government periodicals and bulletins, 1945–1958 at Cornell University. Ithaca, N.Y., Southeast Asia Program, Dept. of Far Eastern Studies, Cornell Univ., 1959. 69p. (Cornell University. Dept. of Far Eastern Studies. Southeast Asia Program. Data paper, no.33) **AF56**

Ireland

See also Great Britain, p.137.

U.S. Dept. of State. A checklist of periodicals published in the Republic of Ireland (including newspapers but excluding annuals). [Wash., Dept. of State], 1952. 33p. (Its Publications report. Notes on foreign publications. Report no.IAD-F-27) **AF57**

Gives title, publisher, address, frequency, price, and a few notes indicating discontinuance, suspension, Gaelic-language publications, etc.

Italy

Italy. Consiglio Nazionale delle Ricerche. Periodici italiani scientifici, tecnici e di cultura generale. 5. ed. interamente rinnovata. 1939. Roma, Arti Grafiche Trinacria, 1939. 3v. **AF58**

Detailed information about Italian periodicals current in the 1930's.

Majolo Molinari, Olga. La stampa periodica romana dell' Ottocento. Roma, Instit. di Studi Romani, 1963. 2v. **AF59**

A comprehensive bibliography of some 1700 Italian 19th-century periodicals with bibliographical details and descriptive annotations. Arranged alphabetically with indexes: chronological, subject, and name.

Bibliography, v.2, p.1143–88.

Righini, Benvenuto. I periodici fiorentini (1597–1950) catalogo ragionato. Firenze, Sansoni Antiquariato, 1955. 2v. facsims. (Contributi alla Biblioteca bibliografica italica, 7 and 9) **AF60**

Florentine periodicals, 1597–1950, alphabetically arranged with detailed information on title and changes in title, dates of beginning and cessation, place and publisher, format, periodicity, names of editors and, in many cases, contributors, etc. v.2 contains an index of names, a chronological index, a bibliography on Florentine periodicals, etc.

Current

Annuario della stampa italiana, a cura della Federazione Nazionale della Stampa Italiana, 1954/55– . Milano/Roma, Fratelli Bocca, 1954– . Irregular. **AF61**

A continuation of the annual of the same title published 1916–42.

Includes texts of laws on the press, professional organizations, material on journalism in Italy, and lists of periodicals and newspapers, Italian journalists, associations, etc.

Associazione Italiana Editori. Elenco dei quotidiani e periodici italiani, 1951– . Milano, Società Anonima per Pubblicazioni Bibliografico-Editoriali, 1952– . Biennial. **AF62**

Classed arrangement with title index. Gives title, frequency, price, address, editor, etc.

Repertorio analitico della stampa italiana: quotidiani e periodici, 1964– . Milano, Messaggerie Italiane, 1963– . **AF63**

Lists some 8000 periodicals arranged by a simplified Dewey Decimal Classification with title index. The main list gives title, frequency, and city of publication; the title index gives subscription prices.

Japan

Japan. Diet. Library. Directory of Japanese learned periodicals, 1957. Tokyo, Tokyo Lib. Bureau, 1958. unpaged. **AF64**

1st ed. 1953.

This enlarged edition lists "as comprehensively as possible, periodicals and serials of a scientific and scholarly character in the field of generalities, humanities and social sciences," and also in natural and medical sciences and applied sciences and fine arts. These last two parts were originally published separately.

Classified by Universal Decimal Classification. No indexes. Titles are given in romanized script, Japanese characters, English translation in parentheses, with publisher, address, year of first issue, periodicity, size, language of publication, indication of summaries in European languages, price, etc.

Korea

Rhee, Byung Mock. Bibliography of university periodicals of Korea, 1945–1964, with directory of institutions of higher education. Seoul, Dept. of Lib. Science, Yonsei Univ., 1964. 265p. (Library science ser. of Yonsei Univ., no.15) **AF65**

A listing of "all known periodicals which have ever been or are currently published by the higher learning institutions . . . "—*Abstract.*

Latin America

La Plata. Universidad Nacional. Biblioteca. Catálogo de periódicos sudamericanos existentes en la Biblioteca Pública de la Universidad (1791–1861). La Plata, 1934. 231p. **AF66**

Detailed bibliographical information about Latin-American periodicals published 1791–1861.

Pan American Union. Repertorio de publicaciones periódicas actuales latinoamericanas. Directory of current Latin American periodicals. Répertoire des périodiques en cours publiés en Amerique latine. Paris, UNESCO, 1958. 266p. (UNESCO bibliographical handbooks. [8]) **AF67**

Lists 3375 titles, arranged by Universal Decimal Classification, with geographical index and subject indexes in Spanish, English, and French. No title index.

Zimmerman, Irene. A guide to current Latin American periodicals: humanities and social sciences. Gainesville, Fla., Kallman Pub. Co., 1961. 357p. **AF68**

"Primarily an annotated, evaluative bibliography . . . "—*Introd.* Lists 668 active periodicals and 117 on its "casualty list." Includes periodicals published in South and Central

America, Mexico, and the West Indies as well as those published in the United States by Latin Americans and those dealing with Latin-American languages and literatures, etc.

Main arrangement is alphabetical by country, followed by a classified section and a chronological listing. The annotations, given in the first section, are full in descriptive and evaluative information. The "casualty list" records those periodicals from which the author has not been able to elicit recent information.

Malaya

Roff, William R. Guide to Malay periodicals, 1876–1941, with details of known holdings in Malaya. Singapore, 1961. 46p. (Papers on Southeast Asian subjects, no.4) (Distr. by Cellar Book Shop, Box 6, College Park Sta., Detroit 21, Mich.) **AF69**

Published for the Dept. of History in the University of Malaya in Kuala Lumpur by Eastern Universities Pr., Ltd. Chronological listing with title index.

Mexico

Mendoza López, Margarita. Catálogo de publicaciones periódicas mexicanas. México, 1959. 262p. **AF70**

At head of title: Centro Mexicano de Escritores.

Listing is by place of publication, then alphabetically by title. Detailed directory-type information is given, with auxiliary lists of titles on which full information was not available.

Netherlands

List of scientific and learned periodicals in the Netherlands. [2d rev. and enl. ed.] The Hague, Nijhoff, 1953. 63p. (Netherlands Inst. for Documentation and Filing. Publ. no.4 [2d ser.]) **AF71**

1st edition had title *Scientific periodicals in the Netherlands* and was prepared by Dr. A. Gorter. This edition adds periodicals in the humanities, now listing 491 selected titles.

New Zealand

See Australia, p.135.

Nigeria

Ibadan. University College. Library. Nigerian periodicals & newspapers, 1950–1955. Ibadan, 1956. 23p. **AF72**

A list of those received . . . by the library. 306 entries.

To be supplemented by information in annual volume of *Nigerian publications* (AA620).

Pakistan

Moid, A. and **Siddiqui, Akhtar.** A guide to periodical publications and newspapers of Pakistan. Karachi, Pakistan Bibliographical Working Group, Karachi Univ. Lib., 1953. 60p. (Its Publ. no.2) **AF73**

A classified arrangement with very brief information: title, address, frequency, and price.

Poland

Bibliografia czasopism i wydawnictw zbiorowych. 1958– . Warszawa, Biblioteka Narodowa. Inst. Bibliograficzny, 1960– . Annual. **AF74**

1958 also has title *Bibliography of Polish serials*.

An alphabetical listing of almost 1700 periodicals with

three indexes: (1) classified; (2) by organization or institution; (3) by editor.

Danilewicz, Maria and **Sadowska, Genowefa.** Catalogue of periodicals in Polish or relating to Poland and other Slavonic countries published outside Poland since September 1st, 1939. London, 1964. 75p. **AF75**

Added title page in Polish.
Lists 895 titles.

Rumania

Newspapers and periodicals from Rumania. Journaux et périodiques de Roumanie. Zeitungen und Zeitschriften aus Rumänien. 1958– . [Bucharest], Cartimex, 1958– . Annual. **AF76**

Text in English, French, and German.
A classified listing with alphabetical index.

Russia

Lisovskii, Nikolai Mikhailovich. Russkaia periodicheskaia pechat' 1703–1900 gg., bibliografiia i graficheskiia tablitsy. Petrograd, Shumakhore, 1915. 267p. tables. **AF77**

Remains the standard bibliography for 18th- and 19th-century Russian journals and newspapers. Chronologically arranged, with indexes.

—— Bibliografiia russkoi periodicheskoi pechati 1703–1900 gg. (Materialy dlia istorii russkoi zhurnalistiki) Petrograd, 1915. 1067p. **AF78**

A separate printing of the above, in smaller format, without tables.

See also the handbook *Russkaia periodicheskaia pechat'*, 1702–1894 (AF80a).

Leningrad. Publichnaia Biblioteka. Bibliografiia periodicheskikh izdanii Rossii 1901–1916. Pod obshchei red. V. M. Barashenkova [i dr.]. Leningrad, 1958–61. 4v. **AF79**

Title also in English, German, French.

At head of title: L. N. Beliaeva, M. K. Zinov'eva, M. M. Nikiforov.

Full bibliographic description of periodicals, other than illegal publications, published within the territory of pre-1917 Russia. Includes newspapers; excludes annuals and almanacs. Entries arranged alphabetically, with numerous indexes in v.4.

Supersedes checking edition *Predvaritel'nyi spisok periodicheskikh izdanii Rossii,* 1901–1916 (Leningrad, 1949).

Periodicheskaia pechat' SSSR, 1917–1949; bibliograficheskii ukazatel'. Moskva, Vsesoiuznaia Knizhnaia Palata, 1955–63. 10v. in 11. **AF80**

[v.1$^{1-2}$], Zhurnaly, trudy i biulleteni po obshchestvenno-politicheskim i sotsial'no-ekonomicheskim voprosam. 1958. 317p., 267p.

[v.2] ——po estestvennym naukam i matematike. 1956. 219p.

[v.3] ——po tekhnike i promyshlennosti. 1955. 315p.

[v.4] ——po transporty, sviazy i kommunal'nomu delu. 1955. 124p.

[v.5] ——po sel'skomu khoziaistvu. 1955. 230p.

[v.6] ——po kul'turnomy stroitel'stvu, narodnomu obrazovaniiu i prosveshcheniiu. 1956. 198p.

[v.7] ——po zdravookhraneniiu, meditzine, fizicheskoi kul'ture i sportu. 1956. 170p.

[v.8] ——po iazykoznaniiu, literaturovedeniiu, khudozhestvennoi literature i iskusstvu. 1958. 218p.

[v.9] ——po voprosam pechati, bibliotechnogo dela i bibliografii. 1959. 191p.

[v.10], Svodnye ukazateli.

The major retrospective bibliography of periodicals, other than newspapers, published in the USSR in all languages from Nov. 1917 through 1949. Includes numbered series appearing irregularly. Gives full bibliographic information as to periodicity, numbering, title changes, etc. Each volume contains alphabetical index of titles, index of journals in languages other than Russian, index by place of publication, and index of publishers and issuing organizations; master indexes in the last volume.

Continued by *Letopis' periodicheskikh izdanii SSSR,* 1950/ 54–　(AF81).

Russkaia periodicheskaia pechat' (1702–1894); spravochnik. Pod red. A. G. Dement'eva i dr. Moskva, Gospolitizdat, 1959. 835p.　　　　　　　　　**AF80a**

—— (1895–Oktiabr' 1917); spravochnik. Avtory-sost. M. S. Cherapakhov i e. M. Fingerit. Moskva, Gospolitizdat, 1957. 251p.

Chronologically arranged and well-indexed handbooks giving extensive factual information, with political commentary, on the major social and literary periodicals (journals, almanacs, and newspapers) published in and outside of Russia between 1702 and 1917. Includes editor's names, major contributors, special features, and references to supplements and indexes.

Current

Letopis' periodicheskikh izdanii SSSR; bibliograficheskii ukazatel'. 1950/54, 1955/60 (in 2v.). Moskva, Izd-vo Vsesoiuznoi Knizhnoi Palaty, 1955–　. Quinquennial.
　　　　　　　　　　　　　　　　　　　　　AF81

Continues annual volumes from 1933.
Lists all Soviet periodical publications. Pt.1 includes journals, proceedings, bulletins, and those annuals and collections which appear with continuous numbering. Pt.2 lists newspapers geographically, with alphabetical and subject indexes.
Supplements, for continuing titles and for new and changed titles, appear as:

—— Trudy, uchennye zapiski, sborniki i drugie prodolzhaiushchiesia izdaniia. 1961–　. Moskva, 1963–　. Annual.

—— Novye, pereimenovannye i prekrativshiesia zhurnaly i gazety. S. 1 IAnvaria 1961 g. po–　. Moskva, 1963–　. Cumulative.

Bibliography

Leningrad. Publichnaia Biblioteka. Obshchie bibliografii russkikh periodicheskikh izdanii, 1703–1954, i materialy po statistike russkoi periodicheskoi pechati; annotirovannyi ukazatel'. Pod red. P. N. Berkova. Leningrad, 1956. 139p. (Bibliografiia russkoi bibliografii)　　　**AF82**

At head of title: M. V. Mashkova i M. V. Sokurova.
General bibliographies, annotated, of the Russian periodical press, together with statistical material. Supplements the bibliography of book bibliographies by Sokurova (AA56).

Rwandi

See Congo, p.135.

South Africa

Saul, C. Daphne. South African periodical publications, 1800–1875: a bibliography. Capetown, Univ. School of Librarianship, 1949. 45p.　　　　　　　**AF83**

Lists periodicals, almanacs, directories, and yearbooks; excludes newspapers, government publications, and annual reports of societies. Gives usual bibliographical information and locates copies in South African libraries.

Spain

Givanel Mas, Juan. Bibliografía catalana: premsa. Barcelona, [Impr. Altés], 1931–37. 3v. il.　　　　**AF84**

Detailed bibliographical information about periodicals published in Catalonia, 1792–1925, arranged chronologically under cities. v.3 is an alphabetical index with historical notes and many facsimiles.

Madrid. Biblioteca Nacional. Publicaciones periódicas existentes en la Biblioteca Nacional; catálogo redactado y ordenado por Florentino Zamora Lucas y María Casado Jorge. Madrid, Dirección General de Archivos y Bibliotecas. Servicio de Publicaciones del Ministerio de Educación Nacional, 1952. 718p. il.　　　　**AF85**

A classed list of almost 9000 titles with alphabetical index of titles. Gives title, place of publication, volumes in the library, and (sometimes) frequency.

Madrid. Hemeroteca Municipal. Catálogo de las publicaciones periódicas madrileñas existentes en la Hemeroteca Municipal de Madrid, 1661–1930. Madrid, Artes Graficas Municipales, 1933. 360p.　　　**AF86**

Madrid. Instituto de Cultura Hispánica. Departamento de Información. Catálogo de revistas españolas. Madrid, Ed. Cultura Hispánica, 1948. 216p.　　　**AF87**

A classified list of periodicals, omitting those of very limited interest. Gives detailed information for each, including editors, publishers, contributors, size, frequency, etc. but no dates. Subject and title indexes.

Current

Annuario de la prensa española v.1–　. Madrid, 1943–　. (Ministerio de Información y Turismo. Dirección General de Prensa)　　　　　　　　　　　　**AF88**

v.1, 1943; v.2, 1945/46; v.3–5 issued in 2 pts. each: pt.1, Newspapers; pt.2, Periodicals.
Gives detailed information, including address, personnel, format, size, number of copies printed, etc.

Sweden

Lundstedt, Bernhard Wilhelm. Sveriges periodiska litteratur. Bibliografi. Stockholm, Iduns Tryckeri, 1895–1902. 3v.　　　　　　　　　　　　　　　　　　**AF89**

v.1, 1645–1812; v.2, Stockholm, 1813–1894; v.3, Landsorten, 1813–99.
Gives detailed bibliographical information about Swedish newspapers.

Switzerland

Bern. Schweizerische Landesbibliothek. Verzeichnis der laufenden schweizerischen Zeitschriften. Catalogue des périodiques suisses, revues, journaux, annuaires, almanachs, collections, etc., reçus par la Bibliothèque Nationale à Berne. 2. éd. refondue et considérablement augm., publ. par la direction de la Bibliothèque. Bern-Bümpliz, Benteli, 1925. 217p.　　　　**AF90**

—— —— Nachtrag, 1926–30. Bern-Bümpliz, Benteli, 1926–31. 5v.
A classified list with title index.

Schweizerischer Zeitschriften- und Zeitungskatalog. Catalogue des revues et journaux suisses. Olten, Schweizerisches Vereinssortiment, [1945]. 239p.　　　**AF91**

Classed list with title index of periodicals currently published in Switzerland and information on complete title, publisher, address, beginning date, frequency, size, general coverage, etc.

Schweizer Zeitschriftenverzeichnis; Répertoire des périodiques suisses; Repertorio dei periodici svizzeri, 1951/1955, 1956/60. Zürich, Schweizerisches Buchhändler- und Verleger-Vereins, 1956–61. v.1–2. Quinquennial. **AF92**

Forms pt.2 of the *Schweizerische Nationalbibliographie* (AA716).

Gives quite complete bibliographical information for periodicals published in Switzerland. Except for newspapers, lists many kinds of serial publications published at least once a year—i.e., periodicals, annuals, almanacs, etc.—though certain categories are omitted, e.g., annual reports, religious tracts, business bulletins, etc.

Classified arrangement with title index.

Zeitungskatalog der Schweiz. Catalogue des journaux suisses. [Geneva(?), Verband Schweizerischer Annoncen-Expeditionen, 1950–] Annual (Irregular). **AF93**

Directory of Swiss periodicals and newspapers. Text in German and French.

Coverage varies: 1959–61 (semiannual), pt.1, Newspapers; pt.2, Periodicals, professional journals and almanacs. 1962– lists newspapers only.

Yugoslavia

Bibliografija jugoslovenske periodike. jan./mart 1956– . Beograd, Bibliografski Institut FNBJ, 1956– . Quarterly with annual indexes. **AF94**

Title varies.

At head of title, 1962– : Jugoslovenski Bibliografski Institut.

A current listing of periodicals and newspapers.

Jugoslovenski časopisi (izbor). 2. izdanje. Yugoslav periodicals (Selection). 2d ed. Beograd, Jugoslovenski Centar za Tehničku i Naučnu Dokumentaciju, 1955. 108p. **AF95**

Title also in French and German.

A classified list with title index. All headings are given in the four languages: Yugoslavian, English, French, German. Titles are also translated into the four languages. Gives title, publisher, address, beginning date, frequency, price, language of text, etc.

UNION LISTS

❧ A union list of periodicals is a catalog, usually in alphabetical title arrangement, of the periodicals to be found in the libraries of a specific country or region, with indication of the libraries which own any given title. Such lists may be general in scope, including titles of periodicals in all fields, or they may be limited to the periodicals in some particular subject or class. There are two main types of union lists: (1) lists of periodicals currently received; and (2) lists of sets, with exact indication of what portion of each set is in the libraries listed. The first type is useful within the region covered for the location of current issues. Information about the periodical is usually very brief, frequently limited to title and place of publication. The second type is more useful for reference, as details are usually given concerning title, changes of title, place of publication, date of founding (and of last volume if publication has ceased), volume numbers, etc., and exact indication of the portions of each set held by the libraries listed.

The principal use of such lists is for reference and interlibrary loan purposes, but they are also useful to catalogers. Even when periodicals are not available for

interlibrary loan, the knowledge of the location of particular volumes or sets either in this country or in another is frequently useful because of the possibility of obtaining microfilms or photographic copies of the material. For this reason union lists of periodicals in foreign countries, as well as those published in this country, are needed by research libraries.

Because of the comprehensiveness of the *Union list of serials* (AF98) and because of the bibliographies of union lists noted below, regional union lists are not included here, although they should be acquired by libraries according to need and locale. Smaller libraries will need the union lists of their own region; large research libraries will need union lists from many parts of this country and abroad.

United States

Bibliography

Bibliography of union lists of serials, comp. by D. C. Haskell and Karl Brown. (In Union list of serials in libraries of the United States and Canada. 2d ed. N.Y., 1943. p.3053–65) **AF96**

Includes union lists of periodicals and of newspapers.

For newspapers, supersedes the list in *American newspapers, 1821–1936*, (AG5).

U.S. Library of Congress. General Reference and Bibliography Division. Union lists of serials; a bibliography. Comp. by Ruth S. Freitag. Wash., 1964. 150p. **AF97**

Brings up to date the bibliography compiled by Haskell and Brown (AF96). Lists more than 1200 union lists, arranged geographically by region and country. Includes both separately published works and lists published in journals or as parts of books.

Lists

✔**Union list of serials** in libraries of the United States and Canada. 3d ed., ed. by Edna Brown Titus. N.Y., Wilson, 1965. 5v. **AF98**

History: 1st ed. 1927 (Supplements, Jan. 1925–Dec. 1932. 2v.); 2d ed. 1943 (Supplements, Jan. 1941–Dec. 1949. 2v.), ed. by Winifred Gregory. (For a history of the *Union list* and its predecessors, *see* Preface by Howard Rovelstad.)

The 1st edition contained entries for some 75,000 serial titles with location of holdings in 225 libraries in the United States and Canada. The 2d edition was enlarged to some 115,000 titles with locations in 650 libraries. The two supplements brought this record up to Dec. 1949 with additional titles. These two editions proved that this comprehensive union list was indispensable in any American library doing reference work with periodicals. Therefore, under the sponsorship of the Joint Committee on the Union List of Serials, with the cooperation of the Library of Congress, and funded by a grant from the Council on Library Resources, Inc., a 3d edition was prepared.

The 3d edition follows closely the pattern of the 2d, listing the entries in the 2d edition, plus those in the two supplements, with the addition of almost 12,000 new titles which began publication before 1950, thus listing more than 156,000 titles, with holdings in 956 cooperating libraries. For the titles acquired by cooperating libraries since the 2d edition and its supplements, additional locations are reported for "significant titles only—titles not commonly held. Additional locations were not to be listed whenever ten or more locations had already been listed in the second edition and supplements unless considered both desirable and necessary—e.g., geographical considerations."—*Introd.*

Each entry gives catalog description of title (under *latest* form of name), a statement of what constitutes a complete set, and indicates changes of title and exact holdings in reporting libraries, with cross references from all changed titles and alternative entries. Includes all types of serial publications but: government publications (except periodicals and monograph series issued by governments); United Nations publications; administrative reports of societies, universities, corporations, etc.; almanacs; gift books; American newspapers; English and other foreign newspapers after 1820; law reports and digests; publications of agricultural and other experiment stations; local religious, labor, and fraternal organizations; boards of trade; chambers of commerce; national and international conferences and congresses, etc.; house organs (unless of technical and scientific value); alumni, undergraduate, and intercollegiate fraternal publications; trench papers; and in general all titles having a highly limited or ephemeral value. —Cf. *Introd*. It was found to be impractical to incorporate entries for titles in the Far Eastern languages.

This edition, covering up to Dec. 1949, will be the last in this form. Continued for periodicals begun after 1950 by *New serial titles* (AF99).

✓ **New serial titles,** 1950–1960; supplement to the Union list of serials, 3d ed. A union list of serials commencing publication after Dec. 31, 1949—prep. under the sponsorship of the Joint Committee on the Union List of Serials. Wash., Lib. of Congress, 1961. 2v. **AF99**

This "cumulation supersedes all earlier annual volumes, as it includes all of the post-1949 serials listed during the 10 years of publication of *New serial titles* and its predecessor, *Serial titles newly received*. The cumulation contains an extensive section on changes in serials . . ."–U.S. Library of Congress. *Information bulletin* 21, no.16:183. April 16, 1962.

Lists periodicals which began publication in 1950 and later, giving place of publication and statement of beginning date (and closing date if pertinent) with record of holdings in more than 700 United States and Canadian libraries.

Continued by monthly issues and by annual cumulations which are self-cumulative through periods of at least five years; e.g., the 1963 volume cumulates all entries 1961–63 and supplements the 10-year cumulation.

A section at the back of each cumulation lists "Changes in Serials" and notes changes for all serials regardless of their beginning date. "These changes include title changes, changes in the name or catalog entry of corporate authors, cessations, suspensions, resumptions and the like."

New serial titles—classed subject arrangement. Jan./May, 1955– . Wash., Lib. of Congress, Card Division, 1955– . Monthly. No cumulations. **AF100**

Arranged by Dewey Decimal Classification. Indicates holdings in the Library of Congress and occasionally in other libraries.

Indiana. University. Library. Union list of little magazines . . . Chicago, Midwest Inter-Lib. Center, 1956. 98p. **AF101**

Subtitle: Showing holdings of 1037 little magazines in the libraries of Indiana University, Northwestern University, Ohio State University, State University of Iowa, University of Chicago, University of Illinois.

Willging, Eugene Paul and **Hatzfeld, Herta.** Catholic serials of the nineteenth century in the United States; a descriptive bibliography and union list. 2d ser. Wash., Catholic Univ. of America Pr., 1959–65. Pts.1–9. (In progress) **AF102**

Contents: 2d ser., pt.1, Minnesota, North Dakota and South Dakota. 68p.; pt.2, Wisconsin. 125p.; pt.3, Illinois. 164p.; pt.4, Indiana. 47p.; pt.5, Pennsylvania. 183p.; pt.6, Iowa. 44p.; pt.7, Michigan. 74p.; pt.8, California. 69p.; pt.9, Missouri. 102p.

The 1st series, which covers those states with briefer his-

tories, has been appearing in the *Records* of the American Catholic Historical Society of Philadelphia since 1954.

Canada

See also Union list of serials in libraries of the United States and Canada (AF98).

Goggio, Emilio, Corrigan, Beatrice [and] **Parker, Jack H.** A bibliography of Canadian cultural periodicals (English and French from colonial times to 1950) in Canadian libraries. Toronto, Univ. of Toronto, Dept. of Italian, Spanish and Portuguese, 1955. 45p. **AF103**

A union list of Canadian periodicals in the humanities and social sciences, which lists the location of the most complete file found and, when files are fragmentary, the libraries that may supply the deficiencies.

France

Paris. Bibliothèque Nationale. Dépt. des Périodiques. Inventaire des périodiques étrangers reçus en France par les bibliothèques et les organismes de documentation en 1960–1961. [3. éd.] Paris, Bibliothèque Nationale, 1962. 636p. (Direction des Bibliothèques de France. Inventaire permanent des périodiques étrangers en cours) **AF104**

1st ed. 1956.

Lists some 30,000 titles of foreign periodicals in all subject fields received in about 2000 libraries and other depositories. Gives title, subtitle, place of publication, and locations of files. No dates.

—— Périodiques slaves en caractères cyrilliques; état des collections en 1950. Paris, Bibliothèque Nationale, 1956. 2v. (Its Catalogue collectif des périodiques conservés dans les bibliothèques de Paris et dans les bibliothèques universitaires de France) **AF105**

A union list of periodical holdings of 46 libraries of Paris and of French universities. Russian, Ukrainian, Belorussian, Bulgarian, and Serbian titles are listed in one alphabet. Newspapers are excluded. Slavic periodicals in Latin characters will be listed in the general section of the Bibliothèque Nationale's *Catalogue collectif des périodiques* now in progress (processed only, and not yet generally available).

Germany

Bruhn, Peter. Gesamtverzeichnis russischer und sowjetischer Periodika und Serienwerke; hrsg. von Werner Philipp. Wiesbaden, in Kommission bei O. Harrassowitz, [1960–64]. Lfg. 1–8. (Berlin [West Berlin], Freie Universität. Osteuropa Inst. Bibliographische Mitteilungen. 3) (In progress) **AF106**

Contents: Bd.1, A–N. 1962. 663p.; [Bd.2¹], Lfg. 8, O–Pozy.

Locates Russian and Soviet periodicals in libraries of the Federal German Republic and West Berlin. Notable for its broad chronological, linguistic, and geographical coverage. Includes newspapers, yearbooks, almanacs, and numbered series; also publications of official and semiofficial Russian and Soviet groups abroad.

Gesamtverzeichnis ausländischer Zeitschriften und Serien 1939–1958 (GAZS). Bearb. und hrsg. von der Staatsbibliothek der Stiftung Preussischer Kulturbesitz. Wiesbaden, Harrassowitz, 1959– . (In progress) **AF107**

Sponsoring body varies.

Hauptband, 1939–1958. I. Teil, Lfg. 1–10, A–Elh; Lfg. 11–18, Eli–Mater.

An extensive list of non-German periodicals, with holdings in German libraries indicated in detail. Unfortunately, there is no key to the symbols used to indicate libraries; for this, reference must be made to Wolfgang Voigt. *Sigelverzeichnis für die Bibliotheken der Bundesrepublik Deutschland* . . . Wiesbaden, Harrassowitz, 1960.

Previous ed.: *Gesamtverzeichnis der ausländischen Zeitschriften (GAZ) 1914–1924.* Berlin, Staatsbibliothek, 1929. 784p.

Great Britain

British union-catalogue of periodicals; a record of the periodicals of the world, from the seventeenth century to the present day, in British libraries. Ed. for the Council of the British Union-Catalogue of Periodicals by James D. Stewart, with Muriel E. Hammond and Erwin Saenger. N.Y., Academic Pr.; London, Butterworths Scientific Publs., 1955–58. 4v. **AF108**

Lists more than 140,000 titles contained in about 440 libraries with indication of holdings; an important addition to union lists. Includes many periodicals not in the *Union list of serials* (AF98), and the difference in form of entry makes possible a different approach in identifying titles.

Periodicals are listed under the first word of the title, not an article, except that periodicals issued by an organization are entered under the name of the organization unless the title is specific in itself. All periodicals are entered under their *earliest* known names, followed by particulars of all changes of name in chronological sequence. References are given from all later names to the original name. Similarly all academies, societies, and other organizations are entered under their *original* names, with particulars of alternative names, and all changes of organization. References from all variants are given to the original name.

The alphabetization is by the words printed in heavy type; all minor words, articles, prepositions, conjunctions, etc. are printed but ignored. Variant spellings such as "Bollettino" and "Bullettino" are amalgamated. Other details are explained at the beginning of v.1.

All locations for commonly held periodicals are not necessarily given, but in the case of rare periodicals all reported holdings, fragmentary or otherwise, have been included.

Supersedes for most purposes the *Union catalogue of the periodical publications in the university libraries of the British isles.* London, Nat. Central Lib., 1937. 712p.

—— Supplement to 1960. Ed. for the Council of the British Union-Catalogue of Periodicals by James D. Stewart with Muriel E. Hammond and Erwin Saenger. London, Butterworths, 1962. 991p.

Includes entries for new periodicals reported as first appearing since publication of the main volumes, some expanded or amended entries, and some entries for earlier periodicals not previously reported.

British union-catalogue of periodicals, incorporating World list of scientific periodicals. New periodical titles. London, Butterworths, 1964– . v.1– . Quarterly. Annual cumulations. **AF109**

Edited for the National Central Library by Kenneth I. Porter.

Aims to list periodicals and serials which began in or after 1960, changed title, began a new series, or ceased publication. Will serve as a continuing supplement to both the *British union-catalogue* and the *World list* (EA42).

Lists library holdings in British libraries.

Italy

Vatican. Biblioteca Vaticana. Catalogo delle pubblicazioni periodiche esistenti in varie biblioteche di Roma e Firenze. Città del Vaticano, 1955. 495p. **AF110**

Pubblicato con la collaborazione dell' Unione Internazionale degli Istituti di Archeologia, Storia e Storia dell' Arte in Roma.

A union list of some 9000 periodicals to be found in 27 libraries of Rome and Florence, indicating holdings.

Philippines

Quezon, Philippines. University of the Philippines. Institute of Public Administration. Inter-Departmental Reference Service. Union list of serials of government agency libraries of the Philippines. Rev. and enl. ed. Manila, 1960. 911p. **AF111**

Includes nearly 8000 entries of foreign and domestic periodicals, representing the holdings of 79 libraries in the Philippines.

The alphabetical list, which gives full information, is followed by a classified list of the serials included.

Portugal

Centro de Documentação Científica. Publicações periódicas estrangeiras inventariadas nas bibliotecas portuguesas. Lisboa, Inst. Para a Alta Cultura, 1948–58. v.1–5. (In progress) **AF112**

[v.1], Ciências médicas. 1948. 198p.; [v.2], Etnologia, ciências naturais, agro-pecuária. 1953. 738p.; [v.3], Matemática, astronomia, física, química, engenharia, indústria. 1955. 389p.; [v.4], Ciências sociais. 1956. 510p.; v.5, Filosofia, religião, pedagogia, filologia, literatura, belas-artes, geografia, história. 1958. 320p.

Projected to be in 6v., with an index. Gives title, place of publication, beginning date, changes of title, etc., with holdings of Portuguese libraries.

South Africa

Catalogue of Union periodicals, ed. for the National Research Council and National Research Board. . . . Johannesburg, 1943–52. v.1–2. (In progress) **AF113**

v.1, Science and technology. 525p. Supplement, 1949. 522p.; v.2, Humanities. 804p.

A union list of periodicals in some 82 libraries in the Union of South Africa. Gives title, place of publication, date of founding, and symbols showing location.

South Asia

Ranganathan, Shiyali Ramamrita [and others]. Union catalogue of learned periodical publications in South Asia. Pub. with the assistance of UNESCO. Delhi, Indian Lib. Assoc.; London, G. Blunt, 1953– . v.1– . (Indian Library Assoc. English ser. 7) **AF114**

v.1, Physical and biological sciences. 390p.

Lists holdings in libraries of Indonesia, Malaya, Thailand, Burma, Ceylon, and India.

Switzerland

Vereinigung Schweizerischer Bibliothekare. Verzeichnis ausländischer Zeitschriften in schweizerischen Bibliotheken. Répertoire des périodiques étrangers reçus par les bibliothèques suisses. 4. Aufl. Hrsg. von der Vereinigung Schweizerischer Bibliothekare, mit Unterstützung des schweizerischen Nationalfonds zur Förderung der wissenschaftlichen Forschung. Redaktion: Schweizerische Landesbibliothek. Bern, 1955. 620p. **AF115**

1st ed. 1904; 2d ed. 1912; 3d ed. 1925.

P.xix–xl contains a list of institutions reporting, with conditions for lending.

Includes some 34,000 titles—published since 1900—found in Swiss libraries. Indicates holdings. The main list is followed by a geographical index.

—— —— Supplement 1–2. Bern, 1957–62.

The supplements add more than 12,000 new titles, as well as provide many corrections and additions.

INDEXES

See name of subject for the indexes to particular subjects, e.g., for the *Education index see* Education; for the *Art index see* Fine Arts, etc.; *see* Pure and Applied Sciences, p.525–26, for comment on abstract journals.

❧ The cardinal points which determine the value of an index to periodicals are:

  I. Scope of index
  II. Length of period covered
  III. Frequency and promptness of publication
  IV. Completeness of the indexing of the material covered
  V. Quality of indexing

To test an index on these points, note the following:

I. Scope of index
  A. Number and kind of periodicals indexed
    1. Are they substantial, established, likely to be of permanent interest?
    2. Are foreign periodicals included?
    3. Is other material indexed, e.g., pamphlets, documents, books, etc.?
  B. The general index
    1. Is there a balanced representation of periodicals in many fields?
    2. How does the selection compare with other indexes covering the same period?
      a) Is there much overlapping?
      b) Does it emphasize particular types of periodicals?
  C. The index devoted to a particular subject or specialized field
    1. How broad or how narrow is the field covered?
    2. How comprehensive for the periodicals in the field?
    3. Does it overlap other special indexes?

II. Length of period covered
  A. By the whole index? (For anything except current work, an index which covers fifty years is more than twice as useful as a similar one covering only twenty-five years.)
  B. By a single volume? (A cumulative volume for five years is easier to use than five annual volumes.)
  C. Is the index still in progress, or has it been discontinued?

III. Frequency and promptness of publication
  A. How often is the index published?
  B. How often does it cumulate?
    1. Monthly, quarterly, or semiannually?
    2. Annually?
    3. Larger cumulations?
  C. Are issues of periodicals indexed promptly upon appearance or is there a considerable lag?

IV. Completeness of the indexing of the material covered
  A. Are all articles in the periodicals included?
  B. What is the basis of selection if only selected articles are indexed? (As the emphasis on articles and subjects changes with the passage of time, the selective index is much less useful than the complete index. Even the nominally complete index may omit short items, notices, etc.)

V. Quality of indexing
  A. Method of arrangement
    1. By author, title, and subject?

    2. By author and subject?
    3. By author only?
    4. By subject only?
    5. By class?
  B. Convenience of arrangement
    1. Alphabetical
      a) In dictionary form, i.e., authors, titles, and subjects in one alphabet?
      b) In one list or several?
    2. Subject
      a) What types of subjects are used? Is it arranged by a consistent system of subject headings and cross references, or is it by catchword subjects?
      b) Is there an author index?
    3. Classed
      a) Is there a table of contents showing arrangement?
      b) Is there an alphabetical index?
    4. Are there adequate cross references?
    5. Is there a list of periodicals indexed?
      a) Does it show abbreviations used?
      b) Does it show volumes indexed?
    6. Typography
      a) Is the type face clear and legible?
      b) Do headings stand out clearly?
      c) Is differentiation shown in types of headings?
    7. Is the general scheme clear, simple, and easy to use?
  C. Fullness of information for each entry. Does it include:
    1. Author's name in full or with initials?
    2. Full title of article?
    3. Title of periodical (or intelligible abbreviation)?
    4. Volume and inclusive paging?
    5. Date?
    6. Other items of information, e.g., illustrations, portraits, bibliographies, etc.?
  D. Accuracy of entry

Bibliography

New York. Public Library. A check list of cumulative indexes to individual periodicals in the New York Public Library, comp. by Daniel C. Haskell. N.Y., Lib., 1942. 370p.   **AF116**

An alphabetical list of thousands of cumulative indexes to periodicals in various languages, mainly of the 19th and 20th centuries, which are available in the New York Public Library, with the addition of a few not available in the library.

"A cumulative index is to be understood as one which indexes at least 3 volumes . . . and makes at least a slight attempt at the classification of the periodical's contents, either an arrangement by authors or by subjects."

International

Bibliographie der fremdsprachigen Zeitschriftenliteratur; Répertoire bibliographique international des revues; International index to periodicals 1911–24, 1925/26–62/ 64. Gautzsch b. Leipzig, Dietrich, 1911–64. v.1–20, n.F.v.1–51 (Internationale Bibliographie der Zeitschriftenliteratur, Abt. B)   **AF117**

An important index similar in general plan and arrangement to the *Bibliographie der deutschen Zeitschriftenliteratur* (AF148). Indexes about 1400 periodicals and general works in the principal non-German languages. The first series is a subject index only; the second series includes, in addition, author indexes. Beginning with n.F. v.4, some supplementary indexing of material earlier than the covering date of the volume is included.

N.F. v.26–29, 1944–48, not yet published.

With its wide coverage, this index is very useful for finding materials in American and English periodicals, as well as in French, Italian, and other European publications. Because of the lack of French periodical indexes, it is particularly important for French articles.

Merged into *Internationale Bibliographie der Zeitschriftenliteratur* (AF118).

✓ **Internationale Bibliographie der Zeitschriftenliteratur** aus allen Gebieten des Wissens, hrsg. von Otto Zeller. Jahrg. 1– . 1963/64– . Osnabrück, Felix Dietrich, 1965– . v.1– . Semiannual volumes (issued in Lfg.). **AF118**

Title also in English and French: *International bibliography of periodical literature covering all fields of knowledge. Bibliographie internationale de la littérature périodique dans tous les domaines de la connaissance.*

A continuation in combined form of the *Bibliographie der deutschen Zeitschriftenliteratur* (AF148) and the *Bibliographie der fremdsprachigen Zeitschriftenliteratur* (AF117).

A subject index to world periodical literature. The subjects are in German with cross references from English and French forms. Author index.

Lfg. 1 is a list of the more than 7600 periodicals consulted.

United States and Great Britain

✓ **Poole's Index to periodical literature,** 1802–81. Rev. ed. Boston, Houghton, 1891 [pref. 1891, c1882]. 2v. **AF119**

—— Supplements, Jan. 1882–Jan. 1, 1907. Boston, Houghton, [c1887–1908]. 5v.

(Repr. by photo-offset: N.Y., Peter Smith, 1938. 6v. in 7)

Originally edited by William Frederick Poole, continued by him and W. I. Fletcher, with the cooperation of members of the American Library Association.

v.1, 1802–81; 1st suppl., 1882–86; 2d suppl., 1887–91; 3d suppl., 1892–96; 4th suppl., 1897–1901; 5th suppl., 1902–1906.

The pioneer index and, though now discontinued, still an important index to American and English periodicals, since it covers the longest period (105 years) and indexes the large total of about 590,000 articles in 12,241 volumes of 479 American and English periodicals. A subject index only; includes *no author entries.* Authors' names appear frequently as entries, but only as subject entries for biographical or critical articles about them. To make intelligent use of the index the student should remember the following four points: (1) no author entries; (2) all articles having a distinct subject are entered under that subject; (3) articles having no subject, i.e., fiction, poems, plays, are entered under the first word of the title not an article; (4) book reviews are entered in two ways: (a) reviews of a book which has a definite subject are entered under subject of the book; (b) reviews of a book which does not have a distinct subject, i.e., a novel, poetry, a drama, are entered under the name of the author reviewed. Approximately complete for the periodicals covered, except in the following respects: (1) very brief articles, notes, etc. are generally omitted; (2) minor book reviews are not included; and (3) some English periodicals noted in v.1 are incompletely indexed because of failure in collaboration between English and American indexers. Information given about each article includes its title, author's name in parentheses when it was known or could be ascertained, abbreviated title of periodical, and volume and page reference. Neither inclusive paging nor date is given, but the date (year only) can be ascertained from the "Chronological Conspectus" in each volume. Indexes principally periodicals of a general nature, but a few selected periodicals on special subjects are included. In general, the work of both indexing and printing is very accurate, with comparatively few typographical errors. For list

of errata *see Bulletin of bibliography* 2:24–25, 40–41, 56–58, 75–76, 133–34; 3:25; 4:11–12, 72. Jan. 1900–Oct. 1905.

Bell, Marion V. and **Bacon, Jean C.** Poole's Index, date and volume key . . . Chicago, Assoc. of College and Reference Libraries, 1957. 61p. (ACRL monograph no.19) **AF120**

In this "key the 479 periodical titles indexed in the various volumes of *Poole's Index* are thrown into one alphabet," and the date is shown, in tabular form, for each volume number, thus obviating the necessity for checking a title in the "Chronological conspectus" in each volume of Poole.

✓ **Nineteenth century readers' guide** to periodical literature, 1890–1899, with supplementary indexing, 1900–1922, ed. by Helen Grant Cushing and Adah V. Morris. . . . N.Y., Wilson, 1944. 2v. **AF121**

An author, subject, and illustrator index to the material in 51 periodicals (1003 volumes) mainly in the period from 1890 to 1899. Some indexing has been done for volumes published after 1899 "in order to make the indexing of each title complete from the year 1890 to the time when it was added to the list of one of the Wilson indexes. Fourteen of the 51 titles indexed have been indexed beyond 1899, some as far as 1922."—*Pref.*

Periodicals indexed are mainly general and literary, but some are included from special fields. Book reviews are listed under author entry only. More than 13,000 poems are listed under Poems by title. Full entry is under author's name. Poems on particular persons, events, etc. are also under subject.

In some 19th-century periodicals the editorial practice was to publish articles anonymously, e.g., in the *Edinburgh review* and the *Quarterly review.* For many of these articles the authors' names have been ascertained from the publishers' records and are indicated in this index.

These two volumes were planned as part of a larger project to cover the whole 19th century by a modern periodical index in dictionary form, but no further volumes have been published.

✓ **Readers' guide to periodical literature** [cumulated], 1900– . N.Y., Wilson, 1905– . v.1– . **AF122**

A cumulative index, made up of three forms or sections: (1) permanent cumulated volumes (since 1935, two years to a volume; previous volumes varied from three to five years); (2) annual volumes, to be used as supplements to the cumulated volumes until superseded by a new permanent volume; and (3) issues published semimonthly, Sept. to June; monthly, July–Aug., cumulating at intervals until the last number of each current volume, which covers 12 months, forms a new annual volume. A complete set to date consists of all permanent cumulated volumes, all annuals since the last cumulated, and the subsequent numbers for the current year.

The *Readers' Guide* began in 1901 as an index for the small library, covering at first only 15 of the more popular periodicals, and gradually extended until in 1903 it absorbed the *Cumulative index* (1896–1903) and in 1911 took over the work of the *Annual library index* (AF128). List of periodicals indexed varies from volume to volume. Beginning with v.19, 1953, the *Readers' Guide:* (a) indexes U.S. periodicals of broad, general, and popular character, and (b) aims to provide a well-balanced selection of U.S. popular, nontechnical magazines representing all the important scientific and subject fields.

A modern index of the best type. Its special features are: (1) full dictionary cataloging of all articles, i.e., their entry under author, subject, and title when necessary; (2) uniformity of entries, due to the fact that the work is done by a few professional indexers rather than by many voluntary collaborators; (3) use of catalog subject headings instead of catchword subject; (4) full information in the references, i.e., exact date and inclusive paging, illustrations, portraits, etc.; (5) cumulative features which keep the index well up to date without multiplying alphabets to be consulted; (6) indexing of all book reviews, through 1904, under author reviewed; after 1905, reviews are generally omitted because included in the *Book review digest* (AA314); (7) indexing, in the second and third cumulated volumes, of some 597 composite books, thus forming an unofficial continuation of the *A.L.A. index . . . to general literature* (BD144). This book indexing was abandoned after 1914.

Abridged readers' guide to periodical literature, July 1935– . Author and subject index to a selected list of periodicals. N.Y., Wilson, 1936– . v.1– .　**AF123**

An index to 24–30 periodicals, designed especially for school and small public libraries unable to afford the regular *Readers' guide* (AF122). For the public library which is growing and can possibly afford the greater expense, the unabridged Guide is the better investment.

Monthly, cumulating; the May number forms a new annual volume cumulating biennially.

Social sciences and humanities index: formerly International index. N.Y., Wilson, 1916– . v.1– .　**AF124**

Title varies: v.1–2, *Readers' guide to periodical literature supplement;* v.3–52, *International index to periodicals* (with various subtitles); v.53, no.1, June 1965– , *Social sciences and humanities index.*

A cumulative index made up of three forms: (1) permanent cumulated volumes covering four, three, or two years; (2) annual volumes; and (3) current numbers issued quarterly, June, Sept., Dec., and March (frequency varies).

An important index for the large or scholarly library. An author and subject index on the same plan as the *Readers' guide* (AF122) but covering periodicals of a different type, i.e., the more scholarly journals in the humanities and social sciences. Coverage varies, with the transfer of titles to new Wilson subject indexes, etc., and the addition of new titles. Before World War II a number of foreign titles were included, e.g., in v.8, 1937–1940, 221 titles were indexed: 125 American, 39 English, 3 Canadian, 25 French, 20 German, 4 Oriental, 2 Italian, 1 each Dutch, Irish, and Spanish. Since the war, foreign titles have been dropped, as well as psychological and scientific periodicals. Now indexes about 175 American and English periodicals.

Subject index to periodicals, 1915–61. London, Lib. Assoc., 1919–62. Annual. (Quarterly, 1954–61, with annual cumulations)　**AF125**

Ceased publication.

An English index, begun in 1915 under the title *Athenaeum subject index;* title changed, 1919, to *Subject index.* The 1915–16 volume has an author-subject arrangement cumulated from preliminary class lists. Continued by class lists 1917–19, in one set, with a general author index, and 1920–22, one year each, with no author index.

1923–25 not published.

The form was changed in 1926, becoming an alphabetical subject list (with no author index) to articles on definite subjects. Magazine fiction, poetry, and essays not on definite subjects were omitted. Until the time of World War II (approximately 1940), it indexed more than 500 periodicals, principally British and American but including a number of foreign titles. Though duplicating much of the indexing in the *Readers' guide* (AF122) and the then *International index* (AF124), it indexed many periodicals not covered by those indexes, including British local-history periodicals, antiquarian society proceedings, etc.

During the war, the indexing of foreign titles was discontinued, and with the 1947 volume (published 1949), the indexing of American periodicals was also dropped. Later volumes indexed more than 300 titles, entirely British.

Regional lists, including entries of local interest, were collected and issued annually by county, with Scotland as a separate issue.

Ceased publication in this form with the 1961 volume. Continued by indexes covering special subjects: *British hu-*

manities index (AF126), *British education index* (CB25), *British technology index* (EA64).

British humanities index, 1962– . London, Lib. Assoc., 1963– . Quarterly, with annual cumulations.　**AF126**

A continuation in part of the *Subject index to periodicals* above. This section to cover "all material relating to the arts and politics." Quarterly issues are by subject only; annuals are in two parts—a subject section and an author section—each giving full indexing information. Indexes some 275 British periodicals including many in local history.

☙ Among the older and more specialized indexes the following are sometimes useful:

Annual literary index, 1892–1904. Including periodicals, American and English; essays, book-chapters, etc. N.Y., Publishers' Weekly, 1893–1905. 13v.　**AF127**

Annual library index, 1905–1910. Including periodicals, American and English; essays, book-chapters, etc. N.Y., Publishers' Weekly, 1906–11. 6v.　**AF128**

These two indexes, although differing slightly in arrangement, served as a continuation of *Poole* (AF119), forming the basis for the five-year supplements. However, they added author indexing never incorporated in *Poole.* Except for this indexing, they were largely superseded by *Poole* and the *A.L.A. index . . . to general literature* (BD144).

Annual magazine subject index, 1907–49; a subject index to a selected list of American and English periodicals and society publications. Boston, Faxon, 1908–52. 43v.　**AF129**

Ceased publication.

v.1, had title *Magazine subject index* and is a basic volume, indexing 79 periodicals (44 from their first issues to Dec. 31, 1907, and 35 for the year 1907).

An index of subjects only, not of authors or titles, except that fiction when included is indexed under author's name. Indexes material with exact references and indication of illustrations, maps, etc. Intended as a supplement to other indexes and so aims to include no periodicals indexed in established indexes. While the list of periodicals is general in character, about half of the titles relate to history, especially local history; the index specializes also in travel, mountaineering, exploration, outdoor life, and fine arts. Indexes all important articles in the periodicals covered but omits short articles, poetry, and most fiction, though continued stories and short stories by notable writers are included.

Includes many local-history titles, especially transactions of local-history societies indexed in Griffin, *Bibliography of American historical societies* (DB15). As these are often indexed back to the date when Griffin stopped, the index constitutes an informal continuation of Griffin. The only exception to the rule not to index material included elsewhere is in the case of these history periodicals.

The entries in the 43v. are cumulated into one alphabet in:

Cumulated magazine subject index, 1907–1949; a cumulation of the F. W. Faxon Company's Annual magazine subject index . . . Cumulated by G. K. Hall & Co. Boston, Hall, 1964. 2v.　**AF130**

A photographic reproduction of the actual entries originally printed in the *Annual magazine subject index,* clipped and rearranged in one alphabetical sequence. For coverage *see* AF129.

Catholic periodical index; a cumulative author and subject index to a selected list of Catholic periodicals, 1930– . N.Y., Catholic Lib. Assoc., 1939– . Quarterly, with biennial cumulations.　**AF131**

1930–33 forms the first permanent volume in a series of four-year cumulations to June 1948, thereafter biennial.

Indexes, by author and subject, 50 to more than 200 periodicals, published mainly in the United States, Canada, England, and Ireland.

Index to little magazines, 1948– . Denver, Colo., Alan Swallow, 1949– . Annual; biennial. **AF132**

The first issue for 1948 indexes 31 titles; the volume for 1962/63 indexes 51 titles. "A selective list limited to primarily literary periodicals of high quality and with a degree of permanence." Coverage varies from volume to volume.

Index to selected periodicals received in the Hallie Q. Brown Library. Decennial cumulation, 1950–59. Ed., Charlotte W. Lytle. Boston, G. K. Hall, 1961. 501p. **AF133**

Title varies: 1950–Spring 1959, *Index to selected Negro periodicals*.

Supersedes annual volumes for the period. Continued by quarterly and annual issues, compiled jointly by the staffs of the Hallie Q. Brown Library and the Schomburg Collection, New York Public Library.

Covers Negro periodicals not indexed elsewhere. An author-subject index. Book reviews are listed under that heading.

Library Association. Wales and Monmouthshire Branch. Subject index to Welsh periodicals. v.1–6, 1931–1941/45. Swansea, 1934–57. (In progress) **AF134**

Indexes periodicals (excluding newspapers and some denominational publications) published in Wales, in both Welsh and English, and periodicals published elsewhere which include material of Welsh and general Celtic interest.

Review of reviews. Index to the periodicals of 1890–1902. [v.1]–13. London, N.Y., Review of Reviews, 1891–1903. 13v. Annual. **AF135**

Title varies: v.1, *Annual index of periodicals and photographs for 1890;* v.2–4, *Index to the periodical literature of the world*.

Primarily a subject index, but contains a fair number of author entries also, especially in the later volumes. Indexes material under broad subjects and gives full bibliographical information with reference to the volume, month, and page of the *Review of reviews* where a summary or other notice of the article is to be found. Indicates maps and illustrations. Number of periodicals indexed varies from 117 in 1890 to 195 in 1902. Principally useful because it covers many English periodicals (about 100 in the later volumes) not indexed in *Poole* (AF119).

Subject index to children's magazines. Madison 5, Wis., 301 Palomino Lane, 1949– . v.1– . Monthly (except June and July). Semiannual cumulations in Feb. and Aug. **AF136**

Editors vary.

Indexes by subject some 40–50 magazines useful to elementary and junior high libraries.

Australia

Australian periodical index, 1944–1960/63. Sydney, Trustees of the Pub. Lib. of New South Wales, the Mitchell Lib., 1950–[66?]. **AF137**

Title varies. Cumulates under title *Index to periodicals*. Annual, with quadrennial cumulations (slightly irregular). Will cease publication after the 1960/63 cumulation.

Belgium

Bibliographie de Belgique: 2ème partie, Sommaire des périodiques, 1897–1914. Bruxelles, Van Oest, 1897–1914. **AF138**

Title and frequency vary. 1899–1911, is third part of *Biblio-*

graphie de Belgique and has title *Bulletin des sommaires;* 1912–13, is second part and has title *Sommaire des périodiques;* 1899–1911, frequency varied, monthly (sometimes bimonthly or quarterly) with annual author index; 1912–14, semiannual with annual author and subject indexes. Each number is a classed subject index arranged by the Universal Decimal Classification numbers. Indexes a large number of periodicals, giving fairly full information for each article. A cumbersome but usable index supplying material not easily found in any other way.

Discontinued 1915, because of World War I. Continued by the following:

—— 2ème partie, Bulletin mensuel des articles de fond parus dans les revues belges. Janv., 1921–25. Bruxelles, Service de la Bibliographie de Belgique, 1921–25. n.s. v.47–51. Monthly. **AF139**

No more published.

Roemans, Robert. Bibliographie van de moderne Vlaamsche literatuur, 1893–1930. 1. deel. Kortrijk, Steenlandt, 1930–34. Afl. 1–10. **AF140**

No more published.

1. deel: De Vlaamsche tijdschriften.

An index to the literary articles in Flemish periodicals, indexed periodical by periodical with cumulated author indexes to poetry, prose, and critical articles.

Continued by:

—— and **Assche, Hilda van.** Bibliografie van de Vlaamse tijdschriften. Hasselt, Heideland, 1960–64. Reeks I–II. (In progress) **AF141**

Contents: Reeks I, Vlaamse literaire tijdschriften van 1930 tot en met 1958. Afl. 1–7; Reeks II, Vlaamse niet-literaire tijdschriften van 1886 tot en met 1961. Afl. 2– .

Reeks I indexes literary periodicals, poetry, prose, theater, and critical articles; some issues are devoted to a single periodical, some index several. Reeks II indexes periodicals in the fields of linguistics, philology, folklore, history, etc.

Bulgaria

Letopis na periodichniia pechat; mesecher bibliografski biuletin na statii ot spisaniia, vestnitsi i sbornitsi. god. 1– . ian. 1952– . Sofia, 1952– . Monthly. (Bulgarski Bibliografski Inst. Elin Pelin) **AF142**

Monthly issues arranged by classified scheme with author indexes. Annual cumulated author index.

Canada

Canadian periodical index, 1928–47. Toronto, Public Libraries Branch, Ontario Dept. of Educ., 1928–47. **AF143**

Publisher varies.

Set consists of: 1928–30. Quarterly issues; 1931 (pub. 1932). Annual cumulation; 1932. Quarterly issues; 1933–37. Not published; 1938–47. Annual volumes (being cumulations of the quarterly indexes published in the *Ontario library review*).

An author and subject index to Canadian periodicals, most of which are not indexed in other periodical indexes. Covers a varying number of titles, usually between 30 and 40.

Continued by:

Canadian index to periodicals and documentary films; an author and subject index, Jan. 1948–Dec. 1959. Ed. by Margaret E. Wodehouse [and] Ruth Mulholland. Ottawa, Canadian Lib. Assoc., 1962. 1180p. **AF144**

Added title page in French: *Index de périodiques et de films documentaires canadiens.*

Cumulation, which supersedes annual volumes, published as *Canadian index; a guide to Canadian periodicals and films.*

A bilingual index by author and subject to some 60 Canadian periodicals. Subject headings are in English, but French cross references are given to the English headings. Includes documentary films. Book reviews are listed under the form heading "Book reviews."

Kept to date by monthly and annual volumes. 1960–63. v.13–16.

Title change with v.17 as follows:

Canadian periodical index. Index de périodiques canadiens. v.17– . Ottawa, Canadian Lib. Assoc., 1964– . Monthly, with annual and quinquennial cumulations.   **AF145**

The monthly issues are a subject index to Canadian periodicals. The cumulations are to be by author and subject and follow the plan of the *Canadian index to periodicals* above.

The listing of films formerly in this index has been taken over by the National Library and will appear in *Canadiana* (AA402).

Denmark

Copenhagen. Kommunebiblioteker. Danske blandede Tidsskrifter, 1855–1912; indholdsoversigt til 27 danske Tidsskrifter, udarb. af Ellen Bruun [and others]; red. af Svend Thomsen. København, Bianco Lunos, 1928–29. 2v.   **AF146**

A classified subject index of articles contained in 27 general periodicals, arranged by a decimal classification, with author and alphabetical subject indexes to the classified part. Useful as supplying indexing of some material earlier than that covered by the more comprehensive *Dansk Tidsskrift-Index,* 1915– (AF147). Later indexing of 5 of the 27 periodicals covered is given in the *Dansk Tidsskrift-Index.*

Dansk Tidsskrift-Index, 1– , 1915– , udg. af Statens Bibliotekstilsyn. København, Dansk Bibliografisk Kontor, 1916– . v.1– .   **AF147**

Publisher varies.

A classified subject index. Later volumes include subject and author indexes. Number of periodicals indexed varies: v.1, 165; v.48 (1962), about 300 (Danish and other Scandinavian).

Each volume contains a section of *Personal Historie* listing biographical articles.

Germany

Bibliographie der deutschen Zeitschriftenliteratur, mit Einschluss von Sammelwerken. . . . 1896–64. Gautzsch b. Leipzig, 1897–64. v.1–128. Semiannual. (Internationale Bibliographie der Zeitschriftenliteratur, Abt. A)   **AF148**

Title varies.

A comprehensive index valuable because of the large number of important German periodicals, transactions, yearbooks, and other composite works indexed. Semiannual volumes with no cumulation necessitate the consultation of many alphabets. Except in the case of v.34–35, 40, 40a–41, and 43–46, for which combined author indexes in three separate volumes have been published, each volume consists of: (1) a subject index arranged alphabetically by rather large subjects, giving for each article indexed its title, author's name in parentheses when known, reference to periodical by key number (instead of title), page, and sometimes volume; and (2) an author index to the subject index (omitted in some volumes). The number of periodicals indexed is large, ranging from 275 in the first volume to some 4500 in later volumes. The retrospective indexing of the *Ergänzungsbände* carries the work back to 1861. Important in university work and in large libraries which have many German periodicals, but not generally recommended for other libraries. Often

especially important for biography because it indexes many yearbooks of learned societies containing obituary notices.

In 1965 merged into *Internationale Bibliographie der Zeitschriftenliteratur* (AF118).

—— Gesamt-register der Schlagworte aus Bd.66–75, 76–85. Leipzig, Dietrich, 1940–43. 2v.

—— Gesamt-register der Schlagworte zu Abt. A. *Bibliographie der deutschen Zeitschriftenliteratur.* Bd.97–113, und Abt. B. *Bibliographie der fremdsprachigen Zeitschriftenliteratur,* n.F., Bd.30–39. Osnabrück, Dietrich, 1957. 533p.

A combined catchword index to Abt. A and Abt. B (AF148, AF117) in one alphabet.

—— Ergänzungsband 1– . Gautzsch b. Leipzig, Dietrich, 1908– . v.1– .

Numbered in set as v.22A, 24A, 28A, 30A, 32A, 33A, 35A, 35B, 36B, 37A, 39B, 41A, 42A, 72A, 78A, 80A, 82A.

Contents: Ergbd. 1, 1896–98; 2, 1896–1908; 3, 1893–95; 4, 1891–92; 5, 1889–90; 6, 1911–13; 7, 1887–88; 8, 1913–14; 9, 1885–86; 10, 1914–15; 11, 1883–84; 12, 1881–82; 13, 1915–17; 14, 1879–81; 15, 1876–78; 16, 1873–75; 17, 1870–73; 18, 1868–70; v.19, 1865–67; v.20, 1861–67.

Germany, East

Gesamtinhaltsverzeichnis der wissenschaftlichen Zeitschriften der Universitäten und Hochschulen der Deutschen Demokratischen Republik. 1.–2. Fünfjahrverzeichnis, 1951/52–1955/56; 1956/57–1961. Berlin, 1959–63. 2v.   **AF149**

Indexes the periodicals issued by selected universities and Hochschulen of Eastern Germany; the first five-year index covers 15 of these institutions, and the second, 22.

Classified arrangement with author index.

Great Britain

See United States and Great Britain, p.145.

Hungary

Magyar folyóiratok repertóriuma; Repertorium bibliographicum periodicorum hungaricorum. Kiadja az Országos Széchényi Könyvtár. A magyar nemzeti bibliográfia melléklete. 1– füzet, Jan.–Jun. 1946– . Budapest, 1946– . Monthly.   **AF149a**

A supplement to *Magyar nemzeti bibliográfia* (AA540). Originally appeared quarterly.

A monthly classified index to about 125 periodicals, with monthly and annual author indexes.

India

Guide to Indian periodical literature. March 1964– . Gurgaon (PB), India, Prabhu Book Service, 1964– . v.1– . Monthly, with annual cumulation.   **AF150**

A subject guide to articles published in selected Indian and foreign periodicals.

India (Republic). Parliament. Abstracts and index of articles, v.1, no.1, Jan. 1958–62. New Delhi, Lok Sabha Secretariat, 1958–62. Monthly.   **AF151**

Incorporates the "Abstracting Service" and the "Monthly List of Selected Articles," which were issued as separate periodicals.

In two parts: pt.1, Abstracts, giving "digests of important articles on political, economic, social, legal, parliamentary, and other subjects"; pt.2, an index to the contents of periodicals and newspapers received in the Parliament Library.

Ceased publication and merged with its *Abstracts of reports* to form its *Abstracts and index of reports and articles* (AH67).

Italy

Italy. Parlamento. Camera dei Deputati. Biblioteca. Catalogo metodico degli scritti contenuti nelle pubblicazioni periodiche italiane e straniere. Parte 1. Scritti biografici e critici. Roma, 1885–1935. 10v. and index.   **AF152**

For full information *see* AJ6.

Italy. Provveditorato Generale dello Stato. Pubblicazioni edite dallo stato o col suo concorso: Spoglio dei periodici e delle opere collettive 1901– . Roma, Libreria dello Stato, 1926– . v.1– .   **AF153**

Basic work, 1901–25, 2v. 1926; 1926–30, 2v. 1931; 1931–35, 2v. 1937; 1936–40, 2v. 1942.

A subject index to more than 200 Italian periodicals and collected works which are either government publications or issued under government auspices or aid. Each volume in two parts: (1) Index to biographical and critical articles arranged alphabetically by name of person written about, and (2) Subject index, arranged by large classes, e.g., agriculture, archaeology, etc., with subdivisions under each, and an alphabetical index of small topics referring to the large classes. Entries in the biographical section are repeated in the classed section. Information given about each article is full, including author and title of article, and title, volume, inclusive paging, and date of the volume in which it appears.

Latin America

Índice general de publicaciones periódicas latino-americanas. Humanidades y ciencias sociales. Index to Latin American periodicals. Humanities and social sciences. v.1, 1961– . Boston, Hall, 1962– . Quarterly, with annual cumulations.   **AF154**

Prepared by the Columbus Memorial Library of the Pan American Union and the New York Public Library. Ed., Jorge Grossmann.

"A guide to articles appearing in selected Latin American periodicals in the humanities and social sciences."—*Introd.* More than 300 periodicals are listed, though less than half are completely indexed. The index offers both author and subject approach, subject headings appearing in Spanish, with an auxiliary list of corresponding English terms.

Leavitt, Sturgis E. Revistas hispanoamericanas: índice bibliográfico, 1843–1935. Recopilado . . . con la colaboración de Madaline W. Nichols y Jefferson Rea Spell. Santiago de Chile, Fondo Histórico y Bibliográfico José Toribio Medina, 1960. 589p.   **AF155**

"Homenaje al Sesquicentenario de la independencia nacional, 1810–1960."

A classified index to the material in 56 Spanish-American periodicals, primarily in literature, linguistics, and folklore. Name index. An appendix lists those libraries in the United States holding complete sets of the periodicals indexed.

Pan American Union. Columbus Memorial Library. Index to Latin American periodical literature, 1929–1960. Boston, Hall, 1962. 8v.   **AF156**

Photoreproduced from catalog cards, this set is compiled from index cards prepared at the Library of the Pan American Union and includes "approximately 250,000 entries of authors, subjects and other secondary entries. Until 1951 . . . only entries by subject were made, except for well-known authors and authors of articles having literary value."—*Pref.* Indexing is on a broad, selective basis from an estimated 3000 different periodical titles mainly of Latin-American origin.

Netherlands

Nijhoff's Index op de Nederlandse en Vlaamse periodieken. 'sGravenhage, Nijhoff, 1910– . v.1– . Monthly.   **AF157**

Title varies.

The number of periodicals indexed varies from 19 in the earlier volumes to more than 60.

Monthly index to general periodicals, including a few newspapers. Each number contains authors and subjects in one alphabet with a separate list of book reviews at the end. No cumulations, but beginning with the volume for 1925, there is an annual author index and a catchword subject index.

New Zealand

Index to New Zealand periodicals, 1940–49. Wellington, New Zealand Lib. Assoc., 1940–50.   **AF158**

1940 issue, prep. by the Otago Branch of the Library Association as a preliminary index to 12 periodicals; v.1–2, 1941–42, issued quarterly, cumulated annually; v.3, no.1, Jan.–June 1943; publication suspended July 1943–Dec. 1946; 1947–49 published semiannually with annual cumulation. Indexes 38 periodicals.

Continued by:

Index to New Zealand periodicals and Current national bibliography of New Zealand books and pamphlets, 1950– . Wellington, New Zealand Lib. Assoc., 1951– . Annual.

The first volume to include the *Current national bibliography*.

The periodical index sections for 1958–60 inclusive were cumulated into one volume (pub. 1961) with the *Current national bibliography* for 1960, but the national bibliography sections were not cumulated. This is a subject index with cross references from author entries to the subject listing.

1961–62 also cumulated into one volume.

Norway

Deichmanske Bibliotek. Register til norges tidsskrifter, v.1–2. Kristiania, Cammermeyer, 1908–11. 2v.   **AF159**

Contents: v.1, Topografi; v.2, Norsk biografi.

Arranged by subject, each volume indexing one subject. v.1 (1908) indexes the topographical articles in 75 periodicals of varying dates from about the beginning of the 19th century to 1907; v.2 indexes nearly 15,000 biographical articles in more than 700 periodicals of the 19th and the first part of the 20th century, giving not only references to periodicals, but also dates of birth and death and very brief characterization for each name indexed. The list of periodicals included in v.2 furnishes a nearly complete bibliography of Norwegian periodicals.

Norsk tidsskriftindex, 1918– , systematisk fortegnelse over indholdet av norske periodiske skrifter. Oslo, Steenske Forlag, 1919–35; Fabritius, 1936– . v.1–   **AF160**

Subtitle varies.

A classified subject index with an alphabetical subject index to some 250 Norwegian periodicals.

Issued in annual volumes, with a general title page, list of abbreviations and periodicals indexed, and alphabetical subject index to the classed lists for v.1–3 (1918–20); v.4–8 (1921–25); v.9–13 (1926–30); v.14–18 (1931–35); v.19–23 (1936–40); v.24–25 (1941–42); v.26–28 (1943–45); v.29–33 (1946–50).

Beginning with v.18, 1935, the publisher changed from Steenske Forlag to Fabritius & Sønner, and the index became a part of the bibliographical series *Norsk bibliografisk bibliotek*, v.18 being numbered as bd. 1, hft.5 in that series (with retrospective numbering of v.14–17 as bd.1, hft.1–4), and v.19–23 as bd.4. The detailed indexing of articles of individual biography, formerly a feature of the index under the heading *"Personalhistorie,"* is omitted there from 1931– and included, instead, in a separate series, the first volume of which is *Biografiske artikler i norske tidsskrifter 1931–35,* numbered as bd.2, hft.3 of the *Norsk bibliografisk bibliotek* (AJ215).

Philippines

Index to Philippine periodicals. Manila, Inter-Departmental Reference Service, Inst. of Public Administration, Univ. of the Philippines, 1956– . v.1– . Semiannual, with annual cumulations. **AF161**

Frequency varies. Indexes from 50 to 120 periodicals, by author, subject and distinctive title, in one alphabet.

Selected Philippine periodical index. Jan. 1956– . (In Silliman journal, v.3– . Quarterly) **AF162**

Title and editors vary. Since 1962, edited by Gorgonio D. Siega and E. P. Bañas.

An author-subject index to 35–40 Philippine periodicals in English.

South Africa

Index to South African periodicals, 1940–49, 1950–59. Johannesburg, Pub. Lib., 1953–62. 4v.; 3v. **AF163**

Added title page in Afrikaans.

1940/49,v.1–2, Subject list of English articles; v.3, Subject list of Afrikaans articles; v.4, Author section. Cumulates and supersedes annual volumes for the period. 1950/59, arranged in single alphabetical sequence combining author and subject entries.

—— v.20– . 1960– . Annual.

Issued annually with projected 10-year cumulations.

Indexes some 300 South African periodicals: the scholarly and scientific quite fully, others selectively.

Spain

Colección de índices de publicaciones periódicas, dirigida por Joaquín de Entrambasaguas. Madrid, Inst. "Nicolás Antonio" del Consejo Superior de Investigaciones Científicas, 1946–53. v.1–16. **AF164**

Each volume is an index to an individual periodical, usually from the 19th century. In some cases extracts from articles or annotations are included. Usually gives: name, place, subject, title, first-line index, and a selection of plates of illustrations in each issue.

Spain. Consejo Superior de Investigaciones Científicas. Biblioteca General. Materiales de investigación: índice de artículos de revistas (1939–1949), pub. bajo la dirección de A. Tortajada y C. de Amaniel. Madrid, 1952. 2v. **AF165**

Arranged alphabetically by author and subject. Indexes some 125 periodicals in both the humanities and the sciences.

Turkey

Türkiye makaleler bibliyoğrafyasī. Bibliographie des articles parus dans les périodiques turcs. Mart 1952– . Ankara, Türk Tarih Kurumu Basimevi, 1952– . (Millî Kütüphane Bibliyoğrafya Enstitüsü. Yayinlari. Bibliothèque Nationale, Inst. de Bibliographie. Publ.) Quarterly. **AF166**

Place, publisher, series, and frequency vary.

Text in Turkish and French.

Indexes articles in periodicals, annuals, and society publications appearing in Turkey. Arrangement is classified, with annual author index. All titles are given in both languages, and very brief annotations are given in some cases. Reviews are included.

Yugoslavia

Bibliografija jugoslavije: članci i prilozi u časopisima, novinama i zb'irnim delima, Jan./Mart, 1950– . Beograd, Bibliografski Inst. FNRJ, [1950–]. Quarterly. **AF167**

A classified index to Yugoslav periodicals in all fields. Beginning with the first issue of 1952, it appears in sections, of which Series A covers social sciences; Series B, natural and applied sciences; Series C, philology, art, sport, literature, music.

Bibliografija rasprava, članaka i književnih radova u časopisima Narodne Republike Hrvatske, 1945/46– . Zagreb, Jugoslovenska Akademija Znanosti i Umjetnosti, 1948– . Annual. **AF168**

Index to Croatian periodicals; classified, with alphabetical indexes by author and subject. The first volume covers the years 1945 and 1946; subsequent issues are annual.

Bibliografija rasprava, članaka i književnih radova. [Glavni redaktor: Mate Ujević] Zagreb, Leksikografski Zavod, 1956–63. v.1–7. (In progress) **AF169**

A retrospective periodical index, planned to be in 25v., to form a comprehensive record of articles published in Yugoslavia since 1800 in magazines, newspapers, yearbooks, and collections. Arrangement is by large classifications with indexes. The first 7v. cover various categories of literature.

A G

Newspapers

Newspapers are important in certain lines of reference work. Current issues are helpful on questions of the day, events, policies, opinion, politics, personalities, and many others. Back volumes serve the same purpose for the contemporary history of an earlier period, and often record details of a situation, or information local in its application, that are not found in general reference books. Bound files of newspapers have always been valuable additions to the reference equipment of a library that could afford them. However, they created many problems because of the difficulties and expense of binding, shelving, and preserving them, particularly because of the rapid deterioration of newsprint. In recent years many files of important papers have been microfilmed, and in this form are available for purchase or interlibrary loan. For a record of newspapers available on microfilm, *see* the checklist by George A. Schwegmann, listed below (AG12).

To make intelligent use of newspapers the reference worker needs the same type of reference aids that he needs for periodicals, i.e.: (1) indexes, (2) bibliographies, and (3) lists of holdings of other libraries. These differ in some ways from the corresponding aids for periodicals. For example, no general index to newspapers similar to the *Readers' guide* (AF122) is available. Such a work would be a practical impossibility, and it is not so necessary as an index to periodicals. Since most metropolitan newspapers publish reports of important events at approximately the same time, the date of an event is the clue needed, and an index of dates, or an index of one newspaper, will furnish a workable index to most newspapers for subjects of general interest—but not, of course, for purely local or special articles, editorials, and many obituaries.

The most used newspaper indexes in American libraries are the *New York Times index* (AG32) and the *Times* (London) *index* (AG37).

BIBLIOGRAPHIES AND UNION LISTS

Many directories list both newspapers and periodicals, and such directories are listed under Periodicals—Bibliography, p.133.

Local union lists, and union lists of papers in single libraries, have been omitted here. For lists of these, *see* Theodore Besterman. *A world bibliography of bibliographies.* 3d. ed. 1955–56 (AA13), under "Periodical publications," v.3, col.3008–14, 3026–29; for lists of newspapers of particular states, *see ibid.*, col.3119–30.

International

Internationaler Pressekatalog; Handbuch der Zeitungswerbung in Europa. 1961/62– . Hrsg.: J. Schäfer und R. Wittgen. Frankfurt am Main, Verlag J. Schäfer, 1961– . v.1– . il. **AG1**

In German, English, and French. Lists about 3000 newspapers from more than 20 European countries with information on advertising practices.

Merrill, John C., Bryan, Carter R. and **Alisky, Marvin.** The foreign press. [Baton Rouge], Louisiana State Univ. Pr., 1964. 256p. **AG2**

1st edition, 1959, had title *Handbook of the foreign press.*

After an introductory section surveying the general picture, discusses the situation of the press, country by country, giving a general survey with statistics, and information about leading newspapers, etc. Selected source materials, p.243–49.

U.S. Library of Congress. Periodicals Division. Check-list of foreign newspapers in the Library. . . . newly comp. under the direction of H. S. Parsons. Wash., Govt. Prt. Off., 1929. 209p. **AG3**

1st ed. 1904.

Arranged geographically by place of publication, and under each place alphabetically by title of newspaper. Gives for each paper exact statement of Library of Congress files. Includes almost 2700 titles, published in 79 countries in 21 languages.

U.S. Library of Congress. Serial Division. Postwar foreign newspapers; a union list. Wash., 1953. 231p. **AG4**

Includes Russian but not Latin-American newspapers. (The latter will be covered in a union list to be published by Pan American Union. Library.) Arrangement is alphabetical by country, with a title index. Frequency and date of establishment are given where known. Reports the holdings of 76 libraries in the United States.

United States

See also Ayer's Directory (AF13); *Editor and publisher* (AF14); *Working press of the nation* (AF19).

American newspapers, 1821–1936; a union list of files available in the United States and Canada, ed. by Winifred Gregory under the auspices of the Bibliographical Society of America. N.Y., Wilson, 1937. 791p. **AG5**

A union list of first importance which lists the exact holdings of newspapers in nearly 5700 depositories, such as libraries, county courthouses, newspaper offices, and private collections. In addition to the main union list, contains (p.787–89) "A bibliography of union lists of newspapers," compiled by Karl Brown and Daniel C. Haskell.

Arndt, Karl J. R. and **Olson, May E.** German-American newspapers and periodicals, 1732–1955: history and bibliography. Heidelberg, Quelle & Meyer, 1961. 794p. il. (Deutsche Presseforschung. 3) (Distr. in U.S. by Clark Univ. Pr., Worcester, Mass.) **AG6**

Added title page and introduction in German: *Deutsch-amerikanische Zeitungen und Zeitschriften.*

Arranged by state and then by city; lists some 5000 German-American newspapers and periodicals published in this country from 1732 to 1955, giving, whenever possible, changes of titles, names of editors and publishers, frequency, sometimes circulation, size, etc. Occasionally brief annotations are included. Locations of files are indicated in American and European libraries.

Brayer, Herbert O. Preliminary guide to indexed newspapers in the United States, 1850–1900. (Repr. from the Mississippi Valley historical review 33, no.2: 237–58. Sept. 1946) **AG7**

Arranged by state and then by library or other depository. Indicates indexes to files of newspapers, dates covered, and physical nature of index, i.e., cards, manuscript, or printed.

Brigham, Clarence S. History and bibliography of American newspapers, 1690–1820. Worcester, Mass., Amer. Antiquarian Soc., 1947. 2v. (Repr.: Hamden, Conn., Archon, 1962. 2v. [incl.] Additions and corrections) **AG8**

Originally published in the *Proceedings* of the American Antiquarian Society, 1913–27. This cumulated edition, a work of the first importance, includes corrections, additions, and more detailed listings. Arranged alphabetically by state and town, it lists 2120 newspapers published between 1690 and 1820 with indication of location of files in all parts of the country. Historical notes for each paper give title, date of establishment, exact dates of changes of titles, names of editors and publishers, frequency, etc.

The bibliography is followed by lists of libraries and private owners, an index of titles, and an index of printers.

With *American newspapers,* 1821–1936 (AG5), this forms a comprehensive record of American newspaper files from 1690–1936.

——— Additions and corrections. 1961. 50p. (Repr. from the *Proceedings* of the American Antiquarian Society, April 1961)

Hebrew Union College—Jewish Institute of Religion. American Jewish Periodical Center. Jewish newspapers and periodicals on microfilm, available at the American Jewish Periodical Center. Cincinnati, 1957. 56p. **AG9**

The Center is attempting to microfilm every Jewish newspaper in any language, published in the United States up to 1925, with a selected number after that date. These films are available on interlibrary loan.

——— 1st supplement by Herbert C. Zafren. 1960. 28p.

North, Simon Newton Dexter. History and present condition of the newspaper and periodical press of the United States, with a catalogue of the publications of the census year. Wash., Govt. Prt. Off., 1884. 446p. maps. (U.S. Census Office. 10th Census. v.8)   **AG10**

A history of the newspaper and periodical press 1639–1880, with maps and statistical tables; a catalog of periodical publications issued during the census year June 1, 1879—May 31, 1880; and a chronological history.

U.S. Library of Congress. Periodicals Division. Check list of American 18th century newspapers in the Library of Congress, originally comp. by John Van Ness Ingram. New ed. rev. and enl. under the direction of Henry S. Parsons. Wash., Govt. Prt. Off., 1936. 401p.   **AG11**

1st ed. 1912.

Arranged alphabetically by state, subdivided by town. Gives for each newspaper: date of establishment; changes in title; names of printers, publishers, and editors; and a statement of the Library of Congress file. Title index, and index to printers, publishers, and editors.

U.S. Library of Congress. Union Catalog Division. Newspapers on microfilm. 5th ed. Comp. under the direction of George A. Schwegmann. Wash., 1963. 305p.   **AG12**

A union list of negative and positive microfilms of newspapers to be found in libraries of the United States and Canada. Contains approximately 16,000 entries, including about 4000 foreign newspapers.

"The listing of microfilms of Russian newspapers which appeared in Paul L. Horecky's *Russian, Ukrainian, and Belorussian newspapers, 1917–1953* [AG28] has been supplemented to include the year 1957, and the additional titles are included here."—*Pref.*

Africa

U.S. Library of Congress. Serial Division. African newspapers in selected American libraries. 2d enl. ed. Wash., 1962. 68p. Addenda, 2p.   **AG13**

1st ed. 1956.

Records issues in 20 American libraries.

Australia

Union list of newspapers in Australian libraries . . . comp. by the Australian Bibliographical Centre, Commonwealth National Library. Canberra, Australian Advisory Council on Bibliographical Services, 1959–61.   **AG14**

Pt.1, Newspapers published outside Australia, 1959. Suppl. 1–2, 1960–61; pt.2, Newspapers published in Australia. 1960. Suppl.1, 1961.

Pt.2 gives information about Australian newspapers, including date of establishment, frequency, changes in title, etc.

Belgium

Annuaire officiel de la presse belge. Officieel jaarboek van de Belgische pers. [Bruxelles], Assoc. Générale de la Presse Belge, 1950– . Irregular.   **AG15**

1st ed. 1921; 1950 is the first postwar edition. Gives detailed information about journalism and press associations in Belgium, and a list of daily papers by place of publication.

Canada

Canadian Library Association. Microfilm Committee. Canadian newspapers on microfilm. Catalogue de journaux canadiens sur microfilm. Comp. . . . under the supervision of Sheila A. Egoff. Ottawa, Assoc., 1959. v.1– . Loose-leaf.   **AG16**

Contents: pt.1, Cumulative catalogue of microfilms of the Canadian Library Association; pt.2, Other Canadian newspapers on microfilm.

In each section, Canadian newspapers are listed first—by province—followed by a small group of foreign newspapers, with a title index for each section.

Supersedes *Newspaper microfilming project,* no.1–6, 1948–57.

Czechoslovakia

Potemra, Michal. Bibliografia slovenských novín a časopisov do roku 1918. V Martine, Matica Slovenská, 1958. 145p. (Slovenská narodná bibliografia. Séria B. Periodiká, zväzok la)   **AG17**

At head of title: Štátna vedecká knižnica v Košiciach.

Bibliography of Slovak newspapers and journals up to 1918, including those of the resistance movement abroad and handwritten publications, with locations in libraries. Geographical, name, and chronological indexes; summaries in Russian, French, English, and German.

France

Paris. Bibliothèque Nationale. Département des Périodiques. Répertoire collectif des quotidiens et hebdomadaires publiés dans les départements de la France métropolitaine de 1944 à 1956 et conservés dans les archives et bibliothèques de France. Paris, Univ. de Paris, Inst. Français de Presse, 1958. 153p.   **AG18**

Cover title: Journaux français, 1944–1956.

Gives title, place of publication, date of first issue, and location of files.

Great Britain

British Museum. Dept. of Printed Books. Catalogue of printed books. Supplement: Newspapers published in Great Britain and Ireland, 1801–1900. London, Clowes, 1905. 532col.   **AG19**

Contents: (1) London papers; (2) English and Welsh provincial papers: (a) by place of publication, (b) alphabetical title list; (3) Scotch newspapers: (a) by place, (b) alphabetical list; (4) Irish newspapers: (a) by place, (b) alphabetical list.

A valuable record of 19th-century newspapers; not included in this form in the revised British Museum catalog.

Hewitt, Arthur Reginald. Union list of Commonwealth newspapers in London, Oxford and Cambridge. London, pub. for the Inst. of Commonwealth Studies by the Athlone Pr., Univ. of London, 1960. 101p.   **AG20**

Based on the holdings of the British Museum; indicates files—in 62 libraries and newspaper offices—of newspapers published in the Commonwealth nations. Arrangement is alphabetical by country and territory of origin. Title index.

Times, London. Tercentenary handlist of English & Welsh newspapers, magazines and reviews. London, Times, 1920. 324p.   **AG21**

Contents: Sec. I: London and suburban press, arranged chronologically, 1620–1919. Separate list, periodicals in Armenian, Hebrew, Yiddish, Russian, and Turkish. Title index to Sec. I; Sec. II: The provincial press, arranged chronologically by date of the first known issue, 1701–1919. Title index to Sec. II.

A chronological bibliography of English periodicals from 1620 to 1919, which attempts to include all types of periodicals except: (1) official periodicals issued during the war; (2) annuals and yearbooks; (3) publications of societies classed as academies in the British Museum; and (4) local church periodicals. While avowedly incomplete for the difficult period of the 18th century, claims to be nearly exhaustive for the 17th and 19th centuries. Based upon the collections of the British Museum. Each title is listed under the date of the earliest copy which has been found for examination, and the information given for it includes: number and date of the earliest issue; date of discontinuance, if known; and in some cases name of printer, editor, distributor, and a reference to the library or collection if it is other than the British Museum's general collection.

Useful as a means of identifying titles, and as showing, by its chronological arrangement, what periodicals are available for a given date.

Ireland

Munter, R. L. A handlist of Irish newspapers, 1685–1750. London, Bowes & Bowes, 1960. 35p. (Cambridge Bibliographical Society. Monograph no.4) **AG22**

Listing is by place of publication, then chronological. Locates files of the papers in Irish and English libraries.

New Zealand

New Zealand. General Assembly. Library. A union catalogue of New Zealand newspapers preserved in public libraries, newspaper offices, etc. G. H. Scholefield, Chief Librarian. Wellington, E. V. Paul, Govt. Pr., 1938. 38p. **AG23**

Arranged by city. Gives title, dates of beginning and termination, frequency, size, and holdings in New Zealand libraries.

Pakistan

Pakistan. Press Information Dept. General list of newspapers and periodicals published in Pakistan. Karachi, Manager, Govt. of Pakistan Pr., 1956?– . Semiannual. (Its Reference ser. no.1) **AG24**

"A general list of the newspapers published in Pakistan and known to have been in existence in the last six months: giving periodicity, place of publication and name of the editor. . . ."—*Note.* Frequency and title vary slightly.

Pakistan press year book, 1956– . Karachi, Express Pub., 1956– . Annual (?). **AG25**

On cover: A reference book on press and advertising in Pakistan.

A handbook including articles on the press; lists of news agencies, press associations, press delegations, and advertising agencies, etc.; lists of periodicals and newspapers with details of publication, etc.

Poland

"Prasa," Robotnicza Spółdzielnia Wydawnicza, Warsaw. Zakład Badań Prasoznawczych. Materiały do bibliografii dziennikarstwa i prasy w Polsce, w latach 1944–1954; wybór. [Opracował Zespół Biblioteki Stowarzyszenia Dziennikarzy Polskich: Maria Bzowska (et al.). Pod redakcja Jana Halperna] Warszawa, Państwowe Wydawnictwo Naukowe, 1957. 788p. **AG26**

An extensive bibliography of more than 10,000 titles on the history and organization of journalism and the press in Poland.

Russia

Leningrad. Publichnaia Biblioteka. Gazety Otdel'. Alfavitnyi sluzhebnyi katalog russkikh dorevoliutsionnykh gazet, 1703–1916. Leningrad, 1958. 279p. **AG27**

The Leningrad Public Library's holdings of Russian newspapers published between 1703 and 1916, listed alphabetically, with a geographical-chronological index. Omitted are illegal publications included in the library's *Volnaia russkaia pechat',* Peterburg, 1920; and newspapers published abroad in Russian, except those published in Harbin and Port Arthur.

U.S. Library of Congress. Slavic and East European Division. Russian, Ukrainian, and Belorussian newspapers, 1917–1953; a union list. Comp. by Paul L. Horecky. Wash., 1953. 218p. **AG28**

Holdings as of May 1953 are given for 39 participating libraries, degree of completeness being indicated as poor, moderate, substantial, or extensive, without listing actual issues held. Microfilm files are included; these are continued in AG12.

U.S. Library of Congress. Newspapers of the Soviet Union in the Library of Congress (Slavic, 1954–1960; non-Slavic, 1917–1960). Prep. by Paul L. Horecky [and others]. Wash., Slavic and Central European Division, Reference Dept. (Govt. Prt. Off.), 1962. 73p. **AG29**

Switzerland

Blaser, Fritz. Bibliographie der schweizer Presse mit Einschluss der Fürstentums Liechtenstein. Bibliographie de la presse suisse. Bibliografia della stampa svizzera. Basel, Birkhäuser Verlag, 1956–58. 1v. in 2 (1441p.). (Quellen zur schweizer Geschichte. n.F. IV.Abt.: Handbücher, Bd.VII) **AG30**

An extensive listing of the Swiss and Liechtenstein press which attempts to include all dailies and periodicals published before 1803 and all political papers and periodicals after 1803; omits scientific and literary periodicals. Gives detailed information about each title. Arranged alphabetically with chronological and geographical indexes.

Title and introductory material in German, French, and Italian, with the annotation in the language of the periodical.

Tanganyika

Tanganyika press directory. (Rev. ed.) Dar es Salaam, Tanganyika Information Services, 1962. 18p. **AG31**

Lists daily, weekly, fortnightly, monthly, and quarterly newspapers indicating for each: title, price, language, circulation, owner, editor, and editorial address.

INDEXES

United States

New York Times index, v.1– . 1913– . N.Y., Times, 1913– . v.1– . Semimonthly, with annual cumulation. **AG32**

Frequency varies; 1913–29, quarterly with no cumulations, the four quarterly parts constituting a volume; 1930, monthly with quarterly cumulations and an annual cumulated volume; 1931–47, monthly with annual cumulations; 1948– , semimonthly with annual cumulations.

A carefully made subject index giving exact reference to date, page, and column, and plentiful cross references to names and related topics. The brief synopses of articles answer some questions without reference to the paper itself. Indexes the Late City edition of the *New York Times,* the edition that is microfilmed and used for bound files, but also serves as an independent index to dates and even as a guide to the reporting of current happenings in other newspapers.

An earlier index—originally issued in columnar form, covering 1851–58, 1860, 1863–June 1905—is now available on microfilm.

Christian Science monitor. Subject index of the Christian Science monitor, v.1– . Jan. 1960– . Boston, 1960– . Monthly, with semiannual and annual cumulations.
AG33

The Western and New England editions are indexed for the period Jan. 1960–June 1961; beginning with July 1961, the Eastern edition is added. From Jan. 1962 on, the Eastern, Western, and Midwestern editions are indexed.

New York Daily Tribune index, 1875–1906. N.Y., Tribune Assoc., 1876–1907. 31v. **AG34**

Annual; no more published. A much briefer index than the *New York Times index* (AG32), but useful for the period covered.

Denmark

Avis-Kronik-Index, udgivet af Folkebibliotekernes bibliografiske Kontor med Støtte af Undervisningsministeriet og Pressen. Red. af E. A. Jensen og K. H. Nielsen. København, Munksgaard, 1940– . Aarg. 1– . Monthly.
AG35

A monthly index of the main contents of 35–50 Danish daily newspapers. Especially valuable for biographical material and literary reviews. Annual indexes by authors, artists, plays, films, book reviews, and biographical articles.

Germany

Monatliches Verzeichnis von Aufsätzen aus deutschen Zeitungen in sachlich-alphabetischer Anordnung, mit Jahres-Gesamt-Sach-und-Verfasser-Register, 1909–44. Gautzsch bei Leipzig, Dietrich, 1909–44. v.1–31. (Bibliographie d. deutschen Zeitschriftenliteratur, Abt. A. Beilage Bde.) **AG36**

Ceased publication.

Weekly, 1928–29; fortnightly, 1909–22, 1930–33; monthly, 1934–44. An index to the principal articles in German and some Austrian papers. The issues for one year form a volume, with a subject and an author index to the volume. Not published 1923–27; during that period indexing of the same papers was included in the *Bibliographie der deutschen Zeitschriftenliteratur* (AF148).

Great Britain

Times, London. Index to the Times. 1906– . London, Times, 1907– . v.1– . **AG37**

Title varies: 1906–13, *The annual index;* 1914–Jan./Feb. 1957, *The official index.*

Monthly, 1906–June 1914, with annual cumulations for 1906–13 and semiannual cumulation Jan.–June 1914; quarterly, July 1914–1956; bimonthly 1957– . No cumulations.

Detailed alphabetical index referring to date, page, and column. Very useful. Indexes the Final edition of *The Times,* as well as matter appearing in earlier editions but not in the final issue. Indexes book reviews both under author's name and under heading "Books reviewed."

Indexed the *Times literary supplement* from 1906 to 1921.

—— Palmer's Index to the Times newspaper, 1790–June 1941. London, Palmer, 1868–1943. (Repr.: N.Y., Kraus, 1965) **AG38**

Quarterly, beginning with the index covering Oct.–Dec. 1867, published in 1868. The indexes for preceding volumes have been issued in the reverse order, beginning with the one covering July–Sept. 1867, published in 1875.

Much briefer than *The official index* noted above, but useful because of the importance of the newspaper and the long period covered by the index. The indexing of obituary, death,

and funeral notices under the heading "Deaths," in each volume, frequently supplies biographical material difficult to find elsewhere.

Union of Soviet Socialist Republics

Current digest of the Soviet press. v.1– . Feb. 1, 1949– . N.Y., Joint Committee on Slavic Studies, 413 West 117th St., 1949– . Weekly. **AG39**

For full information *see* DA16.

—— Quarterly index, 1949– .

Issued as a supplement to the *Current digest of the Soviet press;* indexes articles as translated in the *Current digest,* and also in the English-language Soviet periodical *International affairs.*

JOURNALISM

Bibliography

Price, Warren C. The literature of journalism, an annotated bibliography. Minneapolis, Univ. of Minn. Pr., 1959. 489p. **AG40**

Lists more than 3000 items (in English), most of them annotated. "The base of the work is frankly historical and biographical, with more than two-fifths of all the titles in these two categories" (*Foreword*), but sections are included for selected works on press management, public opinion, radio and television, foreign press, etc.

Classified arrangement with author, subject, and anonymous title index.

Swindler, William F. A bibliography of law on journalism. N.Y., Columbia Univ. Pr., 1947. 191p. **AG41**

Classed, with author and subject indexes.

Wolseley, Roland Edgar. The journalist's bookshelf; an annotated and selected bibliography of United States journalism. 7th ed. Philadelphia, Chilton, 1961. 225p. **AG42**

1st ed. 1939.

Originally intended to supplement Carl L. Cannon. *Journalism: a bibliography.* N.Y., N.Y. Pub. Lib., 1924. 360p.

Now, in view of the publication of the Price bibliography (AG40), this work aims to present a selected, annotated bibliography of United States journalism, including new titles not in Price, plus some categories (e.g., high school journalism, fiction relating to journalism) not covered by Price.

Classed arrangement, with indexes of authors and titles.

Encyclopedias

Handbuch der Zeitungswissenschaft, hrsg. von Walther Heide, bearb. von Ernst Herbert Lehmann. Leipzig, Hiersemann, 1940–43. Lfg. 1–7. il. **AG43**

No more published.

Lfg. 1–7, A–Kommunistische Presse.

Deals with the history and practices of the newspaper press. Long, signed articles with extensive bibliographies.

History

Mott, Frank Luther. American journalism; a history, 1690–1960. 3d ed. N.Y., Macmillan, 1962. 901p. il. **AG44**

1st ed. 1941.

A detailed history with bibliographical notes.

A H

Government Publications

❧ Much important reference material is to be found in the reports, bulletins, and other publications issued by the various national, state, and municipal governments. These publications, generally known as "government publications" or "public documents," cover topics in nearly the whole field of knowledge, but are most important for subjects in the fields of social and political science, economics, finance, labor, industry, statistics, education, history, etc., and in certain sciences such as agriculture, ethnology, geology, meteorology, aeronautics and related technologies, etc., to the study and promotion of which certain government bureaus or commissions are devoted. No extended reference work can be done in questions of labor conditions in America, for example, without the use of some of the publications of the U.S. Department of Labor, or in American geology without those of the U.S. Geological Survey.

Public documents are popularly supposed to be difficult to use and understand, and because this difficulty is overrated, reference workers often fail to make the best use of such material. The documents are published in complicated forms and sets, and must be located through the printed catalogs, bibliographies, and indexes provided for the purpose, but for the periods covered by modern indexes, they are no harder to find than periodical literature which has to be found through periodical indexes. For explanations of the use of United States government publications and their indexes, consult especially Boyd (AH7) and Schmeckebier (AH9).

For indexes and bibliographies relating to special subjects, *see* those subjects. Listed below are some of the most important general guides and indexes for the United States and Great Britain, and also a few bibliographies for other countries that have been published since 1942, when the 3d edition of the bibliography by Childs (AH2) was issued. The latter lists and describes document bibliographical work in the various countries at that time and is still useful for historical purposes. A more up-to-date listing is the UNESCO publication *A study of current bibliographies of national official publications,* 1958 (AH3).

INTERNATIONAL

Guides

Brown, Everett S. Manual of government publications: United States and foreign. N.Y., Appleton, 1950. 121p.   **AH1**

A brief manual which discusses the government publications of the various countries of the world. Emphasis is

on the United States, Great Britain, and international affairs, particularly the League of Nations and the United Nations.

Bibliography

Childs, James Bennett. Government document bibliography in the United States and elsewhere. 3d ed. Wash., Govt. Prt. Off., 1942. 78p. (Repr.: N.Y., Johnson Reprint Corp., [1964])   **AH2**

At head of title: The Library of Congress, Division of Documents.

In five sections: (1) United States; (2) Confederate States of America; (3) States; (4) Foreign Countries; and (5) League of Nations. The catalogs, indexes, and guides to the documents of each country are listed, sometimes with brief annotations.

International Committee for Social Sciences Documentation. Étude des bibliographies courantes des publications officielles nationales: guide sommaire et inventaire. A study of current bibliographies of national official publications; short guide and inventory. Comp. by Jean Meyriat. [Paris], UNESCO, 1958. 260p. (UNESCO bibliographical handbooks. 7)   **AH3**

Introductory matter in French and English. Annotations sometimes in one, sometimes in the other.

Lists national bibliographies, official journals, document bibliographies, legislative publications, etc. of all independent states.

New York. Public Library. National and Local Gazettes Microfilming Program. Cumulative list of national and local gazettes filmed. Jan. 1, 1961–   . N.Y., 1961–   . Irregular.   **AH4**

2d ed. 1962. Includes 236 national and local gazettes available on film at the end of 1961. Lists additional gazettes from many parts of the world, and makes a special effort to include gazettes of those African and Asian countries that attained independence in 1962.

————— ——— Supplement. Dec. 1962. 27p.

United Nations. Library. Geneva. Répertoire des données publiées régulièrement dans les journaux officiels. Analysis of material published regularly in official gazettes. Genève, 1958. 39p. (Its Listes bibliographiques, nouv. sér., no.1)   **AH5**

Revised and expanded edition of an earlier list published by the League of Nations Library in 1935.

In three sections: (1) analysis by country; (2) subject index; (3) inventory of the entire collection of official gazettes.

Union lists

List of the serial publications of foreign governments, 1815–1931, ed. by Winifred Gregory, for the American Council of Learned Societies, American Library Association, National Research Council. N.Y., Wilson, 1932. 720p.   **AH6**

A union list, on the same general plan as the *Union list of serials* (AF98), for a type of serial publication excluded from that list, i.e., government serials, including only genuine government serials and omitting publications of universities, societies, etc. which are subsidized by a government. Arranged alphabetically by country name (except that Russia is in a separate list at the end), with subarrangement by government departments, bureaus, etc., and with indication of holdings of the various publications in some 85 American libraries.

UNITED STATES

Guides

Boyd, Anne Morris. United States government publications. 3d ed. rev. by Rae Elizabeth Rips. N.Y., Wilson, 1949. 627p.   **AH7**

1st ed. 1931; 2d ed. 1940.

After a discussion of the nature, printing, and distribution of catalogs and indexes of United States government publications, the arrangement of material then follows that of the organization of the government, i.e., the legislative, judicial, and executive branches, each subdivided by major divisions: Congress; the courts; the 10 Departments; and independent agencies and institutions.

Lists and describes the important and typical publications of each, but does not attempt to be complete. Originally planned as a library-school textbook, this edition has been extended to increase its usefulness in a reference department, and revised to include the many changes in government departments and agencies made during the war and postwar years to July 1, 1948.

Leidy, W. Philip. A popular guide to government publications. 2d ed. N.Y., Columbia Univ. Pr., 1963. 291p.   **AH8**

The 1st edition, 1953, covered some 2500 titles published 1940–50.

The 2d edition includes about 2300 titles, published mainly by the U.S. Government Printing Office, between 1951 and 1962; arrangement is by broad subject, with a detailed subject index. Complete information is given, and some items are annotated. A guide for the public library and for the citizen seeking low-cost, authoritative information on a wide variety of subjects.

Schmeckebier, Laurence Frederick and **Eastin, Roy B.** Government publications and their use. Rev. ed. Wash., Brookings Inst., 1961. 476p.   **AH9**

1st ed. 1936.

A useful guide to government publications with descriptions, including classification and distribution, of catalogs and indexes, bibliographies, Congressional publications, Constitutions (federal and state), laws (federal and state), court decisions, administrative regulations, presidential papers, foreign affairs, reports, organization and personnel, maps, etc. Includes list of government periodicals, and microfacsimile editions of government publications.

Answers many questions as to what was published, when, by whom, in what form, etc.

Tompkins, Dorothy C. Materials for the study of federal government. Chicago, Public Admin. Service, 1948. 338p.   **AH10**

Treats government publications dealing with federal administration, covering: the Constitution; laws and codes; publications of the legislative, executive, and judicial branches, and the President; the federal budget; government statistics; the New Deal; and World War II.

Bibliography

Andriot, John L. Guide to U.S. government serials and periodicals. [McLean, Va.], Documents Index, 1962– . v.1– . (In progress)   **AH11**

To be in 3v.

Contents: v.1, Current serials and periodicals of Washington agencies; v.2, to include releases and other ephemeral material; v.3, to list publications of agencies outside Washington.

Catalogs and indexes

The Serial set

☙ The collected edition of United States government publications is known as the *Congressional edition* or *Serial set.* It includes Senate and House journals (through the 82d Congress, 1952), Senate and House documents, and Senate and House reports. The documents include a large variety of reports from executive departments and independent bodies which are printed in the set by order of Congress. (For further description of this set, *see* Schmeckebier, p.135–39 [AH9].)

For purposes of easy arrangement, each bound volume is given a serial number. (A volume may include from one to several individual items.) Volumes are numbered consecutively beginning with the 15th Congress (1817). In many libraries documents are arranged on the shelves by these serial numbers, and the number must be ascertained in order to find a particular document. These serial numbers are included in many of the lists and indexes noted below, sometimes in numerical lists and sometimes under specific entries. A complete record, with some overlapping, can be found in the following: 15th–60th Congress (1817–1909) in the *Checklist* (AH16); 54th–76th Congress (1895–1940) in the *Document catalog* (AH17) under "Congressional documents" list; 73d Congress (1933/34–) in the *Numerical lists* (AH19).

The *American state papers,* which contain reprints of the documents of the first 14 Congresses (1789–1817), grouped by class into 38v., have been assigned special serial numbers from 01–038. These numbers can be found in the *Checklist* (AH16).

Early period to 1893

Greely, Adolphus Washington. Public documents of the first fourteen Congresses, 1789–1817. Papers relating to early Congressional documents. Wash., Govt. Prt. Off., 1900. 903p. (56th Cong., 1st sess. Senate doc. 428)   **AH12**

—— —— Supplement. Wash., Govt. Prt. Off., 1904.

Reprinted from the *Annual report* of the American Historical Association, 1903, 1:343–406.

Poore, Benjamin Perley. A descriptive catalogue of the government publications of the United States, Sept. 5, 1774—March 4, 1881, comp. by order of Congress. Wash., Govt. Prt. Off., 1885. 1392p. (48th Cong., 2d sess. Senate. Misc. doc. 67) (Repr.: Ann Arbor, Mich., Edwards, 1953)   **AH13**

Arranged chronologically, with general index. For each document gives full title, author, date, and a brief abstract of contents. Exact reference is given to the series in which each document appears. Contains much valuable material, but is difficult to use for quick reference because the index is not sufficiently complete, detailed, or specific.

Ames, John Griffith. Comprehensive index to the publications of the United States government, 1881–1893. Wash., Govt. Prt. Off., 1905. 2v. (58th Cong., 2d sess. House doc. 754) (Repr.: Ann Arbor, Mich., Edwards, 1953. 2v. in 1)   **AH14**

The *Comprehensive index,* 1889–93, by J. G. Ames, published in 1894, is superseded by this work.

Bridges the gap between Poore's *Descriptive catalogue* (AH13), and the first volume of the *Document catalog* (AH17).

Arranged in three columns. In the first is given the author

of the document or the department by which it was issued; in the second, a list of the documents arranged alphabetically by the key word in the title; in the third, if the document is in the serial set, reference is made to the Congress, session, and volume of the series in which each is embraced, and the number of the document. Personal name index.

Although not entirely complete, a good usable index, but less minute and detailed than the *Document catalog*. Indicates the different editions in which a document was issued and gives serial numbers in a table under the heading "Congressional documents."

U.S. Superintendent of Documents. Tables of and annotated index to the Congressional series of United States public documents. Wash., Govt. Prt. Off., 1902. 769p. **AH15**

In two parts: (1) tables of the American state papers and the documents of the 15th through the 52nd Congress, arranged by serial number; and (2) minute alphabetical subject index to these documents. The first part is now superseded by the third edition of the *Checklist* noted below, but the subject index is still useful as a key to the Congressional set before 1893.

—— Checklist of United States public documents, 1789–1909. 3d ed. rev. and enl. Wash., Govt. Prt. Off., 1911. v.1. 1707p. (Repr.: N.Y., Kraus, 1962, v.1) **AH16**

v.1, Lists of Congressional and departmental publications; v.2 was to have been an index, but was never issued.

A checklist, not a catalog, covering Congressional documents through the 60th Congress, and department and bureau publications to the end of 1909. Lists: (1) American state papers, with serial numbers; (2) Congressional documents, 15th–60th Congresses, with serial numbers; (3) Department publications arranged alphabetically by government author; (4) Proceedings of Congress; (5) Miscellaneous publications of Congress, committee reports, etc.; (6) Papers of Revolutionary period and first 14 Congresses. The list of departmental publications gives, for periodical publications, a statement of the volumes and dates which constitute a complete set, and the serial numbers if the publication is contained also in the serial set; for separate publications the full title and date are given, and the serial number if the document appears also in the serial set. The preface contains a list and description of previous indexes and catalogs of United States documents. This edition replaces the 2d edition of the *Checklist* and the tables of the *Tables and index* (AH15), but not its index.

A brief errata list is printed in the *Monthly catalog*, May 1912, p.720–721 (AH18).

1893–1940

U.S. Superintendent of Documents. Catalog of the public documents of Congress and of all departments of the government of the United States for the period March 4, 1893—Dec. 31, 1940. Wash., Govt. Prt. Off., 1896–1945. v.1–25. **AH17**

The "comprehensive index" provided for by the act approved Jan. 12, 1895. Publication terminated with v.25.

This index, which is generally referred to by its binder's title as the *Document catalog,* forms for the years 1893 to 1940 the permanent and complete catalog of all government publications both Congressional and departmental. It is a dictionary catalog in form, listing all documents under author (governmental or personal), subject, and, when necessary, title, and giving full catalog information for each book or pamphlet included. Includes a large amount of analysis; refers to all editions in which a document has appeared; and gives serial numbers for documents in the serial set, as follows: in v.1–4, serial numbers are given only in the table under the entry "Congressional documents"; beginning with v.5, serial numbers are *also* given throughout the list under the

main (i.e., author) entry for each document, but not under the analytical entries.

1940 to date

U.S. Superintendent of Documents. Monthly catalog of United States government publications. 1895– . Wash., Govt. Prt. Off., 1895– . Monthly. **AH18**

Title varies: 1895–June 1907, *Catalogue of the United States public documents;* July 1907–1939, *Monthly catalog, United States public documents;* 1940–50, *United States government publications: monthly catalog.*

A current bibliography of publications issued by all branches of the government, including both the Congressional and the department and bureau publications. Each issue contains general instructions for ordering documents, and a list of the documents published during the month arranged by the department and bureau, with indication, for each publication, of its full title, date, paging, price, Library of Congress card number, etc. An annual index is in each volume and, beginning with July 1945, a monthly index in each issue. An added feature is a section called "Previews," which lists important titles before they are issued, so that prepublication orders may be placed. *A directory of United States government periodicals and subscription publications* (title varies) was published semiannually 1951–60 (usually Feb. and Aug.); annual 1961– (with Feb. issue).

—— —— Supplements: 1941–1942, 1943–1944, 1945–1946. Wash., Govt. Prt. Off., 1947–48. 3v.

Include publications received by the Public Documents Division Library, not listed previously in any Superintendent of Documents catalog. No further supplements published, as, beginning in April 1947, all documents are listed in the *Monthly catalog* as received, regardless of publication date.

—— —— Decennial cumulative index, 1941–1950 . . . Wash., Govt. Prt. Off., 1953. 1848p.

"Index to the monthly issues from January 1941 to December 1950 and the Supplements for 1941–42, 1943–44, and 1945–46."—*Title page.*

—— Numerical lists and schedule of volumes of the reports and documents of the 73rd Congress, 1933/34– . Wash., Govt. Prt. Off., 1934– . **AH19**

Usually a separate volume appears for each session of Congress.

Prior to 1941, the set is superseded by the "Congressional documents" tables in the *Document catalog* (AH17). From the 77th Congress, 1st sess., Jan. 3, 1941, on, it must be used to obtain serial numbers for the Congressional reports and documents which are now listed only in the *Monthly catalog* (AH18), and without serial number.

—— Price lists. Wash., Govt. Prt. Off. no.1– . 1898– . Frequently revised. **AH20**

Sales catalogs of government publications, arranged by subject field. Include no material not already listed in the more general publications noted above, but present the same material in a different arrangement and grouping which are sometimes more convenient for quick reference. Give prices, indicate material still in print, and sometimes supply useful annotations.

Contents (of numbers in active stock and on current topics; frequently revised): no.10, Laws; 11, Home economics; 15, Geology; 19, Army; 21, Fish and wildlife; 25, Transportation, highways, roads, and postal service; 28, Finance; 31, Education; 33, Labor; 33A, Occupations; 35, National parks; 36, Government periodicals and subscription services; 37, Tariff and taxation; 38, Animal industry; 41, Insects; 42, Irrigation, drainage, water power; 43, Forestry; 44, Plants; 46, Soils and fertilizers; 48, Weather, astronomy, and meteorology; 50, American history; 51, Health and hygiene; 51A, Diseases;

53, Maps; 54, Political science; 55, Indians; 58, Mines; 59, Interstate commerce; 60, Guam, Puerto Rico, Samoa, and Virgin Islands; 62, Commerce; 63, Navy; 64, Scientific tests, standards; 65, Foreign relations of U.S.; 67, Immigration, naturalization, and citizenship; 68, Farm management; 70, Census; 71, Children's Bureau; 72, Homes; 78, Industrial workers; 79, Aviation; 81, Posters and charts; 82, Radio and electricity; 83, Library of Congress; 84, Atomic energy and civil defense; 85, Defense; 86, Consumer information.

United States government publications (non-depository). Jan. 1953– . N.Y., Readex Microprint, 1953– . Monthly. **AH21**

Consists of all nondepository items, reproduced in full in microprint, on cards measuring 6 by 9 inches, for use in a Readex Microprint reader. Arrangement is by *Monthly catalog* entry number (AH18).

Cards are issued somewhat later than the *Monthly catalog*.

Readex Microprint Corporation. Index to Readex microprint edition of JPRS reports (Joint Publications Research Service), prep. by Mary Elizabeth Poole. N.Y., Corporation, [1964?]. 137p. **AH22**

The JPRS reports, which are mainly translations of a wide variety of articles and technical writings from Communist-bloc countries, are listed in the *Monthly catalog* (AH18) and thus are reproduced in the microprint edition of nondepository publications. This index is a correlation of the JPRS numbers and the *Monthly catalog* numbers under which they are arranged in the microprint edition. Its use will obviate the necessity of checking a report under author or subject in the *Monthly catalog* when the JPRS number is known.

American Library Association. Interdivisional Committee on Public Documents. United States government publications: a partial list of non-GPO imprints, prep. . . . by Jennings Wood. Chicago, Assoc., 1964. 86p. **AH23**

A listing by agency of nonclassified publications issued by department or agency on their own equipment rather than by the Government Printing Office. Covers mainly 1962–64.

Congressional committee hearings

U.S. Congress. Senate. Library. Index of Congressional committee hearings (not confidential in character) prior to Jan. 3, 1935, in the United States Senate Library. Wash., Govt. Prt. Off., 1935. 1056p. **AH24**

—— Cumulative index of Congressional committee hearings (not confidential in character) from 74th Congress (Jan. 3, 1935) through 85th Congress (Jan. 3, 1959) in the United States Senate Library. Indexed and comp. under the direction of Felton M. Johnston, secretary of the Senate, by Richard D. Hupman, librarian [and others]. Wash., Govt. Prt. Off., 1959. 823p.

—— Quadrennial supplement to Cumulative index of Congressional committee hearings (not confidential in character) from 86th Congress (Jan. 7, 1959) through 87th Congress (Jan. 3, 1963) together with selected committee prints in the United States Senate Library, comp. and indexed by Mary F. Sterrett. Wash., Govt. Prt. Off., 1963. 762p.

U.S. Congress. House. Library. Index to Congressional committee hearings in the Library of the United States House of Representatives prior to Jan. 1, 1951. Comp. by Russell Saville, under the direction of Lyle O. Snader, clerk of the House of Representatives. Wash., Govt. Prt. Off., 1954. 485p. **AH25**

—— Supplemental index to Congressional committee hearings, Jan. 3, 1949 to Jan. 3, 1955; 81st, 82d, and 83d Congresses, in the Library of the United States House of Representatives. Comp. by John A. Cooper under the

direction of Ralph R. Roberts. Wash., Govt. Prt. Off., 1956. 127p.

The Senate and House lists differ, neither being complete but including only the hearings in these specific libraries. However, coverage, especially for recent years, is fairly complete.

Legislative debates

U.S. Congress. Congressional record: containing the proceedings and debates of the 43d Congress– . March 4, 1873– . Wash., Govt. Prt. Off., 1873– . v.1– . **AH26**

Issued daily while Congress is in session; revised and issued in bound form at the end of the session. The issue for each session is numbered as one volume and paged continuously though bound in several parts. There are frequent indexes during the session and a final index to the whole volume, this index sometimes bound separately, sometimes included in the last bound part.

Contains the Presidents' messages, Congressional speeches and debates in full, and record of votes. Does not include text of bills. Each index is in two parts: (1) Alphabetical index of names and subjects, giving (under subject) bills and bill number, and (2) History of bills and resolutions, arranged by number. This second index is the one to use for full information about a bill, as it gives page references to all material in the *Record* about the bill, from its introduction to its final passage and signing. Beginning with the 80th Congress, March 17, 1947, a section "Daily Digest" is included.

For material before 1873 the following earlier compilations should be consulted: (1) *Debates and proceedings* (generally known by its binder's title *Annals of Congress*), 1st–18th Congress, 1789–1824. 42v. (1834–56); (2) *Register of debates,* 18th Congress, 2d sess.—25th Congress, 1st sess., 1824–37. 14v. in 29. (1825–37); and (3) *Congressional globe,* 23d–43d Congress, 1833–73. 46v. in 108 (1834–73).

For further information concerning the *Congressional record, see* Schmeckebier, *Government publications* (AH9).

Executive branch

U.S. President. A compilation of the messages and papers of the Presidents . . . (with additions and encyclopedic index by private enterprise). N.Y., Bureau of Nat. Literature, [19?]. 20v. **AH27**

Originally published: Wash., Govt. Prt. Off., 1896–99. 10v. (House misc. doc. 210, 53d Cong., 2d sess.), covering 1789–1897. Published by authority of Congress by James D. Richardson.

Additional volumes bring the record through the terms of Calvin Coolidge, 1929. These were commercially published in various editions with varying volume numbers, usually without publication dates. (For record *see* Schmeckebier, p.308–18 [AH9].)

Commercially published Presidential messages cover the administrations of Herbert Hoover, 1929–33, and Franklin D. Roosevelt, 1933–45.

Continued officially by:

—— Public papers of the Presidents of the United States, containing the public messages, speeches, and statements of the President. Wash., 1958– . Annual. **AH28**

Contents: Harry S. Truman, 1945–48. 4v. (1961–64); Dwight D. Eisenhower, 1953–61. 8v. (1958–61); John F. Kennedy, 1961–63. 4v. (1962–64).

Published by the Office of the Federal Register, National Archives and Record Service, General Services Administration.

A series designed to include the public messages and statements of the Presidents. Annual volumes are published soon after the close of each calendar year, and at the same time volumes covering previous years are compiled.

U.S. Library of Congress. Legislative Reference Service. Table of executive orders appearing in the Federal Register and the Code of Federal Regulations. Wash., Reference Dept., Lib. of Congress, 1955. 76p. **AH29**

Prepared by Margaret Fennell of the American Law Division.

An index, by Executive Order number, to the volume and page of the *Federal register* or *Code of federal regulations* in which the Order was printed.

Covers 1936–54, and supplements the compilation of the Historical Records Survey, *Presidential executive orders* (1944. 2v.) and the *List and index of Presidential executive orders* (unnumbered ser., 1942), issued by the Historical Records Survey of New Jersey.

U.S. Congress. Senate. Library. Presidential vetoes . . . Comp. by the Senate Library under the direction of Felton M. Johnston and Richard D. Hupman. Wash., Govt. Prt. Off., 1961. 244p. **AH30**

Subtitle: List of bills vetoed and action taken thereon by the Senate and House of Representatives, First Congress through Eighty-sixth Congress, 1789–1961.

State publications

Guides

Wilcox, Jerome Kear. Manual on the use of state publications. Chicago, Amer. Lib. Assoc., 1940. 342p. **AH31**

Sponsored by the American Library Association's Committee on Public Documents. Each section is written by a specialist. Contains general descriptions plus bibliographies of "Basic state publications."

Bibliography

National Association of State Libraries. Public Documents Clearing House Committee. Check-list of legislative journals of the states of the United States of America; comp. by Grace E. Macdonald. Providence, R.I., Oxford Pr., 1938. 274p. **AH32**

—— —— Supplement; comp. by William S. Jenkins. Boston, 1943. 107p.

Continued by:

Pullen, William Russell. A check list of legislative journals issued since 1937 by the states of the United States of America. Chicago, Amer. Lib. Assoc., 1955. 59p. **AH33**

U.S. Library of Congress. Processing Dept. Monthly checklist of state publications, v.1, 1910– . Wash., Govt. Prt. Off., 1910– . Monthly. **AH34**

Sponsoring division of the Library of Congress varies.

A current bibliography, arranged alphabetically by states' names, of the publications of the states, territories, and insular possessions of the United States. Though limited to the publications received by the Library of Congress, it is approximately complete, as the Library aims to acquire all such material issued. Each title is given with full cataloging information, including contents in the case of composite reports. Since the annual index refers to the contents notes as well as to the main titles, the list can be made to serve as a subject index as well as a bibliography. Beginning in 1963, periodicals are listed semiannually in the June and Dec. issues, with the Dec. list cumulative for the year.

AFRICA

U.S. Library of Congress. African Section. Official publications of British East Africa, comp. by Helen F. Conover and Audrey A. Walker. Wash., 1960–63. 4v. **AH35**

Contents: pt.1, The East Africa High Commission and other regional documents. 67p.; pt.2, Tanganyika. 134p.; pt. 3, Kenya and Zanzibar. 162p.; pt.4, Uganda. 100p.

—— Official publications of French Equatorial Africa, French Cameroons, and Togo, 1946–1958, comp. by Julian W. Witherell. Wash., 1964. 78p. **AH36**

A list of publications of the various governments concerned with A.E.F. (Afrique Equatoriale Française)—Chad, Gabon, Middle Congo, Ubangi-Shari, French Cameroons, Togo, France, French Union—and United Nations publications bearing directly on French Cameroons and Togo.

U.S. Library of Congress. General Reference and Bibliography Division. Official publications of French West Africa, 1946–1958; a guide comp. by Helen F. Conover. Wash., 1960. 88p. **AH37**

A listing of the official publications of French West Africa issued during the Fourth French Republic, covering the documents of the Gouvernement Général, and of the eight territories—Dahomey, French Guinea, Ivory Coast, Mauritania, Niger, Senegal, French Sudan, and Upper Volta—as well as a selection of French official papers dealing with the region.

AUSTRALIA

Canberra, Australia. National Library of Australia. Australian government publications. 1961– . Canberra, Commonwealth Govt. Pr., 1962– . Annual. **AH38**

Supersedes its *Monthly list of Australian government publications,* 1952–1960, and its annual cumulation in its *Annual catalogue of Australian publications.*

CANADA

Guides

Higgins, Marion Villiers. Canadian government publications; a manual for librarians. Chicago, Amer. Lib. Assoc., 1935. 582p. il. **AH39**

Beginning with the French regime, 1608–1760, lists Canadian government publications to 1935, including a historical summary of issuing bodies. Arrangement is by department with subject and author index.

Bibliography

Canada. Dept. of Public Printing and Stationery. Canadian government publications: catalogue, 1953– . Ottawa, Queen's printer, 1954– . v.1– . Annual. **AH40**

—— —— Monthly catalogue, Jan. 1953– . Ottawa, Queen's printer, 1953– . Monthly.

Succeeds the *Catalogue of official publications of the Parliament and government of Canada,* 1928–1948.

The *Monthly catalogue* cumulates the listings of the *Daily checklist,* and is itself cumulated into the *Catalogue* (title varies slightly).

Bilingual. Each issue lists publications in English and French; each part subdivided into (1) parliamentary publications, and (2) departmental publications, followed by international publications and an index.

Bishop, Olga Bernice. Publications of the government of

the Province of Canada, 1841–1867. Ottawa, Nat. Lib. of Canada, 1963. 351p. **AH41**

—— Publications of the governments of Nova Scotia, Prince Edward Island, New Brunswick, 1758–1952. Ottawa, Nat. Lib. of Canada, 1957. 237p. **AH42**

Holmes, Marjorie C. Publications of the government of British Columbia, 1871–1947. Victoria, Provincial Lib., [1950]. **AH43**

A complete revision and enlargement of *Publications of the government of British Columbia, 1871–1937*, by Sydney Weston.

MacDonald, Christine. Publications of the governments of the Northwest Territories, 1876–1905 and of the Province of Saskatchewan, 1905–1952. Regina, Sask., Legislative Lib., 1952. 109p. **AH44**

DENMARK

Bibliografi over Danmarks offentlige Publikationer. Årg. 1– . 1948– . København, Dansk Bibliografisk Kontor, 1949– . Annual. **AH45**

At head of title: Impressa publica regni danici 1948– .

Title varies: 1948–59, *Bibliografi Fortegnelse over statens Tryksager og statsunderstøttede Publikationer*.

An index of government publications arranged under issuing office, with indexes by subject and person.

FRANCE

Bibliographie de la France. Suppl. F., Publications officielles. Sept. 1950– . Paris, Cercle de la Librairie, 1950– . Irregular. **AH46**

A supplement to the *Bibliographie* (AA473), which includes national, local, and overseas government publications. Annual index.

Dampierre, Jacques de. Les publications officielles des pouvoirs publics: Étude critique et administrative. Paris, Picard, 1942. 628p. **AH47**

Contains a detailed historical description of the official publications of France. Those of a few of the major countries of the world—e.g., United States, Great Britain, the Netherlands, Italy, and Germany—are briefly noted.

Journal officiel de la République Française. Éd. complète. 1870– . **AH48**

Preceded by: *Gazette nationale, ou Moniteur universel*, 1789–1810; *Moniteur universel, journal officiel*, 1811–68; *Journal officiel de l'Empire Français*, 1869–4 sept. 1870.

From 1881, in several parts, the main ones being: (1) Lois et décrets; (2) Débats parlementaires: (a) Sénat, and (b) Assemblée Nationale; (3) Documents parlementaires; (4) Bulletin annexe.

Designations vary.

Appears daily except Mondays and holidays; contains texts of national laws and decrees, important administrative orders and proclamations, and parliamentary debates and committee reports.

Indexes (Tables) published annually.

For more complete information, *see* UNESCO, *Étude des bibliographies courantes des publications officielles nationales* (AH3).

GERMANY

Guides

Childs, James Bennett. German Federal Republic official publications, 1949–1957, with inclusion of preceding

zonal official publications; a survey. Wash., Lib. of Congress, Reference Dept., Serial Division, 1958. 2v. in 1 (887p.). **AH49**

Contents: v.1, Bundespräsident—Bundesministerium der Justiz; v.2, Bundesministerium für das Post- und Fernmeldewesen—Zonal period. Describes the agencies of the Federal Republic and of the Zonal organization with lists of their publications. Those of the member states are not included. Both serial and monographic publications are listed with indications of Library of Congress holdings as of Oct. 1957.

Bibliography

Deutsche Bibliographie: Verzeichnis amtlicher Druckschriften. 1957/58– . Frankfurt a. M., Buchhändler-Vereinigung, 1962– . Biennial. **AH50**

Lists official publications of the government—legislative bodies and institutions—as well as publications of semiofficial institutions of the German Federal Republic and West Berlin.

Leipzig. Deutsche Bücherei. Monatliches Verzeichnis der reichsdeutschen amtlichen Druckschriften . . . v.1–17, no.6, 1928–1944. Berlin, Reichs- und Staatsverlag G.M.B.H., 1928–44. 17v. **AH51**

GREAT BRITAIN

Guides

Ford, Percy and **Ford, Grace.** A guide to parliamentary papers; what they are: how to find them: how to use them. Oxford, Blackwell, 1955. 79p. **AH52**

A useful introductory guide, giving a brief history and description of the contents of the papers and indexes. The appendix includes a list of collections of papers, indexes, and catalogs.

Gt.Brit. Stationery Office. Published by HMSO; a brief guide to official publications. London, 1960. 58p. il. **AH53**

Not a catalog but a guide, under broad subject headings, to publications issued and sold by H.M. Stationery Office.

Horrocks, Sidney. The state as publisher. A librarian's guide to the publications of His Majesty's Stationery Office. London, Lib. Assoc., 1952. 32p. (Library Assoc. pamphlet, no.10) **AH54**

A brief but clear outline by the reference librarian of the Manchester Public Libraries, explaining the historical development of the Stationery Office and the present status of publications. Includes advice on arrangement and preservation of documents, as well as on their cataloging in both small and large collections.

Lees-Smith, H. B. A guide to parliamentary and official papers. London, Oxford Univ. Pr., 1924. 23p. **AH55**

A clear, concise description of the official documents of the British government. Somewhat out of date but still valuable.

Catalogs and indexes

18th century

Gt.Brit. Parliament. House of Commons. Catalogue of parliamentary reports and a breviate of their contents, arranged under heads according to the subjects, 1696–1834. [London], 1834. 220p. (Repr.: Oxford, Blackwell, 1953) **AH56**

Indexes the "1st series" of parliamentary reports (15v.),

the reports in the *Journals,* and those in the *Sessional papers,* 1801–34.

—— Catalogue of papers printed by order of the House of Commons for the year 1731 to 1800, in the custody of the Clerk of the Journals. [London], 1807. [v.p., i.e., 101p.] **AH57**

Consists of three chronological lists, each with its own subject index: (1) Bills; (2) Reports; and (3) Accounts and Papers.

19th and 20th centuries

Gt.Brit. Parliament. House of Commons. General alphabetical index to the bills, reports, estimates, accounts and papers printed by order of the House of Commons and to the papers presented by command, 1801–1948/49. London, Stat. Off., 1853–1960. 4v. (In progress) **AH58**

Consists of the following four unnumbered volumes: (1) General index to the accounts and papers, reports of commissioners, estimates, etc., 1801–1852; (2) Indexes to bills and reports, 1801–1852, in two sections: General index to the bills, and General index to the reports of select committees; (3) General index, 1852–1899; and (4) General index, 1900–1948/49.

An index to the documents included in the parliamentary papers of the House of Commons, not including the papers of the House of Lords except insofar as these are duplicated in the Commons papers, and not including the publications of bureaus and departments. Arranged alphabetically by rather large subjects; does not include many analytical entries. Gives fairly full information about each paper, including its full title, date, and bill, document, or command number, and a reference to the year and volume of the sessional papers in which it is to be found, and the paging as made up for the House of Commons set.

For most purposes these indexes supersede the decennial and annual indexes for the periods covered, although the latter may still be useful for analyses of comprehensive series and for the numerical lists of command papers.

—— General alphabetical index to the bills, reports, estimates, accounts and papers printed by order of the House of Commons and to the papers presented by command, 1950–1958/59– . London, Stat. Off., 1963– .

Decennial cumulation of the annual indexes. Does not include the numerical lists. A continuation of the decennial indexes, 1870–1949, now superseded by the 50-year indexes.

—— List of the bills, reports, estimates, and accounts and papers printed by order of the House of Commons and of the papers presented by command . . . with a general alphabetical index thereto, 1801– . London, Stat. Off. Annual. **AH59**

Issued annually as the final volume for each session of the *Sessional papers* of the House of Commons.

From 1828, contains not only an index, but also a list of bills and papers in their numerical order; in 1834, a list of command papers is added, and, in 1867, a preliminary list showing the make-up of the set for each session.

The index section is superseded through 1958/59 by the 50-year and 10-year indexes described above, but the numerical lists are still the only ones available, and are useful for identifying command papers often asked for by number only.

Gt.Brit. Parliament. House of Lords. General index to sessional papers printed by order of the House of Lords or presented by special command. London, Eyre, 1860–86. 3v. **AH60**

Publisher varies. v.1 reprinted: London, Stat. Off., 1938. v.1, 1801–59; v.2, 1859–70; v.3, 1871–85.

From 1886 to 1920, annual indexes were published. Subsequently the only lists printed are unnumbered annual lists of titles.

Gt.Brit. Stationery Office. Catalogue of government publications. 1922– . London, Stat. Off., 1923– . Annual. **AH61**

Title varies: *Consolidated list of parliamentary and Stationery Office publications,* 1922; *Consolidated list of government publications,* 1923–50; *Government publications: consolidated list,* 1951–53; *Government publications: catalogue,* 1954–55; *Catalogue of government publications,* 1956– .

Continues the *Quarterly list . . . of official publications.* London, Stat. Off., 1897–1922.

—— Consolidated index to government publications, 1936/40– . London, Stat. Off., 1952– . Quinquennial. **AH62**

Four of these 5-year indexes have now appeared and consolidate the indexing of the annual lists, which are consecutively paged in anticipation of the publication of the indexes.

—— Government publications monthly list. London, Stat. Off. Monthly. **AH63**

Intended primarily as sales catalogs, these are superseded by the *Catalogue of government publications* (AH61).

Select lists

Ford, Percy and **Ford, Grace.** Select list of British parliamentary papers, 1833–1899. Oxford, Blackwell, 1953. 165p. **AH64**

Arranged by subject, with an alphabetical index. Includes the "reports and all other material issued by committees and commissions or similar bodies of investigation into economic, social and constitutional questions, and matters of law and administration."—*Introd.*

Supplements the *Catalogue of parliamentary reports . . . 1696–1834* (AH56).

—— A breviate of parliamentary papers 1900–1916; the foundation of the welfare state. Oxford, Blackwell, 1957. 470p. **AH65**

A guide, with abstracts, to 1048 reports of British royal commissions and other committees of inquiry, in the fields of constitutional, economic, financial, and social policy and of legal administration. Arrangement is by broad subject field, with an outline of this subject classification, a detailed subject list of individual documents, and an index. The abstracts will be a useful supplement to small collections of parliamentary papers, as well as a guide to more complete sets.

—— A breviate of parliamentary papers, 1917–1939. Oxford, Blackwell, 1951; N.Y., Macmillan, 1952. 571p.

A guide to 1200 reports selected and arranged as the one above.

—— A breviate of parliamentary papers, 1940–1954; war and reconstruction. Oxford, Blackwell, 1961. 515p.

"Follows the same general pattern as the two previous breviaries."—*Introd.*

Parliamentary debates

Gt.Brit. Parliament. Parliamentary debates, v.1–41 (1803–20); n.s. v.1–25 (1820–30); 3d ser. v.1–356 (1830–90/91); 4th ser. v.1–199 (1892–1908); 5th ser.: Commons, v.1– . (1909–); Lords, v.1– . (1909–). London, 1804– . **AH66**

Generally cited as *Hansard.* Publisher varies.

There is a general index to the 66v. of the 1st–2d series (London, Baldwin, 1834. 2v.); for series 3–5 the sessional indexes—sometimes in separate volumes, sometimes included in the last volume of debates of the session—must be used.

The 5th series is official and contains complete and verbatim reports of debates, and all division lists. The 1st–4th series were unofficial; their reports of debates are neither complete nor verbatim, and not all division lists are given in full. For an interesting account of parliamentary debates of the 19th to the 20th century *see* H. D. Jordan. "Reports of parliamentary debates 1803–1908," in *Economica* 11:437–49. Nov. 1931.

The period before 1803 is covered by Cobbett's *Parliamentary history of England from the earliest period to the year 1803* (London, Hansard, 1806–20. 36v.), which is, of course, a retrospective compilation rather than a current record. For an interesting account of sources upon which it is based, or which are available for the early period, *see* "General collections of reports of parliamentary debates for the period since 1660," in London. University. *Bulletin of the Institute of Historical Research* 10:171–77. Feb. 1933.

INDIA

India (Republic). Parliament. Abstracts and index of reports and articles. Jan./March 1963– . New Delhi, Lok Sabha Secretariat, 1963– . Quarterly.   **AH67**

Formed by the merger of its *Abstracts of reports, 1955–1962*, and its *Abstracts and index of articles, 1958–62* (AF 151).

Each issue in four parts: (1) Abstracts of reports; (2) Abstracts of articles; (3) Index of reports; (4) Index of articles.

JAPAN

Japan. Diet Library. Branch Libraries Division. List of Japanese government publications in European languages, 1945–1955. [Tokyo, 1956?] 53p.   **AH68**

Titles and abstracts are in European languages.

Includes publications of all government agencies, as well as those of the Japan Monopoly Corporation, the Japanese National Railways, the Nippon Telegraph and Telephone Public Corporation, and the Bank of Japan; also a list of SCAP (Supreme Commander for the Allied Powers) publications, 1946–52, owned by the American Embassy Library and the National Diet Library (7p.).

LATIN AMERICA

Hill, Roscoe R. The national archives of Latin America; ed. for the Joint Committee on Latin American Studies of the National Research Council, the American Council of Learned Societies, and the Social Science Research Council. Cambridge, Harvard Univ. Pr., 1945. 169p. il. (Joint Committee on Latin American Studies. Misc. publ. no.3)   **AH69**

Survey of the history, housing, personnel, and contents of the national archives of each of the 20 Latin-American republics.

U.S. Library of Congress. A guide to the official publications of the other American republics. James B. Childs, gen. ed. Wash., Govt. Prt. Off., 1945–49. v.1–19. (Latin Amer. ser.)   **AH70**

Contents: v.1, Argentina. 1945. 124p.; v.2, Bolivia. 1945. 66p.; v.3, Brazil, comp. by John De Noia. 1948 (1949). 223p.; v.4, Chile, comp. by Otto Neuburger. 1947. 94p.; v.5, Colombia, [comp. by] James B. Childs. 1948. 89p.; v.6, Costa Rica, comp. by Henry V. Besso. 1947. 92p.; v.7, Cuba. 1945. 40p.; v.8, Dominican Republic, comp. by John De Noia. 1947. 40p.; v.9, Ecuador, comp. by John De Noia. 1947. 56p.; v.10, El Salvador, comp. by John De Noia. 1947. 64p.; v.11, Guate-

mala, comp. by Henry V. Besso. 1947. 88p.; v.12, Haiti. 1947. 25p.; v.13, Honduras. 1947. 31p.; v.14, Nicaragua, comp. by John De Noia. 1947. 33p.; v.15, Panama, comp. by John De Noia. 1947. 34p.; v.16, Paraguay, [comp. by] James B. Childs. 1947. 61p.; v.17, Peru, comp. by John De Noia. 1948 (1949). 90p.; v.18, Uruguay, comp. by John De Noia and Glenda Crevenna. 1948 (1949). 91p.; v.19, Venezuela, comp. by Otto Neuburger. 1948 (1949). 59p.

A series of guides, each of which gives information about general publications, including official gazettes, session laws, codes, constitution, etc., followed by the publications of the legislative, executive, and judicial branches.

NEW ZEALAND

New Zealand. National Archives. A guide to the Dominion archives. Wellington, Dept. of Internal Affairs, 1953. 27p.   **AH71**

Includes a section on government publications and bibliography, p.25–27.

Earlier name of issuing body: Dominion Archives.

—— Preliminary inventory. no.1– . Wellington, Dept. of Internal Affairs, 1953– .   **AH72**

An annotated list of governmental archival material dating from 1840, arranged chronologically.

NIGERIA

U.S. Library of Congress. General Reference and Bibliography Division. Nigerian official publications, 1869–1959: a guide, comp. by Helen F. Conover. Wash., 1959. 153p.   **AH73**

A listing of more than 1200 titles: pt.1 covers 1947–1959; pt.2, 1923–1946; pt.3, 1861–1922.

NORWAY

Oslo. Universitet. Bibliotek. Bibliografi over norges offentlige publikasjoner, 1956– . Oslo, Universitetsforlaget, 1957– . v.[1]– . Annual.   **AH74**

"Comprises both government publications and publications edited with grants from government."—*Note.*

PAKISTAN

Moreland, George B. and **Siddiqui, Akhtar H.** Publications of the government of Pakistan, 1947–1957. [Karachi], Inst. of Public and Business Admin., Univ. of Karachi, 1958. 187p.   **AH75**

Attempts to bring together the official publications of the government of Pakistan which are for sale, and also many government documents not for sale, by the Manager of Publications.

Pakistan. Catalogue of the government of Pakistan publications. 1962– . Karachi, Manager of Publ., 1962– . Annual.   **AH76**

Arranged by departments; lists publications beginning with 1949. Includes a separate list of periodicals.

Kept up to date by supplements.

PHILIPPINES

Philippine Islands. Philippine Library and Museum. Legislative Reference Division. Checklist of publications of the government of the Philippine Islands, Sept. 1, 1900 to Dec. 31, 1917, comp. by Emma O. Elmer. Manila, 1918. 288p. **AH77**

Continued by:

Bibliographical Society of the Philippines. Checklist of Philippine government documents, 1917–1949, comp. by Consolacion B. Rebadavia . . . Quezon City, Univ. of the Philippines Lib., 1960. 817p. **AH78**

A retrospective bibliography of more than 6000 items.

—— Checklist of Philippine government documents, 1950. Wash., Lib. of Congress, 1953. 62p.

755 numbered items.

Quezon, Philippines. University of the Philippines. Institute of Public Administration. Library. List of Philippine government publications, 1945–1958, comp. by Andrea C. Ponce and Jacinto C. Yatoo. Manila, 1959– . Pt. 1– . (In progress) **AH79**

Contents: pt.1, Publications of agencies under the Dept. of Agriculture and Natural Resources, Dept. of Commerce and Industry, Dept. of Education, and Dept. of Labor.

Philippines (Republic). Bureau of Public Libraries. Philippine government publications. v.1, no.1, Jan. 1958– . Manila, 1958– . Monthly or bimonthly. **AH80**

The first current record of the government publications of the Republic of the Philippines.

SIERRA LEONE

U.S. Library of Congress. African Section. Official publications of Sierra Leone and Gambia, comp. by Audrey A. Walker. Wash., 1963. 92p. **AH81**

A listing of some 700 titles, 500 having to do with Sierra Leone and 200 with Gambia. Historical notes accompany each section.

SOMALILAND

U.S. Library of Congress. General Reference and Bibliography Division. Official publications of Somaliland, 1941–1959; a guide, comp. by Helen F. Conover. Wash., 1960. 41p. **AH82**

Has separate sections for Somaliland under Italian administration, British Somaliland, and French Somaliland. Subject index.

Lists about 170 titles, including a bibliography of chief sources.

SWEDEN

Sweden. Riksdagen. Bibliotek. Årsbibliografi över Sveriges offentliga publikationer, utg. av Riksdagsbiblioteket. 1931/33– . Stockholm, Beckmans, 1934– . Annual. **AH83**

TUNIS

Pilipenko, Hélène and **Rousset de Pina, Jean.** Récapitulation des périodiques officiels parus en Tunisie de 1881 à 1955. Tunis, 1956. 108p. **AH84**

At head of title: Royaume de Tunis, Ministère de l'Éducation Nationale, Bibliothèque Nationale de Tunisie.

A detailed listing of official periodical publications arranged by issuing agency, with title, name, and agency indexes.

A I

Dissertations

❧ Dissertations for the doctorate form a special class of publications, and catalogs or bibliographies of these dissertations, both American and foreign, assume definite importance in university, reference, or special libraries where much use is made of thesis material. As the doctor's degree is given only for original work, and as each doctoral dissertation must deal with some aspect of a subject not previously treated, the value of a dissertation to the reader interested in the subject is obvious.

While some dissertations are issued by commercial publishers, and some are privately printed, many are available only in typewritten form or on microfilm. Only those issued by commercial publishers appear in the trade bibliographies; the others are listed in special bibliographies of dissertations, of which there are various types:

I. National
  A. Completed
    1. General—covering the dissertations of all the universities of a given country
      a) Cumulative—covering a number of years
      b) Annual
    2. Subject—covering the theses of all universities in a given country in a particular subject field
  B. In progress
II. Individual university
  A. Lists
  B. Abstracts

These bibliographies are of primary importance in research libraries: (1) to show the student trying to select a thesis subject whether that subject has already been treated or is being worked on; (2) to show at what university a particular dissertation was written; (3) to show the acquisitions department whether a publication not listed in the trade lists is a dissertation; (4) to show the research worker what material has been written on very special subjects; (5) to provide biographical data, about the authors of dissertations, which are included in some of the lists.

The general practice used to be to distribute printed dissertations to university libraries and to special libraries interested in particular subjects. Now most dissertations are submitted in manuscript and are available, on interlibrary loan or for purchase, either on microfilm or on Xerox (*see Dissertation abstracts*, AI11). Many of these may be purchased from University Microfilms, Ann Arbor, Mich., but in some cases it is necessary to write directly to the university where the dissertation was written.

For current work, especially in university libraries where it is essential to keep informed of research being done, the various lists of "dissertations in progress" are very useful.

In the following lists only the national bibliographies of completed dissertations are included, except (1) in a few cases, e.g., Germany, where extensive lists of individual universities precede the years covered by the national lists; and (2) in the case of small countries, e.g., Norway, where there is no national list, and therefore the list of the main university serves as such.

Abstracts and lists from individual universities will at times provide information not found in the general bibliographies. For bibliographies of theses from American universities *see* Thomas R. Palfrey and Henry E. Coleman, *Guide to bibliographies of theses, United States and Canada* (2d ed. Chicago, Amer. Lib. Assoc., 1940) and its supplement by Ralph P. Rosenberg, in *Bulletin of bibliography* 18:181–82, 201–3. Sept./Dec. 1945—Jan./April 1946.

For lists of dissertations—both completed and in progress—in particular subjects, *see* under subject.

MANUALS

Campbell, William Giles. Form and style in thesis writing. Boston, Houghton, 1954. 114p. il.　　　　**AI1**
　　1st ed. 1939.

Dugdale, Kathleen. A manual of form for theses and term reports. (Rev.) Bloomington, Ind., Author, 1955. 58p. il.　　**AI2**
　　Includes many sample pages.
　　"Designed to help the student and the typist prepare a completed research study in acceptable typewritten form."—*Introd.*

Hurt, Peyton. Bibliography and footnotes; a style manual for college and university students, rev. and enl. by Mary L. Hurt Richmond. Berkeley, Los Angeles, Univ. of California Pr., 1949. 167p.　　**AI3**
　　Very useful for form of footnotes, etc.

Turabian, Kate L. A manual for writers of term papers, theses, and dissertations. Rev. ed. Chicago, Univ. of Chicago Pr., 1955. 82p.　　**AI4**
　　1st ed. 1937.
　　Also published by Phoenix Books. Univ. of Chicago Pr., 1955. 109p.
　　A well-organized and widely used manual, primarily for graduate students.

—— Student's guide for writing college papers. Chicago, Univ. of Chicago Pr., 1963. 172p. (Phoenix books. P134)　　**AI5**
　　Primarily for undergraduates.

BIBLIOGRAPHY

International

Oxford. University. Bodleian Library. Catalogus dissertationum academicarum quibus nuper aucta est Bibliotheca Bodleiana MDCCCXXXII. Oxford, Typ. Acad., 1834. 448p., 63p.　　**AI6**

A listing of all dissertations in the Bodleian Library in 1832 from various universities.

Paris. Bibliothèque Nationale. Dépt. des Imprimés. Catalogue des dissertations et écrits académiques provenant des échanges avec les universités étrangères et reçus par la Bibliothèque Nationale, 1882–1924. Paris, Klincksieck, 1884–1925. t.1–43.　　**AI7**
　　Dissertations received by the Bibliothèque Nationale from European universities, arranged by university.

United States

U.S. Library of Congress. Catalog Division. List of American doctoral dissertations printed in 1912–38. Wash., Govt. Prt. Off., 1913–40. 26v.　　**AI8**
　　Contents of each volume: (1) Alphabetical list of theses printed during the year; (2) Classified list, arranged under the broad classes of the Library of Congress scheme; (3) Index of subjects; (4) Doctors whose theses have been printed during the year, arranged by institutions.
　　Lists 1 and 2 give full catalog information and, in case of reprints, indicate the periodical or other publication in which the thesis was first printed. Includes the *printed* theses of about 45 colleges and universities. No more published.

✓**Doctoral dissertations accepted by American universities,** 1933/34–1954/55. Comp. for the Assoc. of Research Libraries. N.Y., Wilson, 1934–56. no.1–22.　　**AI9**
　　Ceased publication.
　　A list of dissertations (United States and Canada) arranged by subject and then by university, giving for each dissertation its author, title, and—in the case of those printed— bibliographical data as to separate publication or inclusion in some periodical or collection. Alphabetical author index, and subject index.
　　Continued by:

✓**Index to American doctoral dissertations,** 1955/56– . Comp. for the Assoc. of Research Libraries. Ann Arbor, Mich., Univ. Microfilms, 1957– . Annual. (Being *Dissertation abstracts,* v.16, no.13, and cont.)　　**AI10**
　　Issued annually as no.13 of *Dissertation abstracts,* it consolidates into one list dissertations for which doctoral degrees were granted in the United States and Canada during the academic year covered, as well as those available on microfilm.
　　Arranged by subject classification with author indexes. The subject classification must be used with care, as there are not sufficient subject breakdowns to make it easy to discover what has been done in a particular field.
　　Preliminary tables give information on the publication and lending of dissertations, and the distribution of doctorates by university and subject field.

✓**Dissertation abstracts;** abstracts of dissertations and monographs in microform. Ann Arbor, Mich., Univ. Microfilms, 1952– . v.12– . Monthly.　　**AI11**
　　v.1–11, 1935–51, issued as *Microfilm abstracts,* with a cumulative author index.
　　Subtitle varies. Coverage varies.
　　A compilation of abstracts of doctoral dissertations submitted to University Microfilms, Inc., by a varying number of cooperating universities (140 in 1963). The dissertations themselves are microfilmed and are available for purchase from University Microfilms. For each, an abstract is included in *Dissertation abstracts.* The main list is arranged alphabetically by subject field and then by university; each listing includes title, order number, author's name, university, date, name of supervisor, abstract, prices of microfilm and of Xerox copy, and number of pages. Each issue includes a subject index and an author index. Pt.2 of no.12 (June) of each year, since 1961/62, is a cumulated subject and author index for the year. This includes *only* the dissertations ab-

stracted and not those in the *Index to American doctoral dissertations* (AI10).

Dissertations of the sixties. Ann Arbor, Mich., Univ. Microfilms, 1964– . Annual. **AI12**

A new series by subject field; (1) Psychology, 1963– lists about 1800 titles.

Masters abstracts: abstracts of selected masters theses on microfilm. Ann Arbor, Mich., Univ. Microfilms, 1962– . v.1– . Quarterly. **AI13**

v.1, 1962/63, semiannual; v.2, 1964, quarterly.

Published abstracts of a selected list of master's essays, from various universities, available on microfilm. Classified arrangement. No indexes announced.

Yüan, T'ung-li. Guide to doctoral dissertations by Chinese students in America, 1905–1960. Wash., Sino-American Cultural Soc., 1961. 248p. **AI14**

Lists almost 2800 dissertations. Contents: pt.1, Humanities, social and behavioral sciences; pt.2, Physical, biological, and engineering sciences; pt.3, Canadian dissertations, 1926–1960. Alphabetical by author within each part.

Australia

Marshall, Mary Jacqueline. Union list of higher degree theses in Australian university libraries. Hobart, Univ. of Tasmania Lib., 1959. 237p. **AI15**

A union list from nine university libraries, through 1958. Includes both master's and doctor's theses in classified arrangement, with author and subject indexes.

Austria

Vienna. Universität. Philosophische Fakultät. Verzeichnis über die seit dem Jahre 1872 an der Philosophischen Fakultät der Universität in Wien eingereichten und approbierten Dissertationen. Wien, 1935–36. 3v. **AI16**

Arranged by large subjects, with a catchword subject index at end of each group and an author index at end of each volume.

—— —— Bd.4, Nachtrag: Verzeichnis der 1934 bis 1937 an der Philosophischen Fakultät der Universität in Wien u. der 1872 bis 1937 an der Philosophischen Fakultät der Universität in Innsbruck eingereichten und approbierten Dissertationen. . . . Wien, [c1937]. 292p.

v.4 of the basic set listed above; providing a 1934–37 supplement to the Vienna list and a basic list for Innsbruck.

Continued by:

Alker, Lisl. Verzeichnis der an der Universität Wien approbierten Dissertationen, 1937/1944– . Wien, Kerry, 1954. **AI17**

1937/1944 (pub. 1954); 1945/1949 (pub. 1952); 1950/1957 (pub. 1959).

Classified, with combined author and subject index.

Canada

See also AI9, AI10, AI11.

Ottawa. Canadian Bibliographic Centre. Canadian graduate theses in the humanities and social sciences, 1921–1946. Ottawa, Printer to the King, 1951. 194p. **AI18**

3043 theses, arranged by subject and then by institution, with an author index and English and French subject indexes. Information given usually includes: author, title, pagination, degree, date, professor in charge, and a very brief note on scope and content. Tables at the end give distribution of theses by subject, etc., and library practice with regard to loan of theses.

Ottawa. National Library of Canada. Canadian theses. Thèses canadiennes, 1960/61– . Ottawa, 1962– . Annual. **AI19**

A previous list was issued for 1952 in 1953. Now expected to be annual. Arranged by broad classification based on the Dewey Decimal Classification, then by university. Author index.

Denmark

Copenhagen. Universitet. Bibliotek. Danish theses for the doctorate and commemorative publications of the University of Copenhagen, 1836–1926, a bio-bibliography. Copenhagen, Levin and Munksgaard, 1929. 395p. **AI20**

In two parts: (1) class list, arranged by the main classes of the Decimal Classification; (2) alphabetical author list, which gives brief biographies of the authors with references to fuller biographies elsewhere, and also serves as an author index to the class list. Bibliographical detail given for each thesis includes: author's name, title, English translation of a Danish title sometimes with brief abstract in English, date, paging, illustrations, date of oral defense. Subject index.

Continued by:

—— Danish theses for the doctorate, 1927–1958; a bibliography . . . Copenhagen, Univ. Lib., 1962. 249p.

Arranged alphabetically by author with subject index.

Finland

See also Sweden, AI48–AI50.

Hjelt, Otto Edvard August. Det Finska universitetets disputations- och program-litteratur under åren 1828–1908 systematiskt ordnad. Dissertationes academicae et programmata Universitatis litterarum Fennorum Helsingforsiae annis 1828–1908 edita. Helsingfors, Helsingfors Centraltryckeri, 1909. 162p. **AI21**

Kärmeniemi, Kaija. Opinnäytteiden bibliografia; luettelo Helsingin yliopistossa, Turun yliopistossa ja Yhteiskunnallisessa Korkeakoulussa vuoteen 1956 mennessä humanististen tietei den aloilta laadituista tutkielmista. Helsinki, Suomalaisen Kirjallisuuden Seura, 1959. 164p. (Tietolipas no.15) **AI22**

Finnish dissertations up to 1956.

Vallinkoski, J. Turun akatemian väitöskirjat, 1642–1828. Die dissertationen der alten universität Turku (Academia Aboënsis) 1642–1828. Helsinki, 1962–64. no.1–3. (In progress) (Helsingin yliopiston kirjaston julkaisuja. 30. Publications of the University Library at Helsinki, 30) **AI23**

Contents: 1–3, A–Aeschillus.

A listing of dissertations written at the old Finnish university at Turku (now Åbo).

France

Maire, Albert. Répertoire alphabétique des thèses de doctorat ès lettres des universités françaises, 1810–1900. Paris, Picard, 1903. 226p. **AI24**

List of 2182 theses, arranged alphabetically by author. Gives for each: author, title, place, publisher, date, paging, university, and whether published in any other form. Marks rejected theses.

Includes a chronological list by universities and a subject index.

Mourier, Athénaïs and **Deltour, F.** Notice sur le doctorat ès lettres, suivie du Catalogue et de l'analyse des thèses françaises et latines admises par les facultés des lettres depuis 1810. 4. éd., corr. et considérablement augm. Paris, Delalain, 1880. 442p. **AI25**

—— Catalogue et analyse des thèses latines et françaises. Paris, Delalain, 1882–1901. 21v. **AI26**

The main list and the 21 annuals, together covering 1810–1900, include practically the same theses as Maire's *Répertoire* (AI24), but arrange them by years and universities instead of alphabetically, and give, in addition to title and paging, full contents of each thesis and very brief biographical data. Main use is for contents. Indexes: (1) subjects, and (2) authors.

France. Ministère de l'Éducation Nationale. Catalogue des thèses de doctorat soutenues devant les universités françaises. 1884/85– . Paris, [etc.], 1885– . **AI27**

1884/85–1930/31 published by the Ministère de l'Instruction Publique.

Title varies: *Catalogue des thèses et écrits académiques,* 1884–1959.

Issued annually, 5 annuals forming a volume. The official French list. Each annual issue, 1885–1913, is arranged alphabetically by university, with subarrangement by *faculté;* beginning with 1914, the arrangement is by *faculté,* with author indexes since 1957. Gives for each thesis: author's name, full title, place, publisher, and since 1930/31, date, size, and paging. v.1–9 (1884/89–1928/29) have author and subject indexes. Of great value in the university library, as the French theses are among the most important published.

The *Bibliographie de la France* (AA473) contains an alphabetical list of dissertations 1930– , published as preliminary supplements to the *Bibliographie,* pt.1, 1932– .

Germany

Berlin. Universität. Bibliothek. Verzeichnis der Berliner Universitätsschriften, 1810–85. Berlin, Weber, 1899. 848p. **AI28**

Arranged by faculty with author index.

Milkau, Fritz. Verzeichniss der Bonner Universitätsschriften, 1818–1885. Bonn, Cohen, 1897. 440p. **AI29**

Pretzsch, Karl. Verzeichnis der Breslauer Universitätsschriften, 1811–1885. Breslau, Korn, 1905. 387p. **AI30**

Mundt, Hermann. Bio-bibliographisches Verzeichnis von Universitäts- u. Hochschuldrucken (Dissertationen) vom Ausgang des 16. bis Ende des 19. Jahrhunderts. Bd.1–2. Leipzig, Carlsohn, 1936–42. **AI31**

Bd.1, A–Kühn (appeared as Lfg. 1–9, 1934–36). [Bd.2], Kühn-Ritter (appeared as Lfg. 10–13, 1937–42). Incomplete.

A list of theses containing brief biographical data about the various persons connected with them, arranged alphabetically by respondent. Chiefly German, with some Dutch and Scandinavian dissertations.

Klussmann, Rudolf. Systematisches Verzeichnis der Abhandlungen welche in den Schulschriften sämtlicher an dem Programmtausche teilnehmenden Lehranstalten erschienen sind. Leipzig, Teubner, 1889–1916. 5v. **AI32**

Classified, with index of places and index of authors. Covers 1876–1910.

Pennsylvania. University. Library. Catalog of the Programmschriften collection. Boston, Hall, 1961. 117p., 260p. **AI33**

Approximately 5000 scholarly pamphlets, largely in the humanities, selected from a much larger collection. A subject index is the key to the reproduced typed cards, arranged by author.

Annuals

Bibliographischer Monatsbericht über neu erschienene Schul-, Universitäts- und Hochschulschriften, 1889/90–1942/43. Leipzig, Fock, 1890–1943. Jahr.1–54. **AI34**

Ceased publication with v.54, no.1/2, June 1943.

Classified arrangement, with annual author index, and, from v.4 on, an annual *Sachregister.*

Superseded for most purposes by the *Jahresverzeichnis der deutschen Hochschulschriften* (AI36).

Jahresverzeichnis der an den deutschen Schulanstalten erschienenen Abhandlungen, 1889–1930. Berlin, de Gruyter, 1890–1931. v.1–28. **AI35**

Publisher varies.

v.1–27 cover one year each, 1889–1915; v.28 covers the 15 years, 1916–30.

Arranged alphabetically by author with subject indexes.

Jahresverzeichnis der deutschen Hochschulschriften, 1885– . Bearb. von der Deutschen Bücherei. Leipzig, VEB Verlag für Buch- und Bibliothekswesen, 1887– . Bd.1– . **AI36**

Publisher varies.

Title varies: 1924–35, *Jahresverzeichnis der an den deutschen Universitäten und Hochschulen erschienen Schriften.*

The standard official German list including the theses of all the German universities from 1885, the theses of the Technische Hochschulen from 1913, and the theses of the Hochschulen der Länder from 1924. Arranged by universities, with an author index in each volume, a separate subject index for Bd.1–5, and a subject index in each volume, Bd.6– . Gives for each thesis: author's full name, title of thesis, date, publisher, paging, size, and whether reprinted from some scientific journal, report, etc.

Great Britain

Index to theses accepted for higher degrees in the universities of Great Britain and Ireland. v.1, 1950/51– . London, ASLIB, 1953– . v.1– . Annual. **AI37**

Classified arrangement, and alphabetically by university under these heads. Subject and author indexes.

Cambridge. University. Abstracts of dissertations approved for the Ph.D., M.Sc., and M.Litt. degrees in the University of Cambridge . . . 1925/26–1956/57. Cambridge, Univ. Pr., 1927–59. **AI38**

Ceased publication. Continued by:

—— Titles of dissertations approved for the Ph.D., M.Sc., and M.Litt. degrees in the University of Cambridge, 1957/58– . Cambridge, Univ. Pr., 1958– . v.1– . Annual. **AI39**

Oxford. University. Committee for Advanced Studies. Abstracts of dissertations for the degree of doctor of philosophy. v.1–13, 1925/28–1940. Oxford, Univ. Pr., 1928–47. 13v. **AI40**

—— Successful candidates for the degree of D.Phil., B.Litt., and B.Sc., with titles of their theses. v.1– , 1940/49– . Oxford, 1950– . Annual. **AI41**

Netherlands

Utrecht. Reichsuniversiteit. Bibliothek. Catalogus van academische geschriften in Nederland verschenen, jaarg. 1– , 1924– . Utrecht, 1925– . **AI42**

Issuing body varies. Title varies; through 1945, included Nederlands Indie.

Arranged by university.

Combined author and subject index for jaarg.1–5, 1924–28, which form v.1; jaarg.6– , 1929– , have author index only.

New Zealand

Jenkins, D. L. Union list of theses of the University of New Zealand, 1910–1954. Wellington, New Zealand Lib. Assoc., 1956. unpaged. **AI43**

Arranged by subject field, then chronologically. Author index.

Norway

Andresen, Gunnar W. Doctores kreert ved Universitet i Oslo, 1817–1961; en bibliografi . . . med en historisk innledning; om doktorgraden ved vårt universitet av Leiv Amundsen. Oslo, Universitets Forlaget, 1962. 100p. **AI44**

Doctor's dissertations from the University of Norway arranged by faculty, with author index.

South Africa

Robinson, Anthony Meredith Lewin. Catalogue of theses and dissertations accepted for degrees by the South African universities; Katalogus van proefskrifte en verhandelinge vir grade deur die Suid-Afrikaanse universiteite goedgekeur, 1918–1941. . . . (Pub. with the assistance of the National Research Board) . . . Cape Town, 1943. 155p. **AI45**

1757 items. Classified, with subject and author indexes.
Continued by:

Malan, Stephanus I. Gesamentlike katalogus van proefskrifte en verhandelinge van die Suid-Afrikaanse universiteite. Union catalogue of theses and dissertations of the South African universities, 1942–1958. Potchefstroom, Univ. for Christian Higher Education, 1959. 216p. **AI46**

Title page and introductory materials in Afrikaans and English.
A classified list with author index.

Spain

Madrid. Universidad. Catálogo de las tesis doctorales manuscritas existentes en la Universidad de Madrid. Madrid, González, 1952. 36p. **AI47**

Entries cover the total holdings of manuscript doctoral theses, and are arranged alphabetically under broad subject. No author or subject index.

Sweden

Marklin, Gabriel. Catalogus disputationum in academiis Scandinaviae et Finlandiae Lidenianus continuatus a Gabr. Marklin. Upsaliae, Reg. Academiae Typ., 1820. 3 pts. **AI48**

Covers 1778–1819.
Contents: (1) Disputationes upsalienses; (2) Disputationes lundenses. Disputationes christianienses; (3) Disputationes aboënses.

—— —— Ad Catalogum disputationum in academiis et gymnasiis Sueciae Lidenianum supplementa addidit Gabr. Marklin. Upsaliae, Reg. Academiae Typ., 1820. 117p.

—— Catalogus disputationum in academiis continuatus a Gabr. Marklin. . . . Stockholm, 1874. 3v. in 1. **AI49**

First issued Upsaliae, 1856.
Covers 1820–55.
Contents: (1) Disputationes upsalienses; (2) Disputationes lundenses; (3) Disputationes fennorum.

Josephson, Aksel Gustav Salomon. Avhandlingar ock program, uitg. vid svenska ock finska akademier ock skolor, 1855–1890. Uppsala, [1891–1897]. 2v. **AI50**

Author list with classified index.
Continued by:

Nelson, Axel Herman. Akademiska afhandlingar vid sveriges universitet och högskolor läsåren 1890/91–1909/

10 jämte förteckning öfver svenskars akademiska afhandlingar vid utländska universitet under samma tid. Uppsala, Akademiska Bokhandeln, [1911–12]. 149p. **AI51**

An author list with classified index.
Continued by:

Tuneld, John. Akademiska avhandlingar vid sveriges universitet och högskolor, läsåren 1910/11–1939/40; bibliografi. Lund, [Ohlsson], 1945. 336p. **AI52**

An author list with classified index.

Switzerland

Jahresverzeichnis der schweizerischen Hochschulschriften, 1897– ; Catalogue des écrits académiques suisses, 1897– . Basel, Verlag der Universitätsbibliothek, 1898– . Bd.1– . Annual. **AI53**

Publisher varies. Title varies.
Arranged by university. Each issue has an author index (1925, Personen-Register) and, 1926– , a catchword subject index.

—— Verfasser-Register zu den Jahrgängen 1897/98–1922/23. Basel, Univ.-Bibliothek, 1927. 87p.

Union of Soviet Socialist Republics

Moscow. Publichnaia Biblioteka. Katalog kandidatskikh i doktorskikh dissertatsii, postupivshikh v Biblioteku imeni V. I. Lenina i Gosudarstvennuiu Tsentral'nuiu Nauchnuiu Meditsinskuiu Biblioteku. 1957, 2–oe polugodie– . Moskva, 1958– . Quarterly (1957–58, semiannual). **AI54**

The principal current bibliography for the texts of Soviet dissertations in all fields, as deposited with the Lenin Library and the Central State Library of Medicine.

Current bibliographic listing of the authors' printed summaries of 15–50 pages in length is provided by: "*Avtoreferaty dissertatsii*," in *Knizhnaia letopis'; dopolnitel'nyi vypusk* [AA672a] for the years 1961, 1964– .

For a history of these titles and related lists, *see* Eleanor Buist. "Soviet dissertation lists since 1934," in *Library quarterly* 33: 192–207. April 1963.

A J

Biography

✤ Dictionaries of biography are among the most used reference books in any collection, and even a small library will need several works in this class. There are three main types of biographical dictionaries: (1) general; (2) national or regional; and (3) professional or occupational. Each of these may be subdivided into (1) general or retrospective, and (2) contemporary.

In this section are listed general biographical works, both retrospective and current, from various countries. For biographical dictionaries in specialized fields, *see* those subjects, e.g., Education, Medical Sciences, etc.

The basic works needed in almost any American library

would include: the *Dictionary of American biography* (AJ32); the latest, or at least a recent, edition of *Who's who in America* (AJ45); *Current biography* (AJ28); and *Webster's Biographical dictionary* (AJ25). To these would probably be added the appropriate regional who's who and, where possible, the *Biography index* (AJ2). Many libraries will need professional and occupational works such as *American men of science* (EA183); the *Directory of American scholars* (AJ52); Theodore Baker's *Biographical dictionary of musicians* (BH43), etc.; and the large library will want many of the works from other countries.

In examining biographical dictionaries, they should be tested for the points enumerated in the general instructions for examining reference books, and, in addition, any evidence noted carefully of lack of objectivity in the selection of names. Unscrupulous publishers will sometimes include padded or unduly eulogistic articles on comparatively unknown persons, with the expectation, or on condition, that these persons will pay for inclusion or will subscribe for the book. The inclusion of such articles puts the book in the commercial or "vanity" class and casts doubt upon the authority of all articles. Such books are not necessarily to be rejected if they happen to be the only ones in their field, but they must always be used with caution.

GENERAL WORKS

Indexes

Arnim, Max. Internationale Personalbibliographie, 1800–1943. 2. verb. und stark verm. Aufl. Leipzig, Hiersemann, 1944–52. 2v. **AJ1**

Primarily an index to bibliographies of individuals, but as many of the bibliographies indexed have accompanying biographical data, the work serves also as an index to biographical articles. For full description *see* AA11.

Biography index; a cumulative index to biographical material in books and magazines. N.Y., Wilson, 1947– . v.1– . (In progress) **AJ2**

A quarterly index to biographical material, published in Nov., Feb., May, and Aug. with annual and three-year cumulations in August. "It includes current books in the English language wherever published; biographical material from the 1500 periodicals now regularly indexed in the Wilson indexes, plus a selected list of professional journals in the fields of law and medicine; obituaries of national and international interest from the *New York Times*. All types of biographical material are covered: pure biography, critical material of biographical significance, autobiography, letters, diaries, memoirs, journals, genealogies, fiction, drama, poetry, bibliographies, obituaries, pictorial works and juvenile literature. Works of collective biography are fully analyzed. Incidental biographical material such as prefaces and chapters in otherwise non-biographical books is included. Portraits are indicated when they appear in conjunction with indexed material. . . ."—*Pref.*

Index is in two sections: (1) Name alphabet, giving for each biographee, insofar as possible, full name, dates, nationality, and occupation or profession with index references; (2) Index by profession and occupation. Large categories, such as authors, are divided by nationality.

The first volume indexes back to Jan. 1, 1946.

Chevalier, Cyr Ulysse Joseph. Répertoire des sources historiques du Moyen Âge; bio-bibliographie. Nouv. éd. refondue, corr. et considérablement augm. Paris, Picard, 1903–7. 2v. **AJ3**

The most complete and important work for the medieval period, arranged alphabetically, giving under the French form of each name: (1) brief biographical data, i.e., characterizing phrase and dates of birth and death, and (2) references to books, periodicals, society transactions, etc., where some account of the personage may be found. Very useful for out-of-the-way names, or for complete lists of references on more familiar names; less useful for quick reference work on more familiar names because too much material is given for the ordinary reader. For the large and university library.

For complete set *see* DA104.

Essay and general literature index. N.Y., Wilson, 1934– . **AJ3a**

Contains a large amount of analytical material for biography and criticism of individuals and so often serves as an index of biography. For full description *see* BD145.

Hefling, Helen and **Richards, Eva.** Index to contemporary biography and criticism. New ed. rev. and enl. by Helen Hefling and Jessie W. Dyde . . . introd. by M. E. Hazeltine. Boston, Faxon, 1934. 229p. (Useful reference ser., no.50) **AJ4**

An index to biographical material about persons born since the mid-19th century. Some 420 collections of biography and criticism have been indexed, omitting such strictly reference works as the various Who's who's.

Hyamson, Albert Montefiore. A dictionary of universal biography of all ages and of all peoples. 2d ed. entirely rewritten. N.Y., Dutton, 1951. 679p. **AJ5**

1st ed. 1916.

Not a biographical dictionary in the general sense of the term, but an index to the persons appearing in 24 standard biographical dictionaries of various countries. Most of the entries consist of a single line, giving name, dates, nationality, profession, and symbol for source.

Italy. Parlamento. Camera dei Deputati. Biblioteca. Catalogo metodico degli scritti contenuti nelle pubblicazioni periodiche italiane e straniere. Parte 1. Scritti biografici e critici. Roma, Tip. della Camera dei Deputati, 1885–1935. 10v. and index. **AJ6**

Contents: v.1, to 1883; suppl. 1, 1884–87 and earlier; suppl. 2, 1887–88 and earlier; suppl. 3, 1889–94; suppl. 4, 1895–1900; suppl. 5, 1901–6; n.s. v.1, 1907–12; n.s. v.2, 1913–18; n.s. v.3, 1919–24; n.s. v.4, 1925–30. Indice generale, a tutto l'anno 1906. 1909. 117p.

Not a general index but a subject catalog of biographical articles in the sets of periodicals (19,785 volumes) contained in the library of the Italian Chamber of Deputies. Each volume has: (1) a main subject list, arranged by name of biographee, which gives for each article indexed its title, author, and the title and volume or year of the periodical in which it is to be found, and (2) a brief author index referring to the subject list. The supplements index the volumes added during the period covered and earlier material omitted from the first volume. The *Indice generale* refers to all names included in the subject lists of the first volume and supplements 1–5. Sets indexed include the principal Italian periodicals and society transactions and also many important English, French, German, and Spanish titles.

Oettinger, Eduard Maria. Bibliographie biographique universelle. Dictionnaire des ouvrages relatifs à l'histoire de la vie publique et privée des personnages célèbres de tous les temps et de toutes les nations, depuis le commencement du monde jusqu'à nos jours . . . enrichi du répertoire des bio-bibliographies générales, nationales et spéciales. Bruxelles, Stienon, 1854. 2v. (Repr.: Paris, Lacroix, 1866) **AJ7**

Arranged alphabetically by biographee with dates and brief identifying phrase, this lists, in chronological order, separately published works about a large number of eminent persons of all times and of all countries.

v.2 includes lists of general, national and local, and subject biographical dictionaries.

O'Neill, Edward Hayes. Biography by Americans, 1658–1936; a subject bibliography. Philadelphia, Univ. of Pa. Pr.; London, Milford, 1939. 465p. **AJ8**

Attempts to record all known biographies written by Americans, except that in the case of particularly famous men only the more important books are listed. The main section, arranged alphabetically by the subject of the biography, lists separately published works and analyzes the 707 collective biographies listed in the second part.

Phillips, Lawrence Barnett. Dictionary of biographical reference; containing over 100,000 names; together with a classed index of the biographical literature of Europe and America. New ed. rev., corr., and augm. with supplement to date, by Frank Weitenkampf. [3d ed.] London, Low; Philadelphia, Gebbie, 1889. 1038p. **AJ9**

1st ed. 1871. 1020p.; 2d ed., under title *Great index of biographical reference,* 1881. 1036p.

International in scope and covers all periods. Gives full name, identifying phrase, dates, and reference to collections where biographical material can be found. Indexes some 40 biographical collections and other works.

Riches, Phyllis M. Analytical bibliography of universal collected biography, comprising books published in the English tongue in Great Britain and Ireland, America and the British dominions . . . London, Lib. Assoc., 1934. 709p. **AJ10**

An index to biographies of persons of various periods and nationalities in collected works in the English language. In four sections: (1) analytical index, arranged alphabetically by biographee; (2) a bibliography of the works analyzed; (3) a chronological list of the biographees; and (4) a list arranged by profession or trade.

Ungherini, Aglauro. Manuel de bibliographie biographique et d'iconographie des femmes célèbres . . . Turin, Roux; Paris, Nilsson, 1892–1905. 3v., i.e., main work, 896col.; 1st suppl., 634col.; 2d suppl., 758col. **AJ11**

A useful index to material about women of all countries and all periods. Gives an identifying phrase with dates of birth and death, lists monographic biographies in various languages, and cites portraits, autographs, etc. A cumulated index in the second supplement.

U.S. Library of Congress. General Reference and Bibliography Division. Biographical sources for foreign countries. Wash., 1944–45. no.1–4. **AJ12**

Pt.1, General, comp. by Helen D. Jones; pt.2, Germany and Austria, comp. by Nelson R. Burr; pt.3, The Philippines, comp. by Helen D. Jones; pt.4, The Japanese Empire, comp. by Nelson R. Burr.

Annotated bibliographies "designed to present a record of sources for biographical information on living persons in foreign countries. . . . In general . . . restricted to publications issued within the past twenty years."

In addition to general dictionaries of biography, includes a wide variety of sources, e.g., monographs, registers of national and local governments, official gazettes, city directories, yearbooks and membership lists of professional and technical associations, proceedings of conventions and congresses, periodicals, school directories, etc.

Classed arrangement with author and subject indexes.

INTERNATIONAL

Biographie universelle (Michaud) ancienne et moderne. Nouv. éd., publiée sous la direction de M. Michaud, rev., corr. et considérablement augm. d'articles omis ou nou-

veaux; ouvrage rédigé par une société de gens de lettres et de savants. Paris, Mme. C. Desplaces, 1843–65. 45v. **AJ13**

Usually cited as *Michaud.*

The 1st edition, in 84v. including supplements, was published 1811–57. Issue of the new edition, revised and enlarged, was begun in 1843. Its publication was interrupted in 1852 by a law suit undertaken by Mme. Desplaces, its publisher, against the firm of Didot Frères, which had started a rival dictionary, the *Nouvelle biographie universelle ancienne et moderne,* edited by Hoefer (AJ20), and had incorporated many articles taken in whole or in part from *Michaud.* After various decisions and reversals, the suit was finally won by Mme. Desplaces in 1855, Didot was forbidden to copy any more, and the publication of *Michaud* was resumed. The Didot dictionary, under a changed title and without the pirated articles, was also continued. For an interesting account of this famous suit, by R. C. Christie, *see Quarterly review* 157: 204–26; reprinted in his *Selected essays and papers.* London, Longmans, 1902.

The most important of the large dictionaries of universal biography, still very useful. While *Michaud* and the rival work by Hoefer cover much the same ground, there are definite and well-recognized differences. In spite of various inaccuracies, *Michaud* is more carefully edited; its articles, signed with initials, are longer and often better than those in *Hoefer;* its bibliographies (except in one point) are better; and it contains more names in the second half of the alphabet, N–Z. *Hoefer* contains more names, especially minor ones, in the part A–M; has some articles which are better than the corresponding articles in *Michaud;* and in the bibliographies gives titles in the original, whereas *Michaud* translates into French.

Chambers's Biographical dictionary. New ed., ed. by J. O. Thorne. Edinburgh, Chambers, 1961; N.Y., St. Martin's, 1962. 1432p. **AJ14**

A good small dictionary, covering the great of all nations and of all times, first published in 1897 and reprinted several times with changes.

This enlarged edition shows considerable revision and has many new listings, especially of contemporaries. Bibliographic references are more extensive and include many recent titles. Pronunciation of difficult names is often indicated. Subject index, p.1398–1432.

Grimal, Pierre. Dictionnaire des biographies. [1. éd.] Paris, Presses Universitaires de France, 1958. 2v. il. **AJ16**

A general biographical dictionary containing sketches of persons who have contributed to Western culture and life, from the time of the Greeks to modern times, but not including living persons. Usually one bibliographic citation is given for each entry and often a reference to portraits.

Heinzel, Erwin. Lexikon historischer Ereignisse und Personen in Kunst, Literatur und Musik. Wien, Hollinek, 1956. 782p. il. **AJ17**

Confines its listings to those historically important persons and events of many countries that have subsequently received substantial treatment in literature, music, or art. For each person or event, gives a statement of biographical or historical background and a summary of the extent and nature of the treatment the subject has received in the arts. These are followed by the literary, musical, and artistic works concerning the subject (e.g., poems, novels, dramas, operas, symphonies, portraits, busts, etc.).

Jöcher, Christian Gottlieb. Allgemeines Gelehrten-Lexicon, darinne die Gelehrten aller Stände sowohl männals weiblichen Geschlechts, welche vom Anfange der Welt bis auf ietzige Zeit gelebt, und sich der gelehrten Welt bekannt gemacht, nach ihrer Geburt, Leben, merckwürdigen Geschichten, Absterben und Schrifften aus den glaubwurdigsten Scribenten in alphabetischer

Ordnung beschrieben werden. Leipzig, Gleditsch, 1750–51. 4v. **AJ18**

v.1–4, A–Z.

—— —— Fortsetzung und Ergänzungen. . . . Leipzig, Gleditsch, 1784–87; Delmenhorst, Jöntzen, 1810; Bremen, Heyse, 1813–19; Leipzig, Selbstverlag der Deutschen Gesellschaft, 1897. v.1–7. (Repr.: Hildesheim, Georg Olms Verlagsbuchhandlung, 1961)

v.1–7, A–Romuleus (no more published).

v.1–2 by J. C. Adelung; v.3–6 by H. W. Rotermund; v.7 by Otto Günther.

A comprehensive and still very useful compilation of biographical sketches of persons of many nationalities and periods but particularly strong for the Middle Ages. The original work includes those living before 1750; the supplement adds more from this period, as well as others of a slightly later date. References are given to sources, and bibliographies, especially in the supplement, are quite full.

New Century cyclopedia of names, ed. by Clarence L. Barnhart with the assistance of William D. Halsey [and others]. N.Y., Appleton, 1954. 3v. **AJ19**

A complete modernization and revision of the *Century cyclopedia of names,* originally issued as v.11 of the *Century dictionary and cyclopedia* (AE4).

More than twice as large as the previous work, this edition contains entries for more than 100,000 proper names: "persons, places, historical events, plays and operas, works of fiction, literary characters, works of art, mythological and legendary persons and places and any other class of proper names of interest or importance today." Pronunciation is indicated; articles vary in length from two lines to more than half a page. Numerous appendixes, including a chronological table of world history, lists of rulers, genealogical charts, and a list of prenames with pronunciations.

Nouvelle biographie générale depuis les temps plus reculés jusqu'à nos jours, avec les renseignements bibliographiques et l'indication des sources à consulter; publiée par MM. Firmin Didot Frères, sous la direction de M. le Dr. Hoefer. Paris, Firmin Didot, 1853–66. 46v. (Repr.: Copenhague, Rosenkilde & Bagger, 1963– . In progress) **AJ20**

Usually cited as *Hoefer.*

Begun in 1852 under the title *Nouvelle biographie universelle;* title later changed to *Nouvelle biographie générale.* There are three editions of v.1–2: (1) edition with the title *Nouvelle biographie universelle ancienne et moderne,* containing the 405 pirated articles from *Michaud* (see AJ13); (2) edition with title *Nouvelle biographie universelle depuis les temps les plus reculés,* with those articles omitted; (3) edition with title *Nouvelle biographie générale.* This last is the one usually found in libraries.

Planned to be more concise and more comprehensive than *Michaud,* to include names of people then living, and to list many minor names omitted in *Michaud.* It does include more names in the first part of the alphabet. For other points of comparison *see Biographie universelle* (AJ13).

Oettinger, Eduard Maria. Moniteur des dates. Biographisch-genealogisch-historisches Welt-Register enthaltend die Personal-Akten der Menschheit . . . von mehr als 100,000 geschichtlichen Persönlichkeiten aller Zeiten und Nationen von Erschaffung der Welt bis auf den heutigen Tag. . . . Leipzig, Denicke, 1869–73; Hermann, 1873–82. 9v. **AJ21**

v.1–6, A–Z; v.7–9, Supplément.

v.1–6, edited by Oettinger, published in parts, 1866–68, with title *Moniteur des dates, contenant un million de renseignements biographiques, généalogiques et historiques;* v.7–9 have title *Moniteur des dates . . . Supplément;* commencé par Edouard-Marie Oettinger, considérablement augm. . . . réd. et éd. par Hugo Schramm.

Articles are very brief, usually three or four lines, but work

is very comprehensive and includes some names not easily found elsewhere.

Répertoire des médiévistes européens. Supplément aux Cahiers de civilisation médiévale. Poitiers, Université, Centre d'Études Supérieures de Civilisation Médiévale, 1960. 271p. **AJ22**

Earlier edition entitled *Répertoire des médiévistes d'Europe.* Paris, [1954?]. 95p.

Lists nearly 1700 scholars, with present occupation and address, specialty, and publications since 1954, including articles as well as books. A list of institutes and centers of medieval study is appended.

Thomas, Joseph. Universal pronouncing dictionary of biography and mythology. 5th ed. Philadelphia, London, Lippincott, [c1930]. 2550p. **AJ23**

Usually cited as *Lippincott's Biographical dictionary.*

1st ed. 1870; 3d ed. 1901.

A useful general biographical dictionary in English. Comprehensive—includes men and women of all nations and periods, and names from the Greek, Roman, Teutonic, Sanskrit, and other mythologies. Articles in general are brief, though a few are long; particular attention is given to pronunciation; and there is some bibliography, though this is a minor feature. Appendixes: (1) Vocabulary of Christian (or first) names, with pronunciation, and equivalents in the principal foreign languages; (2) Disputed or doubtful pronunciations.

Vapereau, Gustave. Dictionnaire universel des contemporains contenant toutes les personnes notables de la France et des pays étrangers . . . Ouvrage rédigé et tenu à jour avec le concours d'écrivains de tous les pays. 6. éd. entièrement refondue et considérablement augm. Paris, Hachette, 1893. 1629p. **AJ24**

—— —— Supplément. Paris, Hachette, 1895. 103p.

A dictionary of notable persons of the latter half of the 19th century, of Europe and the Americas.

Webster's Biographical dictionary; a dictionary of names of noteworthy persons, with pronunciations and concise biographies. Merriam-Webster. Springfield, Mass., Merriam, [1962]. 1697p. **AJ25**

1st ed. 1943.

William Allan Neilson, ed. in chief.

A pronouncing biographical dictionary of "upwards of 40,000" names, not restricted by period, nationality, race, religion, or occupation. Includes living persons. Gives brief, condensed biographical sketches and makes a particular point of showing syllabic division and pronunciation of all names. A pronouncing list of prenames is given, p.1628–68; p.1669–97 includes tables of the presidents, vice-presidents, justices of the Supreme Court, cabinet officers, diplomatic agents, etc. of the United States; rulers of the British Empire and some other countries; lists of popes, etc.

Who's who in central and east Europe. 1933/34, 1935/36, ed. by Stephen Taylor. Zurich, Central European Times Pub. Co., [1935–37]. 2v. **AJ26**

Subtitle: A biographical dictionary containing . . . biographies of prominent people from Albania, Austria, Bulgaria, Czechoslovakia, Danzig, Estonia, Finland, Greece, Hungary, Latvia, Liechtenstein, Lithuania, Poland, Rumania, Switzerland, Turkey and Yugoslavia.

Now much out of date and partially replaced by some of the publisher's other works covering specific countries, but still useful for names difficult to find elsewhere.

Contemporary

Contemporary authors; a bio-bibliographical guide to current authors and their works. James M. Ethridge, ed. Detroit, Gale Research Co., 1962– . v.1– . Semi-annual. **AJ27**

Frequency varies, v.1–4, quarterly. Cumulated index, v.1–8. Indexes to cumulate every two years.

Published to give an up-to-date source of biographical information on current authors in many fields—humanities, social sciences, and sciences—and from many countries.

Sketches attempt to give, as pertinent: personal facts (including names of parents, children, etc.), career, writings (as complete a bibliography as possible), work in progress, sidelights, and sometimes biographical sources.

Current biography. v.1, 1940– . N.Y., Wilson, 1940– . il. Monthly (except Aug.). **AJ28**

Published monthly with a bound annual cumulation, *Current biography yearbook,* which includes all biographical sketches and obituary notices, revised and brought up to date. Each issue carries a cumulative index for all issues of the current year, and each volume includes a cumulated index to all preceding volumes for 10-year periods.

This service includes an average of 300–350 biographies annually of persons of various nationalities. Information given generally includes: full name, dates of birth and death, occupation and reason for newsworthiness, address, a biographical sketch of three to four columns, with portrait and references to sources for further information. Each issue, including the cumulations, contains a classified list by occupations.

International who's who, 1935– . London, Europa Publs. and Allen & Unwin, 1935– . Annual (slightly irregular in dating). **AJ29**

Contains short biographies, of who's who type, of persons prominent in Europe, North and South America, Asia, Australia, etc.

Who's who in world Jewry; a biographical dictionary of outstanding Jews. White Plains, N.Y., Who's Who in World Jewry, Inc. (distr. by McKay), 1965. 1087p. **AJ30**

1st ed. 1955.

Includes about 11,000 sketches of prominent Jews in various parts of the world; more than one half are from the United States, with large representations from Argentina, Australia, Canada, Mexico, western Europe, Israel, and South Africa, and smaller numbers from the Middle and the Far East. The USSR and associated countries are excluded, with the exception of Yugoslavia and Hungary.

Inclusion is based exclusively on record of achievement except that high officials in all branches of government, including the armed forces, and academicians with the rank of assistant professor or higher are automatically listed.

UNITED STATES

Appleton's Cyclopaedia of American biography, ed. by J. G. Wilson and John Fiske. N.Y., Appleton, 1887–1900. 7v. il. **AJ31**

v.1–6, A–Z, suppl. A–Z, analytical index; v.7, suppl. A–Z; Pen names, nicknames, sobriquets; Lists of deaths in v.1–6; Signers of the Declaration of Independence, presidents of the Continental Congress, presidents, vice-presidents, unsuccessful candidates for those offices, cabinets, 1789–1897; analytical index to v.7.

Includes names of native and adopted citizens of the United States, including living persons, from the earliest settlement; eminent citizens of Canada, Mexico, and other countries of North and South America; and names of men of foreign birth closely identified with American history.

Contains fairly long articles; little bibliography; many portraits, principally small cuts in the text; and many facsimiles of autographs. A peculiarity of arrangement to be remembered is that under each family name arrangement is not alphabetical but by seniority in the family. The analytical index

is useful for subjects and for names not treated separately. Practically superseded by the *Dictionary of American biography* (AJ32), but still useful for names and certain types of information not given there. Not entirely accurate; for interesting accounts of some curious fictitious biographies *see:* (1) J. H. Barnhart. "Some fictitious botanists," *Journal of the N.Y. Botanical Garden* 20: 171–81. Sept. 1919; (2) Margaret Castle Schindler. "Fictitious biography," *American historical review* 42:680–90. July 1937; and (3) "84 phonies," *Letters* 3, no.19, 1–2. Sept. 14, 1936.

An edition entitled *Cyclopedia of American biography* (N.Y., Press Assoc. Compilers, 1915. 6v.), a new enlarged edition of *Appleton's Cyclopaedia of American biography,* is printed from the same plates as the original edition, with the omission of some of the older articles, the inclusion of some new ones, and the addition of a supplementary list at the end of each volume. Six supplementary (nonalphabetical) volumes to this edition, numbered as volumes 7–12, 1918–31, were sold separately.

No cumulated index.

Dictionary of American biography. Published under the auspices of the American Council of Learned Societies. N.Y., Scribner; London, Milford, 1928–37. 20v. and Index. (Repr.: N.Y., Scribner, 1943. 21v.; 1946, 11v. on thin paper) **AJ32**

The scholarly American biographical dictionary designed on the lines of the English *Dictionary of national biography* (AJ144) with signed articles and bibliographies. Planned to include noteworthy persons of all periods who lived in the territory now known as the United States, excluding British officers serving in America after the colonies declared their independence. Does not include living persons.

As compared with the other principal dictionaries in this field the *DAB* is narrower in scope than *Appleton's* (AJ31), which includes Canadian and Latin-American names, and less inclusive than the *National cyclopaedia* (AJ34), which includes many more minor names. However, it has articles of more distinction than either of those works and much more bibliography. In most cases, the articles are excellent, but there are occasional inaccuracies in both articles and bibliographies.

The reprint edition listed above has a list of errata, v.1, p.xiii–xxxi, with this note: "In making this reprinting of the *Dictionary of American biography,* such corrections as have so far come to the attention of the editors have been made either in the plates or in the following list."

Editors: v.1–3, Allen Johnson; v.4–7, Allen Johnson and Dumas Malone; v.8–20, Dumas Malone; Suppl. 1, Harris E. Starr; Suppl. 2, Robert L. Schuyler and Edward T. James.

——— Supplements 1–2. N.Y., Scribner, 1944–58.

v.1, to Dec. 31, 1935; v.2, 1936–1940.

——— Index. N.Y., Scribner, 1937. 613p.

Contains six separate indexes: (1) Names of subjects of biographies, with authors; (2) Contributors, with subjects of their articles; (3) Birthplaces, arranged alphabetically by (a) states, and (b) foreign countries; (4) Schools and colleges attended by persons included in the dictionary; (5) Occupations; (6) Topics.

Prepared by the publishers, not by the editors, of the dictionary.

——— **Concise dictionary of American biography.** N.Y., Scribner, 1964. 1273p. **AJ33**

Presents the essential facts of every article in the *Dictionary of American biography* in summary form. As in the original, no subject who died later than 1940 is included, but in a few cases, where recent scholarship has revealed new information, some revisions have been made by the writers of the original articles. Entries from the two supplements have been incorporated into the alphabetical arrangement with reference to original location.

Outstanding titles by authors are listed, but bibliographical sources are omitted.

National cyclopaedia of American biography. N.Y., White, 1892–1965. v.1–47. il. (In progress) Some volumes issued in rev. ed. **AJ34**

The most comprehensive American work, less limited and selective than the *Dictionary of American biography* (AJ32), and more up to date than *Appleton's* (AJ31). Articles are unsigned, in general being written by members of an office force from questionnaires and other information supplied by families of the biographees. No bibliography. The special reference use of the *National cyclopaedia* is in its comprehensiveness. Not alphabetically arranged, so must be used through the general indexes. Each volume is also separately indexed.

—— Current volumes, A–J. N.Y., White, 1930–64. il. (In progress)

v.J covers 1960–63.

Includes living persons only, the biographies given being considerably longer than those in *Who's who in America.* Each volume is separately indexed, and all are cumulatively indexed in pt.3 of the general index.

—— Indexes.... N.Y., White, 1945– . Loose-leaf.

Subtitle: Personal and topical indexes to the published volumes of the *National cyclopaedia of American biography,* including the first and revised editions.

Pt.1, v.1–30; pt.2, v.31 and subsequent volumes; pt.3, Current volumes.

Loose-leaf. Pts.2–3 revised as new volumes appear.

Indexes not only the main biographical articles but also names, institutions, events, and other subjects mentioned in the articles.

White's Conspectus of American biography; a tabulated record of American history and biography. 2d ed. Rev. and enl. ed. of A conspectus of American biography. Comp. by the editorial staff of the National Cyclopaedia of American Biography. N.Y., White, 1937. 455p. **AJ35**

A revised edition of the Conspectus part of the Conspectus and index volume (1906) of the *National cyclopaedia of American biography* (AJ34). Includes many chronological lists of officeholders of various kinds—e.g., presidents, cabinet members, bishops, presidents of societies and colleges, recipients of literary and other awards and medals—and various alphabetical lists, e.g., pseudonyms and sobriquets; Americans in fiction, poetry, and drama, etc. Useful both as a classified index to the *National cyclopaedia* and as an independent handbook of information.

Sabine, Lorenzo. Biographical sketches of loyalists of the American Revolution, with an historical essay. Boston, Little, 1864. 2v. **AJ36**

Sketches on the Tories, varying in length from a few lines to two or three pages. Frequently give genealogical information.

Warner, Ezra J. Generals in gray; lives of the Confederate commanders. Baton Rouge, Louisiana State Univ. Pr., 1959. 420p. il. **AJ37**

Includes biographical sketches of the 425 general officers of the Confederate Army, with emphasis on military careers during the Civil War.

Willard, Frances Elizabeth and **Livermore, Mary A.** A woman of the century; 1470 biographical sketches accompanied by portraits of leading American women in all walks of life. Buffalo, N.Y., Charles Wells Moulton, 1893. 812p. il. **AJ38**

Useful for biographies of American women of the 19th century, many of whom do not appear in other biographical reference works.

Who was who in America: Historical volume, 1607–1896. A component volume of Who's who in American history. Chicago, Marquis, 1963. 670p. **AJ39**

Subtitle: A compilation of sketches of individuals, both of the United States of America and other countries, who have made contribution to, or whose activity was in some manner related to the history of the United States, from the founding of the Jamestown Colony to the year of continuation by volume 1 of *Who was who.*

Includes tables of presidents and vice-presidents of the United States, cabinet officers, justices of the Supreme Court, first governors and years of admission of the several states, some major events in United States history, etc.

Who was who in America; a companion biographical reference work to Who's who in America. Chicago, Marquis, 1942–60. v.1–3. (In progress) **AJ40**

Contents: v.1, 1897–1942; v.2, 1943–1950; v.3, 1951–1960.

Includes sketches removed because of death from *Who's who in America,* with dates of death, and often interment location, appended.

With the *Historical volume, 1607–1896,* these volumes form a series entitled *Who's who in American history.*

College graduates

A library doing much reference work in American biography will do well to build up as comprehensive a collection as possible of biographical registers of American schools and colleges. While many alumni directories include only names and addresses, the biographical and historical registers frequently include more detailed information than can readily be found elsewhere. Two outstanding examples of these registers are listed below:

Dexter, Franklin Bowditch. Biographical sketches of the graduates of Yale college. N.Y., Holt, 1885–1912. 6v. **AJ41**

v.1–6, 1701–1815.

Good biographies with full bibliographies of works by authors and references to authorities.

—— Biographical notices of graduates of Yale college, including those graduated in classes later than 1815, who are not commemorated in the annual obituary records. Issued as a supplement to the Obituary Record. New Haven, Conn., 1913. 411p. **AJ42**

Covers the years 1815–84. Continued by the following:

Yale University. Obituary record of graduates . . . 1859–1951. New Haven, Conn., 1860–1951. no.1–110. Annual. **AJ43**

Ceased publication.

Sibley, John Langdon. Biographical sketches of those who attended Harvard College with bibliographical and other notes. Boston, Mass. Historical Soc., 1872–1962. v.1–12. il. (In progress) **AJ44**

v.1–3 have title *Biographical sketches of graduates of Harvard University.*

v.4–12, ed. by C. K. Shipton.

v.1–12, 1642–1750.

Contemporary

Who's who in America (AJ45) is the best-known and generally the most useful of the current biographical works for information about persons of national prominence. For persons not listed there or for whom additional information is desired, other compilations of various kinds are available, only a few of which can be listed here. Most of these fall into one of the following categories:

1. *National.* Other national works are of varying degrees of worth and usefulness. Some of them include longer,

more discursive biographies than *Who's who in America,* such as those in *Current biography* (AJ28). Others of the commercial or "vanity" type must be used with caution.

2. *Local.* These include both sectional and state. The A. N. Marquis Company is now publishing a series of sectional compilations to include *Who's who in the East* (AJ46); *Who's who in the Midwest* (AJ47); *Who's who in the South and Southwest* (AJ48); and *Who's who in the West* (AJ49). These are listed below. Various state publications are also available, e.g., *Who's who in New York* (13th ed. N.Y., Lewis, 1960); *Who's who in Oklahoma* (Muskogee, 1964). These are not listed here but will be needed in libraries according to location.
3. *Professional or business,* e.g., *World who's who in commerce and industry* (CH121); *American men of science* (EA183). These will be found under their proper subject in this book.
4. *Foreign-American,* e.g., *Italian-American who's who* (AJ53). These should be acquired by libraries according to local need.
5. *Religious or Racial,* e.g., *American Catholic who's who* (AJ50); *Who's who in American Jewry* (AJ54); *Who's who in colored America* (AJ55); and various denominational works listed under Religion, p.203.

Who's who in America, a biographical dictionary of notable living men and women. Chicago, Marquis, 1899– . v.1– . Biennial. **AJ45**

The standard dictionary of contemporary biography, containing concise biographical data, prepared according to established practices, with addresses and, in case of authors, lists of works. Issued biennially and constantly expanded since 1899. The standards of admission are high, aiming to include the "best-known men and women in all lines of useful and reputable achievement" including (1) those selected on account of special prominence in creditable lines of effort . . . and (2) those included arbitrarily on account of official position."

The 33d edition (1964/65) lists more than 58,000 names, approximately 9000 for the first time. Includes the names of some outstanding persons of other countries and of representatives to the United Nations. Each edition is thoroughly revised, new biographies added, and others dropped. For names of persons dropped because of death *see Who was who* (AJ40). For those dropped for other reasons, *see* "Noncurrent listings" in *Indices and necrology* (below).

Volumes up to v.22 (1942/43) included geographical indexes. Since then a few have been published separately; *see Indices and necrology* below.

—— Indices and necrology. [v.1], 1952; [v.2], 1954; [v.3], 1958.

Contents: Non-current listings from v.1–22, 23–26 (1899–1950/51) in [v.1]; from v.27–30 (1952/53–1958/59) in [v.3].

Vocational-geographical index to v.26 (1950/51) in [v.1]; to v.28 (1954/55) in [v.2]; to v.30 (1958/59) in [v.3].

Necrology, v.28 (1954/55) in [v.2]; v.29 (1956/57) in [v.3].

—— Monthly supplement and international who's who. Current biographical reference service. Dec. 1939–Aug. 1959. Chicago, Marquis, 1939–59. 9v. Monthly (Quarterly). **AJ45a**

Ceased publication. Title varies.

A supplementary service to *Who's who in America,* and other Marquis publications, which gave sketches of "Who's who in world news—and why," with cross references to other works. International in scope. Averaged about 400 names per month.

Cumulated index to v.1–10, 1939–1949, published separately and also in *Who was who* 2: 605–54. Later volumes have cumulated annual indexes.

The Marquis sectional who's whos are designed to supplement *Who's who in America* (AJ45) and to give representative coverage of a region. Each volume averages some 14,000 names, selected on the same principles of "reference usefulness" used for the national work; a few of these, deemed especially newsworthy, are duplicated in *Who's who in America* and in the regional volume. Each volume includes a list indicating names from the area to be found in *Who's who in America* which are not duplicated, as well as names about which data are available in the Marquis National Biographical Reference files, even though sketches are not in print.

Who's who in the East (and eastern Canada); a biographical dictionary of noteworthy men and women of the Middle Atlantic and northeastern states and eastern Canada. v.1, 1942/43– . Chicago, Marquis, 1943– . v.1– . Biennial (slightly irregular). **AJ46**

Publisher varies; subtitle varies; coverage varies. 1964/65 called 9th ed. and scope broadened to include eastern Canada.

Covers the New England states, and Delaware, Maryland, New Jersey, New York, Pennsylvania, West Virginia; and in Canada: New Brunswick, Newfoundland, Nova Scotia, Prince Edward Island, and Quebec.

Who's who in the Midwest; a biographical dictionary of noteworthy men and women of the central and midwestern states. 1st ed., 1949– . Chicago, Marquis, 1949– . Biennial (slightly irregular). **AJ47**

1963/64 called 8th ed.

Covers Illinois, Indiana, Iowa, Kansas, Michigan, Minnesota, Missouri, Nebraska, North Dakota, Ohio, South Dakota, and Wisconsin.

Who's who in the South and Southwest; a biographical dictionary of noteworthy men and women of the southern and southwestern states. Chicago, Marquis, 1950– . v.1– . Biennial (slightly irregular). **AJ48**

1963/64 called 8th ed.

Covers Alabama, Arkansas, the District of Columbia, Florida, Georgia, Kentucky, Louisiana, Mississippi, North Carolina, Oklahoma, South Carolina, Tennessee, Texas, and Virginia.

Who's who in the West; a biographical dictionary of noteworthy men and women of the Pacific coastal and western states. Chicago, Marquis, 1949– . Biennial (slightly irregular). **AJ49**

1962 called 8th ed.

Title varies: *Who's who on the Pacific coast, Who's who in the Far West.*

Covers Alaska, Arizona, California, Colorado, Hawaii, Idaho, Montana, Nevada, New Mexico, Oregon, Utah, Washington, and Wyoming.

American Catholic who's who, 1934/35– . Detroit, Walter Romig, [1934]– . Biennial. **AJ50**

An earlier edition, edited by G. P. Curtis, was published in 1911 by B. Herder in St. Louis.

Current biography. N.Y., Wilson, 1940– . **AJ51**

For full description *see* AJ28.

Directory of American scholars; a biographical directory. Ed. by the Jaques Cattell Press. 4th ed. N.Y., Bowker, 1963–64. 4v. **AJ52**

1st ed. 1942; 2d ed. 1951; 3d ed. 1957.

The 4th edition is published in 4v.: v.1, History; v.2, English, Speech and Drama; v.3, Foreign languages—modern and classical, Linguistics and Philology; v.4, Philosophy, Religion and Law.

Includes sketches of proven scholars in the various categories noted, with cross references from one volume to another or to *American men of science* (EA183).

Italian-American who's who; a biographical dictionary of Italian-American leaders, ed. by Giovanni Schiavo. v.1, 1935– . N.Y., Vigo Pr., [1935]– . il. Annual (slightly irregular). **AJ53**

Subtitle varies slightly.

Who's who in American Jewry; a biographical dictionary of living Jews of the United States and Canada. v.3, 1938–39. Ed. by John Simons. N.Y., Nat. News Assoc., [c1938]. 1177p. il. **AJ54**

v.1, 1926; v.2, 1928. Publisher and subtitle vary.

As comparatively few of the names included are also in *Who's who in America* (AJ45), this may still be useful for the period covered.

Contains a geographical index (p.xi–l), and an *Addenda* list (p.li–lv).

Who's who in colored America; an illustrated biographical directory of notable living persons of African descent in the United States. 1st ed., 1927– . Yonkers, N.Y., Burckell, 1927– . v.1– . il. **AJ55**

Published at irregular intervals. 6th ed. 1941–44; 7th ed. 1950.

Publisher varies; subtitle varies.

Biographical sketches of Negroes outstanding in all fields and professions. Includes a geographical listing and a vocational listing.

Who's who of American women: a biographical dictionary of notable living American women. v.1, 1958/1959– . Chicago, Marquis, 1958– . Biennial. **AJ56**

3d ed. 1964/65.

A who's who listing "women outstanding as women." Includes all American women listed in the last issue of *Who's who in America,* and others chosen as women most likely to be of potential reference interest.

An earlier work, by a different publisher, entitled *American women* was published in three editions: 1935/36, 1937/38, 1939/40. Los Angeles, American Publ., 1935–39.

Bibliography

Dargan, Marion. Guide to American biography. Albuquerque, Univ. of New Mexico Pr., 1949–52. 2v. **AJ57**

Pt.1, 1607–1815; pt.2, 1815–1933.

Arranged by chronological periods, subdivided by geographical regions. Under each person lists original sources, separately published biographies, references to collective biography, special aspects, etc. Includes only the outstanding names (179 in pt.1; 380 in pt.2).

Kaplan, Louis. A bibliography of American autobiographies . . . in association with James Tyler Cook, Clinton E. Colby, Jr., Daniel C. Haskell. Madison, Univ. of Wisconsin Pr., 1961. 372p. **AJ58**

6377 numbered entries arranged alphabetically by author. The subject index indicates occupation, locale, and important historical events, as well as some other categories. Many of the headings are subdivided by period, e.g., Doctors: (–1800), (1800–1850), (1850–1900), (1900–1945).

AFRICA

Segal, Ronald. Political Africa; a who's who of personalities and parties. London, Stevens & Sons, 1961. 475p. **AJ59**

For full description *see* CI84.

ARGENTINA

Muzzio, Julio A. Diccionario histórico y biográfico de la Républica Argentina. Buenos Aires, Roldán, 1920. 2v. (445p.) **AJ60**

Covers all periods. Primarily biographical.

Udaondo, Enrique. Diccionario biográfico argentino. . . . Buenos Aires, Casa Ed. "Coni," 1938. 1151p. **AJ61**

At head of title: Institución Mitre.

Contains some 3300 biographies in the period 1800–1920. Little or no bibliography.

—— Diccionario biográfico colonial argentino. Obra prologada por Gregorio Araoz Alfaro. . . . Buenos Aires, Ed. Huarpes, 1945. 980p. il. **AJ62**

At head of title: Institución Mitre.

Covers the colonial period of Argentina from the discovery and conquest of the Rio de la Plata to 1810. A companion volume to the preceding.

Yaben, Jacinto R. Biografías argentinas y sudamericanas; introducción del Juan B. Terán. . . . Buenos Aires, Ed. "Metrópolis," 1938–40. 5v. il. **AJ63**

v.1, 2, and 4 contain lists of works used.

A large proportion of the work is devoted to biographies of military and naval men.

v.5 includes a supplement containing new biographies and additional material on biographies already published.

Contemporary

Quién es quién en la Argentina; biografías contemporáneas. 5. ed. 1950. Buenos Aires, Kraft, [1950]. 628p. **AJ64**

1. ed. 1939.

For additional works on Argentine biography *see* Sabor, *Manual de fuentes de información,* p.211–19 (AA306).

AUSTRALIA

Mennell, Philip. Dictionary of Australasian biography; comprising notices of eminent colonists from the inauguration of responsible government down to the present time (1855–1892) . . . London, Hutchinson, 1892. 542p. **AJ66**

Serle, Percival. Dictionary of Australian biography. Sydney, Angus and Robertson, 1949. 2v. **AJ67**

Patterned on the *Dictionary of national biography* (AJ144), this contains "1030 biographies of Australians, or men who were closely connected with Australia, who died before the end of 1942." The sketches average two to three columns in length and include bibliographies of source material at the end of each.

Contemporary

Who's who in Australia. 16th ed. 1959. . . . Melbourne, Herald and Weekly Times, 1959. 896p. Triennial (Irregular). **AJ68**

Incorporating John's *Notable Australians,* which was first published in 1906.

Subtitle: An Australian biographical dictionary and register of titled persons.

AUSTRIA

Wurzbach, Constantin, *Ritter von Tannenburg.* Biographisches Lexikon des Kaiserthums Oesterreich, enthaltend die Lebensskizzen der denkwürdigen Personen, welche seit 1750 in den österreichischen Kronländern geboren wurden oder darin gelebt und gewirkt haben. Wien, Zamarski, 1856–91. 60v.   **AJ69**

Subtitle and imprint vary.

The standard Austrian work covering the period from 1750. Contains 24,254 biographies of inhabitants of the various lands included in the former Austrian Empire. Gives biographies of some length, and bibliographies.

—————— Register zu den Nachträgen in Wurzbachs 'Biographischem Lexikon d. Kaiserthums Österreich' . . . Wien, Gilhofer, 1923. 16p.

An index to the supplements included in v.9, 11, 14, 22, 23, 24, 26, and 28.

Akademie der Wissenschaften, Vienna. Österreichisches biographisches Lexikon, 1815–1950. Hrsg. von der Österreichischen Akademie der Wissenschaften. Nach Vorarbeiten von Anton Bettelheim und Oswald Redlich unter Mitwirkung bewährter Sachkenner und der Leitung von Leo Santifaller, bearb. von Eva Obermayer-Marnach. Graz-Köln, Böhlaus, 1954–63. Lfg. 1–13. (In progress)   **AJ70**

Bd.1–2 (Lfg. 1–10), A–Hubl; Bd.3 (Lfg. 11–13), incompl. Hubl–Keller.

Designed to continue Wurzbach, *Biographisches Lexikon* (AJ69) and *Neue österreichische Biographie* (AJ71). Includes sketches of prominent persons of the former Austro-Hungarian Empire and the succeeding state of Austria who were prominent in the arts, sciences, and politics, and who died prior to 1951.

Brief sketches, unsigned, with bibliographies of works both by and about.

Neue österreichische Biographie ab 1815. Wien, Amalthea-Verlag, 1923–63. Abt. 1, v.1–15; Abt. 2, v.1. (In progress)   **AJ71**

v.1–8 had title *Neue österreichische Biographie, 1815–1918.*

Bd.10–15 have subtitle *Grosse Österreicher* (varies slightly).

Long, signed articles with bibliographies—and in many cases portraits—of 19th- and 20th-century Austrians. Not alphabetically arranged but with a cumulated index at the back of each volume beginning with v.8.

Abt. 2, Bd.1 is a bibliography listing biographical dictionaries and collective biography in two parts: (1) by subject or specialty; and (2) by geographical division.

"Wer ist wer"; Lexikon österreichischer Zeitgenossen. Wien, Selbst-Verlag "Wer ist wer," 1937. 420p.   **AJ72**

Contains about 1500 biographies of personalities prominent before World War II with a subject index by professions, specialties, etc.

Contemporary

Österreicher der Gegenwart; Lexikon schöpferischer und schaffender Zeitgenossen. Wien, Österreichische Staatsdruckerei, 1951. 419p.   **AJ73**

Published by Österreich-Institut.

Bio-bibliographical data on about 2650 living Austrians, with vocational index.

Wer ist wer in Österreich. Wien, Huttern, 1951. 224p. il.   **AJ74**

An alphabetical listing of 1736 Austrians, with no subject index. Little or no bibliography.

Who's who in Austria; a biographical dictionary containing about 4000 biographies of prominent personalities from and in Austria, ed. by Stephen Taylor. Ed. 1– . Zurich, Central European Times Pub. Co., 1954– . Biennial.   **AJ75**

Subtitle varies slightly. v.1, 1955; v.2, 1957/58; v.3, 1959/60.

In English. Each volume in two parts: (1) Who's who section; and (2) Directory of organizations, institutes, associations, and enterprises.

BELGIUM

Académie Royale des Sciences, des Lettres, et des Beaux-arts de Belgique. Biographie nationale. Bruxelles, Bruylant-Christophe, 1866–1944. 28v. v.29– , 1956– . (In progress)   **AJ76**

v.1–27, A–Z; v.28, Table générale; v.29–32, Supplément (v.1–4¹). 1956–64.

Long, signed articles by specialists, with bibliographies. Includes no living persons and, as names were not selected for inclusion until a person had been dead 10 years, the earlier volumes contain mainly persons who died before 1850. The supplement includes both early names and names of the 19th and 20th centuries. For names of a later date this dictionary may be supplemented usefully by the long, signed obituaries, with detailed bibliographies, often with portraits, in the *Annuaire* of the Académie Royale. For these obituaries before 1914, the following general index is helpful.

—————— Annuaire: Table des notices biographiques publiées dans l'Annuaire (1835–1914). Bruxelles, Hayez, 1919. 55p.   **AJ77**

Also included in the issue of the *Annuaire* for 81ᵉ–85ᵉ années, 1915–1919, p.113–67; complément, 1915–1926, in *Annuaire* 92ᵉ année, 1926, p.129–33.

—————— Notices biographiques et bibliographiques concernant les membres, les correspondants et les associés. 1.–5. éd. 1854–1909. Bruxelles, Hayez, 1855–1909. 5v.   **AJ78**

Brief biographical sketches with long bibliographies. Each edition includes some names from the previous edition, but also omits and adds other names.

Académie Royale des Sciences d'Outre-Mer, Brussels. Biographie coloniale belge. Belgische koloniale biografie. Bruxelles, Académie, 1948–58. v.1–5. il. (In progress)   **AJ79**

Publisher varies.

Devoted to persons, mostly but not exclusively Belgians, who contributed to the history and development of the Belgian Congo. No name is chosen for inclusion until at least 10 years after the person's death. Sketches vary in length, but all are signed and dated and many include bibliographies. Each volume is a separate alphabetical listing, with a cumulative index to preceding volumes.

Seyn, Eugène de. Dictionnaire biographique des sciences, des lettres et des arts en Belgique. Bruxelles, Éd. l'Avenir, 1935–36. 2v. il.   **AJ80**

Covers all periods, and includes living persons. Articles are brief, with many portraits but little or no bibliography *about* the names included, although, in the case of articles about writers, lists of works by those writers are given. Many of the biographies of writers are adapted from the articles in the *Dictionnaire des écrivains belges,* by Eugène de Seyn (BD646).

Contemporary

Who's who in Belgium and Grand Duchy of Luxembourg. 2d ed. Ed. by F. Michielsen and Stephen S. Taylor. Brussels, N.Y., Intercontinental Book and Pub. Co., 1962. (Belgian ed., Les Éditions Biographiques, Brussels) 1343p.   **AJ81**

1st edition, 1957/58, had title *Who's who in Belgium, including the Belgian Congo.*

Subtitle: A biographical dictionary containing about 7000 biographies of prominent people in and of Belgium and the Grand Duchy of Luxembourg.

Wie is dat in Vlaanderen? Biografisch lexicon van bekende tijdgenoten in Vlaams-Belgie op politiek, administratief, rechtskundig, godsdienstig, sociaal, militair, sportief, economisch, wetenschappelijk en artistiek gebied. Brussels, Amsterdam, Elsevier, 1953. 284p.   **AJ82**

A who's who for Flemish Belgium.

Bibliography

Dhondt, Jan and **Vervaeck, Solange.** Instruments biographiques pour l'histoire contemporaine de la Belgique. Louvain, Éd. Nauwelaerts; Paris, Béatrice-Nauwelaerts, 1960. 80p. (Centre Inter-universitaire d'Histoire Contemporaine. Cahier 13)   **AJ83**

A bibliography of general and specialized sources for Belgian biography.

BOLIVIA

Quién es quién en Bolivia, por Julio César Chávez y Miguel Ángel Gatti. [La Paz?], Ed. Quién es Quién en Bolivia, 1942. 257p.   **AJ84**

BRAZIL

Bear, Ely. Vultos do Brasil; dicionário biobibliográfico brasileiro. São Paulo. Livraria Exposiçào do Livro, [1961?]. 286p. il.   **AJ85**

Short sketches of some 300 outstanding men of Brazil of the 19th and 20th centuries.

Brazil. Ministério da Viação e Obras Públicas. Serviço de Documentação. Dados biográficos dos ministros, 1861–1961. [Rio de Janeiro], [1962?]. 164p.   **AJ86**

Biographical sketches of a number of Brazilian cabinet members since 1861.

Segadas Machado-Guimarães, Argeu de. Diccionario bio-bibliographico brasileiro, de diplomacia, politica externa e direito internacional, por Argeu Guimarães. Rio de Janeiro, Autor, 1938. 482p.   **AJ87**

A biographical dictionary of Brazilian statesmen and a bibliography of Brazilian foreign relations, all in one alphabetical arrangement. Primarily 19th and 20th centuries but includes some earlier material.

Velho Sobrinho, João Francisco. Dicionário bio-bibliográfico brasileiro. Rio de Janeiro, Ministério da Educação e Saude, 1937–40. v.1–2. il. (In progress?)   **AJ88**

v.1–2, A–Buxton.

Fairly long sketches with bibliographies.

Contemporary

Coutinho, Afrânio. Brasil e brasileiros de hoje. Rio de Janeiro, Ed. Sul Americana, 1961. 2v.   **AJ89**

About 7000 who's who–type sketches of contemporary Brazilians.

Quem é quem no Brasil; biografias contemporaneas. v.4,

1955. São Paulo, Soc. Brasileira de Expansão Commercial, 1955. 740p., xxxviiip.   **AJ90**

Who's who sketches in classified arrangement, with alphabetical index. Also includes an index to the sketches in v.1–3.

CANADA

Allaire, Jean Baptiste Arthur. Dictionnaire biographique du clergé canadien-français. St.-Hyacinthe, [Québec], Impr. de "La Tribune," 1908–20. 4v. il.   **AJ91**

v.1, Les anciens; v.2, Les contemporains; v.3, Suppléments, 1–6; v.4, Le clergé canadien-français, revue mensuelle; Table générale des quatre volumes.

Consists of two main volumes—six supplements forming one volume—and 24 monthly numbers. The general index at the end of v.4 links together these 32 alphabets. Short articles, many small portraits.

Morice, Adrien Gabriel. Dictionnaire historique des Canadiens et des métis français de l'Ouest. Québec, Garneau, 1908. 329p.   **AJ92**

A historical biographical dictionary of the French explorers to the Canadian Northwest.

Standard dictionary of Canadian biography; the Canadian who was who. Eds., Charles G. D. Roberts and Arthur L. Tunnell. Toronto, Trans-Canada Pr., 1934–38. 2v.   **AJ93**

Contains fairly long biographies, with bibliographies, of Canadians who died 1875–1937. Articles are signed with initials.

Each volume is arranged alphabetically with a list in v.2 of the sketches in v.1.

Wallace, William Stewart. The Macmillan dictionary of Canadian biography. 3d ed. rev. and enl. London, Toronto, Macmillan; N.Y., St. Martin's, 1963. 822p.   **AJ94**

1st ed. 1926.

The best general dictionary of Canadian biography of all periods and all classes, exclusive of living persons. Contains concise biographical sketches with bibliographies.

Contemporary

Les biographies françaises d'Amérique. Les Journalistes Associés, éditeurs. 2. éd. Sherbrooke, Québec, 1950. 913p. il.   **AJ95**

1st ed. 1942.

Nonalphabetical; grouped by profession or occupation, with index. Lists living persons of the French ethnic groups.

Canadian who's who. . . . v.1– . 1910, 1938– . Toronto, Trans-Canada Pr., c1910– . v.1– . (v.9, 1961/63)   **AJ96**

Subtitle: With which is incorporated 'Canadian men and women of the time.' A biographical dictionary of notable living men and women.

Publisher varies.

v.1, 1910; v.2, 1936–37. Alphabetical arrangement with a classified index. Includes biographies of some persons in *Who's who in Canada* (AJ97), but each work includes names not in the other.

Who's who in Canada. An illustrated biographical record of men and women of the time, ed. by B. M. Greene. Toronto, Internat. Pr., 1922– . il. Biennial.   **AJ97**

Subtitle varies.

Continues, with same volume numbering, *Who's who and why.* 1921 issue called 15th year of issue.

Nonalphabetical but includes an alphabetical index.

Who's who in the East (and eastern Canada); a biographical dictionary of noteworthy men and women of the Middle Atlantic and northeastern states and eastern Canada. Chicago, Marquis, 1963– . **AJ98**

For main entry *see* AJ46.

With the 9th edition, 1964/65, coverage was broadened to include eastern Canada: New Brunswick, Newfoundland, Nova Scotia, Prince Edward Island, and Quebec.

CARIBBEAN COUNTRIES

British Caribbean who, what, why. 1st ed. Ed. and pub., Lloyd Sydney Smith. Glasgow, Scot., Bell and Bain, 1956– . v.1, 1955/56– . **AJ99**

Covers: Jamaica, Trinidad, Barbados, British Guiana, British Honduras; (Windward Islands) Grenada, St. Lucia, St. Vincent, Dominica; (Leeward Islands) Antigua, St. Kitts-Nevis, Montserrat, and British Virgin Islands.

In five sections: (1) General material on government, organizations, and geography; (2) Who's who, arranged by country and subdivided by profession or business; (3) Colonial affairs; (4) Directory of business firms; (5) Overseas business organizations trading with the British Caribbean. A detailed table of contents and a name index are included.

CHILE

Figueroa, Pedro Pablo. Diccionario biográfico de Chile. 4. ed. Santiago, Impr. y Encuadernación Barcelona, 1897–1902. 3v. il. **AJ100**

1st ed. 1887; 2d ed. 1888; 3d ed. 1891.

Earlier editions include names dropped from later editions, and the later editions add new names, as well as corrections and additional information, to names previously included.

Primarily 19th century with a few earlier names.

—— Diccionario biográfico de estranjeros en Chile. Santiago, Impr. Moderna, 1900. 258p. **AJ101**

Biographies of foreigners who lived in Chile.

Figueroa, Virgilio. Diccionario histórico, biográfico y bibliográfico de Chile, por Virgilio Figueroa (Virgilio Talquino), 1800–1930. Santiago, "Balcells and Co.," 1925–31. 5v. in 4. il. **AJ102**

Title varies: v.1 has title *Diccionario histórico y biográfico de Chile, 1800–1925.*

Arranged alphabetically by family name and then by seniority in the family rather than alphabetically. Most articles conclude with bibliographies of source materials.

Medina, José Toribio. Diccionario biográfico colonial de Chile. Santiago, Impr. Elzeviriana, 1906. 1004p. il. **AJ103**

—— —— Muestras de errores y defectos del "Diccionario biográfico colonial de Chile por José Toribio Medina," [por] Luis Francisco Prieto. Santiago, Impr. y Encuadernación Chile, 1907. 124p.

A biographical dictionary covering from the age of discovery through the 18th century.

CHINA

☙ Biographical sections are frequently included in the yearbooks listed under Statistics, e.g., *China yearbook* (CG82).

The following list includes some works on Chinese biography in languages other than Chinese:

Giles, Herbert Allen. A Chinese biographical dictionary. London, Quaritch, 1898; Shanghai, Kelly and Walsh (repr. 1939). 1022p. **AJ104**

A standard dictionary in English, not completely superseded by the Library of Congress volumes listed below. May be supplemented and corrected on certain points by the use of the following: E. von Zach. "Einige Verbesserungen zu Giles' Chinese biographical dictionary." *Asia major* 3:545–68. 1926; Paul Pelliot. "A propos du 'Chinese biographical dictionary' de M. H. Giles." *Ibid.* 4:377–89. 1927; Paul Pelliot. "Les Yi nien lou." *T'oung pao* 25:65–81. 1927.

Perleberg, Max. Who's who in modern China (from the beginning of the Chinese Republic to the end of 1953) ... Hong Kong, Ye Olde Printerie, 1954. 428p. il. **AJ105**

Subtitle: Over two thousand detailed biographies of the most important men who took part in the great struggle for China, including detailed histories of the political parties, government organizations, a glossary of new terms used in contemporary Chinese together with a double index in Chinese and English and two charts.

Includes persons both living and dead. Now out of date, but may be useful for period covered. Entries are of the usual who's who type, with much additional information on government structure and personnel for both Nationalist and Communist China. The indexes cover only the biographical sections. Text is in English.

U.S. Library of Congress. Orientalia Division. Eminent Chinese of the Ch'ing period (1644–1912). Ed. by Arthur W. Hummel. Wash., Govt. Prt. Off., 1943–44. 2v. **AJ106**

v.1, A–O. 604p.; v.2, P–Y. p.605–1103.

Designed to include some 800 sketches of eminent Chinese of the last 300 years, primarily of the epoch ruled by the Ch'ing dynasty (1644–1912). A very useful reference work, with detailed, authoritative, signed articles and references to sources. "No independent sketches are included for persons who died after 1912; but it was found possible to incorporate information, sometimes in considerable detail, of many men who lived after that date, and of not a few who are still living."—*Editor's note.*

Who's who in China; biographies of Chinese leaders. Shanghai, China Weekly Review, 1918–40. v.1–5. il. **AJ107**

1st ed. 1918; 2d ed. 1920; 3d ed. 1925; 3d ed. Suppl. [1928?]; 4th ed. 1932; 4th ed. Suppl. 1933; 5th ed. 1936; 5th ed. Suppl. 1940.

The 5th edition is the first in the series to include biographies of women.

Bibliography

Wu, Wen-Chin. Leaders of twentieth-century China; an annotated bibliography of selected Chinese biographical works in the Hoover Library, by Eugene Wu. Stanford, Calif., Stanford Univ. Pr., 1956. 106p. (Hoover Institute and Library. Bibliographical ser. 4) **AJ108**

Approximately 500 items, including collections, dictionaries, and serials, as well as individual biographies. Names are listed first in roman type, followed by Chinese characters.

COLOMBIA

Ospina, Joaquín. Diccionario biográfico y bibliográfico de Colombia. . . . Bogotá, Ed. de Cromos (v.2–3, Ed. Aguila), 1927–39. 3v. il. **AJ109**

Covers from the Spanish conquest to the 20th century. Includes persons of many professions who contributed to the development of the country.

Quién es quién en Colombia. 2. ed. con datos controlados hasta el 14 mayo de 1948. Bogotá, Oliverio Perry, 1948. 540p. **AJ110**

1. ed. 1944.

Includes who's who type of sketch for 1579 persons. Contains a professional directory by city and by profession. Largely superseded by *Quién es quién en Venezuela, Panama, Ecuador, Colombia* (AJ188).

CONGO

Artigue, Pierre. Qui sont les leaders congolais? Bruxelles, Éd. Europe-Afrique, 1961. 375p. (Collection "Carrefours africains") **AJ111**

1st ed. 1960.

The 2d edition is more political than the first and includes more than 800 biographical sketches of senators, deputies, ministers, and other officials, business leaders, journalists, etc.

CUBA

Cuba en la mano: enciclopedia popular ilustrada. La Habana, [Ucar, Garcia], 1940. 1302p. il. **AJ112**

Índice biográfico, p.787–1033.
For full description *see* DB164.

Peraza Sarausa, Fermín. Diccionario biográfico cubano. Habana, Ed. Anuario Bibliográfico Cubano, 1951–60. v.1–11. (In progress) **AJ113**

v.1–7, Abad–Z; v.8–11, A–Iz.

A preliminary issue, in mimeographed form, of a collection of Cuban biographies which originally appeared in *El mundo* (Havana). Only persons no longer living are included.

—— Personalidades cubanas. Habana, Ed. Anuario Bibliográfico Cubano, 1957–65. v.1–8. (In progress) **AJ114**

v.1–7 cover 1957–59; v.8 is *Cuba en el exilio.*
A companion work to the preceding; gives brief sketches of living persons. v.7 includes an index to v.1–7.

CZECHOSLOVAKIA

Kuhn, Heinrich and **Böss, Otto.** Biographisches Handbuch der Tschechoslowakei. München, R. Lerche, 1961. 640p. (Veröffentlichungen des Collegium Carolinum) **AJ116**

In German. Preliminary sections, giving personnel of party and state organizations, societies, institutions, universities, etc., are followed by the biographical section with sketches of the who's who type.

DENMARK

Dansk biografisk Haandleksikon, redig, af Svend Dahl og P. Engelstoft. Kjøbenhavn, Gyldendal, 1920–26. 3v. il. **AJ117**

Less comprehensive than Bricka (AJ118), this work includes some 6000 rather brief biographical sketches, signed, with bibliographies and small illustrations. Covers from early times to the present and includes living persons.

Dansk biografisk Leksikon, grundlagt af C. F. Bricka, redig. af Povl Engelstoft under Medvirkning af Svend Dahl; udg. med Støtte af Carlsbergfondet. København, Schultz, 1933–44. 27v. **AJ118**

v.1–26, A–Østrup; v.27, Supplement.

Signed articles with bibliographies, covering from early times to the present day. Includes names of living persons. A revised, much enlarged edition of C. F. Bricka, *Dansk biografisk Lexikon* (1887–1905. 19v.), although some names recorded there were not taken over into the new edition.

Marquard, Emil. Danske Gesandter og Gesandtskabspersonale indtil 1914. Udg. af rigsarkivet. København, I Kommission hos Ejnar Munksgaards Forlag, 1952. 493p. **AJ119**

A biographical dictionary of Danish diplomats, in two parts: (1) up to 1648, and (2) 1648–1914. Each section is arranged by the country to which the diplomats were assigned. Name index.

Contemporary

Kraks blaa Bog, nulevende danske maend og kvinders Levnedsløb. København, Krak, 1910– . v.1– . Annual. (v.55, 1964) **AJ120**

The standard Danish who's who. 1959 has a general index to the names included in v.1–49, 1910–58.

Bibliography

Erichsen, Balder and **Krarup, Alfred.** Dansk personalhistorisk Bibliografi; systematisk Fortegnelse over Bidrag til Danmarks Personalhistorie (i Tilslutning til Bibliotheca danica). København, Gads, 1917. 806p. (Dansk historisk Bibliografi. 3. Bd.) **AJ121**

Includes books and analytical material, indexing many articles in periodicals. Lists more than 15,000 references. As it gives, in most cases, dates of birth or death and some characterizing phrase, it can be used for such direct biographical information, as well as for its bibliographical references.

Continued informally by the indexing of biographical articles, also with dates and characterizing phrases, given in the *Dansk Tidsskrift-Index,* 1915– , under the heading *Personalhistorie.* For description *see* AF147.

ECUADOR

Pérez Marchant, Braulio. Diccionario biográfico del Ecuador. Quito, Escuela de Artes y Oficios, 1928. 515p. il. **AJ122**

Covers all periods, but is mainly 19th century.

ENGLAND

See Great Britain, p.180.

FINLAND

Finsk biografisk handbok, under medvärkan af fackmän utg. af Tor Carpelan. Helsingfors, Edlunds Förlag, 1903. 2v. **AJ123**

Issued in parts, 1895–1903.
Adequate signed biographies, little bibliography.

Heikinheimo, Ilmari. Suomen elämäkerrasto. Porvoo, Helsinki, Werner Söderström, 1955. 855p. il. **AJ124**

Fairly brief sketches of all periods with many portraits. Particularly strong for the 18th and 19th centuries.

Contemporary

Kuke kukin on (Aikalaiskirja). Who's who in Finland. Henkilötietoja nykypolven suomalaisista. 1960. Helsingissä, Kustannusosakeyhtiö Otava, 1960. 1098p. **AJ125**

Earlier editions published with title *Aikalaiskirja.*

Vem och vad? Biografisk handbok, 1948. Under redaktion av J. O. Tallquist och Ola Zweygbergk. Helsingfors, H. Schildt, 1948. 879p. **AJ126**

1st ed. 1920. Usually published every five years, but because of the war the volume due in 1946 was not published until 1948.

Earlier volumes edited by H. R. Söderström.

FRANCE

☘ The principal 19th-century dictionaries of French biography are the international works: *Biographie universelle* (*Michaud*) (AJ13) and *Nouvelle biographie générale* (Hoefer) (AJ20). *See also* Paris. Bibliothèque Nationale. *Répertoire de l'histoire de la Révolution Française.* v.1, *Personnes* (DC61).

Académie des Sciences, Paris. Index biographique des membres et correspondants de l'Académie des Sciences du 22 décembre 1666 au 15 novembre 1954. Paris, Gauthier-Villars, 1954. 534p. **AJ127**

Lists, with brief biographical information, all persons who have been members or *correspondants* of the Academy since its origin in 1666. Supersedes earlier editions.

Dictionnaire de biographie française. Paris, Letouzey, 1933–63. v.1–9, 10$^{1-2}$. (In progress) **AJ128**

v.1–10, fasc.2, A–Delbos.

Editors vary.

An important new dictionary of national biography; planned to be a much more extensive work than the corresponding dictionaries of English and American biography. Articles, which in the main are shorter than those in the *Dictionary of national biography* (AJ144), are signed with the writers' names, not merely initials, and nearly all have bibliographies, some of which are very extensive.

Haag, Eugène and **Haag, Émile.** La France protestante; ou, Vies des protestants français qui se sont fait un nom dans l'histoire depuis les premiers temps de la Réformation jusqu'à la reconnaissance du principe de la liberté des cultes par l'Assemblée Nationale. Paris, Genève, Cherbuliez, 1846–59. 10v. **AJ129**

There is a later edition of which only v.1–6 (A–Gasparen) were ever published (Paris, Sandoz, 1877–88).

Sketches vary in length from a few lines to several pages. Bibliographies are composed largely of material by, rather than about, the biographee, but these are extensive.

v.10 consists of *Pièces justificatives,* and includes the texts of edicts, laws, and other source materials relating to Protestantism in France.

Kuscinski, August. Dictionnaire des conventionnels. Paris, Au Siège de la Société, 1916–19. 615p. (Société de l'Histoire de la Révolution Française) **AJ129a**

Biographical sketches of the members of the National Convention, 1792–95.

Robert, Adolphe [and others]. Dictionnaire des parlementaires français, comprenant tous les membres des assemblées françaises et tous les ministres français depuis le 1er mai 1789 jusqu'au 1er mai 1889. Paris, Bourloton, 1891. 5v. il. **AJ130**

Continued by *Les parlementaires français,* by René Samuel and Georges Bonét-Maury. Intended to be published in two parts—1889–1900 and 1900–14—of which only the second appeared (Paris, Roustan, 1914).

Biographical sketches of French parliamentarians and ministers.

For complete record *see* CI103, CI104.

Contemporary

Dictionnaire biographique français contemporain. 2. éd. 1954–55. Paris, Pharos, Agence Internat. de Documentation Contemporaine, 1954. 708p. il. **AJ131**

1st ed. 1950. A dictionary of contemporary French biography, with an index, classified by profession, society membership, etc. Bibliographies are usually given of works by a writer, but only occasionally are works about a person listed. The 2d edition is considerably larger than the 1st.

—— Supplements 1–2, 1955–1956.

Each of these include a few new sketches, and brief notes bringing to date some of the biographies in the main work.

Nouveau dictionnaire national des contemporains, 1961/ 62– . Paris, Éd. du Nouveau Dictionnaire National des Contemporains, 1962– . Irregular (?). **AJ132**

An illustrated biographical dictionary of contemporary personalities with fairly long sketches in the general style and format of the *Dictionnaire national des contemporains* dirigé par Nath Imbert (Paris, Lajeunesse, 1936–39. 3v. il.), which included more than 3000 names of persons prominent in the 1930's.

Who's who in France: dictionnaire biographique, 1953/ 54– . Paris, Lafitte, 1953– . Biennial. **AJ133**

1st edition, 1953/1954, had title *Who's who in France: Paris,* and was restricted to persons living in Paris.

Later editions cover all of France, as well as French persons overseas and French-speaking peoples in African nations, etc. Sketches are of the usual who's who type. In spite of the English title, sketches and text are in French.

In two main parts: (1) Notices biographiques, and (2) Les grands entreprises, which gives information about large business firms.

An earlier *Qui êtes-vous?* (Paris, Delagrave) appeared in three editions: 1908, 1909, and 1924.

Regional

☘ Many dictionaries of local biography have been published. Titles of some of these may be found in Schneider's *Handbuch der Bibliographie,* p.502–3 (AA8).

GERMANY

Allgemeine deutsche Biographie; hrsg. durch die Historische Commission bei der K. Akademie der Wissenschaften. Leipzig, Duncker, 1875–1912. 56v. **AJ134**

v.1–45, A–Z; v.46–55, Nachträge bis 1899, Andr–Z (A–Ad included in v.45); v.56, General Register.

The outstanding German biographical dictionary, containing long, signed articles, with bibliographies, on persons from early times to the end of the 19th century. Does not include living persons. As there are supplementary sections in many volumes, it is essential that the index be used to find the complete record.

For biographies of persons deceased since the compilation of this work the following may be used as informal supplements:

Biographisches Jahrbuch und deutscher Nekrolog, 1896– 1913; hrsg. von Anton Bettelheim. Berlin, Reimer, 1897– 1917. v.1–18 and separate index volume. Annual. **AJ135**

Each volume contains: (1) section of long, signed articles, with bibliographies, on prominent Germans who died during the year; (2) a necrology of briefer notices; and (3) index. The index volume is a combined index to v.1–10 (1896–1905).

Continued by:

Deutsches biographisches Jahrbuch, hrsg. vom Verbande der Deutschen Akademien, 1914–23, 1928–29. Berlin, Deutsche Verlagsanstalt, 1925–32. v.1–5, 10–11. **AJ136**

v.1, 1914–16; v.2, 1917–20; v.3, 1921; v.4, 1922; v.5, 1923; v.10, 1928; v.11, 1929.

Also contains long, signed articles, many with bibliographies, and a necrology list of briefer notices. No cumulated index.

Die grossen Deutschen: deutsche Biographie, hrsg. von Hermann Heimpel, Theodor Heuss, Benno Reifenberg. Berlin, im Propyläen-Verlag bei Ullstein, 1957–58. (v.1–2, 1958) 5v. il. **AJ137**

Nonalphabetical; gives in chronological order signed biographies, several pages in length, of 234 figures outstanding in German cultural, religious, military history, etc. from 672 to date.

The original edition was edited by Willy Andreas and Wilhelm von Scholz (1935–37). The new edition is greatly rewritten, many articles are by different authors, and the illustrations—some in color, some facsimiles—have been changed.

v.5 is a supplementary volume with a cumulated index to v.1–5.

Mitteldeutsche Köpfe: Lebensbilder aus einem Jahrtausent. Frankfurt am Main, Verlag Wolfgang Weidlich, 1959. 239p. **AJ138**

Brief biographical sketches of persons prominent in the cultural, business, and political life of central Germany from the Middle Ages to the present day.

✓ **Neue deutsche Biographie,** hrsg. von der Historischen Kommission bei der Bayerischen Akademie der Wissenschaften . . . Berlin, Duncker und Humblot, 1953–61. Bd.1–5. (In progress) **AJ139**

Bd.1–5, Aachen–Fyn.

A new work, not intended to supersede the *Allgemeine deutsche Biographie* (AJ134), although many of the same names appear in it, with persons who have died since the older work was published and some additional names from earlier periods. Articles are signed, and bibliographies, including materials by and about biographees, are given at the end of each article. References to portraits are sometimes noted. An index in each volume, covering the part of the alphabet contained in the volume, includes references to all entries in the *Allgemeine deutsche Biographie,* thus calling attention to articles omitted from the new work.

Rössler, Hellmuth and **Franz, Günther.** Biographisches Wörterbuch zur deutschen Geschichte. München, Oldenburg, 1952. 968p. **AJ139a**

Includes some 2000 individual biographies, in all fields and from Roman times to 1933, mainly of Germans but also of some foreigners important in the history of Germany. Brief bibliographical notes.

P.ix–xix, index by period; p.xx–xxxi, index by field or profession (subdivided by period); p.xxxii–xlviii, index by region (subdivided by period).

Contemporary

Kürschners deutscher Gelehrten-Kalender, 1961. 9. Ausg. Berlin, de Gruyter, 1961. 2v. **AJ140**

1st ed. 1925; 2d ed. 1926; 3d ed. 1928; 4th ed. 1931; 5th ed. 1935; 6th ed. 1940/41; 7th ed. 1950; 8th ed. 1954.

A biographical dictionary of German scholars in the non-

literary fields, an offshoot of *Kürschners deutscher Literatur-Kalender* (BD578).

The editions vary considerably in size and content, both as to names included and as to supplementary information. The 1961 edition is in 2v., treating about 17,000 personalities. Extensive bibliographical listings.

Wer ist wer? Das deutsche who's who. 14. Ausg. von Degeners Wer ist's? Hrsg. von Walter Habel. Berlin-Grunewald, Arani Verlags-GMBH, 1962. Now quadrennial. **AJ141**

v.14, Bd.1, Bundesrepublik Deutschland und West Berlin. 1789p.

Title varies: v.1–9 (1905–28), *Wer ist's?;* v.10 (1935), *Degener's Wer ist's?.*

A continuation of the standard German who's who. This edition to be in two parts, the second to cover Mittel- und Ostdeutschland.

This volume includes sketches for more than 22,000 personalities in all fields.

Who's who in Germany: a biographical dictionary containing about 11,000 biographies of prominent people in and of Germany and 2400 organizations, ed. by Horst C. Kliemann and Stephen S. Taylor. 2d ed. Munich, Oldenbourg, 1960. 1618p., 140p. **AJ142**

1st ed. 1955.

Another in the English-language series of who's whos of European countries. Includes biographical sketches and a directory of organizations, associations, and institutions in the Federal Republic of Germany.

Regional

☙ Many dictionaries and collections of local biography often contain names or information not given in the general dictionaries of German biography. A useful list of these regional works is given in Schneider's *Handbuch der Bibliographie,* p.485–97 (AA8).

GERMANY, EAST

SBZ-Biographie; ein biographisches Nachschlagebuch über die Sowjetische Besatzungszone Deutschlands. Hrsg. vom Bundesministerium für gesamtdeutsche Fragen. Bonn, Deutscher Bundes-Verlag, 1964. 406p. **AJ143**

Title varies. 1958, *Wer ist wer in der SBZ?*

Biographical sketches of persons in East Germany.

GREAT BRITAIN

Dictionary of national biography, ed. by Leslie Stephen and Sidney Lee. Reissue. London, Smith, Elder, 1908–9. 22v. (1938 repr. 22v.) **AJ144**

v.1–21, A–Z; v.22, 1st suppl., Additional names, 1901.

—— 2d–6th supplements. Oxford, Univ. Pr., 1912–59. 5v.

2d suppl., 1901–11, ed. by Sir Sidney Lee. 1912; 3d suppl., 1912–21, ed. by H. W. C. Davis and J. R. H. Weaver. 1927; 4th suppl., 1922–30, ed. by J. R. H. Weaver. 1937; 5th suppl., 1931–40, ed. by L. G. Wickham Legg. 1949; 6th suppl., 1941–50, ed. by L. G. Wickham Legg and E. T. Williams. 1959.

—— Index and epitome, ed. by Sir Sidney Lee. London, Smith, Elder, 1903–13. 2v.

Contents: Index and epitome to main set and 1st suppl. (22v.) 2d ed. 1906. 1456p.; Index . . . to 2d suppl. 1913. 129p.

History: Founded by George Smith of the London firm of Smith, Elder and Co., and originally published by that firm as follows: Main work and 1st suppl. 63v. 1885–1901; Index and epitome to v.1–63. 1903. 1456p.; Errata for v.1–63. 1904. 299p.; 2d suppl. 3v. 1912; Index and epitome to 2d suppl. 1913. 129p.; Reissue of 63v. ed., on thinner paper, with the incorporation in the text of the material in the Errata volume. 22v. 1908–9. Presented, 1917, by the heirs of George Smith, to the Oxford University Press, to be continued by that institution. In 1920 the Press reissued the 2d supplement, on thin paper, in 1v. and has continued the work by publishing the 3d–6th supplements and *The concise dictionary*. Though the original work is not being revised by the present publisher, an informal revision of many articles is to be found in the Errata notes published in the *Bulletin* of the Institute of Historical Research of London University, 1923–   .

Constitutes the most important reference work for English biography, containing signed articles by specialists, and excellent bibliographies; important names are treated at great length, minor names more briefly, and all are generally reliable and scholarly. Scope includes all noteworthy inhabitants of the British Isles and the Colonies, exclusive of living persons; also noteworthy Americans of the colonial period. The supplements bring the record down to 1950.

Each supplement includes a cumulative index covering all entries from 1901 in one alphabetical sequence.

—— The concise dictionary. Oxford, Univ. Pr., 1903 (repr. 1953–61). 2v.

Pt.1, From the beginnings to 1900: being an epitome of the main work and its supplement. 1503p.

The 1953 reprint lists, on p.1457–1503, corrections and additions, which in many cases correct or amplify the main work.

Pt.2, 1901–1950: being an epitome of the twentieth century *D.N.B.* down to the end of 1950. 528p.

Includes a Select Subject Index, p.485–528.

The concise dictionary serves a double purpose, i.e., it is both an index and also an independent biographical dictionary, as it gives abstracts, each about one fourteenth of the length of the original article.

❦ The following publications, although more limited in scope than the *Dictionary of national biography*, are often useful for names or types of information not given there:

Boase, Frederic. Modern English biography, containing many thousand concise memoirs of persons who have died since 1850, with an index of the most interesting matter. Truro, Netherton, 1892–1921. 6v. (Repr.: London, Frank Cass, 1964. 6v.) **AJ145**

v.1–3, A–Z, Index; v.4–6 (suppl. v.1–3), A–Z.

A useful work, particularly for minor 19th-century names not included in the *Dictionary of national biography* (AJ144). Good subject index, including lists of pseudonyms, fancy names, class lists, etc.

Burke's Handbook to the most excellent Order of the British Empire; containing biographies, a full list of persons appointed to the Order . . . ed. by A. Winton Thorpe. London, Burke, 1921. 703p. il. **AJ146**

This order was established by Letters Patent on June 4, 1917, its members to be those who in either civil or military capacities rendered important services to the Empire. Therefore, this is a volume devoted primarily to the outstanding persons of the First World War.

Catholic who's who, 1908–52. London, Burns, 1908–52. Annual (slightly irregular). **AJ147**

Until 1935, title was *Catholic who's who and yearbook*. Suspended 1943–51. Ceased publication (?).

Gillow, Joseph. A literary and biographical history; or,

Bibliographical dictionary of the English Catholics from the breach with Rome, in 1534, to the present time. London, Burns; N.Y., Catholic Pub. Soc., [1885–92]. 5v. (Repr.: N.Y., Burt Franklin, 1961) **AJ148**

Gives some 2000 biographies. Useful for names not included in the *Dictionary of national biography* and for more information about some names which are there. Especially useful for the bibliographies which are very full.

May be supplemented for the 18th century by:

Kirk, John. Biographies of English Catholics in the eighteenth century, by the Rev. John Kirk, being part of his projected continuation of Dodd's Church history, ed. by J. H. Pollen and Edwin Burton. London, Burns, 1909. 293p. **AJ149**

Ward, Thomas Humphry. Men of the reign; a biographical dictionary of eminent persons of British and colonial birth who have died during the reign of Queen Victoria. London, Routledge, 1885. 1020p. **AJ150**

A concise biographical dictionary of 19th-century personalities, containing some names not included in either the *Dictionary of national biography* (AJ144) or Boase, *Modern English biography* (AJ145).

Wedgwood, Josiah Clement. History of Parliament, 1439–1509. v.1, Biographies of the members of the Commons House. London, Stat. Off., 1936. v.1 (984p.). col. coats of arms. **AJ151**

A list of 2600 men, out of a possible total of 3800 known to have been elected members of 29 Parliaments, 1439–1509, with biographical data about each and many bibliographical footnotes referring to sources. As only 60 of the 2600 names are included in the *Dictionary of national biography,* this work is important for British biography as well as for Parliamentary history.

For description of set *see* CI131.

Who was who, 1897–1915, 1916–1928, 1929–1940, 1941–1950, 1951–1960; a companion to Who's who; containing the biographies of those who died during the period. London, Black, 1929–61. 5v. **AJ152**

1897–1915 has been published in four editions: 1st ed. June 1920; 2d ed., with addenda and corrigenda, 1929; 3d ed., with rev. corrigenda, 1935; 4th ed., with rev. addenda and corrigenda, 1953.

For the most part the original sketches as they last appeared in *Who's who* (AJ155) are reprinted with the date of death added, but in a few instances additional information has been added.

Who's who in history by C. R. N. Routh. Oxford, Blackwell, 1960–64. v.1–2. il. (In progress) **AJ153**

Contents: v.1, British Isles, 55 B.C.–1485. 269p.; v.2, England, 1485–1603. 476p.

To be a 4v. British biographical dictionary covering from 55 B.C. through the Victorian period. Popularly written sketches, averaging two to three pages, arranged chronologically by death date.

Contemporary

Kelly's Handbook to the titled, landed, and official classes, 1880–   . London, Kelly Directories, 1880–   . v.1–   . Annual. **AJ154**

Brief biographical sketches of those who have hereditary or honorary titles; members of Parliament; government officials; landed proprietors; distinguished members of the dramatic, literary, and artistic worlds; and leaders in commerce and industry.

Who's who, an annual biographical dictionary, with which is incorporated "Men and women of the time." London, Black; N.Y., St. Martin's, 1849–   . v.1–   . Annual. **AJ155**

The pioneer work of the who's who type and still one of the most important. Until 1897, it was a handbook of titled and official classes and included lists of names rather than biographical sketches. With 1897, called "First year of new issue," it changed its character and became a biographical dictionary of prominent persons in many fields. It has been developed and enlarged along these lines ever since. It is principally British, but a few prominent names of other nationalities are included. Biographies are reliable and fairly detailed; they give main facts, addresses, and, in case of authors, lists of works.

For a compilation of biographies of deceased persons selected from the volumes 1897–1960, *see Who was who* (AJ 152).

Bibliography

Hart, Hester E. R. and **Johnston, Marjorie.** Bibliography of the registers (printed) of the universities, inns of court, colleges and schools of Great Britain and Ireland. (In London. University. Inst. of Historical Research. Bull. 9:19–30, 65–83, 154–70. June, Nov. 1931; Feb. 1932; 10:109–13. Nov. 1932)   **AJ156**

A bibliography of registers, most of which include some biographical material. Pt.1, Universities, inns of court, colleges, and other similar institutions; pt.2, Schools; Addenda and corrigenda.

Matthews, William. British autobiographies; an annotated bibliography of British autobiographies published or written before 1951. Berkeley, Los Angeles, Univ. of Calif. Pr., 1955. 376p.   **AJ157**

Information given includes full name of author, abbreviated title, and date of publication with brief and pithy annotations. Arranged alphabetically by author with an index under headings indicating professions and occupations, places and regions, reminiscences, wars, and general topics.

Royal Commonwealth Society. Library. Biography catalogue, by Donald H. Simpson. London, Soc., 1961. 511p.   **AJ158**

An index of biographical materials contained in the Society's library about persons in the Empire and the Commonwealth, and those in the United Kingdom and elsewhere connected with British imperial affairs. Books and periodical articles are both included. There is an extensive listing and index, by country, of works of collective biography, and an index of authors.

Stauffer, Donald Alfred. The art of biography in 18th century England: Bibliographical supplement. Princeton, N.J., Princeton Univ. Pr., 1941. 293p. 2v.   **AJ159**

A subject and author index of biographies and autobiographies written or translated in England 1700–1800, with a "chronological table of the most important biographical works in England, 1700–1800." A supplement to the author's *The art of biography in 18th century England.* Princeton Univ. Pr., 1941.

Preceded by his *English biography before 1700* (Cambridge, Harvard Univ. Pr., 1930), which included a bibliography of early biographies published before 1700, p.289–372.

Indexes

Index Society, London. An index to the biographical and obituary notices in the Gentleman's magazine, 1731–1780. London, British Record Soc., 1886–91. 677p. (Publ. of the British Record Soc. . . . Index Soc., v.15)   **AJ160**

Musgrave, *Sir* **William.** Obituary prior to 1800 (as far as relates to England, Scotland, and Ireland) comp. by Sir William Musgrave . . . and entitled by him "A general nomenclator and obituary, with reference to the

books where the persons are mentioned, and where some account of their character is to be found." Ed. by Sir George J. Armytage. London, 1899–1901. 6v. (Publ. of the Harleian Soc., v.44–49)   **AJ161**

An alphabetical index to a large number of obituaries and biographies, found in some 85 works.

Gives name, date of death, sometimes a characterizing word or phrase, and reference to the book or other publication where a biography or obituary notice may be found. Very useful, especially for names not included in the *Dictionary of national biography* (AJ144).

HONG KONG

Hong Kong who's who: an almanac of personalities and their history. 1958/1960. Rola Luzzatto, ed. and pub.; Rennie Remedios, asst. ed. Hong Kong, [1959?]. 288p.   **AJ162**

Includes biographical sketches of prominent personalities, both oriental and occidental.

HUNGARY

[Jásznigi, Alexander] and **Parlagi, Imre.** Das geistige Ungarn, biographisches Lexikon, hrsg. von Oskar von Krücken [pseud.] u. Imre Parlagi. Wien, Braumüller, [1918]. 2v.   **AJ163**

Includes principally writers, artists, and men in public life.

Szinnyei, József. Magyar írók élete és munkái a Magyar Tudományos Akadémia megbízásából. Budapest, Hornyánszky V., 1891–1914. 14v.   **AJ164**

Continued by the following:

Gulyás, Pál. Magyar írók; élete és munkái. Új sorozat. Budapest, Magyar Könyvtárosok és Levéltárosok Egyesülete, 1939–1944. v.1–6.   **AJ165**

v.1–6, A–Dzurányi. Ceased publication (?).

Based on principles of *DNB,* it includes biographies of all notable Hungarians. More comprehensive than Jásznigi (AJ 163).

See also Wurzbach's *Biographisches Lexikon des Kaiserthums Oesterreich* (AJ69), which includes biographies of 3344 Hungarians.

Szy, Tibor. Hungarians in America; a biographical directory of professionals of Hungarian origin in the Americas. N.Y., Hungarian Univ. Assoc., 1963. 606p.   **AJ166**

ICELAND

Ólason, Páll Eggert. Íslenzkar æviskrár frá landnámstímum til ársloka 1940. Reykjavík, Íslenzka Bókmenntafélags, 1948–52. 5v.   **AJ167**

A national biographical dictionary covering all periods up to 1940. Living persons are not included. Entries are brief but include bibliography. Biographees are entered under first name according to Icelandic usage.

INDIA

Buckland, Charles Edward. Dictionary of Indian biography. London, Sonnenschein, 1906. 494p.   **AJ168**

Contains about 2600 concise biographies of persons—English, Indian, or foreign—noteworthy in the history, service, literature, or science of India since 1750.

Rao, C. Hayavadana. Indian biographical dictionary, 1915. Madras, Pillar, [1915?]. 472p., 31p. **AJ169**

Brief biographies, of the who's who type, of both natives and Europeans. Supplements give warrant of precedence, New Year's and Birthday honors, list of clubs, etc.

Who's who in India, containing lives and portraits of ruling chiefs, nobles, titled personages and other eminent Indians. Popular ed. Lucknow, Newul Kishore Pr., 1911–14. 1610p. and 2 suppl. il. **AJ170**

Contains eight separate biographical lists, classified by states and provinces, each list arranged in general order of precedence, not alphabetically. General alphabetical index at end. Many portraits. Only native Indians included.

Who's who in India, Burma and Ceylon, (illus.) ed. and comp. by Thomas Peters. [9th ed.] Poona, Sun Pub. House, [1938]. 818p., 48p., xxiiip. il. **AJ171**

Title varies: *Who's who in India.*

Contents: The royal family and provincial governors, p.1–34; Indian princes and chiefs, p.37–122; General, p.125–818; Who's who in Indian industries and commerce, p.1–48; Index, p.i–xxiii.

IRELAND

Crone, John Smith. Concise dictionary of Irish biography. Rev. and enl. ed. Dublin, Talbot Pr.; N.Y., Longmans, 1937. 290p. **AJ172**

1st ed. 1928.

Brief biographical sketches of "notable Irish men and women in every sphere of activity," from the early days to the 20th century. Does not include living persons. This edition includes an appendix, p.271–90.

Ryan, Richard. Biographia hibernica. A biographical dictionary of the worthies of Ireland, from the earliest periods to the present time. London, Ryan, 1819–21. 2v. **AJ173**

Long, discursive sketches of persons known and unknown.

Thom's Irish who's who: a biographical book of reference of prominent men and women in Irish life at home and abroad. Dublin, Thom, 1923. 266p. **AJ174**

No more published.

Brief who's who–type sketches of Irishmen prominent in 1923.

ISRAEL

Contemporary

Who's who: Israel 1952–   . Tel Aviv, Who's Who in the State of Israel Pub. House, 1952–   . il. Annual. **AJ175**

Previous editions called: *Palestine and Transjordan who's who,* 1945; *Palestine personalia,* 1947; *Who's who in the State of Israel,* 1949.

Text in English.

Pt.1 is the who's who section, with brief sketches of outstanding personalities; pt.2—Public bodies and enterprises—gives information on national institutions and political parties, cultural and educational institutions, banking and finance, industry, etc.

ITALY

Dizionario biografico degli italiani. [Redazione, direttorei Alberto M. Ghisalberti] Roma, Istit. della Enciclopedia Italiana, 1960–64. v.1–5. (In progress) **AJ176**

Contents: v.1–5, Aaron–Baratta.

A scholarly dictionary of national biography with signed biographies of Italians from the 5th century to the present, exclusive of living persons. A bibliography of source material is included for each sketch. The plan is to publish about 2v. a year, the completed set to comprise some 40,000 biographies.

Enciclopedia biografica e bibliografica "Italiana." . . . Milano, Istit. Ed. Italiano, Bernardo Carlo Tosi, 1936–44. ser. 4–50. il. (Incompl.) **AJ177**

Announced for publication in 48 series, each devoted to a special class, e.g., writers, soldiers, scientists, actors, etc. Includes biographies of medium length, unsigned, but supplied with bibliographies and with many illustrations taken from contemporary sources. Planned on a large scale but never carried to completion. Series were published in irregular order, and many were never issued.

Savino, Edoardo. La nazione operante; albo d'oro del fascismo profili et figure . . . 3. ed. riv. e amp. Novara, Istit. Geografico de Agostini, 1937. 784p. il. **AJ178**

Contains some 2150 biographies of prominent Fascists in all fields.

Contemporary

Chi è? Dizionario degli italiani d'oggi. 7. ed. Rome, Scarano, 1961. 714p. **AJ179**

1. ed. 1928. Suppl. 1929; 2. ed. 1931; 3. ed. 1936; 4. ed. 1940; 5. ed. 1948; 6. ed. 1957.

Another work with the same title was issued in 1908 by Guido Biagi.

A who's who of current Italian personalities.

Vaccaro, Gennaro. Panorama biografico degli italiani d'oggi. Roma, Armando Curcio Editore, 1956. 2v. (1648p.) **AJ180**

Contains some 25,000 biographical sketches of living Italians.

Who's who in Italy, [1st ed.] 1957/1958. A biographical dictionary containing about 7000 biographies of prominent people in and of Italy and 1400 organizations, ed. by Igino Giordani and Stephen S. Taylor. Milano, Intercontinental Book and Pub. S.r.1., 1958. 1137p. **AJ181**

Another in the series of who's whos published in English by this company, which has branches in various countries (e.g., Central European Times Publishing Co., Zurich).

Follows the pattern of others in the series: pt.1, Biographies; pt.2, Directory of organizations: cultural, religious, and economic institutions; trade unions; etc.

Bibliography

Pizzi, Francesco. Italica gens; repertori a stampa di biografia generale italiana. Cremona, Moschetti, 1934. 131p. **AJ182**

A bibliography of 1238 biographical works in three parts: (1) general; (2) arranged by locality; and (3) arranged by subject. Author index.

JAMAICA

Who's who, Jamaica, British West Indies. An illustrated biographical record of outstanding people in Jamaica. Kingston, Who's Who (Jamaica), 1935–   . v.1, 1934/35–   . (9th ed. 1957) **AJ183**

Title varies: 1934/35–1939/40, *Who's who and why in Jamaica;* 1941/46–   , *Who's who, Jamaica, British West Indies.* Subtitle varies.

JAPAN

Iseki, K. R. Who's who in "Hakushi" in great Japan. Tokyo, Hattensha, [1921–30]. v.1–5. il.   **AJ184**

A dictionary of contemporary biography of Japanese who are *Hakushi,* or holders of the doctor's degree in various fields. Articles are in Japanese and English. Arranged by subjects: v.1, Law, Pharmacology; v.2–4, Medicine; v.5, Engineering.

Who's who in Japan, 1912–40/41, by Tsunesaburo Kamesaka. Tokyo, Who's Who in Japan Pub. Off., 1911–40. v.1–21. Annual (slightly irregular).   **AJ185**

Editor varies.

In English, on the general plan of the English *Who's who.*

Japan biographical encyclopedia and who's who. [1st ed.–] Tokyo, Japan Biographical Research Dept., Rengo Pr., 1958–   . Triennial.   **AJ186**

1st ed. 1958; 2d ed. 1961; 3d ed. 1964/65. 2377p.

Gives, in English, concise biographical sketches of notables in all fields, of all periods, living and dead, with names of religious, mythical, and legendary beings and a very few foreigners. Appendixes list: additional names, members of Japanese diets and cabinets, emperors, diplomatic representatives to and from other countries, a chronology of Japanese history, etc.

Who's who of contemporary Japan. 1963. Tokyo, Japanese Politics Economy Research Inst., 1963. 466p. **AJ187**

Sketches in English of persons prominent in various fields.

LATIN AMERICA

Quién es quién en Venezuela, Panama, Ecuador, Colombia. Bogotá, Oliverio Perry, [1952]. 1074p. il.   **AJ188**

Each country is separately treated, with (in all) some 5000 biographical sketches of the who's who type alphabetically arranged; many of the entries are accompanied by small portraits of varying quality. Includes lists of pseudonyms and of biographees by occupation, and an index—all divided by country and then arranged alphabetically.

Who's who in Latin America; a biographical dictionary of notable living men and women of Latin America. Founded in 1935 by Percy Alvin Martin. (3d ed. rev. and enl.) . . . ed. by Ronald Hilton. . . . Stanford, Calif., Stanford Univ. Pr.; Chicago, Marquis, [c1945–51]. 7v.   **AJ189**

Contents: pt.1, Mexico; pt.2, Central America and Panama; pt.3, Colombia, Ecuador, and Venezuela; pt.4, Bolivia, Chile, and Peru; pt.5, Argentina, Paraguay, and Uruguay; pt.6, Brazil; pt.7, Cuba, Dominican Republic, and Haiti.

The first two editions, 1935 and 1940, 1v. each, were edited by P. A. Martin. This edition, revised and reorganized, includes some 8000 biographies, whereas the 2d edition included only slightly over 1500. However, as each country is treated separately, the great disadvantage of this edition is the number of alphabets which must be checked if the country of the person searched for is not known.

Bibliography

Jones, Cecil Knight. A bibliography of Latin American bibliographies. 2d ed. rev. and enl. by the author with the assistance of James A. Granier. Wash., Govt. Prt. Off., 1942. 311p. (U.S. Library of Congress. Latin Amer. ser., no.2)   **AJ190**

Includes collective biographies. For full description *see* AA44.

Toro, Josefina del. A bibliography of the collective biog-raphy of Spanish America. . . . Río Piedras, P.R., Univ., 1938. 140p. (University of Puerto Rico. Bull., ser. IX, no.1, Sept. 1938)   **AJ191**

A very useful annotated list of 488 works of collective biography, arranged by country with author index.

LITHUANIA

Biržiška, Vaclovas. Aleksandrynas: biographies, bibliographies, and bio-bibliographies of old Lithuanian authors to 1865. Chicago, Lithuanian-Amer. Cultural Fund, 1960–63. v.1–2. (In progress)   **AJ192**

Added title page and text in Lithuanian.

Contents: v.1, 16th–17th centuries, with a preface in English. 431p.; v.2, 18th–19th centuries. 497p.

LUXEMBOURG

Biographie nationale du pays de Luxembourg, depuis ses origines jusqu'à nos jours; collection présentée par Jules Mersch. Luxembourg, Impr. de la Cour Victor Buck, 1947–63. v.1–6 (fasc.1–12). il. (In progress)   **AJ193**

Nonalphabetical. Each fascicule includes some six to nine long articles on persons or families of various periods in the history of Luxembourg, often with bibliographies and many illustrations. Two fascicules form a volume, continuously paged and including an index to the names appearing in the articles in each volume. No cumulations.

Fasc.1 was published in a revised and corrected edition, 1957.

Who's who in Belgium and Grand Duchy of Luxembourg. 2d ed. Brussels, Intercontinental Book and Pub. Co., 1962.   **AJ194**

For full record *see* AJ81.

MALAYA

Leaders of Malaya and who's who, 1956–   , ed. and pub. by J. Victor Morais. Kuala Lumpur, Economy Printers, 1956–   . il. Biennial.   **AJ195**

The 3d edition, 1959/60, contains some 5000 biographical sketches.

MEXICO

Beristain de Souza, J. M. Biblioteca hispano americana septentrional. [3d ed.] México, Ed. Fuente Cultural, 1947. 5v. il.   **AJ196**

For full record *see* AA588.

Includes bio-bibliographical information about authors.

Mestre Ghigliazza, Manuel. Efemérides biográficas (de-funciones-nacimientos). México, Antigua Librería Robredo, J. Porrúa, 1945. 347p.   **AJ197**

A chronological arrangement, by year of death, of outstanding Mexicans who died between 1822 and 1945. Gives field of activity or title, place and date of birth and death. Alphabetical index.

Peral, Miguel Angel. Diccionario biográfico mexicano. México, Ed. P.A.C., [1944]. 2v. and Apéndice. **AJ198**

v.1–2, paged continuously. 894p.; Apéndice. 465p.

Covers 544 to 1944, and gathers much material in one place but with certain weaknesses, e.g., date of birth and death are frequently omitted and no bibliographical data or references to sources are given.

Sosa, Francisco. Biografías de Mexicanos distinguidos. Ed. de la Secretaría de Fomento. México, Oficina Tipográfica de la Secretaría de Fomento, 1884. 1115p. **AJ199**

Fairly long sketches. Covers all periods. No bibliography.

Valverde Tellez, Emeterio. Bio-bibliografía eclesiástica mexicana (1821–1943). México, Ed. Jus, 1949. 3v. **AJ200**

Contents: v.1–2, Obispos; v.3, Sacerdotes.
Biographical sketches with long bibliographies of the bishops and other clergy.

Bibliography

Iguíniz, Juan B. Bibliografía biográfica mexicana: t.1. Repertorios biográficos. México, [Impr. de la Secretaría de Relaciones Exteriores], 1930. 546p. (Monografías bibliográficas mexicanas, núm. 18) **AJ201**

A list of 703 works of collective biography with full contents notes, including names of persons. Contains, p.361–546, a full index to all names mentioned in notes, which serves therefore as an index to biographical material on some 7000 Mexicans of all periods.

MIDDLE EAST

Recueil des archives biographiques permanentes du monde arabe. 2. éd. Damas, Bureau des Documentations Arabes, 1959–61. 2v. Loose-leaf. (In progress) **AJ202**

For each of the major Arab countries biographical information is given, in tabulated form, on a number of persons connected with the government.

Kept up to date by *Collection trimestrielle d'additifs et rectificatifs biographiques.* (Loose-leaf)

Who's who in U.A.R. and the Near East: the greatest biographical work in the Middle and Near East. Cairo, 1959. Annual. **AJ203**

Ceased publication.
Title varies: 19?–47, *Le mondain égyptien, The Egyptian who's who;* 1948–51, *Who's who in Egypt and the Middle East;* 1952–57/58, *Who's who in Egypt and the Near East.* (Title also in Arabic and in French: *Le mondain égyptien et du Proche-Orient.*)
1959 called 24th edition. Includes U.A.R., Sudan, Iran, Libya, Cyprus, Lebanon, Jordan, Iraq, Saudi-Arabia, India, Pakistan, Ceylon, Indonesia, Ethiopia, and Aden.

The first section is arranged by country, giving brief descriptive information with names of governmental officials, diplomatic representatives, and business firms, followed by an alphabetical listing of persons with addresses and brief biographical information.

NETHERLANDS

Aa, Abraham Jacobus van der. Biographisch woordenboek der Nederlanden. Nieuwe uitg. Haarlem, Brederode, 1852–78. 12v. il. **AJ204**

A valuable work including sketches on persons from medieval times to mid-19th century. The length of articles varies from a few lines to two or three columns. Includes considerable bibliography both by and about.

Nieuw Nederlandsch biografisch woordenboek, onder red. van P. C. Molhuysen, P. J. Blok en Fr. K. H. Kossmann. Leiden, Sijthoff, 1911–37. 10v. **AJ205**

Each volume is arranged alphabetically and has a cumulated index to all previous volumes. v.10 has an index to the set. Adequate signed articles, bibliographies.

Persoonlijkheden in het koninkrijk der Nederlanden in woord en beeld; Nederlanders en hun werk met een inleidung van H. Brugmans; mede bevattende de biografieen van de leden van het koninklijk huis door N. Japikse. Amsterdam, Van Holkema & Warendorf, 1938. 1748p. il. **AJ206**

Includes some 5000 biographies of living persons with portraits.

Contemporary

Wie is dat? Biografische gegevens van Nederlanders die een vooraanstaande plaats in het maatschappelijk leven innemen met vermelding van adressen. [6. uitg.] 's-Gravenhage, Nijhoff, 1956. 703p. **AJ207**

1st ed. 1931; 2d ed. 1932; 3d ed. 1935; 4th ed. 1938; 5th ed. 1948.
Subtitle varies.
The Netherlands who's who.

NEW ZEALAND

Scholefield, Guy Hardy. A dictionary of New Zealand biography. Wellington, Dept. of Internal Affairs, 1940. 2v. **AJ208**

"Bibliography," v.1, p.xviii–xxix.
A national biographical dictionary, modeled on the *Dictionary of national biography* (AJ144), of persons who have distinguished themselves in the history of New Zealand since organized European migration began approximately 100 years ago. Includes bibliography.

Contemporary

Who's who in New Zealand. (Established 1908) 7th ed. Wellington, Reed, 1961. 307p. **AJ209**

Subtitle varies.
Contains preliminary directory material, including officials of government, church, and education, and diplomatic representatives; election returns; titles and dignities, etc. Biographies are of usual who's who type.

NIGERIA

Who's who in Nigeria; a biographical dictionary. A "Daily Times" publication. Lagos, Nigerian Printing and Pub. Co., 1956. 278p. **AJ210**

1st ed.
"Includes the biographies of more than 1500 prominent people in the day to day life of this country."—*Pref.* Both native Nigerians and Europeans.

NORWAY

Norsk biografisk leksikon. Redaktion: Edv. Bull, Anders Krogvig, Gerhard Gran. Oslo, Aschehoug, 1923–64. v.1–15$^{1-2}$ (hft.72). (In progress) **AJ211**

v.1–15$^{1-2}$ (hft.72), A–Størmer.
Imprint and editors vary.
Long articles signed by specialists; with bibliographies.
Covers from the earliest times to the present and includes living persons.

Contemporary

Hvem er hvem? 1964 [9. utg.] Oslo, Aschehoug, 1964. 686p. **AJ212**

1st ed. 1912; 2d ed. 1930; 3d ed. 1934; 4th ed. 1938; 5th ed. 1948; 6th ed. 1950; 7th ed. 1955; 8th ed. 1959.

The Norwegian who's who. The 9th edition includes 3840 biographical sketches.

Bibliography

Andresen, Harald. Norsk biografisk oppslagsliteratur; katalog utarb. for Norsk Slektshistorisk Forening. [Oslo], Cammermeyer, [1945]. 218p. [Slektshistorisk bibliotek] **AJ213**

A bibliography of Norwegian sources for biographical materials, arranged by fields of specialization.

Deichmanske Bibliotek. Register til norges tidsskrifter: v.2, Norsk biografi (til 31/12 1909). Kristiania, Cammermeyer, 1911. 599p. **AJ214**

Lists nearly 15,000 names giving for each: dates of birth or death, some characterizing phrase, and references to biographical articles in Norwegian periodicals. Because of the dates and characterizing phrases the work can be used for some direct biographical information as well as for its indexing.

Continued informally by similar indexing, also with dates and characterizing phrases, in the *Norsk tidsskriftindex,* 1921–30 (AF160), under the heading *Personalhistorie;* from 1931–40 in:

Biografiske artikler i norske tidsskrifter, 1931–1935, 1936–1940. Oslo, Fabritius, 1936–47. 2v. (Norsk bibliografisk bibliotek, bd.2, hft.3, bd.7) **AJ215**

Ed.: 1931/35, W. P. Sommerfeldt; 1936/40, Vilhelm Haffner.

PAKISTAN

Biographical encyclopedia of Pakistan, 1960/61. [2d ed.] Lahore, Biographical Research Inst., Pakistan, for Internat. Pub., 1960. 936p. **AJ216**

1st ed. 1955/56.

Chief ed., Khan Tahawar Ali Khan.

Biographical data of important contemporary figures in Pakistan. Arranged in 12 large occupational groups with alphabetical index.

In part of the edition a supplementary section of additional names was included, but not all copies include this.

PARAGUAY

Quién es quién en el Paraguay? Buenos Aires, Ed. F. Monte Domecq, 1941–46. v.1–4. il. Annual (slightly irregular). **AJ217**

Later volumes omit names included in earlier volumes and add others, making it necessary to consult all volumes. Includes commercial directories.

PERU

[Beltroy, Manuel]. Peruanos notables de hoy; biografías de peruanos representativos contemporáneos. 1. ed. 1957. Lima, Sanmarti, [1957?]. 202p. **AJ218**

Who's who type of sketch on outstanding personalities. Includes a classified list.

Diccionario biográfico del Perú . . . Raúl Garbin Diaz, Raúl Garbin, Jr., Julio Cárdenas Ramírez. 1. ed. 1943–44. . . . [Lima, "Escuelas Americanas," 1944]. 977p. il. **AJ219**

A combination who's who, commercial directory, and government roster.

Mendiburu, Manuel de. Diccionario histórico-biográfico del Perú. 2. ed. con adiciones y notas bibliográficas publicada por Evaristo San Cristóval. . . . Lima, "Enrique Palacios," 1931–35. 11v. il. **AJ220**

"Catálogo de las obras y manuscritos que deben consultarse para la historia de la América latina y particularmente del Perú."—v.1, p.15–52.

Historical and biographical articles in one alphabet, with a subject index in each volume and a general index at the end. Includes fairly long articles with references to sources.

———— Apéndice. Lima, Gil, 1935–36. v.1–3, A–N.

Paz-Soldán, Juan Pedro. Diccionario biográfico de peruanos contemporáneos. Nueva ed. corr. y aum. Lima, Lib. e Impr. Gil, 1921. 449p. il. **AJ221**

Biographical sketches with bibliographies of writings by, but not about, biographees.

PHILIPPINES

Manuel, E. Arsenio. Dictionary of Philippine biography. Quezon City, Filipiniana Pub., 1955– . v.1– . il. (In progress) **AJ222**

v.1, A–Z.

The first volume of a proposed series planned to include nonliving individuals who have contributed significantly to Philippine history and culture. v.1 contains biographical sketches not limited to any particular period and varying in length from half a page to about 30 pages. Fairly extensive bibliographies of works by and about the persons.

POLAND

Akademja Umiejętności, Kraków. Polski słownik biograficzny. Kraków, Nakł. Polskiej Akademja Umiejętności, 1935–64. v.1–10, pt.4. (In progress) **AJ223**

v.1–10, pt.4, A–Jarosiński.

A scholarly dictionary with signed articles and long bibliographies.

PORTUGAL

Quem é alguém (Who's who in Portugal). Dicionário biográfico das personalidades em destaque do nosso tempo. 1947– . Lisboa, Portugália Editora, [1947]– . v.1– . **AJ224**

No more published (?).

A who's who of contemporary personalities.

❦ As there is no national biographical dictionary for Portugal, Portuguese encyclopedias should be consulted for biographical articles. *See also* I. F. da Silva, *Diccionario bibliográphico portuguez* (1858–1923. 22v.) (AA652) for the biographical notes given for authors.

PUERTO RICO

Quién es quién en Puerto Rico; diccionario biográfico de record personal. Dir. y ed., Conrado Asenjo. 4. ed. 1948–49. San Juan, Impr. Venezuela, 1947. 216p.   **AJ225**
1. ed. 1933–34; 2. ed. 1936–37; 3. ed. 1941–42.

SALVADOR

García, Miguel Angel. Diccionario histórico-enciclopédico de la República de El Salvador. San Salvador, 1927–51. v.1–13. (In progress)   **AJ226**
v.1–13, A–Col.
Includes biography. For full description *see* DB151.

SCOTLAND

Anderson, William. The Scottish nation; or, The surnames, families, literature, honours and biographical history of the people of Scotland. Edinburgh, Fullarton, 1878–80. 3v. il.   **AJ227**
Fairly long articles giving the histories of families and biographies of individuals, illustrated by woodcuts and steel engravings and often with facsimiles of autographs.

SLAVIC COUNTRIES

Munich. Universität. Slavisches Seminar. Kleine slavische Biographie. Wiesbaden, Harrassowitz, 1958. 832p.   **AJ228**
Biographical sketches of persons from the various Slavic cultures, primarily in the arts and professions, from the 18th century to the present.

SOUTH AFRICA

Who's who of southern Africa (incorporating South African who's who and the Who's who of the Federation of Rhodesia and Nyasaland, Central and East Africa). Johannesburg, Wootton & Gibson, 1907–   . Annual.   **AJ229**
1st ed. 1907. Title varies: 1907–58, *South African who's who.*
Subtitle, 1963: An illustrated biographical sketch book of personalities in southern Africa with separate sections for the Republic of South Africa, South-West Africa, Southern Rhodesia, Northern Rhodesia (Zambia), Nyasaland (Malawi), Central and East Africa and Mauritius.

SOUTH PACIFIC

O'Reilly, Patrick. Calédoniens; répertoire bio-bibliographique de la Nouvelle-Calédonie . . . Paris, Musée de l'Homme, 1953. 305p. il. (Publications de la Société des Océanistes, no.3)   **AJ230**
Includes persons, no longer living, who have contributed to the growth and prosperity of the colony: administrators, scientists, engineers, travelers, missionaries, etc., and also the principal Caledonian chiefs. Gives titles of works by authors, but no references to sources. Index includes names mentioned in sketches as well as in main listings. Also an index by professions.

—— Hébridais; répertoire bio-bibliographique des Nouvelles-Hébrides. Paris, Musée de l'Homme, 1957. 287p. il. (Publications de la Société des Océanistes, no.6)   **AJ231**
Several hundred biographical sketches of people of all periods connected with the life of the New Hebrides, European as well as native. Gives titles of works by authors but no references to sources. Includes an index by professions.

—— and **Teissier, Raoul.** Tahitiens; répertoire bio-bibliographique de la Polynésie française. Paris, Musée de l'Homme, 1962. 534p. (Publications de la Société des Océanistes, no.10)   **AJ232**
Includes fairly long articles on people of all periods connected with Tahiti, native and European, and an index by professions.

SPAIN

☙ No general modern dictionary of national biography is available for Spain. The large Spanish encyclopedias, and especially the *Espasa* (AD68), include many biographies of Spaniards and Spanish-Americans. For names and information not found there, works of collective biography and the numerous regional and special biographical dictionaries should be consulted. A useful bibliography of older regional and special works is given in the following:

Foulché-Delbosc, Raymond and **Barrau-Dihigo, Louis.** Manuel de l'hispanisant. N.Y., Putnam, 1920–25. 2v.   **AJ233**
v.1 includes: List of general biographies, p.41–60; Regional biographies, arranged by place, p.60–81; List of biographical works on special classes, e.g., artists, etc., p.81–119.
For full description *see* AA50.

Couceiro Freijomil, Antonio. Diccionario bio-bibliográfico de escritores. Santiago de Compostela, Ed. de los Bibliófilos Gallegos, 1951–54. 3v. (Enciclopedia gallega, 1)   **AJ234**
Brief biographical sketches of authors of Galicia in various subject fields, with extensive bibliographies. Covers all periods down to the present day.

Esperabé Arteaga, Enrique. Diccionario enciclopédico ilustrado y crítico de los hombres de España. [Nueva ed., reformada, ampliada y completada] Madrid, Artes Gráficas Ibarra, [1957?]. 530p.   **AJ235**
Brief biographical sketches of Spaniards of various periods including living persons. Illustrations are poor. No bibliographies.

Contemporary

Figuras de hoy; enciclopedia biográfica nacional ilustrada de las personalidades de la actualidad. 2. ed. Madrid, Ed. Ciencia y Cultura, 1950–   . v.1–   . il.   **AJ236**
Cover title: *Enciclopedia figuras de hoy.*
Brief sketches of contemporary persons.

Who's who in Spain. 1st ed. A biographical dictionary containing about 6000 biographies of prominent people in and of Spain and 1400 organizations, ed. by S. Olives Canals and Stephen S. Taylor. Barcelona, Intercontinental Book and Pub. Co., 1963. 998p.   **AJ237**
In English. Biographical section, p.3–926; Directory of organizations, associations, and institutions, p.929–98.

SUDAN

Hill, Richard Leslie. A biographical dictionary of the Anglo-Egyptian Sudan. Oxford, Clarendon Pr., 1951. 391p.   **AJ238**

"Contains over 1,900 short notices of people who have died before 1948 and who have contributed, each after his fashion, to the story of the Sudan."—*Pref.*

SWEDEN

Svenska män och kvinnor; biografisk uppslagsbok. Stockholm, Bonnier, 1942–55. 8v. il.   **AJ239**

Covers from the earliest times to the present and includes living persons. Articles are brief but are signed. Almost no bibliography except for the titles of books written by persons included. Differs from the *Svenskt biografiskt lexikon* (AJ240) in the brevity of its sketches and its lack of bibliography. Should be useful in libraries which do not need the extensive information given in the larger work, and in all libraries until that is completed.

Svenskt biografiskt lexikon. Redaktionskommitté: J. A. Almquist [o.a.]. Redaktör: Bertil Boëthius. Stockholm, Bonnier, 1917–64. v.1–16, hft.1–2 (hft.77). il. (In progress)   **AJ240**

v.1–16$^{1-2}$, A–Forselles. A chronological index to v.1–10 is included in v.10, p.769–94.

Excellent work with long, signed articles, bibliographies, and many portraits. Includes persons of all periods but no longer covers living persons, although these were in v.1–10.

Contemporary

Vem är det. Svensk biografisk handbok 1912– . Stockholm, Norstedt, 1912– . v.1– . Biennial. (3 years between 1920–23)   **AJ241**

Subtitle varies.

The standard Swedish who's who.

Bibliography

Ägren, Sven. Svensk biografisk uppslagslitteratur; bibliografisk förteckning. Uppsala, Almqvist & Wiksell, 1929. 423p. (Added title page: Svenska bibliotekariesamfundets skriftserie. I)   **AJ242**

Classified, with author and subject index.

Includes material dealing with Swedish Finland (to 1809) and other Swedish possessions, as well as with Swedes in foreign countries.

A comprehensive classified bibliography of more than 2000 titles of biographical dictionaries, registers, collective biographies, etc., which include Swedish biography.

SWITZERLAND

Dictionnaire historique et biographique de la Suisse. . . . Neuchâtel, Admin. du Dictionnaire, 1921–34. 7v. and suppl. il.   **AJ243**

Contains a large amount of genealogy and biography, including persons still living. For full description *see* DC246.

Keller, Willy. Schweizer biographisches Archiv. Zürich, Verlag Internat. Publikationen, 1951–58. 6v. il. **AJ244**

A dictionary of contemporary Swiss biography. Each volume is arranged alphabetically from A to Z, distribution of biographies among the volumes being arbitrary. Sketches, of the usual who's who type, are in that one of the four official national languages used by the biographee; excellent photographs (in a separate section of plates at the end of each volume) accompany most of the sketches. v.6 includes a cumulated index to the set.

Neue schweizer Biographie; nouvelle biographie suisse; nuova biografia svizzera. Chefredaktion, A. Bruckner. Basel, Buchdruckerei sum Basler Berichthaus, 1938. 612p. il.   **AJ245**

Contains about 5000 biographies of contemporary native Swiss, the majority with pictures. Sketches are in the language of the subject: German, French, or Italian.

Schweizer Schriftsteller der Gegenwart; Écrivains suisses d'aujourd'hui; Scrittori svizzeri d'oggi; Scriptuors svizzers da noss dis. Bern, Francke Verlag, 1962. 200p. **AJ246**

Gives who's who type of information, including lists of the authors' works. Sketches are, as far as possible, in the language of the individual author.

Schweizerisches Zeitgenossen-Lexikon. Lexique suisse des contemporains. Lessico svizzero dei contemporanei. Begründet und redigiert von Hermann Aellen. 2. Ausg. Bern und Leipzig, Gotthelf-Verlag, [1932]. 1023p.   **AJ247**

1st ed. 1921. 764p.; Suppl. 1926. 200p.

Language of sketch is that used by the biographee: German, French, or Italian. Who's who type of sketch.

Contemporary

Who's who in Switzerland, including the Principality of Liechtenstein, 1962/63. [4. ed.] A biographical dictionary containing about 2600 biographies of prominent people in and out of Switzerland (including the Principality of Liechtenstein), ed. by Louis Nagel [and] Stephen Taylor. Geneva, Nagel, 1962/63. 534p.   **AJ248**

1st ed. 1950/51.

In English. Who's who section only.

This edition omits the directory of organizations included in the earlier editions.

Bibliography

Barth, Hans. Bibliographie der schweizer Geschichte. Basel, Basler Buch- und Antiquariatshandlung, 1914–15. 3v.   **AJ249**

A very full bibliography of separately published biographies is given in v.2, p.116–404. For full description *see* DC242.

Bern. Schweizerische Landesbibliothek. Katalog . . . Personenkatalog, 1901–1920, 1921–1930, 1931–1940, 1941–1947. Bern, Huber, 1929–51. 4v. (In its Systematisches Verzeichnis der schweizerischen oder die Schweiz betreffenden Veröffentlichungen)   **AJ250**

Lists of biographical works published in Switzerland during the period, arranged alphabetically by the name of the biographee.

For description of complete work *see* AA715.

Bibliographie der Schweizergeschichte, Jahrg.1913– . Zurich, Leemann, 1914– . Annual.   **AJ251**

This current bibliography of Swiss history has a section *Personengeschichte* which, particularly in its earlier volumes, is very full in its indexing of biographical and obituary articles on natives and residents of Switzerland.

For full description *see* DC245.

Repertorium über die in Zeit- und Sammelschriften der Jahre 1812–1890, 1891–1900, enthaltenen Aufsätze und Mitteilungen schweizergeschichtlichen Inhaltes. Basel, Basler Buch- und Antiquariatshandlung, 1892–1906. 2v.
                                                      AJ252

Each volume contains a list of biographical articles and obituaries in more than 300 periodicals and other collective works, which—as it gives dates of birth and death and, in many cases, a brief characterizing phrase—furnishes some direct information as well as the references to the articles indexed. For full description *see* DC244.

TURKEY

Who's who in Turkey, 1960. [2d ed.] Comp. and ed. by Afşin Oktay. Ankara, Oktay, 1960. 192p.   **AJ253**
 1st ed. 1958.
 Includes sketches of some 900 persons prominent in the life of contemporary Turkey. In English.

UNION OF SOVIET SOCIALIST REPUBLICS

Akademiia Nauk, SSSR. Materialy dlia biograficheskago slovaria dieistvitel'nykh chlenov Imperatorskoi Akademii Nauk. Petrograd, 1915–17. 2v. (Imperatorskaia Akademiia Nauk, 1889–1914. v.3)   **AJ254**
 Extensive biographical sketches of academicians, with detailed bibliographies.

Deiateli revoliutsionnogo dvizheniia v Rossii; bio-bibliograficheskii slovar'. Ot predshestvennikov dekabristov do padeniia tsarizma. Pod red. V. Vilenskogo-Sibiriakova i dr. Moskva, 1927–34.   **AJ255**
 v.1–2, 3$^{1-2}$, 5$^{1-2}$. il.
 At head of title: Vsesoiuznoe obshchestvo politicheskikh katorzhan i ssyl'nopselentsev.
 Biographical dictionary of the Revolutionary movement.

Munich. Osteuropa Institut. 5000 Sowjetköpfe; Gliederung und Gesicht eines Führungskollektivs. Hrsg. von Hans Koch. Köln, Deutsche Industrie-Verlag, 1959. 862p. (Bücher des Deutschen Industrie-Instituts) **AJ256**
 Biographical sketches, compiled abroad—an expansion of the section *"Sowjetköpfe"* in the Institute's *Sowjetbuch.* Contains a directory of organizations with the names of leading personnel.

Porträts der UdSSR-Prominenz. München, Inst. zur Erforschung der UdSSR, 1960–61. Nr.1–24. Loose-leaf.
   AJ257
 Approximately 500 biographies of prominent persons of the Soviet Union, with references to printed sources.

Russkii biograficheskii slovar' . . . izdan pod nabliudeniem predsiedatelia I. Russkago Istoricheskago Obshchestva A. A. Polovtsova. S.-Peterburg, "Kadima," 1896–1918. 25v.   **AJ258**
 Publisher varies.
 Arranged alphabetically but not published in that order, some volumes in last of alphabet appearing before earlier letters; parts of the alphabet not yet covered when work was discontinued are the letters V, Gog–Gia, E, M, Nik–Nia, Tk–Tia, U; volumes after v.2 are not numbered. Contains signed articles of some length with bibliographies; especially strong for material about the upper and ecclesiastical classes of pre-Revolutionary Russia.
 A preliminary list with additional names and brief identification appeared in Russkoe Istoricheskoe Obshchestvo, *Sbornik*, v.60–62.

Contemporary

Who's who in the U.S.S.R. 1961/62– . Montreal, Intercontinental Book and Pub. Co., 1962– .   **AJ259**

Subtitle: A biographical dictionary containing about 4000 biographies of prominent personalities in the Soviet Union, comp. by the Institute for the Study of the USSR, Munich, Germany.
 In English. Names and titles of works are transliterated.
 The Institute's earlier compilation, not entirely superseded because of different coverage, appeared as *Biographic directory of the USSR*. N.Y., Scarecrow, 1958. 782p.

Bibliography

Kaufman, Isaak Mikhailovich. Russkie biograficheskie i biobibliograficheskie slovari. Moskva, Gos. Izd-vo Kul'turno-Prosvet. Lit-ry, 1955. 751p.   **AJ260**
 1st ed. 1950.
 A valuable guide to Russian biography and bio-bibliography from the 18th century through 1954.

URUGUAY

Scarone, Arturo. Uruguayos contemporáneos; nuevo diccionario de datos biográficos y bibliográficos. Montevideo, Barreiro y Ramos, 1937. 610p.   **AJ261**
 1st ed. 1918. This edition completely revised and rewritten. Includes more than 1200 names in the main alphabet. The 71 names in the appendix are of persons who have died since the publication of the 1st edition.

VENEZUELA

Diccionario biográfico de Venezuela. Eds.: Garrido Mezquita y Compañia, pub. bajo la dirección técnica de Julio Cárdenas Ramirez. 1.ed. Madrid, Bláss, 1953. 1558p. il., maps.   **AJ262**
 Besides biographical sketches, contains much statistical and gazetteer information interspersed with the who's who. Persons, associations, and states are arranged in a single alphabet, with a commercial and industrial directory by trade, and indexes by profession to the biographical section. Lists mainly living persons, but has some full-page articles on Venezuelans of historic importance. In spite of the confusing arrangement, this is valuable for the great amount of information included.

WALES

Y bywgraffiadur Cymreig hyd 1940; paratowyd dan nawdd Anrhydeddus Gymdeithas y Cymmrodorion. Llundain, 1953. 1110p.   **AJ263**
 A biographical dictionary in Welsh planned on the lines of the *D.N.B.* and covering A.D. 400–1940, but not including living persons. Articles are written by specialists; are signed; and include references to sources and, for writers, extensive bibliographies.
 Largely supersedes earlier works but, if needed, the list of abbreviations, p.xxx–lii, serves as a bibliography of these.

Dictionary of Welsh biography down to 1940, under the auspices of the Honourable Society of Cymmrodorion. Oxford, Blackwell, 1959. 1157p.   **AJ264**
 "The present English edition is not a mere translation of the Welsh volume. The intervening years have enabled the Editors to pick up the fruits of later research and to make many corrections."—*Pref.*

YUGOSLAVIA

Ko je ko u Jugoslaviji; biografski podaci o jugoslovenskim savremenicima. 1. izd. Beograd, [Izd. "Sedme Sile"], 1957. 810p.   **AJ265**

The first postwar who's who for Yugoslavia. A previous *Ko je ko u Jugoslaviji* was published in 1928.

Slovenski biografski leksikon . . . Ljubljana, [Slovenska Akademija Znanosti in Umetnosti], 1925–60. v.1–3, pt.1. (In progress)   **AJ266**

v.1, A–Lužar. 1925–1932; v.2, Maas–Qualle. 1933–1952; v.3¹, Raab–Schmid, 1960– .

Publisher varies.

Long, signed articles, many with bibliographies.

A K

Genealogy

❧ Genealogy is the study of family history and as such may require special techniques and the searching of records of many kinds. Guides, such as G. H. Doane, *Searching for your ancestors* (AK2), and N. C. Stevenson, *Search and research* (AK4), may be helpful, but the average library will not find it possible to have available the materials necessary for detailed genealogical research, including the genealogies of individual families, local histories, parish registers, etc. Some large libraries have extensive genealogical collections, notably the Library of Congress, the New York Public Library, the Newberry Library in Chicago, and the Los Angeles Public Library, and some special libraries are also devoted to this work, such as the Genealogical Society Library in Salt Lake City. Local libraries often collect material relating to their own community or area, and may have sources not available in larger collections. When a library cannot supply a reader with genealogical material, it should refer him to one or more of the specialized libraries. Lists will be found in the library directories, e.g., Lee Ash, *Subject collections* (AB78).

This section includes some of the guides and bibliographies useful in American and English genealogy; a selection of peerages and other compilations of European nobility; and reference works on heraldry, orders and decorations, flags, and personal names.

UNITED STATES

Guides

American Society of Genealogists. Genealogical research; methods and sources. Ed., Milton Rubincam. Wash., 1960. 456p. il.   **AK1**

Discussions of methods, interpretation, rules of evidence; materials for research: original sources, public records, institutional records, secondary materials; regional genealogy: state and local records; pre-American ancestry.

Doane, Gilbert Harry. Searching for your ancestors; the how and why of genealogy. [3d ed.] Minneapolis, Univ. of Minn. Pr., 1960. 198p. il.   **AK2**

1st ed. 1937.

A manual and guide to genealogical searching, with chapters on such subjects as the finding and use of family papers, town records, cemeteries, church records; how to arrange a genealogy; getting ready to cross the Atlantic, etc.

Includes a useful bibliography of the most used guides and materials, p.165–82, and a bibliography of lists, registers, rolls, and rosters of Revolutionary War soldiers, p.189–93.

Pine, Leslie Gilbert. American origins. Garden City, N.Y., Doubleday, 1960. 357p.   **AK3**

A handbook of European genealogical sources intended for the American inquirer who has ascertained his first immigrant ancestor and wishes to trace that ancestor in Europe. Chapters are devoted to genealogical research in individual countries, with accounts of the types of records and sources available.

Stevenson, Noel C. Search and research, the researcher's handbook; a guide to official records and library sources for investigators, historians, genealogists, lawyers and librarians. Rev. ed. Salt Lake City, Deseret Book Co., 1964. 364p.   **AK4**

1st ed. 1951.

A manual of genealogical research including chapters on where and how, with lists of sources. Under names of states lists: libraries, historical societies and archives, research suggestions, reference books, military records, official records, census records, etc. Also gives sources for Canada, England and Wales, Scotland, Northern Ireland, and Eire.

Bibliographies and indexes

American genealogical index; Fremont Rider, ed. . . . pub. by a committee representing the cooperating subscribing libraries. . . . Middletown, Conn., 1942–52. 48v.   **AK5**

Begun in 1936 as a surname index printed on cards; now issued in book form giving full name entries.—Cf. *Pref.*

v.1–48, A–Z.

This will be superseded by:

American genealogical-biographical index to American genealogical, biographical and local history materials. . . . Pub. . . . by the Godfrey Memorial Library. Fremont Rider, ed. Middletown, Conn., 1952–64. v.1–47. (In progress)   **AK6**

Series 2 of AK5 above. v.1–47, A–Eames, A.

Cappon, Lester Jesse. American genealogical periodicals: a bibliography with a chronological finding-list. [2d printing with additions] N.Y., N.Y. Pub. Lib., 1964. 32p.   **AK7**

1st printing 1962.

Detailed bibliographical descriptions of national and local genealogical periodicals. The 2d printing adds a geographical finding list by state.

Colket, Meredith B. and **Bridgers, Frank E.** Guide to genealogical records in the National Archives. Wash., Govt. Prt. Off., 1964. 145p. (National Archives publ., no.64–8)   **AK8**

A guide, not to genealogical records as such, but to those that may be useful to the genealogist, e.g., population and mortality census schedules; passenger arrival lists; military, naval, and marine records, etc.

Genealogical periodical annual. Index, 1962– , ed. by Ellen Stanley Rogers. Bladensburg, Md., Genealogical Recorders, 1963– .   **AK9**

Aims to index the contents of genealogical periodicals with some inclusion of articles of like interest from other periodicals.

Hotten, John Camden. Original lists of persons of quality, emigrants, religious exiles, political rebels . . . and others who went from Great Britain to the American plantations. N.Y., Bouton; London, Chatto, 1874. 580p. (Repr.: N.Y., G. A. Baker, 1931) **AK10**

Index to American genealogies; and to genealogical material contained in all works such as town histories, county histories, local histories, historical society publications, biographies, historical periodicals, and kindred works, alphabetically arranged. 5th ed. rev., improved, and enl. Albany, N.Y., Munsell, 1900. 352p. and suppl. 1908. 107p. **AK11**

Basic volume (1900) indexes about 50,000 references; supplement continues indexing for 1900–1908.

Cover title: *Munsell's genealogical index.*

Jacobus, Donald Lines. Index to genealogical periodicals. New Haven, Conn., Jacobus, 1932–53. 3v. (Repr.: Baltimore, Genealogical Pub. Co., 1963. v.1) **AK12**

v.1 covers through 1931; v.2, 1932–46; v.3, 1947–52.

Lancour, Harold. A bibliography of ship passenger lists, 1538–1825; being a guide to published lists of early immigrants to North America. 3d ed. rev. and enl. by Richard J. Wolfe. With a list of passenger arrival records in the National Archives by Frank E. Bridgers. N.Y., N.Y. Pub. Lib., 1963. 137p. **AK13**

1st edition, 1937, had title *Passenger lists of ships coming to North America, 1607–1825.*

Emigration lists of persons who came to America before 1826. The new edition has been revised, new material added, and, in some parts, restyled. Index of ship names.

Newberry Library, Chicago. The genealogical index. Boston, G. K. Hall, 1960. 4v. **AK14**

A photographic reproduction of a valuable index containing more than 400,000 surnames with references to sources in which the name appears, e.g., town and county histories, vital records, printed genealogies, etc.

U.S. Library of Congress. American and English genealogies in the Library. . . . 2d ed. Wash., Govt. Prt. Off., 1919. 1332p. **AK15**

Contains some 7000 entries.

—— American and English genealogies in the Library of Congress. Comp. by Dr. and Mrs. C. K. Jones. 1954. 67 cards.

"Microcarded from Library of Congress card copy."

Dictionaries and compendiums

Burke's Distinguished families of America; the lineages of 1600 families of British origin now resident in the United States of America. London, Burke's Peerage, 1948. p.2539–3021. col. coats of arms. **AK16**

Issue for 1948 originally published as the American section of Burke's *Genealogical and heraldic history of the landed gentry, 1939.*

Savage, James. Genealogical dictionary of the first settlers of New England showing three generations of those who came before May, 1692, on the basis of Farmer's Register. Boston, Little, 1860–62. 4v. (Repr.: Baltimore, Genealogical Pub. Co., 1965) **AK17**

v.4 of the reprint includes also:

—— Genealogical notes and errata to Savage's Genealogical dictionary . . . by C. H. Dall. Lowell, Mass., Elliott, 1881. 8p.

—— A genealogical cross index of . . . the Genealog-

ical dictionary of James Savage, by O. P. Dexter. N.Y., Dexter, 1884. 38p.

U.S. Bureau of the Census. Heads of families at the first census, 1790. Wash., Govt. Prt. Off., 1907–9. 12v. (Repr.: Spartanburg, S.C., Reprint Co., 1960–64. 12v.) **AK18**

Contents: Maine, New Hampshire, Vermont, Massachusetts, Rhode Island, Connecticut, New York, Pennsylvania, Maryland, Virginia, North Carolina, South Carolina. The statistics for Virginia are from the state census of 1782–85; those for all other states, from the federal census of 1790. Of great value for genealogical reference work, in that it shows in what towns families of any given surname were living in the year 1790, and so indicates what local records should be examined for further information.

CANADA

Godbout, Archange. Nos ancêtres au XVIIᵉ siècle: dictionnaire généalogique et bio-bibliographique des familles canadiennes. Livr. 1–5. (Extrait du Rapport de l'Archiviste de la Province de Québec, 1951/53–1960) (In progress) **AK19**

Contents: Livr. 1–5, A–Bosquet.

A reedited edition of v.1 of Tanguay (AK20) on a different plan, designed to give the genealogical origins of those Canadian families founded before 1700 which have current-day descendants.

Tanguay, Cyprien. Dictionnaire généalogique des familles canadiennes, depuis la fondation de la colonie jusqu'à nos jours. Québec, Eusèbe Senécal, 1871–90. 7v. **AK20**

1st ser., v.1, 1608–1700; 2d ser., v.2–7, 1701–1763.

The 2d series includes some entries later than 1763 belonging to a projected 3d series.

EUROPE

Almanach de Gotha, annuaire généalogique, diplomatique et statistique, 1763– . Gotha, Perthes, 1763– . Annual. **AK21**

For full description *see* CI75.

The first section was very useful for the genealogies of the royal and princely houses of Europe, up to 1940, which is now for the most part continued in the *Genealogisches Handbuch des Adels* (AK22).

Many other annuals of the nobility of the various countries of Europe have been published, most of which were suspended or discontinued before World War II. Some of the most important were the various series of the *Gothaisches genealogisches Taschenbuch* (Gotha, Justus Perthes), issued to cover various periods from 1765–1944. They included series on the Fürstliche Häuser, Adelige Häuser, Freiherrliche Häuser, Gräfliche Häuser, etc.

Others include: *Annuaire de la noblesse de France* (Paris, Au Bureau de la Publication), 1843– (pub. in an English ed., *World nobility and peerage,* 1954 and 1960); *Annuaire de la noblesse de Belgique* (Bruxelles), 1847–1941; *Annuario della nobilità italiana* (Bari), 1879–1905; *Nederland's adelsboeks* ('sGravenhage, Van Stockum), 1903– ; *Svensk adelskalender* ('Stockholm, Norstedt), 1899– ; *Danmarks adels Aarbog* (Kjøbenhavn, Vilk. Trydes), 1884– ; *Anuario de la nobleza de España* (Madrid), 1908– .

Genealogisches Handbuch des Adels, bearb. unter Aufsicht des Ausschusses für adelsrechtliche Fragen der deutschen Adelsverbände in Gemeinschaft mit dem Deutschen Adelsarchiv. Limburg a.d. Lahn, C. A. Starke, 1951–65. v.1–33. il. (In progress) **AK22**

Issued in four series: the first treats the reigning houses of Europe, the others include German families only. Information is detailed, and lineage is indicated from the earliest dates.

Contents: Fürstliche Häuser (Royal houses), v.1–7, 1951–64 (the reigning houses of Europe); Adelige Häuser (Nobility): A, v.1–7, 1954–65; B, v.1–6, 1953–64; Freiherrliche Häuser (Barons): A, v.1–5, 1952–63; B, v.1–3, 1954–63; Gräfliche Häuser (Counts): A, v.1–4, 1952–62; B, v.1–2, 1953–60.

Each volume has an index of all names in that volume; most have also an index of families in previously published volumes of their series.

International register of nobility. Bruxelles, Internat. Off. of Publicity, 1955– . v.1– . **AK23**

v.1, 1955. 223p.; v.2, 1959–1960. 1604p.

v.2 bears the subtitle: Dictionnaire généalogique de la noblesse européenne, and is in four parts: (1) Maisons souveraines; (2) Maisons ex-souveraines; (3) Noblesse européenne; (4) Ordres de chevalerie.

Text in French.

Isenburg, Wilhelm Karl, *Prinz von.* Stammtafeln zur Geschichte der europäischen Staaten (Europäische Stammtafeln). Berichtigter und ergänzter Abdruck der 2. verb. Aufl. von 1953, hrsg. von Frank *Baron* Freytag von Loringhoven. Marburg, Stargardt, 1958–61. 4v. in 3. (v.3, 1958) **AK24**

Contents: Bd.1, Die deutschen Staaten. 198 tables; Bd.2, Die ausserdeutschen Staaten. 144 tables (combined index to Bd.1–2); Bd.3–4, Europäische Stammtafeln. 159 tables, 160 tables (separately indexed).

Genealogical tables of the kings and rulers of Germany and other European states.

Ruvigny and Raineval, Melville Amadeus Henry Douglas Heddle de la Caillemotte de Massue de Ruvigny, *9th Marquis of.* Titled nobility of Europe. An international peerage, or "Who's who," of the sovereigns, princes and nobles of Europe. London, Harrison, 1914. 1598p. il. (coats of arms) **AK25**

Contains fairly full accounts of existing titles of nobility and biographies of living members (in 1914) of each family included in one international list, arranged alphabetically under the chief title borne by the head of the house. With a full index to surnames, variations in spelling, merged titles, and titled members of a family whose names differ from that of the head of the house. Claims to be fairly complete for all British, Spanish, Belgian, and Portuguese titles; for French ducal titles; and for Austrian, German, Hungarian, Swedish, Dutch, Danish, and Finnish titles above the rank of baron.

FRANCE

Saffroy, Gaston. Bibliographie des almanachs et annuaires administratifs, ecclésiastiques et militaires français de l'ancien régime; et des almanachs et annuaires généalogiques et nobilaires du XVIᵉ siècle à nos jours. Paris, Librairie Gaston Saffroy, 1959. 109p. **AK26**

806 numbered entries, most of them annotated. Useful for the historian as well as for the specialist in genealogy.

Gives detailed accounts of the *Almanach de Gotha* (AK21) and other genealogical almanacs.

La Chesnaye-Desbois, François Alexandre Aubert de. Dictionnaire de la noblesse . . . de la France. . . . 3. éd. Paris, Schlesinger, 1863–76. 19v. **AK27**

Subtitle: Contenant les généalogies, l'histoire & la chronologie des familles nobles de la France, l'explication de leurs armes et l'état des grandes terres du royaume. . . . On a joint à ce dictionnaire le tableau généalogique et historique des maisons souveraines de l'Europe et une notice des familles étrangères, les plus anciennes, les plus nobles et les plus illu-

stres. 3. éd. entièrement refondue . . . & augm. d'une table générale de tous les noms de familles, de terres, de fiefs, d'alliances cités dans le cours de l'ouvrage.

v.1–19, A–Z.

Lorenz, 6: 58 (AA470), states that the work was to extend to 22v., with an armorial; v.20–22 and the armorial were, however, never published.

Woelmont, Henri de. Notices généalogiques, 1.–7. sér. Paris, Champion, 1923–30. v.1–7 and suppl. volume. **AK28**

The seven series contain notices of 1078 noble French families, some still in existence and some extinct, giving for each: description of the arms, bibliography, brief history of the family, and the genealogy. Each volume is arranged alphabetically by family names. No general index, each volume having its own index to all names mentioned in articles as well as those used for headings. The supplementary volume contains additions et corrections to ser. 1–5.

GERMANY

Familiengeschichtliche Bibliographie, hrsg. unter dem Schutze der Arbeitsgemeinschaft der deutschen familien- und wappenkundlichen Vereine, 1900– . . . . Leipzig, Zentralstelle für Deutschen Personen u. Familiengeschichte, 1928–62. v.1–7¹⁻⁵, 11¹⁻². (In progress) **AK29**

v.1, 1900–1920, a basic volume for the 20-year period, by Friedrich Wecken, containing 13,912 entries. v.2, 1921–26, by Friedrich Wecken, annual lists for each year, the six lists totaling 8033 entries. v.3, 1927–30, by Johannes Hohlfeld, annual lists for each of the four years. v.4, 1931/32, 1933, 1934. Register. v.5: pt.1, Bibliographie, 1935, by Johannes Hohlfeld; pt.2, Bibliographie, 1897–99, by Gunther Preuss-Tantzen; pt.3, Heraldischer Bibliographie, by Egon *Freiherr* von Berchem. v.6: pt.1–2, Bibliographie, 1936/37, by Johannes Hohlfeld; pt. 3, Gesamtregister zur familiengeschichtlichen Bibliographie 1897–1937 und zur Heraldischen Bibliographie, Bd.1, by Johannes Hohlfeld und Fritz Ranitzsch. v.7, pts.1–5, 1938–1945, by Johannes Hohlfeld. v.11, pts.1–2, 1960–61, by Heinz F. Friederichs. v.8–10 not yet published.

Kneschke, Ernest Heinrich. Neues allgemeines deutsches Adels-Lexicon im Vereine mit mehreren Historikern. Leipzig, Degener, 1929/30. 9v. **AK30**

Unchanged reprint of Leipzig, F. Voigt, 1859–70.

A biographical dictionary of the German nobility with bibliographies. Alphabetically arranged.

GREAT BRITAIN

Bibliography

Burke, Arthur Meredyth. Key to the ancient parish registers of England and Wales. London, Sackville Pr., 1908. 163p. (Repr.: Baltimore, General Book Co., 1962) **AK31**

"The object of this work is to provide those who have reason to consult the Parish Registers with an easy and reliable guide to the accessibility or otherwise of these national records."—*Pref.*

An alphabetical list of all the parishes in England and Wales which have records beginning before 1813. For each register it gives the date of the earliest entry, and notes all transcripts which have been printed. Useful.

Harrison, Howard Guy. A select bibliography of English genealogy with brief lists for Wales, Scotland and Ireland. (A manual for students) London, Phillimore, 1937. 167p. **AK32**

A general section of sources is followed by an arrangement by counties.

Marshall, George William. The genealogist's guide. Guildford, Billing, 1903. 884p. **AK33**

Includes supplement, p.683–884. The standard guide, arranged alphabetically by family name with indication of sources.

Continued by:

Whitmore, John Beach. A genealogical guide; an index to British pedigrees, in continuation of Marshall's "Genealogist's guide (1903)." London, Walford, 1953. 658p. **AK34**

Dictionaries and compendiums

Burke, *Sir* John Bernard. Burke's Genealogical and heraldic history of the peerage, baronetage, and knightage. London, Burke, 1826– . il. (coats of arms). Annual, 1851–1940; quadrennial since 1949 (slightly irregular). **AK35**

Title, publisher, and frequency vary.

Contents vary. 1963: Special articles; Royal family; Peerage and baronetage, arranged alphabetically by title, giving brief account of present holder of title, names of wife, children, heir, lineage, date of creation, arms (both illustration and description), residence; Archbishops and bishops; Knightage, companionage, and Privy Council; Peerages in order of precedence, Extinct titles, etc.

The only one of the currently published peerages which gives full lineage.

—— Genealogical and heraldic history of the colonial gentry. London, Harrison, 1891–95. 2v. il. **AK36**

—— Burke's Genealogical and heraldic history of the landed gentry, founded by John Burke and Sir Bernard Burke. 17th ed., ed. by L. G. Pine. London, Burke's Peerage, 1952. clxxviiip., 2840p. il. (coats of arms). **AK37**

History: 1st ed., *Burke's Commoners*, 1837. 2v.; 2d ed., *Landed gentry of Great Britain and Ireland*, 1847–52. 3v. After the 9th edition, 1898, Irish families were omitted and included, instead, in a separate work, *Landed gentry of Ireland* (AK44).

While the avowed purpose of the work is for genealogical and heraldic information, it is often very useful for biographical data on facts or names omitted in the biographical dictionaries.

Gives brief sketch of present head of family, names of wife and children, lineage, arms (both illustration and description), and seat.

—— Genealogical history of the dormant, abeyant, forfeited, and extinct peerages of the British Empire. New ed. London, Harrison, 1883. 642p. coats of arms. (Repr.: London, Wm. Clowes for Burke's Peerage, 1962) **AK38**

1st ed. 1831.

Cokayne, George Edward. Complete baronetage. Exeter, Pollard, 1900–1909. 5v. and index volume. **AK39**

v.1, English baronetcies, 1611–25, and Irish, 1619–25; v.2, English, Irish and Scottish, 1625–49; v.3, English, Irish and Scottish, 1649–64; v.4, English, Irish and Scottish, 1665–1707; v.5, Great Britain and Ireland, 1707–1800; Index volume: Index and appendix.

—— The complete peerage; or, A history of the House of Lords and all its members from the earliest times . . . rev. and much enl. London, St. Catherine Pr., 1910–59. 13v. in 14. **AK40**

Title and editors vary.

v.1–5 had title *Complete peerage of England, Scotland, Ireland, Great Britain, and the United Kingdom, extant, extinct, or dormant.*

v.1–12, 14, A–Z; v.13 (1940), *Peerage creations and promotions from 22 Jan. 1901 to 31 Dec. 1938.*

The most complete record of the British peerage, giving full accounts, with bibliographical references to sources of information and many biographical details. Important as a supplement to biographical dictionaries as well as for genealogical information.

Debrett's Peerage, baronetage, knightage and companionage. London, Kelly's Directories, 1713– . il. Annual. **AK41**

Editors and publishers vary.

Subtitle 1964: Comprises information concerning persons bearing hereditary or courtesy titles, privy councillors, knights, companions of the various orders, and the collateral branches of peers and baronets.

Gives biographical data, arms (illustration and description), living children, living collateral branches, predecessors, etc.

Doyle, James Edmund. Official baronage of England, showing the succession, dignities, and offices of every peer from 1066 to 1885. London, Longmans, 1886. 3v. il. **AK42**

Haydn, Joseph Timothy. The book of dignities . . . 3d ed. London, W. H. Allen, 1894. xxviiip., 1170p. **AK43**

Subtitle: Containing lists of the official personages of the British Empire, civil, diplomatic, heraldic, judicial, ecclesiastical, municipal, naval and military . . . with the sovereigns and rulers of the world from the foundation of their respective states; the orders of knighthood of the United Kingdom and India, etc. etc.

IRELAND

Burke, *Sir* John Bernard. Burke's Genealogical and heraldic history of the landed gentry of Ireland. Ed. by L. G. Pine. 4th ed. London, Burke's Peerage, 1958. 778p. il. **AK44**

1st ed. 1899.

MacLysaght, Edward. Irish families; their names, arms, and origins. Dublin, H. Figgis, 1957. 366p. il. **AK45**

—— More Irish families. Galway, O'Gorman, 1960. 320p. il. **AK45a**

The author's aim is "to correct errors long current and to present in easily accessible form essential facts about Irish nomenclature and families."—*Pref.*

—— —— Supplement to Irish families. N.Y., Genealogical Pub. Co., 1964. 163p.

Contains information on some 500 additional names as well as further material on some names previously included.

ITALY

Spreti, Vittorio, *Marchese.* Enciclopedia storico-nobiliare italiana; famiglie nobili e titolate viventi riconosciute dal R. governo d'Italia compresi: città, communità, mense vescovili, abazie, parrocchie ed enti nobili e titolati riconosciuti. Milano, Ed. Encic. Stor.-Nob. Ital., 1928–35. 6v. and Appendix, v.1–2. il. (coats of arms) **AK46**

A historical, biographical encyclopedia of titled Italian families.

—— and **Azzi Vitelleschi, Giustiniano degli.** Saggio di bibliografia araldica italiana. Supplemento a l'Enciclopedia storico-nobiliare italiana. Milano, Ed. Encic. Stor.-Nob. Ital., 1936. 230p. **AK47**

A bibliography of Italian heraldry and nobility.

SCOTLAND

Ferguson, Joan P. S. Scottish family histories held in Scottish libraries. Edinburgh, Scottish Central Library, 1960. 194p.   **AK48**

Locates copies of published works and a few manuscripts. Arranged by family name.

Stuart, Margaret. Scottish family history: a guide to works of reference on the history and genealogy of Scottish families. Edinburgh, Oliver & Boyd, 1930. 386p.   **AK49**

Includes books, pamphlets, and a large amount of analysis of periodicals, composite books, collections, etc.

Clans and tartans

Adam, Frank. The clans, septs, and regiments of the Scottish Highlands, rev. by Sir Thomas Innes of Learney. 4th ed. Edinburgh, London, W. & A. K. Johnston, 1952. 624p. il.   **AK50**

Includes colored plates of tartans.

Covers the history and structure of the clan system, Celtic culture, the Highland regiments, clan insignia and heraldry, clan lists and statistics, etc.

Innes, *Sir* Thomas. The tartans of the clans and families of Scotland. 6th ed. Edinburgh, Johnston, 1958. 300p. il. (116 col. plates of tartans).   **AK51**

1st ed. 1938.

Introductory chapters discuss the clan system, order of succession, etc., followed by clans arranged alphabetically, with one-page histories, and colored plates of the tartans.

SPAIN

Instituto Internacional de Genealogía y Heráldica. Índice nobiliario español. Recop. y redac. por Vicente de Cadenas y Vicent [et al.]. Madrid, Ed. Hidalguía, 1955. 754p. (Guía nobiliaria universal. Sección española)   **AK52**

Brief listings of the Spanish nobility indicating titles, etc., and a section on military orders, societies of nobles, etc.

FORMS OF ADDRESS

Titles and forms of address: a guide to their correct use. 10th ed. London, Black; N.Y., Macmillan, 1958. 164p.   **AK53**

A useful handbook to correct English usage for the titled classes and for the church, the armed services, the law, the universities, the government services, etc. Also includes lists of abbreviations and of the pronunciation of proper names.

❧ Somewhat similar lists to those in AK53, included in larger reference books, are: modes of addressing persons of title, included regularly in the introductory parts of the peerages; and sections on forms of address in the various books on etiquette.

A useful list for American forms is found in S. A. Taintor and K. M. Monro, *Secretary's handbook,* 1958, p.287–331 (CH143); another is in *Webster's New international dictionary,* 2d ed., 1961, p.3012–14 (AE7); 3d ed., 1961, p.51a–54a (AE8), under "Forms of address."

HERALDRY

Bolton, Charles Knowles. Bolton's American armory; a record of coats of arms which have been in use within the present bounds of the United States. Boston, Faxon, 1927. 223p. (Useful reference ser.) (Repr.: Baltimore, Heraldic Book Co., 1964)   **AK54**

Boutell, Charles. Heraldry. Rev. by C. W. Scott-Giles and J. P. Brooke-Little. [New rev. ed.] London, N.Y., Warne, [1963]. 316p. il. (part col.), coats of arms (part col.).   **AK55**

Based on Boutell's *Manual of heraldry* (1863) and *English heraldry* (1867).

Burke, *Sir* John Bernard. General armory of England, Scotland, Ireland, and Wales, comprising a registry of armorial bearings from the earliest to the present time. With a supplement. London, Harrison, 1884. 1185p. il. (Repr.: London, Wm. Clowes for Burke's Peerage, 1961)   **AK56**

An enlarged edition (first pub. 1842) of *Encyclopaedia of heraldry; or, General armory of England, Scotland and Ireland,* published in many editions.

Fairbairn, James. Book of crests of the families of Great Britain and Ireland. 4th ed. rev. and enl. by A. C. Fox-Davies. Edinburgh, Jack, 1905. 2v. il.   **AK57**

1st ed. 1859. Rev. ed. 1860. 2v. (American ed.: N.Y., 1911. Repr.: Baltimore Genealogical Pub. Co., 1963. 2v. in 1 [137p., 613p.])

A volume of plates with an index to crests arranged by surnames; a glossary; and a section of mottoes.

Fox-Davies, Arthur Charles. Armorial families, a directory of gentlemen of coat-armour. 7th ed. London, Hurst and Blackett, 1929. 2v. il.   **AK58**

Arranged by families with descriptions of coats of arms, mottoes, etc.

—— Book of public arms, a complete encyclopaedia of all royal, territorial, municipal, corporate, official and impersonal arms. New ed., containing over 1300 drawings. London, Jack, 1915. 876p. il.   **AK59**

—— Complete guide to heraldry. Rev. ed. London, Nelson, 1949. 647p. il. (Repr. 1961)   **AK60**

Founded upon the author's *Art of heraldry,* 1904. First pub. 1909; repr. with revisions by C. A. H. Franklyn.

Gayre of Gayre and Nigg, Robert and **Gayre of Gayre and Nigg, Reinold.** Roll of Scottish arms. London, Armorial, 1964– . v.1– . (In progress)   **AK61**

Contents: v.1, A–G.

"A complete roll of Scottish armorial bearings arranged alphabetically, giving the names, ranks, titles, designations and blazons as they appear in the original manuscript."— *Introd.*

Innes, Thomas. Scots heraldry, a practical handbook on the historical principles and modern application of the art and science . . . 2d ed. rev. and enl. Edinburgh, Oliver and Boyd, 1956. 258p. il.   **AK62**

1st ed. 1934.

Jougla de Morenas, Henri. Grand armorial de France; catalogue général des armoiries des familles nobles de France. Paris, Éd. Héraldiques, 1939–49. 6v. il.   **AK63**

—— —— Supplément. Paris, Soc. du Grand Armorial de France, 1952. 447p. il.

New England Historic Genealogical Society. Heraldic Committee. Roll of arms. Boston, 1928–58. Pts.1–7. coats of arms. (In progress)   **AK64**

Of first importance. Names of American families having registered arms, with descriptions and line drawings. Arranged by registration number, with an alphabetical index of surnames in each part.

Rietstap, Jean Baptiste. Armorial général; precédé d'un dictionnaire des termes du blason. 2. éd. Gouda, van Goor, 1884–87. 2v. il. (Repr.: N.Y., Barnes & Noble, 1965) **AK65**

Publisher varies.

A general work on European arms, dealing with more than 100,000 families entitled to hereditary honors.

—— —— Armoiries des familles contenues dans l'Armorial général. Paris. Inst. Héraldique Universel, 1903–26. 6v. il.

Plates of coats of arms (blazons) described in the *Armorial général,* arranged in alphabetical order. v.2–6 have title *Planches de l'Armorial général,* par H. and V. Rolland. v.5–6 have imprint: La Haye, Nijhoff, 1921–26.

—— —— General illustrated armorial, by V. and H. Rolland. [3d ed.] Lyon, Soc. de Sauvegarde Historique, [1953?]. 6v.

A 3d edition of the above, published with the text material in English.

—— —— Supplément par V. [and] H. Rolland. La Haye, Nijhoff, 1926–54. v.1–7. il. (In progress)

v.1–2 issued in 36 pts., 1904–26. v.2 bound in 2v.

—— —— —— Table du supplément, par Henri Rolland. Lyon, Soc. de Sauvegarde Historique, 1951. 1v. (unpaged)

Indexes v.1–6 of the *Supplément.* These 6v. (bound in 7) are called v.1–7 in the index.

The supplements include both illustrations and blazons.

Terminology

Gough, Henry. Glossary of terms used in heraldry. New ed. Oxford, Parker, 1894. 659p. il. **AK66**

Still one of the more useful glossaries.

Stalins, Gaston Ferdinand Laurent, *Baron.* Vocabulaire-atlas héraldique en six langues; français-English-deutsch-español-italiano-Nederlandsch, par le baron Stalins avec la collaboration de René le Juge de Segrais [et al.]. Paris, Soc. du Grand Armorial de France, 1952. 119p. il. **AK67**

At head of title: Academie Internationale d'Héraldique. Pt.1 (p.10–39) gives the principal terms used in heraldry, in six languages, in table form and numbered; the numbers correspond to the illustrations in the plates. Pt.2 (p.42–71) gives an alphabetical listing of terms for each of the six languages, with the number of its representation in the plates. Pt.3 (p.75–119) consists of 23 black-and-white plates, each containing several small but clear figures representing the heraldic terms in pts.1–2. A clear, concise guide to heraldic terminology.

ORDERS AND DECORATIONS

☙ Information on orders and decorations is given in many genealogical annuals, such as the *Almanach de Gotha* (AK21), Burke's *Peerage* (AK35), etc., and in the older official registers, such as the French *Almanach national* (CI98), the Belgian *Almanach royal officiel* (CI88), etc.

American Numismatic Society. Numismatic notes and monographs, no.11, 20, 31, 36, 51, 56, 89, 106. N.Y., Soc., 1922–45. 8v. il. **AK68**

no.11, *French* orders and decorations. 1922. 110p.; no.20, *Italian* orders of chivalry and medals of honor. 1923. 146p.; no.31, *Spanish* orders of chivalry and decorations of honor.

1926. 165p.; no.36, Decorations and medals of the *French colonies* and protectorates. 1928. 62p.; no.51, *Russian* imperial orders. 1932. 101p.; no.56, *South American* decorations and war medals. 1932. 178p.; no.89, *Mexican* decorations of honor. 1940. 53p.; no.106, *British* orders and decorations. 1945. 124p.

no.51, by Alan W. Hazelton; no.106, by James C. Risk; the others by Harrold E. Gillingham.

Burke, *Sir* **John Bernard.** The book of orders of knighthood and decorations of honour of all nations, comprising an historical account of each order, military, naval, and civil, from the earliest to the present time, with lists of the knights and companions of each British order. London, Hurst and Blackett, 1858. 411p. 100 col. pl. **AK69**

Jocelyn, Arthur. Awards of honour; the orders, decorations, medals and awards of Great Britain and the Commonwealth from Edward III to Elizabeth II. London, Adam & Charles Black, 1956. 276p. col. plates. **AK70**

Contains descriptions of the orders, decorations, etc., with colored plates.

Nicolas, *Sir* **Nicholas Harris.** History of the orders of knighthood of the British Empire; of the Order of the Guelphs of Hanover; and of the medals, clasps, and crosses, conferred for naval and military services. London, Hunter, 1842. 4v. il. **AK71**

Wyllie, Robert E. Orders, decorations and insignia, military and civil; with the history and romance of their origin and a full description of each . . . with 367 illustrations (over 200 in colour). N.Y., London, Putnam, [c1921]. 269p. il. **AK72**

Contains historical and descriptive information, with many excellent illustrations of the medals, ribbons, badges, etc., of the United States, Great Britain, Belgium, China, Cuba, Czechoslovakia, France, Greece, Hawaii, Italy, Japan, Monaco, Montenegro, Panama, Poland, Portugal, Rumania, Russia, and Serbia. Includes also information on shoulder insignia, insignia of rank, and insignia and colors of arms of service.

FLAGS

Brown, James LaSalle. The flag of the United States, its use in commerce. Wash., Govt. Prt. Off., 1941. 51p. (U.S. Bureau of Foreign and Domestic Commerce. Trade promotion ser., no.218) **AK73**

Contains the text of the federal, state, and territorial laws on the use of the flag, with special attention to its use in the business world.—Cf. *Foreword.*

Carr, Harold Gresham. Flags of the world. [Rev. ed.] . . . London, N.Y., Warne, 1961. 329p. il. **AK74**

1st ed. 1953.

Histories and descriptions of the flags and standards of the various countries of the world with special emphasis on British flags.

Gt.Brit. Admiralty. Flags of all nations. [Rev. ed.] London, Stat. Off., 1955–58. v.1–2. il. Loose-leaf. (In progress) **AK75**

Contents: v.1, National flags and ensigns. v.2, Standards of rulers, sovereigns and heads of state; Flags of heads of ministries, and of naval, military and air force officers. Amendment no.1 incorporated in main volume. Amendment no.2, June 15, 1956. Amendment no.3, April 4, 1958.

To be in 3v.

Consists of colored plates, little or no text.

Previous edition entitled *Drawings of the flags of all nations* (1930).

Kannik, Preben. The flag book. Illus. in color by Wilhelm Petersen. N.Y., Barrows, 1959 [i.e., 1960]. 196p. il.

AK76

Translation of the author's *Alverdens flag i farver.* København, Politikens Forlag, 1956.

Gives illustrations of some 800 official flags of the present day arranged geographically, 80 national coats of arms, and older flags of historical interest.

Quaife, Milo M., Weig, Melvin J. and **Appleman, Roy E.** The history of the United States flag from the Revolution to the present, including a guide to its use and display. [1st ed.] N.Y., Harper, 1961. 190p. il. **AK77**

Gives the history of the flag and other United States symbols, e.g., the seal; use and display, etc.

Shankle, George Earlie. State names, flags, seals, . . . and other symbols. Rev. ed. N.Y., Wilson, 1941. 524p. il.

AK78

Subtitle: A study based on historical documents giving the origin and significance of the state names, nicknames, mottoes, seals, flags, flowers, birds, songs, and descriptive comments on the capitol buildings and on some of the leading state histories, with facsimiles of the state flags and seals.

U.S. Office of Naval Operations. Flags of the United States and other countries, 1938. . . . Wash., U.S. Navy Dept., Hydrographic Off., 1938. 1v. il. Loose-leaf. (Hydrographic Office. [Publ.] 89) **AK79**

Colored plates.

" . . . Supersedes the flag supplement to H.O.87 issued in 1933, and also chapter 28 of the Communication Instructions, 1929."

NAMES

Bibliography

Smith, Elsdon Coles. Personal names, a bibliography. N.Y., N.Y. Pub. Lib., 1952. 226p. **AK80**

Reprinted from the *Bulletin* of the New York Public Library, 1950–51.

A classified bibliography of 3415 monographs and periodical articles on names, with brief, critical annotations. Library locations are given. Alphabetical index.

Christian names

Audebert, Antoine. Dictionnaire analytique des prénoms. Paris, Calmann-Lévy, 1956. 229p. **AK81**

Egger, Carolus. Lexicon nominum virorum et mulierum. Romae, Soc. Libraria "Studium," 1957. 197p. **AK82**

A dictionary of personal names with their Latin equivalents and etymologies.

Loughead, Flora Haines. Dictionary of given names, with origins and meanings. 2d ed. rev. and corr. Glendale, Calif., Arthur H. Clark, 1958. 248p. **AK83**

1st ed. 1933.

Wells, Evelyn. What to name the baby (a treasury of names). 15,000 names to choose from. Garden City, N.Y., Doubleday, 1953. 326p. **AK84**

1st edition, 1946, had title *A treasury of names.*

A useful guide for quick reference to foreign equivalents of American forenames.

Withycombe, Elizabeth Gidley. Oxford dictionary of English Christian names. Oxford, Clarendon Pr., 1945. 136p. **AK85**

Gives sources for earliest usage.

Yonge, Charlotte Mary. History of Christian names. New ed. rev. London, Macmillan, 1884. 476p. **AK86**

Contains a glossary of Christian names (Preface, p.19–144) which gives the meaning and refers to the body of the book where a full description will be found with derivations, forms in various languages, etc.

Surnames

British

Fransson, Gustav. Middle English surnames of occupation, 1100–1350, with an excursus on toponymical surnames. Lund, Gleerup; London, Williams & Norgate, 1935. 217p. (Lund studies in English, no.3) **AK87**

Reaney, Percy Hide. A dictionary of British surnames. London, Routledge and Paul, 1958. 366p. **AK88**

Gives etymologies, origins, different forms, and references to sources. Includes about 10,000 entries.

To some extent supersedes Charles W. Bardsley, *Dictionary of English and Welsh surnames* (London, Frowde, 1901. 837p.), although this may still be useful.

Canadian

Dionne, Narcisse Eutrope. Les Canadiens-Français. Origine des familles émigrées de France, d'Espagne, de Suisse, etc., pour venir se fixer au Canada, depuis la fondation de Québec jusqu'à ces derniers temps et signification de leurs noms. Québec, Garneau; Montréal, Granger, 1914. 611p. **AK89**

French

Chapuy, Paul. Origine des noms patronymiques français (donnant l'étymologie de 10,000 noms de famille) suivi d'une étude sur les noms de famille basques. Paris, Dorbon-Aîné, 1934. 350p. **AK90**

Dauzat, Albert. Dictionnaire étymologique des noms de famille et prénoms de France. Paris, Larousse, 1951. 604p. **AK91**

German

Bach, Adolf. Deutsche Namenkunde. 2. stark erw. Aufl. Heidelberg, Winter, 1952–53. v.1– . (In progress)

AK92

Bd.1, Die deutschen Personennamen; Hlbbd. 1, Einleitung. Zur Laut- und Formenlehre, Wortfügung, -bildung und -bedeutung der deutschen Personennamen; Hlbbd. 2, Die deutschen Personennamen in geschichtlicher, geographischer, soziologischer und psychologischer Betrachtung.

For Bd.2, Die deutschen Ortsnamen, *see* CK104.

1st edition of Bd.1 appeared in 1943 as v.18 of Paul's *Grundriss der germanischen Philologie* (BC36).

—— —— Registerband, bearb. von Dieter Berger. Heidelberg, Winter, 1956. 457p.

Brechenmacher, Josef Karlmann. Etymologisches Wörterbuch der deutschen Familiennamen. 2. von Grund auf neubearb. Aufl. der "Deutschen Sippennamen." Limburg/ Lahn, Starke, 1957–63. 2v. **AK93**

The most comprehensive dictionary of German family names, including more than 28,500 names.

Gottschald, Max. Deutsche Namenkunde: unsere Familiennamen nach ihrer Entstehung und Bedeutung. 3. verm. Aufl., besorgt von Eduard Brodführer. Berlin, de Gruyter, 1954. 630p. **AK94**

1st ed. 1932; 2d ed. 1942.
Gives origins and meanings of German surnames.

Irish

MacLysaght, Edward. A guide to Irish surnames. Baltimore, Genealogical Pub. Co., 1964. 248p. **AK95**

Bibliography of Irish family history, p.207–47.

Largely supersedes Patrick Woufle, *Irish names and surnames*. Dublin, Gill, 1923. Treats some 2500 names, listing them in modern form followed by the Gaelic-Irish.

Italian

Bongioanni, Angelo. Nomi e cognomi; saggio di ricerche etimologiche e storiche. Torino, Bocca, 1928. 268p. (Piccola biblioteca di scienza moderne, no.367) **AK96**

Fucilla, Joseph Guerin. Our Italian surnames. Evanston, Ill., Chandler's, 1949. 299p. **AK97**

Includes bibliographies.

Russian

Benson, Morton. Dictionary of Russian personal names, with a guide to stress and morphology. Philadelphia, Univ. of Pa. Pr., 1964. 175p. (Univ. of Pennsylvania. Studies in East European languages and literatures) **AK98**

A chapter on the stress and declension of surnames is followed by a list of surnames with accents; a chapter on Russian given names with lists and explanations of diminutives; and a brief bibliography.

Scottish

Black, George Fraser. The surnames of Scotland; their origin, meaning, and history. N.Y., N.Y. Pub. Lib., 1962. 838p. (Repr. from the New York Public Library. Bull. Aug. 1943–Sept. 1946) **AK99**

Revision of the 1946 ed., with new amendments and additions, p.831–34, by Mary Elder Black.

A monumental work giving origin, meaning, and history of Scottish surnames from the earliest times, with references to sources.

Spanish

Gosnell, Charles Francis. Spanish personal names; principles governing their formation and use which may be presented as a help for catalogers and bibliographers. N.Y., Wilson, 1938. 112p. **AK100**

Bibliography, p. 89–101.

B

THE

HUMANITIES

✤ The meaning of the term "the humanities" has changed and developed during recent years. In the nineteenth century it meant primarily the Greek and Roman classics, with the inclusion at times of rhetoric, grammar, and belles-lettres. As recently as 1934, the Second Edition of Webster's *New international dictionary* (AE7) defined it as "the branches of polite learning regarded as primarily conducive to culture; esp., the ancient classics and belles-lettres . . . ." The term now seems to include those branches of learning having a cultural character as distinguished from the social and physical sciences. The interpretation used in this *Guide* is that developed in many subject-arranged libraries and embraces the following: philosophy, religion, linguistics and philology, literature, the fine arts, applied arts, theater arts, and music.

In many of these categories there are guides to the literature—e.g., Wilhelm Totok, *Bibliographischer Wegweiser der philosophischen Literatur* (BA1); Mary W. Chamberlin, *Guide to art reference books* (BE1); Vincent H. Duckles, *Music reference and research materials* (BH1)—which should be consulted for titles not listed in the present work. In the field of comparative literature, Fernand Baldensperger and Werner P. Friederich, *Bibliography of comparative literature* (BD1), will be helpful, and under specific literatures will be found such useful guides as: Howard M. Jones and Richard M. Ludwig, *Guide to American literature and its backgrounds since 1890* (BD204); Richard D. Altick and Andrew Wright, *Selective bibliography for the study of English and American literature* (BD302); Donald F. Bond, *A reference guide to English studies* (BD303); Chauncey Sanders, *An introduction to research in English literary history* (BD305); Johannes Hansel, *Bücherkunde für Germanisten* (BD556); and Thomas R. Palfrey [and others], *A bibliographical guide to the Romance languages and literatures* (BD638).

B A

Philosophy

❦ Reference works in philosophy are almost entirely bibliographical, with some encyclopedias and dictionaries; therefore, general histories and textbooks are especially needed as supplementary materials. In the average American library the most useful reference work in this class is probably Baldwin's *Dictionary of philosophy and psychology* (BA26), v.3 of which is Rand's *Bibliography of philosophy, psychology, and cognate subjects* (BA13). Rand is now much out of date but is still useful for material up to the end of the 19th century. A bibliography to cover 1900–1932 has been in process for many years but has not yet been published. The *Journal of philosophy* published an annual bibliography from 1933 to 1936 (BA8), when the record was taken over by the *Bibliographie de la philosophie* (BA5, BA6), published by the Institut International de Philosophie. Together these give a fairly comprehensive record for this period. Several bibliographies are also published in other European countries which will be useful in large or more specialized libraries.

GUIDES

Totok, Wilhelm. Bibliographischer Wegweiser der philosophischen Literatur. Frankfurt am Main, Klostermann, 1959. 35p. **BA1**

A brief guide to bibliographies and encyclopedias in the field of philosophy.

BIBLIOGRAPHY

International

Albert, Ethel M., Kluckhohn, Clyde [and others]. A selected bibliography on values, ethics, and esthetics in the behavioral sciences and philosophy, 1920–1958. Glencoe, Ill., Free Pr., 1959. 342p. **BA2**

At head of title: Harvard University, Laboratory of Social Relations, Cambridge, Mass. and Center for Advanced Study in the Behavioral Sciences, Stanford, Calif.

A listing of some 2000 titles of books and periodical articles published during the period covered.

Berg, Jan. Selektiv bibliografi i teoretisk filosofi. Stockholm, 1960. 81p. (Filosofisker studier utg. av Filosofiska Inst. vid Stockholms Universitet, Häfte 5) **BA3**

———— ———— Supplement. 1961. 7p.

A classified bibliography of books and periodical articles in various languages, primarily from the 20th century. Covers mathematical logic, scientific theory, and the philosophy of the history of ideas.

Bibliographia philosophica, 1934–1945. Ed., G. A. de Brie. Bruxellis, Ed. Spectrum, 1950–54. 2v. **BA4**

v.1, Bibliographia historiae philosophiae. 664p.; v.2, Bibliographia philosophiae. 798p.

A comprehensive bibliography which aims to list all philosophical literature, books, periodicals, and many book reviews, published from 1934 to 1945, in Danish, Dutch, English, French, German, Italian, Latin, Norwegian, Portuguese, Spanish, and Swedish.

v.1 (no.1–23057) is arranged chronologically according to the lives of the philosophers of different historical periods and schools.

v.2 (no.23058–48178) lists publications treating philosophy in its doctrinal aspects, in a classified arrangement. Combined name index to both volumes.

Bibliographie de la philosophie . . . 1–10. 1937–52/53. Paris, Vrin, 1937–58. 10v. **BA5**

At head of title: Institute International de Philosophie.

Publication suspended, juil. 1939–déc. 1945. Resumed publication, v.4, 1946.

An international bibliography of books, periodical articles, and doctoral dissertations.

Superseded by:

———— Bulletin trimestrial. Bibliography of philosophy, a quarterly bulletin. International Institute of Philosophy. Paris, Vrin, 1954– . v.1– . Quarterly. **BA6**

Published for the International Federation of Philosophical Societies under the auspices of the International Council of Philosophy and Humanistic Studies with the aid of UNESCO and of the French National Centre for Scientific Research.

Title page and preliminary matter in French and English.

Now an abstract journal dealing with books only. The abstracts are usually in the language of the original article but with translations into either English or French.

Bibliographische Einführungen in das Studium der Philosophie, hrsg. von I. M. Bochenski. Bern, Francke, 1948– . no.1–23. (In progress) **BA7**

A series of brief bibliographies on various aspects of philosophy—for the most part of 20th-century materials.

Contents: (1) I. M. Bochenski and F. Monteleone. Allgemeine philosophische Bibliographie. 42p.; (2) Ralph B. Winn. Amerikanische Philosophie. 32p.; (3) E. W. Beth. Symbolische Logik und Grundlegung der exakten Wissenschaften. 28p.; (4) Régis Jolivet. Kierkegaard. 33p.; (5) Olaf Gigon. Antike Philosophie. 52p.; (6) P. J. de Menasce. Arabische Philosophie. 49p.; (7) M. F. Sciacca. Italienische Philosophie der Gegenwart. 36p.; (8) M. D. Phillippe. Aristoteles. 48p.; (9) Régis Jolivet. Französische Existenzphilosophie. 36p.; (10) M. F. Sciacca. Augustinus. 32p.; (11) Karl Dürr. Der logische Positivismus. 24p.; (12) Olaf Gigon. Platon. 30p.; (13/14) Paul Wyser. Thomas von Aquin. 78p.; (15/16) Paul Wyser. Der Thomismus. 120p.; (17) F. van Steenberghen. Philosophie des Mittelalters. 52p.; (18) Othmar Perler. Patristische Philosophie. 44p.; (19) Georges Vajda. Jüdische Philosophie. 40p.; (20/21) C. Regamey. Buddhistische Philosophie. 86p.; (22) Odulf Schäfer. Johannes Duns Scotus. 34p.; (23) Otto Friedrich Bollnow. Deutsche Existenzphilosophie. 40p.

Bibliography of philosophy, 1933–36. N.Y., Journal of Philosophy, 1934–37. v.1–4. **BA8**

Reprinted from *Journal of philosophy.*

Annual classified lists with alphabetical name indexes. Intended to include all the scholarly philosophical literature published during the year in English, French, German, and Italian, with some items in other languages.

No more published.

Buenos Aires. Universidad Nacional. Instituto Bibliotecológico. Bibliografía filosófica del siglo XX; catálogo de la Exposición Bibliográfica Internacional de la Filosofía del Siglo XX. Buenos Aires, Ed. Peuser, [1952]. 465p. **BA9**

A classified list of some 4000 20th-century philosophical

writings in various languages, showing location of copies in 6 Argentinian libraries. No annotations.

France. Centre National de la Recherche Scientifique. Bulletin signalétique. 19, Sciences humaines: Philosophie. Paris, Centre de Documentation du C.N.R.S., 1947– . v.1– . Quarterly.　　**BA10**

For full contents of *Bulletin signalétique, see* EA71.

Title varies: v.1–9, Bulletin analytique: Philosophie; v.10–14, Bulletin signalétique: Philosophie. Sciences humaines; v.15– , Sciences humaines: Philosophie.

An exhaustive classified index to periodicals from countries all over the world. Brief abstracts are given in French.

Covers philosophy, religion, logic, aesthetics, archaeology, and the history of art, psychology, pedagogy, sociology, sciences of language, history of science, and technology.

Hoffmans, Jean. La philosophie et les philosophes: ouvrages généraux. Bruxelles, Van Oest, 1920. 395p. **BA11**

Contents: Dictionaries; treatises and manuals; histories: general, by periods, by countries, by systems, etc.; editions and translations of philosophical works, periodicals, bibliographies.

Lists works on philosophical subjects published in western languages from about the 17th to the early 20th centuries.

Philosophic abstracts. N.Y., Philosophic Abstracts, 1939–54. v.1–16. (Index v.1–12)　　**BA12**

No more published.

An abstract journal giving abstracts in English of philosophical works published in various countries.

Rand, Benjamin. Bibliography of philosophy, psychology, and cognate subjects. N.Y., Macmillan, 1905. 2v. (Repr.: N.Y., Peter Smith, 1949)　　**BA13**

Forms v.3 of Baldwin's *Dictionary of philosophy* (BA26); also sold separately. The most important bibliography of the subject in English, although now out of date.

Contents: I, General; II, History of philosophy. Bibliographies of individual philosophers of all periods (arranged alphabetically); III, Systematic philosophy, logic, aesthetics, philosophy of religion, ethics, psychology.

Répertoire bibliographique de la philosophie, t.1– , fév. 1949– . Louvain, Éd. de l'Inst. Supérieur de Philosophie, 1949– . Quarterly.　　**BA14**

At head of title: Société Philosophique de Louvain.

Publié sous les auspices de l'Institut International de Philosophie avec le patronage de l'UNESCO.

A comprehensive bibliography of books and articles on philosophy appearing in various countries. Classified lists with annual author indexes. A list of book reviews appears annually in the November issue.

Continues *Répertoire bibliographique* which appeared quarterly as a supplement to *Revue philosophique de Louvain,* 1934–48.

Société Internationale pour l'Étude de la Philosophie Médiévale. Bulletin. Louvain, Secrétariat de la S.I.E.P.M., 1959– . v.1– . Annual.　　**BA15**

v.5, 1963, contains: (1) Information concerning S.I.E.P.M.; (2) Notices concerning institutions and associations specially concerned with the study of medieval thought; (3) Notices of work in progress; (4) Miscellaneous information (including list of doctoral dissertations by country); (5) Notes of interest arranged by country, etc.; (6) Index of names of medieval authors cited in no.5 of the *Bulletin.*

Varet, Gilbert. Manuel de bibliographie philosophique. Paris, Presses Universitaires de France, 1956. 2v. (Logos: introduction aux études philosophiques)　　**BA16**

Contents: v.1, Les philosophies classiques. 494p.; v.2, Les sciences philosophiques. p.496–1058.

A useful manual comprising a comprehensive selection of materials in various languages, listing books and periodical articles—covering ancient, medieval, and modern philosophies—broadly interpreted.

Annotated.

Periodicals

U.S. Library of Congress. General Reference and Bibliography Division. Philosophical periodicals, an annotated world list by David Baumgardt. Wash., 1952. 89p. **BA17**

Lists periodicals from 71 political areas, with brief annotations. Frequency, date of inception, editor, and publisher (with complete address) are given for each title. Alphabetical index of titles.

Zampetti, Enrico. Bibliografia ragionata delle riviste filosofiche italiane dal 1900 al 1955. Roma, Università, 1956. 136p. (Istituto di Studi Filosofici, Roma)　　**BA18**

Reprinted from v.4 of the *Bibliografia filosofica italiana* dal 1900 al 1950 (BA19).

Gives detailed descriptions of Italian philosophical periodicals of the period covered.

Italy

Bibliografia filosofica italiana dal 1900 al 1950 . . . Roma, Ed. Delfino, 1950–56. 4v.　　**BA19**

"A cura dell' Istituto di Studi Filosofici e del Centro Nazionale di Informazioni Bibliografiche, con la collaborazione del Centro di Studi Filosofici Cristiani di Gallarate."—*Title page.*

Covers books and periodical articles published in Italy between Jan. 1900 and Dec. 1949; arrangement is alphabetical by author, with writings *on* an author following those *by* him.

v.4 includes: Additions and corrections; Anonyms and pseudonyms; and *Bibliografia ragionata delle riviste filosofiche italiane dal 1900 al 1955* a cura di Enrico Zampetti. This last is also published separately; *see* BA18.

Continued by:

—— anno 1949– . Milano, Carlo Marzorati, 1951– . Annual.　　**BA20**

"Centro di Studi Filosofici Cristiani di Gallarate" . . . .

Annual bibliography of Italian writings in the field, including periodical articles as well as monographs.

Netherlands

Poortman, Johannes Jacobus. Repertorium der Nederlandse wijsbegeerte. Amsterdam, Antwerp, Wereldbibliotheek, 1948. 403p.　　**BA21**

A bibliography of philosophical works printed in Dutch in the Netherlands regardless of the nationality of the author, and of works by Netherlanders wherever printed. In two parts: (1) alphabetical by subject; and (2) alphabetical by philosopher.

—— —— Supplement 1. Amsterdam, 1958. 168p.

Lists material published 1947–57.

Poland

Polska Akademia Nauk. Komitet Filozoficzny. Bibliografia filozofii polskiej. . . . [Opracowała Alicja Kadler] Wyd. 1. Warszawa, Państwowe Wydawnictwo Naukowe, 1955–60. 2v.　　**BA22**

Contents: 1750–1830; 1831–1864.

Each volume is arranged alphabetically by philosopher, listing writings both by and about.

At head of title of v.2: Polska Akademia Nauk. Instytut Filozofii i Socjologii.

Spain

Martínez Gómez, Luis. Bibliografía filosófica española e hispanoamericana (1940–1958). Barcelona, Juan Flors, 1961. 500p. (Libros "Pensamiento." Serie: Difusión, no.1) **BA23**

A classified listing of more than 10,000 items—books and articles—primarily a cumulation of the bibliographic sections of the Spanish philosophical journal *Pensamiento*. Name index.

Switzerland

Schweizerische Philosophische Gesellschaft. Bibliographie der philosophischen, psychologischen und pädagogischen Literatur in der deutschsprachigen Schweiz, 1900–1940, hrsg. von E. Heuss, [u.A.]. Basel, Verlag für Recht und Gesellschaft, 1944. 207p. (Its Jahrbuch ... Beihefte II) **BA24**

—— [Supplement], 1941–1944, von Hans Zantop. 1945. p.218–78. (Its Jahrbuch, v.5. Separatum)

Lists alphabetically, by author, books and periodical articles on philosophy, psychology, and education published in German-speaking Switzerland. The main part of the work includes German works only; the supplement covers German, French, and Italian.

Union of Soviet Socialist Republics

Bibliographie der sowjetischen Philosophie. Freiburg/Schweiz, Ost-Europa Inst., [1959–62]. v.1–3. (Sovietica; Veröffentlichungen des Ost-Europa Instituts, Universität Freiburg/Schweiz, 1–2, 6) **BA25**

Vorwort signed I. M. Bochenski.

Contents: v.1, Die "Voprosy Filosofii," 1947–1956; v.2, Bücher, 1947–1956. Bücher und Aufsätze, 1957–1958. Namenverzeichnis, 1946–1958; v.3, Bücher und Aufsätze, 1959–1960.

Lists major books and articles in philosophy published in the Soviet Union after 1947. Author and subject indexes.

DICTIONARIES AND ENCYCLOPEDIAS

Baldwin, James Mark. Dictionary of philosophy and psychology, including many of the principal conceptions of ethics, logic, aesthetics, philosophy of religion, mental pathology, anthropology, biology, neurology, physiology, economics, political and social philosophy, philology, physical science and education, and giving a terminology in English, French, German and Italian. N.Y., Macmillan, 1901–5. 3v. in 4. il. (Repr.: Gloucester, Mass., Peter Smith, 1960) **BA26**

v.1–2, A–Z. Indexes: (1) Greek terms, (2) Latin terms, (3) German terms, (4) French terms, (5) Italian terms; v.3, Bibliography of philosophy (*see* Rand, BA13).

The only encyclopedia of the subject in English, excellent and authoritative when first issued and still useful for many topics though now out of date for modern developments. Concise rather than exhaustive in treatment, with signed articles by specialists and many bibliographies. Covers the whole field but is fuller for modern than for earlier aspects of the subject and does not attempt to cover the whole of Greek and scholastic philosophy. Includes very brief biographies of men no longer living. Special features are the inclusion of French, German, and Italian equivalents of English terms, used as entries, and the indexes of foreign terms used in the articles.

A new edition, 1910, differed from the original only in the correction of a few typographical errors.

Blanc, Elie. Dictionnaire de philosophie ancienne, moderne et contemporaine. Paris, Lethielleux, 1906. 1248 col.

—— —— Supplément ... années 1906, 1907, 1908. Paris, 1908. 154col. **BA27**

Explanations of philosophical terms and schools, and brief biographical sketches of philosophers of all periods.

Brugger, Walter. Philosophisches Wörterbuch. 4. Aufl. ... Freiburg, Herder, 1951. 544p. (Mensch. Welt. Gott; ein Aufbau der Philosophie in Einzeldarstellung, Ergänzungsbd.) **BA28**

Explanations of philosophical terms, with bibliographies.

Includes an outline of the history of philosophy from ancient times to the present day.

Eisler, Rudolf. Handwörterbuch der Philosophie. 2. Aufl. neuhrsg. von Richard Müller-Freienfels. Berlin, Mittler, 1922. 785p. (Repr: Düsseldorf, Mikrobuch- und Film Gesellschaft, 1949) **BA29**

1st ed. 1913.

A condensation of the author's *Wörterbuch der philosophischen Begriffe* (BA30), utilizing also some material from his *Philosophen-Lexikon* (BA39). An excellent small work—useful where short, concise articles are wanted, but not a substitute in a research library for the two larger works. Includes bibliographies.

—— Wörterbuch der philosophischen Begriffe, historisch-quellenmässig. 4. völlig neubearb. Aufl. hrsg. unter Mitwirkung der Kantgesellschaft. Berlin, Mittler, 1927–30. 3v. **BA30**

1st ed. 1889. 1v.; 2d ed. 1904. 2v.; 3d ed. 1910. 3v.

Scholarly articles with bibliographies, on philosophical concepts and terms, tracing their use, meanings, and treatment through the writings of the philosophers, and giving many references to sources. For the specialist, not the general reader. Of first importance in advanced work.

Literatur-Verzeichnis, v.3, p.695–906.

Enciclopedia filosofica. Venezia, Roma, Istit. per la Collaborazione Culturale, 1957. 4v. il. **BA31**

At head of title: Centro di Studi Filosofici di Gallarate.

A scholarly encyclopedia with signed articles and bibliographies. Treats philosophical concepts and schools and relevant matters in literature, science, law, etc. Includes many biographical articles. Three main indexes at the end of v.4: (1) classified by theoretical concept; (2) classified by historical development; and (3) an analytical index of terms and personal names referred to in the text but not used as entries.

Ferrater Mora, José. Diccionario de filosofía. 4. ed. Buenos Aires, Ed. Sudamericana, 1958. 1481p. **BA32**

1st ed. 1941.

A useful general encyclopedia with many biographical sketches (including living persons), and articles on philosophical schools, concepts, etc. Not limited by country or period. Extensive bibliographies.

Foulquié, Paul. Dictionnaire de la langue philosophique ... avec la collaboration de Raymond Saint-Jean. Paris, Presses Universitaires de France, 1962. 776p. **BA33**

Lists words in groups under main root word, with cross references from derivative forms. Each entry gives etymology and definitions, indicating various areas of usage; synonyms; and illustrative quotations from the literature, with brief references to sources.

Unfortunately, no bibliography of these sources is included, and the quotations are not dated.

Hoffmeister, Johannes. Wörterbuch der philosophischen Begriffe. 2. Aufl. Hamburg, Felix Meiner, 1955. 687p. (Die philosophische Bibliothek, Bd.225) **BA34**

1st ed. 1944.

Based on the work previously edited by Friedrich Kirchner and Carl Michaelis.

Concise articles on philosophical terms and concepts with some bibliography. Does not include biography.

Lalande, André. Vocabulaire technique et critique de la philosophie, revu par MM. les membres et correspondants de la Société Française de Philosophie, et publié avec leurs corrections et observations. 7. ed. rev. et augm. Paris, Presses Universitaires de France, 1956. 1323p.　　**BA35**

1st ed. 1926.

Defines and discusses philosophical terms, giving equivalents in various languages, references to sources, etc.

Urmson, James Opie. The concise encyclopedia of Western philosophy and philosophers. London, Hutchinson; N.Y., Hawthorn, 1960. 431p. incl. plates.　　**BA36**

Articles, although not signed, have been contributed by nearly 50 scholars, most of them British (representing Oxford philosophy), and are written primarily for the "intelligent layman." Coverage is selective, but the work includes biographical articles, general descriptions of the main philosophical concepts, and definitions of terms.

No bibliography.

Wuellner, Bernard. Dictionary of scholastic philosophy. Milwaukee, Bruce, 1956. 138p.　　**BA37**

A dictionary giving explanations and definitions of terms with some references to sources. Includes charts and diagrams.

HISTORY

✓**Ueberweg, Friedrich.** Grundriss der Geschichte der Philosophie. 11.–12. Aufl. hrsg. von Karl Praechter. Berlin, Mittler, 1923–28. 5v. (Repr.: Basel, B. Schwabe, 1957)　　**BA38**

Important reference history, particularly useful for its full bibliographies and its biographical information.

Covers ancient; patristic and scholastic; and modern philosophy. Written by specialists.

BIOGRAPHY

Philosophen-Lexikon; Handwörterbuch der Philosophie nach Personen, verf. und hrsg. von Werner Ziegenfuss und Gertrud Jung. Berlin, de Gruyter, 1949–50. 2v.　　**BA39**

A biographical dictionary of philosophers of all periods and all countries, but with the emphasis on philosophy since Hegel. Includes living persons. Planned to take the place of the earlier *Philosophen-Lexikon* by Rudolf Eisler (Berlin, Mittler, 1912. 889p.) and on the same general plan as that work, but with longer articles, inclusion of additional names, and considerable additional material on names included by Eisler. Nearly all articles, even the short ones, have bibliographies.

The first six parts, A–Juvalta, were published in 1937, but further publication was prohibited on political grounds. The present text of both volumes remains almost unaltered except for the addition of some later death dates and of bibliographical data: to 1945 for German publications, to 1939 for other countries.

Riedl, John O. Catalogue of Renaissance philosophers (1300–1650), comp. by Robert A. Baker [and others] under the direction of John O. Riedl. Milwaukee, Marquette Univ. Pr., 1940. 179p.　　**BA40**

Arranged by schools with alphabetical author index. Gives biographical notes and bibliographies of writings.

INDIVIDUAL PHILOSOPHERS

See also Greek—Individual Authors, p.300; Latin—Individual Authors, p.302.

Aristotle

Aristoteles. Aristotle dictionary, ed. by Thomas P. Kiernan. N.Y., Philosophical Lib., 1962. 524p.　　**BA41**

Introduction by Theodore E. James, p.7–163.

"References are made to the appropriate *loci* of the quotations . . . in the Bekker edition of the Greek published in 1831."

Arranged by subject word in English, with exact references to sources.

Augustine

Andresen, Carl. Bibliographia Augustiniana. Darmstadt, Wissenschaftliche Buchgesellschaft, 1962. 127p.　　**BA42**

Preface in German and Latin.

"Sonderdruck aus: Zum Augustin-Gespräch der Gegenwart (Wege der Forschung Bd.V.)."

Material by and about St. Augustine.

Classified arrangement. No index.

Croce

Cione, Edmondo. Bibliografia crociana. [Roma], Bocca, 1956. 481p. (Biblioteca di scienze moderne. 155)　　**BA43**

Lists works by and about Croce.

Descartes

Sebba, Gregor. Bibliographia Cartesiana: a critical guide to the Descartes literature, 1800–1960. The Hague, Nijhoff, 1964. 510p. (Archives internationales d'histoire des idées. International archives of the history of ideas. 5)　　**BA44**

Supersedes the author's *Descartes and his philosophy: a bibliographical guide . . . 1800–1958* (Athens, Ga., 1959. v.1; no more published).

Contents: pt.1, Introduction to Descartes studies. no.1–562; pt.2, Alphabetical bibliography, 1800–1960. no.1001–3612; pt.3, Indices: systematic and analytical.

Lists books and periodical articles in many languages.

Dewey

Thomas, Milton Halsey. John Dewey; a centennial bibliography. Chicago, Univ. of Chicago Pr., 1962. 370p.　　**BA45**

"First pub. as *A bibliography of John Dewey . . . 1929, . . . A bibliography of John Dewey, 1882–1939.* 1939."

In two sections: (1) Writings of John Dewey (intended to be exhaustive and listing for each book: editions, translations, and reviews); (2) Writings about John Dewey.

Duns Scotus

Schäfer, Odulf. Bibliographia de vita, operibus et doctrina Iohannis Duns Scoti, doctoris subtilis ac Mariani, saec. XIX–XX. Romae, Orbis Catholicus-Herder, 1955. 223p.　　**BA46**

An alphabetical listing of 4506 numbered entries—including books and periodical articles—about Duns Scotus. Name and analytical indexes.

Epictetus

Oldfather, William Abbott. Contributions toward a bibliography of Epictetus; appendix: Jacob Schenk's Translation of the Encheiridion, Basel 1534, facsimile reproduction from the copy in the British Museum. Urbana, Univ. of Illinois, 1927. 201p.   **BA47**

—— —— A supplement, ed. by Marian Harman, with a preliminary list of Epictetus manuscripts by W. H. Friedrich and C. U. Faye. Urbana, Univ. of Illinois, 1952. 177p.

For full information *see* BD942.

Erasmus

Haeghen, Ferdinand van der. Bibliotheca Erasmiana: répertoire des œuvres d'Érasme. Nieuwkoop, B. de Graaf, 1961. 3 pts. in 1v. (Repr. of the Gand, 1893, ed.)   **BA48**

Contents: 1. sér., Liste sommaire et provisoire des diverses éditions de ses œuvres. 186p.; 2. sér., Auteurs publiés, traduits ou annotés par Érasme. Liste sommaire et provisoire. 67p.; 3. sér., Sources. Biographies d'Érasme et écrits le concernant; ouvrages qui contiennent des notes d'Érasme, des extraits de ses œuvres, etc. 65p.

Margolin, Jean Claude. Douze années de bibliographie érasmienne, 1950–1961. Paris, Vrin, 1963. 204p.   **BA49**

Hume

Jessop, Thomas Edmund. A bibliography of David Hume and of Scottish philosophy from Francis Hutcheson to Lord Balfour. London, A. Brown, 1938. 201p.   **BA50**

Lists works by and about Hume, p.5–71; other Scottish philosophers, p.75–189.

Kant

Eisler, Rudolf. Kant-Lexikon; Nachschlagewerk zu Kants sämtlichen Schriften, Briefen und handschriftlichen Nachlass; hrsg. unter Mitwirkung der Kantgesellschaft. Berlin, Mittler, 1930. 642p.   **BA51**

Arranged by German word with explanations and exact references to sources.

Kierkegaard

Himmelstrup, Jens. Søren Kierkegaard; international bibliografi. København, Nyt Nordisk Forlag, Arnold Busck, 1962. 216p.   **BA52**

Added title page in English.

Lists material by and about Kierkegaard in various languages covering 1835–1955.

Nietzsche

Reichert, Herbert William and **Schlechta, Karl.** International Nietzsche bibliography. Chapel Hill, N.C., Univ. of North Carolina Pr., [1960]. 133p. (North Carolina. University. Studies in comparative literature, no.29)   **BA53**

A total of 3973 items—books and periodical articles—about Nietzsche. Arranged by language, alphabetical by author within each language group.

Thomas Aquinas

Deferrari, Roy Joseph and **Barry,** *Sister* **M. Inviolata.** A lexicon of St. Thomas Aquinas based on the Summa theologica and selected passages of his other works. . . . With the technical collaboration of Ignatius McGuiness. [Wash., Catholic Univ. of America Pr., 1948–49] 1185p.   **BA54**

Arranged by Latin words, with their different English meanings and with Latin quotations from the *Summa theologica* and indications of exact sources.

—— A complete index of the Summa theologica of St. Thomas Aquinas. Wash., Catholic Univ. of America Pr., 1956. 386p.   **BA55**

An *index verborum,* prepared in conjunction with the authors' *Lexicon of St. Thomas Aquinas* (BA54).

Mandonnet, Pierre and **Destrez, J.** Bibliographie thomiste. La Saulchoir, Kain (Belgique), Revue des Sciences Philosophiques et Théologiques, 1921. 116p. (Bibliothèque tomiste, I)   **BA56**

Lists more than 2200 items in various languages. Supplemented by:

Bourke, Vernon Joseph. Thomistic bibliography, 1920–1940. . . . The modern schoolman, supplement to v.21. St. Louis, 1945. 312p.   **BA57**

Lists more than 6660 books and periodical articles in various languages. Classified arrangement with indexes.

BB

Religion

❧ In the field of religion, both Christian and non-Christian, reference materials are very extensive. They include encyclopedias, dictionaries, directories, and manuals in English and in other languages, which should be acquired by libraries according to need.

A basic working collection of materials in English might include: *Encyclopaedia of religion and ethics* (BB12); *Catholic encyclopedia* (BB201); *Universal Jewish encyclopedia* (BB302); one or more editions of the Bible (*see* BB72); Strong, *Exhaustive concordance of the Bible* (BB95); Stevenson, *Home book of Bible quotations* (BB103); Hastings, *Dictionary of the Bible* (BB113); Julian, *Dictionary of hymnology* (BB70); *Yearbook of American churches* (BB147); and whatever denominational yearbooks are needed.

Large libraries, and libraries specializing in religious materials, will need to add many of the more specialized works, including some of those in foreign languages.

GENERAL WORKS

Bibliography

Barrow, John Graves. A bibliography of bibliographies in religion. Ann Arbor, Mich., Edwards Bros., 1955. 489p. (For sale by Author, 716 Brown Bldg., Austin 1, Tex.)   **BB1**

Based upon the author's Ph.D. dissertation, Yale University, 1930.

A comprehensive work attempting "to bring together all separately published bibliographies in the field of religion," from the 15th century to the present, and in many languages. Primarily Christian but with a brief section on non-Christian religions. Brief annotations.

Chronological under subject field with author index. Locates copies in numerous American and European libraries.

Diehl, Katharine Smith. Religions, mythologies, folklores: an annotated bibliography. 2d ed. N.Y., Scarecrow, 1962. 573p.   **BB2**

1st ed. 1956.

An annotated bibliography covering the "literature of faith and practice in all cultures. It includes books of general and specific reference, literatures, literary and historical guides, various scriptures and commentaries, records of institutional accomplishment, and biographies."—*Pref.*

Classified arrangement with author and title index.

International bibliography of the history of religions. Bibliographie internationale de l'histoire des religions . . . 1952– . . . . Leiden, E. J. Brill, 1954– . v.1– . Annual.   **BB3**

Under the supervision of C. J. Bleeker, comp. by Henriette Boas. Published in connection with the periodical *Numen,* with the support of UNESCO and under the auspices of the International Council for Philosophy and Humanistic Studies, by the International Association for the History of Religions.

Lists books and articles published during the year on the history of the various religions of the world. Classified arrangement. No author indexes until 1958/59.

Morris, Raymond P. A theological book list. Produced by the Theological Education Fund of the International Missionary Council for theological seminaries and colleges in Africa, Asia, Latin America and the Southwest Pacific. Oxford, Blackwell; Naperville, Ill., Allenson's, 1960. 242p.   **BB4**

Continued by:

A theological book list . . . produced by the Theological Education Fund, a service of the Commission on World Mission and Evangelism of the World Council of Churches, for theological seminaries and colleges in Africa, Asia, Latin America and the Southwest Pacific. Oxford, Blackwell; Naperville, Ill., Allenson's, 1963. [v.p.]   **BB5**

Contents: Works in English, comp. by A. Marcus Ward; French, comp. by Frank Michaeli; German, comp. by Hanswerner Gensichen; Portuguese, comp. by Aharon Sapsezian; Spanish, comp. by Carlos Gattinoni.

Dissertations

Council on Graduate Studies in Religion. Doctoral dissertations in the field of religion, 1940–1952: their titles, location, fields, and short précis of contents. [N.Y.], Columbia Univ. Pr. for the Council, 1954. 194p.   **BB6**

Published as a supplement to the *Review of religion,* v.18.

————— Supplement. 1952– .

The main work is an alphabetical list by author of 425 dissertations with brief abstracts. The supplements are annual author lists only.

Little, Lawrence Calvin. Researches in personality, character and religious education: a bibliography of American doctoral dissertations, 1885 to 1959. With an index prep. by Helen-Jean Moore. Pittsburgh, Pa., Univ. of Pittsburgh Pr., 1962. 215p.   **BB7**

Cover title: Bibliography of American doctoral dissertations in religious education, 1885 to 1959.

A listing of more than 6300 doctoral dissertations arranged alphabetically by author with subject index.

Indexes and abstract journals

American Theological Library Association. Index to religious periodical literature; an author and subject index to periodical literature, 1949/1952– , including an author index to book reviews. Prep. by libraries of the American Theological Library Association. Chicago, Amer. Theological Lib. Assoc., 1953– . v.1– .   **BB8**

Annual with cumulated volumes: v.1, 1949–52; v.2, 1953–54; v.3, 1955–56; v.4, 1957–59. Triennial cumulations thereafter.

Indexes religious and archaeological periodicals from the United States, Canada, England, France, Germany, Japan, Scotland, and other countries. Coverage and number of periodicals indexed vary. Each volume includes a listing of book reviews.

Protestant in viewpoint, but indexes some Catholic and Jewish periodicals.

Christian Librarian Fellowship. Christian periodical index: a subject index to periodical literature, 1958– . Prep. by the librarians of the Christian Librarian Fellowship. Buffalo, N.Y., distr. by Buffalo Bible Inst. Bookstore, 1958– . v.1– . Annual.   **BB9**

Five-year cumulated volume covers 1956–60.

Indexes about 20 evangelical and fundamentalist periodicals from the United States, Canada, and England.

Religious and theological abstracts. Youngstown, Ohio, Theological Pub., 1958– . v.1– . Quarterly.   **BB10**

A nonsectarian abstracting service, giving brief abstracts in English of articles appearing in a selected list of religious periodicals—including Christian, Jewish, and Muslim journals—in various languages.

Author, subject, and Biblical indexes for each volume.

Richardson, Ernest Cushing. Periodical articles on religion; an alphabetical subject index and index encyclopaedia to periodical articles on religion, 1890–1899. N.Y., Scribner, 1907–11. 2v.   **BB11**

Title varies.

Subject volume, 1907. 1168p.; author volume, 1911. 876p.

An index to 58,000 articles by 21,000 writers, in more than 600 periodicals and transactions in English and the principal foreign languages, on the religions of the world. The subject volume, arranged alphabetically, has a special feature not ordinarily found in indexes, i.e., each heading used is briefly defined, or a person or place is identified and followed by a reference to some encyclopedia article. The author volume indexes the same articles as the subject volume.

Encyclopedias

Encyclopaedia of religion and ethics; ed. by James Hastings, with the assistance of John A. Selbie and Louis H. Gray. Edinburgh, Clark; N.Y., Scribner, 1908–27. 12v. and index. il.   **BB12**

Low-priced edition on thinner paper, 7v.

The most comprehensive work in this class, in English, including articles on all religions; ethical systems and movements; religious beliefs and customs; philosophical ideas; moral practices; related subjects in anthropology, mythology, folklore, biology, psychology, economics, and sociology; and names of persons and places connected with any of these subjects. Signed articles, full bibliographies.

Herzog, Johann Jakob. Realencyklopädie für protestantische Theologie und Kirche, begründet von J. J. Herzog; in 3. verb. und verm. Aufl. . . . hrsg. von Albert Hauck. Leipzig, Hinrichs, 1896–1913. 24v.   **BB13**

v.1–21, A–Z; v.22, Index; v.23–24, Supplement, A–Z.

Long, signed articles by specialists, and full bibliographies. The most extended German work—and one of the most important in any language from the Protestant point of view.

Formed the basis for the *New Schaff-Herzog* (BB18). Of value in the theological, university, or large reference library.

Lexikon für Theologie und Kirche; begründet von Michael Buchberger. 2. völlig neubearb. Aufl. . . . hrsg. von Josef Höfer und Karl Rahner. Freiburg, Herder, 1957–64. v.1–9. (In progress)   **BB14**

   Contents: v.1–9, A–Tetzel.

   1st ed. 1930–38. 10v.

   Signed articles, some of considerable length, with bibliographies, covering various religions, practices, faiths, and rituals. Includes biography. From the Roman Catholic point of view.

Mathews, Shailer and **Smith, Gerald Birney.** Dictionary of religion and ethics. N.Y., Macmillan, 1921. 513p.   **BB15**

   A dictionary, not a detailed encyclopedia, which aims to define all terms definitely connected with the subjects of religion and ethics and to discuss fully the more important terms, especially those in primitive and ethnic religions. Includes biographies of persons not living. The longer articles are signed. Classified bibliography at the end of the volume.

Nordisk teologisk uppslagsbok för kyrka och skola. Redaktion: Ragnar Askmark [et al.]. Lund, Gleerup; Köbenhavn, Munksgaard, 1952–57. 3v. il.   **BB16**

   v.1–3, A–Ö; Register.

   Published in Denmark and Norway with the title *Nordisk teologisk leksikon.*

   A general religious encyclopedia with signed articles and fairly extensive bibliographies listing works in various languages. Includes biographies.

Die Religion in Geschichte und Gegenwart; Handwörterbuch für Theologie und Religionswissenschaft. 3. völlig neubearb. Aufl. . . . hrsg. von Kurt Galling. Tübingen, J. C. B. Mohr (Paul Siebeck), 1956–62. 6v. il.   **BB17**

   1st ed. 1909–13; 2d ed. 1927–32.

   Cited as *RGG;* an authoritative work containing long, signed articles by specialists. From an advanced Protestant point of view but includes articles on Catholic doctrines. Full bibliographies. Many biographical sketches, including articles on living persons.

Schaff-Herzog encyclopedia. New Schaff-Herzog encyclopedia of religious knowledge, embracing Biblical, historical, doctrinal and practical theology and Biblical, theological and ecclesiastical biography, from the earliest times to the present day; based on the 3d ed. of the Realencyklopädie founded by J. J. Herzog and ed. by Albert Hauck. S. M. Jackson, ed. in chief. N.Y., Funk & Wagnalls, 1908–12. 12v. and index. (Repr.: Grand Rapids, Mich., Baker Book House, 1949–50. 13v.)   **BB18**

   One of the most important reference books on its subject in English. Based upon the 3d edition of the Herzog-Hauck *Realencyklopädie* (BB13) and thus Protestant in tone, it is not a mere translation of the German work since much of the material has been condensed, fresh material added, and the bibliographies extended and improved. Not limited to the Christian religion but includes articles on other religions and religious leaders. Covers the whole field of Biblical, historical, and contemporary theology, including separate articles on all sects, denominations and churches, organizations and societies, missions, doctrines, controversies, etc. Biographical notices include those of men living at the time the work was published. The bibliography is in three forms: (1) general bibliographical survey, with critical comment, in the preface (p.xii–xiv); (2) bibliographical appendix at the beginning of each volume listing recent literature; and (3) bibliographies appended to each article.

   Supplemented by:

Twentieth century encyclopedia of religious knowledge: an extension of the New Schaff-Herzog encyclopedia of religious knowledge. Ed. in chief, Lefferts A. Loetscher.

Grand Rapids, Mich., Baker Book House, 1955. 2v.   **BB19**

   These volumes may be used either with the set or independently. They include biographical sketches of persons both living and dead; articles on new subjects; and articles which bring up to date subjects previously treated. Articles are signed and usually include bibliographies.

Sacred books

Champion, Selwyn Gurney. The eleven religions and their proverbial lore, a comparative study. . . . Foreword to the American ed. by Rufus M. Jones. . . . A reference book to the eleven surviving major religions of the world, with introductions by thirteen leading authorities. N.Y., Dutton, 1945. 340p.   **BB20**

   A book of quotations arranged under religion by key word, with subject-matter index and alternative chief-word index. Bibliography, p.336–60.

Hume, Robert Ernest. Treasure house of the living religions; selections from their sacred scriptures. N.Y., Scribner, 1932. 493p.   **BB21**

   A classified anthology of 3,074 selected quotations from the sacred books of the eleven great historical religions—Buddhism, Christianity, Confucianism, Hinduism, Islam, Jainism, Judaism, Shinto, Sikhism, Taoism, and Zoroastrianism—with exact indication of source of each quotation; a full "Bibliography showing the canonical order of constituent documents of the several sacred scriptures together with the English translations of each document," p.405–43; and an alphabetical topical index. A work of wide and precise scholarship, useful to the general reader for the interest of the selections and to the specialist for both selections and bibliographical materials.

Sacred books of the East, tr. by various oriental scholars and ed. by F. Max Müller. Oxford, Clarendon Pr., 1879–1910. 50v.   **BB22**

   v.1, 15, The Upanishads, tr. by F. Max Müller; v.2, 14, The sacred laws of the Âryas, tr. by George Bühler; v.3, 16, 27, 28, The sacred books of China, the texts of Confucianism, tr. by James Legge; v.4, 23, 31, The Zend-Avesta, tr. by James Darmesteter and L. H. Mills; v.5, 18, 24, 37, 47, Pahlavi texts, tr. by E. W. West; v.6, 9, The Qur'ân, tr. by E. Palmer; v.7, The Institutes of Vishnu, tr. by Julius Jolly; v.8, The Bhagavadgîtâ, with the Sanatsugâtîya and the Anugîtâ, tr. by Kâshinâth Trimbak Telang; v.10, The Dhammapada, tr. from Pâli by F. M. Müller; The Sutta-nipâta, tr. from Pâli by V. Fausböll; v.11, Buddhist suttas, tr. from Pâli by T. W. Rhys Davids; v.12, 26, 41, 43, 44, The Satapathabrâhmana, tr. by Julius Eggeling; v.13, 17, 20, Vinayā texts, tr. from the Pâli by T. W. Rhys Davids and Hermann Oldenberg;

   v.19, The Fo-sho-hing-tsan-king by Asvaghosha, tr. by Samuel Beal; v.21, The Saddharma-pundarika, tr. by H. Kern; v.22, 45, Gaina sûtras, tr. from Prâkrit by Herman Jacobi; v.25, The laws of Manu, tr. by G. Bühler; v.29, 30, The Grihya-sûtras, tr. by Hermann Oldenberg; v.32, 46, Vedic hymns, tr. by F. M. Müller and H. Oldenberg; v.33, The minor law books, pt.1, tr. by Julius Jolly; v.34, 38, 48, The Vedânta sûtras, tr. by George Thibaut; v.35, 36, The questions of King Milinda, tr. by T. W. Rhys Davids; v.39, 40, The sacred books of China, the texts of Tâoism, tr. by James Legge; v.42, Hymns of the Atharva-veda, tr. by Maurice Bloomfield; v.49, Buddhist Mâháyana texts, tr. by E. B. Cowell; v.50, General index, by M. Winternitz.

   Includes all the most important works of the seven non-Christian religions that have influenced the civilization of Asia: the Vedic-Brahmanic system, Buddhism, Jainism, Islam, Confucianism, Taoism, and the Parsi religion. The excellent and detailed general index can be used for both large and small topics, beliefs, myths, names of deities, etc. Index also issued separately, as follows:

Winternitz, Moriz. Concise dictionary of Eastern religion, being the index volume to the Sacred books of the East. Oxford, Clarendon Pr., 1910. 683p. **BB23**

Published also under the title *A general index to the names and subject matter of the Sacred books of the East*.

CHRISTIANITY

General works

Bibliography

Allison, William Henry. History of Christianity. (Sec. 5 of *A guide to historical literature*, ed. by G. M. Dutcher and others. N.Y., Macmillan, 1931. p.233–75. [*see* DA1]) **BB24**

A useful annotated bibliography covering the basic works on the history of the Christian religion and church, including reference works and general and special histories.

Continued by: Sec. D, "History of religions—Christianity," in American Historical Association's *Guide to historical literature* (1961), p.65–74 (DA1).

Burr, Nelson Rollin. A critical bibliography of religion in America. Princeton, N.J., Princeton Univ. Pr., 1961. 2v. (Princeton studies in American civilization, no.5) **BB25**

The final volume (bound in 2v.) of a series of 4v., *Religion in American life,* by James Ward Smith and A. Leland Jamison. A very comprehensive bibliography in classified arrangement with running commentary. Main divisions: pt.1, Bibliographical guides: general surveys and histories; pt.2, Evolution of American religion; pt.3, Religion and society; pt.4, Religion in the arts and literature; pt.5, Intellectual history, theology, philosophy, and science. Tables of contents, and an author index, but no subject index.

New York (City). Union Theological Seminary. Library. Catalogue of the McAlpin collection of British history and theology; comp. and ed. by Charles Ripley Gillett. N.Y., 1927–30. 5v. **BB26**

v.1–4, 1500–1700; v.5, Index.

A rich collection of material including many pamphlets on British theology and history.

Theologischer Jahresbericht, 1881–1913. Tübingen, Mohr, 1882–1916. v.1–33. **BB27**

An important serial bibliography of books and periodical material; for the university, theological, or large reference library. Discontinued after the outbreak of World War I.

Theologische Literaturzeitung, 1., 1876– . Leipzig, Hinrichs, 1876– . Biweekly. **BB28**

—— Bibliographisches Beiblatt. Die theologische Literatur des Jahres 1922–42. Leipzig, Hinrichs, 1922–43. Biweekly, 1922–24; semiannual, 1925–35; annual, 1936–42.

A comprehensive survey of book and periodical material in many languages.

Encyclopedias and dictionaries

❧ For most questions asked by English-speaking readers, the *Encyclopaedia of religion and ethics* (BB12) and the *New Schaff-Herzog* (BB18) will be adequate. In the large reference library it will often be necessary to use some of the foreign works, especially for topics in foreign church history, foreign religious biography, etc. The most extended modern work of reference in the field of theology is the great French series now in course of publica-

tion under the general title *Encyclopédie des sciences religieuses,* composed of the following separate works: *Dictionnaire d'archéologie chrétienne* by Cabrol (BB34); *Dictionnaire d'histoire et de géographie ecclésiastiques* by Baudrillart (BB29); *Dictionnaire de théologie catholique* by Vacant and Mangenot (BB202); *Dictionnaire de la Bible* by Vigouroux (BB125); and *Dictionnaire de droit canonique* (CJ89). These are listed separately under their subjects. Parts of this series contain the finest material on the subject published in any language, and the work as a whole represents the highest level of French Catholic scholarship. The price of the sets puts them beyond the reach of the small or medium-sized library, and the work is too special to be of much use except in a theological library, a large general reference library, or a library specializing in medieval and ecclesiastical history and literature.

Baudrillart, Alfred. Dictionnaire d'histoire et de géographie ecclésiastiques, commencé sous la direction de Mgr. Alfred Baudrillart, continué par A. de Meyer et Ét. van Cauwenbergh, avec le concours d'un grand nombre de collaborateurs. Paris, Letouzey, 1912–64. v.1–15. il. (In progress) **BB29**

v.1–15, A–Eusébie. From v.14, edited by R. Aubert and É. van Cauwenbergh.

Scope of the work covers all subjects in the history of the Roman Catholic church, and other churches as they affect the Roman church, from the beginning of Christianity to the present time. The geographical material includes separate articles on towns and other small divisions, past and present, indicating the connection of the place with ecclesiastical history, its present ecclesiastical status, a list of its religious institutions, and (in case it is or has been an espiscopal see) a list of the bishops, etc. Includes biographical articles on: all important and some minor names in the Roman Catholic church; members of other churches who have had any effect on the Roman church; ecclesiastical and theological writers; saints in the Russian and other churches; ecclesiastical musicians, artists, etc. Signed articles, good bibliographies.

Evangelisches Kirchenlexikon; kirchlich-theologisches Handwörterbuch . . . hrsg. von Heinz Brunotte u. Otto Weber. Göttingen, Vandenhoeck und Ruprecht, 1955–61. 4v. **BB30**

A German Protestant encyclopedia designed as a modern supplement to older works of reference on Christian theology and church affairs, emphasizing recent literature.

Entries include theological concepts, clerical terms, national and geographical areas—with emphasis on their religious history—and biographies. Long articles are signed and include bibliographies.

v.4, the *Register,* contains a list of the several hundred contributors to the set, a subject index, and an extensive *Biographischer Anhang.* The last gives brief biographical information on nearly 15,000 persons connected with Christianity through the ages, with references to citations in the main set.

Malloch, James M. A practical church dictionary, ed. by Kay Smallzried. N.Y., Morehouse-Barlow, 1964. 520p. **BB31**

A dictionary prepared from the viewpoint of the Episcopal church but with an ecumenical approach that includes other Protestant, Roman Catholic, and Eastern Orthodox churches. Definitions were written by Dr. Malloch. No bibliography with the articles. "Books for further reference," p.517–20.

Oxford dictionary of the Christian church, ed. by F. L. Cross. London, Oxford Univ. Pr., 1957. 1492p. (Repr. with corrections, 1961) **BB32**

A useful, 1v. work containing more than 6000 articles, some of considerable length. Although about half of the entries were written by contributing scholars, in the interests of uniformity none are signed. Bibliographies are appended to most articles. Coverage is broad, including historical and doctrinal development, many biographies, definitions of ecclesiastical terms and customs, etc.

Viller, Marcel. Dictionnaire de spiritualité, ascétique et mystique, doctrine et histoire, fondé par Marcel Viller, F. Cavallera et J. de Guibert, . . . avec le concours d'un grand nombre de collaborateurs. Paris, Beauchesne, 1932–64. Fasc.1–38. (In progress) **BB33**

v.1–5, A–Fyot.

Long, signed articles with bibliographies and references to sources; includes many biographies.

Editors vary.

Christian antiquities

Cabrol, Fernand and **Leclerq, Henri.** Dictionnaire d'archéologie chrétienne et de liturgie, publié sous la direction de Henri Marrou. Paris, Letouzey, 1907–53. 15v. il. **BB34**

Issued in parts.

Excellent signed articles, with full bibliographies, on institutions, manners, and customs of primitive Christianity, and on the architecture, Christian art, iconography, symbols, epigraphy, paleography, numismatics, liturgy, rites, and ceremonies of the early church to the time of Charlemagne. Covers about the same ground as Smith's *Dictionary of Christian antiquities* (BB37) but with fuller and more up-to-date treatment.

Corswant, Willy. Dictionnaire d'archéologie biblique. Revu et illustré par Édouard Urech. Neuchâtel, Paris, Delachaux et Niestlé, 1956. 324p. il. **BB35**

Planned especially as an aid to teachers of the Bible; is concerned with the private, civil, and religious life of the Jews and early Christians, and with the flora, fauna, and minerals of Israel. Written in nontechnical language, illustrated with line drawings. At the end of each article, references are given to the Biblical texts.

Reallexikon für Antike und Christentum; Sachwörterbuch zur Auseinandersetzung des Christentums mit der antiken Welt. In Verbindung mit Franz Joseph Dolger, Hans Lietzmann, [and others], hrsg. von Theodor Klauser. Stuttgart, Hiersemann, 1950–64. v.1–6 (incompl.). (In progress) **BB36**

Bd.1–6 (Lfg. 41–43), A–Erz.

Long, signed articles by many scholars dealing with the relationship of the ancient world to Christianity up to the 6th century A.D.

Smith, *Sir* **William** and **Cheetham, Samuel.** Dictionary of Christian antiquities, being a continuation of the "Dictionary of the Bible." London, Murray; Boston, Little, 1876–80. 2v. il. **BB37**

Treats subjects connected with the organization of the church: its officers, legislation, discipline, and revenues; social life; ceremonials, church music, vestments, instruments, and insignia; ecclesiastical architecture and art and their symbolism; sacred days, burial places, etc. Omits literature, sects, doctrines, heresies, etc., as such subjects are covered in the companion work *Dictionary of Christian biography* (BB38). Covers period to the age of Charlemagne. Long, signed articles; exact references to many sources; bibliographies. Not abreast of modern scholarship but still useful on many points.

Smith, *Sir* **William** and **Wace, Henry.** Dictionary of Christian biography, literature, sects, and doctrines. London, Murray; Boston, Little, 1877–87. 4v. **BB38**

A companion work to the entry above.

Aims to supply an adequate account, based upon original authorities, of all persons connected with the church—down to the age of Charlemagne—about whom anything is known, of all literature connected with them, and of the controversies about doctrine and discipline in which they were engaged. Pays special attention to subjects and names in English, Scottish, and Irish church history. Signed articles; bibliographies.

Wace, Henry and **Piercy, William C.** Dictionary of Christian biography and literature to the end of the sixth century, A.D., with an account of the principal sects and heresies. London, Murray; Boston, Little, 1911. 1028p. **BB39**

A revised and abridged edition of Smith's *Dictionary of Christian biography* (BB38). Adds later references but does not supersede Smith, which must still be used for long articles, for minor names, and for subjects of the 7th and 8th centuries, as this new edition covers only the first six centuries.

Terms

Purvis, John Stanley. Dictionary of ecclesiastical terms. London, Nelson, 1962. 204p. **BB40**

Gives definitions of ecclesiastical terms, primarily as used in England, including those used in the Church of England and in the Roman Catholic and Eastern Orthodox churches.

White, Richard Clark. The vocabulary of the church: a pronunciation guide. N.Y., Macmillan, 1960. 178p. **BB41**

Emphasis is on proper nouns and Biblical words; gives word and pronunciation only. "The standard pronunciation is American religious usage."—*Introd.*

Biography

Haag, Eugène and **Haag, Émile.** La France protestante; ou, Vies des protestants français qui se sont fait un nom dans l'histoire . . . Paris, Cherbuliez, 1846–59. 10v. **BB42**

For description *see* AJ129.

Moyer, Elgin S. Who was who in church history. Chicago, Moody Pr., 1962. 452p. **BB43**

Biographical sketches of some 1700 personalities "who have made a definite contribution to the history of the Christian church since the apostolic age."—*Pref.* Does not treat living persons, but does include many 20th-century names.

Sprague, William Buell. Annals of the American pulpit; or, Commemorative notices of distinguished American clergymen of various denominations, from the early settlement of the country to the close of the year 1855. With historical introductions. N.Y., R. Carter, 1857–[69]. 9v. il. **BB44**

v.1–2, Trinitarian Congregational; v.3–4, Presbyterian; v.5, Episcopalian; v.6, Baptist; v.7, Methodist; v.8, Unitarian Congregational; v.9, Lutheran. Reformed Dutch. Associate. Associate Reformed. Reformed Presbyterian.

A useful work of sketches, averaging two to three pages in length, with extensive bibliographies of the publications by the biographee. Has an alphabetical index for each denomination but no general index.

Creeds

Schaff, Philip. The creeds of Christendom; with a history and critical notes. 6th ed. rev. and enl. N.Y., London, Harper, 1919. 3v. (Bibliotheca symbolica ecclesiae universalis). **BB45**

v.1, History of creeds, church by church, with many bibliographical references; v.2, Creeds of the Greek and Latin churches, giving for each the full Greek or Latin text and an English translation in parallel columns, with an index of subjects; v.3, Creeds of the Evangelical Protestant churches, in language of original with parallel English translations, with index of subjects.

Costume

Norris, Herbert. Church vestments: their origin and development. London, Dent, 1949. 190p. il.   **BB46**

Illustrated with plates and line drawings. Based on the author's *Costume and fashion,* it treats the history and development of the classical garments used in the church.

Church history and expansion

History

American church history series, consisting of a series of denominational histories published under the auspices of the American Society of Church History. Gen. eds.: Philip Schaff, H. C. Potter, S. M. Jackson. N.Y., Christian Literature Co. (Scribner), 1893–1901. 13v.   **BB47**

Now much out of date but still occasionally useful. Consists of separate histories of major denominations by various authors. Includes a bibliography of American church history, 1820–93, in v.12.

Mayer, Frederick Emanuel. The religious bodies of America. 2d ed. St. Louis, Concordia Pub. House, 1956. 591p.   **BB48**

A treatise on the doctrines, practices, and historical development of the churches of America, arranged by church groupings, with description and bibliography for each denomination, sect, and organization. Includes many references to authorities.

Rouse, Ruth and **Neill, Stephen Charles.** A history of the ecumenical movement, 1517–1948. London, pub. on behalf of the Ecumenical Institute by the Soc. for Promoting Christian Knowledge. Philadelphia, Westminster Pr., 1954. 822p.   **BB49**

Bibliography, p.745–86.
A survey history from the period of the Reformation to 1948, each section written by a specialist.

Schaff, Philip. History of the Christian church. N.Y., Scribner, 1889–1910. 7v. in 8. il.   **BB50**

A detailed, documented history.

Sweet, William Warren. Religion on the American frontier. A collection of source material. Chicago, Univ. of Chicago Pr., 1931–46. v.1–4. il.   **BB51**

Publisher varies. No more published.
Contents: [v.1], The Baptists, 1783–1830. 1931; v.2, The Presbyterians, 1783–1840. 1936; v.3, The Congregationalists, 1783–1850. 1939; v.4, The Methodists, 1783–1840. 1946.
Each volume includes bibliography.

Vekené, E. van der. Bibliographie der Inquisition; ein Versuch. Hildesheim, Georg Olms, 1963. 323p.   **BB52**

A bibliography of 1950 numbered entries arranged chronologically from about 1483 to 1961. Includes works in Western languages and locates copies in European libraries.

Source books

Ayer, Joseph Cullen. A source book for ancient church history, from the apostolic age to the close of the conciliar period. N.Y., Scribner, 1913. 707p.   **BB53**

A standard work.

Bell, George Kennedy Allen. Documents on Christian unity. London, N.Y., Oxford Univ. Pr., 1929–58. 4v.   **BB54**

Ser. 1, 1920–24; ser. 2, 1924–30; ser. 3, 1930–48; ser. 4, 1948–57.

A selection of documents from the 1st and 2d series, 1920–30, was published in 1955.
A collection of documents designed to illustrate the growth of the ecumenical movement throughout the world.

Gee, Henry and **Hardy, William John.** Documents illustrative of English church history, comp. from original sources. London, N.Y., Macmillan, 1896. 670p.   **BB55**

Covers A.D. 314–1700.

Kidd, Beresford James. Documents illustrative of the history of the church. London, Soc. for Promoting Christian Knowledge; N.Y., Macmillan, 1920–41. v.1–3.   **BB56**

Contents: v.1, to A.D. 313; v.2, 313–461; v.3, ca. 500–1500.
Partially superseded by James Stevenson. *A new Eusebius; documents illustrative of the history of the church to* A.D. *337. Based upon the collection ed. by B. J. Kidd.* London, S.P.C.K., 1957. 427p.

Missions

❧ No single comprehensive bibliography of Protestant missions is available comparable to Streit's *Bibliotheca missionum* (BB61) which treats Catholic missions. For a listing of various bibliographies, largely specialized, *see* John G. Barrow. *A bibliography of bibliographies in religion,* p.286–301 (**BB1**).

Bibliografia missionaria, anno 1– . Comp. dal Giovanni Rommerskirchen [and others]. Roma, Pontificia Universitaria di Propaganda Fine, 1935– . v.1– . Annual.   **BB57**

v.1 covers Jan. 1, 1933—June 30, 1934; v.2, July 1, 1934—Dec. 31, 1935; v.10, 1943–46. Other volumes are annual, with four-year cumulated indexes.
A bibliography of Catholic missions. Classified arrangement with author and subject indexes.

Latourette, Kenneth Scott. A history of the expansion of Christianity. N.Y., Harper, 1937–45. 7v. maps.   **BB58**

A comprehensive survey of missions from the earliest times to the present, with an extensive bibliography in each volume.

Laures, Johannes. Kirishitan bunko; a manual of books and documents on the early Christian missions in Japan ... 3d rev. and enl. ed. Tokyo. Sophia Univ., 1957. 536p. il. (Monumenta nipponica monographs, no.5)   **BB59**

Subtitle: With special reference to the principal libraries in Japan and more particularly to the collection at Sophia University, Tokyo; with an appendix of ancient maps of the Far East, especially Japan.
1st ed. 1940.
"Kirishitan Bunko is a bibliography, *Kirishitan* literature, i.e. of documents (books, articles, manuscripts) relating to the Christian missions from their beginnings [in the 16th century] to the first years after the reopening of Japan to foreign intercourse" (*Foreword*), which are to be found in Japan, with indication of location.
Catholic viewpoint.

N.Y. (City) Missionary Research Library. Directory of North American Protestant foreign missionary agencies. 3d ed. N.Y., 1958. 92p.   **BB60**

1st ed. 1953.
Lists nearly 350 agencies grouped by type, with indexes by name of agency, location of headquarters, and geographical fields of service.

Streit, Robert. Bibliotheca missionum, begonnen von P. Robert Streit, fortgeführt von P. Johannes Dindinger. Freiburg, Herder, 1916–63. v.1–22. (Veröffentlichungen des Internationalen Inst. für Missionswissenschaftliche Forschung)   **BB61**

Imprint varies.

The great Catholic bibliography of missions.

Includes voyages, relations, official documents, etc. Gives full bibliographical details, critical estimates, annotations, references to sources, and (in many cases) location of copies in European libraries.

v.1, Grundlegender und allgemeiner Teil; v.2–3, Amerikanische Missionsliteratur, 1493–1699, 1700–1909; v.4–5, Asiatische Missionsliteratur, 1245–1599, 1600–1699; v.6, Missionsliteratur Indiens, der Philippinen, Japans und Indochinas, 1700–1799; v.7, Chinesische Missionsliteratur, 1700–1799; v.8, Missionsliteratur Indiens und Indonesiens, 1800–1909; v.9, Missionsliteratur der Philippinen, 1800–1909; v.10, Missionsliteratur Japans und Koreas, 1800–1909; v.11, Missionsliteratur Indochinas, 1800–1909; v.12–14, Chinesische Missionsliteratur, 1800–1884, 1885–1909, 1910–1950; v.15–20, Afrikanische Missionsliteratur, 1053–1599, 1600–1699, 1700–1879, 1880–1909, 1910–1940, t.1; v.21, Missionsliteratur von Australien und Ozeanien, 1525–1950; v.22, Grundlegender und allgemeiner Teil, 1910–1935, und Nachtrag zu Bd.1.

Statistics

National Council of the Churches of Christ in the U.S.A. Bureau of Research and Survey. Churches and church membership in the United States; an enumeration and analysis by counties, states and regions. N.Y., Council, 1956–58. Ser. A–ser. E. **BB62**

Contents: ser. A, no.1–4, Major faiths by regions, divisions, and states; ser. B, no.1–8, Denominational statistics by regions, divisions, and states; ser. C, no.1–59, Denominational statistics by states and counties; ser. D, no.1–6, Denominational statistics by metropolitan areas; ser. E, no.1–3, Socio-economic characteristics.

U.S. Bureau of the Census. Religious bodies: 1936. Wash., Govt. Prt. Off., 1941. 3v. **BB63**

v.1, Summary and detailed tables; v.2–3, Separate denominations: statistics, history, doctrine, organization, and work.

Statistics given are, as nearly as possible, those for the year 1936, and cover, for the continental United States: membership, church edifices and parsonages, value of church property and debt on same, expenditures, and Sunday schools.

Previous full reports for this century covered 1906, 1916, and 1926.

Since 1936, full reports have not been made by the Bureau of the Census, although very abbreviated statistics are given in its *Population characteristics*, P20, no.79. More detailed figures are included in the *Yearbook of American churches* (BB147).

World Christian handbook, [no.1]– . 1949– . London, World Dominion Pr., 1949– . Irregular. **BB64**

Editions published 1949, 1952, 1957, 1962.

Each edition includes survey articles and statistics on church membership for various countries of the world.

Atlases

Freitag, Anton [and others]. Atlas du monde chrétien; l'expansion du christianisme à travers les siècles. Paris, Bruxelles, Elsevier, 1959. 215p. il. 34cm. **BB65**

The historical maps (in color) are far outnumbered by the pages of photographs (of people, places, works of art) and explanatory text. Index of proper names.

Translated as:

—— The twentieth century atlas of the Christian world; the expansion of Christianity through the centuries. N.Y., Hawthorn, 1963, i.e., 1964. 199p. il. maps. 35cm. **BB66**

A pictorial atlas, from the Catholic point of view.

Gaustad, Edwin Scott. Historical atlas of religion in America. N.Y., Harper, 1962. 179p. maps, charts. 31cm. **BB67**

A work which—by maps, charts, tables, and text—shows the expansion and development of the churches and membership of the various denominations from 1650 to 1960.

Meer, Frederic van der and **Mohrmann, Christine.** Atlas of the early Christian world; tr. and ed. by Mary F. Hedlund and H. H. Rowley. London, Nelson, 1958. 215p. incl. 42 maps. il. 36cm. **BB67a**

A translation of the work originally published as the *Atlas van de oudchristelijke wereld.* Amsterdam, Elsevier, 1958. Includes 620 plates illustrating the history of Christianity for the first six centuries, covering sculpture, architecture, mosaics, Christian cities, etc. The 42 maps are the work of Prof. Van der Meer and show in great detail the various parts of the Roman Empire, with plans of important cities and regions, churches, monuments, dioceses, etc.

The text comments on the historical and geographical background and describes the illustrations.

Indexed.

Hymnology

Analecta hymnica medii aevi, hrsg. von Guido Maria Dreves und Clemens Blume. Leipzig, Reisland, 1886–1922. v.1–55. (Repr.: N.Y., Johnson Reprint Corp., 1961. v.1–55) (Also available on microcards. 55v. on 186 cards) **BB68**

A very comprehensive collection, giving texts of hymns and detailed historical and bibliographical notes.

Chevalier, Cyr Ulysse Joseph. Repertorium hymnologicum. Catalogue des chants, hymnes, proses, séquences, tropes en usage dans l'église latine depuis les origines jusqu'à nos jours. Louvain, Bruxelles, Soc. des Bollandistes, 1892–1920. 6v. (Facsimile repr.: Louvain, Lefever, 1959?) **BB69**

Published in parts as a separately paged supplement to the *Analecta bollandiana,* 1889–1920. (BB223).

For each hymn gives *incipit,* saint or feast of the church to which the hymn belongs and its place in the office, number of strophes, author's name, date of composition if known, and reference to manuscripts or printed sources in which the hymn is found.

Julian, John. A dictionary of hymnology setting forth the origin and history of Christian hymns of all ages and nations. Rev. ed. with new supplement. London, Murray; N.Y., Scribner, 1907. 1768p. (Repr.: N.Y., Dover, 1957) **BB70**

1st ed. 1892; the revised edition corrects some typographical errors and adds a new supplement of 131 pages to cover later information, and new indexes.

Contents: (1) Dictionary; (2) Cross reference index to first lines in English, French, German, Latin, etc.; (3) Index of authors, translators, etc.; (4) Appendix, A–Z, late articles; (5) Appendix, A–Z, additions and corrections to articles in main part; (6) New supplement; (7) Indexes to appendixes and supplement.

Deals with Christian hymns of all ages and nations, with special reference to those in the hymnbooks of English-speaking countries. Articles on subjects in hymnology, hymn writers, and separate hymns—all in one alphabet; important subjects are treated at considerable length. Signed articles; bibliographies.

McCutchan, Robert Guy. Hymn tune names; their sources and significance. N.Y., Nashville, Abingdon, 1957. 206p. **BB71**

An alphabetical list of the names of hymn tunes, indicating melody and time, and giving the origin and history of the name.

The Bible

Texts

☙ While the Bible is not a reference book in the ordinary sense of the term, at least one copy should be in even the small reference collection, and others should be acquired as needed. In recent years, many new translations and versions have been made directly from the original Hebrew and Greek manuscripts and based on modern archaeological discoveries. For a bibliography of English Bibles, *see* Margaret T. Hills, *The English Bible in America* (BB77).

Bible. Various versions.   **BB72**

The principal versions in English at present are:

1. *King James* or *Authorized version* (1611), still the most used Bible among Protestants.
2. *American Revised version* (1901), which differs on some points from the *English Revised version* (1885).
3. *Revised Standard version* (N.Y., Nelson, 1952). The New Testament appeared first, in 1946. Translated into modern English by a group of American scholars under the general editorship of Luther A. Weigle.
4. *New English Bible: New Testament* (N.Y., Oxford Univ. Pr. and Cambridge Univ. Pr., 1961). Undertaken to provide "a faithful rendering of the best available Greek text into current speech of our own time."—*Introd.*
5. *Douay Bible,* a translation of the Latin Vulgate, the Bible used by Roman Catholics. It differs from the Protestant Bible in the number and order of the books, and in the fact that the Apocryphal books are accepted as canonical and are interspersed with the other books in both the Old and the New Testaments.
6. *Old Testament, Confraternity edition,* "translated from the original languages . . . by members of the Catholic Biblical Association of America; sponsored by the Episcopal Committee of the Confraternity of Christian Doctrine" (Paterson, N.J., St. Anthony Guild Pr., 1952–61. v.1, 3–4.) is intended to replace the Douay Bible for the American reader.
   New Testament, Confraternity edition (a revision of the Challoner-Rheims version), first published in 1941, is available separately or in a "New Catholic edition" which combines the Old Testament in the Douay version with the Psalms and the New Testament in the Confraternity edition.
7. *Jewish version.* Good reference editions of the English translation of the Old Testament, first published in 1917, are available from the Jewish Publication Society, Philadelphia. A revised translation with modern text is in preparation.

A convenient collection of various English translations of the New Testament is the *New Testament octapla,* ed. by Luther A. Weigle (N.Y., Nelson, 1962). Versions represented are: Tyndale, Great Bible, Geneva Bible, Bishops' Bible, Rheims, King James, American Standard, Revised Standard.

Among other good modern translations of the Bible the following are notable: *Moffatt Bible.* N.Y., Harper, 1925; *Complete Bible, an American translation:* the Old Testament, tr. by J. M. Powis Smith; the Apocrypha and New Testament, tr. by Edgar J. Goodspeed. Univ. of Chicago Pr., 1939; *New Testament in modern English,* tr. by J. B. Phillips. N.Y., Macmillan, 1958; and the translation from the Latin Vulgate, by Ronald A. Knox. N.Y., Sheed & Ward, 1954, 1950.

The Apocrypha   **BB73**

Among the various editions and versions of the Apocrypha are:

1. *Apocrypha and pseudepigrapha of the Old Testament in English,* with introductions and critical and explanatory notes to the several books. 2d ed. Oxford, Univ. Pr., 1963. 1st ed. 1913.
2. *Apocrypha, according to the Authorized version,* ed. by Robert H. Pfeiffer. N.Y., Harper, 1953. 295p.
3. *Apocrypha of the Old Testament.* Revised Standard version. N.Y., Nelson, 1957. 250p.
4. *New Testament Apocrypha,* by Edgar Hennecke, ed. by William Schneemelcher. English translation by A. J. B. Higgins [and others], ed. by R. McL. Wilson. Philadelphia, Westminster, 1963– . v.1– . (In progress) v.1, Gospels and related writings; tr. from the completely revised 3d German edition.

Bibliography

British and Foreign Bible Society. Library. Historical catalogue of the printed editions of Holy Scripture in the library of the . . . Society. Comp. by T. H. Darlow and H. F. Moule. London, Bible House, 1903–11. 2v. in 4.   **BB74**

Contents: v.1, English; v.2, Polyglots and languages other than English: pt.1, Polyglots. Acawoio–Grebo; pt.2, Greek–Opa; pt.3, Ora–Zulu. Indexes.

An indispensable catalog of editions of the Bible, arranged chronologically under each language; annotated. Five indexes: (1) Languages and dialects (more than 600); (2) Translators, revisers, editors, etc.; (3) Printers, publishers, etc.; (4) Places of printing; and (5) General subjects (names of Bibles, etc.).

British Museum. Dept. of Printed Books. General catalogue of printed books. Photolithographic ed. to 1955. v.17–19: Bible. London, Museum, 1965. 3v.   **BB75**

An extensive collection of the Bible: (1) Complete editions by language, chronologically under language; (2) Selections; (3) Old Testament, followed by sections and individual books; (4) Books of the Apocrypha; (5) New Testament, sections, individual books, N.T. Apocrypha; (6) Appendix; (7) Index by language; (8) Select index of titles.

Burchard, Christoph. Bibliographie zu den Handschriften vom Toten Meer. Berlin, Alfred Töpelmann, 1957. 118p. (Beihefte zur Zeitschrift für die alttestamentliche Wissenschaft, 76)   **BB76**

A bibliography of books and periodical articles on the Dead Sea Scrolls, published 1948–55 in various languages.

Hills, Margaret Thorndike. The English Bible in America: a bibliography of editions of the Bible and the New Testament published in America, 1777–1957. N.Y., Amer. Bible Soc. and the N.Y. Pub. Lib., 1961. 477p.   **BB77**

A chronological, annotated listing of Bibles in the English language published in the United States and Canada, with indication of locations of copies. Six indexes: (1) geographical of publishers and printers; (2) alphabetical of publishers and printers; (3) translations, translators, and revisers; (4) editors and commentators; (5) edition titles; and (6) general index.

Metzger, Bruce M. Index of articles on the New Testament and the early church published in Festschriften. Philadelphia, Soc. of Biblical Literature, 1951. 182p. (Journal of Biblical literature. Monograph ser., v.5)   **BB78**

An index to some 2350 articles to be found in 640 collections of *Festschriften* published up to the end of 1950 in various languages. From these collections only articles pertinent to the subject have been included.

———— ——— Supplement. 1955. 20p.

North, Eric McCoy. The book of a thousand tongues; being some account of the translation and publication of all or part of the Holy Scriptures into more than a thousand languages and dialects with over 1100 examples from the text. Pub. for the American Bible Society. N.Y., Harper, 1938. 386p. il. **BB79**

Descriptive notes and facsimiles of extracts from printed Bibles in more than a thousand languages. Particularly useful for identifying Bibles in varying tongues, including many versions in English. Includes chronological lists of the languages in which the Bible has been published in whole or in part.

Pope, Hugh. English versions of the Bible. Rev. and ampl. by Sebastian Bullough. St. Louis, Herder, 1952. 787p. **BB80**

A history of both Catholic and Protestant versions, with a bibliography of books about the Bible.
Bibliography, p.686–718.

Rumball-Petre, Edwin A. R. America's first Bibles, with a census of 555 extant Bibles. Portland, Me., Southworth-Anthoensen Pr., 1940. 184p. **BB81**

Descriptions of America's first Bibles, with a census showing location of copies.

—— Rare Bibles: an introduction for collectors and a descriptive check list. 2d ed. N.Y., Philip C. Duschnes, 1963. 60p. **BB82**

1st ed. 1938.
An annotated bibliography of rare copies of the Bible in various languages.

San Francisco Theological Seminary, San Anselmo, California. Dept. of New Testament Literature. Graduate Seminar in New Testament. Bibliography of New Testament literature, 1900–1950. Prep. by the Graduate Seminar in New Testament (1952–1953), under the direction of John Wick Bowman . . . Ed. by Tadashi Akaishi. San Anselmo, Seminary Cooperative Store, [1953]. 312p. **BB83**

A classified, annotated bibliography of nearly 2400 books and some periodical articles in the English language.

Society for Old Testament Study. Eleven years of Bible bibliography; the book lists of the Society for Old Testament Study, 1946–56. Ed. by H. H. Rowley. Indian Hills, Colo., Falcon's Wing Pr., 1957. 804p. **BB84**

Reprints of the annual classified, annotated book lists on the Old Testament and related subjects, published by the Society for Old Testament Study, with a cumulated author index.

The annual lists comprise books published in various languages with notes written by contributing scholars. The cumulated volume is continued by the *Book list* (Durham, Eng., Soc., 1957–).

Stegmüller, Friedrich. Repertorium biblicum medii aevi. Madrid, Consejo Superior de Investigaciones Científicas, Inst. Francisco Suárez, 1940 [i.e., 1950]–61. 7v. **BB85**

Contents: v.1, Initia biblica. Apocrypha. Prologi; v.2–5, Commentaria: Auctores; v.6–7, Commentaria: Anonyma (arranged alphabetically by place of publication).

v.1 contains a long treatment of apocryphal writings (p.25–250) and a list of prefaces to the Bible (p.253–306). v.2–7 list patristic and medieval commentaries on the Bible, with *incipits* and *explicits,* editions, manuscripts, and bibliography.

Abstract journals

Internationale Zeitschriftenschau für Bibelwissenschaft und Grenzgebiete; International review of Biblical studies; Revue internationale des études bibliques, 1951/52– . Stuttgart, Verlag Katholisches Bibelwerk, 1952– . Bd.1– . Biennial. **BB86**

An international bibliography and abstract journal of Biblical studies. Classed arrangement with author indexes. Most of the abstracts are in German.

New Testament abstracts; a record of current periodical literature issued by the Theological Faculty of Weston College. Weston, Mass., 1956– . v.1– . 3 times per year. **BB87**

Presents abstracts in English of articles on the New Testament which have appeared in Catholic, Protestant, and Jewish periodicals in many languages.

Each volume includes an index of Scripture texts and an index of authors.

History

Cambridge history of the Bible: the West from the Reformation to the present day, ed. by S. L. Greenslade. Cambridge, Univ. Pr., 1963. 590p. il., plates. **BB88**

A history of the Bible, its translations into Western languages, and its various versions. Includes chapters by scholars on Continental versions to 1600 (German, Italian, French, Dutch, Spanish, East-Central European, Scandinavian); English versions, 1525–1611; the rise of modern Biblical scholarship, with discussion of modern Continental translations and English versions since 1611. Appendixes list aids to Bible study and commentaries. Bibliography, p.536–49.

A volume to precede this chronologically—*From Jerome to the Renaissance,* ed. by G. W. H. Lampe—is in preparation.

Concordances

Cruden, Alexander. Complete concordance to the Old and New Testament . . . with . . . a concordance to the Apocrypha . . . London, Warne, [pref. 1737]. 719p. **BB89**

1st ed. 1737. Frequently reprinted by various publishers. Contents: (1) Common words; (2) Proper names; (3) Aprocyphal books.

A well-known older concordance, issued in various editions by different publishers. Not complete, and now superseded, as far as the canonical books are concerned, by the later concordances noted below, but still useful for its concordance to the Apocrypha. Some modern reprints omit the Apocrypha.

Gant, William John. The Moffatt Bible concordance; a complete concordance to: The Bible, a new translation by James Moffatt. N.Y., Harper, 1950. 550p. **BB90**

Also published in London by Hodder and Stoughton with title *Concordance of the Bible in the Moffatt translation.*

Hazard, Marshall Custis. A complete concordance to the American Standard version of the Holy Bible. N.Y., Nelson, 1932. 1234p. **BB91**

Subtitle: Contains about 300,000 references, arranged under 16,000 headings and subheadings; includes the alternative marginal readings; gives the pronunciation and meaning of all proper names and places, with biographical and geographical information which make it serve as a Bible dictionary as well as a concordance.

Joy, Charles Rhind. Harper's Topical concordance. Rev. and enl. ed. N.Y., London, Harper, 1962. 628p. **BB92**

1st ed. 1940.
Some 25,000 texts arranged under more than 2100 topics, with cross references. Designed for the person looking for texts or quotations on a given subject.

Metzger, Bruce Manning and **Metzger, Isobel M.** The Oxford concise concordance to the Revised Standard version of the Holy Bible. N.Y., Oxford Univ. Pr., 1962. 158p. **BB93**

Prepared for the general reader; selection of words and passages was planned to include the most significant and noteworthy. Proper names are included in the main alphabet, and brief digests of biographical or geographical facts are often given.

Nelson's Complete concordance of the Revised Standard version Bible, comp. under the supervision of John W. Ellison. N.Y., Nelson, 1957. 2157p. **BB94**

Prepared with the help of a computer, the concordance is exhaustive, listing the context and location of each word, except for some 150 frequently used words which would seldom, if ever, be the key words in a passage.

Also, *Nelson's Concise concordance* (1961), listing the principal words.

Strong, James. Exhaustive concordance of the Bible. London, Hodder; N.Y., Hunt, 1894 [c1890]. 1340p., 262p., 126p., 79p. **BB95**

Frequently reprinted.

N.Y., Abingdon, 1963.

The most complete concordance, giving every word of the text of the King James version and a comparative concordance of the Authorized and Revised versions, also brief dictionaries of the Hebrew and Greek words of the original, with references to the English words. 47 very common words are cited in the appendix by reference only and are not given in the main concordance.

Thompson, Newton Wayland and **Stock, Raymond.** Complete concordance to the Bible (Douay version). St. Louis, London, Herder, 1945. 1914p. **BB96**

First published in 1942 under title *Concordance to the Bible* (*Douay version*).

This edition is much enlarged, with many additional words and additional references to words included in the 1st edition.

Young, Robert. Analytical concordance to the Bible . . . about 311,000 references, subdivided under the Hebrew and Greek originals with the literal meaning and pronunciation of each . . . Also index lexicons to the Old and New Testaments . . . and a complete list of Scripture proper names. 22d American ed. rev. by W. B. Stevenson. N.Y., Funk & Wagnalls, 1955. 1090p., 93p., 23p., 51p. **BB97**

1st ed. 1879; rev. ed., rev. by W. B. Stevenson, 1902; editions of later date are reprints of this, with some slight revision, and include a supplement entitled "Recent discoveries in Bible lands," by William F. Albright.

☙ The following concordances to the Latin, Greek, and Hebrew texts are useful in the large reference library:

Bechis, Michael. Repertorium biblicum, seu totius Sacrae Scripturae concordantiae juxta Vulgatae editionis exemplar. Augustae Taurinorum, in Officina Salesiana, 1899. 2v. **BB98**

A concordance to the Latin Vulgate.

Hatch, Edwin and **Redpath, Henry A.** A concordance to the Septuagint and the other Greek versions of the Old Testament (including the Apocryphal books). Oxford, Clarendon Pr., 1897–1906. 2v. and suppl. (Photomech. repr.: Graz, Akademische Druck- und Verlagsanstalt, 1954. 2v.; Supplement by Henry A. Redpath. 272p.) **BB99**

Lisowsky, Gerhard. Konkordanz zum hebräischen Alten Testament, nach dem von Paul Kahle in der Biblia hebraica edidit R. Kittel, besorgten masoretischen Text unter verantwortlicher Mitwirkung von Leonhard Rost. Stuttgart, Privilegierte Württembergische Bibelanstalt, 1958. 1672p. (Concordantiae Veteris Testamenti hebraicae atque aramaicae) **BB100**

Published in 12 Lfg. 1955–57. Follows the Masoretic text.

In Hebrew, with translation of many words into German, Latin, and English. Prefatory matter in German, Latin, and English.

Mandelkern, Salomon. Veteris Testamenti concordantiae hebraicae atque chaldaicae, quibus continentur cuncta quae in prioribus concordantiis reperiuntur vocabula, lacunis omnibus expletis, emendatis cuiusquemodi vitiis, locis ubique denuo excerptis atque in meliorem formam redactis, vocalibus interdum adscriptis, particulae omnes adhuc nondum collatae, pronomina omnia hic primum congesta atque enarrata, nomina propria omnia separatim commemorata, servato textu masoretico librorumque sacrorum ordine. Editio altera locupletissime aucta et emendata. Berlin, Margolin, 1937. 1532p., 16p. (Repr.: Jerusalem, Tel Aviv, Margolin, 1955. 2v.) **BB101**

Hebrew and Latin.

Added title page (1955): Concordance on the Bible. New ed., rev., corr., and completed by Chaim Mordecai Brecher, with supplementary corrections and notes by Abraham Avrunin. With an English introduction by Harry Freedman and incorporating *Otzar halexicografia halvrit* by A. R. Malachi.

Moulton, William Fiddian and **Geden, A. S.** Concordance to the Greek Testament, according to the texts of Westcott and Hort, Tischendorf and the English revisers. 3d ed. Edinburgh, Clark; N.Y., Scribner, 1926. 1033p. **BB102**

Quotations

Stevenson, Burton Egbert. The home book of Bible quotations. N.Y., Harper, 1949. 645p. **BB103**

Quotations are arranged under subject with many cross references, with a word concordance index to the whole. Based on the King James version, with a few references to variations in the Revised version. Includes the Apocrypha of both the Old and the New Testaments. Exact citation is given to book, chapter, and verse.

Dictionaries and handbooks

Allmen, Jean Jacques von. A companion to the Bible. N.Y., Oxford Univ. Pr., 1958. 479p. **BB104**

A translation of the author's *Vocabulaire biblique* (2. éd. Neuchâtel, Delachaux, 1956. 318p.). Prepared as a "popular manual of Biblical theology the principal ideas of which are classified alphabetically."—*Pref.* Articles are written and signed by a group of French and Swiss Protestant scholars.

Scripture quotations are from the Revised Standard version of the Bible.

Bridges, Ronald and **Weigle, Luther A.** The Bible word book concerning obsolete or archaic words in the King James version of the Bible. N.Y., Nelson, 1960. 422p. **BB105**

Prepared for the general reader; has articles on 827 obsolete or archaic words used in the King James version, the meanings of which have changed. Explains the original meanings and shows what words have been used to replace them in the Revised Standard version; with an index to the words and phrases from the Revised version.

Cheyne, Thomas Kelly and **Black, J. S.** Encyclopaedia biblica; a critical dictionary of the literary, political, and religious history, the archaeology, geography, and natural history of the Bible. N.Y., Macmillan, 1899–1903. 4v. il. **BB106**

Reprinted in 1v. on India paper, with rectification of some typographical errors, 1914.

Signed articles by specialists, with bibliographies. Prepared with the cooperation of many foreign scholars, primarily for the scholar and professional Bible student. Standpoint is that of advanced higher criticism.

Davis, John D. The Westminster dictionary of the Bible . . . rev. and rewritten, by Henry Snyder Gehman. . . . Philadelphia, Westminster Pr., 1944. 658p. il. (Westminster aids to the study of the Scriptures) **BB107**

Previously published under title *A dictionary of the Bible.* A scholarly 1v. dictionary of the Bible, conservative in interpretation. Indicates pronunciation. Concludes with a section of 16 historical maps, ed. by G. E. Wright and F. V. Filson.

Deen, Edith. All of the women of the Bible. N.Y., Harper, 1955. 410p. **BB108**

In three main sections: (1) Searching studies of women in the foreground; (2) Alphabetical listing of named women; (3) Chronological listings of nameless women in the background.

Dheilly, Joseph. Dictionnaire biblique. Tournai, Desclée, 1964. 1260p. **BB109**

Deals with Biblical themes, people, and institutions, and the history and geography of Biblical places, with references to recent archaeological research. Articles range in length from a single line to several pages.

Douglas, James Dixon [and others]. The new Bible dictionary. Bungay, Suffolk, Richard Clay; Grand Rapids, Mich., Eerdmans, 1962. 1375p. il. maps. **BB110**

2300 articles written specifically for this new dictionary by a group of British scholars (with some collaboration from scholars in other countries). Each article is signed, and many conclude with bibliographies. Will be of especial interest to the Protestant layman.

Encyclopedic dictionary of the Bible, tr. by Louis F. Hartman. N.Y., McGraw-Hill, 1963. 2634col. il. **BB111**

Subtitle: A translation and adaptation of A. van den Born's *Bijbels woordenboek.* 2d rev. ed. 1954–1957.

A Catholic Bible dictionary. Modern scholarship.

Hastings, James. Dictionary of the Bible, dealing with its language, literature, and contents, including the Biblical theology. Edinburgh, Clark; N.Y., Scribner, 1898–1904. 5v. il. **BB112**

v.5 is an "extra" volume, containing indexes, maps, and some articles not alphabetically arranged.

A standard older work with signed articles and bibliographies. From a less advanced point of view than *Cheyne* (BB106), and intended for use by the general reader as well as by the professional Bible student.

—— Dictionary of the Bible. Rev. ed. by Frederick C. Grant and H. H. Rowley. N.Y., Scribner, 1963. 1059p. il. **BB113**

1st ed. 1909. Frequently reprinted. An independent work, not a condensation of Hastings' larger work above.

This edition has been thoroughly revised in the light of modern discoveries and scholarship. References are to the Revised Standard version of the Bible with cross references from the Authorized version and the Revised version.

—— Dictionary of Christ and the Gospels. N.Y., Scribner; Edinburgh, Clark, 1906–8. 2v. il. **BB114**

Complementary to Hastings' *Dictionary of the Bible* (BB 112). Purpose is to give an account of (1) everything relating to the person, life, work, and teaching of Christ, whether found in the Gospels or elsewhere, and (2) everything contained in the Gospels. Planned especially for preachers; most of the articles are written by men who are or have been preachers. Signed articles; bibliographies.

—— Dictionary of the Apostolic church. N.Y., Scribner; Edinburgh, Clark, 1916. 2v. **BB115**

A continuation of the above, doing for the rest of the New Testament what that work did for the Gospels.

International standard Bible encyclopedia; James Orr, gen. ed. [Rev. ed.] Chicago, Howard-Severance, 1930. 5v. il. (Repr.: Grand Rapids, Mich., Eerdmans, 1960) **BB116**

Represents the conservative point of view and useful, there-fore, for readers for whom Hastings (BB112) and Cheyne (BB106) are too advanced.

Articles are signed by specialists and include bibliographies. In some cases various viewpoints by leading scholars are given on moot issues.

The interpreter's dictionary of the Bible; an illustrated encyclopedia identifying and explaining all proper names and significant terms and subjects in the Holy Scriptures, including the Apocrypha, with attention to archaeological discoveries and researches into the life and faith of ancient times. N.Y., Nashville, Abingdon, 1962. 4v. **BB117**

George Arthur Buttrick, ed.

A scholarly encyclopedic dictionary designed for the preacher, scholar, student, teacher, and general reader, based on recent discoveries and referring to both the King James version and the Revised Standard version, to the Apocrypha, the Pseudepigrapha, the Dead Sea Scrolls, and other ancient manuscripts. Articles have been contributed by scholars from many countries, are signed, and usually include bibliographies. The illustrations, both in color and in black and white, are good and pertinent, and there is a section of colored maps, as well as outline maps inserted in the text. Indispensable for modern Biblical study.

Lockyer, Herbert. All the men of the Bible: a portrait gallery and reference library of more than 3000 Biblical characters. Grand Rapids, Mich., Zondervan, 1958. 381p. **BB118**

An alphabetical listing of Biblical men, giving pronunciation and meaning of the names, Biblical citation, and, in many cases, a brief history of the character.

Miller, Madeleine Sweeney and **Miller, John Lane.** Harper's Bible dictionary. N.Y., Harper, 1952. 851p. il. **BB119**

Published in England as *Black's Bible dictionary.* London, Black, 1954.

A useful and usable, 1v., alphabetically arranged, encyclopedic dictionary, though not so comprehensive as Hastings (BB 113). Treats the archaeology, geography, and chronology of the Bible, including names of persons and places, ideas, books of the Bible, phrases, objects, etc. Pronunciation is indicated for some, but not all, difficult or unusual words or phrases. Illustrated with photographs, line drawings, and maps.

Osterloh, Edo and **Engelland, Hans.** Biblisch-theologisches Handwörterbuch zur Lutherbibel und zu neueren Übersetzungen. Mit einem Querregister. 2. durchg. und erg. Aufl. Göttingen, Vandenhoeck und Ruprecht, 1959. 752p. **BB120**

1st ed. 1954.

More than 30 persons from all branches of the Evangelical church in Germany have collaborated in the compilation of this new dictionary, based on the terminology of the Luther Bible. Many cross references are given from terms used in other German Bibles, and there is also (in Lfg. 2) a cross index of words from *Das Neue Testament deutsch,* the *Menge-Bibel,* and the *Zürcher-Bibel.* Articles vary in length from a few lines to several pages. Exact references are given for Bible citations, but there is little bibliography.

Reicke, Bo Ivar and **Rost, Leonhard.** Biblisch-historisches Handwörterbuch; Landeskunde, Geschichte, Religion, Kultur, Literatur. Göttingen, Vandenhoeck und Ruprecht, 1962–64. v.1–2. il. (In progress) **BB121**

Contents: v.1–2, A–O.

A scholarly encyclopedia with signed articles and bibliographies. Emphasis is on understanding Biblical and related terms, including personal and place-names in their historical context and in the light of recent scholarship and archaeological research. Plates, line drawings, and maps illustrate the text.

Richardson, Alan. A theological word book of the Bible. N.Y., Macmillan, 1951. 290p. **BB122**

Aims "to elucidate the distinctive meanings of the key-words of the Bible" from the theological point of view. Articles are written by specialists, mainly British, and are signed.

Steinmueller, John E. and **Sullivan, Kathryn.** Catholic Biblical encyclopedia. N.Y., Joseph F. Wagner, 1956. 2v. in 1. il. **BB123**

Contents: Old Testament, introd. by Athanasius Miller. 1956. 1163p.; New Testament, introd. by the late James M. Vosté. 1950. 679p., xiiip.

The second part was originally published separately. Intended "for the great majority of educated people" rather than for the Biblical specialist. Articles vary in length from a few lines to several pages, and include biographical, geographical, archaeological, and dogmatic subjects. Pronunciation is indicated. A special chapter on Mariology is appended to the volume.

Theological dictionary of the New Testament, ed. by Gerhard Kittel. Tr. and ed. by Geoffrey W. Bromiley. Grand Rapids, Mich., Eerdmans, 1964– . v.1–2. (In progress) **BB124**

Tr. from *Theologisches Wörterbuch zum Neuen Testament.*

v.1–2, A–Eta.

Vigouroux, Fulcran Grégoire and **Pirot, Louis.** Dictionnaire de la Bible, contenant tous les noms de personnes, de lieux, de plantes, d'animaux mentionnés dans les Saintes Écritures, les questions théologiques, archéologiques, scientifiques relatives à l'Ancien et au Nouveau Testament et des notices sur les commentateurs anciens et modernes. Paris, Letouzey, 1907–63. 5v. and supp. v.1–7¹⁻³ (fasc.36–38). il. (In progress) **BB125**

v.1–5, A–Z. 1907–12; Supplement, ed. by Louis Pirot [and others], v.1–7¹⁻³, A–Pentateuque. 1928–63.

The standard Bible dictionary from the French Catholic point of view, containing long, signed articles by Catholic scholars, good bibliographies, and excellent illustrations. Differs from Hastings' *Dictionary of the Bible* (BB112) and Cheyne's *Encyclopaedia biblica* (BB106) on several points, notably in the inclusion of separate biographical articles, with bibliographies, on the various commentators on the Bible: ancient, modern, Catholic, Protestant, and Jewish.

Walker, Winifred. All the plants of the Bible. N.Y., Harper, 1957. 244p. il. **BB126**

Illustrated by photographs giving the English, Latin, and Hebrew names for each plant, Biblical reference, characteristics, and lore.

Commentaries

Anchor Bible. Garden City, N.Y., Doubleday, 1964– . v.1– . (In progress) **BB127**

To be in 38v.

Contents: v.1, Genesis, tr. by E. A. Speiser. 1964; v.15, Job, tr. by Marvin H. Pope. 1964; v.21, Jeremiah, tr. by John Bright. 1965; v.37, The epistles of James, Peter and Jude, tr. by Bo Reicke. 1964.

A project of Protestant, Catholic, and Jewish scholars. New translations of the books of the Bible with extensive commentary.

Eiselen, Frederick Carl, Lewis, Edwin and **Downey, David G.** Abingdon Bible commentary. N.Y., Abingdon, 1929. 1452p. maps. **BB128**

The general introductory chapters, and those on each book of the Bible, have been written by specialists from various parts of the English-speaking world.

Grant, Frederick Clifton. Nelson's Bible commentary, based on the Revised Standard version. N.Y., Nelson, 1962– . v.4, 6–7. (In progress) **BB129**

Announced contents: v.1, The Hexateuch, by Cuthbert A.

Simpson; v.2, The historical books, by Norman W. Porteus; v.3, The poetical books, by James Muilenburg; v.4, The prophets, by Emil G. Kraeling. 1963; v.5, The Apocrypha, by Allen Wikgren; v.6, The New Testament, by Frederick C. Grant: The Gospels and the Acts of the Apostles. 1962; v.7, The Letters and the Revelation to John. 1962.

International critical commentary on the Holy Scriptures, under the editorship of the Rev. Samuel Rolles Driver, the Rev. Alfred Plummer and the Rev. Charles Augustus Briggs. Edinburgh, Clark; N.Y., Scribner, 1896–1937. v.1–45. **BB130**

Commentaries on individual books of the Bible, each by an authority.

Interpreter's Bible: The Holy Scriptures in the King James and Revised Standard versions with general articles and introduction, exegesis, exposition for each book of the Bible. N.Y., Nashville, Abingdon, 1951–57. 12v. **BB131**

A guide and commentary to the Bible by some 125 scholars, prepared for the general reader, the teacher, and the preacher. Includes long introductions with bibliographies to the whole Bible, to each Testament, and to each book. Each is written and signed by an individual scholar. The working page is in three parts: (1) at the top, the King James version and the Revised Standard version are side by side; (2) in the center of the page is the Exegesis; (3) at the bottom of the page is the Exposition.

The layman's Bible commentaries. London, SCM Pr., 1960–65. 25v. **BB132**

Prepared by Protestant scholars; presents clearly written commentaries on each book of the Bible. Aimed at the layman.

Moffatt New Testament commentary, based on the new translation by James Moffatt. N.Y., Harper, 1927–50. 17v. **BB133**

Scholarly commentaries, in readable style, on each book of the New Testament.

Neil, William. Harper's Bible commentary. N.Y., Harper, 1962. 544p. **BB134**

A companion work to *Harper's Bible dictionary.* Designed to be read with both the Revised Standard version and the King James version. An excellent 1v. commentary.

First published in England with title *One volume Bible commentary.* 1962.

Orchard, Bernard. A Catholic commentary on Holy Scripture. Ed. Committee, Dom Bernard Orchard [and others]. London, N.Y., Thomas Nelson, 1953. 1312p. maps. **BB135**

Based on the current Douay version but designed to be read with any other translation. Includes general introductory articles to the whole work, to the Old Testament, and to the New Testament, each signed by a scholar. The commentaries are also signed. Selective bibliographies include works by Catholic and non-Catholic authors. An extensive index.

Peake's Commentary on the Bible. Gen. ed. and New Testament ed., Matthew Black. Old Testament ed., H. H. Rowley. London, N.Y., Nelson, 1962. 1126p. maps. **BB136**

1st ed. by Arthur Samuel Peake. 1919: Supplement. 1936.

The new edition is brought up to date in the light of modern discoveries and scholarship and is based on the Revised Standard version. Contributions are by specialists from the British Commonwealth and the United States.

Hebrew interpretation

Encyclopaedia biblica [Entsiqlopëdiyah Miqrä'ït]; thesaurus rerum bibliocarum alphabetico ordine. Digestus ... Hierosolymis, Sumptibus Inst. Bialik, 1950–58. v.1–3. il. (In progress) **BB137**

The product of modern Hebrew scholarship, this new Bible encyclopedia is being published under the auspices of the Jewish Agency of Palestine and the Museum of Jewish Antiquities of the Hebrew University in Jerusalem. The contributors are, for the most part, Israeli scholars and are authorities in their fields. The articles, written entirely in modern literary Hebrew, are signed with initials, and usually are accompanied by bibliographies which list books both in Hebrew and in western European languages.

Kasher, Menahem M. Encyclopedia of Biblical interpretation, a millenial anthology. Tr. under the editorship of Rabbi Dr. Harry Freedman. N.Y., Amer. Biblical Encyclopedia Soc., 1953–62. v.1–5. (In progress)   **BB138**

v.1–5 treat Genesis I–XLIV.

A monumental collection of Jewish interpretations of the Bible, giving an anthology of passages drawn from the Talmudic-Midrashic literature pertaining to each verse of the Bible, with indication of sources, and a commentary containing exegetical passages from ancient and modern sources with notes and subject indexes.

Atlases

Grollenberg, Luc H. Atlas of the Bible. Tr. and ed. by Joyce M. H. Reid and H. H. Rowley. [London], N.Y., Nelson, 1956. 165p. il., maps.   **BB139**

A translation of the 2d Dutch edition, *Atlas van de Bijbel* (Amsterdam, Elsevier, 1954), published with Catholic imprimatur. A scholarly work, with a wealth of illustrations and a text summarizing Biblical history, geography, and archaeology, including a discussion of the Dead Sea Scrolls. 35 maps, well conceived and executed. A gazetteer index contains the names of geographical features, towns, and peoples, and the names of individuals who played especially important roles in Biblical history.

Kraeling, Emil Gottlieb Heinrich. Rand McNally Bible atlas. Chicago, Rand McNally, [c1956]. 487p. il., maps.   **BB140**

For the general reader. The extensive text is primarily a historical discussion of geographical references in the Bible, told in the sequence of the Books of the Bible with archaeological and historical background. Many illustrations in black and white and a section of 22 maps in the center of the volume, with a geographical index to the place-names appearing on the maps and in the text.

—— Rand McNally historical atlas of the Holy Land. Chicago, 1959. 88p. il., maps. 26cm.   **BB141**

An abridged edition of the above.

May, Herbert Gordon. Oxford Bible atlas . . . with the assistance of R. W. Hamilton and G. N. S. Hunt. London, N.Y., Oxford Univ. Pr., 1962. 144p. il., maps.   **BB142**

A well-illustrated work with attractive maps, textual explanations, etc. The text is not so extensive as in the Rand McNally; Westminster; or Grollenberg atlases, but it is a useful, inexpensive atlas.

Smith, George Adam. Atlas of the historical geography of the Holy Land. London, Hodder, 1915. 60p., 12p. 57 col. maps. 38cm.   **BB143**

A standard, older atlas, still useful for its excellent maps although not abreast of modern scholarship.

Wright, George Ernest and **Filson, Floyd Vivian.** The Westminster historical atlas to the Bible. Rev. ed. Philadelphia, Westminster, 1956. 130p. il., maps.   **BB144**

1st ed. 1945.

A scholarly atlas, with much archaeological information, historical discussion, and illustrations. The maps are clear and well drawn. Three indexes: (1) to the text; (2) to the maps, including a topographical concordance to the Bible; and (3) to Arabic names identified with Biblical places in Syria and Palestine.

Protestant denominations

General

Handbooks

Mead, Frank Spencer. Handbook of denominations in the United States. 2d rev. ed. N.Y., Abingdon, 1961. 272p.   **BB145**

1st ed. 1951.

Attempts to give brief, impartial accounts of the various religious bodies in the United States, including history, doctrines, present membership, etc.

Yearbooks

Annuaire protestant, 1880–   ; La France protestante et le Protestantisme de langue française. Paris, Fischbacher, 1880–   . v.1–   . Annual.   **BB146**

Subtitle varies.

Directory and institutional information; no biography.

Yearbook of American churches, 1916–   . Pub. by the National Council of the Churches of Christ in the U.S.A. N.Y., 1916–   . Annual.   **BB147**

Editor since 1952, B. Y. Landis.

Title, publisher, and frequency vary. v.1–2, *Federal Council year book;* v.3–8, *Year book of the churches;* v.9 (1927), *Handbook of the churches.* Now covers the organizations and activities of all faiths. Some issues contain a biographical section.

❧ Many denominations publish annuals and/or directories; only a few of the larger denominations are listed here, and many of these have been formed by mergers of various bodies. For information about other denominations *see* the *Yearbook of American churches* (BB147), and the annual reports or yearbooks of individual denominations; the latter are useful for denominational facts and figures, lists of ministers, etc.

Baptist

Encyclopedia of Southern Baptists. Nashville, Broadman, 1958. 2v. il.   **BB148**

Signed articles with bibliographies, including many biographical sketches. Covers the history, method, and work of the Southern Baptists including organizations, institutions, colleges, newspapers, etc., as well as articles on their viewpoint on religious beliefs and practices.

Starr, Edward Caryl. A Baptist bibliography, being a register of printed material by and about Baptists, including works written against the Baptists. Rochester, N.Y., Amer. Baptist Historical Soc., 1947–64. v.1–9. (In progress)   **BB149**

Imprint varies.

v.1–9, A–Halko.

Arranged alphabetically by author, with an index in each volume to joint authors, translators, Baptist publishers, distinctive titles, and subjects. Locates copies.

Whitley, William Thomas. A Baptist bibliography; being a register of the chief materials for Baptist history, whether in manuscript or in print, preserved in Great Britain, Ireland, and the Colonies . . . comp. for the Baptist Union of Great Britain and Ireland. London, Kingsgate Pr., 1916–22. 2v.   **BB150**

v.1, 1526–1776; v.2, 1777–1837. Addenda, 1613–53. Indexes: (1) Anonymous pamphlets, (2) Authors, (3) Places, (4) Subjects.

Locates copies in 31 libraries, mainly British.

Yearbooks

American Baptist Convention. Yearbook, 1950– . Philadelphia, Amer. Baptist Pub. Soc., 1950– . il. Annual. (1964/65)   **BB151**

Previously published as *Yearbook* of the Northern Baptist Convention, combining its *Annual* and the *American Baptist year book.*

Name changed from Northern Baptist Convention in 1950.

Includes minutes of the annual conventions; historical documents and tables; directories of councils and committees; cooperating, affiliated, and associated organizations; and churches, ministers, and missionaries.

Southern Baptist Convention. Executive Committee. Annual. Nashville, Tenn., 1847?– . Annual (Biennial until 1866). (v.107, 1964)   **BB152**

Includes statistics, directory information, etc.

Church of England

Yearbooks

Church of England. National Assembly. Official year book, 1883– . London, Soc. for Promoting Christian Knowledge, 1883– . Annual.   **BB153**

Title varies. Cover title: *Church of England year book.*

General directory information. Gives brief biographies of members of the church assembly.

Crockford's Clerical directory, 1858– . Oxford, Univ. Pr., 1858– . v.1– . il. Annual.   **BB154**

Subtitle varies. For 1961/62: A reference book of the clergy of the Church of England and of other churches in communion with the See of Canterbury.

Includes biographical sketches for Church of England clergy in the British Isles and overseas, as well as statistical and directory information.

History

LeNeve, John. Fasti ecclesiae anglicanae; or, A calendar of the principal ecclesiastical dignitaries in England and Wales, and of the chief officers in the universities of Oxford and Cambridge, from the earliest time to the year MDCCXV . . . corrected and continued to the present time by T. Duffus Hardy. Oxford, Univ. Pr., 1854. 3v.   **BB155**

Lists of ecclesiastical dignitaries, bishops, archdeacons, prebendaries, etc. arranged by diocese, with alphabetical indexes of names. Some biographical information. + *alunei directories*

—— Fasti ecclesiae anglicanae, 1300–1541. London, Univ. of London, Inst. of Historical Research, Athlone Pr., 1962–65. v.1–11. (In progress)

Ollard, Sidney Leslie, Crosse, Gordon and **Bond, M. F.** Dictionary of English church history. [3d ed. rev.] London, Mowbray; N.Y., Morehouse, 1948. 698p.   **BB156**

1st ed. 1912; 2d ed. 1919.

Scope of this work is strictly that of the English church, i.e., the provinces of Canterbury and York, and does not include discussion of the church in Ireland, Scotland, or America. Good signed articles with brief bibliographies (usually undated) on history, beliefs, controversies, architecture, costume, music, etc., of the church. Many biographies of persons deceased. A special feature is the list of bishops under the name of each see. High Church point of view.

Book of Common Prayer

Church of England. Book of Common Prayer. The Book of common prayer and administration of the sacraments, and other rites and ceremonies of the church according to the use of the Church of England. . . . Oxford, Univ. Pr.   **BB157**

For editions *see* current issues of the *Oxford Bible catalogue* of the Oxford University Press.

—— Annotated Book of common prayer, being an historical, ritual and theological commentary on the devotional system of the Church of England by John Henry Blunt. New impression, 1899; reissue, with additions and corrections. London, Longmans, 1903 [pref. 1883]. 732p.   **BB158**

Bibliography

Benton, Josiah Henry. The Book of common prayer and books connected with its origin and growth; catalogue of the collection of Josiah Henry Benton. . . . 2d ed. prep. by William Muss-Arnolt. Boston, priv. pr., 1914. 142p.   **BB159**

A collection of books of common prayer of the Churches of England, Ireland, and Scotland; the Protestant Episcopal church of the United States; and others.

Muss-Arnolt, William. The Book of common prayer among the nations of the world; . . . a study based mainly on the collection of Josiah Henry Benton. London, Soc. for Promoting Christian Knowledge, 1914. 473p. **BB160**

Subtitle: . . . a history of translations of the prayer book of the Church of England and of the Protestant Episcopal church of America.

Dictionaries

Harford, George and **Stevenson, Morley.** The Prayer book dictionary. London, Pitman, 1912. 832p.   **BB161**

Treats principally the English prayer book, with slight information about the prayer book of the Protestant Episcopal church.

An alphabetical dictionary dealing with the "origins, history, use and teaching of the several authorized editions of the Book of Common Prayer . . . all accompanying ceremonies and supplementary rites . . . [etc.]"—*Introd.*

Church of Ireland

Phillips, Walter Alison. History of the Church of Ireland, from the earliest times to the present day. Oxford, Univ. Pr., 1933–34. 3v.   **BB162**

Bibliography in each volume.

Church of Scotland

Macgregor, Malcolm B. The sources and literature of Scottish church history. Glasgow, McCallum, 1934. 260p.   **BB163**

An annotated bibliography of sources and secondary materials. Includes biographical sketches of outstanding persons in Scottish religious history from the earliest times to the present.

Scott, Hew. Fasti ecclesiae scoticanae; the succession of ministers in the Church of Scotland from the Reformation. New ed., rev. and continued to the present time under the superintendence of a committee appointed by the General Assembly. Edinburgh, Oliver and Boyd, 1915–28. 7v.; v.8, 1950.   **BB164**

1st ed. 1866–71; 3v. in 6.

v.1–7 cover from 1560–1914. A brief historical sketch of each minister is given, with a list of his writings and bibliographical references where such are available. Each volume has a bibliography of local and parish histories. Number of biographies is more than 15,000.

v.8 is a supplementary volume, covering 1914–28, and addenda and corrigenda, 1560–1949.

Congregational

See United Church of Christ, p.218.

Disciples of Christ

See United Church of Christ, p.218.

Friends, Society of

Quaker records; being an index to "The annual monitor," 1813–92, containing over 20,000 obituary notices of members of the Society of Friends, alphabetically and chronologically arranged. Ed. by Joseph J. Green. London, Hicks, 1894. 458p. il. **BB165**

Gives name, residence, year of death, age at death, and reference to the obituary in *The annual Monitor.*

Smith, Joseph. Descriptive catalogue of Friends' books, or books written by members of the Society of Friends . . . from their first rise to the present time . . . with critical remarks and occasional biographical notices. London, J. Smith, 1867. 2v. **BB166**

—————— Supplement. London, Hicks, 1893. 364p.

An alphabetical catalog of books about Quakers, or written by Quakers, including "all writings by authors before joining, and by those after having left the society." Full entries, sometimes with annotations. Many biographical notes.

—————— Bibliotheca anti-Quakeriana; or, A catalogue of books adverse to the Society of Friends, alphabetically arranged, with biographical notices of the authors, together with the answers which have been given to some of them. . . . London, J. Smith, 1873. 474p. **BB167**

Includes the definitive "Muggletonian" bibliography (on Ludowick Muggleton, an English sectarian and critic of Quakerism).

—————— Bibliotheca Quakeristica, a bibliography of miscellaneous literature relating to the Friends (Quakers), chiefly written by persons not members of their society; also of publications by authors in some way connected; and biographical notices. London, J. Smith, 1883. 32p. **BB168**

Lutheran

Lutheran cyclopedia. Erwin L. Lueker, ed. in chief. St. Louis, Mo., Concordia Pub. House, 1954. 1160p. **BB169**

A general religious encyclopedia prepared under the auspices of the General Literature Board of the Lutheran Church, but not restricted to matters concerning Lutheranism. Includes articles on Bible interpretation, systematized theology, church history, biography, archaeology, life and worship in the church, etc. Although biographies of persons of many denominations and periods are included, it is particularly strong in Lutherans. For the most part, living persons are omitted.

American Lutheran Church. Yearbook, 1961– . Minneapolis, Augsburg Pub. House, 1960– . Annual. **BB170**

Statistical and directory information.

Corporate body organized in 1960, combined the American Lutheran Church, the Evangelical Lutheran Church, and the United Evangelical Lutheran Church.

Mennonite

Bender, Harold Stauffer. Two centuries of American Mennonite literature, a bibliography of Mennonitica Americana, 1727–1928. Goshen, Ind., Mennonite Historical Soc., Goshen College, 1929. 181p. incl. facsims. (Studies in Anabaptist and Mennonite history, no.1) **BB171**

Chronologically arranged by date of publication under the distinct groups of Mennonites, with author and title indexes.

The Mennonite encyclopedia; a comprehensive reference work on the Anabaptist-Mennonite movement. Scottdale, Pa., Mennonite Pub. House, 1955–59. 4v. il. **BB172**

Index of titles issued in lithographed form. 1960. 132p.

Treats historical and contemporary topics relating to the Anabaptist-Mennonite movement from its beginning in the 16th century to the present time. Covers theology, ethics, history, and biography with special emphasis on existing and extinct congregations and institutions. Articles vary in length from a few lines to several columns, are signed, and include bibliographies.

Mennonitisches Lexikon, hrsg. von Christian Hege und Christian Neff. Frankfort am Main, Authors, 1913–64. v.1–4. (incompl.). (In progress) **BB173**

v.1–3, A–R; v.4 (Lfg. 43/44–51/52), S–Wehrlostigkeit.

Signed articles with bibliographies.

Methodist

Methodist Church. Dept. of Research and Statistics. General minutes of the annual conferences. Evanston, Ill., 1940?– . **BB174**

Statistical and directory information.

Corporate body was formed in 1939 by a merger of the Methodist Episcopal Church; the Methodist Episcopal Church, South; and the Methodist Protestant Church.

Presbyterian

United Presbyterian Church in the United States of America. General Assembly. Minutes of the General Assembly. Philadelphia, 1958– . **BB175**

Since the 6th ser., v.1, 1958, the *Minutes* have been published in three volumes: v.1, Journals; v.2, Annual reports; v.3, Statistics, including the synod and presbytery rolls (useful for its statistical and directory information).

Corporate body united (1958) the Presbyterian Church in the U.S.A. and the United Presbyterian Church of North America.

Protestant Episcopal

Yearbooks

Clerical directory of the Protestant Episcopal church in the United States of America. N.Y., Church Hymnal Corp., 1898– . **BB176**

Previous titles: *Lloyd's Clerical directory* and *Stowe's Clerical directory.*

Contains biographical sketches of the clergymen of the Protestant Episcopal church throughout the world; issued approximately every third year.

None issued between 1941 and 1947.

The Episcopal church annual, 1830– . N.Y., Morehouse-Gorham Co., 1830– . Annual. **BB177**

Established in 1830 as *The churchman's almanac;* 1882–1952, *The living church annual.* Title varies somewhat through the years. In 1953 assumed the present title.

General directory and institutional information, with clergy list.

Book of Common Prayer

❧ The *Book of common prayer* of the Protestant Episcopal Church of the United States was adopted after the

Revolution and put into use in 1790. There have been two revisions: in 1892 and in 1928. The 1928 revision made numerous changes in arrangement of material, the addition of new prayers, and the rewriting of others. In 1934 a standardized paging was approved for the main part of the book, i.e., from Morning Prayer to the end of the Articles of Religion. In 1943, additional material was added to the prefatory paging, which uses roman numerals. The *Index* noted below (BB178) is based on these latest revisions.

Pepper, George Wharton. An analytical index to the Book of common prayer; and a brief account of its evolution. Together with a revision of Gladstone's Concordance to the Psalter. Philadelphia. Winston, 1948. 251p.   **BB178**

Based on the 1928 revision, with the prefatory matter paged according to the resolution of 1943 and the remainder upon the pagination provided for by the resolution of 1934.

Includes a table showing the principal changes in the Psalter made in the revision of 1928, and a concordance to the Psalter.

Protestant Episcopal Church in the U.S.A. Book of Common Prayer. Book of common prayer and administration of the sacraments and other rites and ceremonies of the church, according to the use of the Protestant Episcopal church in the United States of America, together with the Psalter or Psalms of David. N.Y., Oxford Univ. Pr., 1944. 611p.   **BB179**

The latest revision, adopted 1928, paged according to the Standard prayer book.

For other editions *see* current issue of the *Oxford Bible catalogue* of the Oxford University Press.

Reformed

Corwin, Charles Edward. Manual of the Reformed Church in America (formerly Reformed Protestant Dutch Church) 1628–1933. 5th ed. rev. N.Y., Board of Publ. of the Reformed Church in America, 1922–33. 782p. and suppl., 60p. il.   **BB180**

1st–4th eds. by Edward Tanjore Corwin.

Not a dictionary, but contains a large amount of useful reference information; especially helpful for its biographies.

Contents: pt.1, History of the Reformed Church in America; pt.2, The ministry, biographical sketches alphabetically arranged, with bibliographies, and many references to biographies in earlier editions, p.235–606; pt.3, Churches, alphabetically arranged. Appendix: chronological list of ministers 1628–1922, chronological list of churches; Supplement, 1923–33.

United Church of Christ

Dexter, Henry Martyn. The Congregationalism of the last 300 years, as seen in its literature . . . with a bibliographical appendix. N.Y., Harper, 1880. 716p., 326p.   **BB181**

Includes *Collections toward a bibliography of Congregationalism.* 326p. 7250 entries.

The bibliography is still the most extensive one on Congregationalism.

Peel, Albert. The Congregational two hundred, 1530–1948. London, Independent Pr., 1948. 288p.   **BB182**

Incorporates *A hundred eminent Congregationalists,* 1927.

Biographical sketches of 200 outstanding Congregationalists in England and America.

Spencer, Claude Elbert. An author catalog of Disciples of Christ and related religious groups. Canton, Mo., Disciples of Christ Historical Soc., 1946. 367p.   **BB183**

A catalog of works on many subjects by members of the Disciples of Christ. Gives dates and places of birth and death of the authors, when known.

United Church of Christ. Yearbook. Philadelphia, Church, 1962– . (1964, statistics for 1963)   **BB184**

Statistical and directory information.

Corporate body united, in 1957, the Congregational Christian churches with the Evangelical and Reformed Church. Continues the *Yearbook* of the Congregational Christian churches, which had been a continuation of the *Congregational yearbook* and the *Christian annual.*

Roman Catholic church

Bibliography

Ellis, John Tracy. A guide to American Catholic history. Milwaukee, Bruce, 1959. 147p.   **BB185**

A classified, annotated list of nearly 800 titles, including dissertations. Supplementary sections give manuscript depositories, historical associations, and relevant periodicals. Author, title, and subject index.

Guide to Catholic literature, 1888–1940. Detroit, Romig, 1940. 1240p.   **BB186**

Issued in 5 pts., A–Z.

Subtitle: An author-subject-title index in one straight alphabet of books and booklets, in all languages, on all subjects by Catholics or of particular Catholic interest, published or reprinted during the fifty-two years, January 1, 1888 to January 1, 1940, with more than a quarter of a million biographical, descriptive, and critical notes, each with complete reference to its authoritative source for further reference, reading, and study.

Under the author entry, material is entered in this order: (1) biography of the author, (2) books by him, (3) books and appreciable parts of books about him and his works, and (4) magazine articles about him and his works. Critical annotations and brief extracts from reviews, with exact citations, are included. Subject and title entries are cross references to the author entry.

—— v.2– , 1940– , . . . ed. by Walter Romig. Detroit, Romig, [1945–].

Annual volumes cumulate every four years into quadrennial supplements.

On the same plan as the basic volume.

Parsons, Wilfrid. Early Catholic Americana; a list of books and other works by Catholic authors in the United States, 1729–1830. . . . N.Y., Macmillan, 1939. 282p.   **BB187**

Includes 1187 numbered entries, in chronological arrangement, with author index. Locates copies.

Supersedes, except for the notes and comment, the *Bibliotheca Catholica Americana* of J. M. Finotti (1872).

Bowe, Forrest. List of additions and corrections to Early Catholic Americana. Contribution of French translations (1724–1820). N.Y., Franco-Americana, 1952. 101p. il.   **BB188**

A supplement of French translations to Parsons above.

Regis, *Sister.* The Catholic bookman's guide; a critical evaluation of Catholic literature. N.Y., Hawthorn, 1962. 638p.   **BB188a**

For full information *see* AA270.

Vollmar, Edward R. The Catholic church in America: an historical bibliography. 2d ed. New Brunswick, N.J., Scarecrow, 1963. 399p.   **BB189**

Lists, alphabetically by author, books and periodical articles covering the period 1850–1961, including master's essays and doctoral dissertations dealing with the history of the Catholic church in America. Only theses from the regular degree-granting Catholic colleges have been included. Subject index.

Liturgy and ritual

✤ "The official books of the Roman Rite are seven— the Missal, Pontifical, Breviary, Ritual, Caerimoniale Episcoporum, Memoriale Rituum, and Martyrology. These contain all and only the liturgical services of this rite. Several repeat matter also found in others . . . (a) The Roman Missal (*Missale Romanum*) [contains the rites for the celebration of the Mass] . . . (b) The Pontifical (*Pontificale Romanum*) is the bishop's-book . . . (c) The Breviary (*Breviarium Romanum*) contains all the Divine Office without chant . . . (d) The Ritual (*Rituale Romanum*) contains all the services a priest needs besides those of the Missal and Breviary . . . (e) The Ceremonial of Bishops (*Caerimoniale Episcoporum*) in spite of its title contains much matter needed by other people than bishops. It is entirely a book of rubrical directions. . . . Much of it is already contained in the Missal, Pontifical and Ritual . . . (f) The Memorial of Rites (*Memoriale Rituum*) or Little Ritual (*Rituale parvum*) . . . gives directions for certain rites (the blessing of candles, ashes, palms, the Holy Week services) in small churches where there are no ministers (deacon and subdeacon) . . . (g) The Martyrology (*Martyrologium Romanum*) is an enlarged calendar giving the names and very short accounts of all saints (not only martyrs) commemorated in various places each day."—"Liturgical books," *Catholic encyclopedia* 9:300–302.

For fuller description of these books *see* the above article in the *Catholic encyclopedia* (BB201). For ordinary reference purposes, complete editions of four of these books, although not covering the whole rite of the Church, are adequate for most questions. Good editions of these four are the following:

Catholic Church. Liturgy and Ritual. Breviary. Breviarium Romanum ex decreto Sacrosancti Concilii Tridentini restitutum S. Pii V Pontificis Maximi jussu editum aliorumque pontificum cura recognitum Pii Papae X, auctoritate reformatum. Editio vigesima juxta typicam. Rome, Paris, Deslée & Soch, 1948. 4v.   **BB190**

Issued in four unnumbered volumes covering the four seasons, i.e., *Pars verna* (spring); *Pars aestiva* (summer); *Pars autumnalis* (autumn); *Pars hiemalis* (winter).

Only editions since 1908 contain the revised forms now in use. For historical questions, older editions treating older forms will have to be used.

—— Roman breviary in English, restored by the Sacred Council of Trent . . . Ed. by Joseph A. Nelson. N.Y., Benziger, [1950–51]. 4v.   **BB191**

Catholic Church. Liturgy and Ritual. Ritual. Rituale Romanum Pauli V Pontificis Maximi jussu editum, aliorumque pontificum cura recognitum, atque auctoritate Ssmi D. N. Pii Papae XI ad normam codicis juris canonici accommodatum; cui accedit benedictionum et instructionum appendix. Editio quinta post typicam. Turonibus, Typ. A. Mame; N.Y., Benziger, 1928. 710p., 29p. **BB192**

Gives the complete Latin text. A usable edition of selections only—with text in Latin, English, French, and German —is *The sacristy manual*, containing the portions of the Roman ritual most frequently used in parish church functions; comp. by Rev. Paul Griffith. Baltimore, Murphy, [c1905]. 80p.

—— The Roman ritual, in Latin and English . . . tr. and ed. . . . by Philip T. Weller. Milwaukee, Bruce, [1947–52]. 3v.   **BB193**

Catholic Church. Liturgy and Ritual. Missal. English. Saint Andrew Bible missal. Prep. by a missal commission of St. Andrew's Abbey. Bruges, Biblica, 1962. 1535p. **BB194**

Catholic Church. Liturgy and Ritual. Martyrology. English. The Roman martyrology, in which are to be found the eulogies of the saints and blessed approved by the Sacred Congregation of Rites up to 1961. An English tr. from the 4th edition after the typical edition (1956) approved by Pope Benedict XV (1922). Ed. by J. B. O'Connell. London, Burns & Oates; Westminster, Md., Newman Pr., [1962]. 412p.   **BB195**

Bohatta, Hanns. Bibliographie der Breviere, 1501–1850. Leipzig, Hiersemann, 1937. 349p.   **BB196**

A bibliography of breviaries, including Roman breviaries and those of the various orders. Indexes by title, date, printer or publisher, and place of publication.

—— Bibliographie der Livres d'Heures (Horae B.M.V.), officia, hortuli animae, coronae B.M.V., rosaria und cursus B.M.V., des XV. und XVI. Jahrhunderts. 2. verm. Aufl. Wien, Gilhofer & Ranschburg, 1924. 92p. **BB197**

An annotated, classified list of Books of Hours of the 15th and 16th centuries.

Britt, Matthew. A dictionary of the Psalter, containing the vocabulary of the Psalms, hymns, canticles and miscellaneous prayers of the breviary Psalter. N.Y., Benziger, 1928. 299p.   **BB198**

A dictionary of the Latin words, with English equivalents, and quotations given in each language. Concerned primarily with the Vulgate text, but translations of the Hebrew text are given when they throw light on obscure terms in the Vulgate text.

Weale, William Henry James. Bibliographia liturgica; catalogus missalium, ritus latini ab anno MCCCCLXXIV impressorum, iterum edidit H. Bohatta. London, Quaritch, 1928. 380p.   **BB199**

A listing of Latin missals by: pt.1, place-name; pt.2, order. Chronological and typographical indexes.

History

Ellis, John Tracy. Documents of American Catholic history. [2d ed.] Milwaukee, Bruce, 1962. 667p.   **BB200**

A documentary source book, reprinting documents from 1493 to 1961, with references to sources.

Encyclopedias

Catholic encyclopedia; an international work of reference on the constitution, doctrine, discipline and history of the Catholic church. N.Y., Catholic Encyclopedia Pr., [c1907–22]. 17v. il.   **BB201**

v.1–15, A–Z. Errata; v.16, Additional articles. Index; v.17, Supplement.

Authoritative work with long, signed articles by specialists, and good bibliographies and illustrations. Very useful for many questions on subjects in medieval literature, history, philosophy, art, etc., as well as for questions of Catholic doctrine, history, biography. The standard work in English, but for very full information it is often not so complete as the great French Catholic works, and now somewhat out of date.

Need for a revision was felt, and, in 1936, v.1 of a revised and enlarged edition was published by the Gilmary Society in New York, but no more volumes have appeared.

—— Supplement II. Ed. by Vincent C. Hopkins. N.Y., Gilmary Soc., 1950– . Loose-leaf.

Supplement II also called v.18.

A record of events since the original publication in 1913 and the first Supplement in 1922. Consists of signed articles by scholars from many countries, dealing largely with events arranged by country. Other articles treat special dogmas, orders, persons, etc. Usually include bibliography.

Dictionnaire de théologie catholique contenant l'esposé des doctrines de la théologie catholique, leurs preuves et leur histoire, commencé sous la direction de A. Vacant et E. Mangenot continué sous celle de É. Amann. . . . Paris, Letouzey, 1909–50. 15v. il.   **BB202**

Authoritative; long, signed articles and excellent bibliographies. More exhaustive in treatment than the *Catholic encyclopedia* (BB201). Good for topics and names in scholastic and medieval philosophy. More recent information on topics treated in the earlier volumes is frequently given under allied subjects in later volumes.

—— Table analytique, t.1–9, A–L (inclus.). 1929. 143p.

—— Tables générales, par Bernard Loth et Albert Michel. Paris, Letouzey, 1951–63. [Fasc.1–11] (In progress)

Fasc.1–11 Aaron–Juvernay.

A synthesis of materials in the encyclopedia brought together under specific headings arranged alphabetically. In some cases new material, principally bio-bibliographical, has been inserted in the index in order to bring matter in the earlier volumes up to date.

✓ **Enciclopedia cattolica.** Città del Vaticano, Enciclopedia Cattolica, 1948–54. 12v. il.   **BB203**

An entirely new work of major importance. Written in Italian and mainly by Italian scholars, it deals with all matters pertaining to the Catholic church, historical and contemporary. Articles vary in length from a few lines to several pages, are signed, and include long bibliographies which give dates and exact references. Profusely illustrated.

v.12 includes *Indice sistematico,* col.1840–2134.

Enciclopedia ecclesiastica, pubblicata sotto la direzione dell' Eccellenza Mons. Adriano Bernareggi. Milano, Vallardi, 1942–55. v.1–6. il. (In progress)   **BB204**

v.1–6, A–Mignot.

An Italian Catholic encyclopedia which includes brief articles on all phases of religion—dogmas, rites, customs, philosophies, history, canon law, architecture, archaeology and art, etc.—and a large amount of biography. Bibliographies at end of most articles.

Migne, Jacques Paul. Encyclopédie théologique. 1.–3. sér. Dictionnaires sur toutes les parties de la science religieuse. Paris, Migne, 1844–66. 168v. in 171. **BB205**

The various dictionaries in this set are unequal in value—some of them were uncritical even when new—and many of them are now entirely superseded by later and more scholarly works. They cover a wide field, however; include some subjects for which there are no comprehensive modern dictionaries (e.g., the *Dictionnaire des mystères*); and some of them contain a large amount of minor biography. Such dictionaries may still be useful even though they do not give the latest critical information. For complete contents *see* Paris. Bibliothèque Nationale. *Catalogue général des livres imprimés,* v.114, col.948–62 (AA72) or Lorenz, *Catalogue général,* v.3 and 6 (AA470).

Wetzer, Heinrich Joseph. Wetzer und Welte's Kirchenlexikon, oder Encyklopädie der katholischen Theologie und ihrer Hülfswissenschaften. 2. Aufl. in neuer Bearb. unter Mitwirkung vieler katholischen Gelehrten begonnen von Joseph, cardinal Hergenröther, fortgesetzt von Franz Kaulen. Freiburg im Breisgau, Herder, 1882–1901. 12v. and index.   **BB206**

The standard German Catholic encyclopedia, with signed articles.

Namen- und Sachregister. 1903. 604p.

Dictionaries

Addis, William E. and **Arnold, Thomas.** A Catholic dictionary, containing some account of the doctrine, discipline, rites, ceremonies, councils, and religious orders of the Catholic church. [16th ed.] Rev. by T. B. Scannell [and others]. London, Routledge and Paul, 1957. 859p.   **BB207**

1st ed. 1883.

A 1v. dictionary of Catholic doctrines prepared by British scholars.

A Catholic dictionary (The Catholic encyclopaedic dictionary). Ed. by Donald Attwater. 3d ed. N.Y., Macmillan, 1961. 552p.   **BB208**

Originally published in 1931 under the title *The Catholic encyclopaedic dictionary.*

Includes definitions and meanings of terms, names, and phrases in the philosophy, theology, canon law, liturgy, institutions, etc. of the Catholic church. Omits biography except for the saints in the general calendar of the Roman church.

A Catholic dictionary of theology. A work projected with the approval of the Catholic hierarchy of England and Wales. London, N.Y., Nelson, 1963– . v.1– . (In progress)   **BB209**

Contents: v.1, A–casuistry.

Prepared as a companion work to the *Catholic commentary on Holy Scripture* (BB135); presents "Catholic doctrines with the sources from which they are drawn in Scripture and Tradition" but does not "enter into matters of Catholic discipline, or the Canon Law which governs them, except when these have doctrinal importance."—*Pref.* Articles, which vary in length from one column to several pages, are signed and usually include references to sources and bibliographies.

Catholic encyclopedia dictionary; containing 8,500 articles on the beliefs, devotions, rites, symbolism, tradition and history of the church; her laws, organizations, dioceses, missions, institutions, religious orders, saints; her part in promoting art, science, education and social welfare. Comp. and ed. under the direction of the editors of the Catholic encyclopedia. N.Y., Gilmary Soc., 1941. 1095p. il.   **BB210**

A reissue, with no revision, of the *New Catholic dictionary,* published in 1929 by the Universal Knowledge Foundation.

Concise articles, many of them signed, on all phases of Catholic life. Includes biography.

Biography

Delaney, John J. and **Tobin, James Edward.** Dictionary of Catholic biography. Garden City, N.Y., Doubleday, 1961. 1245p.   **BB211**

Includes biographical sketches of some 15,000 persons who have contributed to the development of the Catholic church from the beginning to 1961, but does not include living persons.

American Catholic who's who, 1934/35– . *See* AJ50.

Catholic who's who, 1908– . London. *See* AJ147.

Yearbooks and directories

Annuario pontificio, 1716– . Roma, Tipografia Poliglotta Vaticana, 1716– . il. Annual.   **BB212**

Contains list of popes from St. Peter on: Roman Catholic hierarchy at Rome and throughout the world, with brief biographical notes; institutions and offices at Rome; list of religious orders with dates of founding and name of present head; Latin names of sees according to the Roman Curia, with classical Latin and vernacular names; Latin names of religious orders; index of personal names, etc.

Catholic directory for 1838– . London, Burns, 1838– . v.1– . maps. Annual.   **BB213**

"The official handbook of the Catholic church in England and Wales."—*Pref.*

Gives directory information: church, clergy, institutions, schools, etc.

National Catholic almanac . . . comp. by the Franciscan Clerics of the Holy Name Province, Washington, D.C. Paterson, N.J., St. Anthony's Guild, 1904– . Annual. **BB214**

Title, imprint, and sponsoring body vary. Former titles: *St. Anthony's almanac* and *Franciscan almanac*.

Includes much miscellaneous information, e.g., annual survey of news, ecclesiastical calendar, glossary of terms in Catholic use, the Catholic church in various countries of the world, statistics, directory information, etc.

Official Catholic directory, 1886– . N.Y., Kenedy, 1886– . il. Annual. **BB215**

Titles varies, imprint varies.

Useful annual, containing a large amount of detailed directory, institutional, and statistical information about the organization, clergy, churches, missions, schools, religious orders, etc. of the Catholic church in the United States and its possessions, Great Britain and Ireland, Australia, New Zealand, Oceania, Bermuda, Canada and other parts of British America, Cuba and Mexico, and the Philippines.

Coverage varies.

Atlases

Streit, Karl. Atlas hierarchicus. Descriptio geographica et statistica S. Romanae Ecclesiae tum occidentis tum orientis juxta statum praesentem accedunt nonnullae notae historicae necnon ethnographicae. . . . ed. 2. Paderborn, St. Boniface Pr.; Fribourg im Breisgau, Herder, 1929. 68 (i.e., 132) p., 47p. pl., maps, tables. 40cm. **BB216**

Contains text giving descriptive, historical, and ethnographical information; 38 large maps; and an index (9p.). Preface and text are given in German, Italian, French, and Spanish. 1st edition, 1913, contained English text also and a list of sources omitted in the 2d edition. An English issue of the revised edition appeared under the title *Catholic world atlas containing a geographical and statistical description with maps of the Holy Roman Catholic church* . . . Paderborn, St. Boniface Pr.; N.Y., Soc. for the Propagation of the Faith, 1929.

Saints

Baring-Gould, Sabine. The lives of the saints, with introduction and additional lives of English martyrs, Cornish, Scottish, and Welsh saints, and a full index to the entire work. New and rev. ed. illustrated by 473 engravings. Edinburgh, Grant, 1914. 16v. il. **BB217**

v.1–15, Jan.–Dec. (July, Oct., and Nov. in 2v. each); v.16, Appendix; indexes.

A standard work on the lives of the saints arranged day by day throughout the year.

Book of saints, a dictionary of servants of God canonized by the Catholic church: extracted from the Roman and other martyrologies, comp. by the Benedictine monks of St. Augustine's Abbey, Ramsgate. 4th ed. rev. and enl. with a calendar of saints. London, Black; N.Y., Macmillan, 1947. 708p. **BB218**

1st ed. 1921; 3d ed. 1934.

A concise handbook which includes all saints in the Roman martyrology and some others, especially those who have given place-names to towns and villages in the British Isles.

The 4th edition is thoroughly revised and rewritten with additional material, omitting some matter included in the 3d edition.

Butler, Alban. Lives of the saints, new ed. rev. and co-

piously supplemented by Herbert Thurston. London, Burns and Oates; N.Y., Kenedy, 1925–38. 12v. **BB219**

—— —— Complete ed., rev. and supplemented by Herbert Thurston and Donald Attwater. N.Y., Kenedy, 1956. 4v.

The 12v. edition was thoroughly revised by Thurston. In the 4v. edition, revised by Attwater, many sketches have been included without alteration, some brief ones have been omitted, and a few sketches of recently canonized saints have been added. The homilies originally included have been omitted.

—— A dictionary of saints; being also an index to the rev. ed. of Butler's Lives of the saints, comp. by Donald Attwater. N.Y., Kenedy, 1938. 319p. **BB220**

The saints: a concise biographical dictionary, ed. by John Coulson. London, Burns and Oates; N.Y., Hawthorn, 1958. 496p. il. **BB221**

Contains brief biographies of more than 2200 saints. Many of the articles, although not signed, are contributed by authorities in the field. Profusely illustrated with colored and black-and-white plates.

❧ The foregoing are popular works, useful for ordinary purposes. For research use, however, the indispensable works are the *Acta sanctorum* and other publications of the Bollandists described below. For an account of the *Acta sanctorum see* the *Catholic encyclopedia* 2:630–39.

Acta sanctorum quotquot toto orbe coluntur, vel a catholicis scriptoribus celebrantur, quae ex Latinis et Graecis, aliarumque gentium antiquis monumentis collegit, digessit, notis illustravit Joannes Bollandus . . . operam et studium contulit Godefridus Henschenius. . . . Editio novissima curante Joanne Carnandet. Parisiis, Palmé, 1863–1940. Jan.–Dec. 85v. in 67. **BB222**

Contents: Jan.–Apr., 3v. each; May, 7v. and Propylaeum; June–July, 7v. each; Aug., 6v.; Sept., 8v.; Oct., 13v. in 14; Nov., v.1–4 and Propylaeum; Dec., Propylaeum.

—— Ad Acta sanctorum . . . supplementum, volumen complectens Auctaria Octobris et Tabulas generales. Scilicet ephemerides et indicem alphabeticum decem priorum mensium . . . cura et opere L. M. Rigollot. Parisiis, 1875. 2v.

—— Supplément aux Acta sanctorum pour des vies de saints de l'époque mérovingienne par M. l'Abbé C. Narbey. . . . Paris, Le Soudier, 1899–1900. v.1–2.

Supplemented by:

Analecta bollandiana, v.1– . Bruxelles, Soc. des Bollandistes; Paris, Picard, 1882– . Quarterly. **BB223**

Gives the current bibliography of the subject, with critical reviews of new publications, and supplements the *Acta sanctorum* (BB222) by printing texts, commentaries, etc. not included in the *Acta*.

—— Indices in tomos I–XX (1882–1901), XXI–XL (1902–1922), XLI–LX (1923–1942). Bruxelles, Soc. des Bollandistes, 1904–45. 3v.

—— Table générale des articles publiés en 80 ans, 1882–1961. Bruxelles, 1962. 33p.

Bibliotheca hagiographica graeca. 3. éd. mise à jour et considérablement augmentée par François Halkin. Bruxelles, Soc. des Bollandistes, 1957. 3v. (Subsidia hagiographica, no.8a) **BB224**

Contents: t.1–2, A–Z; t.3, Supplément, appendices, et tables.

1st ed. 1895; 2d ed. 1909.

This revision brings up to date the listing of Greek hagiographical manuscripts and documents, and includes numerous items and early editions not previously listed.

Bibliotheca hagiographica latina antiquae et mediae aetatis. Ed. Socii Bollandiani. Bruxellis, 1898–1901. 2v. (1304p.) (Subsidia hagiographica, no.6, 12)   **BB225**

Réimpression anastatique. Bruxelles, Soc. des Bollandistes, 1949. 2v.

—— Supplementi. Ed. altera auctior. 1911. 355p.

Bibliotheca hagiographica orientalis. Ed. Socii Bollandiani. Bruxellis, Impr. Catholique, 1910. 287p. (Studia hagiographica. 10)   **BB226**

Réproduction photomécanique, 1954.

Popes, cardinals, bishops

Eubel, Conrad. Hierarchia catholica medii et recentioris aevi; sive, Summorum pontificum S.R.E. cardinalium, ecclesiarum antistitum series, e documentis tabularii praesertim Vaticani collecta, digesta, edita. 2d ed. Monasterii, Sumptibus et Typis Librariae Regensbergianae; Patavia, "Il Messaggero di S. Antonio," 1913–58. v.1–6. (In progress)   **BB227**

v.1–6, 1198–1799.
v.1–3 have title *Hierarchia catholica medii aevi.*
Chronological lists of the popes and cardinals, and of the bishops in all countries, arranged alphabetically by the Latin name of the diocese. Index by modern name.

Gams, Pius Bonifacius. Series episcoporum ecclesiae Catholicae, quotquot innotuerunt a Beato Petro Apostolo. Ratisbonae, G. J. Manz, 1873–86. 963p. and suppl., 148p. (Repr.: Leipzig, Hiersemann, 1931. 2v.)   **BB228**

Historical list of the bishops of each see from the beginning. Useful in the large or research library. Supplement covers 1870–85.

Mann, Horace Kinder. Lives of the popes in the early Middle Ages. . . . London, Kegan Paul, 1902–32. v.1–18 in 19.   **BB229**

A documented history covering the years 590–1305.
v.6–18 have title *Lives of the popes in the Middle Ages.*

Pastor, Ludwig, *Freiherr von.* History of the popes, from the close of the Middle Ages. Drawn from the secret archives of the Vatican and other original sources. From the German. Tr. and ed. by F. I. Autrobus, E. F. Peeler [and others]. London, Hodges, 1891–1953. 40v.   **BB230**

Imprint varies.
English translation of the author's *Geschichte der Päpste.*
Covers from 1305 to 1799.

Papal pronouncements

Carlen, Mary Claudia, *Sister.* Dictionary of papal pronouncements: Leo XIII to Pius XII, 1878–1957. N.Y., Kenedy, 1958. 216p.   **BB231**

Includes all encyclicals from 1878 through 1957 and a selection of documents in other categories. Arranged alphabetically by title; gives the first few words of the original text, followed by the type of document, date, occasion or group addressed, and a statement of content. Index of subjects and personal and corporate names.

Catholic Church. *Pope.* The Papal encyclicals in their historical context, by Anne Fremantle. N.Y., Putnam, 1956. 317p.   **BB232**

Includes excerpts in English from important encyclicals from earliest times to 1954, and includes a complete chronological list since 1740.

Patrology

For certain kinds of reference work—especially in large reference libraries, theological libraries, and in college and university work in medieval history, literature, and philosophy—the writings of the Fathers of the Church, either in the original Latin or Greek, or in English translation, are often wanted. The following are important collections for such needs:

Migne, Jacques Paul. Patrologiae cursus completus, seu Bibliotheca universalis . . . omnium SS. patrum, doctorum, scriptorumque ecclesiasticorum. . . . Series latina . . . a Tertulliano ad Innocentium III. Parisiis, Migne, 1844–80. 221v.   **BB233**

Contents: v.1–217, Texts; v.218–221, Indexes.

—— —— Supplementum, accurante Adalberto Hamman. Paris, Garnier, 1958–63. v.1–3.

—— —— Series graeca . . . a S. Barnaba ad Photium. Parisiis, Migne, 1857–66. 161v. in 166.   **BB234**

—— —— —— Indices digessit Ferdinandus Cavallera. Parisiis, Garnier, 1912. 218p.

—— —— —— Index locupletissimus [by] Theodorus Hopfner. Paris, Geuthner, 1928–45. 2v.

Monumental sets, useful both for the large amount of material included and for the indexes, especially the full subject indexes of many kinds included in v. 218–221 of the *Series latina,* and the place index to the *Series graeca.* Texts included are all reprints; those in the *Series graeca* are given both in Latin and in Greek, in parallel columns.

Altaner, Berthold. Patrologie: Leben, Schriften und Lehre der Kirchenvater. 5. völlig neubearb. Aufl. Freiburg, Herder, 1958. 507p.   **BB235**

An extensive bibliographical work with comments on the lives, writings, and teachings of the Church Fathers. Translated into French, Spanish, and Italian; and into French as *Patrology,* tr. by Hilda C. Graef. N.Y., Herder, 1960. 659p.

Ante-Nicene Fathers; translations of the writings of the Fathers down to A.D. 325. Alexander Roberts and James Donaldson, eds. American repr. of the Edinburgh ed., rev. and chronologically arranged with brief prefaces and occasional notes by A. C. Coxe. N.Y., Christian Literature Co., 1896–97. 10v. (Repr.: Grand Rapids, Mich., Eerdmans, 1956)   **BB236**

The Edinburgh edition, with title *Ante-Nicene Christian library,* was published by Clark. 24v.
A collection of the writings of the Apostolic Fathers down to 325 A.D., in English translation. Contents of American edition: v.1–8, Text; v.10, Additional volume, containing early Christian works . . . and selections from the commentaries of Origen, etc.; v.9, Bibliographical synopsis, by E. C. Richardson. General index to v.1–8, by Bernard Pick.

Select library of Nicene and post-Nicene Fathers of the Christian church, ed. by Philip Schaff. 1st–2d ser. tr. into English. N.Y., Christian Literature Co., 1886–1900. 28v.   **BB237**

English translations of the "most important works of Greek Fathers from Eusebius to Photius, and of the Latin Fathers from Ambrose to Gregory the Great."

Bardenhewer, Otto. Patrology; the lives and works of the Fathers of the church. Tr. from the 2d ed. by Thomas J. Shahan. Freiburg im Breisgau; St. Louis, Herder, 1908. 680p.   **BB238**

A useful reference manual intended primarily for Catholic seminary students but helpful for others. Gives for each of the Fathers: (1) a brief biographical sketch, (2) a general statement about his writings, their character, doctrine, etc., and (3) bibliography, indicating complete editions, selections and separate works, translations, and works about.

Bibliographia patristica: internationale patristische Bibliographie . . . hrsg. von W. Schneemelcher, 1956– . Berlin, de Gruyter, 1959– . v.1– . Annual.   **BB239**

A committee of patristic scholars of various confessions contributes to this listing of studies about the early Christian Fathers and related historical and theological topics. Each volume contains more than 1000 entries from some 900 journals and series. Includes book reviews.

Dekkers, Eligius. Clavis patrum latinorum, qua in novum corpus Christianorum edendum optimas quasque scriptorum recensiones a Tertulliano ad Bedam; commode recludit Eligius Dekkers; opera usus qua rem praeparavit et iuvit Aemilius Gaar, Vindobonensis. Ed. altera, aucta et emendata. Steenbrugis, In Abbatia Sancti Petri, [1961]. 640p. (Sacris erudiri; jaarboek voor godsdienstwetenschappen. 3, 1961) **BB240**

1st ed. 1951.

A key to the Latin writings of the Church Fathers that have appeared in collections and periodicals. Three indexes: (1) Index nominum et operum; (2) Index systematicus; (3) Initia.

Religious orders

☙ For a comprehensive listing of bibliographies and bio-bibliographies of religious orders of all periods, *see* John G. Barrow, *A bibliography of bibliographies in religion*, p.236–56 (BB1).

Cottineau, L. H. Répertoire topo-bibliographique des abbayes et prieurés. Macon, Protat, 1935–38. 2v. **BB241**

Arranged by the place where the religious house is situated; gives variant forms of name, location with reference to larger places, order to which religious house belongs, sometimes brief history of the house, and references to sources of information.

Hélyot, Pierre. Dictionnaire des ordres religieux. Paris, Migne, 1859–63. 4v. il. (1ᵉʳᵉ encyclopédie théologique, pub. par M. l'Abbé Migne, t.20–23) **BB242**

Subtitle: Histoire des ordres monastiques, religieux et militaires, et des congrégations séculières de l'un et de l'autre sexe, qui ont été établies jusqu'à présent. . . . Mise par ordre alphabétique, corr. et augm. . . . d'un supplément où l'on trouve l'histoire des congrégations omises par Hélyot, et l'histoire des sociétés religieuses établies depuis que cet auteur a publié son ouvrage, par Marie-Léandre Badiche.

An older work, useful in the absence of a later dictionary of the subject.

Kapsner, Oliver Leonard. Catholic religious orders; listing conventional and full names in English, foreign language, and Latin, also abbreviations, date and country of origin and founders, comp. . . . with the sponsorship of the Catholic Library Association; 2d ed. enl. Collegeville, Minn., St. John's Abbey Pr., 1957. 594p. **BB243**

A listing of names of orders primarily for the use of library catalogers, but with its many cross references from the variant forms it may also serve as a handy guide for others. Information under the main entry includes variant forms of name, abbreviation, founder, date, and country of founding.

Knowles, David and **Hadcock, Richard Neville.** Medieval religious houses, England and Wales. London, Longmans, 1953. 387p. maps. **BB244**

Based on Knowles's *Religious houses of medieval England* (London, 1940). Houses are grouped by religious order, with information on history, rank, wealth, numerical strength, architectural remains, etc. Extensive documentation, index, tables, maps.

Orthodox Eastern churches

Attwater, Donald. The Christian churches of the East. [Rev. ed.] Milwaukee, Bruce, 1947–48. 2v. **BB245**

Contents: v.1, Churches in communion with Rome; v.2, Churches not in communion with Rome.
Includes bibliographies.
A revision of the author's *The Catholic Eastern churches* (1935) and *The dissident Eastern churches* (1937).

Fortescue, Adrian. The lesser Eastern churches. London, Catholic Truth Soc., 1913. 468p. il. **BB246**

Treats the various churches of the Nestorians; the Copts; the Abyssinians, Jacobites, and Malabar Christians; and the Armenians.

A continuation of the author's *Orthodox Eastern church* (BB247).

—— The Orthodox Eastern church. 3d ed. London, Catholic Truth Soc., 1911. 451p. il. **BB247**

Frequently reprinted.

—— The Uniate Eastern churches; the Byzantine rite in Italy, Sicily, Syria, and Egypt, ed. by George D. Smith. London, Oates and Washbourne; N.Y., Benziger, 1923. 244p. (Repr.: N.Y., Ungar, 1957) **BB248**

"List of books," p.xi–xxi.

Dictionaries

Langford-James, Richard Lloyd. A dictionary of the Eastern Orthodox church. London, Faith Pr., 1923. 144p. **BB249**

An alphabetical dictionary of the rites, customs, and ceremonies of the Eastern Orthodox church.

Liturgy and ritual

Greek Church. Liturgy and Ritual. Service book of the Holy Orthodox-Catholic Apostolic church, comp., tr. and arr. from the Old Church-Slavonic service books of the Russian church, and collated with the service books of the Greek church, by Isabel Florence Hapgood. Rev. ed., with endorsement by Patriarch Tikhon. 3d ed. Brooklyn, N.Y., Syrian Antiochian Orthodox Archdiocese of New York and all North America, 1956. 615p. il. **BB250**

BUDDHISM

Bibliography

A bibliography on Japanese Buddhism, ed. by Bandō Shōjun [and others]. Tokyo, CIIB Pr., 1958. 180p. **BB251**

A classified bibliography listing books and periodical articles (1660 numbered items) written mainly in European languages up to July 1958. Locates copies in Japanese libraries.

Hanayama, Shinsho. Bibliography on Buddhism; ed. by the Commemoration Committee for Prof. Shinsho Hanayama's sixty-first birthday. Tokyo, Hokuseido Pr., 1961. 869p. [Distr., N.Y., Perkins Oriental, 1962] **BB253**

An extensive bibliography of 15,073 numbered entries, arranged alphabetically with subject index. Lists books and articles in Western languages primarily of the 19th and 20th centuries—prior to 1928 when the *Bibliographie bouddhique* (BB254) was started.

Current

Bibliographie bouddhique, 1928/29–1954/58. Paris, Librairie d'Amérique et d'Orient, 1930–61. Fasc.1–28/31. Annual. **BB254**

Indexes: fasc.1–6, 1928–34, in fasc.6; fasc.7–23, 1934–50, in fasc.23 bis.

An important annual annotated bibliography which includes both books and the indexing of some 200 periodicals in many languages. Some issues include special retrospective author bibliographies, e.g., Léon Feer (v.2); J. Ph. Vogel (v.3); Paul Pelliot (v.4–5); Sylvain Lévi (v.7–8); Louis de La Vallée Poussin (v. 22 bis).

Encyclopedias and dictionaries

Encyclopaedia of Buddhism, ed. by G. P. Malalasekera. Colombo, Govt. Pr., 1961–63. Fasc.1–2. il. (In progress)
BB255

Fasc.1–2, A–Ākan.
Designed as a scholarly and definitive work and produced under the aegis of the government of Ceylon.

Arrangement is in dictionary form with articles on all aspects of Buddhist thought, history, and civilization, including personal and place-names, literary titles, and, especially, religious and moral concepts. Articles vary in length; many of the longer ones are signed, others have initials only. For some, bibliographies are appended, but in many others, references are cited only within the text.

Hackmann, Heinrich. Erklärendes Wörterbuch zum chinesischen Buddhismus, Chinesisch-Sanskrit-Deutsch. Nach seinem handschriftlichen Nachlass überarb. von Johannes Nobel. Leiden, Brill, 1951– . Lfg. 1–8. (In progress?)
BB255a

Lfg. 1–8, A–Lieu.
The first issues of an important new Buddhist encyclopedia to be complete in 12 fascicles.

Humphreys, Christmas. A popular dictionary of Buddhism. London, Arco, 1962. 223p.
BB256

Based on *A brief glossary of Buddhist terms,* by Arthur Charles March (London, Buddhist Lodge, 1937), later expanded for inclusion in *A Buddhist student's manual,* 1956.

A popular dictionary designed for the English-speaking student of Buddhism who is not a trained scholar, and including those English terms of special meaning found in books on Buddhism.

Soothill, William Edward and **Hodous, Lewis.** A dictionary of Chinese Buddhist terms, with Sanskrit and English equivalents and a Sanskrit-Pali index. London, Kegan Paul, 1937. 510p.
BB257

Definitions in English.

HINDUISM

Bibliography

Dandekar, Ramchandra Narayan. Vedic bibliography. Bombay, Karnatak Pub. House; Poona, Univ. of Poona, 1946–61. v.1–2. (In progress)
BB258

Subtitle of v.1: An up-to-date, comprehensive, and analytically arranged register of all important work done since 1930 in the field of the Veda and allied antiquities including Indus Valley civilisation.

v.2 continues the record, 1946 to about 1960, listing nearly 6000 books and periodical articles.

May be regarded as a continuation of Renou, *Bibliographie védique* (BB259).

Renou, Louis. Bibliographie védique. Paris. Adrien-Maisonneuve, 1931. 339p.
BB259

A classed bibliography listing materials in many languages on the Vedas and the history of Hinduism, primarily of the 19th and 20th centuries.

Concordances and indexes

Bloomfield, Maurice. A Vedic concordance, . . . Cambridge, Harvard Univ. Pr., 1906. 1078p. (Harvard oriental ser. v.10)
BB260

Subtitle: Being an alphabetic index to every line of every stanza of the published Vedic literature and to the liturgical formulas thereof, that is, an index to the Vedic mantras; together with an account of their variations in the different Vedic books.

Macdonnell, Arthur Anthony and **Keith, A. B.** Vedic index of names and subjects. London, Murray, pub. for the Govt. of India, 1912. 2v.
BB261

An index by proper name and subject to Vedic literature from its earliest forms (*ca.* 1200 B.C.) to the rise of Buddhism (*ca.* 500 B.C.). Includes personal and geographical names and subjects, e.g., agriculture, caste, economic conditions, customs, law, position of women, and many others.

Dictionaries

Dowson, John. A classical dictionary of Hindu mythology and religion, geography, history, and literature. 8th ed. London, Routledge and Paul, 1953. 411p. (Trübner's oriental ser.)
BB262

1st ed. 1879. Frequently reprinted without much change.
Includes names of gods, personal and geographical names, and subjects.

ISLAM

Bibliography

Gabrieli, Giuseppe. Manuale di bibliografia musulmana. Parte 1. Bibliografia generale. Roma, Tipografia dell' Unione Editrice, 1916. 491p.
BB263

A comprehensive bibliography of books and periodical materials, in many languages, on all phases of Moslem life and culture. Includes comparative tables of Mussulman and Christian calendars.

Pearson, James Douglas. Index Islamicus, 1906–1955: a catalogue of articles on Islamic subjects in periodicals and other collective publications, comp. . . . with the assistance of Julia F. Ashton. Cambridge, Eng., W. Heffer, 1958. 897p.
BB264

Indexes more than 26,000 articles appearing in periodicals, *Festschriften,* and other collected works, published 1906–55. Periodicals devoted to the field of Islam are indexed completely; other periodicals in many languages are indexed for articles on Islamic subjects. Articles are arranged by a detailed classification system with an author index.

———— —— Supplement, 1956–1960. 1962. 316p.

Pfannmüller, Gustav. Handbuch der Islam-Literatur. Berlin, de Gruyter, 1923. 436p.
BB265

A comprehensive, critical manual with bibliographies listing materials in various languages on Islamic religious literature.

Sauvaget, Jean. Introduction à l'histoire de l'Orient musulman: éléments de bibliographie. Éd. refondue et complétée par Cl. Cahen. Paris, Adrien-Maisonneuve, 1961. 256p.
BB266

A practical manual, with bibliographies, for the student of the history of Islam.

Encyclopedias and handbooks

Encyclopaedia of Islam. New ed. . . . ed. by H. A. R. Gibb, J. H. Kramers, E. Lévi-Provençal, J. Schacht . . .

under the patronage of the International Union of Academies. Leiden, Brill; London, Luzac,1954–64. v.1–2. (In progress) **BB267**

    1st ed. 1911–38. 4v. and suppl.

    Contents: v.1–2 (fasc.23–36), A–F'il.

    A completely new edition of the most important reference work in English on Islamic subjects.

    A work of high scholarship and authority, containing signed articles, with bibliographies, on subjects in biography, history, geography, religious beliefs, institutions, manners and customs, tribes, industries, sciences, and terms of different sorts; with special emphasis in the new edition on economic and social topics and on artistic production. Geographical material includes separate articles on towns and larger political divisions in the Ottoman Empire, and in foreign countries in which Islam is of importance. More cross references in English and French have been introduced to facilitate usage by non-Orientalists.

    Until this edition is completed, it will be necessary to continue use of the 1st edition.

Shorter Encyclopaedia of Islam, ed. on behalf of the Royal Netherlands Academy by H. A. R. Gibb and J. H. Kramers. Leiden, Brill; London, Luzac, 1953. 671p. il. **BB268**

    Consists mainly of articles on the religion and law of Islam taken from the first edition of the *Encyclopaedia of Islam* (4v. and suppl. 1911–38), with the addition of some new entries and the revision of some of the older material. Bibliographies have often been brought up to date, and there is a useful "Register of subjects" which indexes the entries under English-language headings.

Handwörterbuch des Islam, im Auftrag der K. Akademie van Wetenschappen. Amsterdam, hrsg. von A. J. Wensinck und J. H. Kramers. Leiden, Brill, 1941. 833p. il. **BB269**

    A scholarly 1v. work with long, signed articles and extensive bibliographies.

Annuaire du monde musulman, statistique, historique, social et économique, rédigé par Louis Massignon. 4. éd. rev. et mise à jour avec le concours de V. Monteil. 1954. Paris, Presses Universitaires de France, 1955. 428p. **BB270**

    1. éd. 1923; 2. éd. 1925; 3. éd. 1929.

    Contains descriptive and statistical information on the population, religion, government, and economic and social conditions of the various countries of the Moslem world, primarily in Asia and Africa, with brief records of Moslems in Europe and other countries.

Atlases

Hazard, Harry W. Atlas of Islamic history. Maps executed by H. Lester Cooke, Jr., and J. McA. Smiley. 3d ed. rev. and corr. Princeton, N.J., Princeton Univ. Pr., 1954. 49p. (Princeton oriental studies. v.12) **BB271**

    Traces the development of the Islamic Empire from the first Islamic century (600 A.D.) to the present century. A summary of the important historical events during each century in Europe, Africa, and Asia is given on the page facing each map.

    At the end of the atlas is a conversion table of Christian and Moslem dates, followed by an index of place-names appearing on the maps.

Historical atlas of the Muslim peoples, comp. by Roelof Roolvink [and others]. Amsterdam, Djambatan; Cambridge, Harvard Univ. Pr., 1957. 40p. col. maps. 29cm. **BB271a**

    Clear, well-produced maps.

Koran

Koran; tr. from the Arabic by J. M. Rodwell. 2d rev. and amended ed. London, Quaritch, 1876. 562p. (Frequently repr. in Everyman's library with introd. by G. Margoliouth. London, Dent; N.Y., Dutton, 1953. 506p.) **BB272**

JAINISM

Guérinot, Armand Albert. Essai de bibliographie Jaina, répertoire analytique et méthodique des travaux relatifs au Jainisme. Paris, Leroux, 1906. 568p. il. (Ministère de l'Instruction Publique. Annales Musée Guimet. Bibliothèque d'études, t.22) **BB273**

    A classed bibliography of 852 works on Jainism.

    Supplemented by *Notes de bibliographie jaina* in *Journal asiatique,* 10. sér., 10:47–148. 1909.

JUDAISM

Bibliography

See also Barrow, *A bibliography of bibliographies in religion* (BB1).

Benjacob, Isaac. Ozar Ha-Sepharim (Bücherschatz). Bibliographie der gesammten hebraeischen Literatur mit Einschluss der Handschriften (bis 1863). Wilna, Benjacob, 1880. 678p. **BB275**

    Title pages in Hebrew, Russian, German, and Latin. Text in Hebrew. Arranged alphabetically. Includes entries for 17,000 Hebrew books and manuscripts published up to 1863.

Blumenkranz, Bernhard. Bibliographie des Juifs en France. Paris, Centre d'Études Juives, 1961. 188p. (École Pratique des Hautes Études, Sorbonne. 6. sec.: Sciences économiques et sociales. Études juives. Volume hors-série) **BB276**

    Lists some 4400 entries in various languages—including books, theses, and articles in periodicals and general Jewish encyclopaedias—on Jews in France. Alphabetical by author; no subject index.

Braham, Randolph L. The Hungarian Jewish catastrophe; a selected and annotated bibliography. N.Y., [Marstin Pr.], 1962. 86p. (Jerusalem. Yad va-shem. Joint documentary projects. Bibliographical ser., no.4) **BB277**

    Sponsored jointly by Yad Washem Martyrs' and Heroes' Memorial Authority, Jerusalem, and the Yivo Institute for Jewish Research.

    A selected, classified bibliography of books and articles in various languages.

Cohen, Y. Yosef. Jewish publications in the Soviet Union, 1917–1960. Bibliographies comp. and arr. by Y. Y. Cohen with the assistance of M. Piekarz . . . ed. by Kh. Shmeruk. Jerusalem, Historical Soc. of Israel, 1961. 502p. **BB278**

    In Hebrew. Added title page, preface, and table of contents in English.

    Lists Hebrew and Yiddish publications of the Soviet Union for the period.

Eichstädt, Volkmar. Bibliographie zur Geschichte der Judenfrage. Bd.1, 1750–1848. Hamburg, Hanseatische Verlagsanstalt, 1938. 267p. (Schriften des Reichsinstitutes für Geschichte des Neuen Deutschlands) **BB279**

    No more published.

    A classified bibliography of more than 3000 books and articles, primarily in German, published from 1750 to 1848 on the Jewish question.

Frankfurt am Main. Stadtbibliothek. Katalog der Judaica und Hebraica. Frankfurt am Main, M. Lehrberger, 1932. v.1. 646p.   **BB280**

No more published.

Edited by A. Freimann.

v.1, Judaica.

An extensive classified catalog of materials on Jews and Judaism.

Friedberg, B. Bet eked sepharim. Lexique bibliographique de tous les ouvrages de la littérature hébraïque et judéo-allemande . . . imprimés et publiés de 1475–1900. Anvers, [Delplace, Koch], 1928–31. 844p.   **BB281**

Includes Arabic, Greek, Italian, Persian, Samaritan, Spanish-Portuguese, and Tartarian. Entirely in Hebrew.

Title page in English and German.

Friedman, Philip. Bibliography of books in Hebrew on the Jewish catastrophe and heroism in Europe. Jerusalem, 1960. 433p. (Jerusalem. Yad va-shem. Joint documentary projects. Bibliographical ser., no.2)   **BB282**

Sponsored jointly by Yad Washem, Remembrance Authority of Disaster and Heroism, Jerusalem, and the Yivo Institute for Jewish Research, New York (names vary).

In Hebrew. Added title page, introduction, and index in English.

"Lists the books published in Hebrew both in Israel and abroad, including translations into Hebrew. It also lists books written partly in Hebrew . . ."—*Foreword.* Includes monographic works only. A separate volume will be devoted to articles.

Covers mainly 1933–45, with some listings preceding and following.

Friedman, Philip and **Gar, Joseph.** Bibliography of Yiddish books on the catastrophe and heroism. N.Y., [Marstin Pr.], 1962. 330p. (Jerusalem. Yad va-shem. Joint documentary projects. Bibliographical ser., no.3)   **BB283**

Sponsored jointly by Yad Washem Martyrs' and Heroes' Memorial Authority, Jerusalem, and the Yivo Institute for Jewish Research, New York.

Text in Yiddish. Added title page, introduction, and index in English.

A classified bibliography in five main divisions: (1) documentation, (2) research, (3) belles-lettres and art, (4) resistance, (5) reflections on the catastrophe. Covers mainly 1933–45 with some later entries.

Hebrew Union College—Jewish Institute of Religion. Library. Jewish Americana . . . A supplement to A. S. W. Rosenbach, An American Jewish bibliography. Cincinnati, Ohio, Amer. Jewish Archives, 1954. 115p. facsims. (Monographs of the American Jewish archives, no.1) **BB284**

Subtitle: A catalogue of books and articles by Jews or relating to them printed in the United States from the earliest days to 1850 and found in the Library of the Hebrew Union College—Jewish Institute of Religion in Cincinnati.

For Rosenbach *see* BB291.

Continued by:

Levine, Allan E. An American Jewish bibliography. Cincinnati, Ohio, Amer. Jewish Archives, 1959. 100p. (Monographs of the American Jewish archives, no.11) **BB285**

Subtitle: A list of books and pamphlets by Jews or relating to them printed in the United States from 1851 to 1875, which are in the possession of the Hebrew Union College—Jewish Institute of Religion Library in Cincinnati.

Lehmann, Ruth Pauline. Nova bibliotheca anglo-judaica; a bibliographical guide to Anglo-Jewish history 1937–1960. London, Jewish Historical Soc. of England, 1961. 232p.   **BB286**

Brings up to date the *Magna bibliotheca anglo-judaica* by Cecil Roth (BB292).

A selective rather than an exhaustive bibliography of books and periodical articles published since 1937 bearing on Anglo-Jewish history. No attempt has been made to supplement Part II, listing primary sources, of the *Magna bibliotheca.*

Marcus, Jacob R. and **Bilgray, Albert.** An index to Jewish Festschriften. Cincinnati, Ohio, Hebrew Union College, 1937. 154p.   **BB287**

Indexes the contents of 53 *Festschriften,* published before 1936, by author, title, and subject.

Milano, Attilio. Bibliotheca historica italo-judaica. Firenze, Sansoni Antiquariato, 1954. 209p. (Contributi alla Biblioteca bibliografica italica. 6)   **BB288**

A bibliography of books and periodical articles on the Jew in Italy. Indexes by locality, by subject, and by author.

New York Public Library. Jewish Collection. Dictionary catalog of the Jewish collection. Boston, G. K. Hall, 1960. 14v.   **BB289**

A photographic reproduction of the card catalog of one of the great Jewish collections of the world. Contains some 250,000 entries for books, periodicals, and analytics. Lists works in Hebrew and Yiddish, and in European languages, on the history and tradition of the Jewish people of all times and in all countries.

Robinson, Jacob and **Friedman, Philip.** Guide to Jewish history under Nazi impact. N.Y., [Marstin Pr.], 1960. 425p. (Jerusalem. Yad va-shem. Joint documentary projects. Bibliographical ser., no.1)   **BB290**

Sponsored jointly by Yad Washem Martyrs' and Heroes' Memorial Authority, Jerusalem, and the Yivo Institute for Jewish Research, New York (names vary).

This comprehensive work, the first volume of a bibliographical series on this subject, contains 3841 entries in 24 languages in a classified arrangement. In four main parts: pt.1, The Jewish catastrophe in historical perspective; pt.2, Reference books; pt.3, Research: institutions, methods, and techniques; pt.4, Documentation.

Introductory paragraphs and annotations make this a manual as well as a bibliography, and various types of indexes add to its usefulness.

Rosenbach, Abraham Simon Wolf. An American Jewish bibliography; being a list of books and pamphlets by Jews or relating to them printed in the United States from the establishment of the press in the colonies until 1850. Baltimore, Lord Baltimore Pr., 1926. 486p. facsims. (Publ. of the American Jewish Historical Soc., no.30)   **BB291**

A detailed bibliography of almost 700 items, arranged chronologically, with author index. Locates copies.

Continued by BB284 and BB285.

Roth, Cecil. Magna bibliotheca anglo-judaica; a bibliographical guide to Anglo-Jewish history. New ed. rev. and enl. London, Jewish Historical Soc. of England, Univ. College, 5698 (1937). 464p.   **BB292**

Classified.

A revised edition of *Bibliotheca anglo-judaica,* comp. by Joseph Jacobs and Lucien Wolf (London, 1888). In two parts: pt.1, "Histories," consisting largely of secondary works; pt.2, "Historical material," listing primary sources usually up to the year 1837, though material on the reform movement is extended to 1842 and on Jewish emancipation to 1858.

Continued by Lehmann, *Nova bibliotheca anglo-judaica* (BB286).

Shunami, Shlomo. Bibliography of Jewish bibliographies. Jerusalem, Univ. Pr., 1936. 399p.   **BB293**

Includes works in many languages. Classified, with index of names and subjects and an index of Hebrew titles.

Lists bibliographies on editions of the Bible and its parts, commentaries, versions, etc.; history and religion of Israel, literature, etc.

Szajkowski, Zosa. Franco-Judaica; an analytical bibliography of books, pamphlets, decrees, briefs and other printed documents pertaining to the Jews in France, 1500–1788. N.Y., Amer. Academy for Jewish Research, 1962. 160p. **BB294**

An annotated bibliography of more than 1700 entries.

Wiener Library, London. German Jewry: its history, life and culture. London, Vallentine, Mitchell, 1958. 279p. (Wiener Library. Catalogue ser., no.3) **BB295**

A classified catalog of materials relating to the history and life of the German-speaking Jews of Central Europe. Although some earlier works are included, most of the titles have been published since World War I.

Indexes

Index to Jewish periodicals; an author and subject index to selected American and Anglo-Jewish journals of general and scholarly interest. v.1, June 1963– . Cleveland, Ohio (16620 Lomond Blvd.), 1963– . Quarterly (with annual cumulations). **BB296**

Cumulated volume, June 1963–May 1964, indexes some 24 periodicals. Includes book reviews.

Encyclopedias

Ausubel, Nathan. The book of Jewish knowledge: an encyclopedia of Judaism and the Jewish people, covering all elements of Jewish life from Biblical times to the present. N.Y., Crown, 1964. 560p. il. **BB297**

An alphabetical encyclopedia dealing with the history, culture, and ethics of the Jews from Biblical to modern times.

Encyclopaedia Judaica; das Judentum in Geschichte und Gegenwart. Berlin, Verlag Eschkol, [c1928–34]. v.1–10. il. **BB298**

v.1–10, A–Lyra. No more published.

v.1–2, only, issued also in an edition in Hebrew.

A scientific work of high scholarship, with signed articles and valuable bibliographies, covering all aspects of Jewish life, thought, literature, religion, customs, history, etc., especially full in biography.

Jewish encyclopedia; a descriptive record of the history, religion, literature, and customs of the Jewish people from the earliest times to the present day; prep. under the direction of Cyrus Adler [and others] . . . Isidore Singer, managing ed. N.Y., Funk & Wagnalls, 1901–6. 12v. il. **BB299**

A standard encyclopedia in English, with signed articles by specialists and with bibliographies. Now out of date, but still useful for its biographies and other historical information.

Jüdisches Lexikon; ein enzyklopädisches Handbuch des jüdischen Wissens . . . begr. von Georg Herlitz und Bruno Kirschner. Berlin, Jüdischer Verlag, [c1927–30]. 4v. in 5. il. **BB300**

More popular in character than the *Encyclopaedia Judaica* (BB298), with brief signed articles and some bibliography. Lavishly illustrated.

Standard Jewish encyclopedia. Cecil Roth, ed. in chief. Garden City, N.Y., Doubleday, 1959. 1978col. il. **BB301**

A compilation of concise factual and biographical information, intended primarily as a work of contemporary reference, placing special emphasis on recent developments in Jewish history, and on the American community and the State of Israel, but also "covering every phase of Jewish life, literature, and thought from their beginning."—*Pref.*

Biographical sketches include living persons.

Universal Jewish encyclopedia . . . an authoritative and popular presentation of Jews and Judaism since the earliest times; ed. by Isaac Landman . . . N.Y., Universal Jewish Encyclopedia, Inc., 1939–44. 10v. and reading guide and index (78p.). il. **BB302**

A useful, modern encyclopedia, more popular in treatment than the scholarly *Jewish encyclopedia* (BB299) but more up to date. Especially strong in its treatment of American subjects and of the 20th century. Contains many biographies, including living persons. Many articles signed, with bibliographies.

Biography

☙ All of the encyclopedias listed above include biographies, in some cases of considerable reference importance. In some cases the yearbooks (BB308–BB312) include contemporary biography. The following two entries are limited to biography and include many names not given in the more general works:

Rosenbloom, Joseph R. A biographical dictionary of early American Jews: colonial times through 1800. (Lexington], Univ. of Kentucky Pr., 1960. 175p. **BB303**

Attempts to list all persons identifiable as Jews in America before 1800, with such biographical facts as can be found in manuscript and printed sources.

Wininger, Salomon. Grosse jüdische National-Biographie, mit mehr als 12,000 Lebensbeschreibungen namhafter jüdischer Männer und Frauen aller Zeiten und Länder. Ein Nachschlagewerk für das jüdische Volk und dessen Freunde. Cernauti, "Arta," 1928–37. v.1–7$^{1-7}$. **BB304**

v.1–5, A–St; v.6, St–Z; Nachträge, A–Geldern; v.7 (incompl.), Geiler–Z; 2. Nachträge, A–Fink.

No more published.

An international biographical dictionary of Jews primarily from the Middle Ages to the 20th century, with a few of earlier date. The number of sketches noted in the title varies from 8000 to 12,000.

Who's who in American Jewry, *see* AJ54.

History

Baron, Salo Wittmayer. A social and religious history of the Jews. 2d ed. rev. and enl. N.Y., Columbia Univ. Pr., 1952–60. 8v. and index. **BB305**

1st ed. 1937. 3v.

Covers from ancient times to 1200. Each volume includes "Notes" (explanations, descriptions, and references to sources).

Contents: v.1–2, Ancient times; v.3–8, High Middle Ages, 500–1200: v.3, Heirs of Rome and Persia; v.4, Meeting of East and West; v.5, Religious controls and discussions; v.6, Laws, homilies, and the Bible; v.7, Hebrew language and letters; v.8, Philosophy and science.

Handbooks

Birnbaum, Philip. A book of Jewish concepts. N.Y., Hebrew Pub. Co., 1964. 719p. **BB306**

Aims to set forth in English the essential teachings of Judaism, with entries for each book of the Hebrew Bible, terms from Talmudic-Midrashic literature, and Jewish codes of law and ethics. Arrangement is alphabetical by Hebrew terms, with both English and Hebrew indexes.

Federbusch, Simon. World Jewry today. N.Y., Yoseloff, 1959. 748col. **BB307**

Published in Jerusalem by Massadah Pub. Co.

Arranged geographically, giving brief descriptions of the Jewish communities in each country with lists of organizations, periodicals, etc.

Yearbooks

American Jewish year book, 5660– , Sept. 5, 1899– . Philadelphia, Jewish Pub. Soc., 1899– . v.1– . Annual.
BB308

Contains important directory and statistical information, and a review of the year's events in America and other countries. Each volume contains special articles, biographies, necrologies, and bibliographies. Many of these from earlier issues continue to have reference value. v.40 contains a subject index to special articles in v.1–40. Beginning with v.44, each volume contains an American Jewish bibliography.

American synagogue directory. Publisher, Lawrence Frenkel. N.Y., Frenkel Mailing Service, 1957– . Annual.
BB309

Arranged by state and city; lists synagogues with addresses and names of rabbis and presidents of the congregations.

Jewish year book, 5657– . (1896–). London, "Jewish Chronicle," 1896– . v.1– . (1963)
BB310

Contains statistical and institutional information for the British Commonwealth, bibliographies, and a who's who.

Standard American-Jewish directory, 1960– . [N.Y., Barkai & Hudes], 1960– . il. v.1– .
BB311

Directory information on congregations, institutions, and organizations; trades and services; general information including holidays and feast days, statistics, etc.

Zionist yearbook. Ed., Joseph Litvin. London, Zionist Federation of Great Britain and Ireland, 1951/52– . Annual. (1962/63)
BB312

Includes directory information about Zionist organizations in Great Britain and abroad; governmental information about Israel; and biographical notices.

SHINTOISM

Kato, Genchi, Reitz, Karl and **Schiffer, William.** A bibliography of Shinto in Western languages, from the oldest times to 1952. Tokyo, Meiji Jungu Shamusho, 1953. 58p.
BB313

Alphabetical arrangement. No annotations.

ZOROASTRIANISM

Dhalla, Maneckji N. History of Zoroastrianism. London, N.Y., Oxford Univ. Pr., 1938. 525p.
BB314

A documented history of Zoroastrianism and its literature and beliefs from earliest to modern times. The bibliography lists translations of the sacred texts into Western languages as well as works about Zoroastrianism.

BC

Linguistics and Philology

❦ This section includes works dealing with the study of language: survey histories such as Mencken's *American language* (BC24), Brunot's *Histoire de la langue française* (BC45), and Cejador y Frauca's *Historia de la lengua y literatura castellana* (BC56); guides to groups of languages, e.g., De Bray's *Guide to the Slavonic languages* (BC69); bibliographies of language groups, e.g., Loewenthal's *Turkic languages and literatures of Central Asia* (BC74) and LaSor's *Basic Semitic bibliography* (BC76); and, of particular importance, the various annual bibliographies. Von Ostermann's *Manual of foreign languages* (BC2) is very useful to the worker who needs to know the alphabets, transliteration, and basic grammatical rules of many languages.

Many of the bibliographies of literature include works on language. For these consult Section BD, Literature. Dictionaries and bibliographies of dictionaries will be found in Section AE, Dictionaries.

INTERNATIONAL

Manuals

Gleichen, *Lord* **Edward** and **Reynolds, John H.** Alphabets of foreign languages. [New ed.] London, Stanford, for Permanent Committee on Geographical Names for British Official Use, 1956. 82p.
BC1

1st ed. 1921.
Treats 78 languages in 11 groups.

Von Ostermann, Georg F. Manual of foreign languages for the use of librarians, bibliographers, research workers, editors, translators, and printers. 4th ed. rev. and enl. N.Y., Central Book Co., 1952. 414p.
BC2

A useful manual of concise information about some 130 languages and dialects, giving: the alphabet in the original letters or characters in varying forms, with transliteration into English and pronunciation; brief rules for punctuation, capitalization, syllabication, transliteration, phonetics, and grammar; cardinal and ordinal numbers; years, seasons, months, days, etc.

3d edition, 1936, published by the U.S. Government Printing Office.

"All portions of the third edition not requiring change have been reproduced in this new edition by the photographic process. Corrections and minor additions have been 'stripped' in, and all new material, set in type for the first time, is presented in a format approximating as closely as possible that used in the third and prior edition."—*Pref.*

Some languages have undergone extensive revision, and Estonian has been added.

Wemyss, Stanley. The languages of the world, ancient and modern. Philadelphia, Stanley Wemyss, 1950. 237p.
BC3

Subtitle: The alphabets, ideographs, and other written characters of the languages of the world, in sound and symbol.

Bibliography

Akademiia Nauk SSSR. Institut IAzykoznaniia. Bibliograficheskii ukazatel' literatury po iazykoznaniiu, izdannoi v SSSR s 1918 po 1957 god. Sost.: N. P. Debets i dr. Moskva, 1958. v.1. **BC4**

Ceased publication (?).

A bibliographic index, planned in 5v., of the literature in all branches of linguistics published in the USSR between 1918 and 1957. v.1 covers books, collections, and doctoral dissertations in Russian, to 1955.

—— Bibliograficheskii ukazatel' literatury po russkomu iazykoznaniiu s 1825 po 1880 god. Glav. redaktor V. V. Vinogradov. Moskva, 1954–59. 8v. **BC5**

An annotated bibliographic index to the literature on linguistics published in Russia between 1825 and 1880.

v.8 contains a general index.

Gipper, Helmut and **Schwarz, Hans.** Bibliographisches Handbuch zur Sprachinhaltsforschung; Schriftum zur Sprachinhaltsforschung in alphabetischer Folge nach Verfassern, mit Besprechungen und Inhaltshinweisen. Hrsg. [von] Leo Brandt. Köln, [1961?]–62. Lfg. 1–6. (Wissenschaftliche Abhandlungen der Arbeitsgemeinschaft für Forschung des Landes Nordhein-Westfalen, Bd.16a) (In progress) **BC6**

"Die Arbeitsgemeinschaft für Forschung vorgelegt von Jost Trier und Leo Weisgerber."—*Verso of title page.*

Lfg. 1–6, A–Gul.

An extensive annotated bibliography of works in various languages on semantics.

Guiraud, Pierre. Bibliographie critique de la statistique linguistique. Revisée et complétée par Thomas D. Houchin, Jaan Puhvel et Calvert W. Watkins, sous la direction de Joshua Whatmough. Utrecht, Éd. Spectrum, 1954. 123p. (Comité International Permanent de Linguistes. Publications du Comité de la Statistique Linguistique. II) **BC7**

A classified list of scholarly books and articles in many languages on a variety of statistical approaches to linguistic studies (e.g., word counts, rhyme frequencies, etc.).

Moscow. Publichnaia Biblioteka. Otdel Spravochno-Bibliograficheskoi i Informatsionnoi Raboty. Bibliografiia bibliografii po iazykoznaniiu; annotirovannyi sistematicheskii ukazatel' otechestvennykh izdanii. [Sost.: E. I. Kukushkina i A. G. Stepanova] Moskva, 1963. 411p. **BC8**

A bibliography of bibliographies published in Russia and the USSR in all fields of linguistic study.

Nostrand, Howard Lee [and others]. Research on language teaching; an annotated international bibliography for 1945–61. . . . Seattle, Univ. of Wash. Pr., 1962. 280p. (Univ. of Washington publ. on language and learning. v.1) **BC9**

An annotated, classified listing of books and periodical articles on methods, material, equipment, psychology of language learning, teaching at various levels, etc. Includes a list of bibliographies and one of periodicals and serials.

For current listings in this subject, *see Education index* (CB27).

Pop, Sever. Bibliographie des questionnaires linguistiques. Louvain, Commission d'Enquête Linguistique, [1955]. 168p. (Comité International Permanent de Linguistes. Publications de la Commission d'Enquête Linguistique. VI) **BC10**

A chronological listing of questionnaires employed in linguistic field work, with annotations and sources of reference for each item. Indexes of names and subjects.

Current

Bibliographie linguistique des années 1939–1947, publiée par le Comité International Permanent de Linguistes. Utrecht, Spectrum, 1949– . v.1– . Annual. (v.16, 1961) **BC11**

Added title page in English: Linguistic bibliography for the year.

1939/47 in 2v.: v.1 lists books, reviews, and periodical articles on various branches of linguistics appearing in South Africa, Belgium (publications in Flemish), Czechoslovakia, Finland, France, Italy, the Netherlands, Norway, Poland, Spain, and Switzerland; v.2 includes contributions from Austria, Belgium (French), Denmark, England, Greece, India, Ireland, Portugal, Russia, Sweden, Turkey, and the U.S.A. etc., with an author index to both volumes.

Materials are grouped under large classes, with subdivisions, e.g., General linguistics: Indo-European, Asianic and Mediterranean, Finno-Ugrian, Basque, Hamito-Semitic, Negro-African, Caucasian, Turkish and Mongolian, Eastern Asia [and others]. Continued by annual volumes, with slightly enlarged coverage.

Bulletin signalétique. Sec. 21:Sociologie. Sciences du langage. Paris, Centre National de la Recherche Scientifique, 1961– . Quarterly. **BC12**

An international abstract journal with very comprehensive coverage. For complete set *see* EA71. The language section includes the philosophy of language, historical linguistics and comparative grammar, philology, and stylistics.

Modern Language Association of America. MLA international bibliography, 1921– . **BC13**

For full information *see* BD9.

Year's work in modern language studies, by a number of scholars. 1929/30– . Oxford, Univ. Pr., 1931– . v.1– . Annual. **BC14**

v.11 covers 1940–49 in one composite volume.

Coverage varies. Usually includes material on language and literature in: (1) Medieval Latin; (2) Romance languages; (3) Germanic languages; and (4) Slavonic languages.

Covers from medieval times to the present day.

Periodicals

Ulving, Tor. Periodica philologica abbreviata; a list of initial abbreviations of periodicals in philology and related subjects. Stockholm, Almqvist & Wiksell, 1963. 137p. **BC15**

An international list of initial abbreviations for more than 3000 periodicals, with full name of periodical and place of publication.

Dissertations

Varnhagen, Hermann. Systematisches Verzeichnis der Programmabhandlungen, Dissertationen und Habilitationsschriften aus dem Gebiete der romanischen und englischen Philologie sowie der allgemeinen Sprach- und Litteraturwissenschaft und der Pädagogik und Methodik. 2. vollst. umgearb. Aufl. Besorgt von Johannes Martin. Leipzig, Koch, 1893. 296p. **BC16**

German dissertations in literature and language.

Surveys

Bodmer, Frederick. The loom of language. Lancelot Hogben, ed. N.Y., Norton, [c1944]. 692p. il. **BC17**

A survey of the interrelationships of language in four main parts: (1) The natural history of language; (2) Our hybrid heritage; (3) The world language problem; (4) Language museum.

The last part includes word lists, giving basic vocabularies in Teutonic and Romance languages, and a list of Greek words with roots which survive in English and in international scientific terms.

Meillet, Antoine and **Cohen, Marcel.** Les langues du monde, par un groupe de linguistes. Nouv. éd. Paris, Centre National de la Recherche Scientifique, 1952. 1294p. maps (in pocket).   **BC18**

1st ed. 1924.

At head of title: Société de Linguistique de Paris.

A basic work treating the languages and dialects of the world under language groupings. Under each section gives information on the locale, numbers of persons who speak the language, classification, characteristics, and, for each language, phonetics, morphology, vocabulary, etc. Extensive bibliographies with each group.

Bibliography: (1) Classification des langues, p.xvii–xxxv; (2) Linguistique générale, p.xxxvi–xlii. (The bibliographies include titles in various languages published from the 10th century to 1951.)

Index des langues, p.1210–1273.

Atlas des langues du monde (folded maps in pocket) indicates the languages and language groupings of the various countries of the world.

Pop, Sever. La dialectologie; aperçu historique et méthodes d'enquêtes linguistiques. Louvain, Bibliothèque de l'Université, Bureau du Recueil, 1950. 2v. (1334p.). maps. (Université de Louvain. Recueil de travaux d'histoire et de philologie, 3. sér., fasc.38–39)   **BC19**

Contents: 1. pt., Dialectologie romane: Le français, Le domaine franco-provençal, Le provençal, Le catalan, L'espagnol, Le portugais, L'italien, Le romanche, Le dalmate, Le roumain; 2. pt., Dialectologie non romane. Langues germaniques: Allemagne, Suisse, Grand-Duché de Luxembourg, Belgique et Pays-Bas. Les pays scandinaves, Grande-Bretagne, États-Unis et Canada. Langues celtiques, Langues slaves, Langues finno-ougriennes. Le grec modern. L'albanais. Le domaine berbère. Le domaine bantou. Le domaine arabe. Le chinois. Les langues de l'Inde. Le coréen.

A comprehensive historical survey covering dialectal research and methods employed. Fully documented throughout text and in footnotes. Detailed indexes by year, place, persons, geographical names, and subjects. List of illustrations. Table of contents. Chronological list of linguistic atlases, 1880–1948, p.1194–97.

Dictionaries

Pei, Mario Andrew and **Gaynor, Frank.** Dictionary of linguistics. N.Y., Philosophical Lib., 1954. 238p.   **BC20**

Brief definitions of the grammatical, historical, and descriptive terms used in linguistics. Includes "the names, affiliations, and very brief descriptions of the major languages and dialects of the world, both past and present."—*Pref.*

Directories

Pop, Sever and **Pop, Rodica Doina.** Premier répertoire des instituts et des sociétés de linguistique du monde. Louvain, Commission d'Enquête Linguistique, 1958. 294p. il. (Publications de la Commission d'Enquête Linguistique, 8)   **BC21**

At head of title: Comité International Permanent des Linguistes.

Lists linguistics societies from 57 countries of Africa, Asia, Europe, and the Americas, with descriptions of policies and activities.

ENGLISH

Bibliography and history

Baugh, Albert Croll. A history of the English language. 2d ed. rev. N.Y., Appleton, 1959. 506p. il.   **BC22**

Primarily a textbook for college students, which aims to present the historical development of the English language against a background of the political, social, and intellectual history of England from early times to the present day. Includes the English language in America. Bibliographies at ends of chapters.

Kennedy, Arthur Garfield. A bibliography of writings on the English language from the beginning of printing to the end of 1922. Cambridge, Harvard Univ. Pr.; New Haven, Yale Univ. Pr., 1927. 517p.   **BC23**

A very comprehensive list of 13,402 numbered items. Classified, with indexes to authors and reviewers and to subjects. A "Review with a list of additions and corrections" by Arvid Gabrielson was published in *Studia neophilologica* 2: 117–68. 1929.

Mencken, Henry Louis. The American language; an inquiry into the development of English in the United States. 4th ed. corr., enl., and rewritten. N.Y., Knopf, 1936. 769p.   **BC24**

——— Supplements 1–2. N.Y., Knopf, 1945–48. 2v.

A historical treatment of the development of the English language in the United States covering such subjects as: the two streams of English; the beginning and growth of the American language; pronunciation and spelling; the common speech; proper names in America; American slang, etc. Appendix: Non-English dialects in America. List of words and phrases. Index.

The supplements follow the same plan as the original work, the first containing supplemental material to Chapters 1–6 and the second to Chapters 7–11 and the appendix, with cross references to the main volume.

Each volume includes copious footnotes, references to sources, a list of words and phrases with reference to the text, and an index.

——— The American language; an inquiry into the development of English in the United States. The 4th ed. and the two supplements, abridged, with annotations and new material, by Raven I. McDavid, Jr. With the assistance of David W. Maurer. [1st abridged ed.] N.Y., Knopf, 1963. 777p., cxxivp.   **BC25**

Not a revision but a briefer form of the 3v. work with some modifications required by recent changes in the language, "and in the civilization which the language reflects."—*Introd.*

Scheurweghs, Gustave. Analytical bibliography of writings on modern English morphology and syntax, 1877–1960. Louvain, Belgium, Nauwelaerts, 1963–65. v.1–2. (In progress) (Publications of the University of Louvain)   **BC26**

Contents: v.1, Periodical literature and miscellanies of the United States of America and western and northern Europe. With an appendix on Japanese publications by Hideo Yamaguchi (Fukui, Japan); v.2, Studies in book form, including dissertations and *Programmabhandlungen* published in the United States of America and western and northern Europe. With appendixes on Japanese publications by Hideo Yamaguchi, and on Czechoslovak publications by Ján Šimko (Bratislava).

Annotated, classified bibliographies with author and subject indexes.

Current bibliography

Abstracts of English studies: an official publication of the National Council of Teachers of English. Boulder, Colo., 1958– . v.1– . **BC27**

For full information *see* BD312.

Modern Humanities Research Association. Annual bibliography of English language and literature, 1920– . Cambridge, Univ. Pr., 1921– . v.1– . **BC28**

For full information *see* BD313.

Atlases

Kurath, Hans. Linguistic atlas of New England . . . Hans Kurath, dir. and ed.; Miles L. Hanley, assoc. dir.; Bernard Bloch, asst. ed.; Guy S. Lowman, Jr., principal field investigator; Marcus L. Hansen, historian. Sponsored by the American Council of Learned Societies and assisted by universities and colleges in New England. Providence, R.I., Brown Univ., 1939–43. v.1–3 in 6v. 56cm. double maps. (Linguistic atlas of the U.S. and Canada) **BC29**

Each volume in two parts. Maps numbered consecutively, 1–734.

—— —— Handbook of the linguistic geography of New England. Providence, R.I., Brown Univ., 1939. 240p. maps. **BC29a**

Bibliography of linguistic geography, p.54–61; Bibliography of New England history, p.105–21.

IRISH

Dublin. National Library of Ireland. Bibliography of Irish philology and of printed Irish literature. Dublin, Stat. Off., 1913. 307p. **BC30**

Compiled by R. I. Best and supplemented by:

Best, Richard Irvine. Bibliography of Irish philology and manuscript literature; publications 1913–1941. Dublin, Dublin Inst. for Advanced Studies, 1942. 253p. **BC31**

Bibliographies of printed works relating to the Irish language and literature, comprising the works of native Irish writers down to the latter part of the 19th century.

SCOTTISH

Woolley, John S. Bibliography for Scottish linguistic studies. Pub. for the University of Edinburgh, Linguistic Survey of Scotland. Edinburgh, James Thin, 1954. 37p. **BC32**

A list designed primarily "for those interested in the study of modern Scottish dialects."

GERMANIC LANGUAGES

Jahresbericht über die Erscheinungen auf dem Gebiete der germanischen Philologie hrsg. von der Gesellschaft für Deutsche Philologie in Berlin, 1879–1936/39. Berlin, de Gruyter, 1880–1954. 58v. **BC33**

Useful annual bibliography, listing the new book, pamphlet, and dissertation literature, and also indexing articles in a large number of important periodicals.

1936/39 (pub. 1954) brings the record up to the beginning of World War II.

Superseded by *Jahresbericht für deutsche Sprache und Literatur* (BD566).

Knobloch, Johann. Sprachwissenschaftliches Wörterbuch. Heidelberg, Winter, 1961–63. Lfg. 1–2. (Indogermanische Bibliothek. II. Reihe. Wörterbücher) (In progress) **BC34**

Lfg. 1–2, a–Artikel.

A scholarly dictionary of general and comparative linguistics, with emphasis on German terms and scholarship.

Loewenthal, Fritz. Bibliographisches Handbuch zur deutschen Philologie. Halle, Niemeyer, 1932. 217p. **BC35**

A classified bibliography of more than 2000 titles, some annotated. Name and subject index. Includes chapters on the Scandinavian languages.

Paul, Hermann. Grundriss der germanischen Philologie. 2. verb. und verm. Aufl. Strassburg, Trübner, 1900–1909. 3v. maps. **BC36**

For advanced workers only. Not alphabetically arranged, but in chapters with detailed alphabetical indexes, and many important bibliographical references. Covers the fields of language, literature, and allied subjects, e.g., myths, legends, manners and customs, etc.

A 3d edition has begun to appear, as follows:

—— Grundriss der germanischen Philologie unter Mitwirkung zahlreicher Fachgelehrter, begründet von Hermann Paul. Berlin, de Gruyter, 1913–64.

v.1 ^{1}, 2–10, 11 $^{1-3}$, 12 $^{1-2}$, 13 $^{1-4}$, 14–16, 17, 18 ^{1} (in progress).

An extensive revision; each volume edited by a specialist and covering a particular period or phase of Germanic philology.

Stroh, Friedrich. Handbuch der germanischen Philologie. Berlin, de Gruyter, 1952. 820p. il. **BC37**

Includes a historical outline of Germanic philology in general, and studies of the philology of individual fields, such as law, religion, literature, art. A considerable amount of bibliographical material is included throughout, but there is no separate bibliography. Sources cited are included in the general index.

Atlases

Deutscher Sprachatlas; auf Grund des Sprachatlas des Deutschen Reichs von Georg Wenker begonnen von Ferdinand Wrede, fortgesetzt von Walther Mitzka und Bernhard Martin. Marburg (Lahn), N. G. Elwert, 1927–56. 335p. 25cm., and atlas of 128 maps 63x68cm. In portfolio. **BC38**

Issued in parts.
Subtitle varies.

Dutch

Haeringen, Coenraad Bernardus van. Netherlandic language research; men and works in the study of Dutch. 2d ed. Leiden, Brill, 1960. 120p. **BC39**

1st ed. 1954.

A survey of 20th-century research on the history of the language of the Netherlands, with some critical evaluation of selected works in the field. Includes a chapter on reference works and periodicals.

Scandinavian

Bibliographie der nordischen Philologie, 1, 1925/26– . (Appears annually in *Acta philologica scandinavica*) **BC40**

A bibliography of Scandinavian philology and linguistics. Some issues cover more than one year. Lists books and periodical articles.

ROMANCE LANGUAGES

Gröber, Gustav. Grundriss der romanischen Philologie. 1st–2d ed. Strassburg, Trübner, 1897–1906. v.1–2 in 4.
BC41

v.1 is 2d edition, 1904–6.

Important reference book on the history and development of Romance philology and linguistics, for advanced workers only. Not alphabetically arranged, but in chapters, with detailed indexes and many bibliographical references.

—— —— Neue Folge. Abt. 1. Geschichte der französischen Literatur. Berlin, de Gruyter, 1933–38. v.3–5.

Contents: v.3–4, Geschichte der mittelfranzösischen Literatur: I, Vers- und Prosadichtung des 14. Jahrhundert, Drama des 14. und 15. Jahrhunderts. 2. Aufl. bearb. von Stefan Hofer; II, Vers- und Prosadichtung des 15. Jahrhundert. 2. Aufl. bearb. von Stefan Hofer; v.5, Frankreichs Literatur im 16. Jahrhundert, von Walter Mönch.

v.1–2 were to cover Altfranzösischen Dichtung; v.6– , 17. Jahrhundert– .

Jahrbuch für romanische und englische Sprache und Literatur. Berlin, Brockhaus, 1859–76. 15v.
BC42

None published 1872–73. Publisher varies. Contains a systematic bibliography of Romance languages and literatures.

Kritischer Jahresbericht über die Fortschritte der romanischen Philologie, 1890–1912. Erlangen, Junge, 1892–1915. v.1–13.
BC43

An important bibliography of books and articles on Romance philology, i.e., language and literature. In chapters, not in list form, and so somewhat difficult to use for purposes of quick reference, but important for the large amount of material included and for the analysis of periodicals. Discontinued.

Zeitschrift für romanische Philologie. Supplement Heft: Bibliographie, 1875– . Halle, 1878– .
BC44

v.39–43, 1914–23, never published.

A significant current bibliography listing books and periodical articles on the language and literature of the various Romance languages.

1940–50 issued in 1v. (14 Lfg.), 1952–57; 1951–55 issued in 1v. (2 Lfg.), 1961.

French

Brunot, Ferdinand. Histoire de la langue française, des origines à 1900. Paris, Colin, 1905– . v.1– . (In progress)
BC45

Contents: v.1, De l'époque latine à la Renaissance [rev. and corr. ed., 1924]. 547p.; v.2, Le seizième siècle. 1906. 504p.; v.3, La formation de la langue classique (1600–1660). 1909–11. 2v.; v.4, La langue classique (1660–1715). 1913–24. 2v.; v.5, Le français en France et hors de France au XVIIᵉ siècle. 1917. 443p.; v.6, Le XVIIIᵉ siècle. 1930–33. 2v. in 4; v.7, La propagation du français en France jusqu'à la fin de l'ancien régime. 1926. 360p.; v.8, Le français hors de France au XVIIIᵉ siècle. 1934–35. 2v. in 3; v.9, La Révolution et l'Empire. 1927–37. 2v.; v.10, La langue classique dans la tourmente. 1939–43. 2v.; v.11, Le français au dehors sous la Révolution, le Consulat et l'Empire (in prep.); v.12, L'époque romantique (1815–52), par Charles Bruneau. 1948. 593p.; v.13, L'époque réaliste (1852–86), par Charles Bruneau. 1953– . pt.1 (pt.2 in prep.); v.14, Le symbolisme (1886–1914), par Charles Bruneau (in prep.).

A monumental documented history of the French language.

Golden, Herbert Hershel and **Simches, Seymour O.** Modern French literature and language; a bibliography of homage studies. Cambridge, Harvard Univ. Pr., 1953. 158p.
BC46

For full information *see* BD653.

Horluc, Pierre and **Marinet, Georges.** Bibliographie de la syntaxe du français (1840–1905). Lyon, A. Rey; Paris, A. Picard, 1908. 320p. (Annales de l'Université de Lyon. n.s. II. Droit, lettres, fasc.20)
BC47

Lists materials published 1840–1905 on the history and treatment of French syntax from the Middle Ages through the 19th century.

Petit de Julleville, Louis. Histoire de la langue et de la littérature française des origines à 1900. Paris, Colin, 1896–99. 8v. il.
BC48

For full information *see* BD692.

Wagner, Robert-Léon. Introduction à la linguistique française. Genève, Droz; Lille, Giard, 1947. 142p. (Soc. de Publications Romanes et Françaises, v.27)
BC49

Includes bibliographies, p.59–139.

—— —— Supplément bibliographique. 1955. 71p. (Soc. de Publications Romanes et Françaises, v.47)

Atlases

Gilliéron, Jules and **Edmont, Edmond.** Atlas linguistique de la France . . . Paris, H. Champion, 1902–10. 1920 (i.e., 2048) maps in 17 portfolios. 55cm. Issued in 35 pts.
BC50

—— —— Notice servant à l'intelligence des cartes. Paris, H. Champion, 1902. 55p. 27cm.

—— —— Table. Paris, Champion, 1912. 519p.

—— —— Suppléments. Paris, Champion, 1920– .

—— Atlas linguistique de la France . . . Corse. Paris, Champion, 1914–15. Pts.1–4. 799 maps. 55cm.

An appendix to the author's *Atlas linguistique de la France*.

Italian

Golden, Herbert Hershel and **Simches, Seymour O.** Modern Italian language and literature; a bibliography of homage studies. Cambridge, Harvard Univ. Pr., 1959. 207p.
BC51

For full information *see* BD754.

Hall, Robert Anderson. Bibliografia della linguistica italiana. 2. ed. riv. e aggiornata. Firenze, Sansoni, 1958. 3v. (Biblioteca bibliografica italica, 13–15)
BC52

A major revision of the 1941 edition published as *Bibliography of Italian linguistics* (Baltimore, Linguistic Soc. of Amer.). This 2d edition contains some 6900 items, about twice the number in the 1st edition.

Includes material published since about 1860, arranged in four main sections: (1) History of the Italian language, (2) Description of the Italian language, (3) Italian dialectology, and (4) History of Italian linguistics. Five indexes: author and title, regions and dialects, words, etyma, and general subjects.

Atlases

Jaberg, Karl and **Jud, Jakob.** Sprach- und Sachatlas italiens und der Südschweiz . . . ; die Mundartaufnahmen wurden durchgeführt von P. Scheuermeier, G. Rohlfs und M. L. Wagner . . . Zofingen (Schweiz), Ringier, 1928–40. 8v. in 16. plates, fold. maps, tables. 46cm.
BC53

Latin

Cousin, Jean. Bibliographie de la langue latine, 1880–1948. Paris, Soc. d'Édit. "Les Belles Lettres," 1951. 375p.

(Collection de bibliographie classique par J. Marouzeau) **BC54**

A classified bibliography, in many languages, of books and periodical articles on the Latin language.

Portuguese

Paiva Boléo, Manuel de. Introdução ao estudo da filologia portuguesa. Lisboa, Rev. de Portugal, 1946. 150p. **BC55**

"Extr. dos nos. 34 a 43 da *Revista de Portugal*."

Includes bibliographies on the various Romance languages with emphasis on the Portuguese; covers phonetics, etymological dictionaries, historical grammars, etc.

Spanish

Cejador y Frauca, Julio. Historia de la lengua y literatura castellana. Madrid, 1915–22. 14v. il. **BC56**

For full information *see* BD812.

Enciclopedia lingüística hispánica, dirigida por M. Alvar [and others]. Madrid, Consejo Superior de Investigaciones Científicas, 1960–62. v.1–   and suppl. to v.1–   . (In progress) **BC57**

Contents: v.1, Antecedentes, onomastica. 656p.; Suppl. to v.1, La fragmentación fonética peninsular.

To be in 6v.

Nonalphabetical.

A scholarly treatment of the Spanish language. Chapters by specialists with bibliographical footnotes.

Golden, Herbert Hershel and **Simches, Seymour O.** Modern Iberian language and literature; a bibliography of homage studies. Cambridge, Harvard Univ. Pr., 1958. 184p. **BC58**

For full information *see* BD802.

Hall, Pauline Cook. A bibliography of Spanish linguistics: articles in serial publications. Baltimore, Linguistic Soc. of Amer., 1957. 162p. (Language dissertation, no.54. Supplement to *Language,* v.32, no.4, pt.2, Oct.–Dec. 1956) **BC59**

(Thesis, State University of Iowa.)

"Articles on the Spanish language available to scholars in this country." A classified list of 1930 items, with indexes of authors, words, and subjects.

Viñaza, Cipriano Muñoz y Manzano, *Conde de.* Biblioteca histórica de la filología castellana. Madrid, Manuel Tello, 1893. 1115p. **BC60**

An extensive bibliography—covering the years 1492–1893—on Castilian philology. Classified arrangement, and then chronological. A valuable historical work.

Woodbridge, Hensley Charles and **Olson, Paul Richard.** A tentative bibliography of Hispanic linguistics [based on the studies of Yakov Malkiel]. Urbana, Dept. of Spanish and Italian, Univ. of Illinois, 1952. 203p. **BC61**

Excludes Latin-American linguistics.

Lists 1879 items covering Hispanic linguistics from the Vulgar and medieval Latin period to the present day. Classified arrangement with author and word indexes. Includes both books and periodical articles.

Spanish American

Marino Flores, Anselmo. Bibliografía lingüística de la República Mexicana. México, Inst. Indigenista Interamericano, 1957. 95p. **BC62**

Lists books and articles on the various languages and dialects of Mexico.

Nichols, Madaline W. A bibliographical guide to materials on American Spanish. Cambridge, Harvard Univ.

Pr., 1941. 114p. (Committee on Latin Amer. studies, Amer. Council of Learned Societies, Misc. publ., no.2) **BC63**

1201 annotated items—books and periodical articles—on the philology of American Spanish, including general material and material under each country. Records official philological academies and organizations and the learned journals.

Tovar, Antonio. Catálogo de las lenguas de América del Sud; enumeración, con indicaciones tipológicas, bibliografía y mapas. Buenos Aires, Ed. Sudamericana, 1961. 406p. il. **BC64**

A discussion of the languages and dialects of South America is followed by a bibliography, p.203–370.

GREEK

Logos; monografías y síntesis bibliográfica de filología griega por Sebastian Cirac Estopañan. Barcelona, Univ. de Barcelona, 1960–   . v.1–   . (Facultad de Filosofía y Letras. Cátedra de Filología Griega. Sección de Filología Griega y Bizantinistica del C. S. de I. Científicas) Annual. **BC65**

v.1, 1960 (577p.), is an annotated listing of some 4600 books and articles in various languages on Greek philology.

Swanson, Donald Carl Eugene. Modern Greek studies in the West; a critical bibliography of studies on modern Greek linguistics, philology, and folklore, in languages other than Greek. N.Y., N.Y. Pub. Lib., 1960. 93p. **BC66**

Includes books and periodical articles, with brief annotations and references to reviews. Indexes to authors, words discussed, Greek regions, etc.

ARABIC

Sobelman, Harvey [and others]. Arabic dialect studies: a selected bibliography. Wash., Center for Applied Linguistics of the Modern Language Assoc. and the Middle East Inst., 1962. 100p. **BC67**

Discussion and bibliography of Syrian, Egyptian, Arabian Peninsula, Iraqi, North African, and Maltese Arabic studies.

SLAVIC

Akademiia Nauk SSSR. Institut Russkogo Iazyka. Slavianskoe iazykoznanie; bibliograficheskii ukazatel' literatury, izdannoi v SSSR s 1918 po 1960 gg. Red. S. B. Bernshtein. Moskva, 1963. 2v. **BC68**

A bibliography of books, articles, surveys, and reviews published in the Soviet Union on the subject of Slavic linguistics.

De Bray, Reginald G. A. Guide to the Slavonic languages. London, Dent, [1951]. 797p. [Repr.: London, Dent; N.Y., Dutton, 1963] **BC69**

An attempt to give an overall view of the Slavonic languages to those who are already familiar with one of the group. Each language is treated in a separate section, introduced by a brief history of the language followed by a more-or-less detailed examination of the alphabet, pronunciation, morphology, word order, and features characteristic of the language, and brief passages from its literature. The bibliography at the end of the book, while not attempting to be exhaustive, lists grammars, dictionaries, and other aids to study in the field, including works in English, French, and German. A detailed table of contents but no index.

Hille, Annemarie. Bibliographische Einführung in das Studium der slawischen Philologie. Halle (Saale), Max Niemeyer Verlag, 1959. 149p. **BC70**

A selection of reference books, bibliographies, and studies in Slavic linguistics and literature, organized as a guide for students.

International Organization for Standardization. International system for the transliteration of Cyrillic characters. 1st ed. Oct. 1955. Printed in Switzerland. 7p. (ISO Recommendation, R9) **BC71**

Presents a system resembling European practice, rather than the U.S. Library of Congress system, for transliteration into Latin characters from Russian, Bulgarian, Ukrainian, Belorussian, and Serbian. The Recommendation was approved by 20 out of 34 member bodies of ISO, as of 1953. Adopted by UNESCO in 1956 for its bibliographical publications.

For discussion and tables of seven Anglo-American systems of transliteration from Russian, *see* R. Neiswender, *Guide to Russian reference and language aids,* p.63–66 (AA303).

Sadnik, Linda and **Aitzemüller, Rudolf.** Vergleichendes Wörterbuch der slavischen Sprachen. Wiesbaden, Harrassowitz, 1963–64. (In progress) **BC72**

Lfg. 1–2, A–Ble.

A comparative dictionary for Slavic languages.

Unbegaun, Boris Ottokar. A bibliographical guide to the Russian language, with the collaboration of J. S. G. Simmons. Oxford, Clarendon Pr., 1953. 174p. **BC73**

A practical guide to publications dealing with the Russian language and its history, listing 1043 titles, many of them annotated, under three main divisions: (1) (General), works of a general bibliographical nature; (2) (Historical), relating to the prehistory and history of the Russian language; and (3) (Descriptive), grammar and vocabulary of modern literary Russian, and works on dialects, slang, jargons, etc. Titles are given in full and in the original language. Index.

TURKIC

Loewenthal, Rudolf. The Turkic languages and literatures of Central Asia; a bibliography. 's-Gravenhage, Mouton, 1957. 212p. (Central Asiatic studies. I) **BC74**

A classified list of 2093 books and articles. Author index. Covers Old, Middle, and Modern Turkic languages.

Sovietico-Turcica: Beiträge zur Bibliographie der türkischen Sprachwissenschaft in rüssischer Sprache in der Sowjetunion, 1917–1957. Budapest, Akadémiai Kiadó, 1960. 319p. (Bibliotheca orientalis hungarica. IX) **BC75**

"Mit Unterstützung der Ungarischen Akademie der Wissenschaften und unter Mitwirkung einer Arbeitsgemeinschaft des Turkologischen Instituts der Universität Budapest red. von Georg Hazai, übers. von A. T.-Varga . . . "—*Verso of title page.*

More than 2700 items, alphabetically listed by main entry in Russian, with German translation of title following each listing. Subject index in German.

SEMITIC

LaSor, William Sanford. A basic Semitic bibliography. (Annotated) Wheaton, Ill., Van Kampen Pr., 1950. 56p. **BC76**

A selected bibliography arranged by Semitic language. Under each language there is a brief introduction and then, insofar as possible, are listed texts, grammars, and lexicons, historical and general. Basic works are included in English and other western European languages. Titles are annotated briefly.

YIDDISH

Weinreich, Uriel and **Weinreich, Beatrice.** Yiddish language and folklore; a selective bibliography for research. 's-Gravenhage, Mouton, 1959. 66p. (Janua linguarum, no.10) **BC77**

In two parts: pt.1, Yiddish language (253 items); pt.2, Yiddish folklore (items 254–481).

EAST AFRICAN

Whiteley, W. H. and **Gutkind, A. E.** A linguistic bibliography of East Africa. Rev. ed. Kampala, East African Swahili Committee and East African Inst. of Social Research, 1958. 1v. Loose-leaf. **BC78**

The 1st edition attempted to bring together "in one easily accessible publication a list of all that was known to have been written on the grammar and lexicon of the East African languages." This edition incorporates the listings from the 1954 volume and its supplements, with additional material: books, periodical articles, and manuscripts. Sections are devoted to the languages of Tanganyika, Kenya, and Uganda, with a special section for Swahili.

OCEANIC

Hollyman, K. J. A checklist of Oceanic languages (Melanesia, Micronesia, New Guinea, Polynesia). Auckland, Linguistic Soc. of New Zealand, 1960. 32p. (Te Reo monographs) **BC79**

A list of more than 1500 languages and dialects, with abbreviated references to the linguistic family from which derived, the areas in which spoken, and a bibliographic citation for further information.

Klieneberger, H. R. Bibliography of Oceanic linguistics. London, Oxford Univ. Pr., 1957. 143p. (London oriental bibliographies, v.1) **BC80**

Includes "printed books, periodical articles, and reviews dealing with Oceanic (i.e., Polynesian, Micronesian, Melanesian, and Papuan) languages . . . [and] dictionaries, vocabularies, grammars, and other linguistic contributions but excludes writings in the individual languages themselves." Arranged by region, subdivided by language.

Kunz, Egon F. An annotated bibliography of the languages of the Gilbert Islands, Ellice Islands and Nauru. Sydney, Trustees of the Pub. Lib. of New South Wales, 1959. 202p. **BC81**

Locates copies, some in libraries outside Australia.

Teeuw, A. and **Emanuels, H. W.** A critical survey of studies on Malay and Bahasa Indonesia. s'-Gravenhage, Nijhoff, 1961. 176p. (Koninklijk Instituut voor Taal-, Land- en Volkenkunde. Bibliographical ser., 5) **BC82**

A survey with bibliography of linguistic materials, including a history of dictionaries; dialects; grammars, etc.

BD

Literature

☙ In the general library many of the questions asked at the reference desk pertain to some phase of literature, e.g., biographies of authors; reviews of books; quotations; identifications of partly remembered titles; characters; plots; location of poems, plays, short stories, essays; or the history and development of literature by form or by nationality. To answer these questions the general as well as the special reference works must be remembered. National bibliographies and biographical dictionaries, indexes to periodicals and book reviews, encyclopedias and dictionaries, are of basic importance. However, to supplement the general works, a large number of special aids are available, some international in scope and others devoted to the literature of a particular country.

The needs of libraries will vary, but basic equipment for an average American library would include: for **history and bibliography,** *Cambridge bibliography of English literature* (BD309), *Cambridge history of English literature* (BD344), *Cambridge history of American literature* (BD221), and *Literary history of the United States* (BD222); **dictionaries and handbooks,** *Columbia dictionary of modern European literature* (BD20), Kunitz and Haycraft's *Twentieth century authors* (BD68), *Contemporary authors* (BD64), *American authors* (BD224), *British authors* (BD349, BD350), *Oxford companion to American literature* (BD216), and *Oxford companion to English literature* (BD335); **plots,** Keller's *Reader's digest of books* (BD36), or Magill's *Masterpieces of world literature* (BD37); **quotations and proverbs,** Bartlett's *Familiar quotations* (BD75), Hoyt's *New cyclopedia of practical quotations* (BD77), *Oxford dictionary of quotations* (BD80), *Oxford dictionary of English proverbs* (BD124), Stevenson's *Home book of quotations* (BD83) and his *Home book of proverbs* (BD125); and the **various indexes** to poetry, plays, short stories, essays, etc.

Anthologies and collections of poetry, plays, short stories, and other forms of literature may be shelved in the reference room or may be made available elsewhere in the library. Materials in foreign literature should be acquired according to need. Libraries much used by students will need several of the annual bibliographical surveys, e.g., *MLA International bibliography* of the Modern Language Association (BD9), *Annual bibliography* of the Modern Humanities Research Association (BD313), *Year's work in English studies* (BD314), and many of the more specialized works.

GENERAL WORKS

Bibliography

Baldensperger, Fernand and **Friederich, Werner P.** Bibliography of comparative literature. Chapel Hill, Univ. of North Carolina Pr., 1950. 701p. (Univ. of North Carolina studies in comparative literature, no.1) **BD1**

An extensive compendium attempting to cover literary influences from early to modern times. Arranged in four books: the first and third dealing with generalities (including themes, motifs, genres, international literary relations, etc.); the second and fourth with specific literatures and their contributions, listed according to country or author exerting influence.

Bibliographical citations are very brief. A detailed table of contents but no index.

For continuation *see Yearbook of comparative and general literature* (BD12).

Betz, Louis Paul. La littérature comparée. Essai bibliographique. Introd. par Joseph Texte. 2. éd. augm., pub., avec un index méthodique, par Fernand Baldensperger. Strasbourg, Trübner, 1904. 386col., 389–410p. **BD2**

A bibliography of books and periodical articles on comparative literature from the Middle Ages through the 19th century.

Still useful for the large amount of 19th-century material not included in Baldensperger (BD1).

Edwardes, Marian. Summary of the literatures of modern Europe (England, France, Germany, Italy, Spain) from the origins to 1400. London, Dent, 1907. 532p. **BD3**

Arranged by country and under each by century, from the earliest times through the 13th century; for each century notes the principal writers, list of works, notes about works, and bibliographical references to editions, translations, and critical works and articles. Gives information about the historical romances, the cycles, the *chansons de geste,* etc.

Farrar, Clarissa Palmer and **Evans, Austin Patterson.** Bibliography of English translations from medieval sources. N.Y., Columbia Univ. Pr., 1946. 534p. (Records of civilization; sources and studies, no.39) **BD4**

"Aims to include English translations of important literary sources produced during the period from Constantine the Great to the year 1500 within an area roughly inclusive of Europe, northern Africa and western Asia."—*Pref.* Lists works published through 1942, with a few items published later which were inserted in proof.

An outstanding work including almost 4000 entries arranged alphabetically by author, with many annotations describing content, translator's comment, editions or reprints of a given translation, adequacy of translation, etc. Extensive index to authors, translators, editors, titles, subjects, etc.

International Federation of Modern Languages and Literatures. Répertoire chronologique des littératures modernes, publié par la Commission Internationale d'Histoire Littéraire Moderne. [Ed.], Paul Van Tieghem. Paris, E. Droz, 1935. 413p. **BD5**

Issued in parts, 1935–37.

Arranged chronologically; under each year lists the principal writings and literary events by country. Covers 1455–1900. Index.

Reuss, Jeremias David. Repertorium commentationum a societatibus litterariis editarum. Secundum disciplinarum ordinem . . . T.8–9. Gottingae, Dieterich, 1810. (Repr.: N.Y., Burt Franklin, 1961) **BD6**

Contents: T.8, Historia . . . Historia litteraria; T.9, Philologia, Linguae, Scriptores graeci, Scriptores latini, Litterae elegantiores, Poesis, Rhetorica, Ars antique, Pictura, Musica.

A valuable index to the publications of the learned societies of various countries up to 1800. Classed arrangement with author index.

For complete contents of v.8 *see* DA13; for description of complete set *see* EA15.

Current

Bibliographie générale de littérature comparée, années 1949/1950–1957/1958. Paris, Boivin, 1951–59. Biennial. **BD7**

Publiée avec le concours de l'UNESCO.
Ceased publication (?).
Reprints of the quarterly bibliographies in *Revue de littérature comparée,* issued in this form to supplement Baldensperger (BD1).

Literature of the Renaissance. (In Studies in philology, v.14, 1917–   ) Annual.   **BD8**

Through 1952 called *Recent literature of the Renaissance.* Until 1938 covered works on the English Renaissance only. From 1939 covers English, French, Germanic, Italian, Neo-Latin, Spanish, and Portuguese (slight variations). Includes index of proper names.

Modern Language Association of America. MLA International bibliography, 1921–   . (Pub. as supplements to PMLA, v.39–   ) Annual.   **BD9**

1921–1954/55, repr. as *MLA American bibliography;* 1956, repr. as *MLA International bibliography of books and articles on the modern languages and literatures.* N.Y., Kraus, 1964.

A very useful annual bibliography; from 1921 to 1955 entitled *American bibliography* and limited to writings by Americans on the literatures of various countries, e.g., English, American, French, Italian, Spanish, Portuguese, and Germanic. Coverage varied. 1956–62, title changed to *Annual bibliography* and coverage extended to include writers in other languages. 1963–   , title changed to *MLA International bibliography* (this title used in reprint edition as noted above). Selections are made from various book sources and from a basic master list of about 1150 periodicals in the field of modern languages and literatures. By 1963 the work listed books and articles in English, French, German, Spanish, Italian, Portuguese, Rumanian, Scandinavian, Dutch, Celtic, and a selection of 10 East European languages.

Classified arrangement with author indexes. No cumulations.

Progress of medieval and Renaissance studies in the United States and Canada. Bull. no.1–25. Boulder, Colo., 1923–60.   **BD10**

Title varies. Publication suspended.

Renaissance studies added with no.15. Each number contains lists of papers, publications, projects, doctoral dissertations, and a list of medieval and Renaissance scholars, with their publications.

The Romantic movement: A selective and critical bibliography for 1936–48. (In ELH, a journal of English literary history. 1937–49; 1949–   , in Philological quarterly, 1950–   ) Annual.   **BD11**

Editors vary.

"Designed to cover a 'movement' " rather than a period. English section limited to 1800–37; other sections not so limited. Covers English, French, German, Spanish, and Portuguese.

Yearbook of comparative and general literature. Bloomington, Indiana Univ., 1952–   . v.1–   . Annual. **BD12**

Published in collaboration with the Comparative Literature Committee of the National Council of Teachers of English; the American Comparative Literature Association; and the Comparative Literature Section of the Modern Language Association.

Includes articles, news items, biographical sketches, and an *Annual bibliography* designed to serve as a supplement to Baldensperger, *Bibliography of comparative literature* (BD1).

General collections and anthologies

Great books of the Western world and the great ideas. Ed. in chief, Robert Maynard Hutchins; assoc. ed., Mortimer J. Adler. Chicago, Encyclopaedia Britannica, 1952. 54v. il.   **BD13**

Advisory board: Stringfellow Barr, Scott Buchanan, John

Erskine, Clarence H. Faust, Alexander Meiklejohn, Joseph J. Schwab, and Mark Van Doren. Editorial consultants: A. F. B. Clark, F. L. Lucas, and Walter Murdoch.

A collection of the great books from Homer to Freud, each given in English in its entirety (with three exceptions).

v.2–3, entitled *The great ideas: Syntopicon* (Mortimer J. Adler, ed. in chief; William Gorman, gen. ed.), are an index and a guide to reading. The great ideas are arranged in 102 topical chapters, each with an introduction, an outline of topics, references, cross references, and additional readings. The citations under each topic are in chronological order, with references to the specific parts of works dealing with the various phases of the topic.

v.3 closes with a bibliography of additional readings, a chapter on the principles and methods of syntopical construction, and an inventory of terms.

The Syntopicon may serve as an index to the set, a guide to writings on certain topics, or even as an index to quotations. However, its complex structure will detract from its use as a quick reference aid.

The Harvard classics, ed. by Charles W. Eliot. N.Y., Collier, 1909. 50 (i.e., 52) v. il.   **BD14**

A collection of writings chosen as representations of the world's great literature in all fields. With a few exceptions, such as the Bible and Shakespeare, the works are complete, not selections. Chronologically the material covers from ancient to modern times: from the sacred books of the early religions, through the literature of Greece and Rome, the Middle Ages in the Orient and Europe, the Renaissance, and the 19th century, in Europe and America.

v.50 contains an analytical author, subject, and title index to all of the material contained in the set, as well as an index to first lines of poems, songs and choruses, hymns, and psalms. There are two additional unnumbered volumes: (1) Reading guide and (2) Lectures on the Harvard Classics, edited by William Allan Neilson.

The set is useful in libraries particularly for its comprehensive index, and also because it may provide additional copies of standard works.

——— The idexicon, a guide to the great ideas of the Eastern and Western worlds. N.Y., Crowell-Collier, 1961. 470p.   **BD14a**

An index to the authors included, and the ideas and subjects treated, in the 50v. of the *Harvard classics.* Intended to aid in the tracing of the development of ideas and concepts by different writers through the centuries.

Warner library . . . Eds.: John W. Cunliffe, Ashley H. Thorndike, N.Y., Warner Lib. Co., 1917. 30v. il. **BD15**

Contents: v.1–26, World's best literature (sketches and selections); v.27, Book of songs and lyrics; v.28, Reader's dictionary of authors, ed. by H. M. Ayres; v.29, Reader's digest of books, ed. by H. R. Keller; v.30, Students' course in literature, by G. R. Lomer. General index: authors, titles, subjects, etc.

A useful popular collection of representative selections from writers of all periods and countries, with considerable popular reference material in the way of critical notices, biographies, synopses of books, etc. Issued in three different editions. The 1st edition, ed. by Charles Dudley Warner (N.Y., Peale, 1896–97. 30v.), had title *Library of the world's best literature.* The 1917 edition is a reprint from plates of v.1–27 of the 1st edition, with changes and the addition of considerable new material on new pages inserted throughout in their proper places and fitted into the original paging by the use of subletters a,b,c, etc.; v.28–30 of this edition are entirely reset. A later, entirely rearranged edition, with the title *Columbia University course in literature, based on the World's best literature,* utilized considerable material from the 1917 edition; was arranged by countries and periods rather than by authors; and added selections and notices, but omitted the three special reference volumes of the 1917 edition, i.e., *Dictionary of authors, Reader's digest,* and *General index.* The

Reader's digest which forms v.29 of the 1917 edition is also published separately by Macmilllan; for new, enlarged edition *see* BD36. The critical and biographical notices in v.1–26 of the 1917 edition and in the *Columbia University course in literature,* but not the selections, are indexed in the *Essay . . . index.* N.Y., Wilson, 1934 (BD145)

Dictionaries and encyclopedias

Barnet, Sylvan, Berman, Morton and **Burto, William.** A dictionary of literary terms. Boston, Little, 1960. 96p.
BD16

Originally published (1960) as a portion of the authors' *The study of literature; a handbook of critical essays and terms.*

A brief handbook. Major literary forms and concepts are explained in some detail. Many cross references from specific terms to the longer articles.

Beckson, Karl and **Ganz, Arthur.** A reader's guide to literary terms: a dictionary. N.Y., Noonday, 1960. 230p.
BD17

Not only gives definitions but discusses meanings of literary terms, often with examples and references to literature.

Benét, William Rose. The reader's encyclopedia. 2d ed. N.Y., Crowell, 1965. 1118p. il.   **BD18**

1st ed. 1948.

A comprehensive work containing brief articles on writers, scientists, philosophers, etc., of all nations and all periods; allusions and literary expressions and terms; literary schools and movements; plots and characters; descriptions of musical compositions and works of art, etc.

The 2d edition emphasizes world literature with emphasis on areas of growing interest, e.g., the Orient, the Soviet Union, Latin America, and the Near East; and the literary developments since 1948 when the 1st edition was published.

Cassell's Encyclopaedia of literature. Ed., Sigfrid Henry Steinberg. London, Cassell, 1953. 2v.(2086p.).   **BD19**

Also published as *Cassell's Encyclopaedia of world literature.* N.Y., Funk & Wagnalls, 1954.

Contents: pt.1, Histories of the literatures of the world and general literary subjects, p.1–574; pt.2, Biographies of authors who died before 1 August 1914, p.575–1670; pt.3, Biographies of authors who were living on 1 August 1914 or who were born after that date, p.1671–2086.

Articles in pt.1 vary in length from brief definitions of literary terms to several pages and are signed; bibliographies are included.

Biographical sketches are brief, include bibliographies of works by and about, and are also signed.

Columbia dictionary of modern European literature. Horatio Smith, gen. ed. N.Y., Columbia Univ. Pr., 1947. 899p.   **BD20**

"The intention of this Dictionary is to provide a record and signed evaluations of the chief books of the important literary artists of all continental Europe—in the twentieth century and the immediately preceding and closely related decades. . . . "—*Pref.*

A scholarly dictionary, including biographical sketches with critical evaluations covering 200 French, 150 German, 100 Russian, 100 Italian, 100 Spanish, 50 Polish, 40 Czech writers, etc., and survey articles with bibliographies of the 31 literatures of the Continent, each written and signed by an authority. 239 specialists have written the 1167 articles. For the most part, careful editing has achieved a balance in choice and treatment of subjects, and in bibliographical form, without formalizing the style of the individual writer, though, as in any cooperative undertaking, the result is sometimes uneven.

Dizionario letterario Bompiani delle opere e dei personaggi di tutti i tempi e di tutte le letterature. Milan, Bompiani, 1947–50. 9v.   **BD21**

Contents: v.1–7, A–Z; v.8, a dictionary of literary characters; v.9, indexes.

A dictionary, listing and describing the works of all times and all countries in literature, art, and music. Although the emphasis is on literature, musical works and many famous pictures are described. Lavishly illustrated with many colored plates and black-and-white illustrations. The first half of v.1 is devoted to 58 *movimenti spirituali,* arranged alphabetically, e.g., Dadaism, euphuism, mysticism. The main part of the work consists of signed articles, arranged alphabetically by the Italian form of the title of the work followed by the original title in brackets. Brief biographical notes are usually included in the articles, but there are no author entries.

v.8 is a dictionary of literary characters alphabetized according to the Italian form of the name. The scope is broad, ranging from Adam to Superman. v.9 includes synoptic tables showing literary development in all parts of the world; a list of titles in the original languages with their Italian equivalents; an index of authors; and an index of illustrations by artist.

—— Appendice. Milan, Bompiani, 1964– . v.1– . (In progress)

Contents: v.1, A–M.

Dizionario universale delle letteratura contemporanea. [Direttore: Alberto Mondadori] Milano, Mondadori, 1959–63. 5v. il.   **BD22**

An encyclopedia of world literature covering 1870–1960 and supplementing Bompiani. Arranged alphabetically, it includes authors ("non-literary" as well as men of letters), literary movements, periodicals, national literatures, etc. Bibliographies are generally substantial and include works by and about an author. Extensively illustrated in black and white and in color.

v.5 includes chronological tables, 1870–1961, and various indexes: authors, titles both in Italian and in the original language; works not translated; illustrations; etc.

Dictionnaire des œuvres de tous les temps et de tous les pays: littérature, philosophie, musique, sciences par Laffont-Bompiani. [3d ed.] Paris, Soc. d'Édit. de Dictionnaires et Encyclopédies, 1958. 4v. and index. il.   **BD23**

1st ed. 1952–54.

An abridged French edition of Bompiani (BD21), omitting the section on literary movements and literary characters. Listing is by French form of the titles, with an author index volume.

—— Supplément, 1959. Paris, S.E.D.E., 1959. 5 fasc., each 16p.

Addenda to v.1–4 and index of authors.

Dictionnaire des personnages littéraires et dramatiques de tous les temps et de tous les pays: poésie, théâtre, roman, musique. Laffont-Bompiani. Paris, Soc. d'Édit. de Dictionnaires et Encyclopédies, 1960. 664p. il.   **BD24**

A companion volume to the *Dictionnaire des œuvres de tous les temps et de tous les pays* (BD23); identifies and describes characters of fiction, poetry, music, and drama. Historical persons are included only if they have become literary characters. Cross references are made to works in the *Dictionnaire des œuvres.*

Dictionnaire universel des lettres, publié sous la direction de Pierre Clarac. Paris, Soc. d'Édit. de Dictionnaires et Encyclopédies, 1961. 952p. il.   **BD25**

At head of title: Laffont-Bompiani.

A concise encyclopedia of authors, works, literary terms, and movements, arranged in one alphabet. Much of the material is based on fuller articles appearing in other sets of the same publisher, themselves based on or related to Bompiani (BD21); other articles are new.

Eppelsheimer, Hanns Wilhelm. Handbuch der Weltliteratur, von den Anfängen bis zur Gegenwart. 3. neubearb. und ergänzte Aufl. Frankfurt am Main, Klostermann, 1960. 808p.   **BD26**

1st ed. 1937; 2d ed. 1947–50. 2v.

Covers the literatures of East Asia, India, the ancient Near East, Islam, Greece and Rome, the Middle Ages, and Europe, the latter arranged by century and then by country.

Each section has a brief introduction followed by bibliography, with biographical sketches of authors, giving editions, translations, criticism, etc.

Frauwallner, Erich, Giebisch, Hans and **Heinzel, E.** Die Weltliteratur; biographisches, literarhistorisches und bibliographisches Lexikon in Übersichten und Stichwörtern. Wien, Hollinek, 1951–54. 3v.   **BD27**

A scholarly German encyclopedia of world literature from the earliest times to 1951, giving concise information about national literatures, literary forms, and outstanding authors, alphabetically arranged with many cross references. Articles include bibliographies; for personal names, these include both works by and about the authors.

v.3 includes an appendix and an index.

Lexikon der Weltliteratur im 20. Jahrhundert. 2. Aufl. Freiburg, Herder, 1960–61. 2v. il.   **BD28**

v.1, 2. Aufl.; v.2, 1. and 2. Aufl.

Includes some 1900 signed articles on authors of many nationalities, national literatures, and literary movements. Biographical articles average one to two columns in length, with some much longer, and include bibliographies of works by and about the writers. The more general articles also include bibliographies.

Meyers Handbuch über die Literatur. Hrsg. und bearb. von den Fachredaktion des Bibliographischen Instituts. Mannheim, Allgemeiner Verlag, 1964. 959p. il., facsims.   **BD29**

In two main sections: (1) "Sachwörterbuch zur Literatur" and (2) "Lexikon der Dichter und Schriftsteller." Includes chronologies of various national literatures, miscellaneous tables, and reproductions of handwritten manuscripts of selected authors.

Sáinz de Robles, Federico Carlos. Ensayo de un diccionario de la literatura. Madrid, Aguilar, 1949–50. 3v.   **BD30**

Contents: t.1, Términos y conceptos literarios; t.2, Escritores españoles e hispanoamericanos; t.3, Escritores extranjeros.

The entries in v.1 range from definitions of terms to extensive articles on literary concepts with bibliographies. The bio-bibliographical articles in v.2–3 include sketches of authors of all periods.

Schneider, Georg. Die Schlüsselliteratur. Stuttgart, Hiersemann, 1951–53. 3v.   **BD31**

Contents: Bd.1, Das literarische Gesamtbild; Bd.2, Entschlüsselung deutscher Romane und Dramen; Bd.3, Entschlüsselung ausländischer Romane und Dramen.

A key to the identities of real characters and events appearing in literature under fictitious names. Not all-inclusive but treats the significant works of many literatures. v.1 gives general explanations and definitions, history, and discussion with indexes of authors and prototypes; v.2 is devoted to German fiction and drama; v.3, to non-German literature.

Thrall, William Flint and **Hibbard, Addison.** A handbook to literature, rev. and enl. by C. Hugh Holman. N.Y., Odyssey, 1960. 598p.   **BD32**

1st ed. 1936.

Explanations of terms, concepts, schools, and movements, alphabetically arranged with many cross references.

An "Outline of literary history, English and American" (p.519–598) lists in tabular form outstanding English literary events from Celtic Britain to 1959, and, for American literature, from 1607 to 1959.

Wilpert, Gero von. Sachwörterbuch der Literatur. 2. verb. und erw. Aufl. Stuttgart, Kröner, 1959. 701p. (Kröners Taschenausgabe. Bd.231)   **BD33**

A dictionary of literary terms, giving definition, frequently etymology, usage, and bibliography.

Digests

Various handbooks and compilations which give plots of novels, and synopses and digests of well-known books, should be represented in the general reference collection, although occasionally, when a student asks for an outline to save the trouble of reading assigned work, the librarian will need to exercise discretion in supplying or withholding material. Synopses are found in many author dictionaries and handbooks: in such works as the *Oxford companions* (BD216, BD335) and Brewer's *Reader's handbook* (BD49) (these are comparatively brief); and in some encyclopedias such as Larousse, *Grand dictionnaire* (AD28). Critical reviews also often give outlines of the works reviewed. For other aids see the following:

Downs, Robert B. Famous books, ancient and medieval. N.Y., Barnes & Noble, 1964. 329p.   **BD34**

Outlines of 108 works that have shaped modern civilization, from the *Book of the dead* to *Canterbury tales*. Includes biographical information, summaries, and discussions of influence.

Haydn, Hiram and **Fuller, Edmund.** Thesaurus of book digests: digests of the world's permanent writings from the ancient classics to current literature. N.Y., Crown, 1949. 831p.   **BD35**

Very concise digests arranged by title, with an author index and an index to characters. In some cases, when authors are remembered for the body of their work rather than for a particular title, discussion is given under the author's name.

Keller, Helen Rex. Reader's digest of books. New and greatly enl. ed. N.Y., Macmillan, 1929. 1447p.   **BD36**

Frequently reprinted.

Earlier edition (1917. 941p.) was also issued as v.29 of the *Warner library* (BD15). Separately published in 1922.

Synopses of the outstanding works, fiction and nonfiction, of many countries and periods. In two alphabets; the supplementary alphabet, p.925–1423, contains the new material added in the 1929 edition, and is indexed in a separate index.

Magill, Frank Northen. Masterpieces of world literature in digest form. N.Y., Harper, 1952–60. v.1–3.   **BD37**

1st ser., 1952; 2d ser., 1956; 3d ser., 1960.

Also published as *Masterplots . . . plots in story form from the world's fine literature* (N.Y., Salem Pr., 1954–60. 6v.), and in various combinations.

Each volume arranged alphabetically by title of work. Indicates type of work, author, time, locale, date first published, principal characters, critique, the story.

Masterplots annual volume, 1954– . Ed. by Frank N. Magill. N.Y., Salem Pr., 1955– . v.1– .   **BD38**

Title varies: 1954, *Masterplots annual review*.

"Essay-reviews of 100 outstanding books published in the United States . . . ."

Signed reviews.

Masterplots annuals. Masterplots; best masterplots, 1954–1962. 175 essay-reviews from Masterplots annuals since 1954. Ed. by Frank N. Magill and Dayton Kohler. N.Y., Salem Pr., 1963. lviiip., 625p.   **BD39**

Olbrich, Wilhelm. Der Romanführer. Stuttgart, Hiersemann, 1950–64. v.1–13. (In progress)   **BD40**

A compilation of digests in German of novels and short stories from many countries.

Directories

Author's and writer's who's who, ed. by L. G. Pine. 5th ed. London, Burke's Peerage Ltd., 1963. 540p.　　**BD41**

1st ed. 1934.

Includes not only authors of books but also editors, feature writers, and other journalists. Limited to writers in the English-speaking world.

Literary market place, 1940– . The business directory of American book publishing. N.Y., Bowker, 1940– . Annual. (1964/65)　　**BD42**

For full information *see* AA217.

Writers' and artists' year book, 1906– , a directory for writers, artists, playwrights, writers for film, radio and television, photographers and composers. London, Black; N.Y., Macmillan, 1906– . v.1– . (v.57, 1964) **BD43**

Subtitle varies slightly.

Contains lists of English, Commonwealth, and American journals and magazines, with statement of kind of material accepted by each and rate of payment, lists of publishers, literary agents, markets for writers, plays, films, broadcasting artists, photographers, musicians, etc., and other kinds of directory material useful to writers desiring to place manuscripts.

Writer's handbook, 1936– . Boston, Writer, 1936– . Annual.　　**BD44**

In two parts. Pt.1 is made up of articles by various writers, which appeared originally in *The writer,* on various phases of professional writing including fiction, nonfiction, and specialties. Some articles are carried over from earlier editions, some are new, none are dated.

Pt.2 is a market guide, mainly to the periodical field, giving for each periodical: address, editor, and type of material accepted with indication of rate of payment. Also has section for radio and television, and for book publishers.

Literary awards

Clapp, Jane. International dictionary of literary awards. N.Y., Scarecrow, 1963. 545p.　　**BD45**

" . . . A selected list of major literary honors granted internationally and in countries other than the United States, Canada, and the United Kingdom."—*Pref.*

Each award is described, and a list of winning authors with titles of winning works is given.

Literary and library prizes. N.Y., Bowker, 1959. 259p.　　**BD46**

1st ed. 1935. Title varies. 1935 and 1939 editions were edited by Bessie Graham with title *Famous literary prizes and their winners.*

[3d edition], 1946, had title *Literary prizes and their winners.* This, the 4th edition, lists literary prizes, both American and foreign, giving some explanations and background of the award and a record of the recipients for each since its establishment. Library prizes are included for the first time.

Handbooks

Ackermann, Alfred Seabold Eli. Popular fallacies; a book of common errors explained and corrected, with copious references to authorities. 4th ed. London, Old Westminster Pr., 1950. 843p.　　**BD47**

An informative and sometimes amusing potpourri of facts arranged under broad headings, such as food, weather, literature, etc. Subject index.

Brewer, Ebenezer Cobham. Brewer's Dictionary of phrase and fable, rev. and enl. London, Cassell, 1952; N.Y., Harper, 1953. 977p.　　**BD48**

1st ed. 1870. Frequently revised.

Includes colloquial and proverbial phrases, biographical and mythological references, fictitious characters, titles, etc. This is an entirely revised edition of the 1923 edition, including many terms used in World War II. Many articles have been rewritten, shortened, or omitted. The 1923 edition will often be needed since much useful material has been dropped.

—— Reader's handbook of famous names in fiction, allusions, references, proverbs, plots, stories, and poems. New ed. rev. and greatly enl. London, Chatto; Philadelphia, Lippincott, 1898. 1501p.　　**BD49**

Still one of the best of these handbooks. Appendixes, p.1245–1501, contain: (1) List of English authors and their works, and (2) Title list of dramas and operas, giving authors and dates.

Later issues omit the appendixes.

Freeman, William. Dictionary of fictional characters. London, Dent; N.Y., The Writer, 1963. 458p.　　**BD50**

A listing of some 20,000 fictitious characters, from approximately 2000 books, by some 500 British, Commonwealth, and American authors written in the last 600 years. Covers novels, short stories, poems, and nonmusical plays. Does not include Gilbert and Sullivan or John Gay.

Hyamson, Albert Montefiore. Dictionary of English phrases. London, Routledge; N.Y., Dutton, 1922. 365p.　　**BD51**

Subtitle: Phraseological allusions, catchwords, stereotyped modes of speech and metaphors, nicknames, sobriquets, derivations from personal names, etc. With explanations and thousands of exact references to their sources or early usage.

Magill, Frank N. Cyclopedia of literary characters. N.Y., Harper, 1963. 1280p., xivp., 50p.　　**BD52**

"Also appears under title of *Masterplots cyclopedia of literary characters.*"

Arranged by title of work; gives the characters of each book with brief descriptions of each. Includes books of all periods from the ancient Greeks to the 20th century, with an author index and a character index.

Reader's companion to world literature. Gen. ed., Calvin S. Brown; ed., Lillian Herlands Hornstein . . . N.Y., Dryden, 1956. 493p.　　**BD53**

A compact, well-edited encyclopedia of authors, titles, characters, themes, terminology, etc.

Shankle, George Earlie. American nicknames, their origin and significance. 2d ed. N.Y., Wilson, 1955. 524p. **BD54**

1st ed. 1937.

Not limited to nickname of persons, but includes also those applied to places, institutions, or objects, arranged by real names with cross references from nicknames. Information under the real names includes some explanation of the nicknames and their origin, and gives references to sources of information in footnotes.

Walsh, William Shepard. Handy book of curious information comprising strange happenings in the life of men and animals, odd statistics, extraordinary phenomena and out-of-the-way facts concerning the wonderlands of the earth. Philadelphia, London, Lippincott, [1913]. 942p.　　**BD55**

—— Handy-book of literary curiosities. Philadelphia, London, Lippincott, 1909. 1104p.　　**BD56**

One of the most useful of the older handbooks.

Wheeler, William Adolphus. Familiar allusions; a handbook of miscellaneous information. 5th ed. Boston, Houghton, 1890 [c1881]. 584p.　　**BD57**

"Including the names of celebrated statues, paintings, palaces, country-seats, ruins, churches, ships, streets, clubs, natural curiosities, and the like."

✣ The above are popular handbooks, useful mainly as first aids. Important information will also be found in periodicals of the "notes and queries" type. The following may be especially helpful:

⌐American notes and queries. New Haven, Conn., 1962– . v.1– . Monthly (except July and Aug.). Annual index. **BD58**

Ed., Lee Ash.

A new publication unrelated to an earlier *American notes and queries,* ed. by Walter Pilkington and B. Asterlund (North Bennington, Vt., 1941–50. 8v.).

Includes questions and answers, mainly literary; book reviews; notes on foreign reference books; etc.

✓ **Intermédiaire des chercheurs et curieux,** correspondance littéraire, historique et artistique, questions et réponses, lettres et documents inédits . . . Paris, 1864–1940. v.1– 103. il. Semimonthly; frequency varies. **BD59**

—— Table générale (t.1–34, 1864–96; t.35–82, 1897– 1920; t.83–96, 1921–33). Paris, 1897, 1924, 1935. 3v. Ceased publication.

✓ **L'intermédiaire des chercheurs et curieux;** mensuel de questions et réponses historiques, littéraires, artistiques et sur toutes autres curiosités. Paris, Chercheurs et Curieux, 1951– . année 1– . Monthly. **BD60**

Title varies. 1951–55, *Chercheurs et curieux.*

A monthly, beginning with April 1951, modeled on the preceding. Designed to print answers to questions asked by readers. The Dec. issue includes an annual index by key words.

✓ **Notes and queries,** for readers and writers, collectors and librarians, 1849– . London, Oxford Univ. Pr., 1850– . v.1– . Monthly. **BD61**

Imprint and title vary; earlier subtitle: A medium of communication for literary men, artists, antiquarians and genealogists.

Weekly until June 1942; fortnightly July 1942–1952. Formerly grouped in series of 12v. each, but since the beginning of the thirteenth series (1923) volumed continuously. An index to each volume, and a general index each six years until 1935. The index for July 1935–Dec. 1947 was published in 1v. in 1955.

Contains a large amount of interesting and often very valuable information on out-of-the-way questions—usually small points in general and local history and literature, bibliography, manners, customs, folklore, local observances, quotations, proverbs, etc. Much of the information is in the form of signed answers to questions from readers, and sources of information are given. Indexes are well made and detailed, and should be used constantly as supplements to the handbooks of allusions, quotations, proverbs, etc.

✣ Local periodicals of this type are also useful for small points in the literature, biography, history, etc. of their special localities. For titles of English county "Notes and queries," *see Bibliography of British history: Tudor period,* ed. by Conyers Read, 2d ed. 1959, p.355–409 (DC110).

Biographies of authors

✣ The main sources for biographical sketches of authors of any country are the encyclopedias and national biographical dictionaries of the country. For special dictionaries of authors of a particular country, *see* the name of that country in this section. *See also* Dictionaries and encyclopedias, p.237. Following is a brief list of author dictionaries which are international in scope:

Biographisches Jahrbuch für Altertumskunde, 1878– 1943. Berlin, Calvary, 1879–98. Leipzig, Reisland, 1899– 1944. v.1–63. **BD62**

Annual, except that no volume was published for 1912. Issued as part of the *Jahresbericht über die Fortschritte der klassischen Altertumswissenschaft.* No biographical section since 1943.

Contains signed obituaries of classical philologists; articles are of some length, with bibliographies.

Browning, David Clayton. Everyman's dictionary of literary biography, English and American, comp. after John W. Cousin . . . Rev. ed. London, Dent; N.Y., Dutton, 1960. 769p. **BD63**

For full information *see* BD348.

Contemporary authors; a bio-bibliographical guide to current authors and their works. James M. Ethridge, ed. Detroit, Gale Research, 1962– . v.1– . Semiannual. v.8 includes cumulated index to v.1–8. **BD64**

A series giving bio-bibliographical sketches of living authors who, for the most part, write in the English language. A few foreign writers are included. For full information *see* AJ27.

Dizionario letterario Bompiani degli autori, di tutti i tempi e di tutte le letterature. Milano, Bompiani, 1956– 57. 3v. il. **BD65**

A companion set to the *Dizionario letterario Bompiani delle opere e dei personaggi* . . . (BD21). Contains biographical and critical sketches of some 6000 authors, with listings of their important works but not works about them. Profusely illustrated.

An edition in French was published as:

Dictionnaire biographique des auteurs de tous les temps et de tous les pays [par] Laffont-Bompiani. Paris, Soc. d'Édit. de Dictionnaires et Encyclopédies [1957–58]. 2v. **BD66**

Gubernatis, Angelo de. Dictionnaire international des écrivains du monde latin. Rome, Auteur, 1905. 1506p. **BD67**

—— —— Supplément et index. Rome, Auteur, 1906. 254p.

With a subject index to both volumes.

Includes contemporary writers of Latin nationality—i.e., Belgian, French, Italian, Latin-American, Portuguese, Rumanian, and Spanish, whatever the subject of their works— and non-Latin authors who have written on Latin subjects. Especially full for Italian names.

Kunitz, Stanley Jasspon and **Haycraft, Howard.** Twentieth century authors, a biographical dictionary of modern literature; complete in one volume with 1850 biographies and 1700 portraits. N.Y., Wilson, 1942. 1577p. il. (Authors ser.) **BD68**

Popularly written sketches, usually of some length, aiming to give information on "writers of this century of all nations, whose books are familiar to readers of English. No attempt has been made to include foreign authors on the basis of their reputation in their native lands or tongues; the criterion, in general, has been the degree of acceptance of their translated works in the United States and England."—*Pref.* Includes bibliographies by and about the author.

Kunitz, Stanley Jasspon and **Colby, Vineta.** First supplement. N.Y., Wilson, 1955. 1123p.

700 new subjects have been added, and biographies and bibliographies in the basic volume have been brought up to date.

Lennartz, Franz. Ausländische Dichter und Schriftsteller unserer Zeit: Einzeldarstellungen zur schönen Literatur in fremden Sprachen. Stuttgart, Kröner, 1955. 749p. (Kröners Taschenausgabe 217) **BD69**

A companion volume to the author's *Deutsche Dichter und Schriftsteller* (BD581). Gives biographical sketches, with bibliographies, of some 300 non-German writers.

Magill, Frank N. Cyclopedia of world authors. Assoc. ed., Dayton Kohler. N.Y., Harper, 1958. 1198p. **BD70**

"Also appears under the title of *Masterplots cyclopedia of world authors*."

Treats the life and works of more than 750 authors represented in the *Masterpieces of world literature in digest form* (BD37) (also entitled *Masterplots*).

Gives place and date of birth and death (when appropriate), list of works, a biographical sketch varying in length from 200 words to 1000, followed by a section of bibliographical references to biographical information.

New Century cyclopedia of names, ed. by Clarence L. Barnhart with the assistance of William D. Halsey [and others]. N.Y., Appleton, 1954. 3v.(4342p.). **BD71**

A complete modernization and revision of the *Century cyclopedia of names*.

For annotation, *see* AJ19.

Perdigão, Henrique. Dicionário universal de litteratura (bio-bibliográfico e cronológico). 2. ed. Pôrto, Lopes da Silva, 1940. 1038p. il. **BD72**

Covers all countries and all periods but is especially strong in Portuguese and Brazilian names.

Includes a chronological index by nationalities and an alphabetical index.

Sharp, Robert Farquharson. Short biographical dictionary of foreign literature. London, Dent; N.Y., Dutton, [1933]. 302p. (Everyman's library. Reference. no.900) **BD73**

A concise dictionary of some 550 "European-non-English" authors with brief biographical notes and lists of works, including date of publication. May be useful in libraries which do not have the larger foreign biographical dictionaries.

Quotations

☙ Books of quotations are important in any reference collection for: (1) identifying a given quotation and verifying the wording; (2) suggesting quotations about a particular subject or suitable for a special occasion; and (3) supplying quotable passages from the writings of a given author. The first is probably the most frequent need in libraries. As every book of quotations is necessarily selective, and as each includes something not given in the others, the large library should keep the older works even when new and seemingly more comprehensive books are added to the reference collection. The small library, however, will find a much more limited supply quite adequate. If it has fairly recent editions of Bartlett's *Familiar quotations* (BD75) as the best chronological author list, and Stevenson's *Home book of quotations* (BD83), Hoyt's *New cyclopedia of practical quotations* (BD77), and the *Oxford dictionary of quotations* (BD80), as useful subject lists, it is well equipped for ordinary reference work for English as well as for a general selection of foreign quotations.

The reference value of a book of quotations depends upon three things: (1) the comprehensiveness of the collection and the care and judgment with which the quotations have been chosen; (2) the exactness of reference with which the quotations are given, i.e., the reference should be not merely to the author, but to the special work and its chapter, section, stanza, etc.; and (3) the *completeness of the index*. As the most frequent use of such books is for the purpose of locating a given quotation, the index should include every word in each quotation which a reader is at all likely to remember.

Additional sources for quotations which should not be overlooked are: (1) the unabridged dictionary which gives quotations to show the history and usage of words, e.g., the *Oxford English dictionary* (AE21), which is a prime source for quotations from medieval times through the 19th century; (2) question-and-answer periodicals, such as *Notes and queries* (BD61) and *L'intermédiaire des chercheurs* (BD60), through which many quotations are located; and (3) author concordances and dictionaries, helpful when the author is known or surmised.

General collections

Adams, Franklin Pierce. FPA book of quotations: a new collection of famous sayings, reflecting the wisdom and the wit of times past and present and including the virtuous, humorous and philosophic commentary on life by men and women of every age together with riches from the profound wells of the Bible, proverbs, and anonymity. N.Y., Funk & Wagnalls, 1952. 914p. **BD74**

A general collection including more than 15,000 quotations grouped under topic, and under topic arranged alphabetically by author. There is an index of topics with cross references and an index of authors, but no word index. The selection is broad, with quotations from well-known sources as well as from lesser-known writers, and a fair number from modern writers and speakers. In some cases, references to sources are given in full, and in others, reference is to author and title or author only. Dates of birth and death are given for authors.

Bartlett, John. Familiar quotations; a collection of passages, phrases and proverbs traced to their sources in ancient and modern literature. 13th and Centennial ed., completely rev. Boston, Little, 1955. 1614p. **BD75**

1st ed. 1855; 11th ed., rev. by Christopher Morley and L. D. Everett, 1937; 12th ed., rev. and enl. by Morley and Everett, 1948.

A standard collection, comprehensive and well selected. Arranged by authors chronologically, with exact references. One of the best books of quotations with a long history. The 11th edition almost doubled the size of the 10th edition; the 12th edition is the same as the 11th up to p.787, but after that it is reedited to include new authors, particularly contemporary authors, additional quotations, etc. The miscellaneous section, Addenda, is also enlarged by the inclusion of both old and new quotations. Comprises many interesting footnotes, tracing history or usage of analogous thoughts, the circumstances under which a particular remark was made, etc.

The index is especially fine, containing an average of four or five entries per quotation, and was entirely remade to include all of the additional material in the 12th edition.

The 13th, or Centennial, edition has been thoroughly revised by the staff of the publishing firm. The chronological arrangement by author has been maintained, and all quotations have been integrated into one listing except for quotations from (1) anonymous works, (2) the Bible, (3) the Book of Common Prayer, and (4) the Koran.

Many quotations previously included have been omitted, and many new ones added. Earlier editions, particularly the 12th, should not be discarded, as they will include quotations omitted from the latest edition.

Benham, *Sir* William Gurney. Benham's Book of quotations, proverbs, and household words. New and rev. ed. with suppl. and full indexes. N.Y., Putnam, 1949. 1384p. **BD76**

1st ed. 1907; 2d rev. ed. 1936.

Contains: (1) Quotations, British and American, p.1–440; (2) Bible and Book of Common Prayer, p.441–65; (3) "Waifs and strays," e.g., political phrases, epitaphs, London street sayings, bell inscriptions, etc., p.466–512; (4) Foreign (Greek, Latin, French, German, Italian, Spanish, Dutch), p.513–764; (5) Proverbs, p.765–928; and (6) Index, p.929–1259.

Includes about 30,000 quotations.

Frequently reprinted with little change. In the 1949 edition, the main part of the work is substantially the same as in the 1936 edition, with some errors corrected and dates of death added. A supplement with its own index has been added, p.1261–1322 (index p.1323–84). While this supplement includes a few recent quotations of modern authors, it is largely devoted to additional quotations of authors included in the main work.

Hoyt, Jehiel Keeler. Hoyt's New cyclopedia of practical quotations drawn from the speech and literature of all nations, ancient and modern, classic and popular, in English and foreign text. With . . . copious indexes; compl. rev. and greatly enl. by Kate Louise Roberts. N.Y., London, Funk & Wagnalls, 1922. 1343p. **BD77**

1st ed. 1882; 2d ed. enl. 1896. Reissued in 1940 with a few corrections and the addition of death dates for some authors in the author list. The "New 1947 Edition" published by Somerset Books, N.Y., is practically unchanged.

Contents: (1) Quotations, arranged alphabetically by general subjects; (2) Index of quoted authors, with brief biographical data; (3) Concordance of quotations.

A very comprehensive collection of some 21,000 quotations given with exact references. Omits quotations from the Bible. The indexes are excellent. Though now more than 40 years old, still useful except for contemporary writers.

Kenkyusha dictionary of English quotations with examples of their use by modern authors, ed. by Sanki Ichikawa, Masami Nishikawa, Mamoru Shimizu. Tokyo, Kenkyusha, 1952. 968p. **BD78**

The three main sections list quotations from the Bible, from Shakespeare, and from other authors, and give under each quotation a number of passages from modern works (including periodicals) where the quotations have been used. Arrangement under the main headings is by original source (e.g., the Bible from Genesis to Revelation), the authors in the third section being listed alphabetically. Includes an alphabetical index of quotations, usually by catchwords, and a list of the modern authors and works cited.

Mencken, Henry Louis. A new dictionary of quotations on historical principles from ancient and modern sources. N.Y., Knopf, 1942. 1347p. **BD79**

A comprehensive collection with emphasis on the lesser-known quotations. Includes many proverbs and some foreign quotations, mainly in English translation. Arranged by rubric with many cross references to allied headings. Quotations are dated whenever possible and arranged chronologically under rubric. An attempt has been made to trace each quotation to its earliest usage. No index. Gives name of author and title of work but not exact reference.

Oxford dictionary of quotations. 2d ed. London, N.Y., Oxford Univ. Pr., 1953. 1003p. **BD80**

The 2d edition includes in one alphabetical sequence: authors writing in English, foreign authors, the Prayer Book, the Bible, and other anonymous works.

A comprehensive collection of quotations chosen for their familiarity. Gives exact references to sources. Omits proverbs and phrases because these are given in the *Oxford dictionary of English proverbs* (BD124). The 2d edition omits some 250 quotations, and adds about 1300 new ones. Indexed by key words. "The index has been entirely remade and is somewhat fuller than that to the first edition. Greek quotations are indexed separately."—*Note to 2d edition.*

Seldes, George. The great quotations. N.Y., Stuart, 1960. 893p. (A Caesar-Stuart book) **BD81**

A collection, primarily of prose quotations, concerned with the play of ideas, many controversial. Arranged alphabetically by author with index by "ideas." Includes writers of many countries but all in English. Citations are to name of work only, without exact reference and at times no source is given. Omits most poetry and all Bible and Shakespeare because they are fully covered elsewhere.

Simpson, James Beasley. Contemporary quotations. N.Y., Crowell, 1964. 500p. **BD82**

Contemporary quotations (since 1950) gleaned from newspapers, magazines, speeches, sermons, the theater, television, etc., arranged by large classifications—The nation; The world; Man; Communications and the arts—with subheadings. Source and subject indexes.

Stevenson, Burton Egbert. Home book of quotations, classical and modern. 9th ed. rev. N.Y., Dodd, 1964. 2817p. **BD83**

1st ed. 1934.

A comprehensive and well-chosen collection of more than 50,000 quotations, arranged alphabetically by subject with subarrangement by smaller topics. Usually gives exact citation. Includes an index of authors—giving full name, identifying phrase, and dates of birth and death, with references to all quotations cited—and a word index, which indexes the quotation by leading words, usually nouns, though in some cases verbs and adjectives are also used. Boldface entries are given for some of the smaller subjects. The quotations under these are not indexed separately, and one must, therefore, turn to the subject and run through the entries. This practice must be remembered when using this index.

The 9th edition includes two appendixes: I, p.2273–98 (for the most part, added in the 5th edition); and II, p.2298j–z, p.2299a–h (added in the 9th edition). The quotations on these pages are indexed in a separate section at the end of the main index, p.2811–17.

The 3d edition (1937) was a thorough revision of the first two editions, with the addition of more than 1000 quotations, revision of notes, etc., and a much enlarged index.

Of other editions, the 5th (1947) and the 9th include the most revision. The 9th adds over 500 new entries, with clarification of others. The changes are in the appendixes and the separate index. Not all of the new authors have been added to the author index.

Foreign and classical

❧ For some questions concerned with foreign and classical quotations the great dictionaries of the language, the special dialect or period dictionaries, and the dictionaries or concordances of individual authors are the most useful sources. For example, the *Thesaurus linguae latinae* (AE395) contains many more quotations than could be found in even a very comprehensive dictionary of Latin quotations; Wetmore's *Index verborum Vergilianus* (BD977) can be used to locate more Vergil quotations than would be found in a quotation book, etc. The books of foreign quotations listed below are the easy first aids; for material not found in them, dictionaries within the various fields should be consulted.

Arabic and Persian

Field, Claud. Dictionary of oriental quotations (Arabic and Persian). London, Sonnenschein; N.Y., Macmillan, 1911. 351p. **BD84**

Gives quotations in transliteration, arranged alphabetically by first word, with translations. Index of authors and index of subjects and catchwords, the latter not very full. Includes 85 authors.

Canadian

Hamilton, Robert M. Canadian quotations and phrases, literary and historical. Toronto, McClelland and Stewart, 1952. 272p. **BD85**

A collection of quotations and phrases from Canadian authors and from non-Canadians on subjects distinctly Canadian. Arranged by topic with author index. Reference is usually, but not always, to exact source.

Chinese

Ch'êng Yü K'ao. A manual of Chinese quotations, being a translation of the Ch'êng Yü K'ao. With the Chinese text, notes, explanations and English and Chinese indices for easy reference by J. H. Stewart Lockhart. Hong Kong, Kelly and Walsh, 1903. 645p., cxviip.   **BD86**

Scarborough, William. Collection of Chinese proverbs, rev. and enl. by the addition of some six hundred proverbs, by C. Wilfrid Allan. Shanghai, Presbyterian Mission Pr., 1927. 381p.   **BD87**

Classified arrangement. Subject index.

Dutch

Laan, Kornelis ter. Nederlandse spreekworden, spreuken, en zegswijzen. 'sGravenhage, G. B. Van Goor Zonen's Uitgeversmaatsch, 1950. 332p.   **BD88**

A collection of Dutch proverbs and sayings, including many translated from other languages. Arranged alphabetically by key word. Reference is usually given to source.

Margadant, S. W. F. Twintigduizend citaten, aphorismen en spreekwoorden. [2. druk] 'sGravenhage, Leopolds, Uitgeversmij, 1952. 741p.   **BD89**

1st ed. 1935.

Includes some 20,000 quotations in Dutch, many of them translations from other languages for which the original is usually given. Sources include ancient and modern literatures, proverbs, maxims, etc. Arranged by topic with some cross references. No word index.

French

Dupré, Paul. Encyclopédie des citations. Comité de Rédaction sous la présidence de Fernand Keller. Paris, Éd. de Trévise, 1959. 701p.   **BD90**

Includes quotations from many languages and periods, all translated into French. References are usually to exact sources. An index of personal names, one by key words, and one by ideas.

Genest, Émile. Dictionnaire des citations; dictionnaire des phrases, vers et mots célèbres employés dans le langage courant, avec précision de l'origine. Paris, Nathan, 1954. 423p.   **BD91**

Arranged alphabetically by first word of quotation with indexes by author and by subject. Citation is usually to exact reference.

Apparently a somewhat enlarged edition of the author's *Où est-ce donc?* Paris, Nathan, 1925.

Another of the author's earlier works is *Les belles citations de la littérature française.* Paris, Nathan, 1923–27. 2v.

Guerlac, Othon Goepp. Les citations françaises; recueil de passages célèbres, phrases familières, mots historiques. 2. éd. rev. et augm. Paris, Colin, 1933. 458p.   **BD92**

Arranged in main by authors, chronologically, with two alphabetical indexes: (1) authors; (2) catchwords. Includes modern as well as older quotations, gives exact references, and has many footnotes giving additional facts, e.g., parallel passages in other writers, etc.

The most generally useful of the French quotation books.

Guterman, Norbert. A book of French quotations with English translations. Garden City, N.Y., Doubleday, 1963. 442p.   **BD93**

Arranged chronologically by author, French quotations and English translations on opposite pages. Brief descriptive notes in English are given on the authors. Indexes of authors, of first lines in French, and of first lines in English.

Harbottle, Thomas Benfield and **Dalbiac, P. H.** Dictionary of quotations (French and Italian). London, Sonnenschein; N.Y., Macmillan, 1901. 565p. (Repr.: N.Y., Ungar, 1958)   **BD94**

Under each language arranged alphabetically by first word of quotation. Gives exact references to sources. Index of authors and of subjects.

Ramage, Craufurd Tait. Beautiful thoughts from French and Italian authors; with English translations. 4th ed. London, Routledge, 1884. 619p.   **BD95**

Also published under title *Familiar quotations from French and Italian authors.*

Under each language arranged alphabetically by author, giving quotation in the original with English translation. Indexes in each of the three languages.

German

Büchmann, Georg. Geflügelte Worte; der Zitatenschatz des deutschen Volkes. Fortgesetzt von Walter Roberttornow, Konrad Weidling [u.A.]. 28. Aufl. neubearb. von Gunther Haupt und Werner Rust. Berlin, Max Paschke, 1937. 788p.   **BD96**

Arranged by country of origin with a name index and word indexes.

A shortened and modernized edition was published as *Geflügelte Worte und Zeitenschatz* (Zürich, Clasen, 1946. 425p.), and another, edited by Hanns Martin Elster, as *Geflügelte Worte* (Stuttgart, Reclam, 1957. 630p.).

Dalbiac, Lilian. Dictionary of quotations (German) with author and subject indexes. London, Sonnenschein; N.Y., Macmillan, 1906. 485p. (Repr.: N.Y., Ungar, 1958)   **BD97**

German quotations arranged alphabetically, with English translations; indexes by subject in English and German, and by author.

Peltzer, Karl. Das treffende Zitat: Gedankengut aus drei Jahrtausenden nach Stichwörtern geordnet. Thun und München, Ott Verlag, [1957]. 740p.   **BD98**

A general quotation book in German, arranged in one catchword alphabet. In most cases sources are indicated.

Ramage, Craufurd Tait. Beautiful thoughts from German and Spanish authors. New rev. ed. London, Routledge, 1884. 559p.   **BD99**

Also published under title *Familiar quotations from German and Spanish authors.*

Arranged under author by English rubric, with quotation in the original and English translation. Subject index in each language.

Zoozmann, Richard. Zitatenschatz der Weltliteratur; eine Sammlung von Zitaten, Sentenzen, Aphorismen, Epigrammen, Sprichwörtern, Redensarten und Aussprücken. Nach Schlagwörten geordnet. 9. unveränd. Aufl. Berlin, Verlag Praktisches Wissen, Peters, 1956. 922p.   **BD100**

Sayings, aphorisms, etc. from various countries arranged alphabetically by catchword. No indexes.

Italian

Finzi, Giuseppe. Dizionario di citazioni latine ed italiane. Milano, Sandron, 1902. 967p.   **BD101**

Subtitle: Citazioni latine; Detti proverbiali; Frasi e versi curiosi; Versi leonini e salernitani; Detti e motti storici e allegorici; Massime di diritto romano; Citazioni italiane.

8560 entries arranged by rubric. Key-word index. References are usually to exact sources.

Fumagalli, Giuseppe. Chi l'ha detto? Tesoro di citazioni italiane e straniere, di origine letteraria e storica. Aggiunte le frasi storiche della guerra 1914–18. 9. ed. Milano, Hoepli, 1946. 841p. **BD102**

1st ed. 1894.

Covers quotations in different languages, arranged by subject, with references to exact sources and some explanatory notes. Indexes: (1) authors; (2) quotations.

Giusti, Giuseppe and **Capponi, Gino.** Dizionario dei proverbi italiani. Milano, Veronelli, 1956. 483p. **BD103**

Earlier editions had title *Raccolta de' proverbi toscani*. 1st edition, 1852, frequently reprinted up to 1913. This reprinting, with different title, is without significant change; paging and indexing seem to check exactly with 1871 edition.

Palazzi, Fernando and **Spaventa Filippi, Silvio.** Il libro dei mille savi: massime, pensieri, aforismi, paradossi di tutti i tempi e di tutti i paesi, accompagnati dal testo originale e dalle citazione delle fonti. 4. ristampa della 2. ed. con l'aggiunta di circa altri mille aforismi. Milano, Hoepli, 1955. 1095p. **BD104**

All quotations given in Italian, with general source (not exact citation); quotations in original language given in footnotes. Index of authors but no word index. Arranged by subject.

Ramage, Craufurd Tait. Beautiful thoughts from French and Italian authors. London, Routledge, 1884. 619p. **BD105**

For full record *see* BD95.

Latin and Greek

Harbottle, Thomas Benfield. Dictionary of quotations (classical). London, Sonnenschein, 1906. 678p. (Repr.: N.Y., Ungar, 1958) **BD106**

The best dictionary of Latin and Greek quotations. Gives each in the original, with exact reference to source, and an English translation with name of translator. Indexes: (1) authors; (2) subjects, Latin; (3) subjects, Greek; (4) subjects, English.

This edition includes an appendix, p.649–78.

Ramage, Craufurd Tait. Beautiful thoughts from Greek authors, with English translations. London, Routledge, 1895. 589p. **BD107**

Also published under title *Familiar quotations from Greek authors*.

Arranged alphabetically by author, with quotations in Greek and in English translation. Exact citations to sources. English index.

—— Beautiful thoughts from Latin authors, with English translations. London, Routledge, 1895. 855p. **BD108**

Also published under title *Familiar quotations from Latin authors*.

Arranged alphabetically by author, with quotations in Latin and in English translation. Exact citations to sources. Latin and English indexes.

Persian

See Arabic and Persian, p.242.

Scandinavian

Langlet, Valdemar. Bevingade ord och slagord; efter olika källor sammanställda och förklarade. Stockholm, Geber, 1925–28. 2v. **BD109**

v.1, Citat från främmande sprak. 499p.; v.2, Svenska citat. 680p.

Voss, Fridtjof. Norsk sitatleksikon. 6000 bevingede ord.

2. rev. utgave. Stavanger, Stabenfeldt Forlag, [1955]. 680col. **BD110**

A general quotation book including not only Norwegian but quotations from various languages translated into Norwegian, followed by the original. Alphabetical by catchword subject. First-line indexes in Norwegian and in each of the other languages. Author index.

Spanish

Borras, Tomás and **Sáinz de Robles, Federico Carlos.** Diccionario de sabiduría; frases y conceptos. [2. ed.] Madrid, Aguilar, 1956. 1369p. **BD111**

1st ed. 1953.

Arranged by subject, giving only name of author and no further citation of source. Subject and author indexes.

Harbottle, Thomas Benfield and **Hume, Martin.** Dictionary of quotations (Spanish) with subject and author's index. London, Sonnenschein; N.Y., Macmillan, 1907. 462p. (Repr.: N.Y., Ungar, 1958) **BD112**

Martínez Kleiser, Luis. Refranero general, ideológico español. Madrid, Real Academia Española, 1953. 783p. **BD113**

More than 65,000 entries arranged under concepts; gathered from other collections of proverbs with references to the collections.

Mir y Noguera, Juan. Diccionario de frases de los autores clásicos españoles, 1. ed. argentina con más de 70,000 locuciones. Buenos Aires, Gil, 1942. 1328p. **BD114**

This Argentinian edition of a work, previously published in Madrid in 1899, was revised, and an index of authors and works from which the phrases were taken was added.

Arranged by rubric. Gives exact references to sources.

Ramage, Craufurd Tait. Beautiful thoughts from German and Spanish authors. London, Routledge, 1884. **BD115**

For full information *see* BD99.

Rodríguez Marín, Francisco. Más de 21,000 refranes castellanos no contenidos en la copiosa collección del Maestro Gonzálo Correas. Madrid, Rev. de Archivos, Bibliotecas y Museos, 1926. 519p. **BD116**

—— 12,600 refranes más. 1930. 344p.

—— Los 6,666 refranes. 1934. 198p.

—— Todavía 10,700 refranes más. 1941. 317p.

Sbarbi y Osuna, José María. Gran diccionario de refranes de la lengua española; refranes, adagios, proverbios, modismos, locuciones y frases proverbiales . . . corr. y pub. bajo la dirección de Manuel J. García. Buenos Aires, Gil, 1943. 1028p. **BD117**

Published 1922 under title *Diccionario de refranes, adagios* [*etc.*].

Arranged by rubric. No indexes.

Vega, Vicente. Diccionario ilustrado de frases célebres y citas literarias. Barcelona, Gustavo Gili, 1952. 939p. il. **BD118**

Quotations, in various languages, arranged alphabetically under subjects, with indexes by topic, first word of quotation, and author. When phrases are given in other languages, Spanish translations are included. In some cases quotations are translated into Spanish and are not given in the original. Citations to exact sources are given irregularly.

Proverbs

🌿 Many types of books of proverbs, like those of quotations, are available. A number of the older works may still prove useful for historical purposes, but the very comprehensive Stevenson, *Home book of proverbs, maxims and familiar phrases* (BD125), and the *Oxford dictionary of English proverbs* (BD124), will now answer most of the general questions in this field. For books of proverbs of particular countries, *see* books of quotations of the country.

Bibliography

Moll, Otto E. Sprichwörterbibliographie. Frankfurt am Main, Klostermann, [1957–58]. 630p.　　　**BD119**

An extensive bibliography of more than 9000 items, arranged first by language, then by period, locality, etc. Besides the languages of Europe and America includes those of Asia, Africa, the Pacific islands, etc. Contains dialect dictionaries as well as collections of proverbs. Author index.

Stephens, Thomas Arthur. Proverb literature; a bibliography of works relating to proverbs, ed. by Wilfrid Bonser . . . comp. from materials left by the late T. A. Stephens. . . . London, W. Glaisher, 1930. 496p. ([Folk-lore Society. Publ.] 89)　　　**BD120**

An annotated bibliography of more than 4000 works on the proverbs of all nations, including collections of particular localities and special subjects.

Collections

Apperson, George Latimer. English proverbs and proverbial phrases; a historical dictionary. . . . London, Dent; N.Y., Dutton, 1929. 721p.　　　**BD121**

Traces the history of English proverbs and proverbial phrases, through references to the literature.

In one alphabetic arrangement, but in a twofold manner: (1) all proverbs which classify naturally under such headings as months and seasons, animals, birds, God, the Devil, sun, moon, rain, fool, time, money, war, etc., etc. are listed under these headings; (2) all other proverbs are alphabetical under their first main word.

Champion, Selwyn Gurney. Racial proverbs; a selection of the world's proverbs arranged linguistically . . . with authoritative introductions to the proverbs of 27 countries and races. London, Routledge; N.Y., Macmillan, 1938. cxxixp., 767p.　　　**BD122**

"Embodies the first and second series of [his] 'Wayside sayings.' "—*Introd.*

"Authorities consulted," p.cix–cxxix.

Arranged by country with the following four indexes: (1) Linguistic and geographical, (2) Subject-matter, (3) Race, and (4) Alternative chief-word.

The introduction to the proverbs of each country or race is by a specialist.

Davidoff, Henry. A world treasury of proverbs, from twenty-five languages. N.Y., Random, 1946. 526p. (Garden City Pub. Co., 1948)　　　**BD123**

More than 15,000 proverbs and sayings from 25 languages, arranged by rubric with subject and author indexes.

Smith, William George. Oxford dictionary of English proverbs; introd. by Janet E. Heseltine. 2d ed. rev. throughout by Sir Paul Harvey. Oxford, Clarendon Pr., 1948. 740p.　　　**BD124**

The 1st edition (1935) contained about 10,000 proverbs, arranged alphabetically by first word, including "a," "an," "the." This edition has been somewhat enlarged and some earlier sources noted, but its main improvement lies in its new arrangement. Proverbs are now alphabetized under significant words (usually the first), with the preceding words, if any, transferred to the end or, occasionally, to an intermediate point. Liberal cross references are included from all other

significant words, usually with enough of the phrase so that it is readily identifiable.

Dated references are given for each proverb to the earliest uses and sources found, with variant usages at succeeding times, shown by examples from the literature in the manner of the *Oxford dictionary*. The introduction includes a brief survey of proverb collections.

Stevenson, Burton. Home book of proverbs, maxims and familiar phrases. N.Y., Macmillan, 1948. 2957p. **BD125**

Attempts to trace back, to their sources, proverbs, maxims, and familiar phrases in ordinary English and American use and to show their development.

Follows the pattern of the author's *Home book of quotations* (BD83), with subject arrangement and detailed word index. Very comprehensive, including more than 73,000 expressions from many languages and periods; many of them might be considered quotations, as the interpretation of proverb and maxim is very broad. Dates for proverbs are noted, and those from foreign sources are given in English translation followed by the original language (except for the oriental). Indexes at least one and sometimes more key words.

Taylor, Archer. The proverb. Cambridge, Harvard Univ. Pr., 1931. 223p.　　　**BD126**

―――― Index. Helsinki, Suomalainen Tiedeakatemia, 1934. 105p. (FF [Folklore Fellows] communications, no.113) (Repr. in 1v. Hatboro, Pa., Folklore Associates; Copenhagen, Rosenkilde & Bagger, 1962. 223p., 105p.)

The main volume discusses the origin, content, and style of proverbs. The index lists the proverbs mentioned with reference to page and also to the treatment in other collections of proverbs.

―――― and **Whiting, Bartlett Jere.** A dictionary of American proverbs and proverbial phrases, 1820–1880. Cambridge, Belknap Pr. of Harvard Univ. Pr., 1958. 418p.　**BD127**

An alphabetically arranged dictionary, listing proverbs by what is considered the most important word, illustrated with many examples from American literature, 1820–80.

Tilley, Morris Palmer. A dictionary of the proverbs in England in the 16th and 17th centuries; a collection of the proverbs found in English literature and the dictionaries of the period. Ann Arbor, Univ. of Michigan Pr., 1950. 854p.　　　**BD128**

Contains some 11,780 proverbs arranged by catchword. Each proverb is followed by citations arranged chronologically. Contains a bibliography of the works cited, an index of Shakespearean quotations appearing in the text, and an index of significant words in the proverbs.

Drama

See also Theater Arts, p.324, and subhead "Drama" under the various national literatures.

Bibliography

Clarence, Reginald. "The Stage" cyclopaedia; a bibliography of plays. London, "The Stage," 1909. 503p. **BD129**

Subtitle: An alphabetical list of plays and other stage pieces of which any record can be found since the commencement of the English stage . . . with descriptions, authors' names, dates and places of production, and other useful information comprising in all nearly 50,000 plays and extending over a period of upwards of 500 years.

A title up list with some form entries (e.g., Greek plays), aiming to be complete for English drama and selective for the better-known foreign plays.

Drury, Francis Keese Wynkoop. Drury's Guide to best plays. Wash., Scarecrow, 1953. 367p.　　　**BD130**

Contents: pt.1, Author list; pt.2, Title index; pt.3, Subject index; pt.4, Abbreviations used for citing collections. ". . . includes more than 1200 plays available in English" (*Introd.*), giving dates of first production or printing, editions (including collections), description, plot, and data for actors.

Horn-Monval, Madeleine. Répertoire bibliographique des traductions et adaptations françaises du théâtre étranger du XVe siècle à nos jours. Paris, Centre National de la Recherche Scientifique, 1958–64. v.1–6. (In progress)
BD131

v.1, Théâtre grec antique. 122p.; v.2, Théâtre latin antique. Théâtre latin médiéval et moderne. 112p.; v.3, Théâtre italien. Opéras italiens (livrets). 179p.; v.4, Théâtre espagnol; Théâtre de l'Amérique latine; Théâtre portugais. 126p.; v.5, Théâtre anglais; Théâtre américain. 284p.; v.6, Théâtre allemand; Théâtre autrichien; Théâtre suisse. 177p.

To be in 8v.; later volumes to treat French translations and adaptations of German, Flemish, Dutch, and Scandinavian; Slavic, Near Eastern, and Oriental dramas.

Schwanbeck, Gisela. Bibliographie der deutschsprachigen Hochschulschriften zur Theaterwissenschaft von 1885 bis 1952. Berlin, Selbstverlag der Gesellschaft für Theatergeschichte, 1956. 563p. (Gesellschaft für Theatergeschichte. Schriften. Bd.58)   **BD132**

A classified list of 3309 German dissertations on the drama and theater from antiquity to the present. Author and catchword index.

Shipley, Joseph Twadell. Guide to great plays. Wash., Public Affairs Pr., [1956]. 867p.   **BD133**

A listing, by author, of several hundred "great" plays of all periods. For each a plot synopsis is given, with additional information on the play's history and production, excerpts from reviews, notes on famous casts, etc.

Stratman, Carl Joseph. Bibliography of medieval drama. Berkeley, Los Angeles, Univ. of Calif. Pr., 1954. 423p.
BD134

Attempts to cover early liturgical forms, mystery and miracle plays, moralities, interludes, etc. Lists manuscripts, texts, and various editions of individual plays, with critical studies of them, including dissertations. The general sections are followed by chapters devoted to English, French, German, Italian, Latin, and Spanish drama.

Locations are given for most book entries, and there is a finding list of files of periodicals.

Indexes

American Library Association. Board on Library Service to Children and Young People. Subject index to children's plays, comp. by a Subcommittee, Elizabeth D. Briggs, chairman. Chicago, Assoc., 1940. 277p.   **BD135**

A subject index of plays found in 202 collections, suitable for children in grades 1–8.

Dramatic index for 1909–49, covering articles and illustrations concerning the stage and its players in the periodicals of America and England and including the dramatic books of the year. Boston, Faxon, 1910–52. 41v. Annual.
BD136

Ceased publication.

Issued separately, and also as pt.2 of the *Annual magazine subject index,* 1909–49 (AF129). Contains the cumulation of the *Dramatic index* published in the quarterly numbers of the *Bulletin of bibliography.* v.1–8, 11–41 have appendix *Dramatic books and plays* (*in English*) published 1912–16, 1919–49.

An annual subject index to articles about the drama, the theater, actors and actresses, playwrights, librettists, managers, etc.; to synopses of plays; to reviews; and to stage and dramatic portraits, scenes from plays, and other theatrical illustrations contained in English and American periodicals; and to texts of plays whether published in book or magazine

form. Magazine articles are entered under subject only; texts of plays are under title, or under the form heading "Dramas" with cross reference from author; costume portraits are under both the actor and the character. While the index nominally begins with 1909, some retrospective indexing is included. From 1912, the dramatic books of the year are indexed both in the main index and in the appendix, *Dramatic books and plays,* which consists of (1) author list of books about the theater, (2) author list of play texts, and (3) title list of texts.

Firkins, Ina Ten Eyck. Index of plays, 1800–1926. N.Y., Wilson, 1927. 307p.   **BD137**

A comprehensive index of 7872 plays by 2203 authors, showing where the text of each can be found in collections or other publications. Indexes only plays in English but includes translations of foreign plays. In two parts: (1) author index, giving full bibliographical information about each play, and, in many cases, number of acts and brief characterizations, as, comedy, tragedy, social, domestic, etc.; (2) title and subject index, referring to the author list.

—— —— Supplement, [1927–34]. N.Y., Wilson, 1935. 140p.

Indexes 3284 plays by 1335 authors.

Index to the Best plays series, 1899–1950, 1949–1960. N.Y., Dodd, 1950–61. 147p., 46p.   **BD138**

For description *see* BD235.

Ireland, Norma Olin. An index to skits and stunts. Boston, Faxon, 1958. 348p. (Useful reference ser., no.88)
BD139

An author, title, and subject index to 148 collections (books and pamphlets). Some 800 subject headings are used, and cross references are numerous.

Logasa, Hannah and **Ver Nooy, Winifred.** Index to one-act plays. Boston, Faxon, 1924–58. 5v. (Useful reference ser., no.30, 46, 68, 78, 87)   **BD140**

Basic volume: Plays written in English or translated into English, published since 1900. 327p.; Suppl., 1924–31. 432p.; 2d Suppl., 1932–40. 556p.; 3d Suppl., 1941–48. 318p.; 4th Suppl., 1948–57. 245p.

Title, author, and subject indexes to one-act plays in collections, and also to separately published pamphlets. The 3d supplement includes radio plays; the 4th, radio and television. 3d and 4th supplements by Hannah Logasa.

Ottemiller, John Henry. Index to plays in collections; an author and title index to plays appearing in collections published between 1900 and 1962. 4th ed. rev. and enl. N.Y., Scarecrow, 1964. 370p.   **BD141**

1st ed. 1943.

Contents: (1) Author index, giving name and dates, title of play, date of first production, references from original titles and variant translated titles, references from joint authors and translators, etc.; (2) List of collections analyzed and key to symbols; and (3) Title index, referring from all forms of titles, translated titles, and subtitles.

Lists 6993 copies of 2536 different plays by 1300 authors in 814 collections appearing between 1900 and 1962 in England and the United States. Includes plays from ancient to modern times. All editions of the same collection have been included when the contents of successive editions vary. Does not include collections of children's plays, amateur plays, one-act plays, holiday and anniversary plays and pageants, and radio and television plays, but such plays are indexed if they appear in one of the collections that is included. Partial and selected texts are omitted.

Play index, 1949–1952, 1953–1960. N.Y., Wilson, 1953–63. 2v.   **BD142**

1949–1952, an index to 2616 plays in 1138 volumes, ed. by Dorothy H. West and Dorothy M. Peake; 1953–1960, an index to 4592 plays in 1735 volumes, ed. by Estelle A. Fidell and Dorothy M. Peake.

Each volume in four parts: (1) the main list, arranged by author, title, and subject; (2) a list of the collections indexed; (3) cast analysis, listing each play under type of cast (male, female, mixed, puppet) and further by the number of characters; (4) directory of publishers.

All types of plays are indexed, including translations into English. The dictionary catalog arrangement and the large amount of subject indexing are particularly helpful.

Thomson, Ruth Gibbons. Index to full length plays, 1895 to 1925. Boston, Faxon, 1956. 172p. (Useful reference ser., no.85)   **BD143**

——— ——— 1926–1944. Boston, Faxon, 1946. 305p. (Useful reference ser., no.71)

Each of these companion volumes includes a title index—giving author, translator, number of acts, number of characters, subject, and scene—followed by author and subject indexes referring to the title index and a bibliography giving publisher, date, etc.

Essays

Indexes

A.L.A. index . . . to general literature. 2d ed. enl. . . . Boston, Chicago, Amer. Lib. Assoc. Pub. Board, 1901–14. 679p. and suppl., 223p.   **BD144**

Basic volume, covering material to Jan. 1, 1900. 679p. 1901; Supplement, 1900–1910. 223p. 1914.

A subject index which attempts to do for books of essays and general literature what *Poole's Index* (AF119) does for periodicals. Indexes books belonging to the following classes: (1) Essays and similar collections of critical, biographical, and other monographs; (2) Books of travel and general history whose chapters or parts are worthy of separate reference; (3) Reports and publications of boards and associations dealing with sociological matters, and of historical and literary societies; and (4) Miscellaneous books and some public documents.

Includes only books in English. Indexing is by catchword subject, not by modern catalog subject.

Continued by the *Essay index* (BD145), which indexes collections published since 1900. Some of the books indexed in the *Supplement*, 1900–1910, have been taken over by the *Essay index*, but others, particularly those on travel, have not been reindexed; therefore, the *Supplement* has not been entirely superseded. For a more detailed discussion of the relationship of the two indexes, *see* the preface to the *Essay index,* p.v–vi.

Essay and general literature index, 1900–1933; an index to about 40,000 essays and articles in 2144 volumes of collections of essays and miscellaneous works, ed. by Minnie Earl Sears and Marian Shaw. N.Y., Wilson, 1934. 1952p.   **BD145**

Kept up to date by supplements: (1) 7-year cumulations, 1934–1940, 1941–1947, 1948–1954; (2) 5-year cumulations, 1955/1959– ; and (3) semiannual and annual cumulations. Frequently cited as the *Essay index.*

Index, p.1–1890; List of books indexed, p.1893–1952.

The basic volume is a detailed index, by authors, subjects, and some titles, to essays and articles published 1900–1933 and also to earlier essays if included in collections published since 1900. Indexing is given with exact reference; in the case of many essays first printed in periodicals, the reference to the periodical is given also, and variant titles for the same essay are indicated.

A monumental work, useful in several departments of library service. In *cataloging,* it provides a usable substitute for a large amount of analysis, the cost of which would be prohibitive in the average card catalog. As a *reference* aid, it serves many purposes, showing, e.g., (1) list of essays by a given author, (2) authorship of an essay when only title is

known, (3) analytical material on a given subject, particularly small, unusual, or intangible subjects not covered by whole books, (4) biographical and critical matter about persons, (5) criticisms of individual books, and (6) different places or collections in which an essay is printed (an important point in school or college libraries when it is necessary to supply many copies of some recommended reading). For purposes of *selection of books,* the list of books indexed serves as a good guide to the worthwhile essay and other composite-book material of the 20th century.

The supplements, 1934–59, index more than 109,000 essays and articles in more than 5500 collections.

Standard catalog for public libraries, 1940 ed.– . N.Y., Wilson, 1940– .   **BD146**

Primarily a catalog rather than an index, but serves as the latter also, as its index includes entries for analyzed material in hundreds of books of a composite character. For full description *see* AA272.

Fiction

Bibliography

Baker, Ernest Albert and **Packman, James.** Guide to the best fiction, English and American, including translations from foreign languages. New and enl. ed. London, Routledge; N.Y., Macmillan, 1932. 634p.   **BD147**

1st ed. 1903; 2d ed. 1913. The 3d edition is much enlarged from the 2d by the addition of material from 1911 through 1930, and differs from the 2d edition in arrangement, i.e., has one alphabetical list instead of national lists with chronological subdivisions.

A comprehensive and very useful work, with good annotations and a detailed and useful general index of authors, titles, subjects, historical names, allusions, places, characters, etc.

Baker, Ernest Albert. Guide to historical fiction. London, Routledge; N.Y., Macmillan, 1914. 566p.   **BD148**

Lists about 5000 novels which in any way portray the life of the past, including medieval romances and novels of manners, as well as avowedly historical novels. Arrangement is first by country and then chronologically by the historical period; descriptive notes indicate briefly the plot and scene of each story, its historical characters, etc. Full index (148p.) of authors, titles, historical names, places, events, allusions, etc.

Bleiler, Everett Franklin. The checklist of fantastic literature: a bibliography of fantasy, weird, and science fiction books published in the English language. Chicago, Shasta, 1948. 452p.   **BD149**

Arranged alphabetically by author, with title index. No subject approach.

Fiction catalog: 7th ed. 1960. A list of 4097 works of fiction in the English language with annotations. Ed. by Estelle A. Fidell and Esther V. Flory. N.Y., Wilson, 1961. 650p. (Standard catalog ser.)   **BD150**

Continued by annual supplements.

The 7th edition in a series listing fiction titles of various periods in the English language, chosen by a group of consultant librarians and specialists. Earlier editions were dictionary in form; this form has been changed to a divided catalog: pt.1, an author alphabet with full bibliographical information and annotations; pt.2, a title and subject index to pt.1.

Designed as an aid in book selection (purchasing, rebinding, discarding, replacing, etc.) and as a reference tool listing outstanding novels with critical annotations, usually giving plot outline, and supplying a subject and geographical approach as well as title indexing. Titles especially recommended are starred and double-starred, and books suitable for young adults are indicated.

Gardner, Frank M. Sequels, incorporating Aldred and Parker's Sequel stories. [4th ed.] London, Assoc. of Assist. Librarians, 1955. 189p. **BD151**

1st ed. 1922.

Lists more than 14,000 titles of sequels in the English language including translations. More general in scope than Kerr (BD153), but omits bibliographical data and works in foreign languages.

Gove, Philip Babcock. The imaginary voyage in prose fiction; a history of its criticism and a guide for its study, with an annotated check list of 215 imaginary voyages from 1700 to 1800. N.Y., Columbia Univ. Pr., 1941. 445p. (Columbia Univ. studies in English and comparative literature, no.152) **BD152**

Thesis (Ph.D.), Columbia University, 1940.
Bibliography, p.[403]–20.
Pt.2, p.180–402, is a detailed bibliography with full annotations of imaginary voyages in various languages: English, French, German, Dutch, Swedish, Danish, Latin, Japanese, etc. Locates copies.

Kerr, Elizabeth Margaret. Bibliography of the sequence novel. Minneapolis, Univ. of Minn. Pr., 1950. 126p. **BD153**

Attempts to list all the novels in series in which the sequence of the volumes depends upon the development of characters and themes.

Divided into the following language groups: British-American, Romance, Teutonic, and Slavic. The foreign sections of the bibliography are more selective than complete. For the 20th century, entries have been brought up to the end of 1948.

Lenrow, Elbert. Reader's guide to prose fiction; an introductory essay, with bibliographies of 1500 novels selected, topically classified, and annotated for use in meeting the needs of individuals in general education . . . for the Commission on Secondary School Curriculum. N.Y., London, Appleton, 1940. 371p. **BD154**

Divided into three main sections: pt.1, The individual's need for entertainment and escape; pt.2, The individual and his personal environment; pt.3, The individual and his social environment. Each of these is divided into topical classifications. Full annotations, and an author, title, and subject index.

Logasa, Hannah. Historical fiction: guide for junior and senior high schools, and colleges, also for general reader. 8th rev. and enl. ed. Philadelphia, McKinley, 1964. 368p. (McKinley bibliographies, v.1) **BD155**

A classified list, with author and title index, of historical fiction. Earlier editions also included nonfiction, which is now treated separately (*see* DA10).

McGarry, Daniel D. and **White, Sarah Harriman.** Historical fiction guide: annotated, chronological, geographical, and topical list of five thousand selected historical novels. N.Y., Scarecrow, 1964. 628p. **BD156**

Arranged by chronological period and then geographically; lists almost 5000 fictional works in English including translations into English. Covers from ancient times to 1900. Author and title but no subject index.

Nield, Jonathan. Guide to the best historical novels and tales. [5th ed. rev., enl., rearranged, and mostly rewritten] London, Mathews; N.Y., Macmillan, [1929]. 424p. **BD157**

1st ed. 1902.

Includes: Chronological lists for pre-Christian Era and 1st–20th centuries; Supplementary list of semihistorical novels; Bibliography of books and articles about historical fiction; Index of: (1) authors, (2) titles, and (3) subjects.

A comprehensive list of 2392 titles, mainly English but including some foreign material in English translation or in the original. Differs from the 1911 edition in the elimination of some 1400 titles, and in the addition of 1160 not previously included.

Criticism

Thurston, Jarvis A. [and others]. Short fiction criticism: a checklist of interpretation since 1925 of stories and novelettes (American, British, Continental) 1800–1958. Denver, Alan Swallow, 1960. 265p. **BD158**

Sources consulted, p.209–65.

A listing of critical articles published in books and periodicals, including "little magazines," on stories and novelettes no longer than 150 pages. Confined to material in English.

Walker, Warren S. Twentieth-century short story explication: interpretations, 1900–1960 inclusive, of short fiction since 1800. Hamden, Conn., Shoe String, 1961. 369p. **BD159**

"A bibliography of short story explication . . . in books, monographs and periodicals."—*Pref.* Most items were written after 1920, and most are in English. Except for the most recent items, the references unfortunately duplicate a large percentage of those in Thurston's *Short fiction criticism* (BD158).

—— —— Supplement: interpretations, since 1960, of short fiction since 1800. Hamden, Conn., 1963. 131p.

". . . carries the bibliography forward to April 1, 1963."—*Pref.*

Indexes

Cook, Dorothy Elizabeth and **Monro, Isabel Stevenson.** Short story index; an index to 60,000 stories in 4320 collections. N.Y., Wilson, 1953. 1553p. **BD160**

"Supersedes the *Index to short stories* compiled by Ina Ten Eyck Firkins (1923) and its Supplements (1929 and 1936)."—*Pref.*

Indexes—by author, title, and, in many cases, subject—some 60,000 stories published in 1949 or earlier. The list of collections indexed is given in pt. II, by author and title.

—— —— Supplement, 1950–1954, 1955–1958. N.Y., Wilson, 1956–60. 2v.

Contents: 1950–1954, comp. by D. E. Cook and Estelle A. Fidell. Indexes 9575 stories in 549 collections. 394p.; 1955–1958, comp. by Estelle A. Fidell and Esther V. Flory. Indexes 6392 stories in 376 collections. 341p.

Cotton, Gerald Brooks and **Glencross, Alan.** Cumulated fiction index, 1945–1960. (Fiction index three) . . . London, Assoc. of Assist. Librarians, 1960. 552p. **BD161**

Subtitle: A guide to more than 25,000 works of fiction, including short story collections, anthologies, omnibus volumes, extracts and condensed books, mainly available between January 1945 and February 1960, arranged under 3000 subject headings with numerous references, and intended for use in public and circulating libraries, schools and bookshops and by the general reader.

1st ed., *Fiction index 1*, 1953. A supplement was published in 1957.

"This volume is a revised cumulation of the first two, with new material added for books published between 1957 and 1960."—*Pref.* Subject approach only. No dates or publishing information.

Eastman, Mary Huse. Index to fairy tales, myths and legends. 2d ed. rev. and enl. Boston, Faxon, 1926. 610p. (Useful reference ser., no.28) **BD162**

—— —— Supplement, 1937. 566p. (Useful reference ser., no.61)

—— —— 2d Supplement, 1952. 370p. (Useful reference ser., no.82)

A title index—with entry under best-known title and cross references from variant titles—to the fairy tales and legends included in a large number of collections. Principally useful in public libraries and as a help to the children's librarian, but of some value also to the special student of folklore.

Hannigan, Francis J. Standard index of short stories, 1900–1914. Boston, Small, 1918. 334p. **BD163**

An author and title index to stories published in 24 American magazines, 1900–14. Contains some 35,000 entries for stories by about 3000 authors. Although there is much duplication, it does include titles not found in the *Short story index* (BD160) or in the *Readers' guide* (AF122).

Poetry
Indexes

American Library Association. Subject index to poetry for children and young people, comp. by Violet Sell [and others]. Chicago, Assoc., 1957. 582p. **BD164**

Intended for librarians and others to use with children and young people from kindergarten through high school; indexes poems in 157 collections on "specific topics, universal concepts, persons, places, and things, as well as . . . for special occasions or programs."—*Pref.*

Braithwaite, William Stanley Beaumont. Anthology of magazine verse, 1913– . N.Y., Gomme, 1913– . **BD165**

For full record *see* BD258.

Includes an annual index to poems published in magazines.

Brewton, John Edmund and **Brewton, Sara Westbrook.** Index to children's poetry; a title, subject, author, and first line index to poetry in collections for children and youth. N.Y., Wilson, 1942. 965p. **BD166**

"A dictionary index to 130 collections of poems for children and youth, with title, subject, author and first line entries. More than 15,000 poems by approximately 2500 different authors are classified under more than 1800 different subjects."—*Introd.*

—— —— First supplement. N.Y., Wilson, 1954. 405p.

Indexes 66 collections published between 1938 and 1951. "More than 7000 poems by approximately 1300 different authors are classified under more than 1250 different subjects." —*Introd.*

A smaller work, *Children's poetry index* by Maud R. Macpherson (Boston, Faxon, 1938. 453p.), indexes 50 collections, 18 of which are not included in Brewton, and therefore may occasionally be useful.

Bruncken, Herbert. Subject index to poetry; a guide for adult readers. Chicago, Amer. Lib. Assoc., 1940. 201p. **BD167**

Indexes 215 anthologies of prose and poetry under specific subjects. Attempts to supply material for "(1) the location of poetry on specific subjects, (2) the location of a poem, the topical matter or dominant idea of which is known, but not author, title or first line, (3) the location of a poem whose author, title or first line is not known, but a line or fragment of a line of which is known."—*Pref.*

Cushing, Helen Grant. Children's song index. N.Y., Wilson, 1936. 798p. **BD168**

Includes poems set to music. For full description *see* BH110.

Granger's Index to poetry. 5th ed. compl. rev. and enl., indexing anthologies published through June 30, 1960. Ed. by William F. Bernhardt. N.Y., Columbia Univ. Pr., 1962. 2123p. **BD169**

1st ed. 1904; 2d ed. 1918; 3d ed. 1940; 4th ed. 1953, with intervening supplements.

A very useful index important in public, college, and school libraries as it indexes a large number of standard and popular collections of poetry (the 1st–3d editions also indexed prose selections). In the 4th and 5th editions, the title and first-line indexes are combined, followed by an author index and a subject index.

Each edition includes some anthologies previously indexed, drops some, and adds others. The 5th edition treats 574 anthologies including 110 new titles. Because of the number of titles indexed in earlier editions, but omitted in later ones, most libraries will find it advantageous to keep all.

Hastings, Henry C. Spoken poetry on records and tapes; an index of currently available recordings. Chicago, Assoc. of College and Reference Libraries, 1957. 51p. (ACRL monographs, no.18) **BD170**

Main listing is alphabetical by poet or anonymous title; a second section contains anthologies, to which the appropriate items in the main listing are keyed.

Ireland, Norma Olin. An index to monologs and dialogs. Rev. and enl. ed. Boston, Faxon, 1949. 171p. (Useful reference ser., no.77) **BD171**

1st ed. 1939.

An author, subject, and title index to 140 collections—51 more than in the 1st edition.

—— —— Supplement. Boston, Faxon, 1959. 133p. (Useful reference ser., no.89)

Indexes 127 additional collections.

Sears, Minnie Earl. Song index. An index to more than 12,000 songs in 177 song collections. N.Y., Wilson, 1926–34. 2v. **BD172**

Includes poems which have been set to music. Indexes many titles not included in Granger (BD169), especially foreign poems in either original or translation.

For full description *see* BH112.

U.S. Library of Congress. General Reference and Bibliography Division. Archive of recorded poetry and literature; a checklist. Wash., 1961. 132p. **BD173**

Checklist of recordings in the Library's archives, arranged by recording artist, with index of authors whose works are not read by themselves. Sales catalog may be obtained from the Library's recording laboratory.

Romances and epics

See also French—Bibliography—Medieval, p.283.

Ackerman, Robert William. An index of the Arthurian names in Middle English. Stanford, Calif., Stanford Univ. Pr., 1952. 250p. (Stanford Univ. publs. University ser. Language and literature. v.10) **BD174**

British Museum. Dept. of Manuscripts. Catalogue of romances in the Dept. of Manuscripts in the British Museum. London, Trustees, 1883–1910. 3v. **BD175**

v.1–2, by H. L. D. Ward; v.3, by J. A. Herbert.

The most important reference book in English on the subject. For each romance it gives, in addition to the description of the manuscript in the British Museum, some account of the tale, its outlines, different versions, other manuscripts, authorship, history, etc., and important bibliographical references both to printed texts and to critical comment.

Chapman, Coolidge Otis. An index of names in Pearl, Purity, Patience, and Gawain. Ithaca, N.Y., Cornell Univ. Pr., 1951. 66p. (Cornell studies in English, v.38) **BD176**

An index of proper names in four medieval poems, with line references and biographical and geographical information.

Guerber, Hélène Adeline. Book of the epic; the world's great epics told in story. London, Harrap, 1919. 631p. il. **BD177**

Gives synopses of the stories of the great Greek, Latin, French, Spanish, Portuguese, Italian, British, German, Dutch, Scandinavian, Russian and Finnish, Balkan, Hebrew and

Early Christian, Arabian and Persian, Indian, Chinese and Japanese, and American epics.

Newberry Library, Chicago. The Arthurian legend: a check list of books in the Newberry Library, comp. by Jane D. Harding. Chicago, Lib., 1933. 120p.   **BD178**

Contents: Texts (classified by language) and critical works; Index to titles, editors, and translators of texts.

—— —— Supplement, 1938. 90p.

Northup, Clark Sutherland and **Parry, John J.** The Arthurian legends: modern retellings of the old stories, an annotated bibliography. (In Journal of English and Germanic philology 43:173–221. April 1944)   **BD179**

—— —— Supplement, by Paul A. Brown. (In Journal of English and Germanic philology 49:208–16. April 1950)

Lists bibliographies and discussions of modern versions; new versions of the Arthurian stories; doubtful items; and items rejected because the Arthurian connection is too slight or wholly lacking in spite of the titles.

Parry, John J. and **Schlauch, Margaret.** A bibliography of critical Arthurian literature ... 1922–35. N.Y., Modern Language Assoc., 1931–36. 2v.   **BD180**

v.1, 1922–29; v.2, 1930–35.

Supplemented by lists appearing in the *Modern language quarterly*, the first covering 1936–39, annual thereafter, prepared by John J. Parry; 1955 on, prepared by Paul A. Brown.

A listing of books with references to reviews and periodical articles in various languages. Items are numbered consecutively from the beginning. In the forty years 1922–1961, 5135 items have been listed.

See also the *Critical bibliography of French literature*, v.1, The mediaeval period, Chapters 6–11 (BD651).

Société Internationale Arthurienne. Bulletin bibliographique. Paris, 1949– . no.1– . Annual.   **BD181**

Title also in English: *Bibliographical bulletin* of the International Arthurian Society.

An international annual bibliography of Arthurian writings, including books, periodical articles, dissertations, works in progress, etc. References to reviews are frequently given. Listings are arranged by country of origin.

Some numbers include special articles on Arthurian subjects and lists of members.

Spence, Lewis. Dictionary of medieval romance and romance writers. London, Routledge; N.Y., Dutton, 1913. 395p.   **BD182**

A list, in one alphabet, of the titles and characters of the principal British, Celtic, French, Italian, Scandinavian, Spanish, and Teutonic romances from the 11th to the 14th centuries. Gives: (1) under title, a fairly detailed synopsis of the story of the romance with some bibliographical references but no full list of editions, and (2) under character, a brief description of the character, and the title of the romance in which it appears.

Speech

Bibliography

Cleary, James W. and **Haberman, Frederick W.** Rhetoric and public address: a bibliography, 1947–1961. Madison and Milwaukee, 1964. 487p.   **BD183**

Based on the annual bibliographies published in the *Quarterly journal of speech*, 1947–51, and in *Speech monographs*, 1952–61, but is not merely a cumulation of these. The entries were reviewed, some corrected, some dropped, and about 1500 items added.

An alphabetically arranged list of 8035 items with subject index. Also a list of practitioners and theorists, and an index of reviewers.

Continued by the *Bibliography of rhetoric and public address* appearing annually in *Speech monographs*.

Dissertations

Auer, John Jeffery. Doctoral dissertations in speech: work in progress, 1951– . (In Speech monographs, v.18–) Annual.   **BD184**

Lists dissertations in progress, arranged by subject.

Dow, Clyde W. Abstracts of theses in the field of speech. (In Speech monographs, v.13, 1946–) Annual. **BD185**

An annual listing giving abstracts of doctor's dissertations and master's essays.

Knower, Franklin H. Graduate theses; an index of graduate work in speech. (In Speech monographs, v.2, 1935–)   **BD186**

The first installment covers 1902–34; annual thereafter. Includes both doctor's and master's theses completed.

Indexes

Sutton, Roberta Briggs. Speech index; an index to 64 collections of world famous orations and speeches for various occasions. N.Y., Wilson, 1935. 272p.   **BD187**

A dictionary catalog with entries for each oration under author, subject, and type of speech.

—— —— 1935–1955. New Brunswick, N.J., Scarecrow, 1956. 448p.

Indexes 70 collections in same general way.

—— —— 1956–1961. N.Y., Scarecrow, 1962. 219p.

"Includes 32 new titles or revised editions of titles previously indexed, and 12 older titles in print during the years 1956–1961."

new ed → 1935-1965

Collections and handbooks

Baird, Albert Craig. Representative American speeches. 1937/38– . N.Y., Wilson, 1938– . Annual.   **BD188**

Representative speeches of the year. Issued each year as one number of the *Reference shelf* (BD201).

Brewer, David Josiah [and others]. World's best orations; from the earliest period to the present time. St. Louis, Mo., Kaiser, 1899–1901. 10v. il.   **BD189**

Arranged alphabetically by author. Gives for each a brief biographical sketch and selected orations. Indexes: (1) orators; (2) subjects; (3) chronological index of orators; (4) chronological index of periods and events; (5) chronological indexes of law, government, and politics, of religion and philosophy, of literature; (6) general index of orators, subjects, events, etc.

Prochnow, Herbert Victor. 1400 ideas for speakers and toastmasters: how to speak with confidence. Natick, Mass., W. A. Wilde, 1964. 158p.   **BD190**

A collection of humorous stories, epigrams, unusual facts and illustrations, selections from speeches, quotations, and unusual comments, etc.

—— Speaker's handbook of epigrams and witticisms. N.Y., Harper, 1955. 332p.   **BD191**

Some 5000 expressions arranged by rubric. Sometimes indicates author but does not give exact citation.

—— The toastmaster's handbook. N.Y., Prentice-Hall, 1949. 374p.   **BD192**

A manual on the responsibilities and techniques of the toastmaster with samples of introductions, quotations, stories, etc.

Speech Association of America. A history and criticism

of American public address. 1st ed. N.Y., McGraw-Hill, 1943–55. 3v. **BD193**

v.1–2, ed. by W. N. Brigance; v.3, ed. by M. K. Hochmuth and associates: W. N. Brigance and D. Bryant.

Chapters written by specialists treat the great speakers of America, from Jonathan Edwards to Franklin Delano Roosevelt, with extensive footnotes and bibliographies.

Vital speeches of the day. v.1, Oct. 8, 1934– . N.Y., City News Pub. Co., 1934– . Monthly. **BD194**

Prints in full the important addresses of contemporary leaders of public opinion in the fields of economics, politics, education, sociology, business, labor, etc.

—— 25 year index, Oct. 8, 1934—Oct. 1, 1959. Pelham, N.Y., City News Pub. Co., 1963. 137p.

Debating

Bibliography

Kruger, Arthur N. A classified bibliography of argumentation and debate. N.Y., Scarecrow, 1964. 400p. **BD195**

A comprehensive, classified bibliography of books and articles in English, primarily of the 20th century. Covers all phases of debating. Includes master's and doctor's theses.

Indexes

Debate index, comp. by Edith M. Phelps. New ed. rev. N.Y., Wilson, 1939. 130p. (Reference shelf, v.12, no.9) **BD196**

—— Supplement, comp. by Julia E. Johnsen. (Reference shelf, v.14, no.9, 1941)

—— 2d supplement, comp. by Joseph R. Dunlap and Martin A. Kuhn. (Reference shelf, v.36, no.3, 1964)

A subject index to debates, briefs, bibliographies, and collections of articles on public questions.

Handbooks

❦ Numerous manuals and texts on the conduct and technique of debates and discussions have been published. The following are representative examples; for others, *see* Kruger (BD195).

Auer, John Jeffery and **Ewbank, Henry Lee.** Handbook for discussion leaders. Rev. ed. N.Y., Harper, 1954. 153p. **BD197**

Methods of organizing, conducting, and evaluating group discussions, panels, symposiums, lectures, debates, forums.

Baird, Albert Craig. Argumentation, discussion, and debate. 1st ed. N.Y., McGraw-Hill, 1950. 422p. (McGraw-Hill ser. in speech) **BD198**

Ewbank, Henry Lee and **Auer, John Jeffery.** Discussion and debate; tools of a democracy. 2d ed. N.Y., Appleton, 1951. 492p. **BD199**

1st ed. 1941.
A textbook for colleges and universities.

Quimby, Brooks. So you want to discuss and debate. [A manual for debaters] [2d ed.] Portland, Me., J. Weston Walch, 1954. 230p. il. **BD200**

Reference shelf. N.Y., Wilson, 1922– . v.1– . **BD201**

Issued 6 numbers to a volume.
Each number is devoted to a timely controversial question, with reprints of selected articles from books and periodicals giving background information and pro and con arguments, followed by a comprehensive bibliography.

Walch, John Weston. Complete handbook on . . . Portland, Me., J. Weston Walch, [19?–]. Annual. **BD202**

Issued annually in two series: (1) on the topic for the collegiate debate of the year; (2) on the topic of the high school debate of the year.

Gives background information, arguments pro and con, and statistics, facts, and opinions on the subject. Quotations are given with exact citations to sources. Annotated bibliographies.

ENGLISH LANGUAGE

American

Bibliography

❦ In addition to the bibliographies listed below, those listed under United States, p.31–34, should be consulted. Northup's *Register of bibliographies* (AA22), Besterman's *World bibliography of bibliographies* (AA13), and the *Bibliographic index* (AA14) refer to many individual bibliographies, either issued separately or included in periodicals or other composite works.

Blanck, Jacob Nathaniel. Bibliography of American literature, comp. . . . for the Bibliographical Society of America. New Haven, Yale Univ. Pr., 1955–63. v.1–4. (In progress) **BD203**

Contents: v.1–4, A–Ingraham.

A selective bibliography of American authors, which, when completed, will include the works published in book form of approximately 300 writers from the beginning of the Federal period up to and including persons who died before the end of 1930. Authors whose writings do not have literary interest or are not of the character of belles-lettres are excluded.

Material for each author is arranged chronologically and includes: (1) First editions of books and pamphlets, and any other book containing the first appearance of any work; (2) Reprints containing textual or other changes; and (3) A selected list of biographical, bibliographical, and critical works. Periodical and newspaper publications, later editions, translations, and volumes containing isolated correspondence are not included. Location is indicated for the copies examined.

Jones, Howard Mumford and **Ludwig, Richard M.** Guide to American literature and its backgrounds since 1890. 3d ed. rev. and enl. Cambridge, Harvard Univ. Pr., 1964. 240p. **BD204**

1st ed., 1953, by Howard Mumford Jones.
A guide listing works presenting the intellectual, sociological, and political backgrounds of American literary history, followed by reading lists (p.121–223) on various aspects and schools in American literature since 1890.

Leary, Lewis Gaston. Articles on American literature, 1900–1950. Durham, N.C., Duke Univ. Pr., 1954. 437p. **BD205**

A very useful bibliography—a revision and extension of the author's earlier work which covered 1920–45 (pub. 1947) —based on the bibliographies published quarterly in *American literature* since 1929, and annually in *PMLA* since 1922. The coverage has been broadened as well as extended backward to 1900 by the examination of periodicals and other bibliographies.

Literary history of the United States. 3d ed. rev. v.2, Bibliography. N.Y., Macmillan, 1963. 790p., 268p. **BD206**

For full description see BD222.

Millett, Fred Benjamin. Contemporary American authors; a critical survey and 219 bio-bibliographies. N.Y., Harcourt, 1940. 716p. **BD207**

This edition, based on *Contemporary American literature,* by J. M. Manly and Edith Rickert (1st ed. 1922; 2d ed. 1929); though now out of date, is still useful. P.1–204 contain a critical survey of contemporary American literature since 1900; p.207–666 contain the bio-bibliographical sketches, which give brief biographies followed by bibliographies of works by the author and a list of studies and articles about the author.

Rusk, Ralph Leslie. The literature of the middle western frontier. N.Y., Columbia Univ. Pr., 1925. 2v. (Columbia Univ. studies in English and comparative literature, v.83) (Repr.: N.Y., Ungar, 1963) **BD208**

v.1, History and survey to 1840; v.2, Bibliographies. v.2, classified according to the treatment in v.1, covering cultural beginnings, travel, newspapers and magazines, controversial writings, scholarly writings and schoolbooks, fiction, poetry and drama. Locates copies.

Thompson, Ralph. American literary annuals and gift books, 1825–1865. N.Y., Wilson, 1936. 183p. **BD209**

Contains a history and discussion of representative American annuals and gift books, p.1–101, and a catalog, p.102–63, describing, with fuller data than that given in Faxon (*Literary annuals and gift-books.* Boston, Boston Book Co., 1912), some 230 titles with detailed information as to the different editions of each, location of copies, indication as to whether the annual is for juvenile or adult readers, and many notes as to reprints under changed titles. Index includes these variant titles.

Largely supersedes the earlier list by Faxon.

Dissertations

Woodress, James Leslie. Dissertations in American literature, 1891–1955, with supplement, 1956–1961. Durham, N.C., Duke Univ. Pr., 1962. 138p. **BD210**

The original list, arranged by subject, and published in 1957, covered 1891–1955 and listed more than 2500 theses written at approximately 100 universities. This list is reprinted here with a supplement covering 1956–61, adding 809 new titles and 150 others previously reported as in progress. A cumulated author index to both sections.

newly rev. + enl. mikaas of .

Manuscripts

manian koutz
.1891– 64

Modern Language Association of America. American Literature Group. Committee on Manuscript Holdings. American literary manuscripts: a checklist of holdings in academic, historical and public libraries in the United States. Austin, Univ. of Texas Pr., 1960. 421p. **BD211**

Lists some 2350 American writers indicating, by Library of Congress symbol for nearly 300 participating libraries, the holdings of manuscripts of creative works, journals or diaries, letters to and from the author, special collections, etc. Type and extent of holdings are shown by "category-symbols," with, when possible, indication of the number of pieces.

Translations

Brown, Glenora W. and **Brown, Deming B.** A guide to Soviet Russian translations of American literature. N.Y., King's Crown Pr., Columbia Univ., 1954. 243p. (Columbia Slavonic studies) **BD212**

Includes translations of American works—novels, short stories, poems, plays, biographies, memoirs, essays, movie scenarios, and certain journalistic and historical writings—published in book and periodical form in the USSR, 1917–47.

In two parts; (1) anthologies and (2) individual authors. Each entry includes Russian and American title, translator, publisher or periodical title, place and date of publication,

pagination, number of copies published, and Russian source. Author and American title indexes.

Mummendey, Richard. Die schöne Literatur der Vereinigten Staaten von Amerika in deutschen Übersetzungen; eine Bibliographie. Bonn, Bouvier; Charlottesville, Bibliographical Soc. of the Univ. of Virginia, 1961. 199p. **BD213**

Title on spine: American belles-lettres in German translations; on added title page: Belles-lettres of the United States of America in German translations; a bibliography.

Prefatory matter in English and German.

"Lists the literary works of American authors published originally in the English language which have been translated into German and have appeared as separate volumes."—*Pref.* Covers from the early period through 1957 and lists as many translations as could be found.

Dictionaries and handbooks

Burke, William Jeremiah and **Howe, Will D.** American authors and books, 1640 to the present day. Augm. and rev. by Irving R. Weiss. N.Y., Crown, 1962. 834p. **BD214**

"The purpose of this handbook is to present the most useful facts about the writing, illustrating, editing, publishing, reviewing, collecting, selling and preservation of American books from 1640 to 1940."—*Pref. to 1st ed.* The new edition brings the material up to date, particularly in information about authors and their works. It includes, in alphabetical order, concise articles—with cross references to related subjects —on authors, books, periodicals, newspapers, publishing firms, literary societies, regions and localities, etc. Limited to the continental United States. Its biographical sketches, which include those of many minor writers, are brief, and usually give complete dates of birth and death, principal occupations, and titles of works. Lists many titles of novels, plays, short stories, poems, essays, orations, songs, hymns, etc., with author and publication date and sometimes brief synopses; and gives information on magazines, including "little magazines," and a selected list of newspapers. The coverage is larger than that in the *Oxford companion to American literature* (BD 216), but the articles are much shorter.

Duyckinck, Evert Augustus and **Duyckinck, G. L.** Cyclopaedia of American literature. Ed. to date by M. L. Simons. Philadelphia, Baxter, 1875. 2v. il. **BD215**

1st ed. 1855.

Various printings.

Subtitle: Embracing personal and critical notices of authors, and selections of their writings, from the earliest period to the present day, with portraits, autographs, and other illustrations.

Standard collection, arranged chronologically, 1626–1875. Still useful, especially for minor earlier writers.

Hart, James David. The Oxford companion to American literature. 3d ed. [rev. and enl.] N.Y., Oxford Univ. Pr., 1956. 890p. **BD216**

"In alphabetical arrangement the work includes . . . short biographies, and bibliographies of American authors, with information regarding their style and subject matter; nearly 900 summaries and descriptions of the important American novels, stories, essays, poems and plays; definitions and historical outlines of literary schools and movements; and information on literary societies, magazines, anthologies, co-operative publications, literary awards, book collectors, printers, etc."—*Pref.* Includes some Canadian material. There are not so many entries as in Burke and Howe, *American authors and books* (BD214), but the articles are longer; likewise, the biographical sketches are longer and give more facts. But while Burke and Howe gives complete dates of birth and death, this gives years only; its synopses are also longer, and more space is given to the social and cultural background of American literature and to biographies and discussions of men and movements—social, economic, scientific, military, political, and religious—in their effects upon literature.

Chronological index gives, in parallel columns, the literary and social history of America from 1000 to 1955, p.863–90.

Herzberg, Max J. The reader's encyclopedia of American literature . . . N.Y., Crowell, 1962. 1280p. il.   **BD217**

A comprehensive dictionary of American authors, critics, literary movements, synopses of books, literary characters, periodicals, geographical features which have influenced literature, etc. Not so scholarly as the *Oxford companion* but more inclusive.

White's Conspectus of American biography; a tabulated record of American history and biography. 2d ed. N.Y., White, 1937. 455p.   **BD218**

Includes many lists relating to American literature, e.g., Americans in fiction, poetry, and the drama; pseudonyms and sobriquets; recipients of awards, etc.

For full description *see* AJ35.

Criticism

See also Fiction—Criticism, BD158, BD159, BD248.

Nyren, Dorothy. A library of literary criticism: modern American literature. 3d ed., with index to critics, and supplement. N.Y., Ungar, 1964. 620p.   **BD219**

1st ed. 1960.

Planned as a successor, for American literature, to Moulton's *Library of literary criticism* (BD339); gives excerpts, from critical material found in popular and scholarly journals and in books, on American authors who wrote or became prominent after 1904. Definite citation is given for each review.

The 3d edition includes the 170 authors in the earlier edition and adds a supplement, p.555–92, covering 4 new authors and additional material for 16 authors in the main work. An index to the supplement is also added.

Stovall, Floyd. Eight American authors; a review of research and criticism. N.Y., Modern Language Assoc. of Amer., 1956. 418p.   **BD220**

Eight essays, each by a different scholar, discussing the published bibliographies, editions, biographies, and critical studies of the author treated.

Contents: Poe, by Jay B. Hubbell; Emerson, by Floyd Stovall; Hawthorne, by Walter Blair; Thoreau, by Louis Leary; Melville, by Stanley T. Williams; Whitman, by Williard Thorp; Mark Twain, by Harry Hayden Clark; Henry James, by Robert E. Spiller.

———— ———— Bibliographical supplement by **J.** Chesley Mathews. N.Y., Norton, 1963. p.420–66.

Lists selected books and articles published 1955–62 **to** supplement the above.

History

Cambridge history of American literature, ed. by William Peterfield Trent, John Erskine, Stuart P. Sherman, Carl Van Doren. N.Y., Putnam, 1917–21. 4v.   **BD221**

v.1, Colonial and Revolutionary literature. Early national literature, pt.1; v.2, Early national literature, pt.2. Later national literature, pt.1; v.3–4, Later national literature, pts.2–3.

Still an important history of American literature, necessary in all types of general libraries. Covers the early period with unusual thoroughness; treats the ordinary literary forms and subjects, standard writers, etc. with great detail; and includes adequate treatment of many subjects not covered in the customary literary histories, e.g., accounts of the early travelers, explorers, and observers; colonial newspapers; literary annuals and gift books; later magazines and newspapers;

children's literature; oral literature; the English language in America; non-English writings, i.e., German, French, Yiddish, aboriginal. Each chapter is by a specialist, and the bibliographies, arranged by chapters at the ends of v.1, 2, and 4, are very full, although not now up to date; in all, the bibliography covers more than 500 pages. Author, title, and subject index in v.1, 2, and 4 (the latter covers v.3–4). The bibliographies are indexed in Northup's *Register* (AA22).

Available in two different editions: (1) the complete edition, originally published by Putnam; and (2) an inexpensive reprint, complete as to text but lacking the bibliographies (Macmillan, 1933. 3v.). This reprint naturally lacks the reference value of the complete edition with the bibliographies, but is useful in the small library not able to afford the full edition, or in the larger library as an extra set for circulation.

Literary history of the United States. Eds.: Robert E. Spiller [and others]. 3d ed. rev. N.Y., Macmillan, 1963. 2v.   **BD222**

1st ed. 1948. 3v.

Contents: v.1, History; v.2, Bibliography.

The first comprehensive history since the *Cambridge history of American literature* (BD221). v.1 (originally published in 2v.) presents a survey from colonial times to the present day in a series of chapters written by authorities and integrated into a whole by a board of editors. The chapters are not signed, but a list of them with the author of each is given on p.1442–45. No footnotes. In the 3d edition, the main text remains the same except for minor corrections, but two chapters have been added: one covering the period between the two World wars, the other the period since 1945. Also includes a highly selected bibliography for the general reader, p.1446–81.

v.2, *Bibliography,* consists of bibliographical essays organized to develop the treatment of the text. Divided into four main sections: (1) Guide to resources; (2) Literature and culture; (3) Movements and influences; and (4) Individual authors. This fourth section furnishes information on 207 authors, usually listing separate and collected works, edited texts and reprints, biography and criticism, primary sources (including location of manuscripts), and bibliographies. Gives valuable critical and evaluative comments on editions, biographies, etc. In the revised edition, a *Bibliography supplement,* originally published in 1958, has been added to the main bibliography. It follows the same arrangement and adds 16 new individual author bibliographies. The index has been cumulated to serve both the main bibliography and the supplement.

This comprehensive bibliography is sometimes difficult to use because of its paragraph form and its inadequate index. The index lists names of literary authors treated, titles of periodicals, and some subject and form headings, e.g., Anthologies, Negro writers and writing, Regionalism and local color, etc. No consistency is evident in the indexing of authors of critical or bibliographical works; sometimes they are included, sometimes not.

Hubbell, Jay Broadus. The South in American literature, 1607–1900. Durham, N.C., Duke Univ. Pr., 1954. 987p.   **BD223**

An extensive survey history.

Bibliography, p.883–974. Includes topical, annotated bibliographies, and bibliographies on individual writers.

Biographies of authors

Kunitz, Stanley J. and **Haycraft, Howard.** American authors, 1600–1900; a biographical dictionary of American literature, complete in one volume with 1300 biographies and 400 portraits. N.Y., Wilson, 1938. 846p. il.   **BD224**

Popularly written biographies with brief bibliographies of works by and about the authors.

———— The junior book of authors. 2d ed. rev. N.Y., Wilson, 1951. 309p. il.   **BD225**

The 1st edition, 1934, included biographical or autobiographical sketches of some 268 writers and illustrators (living and deceased) for younger readers. The 2d edition contains 289 sketches, of which 160 are repeated with revisions; the remaining 129 are new names which have come into prominence since 1934. The 108 dropped names are largely in the field of the classics, e.g., Louisa M. Alcott, and the borderline group of books between adult and juvenile. All of these names are to be found in other Wilson biographical dictionaries, but libraries may wish to keep both editions on their shelves.

Fuller, Muriel. More junior authors. N.Y., Wilson, 1963. 235p. portraits.   **BD226**

Companion volume to the above.

Includes sketches, many of them autobiographical, of 268 authors and illustrators of books for children and young people.

General collections and anthologies

Fadiman, Clifton. The American treasury, 1455–1955, selected, arr., and ed. by Clifton Fadiman, assisted by Charles Van Doren. N.Y., Harper, 1955. 1108p. **BD227**

An unconventional anthology, "a collection of interesting, diverting, beautiful or inspiring statements made by 1300 Americans."—*Pref.* In a systematic arrangement; includes some 6000 quotations or passages, sometimes of some length, on life in America.

The indexes by subject, familiar word, author, and title aid in the use of the volume as a reference work, although sources are to author only and not to exact citation.

✓**Library of southern literature;** comp. under the direct supervision of southern men of letters. E. A. Alderman, J. C. Harris, editors in chief. New Orleans, Martin and Hoyt, [c1908–23]. 17v. il.   **BD228**

v.1–13, Biographical and critical sketches, and selected extracts arranged alphabetically by the authors discussed; v.14, Miscellanea: poems, anecdotes, letters, epitaphs and inscriptions, quotations, bibliography; v.15, Biographical dictionary, ed. by Lucian Lamar Knight, containing 3800 sketches; v.16, Historical side lights, 50 reading courses. Bibliography, references to bibliographies in v.1–13, and supplementary lists. Index of authors, titles, and subjects; v.17, Supplement.

A useful collection, but with various inaccuracies in the biographical sections.

✓**Stedman, Edmund Clarence** and **Hutchinson, Ellen Mackay.** Library of American literature from the earliest settlement to the present time. N.Y., Webster, 1891 [c1887–90]. 11v. il.   **BD229**

Frequently reprinted.

Gives selections which are characteristic examples of the work of the principal American writers 1607–1889; a biographical dictionary of the writers included is given in v.11, p.467–614, and there is a general index of persons, subjects, and some titles, the latter grouped under form headings such as poetry, essays, etc.; quotations are brought out in index under heading, "Noted sayings."

Drama

Bibliography

See also BD238, BD239.

Bergquist, G. William. Three centuries of English and American plays; a checklist. England, 1500–1800; United States, 1714–1830. N.Y., London, Hafner, 1963. 281p. **BD230**

For complete record *see* BD352.

Hill, Frank Pierce. American plays printed 1714–1830;

a bibliographical record. Stanford, Calif., Stanford Univ. Pr.; Oxford, Univ. Pr., 1934. 152p.   **BD231**

Based primarily upon the 2d edition of Wegelin (BD234); and upon the typewritten catalog prepared by F. W. Atkinson, 1918, of published plays in his library.

Arranged alphabetically by author and anonymous title, with title index and chronological list.

Roden, Robert F. Later American plays, 1831–1900; being a compilation of the titles of plays by American authors published and performed in America since 1831. N.Y., Dunlap Soc., 1900. 132p. (Publ. of the Dunlap Soc., n.s. 12)   **BD232**

Gives brief biographical notes, followed by a listing of published plays.

U.S. Copyright Office. Dramatic compositions copyrighted in the United States, 1870 to 1916. Wash., Govt. Prt. Off., 1918. 2v.(3547p.).   **BD233**

A list of about 60,000 plays registered for copyright July 21, 1870—Dec. 31, 1916. The main list is arranged alphabetically by title and gives, for each title, author's name, number of acts, number of pages, place published and date of a published play (or the word "typewritten" to indicate the typed manuscript of an unpublished play), date of copyright, holder of copyright, number of copies deposited, etc. Cross references from alternative, secondary, and translated titles are given in the main alphabet. Also includes a supplementary alphabet of recent titles (1915–16), and a detailed author index containing names of authors, joint authors, editors, translators, and copyright proprietors, pseudonyms, etc. A very useful list for questions as to authorship, publication, etc. of plays.

For titles of plays copyrighted later than 1916, the *Catalog of copyright entries* (AA353) should be consulted.

Wegelin, Oscar. Early American plays, 1714–1830; a compilation of the titles of plays and dramatic poems written by authors born in or residing in North America previous to 1830. 2d ed. rev. N.Y., Literary Collector Pr., 1905. 94p.   **BD234**

Brief biographical sketches are followed by titles of plays.

Annuals

Best plays of 1894/99–   and **Year book of the drama in America.** Boston, Small, 1920–25; N.Y., Dodd, 1926– . il. Annual. (1963–64)   **BD235**

Title varies: 1899/1909—1946/47, *Best plays . . .*; 1947/48—1949/50, *Burns Mantle best plays;* 1950/51– , *Best plays . . . .*

1894/99 (pub. 1955), 1899/1909 (pub. 1944), and 1909/19 (pub. 1933) are basic volumes edited by Burns Mantle and G. P. Sherwood, giving selected plays, and chronological lists of plays produced, with date, theater, and cast.

Contents of the annual volumes vary somewhat but include such sections as: (1) Digests with critical comment of selected plays of the year; (2) Title list of plays produced in New York during the year, giving for each: title, author, number of performances, theater, cast of characters, and brief outline of plot; (3) Plays produced outside of New York; (4) Shakespeare festivals; (5) Statistics of runs; (6) List of actors with place and date of birth of each; (7) Prizes and awards; and (8) Index of authors, Index of plays and casts, Index of producers, directors, designers.

——— Index, 1899–1950, 1949–60. N.Y., Dodd, 1950–61. 147p., 46p.

Include indexes, by title, to the plays appearing in the annual volumes, and indexes to authors, adapters, composers, and lyricists. Symbols indicate one of the "ten best," a Pulitzer-prize play, and a New York Drama Critics Circle award play.

Daniel Blum's Theatre world. 1944/45– . N.Y., Theatre World, 1945– . v.1– . il. Annual.   **BD236**

For complete record *see* BG13.

Digests

Lovell, John. Digests of great American plays; complete summaries of more than 100 plays from the beginnings to the present. N.Y., Crowell, 1961. 452p. il. (A Crowell reference book)   **BD237**

Chronologically arranged. Gives for each play: plot summary, cast, and other pertinent facts. Indexes of titles and of authors, and a number of supplementary lists: songs, famous actors, historical characters, etc.

History

Quinn, Arthur Hobson. History of the American drama, from the beginning to the Civil War. 2d ed. N.Y., Crofts, 1943. 530p.   **BD238**

"A list of American plays," p.423–97. Bibliography, p.393–421.

—— A history of the American drama from the Civil War to the present day. [Rev. ed.] N.Y., London, Crofts, 1937. 2v. in 1. 296p., 432p. il.   **BD239**

General bibliography and list of American plays, 1860–1936, p.305–402.

Fiction

Bibliography

Coan, Otis Welton and **Lillard, Richard Gordon.** America in fiction, an annotated list of novels that interpret aspects of life in the United States. 4th ed. Stanford, Calif., Stanford Univ. Pr., [1956]. 200p.   **BD240**

1st ed. 1941.

Lists novels and collections of short stories by phase or aspect of American life, with brief annotations indicating subject matter and treatment. Recommended titles are starred.

Dickinson, Arthur Taylor. American historical fiction. 2d ed. N.Y., Scarecrow, 1963. 364p.   **BD241**

1st ed. 1958.

The 2d edition lists 1909 novels dealing with American history from colonial days to the Cold War, for the most part works published 1917–61, with a few earlier standard titles. Chronological arrangement with author, title, and subject index.

Johannsen, Albert. The House of Beadle and Adams and its dime and nickel novels: the story of a vanished literature. Norman, Univ. of Oklahoma Pr., 1950–62. 3v. il.   **BD242**

Contents: v.1, A history of the firm. Numerical lists of the various series of Beadle novels; v.2, The authors and their novels. Appendix. (Gives biographical sketches of the authors, and lists of their books; general alphabetical index of titles and subtitles; index of principal localities, characters, etc.); v.3, Supplement, Addenda, Corrigenda. 108p. (Includes an index of songs giving the titles of the songs in the Beadle *Songsters*.)

Johnson, James Gibson. Southern fiction prior to 1860; an attempt at a first-hand bibliography. Charlottesville, Va., Michie Co., 1909. 126p.   **BD243**

Thesis (Ph.D.), Univ. of Virginia.

Arranged alphabetically, followed by a chronological list 1765–1860.

New York. Public Library. Beadle collection of dime novels given to the . . . library by Dr. Frank P. O'Brien. N.Y., Lib., 1922. 99p. il.   **BD244**

A list of some 1400 novels, arranged alphabetically by series, with indexes of: (1) authors, and (2) titles.

Queen, Ellery, *pseud.* The detective short story: a bibliography. Boston, Little, 1942. 146p.   **BD245**

Lists, usually with brief annotations, short stories averaging 6000–8000 words in length, with some longer ones, dealing with crime and detection.

Wright, Lyle Henry. American fiction, 1774–1850; a contribution toward a bibliography. Rev. ed. San Marino, Calif., 1948. 355p. (Huntington Lib. publ.)   **BD246**

1st ed. 1939.

This edition has been thoroughly revised and enlarged by some 600 titles to a total of 2772 entries, and a useful chronological index has been added. Lists novels, romances, short stories, fictitious biographies, travels, allegories, and tractlike tales, written by Americans. Locates copies in 19 libraries and 2 private collections.

—— American fiction, 1851–1875; a contribution toward a bibliography. San Marino, Calif., Huntington Lib., 1957. 413p. il. (Huntington Library publ.)   **BD247**

A companion volume to the above, listing 2832 titles. Locates copies in 18 libraries and 1 private collection.

Criticism

Gerstenberger, Donna Lorine and **Hendrick, George.** The American novel, 1789–1959; a checklist of twentieth-century criticism. Denver, Alan Swallow, 1961. 333p.   **BD248**

Arranged alphabetically by novelist, with listings of criticism arranged under individual novels, general studies, and bibliographies. A second section of the book lists general studies of the American novel by century.

Bibliography, p.296–333.

Annuals

Best American short stories of 1915– , and the Yearbook of the American short story. Boston, Houghton, 1915– . v.1– . Annual. (1964)   **BD249**

Title varies: 1915–41, *Best short stories;* 1942– , *Best American short stories.*

Eds.: 1915–41, E. J. O'Brien; 1942–57, Martha Foley; 1958– , Martha Foley and David Burnett.

Each volume contains: (1) Text of selected short stories of the year, and (2) Yearbook. Contents of yearbooks vary; in recent years are much reduced in extent.

Indexes

Day, Donald Byrne. Index to the science-fiction magazines, 1926–1950. Portland, Ore., Perri Pr., 1952. 184p.   **BD250**

Indexes 55 American and 3 British periodicals from their first issue through 1950. Includes an index by authors, one by titles, and a checklist of the magazines indexed with a record of all issues.

History

Quinn, Arthur Hobson. American fiction; an historical and critical survey. N.Y., Appleton, 1936. 805p.   **BD251**

A chronological treatment of the novel and short story from 1770 to 1935.

Bibliography, p.726–72.

Poetry

Bibliography

Brown University. Library. The Anthony memorial; a catalogue of the Harris collection of American poetry with biographical and bibliographical notes by John C. Stockbridge. Providence, R.I., 1886. 320p. **BD252**

The catalog of a notable 19th-century collection of American poetry, presented to the library by H. B. Anthony.

Irish, Wynot R. The modern American muse; a complete bibliography of American verse, 1900–1925. Syracuse, N.Y., Syracuse Univ. Pr., 1950. 259p. **BD253**

Lists 6906 separately published books of verse appearing in the first quarter of this century. Many of them are books of fugitive verse which were privately printed in small editions, and in many cases not listed in the usual publications of the book trade. Also included are the works of the better-known American poets published by the standard publishers.

Items are arranged chronologically by year of publication, and alphabetically by author under the year. Unfortunately there is no index, either by author or by title.

Porter, Dorothy Burnett. North American Negro poets; a bibliographical checklist of their writings, 1760–1944. Hattiesburg, Miss., The Book Farm, 1945. 90p. (Heartman's Historical ser., no.70) **BD254**

An expansion of *A bibliographical checklist of American Negro poetry,* by Arthur A. Schomburg, 1916, listing writings of American Negro poets and indicating location of copies.

U.S. Library of Congress. General Reference and Bibliography Division. Sixty American poets, 1896–1944: selected with preface and critical notes, by Allen Tate. Rev. ed. prep. by Kenton Kilmer. Wash., 1954. 155p. **BD255**

A brief critical note about each author is followed by titles of works with location in at least one American library; works edited and translated; titles of books containing bibliographies; and often location of manuscript collections, recordings, etc.

Wegelin, Oscar. Early American poetry; a compilation of the titles of volumes of verse and broadsides by writers born or residing in North America, north of the Mexican border. 2d ed. rev. and enl. N.Y., Peter Smith, 1930. 2v. in 1. il. **BD256**

Covers 1650–1820, listing 1379 titles.

Dictionaries

Spender, Stephen and **Hall, Donald.** The concise encyclopedia of English and American poets and poetry. N.Y., Hawthorn, 1963. 415p. il. **BD257**

For complete record *see* BD395.

Anthologies

Braithwaite, William Stanley Beaumont. Anthology of magazine verse for 1913–1929, 1958– , and Yearbook of American poetry. N.Y., Gomme, 1913–29, 1959– . Annual. (1958) **BD258**

Publisher varies. Publication suspended, 1930–57.

Each volume consists of two parts: (1) the anthology, and (2) the yearbook. Contents of the yearbook vary somewhat, but in general include an author index to poems published in magazines, an author list of magazine reviews and articles on poetry, an author list of new volumes of poems, and a selected list of books about poets and poetry. The 1926 volume contains a separately paged *Biographical dictionary of poets in the United States.*

The 1958 volume includes *Anthology of poems from the seventeen previously published Braithwaite anthologies,* ed. by Margaret Haley Carpenter.

Oxford book of American verse, chosen and with an introd. by F. O. Matthiessen. N.Y., Oxford Univ. Pr., 1950. 1132p. **BD259**

Stedman, Edmund Clarence. American anthology, 1787–1900; selections illustrating the editor's critical review of American poetry in the nineteenth century. Cambridge, Mass., Houghton, 1900. 878p. **BD260**

Includes biographical notes, index of first lines, and index of titles.

Stevenson, Burton Egbert. Home book of verse, American and English; with an appendix containing a few well-known poems in other languages. 9th ed. N.Y., Holt, 1953. 2v. (lxxxivp., 4012p.) **BD261**

—— Home book of modern verse. 2d ed. rev. N.Y., Holt, 1953. 1124p. **BD262**

For description of these two valuable anthologies, *see* BD402, BD403.

Untermeyer, Louis. Modern American poetry, a critical anthology. New and enl. ed. [i.e., 8th.]. N.Y., Harcourt, 1962. 701p. **BD263**

1st ed. 1919.

A revised edition including biographical and critical paragraphs, with selections of poems from 76 poets from Walt Whitman to Sexton, including 13 who appear for the first time in this anthology.

Published also in a combined edition with the author's *Modern British poetry* (BD404).

Parodies

See English—Parodies, BD411–BD413.

Diaries and letters

Matthews, William. American diaries, an annotated bibliography of American diaries written prior to the year 1861, . . . with the assistance of Roy Harvey Pearce. Berkeley, Los Angeles, Univ. of Calif. Pr., 1945. 383p. (Univ. of California publ. in English, v.16, 1945) (Repr.: Boston, J. S. Canner, 1959) **BD264**

A chronological list of diaries written prior to 1861 with annotations giving full name, occupation, dates, and home of author, and brief notes as to subject content of diary and record of printed source. Manuscript diaries not included.

Weiss, Harry Bischoff. American letter-writers, 1698–1943. N.Y., N.Y. Pub. Lib., 1945. 54p. **BD265**

"Reprinted from the *Bulletin* of the New York Public Library of Dec. 1944 and Jan. 1945."

A bibliography of handbooks of model letter-writing for the "average" person. Locates copies.

Individual authors

The following list does not include all the authors for whom separately published bibliographies are available. It includes only a selection of those of major authors and of writers for whom concordances, dictionaries, or handbooks as well as bibliographies have been published. For additional titles consult the bibliographies listed under American—Bibliography, p.251–52.

Clemens

Asselineau, Roger. The literary reputation of Mark Twain from 1910 to 1950; a critical essay and a bibliography.

Paris, Didier, 1954. 240p. (Publications de la Faculté des Lettres de l'Université de Clermont. Fasc. hors-série) **BD266**

Johnson, Merle. A bibliography of the works of Mark Twain, Samuel Langhorne Clemens. Rev. and enl. N.Y., Harper, 1935. 274p. **BD267**

Subtitle: A list of first editions in book form and of first printings in periodicals and occasional publications of his varied literary activities.

Harnsberger, Caroline Thomas. Mark Twain at your fingertips. N.Y., Beechhurst Pr., 1948. 559p. **BD268**

Quotations from Mark Twain arranged alphabetically by subject matter, followed by a brief bibliography, a topical index with cross references, and a correlated subject index.

Ramsay, Robert L. and **Emberson, Frances Guthrie.** A Mark Twain lexicon. Columbia, Univ. of Missouri Pr., 1938. 278p. (Univ. of Missouri studies, v.13, no.1) **BD269**

Includes a classification of Mark Twain's vocabulary—Americanisms, new words, archaisms, and miscellaneous groups—and a lexicon of words with exact references to his works.

Dickinson

Rosenbaum, Stanford Patrick. A concordance to the poems of Emily Dickinson. Ithaca, N.Y., Cornell Univ. Pr., 1964. 899p. **BD270**

Computer-produced concordance.

Eliot

Gallup, Donald Clifford. T. S. Eliot; a bibliography, including contributions to periodicals and foreign translations. London, Faber and Faber, 1952; N.Y., Harcourt, 1953. 177p. **BD271**

A revision and extension of the author's *A bibliographical checklist of the writings of T. S. Eliot* (1947).

Emerson

Bryer, Jackson R. and **Rees, Robert A.** A checklist of Emerson criticism, 1951–1961, with a detailed index. Hartford, Conn., Transcendental Books, 1964. 50p. il. **BD272**

Cooke, George Willis. Bibliography of Ralph Waldo Emerson. Boston, Houghton, 1908. 340p. **BD273**

Includes works both by and about Emerson.

Hubbell, George Shelton. Concordance to the poems of Ralph Waldo Emerson. N.Y., Wilson, 1932. 478p. **BD274**

Based on the text of v.9 of the Centenary edition of Emerson (Houghton) and thus incomplete, as it covers only the poems collected in that volume and does not include uncollected poems scattered through other volumes of the edition. Gives all occurrences of words listed except in the case of some 172 common words for which only selected references are given.

Carpenter, Frederic Ives. Emerson handbook. N.Y., Hendricks House, 1953. 268p. **BD275**

A treatment and exposition with bibliographies.

Faulkner

Meriwether, James B. The literary career of William Faulkner; a bibliographical study. Princeton, N.J., Princeton Univ. Lib., 1961. 192p. il. **BD276**

Comprises an extensive catalog of a Faulkner exhibit held

at Princeton in 1957, and a classified bibliography of his work. Title index.

Runyan, Harry. A Faulkner glossary. N.Y., Citadel, 1964. 310p. **BD277**

Tuck, Dorothy. Crowell's Handbook of Faulkner . . . Lewis Leary, advisory ed. N.Y., Crowell, 1964. 259p. **BD278**

Hawthorne

Browne, Nina Eliza. Bibliography of Nathaniel Hawthorne. Boston, Houghton, 1905. 215p. **BD279**

Includes material both by and about Hawthorne.

O'Connor, Evangeline M. Analytical index to the works of Nathaniel Hawthorne. Boston, Houghton, [c1882]. 294p. **BD280**

Holmes

Currier, Thomas Franklin. A bibliography of Oliver Wendell Holmes . . . ed. by Eleanor M. Tilton for the Bibliographical Society of America. N.Y., New York Univ. Pr.; London, Oxford Univ. Pr., 1953. 707p. il. **BD281**

An extensive and detailed bibliography of materials by and about Holmes.

James

Edel, Leon and **Laurence, Dan H.** A bibliography of Henry James. 2d ed. rev. London, Hart-Davis, 1961. 427p. (Soho bibliographies, no.8) **BD282**

Poe

Heartman, Charles Frederick and **Canny, James R.** A bibliography of first printings of the writings of Edgar Allan Poe, together with a record of first and later printings of his contributions to annuals, anthologies, periodicals and newspapers issued during his lifetime, also some spurious Poeana and fakes. Rev. ed. Hattiesburg, Miss., The Book Farm, 1943. 294p. (Heartman's Historical ser., no.53 repr.) **BD283**

First published 1940, this is a revised edition of *A census of first editions and source materials by Edgar Allan Poe in American collections* . . . comp. by Charles F. Heartman and Kenneth Rede, pub. in 1932.—Cf. *Pref.* to 1940 edition.

Robertson, John W. Bibliography of the writings of Edgar A. Poe. San Francisco, Grabhorn, 1934. 2v. il. **BD284**

v.1, Bibliography [works by Poe]; v.2, Commentary on the bibliography.

Booth, Bradford Allen and **Jones, Claude Edward.** A concordance of the poetical works of Edgar Allan Poe. Baltimore, Johns Hopkins Pr., 1941. 211p. **BD285**

Pound

Gallup, Donald Clifford. A bibliography of Ezra Pound. London, Hart-Davis, 1963. 454p. (Soho bibliographies) **BD286**

Thoreau

Allen, Francis H. A bibliography of Henry David Thoreau. Boston, Houghton, 1908. 201p. **BD287**

Includes works both by and about Thoreau.
Supplemented by:

White, William. A Henry David Thoreau bibliography, 1908–1937. Boston, Faxon, 1939. 51p. (Bulletin of bibliography pamphlets, no.35) **BD288**

Harding, Walter Roy. A Thoreau handbook. N.Y., New York Univ. Pr., 1959. 229p.   **BD289**

Contains five chapters surveying: (1) the literature of Thoreau's life (with evaluation of biographies), (2) his individual works, (3) his sources, (4) his ideas, and (5) the course of his fame. The general evaluative discussion in each chapter is followed by a critical, annotated bibliography.

Includes doctoral dissertations.

Whitman

Duke University, Durham, N.C. Library. Catalogue of the Whitman collection in the Duke University Library being a part of the Trent collection given by Dr. and Mrs. Josiah C. Trent, comp. by Ellen Frances Frey. . . . Durham, N.C., Duke Univ. Lib., 1945. 148p. il. **BD290**

Includes material both by and about Whitman.

Wells, Carolyn and **Goldsmith, Alfred F.** A concise bibliography of the works of Walt Whitman with a supplement of fifty books about him. Boston, Houghton, 1922. 106p.   **BD291**

Eby, Edwin Harold. Concordance of Walt Whitman's Leaves of grass and selected prose writings. Seattle, Univ. of Wash. Pr., 1949–54. 964p.   **BD292**

Subtitle: Including Democratic vistas; A backward glance o'er travel'd roads; Preface to the 1855 edition; Preface, 1872; Preface, 1876; and Preface note to 2d appendix.

Issued in 5 fascicules.

Name on title page, Harold Edwin Eby, corrected by errata slip to Edwin Harold Eby.

Allen, Gay Wilson. Walt Whitman handbook. Chicago, Packard, 1946. 560p.   **BD293**

Chapters discuss Whitman biography, the growth of *Leaves of grass,* the *Prose works,* Whitman's ideas and techniques, and his relation to world literature. Each chapter followed by a selected bibliography.

Australian and New Zealand

Cuthbert, Eleanora Isabel. Index of Australian and New Zealand poetry. N.Y., Scarecrow, 1963. 453p.   **BD294**

In three parts: (1) authors, (2) titles, and (3) first lines. Indexes 22 collections.

Miller, Edmund Morris. Australian literature; a bibliography to 1938. Extended to 1950, ed. with a historical outline and descriptive commentaries by Frederick T. Macartney. Sydney, Angus and Robertson, [1956]. 503p.   **BD295**

An extensive revision of the author's *Australian literature* . . . (1940). Historical treatment of the writers and literature of Australia with extensive bibliographies. Arranged alphabetically by author. Contains considerable biographical material. Indexes that were useful in the earlier edition because of the chronological arrangement have been eliminated.

New Zealand Authors' Week Committee. Annals of New Zealand literature; being a preliminary list of New Zealand authors and their works with introductory essays and verses. [n.p.], Committee, 1936. 117p. il.   **BD296**

A checklist with names of authors, titles, and dates of their works.

Canadian

Garvin, John William. Canadian poets. Rev. ed. Toronto, McClelland, [c1926]. 536p. il.   **BD297**

Gives selections from poems of 75 authors with biography of each. Includes 28 poets (212 poems) not included in the 1916 edition.

Sylvestre, Guy, Conron, Brandon and **Klinck, Carl F.** Canadian writers; Écrivains canadiens. Toronto, Ryerson Pr., 1964. 163p.   **BD298**

A biographical dictionary containing information on about 300 Canadian authors. Articles appear in English or French according to the language of the biographee's writings. Includes a literary chronology, a brief general bibliography, and a useful index of titles of literary works mentioned in the biographies.

Thomas, Clara. Canadian novelists, 1920–1945. Toronto, N.Y., Longmans, [1946]. 129p.   **BD299**

Bio-bibliographical sketches of 122 contemporary authors born in, or residents of, Canada.

Wallace, William Stewart. The Macmillan dictionary of Canadian biography. 3d ed. rev. and enl. Toronto, Macmillan, 1963. 822p.   **BD300**

"Especial efforts have been taken to make the book useful as an author dictionary."—*Pref.* For full description *see* AJ94.

Watters, Reginald Eyre. A check list of Canadian literature and background materials, 1628–1950. . . . Comp. for the Humanities Research Council of Canada. Toronto, Univ. of Toronto Pr., 1959. 789p.   **BD301**

Subtitle: Being a comprehensive list of the books which constitute Canadian literature written in English together with a selective list of other books by Canadian authors which reveal the backgrounds of that literature.

Pt.1 "attempts to record all known titles in the recognized forms of poetry, fiction, and drama that were produced by English-speaking Canadians up to 1950"; pt.2 is a selective listing of books by Canadians on biography, literary criticism, local history, religion, bibliography, etc. which might serve as background material.

English

Guides

Altick, Richard Daniel and **Wright, Andrew.** Selective bibliography for the study of English and American literature. 2d ed. N.Y., Macmillan, 1963. 149p. (Alternate pages blank)   **BD302**

1st ed. 1960.

A highly selective guide to research materials; classified arrangement with author, title, and subject index.

Bond, Donald Frederick. A reference guide to English studies. Chicago, Univ. of Chicago Pr., 1962. 171p.   **BD303**

A manual designed for the graduate student. A successor to Tom Peete Cross's *Bibliographical guide to English studies* (10th ed. Univ. of Chicago Pr., 1951) which follows the same plan, with slight variations, but almost doubles the number of entries.

Kennedy, Arthur Garfield and **Sands, Donald B.** A concise bibliography for students of English. 4th ed. Stanford, Calif., Stanford Univ. Pr., 1960. 467p.   **BD304**

1st ed. 1940.

A listing of more than 5000 titles in a classified arrangement. Includes material on various literary forms; periodicals and series; folklore; language; methods and style of writing; printing and the book trade; bibliographical and reference guides, etc. Almost no annotations. Indexes by author and by subject.

Sanders, Chauncey. An introduction to research in English literary history; with a chapter on research in folklore by Stith Thompson. N.Y., Macmillan, 1952. 423p. il.   **BD305**

A manual and textbook for courses in bibliography and method, dealing with such subjects as the materials, the tools, and the methods of research; covers problems of editing, biography, authenticity and attribution, source study, chronology, success and influence, interpretation, technique, and the history of ideas and folklore, with a final chapter of suggestions on thesis writing.

Bibliography

❧ In addition to the guides and bibliographies listed here, those listed under Great Britain, p.45–48, should be consulted. The bibliographies in the *Dictionary of national biography* (AJ144) will also be helpful. Northup's *Register* (BD306), Besterman's *World bibliography of bibliographies* (AA13), and the *Bibliographic index* (AA14) refer to many individual bibliographies, either issued separately or (except for Besterman) included in periodicals or other composite works.

Bibliography

Northup, Clark Sutherland. Register of bibliographies of the English language and literature. New Haven, Yale Univ. Pr., 1925. 507p. (Cornell studies in English, 9) **BD306**

A still-useful list of bibliographies, both of those separately published and of those in periodicals, books, etc.

For full entry *see* AA22.

Van Patten, Nathan. Index to bibliographies and bibliographical contributions relating to the work of American and British authors, 1923–1932. Stanford, Calif., Stanford Univ. Pr.; London, Milford, 1934. 324p. **BD307**

Chronologically, this continues the work of Northup's *Register* (AA22). Arranged alphabetically under the name of the subject of each bibliography, with index to authors and compilers of the bibliographies.

General

Allibone, Samuel Austin. Critical dictionary of English literature and British and American authors, living and deceased, from the earliest accounts to the latter half of the nineteenth century. Containing over 46,000 articles (authors), with forty indexes of subjects. Philadelphia, Lippincott, 1858. 3v. (3140p.) **BD308**

A standard, older work very useful in spite of the fact that it is not entirely accurate and so must often be checked for important points. Based in part upon Watt's *Bibliotheca Britannica* (AA493) and reflects Watt's inaccuracies. Arranged alphabetically by authors, giving for each: brief biographical sketch, list of works with dates, and references to critical comments or reviews.

———— Supplement . . . containing over 37,000 articles (authors), and enumerating over 93,000 titles, by John Foster Kirk. Philadelphia, Lippincott, 1891. 2v. (1562p.)

Cambridge bibliography of English literature, ed. by F. W. Bateson. . . . Cambridge, Univ. Pr., 1940–57; N.Y., Macmillan, 1941–57. 5v. **BD309**

v.1–3, 600–1900; v.4, Index; v.5, Supplement.

The most extensive and comprehensive bibliography in its field, which covers with fullness and considerable detail, though avowedly not with actual completeness, the Old English, Middle English, modern English, and Latin literature of the British Isles, with briefer treatment of the English literature of the Dominions and India; does not include American literature or the French literature of Canada, and gives only incidental inclusion of Welsh, Gaelic, or Celtic material. Sections on the literatures of the Dominions are comparatively brief.

Arranged chronologically, and under periods by literary forms, e.g., Poetry, Drama, Periodicals, etc., and large class

groups, such as History, Philosophy, etc., with further subdivision under forms and groups by special topics and by the individual authors treated. References given under each author vary according to his importance or to the amount of material available, but include generally: *bibliographies* of that author, either separately published or included in some periodical or other work; *collected editions* of his works; *separate works,* with date of first edition and of subsequent editions within the next 50 years, with references to later editions having special features or editing; and a selection of *biographical and critical works* about the author.

Under the form group "Drama," a useful reference feature is the analytical reference to texts of separate plays as printed in the standard collections of plays, such as Dodsley, Bell, French, Lacy, etc. A somewhat similar feature is the reference under some poets to anthologies containing examples of their work. Throughout, entries are given compactly and with considerable abbreviation, but there is no one complete list of the abbreviations used. A key to the most frequently used abbreviations is given at the beginning of v.1, but other abbreviations, particularly within certain sections, are explained only at the beginning of such sections. The Index volume (287p.) includes *subject* entries for literary topics; *titles* of periodicals and anonymous books; and *author names* in the case of authors treated as part of the subject matter of the bibliography, but not in the case of authors of the biographical or critical references cited. The Supplement lists publications on the study of English language and literature, down to 1900, which have appeared approximately from 1940 to 1955.

Indispensable as a first-aid reference bibliography in all college, university, and large public libraries, and also in medium-sized public libraries doing much work in English literature. For research work it will naturally need to be supplemented by various specialized works. Its value as a guide to the selection of books in the building up of library collections is obvious.

Watson, George. Concise Cambridge bibliography of English literature, 600–1950. Cambridge, Univ. Pr., 1958. 271p. **BD310**

Treats in compressed form about 400 authors regarded as "major," selected from the *Cambridge bibliography of English literature* (BD309), with the addition of a section covering 1900–1950. Divided into six chronological sections, preceded by a general introductory section giving bibliographies, literary history and criticism, collections, dictionaries, etc. The bibliographies of each author are condensed and selected, but include works both by and about the writer.

Church, Elihu Dwight. A catalogue of books, consisting of English literature and miscellanea, including many original editions of Shakespeare, forming a part of the library of E. D. Church, comp. and annotated by George Watson Cole. . . . N.Y., Dodd, 1909. 2v. il. **BD311**

An admirably made catalog of rare books, especially important for its very fine bibliographical notes, and location of copies of the books described. Includes examples from the time of Caxton to the latter part of the 19th century.

Current

Abstracts of English studies: an official publication of the National Council of Teachers of English. Boulder, Colo., 1958– . v.1– . Monthly (except July and Aug.). **BD312**

Address: Business, National Council of Teachers of English, 508 S. Sixth St., Champaign, Ill.; Editorial, c/o Dept. of English, Ohio University, Athens, Ohio.

Numbered abstracts of articles in American and foreign periodicals on English, Commonwealth, and American literature and on English philology. Arranged by periodical, with a rather sketchy subject index in each issue.

Modern Humanities Research Association. Annual bib-

liography of English language and literature, 1920– .
Cambridge, Univ. Pr., 1921– . v.1– . Annual (some
volumes cover 2–3 years). (v.36, 1961, pub. 1964)
BD313

An excellent annual bibliography of English and American literature, including books, pamphlets, and periodical
articles and referring to reviews of works listed.

The language section is arranged according to subject; the
literature section is arranged chronologically. Name index.

Year's work in English studies, 1919/20– , pub. for the
English Association. London, Murray, 1921– . v.1–
Annual. (v.43, 1962, pub. 1964)   **BD314**

A selective, critical survey of studies of English literature
appearing in books and articles published in Britain, Europe,
and America, grouped by chronological periods. Also includes
material on English language, and, since 1954, a final chapter
on American literature. Indexes by author and subject. Covers much the same ground as the preceding entry, listing fewer
titles, but giving running comment on their importance or
character.

Dissertations

Mummendey, Richard. Language and literature of the
Anglo-Saxon nations as presented in German doctoral
dissertations, 1885–1950; a bibliography. Bonn, Ger.,
Bouvier; Charlottesville, Bibliographical Soc. of the Univ.
of Virginia, 1954. 200p.   **BD315**

Added title page in German; prefatory matter and captions in English and German.

Lists 2989 items arranged by subject field, with a name and
subject index.

Old and Middle English

Heusinkveld, Arthur H. and **Bashe, Edwin J.** A bibliographical guide to Old English; a selective bibliography of
the language, literature, and history of the Anglo-Saxons.
Iowa City, Univ. of Iowa, 1931. 153p. (Univ. of Iowa
humanistic studies, v.4, no.5)   **BD316**

A selective bibliography of books and periodical articles
covering general bibliography, the people and their institutions, language, paleography, literature, etc.

Wells, John Edwin. Manual of the writings in Middle
English, 1050–1400, pub. under the auspices of the Con-
necticut Academy of Arts and Sciences. New Haven, Yale
Univ. Pr., 1916–51. 941p. and suppl. 1–9.   **BD317**

Main work, covering bibliography to Sept. 1915, 941p.;
Suppl. 1–9, Additions and rectifications, Sept. 1915–Dec.
1945, paged continuously with main work, p.947–1938. Suppl.
8 includes an index to pieces first treated in Suppl. 1–8.

"This manual makes the first attempt to treat all the extant
writings in print, from single lines to the most extensive pieces,
composed in English between 1050 and 1400. At times, as
with the Romances, the Legends, and the Drama, a desire
for greater completeness has led to the inclusion of pieces later
than 1400.

"The work is not a history, but a handbook. It seeks to
record the generally accepted views of scholars on pertinent
matters, and does not pretend to offer new theories or investigations."—*Pref.*

Gives for each piece listed: its probable date, MS or MSS,
form and extent, dialect in which first composed, source or
sources when known, bibliography, and—in case of the longer
works—comment and abstract also.

An important handbook, indispensable in any library doing
reference work in this field.

To 1700

Hazlitt, William Carew. Handbook to the popular, poetical, and dramatic literature of Great Britain, from the
invention of printing to the Restoration. London, J. R.
Smith, 1867. 701p. (Repr.: N.Y., Burt Franklin, 1961)
BD318

Revised and supplemented by:

——— Bibliographical collections and notes on early English literature, 1474–1700. London, Quaritch, 1876–
1903. 6v. (Repr.: N.Y., Burt Franklin, 1961)   **BD319**

1st series has title, *Collections and notes.*

1st ser., 498p. 1876; 2d ser., 717p. 1882; 3d ser., 315p.
1887; suppl. to 3d ser., 181p. 1889; 2d suppl. to 3d ser., 106p.
1892; 4th ser., 446p. 1903.

Bibliography and notes on English literature comprising
many thousand titles.

——— General index to Hazlitt's Handbook and his Bibli-
ograpical collections (1867–1889), by G. J. Gray. London, Quaritch, 1893. 866p. (Repr.: N.Y., Burt Franklin,
1961)   **BD320**

Indexes the *Handbook* (BD318) and all volumes of the
Bibliographical collections (BD319), except the 4th series
and the 2d supplement to the 3d series.

Tannenbaum, Samuel A. and **Tannenbaum, Dorothy R.**
Elizabethan bibliographies. [Concise bibliographies] N.Y.,
Author, 1937–50. no.1–41 and suppls.   **BD321**

no.1, Christopher Marlowe. 1937. 95p.—Suppl. 1, 1937.
[5p.]—Suppl. 2, 1947. 99p.; no.2, Ben Jonson. 1938. 151p.;
no.3, 4, 5, Beaumont and Fletcher. 1938. 94p.—Philip Mas-
singer. 1938. 39p.—George Chapman. 1938. 40p.—Suppl. to
no.3. 1946. 23p.—Suppl. to no.5. 1946. 17p.; no.6,7, Thomas
Heywood. 1939. 43p.—Thomas Dekker. 1939. 46p.—Suppl.
to no.7. 1945. 14p.; no.8, Robert Greene. 1939. 58p.—Suppl.
to no.8, 1945. 17p.; no.9, Shakspere's Macbeth. 1939. 165p.;
no.10, Shakspere's sonnets. 1940. 88p.; no.11, Thomas Lodge.
1940. 30p.; no.12, John Lyly. 1940. 38p.; no.13, Thomas
Middleton. 1940. 35p.; no.14, John Marston. 1940. 34p.; no.
15, George Peele. 1940. 36p.; no.16, Shakspere's King Lear.
1940. 101p.; no.17, Shakspere's The Merchant of Venice.
1941. 140p.; no.18, Thomas Kyd. 1941. 34p.; no.19, John
Webster. 1941. 38p.; no.20–21, John Ford. 1941. 26p.—
Thomas Nashe. 1941. 31p.;

no.22, Michael Drayton. 1941. 54p.; no.23, Sir Philip Sidney. 1941. 69p.; no.24, Michel Eyquem de Montaigne. 1942.
137p.; no.25, Samuel Daniel. 1942. 37p.; no.26, George Gas-
coigne. 1942. 22p.; no.27, Anthony Mundy, including the
play of "Sir Thomas Moore." 1942. 36p.; no.28, Shakspere's
Othello. 1943. 132p.; no.29, Shakspere's Troilus and Cressida.
1943. 44p.; no.30–32, Marie Stuart, Queen of Scots. 1944–
46. 3v.; no.33, Cyril Tourneur. 1946. 14p.; no.34, James Shirley. 1946. 42p.; no.35, George Herbert. 1946. 55p.; no.36,
John Heywood. 1946. 31p.; no.37, Roger Ascham. 1946. 27p.;
no.38, Thomas Randolph. 1946. 24p.; no.39, Nicholas Breton.
1947. 34p.; no.40, Robert Herrick. 1949. 58p.; no.41, Shakspere's Romeo and Juliet. 1950. 133p.

18th century

Tobin, James Edward. Eighteenth century English literature and its cultural background; a bibliography. N.Y.,
Fordham Univ. Pr., 1939. 190p.   **BD322**

Contents: pt.1, Cultural and critical background, p.1–64;
pt.2, Bibliographies of individual authors, p.67–180.

The individual bibliographies list works by the author in
very brief form, and books and articles about the author. No
annotations.

English literature, 1660–1800; a bibliography of modern
studies comp. for Philological quarterly, by Ronald S.
Crane [and others]. Princeton, Princeton Univ. Pr.,
1950– . v.1– . (In progress)   **BD323**

Contents: Studies published: v.1, 1925–1937; v.2, 1938–
1949; v.3, 1950–1955; v.4, 1956–1959.

Reprints of the annual bibliographies published in the

Philological quarterly, 1926–60. Many entries include reviews or annotations.

v.2 includes a name, subject, and topical index to v.1–2; v.4 includes a similar index to v.3–4.

Continued annually in the *Philological quarterly.*

Translations

Rochedieu, Charles Alfred. Bibliography of French translations of English works, 1700–1800. Chicago, Univ. of Chicago Pr., 1948. 387p. **BD324**

Lists the works of some 900 authors under the author's name and the English title, with cross reference from the French title.

19th century

The Romantic movement: a selective and critical bibliography. (In ELH, a journal of English literary history, 1937–49; in Philological quarterly, 1950–) **BD325**

For full record *see* (BD11).

Bibliographies of studies in Victorian literature for the thirteen years 1932–1944, ed. by William Darby Templeman. Urbana, Univ. of Illinois Pr., 1945. 450p. **BD326**

A photoprint of bibliographies published originally in the May issues of *Modern philology,* 1933–45, and therefore arranged by year. Includes an index of Victorian authors mentioned in Sec. IV of each year and in the first three sections of the bibliography for 1932, which was differently arranged.

Continued by:

——— for the ten years 1945–54, ed. by Austin Wright. Urbana, Univ. of Illinois Pr., 1956. 310p. **BD326a**

Reprints of the annual *Victorian bibliographies,* 1945–54, published in *Modern philology.*

Continued in *Modern philology,* 1955–56.

Continued by:

Victorian bibliography. Francis G. Townsend, ed. 1957– . (In Victorian studies, v.1, June 1958–) **BD327**

Continues the list previously published in *Modern philology.*

Lists books, usually with references to reviews, and periodical articles.

Dissertations

Altick, Richard Daniel and **Matthews, William R.** Guide to doctoral dissertations in Victorian literature, 1886–1958. Urbana, Univ. of Illinois Pr., 1960. 119p. **BD328**

2105 dissertations from universities in the United States, United Kingdom, Germany, France, Austria, and Switzerland. Classifications include generalities, literary forms, literary criticism, and then individual authors. Author index.

20th century

Longaker, John Mark and **Bolles, Edwin Courtlandt.** Contemporary English literature. N.Y., Appleton, 1953. 526p. il. **BD329**

An introductory survey covering 1890–1950, with individual authors arranged chronologically within topical divisions (poetry, novel, drama, miscellaneous prose). Author bibliographies are sometimes full, sometimes selective; reviews and newspaper notices are not included.

Millett, Fred Benjamin. Contemporary British literature; a critical survey and 232 author bibliographies. 3d rev. and enl. ed., based on the 2d rev. and enl. ed. by J. M. Manley and Edith Rickert. N.Y., Harcourt, 1935. 556p. **BD330**

This edition is brought up to about 1934; adds new bib-

liographies of some 40 authors not included in the 2d edition, but omits about 30.

Current bibliography [of twentieth-century literature, 1954–]. (In Twentieth-century literature: a scholarly and critical journal, 1955/56–) Quarterly. **BD331**

A quarterly annotated listing of articles from periodicals in English and some foreign languages on 20th-century literature. No cumulations.

Manuscript sources

Early English manuscripts in facsimile. Copenhagen, Rosenkilde & Bagger; Baltimore, Johns Hopkins Pr., [1951]–63. v.1–12. (In progress) **BD332**

v.1, Beowulf (British Museum. MS. Cotton. Vitellius A.XV). The Thorkelin transcripts. Ed. by Kemp Malone. 1951.

v.2, Beda Venerabilis. Historia ecclesiastica gentis anglorum. (Leningrad. Public Library. MS. Q.V.I.18) The Leningrad Bede, an eighth century manuscript. Ed. by O. Arngart. 1952.

v.3, Orosius, Paulus. Historia adversum paganos. English. (British Museum. Add. MS. 47967) The Tollemache Orosius. Ed. by Alistair Campbell. 1953.

v.4, Anglo-Saxon Chronicle. (Oxford. Bodleian Library. MS. Laud misc. 636) The Peterborough chronicle. Ed. by Dorothy Whitelock. 1954.

v.5, Laece boc. (British Museum. Royal MS. 12D.XVII) Bald's Leechbook. Ed. by C. E. Wright with an appendix by Randolph Quirk. 1955.

v.6, Gregorius I, the Great, Saint, Pope. Regula pastoralis. English. (Oxford. Bodleian Library. MS. Hatton 20; British Museum. MS. Cotton. Tiberius. B.XI; Kassel. Landesbibliothek. MS. Anhang 19) The pastoral care; King Alfred's translation. Ed. by N. R. Ker. 1956.

v.7, Textus Roffensis. (Rochester Cathedral. Library. MS. A.3.5. pt.I) Textus Roffensis. Ed. by Peter Sawyer. 1957. For pt.II, *see* no.11.

v.8, Catholic Church. Liturgy and ritual. Psalter. "Paris Psalter." (Paris. Bibliothèque Nationale. Fonds latin. MS. 8824) The Paris psalter. Pref. by various contributors. Collected by Bertram Colgrove. 1958.

v.9, Beda Venerabilis. Historia ecclesiastica gentis anglorum. (Cambridge. University Library. MS. Kk.5.16) The Moore Bede, an eighth century manuscript. Ed. by Peter Hunter Blair with contribution by Roger A. B. Mynors. 1959.

v.10, Blickling Homilies. (Princeton, N.J. Scheide Library. MS. 66) The Blickling homilies. Ed. by Rudolph Willard. 1960.

v.11, Textus Roffensis. (Rochester Cathedral. Library. MS. A.3.5. pt.II) Textus Roffensis. Ed. by Peter Sawyer. 1957. For pt.I, *see* no.7.

v.12, Nowell Codex. (British Museum. MS. Cotton. Vitellius A.XV.2d MS) The Nowell codex. Ed. by Kemp Malone. 1963.

Dictionaries and handbooks

Chamber's Cyclopaedia of English literature. Ed. by David Patrick and rev. by J. Liddell Geddie. London, Chambers; Philadelphia, Lippincott, 1922–38. 3v. il. **BD333**

1st ed. 1844. 2v.; rev. ed. 1901. 3v.; v.1 rev. 1927, v.2 rev. 1938, v.3, 1922.

A chronological, not an alphabetical, encyclopedia, containing a large number of articles on individual writers and some articles on literary forms, periods, and subjects. For each writer treated gives biography, comment on his writings, some specimens of his works, a bibliography, and in many cases a portrait. Some articles are signed; general alphabetical index of authors and titles is in v.3.

The 1922 issue contains six additional pages at the end of

v.3, adding 143 new names, and shows some revision throughout.

Freeman, William. Dictionary of fictional characters. London, Dent; N.Y., The Writer, 1963. 458p. **BD334**

For full information *see* BD50.

Harvey, *Sir* Paul. Oxford companion to English literature. 3d ed. Oxford, Clarendon Pr., 1946. 931p. **BD335**

1st ed. 1932; 2d ed. 1937.

A very useful dictionary of brief articles on authors; literary works; characters in fiction, drama, etc.; and literary allusions commonly met with in English literature. This edition has been revised and reset with some new and some rewritten articles.

—— Concise Oxford dictionary of English literature. Oxford, Clarendon Pr., 1939. 567p. **BD336**

An abridgment of the above, prepared by John Mulgan. It retains the entries which deal with the main aspects of English literature, though often in shortened form. Articles have been added which summarize, concisely, periods of literary history and general literary subjects.—Cf. *Pref.*

New Century handbook of English literature, ed. by Clarence L. Barnhart, with the assistance of William D. Halsey. N.Y., Appleton, [1956]. 1167p. **BD337**

An encyclopedia in dictionary form comprising 14,000 entries for authors, titles, plots, characters, place-names, movements, literary terms, etc. Many of the articles are taken from the *New Century cyclopedia of names* (AJ19) and give detailed information; in others there seems little relevance to the subject and often a curious imbalance in relative length of articles.

Criticism

Juchhoff, Rudolf. Sammelkatalog der biographischen und literarkritischen Werke zu englischen Schriftstellern des 19. und 20. Jahrhunderts (1830–1958). Verzeichnis der Bestände in deutschen Bibliotheken. Unter Mitarbeit von Hildegard Föhl. Krefeld, Scherpe Verlag, [1959?]. 272p. **BD338**

A listing of several hundred English authors (1830–1958) with indication of biographical and critical material about them. Includes books, dissertations, essays, and chapters in books, but not periodical articles. Coverage is international with a large number of German items. Holdings are given for some 60 German libraries.

Moulton, Charles Wells. Library of literary criticism of English and American authors. Buffalo, Moulton Pub. Co., 1901–5. 8v. il. (Repr.: N.Y., Peter Smith, 1934) **BD339**

A compilation of quoted material, not an encyclopedia of original articles. Covers the years 680–1904. For each author treated gives brief biographical data and then selected quotations from criticisms of his work, grouped as: (1) personal, (2) individual works, (3) general. Extracts are of some length and are given with exact references, so that the work serves both as an encyclopedia of critical comment and as an index of literary criticisms.

For continuation for American literature, *see* Dorothy Nyren's *A library of literary criticism* (BD219).

Outlines

Annals of English literature, 1475–1950; the principal publications of each year together with an alphabetical index of authors and their works. 2d ed. Oxford, Clarendon Pr., 1961. 380p. **BD340**

1st ed. 1935, comp. by J. G. Ghosh and E. G. Withycombe; 2d ed. rev. and brought up to date by R. W. Chapman.

A chronological list giving, under each year, authors and

brief titles of outstanding books published that year, and, in parallel columns, important literary or historical events of the same year. Detailed author index, p.268–340.

Ryland, Frederick. Chronological outlines of English literature. London, Macmillan, 1914. 351p. **BD341**

First publ. 1890. Frequently reprinted with slight alterations, but without any extension of the tables beyond the original date, 1889.

A handbook which does for English literary history what the various "tabular views" do for political history. In two parts: pt.1 presents, in chronological arrangement, the principal periods and events of English literature and shows, in parallel columns, contemporary events in foreign literatures, political history, and (after 1500) the principal biographical dates; pt.2 is an alphabetical list of English authors with titles and dates of their principal works.

Atlases

Briscoe, John D'Auby, Sharp, Robert Lathrop and **Borish, Murray Eugene.** A mapbook of English literature. N.Y., Holt, 1936. 47p. **BD342**

Maps of Great Britain and London by chronological period with biographical and literary notes. Special maps of the Lake country, Hardy's Wessex, Oxford, Cambridge, Ireland, and the travels of English writers on the continent of Europe.

Goode, Clement Tyson and **Shannon, Edgar Finley.** An atlas of English literature. N.Y., Century, 1925. 136p., incl. maps. **BD343**

Gives outline maps by periods, with tables of authors and place-names associated with them.

History

Cambridge history of English literature, ed. by A. W. Ward and A. R. Waller. Cambridge, Univ. Pr.; N.Y., Putnam, 1907–33. 15v. **BD344**

The most important general history of the literature, covering from the earliest times to the end of the 19th century; each chapter is by a specialist. Includes extended and very useful bibliographies which are indexed in Northup's *Register* (AA22).

Available in different editions which show some variations in text and content. The English edition has made corrections in text from time to time, and has issued errata sheets containing further corrections and also additions to the bibliographies; the American edition (originally Putnam, now Macmillan) differs in paging and lacks the corrections in text and the errata lists of the English edition, except that some of these errata, but not the additions to the bibliographies, have been listed in the index volume published in 1933. Inexpensive reprints of both the English and the American editions (Macmillan) are reprints of the full text and index, but omit the bibliographies, thus losing much of their value for reference purposes. However, these reprints are useful in the small library unable to afford either of the complete editions, and in the large library as an extra set for circulation.

Garnett, Richard and **Gosse, Edmund.** English literature, an illustrated record. London, Heinemann; N.Y., Macmillan, 1903. 4v. il. (Repr.: 4v. in 2. 1935) **BD345**

Gives literary history, biographical and critical sketches of authors, account and criticism of various works of literature, some illustrative extracts and quotations, and many illustrations—some in color, largely from contemporary prints—illuminations, portraits, etc. The special reference value of the work is in these illustrations.

A new edition, 1923, differs only in having a supplementary chapter by John Erskine on the literature of 1902–22. This is the edition reprinted in 1935.

Oxford history of English literature, ed. by Frank Percy Wilson and Bonamy Dobrée. Oxford, Clarendon Pr., 1945–63. v.2¹⁻²–3, 5, 7, 9–10, 12. (In progress)   **BD346**

To be in 12v. in 14. A standard reference history. Each volume includes extensive bibliographies, but these are not indexed in the indexes in each volume.

Contents: v.1, pt.1, Before the Norman Conquest. In prep.; v.1, pt.2, Middle English literature. In prep.; v.2, pt.1, H. S. Bennett. Chaucer and the 15th century. 1947. Repr. with corrections, 1948, 1954; v.2, pt.2, E. K. Chambers. The close of the Middle Ages. 1945. 2d impr. with corrections, 1947; v.3, C. S. Lewis. The 16th century, excluding drama. 1954; v.4, English drama, *ca.* 1485–1642. In prep.; v.5, Douglas Bush. The earlier 17th century, 1600–1660. 1945. 2d ed. rev. 1962; v.6, The late 17th century. In prep.; v.7, Bonamy Dobrée. The early 18th century, 1700–1740. 1959; v.8, The mid-18th century. In prep.; v.9, W. L. Renwick. 1789–1815. 1963; v.10, Ian Jack. 1815–1832. 1963; v.11, The mid-19th century. In prep.; v.12, J. I. M. Stewart. Eight modern writers. 1963.

Biographies of authors

❧ In many cases the best biographical sketches of English authors will be found in the *Dictionary of national biography* (AJ144) and other works listed under Great Britain, p.180–82. In the absence of those works, or for names or information not included in them, the following smaller works may be useful:

Allibone, Samuel Austin. Critical dictionary of English literature and British and American authors. Philadelphia, Lippincott, 1858–91. 5v.   **BD347**

For full description *see* BD308.

Browning, David Clayton. Everyman's dictionary of literary biography, English and American, comp. after John W. Cousin . . . Rev. ed. London, Dent; N.Y., Dutton, 1960. 769p. (Everyman's reference library)   **BD348**

1st ed. 1958.

Substantially a new work, although based on Cousin's *Short biographical dictionary of English literature* (1910). Brief biographical sketches of more than 2000 authors, including contemporaries. Principal works with dates are noted, but no critical references.

Kunitz, Stanley J. and **Haycraft, Howard.** British authors before 1800; a biographical dictionary. Complete in one volume with 650 biographies and 220 portraits. N.Y., Wilson, 1952. 584p. il.   **BD349**

—— British authors of the 19th century. Complete in one volume with 1000 biographies and 350 portraits. N.Y., Wilson, 1936. 677p. il.   **BD350**

Both volumes contain sketches which are informal and popular in nature, the length of the articles ranging from 300 to 1500 words, depending on the importance of the writer. Bibliographies of principal works are included with brief citations for works about the author.

Russell, Josiah Cox. Dictionary of writers of thirteenth century England. London, N.Y., Longmans, [1936]. 210p. (London. University Inst. of Historical Research. Bull. Special suppl. 3)   **BD351**

Quite detailed sketches with many bibliographical references to sources.

Drama

Bibliography

Bergquist, G. William. Three centuries of English and American plays; a checklist. England, 1500–1800; United States, 1714–1830. N.Y., London, Hafner, 1963. 281p.   **BD352**

". . . originally compiled to serve as an index to the contents of the microprint edition of the *Three centuries of English and American plays . . .*"—*Foreword*. This is a more complete listing of the dramatic literature of the period than can be found in other works. Arranged alphabetically by author and title; notes approximately 5500 plays.

British Museum. Dept. of Manuscripts. Catalogue of additions to the manuscripts: plays submitted to the Lord Chamberlain, 1824–1851. London, Museum, 1964. 359p.   **BD353**

A continuation of the chronological listing of plays contained in the Larpent collection (BD359). The plays submitted 1824–1900 are in the British Museum, and this is the record of some 4250 plays submitted to the Lord Chamberlain, 1824–1851. Arranged chronologically; author and title indexes.

Greg, *Sir* **Walter Wilson.** A bibliography of the English printed drama to the Restoration. London, pr. for the Bibliographical Society at the Univ. Pr., Oxford, 1939–59. 4v. (1752p.). il. facsim. (Illustrated monographs, no.24)   **BD354**

Arranged according to the supposed date of the earliest surviving edition. Locates copies in British and American libraries.

Contents: v.1, Stationers' records. Plays to 1616, no.1–349; v.2, Plays, 1617–1689, no.350–836. Latin plays. Lost plays; v.3, Collections, appendix, reference lists; v.4, Introduction, additions, corrections, index of titles.

—— A list of English plays written before 1643 and printed before 1700. London, Bibliographical Soc., 1900. 158p.   **BD355**

Arranged alphabetically by author with indexes by author and by title. Locates copies.

—— List of masques, pageants, etc., supplementary to a List of English plays. London, Bibliographical Soc., 1902. 35p., cxxxip.   **BD356**

List of masques, pageants, etc.; Index of authors; Index of titles; Appendixes; Advertisement lists; The early play lists; A list of English plays (Addenda and corrigenda).

Harbage, Alfred. Annals of English drama, 975–1700; an analytical record of all plays, extant or lost, chronologically arranged and indexed by authors, titles, dramatic companies, etc. Rev. by S. Schoenbaum. London, Methuen, 1964. 323p.   **BD357**

1st ed. 1940.

Chronologically arranged in tabular form indicating author, title, date of first performance, type (i.e., mask, tragedy, tragicomedy, etc.), auspices, first edition, and last edition. Indexes of playwrights, English plays, foreign plays translated or adapted, dramatic companies. List of theaters. Appendix: Extant play manuscripts, 975–1700, their location and catalog numbers.

About 100 new entries have been added, and the indexes made fuller and more detailed.

Hazlitt, William Carew. Manual for the collector and amateur of old English plays. Ed. from the material formed by Kirkman, Langbaine, Downes, Oldys, and Halliwell-Phillipps, with extensive additions and corrections. London, Pickering and Chatto, 1892. 284p. **BD358**

A listing of plays, alphabetically by title, and index of names, theaters, theatrical companies, city guilds, etc.

Henry E. Huntington Library. Catalogue of the Larpent plays in the Huntington Library, comp. by Dougald MacMillan. San Marino, Calif., 1939. 442p. (Huntington Library lists, no.4)   **BD359**

"The licensing act of 1737 required that copies of all plays and other entertainments designed to be performed on the stage in Great Britain be submitted . . . for license." John

Larpent was appointed Examiner on Nov. 20, 1778, and "died in office on Jan. 18, 1824. The official copies of plays submitted to the Examiner between 1737 and Jan. 1824, in Larpent's possession at the time of his death were bought about 1832 by John Payne Collier and Thomas Amyot."—*Pref. note.* These copies are now in the Huntington Library.

The list is chronological with author and title indexes. For continuation *see* BD353.

The London stage, 1660–1800: a calendar of plays, entertainments and afterpieces, together with casts, box-receipts and contemporary comment, comp. from the playbills, newspapers and theatrical diaries of the period. Carbondale, Ill., Southern Illinois Univ. Pr., 1960–62. Pts.2–4. (In progress)   **BD360**

For full record *see* BG29.

Nicoll, Allardyce. A short-title alphabetical catalogue of plays produced or printed in England from 1660–1900. Cambridge, Univ. Pr., 1959. 569p. (v.6 of his History of English drama)   **BD361**

For complete record *see* BD373.

Sibley, Gertrude Marian. The lost plays and masques, 1500–1642. Ithaca, N.Y., Cornell Univ. Pr., 1933. 205p. (Cornell studies in English, v.19)   **BD362**

Contents: The lost plays and masques; Lost masques with known titles; English plays with known titles acted in Germany; Index of playwrights.

Steele, Mary Susan. Plays and masques at court during the reigns of Elizabeth, James and Charles. New Haven, Yale Univ. Pr.; London, Milford, 1926. 300p. (Cornell studies in English, [10])   **BD363**

Lists court plays and masques for the years 1558–1642.

Summers, Montague. Bibliography of the Restoration drama. London, Fortune Pr., [1935]. 143p.   **BD364**

Alphabetical by author; no index. Lists plays, acted and unacted, printed and unprinted, from 1660 to 1700.

Woodward, Gertrude Loop and **McManaway, James Gilmer.** A check list of English plays, 1641–1700. Chicago, Newberry Lib., 1945. 155p.   **BD365**

"Its purpose is to record the plays and masques, with the variant editions and issues, printed in the English language in the British Isles or in other countries during the years 1641 to 1700, inclusive, and to give the location of copies in [15] American libraries."—*Pref.*

—— —— Supplement, comp. by Fredson Bowers. Charlottesville, Univ. of Virginia, 1949. 22p.

Locates copies.

Periodicals

Stratman, Carl Joseph. A bibliography of British dramatic periodicals, 1720–1960. N.Y., N.Y. Pub. Lib., 1962. 58p.   **BD366**

A chronological listing, with title and place index, of 674 British dramatic periodicals with location of copies in American and British libraries.

History and biography

Baker, David Erskine. Biographia dramatica. . . . London, Longmans, 1812. 3v. in 4.   **BD367**

Subtitle: A companion to the playhouse: containing historical and critical memoirs, and original anecdotes, of British and Irish dramatic writers, from the commencement of our theatrical exhibitions; among whom are some of the most celebrated actors. Originally comp. to the year 1764, by D. E. Baker. Continued to 1782, by Isaac Reed, and brought down to the end of November, 1811, with very considerable additions and improvements throughout, by Stephen Jones.

v.1, pts.1–2, Authors and actors, A–Z; v.2, Names of

dramas, A–L; v.3, Names of dramas, M–Z. Latin plays by English authors. Oratorios.

An older work, but still important for its biographies of dramatists and long lists of their works.

Bentley, Gerald Eades. The Jacobean and Caroline stage. Oxford, Clarendon Pr., 1941–56. v.1–5. (In progress)   **BD368**

Contents: v.1–2, Dramatic companies and players; v.3–5, Plays and playwrights.

A final volume was projected to treat theaters and theatrical customs, and to include an index to the 6v.

Chambers, Edmund Kerchever. The mediaeval stage. Oxford, Clarendon Pr., 1903. 2v.   **BD369**

Contents: v.1, Minstrelsy. Folk drama; v.2, Religious drama. The interlude. Appendices. Subject index.

—— The Elizabethan stage. Oxford, Clarendon Pr., 1923. 4v. il. (Repr. with corrections, 1951)   **BD370**

Partial contents: v.1, The court. The control of the stage; v.2, The companies. The play-houses; v.3, Plays and playwrights; v.4, Anonymous works. Appendices. Indexes (by plays, persons, places, subjects).

—— —— Index, comp. by Beatrice White, to "The Elizabethan stage" and "William Shakespeare: A study of facts and problems." Oxford, Clarendon Pr., 1934. 161p.

Published by arrangement with the Shakespeare Association, for whose members the index was made.

Fleay, Frederick Gard. Biographical chronicle of the English drama, 1559–1642. London, Reeves, 1891. 2v. (Repr.: N.Y., Burt Franklin, 1962. 2v.)   **BD371**

A list of authors, arranged alphabetically, giving for each: (1) brief biographical data, and (2) a list of plays in the order of original production. Appendixes in v.2 cover: Plays by anonymous authors, Masques by anonymous authors, University plays in English, University plays in Latin, Translations.

Genest, John. Some account of the English stage, from the Restoration in 1660 to 1830. Bath, pr. by H. E. Carrington, 1832. 10v.   **BD372**

A valuable early history of plays, players, and playwrights of the period covered.

Nicoll, Allardyce. A history of English drama, 1660–1900. Cambridge, Univ. Pr., 1952–59. 6v.   **BD373**

Contents: v.1, Restoration drama, 1660–1700. 4th ed. 462p.; v.2, Early 18th century drama, [1700–1750]. 3d ed. 467p.; v.3, Late 18th century drama, 1750–1800. 2d ed. 423p.; v.4, Early 19th century drama, 1800–1850. [2d ed.] 668p.; v.5, Late 19th century drama, 1850–1900. [2d ed.] 901p.; v.6, A short-title alphabetical catalogue of plays produced or printed in England from 1660–1900. 569p.

Each historical volume is on the same general plan, giving: (1) history, and (2) appendixes, containing such useful reference material as lists of theaters and handlists of plays produced during the period covered.

v.6 not only serves as a title index to plays recorded in the earlier volumes, but provides additional information on some plays and lists others not previously mentioned; includes numerous cross references from alternate titles.

Ward, *Sir* **Adolphus William.** History of English dramatic literature to the death of Queen Anne. New and rev. ed. London, N.Y., Macmillan, 1899. 3v.   **BD374**

A well-documented history with detailed index.

Fiction

Bibliography

Block, Andrew. The English novel, 1740–1850; a catalogue including prose romances, short stories, and translations of foreign fiction. [New and rev. ed., i.e., 2d ed.] London, Dawsons of Pall Mall, 1961; N.Y., Oceana, 1962. 349p. **BD375**

1st ed. 1939.
Arranged alphabetically by author or, if anonymous or pseudonymous, by title. Title index.

Clarke, Ignatius Frederick. The tale of the future, from the beginning to the present day . . . London, Lib. Assoc., 1961. 165p. il. (Library Association bibliographies, no.2) **BD376**

Subtitle: A check-list of those satires, ideal states, imaginary wars and invasions, political warnings and forecasts, interplanetary voyages and scientific romances—all located in an imaginary future period—that have been published in the United Kingdom between 1644 and 1960.
Chronological arrangement of nearly 1000 titles. Indexes of authors and titles.

Esdaile, Arundell. List of English tales and prose romances printed before 1740. London, pr. for the Bibliographical Society by Blades, East and Blades, 1912. 329p. **BD377**

Pt.1, 1475–1642; pt.2, 1643–1739. Each part is arranged alphabetically by author and title, with plentiful cross references. Gives full title and imprint, list of editions, libraries in which the copies included were seen, and bibliographies in which the work is described. Scope of list includes both English tales and English translations of foreign works. Notes are bibliographical, not critical. Of value to the specialist, the bibliographer, and the cataloger.

Leclaire, Lucien. A general analytical bibliography of the regional novelists of the British Isles, 1800–1950. Paris, "Les Belles Lettres," 1954. 399p. maps. **BD378**

Divided into three main periods: 1800–1830, 1830–1870, and after 1870. For each author gives a brief biographical note, a list of the novels pertinent to the scope of the work, their various editions, and the scene of each novel. Coverage uneven. Three indexes: by author, by place-name, and by region.

McBurney, William Harlin. A check list of English prose fiction, 1700–1739. Cambridge, Harvard Univ. Pr., 1960. 154p. **BD379**

A listing of some 400 titles of works comprising the prose-fiction background from which the English novel grew. Arrangement is chronological by year, with, for each item, author, full title and imprint, price (where available), later editions to 1739, and at least one library location if possible, here or abroad.

O'Dell, Sterg. A chronological list of prose fiction in English printed in England and other countries, 1475–1640. Cambridge, Mass., Technology Pr. of M.I.T., 1954. 147p. **BD380**

Author index.
Locates copies and includes references to *S.T.C.* number (AA498).

Summers, Montague. A Gothic bibliography. London, Fortune Pr.; N.Y., Columbia Univ. Pr., 1941. 621p. il. **BD381**

Contents: Index of authors, p.1–219; Title index, p.220–568; Addenda, p.569–620.
A bibliography of the English romantic novel from 1728 to 1916. Usually omits the well-known writers for whom there are already standard bibliographies.

Criticism

Bell, Inglis Freeman and **Baird, Donald.** The English novel, 1578–1956: a checklist of twentieth-century criticisms. Denver, Alan Swallow, 1959. 169p. **BD382**

A selective listing of 20th-century criticisms of English novels from Lyly to date, including citations to books and periodicals. Arrangement is alphabetical by novelist's name, then by title of the novel.

Stevenson, Lionel [and others]. Victorian fiction; a guide to research. Cambridge, Harvard Univ. Pr., 1964. 440p. **BD383**

A companion to Faverty's *Victorian poets* (BD392). Separate chapters on each of the principal novelists provide a survey of research and a critical evaluation of selected writings in the field.

Translations

Streeter, Harold Wade. The eighteenth century English novel in French translation; a bibliographical study. N.Y., Inst. of French Studies, 1936. 256p. **BD384**

Thesis (Ph.D.), Columbia University, 1936.
A general bibliographical study is followed by a bibliography of French translations of English novels, 1700–1805.

History

Baker, Ernest Albert. History of the English novel. London, Witherby, 1924–39. 10v. (Repr.: N.Y., Barnes & Noble, 1950) **BD385**

From the beginnings to the early 20th century.
Brief bibliographies and an index in each volume.

Poetry

Bibliography

Boys, Richard Charles. A finding-list of English poetical miscellanies 1700–48 in selected American libraries. [Baltimore, 1940] (Repr. from ELH, a journal of English literary history 7:144–62. June 1940) **BD386**

Based on Case's *Bibliography* (BD390); a chronological list showing location in 14 American libraries, with the addition of some other libraries not checked systematically.

Brown, Carleton Fairchild. Register of Middle English religious and didactic verse. Oxford, pr. for the Bibliographical Society at the Univ. Pr., 1916–20. 2v. [Bibliographical Soc., London. Publ.] **BD387**

Pt.1, List of manuscripts; pt.2, Index of first lines and index of subjects and titles.
Pt.1 lists manuscripts arranged by the library in which they are found. Includes religious and didactic verse written between 1200 and 1500.

—— and **Robbins, Rossell Hope.** Index of Middle English verse. N.Y., pr. for the Index Society, by Columbia Univ. Pr., 1943. 785p. **BD388**

A scholarly index to all poems published in England before 1500. Designed to complete the work by Carleton Brown, above. The 2273 entries in the *Register,* in about 1100 manuscripts, have been increased in this *Index* to 4365 entries in more than 2000 manuscripts.
Includes a subject and title index and a list of locations of privately owned manuscripts.
Supplemented by:

Ringler, William. A bibliography and first-line index of English verse printed through 1500: a supplement to Brown and Robbins' "Index of Middle English verse." (In Papers of the Bibliographical Soc. of America 49:153–80. 1955) **BD389**

Case, Arthur Ellicott. Bibliography of English poetical miscellanies, 1521–1750. Oxford, pr. for the Bibliographical Society at the Univ. Pr., 1935 (for 1929). 386p. **BD390**

Arranged chronologically by date of the earliest-known edition, with descriptions of subsequent editions to 1750. Indexes by title, by year, and by persons. Locates copies in British and American libraries.

Green, David Bonnell and **Wilson, Edwin Graves.** Keats, Shelley, Byron, Hunt, and their circles; a bibliography, July 1, 1950–June 30, 1962. Lincoln, Univ. of Nebraska Pr., 1964. 323p.   **BD391**

A collection of the twelve annual bibliographies originally published in the *Keats-Shelley journal,* reprinted with a cumulated index. The intent has been to include all new editions, reprints, translations, etc., and all books and articles relating to any one or all of these poets and of the contemporaries in their circles.

Criticism

Faverty, Frederic Everett. The Victorian poets; a guide to research. Cambridge, Harvard Univ. Pr., 1956. 292p.   **BD392**

A handbook of "bibliography, scholarship and criticism in the field."—*Pref.* Chapters by specialists treat major poets separately, minor poets and movements collectively.

Houtchens, Carolyn Washburn and **Houtchens, Lawrence Huston.** The English romantic poets and essayists: a review of research and criticism. N.Y., Modern Language Assoc. of Amer., 1957. 363p.   **BD392a**

A companion volume to Raysor, *The English romantic poets* (BD394). A critical evaluation of the material about 10 romantic poets and essayists, covering, as pertinent, bibliographies, editions, biographies, and criticism.

Kuntz, Joseph Marshall. Poetry explication; a checklist of interpretation since 1925 of British and American poems past and present. Rev. ed. Denver, Alan Swallow, 1962. 331p.   **BD393**

1st ed., by George Arms and Joseph M. Kuntz, 1950.

Indexes explications in a selected group of composite volumes and literary periodicals.

The 2d edition, covering the period 1925 through 1959, is an extension of the 1st edition in that it incorporates explications published from 1950 to 1959, with some few corrections of the earlier work.

Raysor, Thomas Middleton. The English romantic poets; a review of research, by Ernest Bernbaum [and others]. Rev. ed. N.Y., Modern Language Assoc. of Amer., 1956. 307p.   **BD394**

1st ed. 1950.

A companion volume to Faverty (BD392), with a general chapter on the romantic movement and special chapters on Wordsworth, Coleridge, Byron, Shelley, and Keats.

Dictionaries

Spender, Stephen and **Hall, Donald.** The concise encyclopedia of English and American poets and poetry. N.Y., Hawthorn, 1963. 415p. il.   **BD395**

Biographical sketches of poets, with brief articles on literary movements, forms, etc.

History

Courthope, William John. History of English poetry. N.Y., London, Macmillan, 1895–1910. 6v.   **BD396**

A standard work covering from the Middle Ages to the romantic movement. Each volume includes an analytical table of contents, and there is a cumulated index in v.6.

Anthologies

Arber, Edward. British anthologies. London, Frowde, 1900–1901. 10v.   **BD397**

v.1, Dunbar anthology, 1401–1508; v.2, Surrey and Wyatt anthology, 1509–47; v.3, Spenser anthology, 1548–91; v.4, Shakespeare anthology, 1592–1616; v.5, Jonson anthology, 1617–37; v.6, Milton anthology, 1638–74; v.7, Dryden anthology, 1675–1700; v.8, Pope anthology, 1701–44; v.9, Goldsmith anthology, 1745–74; v.10, Cowper anthology, 1775–1800.

Includes about 2500 entire poems, by about 300 authors. Each volume has an author index, and an index of first lines, with notes and a glossary; v.10 has also a general index of first lines for the 10v.

Oxford book of Christian verse, chosen and ed. by Lord David Cecil. Oxford, Clarendon Pr., 1940. 560p. **BD398**

Covers from the 13th to the early 20th centuries.

Oxford book of English verse, 1250–1918, chosen and ed. by Sir Arthur Quiller-Couch. New ed. Oxford, Clarendon Pr., 1939. 1171p.   **BD399**

Includes 966 poems against 883 in the earlier edition, which stopped with 1900. Many new poems have been included, some for new authors and some as additions to and in some cases alterations to the selections of poets included before.

Complemented by a series of *Oxford books* each devoted to a particular period or century, as follows: *English mystical verse,* chosen by D. H. S. Nicholson and A. H. E. Lee, 1916. 644p.; *Sixteenth century verse,* chosen by E. K. Chambers, 1932. 905p.; *Seventeenth century verse,* chosen by H. J. C. Grierson and G. Bullough, 1934. 974p.; *Eighteenth century verse,* chosen by David Nichol Smith, 1926. 727p.; *Regency verse,* 1798–1837, chosen by H. S. Milford, 1928. 888p.; *Victorian verse,* chosen by Arthur Quiller-Couch, 1912. 1023p.; *Modern verse,* 1892–1935, chosen by W. B. Yeats. 1936. 454p.

Useful collections for the selection of poems, though with little reference apparatus beyond indexes of authors and first lines.

Oxford book of light verse, chosen by W. H. Auden. Oxford, Clarendon Pr., 1938. 553p.   **BD400**

"Three kinds of poetry have been included: (1) Poetry written for performance, to be spoken or sung before an audience, e.g., Folk-songs, the poems of Tom Moore, (2) Poetry intended to be read, but having for its subject matter the everyday social life of its period or the experiences of the poet as an ordinary human being, e.g., the poems of Chaucer, Pope, Byron, (3) Such nonsense poetry as, through its properties and technique, has a general appeal, e.g., Nursery rhymes, the poems of Edward Lear."—*Introd.*

To avoid overlapping, the work does not include poems which are in the *Oxford book of English verse* (BD399).

Oxford dictionary of nursery rhymes, ed. by Iona and Peter Opie. Oxford, Clarendon Pr., 1951. 467p. il. **BD401**

Said to be the most comprehensive and authoritative work ever published on English nursery rhymes; includes 550 rhymes (all current today or until recently), arranged alphabetically by the most prominent word or, in the case of nonsense jingles, by the opening phrase. The standard version of each nursery rhyme is given first, followed by the earliest recorded version (where available), and bibliographical references. Two indexes: (1) "notable figures associated with the invention, diffusion or illustration of nursery rhymes," and (2) first lines of both standard and other versions. Contains many prints of drawings and texts taken from famous old nursery-rhyme books, and a 45-page introduction.

Stevenson, Burton Egbert. Home book of verse, American and English; with an appendix containing a few well-known poems in other languages. 9th ed. N.Y., Holt, 1953. 2v. (lxxxivp., 4012p.)   **BD402**

1st ed. 1912.

One of the most extensive collections, with coverage from the last part of the 16th century to the first part of the 20th century. Arranged by large subjects, with full indexes of authors, titles, and first lines.

Continued by:

—— Home book of modern verse; an extension of The home book of verse, being a selection from American and English poetry of the 20th century. 2d ed. rev. N.Y., Holt, 1953. 1124p. **BD403**

1st ed. 1925. The 2d edition is not noticeably changed except by the addition of "Corrigenda to Index of authors," p.1123–24.

A well-selected collection from early 20th-century poets. Arranged by large subjects with indexes by authors, first lines, and titles.

Untermeyer, Louis. Modern British poetry. New and enl. ed. N.Y., Harcourt, 1962. 541p. **BD404**

Published also in a combined edition with the author's *Modern American poetry* (BD263).

Includes biographical sketches of the 79 authors. Arranged chronologically by birth dates, Hardy to Tomlinson.

—— A treasury of great poems, English and American, from the foundations of the English spirit to the outstanding poetry of our own time, with lives of the poets and historical settings selected and integrated. N.Y., Simon & Schuster, 1942. 1288p. **BD405**

An anthology of almost 1000 poems with interspersed comments on the poets, the origin and source of a poem, seeming obscurities, etc. Index of authors and titles. Index of first lines.

Ballads

Bibliography

Crawford, James Ludovic Lindsay, *26th Earl of*. Bibliotheca Lindesiana. Catalogue of a collection of English ballads of the XVIIth and XVIIIth centuries, printed for the most part in black letter. [Aberdeen], priv. pr. [Aberdeen Univ. Pr.], 1890. 686p. **BD406**

Records more than 1400 ballads by first line, with list of printers and index.

London. Stationers' Company. An analytical index to the ballad-entries (1557–1709) in the Registers of the Company of Stationers of London, comp. by Hyder E. Rollins. Chapel Hill, Univ. of North Carolina Pr., 1924. 324p. **BD407**

Indexes ballads by title, by first line, and by names and subjects.

Anthologies

Child, Francis James. English and Scottish popular ballads. Boston, Houghton, 1883–98. 5v. (Repr. 1956. 5v. in 3) **BD408**

The great collection of English ballads. Contains text of 305 distinct ballads, each given in all its extant versions. For each ballad includes a historical and bibliographical introduction, with full account of parallels in other languages, the diffusion of the story, etc. Appendix in v.5 contains: Glossary, Sources of the text, Index of published airs of English and Scottish ballads, Ballad airs [46] from manuscript, Index of ballad titles, Titles of collections of ballads briefly noted in this work, Index of matters, Bibliography. For the tunes of these ballads *see* BH114.

For the large reference or university library; for the smaller library the following abridgment is sufficient:

—— English and Scottish popular ballads, ed. from the collection of Francis James Child by Helen Child Sargent and George Lyman Kittredge. Boston, Houghton, 1904. 729p. **BD409**

An abridgment of the above, sufficient for ordinary purposes. Gives each of the 305 ballads (except no.33, 279, 281, 290, and 299) in one or more versions, without the *apparatus criticus*, and with briefer notes. Contains a briefer glossary, full list of sources, and an index of titles.

Oxford book of ballads, chosen and ed. by Sir Arthur Thomas Quiller-Couch. Oxford, Clarendon Pr., 1910. 871p. **BD410**

An anthology for reading rather than for reference. A selected list which includes only one version of each ballad, i.e., the one considered the best for the general reader. Index to first lines.

Parodies

Hamilton, Walter. Parodies of the works of English and American authors, collected and annotated. London, Reeves, 1884–99. 6v. il. **BD411**

The most comprehensive collection; many parodies are given in full, some only mentioned.

Includes bibliographies. Index in each volume.

Lowrey, Burling. Twentieth century parody: American and British. N.Y., Harcourt, 1960. 304p. **BD412**

Macdonald, Dwight. Parodies: an anthology from Chaucer to Beerbohm—and after. N.Y., Random, 1960. 574p. **BD413**

British and American parodists grouped in three periods, and a section of "Specialties."

Diaries and letters

Matthews, William. British diaries; an annotated bibliography of British diaries written between 1442 and 1942. Berkeley, Univ. of Calif. Pr., 1950. 339p. **BD414**

Diaries, both in published and manuscript form (and including those reproduced in periodicals), are listed chronologically by year of first entry. Brief annotations suggest the contents: religious, military, personal, social, etc. Author index. For unpublished items, owner or library location is given.

Individual authors

☙ The following list does not include all the authors for whom separately published bibliographies are available. It includes only a selection of those of major authors and of writers for whom concordances, dictionaries, or handbooks as well as bibliographies have been published. For additional titles consult the bibliographies listed under English—Bibliography, p.259–61.

Arnold

Parrish, Stephen Maxfield. A concordance to the poems of Matthew Arnold. Ithaca, N.Y., Cornell Univ. Pr., 1959. 965p. (The Cornell concordances) **BD415**

The first of a new series of concordances to be issued at Cornell, produced by machine method. The preface indicates its distinctive features: lack of punctuation, words omitted, inclusion of variants, etc. An appendix lists words in order of their frequency.

Austen

Chapman, Robert William. Jane Austen; a critical bibliography. Oxford, Clarendon Pr., 1953. 62p. **BD416**

Excludes reprints of the novels published since 1890, but includes all editions prior to that date, also translations. Biography and criticism section (p.19–57) is arranged by broad period divisions from 1785 to date.

Keynes, Geoffrey. Jane Austen; a bibliography. London, Nonesuch Pr., 1929. 289p. **BD417**

Beowulf

Cook, Albert Stanburrough. Concordance to Beowulf. Halle, Niemeyer, 1911. 436p. **BD418**

Based upon the text of Wyatt's 2d edition (Cambridge, 1898). Omits numerals, prepositions, many pronouns, and 62 other common words.

Brontë

Wise, Thomas J. A bibliography of the writings in prose and verse of the Brontë family. London, priv. circ., 1917. 255p. il. **BD419**

Wroot, Herbert E. Persons and places of the Brontë novels. Bradford, Eng., Brontë Soc., 1906. 237p. (Brontë Soc. transactions, v.3) **BD420**

Not a formal dictionary, but gives for a selected list of characters and places the same kind of information as that given in regular author dictionaries. Covers only the four novels of Charlotte Brontë.

A reprint, with amplifications and corrections, has title, *Sources of Charlotte Brontë's novels; persons and places.* Shipley, Outhwaite, 1935. 214p. (Brontë Soc. publ., v.8, no.4, Suppl. pt.)

Browning

Broughton, Leslie Nathan, Northup, Clark Sutherland and **Pearsall, Robert.** Robert Browning: a bibliography, 1830–1950. Ithaca, N.Y., Cornell Univ. Pr., 1953. 446p. (Cornell studies in English, v.39) **BD421**

Includes Browning's writings (854 items); reference works on Browning; biography and criticism (4538 items, arranged chronologically); verse criticism, appreciation, parody; a calendar of letters; musical settings to Browning's poems; index.

Broughton, Leslie Nathan and **Stelter, Benjamin F.** Concordance to the poems of Robert Browning. N.Y., Stechert, 1924–25. 2v. **BD422**

Complete, except in the case of 70 very common words which are either omitted altogether or represented by selected references. Based upon the text of the Globe edition.

For libraries not having this complete concordance, the smaller *Phrase book* by Marie Ada Molineux (Boston, Houghton, 1896. 520p.) is useful for the more familiar Browning quotations.

Berdoe, Edward. Browning cyclopaedia. 8th ed. London, Allen; N.Y., Macmillan, 1916. 577p. **BD423**

1st ed. 1892. The 8th edition has an appendix of 5 pages.

DeVane, William Clyde. A Browning handbook. 2d ed. N.Y., Appleton, 1955. 594p. il. **BD424**

1st ed. 1935.

A handbook giving detailed descriptions of each poem, arranged chronologically in the order in which the poems were written.

Includes a brief bibliography and an index.

Orr, Alexandra Leighton. Handbook to the works of Robert Browning. 6th ed. rev. London, Bell, 1892. 420p. **BD425**

Frequently reprinted.

Burns

Egerer, J. W. A bibliography of Robert Burns. Edinburgh, London, Oliver & Boyd, 1964. 396p. **BD426**

Lists editions and translations of Burns's works. Chronological arrangement with full description for editions 1786–1802, and briefer listings for later editions.

Reid, J. B. Complete word and phrase concordance to the poems and songs of Robert Burns. Glasgow, Kerr, 1889. 561p. **BD427**

Lindsay, John Maurice. The Burns encyclopedia. London, Hutchinson, 1959. 287p. il. **BD428**

An alphabetical listing of articles about "people whom Burns met or referred to in his letters and in his poems," together with information on places which figured in his life. Index.

Ross, John Dawson. Burns handbook. Stirling, Mackay, [1931]. 378p. **BD429**

A popular dictionary of allusions, names, etc., either referred to in the poems or having some connection with the poet's life and works. A companion volume to the same author's *Who's who in Burns* (Stirling, Mackay, 1927). Has a map of the Burns country on the endpapers.

Chaucer

Hammond, Eleanor Prescott. Chaucer: a bibliographical manual. N.Y., Macmillan, 1908. 579p. **BD430**

Describes sources, manuscripts, editions, modernizations, translations, etc.

Griffith, Dudley David. Bibliography of Chaucer, 1908–1953. Seattle, Univ. of Wash. Pr., 1955. 398p. **BD431**

Planned as a supplement to Hammond above. The section on "Influence and allusions" supplements C. F. E. Spurgeon (BD432).

Supersedes the author's earlier bibliography, which covered 1908–24.

Spurgeon, Caroline Frances Eleanor. Five hundred years of Chaucer criticism and allusion (1357–1900). London, pub. for the Chaucer Society by K. Paul, 1914–[25]. 7v. (Chaucer Soc. [Publ.], 2d ser., 48–50, 52–56) **BD432**

Issued also in 3v. by the Cambridge University Press, 1925.

Contents: pt.1, Foreword to pt.1. Text of allusions (1357–1800); pt.2, Text of allusions (1801–1850); pt.3, Text of allusions (1851–1900); pt.4, Appendix A: Additional English and Latin references, with notes on the debt of some writers to Chaucer; pt.5, Appendixes B and C: French and German allusions; [pt.6], Introductions; [pt.7], Index.

—— —— Supplement containing additional entries 1868–1900. London, priv. pr., 1920. 171p.

Tatlock, John Strong Perry and **Kennedy, Arthur G.** Concordance to the complete works of Geoffrey Chaucer and to the Romaunt of the Rose. Wash., Carnegie Inst., 1927. 1110p. (Carnegie Inst. publ. 353) **BD433**

Complete, except in the case of about 150 very common words, for which only selected references are given. Based upon the text of the Globe edition.

French, Robert Dudley. A Chaucer handbook. 2d ed. N.Y., Crofts, 1947. 402p. **BD434**

1st ed. 1929. The revision is mainly in the bibliography and in the footnotes, with occasional changes in the text. The bibliography has been increased from about 12 to 29 pages.

Magoun, Francis Peabody. A Chaucer gazetteer. Chicago, Univ. of Chicago Pr., 1961. 173p. **BD435**

"A listing and discussion of all geographical names and names (uncapitalized) of geographical origin or with geographical connections . . . used by Chaucer."—*Pref.*

Corson, Hiram. Index of proper names and subjects to Chaucer's Canterbury tales, together with comparisons and similies, metaphors and proverbs, maxims, etc., in the same. [London], pub. for the Chaucer Society by K. Paul, 1911, for the issue of 1884. 121p. (Chaucer Soc. [publ.], 1st ser., 72) **BD436**

Coleridge

Kennedy, Virginia Wadlow and **Barton, Mary Neill.** Samuel Taylor Coleridge; a selected bibliography of the best available editions of his writings, of biographies and criticisms of him and of references showing his relations with contemporaries, for students and teachers. Baltimore, Enoch Pratt Free Lib., 1935. 151p.   **BD437**

Logan, Eugenia, *Sister.* A concordance to the poetry of Samuel Taylor Coleridge. St. Mary-of-the-Woods, Ind., priv. pr., 1940. 901p.   **BD438**

Based on the text edition by Ernest Hartley Coleridge. Oxford, Univ. Pr., 1912. 2v.

Conrad

Lohf, Kenneth A. and **Sheehy, Eugene P.** Joseph Conrad at mid-century; editions and studies, 1895–1955. Minneapolis, Univ. of Minn. Pr., [1957]. 114p.   **BD439**

A bibliography of works by and about Conrad.

Dickens

Eckel, John C. First editions of the writings of Charles Dickens and their values; a bibliography. . . . London, Chapman, 1913. 296p. il.   **BD440**

Miller, William. The Dickens student and collector; a list of writings relating to Charles Dickens and his works, 1836–1945. Cambridge, Harvard Univ. Pr., 1946. 351p.   **BD441**

A comprehensive bibliography of writings about Dickens and his works, arranged by subject, and chronologically under subject. Detailed index.

Hayward, Arthur L. Dickens encyclopaedia; an alphabetical dictionary of references to every character and place mentioned in the works of fiction with explanatory notes on obscure allusions and phrases. London, Routledge; N.Y., Dutton, 1924. 174p. il.   **BD442**

Includes, in one alphabet, synopses of plots, descriptions of characters and scenes with references to all chapters in which these occur, and articles on miscellaneous subjects, e.g., illustrators of Dickens' works. Includes fewer names of characters than Philip (BD443), but is fuller for information about real persons and places. Good illustrations.

Philip, Alexander J. and **Gadd, W. L.** Dickens dictionary. 2d ed. rev. and greatly enl. Gravesend, "The Librarian," 1928. 375p. il.   **BD443**

Contains: (1) synopses of plots; (2) alphabetical list of characters and places; (3) index of originals. Includes names from all Dickens' works except the *Child's history of England.* Differs from Pierce's *Dickens dictionary* (BD444) in having all names in one alphabetical list, instead of in separate lists for each novel; in referring only to the first chapter in which a character appears; and in omitting quotations. Differs from the 1st edition in including all notes about originals in the Index.

Pierce, Gilbert Ashville. Dickens dictionary; a key to the characters and principal incidents in the tales of Charles Dickens, with additions by W. A. Wheeler. Boston, Houghton; London, Chapman, [c1872, 1900]. 573p. il.   **BD444**

Arranged by books, not in one alphabet; an older work, but not superseded by more recent works. Gives description of each character, its connection with the plot, quotations, and exact chapter references for all chapters in which the character appears.

Dodgson

Williams, Sidney Herbert and **Madan, Falconer.** The Lewis Carroll handbook . . . rev., augm. and brought up to 1960 by Roger Lancelyn Green. London, Oxford Univ. Pr., 1962. 307p.   **BD445**

"First pub. in 1931."

Being a new version of *A handbook of the literature of the Rev. C. L. Dodgson.*

Contents: pt.1, A list, with notes, of all pieces and editions printed or issued by Dodgson from 1845 to 1898, and editions of his work containing new material or reprints of exceptional interest from 1898 to 1960, in order of date; pt.2, Notes of ordinary editions . . . issued from 1898 to 1960, with American editions of any date; pt.3, Memoirs, reminiscences, memorials, bibliographies, etc.

Donne

Keynes, Geoffrey. A bibliography of Dr. John Donne, dean of Saint Paul's. 3d ed. Cambridge, Univ. Pr., 1958. 285p.   **BD446**

1st ed. 1914; 2d ed. 1932. Includes materials by and about Donne.

Combs, Homer Carroll and **Sullens, Zay Rusk.** Concordance to the English poems of John Donne. Chicago, Packard, 1940. 418p.   **BD447**

Based on *The poems* of John Donne, ed. by H. J. C. Grierson. Rev. ed. Oxford, Univ. Pr., 1929.

Doyle

Christ, Jay Finley. An irregular guide to Sherlock Holmes of Baker Street. N.Y., Argus Books; Summit, N.J., Pamphlet House, 1947. 118p.   **BD448**

An index to words, ideas, personal names, etc., with reference to the stories in which they appear.

Dryden

Macdonald, Hugh. John Dryden; a bibliography of early editions and of Drydeniana. Oxford, Clarendon Pr., 1939. 358p. il.   **BD449**

Gives detailed bibliographical descriptions with notes.

—— and **Osborn, James Marshall.** Macdonald's Bibliography of Dryden; an annotated check list of selected American libraries. [Chicago, Univ. of Chicago Pr., 1941] (Extract from Modern philology 39:69–98, 197–212. Aug. and Nov. 1941)   **BD449a**

Locates copies in 10 American libraries and incorporates "notes of additions and corrections to more than a third of Macdonald's descriptions."

Aden, John M. The critical opinions of John Dryden: a dictionary. Nashville, Vanderbilt Univ. Pr., 1963. 290p.   **BD450**

Arranged alphabetically by topic, chronologically under topic; gives quotations from Dryden's prose works expressing his critical opinions.

Montgomery, Guy. Concordance to the poetical works of John Dryden . . . assisted by Mary Jackman and Helen S. Agoa. Berkeley, Univ. of Calif. Pr., 1957. 722p.   **BD451**

"Based on the Cambridge ed. of the *Poetical works* of John Dryden, ed. by George Rapall Noyes . . . rev. and enlarged in 1950."

Eliot

Mudge, Isadore Gilbert and **Sears, Minnie Earl.** A George Eliot dictionary, the characters and scenes of the novels, stories and poems alphabetically arranged. London, Routledge; N.Y., Wilson, 1924. 260p.   **BD452**

Contains: (1) synopses; (2) main dictionary of fictitious and historical characters, places, etc., with descriptions, illustrative quotations, notations as to originals, and many historical notes on the real characters and scenes, especially those in *Romola;* (3) list of books mentioned in the novels and stories, with identifications; and (4) index of originals.

FitzGerald

Tutin, John Ramsden. Concordance to FitzGerald's translation of the Rubáiyát of Omar Khayyám. London, N.Y., Macmillan, 1900. 169p. **BD453**

Indexes every word in the last edition issued during Fitz-Gerald's lifetime; every word in the 1st edition, 1859; and all variations in the 2d, 3d, and other editions—forming a practically complete index to the entire work in its distinct forms. References are to edition, quatrain, and line.

Gray

Northup, Clark Sutherland. Bibliography of Thomas Gray. New Haven, Yale Univ. Pr., 1917. 296p. (Cornell studies in English, 1) **BD454**

Starr, Herbert Willmarth. A bibliography of Thomas Gray, 1917–1951; with material supplementary to C. S. Northup's Bibliography of Thomas Gray. Philadelphia, Univ. of Pa. Pr. for Temple Univ. Publs., 1953. 152p. **BD455**

Includes works by and about Gray. Locates copies.

Cook, Albert Stanburrough. Concordance to the English poems of Thomas Gray. Boston, Houghton, 1908. 160p. **BD456**

Omits 47 common words, but is otherwise complete. Based upon Gosse's edition.

Hardy

Purdy, Richard Little. Thomas Hardy, a bibliographical study. London, N.Y., Geoffrey Cumberlege, Oxford Univ. Pr., 1954. 386p. **BD457**

A comprehensive, detailed bibliography of works by Hardy.

Saxelby, F. Outwin. A Thomas Hardy dictionary; the characters and scenes of the novels and poems alphabetically arranged and described. London, Routledge; N.Y., Dutton, 1911. lxxviiip., 238p. **BD458**

Contains: (1) Biographical sketch; (2) List of 1st editions; (3) Bibliography of the novels; (4) List of books about Hardy and Wessex; (5) Map: "Heart of Wessex"; (6) List of fictitious place names followed by real names; (7) Synopses of the novels; and (8) Dictionary of characters and places.

Johnson

Clifford, James L. Johnsonian studies, 1887–1950; a survey and bibliography. Minneapolis, Univ. of Minn. Pr., 1951. 140p. **BD459**

Lists editions, criticisms, etc.

Joyce

Slocum, John J. and **Cahoon, Herbert.** A bibliography of James Joyce, 1882–1941. London, Hart–Davis, 1953. 195p. (Soho bibliographies, 5) **BD460**

Does not include critical works about Joyce. Based on the Slocum collection of Joyce materials now in the Yale University Library.

Hart, Clive. A concordance to Finnegans wake. Minneapolis, Univ. of Minn. Pr., 1963. 516p. **BD461**

Keats

MacGillivray, J. R. Keats: a bibliography and reference guide with an essay on Keats' reputation. Toronto, Univ.

of Toronto Pr., 1949. 210p. (Univ. of Toronto. Dept. of English. Studies and texts, no.3) **BD462**

Baldwin, Dane Lewis, Broughton, L. N. [and others]. Concordance to the poems of John Keats. Wash., Carnegie Inst., 1917. 437p. **BD463**

Based on the Buxton Forman editions of 1910 and 1914. Gives a complete record of all words used by Keats, except 59 common words omitted altogether and 10 others recorded only partially.

Kipling

Stewart, James McG. Rudyard Kipling: a bibliographical catalogue . . . ed. by A. W. Yeats. Toronto, Dalhousie Univ. Pr. and Univ. of Toronto Pr., 1959. 673p. il. **BD464**

A descriptive bibliography of Kipling's published works appearing in book form. Appendixes include: Items in sales catalogues; Uncollected prose and verse; Works in anthologies and readers; Collected sets; Musical settings; and Unauthorized editions.

Young, W. Arthur. Dictionary of the characters and scenes in the stories and poems of Rudyard Kipling, 1886–1911. London, Routledge; N.Y., Dutton, [1911]. 231p. **BD465**

Contains: (1) Summary of the books (giving synopses of plots); and (2) Dictionary proper, which gives names of the characters and titles of books, stories, and poems in one alphabet.

Lawrence

Roberts, Warren. A bibliography of D. H. Lawrence. London, Hart-Davis, 1963. 399p. (Soho bibliographies, 12) **BD466**

Marlowe

Crawford, Charles. The Marlowe concordance. Louvain, Uystpruyst [etc.], 1911–32. 1453p. (Materialien zur Kunde des älteren englischen Dramas, begr. u. hrsg. von W. Bang, v.34, pts.1–3; Materials for the study of the Old English drama; ed. by Henry DeVocht, n.s. v.2–3, 6–7) **BD467**

"Very few words have been omitted from the concordance, and only those which are of little aid to study, such as auxiliary verbs, pronouns, and insignificant prepositions and conjunctions."—*Pref.*

Milton

Stevens, David Harrison. Reference guide to Milton; from 1800 to the present day. Chicago, Univ. of Chicago Pr., 1930. 302p. **BD468**

Lists editions, translations, biography, criticism, etc., from 1800 to about 1928.

Fletcher, Harris Francis. Contributions to a Milton bibliography, 1800–1930, being a list of addenda to Stevens' Reference guide to Milton. Urbana, Univ. of Illinois Pr., 1931. 166p. (Univ. of Illinois studies in language and literature. v.16, no.1) **BD469**

Huckabay, Calvin. John Milton: a bibliographical supplement, 1929–1957. Pittsburgh, Duquesne Univ. Pr., 1960. 211p. (Duquesne studies. Philological ser. I) **BD470**

Designed to supplement the bibliographies by David H. Stevens, *Reference guide to Milton* (BD468), and Harris F. Fletcher, *Contributions to a Milton bibliography* (BD469).

Lists significant books and articles of the period covered and includes some doctoral dissertations and master's essays.

Reviewers point out an unusual number of omissions and typographical errors. (*See*, e.g., *Renaissance news* 14:121–24. 1961 and *Modern philology* 58:281–82. 1961)

Patterson, Frank Allen. An index to the Columbia edition of the Works of John Milton, by Frank Allen Patterson assisted by French Rowe Fogle. N.Y., Columbia Univ. Pr., 1940. 2v. 2141p.   **BD471**

Uniform with the Columbia *Works of John Milton* but sold separately. A detailed, analytical index to the works of Milton, including references to names, ideas, and subjects. Serves also as a word index. May be used with other editions of Milton, although the page references are to the Columbia *Milton*.

Bradshaw, John. Concordance to the poetical works of John Milton. London, Sonnenschein, 1894. 412p. **BD472**

Based upon the Aldine edition (Bell, 1894); includes all the poems except the Psalms and the translations in the prose works; omits the commoner pronouns, conjunctions, adverbs, and prepositions.

Cooper, Lane. Concordance to the Latin, Greek and Italian poems of John Milton. Halle, Niemeyer, 1923. 212p.   **BD473**

Based mainly upon Beeching's reprint of 1900, with some use of the Oxford miniature edition and of two poems from Masson's edition.

Gilbert, Allan H. Geographical dictionary of Milton. New Haven, Yale Univ. Pr., 1919. 322p.   **BD474**

Gives all place-names mentioned in all of Milton's prose and poetry (except the addresses of the *Letters of state* and the Biblical quotations in *De doctrina christiana*), with exact references to all passages where they occur and explanation of what they meant to Milton. References are to the Oxford edition of the *Poems,* edited by Beeching, and to the edition of the *Prose works* published by Pickering, 1851.

Hanford, James Holly. A Milton handbook; 4th ed. N.Y., Crofts, 1946. 465p.   **BD475**

1st ed. 1926; 3d ed. 1940. The 4th edition adds new appendixes, along with revisions and additions in text, footnotes, and bibliography.

A survey companion to Milton studies for the advanced student. Discusses Milton's life and works with references to source materials. Bibliography, p.421–47.

More

Gibson, R. W. St. Thomas More: a preliminary bibliography of his works and of Moreana to the year 1750. With a bibliography of Utopiana comp. by R. W. Gibson and J. Max Patrick. New Haven, Yale Univ. Pr., 1961. 499p. facsims.   **BD476**

A preliminary bibliography, published in connection with the projected edition of More's works now in preparation at Yale. A revised edition, to include new materials discovered by the editors, will be issued upon the completion of the work some 10 years hence.

Includes works by and about More published up to 1750.

Pope

Griffith, Reginald Harvey. Alexander Pope; a bibliography. Austin, Univ. of Texas, 1922–27. v.1, pts.1–2.   **BD477**

v.1, pts.1–2, Pope's own writings, 1709–51; v.2—to cover material about Pope—was never published.

Abbott, Edwin. Concordance to the works of Alexander Pope. N.Y., Appleton, 1875. 365p.   **BD478**

Based upon Warburton's edition, 1751; includes all words in poems in that edition except the translations from the Greek and Latin, the adaptations from Chaucer, and the imitations of the English poets.

Scott

Corson, James Clarkson. Bibliography of Sir Walter Scott; a classified and annotated list of books and articles relating to his life and works, 1797–1940. Edinburgh, Oliver & Boyd, 1943. 428p.   **BD479**

Ruff, William. A bibliography of the poetical works of Sir Walter Scott, 1796–1832. Edinburgh, Edinburgh Bibliographical Soc., 1938. p.99–239, 279–81. (Repr. from Edinburgh Bibliographical Soc., Transactions v.1, 1937–38)   **BD480**

Husband, M. F. A. Dictionary of the characters in the Waverley novels of Sir Walter Scott. London, Routledge; N.Y., Dutton, 1910. 287p.   **BD481**

Gives the characters and scenes of all the novels in one alphabetical list, but contains no outlines of plots. Differs from Rogers' *Waverley dictionary* (BD482) in having the one list instead of a separate list for each novel and in referring only to the title of the story in which a character appears, not to specific chapters. In this latter respect, less useful than Rogers, although it lists more characters.

Rogers, May. Waverley dictionary. 2d ed. Chicago, Griggs, 1885 [c1878]. 357p.   **BD482**

An alphabetical arrangement of all the characters in the Waverley novels, with a descriptive analysis of each character and illustrative selections from the text. Gives exact chapter references.

Shakespeare

❧ For many questions on Shakespeare the elaborate notes given in the New Variorum edition (Philadelphia, Lippincott, 1871–1955. v.1–27. In progress) furnish excellent reference material.

Bibliography

Jaggard, William. Shakespeare bibliography; a dictionary of every known issue of the writings of our national poet and of recorded opinion thereon in the English language, with historical introduction. Stratford-on-Avon, Shakespeare Pr., 1911. 729p. il.   **BD484**

Bartlett, Henrietta C. Mr. William Shakespeare; original and early editions of his quartos and folios, his source books and those containing contemporary notices. New Haven, Yale Univ. Pr., 1922. 217p.   **BD485**

——— and **Pollard, Alfred W.** A census of Shakespeare's plays in quarto, 1594–1709, rev. and extended. New Haven, Yale Univ. Pr.; London, Milford, 1939. 165p.   **BD486**

Records and describes all separate editions and issues before 1709. Every known copy of each edition and issue is described, and its history from publication to Jan. 1939 given as fully as possible. The index includes all names of owners, booksellers, auctioneers, and binders found in the census.

Ebisch, Walther and **Schücking, Levin L.** Shakespeare bibliography. . . . Oxford, Clarendon Pr., 1931. 294p. [Sächsische Forschungsinstitut in Leipzig. Forschungsinstitut für Neuere Philologie. III. Anglistische Abt. Extra volume]   **BD487**

A selective bibliography of material about Shakespeare, his times, life, personality, texts, sources, literary influences, language, art, production, influence, individual plays, etc.

——— ——— Supplement for the years 1930–35. Oxford, Clarendon Pr., 1937. 104p.

Smith, Gordon Ross. A classified Shakespeare bibliography, 1936–1958. University Park, Pa. State Univ. Pr., 1963. 784p.   **BD488**

In effect, a continuation of Ebisch and Schücking (BD487).

Shakespeare Association of America. [Annual bibliography of Shakespeareana], 1925– . **BD489**

Bibliographies for 1925–48 appeared under varying titles in the *Shakespeare Association bulletin,* v.1–24, 1926–49. Bibliographies for 1949– have title *Shakespeare: an annotated bibliography,* and are continued in the *Shakespeare quarterly,* v.1– , 1950– .

A subject bibliography of books, pamphlets, and periodical material, including much analysis of periodicals. Before 1949, the bibliography was not annotated.

Shakespeare survey; an annual survey of Shakespearian study and production, v.1– , 1948– . Cambridge, Univ. Pr., 1948– . il. (v.17, 1964) **BD490**

Ed., Allardyce Nicoll.

"Issued under the sponsorship of the University of Birmingham, the University of Manchester, the Royal Shakespeare Theatre, [and] the Shakespeare Birthplace Trust" (varies).

Each volume has a specific theme and includes articles related to some particular aspect of Shakespeare study. International in scope, with information on productions, etc., and an annual critical survey of "The year's contributions to Shakespearian study."

v.17, published in honor of the quartercentenary year, has special title *Shakespeare in his own age.* Intended to stand as an independent study of the Elizabethan period, it dispenses with such usual features as "International notes" and the reviews.

Concordances

Bartlett, John. New and complete concordance or verbal index to words, phrases, and passages in the dramatic works of Shakespeare with a supplementary concordance to the poems. London, Macmillan, 1894. 1910p. **BD491**

Based upon the text of the Globe edition; gives full context for each word listed, with exact reference to act, scene, and line as numbered in the Globe edition, 1891. The best and most comprehensive Shakespeare concordance.

Stevenson, Burton Egbert. Home book of Shakespeare quotations, being also a concordance and a glossary of the unique words and phrases in the plays and poems. N.Y., London, Scribner, 1937. 2055p. **BD492**

Dictionaries

Baker, Arthur Ernest. A Shakespeare commentary . . . v.1. Taunton, Eng., Author, 1938. 965p. tables. **BD493**

Subtitle: Dates of composition and first publication; sources of the plots and detailed outlines of the plays; together with the characters, place-names, classical, geographical, topographical and curious historical and folk allusions, with glosses; to which are added appendices, giving extracts from Holinshed, Plutarch, and the various romances, novels, poems and histories used by Shakespeare in the formation of the dramas.

Pub. in 15 pts., 1917–38. Pts.1–13 had title *Shakespeare dictionary.*

Contents: pt.1, Julius Caesar; pt.2, As you like it; pt.3, Macbeth; pt.4, The Tempest; pt.5, Hamlet; pt.6, King Lear; pt.7, King John; pt.8, Merchant of Venice; pt.9, King Richard II; pts.10–11, King Henry IV; pt.12, King Henry V; pt.13, King Henry VI, pt.1; pt.14, King Henry VI, pt.2; pt.15, King Henry VI, pt.3.

A popular dictionary of characters, place-names, and allusions, each part in a separate alphabet.

Halliday, Frank Ernest. A Shakespeare companion. 1564–1964. N.Y., Schocken, 1964. 569p. il. **BD494**

1st ed. 1952. 742p.

A thoroughly revised edition of this detailed dictionary to the plots and characters of Shakespeare's plays; the productions; sources, spelling, and pronunciation of Elizabethan English; his life, etc., etc.

Use of a two-column page and smaller type largely accounts for the reduced number of pages in the revised edition.

Onions, Charles Talbut. Shakespeare glossary. 2d ed. rev. Oxford, Clarendon Pr., 1919. 259p. **BD495**

An excellent small dictionary, by a man who was for many years on the staff of the *New English dictionary* (AE20). The aim of the glossary is to supply: (1) definitions or illustrations of words or senses now obsolete or surviving only in archaic or provincial use; (2) explanations of other words involving allusions not generally familiar; and (3) explanations of proper names carrying with them some connotative significance, etc. Includes also obsolete and technical terms which occur only in the stage directions.

Stokes, Francis Griffin. Dictionary of the characters and proper names in the works of Shakespeare, with notes on the sources and dates of the plays and poems. London, Harrap; Boston, Houghton, 1924. 359p. (Repr.: N.Y., Peter Smith, 1949) **BD496**

Includes, in one alphabet, titles of Shakespeare's works, with brief account of first editions, sources, etc.; names of all characters—historical, legendary, and fictitious—with brief analysis of the dramatic action of each; names used as allusions; place-names; and miscellaneous names, such as seasons, planets, etc. Gives exact reference to play, act, and line, and some bibliographical references to sources of further information.

Sugden, Edward Holdsworth. Topographical dictionary to the works of Shakespeare and his fellow dramatists. Manchester, Univ. Pr.; London, N.Y., Longmans, 1925. 580p. il. maps. (Publ. of the University of Manchester, 168) **BD497**

Lists of place-names, i.e., countries, towns, rivers, and streets, with brief article about each and exact reference to the play in which it occurs, and references to sources of further information. Includes also the place-names of Milton and some references to Spenser.

Plots

Guerber, H. A. Stories of Shakespeare's comedies. N.Y., Dodd, 1910. 336p. **BD498**

—— Stories of Shakespeare's tragedies. N.Y., Dodd, 1911. 349p. **BD499**

—— Stories of Shakespeare's English history plays. N.Y., Dodd, 1912. 315p. **BD500**

Three companion volumes, inferior in literary form to Lamb's *Tales from Shakespeare,* but useful for reference purposes because they give simple, clear outlines, act by act, of the 14 comedies, the 12 tragedies, and the 8 English-history plays.

Shaw

Broad, C. Lewis and **Broad, Violet M.** Dictionary to the plays and novels of Bernard Shaw, with bibliography of his works and of the literature concerning him, with a record of the principal Shavian play productions. London, Black, [1929]. 230p. **BD501**

Shelley

Wise, Thomas James. Shelley library, a catalogue of printed books, manuscripts and autograph letters by Percy Bysshe Shelley, Harriet Shelley and Mary Wollstonecraft Shelley. London, pr. for priv. circ., 1924. 164p. facsim. **BD502**

Ellis, Frederick S. Lexical concordance to the poetical works of Percy Bysshe Shelley. London, Quaritch, 1892. 818p. **BD503**

Based upon the text of the Forman edition, 1880.

Spenser

Carpenter, Frederic Ives. Reference guide to Edmund Spenser. Chicago, Univ. of Chicago Pr., 1923. 333p. **BD504**

Atkinson, Dorothy F. Edmund Spenser, a bibliographical supplement. Baltimore, Johns Hopkins Pr.; Oxford, Univ. Pr., 1937. 242p. **BD505**

Designed as a supplement to Carpenter, above.

McNeir, Waldo F. and **Provost, Foster.** Annotated bibliography of Edmund Spenser, 1937–1960. Pittsburgh, Duquesne Univ. Pr., 1962. 255p. (Duquesne studies. Philological ser., 3) **BD506**

Covers period since Atkinson's *Supplement* to Carpenter (BD505).

Johnson, Francis R. A critical bibliography of the works of Edmund Spenser printed before 1700. Baltimore, Johns Hopkins Pr., 1933. 61p. il. **BD507**

Osgood, Charles Grosvenor. Concordance to the poems of Edmund Spenser. Wash., Carnegie Inst., 1915. 997p. (Repr.: Gloucester, Mass., Peter Smith, 1963) **BD508**

Complete, except in the case of 174 very common words for which only selected references are given; based upon the text of Morris' edition (Globe ed. 1869) corrected by the text of R. E. Neil Dodge's edition (Cambridge ed. 1908), with record of all variants in the Oxford edition, 1909–10.

Whitman, Charles Huntington. Subject-index to the poems of Edmund Spenser, pub. under the auspices of the Connecticut Academy of Arts and Sciences. New Haven, Yale Univ. Pr., 1918. 261p. **BD509**

A subject index of names of persons, places, animals, and things, with some dictionary features also, as it includes brief allegorical and other explanations, when necessary. Based upon the Cambridge text, edited by R. E. Neil Dodge, but the table of abbreviations also gives page references for each poem to the Cambridge, Globe, Smith, and De Selincourt editions.

Swift

Teerink, Herman. A bibliography of the writings of Jonathan Swift. 2d ed. rev. and corr. Ed. by Arthur H. Scouten. Philadelphia, Univ. of Pa. Pr., 1963. 453p. il. **BD510**

First published 1957 under title *A bibliography of the writings in prose and verse of Jonathan Swift.*

Tennyson

Wise, Thomas James. Bibliography of the writings of Alfred, Lord Tennyson. London, pr. for priv. circ., 1908. 2v. il. **BD511**

Baker, Arthur Ernest. Concordance to the poetical and dramatic works of Alfred, Lord Tennyson. London, K. Paul; N.Y., Macmillan, 1914. 1212p. **BD512**

Complete except for about 250 common words; in four alphabets. Based upon the Macmillan edition (6v.) but covers also the poems included in the *Life of Lord Tennyson* by his son, and in the *Suppressed poems* edited by J. C. Thomson.

Supplemented by the same compiler's *Concordance to The devil and the lady, by Alfred Tennyson.* London, Golden Vista Pr., 1931. 247p.

—— Tennyson dictionary, the characters and place-names contained in the poetical and dramatic works of the poet alphabetically arranged and described. London, Routledge; N.Y., Dutton, [1916]. 296p. **BD513**

Contents: (1) Brief synopses of poems and plays; and (2) Dictionary of characters and places, and of names referred to.

Thackeray

Van Duzer, Henry Sayre. Thackeray library; first editions and first publications, portraits, water colors, etchings, drawings and manuscripts . . . a few additional items are included, forming a complete Thackeray bibliography; with twenty-three illustrations. N.Y., priv. pr. [De Vinne Pr.], 1919. 198p. il. **BD514**

Mudge, Isadore Gilbert and **Sears, Minnie Earl.** A Thackeray dictionary; the characters and scenes of the novels and short stories alphabetically arranged. London, Routledge; N.Y., Dutton, 1910. xlvp., 304p. **BD515**

Contains: (1) Synopses; (2) Main alphabetical list of historical and fictitious characters and place names; and (3) Index of originals.

Trollope

Gerould, Winifred Gregory and **Gerould, James Thayer.** A guide to Trollope. Princeton, N.J., Princeton Univ. Pr., 1948. 256p. **BD516**

"An alphabetical record of characters and places having a significant role in the novels and stories." Includes brief plots.

Woolf

Kirkpatrick, Brownlee Jean. A bibliography of Virginia Woolf. London, Hart-Davis, 1957. 180p. (Soho bibliographies, 9) **BD517**

Comprises only works by Mrs. Woolf.

Wordsworth

Cornell University. Library. The Cornell Wordsworth collection; a catalogue of books and manuscripts presented to the University by Mr. Victor Emanuel, comp. by George Harris Healey. Ithaca, N.Y., Cornell Univ. Pr., 1957. 458p. il. **BD518**

A new work listing some 3000 items—not merely a revision of the 1931 list based on the same collection.

Wise, Thomas James. Bibliography of the writings in prose and verse of William Wordsworth. London, pr. for priv. circ., 1916. 268p. il. **BD519**

Logan, James Venable. Wordsworthian criticism; a guide and bibliography. Columbus, Ohio State Univ., 1947. 304p. (Graduate School monographs. Contributions in languages and literature, no.12) **BD520**

2d impression, 1961.

Henley, Elton F. and **Stam, David H.** Wordsworthian criticism, 1945–1959; an annotated bibliography. N.Y., N.Y. Pub. Lib., 1960. 61p. **BD521**

Supplements Logan, above, for bibliography.

Cooper, Lane. Concordance to the poems of William Wordsworth, ed. for the Concordance Society. London, Smith, Elder; N.Y., Dutton, 1911. 1136p. **BD522**

Based upon the text of the Oxford *Wordsworth* edited by Hutchinson, 1907. Gives complete list of references for all words, except that all references for 52 of the most common words are omitted, and only a selection given for 195 other very common words.

Tutin, J. R. Wordsworth dictionary. Hull [Eng.], Tutin, 1891. 216p. and suppl., 20p. **BD523**

Contents: (1) Dictionary of persons with indication of the poems in which they are mentioned; (2) Dictionary of places; (3) Familiar quotations; (4) Chronological list of best poems; (5) Birds, trees and flowers of Wordsworth. Supplement: Index to the animal and vegetable kingdom of Wordsworth (Hull, 1892. 20p.).

Yeats

Parrish, Stephen Maxfield. A concordance to the poems of W. B. Yeats . . . programmed by James Allan Painter. Ithaca, N.Y., Cornell Univ. Pr., 1963. 967p. **BD524**

Based on the *Variorum edition of the poems* . . . ed. by Peter Allt and R. K. Alspach (Macmillan, 1957). A Cornell concordance produced with the aid of an electronic computer.

Wade, Allan. A bibliography of the writings of W. B. Yeats. [2d ed. rev.] London, Hart-Davis, 1958. 449p. (Soho bibliographies, 1) **BD525**

Includes brief list of books about Yeats.

Indian

Singh, Bhupal. Survey of Anglo-Indian fiction. Oxford, Univ. Pr., 1934. 344p. **BD526**

A survey and criticism of the Anglo-Indian novel is followed by a Bibliography: A, Anglo-Indian novels, p.311–34; B, Criticism and biography, p.334–35; C, Articles and reviews, p.335–36.

Spencer, Dorothy Mary. Indian fiction in English: an annotated bibliography. Philadelphia, Univ. of Pa. Pr., 1960. 98p. **BD527**

Contents: Introductory essay on Indian society, culture and fiction, p.9–42; Annotated list of fiction and autobiography written by Indians in English or translated into English, p.43–98.

Lists some 200 works of fiction and about 45 autobiographies, about three quarters of which are written in English.

Winternitz, Moriz. A history of Indian literature . . . Calcutta, Univ. of Calcutta, 1927–63. v.1–3, pt.1. (In progress) **BD528**

Translated from the author's *Geschichte der indischen Litteratur*. Leipzig, Amelang, 1908–22.

Contents: v.1, Introduction, Veda, National epics, Purānas, and Tantras. 1927; v.2, Buddhist literature and Jaina literature. 1933; v.3, pt.1, Classical Sanskrit literature. 1963.

A heavily documented history.

Who's who of Indian writers. New Delhi, Sahitya Akademi, 1961. 410p. **BD529**

"Contains basic biographical and bibliographical information about living Indian authors in all Indian languages including English."—*Pref.*

Irish

Brooke, Stopford Augustus and **Rolleston, T. W.** Treasury of Irish poetry in the English tongue. Rev. and enl. N.Y., Macmillan, 1932. 610p. **BD530**

1st ed. 1900.

Gives 344 poems from the works of 119 authors, with biographical and bibliographical notes, occasionally of some length and signed.

Brown, Stephen James. A guide to books on Ireland. Pt.1, Prose literature, a poetry, music and plays. Dublin, Figgis; London, Longmans, 1912. 371p. **BD531**

No more published.

An annotated bibliography of Irish literature.

—— Ireland in fiction; a guide to Irish novels, tales, romances, and folk-lore. New ed. . . . Dublin, London, Maunsel, 1919. 362p. **BD532**

"Includes all works of fiction published in volume form, and dealing with Ireland or with the Irish abroad, and such works only."—*Pref.*

An author list of 1713 novels in the English language, with descriptive annotations and brief biographical notes. Appendixes contain: some useful works of reference; publishers and series; classified lists of novels (e.g., historical fiction, legends, Catholic clerical life, etc.); Irish fiction in periodicals. Index of titles and subjects. Has more titles, and about 550 more notes, than the edition of 1916.

O'Donoghue, David James. Poets of Ireland; a biographical and bibliographical dictionary of Irish writers of English verse. Dublin, Figgis; London, Frowde, 1912. 504p. **BD533**

Biographical sketches with bibliographies. Restricted to Irish poets who wrote in the English language.

Scottish

Dixon, William Macneile. Edinburgh book of Scottish verse, 1300–1900. London, Meiklejohn; N.Y., Oxford Univ. Pr., 1910. 938p. **BD534**

Bibliographical notes; glossary; index of authors; index of first lines and some titles.

Geddie, William. A bibliography of middle Scots poets; with an introduction on the history of their reputations. Edinburgh, pr. for the Scottish Text Society by Blackwood, 1912. 364p. (Scottish Text Soc. [Publ. 61]) **BD535**

Lists editions, citations to biography and criticism, etc.

GERMANIC LANGUAGES

Dutch

Baur, Frank [and others]. Geschiedenis van de letterkunde der Nederlanden. 's Hertogenbosch, Teulings' Uitgevers-Maatschappij L. C. G. Malmberg, 1939–59. v.1–5, 7, 9. il. (In progress) **BD536**

To be in 9v.

Each volume by a specialist. An illustrated history with bibliographies throughout.

Brussels. Bibliothèque Royale de Belgique. De Nederlandsche letterkunde in België, 1830–1930. Ronse, Leherte-Courtin, 1932. 172p. il. **BD537**

Brief biographical sketches with bibliographies.

List of 189 periodicals.

Buisman, M. Populaire prozaschrijvers van 1600 tot 1815: romans, novellen, verhalen, levensbeschrijvingen, Arcadia's, sprookjes. Alphabetische naamlijst. Amsterdam, B. M. Israël, [1960?]. 508p. **BD538**

A comprehensive bibliography of novels, short stories, biographies, Utopias, and fairy tales, published from 1600 to 1815, in Dutch as well as translations into Dutch.

Frederiks, Johannes Godefridus and **Branden, F. J. van den.** Biographisch woordenboek der Noord- en Zuidnederlandsche letterkunde. 2. omgew. druk. Amsterdam, Veen, 1888–92. 918p. **BD539**

A biographical dictionary useful especially for the 18th and 19th centuries and including writers from both Holland and Belgium.

Jong, Dirk de. Het vrije boek in onvrije tijd; bibliografie van illegale en clandestiene bellettrie. Leiden, Sijthoff, 1958. 341p. **BD540**

An author listing of more than 1000 items of belles-lettres

published clandestinely in the Netherlands during the German occupation in World War II.

Lectuur-Repertorium ... 2. en definitieve uitgave. Uitgave van het Algemeen Secretariaat voor Katholieke Boekerijen. Antwerpen, Vlaamsche Boekcentrale, 1952–54. 3v. **BD541**

Subtitle: Auteurslijst bevattende 23,000 bio-bibliografische nota's en 3000 portretten van auteurs behorende tot de Nederlandse en de algemene literatuur, met waarde- en vakaanduiding van 90,000 literaire en vulgariserende werken, samengesteld door het A.S.K.B. onder redactie van Joris Baers.

Supersedes the earlier edition (1932–36) and its supplements (1939–46). A detailed bio-bibliography of major authors writing in or translated into Dutch. Individual titles are keyed to a classification scheme to indicate moral values and literary type.

Petit, Louis David. Bibliographie der Middelnederlandsche taal- en letterkunde. Leiden, Brill, 1888–1910. 2v. **BD542**

Contents: v.1, Works appearing before 1888; v.2, Works appearing from 1888–1910.
Bibliography of Middle Dutch language and literature.

Winkel, Jan te. De ontwikkelingsgang der Nederlandsche letterkunde. 2. druk. Haarlem, Bohn, 1922–27. 7v. **BD543**

1st ed. 1908–21.
An important reference history.

Afrikaans

Nienaber, Petrus Johannes. Bronnegids by die studie van die Afrikaanse taal en letterkunde. Johannesburg, Nienaber, 1947. 422p. **BD544**

——— ——— Deel II, 1947–1951. 1952. 193p.
Bibliography of Afrikaans literature and language.

Flemish

Arents, Prosper. De Vlaamse schrijvers in het Engels vertaald, 1481–1949. Gent, Erasmus, 1950. 466p. (Koninklijke Vlaamse Academie voor Taal- en Letterkunde) **BD545**

A bibliography of translations into English from the Flemish, with detailed bibliographical information and location of copies in American and European libraries.

——— Flemish writers translated (1830–1931); bibliographical essay. The Hague, Nijhoff, 1931. 191p. **BD546**

A listing of Flemish works translated into various languages; classified arrangement with indexes of authors, translators, illustrators, etc.

Coppe, Paul and **Pirsoul, Léon.** Dictionnaire bio-bibliographique des littérateurs d'expression wallonne, 1622 à 1950. Gembloux, Duculot, 1951. 415p. **BD547**

Includes 1325 sketches and lists some 25,000 titles of works in the Walloon dialect. The sketch of each author indicates place and date of birth and death; pseudonym, if any; profession; and a concise critical note on the value of his contribution and the titles of his works. Bibliographical information is brief, usually consisting of title and date (in some cases dates are omitted).

Roemans, Robert. Bibliographie van de moderne Vlaamsche literatuur, 1893–1930. 1. deel. Kortrijk, 1930–34. Afl. 1–10. **BD548**

——— and **Assche, Hilda van.** Bibliografie van de Vlaamse tijdschriften. Reeks 1: Vlaamse literaire tijdschriften van 1930 tot en met 1958. Hasselt, Heideland, 1960–63. Reeks 1–2. (In progress) **BD549**

For full information *see* AF140–AF141.

Friesian

Aarhus, Denmark. Statsbiblioteket. Friserne, Land og Folk Sprog og Litteratur. Aarhus, 1933–59. 2v. il. **BD550**

Contents: v.1, To 1933; v.2, 1934–59.
Lists works on the history, language, and literature of Friesland.

Friesland. Provinciale Bibliotheek. Catalogus der Friesche taal- en letterkunde en overige Friesche geschriften. Leeuwarden, Noordnederlandsche Boekhandel, 1941. 859p. **BD551**

A classified catalog with extensive indexes.

Wumkes, G. A. Bodders yn de Fryske striid. Boalsert, Osinga, 1926. 751p. il. **BD552**

A collection of bio-bibliographical articles with extracts from writings.

——— Paden fen Fryslan; samle opstellen. Boalsert, Osinga, 1932–43. 4v. il. **BD553**

A history of Friesian literature, with bibliographical notes interspersed.

German

Bibliography

Arnold, Robert Franz. Allgemeine Bücherkunde zur neueren deutschen Literaturgeschichte. 3. neubearb. und stark verm. Aufl. Berlin, de Gruyter, 1931. 362p. **BD554**

1st ed. 1910; 2d ed. 1919.
A useful small bibliography, covering more than the field of German literature as it is ordinarily understood. In addition to editions, histories, criticisms, etc., it treats more general reference books—such as encyclopedias, biographical dictionaries, special encyclopedias—and attempts to indicate their special value to the student of German literature.

Goedeke, Karl. Grundriss zur Geschichte der deutschen Dichtung aus den Quellen. 2. ganz neubearb. Aufl. Dresden, Ehlermann, 1884–1959. 14v. **BD555**

Contents: v.1, Das Mittelalter. 1884; v.2, Reformationszeitalter. 1886; v.3, Vom dreissigjährigen bis zum siebenjährigen Kriege. 1887; v.4–5, Vom siebenjährigen bis zum Weltkriege. 1891–93; v.6–7, Zeit des Weltkrieges. 1898–1900; v.8–14, Vom Weltfrieden, 1815 bis zur französischen Revolution 1830. 1905–59.

The most complete bibliography of German literature, indispensable in the large reference library or for university work, but too exhaustive and special for the small library. Gives some biographical and critical comment on authors; critical and other notes on individual works, sources, etc.; and exhaustive bibliographies of editions, treatises, histories, biographical and critical articles, etc. No cumulated index but detailed index in each volume.

——— ——— 3. neubearb. Aufl. nach dem Tode des Verfassers in Verbindung mit Fachgelehrten fortgeführt von Edmund Goetze. Dresden, Ehlermann, 1906–60. v.4, pts.1–5.

This is the only volume published in a 3d edition.
Pts.1–4, 1906–13; pt.5, pub. Berlin, Akademie Verlag, 1957–60.
Contents: Bd.4, Abt. 1, Vom siebenjährigen bis zum Weltkriege: Nationale Dichtung. Bd.4, Abt. 2–5, Goethe: Abt. 2, Goethe's Leben, Allgemeine Bibliographie; Abt. 3, Bibliographie der Werke Goethe; Abt. 4, Nachträge, Berichtigungen

und Register zu Abt. 2–3; Abt. 5, Goethe-Bibliographie, 1912–1950.

An extensive bibliography on Goethe's life and works. Abt. 5 is *Goethe-Bibliographie, 1912–1950,* by Carl Diesch and Paul Schlager. For materials after 1950, *see Goethe,* published by the Goethe-Gesellschaft (BD599).

—— —— Neue Folge. (Fortführung von 1830 bis 1880), hrsg. von der Deutschen Akademie der Wissenschaften zu Berlin unter Leitung von Leopold Magon . . . bearb. von Georg Minde-Pouet und Eva Rothe. Berlin, Akademie Verlag, 1955–62. Bd.1– . (In progress)

Contents: Bd.1, Bibliographie der Literatur über die deutsche Dichtung im Zeitraum 1830 bis 1880; Die Schriftsteller in alphabetischer Folge, A–Ays. 733p.

Hansel, Johannes. Bücherkunde für Germanisten: Wie sammelt man das Schrifttum nach dem neuesten Forschungsstand? Berlin, Erich Schmidt Verlag, 1959. 233p. **BD556**

A guide to basic works for research in Germanic philology and literature, including guides, bibliographies, general histories, annual surveys, etc.; a section on manuscripts; and author/title and subject indexes. German-language works predominate, but some titles in other languages are given.

Körner, Josef. Bibliographisches Handbuch des deutschen Schrifttums. 3. völlig umgearb. und wesentlich verm. Aufl. Bern, Francke, 1949. 644p. **BD557**

Previously published as an appendix to Wilhelm Scherer and Oskar Walzel, *Geschichte der deutschen Literatur.* 4. Aufl. Berlin, Askanischer Verlag, 1928. Lists books and periodical articles dealing with German literature and authors from ancient times to World War II. Arrangement is chronological by periods, each subdivided by subject. Subject and name indexes, though the latter lists only the names treated, not the authors of articles.

In the research library this work will not be a substitute for Goedeke (BD555), but will supplement it for more recent materials. Should be useful in the smaller library not needing the wealth of detail given in Goedeke.

Olzien, Otto. Bibliographie zur deutschen Literaturgeschichte. Stuttgart, Metzler, 1953. 156p. (Annalen der deutschen Literatur. Ergänzungsheft 2) **BD558**

Includes some sources covered by more comprehensive bibliographies, but emphasis is here placed on work published since Körner's *Bibliographisches Handbuch des deutschen Schrifttums,* 1949 (BD557)—through the end of 1952. Includes bibliographies of individual authors arranged alphabetically.

—— —— Nachträge, 1953–1954, mit Ergänzungen und Berichtigungen. Stuttgart, Metzler, 1955. 24p.

Schmitt, Franz Anselm. Stoff- und Motivgeschichte der deutschen Literatur: eine Bibliographie begründet von Kurt Bauerhorst. Berlin, de Gruyter, 1959. 226p. **BD559**

Based on and supersedes the *Bibliographie der Stoff- und Motivgeschichte der deutschen Literatur* by Kurt Bauerhorst. Berlin, 1932.

A bibliography of scholarly studies, mostly German, on the use of themes and motifs in German literature. Arrangement is alphabetical by *Stoff* or *Motiv,* with some 3700 titles under 1000 headings. Lists books, periodical articles, dissertations, chapters in books, and *Festschriften.* Author index.

Sternfeld, Wilhelm and **Tiedemann, Eva.** Deutsche Exil-Literatur, 1933–1945; eine Bio-bibliographie. Heidelberg, Lambert Schneider, 1962. 405p. (Deutsche Akademie für Sprache und Dichtung. Veröffentlichungen. 29) **BD560**

Very brief biographical sketches of German exiles are followed by lists of books and periodical articles.

Yale University. Library. Yale Collection of German

Literature. German Baroque literature; a catalogue of the collection in the Yale University Library, by Curt von Faber du Faur. New Haven, Yale Univ. Pr., 1958. 496p. il. (Bibliographical ser. from the Yale University Library collections) **BD561**

" . . . an attempt to present an outline of literary history based on a catalogue of a collection of books" for the period (*ca.* 1575–1740).—*Pref.* Classified arrangement with detailed bibliographic information. Indexes of authors, composers, and illustrators.

Current

Bibliographie der deutschen Literaturwissenschaft, Bd. 1– , 1945/53– . Frankfurt am Main, Klostermann, 1957– . Biennial since 1957/58. **BD562**

Ed.: v.1, 1945/53, Hanns W. Eppelsheimer; v.2, 1954/56– , Clemens Köttelwesch.

A comprehensive bibliography of Western-language materials: books, pamphlets, articles, dissertations, reviews, etc. Basic arrangement is by literary period, with author and subject indexes.

Germanistik: internationales Referatenorgan mit bibliographischen Hinweisen. Tübingen, Niemeyer, 1960– . v.1– . Quarterly. **BD563**

1. Jahrg., Hft.1, Jan. 1960– .

An international bibliography of materials, from many countries, on German literature. Lists books, periodical articles, and analytics.

Arranged chronologically by period; some entries carry annotations. Hft.4 of each volume includes an author-subject index.

Jahresberichte für neuere deutsche Literaturgeschichte, 1890–1915. Berlin, Behr, 1892–1919. v.1–26, pt.1. **BD564**

An important annual survey, including books, pamphlets, theses, and periodical articles. Continued by:

Jahresbericht über die wissenschaftlichen Erscheinungen auf dem Gebiete der neueren deutschen Literatur, hrsg. von der Literaturarchivgesellschaft in Berlin, 1921–36/39. Berlin, de Gruyter, 1924–56. n.F., v.1–16/19. **BD565**

Continued in:

Jahresbericht für deutsche Sprache und Literatur, bearb. unter Leitung von Gerhard Marx. Berlin, Akademie-Verlag, 1960– . Bd.1– . (Deutsche Akademie der Wissenschaften zu Berlin. Inst. für Deutsche Sprache und Literatur) **BD566**

Bd.1, Bibliographie, 1940–1945. 979p.

A continuation in combined form of two bibliographical series, the *Jahresbericht über die Erscheinungen auf dem Gebiete der germanischen Philologie* (BC33) and the *Jahresbericht über die wissenschaftlichen Erscheinungen auf dem Gebiete der neueren deutschen Literatur* (BD565).

A comprehensive bibliography of books and periodical articles on German language and literature of all periods. Includes works in European languages (except Slavic) from European and American periodicals.

Classified arrangement with extensive indexes.

Manuscripts

Frels, Wilhelm. Deutsche Dichterhandschriften von 1400 bis 1900. Leipzig, Hiersemann, 1934. 382p. (Bibliographical publ. Germanic section. Modern Language Assoc. of America. v.2) **BD567**

Subtitle: Gesamtkatalog der eigenhändigen Handschriften deutscher Dichter in den Bibliotheken und Archiven Deutschlands, Österreichs, der Schweiz und der ČSR.

Translations into English

Goodnight, Scott Holland. German literature in American magazines prior to 1846. Madison, 1907. 264p. (Bull. of the Univ. of Wisconsin, no.188. Philology and literature ser., v.4, no.1) **BD568**

Includes a bibliography, arranged chronologically and by magazines, p.108–242; and index of (1) authors, and (2) magazines.

Haertel, Martin Henry. German literature in American magazines, 1846 to 1880. Madison, 1908. 188p. (Bull. of the Univ. of Wisconsin, no.263. Philology and literature ser., v.4, no.2) **BD569**

Bibliography, p.95–178; index of (1) authors, and (2) magazines.

Morgan, Bayard Quincy. A critical bibliography of German literature in English translation, 1481–1927, with supplement embracing the years 1928–1935 . . . 2d ed. compl. rev. and greatly augm. Stanford, Calif., Stanford Univ. Pr.; London, Milford, 1938. 773p. **BD570**

1st ed. 1922.

The main list contains 10,797 numbered titles, and is followed by List A, Anonyms. 587 titles; List B, Bibliographies. 50 titles; List C, Collections. 577 titles; Index of translators, p.631–90; Supplement (1928–35), p.693–773.

—— and **Hohlfeld, A. R.** German literature in British magazines, 1750–1860. Madison, Univ. of Wisconsin Pr., 1949. 364p. **BD571**

1750–1810 by Walter Roloff; 1811–1835 by Morton E. Mix; 1836–1860 by Martha Nicolai.

A chronological list of magazine references with an alphabetical list of the German authors named. Preceded by a historical introduction giving a survey of magazine reflection of the British reception of German literature, 1750–1860.

Dictionaries of authors and literature

Albrecht, Günter [et al.]. Deutsches Schriftstellerlexikon von den Anfängen bis zur Gegenwart. 2. bearb. und verb. Aufl. Weimar, Volksverlag Weimar, 1961. 651p. **BD572**

Biographical sketches, with bibliographies, of German writers from early times to the present. Includes living persons.

Brümmer, Franz. Lexikon der deutschen Dichter und Prosaisten vom Beginn des 19. Jahrhunderts bis zur Gegenwart. 6. völlig neubearb. Aufl. Leipzig, Reclam, 1913. 8v. **BD573**

A useful handbook containing brief biographical sketches and lists of works of some 9900 German, Austrian, and Swiss authors. Very strong in pseudonyms. Supplement in v.8 brings the work down to end of 1912.

Frenzel, Herbert Alfred and **Frenzel, E.** Daten deutscher Dichtung: chronologischer Abriss der deutschen Literaturgeschichte von den Anfängen bis zur Gegenwart. 2. verb. und verm. Aufl. Köln-Berlin, Kiepenheuer und Witsch, 1959. 484p. **BD574**

Arranged under broad period divisions, followed by an alphabetical list of authors of the period, and then by a chronological list of outstanding works. Brief biographical notes are given for authors, with a résumé for each title.

Giebisch, Hans, Pichler, L. and **Vancsa, K.** Kleines österreichisches Literaturlexikon. Wien, Hollinek, 1948. 548p. (Buchreihe "Österreichische Heimat," Bd.8) **BD575**

Biographical sketches of writers, titles of works, definitions and descriptions of literary expressions, etc., in one alphabet.

Kosch, Wilhelm. Deutsches Literatur-Lexikon; biographisches und bibliographisches Handbuch. 2. vollständig neubearb. und stark erw. Aufl. Bern, Francke, 1947–58. 4v. **BD576**

1st ed. 1927–30.

Primarily a dictionary of German authors of all periods. Includes living persons. Extensive bibliographies cite both original and critical works. Includes entries on literary forms, titles, allusions, places, etc.

—— Deutsches Literatur-Lexikon. Ausgabe in einem Band. Bearb. von Bruno Berger. Bern, München, Francke Verlag, 1963. 511p. **BD577**

Derived from the preceding work; consists almost entirely of biographical sketches of German writers, omitting most of the subject entries found in the larger work. The biographical articles give brief biographical facts and often extensive bibliographies, both by and about the writers. Occasional inaccuracies in dates, etc.

Kürschners deutscher Literatur-Kalender, hrsg. von Gerhard Lüdtke. Berlin, de Gruyter, 1879– . v.1– . Annual. **BD578**

Title and imprint vary.

v.39, 1917; v.40, 1922; v.41, 1924. Beginning with v.42, 1925, work is issued in two series: one continuing the *Literatur-Kalender,* the other becoming *Kürschners deutscher Gelehrten-Kalender* (AJ140).

A useful biographical record of German authors.

Kürschner Nekrolog, 1901–1935, hrsg. von Gerhard Lüdtke. Berlin, de Gruyter, 1936. 976col. **BD579**

Contents: Biographies reprinted from the *Literatur-Kalender* (BD578)—with date and place of death added— of some 3700 authors who died 1901–35; two chronological lists, arranged by years, of (1) births, and (2) deaths.

Kutzbach, Karl August. Autorenlexikon der Gegenwart. Bonn, Bouvier, 1950– . v.1– . (In progress) **BD580**

v.1, Schöne Literatur verfasst in deutscher Sprache mit einer Chronik seit 1945.

Bio-bibliographical sketches of about 1000 contemporary writers of German-language belles-lettres, with indexes by form of writing, region, religious or philosophical outlook, etc. Annual records (1945–49) of obituaries, anniversaries, awards, and foundation or reinstatement of societies and publications. A second volume was planned for writers in other fields.

Lennartz, Franz. Deutsche Dichter und Schriftsteller unserer Zeit: Einzeldarstellungen zur Schönen Literatur in deutscher Sprache. 8. erw. Aufl. Stuttgart, Kröner, 1959. 835p. (Kröners Taschenausgabe Bd.151) **BD581**

1st ed. 1938 (title varies).

Includes biographical and critical sketches, averaging two to three pages in length, with bibliographies.

Lexikon sozialistischer deutscher Literatur, von den Anfängen bis 1945; monographisch-biographische Darstellungen. Halle, Verlag Sprache und Literatur, 1963. 592p. **BD582**

An alphabetically arranged dictionary of articles on socialist writers, newspapers, collections, etc. Articles include bibliographies.

Petry, Karl. Handbuch zur deutschen Literaturgeschichte. Köln, B. Pick, 1949. 2v. **BD583**

—— —— Titel- und Namenregister, 27p., inserted at back of v.2.

A handbook of German literature from the beginning to the mid-20th century, arranged chronologically by period. Includes biographical sketches which list works by an author as well as book and periodical material about him.

Reallexikon der deutschen Literaturgeschichte, begründet von Paul Merker und Wolfgang Stammler. 2. Aufl. Berlin, de Gruyter, 1955–65. v.1–2$^{1–10}$. (In progress) **BD584**

v.1–2 [1–10], A–Ossianische Dichtung.

An alphabetically arranged dictionary with signed articles and extensive bibliographies on periods, types, schools, and kinds of German literature. No entries under personal names.

Schmitt, Fritz. Deutsche Literaturgeschichte in Tabellen. Bonn, Athenäum-Verlag, 1949–52. 3v. **BD585**

Contents: T.1, Die Literatur des Mittelalters, 750–1450; T.2, Renaissance, Barock, Klassizismus, 1450–1770; T.3, 1770 bis zur Gegenwart.

A detailed outline of German literature, giving brief biographical and bibliographical facts, with references to manuscripts, source materials, and critical studies.

Includes information on comparative literature and the influence of foreign literatures on the German.

Schneider, Max. Deutsches Titelbuch. Ein Hilfsmittel zum Nachweis von Verfassern deutscher Literaturwerke. 2. verb. und wesentlich verm. Aufl. Berlin, Paschke, 1927. 798p. **BD586**

1st edition had title *Von wem ist das doch?* 1907–9.

German titles and first lines of poems arranged alphabetically with attribution to author. Primarily of the 19th century with occasional 18th- and 20th-century titles. Index of subjects.

Schriftsteller der Deutschen Demokratischen Republik. Leipzig, Verlag für Buch- und Bibliothekswesen, 1961. 196p. **BD587**

Brief sketches of current authors, giving date and place of birth, position, address, and lists of works.

Stammler, Wolfgang. Die deutsche Literatur des Mittelalters; Verfasserlexikon; unter Mitarbeit zahlreicher Fachgenossen. Berlin, de Gruyter, 1933–55. 5v. **BD588**

Issued in parts. v.3–5, ed. by Karl Langosch.

Long, scholarly articles signed by specialists, with detailed bibliographies of works by and about German medieval authors and writings. Includes works in medieval Latin of significance in German literature, and also anonymous works.

History

Könnecke, Gustav. Bilderatlas zur Geschichte der deutschen Nationallitteratur. Eine Ergänzung zu jeder deutschen Litteraturgeschichte. 2. verb. und verm. Aufl. Marburg, Elwert, [1895]. 423p. il. **BD589**

German literature from earliest times to the end of the 19th century, depicted in illustrations and facsimiles. Includes pictures of authors—many times with autographs and samples of handwriting—biographical sketches, etc.

Drama

Allgayer, Wilhelm. Dramenlexikon: ein Wegweiser zu etwa 10,000 urheberrechtlich geschützten Bühnenwerken der Jahre 1945–1957; 1957–1960. Begründet von Friedrich Ernst Schulz. Köln, Berlin, Kiepenheuer und Witsch, 1958–62. 2v. **BD590**

Original ed., 1942, ed. by F. E. Schulz.

A listing of German plays or plays translated into German. Alphabetical by title, with various data on production and publication. Author indexes.

Gregor, Joseph. Der Schauspielführer. Stuttgart, Hiersemann, 1953–57. 6v. **BD591**

Contents: Bd.1, Das deutsche Schauspiel vom Mittelalter bis zum Expressionismus. 1953. 375p.

Bd.2, Das deutsche Schauspiel der Gegenwart; Das Schauspiel der romanischen Völker, T.1. 1954. 355p.

Bd.3, Das Schauspiel der romanischen Völker, T.2; Das niederländische Schauspiel, Das englische Schauspiel, T.1–2. 1955. 307p.

Bd.4, Das englische Schauspiel, T.3: Nordamerika; Das Schauspiel der nordischen Völker; Das Schauspiel der slavischen Völker: A, Russland; B, Ukraine. 1956. 332p.

Bd.5, Das Schauspiel der slavischen Völker: Polen, Tschechoslowakei, Kroatien, Dalmatien, Slowenien, Serbien; Das Schauspiel Ungarns und Griechenlands, des Nahen und Fernen Ostens; Die antiken dramatischen Kulturen. 1957. 323p.

Bd.6, Nachträge zu Bd.I–V; vergleichender Abriss der dramatischen Weltliteratur; Gesamtregister zu Bd.I–VI. 1957. 324p.

A guide to more than 1000 years of German drama, and German translations of foreign drama, giving outlines of individual works with critical and historical notes. Arrangement is by period or school, with indexes by author, title, and date of first publication.

Johns Hopkins University. Library. Fifty years of German drama; a bibliography of modern German drama, 1880–1930, based on the Loewenberg collection. Baltimore, Johns Hopkins Pr., 1941. 111p. **BD592**

A collection of some 3000 volumes, nearly all 1st editions.

Fiction

Luther, Arthur and **Friesenhahn, Heinz.** Land und Leute in deutscher Erzählung. Ein bibliographisches Literaturlexikon neubearb. . . . 3. gänzlich veränd. und erg. Aufl. Stuttgart, Hiersemann, 1954. 555p. **BD593**

A complete revision of Luther's *Deutsches Land in deutscher Erzählung* (2d ed. 1936) and his *Deutsche Geschichte in deutscher Erzählung* (2d ed. 1943).

In two parts: pt.1, approximately 8000 novels are listed under 440 place-names; pt.2, some 2200 novels are listed under the names of 680 historical personages.

Indexes: (1) Places; (2) Chronological list of the historical characters; and (3) Authors.

Schmitt, Franz Anselm. Beruf und Arbeit in deutscher Erzählung; ein literarisches Lexikon. Stuttgart, Hiersemann, 1952. 668col. **BD594**

German novels of the last two centuries arranged according to the protagonist's trade or profession, with alphabetical author index.

Individual authors

Goethe

Goedeke, Karl. Grundriss zur Geschichte der deutschen Dichtung aus den Quellen. 3. neubearb. Aufl. Dresden, Ehlermann, 1906–60. v.4, pts.1–5. **BD595**

An extensive bibliography on Goethe. For full information *see* BD555.

Kippenberg, Anton. Katalog der Sammlung Kippenberg. 2. Ausg. Leipzig, Insel-Verlag, 1928. 2v. and index. il. **BD596**

Includes Goethe manuscripts, editions, translations, etc.

Pyritz, Hans. Goethe-Bibliographie . . . unter redaktioneller Mitarbeit von Paul Raabe. Heidelberg, Carl Winter, 1955–64. Lfg. 1–9. (In progress) **BD597**

Classified listing of scholarly materials useful for Goethe research, more selective than Goedeke (BD555). Includes books, parts of books, articles, theses, etc., with excellent bibliographic information and some brief annotations.

Yale University. Library. William A. Speck Collection of Goetheana. Goethe's works with the exception of Faust; a catalogue comp. by members of the Yale University Library Staff, ed., arr., and supplied with literary notes and preceded by an introduction and a biographical sketch of William A. Speck by Carl Frederick Schreiber. . . . New Haven, Yale Univ. Pr., 1940. 239p. facsim. **BD598**

The first volume of a comprehensive catalog of the William A. Speck collection of Goetheana. As planned, v.2 was to contain the record of the material on Faust; v.3, biographical material; and v.4, addenda and general index.

Goethe. 1. Bd., 1936– . Weimar, Böhlaus, 1936– . **BD599**

Frequency varies; subtitle varies. None published 1945–46. "Neue Folge des Jahrbuchs der Goethe-Gesellschaft." Supplements, with the title *Goethe-Bibliographie,* accompany each issue, 1952/53–.

Fischer, Paul. Goethe-Wortschatz, ein sprachgeschichtliches Wörterbuch zu Goethes sämtlichen Werken. Leipzig, E. Rohmkopf, 1929. 905p. **BD600**

Goethe-Handbuch: Goethe, seine Welt und Zeit in Werk und Wirkung. 2. vollkommen neugestaltete Aufl. unter Mitwirkung zahlreicher Fachgelehrter, hrsg. von Alfred Zastrau. Stuttgart, Metzler, 1955–61. v.1, v.4. **BD601**

v.1, Aachen–Farbenlehre (issued in 14 Lfg.).
v.4, Karten der Reisen Goethes (Index and maps in portfolio).
A new and considerably expanded reworking of the 1916–18 edition by Julius Zeitler. Signed articles with bibliographies.

Hegel

Glockner, Hermann. Hegel-Lexikon. 2. verb. Aufl. Stuttgart, Frommann, 1957. 2v. (Added title page: Georg Wilhelm Friedrich Hegel. Sämtliche Werke. Jubiläumsausgabe . . . 23.–26. Bd.) **BD602**

1st ed. 1935–39. 4v.

Heine

Arnold, Armin. Heine in England and America; a bibliographical check-list. London, Linden Pr., 1959. 80p. **BD603**

Aims "to provide an adequate bibliography of the English translations of Heine and of English and American criticism of Heine."—*Pref.*

Wilhelm, Gottfried. Heine Bibliographie. Unter Mitarbeit von Eberhard Galley. Weimar, Arion Verlag, 1960. 2v. **BD604**

Contents: T.I, Primärliteratur, 1817–1953. 191p.; T.II, Sekundärliteratur, 1822–1953. 294p.
T.I lists 2011 numbered items (including translations of Heine's writings); T.II lists 4032 items relating to the man and his work. The volumes are separately indexed.

Kafka

Järv, Harry. Die Kafka-Literatur; eine Bibliographie. Malmö, Lund, Bo Cavefors Verlag, 1961. 380p. **BD605**

An extensive listing by author of books and articles about Kafka in many languages. Supplementary lists of lectures on Kafka; Swedish translations of his works; and indexes of persons, titles, and journals mentioned.

Mann

Burgin, Hans. Das Werk Thomas Manns: eine Bibliographie unter Mitarbeit von Walter A. Reichart und Erich Neumann. Frankfurt am Main, S. Fischer Verlag, 1959. 319p. **BD606**

Lists editions, translations, contributions to periodicals in various languages, and a few special items such as drawings and records. Does not include works about Mann.

Jonas, Klaus W. Fifty years of Thomas Mann studies; a bibliography of criticism. Minneapolis, Univ. of Minn. Pr., 1955. 217p. **BD607**

Lists 3010 books, articles, and dissertations in various languages.

Schiller

Vulpius, Wolfgang. Schiller Bibliographie, 1893–1958. Weimar, Arion Verlag, 1959. 569p. (Weimar. Nationale Forschungs- und Gedenkstätten der Klassischen Deutschen Literatur. Bibliographien, Kataloge und Bestandsverzeichnis) **BD608**

Lists some 1800 citations for Schiller's works and more than 5500 books, articles, and dissertations about him.

London. University. Institute of Germanic Languages and Literatures. Schiller in England, 1787–1960, comp. under the direction of R. Pick. Leeds, Maney, 1961. 127p. (Publications of the English Goethe Society, n.s. v.30, 1961) **BD609**

Includes texts, translations, and critical and biographical accounts in books and periodicals.

Rudolph, Ludwig. Schiller-Lexikon; erläuterndes Wörterbuch zu Schiller's Dichterwerken, unter Mitwirkung von Karl Goldbeck. 2. Ausg. Berlin, Nicolay, 1890. 2v. **BD610**

Scandinavian

See also under the four individual languages following: Danish, Icelandic, Norwegian, Swedish.

Arntz, Helmut. Bibliographie der Runenkunde: mit Unterstützung des Archäologischen Instituts des Deutschen Reiches. Leipzig, Harrassowitz, 1937. 293p. **BD611**

Zeitschriften und (bio)- bibliographische Hilfsmittel, p.265–76.
An extensive bibliography of materials in various languages on runic antiquities, inscriptions, etc. in Scandinavia, Iceland, England, and other places.

Bibliography of Old Norse-Icelandic studies, 1963– . v.1– . Copenhagen, Munksgaard, 1964– . **BD612**

Annual.
Selective bibliography catering to the interests of students "of Old Norse language and literature, medieval Norwegian and Icelandic history and related subjects."—*Pref.* Arrangement is alphabetical by author with a subject index. Preface and introductory essay in English.

Marquardt, Hertha. Bibliographie der Runeninschriften nach Fundorten. Hrsg. von Skandinavischen Seminar der Universität Göttingen im Auftrag von Wolfgang Krause. Göttingen, Vandenhoeck und Ruprecht, 1961. T.1– . (Abhandlungen der Akademie der Wissenschaften in Göttingen. Phil.-Hist. Kl., 3. Folge, Nr.48) (In progress) **BD613**

1. T., Die Runeninschriften der Britischen Inseln. 168p.
An extensive bibliography of articles and books on runic inscriptions and allied archaeological remains. This first volume deals with the British Isles.

Hollander, Lee Milton. A bibliography of skaldic studies. Copenhagen, Munksgaard, 1958. 117p. **BD614**

Lists editions and collections of skaldic verse, as well as books and articles about it. Index of authors, editors, and translators.

Nordische Bibliographie, hrsg. von dem Nordischen Institut der Universität Greifswald. I. Reihe, Norwegen; II. Reihe, Schweden. Braunschweig, Westermann, 1928–31. v.1$^{1-3}$–2^1. **BD615**

Contents: I. Reihe, Norwegen: 1. Hft., Ibsen-Bibliographie, bearb. von Fritz Meyen. 1928; 2. Hft., Norwegische Literatur (ausser Ibsen), bearb. von Fritz Meyen. 1928; 3. Hft., Hamsun-Bibliographie, bearb. von Fritz Meyen. 1931; II. Reihe, Schweden: 1. Hft., Lagerlöf-Bibliographie. 1930.

No more published.

Ehrencron-Müller, Holger. Forfatterlexikon omfattende Danmark, Norge og Island indtil 1814. København, Aschehoug, 1924–39. v.1–12; Suppl. 2.   **BD616**

v.1–8, A–Weg; v.9, Wei–Ø. Supplement; v.10–12, Bibliografi over Holbergs Skrifter. Supplement 2. The latter includes corrections and additions to all volumes including the Holberg bibliography.

An authoritative work, giving brief biographical data and full lists of writings for each author. Similar in plan to the dictionaries by Erslew (BD622) and Halvorsen (BD628), and linked to those two works by cross references in the case of many authors whose activity extended into the period after 1814.

Blankner, Frederika. The history of the Scandinavian literatures . . . based in part on the work of Giovanni Bach with additional sections by Richard Beck, Adolph B. Benson, Axel Johan Uppvall and others. N.Y., Dial, 1938. 407p.   **BD617**

Subtitle: A survey of the literatures of Norway, Sweden, Denmark, Iceland and Finland, from their origins to the present day, including Scandinavian-American authors, and selected bibliographies.

The sections on Norwegian, Swedish, and Danish literature are based on the work of Giovanni Bach, translated and enlarged by Frederika Blankner. Other sections are by other specialists.

Selected bibliographies of books and articles, especially in English, p.321–78.

Danish

Bibliography

Bredsdorff, Elias. Danish literature in English translation; with a special Hans Christian Andersen supplement: a bibliography. Copenhagen, Munksgaard, 1950. 198p.   **BD618**

Covers translations of Danish literature into English from 1533 to 1949 and also lists materials in English about Danish literature.

The Supplement, p.119–98, is "A bibliography of Hans Christian Andersen's works in English translation, and of books and articles relating to H. C. Andersen."

Elkjaer, Kjeld, Haraldsted, Ib [and others]. Skønlitteratur i danske Tidsskrifter, 1913–1942; en Bibliografi. København, Folkebibliotekernes Bibliografiske Kontor, 1946. 236p.   **BD619**

Largely devoted to Danish literature, but also includes references to articles that have appeared in Danish periodicals on foreign literatures.

Mitchell, Philip Marshall. A bibliographical guide to Danish literature. Copenhagen, Munksgaard, 1951. 62p.   **BD620**

A bibliography intended to indicate the most important works of Danish literature, literary history, and criticism, showing standard editions, translations, biographical and critical works, etc. The works considered most significant are starred.

Dictionaries of authors

Dansk skønlitteraert Forfatterleksikon, 1900–1950. Bibliografisk red., Svend Dahl; Medredaktører, Ludvig

Bramsen og Mogens Haugsted; Biografisk red., Povl Engelstoft. København, Grønholt Pedersen, 1959–64. 3v.   **BD621**

A bio-bibliographical dictionary which treats some 3500 20th-century Danish literary figures. The bibliographies, though presented in abbreviated form, appear to be very comprehensive. Data are meant to be complete through 1950, with some later listings.

Erslew, Thomas Hansen. Almindeligt Forfatter-Lexicon for Kongeriget Danmark med tilhørende Bilande, fra 1814 til 1840. Kjøbenhavn, Forlagsforeningens Forlag, 1843–53. 3v.   **BD622**

—— —— Supplement . . . indtil Udgangen of Aaret 1853. Kjøbenhavn, 1858–68. 3v.

An older, but still standard, dictionary giving biographical sketches of Danish authors with bibliographies, for the period 1814–53.

Woel, Cai Mogens. Dansk Forfatterleksikon; 338 Biografier over nulevende danske Forfattere. [København], Nordiske Landes Bogforlag, 1945. 360p. il.   **BD623**

Biographical sketches with bibliographies of living authors.

History

Petersen, Carl Sophus and **Andersen, Vilhelm.** Illustreret dansk Litteraturhistorie. Kjøbenhavn, Gyldendal, 1924– 34. 4v. il.   **BD624**

v.1, 1929; v.2, 1934; v.3, 1924; v.4, 1925. Issued in parts.

Planned as a 3d revised edition of Peter Hansen's *Illustreret dansk Litteraturhistorie*, the standard illustrated history of Danish literature, with extensive bibliographies at the end of each volume.

Icelandic

See also Iceland, p.50.

Hall, Gunnar. Bókaskrá Gunnars Hall. Catalogue of the library of Gunnar Hall. Akureyri, Prentad i Prentsmidju Björns Jónssonar, 1956. 520p.   **BD625**

A classified listing of an extensive collection of Icelandic and Old Norse literature.

Hermannsson, Halldór. Icelandic authors of today; with an appendix giving a list of works dealing with modern Icelandic literature. Ithaca, Cornell Univ. Lib., 1913. 69p. (Islandica, v.6)   **BD626**

An excellent small biographical dictionary in English for authors of some importance who were living at the time of writing. Gives biographical data, list of works, and references to books or periodicals containing fuller information.

Norwegian

Bibliography

Øksnevad, Reidar. Norsk litteraturhistorisk bibliografi, 1900–1945. Oslo, Gyldendal Norsk Forlag, 1951. 378p.   **BD627**

—— —— 1946–1955. 1958. 139p.

A bibliography of books and periodical articles in various languages published in the 20th century on Norwegian literature and authors.

Dictionaries of authors

Halvorsen, Jens Braage. Norsk forfatter-lexikon, 1814– 1880. Paa grundlag af J. E. Krafts og Chr. Langes "Norsk forfatter-lexikon 1814–1856" samlet, redig. og udg. med understøttelse af statskassen. Kristiania, Norske Forlagsforening, 1885–1908. 6v. **BD628**

Biographical sketches with bibliographies of Norwegian authors. Preceded in time by Ehrencron-Müller (BD616).

History

Elster, Kristian. Illustreret norsk litteratur historie. 2. utg. Oslo, Gyldendal, 1934–35. 6v. il. **BD629**

A standard illustrated history with bio-bibliographies.

Swedish

Bibliography

Svensk litteraturhistorisk bibliografi, 1900–1935. Uppsala, Svenska Litteratursällskapet, 1939–50. 522p. (Skrifter utg. af Svenska Litteratursällskapet) **BD630**

Classed catalog. A cumulation of the material for 1900–1935 appearing in the following annual, with author index:

Svensk litteraturhistorisk bibliografi, no.1, 1880– . (Issued as a separately paged supplement to *Samlaren: Tidskrift för svensk litteraturhistorisk forskning,* 1880–) **BD631**

An annual classified bibliography.

Dictionaries of authors

Ahlén, Bengt. Svenskt författarlexikon, 1900–1940: bio-bibliografisk handbok till Sveriges moderna litteratur. . . . Stockholm, Svenskt Författarlexikons Förlag, 1942. 3v. portraits. **BD632**

v.1–2 are an alphabetical biographical dictionary with brief biographical sketches and lists of works by and about the authors. v.3 is a title index to works mentioned in the first 2v.

—— —— 1941–1950. Stockholm, Rabén och Sjögrens Förlag, 1953. 690p. portraits.

Runnquist, Åke. Moderna svenska författare. Stockholm, Forum, 1959. 176p. il. **BD633**

Brief biographical sketches of modern Swedish writers grouped by period—authors of prominence in the thirties, the forties, and the fifties—with an alphabetical name index.

Svenskt litteraturlexikon. Lund, Gleerup, 1964. 620p. **BD634**

A handbook offering biographical sketches of Swedish authors together with definitions of literary terms. Some articles include bibliographical references. Contains an index of titles mentioned in the biographical sketches.

History

Böök, Fredrik, Castrén, Gunnar [and others]. Svenska litteraturens historia. Ny omarb. uppl. Stockholm, Norstedt, 1929. 3v. il. **BD635**

A general history with bibliographies.

Ny illustrerad svensk litteraturhistoria. Huvudredaktör, E. N. Tigerstedt. Stockholm, Natur och Kultur, 1955–58. 5v. **BD636**

Contents: v.1–4, From early times through the 19th century; v.5, Four decades of the 20th century, by Erik Hjalmar Linder. 3. bearb. och utökade uppl.

A new illustrated history of Swedish literature designed to supersede the standard *Illustrerad svensk litteraturhistoria* by Henrik Schück and Karl Warburg (3. uppl. 1926–32. 7v.**).**

The new work is completely rewritten, each section by a specialist, with substantial bibliographies at the end of each

volume. v.5, covering 1900–1940, was first published in 1949 (2d ed. 1952) as an 8th volume to Schück and Warburg. The 3d edition is considerably revised.

Sveriges national-litteratur, 1500–1900, planlagdt af Oscar Levertin, utg. af Henrik Schück och Ruben G:son Berg. Stockholm, Bonnier, [1907–19]. v.1–25$^{1-2}$. il. **BD637**

An extensive collection of prose, poetical, and dramatic selections, with biographies of some of the authors represented. The arrangement is roughly chronological, some volumes being devoted to only one author, others including a number of authors. The lack of a general index makes the set difficult to use for quick reference.

ROMANCE LANGUAGES

General works

Guides

Palfrey, Thomas Rossman, Fucilla, Joseph Guerin and **Holbrook, William Collar.** A bibliographical guide to the Romance languages and literatures. 5th ed. Evanston, Ill., Chandler, 1963. 122p. **BD638**

1st ed. 1939.

Contents: (1) General Romance bibliography; (2) French language and literature (including Provençal, French-Swiss, Belgian); (3) Italian; (4) Portuguese and Brazilian; (5) Spanish, Catalan, Spanish-American; (6) Roumanian.

Bibliography

Hatzfeld, Helmut. Bibliografía crítica de la nueva estilística, aplicada a las literaturas románicas. Madrid, Ed. Gredos, 1955. 660p. (Biblioteca románica hispánica. I. Tratados y monografías. 6) **BD639**

A survey bibliography of style investigation, treating general studies, stylistic comparison, the language of individual authors, history of style, theory of style, and many specialized aspects of stylistics. Two indexes: (1) style investigators; and (2) proper names, titles, problems, terms, etc.

The 1st edition in English was entitled *A critical bibliography of the new stylistics applied to the Romance literatures,* 1900–1952. Chapel Hill, N.C., 1953. 302p. This Spanish version is equivalent to a considerably expanded 2d edition.

—— and **LeHir, Yves.** Essai de bibliographie critique de stylistique française et romane (1955–1960). Paris, Presses Universitaires de France, 1961. 313p. (Université de Grenoble. Faculté des Lettres et Sciences Humaines. 26) **BD640**

Serves as a supplement to the above, covering publications of the years 1955–60.

Belgian writers
(French)

Charlier, Gustave and **Hanse, Joseph.** Histoire illustrée des lettres françaises de Belgique. Bruxelles, Renaissance du Livre, 1958. 656p. il. **BD641**

A lavishly illustrated history of the literature of Belgium, in French, from the earliest times to the present day. Chapters are written by specialists and include bibliographies.

Culot, Jean-Marie. Bibliographie des écrivains français de Belgique, 1881–1950. Bruxelles, Palais des Académies, 1958– . v.1– . (Academie Royale de Langue et de Littérature Françaises de Belgique) (In progress) **BD642**

v.1 contains two introductory sections: (1) Ouvrages d'histoire littéraire et de critique d'une portée générale ou relatifs à plusieurs écrivains, 1880–1950, p.1–29; (2) Anthologies et ouvrages collectifs, p.31–65. These are followed by the alphabetical author list, A–Destrée, p.67–304.

Planned to continue the *Bibliographie nationale* (AA373) for writers on literature.

For each writer gives: dates, works by, and periodicals and collections to which he has contributed, with a list of works to consult.

Doutrepont, Georges. Histoire illustrée de la littérature française en Belgique; précis méthodique. Bruxelles, Didier, 1939. 398p. il. **BD643**

Includes many bio-bibliographies.

Dumont-Wilden, Louis. Anthologie des écrivains belges, poètes et prosateurs. Paris, Georges Crès, 1917. 2v. il. **BD644**

Gives prose and poetical selections from Belgian authors who wrote in French, and biographies and bibliographies of authors included.

Hanlet, Camille. Les écrivains belges contemporains de langue française, 1800–1946. Liége, Dessain, 1946. 2v. (1302p.). il. **BD645**

An extensive survey of all Belgian authors writing in French from the 18th century to 1946. The length of the biography and critical annotation varies from a few lines to several pages. For many writers, bibliographies of works about the person are included.

Seyn, Eugène de. Dictionnaire des écrivains belges, bio-bibliographie. Bruges, Éd. "Excelsior," 1930–31. 2v. il. **BD646**

Includes bio-bibliographical sketches of writers considered to be Belgian, from early to modern times. Gives little or no bibliography about the writers.

Canadian writers

(French)

See also English Language—Canadian p.258.

British Columbia. University. Library. A check list of printed materials relating to French Canadian literature. Liste de référence d'imprimés relatifs à la littérature canadienne-française, [par] Gerard Tougas. Vancouver, Canada, 1958. 93p. **BD647**

Arranged alphabetically by author; lists novels, poetry, drama, short stories, chronicles, literary criticism, and biographies dealing with authors; parliamentary oratory; travelers' chronicles; and folklore. Excludes history, philosophy, and pulpit oratory.

Represents the holdings of the University of British Columbia library.

Drolet, Antonio. Bibliographie du roman canadien-français, 1900–1950. Québec, Presses Universitaires de Laval, 1955. 125p. **BD648**

An author listing of 886 titles of French-Canadian novels, preceded by a list of critical studies on the subject. Title index.

French

Guides

Langlois, Pierre and **Mareuil, André.** Guide bibliographique des études littéraires. Éd. rev. et augm. d'un appendice: Contribution de la critique étrangère. Paris, Hachette, 1960. 254p., xxxiip. **BD649**

1st ed. 1958.

A manual and guide prepared especially for small colleges in France, dealing with French literature from the Middle Ages to the 20th century, preceded by a chapter on classical authors.

Sources

Gallet-Guerne, Danielle. Les sources de l'histoire littéraire aux Archives Nationales. Paris, Impr. Nationale, 1961. 161p. **BD650**

At head of title: Ministère d'État Chargé des Affaires Culturelles. Direction des Archives de France. Archives Nationales.

A guide to the manuscript materials concerning French authors to be found in the various archives.

Bibliography

General

Critical bibliography of French literature; David C. Cabeen, gen. ed. Syracuse, Syracuse Univ. Pr., 1947–61. v.1–4. (In progress) **BD651**

Contents: v.1, Urban T. Holmes. The mediaeval period. 1947 (enl. ed. 1952). 256p.; v.2, Alexander H. Schutz. The sixteenth century. 1956. 365p.; v.3, Nathan Edelman. The seventeenth century. 1961. 638p.; v.4, George R. Havens and Donald F. Bond. The eighteenth century. 1951. 411p.

With v.3, Jules Brody became joint general editor.

A selective, evaluative, and annotated bibliography compiled by contributing specialists. Arranged by chronological periods; lists books, dissertations, and periodical articles, with references to reviews. Of first importance.

Giraud, Jeanne. Manuel de bibliographie littéraire pour les XVIᵉ, XVIIᵉ et XVIIIᵉ siècles français, 1921–1935. 2. éd., conforme à la première. Paris, Vrin, 1958. 304p. (Publications de la Faculté des Lettres de l'Université de Lille, II) **BD652**

Reprint of work originally pub. 1939.

——— 1936–1945. Paris, Nizet, 1956. 270p.

Designed to serve as a supplement, for works published during these periods, to Lanson (BD655) and to Thieme (BD672).

Golden, Herbert Hershel and **Simches, Seymour O.** Modern French literature and language; a bibliography of homage studies. Cambridge, Harvard Univ. Pr., 1953. 158p. **BD653**

Indexes articles in *Festschriften* and homage volumes, with chief emphasis on studies dealing with French language and literature from 1500 to the present.

The first section lists the 309 homage volumes indexed.

Klapp, Otto. Bibliographie der französischen Literaturwissenschaft. Bd.1, 1956/58– . Frankfurt am Main, Klostermann, 1960– . v.1– . Biennial. **BD654**

Added title page in French: Bibliographie d'histoire littéraire française; introduction and headings in French.

Planned as a companion to H. W. Eppelsheimer, *Bibliographie der deutschen Literaturwissenschaft* (BD554a), this work interprets French literature in a broad sense. Lists books, articles, and theses published during the period covered, analyzing in each volume some 400 periodicals and more than 150 collections. Arrangement is chronological, from the Middle Ages to the 20th century, with indexes by name and by subject.

Lanson, Gustave. Manuel bibliographique de la littérature française moderne, XVIᵉ, XVIIᵉ, XVIIIᵉ, et XIXᵉ siècles. Nouv. éd., rev. et augm. Paris, Hachette, 1921. 1820p. **BD655**

1st ed. in 5v. 1909–12; rev. ed. with suppl., 1v. 1914.

1746p. The 1921 edition contains a brief section on the beginning of the 20th century and the *"Littérature de la guerre."*

An important bibliography of French literature—selective, not complete—comprising more than 23,000 entries. Indexes a considerable amount of analytical material including articles from more than 800 periodicals.

For continuation *see* Giraud (BD652).

Rudel, Yves-Marie. Panorama de la littérature bretonne des origines à nos jours, écrivains de langue bretonne et de langue française. Rennes, Impr. Bretonne, 1950. 154p.   **BD656**

A brief survey of the writers of the literature of Brittany, giving bio-bibliographical sketches of both those who have written in the Breton language and those who have written in French.

Medieval

Bédier, Joseph. Les légendes épiques; recherches sur la formation des chansons de geste . . . 3. éd. . . . Paris, Champion, 1926–29. 4v. il.   **BD657**

A history of the *chansons de geste* with bibliographical references. Gives descriptions of texts and discusses modern theories of the origins of the *chansons*.

Bossuat, Robert. Manuel bibliographique de la littérature française du Moyen Âge. Melun, Librairie d'Argences, 1951. 635p. (Bibliothèque Elzévirienne. Nouv. sér. Études et documents)   **BD658**

A bibliographical manual of the French literature of the Middle Ages, listing material in French and other western European languages. After an introduction giving general works, the book is divided into two sections: *L'ancien français* and *Le moyen français*. For each work, the principal editions are listed, followed by translations and adaptations, and critical works. The latter include both books and periodical articles.

—— —— Supplément, 1949–1953, avec le concours de Jacques Monfrin. 1955. 150p.

—— —— 2d supplément, 1954–1960. 1961. 132p.

Flutre, Fernand. Table des noms propres avec toutes leurs variantes figurant dans les romans du Moyen Âge écrits en français ou en provençal et actuellement publiés ou analysés. Poitiers, Centre d'Études Supérieures de Civilisation Médiévale, 1962. 324p. (Publications du C.E.S.C.M., II)   **BD659**

A listing of proper names, in their variant forms, appearing in medieval romances written in French and Provençal, in two parts: (1) personal names, and (2) geographic, including ethnic, names. Gives citations to texts and a bibliography of the editions used.

Gautier, Léon. Bibliographie des chansons de geste. (Complément des Épopées françaises) Paris, Welter, 1897. 315p.   **BD660**

Forms v.5 of the author's *Les épopées françaises* (BD686).

A valuable comprehensive bibliography in two parts. The first part is a classed list of general works; the second is devoted to works about individual *chansons*.

Jeanroy, Alfred. Bibliographie sommaire des chansonniers français du Moyen Âge (manuscrits et éditions). Paris, Champion, 1918. 75p. (Les classiques français du Moyen Âge)   **BD661**

Issued as a complement to Raynaud (BD663). Pt.1 lists manuscripts with brief descriptions and bibliographical references; pt.2 lists printed editions. The appendix gives additions and corrections to Raynaud.

Langlois, Ernest. Table des noms propres de toute nature compris dans les chansons de geste imprimées. Paris, Bouillon, 1904. 674p.   **BD662**

A useful list of personal and geographical names arranged in one alphabet.

Raynaud, Gaston. Bibliographie des chansonniers français des XIIIe et XIVe siècles. Paris, Vieweg, 1884. 2v.   **BD663**

v.1 lists manuscripts with brief descriptions; v.2 lists individual poems in alphabetical order of rhymes, giving references to manuscripts.

Woledge, Brian. Bibliographie des romans et nouvelles en prose française antérieurs à 1500. Genève, Droz, 1954. 180p. (Société de Publications Romanes et Françaises sous la direction de Mario Roques, XLII)   **BD664**

Lists 190 early French romances, with indication of manuscripts, printings, sources, etc. Supplementary lists of manuscripts are arranged by city, printers, authors, titles, literary themes, etc.

16th–18th centuries

Cioranescu, Alexandre. Bibliographie de la littérature française du seizième siècle. Collaboration et préface de V.-L. Saulnier. Paris, Klincksieck, 1959. 745p.   **BD665**

In two parts: (1) *Généralités,* and (2) individual authors. Pt.2, the larger section, is arranged alphabetically by 16th-century author, listing works by him followed by a record of studies about him, including books and articles published through 1950. The explanation of the coverage of the index should be noted. In general, it includes the names of authors or persons *not* included in alphabetical order in the main work, names of places, anonymous works, literary themes, etc. It does not index the main entries for 16th-century works or the names of the modern authors of books and periodical articles.

Will, Samuel F. A bibliography of American studies on the French Renaissance (1500–1600). Urbana, Univ. of Illinois Pr., 1940. 151p. (Illinois studies in language and literature, v.26, no.2)   **BD666**

Includes books and periodical articles, published in America or by Americans from 1886 to 1937, on France in the 16th century. 1895 items.

Bibliography of French seventeenth century studies, 1953– . Pub. for the French III Committee, Modern Language Assoc. of America, Bloomington, Ind., 1953– . Annual.   **BD667**

Lists books and articles.

Escoffier, Maurice. Le mouvement romantique, 1788–1850: essai de bibliographie synchronique et méthodique. Paris, Maison du Bibliophile, 1934. 428p.   **BD668**

Arranged chronologically. Under each year works are listed by type: poetry, fiction, religion, philosophy, history, science, etc. Indexes of authors, anonymous works, collections and keepsakes, periodicals, and binders.

19th and 20th centuries

Flasche, Hans. Die Sprachen und Literaturen der Romanen im Spiegel der deutschen Universitätsschriften, 1885–1950; eine Bibliographie. Bonn, Bouvier, 1958. 299p. (Bonner Beiträge zur Bibliotheks- und Bücherkunde, Bd.3)   **BD669**

In German, French, and English.

Published also by the Bibliographical Society of the University of Virginia under the title *Romance languages and literatures as presented in German doctoral dissertations, 1885–1950; a bibliography.*

A listing of more than 4600 German dissertations, in classified arrangement with author and subject indexes.

A companion volume to Mummendey (BD315).

Lachèvre, Frédéric. Bibliographie sommaire des keepsakes et autres recueils collectifs de la période romantique,

1823–1848. Paris, Giraud-Badin, 1929. 2v. (Les bibliographies nouvelles. Collection du Bulletin du bibliophile) **BD670**

A bibliography of French keepsakes or gift books, which include the early writings of many authors (often difficult to find elsewhere), with comprehensive indexes by title and by author.

✓✓ **Talvart, Hector** and **Place, Joseph.** Bibliographie des auteurs modernes de langue française (1801–1962). Paris, Éd. de la Chronique des Lettres Françaises, 1928–1964. v.1–15. (In progress) **BD671**

v.1–15, A–Mirbeau.

An invaluable bibliography of French authors, planned on a large scale. Arranged alphabetically by author, giving generally for each: (1) a biographical sketch; (2) list of writings and editions; (3) minor literary works, i.e., addresses, prefaces, journals edited, etc.; and (4) lists of biographical and critical works and articles about the author, including a large amount of analytical material.

Each volume comprises material published up to the year of its publication, i.e., v.1 covers 1801–1927; v.15, 1801–1962.

✓ **Thieme, Hugo Paul.** Bibliographie de la littérature française de 1800 à 1930. . . . Paris, E. Droz, 1933. 3v. **BD672**

1st ed. 1907.
v.1–2, A–Z; v.3, Civilization.

An important reference bibliography, arranged alphabetically by author, listing both works by an author and extensive bibliographies of biographical and critical material about him. v.3 lists books and articles on the history of the language, literature, and culture of France.

See also Giraud (BD652).

Continued by:

✓ **Dreher, Silpelitt** and **Rolli, Madeline.** Bibliographie de la littérature française, 1930–1939. Complément à la Bibliographie de H. P. Thieme. Genève, Droz, 1948–49. 438p. **BD673**

Includes material published 1930–39 on the authors treated by Thieme (BD672).

Continued by:

✓ **Drevet, Marguerite L.** Bibliographie de la littérature française, 1940–1949. Complément à la Bibliographie de H. P. Thieme. Genève, Droz, 1954–55. 644p. **BD674**

✓ **French VI bibliography:** Critical and biographical references for the study of nineteenth-century French literature. 1954/55– . N.Y.?, 1956– . (Modern Language Assoc. of America. French VI) Biennial. **BD675**

Title varies. Frequency varies.
Patterned on *French VII* (BD677). v.1, no.4, covers 1958–61. Lists books and periodical articles by: (1) General subjects; (2) Author-subjects.

✓ **Alden, Douglas W., Jasper, G. R.** and **Waterman, R. P.** Bibliography of critical and biographical references for the study of contemporary French literature. Books and articles published from 1940 to 1948. N.Y., Stechert-Hafner, 1949. 106p. (Modern Language Assoc. of America. French VII, Publ. no.1) **BD676**

A very useful bibliography of material on 20th-century French literature. In two parts: pt.1, General subjects in a classified arrangement; pt.2, Author-subjects arranged alphabetically.

Includes both books and periodical articles.

Continued by annual supplements as follows:

French VII bibliography: critical and biographical references for the study of contemporary French literature. N.Y., Stechert-Hafner, 1949– . (Modern Language Assoc. of America. French VII, Publ.2–) Annual (noncumulative). **BD677**

v.1, 1949–1953; v.2, 1954–1958. General index to v.1–2; v.3, 1959–1963.

Arranged in same manner as basic volume. Items are numbered consecutively throughout, and cross references by item number link materials under author's names and those under subject fields.

Translations

Fromm, Hans. Bibliographie deutscher Übersetzungen aus dem Französischen, 1700–1948. Baden-Baden, Verlag für Kunst und Wissenschaft, 1950–53. 6v. **BD678**

For full record *see* AA90.

Dictionaries and handbooks

Boisdeffre, Pierre de. Dictionnaire de littérature contemporaine, [par] R. M. Albérès, [pseud., et al.]. Nouv. éd. mise à jour. Paris, Éd. Universitaires, 1963. 687p. **BD679**

1. éd. 1962.

Bio-bibliographies of 20th-century French writers, preceded by several introductory chapters on various literary forms and movements.

Braun, Sidney David. Dictionary of French literature. N.Y., Philosophical Lib., 1958. 362p. il. **BD680**

In alphabetical order; gives biographical sketches of authors, brief digests of important works, surveys of literary genres and movements, definitions of literary terms, and articles on language. Covers French literature from the earliest times to the contemporary period.

✓ **Dictionnaire des lettres françaises,** publié sous la direction du Cardinal Georges Grente. Paris, Arthème Fayard, 1951–64. [v.1–4] (In progress) **BD681**

Contents: Le Moyen Âge. 1964. 765p.; Le seizième siècle. 1951. 718p.; Le dix-septième siècle. 1954. 1030p.; Le dix-huitième siècle. 1960. 2v.

Each period alphabetically arranged. This scholarly dictionary includes articles, varying from a few lines to several pages, on persons, academies, universities, and literary subjects. Articles are signed and contain extensive bibliographies of the works of authors and of materials to consult about persons or subjects.

Harvey, Sir Paul and **Heseltine, Janet E.** The Oxford companion to French literature. Oxford, Clarendon Pr., 1959. 771p. **BD682**

Covers French literature from medieval times to approximately 1939, in the manner of other Oxford *Companions,* including: (1) articles on authors, critics, historians, religious writers, savants, scientists, etc.; (2) articles on individual works, allusions, places, and institutions; and (3) general survey articles on phases or aspects of French literary life, movements, etc.

Pingaud, Bernard. Écrivains d'aujourd'hui, 1940–1960. Dictionnaire anthologique et critique. Paris, Grasset, 1960. 539p. il. **BD683**

Gives brief biographical sketches, brief bibliographies of works by the authors, two or three pages of extracts of writings, and sometimes a few references to works about the writers.

History

✓ **Bédier, Joseph** and **Hazard, Paul.** Littérature française. Nouv. éd. ref. et augm. sous la direction de Pierre Martino. Paris, Larousse, 1948–49. 2v. il. **BD684**

1st edition, 1923, had title *Histoire de la littérature française illustrée.* This edition thoroughly revised and reset. Lavishly illustrated.

Calvet, J. Histoire de la littérature française. Paris, de Gigord, 1955–64. v.1–10. il. (In progress) **BD685**

Contents: v.1, Le Moyen Âge, par Robert Bossuat. 1955; v.2, La Renaissance, par Raoul Morçay and Armand Müller. 1960; v.3, Le préclassicisme, d'après Raoul Morçay, par Pierre Sage. 1962; v.4, Les écrivains classiques, par H. Gaillard de Champris. 1960; v.5, La littérature religieuse de François de Sales à Fénelon, par J. Calvet. 1956; v.6, De Télémaque à Candide, par Albert Cherel. 1958; v.7, De Candide à Atala, par Henri Berthaut. 1958; v.8, Le romantisme, par Pierre Moreau. 1957; v.9, Le réalisme et le naturalisme, par René Dumesnil. 1955; v.10, Les lettres contemporains, par Louis Chaigne. 1964.

Originally published 1931–38; all volumes have been revised, some completely rewritten. A valuable survey from the Catholic point of view, with much bibliography.

Gautier, Léon. Les épopées françaises. Étude sur les origines et l'histoire de la littérature nationale. 2. éd., entièrement refondue. Paris, Palme, 1878–97. 5v.
BD686

Contents: t.1–2, 1. pt., Origine et histoire; t.3–4, 2. pt., Légende et héros. Livre 1, Geste du roi. Livre 2, Geste de Guillaume; t.5, Bibliographie des chansons de geste.
A documented history of first importance.

Godefroy, Frédéric Eugène. Histoire de la littérature française depuis le 16ᵉ siècle jusqu'à nos jours. 2. éd. Paris, Gaume, 1878–1881. 10v.
BD687

A standard 19th-century history.

Histoire littéraire de la France; ouvrage commencé par des religieux bénédictins de la Congrégation de Saint Maur, et continué par des membres de l'Institut (Académie des Inscriptions et Belles-Lettres). Paris, Impr. Nationale, 1733–1962. v.1–39. (In progress) **BD688**

Title and imprint vary.
12v. of this work were published by the Maurists, 1733–63. v.11 and 12 were reprinted in 1841 and 1830.
Index to v.9–15 in v.15; to v.16–23 in v.23; to v.25–32 in v.32; to v.33–38 in v.38.
The most detailed history of French literature, beginning with the earliest period and so full that v.39 has advanced only part way through the 14th century. Comprises signed contributions by specialists, containing very detailed information and, especially in the later volumes, very full bibliographical references. Includes some articles on literary subjects, forms, movements, etc., but consists in the main of biographical and critical articles on individual authors, including many not treated in other histories.

Lanson, Gustave. Histoire de la littérature française. Remaniée et complétée pour la période 1850–1950 par Paul Tuffrau. Paris, Hachette, [1952]. 1441p. **BD689**

A standard work frequently reprinted.

—— Histoire illustrée de la littérature française; le Moyen Âge, du Moyen Âge à la Renaissance, le XVIᵉ siècle, le XVIIᵉ siècle, le XVIIIᵉ siècle, époque contemporaine. Paris, Hachette, [c1923]. 2v. il. **BD690**

This edition profusely illustrated. Also frequently reprinted, without the illustrations, in a 1v. edition. A standard work.

Niceron, Jean-Pierre. Mémoires pour servir à l'histoire des hommes illustres dans la république des lettres, avec un catalogue raisonné de leurs ouvrages. Paris, Briasson, 1727–45. 43v. **BD691**

Beginning with v.31, each volume contains an index which includes articles in the preceding volumes.

Petit de Julleville, Louis. Histoire de la langue et de la littérature française des origines à 1900. Paris, Colin, 1896–99. 8v. il. **BD692**

A history still useful for reference use; chapters written by different authorities. Bibliographies, many good illustrations.

Anthologies

✣ Many anthologies of French poetry and prose are particularly useful for their bio-bibliographical notes on the authors included. Much of this information is not easily found elsewhere. Only a few of these collections are included here; others will be found listed in Thieme (BD672), Lanson (BD655), etc.

Ali-Bert. Anthologie des poètes néoclassiques; morceaux choisis, précédes de notices bio-bibliographiques. Paris, Messein, [1932–33]. 2v. **BD693**

Bio-bibliographical notes precede selected poems.

Anthologie des essayistes français contemporains. Paris, Éd. Kra, [1934]. 550p. **BD694**

Bio-bibliographical notes.

Association des Écrivains Combattants. Anthologie des écrivains morts à la guerre, 1914–1918. . . . Amiens, Malfère, 1924–26. 5v. **BD695**

Gives fairly long biographies and bibliographies; includes many minor names.

Bever, Adolphe van. Les poètes du terroir du XVᵉ siècle au XXᵉ siècle, textes choisis, accompagnés de notices biographiques, d'une bibliographie et de cartes des anciens pays de France. Paris, Delagrave, 1909–14. 4v. il.
BD696

A useful regional anthology, grouped by the names of the old provinces. For each author represented a biographical sketch, a bibliography, and selected poems are given. The biographies and bibliographies are especially useful. General index of authors and places in v.4.

Mazade, Fernand. Anthologie des poètes français des origines à nos jours. Paris, Librairie de France, [1926–28]. 4v. il. **BD697**

Includes biographical sketches.

Walch, Gerard. Anthologie des poètes français contemporains; le Parnasse et les écoles postérieures au Parnasse (1866 à nos jours). Morceaux choisis, accompagnés de notices bio- et bibliographiques et de nombreux autographes. Paris, Delagrave, 1958–59. 5v. il. **BD698**

Earlier ed. 1932–34.

Drama

Brenner, Clarence Dietz. A bibliographical list of plays in the French language, 1700–1789. Berkeley, Calif., 1947. 229p. **BD699**

Lists more than 11,000 dramatic compositions by author and title. Analyzes many collections.

Champion, Edouard. La Comédie-Française, 1927–37. Nogent-le-Rotrou, Daupeley-Gouveneur, 1934–39. v.1–5. il. **BD700**

1927–32; 1933–34; 1935; 1936; 1937.
A continuation of Joannidès (BD701).

Joannidès, A. La Comédie-Française de 1680 à 1900. Dictionnaire général des pièces et des auteurs, avec une préface de Jules Claretie. Paris, Plon-Nourrit, 1901. 136p., 274p. 19 facsim. **BD701**

Contents: (1) Alphabetical title list of plays, giving title, author's name, date of first performance; (2) Alphabetical list of authors with short-title list of their works; (3) Chronological list, showing plays given each year and number of performances of each; and (4) Appendixes, giving plays of the Comédie Française presented at the Odéon, in the provinces, or at London; list of poems recited at the Comédie, etc.

—— La Comédie-Française, 1680 à 1920. Tableau des représentations par auteurs et par pièces. Paris, Plon-Nourrit, 1921. 138p. **BD702**

Contents: (1) Author list, giving short titles of plays, date of first performance, and total number of times each has been played down to 1920; (2) Title index.

Lancaster, Henry Carrington. The Comédie Française, 1680–1701; plays, actors, spectators, finances. Baltimore, Johns Hopkins Pr.; London, Milford; Paris, Les Belles-Lettres, 1941. 210p. (Johns Hopkins studies in Romance literatures and languages. Extra v.17)   **BD703**

Arranged chronologically, giving in tabular form: name of play, number of spectators, receipts, etc.

—— History of French dramatic literature in the 17th century. Baltimore, Johns Hopkins Pr.; Paris, Presses Universitaires, 1929–42. 5v. in 9.   **BD704**

A detailed history with lists of plays, bibliographical footnotes, etc. v.5 includes a subject index, a finding list of plays, and a general index to all 5v.

—— Sunset, a history of Parisian drama in the last years of Louis XIV, 1701–1715. Baltimore, Johns Hopkins Pr.; London, Milford; Paris, Les Belles-Lettres, 1945. 365p.   **BD705**

A sequel to the foregoing, compiled on the same plan, devoted primarily to plays acted or published in or near Paris. Includes additions and corrections to the *History . . . in the 17th century* (BD704), and a list of plays acted at the Comédie Française, 1701–Sept. 1715, supplementing the author's work on the *Comédie Française, 1680–1701* (BD703).

Continued by:

—— French tragedy in the time of Louis XV and Voltaire, 1715–1774. Baltimore, Johns Hopkins Pr.; London, Oxford Univ. Pr., 1950. 2v.   **BD706**

Continued by:

—— French tragedy in the reign of Louis XVI and the early years of the French Revolution, 1774–1792. Baltimore, Johns Hopkins Pr., 1953. 181p.   **BD707**

Soleinne, Martineau de. Bibliothèque dramatique de Monsieur de Soleinne. Catalogue rédigé par P. L. Jacob, bibliophile. Paris, Alliance des Arts, 1843–45. 7v. **BD708**

t.1, Théâtre oriental; grec et romain; latin moderne; ancien théâtre français; théâtre français moderne depuis Jodelle jusqu'à Racine. Supplément; t.2, Théâtre français depuis Racine jusqu'à Victor Hugo. Théâtre des provinces. Théâtre français a l'étranger; t.3, Suite du théâtre français; recueils manuscrits; recueils divers; théâtre de la cour; ballets; répertoires des théâtres de Paris; théâtre burlesque; théâtre de société; proverbes dramatiques; théâtre d'éducation; pièces satiriques; pièces en patois; dialogues. Appendice. Autographes; t.4, Théâtre italien; espagnol et portugais; allemand; anglais; suédois, flamand et hollandais, russe et polonais, turc, grec et valaque; t.5, 1. pt., Écrits relatifs au théâtre. 2. pt., Estampes et dessins; [t.6], Livres doubles et livres omis; [t.7], Table générale.

The catalog of a very useful collection covering the theater from ancient times through the first part of the 19th century. Particularly strong in all forms of the French theater, including drama, ballets, burlesque, etc. Also includes works of the theater in many other European countries.

—— —— Table des pièces de théâtre décrites dans le catalogue de la bibliothèque de M. de Soleinne, par Charles Brunet. Pub. par Henri de Rothschild. Paris, D. Morgand, 1914. 491p.

Useful title index to more than 5000 plays giving for each title brief information: whether prose or verse, kind of play (comedy, tragedy, etc.), number of acts, author's name, and reference to its number in the Soleinne catalog.

Wicks, Charles Beaumont and **Schweitzer, Jerome W.** The Parisian stage: alphabetical indexes of plays and authors. University, Ala., Univ. of Alabama Pr., 1950–61. v.1–3. (In progress)   **BD709**

Contents: pt.1, 1800–1815. 1950. 88p.; pt.2, 1816–1830. 1953. 105p.; pt.3, 1831–1850. 1961. 287p.

Pts.1–2 by C. B. Wicks.

Each part is in two sections: (1) an alphabetical list by title, and (2) an author index.

Attempts to be a complete list of dramatic productions presented in Paris in the 19th century, giving where possible: title, subtitle, type of play, number of acts, whether in prose or verse, real names of authors, theater and date of first performance in Paris.

Fiction

DeJongh, William Frederick Jekel. A bibliography of the novel and short story in French from the beginning of printing till 1600. Albuquerque, Univ. of New Mexico Pr., 1944. 79p. (Univ. of New Mexico. Bull. Bibliographical ser., v.1, no.1)   **BD710**

336 items arranged chronologically.

Jones, Silas Paul. A list of French prose fiction from 1700–1750, with a brief introd. N.Y., Wilson, 1939. 150p.   **BD711**

Annotated chronological list with detailed index to authors, titles, and pseudonyms. Locates copies.

Williams, Ralph Coplestone. Bibliography of the 17th-century novel in France. N.Y., Century, 1931. 355p.   **BD712**

An alphabetical list, followed by a chronological list. Additions and corrections are given in an article by F. P. Rolfe, "On the bibliography of 17th-century prose fiction," *PMLA* 49:1071–86. Dec. 1934.

Poetry

Lachèvre, Frédéric. Bibliographie des recueils collectifs de poésies du XVIe siècle (du Jardin de plaisance, 1502, aux Recueils de Toussaint du Bray, 1609). . . . Paris, Champion, 1922. 613p. il.   **BD713**

Subtitle: Donnant: (1) La description et le contenu des recueils; (2) Une table générale des pièces anonymes ou signées d'initiales de ces recueils (titre et premier vers), avec l'indication du nom des auteurs pour celles qui ont pu être attribuées.

A description of the contents of a large number of collections of poetry, with identification of many anonymous items.

—— Bibliographie des recueils collectifs de poésies publiés de 1597 à 1700. . . . Paris, Leclerc, 1901–5. 4v.   **BD714**

Subtitle: Donnant: (1) La description et le contenu des recueils; (2) Les pièces de chaque auteur classées dans l'ordre alphabétique de premier vers, precedées d'une notice bio-bibliographique, etc.; (3) Une table générale des pièces anonymes ou signées d'initiales (titre et premier vers) avec l'indication des noms des auteurs pour celles qui ont pu leur être attribuées; (4) La reproduction des pièces qui n'ont pas été relevées par les derniers éditeurs des poètes figurant dans les recueils collectifs; (5) Une table des noms cités dans le texte et le premier vers des pièces des recueils collectifs. Etc., etc.

v.1–3 arranged chronologically, 1597–1700; v.4, Supplément, additions, corrections, tables générales.

A monumental work describing the collections, giving bio-bibliographical notices of the authors, with attributions for many anonymous poems, some of which have been disputed.

—— Les recueils collectifs de poésies libres et satiriques publiés depuis 1600 jusqu'à la mort de Théophile (1626). Bibliographie de ces recueils et bio-bibliographie des auteurs qui y figurent. . . . Paris, Champion, 1914–22. 597p. and suppl., 95p. (The author's Le libertinage au XVIIe siècle.—IV)   **BD715**

Supplements the preceding work.

—— Bibliographie sommaire de l'Almanach des muses (1765–1833). . . . Paris, Giraud-Badin, 1928. 206p. (Les bibliographies nouvelles. Collection du Bulletin du bibliophile. no.12)   **BD716**

Arranged chronologically; lists literary almanacs of this period, with detailed indexes.

Mendès, Catulle. Le mouvement poétique français de 1867 à 1900. Rapport . . . suivi d'un Dictionnaire bibliographique et critique et d'une Nomenclature chronologique de la plupart des poètes français du XIXᵉ siècle. Paris, Impr. Nationale, E. Fasquelle, 1903. 218p., 340p. **BD717**

The survey report is followed by the *Dictionnaire,* arranged alphabetically, and listing for each poet the titles of his works and extracts from critical opinions with references to sources.

Individual authors

❧ The following list does not include all French authors for whom important reference bibliographies have been published. In the main, it lists those for whom two types of reference aids are available: bibliographies and dictionaries. Bibliographies of many authors are listed in Lanson's *Manuel bibliographique* (BD655); and the lists of works given under authors' names in the *Catalogue général* of the Bibliothèque Nationale (AA72) serve as useful bibliographies, especially in the case of voluminous authors (e.g., Balzac, Dumas, etc.) for whom title indexes are given in that catalog. Often, these author bibliographies have been published as separates by the Bibliothèque Nationale and can be acquired by libraries which do not have the full catalog.

Balzac

Royce, William Hobart. Balzac bibliography. . . . Chicago, Univ. of Chicago Pr., [c1929–30]. 2v. **BD718**
v.1, Writings relative to the life and works of Balzac; v.2, Indexes: (1) by periodicals, and (2) topical index.

George, Albert Joseph. Books by Balzac. A checklist of books by Honoré de Balzac, comp. from the papers of William Hobart Royce, presently in the Syracuse University collection. Syracuse, Syracuse Univ. Pr., 1960. 90p. **BD719**
The Royce collection has now been acquired by Syracuse University, and a new edition of the *Balzac bibliography* (BD 718) is in preparation. This checklist "has been preprinted as a separate issue for the convenience of Balzacians."—*Pref.*

Cerfberr, Anatole and **Christophe, Jules.** Répertoire de la Comédie humaine de H. de Balzac. Paris, Lévy, 1887. 563p. **BD720**
A dictionary of characters. Gives a brief description for each character, indicates its connection with the plot of the story, and refers to title of the novel or story in which the character appears; does not refer to chapters.
Two English translations have been published as follows:

—— Repertory of the Comédie humaine, tr. by J. W. McSpadden. Philadelphia, Avil Pub. Co., 1902. 522p. (Balzac. Works. Popular lib. ed. v.36) **BD721**

—— Compendium, H. de Balzac's Comédie humaine, tr. and ed. by J. Rudd. Philadelphia, Gebbie Pub. Co., 1899. 583p. **BD722**

Lotte, Fernand. Dictionnaire biographique des personnages fictifs de la Comédie humaine. Paris, José Corti, 1952. 676p. **BD723**
An alphabetical listing of the fictitious characters in Balzac's *La comédie humaine,* giving biographical information and citations to the books in which the characters appear.
A companion volume of the real characters is said to be in preparation.

—— —— Anonymes. Paris, José Corti, 1956. 91p. **BD724**
A listing, with brief descriptions, of Balzacian characters which are not named.

—— Armorial de la Comédie humaine. Ouvrage illustré de 65 reproductions. Paris, Garnier, 1963. 107p. **BD725**
Descriptions of arms, with illustrations, and a glossary of terms.

Beyle

Cordier, Henri. Bibliographie stendhalienne. . . . Paris, Champion, 1914. 416p. il. (Half title: Œuvres complètes de Stendhal, pub. sous la direction d'Édouard Champion) **BD726**

Bibliographie stendhalienne, 1928/29– . Grenoble, Arthaud, 1930– . Biennial. (1957/60, pub. 1962) **BD727**

Martineau, Henri. Petit dictionnaire stendhalien. Paris, Le Divan, 1948. 501p. **BD728**

Camus

Bollinger, Renate. Albert Camus: eine Bibliographie der Literatur über ihn und sein Werk. Köln, Greven Verlag, 1957. 50p. (Bibliothekar-Lehrinstitut des Landes Nordrhein-Westfalen. Bibliographische Hft.1) **BD729**
Lists some 550 items—books and periodical articles—on Camus and his works. The files of almost 250 periodicals in various languages were checked, many not in Crépin (BD 730).

Crépin, Simone. Albert Camus; essai de bibliographie. Bruxelles, Commission Belge de Bibliographie, 1960. 239p. (Bibliographia belgica, 55) **BD730**
Lists more than 1150 books and articles by and about Camus. About 150 periodicals were checked for articles, many not in Bollinger (BD729). Includes translations of Camus' works.

Corneille

Picot, Émile. Bibliographie cornélienne; ou, Description raisonnée de toutes les éditions des œuvres de Pierre Corneille, des imitations ou traductions qui en ont été faites, et des ouvrages relatifs à Corneille et à ses écrits. Paris, Fontaine, 1876. 552p. **BD731**

Le Verdier, Pierre and **Pelay, E.** Additions à la Bibliographie cornélienne. Rouen, Lestringant, 1908. 251p. **BD732**

Marty-Laveaux, Charles Joseph. Lexique de langue de Pierre Corneille. Paris, Hachette, 1868. 2v. **BD733**
v.11–12 of the *Grands écrivains* edition of Corneille.

Gide

Naville, Arnold. Bibliographie des écrits de André Gide (depuis 1891 jusqu'en 1952). [Nouvelle éd., mise à jour par Jacques Naville] Paris, Guy Le Prat, H. Matarasso, 1949 [i.e., 1962]. 223p., [8]p. **BD734**
Main section ends June 30, 1949; "Complément bibliographique, 1949–1952," last 8 unnumbered pages.
Includes works both by and about Gide.

La Fontaine

Rochambeau, Achille Lacroix de Vimeur, *Comte de.* Bibliographie des œuvres de La Fontaine. Paris, Rouquette, 1911. 669p. **BD735**

Regnier, Henri. Lexique de la langue de J. de La Fontaine, avec une introduction grammaticale. Paris, Hachette, 1892. 2v. **BD736**
v.10–11 of the *Grands écrivains* edition of La Fontaine.

La Rochefoucauld

Marchand, Jean. Bibliographie générale raisonnée de La Rochefoucauld. Paris, Giraud-Badin, 1948. 296p. **BD737**

Regnier, Henri. Lexique de la langue de La Rochefoucauld, avec une introduction grammaticale. Paris, Hachette, 1883. 464p. **BD738**

v.3² of the *Grands écrivains* edition of La Rochefoucauld.

Molière

Desfeuilles, Arthur. Notice bibliographique. Paris, Hachette, 1893. 326p. **BD739**

v.11 of the *Grands écrivains* edition of Molière.

—— and **Desfeuilles, Paul.** Lexique de la langue de Molière, avec une introduction grammaticale. Paris, Hachette, 1900. 2v. **BD740**

v.12–13 of the *Grands écrivains* edition of Molière.

Guibert, Albert-Jean. Bibliographie des œuvres de Molière publiées au XVIIᵉ siècle. Paris, Éd. du Centre National de la Recherche Scientifique, 1961. 2v. il. **BD741**

A detailed and scholarly listing of separate plays, collected works, Dutch editions, ballets, poems, miscellaneous works, etc. Full bibliographic information and many explanatory notes.

Saintonge, Paul Frédéric and **Christ, Robert Wilson.** Fifty years of Molière studies, a bibliography, 1892–1941. Baltimore, Johns Hopkins Pr.; London, Milford, 1942. 313p. (Johns Hopkins studies in Romance literatures and languages. Extra v.19) **BD742**

3316 numbered items.

Montaigne

Richou, Gabriel. Inventaire de la collection des ouvrages et documents réunis par J. F. Payen et J. B. Bastide sur Michel de Montagne. . . . Paris, Téchener, 1878. 396p. **BD743**

Villey-Desmeserets, Pierre. Lexique de la langue des Essais, et index des noms propres, . . . avec la collaboration de Grace Norton. Bordeaux, Impr. Nouvelle F. Pech, 1933. 727p. (Montaigne, M. E. de. Les essais . . . pub. d'après l'exemplaire de Bordeaux, 1933. v.5) **BD744**

Contents: Lexique, p.5–697; Index du noms propres contenus dans les essais, p.699–727.

Forms v.5 of the *Édition municipale de Bordeaux* of Montaigne.

Proust

Spalding, P. A. A reader's handbook to Proust; an index guide to Remembrance of things past. London, Chatto and Windus, 1952. 303p. **BD745**

Includes a synopsis, an index to characters, a general index, principal dates in Proust's life and work, and a brief note on Proust's sources.

Racine

Williams, Edwin E. Racine depuis 1885; bibliographie raisonnée des libres—articles—comptes-rendus critiques relatifs à la vie et l'œuvre de Jean Racine, 1885–1939. Baltimore, Johns Hopkins Pr.; London, Milford, 1940. 279p. (Johns Hopkins studies in Romance literatures and languages. Extra v.16) **BD746**

Marty-Laveaux, Charles Joseph. Lexique de la langue de J. Racine, avec une introduction grammaticale, précédé d'une étude sur le style de Racine par P. Mesnard et suivi des tableaux des représentations de Corneille et de Racine

par E. Despois. Paris, Hachette, 1873. cxlivp., 616p. **BD747**

v.8 of the *Grands écrivains* edition of Racine.

Rousseau

Sénelier, Jean. Bibliographie générale des œuvres de J.-J. Rousseau. Paris, Presses Universitaires de France, 1950. 282p. **BD748**

Ouvrage publié avec le concours du Centre National de la Recherche Scientifique.

Voltaire

Bengescu, George. Voltaire. Bibliographie de ses œuvres. Paris, Perrin, 1882–90. 4v. **BD749**

—————— Table de la Bibliographie de Voltaire par Bengesco, établie par Jean Malcolm. Genève, Inst. et Musée Voltaire, 1953. 127p.

Barr, Mary Margaret. A bibliography of writings on Voltaire, 1825–1925. N.Y., Inst. of French Studies, 1929. 123p. **BD750**

Zola

Patterson, J. G. Zola dictionary; the characters of the Rougon-Macquart novels of Émile Zola, with a biographical and critical introduction, synopses of the plots, bibliographical note, map, genealogy, etc. London, Routledge; N.Y., Dutton, 1912. 232p. **BD751**

Contains note on the French editions and the English translations, short synopses of plots, the dictionary of characters, and an alphabetical list of principal scenes. The dictionary gives brief descriptions of each character but no illustrative quotations, and refers only to the title of the story in which a character appears, not to specific chapters.

Italian

Guides

Mazzoni, Guido. Avviamento allo studio critico delle lettere italiane. 4. ed. riv. e aggiorn. per cura di Carmine Jannaco, con prefazione di Francesco Maggini e appendici di Pio Rajna e Ernesto Giacomo Parodi. Firenze, Sansoni, 1951. 238p. (Manuali di filologia e storia. ser. II, v.3) **BD752**

1st ed. 1892.

A bibliographical handbook, still useful primarily for its comments on older materials.

Ramat, Raffaello. Orientamento bibliografico per lo studio della letteratura italiana. Roma, Ausonia, 1954. 170p. **BD753**

A guide for students of Italian literature.

Bibliography

Golden, Herbert Hershel and **Simches, Seymour Oliver.** Modern Italian language and literature; a bibliography of homage studies. Cambridge, Harvard Univ. Pr., 1959. 207p. **BD754**

Indexes 1966 *Festschriften,* in 474 collections, on modern Italian language and literature from the Renaissance to 1957. Index of authors of the articles and of persons, works, and subjects treated.

Prezzolini, Giuseppe. Repertorio bibliografico della storia e della critica della letteratura italiana dal 1902 al 1932, prep. nella Casa Italiana della Columbia University e con l'aiuto del Council on Research in the Humanities, New York, 1930–1936. Roma, Ed. Roma, 1937–39. 2v. **BD755**

Arranged alphabetically by names of authors written about or commented on, and by literary forms and subjects, with exact references to an enormous amount of critical and biographical material in books, periodicals, society publications, etc.

—— Repertorio bibliografico della storia e della critica della letteratura italiana dal 1933 al 1942. N.Y., Vanni, 1946–48. 2v.

This section follows the same general plan as the first 2v., giving references under authors, literary forms, etc. Many form headings have geographical subdivisions.

Repertorio bibliografico della letteratura italiana, a cura della Facoltà di Magistero di Roma, sotto la direzione di Umberto Bosco. Firenze, Sansoni, 1953–60. v.1–2. (In progress) **BD756**

v.1, 1948–1949; v.2, 1950–1953.
A continuation of Prezzolini (BD755).
The years 1943–47 are still to be filled in.
These volumes are arranged alphabetically by author, with subject indexes, and list both books and periodical articles.

Translations

Shields, Nancy Catchings. Italian translations in America. N.Y., [1931]. 410p. (Inst. of French Studies. Comparative literature ser.) **BD757**

Translations of Italian works arranged chronologically by date of publication, covering the period 1751–1928. Each title is located in one library or, if not found, the original source of entry is indicated.

Dictionaries

Fusco, Enrico M. Scrittori e idee: dizionario critico della letteratura italiana. [Torino], Società Ed. Internazionale, 1956. 626p. **BD758**

Includes biographical sketches, with bibliographies, of writers of all periods, and brief articles on movements, literary forms, etc.

Renda, Umberto and **Operti, Piero.** Dizionario storico della letteratura italiana. Ed. riv. e aggiorn. sul testo originale di Vittorio Turri. Torino, Paravia, 1952. 1188p. **BD759**

1st ed. 1900; nuova ed., 1941, by Vittorio Turri and U. Renda.
A bio-bibliographical dictionary containing some 1400 entries, many quite extensive, including living Italian writers, as well as articles on literary forms and movements, etc.

History

Sanctis, Francesco de. Storia della letteratura italiana, a cura di Benedetto Croce. 6. ed. Bari, Laterza, 1958. 2v. (The author's Opere, I–II) **BD760**

A standard history published in many editions. English translation by Joan Redfern. N.Y., Basic Books, 1960. 2v.

Biography

Ferrari, Luigi. Onomasticon; repertorio biobibliografico degli scrittori italiani dal 1501 al 1850. Milano, Hoepli, 1947. 708p. (Bibliotheca veneta, collana di opere erudite a cura della Scuola Storico-Filologica delle Venezie . . . della R. Università di Padova. [v.1]) **BD761**

An index to almost 50,000 individual biographies of authors contained in some 375 collections: general and local. The list of these collections, p.xxi–xliv, forms a bibliography of collected works of Italian biography, with indication of location in an Italian library.

Fucilla, Joseph Guerin. Universal author repertoire of Italian essay literature. N.Y., Vanni, 1941. 534p. **BD762**

An index to biographical and critical articles on authors, primarily Italian, but also including non-Italian writers of many countries, contained in 1697 collections of Italian essays. Arranged alphabetically by subject.
Continued by:

—— Saggistica letteraria italiana; bibliografia per soggetti: 1938–1952. Firenze, Sansoni, 1956. 281p. **BD763**

A bibliography of studies on Italian and foreign authors and their works, contained in collections of miscellaneous essays printed in Italy 1938–52.

Gastaldi, Mario and **Scano, Carmen.** Dizionario delle scrittrici italiane contemporanee (arte, lettere, scienze). Milano, Gastaldi Editore, 1957. 247p. il. **BD764**

A dictionary of Italian women writers, usually giving place of birth, educational degrees, position or occupation, and a bibliography of writings.

Drama

Toronto. University. Library. Catalogue of Italian plays, 1500–1700, in the Library of the University of Toronto, comp. by Beatrice Corrigan. Toronto, Univ. of Toronto Pr., 1961. 134p. **BD765**

Arranged alphabetically by author with title index, giving bibliographical information, form, dedication, and (in many cases) brief annotations.

Individual authors

❦ This list does not attempt to include all authors for whom important reference bibliographies have been published. It contains only a selection of those of major authors and of writers for whom dictionaries or concordances as well as bibliographies are available.

D'Annunzio

Falqui, Enrico. Bibliografia dannunziana. 2. ed. aum. Firenze, Le Monnier, 1941. 198p. **BD766**

Forcella, Roberto. D'Annunzio, 1863–1886. Roma, Fond. Leonardo, 1926–36. v.1–3. **BD767**

Contents: v.1, 1863–83; v.2, 1884–85; v.3, 1886.

Passerini, Giuseppe Lando, *Conte.* Il vocabolario dannunziano, con un autografo e un ritratto del poeta. Firenze, Sansoni, [1928]. 971p. il. **BD768**

1st edition, 1912–13, was in two alphabets: v.1, poetry; v.2, prose. The 2d edition rearranges the material in one alphabet.

Ariosto

Fatini, Giuseppe. Bibliografia della critica ariostea (1510–1956). Firenze, Felice Le Monnier, 1958. 722p. (Istit. Nazionale de Studi sul Rinascimento) **BD769**

An extensive bibliography of books and periodical articles arranged chronologically, with subject and author indexes.

Casanova

Childs, James Rives. Casanoviana, an annotated world bibliography of Jacques Casanova de Seingalt and of works concerning him. Vienna, Christian M. Nebehay, 1956. 396p. il. **BD770**

Privately printed for the Casanova Society of Virginia.

A detailed, annotated bibliography. The subject section includes articles as well as books.

Dante

Bibliography

✓ **Cornell University. Library.** Catalogue of the Dante collection presented by Willard Fiske, comp. by Theodore Wesley Koch. Ithaca, N.Y., Lib., 1898–1921. 2v. and suppl., 152p. **BD771**

v.1, Dante's works, Works on Dante (A–G); v.2, Works on Dante (H–Z), supplement, indexes, appendix; Supplement, additions 1898–1920.

Supplemented for some points by the following:

Koch, Theodore Wesley. List of Danteiana in American libraries supplementing the catalogue of the Cornell collection. Boston, Ginn, 1901. 67p. **BD772**

Repr. from the 18th *Annual report* of the Dante Society, Cambridge, Mass.

—— Dante in America; a historical and bibliographical study. Boston, Ginn, 1896. 150p. **BD773**

Repr. from the 15th *Annual report* of the Dante Society, Cambridge, Mass.

—— —— [Supplement], May 1896–May 1908. (In Dante Society, Cambridge, Mass. 28th Annual report, 1909. Boston, Ginn, 1910. p.11–35)

Evola, Niccolò Domenico. Bibliografia dantesca (1920–1930). Firenze, Olschki, 1932. 260p. (Giornale dantesco ... v.33, n.s. 3. Annuario dantesco 1930. Supplemento) **BD774**

Supplemented by *Bibliografia dantesca*, 1931/37–1938/39, published in *Il giornale dantesco*, v.39–41, and by:

Vallone, Aldo. Gli studi danteschi dal 1940 al 1949. Firenze, Olschki, 1950. 138p. (Biblioteca di bibliografia italiana. 19) **BD775**

La Piana, Angelina. Dante's American pilgrimage; a historical survey of Dante studies in the United States, 1800–1944. New Haven, pub. for Wellesley College by Yale Univ. Pr., 1948. 310p. **BD776**

Bibliography in footnotes. Author index.

Mambelli, Giuliano. Gli annali delle edizioni dantesche con XLVI tavole fuori testo; contributo ad una bibliografia definitiva. Bologna, Zanichelli, 1931. 424p. il. **BD777**

Manna, Anna M. La raccolta dantesca della Biblioteca Universitaria di Napoli. Firenze. Olschki, 1959. 2v. (Biblioteca di bibliografia italiana. 34) **BD778**

Lists books both by and about Dante in the collection, with author and subject indexes.

Toynbee, Paget. Britain's tribute to Dante in literature and art; a chronological record of 540 years (ca. 1380–1920). London, pub. for the British Academy by H. Milford, [1921]. 212p. **BD779**

Concordances

Fay, Edward Allen. Concordance of the Divina commedia. Cambridge, [Mass.], Dante Soc.; Oxford, Univ. Pr., 1888. 819p. **BD780**

Based upon the text of Witte's edition (Berlin, 1862), but adds variants from the edition of Niccolini (Capponi Borghi and Becchi, Florence, 1837). Includes all words used by Dante but omits context and reference for some of the more common pronouns, prepositions, adverbs, and conjunctions and the more frequently recurring forms of the verbs *avere* and *essere*.

Sheldon, Edward Stevens and **White, A. C.** Concordanza delle opere italiane in prosa e del Canzoniere di Dante Alighieri pubblicata per la Società Dantesca di Cambridge, Mass. Oxford, Univ. Pr., 1905. 740p. **BD781**

Gordon, Lewis H. Supplementary concordance to the minor Italian works of Dante. Cambridge, pub. for the Dante Society, Harvard Univ. Pr., 1936. 38p. **BD782**

Supplementary to the preceding work.

Rand, Edward Kennard and **Wilkins, Ernest Hatch.** Dantis Alagherii opervm latinorvm concordantiae. Oxford, Clarendon Pr., 1912. 577p. **BD783**

Based on the text of the 3d Oxford edition, 1904.

Dictionaries and handbooks

Gustarelli, Andrea. Dizionario dantesco, per lo studio della Divina commedia. Milano, Malfasi, 1946. 253p. **BD784**

Alphabetical dictionary to names, places, some phrases, etc., with exact references to sources and biographical, historical, descriptive notes, etc.

Scartazzini, Giovanni Andrea. Enciclopedia dantesca; dizionario critico e ragionato di quanto concerne la vita e le opere di Dante Alighieri. Milano, Hoepli, 1896–1905. 3v. **BD785**

v.1–2, A–Z. v.3, Vocabolario-concordanza delle opere latine e italiane di Dante Alighieri, preceduto dalla biografia di G. A. Scartazzini.

Siebzehner-Vivanti, Giorgio. Dizionario della Divina commedia, a cura di Michele Messina. Firenze, Olschki, 1954. 655p. **BD786**

Snell, Frederick John. Handbook to the works of Dante. London, Bell; N.Y., Macmillan, 1909. 378p. **BD787**

A handbook, not a dictionary; useful for the more popular questions.

Toynbee, Paget. Concise dictionary of proper names and notable matters in the works of Dante. Oxford, Clarendon Pr., 1914. 568p. **BD788**

Based upon the author's larger *Dictionary* ... (1898) but not a mere abridgment, as it includes some names and material not included in the earlier work; omits names in one poem now known not to have been written by Dante; and brings other matter in line with more recent information. Conciseness is attained by judicious condensation rather than by omission of any vital material.

Petrarch

✓ **Cornell University. Library.** Catalogue of the Petrarch collection bequeathed by Willard Fiske, comp. by Mary Fowler. London, Milford, 1916. 547p. **BD789**

McKenzie, Kenneth. Concordanza delle rime di Francesco Petrarca. Oxford, Univ. Pr.; New Haven, Yale Univ. Pr., 1912. 519p. **BD790**

Based upon the text of the Salvo-Cozzo edition, 1904. Gives context and references for all important words, and references only for certain minor words of frequent occurrence.

Portuguese

(including Brazilian)

Bibliography

Carpeau, Otto Maria, [pseud.] Pequena bibliografia crítica da literatura brasileira. 3. ed. rev. e aum. Rio de Janeiro, Ed. Letras e Artes, 1964. 335p. **BD791**

1st ed. 1951.

Arranged chronologically by literary movements and genres, with bibliographical listings of works by and about the authors. Covers from the colonial period to the 20th century.

Newberry Library, Chicago. A catalog of the William B. Greenlee collection of Portuguese history and literature and the Portuguese materials in the Newberry Library, comp. by Doris Varner Welsh. Chicago, Newberry Library, 1953. 342p. **BD792**

For annotation *see* DC219.

Simões dos Reis, Antônio. Bibliografia da História da literatura brasileira de Sílvio Romero. Rio [de Janeiro], Zelio Valverde, 1944. 305p. **BD793**

No more published.

Bibliography to accompany Sylvio Romero's *História da literatura brasileira.* 3. ed. Rio de Janeiro, Olympio, 1943. 5v.

Contents: Fatores da literatura brasileira: v.1, Trabalhos estrangeiros e nacionais sobre a literatura brasileira.

Topete, José Manuel. A working bibliography of Brazilian literature. Gainesville, Univ. of Florida Pr., 1957. 114p. **BD794**

A supplement to the author's *Working bibliography of Latin American literature* (BD841), which included no chapter on Brazil.

Aims "to present a complete picture of its major writers both bibliographically and critically, to bring together all known critical works on the subject, and to include as many of the contemporary writers as space and economy permit." —*Pref.*

Wogan, Daniel S. A literatura hispano-americana no Brasil: 1877–1944; bibliografia de crítica, história literária e traduções. Baton Rouge, Louisiana State Univ. Pr., 1948. 98p. **BD795**

An annotated bibliography of 822 items, listing the contributions that Brazilians have made to the history and criticism of the literatures of Spanish America. Arranged by country; includes books and articles published from 1877 to 1945. Portuguese translations of Spanish-American novels, plays, short stories, and poems are included under each country.

Current

Anuario da literatura brasileira. Ano I, 1960– . Rio de Janeiro, 1960– **BD796**

An annual containing a calendar of literary events, articles, and bibliographies.

History

Forjaz de Sampaio, Albino. História da literatura portuguesa ilustrada, publicada . . . com a colaboração dos senhores Afonso Lopes Vieira, Agostinho de Campos, [e outros]. Paris, Aillaud, [1929–42]. 4v. il. **BD797**

A lavishly illustrated history, covering from medieval times to the 19th century with a brief chapter on the 20th century. Each chapter begins with an extensive bibliography. Illustrations include many facsimiles of title pages, manuscripts, etc.

Motta, Arthur. História da litteratura brasileira. . . . São Paulo, Companhia Ed. Nacional, 1930. 2v. **BD798**

v.1, 16th–17th centuries; v.2, 18th century.

Includes bibliography.

Spanish

Bibliography

Bibliographie hispanique, 1905–17. N.Y., Hispanic Soc., [1909–19]. 13v. **BD799**

Annual bibliography including both books and periodical articles, and covering the languages, literature, and history of the Spanish and Portuguese countries, both in Europe and elsewhere.

No more published.

Fitzmaurice-Kelly, James. Spanish bibliography. London, Oxford Univ. Pr., 1925. 389p. (Hispanic notes and monographs issued by the Hispanic Society of America. Bibliography ser. II) **BD800**

A much expanded English edition of the author's *Bibliographie de l'histoire de la littérature espagnole.* Paris, Colin, 1913. 78p.

Lists general works, collections, etc., then works by and critical studies about Spanish literary authors.

Foulché-Delbosc, Raymond and **Barrau-Dihigo, Louis.** Manuel de l'hispanisant. N.Y., Putnam, 1920; Hispanic Soc. of America, 1925. v.1–2. **BD801**

For full description *see* AA50.

Golden, Herbert Hershel and **Simches, Seymour O.** Modern Iberian language and literature: a bibliography of homage studies. Cambridge, Harvard Univ. Pr., 1958. 184p. **BD802**

Indexes articles in *Festschriften* and homage volumes; concerned primarily with the Catalan, Portuguese, and Spanish languages and literatures, with some articles relating to Spanish America and Brazil. Covers studies from approximately 1500. 424 books in various languages, published through 1956, are indexed.

Handbook of Latin American studies; a guide to the material published . . . in 1935– . Cambridge, Harvard Univ. Pr., 1936– . v.1– . Annual. **BD803**

Each volume includes a section on literature. For full description *see* DB102.

Millares Carlo, Augustín. Ensayo de una biobibliografía de escritores naturales de las islas Canarias (siglos XVI, XVII y XVIII). Madrid, Tipografía de Archivos, 1932. 716p. **BD804**

Includes biographical sketches and extensive bibliographies.

Serís, Homero. Manual de bibliografía de la literatura española. Syracuse, N.Y., Centro de Estudios Hispánicos, 1948–54. v.1 in 2v. (Publicaciones del Centro de Estudios Hispánicos, 2) (In progress)? **BD805**

Pt.1: fasc.1, Obras generales, 422p. 1948; fasc.2, p.423–1086. 1954.

The first volume of a very comprehensive bibliographical manual of Spanish literature. This volume includes 8779 numbered items with a full alphabetical index and a general table of contents. Lists both books and periodical articles, some with annotations.

Later parts were announced to cover: (2) Lengua; (3) Edad media; (4) Siglos XVI y XVII; (5) Siglo XVIII; (6) Siglo XIX; and (7) Siglo XX, suplemento e índices. Publication, however, has been suspended.

Simón Díaz, José. Bibliografía de literatura hispánica. Madrid, Consejo Superior de Investigaciones Científicas,

Inst. "Miguel de Cervantes" de Filología Hispánica, 1950–61. v.1–6. (v.1 pub. in 2d ed., 1960. 749p.) (In progress) **BD806**

Contents: v.1, Literatura castellana; Literatura catalana; Literatura gallega; Literatura vasca. 2d. ed. 1960; v.2, Bibliografías de bibliografías; Bio-bibliografías; Índices de publicaciones periódicas; Historia de la imprenta. 1951; v.3, Literatura castellana: Edad media, Siglos XI–XV. 1953; v.4, Siglos de oro: Fuentes generales: Autores, A–Agustin. 1955; v.5, Alaba–Arce. 1958; v.6, Aria–Buzio. 1961.

A comprehensive bibliography of all the Hispanic literatures. The 2d edition of the 1st volume—general historical and critical works, containing 5835 entries—is divided broadly by language (Castilian, Catalan, Galician, and Basque), the Castilian being further subdivided to differentiate between the literatures of Spain and those of the Latin-American countries. Books, periodical articles, and unpublished works such as theses and lectures are included; in some cases, references are given to reviews of books. Library locations, chiefly in Spanish libraries, are noted in many instances. Author and library indexes. v.2 contains 2124 entries, mainly general bibliographies in the field of literature; bio-bibliographies; a list of periodical indexes, etc. The third and subsequent volumes are devoted to individual bibliographies arranged by author, with comprehensive indexes by: (1) author, (2) first lines of poems, (3) libraries, and (4) subjects in each volume.

—— Manual de bibliografía de la literatura española. Madrid, Ed. Gustavo Gili, 1963. (Distr. in U.S. by Bowker) 603p. **BD807**

A selective guide to more than 15,000 titles of books published in Spain from the Middle Ages to the 20th century. Not an abridgment of the author's larger work, but a more compact listing and more limited in scope.

Arranged chronologically by centuries. Under each century, general works are followed by the names of individual authors arranged alphabetically, with the titles of their works and of biographical and critical works about them. Name and subject indexes.

Vera, Francisco. La cultura española medieval. Datos bio-bibliográficos para su historia. Madrid, Victoriano Suárez, 1933–34. 2v. **BD808**

A bio-bibliographical dictionary of the writers of medieval Spain.

Translations into English

Pane, Remigio Ugo. English translations from the Spanish, 1484–1943, a bibliography. New Brunswick, N.J., Rutgers Univ. Pr., 1944. 218p. (Rutgers Univ. studies in Spanish, no.2) **BD809**

An unannotated, alphabetical list of 2682 items of peninsular-Spanish literature and history. A review with corrections and additions by W. K. Jones was published in *Hispanic review* 13: 174–77. April 1945.

Dictionaries and encyclopedias

Diccionario de literatura española. 2. ed. Madrid, Revista de Occidente, 1953. 926p. **BD810**

1st ed. 1949.

The 2d edition is reset, with much additional material and many new entries.

An extensive dictionary covering Spanish literature from 710 to 1931, including biographies, with bibliographies, articles on forms of literature, literary terms, etc. All articles are signed. An index of titles mentioned in the text and a chronological index.

Newmark, Maxim. Dictionary of Spanish literature. N.Y., Philosophical Lib., 1956. 352p. **BD811**

Prepared as a concise and factual guide for American students of Spanish and Spanish-American literature. Includes brief biographical sketches, definitions of terms, and a few references to associations and periodicals.

History

Cejador y Frauca, Julio. Historia de la lengua y literatura castellana. Madrid, "Revista de Archivos, Bibliotecas y Museos," 1915–22. 14v. il. **BD812**

v.1–4 have appeared in a 2d edition, 1927–35, and v.1 in a 3d edition, 1932–33.

A standard history covering from the time of Charles V to 1920. Includes bibliographies.

Díaz Plaja, Guillermo. Historia general de las literaturas hispánicas. Con una introducción de Ramón Menéndez Pidal. Barcelona, Ed. Barna, 1949–58. v.1–5. il. (In progress) **BD813**

Each section written by a specialist, with extensive bibliographies.

Covers not only Spanish literature but others, such as Arab, Catalan, Hebrew, and Latin which have flourished in Spain, and the literatures of other Spanish-speaking countries in the Americas, Philippines, etc.

Fitzmaurice-Kelly, James. A new history of Spanish literature. Oxford, Milford, 1926. 551p. **BD814**

1st ed. 1898.

A useful history in English, although now out of date; contains considerable bibliography, including many bibliographical footnotes throughout and a brief general bibliography, p.520–28.

Also published in Spanish, French, and German editions.

Rio, Angel del. Historia de la literatura española. N.Y., Dryden, 1948. 2v. **BD815**

Contents: v.1, Desde las orígenes hasta 1700; v.2, Desde 1700 hasta nuestros días.

Extensive bibliography at the end of each chapter.

Salcedo y Ruiz, Angel. La literatura española; resumen de historia crítica. 2. ed. ref. y muy aum. Madrid, Calleja, 1914–17. 4v. il. **BD816**

v.1, La edad media; v.2, El siglo de oro; v.3, El classicismo; v.4, Nuestros días.

An illustrated history with bibliographical footnotes.

Anthologies

Biblioteca de autores españoles, desde la formación del languaje hasta nuestros días. Madrid, Rivadeneyra, 1846–86; Real Academia Española, 1954–64. v.1–176. (In progress) **BD817**

v.1–71, 1846–86; renewed publication, v.72, 1954. Various reprints issued during interim.

v.71, General indexes, v.1–70: (1) Index classified by literary forms; (2) Index to titles; (3) Index to first lines; (4) Author index.

A collection of the writings of Spanish authors from earliest times to the present day.

De Onís, Federico. Antología de la poesía española e hispanoamericana (1882–1932). Madrid, Impr. Hernando, 1934. 1212p. (Publicaciones de la Revista de filología española, v.10) (Repr. with corrections: N.Y., Las Américas Pub. Co., 1961. 1207p.) **BD818**

Includes selections from about 160 poets, with bibliography and biography for each.

Torrente Ballester, Gonzalo. Panorama de la literatura española contemporánea. 2. ed. Madrid, Ed. Guadarrama, 1961. 2v. **BD819**

v.2 includes *Bibliografía* by Jorge Campos, p.913–1078.

An anthology of poetical and prose selections from contemporary Spanish authors. The bibliography lists books by and about the authors.

Walsh, Thomas. Hispanic anthology; poems translated from the Spanish by English and North American poets. N.Y., Putnam, 1920. 779p. il. (Hispanic notes and monographs. Peninsular ser., IV) **BD820**

Includes brief biographical notes.

Drama

Coe, Ada May. Catálogo bibliográfico y crítico de las comedias anunciadas en los periódicos de Madrid desde 1661 hasta 1819. Baltimore, Johns Hopkins Pr.; London, Milford, 1935. 270p. (Johns Hopkins studies in Romance literatures and languages, extra v.9) **BD821**

A list of plays noted in the periodicals of Madrid from 1661 to 1819, arranged alphabetically by title, with author index.

Cotarelo y Mori, Emilio. Catálogo descriptivo de la gran colección de Comedias escogidas que consta de cuarenta y ocho volúmenes, impresos de 1652 a 1704. Madrid, Tipografía de Archivos, 1932. 266p. **BD822**

Contains full descriptions of each volume of the *Comedias nuevas escogidas de los mejores ingenios de España,* with contents and author and title indexes.

—— Teatro español; catálogo abreviado de una colección dramática española, hasta fines del siglo XIX y de obras relativas al teatro español. Madrid, V. e H. de J. Ratés, 1930. 164p. **BD823**

A listing of more than 1800 plays and works about the Spanish theater.

O'Brien, Robert Alfred. Spanish plays in English translation; an annotated bibliography. N.Y., pub. for the American Educational Theatre Association by Las Américas Pub. Co., 1963. 70p. **BD824**

Annotations on authors and plays. Includes information for producers on number of acts, number of men and women in cast, royalty requirements, etc.

Rogers, Paul Patrick. Spanish drama collection in the Oberlin College Library; a descriptive catalogue. Oberlin, Ohio, Oberlin College, 1940. 468p. **BD825**

Covers the period from the last quarter of the 17th century to the year 1924. Includes 7530 numbered items, arranged alphabetically by author.

—— —— Supplementary volume, containing reference lists. 1946. 157p.

Contents: no.7531–7644, Anonymous plays; Title list; Composers; Printers; List of theaters.

Toronto. University. Library. A bibliography of *comedias sueltas* in the University of Toronto library, comp. by J. A. Molinaro, J. H. Parker and Evelyn Rugg. Toronto, Univ. of Toronto Pr., 1959. 149p. **BD826**

Lists the *sueltas* in a special collection presented to the university; includes principally 18th-century editions of more than 700 Spanish plays from 1703 to 1825. Arrangement is alphabetical by title, with indexes by author, and by publishers and booksellers.

Fiction

Brown, Reginald F. La novela española, 1700–1850. Madrid, Dirección General de Archivos y Bibliotecas. Servicio de Publicaciones del Ministerio de Educación Nacional, 1953. 221p. (Bibliografías de archivos y bibliotecas) **BD827**

Arranged chronologically with an author index.

Individual authors

Cervantes

Grismer, Raymond Leonard. Cervantes: a bibliography. Books, essays, articles and other studies on the life of Cervantes, his works, and his imitators. N.Y., Wilson, 1946. 183p. **BD828**

Madrid. Biblioteca Nacional. Catálogo bibliográfico de la sección de Cervantes de la Biblioteca Nacional, por Gabriel-Martin del Rio y Rico. . . . Madrid, "Revista de Archivos, Bibliotecas y Museos," 1930. 915p. **BD829**

Rius y de Llosellas, Leopoldo. Bibliografía crítica de las obras de Miguel de Cervantes Saavedra. Madrid, Murillo, 1895–1905. 3v. il. **BD830**

Sedó Peris-Mencheta, Juan. Catálogo de la colección cervantina Sedó (redactado por Luis María Plaza Escudero). Barcelona, José Porter, 1953–55. 3v. **BD831**

Contents: v.1, Ediciones del Quijote; v.2, Obras de Cervantes (excepto Don Quijote), Obras de Cervantes completas y selectas, Obras de inspiración cervantina, Novelistica caballeresca y sentimental; v.3, Crítica cervantina, catálogos, conmemoraciones, varia. Índices.

—— —— Suplemento. 1955. 27p.

—— —— Guía del lector. Resumen estadístico de las ediciones del Quijote. Adiciones últimas. [8p.]

—— —— Fe de erratas. [6p.]

Suñé Benages, Juan and **Suñé Fonbuena, Juan.** Bibliografía crítica de ediciones del Quijote, impresas desde 1605 hasta 1917 . . . continuado hasta 1937 por el primero de los citados autores y ahora redactada por J. D. M. Ford y C. T. Keller. Cambridge, Harvard Univ. Pr., 1939. 73p. **BD832**

Added title page in English.

Cayón Fernandez, Luis. Diccionario de El ingenioso hidalgo Don Quijote de La Mancha. Madrid, Ed. Tesoro, 1962. 387p. **BD833**

Predmore, Richard L. An index to Don Quijote including proper names and notable matters. New Brunswick, N.J., Rutgers Univ. Pr., 1938. 102p. (Rutgers Univ. studies in Spanish, 1) **BD834**

Spanish American

Bibliography

Grismer, Raymond Leonard. A new bibliography of the literatures of Spain and Spanish America, including many studies on anthropology, archaeology, art, economics, education, geography, history, law, music, philosophy and other subjects. Minneapolis, Perine Book Co., 1941–46. v.1–7. **BD835**

v.1–7, A–Cez.

Publisher varies. No more published.

Intended to replace the author's two earlier volumes of bibliography on the literatures of Spain and Spanish America, published 1933 and 1935.

Arranged alphabetically by author and subject. Includes books, and articles in periodicals and collections.

—— A reference index to twelve thousand Spanish American authors; a guide to the literature of Spanish America. N.Y., Wilson, 1939. 150p. (Inter-American Bibliographical and Library Assoc. publ. ser.3, v.1) **BD836**

An index to more than 125 books of literary history, biography, bibliography, etc. containing material about Spanish-American authors. Arranged alphabetically by author.

Harvard Council on Hispano-American Studies. Bibliographies of the belles-lettres of Hispanic America. Cambridge, Harvard Univ. Pr., 1947. 3v.   **BD837**

Reprints of some of the Council's bibliographies, mainly the "tentative bibliographies of belles-lettres" of the various Latin-American countries, originally published separately, 1931–35. These may still be occasionally useful, especially for those countries for which no more recent bibliographies have been published.

Leguizamón, Julio A. Bibliografía general de la literatura hispanoamericana. Buenos Aires, Ed. Reunidas, 1954. 213p.   **BD838**

A much expanded revision of the bibliography which appeared originally in the author's *Historia de la literatura hispano-americana.* Buenos Aires, Ed. Reunidas, 1945. 2v. Classed arrangement with name index.

Sánchez, Luis Alberto. Repertorio bibliográfico de la literatura latino-americana. [Santiago], Universidad de Chile, 1955–57. t.1–2. (In progress)   **BD839**

Contents: t.1, fasc.1, Historia y crítica generales; antologías generales. fasc.2, Historia y crítica nacionales: América Central, Argentina; t.2, Brasil, Bolivia.

Aims to be, when complete, a comprehensive bibliography of books and articles on Latin-American literature. To be in five main sections: (1) history, criticism, and anthologies; (2) bibliographies; (3) literary forms; (4) literary themes; (5) translations.

Simmons, Merle Edwin. A bibliography of the *romance* and related forms in Spanish America. Bloomington, Indiana Univ. Pr., 1963. 396p. (Indiana Univ. folklore ser., no.18)   **BD840**

A bibliography of books and articles on the romances, ballads, and folklore of South American countries. Lists more than 2100 items.

Topete, José Manuel. A working bibliography of Latin American literature, published by Walter B. Fraser, chairman of the Inter-American Center of Florida, in cooperation with the Inter-American Bibliographical and Library Association and the School of Inter-American Studies, University of Florida. St. Augustine, Fla., 1952. 162p. (Inter-American Bibliographical and Library Assoc. ser.1, v.12)   **BD841**

Arranged by country; lists histories of literature, anthologies, bibliographies, criticism, translations, etc. Author index.

Yale University. Library. Spanish American literature in the Yale University Library; a bibliography [by] Frederick Bliss Luquiens. . . . New Haven, Yale Univ. Pr.; London, Milford, 1939. 335p.   **BD842**

Contains 5668 numbered entries. "The word *literature* . . . is to be understood in the broad sense of 'good writing.' "— *Introd.* Arranged by the countries of Spanish America, with index to the whole.

Periodicals

Carter, Boyd George. Las revistas literarias de Hispanoamérica: breve historia y contenido. México, Ed. de Andrea, 1959. 282p. (Colección studium, 24)   **BD843**

Contents: pt.1, A brief history of literary periodicals of Spanish America; pt.2, Short studies of 50 literary periodicals; pt.3, A selected bibliography of articles from 125 literary periodicals; pt.4, General bibliography.

Translations into English

Jones, Willis Knapp. Latin American writers in English translation; a tentative bibliography. Wash., Pan Amer. Union, 1944. 141 (i.e., 142) p. ([Pan American Union. Columbus Memorial Library] Bibliographic ser., no.30)   **BD844**

"This bibliography is intended to list all Latin American writing from the time of Columbus and Cortes to the present, that has been translated into English."—*Introd.* Arranged by class with country subdivision. Includes history and travel, essays, poetry, drama, and fiction. Author index.

Leavitt, Sturgis E. Hispano-American literature in the United States; a bibliography of translations and criticisms. Cambridge, Harv. Univ. Pr., 1932. 54p. (Harvard Council on Hispano-American Studies)   **BD845**

A chronological listing of books and periodical articles published in the United States on Hispano-American literature from 1827 to 1931. Author index.

Anthologies

Fitts, Dudley. Anthology of contemporary Latin-American poetry. Norfolk, Conn., New Directions, 1947. 677p.   **BD846**

Added title page: Antología de la poesía americana contemporánea.

English and original text (Spanish, Portuguese, or French) on opposite pages.

"Biographical and bibliographical notes, by H. R. Hays": p.588–649.

Dictionaries

Pan American Union. Letters Section. Diccionario de la literatura latinoamericana. [Ed. provisional] Wash., Unión Panamericana, [1958–61]. [v.1–4] (In progress)   **BD847**

v.1, Bolivia. 121p.; v.2, Chile. 1958. 234p.; v.3, Colombia. 1959. 179p.; v.4, Argentina. 1960–61. 2 pts. 398p.

The final work, now published in a provisional edition, aims to present a comprehensive encyclopedia of Latin-American literature with emphasis on the critical evaluation of each writer. Each fascicule is a dictionary of authors, giving for each a biographical sketch, an evaluative critical summary, and a bibliography of works by and about.

History

Hamilton Depassier, Carlos. Historia de la literatura hispanoamericana. [1. ed.] N.Y., Las Américas Pub. Co., 1960–61. 2v.   **BD848**

Contents: v.1, Colonia y siglo XIX; v.2, siglo XX.

Individual countries

❧ Only a few of the Spanish-American countries are listed here—those for which fairly recent bibliographies of literature have been found. For other material on these and on the other countries, consult the general bibliographies BD835–BD842 and the *Handbook of Latin American studies,* DB102.

Argentinian

Arrieta, Rafael Alberto. Historia de la literatura argentina. [1. ed.] Buenos Aires, Ed. Peuser, 1958–60. v.1–6. il.   **BD849**

Includes bibliography.

Chilean

Castillo, Homero and **Silva Castro, Raúl.** Historia bibliográfica de la novela chilena. México, Ed. de Andrea; Charlottesville, Bibliographical Soc. of the Univ. of Virginia, 1961. 214p.   **BD850**

Added title page in English: Bibliography of the Chilean novel.

Arranged alphabetically by author; lists more than 4000 titles, including short stories in collections.

Durán Cerda, Julio. Repertorio del teatro chileno; bibliografía, obras inéditas y estrenadas. Santiago de Chile, [Ed. Universitaria], 1962. 247p. (Universidad de Chile. Facultad de Filosofía y Educación. Publicaciones del Inst. de Literatura Chilena. ser. C, no.1) **BD851**

The "works" section lists 1710 items alphabetically by author; a selective list of studies, and author and title indexes, are appended.

Solar, Hernán del. Índice de la poesía chilena contemporánea. Santiago de Chile, Ed. Ercilla, 1937. 298p. **BD852**

Anthology with bio-bibliographical notes.

Colombian

Englekirk, John Eugene and **Wade, Gerald E.** Bibliografía de la novela colombiana. México, Impr. Universitaria, 1950. 131p. **BD853**

An annotated bibliography of the Colombian novel from about 1836.

Ortega Torres, José Joaquín. Historia de la literatura colombiana, con prólogos de Antonio Gómez Restrepo y de Daniel Samper Ortega. 2. ed. aum. . . . Bogotá, Ed. Cromos, 1935. 1214p. il. **BD854**

Contains some general literary history, but the greater part of the book consists of biographies and bibliographies, with extracts from the works of some 180 Colombian authors.

Costa Rican

Sotela, Rogelio. Escritores de Costa Rica. San José, Lehmann, 1942. 876p. **BD855**

An anthology of prose and poetry with biographical notes.

Cuban

Arrom, José Juan. Historia de la literatura dramática cubana. New Haven, Yale Univ. Pr., 1944. 132p. il. (Yale Romanic studies, v.23) **BD856**

Bibliografía general, p.93–94; Apéndice bibliográfico de obras dramáticas cubanas, p.95–127. This appendix is a useful bibliography of the Cuban theater. Locates copies in four libraries in the United States and in five in Cuba.

Remos y Rubio, Juan J. Historia de la literatura cubana. Habana, Cardenas, 1945. 3v. **BD857**

A comprehensive history of Cuban literature from its origin to the present day. Includes biographies and bibliographies.

Ecuadorian

Rolando, Carlos A. Las bellas letras en el Ecuador. Guayaquil, Impr. i Talleres Municipales, 1944. 157p. **BD858**

Running title: Bibliografía de autores nacionales-literatura.

A bibliography of literary works printed in Ecuador from colonial times to the present. Arranged by class, including bibliography, library economy, periodicals, poetry, fiction, drama, essays, etc. Author index.

Mexican

González Peña, Carlos. Historia de la literatura mexicana desde los orígenes hasta nuestros días. 7. ed. corr. México, Ed. Porrua, 1960. 463p. **BD859**

Bibliography, p.445–47.

Iguiniz, Juan Bautista. Bibliografía de novelistas mexicanos. Ensayo biográfico, bibliográfico y crítico. Precedido de un estudio histórico de la novela mexicana por Francisco Monterde García Icazbalceta. México, Impr. de la Secretaría de Relaciones Exteriores, 1926. 432p. (Monografías bibliográficas mexicanas, núm.3) **BD860**

Bio-bibliographies of Mexican novelists, with a title index and a list of pseudonyms.

Lamb, Ruth S. Bibliografía del teatro mexicano del siglo XX. Claremont, Calif., Claremont Colleges; México, Ed. de Andrea, 1962. 143p. (Colección studium, 33) **BD861**

An alphabetical listing by author. No title index.

Leal, Luis. Bibliografía del cuento mexicano. Emory, Ga., Emory University; México, Ed. de Andrea, 1958. 162p. (Colección studium, 21) **BD862**

A bibliography of the Mexican short story arranged alphabetically by author. Indexes various collections of stories and lists separately published stories and those published in periodicals.

Monterde García Icazbalceta, Francisco. Bibliografía del teatro en México. México, Impr. de la Secretaría de Relaciones Exteriores, 1933 (i.e., 1934). lxxxp., 649p. facsim. (Monografías bibliográficas mexicanas, 28) **BD863**

A bibliography of works by Mexican authors and by others who lived in Mexico, including original works; translations and adaptations; foreign works printed in Mexico or on Mexican subjects; and works containing studies on the Mexican theater.

Moore, Ernest Richard. Bibliografía de novelistas de la revolución mexicana. México, [priv. pr.], 1941. 190p. **BD864**

Locates copies in Mexican, American, and European libraries.

Puerto Rican

Rivera de Álvarez, Josefina. Diccionario de literatura puertorriqueña. [Rio Piedras], Universidad de Puerto Rico, [1955]. 499p. (Ediciones de la Torre. Manuales y tratados) **BD865**

In two main sections: the first, a textual history with a lengthy bibliography; the second, a bio-bibliography of authors.

SLAVIC AND EAST EUROPEAN LANGUAGES

☙ Only a few works in these literatures can be listed here. For more detailed bibliographies, *see* Horecky, *Basic Russian publications* (1962) (DC253) and *Russia and the Soviet Union* (1965) (DC254); Strakhovsky, *Handbook of Slavic studies* (1949) (DC17); *Columbia dictionary of modern European literature*, ed. by Horatio Smith (1947) (BD20); Kerner, *Slavic Europe* (1918) (DC9); etc. The *Slavic review*, the *Slavonic and East European review*, and *Revue des études slaves* include survey and bibliographical articles which are helpful.

General works

Guides

Jena. Universität. Bibliothek. Slavica-Auswahl-Katalog der Universitätsbibliothek Jena; ein Hilfsbuch für Slawisten und Germanoslavica-Forscher. Weimar, H.

Böhlaus Nachfolger, 1956–59. 2v. in 3. (Claves Jenenses 4–6)   **BD866**

Contents: v.1, Allgemeine Literatur, Tschechoslowakei und Polen; v.2: pt.1, Russland und Sowjetunion; pt.2, Jugoslawien und Bulgarien. Hochschul- Gymnasial- und Gelegenheitsschriften der UB Jena vom 16. bis 18. Jahrhundert, mit persönlichem oder sachlichem Bezug auf Südost- und Osteuropa. Nachträge.

A catalog of 7400 of the Slavic and Germano-Slavic holdings of Jena University Library, particularly strong in 17th- and 18th-century literature. Arrangement is in the form of a bibliographic handbook for Slavic studies. Appendix and author index in v.3.

Czech

Balášová, Olga [and others]. Bibliografie české literární vědy, 1945–1955. Práce o české literatuře. Praha, Státní Pedagogické Nakl., 1964. 693p.   **BD867**

Lists 5590 items on Czech literature of all periods published 1945–55.

Jelinek, Hanus. Histoire de la littérature tchèque. 4. éd. Paris, Éd. du Sagittaire, 1930–35. 3v.   **BD868**

v.1–3, Des origines à nos jours.

Kunc, Jaroslav. Česká literární bibliografie, 1945–1963. Soupis článků, statí a kritik z knižních publikací a periodického tisku let 1945–1963 o dílech soudobých českých spisovatelů. [Praha], Státní Knihovna ČSSR-Národní Knihovna v Praze, 1963– . portraits. (In progress)   **BD869**

(Bibliografický katalog ČSSR, České knihy 1963. Zvláštní sešit 6, prosinec 1963)

Pt.1, A–M (623p.). List of works by and about Czech literary authors.

—— Slovník soudobých českých spisovatelů; krásné písemnictví v letech 1918–45. Praha, Orbis, 1945–46. 2v. il.   **BD870**

A dictionary of contemporary Bohemian writers, Oct. 28, 1918—May 5, 1945. Restricted to belles-lettres.

Continued by:

—— Slovník českých spisovatelů beletristů, 1945–1956. Praha, Státní Pedagogické Nakl., 1957. 483p. (Ed. Národní Knihovny v Praze. Sv.6)   **BD871**

A biographical dictionary of 478 Czech literary figures.

Hungarian

Irodalomtörténeti munkásság, 1939–44. Összeállitotta Kozocsa Sándor. Budapest, Országos Széchényi Könyvtár, 1941–46. 6v.   **BD872**

Continued by:

Magyar irodalom bibliográfiája, 1945/49– . Összeállitotta Kozocsa Sándor. Budapest, 1950– . v.1– . Annual.   **BD872a**

Publisher varies.

Contents: Literary criticism, linguistics, bibliographies; Collections; Works by and about Hungarian authors.

Tezla, Albert. An introductory bibliography to the study of Hungarian literature. Cambridge, Harvard Univ. Pr., 1964. 290p.   **BD872b**

1295 numbered entries of secondary and primary sources published through 1960, designed primarily for students in the United States. Classified arrangement with name index. Titles are annotated, and there are numerous cross references. Locates copies in American and European libraries.

Lithuanian

Biržiška, Vaclovas. Lietuvių bibliografija, [1517–1904]. Kaunas, Svietmo Ministerijos Leidinys, 1924–29. 3v.   **BD873**

Tarybinė lietuvių literatūra ir kritika. Bibliografija. 1945/1955– . Vilnius, 1957– . (Lietuvos TSR Mokslu Akademija, Lietuvių Kalbos ir Literatūros Inst.)   **BD874**

Bibliography of Soviet-Lithuanian literature and literary criticism, in Lithuanian and Russian.

Polish

Czachowski, Kasimierz. Obraz współczesnej literartury polskiej, 1884–1933. Lwów, Nakł. Państwowego Wydawnictwa Książek Szkolnych, 1934–36. 3v.   **BD875**

Includes extensive bibliographies, chronology, and index.

—— Najnowsza twórczość literacka, 1935–37. Lwów, 1938. 273p. il.

Lorentowicz, Jan. La Pologne en France; essai d'une bibliographie raisonnée . . . avec la collaboration de A. M. Chmurski. . . . Paris, Champion, 1935–38. 2v. (v.2, Institut d'Études Slaves de l'Université de Paris. Bibliothèque Polonaise. IV)   **BD876**

v.1, Littérature, théâtre, beaux-arts; v.2, Encyclopédies, langue, voyages, histoire.

French writings concerning Poland including both book and periodical articles.

Classified, with author and title indexes.

Polska Akademia Nauk. Instytut Badań Literackich. Bibliografia literatury polskiej okresu odrodzenia (materiały). Opracowali: Kazimierz Budzyk, Roman Pollak, Stanisław Stupkiewicz. [Warszawa], Państwowy Inst. Wydawniczy, 1954. 463p.   **BD877**

A bibliography of Polish literature during the Renaissance and Reformation, and of later studies of the subject in all languages. Biographical articles on the major authors.

Korbut, Gabrjel. Literatura polska od początków do wojny światowej; ksiażka podręczna informacyjna dla studjujących naukowo dzieje rozwoju piśmiennictwa polskiego. . . . Wyd. 2., powiększone. Warszawa, Skład Głowny w Kasie Im. Mianowskiego, 1929–31. 4v.   **BD878**

v.1, 10th–17th centuries; v.2, 18th century–1820; v.3, 1820–63; v.4, 1864–1914.

Korzeniewska, Ewa. Słownik współczesnych pisarzy polskich. Warszawa, Państwowe Wydawnictwo Naukowe, 1963–64. 3v. (Instytut Badań Literackich Polskiej Akademii Nauk. Bibliografia literatury polskiej "Nowy Korbut")   **BD879**

Continuation of Korbut, above.

A bio-bibliographical work of 20th-century Polish authors, giving brief biographical sketches followed by lists of works by and about the authors.

Pollak, Roman. Piśmiennictwo staropolskie. Warszawa, Państwowy Inst. Wydawniczy, 1963–64. v.1$^{1-2}$. (Instytut Badań Literackich Polskiej Akademii Nauk. Bibliografia literatury polskiej "Nowy Korbut") (In progress)   **BD880**

Continuation of Korbut above.

Contents: pt.1, Hasła ogólne i anonimowe; pt.2, Hasła osobowe, A–M.

The first part consists of a bibliography of general and anonymous works of old Polish literature. The second part is a bio-bibliography of Polish writers from the beginning to the 18th century.

Translations

Coleman, Marion Moore. Polish literature in English translation; a bibliography. Cheshire, Conn., Cherry Hill Books, 1963. 180p. **BD881**

Arranged by author; lists translations of novels, poems, short stories, dramas, etc., dating from the 16th century to 1960. Some references to reviews. Index of translators included.

Rumanian

Adamescu, Gheorghe. Contribuțiune la bibliografia românească. Fasc.1–3. București, Cartea Românească, 1921–28. 3 pts. **BD882**

Fasc.1–3, Istoria literaturii române. Texte și autori, 1500–1921/25.

An important bibliography of Rumanian literature, in chronological order by the birth dates of the writers.

Călinescu, George. Istoria literaturii române dela origini până in prezent. București, Fundația Regală Pentru Literatură și Artă, 1941. 948p. il. **BD883**

A comprehensive survey of Rumanian literature from the 16th to the early 20th centuries, arranged by periods. Treats many authors at length. Copiously illustrated. Extensive bibliography; alphabetical index of authors.

Georgescu-Tistu, Nicolae. Bibliografia literară română. București, Impr. Națională, 1932. 254p. il. (Academia Română. Studii și cercetări, v.18) **BD884**

Resumé in French, p.229–36.

Russian

Guides

Fomin, Aleksandr Grigor'evich. Putevoditel' po bibliografii, biobibliografii, istoriografii, khronologii i entsiklopedii literatury; sistematicheskii, annotirovannyi ukazatel' russkikh knig i zhurnal'nykh rabot, napechatannykh v 1736–1932 gg. Leningrad, Goslitizdat, 1934. 334p. **BD885**

An important guide to Russian bibliographies and reference works in the field of literature.

Bibliography

Akademiia Nauk SSSR. Institut Russkoi Literatury. Bibliografiia drevnerusskoi povesti. Sost. A. A. Nazarevskii. Moskva, 1955. 191p. **BD886**

A bibliography of the early Russian folktale, listing manuscripts, published texts, and research.

—— Bibliografiia sovetskikh russkikh rabot po literature XI–XVII vv. za 1917–1957 gg. Sost.: N. F. Dobrolenkova. Moskva, 1961. 434p. **BD887**

Chronologically arranged by year of publication; lists Soviet research published in Russian on the history of Russian literature of the 11th through the 17th centuries, and 18th-century manuscript material relevant to the earlier period. Name and subject indexes.

—— Istoriia russkoi literatury XIX veka; bibliograficheskii ukazatel'. Pod red. K. D. Muratovoi. Leningrad, Izd-vo Akademii Nauk SSSR, 1962. 965p. **BD888**

—— Istoriia russkoi literatury kontsa XIX nachala XX veka; bibliograficheskii ukazatel'. Pod red. K. D. Muratovoi. Leningrad, Izd-vo Akademii Nauk SSSR, 1963. 516p. **BD889**

Two major bibliographies for Russian literature of the 19th and 20th centuries. Introductory sections deal with history of Russian literature and criticism, journalism, censorship, and related themes. Personal bibliographies for more than 450 authors are given, listing editions of complete works, and published letters, biographical materials, critical literature, and additional bibliographic and reference materials. Name and subject indexes.

Harvard University. Library. The Kilgour collection of Russian literature, 1750–1920, with notes on early books and manuscripts of the 16th and 17th centuries. Cambridge, Harvard College Lib., distr. by the Harvard Univ. Pr., 1959. 1v. unpaged. il. **BD890**

A catalog of 1348 first editions ". . . from Lomonosov to Blok . . . the holdings of Pushkin being particularly notable."— *Pref.* All title pages are reproduced in facsimile, with translations, collation, and notes to facilitate comparison and identification of editions by persons with limited knowledge of the language. Bookplates, labels, and stamps are also reproduced.

Leningrad. Publichnaia Biblioteka. Russkie sovetskie pisateli-prozaiki: bio-bibliograficheskii ukazatel'. [Sost.: V. M. Akimov i dr.] Leningrad, 1959–64. v.1–3. (In progress) **BD891**

T.1–3, Avdeenko–M. Prishvin.

Biography and bibliography for a selection of Russian prose writers of the Soviet period.

Matsuev, Nikolai Ivanovich. Khudozhestvennaia literatura, russkaia i perevodnaia; bibliografiia 1917/25–1938/53$^{1-2}$. Moskva, Gos. Izd-vo Khudozh. Lit-ry, 1926–59. (In progress) **BD892**

The four volumes for the years 1917–37 cover belles-lettres, criticism, and studies in literature written in Russian or translated into Russian from any other language. With the establishment of *Sovetskaia khudozhestvennaia literatura i kritika* (BD898), the two volumes continuing the present title are limited to pre-Revolutionary Russian authors in current editions and literary studies, and translations into Russian from foreign literatures.

Moscow. Publichnaia Biblioteka. Russkie pisateli vtoroi poloviny XIX nachala XX vv. (do 1917 g.); rekomendatel'nyi ukazatel' literatury. Moskva, 1958–63. v.1–3. (In progress) **BD893**

A selective, annotated bibliography of writings by and about Russian authors of the second half of the 19th century and up to 1917, useful for listing of editions and Soviet criticism. Continues chronologically *Russkie pisateli XVIII veka* (1954) and *Russkie pisateli pervoi poloviny XIX veka* (1951).

Smirnov-Sokol'skii, Nikolai Pavlovich. Russkie literaturnye al'manakhi i sborniki XVIII–XIX vv.; predvaritel'nyi spisok. Moskva, 1956. 162p. **BD894**

At head of title: Vsesoiuznaia Knizhnaia Palata.

A preliminary list of 1285 Russian literary almanacs of the 18th and 19th centuries, including humorous almanacs after 1867 and children's almanacs and collections.

Startsev, Ivan Ivanovich. Khudozhestvennaia literatura narodov SSSR v perevodakh na russkii iazyk; bibliografiia. Moskva, Gos. Izd-vo Khudozh. Lit-ry, 1957–64. v.1–2. (In progress) **BD895**

A bibliography of the literature of language groups of the USSR as translated into Russian.

Contents: v.1, 1934–54; v.2, 1955–59.

Struve, Gleb. Soviet Russian literature, 1917–50. [1st ed.] Norman, Univ. of Okla. Pr., 1951. 414p. **BD896**

Bibliography, p.373–400.

Based on the author's *Soviet Russian literature,* first published London, Routledge, 1935.

A reliable history, with extensive bibliography.

Vsesoiuznaia Knizhnaia Palata. Literaturno-khudozhest-

vennye al'manakhi i sborniki; bibliograficheskii ukazatel'. Moskva, 1957–60. v.1–4. **BD897**

v.1, 1900–1911, comp. by O. D. Golubeva; v.2, 1912–17,
and v.3, 1918–27, comp. by N. P. Rogozhin; v.4, 1928–37,
comp. by O. D. Golubeva.

Analyzes the contents of Russian literary almanacs and
related works; chronologically arranged, with various indexes.

Current

Matsuev, Nikolai Ivanovich. Sovetskaia khudozhestvennaia literatura i kritika, 1938/48; 1949/51– ; bibliografiia. Moskva, Sovetskii Pisatel', 1952– . Biennial
after 1949/51. **BD898**

Current bibliography, with reviews, for contemporary Russian literature and criticism, and the literatures of other nationalities in the Soviet Union as translated into Russian.

Continues, in part, *Khudozhestvennaia literatura, russkaia
i perevodnaia* (BD892).

Translations

Ettlinger, Amrei and **Gladstone, Joan M.** Russian literature, theatre and art; a bibliography of works in English,
pub. 1900–1945. London, Hutchinson, [pref. 1945]. 96p.
BD899

Designed to supplement Philip Grierson's *Books on Soviet
Russia, 1917–42* (DC252). Contains classified lists of books
on studies in English on Russian literature, theater, and art,
and Russian literature in English translation from the 19th
century to the present time. No index.

Line, Maurice B. A bibliography of Russian literature in
English translation to 1900 (excluding periodicals). London, Lib. Assoc., 1963. 74p. **BD900**

Proizvedeniia sovetskikh pisatelei v perevodakh na inostrannye iazyki; otdel'nye zarubezhnye izdaniia 1954–
1957; bibliograficheskii ukazatel'. Moskva, 1959. 277p.
BD901

At head of title: Soiuz Pisatelei SSSR i Vsesoiuznaia Gosudarstvennaia Biblioteka Inostrannoi Literatury.

Bibliography of translations of the works of Soviet Russian
and other Soviet writers published abroad as separate books.
Does not include translations in anthologies or collections or
in periodical literature. Lists 5300 titles, primarily literary,
by 920 authors, published during the years 1954–57 in 48
languages.

Continues work of the same title for 1945–53 imprints
(Moskva, 1954).

Encyclopedias and dictionaries

Kratkaia literaturnaia entsiklopediia. Glav. red. A. A.
Surkov. Moskva, Sovetskaia Entsiklopediia, 1962–64.
(Entsiklopedii, slovari, spravochniki) (In progress)
BD902

v.1–2, Aarne–Ziul'figar Shirvani.

A general literary encyclopedia, in Russian, particularly
useful for the inclusion of writers of the Soviet period and
those of the various national minority groups of the Soviet
Union.

Literaturnaia entsiklopediia. Redaktsionnaia kollegiia: P.
I. Lebedev-Polianskii, I. M. Nusinov. Moskva, "Khudozhestvennaia Literatura," 1929–39. v.1–9, 11. il. (Repr.
1948. American Council of Learned Societies reprints.
Russian ser., no.20) **BD903**

An extensive treatment of world literature from a current
Marxist-Leninist standpoint, with special emphasis on the
literatures of Russia and other portions of the USSR.

Vengerov, S. A. Istochniki slovaria russkikh pisatelei.

Sanktpeterburg, Tip. Imp. Akademiia Nauk, 1900–1917.
v.1–4. **BD904**

v.1–4, A–Nekrasov.

A dictionary of Russian writers with references to sources.
No more published.

Individual authors

Dostoevski

Muchnic, Helen. Dostoevsky's English reputation, 1881–
1936. Northampton, Mass., 1939. 219p. (Smith College
studies in modern languages, v.20, no.3–4) **BD905**

A survey of English and American criticism.
Bibliography, p.194–209.

Seduro, Vladimir. Dostoyevski in Russian literary criticism, 1846–1956. N.Y., Columbia Univ. Pr., 1957. 411p.
BD906

A survey history with bibliography, p.346–99.

Tolstoi

**Moscow. Vsesoiuznaia Gosudarstvennaia Biblioteka Ino-
strannoi Literatury.** Khudozhestvennye proizvedeniia L.
N. Tolstogo v perevodakh na inostrannye iazyki; otdelnye
zarubezhnye izdaniia. Bibliografiia. [Otv. red. T. L. Moty-
leva] Moskva, Izd-vo Vsesoiuznaia Knizhnoi Palaty,
1961. 588p. **BD907**

A bibliography of translations of Tolstoi's literary works
published in 48 languages between 1862 and early 1960.
Omits translations into non-Russian languages of the Soviet
Union. Indexes for Russian titles, foreign titles, dramatiza-
tions and scenarios, translators, and languages.

Turgenev

Yachnin, Rissa and **Stam, David H.** Turgenev in English;
a checklist of works by and about him. N.Y., N.Y. Pub.
Lib., 1962. 55p. **BD908**

Ukrainian

Ukrains'ki pys'mennyky; biobibliohrafichnyi slovnyk u
p'iaty tomakh. Red. O. I. Bilets'kyi. Kyiv, Derzh. Vyd-vo
Khudozh. Lit-ry, 1960–63. v.1–3. (In progress) **BD909**

Bio-bibliography, with a wide range of early texts, source
materials, and criticism for Ukrainian and related literature
of the 11th–18th centuries cited in the first volume. v.2–3
contain alphabetical list of authors of the 19th and early-
20th centuries.

Yugoslavian

Vuković, Milan T. Mali knjižarski leksikon: bibliograf-
sko, bibliofilsko, bibliotekarski priručnik. Beograd, 1959.
793p. **BD910**

CLASSICAL LANGUAGES

General works

Bibliography

Fabricius, Johann Albert. Bibliotheca graeca . . . Ed. 4
variorum curis emendatior atque auctior. Hamburgi,
Bohn, 1790–1809. 12v. **BD912**

—— —— Index. Lipsiae, Cnobloch, 1838. 94p.

—— Bibliotheca latina, mediae et infimae aetatis, cum supplemento Christiani Schoettgenii jam a p. Joanne Dominico Mansi. Florentiae, Baracchi, 1858–59. 6v. in 3. **BD913**

Still useful bio-bibliographical dictionaries of Greek authors and Latin authors of the Middle Ages.

Engelmann, Wilhelm. Bibliotheca scriptorum classicorum; 8. Aufl. umfassend die Literatur von 1700 bis 1878, neubearb. von E. Preuss. Leipzig, Engelmann, 1880–82. 2v. (Photoreprint: Hildesheim, G. Olms, 1959. 2v.) **BD914**

v.1, Greek; v.2, Latin.

The standard bibliography, useful for information about editions of collected works and separate works, translations, and works about. Of first importance in the large reference or college library. Continued by the following:

Klussmann, Rudolf. Bibliotheca scriptorum classicorum et graecorum et latinorum. Die Literatur von 1878 bis 1896 einschliesslich umfassend. Leipzig, Reisland, 1909–13. 2v. in 4. **BD915**

v.1, Greek; v.2, Latin.

Also published as v.146, 151, 156, and 165 of *Jahresbericht über die Fortschritte der klassischen Altertumswissenschaft* (Berlin, 1909, 1911–13).

Lambrino, Scarlat. Bibliographie de l'antiquité classique, 1896–1914. Paris, Soc. d'Édit. "Les Belles-Lettres," 1951– . pt.1– . (Collection de bibliographie classique) **BD916**

1. pt., Auteurs et textes.

A much needed work designed to fill the gap in the bibliographical record of classical studies between the works of Engelmann (BD914) and Klussmann (BD915), which together cover 1700–1896, and the *Dix années de bibliographie classique* of Marouzeau, 1914–1924 (BD917). Following the same plan as the latter, v.1, *Auteurs et textes*, 1896–1914, lists editions, translations, and works about classical writers in books and periodicals. The coverage is not limited to literature but includes all phases of Greco-Latin antiquity from prehistory to the Byzantine and Gallo-Roman periods. As in Marouzeau, the second volume was to be concerned with *Matières et disciplines*.

Marouzeau, Jules. Dix années de bibliographie classique; bibliographie critique et analytique de l'antiquité gréco-latine pour la période 1914–1924. Paris, Soc. d'Édit. "Les Belles-Lettres," 1927–28. 2v. **BD917**

v.1, Auteurs et textes; v.2, Matières et disciplines.

The subject volume covers the whole field of history and culture of the classical world.

Continued by *L'année philologique* (BD920).

Nairn, John Arbuthnot. Classical hand-list, ed. by B. H. Blackwell, Ltd. 3d ed. rev. and enl. Oxford, Blackwell, 1953. 164p. **BD918**

1st edition, 1931, had title *A hand-list of books relating to the classics and classical antiquity*.

A convenient listing of texts and translations of Greek and Latin authors and books relating to classical antiquity.

Ooteghem, Jules van. Bibliotheca graeca et latina à l'usage des professeurs des humanités gréco-latine. 2. éd. rev. et aug. Namur, Éd. de la Revue "Les études classiques," [1946]. 386p. **BD919**

The 1st edition appeared in *Les études classiques* in April and Oct. 1936. Compiled especially for teachers in the secondary schools and, therefore, treats mainly the authors taught in the schools, with other authors receiving less attention. Lists editions, translations, dictionaries, and critical studies under each author.

Current

L'année philologique; bibliographie critique et analytique de l'antiquité gréco-latine, pub. sous la direction de J. Marouzeau [and others], 1924/26– . Paris, Soc. d'Édit. "Les Belles-Lettres," 1928– . Annual. **BD920**

A very useful survey, in classified order. Some volumes cover more than one year, and all include additional references to previous years.

A continuation of Marouzeau (BD917).

Bibliotheca philologica classica, 1874–1938. Leipzig, Reisland, 1875–1941. 65v. Annual. (Beiblatt zum Jahresbericht über die Fortschritte der klassischen Altertumswissenschaft) **BD921**

Annual survey. No more published. Wider in scope than Engelmann (BD914) or Klussmann (BD915).

Bibliotheca classica orientalis: Documentation der altertumswissenschaftlichen Literatur der Sowjetunion und der Länder der Volksdemokratie. Berlin, Akademie Verlag, 1956– . 1. Jahrg.– . Quarterly. **BD922**

Hrsg. vom Institut für Griechisch-römische Altertumskunde bei der Deutschen Akademie der Wissenschaften zu Berlin.

A classed collection of original reviews of scholarly books and articles in the field and of notices of other reviews.

Klassieke bibliographie, 1.–22. jaarg., 1929–1950. Maandlijsten van tijdschriftartikelen met driemaandelijksche lijsten van nieuwe boekwerken in die Buma-Bibliotheek en in andere Nederlandsche bibliotheken. Utrecht, 1930–50. Annual. **BD923**

Publication suspended.

Books and periodical articles, arranged by subject. Published also on cards.

Year's work in classical studies. v.1–34, 1906–1945/47, ed. for the Classical Journals Board. London, Arrowsmith, 1907–50. Annual. **BD924**

Ceased publication. An annual survey in English, not so comprehensive as the *Bibliotheca philologica classica* (BD921) or *L'année philologique* (BD920).

Periodicals

Southan, Joyce E. A survey of classical periodicals; union catalogue of periodicals relevant to classical studies in certain British libraries. London, Univ. of London Inst. of Classical Studies, 1962. 181p. (London University Inst. of Classical Studies. Bull. supplement 13) **BD925**

A union list of classical periodicals in some 50 British libraries, giving dates of publication, changes of title, etc.

Translations into English

Foster, Finley Melville Kendall. English translations from the Greek, a bibliographical survey. N.Y., Columbia Univ. Pr., 1918. 146p. (Columbia Univ. studies in English and comparative literature. [62]) **BD926**

A list of translations from 1476 to 1917.

Smith, F. Seymour. The classics in translation; an annotated guide to the best translations of the Greek and Latin classics into English. London, N.Y., Scribner, 1930. 307p. **BD927**

An annotated guide. Translations especially recommended are starred.

Handbooks

Feder, Lillian. Crowell's Handbook of classical literature. N.Y., Crowell, 1964. 448p. maps. **BD928**

Subtitle on jacket: A modern guide to the drama, poetry, and prose of Greece and Rome, with biographies of their authors.

An alphabetical dictionary of names, titles, mythological characters, etc. Gives detailed summaries of individual works, occasional commentaries, etc.

Harsh, Philip Whaley. A handbook of classical drama. Stanford, Calif., Stanford Univ. Pr., 1944. 526p. **BD929**

Discussions of Greek and Roman dramatists and their plays, "designed to be a modern appreciation of the plays as literature and a convenient brief guide to further critical material."

Bibliography, p.497–511, lists texts in the original language and English translations with annotations. Recommended translations are starred.

Harvey, Sir **Paul.** Oxford companion to classical literature. Oxford, Clarendon Pr., 1937. 468p. **BD930**

Frequently reprinted.

A useful handbook of concise information on classical writers, literary forms and subjects, individual works, names and subjects in Greek and Roman history, institutions, religion, etc., about which the student or reader of classical literature may need information.

Thompson, Sir **Edward Maunde.** An introduction to Greek and Latin palaeography. Oxford, Clarendon Pr., 1912. 600p. il., facsims. **BD931**

An enlarged edition of the author's *Handbook of Greek and Latin palaeography* (3d ed. 1906).

For full information *see* AA153.

Collections

Loeb classical library, founded by James Loeb. Cambridge, Harvard Univ. Pr., 1912– .v.1– . (In progress) **BD932**

Publisher varies.

An extensive collection of several hundred volumes in two series: (1) Greek, and (2) Latin.

Each volume gives parallel texts of original and English translation, has a brief introduction, and a bibliography. No general index as yet, but indexes to individual authors, though varying in kind and value, are frequently useful for locating a subject or specific passage.

Greek

Bibliography

Riesenfeld, Harald and **Riesenfeld, Blenda.** Repertorium lexicographicum graecum: a catalogue of indexes and dictionaries to Greek authors. Stockholm, Almqvist and Wiksell, 1954. 95p. **BD933**

A companion volume to Paul Faider's *Répertoire des index et lexiques d'auteurs latins* (1926) (BD953), listing indexes and dictionaries "bearing upon Greek literature from its beginning to the end of the Byzantine epoch," including the Greek Bible. Both separately published works and parts of volumes are listed. Preface and notes are in English.

History

Croiset, Alfred and **Croiset, Maurice.** Histoire de la littérature grecque. 2.–4. éd. Paris, Boccard, 1899–1929. 5v. **BD934**

v.1, 4th ed., 1928; v.2–3, 3d ed., 1914–1929; v.4, 4th ed., 1947; v.5, 3d ed., 1928.

Important reference history; many bibliographies.

Schmid, Wilhelm and **Stählin, Otto.** Geschichte der grie-

chischen Literatur. München, Beck, 1929–48. v.1$^{1-5}$. (Handbuch der Altertumswissenschaft, begründet von Iwan von Müller . . . 7 Abt.) **BD935**

A well-documented history, based on the standard German work, *Geschichte der griechischen Literatur,* by Wilhelm von Christ. 6. Aufl. München, Beck, 1912–24. 2v. in 3.

Individual authors

For other indexes and dictionaries *see* Riesenfeld, BD933.

Aeschylus

Italie, Gabriel. Index Aeschyleus. Leiden, Brill, 1954–55. 336p. **BD936**

Aristophanes

Dunbar, Henry. Complete concordance to the comedies and fragments of Aristophanes. Oxford, Clarendon Pr., 1883. 342p. **BD937**

Based upon the text of Dindorf's edition of Aristophanes (Oxford, 1835), and Meineke's edition of the *Fragments* (Berlin, 1840).

Todd, Otis Johnson. Index Aristophanevs. Cambridge, Harvard Univ. Pr.; Oxford, Univ. Pr., 1932. 275p. **BD938**

Aristotle

Bonitz, Hermann. Index Aristotelicus. Berlin, Reimer, 1870. 878p. (Repr.: Graz, Akademische Druck- und Verlagsanstalt, 1955) **BD939**

Forms part of v.5 of the Bekker edition of Aristotle (Berlin, 1831–70).

Organ, Troy Wilson. An index to Aristotle in English translation. Princeton, N.J., Princeton Univ. Pr., 1949. 181p. **BD940**

Based on the translation by W. D. Ross and J. A. Smith. Oxford, Univ. Pr., 1908–31. 11v. Does not include the *Fragments* or the *Constitution of Athens.*

Boethius

Cooper, Lane. Concordance of Boethius; the five theological tractates and the Consolation of philosophy. Cambridge, Mass., Mediaeval Academy of America, 1928. 467p. (Mediaeval Academy of America. Publ. 1) **BD941**

Epictetus

Oldfather, William Abbott. Contributions toward a bibliography of Epictetus; appendix: Jacob Schenk's Translation of the Encheiridion, Basel 1534, facsimile reproduction from the copy in the British Museum. Urbana, Univ. of Illinois, 1927. 201p. **BD942**

————— A supplement, ed. by Marian Harman, with a preliminary list of Epictetus manuscripts by W. H. Friedrich and C. U. Faye. Urbana, Univ. of Illinois, 1952. 177p.

The main work lists more than 1175 entries of works and translations. Locates copies. The supplement follows the arrangement of the earlier volume, and adds information found in the examination of volumes in European libraries and elsewhere.

Euripides

Allen, James Turney and **Italie, Gabriel.** A concordance to Euripides. Berkeley, Los Angeles, Univ. of Calif. Pr.; London, Cambridge Univ. Pr., 1954. 686p. **BD943**

Based on various texts; includes all occurrences of every word except for the very common prepositions, conjunctions, etc.

Herodotus

Powell, John Enoch. A lexicon to Herodotus. . . . Cambridge, Univ. Pr., 1938. 391p. **BD944**

Based on the 3d Oxford text of Hude (1926).—Cf. *Pref.*

Homer

Cunliffe, Richard John. Lexicon of the Homeric dialect. London, Blackie, 1924. 445p. **BD945**

Supplemented by:

—— Homeric proper and place names. London, Blackie, 1931. 42p. **BD946**

Dunbar, Henry. A complete concordance to the Odyssey of Homer. New ed., compl. rev. and enl. by Benedetto Marzullo. Hildesheim, G. Olms, 1962. 398p. **BD947**

1st ed. 1880.

A companion to Prendergast (BD948), intended to form with that work a complete concordance to Homer.

Prendergast, Guy Lushington. Complete concordance to the Iliad of Homer. New ed., compl. rev. and enl. by Benedetto Marzullo. Hildesheim, G. Olms, 1962. 427p. **BD948**

1st ed. 1875.

Compiled from Priestley's edition of Heyne's *Homer,* 1834.

Plato

Ast, Friedrich. Lexicon Platonicum; sive, Vocum Platonicarum index. Lipsiae, Weidmann, 1835–38. 3v. **BD949**

Zürcher, Josef. Lexicon academicum. Paderborn, Verlag Ferdinand Schöningh, 1954. 36p. **BD950**

A dictionary of proper names, in Greek, supplementing Ast, above.

Sophocles

Ellendt, Friedrich Theodor. Lexicon Sophocleum, adhibitis veterum interpretum explicationibus, grammaticorum notationibus, recentiorum doctorum commentariis. Ed. altera emendata. Curavit Hermannus Genthe. Berlin, Borntraeger, 1872. 812p. (Repr.: Hildesheim, Olms, 1958) **BD951**

—— —— Index commentationum Sophoclearum ab A. 1836 editarum triplex. Berlin, Borntraeger, 1874. 134p.

Latin

Bibliography

Caes, Lucien and **Henrion, R.** Collectio bibliographica operum ad ius romanum pertinentium. Bruxelles, Office Internat. de Librairie, 1949–64. (In progress) **BD952**

For contents and annotation *see* CJ8.

Faider, Paul. Répertoire des index et lexiques d'auteurs latins. Paris, Soc. d'Édit. "Les Belles-Lettres," 1926. 56p. **BD953**

Lists dictionaries and indexes of Latin authors.

For similar list of Greek dictionaries *see* Riesenfeld, BD933.

Herescu, Niculae I. Bibliographie de la littérature latine. Paris, Soc. d'Édit. "Les Belles-Lettres," 1943. 426p. (Collection de bibliographie classique, pub. sous la direction de J. Marouzeau) **BD954**

An analytical, selective bibliography of materials on Latin

subjects. Arranged by period with an alphabetical index to Latin authors. No index to secondary authors. Under each author, material is arranged under such subheadings as manuscripts, editions, extracts, translations, dictionaries and indexes, studies. In works of voluminous authors these may be further subdivided.

Useful because it brings together in a convenient form a large amount of material that is otherwise scattered. Covers to approximately 1940.

—— —— Notes additionnelles. Paris, Inst. Roumain d'Études Latines, 1951. 15p.

Kristeller, Paul Oskar. Catalogus translationum et commentariorum: medieval and Renaissance Latin translations and commentaries. Annotated lists and guides. v.1– . Ed. in chief, Paul Oskar Kristeller. Wash., Catholic Univ. of America Pr., 1960– . 249p. **BD955**

At head of title: Union Académique Internationale.

This series "will list and describe the Latin translations of ancient Greek authors and the Latin commentaries on ancient Latin (and Greek) authors up to the year 1600 . . . "—*Pref.*

The first issue includes extensive lists of the extant Greek and Latin authors (most of whom the series intends to treat), followed by a first group of bio-bibliographical sketches on nine specific classical writers. Chapters will appear as they are completed, rather than in any alphabetical or chronological sequence, and "alphabetical indices of ancient authors will be added when necessary."

—— Latin manuscript books before 1600; a list of the printed catalogues and unpublished inventories of extant collections. New ed. rev. N.Y., Fordham Univ. Pr., [1960]. 234p. **BD956**

For complete record *see* AA141.

Menéndez y Pelayo, Marcelino. Bibliografía hispanolatina clásica, edición prep. por Enrique Sánchez Reyes. Santander, Aldus S.A. de Artes Gráficas, 1950–1953. 10v. (Edición nacional de las obras completas de Menéndez Pelayo dir. por Angel González Palencia. t.44–53) **BD957**

A bibliography listing Spanish editions of the Latin classics including: manuscripts, editions, commentaries, translations, critical works, imitations, and works showing the influence of Latin classics on Spanish literature. Comments, extracts, etc., are given throughout. Actual bibliographical information is not always complete.

Indexes in last volume.

History

Manitius, Maximilianus. Geschichte der lateinischen Literatur des Mittelalters. München, Beck, 1911–31. 3v. (Handbuch der klassischen Altertumswissenschaft . . . hrsg. von I. von Müller. 9. Bd., 2. Abt., 1.–3. Teil) **BD958**

v.1, Von Justinian bis zur Mitte des 10. Jahrh.; v.2, Von der Mitte des 10. Jahrh. bis zum Ausbruch des Kampfes zwischen Kirche u. Staat; v.3, Vom Ausbruch des Kirchenstreites bis zum Ende des 12. Jahrh.

The standard history of medieval Latin literature, indispensable in the large reference library.

Schanz, Martin. Geschichte der römischen Literatur bis zum Gesetzgebungswerk des Kaisers Justinian. 1.–4. ganz umgearb. und stark verm. Aufl. München, Beck, 1911–35. 4v. in 5. (Handbuch der klassischen Altertumswissenschaft . . . hrsg. von I. von Müller. 8. Bd.) **BD959**

v.1–2, 4th ed., 1927–35; v.3, 3d ed., 1912; v.4¹, 2d ed., 1914; v.4², 1st ed., 1920 (v.3–4 repr. 1959).

v.1, Die römische Literatur in der Zeit der Republik; v.2, Die römische Literatur in der Zeit der Monarchie bis auf Hadrian; v.3, Die Zeit von Hadrian 117 bis auf Constantin 324; v.4, Von Constantin bis zum Gesetzgebungswerk Justinians: 1. Hälfte, Die Literatur des vierten Jahrhunderts; 2. Hälfte, Die Literatur des fünften und sechsten Jahrhunderts.

An extensively documented history. Continued by Manitius, above.

Teuffel, Wilhelm Sigismund. History of Roman literature, rev. and enl. by Ludwig Schwabe. Authorized tr. from the 5th German ed. by George C. W. Warr. London, Bell, 1891–92. 2v. **BD960**

Contents: v.1, The Republican period; v.2, The Imperial period.

A bibliographical account of Roman history from earliest times to the 6th century A.D.

A 6th German edition, *Geschichte der römischen Literatur,* was published. Leipzig, Teubner, 1910–16. 3v.

Individual authors

For other dictionaries and indexes *see* Faider, BD953.

Caesar

Merguet, Hugo. Lexikon zu den Schriften Cäsars und seiner Fortsetzer mit Angabe samtlicher Stellen. Jena, Fischer, 1886. 1142p. **BD961**

Catullus

Wetmore, Monroe Nichols. Index verborvm Catvllianvs. New Haven, Yale Univ. Pr., 1912. 115p. **BD962**

A complete word index to the poems of Catullus, based upon the Ellis edition, 1906, and including also the variants found in the editions of Baehrens-Schulze, 1893; Haupt-Vahlen, 1904; Riese, 1884; Mueller, 1892; Friedrich, 1908; and Merrill, 1893.

Cicero

Abbott, Kenneth Morgan, Oldfather, William Abbott and **Canter, Howard Vernon.** Index verborum in Ciceronis Rhetorica; necnon incerti auctoris libros Ad Herennium. Urbana, Univ. of Illinois Pr., 1964. 1160p. **BD963**

"Based on the editions of Cicero's *Rhetorica* by A. S. Wilkins, *De inventione* by Eduard Stroebel, and the 2d ed. of *Ad Herennium* by Friedrich Marx."

Includes a bibliography of critical materials and an *"Additamentum ad Apparatum Criticum"* which attempts "to record the critical contributions or comments on the text which have been published since the appearance of the earliest of our basic texts in 1900."

Spaeth, John William. Index verborum Ciceronis Poeticorum fragmentorum. Urbana, Univ. of Illinois Pr., 1955. 130p. **BD964**

"Based on the text of Aemilius Baehrens."

Oldfather, William Abbott, Canter, Howard Vernon and **Abbott, Kenneth Morgan.** Index verborum Ciceronis Epistularum. Urbana, Univ. of Illinois Pr., 1938. 583p. **BD965**

Based on the edition by L. C. Purser in Oxford Classical Texts, 1901–3.

Horace

Cooper, Lane. Concordance to the works of Horace. Wash., Carnegie Inst., 1916. 593p. (Repr.: Barnes & Noble, 1961) **BD966**

Juvenal

Kelling, Lucile and **Suskin, Albert.** Index verborum Juvenalis. Chapel Hill, Univ. of North Carolina Pr., 1951. 139p. **BD967**

Lists the words in all the satires of Juvenal.

Lucan

Deferrari, Roy Joseph, Fanning, *Sister* **Maria Walburg** and **Sullivan,** *Sister* **Anne Stanislaus.** A concordance of Lucan. . . . Wash., Catholic Univ. of America Pr., 1940. 602p. **BD968**

"Based on the text of A. E. Housman (Oxford, Blackwell, 1927)."—*Pref.*

Lucretius

Gordon, Cosmo Alexander. A bibliography of Lucretius. London, Hart-Davis, 1962. 318p. il. (Soho bibliographies, 12) **BD969**

Lists text editions, annotated editions, pocket editions, translations, illustrated editions, selections and extracts, ghosts, etc.

Paulson, Johannes. Index Lucretianus continens copiam verborum quam exhibent editiones Lachmanni, Bernaysi, Munronis, Briegeri et Giussani. (Ut manu scriptus prelo datus) Gotoburgi, Zachrisson, 1911. 177p. **BD970**

Ovid

Deferrari, Roy Joseph, Barry, *Sister* **M. Inviolata** and **McGuire, Martin Rawson Patrick.** A concordance of Ovid. Wash., Catholic Univ. of America Pr., 1939. 2220p. **BD971**

"A combination of a concordance and an index verborum . . . based exclusively on the Teubner edition of Ovid."—*Pref.*

Paratore, Ettore. Bibliografia Ovidiana. Sulmona, Comitato per le Celebrazioni del Bimillenario, 1958. 169p. **BD972**

Lists incunabula, editions, translations, dissertations, critical works, articles, and dictionaries. Each section arranged chronologically. No index.

Plautus

Lodge, González. Lexicon Plavtinvm. Leipzig, Teubner, 1904–33. 2v. **BD973**

Prudentius

Deferrari, Roy Joseph and **Campbell, James Marshall.** Concordance of Prudentius. Cambridge, Mass., Mediaeval Academy of America, 1932. 833p. (Mediaeval Academy of America. Publ. 9) **BD974**

Seneca

Oldfather, William Abbott, Pease, Arthur Stanley and **Canter, Howard Vernon.** Index verborum quae in Senecae fabulis necnon in Octavia praetexta reperiuntur. Urbana, Univ. of Illinois, 1918. 272p. (Univ. of Illinois studies in language and literature. v.4, no.2–4) **BD975**

Vergil

Mambelli, Giuliano. Gli studi Virgiliani nel secolo XX. Contributo ad una bibliografia generale. Firenze, Sansoni, 1940. 2v. (Guide bibliografiche dell' Istit. Nazionale di Cultura Fascista. VII) **BD976**

An annotated bibliography of books and periodical articles in many languages.

Wetmore, Monroe Nichols. Index verborum Vergilianus. [2d ed.] New Haven, Yale Univ. Pr., 1930. 554p. **BD977**

1st ed. 1911.

A word index to the *Eclogues,* the *Georgics,* the *Aeneid,* and the poems usually included in the *Appendix Vergiliana.*

ORIENTAL LANGUAGES

General works

Bibliography

Senny, Jacqueline. Contributions à l'appréciation des valeurs culturelles de l'Orient: traductions françaises de littératures orientales. Bruxelles, Commission Belge de Bibliographie, 1958. 299p. (Bibliographia belgica, 37) **BD978**

Mémoire présenté à l'École Provinciale de Bibliothécaires du Brabant, session 1954.

A list of 2466 oriental works translated into French since the 17th century. Includes all of the Orient—the Near East as well as the Far East.

Arabic

Brockelmann, Carl. Geschichte der arabischen Litteratur. 2. den Supplementbände angepasste Aufl. Leiden, Brill, 1943–49. 2v. **BD979**

Particularly useful for its extensive bibliographies.

A new edition of this standard work "fitted to the *Supplementband*" (Leiden, Brill, 1936–42. 3v.).

Chauvin, Victor. Bibliographie des ouvrages arabes ou relatifs aux arabes publiés dans l'Europe chrétienne de 1810 à 1885. Liége, Vaillant-Carmanne, 1892–1922. 12v. **BD980**

Contents: (1) Préface. Table de Schnurrer. Les proverbes; (2) Kalîlah; (3) Louqmâne et les fabulistes. Barlaam. 'Antar et les romans de chevalerie; (4–7) Les mille et une nuits; (8) Syntipas; (9) Pierre Alphonse. Secundus. Recueils orientaux. Tables de Henning et de Mardrus. Contes occidentaux. Les maqâmes; (10) Le Coran et la tradition; (11) Mahomet; (12) Le Mahométisme.

No general index but some parts have alphabetical or subject indexes, some are arranged alphabetically.

Chinese

Davidson, Martha. A list of published translations from Chinese into English, French and German . . . (Tentative edition). Ann Arbor, Mich., J. W. Edwards for the American Council of Learned Societies, 1952–57. Pts. 1–2. (In progress) **BD981**

Pt.1, Literature, exclusive of poetry. 179p.; pt. 2, Poetry. 462p.

The series is planned to cover all fields in the humanities and the social sciences.

Legge, James. Chinese classics; with a translation, critical and exegetical notes, prolegomena and copious indexes. 2d ed. rev. Oxford, Clarendon Pr., 1893–95. 5v. in 8. maps. (Repr.: Hong Kong, Hong Kong Univ. Pr., 1960. 5v.) **BD982**

v.1–2, 2d ed., revised, 1893–95, printed at the Clarendon Press, Oxford; v.3–5—printed at the London Missionary Society's Printing Office, Hong Kong—are a reissue of the older edition with new title page and imprint: London, H. Frowde, [n.d.].

The volumes originally planned were "to embrace all the books in 'The Thirteen king,'" but v.6–7 were never published. English translations of the *Yih king* and the *Li ki* appeared, respectively, as v.16 and v.27–28 of the series *Sacred books of the East* (BB22). A translation of the *Hsiao king* appeared in v.3 of the same series.

v.1, Confucian analects, the Great learning, and the Doctrine of the mean; v.2, The works of Mencius; v.3, The Shoo-king, or the Book of historical documents: pt.1, The first parts of the Shoo-king, or the Books of T'ang, the Books of Yu, the Books of Hea, the Books of Shang, and the Prolegomena; pt.2, The fifth part of the Shoo-king, or the Books of Chow, and the indexes; v.4, The She-king, or the Book of poetry: pt.1, The first part of the She-king, or the Lessons from the states, and the Prolegomena; pt.2, The second, third, and fourth parts of the She-king, or the Minor odes of the kingdom, the Greater odes of the kingdom, the Sacrificial odes and praise-songs, and the indexes; v.5, The Ch'un ts'ew, with the Tso chuen: pt.1, Dukes Yin, Hwan, Chwang, Min, He, Wan, Seuen, and Ch'ing, and the Prolegomena; pt.2, Dukes Seang, Ch'aou, Ting, and Gae, with Tso's appendix, and the indexes.

Schyns, Joseph. 1500 modern Chinese novels and plays. Peiping, Catholic Univ. Pr., 1948. 484p. **BD983**

Subtitle: "Present day fiction and drama in China by Su Hsueh-Lin; Short biographies of authors by Chao Yen-Sheng."

Study of contemporary Chinese literature; gives reviews in English of 1500 novels and plays and about 200 biographies. Names and titles are given in Anglicized form and in Chinese characters.

Coptic

Kammerer, Winifred. A Coptic bibliography, comp. . . . with the collaboration of Elinor Mullet Husselman and Louise A. Shier. Ann Arbor, Univ. of Michigan Pr., 1950. 205p. (Univ. of Michigan. General library publ., no.7) **BD984**

Contains more than 3000 references to Coptic texts and to books and periodicals on Coptic philology, literature, history, religion, and art published in all countries through 1948. Early works are included, although most items are from the late-19th and the 20th centuries. Many entries contain brief, descriptive annotations; and some, references to important reviews. Arrangement is classified, with an author index.

Hebrew and Yiddish

Benjacob, Isaac. Ozar Ha-Sepharim (Bücherschatz). Bibliographie der gesammten hebraeischen Literatur mit Einschluss der Handschriften (bis 1863). Wilna, Benjacob, 1880. 678p. **BD985**

For full information *see* BB275.

Reisen, Zalman. Leksikon fun der yidisher literatur. . . . Wilno, Kleckin, 1927–29. 4v. il. **BD986**

In Yiddish.

Schwab, Moïse. Répertoire des articles relatifs à l'histoire et à la littérature juives, parus dans les périodiques, de 1665 à 1900. Paris, Geuthner, 1914–23. 539p. **BD987**

An extensive bibliography of articles in many languages on the history and the literature of the Jews. Arranged alphabetically by author.

Shunami, Shlomo. Bibliography of Jewish bibliographies. Jerusalem, Univ. Pr., 1936. 399p. **BD988**

For description *see* BB293.

Waxman, Meyer. A history of Jewish literature from the close of the Bible to our own days. N.Y., Bloch, 1930–41. 4v. il. **BD989**

v.2 and v.4 published in 2d edition, enlarged and corrected, 1943–47.

A detailed history of Jewish literature in its various forms and in various countries from about 200 B.C. to 1935.

Indic

Emeneau, Murray Barnson. A union list of printed Indic texts and translations in American libraries. New Haven,

Amer. Oriental Soc., 1935. 540p. (American Oriental ser., v.7) **BD990**

"List includes all books in Sanskrit, Pali, Prakrit, and Apabhramśa, and most of the books in the older stages of the vernaculars . . . Translations of the texts are also included."— *Introd.* Does not include secondary works. Locates copies in 15 American libraries.

Farquhar, John N. An outline of the religious literature of India. London, N.Y., Oxford Univ. Pr., 1920. 451p. (The religious quest of India) **BD991**

Bibliography, p.362–405. Lists the main histories of the literatures, and treats Hindu and Buddhist literatures in detail, giving references to histories, original texts, translations, etc.

Iranian

Afshar, Iraj. A bibliography of bibliographies on Iranian studies. [Tihrān, 1964?] 217p. **BD992**

Main title page and text in Iranian, with some titles in Western languages, and indexes in both.

Browne, Edward Granville. A literary history of Persia. Cambridge, Univ. Pr., 1953–56. (v.1, 1956) 4v. il. **BD993**

Contents: v.1, From the earliest times to Firdawsí; v.2, From Firdawsí to Sa'di; v.3, The Tartar dominion (1265–1502); v.4, Modern times (1500–1924).

Reissue, not a new edition, of volumes originally published separately, some with slightly different title.

Storey, Charles Ambrose. Persian literature; a bio-bibliographical survey. London, Luzac, 1927–58. v.1 in 2; v.2, pt.1. (In progress) **BD994**

Contents: v.1, Qur'anic literature. History and biography: pt.1, General history. The prophets and early Islam. History of India. 1927–39; pt.2, Biography. Additions and corrections. Indexes. 1953; v.2., pt.1, Mathematics. Weights and measures. Astronomy and astrology. Geography. 1958.

Japanese

Bonneau, Georges. Bibliographie de la littérature japonaise contemporaine. Paris, Geuthner; Tókyô, Mitsukoshi, 1938. 280p. (Bull. de la Maison Franco-Japonaise, t.9, no.1–4, 1937) **BD995**

"5ème supplément à la *Bibliographie des principales publications editées dans l'Empire japonais.*"

A valuable bibliography. Pt.1, Introduction, gives important sources, Japanese and Western; list of translations from Western works into Japanese; and classification of authors as to type or school. Pt.2, *Bibliographie des œuvres représentatives originales de la littérature japonaise contemporaine,* arranged alphabetically by author, gives English transliteration; Japanese characters; date and place of birth and death; subject arrangement of works with title in transliteration, Japanese characters, and translation into French; place and date. Includes magazine articles. Pt.3, Index to names in Introduction and *Bibliographie.*

Japan. National Commission for UNESCO. Who's who among Japanese writers. Tokyo, Kasai Pub. and Prt. Co., 1957. 140p. **BD996**

Biographical sketches of contemporary Japanese writers. Issued in cooperation with the Japan P.E.N. Centre.

P.E.N. Club, Japan. Japanese literature in European languages. [2d ed.] Tokyo, 1961. 98p. **BD997**

An attempt to list "all materials relative to Japanese literature that have been written in European languages and published by the end of 1956."—*Introd.*

Contents: General; Classical literature; Classical theater; Modern literature; Juvenile and folk literature.

Lists translations and shows the original Japanese titles in both Japanese characters and roman letters.

Philippine

Yabes, Leopoldo Y. Philippine literature in English: 1898–1957; a bibliographical survey. Quezon City, Univ. of the Philippines, 1958. p.343–434. (Repr. from Philippine social sciences and humanities review 22:343–434. Dec. 1957) **BD998**

Syriac

British Museum. Dept. of Oriental Printed Books and Manuscripts. Catalogue of Syriac printed books and related literature in the British Museum. Comp. by Cyril Moss. London, Museum, 1962. 1174col., 206col., 272 col. **BD999**

Not merely a catalog but an extensive listing of Syriac texts and of books and periodical articles on Syriac studies. The first published record of Syriac materials in the British Museum.

Yiddish

See Hebrew and Yiddish, p.303.

B E

Fine Arts

❧ The field of the Fine Arts is one in which the specialized library rather than the general library is often needed, because while the general library provides many reference books—bibliographies, dictionaries, indexes, etc., in painting, sculpture, and architecture—many times the large textbooks, histories, and collections of plates will be wanted. Because of their size and expense, these will usually be found only in the special library.

A general reference collection will need such works as: *Art index* (BE25); *Encyclopedia of world art* (BE33) or *Harper's Encyclopedia of art* (BE34); *American art directory* (BE42); some histories of art, e.g., Gardner, *Art through the ages* (BE55), Robb and Garrison, *Art in the Western world* (BE63), and Upjohn (and others), *History of world art* (BE65); *Who's who in American art* (BE78); and perhaps some of the art reproductions as listed in BE101–BE113.

For additional titles and further information, the *Guide to art reference books,* by Mary W. Chamberlin (BE1), should be consulted.

GENERAL WORKS

Guides

Chamberlin, Mary Walls. Guide to art reference books. Chicago, Amer. Lib. Assoc., 1959. 418p. **BE1**

Organizes and appraises reference sources for the history of art. Lists more than 2500 titles, ranging from ready-reference to highly specialized works, in the Fine Arts (N) section of the Library of Congress classification scheme, i.e., architecture, painting, sculpture, prints and engravings, drawings, and the applied arts. Omits monographs on individual artists, and specialized subjects, catalogs of museums and private collections, guidebooks, and all but a few picture books. Arrangement is basically by subject, preceded by general chapters by form, e.g., bibliographies, directories, encyclopedias, iconography, etc. Annotations are descriptive and often evaluative.

The last three chapters describe: Documents and sources; Periodicals (some 250 titles, omitting museum bulletins); Series of art books (more than 100 titles of the most used series). The Appendix describes the holdings of the most important special art collections and libraries of the United States and western Europe.

Bibliography

Bibliografia del libro d'arte italiano. Roma, Bestetti, [1952–64]. v.1–2. il. (In progress) **BE2**
v.1, comp. by Erardo Aeschlimann; v.2, by C. E. Tanfani. Contents: v.1, 1940–1952. 380p.; v.2, 1952–1962. 2v.
Classified arrangement, with author and subject index in each volume.

Amsterdam. Rijksmuseum. Kunsthistorische Bibliotheek. Catalogus. Amsterdam, Dept. van Onderwijs, Kunsten en Wetenschappen, 1934–36. 4v. **BE3**
Classified, with indexes in v.4. The catalog of the library's collection, covering art in general with emphasis on painting and drawing.

Bibliographie zu Kunst und Kunstgeschichte; Veröffentlichungen im Gebiet der Deutschen Demokratischen Republik. Leipzig, Verlag für Buch- und Bibliothekswesen, [1956–]. v.1– . Triennial (?). **BE4**
v.1, 1945/53; v.2, 1954/56.
Classified lists of books and periodical articles published in East Germany. Indexes in each volume for: periodicals, artists, place-names, catchwords, personal names, and authors. v.2 also contains a supplement of 1945–53 publications.

Borroni, Fabia. "Il Cicognara"; bibliografia dell' archeologia classica e dell' arte italiana. Firenze, Sansoni, 1954–65. v.1–(2⁵) in 10v. il. (Biblioteca bibliografica italica. 6–7, 10–11, 19, 23, 25, 27, 29, 31) (In progress) **BE5**
A comprehensive, annotated bibliography of classical archaeology and Italian art. Arranged under large form categories and then chronologically. v.1 includes: bibliography, catalogs of art libraries and of art books, encyclopedias and dictionaries, aesthetics, academic dissertations and conferences, didactic poems, technical aspects, and conservation and restoration, with an analytical index and an index to facsimiles. v.2 has title Archeologia classica and includes: treatises and descriptive literature, methods, manuals and general works, congresses and conferences, catalogs, museums, periodicals, travels, and topography.

Creswell, Keppel Archibald Cameron. A bibliography of the architecture, arts and crafts of Islam to 1st Jan. 1960. Cairo, American Univ. at Cairo Pr., 1961. (Distr. by Oxford Univ. Pr.) 1330p., xxvp. **BE6**
A monumental bibliography of books and periodical articles intended to cover every branch of Muslim architecture and art except numismatics, listing some 12,300 items.
Contents: pt.1, Architecture (divided by country), p.1–478; pt.2, Arts and crafts (divided by craft or material, each subdivided by country), p.479–1330.
Index of authors, p.i–xxv.

Deutscher Kunstrat. Schrifttum zur deutschen Kunst des 20. Jahrhunderts; eine Bibliographie, bearb. von Ernst

Thiele. 2. Aufl. Köln, Oda-Verlag, 1960– . v.1– . (In progress) **BE7**
An annotated bibliography of German art of the 20th century, containing material published in Germany and elsewhere since 1945. v.1 lists monographs and parts of books on individual artists, arranged alphabetically by artist with an author index. Later volumes will contain periodical articles, exhibition catalogs, and works on applied arts and architecture.

Gettens, Rutherford John and **Usilton, Bertha M.** Abstracts of technical studies in art and archaeology, 1943–1952. Wash., 1955. 408p. (Freer Gallery of Art. Occasional papers, v.2, no.2) **BE8**
Preceded by Technical studies in the field of the fine arts (quarterly), published for the Fogg Art Museum, Harvard University, 1932–42. 10v.
Lists some 1400 books and periodical articles in various languages dealing with the application of science and technology to the fields of art and archaeology. The abstracts are signed and are of varying length. Author and subject index.
Continued by:

I.I.C. abstracts; abstracts of the technical literature on archaeology and the fine arts. Issued by the International Institute for Conservation of Historic and Artistic Works. London, 1955– . v.1– . Semiannual. **BE9**
Abstracts and bibliography in English and French.
Before 1959, name of Institute was International Institute for the Conservation of Museum Objects.

Hall, H. van. Repertorium voor de geschiedenis der Nederlandsche schilder- en graveerkunst, sedert het begin der 12de eeuw. 's-Gravenhage, Nijhoff, 1936–49. 2v. **BE10**
A classed bibliography of books and periodical articles, with author and subject index in each volume. v.1, 12th century to 1932, includes also material on Belgian painters and engravers to 1500; v.2, 1933–46.
Continued by Netherlands. Rijksbureau voor Kunsthistorische Documentatie, Bibliography of the Netherlands Institute for Art History (BE16).

Hammond, William Alexander. A bibliography of aesthetics and of the philosophy of the fine arts, 1900–1932. Rev. and enl. ed. N.Y., Longmans, 1934. 205p. **BE11**
1st edition published as a supplement to the May 1933 issue of the Philosophical review.
Classified and annotated, with author index.

Internationale Bibliographie der Kunstwissenschaft, 1902–17/18. Berlin, Behr, 1903–20. 15v. Annual. **BE12**
Useful classified bibliography for the large or special library. Includes books and periodical articles in various languages. Author and subject indexes for each year.

Lebel, Gustave. Bibliographie des revues et périodiques d'art parus en France de 1746 à 1914. Introd. par Georges Wildenstein. Paris, N.Y., 1951. 64p. il. (Gazette des beaux-arts, janv.–mars 1951. 6ᵉ pér., t.38) **BE13**
Arranged by title; includes date of first issue, frequency, editor, location (Bibliothèque Nationale or Bibliothèque d'Art et d'Archéologie de l'Université de Paris). Many entries have annotations. Chronological index.

London. University. Courtauld Institute of Art. Bibliography of the history of British art. v.1–6, 1934–1946/48. Cambridge, Univ. Pr., 1936–56. 6v. **BE14**
Title varies: 1934–37, Annual bibliography of the history of British art.
Lists books and periodical articles in subject arrangement with an index in each volume. Includes Celtic and Viking art but not Roman. Covers architecture, painting, sculpture, the graphic arts, and applied arts. Writings on British museums and private collections are included, though the arts discussed may not be British, also writings on foreign artists working in Great Britain. After v.3, sections are omitted or curtailed

when the subjects are covered by other bibliographical publications.

Lucas, Edna Louise. The Harvard list of books on art. Cambridge, Harvard Univ. Pr., 1952. 163p.   **BE15**

Brief subject listing of English and foreign titles, excluding periodicals, with author and artist index. A revision of the author's *Books on art,* 1936, omitting some out-of-print titles and including new titles through 1950. The older edition, intended as a foundation list suitable for a college library, is not entirely superseded since the omissions from the 1952 edition include many important older titles and much background material.

Netherlands. Rijksbureau voor Kunsthistorische Documentatie. Bibliography of the Netherlands Institute for Art History. v.1, 1943/45– . Hague, 1943– . v.1– . (v.8², 1955/56)   **BE16**

Intended "as a supplement to the '*Mededeelingen*' of the Rijksbureau voor Kunsthistorische Documentatie. . . . A continuation . . . of the work done by van Hall [Repertorium]" (BE10).—*Note in v.1, no.1.*

Each volume—in several parts, irregularly issued—has classed and annotated lists of books and periodical articles on Dutch and Flemish art of every period (not including architecture).

New York. Metropolitan Museum of Art. Library. Library catalog. Boston, G. K. Hall, 1960. 25v.   **BE17**

——— ——— Supplement. 1st– . 1962– .

A photographic reproduction of the dictionary card catalog of this important collection. v.1–23 cover the books and periodicals; v.24–25, the sales catalogs. The first supplement reproduces some 21,000 cards representing additions to the collection since 1960.

Rave, Paul Ortwin. Kunstgeschichte in Festschriften; allgemeine Bibliographie kunstwissenschaftlicher Abhandlungen in den bis 1960 erschienenen Festschriften . . . unter Mitarbeit von Barbara Stein. Berlin, Mann, 1962. 314p.   **BE18**

Contains: (1) a list of the *Festschriften* indexed; (2) a list, arranged by subject, of the 5865 essays on art included in them; and (3) indexes of the titles of the *Festschriften,* of the authors of the art essays, of artists and others, and of places written about.

Reisner, Robert George. Fakes and forgeries in the fine arts; a bibliography. N.Y., Special Libraries Assoc., 1950. 58p.   **BE19**

Arranged mainly by field, i.e., painting, prints, sculptures, etc., with a general section on fakes and forgeries in more than one art form, and works on the moral, ethical, philosophical, and psychological aspects of forgery. Covers books and periodical articles published 1848–1948. Separate bibliography of articles from the *New York Times,* 1897–1950 (p.37–54). Author index.

Répertoire d'art et d'archéologie, dépouillement des périodiques et des catalogues de ventes, bibliographie des ouvrages d'art français et étrangers, fasc.1, 1910– . Paris, Morancé, 1910– . v.1– . (v.64, 1960)   **BE20**

Annual except for 1914/19. Some annual numbers are combined. Subtitle varies. Indexes: for 1910–1914/19 and 1925 to date, each volume has an index of authors, subjects, places; for 1920–24 a combined index was published as fasc.29, 1927.

Published under the auspices of the Bibliothèque d'Art et d'Archéologie of the University of Paris and, since 1945, of the Comité International d'Histoire de l'Art.

A bibliography of books and periodical articles from various countries, classified by large subject (mainly period and country), with a separate section for sales catalogs.

Rowland, Benjamin. The Harvard outline and reading lists for Oriental art. Rev. ed. Cambridge, Harvard Univ. Pr., 1958. 74p.   **BE21**

"A complete revision of the edition published in 1952 which itself was a revision of the *Outline and bibliographies of Oriental art . . . 1938.*"—*Pref.*

Very brief chronological outlines by country are followed by the bibliographical lists, with no indexes.

Schlosser, Julius, *Ritter von.* La letteratura artistica, manuale delle fonti della storia dell' arte moderna. Trad. di Filippo Rossi. 2. ed. italiana aggiorn. da Otto Kurz. Firenze, Nuova Italia, 1956. 766p. (Il pensioro storico, 12)   **BE22**

At head of title: Julius Schlosser Magnino.

Translation of *Die Kunstliteratur; ein Handbuch zur Quellenkunde der neueren Kunstgeschichte* (Wien, Schroll, 1924). Originally published under title *Materialien zur Quellenkunde der Kunstgeschichte* (Wien, 1914–20). An Italian translation with additions by the author was published in 1935, and an appendix by Otto Kurz in 1937.

A valuable manual for the literature of art history up to the early-19th century. Kurz's additions of later material are enclosed in brackets. Indexes of artists and authors.

South Kensington Museum, London. National Art Library. First proofs of the Universal catalogue of books on art. London, Chapman & Hall, 1870. 2v. (Repr.: N.Y., Burt Franklin, 1964?. 2v. and suppl.)   **BE23**

——— ——— Supplement to the Universal catalogue of books on art. London, Eyre & Spottiswoode, 1877. 654p.

"Not only the books in the library, but all books printed and published at the date of the issue of the Catalogue, that could be required to make the library perfect."—*v.1, p.i.*

Indexes

A.L.A. portrait index; index to portraits contained in printed books and periodicals; ed. by W. C. Lane and N. E. Browne. Wash., Lib. of Congress, 1906. 1601p.   **BE24**

An index to portraits contained in 1181 sets (6216 volumes), including both books and periodicals through the year 1904. Indexes some 120,000 portraits of about 40,000 persons. Information given includes: (1) dates of birth and death, and brief characterization of the person, artist, engraver, etc., of the portrait; and (2) volume and page of the work where the portrait may be found. Does not index portraits in local histories, genealogical works, or collections of engravings as such, or portraits of writers included in sets of their collected works.

Art index, Jan. 1929– , a cumulative author and subject index to a selected list of fine arts periodicals. N.Y., Wilson, 1933– . v.1– .   **BE25**

2-year cumulations; annual cumulations in Oct.; and quarterly numbers issued Jan., April, July, Oct. (varies slightly).

Through Oct. 1957 indexes museum bulletins. Fields covered vary; now indexes American and foreign periodicals in the fields of archaeology, architecture, art history, arts and crafts, fine arts, graphic arts, industrial design, interior decoration, photography and films, planning and landscape design, and related subjects. Method of indexing, which differs somewhat from that followed in the other special indexes issued by the same publisher, is as follows: (1) ordinary articles are indexed under author and subject or subjects; (2) book reviews are indexed under the author *reviewed* and under subject or subjects; (3) exhibitions are indexed under the artist; (4) illustrations accompanying an article are listed in the entry for that article but not indexed individually; illustrations without text are indexed under the artist's name.

Chicago. Art Institute. Ryerson Library. Index to art periodicals. Boston, G. K. Hall, 1962. 11v.   **BE26**

Photographic reproduction of the library's card file. All

entries are by subject, alphabeted within the subject by periodical. Material which appears in the *Art index* (BE25) is excluded.

Clapp, Jane. Art in *Life*. N.Y., Scarecrow, 1959. 504p.
BE27

Indexes—by author, title, and subject—the reproductions of paintings and graphic arts in *Life* (the periodical), 1936–56. Includes also selected photographs of architecture, sculpture, and the decorative arts, and portraits of artists and of historic and literary personages.

Ellis, Jessie Croft. Nature and its applications; over 200,000 selected references to nature forms and illustrations of nature as used in every way. Boston, Faxon, 1949. 861p. (Useful reference series, no.74) **BE28**

A revised and very much enlarged edition of the author's *Nature index* (1930), broader in scope and in coverage. Indexes illustrations in about 130 books and periodicals, including some encyclopedias. Indexed works are mainly in English, but a few foreign works are included.

—— Travel through pictures: references to pictures, in books and periodicals, of interesting sites all over the world. Boston, Faxon, 1935. 699p. (Useful reference ser., no.53) **BE29**

Monro, Isabel Stevenson and **Monro, Kate M.** Index to reproductions of American paintings; a guide to pictures occurring in more than eight hundred books. N.Y., Wilson, 1948. 731p. **BE30**

—— —— Supplement. 1st– . 1964– .

The main work "lists the work of artists of the United States occurring in 520 books and in more than 300 catalogues of annual exhibitions held by art museums. The paintings are entered (1) under name of the artist, followed by his dates when obtainable, by title of the picture, and by an abbreviated entry for the book in which the reproduction may be found; (2) under titles; and (3) in some cases under subjects. Locations of pictures in permanent collections have also been included whenever this information was available."—*Pref.*

The first supplement lists paintings in more than 400 books and catalogs, most of these published between 1948 and 1961.

—— Index to reproductions of European paintings; a guide to pictures in more than three hundred books. N.Y., Wilson, 1956. 668p. **BE31**

"A guide to pictures by European artists that are reproduced in 328 books. The paintings are entered (1) under name of artist, followed by his dates when obtainable, by the title of the picture, and by an abbreviated entry of the book in which the reproduction may be found; (2) under titles; and (3) in some cases under subjects. Whenever permanent locations could be determined this information has been recorded by symbols."—*Pref.*

Encyclopedias and dictionaries

Enciclopedia dell' arte antica: classica e orientale. Roma, Istit. della Enciclopedia Italiana, 1958–63. v.1–5. il. (In progress) **BE32**

v.1–5, A–Paz.

Ed. in chief, Ranuccio Bianchi Bandinelli.

A handsomely illustrated encyclopedia with signed articles and bibliographies, treating the art history and iconography of the countries of classical antiquity, i.e., Asia, Northern Africa, and Europe, from prehistory to about 500 A.D.

Encyclopedia of world art. N.Y., McGraw-Hill, 1959–64. v.1–9. il. (In progress) **BE33**

Contents: v.1–9, A–Micronesian cultures.

Published simultaneously in Italian (*Enciclopedia universale dell' arte*. Firenze, Sansoni, 1958–) and English; the original articles were written in various languages and translated into English.

The English-language edition corresponds to the Italian, with some minor changes and three major differences: (1) more cross references; (2) a more extensive article on the art of the Americas; (3) some 300 separate, short biographies added to give more ready access to information about persons treated in longer monographic articles.

Contributors are specialists from many parts of the world. Articles are signed and include extensive bibliographies. The subject matter covers "architecture, sculpture, and painting, and every other man-made object that, regardless of its purpose or technique, enters the field of esthetic judgment because of its form or decoration."—*Pref.* Includes all countries and all periods.

Approximately the last half of each volume consists of plates arranged to illustrate the articles in the first half.

Harper's Encyclopedia of art; architecture, sculpture, painting, decorative arts, based on the work of Louis Hourticq . . . and tr. under the supervision of Tancred Borenius . . . fully rev. under the supervision of J. Leroy Davidson and Philippa Gerry, with the assistance of the staff of the Index of Twentieth-Century Artists, College Art Association, New York City. . . . N.Y., London, Harper, 1937. 2v. il. **BE34**

Reprinted as *New standard encyclopedia of art*. N.Y., Garden City Pub. Co., 1939. 2v. in 1.

Based on the following work by Louis Hourticq (BE35). Comprises short articles, brief bibliographies, and biographies including living persons.

Hourticq, Louis. Encyclopédie des beaux-arts; architecture, sculpture, peinture, arts décoratifs. [Paris], Hachette, [c1925]. 2v. il. **BE35**

At head of title: Bibliothèque Omnium.

Aims to be a dictionary, a history, and an album. Each page includes a part of the dictionary of terms and biographies in entries of widely varying length; a part of the general history which covers world art through the 19th century; and one or more small reproductions. There are also 130 plates, some in color.

Koch, Willi August. Musisches Lexikon: Künstler, Kunstwerke und Motive aus Dichtung, Musik und bildender Kunst. Stuttgart, Kröner, 1956. 1044col. il. **BE36**

A concise encyclopedia of the arts of the Western world, including literature and music, unrestricted by period or nationality. Index of names, places, and titles.

Runes, Dagobert David and **Schrickel, Harry G.** Encyclopedia of the arts. N.Y., Philosophical Lib., [1946]. 1064p. **BE37**

Contains definitions of terms, and longer articles on schools of art, forms, phases, etc., including music with the other arts. Many articles signed. Coverage and treatment uneven. Does not include biography.

Schmitt, Otto. Reallexikon zur deutschen Kunstgeschichte. Stuttgart, Metzler, 1937–62. Bd.1–5 (Lfg. 1–55). il. (In progress) **BE38**

Bd.1–[5] (Lfg. 49–55): A–Epitaph.

Imprint varies: Bd.2– , Stuttgart, Druckenmüller.

Long, signed articles, with bibliographies and many illustrations, on subjects in art history and on specific works of art. Biographies are excluded. Covers countries and regions with predominantly German culture from the early Middle Ages to the mid-19th century. v.3 contains an index of catchwords in German, French, English, and Italian covering the first 3v. Beginning with v.4, each volume is to contain such an index covering the single volume. v.4 also contains a supplement (columns 1443–1544).

Terms

Adeline, Jules. Art dictionary, containing a complete index of all terms used in art, architecture, heraldry, and archaeology. Tr. from the French and enl. N.Y., London, Appleton, 1927. 422p. il. (Repr.: Ann Arbor, Mich., Edwards, 1953) **BE39**

"A large amount of information has been incorporated from F. W. Fairholt's *Dictionary of terms in art* [London, Virtue, 1854]."—*Introd.*

A standard work which has appeared in many editions since it was first published in 1891.

Hansford, Sidney Howard. A glossary of Chinese art and archaeology. [2d ed. rev.] London, China Soc., 1961. 104p. il. (China Soc. Sinological ser., no.4) **BE40**

1st ed. 1954.

A small dictionary of technical terms covering a wide variety of fields, including bronzes, gems and gem stones, sculpture in stone, painting, ceramics, lacquer, etc.

Words are given in Chinese characters, Chinese transliteration, and English equivalent, with (in many cases) an explanation or definition.

Réau, Louis. Dictionnaire polyglotte des termes d'art et d'archéologie. Paris, Presses Universitaires de France, 1953. 247p. **BE41**

At head of title: Comité International d'Histoire de l'Art. "Ouvrage publié avec le concours de l'UNESCO."

Unlike the 1928 ed. (*Lexique polyglotte*), which was grouped by 12 languages with the equivalent French term for each entry, this edition has a single alphabet of common French terms (technical and iconographical) with the equivalent terms for each in Greek, Latin, Italian, Spanish, Portuguese, English, German, Dutch, Danish, Swedish, Czech, Polish, and Russian. No definitions are given.

Directories

For directories of museums *see also* Pure and Applied Sciences, p.539–40.

American art directory. v.1– . 1898– . N.Y., Bowker, 1899– . il. Triennial, 1952– . (v.42, 1964) **BE42**

Frequency varies.

Title varies: v.1–37, 1898–1945/48, *American art annual.* Since 1913 published by or for the American Federation of Arts. *Who's who in American art,* v.1–4, 1936–47 (BE78), was issued as pt.2 of v.33–36 of the *American art annual* which, in v.1–32, 1898–1935, had included various biographical lists.

Covers "museums, art organizations, universities and colleges having art departments and museums of their own, art schools and classes in the United States, Canada and abroad. In addition, there are sections listing art magazines; newspapers carrying art notes, and their critic; traveling exhibitions with booking agencies and type of material and their sources; children's and junior museums; scholarships and fellowships available . . . supervisors and directors of art education in the school systems of the nation."—*v.42, Editor's note.*

Cartwright, W. Aubrey. Guide to art museums in the United States. N.Y., Duell, 1958– . v.1– . il. **BE43**

"The first in a series intended as a guide to works of art in American collections."—*Pref.* This volume covers *The East coast—Washington to Miami.*

Faison, Samson Lane. A guide to the art museums of New England. [1st ed.] N.Y., Harcourt, 1958. 270p. il. **BE44**

A selective guide to the art treasures in some 60 museums and collections in the New England States. Arranged by state and by location within the state. For each museum a brief description is given, followed by several lines or paragraphs of comment on a few of its works, accompanied by small reproductions of the works chosen.

International directory of arts. Internationales Kunst-Adressbuch. Annuario internazionale delle belle arti.

1952/53– . Berlin, Deutsche Zentraldruckerei, [1952 –]. v.1– . Annual. **BE45**

Absorbed *Deutsches Kunst-Adressbuch* which began publication autumn of 1949.

Title page also in French and Spanish. Order and number of languages vary. Prefatory text and table of contents in German, English, French, and variously in Italian or Spanish.

Imprint varies: Ed.1, Berlin, Kaupertverlag.

The 7th ed. (1963/64 in 2v.) includes lists with addresses, arranged by country, of: museums, art galleries, libraries, associations, universities, colleges and academies offering art courses, auctioneers, restorers, dealers, booksellers, publishers, and periodicals. Listed in single alphabets: artists, and private collectors. An index of experts named in the various lists, arranged by subject.

Mastai's National classified directory of American art & antique dealers. 1943– . N.Y., Mastai, 1942– . v.1– . Irregular. (7th ed. 1961) **BE46**

Title varies: 1st–6th ed., *Mastai's Classified directory of American art & antique dealers.*

Dealers in the United States make up the main list, arranged by state, city, and specialty. (Brief lists of Canadian and Latin-American dealers appeared in the first three editions.) The list of major art museums, by country, has grown from the first-edition list for the United States and Canada to include also Mexico and six European countries. A third section, begun in the 2d edition, 1944, lists paintings sold at auction, giving sale price and place and date of sale.

Year's art, 1880–1947, a concise epitome of all matters relating to the arts of painting, sculpture, engraving and architecture, and to schools of design, which have occurred during the year together with information respecting the events of the year. London, Hutchinson, 1880– 1947. 64v. il. Annual. **BE47**

v.63 covers 1942–44; v.64, 1945–47.

Includes lists of museums, associations, and schools in Great Britain and the major ones in the Dominions and the United States; information on sales and exhibitions; a directory of artists and dealers; obituaries; and information on a variety of other pertinent subjects.

Sales

Art prices current . . . a record of sale prices at the principal London, Continental and American auction rooms. London, Art Trade Pr., 1908– . v.1–9 (1907/08–1915/ 16); n.s. v.1– , 1921/22– . (v.39, 1961/62) **BE48**

Subtitle varies. Publication suspended 1917–20. Arranged by medium: pt.A, Paintings, drawings, and miniatures; pt.B, Engravings and prints. Each part is arranged chronologically by sales, with items within the part consecutively numbered and covering artist, title, size, purchaser, price, sometimes condition. Indexes of artists, engravers, and collectors.

Cote des tableaux; ou, Annuaire des ventes de tableaux, dessins, aquarelles, pastels, gouaches, miniatures; guide du marchand, de l'amateur. t.1–11. Tous les prix des ventes de l'année, oct. 1918–fin juil. 1929. Paris, L. Maurice, [1919–31]. v.1–11. il. **BE49**

Title varies: 1918–22, *Annuaire des ventes de tableaux;* 1923–29, *Cote des tableaux.*

Lists: (1) sales of the year chronologically arranged, and (2) paintings, etc. sold, arranged alphabetically by artist and giving size, price, date, and place of sale.

Lancour, Harold. American art auction catalogues, 1785– 1942; a union list. N.Y., N.Y. Pub. Lib., 1944. 377p. **BE50**

"Reprinted with revisions and additions from the *Bulletin* of the New York Public Library, Jan. 1943–Feb. 1944."

A union checklist of more than 7000 catalogs of auction sales of art objects including paintings, drawings, statuary, furniture, rugs, jewelry, textiles, musical instruments, curios, etc. Excludes books, maps, bookplates, stamps, and coins. Locates copies in 21 libraries. Includes list of auction houses and an index of owners.

Lugt, Frits. Répertoire des catalogues de ventes publiques intéressant l'art ou la curiosité. La Haye, Nijhoff, 1938–64. v.1–3. (Publications du Rijksbureau voor Kunsthistorische en Ikonografische Documentatie) (In progress) **BE51**

A chronological list of more than 58,000 catalogs of art sales held throughout Europe: v.1 covers 1600–1825; v.2, 1826–60; v.3, 1861–1900. Information for each entry includes: date and place of sale, provenance, contents, number of items and pages, auctioneers, and location of copies in libraries. Index of names of collections sold.

Print prices current; being a complete alphabetical record of all engravings, etchings and Baxter prints sold by auction in Great Britain and America, each item annotated with the date of sale, price realised and the quality and condition of the prints. v.1–21, Oct. 1918–Aug. 1939. London, F. L. Wilder, 1919–40. 21v. Annual. **BE52**

Subtitle varies slightly.

American prices included for the first time in v.13, 1930/31. Arranged by engravers, with index by artists.

World collectors annuary. v.1, 1946/49– . Delft, Brouwer [etc.], 1950– . il. Annual. (v.15, 1963) **BE53**

Editor, 1946/49– , F. A. van Braam.

Index to v.1–11, 1946–59.

Lists alphabetically by artist the paintings, watercolors, and drawings sold at auction in Europe and the United States, giving description, place and date of sale, and price paid. In v.1–3 the list includes prints. Prints are not included in v.4, but they are separately listed beginning with v.5–8, 1953/56 (in 1v.). Furniture, porcelain, etc. are listed only in v.5–10. All volumes include a section of reproductions of selected works sold during the year.

History

Cossío, Manuel Bartolomé and **Pijoán y Soteras, José.** Summa artis, historia general del arte . . . 1. ed. Bilbao, Madrid, Espasa-Calpe, 1931–61. v.1–18. il. (In progress) **BE54**

A comprehensive history with profuse and excellent illustrations and bibliographies. Discusses (1) the arts of primitive peoples throughout the world, and (2) art in Asia, Egypt, Greece, and the various countries of Europe from ancient times through the 18th century.

Gardner, Helen. Art through the ages. 4th ed. rev. under the editorship of Sumner McK. Crosby by the Dept. of the History of Art, Yale University. N.Y., Harcourt, 1959. 840p. il. **BE55**

1st ed. 1926.

Intended for high school and college students and the general reader. This edition, differing from the organization of the 3d edition, has an introduction on the vocabulary and principles of art history, and sections on Ancient, European, Non-European, and Modern art. 832 illustrations. Bibliographies at ends of chapters; Glossary, p.789–99; Index.

Hauser, Arnold. The social history of art. [Tr. in collaboration with the author by Stanley Godman] N.Y., Knopf, 1951. 2v. (1022p.). il. (Repr.: N.Y., Vintage, 1958–60. 4v.) **BE56**

Bibliography given in brief form as "Notes" to chapters at the end of each volume, with no systematic arrangement. Indexes of subjects and names at the end of v.2.

Janson, Horst Woldemar and **Janson, Dora Jane.** History of art; a survey of the major visual arts from the dawn

of history to the present day. N.Y., Abrams, 1962. 572p. il. (part col.) **BE57**

A handsomely illustrated summary of Western painting, sculpture, and architecture, up to the 19th century, with a brief postscript on Oriental and Pre-Columbian art.

Bibliography, p.554–60.

—— Key monuments of the history of art: a visual survey. Englewood Cliffs, N.J., Prentice-Hall; N.Y., Abrams, 1959. 1068p. il. **BE58**

A selection of more than 1200 reproductions of historically significant works covering architecture, sculpture, and painting of the world, from prehistoric to modern times.

Larkin, Oliver Waterman. Art and life in America. Rev. and enl. ed. N.Y., Holt, [1960]. 559p. il. (part col.) **BE59**

1st ed. 1949.

A survey of American architecture, painting, and sculpture. "What part the visual plastic arts have played in our society." —*Author's foreword.*

"Bibliographical notes," p.491–525.

Michel, André. Histoire de l'art depuis les premiers temps chrétiens jusqu'à nos jours. . . . Paris, Colin, [c1905–29]. 8v. in 17. il. **BE60**

—— —— Index d'ensemble. Noms d'artistes, noms de lieux, sujets et table générale par Louise Lefrançois-Pillion. Paris, Colin, [c1929]. 279p.

A fundamental history with good bibliographies and index.

v.1–7, each in two parts, cover European art through the 18th century. v.8, in three parts, covers art in Europe and America in the 19th and early-20th centuries. Each section, written by one of the numerous collaborating scholars, is signed and includes bibliographies.

Pelican history of art, ed. by Nikolaus Pevsner. Baltimore, Penguin, 1953–62. v.1–21 (Z1–Z21). il. (In progress) **BE61**

A series expected to be in 50v., covering world art and architecture of all periods, each written by a specialist and containing substantial bibliographies and many plates. Volumes are not published in chronological or regional sequence. The series numbering is in the order of publication:

Z1. Waterhouse, E. K. *Painting in Britain, 1530 to 1790.* [1953]

Z2. Rowland, B. *The art and architecture of India: Buddhist, Hindu, Jain.* [1953]

Z3. Summerson, J. N. *Architecture in Britain, 1530 to 1830.* [4th rev. and enl. ed. 1963] (1st ed. 1954)

Z4. Blunt, A. *Art and architecture in France, 1500–1700.* [1954]

Z5. Rickert, M. *Painting in Britain: the Middle Ages.* [1954]

Z6. Hamilton, G. H. *The art and architecture of Russia.* [1954]

Z7. Frankfort, H. *The art and architecture of the ancient Orient.* [1955]

Z8. Paine, R. T. and Soper, A. *The art and architecture of Japan.* [1955]

Z9. Stone, Lawrence. *Sculpture in Britain: the Middle Ages.* [1955]

Z10. Sickman, L. C. S. and Soper, A. *The art and architecture of China.* [1956]

Z11. Lawrence, A. W. *Greek architecture.* [1957]

Z12. Webb, G. F. *Architecture in Britain: the Middle Ages.* [1956]

Z13. Conant, K. J. *Carolingian and Romanesque architecture, 800 to 1200.* [1959]

Z14. Smith, W. S. *The art and architecture of ancient Egypt.* [1958]

Z15. Hitchcock, H. R. *Architecture: nineteenth and twentieth centuries.* [2d ed. 1963] (1st ed. 1958)

Z16. Wittkower, R. *Art and architecture in Italy, 1600 to 1750.* [1958]

Z17. Kubler, G. and Soria, M. *Art and architecture in Spain*

and Portugal and their American dominions, 1500 to 1800.
[1959]
Z18. Gerson, H. and Kuile, E. H. ter. *Art and architecture in Belgium, 1600 to 1800.* [1960]
Z19. Frankl, P. *Gothic architecture.* [1962]
Z20. Novotny, F. *Painting and sculpture in Europe, 1780 to 1880.* [1960]
Z21. Kubler, G. *The art and architecture of ancient America: the Mexican, Maya and Andean peoples.* 1962.

Pijoán y Soteras, José. History of art; Foreword by R. B. Harshe, tr. by R. L. Roys. 2d ed. London, Batsford, 1933. 3v. il.   **BE62**
Spanish ed. 1914–16; 2d ed. 1923.
Also published in a cheaper edition with title *An outline history of art.* Chicago, Univ. of Knowledge, 1938. 3v.
Good reference history, with bibliography at end of each chapter, and many illustrations, some colored. Indexes: (1) alphabetical list of artists, archaeologists, etc.; (2) list of illustrations; and (3) alphabetical index of all works of art reproduced or mentioned in the text.

Robb, David Metheny and **Garrison, Jessie J.** Art in the Western world. 4th ed. N.Y., Harper, 1963. 782p. il.   **BE63**
1st ed. 1935.
A standard introduction to the whole field of art. Separate sections on architecture, sculpture, painting, and the minor arts. Also contains: a chronological and topical concordance, glossary, bibliography, chronological table, index to the 652 illustrations, and a general index.

Springer, Anton. Handbuch der Kunstgeschichte. . . . Leipzig, Kröner, 1918–29. 6v. il.   **BE64**
1st ed. 1875; frequently republished and revised.
A standard history covering art from ancient times to the 20th century, primarily European. Well illustrated. Each volume is separately indexed.

Upjohn, Everard M., Wingert, Paul Stover and **Mahler, Jane Gaston.** History of world art. 2d ed. rev. and enl. N.Y., Oxford, 1958. 876p. 671 il. 17pl.(col.)   **BE65**
1st ed. 1949.
A survey history of painting, sculpture, and architecture designed for introductory college courses. In this edition the chapters on the 20th century have been rewritten; chapters added on prehistoric, primitive, and Pre-Columbian art; and reproductions put at the point of discussion of the works of art. Suggested readings, p.841–50; glossary, p.831–39; index.

Biography

❦ Here are listed some of the more important biographical dictionaries, general in scope and international in coverage. Dictionaries devoted to a particular country, except those for the United States, are omitted. For lists of these *see* Chamberlin, *Guide to art reference books,* p.40–49 (BE1).

Bénézit, Emmanuel. Dictionnaire critique et documentaire des peintres, sculpteurs, dessinateurs et graveurs de tous les temps et de tous les pays, par un groupe d'écrivains spécialistes français et étrangers. Nouv. éd. entièrement refondue, rev. et corr. Paris, Gründ, [1956–61; c1948–55]. 8v. il.   **BE66**
1st ed. 1911–23. 3v.
A comprehensive list, covering artists from the 1st to the mid-20th centuries, including many minor names. Includes both Western and Eastern art. Entries, varying in length from a few lines to several columns, usually include a list of chief works, museums where displayed, and (in some instances) prices paid for works. Symbols and signatures are reproduced in facsimile, and at the end of each key letter of the alphabet a list of the signatures used by anonymous artists appears.

Édouard-Joseph, René. Dictionnaire biographique des artistes contemporains, 1910–1930, avec nombreux portraits, signatures et reproductions. Paris, Art & Édition, 1930–34. 3v. il.   **BE67**
Publisher varies.
Intended to include primarily artists living or exhibited in France from 1910 to 1930.
—— —— Supplément. Paris, 1936. 162p. il.

Kaltenbach, Gustave Émile. Dictionary of pronunciation of artists' names, with their schools and dates, for American readers and students. [2d ed.] Chicago, Art Inst., [1938]. 74p.   **BE68**
1st ed. 1934.
Includes more than 1500 names.

Mallett, Daniel Trowbridge. Mallett's Index of artists; international—biographical; including painters, sculptors, illustrators, engravers and etchers of the past and the present. N.Y., Bowker, 1935. 493p.   **BE69**
—— —— Supplement. 1940. 319p.
Both volumes repr.: N.Y., Peter Smith, 1948.
"Covers all the artists whose works are exhibited in leading galleries or inquired about by modern students."—*Foreword.* Entries give basic biographical data. For further information, entries also include a key to one or more of the 22 general reference works and more than 1000 specialized works listed as "Sources of biographical information." The Supplement includes entries for artists of all countries and periods not in the 1935 *Index;* a Necrology, 1935–40; and a list of early American silversmiths. The entries, in cases of artists not found in the listed sources, refer to the art gallery, museum, library, etc. from which data may be obtained.
Very useful as a first aid in biographical search, but should be used with some caution as it contains various inaccuracies.

Müller, Hermann Alexander and **Singer, Hans W.** Allgemeines Künstler-Lexicon. Leben und Werke der berühmtesten bildenden Künstler. 3. umgearb. u. bis auf die neueste Zeit ergänzte Aufl. Frankfurt a. M., Rütten, 1895–1901. 5v.   **BE70**
—— —— Nachträge und Berichtigungen. 1906. 295p.
Short biographical entries. A 5th edition (not revised) was issued in 1921–22 in 6v. v.6 contains a 2d supplement with corrections.

Thieme, Ulrich and **Becker, Felix.** Allgemeines Lexikon der bildenden Künstler von der Antike bis zur Gegenwart, unter Mitwirkung von etwa 400 Fachgelehrten des In- und Auslandes. Lepzig, Seemann, 1907–50. 37v.   **BE71**
Binder's title: Künstler Lexikon.
Imprint varies: v.1–4, Leipzig, Engelmann.
v.1–36, A–Z; v.37, Meister mit Notnamen und Monogrammisten. v.16–37, edited by Hans Vollmer.
The most complete and authoritative dictionary of painters, sculptors, engravers, etchers, and architects. Includes living persons. Locations of works of art are frequently given. Good bibliographies, and the longer articles are signed. Some 400 contributing specialists.

Vollmer, Hans. Allgemeines Lexikon der bildenden Künstler des XX. Jahrhunderts. Unter Mitwirkung von Fachgelehrten des In- und Auslandes. Leipzig, Seemann, 1953–62. 6v.   **BE72**
Half title: Künstlerlexikon des XX. Jahrhunderts.
A continuation of Thieme, above. Includes some overlap from the 19th century. Gives brief biographical notes, lists of works, and bibliographical references.
Bd.1–5, A–Z. Nachträge, A–G; Bd.6, Nachträge, H–Z.

Who's who in art. Biographies of leading men and women in the world of art today. 1st ed.– . London, Art Trade Pr., 1927– . Biennial. (12th ed. 1964)   **BE73**
1st–3d ed., 1927, 1929, 1934; 4th ed.– , 1948– .

Includes artists, designers, craftsmen, critics, writers, teachers, collectors, and curators, with appendixes of monograms and signatures, and obituary. British names predominate.

United States

Fielding, Mantle. Dictionary of American painters, sculptors and engravers. Philadelphia, 1926. 433p. il. (Repr.: N.Y., Struck, 1945) **BE74**

Brief biographical sketches of nearly 8000 American artists. Bibliography, p.424–33.

Index of twentieth century artists. v.1–4, no.7, Oct. 1933–April 1937. N.Y., College Art Assoc., 1933–37. 4v.
BE75

Each monthly number contains detailed information about one or more American artists, including for each artist: biographical data, awards and honors, membership in associations, museums containing his work, exhibitions in which he was represented, and bibliographical references—with reproductions of his work—in books and periodicals. The last number (Sept.) of each year is called a supplement, and consists of additions and revisions of material previously published. Cumulated index to v.1–3 in v.3. A typed table of contents for the 4v. set was issued. Total number of artists included in the 4v., 120.

New York Historical Society. Dictionary of artists in America, 1564–1860, by George C. Groce and David H. Wallace. New Haven, Yale Univ. Pr., 1957. 759p. **BE76**

"A documented biographical dictionary of painters, draftsmen, sculptors, engravers, lithographers, and allied artists, either amateur or professional, native or foreign-born, who worked within the present continental limits of the United States between the years 1564 and 1860 inclusive."—*Introd.*

Includes almost 11,000 names. Bibliography, p.713–59.

Smith, Ralph Clifton. A biographical index of American artists. . . . Baltimore, Williams and Wilkins, 1930. 102p.
BE77

Some 4700 American artists are listed, with references to material in 42 reference works. The index gives for each artist: place and date of birth and death, medium in which he worked, and references to biographical information.

Who's who in American art. v.1, 1936/37– . N.Y., Bowker, 1935– . Biennial (Irregular). (v.8, 1962)
BE78

Issued by the American Federation of Arts.

v.1–4, 1936/37–1940/47, were issued as pt.2 of the *American art annual* (BE42), v.33–36, 1936–1940/47. Subtitle, v.1–4, varies slightly.

A biographical directory of painters, sculptors, graphic artists, craftsmen, historians, critics, editors, museum personnel, educators, lecturers, etc. Sections include: American biographies, Canadian biographies, Geographical index, and Obituaries. v.2 contains a Necrology, Oct. 1927–Oct. 1935, which continues the Necrology, 1897–1927, in v.25 of the *American art annual.* The Obituaries sections continue the record. v.4, p.611–53, contains a bibliography on American art by Elizabeth McCausland.

Symbolism in art

See also Mythology, p.368; Classical Antiquities, p.469; Saints, p.221.

Aurenhammer, Hans. Lexikon der christlichen Ikonographie. Wien, Br. Hollinek, 1959–62. Lfg. 1–4. (In progress) **BE79**

Lfg. 1–4, A–Blasius.

A scholarly dictionary of Christian iconography, giving under each subject (1) sources, (2) symbols, and (3) attributes, with references to representations in art. Almost all articles have bibliographies.

Bailey, Henry Turner and **Pool, Ethel.** Symbolism for artists, creative and appreciative. Worcester, Mass., Davis Pr., 1925. 247p. il. **BE80**

Alphabetical list of elements and their meanings, with illustrations (46 plates). Includes a list of College and university colors, p.222–35; Bibliography, p.236–38; Plate and figure references, p.239–47.

Bles, Arthur de. How to distinguish the saints in art by their costumes, symbols and attributes. N.Y., Art Culture Publ., 1925. 168p. il. **BE81**

Contents: (1) Chapters 1–12, symbolism in general and for different groups, e.g., Virgin Mary, Evangelists, monastic orders, etc., with illustrations and explanations of pictures showing symbols; (2) Appendixes: Alphabetical table of martyrdoms; Tables of saints classified by habitual costume; Saints classified by categories; Alphabetical table of symbols and attributes with names of those who bear them; Chronological tables of bishops and popes of Rome; List of illustrations; General index.

Drake, Maurice and **Drake, Wilfred.** Saints and their emblems. London, Laurie; Philadelphia, Lippincott, 1916. 235p. il. **BE82**

(1) Dictionary of saints; (2) Dictionary of emblems; (3) Appendixes: Patriarchs and prophets; Sibyls; Patron saints of arts, trades, and professions; Other patron saints.

Droulers, Eug. Dictionnaire des attributs, allégories, emblèmes et symboles. Turnhout, Brepols, [1948?]. 281p. il. **BE83**

Alphabetical arrangement, including names of people, attributes, allegorical figures, etc. Definitions vary in length from a few sentences to several paragraphs. The illustrations in the text and in a section at the end are indexed, and there is a bibliography of sources.

Jameson, Anna Brownell (Murphy). The history of Our Lord as exemplified in works of art; with that of His types; St. John the Baptist; and other persons of the Old and New Testament. Cont. and compl. by Lady Eastlake. 2d ed. London, Longmans, 1865. 2v. il. **BE84**

Discusses early symbolic forms in Christian art as found in murals, mosaics, doors of churches, miniatures, etc. Describes specific works of art depicting incidents and characters of the Bible.

—— Legends of the Madonna, ed. with additional notes by E. M. Hurll. Boston, Houghton, 1896. 372p. il. **BE85**

1st ed. 1852. Frequently reprinted.

Divided into devotional and historical subjects. The historical development of symbols, and of traditional characteristics of representations in art of the Madonna, are discussed and specific works of art described or referred to with many photographs and line drawings. Indexes of artists; galleries and churches; and a general index.

—— Legends of the monastic orders as represented in the fine arts, forming the second series of Sacred and legendary art. [2d ed.] London, N.Y., Longmans, 1900. 461p. il. **BE86**

1st ed. 1850.

The introduction discusses the different orders, the character and influence of monastic art, and the principal churches and other buildings of the orders. Grouped by order: Benedictine, Augustine, Mendicant, Jesuit, and Visitation of St. Mary. Saints of the orders are discussed in relation to paintings and sculptures which represent them.

—— Sacred and legendary art, ed. with additional notes by E. M. Hurll. Boston, Houghton, 1896. 2v. il. **BE87**

1st ed. 1848.

Considers representations in art of angels, the Evangelists, the apostles, doctors of the church, patron saints, hermit and warrior saints, martyrs, early bishops, etc.

Künstle, Karl. Ikonographie der christlichen Kunst. Freiburg im Breisgau, Herder, 1926–28. 2v. il. (v.1, 1928)   **BE88**

v.1 discusses: (1) the history of symbolism in Christian art from the early church through the Middle Ages; (2) animal and other nature symbolism; (3) representations of subjects from the Old and New Testaments. v.2, which has a separate title page, *Ikonographie der Heiligen,* is a dictionary of saints, with brief biographical data; indication of their emblems; how and where depicted in mosaics, paintings, etc.; and bibliographical references to printed descriptions of these representations. Important for the art, theological, or large reference library.

Lehner, Ernst. Symbols, signs and signets. Cleveland, World, [1950]. 221p. il.   **BE89**

No attempt at completeness. Clear reproductions of signs and symbols are given under such headings as "Symbolic gods and deities," "Astronomy and astrology," "Heraldry," "Monsters," etc.; each section is preceded by a brief introduction. Some sections are indexed, but there is no general index. Bibliography, p.217–21.

Marle, Raimond van. Iconographie de l'art profane au Moyen-Âge et à la Renaissance et la décoration des demeures. La Haye, Nijhoff, 1931–32. 2v. il.   **BE90**

[v.1], La vie quotidienne; [v.2], Allégories et symboles. Includes bibliographies and many illustrations.

Pigler, Andor. Barockthemen: eine Auswahl von Verzeichnissen zur Ikonographie des 17. und 18. Jahrhunderts. [Budapest], Verlag der Ungarischen Akademie der Wissenschaften, 1956. 2v. il.   **BE91**

A listing of themes represented in the baroque art of the 17th and 18th centuries, with references to the artists who have treated them (including artists of the 15th and 16th centuries); indication of where the work may be found; and notation where an illustration may be located in book or periodical. Usually includes the artists of Italy, France, Germany, and the Netherlands.

v.1 contains religious representations; v.2, secular representations in Greek and Roman history, legends, and folklore, and in general history, allegories, etc. General index in v.2.

Réau, Louis. Iconographie de l'art chrétien. Paris, Presses Universitaires de France, 1955–59. 3v. in 6. il.   **BE92**

Contents: v.1, Introduction générale; v.2, Iconographie de la Bible: pt.1, Ancien Testament. pt.2, Nouveau Testament; v.3, Iconographie des saints.

Classifies iconographic themes, indicates their variations and evolution, and lists principal works of art representing them. Covers medieval Western and Byzantine art. Includes bibliographies and many illustrations.

Waters, Clara (Erskine) Clement. Handbook of legendary and mythological art. 23d ed. Boston, Houghton, 1892 [c1871–86]. 575p. il.   **BE93**

1st ed. 1871.

Contents: Symbolism in art; Legends and stories illustrated in art; Legends of place; Ancient myths illustrated in art. Catalogue of pictures.

The first two parts incorporate the text of the author's *Handbook of Christian symbols and stories of the saints as illustrated in art* (1886).

Webber, Frederick Roth. Church symbolism; an explanation of the more important symbols of the Old and New Testament, the primitive, the mediaeval and the modern church . . . introd. by Ralph Adams Cram. 2d ed. rev. Cleveland, J. H. Jansen, 1938. 413p. il.   **BE94**

Glossary of the more important symbols, p.357–88; Bibliography, p.389–94.

Whittick, Arnold. Symbols, signs and their meaning. Newton, Mass., Branford; London, L. Hill, 1960. 408p. il.   **BE95**

Contents: pt.1, Introduction; pt.2, Symbolism in its precise and applied forms and its practical uses; pt.3, Encyclopaedic dictionary: Traditional and familiar symbols, their origin, meaning and history; pt.4, Individual and collective expression—instinctive, creative and imaginative symbolism.

Confined "to visual symbols and symbolism and mainly to Western uses and examples, including only the better known Oriental examples."—*Pref.*

Buddhist

Akiyama, Aisaburo. Buddhist hand-symbol. Yokohama, Yoshikawa Book Store, 1939. 86p. il.   **BE96**

Text in English and Japanese. An illustration is given for each symbol.

Bhattacharyya, Benoytosh. The Indian Buddhist iconography, mainly based on the Sādhanamālā and cognate Tāntric texts of rituals. [2d ed. rev. and enl., with 357 illus.] Calcutta, Mukhopadhyay, 1958. 478p. il.   **BE97**

1st ed., Oxford Univ. Pr., 1924.

This comprehensive work is illustrated by more than 350 pictures and line drawings.

Chinese

Williams, Charles Alfred Speed. Encyclopedia of Chinese symbolism and art motives; an alphabetical compendium of legends and beliefs, as reflected in the manners and customs of the Chinese throughout history. N.Y., Julian, 1960. 468p.   **BE98**

"A re-issue of the . . . work originally titled *Outlines of Chinese symbolism and art motives* published 1931, rev. 1932."

Hindu

Banerjea, Jitendra Nath. The development of Hindu iconography. [2d ed. rev. and enl.] Calcutta, Univ. of Calcutta, 1956. 653p. il. (49pl.)   **BE99**

1st ed. 1941.

A comprehensive history dealing with the development and manifestations of Hindu iconography from ancient times.

Gopinātha Rāu, T. A. Elements of Hindu iconography. Madras, Law Printing House, 1914–16. 2v. in 4. il.   **BE100**

In Sanskrit and English.

Art reproductions

American Library Color Slide Company, Inc., New York. The American Library compendium and index of world art: architecture, sculpture, painting and the minor arts as comp. from the archives of the American Library of Color Slides. N.Y., Amer. Archives of World Art, 1961. 465p.   **BE101**

A compendium of "over 60,000 listings . . . derived from 30,000 works of art," covering architecture, sculpture, painting, and the minor arts arranged by period and then by country. When known, the names and dates of the artist are given as well as the present location of individual works. Includes special sections of survey sets and basic slide libraries.

Slides may be obtained from the American Library Color Slide Co., 222 West 23rd St., New York, N.Y. 10011.

Brooke, Milton and **Dubester, Henry J.** Guide to color prints. Wash., Scarecrow, 1953. 257p.   **BE102**

A comprehensive listing of some 5000 color reproductions available for purchase in the United States. The main list is arranged alphabetically by the more than 1000 painters represented. Size, publisher, and price of the prints are given. A second list includes about 150 portfolios and sets of color prints. Indexes by title and by artist.

Clapp, Jane. Art reproductions. N.Y., Scarecrow, 1961. 350p. **BE103**

"List of art reproductions available from ninety-five museums in the United States and Canada.... Arrangement ... is by media (as painting, graphic arts ... [etc.]). Under media, reproductions are arranged by locale ... The index includes names of artists, ... of individuals portrayed, locations depicted, and a few subjects."—*p.[3]*. Gives a list of the museums and a list of additional sources.

New York Graphic Society. Fine art reproductions of old & modern masters. Greenwich, Conn., [1962, c1961]. 443p. il. **BE104**

A catalog of color prints published by this company. Arranged by broad group (i.e., American painting, Old masters, Seascapes, etc.), with indexes by artist and by subject. Each entry includes: a small color reproduction, name and dates of artist, his nationality if not indicated by group, title with date and location of the original, catalog number, size and sale price of the print.

Nunn, George Walter Arthur. British sources of photographs and pictures. London, Cassell, 1952. 220p. **BE105**

Lists: (1) photographers and photographic agencies with addresses and brief descriptions of their collections; (2) libraries, museums and art galleries, art institutions, and societies; and (3) art journals, photographic journals, etc., with subject index.

Pierson, William Harvey and **Davidson, Martha.** Arts of the United States: a pictorial survey. N.Y., McGraw-Hill, [c1960]. 452p. il. **BE106**

"Based on a collection of color slides assembled by the University of Georgia under a grant by Carnegie Corporation of New York."—*Title page*.

The authors (executive secretary and coordinating editor of the Carnegie project) explain its purposes: (1) to compile and document material representing the history of American art in most of its phases from the beginning to the present; (2) to select from this material some 4000 works to be reproduced in high-quality color slides, intended for use in schools, museums, and libraries, here and abroad. The catalog of these slides—arranged by subject and giving number, identifying information, and a small reproduction in black and white for each entry—is preceded by essays on each subject group written by the specialists who chose the material. An index of artists, titles, and subjects.

Ploetz, Gerhard. Bildquellen-Handbuch; der Wegweiser für Bildsuchende. 1. Ausg. Wiesbaden, Chmielorz, [1961]. 611p. il. **BE107**

A guide to photographic sources (including archives, commercial firms, museums, and learned societies) and types of photographic illustrations for widely ranging pictorial purposes.

Pt.1 consists of indexes of subjects, countries, places, people, and artists, listing with each entry the number of the collection in which photographs on the subject are found. Pts. 2–5 (p.257–562) contain a list of 4000 picture archives and collections, grouped in 20 categories (firms, libraries, etc.) arranged by country and place; a list of photography societies arranged by country and place and including addresses, officers, and in some cases members; and indexes to these lists by country and by firm, museum, etc. owning the collection. Pt.6 has 9 brief articles on photography, and pt.7 has brief indexes to the sections.

Special Libraries Association. Picture Division. Picture sources. Celestine G. Frankenberg, ed. 2d ed. N.Y., [1964]. 216p. **BE108**

1st ed. 1959.

A directory intended for picture researchers, librarians, editors, artists, and all other professional users of pictures. Includes 703 sources (libraries, museums, business firms, etc., having picture collections), listed alphabetically within 11 large subject groups. Address and description of the collection and its use are given for each source listed. Also contains an alphabetical and a geographical list of sources and a subject index. 33 of the entries are for sources outside North America.

✔**United Nations Educational, Scientific and Cultural Organization.** The Unesco catalogue of colour reproductions of paintings prior to 1860. [6th ed. rev. and enl.] N.Y., Internat. Documents Service, 1962. 323p. il. **BE109**

1st ed. 1950. Revised approximately biennially.

—— Catalogue de reproductions en couleurs de peintures, 1860 à 1963. Catalogue of colour reproductions of paintings, 1860 to 1963. Catálogo de reproducciones en color de pinturas, 1860 a 1963. Paris, UNESCO, 1963. 519p. il. **BE110**

1st ed. 1949. Revised approximately biennially.

Title page and preface in French, English, and Spanish.

The choice of prints is based on fidelity of color reproduction, significance of artist, and importance of painting. The entries, arranged by artist, include a small reproduction in black and white; the name of the painter; dates and places of birth and death; the title of the original and its date, medium, size, and location. For the reproductions are given: the printing process, size, publisher, price, and UNESCO archives number. Index of painters and lists of publishers and printers.

—— Répertoire international des archives photographiques d'œuvres d'art. International directory of photographic archives of works of art. Paris, Dunod, 1950–54. 2v. **BE111**

v.1, 1950, gives information on 1195 photographic collections from 87 countries with a supplement listing 19 additional collections. v.2 adds 100 collections in 24 countries not mentioned in v.1. Each volume is arranged by the French names of the countries, and includes indexes of subjects and of countries.

U.S. Library of Congress. Reference Dept. Guide to the special collections of prints and photographs in the Library of Congress, comp. by Paul Vanderbilt. Wash., 1955. 200p. **BE112**

Lists 802 collections arranged alphabetically by name of originator or subject designation, with sufficient annotation to make clear each collection's origin, nature, and scope. Index of proper names and broad subjects.

University Prints, Cambridge, Mass. The University prints; fine art reproductions for students ... Complete catalogue. Cambridge, Mass., 1965. 262p. il. **BE113**

Subtitle: Listing by period, school and artist all 6600 different fine arts subjects—architecture, painting, sculpture—available both as slides and as prints. All prints a uniform 5½ x 8 inches ... in black and white ... 200 in color. Available loose-leaf or custom-bound.

A collection suitable for college-level teaching, selected and frequently revised by authorities on the various subjects.

ARCHITECTURE

Bibliography

✔**Columbia University. Libraries. Avery Architectural Library.** Catalog. James Grote van Derpool, Avery librarian. Boston, Microphotography Co., 1958. 6v. (11,534p.) **BE114**

The first catalog was published in 1895.

The Avery Library is one of the outstanding architectural collections in the United States. This photographic reproduction of all cards in the library's catalog, before May 1958, includes not only the Avery collection but all architectural and art books on the Columbia University campus.

Hitchcock, Henry Russell. American architectural books; a list of books, portfolios, and pamphlets on architecture and related subjects published in America before 1895. Minneapolis, Univ. of Minn. Pr., 1962. 130p.   **BE115**

Reprint of 3d revised edition, 1946, which lists 1461 items, distinguishing editions and locating copies in more than 130 public and private libraries. A new preface presents 30 emendations (8 being new titles or editions, the rest minor corrections of collations and imprints).

Roos, Frank John. Writings on early American architecture; an annotated list of books and articles on architecture constructed before 1860 in the eastern half of the United States. Columbus, Ohio State Univ. Pr., 1943. 271p. (Ohio. State Univ., Columbus. Graduate school studies. Contributions in fine arts, no.2)   **BE116**

Almost 2800 entries arranged by states within regional areas (New England, Middle Atlantic States, Southern States, North Atlantic States), preceded by: Colonial and Early Republican periods; Architects; General references and bibliographies. A general index includes names, places, and subjects.

Royal Institute of British Architects, London. Library. Catalogue of the . . . library. London, 1937–38. 2v.   **BE117**

v.1, Authors; v.2, Classified index and alphabetical subject index of books and manuscripts.

The catalog of an important library which has trebled in size since its last preceding general catalog was published, 1889–99.

Indexes

Columbia University. Libraries. Avery Architectural Library. Avery index to architectural periodicals. Boston, G. K. Hall, 1963. 12v.   **BE118**

Photographic reproduction of the library's card file. Indexes articles on architecture in its widest sense, including archaeology, decorative arts, interior decoration, furniture, landscape architecture, city planning, and housing. Periodicals in non-Western alphabets are not included. Projected supplements will contain current material.

Encyclopedias and dictionaries

Architectural Publication Society. Dictionary of architecture. London, Richards, 1852–92. 6v. il.   **BE119**

Still an important work, including terms; architectural forms and subjects; places with some account of their architectural features; and biographies of architects. Bibliographical references.

Briggs, Martin Shaw. Everyman's concise encyclopaedia of architecture. London, Dent; N.Y., Dutton, 1959. 372p. il.   **BE120**

An alphabetically arranged dictionary of terms and biographies with line drawings and a section of 32 plates.

Hatje, Gerd. Encyclopaedia of modern architecture. London, Thames & Hudson, [1963]. 336p. il.   **BE121**

Originally published as *Knaurs Lexikon der modernen Architektur.* München, Droemersche Verlagsanstalt. T. Knaur Nachf. [1963].

Articles, except very brief ones, are signed, and many include bibliographical references. They present those architects, schools, styles, associations, countries, construction terms, and materials which, since the mid-19th century, have contributed to the development of modern architecture.

Osborne, Arthur Leslie. A dictionary of English domestic architecture. London, Country Life, [1954]. 112p. il.   **BE122**

Dictionary of terms. Articles range from brief definitions to encyclopedic length. Line drawings are especially clear and attractive.

Planat, Paul Amédée. Encyclopédie de l'architecture et de la construction. Paris, Dujardin, [1888–92]. 6v. in 12. il.   **BE123**

At head of title: Bibliothèque de la construction moderne, publiée sous la direction de M. P. Planat.

Intended as a summing up of the whole of architectural knowledge at the end of the 19th century, covering architectural history, principles, and legislation, and the technical phases of construction. Contributors are architectural scholars and practicing architects. Articles on broad subjects are long and signed. Brief biographies of great architects and builders are included.

Saylor, Henry Hodgman. Dictionary of architecture. N.Y., Wiley, 1952. 221p. 16pl.   **BE124**

A dictionary of terms which indicates pronunciation and gives brief definitions. American in viewpoint.

Sturgis, Russell. Dictionary of architecture and building, biographical, historical, and descriptive. N.Y., Macmillan, 1901. 3v. il.   **BE125**

The standard dictionary in English, in spite of its age. Written in collaboration with many specialists: American and foreign. Longer articles and biographies are signed. Illustrations consist of line drawings, and plates which reproduce photographs. Bibliographies at the ends of many entries, and a bibliography of sources at end of v.3.

Viollet-Le-Duc, Eugène Emmanuel. Dictionnaire raisonné de l'architecture française du XIᵉ au XVIᵉ siècle. Paris, Bance, 1854–68. 10v. il.   **BE126**

Imprint varies: v.7–10, pub. by A. Morel.

—— —— Table analytique et synthétique, avec table alphabétique des noms de lieux par départements, pour la France et par contrées, pour l'étranger, [par] Henri Sabine. Paris, Librairie des Imprimeries Réunies, 1889. 387p.

Long articles in dictionary arrangement, including some on sculpture.

Ware, Dora and **Beatty, Betty.** A short dictionary of architecture, including some common building terms; with an introduction on the study of architecture by John Gloag. [3d ed. rev. and enl.] London, Allen & Unwin, 1953. 136p. il.   **BE127**

1st ed. 1944; 2d ed. 1946.

A useful small dictionary of terms commonly used in classical and modern architecture, well illustrated with line drawings.

Wasmuths Lexikon der Baukunst. Berlin, Wasmuth, [c1929–37]. 5v.   **BE128**

"Unter Mitwirkung zahlreicher Fachleute hrsg. von Günther Wasmuth . . ."

Covers both the practical and the art aspects of architecture, including terms, encyclopedic articles (often signed), many biographies, and excellent illustrations. No exhaustive bibliographies, but many short bibliographical references.

Handbooks

American Institute of Architects. Handbook of architectural practice. [8th ed.] Wash., 1958. [v.p.] il.   **BE129**

1st ed. 1920.

Includes sections on: building and architecture (elements, qualifications, organizations, ethics, legal and other problems of the profession); office procedure; project procedures; Appendix (with various forms, a list of building organizations, and bibliography).

History

Fletcher, *Sir* **Banister Flight.** A history of architecture on the comparative method, for students, craftsmen & amateurs. 17th ed. rev. by R. A. Cordingley. N.Y., Scribner; London, Athlone Pr., 1961. 1366p. il. **BE130**

A profusely illustrated standard reference work first published 1896. Though little changed in general form since the 9th edition, 1931, this 17th edition by the Royal Institute of British Architects and the University of London has major revisions of text.

Pt.1, Ancient architecture and the Western succession; pt.2, Architecture in the East. Each style is considered under five sections: (1) influences, (2) characteristics, (3) examples, (4) comparative analysis of structural patterns, and (5) reference books.

Gloag, John. Guide to Western architecture. With 279 illustrations in the text of which 161 were drawn by Hilton Wright. London, Allen & Unwin, 1958. 407p. il., maps. **BE131**

A summary outline from the 6th century B.C. to the present. Includes bibliography and a list of "the principal architects and their works, from the seventh century B.C. to the end of the Renaissance."

Hamlin, Talbot Faulkner. The American spirit in architecture. New Haven, Yale Univ. Pr., 1926. 353p. il. (Pageant of America. v.13) **BE132**

Useful as a pictorial history. The first half of the book is in chronological arrangement. The second half concerns types of buildings. Each chapter has many architectural illustrations with explanatory captions, preceded by one to three pages of text summarizing social and architectural developments.

—— Architecture through the ages. [Rev. ed.] N.Y., Putnam, [1953]. 684p. il. **BE133**

1st ed. 1940.

An excellent survey history from the social point of view. The Introduction, p.vii–viii, contains a selection of postwar publications describing recent discoveries and illuminating new evaluations and interpretations.

—— Forms and functions of twentieth-century architecture. N.Y., Columbia Univ. Pr., 1952. 4v. il. **BE134**

"Prepared under the auspices of the School of Architecture of Columbia University."

v.1, The elements of building; v.2, The principles of composition; v.3–4, Building types.

An important work, which largely supersedes Julien Guadet's *Éléments et théorie de l'architecture* (3. éd. 1909). Many specialists collaborated, and each building type is dealt with by an outstanding architect. Each chapter has a list of suggested additional readings; v.4 includes a general index and also one of architectural works described or illustrated. More than 2500 illustrations.

Jones, Cranston. Architecture today and tomorrow. N.Y., McGraw-Hill, 1961. 243p. il. **BE135**

The development of modern architecture treated by the analysis of the works of some 24 outstanding architects from the early-20th century to date, in various countries of the world. Lavishly illustrated, part in color.

Biography

American architects directory. 1st–2d ed., 1956–62. N.Y., Bowker, 1955–62. v.1–2. **BE136**

"Published under the sponsorship of American Institute of Architects."

Alphabetical listing of names and addresses with brief biographical information when available. Members of the American Institute of Architects are included automatically; other architects of established reputation from whom biographical

details have been obtained are also included. Contains a geographical index; lists of officers and regional directors of the Institute, its honorary members, fellows, and award winners; and appendixes giving standards, schedules, etc.

Colvin, Howard Montagu. A biographical dictionary of English architects, 1660–1840. London, Murray; Cambridge, Harvard Univ. Pr., 1954. 821p. **BE137**

Includes sketches of more than 1000 architects of the classical period. Sketches vary in length from a few lines to three or four pages and frequently include lists of the buildings which the architect designed, with bibliographical references. Two indexes: (1) persons mentioned anywhere in the dictionary; and (2) an index of places with references to buildings in each.

Harvey, John Hooper. English mediaeval architects, a biographical dictionary down to 1550. London, Batsford, 1954. 411p. **BE138**

Subtitle: . . . including master masons, carpenters, carvers, building contractors and others responsible for design.

Painstaking details about some 1300 persons, with references to sources.

Withey, Henry F. and **Withey, Elsie Rathburn.** Biographical dictionary of American architects (deceased). Los Angeles, New Age Pub. Co., 1956. 678p. **BE139**

Brief biographical sketches of nearly 2000 men and women, working *ca.* 1740–1952, now deceased. Usually indicates best-known works, and cites references at the ends of its articles.

City planning

Bestor, George Clinton and **Jones, Holway R.** City planning: a basic bibliography of sources and trends. Sacramento, California Council of Civil Engineers and Land Surveyors, 1962. 195p. **BE140**

An annotated bibliography of more than 1000 entries alphabetically arranged by title within subject groups. The main section concerns the functions and processes of contemporary city planning; others cover the nature of cities, history of planning, education for planning, and general bibliographies. Emphasis is on English-language publications. Special lists include: Some major city planning collections in the United States; A basic library for planning commissions; A selected list of services and periodicals.

International Federation for Housing and Town Planning. International glossary of technical terms used in housing and town planning . . . 2d rev. and enl. ed. Ed., H. J. Spiwak. Amsterdam, [1951]. 144p. **BE141**

Title page and text in English, French, German, Italian, and Spanish.

Gardens

Frohman, Louis H. and **Elliot, Jean.** A pictorial guide to American gardens. N.Y., Crown, [1960]. 364p. il. (part col.) **BE142**

A guide to famous gardens in the United States, grouped by region.

PAINTING

Bibliography

McColvin, Eric Raymond. Painting: a guide to the best books with special reference to the requirements of public libraries. London, Grafton, 1934. 216p. **BE143**

A brief introduction discusses principles of book selection and questions of practical administration. The bibliography—annotated, with most useful titles starred—is arranged by subject within four groups: (1) Theory and practice, (2)

Art galleries, (3) General history, and (4) Schools of painting. Indexes by subject, schools of painting, artists, and authors.

Dictionaries and encyclopedias

Berckelaers, Ferdinand Louis. A dictionary of abstract painting, with a history of abstract painting [by] Michel Seuphor, [pseud.]. N.Y., Tudor, 1957; London, Methuen, 1958. 305p. il.   **BE144**

Translated from the French *Dictionnaire de la peinture abstraite.* Paris, Hazan, 1957.

The history is followed by a "Chronological table of abstract art," p.[106–13], and the Dictionary, p.117–294, which gives brief biographical entries for some 500 artists. Many small, colored illustrations. Bibliography, p.297–[305].

Dictionary of modern painting. General eds.: Carlton Lake and Robert Maillard. [3d ed. rev. and enl.] N.Y., Tudor, 1964. 416p. il. (part col.)   **BE145**

1st American ed. 1955.

Original French ed.: *Dictionnaire de la peinture moderne.* Paris, Hazan, 1954. 328p. German translation: *Knaurs Lexikon moderner Kunst.* Munich, Knaur, 1955. 336p.

Includes, in alphabetical order, articles on persons, schools of painting, art movements, places, etc. The English version has some additional entries and illustrations.

Covers the period from the Impressionists to approximately World War II, i.e., the only living painters to be included are those who had made their mark before the outbreak of the Second World War.

Encyclopedia of painting: painters and painting of the world from prehistoric times to the present day. Bernard S. Myers, ed. N.Y., Crown, 1955. 511p. il.   **BE146**

A 1v. encyclopedia which attempts in a "portable and not too costly volume . . . to give an over-all picture of the outstanding painters, movements, styles and techniques from the most ancient times to the present day."—*Pref.* Arranged alphabetically with the partial exception of oriental painters; these are grouped by period under the headings: Chinese, Japanese, Indian, and Persian. Includes almost 1000 illustrations, many in color.

Gaunt, William. Everyman's dictionary of pictorial art. London, Dent; N.Y., Dutton, [1962]. 2v. il.   **BE147**

"The aim is to provide in concise form and within the limits of 250,000 words and 1,000 illustrations a handy reference to painters and periods, forms and techniques of pictorial art in all parts of the world . . . from the earliest times to the present."—*Introd.*

Includes biographical sketches of some 1200 artists; descriptions of the main periods and schools of art; galleries; definitions of terms; descriptions of some famous paintings, etc. Supplementary lists of British and American artists are included in v.2.

Morse, John D. Old masters in America, a comprehensive guide; more than two-thousand paintings in United States and Canada by forty famous artists. Chicago, Rand McNally, [1955]. 192p. il.   **BE148**

"A complete listing of every picture now on display in America by forty of Europe's old masters."—*Foreword.* Arranged by artist. Under each a biographical sketch, brief comment on his work, and a list of his paintings in America, arranged by place and art gallery. A geographical index to the galleries is by state and city.

History

❧ The history of painting is usually well covered in the general histories of art. For more detailed histories consult Chamberlin, p.164–202 (BE1) and the bibliographies in Robb and Garrison (BE63) and in Upjohn, Wingert,

and Mahler (BE65). A few of the most generally useful histories are:

Barker, Virgil. American painting, history and interpretation. N.Y., Macmillan, 1950. 717p. il.   **BE149**

Covers the history to the end of the 19th century. Bibliographical references are given for each chapter at the end of the volume, and there is a brief list of general sources. The index includes a section on the owners of the paintings mentioned.

Isham, Samuel. The history of American painting. New ed. with supplementary chapters by Royal Cortissoz. N.Y., Macmillan, 1927. 608p. il. (Reissue 1942) **BE150**

A standard work first published 1905, as v.3 of *The history of American art,* ed. by J. C. Van Dyke. Traces the development and the appreciation of painting in America to the latter part of the 19th century. The five chapters by Cortissoz continue the history for another quarter century. Bibliography, compiled by Henry Meier, p.593–600.

Mather, Frank Jewett. Western European painting of the Renaissance. N.Y., Holt, 1939. 873p. il. (Repr.: N.Y., Tudor, 1948)   **BE151**

A comprehensive survey.

Muther, Richard. History of painting from the IVth to the early XIXth century. Authorised English ed., tr. from the German and ed. with annotations by George Kriehn. N.Y., Putnam, 1907. 2v. il.   **BE152**

An older standard work. Original work: *Geschichte der Malerei.* Leipzig, 1900.

—— History of modern painting. Rev. ed. . . . to the end of the XIX century. London, Dent; N.Y., Dutton, 1907. 4v. il.   **BE153**

Original work: *Geschichte der Malerei im neunzehnten Jahrhundert.* München, 1893–94. 3v. The English translation was first published 1895–96. A detailed history of 19th-century European painting. Includes bibliographies and an index of artists.

Read, *Sir* Herbert Edward. A concise history of modern painting. London, Thames & Hudson, [1959]. 376p., incl. 485 il.   **BE154**

A brief survey covering painting from Cezanne to the present, which, because of its illustrations, documentation, and bibliography, may be useful for reference purposes.

Richardson, Edgar Preston. Painting in America; the story of 450 years. N.Y., Crowell, 1956. 447p. il. (The growth of America ser.)   **BE155**

A usable survey treatment, including much biographical and critical material. Bibliography, p.417–27; index, p.429–47.

—— A short history of painting in America; the story of 450 years. N.Y., Crowell, 1963. 348p. il.   **BE156**

"An abridgment, with a new concluding chapter and other new matter . . ."

Bibliography, p.319–33.

Robb, David Metheny. The Harper history of painting: the Occidental tradition. N.Y., Harper, [1951]. 1006p. il.   **BE157**

Covers painting in the West from preclassic to contemporary times. Includes a glossary of brief identifications and definitions, p.945–63, and a selected bibliography, p.965–83. Colored plates.

Biography

For biographical works for particular nationalities, *see* Chamberlin, *Guide to art reference books,* p.161–64 (BE1).

Aeschlimann, Erardo and **Ancona, Paolo d'.** Dictionnaire des miniaturistes du Moyen Âge et de la Renaissance dans les différentes contrées de l'Europe. 2. éd. rev. et augm. Milan, Hoepli, 1949. 239p. 155pl. (part col.) **BE158**

Brief biographical notes with bibliographical references. The 2d edition has been revised, with some new names and additional references. 13 new plates have been added, but the plates in the 1st edition seem definitely superior to those in the 2d. An index, arranged by epochs subdivided by country, is new in the 2d edition. The 1st edition was published in 1940 under the name of Aeschlimann; "Le nom de M. Paolo D'Ancona ne pouvait figurer en raison des lois raciales qui étaient en rigueur en Italie à cette époque."—*Pref. 2d edition.*

Bradley, John William. A dictionary of miniaturists, illuminators, calligraphers, and copyists, with references to their works, and notices of their patrons, from the establishment of Christianity to the eighteenth century. Comp. from various sources, many hitherto unedited. London, Quaritch, 1887–89. 3v. (Repr.: N.Y., Burt Franklin, [1958]) **BE159**

Entries include: name of artist, his century, his designation (whether miniaturist or other), and brief comment on his work with sources. An appendix lists supplementary names.

Bryan, Michael. Bryan's Dictionary of painters and engravers. [4th ed.] rev. and enl. under the supervision of G. C. Williamson. London, Bell; N.Y., Macmillan, 1903–5. 5v. il. (Repr.: London, Bell, 1926–34 [v.1, 1930]; Port Washington, N.Y., Kennikat, 1964) **BE160**

1st ed. 1816. 2v.; 2d ed. rev. 1849. 1v.; Supplement 1876; new ed. rev. 1884–89. 2v.

A standard biographical dictionary which usually lists works and frequently indicates location.

Monograms of painters and engravers, v.5, p.421–25.

Champlin, John Denison and **Perkins, Charles C.** Cyclopedia of painters and paintings. N.Y., Scribner, 1892 [c1885–87]. 4v. il. (Repr.: N.Y., Empire State Book Co., 1927) **BE161**

Gives, in one alphabet, biographical articles on painters and descriptive articles on famous paintings. The biographies give main facts of the artist's life; list of his paintings, with reference to the museums or collections where they are located; and some bibliography. Articles on paintings give brief description, some facts of history, museum, a statement of whether engraved and by whom, and some bibliographical references. Illustrated by outline drawings and plates. Includes numerous facsimiles of monograms and signatures.

PRINTS AND ENGRAVINGS

History

Delteil, Loÿs. Manuel de l'amateur d'estampes du XVIIIᵉ siècle. Paris, Dorban-Aîné, [1910]. 447p. 106pl. **BE162**

Manuel, p.1–364; Table alphabétique des ventes publiques, avec noms des propriétaires, mentionnées au cours du Manuel, p.365–68; Table des noms d'artistes et des estampes cités, p.369–442.

A detailed history of 18th-century engraving, chiefly in France but including other European work. Prints cited in the text are noted at the bottom of the page, often with information on sales and prices.

—— Manuel de l'amateur d'estampes des XIXᵉ et XXᵉ siècles (1801–1924). Paris, Dorbon-Aîné, [1925]. 2v. il. **BE163**

A history of 19th- and 20th-century engraving. In organization and format similar to the previous title. v.2 contains a bibliography, p.[547]–56, and indexes (1) of sales mentioned in the text, and (2) of artists and titles cited.

—— 700 reproductions d'estampes des XIXᵉ et XXᵉ

siècles pour servir de complément au *Manuel* . . . [1925]. 2v. il. **BE164**

Plates are chronologically arranged, each marked with name of artist, title, and page reference to the *Manuel*. Index of artists and titles.

Hind, Arthur Mayger. History of engraving and etching, from the 15th century to the year 1914; being the 3d and fully rev. ed. of "A short history of engraving and etching." Boston, Houghton, [1923]. 487p. il. (Repr.: N.Y., Dover, 1963) **BE165**

Appendixes: (1) Classified list of engravers; (2) General bibliography; and (3) Index of engravers and individual bibliography.

Still the best history of engraving.

—— An introduction to a history of woodcut, with a detailed survey of work done in the fifteenth century . . . with frontispiece and 483 illustrations in the text. London, Constable; Boston, Houghton, 1935. 2v. il. **BE166**

A standard work with clear and detailed treatment. Includes chapters on technique, and historical surveys of the work in various countries. Includes bibliography.

Biography

Beraldi, Henri. Les graveurs du XIXᵉ siècle; guide de l'amateur d'estampes modernes. Paris, Conquet, 1885–92. 12v. il. **BE167**

Intended as an inventory of 19th-century prints. Some 2000 artists are listed alphabetically with very brief biographical information, lists of their prints as complete as possible, and critical comment on the more important works.

Fielding, Mantle. American engravers upon copper and steel; biographical sketches and check lists of engravings, a supplement to David McNeely Stauffer's American engravers. Philadelphia, priv. pr., 1917. 365p. il. (Repr.: N.Y., Burt Franklin, 1964) **BE168**

Checklists of 1932 engravings with biographical information not found in Stauffer (BE170). Includes an index by subject of engraving.

Monod, Lucien. Aide-mémoire de l'amateur et du professionnel. Le prix des estampes, anciennes et modernes, prix atteints dans les ventes, suites et états, biographies et bibliographies. Paris, Morancé, 1920–31. 9v. **BE169**

A dictionary of artists and their works with very brief biographical data, bibliography, and record of prices realized at various sales.

v.1–9, A–Z; v.9 contains also: Graveurs identifiés par leurs monogrammes ou par des désignations particulières (XVᵉ et XVIᵉ siècles), p.61–73; Bibliographie générale, p.77–109; Nomenclature des estampes par catégories et par sujets (indication des planches typiques, bibliographies, planches anonymes), p.113–281.

Stauffer, David McNeely. American engravers upon copper and steel. N.Y., Grolier Club, 1907. 2v. il. (Repr.: N.Y., Burt Franklin, 1964) **BE170**

—— —— An artist's index to Stauffer's "American engravers," by Thomas Hovey Gage. Worcester, Mass., Amer. Antiquarian Soc., 1921. 49p. (Repr. from Proceedings of the American Antiquarian Soc., Oct. 1920)

A pioneer work on engravers working in America before 1825. v.1 includes some 700 biographical sketches and an index of the engravings described, also a brief introduction on copperplate engraving in the United States, and a short section of advertisements about prints found in early American newspapers. v.2 is a checklist of 3438 works arranged by engraver.

See also Mantle Fielding, *American engravers upon copper and steel . . . a supplement to . . . Stauffer's American engravers* (BE168).

SCULPTURE

History

Bieber, Margarete. The sculpture of the Hellenic Age. Rev. ed. N.Y., Columbia Univ. Pr., 1961. 259p. il. **BE171**
1st ed. 1955.
A scholarly work covering the period from the beginning of the 4th century to almost the end of the 1st century B.C.

Chase, George Henry and **Post, Chandler Rathfon.** History of sculpture. N.Y., London, Harper, [c1924]. 582p. il. **BE172**
A standard handbook. The final chapter is on sculpture of the Orient. "Bibliographical note" at end of each chapter. Indexes of sculptors, monuments, and places.

Post, Chandler Rathfon. History of European and American sculpture from the early Christian period to the present day. Cambridge, Harvard Univ. Pr., 1921. 2v. il. **BE173**
A standard work. Bibliography, v.2, p.271–89.

Biography

Bessone-Aurelj, Antonietta Maria. Dizionario degli scultori ed architetti italiani. Genova, Roma, Ed. Dante Alighieri, 1947. 523p. **BE174**
Very brief biographical information without bibliographies.

Dictionary of modern sculpture. Gen. ed., Robert Maillard. N.Y., Tudor; London, Methuen, [1962, c1960]. 310p. il. **BE175**
Translated from the French *Dictionnaire de la sculpture moderne.* Paris, Hazan, 1960.
Biographical and critical sketches of 412 sculptors representing the principal movements since Rodin. 453 works reproduced.

Gunnis, Rupert. Dictionary of British sculptors, 1660–1851. London, Odhams, [1953]. 514p. 32pl. **BE176**
Gives the lives and known work of more than 1700 sculptors; more attention given, when possible, to the lesser-known men than to those for whom biographies already exist. Includes indexes of places and names.

Lami, Stanislas. Dictionnaire des sculpteurs de l'école française. Paris, Champion, 1898–1921. 8v. **BE177**
Contents (not volumed as a set): Du moyen âge au règne de Louis XIV. 1898. 581p.; Sous le règne de Louis XIV. 1906. 504p.; Au 18e siècle. 1910–11. 2v.; Au 19e siècle. 1914–21. 4v.
Each period arranged alphabetically by artist, giving biographical sketch, list of works, and bibliography. The volumes for the 19th century include only artists deceased before 1914.

B F

Applied Arts

☙ Many of the subjects in this grouping of Applied Arts are highly specialized, and often the publications consist of illustrated texts rather than the more usual dictionary or handbook material. General libraries will want to acquire such works on a limited, selective basis, referring the more specialized questions to the special library. Only a small selection is listed here. For much more extensive lists in these fields, consult Chamberlin, p.224–68 (BE1).

ANTIQUES

Baker, Mary Gladys Steel. A dictionary of antiques, by Sheila Stuart, [pseud.] (Mrs. Howard Baker). Edinburgh, London, Chambers, 1953. 263p. il. **BF1**
Covers: furniture, smaller antiques, pottery and china, glass, silver and Sheffield plate, and pewter.

Boger, Louise Ade and **Boger, H. Batterson.** The dictionary of antiques and the decorative arts. Illus. by I. N. Steinberg and associates. N.Y., Scribner, 1957. 566p. il. **BF2**
Subtitle: A book of reference for glass, furniture, ceramics, silver, periods, styles, technical terms, etc.
Bibliography, p.559–66.

Connoisseur. The complete encyclopedia of antiques. Ed., L. G. G. Ramsey. London, Connoisseur; [N.Y., Hawthorn], [1962]. 1472p. il. 512pl. **BF3**
Adapted from the Connoisseur's *Concise encyclopaedia of antiques* (5v. 1954–61) and *The concise encyclopaedia of American antiques,* by Helen Comstock (2v. 1958). The random grouping of chapters by some 100 contributors in the previous volumes has been changed to bring like subject material together under 17 headings. Many of the chapters contain glossaries. Includes a list of major museums in Great Britain, Europe, and the United States arranged under the 17 subjects represented. Bibliography, p.1410–22.

Macdonald-Taylor, Margaret Stephens. A dictionary of marks: metalwork, furniture, ceramics; the identification handbook for antique collectors. [1st ed.] N.Y., Hawthorn; London, Connoisseur, 1962. 318p. il. **BF4**
Marks on English and American silver and pewter, English and French furniture, Flemish and French tapestry, English and European pottery, etc.

CERAMICS

Barber, Edwin Atlee. Ceramic collectors' glossary. N.Y., Walpole Soc., 1914. 119p. il. **BF5**
A dictionary of terms only, frequently with small line drawings.

Chaffers, William. Marks and monograms on European and Oriental pottery and porcelain, with historical notices of each manufactory; over 5,000 potters' marks and illustrations, ed. by Frederick Litchfield . . . 14th ed. . . . London, Reeves, 1932. 1095p. il. (Repr. with new title page: Los Angeles, Borden Pub. Co., 1946) **BF6**
The standard work in English.

—— Collector's handbook of marks and monograms on pottery and porcelain of the Renaissance and modern periods, with upwards of 5,000 marks. Rev. and considerably augm. by Frederick Litchfield. 3d ed. London, Reeves, 1952. 367p. il. **BF7**
An abridgment of the above.

—— New keramic gallery, containing 700 illustrations of rare, curious and choice examples of pottery and porcelain from early times to the beginning of the twentieth century . . . 3d ed., enl. by over 100 additional illustrations, with descriptions . . . rev. and ed. by H. M. Cundall. London, Reeves, 1926. 2v. il. **BF8**

A pictorial supplement to the 13th edition of the author's *Marks and monograms on . . . pottery and porcelain.*

Cushion, John Patrick and **Honey, William Bowyer.** Handbook of pottery and porcelain marks. London, Faber, 1956. 476p. il., maps. **BF9**

An aid to the identification of pottery and porcelain. Contains some 3500 factory marks. Especially strong in English marks, but includes also some from Europe, China, and Japan. Many of the 19th- and 20th-century marks have not been recorded previously. *252 + 253*

Garnier, Édouard. Dictionnaire de la céramique; faïences —grès—poteries . . . Aquarelles, marques et monogrammes d'après les dessins de l'auteur. Paris, Librairie de l'Art, [1893]. 258p. il., col. pl. (Bibliothèque Internat. de l'Art. Guides du collectionneur) **BF10**

Includes biography.

Solon, Louis Marc Emmanuel. Ceramic literature; an analytical index to the works published in all languages on the history and the technology of the ceramic art; also to the catalogues of public museums, private collections, and of auction sales . . . and to the most important price-lists of the ancient and modern manufactories. . . . London, Griffin, 1910. 660p. **BF11**

Pt.1, Author list, annotated; pt.2, Classified list.

CLOCKS AND WATCHES

Baillie, Granville Hugh. Clocks and watches; an historical bibliography. London, N.A.G. Pr., 1951. 414p. il. **BF12**

Foreword by Sir Harold Spencer-Jones, Astronomer Royal. Comprehensive chronological list of books, pamphlets, manuscripts, and periodical articles—published up to 1800— on mechanical timepieces only. Introductory section gives a brief history of horology, with a list of earlier bibliographies on the subject and indications of London libraries rich in the field. Annotations are exceptionally full, with biographical notes on authors, locations of copies, outlines of contents, and quotations and illustrations from many items listed.

—— Watchmakers and clockmakers of the world. [2d ed.] London, N.A.G. Pr., [1947]. 388p. maps. **BF13**

1st ed. 1929.

An alphabetical directory giving name, place, dates, type of clock or watch, and sometimes other brief information. Lists makers to 1825 with a few outstanding later names. The 2d edition includes some 35,000 names—10,000 more than the 1st edition.

Britten, Frederick James. Old clocks and watches and their makers; a historical and descriptive account of the different styles of clocks and watches of the past in England and abroad, containing a list of nearly fourteen thousand makers. 7th ed. by G. H. Baillie, C. Clutton, and C. A. Ilbert. London, Spon; N.Y., Dutton, 1956. 518p. il. **BF14**

1st ed. 1899.

Glossary of technical terms, p.297–308; Hallmarks, p.309–11; Bibliography, p.312–17; List of former clock and watch makers (with dates and places of work), p.319–505.

Drepperd, Carl William. American clocks and clockmakers. enl. [i.e., 2d] ed. Boston, Branford, 1958 [c1947]. 312p., 52p. il. **BF15**

Reproduces the 1st edition of 1947 (which includes historical chapters; a list of American clockmakers, p.196–293; a list of terms with explanations, p.[295]–312; and a bibliography, p.312), and inserts at the end a 52p. supplement, "Additional names of clockmakers."

COSTUME

Bibliography

Colas, René. Bibliographie générale du costume et de la mode. Description des suites, recueils, séries, revues et livres français et étrangers relatifs au costume civil, militaire et religieux, aux modes, aux coiffures et aux divers accessoires de l'habillement. Avec une table méthodique et un index alphabétique. Paris, Colas, 1933. 2v. (Repr.: N.Y., Hacker Art Books) **BF16**

The 3121 entries are listed by author. The bibliographical information for each item includes references to important bibliographies in which it appears.

Hiler, Hilaire and **Hiler, Meyer.** Bibliography of costume; a dictionary catalog of about eight thousand books and periodicals . . . ed. by Helen Grant Cushing, assisted by Adah V. Morris. N.Y., Wilson, 1939. 911p. **BF17**

Lists "approximately eighty-four hundred works on costume and adornment, including books in all languages."— *Pref.*

Lipperheide, Franz Joseph, *Freiherr von.* Katalog der Freiherrlich von Lipperheide'schen Kostümbibliothek. Berlin, Lipperheide, 1896–1905. 2v. il. (N.Y., Hacker Art Books) **BF18**

Classed catalog of an important collection which became the property of the Staatliche Kunstbibliothek, Berlin.

Indexes

Monro, Isabel Stevenson and **Cook, Dorothy E.** Costume index; a subject index to plates and to illustrated texts. N.Y., Wilson, 1937. 338p. **BF19**

—— —— Supplement. Ed. by I. S. Monro and K. M. Monro. 1957. 210p.

An important index to more than 600 works either wholly on costume or containing much material on the subject. Indexing is specific and detailed: under countries and localities, under classes of persons having special types of costume, and under details of costume—e.g., shoes, hats, etc.—with chronological subdivisions under important or large classes. The list of books indexed marks location of copies in some 33 libraries. The supplement indexes 347 books.

Dictionaries and encyclopedias

Cunnington, Cecil Willett, Cunnington, Phillis and **Beard, Charles.** A dictionary of English costume [900–1900]. London, A. & C. Black; Philadelphia, Dufour, 1960. 281p. il. **BF20**

An alphabetically arranged dictionary of terms illustrated with numerous line drawings. Has a separate "glossary of materials," p.241–80, and one page of "obsolete colour names (prior to 1800)." The medieval items are chosen from material collected by Charles Beard.

Picken, Mary (Brooks). The fashion dictionary: fabric, sewing, and dress as expressed in the language of fashion. N.Y., Funk & Wagnalls, [1957]. 397p. il. **BF21**

Based on the author's *Language of fashion* (1939). Includes more than 10,000 terms and names associated with wearing apparel, with many line drawings and photographic illustrations. Indicates pronunciation.

History and illustration

Brooke, Iris. Western European costume and its relation to the theatre. London [etc.], Harrap, [1939–40]. 2v. il., col. pl. **BF22**

2d ed.: N.Y., Theatre Arts Books, 1964 [c1963]. v.1.

v.1, 13th to 17th century; v.2, 17th to mid-19th century.

The 176 line drawings and 32 color plates are drawn by the author. "The aim and scope of this book is to point out differences in costume, and the manner in which those costumes were worn at corresponding dates in the more important countries of Western Europe . . . also to give their connexions in relations to the theatre and dramatists contemporary with them."—v.1, p.17.

Davenport, Millia. The book of costume. N.Y., Crown, [1948]. 2v.(958p.). il.   **BF23**

A chronological survey from early times to the end of the American Civil War. The almost 3000 illustrations (partly in color) are mainly from contemporary paintings, engravings, sculpture, etc. Location of the originals is usually given.

Evans, Mary. Costume throughout the ages. [Rev. ed.] Philadelphia, Lippincott, [1950]. 360p. il.   **BF24**

1st ed. 1930.

Brief account of: (1) the historic dress of the ancients, the French, English, and Americans, and (2) typical regional costumes of Europe, North Africa, Asia, and the Americas. Includes many small photographic illustrations, most of them showing paintings, sculpture, etc. Bibliographies and lists of painters whose works illustrate historic costume. Intended as a school text.

Lester, Katherine Morris and **Oerke, Bess Viola.** Illustrated history of those frills and furbelows of fashion which have come to be known as: accessories of dress; drawings by Helen Westermann. Peoria, Ill., Manual Arts, [1940]. 587p. il.   **BF25**

Cover title: Accessories of dress.

Treats in groups the accessories worn or carried in connection with the costume: hats, veils, earrings, combs, fans, bracelets, walking sticks, muffs, buttons, buckles, etc.

McClellan, Elisabeth. History of American costume, 1607–1870; with an introductory chapter on dress in the Spanish and French settlements in Florida and Louisiana. N.Y., Tudor, 1937. 661p. il.   **BF26**

First published as *Historic dress in America 1607–1800* (Philadelphia, Jacobs, [1904]) and *Historic dress in America 1800–1870* (Philadelphia, Jacobs, [1910]).

Planché, James Robinson. Cyclopaedia of costume; or, Dictionary of dress. London, Chatto and Windus, 1876–79. 2v. il.   **BF27**

Subtitle: Including notices of contemporary fashions on the Continent; a general chronological history of the costumes of the principal countries of Europe, from the commencement of the Christian era to the accession of George the Third.

v.1, Dictionary of terms, garments, weapons, fabrics, etc.; v.2, History of costume in Europe to 1760. Many illustrations, some in color.

Racinet, Albert Charles Auguste. Le costume historique. Paris, Firmin-Didot, 1888. 6v. 500pl. (part col.) **BF28**

v.1 is mainly text: a general introduction; a summary of the four parts (L'antiquité classique, Le monde en dehors de l'Europe, Le monde européen à partir du moyen âge, L'Europe des temps modernes); an index of plates; a geographical and ethnographical index; a bibliography; etc. v.2–6 are plates with explanatory text, covering clothing, furniture, arms, etc.

Truman, Nevil. Historic costuming. London, Pitman, 1936. 152p. il. (part col.)   **BF29**

Planned for the theatrical costumer but useful also for anyone interested in accurate details of historical costume, as it describes details of costumes of ancient Greece and Rome and of Britain from the 5th-century Saxons to 1910. Includes ecclesiastical costume, and armor.

FURNITURE AND INTERIOR DESIGN

Aronson, Joseph. The encyclopedia of furniture. N.Y., Crown, 1938. 202p. il.   **BF30**

Alphabetical arrangement of short articles, illustrated with 1115 photographs and many line cuts.

Bibliography, p.201–2.

Bajot, Édouard. Encyclopédie du meuble du XVᵉ siècle jusqu'à nos jours. Recueil de planches contenant des meubles de style de toutes les époques et de tous les pays, depuis le XVᵉ siècle . . . classées par ordre alphabétique . . . 2000 meubles de style reproduits à grande échelle. Paris, C. Schmid, [1901–9]. 20 pts. in 19v. 600pl. **BF31**

More than 500 engraved plates arranged by type of furniture. Text is limited to very brief captions on the plates—identifying material, country, and period—and a *Table analytique des planches*" and a *Notice*" in v.1. Both list the 54 types of furniture alphabetically, the *Notice*" giving a short historical paragraph for each type.

Connoisseur. The Connoisseur period guides to the houses, decoration, furnishing and chattels of the classic periods, ed. by Ralph Edwards & L. G. G. Ramsey. [London, 1956–58]. 6v. il. (part col.)   **BF32**

Each volume has special title page: [v.1], The Tudor period, 1500–1603; [v.2], The Stuart period, 1603–1714; [v.3], The early Georgian period, 1714–1760; [v.4], The late Georgian period, 1760–1810; [v.5], The Regency period, 1810–1830; [v.6], The early Victorian period, 1830–1860.

Gloag, John. A short dictionary of furniture, containing 1764 terms used in Britain and America. London, Allen & Unwin, 1952. 565p. il.   **BF33**

Brief but clear definitions and descriptions, with many line drawings. Preliminary sections cover: (1) description and (2) design of furniture. The dictionary is followed by lists of British and American furniture makers and designers, and British clockmakers; bibliography; and tabulated lists of periods, types of furniture, materials, and craftsmen from 1100 to 1950. Emphasis is mainly British.

Heal, *Sir* **Ambrose.** The London furniture makers from the Restoration to the Victorian era, 1660–1840 . . . London, Batsford, [1953]. 276p. il.   **BF34**

Subtitle: A record of 2500 cabinet-makers, upholsterers, carvers and gilders with their addresses and working dates illustrated by 165 reproductions of makers' trade-cards, with a chapter by R. W. Symonds on the problem of identification of the furniture they produced illustrated by some hitherto unpublished examples of authenticated pieces.

Hinckley, F. Lewis. A directory of antique furniture: the authentic classification of European and American designs for professionals and connoisseurs. N.Y., Crown, [1953]. xxxivp., 355p. of il.   **BF35**

1099 illustrations with descriptive captions, grouped as French, English, Irish, American furniture, and furniture related to the French and to the English school. Preceded by a 26p. text on the interrelation of design, the spread of French and English design influences, and structural methods.

Johnson, Axel Petrus and **Sironen, M. K.** Manual of the furniture arts and crafts, ed. by W. J. Etten. Grand Rapids, Mich., A. P. Johnson, 1928. 899p. il.   **BF36**

A handbook of brief information on furniture history, period styles, woods and veneers, manufacturing and merchandising, museum collections in the United States, etc. Gives bibliographical references throughout and contains a general bibliography based on the collection of the Grand Rapids Public Library, and a glossary of furniture terms based, with additions, on the Penderel-Brodhurst Glossary (BF40).

Lackschewitz, Gertrud. Interior design and decoration; a bibliography comp. for the American Institute of Decorators. N.Y., N.Y. Pub. Lib., 1961. 86p. **BF37**

A selective list covering the history of architecture and the applied arts as well as 20th-century concepts of design. Arranged by subject with author index. Some entries have a brief descriptive comment.

Macquoid, Percy and **Edwards, Ralph.** Dictionary of English furniture, from the Middle Ages to the late Georgian period. [2d ed.] rev. and enl. by Ralph Edwards. London, Country Life, [1954]. 3v. il. (part col.) **BF38**

Of first importance. "A drastic revision of the former text, [1924–27. 3v.] with the addition of numerous sections and a very !arge *corpus* of illustrations."—*Foreword.*

Nutting, Wallace. Furniture treasury (mostly of American origin). All periods of American furniture with some foreign examples in America, also American hardware and household utensils. Framingham, Mass., Old America Co., [1928–33]. 3v. il. **BF39**

v.1–2 reissued: N.Y., Macmillan, 1948. 2v. Also reissued as 2v. in 1: N.Y., Macmillan, 1954.

v.1–2 include 5000 plates, arranged by type with descriptions and often dimensions and owners, covering styles to the end of the Empire period; index in v.2. v.3 has subtitle: Being a record of designers, details of designs and structure, with lists of clock makers in America, and a glossary of furniture terms, richly illustrated. It is intended to supplement the first two volumes by supplying fuller details.

Penderel-Brodhurst, James George Joseph and **Layton, Edwin J.** Glossary of English furniture of the historic periods. London, Murray, 1925. 196p. **BF40**

Defines terms and identifies prominent cabinetmakers and authors (French and English). Bibliographical sources are included in entries.

Viollet-Le-Duc, Eugène Emmanuel. Dictionnaire raisonné du mobilier français de l'époque carlovingienne à la Renaissance. Paris, Morel, 1871–75. [v.1, 1872] 6v. il. **BF41**

v.1, pt.1, Meubles. v.2: pt.2, Ustensiles; pt.3, Orfèvrerie; pt.4, Instruments de musique; pt.5, Jeux, passetemps; pt.6, Outils, outillages. v.3–4, pt.7, Vêtements, bijoux de corps, objets de toilette. v.5–6, pt.8, Armes de guerre offensives et défensives.

Index in each volume, with one for the whole work in v.6.

LACE

Jackson, [Emily]. History of hand-made lace. Dealing with the origin of lace, the growth of the great lace centres, the mode of manufacture, the methods of distinguishing and the care of various kinds of lace, by Mrs. F. Nevill Jackson, with suppl. information by Ernesto Jesurum. London, Gill; N.Y., Scribner, 1900. 245p. il. **BF42**

Bibliography, p.98–105; "Dictionary of lace," p.[107]–206; "Glossary relating to hand-made lace," p.[207]–19.

Powys, Marian. Lace and lace-making. Drawings by the author. Boston, Branford, 1953. 219p. il. **BF43**

A practical handbook, giving descriptions of various types of lace with methods of identification; also directions for making, mending, and cleaning lace.

Whiting, Gertrude. Lace guide for makers and collectors; with bibliography and five-language nomenclature, profusely illustrated with halftone plates and key designs. N.Y., Dutton, [c1920]. 415p. il. **BF44**

Nomenclature in English, French, Italian, Spanish, and German, p.38–68. Bibliography, p.243–401. Illustrations and instructions for making various types of lace.

METAL ARTS

Gold and silver

Chaffers, William. Hall marks on gold and silver plate, illus. with revised tables of annual date letters employed in the assay offices of England, Scotland and Ireland. 10th ed. extended and enl. and with the addition of new date letters and marks, and a bibliography. Also incorporating makers' marks from the *"Gilda aurifabrorum."* Ed. by C. A. Markham. London, Reeves, 1922. 395p. il. **BF45**

Includes also material on English gold- and silversmiths, tables of statutes and ordinances, chronological list of English plate, etc., and a general index.

Jackson, *Sir* Charles James. English goldsmiths and their marks: a history of the goldsmiths and plate workers of England, Scotland, and Ireland; with over thirteen thousand marks, reproduced in facsimile from authentic examples of plate, and tables of date-letters and other hallmarks used in the assay offices of the United Kingdom. 2d ed. rev. and enl. London, Macmillan, 1921. 747p. il. (Repr.: N.Y., Dover, 1964) **BF46**

1st ed. 1905.

"The term 'Goldsmith' is used, as it formerly was, not only with reference to the worker in gold, but as comprising the Silversmith and the worker in both gold and silver."—*Introd.*

Nocq, Henry. Le poinçon de Paris; répertoire des maîtres-orfèvres de la juridiction de Paris depuis le Moyen-Âge jusqu'à la fin du XVIIIe siècle. Paris, H. Floury, 1926–31. 5v. il. **BF47**

Arranged alphabetically by name of the gold- or silversmith, giving brief information and mark. v.1–4, A–Z. v.4 includes also a *"Résumé chronologique"* and other historical lists and notes. v.5 contains "Errata et addenda" and three indexes.

Okie, Howard Pitcher. Old silver and old Sheffield plate. . . . Garden City, N.Y., Doubleday, 1928. 420p. il. **BF48**

Subtitle: History of the silversmith's art in Great Britain and Ireland, with reproductions in facsimile of about thirteen thousand marks; tables of date letters and other marks; American silversmiths and their marks; Paris marks and Paris date letters with a description of the methods of marking employed by the Paris Guild of Silversmiths; hallmarks, and date letters when used, of nearly all the countries of continental Europe, reproduced in facsimile; a history of Old Sheffield Plate and a description of the method of its production, with the names and marks in facsimile of every known maker.

Rosenberg, Marc. Der goldschmiede Merkzeichen. 3. erweit. u. illus. Aufl. Frankfurt a.M., Frankfurter Verlags-Anstalt, 1922–28. 4v. il. (Repr. 1955) **BF49**

v.1–3, *Deutsches Reich,* are arranged by city with its goldsmiths chronologically arranged. v.4, *Das europäische Ausland,* is arranged by country, then city. It includes Byzantine goldsmiths. Indexes of marks and names in each volume.

Pewter

Cotterell, Howard Herschel. Old pewter; its makers and marks in England, Scotland and Ireland. An account of the old pewterer and his craft, illustrating all known marks and secondary marks of the old pewterers with a series of plates showing the chief types of their wares. London, Batsford; N.Y., Scribner, 1929. 432p. il. (Repr.: London, Batsford; Rutland, Vt., Tuttle, 1963) **BF50**

Alphabetical list of pewterers with illustrations of their marks where known, p.145–344; Initialled marks, alphabetical list, p.345–83; Illustrations of those marks which bear neither their owner's names nor initials, p.384–89; Index to the devices, p.390–415; Index to the "Hallmarks," p.416–21; General index, p.425–32.

Laughlin, Ledlie Irwin. Pewter in America, its makers and their marks. Boston, Houghton, 1940. 2v. il. 78pl.   **BF51**

A standard work, giving history, problems for the collector, and biographical sketches of pewterers working in America prior to 1850, grouped geographically, then chronologically. Contains a "Check list of American makers of pewter, britannia or block tin . . . prior to 1850"; a list of "Dethroned pewterers" (names from previous lists omitted for cause); and a bibliography, v.2, p.[161]–[92].

RUGS

Faraday, Cornelia Bateman. European and American carpets and rugs. . . . With more than 400 illustrations of antique and modern European and American carpets and rugs, with 32 plates in full color. Grand Rapids, Mich., Dean-Hicks Co., 1929. 382p. il.   **BF52**

Subtitle: A history of the hand-woven decorative floor coverings of Spain, France, Great Britain, Scandinavia, Belgium, Holland, Italy, the Balkans, Germany, Austria, and early America; and of the machine-made carpets and rugs of modern Europe and of the United States.

A standard work on carpets other than the Oriental.

Lewis, George Griffin. The practical book of Oriental rugs. . . . [6th] rev. ed., with 32 color plates, 80 halftones and numerous line designs. Philadelphia, Lippincott, 1945. 317p. il.   **BF53**

1st ed. 1911.

A useful handbook on the classification of Oriental rugs and their identification, materials, dyes, weaving, designs and their symbolism, etc.

COINS AND CURRENCY

Bowker, Howard Franklin. A numismatic bibliography of the Far East; a check list of titles in European languages. N.Y., Amer. Numismatic Soc., 1943. 144p. (Numismatic notes and monographs, no.101)   **BF54**

910 bibliographical items plus 71 dealers' catalogs dealing with the currency of China, Annam, Korea, Tibet, and Japan and the coinages of Nepal, Siam, and Mexico.

Bullowa, David M. The commemorative coinage of the United States, 1892–1938. . . . N.Y., Amer. Numismatic Soc., 1938. 192p. il. (Numismatic notes and monographs, no.83)   **BF55**

Continues and amends the *Commemorative coinage of the United States* by Howland Wood (N.Y., 1922). "From . . . 1892 to . . . 1922, the present text is still substantially as it originally appeared. . . ."—*Pref.*

Forrer, Leonard. Biographical dictionary of medallists: coin, gem, and seal-engravers, mintmasters, etc., ancient and modern, with references to their works B.C. 500–A.D. 1900. London, Spink, 1902–30. 8v. il.   **BF56**

v.1–6, A–Z; v.7–8, Supplement, A–Z. v.8 contains also a 2d supplement and an index of illustrations.

Frey, Albert Romer. Dictionary of numismatic names, with Glossary of numismatic terms in English, French, German, Italian, Swedish, by Mark M. Salton. N.Y., Barnes & Noble, [1947]. 311p., 94p.   **BF57**

A reprint of a work originally published in 1917 as v.50 of the *American journal of numismatics;* gives information about terms used in numismatic works in English and foreign languages. Includes a list of principal authorities cited, p.[vii]–ix; a geographical index; and a paper money index. The Glossary includes 2800 numismatic terms without explanations.

Friedberg, Robert. Paper money of the United States; a complete illustrated guide with valuations. 5th ed. Chicago, Follett, [1964]. 305p. il.   **BF58**

Subtitle: Large size notes, fractional currency, small size notes, encased postage stamps from the first year of paper money, 1861, to the present.

A supplementary section includes national bank notes by states, years of issue of charter numbers, and a list of national banks.

Mayer, Leo Ary. Bibliography of Moslem numismatics, India excepted. 2d considerably enl. ed. London, Royal Asiatic Soc., 1954. 283p. (Oriental Translation Fund. Publ. New ser. v.35)   **BF59**

Lists more than 2000 titles arranged alphabetically. The annotation after each title gives the names of the dynasties mentioned in the relevant book or article. In many cases references are given to reviews.

Raymond, Wayte. Coins of the world; 19th century issues. 2d ed. N.Y., Raymond, [1953]. 251p. il.   **BF60**

Subtitle: Containing an extensive list of the silver and minor coins issued by the countries of the whole world, their colonies or dependencies, with illustrations of the principal or most interesting types and giving the average valuation among collectors and dealers.

—— Coins of the world; 20th century issues, 1901–1954. 5th ed. N.Y., Raymond, 1955. 326p. il.   **BF61**

Subtitle: Containing a complete list of all the coins issued by the countries of the whole world, their colonies or dependencies, with illustrations of most of the types and the average valuation among collectors and dealers.

—— Standard catalogue of United States coins and tokens from 1652 to present day. 1935–57. N.Y., Raymond, 1934–57. 18v. il. Annual. (1957)   **BF62**

Ceased publication.

Title varies. 1935–38 published by the Scott Stamp and Coin Co. Not published: 1943, 1948, 1955–56.

—— Standard paper money catalogue; early colonial notes, state issues, continental currency; bills of the Confederacy and southern states; notes of cities and towns. Giving the average valuations among collectors and dealers for the notes usually obtainable, with many illustrations. Comp. and pub. by Wayte Raymond, Inc. N.Y., 1940. 106p. il. (facsim.)   **BF63**

—— —— Pt.2, 1946. U.S. notes and fractional currency. New ed. 48p.

Schlickeysen, F. W. A. and **Pallmann, Reinhold.** Erklärung der Abkürzungen auf Münzen der neueren Zeit, des Mittelalters und des Altertums, sowie auf Denkmünzen und münzartigen Zeichen. 4. Aufl. Graz, Akademische Druck- u. Verlagsanstalt, 1961. 511p.   **BF64**

Reprint of *3. verb. und verm. Aufl. bearb. von Reinhold Pallmann* (Berlin, Spemann, 1896). 1st ed. 1855; 2d ed. 1882.

The section on medieval and modern coins includes 4p. on marks on Russian coins. The section on antiquity concerns Greek and Roman coins.

Schrötter, Friedrich, *Freiherr von.* Wörterbuch der Münzkunde, in Verbindung mit N. Bauer, K. Regling [u.A.]. Berlin, de Gruyter, 1930. 777p. il.   **BF65**

An encyclopedia of numismatics from ancient to modern times.

Vermeule, Cornelius Clarkson. A bibliography of applied numismatics in the fields of Greek and Roman archaeology and the fine arts. London, Spink, 1956. 172p.   **BF66**

1309 numbered items, both books and periodical articles.

Yeoman, Richard S. A catalogue of modern world coins. 1st ed.– . Racine, Wis., Whitman, 1957– . il. (5th ed. 1962) **BF67**

Coins of all countries, in all metals, issued during approximately the past 100 years. Estimated value given. "Alphabetical index of world coin denominations," p.502–5. Photographic illustrations.

—— Red book of United States coins; a guide book. 1st ed.– . Racine, Wis., Whitman, 19?– . il. Annual. (18th ed. 1965) **BF68**

Illustrated catalog and retail price list of coins 1616 to date.

For average prices paid by dealers, *see* the author's *Blue book of United States coins.*

POSTAGE STAMPS

Brookman, Lester G. The 19th century postage stamps of the United States. [1st ed.] N.Y., Lindquist, 1947. 2v. il. **BF69**

Historical and technical information with many illustrations of stamps.

Crawford, James Ludovic Lindsay, *26th Earl of.* Catalogue of the philatelic library of the Earl of Crawford, by E. D. Bacon. London, Philatelic Literature Soc., 1911. 924col. **BF70**

—— —— Supplement. 1926. 136col.

—— —— Addenda to the Supplement. 1938. 8p.

The *Catalogue* was originally published for private distribution: J. L. L. Crawford. *Bibliotheca Lindesiana,* v.7; *A bibliography of the writings, general, special, and periodical, forming the literature of philately.* Aberdeen, Univ. Pr., 1911. 924col. (AA77). The Supplement contains corrections and additions of separate works published to the end of 1908, and of periodicals and auction catalogs to the end of 1906, the same closing dates as those of the Catalogue. The Addenda was issued as a supplement to the March 1938 issue of the *London philatelist,* official journal of the Philatelic Literature Society.

Gibbons, Stanley, Ltd., London. Priced postage stamp catalogue. London, S. Gibbons. **BF71**

Issued in a varying number of parts, each with edition numbering in its own sequence. Not all parts are issued annually, e.g., 1954 to date, work was issued in three parts: pt.1, issued annually; pts.2–3, issued biennially in alternate years. Supplements to the catalog appear in *Gibbons Stamp monthly.*

Pt.1, British Commonwealth, Ireland and South Africa. 1965. 67th ed. c1964; pt.2, Europe and colonies. 1965. 55th ed. c1964; pt.3, America, Asia and Africa. 1964. 54th ed. c1963.

Konwiser, Harry Myron. American philatelic dictionary and Colonial and Revolutionary posts. N.Y., Minkus, 1947. 152p., 56p. il. **BF72**

Colonial and Revolutionary posts, a history of the American postal systems (56p., at end) is a partial reprint of a work with the same title published in 1931 (Richmond, Va., Dietz Pub. Co.).

Scott Publications, Inc., N.Y. Standard postage stamp catalogue (the encyclopedia of philately). 16th ed.– . 1868– . N.Y., Scott Publ., 1867– . Annual. (121st ed. 1965) **BF73**

Title varies slightly. Publisher's name varies: Scott and Co.; Scott Stamp and Coin Co., Ltd.; etc.

Since 1939 each issue is in 2v. Volume subtitles vary. For 1965: v.1, United States and possessions, United Nations, British Commonwealth of Nations, Latin America; v.2, European countries and colonies and the independent nations of Africa and Asia.

Supplements to this catalog appear in *Scott's monthly stamp journal.*

Gives illustrations, description, denominations, and value of the principal stamps, used and unused, of all countries.

U.S. Post Office Dept. Division of Philately. Postage stamps of the United States. Wash., 1927– . Biennial (Irregular). (1963) **BF74**

Title varies: *A description of United States postage stamps issued . . . from July 1, 1847* (varies slightly).

Description of stamps starts in each volume with series of 1847.

PHOTOGRAPHY

Bibliography

Boni, Albert. Photographic literature; an international bibliographic guide to general and specialized literature on photographic processes; techniques; theory; chemistry; physics; apparatus; materials and applications; industry; history; biography; aesthetics. Associate eds., Hubbard Ballou [and others]. N.Y., Morgan and Morgan, in assoc. with R. R. Bowker Co., 1962. 335p. **BF75**

A listing under subject headings, with numerous cross references, of some 12,000 books, pamphlets, and periodical articles on the many technical aspects of photography noted in the title. Author index. Material is mainly in English, German, and French.

Columbia University. Library. Epstean Collection. A catalogue of the Epstean collection on the history and science of photography and its applications especially to the graphic arts. N.Y., Columbia Univ. Pr., 1937. 109p. il. **BF76**

—— —— Authors and short title index. Corrected, with additions, to May 1, 1938. N.Y., 1938. 31p.

—— —— Accessions, May 1938–Dec. 1941 with addenda 1942. N.Y., 1942. 29p.

The catalog of a comprehensive collection of scientific and applied photography.

Abstract journals

Abstracts of photographic science and engineering literature, pub. by the Society of Photographic Scientists and Engineers. N.Y., Engineering Index, 1962– . v.1 (March 1962)– . Monthly. **BF77**

Supersedes *Ansco abstracts* and *Kodak monthly abstract bulletin.*

Publisher varies.

Aims to present abstracts of "world literature dealing with the science, engineering and technology of photography, motion pictures, television, photogrammetry and related fields . . ."—*Introd.*

Encyclopedias

Focal encyclopedia of photography. London, Focal Pr.; N.Y., Macmillan, 1956. 1298p. il. (Repr.: 1960, omitting the illustrations) **BF78**

A combination dictionary and encyclopedia bringing together definitions of terms and articles on the history, techniques, art, and application of photography. A panel of some 200 authors, representing many countries, contributed the longer, signed articles. Emphasis is on British practice, but attention is called to American variants. Illustrated with plates and line drawings.

Lester, Henry M. Photo-lab-index; the cumulative formulary of standard recommended photographic procedures. [22d ed.] N.Y., Morgan and Lester, 1963– . Loose-leaf annual with quarterly suppl.   **BF79**

Basic set published June 1939.

A basic manual of "recommended photographic procedures in a standardized form," divided into 24 sections. Sec. 1–7 treat photographic materials by their manufacturers; sec. 8–24 contain general facts and data by subject area.

Modern encyclopedia of photography; a standard work of reference for amateur and professional photographers. Gen. ed., S. G. Blaxland Stubbs; assoc. eds., F. J. Mortimer and Gordon S. Malthouse. . . . Boston, Amer. Photographic Pub. Co., [1938?]. 2v. il.   **BF80**

Paged continuously.

Contents: v.1, Aberration–Epidiascope; v.2, Exakta–Zoo. Bibliography, p.1330–33. General index, p.1334–50.

An English work, printed in England, distributed in America under an American imprint; therefore, the differences between English and American terminology must be borne in mind. Contributors are largely British authorities in various fields of photography. Some 60 percent of the articles are signed. The style is generally popular. Illustrations are good. Arrangement is usually alphabetical under broad headings, but there are also many short articles on small subjects.

Dictionaries

Fenner, Frank, Jr. A glossary for photography defining over 3000 words having a photographic significance. Chicago, Ziff-Davis, 1939. 147p. (Little technical library)   **BF81**

Ten Eyck, Hendrix. Glossary of terms used in microreproduction. Hingham, Mass., Nat. Microfilm Assoc., 1955. 88p.   **BF82**

B G

Theater Arts

❧ In many libraries there is considerable interest in the theater, both professional and amateur, historical and current. In this section are listed works dealing with the performing arts: (1) the theater itself—production, staging, management, players, etc.—as opposed to plays and history of the drama, which are treated in Section BD, Literature; (2) the dance; and (3) motion pictures.

A basic collection might include the *Oxford companion to the theatre* (BG17), and, for those libraries which can afford it, the *Enciclopedia dello spettacolo* (BG16); *Who's who in the theatre* (BG43); Chujoy, *The dance encyclopedia* (BG55); the *International motion picture almanac* (BG71); and one or more of the handbooks on amateur production (BG44–BG47).

GENERAL WORKS

See also Drama, p.245, and subhead "Drama" under the various national literatures in Section BD, Literature.

Bibliography

American Educational Theatre Association. A bibliography on theatre and drama in American colleges and universities, 1937–1947, comp. and ed. by Committee on Research, John H. McDowell, Chairman. [N.Y., 1949] 124p. (Speech monographs, v.16, no.3)   **BG1**

Contains 2522 entries including books, articles, published original plays and designs, and theses and dissertations. Arranged by subject. Includes author index.

Continued by:

Theatre arts publications available in the United States. 1947/52– . Wash., Amer. Educ. Theatre Assoc., 1959– .   **BG2**

Compiler: 1947/52, William W. Melnitz; 1953/57– Roger M. Busfield.

Title varies slightly.

1947/52 volume includes 4063 entries (books and articles) on the theater, motion pictures, and television, published in the United States and Canada. Does not include theses and dissertations.

1953/57 volume contains 8089 entries (books and articles) "available" in the United States, thus including some foreign publications. Also omits theses and dissertations.

Arrangement is by subject, then alphabetically by author. Author index included.

Baker, Blanch M. Theatre and allied arts: a guide to books dealing with the history, criticism, and technic of the drama and theatre and related arts and crafts. N.Y., Wilson, 1952. 536p.   **BG3**

Based on the author's *Dramatic bibliography*. N.Y., Wilson, 1933. An annotated listing of about 6000 titles in three parts: (1) Drama, theatre and actors; (2) Stagecraft and allied arts of the theatre; (3) Miscellaneous reference material. Each part is subdivided by subject or geographical region. Items included were published between 1885 and 1948, with a few later titles, and are almost all available in English. Indexes by author and subject.

Boston. Public Library. Allen A. Brown Collection. Catalogue of the Allen A. Brown collection of books relating to the stage. Boston, 1919. 952p.   **BG4**

A dictionary catalog of a rich collection of works relating to the history of the stage, followed by an author list of works on the drama, and a brief supplementary list of titles added during the printing of the catalog.

British Drama League. Library. Player's library, the catalogue of the Library of the British Drama League, with an introd. by Frederick S. Boas. London, Faber & Faber, for the British Drama League, 1950. 1115p.   **BG5**

Supersedes the library's first catalog (1930) and its supplement (1934), and includes also the majority of books added to the library through 1950. Arrangement of the catalog of plays is by author, with brief descriptive information. This is followed by a subject listing of books on the theater, a title index of plays, and an author index to the bibliography of the theater.

—— —— 1st–3d supplements, 1951–56. 128p.; 256p.; 256p.

Lowe, Robert William. Bibliographical account of English theatrical literature from the earliest times to the present day. London, Nimmo, 1888. 384p.   **BG6**

An annotated listing of theatrical literature as distinguished from dramatic literature, thus omitting plays and critical accounts of them.

National Council of Teachers of English. Committee on Playlist. Guide to play selection. 2d ed. N.Y., Appleton, 1958. 178p. il.   **BG7**

1st ed., by Milton M. Smith, 1934.

A revised edition which includes some of the plays of the

earlier edition but replaces others with plays published since 1934. Lists 430 long plays and 294 short plays, "suitable for production by school, college and community theatres." Gives brief summaries, with staging needs, royalties, etc.

Santaniello, A. E. Theatre books in print. N.Y., Drama Book Shop, 1963. 266p. **BG8**

Annotated list of books, mostly in English, on the theater and drama; technical arts of the theater; and motion pictures, television, and radio. Does not usually include plays, or collections of plays, or books on the dance, but does include books on the musical theater.

Stott, Raymond Toole. Circus and allied arts; a world bibliography, 1500–1957: based mainly on circus literature in the British Museum, the Library of Congress, the Bibliothèque Nationale and on his own collection. Derby, Eng., Harpur & Sons, 1958–62. 3v. il. **BG9**

Lists books and pamphlets in various languages dealing with circus history and biography; technical aspects of performances; and the circus in drama, literature, art, and fiction.

Indexes

Guide to the performing arts, 1957– . Comp. by S. Yancey Belknap. N.Y., Scarecrow, 1960– . Annual. **BG10**

Indexes articles and illustrations in 30–40 periodicals, primarily in the English language but also including a few in French, Italian, and Spanish.

Each volume is in two sections: (1) the main section, and (2) a section devoted to the television arts.

Began as a supplement to *Guide to the musical arts.* 1953–56 (BH41).

Theatre magazine (indexes): A selective index to Theatre magazine, by Stan Cornyn. N.Y., Scarecrow, 1964. 289p. **BG11**

Indexes the *Theatre magazine* from 1900 to 1930.

Annuals

Annales du théâtre et de la musique. 1.–41. année. 1875–1916. Paris, Charpentier, 1876–1916. 41v. **BG12**

An annual survey of the plays, operas, and concerts of Paris, giving for each theater a record, with some comment, of the works produced there during the year and, in case of new works, cast of characters and synopsis of plot.

Daniel Blum's Theatre world. 1944/45– . N.Y., Theatre World, 1945– . v.1– . il. Annual. **BG13**

Annual survey of the theater, with many illustrations, listing plays that appeared on Broadway, with casts, dates of opening and closing, etc., but with no critical comment. Brief biographical sketches of outstanding players, producers, designers, etc. Obituaries.

Theatre world annual (London); a pictorial review of West End productions with a record of plays and players. no.1– . 1949/50– . London, Rockliff, 1950– . il. Annual. **BG14**

Subtitle varies.

World premières. v.1– . Oct. 1949– . Paris, Internat. Theatre Inst., 1949– . Monthly. **BG15**

Subtitle: Monthly bulletin of the International Theatre Institute.

Contains brief accounts of new theatrical productions, including plays, operas, and ballets, as reported by the national centers of some 50 countries.

Encyclopedias and dictionaries

Enciclopedia dello spettacolo. Roma, Casa Ed. le Maschere, 1954–62. 9v. il. **BG16**

Similar in format and in profusion of illustration to the *Enciclopedia italiana* (AD48), and designed to cover the "grand spectacle" from antiquity to the present. Includes the theater, opera, ballet, motion pictures, vaudeville, the circus, etc. Treats performers, authors, composers, directors, designers, etc.; types of entertainment; dramatic themes; historical and technical subjects; organizations and companies; and pertinent place-names.

—— Appendice di aggiornamento. Cinema. [Venezia, Istit. per Collaborazione Culturale, 1963] 173p. il.

Hartnoll, Phyllis. Oxford companion to the theatre. 2d ed. [with illustrated supplement]. London, N.Y., Oxford Univ. Pr., 1957. 887p., 32p. il. **BG17**

1st ed. 1951.

A reprint of the 1st edition with the addition of a 32p. supplement, including new bibliography, and 150 photographic illustrations.

International in scope and covering all periods of history, with emphasis on the popular rather than on the literary theater and on the actor rather than on the dramatist. Opera and ballet are each treated in a single article; the cinema, not at all. Arrangement is similar to that of other Oxford Companions.

Bibliography, p.856–88.

Melchinger, Siegfried. The concise encyclopedia of modern drama. Tr. by George Wellwarth . . . N.Y., Horizon, [1964]. 288p. il. **BG18**

Contains information on contemporary plays, playwrights, and theatrical productions in America and Europe. Includes a glossary of modern dramatic theory, chronology of first performances, and bibliography.

Copiously illustrated.

Terms

Bowman, Walter Parker and **Ball, Robert Hamilton.** Theatre language: a dictionary of terms in English of the drama and stage from medieval to modern times. N.Y., Theatre Arts, 1961. 428p. **BG19**

Contains more than 3500 definitions of words and phrases of the legitimate drama and stage. For the most part, excludes terms peculiar to grand opera and ballet.

Rae, Kenneth and **Southern, Richard.** An international vocabulary of technical theatre terms in eight languages: American, Dutch, English, French, German, Italian, Spanish, Swedish. N.Y., Theatre Arts Books, [1959]. 139p. **BG20**

Added title page in French.

In two parts: pt.1, numbered list of terms in English, alphabetically arranged, with equivalent terms in other languages; pt.2, indexes in the other seven languages keyed to numbered pt.1.

Handbooks

Herman, Lewis and **Herman, Marguerite Schalett.** Foreign dialects; a manual for actors, directors and writers. N.Y., Theatre Arts Books, [1959]. 415p. il. **BG21**

First published in 1943 as *Manual of foreign dialects for radio, stage and screen.*

—— American dialects; a manual for actors, directors and writers. N.Y., Theatre Arts Books, [1959]. 328p. **BG22**

First published in 1947 as *Manual of American dialects for radio, stage, screen and television.*

Sobel, Bernard. The new theatre handbook and digest of plays. [8th ed. compl. rev.] N.Y., Crown, 1959. 749p.   **BG23**

1st edition, 1940, had title *The theatre handbook and digest of plays.*

Includes, in one alphabetical arrangement, theatrical terms, biographical notices, and digests of plays. Covers all periods and all countries.

In this edition many articles remain unchanged, a few have been updated, and a few new entries have been added, but comparatively few digests of plays of the 1950's have been included. The short essays signed by specialists, which appeared in earlier editions, have been omitted.

Bibliography, comp. by George Freedley, p.727–49, largely unchanged; includes only a scattering of works published since 1950.

Directories

Gilder, Rosamond and **Freedley, George.** Theatre collections in libraries and museums: an international handbook. N.Y., Theatre Arts, Inc., 1936. 182p.   **BG24**

Arranged geographically. Describes the theater collections in this country and abroad.

Published under the auspices of the New York Public Library and the National Theatre Conference, with the cooperation of the American Library Association.

International Federation of Library Associations. Bibliothèques et musées des arts du spectacle dans le monde. Rédacteurs: Marie-Françoise Christout et Denis Bablet. Traducteur en anglais, George Miller. Paris, Centre National de la Recherche Scientifique, 1960. 761p.   **BG25**

Added title page in English: Performing arts collections: an international handbook.

Text in French and English.

Detailed information about the performing arts collections in public and private libraries and museums in 36 countries. Gives size and nature of holdings, regulation of use, hours, etc. Includes subject and name index, etc.

Mander, Raymond and **Mitchenson, Joe.** The theatres of London. Illus. by Timothy Birdsall. London, Hart-Davis, 1961. 292p. il.   **BG26**

Descriptions and histories of the theaters now existing in London.

Simon's Directory of theatrical materials, services and information, comp. by Bernard Simon. 1963 ed. N.Y., Package Publicity Service, [c1962]. 160p. il.   **BG27**

1st ed. 1956.

A miscellany of information giving sources of personnel and supplies used in stage productions and the management of theaters, e.g., actors agents, ticket brokers, publishers, costumes, wigs, tents, etc.

History

Hogan, Charles Beecher. Shakespeare in the theatre, 1701–1800. Oxford, Univ. Pr., 1952–57. 2v.   **BG28**

v.1, A record of performances in London, 1701–1750; v.2, A record of performances in London, 1751–1800.

Each volume is in two parts: pt.1, List of performances arranged chronologically; pt.2, An alphabetical list of the plays, giving insofar as possible the complete casts for every performance. Appendixes in each volume include, for the period covered: Shakespeare's popularity in the theatre; Order of popularity of Shakespeare's plays; and London theatres in use.

Indexes in each volume: (1) Actors (giving full name of each, dates when he was "flourishing" as a Shakespearean actor, or of birth and death, and the parts he performed); (2) Characters, with names of all actors who played the parts.

London stage, 1660–1800: a calendar of plays, entertainments and afterpieces, together with casts, box-receipts and contemporary comment, comp. from the playbills, newspapers and theatrical diaries of the period. Carbondale, Ill., Southern Illinois Univ. Pr., 1960–62. Pts.2–4 in 7v. (In progress)   **BG29**

Contents: pt.1, 1660–1700, ed. by William Van Lennep. (in prep.); pt.2, 1700–1729, ed. by E. L. Avery. 2v.; pt.3, 1729–1747, ed. by A. H. Scouten. 2v.; pt.4, 1747–1776, ed. by G. W. Stone. 3v.; pt.5, 1776–1800, ed. by C. B. Hogan (in prep.).

The theatrical seasons are arranged chronologically, listing plays, casts, etc., with an index in each volume.

Mantzius, Karl. History of theatrical art in ancient and modern times, with an introd. by William Archer; authorized translation by Louise von Cossel. London, Duckworth; Philadelphia, Lippincott, 1903–21. 6v. il. (Repr.: N.Y., Peter Smith, 1937)   **BG30**

v.1, Earliest times; v.2, Middle Ages and Renaissance; v.3, Shakespearean period in England; v.4, Molière and his times; the theatre in France in the 17th century; v.5, The great actors of the 18th century; v.6, Classicism and romanticism, tr. by C. Archer.

Nagler, Alois Maria. Sources of theatrical history. N.Y., Theatre Annual, [1952]. 611p. il.   **BG31**

Lists primary sources, with long annotations, from the Greek classical theater to the end of the 19th century.

Nicoll, Allardyce. The development of the theatre: a study of theatrical art from the beginnings to the present day. 4th ed. rev. with 319 illus. N.Y., Harcourt, [1958]. 318p. il.   **BG32**

Concerned mainly with theatrical buildings, designs, arrangements, and equipment. Particular attention is given to the English stage. Good illustrations.

—— Masks, mimes and miracles: studies in the popular art. N.Y., Harcourt, 1931. 407p. il. (Repr.: N.Y., Cooper Square, 1963)   **BG33**

A historical survey from the earliest times through the 17th century with special emphasis on the *commedia dell' arte.* Contains 225 excellent illustrations.

Appendix (p.351–90) devoted to the *commedia dell' arte;* includes lists of chief character parts and chief actors with bibliographical references, and alphabetical list of scenarii.

Odell, George Clinton Densmore. Annals of the New York stage. N.Y., Columbia Univ. Pr., 1927–49. 15v. il.   **BG34**

v.1–15 cover approximately 1699–1894.

A very full account of the history of the stage in New York City, covering actors, plays, theaters, etc., with the historical background of each period.

—— —— Index to the portraits in Odell's Annals of the New York stage, transcribed from the file in the Theatre Collection at Princeton University. [N.Y.], Amer. Soc. for Theatre Research, 1963. 179p.

Biography

Eisenberg, Ludwig Julius. Grosses biographisches Lexikon der deutschen Bühne im XIX. Jahrhundert. Leipzig, List, 1903. 1180p.   **BG35**

Fairly long sketches but no references to sources.

Kosch, Wilhelm. Deutsches Theater-Lexikon; biographisches und bibliographisches Handbuch. Klagenfurt, Kleinmayr, 1951–60. Lfg. 1–18. (In progress)   **BG36**

Lfg. 1–18, A–Pallenberg, M. (completes v.1–2).

Bio-bibliographical information on persons connected with the theater, and articles on dramatic history, theories, and themes. Bibliographical notes include material in newspapers and periodicals as well as in books.

Kürschners biographisches Theater-Handbuch: Schauspiel, Oper, Film, Rundfunk. Deutschland, Österreich, Schweiz, hrsg. von Herbert A. Frenzel und Hans Joachim Moser. Berlin, Walter de Gruyter, 1956. 840p. **BG37**

Includes biographical material on German, Austrian, and Swiss personalities in the fields of opera, film, and radio, including writers and directors as well as performing artists.

Lyonnet, Henry. Dictionnaire des comédiens français (ceux d'hier): biographie, bibliographie, iconographie. Genève, Bibliothèque de la Revue Universelle Internationale Illustrée, 1911–12. 2v. il. **BG38**

Issued in 80 pts., 1902–12.

Does not include living persons. Biographies are of some length with many bibliographical references. Some portraits and facsimiles of autographs included.

Mongrédien, Georges. Dictionnaire biographique des comédiens français du XVII siècle, suivi d'un inventaire des troupes (1590–1710), d'après des documents inédits. Paris, Centre National de la Recherche Scientifique, 1961. 239p. **BG39**

Brief listings of actors, with numbered references to items in an extensive supplementary bibliography.

Lists and gives information concerning acting companies sponsored by French royal houses, foreign royal houses, independent companies, and companies in various French cities.

Nungezer, Edwin. Dictionary of actors and of other persons associated with the public representation of plays in England before 1642. New Haven, Conn., Yale Univ. Pr.; London, Milford, 1929. 438p. (Cornell studies in English, 13) **BG40**

Rasi, Luigi. I comici italiani; biografia, bibliografia, iconografia. Firenze, Bocca, 1897–1905. 2v. il. **BG41**

A comprehensive work, covering the mid-16th through the 19th centuries, and containing many articles of considerable length. Copiously illustrated with portraits, stage designs, etc.

Sundström, Einer. Svenska konstnärer inom teaterns, musikens och filmens värld . . . för teateravdelningen, Arne Lindenbaum; för musikavdelningen, Ake Vretblad. . . . Stockholm, Mimer, [1943]. 531p. il. **BG42**

A historical section, including a sketch of the Swedish theater from 1500 to 1900 and sketches of Swedish music, opera, films, ballet, etc., is followed by a biographical section, p.209–527, giving biographical sketches with portraits of the outstanding persons in these fields, primarily of the 20th century.

Who's who in the theatre; a biographical record of the contemporary stage. Ed. by Freda Gaye. 13th ed. London, Pitman, 1961. 1594p. **BG43**

Originally comp. by John Parker.

1st ed. 1912; 12th ed. 1957.

Fairly detailed biographies of persons connected with the modern theater, including actors, actresses, dramatists, composers, critics, managers, scenic artists, historians, and biographers.

Contents: (1) London play bills, 1956–60; (2) Biographies; (3) Names in previous editions; (4) Miscellaneous lists, e.g., Title list of notable productions on the London stage, Title list of long runs in London and New York, Obituary, etc.

Amateur production and dramatic technique

Bailey, Howard. The ABC's of play producing: a handbook for the nonprofessional. N.Y., McKay, 1955. 276p. il. **BG44**

Information on selecting the play, casting, rehearsing, producing, costuming, lighting, and scenic construction. Discusses theaters-in-the-round, pageants, and religious dramas. Contains a list of recommended plays, p.233–69.

Gassner, John. Producing the play, with the New scene technician's handbook, by Philip Barber. Rev. ed. N.Y., Dryden, [c1953]. 915p. il. **BG45**

1st ed. 1941.

A useful handbook on all phases of play production, combining the aesthetic and practical aspects. Some chapters have been contributed by specialists. The last section is a technical handbook on scenery construction, making of costumes, lighting, acoustics, etc.

Heffner, Hubert C., Selden, Samuel and **Sellman, Hunton D.** Modern theatre practice; a handbook of play production. 4th ed. N.Y., Appleton, 1959. 662p. il. **BG46**

1st ed. 1935.

A standard, authoritative text treating play selection, production, direction, stage scenery, lighting, costuming, etc. Contains glossaries, annotated bibliography, and index.

Smith, Milton. Play production for little theatres, schools, and colleges. N.Y., Appleton, [1948]. 482p. il. **BG47**

A very practical book covering play selection; directing and acting; stagecraft and design; organization and management. Includes annotated bibliography, p.467–71.

THE DANCE

Bibliography

Beaumont, Cyril William. A bibliography of dancing. N.Y., B. Blom, [1963]. 228p. **BG48**

An annotated list, arranged by author, selected from the holdings of the British Museum Library. Includes a detailed subject index.

Magriel, Paul David. A bibliography of dancing; a list of books and articles on the dance and related subjects. N.Y., Wilson, 1936. 229p. il. **BG49**

——— 4th cumulated supplement, 1936–40. 1941. 104p.

"A comprehensive list of references on the dance in all of its phases, and of the arts relating to it, as music, decor, costume, masques, mime and pantomime."—*Pref.*

Locates copies.

Indexes

Guide to dance periodicals. v.1– . 1931/35– . N.Y., Scarecrow, 1948– . Quinquennial, 1931/35–1946/50; Biennial, 1951/52– . (Irregular) **BG50**

v.1, covering 1931/35, pub. 1959; v.2, 1936/40, pub. 1950. Comp. by S. Y. Belknap.

Publisher varies.

Indexes—by author and subject—some 18 periodicals devoted to the dance.

Minneapolis Public Library. Music Dept. Index to folk dances and singing games. Chicago, Amer. Lib. Assoc., 1936. 202p. **BG51**

Includes folk dances, singing games, classic dances, tap and clog dances, and some earlier square- and contradances.

——— Supplement. 1949. 98p.

Indexes 60 collections published 1936–48.

Annuals

Ballet annual; a record and year book of the ballet. 1st–18th, 1947–1963. N.Y., Macmillan; London, A. & C. Black, 1947–63. 18v. Annual.   **BG52**

Ceased publication.

Contains a list of "outstanding events of the year"; articles on various aspects of the ballet by well-known authorities and critics; and a checklist of ballet performances in European centers and America, chiefly New York.

Encyclopedias and handbooks

Beaumont, Cyril William. Complete book of ballets; a guide to the principal ballets of the nineteenth and twentieth centuries. [Rev.] London, Putnam, [1951]. 1106p. il.   **BG53**

1st ed. 1938.

Gives stories of ballets, including information concerning first productions and excerpts of reviews.

———— Supplement. 1945. [Repr. 1952] 212p. il.
Includes works not in the main volume.

———— Ballets of today . . . 2d supplement. London, Putnam, [1954]. 250p. il.   **BG53a**

———— Ballets past and present . . . 3d supplement. London, Putnam, [1955]. 259p. il.   **BG53b**

Bowers, Faubion. Theatre in the East; a survey of Asian dance and drama. N.Y., Nelson, [c1956]. 374p. il. **BG54**

Arranged in 14 chapters devoted to the countries of: India, Ceylon, Burma, Thailand, Cambodia, Laos, Malaya, Indonesia, Philippines, China, Vietnam, Hong Kong, Okinawa, and Japan. Gives history of the dance, and describes folk, traditional, and modern forms. Well illustrated.

✓ **Chujoy, Anatole.** The dance encyclopedia. N.Y., Barnes, 1949. 546p.   **BG55**

Includes long, encyclopedic articles on various forms of the dance, written by specialists, in the same alphabet with briefer articles covering biography, special ballets, types of dances, terms used in dancing, ballet, etc. Appendixes include a bibliography of books in English on the dance and a discography of theater dance music.

✓ **De Mille, Agnes.** The book of the dance. N.Y., Golden Pr., [c1963]. 252p. il.   **BG56**

An encyclopedic work on the development of the dance with examples from all periods and many countries. Gives definitions, types, and methods of choreography. Treats the classical ballet and modern dance in detail, including brief biographies of performers. Profusely illustrated with excellent photographs, many in color. Includes list of principal ballets of leading choreographers and an index.

Dictionary of modern ballet. Gen. eds., Francis Gadan and Robert Maillard; American ed., Selma Jeanne Cohen. [Tr. from the French by John Montague and Peggie Cochrane] Introd. by John Martin. N.Y., Tudor, 1959. 360p. il.   **BG57**

Originally pub. Paris, 1957; London, 1959.

In one alphabet gives descriptions of ballets; famous ballet organizations and companies, etc.; and biographical sketches of dancers, composers, designers, choreographers, etc.

Grant, Gail. The technical manual and dictionary of classical ballet. N.Y., Kamin Dance Pub., 1950. 87p. il.   **BG58**

Gives pronunciation and brief definitions of dance terms, with small line drawings of main positions.

✓ **Lawrence, Robert.** The Victor book of ballets and ballet music. N.Y., Simon & Schuster, 1950. 531p. il. music.   **BG59**

A brief, general outline of the history of ballet, followed by the stories of individual ballets, alphabetically arranged, and including musical themes. Contains a selective discography of RCA Victor recordings, and indexes by choreographer and composer as well as a general index.

✓ **Raffé, Walter George.** Dictionary of the dance. N.Y., Barnes; London, T. Yoseloff, [c1964]. 583p. il.   **BG60**

Defines numerous terms relating to dances and dancing in all countries and periods. Describes in some detail specific dances and types of dances. No entries for individual dancers, choreographers, etc.

A geographical index lists dances by country and culture of origin.

Well illustrated.

Shaw, Lloyd. Cowboy dances, a collection of western square dances; with a foreword by Sherwood Anderson. Caldwell, Idaho, Caxton, 1948. 411p. il. music.   **BG61**

Contains history and description of the dances, directions, and calls. Includes glossary of terms. Appendix contains cowboy dance tunes, arranged by Frederick Knorr. Excellent illustrations.

✓ **Wilson, George Buckley.** A dictionary of ballet. Rev. ed. London, Cassell, [1961]. 312p. il.   **BG62**

Gives definitions of terms; history; information on individual ballets; companies; and brief biographies of leading dancers, composers, and choreographers. Concerned chiefly with classical ballet but includes some information on modern, Spanish, and Indian dances.

A useful book moderately priced.

History

✓ **Martin, John Joseph.** Book of the dance. N.Y., Tudor, 1963. 192p. il.   **BG63**

Published in 1947 under title *The dance*.

An expanded and revised edition of the earlier work, with much new material added.

The main part, preceded by two short sections on basic dance movements and primitive dances, treats in detail the development of the classic ballet and modern dance. Special emphasis on contemporary American dance. Includes numerous excellent illustrations.

Name and subject index.

✓ **Sachs, Curt.** World history of the dance. Tr. by Bessie Schönberg. N.Y., Norton, [c1937]. 469p. il. music. **BG64**

Published in Germany under title *Eine Weltgeschichte des Tanzes.*

MOTION PICTURES

Bibliography

Brussels. Cinémathèque de Belgique. Répertoire mondial des périodiques cinématographiques. World list of film periodicals and serials. 2d ed. Bruxelles, 1960. unpaged.   **BG65**

"Published . . . with the aid of La Commission Nationale Belge de l'U.N.E.S.C.O. (Sous-Commission du Cinéma) [and] La Fédération Internationale des Archives du Film (International Federation of Film Archives)."

1st ed. 1955.

Lists 769 titles, arranged by country. Brief annotations; indexes of titles, issuing agencies, subjects, and geographical areas.

Padua. Università. Centro Cinematografico. Bibliografia generale del cinema. Bibliographie générale du cinéma. General bibliography of motion pictures, a cura di Carl

Vincent [and others]. Roma, Ed. dell'Ateneo, 1953. 251p.
BG66

Classified arrangement with name index. A general bibliography of works in various languages from the origin of motion pictures to approximately 1952.

U.S. Copyright Office. Motion pictures 1894–1912 identified from the records of the United States Copyright Office by Howard Lamarr Walls. Wash., Copyright Off., Lib. of Congress, 1953. 92p.   **BG67**

Lists 8506 works, representing about 6000 titles registered in the Copyright Office.

Continued by:

—— Motion pictures, 1912–1939 (1951); 1940–1949 (1953); 1950–1959 (1960). (Catalog of copyright entries. Cumulative ser.)

Each catalog consists of three parts: (1) a title list of all motion pictures copyrighted, with full information on date of production, number of reels, source of story, credits, and name of company owning the copyright; (2) an index of names; and (3) a series list.

U.S. Library of Congress. Library of Congress catalog—Motion pictures and filmstrips, 1953–1957, 1958–1962. Ann Arbor, Mich., J. W. Edwards, 1958–63. 1088p.; 2v. (800p., 402p.).   **BG68**

Subtitle: A cumulative list of works represented by Library of Congress printed cards.

Published as v.28 of the *National union catalog,* 1953–1957 (AA65), and v.53–54 of the *Catalog,* 1958–1962.

Quinquennial cumulations of the title published quarterly, cumulating annually, and then cumulating quinquennially in the *National union catalog.*

Preceded by v.24 (Films) of *Library of Congress author catalog.* 1948–1952 (AA64).

"Includes entries for all motion pictures and filmstrips (but not for microfilms) currently cataloged or recataloged on L.C. printed cards . . . Attempts to cover all educational motion pictures and filmstrips released in the United States and Canada . . . "—*Introd.* Other coverage varies.

Writers' Program. The film index: a bibliography. v.1, The film as art, comp. by workers of the Writers' Program of the Work Projects Administration in the City of New York. N.Y., Museum of Modern Art Film Lib. and the Wilson Co., 1941. 723p.   **BG69**

An extensive, annotated, classified bibliography of books and articles on the history and technique, and the types, of motion-picture films. Based on the collections in the Museum of Modern Art, the New York Public Library, and other libraries. Index of names and titles.

Annuals

Daniel Blum's Screen world, 1949– . Philadelphia, N.Y., Chilton, 1950– . v.1– . il. Annual.   **BG70**

Publisher varies.

Annual survey of the pictures of the year, with many illustrations, and casts. No comment. List of obituaries.

International motion picture almanac, 1929– . N.Y., Quigley, 1929– . il. Annual.   **BG71**

1965 *Almanac* includes sections on: who's who in motion pictures; corporations; theater circuits; pictures; services; theater equipment and supplies; talent and literary agencies; organizations; codes and censorship; world market; the press; nontheatrical motion pictures, etc.

Annuaire du spectacle: théâtre, cinéma, musique, radio, télévision. Paris, Raoult, 1942/43– . v.1– .   **BG72**

Title varies: 1945–1955, *Annuaire du théâtre.*

A directory of theaters, producers, directors, actors, etc. in the above categories, in France, Belgium, French-speaking Switzerland, etc.

Encyclopedias

Filmlexicon degli autori e delle opere. Roma, Ed. di Bianco e Nero, 1958–64. v.1–6. (In progress)   **BG73**
v.1–6, A–S.

Introduction in Italian, French, English, German, and Spanish. Text in Italian.

International in scope. To be in two sections: (1) authors, and (2) works. The term "authors" includes "directors, story and script-writers, producers, actors, cameramen, composers, art directors and costume designers" of both silent and sound cinematography of the world. Entries contain biographical sketches, "filmographies" (which list film titles, principals, and dates), and, for the more important names, bibliographies.

Dictionaries

Elsevier's Dictionary of cinema, sound and music, in six languages: English/American, French, Spanish, Italian, Dutch, and German. Comp. and arr. on an English alphabetical base by W. E. Clason. Amsterdam, Elsevier, 1956. (Distr. in U.S. by Van Nostrand) 948p. (Elsevier's Multilingual dictionaries)   **BG74**

TELEVISION AND RADIO

See Communication—Mass Media, p.402.

B H

Music

❦ In this specialized field an excellent guide is available: *Music reference and research materials: an annotated bibliography,* by V. H. Duckles (BH1), which should be consulted for extensive and detailed information.

An attempt has been made below to list a substantial selection of works about which information may be sought in a general library. Bibliographical sources both for books about music and for music itself are abundant, as are various encyclopedias and biographical dictionaries, e.g., Grove's *Dictionary of music and musicians* (BH53), long the standard work in English; Baker's *Biographical dictionary of musicians* (BH43); and Blom's *Everyman's dictionary of music* (BH44).

Most libraries will need at least one or two books on the opera and opera plots, e.g., Ewen's *Encyclopedia of the opera* (BH91); Rosenthal's *Concise Oxford dictionary of opera* (BH95); and Kobbé's *Complete opera book* (BH100).

Sears's *Song index* (BH112) is essential; and some of the catalogs of recorded music, those of historical interest as well as those of current listings, will probably be needed.

GENERAL WORKS

Guides

Duckles, Vincent Harris. Music reference and research materials; an annotated bibliography. London, [N.Y.], Free Pr., [1964]. 331p. **BH1**

An excellent guide for teachers and students of musicology and for reference librarians. Contains 1155 annotated entries with complete bibliographical information. Arranged by form: dictionaries, encyclopedias, catalogs, histories, etc. Reviews are cited for recent items. Includes author index.

Haydon, Glen. Introduction to musicology; a survey of the fields, systematic and historical, of musical knowledge and research. N.Y., Prentice-Hall, 1941. 329p. (Repr.: Univ. of North Carolina Pr., 1959) **BH2**

Bibliographies at the end of each chapter and a general bibliography, p.301–13.

Spiess, Lincoln Bunce. Historical musicology; a reference manual for research in music, with articles by Ernst C. Krohn [and others]. Brooklyn, Inst. of Mediaeval Music, [c1963]. 294p. **BH3**

Intended as a guide to students of musicology; includes 1980 numbered items in its bibliography. Not annotated. Particularly useful is the list of current American and foreign music publishers.

Bibliography

Books

Blum, Fred. Music monographs in series. N.Y., Scarecrow, 1964. 197p. **BH4**

Subtitle: A bibliography of numbered monograph series in the field of music current since 1945.

Lists more than 250 series from some 30 countries, arranged alphabetically by title of series or issuing organization. Entries for each volume give author, title, and date. Includes list of publishers and their agents; alphabetical list of series and issuing organizations; and index of names.

Boston. Public library. Catalogue of the Allen A. Brown collection of music in the Public Library of the City of Boston. Boston, Lib., 1908–16. 4v. **BH5**

v.1–3, A–Z; v.4, suppl.

A dictionary catalog of an important collection, devoted especially to 19th-century music.

Includes many analytics.

British Museum. Dept. of Printed Books. Hirsch Library. Books in the Hirsch Library, with supplementary list of music. London, Trustees of the British Museum, 1959. 542p. (Catalogue of printed books in the British Museum. Accessions, 3d ser., pt.291B) **BH6**

A catalog of more than 12,000 books, forming part of the Hirsch Library acquired in 1946. Entries are brief but generally adequate, with German titles most strongly represented. For the German catalog *see* BH10.

A catalog of the music in the collection was issued in 1951 (BH29). A supplement to that catalog is included as an appendix in the present volume.

Chase, Gilbert. A guide to the music of Latin America. 2d ed. rev. and enl. A joint publication of the Pan American Union and the Library of Congress. Wash., Pan Amer. Union, 1962. 411p. **BH7**

1st edition had title *Guide to Latin American music* (1945).

An annotated bibliography with introductory comments for each country. Subheadings for each country vary somewhat but usually include: Introduction; General and miscellaneous;

Biography and criticism; National anthem; Folk and primitive music.

Coover, James B. Music lexicography. Denver, Colo., Bibliographical Center for Research, 1958. 126p. **BH8**

1st edition, 1952, had title *A bibliography of music dictionaries*.

Contains biographical as well as terminological works.

The 2d edition includes an essay on lacunae in music bibliography between 1500 and 1700, and has been enlarged to include more than 1300 "lexicographic works," including autonomous works as well as portions and appendixes of larger works and some periodical articles.

Eitner, Robert. Biographisch-bibliographisches Quellen-Lexikon der Musiker und Musikgelehrten der christlichen Zeitrechnung bis zur Mitte des neunzehnten Jahrhunderts. Leipzig, Breitkopf, 1900–4. 10v. (Repr.: N.Y., Musurgia, 1947. 10v.) **BH9**

Gives brief biographies and full bibliographies; the most important work for bibliographies of manuscripts, early editions, etc. of authors and composers. In many cases indicates location of the items in European libraries. A criticism by Michel Brenet (Marie Bobillier) in *La revue musicale* (1905), p.480–89, contains various corrections. Corrections and additions are also included in the *Miscellanea musicae bio-bibliographica: Musikgeschichtliche Quellennachweis*, by Hermann Springer (published quarterly, 1912–16).

Will be superseded by *Répertoire international des sources musicales* (BH16) when that work is completed.

Hirsch, Paul. Katalog der Musikbibliothek Paul Hirsch. Frankfurt am Main, hrsg. von Kathi Meyer und Paul Hirsch. Berlin, M. Breslauer, 1928–47. 4v. **BH10**

v.4 has imprint: Cambridge Univ. Pr.

Contents: Bd.1, Theoretische Drucke bis 1800; Bd.2, Opern-Partituren; Bd.3, Instrumental- und Vokalmusik bis etwa 1830; Bd.4, Erstausgaben, Chorwerke in Partitur, Gesamtausgaben, Nachschlagewerke, etc. Ergänzungen zu Bd. 1–3.

A catalog of one of the largest and finest libraries of music of Europe, acquired by the British Museum in 1946 (*see* BH6, BH29). For description *see* P. H. Muir, "The Hirsch catalogue," in *Music review* 9:102–7. 1948.

Kahl, Willi and **Luther, Wilhelm-Martin.** Repertorium der Musikwissenschaft. Musikschrifttum. Denkmäler und Gesamtausgaben in Auswahl (1800–1950). Mit Besitzvermerken Deutscher Bibliotheken und Musikwissenschaftlicher Institute. Im Auftr. der Gesellschaft für Musikforschung bearb. . . . Kassel und Basel, Bärenreiter-Verlag, 1953. 271p. **BH11**

A list of 2795 items, in classified arrangement, representing holdings of German libraries. Includes name and subject indexes, and an index to national and folk music.

Kassel. Deutsches Musikgeschichtliches Archiv. Katalog der Filmsammlung. Bd.1, Nr.1–6. Kassel, Bärenreiter, 1955– . Bd.1– . (Irregular) (In progress) **BH12**

Catalog of music and treatises on the history of German music for the period *ca.* 1450–1700 now available on microfilm. For description of the *Archiv, see* Music Library Association, *Notes,* 2d ser., 16:38–39. 1958.

Merriam, Alan P. A bibliography of jazz . . . with the assistance of Robert J. Brenford. Philadelphia, Amer. Folklore Soc., 1954. 145p. (Publ. of the American Folklore Soc. Bibliographical ser., v.4) **BH14**

Contains 3324 items, arranged alphabetically by author, followed by a list of periodicals devoted to jazz, a subject index, and an index to periodical entries cited.

National Association of Schools of Music. List of books on music. Memphis, Tenn., Assoc., [1935]. 57p. **BH15**

Caption title: A musical literature list for music school libraries.

—— —— Supplement. [1st]–10th, Sept. 1936–1957.

—— A cumulative index of the List of books on music and the seven supplements. 1952. (Its Bull. no.33)

A subject index, covering 1935–Feb. 1951.

Ceased publication.

Répertoire international des sources musicales. [Série systématique] München, G. Henle, 1960–64. [2v. unnumbered, now called BI¹, BIII¹] v.BII, BV¹. (In progress) **BH16**

"Publié par la Société Internationale de Musicologie et l'Association Internationale des Bibliothèques Musicales."

Title and introductory matter also in German and in English.

Referred to as *RISM,* it is "intended to provide a catalogue of all available bibliographical musical works, writings about music and textbooks on music from all countries of the world . . . from the earliest times to the year 1800."—*Fore-word.*

The first 2v. to be published were unnumbered. It was announced in v.BII that the volumes of the general alphabetical series would be denoted by the symbol A, followed by the number of the volume in roman figures. The volumes of the classified series would bear the symbol B, followed by the number of the volume in roman figures.

Contents: [BI¹], Recueils imprimés, XVIᵉ–XVIIᵉ siècles; liste chronologique . . . sous la direction de François Lesure. Lists some 2700 collections of the period, with standard bibliographical data, followed by names of the composers included and library locations; [BIII¹], The theory of music from the Carolingian era up to 1400; a descriptive catalogue of manuscripts . . . ed. by Joseph Smits van Waesberghe [and others]. A descriptive catalog of early manuscripts on musical theory, arranged by present location; BII, Recueils imprimés XVIIIᵉ siècle. Lists some 1800 collections printed between 1701 and 1801, arranged alphabetically by title. Locates copies; BV¹, Tropen- und Sequenzenhandschriften, von Heinrich Husman. A catalog of tropes and sequence manuscripts, arranged by country where presently located. Gives full bibliographical description.

Indexes included with each volume.

Sendrey, Alfred. Bibliography of Jewish music. N.Y., Columbia Univ. Pr., 1951. 404p. **BH17**

This comprehensive bibliography of almost 10,000 items is in two separate listings: (1) literature on the subject, and (2) the music itself, including records. Author indexes for both sections.

Current

Bibliographie des Musikschrifttums. 1936– . Leipzig, Frankfurt am Main, Hofmeister, 1936– . Biennial. **BH18**

Frequency varies.

Not published 1940–49. v.1936–39 called "1–4. Jahrg."

A classified bibliography of books and "serious" periodical articles. Though emphasis is on German publications, coverage is international.

British catalogue of music [no.1], Jan./March, 1957– . London, Council of the British National Bibliography, 1957– . Quarterly, with annual cumulation. **BH19**

"A record of music and books about music recently published in Great Britain based upon the material deposited at the Copyright Receipt Office of the British Museum."—*Title page.* Classified arrangement, preceded by an index of composers, titles, arrangers, etc. Excludes various types of modern popular music.

Jahresverzeichnis der deutschen Musikalien und Musik-schriften. Leipzig, Hofmeister, 1852– . v.1– . Annual. **BH20**

Title varies: 1852–53, *Kurzes Verzeichnis sämmtlicher in*

Deutschland und den angrenzenden Ländern gedruckter Musikalien . . . ; 1854–1928, *Verzeichnis der im Jahre . . . erschienen Musikalien;* 1929–42, *Hofmeisters Jahresverzeichnis.*

In three parts: [pt.1], Musikalien, Musikschriften, Zeitschriften und Jahrbücher in one alphabet; [pt.2], Systematischer und Register-Teil; [pt.3], Titel und Textregister.

☙ Useful current listings of new music materials are to be found in: (1) Music Library Association, *Notes: A magazine devoted to music and its literature with bibliographies and reviews of books, records, music;* (2) *Music and letters;* (3) *Musical quarterly;* and (4) *Fontes artis musicae, Review of the International Association of Music Libraries.*

Many of the encyclopedias and bibliographies of music include lists and descriptions of libraries and collections with indication of printed catalogs. Among the more useful are (1) "Libraries and collections," *Grove's Dictionary of music and musicians* (BH53); (2) Lionel Roy McColvin and Harold Reeves. *Music libraries: their organization and contents, with a bibliography of music and musical literature.* London, Grafton, 1937–38. 2v. (v.2, p.213–92); (3) *Die Musik in Geschichte und Gegenwart* (v.9, col.1034–48) (BH58); (4) Willi Apel, *Harvard dictionary of music,* p.398–404 (BH66).

Periodicals

Thoumin, Jean-Adrien. Bibliographie rétrospective des périodiques français de littérature musicale, 1870–1954. Paris, Éd. Documentaires Industrielles et Techniques, 1957. 179p. **BH21**

On cover: Union française des organismes de documentation.

A list of 600 titles with locations indicated. Indexes by year and by editors.

Dissertations

Doctoral dissertations in music and music education, 1949–1956, prep. by W. S. Larson. (In Journal of research in music education 5, no.2:61–225. Fall 1957)

—— 1957–1963, [by] Roderick D. Gordon. (In Journal of research in music education 12, no.1:7–112. Spring 1964) **BH22**

Continues: *Bibliography of research studies in music education, 1932–1948.* [Rev. ed.] prep. by W. S. Larson. Chicago, Music Educators' Nat. Conference, [1949]. 119p.

Doctoral dissertations in musicology. 3d ed. comp. by Helen Hewitt. Philadelphia, Amer. Musicological Soc., 1961. 113p. **BH23**

1st ed. 1952; 2d ed. 1957.

Lists 829 dissertations completed, or in progress, for the doctorate in music from 1905 through April (?) 1961. Arranged by period, followed by several broad subjects. Includes author and subject indexes.

The 1st edition included dissertations in musicology and related fields, e.g., music education, psychology of music, and acoustics. The 2d and 3d editions are limited to "musicology . . . research in the history of music."

Kept up to date by supplements, appearing annually in the 3d number of the *Journal* of the American Musicological Society.

Schaal, Richard. Verzeichnis deutschsprachiger musikwissenschaftlicher Dissertationen 1861–1960. Kassel, Bärenreiter, 1963. 167p. **BH24**

Contains 2819 dissertations in German, listed alphabetically by author. Includes subject index.

Manuscript and published music

Albrecht, Otto Edwin. A census of autograph music manuscripts of European composers in American libraries. Philadelphia, Univ. of Pa. Pr., 1953. 331p. **BH25**

Lists 2017 manuscripts by more than 500 European composers. Gives full bibliographical information. Includes list of owners.

American Society of Composers, Authors and Publishers. ASCAP index of performed compositions. N.Y., Soc., 1952. 2v. **BH26**

An alphabetical listing by title of compositions in the ASCAP repertory, including composer and publisher.

—— ASCAP supplementary index. 1954. 1v. [v.p.]

British Museum. Dept. of Manuscripts. Catalogue of manuscript music in the British Museum, by Augustus Hughes-Hughes. London, pr. by order of the Trustees, 1906–9. 3v. **BH27**

Classified list, with author, subject, and title indexes in each volume.

Contents: v.1, Sacred vocal music; v.2, Secular vocal music; v.3, Instrumental music, treatises, etc.

British Museum. Dept. of Printed Books. Catalogue of printed music published between 1487 and 1800 now in the British Museum, by W. Barclay Squire. London, pr. by order of the Trustees, 1912. 2v. **BH28**

v.2 includes 1st supplement.

—— —— 2d supplement, by William C. Smith. Cambridge, Univ. Pr., 1940. 85p.

British Museum. Dept. of Printed Books. Hirsch Library. Music in the Hirsch Library. London, Trustees of the British Museum, 1951. 438p. (British Museum. Dept. of Printed Books. Catalogue of printed music in the British Museum. Accessions. Pt.53) **BH29**

Contains vocal scores, operas, orchestral scores, chamber music, and collections of early editions, totaling nearly 9000 entries, many of which are not listed in the original 4v. catalog (BH10).

British union-catalogue of early music printed before the year 1801: a record of the holdings of over one hundred libraries throughout the British Isles; ed., Edith B. Schnapper. London, Butterworth, 1957. 2v. **BH30**

A scholarly bibliography which has drawn on the 1912 British Museum (Squire's) *Catalogue* . . . (BH28), but which is essentially an entirely new work. Listing is generally by composer or anonymous title; periodicals are grouped under "Periodical publications." Extensive index of song titles.

Dichter, Harry and **Shapiro, Elliott.** Early American sheet music, its lure and its lore, 1768–1889; including a directory of early American music publishers. . . . N.Y., Bowker, 1941. 287p. 32 facsim. (incl. music) **BH31**

"Famous American musical firsts," p.xxv–xxvii.

Pt.3, "Lithographers and artists working on American sheet music before 1870, by Edith A. Wright and Josephine A. McDevitt," p.249–57.

Arranged by class in chronological periods. Each piece is described with bibliographical details, illustrations, etc.

Heyer, Anna H. Historical sets, collected editions and monuments of music, a guide to their contents. Chicago, Amer. Lib. Assoc., 1957. 485p. **BH32**

Main part lists complete editions of individual composers and most of the major collections, indicating contents and giving complete bibliographical information. Includes index of composers and subjects.

Hofmeisters Handbuch der Musikliteratur; oder, Allgemeines systematisch-geordnetes Verzeichnis der in Deutschland und in den angrenzenden Ländern gedruckten Musikalien auch musikalischen Schriften und Abbildun- gen, mit Anzeige der Verleger und Preise. 3., bis zum Anfang des Jahres 1844 ergänzte Aufl. Bearb. und hrsg. von Adolf Hofmeister. Leipzig, Hofmeister, 1844–45. 3v. **BH33**

First published in Leipzig by Anton Meysel, 1817, covering music and music literature to 1815, with nine supplements to 1825.

Karl Friedrich Whistling issued a revised 2d edition in 1828 with three supplements: 1829, 1834, and 1839.

Adolf Hofmeister edited this 3d edition, called *C. F. Whistling's Handbuch*, with supplementary volumes, as follows: *Handbuch der musikalischen Literatur; oder, Verzeichnis der im Deutschen Reiche, in den Ländern deutscher Sprachgebietes, sowie der für den Vertrieb im Deutschen Reiche wichtigen, im Auslande erschienenen Musikalien auch musikalischen Schriften, Abbildungen und plastichen Darstellungen, mit Anzeige der Verleger und Preise. 4.–19.* (incompl.) Bd. 1844–1940. . . . Leipzig, Hofmeister, 1852– 1943.

Bd.19, Lfg. 1–8, A–L. Ceased publication.

Deutsche Musikbibliographie. Jahrg.1– . Leipzig, Hofmeister, 1829– . Monthly. **BH34**

Supersedes *Handbuch der musikalischen Literatur,* 1817– 29.

Title varies: 1829–1907, *Musikalisch-literarischer Monatsbericht;* 1908–42, *Hofmeisters Musikalisch-literarischer Monatsbericht.*

An alphabetical list, by composer or author, of music and musical writings published in German. Gives place of publication, publisher, and price. Indexed by subject and by publisher. Cumulated in Hofmeister's *Jahresverzeichnis der deutschen Musikalien und Musikschriften* (BH20).

Philadelphia. Free Library. The Edwin A. Fleisher music collection in the Free Library of Philadelphia. Philadelphia, priv. print., 1933–45. 2v. **BH35**

Catalog of a loan collection containing more than 4000 compositions for orchestras and about 2500 for solo instruments with orchestra. Arranged in 15 classes, then alphabetically by composer. Information includes dates of composers; title of each work in original language, with English translation; publisher; instrumentation; length of time required for performance; date of composition; and first performance information. Index of composers and arrangers.

—— —— Supplementary list, 1945–1955. [Philadelphia, 1955?] 33p.

Sonneck, Oscar George Theodore. Bibliography of early secular American music (18th century). Rev. and enl. by William Treat Upton. Wash., Lib. of Congress, Music Division, 1945. 616p. il. (Repr., with a pref. by Irving Lowens: N.Y., Da Capo Pr., 1964) **BH36**

1st ed. 1905.

Revised edition adds much new material. Lists by title— with complete bibliographical information, including first lines—secular music issued by the American press prior to the 19th century. Also contains a list of articles and essays relating to music, and a list of composers, including their works. Locates copies.

U.S. Copyright Office. Catalog of copyright entries . . . pt.3: Musical compositions. Wash., Govt. Prt. Off., 1906– 46. n.s. v.1–41. Monthly, 1906–45; annual, 1946. **BH37**

Through 1945, all musical compositions (published and unpublished) were entered by title in one alphabet in each monthly issue, followed by the list of renewals, with an annual index.

In 1946 the catalog was divided into four groups: (1) Unpublished music; (2) Published music; (3) Renewals; (4) Title index to groups 1 and 2.

—— Catalog of copyright entries. 3d ser. Pt.5: Music. v.1– . Jan./June, 1947– . Wash., Govt. Prt. Off., 1947– . Semiannual. **BH37a**

Issued in three parts, 1947–56: pt. 5A, Published music; pt.5B, Unpublished music; pt.5C, Renewal registrations. (Pt.C issued as pt.14B, 1947–50) Each part published in two numbers per year: (1) Jan./June, and (2) July/Dec.

Beginning with Jan./June, 1957 (3d ser. v.11, pt.5, no.1), the three parts are combined and issued as pt.5, in three groupings: (1) current registrations, (2) renewal registrations, and (3) name index.

Lists all music published in the United States and foreign countries deposited for copyright registration during the period covered. Arrangement is by title. The index to names lists names of composers, authors of words, editors, compilers, arrangers, etc. as given in the main entry.

The most comprehensive bibliography of music available.

For full description of the *Catalog of copyright entries, see* AA353.

U.S. Library of Congress. Library of Congress catalog— Music and phonorecords, 1953– . Wash., 1953– . Semiannual. **BH38**

Subtitle: A cumulative list of works represented by Library of Congress printed cards.

Issued semiannually with annual and quinquennial cumulations. For preceding listings, *see* the Library's *Author catalog* (AA64).

"Contains entries for music scores in the broadest sense, i.e., music intended for performance, regardless of its classification. It includes also phonorecords, e.g., sound recordings, musical or non-musical, reproduced on all kinds of material, including cylinders, discs, tape, and wire."—*Introd.*

Wolfe, Richard J. Secular music in America, 1801–1825; a bibliography. Introd. by Carleton Sprague Smith. N.Y., N.Y. Pub. Lib., 1964. 3v. **BH39**

Lists approximately 10,000 titles and editions of secular music published in America, though not confined to American composers. Includes sacred music, when printed in secular collections or in series, and religious pieces, written by American composers and published in sheet-music form. Arranged alphabetically by composer or anonymous title with detailed bibliographical information. Gives short biographical sketches of lesser-known composers.

Contains indexes of titles, first lines, publishers, etc., and a general index.

A scholarly work useful to research workers and students of American history, as well as to music scholars.

Locates copies.

Indexes

Music index; the key to current music periodical literature. Detroit, Mich., Information Service, 1949– . Monthly (cumulating annually). **BH40**

Indexes, by author and subject, approximately 180 periodicals representing various aspects of the music field, ranging from musicology to the retailing of music. Gives complete indexing for musical periodicals, and indexes articles pertinent to music in some more general ones. All first performances and all obituaries are indexed. Music reviews are listed under composer, title, and medium.

Belknap, Sara Yancey. Guide to the musical arts; an analytical index of articles and illustrations, 1953–56. N.Y., Scarecrow, 1957. unpaged. **BH41**

Lists some 15,000 articles and 6000 illustrations, the former under both author and subject, in journals dealing with music, opera, the dance, and the theater. A considerable amount of the material unfortunately duplicates listings in the *Music index* (BH40).

For continuation, *see* the author's *Guide to the performing arts* (BG10).

Krohn, Ernst C. The history of music; an index to the literature available in a selected group of musicological publications. St. Louis, Mo., Washington Univ., 1952.

463p. (Washington University Library studies, no.3) (Repr.: St. Louis, Baton Music Co., 1958) **BH41**

An index to material on the history of music appearing in some 40 periodicals, mainly German and English. Arrangement is by broad period divisions, further subdivided under such headings as "General studies," "Composers," and the various musical forms. Includes book reviews. Indexes by authors and composers. The material was collected in card-index form by the compiler over about 25 years, but the periodicals covered are not confined to that period.

Encyclopedias and biographical dictionaries

American Society of Composers, Authors and Publishers. The ASCAP biographical dictionary of composers, authors, and publishers. Ed. by Daniel I. McNamara. 2d ed. N.Y., Crowell, 1952. 636p. **BH42**

1st ed. 1948.

Includes sketches of 2171 writers of lyrics and composers (1400 of whom are writers of popular music) and 402 publishers of music who are members of the American Society of Composers, Authors and Publishers.

Baker, Theodore. Biographical dictionary of musicians. 5th ed. compl. rev. by Nicolas Slonimsky. N.Y., Schirmer, 1958. 1855p. **BH43**

1st ed. 1900; 4th ed. 1940.

A useful and reliable dictionary, giving compact biographies—varying from a few lines to several pages—of musicians of all ages and nations, with bibliographies of the musician's own works and titles about him. Indicates pronunciation of foreign names.

This edition extensively revised, including 2300 new biographies, past and contemporary. Strong in factual data, i.e., corrections of previously published misinformation. Bibliographies generally up to date.

Blom, Eric. Everyman's dictionary of music. 4th ed. Rev. by Jack Westrup. London, Dent; N.Y., Dutton, [1962]. 687p. **BH44**

An excellent popular dictionary for quick reference, not for the specialist. Deals with Western music of the Christian Era. Includes terms, works, places, and biographical sketches but omits living performers.

Bull, Storm. Index to biographies of contemporary composers. N.Y., Scarecrow, 1964. 405p. **BH45**

Indexes 69 sources containing biographical information on composers who are living or who were born in 1900 or later, or, if deceased, who died after 1949.

Canadian Broadcasting Corporation. Catalogue of Canadian composers. Ed. by Helmut Kallmann. Rev. and enl. ed. [Toronto], Corporation, [1952]. 254p. **BH46**

1st ed. 1947.

Bio-bibliographical notes on 356 composers, many of whom are living. Contains a historical outline of music in Canada; bibliographies of musical biography and the folk song in Canada; and a directory of musical publications.

Enciclopedia della musica. Direttore, Claudio Sartori. [Milano], Ricordi, [1963–64]. 4v. il. music. **BH47**

Covers terms, forms, history, biographies, etc. Articles are written by some 230 musical authorities from several countries but are unsigned. Treatment is somewhat brief, but bibliographies are included throughout and composers' works are listed. Especially strong in biographies of recent composers and performers. Profusely illustrated in black-and-white photographs and colored plates.

Encyclopédie de la musique. [Publié sous la direction de François Michel en collaboration avec François Lesure et Vladimir Féderov et un comité de rédaction composé de Nadia Boulanger et al.] Paris, Fasquelle, 1958–61. 3v. il.   **BH48**

v.1–3, A–Z.

A general music encyclopedia particularly strong in biography, including contemporary Europeans. The biographical articles are not only more numerous but are usually longer than in Larousse (BH56). Illustrations in black and white and in color include facsimiles of music and manuscripts. Bibliographies are included with the articles; longer articles are signed.

v.1 includes much "preliminary matter" (e.g., sections on the work of contemporary composers, discology, music libraries, institutions, organizations, chronologies, etc.).

Ewen, David. Complete book of the American musical theater . . . . N.Y., Holt, 1958. 447p. il.   **BH49**

Subtitle: A guide to more than 300 productions of the American musical theater from *The black crook* (1866) to the present, with plot, production history, stars, songs, composers, librettists and lyricists, illustrated with photographs.

Presented in textual form arranged alphabetically by composer. Lists of shows and songs; full index.

—— Living musicians. N.Y., Wilson, 1940. 390p. il.   **BH50**

Biographies of 500 living musicians, including singers, instrumentalists, and conductors. Primarily those who would be of interest to the American public. Includes articles on such musical organizations as quartets, chamber-music ensembles, etc.

—— —— Supplement. 1– . 1957– .

The 1st supplement adds approximately 150 new biographies and brings up to date about half of the 500 biographies in the original volume.

Feather, Leonard G. Encyclopedia of jazz. Rev. and enl. with appreciations by Duke Ellington, Benny Goodman and John Hammond. N.Y., Horizon Pr., [c1960]. 527p. il., music.   **BH51**

1st ed. 1955. Title varies.

Contains biographical sketches of more than 2000 jazzmen with a guide to their recordings; history of jazz on records; recommended jazz records; bibliography and discography.

Fétis, François Joseph. Biographie universelle des musiciens et bibliographie générale de la musique. 2. éd. entièrement refondue et augm. de plus de moitié. Paris, Didot, 1867–70. 8v.   **BH52**

—— —— Supplément et complément publiés sous la direction de Arthur Pougin. Paris, Didot, 1878–80. 2v.

(Repr. of the complete 10v. series: Bruxelles, Culture et Civilisation, [1964])

✓**Grove, *Sir* George.** Dictionary of music and musicians. 5th ed., ed. by Eric Blom. N.Y., St. Martin's, 1955 [c1954]. 9v. il.   **BH53**

1st ed., 4v. 1879–89; 2d ed., ed. by J. A. Fuller-Maitland, 5v. 1904–8. American suppl. to 2d ed., N.Y., 1920. 412p.; 3d ed., ed. by H. C. Colles, 5 v. 1927–28; 4th ed., ed. by H. C. Colles, 6v. 1940.

The standard encyclopedia in English covering the whole field from 1450, with special emphasis, however, on English subjects. Includes musical history, theory, and practice; terms; biographies; songs and operas, etc. Does not give opera plots. Signed articles by specialists. Bibliographies in this edition have been improved by the inclusion of periodical articles.

For review comparing this edition with earlier ones, *see Notes*, 2d ser., 12, no.1:85–92. 1954.

—— —— Supplementary volume. N.Y., St. Martin's, 1961. 492p.

Includes corrections, additions to existing articles, some rewritten articles, and new entries for persons and subjects.

Historical Records Survey, District of Columbia. Bio-

bibliographical index of musicians in the United States of America since colonial times. 2d ed. Wash., Music Section, Pan Amer. Union, 1956. 439p.   **BH54**

1st ed. 1941. 2d edition shows little change.

Title, forewords, and introduction in English, Spanish, and Portuguese.

Indexes biographical material in about 65 books giving biographies of musicians in the United States. Names are given in as complete form as possible, followed by dates of birth and death when ascertainable and references to works in which biographical material is to be found.

"A list of special studies, biographies and autobiographies pertaining to the persons whose names appear in the Index," p.421–39.

Kürschners deutscher Musiker-Kalender, 1954. 2. Ausg. des Deutschen Musiker-Lexikons. Hrsg.: Hedwig und E. H. Mueller von Asow. Berlin, de Gruyter, 1954. 1702col.   **BH55**

The 1st edition, *Deutsches Musiker-Lexikon*, by Erich Hermann Müller, was published in 1929.

Gives brief biographical data for approximately 4500 musicians—primarily German, Swiss, and Austrian—whose birth dates range from 1854 to 1939. Performing artists and composers of international reputation are included. An appendix lists 1500 musicians who have died since the 1st edition.

Larousse de la musique. Publié sous la direction de Norbert Dufourcq avec la collaboration de Félix Raugel et Armand Machabey. Paris, Larousse, 1957. 2v. il. (Maps, music, and records in each volume)   **BH56**

An international encyclopedia with articles on musical terminology, subjects, places, performing groups (such as orchestras), etc. Primarily a dictionary of subjects rather than of persons, although there are many biographical sketches, usually brief. Little on contemporary musicians or artists; for these the *Encyclopédie de la musique* (BH48) is much fuller. Articles are well balanced in length, and some are signed. Illustrations in black and white and in color are profuse and usually well reproduced.

Lists of works by a composer are given under his name; other bibliographic references are at the end of each volume.

Mayer-Serra, Otto. Música y músicos de Latino-america. México, Ed. Atlante, 1947. 2v. il.   **BH57**

An alphabetical encyclopedia covering history, biography (including living persons), folklore, religious music, musical instruments, terminology, legislation, etc., of all the countries of Spanish America. In some cases full bibliographies are given for composers. Includes portraits; musical examples; words and music of the national hymns of the various countries, etc.

Die Musik in Geschichte und Gegenwart. Allgemeine Enzyklopädie der Musik. Unter Mitarbeit zahlreicher Musikforscher des In- und Auslandes hrsg. von Friedrich Blume. Kassel/Basel, Bärenreiter, 1949–64. v.1–12. il. (In progress)   **BH58**

v.1–11, A–Schnyder von Wartensee; v.12 (Lfg. 110/111–114/115), Scho–Stam.

A scholarly, comprehensive work, international in scope with long, signed articles by specialists, including extensive bibliographical notes. Profusely illustrated. An indispensable reference book in its field.

Pena, Joaquín. Diccionario de la música Labor; iniciado por Joaquín Pena, continuado por Higinio Anglés, con la colaboración de Miguel Querol . . . Barcelona, Labor, 1954. 2v. il. music.   **BH59**

Bio-bibliographical dictionary, covering all periods, places, and persons, but especially strong on Spanish and Latin-American musical life. Articles are fairly extensive, including lists of works and bibliographies. Contains numerous portraits.

Riemann, Hugo. Riemann musik Lexikon. 12. völlig

neubearb. Aufl., hrsg. von Wilibald Gurlitt. Mainz, B. Schott's Söhne; N.Y., Schott Music Corp., 1959–61. v.1–2. (In progress) **BH60**

1st ed. 1882.

Contents: v.1, Personenteil, A–K; v.2, Personenteil, L–Z. A considerably revised edition of a standard work, with text and bibliographies brought up to date. The first 2v. include articles on persons only; v.3 will be devoted to subjects. Covers all periods and places with strong emphasis on German music. Includes lists of works throughout text and bibliographies.

—— Dictionnaire de musique. Tr. par Georges Humbert. 3. éd. entièrement refondue et augm. sous la direction de A. Schaeffner, avec la collaboration de M. Pincherle, Y. Rokseth, A. Tessier. Paris, Payot, 1931. 1485p. il. **BH60a**

This French edition has reduced the amount of space given to German subjects and has increased that for French, English, and Italian musicians—particularly of the 16th, 17th, and 18th centuries—and for the Spanish and Russian schools.

Scholes, Percy A. The Oxford companion to music, self-indexed and with a pronouncing glossary and over 1,100 portraits and pictures. 9th ed., compl. rev. and reset and with many additions to text and illustrations. London, N.Y., Oxford Univ. Pr., 1955. 1195p. **BH61**

1st ed. 1938.

A comprehensive, alphabetical dictionary on all phases of music containing long, encyclopedic articles; some short articles; and many definitions. Contains more than 1500 biographical articles. Includes a pronouncing glossary of foreign terms and names.

No bibilographies in this edition.

Sohlmans musiklexikon. Nordiskt och allmänt uppslagsverk för tonkonst, musikliv och dans. Stockholm, Sohlman, 1948–52. 4v. il. **BH62**

Generally brief, signed articles with lists of works and bibliographical notes. Coverage is international with emphasis on Scandinavian music. Includes many portraits.

Thompson, Oscar. International cyclopedia of music and musicians. 9th ed. by Robert Sabin. N.Y., Dodd, 1964. 2476p. il. (music) **BH63**

Alphabetically arranged. Most of the articles are short, but there are also included, in the same alphabet, signed monographs of considerable length—written by authorities—on the more important composers and also on special subjects such as the history of music, music criticism, folk music, opera, etc. Each of the biographical articles is followed by a calendar of the composer's life and a classified list of his works. The work is strong in biography, and many contemporary names are included. Appearing in earlier editions, but omitted in this edition, are the appendixes: Plots of operas, and Bibliography. The section "Pronunciation of names and titles," by W. B. S. Smith, p.2455–76, has been retained.

1st ed. 1939. Later editions show spotty revision, adding dates of death, some corrections, and additional material in the appendixes.

Westrup, Jack Allan and **Harrison, F. Ll.** The new college encyclopedia of music. N.Y., Norton, 1950. 739p. music. **BH64**

Published in England under title *Collins Music encyclopaedia.* London, Collins, 1959.

Generally well edited and should prove useful to the interested amateur. Contains entries for: composers, including their works; performers; titles; general and specialized musical terms; and associated items.

Who's who in music and musicians' international directory, ed. by Peter Townend and David Simmons. 4th ed. N.Y., Hafner, 1962. 331p. **BH65**

1st ed. 1935.

Introductory material on a number of British musical or-

ganizations precedes the main section. Contains short biographical sketches of a large number of musicians, mostly British. Includes lists of journals, publishers, festivals, organizations, etc.

Dictionaries of terms

Apel, Willi. Harvard dictionary of music. Cambridge, Harvard Univ. Pr., 1944. 824p. il. **BH66**

Emphasis is on the historical point of view. Omits biographical articles because other dictionaries cover that field. Contains definitions of all kinds, including many used in musical performance, and articles on music history, aesthetics, theory, etc. The bibliographies list books, periodical articles, and references to examples of music.

—— and **Daniel, Ralph T.** The Harvard brief dictionary of music. Cambridge, Harvard Univ. Pr., 1960. 341p. **BH67**

Brief articles for the nonspecialist who does not require the lengthier explanations of the *Harvard dictionary of music* (BH66).

Includes opera plots, songs, and compositions, but no composers.

Baker, Theodore. Dictionary of musical terms . . . with a supplement containing an English-Italian vocabulary for composers. N.Y., Schirmer, 1923. 257p. music. **BH68**

Subtitle: Containing upwards of 9,000 English, French, German, Italian, Latin and Greek words and phrases used in the art and science of music, carefully defined, and with the accent of the foreign words marked; preceded by rules for the pronunciation of Italian, German and French.

"24th issue thoroughly revised, and augmented by an appendix of 700 additional words and phrases."

Bobillier, Marie. Diccionario de la música, histórica y técnico. Traducción de la última edición francesa, rev. y notablemente ampliada con multitud de artículos nuevos . . . Terminología y folklore español y americano . . . Barcelona, Iberia, [1946]. 548p. il. music. **BH69**

Translation of the author's *Dictionnaire pratique et historique de la musique* par Michel Brenet, [pseud.]. Paris, Colin, 1926.

This profusely illustrated edition includes many terms not in the French edition.

Gold, Robert S. A jazz lexicon. N.Y., Knopf, [c1964]. 363p. **BH70**

Current and obsolete terms commonly used in the jazz world with definitions according to historical usage.

Read, Gardner. Thesaurus of orchestral devices. N.Y., London, Pitman, [1953]. 631p. il. **BH71**

A lexicon of instrumentation, including index of nomenclature and terminology in English, Italian, French, and German; abbreviations; list of composers and works; and list of music publishers.

Vannes, René. Essai de terminologie musicale. Dictionnaire universel comprenant plus de 15,000 termes de musique en italien, espagnol, portugais, français, anglais, allemand, latin et grec, disposés en un alphabet unique. Thann, "Alsatia," 1925. 230p. **BH72**

Terms arranged in one alphabet by original language, with brief definitions and equivalents in the other languages.

Handbooks

Berkowitz, Freda Pastor. Popular titles and subtitles of musical compositions. N.Y., Scarecrow, 1962. 182p. **BH73**

A listing of some 500 titles associated with works of serious music from 1600 to the present, with notes as to origin of name. Arranged alphabetically in English except where the foreign-language title is well known. Includes bibliography and list of composers.

History

Collaer, Paul and **Linden, Albert vander.** Atlas historique de la musique. Paris, Elsevier, 1960. 179p. il. maps.
BH74

Maps and plates, with accompanying text, to illustrate the history of music from primitive times to the present.

Grout, Donald Jay. A history of Western music. N.Y., Norton, [1960]. 742p. il. music.
BH75

A survey intended as a text for music students, or for the general reader. Contains glossary, bibliography (p.668–98), and music chronology. Numerous illustrations throughout. Has title, subject, and name index.

Kinsky, Georg. History of music in pictures, ed. . . . with the cooperation of Robert Haas, Hans Schnoor and other experts, with an introd. by Eric Blom. N.Y., Dover, [c1951]. 363p.
BH76

A collection of approximately 1500 illustrations—portraits, instruments, facsimiles, etc.—forming a pictorial history of music from the earliest times to the present. The pictures constitute the main part of the work, the brief text consisting merely of: (1) explanatory notes on each plate of illustrations, (2) indexes and contents, and (3) introduction and foreword. Issued in three editions: (1) original German edition, with title *Geschichte der Musik in Bildern* (Leipzig, Breitkopf, 1930); (2) French edition with title *Album musical* (Paris, Delagrave, 1930), printed from same plates of pictures with notes, indexes, etc., translated into French and a new French introduction; and (3) the English edition originally published London, Dent, 1930, also printed from the original German plates with translation of text.

Mattfeld, Julius. Variety music cavalcade, 1620–1961; a chronology of vocal and instrumental music popular in the United States. Rev. ed. Englewood Cliffs, N.J., Prentice-Hall, [1962]. 713p.
BH77

Originally appeared, in a modified form, first in the *Variety radio directory*, 1938–39, then in weekly issues of *Variety*. Lists popular music chronologically, with a brief account of various events occurring each year. Also includes hymns; secular and sacred songs; choral compositions; and instrumental and orchestral works. Only the musical items are indexed.

[**Norton history of music.** N.Y., Norton, 1940–   ] il.
BH78

While the following volumes do not carry a series note, together they form a comprehensive historical survey:
Curt Sachs. The rise of music in the ancient world, east and west. 1943. 324p.; Gustave Reese. Music in the Middle Ages, with an introd. on the music of ancient times. 1940. 502p. (Bibliography, p.425–63. Record list, p.465–80); Gustave Reese. Music in the Renaissance. [1954] Rev. ed. [1959]. 1022p. (Bibliography, p.884–946); Manfred F. Bukofzer. Music in the Baroque era from Monteverdi to Bach. 1947. 489p. (Checklist of Baroque books on music, p.433–59); Alfred Einstein. Music in the Romantic era. 1947. 371p.; A. Salazar. Music in our time. 1946. 367p.

Oxford history of music. 2d ed. Oxford Univ. Pr., 1931–38. v.1–7 and introd. volume. il. (incl. music)
BH79

Contents: Introd. volume, ed. by Percy C. Buck. Early history, Middle Ages, Folk song, etc. 1929; v.1–2, Polyphonic period, by H. E. Woolridge. 2d ed. rev. by Percy C. Buck. 1929–32; v.3, Music of the 17th century, by C. H. H. Parry. 2d ed. with revisions and introd. note by E. J. Dent. 1938; v.4, Age of Bach and Handel, by J. A. Fuller-Maitland. 2d ed. 1931; v.5, Viennese period, by Sir W. H. Hadow. 2d ed. 1931;

v.6, Romantic period, by E. Dannreuther. 2d ed. 1931; v.7, Symphony and drama, 1850–1900, by H. C. Colles. 1934.
Originally published 1901–5, 6v.; v.1–3, revised and reissued, 2d ed., 1929–38; the new *Introductory volume* was issued with the 2d edition to serve as an introduction to the study of the history of music; v.7 is new, but other volumes (i.e., v.4–6), though called 2d editions, are virtual reprints of original editions, without revision.
Important history, indispensable in any library doing much reference work in musical history.

New Oxford history of music. London, Oxford Univ. Pr., 1954–60. (v.1, 1957) v.1–3. (In progress)
BH80

v.1, Ancient and oriental music, ed. by Egon Wellesz. 1957. 530p.; v.2, Early medieval music up to 1300, ed. by Dom Anselm Hughes. 1954. 434p.; v.3, Ars nova and the Renaissance, 1300–1540, ed. by Dom Anselm Hughes and Gerald Abraham. 1960. 565p.
Planned to be in 10v., plus an index volume, as an entirely new survey of music from the earliest times to the present. Written by outstanding authorities in their fields.

—— History of music in sound. RCA Victor. 10v. **BH80a**
A series of gramophone records presenting compositions from the earliest times to the present with specimens of the music of primitive and oriental peoples.
Recorded as a sound companion to the above.

Slonimsky, Nicolas. Music since 1900. 3d ed. rev. and enl. N.Y., Coleman-Ross, 1949. 759p.
BH81

1st ed. 1938.
Contents: Tabular views of stylistic trends in music, 1900–1948; Descriptive chronology, 1900–1948; Letters and documents.

MUSICAL FORMS

Cobbett, Walter Wilson. Cyclopedic survey of chamber music . . . with supplementary material ed. by Colin Mason. 2d ed. N.Y., Oxford, 1963. 3v.
BH82

1st ed. 1929–30. 2v.
v.1 and 2 of the 2d edition are reissues of the 1929–30 edition except for a few amendments to the text, and the insertion of symbols in the margin, which indicate a further reference in v.3.
Contents: v.1–2, A–Z. Contain signed articles on subjects concerned with chamber music: topics, persons, instruments, organizations, etc. Include biographies with lists of composers' works. v.3 is a selective survey of chamber music since 1929, with a bibliography, additions and corrections to the original edition, and an index of composers.

Ewen, David. Encyclopedia of concert music. N.Y., Hill & Wang, 1959. 566p.
BH83

A companion volume to the author's *Encyclopedia of the opera* (BH91), addressed primarily to the amateur concertgoer and record collector. Includes, in a dictionary arrangement, some "1500 of the best known compositions in all branches of instrumental music, past and present" (*Pref.*); biographies of composers, conductors, and performers; information on famous orchestras, ensembles, festivals, etc.; musical terms, forms, styles, and literary sources.

Green, Stanley. The world of musical comedy; the story of the American musical stage as told through the careers of its foremost composers and lyricists. N.Y., Ziff-Davis, 1960. 391p. il.
BH84

Arranged by composer, with detailed records of productions of works. Appendixes include a list of shows with data on production, casts, and discography.

Coffin, Berton. Singer's repertoire. 2d ed. N.Y., Scarecrow, 1960–62. 5v.
BH85

1st ed. 1956.

Contents: v.1, coloratura soprano, lyric soprano, and dramatic soprano; v.2, mezzo-soprano and contralto; v.3, lyric and dramatic tenor; v.4, baritone and bass; v.5, program notes for the singer's repertoire, by Berton Coffin and Werner Singer.

A list of approximately 8000 songs, arranged by vocal classification and further subdivided by nationality, mood, etc.

Jacobs, Arthur. Choral music: a symposium. Baltimore, Penguin, [1963]. 444p. il. **BH86**

22 essays, by specialists, surveying the history of choral music, followed by bibliographies of recommended: books, p.405–13; musical editions, p.416–26; and gramophone records, p.427–36.

Themes

Barlow, Harold and **Morgenstern, Sam.** A dictionary of musical themes; introd. by John Erskine. N.Y., Crown, 1948. 656p. **BH87**

The "Bartlett" for musical themes; contains some 10,000 themes of instrumental music arranged by composers, with a notation index arranged alphabetically by the first notes of the themes. Index of titles.

—— Dictionary of vocal themes. N.Y., Crown, 1950. 547p. **BH88**

Companion volume to the above. Contains themes from operas, oratorios, cantatas, art songs, and miscellaneous vocal works. Includes index to songs and first lines.

Music Library Association. Committee on Thematic Indexes. A checklist of thematic catalogues. N.Y., N.Y. Pub. Lib., 1954. 37p. (Repr. from New York Public Library. Bull. Jan.–March 1953) **BH89**

Lists 362 items, "including catalogues of 129 individual composers, 63 collections, 22 libraries, and 13 publishers."— *Introd.*

Opera

Eaton, Quaintance. Opera production, a handbook. Minneapolis, Univ. of Minn. Pr., [1961]. 266p. **BH90**

Information on the production of 259 contemporary and standard operas, with brief information on some 260 in the supplementary list. Includes synopsis, time, requirements of roles, chorus, orchestra, sources of scores, list of performing companies in America, etc.

Ewen, David. Encyclopedia of the opera. New enl. ed. N.Y., Hill & Wang, [1963]. 594p. **BH91**

Aims to be a comprehensive source book about opera and opera performance. In one alphabet it covers: stories of operas; characters; excerpts from operas; biographies (composers, librettists, singers, conductors, stage directors, impresarios, teachers, critics, musicologists, etc.); history of opera; opera houses and festivals; literary sources; special types of opera; technical terms. Pronunciation guide, p.557–94.

Identical to the 1955 edition except for supplement of 19 pages preceding the text.

Johnson, Harold Earle. Operas on American subjects. N.Y., Coleman-Ross, 1964. 125p. **BH92**

Covers operas on American subjects, written in America and abroad from 1658 to 1964. Arranged alphabetically by composer. Gives title, date, librettist, source, story, first performance with conductor, cast; cites reviews; includes publisher of vocal score. Subject index by topic and locale, and an index to titles.

Loewenberg, Alfred. Annals of opera, 1597–1940; comp. from the original sources. 2d ed. rev. Genève. Societas Bibliographica, 1955. 2v. **BH93**

Contents: v.1, text; v.2, indexes.

Lists nearly 4000 operas, arranged chronologically according to the dates of first performance, followed by the name of the composer and title of the opera (titles are given in the form in which they first appeared and in the original language; except for Italian, French, and German titles, a translation has been included), name of town where first performed, sometimes name of theater, and a history of performances. References to translations, revivals, etc.

Indexes: (1) Operas; (2) Composers, with dates of birth and death, giving the names of operas by each with dates; (3) Librettists; and (4) General index.

Mattfeld, Julius. A handbook of American operatic premières, 1731–1962. [Detroit, Mich., Information Service], 1963. 142p. (Detroit studies in music bibliography, no.5) **BH94**

Listed alphabetically by title; gives premières of nearly 2000 operas in the United States. Includes index of composers.

Rosenthal, Harold and **Warrack, John.** Concise Oxford dictionary of opera. London, Oxford Univ. Pr., 1964. 446p. **BH95**

Includes entries for terms and characters in opera; brief synopses of operas; and biographical notes on composers, conductors, directors, producers, and singers.

A very useful, up-to-date, 1v. dictionary, especially for recent composers. Older composers are treated more briefly. Contains many literary references.

Ross, Anne. The opera directory. N.Y., Sterling, 1961. 566p. il. **BH96**

An international directory of all aspects of opera today, with lists of: singers (classified by voice), conductors, producers, technical staff, living composers, opera houses, festivals, music organizations, colleges and schools of music, casting index, etc.

Introductory material and table of contents in English, French, German, Italian, Spanish, and Russian.

Seltsam, William H. Metropolitan opera annals; a chronicle of artists and performances. N.Y., Wilson, 1947. 751p. il. **BH97**

A chronological record of the casts and of the operas performed from the first season of the Metropolitan in 1883/84 through 1946/47. Also gives excerpts from press reviews for each season, especially those covering important debuts and first performances.

Profusely illustrated with photographs of the leading singers in typical roles. The index traces all references to artists, performances, reviews, and portraits.

—— —— Supplements. 1– , 1947/57– . N.Y., Wilson, 1957– .

U.S. Library of Congress. Music Division. Catalogue of opera librettos printed before 1800, prep. by O. G. T. Sonneck. Wash., Govt. Prt. Off., 1914. 2v. **BH98**

v.1, Title catalogue; v.2, Author list, composer list, and aria index.

A detailed catalog giving for each libretto: full cataloging information, date and place of first performance, and valuable bibliographical and historical notes. Entry is first by original title, and then by replicas and translations, with reference from alternative, later, and translated titles.

—— Dramatic music . . . catalogue of full scores, comp. by O. G. T. Sonneck. Wash., Govt. Prt. Off., 1908. 170p. **BH99**

Arrangement is alphabetical by composer.

Plots

❧ Many books, old and new, give plots or synopses of operas. They vary considerably in the operas covered and in general treatment: some have short notes, some long, some discuss the music, some the performances, etc.

Only a few of the most comprehensive and more recent are listed here. Various others, however, will be found in many libraries.

Kobbé, Gustave. Kobbé's Complete opera book, ed. and rev. by the Earl of Harewood. London, N.Y., Putnam, [1963]. 1262p. il.　　　　**BH100**

1st ed. 1935; rev. 1954.

Discusses the development of opera, giving the stories of more than 200 operas, brief notes on the composers, musical motives, etc. Includes older operas which are still being produced, and modern works which will probably "be seen by English-speaking audiences during, say, the next ten or fifteen years." The most complete general guide available. This edition is substantially the same as the 1954 edition.

Lubbock, Mark Hugh. The complete book of light opera. With an American section by David Ewen. N.Y., Appleton, [1963]. 953p. il. music.　　　　**BH101**

Intended to serve as a companion volume to Kobbé's *Complete opera book* (BH100). Selection limited to lightest genre of light opera, dating from mid-19th century to 1961. Contains some 300 "musicals" which "the visitor is likely to encounter" in Paris, Vienna, Berlin, London, and New York. Arranged by these places. Gives title, composer, story, source, and first-production information.

Martens, Frederick H. A thousand and one nights of opera. N.Y., London, Appleton, 1926. 487p.　　**BH102**

A most comprehensive book of opera synopses, including some 1550 operas and ballets. Arranged chronologically by historical period of the subject. Synopses vary in length, some being very brief. Indexed by composer and title.

Rieck, Waldemar. Opera plots. An index to the stories of operas, operettas, ballets, etc., from the 16th to the 20th century. N.Y., N.Y. Pub. Lib., 1927. 102p. (Repr. from the New York Public Library. Bull. Jan.–April 1926)　　　　**BH103**

An index by composers' names—with added detailed index of titles—to the outlines of plots contained in more than 200 books of synopses published in English, French, German, and Danish. The list of books indexed forms a useful bibliography of books of synopses.

Gilbert and Sullivan

Searle, Townley. Sir William Schwenck Gilbert; a topsy-turvy adventure. London, Alexander-Ousley, 1931. 105p. il.　　　　**BH104**

A bibliography of the works of Gilbert and of the Gilbert and Sullivan operas.

Dunn, George E. A Gilbert and Sullivan dictionary. N.Y., Oxford Univ. Pr., 1936. 175p.　　　　**BH104a**

Includes obscure words, phrases, allusions, foreign and colloquial words, names of persons, places and incidents, characters, original creators, successors, etc. Lists the operas with dates and theaters of first productions, etc.

Poladian, Sirvart. Sir Arthur Sullivan: an index to the text of his vocal works. [Detroit, Mich., Information Service], 1961. 91p. (Detroit studies in music bibliography, no.2)　　　　**BH104b**

In two parts: pt.1, index to operettas and other large vocal works by title, repeated catchy refrains, and important musical sections; pt.2, index to single songs, hymns, and miscellania by title, first line, and tune name.

Songs

Chipman, John H. Index to top-hit tunes, 1900–1950. With a foreword by Arthur Fiedler. Boston, B. Humphries, [1962]. 249p.　　　　**BH105**

Contains 3000 titles of American popular songs which have sold at least 100,000 copies of sheet music or 100,000 records. Listed by title alphabetically, and chronologically. Gives composer, publisher, and date, and indicates if featured in a film or musical.

Day, Cyrus Lawrence and **Murrie, Eleanore Boswell.** English song-books, 1651–1702; a bibliography with a first-line index of songs. London, pr. for the Bibliographical Society at the Univ. Pr., Oxford, 1940 (for 1937). 439p. il. music.　　　　**BH106**

"The aim of this volume is to list, describe and index all the secular song-books published in England and Scotland between 1651 and 1702. The term secular song-book, as it is here somewhat arbitrarily used, means any publication containing the words and music of two or more secular songs."—*Introd.*

Contents: A detailed chronological bibliography of 252 numbered items, p.17–159, with indexes by first lines and by composers, authors, singers and actors, tunes and airs, sources, songbooks, printers, publishers, and booksellers.

Lewine, Richard and **Simon, Alfred.** Encyclopedia of theatre music: a comprehensive listing of more than 4000 songs from Broadway and Hollywood, 1900–1960. N.Y., Random, 1961. 247p.　　　　**BH107**

Contents: Theatre songs, 1900–1924; Theatre songs, 1925–1960; Motion picture songs; Show chronology, 1925–1960; Complete vocal scores published. Index.

The lists of songs are arranged alphabetically by title, giving composer, lyricist, show, and year. The show chronology gives dates of Broadway openings and the songs from each show.

Shapiro, Nat. Popular music; an annotated index of American popular songs. N.Y., Adrian Pr., [c1964]–　．v.1–　．　　　　**BH108**

A selective list of popular songs, published 1950–59. Arranged by year, then alphabetically by title; gives author, composer, publisher, and first or best-selling record, indicating performer and record company.

Stechenson, Anthony and **Stechenson, Anne.** The Stechenson classified song directory. Hollywood, Calif., Music Industry Pr., [1961]. 503p.　　　　**BH109**

Arranged under some 400 catchwords and composers; gives titles, publishers, and sometimes dates, of about 100,000 popular songs. Includes list of publishers with addresses. Does not include title index.

Indexes

Cushing, Helen Grant. Children's song index; an index to more than 22,000 songs in 189 collections comprising 222 volumes . . . N.Y., Wilson, 1936. xliip., 798p. **BH110**

In general, similar in plan to Sears's *Song index* (BH112), except that subject entries are added. Main entry, with full information, is under title, with *cross references* from alternate titles, different titles in different collections, translated titles, and original titles in certain languages (e.g., Russian), and from first lines and sometimes first line of chorus; and with *added entries* under composer of music, author of words, and subject.

Leigh, Robert. Index to song books. Stockton, Calif., Author, 1964. 237p.　　　　**BH111**

Subtitle: A title index to over 11,000 copies of almost 6,800 songs in 111 song books published [in the United States] between 1933 and 1962.

A title index to songs in books containing words and music. No entries for authors or composers. Serves as a partial continuation of Sears's *Song index* (BH112).

Sears, Minnie Earl. Song index. An index to more than 12,000 songs in 177 song collections comprising 262 volumes. Ed. by M. E. Sears, assisted by Phyllis Crawford. N.Y., Wilson, 1926. 650p. **BH112**

———— Supplement; an index to more than 7,000 songs in 104 song collections comprising 124 volumes. N.Y., Wilson, 1934. 367p.

An important index, useful in the public, college, or school library, as well as in the music library. Contains titles, first lines, authors' names, and composers' names in one alphabet. Each song is indexed fully under its title, with added entry under composer and author, and cross references from first line and from variant or translated titles. Useful for finding: (1) words and music of a wanted song; (2) lists of songs by a given author or composer; (3) authorship of a poem when only its title or first line is known; and (4) whether or not a song has been translated, or is itself a translation, etc.

As many songs were originally poems which have been set to music, this index serves also as an index to poetry, especially for poems and translations not included in *Granger's Index to poetry* (BD169).

☙ Various reference books listed elsewhere in this book, while not primarily concerned with songs, are frequently useful for supplementing the above indexes. *Notes and queries* (BD61) notes songs under the heading "Songs and ballads" in its indexes, and gives a considerable amount of information about these, sometimes with references to their location in collections not included in Sears's *Song index* (BH112). Larousse, *Grand dictionnaire universel* (AD28), has separate articles on about 600 songs entered under the French title, usually giving some information about the song and its author, the words in French, and the music (air only). The fine catalog of the Allen A. Brown collection of the Boston Public Library (BH5) analyzes many songs included in song collections. Two printed catalogs of the British Museum are very useful. Its *Catalogue of printed music . . .* 1487–1800 (BH28) analyzes many songs printed in periodicals, and its *Catalogue of manuscript music* (BH27) has two important indexes—one of sacred vocal music, and the other of secular vocal music—which give title and first-line indexing for many thousand songs. The Library of Congress *Catalogue of opera librettos* (BH98) has an aria index which serves as a key to songs included in operas.

De Charms + Beede Songs in Collection 1966

Folk music

Bibliography

Akademiia Nauk SSSR. Institut Mirovoi Literatury. Russkaia narodnaia pesnia; bibliograficheskii ukazatel' 1735–1945. [Comp. by] Viktor M. Sidel'nikov. Moskva, Izd. Akademii Nauk SSSR, 1962. 169p. **BH113**

In two parts, chronologically arranged: pt.1, list of folk songs and poetry; pt.2, books and articles about Russian folk songs in Russian.

Bronson, Bertrand Harris. The traditional tunes of the Child ballads, with their texts according to the extant records of Great Britain and America. Princeton, N.J., Princeton Univ. Pr., 1959. v.1–2. music. (In progress) **BH114**

Contents: v.1, Ballads, 1–53; v.2, Ballads, 54–113.

An exhaustive, scholarly work including all known variants of the texts. Each ballad preceded by historical notes.

For Child's *English and Scottish popular ballads, see* BD408.

Dean-Smith, Margaret. A guide to English folk song collections, 1822–1952, with an index to their contents, his-

torical annotations and an introduction. Liverpool, Univ. Pr. of Liverpool, in assoc. with the English Folk Dance and Song Soc., 1954. 120p. **BH115**

Indexes some 60 collections.

International Folk Music Council. International catalogue of recorded folk music; ed. by Norman Fraser, with a preface by R. Vaughan Williams . . . London, Pub. for UNESCO by Oxford Univ. Pr., 1954. 210p. (Archives of recorded music, ser. C: Ethnographical and folk music. v.4) **BH116**

Text in English and French.

In two parts: pt.1, Commercial records, i.e., records that may be purchased; pt.2, Recordings held by institutions. Locates collections of authentic folk music in various countries.

Kunst, Jaap. Ethnomusicology, a study of its nature, its problems, methods and representative personalities. 3d enl. ed. The Hague, Nijhoff, 1959. 303p. il. music. **BH117**

1st ed., 1950, pub. under title *Musicologica*.

Contains bibliography (p.79–215), consisting of books and articles published before Sept. 1958 on music and musical instruments of non-Western people, on ancient and early European music and music instruments, and on Western folk music. Includes some 5000 entries. Has indexes of subjects; peoples and regions studied; authors; collectors; musicians; and periodicals.

Locates copies.

———— Supplement. The Hague, Nijhoff, 1960. 45p.

Adds additional titles to the bibliography, all issued before Sept. 1958.

Lawless, Ray McKinley. Folksingers and folksongs in America; a handbook of biography, bibliography and discography. N.Y., Duell, [1960]. 662p. il. **BH118**

A variety of useful material on the subject, including biographical sketches of singers; an annotated bibliography of collections of folk songs; check lists of titles and discography; and chapters on instruments, societies, and festivals. Indexes of names, titles, and subjects.

Lomax, Alan and Cowell, Sidney Robertson. American folk song and folk lore, a regional bibliography . . . [N.Y., Progressive Educ. Assoc., 1942] 59p. (P.E.A. Service Center pamphlet, no.8) **BH119**

Annotated list of books and articles, arranged by regions and by work, dance, and worship songs. Included is a list of periodicals and of bibliographies.

Nettl, Bruno. Reference materials in ethnomusicology. [Detroit, Mich., Information Service], 1961. 46p. (Detroit studies in music bibliography, no.1) **BH120**

At head of title: A bibliographic essay on primitive, oriental, and folk music.

Surveys and evaluates approximately 130 collections, periodicals, directories, bibliographies, and discographies, including books and articles.

U.S. Library of Congress. Music Division. Folk music; catalog of folk songs, ballads, dances, instrumental pieces, and folk tales of United States and Latin America on phonograph records. Wash., [1964]. 110p. **BH121**

Lists 166 discs containing 1240 titles, representative of the best of more than 16,000 records in the collection of the Archive of American Folk Song. These records are sold only by the Library of Congress.

U.S. Library of Congress. Music Division. Archive of American Folk Song. Check-list of recorded songs in the English language in the Archive of American Folk Song to July, 1940. Alphabetical list with geographical index. Wash., Lib., 1942. 3v. **BH122**

The alphabetical list, comprising v.1–2, gives title, name of singer, collector, and place and date of recording.

v.3 is a geographical index of titles, arranged by state and county.

INSTRUMENTS

Boston. Museum of Fine Arts. Leslie Lindsey Mason Collection. Ancient European musical instruments . . . by Nicholas Bessaraboff. [Cambridge], pub. for the Museum of Fine Arts by Harvard Univ. Pr., 1941. 503p. il. music. **BH123**

An authoritative historical study with excellent illustrations. Includes a useful bibliography of books about musical instruments and catalogs of collections.

Marcuse, Sibyl. Musical instruments, a comprehensive dictionary. Garden City, N.Y., Doubleday, 1964. 608p. il. **BH124**

Describes musical instruments used throughout the world from earliest times to the present. Gives names in English with foreign equivalents. Includes numbered list of sources referred to throughout text. Excellent illustrations, though limited to 24 plates.

Sachs, Curt. History of musical instruments. N.Y., Norton, 1940. 505p. il. **BH125**

Bibliography, p.469–87.

—— Real-Lexikon der Musikinstrumente, zugleich ein Polyglossar für das gesamte Instrumentengebiet; mit 200 Abbildungen. Berlin, Bard, 1913. 442p. il. (Repr.: Hildesheim, G. Olms, 1962; N.Y., Dover, 1964) **BH125a**

A comprehensive historical dictionary of instruments of all countries.

RECORDED MUSIC

Bauer, Robert. The new catalogue of historical records, 1898–1908/09. [2d ed.] London, Sidgwick and Jackson, 1947. 494p. **BH126**

A listing of records of internationally famous opera and concert singers, arranged by name of performer. Includes brief listings of: the Cappella Sistina, talking records, instrumentalists, and complete operas.

Clough, Francis F. and **Cuming, G. J.** The world's encyclopaedia of recorded music. London, Sidgwick and Jackson; N.Y., London Gramophone Corp., 1952. 890p. **BH127**

Based on Darrell's *Gramophone Shop encyclopedia of recorded music* (1936). A comprehensive listing of all electrically recorded music of interest to June 1951, and of pre-electrical recordings of unique value. Information is detailed, and the arrangement convenient. Will be indispensable in any collection interested in recorded music.

—— —— 1st supplement (April 1950—May/June 1951). p.725–90. Bound with main volume.

—— —— 2d supplement (1951–1952). 1953. 262p.

—— —— 3d supplement (1953–1955) [1957]. 564p.

Delaunay, Charles. New hot discography; the standard directory of recorded jazz, ed. by Walter E. Schaap and George Avakian. N.Y., Criterion, 1948. 608p. **BH128**

In two parts: (1) the originators and pioneers of jazz; (2) alphabetical listing of the important artists and recording groups organized after 1930.

Gives detailed information about each record, including: personnel, plan of recording, date of session, instruments involved, "discode" numbers, matrix numbers, company catalog numbers, etc. Alphabetical index to all names.

Guide to long-playing records. N.Y., Knopf, 1955. 3v. **BH129**

v.1, Irving Kolodin. Orchestral music. 268p.; v.2, Philip Lieson Miller. Vocal music. 381p.; v.3, Harold C. Schonberg. Chamber and solo instrument music. 280p.

Annotated lists of serious music available on long-playing records presented by three recognized experts. Listing is by composer, with subdivisions by musical form; supplementary listings in v.2–3 of individual performers in collections, miscellanies, etc. Relative merits of the several performances of a given work are indicated. Includes some early 1955 releases.

Hall, David. The record book; international edition. A guide to the world of the phonograph. N.Y., Durrell, 1948. 1394p. **BH130**

Contents: pt.1, General information, p.3–195; pt.2, Record reviews, p.199–1365. Index to pt.1. Index of composers in pt.2.

Pt.1 includes general historical information, discussion of phonographs, recordings, record catalogs, etc. Pt.2 is arranged alphabetically by composers with critical notes on recordings.

Written before long-playing records were on the market, and therefore dated, but still of historical interest to collectors, especially for its annotations.

Moses, Julian Morton. Collectors' guide to American recordings, 1895–1925; foreword by Giuseppe de Luca. N.Y., Amer. Record Collectors Exchange, [1949]. 199p. **BH131**

Arranged by some 235 performers; lists more than 7000 recordings, giving serial or matrix numbers. Includes brief biographical notes for each artist.

—— Price guide to collectors' records. N.Y., Amer. Record Collectors Exchange, [1952]. 31p. **BH132**

An aid "to those desiring to collect, buy or sell rare phonograph records." Referring to numbers in preceding volume, gives average prices for original copies in good condition.

New York Library Association. Children's and Young Adult Services Section. Recordings for children; a selected list . . . 2d ed. rev. [N.Y.], 1964. (Distr. by N.Y. Pub. Lib., Office of Children's Services) 43p. **BH133**

1st ed. 1961.

A wide selection of available records intended "for the home and recreational collections," including stories, poetry, folk songs, games, music, and documentaries.

Pearson, Mary D. Recordings in the public library. Chicago, Amer. Lib. Assoc., 1963. 153p. **BH134**

An excellent handbook on the organization and use of a record collection with up-to-date bibliographies on selection aids, publishers, equipment, cataloging, etc.

Current

Schwann artist issue catalog. Schwann, Boston, 1963. 275p. **BH135**

Title varies slightly. Published at irregular intervals.

Lists currently available records by performer, orchestras, trios, quartets, etc., and by conductors, soloists, and choral groups. Includes price list.

Schwann long playing record catalog. v.1, no.1– . Boston, W. Schwann, Jan. 1949– . Monthly. **BH136**

Title varies: earlier title, *Schwann record catalog*.

A listing of currently available long-playing records, revised each month. Arranged by composer. Includes price list.

—— Supplement. Spring, 1965. [Feb. 1965] 68p.

"A comprehensive listing of imports and other records not listed in the monthly catalog, including popular music of other countries and the children's record section."—*Pref.*

Stereo record guide. v.1– . N.Y., Taplinger, 1960– . continuous paging. Annual. **BH137**

Prep. by Edward Greenfield, Ivan March, and Denis Stevens.

Annotated selection of stereo records including all forms of music, plays, and the spoken word, and a recommended list as a basis for a stereo collection.

Reviews

Index of record reviews, comp. by Kurtz Myers [and others]. March 1948– . (In Notes. 2d ser. v.5, no.2–) Quarterly.   **BH138**

Indexes reviews in some 25 to 30 American and English periodicals with indication of the reviewer's opinion of the quality of the performance: excellent, adequate, or inadequate.

Myers, Kurtz. Record ratings; the Music Library Association's index of record reviews. Ed. by Richard S. Hill. N.Y., Crown, [1956]. 440p.   **BH139**

Cumulation of "Index of record reviews," originally appearing in quarterly issues of *Notes*. Lists each release with complete information, and gives references to reviews in 28 reviewing media. In two parts: pt.1, composer and subject; pt.2, composite releases. Includes performer index.

Polart index to record reviews. 1960– . Detroit, Polart, [c1961] – . Annual.   **BH140**

Indexes reviews published in 14 periodicals. Since 1962, has included tapes. Arranged by composer, collections, miscellaneous, and several broad subjects.

Records in review. 1955– . v.1– . Great Barrington, Mass., Wyeth, [1955]– . Annual.   **BH141**

Title and publisher vary. *High fidelity record annual.* Philadelphia, Lippincott, 1955–56.

Long, critical, signed reviews of serious musical recordings, comp. from *High fidelity* magazine. Arranged by composer; includes section of "Recitals and miscellany." Index of performers.

C

SOCIAL

SCIENCES

🌿 The term "social sciences" embraces a large number of subjects which deal with the relationship of man to society. In this *Guide*, the term is used to cover the works concerned with education; sociology, including social welfare and social conditions; anthropology; mythology; folklore and popular customs; statistics; economics and business; political science and government; law; and geography.

Only a few reference works deal with the social sciences as a whole, but a recent manual by Carl M. White, *Sources of information in the social sciences* (CA6), is a guide to the literature in most of the above fields. This should be consulted for many sources not listed here. Both the *London bibliography of the social sciences* (CA12), the most extensive bibliography in English in this area, and its French counterpart by Grandin (CA9) will be needed in the large library. The *Encyclopaedia of the social sciences* (CA27), long an authoritative work, is still useful for many purposes although now out of date. A new edition is in preparation.

C A

General Works

GUIDES

Frykholm, Lars. Översikt över samhällsvetenskapliga bibliografiska hjälpmedel. A survey of the bibliographical aids in the social sciences. Stockholm, C. E. Fritzes Kungl. Hovbokhandel, 1960. 160p.   **CA1**

A classed list of some 2000 items, mainly bibliographies,

devoted to various branches of the social sciences. Works international in scope comprise the first half, followed by lists relating to national areas. Author and title index.

Lewis, Peter R. The literature of the social sciences; an introductory survey and guide. London, Lib. Assoc., 1960. 222p. **CA2**

A student's guide to the literature of the field (history as such excluded), listing important texts as well as bibliographic and reference tools, with emphasis on British materials. Governmental and international documents well represented. Annotations are generally brief.

McCormick, Thomas Carson and **Francis, Roy G.** Methods of research in the behavioral sciences. N.Y., Harper, 1958. 244p. il. **CA3**

A manual designed particularly to help the graduate student "from the initial decision to do research, to the selection of the problem, and subsequently, step by step through the publication of findings."—*Pref.*

Covers library usage and methods, such as interviews, sampling, tabulation, etc.

Maunier, René. Manuel bibliographique des sciences sociales et économiques. Paris, Sirey, 1920. 228p. **CA4**

An older guide to bibliographies and reference books of the social sciences and economics, particularly useful for historical purposes as it includes many 18th- and 19th-century publications. Includes works in French, English, German, and Italian.

Mukherjee, Ajit Kumar. Annotated guide to reference materials in the human sciences. N.Y., Asia Pub. House, [1963, c1962]. 267p. **CA5**

Lists almost 1200 titles of works pertaining to anthropology, sociology, and social psychology, with main emphasis on reference works—bibliographies, abstracts, dictionaries, encyclopedias, handbooks, etc.—with additional treatment of source materials and standard treatises. Classified, with author and subject indexes.

White, Carl M. and associates. Sources of information in the social sciences; a guide to the literature. Totowa, N.J., Bedminster Pr., 1964. 498p. **CA6**

A guide to the literature of the social sciences which, although designed primarily for graduate library school students, should be useful to research workers as well. Eight principal chapters treat, respectively: social science in general; history; economics and business; sociology; anthropology; psychology; education; and political science. Each consists of two main sections: (1) a bibliographic essay written by a specialist to explain the history and methodology of the discipline, and to cite, as applicable, a substantial number of pertinent, significant monographs; (2) annotated lists of reference sources, grouped by form, type, or specialized aspect, e.g., guides to the literature, abstracts, bibliographies, encyclopedias, handbooks, etc. Periodicals are listed in each category. Author and title index but no subject index.

Sources of information in the social sciences should be consulted for many specialized sources not included in the present *Guide.*

BIBLIOGRAPHY

Barbano, Filippo and **Viterbi, Mario.** Bibliografia della sociologia italiana (1948–1958). Torino, Ramella, 1959. 168p. (Torino. Università. Istituto di Scienze Politiche. Pubblicazioni. VI) **CA7**

At head of title: Centro Nazionale di Prevenzione e Difesa Sociale [e] Associazione Italiana di Scienze Sociali.

A classified bibliography of more than 1600 books and periodical articles on general sociology and the sociology of law, religion, education, industry, human relations, public relations, and rural and urban sociology. Author index.

Behrendt, Richard F. Modern Latin America in social science literature. Albuquerque, Univ. of New Mexico Pr., 1949. 152p. **CA8**

Subtitle: A selected annotated bibliography of books, pamphlets, and periodical articles in English in the fields of economics, politics, and sociology of Latin America.

———— Supplement I, pts.1–2. Wash., Pan Amer. Union, Social Science Section, Dept. of Cultural Affairs, 1950. (Repr. from Ciencias sociales 5:83–95, Sept. 1950 and 6:107–22, Nov. 1950)

Grandin, A. Bibliographie générale des sciences juridiques, politiques, économiques et sociales de 1800 à 1925/26. Paris, Recueil Sirey, 1926. 3v. **CA9**

v.1–2, classified bibliography; v.3, indexes of authors, titles, and subjects.

———— 1.–19. Suppléments, 1926–50. Paris, Recueil Sirey, 1928–51. v.1–19.

No more published (?).

A very comprehensive bibliography of French monographic works in the fields of law, and of the political, economic, and social sciences. International in scope, with special emphasis on French-speaking countries.

Continued for economic materials by Mossé, *Bibliographie d'économie politique* (CH18).

International Committee for Social Sciences Documentation. Retrospective bibliography of social science works published in the Middle East: U.A.R., Iraq, Jordan, Lebanon, 1945–1955. Cairo, UNESCO Middle East Science Cooperation Off., 1959. 299p. **CA10**

Title and headings in English and French.

Prepared with the cooperation of the United Arab Republic National Commission for UNESCO.

Classified arrangement under each country. Covers sociology, sociocultural anthropology, social psychology, political science, and economics.

Cumulated author index.

Continued by:

United Nations Educational, Scientific and Cultural Organization. Middle East Science Cooperation Office. Middle East social science bibliography; books and articles on the social sciences pub. in Arab countries of the Middle East in 1955–1960. Cairo, 1961. 152p. **CA11**

Cover title: Social science bibliography: Arab countries of the Middle East.

A classified listing of some 1200 items, in Western languages as well as in Arabic (transliterated). Author index.

London bibliography of the social sciences . . . comp. under the direction of B. M. Headicar and C. Fuller, with an introd. by Sidney Webb (Lord Passfield). London, London School of Economics, 1931–32. 4v., and suppl. (v.5–11), 1934–60. (London School of Economics. Studies in economics and political science: Bibliographies, no.8) **CA12**

The most extensive subject bibliography in its field; important to all large libraries and research workers. International in scope, recording books, pamphlets, and documents in many languages. Arranged alphabetically by subject, with brief but adequate information: author, title (often abbreviated), paging, date, location, and information as to whether the work contains a bibliography; has many cross references.

Author indexes are included in v.4 (to v.1–3) and in v.5 and v.6 but not in later volumes.

Coverage varies. v.1–5 include holdings of nine London libraries and special collections; the supplements, 1931–36, 1936–50, 1950–55, list additions—other than works in the Russian language—to the British Library of Political and Economic Science, and the Edward Fry Library of International Law (some variation). v.10–11, 1950–55, include additions in Russian, 1936–50, to the two libraries noted.

Ouvrages cyrilliques concernant les sciences sociales; liste des reproductions disponibles; Cyrillic publications concerning the social sciences; current list of reproductions. Paris, Mouton, 1964. 138p. (Cahiers du monde russe et soviétique. Suppl. I) **CA12a**

Compiled from publishers' catalogs to provide comparative information on hard-copy reprint and microform reproductions of books and periodicals, primarily in Russian. In addition to social sciences, includes literature, linguistics, early texts, and criticism. Classified arrangement, without index. An announced second volume will contain an alphabetical index to both volumes.

Social Science Research Council of Australia. Bibliography of research in the social sciences in Australia, 1957–1960. Canberra, Council, 1961. 67p. **CA13**

In two parts: (1) "Research," including master's and doctor's theses, and (2) "Publications," each divided by subject field. The second part consists of books, reports, journal articles, and other published material. Index of authors and one by university, classified according to subject of the research done.

U.S. Dept. of State. Bureau of Intelligence and Research. External Research Staff. External research list, no.1– . Wash., Dept. of State, 1952– . Semiannual. **CA14**

Title and issuing body vary slightly.

These lists of published and unpublished works, completed or in progress, are "based on the External Research Staff's catalog of social science research on areas outside the United States and its territories and the international relations of those areas. This cooperative catalog project is . . . contributed to by faculty and graduate students throughout the country and maintained for the benefit of people whose research can be facilitated by this service."

Lists are published for each area twice a year; the spring list covers *Studies currently in progress;* the fall list, *Recently completed studies.*

Coverage varies. Recent years comprise: (1) The USSR and Eastern Europe; (2) East Asia; (3) Southeast Asia and Southwest Pacific; (4) South Asia; (5) Western Europe; (6) Middle East; (7) Africa; (8) American Republics; (9) Great Britain and Canada; (10) International affairs.

Periodicals

United Nations Educational, Scientific and Cultural Organization. Liste mondiale des périodiques spécialisés dans les sciences sociales . . . World list of social science periodicals. 2d ed. rev. and enl. . . . Prep. by the International Committee for Social Sciences Documentation. [Paris], UNESCO, [1957]. 209p. (Its Documentation in the social sciences) **CA15**

1st ed. 1953.

In French and English. Arranged by country, in alphabetical order, with indexes by title, by scientific institution, by subject, and by "branch," i.e., general subject area, such as statistics, sociocultural sciences, etc.

Includes periodicals published to the end of 1955.

U.S. Bureau of the Census. Bibliography of social science periodicals and monograph series, by Foreign Manpower Research Office . . . under grant from Office of Science Information Service, National Science Foundation. Wash., 1961– . no.1– . (Its Foreign social science bibliographies, ser. P-92, no.1–) (In progress) **CA16**

Contents: no.1, Rumania, 1947–1960. 1961. 27p.; no.2, Bulgaria, 1944–1960. 1961. 36p.; no.3, Mainland China, 1949–1960. 1961. 32p.; no.4, Republic of China, 1949–1961. 1962. 24p.; no.5, Greece, 1950–1961. 1962. 19p.; no.6, Albania, 1944–1961. 1962. 12p.; no.7, Hong Kong, 1950–1961. 1962. 13p.; no.8, North Korea, 1945–1961. 1962. 12p.; no.9, Republic of Korea, 1945–1961. 1962. 48p.; no.10, Iceland, 1950–1962. 1962. 10p.; no.11, Denmark, 1945–1961. 1963. 111p.; no.12, Finland, 1950–1962. 1963. 85p.; no.13, Hungary, 1947–1962. 1964. 137p.; no.14, Turkey, 1950–1962. 1964. 88p.; no.15, Norway, 1945–1962. 1964. 59p.; no.16,

Poland, 1945–1962. 1964. 312p.; no.17, U.S.S.R., 1950–1963. 1965. 443p.

When complete, will cover 22 countries in the Communist bloc or other areas using "difficult languages." Each number is a classified listing of titles available in the Library of Congress. Annotations (or tables of contents), and indexes by subject, title, and issuing agency, are supplied.

Dissertations

United Nations Educational, Scientific and Cultural Organization. Thèses de sciences sociales; catalogue analytique international de thèses inédites de doctorat, 1940–1950. Theses in the social sciences; an international analytical catalogue of unpublished doctorate theses, 1940–1950. [Paris], UNESCO, [1952]. 236p. **CA17**

Contains listings from 30 member states and from Germany, which was not a member at the time of the survey. Titles have been translated, when necessary, into French or English. Listings are under broad subject, and then alphabetical by the French version of a country's name. An index to authors and an index to the broad subjects used.

INDEXES AND ABSTRACT JOURNALS

Australian public affairs information service; a subject index to current literature. no.1– , July 1945– . Canberra, Commonwealth National Lib., 1945– . Monthly (Annual cumulations). **CA18**

Subject index of selected articles on Australian political, economic, social, and cultural affairs. New books, pamphlets, current periodical articles, and government publications from all English-speaking countries are included.

"In addition, 102 important Australian periodicals have been chosen for regular comprehensive indexing of articles whatever their subject." These are mainly in the social sciences and humanities.

Bibliographie der Sozialwissenschaften; internationale Documentation der Buch- und Zeitschriftenliteratur des Gesamtgebiets der Sozialwissenschaften, 1905– . Göttingen, Vandenhoeck & Ruprecht, 1906– . Annual (previously monthly). **CA19**

Frequency varies. Publisher varies.

Title varies: usually *Bibliographie der Sozialwissenschaften,* with variant subtitles, through 1936; *Bibliographie der Staats- und Wirtschaftswissenschaften,* 1937–43; suspended, 1943–47; *Bibliographie der Sozialwissenschaften,* 42. Jahrg. N.F. Jahrg.1– . 1950– .

N.F. v.1 covers 1948/49.

Now published in parts bound with the *Jahrbuch für Sozialwissenschaft.*

A classified list with annual author and subject indexes, listing both books and periodicals in a large range of the political and social sciences in various languages. A comprehensive and very valuable bibliography in these fields.

Fondation Nationale des Sciences Politiques. Bulletin analytique de documentation politique, économique et sociale contemporaine. 1. année– . Paris, Presses Universitaires de France, 1946– . Monthly. (Frequency varies) **CA20**

Selective indexing from more than 1200 French and foreign periodicals on political, economic, and social questions, frequently with a very brief descriptive note. Gives exact citations with inclusive paging. Arranged by class with annual subject index. No author index.

France. Centre National de la Recherche Scientifique. Bulletin signalétique. Sec. 21. Sociologie. Sciences du langage. Paris, Centre du Documentation du C.N.R.S., 1961– . v.15– . Quarterly. **CA21**

A comprehensive, international abstract journal. For complete set *see* EA71.

Public Affairs Information Service. Bulletin of the Public Affairs Information Service. 1st– , annual cumulations. N.Y., Service, 1915– . v.1– . **CA22**

Usually cited as *PAIS*. Issued in three forms: (1) weekly bulletins; (2) cumulations published five times a year; the fifth cumulated issue forming (3) the permanent annual volume.

A subject index to the current literature in its field: books, documents, pamphlets, reports of public and private agencies, articles in periodicals, multigraphed material, etc. Includes selective indexing to more than 1000 periodicals published in English throughout the world.

A very useful index for political science, government, legislation, economics, sociology, etc. Indispensable in the large library.

Social science abstracts; a comprehensive abstracting and indexing journal of the world's periodical literature in the social sciences. N.Y., Social Science Abstracts, Columbia Univ., 1929–33. 5v. **CA23**

Ceased publication.

v.1–4, Abstracts, 1929–32; v.5, Indexes: Subject, p.1–548. Authors, p.551–677. List of periodicals and serials in the social sciences, p.681–725.

An extensive bibliography with abstracts written by specialists. Covers practically the same fields as the *Encyclopaedia of the social sciences* (CA27).

Sociological abstracts, pub. under the co-sponsorship of the Eastern Sociological Society and the Midwest Sociological Society. N.Y., Sociological Abstracts, 1952– . v.1– . 9 times a year. **CA24**

Frequency varies. With 1964, issued 9 times a year, the Dec. issue being the index number. Some years without cumulated indexes.

A classified abstract journal, covering a broad range of sociological articles in periodicals in various languages.

Southern Asia social science bibliography (with annotations and abstracts). no.8, 1959– . Calcutta, Research Centre on the Social Implications of Industrialization in Southern Asia, 1960– . Annual. **CA25**

Formed by the merger, and continuing the numbering, of: *Social science bibliography: India* (1952–58) and *South Asia social science abstracts* (1954–58), both formerly published by UNESCO, Field Service Cooperation Office for South Asia.

A combination bibliography and abstract journal listing books, pamphlets, and periodical articles published in English in South Asia, and, in the case of Vietnam, those published in French. Countries covered: India, Pakistan, Ceylon, Burma, Indonesia, Malaya and Singapore, the Philippines, Thailand, and Vietnam.

Classed arrangement with author and subject indexes.

ENCYCLOPEDIAS AND DICTIONARIES

Dictionnaire de sociologie, familiale, politique, économique, spirituelle, générale, publié sous la direction de G. Jacquemet avec le concours de nombreux collaborateurs. Paris, Letouzey, 1931–39. v.1–4 (incompl.) **CA26**

No more published.

v.1–3, A–Bouclier; v.4 (fasc.19–22), Boud–Cercles.

A scholarly encyclopedia with long, signed articles, often with bibliographies. Contains biographies, and many short articles on tribes, clans, etc. From the Catholic point of view.

Encyclopaedia of the social sciences; ed. in chief, E. R. A. Seligman; assoc. ed., Alvin Johnson. N.Y., Macmillan, 1930–35. 15v. **CA27**

v.1 includes Introductions: I, Development of social thought and institutions (12 articles), p.3–228; II, The social sciences as disciplines by country (11 articles), p.231–49. Index in v.15.

The first comprehensive encyclopedia of the whole field of the social sciences, projected and prepared under the auspices of 10 learned societies. Aims to cover all important topics in the fields of political science, economics, law, anthropology, sociology, penology, and social work, and the social aspects of ethics, education, philosophy, psychology, biology, geography, medicine, art, etc. International in scope and treatment, but fuller for the English-speaking world and western Europe than for other regions or interests. Articles are by specialists and signed; bibliographies in the main are adequate and in unusually good form. About 50 percent of the articles are biographical; includes many biographies of deceased persons. New edition in preparation.

Hamburg. Welt-Wirtschafts-Archiv. Länderlexikon. 1. Aufl. Hamburg, Verlag Weltarchiv GMBH, 1955–60. 3v. il. **CA28**

Pub. in parts, 1953–60.

Contents: v.1, Western, Central, and Southern Europe; v.2, Northern and Eastern Europe, Africa, the Near East; v.3 [2. Aufl.], the Near East (*cont.*), Asia, Oceanica, North America, Central America and the West Indies, South America, Antarctica.

Treats the social and economic structure of the countries of the world. Arrangement is by country with articles of substantial length, e.g. for Great Britain, 150 pages. Emphasis is on the present. Topics include governmental structure, politics, social organization, geography, economics, finance, agriculture, trade, industry, and education.

Includes tables, statistics, and extensive bibliographies.

Handwörterbuch der Soziologie, in Verbindung mit G. Briefs, F. Eulenburg [u. Anderen], hrsg. von Alfred Vierkandt. Stuttgart, Enke, 1931. 690p. **CA29**

Contains long, signed articles on rather large subjects in the social and political fields, with brief bibliographies, including mainly German titles. Two indexes: (1) names, and (2) smaller subjects.

Karrenberg, Friedrich. Evangelisches Soziallexikon, im Auftrag des Deutschen Evangelischen Kirchentages. Stuttgart, Kreuz-Verlag, 1954. 1176col. **CA30**

Prepared by 160 German-Protestant social scientists who attempt to trace historical developments, presenting Catholic and secular viewpoints as well as Protestant.

Covers such topics as sociology and social work, and the social aspects of biology, economics, law, medicine, etc. Includes bibliographies.

Smith, Robert E. F. A Russian-English dictionary of social science terms. London, Butterworth, 1962. 493p. **CA31**

Aims to provide an aid to the translation of Russian social science texts, in the fields of sociology, politics, economics, accounting, public administration, welfare, and education.

Suavet, Thomas. Dictionnaire économique et social. Paris, Économie et Humanisme, Les Éd. Ouvrières, 1962. 453p. (Initiation économique 3) **CA32**

For full information *see* CH38.

Willems, Emilio. Dictionnaire de sociologie; adaptation française par Armand Cuvillier. Paris, Marcel Rivière, 1961. 272p. **CA33**

Originally published in 1950 in Portuguese as *Dicionário de sociologia*. The French translation has been revised and brought up to date. A combination, in one alphabet, of definitions of sociological terms and concepts with biographical sketches of world social scientists. About half of the entries are biographical.

Zadrozny, John Thomas. Dictionary of social science. Wash., Public Affairs Pr., 1959. 367p.   **CA34**

Brief definitions of several thousand terms, primarily in sociology, political science, and economics, with lesser listings in related fields.

DIRECTORIES

Foundation directory, prep. by the Foundation Library Center. Ed. 2. N.Y., Russell Sage Foundation, 1964. 1000p.   **CA35**

1st ed. 1960.

Eds.: Ann D. Walton and Marianna O. Lewis.

Replaces *American foundations and their fields* (eds.1–7, 1930–55, published by the Twentieth Century Fund and Raymond Rich Associates).

An invaluable compilation of detailed information on more than 6000 foundations, listed geographically, with indexes of field of interest, personnel, and corporate title. Extensive prefatory material on foundation organization and operation.

Supplemented by *Foundation news.* N.Y., Foundation Lib. Center, 1960– . Bimonthly.

United Nations Educational, Scientific and Cultural Organization. Coordinating Committee on Documentation in the Social Sciences. International repertory of social science documentation centres. Paris, UNESCO, 1952. 42p.   **CA36**

Centers are listed under countries, alphabetically arranged; information includes officers, subjects covered, services, publications, organization. No indexes. A second volume, to cover countries omitted here, was projected.

United Nations Educational, Scientific and Cultural Organization. Social Science Clearing House. Foundations with social science activities; an international catalogue. Paris, 1957. 89p. (Its Reports and papers in the social sciences, no.7)   **CA37**

Gives fairly detailed information, as of 1956, on structure and activities, financial data, donors and staff, etc. for foundations interested in the social sciences in various countries of the world.

—— International organizations in the social sciences; a summary description of the structure and activities of nongovernmental organizations in consultative relationship with Unesco and specialized in the social sciences. Rev. and augm. ed. with an introd. by Jean Meynaud. Paris, UNESCO, 1961. 145p.   **CA38**

1st ed. 1956.

Gives detailed information on 18 nongovernmental organizations "approved for consultative relationship with Unesco."

—— Research councils in the social sciences. Paris, 1955. 54p. (Its Reports and papers in the social sciences, no.3)   **CA39**

Gives information about the social science research councils, arranged by country.

BIOGRAPHY

American men of science: a biographical directory. 10th ed. [v.5], The social and behavioral sciences. Tempe, Ariz., Jaques Cattell Pr., 1962. 1220p.   **CA40**

Contains more than 22,000 biographical sketches of persons outstanding in the fields of economics, sociology, political science, statistics, psychology, geography, and anthropology. (Historians are included in the *Directory of American scholars, AJ52.*)

For information on complete set *see* EA183.

Bernsdorf, Wilhelm. Internationales soziologen Lexikon, unter Mitarbeit zahlreicher Fachleute des In- und Aus-

landes . . . in Verbindung mit Horst Knospe. Red. für USA: Joseph Maier. Stuttgart, Ferdinand Enke, 1959. 662p.   **CA41**

This biographical dictionary, a companion volume to the author's *Wörterbuch der Soziologie* (CC4), includes sketches of more than 1000 persons, unrestricted by period or nationality. *Soziologen* is broadly interpreted to include social scientists in a variety of fields. Articles are signed and include bibliographies.

United Nations Educational, Scientific and Cultural Organization. Social scientists specializing in African studies; Africanistes spécialistes de sciences sociales. Paris, La Haye, Mouton, 1963. 375p. (École Pratique des Hautes Études, 6. sec., Sciences économiques et sociales: 4. sér. v.5. Bibliographies et instruments de travail. Monde d'outre-mer passé et présent)   **CA42**

A biographical dictionary of 2072 social scientists from the whole African continent, and from countries all over the world, who specialize in African studies. The term "social science" is interpreted in its broadest aspects. A geographical index and one by subject specialty.

Who's who in Soviet social sciences, humanities, art and government, comp. by Ina Telberg. N.Y., Telberg Book Co., 1961. 147p.   **CA43**

"Based on the information in the 3d ed. of 'Malaia sovetskaia entsiklopediia,' Moscow, 1958–1961."—*Pref.* (AD61). Provides brief biographical sketches in English of some 700 living persons. Alphabetical by transliterated form of the name, with a Russian index and an index by professions.

C B

Education

☙ For the education materials library a useful guide is *How to locate educational information and data,* by Alexander and Burke (CB1). The general library, even a small library, will need at least one educational directory, e.g., the U.S. Office of Education's *Education directory* (CB73), an inexpensive work with broad coverage. To this should be added *American universities and colleges* (CB75) and its companion volume, *American junior colleges* (CB74), and whatever other directories seem pertinent. In the larger library the *World of learning* (CB69), which gives information about educational institutions and societies in other countries, will be needed.

Bibliographies, indexes—particularly the *Education index* (CB27)—and dictionaries such as Good's *Dictionary of education* (CB31) should be added as required.

For materials in the audio-visual field *see* AA317–AA327.

GENERAL WORKS

☙ Much useful material may be found in the publications of the U.S. Office of Education, in such fields as: administration, curricula, directories, financial aid, guidance, salaries, vocational education, etc. For titles consult its *List of publications* (CB13); for indexes, lists, and types of materials, *see* Chapter 15 of Alexander and Burke, *How to locate educational information and data* (CB1).

Guides

Alexander, Carter and **Burke, Arvid J.** How to locate educational information and data; an aid to quick utilization of the literature of education. 4th ed. rev. N.Y., Bureau of Publs., Teachers College, Columbia Univ., 1958. 419p. il. **CB1**

1st ed. 1935.

This edition has been extensively revised. Like the earlier editions, it is arranged to be used as a textbook for individual or class study. In two main sections: pt.1, Basic techniques of library utilization; pt.2, Special applications of library utilization techniques. The first covers such subjects as procedures for library searching; the card catalog; locating books and periodicals; using the *Education index* (CB27); making a bibliography; note-taking, etc. The second takes up reference books, evaluation of books, government documents, biographical information, quotations, statistics and statistical methodology, etc.

Bibliography

Blessing, James Hartman. Graduate education; an annotated bibliography. Wash., U.S. Dept. of Health, Education, and Welfare, Office of Education, 1961. 151p. (Its Bull. 1961, no.26) **CB2**

Lists almost 900 books, pamphlets, and periodical articles in classified arrangement, with index of names, institutions, and principal topics.

Eells, Walter Crosby and **Hollis, Ernest V.** The college presidency, 1900–1960; an annotated bibliography. Wash., Dept. of Health, Education, and Welfare, Office of Education, 1961. 143p. (Its Bull. 1961, no.9) **CB3**

Contains 700 numbered references to books, periodicals, theses, reports, etc., with annotations. Arranged in six broad topics. Includes index of names and subjects.

Eells, Walter Crosby. College teachers and college teaching; an annotated bibliography on college and university faculty members and instructional methods. Atlanta, Ga., Southern Regional Educ. Board, 1957. 282p. **CB4**

Contains nearly 2700 entries of books, monographs, and periodical articles, published in 1945 and later, with a few exceptions. Arranged by subject with author index.

—— —— Supplement. 1959. 134p.

France. Ministère de l'Éducation Nationale. Répertoire des ouvrages pédagogiques du siècle. (Bibliothèques de Paris et des départements) Nieuwkoop, B. de Graaf, 1962. 733p. **CB5**

"Unchanged photomechanical reprint of the edition Paris, 1886."

Preface signed: L'inspecteur général, directeur de l'enseignement primaire, F. Buisson.

Arranged by author with broad subject index. Brief note of author's life and work often included.

Harris, Robin S. and **Tremblay, Arthur.** A bibliography of higher education in Canada. Bibliographie de l'enseignement supérieur au Canada. Toronto, Univ. of Toronto Pr., Presses Universitaires Laval, 1960. 158p. (Studies in higher education in Canada, no.1) **CB6**

Title page and introduction in English and French.

Pt.1 provides references on the Canadian cultural and educational background; pt.2 has sections on history and organization of the institutions; curriculum and teaching (with sub-

divisions for specific fields of study); the professor; and the student.

Mezirow, Jack D. and **Berry, Dorothea.** The literature of liberal adult education, 1945–1957. N.Y., Scarecrow, 1960. 308p. **CB7**

Compiled for the Center for the Study of Liberal Education for Adults.

1027 entries, most of them annotated, including "journal articles, government publications, pamphlets, books [and dissertations] published in certain major sections of the field since World War II in the United States, Great Britain and Canada."—*Introd.*

Monroe, Walter Scott and **Shores, Louis.** Bibliographies and summaries in education to July 1935; a catalog of more than 4000 annotated bibliographies and summaries listed under author and subject in one alphabet. N.Y., Wilson, 1936. 470p. **CB8**

Schweizerische Philosophische Gesellschaft. Bibliographie der philosophischen, psychologischen und pädagogischen Literatur . . . 1900–1940, 1941–44. Basel, 1944–45. **CB9**

For full record *see* BA24.

United Nations Educational, Scientific and Cultural Organization. International guide to educational documentation, 1955–1960. Paris, 1963. 700p. **CB10**

Covers books, pamphlets, periodicals, occasional papers, film and sound recordings, etc., published from 1955 to 1960. Pt.1 is a list of international sources and international organizations issuing educational material. Pt.2 (the main section) is an alphabetical arrangement under the 95 countries and territories included. Gives complete bibliographical information with annotations of varying length.

Most countries which publish a considerable volume of documentation are included, notable exceptions being Canada, China, Indonesia, and Italy.

Author, title, and name index.

Subsequent edition to cover the period 1960–65 planned for publication in 1966 or 1967.

U.S. Office of Education. CRP: Cooperative research projects; a seven year summary, July 1, 1956—June 30, 1963. Wash., Govt. Prt. Off., [1964]. 75p. (Its Circular no.736) **CB11**

"Compilation of projects . . . approved for federal funding under the auspices of the Cooperative Research Program."—*Foreword.*

Arranged by number; gives name and location of investigator and title of project. Includes name and subject index and index of institutions conducting research.

Locates copies of final reports.

—— Index to the Reports of the Commissioner of Education: 1867–1907. Wash., Govt. Prt. Off., 1909. 103p. (Bull. 1909, no.7) **CB12**

—— List of publications, 1867–1910. Wash., Govt. Prt. Off., 1910. 55p. (Bull. 1910, no.3) Repr. 1940. **CB13**

—— List of publications, 1910–1936; including those of the former Federal Board for Vocational Education for 1917–1933, with author and subject indexes. Wash., Govt. Prt. Off., 1937. 158p. (Bull. 1937, no.22) **CB13a**

—— Publications, Office of Education, 1937–1959. Wash., Govt. Prt. Off., 1960. 157p. (Bull. 1960, no.3) **CB13b**

—— Publications of the Office of Education. 1959– . Wash., Govt. Prt. Off., 1959– . Annual. (Its Bull. 1959–) **CB13c**

An annotated list of currently available publications, arranged by subject. Includes title index. Not to be confused with publications of same title listing all works ever published by the Office of Education for a certain period.

Current

Center for Programed Instruction, New York. Programs; a guide to programed instructional materials available to educators. Wash., Govt. Prt. Off., 1962– . il. Annual. (U.S. Office of Education. Bull.) **CB14**

Title of each volume includes the year of issue.

List comprises programed instructional materials with descriptions, sample frames, and available sources. No attempt is made at evaluation. Arranged by subject. Includes author and publisher index.

International Bureau of Education, Geneva. Annual educational bibliography. Geneva, 1955– . Annual. **CB15**

An annotated bibliography, arranged by class, of the books received in the International Education Library during the year. Includes publications from many countries on all aspects of education.

Outstanding education books. (In NEA journal. 1924– . Wash., 1925–) **CB16**

Appears annually, usually in the May issue.

An annotated list, selected from a comprehensive list, *Educational books . . .* , Enoch Pratt Library, Baltimore, published annually since 1928; since 1954, in *Educational horizons.*

Dissertations

Blackwell, A. M. A list of researches in education and educational psychology, presented for higher degrees in the universities of the United Kingdom, Northern Ireland, and the Irish Republic . . . classified according to a modification of the Dewey Decimal System. . . . London, pub. for the Foundation by Newnes Educ. Pub. Co., 1950–52. (National Foundation for Educational Research in England and Wales. Publ. no.1, 5, 7, 9, 11) **CB17**

v.1, 1918–48; v.2, 1949–51.
Suppl. no.1–3, 1952/53–56/57.

Eells, Walter Crosby. American dissertations on foreign education . . . 1884–1958. Wash., Committee on Internat. Relations, Nat. Educ. Assoc. of the U.S., 1959. 300p. **CB18**

Subtitle: Doctor's dissertations and master's theses written at American universities and colleges concerning education or educators in foreign countries and education of groups of foreign birth or ancestry in the United States.

Lists nearly 5700 titles, arranged by country, with author and subject indexes.

Gray, Ruth A. Doctors' theses in education; a list of 797 theses deposited with the Office of Education and available for loan. Wash., Govt. Prt. Off., 1935. 69p. (U.S. Office of Education. Pamphlet no.60) **CB19**

"Includes all doctors' theses in Education deposited in the Office of Education prior to September 15, 1934. Arranged alphabetically by author, subject and institution."— *Foreword.*

Iowa. State Teachers College, Cedar Falls. Bureau of Research. Master's theses in education, 1951/52– . Cedar Falls, 1953– . Annual. **CB20**

A general list of master's essays in education from many institutions.

Little, Lawrence C. A bibliography of doctoral dissertations on adults and adult education. Rev. ed. Pittsburgh, Univ. of Pittsburgh Pr., 1963. 163p. **CB21**

A list of some 2500 doctoral dissertations, arranged alphabetically by author. No subject approach.

Research studies in education; a subject and author index of doctoral dissertations, reports and field studies; and a research methods bibliography, comp. by Mary Louise Lyda [and others]. 1953– . Bloomington, Ind., Phi Delta Kappa, 1955– . Annual. **CB22**

Preceded by *Research studies in education; a subject index of doctoral dissertations, reports and field studies,* 1941–51. Phi Delta Kappa, 1953.

Includes doctoral dissertations underway.

U.S. Office of Education. Library. Bibliography of research studies in education, 1926/27–1939/40. Prep. in the Library Division, Office of Education. Wash., Govt. Prt. Off., 1929–42. v.1–14. Annual. (U.S. Bureau of Education. Bull.) **CB23**

Ceased publication.

Lists doctoral dissertations, master's essays, and other research studies. A classed list with institution, author, and subject indexes.

Periodicals

Educational Press Association of America. America's educational press: a classified list of educational publications issued in the U.S. together with an international list of educational periodicals. Glassboro, N.J., Assoc. and UNESCO, 1926– . Biennial. **CB24**

Pub. annually 1925–48.

1963 is the 2d edition of *An international list of educational periodicals* and the 28th *Yearbook* of the Educational Press Association.

Contents: pt.1, International list in English, French, Spanish, p.21–150; pt.2, Educational periodicals issued in the United States, p.151–235.

Title index.

Indexes and abstract journals

British education index. v.1– . 1954/58– . London, Lib. Assoc., [1961]– . 3 times a year. Cumulates biennially. **CB25**

Comp.: 1954/58– . The Librarians of Institutes of Education.

v.1, Aug. 1954–Nov. 1958. 1961. 122p.; v.2, Dec. 1958–Dec. 1961. [1963]. 115p.

Indexes some 50 British periodicals by subject. Includes an author index.

Education abstracts. v.1–16. Paris, UNESCO, Educ. Clearing House, 1949–65. Quarterly (Irregular). **CB26**

Ceased publication.

Title varies: v.1–3, 1949–51, *Fundamental education abstracts;* v.4, 1952–v.16, 1964/65, *Education abstracts.*

Frequency varies: v.1–12, 1949–60, monthly; v.13, 1961–65, quarterly.

Not an abstract journal in the usual sense. Beginning with v.6, each issue is devoted to a particular topic, including bibliographies on special subjects, education in various countries, etc.

Education index, Jan. 1929– ; a cumulative subject index to a selected list of educational periodicals, proceedings, and yearbooks. N.Y., Wilson, 1932– . Monthly (except July and Aug.), cumulating throughout the year with annual and biennial cumulations. **CB27**

v.1–8, 1929–May 1953, issued with triennial cumulations.

Subtitle varies: through v.12, July 1959–June 1961, *A cumulated author and subject index to a selected list of educational periodicals, books and pamphlets.*

Indexes more than 200 periodicals covering all phases of education, varying somewhat from volume to volume and, until June 1961, including many references to books, pamphlets, and analytics in books and society transactions. Also until June 1961, articles were indexed under both author and subject. Now under subject only, and nonperiodical material is no longer included.

State education journal index. v.1, no.1, Sept./Dec., 1963– . Ed. by L. Stanley Ratliff. Fort Collins, Colo., 1964– . Semiannual. **CB28**

Subtitle: An index to materials in the field of education.

Indexes some 50 state and association publications, only 10 of which are indexed in the *Education index*. Plans to increase coverage.

Arrangement is by subject.

Dictionaries and encyclopedias

Educational encyclopedia; thesaurus of Jewish and general education. Martin M. Buber, ed. in chief. Jerusalem, Ministry of Education and Culture and the Bialik Inst., 1959–61. v.1–2. il. (In progress) **CB29**

Added title page in Hebrew; text in Hebrew.

Planned to be in 5v. v.1, Principles of education; v.2, Ways of education.

Announced: v.3, Organization of education; v.4, History of education—Comparative education; v.5, Educational psychology, sociology and biology.

Each volume arranged in alphabetical order. Bibliographies refer to works in several languages.

Encyclopedia of modern education; ed., Harry N. Rivlin . . . assoc. ed., Herbert Schueler. . . . N.Y., Philosophical Lib., 1943. 902p. **CB30**

Includes signed articles on educational trends, policies, and activities.

Useful as a first aid, although information given frequently needs to be checked. The brief bibliographies are almost entirely to publications in the English language, often to secondary rather than to primary sources.

Contains biographies of eminent teachers, psychologists, and philosophers engaged in education.

Good, Carter V. Dictionary of education, prep. under the auspices of Phi Delta Kappa. Ed. with the assistance of Winifred R. Merkel. 2d ed. N.Y., McGraw-Hill, 1959. 676p. **CB31**

1st ed. 1945.

A scholarly dictionary of terms and words that have special meaning in the educational field. More than 100 specialists and some 100 reviewing committees selected, wrote, and evaluated the definitions. "The terms defined and cross-references total approximately 25,000, but the individual definitions are less by several thousand."—*Pref.*

Pronunciation is given for difficult words. Educational terms used in foreign countries are grouped at the end of the book: Canada, p.613–22; England, p.623–32; France, p.633–49; Germany, p.650–58; Italy, p.659–76.

International Federation of University Women. Lexique international des termes universitaires. [Paris], Fédération Internat. des Femmes Diplômées des Universités, 1939. 755p. **CB32**

Title on cover: *International glossary of academic terms.*

Explains in French and English, but does not translate, the official titles and technical terms used by the various universities of the world. Arranged by country with an alphabetical index to terms. South America and the Far East are not included. Also omits, because lists were not received, Greece, Portugal, and Spain.

Lexikon der Pädagogik. Bern, A. Francke, 1950–52. 3v. **CB33**

v.1–2, A–Z; v.3, Überblick über die Geschichte der Pädagogik. Biographien in alphabetischer Reihenfolge. Erziehungswesen einzelner Staaten. Nach Autoren geordnetes Artikel-Register.

An extensive encyclopedia with signed articles and bibliographies. v.3 includes a biographical section, p.19–496, giving sketches of 1277 personalities of all periods and countries.

Monroe, Paul. Cyclopedia of education, ed. . . . with the assistance of departmental editors and more than 1000 individual contributors. N.Y., Macmillan, 1911–13. 5v. il. **CB34**

Excellent when issued, though now out of date, it is still useful, particularly for historical and biographical articles. Has signed articles by specialists, good bibliographies, and excellent illustrations, some in color. The scope of the work is general, including education in all countries and all periods, but American subjects receive somewhat fuller treatment than foreign topics. Analytical index in v.5 groups articles by larger subjects than those used in the main alphabet.

Psykologisk pedagogisk uppslagsbok. Stockholm, Natur och Kultur, 1943–46. 3v. and Supp. 1–och Registerband. il. **CB35**

Long, signed articles with bibliographies. Contains biography including living persons. The supplement volume includes a *Svensk-engelsk-fransk-tysk ordlista.*

Watson, Foster. Encyclopaedia and dictionary of education . . . principles and practice . . . types of teaching institutions and educational systems throughout the world. London, Pitman, 1921–22. 4v. il. **CB36**

General in scope, but most useful for British subjects, as they are treated with much greater fullness. Rather popular in treatment; longer articles are signed; brief bibliographies often given without dates of publication. Includes considerable biography and many illustrations.

Now out of date, but no other British encyclopedia is available.

Handbooks

Encyclopedia of educational research; a project of the American Educational Research Association, ed. by Chester W. Harris, with the assistance of Marie R. Liba. 3d ed. N.Y., Macmillan, 1960. 1564p. **CB37**

1st ed. (1940) and rev. ed. (1950), edited by Walter S. Monroe.

The 3d edition is completely rewritten. Not an encyclopedia in the usual sense, it aims to evaluate and put into new perspective the findings of educational research. Arranged alphabetically by subject; articles are written by specialists, signed, and dated. Its long, selective bibliographies are particularly useful. A 14p. subject index on yellow paper has been inserted in the middle of the volume.

May be supplemented by the surveys of research with bibliographies in the *Review of educational research.* Wash., Educ. Research Assoc., 1931– .

Flack, Michael J. Sources of information on international educational activities; an explanatory survey . . . Wash., Amer. Council on Education, [1958]. 114p. **CB38**

Prepared for the Commission on Education and International Affairs of the American Council on Education.

Preliminary chapters include general information for United States students and faculty abroad, and for foreign students and faculty in the United States. These are followed by a directory of private organizations and governmental agencies with indication of their programs, policies, requirements, and procedures in the field of international education.

Gage, Nathaniel Lees. Handbook of research on teaching; a project of the American Educational Research Association. Chicago, Rand McNally, [1963]. 1218p. il. **CB39**

A long, scholarly work designed especially for the advanced student preparing to do research on teaching. Summarizes and critically analyzes research in the field. Written by 31 specialists; contains lengthy articles on method, variables, areas, grade levels, and subject fields. Arranged in 23 chapters with extensive bibliographies. Includes a name and subject index.

Handbook of adult education in the United States. Malcolm S. Knowles, ed. 4th ed. Chicago, Adult Educ. Assoc. of the U.S.A., 1960. 624p. **CB40**

1st ed. 1934.

Editor and sponsor vary.

Survey articles by specialists on various aspects and areas of adult education, p.1–561. Directory information of organizational agencies (p.565–603) is particularly helpful, giving detailed information about each organization.

Each article has list of suggested readings.

Sasnett, Martena Tenney. Educational systems of the world; interpretations for use in evaluation of foreign credentials. [Los Angeles], Univ. of Southern Calif. Pr., 1952. 838p. **CB41**

Bibliography, p.754–838.

Gives detailed information on the educational system of each country, with indications of equivalent evaluation in the United States.

School executive's guide. Prep. by the Prentice-Hall editorial staff and a board of 46 contributors. Englewood Cliffs, N.J., Prentice-Hall, [c1964]. 1171p. il. **CB42**

A comprehensive work describing up-to-date practices and procedures of administration in public schools; e.g., personnel, finance, community needs. Includes such current topics as the language laboratory, uses of computers for instruction, and effective guidance programs.

Articles are written by specialists and include references.

U.S. Office of Education. Accreditation in higher education, organized and ed. by Lloyd E. Blauch. Wash., Govt. Prt. Off., 1959. 247p. **CB43**

A discussion of the nature and standards of accreditation, and of state and regional agencies of accreditation, with chapters on accreditation of education for the professions.

Includes bibliographies.

United Nations. Secretary-General. Progress of the non-self-governing territories under the charter. v.4, Educational conditions. N.Y., United Nations, 1960–62. 126p. (UN publ. ST/TRI/SER.A/15/v.4) **CB44**

In two chapters: (1) Education: policy; financing; primary, secondary and higher education; technical and vocational training; compulsory schooling; the status of teachers; fundamental and adult education; illiteracy; the use of audio-visual educational media; (2) Cultural and scientific institutions: scientific research, libraries, museums.

United Nations Educational, Scientific and Cultural Organization. Educational publishers. Paris, 1962. 141p. (Its International directories of education, 2) **CB45**

In English, French, and Spanish.

In two sections: pt.1 lists international and national publishers' associations; pt.2 deals with educational publishers and producers of teaching materials.

Contains information on almost 2000 firms from 82 countries, including name, address, subjects with educational level of materials, and total output.

World survey of education. v.1– . Paris, UNESCO, 1955– . Triennial. **CB46**

Supersedes *World handbook of educational organization and statistics.* 1951.

Contents: v.1, Handbook of educational organization and statistics. 1955. 943p.; v.2, Primary education. 1958. 1387p.; v.3, Secondary education. 1961. 1482p.; v.4 is to be on higher education.

Covers some 200 countries, including states not members of UNESCO.

Arranged by country; contains surveys, statistics, bibliographies, etc. Glossary of terms in various languages and an index.

Annuals

Indian yearbook of education. 2d ed. Prep. by the National Institute of Education of the National Council of Educational Research and Training. New Delhi, 1964. 749p. **CB47**

The 1st edition was a review of educational development in India in the postindependence period (1947–61); the 2d is devoted to an examination of problems of elementary education in India.

Contains statistical tables, p.621–730. Name and subject index.

International yearbook of education. 10th– . 1948– . Paris, UNESCO, 1948– . Annual. **CB48**

Assumes the volume numbering of *Annuaire international de l'éducation et de l'enseignement,* 1933–1947 (suspended publication, 1940–45).

The 1962 issue surveys current educational conditions in 87 countries, preceded by a general survey of the principal events in the current school year.

Issued jointly by UNESCO and the International Bureau of Education.

Manual on certification requirements for school personnel in the United States. 1st ed., 1951– . Wash., Nat. Educ. Assoc., 1955– . Biennial. **CB49**

First two editions (1951 and 1953) compiled and published jointly by the Office of Education and the National Commission on Teacher Education and Professional Standards.

Volumes for 1951– prepared by W. E. Armstrong and T. M. Stinnett.

Includes requirements in the 50 states, the District of Columbia, and Puerto Rico; military overseas dependent schools; territorial schools; exchange and study abroad.

Bibliographies.

Woellner, Elizabeth H. and **Wood, M. Aurilla.** Requirements for certification of teachers, counselors, librarians, and administrators for elementary schools, secondary schools, junior colleges. v.1, 1935– . Chicago, Univ. of Chicago Pr., 1935– . Annual. **CB50**

Title varies.

Covers initial certification requirements for the several states; recommendations of regional and national accrediting associations; and information regarding teacher applications in the United States possessions and territories.

Year book of education. 1953– . N.Y., Harcourt, 1953– . Annual. **CB51**

Issued under the auspices of the University of London, Institute of Education; and Teachers College, Columbia University, 1953– .

Continues the *Yearbook of education,* 1932–53. London, Evans Bros., Ltd., 1931–52. Publication suspended 1941–47.

Long articles dealing with selected problems of higher education throughout the world, written by authorities from various countries. Volumes from 1953– have distinctive titles: e.g., Status and position of teachers; Education and technological development; Guidance and counseling.

Associations

Bowyer, Carlton Herbert. The directory of education associations. Emporia, Kan., Teachers College Pr., [c1962]. 157p. **CB52**

Arranged by subject; covers more than 400 American educational associations. In addition to the usual directorial information, includes history and purposes. Name index.

U.S. Office of Education. Education directory. Pt.4, Educational associations. Wash., Govt. Prt. Off., 1912– . Annual. **CB53**

A comprehensive listing of associations.

Contents: (1) National and regional education associations, arranged alphabetically; (2) College professional fraternities, honor societies, and recognition societies (national); (3) State education associations; (4) Foundations; (5) Religious education associations; (6) International education associations; (7) Subject index.

For Education directory *see* CB73.

Young, Raymond J. A directory of educational research agencies and studies. 2d rev. ed. Bloomington, Ind., Phi Delta Kappa, 1962. 75p. **CB54**

1st ed. 1957.

A list of institutions, associations, councils, and school systems conducting educational research, with a bibliography of research studies from each agency.

Directories

Bibliography

Guide to American educational directories. 1st ed. N.Y., B. Klein, 1963– . 322p. **CB55**

Prep. by B. Klein.

Some 1300 directories listed under subject, then alphabetically by title with annotations. A useful new work, although the selection of material is uneven and the information not always complete.

International

Directory of Christian colleges in Asia, Africa, the Middle East, the Pacific, Latin America and the Caribbean. Comp. by Clara E. Orr. N.Y., Missionary Research Lib., 1961. 38p. (MRL directory and survey ser., no.13) **CB56**

Lists by continent and then by country the Christian colleges, giving brief description of each. Roman Catholic colleges are not included.

Garraty, John Arthur and **Adams, Walter.** A guide to study abroad: university, summer school, tour, and work-and-study programs, 1962/63 ed. Manhasset, N.Y., Channel, 1962. 288p. **CB57**

A useful source of information about programs, requirements, living conditions, and costs for the student who wishes to study abroad. Includes foreign programs of certain American institutions. Describes in detail 146 typical programs in 26 countries of Europe, Latin America, and the Near and Far East.

Handbook on international study. 1955– . N.Y., Inst. of Internat. Education, 1955– . Triennial. **CB58**

Since 1961, published in two separate volumes: (1) for U.S. nationals; (2) for foreign nationals.

A guide to study, training, and exchange opportunities. Describes educational systems in various countries; scholarship and fellowship programs; and government regulations.

Index generalis, 1st–21st year, 1919–1939; 1952/53–1954/55; general yearbook of universities and of higher educational institutions, academies, archives, libraries, scientific institutes, botanical and zoological gardens, museums, observatories, learned societies . . . Paris, Dunod, 1920–39; 1953–55. Annual. **CB59**

Title varies; 1920–39 in French. Publisher varies. Publication suspended after 1939. Resumed 1953. Ceased 1955.

In six main parts: (1) Universities and schools of science and technology grouped by countries; (2) Observatories; (3) Libraries and archives; (4) Scientific institutes arranged by place; (5) Learned societies and academies arranged by subject; (6) Indexes (geographical and personal).

Gives for each institution: name and address; brief general and statistical information; list of principal professors, directors, etc.

Indispensable for the period between the World Wars; especially useful for its name indexes.

International Association of Universities. Organisations inter-universitaires; inter-university organisations. Paris, Bureau Internat. des Universités, 1954– . Biennial. **CB60**

In French and English.

In two sections: (1) a directory of universities and other institutions of higher education, giving name, address, date of founding, and member colleges; (2) a list of international and national bodies concerned with cooperation in higher education. Name, address, and usually descriptive information are given.

International Labor Office. Trainees abroad. Stages à l'étranger. Trabajadores en el extranjero. Geneva, 1961. 186p. **CB61**

Earlier editions published by UNESCO: the 1st, in 1949, as a chapter of *Study abroad;* in 1957, as v.3 of *Workers abroad.*

Arranged by country; describes the facilities offered to foreign trainees, giving information on national laws and regulations and on public and private programs for receiving trainees. This includes information on occupational fields, qualifications required, financial conditions, procedures to follow, etc.

Minerva. Jahrbuch der gelehrten Welt, 1.–34. Jahrg., 1891/92–1913/14, 1920–38, 1952–56. Strassburg, Trübner, 1891–1914; Berlin, de Gruyter, 1920–38; 1952–56. v.1–34. Annual; 1952–56. Irregular. **CB62**

Suspended 1915–19, 1939–51.

Before World War II this work was a convenient and reliable international directory, arranged by names of towns, giving under each town the names of universities, colleges, technical schools, libraries, museums, archives, and learned societies with information as to their income, size, name of principal officials, publications, etc. Index of personal names. Contents of volumes vary, but the wealth of detail given in the prewar volumes is still useful for historical purposes.

Bd.1, Europa. 1952; Bd.2, Aussereuropa. 1956. 2v.

These include the same type of information about universities and technical colleges, but omit societies, museums, etc.

The scientific and academic world. Essen-Bredeney, Stifterverband für die deutsche Wissenschaft, 1962. 243p. **CB63**

". . . originally published in German under the title *Weltverbundenheit der Wissenschaft* [1959]. The English version has been thoroughly revised and brought up to date."

Gives brief general and statistical information on the academic and scientific life in 14 of the main European countries, Canada, the People's Republic of China, Japan, South Africa, and the U.S.A., in separate chapters. One chapter is devoted to the smaller countries of Eastern Europe and another to international organizations.

"Obtainable from the National Academy of Sciences, Washington 25, D.C."

United Nations Educational, Scientific and Cultural Organization. Education clearing houses and documentation centres; a preliminary international survey. Paris, 1957. 65p. (Its Educational studies and documents, no.22) **CB64**

Arranged by country, giving information on name, address, director, legal status, functions and purpose, annual budget, staff, library, publications, etc.

—— International directory of adult education. [Paris], UNESCO, 1952. 324p. **CB65**

In three parts: (1) international governmental organizations; (2) international non-governmental organizations; (3) some 50 countries, arranged alphabetically.

Under each country includes: descriptive text, a list of organizations and agencies, and a carefully selected bibliography. General index.

—— Teachers' associations. Associations d'enseignants. Asociaciones de personal docente. Paris, UNESCO, 1961. 127p. **CB66**

"Reports on 1274 organizations (of which 605 are treated

fully, and 669 summarily) in 127 countries and territories." —*Introd.* A revision is planned for 1965.

Universities of the world outside U.S.A., ed. by M. M. Chambers. 1st ed. 1950. Wash., Amer. Council on Education, 1950. 924p.   **CB67**

On the same plan as *American universities and colleges* (CB75). Treats more than 2000 institutions of higher education in more than 70 countries outside the United States.

Arranged by country. Each national section is headed by a brief introduction on the educational system of the country, with a bibliography including titles, which for the most part are in English.

The descriptions of the individual institutions generally include: name, location, history, administration, calendar, housing, admission requirements, language of instruction, organization and staff, enrollment, degrees and diplomas, degrees conferred, grading system, student aid, foreign students, foreign faculty members, library, research facilities, buildings and grounds, finances, chief administrative officers.

An index by name of institutions but no personal or subject indexes.

Vacations abroad: international directory of summer courses, study tours, and work camps. [Paris], UNESCO, 1948– . v.1– . Annual.   **CB68**

v.1 and v.5 issued as *Vacation study supplement* to *Study abroad* (CB142).

Title varies.

Title and introduction in English, French, and Spanish; entries are in one of the three.

Arranged by country; gives information on vacation courses, summer schools and seminars, study tours, student and youth hostels, summer work camps and centers, and other opportunities for study and travel abroad.

As far as possible, exact information is given concerning dates, places, agencies, and addresses. Includes geographical index listing localities where activities take place.

World of learning, 1947– . London, Europa Publs., 1947– . Annual.   **CB69**

Continues the section on institutions of learning formerly published in *Europa year book* (CI37). Arranged alphabetically by country. Lists learned societies and research institutions, libraries, museums, universities, and other institutions of higher education. For most institutions gives date of founding, administrative officers, faculties, etc. Fullness of information varies.

An international section contains information on UNESCO and international councils and organizations.

United States

General

College blue book. Ed. by C. E. Burckel. 10th ed. Yonkers, N.Y., College Blue Book, 1962. 3v. (Irregular) **CB70**

1st ed. 1924. 1st–4th eds., H. W. Hurt, ed.

In 3v., consisting of nine parts: v.1, pt.1, American institutions of higher education; pt.2, Educational atlas and college towns; pt.3, American secondary schools; v.2, pt.4, Financial support of American students and scholars; pt.5, Foreign colleges and universities; pt.6, Accreditation and recognition of American education; v.3, pt.7, Organizations register; pt.8, Periodical publications; pt.9, Addenda.

A comprehensive fact book, giving directory and statistical information, much of it in tabular form. Not always accurate or up to date. Omits a general index.

Official guide to Catholic educational institutions. Rockville Centre, N.Y., Catholic Institutional Directory Co., 1959– . il. Annual.   **CB71**

Supersedes *Directory of Catholic colleges and schools in the United States.* 1952.

5th edition, 1963, has cover title *Official guide to Catholic educational institutions and religious communities in the United States.*

A directory of Catholic universities, colleges, junior colleges, nursing schools, secondary boarding schools, and religious orders for men and women in the United States. Includes information on admission requirements, courses offered, facilities, costs, etc.

Patterson's American education. v.[1]– . 1904– . Mount Prospect, Ill., Educ. Directories, 1904– . maps. Annual.   **CB72**

Coverage and arrangement vary. Title varies.

A comprehensive list of public and private schools, colleges, universities, and other special schools in two parts: (1) school systems, arranged first by states, then by towns; (2) directory of schools, colleges, and universities classified by specialty.

Includes officers of state, county, and city educational systems, etc., and a list of educational associations. An alphabetical index of private schools, colleges, and universities refers to the geographical section.

A source guide to educational materials and equipment is included as a supplement, but may be purchased separately.

U.S. Office of Education. Education directory, 1912– . Wash., Govt. Prt. Off., 1912– . v.1– . Annual. **CB73**

Title varies slightly.

A useful annual varying in format and contents. 1961/62– , issued in five parts: (1) State governments; (2) Public school systems; (3) Higher education; (4) Educational associations; (5) Federal government.

Each one of these sections is an outstanding directory, and all should be in all public, school, and college libraries. It may be advisable to catalog or bind them separately so that each will be available with other works in its field; e.g., pts.1 and 2 will be needed for information about organization and personnel of state and local school systems; pt.3 is one of the most convenient directories of colleges and universities; pt.4 is the most useful list of educational associations available; and pt.5, new in 1962/63, lists key educational personnel in the various U.S. government departments and independent agencies, in organizational format.

Higher education

American Council on Education. American junior colleges, ed. by Edmund J. Gleazer, Jr. 6th ed. Wash., Council, 1963. 551p.   **CB74**

The 1st edition (1940) of this excellent handbook was compiled by W. C. Eells. Successive volumes have been revised, expanded, and published as companion volumes to *American universities and colleges* (CB75).

Gives information on 655 junior colleges in the 50 states, District of Columbia, Canal Zone, Guam, and Puerto Rico. Covers enrollment, curricula, admission and graduation requirements, history, fees, student aid, library, foreign students, and publications. Appendixes include American Association of Junior Colleges; classified data for junior colleges; curricula offered by junior colleges, etc.

—— American universities and colleges. 9th ed., ed. by Allan M. Cartter. Wash., Council, 1964. 1339p. **CB75**

Pub. quadrennially since 1928 (except 1944).

The most generally useful educational directory for higher education, presenting a summary of the present resources of American colleges and universities in three main sections: (1) Survey articles on higher education in the United States, including chapters on selecting a college; undergraduate, graduate, and professional education; the federal government and higher education; the foreign student, etc.; (2) Professional education; (3) Descriptions of more than 1100 institutions arranged alphabetically by state, giving for each: definite information about its history, organization, calendar, admission and degree requirements, fees, graduate work, departments and teaching staff, distinctive educational programs and activities, degrees conferred, enrollment, foreign students, library resources, publications, student financial aid, finances, buildings and grounds, administrative officers, etc.

Appendixes include: accreditation in higher education; academic costume code; degree abbreviations; tables of earned doctorates conferred, 1861–1962, etc.

—— A guide to graduate study: programs leading to the Ph.D. degree. Frederick W. Ness, ed. 2d ed. Wash., Council, 1960. 457p. **CB76**

1st ed., 1957, by the Association of American Colleges.

Introductory chapters on graduate study are followed by the listing of universities which offer programs leading to the Ph.D. degree. Arranged alphabetically, giving information on the graduate programs, fields of study, admission requirements, fees, etc. Index by fields of study.

Barron's Profiles of American colleges, ed. by Benjamin Fine. 1964– . Great Neck, N.Y., Barron's Educ. Series, 1964– . **CB77**

A comprehensive guide to more than 1100 American colleges and universities. In addition to giving information as to location, faculty, enrollment, courses offered, financial aid, etc., this directory includes a statement of the college's aims, living arrangements, regulations regarding student life, religious affiliation, and student travel programs. Especially useful to guidance officers.

Arranged alphabetically by state with index of colleges.

College Entrance Examination Board. The college handbook. 1941– . N.Y., Board, 1941– . Biennial. **CB78**

Title varies. Frequency varies.

Detailed descriptions of 504 colleges—members of the Board—giving information about location, size, programs of study, terms of admission, costs, financial assistance, and where to write for further information.

Fine, Benjamin. American college counselor and guide. [2d ed.], 1958/59. Englewood Cliffs, N.J., Prentice-Hall, 1957. 240p. **CB79**

Sec. I and II discuss the choice of a college, availability of scholarships, working one's way through college, admissions and accreditations, kinds of colleges, universities, junior colleges, etc.

Sec. III discusses professional education with lists of professional schools.

Hawes, Gene R. The new American guide to colleges. 2d ed. compl. rev. and enl. N.Y., Columbia Univ. Pr., 1962. 376p. **CB80**

1st ed. 1959.

A guide organized to aid in finding undergraduate colleges with particular characteristics. Arranged by type of college, e.g., Coed liberal arts, State and city colleges, Liberal arts for men, Liberal arts for women, Junior colleges, State universities, Private universities, Engineering and technical, Teachers colleges, Bible and religious studies. Includes listings in Canada and Mexico.

Contains information on type, sponsorship, accreditation, social life, major fields of interest, costs, admission policies, enrollment, etc.

An index by colleges and a "College discovery index," grouped by region, admission policies, and tuition.

Hoopes, Roy. State universities and colleges; a guide for prospective students. Wash., Luce, [c1962]. 481p. **CB81**

Information on 125 large state and public colleges of the United States, having an enrollment of 2500 or more, that offer a four-year, general liberal arts program. Listed alphabetically by state. Gives general description, admission requirements, expenses, housing, etc.

Junior college directory. 1927– . Wash., Amer. Assoc. of Junior Colleges, 1927– . Annual. **CB82**

A directory of all junior colleges, accredited and nonaccredited, with very brief information as to name, location,

administrative head, accreditation, type, enrollment, and number on staff. Includes lists of junior college societies, organizations, etc.

Lovejoy's College guide, comp. by Clarence Earle Lovejoy. 1953/54– . N.Y., Simon & Schuster, 1952– . Biennial. **CB83**

Earlier editions had title: 1940–41, *So you're going to college;* 1948–50/51, *Complete guide to American colleges and universities.*

Subtitle: A complete reference book to . . . American colleges and universities for use by students, parents, teachers, and guidance counselors.

Gives concise information on accreditation, type, enrollment, equipment, expenses, scholarships, degrees, etc.

Advice on how to choose a college, and how to get scholarships, loans, etc., is included.

U.S. Dept. of State. Office of Intelligence Research and Analysis. Area study programs in American universities. Wash., Govt. Prt. Off., 1959. 106p. **CB84**

1st ed. Feb. 1956.

Describes 96 programs of graduate study—on Africa, Asia, Latin America, Russia and Eastern Europe, and Multi-area—indicating size of faculty, degrees offered, course emphasis, languages, library facilities, etc.

U.S. Office of Education. Accredited higher institutions. Wash., Govt. Prt. Off., 1917– . Quadrennial. **CB85**

Issued as numbers of the Office of Education *Bulletin.*

1960 issue in three parts: pt.1, Institutions of higher education accredited by nationally recognized regional accrediting associations; pt.2, Professional and technical schools or departments accredited by nationally recognized agencies; pt.3, Institutions of higher education accredited and approved by state departments of education, state accrediting commissions, and state universities.

Elementary and secondary education

The gifted: educational resources. Boston, Sargent, 1961. 285p. **CB86**

Subtitle: A preliminary survey of primary and secondary schools in the United States which seek through inspiring teaching to realize the capabilities of mentally superior students.

Lists both public and private schools which have special programs for the gifted.

Handbook of private schools. 1915– . Boston, Sargent, 1915– . v.1– . il. Annual. **CB87**

Title varies slightly.

Lists and describes some 2300 private elementary and secondary schools in the United States. Gives information on type, tuition, staff, enrollment, facilities, etc. Contains a directory of summer academic programs and camps; a list of educational associations; and an alphabetical index of schools.

Lovejoy's Prep school guide. Rev. ed., 1963, by Clarence Earle Lovejoy. N.Y., Harper, 1963. 136p. **CB88**

1st ed. 1958.

Subtitle: Independent, private, secondary institutions, nonpublic, boarding and day; a complete reference book that gives facts about 1800 college preparatory schools and is designed for students, parents, teachers, libraries, churches, parish houses, youth agencies, guidance counselors, industrial corporations, foundations, and United States and foreign government bureaus and departments, including embassies.

Private independent schools; the American private schools for boys and girls . . . 4th ed.– . Wallingford, Conn., James E. Bunting, 1951– . il. Annual. **CB89**

First pub. 1943; pub. irregularly—annual since 1951.

Title varies: 1943, *Independent schools, a directory.*

Subtitle: A directory and guide for parents and teachers. Boarding schools, day schools, and military schools, with or without church affiliations and operating for the most part as educational corporations under state charters.

Gives fairly lengthy descriptions of a large selection of private schools and brief listings of others. Includes a list of educational associations.

U.S. Office of Education. Directory of public secondary day schools, 1958/59, showing accreditation status, enrollment, classroom teachers, and other data by Leah W. Ramsey. Wash., Govt. Prt. Off., 1961. 163p. **CB90**

In tabular form shows location and name of school, type of school, years in school, accreditation by state and regional associations, number of classroom teachers, enrollment, and number of graduates 1957–58.

—— Nonpublic secondary schools; a directory showing accreditation status, enrollment, classroom teachers, and other data by Diane B. Gertler and Leah W. Ramsey. 1960/61. Wash., Govt. Prt. Off., 1963. 106p. **CB91**

"Companion volume to *Directory of public secondary day schools.*"

Gives data for independent and church-affiliated schools.

Specialized education

American trade schools directory, 1957–1958, comp. and ed. by Ulrich H. E. Croner. A loose-leaf directory of trade and vocational schools in the United States, classified by trades taught and listed by states and cities. Kept up to date by monthly supplements. Queens Village, N.Y., Croner, 1957– . Loose-leaf. **CB92**

In two parts: the first classified by trades taught, the second listed by state and city. Includes home-study schools. Lists some 3000 schools.

Directory for exceptional children, educational and training facilities . . . 1954– . Boston, Sargent, 1954– . Biennial (Irregular). **CB93**

4th ed. 1962.

Subtitle: Describing schools, homes, clinics, hospitals and services for the socially maladjusted, mentally retarded, emotionally disturbed, orthopedically handicapped, cerebral palsied, speech handicapped, brain-injured, epileptic, cardiac, blind, deaf.

Includes list of associations, societies, and foundations.

Directory of business schools in the United States; a handbook for vocational advisors and guidance officers. 1st ed. 1943– . Wash., Nat. Assoc. and Council of Business Schools, 1943– . **CB94**

v.1–5 issued by the National Council of Business Schools under the title *Directory of private business schools in the United States.*

A directory of private business schools, giving name, address, and other pertinent information. Schools are classified according to the educational standards adopted by the Association.

Jewish education register and directory. Ed. by Judah Pileh. N.Y., Amer. Assoc. for Jewish Education, 1959. 106p. **CB95**

1st ed. 1951; 1959 ed. called v.2. New edition planned for 1965.

A general section on various phases of Jewish education is followed by the directory, which includes educational agencies, schools, libraries, museums, summer camps, periodicals, etc. Covers the United States and Canada.

King, Sam Wilson. Preparatory trade and industrial training programs in public schools; a directory, 1961–62. Wash., Govt. Prt. Off., 1962. 272p. (U.S. Office of Education. Bull. 1963, no.4) **CB96**

Listed by state and city, in alphabetical order; gives schools and programs for both high school and adult students.

Lovejoy, Clarence Earle. Vocational school guide; a hand-

book of job training opportunities. 2d ed. rev. N.Y., Simon & Schuster, 1963. 174p. **CB97**

1st ed. 1955.

In two parts: pt.1 gives brief general information on choosing a vocation and on educational opportunities for those in the armed services; pt.2 gives information on more than 11,000 schools, arranged by vocation, then by state and city.

Miller, Adeline Elizabeth and **Brown, Betty I.** National directory of schools and vocations. 2d ed. North Springfield, Pa., State School Publ., 1963. 703p. **CB98**

1st ed. 1958.

Includes colleges, universities, and technical and trade schools offering courses in training for vocations. Arranged alphabetically by vocation, then by state. Gives degree, diploma, certificate, and length of course. Lists 349 vocations with cross references.

U.S. Office of Education. Education for the professions, organized and ed. by Lloyd E. Blauch. Wash., Govt. Prt. Off., 1955. 317p. **CB99**

Presents discussion and statistics on education for the various professions, with lists of professional schools and brief bibliographies. Statistics and bibliographies need to be brought up to date, but much of the information is still useful.

Canada

Canada. Bureau of Statistics. Canadian institutions of higher education. Institutions d'enseignement supérieur du Canada. 1953/54– . Ottawa, 1954– . Biennial. **CB100**

In English and French.

Title varies: 1st ed. 1954, *List of institutions of higher education in Canada.*

Introduction gives information for prospective student as to admission requirements, degrees, and scholarships. This is followed by lists of institutions in tabular form, arranged by province, with name, address, courses offered, costs, etc.

Canadian universities and colleges. Universités et collèges canadiens. 1948– . Ottawa, Canadian Universities Foundation, 1948– . v.1– . Biennial. **CB101**

In English and French.

Title varies: v.1–3, 1948–52, *Yearbook of Canadian universities. Annuaire des universités canadiennes.* Issued under the auspices of the National Conference of Canadian Universities.

Prepared primarily for students from other nations. Contains information on each university, e.g., administrative officers, history and government, degrees authorized, courses offered, diplomas offered, admission requirements, registration, fees, scholarships, enrollment, etc. Includes list of Canadian degree abbreviations and a glossary of academic terms.

Information is somewhat fuller than that given in the preceding entry.

China, Communist

Kun, Joseph C. Higher educational institutions of Communist China, 1953–1958: a cumulative list. Cambridge, Mass., Center for Internat. Studies, Mass. Inst. of Technology, 1961. 48p. **CB102**

Appendix C of forthcoming study: "Selection and enrollment of students in Communist Chinese higher educational institutions."

For each institution gives name (in English and in Chinese characters), location, length of course in years, and general remarks.

Orleans, Leo O. Professional manpower and education in Communist China. Wash., Govt. Prt. Off., 1961. 260p. il. **CB103**

An analysis and summary of significant data gathered from

available material dealing with education in Communist China. Gives figures and statistical tables pertaining to all levels of education. Contains lists of research institutions and institutions of higher education, showing courses offered.

Includes an alphabetical index by name and subject.

U.S. Library of Congress. Science and Technology Division. Mainland China organizations of higher learning in science and technology and their publications: a selected guide. Comp. by Chi Wang. Wash., 1961. 104p. **CB104**

For full information *see* EA163.

China, Republic of

Taipei, Taiwan. National Central Library. Directory of the cultural organizations of the Republic of China. Taipei, 1961. 114p. il. **CB105**

1st edition of a directory of learned societies; research institutes; libraries; museums and social education centers; universities and colleges; and research departments in public and private enterprises. Full descriptions are given for each organization, including a list of its publications.

France

Index generalis: France 1958, enseignement supérieur, recherche scientifique, observatoires. Paris, Klincksieck, 1959. 175p. **CB106**

Follows the plan of the *Index generalis* (CB59), but gives information only for France.

Germany

Handbuch der deutschen Wissenschaft. Berlin, Koetschau-Verlag, 1949. 2v. **CB107**

v.1 lists, under place: (1) universities, technical schools, and schools of engineering, agriculture, government, theology, and medicine with lists of faculties; (2) learned societies, museums, libraries, etc., with titles of publications; and (3) more than 300 serial publications with editors and addresses arranged by subject.

v.2 gives brief biographical information for some 6000 German scholars.

Great Britain

Commonwealth universities yearbook; a directory of the universities of the British Commonwealth and the handbook of their Association, 1914– . London, Assoc. of Commonwealth Universities, 1914– . v.1– . Annual. **CB108**

Publication suspended 1941–46.

Title varies: 1914–47, *Yearbook of the universities of the Empire;* 1948–57, *Yearbook of the universities of the Commonwealth.*

Gives fairly detailed information about the universities of the British Commonwealth, including names of administrative officers and faculties; general information as to history, library, and museums; requirements for admission and degrees; scholarships; etc. Index of names.

Appendix includes universities of the Republic of Ireland and of South Africa.

Education authorities directory and annual, 1903– . London, School Govt. Pub. Co., 1903– . Annual. **CB109**

Title varies slightly.

Published as *School government handbook,* no.4, 1903–1929/30. With the issue of 1930/31, the Directory ceases to form part of the series.

Includes a large amount of official, institutional, and personal directory material.

Girls' school year book (public schools). The official book of reference of the Association of Head Mistresses. London, Black, 1906– . v.1– . Annual. **CB110**

Counterpart to the *Public and preparatory schools year book* (CB111).

In two sections: pt.1 deals with leading girls' public schools in Great Britain; pt.2 deals with future career opportunities for girls on leaving school.

Includes a list of public secondary schools for girls, with location and name of school.

Public and preparatory schools year book. The official book of reference of the Headmasters' Conference and of the Incorporated Association of Preparatory Schools. London, Black, 1889– . v.1– . Annual. **CB111**

Title varies.

Gives descriptive information, teaching staffs, etc., of public and preparatory schools for boys in Great Britain. Briefer information is included on universities and colleges and non-university educational institutions. Contains a section on careers: Navy, Army, Air Force, Civil Service, Church, Teaching, Law, and other professions.

Schools; a directory of the schools in Great Britain and Northern Ireland, arranged in order of their counties and towns, including statistical information regarding recognized public schools for boys, sections for tutors, career training courses, and schools on the continent of Europe. London, Truman and Knightley, 1924– . v.1– . il. Annual. **CB112**

Title varies.

Directory information for schools for boys and girls.

Latin America

Pan American Union. Division of Education. Documentation and Information Service. Instituciones latinoamericanas de enseñanza superior. 2. ed. rev. y aum. Wash., Union, [1961]. 93p. **CB113**

1st ed. 1960.

A list of Latin-American institutions of higher education arranged alphabetically by country. Gives name, address, sponsorship, faculties, and research institutes for each institution. Includes directory of university associations.

Introduction, glossary, and notes are in Spanish, English, Portuguese, and French.

Middle East

Boardman, Francis. Institutions of higher learning in the Middle East; a tabulation and summary with some historical notes. Wash., Middle East Inst., 1961. 34p. **CB114**

Statistics

National Research Council. Office of Scientific Personnel. Doctorate production in United States universities, 1920–1962, with baccalaureate origins of doctorates in sciences, arts, and professions. Comp. by Lindsay R. Harmon and Herbert Soldy. Wash., Nat. Academy of Sciences—Nat. Research Council, 1963. 215p. (Its Publ. no.1142) **CB115**

Statistical data showing production of "third-level research degrees such as PhD, ScD, EngD, and EdD; professional degrees such as MD, DDS and DVM are not included."—*Pref.*

Tabular arrangement by field, institution, etc.

This volume is the fifth in a series, and cumulates data in the four previous volumes.

UNESCO statistical yearbook. Annuaire statistique.

[1st]– .1963– .[Paris], 1964– . (Distr. by UNESCO Publ. Center, 317 East 34th St., New York 16, N.Y.) tables. Annual. (SS.64/XIV.8/AF) **CB116**

Title page and text in English and French.

Supersedes United Nations Educational, Scientific and Cultural Organization, *Basic facts and figures.*

Contains international statistical data on population, illiteracy, education, libraries and museums, publications, films, and radio and television.

United Nations Educational, Scientific and Cultural Organization. Manual of educational statistics. [Paris], UNESCO, 1961. 241p. **CB117**

Definitions, classifications, and tabulations of educational statistics, as described by the Committee on the International Standardization of Educational Statistics.

U.S. Office of Education. Biennial survey of education, 1916/18–1956/58. Wash., Govt. Prt. Off., 1921– . (In progress) **CB118**

For the 1956–58 survey—still in progress—each chapter is printed as soon as completed. Publication to cease with this survey.

Contains basic data and statistics on education in the United States from kindergarten through the graduate school.

U.S. Office of Education. Division of Educational Statistics. Digest of educational statistics. Wash., Govt. Prt. Off., 1962– . Annual. **CB119**

Pub. in the Office of Education *Bulletin.*

A very useful compilation, giving current statistical information on schools, enrollments, teachers, graduates, educational attainment, finances, federal programs in the field of education, libraries, international education, and research and development.

Replaces the "Statistical summary of education," formerly Chapter 1 in the *Biennial survey.*

School law

Rezny, Arthur Adolph and **Remmlein, Madaline Kinter.** A schoolman in the law library. Danville, Ill., Interstate Printers and Pub., [1962]. 64p. **CB120**

Subtitle: Problems, bibliography, research tools, analysis of a case, glossary of legal terms.

A brief guide to the use of legal research materials, especially useful to school administrators and advanced students of education.

Yearbook of school law, 1950– , by Lee O. Garber. Danville, Ill., Interstate Printers and Pub., 1950– . Annual. **CB121**

Supersedes the *Yearbook of school law.* 1st–10th eds. 1932–42.

Contains digests of court decisions affecting schools, as well as feature articles. Includes a bibliography of recent research studies in the field of school law. Indexed in the *Education index* (CB27).

Biography

American men of science. 10th ed. Tempe, Ariz., Jaques Cattell Pr., 1962. v.5, Social and behavioral sciences. **CB122**

For full information *see* CA40.

Directory of American scholars; a biographical directory. 4th ed. N.Y., Bowker, 1963–64. 4v. **CB123**

For full information *see* AJ52.

Presidents and deans of American colleges and universities, 1958/59– . Robert C. Cook, ed. Nashville, Tenn., Who's Who in Amer. Education, 1958– . Biennial. **CB124**

1st ed. 1933. 2d ed. 1952. Biennial since 1958/59.

Title varies: 1933/34–1952/53, *Presidents of American colleges and universities;* 1955/56, *Trustees and presidents* . . . ; 1958/59, *Trustees, presidents and deans* . . . ; 1960/61– , *Presidents and deans* . . . .

Biographical sketches, usually with pictures, of the administrative heads of colleges and universities.

Who's who in American education; an illustrated biographical dictionary of eminent living educators of the United States and Canada, ed. by Robert C. Cook. Nashville, Tenn., Who's Who in Amer. Education, 1928– . v.1– . il. Biennial. **CB125**

The 21st edition, 1963–64, is much enlarged. Contains sketches of persons active in higher education, and primary and secondary school administrative officers, as well as some persons not directly connected with education, e.g., public relations executives, librarians of public libraries, etc.

GUIDANCE

☙ Many books and pamphlets have been published on the choice of an occupation or vocation, likewise various bibliographies listing such material. The following are typical bibliographies in this field:

Bibliography

Forrester, Gertrude. Occupational literature: an annotated bibliography. 1964. N.Y., Wilson, 1964. 675p. **CB126**

Earlier editions were published in 1946, 1948, 1954, and 1958. Titles vary.

This edition has been enlarged to include some 5100 pamphlets and 1500 references to books. Classified under some 500 occupational titles. Emphasis is on occupational guidance for secondary school and college students.

Guide to guidance . . . an annotated bibliography of . . . publications of interest to deans, counselors, and advisers. v.1–24, 1938–61. Syracuse, N.Y., Syracuse Univ. Pr., 1939–62. 24v. Annual. **CB127**

Ceased publication.

Subtitle and publisher vary.

Classified list of books, pamphlets, and articles with full annotations summarizing the contents. Contains author and title index.

New York Life Insurance Company. Career Information Service. Career opportunities. 5th rev. ed. [New York], 1963. 397p. **CB128**

Subtitle: A series of articles designed to help guide young people to a better future.

1st ed. 1958.

Informative and well-written articles, somewhat detailed, by specialists, on more than 50 occupations and job opportunities. Includes sources to consult for additional information. Arrangement is by name of occupation.

—— Guide to career information: a bibliography of recent occupational literature. N.Y., Harper, 1957. 203p. **CB129**

Lists more than 800 books and pamphlets grouped under 52 occupational categories. Arranged by subject, with brief but good annotations.

U.S. Employment Service. Job guide for young workers. [1950]– . Wash., Govt. Prt. Off., 1950– . Annual. **CB130**

Not pub. 1951–52.

Gives information about jobs that can be obtained after high school graduation.

Directories

Camp, Dolph. Guidance workers certification requirements. Wash., Govt. Prt. Off., 1963. 107p. (U.S. Office of Education. Bull. 1960. no.14 rev.) **CB131**

Lists certification requirements by state.

Directory of vocational counseling services. 1950– . Wash., 1950– . Biennial. **CB132**

Title varies slightly. Frequency varies.

Issuing body varies. American Board on Professional Standards in Vocational Counseling, created by the American Personnel and Guidance Association, 1958– .

A list of approved counseling agencies which give information useful to counselors.

Technician education yearbook. 1st– . 1963/64– . Ann Arbor, Mich., Prakken Pub., [1963]– . il. Annual. **CB133**

Contains a directory of about 800 United States institutions offering technician training; federal laws and regulations concerning technician training; case studies of outstanding programs; occupational information, etc. "Technician" is limited to those technical workers who assist engineers and scientists and do other technical work in industry. Excludes technicians in such fields as medicine, dentistry, etc. Includes a bibliography.

FELLOWSHIPS AND SCHOLARSHIPS

❦ In recent years an increasing number of lists has been published of the scholarships and fellowships available for students in institutions of higher education in the United States and other countries, but only a selection of these can be given here. Many libraries will find state and regional lists particularly useful.

Canada. Bureau of Statistics. Awards for graduate study and research. Ottawa, Queen's Printer, 1957– . Biennial. **CB134**

Formerly titled *Post-graduate scholarships and fellowships open to Canadian students.* 1951–54.

Awards open to Canadians from sources in Canada and abroad, particularly from the United Kingdom and the United States. When possible, it is noted when Canadian awards are open to persons from outside Canada.

Conference Board of Associated Research Councils. Committee on International Exchange of Persons. United States government grants under the Fulbright-Hays Act. University lecturing. Advanced research. Europe, the Near East, the Far East, Africa. Wash., 1953/54– . Annual. **CB135**

Title varies. Countries included vary.

Other leaflets are issued covering: [1] Argentina, Brazil, Chile, Colombia, Ecuador, Mexico, Paraguay, Peru, Uruguay; [2] Australia, New Zealand; and [3] South and Southeast Asia.

Feingold, S. Norman. Scholarships, fellowships and loans. Cambridge, Mass., Bellman, 1949–62. 4v. **CB136**

Lists administering agencies with name and address, and gives information on the student-aid programs each offers. v.2, 3, and 4 contain revised and additional information, but do not repeat all of the data in the previous volumes. Thus they constitute supplements to rather than replacements of these volumes.

Fellowships in the arts and sciences. 1st– . 1957– . Wash., Amer. Council on Education, 1957– . Annual. **CB137**

Title varies: 1957, *Directory of fellowships in the arts and sciences.* Imprint varies. Published 1957–1962/63 by the Association of American Colleges.

Basic information on awards in arts and sciences available from sources outside the universities themselves. Includes predoctoral fellowships, postdoctoral fellowships, and summer study. Appendix cites recent books, pamphlets, and other sources of information, including works listing aid available for study in specialized fields, e.g., accounting, dentistry, librarianship, etc.

Foundation directory, prep. by the Foundation Library Center. Ed.1– . N.Y., Russell Sage Foundation, 1960– . **CB138**

An extensive listing of foundations, many of which award grants or fellowships.

For complete entry *see* CA35.

Mattingly, Richard Curtis. Financial aid for college students: graduate. Wash., Govt. Prt. Off., 1957. 151p. (U.S. Office of Education. Bull. 1957. no.17) (Studies on financial assistance to students in higher education, no.3) (Repr. 1963) **CB139**

Discusses loans and employment available at each college or university in the various fields of study in 1955–56.

Now out of date, but the only national directory which lists aid offered by the institutions themselves.

—— Financial assistance for college students: undergraduate. Wash., Govt. Prt. Off., 1962. 360p. (U.S. Office of Education. Bull. 1962. no.11. College Information Center ser.) **CB140**

Information on institutional scholarships, undergraduate employment, and loans, showing programs active in 1959–60 in 1667 institutions.

National register of scholarships and fellowships, by Juvenal L. Angel. 4th ed. N.Y., World Trade Academy Pr., 1963–64. 2v. **CB141**

v.1, Scholarships and loans. Arranged by state; lists the scholarships and loan funds, primarily undergraduate, offered by private organizations and corporations, educational institutions, and state and city governments. 1964. 494p.

v.2, Fellowships and grants. Arranged by subject field; lists the fellowships and loans available to students "planning to undertake predoctoral or postdoctoral training." 1963. 208p.

Study abroad; international directory of fellowships, scholarships, and awards compiled by UNESCO. v.1– . 1948– . Paris, N.Y., 1948– . Annual. **CB142**

Announced to be published biennially, beginning with the 16th edition to appear at the end of 1965.

Gives details of available fellowships and scholarships for international study, including: name, field of study, value, duration, number available, where to send application, and date limit.

Arranged according to donors of awards, by administering agency or by country in which donor is located. Includes a list of organizations, arranged alphabetically.

In English, French, and Spanish.

ACADEMIC CUSTOMS

Academic costume

Hargreaves-Mawdsley, W. N. A history of academical dress in Europe until the end of the eighteenth century. Oxford, Clarendon Pr., 1963. 235p. il. **CB143**

Gives detailed, historical descriptions of academic costumes in European universities, arranged chronologically by country. Emphasis is on Great Britain but most other countries, except the empires of Russia and Turkey, are included. Contains copious notes, many illustrations, glossary of terms, and bibliography. Index to subjects and names.

Haycraft, Frank W. The degrees and hoods of the world's universities and colleges. [4th ed.] compl. rev. and enl. by E. A. Scabie Stringer. Cheshunt, Herts., Eng., Cheshunt Pr., 1948. 159p. il.   **CB144**

1st ed. 1923.

A useful guide to academic costume primarily for the British Empire. For each institution gives date of founding; list of degrees offered; and descriptions of gowns, cowls, and hoods, with illustrations, some in color. Includes a history of academic dress, and a list of abbreviations of degrees.

Baty, Thomas. Academic colours. Tokyo, Kenkyusha Pr., 1934. 172p.   **CB145**

Descriptions of the academic costumes worn in British universities with additional chapters on other countries. Includes a section on "Hoods classified according to degree and colour."

Sheard, Kevin. Academic heraldry in America. Marquette, Mich., Northern Michigan College Pr., 1962. 78p. il.   **CB146**

Gives descriptions of hoods worn at colleges and universities in the United States. Arranged first by institution, then by color. Includes brief information on academic ceremonies, seals, and flags.

Not a complete listing and not always accurate but useful, as it brings together information in convenient form for ready reference.

Academic degrees

Eells, Walter Crosby and **Haswell, Harold A.** Academic degrees: earned and honorary degrees conferred by institutions of higher education in the United States. Wash., Govt. Prt. Off., 1960. 324p. (U.S. Office of Education. Bull. 1960, no.28)   **CB147**

Provides information on some 2400 degrees (1600 currently in use) conferred by American universities and colleges. Arranged in three principal lists: (1) classified by field, (2) alphabetical by name of degree, and (3) alphabetical by abbreviation.

College colors

Snyder, Henry L. Our college colors. Kutztown, Pa., Kutztown Pub. Co., 1949. 260p.   **CB148**

Gives the colors for each American college and university with date of adoption and brief history, where ascertainable, of the reason for the choice.

Fraternities

Baird, William Raimond. Baird's Manual of American college fraternities. 17th ed. John Robson, ed. Menasha, Wis., George Banta, 1963. 834p. il.   **CB149**

A new edition of the standard manual of American college fraternities. First published 1879. Gives a descriptive analysis, with a detailed account of each fraternity. Includes men's and women's social and professional fraternities, honor societies, and recognition societies.

Prizes and awards

Brook, Herbert. The blue book of awards; a compilation of major prizes, medals, honors and distinctions, including significant graduate scholarships and fellowships, open to citizens of the United States and Canada, indexed by donors and classified by fields. Chicago, Marquis-Who's Who, 1956. 186p.   **CB150**

Lists many types of awards, prizes, medals, competitive scholarships, etc. The main section is arranged alphabetically, giving, where pertinent: date of establishment, purpose, eligi-

bility, what award consists of, when given, address from whom information may be obtained, and (in some cases) recent recipients. Index by donor and a classified index by field.

RECREATION AND SPORTS

Bibliography

Greenwood, Frances Anderson. Bibliography of swimming. N.Y., Wilson, 1940. 308p.   **CB151**

A dictionary catalog of books and periodical articles on swimming and allied subjects, containing approximately 10,000 titles listed by author and classified under 608 subjects. Includes material in various languages published up to June 1938.

The Hague. Koninklijke Bibliotheek. Bibliotheca Van der Linde-Niemeijeriana; a catalogue of the chess collection in the Royal Library, The Hague. The Hague, Staatsdrukkerij, 1955. 342p.   **CB152**

A catalog of several rich collections on chess in the Royal Library, particularly those originally owned by Dr. Antonius Van der Linde and Dr. M. Niemeijer.

Classed, with author index.

Henderson, Robert William. Early American sport; a check-list of books by American and foreign authors published in America prior to 1860, including sporting songs. 2d ed. rev. and enl. N.Y., Barnes, 1953. 234p. il.   **CB153**

1st ed., 1937, pub. by the Grolier Club.

Lists 1217 editions of 628 titles, arranged alphabetically by author (or title, if anonymous) with a subject index. Based on the collection in the Racquet and Tennis Club of New York City.

Locates copies.

Henry E. Huntington Library and Art Gallery, San Marino, Calif. Sporting books in the Huntington Library, comp. by Lyle H. Wright. San Marino, Calif., 1937. 132p. (Huntington Library lists, no.2)   **CB154**

A classed list, with author and title index.

Higginson, Alexander Henry. British and American sporting authors, their writings and biographies . . . with a bibliography by Sydney R. Smith. . . . Berryville, Va., Blue Ridge Pr., 1949. 443p. il.   **CB155**

Biographical sketches, in chronological order, are followed by an alphabetical bibliography (p.399–437), which includes author and title entries. Alphabetical index of authors.

How-to-do-it books; a selected guide. 3d ed. rev. N.Y., Bowker, 1963. 265p.   **CB156**

1st ed. (1950) and 2d ed. (1954) by Robert E. Kingery.

Lists more than 4000 "know-how books, pamphlets, government documents, etc., relating primarily to the non-vocational, spare-time recreational and home-making activities of men, women, and children."—*Introd.* Arranged by subject with detailed index.

Phillips, John Charles. American game mammals and birds; a catalogue of books, 1582–1925, sport, natural history and conservation. Boston, Houghton, 1930. 638p.   **CB157**

Also published under title *A bibliography of American sporting books.* Boston, Morrill, [c1930].

Most of the titles are from the Charles Sheldon Library which now belongs to Yale University.

Gives complete bibliographical information and frequently a brief descriptive note.

Smith, Frank Seymour. Know-how books; an annotated bibliography of do it yourself books for the handyman and of introductions to science, art, history and literature for the beginner and home student. London, Thames & Hudson, 1956. 306p. **CB158**

Printed in N.Y. by Bowker, 1957.

A British counterpart of *How-to-do-it books* (CB156).

Lists some 3000 works classified by the Dewey Decimal system. A subject index but no author index.

Dictionaries and handbooks

Avis, Frederick Compton. The sportsman's glossary. London, Souvenir Pr.; Toronto, Ryerson Pr., 1961. 301p. **CB159**

Brief definitions listed under 15 different sports, almost exclusively British. No index.

Cummings, Parke. The dictionary of sports. N.Y., Barnes, 1949. 572p. il. **CB160**

A dictionary of terms used in sports.

Dictionnaire des jeux, publié sous la direction de René Alleau, avec la collaboration de Renaud Matignon. [Paris?], Réalités de l'Imaginaire, Tchou, [1964]. 544p. il. **CB161**

A comprehensive work describing in detail ancient and modern games and amusements of all countries. Gives history of each game and rules of play. Contains excellent illustrations, some in color.

Foster, Robert Frederick. Complete Hoyle. Rev. and enl. Philadelphia, Lippincott, [1963]. 697p. il. **CB162**

Subtitle: An encyclopedia of games, including all indoor games played to-day, with suggestions for good play, illustrative hands and all official laws to date . . . with the complete laws of contract bridge and canasta.

Gomme, Alice Bertha. Traditional games of England, Scotland, and Ireland; with tunes, singing-rhymes and methods of playing according to the variants extant and recorded in different parts of the Kingdom. London, Nutt, 1894–98. 2v. (Dictionary of British folk-lore, ed. by G. Laurence Gomme, pt.1) (Repr.: Gloucester, Mass., Peter Smith. 2v.; also, N.Y., Dover, [1964]. 2v. **CB163**

Hargrave, Catherine Perry. History of playing cards and a bibliography of cards and gaming; comp. and il. from the old cards and books in the collection of the United States Playing Card Company in Cincinnati. Boston, Houghton; London, Allen and Unwin, 1930. 468p. il. **CB164**

Bibliography, p.369–449.

Hunter's encyclopedia, ed. Raymond R. Camp. Harrisburg, Pa., Stackpole and Heck, [1948]. 1152p. il. **CB165**

A comprehensive work dealing with the game animals and birds of this continent, describing their appearance, characteristics, history, range, etc., with methods of hunting, firearms, game laws, etc. Arranged by groupings with a detailed index.

Contents: Big game; Small game; Animal predators; Winged predators; Small mammals; Upland game birds; Shorebirds; Waterfowl; Color section (colored plates of upland game birds and waterfowl); Firearms; Ammunition; Dogs; Miscellany (including chapters on camping, clothing, various methods of hunting, regulations and laws, etc.).

Lovell, Eleanor Cook and **Hall, Ruth Mason.** Index to handicrafts, model-making, and workshop projects. Boston, Faxon, 1936. 476p. (Useful reference ser., no.57) **CB166**

—— —— Supplement, 1–2. . . . Boston, Faxon, 1943–50. 527p., 593p. (Useful reference ser., no.70, 79)

An index to periodical articles for use in school and home craftwork.

Menke, Frank Grant. The encyclopedia of sports. 3d rev. ed. [Roger L. Treat, ed.] N.Y., Barnes, [1963]. 1044p. il. **CB167**

1st ed. 1939. Title varies slightly.

Covers a wide variety of sports, giving: history, description, basic rules, names and records of champions, and financial statistics, with special attention to the United States.

Quercetani, Roberto L. A world history of track and field athletics, 1864–1964. London, N.Y., Oxford Univ. Pr., 1964. 370p. il. **CB168**

A survey giving all-time records of 20 events. Includes index of names.

Spalding's Official athletic almanac, 1893–1941. Founded by James E. Sullivan. N.Y., Amer. Sports Pub. Co., 1893–1941. (Spalding's Athletic library, no.1R) **CB169**

Gives: (1) world, Olympic, and American track, field, and swimming records for men and women; (2) A.A.U. championships and records; and (3) All-America track and field teams, etc.

Ceased publication with 1941.

Turkin, Hy and **Thompson, S. C.** Official encyclopedia of baseball. 3d rev. ed. N.Y., Barnes; London, Yoseloff, [c1963]. 625p. il. **CB170**

1st ed. 1951.

Includes data on managers and players in regular major-league games since 1871; historical information on baseball; rules and scoring; baseball ballads; glossary of slang terms. No index.

U.S. Children's Bureau. Handbook for recreation. [Rev. ed. Wash.], U.S. Dept. of Health, Education, and Welfare. Social Security Admin., Children's Bureau, 1960. 148p. il., music. (Its Publ. no.231, rev. 1959) **CB171**

Contains information on games, dances, music, storytelling, etc. Especially useful for nonprofessional recreational leaders in charge of group activities. Includes a title index and a classified game and activity index; also, a list of references with brief annotations.

Camping

American Camping Association. Directory of accredited camps for boys and girls. Martinsville, Ind., 1933?– . Annual. **CB172**

Title varies.

All camps listed are members of the American Camping Association and are accredited by it. Arranged by state and then alphabetically. Gives name, date of founding, location, director, number accommodated, length of season, cost, specialties, etc.

Rand McNally guidebook to campgrounds. N.Y., Rand McNally, [c1959]– . Annual. maps. **CB173**

Title varies.

Subtitle: A family camping directory of campgrounds throughout the United States and Canada.

The first part consists of sectional colored maps, showing major highways, cities, and towns with numbered camp locations. Following this section are tables for each state, or province, giving detailed information as to facilities available at each campsite, keyed to location on map.

Rhodes, Glenn and **Rhodes, Dale.** Camping maps U.S.A. and Canada. [Rev. ed.] N.Y., Macmillan, [c1957]– . Annual. **CB174**

A handy guide containing substantially the same information as the *Rand McNally guidebook to campgrounds* but arranged in slightly different form. List of campsites is arranged alphabetically by states, with map for each state and concise information describing facilities, fees, etc.

C C

Sociology

☙ This section deals mainly with reference materials concerned with social conditions and social welfare, criminology, and racial groups. The *International bibliography of sociology* (CC2), an extensive annual listing of materials in many languages, is of first importance in the research library.

The *Encyclopedia of social work* (CC13), formerly the *Social work year book;* Shock's *Classified bibliography of gerontology and geriatrics* (CC23); *Child development abstracts and bibliography* (CC39); *Excerpta criminologica* (CC48); and the bibliographies on crime and criminal justice (CC46–CC57) are useful works in these fields.

GENERAL WORKS

Bibliography

Current sociological research. N.Y., Amer. Sociological Assoc., 1953– . Annual.   **CC1**

"A listing of research in progress as reported by members of the American Sociological Association." Classified arrangement with name index. Does not indicate doctoral dissertations.

International bibliography of sociology. Bibliographie internationale de sociologie. 1951– . London, Tavistock; Chicago, Aldine, 1952– . Annual. (International bibliography of the social sciences)   **CC2**

Publisher varies. 1951–53, pub. in *Current sociology;* v.4–9, Paris, UNESCO; v.10, 1960– , issued as *Publications* of the International Committee for Social Sciences Documentation, as one of the series of the "International bibliography of the social sciences" (series title varies slightly).

In English and French.

An extensive classified listing of books, pamphlets, periodical articles, and official government publications in many languages, including Slavic and Asian languages. Indexes by author and subject (in English and French).

For other bibliographies in the series *see* CH25 (Economics); CI19 (Political science); CD29 (Social and cultural anthropology).

Viet, Jean. Les villes nouvelles: éléments d'une bibliographie annotée; New towns: a selected annotated bibliography. Paris, UNESCO, 1960. 82p. (Reports and papers in the social sciences, no.12)   **CC3**

Classified, annotated list of 900 items—books, articles, documents—on social and technical aspects of newly built communities.

Dictionaries

Bernsdorf, Wilhelm and **Bülow, Friedrich.** Wörterbuch der Soziologie. Stuttgart, Ferdinand Enke, 1955. 640p.   **CC4**

An encyclopedic dictionary of sociological terms with fairly long, signed contributions by 84 German specialists. Most articles contain brief bibliographies.

Fairchild, Henry Pratt. Dictionary of sociology. N.Y., Philosophical Lib., 1944. 342p.   **CC5**

Brief, signed articles giving definitions of sociological terms.

Mihanovich, Clement Simon, McNamara, Robert J. and **Tome, William N.** Glossary of sociological terms. Milwaukee, Bruce, 1957. 36p.   **CC6**

An attempt to give definitions of the terms and concepts used in sociology and related fields, grouped under broad categories.

SOCIAL CONDITIONS AND SOCIAL WELFARE

Social work

Bibliography

Council on Social Work Education. Building a social work library; a guide to the selection of books, periodicals and reference tools. N.Y., 1962. 105p.   **CC7**

A classified listing of books considered basic for a social-work library. No index.

—— United States government publications in social welfare: a selected bibliography. 2d ed. N.Y., 1956. 81p.   **CC8**

—— —— Supplements 1–2/3, 1957, 1960. 24p., 42p.

A classified selection of documents published by various departments of the government.

Joint University Council for Social Studies and Public Administration. Bibliography of social work and administration. London, Council, 1954. 117p.   **CC9**

Subtitle: A classified list of articles from selected British periodicals, 1930–1952, comp. by F. M. Birkett.

No author index.

Otto, Margaret M. A selected bibliography in philanthropy. (In Russell Sage Foundation. Report of the Princeton Conference on the History of Philanthropy in the United States. N.Y., 1956. p.41–84)   **CC10**

An annotated listing of some 500 titles dealing with the historical background and current trends in philanthropy.

Tighe, Leo W. A classified bibliography for the field of social work. Santa Clara, Calif., Premier Publ., 1959. 235p.   **CC11**

A classified bibliography treating counseling and guidance, and social work. Lists some 5500 books, articles, government documents, dissertations, and audio-visual materials.

Dissertations

Doctoral dissertations in social work. (In Social service review, Sept. 1954–) Annual.   **CC12**

Gives abstracts of completed dissertations and lists of those in preparation. Includes only dissertations submitted at graduate schools of social work.

Encyclopedias

Encyclopedia of social work: successor to the Social work year book. N.Y., National Assoc. of Social Workers, 1965– . v.15– .   **CC13**

The *Social work year book* was issued, 1929–49, by the Russell Sage Foundation; 1951–54, by the American Association of Social Workers; 1957–60, by the National Association of Social Workers.

The new title indicates a broadening of the scope and an increase in the number of articles, including biographies of outstanding social workers.

Contents: pt.1, History of social work and social welfare; pt.2, Articles and biographies; pt.3, Statistics (45 tables); pt.4, Directory of agencies. Index.

The second part includes signed articles and biographies of some length, with bibliographies; the fourth part continues the "Directory of agencies" as included in the *Social work year book,* listing international, national, and Canadian agencies, giving: name, date of founding, address, chief officer, membership, purpose and activities, periodicals, etc.

Dictionaries

Lorenzi, Angela. Glossary of social work terms in English-French-German. Köln, Carl Heymann, 1956. 172p. (Schriften des Deutschen Vereins für Öffentliche und Private Fürsorge) **CC14**

A glossary in three sections—English, French, German—translating social-work terms into the other languages.

Young, Erle Fiske. Dictionary of social welfare. N.Y., Social Sciences Pub., 1948. 218p. **CC15**

Gives definitions of technical, psychological, and slang terms.

Directories

Chambers, Merritt Madison. Charters of philanthropies: a study of selected trust instruments, charters, by-laws, and court decisions. N.Y., Carnegie Foundation for the Advancement of Teaching, 1948. 247p. **CC16**

Revised from Edward C. Elliott, and M. M. Chambers, *Charters of philanthropies* (N.Y., 1939), treating some but not all of the same foundations and adding others.

After an introduction discussing charitable foundations in general, the trust instruments, charters, bylaws, etc. of particular foundations are reproduced.

Encyclopedia of social work. N.Y., 1965– . **CC17**

Includes directory of international, national, and Canadian agencies. *See* CC13.

Federation of Protestant Welfare Agencies. Directory: a manual for benefactors and their advisors. 5th ed. N.Y., 1958. 200p. **CC18**

1st ed. 1935. Title varies.

Gives directory and descriptive information, with an index to types of service.

National Social Welfare Assembly, Inc. Service directory of national organizations, affiliated and associated with the . . . assembly, 1951– . N.Y., Assembly, 1951– . il. Annual. **CC19**

Gives territorial responsibility, fields of interest, addresses, and principal officials of the various agencies.

Public welfare directory, 1940– . Chicago, Amer. Public Welfare Assoc., 1940– . il. Annual. **CC20**

Lists federal, state, and local public assistance and welfare agencies, with directors.

For each state includes an introductory statement on its administration of public welfare and on "Where to write" for information on assistance, birth and death records, marriage and divorce records, mental health, correctional institutions, etc.

United Nations. Dept. of Social Affairs. International directory of nation-wide organizations concerned with family, youth and child-welfare. [N.Y.?], United Nations, 1952. 289p. **CC22**

Arranged by country, subdivided into government and voluntary agencies. Only names and addresses of organizations are given, with no indication of officers, scope, activities, etc.

Aging

Shock, Nathan W. A classified bibliography of gerontology and geriatrics. Stanford, Calif., Stanford Univ. Pr., 1951. 599p. **CC23**

———— ———— Supplement I, 1949–1955. 1957. 525p.

———— ———— Supplement II, 1956–1961. 1963. 624p.

Includes monographs and periodical articles—more than 51,000 items—in all languages. Attempts to cover the whole field, from biochemistry to social science and social work as they concern the aged.

Supplements appear in the *Journal of gerontology.*

U.S. Congress. Senate. Committee on Labor and Public Welfare. Directory of voluntary organizations in the field of aging: a report by the Subcommittee on Problems of the Aged and Aging . . . Wash., Govt. Prt. Off., 1961. 365p. **CC24**

An extensive list, classified by type, including state and local branches of national bodies. Often includes comments of officers to the subcommittee. Alphabetical index.

U.S. Dept. of Health, Education, and Welfare. Library. Selected references on aging: an annotated bibliography. Comp. for the Special Staff on Aging. Wash., Govt. Prt. Off., 1959. 110p. **CC25**

On cover: 1961 White House Conference edition.

Earlier editions were issued by the Federal Security Agency Library.

A classified listing with brief annotations.

U.S. National Voluntary Services and Service Organizations. Handbook of national organizations with delegate status at the White House Conference on Aging, with plans, programs, services in the field of aging. Wash., Govt. Prt. Off., 1959– . Annual (?). **CC26**

1st edition, 1959, issued loose-leaf with varying title by Dept. of Health, Education, and Welfare. 2d ed. 1960.

Alphabetical listing of several hundred organizations with information on structure, programs, publications, etc. for each.

U.S. Social Security Administration. Basic readings in social security. 25th anniversary of the Social Security Act, 1935–1960. Comp. . . . by the Library of the U.S. Dept. of Health, Education, and Welfare. Wash., Govt. Prt. Off., 1960. 221p. (Its Publ. no.28) **CC27**

For full information *see* CH263.

Blind

American Foundation for the Blind. Directory of agencies serving blind persons in the United States and Canada, comp. by Hilma Saterlee. 1st ed.– . N.Y., Foundation, 1926– . **CC28**

Pub. irregularly. Title varies: formerly *Directory of activities for the blind in the United States and Canada.*

Gives information on federal agencies, national voluntary agencies, and statewide, local, and regional services, with supplementary lists of various voluntary organizations.

—— Periodicals of special interest to blind persons in the United States and Canada. N.Y., Foundation, 1960. 48p. **CC29**

Has descriptive notes on format and content of each title.

New edition of *Directory of periodicals of special interest to the blind,* 1950.

Graham, Milton D. Social research on blindness: present status and future potentials. N.Y., Amer. Foundation for the Blind, 1960. 177p. **CC30**

Arranged by sections concerning types of activity with the blind. In each, major research projects are outlined in some detail, followed by extensive lists of relevant publications.

Lende, Helga. Books about the blind; a bibliographical guide to literature relating to the blind. New rev. ed. N.Y., Amer. Foundation for the Blind, 1953. 357p. **CC31**

1st ed. 1940.

An annotated bibliography of about 4200 references, more than half of which were not listed in the first edition. The main classes cover: work with the blind; education; psychology; vocations and economic adjustment; social adjustment; literature and reading; special groups; biographies and autobiographies; author index.

U.S. Library of Congress. Division for the Blind. Books on magnetic tape; a catalog of tape recordings which supplement the talking book program. Wash., 1962. 127p. **CC32**

Taped books available for loan to the blind.

—— Catalog of press Braille books provided by the Library of Congress, 1931–1948. Wash., Govt. Prt. Off., 1950. 163p. **CC33**

A classified listing, with author, title, and subject index, of books that the Library of Congress will lend free to the adult blind of the United States and its territories. Almost all titles listed are in Standard English Braille, Grade 2. Moon type books or hand-copied Braille are not included.

—— —— Cumulative supplement, 1948–54. 1955. 59p.

—— Union catalog of hand-copied books in Braille. Wash., Govt. Prt. Off., 1955. 581p. **CC34**

Includes more than 15,000 titles of hand-copied, as distinguished from press-copied, Braille books and indicates location of copies in various libraries of the United States. Complements the *Catalog of press Braille books,* above.

—— —— Supplement. 1960. 105p.

—— Talking books for the blind. Wash., Govt. Prt. Off., 1949– . Annual, with cumulations at intervals. **CC35**

Title varies.

Cumulations: 1934/48, 1948/53.

Classified lists, with author and title indexes, of talking books available without charge from the Library of Congress.

Deaf

DSH abstracts (American Speech and Hearing Association and Gallaudet College). Wash., Deafness, Speech and Hearing Pub., Oct. 1960– . v.1– . Quarterly. **CC36**

Abstracts of articles in the major languages on deafness, speech, and hearing. Titles are given in original language with English translation. Classified with author index. Annual author and subject indexes.

Flint, Richard W., Higgins, Francis C. and **Padden, Donald A.** Doctors' dissertations and masters' theses on the education of the deaf, 1897–1955. Wash., 1955. p.343–417. (Amer. annals of the deaf, v.100, no.4. Sept. 1955) **CC37**

Lists more than 1000 theses by author, with indexes by subject and by college.

Harvard University. Psycho-Acoustic Laboratory. Bibliography on hearing . . . S. S. Stevens, dir.; J. G. C. Loring, comp.; Dorothy Cohen, tech. ed. Cambridge, Mass., Harvard Univ. Pr., 1955. 599p. **CC38**

An enlargement of *A bibliography in audition,* comp. by George A. Miller [and others]. 1950.

This edition contains more than 10,000 titles with emphasis on the period 1938–52, with important materials before 1938. All titles listed in the 1st edition are repeated here; and the coverage has been expanded, particularly in the fields of psychology and the acoustics of music, deafness and the deafened, ultrasonics, and the effects of drugs on human and animal hearing. Arranged alphabetically by author with subject index. Titles are given in the original language with English translation in brackets.

Children and youth
Bibliography

Child development abstracts and bibliography. v.1– . June 1927– . Lafayette, Ind., Purdue Univ., Soc. for Research in Child Development, 1927– . 3 times a year. **CC39**

Title varies slightly. Frequency varies.

Publication of the Committee on Child Development, National Research Council, v.1–9.

Contains abstracts of articles from some 125 American and foreign periodicals and book reviews, usually signed. Arrangement is by subject. Author and subject index cumulates annually.

Menefee, Louise Arnold and **Chambers, Merritt Madison.** American youth, an annotated bibliography, prep. for the American Youth Commission. Wash., Amer. Council on Education, 1938. 492p. **CC40**

Annotated and classified, with alphabetical index.

Supplemented by:

Chambers, Merritt Madison and **Exton, Elaine.** Youth—key to America's future; an annotated bibliography. Wash., Amer. Council on Education, 1949. 117p. **CC40a**

U.S. Children's Bureau. Clearing House for Research in Child Life. Research relating to children. Bulletin, [1]– . Dec. 1948/June 1949– . Wash., Govt. Prt. Off., 1950– . Annual (Irregular). **CC41**

Each issue reports research in progress or very recently completed. Does not repeat studies included in earlier issues. Contains abstracts of studies arranged by broad subjects, and indexes of organizations, investigators, and subjects.

Bulletin 1, Suppl. 1–4. July 1949–Jan./April 1951.

Bulletin 2, Suppl. 1–4. Jan. 1952/March 1954–Feb./Nov. 1955.

No further supplements published.

Directories

Chambers, Merritt Madison. Youth-serving organizations; national non-governmental associations. 3d ed. Prep. for the Committee on Youth Problems. Wash., Amer. Council on Education, 1948. 162p. diagrams. **CC42**

1st ed. 1937.

A comprehensive list of organizations that concern themselves directly or indirectly with youth, arranged by class or type, with an index by names of organizations. For each organization usually gives: information on membership, officers, purpose, activities, publications, staff, and finances.

Tuttle, George. Youth organizations in Canada; a reference manual. Prep. for the Canadian Youth Commission. Toronto, Ryerson Pr., 1946. 110p. **CC43**

Gives name, membership, organization, purpose, activities, publications, staff, finances, etc.

U.S. Children's Bureau. Public training schools for delinquent children: directory. Wash., Govt. Prt. Off., 1940–55. v.1–4. **CC44**

Title varies: 1940– , *Directory of state, county, and municipal training schools caring for delinquent children in the United States.*

Youth organizations of Great Britain. 3d ed. Douglas Cooke, ed. London, Jordan, 1962. 168p. **CC45**

1st ed. 1944/45; 2d ed. 1945/46.

A directory giving organization, personnel, history, description, etc. of the various organizations devoted to youth.

CRIMINOLOGY

Bibliography

Cabot, Phillippe Sidney de Q. Juvenile delinquency; a critical annotated bibliography. N.Y., Wilson, 1946. 166p. **CC46**

972 numbered entries of books and periodical articles covering the period 1914–44. Arranged alphabetically with subject index.

Cumming, *Sir* **John.** A contribution towards a bibliography dealing with crime and cognate subjects. 3d ed. London, pr. by the Receiver for the Metropolitan Police District, New Scotland Yard, 1935. 107p. **CC47**

A classified bibliography of books and some periodical articles, covering approximately 50 years. International in scope but from the British viewpoint. Author index.

Excerpta Criminologica Foundation. Excerpta criminologica. Amsterdam, Foundation, 1961– . Bimonthly. **CC48**

An abstract journal of periodical articles and books on subjects relating to criminology. International in scope.

Greer, Sarah. Bibliography of police administration and police science. N.Y., Inst. of Public Admin., 1936. 152p. **CC49**

An annotated, classified bibliography covering different aspects of police administration and science in the various countries of the world.

International Society of Criminology. Éléments d'une documentation en criminologie. Selected documentation on criminology. Paris, UNESCO, 1961. 114p. (UNESCO. Social Science Clearing House. Reports and papers in the social sciences, no.14) **CC50**

In French and English.

A brief survey of the present state of the bibliography of criminology precedes the bibliography proper. The latter consists of a section of general materials, followed by listings of basic documentation arranged by country. Author index only. Lack of a table of contents reduces the usefulness of the work.

McDade, Thomas M. The annals of murder: a bibliography of books and pamphlets on American murders from colonial times to 1900. Norman, Univ. of Okla. Pr., 1961. 360p. il. **CC51**

Lists "separate publications devoted primarily to a single murder case which took place in what is now the United States and which occurred prior to 1900. . . . It includes trials, confessions, lives of murderers (but generally not of victims), speeches of counsel, etc."—*Pref.* Arranged by murderer when known, otherwise by victim. Name index.

Social Science Research Council. Committee on Survey of Research on Crime and Criminal Justice. Guide to material on crime and criminal justice . . . prep. by Augustus Frederick Kuhlman. . . . N.Y., Wilson, 1929. 633p. **CC52**

"A descriptive, classified, union catalog of books, monographs, and pamphlets in thirteen selected libraries, and of articles listed in the leading periodical indexes relating to all phases of crime and criminal justice in the United States."—*Pref.*

Arranged by class with a subject index.

—— —— Author index, prep. by D. C. Culver. N.Y., Wilson, 1934. 32p.

Issued in form to be inserted in the back of the main volume.

Continued by:

California. University. Bureau of Public Administration. Bibliography of crime and criminal justice, 1927–1931, 1932–1937, comp. by Dorothy Campbell Culver [Tompkins]. N.Y., Wilson, 1934–39. 2v. 413p., 391p. **CC53**

A comprehensive, classified bibliography of books and periodical articles. Includes works in various languages.

—— Sources for the study of the administration of criminal justice, comp. by Dorothy Campbell Tompkins. Sacramento, Calif. State Board of Corrections, 1949. 294p. **CC54**

Includes items published since 1938. Emphasizes material pertinent to conditions in California.

—— Administration of criminal justice, 1949–1956; a selected bibliography, comp. by Dorothy Campbell Tompkins. Sacramento, Calif. State Board of Corrections, 1956. 351p. **CC55**

Tompkins, Dorothy Campbell. The offender; a bibliography. Berkeley, Univ. of Calif. Inst. of Governmental Studies, 1963. 268p. **CC56**

"Covers the years since 1937, and in a measure supplements the Culver *Bibliography of crime and criminal justice, 1932–1937* [CC53]. It draws on the fields of psychiatry, psychology, medicine, education, sociology, social welfare, and criminology."—*Pref.*

Classified, with author-subject index.

—— Probation since World War II; a bibliography. Berkeley, Inst. of Governmental Studies, Univ. of Calif., 1964. 311p. **CC57**

An annotated bibliography of works in English, published since World War II, on probation and parole. Supplements the author's other bibliographies on criminal justice.

Encyclopedias and dictionaries

Branham, Vernon Carnegie and **Kutash, Samuel B.** Encyclopedia of criminology. N.Y., Philosophical Lib., 1949. 527p. **CC58**

Includes some 100 fairly long articles signed by specialists. Bibliographies are appended. Uneven.

Dizionario di criminologia, per opera di numerosi autori ed a cura di Eugenio Florian, Alfredo Niceforo [e] Nicola Pende. Milano, Vallardi, 1943. 2v. il. **CC59**

Long, signed articles with bibliographies; titles primarily in Italian and French.

Elsevier's Dictionary of criminal science, in eight languages: English/American, French, Italian, Spanish, Portuguese, Dutch, Swedish, and German; comp. and arr. on an English alphabetical base by Johann Anton Adler. Amsterdam, Elsevier [distr. by Van Nostrand, Princeton, N.J.], 1960. 1460p. **CC60**

Directories

American Correctional Association. Directory: state and federal correctional institutions of the United States of America, Canada, England and Scotland. N.Y., Assoc., 1955– . Annual. **CC61**

Title varies. Issued until 1954 under the earlier name of the association, American Prison Association.

RACE RELATIONS

Hellmann, Ellen and **Abrahams, Leah.** Handbook on race relations in South Africa. Pub. for the South African Institute of Race Relations. Capetown, London, Oxford Univ. Pr., 1949. 778p.   **CC62**

Survey articles by authorities on various phases of race relations in South Africa. Covers such subjects as: population, government, law, labor, trade unions, agriculture, taxation, education, social welfare, politics, religion, literature, music, art, race cooperation, race attitude, etc. Some documentation in footnotes, but no bibliography.

Thompson, Edgar T. and **Thompson, Alma Macy.** Race and region; a descriptive bibliography. Chapel Hill, Univ. of North Carolina Pr., 1949. 194p.   **CC63**

A comprehensive, annotated, classified bibliography on race relations compiled with special reference to the relations between Whites and Negroes in the United States. Based on collections in Duke University, the University of North Carolina, and North Carolina College in Durham, with indication of location of copies in these libraries.

Viet, Jean. Selected documentation for the study of race relations. Paris, UNESCO, 1958. 81p. (Reports and papers in the social sciences, no.9)   **CC64**

Racial groups

Gypsies

Leeds. University. Library. Brotherton Library. Catalogue of the Romany collection formed by D. U. McGrigor Phillips and presented to the University of Leeds. Edinburgh, pub. for the Brotherton collection by Nelson, 1962. 227p.   **CC65**

A classified bibliography of more than 1200 items, including books and pamphlets, manuscripts, music, letters, playbills, pictures, engravings, etc., relating to Gypsies in many countries. Author and title index.

Indians

American Indian index. Chicago, J. A. Huebner, 1953– . no.1– . (In progress)   **CC66**

No.1–103, A–Z; no.104, May 1963, starts Sec. 2, A– . A subject index to books, periodicals, and documents.

Dockstader, Frederick J. The American Indian in graduate studies; a bibliography of theses and dissertations. N.Y., Museum of the American Indian, Heye Foundation, 1957. 399p. (Contributions from the Museum of the American Indian, Heye Foundation, v.15)   **CC67**

An alphabetical listing of 3684 theses, appearing from 1890 to 1955; "selection has been extended beyond anthropology to include all academic fields . . . such as history, sociology, education, music, art and literature." Many entries have brief explanatory notes. Subject index.

Fenton, William Nelson. American Indian and white relations to 1830: needs and opportunities for study; an essay. A bibliography by L. H. Butterfield, Wilcomb E. Washburn and William N. Fenton. Chapel Hill, Univ. of North Carolina Pr., 1957. 138p.   **CC68**

Published for the Institute of Early American History and Culture, Williamsburg, Va.

The major section is a selective bibliography compiled to serve the needs of graduate students by bringing together, in one list, studies of Indian-white relations both in the humanities and in the social sciences. A section on manuscript sources gives locations of collections in the United States and Canada.

Hargrett, Lester. A bibliography of the constitutions and laws of the American Indians. Cambridge, Harvard Univ. Pr., 1947. 124p.   **CC69**

Arranged by tribe. Annotated. Locates copies in some 50 public and private libraries.

Hodge, Frederick Webb. Handbook of American Indians

north of Mexico. Wash., Govt. Prt. Off., 1907–10. 2v. (Repr.: N.Y., Pageant Books, 1959)   **CC70**
For full description see CD32.

Parra, Manuel Germán and **Moreno, Wigberto Jiménez.** Bibliografía indigenista de México y Centroamérica (1850–1950). México, Inst. Nacional Indigenista, 1954. 342p. (Memorias del Inst. Nacional Indigenista. v.4)   **CC71**

A comprehensive bibliography of books and articles, in various languages, covering all aspects of the life of Indians of Mexico and Central America.

Steward, Julian Haynes. Handbook of South American Indians. . . . Wash., Govt. Prt. Off., 1946–59. 7v. **CC72**
For full description see CD35.

Swanton, John Reed. The Indian tribes of North America. Wash., Govt. Prt. Off., 1952. 726p. maps. (Smithsonian Inst. Bureau of American Ethnology. Bull. 145)   **CC73**

Arranged by state and then by other countries of North America. Gives extensive information on Indian tribes: their location, history, population, connection in which they have become noted, villages, meanings of names, etc. Detailed index.
Bibliography, p.643–82.

Negroes

Bibliography

Dumond, Dwight Lowell. A bibliography of antislavery in America. Ann Arbor, Univ. of Michigan Pr., 1961. 119p.   **CC74**

Prepared to accompany the author's *Antislavery; the crusade for freedom in America* (1961), "this is the literature written and circulated by those active in the antislavery movement and used by the author."—*Note.* Includes works published up to the time of the Civil War.

Hampton Institute, Hampton, Va. Collis P. Huntington Library. A classified catalogue of the Negro collection, comp. by the Writers' Program of the Work Projects Administration in the state of Virginia. Sponsored by Hampton Institute. [n.p.], 1940. 255p., [35]p.   **CC75**

More than 5000 titles on the Negro in Africa and in America. Particularly strong in material on slavery and reconstruction. Classified, with author and title index.

National Urban League (for Social Service among Negroes). Dept. of Research. Selected bibliography on the Negro. 4th ed. June 1951. N.Y., League, 1951. 124p.   **CC76**

A classified, annotated bibliography. No index.

New York. Public Library. Schomburg Collection. Dictionary catalog of the Schomburg collection of Negro literature and history. Boston, G. K. Hall, 1962. 9v.   **CC77**

A photographic reproduction of the cards of a dictionary catalog of "a library and archive of materials devoted to Negro life and history . . . international in scope . . . includes books by authors of African descent, regardless of subject matter or language . . . and all significant materials about peoples of African descent."—*Pref.* Includes more than 36,000 bound volumes.

Texas. Southern University, Houston, Texas. Library. Catalogue, Heartman Negro collection. Houston, [1956?]. 325p.   **CC78**

A collection of approximately 15,000 items, some three fourths of which have been cataloged. "Consists of books, pamphlets, periodicals, maps, broadsides, documents, almanacs, lithographs, oil paintings, musical scores, clippings, cartoons, [etc.] dating from 1600 to 1955."

Arranged by Dewey Decimal Classification. No index.

Work, Monroe Nathan. Bibliography of the Negro in Africa and America. N.Y., Wilson, 1928. 698p.   **CC79**

A comprehensive bibliography of more than 17,000 selected titles of books, pamphlets, and periodical articles. Classified, with author index.

Annuals

Negro year book, 1912–52. Tuskegee Inst., Ala., Dept. of Records and Research, 1912–52. 11v.   **CC80**

Ceased publication with v.11.

Pub. 1912, 1913, 1914/15, 1916/17, 1918/19, 1921/22, 1925/26, 1931/32, 1937/38, 1941/46, 1952.

1st–9th ed., ed. by Monroe N. Work; 10th–11th ed., ed. by Jessie P. Guzman.

Statistics and survey articles on the Negro in the United States—his conditions and achievements.

Biography

Who's who in colored America; a biographical dictionary of notable living persons of African descent in America. Brooklyn, N.Y., Who's Who in Colored America, 1927– .   **CC81**

For full record *see* AJ55.

C D

Anthropology and Ethnology

❧ Few general reference books in anthropology are available, as most works treat specific countries or areas. The *International bibliography of social and cultural anthropology* (CD29) is a comprehensive annual bibliography; the *Atlas for anthropology* (CD43) is useful for its ethnic maps; and Coon's *Origin of races* (CD31) is a well-documented text which may substitute for a reference manual.

BIBLIOGRAPHY

General

Comas, Juan. Historia y bibliografía de los congresos internacionales de ciencias antropológicas: 1865–1954. México, Dirección General de Publicaciones, 1956. 490p. il. (Universidad Nacional Autónoma de México. Inst. de Historia. Publicaciones, 1. ser., núm. 37)   **CD1**

Covers the activities and publications of four major international organizations in anthropology and related fields as well as those of several smaller bodies. The second part is a classified subject bibliography of some 3000 papers which have been published in the reports of the more important congresses.

International catalogue of scientific literature: P, Anthropology. 1st–14th annual issues, 1903–19. London, 1903–20. 14v.   **CD2**

For full description *see* EA12.

Keesing, Felix Maxwell. Culture change; an analysis and bibliography of anthropological sources to 1952 . . . Stanford, Calif., Stanford Univ. Pr.; London, Oxford Univ. Pr., [1953]. 242p. (Stanford anthropological ser., no.1)   **CD3**

The analytical survey (p.1–94) is divided by broad periods, and discusses the trends in research and outstanding publications in each. The bibliography (p.104–242) is chronological from 1820, with items listed alphabetically for each year. Information given is very brief. Periodical articles are included. No index.

Krogman, Wilton Marion. A bibliography of human morphology, 1914–1939. Chicago, Univ. of Chicago Pr., 1941. 385p.   **CD4**

Classed index to materials in more than 900 periodicals under such headings as: osteology, races of man, prehistory of man, craniology, human heredity, nervous system, etc. Author index.

Miller, Mamie Ruth Tanquist. . . . An author, title, and subject check list of Smithsonian Institution publications relating to anthropology. Pub. in cooperation with the School of American Research. . . . Albuquerque, Univ. of New Mexico Pr., 1946. 218p. (Univ. of New Mexico. Bull. Bibliographical ser., v.1, no.2; whole no.405) **CD5**

For publications of the Bureau of American Ethnology, *see* CD8.

Mukherjee, Ajit Kumar. Annotated guide to reference materials in the human sciences. N.Y., Asia Pub. House, [1963, c1962]. 267p.   **CD6**

A guide to materials—primarily in English—in anthropology, sociology, and social psychology.

For full information *see* CA5.

U.S. Bureau of American Ethnology. Bulletin. Index to Bulletins 1–100, with index to Contributions to North American ethnology, Introductions, and Miscellaneous publications, by Biren Bonnerjea. Wash., Govt. Prt. Off., 1963. 726p. (U.S. Bureau of Amer. Ethnology. Bull. 178)   **CD7**

Includes subject, author, and title indexes and index to illustrations.

—— List of publications of the Bureau of American Ethnology, with index to authors and titles, rev. to Dec. 1961. Wash., Govt. Prt. Off., 1962. 130p.   **CD8**

—— General index: Annual reports of the Bureau, v.1–48 (1879–1931) . . . comp. by Biren Bonnerjea. Wash., Govt. Prt. Off., 1933. P.25–1220. (In its 48th Annual report, 1930/31)   **CD9**

Pt.1, Subject index; pt.2, List of annual reports . . . with an index to authors and titles.

Current

Biennial review of anthropology, 1959– . Ed. by Bernard J. Siegel. Stanford, Calif., Stanford Univ. Pr., 1959– . v.1– . Biennial.   **CD10**

Describes and evaluates the more noteworthy recent papers and monographs in anthropology. International in coverage. Arranged in chapters representing fields of current interest; each chapter is written by a specialist and includes a bibliography. Contains a subject index.

The Americas

Baldus, Herbert. Bibliografia crítica da etnologia brasileira. São Paulo, [Ed. São Nicolau Indústria Grafica], 1954.

859p. il. (Comissão do IV Centenário da Cidade de São Paulo. Serviço de Comemoraçoes Culturais)   **CD11**

An annotated bibliography of 1785 titles in various languages.

Bernal, Ignacio. Bibliografía de arqueología y etnografía; Mesoamérica y norte de México, 1514–1960. México, Inst. Nacional de Antropología e Historia, 1962. 634p. maps. (Inst. Nacional de Antropología e Historia. Memorias. 7)   **CD12**

More than 13,000 numbered entries, including books, periodical articles, reports, etc., classified by region and then by subject.

Author index included.

Comas, Juan. Bibliografía selectiva de las culturas indígenas de América. México, 1953. 292p. maps. (Inst. Pan-Americano de Geografía e Historia. Comisión de Historia. Publicación núm. 166. Bibliografías, I)   **CD13**

2014 entries. Classed arrangement, with indexes to indigenous groups and to authors. Lists works in various languages with a preponderance of English titles.

Murdock, George Peter. Ethnographic bibliography of North America. 3d ed. New Haven, Conn., Human Relations Area Files, 1960. 393p. 15 maps. (Behavior science bibliographies)   **CD14**

1st ed. 1941 (Yale anthropological studies, v.1); 2d ed. 1953.

A selective, classified bibliography—organized by areas and within each area by tribal groups—of printed materials on primitive and historical cultures. This edition is completely revised, bringing the record down to 1958 with incomplete coverage of 1959 and early 1960. The number of titles has been increased from some 9400 in the 1st edition to more than 17,300 in the 3d edition.

O'Leary, Timothy J. Ethnographic bibliography of South America. New Haven, Conn., Human Relations Area Files, 1963. 387p. maps. (Behavior science bibliographies)   **CD15**

A listing of books, periodical articles, reports, etc., intended to cover ethnographic literature on continental South America through 1961. No coverage of Panama and the Caribbean Islands except where the latter belong to Colombia or Venezuela. The main part is arranged by areas, and within each area by tribal groups. Includes list of works on general South America and list of bibliographic aids.

Rouse, Irving and **Goggin, John M.** An anthropological bibliography of the eastern seaboard, comp. under the auspices of the Federation. New Haven, Conn., pub. by the Federation at the Yale Peabody Museum, 1947, 1963. 2v. (Eastern States Archeological Federation. Research publ. no.1, 2)   **CD16**

Place of publication varies.

An alphabetical listing by author of books, periodical articles, and reports, arranged in three sections: (1) archaeology, (2) ethnology, and (3) Indian history. Each section is subdivided into regions.

v.2 is a supplement covering 1947–59 publications. After 1959, publications are listed in *Abstracts of New World archaeology* (DA62).

Seville. Universidad. Seminario de Antropología Americana. Publicaciones. v.1–6. Sevilla, 1960–64. (In progress)   **CD17**

Contents: v.1, José Alcina Franch. Bibliografía básica de arqueología americana. 1960. 125p.; v.2, El Americanismo en las revistas: antropología, 1. 1961. 78p.; v.3, Alfredo Jiménez Múñez. Mitos de creación en Sudamérica. 1962. 102p.; v.4, El Americanismo en las revistas: antropología, 2. 1962. 144p.; v.5, Helmuth Fuchs. Bibliografía básica de etnología de Venezuela. 1964. 251p.; v.6, El Americanismo en las revistas: antropología, 3. 1964. 120p.

Africa

Hambly, Wilfrid Dyson. Source book for African anthropology. Chicago, 1937. 2v. (953p.). il. (Anthropological ser., Field Museum of Natural History, v.26. Publ. 394, 396)   **CD18**

Bibliographies, p.728–866.

—— —— Supplement. Bibliography of African anthropology, 1937–1949. Chicago, Natural History Museum, 1952. p.161–292. (Fieldiana: Anthropology, v.37, no.2)

Selective but extensive bibliographies listing both books and periodical articles.

Mylius, Norbert. Afrika Bibliographie, 1943–1951. Wien, Verein Freunde der Volkerkunde, 1952. 237p.   **CD19**

Serves as a supplement to Wieschhoff, *Anthropological bibliography of Negro Africa* (CD22). After general sections which list bibliographies and periodicals, the material is arranged by geographical region and subdivided by subject. Periodical articles are not included.

Rita-Ferreira, A. Bibliografia etnológica de Moçambique (das origens a 1954). Lisboa, Junta de Investigações do Ultramar, 1961. 254p.   **CD20**

Contains approximately 1000 entries, mostly in English, with annotations in Portuguese. Includes books and periodical articles, arranged first by region and then by group.

Schapera, Isaac. Select bibliography of South African native life and problems. Comp. for the Inter-University Committee for African Studies. London, Oxford Univ. Pr., 1941. 249p.   **CD21**

Contains the more important books, periodical articles, and reports, with brief annotations, published prior to 1939. Arranged in sections: physical anthropology, archaeology, ethnology, modern status and conditions, and linguistics. Author index included.

—— —— Supplement. Modern status and conditions. Bibliography, by A. Holden and A. Jacoby. Cape Town, [Univ., School of Librarianship], 1950. 2 pts. in 1v.

—— —— 2d supplement. Modern status and conditions, 1950–1958. A select bibliography, by R. Giffen and J. Back. Cape Town, Univ., School of Librarianship, 1958. 2 pts. in 1v.

Wieschhoff, Heinrich Albert. Anthropological bibliography of Negro Africa. New Haven, Conn., Amer. Oriental Soc., 1948. 461p. (American oriental ser., v.23)   **CD22**

Arranged by name of tribe and geographical area, in alphabetical order.

Asia

Calcutta. National Library. Indian anthropology, comp. by J. M. Kanitkar. Ed., rev., and enl. by D. L. Banerjee and A. K. Ohdedar. Calcutta, 1960. 290p. (A bibliography of Indology, v.1)   **CD23**

More than 2000 books and articles on Indian anthropology and related subjects: sociology, history, geography, etc. Many annotations, some extensive. Arrangement is by geographical region, with a final section on India as a whole. Author and subject indexes.

Field, Henry. Bibliography on southwestern Asia. Coral Gables, Fla., Univ. of Miami Pr., 1953. 106p.   **CD24**

An anthropogeographical bibliography of 3016 items, mainly periodical articles, published between 1940 and 1952. Arrangement is under the two main headings—Anthropogeography and Natural History—the latter being further subdivided into zoology (in seven subsections covering birds, fish, etc.) and botany. Index of authors.

—— —— II–VI. 2d–6th compilations. 1955–59. Annual.

—— —— Subject index. v.1–5.

The annuals follow the same plan as the basic volume.

Fürer-Haimendorf, Elizabeth von. An anthropological bibliography of South Asia, together with a directory of recent anthropological field work. Paris, Mouton & Co., 1958–64. v.1–2. (École Pratique des Hautes Études. 6ᵉ sec. Le monde d'outre-mer passé et présent. 4. sér.: Bibliographies III, IV) **CD25**

Includes books, periodical articles, and unpublished dissertations in Western languages, dealing mainly with the cultural and social aspects of anthropology. Other fields are covered less completely. The geographic area comprises India, Pakistan, Nepal, Sikkim, Bhutan, and Ceylon. Arranged by regional sections with subject subdivisions, each including a directory of field research and an author index. v.1 includes a select list of works published prior to 1940 and works issued 1940–54; v.2 covers 1955–59. Further volumes are planned to appear at five-year intervals.

Kennedy, Raymond. Bibliography of Indonesian peoples and cultures. 2d rev. ed. Rev. and ed. by Thomas W. Maretzki and H. Th. Fischer. New Haven, Conn., Human Relations Area Files, 1962. 207p. maps. (Behavior science bibliographies. Southeast Asia studies, Yale University) **CD26**

For full information *see* DE71.

Australia

Greenway, John. Bibliography of the Australian aborigines and the native peoples of Torres Strait to 1959. Sydney, London, Angus & Robertson, 1963. 420p. **CD27**

An alphabetical listing of 10,283 books and periodical articles, primarily in English but with some titles in other European languages. Indexes by subject and by aboriginal tribe.

Europe

Ripley, William Zebina. Selected bibliography of the anthropology and ethnology of Europe. Boston, Pub. Lib., 1899. 160p. **CD28**

Also published as supplement to the author's *Races of Europe* (N.Y., Appleton, 1899).

Contains nearly 2000 entries, arranged by author, including books and serial publications. Subject index with references to main entries.

INDEXES

International bibliography of social and cultural anthropology. Bibliographie internationale d'anthropologie sociale et culturelle. v.1, 1955– . Prep. by the International Committee for Social Sciences Documentation in cooperation with the International Congress of Anthropological and Ethnological Sciences. London, Tavistock; Chicago, Aldine, 1958– . v.1– . Annual. (International bibliography of the social sciences) **CD29**

Publisher varies. v.1–5, UNESCO, as part of *Documentation in the social sciences;* v.6, as *Publication* of the International Committee for Social Sciences Documentation.

A companion to other UNESCO annual bibliographies in the social sciences: sociology (CC2), economics (CH25), and political science (CI19). Attempts to list scientific works in many languages from many countries. Includes books, periodical articles, and duplicated materials but not unpublished typed theses, etc. Arranged by a special classification scheme, with an author index and subject indexes in both English and French.

Royal Anthropological Institute of Great Britain and Ireland. Library. Index to current periodicals received in the Library of the Royal Anthropological Institute. v.1– . Jan./March 1963– . London, 1962– . Quarterly. **CD30**

Includes a "Specimen issue" Jan./March 1962.

A classified index, arranged regionally, to 400 periodicals, covering all branches of "the science of man."

DICTIONARIES AND HANDBOOKS

Coon, Carleton Stevens. Origin of races. N.Y., Knopf, 1962. 724p. il. maps. **CD31**

A well-documented text. Includes: Statistical appendix, p.[667–84]; Bibliography, p.685–710; Glossary, p.711–24; Index.

Hodge, Frederick Webb. Handbook of American Indians north of Mexico. Wash., Govt. Prt. Off., 1907–10. [Reissued 1912] 2v. il. (U.S. Bureau of American Ethnology. Bull. 30) (Repr.: N.Y., Pageant Books, 1959) **CD32**

"Contains a descriptive list of the stocks, confederacies, tribes, tribal divisions and settlements north of Mexico, accompanied with the various names by which these have been known, together with biographies of Indians of note, sketches of their history, archeology, manners, arts, customs and institutions, and the aboriginal words incorporated in the English language. . . . Accompanying each synonym (the earliest known date always being given) a reference to the authority is noted, and these references form practically a bibliography of the tribe for those who wish to pursue the subject further." —*Pref.*

—— Handbook of Indians of Canada. Pub. as an appendix to the Tenth report of the Geographic Board of Canada. Ottawa, Parmelee, 1913. 632p. maps. **CD33**

A reprint, with some additional material, of the articles in the author's *Handbook of American Indians north of Mexico* (CD32) which relate to Canada.

International dictionary of regional European ethnology and folklore. Copenhagen, Rosenkilde & Bagger, 1960– . v.1– . (In progress) **CD34**

"Under the auspices of the International Council for Philosophy and Humanistic Studies and with the support of UNESCO published by CIAP (International Commission of Folk Arts and Folklore)."

Contents: v.1, Åke Hultkrantz, General ethnological concepts.

An alphabetically arranged dictionary designed "to give definitions of ethnological and folkloristic technical terms and concepts . . ."—*Introd.* Arranged by English term with synonyms in French, Spanish, German, and Swedish, and descriptive definitions and references to the literature of the subject.

Bibliography, p.251–52.

v.2 is to cover folk literature.

Steward, Julian Haynes. Handbook of South American Indians. . . . Prep. in cooperation with the United States Department of State as a project of the Interdepartmental Committee on Cultural and Scientific Cooperation. Wash., Govt. Prt. Off., 1946–59. 7v. il. ([U.S.] Bureau of American Ethnology. Bull. 143) (Repr.: N.Y., Cooper Square Publ., 1963) **CD35**

At head of title: Smithsonian Institution. Bureau of American Ethnology. . . .

v.1, The marginal tribes; v.2, The Andean civilizations; v.3, The tropical forest tribes; v.4, The circum-Caribbean tribes; v.5, The comparative ethnology of South American Indians; v.6, Physical anthropology, linguistics, and cultural geography of South American Indians; v.7, Index.

Anthropological descriptions by American scientists of all phases of life of the tribes considered, with especial attention to the time of a tribe's first contact with Europeans. Well illustrated. Good ethnographical maps. Extensive bibliographies.

U.S. Immigration Commission, 1907. Dictionary of races or peoples. Wash., Govt. Prt. Off., 1911. 150p. maps. (Its Reports, v.5) **CD36**

"While this dictionary treats of more than 600 subjects covering all the important and many of the obscure branches of the human family, it is intended primarily as a discussion of the various races and the peoples indigenous to the countries furnishing the present immigration movement to the United States or which may become sources of future immigration."—*Pref.*

Popular rather than scientific. Has short articles; general bibliography, p.8–12, but no bibliographies in the text; maps; and good cross references.

Winick, Charles. Dictionary of anthropology. N.Y., Philosophical Lib., 1956. 579p. (Repr.: Paterson, N.J., Littlefield, Adams, 1964) **CD37**

A dictionary of anthropological terms, uneven in coverage but useful for the definitions of unusual terms not usually found in general dictionaries.

Wright, Muriel H. A guide to the Indian tribes of Oklahoma. Norman, Univ. of Okla. Pr., 1951. 300p. il. **CD38**

Approximately one third of the total Indian population of the United States is found in Oklahoma, distributed among 65 tribes. Information about each of these tribes is organized under the following headings: origin and meaning of name, linguistic family, present location, numbers, history, organization, life and culture, and ceremonials. Space devoted to each varies from 1 to 20 pages. Includes "Suggested readings" and an extensive bibliography indicating libraries and other locations of material.

DIRECTORIES

International directory of anthropological institutions, ed. by William L. Thomas, Jr., and Anna M. Pikelis . . . N.Y., Wenner-Gren Foundation for Anthropological Research, 1953. 468p. **CD39**

Arrangement is under geographical division, either individual countries or closely related groups of countries (e.g., Netherlands and Belgium, Middle America and the Caribbean). For each of these sections a general outline of the history and scope of anthropological research is given, followed by detailed information on individual institutions, generally including officers, date of foundation, purpose, publications, research facilities, etc. Alphabetical indexes of institutions and of cities and towns.

Pacific anthropologists, 1964. Comp. by Robert N. Bowen and Adrienne L. Kaeppler. Honolulu, Pacific Scientific Information Center, Bernice P. Bishop Museum, [1964]. unpaged. **CD40**

Lists 604 individuals interested in Pacific anthropology. Names arranged alphabetically, with addresses and fields of interest. Includes interest index and residence index.

HISTORY

Penniman, Thomas Kenneth. A hundred years of anthropology. With contributions by Beatrice Blackwood and J. S. Weiner. 2d ed. rev. London, Duckworth, 1952. 512p. **CD41**

Bibliography, p.457–500. Index of subjects and authors.

BIOGRAPHY

International directory of anthropologists. 3d ed. Melville J. Herskovits, ed. . . . Wash., D.C., 1950. 210p. **CD42**

Prepared under the auspices of the Committee on International Relations in Anthropology of the Division of Anthropology and Psychology, National Research Council, American Anthropological Association.

1st ed. 1938; 2d ed. 1940.

A biographical directory in alphabetical arrangement, giving name, address, date of birth, education, positions, areas of interest, and field trips. Russian anthropologists omitted, as no information was available.

ATLASES

Spencer, Robert F. and **Johnson, Elden.** Atlas for anthropology. Dubuque, Iowa, W. C. Brown Co., 1960. 52p. fold. maps. **CD43**

This series of 15 maps, intended as a manual for beginning students, covers tribes and ethnic groups, language areas, Old World prehistory, and New World prehistory.

A useful atlas moderately priced.

C E

Mythology

MUSTS:

Such standard works as Gayley's *Classic myths* (CE10) and the *Mythology of all races* (CE5) have been joined more recently by Edith Hamilton's *Mythology* (CE2) and the *Larousse encyclopedia of mythology* (CE4). Diehl's *Religions, mythologies, folklores* (CE1, BB2) should be consulted for more extensive listings.

INTERNATIONAL

Diehl, Katharine Smith. Religions, mythologies, folklores: an annotated bibliography. 2d ed. N.Y., Scarecrow, 1962. 573p. **CE1**

An extensive bibliography of materials on mythology and folklore; *see* BB2.

Hamilton, Edith. Mythology. Illus. by Steele Savage. Boston, Little, 1942. 497p. **CE2**

Includes both classic and Norse myths with comparisons of the original and the later versions. Family charts, p.457–73.

Haussig, Hans Wilhelm. Wörterbuch der Mythologie. Stuttgart, Ernst Klett, 1961?– . Abt. I, T.I, Lfg. 1–2. il. (In progress) **CE3**

Abt. I, Die alten Kulturvölker: T.I, Vorderer Orient; T.II, Das alte Europa.

The first parts of a work treating the mythologies of the world. Arranged by geographical area, with each section written by a specialist.

The first volume deals with Egypt and the Near East; the second, with the various countries of eastern Europe. Later volumes are announced to cover Iran, Central and East Asia, and early America.

Larousse encyclopedia of mythology. With an introd. by

Robert Graves. [Tr. by Richard Aldington and Delano Ames, and rev. by a panel of editorial advisers from the Larousse mythologie générale, ed. by Felix Guirand] N.Y., Prometheus, 1959. 500p. il.   **CE4**

First published in France in 1935. Presents articles on the mythologies of various countries and civilizations from prehistory to present times. Not an encyclopedia in the usual sense of the term, as the material is presented in essay form with no easy approach to specific points. Includes various aspects of folklore, legend, and religious customs.

Mythology of all races. Louis Herbert Gray, ed.: v.1, 3, 6, 9–12; John Arnott MacCulloch and G. F. Moore, eds.: v.2, 4–5, 7–8, 13. Boston, Archaeological Inst. of America, Marshall Jones Co., 1916–32. 13v. il.   **CE5**

v.1, *Greek and Roman,* by W. S. Fox; v.2, *Eddic,* by J. A. MacCulloch; v.3, *Celtic,* by J. A. MacCulloch. *Slavic,* by Jan Machal; v.4, *Finno-Ugric, Siberian,* by Uno Holmberg; v.5, *Semitic,* by S. H. Langdon; v.6, *Indian,* by A. B. Keith. *Iranian,* by A. J. Carnoy; v.7, *Armenian,* by M. H. Ananikian. *African,* by Alice Werner; v.8, *Chinese,* by J. C. Ferguson. *Japanese,* by Masaharu Anesaki; v.9, *Oceanic,* by R. B. Dixon; v.10, *North American,* by H. B. Alexander; v.11, *Latin-American,* by H. B. Alexander; v.12, *Egyptian,* by W. Max Müller. *Indo-Chinese,* by J. G. Scott; v.13, Index.

An important set which contains valuable reference material in both text and illustrations. The general index makes it the most useful single reference work in the field available in English.

Robinson, Herbert Spencer and **Wilson, Knox.** The encyclopaedia of myths and legends of all nations. [Rev. ed.] by Barbara Leonie Picard. London, Edward Ward, 1962. 244p.   **CE6**

1st edition (Garden City, N.Y., Doubleday, 1950) had title *Myths and legends of all nations.*

Sykes, Egerton. Everyman's dictionary of nonclassical mythology. [3d ed.] London, Dent; N.Y., Dutton, 1961. 280p.   **CE7**

1st ed. 1952. Present edition contains revisions and an appendix.

Several thousand personal and place-names, epithets, concepts, etc. are treated briefly but pointedly. Cross references are indicated, and there is a selective bibliography, arranged by geographical area.

CHINESE

Werner, Edward Theodore Chalmers. Dictionary of Chinese mythology. Shanghai, Kelly, 1932. 627p.   **CE8**

"This dictionary has been written with the object of furnishing, in a compact form, information concerning the entities, animate and inanimate, constituting the Chinese supernal and infernal hierarchies."—*Pref.*

EGYPTIAN

Bonnet, Hans. Reallexikon der ägyptischen Religionsgeschichte. Berlin, de Gruyter, 1952. 883p. il.   **CE9**

An encyclopedic dictionary, giving definitions and descriptions of persons, cults, concepts, etc. in Egyptian religious history and mythology. Bibliographical references are to available rather than to original sources.

GREEK AND ROMAN

Gayley, Charles Mills. Classic myths in English literature and in art, based originally on Bulfinch's Age of fable (1855) accompanied by an interpretative and illustrative commentary. . . . New ed. rev. and enl. Boston, Ginn, [1939]. 597p. il.   **CE10**

A standard text frequently reprinted, treating the classical myths particularly in their relationship to English poetry and to art, with brief chapters on Norse and German mythology. Includes an extensive commentary and detailed indexes.

Grimal, Pierre. Dictionnaire de la mythologie grecque et romaine. 2. éd. corr. Paris, Presses Universitaires de France, 1958. 576p. il.   **CE11**

A compact dictionary of the most generally known myths and legends, with bibliographical references and 40 genealogical tables. An index of mythological, historical, and geographical proper names and another of legendary themes.

Hunger, Herbert. Lexikon der griechischen und römischen Mythologie mit Hinweisen auf das Fortwirken antiker Stoffe und Motive in der bildenden Kunst, Literatur und Musik des Abendlandes bis zur Gegenwart. 5. erw. und erg. Aufl. Wien, Hollinek, 1959. 387p. il. **CE12**

1st ed. 1953.

A concise dictionary of Greek and Roman mythology arranged alphabetically, with bibliographical references to the themes in art, literature, and music.

Roscher, Wilhelm Heinrich. Ausführliches Lexikon der griechischen und römischen Mythologie. Leipzig, Teubner, 1884–1937. 6v. and 3 suppl. il.   **CE13**

v.1–6, A–Z und Nachträge; Supplements: [1] Epitheta deorum ed. by C. F. H. Bruchmann and I. B. Carter, 1893–1902. 2v.; [2] Mythische Kosmographie der Griechen, by E. H. Berger, 1904. 2v.; [3] Geschichte der klassischen Mythologie u. Religionsgeschichte, by Otto Gruppe, 1921. 248p.

Scholarly, signed articles with bibliographies and good illustrations. The most complete work; valuable for large reference or university libraries but not suited to other types.

TEUTONIC

Guerber, Hélène Adeline. Myths of northern lands, narrated with special reference to literature and art. N.Y., Amer. Book Co., 1895. 319p. il.   **CE14**

A useful collection of the Norse myths written in a popular style. Includes numerous poetical quotations with index to same, in addition to glossary and index to names, places, key words, etc.

C F

Folklore and Popular Customs

❦ Libraries of all sizes will need some works on folklore. *Funk and Wagnalls Standard dictionary of folklore, mythology and legend* (CF11) is a good, comprehensive encyclopedia for quick reference. Frazer's *Golden bough* (CF8), a great mine of information, is now abridged into one volume, *The new Golden bough* (CF10).

The *Internationale volkskundliche Bibliographie* (*International folklore bibliography*) (CF4) presents a current record of folklore studies of many countries and of all periods.

GENERAL WORKS

Bibliography

☙ Useful current bibliographies of folklore are published in *Handbook of Latin American studies* (DB102); "MLA International bibliography" in *PMLA* (*see* BD9); "Articles on American literature appearing in current periodicals" in quarterly issues of *American literature;* and the March issues of *Southern folklore quarterly*. *See also* Diehl, BB2.

Aarne, Antti. The types of the folktale; a classification and bibliography . . . tr. and enl. by Stith Thompson. 2d rev. ed. Helsinki, Suomalainen Tiedeakatemia, 1961. 588p. (Folklore Fellows communications, no.184) **CF1**

Original title: *Verzeichnis der Märchentypen*. (FF communications, no.3)

Hague. Koninklijke Bibliotheek. Catalogus van folklore in de Koninklijke Bibliotheek. Den Haag, Drukkerij "Humanitas," 1919–22. 3v. in 2. **CF2**

Contents: 1. deel, Europa; 2. deel, Buiten Europa. Supplement. Registers.

A very rich collection for all countries. Continued chronologically by *Volkskundliche Bibliographie* (CF6).

Haywood, Charles. A bibliography of North American folklore and folksong. 2d rev. ed. N.Y., Dover, 1961. 2v. (1301p.). maps. **CF3**

Contents: v.1, The American people north of Mexico, including Canada; v.2, The American Indians north of Mexico, including the Eskimos.

1st ed. N.Y., Greenberg, 1951.

The Dover edition is a corrected republication of the 1st edition, with the addition of a new Index Supplement: Composers, Arrangers, Performers.

A comprehensive, classified bibliography. Covers material on folklore, folksong, legends, dance, etc., as well as music in printed form and on records. Includes some descriptive and evaluative annotations; detailed tables of contents; an author and subject index with title entries for individual songs; and a new index of composers, arrangers, and performers.

Internationale volkskundliche Bibliographie. International folklore bibliography. Bibliographie internationale des arts et traditions populaires. Ouvrage publié par la Commission Internationale des Arts et Traditions Populaires sous les auspices du Conseil International de la Philosophie et des Sciences Humaines et avec le concours de l'UNESCO. 1939/1941– . Rédigé . . . par Robert Wildhaber. Bâle, Impr. G. Krebs; Bonn, Rudolf Habelt, 1949– . **CF4**

Frequency varies.

Title in German, English, and French. Order on title page varies. Language of subtitle varies. Publisher varies.

Contents: 1939–1941 (1949); 1942–1947 (1950); 1948–1949 (1954); 1950–1951 (1955); 1952–1954 (1959); 1955–1956 (1962). (Biennial thereafter)

An extensive bibliography covering folklore of all countries and of all periods.

Preceded by *Volkskundliche Bibliographie* (CF6).

Ramsey, Eloise. Folklore for children and young people; a critical and descriptive bibliography for use in the elementary and intermediate school. Comp. and annotated . . . in collaboration with Dorothy Mills Howard.

Philadelphia, Amer. Folklore Soc., 1952. 110p. (Publications of the American Folklore Soc. Bibliographical ser., v.3) **CF5**

A selective list of basic materials in folklore chosen to meet the needs and tastes of children and young people. International in scope; only titles showing reliable scholarship have been included. Pt.1 includes basic sources and relevant materials suitable for children, and pt.2 gives selected sources for teachers.

Annotations are long, descriptive, and evaluative.

Volkskundliche Bibliographie, 1917–1937/38. Im Auftrage des Verbandes Deutscher Vereine für Volkskunde mit Unterstützung, begonnen von E. Hoffmann-Krayer, weitergeführt von Paul Geiger. Berlin, de Gruyter, 1919–57. 14v. (1937/38 [pub. 1957] by Robert Wildhaber) **CF6**

International in scope; a very comprehensive bibliography, listing books, periodical articles, and book reviews. Classified arrangement with full author and subject indexes.

Continued by *Internationale volkskundliche Bibliographie* (CF4).

Encyclopedias and handbooks

Brand, John. Popular antiquities of Great Britain. Faiths and folklore . . . [ed.] by W. Carew Hazlitt. London, Reeves, 1905. 2v. il. **CF7**

Subtitle: A dictionary of national beliefs, superstitions and popular customs, past and current, with their classical and foreign analogues, described and illustrated. Forming a new edition of "The Popular Antiquities of Great Britain" by Brand and Ellis, largely extended, corrected and brought down to the present time, and now first alphabetically arranged.

Frazer, *Sir* **James George.** The golden bough; a study in magic and religion. 3d ed. London, Macmillan, 1907–15. 12v. (London, Macmillan; N.Y., St. Martin's, 1955. 13v. including *Aftermath* [CF9]) **CF8**

Various printings.

v.1–2, The magic art and the evolution of kings; v.3, Taboo and the perils of the soul; v.4, The dying god; v.5–6, Adonis, Attis, Osiris—studies in the history of oriental religion; v.7–8, Spirits of the corn and of the wild; v.9, The scapegoat; v.10–11, Balder the Beautiful—the fire festivals of Europe and the doctrine of the external soul; v.12, Bibliography and general index.

Not a reference book in the ordinary sense of the word, but a great storehouse of information about primitive religion. The very detailed general index makes it possible to use the set for ready reference, and the bibliography is extensive.

—— Aftermath; a supplement to the Golden bough. London, Macmillan, 1936. 494p. **CF9**

This supplementary volume contains new matter gathered from works published since 1915, and from some earlier sources not utilized in the basic work.

—— The new Golden bough; a new abridgment of the classic work. Ed., with notes and foreword, by Theodor H. Gaster. N.Y., Criterion, 1959. 738p. **CF10**

A new 1v. abridgment of Frazer's work, bringing it to date in the light of recent discoveries. Includes many of Frazer's original notes, keyed to additional notes by the new editor. Comprehensive index.

Funk and Wagnalls standard dictionary of folklore, mythology and legend. Maria Leach, ed. N.Y., Funk & Wagnalls, 1949–50. 2v. **CF11**

v.1–2, A–Z.

A comprehensive encyclopedia and dictionary dealing with the gods, heroes, tales, motifs, customs, beliefs, songs, dances, games, proverbs, etc. of the cultures of the world, including "survey articles" with bibliographies on regions and on special subjects (ballad, dance, fairy tale, national mythologies, etc.), written and signed by specialists.

Handwörterbuch des deutschen Aberglaubens, hrsg. unter besonderer Mitwirkung von E. Hoffmann-Krayer und Mitarbeit zahlreicher Fachgenossen von Hanns Bächtold-Stäubli. Berlin, de Gruyter, 1927–41. 9v. and Nachträge in v.9. (Handwörterbücher zur deutschen Volkskunde, hrsg. vom Verband Deutscher Vereine für Volkskunde. Abt. I)   **CF12**

A scholarly encyclopedia with long, signed articles by specialists, and extensive bibliographies. Treats German superstitions and popular beliefs, covering religious, sociological, and historical aspects.

Handwörterbuch des deutschen Märchens, hrsg. unter besonderer Mitwirkung von Johannes Bolte und Mitarbeit zahlreicher Fachgenossen von Lutz Mackensen. Berlin, de Gruyter, 1930–40. v.1–2. (Handwörterbücher zur deutschen Volkskunde. . . . Abt. II, Märchen) **CF13**

v.1–2, A–Gyges.

Long, signed articles by specialists—with extensive bibliographies—on the types and motifs of German fairy tales.

Radford, Edwin and **Radford, M. A.** Encyclopaedia of superstitions, ed. and rev. by Christina Hole. [Rev. and enl. ed.] London, Hutchinson, 1961. 384p.   **CF14**

1st ed. 1948.

An alphabetically arranged dictionary describing English superstitions.

Robbins, Rossell Hope. The encyclopedia of witchcraft and demonology. N.Y., Crown, 1959. 571p. il. **CF15**

Bibliography, p.558–71.

Concerned primarily with the witchcraft of 1450–1750 in various countries. Articles are generally brief, but some run to several pages. Although bibliographies are not appended to individual articles, there is a select bibliography of 1140 items with its own subject index.

Thompson, Stith. Motif-index of folk-literature; a classification of narrative elements in folktales, ballads, myths, fables, and mediaeval romances, exempla, fabliaux, jest-books and local legends. Rev. and enl. ed. Bloomington, Indiana Univ. Pr., 1955–58. 6v.   **CF16**

1st ed. 1932–36. 6v.

The new edition has been expanded and almost doubled in size and scope.

A decimal classification scheme devised to index the motifs found in traditional narrative literature: the folktale, myth, ballad, fable, medieval romance, etc. References are usually furnished to one or more works where material about a motif may be found, but the work is planned primarily as an index and is only incidentally a bibliography.

v.6 is a detailed alphabetical index of motifs.

Verband der Vereine für Volkskunde. Handwörterbuch der Sage, hrsg. von Will-Erich Peuckert. Göttingen, Vandenhoeck & Ruprecht, 1961–63. Lfg. 1–3. (In progress)   **CF17**

Contents: Lfg. 1–3, Aa–Aufwachsen.

To be in 8v. (approximately 45 Lfg.).

Intends to provide information on terms in folklore, mythology, and popular religion in their sociological and psychological as well as historical and religious contexts. Lfg. 1 includes an extensive bibliography.

Walsh, William Shepard. Curiosities of popular customs and of rites, ceremonies, observances, and miscellaneous antiquities. Philadelphia, Lippincott, 1898. 1018p. il.
now reprinted   **CF18**

Frequently reprinted.

Descriptions of popular customs in various countries of the world.

HOLIDAYS

Banks, Mary Macleod. British calendar customs: Scotland. . . . London, Folk-Lore Soc., W. Glaisher, 1937–41. 3v. il. (Publ. of the Folk-Lore Soc., 100, 104, 108) **CF19**

Contents: v.1, Movable festivals, Harvest, March riding and Wapynshaws, Wells, Fairs; v.2, The Seasons, the Quarters, Hogmanay, Jan. to May; v.3, June to Dec., Christmas, the Yules.

Customs and observances, with descriptions and anecdotes.

—— British calendar customs: Orkney and Shetland. London, Folk-Lore Soc., W. Glaisher, 1946. 110p. il. (Publ. of the Folk-Lore Soc., 112)   **CF20**

For British calendar customs: England *see* CF32.

Chambers, Robert. Book of days; a miscellany of popular antiquities in connection with the calendar, including anecdote, biography, and history, curiosities of literature, and oddities of human life and character. Philadelphia, Lippincott, 1899. 2v.   **CF21**

1st ed. 1862–64. Later editions show little change.

Arranged by day, giving anecdotes and descriptions of popular customs and observances. A standard work.

Douglas, George William. The American book of days: a compendium of information about holidays, festivals, notable anniversaries and Christian and Jewish Holy Days with notes on other American anniversaries worthy of remembrance. Rev. by Helen Douglas Compton. N.Y., Wilson, 1948. 697p. il.   **CF22**

Descriptive articles for each day of the year.

Gaster, Theodor Herzl. Festivals of the Jewish year; a modern interpretation and guide. N.Y., Sloane, 1953. 308p.   **CF23**

Gives historical outlines of the great Jewish festivals, with descriptions of their observation, comparing them with the customs and ceremonies of other peoples. A bibliography of further readings but no index.

Harper, Howard V. Days and customs of all faiths. N.Y., Fleet, 1957. 399p.   **CF24**

Arranged by month and day, giving brief descriptions of the saints or the religious significance of the day. Includes Protestant, Catholic, and Jewish practices and beliefs.

Hazeltine, Mary Emogene. Anniversaries and holidays; a calendar of days and how to observe them . . . 2d ed., compl. rev. with the editorial assistance of Judith K. Sollenberger. Chicago, Amer. Lib. Assoc., 1944. 316p.   **CF25**

A very useful guide originally published in 1928. pt.1, Calendar; pt.2, Books about holidays, special days, and seasons, including the origin and history of holiday customs, plays and pageants for holidays, programs and program making, entertainments, etc.; pt.3, Books about persons referred to in the calendar; pt.4, Classified index; pt.5, General index.

Hone, William. Every-day book and Table book. . . . London, Tegg, 1838. 3v. il.   **CF26**

Subtitle: Everlasting calendar of popular amusements, sports, pastimes, ceremonies, manners, customs, and events, incident to each of the three hundred and sixty-five days, in past and present times; forming a complete history of the year, months, and seasons, and a perpetual key to the almanac.

Schauffler, Robert Haven. Our American holiday series. N.Y., Moffat, 1907–47. 19v.   **CF27**

Arbor day. 1909; Armistice day, comp. by A. P. Sanford. 1927; Christmas. 1907; Columbus day, comp. by H. C. Paulmier. 1938; Democracy days, comp. by H. C. Paulmier. 1942; Easter, comp. by S. T. Rice. 1916; Flag day. 1912; Good Will days, comp. by H. C. Paulmier. 1947; Hallowe'en. 1933; Independence day. 1912; Lincoln's birthday. 1909; Memorial day. 1911; Mother's day, comp. by S. T. Rice. 1915; Music week. 1935; Pan-American day, comp. by H. C. Paulmier. 1943; Peace days, comp. by H. C. Paulmier. 1946; Roosevelt day (October 27), comp. by H. C. Paulmier. 1932; Thanksgiving day. 1907; Washington's birthday. 1910.

—— The days we celebrate. N.Y., Dodd, 1940. 4v. **CF28**

Designed to bring to date *Our American holidays* (CF27) and *Plays for our American holidays*. Most of the material is of more recent publication than the material in the corresponding volume of the earlier set.

v.1, Christmas, St. Valentine's day, St. Patrick's day, Easter; v.2, New Year's day, All Fools' day, May day, Arbor day, Harvest festival, Thanksgiving; v.3, Lincoln's birthday, Washington's birthday, Memorial day, Flag day, Independence day, Armistice day, Columbus day; v.4, Mother's day, Music week, Graduation day, Father's day, Hallowe'en, Book week.

Spicer, Dorothy Gladys. Festivals of western Europe. N.Y., Wilson, 1958. 275p. **CF29**

Concerned with religious feasts and folk festivals having their basis in church holidays; national and political holidays are excluded. Arrangement is by country, then chronological. Includes notes on origins of many festivals, local customs of celebration, etc.

—— Yearbook of English festivals. N.Y., Wilson, 1954. 298p. **CF30**

A calendar guide to the folk festivals of Great Britain, with a special section on the Easter cycle. Indexed by customs, counties, and regions. Includes a glossary of festival terms.

Weiser, Francis Xavier. Handbook of Christian feasts and customs: the year of the Lord in liturgy and folklore. N.Y., Harcourt, 1958. 366p. **CF31**

Attempts to explain the origin, history, development, and observances of Christian feasts with liturgical aspects and the celebration in folklore, including symbols, customs, and traditions. Includes many references to the literature in the field.

Wright, Arthur Robinson. British calendar customs: England . . . ed. by T. E. Lones. London, Folk-Lore Soc., W. Glaisher, 1936–40. 3v. il. (Publ. of the Folk-Lore Soc., 97, 102, 106) **CF32**

Contents: v.1, Movable festivals; v.2–3, Fixed festivals, January–December. Customs and observances, with descriptions and anecdotes.

For other volumes of British calendar customs *see* CF19–CF20.

ETIQUETTE

Bibliography

Bobbitt, Mary Reed. A bibliography of etiquette books published in America before 1900. N.Y., N.Y. Pub. Lib., 1947. 35p. (Repr. from the New York Public Library. Bull. Dec. 1947) **CF33**

Arrangement is by author, or title when author is unknown. Includes title index. Locates copies.

Newberry Library, Chicago. A check list of courtesy books in the Newberry Library, comp. by Virgil B. Heltzel. Chicago, Lib., 1942. 161p. **CF34**

Contains 1539 entries, including various editions, of works on "courtesy literature" written before 1775.

Handbooks

McCandless, Bruce. Service etiquette. 2d ed. by Brooks J. Harral and Oretha D. Swartz. Rev. by Oretha D. Swartz. Annapolis, U.S. Naval Inst., [1963]. 447p. il. **CF35**

1st ed. 1959.

Subtitle: The guide to correct social usage on official and unofficial occasions for men and women in the Army, Navy, Marine Corps, Coast Guard, and Air Force.

Post, Emily. Etiquette, the blue book of social usage. [10th ed.] N.Y., Funk & Wagnalls, [1960]. 671p. il. **CF36**

First published in 1922 under title *Etiquette in society, in business, in politics, and at home.*

Long a standard work. Particularly useful for formal occasions.

Radlovic, I. Monte. Etiquette and protocol; a handbook of conduct in American and international circles. N.Y., Harcourt, [1956]. 240p. **CF37**

Roosevelt, Eleanor. Book of common sense etiquette. N.Y., Macmillan, [1962]. 591p. **CF38**

An up-to-date, practical book, giving special attention to young people and young families at home, at work, in the community, and abroad.

Contains a useful list of references.

Vanderbilt, Amy. New complete book of etiquette; the guide to gracious living. Garden City, N.Y., Doubleday, [1963]. 733p. il. **CF39**

1st ed. 1952.

Comprehensive manual of current social practices, giving advice and suggestions for all social occasions from christenings to funerals.

C G

Statistics

❧ Reference questions calling for statistics are frequent in any library, and books which furnish reliable and up-to-date statistics are of great importance in any reference collection, especially in libraries where original research in social, political, economic, or industrial questions is done.

Statistical reference works fall into six main classes: (1) general dictionaries or compends, (2) almanacs or annuals of miscellaneous statistics and general information, (3) census reports and bulletins, (4) national yearbooks and statistical annuals limited to the figures of one particular country, (5) periodicals, official and nonofficial, (6) statistics of a particular subject, e.g., agriculture, foreign commerce, etc.

Of these six classes, the first and second are of the easiest and most frequent use for popular questions and are useful within their limitations, although they are usually neither detailed nor authoritative enough for important questions. For reliable and authoritative statistics, works falling in the other classes must be used.

The third class is always official (i.e., prepared by a government), and no attempt has been made to list these here, except for guides to the U.S. census. For information about census reports in various other countries, consult the two bibliographies published by the Census

Library Project of the Library of Congress: *General censuses and vital statistics in the Americas* (1943) (CG37), and *National censuses and vital statistics in Europe, 1918–1939* (1948), with *Supplement, 1940–1948* (1948) (CG9); and the *Bibliography of selected statistical sources of the American nations* (1947) (CG36).

For statistical annuals and national yearbooks, *see* p.374–87. The *Population index* (CG13) and the *Public affairs information service* (CA22) are both useful indexes to the statistical material to be found in periodicals.

For statistics on special subjects *see* names of individual subjects. Frequently recourse must also be had to government publications of varying kinds. Statistics for regions, states, and smaller subdivisions may be found in census publications, regional surveys, state and municipal handbooks, etc. For additional works on statistical method and mathematical statistics, *see* Mathematics, p.570.

GENERAL WORKS

Bibliography

Buros, Oscar Krisen. Research and statistical methodology; books and reviews of 1933–1938. New Brunswick, N.J., Rutgers Univ. Pr., 1938. 100p.　　**CG1**

—— Second yearbook of research and statistical methodology; books and reviews. Highland Park, N.J., Gryphon Pr., 1941. 383p.　　**CG1a**

Covers 1938–41 and contains 1652 excerpts from reviews from 283 periodicals of 346 books.

—— Statistical methodology reviews, 1941–50. N.Y., Wiley, 1951. 457p.　　**CG1b**

Abstracts from 842 reviews in 112 periodicals of 342 books in English.

v.1–2 include books on research methods, scientific methods, social relations of science, collective biographies of scientists, general histories of science, and statistical methodology. v.3 lists only books on statistical methods, probability, and mathematics of statistics. Arrangement is alphabetical by author of the book reviewed. Includes indexes of: (1) publishers, (2) names of authors and reviewers, (3) titles, and (4) broad subjects.

Eldridge, Hope T. The materials of demography: a selected and annotated bibliography. N.Y., 1959. 222p.　　**CG2**

Published by the International Union for the Scientific Study of Population and the Population Association of America (Brown University, Providence, R.I.).

A classified listing of books, articles, and, especially, reports of conferences, special research committees, etc. in English. Many full annotations, and usually listings of individual papers contained in polygraphic works. Author index.

International Statistical Institute. Bibliography of basic texts and monographs on statistical methods, 1945–1960. [2d ed. by William R. Buckland and Ronald A. Fox]. Edinburgh, Oliver & Boyd; N.Y., Hafner, [1963]. 297p.　　**CG3**

1st ed. 1951.

Lists nearly 200 books, written in English, with full bibliographical information, including chapter headings. Gives excerpts of reviews from statistical journals for each entry. Arranged by broad subject. Includes author index.

Kendall, Maurice George and **Doig, Alison G.** Bibliography of statistical literature. N.Y., Hafner, 1962– . v.1– . (In progress)　　**CG4**

3v. are planned.

Contents: v.[1], 1950–58. 297p.; v.2 will cover 1940–49.

An author list of papers, mostly in Western languages, on statistical method, statistical theory, and probability from the 16th century up to the end of 1958. No books are included.

Koren, John. History of statistics, their development and progress in many countries; in memoirs to commemorate the seventy-fifth anniversary of the American Statistical Association. N.Y., Macmillan, 1918. 773p.　　**CG5**

Especially useful for information about the history of official statistical publications.

Schweizerische Bibliographie für Statistik und Volkswirtschaft. Bibliographie suisse de statistique et d'économie politique, bearb. vom Eidgenössischen Statistischen Amt, Bern. 1. Jahrg.– . 1937– . Bern, Schweizerische Gesellschaft für Statistik und Volkswirtschaft, 1938– . Annual (slightly irregular).　　**CG6**

v.20, (1961), pub. 1964.

Classified. Beginning with v.7, has author index.

Includes books, reports, and articles on statistics, primarily by Swiss authors, with a selection of works by foreign authors.

United Nations. Dept. of Economic and Social Affairs. Analytical bibliography of international migration statistics, selected countries, 1925–1950. N.Y., 1955. 195p. (Population studies, no.24)　　**CG7**

An analytical bibliography for 24 selected countries, presenting a list of primary sources and other publications containing statistical data, and "within each major category of departures and arrivals the sources and years for which detailed classification and cross-classifications are available."— *Introd.*

United Nations. Statistical Office. Statistical papers: Series M. N.Y., 1949– . no.1– . Irregular.　　**CG8**

This series contains papers on international statistics, e.g.: no.1, Nomenclature of geographic areas for statistical purposes (1949); no.4, International standard industrial classification of all economic activities (rev. 1958); no.8, International standard definitions for transport statistics (1950); no.18, Bibliography of recent official demographic statistics (1954); no.21, World weights and measures: handbook for statisticians (1955); no.22, Directory of international standards for statistics, including a bibliography on methods (rev. 1960); no.36, Bibliography of industrial and distributive-trade statistics (rev. 1963); no.38, Commodity indexes for the Standard international trade classification (1963).

U.S. Library of Congress. Census Library Project. National censuses and vital statistics in Europe, 1918–1939; an annotated bibliography. Wash., Govt. Prt. Off., 1948. 215p.　　**CG9**

A very useful guide to the national censuses and official statistical publications of the various countries of Europe, for the period between the two World wars.

—— —— 1940–1948 Supplement. 1948. 48p.

—— Statistical bulletins; an annotated bibliography of the general statistical bulletins of major political subdivisions of the world, prep. by Phyllis G. Carter. Wash., 1954. 93p.　　**CG10**

At head of title: U.S. Library of Congress. Reference Dept.; U.S. Dept. of Commerce. Bureau of the Census.

Lists "periodicals issued by an official agency more frequently than annually," covering statistics in several subject fields. Arranged by continent and then by country. Indicates beginning date, frequency, categories of statistical data, holdings in Washington libraries, etc.

—— Statistical yearbooks; an annotated bibliography of the general statistical yearbooks of major political subdivisions of the world. Prep. by Phyllis G. Carter. Wash., 1953. 123p.　　**CG11**

At head of title: U.S. Library of Congress. Reference Dept.; U.S. Dept. of Commerce. Bureau of the Census.

Arranged by continents and then alphabetically by country. Gives full bibliographical data, including dates of first and most recent issues, types of statistics covered, frequency, etc.

Zelinsky, Wilbur. A bibliographic guide to population geography. Chicago, 1962. 257p. (Chicago. Univ. Dept. of Geography. Research paper no.80)   **CG12**

A listing of 2588 items on all phases of population geography, published in various parts of the world from the mid-19th century to mid-1961.

Regional arrangement with author index.

Indexes

Population index. v.1, 1935– . Princeton, N.J., Office of Population Research, Princeton Univ., and the Population Assoc. of America, 1935– . v.1– . Quarterly.   **CG13**

An annotated bibliography of books and periodical literature on all phases of population problems. Arranged by class, with annual cumulated indexes by author and country. Includes special articles and current items.

Title varies: Jan. 1935–Oct. 1936, *Population literature.* v.1, no.1 (rev. May 1, 1935) "replaces 'Review of current research, 1,' including all titles from that publication as well as additional foreign and American citations for 1933. (No 1934 or 1935 titles were added.) The period covered by this number begins Jan. 1, 1933, which terminates the period covered by *Social science abstracts* (1929–1932) [CA23]."—*Note,* v.1, p.1.

v.1–2 were published by the Population Association of America, Washington, D.C.

Directories

Directory of statisticians and others in allied professions, 1961. Wash., Amer. Statistical Assoc., [1962]. 191p.   **CG14**

A combined membership directory of the American Statistical Association, the Biometric Society (Eastern and Western North American regions), and the Institute of Mathematical Statistics. Arranged alphabetically; lists 9400 names, giving dates, address, position, and education. Includes a geographical listing by state and city; also a foreign section by country.

United Nations Educational, Scientific and Cultural Organization. Social Science Clearing House. International repertory of institutions conducting population studies. Paris, UNESCO, 1959. 240p. (Its Reports and papers in the social sciences, no.11)   **CG15**

Title and introduction also in French. Text in English or French.

Arranged by locality. Information on individual organizations varies, but generally includes corporate structure, staff activities, and publications.

Dictionaries

Hungary. Központi Statisztikai Hivatal. Statisztikai szótár; 1700 statisztikai kifejezés hét nyelven. Statistical dictionary; 1700 statistical terms in seven languages. Budapest, [Statisztikai Kiadó Vállalat], 1961. 171p.   **CG16**

Title and introductory material in seven languages: Russian, Hungarian, Bulgarian, Czech, Polish, German, and English. Main listing is in Russian with equivalents in other languages, followed by word indexes of the six non-Russian languages.

International Union for the Scientific Study of Population. Multilingual demographic dictionary. English section. N.Y., United Nations, Dept. of Economic and Social Affairs, 1958. 77p. (United Nations. Population Branch. Population studies, no.29) United Nations. [Document] ST/SOA/Ser.A/29.   **CG17**

Issued also in French and Spanish. Explanations of concepts and technical terms (numbered) used in demography. Alphabetical index is included, referring to number for explanation.

German and Italian editions also published as:

Wilhelm Winkler. *Mehrsprachiges demographischen Wörterbuch.* [Hamburg], Deutsche Akademie für Bevölkerungswissenschaft an der Universität Hamburg, 1960. 147p.

Dizionario demografico multilingue, prep. dallo Commissione del Dizionario Demografico. Milano, A. Gruffe, 1959. 166p.

Kendall, Maurice George and **Buckland, William R.** A dictionary of statistical terms; prep. for the International Statistical Institute with the assistance of the UNESCO. 2d ed. N.Y., Hafner, 1960. 575p.   **CG18**

1st ed. 1957.

Preface in French and English.

A dictionary of terms in current use with glossaries in French, German, Italian, and Spanish, referring to English equivalents.

Kurtz, Albert K. and **Edgerton, Harold A.** Statistical dictionary of terms and symbols. N.Y., Wiley; London, Chapman and Hall, 1939. 191p.   **CG19**

A very good dictionary, giving clear and, when necessary, detailed definitions. Explanations of many symbols are included.

Inter American Statistical Institute. Statistical vocabulary. 2d ed. Wash., Pan Amer. Union, 1960. 83p.   **CG20**

1st ed. 1950.

Title page and text in English, Spanish, Portuguese, and French.

Consists of: (1) a "main list" of more than 1300 English terms with equivalents in Spanish, Portuguese, and French, and (2) separate Spanish, Portuguese, and French alphabetical indexes, each keyed to the English equivalents.

COMPENDIUMS
International

Institut International de Statistique. Revue, 1. année, 1933– . La Haye, 1933– . Quarterly (some numbers combined), 1933–50; 3 numbers a year (some combined), 1951– .   **CG21**

Supersedes: Institut International de Statistique. Office Permanent. *Bulletin mensuel.*

Title page also in English: *Review of the International Statistical Institute.*

Text in English, French, German, Italian, or Spanish, with summaries in English or French (occasionally in both).

Each number includes section, *"Bibliographie statistique internationale."*

An important current bibliography, international in scope.

Institut International de Statistique. Office Permanent. Annuaire international de statistique. La Haye, 1916–21. v.1–8. maps.   **CG22**

Contents: (1) État de la population (Europe), 1916; (2) Mouvement de la population (Europe), 1917; (3) État de la population (Amérique), 1919; (4) Mouvement de la population (Amérique), 1920; (5) État de la population (Afrique, Asie, Océanie), 1921; (6) Salaires et durée du travail, conventions, collectives, chômage, placement, syndicats ouvriers et patronaux, grèves et lock-outs; (7) Enseignement primaire, agriculture, postes, télégraphie et téléphonie, sociétés anonymes, coopératives, habitations, indices des prix de gros; (8) Finances d'états, production, cours des changes.

No more published. v.1–5, continued by:

—— Aperçu de la démographie des divers pays du monde, 1922–36. La Haye, Van Stockum, 1923–39. v.1–[6].   **CG23** v.6, pub. 1939, covers 1929–36.

Contents: (1) État de la population; (2) Mouvement de la population.

—— Statistique internationale des grandes villes. 1927–34. La Haye, Van Stockum, 1927–40. v.1–3.   **CG24**

Title varies.

Continued by:

—— —— 1954– . (In progress)

Series of volumes as follows: A1, Statistiques démographiques des grandes villes, 1946/51, 1954; A2, Statistiques démographiques des grandes villes, 1946/53, 1957; B1, Statistique du logement et de la construction, 1946/53, 1956; B2, Statistique du logement; analyse et tableaux supplémentaires, 1960; C1, Données économiques des grandes villes, 1950/54, 1958; D1, Services publics et transports dans les grandes villes, 1950 et 1955, 1959; E1, Statistique culturelle et des sports, 1951/57, 1961.

—— Annuaire de statistique internationale des grandes villes. v.1– . 1961– . La Haye. Biennial.   **CG25**

Issued also under title *International statistical yearbook of large towns.*

Brings together information appearing in separate volumes of *Statistique internationale des grandes villes.*

Länder der Erde; politisch-ökonomisches Handbuch. 3. völlig neubearb. und erw. Aufl. [Gesamtredaktion: Horst Seydewitz und Otto Brandt] Berlin, Verlag Die Wirtschaft, [1962]. 837p. il.   **CG26**

At head of title: Autorenkollektiv.

1st ed. 1959.

Translated from the Russian: *Zarubezhnye strany.*

Economic and political statistical information on the countries of the world, especially valuable for Iron Curtain countries.

Mulhall, Michael George. Dictionary of statistics. 4th ed. rev. London, Routledge, 1899. 853p.   **CG27**

Pt.1, Statistics from the time of Emperor Diocletian to 1890, arranged alphabetically. Pt.2, 1890–98; List of books of reference; Index to pts.1–2. Does not give authorities for statistics included.

Webb, Augustus Duncan. New dictionary of statistics. London, Routledge; N.Y., Dutton, 1911. 682p.   **CG28**

A supplement, for 1899–1909, to Mulhall's *Dictionary of statistics* (CG27). Arranged on the same general plan as Mulhall, but superior to that work in that authorities for all statistics are given.

Statesman's year-book; statistical and historical annual of the states of the world, 1864– . London, N.Y., Macmillan, 1864– . v.1– .   **CG29**

Not an almanac of miscellaneous statistics, but a concise and reliable manual of descriptive and statistical information about the governments of the world. Contents vary somewhat but usually cover: (1) British Commonwealth; (2) United States; (3) Other countries, arranged alphabetically. For each country gives: information about its ruler, constitution and government, area, population, religion, social welfare, instruction, justice and crime, state finance, defense, production and industry, agriculture, commerce, navigation, communications, banking and credit, money, weights and measures, diplomatic representatives, etc. A valuable feature is the selected bibliography of statistical and other books of reference given for each country. Recent volumes include information on the United Nations.

The most useful of all the general yearbooks; indispensable in any type of library.

Statistical year-book of the League of Nations, 1926–1942/44. Geneva, 1927–45. (Publications of the League of Nations. II, Economic and financial) Annual. **CG30**

Ceased publication with v.17, 1942–44. For continuation *see* United Nations, *Statistical yearbook* (CG32).

Title varies. 1935–1942/44, in French and English.

Annual survey of commerce, finance, and industry in the various countries of the world. Particularly useful for comparative purposes.

United Nations. Statistical Office. Demographic yearbook; Annuaire démographique, 1948– . N.Y., 1949– . Annual.   **CG31**

Compendium of international demographic data including official statistics from almost 250 geographic areas of the world. Covers area, population, natality, mortality, marriage and divorce, and characteristics of the population.

1963 contains a cumulative subject index covering all previous issues.

—— Statistical yearbook; Annuaire statistique, 1948– . N.Y., 1949– . v.1– . Annual.   **CG32**

A summary of international statistics to continue the *Statistical year-book of the League of Nations* (CG30). Covers population, agriculture, mining, manufacturing, finance, trade, social statistics, education, etc. of the various countries of the world, the tables usually covering a number of years. References are given to sources.

"World summary, principal series," has been introduced in v.15, 1963, summarizing tables appearing in various chapters.

Kept up to date in part by:

—— Monthly bulletin of statistics, no.1, Jan. 1947– . N.Y., 1947– . Monthly.   **CG33**

In English and French. Aims to show by statistics the changing economic and social conditions in different countries.

Inter-American

América en cifras. 1960– . Wash., Pan Amer. Union, 1961– . Annual (?).   **CG34**

Introduction, explanatory notes, and preface in English and Spanish.

Basic statistical information on the American nations, 1961, issued in 8 pts. Supplies statistics in the areas of demography, housing, agriculture, forestry, fishing, industrial production, transport, tourism, trade, finance, prices, wages, consumption, and social, labor, and cultural affairs.

Supplement contains: (1) tables of contents of all parts; (2) a subject index; and (3) a general bibliography.

South American handbook, 1924– ; a yearbook and guide to the countries and resources of South and Central America, Mexico and West Indies. London, Trade and Travel Publs., 1924– . maps. Annual.   **CG35**

Continues the *Anglo–South American handbook,* 1921–22. Title and publisher vary.

A very useful handbook giving travel and gazetteer information about each country, also natural resources, government, communications and transportation, etc.

Bibliography

Inter American Statistical Institute. Bibliography of selected statistical sources of the American nations. Bibliografía de fuentes estadísticas escogidas de las naciones americanas. 1st ed. Wash., 1947. 689p.   **CG36**

Subtitle: A guide to the principal statistical materials of the 22 American nations, including data, analyses, methodology, and laws and organization of statistical agencies.

In English and Spanish.

A comprehensive, classified bibliography with annotations. Detailed alphabetical index and a classified index. Gives full information about the statistical publications of each country, including censuses, yearbooks, current serials, and works in special subjects, e.g., economics, labor, etc.

Also includes a section on general statistical works.

Supplemented by quarterly bibliography in *Estadística: journal of the American Statistical Institute.* v.6, 1948– .

U.S. Library of Congress. Census Library Project. General censuses and vital statistics in the Americas; prep. under the supervision of Irene B. Taeuber, chief, Census Library Project. Wash., Govt. Prt. Off., 1943. 151p.
        CG37

Subtitle: An annotated bibliography of the historical censuses and current vital statistics of the 21 American republics, the American sections of the British Commonwealth of Nations, the American colonies of Denmark, France, and the Netherlands, and the American territories and possessions of the United States.

Directories

Inter American Statistical Institute. Directory of statistical personnel in the American nations. Directorio . . . Nominata . . . Répertoire . . . 1955 . . . 5th ed. Wash., 1955. 194p.
        CG38

1st edition issued in *Statistical activities of the American nations* (1940, p.677–737) under the title "Biographical directory of statistical personnel."

Gives biographical information on 740 persons in the American nations, other than the United States, arranged alphabetically by country. Appendixes list: (1) agencies which collect and publish statistics; (2) national committees of vital and health statistics; and (3) statistical societies of America. Includes an alphabetical index of individuals.

United States

Guides and bibliographies

Andriot, John L. Guide to U.S. government statistics. [3d ed. rev. and enl.] Arlington, Va., Documents Index, 1961. 402p.
        CG39

1st ed. 1956.

Title varies: 1956–57, *U.S. government statistics.*

In two parts: "(1) the *Guide,* arranged by Departments and Agencies, listing the various publications containing statistical data with . . . bibliographical information and . . . annotations, and (2) the *Index,* a detailed subject index."— *Foreword.*

Information is given on frequency, availability, price, and ordering procedures. Annotations are pertinent and concise.

U.S. Bureau of the Budget. Office of Statistical Standards. Statistical services of the United States government. Rev. ed. Wash., 1963. 136p.
        CG40

". . . to provide a general description of the economic and social statistical programs of the United States Government— where they are located, how the data are collected, and what data are available in these areas from Federal agencies."

Contains a list of principal statistical publications of federal agencies, with annotations.

U.S. Bureau of the Census. Bureau of the Census catalog, 1946– . Wash., Govt. Prt. Off., 1947– . Quarterly and cumulative to annual with monthly supplements.
        CG41

Title varies as follows: *Census publications: catalog and subject guide,* 1945–51; *Catalog of United States census publications,* 1952–62; *Bureau of the Census catalog of publications,* 1963; *Bureau of the Census catalog,* 1964– .

A listing of published materials of the Bureau of the Census. Beginning with 1964, includes unpublished material available on tapes, punched cards, etc.

U.S. Library of Congress. Census Library Project. Catalog of United States census publications, 1790–1945, prep. by Henry J. Dubester, chief, Census Library Project. Wash., Govt. Prt. Off., 1950. 320p.   **CG42**

Designed to serve both as a "guide to census statistics and to record the historical development of publication patterns." Annotated. In two sections: pt.1, decennial census publications; pt.2, other publications, arranged by subject, e.g., agriculture, business, industry, religious bodies, etc. The index is to the subjects contained in titles and annotations.

For brief information largely supersedes earlier bibliographical surveys and indexes, but the following are sometimes useful for more detailed information: U.S. Bureau of Labor Statistics. *The history and growth of the United States census.* Wash., Govt. Prt. Off., 1900. 967p.; U.S. Office of the Census. *A century of population growth from the first census . . . to the twelfth,* 1790–1900. Wash., Govt. Prt. Off., 1909. 303p.; its *Circular of information concerning census publications, 1790–1916.* Jan. 1, 1917. 124p.; its *Topical index of population census reports, 1900–1930.* 1934. 76p.; its *Periodic and special reports on population, 1930–1939.* 1939. 12p.

Supplemented by:

—— State censuses; an annotated bibliography of censuses of population taken after the year 1790 by states and territories of the United States; prep. by Henry J. Dubester. Wash., Govt. Prt. Off., 1948. 73p.   **CG43**

U.S. National Archives. Federal population censuses, 1840–80; a price list of microfilm copies of the original schedules. Wash., Nat. Archives, Nat. Archives and Records Service, General Services Admin., 1955. 73p. (National Archives publ. no.55–7)   **CG44**

A list of the census schedules of this period which may now be purchased on positive microfilm. The list covering the 1830 census was included in the *List of National Archives microfilm publications* (1953) (DB38).

Compendiums

American yearbook; a record of events and progress, 1910–19, 1925–50. N.Y., Nelson, 1911–50. v.1–36.
        CG45

Publisher varies. Ceased publication.

Long, signed articles, by specialists, give good narrative accounts—including bibliographies and statistics—of the events of the year, covering national and international politics, American government, economics and business, social conditions, science, humanities, etc., with a chronology and a necrology.

Bogue, Donald J. The population of the United States . . . with a special chapter on fertility by Wilson H. Grabill. Glencoe, Ill., Free Pr., 1959. 873p. (Studies in population distribution, no.14)   **CG46**

Extensive tables, diagrams, and text on United States population: growth, distribution, age, sex, mortality, fertility, economics, etc. Includes also estimates for 1960 and later.

Information please almanac, atlas and yearbook, 1947– . Planned and supervised by Dan Golenpaul Associates. N.Y., Simon & Schuster, 1947– . Annual.   **CG47**

Publisher varies. Title varies.

An almanac of miscellaneous information, with a general class arrangement and a subject index. Includes special timely articles in each volume; reviews of the year in books, sports, theater, fiction, screen, music, etc., written by specialists; statistical and historical descriptions of the various countries of the world; sports records; and many kinds of general information.

Sources for many of the tables and special articles are noted. The "Celebrated persons" section is in two groups: (1) those living, and (2) those deceased. Place of birth and dates are given but no other biographical information. Names in this section are not indexed individually in the general index.

Tribune almanac and political register, 1838–1914. N.Y., 1838–1914. 76v.   **CG48**

Title varies: 1838, *Whig almanac and politician's register;*

1839–41, *Politician's register;* 1843–55, *Whig almanac and United States register.*

A reliable and useful almanac for American statistics, especially political statistics, election returns, etc. Includes full texts of party platforms. Discontinued, but still useful for historical information.

U.S. Bureau of the Census. Statistical abstract of the United States, 1878– . Wash., Govt. Prt. Off., 1879– . v.1– . Annual. **CG49**

v.1–25, 1878–1902, prep. by the Bureau of Statistics (Treasury Dept.); v.26–34, 1903–11, by the Bureau of Statistics (Dept. of Commerce and Labor); 1912–37, by the Bureau of Foreign and Domestic Commerce.

A single-volume work presenting quantitative summary statistics on the political, social, and economic organization of the United States. Indispensable in any library; it serves not only as a first source for statistics of national importance but also as a guide to further information, as references are given to the sources of all tables.

Statistics given in the tables cover a period of several years, usually about 15 or 20; some tables run back to 1789 or 1800.

—— —— County and city data book, 1949– . Wash., Govt. Prt. Off., 1952– . (Irregular) **CG50**

A *Statistical abstract* supplement which combines its *Cities supplement,* 1940, and its *County data book,* 1947.

Issued for 1949, 1952, 1956, 1962.

Presents the latest available census figures for each county, and for approximately 400 of the larger cities in the United States. Also has summary figures for states, geographical regions, and standard metropolitan areas.

—— —— Historical statistics of the United States, colonial times to 1957. 1960. 789p. il. **CG51**

A supplement to the *Statistical abstract* (CG49), including comparative historical statistics of the same type as those in the *Abstract.* Prepared with the cooperation of the Social Science Research Council.

A completely revised edition of *Historical statistics of the United States, 1789–1945* (1949). Covers periods from 1610 to 1957.

—— City finances, 1942– . Wash., Govt. Prt. Off., 1944– . Annual. **CG52**

1909–41 issues had title *Financial statistics of cities.*

Includes summary of city government finances, and compendium of city government finances, giving finances of the 43 largest cities in detail.

Form and volume numbering vary.

—— State finances, 1942– . Wash., Govt. Prt. Off., 1944– . Annual. **CG53**

1915–41 issues had title *Financial statistics of states.*

Published annually in parts; form and volume numbering vary, but usually include: individual state reports; topical reports, e.g., budgets, expenditure, debt, tax collections, etc.; statistical compendiums (preliminary and final).

U.S. National Vital Statistics Division. Vital statistics of the United States. 1937– . Wash., Govt. Prt. Off., 1939– . Annual. **CG54**

Contains basic data on natality, marriage, divorce, and mortality. Issued in two volumes: v.1, Natality characteristics for each state, metropolitan area and other geographic areas of the United States, Puerto Rico and the Virgin Islands; v.2, in 2 pts., Mortality data for the United States, Puerto Rico and Virgin Islands.

Supersedes the Division's *Mortality statistics* and its *Birth, stillbirth and infant mortality statistics.*

—— —— Special reports. For details concerning these publications, *see* Andriot, *Guide to U.S. government serials and periodicals* (AH11).

World almanac, and book of facts, 1868– . N.Y., World-Telegram, 1868– . v.1– . Annual. **CG55**

The most comprehensive and most frequently useful of the American almanacs of miscellaneous information. Contains statistics on social, industrial, political, financial, religious, educational, and other subjects; political organizations; societies; historical lists of famous events, etc. Well up to date and, in general, reliable; sources for many of the statistics are given. A useful handbook, and one with which the reference worker should familiarize himself thoroughly. Alphabetical index at the front of each volume. Each issue before 1915 had also a short index of notable articles in preceding volumes.

☙ Statistical annuals and other compendiums are much used, both for historical and for current statistics. For this reason, as many files as possible have been listed below for the nations of the world, and because currency is of particular importance, the latest issue received by the fall of 1964 has been given in parentheses following the entry.

Africa

See also names of individual countries.

Bibliography

France. Institut National de la Statistique et des Études Économiques. Service de Cooperation. Bibliographie démographique, 1945–1962. Paris, Institut, 1963. 33p. **CG56**

List of demographic works published by the Institut on 15 French-African countries: Cameroun, Centrafrique, Congo, Côte-d'Ivoire, Dahomey, Gabon, Guinée, Haute-Volta, Mali, Madagascar, Mauritanie, Niger, Sénégal, Chad, Togo.

United Nations. Economic Commission for Africa Library. Annuals received in the UNECA library. Addis Ababa, 1962. 194p. (United Nations [document] E/CN. 14/Lib/ser. A/2) **CG57**

A selected list of serials arranged in three parts: (1) non-governmental annuals; (2) governmental annuals; (3) United Nations and specialized agencies annuals. Includes author, subject, and title indexes.

A very useful checklist of current statistical annuals, mainly for the countries of Africa. Does not include dates.

U.S. Library of Congress. Census Library Project. Population censuses and other official demographic statistics of Africa (not including British Africa); an annotated bibliography, prep. by Henry J. Dubester. Wash., Govt. Prt. Off., 1950. 53p. **CG58**

—— Population censuses and other official demographic statistics of British Africa; an annotated bibliography, prep. by Henry J. Dubester. Wash., Govt. Prt. Off., 1950. 78p. **CG59**

Compendiums

West Africa annual. 1962– . London, J. Clarke, 1962– . il. Annual. (1962) **CG60**

Ed. by L. K. Jakande.

Under each country gives information on the land and the people, history, population, government, constitution, finance, economic programs, education, etc.

West African directory. 1962– . London, T. Skinner, 1962– . il. Annual. (1963/64) **CG61**

Gives, for the 15 countries of West Africa and the offshore islands of Fernando Po, São Tomé, and Principe, information on geography, climate, peoples, government, education, communication, and tourism. Includes statistics of population, production, finance, and trade; also, a classified business directory.

Arab States

See also United Arab Republic, p.386.

Bibliography

Sirs el Laiyana, Egypt. Arab States Fundamental Education Centre. Social Science Division. Statistical sources of the Arab states; a comprehensive list. Sirs-el-Layyan, Arab States Training Centre for Education for Community Development, 1961. 29p.   **CG62**

"A bibliography of official statistics issued regularly or occasionally by the governments of ten Arab states."—*Pref.*

Argentina

Argentine Republic. Dirección Nacional de Estadística y Censos. Anuario. 1892–1914. Buenos Aires, Compañía Sud-americana de Billetes de Banco, 1892–1914?. **CG63**

—— Anuario estadístico. 1944, 1948– . Buenos Aires, 1947– . Irregular.   **CG64**

1948, in two parts: (1) Compendio; (2) Comercio exterior. 1949/50, in three parts: (1) Compendio; (2) Comercio exterior; (3) Estadística industrial. (Latest single volume 1957) *Comercio exterior* continued annually. (1963)

For further description of statistical yearbooks of Argentina, *see* U.S. Library of Congress, *A guide to the official publications of the other American republics: Argentina,* ed. by James B. Childs, p.52–53 (AH70).

Australia

Australia. Bureau of Census and Statistics. Official year book of the Commonwealth of Australia, 1901/08– . Canberra, 1908– . v.1– . maps. Annual since v.41, 1955. (1963)   **CG65**

The various states of Australia also publish: for New South Wales, South Australia, and Western Australia, *Statistical register* (annual); for Victoria, *Victorian yearbook* (annual); for Queensland, *Queensland yearbook* (annual); for Tasmania, *Statistics of the State of Tasmania* (annual).

Austria

Austria. Statistisches Zentralamt. Statistisches Handbuch für die Republik Österreich. Wien, 1950– . 1. Jahrg., n.F., 1950– . Annual. (v.14, 1963)   **CG66**

Continues *Statistisches Jahrbuch für Österreich.* 1920–38. Jahrg.1–18. Title varies: v.1–17, *Statistisches Handbuch,* published by the Bundesamt für Österreich; v.18, 1938, *Statistisches Jahrbuch für Österreich,* published by the Statistisches Landesamt after the annexation of Austria by Germany.

Österreichisches Jahrbuch, 1919– , hrsg. vom Bundespressedienst. Wien, Staatsdruckerei, 1920– . v.1– . Annual. (v.58, 1963, pub. 1964)   **CG67**

Suspended 1937–44.

A comprehensive summary of the political, economic, social, and cultural life, including statistical data.

Belgium

Belgium. Institut National de Statistique. Annuaire statistique de la Belgique. 1870– . Bruxelles, 1870– . v.1– . maps. Annual. (v.83, 1962)   **CG68**

Issued also in Flemish.

Issuing body and title vary slightly: v.42–80, 1912–59, titled *Annuaire statistique de la Belgique et du Congo belge.*

Brazil

Bibliography

Brazil. Conselho Nacional de Estatística. Bibliografia geográfico-estatística brasileira. Rio de Janeiro, 1956– . (In progress)   **CG69**

v.1, 1936/1950.

A listing of the publications of the Brazilian Institute of Geography and Statistics from 1936 through 1950, arranged by subject. Devoted mainly to economic and geographical aspects of Latin America, but area covered includes various countries of the world.

Compendiums

Brazil. Conselho Nacional de Estatística. Anuário estatístico do Brazil. Ano 1– , 1935– . Rio de Janeiro, 1936– . Annual. (v.24, 1963)   **CG70**

v.5, 1939/40; v.6, 1941/45.

Issuing body varies.

Brazil. Ministério das Relações Exteriores. Brasil. 1st ed.– . 1932– . Brasília, 1932– . il., maps. Irregular. (11th ed. 1960)   **CG71**

In Portuguese; some numbers in English, some also in Spanish.

A lengthy work (1960 issue contains 961p.), giving general information and statistics on area, demography, administration, and the economic, social, and cultural affairs of Brazil. Includes subject index.

Bulgaria

Bulgaria. Tsentralno Statistichesko Upravlenie. Statisticheski godishnik na Narodna Republika Bulgariia. 1947/48– . Sofia, 1948?– . Annual. (1963, pub. 1963)   **CG72**

Supersedes *Statisticheski godishnik na Bulgarskoto Tsarstvo. Annuaire statistique de Royaume de Bulgarie.* Année 1–34, 1909–42. Sofia, 1910–42. (Années 5–14, 1913/22; 15–16, 1923/24; 21–22, 1929/30, issued together).

Russian and English translations of the text to be used with the tables in the main volume are issued separately.

Canada

Canada. Bureau of Statistics. Canada, 1930– . The official handbook of present conditions and recent progress. Ottawa, 1930– . il. Annual. (1964)   **CG73**

Intended to provide a factual survey of the Canadian economy set in a statistical background and copiously illustrated with photographs depicting recent economic, social, and cultural developments.

—— Canada year book, 1905– . The official statistical annual of the resources, history, institutions and social and economic conditions of Canada. Ottawa, 1906– . v.1– . il., maps. Annual. (1963/64)   **CG74**

Subtitle varies.

Some volumes cover two years.

Official data on the physiography, history, constitution and government, institutions, population, production, industry, trade, transportation, finance, labor, administration, and general social and economic conditions.

Includes a useful chapter, "Sources of official information," containing a "Directory of sources" and a bibliography of special materials published in former editions of the *Year book.*

Canadian almanac and directory for the year 1847– . Toronto, Copp Clark Co., 1847– . Annual. (1964)   **CG75**

Title varies.

Contains authentic legal, commercial, statistical, astronomical, departmental, ecclesiastical, financial, educational, and general information.

Supplement gives list of Cabinet officers and members of the House of Commons.

Canadian annual review . . . 1960– . Ed. by John T. Saywell. Toronto, Univ. of Toronto Pr., 1961– . v.1– . Annual. (1963, pub. 1964)   **CG76**

A survey annual covering such fields as: parliament and politics, external affairs and defense, the national economy, life and leisure, obituaries.

Some chapters are in French.

Ceylon

Ceylon. Dept. of Census and Statistics. Statistical abstract of Ceylon, 1949– . Colombo, 1949– . Annual. (1963, pub. 1964)   **CG77**

1949 covers 1937–48.

Contains, with additions, the information formerly appearing in the discontinued *Ceylon blue book:* statistics of population, commerce, industry, education, etc.

Chile

Chile. Dirección de Estadística y Censos. Anuario estadístico, 1848– . Santiago, 1860– .   **CG78**

The general statistics of Chile first appeared in 1860, the initial volumes covering 1848–58, and ran until 1887/88 (26v.). Next published were for 1909 (3v.) and 1910 (3v.). From 1911– , the statistics have appeared in several subseries, e.g., Demografía, Agricultura, Política y administración, etc.

Title varies; some volumes called *Estadística anual.*

Since 1939, an annual summary of statistical data entitled *Sinopsis* is issued as the Dec. number of the monthly periodical *Estadística chilena.*

Chile. Dirección General de Informaciones y Cultura. Anuario DIC. 2d ed. 1956. Santiago de Chile, 1956. il.   **CG79**

1st ed. 1946.

A survey of life and culture in Chile: politics and government; economics; arts and sciences.

China

Bibliography

U.S. Bureau of the Census. The population and manpower of China: an annotated bibliography, by Foreign Manpower Research Office, Bureau of the Census. Wash., Govt. Prt. Off., 1958. 132p. (Its International population statistics reports, ser. P-90, no.8)   **CG80**

Contains materials on Taiwan as well as on Mainland China, and also on Chinese in other sections of southeast Asia.

Compendiums

China. Directorate General of Budgets, Accounts and Statistics. Statistical abstract of the Republic of China. 5th ed. 1955– . [Taipei], Taiwan, 1955– . Irregular.   **CG81**

Earlier eds. issued in 1935, 1945, and 1947.

Imprint varies. 1963 is the 13th since the *Abstract's* beginning and the 9th printed in Taiwan.

Aims to be a comprehensive national yearbook; however, data are primarily for Taiwan.

China yearbook. 1937/43– . Taipei, Taiwan, China

Pub. Co., 1943– . il. Irregular. (1963/64)   **CG82**

Title varies: *China handbook,* 1937/43–1956/57. Imprint varies.

Publication suspended 1947–49.

Attempts to cover the political, economic, social, and cultural activities of the Republic of China.

Contains a who's who.

China year book, 1912–1939. London, Routledge; N.Y., Dutton, 1912–19; Tientsin, Tientsin Pr., 1921–29; Shanghai, North China Daily News, 1931–39. Irregular.   **CG83**

Unofficial but of first importance, while published, for reliable detailed information about the people, government, economic condition, religion, education, products, etc. of China. Includes a "Who's who in China."

Edited by H. G. W. Woodhead and H. T. Montague Bell.

Index to previous issues appears in the 20th issue, 1939.

Chinese yearbook . . . Issue 1–7, 1935/36–1944/45. Prep. from official and other public sources by the Council of International Affairs, Chungking. Bombay, London, Thacker, 1935–46.   **CG84**

Publisher varies.

Contains a large amount of historical, descriptive, industrial, economic, and directory information, as well as statistical material. Differs from the *China year book* (CG83) primarily in being compiled by Chinese authorities; it also contains fuller discussions of some subjects. Does not have a biographical section.

Ceased publication with the 1944/45 issue.

China (People's Republic of China, 1949–). State Statistical Bureau. Ten great years; statistics of the economic and cultural achievements of the People's Republic of China. [Tr. from the Chinese] Peking, Foreign Languages Pr., 1960. 223p. il.   **CG85**

Pub. also in Chinese.

"The aim of this book is to describe, through extensive statistical data presented systematically, the great economic and cultural achievements of the People's Republic of China during the past decade."—*Foreword.*

Colombia

Colombia. Departamento Administrativo Nacional de Estadística. Anuario general de estadística, 1915– . Bogotá, Impr. Nacional, 1915– . Annual. (1961, pub. 1963)   **CG86**

—— Síntesis estadística, 1941– . Bogotá, 1941– . Irregular.   **CG86a**

Issuing body varies. Title varies slightly.

Supersedes *Anuario estadístico,* 1875/76–1884, issued by Oficina de Estadística Nacional, and *Estadística anual de la República de Colombia,* issued by Dirección General de Estadística.

Costa Rica

Costa Rica. Dirección General de Estadística. Anuario estadístico, 1883– . San José, Impr. Nacional, 1884– . (1962)   **CG87**

Suspended between v.10, 1893, and v.11, 1907; 1946–47. Discontinued volume numbering after v.49, 1945.

Czechoslovakia

Czechoslovak Republic. Státní Úřad Statistický. Statistická ročenka Československé Socialistické Republiky, 1957– . Prague, 1957– . Annual. (1963)   **CG88**

At head of title: Ústřední Komise Lidové Kontroly a Statistický.

Title and issuing body vary slightly.

An English translation is issued with the title *Czechoslovak statistical abstract* (1963).

Supersedes *Manuel statistique de la République Tchécoslovaque* (Statistisches Handbuch der Čechoslovakischen Republik), v.1–4, 1920–32; *Annuaire statistique de la Républik Tchécoslovaque*, 1934–38. Published also in German. None published 1939–47. Resumed publication with *Manuel statistique*, 1948; issued also in English, *Statistical digest of the Czechoslovak Republic*, 1948; in Czech, *Statistická příručka CSR*, 1948; and in Russian.

Denmark

Denmark. Statistiske Departement. Statistisk Årbog. Statistical yearbook. 1892– . København, 1896– . v.1– . Annual. (1963/64)   **CG89**

Text in Danish and English, beginning with v.57, 1952. Previously published with text in Danish and French.

Contents: pt.1, Denmark proper; pt.2, The Faroe Islands; pt.3, Greenland; pt.4, International tables.

Dominican Republic

Dominican Republic. Dirección General de Estadística. Anuario estadístico, 1936–54. Trujillo, 1937–57. Annual.   **CG90**

Ceased publication with issue for 1954.

East Africa

Year book and guide to East Africa: Kenya, Uganda, Tanganyika, Zanzibar, Portuguese East Africa, Mauritius, Seychelles, etc. ed. annually for the Union-Castle Mail Steamship Co., 1950– . London, R. Hale, [1950–]. il., maps. Annual. (1964)   **CG91**

For description *see Year book and guide to Southern Africa* (CG184).

Ecuador

Ecuador. Dirección General de Estadística y Censos. Síntesis estadística del Ecuador, 1955/60– . Quito, 1962– . Annual. (1955/62, pub. 1963)   **CG92**

Egypt

See United Arab Republic, p.386.

Finland

Finland. Tilastollinen Päätoimisto. Suomen tilastollinen vuosikirja, uusi sarja. Statistisk årsbok för Finland, ny ser. Statistical yearbook of Finland, n.s., 1902– . Helsinki, 1903– . 1st ed.– . Annual. (1963, pub. 1964)   **CG93**

Continues publication of same title, 1879–1902.

Title and text also in Swedish and French, 1934–52; in Swedish and English, 1953– . Some early issues in Russian and French.

France

Almanach Hachette; petite encyclopédie populaire, 1894– . Paris, Hachette, 1894– . il. Annual. (1964)   **CG94**

A handbook of miscellaneous information.

France. Institut National de la Statistique et des Études Economiques. Annuaire statistique de la France, 1877– . Paris, Impr. Nationale, 1878– . v.1– . Annual. (1963)   **CG95**

v.55, 1941; v.56, 1940–45.

Title varies slightly.

v.1–56 (1878–1940/45), issued by Statistique Générale de la France.

—— Annuaire statistique le l'Union Française Outre-Mer [Statistical yearbook of French Overseas Union] 2d ed. 1939–49. Paris, 1951. 2v.   **CG96**

1st ed., 1939–46, pub. 1949?.

1949–54, pub. 1956; 1958, pub. 1959 with title *Outre-Mer*.

Continued by:

—— Annuaire statistique des territoires d'outre-mer. 1959– . (1961)   **CG96a**

Seine (Dépt.) Préfecture. Cabinet du Préfet. Annuaire statistique de la ville de Paris et communes suburbaines de la Seine. 1.– année, 1880– . Paris, 1881– . Annual. (1961)   **CG97**

Germany

Bibliography

Deutsche Statistische Gesellschaft. Bibliographie der amtlichen westdeutschen Statistik, 1945–1951. München, 1952. 91p. (Einzelschriften der Deutschen Statistischen Gesellschaft. Hft. Nr.3)   **CG98**

Compendiums

Germany (Federal Republic, 1949–). Statistisches Bundesamt, Wiesbaden. Statistisches Jahrbuch für die Bundesrepublik Deutschland, 1952– . Stuttgart-Mainz, Kohlhammer, 1952– . Annual. (1964)   **CG99**

Continues the *Statistisches Jahrbuch für das Deutsche Reich,* 1880–1938, 57v., for the territory under the Federal Government of Germany. Has an added section giving international statistics.

—— Handbook of statistics for the Federal Republic of Germany. Stuttgart, Kohlhammer, 1961– . il. Triennial.   **CG99a**

Supersedes in part the office's *Statistisches Taschenbuch. Pocket book of statistics. Annuaire statistique de poche,* issued in 1958.

Germany (Territory under Allied Occupation, 1945–1955, U.S. Zone). Council of Land Minister-Presidents. Statistisches Handbuch von Deutschland, 1928–44, hrsg. vom Länderrat des Amerikanischen Besatzungsgebiets. München, F. Ehrenwirth, 1949. 640p., 17p.   **CG100**

Designed to provide some statistical information since the 1938 issue of the *Statistisches Jahrbuch für das Deutsche Reich* (CG99). 1928 was chosen as a "normal" year to compare with later available statistics.

Statistisches Jahrbuch deutscher Gemeinden. 1890– . 1. Jahrg.– . Hrsg. vom Deutschen Städtetag, bearb. vom Verband Deutscher Städtestatisker. Braunschweig, Waisenhaus-Buchdr., 1890– . Annual. (1963) **CG101**

Imprint varies.

1890–1933 had title *Statistisches Jahrbuch deutscher Städte.*

None issued 1917–26, 1939–48.

Germany (Democratic Republic, 1949–). Staatliche Zentralverwaltung für Statistik. Statistisches Jahrbuch der Deutschen Demokratischen Republik. 1.– . Jahrg. 1955– . Berlin, Deutscher Zentralverlag, 1956– . Annual. (v.9, 1964)   **CG102**

—— Statistical pocket book of the German Democratic Republic. v.1– . 1959– . Annual.

Also published in German, French, and Russian.

Ghana

Ghana. Central Bureau of Statistics. Statistical yearbook. 1st ed.– . 1961– . Accra, 1962– . Annual. (2d ed., 1962, pub. 1964)   **CG103**

Great Britain

Bibliography

Gt.Brit. Interdepartmental Committee on Social and Economic Research. Guides to official sources. London, Stat. Off., 1953– .   **CG104**

Contents: no.1, Labour statistics. Rev. May 1958. 1958. 78p.; no.2, Census reports of Great Britain, 1801–1931. 1951. 118p.; no.3, Local government statistics. 1953. 34p.; no.4, Agricultural and food statistics. 1958. 71p.; no.5, Social security statistics. 1961. 171p.; no.6, Census of production reports. 1961. 86p.

Gt.Brit. Permanent Consultative Committee on Official Statistics. Guide to current official statistics, being a systematic survey of the statistics appearing in all official publications, 1922–38. London, Stat. Off., 1923–39. v.1–17. Annual.   **CG105**

No more published.

Kendall, Maurice G. The sources and nature of the statistics of the United Kingdom, ed. for the Council of the Royal Statistical Society. London, pub. for the Royal Statistical Society by Oliver & Boyd, 1952–57. 2v. **CG106**

Reprints of 39 articles appearing in the Society's *Journal,* under the general headings "General surveys," "Statistics of particular commodities," "Statistics of transport," and "Miscellaneous."

Compendiums

Gt.Brit. Central Statistical Office. Annual abstract of statistics, v.1, 1840– . London, Stat. Off., 1854– . v.1– . Annual. (1963)   **CG107**

v.1–83, issued by the Board of Trade, as *Statistical abstract of the United Kingdom.* Each of these volumes contained statistics for the preceding 15 years. Coverage varies slightly.

v.83, covering 1924 to 1938, was published in 1940. No volumes were published during World War II, but v.84, with a new title and under a new issuing body, appeared in 1948, and covers 1935–46; v.85, published 1948, covers 1937–47; v.86, published 1949, covers 1938–48; v.87– , 1951– , published annually, cover 1938 and the last 10 years.

Mitchell, Brian R. Abstract of British historical statistics. With the collaboration of Phyllis Deane. Cambridge, Univ. Pr., 1962. 513p.   **CG108**

Presents tables of economic statistics of the United Kingdom, with information on sources and coverage and with introduction and bibliographies for each section. In some cases figures go back to the 17th century and earlier, but most series begin with the 18th and 19th centuries.

Whitaker, Joseph. Almanack; 1869– . London, Whitaker, 1869– . v.1– . Annual. (1964)   **CG109**

Especially full for statistics of the British Commonwealth, with brief statistics for foreign countries.

London. County Council. London statistics. n.s. v.1– . 1945/54– . [London], 1957– . maps. Annual. (v.5, 1951/60, pub. 1963)   **CG110**

Supersedes the Council's *Statistical abstract for London* (1897–1950) and its *London statistics* (1890–1936/38).

Greece

Greece. Ethnikē Statistikē Hypēresia. Statistical yearbook of Greece. 1st ed., 1954– . Athens, Nat. Pr. Off., 1955– . Annual. (1963, pub. 1964)   **CG111**

Title and text in Greek and English.

1st edition, 1954, issued with title *Statistical summary of Greece.*

The first postwar statistical yearbook of Greece.

Continues *Statistikē epēteris tēs Hellados. Annuaire statistique de la Grèce,* 1930–39. Title and text in Greek and French.

Hawaii

Thrum's Hawaiian annual and standard guide, combined with All about Hawaii. 1st– . 1875– . Honolulu, Honolulu Star-Bulletin, 1875– . il. Annual. (1963)   **CG112**

Title varies: 1940/41– , combined with *All about Hawaii.* 1963 issue includes section on the Hawaiian language, p.195–216.

—— Index; v.1–58, 1875–1932.

Hungary

Hungary. Központi Statisztikai Hivatal. Statisztikai évkönyv. Statistical yearbook, 1949/55– . Budapest, 1957– . Annual. (1963)   **CG113**

Pub. in Hungarian and English.

Supersedes the Office's *Magyar statisztikai évkönyv. Statistisches Jahrbuch.* v.1–20, 1871–90; *Annuaire statistique.* Nouv. cours, 1893–1941.

—— Statistical yearbook of Hungary, 1949–1955, comp. by Central Bureau of Statistics; from: Statisztikai évkönyv, Budapest. N.Y., Joint Pub. Research Service, 1958. 443p.   **CG114**

India

India. Office of the Economic Adviser. Guide to current official statistics. . . . Prep. under instructions from the Economic Adviser by S. Subramanian, statistician. Delhi, Manager of Publs., 1943–49. v.1–3.   **CG115**

Contents: v.1, Production and prices (2d ed.); v.2, Trade, transport and communications, and finance (excluding public finance); v.3, Public finance, education, public health, census, labour, consumption of commodities, and miscellaneous.

India (Republic). Central Statistical Organisation. Statistical abstract, India. n.s. no.1– . 1949– . Delhi, 1950– . Annual. (no.11, 1962)   **CG116**

Issuing body varies: n.s. no.1 issued by the Office of Economic Advisers.

Supersedes *Statistical abstract for British India,* 1911/12–1939/40, issued by the Dept. of Commercial Intelligence and Statistics, and the *Statistical abstract* for 1946/47, issued by the Office of the Economic Adviser.

Times of India directory and year book including who's who, 1914– . Bombay, London, Bennett, Coleman, 1914– . Annual. (1963/64)   **CG117**

Title varies: *Indian year book,* 1914–47; *The Indian and Pakistan year book and who's who,* 1949–1952/53; *The Times of India directory and year book including who's who,* 1954/55– .

Unofficial but very useful. Contains a large amount of descriptive and statistical information and, 1918– , a "Who's who in India."

Indonesia

Indonesia. Biro Pusat Statistik. Statistical abstracts, [1950–1955]. Djakarta, Central Bureau of Statistics, 1956. 138p.   **CG118**

—— Statistik. Statistical pocket book of Indonesia. 1st ed.– . 1956– . Djakarta, 1957– . Annual. (7th ed. 1962)   **CG118a**

Issued in Dutch and English editions. Comprises basic statistical information on the economic and social conditions in Indonesia.

Netherlands East Indies. Departement van Landbouw, Nijverheid en Handel. Statistisch Kantoor. Statistisch jaaroverzicht van Nederlandsch-Indie. Statistical abstract for the Netherlands East Indies; new ser. of the Statistical annual of the Netherlands (Colonies), 1922/23–39. Batavia, 1924–40. [17v.?]   **CG119**

Title page and text in both Dutch and English.
1930–39 issues are pt.2 of *Indisch verlag,* 1931–40.

Iran

Iran almanac and book of facts. 1st ed.– . 1961– . Tehran, Echo of Iran, 1961– . Annual. (1963) **CG120**

Though not an official publication, this comprehensive book of general information on Iranian life and culture includes many tables of statistics.

Iraq

Iraq. Principal Bureau of Statistics. Statistical abstract. 1927/28–1937/38—— . Baghdad, 1939– . Annual (slightly irregular). (1962, pub. 1963)   **CG121**

At head of title: Ministry of Economics. Issuing body varies.
Title and text in English and Arabic.

Ireland

Ireland (Eire). Central Statistics Office. Statistical abstract, 1931– . Dublin, Stat. Off., 1931– . v.1– . Annual. (1963)   **CG122**

1931–1947/48 issued by Dept. of Industry and Commerce.

Ireland, Northern

Northern Ireland. General Register Office. Ulster year book, 1926– . Belfast, 1926– . Triennial. (1960/62)   **CG123**

None published 1938–1946.
Presents statistical and other information on social and economic conditions, health, education, etc. Each issue contains a special article: for 1960–62, *Industrial development in Northern Ireland.*

Israel

See also Palestine, p.384.

Israel. Central Bureau of Statistics. Statistical abstract of Israel. no.1– . 1949/50– . Jerusalem, Govt. Printer, 1951– . Annual. (no.14, 1963)   **CG124**

Title and text in Hebrew and English.

Israel economist: Annual . . . a survey of Israel's economy. Jerusalem, E. Kollek, 1948–58. v.1–8. Annual. **CG125**

The first issue, 1948, was titled *The Palestine economist: Annual . . . 1948; a review of Palestine's economy.*
Contains articles summarizing various aspects of the economy, with illustrative statistics. The 1958 issue attempts to

survey the 10-year period, 1948–58. Beginning with the 1951 annual, a statistical supplement is included.

Israel yearbook, 1950/51– . [Tel Aviv], Israel Yearbook Publs., 1951– . Annual. (1964)   **CG126**

Succeeds the *Anglo-Palestine yearbook* (1946, 1947–48) and the *Palestine yearbook and Israeli annual.*
Provides: (1) a comprehensive review of social and economic conditions; (2) diplomatic and commercial directories; and (3) a survey of historical developments, arranged under broad subjects.

Italy

Associazione per lo Sviluppo dell' Industria nel Mezzogiorno. Statistiche sul mezzogiorno d'Italia, 1861–1953. Roma, SVIMEZ, 1954. 1096p.   **CG127**

Focuses on regionalism; gives economic, political, and social statistics for the south of Italy, which is less highly developed industrially than the north and center. Not all tables cover the whole period 1861–1953, but especially full treatment is given to population, transportation, emigration, internal migration, education, etc.

Italy. Istituto Centrale di Statistica. Annuario statistico italiano. 1878– . Roma, Istit. Poligrafico dello Stato, 1878– . Annual (Irregular). (1963, pub. 1964) **CG128**

In five series: ser. 1, 1878–1907; ser. 2, 1911–25; ser. 3, 1927–33; ser. 4, 1934–43; ser. 5, 1944/48– .
Ser. 1–2, issued by the Direzione Generale della Statistica.

—— Compendio statistico italiano, 1927– . Roma, Istit. Poligrafico dello Stato, 1927– . Annual. (1963)   **CG129**

Publication suspended 1943–45.
1946 issue, called ser. 2, v.1, serves as an abridged edition of the *Annuario* (CG128).

—— Sommario statistico delle regioni d'Italia. Roma, 1947. 248p. maps, tables.   **CG130**

Some tables give figures beginning with 1871.

Jamaica

Handbook of Jamaica, 1881– , comprising historical, statistical and general information . . . obtained from official and other reliable records and comp. by the Jamaica Information Service. London, Crown Agents; Jamaica, Govt. Prt. Off., 1881– . v.1– . maps. Irregular. (1962)   **CG131**

Japan

Japan. Bureau of General Statistics. Résumé statistique de l'Empire du Japon, 1884–1940. Tokyo, 1887–1940. v.1–54.   **CG132**

Japanese and French.
A résumé of the Japanese statistical annual published in Japanese.

Japan. Ministry of Finance. Financial and economic annual of Japan. Tokyo, Govt. Prt. Off., 1901–40. v.1–40. maps. Annual.   **CG133**

Includes information on area, population, agriculture, industry, and commerce for the Japanese Empire. Early volumes give figures from 1867/68.

Japan. Prime Minister's Office. Statistics Bureau. Japan statistical yearbook, 1949– . [Tokyo], 1949– . Annual. (1963)   **CG134**

1949 and 1950 were published by the Nihon Statistical Association.
In Japanese and English. To replace the *Statistical yearbook of the Empire of Japan,* which ceased with v.59, 1941.

The 1949 issue attempts to fill the eight-year gap in statistics; from 1950 on, the issues concentrate on annual figures.

Japan economic yearbook. [Tokyo, Oriental economist], 1954– . Biennial (Irregular). **CG134a**

Title page reads: The Oriental economist's Japan economic yearbook.

Japan year book, 1933–1949/52. [Tokyo], Foreign Affairs Assoc. of Japan, [1933–52]. Annual (Irregular). **CG135**

"This year book has no connection with that published by the late Prof. Takenobu under the same title, which is now defunct," but was published, 1906–31, by the Japan Year Book Office.

A detailed review of the economic, social, political, and cultural life of Japan. Of special value for coverage during the war years, including much documentary material, e.g., the Constitution, Supreme Commander for the Allied Powers letters and memoranda, laws and ordinances, and text of the Japanese peace treaty signed Sept. 8, 1951.

Taeuber, Irene B. The population of Japan. Princeton, Princeton Univ. Pr., 1958. 461p. il. **CG136**

A comprehensive work containing statistics from the 12th century to 1950, with projections to 1980.

Annotated bibliography, p.395–461, includes references to statistics for Taiwan, Korea, and Manchoukuo.

Jordan

Jordan. Dept. of Statistics. Statistical yearbook. Amman. no.1– . 1950?– . Annual. (no.13, 1962) **CG137**

Text in English and Arabic.

At head of title: The Hashemite Kingdom of Jordan. Ministry of National Economy.

Korea

Hanguk Ŭnhaeng. Chosabu. Economic statistics yearbook. 1st ed. Seoul, 1960– . Annual. (4th ed. 1963) **CG138**

Added title page in Korean. Text in Korean and English.

Besides economic data, gives statistical information on area, population, agriculture, minerals, education, communications, etc.

Korea (Republic). Puhungbu. Statistical handbook of Korea. Seoul, Bureau of Statistics, Economic Planning Board, [1962]. 116p. il. **CG139**

A compact, useful handbook, containing general information and basic statistical data on economic and social aspects of Korea. Arranged by broad subject. No index.

Latin America

See also names of individual countries.

California. University. University at Los Angeles. Committee on Latin American Studies. Statistical abstract of Latin America. 1955– . [Los Angeles], 1956– . il. Biennial, beginning with 1964/65; previously pub. annually. (1963, pub. 1963) **CG140**

Information on the Latin-American Republics, Puerto Rico, and European dependencies in the Western Hemisphere with the exception of Greenland, St. Pierre, and Miquelon.

Latvia

Latvia. Valsts Statistikā Pārvalde. Latvijas statistikā gada grāmata, 1920–39. Annuaire statistique de la Lettonie. Riga, 1921–39. **CG141**

In Lettish and French.

Latvian S.S.R. Statistikas Pārvalde. Latvijas PSR tautas saimnieciba; statistisko datu krājums. Rīga, Valsts Statistikas Izdevniecība, 1957. 229p. tables. **CG142**

In Lettish and Russian.

Covers period mainly from 1945 to 1956, though some tables begin with 1940 and a few even earlier.

Lithuania

Lithuania. Centralinis Statistikos Biuras. Lietuvos statistikos metraštis. . . . Annuaire statistique de la Lithuanie, 1924/1926–38. Kaunas, 1927–39?. v.1–11. Annual. **CG143**

Luxembourg

Luxemburg. Office de la Statistique Générale. Annuaire statistique. 1955, 1960. Luxembourg, 1956, 1962. v.1–2. (In progress) **CG144**

Before 1940, the annual statistics were published as supplements to the Office's *Annuaire officiel,* 1925–30, under the title *Note statistique;* 1931–40, as *Aperçu statistique.* Publication suspended 1941–45.

Malaya

Malaya (Federation). Official year book. v.1– . 1961– . Kuala Lumpur, pr. at the Govt. Pr., 1961– . Annual. (v.2, 1962) **CG145**

At head of title: Ministry of the Interior.

Malta

Malta. Central Office of Statistics. Annual abstract of statistics. no.1– . 1946– . Valetta, 1947– . Annual. (no.15, 1961) **CG146**

Earlier title: *Statistical abstract of the Maltese islands,* no.1–14, 1946–60.

Malta year book for the year 1953– . . . . St. Julian's, St. Michael's College Publ., [1953–]. il. Annual. (1964) **CG147**

General information, with some summary statistics and articles on various aspects of Maltese history, culture, etc.

Mexico

Bibliography

México. Dirección General de Estadística. Bibliografía mexicana de estadística. México, Talleres Gráficos de la Nación, 1942. 2v. **CG148**

Contents: t.1, Generalidades, teoría y aplicaciones metodológicas, demografía, estadística social, económica, administrativa geografía; t.2, Historia, lingüística, publicaciones periódicas, cartografía, titulos complementarios. Índice general geográfico. Índice onomástico de autores.

—— Catálogo general de las estadísticas nacionales. México, 1960. 127p. **CG149**

1st edition had title *Catálogo de estadística.*

A listing of Mexican statistical publications, arranged by subject, with general index. No dates are included.

—— —— Índice. México, 1960. 44p.

Compendiums

México. Dirección General de Estadística. Anuario estadístico, 1893– . México, 1894– . Annual (Irregular). (1960/61, pub. 1963) **CG150**

Title varies slightly.

None published 1908–29, 1931–37.

Covers population, education, labor, agriculture, industry, communication, commerce, finance, etc.

—— Compendio estadístico. México, 1941– . Irregular. (1962)   **CG151**

A small, compact compendium including fairly broad coverage of statistics.

Middle East

Statistical handbook of Middle Eastern countries: Palestine, Cyprus, Egypt, Iraq, the Lebanon, Syria, Transjordan, Turkey. 2d ed. Jerusalem, Jewish Agency for Palestine, Economic Research Inst., 1945. 183p. **CG152**

1st ed. 1944. Reprinted with the correction of a few misprints and the addition of a supplement containing new figures.

Morocco

Morocco. Service Central des Statistiques. Annuaire statistique du Maroc. v.[1]– . 1925– . Rabat, 1926– . Annual (Irregular). (1960)   **CG153**

Also pub. in Arabic.

v.14 covers period 1939–44.

Title varies slightly. Issuing body varies.

Netherlands

Netherlands. Centraal Bureau voor de Statistiek. Jaarcifers voor Nederland. Statistical year book of the Netherlands. 1881– . s'-Gravenhage, Bureau, [1882]– . Annual. (1961–62, pub. 1964)   **CG154**

Title varies.

Text in Dutch and French, 1884–1939; in Dutch and German, 1940–1941/42; in Dutch and English, 1943/46– .

From 1887 to 1921, each volume consisted of two parts: (1) *"Rijk in Europa,"* and (2) *"Kolonien";* from 1922 to 1939, the *"Kolonien"* section was continued as a separate publication by Netherlands East Indies. Departement van Landbouw (*see* CG119).

—— Statistisch zakboek [Pocket year book]. 's-Gravenhage, 1899– . Annual (Irregular). (1963) **CG155**

In Dutch only.

New Zealand

Bibliography

Neale, Edward Percy. Guide to New Zealand official statistics. 3d ed. enl. and rewritten. Christchurch, Whitcombe and Tombs, [1955]. 195p. (Auckland University college texts, no.2)   **CG156**

1st ed. 1938.

Compendiums

New Zealand. Dept. of Statistics. New Zealand official year-book, 1892– . Wellington, 1892– . v.1– . Annual. (1963)   **CG157**

Covers a wide range of descriptive as well as statistical information. 68th issue, 1963, includes a list of special articles appearing in previous issues, and a select bibliography of New Zealand publications, p.1147–66.

Nicaragua

Nicaragua. Dirección General de Estadística. Anuario estadístico, 1938–1947. Managua, Talleres Nacionales, 1939–47.   **CG158**

Ceased publication with 1947.

Nigeria

Diplomatic Press trade directory of the Federal Republic of Nigeria. 1960– . London, Diplomatic Press and Pub. Co., 1960– . il. Biennial. (1963/64)   **CG159**

Title varies slightly.

In two sections: (1) information on government, natural resources, business and industry, transportation and commerce; (2) a classified list of firms and a brief who's who in commerce and industry.

Norway

Norway. Statistiske Sentralbyrå. Statistisk årbok for Norge, 1880– . Statistical year-book of Norway. Oslo, 1881– . v.1– . Annual. (1964, pub. 1964)   **CG160**

1886–1951, in Norwegian and French; 1952– , in Norwegian and English. v.62–64, 1943–45, pub. in 1v. 1946.

Pakistan

Pakistan. Central Statistical Office. Pakistan statistical yearbook. 1st ed.– . 1952– . Karachi, Manager of Publs., 1954– . Irregular. (5th ed., 1962, pub. 1962)   **CG161**

Continues *Statistical digest of Pakistan,* issued by the Dept. of Commercial Intelligence and Statistics, 1950.

—— Statistical pocket-book of Pakistan. 1st ed.– . 1961– . Annual. (1964)   **CG162**

Palestine

Palestine. Office of Statistics. Statistical abstract of Palestine, 1936–1944/45. Jerusalem, Govt. Printer, 1937–46. Annual (slightly irregular).   **CG163**

Ceased with 8th ed., 1944–45.

Statistical handbook of Jewish Palestine, 1947, comp. under the supervision of D. Gurevich, ed. by A. Gertz. Jerusalem, Dept. of Statistics, 1947. 438p.   **CG164**

Gives statistical data on the development of Jewish Palestine during the previous 30 years.

Panama

Panama. Dirección de Estadística y Censos. Panama en cifras. 1st ed.– . 1961– . Panama, 1961– . Biennial. (1963)   **CG165**

1st edition, 1961, covers 1955–60; 2d edition, 1963, covers 1958–62.

Continues *Nuestro progreso en cifras.* 1st ed. 1953; 2d ed. 1958.

—— Extracto estadístico; estadística general. 1941/43–1953/54. [Panama, 1950?–]   **CG166**

Triennial, 1941/43–1950/52; biennial, 1953/54.

—— Anuario de comercio exterior. 1953– . (1962)   **CG167**

Paraguay

Paraguay. Dirección General de Estadística y Censos. Anuario estadístico, 1886– . Asunción, Impr. Nacional, 1888– . Irregular. Quinquennial since 1948. (1954/59)   **CG168**

Peru

Perú. Dirección Nacional de Estadística y Censos. Anuario estadístico del Perú, 1944/45– . Lima, 1947– . Annual. (1956–57, pub. 1959)   **CG169**

Continues the Office's *Extracto estadístico del Perú.*

Philippines

Bibliography

Philippines. Office of Statistical Coordination and Standards. An annotated bibliography of official statistical publications of the Philippine government. Manila, 1963. 25p. **CG170**

Compendiums

Philippines (Republic). Bureau of the Census and Statistics. Statistical handbook of the Philippines. 1st ed.– . 1953– . Manila, 1953– . Irregular. (5th ed., 1962, pub. 1963) **CG171**

Summary statistics cover demographic, economic, and social aspects of the Philippines. 1962 issue includes data from 1946 in some tables.

—— Philippine statistics, 1903–1959; handbook. Manila, 1960. 144p. il. **CG172**

Includes statistics on area, population, economics, agriculture, fishing, minerals, foreign trade, etc.

Poland

Poland. Głowny Urząd Statystyczny. Rocznik statystyczny [Statistical yearbook], rok 1– . 1920/21– . Warsaw, 1922– . Annual (Irregular). (rok 23, 1963) **CG173**

Title varies: 1920/1921–38, in Polish and French, *Rocznik statystyki Rzeczypospolitej Polskiej—Annuaire statistique de la République Polonaise.*

None published for 1939–46, 1951–54. Resumed with v.15, 1955.

—— Concise statistical yearbook of Poland. v.1– . 1930– . Warsaw, 1930– . Annual (Irregular). (1957) **CG174**

At head of title: Central Statistical Office of the Polish People's Republic.

Title varies. Publication suspended 1940–46.

Published in Polish, English, French, and Russian editions.

For many libraries this concise edition would be adequate.

Portugal

Portugal. Instituto Nacional de Estatística. Anuario estatístico de Portugal. Annuaire statistique. 1875– . Lisboa, 1877– . Annual. (1962) **CG175**

Title and issuing body vary.

Beginning 1938(?), title and text in Portuguese and French.

Final chapter gives data on Portuguese territories: Cabo Verde, Guiné, S. Thomé e Principe, Angola, Moçambique, India, Macau e Timor.

Rhodesia

Rhodesia, Southern. Central African Statistical Office. Official year book of Southern Rhodesia. Salisbury, S. Rhodesia, 1924–1952. **CG176**

v.1, 1924; v.2, 1930; v.3, 1932; v.4, 1952.

Title varies.

"Statistical year books" published in 1938 and 1947, and "Statistical handbooks" published in 1939 and 1945. Cf. *Preface* to v.4, 1952.

v.4 gives statistics mainly up to 1950.

Year book and guide of the Rhodesias and Nyasaland. Salisbury, S. Rhodesia, Rhodesian Pub., 1937– . il. Annual (Irregular). (1962) **CG177**

Rumania

Rumania. Directia Centrală de Statistică. Anuarul statistic al R.P.R. 1957– . Bucureşti, 1957– . Annual. (1964) **CG178**

Volumes for 1957– are accompanied by separate volumes of translation of text: 1957, in Russian, Rumanian, and French; 1958– , in Rumanian and English with title *Statistical yearbook of the R.P.R.* (1964).

Rumania. Institutul Central de Statistică. Anuarul statistic al României. Annuaire statistique de la Roumanie, 1902–1937/38?. Bucureşti, 1904–1939/40?. Irregular. **CG179**

Text and tables in Rumanian and French.

1st issue, 1902; 2d, 1909; 3d, 1912.

El Salvador

Salvador. Dirección General de Estadística y Censos. Anuario estadístico, 1911–23, 1927– . San Salvador, Impr. Nacional, 1912– . Annual. (1962) **CG180**

(1940–43, in 2v.; 1944–48, in 3v.; 1949– , in 2v.)

South Africa

South Africa. Office of Census and Statistics. Official year book of the Union and of Basutoland, Bechuanaland Protectorate and Swaziland, 1917– . Pretoria, Govt. Printer, 1918– . v.1– . maps. Biennial. (no.30, 1960, pub. 1961) **CG181**

An important yearbook, giving detailed statistical, descriptive, and historical information, with bibliographies and lists of government publications.

no.1–2, 1917–18, do not include Basutoland.

—— Uniestatistieke oor vyftig jaar; jubileumuitgawe, 1910–1960 . . . Union statistics for fifty years; jubilee issue. [Pretoria, 1960] 1v. [v.p.] **CG182**

Bilingual throughout. Tables for vital statistics, education, labor, agriculture, industry, etc. Tables of contents and notes for each section, but no general index.

State of South Africa; pictorial, social, economic, financial and statistical year-book for the Republic of South Africa. v.1, 1957– . Johannesburg, Da Gama, 1957?– . il. Annual. (1964) **CG183**

Title and publisher vary.

A comprehensive yearbook on conditions in the Union of South Africa.

Year book and guide to Southern Africa: Republic of South Africa, Federation of Rhodesia and Nyasaland, South West Africa, etc., ed. annually for the Union-Castle Mail Steamship Co. 1st ed., 1901– . London, R. Hale, 1901– . il., maps. Annual. (1964) **CG184**

Title varies. Not pub. 1941–46.

A useful and inexpensive yearbook, containing a large amount of descriptive, statistical, and gazetteer information.

In 1950, the former *South and East African year book and guide* was divided into two separate publications, of which this is one. For the other *see Year book and guide to East Africa* (CG91).

Spain

Spain. Dirección General de Estadística (1938–). Zona de Protectorado y de los Territorios de Soberanía de España en el Norte de Africa. Anuario estadístico, 1941–55. Madrid, 1942–57. il. Annual. **CG185**

Ceased publication.

Spain. Instituto Nacional de Estadística. Anuario estadístico de España, 1912– . Madrid, 1913– . v.1– . Annual (slightly irregular). (1963) **CG186**

Suspended publication 1935–42.

Previously published by varying departments.

—— Edición manual, 1941– . Annual. (1964)

Sweden

Sweden. Statistika Centralbyrån. Statistisk årsbok för Sverige. Statistical yearbook of Sweden. Stockholm, 1914– . Annual. (1963) **CG187**

Title and text in Swedish and English, 1952– ; previously in Swedish and French (French title: *Annuaire statistique de la Suède*).

Includes chapter of comparative international statistics.

Continues *Sveriges officiella statistik i sammendrag,* 1870–1913.

Switzerland

Switzerland. Statistisches Amt. Statistisches Jahrbuch der Schweiz. Annuaire statistique de la Suisse, 1891– . Bern, 1891– . v.1– . Annual. (1964) **CG188**

In place of the yearbook for 1897, the *Graphischstatistischer Atlas der Schweiz,* 1897, was issued.

Some tables give figures for 30 years.

Syria

Syria. Ministry of Planning. Directorate of Statistics. al-Majmū'a al-ihsā'īya. Statistical abstract. 1st ed.– . 1948– . Damascus, Govt. Printer, 1948?– . Annual. (1963) **CG189**

In Arabic and English. 1st and 2d editions in Arabic only.

Tanganyika

Handbook of Tanganyika. 2d ed. Ed. by J. P. Moffett, Commissioner for Social Development. Dar-es-Salaam, Govt. Printer, 1958. 703p. il., maps. **CG190**

1st edition, 1930, issued by the Chief Secretary's Office, edited by Gerald F. Sayers.

"An historical and descriptive account of the territory" with statistics throughout the text.

Bibliography, p.567–677.

Tanganyika. Economic and Statistics Division. Statistical abstract, 1938/51– . Dar-es-Salaam, Govt. Printer, 1953?– . Annual. (1962) **CG191**

1st edition covered 1938–51; 2d edition covered 1938–52. Issuing body varies.

Thailand

Bibliography

Thailand. Central Statistical Office. Statistical bibliography; an annotated bibliography of Thai government statistical publications. [Bangkok], 1961. 34p. **CG192**

Compendiums

Thailand. National Statistical Office. Statistical year book, no.1– . Bangkok, 1916– . Irregular. (no.24, 1963) **CG193**

no.21, 1939/40–1944; no.22, 1945–55; no.23, 1956–58. In Thai and English.
Publisher varies.

Trinidad

Trinidad and Tobago year book, 1865– , containing information obtained from official records and reliable sources. Trinidad, Yuille, 1865– . Annual. (v.98, 1963/ 64) **CG194**

Turkey

Turkey. Istatistik Genel Müdürlüğü. Istatistik yıllığı. Annuaire statistique, 1928– . Ankara, 1928– . v.1– . Annual. (1960) **CG195**

Not pub. 1954–58. Resumed 1959.
Title and text in Turkish and French.

Union of Soviet Socialist Republics

Narodnoe khoziaistvo SSSR; statisticheskii ezhegodnik. Moskva, 1956, 1958– . Annual. (1962, pub. 1963) **CG196**

Issued by Tsentral'noe Statisticheskoe Upravlenie SSSR.

The official statistical annual publication, giving data on area, population, economics, industry, agriculture, health, education, and cultural and social affairs. Most important data include comparative figures for the years 1913, 1928, and 1940, pre-Revolutionary and prewar years.

For further information concerning USSR statistical material, *see* Paul L. Horecky, *Basic Russian publications* (DC 253).

☙ Various translations of *Narodnoe khoziaistvo SSSR* have been issued, e.g.:

Union of Soviet Socialist Republics. Tsentral'noe Statisticheskoe Upravlenie. The national economy of the USSR; a statistical compilation. Moscow, State Official Pub. House, 1956. [unpaged] 270p. of tables. **CG197**

—— National economy of the USSR; statistical returns. Moscow, Foreign Languages Pub. House, 1957. 230p. **CG198**

—— Statistical handbook of the USSR; with introd., additional tables and annotations by Harry Schwartz. Moscow, 1956; N.Y., Nat. Industrial Conference Board, 1957. 122p. **CG199**

—— The national economy of the USSR in 1960; statistical yearbook. Wash., U.S. Joint Publ. Research Service, 1962. 937p. (JPRS ser. 12317) **CG200**

United Arab Republic

Egypt. Government Press. Almanac, 1902–39. Cairo, Govt. Pr., 1902–39. Annual. (1939) **CG201**

Issuing office varies. 1913–26 had title *Egyptian government almanac.*

United Arab Republic (Egypt). Dept. of Statistics and Census. Annuaire statistique. [1.] année– . 1909– . Cairo, 1909– . Annual (Irregular). (1959) **CG202**

In Arabic and French.

1909–1955/56, issued by: Egypt. Ministry of Finance. Statistical Dept.

Title varies slightly.

—— Statistical pocket year-book. 1957– . Cairo, 1957– . Annual. (1963) **CG203**

Uruguay

Uruguay. Dirección General de Estadística y Censos. Anuario estadístico, 1884– . Montevideo, Impr. Nacional, 1885– . Quadrennial (Irregular). (v.54, 1955–60) **CG204**

—— Síntesis estadística, 1918– . Annual (slightly irregular).

Venezuela

Venezuela. Dirección General de Estadística y Censos Nacionales. Anuario estadístico de Venezuela, 1877–1912, 1938– . Caracas, Ed. Grafolit, 1878– . **CG205**
None pub. 1913–37. Irregular (1955–56, pub. 1961?).

West Indies

West Indies and Caribbean year book, 1926/27– . London, Skinner, 1927– . il. Annual. (1964) **CG206**
Title varies.
Covers: Bermuda, Bahamas, Barbados, British Guiana, British Honduras, Jamaica, Cayman Islands, Turks and Caicos Islands, Trinidad and Tobago, Leeward Islands, Windward Islands, Canal Zone (Panama), Colombia, Costa Rica, Cuba, Dominican Republic, El Salvador, French Guiana, French West Indies, Guatemala, Haiti, Honduras, Netherlands Antilles, Nicaragua, Panama, Puerto Rico, Surinam, Venezuela, Virgin Islands.
General information, statistics, and trade directories.

Yugoslavia

Statistički godišnjak FNRJ. 1954– . Beograd, Savezni Zavod za Statistiku, 1954– . Annual. (1963) **CG207**
Includes list of publications of statistical offices.
The Federal Statistical Office of the Federal People's Republic of Yugoslavia also issues *Statistical yearbook of the Federal People's Republic of Yugoslavia . . .* English text. Beograd, 1955– . Annual. (1963)
The latter is a translation key to be used with original tables in *Statistički godišnjak FNRJ.* No figures from the tables are reproduced in this volume.
Also published in French.

—— Statistical pocket-book of Yugoslavia. 1955– . Annual. (1964) **CG208**

Yugoslavia. Direktsīja Drzhavne Statistike. Statistički godišnjak. Annuaire statistique. Knjiga v.1–9, 1929–1938/39. Beograd, 1932–39. **CG209**

C H

Economics

🌿 This area is a large one under which many related subjects are grouped: business and business management, commerce, finance and banking, insurance, labor and industrial relations, and various others. Many large libraries, both public and academic, will have special departments devoted to one or several of these subject fields, and in most large cities there will be pertinent special libraries, usually connected with large business or banking concerns. These libraries will have many more specialized sources than can be listed here.

In this section are included some of the bibliographies, indexes, dictionaries, and handbooks from which, or about which, information may be sought in a large general library.

GENERAL WORKS

Bibliography

🌿 Documents issued by the federal government are particularly useful in the field of economics. Only a few of the many valuable publications of the various departments and bureaus can be listed here. The Bureau of Labor Statistics; the Bureau of the Census; the Department of Commerce and its various bureaus, including the now defunct Bureau of Foreign and Domestic Commerce; and many others are prolific publishers. For further information consult the *Monthly catalog of United States government publications* (AH18).

American University of Beirut. Economic Research Institute. A selected and annotated bibliography of economic literature on the Arabic speaking countries of the Middle East, 1938–1952. Beirut, Gedeon Pr., 1954. 199p. **CH2**

—— —— Supplements, 1953– . Annual.
Covers a selection of economic literature, in Arabic, English, and French, on the Arabic-speaking countries of the Middle East. Classified by country and subject, with brief descriptive annotations.

Batson, Harold Edward. A select bibliography of modern economic theory, 1870–1929. London, Routledge, 1930. 224p. **CH3**
An annotated bibliography of books and periodical articles: pt.1, by subject; pt.2, by author.

Braeuer, Walter. Handbuch zur Geschichte der Volkswirtschaftslehre; ein bibliographisches Nachschlagewerk. Frankfurt am Main, Klostermann, 1952. 224p. **CH4**
An international bio-bibliography of the history of political economy from ancient and medieval times to the modern day, with biographical sketches of important economists. Includes books, dissertations, and periodical articles.

L'economia degli stati italiani prima dell' unificazione. Milano, Feltrinelli, 1962– . v.1– . (In progress) **CH5**
At head of title: Istituto Giangiacomo Feltrinelli.
v.1, Stati Sardi di Terraferma (1700–1860); saggio bibliografico a cura di Francesco Sirugo.
Arranged chronologically with author index.

Hanson, Lawrence William. Contemporary printed sources for British and Irish economic history, 1701–1750. Cambridge, Univ. Pr., 1963. 978p. **CH6**
Includes books, pamphlets, broadsides, etc. totaling more than 6500 items, published 1701–1750 inclusive. Represents the holdings of the principal libraries of Great Britain and eight important libraries of the United States.
Locates copies.

Harvard University. Bureau for Economic Research in Latin America. Economic literature of Latin America, a tentative bibliography. Cambridge, Harvard Univ. Pr., 1935–36. 2v. **CH7**
An extensive bibliography of books, pamphlets, and periodical articles listing a total of 12,520 numbered items. Arranged geographically by country or region, with a subject arrangement under each and a general index of authors for

each volume. Special features are the introductory notes at the heads of important sections; the appendixes on the statistical sources of South America, Mexico, and the Caribbean; and notes on collections of Latin-American economic literature in leading libraries.

Hasse, Adelaide Rosalie. Index of economic material in documents of the states of the United States. Prep. for the Dept. of Economics and Sociology of the Carnegie Institution of Washington. Wash., Carnegie Inst., 1907–22. 13v. in 16.   **CH8**

Volumes issued are:
California, 1849–1904. 1908. 316p.
Delaware, 1789–1904. 1910. 137p.
Illinois, 1809–1904. 1909. 393p.
Kentucky, 1792–1904. 1910. 452p.
Maine, 1820–1904. 1907. 95p.
Massachusetts, 1789–1904. 1908. 310p.
New Hampshire, 1789–1904. 1907. 66p.
New Jersey, 1789–1904. 1914. 705p.
New York, 1789–1904. 1907. 553p.
Ohio, 1787–1904. 1912. 2v.
Pennsylvania, 1790–1904. 1919–22. 3v.
Rhode Island, 1789–1904. 1908. 95p.
Vermont, 1789–1904. 1907. 71p.
No more published.

Includes a comprehensive listing of all economic material (with definite reference to volume and page) to be found in the printed reports of administrative officers, legislative committees, and special commissions of the states, and in the governors' messages, for the period covered.

The word "economic" has been interpreted very liberally to include almost any aspect of American history. Indexing is by general heading and broad subject.

Omits reports of bureaus of labor before 1902, as these are covered in the *Index to all reports issued by bureaus of labor statistics . . . to March 1902,* issued by the U.S. Bureau of Labor.

Hazlewood, Arthur. The economics of "under-developed" areas; an annotated reading list of books, articles and official publications. 2d enl. ed. London, pub. for the Inst. of Commonwealth Studies by Oxford Univ. Pr., 1959. 156p.   **CH9**

1st ed. 1954.

A classified list of 1027 numbered items, mostly published between 1930 and 1958, with indexes by author and place.

—— The economics of development; an annotated list of books and articles published 1958–1962. London, pub. for the Inst. of Commonwealth Studies by Oxford Univ. Pr., 1964. 104p.   **CH10**

A sequel to the above, listing 732 entries in English in classified arrangement. Index by author and place.

Hollander, Jacob Harry. The economic library of Jacob H. Hollander, comp. by Elsie A. G. Marsh. Baltimore, priv. pr., 1937. 324p.   **CH11**

3860 titles, chronologically arranged, 1574–1936. Particularly rich in 18th-century English tracts.

Istituto Nazionale per le Relazioni Culturali con l'Estero. Scienze economiche e sociali. Roma, I.R.C.E., 1941. 167p. (Bibliografie del ventennio)   **CH12**

Works published in Italy in the period between World Wars I and II, arranged by broad subject with separate author index. Not annotated.

Johns Hopkins University. Dept. of Political Economy. A selected bibliography of economic reference works and professional journals. Baltimore, 1956. 50p. (Its Economic library selections. Ser. II. Basic lists in special fields, no.3)   **CH13**

A very useful guide for the selection of basic materials, with full bibliographical data and excellent annotations.

Jones, Tom Bard, Warburton, Elizabeth Anne and

Kingsley, Anne. A bibliography on South American economic affairs; articles in nineteenth-century periodicals. Minneapolis, Univ. of Minn. Pr., 1955. 146p.   **CH14**

For each country, lists material under agriculture, commerce, communications, finance, immigration, industry, labor, mining, and transportation.

Katz, Saul M. and **McGowan, Frank.** A selected list of U.S. readings on development, prep. for the United Nations Conference on the Application of Science and Technology for the Benefit of the Less Developed Areas. Wash., Agency for Internat. Development, [1963]. 363p. (For sale by U.S. Govt. Prt. Off.)   **CH15**

Lists 1195 numbered items including books, documents, and periodical articles, mostly published since 1950. Arranged by broad subject with author index.

Landgren, Karl Gustav. Economics in modern Sweden. Wash., Reference Dept., Lib. of Congress, 1957. 117p.   **CH16**

Not a formal bibliography, but many individual works of leading 20th-century Swedish economists are reviewed in detail. Includes a survey of Swedish economic periodicals and research institutions. Has index of persons.

McCulloch, John Ramsay. Literature of political economy; a classified catalogue of select publications in the different departments of that science, with historical, critical, and biographical notices. London, Longmans, 1845. 407p. (Repr. by the London School of Economics and Political Science. Ser. of reprints of scarce works on political economy, no.5, 1938)   **CH17**

Mossé, Robert. Bibliographie d'économie politique, 1945–1960: histoire des doctrines, statistique et économétrie, géographie économique, économie rurale, économie financière, travail sociologie démographie. Paris, Sirey, 1963. 124p.   **CH18**

A classed bibliography on political economy interpreted broadly. Continues for this area the work of Grandin (CA9).

Novotny, Jan Maria. A library of public finance and economics. Montreal, available from McGill Univ. Book Store; N.Y., Burt Franklin, 1953. 383p. (Burt Franklin bibliographical ser. VI)   **CH19**

A listing of books, comprising about one third of the library collected by the author, in all languages. In three main parts: 1, Books in all languages up to 1850, arranged chronologically; 2, Books from 1851 on, in all languages except Czech and Slovak, arranged alphabetically; 3, Books from 1851 on, in Czech and Slovak, arranged alphabetically. These lists are followed by a fourth part: History, description, and evaluation. Includes an author index to pt.1. Many of the items listed are rare or unique.

Schleiffer, Hedwig and **Crandall, Ruth.** Index to economic history essays in Festschriften, 1900–1950. Cambridge, Mass., pub. by Arthur H. Cole and distr. by Harvard Univ. Pr., 1953. 68p.   **CH20**

Arranged by broad subjects (period and geographical division, followed by history of economic thought and business economics, and economic historiography), with indexes of authors and of proper names.

Schwartz, Harry. The Soviet economy; a selected bibliography of materials in English. Syracuse, N.Y., Syracuse Univ. Pr., 1949. 93p.   **CH21**

A classified, annotated bibliography of books, pamphlets, and periodical material.

—— Russia's Soviet economy. 2d ed. with appendix: The Soviet economy, 1954–58. Englewood Cliffs, N.J., Prentice-Hall, [1958]. 682p. il.   **CH22**

The "Reference index" leads to bibliographic footnotes, which to some extent supplement the above work.

Scientific Council for Africa South of the Sahara. Inventory of economic studies concerning Africa south of the Sahara; an annotated reading list of books, articles and official publications. [Ed., Peter Ady] London, Commission for Technical Cooperation in Africa South of the Sahara, 1960. 301p. (Its Publ. no.30. Joint project, no.4)　　　　　　　　　　　　　　　　**CH23**

Title also in French.

Includes books, articles, and documents published since 1945. Arranged first by geographical region, then by subject subdivision. Many items are annotated, in English or French, or both. A list of the titles, by number, translated into Portuguese, is appended. Author index.

Current

continues CH13

Economics library selections. New books in economics. (Pittsburgh. University. Dept. of Economics) Ser. I. no.1/2–　.　Feb./March 1964–　.　(Distr. by Gordon and Breach Science Pub., N.Y.) Quarterly.　　**CH24**

Supersedes *Economics library selections.* Ser. I. New books in economics, issued by Johns Hopkins Univ., Dept. of Political Economy, 1954–1962.

An annotated list of books published in English, German, French, and Spanish, arranged by subdivisions of economics. Titles are rated for purchase by size and type of library.

International bibliography of economics. Bibliographie internationale de science économique. 1952–　.　London, Tavistock; Chicago, Aldine, 1955–　.　v.1–　.　Annual. (International bibliography of the social sciences) **CH25**

Publisher varies. v.1–8, Paris, UNESCO; v.9, 1960–　, issued as *Publications* of the International Committee for Social Sciences Documentation, as one of the series of the *International bibliography of the social sciences* (series title varies slightly).

In English and French.

An extensive, classified list of books, pamphlets, periodical articles, and official government publications, in various languages, including Slavic and Asian. Indexes by author and subject (in English and French).

For other bibliographies in the series *see* CC2 (Sociology); CI19 (Political science); CD29 (Social and cultural anthropology).

Periodicals

France. Institut National de la Statistique et des Études Économiques. Service Central de la Documentation. Bibliothèque. Catalogue des périodiques français et étrangers conservés à la bibliothèque. [Paris], Person, 1956. 175p.　　　　　　　　　　　　　　　　**CH26**

The periodicals are listed alphabetically by title, subject, and country of origin. Includes a separate list of *Publications* of the Institute published since 1940.

Landskron, William A. Official serial publications relating to economic development in Africa south of the Sahara; a preliminary list of English-language publications. Cambridge, Mass., Center for Internat. Studies, Mass. Inst. of Technology, 1961. 43p.　　**CH27**

Arranged by country of publication, with additional relevant British and UN publications. Date of latest known issue is given, although beginning publication date is not, nor are United States library holdings indicated.

Indexes

American Economic Association. Index of economic journals. Homewood, Ill., Irwin, 1961–62. 5v.　　**CH28**

Contents: v.1, 1886–1924; v.2, 1925–1939; v.3, 1940–1949; v.4, 1950–1954; v.5, 1954–1959.

Lists articles in English from 89 journals in various languages. Arranged by a detailed classification scheme, with author index in each volume. Citations are full and precise.

Abstract journals

Bollettino emerografico di economia internazionale, redatto dall' Istituto di Economia Internazionale. v.1–　, gennaio 1948–　.　Genova, Camera di Commercio, Industria e Agricoltura, 1948–　.　Quarterly.　　**CH29**

Abstracts of outstanding articles from the periodicals of the principal countries of the world. In 1965 contained selections from more than 700 publications from 58 countries and 11 international organizations; these numbers vary considerably. Classified. Gives citation to month of periodical but not to volume or page.

Documentation économique; revue bibliographique de synthèse. Publie les analyses classées par sujets d'articles des principales revues économiques. v.1, 1934–　.　Paris, Press Universitaires de France, 1934–　.　Quarterly.
　　　　　　　　　　　　　　　　　　CH30

Subtitle and publisher vary. Suspended Dec. 1938 through Dec. 1946. Resumed with v.6, 1947.

At head of title: Institut National de la Statistique et des Études Économiques, Association de Documentation Économique et Sociale.

Abstracts articles in American, Dutch, English, French, German, Greek, Italian, Portuguese, Spanish, Swedish, and Russian economic periodicals. Classified by subject with author index. Abstracts are in French.

Economic abstracts; . . . review of abstracts on economics, finance, trade and industry, management and labour. v.1–　, 1953–　.　The Hague, Nijhoff, 1953–　.　Semimonthly.　　　　　　　　　　　　　　　　**CH31**

Prepared by the Library of the Economic Information Service with the collaboration of the Library of the Netherlands School of Economics and the Library of the Ministry of Social Affairs.

Excellent abstracts of books and periodical articles in Dutch (with English summaries), English, French, and German. Detailed subject index in each issue, and cumulative author index for each volume.

Journal of economic abstracts. v.1–　.　1963–　.　Cambridge, Harvard Univ., 1963–　.　Quarterly.　　**CH32**

"An international journal published cooperatively by the contributing journals under the auspices of the American Economic Association."

Rather lengthy abstracts selected from some 35 contributing journals. Arranged by journal, with subject index in each issue and author index appearing annually.

Dictionaries and encyclopedias

Bedrijfseconomische encyclopedie onder algemeene leiding van J. G. Stridiron. Utrecht, W. de Haan, 1947–52. 5v. and index. il.　　　　　　　　　　　　**CH33**

Signed articles with bibliographies. Each volume, A–Z. v.1 treats general economic problems; v.2, business economy in its general aspects; v.3, business economy in its special aspects; v.4, management; v.5, statistics and accounting.

Dictionnaire des sciences économiques, publié sous la direction de Jean Romeuf, avec la collaboration de Gilles Pasqualaggi. Paris, Presses Universitaires de France, 1956–58. 2v. diagrams.　　　　　　　　**CH34**

A dictionary of terms used in the study of economics; international in scope. Includes biographical sketches of significant figures, excluding living persons. Many articles are signed; some have bibliographies.

Holmstrom, J. Edwin. Facts, files and action in business and public affairs. London, Chapman & Hall, 1951–　.　v.1–2. (In progress)　　　　　　　　　　　**CH35**

In three parts: pt.1, Sources and background of facts. 1951. 449p. Index; pt.2, Filing, indexing and circulation. 1953. 227p. il. Index and bibl.; pt.3, The planning and ensuing of action (not yet published).

[handwritten marginalia: "definitions can be found in IESS", "actually an ency of econ", "of economy old term for econ"]

Brief summaries of fields of knowledge for the nonspecialist, with suggestions as to sources of more detailed information.

Palgrave, *Sir* **Robert Harry Inglis.** Palgrave's Dictionary of political economy, ed. by Henry Higgs. London, N.Y., Macmillan, 1923–26. 3v. (Repr.: N.Y., Augustus M. Kelley, 1963. 3v. Reprints of economic classics)   **CH36**

1st ed. 1894–96; reprinted 1910 without change in the text, but with a supplement of new articles in v.3, p.693–803; a reprint of the 1910 edition, issued 1915–18, contains the same supplement but with cross references to the supplement incorporated in the main alphabet. The 1923–26 edition is printed from the stereotyped plates of the 1st edition, with some changes in the plates, and with a supplement which uses some of the material from the earlier supplement and adds some new articles.

The standard English work, including some general and foreign aspects of the subject, but largely limited to developments of economic study in the English-speaking world. Signed articles by specialists, and bibliographies. Useful and authoritative, but unfortunately not up to date.

Sloan, Harold S. and **Zurcher, Arnold J.** A dictionary of economics. 4th ed. rev. N.Y., Barnes & Noble, 1961. 371p. (Everyday handbooks)   **CH37**

1st ed. 1949.

Definitions and explanations of terms covering the fields of economics, international trade, money, banking, business, insurance, etc., with "brief digests and descriptions of the more relevant American statutes and judicial decisions and American and international regulatory agencies."—Cf. *Pref.* Many cross references.

Suavet, Thomas. Dictionnaire économique et social. Paris, Économie et Humanisme, Les Éditions Ouvrières, 1962. 453p. il. (Initiation économique 3)   **CH38**

Very useful, recent 1v. dictionary with rather lengthy definitions. Contains 13 charts, 15 maps, 50 tables, and bibliography.

Winton, John R. A dictionary of economic terms. 3d ed. rev. [London], Routledge & Paul, [1951]. 85p.   **CH39**

Attempts to provide current definitions and terms, and to omit those appearing in previous editions (1st, 1905; 2d, 1936) that are now out of date or rarely used. Has a strong emphasis on British usage.

Wörterbuch der Volkswirtschaft, hrsg. von Ludwig Elster. 4. völlig umgearb. Aufl. Jena, Fischer, 1931–33. 3v. il.   **CH40**

The standard German encyclopedia of economics, supplementary to the *Handwörterbuch der Staatswissenschaften* (CI27) which covers political science. Signed articles, bibliographies, and biographies of deceased persons.

Foreign terms

Benisławski, Juliusz. 5-[i.e., Pięcio-] języczny podręczny słownik ekonomiki przemysłu. Warszawa, Polskie Wydawnictwa Gospodarcze, 1959. 214p. (Inst. Ekonomiki i Organizacji Przemysłu)   **CH41**

Polish, English, French, German, and Russian.

Eichborn, Reinhart von. Wirtschaftswörterbuch. [1. Aufl.] Düsseldorf, Econ-Verlag, [1961–62]. 2v.   **CH42**

Contents: v.1, Englisch-deutsch. 923p. 1961; v.2, Deutsch-englisch. 1080p. 1962.

Paenson, Isaac. Systematic glossary English/French/Spanish/Russian of selected economic and social terms. English-French-Russian text comp. by Isaac Paenson. Spanish translation prep. by Luis de la Plaza. N.Y., Oxford, Pergamon Pr. [distr. in the Western Hemisphere by Macmillan, N.Y.], 1963– . Loose-leaf.   **CH43**

Added title page in French, Spanish, and Russian; preface and introduction in all four languages.

Definitions of economic terms arranged according to the system of ideas they convey, proceeding from the general to the particular. Intended primarily for economists, social scientists, translators, government officials, international civil servants, etc.

Three succeeding volumes are planned: 2, Statistics; 3, Legal terms; 4, Economic aspects of industry, atomic energy, transport, communications, distribution, etc.

Atlases

Ginsburg, Norton Sydney. Atlas of economic development. Chicago, Univ. of Chicago Pr., 1961. 119p. maps. 25x35cm. (Dept. of Geography. Research paper, no.68)   **CH44**

An atlas of world economic geography, picturing population, agriculture, commerce and industry, transportation, etc. Each section of maps has accompanying text.

Pt.8 is a statistical analysis by Brian J. L. Berry.

Kish, George. Economic atlas of the Soviet Union. Ann Arbor, Univ. of Michigan Pr., 1960. 96p. maps. 27cm.   **CH45**

Arranged by region with agricultural, industrial, and commercial maps for each. Other maps treat economic aspects of the entire country. Brief text, bibliography, and index. Typography and layout good.

Oxford University Press. Oxford economic atlas of the world. 2d ed. Prep. by the Economist Intelligence Unit and the Cartographic Dept. of the Clarendon Press. Oxford, Univ. Pr., 1959. 128p., 152p. maps. 27cm. **CH46**

1st ed. 1954.

"Intended to meet the needs of economists, geographers, and other students, and of those engaged in trade, industry, and agriculture who require basic information about world economics."—*Jacket.*

In two parts: pt.1, World commodity maps grouped in 10 sections by commodities; pt.2, Index arranged by country, giving statistics and showing the relative significance of different commodities in the economy of the country.

This world atlas is complemented by the Oxford regional atlases which deal in greater detail with such areas as:

—— The Middle East and North Africa. Prep. by the Economist Intelligence Unit and the Cartographic Dept. of the Clarendon Press. London, Oxford Univ. Pr., 1960. 135p. maps. 27cm. (Oxford regional economic atlas)   **CH47**

65p. of a variety of economic maps, followed by an equal amount of text, mostly in summary or tabular form.

—— The U.S.S.R. and Eastern Europe. Prep. by the Economist Intelligence Unit and the Cartographic Dept. of the Clarendon Press. Oxford, Univ. Pr., 1956. 134p. maps. 27cm. (Oxford regional economic atlas)   **CH48**

This volume covers: USSR, East Germany, Poland, Czechoslovakia, Hungary, Romania, Bulgaria, Albania, Mongolian People's Republic, Yugoslavia.

Annuals

Economic almanac for 1940– ; a handbook of useful facts about business, labor and government in the United States and other areas. N.Y., Nat. Industrial Conference Board [1940–]. Biennial. *[handwritten: since 1967]*   **CH49**

Issued as annual, v.1–10, 1940–50.

A statistical compendium covering such subjects as: prices, banking, finance, national income, resources, manufacturing, communication and transportation, industries, agriculture, labor, foreign trade, international economic statistics, etc.

Includes glossary of terms used in business and economics. A general index is followed by a separate index for Canada.

United Nations. Dept. of Economic and Social Affairs.

World economic survey. N.Y., 1945/47– , no.1– . il. Annual. **CH50**

Title varies: no.1, 1945/47, *Economic report;* no.2–7, 1948–1953/54, *World economic report.*

Comprehensive review of world economic conditions and trends.

Beginning with 1955, pt.1 reports on a long-term problem, e.g., Balance of payments; Growth, stability and the rate of saving; and pt.2 contains an examination of recent events in the world economy.

—— —— Supplements, 1948– . Issued irregularly.

❧ Annual surveys and bulletins reporting on regional economic conditions are issued by: Economic Commission for Africa, Economic Commission for Asia and the Far East, Economic Commission for Europe, Economic Commission for Latin America. For complete list *see Checklist of United Nations documents,* 1946–49 (CJ 158), and *United Nations documents index,* 1950– (CJ159).

ACCOUNTING

Bibliography

Bentley, Harry Clark and **Leonard, Ruth S.** Bibliography of works on accounting by American authors, 1796–1934. Boston, Author, 1934–35. 2v. **CH51**

v.1, Books published 1796–1900; v.2, 1901–1934.

Columbia University. Libraries. Business Library. Montgomery Library of Accountancy; a check list of books, printed before 1850, in the Montgomery Library of Accountancy at Columbia University. N.Y., Columbia Univ. Pr., 1927–30. 2v. **CH52**

v.1, Basic list. 45p.; v.2, Accessions, June 1927–Sept. 1930. 32p.

An alphabetical list by author of some 550 books, published from 1494 to 1850 in Europe and America.

Institute of Chartered Accountants in England and Wales, London. Library. Library catalogue. [Edinburgh], Constable, 1913. 963p. **CH53**

Author and subject catalog of a library founded in 1870. Basic volume supersedes earlier catalogs issued in 1903 and 1911. Lists "books, pamphlets, lectures, papers and principal articles in the various accountancy magazines and accountant-students' transactions."—*Pref.*

—— —— London, Council of the Inst., 1937. 2v.

v.1, Subjects, p.1–148; Authors, p.149–256; v.2, Bibliography of bookkeeping. 259p.

—— —— First supplement. 1939. 36p.

Includes books and pamphlets only.

❧ *See also* Coman, *Sources of business information,* p.133–50 (CH65), for a more extensive list of works on accounting for specialized subjects and interests.

Indexes

Accountants digest, v.1, Sept. 1935– . Burlington, Vt., L. L. Briggs, 1935– . Quarterly. **CH54**

"A quarterly presenting in compact form the substance of outstanding articles selected from leading accounting journals of the English-speaking world."

Includes a subject index to periodical accounting literature.

American Institute of Certified Public Accountants. Accountants' index; a bibliography of accounting litera-

ture. N.Y., Inst., 1921– . Biennial. **CH55**

Basic volume, 1912–20; Supplements: (1), 1921/23– . Frequency varies.

A detailed author and subject bibliography of the book, pamphlet, and periodical literature of the subject, including a large amount of indexing of periodicals, and references to parts of books dealing with specific subjects.

Dictionaries and handbooks

Accountants' handbook; 4th ed., ed. by Rufus Wixon and Walter G. Kell. N.Y., Ronald, 1956. [v.p.] il. **CH56**

1st ed., 1923, ed. by William A. Paton.

This edition, prepared with the assistance of a Board of Contributing Editors, has been thoroughly revised.

For many years the authoritative handbook in the field, providing information on all the major divisions of accounting.

Kohler, Eric L. A dictionary for accountants. 3d ed. Englewood Cliffs, N.J., Prentice-Hall, 1963. 523p. **CH57**

1st ed. 1952.

An unofficial revision and expansion of the 1936 *Accounting terminology* of the American Institute of Accountants' Committee on Terminology, of which the author was chairman. Contains definitions and explanations of 2275 terms.

Lasser (J. K.) Institute, New York. J. K. Lasser's Standard handbook for accountants. N.Y., McGraw-Hill, 1956. [v.p.] il. **CH58**

Subtitle: A modern encyclopedia of auditing, cost control, management, systems design, forecasting, operation of the accounting office, and other phases of business planning; prepared by 62 specialists.

ADVERTISING

Bibliography

Advertising Research Foundation. Sources of published advertising research. N.Y., Foundation, 1960. 65p. il. **CH59**

An annotated list of 135 numbered items selected to aid those engaged in advertising research. Includes books, bibliographies, directories, and periodical abstracts. Author and subject index.

Dictionaries and encyclopedias

Graham, Irvin. Encyclopedia of advertising. N.Y., Fairchild, 1952. 606p. **CH60**

"An encyclopedia containing more than 1100 entries relating to advertising, marketing, publishing, public relations, publicity and the graphic arts, combined with valuable reference material in one conveniently alphabetized working manual for everyday use by advertisers, agencies, advertising practitioners, businessmen and students."—*Title page.*

Has an index to terms by general subject matter, and a directory of associations with brief descriptions of their make-up and work.

International Chamber of Commerce. Dictionary of advertising and distribution in eight languages, prep. by a Committee of Experts of the I.C.C. Basel, Verlag für Recht und Gesellschaft, 1954. 1v. unpaged. (Its I.C.C. document, no.14) **CH61**

1st ed. 1937.

Introductory material in each of the eight languages.

A revised, expanded, and reorganized edition. The terms are given in tabular form, based on the English word with equivalents in French, German, Spanish, Italian, Dutch, Portuguese, and Swedish. Indexes to the main work from each language.

Handbooks

Melcher, Daniel and **Larrick, Nancy.** Printing and promotion handbook; how to plan, produce, and use printing, advertising, and direct mail. 2d ed. N.Y., McGraw-Hill, 1956. 438p. il.   **CH62**

Dictionary arrangement.
For full information *see* AA236.

Services

Standard advertising register, v.1– . N.Y., Nat. Register Pub., 1915– . Issued in parts at various intervals.   **CH63**

Title varies. Imprint varies.
Agency list: quarterly, with weekly supplement, *Weekly special service bulletin.*
Geographic index: annual.
Product edition: annual, with monthly supplements.
Information on more than 16,000 advertisers: name, address, business, executives, agency, advertising appropriations, types of media used, etc.

Standard rate and data service. Skokie, Ill., Standard Rate and Data Service, 1919– .   **CH64**

Title varies. Frequency varies.
Excellent source for information on rates and advertising media. Published in 14 separate sections with various titles. Includes newspapers, magazines, radio and television, films, transportation. Gives Canadian and Mexican rates.
Consult *Directory of business and financial services* (CH71) for full description.

BUSINESS

Guides

Coman, Edwin T., Jr. Sources of business information. Rev. ed. Berkeley, Los Angeles, Univ. of Calif. Pr., 1964. 330p.   **CH65**

1st ed. 1949.
A manual and guide to selected sources, with commentary and annotations, listing: bibliographies, compends, handbooks, yearbooks and annual summary numbers of periodicals, general and specialized books, and periodicals. Covers: generalities, statistics, finance, real estate and insurance, accounting, automation, management, personnel and industrial relations, marketing and advertising, public relations, basic industries, foreign trade, etc.
Limited to American and Canadian publications, with a very few from England.
Should be consulted for additional titles not listed in the present *Guide.*

Manley, Marian Catherine. Business information: how to find and use it. N.Y., Harper, 1955. 265p.   **CH66**

A useful manual by the former business librarian of the Newark Public Library. Pt.1 is a discussion of business information sources, and pt.2 lists sources for special subjects in a classified arrangement. Author, title, and subject index.

Wasserman, Paul. Information for administrators: a guide to publications and services for management in business and government. Ithaca, N.Y., Cornell Univ. Pr., 1956. 375p. (Cornell studies in policy and administration)   **CH67**

A manual covering many types of information sources useful to business administrators, including agencies, libraries, associations, etc., as well as lists of publications.

Bibliography

Harvard University. Graduate School of Business Administration. Baker Library. The Kress Library of Business and Economics. Catalogue, covering material pub. through 1776, with data upon cognate items in other Harvard libraries. Boston, Baker Lib., Harvard Graduate School of Business Admin., [c1940]. 414p.   **CH68**

Arranged chronologically, with alphabetical index of authors and anonymous titles.

——— Supplement, [1955], covering material pub. through 1776 with data upon cognate items in other Harvard libraries. Boston, Harvard Graduate School of Business Admin., 1956. 175p.

——— Catalogue, 1777–1817, giving data also upon cognate items in other Harvard libraries. Boston, 1957. 397p.

Humpert, Magdalene. Bibliographie der Kameralwissenschaften. Köln, Schroeder, 1937. 1184p. (Kölner bibliographischen Arbeiten, 1)   **CH69**

Originally planned to include works published 1727–1835, but starting on p.105, the 16th and 17th centuries are also included, so that the greater part of the work covers 1520–1850.

U.S. Dept. of Commerce. Library. United States Dept. of Commerce publications. Wash., Govt. Prt. Off., 1952. 795p.   **CH70**

A selected list of publications dating from 1790 to 1950. Press releases and materials of similar nature are not usually included.

——— Supplement. 1951/52– . Annual.

Business services

Business is a field which changes so rapidly that reference works pertaining to it soon become out of date, and many types of questions can be answered only by the use of current material. Fundamental for this purpose are the different business and financial "services," most of which are now issued in loose-leaf form. In general, each service is devoted to one specialized subject, and consists of basic material kept up to date by revisions—supplied periodically—covering new laws, regulations, rulings, decisions, etc. Some services are completely factual; others include editorial explanations.

A listing of these services is given in the *Directory of business and financial services* (CH71), and a discussion of their use, with a record of some of the most important services, is given in E. T. Coman's *Sources of business information* (CH65). Although these listings deal primarily with American services, similar enterprises exist in various other countries.

Since these services are quite expensive, they will be out of reach of the smaller library, but any large library which does much work in business will have to have at least some of them. Information about price, form, and frequency may be secured by writing directly to the company concerned.

Directory of business and financial services. 6th ed. Ed. by Mary A. McNierney. N.Y., Special Libraries Assoc., 1963. 187p.   **CH71**

Earlier eds., 1924, 1931, 1939, 1944, 1956.
Title varies: 1924, *Handbook of commercial information services.*
Lists about 1500 business and financial services, arranged by publisher or company. Describes each service giving type, scope, frequency of publication, format, and price. Includes

an index of publishers, services, and authors; also a subject index.

Periodical indexes

Business periodicals index; a cumulative subject index to periodicals in the fields of accounting, advertising, banking and finance, general business, insurance, labor and management, marketing and purchasing, office management, public administration, taxation, specific businesses, industries, and trades. N.Y., Wilson, 1958– . v.1– . Monthly (except July), with annual cumulations. **CH72**

Indexes, by subject, some 120 periodicals.

One of two indexes stemming from the *Industrial arts index* (EA63).

Funk and Scott index of corporations and industries. 1960– . Cleveland, Ohio, Investment Index Co., 1960– . Weekly, with monthly and annual cumulations. **CH73**

An index to periodical articles and other references (e.g., financial and corporation report findings) on industries as a whole, and on individual corporations. Approximately 100 serials are regularly indexed. Coverage includes United States, Canada, Great Britain, and Japan.

Dictionaries and encyclopedias

Alexander Hamilton Institute, New York. 2001 business terms and what they mean. N.Y., Inst., [1962]. 303p. **CH74**

Terms are described as used in various business contexts.

Clark, Donald Thomas and **Gottfried, Bert A.** Dictionary of business and finance. N.Y., Crowell, 1957. 409p. **CH75**

Broad in scope, covering many phases of business and finance.

Handwörterbuch der Betriebswirtschaft, begründet von Heinrich Nicklisch. 3. völlig neubearb. Aufl. Unter Mitarbeit von zahlreichen Fachgelehrten und praktischen Betriebswirten hrsg. von Hans Seischab und Karl Schwantag. Stuttgart, Poeschel, 1956–62. 4v. il. **CH76**

1st ed. 1926–28; 2d ed. 1938–39.

Signed articles, with bibliographies of some length. Not limited to material on Germany.

Prentice-Hall, Inc. Encyclopedic dictionary of business finance, prep. by the editorial staff. Englewood Cliffs, N.J., Prentice-Hall, 1960. 658p. il. **CH77**

Definitions of terms in all branches of finance: theoretical and applied. Many are of considerable length and contain tables, diagrams, explanatory problems, and examples. Cross references are numerous. No bibliographic references.

—— Encyclopedic dictionary of business law, prep. by the editorial staff of Prentice-Hall, Inc. Englewood Cliffs, N.J., Prentice-Hall, 1961. 608p. **CH78**

An attempt to define legal terms and principles applicable to business. Explanations are in nontechnical language and illustrated with examples, forms, and figures.

Schwartz, Robert J. The dictionary of business and industry. N.Y., B. C. Forbes, 1954. 561p. **CH79**

A dictionary of terms, mainly technical and trade. Includes abbreviations.

Foreign terms

French

Kettridge, Julius Orman. French-English and English-French dictionary of commercial and financial terms, phrases and practice. . . . London, Routledge, 1931. 647p. **CH80**

Frequently reprinted.

Subtitle: Comprising mercantile business, exporting and importing, produce exchange transactions, transport and travel by water, land and air, customs, marine insurance, finance, banking, currency, foreign exchange and stock exchange transactions, company work, accountancy, income tax, secretarial and office work, postal, telegraphic and telephonic services, and allied subjects, also abbreviations in common use, conventional signs, weights and measures.

German

Gunston, Charles Arthur and **Corner, Charles Morris.** Deutsch-englisches Glossarium finanzieller und wirtschaftlicher Fachausdrücke. 4. erw. Aufl. Frankfurt/Main, Knapp, 1962. 1059p. **CH81**

1st. ed. 1953.

English edition had title *Glossary of German financial and economic terms.*

Italian

Edler, Florence. Glossary of mediaeval terms of business, Italian series, 1200–1600. Cambridge, Mass., Mediaeval Academy of America, 1934. 430p. **CH82**

"Appendices on business and industrial terms and practices as found in the Medici documents of the fifteenth and sixteenth centuries," p.[333]–426.

Macdonald, George Robert. Italian-English and English-Italian commercial dictionary. London, N.Y., Pitman, 1930. 1166p. **CH83**

Japanese

Kenkyusha's English-Japanese dictionary of commercial and technical terms, by Nintaro Fujita. Tokyo, Kenkyusha, 1948. 1192p. il. **CH84**

First pub. 1941.

Polyglot

Herbst, Robert. Dictionary of commercial, financial and legal terms pertaining to trade and industry. Lucerne, Thali Pub., 1955–59. v.1–2. (In progress) **CH85**

v.1, English-German-French. 1150p.; v.2, German-English-French. 985p.

Added title pages in German and French.

Subtitle: Including terms used in importing, manufacturing, distributing, and marketing, as well as those used in banking, stock exchange dealings, credit, foreign exchange, taxation and customs, traffic including land, sea, and air transport, insurance and mail services, economics, social science, and politics, and covering, in particular, the special terminology as used in all fields of private and public law including the legislative, executive, and judicial branches of government.

Portuguese

Sousa Gomes, Luiz. Dicionário econômico-comercial e financeiro. (Terminologia de econômica, finanças, comércio e contabilidade) 7. ed. rev. Rio de Janeiro, Ed. Civilização Brasileira, 1962. 272p. **CH86**

Subtitle: Com . . . um apendice bio-bibliográfico sobre os principais economistas brasileiros e estrangeiros, e ligeiras referências às suas diretrizes econômicas.

Spanish

Robb, Louis Adams. Dictionary of modern business: Spanish-English and English-Spanish. Wash., Anderson Kramer Assoc., 1960. 610p. **CH87**

Added title page in Spanish.

A glossary of specialized words and phrases used in business, finance, accounting, manufacturing, etc. not generally found in English-Spanish dictionaries. Based on Spanish language as used in Latin America.

Sell, Lewis Lazarus. Comprehensive specialist's dictionary for insurance-finance-law-labor-politics-business. N.Y., McKay, 1955–57. 2v.   **CH88**

Added title pages in Spanish.
Contents: English-Spanish (N.Y., Internat. Dictionary Co.), 1955. 535p.; Spanish-English, 1957. 650p.

Swedish

Gullberg, Ingvar E. Svensk-engelsk fackord bok för näringsliv, förvaltning, undervisning och forskning. Stockholm, P. A. Norstedt & Söners Forlag, 1964. 1246p.   **CH89**

Added title page in English: A Swedish-English dictionary of technical terms used in business, industry, administration, education and research.

Directories

See also Encyclopedia of associations (AC28).

Kelley, Etna M. Business founding date directory. Scarsdale, N.Y., Morgan and Morgan, 1954. 228p. il.   **CH90**

Lists more than 9000 business organizations founded between 1687 and 1915 in the United States, in two sections: (1) alphabetical by name, and (2) chronological by year.

—— —— Supplement, including founding dates, for 1916, 1917, 1918, 1931, 1932, and 1933. 1956. 16p.

U.S. Dept. of Commerce. Office of Technical Services. Directory of national associations of businessmen, by Jay Judkins, 1961. 2d ed. Wash., 1961. 81p.   **CH91**

1st ed. 1960.
Supersedes the Office's *Directory of national trade associations,* 1956.
Lists more than 2000 organizations, giving name, address, chief executives, year founded, membership, etc.

World yearbook of chambers of commerce. Annuaire mondial des chambres de commerce. [v.1–   ] Basel, Verlag für Recht und Gesellschaft, 1953–   . (I.C.C. documents. Les documents de la C.C.I. Document no.13)   **CH92**

Issued in loose-leaf form as a basic publication to be kept up to date by supplements.
Pt.1 gives, by country, general information followed by information on national, regional, and local chambers; pt.2 covers national chambers of commerce abroad, and binational or joint chambers of commerce.
Introductory sections are given in English, French, German, Spanish, Italian, and Portuguese; other textual matter is in English and French. Names of towns are given in the language of the country, and the title of each chamber is also in the national language, transliterated and translated where necessary. 80 countries are included; each country's section has a separate title page.

—— —— Supplement, 1954–56. no.1–2.

❦ Many individual states or regions have industrial directories, e.g., *New York State industrial directory, Directory of New England manufacturers.* These should be consulted for local information.

Bibliography

International

Henderson, George P. Reference manual of directories: an annotated list, index and guide to the directories of all countries. London, Jones and Evans Bookshop, 1957–   . (In progress)   **CH93**

Contents: pt.7, Canada. 1959; pt.11, Burma, Ceylon, Pakistan. 1960; pt.14, Australasia. 1957.
For each country, material is grouped under three headings: general, local, and specialized.

Trade directories of the world, comp. and ed. by Ulrich H. E. Croner. Queen's Village, N.Y., Croner Pub., 1952?–   . v.1–   . Loose-leaf.   **CH94**

Title varies: 1952, *Croner's World register of trade directories.*
Lists about 1300 general, trade, business, and professional directories of the United States and of more than 60 foreign countries. Most entries have annotations. Kept up to date by an amendment service.

U.S. Bureau of Foreign Commerce (1953–61). A guide to foreign business directories. Wash., Govt. Prt. Off., 1955. 132p.   **CH95**

First issued by the U.S. Dept. of Foreign Commerce in 1931, under the title *Foreign directories.*
Arranged by country; lists general, special, and local directories. A separate section lists international directories published in the United States.

United States

American Marketing Association. Industrial Section. Industrial Directories Committee. Industrial directories, by Hugh Britton . . . [and others]. Chicago, Assoc., [1963]. 63p.   **CH96**

Information about available directories with detailed descriptions of one published for each of the 50 states. Future editions of directories will be reviewed in the regular feature section of the *Journal of marketing,* "Marketing articles in review."

Davis, Marjorie Veith. American business directories. 2d ed. April 1947. Wash., Govt. Prt. Off., 1947. 198p. (U.S. Bureau of Foreign and Domestic Commerce. Industrial ser., no.67)   **CH97**

Arranged in two sections: (1) Classed list arranged alphabetically; (2) Names of "general" directories arranged geographically.
Substantially the same material in slightly different arrangement is given in the author's *Guide to American business directories.* Wash., Public Affairs Pr., 1948. 242p.
Still useful, although needing revision. Includes many titles not listed in *Guide to American directories* (CH98).

Guide to American directories, ed. by Bernard Klein. [1956]–   . Englewood Cliffs, N.J., Prentice-Hall, 1956–   . Irregular.   **CH98**

Publisher varies.
1st edition, 1956, entitled *Guide to American directories for compiling mailing lists.*
5th ed. 1962.
A very extensive listing under several hundred categories, with descriptive information and publication data for each title. Educational, philanthropic, governmental, and similar activities are included, as well as business and professional.

Moriarty, John Helenbeck. Directory information material (printed) for New York City residents, 1626–1786; a bibliographical study. N.Y., N.Y. Pub. Lib., 1942. 60p.   **CH99**

Reprinted from the *Bulletin* of the New York Public Library, Oct. 1942.

Spear, Dorothea N. Bibliography of American directories through 1860. Worcester, Mass., Amer. Antiquarian Soc., 1961. 389p.   **CH100**

A geographical listing, with locations, of 1647 business

directories, city and country directories, etc. Many annotations.

Great Britain

Goss, Charles William Frederick. The London directories, 1677–1855; a bibliography with notes on their origin and development. London, Archer, 1932. 146p.   **CH101**

Henderson, George P. Current British directories; a comprehensive guide to the directories of the British Isles, with Commonwealth and international sections. 4th ed. London, pub. for C.B.D. Research, Ltd., by Jones and Evans Bookshop, 1962 (c1961). 261p.   **CH102**

1st ed. 1953.

An extensive list of a variety of British directories, predominantly commercial.

Norton, Jane E. Guide to the national and provincial directories of England and Wales, excluding London, pub. before 1856. London, Royal Historical Soc., 1950. 241p.   **CH103**

Complements C. W. F. Goss, *The London directories, 1677–1855* (CH101).

Includes national, local, and Welsh directories.

Statistics

See also Section CG, Statistics.

Bogue, Donald Joseph and **Beale, Calvin L.** Economic areas of the United States. N.Y., Free Pr. of Glencoe, 1961. 1162p. (Studies in population distribution, no.15)   **CH104**

Arranged by region, subregion, and local area. For each, gives considerable textual, graphic, and statistical information on commercial and industrial activities and potentials. Extensive statistical tables in appendix.

Cole, Arthur Harrison. Measures of business change; a Baker Library index. Chicago, Irwin, 1952. 444p. **CH105**

A basic guide to sources for business statistics, in two parts: pt.1, a finding index covering index numbers of general business activity, commodity prices, construction costs, employment and finance; pt.2, devoted to regional and local data in the United States. For each index gives: subject, title, compiler, frequency of publication, and brief description.

Hauser, Philip Morris and **Leonard, William R.** Government statistics for business use. 2d ed. N.Y., Wiley; London, Chapman and Hall, 1956. 440p. il.   **CH106**

1st ed. 1946.

This edition revised and brought up to date. "Limited to the areas of federal government statistics that are assumed to be of most interest to business."—*Introd.*

Each chapter by a specialist in the field.

"Selected list of international statistical publications," p.402–4.

Snyder, Richard M. Measuring business changes; a handbook of significant business indicators. N.Y., Wiley, 1955. 382p. il.   **CH107**

Describes in detail over 50 of the most important national business indicators and indexes and tells how they may be obtained, directly or in official government publications.

Statistics sources. Ed. by Paul Wasserman [and others]. 1st ed. Detroit, Gale Research, [1962]. 288p.   **CH108**

An index to current statistical data arranged by subject. Emphasis is on American publications and organizations.

United Nations. Statistical Office. The growth of world industry, 1938–1961; national tables. La croissance de l'industrie mondiale, 1938–1961; tableaux par pays. N.Y., United Nations, 1963. 849p. (United Nations. ST/STAT/Ser. P/2)   **CH109**

Detailed statistical tables on various kinds of industrial production for about 100 countries and territories.

"A more current and expanded version of Pt.2 of [its] *Patterns of industrial growth, 1938–1959.*"—*Introd.*

U.S. Bureau of the Census. Census of business, 1933–   . Wash., Govt. Prt. Off., 1934–   .   **CH110**

Published for 1933, 1935, 1939, 1948, 1954, 1958, 1963–   . Censuses for 1929 and 1939 were taken as part of the decennial census; those for 1933 and 1935 were special projects. Published quinquennially, 1958–   .

Number and title of volumes vary. Covers retail and wholesale trade statistics in detail. A series of special reports on certain trades is also issued.

U.S. Council of Economic Advisers. Economic indicators. Wash., Govt. Prt. Off., 1948–   . Monthly.   **CH111**

Prepared for the Joint Economic Committee by the Council of Economic Advisers.

Presents basic statistical series on total output, income, and spending; employment, unemployment, and wages; production and business activity; prices, currency, credit, and security markets; and federal finance.

Supplements, published in 1953 and revised 1955, 1957, 1960, 1962, and 1964, describe each series and give annual data.

U.S. Office of Business Economics. Survey of current business. Wash., Govt. Prt. Off., 1921–   . Monthly, with weekly statistical supplements.   **CH112**

Descriptive and statistical material on basic income and trade developments in the United States. Covers prices, foreign trade, commodities, industries, etc. *Annual review* number issued in Feb., 1939–62; *National income* number in July since 1948.

Special subject supplements issued irregularly. Of particular value: *National income,* an extensive review of the national income and product, 1929–53 (1954); and *Personal income by states* for the years 1929–55 (1956).

——— ——— Business statistics. Wash., Govt. Prt. Off., 1932–   . Biennial.   **CH113**

14th ed. 1963.

Title varies: 1932–42, called *Supplement.*

Publication suspended 1934, 1942–47.

Tables give monthly and quarterly data for 2600 statistical series reported in the *Survey of current business.* Data extend back to 1939.

U.S. President. The economic report of the President transmitted to Congress. Jan. 1947–   . Wash., Govt. Prt. Off., 1947–   . Annual.   **CH114**

Title varies slightly.

Annual, accompanied by a supplementary report, dated July, with title *The mid-year economic report,* 1947–52.

Reports for Jan. 1949–   include *The annual economic review,* by the Council of Economic Advisers.

A review of the nation's economic condition, documented by statistics.

History

Hall, Hubert. Select bibliography for the study, sources, and literature of English mediaeval economic history. London, King, 1914. 350p. (Studies in economics and political science . . . London School of Economics) (Repr.: N.Y., Burt Franklin, 1960. 350p.)   **CH115**

Harvard University. Graduate School of Business Administration. Baker Library. Studies in enterprise; a selected bibliography of American and Canadian company histories and biographies of businessmen. Lorna M. Daniells, comp. Boston, 1957. 169p. (Its Reference list, no.4)   **CH116**

An expanded edition of the library's *Business biographies and company histories.* 1948.

Lists 2080 items in a classified arrangement, with subject and author indexes.

Hamburg. Welt-Wirtschafts-Archiv. Verzeichnis der Fest- und Denkschriften von Unternehmungen und Organisationen der Wirtschaft. Hamburg, 1961. 566p. (Its Veröffentlichung) **CH117**

A listing of more than 4000 *Festschriften* and histories of firms and companies. International in scope, but mainly German. Lists works published in this century that are found in the *Archiv*. In classified arrangement with indexes by: (1) author and personal name; (2) firm; and (3) geographical location.

Particularly strong in the histories of individual companies, many of which are not listed in general and national bibliographies.

Larson, Henrietta Melia. Guide to business history; materials for the study of American business history and suggestions for their use. Cambridge, Harvard Univ. Pr., 1948. 1181p. (Harvard studies in business history, v.12) **CH118**

Contents: (1) Introduction; (2) Historical background and setting of American business; (3) Business administrators: Biographical and autobiographical books, pamphlets and articles; (4) The history of individual business units; (5) History of industries; (6) General topics in business history; (7) Research and reference materials. Index.

4904 entries, annotated. A highly useful compilation and guide to historical study.

Biography

Directory of directors in the city of New York. N.Y., Directory of Directors Co., 1898– . Annual. **CH119**

For each director, gives his name and address and the companies of which he is a director. The second section is a list of corporations and firms with lists of directors.

Similar publications are issued for various other large cities.

Poor's Register of corporations, directors and executives, United States and Canada. N.Y., Standard and Poor's Corp., 1928– . Annual (cumulative supplements issued April, July, and Nov.). **CH120**

Lists corporations with officers and directors, followed by an alphabetical list of directors and executives with brief biographical data and companies of which they are directors. Also contains an obituary and a new-name section.

Geografical section in separate volume.

Who's who in public relations (international), ed. by Robert L. Barbour. 2d ed. Meriden, N.H., PR Pub. Co., 1962. 547p. **CH120a**

1st ed. 1959.

Information, for most persons included, is of usual who's who type. For a number who presumably did not furnish information, only present position and address are given.

World who's who in commerce and industry. 13th ed. Chicago, Marquis, 1963. 1464p. **CH121**

1st ed. 1936.

Title varies: ed.1–11, *Who's who in commerce and industry*.

Gives international coverage of businessmen. Includes index of firms with references to individuals.

BUSINESS MANAGEMENT

Bibliography

American Management Association. Ten-year index of AMA publications (1954–1963). N.Y., Assoc., [c1964]. 187p. **CH122**

A detailed catalog of AMA publications, arranged by subject with author index.

Supplemented by *Management bookshelf*. 1957– . Annual.

Management information systems index. [ed.1–] Detroit, Amer. Data Processing, 1962– . v.1– . Annual. **CH123**

Author, subject, and title index to approximately 250 periodicals that deal with data processing. v.1 has separate section giving reviews of books in the field, published prior to 1962.

Taskier, Charlotte E. Input-output bibliography, 1955–1960. N.Y., United Nations, 1961. 222p. (U.N. doc. ST/STAT/7) **CH124**

A classed bibliography, international in scope, of more than 600 items (books, articles, documents, theses, etc.) in the field, which is defined as "an international term to denote inter-relationships among factors not primarily connected with economics, e.g., relationships in the social and behavioral sciences . . . "—*Foreword*. Author index.

Some of the subjects included are city planning, aeronautics, chemistry, farm economics, agriculture, and electric energy.

Dictionaries

Benn, Alice E. The management dictionary; standardization of definitions and concepts of the terminology in the field of personnel management. N.Y., Exposition, 1952. 375p. **CH125**

"Contains over 4000 references of common usage."—*Title page.*

An attempt to provide standard definitions for terms connected with personnel management.

Elsevier's Dictionary of automation, computers, control, and measuring in six languages: English/American, French, Spanish, Italian, Dutch, and German. Comp. and arr. on an English alphabetical base by W. E. Clason. Amsterdam, Elsevier, 1961. 848p. **CH126**

For full information *see* EI141.

U.S. Bureau of the Budget. Automatic data processing glossary. Wash., Govt. Prt. Off., 1962. 62p. **CH127**

Definitions of some 1400 terms used in automatic data processing.

Handbooks

Aljian, George W. Purchasing handbook: standard reference book on purchasing policies, practices, procedures, contracts and forms. N.Y., McGraw-Hill, 1958. [v.p.] il. **CH128**

Each section edited by specialists in the field.

Brady, George Stuart. Materials handbook; an encyclopedia for purchasing agents, engineers, executives, and foremen. 9th ed. N.Y., McGraw-Hill, [1963]. 968p. il. **CH129**

1st ed. 1929.

Gives chief characteristics, sources, substitutes, and uses of approximately 9000 materials. Includes information on economic geography, weights, measurements, and related subjects.

Brown, Stanley M. and **Doris, Lillian.** Business executive's handbook . . . 4th ed. N.Y., Prentice-Hall, 1953. 1496p. il. **CH130**

1st ed. 1936.

A useful, clearly written handbook covering such subjects as: business mathematics, business letters, direct-mail selling, advertising, credits and collections, financial statements, corporate meetings, etc.

Data processing equipment encyclopedia. Detroit, Gille Associates, 1961. 2v. il.   **CH131**

Gives detailed descriptions and specifications of office data-processing equipment.

Contents: v.1, Electromechanical devices: punched card, punched tape, related systems; v.2, Electronic devices.

Heyel, Carl. The encyclopedia of management. N.Y., Reinhold, [1963]. 1084p. il.   **CH132**

Arranged in dictionary form, A–Z, this comprehensive work attempts to cover all aspects of industrial management. Articles are written by specialists and are signed. Includes lengthy lists of references, cited with suggested sources for further information.

—— The foreman's handbook. 3d ed. compl. rev. with additions. N.Y., McGraw-Hill, 1955. 578p. il.   **CH133**

1st ed. 1943.

Practical handbook, written by 24 authorities in management, personnel relations, and production.

Lasser, Jacob Kay. Business management handbook. Sydney Prerau, ed. 2d ed. N.Y., McGraw-Hill, 1960. 842p.   **CH134**

1st ed. 1952.

Chapters written by specialists in their fields.

A handbook of methods and policies for the executive, applicable to retailing, wholesaling, and manufacturing. Includes useful information on tax laws and legal regulations affecting business. Well indexed.

Lesly, Philip. Public relations handbook. 2d ed. Englewood Cliffs, N.J., Prentice-Hall, 1962. 901p. il.   **CH135**

Practical ideas and fundamental principles by various authorities.

Office management handbook. Ed. by Harry L. Wylie. Staff ed., James Q. Harty. 2d ed. N.Y., Ronald, 1958. [v.p.]   **CH136**

1st ed. 1947.

Developed under the auspices of the National Office Management Association.

A comprehensive work, treating in detail all phases of office management. Excellent illustrations.

Production handbook, ed. by Gordon B. Carson. 2d ed. N.Y., Ronald, 1958. [v.p.] il.   **CH137**

1st ed. 1944.

Prepared with the assistance of a Board of Contributing and Consulting Editors.

Detailed information on the planning, organization, and operation of a manufacturing industry.

Yoder, Dale [and others]. Handbook of personnel management and labor relations. N.Y., McGraw-Hill, 1958. [v.p.] il.   **CH139**

A comprehensive handbook for executives, directors, and managers with emphasis on tested practices. Indexed by: individual name, organizations, companies, unions, and subject.

Secretary's handbooks

Doris, Lillian and **Miller, Besse May.** Complete secretary's handbook. Rev. ed. Englewood Cliffs, N.J., Prentice-Hall, 1960. 582p.   **CH140**

1st ed. 1951.

Parkhurst, Charles Chandler. Business communication for better human relations. 6th ed. Englewood Cliffs, N.J., Prentice-Hall, 1961. 579p. il.   **CH141**

1st edition, 1925, by A. Charles Babenroth, has title *Modern business English.*

By the use of many examples, shows how business letters may be made effective. Reference section includes: grammar, punctuation, words and phrases, telephone and telegram messages, etc.

Strong, Earl Poe and **Weaver, Robert G.** Writing for business and industry: reports, letters, minutes of meetings, memos, dictation. Boston, Allyn & Bacon, 1962. 456p. il.   **CH142**

Includes section on English grammar, p.331–84.

Taintor, Sarah Augusta and **Monro, Kate M.** The secretary's handbook: a manual of correct usage. 8th ed. compl. rev. by Kate M. Monro. N.Y., Macmillan, 1958. 559p. il.   **CH143**

1st ed. 1929?.

This edition revised and reset, with omissions and additions of material designed to conform to modern practice. One of the most useful of the secretary's manuals.

COMMERCE

Commercial products

Commodity year book. v.1, 1939– . N.Y., Commodity Research Bureau, 1939– . v.1– . il. Annual (suspended 1943–47).   **CH144**

Economic information with emphasis on statistical data for more than 100 basic raw commodities and semifinished products.

—— Statistical abstract service. v.1, no.1, Jan. 1964– .

Issued 5 times a year. Brings most series up to date.

Lippert, T. W. 10,000 trade names. 1st ed. N.Y., Iron Age, 1947. 112p.   **CH145**

Subtitle: All American and foreign ferrous and nonferrous metals and alloys, plastics, non-metals, refractories, cements, lubricants, chemicals, plywoods, machine tools, small tools, rolling mills, cranes, bearings, joining devices and other equipment made and used by the metals industry. Also processes, proprietary and otherwise, in the production, shaping, treating and finishing of metals.

Special Libraries Association. Business and Finance Division. Committee on Sources of Commodity Prices. Sources of commodity prices. Comp. by Paul Wasserman, [chairman]. N.Y., Assoc., 1959. 170p.   **CH146**

Locates sources of prices to more than 6800 commodities, in alphabetical arrangement, referring to about 150 periodicals published in the United States and Canada.

Appendix lists periodicals with information as to address of publisher and frequency.

U.S. National Bureau of Standards. National directory of commodity specifications; classified and alphabetical lists and brief descriptions of specifications of national recognition. Wash., Govt. Prt. Off., 1945. 1311p. (Its Miscellaneous publ. M178)   **CH147**

3d ed. Previous eds., 1925 and 1932.

Supersedes the Bureau's Miscellaneous publication, M130.

—— —— Supplement. 1947. 322p.

U.S. Technical Committee on Standard Commodity Classification. Standard commodity classification. Wash., Govt. Prt. Off., 1943–44. 2v. (U.S. Bureau of the Budget. Technical paper, no.26–27)   **CH148**

(1) Standard classified list of commodities; (2) Alphabetical index.

—— —— Supplement to v.2. 1945. 1222p. (U.S. Bureau of the Budget. Technical paper, no.28)

The supplement contains about 50,000 additional commodity items, not listed in v.1–2.

Zimmerman, Oswald Theodore and **Lavine, Irvin.** Industrial Research Service's Handbook of material trade names. 1953 ed. Dover, N.H., Industrial Research Service, 1953. 794p.   **CH149**

1st ed. 1946.

This rewritten and expanded edition lists approximately 15,000 trade names under which products are sold, with manufacturers' names and addresses. Chemical and physical properties of many of the products are given. A classification section lists products according to use.

────── Supplement, 1–3, 1956–60.

❧ Guides to the purchasing of all types of products from the consumer point of view are given in various publications reporting the results of tests of the items, with indication of recommended and nonrecommended brands. Two of the most used of these periodicals are:

Consumer bulletin, Sept. 1931– . Wash., N.J., 1931– . il. Monthly.   **CH150**
 Title varies.
 Each monthly issue includes an abridged cumulative index to the preceding issues of the current year.

Consumer reports, May 1936– . Mt. Vernon, N.Y., Consumer's Union of United States, 1936– . il. Monthly.   **CH151**
 Title varies.
 Dec. issue is annual buying guide.

Foreign trade

Bibliography

Henderson, George P. European companies; a guide to sources of information. Sociétés européennes; répertoire des sources de documentation. Europäische Handelsgesellschaften; Handbuch der Informationsquellen. London, C.B.D. Research, 1962– . 1v. Loose-leaf. **CH152**
 Detailed description for each entry. Excludes: (1) publications giving no information other than addresses and products, and (2) sources limited to a particular industry or service (other than finance).

U.S. Bureau of Foreign Commerce (1953–1961). Sources of information on foreign trade practice. Wash., Govt. Prt. Off., 1959. 47p.   **CH153**
 A revision of the bibliography *Foreign trade practice,* issued by the U.S. Dept. of Commerce in June 1954.
 List of governmental and nongovernmental guides, handbooks, and other studies relating to basic procedures of export and import transactions.

U.S. Bureau of International Business Operations. Commercial Intelligence Division. Sources of information on American firms for international buyers. Rev. ed. Wash., 1963. 26p.   **CH154**
 1st ed. 1962.

Dictionaries

Henius, Frank. Dictionary of foreign trade. 2d ed. compl. rev. and greatly expanded. N.Y., Prentice-Hall, 1947. 959p. il.   **CH155**
 First pub. 1946.
 Includes foreign-trade terms, usages, practices, and procedures.

Woollam, W. G. Shipping terms and abbreviations: maritime, insurance, international trade. Cambridge, Md., Cornell Maritime, 1963. 144p.   **CH156**
 Contains more than 2000 abbreviations.
 Pt.1, Abbreviations, arranged alphabetically; pt.2, Index of terms, arranged alphabetically.

Foreign terms

Eksportno-importnyi slovar'. Glavnyi red. B. T. Kolpakov. Moskva, Vneshtorgizdat, 1952–54. 3v. il.   **CH157**
 An alphabetically arranged encyclopedia with articles ranging from a few lines to several pages. Gives translations of terms into a number of languages, as well as definitions in Russian. Many tables and figures are included in the text, and there are some colored plates. All kinds of commodities are listed.

Motta, Giuseppe. Dizionario commerciale: inglese-italiano, italiano-inglese. Economia, legge, finanza (amministrazione, banca, borsa, assicurazione, scambi, commercio estero e marittimo, transporti, dogane, ecc.). Milano, C. Signorelli, [1961]. 1050p.   **CH158**

Netto, Modestino Martins. Vocabulário de intercâmbio comercial: português-inglês; inglês-português. Com um apêndice contendo abreviaturas comerciais, pêsos e medidas, sistema monetário, modelos de cartas comerciais, etc. Rio de Janeiro, Ed. Civilização Brasileira, 1961. 251p.   **CH159**
 A practical glossary of commercial terms.

Servotte, Jozef V. Dictionnaire commercial et financier: français, néerlandais, anglais, allemand. 2. éd. rev. et augm. Bruxelles, Éd. Brepols. [Distr. N.Y., Simmons, 1962] 955p.   **CH160**
 1st ed. 1956.
 Added title page: Woordenboek voor handel en financien.

Spinelli, Nicola. Dizionario commerciale, italiano-inglese e inglese-italiano; terminologia commerciale contabile, economica, finanziaria, giuridica. Ed. 1957 con un'appendice a cura del Giuseppe Motta. Torino, S. Lattes, [1957]. 464p., 683p., 138p.   **CH161**
 1st ed. 1927.

Handbooks

Allen, Roy George Douglas and **Ely, J. Edward.** International trade statistics. N.Y., Wiley, 1953. 448p.   **CH162**
 Describes and appraises the statistics of the individual countries of the world and indicates how trade statistics are compiled and used. Appendix lists national publications of international trade statistics. Includes bibliography, p.417–39.

Dartnell Corporation. Dartnell international trade handbook, by Gerard R. Richter and others. Leslie Llewellyn Lewis, ed. 1st ed. Pub. in cooperation with the American Institute for Foreign Trade. Chicago, 1963. 1312p. il.   **CH163**
 A revised and expanded version of *The foreign trade handbook,* by E. E. Pratt.
 Covers the organization, management, and financing of foreign trade, and its technical and legal aspects.
 Includes texts of "Export-Import Bank act of 1945, as amended," p.1086–90, and the "Trade-expansion act of 1962," p.1187–1235.
 Bibliography, p.1038–57.

Food and Agriculture Organization of the United Nations. Trade yearbook. Annuaire du commerce. Anuario de comercio. v.12– . 1958– . Rome, [1959–].   **CH164**
 Formerly issued as pt.2 of *Yearbook of food and agricultural statistics,* and continues the yearbook's numbering.

Foreign commerce handbook, 1922/23– . Wash., Foreign Commerce Dept., Chamber of Commerce of the U.S., 1922– . Biennial (Irregular).   **CH165**
 A guide to the sources of export and import services and information.

Lloyd's Calendar, 1898– . London, Lloyd's, 1898– . il. Annual.   **CH166**

A useful yearbook containing much miscellaneous commercial shipping and navigation information: laws affecting commerce and navigation, lists of British chambers of commerce, weights and measures of various nations, legal holidays of the world, etc.

United Nations. Statistical Office. Yearbook of international trade statistics, 1950– . N.Y., 1951– . Annual. **CH167**

Continues *International trade statistics,* issued by the League of Nations, 1933–39.

The 13th issue, for 1962, contains statistics on 138 countries, and also on trade by commodities for 112 countries according to the *Standard international trade classification.*

U.S. Bureau of the Census. Foreign commerce and navigation of the United States, 1821–1946. Wash., Govt. Prt. Off., [1820/21]–1950. Annual. **CH168**

Official statistical data on foreign trade and navigation of the United States.

Publishing body varies. Before 1865, published by the Register of Treasury.

Publication of the annual was suspended after 2v. covering 1946 were issued in 1950.

—— Monthly summary of foreign commerce and navigation. 1866–April 1951. (Cumulated quarterly) **CH168a**

Both annual and monthly publications replaced by:

—— Quarterly summary of foreign commerce. Jan. 1951–June 1961. Wash., Govt. Prt. Off., 1951–63. (Cumulated annually) **CH168b**

Discontinued with the Jan./June 1961 issue.

Contains information, including statistical tables, on imports and exports by commodities, countries, customs districts, economic classes, etc.

U.S. Dept. of Commerce. Office of International Trade. Foreign commerce yearbook, 1948–51. Wash., Govt. Prt. Off., 1950–53. **CH169**

Ceased publication.

Preceded by: U.S. Bureau of Foreign and Domestic Commerce, *Commerce yearbook,* 1922–1932, which included pt.1, United States, and pt.2, Foreign countries. Pt.1 was discontinued in 1932. Pt.2 was continued by the Office's *Foreign commerce yearbook,* 1933–39. Publication suspended 1934, 1940–47.

Detailed information on business conditions in the United States and foreign countries, summarizing statistical information originally collected by government bureaus, trade associations, and trade journals, with references to sources of information.

Directories

Directory of American firms operating in foreign countries, comp. by Juvenal L. Angel. 1955/56– . N.Y., World Trade Academy Pr., 1955– . Annual. **CH170**

In 1953, issued as an appendix to Angel's *Looking for employment in foreign countries* (CH361).

Lists more than 3300 American corporations which operate more than 8500 business enterprises in foreign countries. Pt.I gives geographical distribution by country, but omits addresses. Pt.II is an alphabetical list of corporations with United States addresses.

Exporters' encyclopaedia. 1st ed. 1904– . Containing full and authentic information relative to shipments for every country in the world. N.Y., T. Ashwell, 1904– . Annual, including supplementary bulletins which keep the Encyclopaedia up to date throughout the subscription year. **CH171**

Contents: (1) Alphabetical index of ports and trade centers; (2) Countries (arranged alphabetically), consular regulations, ports and trade centers, shipping routes, mail, radio and cable, telephone, exchange restrictions, money, weights, holidays, etc.; (3) General export information; (4) Ports of the United States, etc.

Ports of the world. London, Shipping World, 1946– . v.1– . il. Annual. **CH172**

Ports are listed alphabetically by country. A separate section gives ports of the United Kingdom. Usually includes: location, population, accommodations, charges, pilotage, imports, and exports.

Until 1946 issued as a section of the *Shipping world year book* (CH173).

Shipping world year book and who's who, ed. by Sir Archibald Hurd, 1883– . London, Shipping World, 1883– . Annual. **CH173**

General maritime information; statistical tables; classified world directories of shipowners, shipbuilders, ship repairers, towing services, marine engine builders, etc.; training for the merchant navy; shipping and shipbuilding organizations; who's who in the shipping world.

U.S. Bureau of Foreign Commerce (1953–1961). A directory of foreign advertising agencies and marketing research organizations for the United States international business community, comp. by Helen Biggane. Wash., 1959. 135p. **CH174**

—— A directory of foreign organizations for trade and investment promotion. [2d ed.] Wash., 1961. 108p. **CH175**

1st edition, 1957, had title *A directory of foreign development organizations for trade and investment.*

Lists by country "the principal governmental and private organizations abroad actively engaged in promoting and facilitating trade and investment in the free world."—*Foreword.*

U.S. Hydrographic Office. World port index; locations and general descriptions of maritime ports and shipping places, with reference to appropriate sailing directions and charts. 2d ed. Wash., Govt. Prt. Off., 1957. 201p. il. (Its H.O. publ. no.950) **CH176**

1st ed. 1953.

Bibliography.

United States

American register of exporters and importers, 1945/46– . N.Y., Amer. Register of Exporters and Importers Corp., 1946– . Annual. **CH177**

Lists some 25,000 active American export and import concerns, and allied lines. Product indexes in English, Spanish, French, and German.

Custom house guide. N.Y., Import Publs., 1862– . Annual (with monthly supplements). **CH178**

United States customs tariff, customs ports, internal revenue code, customs, shipping and commerce regulations, and reciprocal trade agreements.

Monthly supplements called *American import and export bulletin.*

Far East

Directory and chronicle for China, Japan, Straits Settlements, Malaya, Siam, Korea, Indo-China, Netherlands Indies, Borneo, the Philippines with which are incorporated The China directory, The Hongkong directory, and Hong list for the Far East. Hongkong, Hongkong Daily Pr., [1866–1941?]. Annual. (1941, 79th year) **CH179**

Title varies.

Contains texts of treaties; tariffs; much useful gazetteer and descriptive material; directories of residents, officials, merchants, etc.

Japan company directory, 1957– . Tokyo, Oriental Economist, [1956–].   **CH180**

A trade directory in English of Japanese business firms. Includes a section, "Who's who in Japanese business."
Supplements *Japan economic yearbook* (CG134a).

Japan trade guide, with a comprehensive mercantile directory. Tokyo, Jiji Tsushin Sha, [1950?–]. il. Annual.   **CH181**

Frequency varies. Publisher varies.

Includes information on Japanese politics, economic developments, foreign trade, government agencies, and trade organizations. Contains a mercantile directory, but omits a who's who section.

Great Britain

Kelly's Directory of merchants, manufacturers and shippers for Great Britain, and the British Empire with supplement for other countries. London, Kelly's Directory, 1880– . Annual.   **CH182**

Very useful for its directory and descriptive material. Alphabetical and classified lists.

Ireland

O'Neill's Commercial who's who and industrial directory of Ireland. Dublin, Parkside Pr., 1935– . Annual.   **CH183**

Title varies.

"Including: press and advertising directory, general business information year-book, handbook of Irish securities, industrial organisations, banker's year-book, trade marks and trade names" (varies).

Middle East

Owen's African and Middle East commerce & travel and international register. 1953/54– . London, Pan-African Commercial Directory, 1954– . il., maps. Annual.   **CH184**

An international register of manufacturers, merchants, and traders, with descriptive notes on population, resources, finances, commerce, etc. of each country.

1953–54 (pub. 1954) had title *Pan-African commercial directory;* 1955, *Owen's Pan-African & Middle East directory.*

Register of commerce and industry in Israel. 1935– . Tel-Aviv, Israel Directory of Commerce and Industry, 1935– . Annual.   **CH185**

In English and Hebrew.

Title varies: 1935–38, *Register of commerce and industry in Palestine, the Palestine directory;* 1939–48, *The Palestine directory, the register of commerce and industry in Palestine;* 1949– , *The register of commerce and industry in Israel.*

Atlases

Lloyd's Maritime atlas, including a comprehensive list of ports and shipping places of the world, comp. and ed. by the shipping editor at Lloyd's. [4th ed.] London, Lloyd's, 1961. 99p. 16pl. (col. maps)   **CH186**

3d ed. 1958.

Tables of distances

Reed's Tables of distances between ports and places in all parts of the world, comprising over 31,000 distances with a table of contents and complete alphabetical index, comp. by A. B. Purbrick and W. R. Nedham. 12th ed. Sunderland, Eng., Reed, 1953. 176p.   **CH187**

1st ed. 1931.

U.S. Coast and Geodetic Survey. Distances between United States ports. 3d ed. Wash., Govt. Prt. Off., 1961. 43p. il.   **CH188**

Contains tables computed for United States coast pilots.

U.S. Naval Oceanographic Office. Distances between ports. Wash., Govt. Prt. Off., 1964. 132p. (Its Publ. no.151)   **CH189**

Supersedes the U.S. Hydrographic Office, *Tables of distances between ports.* 1943. (Its Publ. 117) First pub. in 1916.

Money, weights, and measures

Doursther, Horace. Dictionnaire universel des poids et mesures, anciens et modernes, contenant des tables des monnaies de tous les pays. Bruxelles, Hayez, 1840. 604p. (Repr.: Amsterdam, Holland, Meridian Pub. Co., 1965)   **CH190**

Out of date, but useful for questions involving historical information because of the many older and unusual terms included.

Elsevier's Lexicon of international and national units; English/American, German, Spanish, French, Italian, Japanese, Dutch, Portuguese, Polish, Swedish, Russian. Comp. and arr. by W. E. Clason. Amsterdam, Elsevier, 1964. 76p. (Elsevier lexica, 2)   **CH191**

A guide to the meaning and value of internationally and nationally used units.

International units, arranged alphabetically by unit, p.1–38; Units used in different countries, arranged by country, p.39–56; Words and indexes, p.58–74; Bibliography, p.75–76.

Naft, Stephen. International conversion tables: weights, measures, gauges, currencies, conversion equivalents and factors, technical units, alphabets, other useful information. Expanded and rev. by Ralph de Sola. N.Y., Duell, 1961. 372p.   **CH192**

1st edition had title *Conversion equivalents in international trade.*

Pick's Currency yearbook. Franz Pick. N.Y., Pick Pub. Corp., 1955– . Annual.   **CH193**

Descriptions of world currencies and monetary conditions in 94 countries. Includes official exchange rates.

Tate, William. Tate's Modern cambist. Centenary ed. 28th ed. by W. F. Spalding. London, Wilson; N.Y., Bankers Pub. Co., 1929. 734p.   **CH194**

Subtitle: A manual of the world's monetary systems, the foreign exchanges, the stamp duties on bills of exchange in foreign countries, the principal rules governing bills of exchange and promissory notes, foreign weights and measures, bullion and exchange operations.

—— Tate's Money manual, being the 1st–2d annual editions of additions, alterations and amendments to the centenary edition of Tate's Modern cambist, by W. F. Spalding. London, Wilson; N.Y., Bankers Pub. Co., [1931–33]. v.1–2.   **CH195**

United Nations. Statistical Office. World weights and measures; handbook for statisticians. Provisional ed. N.Y., 1955. 225p. (Its Statistical papers, ser. M, no.21)   **CH196**

Prepared in collaboration with the Food and Agriculture Organization of the United Nations.

Includes: International systems and units of weight and measure; National systems and units of weight, measure, and currency, arranged by country; Unit weights of selected commodities; National currencies, with equivalents in U.S. currency; Indexes of weights and measures, abbreviations, and currencies.

U.S. National Bureau of Standards. Units of weight and measure (United States customary and metric). Defini-

tions and tables of equivalents. . . . Wash., Govt. Prt. Off., 1960. 62p. (Its Miscellaneous publ. 233)   **CH197**
"Supersedes Misc. publ. 214."

Tariff

Bibliography

Contracting Parties to the General Agreement on Tariffs and Trade. GATT bibliography, 1947–1953. 1st ed. Geneva, GATT Secretariat, 1954. 40p.   **CH198**

Contents: pt.1, Bibliography of texts of the GATT and governmental publications; pt.2, Selected GATT publications; pt.3, Chronological list of references to GATT, arranged alphabetically within each period.

Includes books, pamphlets, articles, periodicals, newspaper reports and editorials, and miscellaneous material.

—— —— Supplement. 1st ed.– . Jan. 1954/June 1955– . Annual.

U.S. Tariff Commission. Publications of the Tariff Commission. 1920– . Wash., Govt. Prt. Off., 1920– . Irregular.   **CH199**

Title varies: Subject index to tariff information surveys and reports, 1920; List of principal subjects investigated and reported upon by the United States Tariff Commission, 1921–27; List of publications of the United States Tariff Commission, 1929–34; Publications of the Tariff Commission, 1939– .

—— The tariff; a bibliography. A select list of references. Wash., Govt. Prt. Off., 1934. 980p. (Miscellaneous ser.)   **CH200**

Classified and annotated list of almost 6500 items, with (1) author index, and (2) subject and title index. Emphasis is on tariff situation in the United States, but material listed furnishes information on the more important countries of the world.

Dictionaries and handbooks

U.S. Tariff Commission. Dictionary of tariff information. Wash., Govt. Prt. Off., 1924. 1036p.   **CH201**

Includes articles on tariff systems, methods, practices, history, biographical articles on men connected with American tariff history, and descriptive and statistical articles on all commodities mentioned in the tariff act of 1922. Contains some bibliography.

—— Trade agreements manual. 3d ed. Wash., Govt. Prt. Off., 1959. 30p.   **CH202**

1st ed. 1955.

Subtitle: A summary of selected data relating to trade agreements negotiated by the United States since 1934.

Transportation

Port of New York Authority. A selected bibliography of the Port of New York Authority, 1921–1962. N.Y., [1962]. 110p.   **CH203**

A list of books, journals, reports, and speeches on transportation as related to the activities of the Port of New York Authority. Partial list of topics includes air traffic, bridges, construction, finance, foreign trade, insurance, legislation, operation and maintenance, ports, railroads, ships and shipping, terminals and tolls. Arranged by subject, with author and subject index.

U.S. Interstate Commerce Commission. Report on transport statistics in the United States, 1887/88– . Wash., Govt. Prt. Off., 1889– . v.1– . Annual.   **CH204**

Title varies: 1887/88–1953, *Annual report on the statistics of railways in the United States.*

1963 issue in seven parts: (1) Railroads, their lessors and proprietary companies; the Pullman Company; and the Railway Express Agency, Inc.; (2) Electric railways; (3) Carriers—by water; (4) Oil pipe lines; (5) Motor carriers; (6) Freight forwarders; (7) Private car lines.

U.S. Library of Congress. Reference Dept. Soviet transportation and communications; a bibliography comp. by Renee S. Janse. Wash., 1952. 330p.   **CH205**

Classified listing, with an author index and Library of Congress classification number if in that library. Holdings also indicated for 46 other libraries. Emphasis is on post-1930 publications, but entries are not limited as to date.

Railroads

Bureau of Railway Economics. Railway economics, a collective catalogue of books in fourteen American libraries. Chicago, Univ. of Chicago Pr., 1912. 446p.   **CH206**

Canada. Bureau of Statistics. Library. Bibliographical list of references to Canadian railways, 1829–1938. Ottawa, 1938. 99p.   **CH207**

Contains 1179 references to books and periodicals, indicating location of copies.

Directory of railway officials and year book, comp. from official sources, 1950/51– . London, Tothill, 1950– . il. Annual.   **CH208**

Supersedes *Universal directory of railway officials and railway year book,* 1895–1950.

Information on railways in Great Britain and Ireland, such as history, officials, and statistics, with briefer information on railways in various countries of the world.

Includes bibliography.

Thomson, Thomas Richard. Check list of publications on American railroads before 1841; a union list of printed books and pamphlets, including state and federal documents, dealing with charters, by-laws, legislative acts, speeches, debates, land grants, officers' and engineers' reports, travel guides, maps, etc. N.Y., N.Y. Pub. Lib., 1942. 250p.   **CH209**

"Reprinted with additions from the *Bulletin* of the New York Public Library of January-July-October 1941."

Includes 2671 numbered entries, arranged chronologically, of works which are predominantly related to railroads, or which have the words "railroad" or "railway" on the title page. Includes books, pamphlets, broadsides (except stock or contract certificates or bonds), and maps. Locates copies in 36 libraries that cooperated in checking the list.

Who's who in railroading in North America. 14th ed. N.Y., Simmons-Boardman, 1959. 703p.   **CH210**

Prior to 1930, known as the *Biographical directory of railway officials of America.*

Ships

Howe, Octavius Thorndike and **Matthews, F. C.** American clipper ships, 1833–1858. Salem, Mass., Marine Research Soc., 1926–27. 2v. il. (Marine Research Soc., Salem, Mass. Publ. 13)   **CH211**

Arranged alphabetically by name of ship, giving description and history of each and often a picture. Index includes names of captains, owners, etc., and of ships not described separately.

Matthews, Frederick C. American merchant ships, 1850–1900. Salem, Mass., Marine Research Soc., 1930. 399p. il. (Marine Research Soc., Salem, Mass. Publ. 21) **CH212**

A companion work to Howe above, on the same general plan.

Lytle, William M. Merchant steam vessels of the United

States, 1807–1868. "The Lytle list," comp. from official merchant marine documents of the United States and other sources. Ed. with an introd. by Forrest R. Holdcamper. Mystic, Conn., Steamship Historical Soc. of America, 1952 [i.e., 1953]. 294p. (Steamship Historical Soc. of America. Publ. no.6) **CH213**

A revision and enlargement of *Steam vessels built in the United States,* 1807–1856, compiled under the author's supervision and issued by the U.S. Bureau of Navigation in 1931. Precedes in date *Merchant vessels of the United States, 1866/67–* , published by the U.S. Bureau of Customs (CH220).

Gives information on name, tonnage, year and place built, first home port, and disposition. A separate list of ships lost, and one of ships converted to steam.

—— —— Supplement [no.1]. Compound name index.

—— —— Supplement [no.2]. Corrections and additions, as of Dec. 31, 1954.

—— —— Supplement no.3 . . . Corrections and additions, Jan. 1, 1955—June 30, 1958.

Smith, Eugene Waldo. Trans-Atlantic passenger ships, past and present. [1st ed.] Boston, Dean, 1947. 350p. il. **CH214**

Deals with the principal passenger ships operating in the North Atlantic 1840–1940. Lists alphabetically some 1000 ships, giving: date of construction, name of builder and owner, tonnage, dimensions, activities, changes of name, and final disposition.

—— Trans-Pacific passenger ships and Appendix to Trans-Atlantic passenger ships, past and present. 1st ed. Boston, Dean, 1953. 266p. il. **CH215**

Attempts "to include all known trans-Pacific passenger ships built from 1860 up to the present time. Includes liners sailing from English ports to New Zealand . . . via the Panama Canal."—*Introd.*

Appendix brings the author's companion volume *Trans-Atlantic passenger ships—past and present* up to date.

Wallace, Frederick William. Record of Canadian shipping. A list of square-rigged vessels, mainly 500 tons and over, built in the eastern provinces of British North America . . . 1786 to 1920. Illus. with photographs, paintings, and drawings. Toronto, Musson, [c1929]. 302p. il. **CH216**

Arranged alphabetically by name of ship.

Annuals

American Bureau of Shipping. Record of the American Bureau of Shipping, "American Lloyds," established 1867 to provide a standard American classification of vessels. N.Y., 1867?– . Annual. **CH217**

—— Supplement. no.1, 1949– . Semimonthly.

Title varies: 1869–1932, *Record of American and foreign shipping.*

Separately paged supplements accompany many volumes.

Lloyd's Register of shipping. Founded 1760, reconstituted 1834, united with the Underwriters' Registry for iron vessels in 1885. London, Lloyd's, 1834– . Annual. **CH218**

1963/64 has 4v.

Contents: v.1, Register of ships: names, classes and general information concerning ships classed by *Lloyd's Register of shipping;* also particulars of all known ocean-going merchant ships in the world of 100 tons gross and upwards. Kept up to date by cumulative monthly supplements; v.2, Appendix: additional particulars, structural details, capacities, etc. for ships other than tankers . . .; v.3, Shipowners: list of owners, and managers of the ships recorded in the *Register* with their fleets; v.4, Directory: list of shipbuilders with existing ships

they have built; marine enginebuilders and boilermakers; dry and wet docks; telegraphic addresses and codes used by shipping firms; marine insurance companies.

Merchant ships. Ed. by Eric Talbot-Booth. . . . N.Y., Macmillan, 1936–59. il. Annual. **CH219**

Ceased publication.

Pictures and line drawings of the merchant ships of the various countries of the world, with pertinent information on tonnage, distinguishing features, history, etc. A continuation and extension of *British merchant ships,* edited by Talbot-Booth. London, Rich and Cowan, 1934. 220p.

U.S. Bureau of Customs. Merchant vessels of the United States (including yachts and government vessels). 1866/67– . Wash., Govt. Prt. Off., 1869– . v.1– . il. Annual. **CH220**

Title varies; issuing office varies.

Includes an alphabetical list of vessels, giving: name, tonnage size, where built, name of owner, home port, etc.; former names of merchant vessels; owners of vessels, etc.

Communication

Postal guides

U.S. Post Office Dept. Directory of post offices. Wash., Govt. Prt. Off., 1955– . Loose-leaf. Annual. **CH221**

Revised and published annually in July in bound form. Kept up to date by weekly *Postal bulletin,* beginning with July 6, 1963, issue. 1963 edition includes ZIP code numbers for the first time.

Replaces the *United States official postal guide,* 1874–1954, pt.1, *Domestic postal service.*

—— Directory of international mail. Wash., [1955–]. 1v. Loose-leaf. **CH222**

Kept up to date by loose-leaf pages.

Reconstitutes *United States official postal guide,* 1937–1954, pt.2, *International postal service.*

"Contains rates and other conditions governing mail to individual foreign countries, arranged alphabetically by countries."—*Pref.*

Canada. Post Office Dept. Canada official postal guide; chief regulations of the Post Office, rates of postage and other information. Ottawa, Queen's Printer, 1875– . Biennial. **CH223**

Title and frequency vary.

—— List of post offices in Canada. Ottawa, Queen's Printer, 1955– . Loose-leaf. **CH223a**

—— Monthly supplement to Canada official postal guide. [Ottawa], 1956– .

Supplements the current *Canada official postal guide* and the *List of post offices.*

Gt. Brit. Post Office Dept. Post office guide. London, Stat. Off., 1856– . **CH224**

From 1856 to 1879, called *British postal guide;* published quarterly. Frequency thereafter varies, usually annually with supplements and, since 1937, associated volumes: *Post offices in the United Kingdom* (pub. irregularly), and *London post offices and streets* (pub. irregularly).

Mass media

Blum, Eleanor. Reference books in the mass media: an annotated, selected booklist covering book publishing, broadcasting, films, newspapers, magazines, and advertising. Urbana, Univ. of Illinois Pr., 1962. 103p. **CH225**

Arranged by broad category, with detailed index.

International television almanac. [1]– . 1956– . N.Y., Quigley, 1956– . il. Annual. **CH226**

A compendium containing information on television performers, producers, distributors, feature releases, directories of services, stations and agencies, television in Great Britain and Canada, the world market, the television code, awards, etc.

McMahon, Harry Wayne. Television production; the creative techniques and language of TV today. N.Y., Hastings, [c1957]. 231p. il. **CH227**

A handbook, arranged by chapters, dealing with aspects of TV production. Throughout the text some 2000 terms used in television are defined. An alphabetical word index refers to the place of definition within the text.

National radio-television news directory; official press guide of the Radio-Newsreel-Television Working Press Assoc., 1954/55– . N.Y., Assoc., 1954– . il. Annual. **CH228**

Former title: *Mike and screen press directory and newsguide.*

Directory and biographical information on networks, newsreels, news services, stations, press clubs, members, etc.

Sparks, Kenneth R. A bibliography of doctoral dissertations in television and radio. Syracuse, N.Y., School of Journalism, Syracuse Univ., [1962]. 32p. **CH229**

An alphabetical listing by author of 352 dissertations completed at American universities through Dec. 1961. Does not include those dealing with engineering aspects of the subject. Contains a list of source material from which the bibliography was compiled.

United Nations Educational, Scientific and Cultural Organization. Dept. of Mass Communication. World communications; press, radio, television, film. [4th ed.] Paris, UNESCO; N.Y., UNESCO Pub. Center, [1964]. 380p. il. **CH230**

1st ed. 1950.

A survey describing the facilities of mass communication media throughout the countries of the world. Text accompanied by statistics. Includes selective bibliography.

United Nations Educational, Scientific and Cultural Organization. Division of Free Flow of Information. Professional association in the mass media; handbook of press, film, radio, television organizations. [Paris], UNESCO, [1959]. 206p. **CH231**

A directory giving detailed information on 1049 national organizations in 93 states and territories, and 64 international associations. Includes history, purpose, membership, publications, etc.

U.S. Foreign Broadcast Information Service. Broadcasting stations of the world . . . 18th ed. Wash., Govt. Prt. Off., 1963. 3v. **CH232**

1st ed. 1947?. Frequently revised.

Contents: pt.1, According to country and city; pt.2, According to frequency; pt.3, Frequency modulation and television stations.

Lists all known radio, broadcasting, and television stations except those on domestic channels in the United States.

FINANCE AND BANKING

Bibliography

Dillen, Johannes Gerardus van. History of the principal public banks, accompanied by extensive bibliographies of the history of banking and credit in eleven European countries, collected by J. G. van Dillen in his quality of Secretary to the International Committee for the Study of the History of Banking and Credit. The Hague, Nijhoff, 1934. 480p. **CH233**

Covers banking history from the end of the 15th century to

1815 in Spain, Italy, Holland, Germany, Sweden, England, France, Poland, Russia, Belgium, and Denmark; chapters— written variously in French, German, English, or Italian— are by different authors.

Extensive bibliographies.

International Association for Research in Income and Wealth. Bibliography on income and wealth, v.1, 1937– 1947, ed. by Daniel Creamer; v.2–8, 1948–1957/60, ed. by Phyllis Deane. Cambridge, Bowes & Bowes, 1952–64. v.1–8. (Annotated international bibliographies) **CH234**

A cooperative work by contributors from many countries. Contains books, pamphlets, and periodical articles, but only when they provide critical or descriptive analysis of the measures used. The arrangement is topical, with geographical subdivision when pertinent; otherwise, under each topic the arrangement is alphabetical by author. Author, geographical area, and subject indexes.

Knox, Vera H. Public finance: information sources. Detroit, Gale Research, [1964]. 142p. (Management information guide, 3) **CH235**

Arranged in chapters covering various aspects of public finance: revenues, expenditures, taxation, fiscal administration, and international public finance. Lists books, periodical articles, and documents, mostly published since 1960, with short annotations when needed. Includes lists of periodicals, services, and indexes. Author and subject indexes.

Masui, Mitsuzo. A bibliography of finance. Kobe, Internat. Finance Seminar in the Kobe Univ. of Commerce, 1935. 1614p., 116p. **CH236**

Contents: British books and articles; Ouvrages françaises; Deutsche Literatur; American books and articles; Author index.

Includes works dating from 15th century to 1933.

Westerfield, Ray Bert. Selected bibliography of money, credit, banking and business finance. Cambridge, Mass., Bankers Pub. Co., 1940. 136p. **CH237**

Includes books, encyclopedias, directories, investment manuals, reports of financial associations and credit agencies, and selected statistical, forecasting, and advisory services. Lists leading financial periodicals, but does not index articles. Subject arrangement with author index.

Old, but valuable historically because of the excellence of the selection.

Dictionaries, encyclopedias, and handbooks

Bogen, Jules Irwin [and others]. Financial handbook. Staff ed., Samuel S. Stripman. 4th ed. N.Y., Ronald, 1964. [v.p.] **CH238**

Earlier editions by Robert Hiester Montgomery.

An indispensable handbook for detailed information on the financial management of a business.

Doris, Lillian. Corporate treasurer's and controller's handbook. N.Y., Prentice-Hall, 1950. 1277p. il. **CH239**

Practical discussion of all duties of these positions, with suggestions on principles for settling specific problems.

Frequently reissued.

Munn, Glenn Gaywaine. Encyclopedia of banking and finance. 6th ed. by F. L. Garcia. Boston, Bankers Pub. Co., 1962. 788p. **CH240**

1st ed. 1924.

Definitions of terms and encyclopedic articles, with bibliographies, on: money; credit; banking practice, history, law, accounting, and organization; trusts and finance; foreign exchange; investments; securities; speculation; business organization; insurance; commodities; markets; brokerage.

Palyi, Melchior and **Quittner, P.** Enzyklopädisches Lexikon für das Geld- , Bank- und Börsenwesen . . . In Gemeinschaft mit 150 Fachleuten aus dem In- und Ausland bearb. von Erich Achterbert [et al.]. Frankfurt am Main, F. Knapp, 1957. 2v. **CH241**

1. ed. *Handwörterbuch des Bankwesens*. 1933.
Includes bibliographies.

Thomson, William. Thomson's Dictionary of banking; a concise encyclopaedia of banking law and practice. 10th ed. by R. W. Jones. Scottish banking by C. J. Shimmins; Irish land laws in their relation to banking by F. T. [i.e., C.] King. London, Pitman; N.Y., Philosophical Lib., 1952. 710p. **CH242**

Contains concise articles on British law and practice, from the business rather than from the historical point of view. Omits American terms and practice.

Wyckoff, Peter. Dictionary of stock market terms. Englewood Cliffs, N.J., Prentice-Hall, 1964. 301p. **CH243**

Defines and explains the use of some 1200 technical terms and expressions used in the stock market. Arranged A–Z, with many cross references.

Foreign terms

Herendi, L. Complete dictionary of banking terms in three languages (English-German-French) with alphabetic system in each of these languages. London, N.Y., Pitman, 1928. 3v. in 1. **CH244**

Kettridge, Julius Orman. French-English and English-French dictionary of commercial and financial terms. . . . London, Routledge, 1931. 647p. **CH245**

For full description *see* CH80.

Steneberg, Wilhelm. Handwörterbuch des Finanzwesens in deutscher und englischer Sprache; wörterbuch des Geld- , Bank- und Börsenwesens sowie verwandter Fachgruppen, unter gleichzeitiger Berücksichtigung amerikanischer und englischer Verhältnisse. 2. durchges. Aufl. Berlin, Siemens, 1947. 2v. (Siemens' wissenschaftliche Fachwörterbücher, Bd.1) **CH246**

T.1, Englisch-deutsch; T.2, Deutsch-englisch.
Added title page in English.
A 2d edition, with only slight changes, of the work with the same title by Karl T. Langguth (1933).

Statistics

International Monetary Fund. Balance of payments yearbook. 1st– . 1938/1947– . Wash., 1949– . Annual. **CH247**

Continues the annual *Balance of payments*, issued 1926–45 by the Secretariat of the League of Nations.

Wholly statistical. Annual volumes, arranged by country, consist of a series of loose-leaf sections issued monthly. Volume for 1958–62, issued 1964, contains data for more than 75 countries.

—— International financial statistics. v.1, 1948– . Wash., Internat. Monetary Fund, 1948– . Monthly. **CH248**

Contains summary tables by subject—e.g., exchange rates, gold production, world trade, etc.—followed by very detailed tables for each country, describing its financial and monetary condition. Data for 86 countries in 1964 volume.

United Nations. Statistical Office and Dept. of Economic and Social Affairs. Yearbook of national accounts statistics. Annuaire de statistiques des comptabiles nationales. 1957– . N.Y., 1958– . Annual. **CH249**

Supersedes the UN's *Statistics of national income and expenditure*. 1938–50.
1957 issue covers 1950–56.
"A comprehensive statistical statement about the economic

activity of a country." 1963 volume shows data for more than 100 countries, and includes some international tables of principal aggregates.

U.S. Board of Governors of the Federal Reserve System. Banking and monetary statistics. Wash., Nat. Capital Pr., 1943. 979p. **CH250**

A compilation of statistics covering, for the most part, 1914–41 inclusive. In addition to all-banks in the U.S. statistics, includes sections on money rates and securities markets, government finance, gold, exchange rates, and other international statistics.

—— —— Supplement. 1962– .

In sections, appearing irregularly. A complete list appears in the *Federal Reserve bulletin* (CH252).

—— All-bank statistics, United States, 1896–1955. Wash., 1959. 1229p. **CH251**

This comprehensive revision, based on *Banking and monetary statistics* (1943), gives statistics for all banks by class of bank and by state, with explanatory text.

—— Federal Reserve bulletin. v.1, 1915– . Wash., 1915– . Monthly. **CH252**

The most complete current information, including statistics, on financial conditions in the United States. Also reports on financial developments in foreign countries.

U.S. Internal Revenue Service. Statistics of income. 1916– . Wash., Govt. Prt. Off., 1918– . Annual. **CH253**

Issued by the Service under earlier names: 1916–26, Office of Commissioner of Internal Revenue; 1927–47, Bureau of Internal Revenue.

1953– , issued in varying number of parts, e.g., (1) Individual income tax returns; (2) Corporation income tax returns; (3) U.S. business tax returns; and (4) Fiduciary, gift and estate tax returns.

—— —— Supplemental report. State and metropolitan area data for individual income tax returns, 1959/61. 1964. (Publ. no.471, 12–64) **CH253a**

"Contains heretofore unpublished statistics related to the operation of our tax system in the various states and the 100 largest standard metropolitan statistical areas."—*Letter of transmittal*.

Annuals and directories

Bankers' almanac and year book . . . full particulars of the principal banks of the world. The standard international banking work of reference. London, Skinner, 1844– . Annual. **CH254**

Subtitle varies.
Directory of foreign banks by country, with emphasis on British banks.

Directory of American savings and loan associations. 1955– . Baltimore, T. K. Sanderson, 1955– . Annual. **CH255**

Arranged by state and then by city.

International Monetary Fund. Annual report of the executive directors. 1946/47– . Wash., Internat. Monetary Fund, 1947– . Annual. **CH256**

Report year for 1946/47 ends June 30; for 1947/48, April 30.
Summary of the international economy—balance of payments developments—followed by financial surveys of the individual country members of the I.M.F.

Polk's Bank directory; the bankers standard guide to the financial world. 1895– . Nashville, Tenn., R. L. Polk & Co., 1895– . **CH257**

Issued semiannually in March and Sept. with supplements.

Title varies: v.1–59, 1895–1924, *The bankers encyclopedia;* v.60–114, 1924–51, *Polk's Bankers encyclopedia.*

Supplemented by *Polk's Daily bank information service.* Covers United States and foreign banks with branches, giving: name, address, officers, directors, financial statement, and other banking data. A history of investment brokers and dealers is included.

Rand McNally international bankers directory; the bankers blue book, 1872– . Chicago, Rand McNally, 1872– . v.1– .   **CH258**

Issued semiannually with monthly supplements.

Information on United States and foreign banks, giving: name, address, official personnel, financial statement, governmental banking agencies, and their officials.

Security dealers of North America. 1922– . N.Y., Standard and Poor's Corp., 1922– . Semiannual.   **CH259**

Lists approximately 10,000 stock and bond dealers in the United States and Canada.

Stock exchange official year-book. London, Skinner, 1934– . Annual.   **CH260**

Since 1949, issued in two volumes: v.1, issued in March, contains all groups of securities appearing in the Stock Exchange Official List, except those reserved for v.2. Also has general information and statistics section. v.2, issued in Sept., contains the commercial, industrial, etc. group of companies, together with a classified list of all companies quoted on the London and Associated stock exchanges and a complete index to both volumes. Also has a supplementary volume: *Register of defunct and other companies removed from the Stock Exchange official year-book,* published annually.

Kept up to date by the *Stock exchange gazette,* which is not officially a part of the service, but is issued by the same publisher.

Supersedes the *Stock exchange year-book* and the *Stock exchange official intelligence.*

Tax Foundation, Inc., New York. Facts and figures on government finance, 1941– . Englewood Cliffs, N.J., Prentice-Hall, 1941– . Biennial.   **CH261**

Title varies. Publisher varies.

12th ed. 1962/63.

Information about taxes, expenditures, and debt at federal, state, and local levels. Statistics also cover selected national economic series, social insurance programs, and government enterprise operations.—Cf. *Foreword.*

INSURANCE

Bibliography

Insurance Society of New York. Library. Life insurance catalog of the Library of the Insurance Society of New York. Boston, G. K. Hall, 1960. 352p.   **CH262**

Subject catalog of a library established in 1901, which in 1960 contained about 80,000 books, pamphlets, and periodicals.

U.S. Social Security Administration. Basic readings in social security. 25th anniversary of the Social Security Act, 1935–1960, comp. for the Social Security Administration by the Library of the U.S. Dept. of Health, Education, and Welfare. Wash., Govt. Prt. Off., 1960. 221p. (Its Publ. no.28)   **CH263**

". . . First issued in Nov. 1936 and listed 46 references."— *Foreword.* Present work contains 1640 items in a classed arrangement. Books, articles, and documents are included. References are annotated. Author index.

Current

Insurance literature. Special Libraries Association. Insurance Division. N.Y., Nov. 1961– . 10 issues a year plus index.   **CH264**

Supersedes *Insurance book reviews.* Its Bull. no.1–41; April 1933–Oct. 1961.

". . . current publications in all branches of insurance, gerontology and social insurance . . . ." Includes books, pamphlets, reprints, statistical annuals, and association proceedings. Author and title index.

Encyclopedias and handbooks

Crobaugh, Clyde J. Handbook of insurance. N.Y., Prentice-Hall, 1949– . v.1– .   **CH265**

A useful, practical dictionary of more than 5000 insurance subjects and terms, first published 1931. Arranged in alphabetical order. v.1 of this revised edition covers: Life insurance and annuities; Accident and health insurance.

Cyclopedia of insurance in the United States, 1891– . N.Y., Index Pub. Co., 1891– . Annual.   **CH266**

Title varies.

Contents of volumes similar but vary somewhat. 1962 includes lists of insurance companies and organizations; important court decisions; definitions of insurance terms; biographical sketches, p.787–1206; and a list of biographical sketches appearing in earlier volumes.

Lincoln, Walter Osborn, Tisdale, George W. and **Babcock, John T. W.** Fire insurance inspection and underwriting; a non-technical encyclopedic handbook. 7th ed., rev., enl., and fully illustrated. N.Y., Spectator Co., 1953. 1338p. il.   **CH267**

Defines terms and gives brief encyclopedic information. Especially useful for fire hazards.

Earlier editions by Charles Carroll Dominge and W. O. Lincoln.

Manes, Alfred. Versicherungslexikon, ein Nachschlagewerk für alle Wissensgebiete der gesamten Individual- und Sozial-Versicherung. 3. wesentlich erw. u. umgearb. Aufl. Berlin, Mittler, 1930. 1934col.   **CH268**

1st ed. Tübingen, Mohr, 1909; Ergänzungsband, 1913; 2d ed. Berlin, Mittler, 1924.

The best encyclopedia of the whole subject of insurance, with signed articles by specialists and bibliographies. Includes biographies of deceased persons. Now out of date, but no other work supersedes it.

Dictionaries

Davids, Lewis E. Dictionary of insurance. Paterson, N.J., Littlefield, Adams, 1959. 217p.   **CH269**

Definitions of terms and phrases selected for the layman, the insurance company employee, and the college student of insurance.

Gallagher, Vincent Leo and **Heath, Gerald R.** Insurance words and their meanings; a glossary of fire and casualty insurance terms. 5th ed. Indianapolis, Ind., Rough Notes Co., 1961. 111p.   **CH270**

1st ed. 1954.

Sachs, Wolfgang. Lebensversicherungstechnisches Wörterbuch: Deutsch-englisch-französisch-italienisch-spanisch. Würzburg, Konrad Triltsch Verlag, 1954, 308p.   **CH271**

Actuarial and life insurance terms.

Shimomura, S. New English, French and German-Japanese insurance dictionary. Tokyo, Taiyodo, 1930. 538p.   **CH272**

Annuals

Insurance almanac; who, what, when and where in insurance, an annual of insurance facts. N.Y., Underwriter Pr. and Pub. Co., 1912– . Annual.   **CH273**

Title varies.

Includes directory material (companies, organizations, state departments, etc.).

Formerly included section "Who's who in insurance," which has been issued as a separate volume since 1948 (CH277).

Insurance directory and year book (Post magazine almanack) containing statistics and facts of ordinary life, industrial life, fire, accident and marine insurance, 1931– . London, Buckley Pr., 1931– . Annual.   **CH274**

Title varies. *Post magazine almanack* established 1840.

Spectator insurance year book, 1874– . Philadelphia, Spectator Co., 1874– . v.1– . Annual.   **CH275**

Title varies: formerly *Insurance year book*.

Number of parts in each annual issue varies. Fire, marine, casualty, and surety volumes ceased with 1953/54 issue. Life insurance, 1951/52– .

Useful and important compilation containing a large amount of directory and statistical information, with some historical lists.

U.S. Social Security Administration. Social security bulletin, v.1– . March 1938– . Wash., Adminis., 1938– . Monthly.   **CH276**

Statistical data for each year, 1939–48, were published in the Administration's *Social Security yearbooks,* 1940–49. Supplements, with data for each year, 1949–54, were included in the Sept. *Bulletin,* 1950–55; beginning with 1955 data, the *Supplement* is a separate publication.

—— —— Annual statistical supplement. 1956– . Annual.

Who's who in insurance; a section of the Insurance almanac. N.Y., Underwriter Pr. and Pub. Co., 1948– . v.1– . Annual.   **CH277**

A continuation of the biographical section formerly appearing in the *Insurance almanac* (CH273).

❧ *See also* Coman, *Sources of business information,* p.119–29 (CH65), for yearbooks and other works on special forms of insurance.

LABOR AND INDUSTRIAL RELATIONS

❧ For many questions on various kinds of labor topics the best information will often be found in publications of the national government, especially in the bulletins and reports of the U.S. Bureau of Labor Statistics and the National Labor Relations Board, and in the publications of state labor boards, factory inspection bureaus, and labor unions. While the publications of the Bureau of Labor Statistics deal primarily with American topics, they contain also some information on foreign aspects of the subject. The *Monthly labor review* (CH312) is especially useful for current information and statistics. The British *Ministry of labour gazette* and the Canadian *Labour gazette* (issued monthly in both French and English editions, by the Canadian Department of Labour) serve much the same purpose for current topics in the field of British and Canadian labor.

Bibliography

Boëthius, Inga. Svensk företagssociologisk bibliografi, 1945–1955; en selektiv och resonerande bibliografi. Uppsala, 1958. 211p. (Svenska bibliotekariesamfundets skriftserie. IV)   **CH278**

A selective, annotated bibliography on industrial relations and labor problems.

Chamberlain, Neil W. Sourcebook on labor. N.Y., McGraw-Hill, 1958. 1104p. il.   **CH279**

Designed to parallel the author's text, *Labor,* this collection includes such documents as union constitutions, collective agreements, laws and court decisions, arbitration awards, etc.; also, excerpts from Congressional hearings on labor problems and from speeches made by labor and management officials. A useful collection but lacks an index.

—— —— Rev. and abridged, with the assistance of Richard Perlman. N.Y., McGraw-Hill, [1964]. 382p.

Adds considerable material to the 1958 edition. No index.

Chamberlin, Waldo. Industrial relations in Germany, 1914–1939; annotated bibliography of materials in the Hoover Library on War, Revolution, and Peace and the Stanford University Library. Stanford, Calif., Stanford Univ. Pr., [1942]. 403p.   **CH280**

Lists 1720 items with full bibliographic information and detailed annotations. Contents: (1) Documents; (2) Society publications; (3) Newspapers and periodical publications; (4–7) Monographs, studies, articles.

An alphabetical index refers to each numbered item.

Ente per la Storia del Socialismo e del Movimento Operaio Italiano. Bibliografia del socialismo e del movimento operaio italiano. Roma, Torino, Ed. E.S.M.O.I., 1956–64. il. v.1–2. (In progress)   **CH281**

Contents: v.1, pts.1–2, Periodici. 1427p.; v.2, Libri, opuscoli, articoli, almanacchi, numeri unici: pt.1, A–D, pt.2, E–M.

To be in 3v.: v.3, Government documents.

v.1 is a comprehensive listing of the serial publications of Italian socialism, labor parties, workers' movements, unions, etc., issued from 1848 to 1950. Based entirely upon the holdings of the Biblioteca Nazionale Centrale di Firenze; includes 3866 items with full bibliographical description. Arranged alphabetically with indexes by political parties, trades, date of founding, place of publication, personal names, etc. v.2 is an alphabetical list—by author or title—of books, pamphlets, articles, and unique items published from 1815 to 1952. Locates copies in 90 Italian libraries.

Gulick, Charles Adams, Ockert, Roy A. and **Wallace, Raymond J.** History and theories of working-class movements; a select bibliography. Berkeley, Calif., Bureau of Business and Economic Research and Inst. of Industrial Relations, Univ. of Calif., [1955]. 364p.   **CH282**

Lists articles, notes, and occasional documents in periodicals culled from the files in the University of California Library, covering the years 1800–1953. Area coverage is worldwide, but only articles in English are included.

Arrangement is by region and country (with approximately one third of the total devoted to Great Britain), subdivided by subject. No items are annotated, and there are no indexes.

International Labor Office, Geneva. Library. Bibliography on labour law. Rev. 1958. Geneva, 1958. 104p. (Its Bibliographical contributions, no.13)   **CH283**

Title page and introduction in English and French.

1st ed. 1953.

A list of important collections of national labor legislation, legal decisions, textbooks, commentaries, and periodicals on labor law for all countries. Arranged by country. Author index.

—— Bibliography on the International Labour Organisation. Geneva, 1959. 138p. (Its Bibliographical contributions, no.19)   **CH284**

Title and introductory material in English and French.

A selected bibliography, prepared to mark the 40th anniversary of the International Labor Office. Includes bibliographies, catalogs of its own publications, reports, monographs, theses, and periodical articles.

—— Catalogue of publications of the International Association for Labour Legislation, International Association on Unemployment, and International Association for Social Progress and their national sections. Geneva, 1962. 134p. (Its Bibliographical contributions, no.22) **CH285**

In English and French.

" . . . a catalogue of the publications of the organisations which preceded the creation of the International Labour Organisation in 1919 . . . "—*Introd.*

Includes subject index.

—— Catalogue of publications in English of the International Labour Office, 1919–1950. Geneva, 1951. 379p. (Its Bibliographic contributions, no.5) **CH286**

Contents: pt.1, Titles and subjects, arranged in one alphabet, A–Z; pt.2, a checklist arranged by conference, committee, or other issuing body, and by series.

—— Catalogue des publications en langue française du Bureau International du Travail, 1919–1950. Geneva, 1951. 411p. (Its Bibliographic contributions, no.6) **CH287**

—— Catalogue des publications en langue française du Bureau International du Travail, 1951–55. Geneva, 1957. 88p. (Its Bibliographic contributions, no.6, Suppl.) **CH287a**

Titles and subjects listed in one alphabet, A–Z.

Mouvements ouvriers et socialistes: chronologie et bibliographie. Collection dirigée par É. Dolléans et M. Crozier. Paris, Les Éditions Ouvrières, 1950–59. [v.1–5] (In progress) **CH288**

[v.1], Angleterre, France, Allemagne, États-Unis, 1750–1918, [par] Édouard Dolléans et Michel Crozier. 1950. 380p.; [v.2], L'Italie, des origines à 1922, [par] Alfonso Leonetti. 1952. 195p.; [v.3], L'Espagne, 1750–1936, [par] Renée Lamberet. 1953. 204p.; [v.4], La Russie, [par] Eugène Zaleski: v.1, 1725–1907. v.2, 1908–1917. 2v.; [v.5], L'Amérique latine, 1492–1936, [par] Carlos M. Rama. 1959. 222p.

Each volume is arranged chronologically by period. Under each period there is a chronology of events important to the labor movement, followed by a bibliography listing documents, newspapers, books, and pamphlets, including official publications. v.1 and 4 have indexes of names cited; the other volumes have no indexes.

Neufeld, Maurice F. A representative bibliography of American labor history. Ithaca, N.Y., Cornell Univ., 1964. 146p. **CH289**

Aims at providing a wide range of types of materials—scholarly to popular, etc.—as well as varied points of view, from "extreme left-wing attitudes to those which are clearly opposed to labor unions."—*Pref.* Classed arrangement with author index.

Princeton University. Industrial Relations Section. A trade union library, 1955, prep. by Martin Horowitz and Hazel C. Benjamin. 6th ed. Princeton, N.J., 1955. 58p. **CH290**

Annotated list, mainly of books and government publications, selected particularly for an industrial relations executive. Includes material on union organization structure, collective bargaining, and government in relation to labor problems. Arranged by subject with author index.

Kept up to date by:

—— —— Selected references. no.1, Jan. 1945– . Bimonthly.

Reynolds, Lloyd George and **Killingsworth, Charles C.** Trade union publications: the official journals, conven-

tion proceedings, and constitutions of international unions and federations, 1850–1941. Baltimore, Johns Hopkins Pr., 1944–45. 3v. **CH291**

Contents: v.1, Description and bibliography; v.2–3, Subject index, A–Z.

Based upon the collections in the U.S. Dept. of Labor Library, the John Crerar Library, and the Johns Hopkins University Library.

Special Libraries Association. Social Science Group. A source list of selected labor statistics. Rev. ed. N.Y., Assoc., 1953. 113p. **CH292**

2d revision.

Includes "statistical series published more than once a year . . . on unemployment, labor force, strikes, labor turnover, labor costs, workmen's budgets, fringe benefits, and cost of living."—*Pref.* Includes federal, state, and nongovernmental sources. Helpful annotations.

U.S. Bureau of Labor. Index of all reports issued by bureaus of labor statistics in the United States prior to March 1902, prep. by Carroll D. Wright. Wash., Govt. Prt. Off., 1902. 287p. **CH293**

Indexes the reports of the federal and various state bureaus, whatever their designation, which published labor statistics.

Periodicals

Milan. Istituto Giangiacomo Feltrinelli. Bibliografia della stampa periodica operaia e socialista italiana (1860–1926). Milano, Feltrinelli, 1956–61. v.1– . (In progress) **CH294**

Contents: I periodici di Milano: bibliografia e storia, 1860–1904, 1905–1926. 1956–61. 2v.; I periodici di Messina: bibliografia e storia, a cura di Gino Cerrito. 1961. 233p.

Arranged chronologically, with full bibliographical detail and historical description of each periodical. Indexed by title, personal name, and place of publication.

Naas, Bernard G. and **Sakr, Carmelita S.** American labor union periodicals: a guide to their location. Ithaca, N.Y., Cornell Univ., 1956. 175p. **CH295**

"Published by the New York State School of Industrial and Labor Relations . . . for the Committee of University Industrial Relations Librarians."

A union list of more than 1700 labor union periodicals to be found in about 20 cooperating libraries. Information is given about interlibrary loan and the photographing policies of each library.

Wisconsin. State Historical Society. Labor papers on microfilm; a combined list. Rev. Sept. 1, 1960. Madison?, 1960. 22p. **CH296**

Although this work lists holdings of only seven libraries, "it is believed that it does cover most of the filming of labor papers that has been done in the United States."—*Pref.*

Includes official proceedings, publications, and journals of various unions, as well as a broad selection of local labor papers.

Indexes and abstract journals

Employment relations abstracts, 1958– . Detroit, Information Service, 1958– . Semimonthly. Loose-leaf. **CH297**

Supersedes *Labor-personnel index,* 1951–58.

Abstracts current books and approximately 120 journals in the field of labor relations. Arranged under 20 broad categories with separate, detailed subject guide.

Index to labor articles, v.1–27. N.Y., Rand School of Social Science, 1926–53. Monthly; bimonthly. **CH298**

Ceased publication with Sept.–Oct. 1953.

Classified arrangement with no cumulations and no author

index. Indexes labor articles in general periodicals and in some labor papers not indexed elsewhere. From the labor point of view.

Index to labor union periodicals: a cumulative subject index to materials from a selected list of newspapers and journals published by major labor unions. Ann Arbor, Univ. of Michigan, Bureau of Industrial Relations, 1960– . v.1– . Monthly.   **CH299**

An annotated subject index to 50 labor union periodicals; cumulates annually.

Encyclopedias and handbooks

American Federation of Labor. American Federation of Labor; history, encyclopedia, reference book . . . pub. by authority of the 1916 and 1917 conventions. Wash., 1919–60. 3v. in 4. il.   **CH300**

Covers subjects considered at conventions of the A.F.L. with abstract of the actions taken or opinion expressed, and references to sources. v.1 includes 1881–1918; v.2, 1919–23; v.3, 1924–55, when the A.F.L. merged with the C.I.O. to form a new union. General index.

International Labor Office, Geneva. The International labour code, 1951; a systematic arrangement of the conventions and recommendations adopted by the International Labour Conference, 1919–1951, with appendices embodying other standards of social policy framed by or with the cooperation of the International Labour Organisation, 1919–1951. Geneva, 1952. 2v.   **CH301**

Prep. by C. Wilfred Jenks.

v.1, Code; v.2, Appendixes.

Lees-Smith, Hastings Bertrand. Encyclopaedia of the labour movement. London, Caxton, 1928. 3v. il. **CH302**

Now out of date, but useful historically.

Peterson, Florence. American labor unions; what they are and how they work. 2d rev. ed. N.Y., Harper, 1963. 271p.   **CH303**

Discusses the history, structure, and internal government of unions; educational and beneficial activities; union and employer relationships, etc.

Directories

International labor directory and handbook, ed. by Jack Schuyler. [2d compl. rev. ed.] N.Y., Praeger, 1955. 1043p.   **CH304**

1st ed. 1950.

Directory information on labor organizations and related groups, such as labor press, labor schools, etc., mainly for the United States, Canada, and Great Britain, with brief information on other countries.

U.S. Bureau of International Labor Affairs. Directory of labor organizations. Rev. ed. Wash., 1959–63. 4v. in 7. Loose-leaf.   **CH305**

Contents: Europe. 1959. 2v.; Western Hemisphere. 1960. 2v.; Africa. 1962. [unpaged]; Asia and Australasia. 1963. 2v.

Each volume contains "the best available data and information on the structure, composition, membership, and international affiliations of labor organizations" in the area covered.

—— Directory of International Confederation of Free Trade Unions (ICFTU). Rev. ed. Wash., Govt. Prt. Off., 1963. 116p., [90]p. il.   **CH306**

Earlier editions published as pt.1 of the Bureau's *Directory of international trade union organizations,* 1954, 1956, 1958.

—— Directory of International Trade Secretariats (ITS). Pub. as pt.2 of the Bureau's *Directory of international trade union organizations,* 1954, [1961].   **CH307**

—— Directory of International Federation of Christian Trade Unions (CISC). Rev. ed. Wash., Govt. Prt. Off., 1963– . Loose-leaf.   **CH308**

Earlier edition published in 1955 as pt.3 of the Bureau's *Directory of international trade union organizations.*

—— Directory of World Federation of Trade Unions (WFTU), Dec. 1958. Wash., 1959. Loose-leaf. **CH309**

1st ed. 1955.

"The great majority of the affiliates of the World Federation of Trade Unions come from Iron Curtain countries and are, for all practical purposes, arms of their governments."— *Foreword.*

U.S. Bureau of Labor Statistics. Directory of national and international labor unions in the United States, 1955– . Wash., Govt. Prt. Off., 1955– . Biennial.   **CH310**

Title and frequency vary: 1943–54, *Directory of labor unions in the United States.*

Supersedes the Bureau's *Directory of A.F.L. unions,* 1939–42, and its *Directory of C.I.O. unions,* 1939–42.

Lists national and international unions, and state labor organizations, with address, officers and, for the unions, information about conventions, publications, membership, etc.

Dictionaries

Commerce Clearing House. Labor terms. Chicago, Commerce Clearing House, 1955. 98p.   **CH311**

Published in 1949 and 1953 under title *CCH dictionary of labor law terms.*

"A dictionary of special words and phrases commonly used in the labor relations field."—*Title page.*

Statistics

Monthly labor review. v.1, July 1915– . Wash., Bureau of Labor Statistics, 1915– . Monthly.   **CH312**

Contains special articles and summaries of special reports in the field of labor. Statistics cover employment, labor turnover, earnings and hours, work stoppages, prices and cost of living, etc. Each issue also contains a bibliography of recent labor literature.

—— Subject index. Wash., Govt. Prt. Off., 1941. 2v. (Its Bull. no.695–96)

Covers v.1–11, July 1915–Dec. 1920; v.12–51, Jan. 1921–Dec. 1940.

Continued by decennial indexes, 1941–50 (Bull. no.1080); 1951–60, (Bull. no.1335).

—— Statistical Supplement, 1959– . Annual.

Presents statistics in more detail than the regular monthly issues.

U.S. Bureau of Labor Statistics. Employment and earnings statistics for the United States, 1909–62. Based on the 1957 Standard Industrial Classification. Wash., 1963. 632p. (Its Bull. no.1312–1)   **CH313**

Statistical tables "providing basic information on the nation's non-farm work force."—*Pref.*

Arranged by industry and by code number, then by year and by month, as statistics are available.

—— Handbook of labor statistics, 1924/26–1950. Supplement, 1951. Wash., Govt. Prt. Off., 1927–51. (Bull. no.439, 491, 541, 616, 694, 916, 1016, 1016 suppl.)   **CH314**

Summarizes material and statistics from the various publications of the Bureau, and from some other government publications, on related subjects.

—— History of wages in the United States from colonial times to 1928. Revision of Bull. no.499 with suppl.,

1929–1933. Wash., Govt. Prt. Off., 1934. 574p. tables. (Its Bull. 604) **CH315**

Annuals

Labor Research Association. Labor fact book. N.Y., Internat. Pub., 1931– . il. Biennial (Irregular). **CH316**

Information on political, economic, and social conditions that have affected the labor movement in America, supported by data largely drawn from standard government, business, and labor publications. Some volumes include a chapter on labor abroad.

Name and subject index.

International Labor Office, Geneva. Yearbook of labour statistics. 1935/36– . Geneva, Internat. Labor Off., 1936– . Annual. **CH317**

Frequency varies: 1936–42, annual; 1943/44–1951/52, biennial; 1952/53– , annual.

Preceded by: v.1, Annual review, 1930; v.2–5, *I.L.O. yearbook,* 1931–1934/35.

Text in French, Spanish, and English.

Summarizes labor statistics for 134 countries.

—— Bulletin of labor statistics. 1st– . March 1965– . Quarterly. **CH318**

Supplements annual data presented in the Office's *Yearbook.*

"Supersedes the statistical supplement included with each monthly issue of the *International labour review* until Dec. 1964."

History

Cole, George D. H. British working class politics, 1832–1914. London, Routledge, [1941]. 320p. **CH319**

A concise history of the labor movement and the rise of the Labour Party in Britain. Contains list of labor representation in Parliament from 1800 to 1914, including data on elections; Labour Party statistics; and bibliography.

Index of persons and general index.

—— A history of the Labour Party from 1914. London, Routledge and Paul, [1948]. 516p. **CH320**

Covers the period 1914–45. A sequel to the preceding work.

Includes an index to subjects and names in alphabetical order.

Bibliography, p.485–500, cites books, publications of the Fabian Society, and a chronological list of Labour Party programs, reports, pamphlets, etc., 1914–47.

Commons, John Rogers. History of labor in the United States. N.Y., Macmillan, 1935–36. 4v. **CH321**

A comprehensive survey of the development of labor organization and legislation in the United States, with introductions by John R. Commons; each part by a specialist. Based on the work following. Includes extensive bibliographies.

Documentary history of American industrial society, ed. by John R. Commons [and others]. N.Y., A. H. Clark, 1910–11. 10v. in 11. (Repr.: with new preface to v.1–2, by Louis Filler. N.Y., Russell & Russell, 1958. 10v.) **CH322**

Prepared under the auspices of the American Bureau of Industrial Research with the cooperation of the Carnegie Institution of Washington.

Contents: v.1–2, Plantation and frontier; v.3–4, Labor conspiracy cases (Supplement to v.4, published separately 1910, included in v.4 in 1958 reprint); v.5–10, Labor movement and index.

A collection of source materials covering from the colonial period to 1880.

Includes extensive bibliographies.

Dulles, Foster Rhea. Labor in America, a history. 2d rev.

ed. N.Y., Crowell, 1960. 435p. (Growth of America ser.) **CH323**

A 1v. history giving a straight chronological account of labor in the United States.

Taft, Philip. Organized labor in American history. N.Y., Harper, 1964. 822p. **CH324**

A 1v. history tracing the development of labor in the United States from colonial times to the present. Well documented, with subject and name index.

Biography

Who's who in labor; the authorized biographies of the men and women who lead labor in the United States and Canada and of those who deal with labor [ed. by Marion Dickerman and Ruth Taylor] . . . authorized ed. N.Y., Dryden, 1946. 480p. **CH325**

Contents: Men and women who lead labor, p.1–390; Men and women who deal with labor, p.391–443; List of international labor unions, p.445–51; Directory of the labor press, p.453–56; List of educational and research directors, p.457–65; Chronology of labor legislation, p.465–66; Glossary of labor terminology, ed. by J. R. Steelman, p.467–72; The constitution of the American Federation of Labor, p.473–78; The constitution of the Congress of Industrial Organizations, p.479–80.

MANUFACTURES

Romaine, Lawrence B. A guide to American trade catalogs, 1744–1900. N.Y., Bowker, 1960. 422p. **CH326**

An extensive listing of trade catalogs in classified arrangement, indicating location of copies.

Clark, Victor Selden. History of manufactures in the United States . . . 1929 ed. N.Y., pub. for the Carnegie Institution of Washington by McGraw, 1929. 3v. il. (Repr.: N.Y., Peter Smith, 1949) **CH327**

"The volumes comprise a revision of . . . *History of manufactures in the United States 1607–1860,* published . . . in 1916 . . . a continuation of this history down to 1914 . . . and additional chapters reviewing the principal facts of our manufacturing development from the beginning of the World War to the present time."—*Pref.*

Stanford Research Institute. International Development Center. Small industry; an international annotated bibliography, comp. by Marian Crites Alexander-Frutschi. Glencoe, Ill., Free Pr., 1960. 218p. **CH328**

1100 titles of books, pamphlets, reports, and periodical articles, mostly published since 1950. Classified arrangement, treating questions of economics, organization, management, etc. of small manufacturing industry. Author index and directory of publishers and periodicals.

U.S. Bureau of the Census. Census of manufactures, 1958– . Wash., Govt. Prt. Off., 1961– . To be issued quinquennially. **CH329**

This census was taken decennially, 1800–1900, except for the year 1830; quinquennially, 1900–1919; and biennially thereafter through 1939. Suspended during World War II. Resumed 1947.

1947, v.1–3 and supplement (1950).

1954, v.1–3 (1957–58).

Contents of volumes vary but cover: General statistics; Statistics by industry; Area statistics; Product supplement.

—— Annual survey of manufactures; 1949/1950– . Wash., Govt. Prt. Off., 1952– . **CH330**

Issued irregularly. Surveys have been published for 1949/1950, 1953, 1955/57, and 1959/61.

Designed to provide summary information for the years not covered by the *Census of manufactures* (CH329).

Directories

Federation of British Industries. FBI register of British manufacturers. 1924– . London, Thomas Skinner, 1924– .　　　　　**CH331**

Title varies slightly. Publisher varies.
Publication suspended 1940/41–1946/47.
37th ed. 1965.
Has sections on: products and services; language glossaries (French, German, and Spanish equivalents of products and services); alphabetical directory of names and addresses of FBI member firms; trade associations; brands and trade names; trademarks; etc.

Thomas' Register of American manufacturers. N.Y., Thomas Pub. Co., [190?]– . Annual.　　**CH332**

Title varies.
1962 in four volumes: v.1–3, Product classifications, A–Z; v.4, A–Z list of leading manufacturers, leading trade names, and commercial organizations: chambers of commerce, boards of trade, etc. Index, Product finding guide to contents and index to advertisers.

[handwritten note in left margin: don't throw away all issues without checking]

U.S. Small Business Administration. Research and development: a list of small business concerns interested in performing research and development. Wash., 1960– . Annual (?).　　　　　**CH333**

"Identifies the research and development interests of 2,674 small business concerns in 33 major categories and over a hundred sub-divisions."—*Foreword.*

Special fields

Brewing

Elsevier's Dictionary of barley, malting, and brewing, in six languages: German, English/American, French, Danish, Italian, Spanish; comp. and arr. on a German alphabetical base by B. D. Hartong [under the auspices of the Council of the European Brewery Convention]. Amsterdam, Elsevier; distr. by Van Nostrand, Princeton, N.J., 1961. 669p.　　　　　**CH334**

Coffee

Mueller, Wolf. Bibliographie des Kaffee, des Kakao, der Schokolade, des Tee und deren Surrogate, bis zum Jahre 1900. Bad Bocklet, Walter Krieg Verlag, 1960. 225p. il. (Bibliotheca bibliographica, Bd.20)　　**CH335**

A historical bibliography listing books in many languages, published before 1900, on coffee, cocoa, chocolate, and tea.

Leather

Hide and leather and shoes' encyclopedia of the shoe and leather industry; a complete reference work covering leather, shoes, technology and terminology of the shoe, leather and associated industries. Ralph B. Bryan, ed. in chief. Chicago, Hide and Leather Pub. Co., 1941. 491p. il.　　　　　**CH336**

Includes, in alphabetical arrangement, brief definitions and descriptions and long articles on various important phases of the industry.

Perfume

Poucher, William Arthur. Perfumes, cosmetics and soaps with a special reference to synthetics. 5th–7th ed. London, Chapman & Hall; N.Y., Van Nostrand, 1941–59. 3v. il.　　　　　**CH337**

v.1, 5th ed., Dictionary of raw materials together with an account of the nomenclature of synthetics. 1941; v.2, 6th ed., Treatise on the production, manufacture and application of perfumes of all types. 1941; v.3, 7th ed., Treatise on modern cosmetics. 1959.

Rubber

Elsevier's Rubber dictionary in ten languages: English/American, French, Spanish, Italian, Portuguese, German, Dutch, Swedish, Indonesian, Japanese; comp. and arr. on an English alphabetical base by "Rubber-Stichting" (Rubber Foundation), Delft (The Netherlands). Amsterdam, London, [etc.], Elsevier, 1959. 1537p.　　**CH338**

Spices

Parry, John William. The spice handbook; spices, aromatic seeds and herbs. Brooklyn, N.Y., Chemical Pub. Co., 1945. 254p. il.　　　　　**CH339**

Under name of each commodity usually gives information about: plant, family, nativity and cultivation, description, properties, uses, adulteration, grinding, packing, government standards, etc. Also includes extracts from the Pure Food Laws, glossary, and index.

Textiles

American Fabrics. AF encyclopedia of textiles, by the editors of American fabrics magazine. Englewood Cliffs, N.J., Prentice-Hall, 1960. 702p. il.　　**CH340**

"A source of . . . up-to-date information for the practical work of creating, designing, producing, selling and advertising textiles and textile products."—*Introd.* Includes text, charts, tables, diagrams, glossaries, and extensive illustrations. Index.
Dictionary of textile terms, p.585–673.

Bendure, Zelma and **Pfeiffer, Gladys.** America's fabrics; origin and history, manufacture, characteristics and uses; photographic layout by Crystal Stephen, fabric photographs by Nat Messik. N.Y., Macmillan, 1946. 688p. il.　　　　　**CH341**

Bibliography, p.xi–xii.
Lavishly illustrated, some plates in color. Text is in nontechnical language. Full index.

Merrill, Gilbert R., Macormac, A. R. and **Mauersberger, H. R.** American cotton handbook, a practical text and reference book for the entire cotton industry. 2d rev. ed. N.Y., Textile Book, [1949]. 943p. il.　　**CH342**

1st ed. 1941.
Covers the history, growing, processing, marketing, weaving, dyeing, etc. of cotton. Omits the "Cotton glossary" included in 1st edition, p.925–70.
Bibliography, p.847–97.

Skinner's Cotton trade directory of the world. London, N.Y., Thomas Skinner, 1923– . Annual.　　**CH343**

Table of contents in French, German, Spanish, Italian, Portuguese.
1960 issue includes information from more than 75 countries on firms exporting, importing, and manufacturing cotton. Special sections on silk and man-made fibers, linen, flax and jute, tufted textiles, and nonwoven fabrics. Includes associations, trade unions, research and testing laboratories, technical colleges, and statistical information. Trademarks section contains more than 5000 trade names. General index.

Von Bergen, Werner. Wool handbook; a text and reference book for the entire wool industry. 3d enl. ed. N.Y., Interscience, 1963– . v.1– . il.　　**CH344**

1st edition, 1938, had title *American wool handbook*.

A useful handbook, including chapters on all phases of the wool industry prepared by a staff of specialists.

Bibliography. Glossary.

Dictionaries

De Vries, Louis. Wörterbuch der Textilindustrie. Wiesbaden, Bradstetter, 1959– . v.1– . (In progress) **CH345**

Bd.1, Deutsch-englisch.

Fabierkiewicz, Wacław. Podręczny słownik włókienniczy w 5 językach: polski, rosyjski, angielski, francuski, niemiecki. Warszawa, Państwowe Wydawnictwa Techniczne, 1955. 305p. **CH346**

English title: Handy textile dictionary in five languages [Polish, Russian, English, French, and German].

Title page, preface, table of contents, and indexes in the five languages.

Polanyi, Michael. Dictionary of textile terms; Textil-Fachwörterbuch. German-English/English-German. London, N.Y., Pergamon, 1956. 328p. **CH347**

Lists current terms in many branches of the textile industry, trade, and allied fields.

Textile Mercury. The "Mercury" dictionary of textile terms. Manchester, Eng., Textile Mercury, [1950?]. 542p. il. **CH348**

A comprehensive dictionary of approximately 12,000 terms, including descriptions of many materials and methods no longer in use.

Tobacco

Jahn, Raymond. Tobacco dictionary. N.Y., Philosophical Lib., 1954. 199p. il. **CH349**

Definitions of terms and explanations of "interesting, curious and necessary facts relating to the history, manufacture and use of tobacco."—*Introd.*

New York. Public Library. Arents Tobacco Collection. Tobacco; a catalogue of the books, manuscripts and engravings acquired since 1942 in the Arents Tobacco Collection . . . from 1507 to the present. Comp. by Sarah Augusta Dickson. N.Y., 1958–62. Pts.1–7. il. (Arents Tobacco Collection publ.) (In progress) **CH350**

Contents: pts.1–7, 1507–1672.

430 items, arranged by imprint date. Full bibliographical description and many annotations.

MARKETING

Bibliography

Clarke, George Timothy. Bibliography of advertising and marketing theses for the doctorate in United States colleges and universities, 1944 to 1959. N.Y., Advertising Educ. Foundation, [1961]. 28p. **CH351**

A list of 393 doctoral theses from 38 educational institutions, arranged under 46 subjects. Entry is by title, followed by author, institution granting the degree, and date. Contains no annotations, no author index.

Gunther, Edgar and **Goldstein, Frederick A.** Current sources of marketing information; a bibliography of primary marketing data. Chicago, Amer. Marketing Assoc., 1960. 119p. (A.M.A. bibliography ser., no.6) **CH352**

An annotated listing of approximately 1200 books, journals, reports, and documents; classified: first by generalities, then according to branch of commercial or industrial activity. Author and corporate entry index.

Revzan, David Allen. A comprehensive classified marketing bibliography. Berkeley, Univ. of Calif. Pr., 1951. v.1–2. (Univ. of Calif. Bureau of Business and Economics Research publ.) (In progress) **CH353**

Pt.1, Books published through 1949; pt.2, Government publications, university research monographs, and articles in professional journals, published through 1949; pt.3 (Announced), Material in technical and trade journals.

Attempts to be comprehensive but not complete. Each volume has an author index.

U.S. Library of Congress. Map Division. Marketing maps of the United States; an annotated bibliography. 3d (rev.) ed. Comp. by Walter W. Ristow. Wash., 1958. 147p. **CH354**

1st ed. 1951; 2d ed. 1952.

" . . . a marketing map is considered specifically as a graphic representation of marketing and distribution data on a base map."

The 3d edition omits "some 150 maps, dated prior to 1940, which were listed in the two earlier editions," but includes many new ones, listing more than 585 maps and marketing atlases, etc.

Handbooks

Aspley, John Cameron. Sales manager's handbook. 9th ed. rev. Chicago, Dartnell, 1962. 1151p. il. **CH355**

1st ed. 1934.

A very useful handbook, emphasizing sales organization, training, methods of selling, and marketing research.

Includes glossary of marketing terms.

—— The sales promotion handbook. 3d ed. rev. Chicago, Dartnell, 1960. 1053p. il. **CH356**

A companion to the above.

Bradford's Survey and directory of marketing research agencies in the United States and the world. N.Y., C. E. Burckel, 1944– . Annual. **CH357**

1960/61–1963/64, ed. 9–10.

Title varies: 1944, *Survey and directory, marketing research agencies in New York City;* 1945, *Survey and directory, marketing research agencies in the United States.* Comp., 1944– , E. S. Bradford.

Lists agencies and individuals engaged in marketing and economic research, etc.

Editor and Publisher. Market guide, v.1, 1924– . N.Y., 1924– . Annual. **CH358**

1963 issue surveys 1500 daily newspaper markets. Arranged by state and city; gives for each city such information as: population, location, trade area, banks, principal industries, colleges and universities, largest department stores, chain stores, retail outlets and sales, newspapers, etc.

Industrial Marketing. Media market planning guide. 1963– . Chicago, Advertising Publs., 1963– . Semiannual. **CH359**

Title varies: *Market data book and directory,* 1921–1925/26; *Market data book,* 1926/27–1936; *Industrial marketing—Market data book number,* 1937–51; *Industrial marketing—Market data and directory number,* 1952–62.

Designed for trade and industrial advertisers and advertising agencies. Contains information on industrial and trade markets and the business publications serving them. Gives the salient facts on format, rates, and specifications of 2000 business papers.

Modern Packaging encyclopedia. N.Y., Modern Packaging, 1945– . Annual. **CH360**

Title varies: 1945, *Packaging catalog.*

Issued as Nov. issue of *Modern packaging.*

Subtitle: Package planning and production information (including technical data charts).

Contains alphabetical index.

OCCUPATIONS

Angel, Juvenal Londoño. Looking for employment in foreign countries. 5th ed. rev. and enl. N.Y., World Trade Academy Pr., 1961. 153p.   **CH361**

An expansion of parts of the author's *National and international employment handbook for specialized personnel,* with some additional information on employment conditions abroad. Includes lists of American firms with foreign branches that offer employment possibilities.

—— National and international employment handbook for specialized personnel; practical handbook for those seeking employment here and abroad. 6th ed. N.Y., World Trade Academy Pr., 1961. 308p.   **CH362**

Information on vocational guidance and the procedures of job seeking, with special sections on employment abroad. Appended are a number of classified lists of corporations and firms for consideration as potential employers.

Occupational index. v.1, 1936– . Jaffrey, N.H., Personnel Services, [c1936–]. v.1– . Quarterly. **CH363**

Publisher varies.

Bibliography with abstracts of current publications on occupational information. Each volume has cumulated author, title, and subject indexes to the abstracts listed during the year.

Monthly through 1940; Jan. 1941– , quarterly.

U.S. Bureau of Labor Statistics. Occupational outlook handbook; employment information on major occupations for use in guidance. 1st ed.– . Wash., 1949– . (Its Bull. no.1375) Biennial.   **CH364**

1963/64. 792p.

Up-to-date employment trends and outlook in more than 700 occupations. Information on nature of work, qualifications, earnings and working conditions, how to enter, where to go for more information, etc.

U.S. Bureau of the Census. Alphabetical index of occupations and industries. Rev. ed. Wash., Govt. Prt. Off., 1960. 649p.   **CH365**

1960 census of population.

Prepared for each decennial census, with occasional editions in between.

—— Classified index of occupations and industries. 1960 census of population. Wash., Govt. Prt. Off., 1960. 383p.   **CH366**

U.S. Employment Service. Dictionary of occupational titles. 2d ed., prep. by Division of Occupational Analysis, U.S. Employment Service. Wash., Govt. Prt. Off., 1949. 2v.   **CH367**

1st ed. 1939–44.

v.1, Definitions of titles. 1518p.; v.2, Occupational classification and industry index. 743p.

—— —— Supplement 1. [March, 1955], 1954. 341p.

Supplement contains 2260 new and revised definitions and 1322 new code numbers. Supersedes all releases to the *Dictionary* since the 2d edition was published.

REAL ESTATE

Babb, Janice B. and **Dordick, Beverly F.** Real estate information sources. Detroit, Gale Research, [1963]. 317p.   **CH369**

Annotated list of books, periodicals, reports, and organization publications, mostly in English, arranged by subject. Includes author and subject index.

Cherney, Richard A. Appraisal and assessment dictionary. Englewood Cliffs, N.J., Prentice-Hall, 1960. 337p. il.   **CH370**

2700 terms defined, "useful to appraisers, assessors and others who must write up reports on properties."—*Pref.* Appendix of financial and mathematical tables.

Holmes, Lawrence G. and **Jones, Carrie M.** The real estate handbook. Englewood Cliffs, N.J., Prentice-Hall, 1948. 783p. il.   **CH371**

Gives information on real estate business, brokerage, appraising, property management, land development, financing, titles, insurance, etc. Chapters include bibliographies. Contains a vocabulary with definitions, p.749–63.

Prentice-Hall, Inc., New York. Encyclopedic dictionary of real estate practice, prep. by the editorial staff. Rev. and enl. Englewood Cliffs, N.J., Prentice-Hall, 1962. 533p. il.   **CH372**

1st ed. 1955.

Terms are not merely defined, but are explained in articles varying from a few lines to several pages, with illustrations and samples.

U.S. Bureau of the Census. Census of housing, 1960. Wash., Govt. Prt. Off., 1961– . (In progress) **CH373**

Taken as a part of the 18th decennial census of the United States.

Contents: v.1, 9 pts., States and small areas; v.2, 7 pts., Metropolitan housing; v.5, 2 pts., suppl. to pt.1, Residential finance; v.6, Rural housing.

Final, detailed results of the 1960 census are available in a separate series of reports and will constitute volumes now in progress. A *Census of housing* was taken as part of the decennial censuses of 1940 and 1950.

C I

Political Science

❧ Political science may be defined as the science dealing with the principles and conduct of government, and of politics. Burchfield's *Guide* (CI1), now 30 years old, is useful only for historical purposes. However, C. M. White's *Sources of information in the social sciences* (CA6) lists many titles in this field. Other guides and bibliographies listed under Social Sciences—General Works (p.342–44) should also be consulted.

GENERAL WORKS

Guides

Burchfield, Laverne. Student's guide to materials in political science. N.Y., Holt, 1935. 426p.   **CI1**

"Designed to introduce the student interested in political science to the more important source materials, finding devices, bibliographies, and general reference works which will be of major assistance to him in prosecuting research."—*Foreword*.

Each section is introduced by an outline and a "general statement." Covers such fields as: national, state, and local government; political parties; administration; public finance; law; international relations; allied fields; and general works. Many titles annotated.

Still useful for older periods as no other work has taken its place for these.

Bibliography

Bibliographies françaises de sciences sociales. Paris, Fondation Nationale des Sciences Politiques, 1960–62. v.1–3. (In progress) **CI2**

Contents: v.1, Jean Meyriat. La science politique en France, 1945–1958: Bibliographie commentée. 1960. 134p.; v.2, Bernard Gournay. L'administration française: pt.1, Administrations centrales, bibliographie commentée. 1961. 153p.; v.3, France. Centre National de la Recherche Scientifique. Centre d'Études Sociologiques. Groupe de Sociologie Rurale. Les sociétés rurales françaises. 1962. 124p.

Classified, annotated bibliographies with author indexes.

Bildungswerk Europäische Politik. Bibliographie zur europäischen Integration. Düsseldorf, Europa-Union Verlag, 1962. 178p. **CI3**

An annotated bibliography of books in various languages on the federation of Europe.

British Council. Public administration; a select list of books and periodicals. London, Longmans, 1964. 120p. **CI4**

A classified list of 1548 titles of books and documents on public administration in the British Commonwealth, primarily by British authors. Name index, including titles of periodicals and yearbooks. No annotations.

Brooks, Alexander D. Civil rights and liberties in the United States; an annotated bibliography . . . with a selected list of fiction and audio-visual materials collected by Albert A. Alexander and Virginia H. Ellison. N.Y., Civil Liberties Educ. Foundation, Inc., 1962. 151p. **CI5**

An annotated bibliography of books on civil and political rights, most of them published since 1945. Prepared specifically for use with high school students; should be useful for others as well. Classified, with no index.

Carnell, Francis. The politics of the new states; a select annotated bibliography with special reference to the Commonwealth. London, pub. for the Institute of Commonwealth Studies by Oxford Univ. Pr., 1961. 171p. **CI6**

Books, articles, and documents, principally on political affairs of new states and territories in Asia and Africa. Classed arrangement, with indexes by author and place. Some brief annotations.

Deutsch, Karl Wolfgang. An interdisciplinary bibliography on nationalism, 1935–1953. Cambridge, Mass., Technology Pr. of M.I.T., 1956. 165p. **CI7**

A selective, classified bibliography—for the most part unannotated—arranged by special fields influencing nationalism (e.g., political science, theory of communication, cultural anthropology, sociology and social psychology, linguistics, history, economics, geography, biology, genetics and race, religion, etc.).

Intended to supplement Pinson (CI10).

France. Institut National d'Études Démographiques. Économie et population; les doctrines françaises avant 1800. [v.2], Bibliographie générale commentée. Paris, Presses Universitaires de France, 1956. 688p. (Its Travaux et documents. Cahier no.28) **CI8**

An annotated bibliography of books published in France before 1800 on subjects relative to population, such as: economics, agriculture, commerce and industry, colonies, finance, labor, social questions, marriage, children, religion, health, law, etc. Most of the works were published in the 18th century, with fewer from the 17th and 16th centuries.

v.1, Text by Joseph J. Spengler, 1954 (Cahier no.21).

Heady, Ferrell and **Stokes, Sybil L.** Comparative public administration; a selective annotated bibliography. 2d ed. Ann Arbor, Univ. of Michigan Pr., 1960. 98p. **CI9**

1st ed. 1957.

An annotated listing of some 950 books and periodical articles. Covers such subjects as: modern bureaucracies; organization and administrative relationships; personnel management; administration and the public; etc.

Pinson, Koppel S. A bibliographical introduction to nationalism. N.Y., Columbia Univ. Pr., 1935. 70p. **CI10**

An annotated bibliography of works in English, French, and German dealing specifically with the problems of nationalism in various parts of the world.

Supplemented by Deutsch (CI7).

Seckler-Hudson, Catheryn. Bibliography on public administration: annotated. 4th ed. Wash., Amer. Univ. Pr., 1953. 131p. **CI11**

A selective bibliography of some 1100 titles primarily in the field of national and international administration, with some materials on local administration. A classified list with author index. Only titles in the English language are included.

An earlier work, *Bibliography of public administration*, by Sarah Greer (N.Y., Nat. Inst. of Public Admin., 1926. 2d ed. of pt.1, 1933) is now chiefly useful for historical purposes.

Smith, Bruce Lannes, Lasswell, Harold D. and **Casey, Ralph D.** Propaganda, communication, and public opinion; a comprehensive reference guide. Princeton, N.J., Princeton Univ. Pr., 1946. 435p. **CI12**

An expansion of *Propaganda and promotional activities; an annotated bibliography*, published in 1935.

This new edition includes four essays on *The science of mass communication*, followed by an annotated, selective bibliography of some 2500 titles arranged by class. Includes books, periodicals, and articles which appeared between the middle of 1934 and early 1943, with a few titles of earlier dates. 150 titles have been starred as "outstanding" and given somewhat fuller annotations than most of the others.

Continued by:

Bureau of Social Science Research, Washington, D.C. International communication and political opinion; a guide to the literature [by] Bruce Lannes Smith and Chitra M. Smith. Prep. for the Rand Corporation. Princeton, N.J., Princeton Univ. Pr., 1956. 325p. **CI13**

A classified, annotated bibliography of 2563 numbered items, in English, French, and German, covering publications from mid-1943 to mid-1955, with some materials up to mid-1956. Has author and subject index.

"It concentrates on materials dealing with *international* propaganda, communication, and opinion, and cites works on *internal* matters only when they are of more than general relevance to international politics. It deals primarily with *political* propaganda and promotional activities."—*Introd.*

United Nations. Technical Assistance Administration. International bibliography of public administration. [New York], 1957. 101p. (UN Doc. ST/TAA/M/11) **CI14**

Title page in English, French, and Spanish.

An expanded version of the UN's *Short international bibliography of public administration,* 1953; now includes some 1500 titles in 12 languages.

U.S. Dept. of State. Publications of the Dept. of State, Oct. 1, 1929 to Jan. 1, 1953. Wash., Govt. Prt. Off., 1954. 207p. (Dept. of State publ. 5059) **CI15**

"A complete list of numbered publications . . . published since October 1, 1929."

———— ——— Jan. 1, 1953—Dec. 31, 1957. 1958. 230p.

———— ——— Jan. 1, 1958—Dec. 31, 1960. 1961. 116p.

Each volume is arranged alphabetically by subject, with an index by series.

U.S. Library of Congress. General Reference and Bibliography Division. A guide to bibliographic tools for research in foreign affairs. 2d ed. with supplement, comp. by Helen F. Conover. Wash., 1958. 145p., 15p.   **CI16**

1st ed. 1956.

The 2d edition adds a 15p. supplement. 351 items are listed —with long annotations—in the two sections, including bibliographies, manuals, indexes, etc.

Current

Atlantic studies; Études atlantiques. Boulogne-sur-Seine, L'Inst. Atlantique, 1964– . no.1– . Semiannual. **CI17**

Lists research projects, proposed and in progress, on economic, political, and military relations among the Atlantic countries and on their relations with other nations of the world. Classed arrangement, with indexes by author and by sponsoring agency. Studies are dropped from the listing when published.

Fondation Nationale des Sciences Politiques. Bulletin analytique de documentation politique, économique et sociale contemporaine. Paris, 1946– . v.1– .   **CI18**

For full record *see* CA20.

International bibliography of political science. Bibliographie internationale des sciences sociales, 1953– . London, Tavistock; Chicago, Aldine, 1954– . v.1– . Annual. (International bibliography of the social sciences)   **CI19**

Publisher varies. v.1–8, Paris, UNESCO; v.9, 1960– , issued as *Publications* of the International Committee for Social Sciences Documentation, as one of the series of the *International bibliography of the social sciences* (series title varies slightly).

In English and French.

An extensive, classified listing of books, pamphlets, periodical articles, and official government publications in various languages, including Slavic and Asian languages. Indexes by author and subject (in English and French).

For other bibliographies in the series, *see* CC2 (Sociology); CH25 (Economics); CD29 (Social and cultural anthropology).

International political science abstracts. Documentation politique internationale. v.1, 1951– . London, Blackwell, 1952– . Quarterly. (v.14, 1964)   **CI20**

Publisher varies.

Prepared by the International Political Science Association in cooperation with the International Committee for Social Sciences Documentation and with the support of UNESCO.

Abstracts are in English or French and are selected from a large number of periodicals published in various countries. Arrangement varies. Recent issues are classified by large groupings, with cumulated annual author and subject indexes.

Literatur-Verzeichnis der politischen Wissenschaften, 1952– . Hrsg. von der Hochschule für Politische Wissenschaften. München, 1952– . Annual. (1964)   **CI21**

A comprehensive, annual bibliography of German writings on political science. Annotated and classified.

Technical co-operation: a monthly bibliography. v.1, no.1– , Jan. 1964– . London, Dept. of Technical Co-operation, 1964– . Monthly.   **CI22**

Concerned with technical cooperation and public administration overseas. "Largely devoted to the official publications

of the Commonwealth, but reports and bulletins from foreign institutes and organizations will also be listed when received.' —*Introd. note.*

———— Supplement. no.1, 1964– .

Lists bills and subsidiary legislation of Commonwealth countries.

Encyclopedias and dictionaries

Académie Diplomatique Internationale. Dictionnaire diplomatique . . . t.6. Pub. sous la direction de A.-F. Frangulis. Genève, Paris, N.Y., [etc.], Académie, 1957. 1268p.   **CI23**

An alphabetical dictionary treating questions relating to diplomacy, with bibliographies. Includes articles on general subjects—e.g., atomic energy, colonialism, communism, prisoners of war, etc.—interfiled with articles on the countries of the world. The latter include descriptive notes; political and diplomatic history with documentation and bibliography; and, in *annexes,* the texts of the principal multilateral treaties concluded by them.

For t.5, a biographical volume, *see* CI44.

Diplomaticheskii slovar'. V trek tomakh. Glavnaia redaktsiia A. A. Gromyko i dr. Moskva, Gos. Izd-vo Politicheskoi Lit-ry, 1960–64. 3v.   **CI24**

1st ed.: Moskva, Gospolitizdat, 1948–50. 2v.

A dictionary of modern diplomacy and international affairs. International in scope with emphasis on Russia. Includes definitions of diplomatic terms and a considerable amount of biography. Many articles on international conferences, treaties, diplomatic proceedings, and the foreign policies of countries. Some articles have bibliographies. v.3 contains an index of subjects arranged by country.

Elliott, Florence and **Summerskill, Michael.** Dictionary of politics. [3d ed.] London, Penguin, 1961. 372p.   **CI25**

A compact dictionary of terms, places, and living persons important in current international affairs up to May 1961.

Handwörterbuch der Sozialwissenschaften. Stuttgart, Fischer, [1952–65]. v.1–11 and v.12, incompl. (In progress)   **CI26**

v.1–11, A–Wert.

For the 4th edition, entitled *Handwörterbuch der Staatswissenschaften,* and description, *see* entry following.

This new edition appeared in fascicules 1952– .

Long, signed articles on places, persons, and subjects, with extensive bibliographies.

Handwörterbuch der Staatswissenschaften, hrsg. von Ludwig Elster, Adolf Weber, Fr. Wieser. 4. gänz. umgearb. Aufl. Jena, Fischer, 1923–29. 8v. and suppl.   **CI27**

1st ed. 1890–94. 6v.; 2d ed. 1898–1901. 7v.; 3d ed. 1909–11. 8v. The 1st–3d editions, edited by J. Conrad, L. Elster, [and others], often are cited as *Conrad's Handwörterbuch.*

The most comprehensive German work, and, in some respects, the finest encyclopedia of political science in any language. Long, signed articles by specialists; bibliographies. Many biographies, excluding those of living men.

Staatslexikon; Recht, Wirtschaft, Gesellschaft, hrsg. von der Görres-Gesellschaft. 6. völlig neubearb. und erw. Aufl. Freiburg, Herder, 1957–63. 8v.   **CI28**

1st ed. 1889–97; 5th ed. 1926–32.

A standard German work written from the Catholic viewpoint. This edition is enlarged and thoroughly revised, articles have been rewritten, and new ones added. Articles are signed and have good, up-to-date bibliographies listing works in various languages.

Theimer, Walter. Encyclopaedia of world politics, ed., rev., and enl. by Peter Campbell. London, Faber, [1950]. 471p.   **CI29**

Encyclopedic articles on political topics as well as on each country.

Also published as *Encyclopaedia of modern world politics.* N.Y., Rinehart, 1950.

White, Wilber Wallace. White's Political dictionary. N.Y., World, 1947. 378p. **CI30**

A popular dictionary, international in scope and general in coverage, including many names and terms of World War II and the postwar years, especially the names of government organizations, conferences, treaties, and political events. The appendixes give the constitutions of the League of Nations and of the United Nations.

Worldmark encyclopedia of the nations: a practical guide to the geographic, historical, political, social, and economic status of all nations, their international relationships, and the United Nations system. N.Y., Worldmark Pr., Harper, 1963. 5v. **CI31**

Contents: [v.1], United Nations; [v.2], Africa; [v.3], Americas; [v.4], Asia and Australia; [v.5], Europe.

The 1st edition, 1960, was in 1v., with all countries in one alphabet. This edition is divided by continents, with countries alphabeted in each volume.

Condensed factual information is given for each country, the new edition showing revision and updating throughout. Bibliographies, often including 1962 titles, are appended to each country. The volume on the United Nations treats its organization and operation and its various subsidiaries.

United States

For current information about government machinery, committees, the work of various bureaus, personnel of the government, etc., consult the *Official Congressional directory* (CI53) and the *United States government organization manual* (CI55).

Cyclopedia of American government; ed. by Andrew C. McLaughlin and Albert Bushnell Hart. N.Y., Appleton, 1914. 3v. il. (Repr.: N.Y., Peter Smith, 1949. 3v.) **CI32**

A useful work although now much out of date. Covers topics in theory or philosophy of political society; forms of political organization and government; international and constitutional law; history of political parties; and other American political topics. Many biographies. Arranged alphabetically by small subjects, with an analytical index. Signed articles by specialists with bibliographies. For the earlier political history of the United States, J. J. Lalor's *Cyclopaedia of political science* (N.Y., Merrill, 1888–90. 3v.) is still occasionally useful.

Plano, Jack C. and **Greenberg, Milton.** The American political dictionary. N.Y., Holt, 1962. 383p. **CI33**

Terms are grouped under 18 topics, e.g., U.S. constitution, civil liberties, the legislative process, finance and taxation, foreign policy, and international affairs. Each section includes definitions and explanations (as appropriate) of terms and important agencies, cases, and statutes. The index allows the work to be used as a dictionary.

Smith, Edward Conrad and **Zurcher, Arnold John.** Dictionary of American politics. N.Y., Barnes & Noble, 1955. 437p. il., maps. **CI34**

1st edition, 1888, by Everit Brown and Albert Strauss; 2d edition, 1924, was almost completely rewritten by Edward C. Smith; 3d edition, 1944 (and 1946), was revised by the present editors. 1949 edition had title *New dictionary of American politics.*

This edition has been completely revised and reset with the addition of some 500 new terms bringing the total to more than 3500. Gives brief, concise definitions and also includes slogans, political slang, nicknames, etc.

Sperber, Hans and **Trittschuh, Travis.** American political

terms; an historical dictionary. Detroit, Mich., Wayne State Univ. Pr., 1962. 516p. **CI35**

An alphabetical dictionary of political terms giving origins and various meanings, with references to sources, showing earliest and developing usage. Includes a bibliography of the literature searched.

Directories

Directory of organizations and individuals professionally engaged in governmental research and related activities, 1935– . N.Y., Governmental Research Assoc., 1935– . (1960/61) **CI36**

Title varies slightly.

Arranged geographically, with alphabetical indexes by organization and individual. Includes local, state, and national agencies, as well as individual members of the Governmental Research Association.

Europa year book, 1959– . 1st ed.– . London, Europa Publs., 1959– . Annual. **CI37**

History: (1) *Europa year book,* 1926–29; *Europa, the encyclopedia of Europe,* 1930–58. (Loose-leaf.) Covered: international organizations, including the United Nations and its specialized agencies; world politics, giving the texts of international documents, etc.; and information on each European country. (2) *Orbis, encyclopaedia of extra-European countries,* 1938–59. (Loose-leaf.) Gave the same type of information for the countries of Africa, the Americas, Asia, and Australia, i.e., surveys and directories of political, industrial, financial, cultural, educational, and scientific organizations.

The new, bound volumes, starting in 1959, supersede the loose-leaf series; 1959 issue, in 1v., superseded *Europa.* Beginning with 1960, issued in 2v.: v.1, covering international organizations and Europe; v.2, covering Africa, the Americas, Asia, and Australia. Beginning with 1963, information on educational and learned societies and institutions is omitted and carried only in *World of learning* (CB69).

Information on the United Nations, its agencies, and other international organizations is followed by detailed information about each country, arranged alphabetically in each volume, giving an introductory survey, a statistical survey, the government, the constitution, religion, press, publishers, radio and television, finance, trade and industry, transport and tourism, atomic energy, and brief list of universities (for full information on universities, *see* the *World of learning*).

Greene, Katrine R. C. Institutions and individuals; an annotated list of directories useful in international administration. Chicago, Public Admin. Clearing House, 1953. 59p. **CI38**

A list of 215 directories of various kinds—biographical, institutional, organizational, etc.—with brief information on scope and contents of each. About half of the titles were published after 1949.

Institute of Electoral Research, London. Parliaments and electoral systems, a world handbook. London, Inst., 1962. [Distr. for trade by the Scorpion Pr., Northwood, Middlesex] 128p. **CI39**

"Prep. . . . by Bridget Bloom."

Brief descriptions of the political organization and functioning of the national governments of the world, arranged alphabetically by country.

International yearbook and statesmen's who's who, 1953– . London, Burke's Peerage, 1953– . Annual. **CI40**

Coverage varies. Usually includes: (1) information on international organizations, and (2) political, statistical, and directory information about each country of the world. A biographical section gives sketches of world leaders in government, church, commerce, industry, and education.

Middle East and North Africa, 1948– . London, Europa Publs., 1948– . il. Annual (Irregular). **CI41**

Coverage varies.

Changed title with 11th edition, 1964/65. Previously covered only the Middle East.

Subtitle (1964/65): A survey and directory of Aden (South Arabia), Algeria, Cyprus, Ethiopia, French Somaliland, Iran, Iraq, Israel, Jordan, Kuwait, Lebanon, Libya, Mali, Mauritania, Morocco, Muscat and Oman, Niger, the Persian Gulf States, Saudi Arabia, Somalia, Spanish North Africa, the Sudan, the Syrian Arab Republic, Tunisia, Turkey, the United Arab Republic (Egypt) and the Yemen, with geographical, historical, and economic surveys, concise information about political, industrial, financial, cultural, and educational organizations, and Who's who in the Middle East and North Africa.

Similar in presentation to *Europa* (CI37).

Political handbook and atlas of the world; parliaments, parties and press . . . Jan. 1, 1927–   . N.Y., Council on Foreign Relations, [c1927–   ]. v.1–   . Annual. (1965)
CI42

Title varies.

Treats the independent governments of the world; usually gives: chief government officials, party programs and leaders, political events, and the press (names of newspapers with political affiliation, proprietor or editor, and in some cases the circulation).

Section of 30 pages of maps added in 1963.

Biography

American Political Science Association. Biographical directory. 4th ed. Ed. by Franklin L. Burdette. Wash., Assoc., 1961. 355p.   **CI43**

1st ed. 1945. Title varies.

Serves as a who's who in political science, giving biographical information on members of the association.

Académie Diplomatique Internationale. [t.5], Dictionnaire diplomatique, comprenant les biographies des diplomates, du Moyen Age à nos jours, constituant un traité d'histoire diplomatique sur six siècles, publié sous la direction de A.-F. Frangulis. Genève, Paris, N.Y., [etc.], Académie, [1954?]. 1261p.   **CI44**

A biographical dictionary of diplomats from the Middle Ages to the present day, international in scope. Some articles signed; some bibliography. Uneven in treatment.

For t.6, *Dictionnaire diplomatique,* see CI23.

Tables

Banks, Arthur S. and **Textor, Robert B.** A cross-polity survey. Cambridge, Mass., Mass. Inst. of Technology Pr., 1963. 118p., [1405p.]   **CI45**

Consists of "computer printout" designed to aid in cross-national research for demographic, economic, political, and social relationships.

Introductory and explanatory matter, 118p.; computer printout, [1405p.].

For review *see American sociological review* 29:635–36. Aug. 1964.

Yearbooks

Annuaire européen, European yearbook. Publié sous les auspices du Conseil de l'Europe. The Hague, Nijhoff, 1955–   . v.1–   . Annual.   **CI46**

"Aim is to promote the scientific study of European organizations and their work" (*Note*), including their constitutions and functions. Contains the Council of Europe, European Coal and Steel Community, and other communities and organizations.

Documents appear in French and English; articles in French with English summaries, or in English with French summaries.

Bibliographies include a section of books, pamphlets, and periodical material of the year on European integration.

Asian annual; the "Eastern World" handbook. [v.1]– 1954–   . London, Eastern World, 1954–   . Annual. (1962)
CI47

Arranged alphabetically by country, giving for each: brief information on geography and climate; population; government, with names of administrative officers; agriculture; industry, etc.; foreign trade; communications; weights and measures, etc. Has section on non-Asian countries: their representation and trade in Asian countries, and Asian representation in them.

Middle East record, 1960–   . Tel Aviv, Israel Oriental Soc., Reuven Shiloah Research Center, 1962?–   . v.1–   . Annual.   **CI48**

A record of the politics and international relations of the countries of the Middle East in three main sections: (1) the Middle East in world affairs—general; (2) views and policies on internal affairs and international relations; and (3) synopses of internal political affairs and economic surveys arranged by country.

United Nations. Dept. of Social Affairs. Yearbook on human rights for 1946–   . Lake Success, N.Y., United Nations, 1947–   . v.1–   . Annual. (1961, pub. 1963)
CI49

Contents vary, but provide surveys of the constitutional and legal provisions of the various countries of the world in regard to the rights of the citizen, his status before the law, right of petition, property rights, rights of the press, assembly, education, religion, culture, status of women, etc.

——— First supplementary volume. Freedom from arbitrary arrest, detention and exile. N.Y., United Nations, 1959. 249p.

Comprises statements from the governments of the individual member nations regarding the application and evolution of the right set forth in Article 9 of the Universal Declaration of Human Rights.

GOVERNMENT

United States

Official registers

Congressional staff directory, 1959–   . . . comp. and ed. by Charles B. Brownson. Wash., Congressional Staff Directory (300 New Jersey Ave., S.E.), 1959–   . Annual.
CI50

Publisher varies.

Useful to supplement the *Official Congressional directory* (CI53) and the *United States government organization manual* (CI55), for listings of Congressional staffs, subcommittees, committee staffs, etc. Includes list of major cities with population over 1500, with the names of their representatives; biographical sketches of key staff personnel; and personal name index.

U.S. Civil Service Commission. Official register of the United States, 1933–59; persons occupying administrative and supervisory positions in the legislative, executive and judicial branches of the federal government, and in District of Columbia government. Wash., Govt. Prt. Off., 1933–59.   **CI51**

Biennial until 1921; not issued 1922–24; annual, 1925–59. Ceased publication.

Before 1861, published by the Dept. of State; 1861–1905, by the Dept. of the Interior; 1907–32, by the Bureau of the Census; 1933–59, by the Civil Service Commission.

The *Official register,* formerly known as the *Blue book,*

was the official list of government employees. In two main parts: (1) a classified list, arranged by departments, agencies, offices, etc., in Washington, and in the territorial possessions, giving names of the principal officials and assistants, showing, for each, official title, salary, legal residence, and place of employment; (2) alphabetical index of names included in the classified list.

Until 1911 the *Official register* included the names of all government employees, including the postal service; from 1913 to 1921 it was complete except for the postal service. The issues from 1925 to 1959 were much reduced in size and included only principal officials.

U.S. Congress. Biographical directory of the American Congress, 1774–1961. Wash., Govt. Prt. Off., 1961. 1863p. (85th Cong., 2d sess. House doc. 442. Ser. set no.12108)   **CI52**

Last previous ed. 1928.

Contents: (1) Lists: Executive officers, 1789–1961; The Continental Congress; Representatives under each apportionment; Members of each Congress, 1st through the 86th, arranged by Congress and then by state; (2) Biographies, arranged alphabetically.

Indispensable in any large library.

—— Official Congressional directory for the use of the U.S. Congress, 1809– . Wash., Govt. Prt. Off., 1809– . il. Irregular. (1965) *each session of Cong.* · **CI53**

From 1865, printed at the Government Printing Office; before that by private firms.

Contents, approximately the same in recent volumes though sometimes varying the order: (1) Biographical sketches of members of Congress, arranged by states; (2) State delegations; (3) Alphabetical list of names; (4) Terms of service; (5) Committees, membership and days of meetings; (6) Congressional commissions, joint committees and boards; (7) Committee assignments; (8) Administrative assistants and secretaries; (9) Statistical information including sessions of Congress; votes cast for senators and representatives; number of representatives under each apportionment; governors of states and territories, present list; Presidents and vice-presidents, 1789– ; (10) The Capitol: officers of the Senate, officers of the House, members' rooms, etc.; Miscellaneous officers; (11) Executive departments; (12) Independent agencies; (13) Judiciary: biographies of members of Supreme Court, lists of the courts; (14) District of Columbia government; (15) International organizations; (16) Foreign diplomatic representatives and foreign consular officers in the United States; (17) U.S. diplomatic and consular offices; (18) Press galleries: representatives of newspapers and periodicals, photographers, radio and television correspondents, members, rules, etc.; (19) Maps of Congressional districts; (20) Individual index.

U.S. Dept. of State. Biographic register, 1870– . Wash., Govt. Prt. Off., 1870– . Annual (some years not pub.). (1964 rev. as of Sept. 1963)   **CI54**

Title varies: 1869–1942, *Register of the Department of State;* 1944–50, some years called *Biographic register;* 1951– , *Biographic register.*

Contents vary. The early *Register* usually contained sections on departmental organization; information about the foreign service of the United States; historical lists; lists of the clerical, administrative, and fiscal service; and a biographical section for administrative and professional employees. The *Biographic register,* published since 1944, includes only the biographical section, and in 1963 provided "information and background on personnel of the Dept. of State and the Foreign Service and of other Federal Government agencies that participate in the field of foreign affairs," including such agencies as the U.S. Mission to the United Nations, Agency for International Development, Peace Corps, U.S. Arms Control and Disarmament Agency, U.S. Information Agency, and Foreign Agricultural Service.

United States government organization manual . . .

1935– . Wash., 1935– . Annual. (Earlier volumes irregular) (1965/66)   **CI55**

Title varies: 1935–48, *United States government manual.* Publisher varies. *76-71 is out*

Loose-leaf, 1935–37.

The official organization handbook of the federal government, giving information on the organization, activities, and current officials of the various departments, bureaus, offices, commissions, etc., with descriptions of quasi-official agencies and selected international organizations; charts of the more complex agencies; and appendixes relating to abolished or transferred agencies, to government publications, etc.

❧ The works noted above are official lists. Earlier, unofficial publications which are occasionally useful are: Charles Lanman, *Biographical annals of the civil government of the United States* (2d ed. 1887); R. B. Mosher, *Executive register of the United States, 1789–1902* (1903); and B. P. Poore, *Political register* (1878).

Legislative procedure

U.S. Congress. Senate. Senate manual, containing the standing rules, orders, laws, and resolutions affecting the business of the United States Senate; Jefferson's Manual; Declaration of Independence; Articles of Confederation; Constitution of the United States, etc. Wash., Govt. Prt. Off., 1820– . (1965)   **CI56**

Title varies. Issued for each session of Congress.

In addition to the items listed in the title, the *Senate manual* includes various tables, e.g., List of the presidents pro tempore of the Senate from the first Congress; Lists of senators from the first Congress; Electoral votes for president and vice-president from 1789; Justices of the Supreme Court, 1789– ; Cabinet officers, 1789– , etc.

—— Senate procedure: precedents and practices, by Charles L. Watkins and Floyd M. Riddick. Wash., Govt. Prt. Off., 1964. 761p. (88th Cong., 1st sess. Senate doc. 44)   **CI57**

". . . a compilation of the rules of the Senate, portions of laws affecting Senate procedure, rulings by the Presiding Officer, and established practices of the Senate."—*Pref.*

Divided into chapters and arranged alphabetically with a detailed index. Contains much, but not all, of the information included in the *Senate manual* and is arranged differently.

U.S. Congress. House. Constitution, Jefferson's Manual and Rules of the House of Representatives. Wash., Govt. Prt. Off., 1824– . (1963)   **CI58**

The House manual. Title varies. Issued for each session of Congress.

Congressional districts

U.S. Bureau of the Census. Congressional district data book. (Districts of the 87th– Congress) [1961/62–] Wash., Govt. Prt. Off., 1961– . maps. Biennial. (A *Statistical abstract* suppl.)   **CI59**

Arranged by state; gives statistics of Congressional districts covering such items as: population and housing; vote cast for President and representative; vital statistics; banking, agriculture, trade, industries, manufactures, etc.; non-white population. Appendixes include historical tables of apportionment. Contains maps of Congressional districts.

—— —— Supplement: Redistricted states. no.1– . Wash., 1965– . (no.7)

Each supplement is limited to a single state, and supersedes the data previously published.

—— Congressional district atlas. 86th– Congress, April 1, 1960– . Wash., Govt. Prt. Off., 1960– . maps. Biennial. (89th Cong., July 1, 1964)   **CI60**

Maps showing the boundaries of the Congressional districts for each Congress are arranged by state, and include maps of selected regions, counties, and cities. Revised maps are issued as changes are made.

Election statistics

America votes; a handbook of contemporary American election statistics. v.1– . [1954/55]– . Pittsburgh, [etc.], Univ. of Pittsburgh Pr., [etc.], 1956– . Biennial. (v.5, 1962)   **CI61**

Ed.: v.1– , Richard M. Scammon.

Issued by Governmental Affairs Institute.

Arranged alphabetically by state. Statistics, by state, of vote since 1945 for president, governor, senator, congressman; statistics, by county and ward, of vote in most recent election for president, governor, senator; with maps of each state and of large cities and Congressional districts, and brief statements of basic political information and special situations in each state.

Burnham, Walter Dean. Presidential ballots, 1836–1892. Baltimore, Johns Hopkins Pr., 1955. 956p.   **CI62**

A historical introduction is followed by tables showing distribution of votes by county, section, state, etc. A very useful compilation, followed in time by:

Robinson, Edgar Eugene. The presidential vote, 1896–1932. Stanford, Calif., Stanford Univ. Pr., 1947. 403p.   **CI63**

—— They voted for Roosevelt; the presidential vote, 1932–1944. Stanford, Calif., Stanford Univ. Pr., 1947. 207p.   **CI63a**

Petersen, Svend. A statistical history of the American presidential elections. N.Y., Ungar, 1963. 247p.   **CI64**

"Containing 133 statistical compilations, including a table of votes and percentages for each presidential election [1789–1960], by states and candidates; a table of votes and percentages for each state, by elections and candidates; a table of votes and percentages, by states and elections, for each historical party (Democratic, Republican, Whig, Prohibition, Socialist Labor, Socialist Workers, Populist, Greenback, Farmer Labor, Communist, and Socialist); and 28 other tables covering interesting sidelights."—*Note.*

U.S. Congress. House. Statistics of the presidential and Congressional election of Nov. 2, 1920– . Wash., Govt. Prt. Off., 1921– . Biennial. (1962)   **CI65**

Subtitle (varies slightly): Showing the highest vote for presidential electors, and the vote cast for each nominee for United States senator, representative, delegate, and resident commissioner to the 67th– Congress, together with a recapitulation thereof, including the electoral vote.

U.S. Congress. Senate. Library. Electoral and popular votes for president and Congressional election statistics. Wash., Govt. Prt. Off., 1948. 24p.   **CI66**

Subtitle: Record of popular and electoral vote for president and vice-president by principal political parties and states, 1900 to 1944, and votes for senators and representatives by parties and states in elections of November 1942, 1944 and 1946, together with excerpts from the Constitution and statutes relating to elections.

❦ Electoral votes for the president and vice-president, from 1789– , are included in the *Senate manual* (CI56).

Political parties

❦ The standard histories of political parties, and the campaign textbooks issued by the principal parties, are the main sources of information in this field. Contents of the campaign textbooks vary, but usually contain party platforms, statements of the party's stand on principal issues, acceptance speeches of candidates, committee members, etc. Political and election statistics, accounts of national conventions, and texts of party platforms were given in the *Tribune almanac* (CG48) to 1914. Statistics and chief points of party platforms are given in the *World almanac* (CG55). Summary election statistics on federal offices are given in *Historical statistics of the United States,* colonial times to 1957 (CG51), and in the *Statistical abstract* (CG49). State manuals and legislative handbooks often give statistics of state and local elections. For these *see also* Charles Press and Oliver Williams, *State manuals,* blue books, and election results* (CI71).

Bain, Richard C. Convention decisions and voting records. Wash., Brookings Inst., 1960. 327p., [110 unnumbered p.].   **CI67**

A handbook of presidential conventions, 1832–1956, with a section on each consisting of the political background, organization of the conventions, platforms adopted, nominations, balloting, etc. Appended are extensive lists of participants, chairmen, and voting records by state.

McKee, Thomas Hudson. National conventions and platforms of all political parties, 1789–1905; convention, popular and electoral vote. Also the political complexion of both houses of Congress at each biennial period. 6th ed. rev. and enl. Baltimore, Friedenwald, 1906. 418p., 33p.   **CI68**

Porter, Kirk H. and **Johnson, Donald Bruce.** National party platforms, 1840–1960. 2d ed. Urbana, Univ. of Illinois Pr., 1961. 640p.   **CI69**

A collection of "authenticated copies of all the platforms of the major parties, and of the principal minor parties."—*Pref.*

—— —— Supplement, 1964. Urbana, 1965. 58p.

Local government

Bibliography

Government Affairs Foundation, Inc., New York. Metropolitan communities: a bibliography, with special emphasis upon government and politics. Chicago, Public Admin. Service, 1957. 392p.   **CI70**

5120 numbered items, annotated.

Pt.1, Government and politics in metropolitan areas dealing with: (1) Functions and problems, (2) Governmental organization, and (3) Politics in metropolitan communities; pt.2, Socioeconomic background dealing with: (1) Social structure and process, (2) Population, and (3) the Metropolitan economy.

Author and subject index.

—— —— Supplement, 1955–1957, comp. by Victor Jones and Barbara Hudson. Chicago, 1960. 229p.

Press, Charles and **Williams, Oliver.** State manuals, blue books, and election results. Berkeley, Inst. of Governmental Studies, Univ. of Calif., 1962. 101p.   **CI71**

Arranged by state. Lists manuals with contents, and gives sources for election results.

Tompkins, Dorothy Campbell. State government and administration; a bibliography. [Berkeley], Bureau of Public Admin., Univ. of Calif., 1954. 269p.   **CI72**

An annotated list of books and periodical articles issued, for the most part, since 1930, arranged by large subject field with author and title index. Covers such areas as state constitutions, laws and codes, documents, legislative organization, judicial administration, etc. Includes a list of state manuals, p.138–42, and other state publications.

Encyclopedias and handbooks

Book of the states, 1935– , v.1– . Chicago, Council of State Governments, 1935– . il. Biennial. (v.15, 1964/65) **CI73**

A comprehensive manual on state activities. Order of presentation varies. Contents 1964/65: (1) Constitutions and elections; (2) Legislatures and legislation; (3) The judiciary; (4) Administrative organization; (5) Finance; (6) Intergovernmental relations; (7) Major state services; (8) Directory of the states and territories (giving officers, statistics, and general information). Index.

Frequency varies. Now issued biennially in the spring of even-numbered years, with emphasis given to the developments of the two preceding years. Two supplements are usually issued in the odd-numbered years: one listing state elective officials and legislators; the other, listing administrative officials classified by functions. + PB supPl.

Municipal year book, 1934– ; the authoritative résumé of activities and statistical data of American cities. Chicago, Internat. City Managers' Assoc., 1934– . v.1– . Annual. (v.32, 1965) **CI74**

Contents vary. 1965 issue: pt.1, Governmental units; pt.2, Municipal personnel; pt.3, Municipal finance; pt.4, Municipal activities; pt.5, Directories of officials.

Pts.1–4 include two types of information: (1) signed annual surveys by various writers, and (2) statistical tables. Bibliographies appended.

National governments

Registers and handbooks

☙ For certain kinds of current information about the governments of the world, the *Statesman's year-book* (CG29) is the most reliable and useful handbook in English. Such publications as the official registers, legislative directories, office lists, etc. of the various governments are useful for many questions about government organization, machinery, duties, and personnel. While books of this sort vary in character, they usually contain information about the departments, bureaus, and other offices of a government; the scope, activities, and histories of these; sometimes references to the laws creating them; lists of officials, sometimes with biographical data; institutions and societies which have some kind of government relation; etc. The biographical material is often important for names not included in the more general biographical dictionaries.

This section contains both official and nonofficial handbooks. In many cases the latest issue examined is noted in parentheses at the end of the entry.

Almanach de Gotha, annuaire diplomatique et statistique, 1763– . Gotha, Perthes, 1763– . Annual. (Not pub. 1945–58) (182. année, 1959/60) **CI75**

A standard handbook in which coverage varies, with extensions and additions. For many years, until 1940, included two main sections: (1) Annuaire généalogique, which gave genealogies of the royal and princely houses of Europe, and (2) Annuaire diplomatique et statistique, which gave statistical and descriptive information about the various countries of the world, with lists of the principal executive, legislative, and diplomatic officials of each.

Publication began in 1763 as the French edition of the *Gothaischer Hof-Kalender zum Nutzen und Vergnügen eingericht.* Publisher varies: 1823–1944 by Justus Perthes.

Title varies: 1942–44, *Gothaisches Jahrbuch für Diplomatie, Verwaltung und Wirtschaft.*

Année 182, 1959/60– , also called *Nouvel almanach du corps diplomatique,* issued in separately paged parts, each covering an individual country. Parts issued: Afghanistan. 1960; Albanie. 1960; Amérique, États-Unis. 1959; Belgique. 1959.

These parts include general information about governmental organization, diplomatic and consular representatives, statistics, genealogies of the royal or governing houses, and biographical notices of government officials; also bibliographies.

1964 edition announced for publication in 1965.

Jameson, John Franklin. A provisional list of printed lists of ambassadors and other diplomatic representatives. . . . Paris, Presses Universitaires de France, [1928]. 16p. **CI76**

Extract from the *Bulletin* of the International Committee of Historical Sciences (no.4, March 1928).

A convenient record of printed lists of diplomats, arranged by country. In some cases the record goes back to the Middle Ages.

Repertorium der diplomatischen Vertreter aller Länder seit dem Westfälischen Frieden (1648). Repertory of the diplomatic representatives of all countries since the Peace of Westphalia (1648). Zürich, Fretz & Wasmuth, 1936–50. v.1–2. (In progress) **CI77**

Imprint varies. Title in German, English, French, Italian, and Spanish.

v.1, 1648–1715, by Ludwig Bittner and Lothar Gross. Berlin, Gerhard Stalling, 1936. 753p.; v.2, 1716–1763, by Friedrich Hausmann. Zürich, Fretz & Wasmuth, 1950. 704p.

Arranged by country to which the envoys were sent; each volume has personal-name and country indexes. v.2 also has *"Nachträge und Berichtigungen zum I Band,"* p.429–504.

Africa

Administration et diplomatie d'Afrique noire et de Madagascar, 1962– . Paris, Europe-Outremer (37, rue Marbeuf) and Ediafric (57, avenue d'Iéna), 1961– . Annual. (1963) **CI78**

A guide to the governments of 15 new African republics in the French Community, including standard organizational and directory information for each. Supplementary material gives directory information on African interstate organizations.

Annuaire de l'Afrique du Nord. v.1, 1962– . Paris, Centre National de la Recherche Scientifique, 1964– . il., maps. Annual. **CI79**

Algérie—Maroc—Tunisie.

Includes papers on various phases of constitutional and economic development; chronologies of diplomatic, political, and economic life; documents; bibliography.

Annuaire des états d'Afrique noire. 1961– . Paris, Ediafric, 1961– . Annual. **CI80**

1. édition, 1961, has special title *Gouvernements et cabinets ministériels des républiques d'expression française;* 2. édition, 1962, has special title *Gouvernements et cabinets ministériels, partis politiques.*

A guide to the governments of the new African states of the French Community, arranged by state. Gives lists of officers, with biographical sketches of heads of states and of ministers and cabinet officers.

Annuaire parlementaire des états d'Afrique noire. Députés et conseillers économiques des républiques d'expression française. 1100 biographies, 1962– . Paris, Annuaire Afrique, 1962– . il. Annual. **CI81**

Gives biographical sketches of the members of the legislative assemblies of the 14 new African republics of the French Community, with the personnel of economic and social commissions, etc. Index of names.

Junod, Violaine I. and **Resnick, Idrian N.** The handbook

of Africa. N.Y., New York Univ. Pr., 1963. 472p. il.
    CI82

"Purpose . . . is to provide comparable factual information on each of the fifty-odd political units of Africa, and to provide basic source material by a thorough process of footnoting."—*Introd.*

Under each country gives brief factual data on geography; history; government; population breakdown; social data including education, health, etc.; and economy.

Kitchen, Helen. A handbook of African affairs. N.Y., Praeger, for the African-American Institute, 1964. 311p. maps.   **CI83**

A handbook in four sections: pt.1, a country-by-country political guide, giving, for each independent state and territory, basic facts on population, area, capital, government, monetary unit, principal languages, etc., followed by a brief description; pt.2, the armies of Africa, by country; pt.3, the organization of African unity; pt.4, contemporary African poetry and prose.

Segal, Ronald. Political Africa; a who's who of personalities and parties. London, Stevens & Sons, 1961. 475p.
    CI84

In two sections: (1) "Personalities," p.1–288, which gives biographical sketches of leaders in all parts of Africa, and (2) "Parties," p.291–475, which describes the political parties of the various countries, arranged alphabetically by country. At the head of each country division, information is given on area and population, with reference to the names of persons from that country who are listed in the first section.

Australia

Australia. Parliament. Joint Library Committee. Parliamentary handbook of the Commonwealth of Australia. 1, 1901/15– . Canberra, Govt. Printer, 1915– . Irregular.   **CI85**

14th edition (1962) covers 1959–62.

Title varies: v.1–7, *Biographical handbook and record of elections;* v.8–11, *Parliamentary handbook and record of elections.*

Biographical sketches and lists of members of parliament, records of parliaments and ministries, records of elections, etc.

Australia. Prime Minister's Dept. Commonwealth of Australia directory to the office of the Governor-General, the parliament, the executive government, the judiciary, departments and authorities, 1961– . Canberra, 1961– . (Irregular?) (1964)   **CI86**

Formerly *The federal guide,* last issued in 1958 with supplement, 1959.

A full directory of all important branches of the Australian central government. Indexes of agencies and of personal names.

Austria

Österreichischer Amtskalender, 1. Jahrg., 1922– . Wien, Staatsdrückerei, 1922– . Annual.   **CI87**

Combines the *Niederösterreichische Amtskalender* and the *Hof- und Staatshandbuch.* Title pages of each issue carry the volume numbering of each of the earlier series as well as the new series.

Suspended publication 1938–48. Resumed with v.17, 1949.

A detailed directory of the departments and personnel of the national and local governments of Austria. An appendix lists banks, insurance societies, etc.

Belgium

Almanach royal officiel, publié depuis 1840. Bruxelles, Guyot, 1840–1938. Annual. (Not pub. 1915–19) **CI88**

Ceased publication.

Detailed directory information of the government of Belgium.

Brazil

Brazil. Archivo Nacional. Organizações e programas ministeriais regime parlamentar no Império. 2. ed. Rio de Janeiro, Dept. de Impr. Nacional, 1962. 469p.   **CI89**

A historical register listing cabinet members, deputies to the national assembly, senators, etc. from 1822 to 1889, first issued in 1889 under title *Organizações e programmas ministeriaes desde 1822 a 1889.* Reissued with corrections in 1962 by Arquivo Nacional.

Canada

Canada. Dept. of the Secretary of State. Organization of the government of Canada, July 1963. Rev. ed. Ottawa, Queen's Printer, 1964. 364p.   **CI90**

1st ed. 1958.

Arranged by department, agency, etc. For each there is textual explanation, a list of principal officeholders, and usually an organizational chart. Includes a section on international organizations of which Canada is a member. Indexes of titles and of personal names.

Canadian parliamentary guide. (Ed. with the patronage of the Parliament of Canada and of the legislatures of the various provinces) by G. Pierre Normandin. Ottawa, Syndicat des Oeuvres Sociales Limité, 1912– . (1963)   **CI91**

Imprint varies. Succeeds *Parliamentary companion,* 1862–1911.

Lists, with biographical sketches, the administrative officials, privy council, the senate, and the house of the government of Canada and of the provinces. Includes election statistics, etc. and lists of diplomatic representatives to and from Canada.

China

See also Statistics—China, p.379.

Communist China yearbook. [v.1], 1962– . Hong Kong, China Research Associates, [1963–]. Annual (?). **CI92**

Chapters on various aspects of life in Communist China in 1961, e.g., major meetings and statements (political, military); people's communes; economic, cultural, educational, and foreign relations. The latter treats, first, general foreign relations, and then relations with individual countries. Includes a directory of Communist China's leadership, and a diplomatic list.

U.S. Dept. of State. Bureau of Intelligence and Research. Directory of Chinese Communist officials. 1960– . [Wash., Govt. Prt. Off.], 1960– . (Its Biographic reference aid)   **CI93**

Title varies: 1960 issue called *Directory of party and government officials of Communist China.* Issuing office varies. 1963 in 2v. At head of title: Biographic reference aid.

Directory only; no other biographical information.

Perleberg, Max. Who's who in modern China . . . Hong Kong, Ye Olde Printerie, 1954. 428p. il.   **CI94**

For full entry and annotation, *see* AJ105.

Contains information on government organization and personnel for both Nationalist and Communist China.

Czechoslovakia

[U.S. Dept. of State. Division of Biographic Information]. Directory of Czechoslovak officials. Wash., 1963. 150p. (Its Biographic reference aid)   **CI95**

No biographic information.

Denmark

Denmark. Kongelig Dansk Hof- og Statskalender. Statshåndbog for kongeriget Danmark for Aaret 1734– ....
København, Schultz, 1734– . Annual. (1965) **CI96**

A detailed directory of the departments and personnel of the Danish government.

Finland

Finlands statskalender för året 1811–1939 utg. av Helsingfors Universitet. Helsingfors, Osakeyhitö Weilin & Göös Aktiebolag, 1811–1938. Annual. **CI97**

Ceased publication.

Directory information of the government of Finland.

France

Almanach national; annuaire officiel de la République Française, 1872–1919. Paris, Berger-Levrault, 1872–1919. v.173–217/221. **CI98**

Pub. since 1700. Earlier volumes had title *Almanach royal, Almanach impérial,* etc.

No more published.

Of first importance for information about the organization and personnel of the government of France to the end of World War I. Gives many official lists, e.g., cabinet, senate, and chamber; principal officers of the various government offices and bureaus; and outlines of the duties and functions of these bureaus. Includes also lists of the Legion of Honor, other orders, courts, departmental prefectures, universities, academies, societies, museums, chambers of commerce, etc.

Annuaire diplomatique et consulaire de la République Française. Paris, Impr. Nationale, 1858–1954. Annual. **CI99**

Title varies.

Ceased publication (?).

Includes a historical list of the ministers of foreign affairs since 1589, and directory information on the diplomatic and consular service of France, with biographical sketches.

Annuaire des ministères. (Numéro spécial de Revue de l'administration française, 1945–) Annual. (1965) **CI100**

Title varies. Frequency varies.

Earlier series published 1936?–40.

Includes lists of administration officials: cabinet officers, Assemblée Nationale, diplomatic corps, and the various ministries, agencies, international organizations, etc.

Dictionnaire des parlementaires français: notices biographiques sur les ministres, sénateurs et députés français de 1889 à 1940. Publié sous la direction de Jean Jolly. ....
Paris, Presses Universitaires de France, 1960–63. v.1–3.
(In progress) **CI101**

Subtitle varies slightly.

Contents: t.1, Chronological and alphabetical lists of ministers from 1871. Alphabetical lists of senators, deputies, etc., 1871–1876. Biographical sketches, A–Azéman; t.2, Babaud–Buyat; t.3, C–Cu.

Planned to continue Robert's *Dictionnaire* (CI103). When completed, will supersede Samuel (CI104). The biographical sketches vary in length, but generally are fairly full.

Duverger, Maurice. Les institutions françaises. Paris, Presses Universitaires de France, 1962. 408p. il. **CI102**

Provides brief descriptions of the political, administrative, and financial institutions of France, together with some historical background. A detailed table of contents, but no index.

Robert, Adolphe, Bourloton, Edgar and **Cougny, Gaston.**
Dictionnaire des parlementaires français, comprenant tous les membres des assemblées françaises et tous les ministres français depuis le l^{er} mai 1789 jusqu'au l^{er} mai

1889, avec leurs noms, état civil, états de services, actes politiques, votes parlementaires, etc. Paris, Bourloton, 1891. 5v. il. **CI103**

Fairly long biographical sketches of members of parliament and ministers, 1789–1889.

Samuel, René Claude Louis and **Bonét-Maury, Géo.** Les parlementaires français, II. 1900–1914. Dictionnaire biographique et bibliographique des sénateurs, députés, ministres ayant siège dans les assemblées législatives. Paris, Roustan, 1914. 479p. **CI104**

Began as a continuation of the preceding work by Robert, but the volume covering 1889–1900 was never published. This volume called v.2. For continuing work which will supersede this, *see Dictionnaire des parlementaires français* (CI101).

Germany

Kosch, Wilhelm. Biographisches Staatshandbuch: Lexikon der Politik, Presse und Publizistik. Bern, München, Francke Verlag, 1959–63. 2v. **CI105**

An extensive biographical dictionary of past and present Germans, Austrians, and Swiss prominent in politics and journalism. Articles are brief and unsigned but include bibliographies. In addition to biographies, contains entries for newspaper and journal titles relating to political affairs.

Germany. Reichsministerium des Innern. Handbuch für das Deutsche Reich, 1874–1936. Berlin, Heymann, 1874–1936. Annual (Irregular). **CI106**

Contents vary but usually give a directory of governmental organizations with personnel. Useful for historical purposes.

Germany, East

Germany (Dem. Rep. 1949–) Volkskammer. Die Volkskammer der Deutschen Demokratischen Republik. Wahlperiode 1– . 1957– . Berlin, Kongress-Verlag, [etc.], 1957– . (Wahlperiode 4, 1964) **CI107**

Title varies: 1957–59, *Handbuch der Volkskammer der Deutschen Demokratischen Republik.*

A handbook giving the constitution and other documents of the German Democratic Republic, as well as biographical sketches and pictures of members of the chamber.

Handbuch der Deutschen Demokratischen Republik.
[1963]– . [Berlin], Staatsverlag der Deutschen Demokratischen Republik, [1964]– . il. **CI108**

Supersedes *Jahrbuch der Deutschen Demokratischen Republik.* 1956–61. 6v.

"Hrsg. vom Deutschen Institut für Zeitgeschichte in Verbindung mit dem Staatsverlag der Deutschen Demokratischen Republik."

Chapters discuss the creation of the German Democratic Republic; its political party and other political groups; the organization and functions of various parts of the government; development of commerce, industry, finance, etc.; national health, education, cultural expression, foreign relations. An appendix includes brief population statistics; topographical information; and a chronological list, 1949–63, of national events. Subject index. Few statistics.

SBZ von A bis Z: ein Taschen- und Nachschlagebuch über die Sowjetische Besatzungszone Deutschlands. Hrsg. vom Bundesministerium für Gesamtdeutsche Fragen. 1. Aufl.– . Bonn, Deutscher Bundes-Verlag, 1953– . Annual (Irregular). (9. Aufl. 1965) **CI109**

A handbook in dictionary arrangement, primarily political and economic, but including biographical listings.

U.S. Dept. of State. Division of Biographic Information.
A guide to the government, political parties, and organizations of the so-called "German Democratic Republic."
Wash., 1961. 62p., xviip. (Its Biographic directory, no. 277) **CI110**

A directory of officials, arranged under ministry, agency, etc.

Germany, West

Die Bundesrepublik, Jahrg.65, 1956/57– , vereinigt mit Handbuch für die Bundesrepublik Deutschland. 65. Jahrg.– . Berlin-Köln, Carl Heymann, 1956– . Biennial. (Jahrg.68, 1964)   **CI111**

Formed by the merger of the *Handbuch für die Bundesrepublik Deutschland,* 1953–54, and the *Taschenbuch für Verwaltungsbeamte,* and assumes numbering from the latter.

Jahrg.67– , issued in Hefte: one for the *Bund,* followed by others for the individual provinces.

A directory of West Germany and of its individual component provinces, listing not only government bodies, but also educational and cultural institutions, banks, etc.

Deutsche Politik, 1950– ; Tätigkeitsbericht der Bundesregierung. Hrsg. von dem Presse- und Informationsamt der Bundesregierung. [Bonn], Deutscher Bundesverlag, 1950– . il. Annual (?).   **CI112**

An extensive survey of the government, foreign relations, economic and social conditions, etc. of West Germany.

Kürschners Volkshandbuch Deutscher Bundestag. 1. Wahlperiode, 1953/57– . Darmstadt, Neue Darmstädter Verlagsanstalt, 1954– . Irregular.   **CI113**

24. Aufl. 1962: 4. Wahlperiode 1961.

Supersedes *Kürschners Deutscher Reichstag,* 1890–1933. Published after each election; gives information on the Bundestag, with biographical sketches and pictures of the members.

Schramm, Friedrich Karl. Der Staatsbürger fragt; Lexikon für den Staatsbürger. 5. Aufl. Wiesbaden, Verlag Chmielorz GMBH, 1961. 372p. il.   **CI114**

A dictionary of terms, agencies, institutions, organizations, etc. relating to the government of the West German republic.

Ghana

Trade directory of the Republic of Ghana, including classified trade index. 1st ed.– , 1959– . London, Diplomatic Pr. and Pub. Co., 1959– . il. Annual. (4th ed. 1964)   **CI115**

Title varies: 1959–61/62, *Directory of Ghana.*

Directory information, with some textual material on government ministries, bureaus, agencies, etc. Includes supplementary list of business firms, and a brief who's who section.

Ghana; an official handbook. 1961– . Accra, Ministry of Information and Broadcasting, 1962– . il. Annual. (1961)   **CI116**

An official directory covering land and people, government, ministries, statutory boards and corporations, arts and culture, the press, etc.

Ghana year book: a Daily Graphic publication. [Accra, Ghana Graphic Co.], 1958– . Annual. (1964)   **CI117**

Continues the *Gold coast year book,* 1953–56.

Includes general directory information of the government and organizations of Ghana, with a brief biographical section.

Great Britain

Directories

British imperial calendar and civil service list. London, Stat. Off., 1809– . Irregular. (1965)   **CI118**

Title varies.

Content varies; usually gives: (1) Royal households, High Commissioners in London, the Cabinet, the Treasury, Officers of the House of Peers and House of Commons, etc.; (2) Public departments: England and Wales. Scotland, Northern Ireland; (3) Alphabetical lists of officers; etc. Gives name, official position, degrees and honors, and salary.

Colonial Office list, 1862– . London, Stat. Off., 1862– . Annual, to 1940; biennial, from 1946– . (1964)   **CI119**

Title varies: 1862–1925, *Colonial Office list;* 1926–40, *Dominions Office and Colonial Office list;* 1946– , *Colonial Office list.* Subtitle varies. Not published 1941–45.

Scope and contents vary, but usually include extensive historical and statistical information on each colony or dominion, with biographical section and maps.

Commonwealth Relations Office list. London, Stat. Off., 1951– . Annual. (1965)   **CI120**

Not pub. 1954.

Supersedes the *India Office and Burma Office list,* issued under varying titles, 1803–1947, and the Dominions Office section, issued 1926–40, of the *Dominions Office and Colonial Office list.* For the *Colonial Office list, see* CI119.

The Commonwealth Relations Office was formed in 1947 by the combination of the Dominions Office and the India Office. The *C.R.O. list* contains historical and current lists of officers and representatives in Commonwealth countries, and constitutional and statistical information of each country, etc. Includes a biographical section.

Dod's Parliamentary companion, 1832– . London, Business Dictionaries, 1832– . Annual. (1965)   **CI121**

Publisher varies.

Includes: Biographies of the Royal family and the members of the House of Lords and the House of Commons; Procedure; Ministries and government departments, etc.

Foreign Office list and diplomatic and consular year book; ed. by members of the staff of the Foreign Office. 1806– . London, Harrison, 1806– . Annual. (1965)   **CI122**

Gives organization of the office, various diplomatic and consular lists, foreign service regulations, "Statement of services" with biographical notices, obituaries, references to biographical notices in earlier volumes, various chronological lists; also foreign embassies, legations, and consulates in the United Kingdom and its colonies, protectorates, trusteeship territories, etc.

Handbooks

Britain, 1948/49– , an official handbook, prep. by the Central Office of Information. London, Stat. Off., 1948– . Annual. (1965)   **CI123**

Publisher varies.

Descriptive articles and figures from various official sources on the administration and the national economy of the United Kingdom. Covers government, social welfare, industry, labor, press and broadcasting, etc. Includes bibliography.

British Commonwealth year book, ed. by Ronald S. Russell. [ed. 1–], 1952/53– . London, Newman Neame, 1952– . Annual. (ed. 10, 1962/63)   **CI124**

Title varies: 1952/53, *Commonwealth co-operation; the Empire and Commonwealth year book;* 1953/54–1959/60, *The Empire and Commonwealth year book.*

Gives general and statistical information concerning the British Empire and the Commonwealth of Nations.

Butler, David E. and **Freeman, Jennie.** British political facts, 1900–1960. London, Macmillan; N.Y., St. Martin's, 1963. 245p.   **CI125**

Detailed lists of ministries, party and election statistics, Parliament, major social legislation, treaties, civil service, armed forces, local government, newspapers, statistics, etc.

Commonwealth year book, 1956–59. London, Europa Publs., 1956–59. v.1–3.   **CI126**

Title varies: ed. 1–2, *The British Commonwealth.*

For each country of the Commonwealth gives area articles on geography, history, and economic conditions, followed by sections on the constitution, government, and administration; legal, religious, and educational life; the press; trade and industry; learned societies, institutes, libraries, museums, universities, etc. Detailed tables of contents.

Parliament

Foster, Joseph. Members of Parliament, Scotland, including the minor barons, the commissioners for the shires, and the commissioners for the burghs, 1357–1882. On the basis of the parliamentary return 1880, with genealogical and biographical notices. 2d ed. rev. and corr. London, priv. pr. by Hazell, Watson and Viney, 1882. 360p. **CI127**

Gt.Brit. Parliament. House of Commons. Members of Parliament . . . [Return of the name of every member of the Lower House of Parliament of England, Scotland and Ireland, with name of constituency represented and date of return, from 1213 to 1874]. London, Stat. Off., 1878–91. 2 pts. in 4. (House of Commons. Reports and papers, 1878. no.69, 69I, 69II; 1892. no.169, also numbered 69III) (Repr.: Index to pt.II, Hamden, Conn., Shoe String, 1961. 300p.) **CI128**

Pt.1, Parliaments of England, 1213–1702, arranged chronologically. Index to pt.1, with appendix and corrigenda; pt.2, Parliaments of Great Britain, 1705–96, Parliaments of the United Kingdom, 1801–74, Parliaments and Conventions of the Estates of Scotland, 1357–1707, Parliaments of Ireland, 1559–1800. Index to pt.2, with appendix, i.e., names and members, 1880–1885, and corrigenda; Parliaments of Great Britain, 1705–1800; Parliaments of the United Kingdom, 1801–85.

A very important record.

Namier, *Sir* **Lewis Bernstein** and **Brooke, John.** The House of Commons, 1754–1790. N.Y., pub. for the History of Parliament Trust by Oxford Univ. Pr., 1964. 3v. **CI129**

At head of title: The history of Parliament.

Contents: v.1, Introductory survey, constituencies, appendixes; v.2–3, Members, A–Y. The latter give brief biographical sketches, with histories of individual parliamentary careers. Includes references to sources.

The Times, London. House of Commons . . . London, The Times, 1945– . [v.1–] (1965) **CI130**

Editions have been issued at intervals following general elections.

Subtitle: With full results of the polling, biographies of members and unsuccessful candidates, photographs of all members, and a complete analysis, statistical tables, and a map of the general election (varies slightly).

Wedgwood, Josiah Clement. History of Parliament, 1439–1509. London, Stat. Off., 1936–38. v.1–2. col. coats of arms, facsim. **CI131**

v.1, Biographies of the members of the Commons House; v.2, Register of the ministers and of the members of both houses, 1439–1509.

The first two of a proposed series of 3v. dealing with the history of Parliament from 1439–1509.

For note on v.1 see AJ151.

v.2, *Register,* contains: introductory chapters on treatment, sources, and analyses; time analysis and lists of parliaments, arranged chronologically; notes on each constituency with alphabetical lists of members; tables and appendixes.

Abraham, Louis Arnold and **Hawtrey, Stephen Charles.** A parliamentary dictionary. 2d [rev.] ed. London, Butterworth, 1964. 241p. **CI132**

1st ed. 1956.

A brief encyclopedia of British parliamentary terms and concepts, giving definitions and, in some cases, longer articles, with many cross references and a serviceable index.

Wilding, Norman W. and **Laundy, Philip.** An encyclopaedia of Parliament. London, Cassell, 1958. 705p. **CI133**

An alphabetically arranged encyclopedia of parliamentary history and procedure. Many brief articles, some long ones. Covers colonial parliaments as well as the Parliament at Westminster.

33 appendixes provide chronological lists of parliaments, ministers, secretaries, etc., and a 25p. bibliography.

Local government

Golding, L. Dictionary of local government in England and Wales. London, English Universities Pr., 1962. 446p. **CI134**

Alphabetically arranged, with brief explanations of a large number of terms, regulations, agencies, etc. pertinent to local government.

Gross, Charles. A bibliography of British municipal history. N.Y., London, Longmans, 1897. 461p. **CI135**

For full entry *see* DC159.

Municipal year book and public utilities directory. London, Municipal Journal, 1897– . v.1– . (1965) **CI136**

Subtitle varies.

Includes: (1) articles on all phases of English local government: finance, power, roads, education, parks, public health, town planning, water supply, etc.; (2) list of associations and societies concerned with local government; and (3) information about municipal corporations with lists of offices; county and district councils, with officers; etc.

India

India; a reference annual. 1953– . Delhi, Ministry of Information and Broadcasting, 1953– . Annual. (1964) **CI137**

"Compiled by the Research and Reference Division."

A general governmental yearbook, comprising considerable directory-type, statistical, and textual information on the major services of the national government, and the activities of the country as a whole.

Rama Rao, T. V. India—at a glance; a comprehensive reference book on India. Comp. by Binani Printers. 2d ed. [Calcutta], Orient Longmans, [1954]. 1756p. il. **CI138**

A comprehensive work covering various phases of life in modern India. Treats the political, constitutional, economic, agricultural, industrial, commercial, educational, and social aspects. Includes biographical sketches of officials, and considerable directory material.

Italy

Annuario politico italiano, 1963– . Milano, Ed. di Comunità, 1963– . [v.1–] Annual. (1964) **CI139**

At head of title: Centro Italiano [di] Ricerche e Documentazione.

An encyclopedic handbook of political and economic information. Includes directory material, documents, statistical tables, and biographical sketches of cabinet officers, deputies, and senators. Bibliography.

Bartolotta, Francesco. Governi d'Italia, 1848–1961. [Roma, Author, 1962?]. 330p. **CI140**

A chronological listing of the ministries of Italy, 1848–1961. No biography.

I deputati e senatori del . . . Parlamento republicano. Roma, La Navicella, 1949– . v.1– . (v.4, 1963) **CI141**

Biographical sketches, with pictures, of the members of each Italian Parliament.

Italy. Parlamento. Camera dei Deputati. Annuario parlamentare, 1948/49– . Roma, Tipografia della Camera dei Deputati, 1948– . Annual. (1963/64)   **CI142**

1961– , issued in 2v.

The official register of the Italian government with lists of officials, agencies, commissions, and local administrations, and information on other countries of the world, the United Nations and other international organizations, etc.

Japan

Political handbook of Japan, 1958. Tokyo, Tokyo News Service, 1958. 133p.   **CI143**

1st ed. 1949.

Political organization, statistics, and texts of some official documents; chapters on mass communication media, the press, etc.; and who's who in politics and the press.

U.S. Embassy. Japan. The government organization of Japan (with names of bureau, division and section chiefs) as of Nov. 20, 1962. Tokyo, Translation Services Branch, Political Section, Amer. Embassy, 1962. 232p.   **CI144**

Ward, Robert Edward and **Watanabe, Hajime.** Japanese political science; a guide to Japanese reference and research materials. Rev. ed. Ann Arbor, Univ. of Michigan Pr., 1961. 210p. (Univ. of Michigan, Center for Japanese Studies. Bibliographical ser., no.1, rev. ed.)   **CI145**

1st ed. 1950.

An annotated, classified list of 1759 numbered items, "confined largely, although not exclusively to works written in Japanese," which deal with political science subjects in Japan since the Meiji Restoration (1868).

Korea

Korea (Republic). Kongbosil (Office of Public Information). A handbook of Korea. [Written by Jai Hyon Lee] Seoul, 1955. 360p.   **CI146**

A handbook describing the land and people, government and administration, agriculture, industry, transport and communications, finance and trade, social welfare, religion and culture.

Netherlands

Parlement en kiezer, jaarboekje, 1911/12– . s'Gravenhage, Nijhoff, 1911– . Annual. (1964/65)   **CI147**

A handbook and register of the government of the Netherlands. Includes brief biographies of members of Parliament.

Staatsalmanak voor het Koninkrijk der Nederlanden, 1808, 1815– . s'Gravenhage, Nijhoff, 1808– . Annual. (1965)   **CI148**

Published by the Departement van Binnenlandsche Zaken. Serves as the official register of the Netherlands.

New Zealand

New Zealand. Dept. of Statistics. Report on the local authority statistics of New Zealand, 1926– . 1st ed.– . Wellington, 1926– . v.1– . Annual. (1962/63) **CI149**

Takes the place of the *Annual statistical report on local government*—issued annually since 1875, biennially 1903–24 —and the *Municipal handbook.*

Title varies: 1926–1959/60, *The local authorities handbook of New Zealand,* issued by the Dept. under its earlier name (to 1954–55), Census and Statistics Dept.

Detailed statistics of local governments in New Zealand.

Nigeria

Trade directory of the Federal Republic of Nigeria, including classified trade index. 1960– . London, Diplomatic Pr. and Pub. Co., 1960– . il. Annual. (1963/64)   **CI150**

Title varies: 1960–62, *Directory of the Federation of Nigeria* . . . .

Directory information with some textual material on government, economic development, finance, education, etc., followed by a trade index, and a brief biographical section.

Norway

Norges statskalender for året 1815– . Oslo, Aschehoug, 1815– . Annual (Irregular). (1964)   **CI151**

A comprehensive, detailed register of the government and governmental departments of Norway.

Philippines

Philippines (Republic). Office of Public Information. Official directory. Manila, Bureau of Printing, 1946?– . Irregular. (1959)   **CI152**

Lists the departments and agencies of the government, with names of personnel.

Poland

U.S. Dept. of State. Division of Biographic Information. Directory of Polish officials . . . Wash., 1960. 623p. (Its Biographic directory, no.274)   **CI153**

Subtitle: Personnel in the political parties, government, and mass organizations of the Polish Peoples Republic, November 1960.

A directory; no biographical information.

Rhodesia and Nyasaland

Rhodesia and Nyasaland. Federal Information Dept. Handbook to the Federation of Rhodesia and Nyasaland, ed. by W. V. Brelsford. London, pub. for the Federal Information Dept. by Cassell, 1960. 803p. il., maps. **CI154**

"The first attempt at producing a handbook covering all three territories, Southern and Northern Rhodesia and Nyasaland that together form the Federation of Rhodesia and Nyasaland."—*Pref.*

Chapters on history, politics, and social, economic, and other aspects of national life, many written by specialists. Includes bibliographies.

Sierra Leone

Sierra Leone year book, 1961– . Freetown, Freetown Daily Mail, 1961– . Annual (?).   **CI155**

Miscellaneous governmental information. Includes also a classified trade directory, and a brief who's who section.

South Africa

Official South African municipal year book, 1909– . Cape Town, Juta (London, E. G. Allen), 1910– . v.1– . il. (1963/64)   **CI156**

General information and statistics of South African municipalities.

Spain

Spain. Presidencia del Gobierno. Oficina de Información. Guía de la administración del estado. Madrid, 1963. 375p.   **CI157**

A guide to the organization of the government and its ministries. Does not include names of officials. Has a section giving addresses and telephone numbers of government agencies and of diplomatic representatives in Madrid.

Sudan

Trade directory of the Republic of the Sudan, including classified trade index. 1st ed.– , 1957/58– . London, Diplomatic Pr. and Pub. Co., 1958– . il. Annual. (7th ed. 1965) **CI158**

Title varies: 1957/58–1962/63, *Directory of the Republic of the Sudan* . . . .

Directory information, with textual material on government, economic development, finance, education, etc., followed by a trade index, and a brief biographical section.

Sudan almanac. Comp. in the Central Office of Information of the Republic of the Sudan. Pub. by the Republic of the Sudan. Khartoum, Govt. Prt. Pr., 1948– . Biennial. (1961) **CI159**

Publisher varies.

Gives information on the diplomatic missions to and from the Sudan, history, religion, geography and climate, government, finance, trade, industry, education, transport, press, etc.

Sweden

Sveriges statskalender för året 1877– . Utg. efter Kungl. Maj:ts nådigste förordnande av dess Vetenskapsakademi. Uppsala och Stockholm, Almquist, 1877– . Annual. **CI160**

Continues *Sveriges och norges statskalender,* 1764–1876.

A comprehensive register of the governmental departments and organizations of Sweden, including academies, learned societies, and universities.

Switzerland

Staatskalender der Schweizerischen Eidgenossenschaft. Annuaire de la Confédération Suisse. Annuario della Confederazione Svizzera. Hrsg. von der Bundeskanzlei. Bern, 1849– . Annual. (1961) **CI161**

The official register of the departments and officials of Switzerland.

Thailand

Siam directory. Bangkok, Thai Co., 1947– . Annual. (1964) **CI162**

Title varies: *Thai directory.*

A general directory covering government and diplomatic officials, trade and industry, education, religion, societies, etc.

Turkey

Turkish government organization manual, 1959– . 1st ed.– . Ankara, 1959– . **CI163**

1st ed. by Dovan Dalmis.

A standard manual, in English, of legislative, judicial, and executive departments and agencies, with textual explanations and lists of officeholders. No index.

Sturm, Albert Lee and **Mihçioğlu, Cemal.** Bibliography on public administration in Turkey, 1928–1957, selective and annotated. Ankara, 1959. 224p. **CI164**

Joint publication of the Faculty of Political Sciences and the Institute of Administrative Sciences of the University of Ankara and the Graduate School of Public Administration and Social Service of New York University.

A classified list of 1100 books and articles, in Western languages and Turkish. Brief annotations; author and subject indexes.

Union of Soviet Socialist Republics

Moskva; kratkaia adresno-spravochnaia kniga. 1954– . Moskva, 1954– . Annual. (1962) **CI165**

A city directory of Moscow, listing addresses and telephone numbers of government offices, scientific and educational institutions, and other organizations in such fields as banking, trade, health and social service, transportation, and communication.

SSSR; administrativno-territorial'noe delenie soiuznykh respublik na 1 Aprelia 1960 goda. Izd. 10-oe. Moskva, 1965. 700p. **CI166**

At head of title: Otdel po Voprosam Raboty Sovetov Presidiuma Verkhovnogo Soveta SSSR.

Official directory of the administrative divisions of the USSR from Union Republic to town, with some statistical information, including population and distances. Alphabetical index of place-names.

U.S. Dept. of State. Division of Biographic Information. Directory of Soviet officials, 1960/61– . Wash., 1961– . (1963) **CI167**

1960/61– , issued in 2v.: v.1, covering USSR and RSFSR; v.2, Soviet Union republics.

At head of title, 1960/61: Biographic directory no.272, 278; 1963– : Biographic reference aid.

A directory; no biographical information.

Apparently a revision of *Soviet political leaders,* which appeared without imprint in 1957.

Venezuela

Diccionario biográfico de Venezuela. Madrid, Garrido Mezquita, 1953. 1558p. il., maps. **CI168**

Contains much statistical and gazetteer information on the individual Venezuelan states. For complete entry and annotation, *see* AJ262.

Parliamentary procedure

Bridge, Lawrence Wilford. The Funk and Wagnalls book of parliamentary procedure; a guide to democratic practice in meetings . . . N.Y., Funk & Wagnalls, 1954. 180p. **CI169**

A manual prepared for quick reference use by the layman, with graphs, charts, and examples of standard parliamentary procedure.

Davidson, Henry Alexander. Handbook of parliamentary procedure. N.Y., Ronald, 1955. 292p. **CI170**

Rules and practices for small organizations.

Robert, Henry M. Robert's Rules of order revised. 75th anniversary ed. Chicago, Scott, Foresman, [1951]. 326p. **CI171**

First published in 1876 with title *Pocket manual of rules of order for deliberative assemblies.* Frequently revised and reprinted.

The standard handbook, although not necessarily the easiest to use.

Pt.1, Rules of order; a compendium of parliamentary law, based upon the rules and practice of Congress; pt.2, Organization and conduct of business; a simple explanation of the methods of organizing and conducting the business of societies, conventions, and other deliberative assemblies.

Sturgis, Alice F. Sturgis standard code of parliamentary procedure. N.Y., McGraw-Hill, 1950. 268p. **CI172**

Pt.1, Procedure—its principles and general rules; pt.2, Organizations—their structure and functions; pt.3, Motions.

A standard code compiled with the advice of legal authorities, and with regard to court decisions and the common law. New edition in preparation.

Communism and Socialism

Bibliography

Andréas, Bert. Le manifeste communiste de Marx et Engels; histoire et bibliographie, 1848–1918. Milano, Feltrinelli, 1963. 429p., 23p. facsim. (Bibliographies par l'Institut Giangiacomo Feltrinelli [6]) **CI173**

Facsimile reproduction of the 1st edition of the *Communist manifesto* (23p.) at end.

A bibliography of 544 items in various languages dealing with the *Communist manifesto*. Detailed notes on special editions.

Bibliography on the Communist problem in the United States. N.Y., Fund for the Republic, 1955. 474p. **CI174**

A companion volume to the *Digest of the public record of Communism in the United States* (CI188).

The *Bibliography* is "primarily devoted to literature relating to Communism in the United States since the birth, in 1919, of the first American parties adopting the Communist label."

Author index, p.1–270, gives very brief descriptive annotations; subject index, p.271–430, arranges same material in a topical outline.

Bravo, Gian Maria. Marx e Engels in lingua italiana, 1848–1960. Milano, Ed. Avanti, 1962. 176p. (Saggi e documentazioni. 10) **CI175**

A bibliography of almost 800 books and articles, in Italian, on Marx and Engels.

Collotti, Enzo. Die kommunistische Partei Deutschlands, 1918–1933; ein bibliographischer Beitrag. Milano, Feltrinelli, 1961. 217p. (Bibliographische Beiträge, hrsg. vom Istituto Giangiacomo Feltrinelli) **CI176**

Arranged by chronological periods. Introduction to each period is followed by a bibliography.

Delaney, Robert Finley. The literature of Communism in America; a selected reference guide. Wash., Catholic Univ. of Amer. Pr., 1962. 433p. **CI177**

A classified, annotated bibliography. The annotations reflect the personal opinions of the writer.

Egbert, Donald Drew and **Persons, Stow.** Socialism and American life. Princeton, N.J., Princeton Univ. Pr., 1952. 2v. il. (Princeton studies in American civilization, no.4) **CI178**

v.1, Essays by various authors; v.2, Bibliography, descriptive and critical. Bibliographer, T. D. Seymour Bassett.

The bibliography, written in essay form, gives references to materials on Socialism in its various manifestations as developed in this country, from the early religious communism to the present day. Detailed table of contents and index to authors and subjects.

Kolarz, Walter. Books on Communism: a bibliography. 2d ed. N.Y., Oxford Univ. Pr., 1964. 568p. **CI179**

1st ed. by R. N. Carew Hunt. 1959.

An annotated bibliography "of some 2500 titles of books in English on the development of Communism in the USSR and China and in all the principal countries of the world."—*Pref.* This edition lists about 700 new entries and covers 1945–62, with some publications of 1963.

Kyriak, Theodore E. International Communist developments, 1957–1961; an index and guide to a collection of U.S. JPRS translations emanating from Africa, Asia, Latin America and western Europe. Annapolis, Md. (P.O. Box 267), Research Microfilms, 1962?. 54p. **CI180**

"The United States Joint Publications Research Service (JPRS) was established in early 1957 to service the various units of the federal government with translations of unclassified foreign documents, scholarly works, research reports, and other selected source material not available in English."—*Introd.*

This work lists the contents of such translations dealing with international Communist developments, 1957–61.

Lauerhass, Ludwig. Communism in Latin America: a bibliography. The post-war years (1945–1960). Los Angeles, Calif., Center of Latin American Studies, 1962. 78p. **CI181**

A listing of books, government publications, and articles, arranged under country. Includes works in English, Spanish, Portuguese, French, German, and Russian.

Lawrynenko, Jurij. Ukrainian Communism and Soviet Russian policy toward the Ukraine: an annotated bibliography, 1917–1953. Ed. by David I. Goldstein. N.Y., Research Program on the U.S.S.R., 1953. 454p. (Research program on the U.S.S.R. Studies on the U.S.S.R., no.4) **CI182**

An annotated, classified bibliography of books and articles. Although some entries are in English, for the most part materials listed are in Russian; titles are given in transliteration with English translation in brackets. Locates copies.

Répertoire international des sources pour l'étude des mouvements sociaux aux XIXe et XXe siècles. Paris, Librairie Armand Colin, 1958–63. v.1–3. (In progress) **CI183**

At head of title: Comité International des Sciences Historiques. Commission Internationale d'Histoire des Mouvements Sociaux et des Structures Sociales.

Publié avec le concours de l'Unesco et sous les auspices du Conseil International de la Philosophie et des Sciences Humaines.

v.1, La première Internationale. Périodiques, 1864–77.

Lists periodicals in various languages with full bibliographical detail, brief description, and location of copies in European and a few American libraries.

v.2, La première Internationale. Imprimés, 1864–1876. Actes officiels du Conseil Général et des Congrès et Conférences de l'Association Internationale des Travailleurs (International Working Men's Association).

Materials arranged by congress. Descriptive notes of contents and index of personal names. A preliminary edition of this section, somewhat different in arrangement, appeared in 1959.

v.3, La première Internationale. Imprimés, 1864–1876. Actes officiels des fédérations et sections nationales de l'Association Internationale des Travailleurs.

Arranged by country. Includes descriptive notes and an index of names. Locates copies.

Rubel, Maximilien. Bibliographie des œuvres de Karl Marx, avec en appendice un répertoire des œuvres de Friedrich Engels. Paris, Marcel Rivière, 1956. 272p. **CI184**

A comprehensive bibliography listing works by Marx, including published works, correspondence, unpublished manuscripts, and *dubiosa,* followed by a bibliography of Engels' works.

————— ———— Supplément. Paris, Marcel Rivière, 1960. 74p.

Stammhammer, Josef. Bibliographie des Socialismus und Communismus. Jena, Fischer, 1893–1909. 3v. **CI185**

A standard bibliography of materials in various languages on Socialism and Communism up to 1908.

Uyehara, Cecil H. Leftwing social movements in Japan, an annotated bibliography. Pub. for the Fletcher School of Law and Diplomacy, Tufts University. Tokyo, Rutland, Vt., Tuttle, 1959. 444p. **CI186**

"Part of the Studies on Japan's Social Democratic Parties prep. by Allan B. Cole, George O. Totten, Cecil H. Uyehara."

An extensive listing of books, periodicals, and documents in Japanese. Arrangement is classified, within chapters, each with a textual introduction. Entries are transliterated, followed by Japanese characters. Locations indicated for 12 United States libraries and several in Japan. Author-title index.

Dictionaries and collections

Dekoster, Lester. The vocabulary of Communism. Grand Rapids, Mich., Eerdmans, 1964. 224p. **CI187**

Subtitle: Definitions of key terms, summaries of central

ideas, short biographies of leading figures, descriptions of significant things and events.

"The classics of Marxism," p.183–99.

"Anti-Marxist classics," p.203–23.

Digest of the public record of Communism in the United States. N.Y., Fund for the Republic, 1955. 753p.　**CI188**

Includes the texts of federal and state statutes and decisions, and public documents, tables of cases, etc.

A companion volume to the *Bibliography on the Communist problem in the United States* (CI174).

Osterroth, Franz. Biographisches Lexikon des Sozialismus. Hannover, Dietz, 1960– . Bd.1– . (In progress)　**CI189**

Bd.1, Verstorbene Persönlichkeiten.

Brief biographical sketches of persons of German-area nationality concerned with any of various socialist movements.

Trevisani, Giulio. Piccola enciclopedia del socialismo e del comunismo. 4. ed. Milano, Soc. Ed. de 'Il calendario del popolo,' 1958. 735p. il.　**CI190**

Alphabetically arranged, with articles on people, places, movements, institutions, and book and journal titles. Articles are unsigned and vary in length, many with brief bibliographies appended. Emphasis on Italian subjects. Numerous cross references.

Yearbooks

Yearbook of the international socialist labour movement, 1956/57– , ed. by Julius Braunthal. London, Lincolns-Prager Internat. Yearbook, 1956– . Irregular. (v.2, 1960/61)　**CI191**

Published "under the auspices of the Socialist International and the Asian Socialist Conference."

Gives data on the socialist and labor parties of each country and on the international socialist organizations.

Armed forces

General

Copenhagen. Marinens Bibliothek. Katalog . . . udarb. . . . af H. A. Ø. Bistrup. København, Levin, 1933–36. 2v.　**CI192**

Contents: v.1, Catalog of literature concerning the discoveries and the explorations of the polar environs and the oceans, whale and seal fisheries; biography; periodicals, anuals, and other periodical papers; v.2, Naval, nautical, and technical literature.

An extensive collection containing books in many languages.

—— —— Aarligt tillæg (Yearly supplement). 1933–1946/47. København, 1934–1948.

1948/52– , cover five years (cumulations of the library's monthly and annual *Erhvervelser*) (1958/62).

Craig, Hardin, Jr. A bibliography of encyclopedias and dictionaries dealing with military, naval and maritime affairs, 1577–1961. 2d ed. Houston, Tex., Fondren Lib., Rice Univ., 1962. 70p.　**CI193**

A chronological arrangement of encyclopedias, dictionaries, and wordbooks, in many languages. Author index.

Pohler, Johann. Bibliotheca historico-militaris. Systematische Uebersicht der Erscheinungen aller Sprachen auf dem Gebiete der Geschichte der Kriege und Kriegswissenschaft seit Erfindung der Buchdruckerkunst bis zum Schluss des Jahres 1880. Leipzig, Lang, 1887–99. 4v. (Repr.: N.Y., Burt Franklin, 1961. 4v.)　**CI194**

An extensive military bibliography of some 50,000 titles, including materials in many languages and covering 26 coun-

tries and all periods from ancient times to mid-19th century. Broad in scope; includes military history and science, tactics, weapons, etc., economics, politics, biography, etc.

Arms control and disarmament; a quarterly bibliography with abstracts and annotations. v.1, no.1– , Winter 1964/65– . Wash., Govt. Prt. Off., 1964– . v.1– . Quarterly.　**CI195**

Compiled by the Arms Control and Disarmament Bibliography Section of the Library of Congress.

Listings include abstracts or brief annotations of books, periodical articles, government documents, and publications of international organizations "selected from a survey of the literature received by the Library of Congress that is likely to be available in the larger research and public libraries in the United States."—*Pref.*

Classed arrangement, with author index and with announcement of a subject and a cumulated author index for no.4.

Periodicals

U.S. Air University. Libraries. Union list of foreign military periodicals. Preliminary ed. Ed. by Paul H. Spence and Helen J. Hopewell. Maxwell Air Force Base, Ala., Air Univ. Lib., 1957. 72p.　**CI196**

A union list of 356 titles in some 30 libraries in the United States and Canada, followed by a geographical index listing titles under country of origin.

United States

Bibliography

Dollen, Charles. Bibliography of the United States Marine Corps. N.Y., Scarecrow, 1963. 115p.　**CI197**

Books and periodical articles, emphasizing the years 1940–60.

Dornbusch, Charles Emil. Histories of American army units: World Wars I and II and Korean conflict, with some earlier histories. Wash., Dept. of the Army, Office of the Adjutant General, Special Services Division, Library and Service Club Branch, 1956. 310p.　**CI198**

A listing of all types of unit histories of the Army, not including the Air Force and the Navy.

—— Regimental publications and personal narratives of the Civil War; a check-list. N.Y., N.Y. Pub. Lib., 1961–62. v.1– . (In progress)　**CI199**

Contents: v.1, Northern states: pt.1, Illinois; pt.2, New York; pt.3, New England states; pt.4, New Jersey and Pennsylvania; pt.5, Indiana and Ohio; pt.6, Iowa, Kansas, Michigan, Minnesota, and Wisconsin; pt.7, Index of names.

"A revision of and supplement to the section on 'Military Organizations' in the 3d ed. of the *Bibliography of state participation in the Civil War,* prepared and published by the War Dept. Library, Wash., D.C. in 1913 as its Subject Catalogue No.6."—*Pref.*

—— Unit histories of the United States Air Forces, including privately printed personal narratives. Hampton Bays, N.Y., Hampton Books, 1958. 56p. il.　**CI200**

Covers World War I and World War II.

U.S. Dept. of the Army. Office of Military History. Unit histories of World War II. United States Army, Air Force, Marines, Navy. Reproduced in collaboration with the New York Public Library. [Wash.], Office of the Chief of Military History, [1950]. 141p.　**CI201**

Lists 1223 unit histories.

—— —— Supplement, 1951. Reproduced in collaboration with the New York Public Library and Office of the Chief of Military History, Dept. of the Army. Wash., Library Section, Special Services Division, Dept. of the Army, Sept. 1951. 50p.

Lists items 1230–1673. Includes some official as well as nonofficial histories.

A preliminary mimeographed edition of a list to be published by the Combat Forces Press.

—— Check list of new unit histories, comp. by C. E. Dornbusch. Wash., 1952–56. 3v. in 1. **CI201a**

U.S. Military Academy, West Point. The centennial of the U.S. Military Academy at West Point, N.Y., 1802–1902. v.2, Statistics and bibliographies. Wash., Govt. Prt. Off., 1904. 433p. **CI202**

Includes: Bibliographies of West Point, 1694–1902; Bibliography of the U.S. Military Academy, 1776–1902; Bibliography of the writings of graduates, 1802–1902; List of graduates (1802–1902).

U.S. Naval Academy, Annapolis. Library. Bibliography of naval literature in the United States Naval Academy Library, comp. by L. H. Bolander. [Annapolis, 1929] 3v. in 1. **CI203**

Pt.1, American naval biography; pt.2, Foreign naval biography; pt.3, Naval history.

"Works dealing with naval strategy, tactics, ordnance, and gunnery, seamanship, and navigation have not been included."

Dictionaries

Ruffner, Frederick G. and **Thomas, Robert C.** Code names dictionary. Detroit, Mich., Gale Research, 1963. 555p. **CI204**

Subtitle: A guide to code names, slang, nicknames, journalese and similar terms: aviation, rockets and missiles, military, aerospace, meteorology, atomic energy, communications and others.

U.S. Air University. Research Studies Institute. The United States Air Force dictionary. Ed. by Woodford Agee Heflin. Princeton, N.J., Van Nostrand, 1956. 578p. **CI205**

With supplements as issued.

Defines more than 16,500 words and abbreviations as used in the Air Forces, including terms in the fields of aeronautics, aerodynamics, meteorology, electronics, atomic energy, supersonics, etc.

U.S. Joint Chiefs of Staff. A dictionary of United States military terms, prep. for joint usage of the Armed Services . . . Wash., Public Affairs Pr., 1963. 316p. **CI206**

Lists and defines modern military terms acceptable to the U.S. Dept. of Defense.

Handbooks

❧ For many years the U.S. Army, Air Force, Marine Corps, and Navy have published various types of lists and registers, e.g., *U.S. Army register, Air Force register, Register of commissioned and warrant officers of the United States Navy and Marine Corps.* Titles and frequency vary. For further information and other titles, *see* A. M. Boyd, *United States government publications* (AH7).

Ageton, Arthur Ainsley and **Mack, William P.** The naval officer's guide. 6th ed. Annapolis, Md., U.S. Naval Inst., 1964. 650p. il. **CI207**

1st ed. 1943.

Air officer's guide. A ready-reference encyclopedia of all military information pertinent to commissioned officers of the United States Air Force. Harrisburg, Pa., Military Service Pub. Co., 1948– . Annual (Irregular). il. (1963) **CI208**

Army almanac; a book of facts concerning the United States Army. [2d ed.] Harrisburg, Pa., Stackpole, 1959. 797p. il. **CI209**

Ed. by Gordon R. Young.

"A new commercial edition of the book first published by the Dept. of the Army in 1950 . . . Now extensively revised and brought up to date . . ."—*Foreword.*

A compilation of facts, records, and statistics, giving information on organization and strength of the Army, with historical and current material on all phases of its activities.

Officer's guide; a ready reference on customs and correct procedures which pertain to officers of the United States Army. Harrisburg, Pa., Stackpole, Military Service Div., 1930– . v.1– . Annual (Irregular). (27th ed. 1961) **CI210**

Decorations and insignia

Kerrigan, Evans E. American war medals and decorations. N.Y., Viking, 1964. 149p. il., 4 col. pl. **CI211**

Descriptions and illustrations, some in color, of decorations, service medals, and awards to civilians.

National Geographic Society. Insignia and decorations of the United States armed forces, by Gilbert Grosvenor [and others] . . . Rev. ed., Dec. 1, 1944. Wash., Nat. Geographic Soc., 1945. 208p. il. **CI212**

Descriptions and illustrations, many in color, of decorations, medals, service ribbons, badges, and other insignia of the United States armed forces.

U.S. Adjutant General's Office. American decorations. A list of awards of the Congressional Medal of Honor, the Distinguished-Service Cross, and the Distinguished-Service Medal, awarded under authority of the Congress of the United States, 1862–1926. Wash., Govt. Prt. Off., 1927. 845p. **CI213**

—— —— Supplements, 1–5, Jan. 1, 1927—June 30, 1941. 1927–41.

No more published.

Ships

U.S. Naval History Division. Dictionary of American naval fighting ships. Wash., 1959–63. v.1–2. il. (In progress) **CI214**

Contents: v.1–2, List of ships, A–F; Appendixes.

To be a multivolume set. "An alphabetical arrangement of the ships of the Continental and United States navies, with a historical sketch of each one."—*Pref.* Appendixes appear in each volume; in v.1, chronological listings of battleships, cruisers, submarines, torpedo boats and destroyers, escort vessels; in v.2, aircraft carriers; Confederate forces afloat (historical sketches).

Biography

Callahan, Edward William. List of officers of the Navy of the United States and of the Marine Corps, from 1775 to 1900; comp. from the official records. N.Y., Hamersly, 1901. 749p. **CI215**

Subtitle: Comprising a complete register of all present and former commissioned, warranted, and appointed officers of the United States Navy, and of the Marine Corps, regular and volunteer.

Cullum, George Washington. Biographical register of the officers and graduates of the U.S. Military Academy at West Point, N.Y., since its establishment in 1802. 3d ed., rev. and extended. Boston, etc., 1891–1950. 9v. **CI216**

Place and publisher vary.

v.1–3, 1802–90; v.4, 1890–1900, ed. by E. S. Holden; v.5, 1900–1910, ed. by Lieut. Charles Braden; v.6, A and B, 1910–20, ed. by Col. Wirt Robinson; v.7, 1920–30, ed. by

Capt. W. H. Donaldson; v.8, 1930–40, ed. by Lt. Col. E. E. Farman; v.9, 1940–50, ed. by Col. Charles N. Branham.
v.4–9 called supplements.

Heitman, Francis Bernard. Historical register of officers of the Continental Army during the war of the Revolution, April 1775 to Dec. 1783. New, rev., and enl. ed. Wash., Rare Book Shop Pub. Co., 1914. 685p. **CI217**

An alphabetical register of officers, with service records and various supplementary lists.

—— Historical register and dictionary of the United States Army from its organization, Sept. 29, 1789, to March 2, 1903. Pub. under act of Congress approved March 2, 1903. Wash., Govt. Prt. Off., 1903. 2v. (57th Cong., 2d sess. House doc. 446) **CI218**

v.1 is primarily an alphabetical dictionary of officers of the U.S. Army, giving their service records with some preliminary lists; v.2 includes an alphabetical list of officers of the regular army who were killed, wounded in action, or taken prisoner; strength of the army and losses in the several wars; dates of certain wars, campaigns; alphabetical list of battles, actions, etc., 1775–1902; chronological list of battles, actions; list of forts, batteries, camps . . . general hospitals, national cemeteries, etc.; and various statistical tables.

Powell, William Henry. List of officers of the army of the United States from 1779–1900 embracing a register of all appointments . . . in the volunteer service during the Civil War and of volunteer officers in the service of the United States June 1, 1900, comp. from the official records. N.Y., Hamersly, 1900. 863p. **CI219**

A list of officers, 1779–1815, is arranged by years, followed by the army list, 1815 to 1900, which is arranged alphabetically by name with brief biographical information; a list of officers of volunteers; general officers of the Revolution; etc. Index of names. Known also as the *United States army list.*

—— Officers of the army and navy (volunteer) who served in the Civil War. Philadelphia, Hamersly, 1893. 419p. il. **CI220**

—— and **Shippen, Edward.** Officers of the army and navy (regular) who served in the Civil War. Philadelphia, Hamersly, 1892. 487p. il. **CI221**

C J

Law

❧ Because law is such a highly specialized subject, most legal research is done in special law libraries. These may be independent or they may be connected with some institution, such as state, legislative research, or university libraries. Few general libraries can buy many law books, both because they are so expensive and because they are so technical that they can be used satisfactorily only by those trained in the law. Therefore, the smaller general library should buy only those books which are needed for supplying the less technical legal information and should refer all other legal questions to a nearby law library.

The larger general library, however, will need at least a small collection of law reference books, as they are needed to answer questions in the fields of history, economics, and political and social science, as well as the more general law questions. The minimum equipment should include: (1) a law dictionary; (2) a set of the *Revised statutes of the United States* (CJ76), and either the *United States code* (CJ78) or the *United States code annotated* (CJ79); (3) the latest revision or compilation of the laws of the home state, with subsequent session laws; (4) the charter and ordinances of the home city; (5) the latest compilation of the United States *Treaties in force* (CJ112) and the *Digest of international law* (CJ93–CJ95). To this minimum the library would add, as public demand and library funds justified, one of the large law encyclopedias and, if the library contained many legal periodicals, the indexes of legal periodicals.

Convenient handbooks in almost any library are Shepard's Citations, Inc., *Table of federal acts by popular names* (CJ61) and *Table of federal and state cases by popular names* (CJ62).

GENERAL WORKS

Guides

Beardsley, Arthur Sydney and **Orman, Oscar C.** Legal bibliography and the use of law books. 2d ed. Brooklyn, N.Y., Foundation Pr., 1947. 653p. **CJ1**

A useful manual covering such topics as: Teaching and use of law books; Classes of law books—constitutional and statutory, judicial and quasi-judicial; Books of reference; Search for authorities; Brief making, etc.

International Association of Law Libraries. The law in the United States of America; a selective bibliographical guide [by] Joseph L. Andrews and others. N.Y., New York Univ. Pr., 1965. 100p. **CJ2**

Intended for law librarians in countries other than the United States; lists important treatises, textbooks, and monographs with very brief annotations. Omits periodicals. Gives full bibliographical information with price, in a subject arrangement. No index. Includes a list of law-book publishers with addresses.

Morgan, Edmund M. and **Dwyer, Francis X.** Introduction to the study of law. 2d ed. Chicago, Callaghan, 1948. 357p. (National textbook ser.) **CJ3**

1st ed., 1926, by E. M. Morgan.

This clear, concise introductory text will answer many questions concerning the organization of the courts of the United States and how the law operates.

Includes an annotated bibliography, p.166–283.

Notz, Rebecca Laurens Love. Legal bibliography and legal research. 3d ed. Chicago, Callaghan, 1952. 396p. **CJ4**

Describes outstanding American and current important English law books. Brief, but useful for quick reference.

Price, Miles Oscar and **Bitner, Harry.** Effective legal research; a practical manual of law books and their use. N.Y., Prentice-Hall, 1953. 633p. **CJ5**

A manual on legal research and bibliography which discusses procedures and literature. Of particular value to librarians will be the chapters on special types of reference works, e.g., indexes, digests, encyclopedias, dictionaries, looseleaf services, etc. The chapter on "Standard legal citation forms" incorporates the essentials of Price's *A practical manual of standard legal citation* (1950).

The appendixes include: American law reports and digests; British and Canadian material; a long list of Anglo-American legal periodicals, p.451–98, giving title, place of publication, period covered, and frequency (when possible); and a list of abbreviations commonly used in Anglo-American law, p.511–620. Numerous illustrations of legal materials and a detailed index.

—— —— Student edition rev. Boston, Little, 1962. 496p.

Written as a textbook, this edition is a simplified form of the earlier work. Omits some important historical material and the bibliographical appendixes.

Putnam, Carlton B. How to find the law; a comprehensive treatment of the problems of legal research with illustrations from various publications, together with a legal bibliography for each state and the federal government. A legal reference handbook. 4th ed. St. Paul, Minn., West Pub. Co., 1949. 740p. maps. **CJ6**

1st ed. by Fred A. Eldean, 1931. Supersedes, to a large extent, *Brief making and the use of lawbooks* by R. W. Cooley (1926), which for many years was a standard guide.

Editors vary. Subtitle varies.

Roalfe, William R. How to find the law. 5th ed. St. Paul, Minn., West Pub. Co., 1957. 207p. **CJ7**

Designed as an aid in introducing law students to legal materials, and does not replace the comprehensive 4th edition (CJ6).

Bibliography

Caes, Lucien and **Henrion, R.** Collectio bibliographica operum ad ius romanum pertinentium. Bruxelles, Office Internat. de Librairie, 1949–64. Ser. I, v.1–14; ser. II, v.1–2. (In progress) **CJ8**

Ser. I, Opera edita in periodicis miscellaneis encyclopaedi-isque, v.1–14, 1949–64.

Ser. II, Theses: v.1, Theses Galliae (1800–1848), 1950; v.2, Theses Germaniae (1885–1958), 1960.

An extensive, scholarly listing of articles in periodicals, collections, miscellanies, *Festschriften,* theses, etc., dating approximately from the mid-19th century. "Law" is broadly interpreted so that a substantial body of classical Latin literature is included. Arrangement of each volume is alphabetical by author, with a subject index.

Grandin, A. Bibliographie générale des sciences juridiques, politiques, économiques et sociales de 1800 à 1925/26. Paris, Recueil Sirey, 1926. 3v. **CJ9**

v.1–2, classified bibliography; v.3, indexes of authors, titles, and subjects.

—— —— 1.–19. supplément, 1926–50. Paris, Recueil Sirey, 1928–51. 19v.

For full description *see* CA9.

Harvard University. Law School. Library. Annual legal bibliography. Cambridge, Mass., 1960/61– . v.1– . Annual. **CJ10**

Includes a listing of monographs and articles received in the Harvard Law School Library, cumulating the items which have appeared in the *Current legal bibliography* with some additional material.

—— Current legal bibliography. Cambridge, Mass., 1960– . 9 times a year. **CJ10a**

International Association of Legal Science. Catalogue des sources de documentation juridique dans le monde. A register of legal documentation in the world. 2d ed. rev. and enl. Prep. by the International Association of Legal Science and the International Committee for Social Sciences Documentation. [Paris], UNESCO, 1957. 423p. (Documentation in the social sciences) **CJ11**

1st ed. 1953.

Under country lists codes, collections, constitutions, legal periodicals, centers of documentation, legal bibliographies, etc. Extent of information varies from country to country.

Jacobstein, J. Myron and **Pimsleur, Meira G.** Law books

in print. South Hackensack, N.J., Glanville Pub., 1957–61. v.1–3. (In progress) **CJ12**

Gives standard bibliographic information, including date, pagination, and price for texts and treatises in law, with selective treatment of works in related fields. Attempts to include all materials in the English language, listed in a single alphabet by author, compiler, editor, subject, title, and series. Periodicals, statutes, reports, digests, government documents, etc. are omitted.

Contents: v.1, United States, British and Canadian materials. 1957; v.2, Books in English published throughout the world. 1959; v.3, Books in English published throughout the world from Jan. 1959 through Dec. 1960. 1961.

Consolidated edition, covering books in print as of Dec. 31, 1964, is in press.

Szladits, Charles. Bibliography on foreign and comparative law; books and articles in English. N.Y., Parker School of Foreign and Comparative Law, Columbia Univ., 1955. (Distr. by Oceana, N.Y.) 526p. **CJ13**

Lists some 14,000 books and periodical articles in English in the broad fields of foreign and comparative law. Does not include the Anglo-American legal systems. Classified, with indexes by authors and by geographic areas.

—— —— 1953–1959. Dobbs Ferry, N.Y., Oceana, 1962. 559p.

Updates the first volume and adds some earlier works omitted from it.

—— —— Supplement, 1960–61. 1963. 181p.

A cumulative volume covering 1960–64 is in preparation.

—— Guide to foreign legal materials; French, German, Swiss. [N.Y.], Oceana, 1959. 599p. **CJ14**

At head of title: Parker School studies in foreign and comparative law.

Contains laws, reports, and books, arranged in three parts: (1) French law, (2) German law, and (3) Swiss law. Includes all branches of the law. A list of legal abbreviations is given at the end of each part.

United Nations. Dag Hammarskjöld Library. Annotated list of official gazettes. Rev. draft ed. N.Y., 1962. 70p. **CJ15**

Includes a list of "some of the more important general collections of legislation or guides to publications containing legislation which deal with the laws, decrees, etc., of more than one country."—*Introd.*

United States

Klein, Fannie J. Judicial administration and the legal profession. N.Y., Oceana, 1963. 650p. **CJ16**

Published for the American Judicature Society and the Institute of Judicial Administration.

An annotated bibliography of almost 6000 entries, including books, reports, pamphlets, and periodicals, on the improvement and strengthening of civil justice in the United States (1938–62).

Includes a list of bibliographies and an author-subject index.

Pimsleur, Meira G. Checklists of basic American legal publications. Pub. for American Association of Law Libraries. South Hackensack, N.J., Fred B. Rothman, 1962– . Loose-leaf. (AALL publ., no.4) (In progress) **CJ17**

Sec. 1 covers *State statutes, revisions, compilations,* and is "a revision and updating of Grace E. Macdonald's *Checklist of statutes of states of the United States of America* (1937)." Sec. 2 covers the *Session laws of the various states of the United States,* and is a revision of Grace E. Macdonald's *Checklist of session laws* (1936). Sec. 3 is intended to be a *Checklist of reports and opinions of the attorneys-general.*

Tompkins, Dorothy Campbell. The Supreme Court of the United States; a bibliography. Berkeley, Bureau of Public Admin., Univ. of Calif., 1959. 217p. **CJ18**

Includes a wide selection of monographs, articles, speeches, reports, etc., most of which have appeared since 1930. Items are grouped under such headings as: Organization, Work of the Court, Justices. Some are annotated. Author index.

U.S. Library of Congress. Law Library. Anglo-American legal bibliographies; an annotated guide by William L. Friend. Wash., Govt. Prt. Off., 1944. 166p. facsim. **CJ19**

A historical survey of Anglo-American legal bibliography is followed by an alphabetical list of all types of legal bibliographical publications except "works devoted exclusively to American statutory materials, and library and publishers' catalogues."

Great Britain

Beale, Joseph Henry. Bibliography of early English law books. Cambridge, Harvard Univ. Pr., 1926. 304p. **CJ20**

—— —— Supplement, comp. for the Ames Foundation, by R. B. Anderson. Cambridge, Harvard Univ. Pr., 1943. 50p.

Arranged under statutes, decisions, treatises, printers and their law books. Material is listed in chronological order, dating from the late 15th to the end of the 16th century. An appendix locates copies found in 25 libraries. The supplement includes revisions and corrections of the original volume and adds new material.

Bibliographical guide to the law of the United Kingdom, the Channel Islands and the Isle of Man. London, Univ. of London, Inst. of Advanced Legal Studies, 1956. 219p. **CJ21**

A selective bibliography prepared mainly to introduce English law to foreign lawyers. Arranged by subject, with short introductions, drawing attention to the unique features of English legal arrangement.

Legal bibliography of the British Commonwealth of Nations. 2d ed. London, Sweet & Maxwell, 1955–64. 7v. **CJ22**

1st edition (1925–49. 7v.) had title *Sweet & Maxwell's Complete law book catalogue.*
v.1, English law to 1800, including Wales, the Channel Islands and the Isle of Man. 1955; v.2, English law from 1801 to 1954, including Wales, the Channel Islands and the Isle of Man. 1957; v.3, Canadian and British-American colonial law from earliest times to Dec. 1956. 1957; v.4, Irish law to 1956. 1957; v.5, Scottish law to 1956, together with a list of Roman law books in the English language. 1957; v.6, Australia, New Zealand and their dependencies, from earliest times to June 1958, with lists of reports of cases, digests, and collections of statutes and rules. 1958; v.7, The British Commonwealth, excluding the United Kingdom, Australia, New Zealand, Canada, India and Pakistan. 1964.
v.1 lists books printed from 1480 to 1954. Contains indexes by subjects, places, and authors and titles. v.2–7 are arranged alphabetically by author, or title, with subject index.

Latin America

Bayitch, Stojan A. Latin America; a bibliographical guide to economy, history, law, politics, and society. Coral Gables, Fla., Univ. of Miami Pr., 1961. (Distr. by Oceana, N.Y.) 335p. (Interamerican legal studies, no.6) **CJ23**

A list of books and articles drawn from approximately 400 periodicals. Contains only works in English with emphasis given to law and related topics, excluding international law and foreign relations. Includes a guide by subjects, a guide by countries, and an alphabetical subject index.

U.S. Library of Congress. Law Library. Guide[s] to the law and legal literature of [Latin American countries]. Wash., Lib. of Congress, 1943–48. **CJ24**

Published as numbers of its Latin American series as follows: no.3, Cuba, the Dominican Republic, and Haiti. 1944. 276p.; no.4, Colombia. 1943. 222p.; no.6, Mexico. 1945. 269p.; no.12, Bolivia. 1947. 110p.; no.13, Mexican states. 1947. 180p.; no.14, Paraguay. 1947. 59p.; no.16, Venezuela. 1947. 128p.; no.18, Ecuador. 1947. 100p.; no.20, Peru. 1947. 188p.; no.26, Uruguay. 1947. 123p.; no.28, Chile. 1917–1946. 1947. 103p.; no.32, Argentina. 1917–1946. 1948. 180p.

—— Legal codes of the Latin American republics. Wash., Lib. of Congress, 1942. 95p. (Latin Amer. ser., no.1) **CJ25**

Includes Spanish and Portuguese translations of the English texts.

Union of Soviet Socialist Republics

Hazard, John Newbold and **Stern, William B.** Bibliography of the principal materials on Soviet law. N.Y., Foreign and Internat. Book Co., 1945. 46p. (American Foreign Law Assoc. Bibliographies of foreign law ser., no.12) **CJ26**

Bibliography of the principal materials on Soviet law published in the English, French, German, and Russian languages to Dec. 31, 1943.

Hazard, John Newbold and **Shapiro, Isaac.** The Soviet legal system; post-Stalin documentation and historical commentary. Dobbs Ferry, N.Y., Oceana, 1962. 3v. in 1. (Columbia Univ. Parker School studies in foreign and comparative law) **CJ27**

Contents: v.1, The Soviet state and its citizens (Bibl., p.165–86); v.2, Administering Soviet socialism (Bibl., p.219–35); v.3, Legal relations between Soviet citizens (Bibl., p.151–55).

Dictionaries

Ballentine, James Arthur. Law dictionary with pronunciations. 1948 ed. Rochester, N.Y., Lawyers Co-operative Pub. Co., 1948. 1494p. **CJ28**

Excellent 1v. dictionary.

—— —— Supplement to Ballentine's pronouncing law dictionary . . . Rochester, N.Y., Lawyers Co-operative Pub. Co., 1954. 253p.

Black, Henry Campbell. Black's Law dictionary; definitions of the terms and phrases of American and English jurisprudence, ancient and modern. 4th ed., by the publisher's editorial staff. St. Paul, Minn., West Pub. Co., 1951. 1882p. **CJ29**

1st edition, 1891, had title *A dictionary of law.*
This comprehensive work is the standard law dictionary for ready reference.

Bouvier, John. Bouvier's Law dictionary and concise encyclopedia, 3d revision (being the 8th ed.) by Francis Rawle. Kansas City, Mo., Vernon; St. Paul, Minn., West Pub. Co., 1914. 3v. **CJ30**

First published in 1839 and long regarded as the authoritative American legal dictionary; has gone through many printings. Now out of date but useful for obsolete terms.
Various revised and condensed editions have been issued for student use.

Jowitt, William Allen Jowitt, *1st Earl.* The dictionary of English law. Ed., Clifford Walsh. London, Sweet & Maxwell, 1959. 2v. (1905p.) **CJ31**

A dictionary "covering English law from earliest times to the present day, giving a definition and an explanation of every legal term old and new."—*Pref.*

Legal secretary's encyclopedic dictionary, prep. by the editorial staff of Prentice-Hall, Inc. Englewood Cliffs, N.J., Prentice-Hall, [1962]. 467p. il.　　　　**CJ32**

Especially useful for its simple explanation of legal terms. Includes many specimen legal forms.

Stroud's Judicial dictionary of words and phrases. 3d ed. Gen. ed., John Burke; asst. gen. ed., Peter Allsop. London, Sweet & Maxwell, 1952–53. v.1–4. (In progress)　**CJ33**

1st ed. 1890; 2d ed. 1903. Various supplements.

To be in 5v.: v.1–4, text; v.5, tables and statutes. Kept up to date by periodical supplements. Not a law lexicon but a "dictionary of the English language so far as that language has received interpretation by the Judges."

—— First supplement, to Jan. 1, 1956. 1956. 117p.

Abbreviations

Kirchner, Hildebert. Abkürzungsverzeichnis der Rechtssprache auf der Grundlage der für den Bundesgerichtshof geltenden Abkürzungsregeln. Berlin, de Gruyter, 1957. 347p.　　　　　　　　　　　　　**CJ34**

The first part lists abbreviations in alphabetical order; the second is in sections arranged alphabetically by title of periodical, law, etc., followed by the abbreviation.

Foreign terms

☙ For many purposes the large, general, bilingual dictionaries are more satisfactory than these books of legal terminology which frequently give synonyms only, without explanatory usage. However, the following may be useful:

Belgian

Wilkin, Robert. Dictionnaire du droit public. Bruxelles, E. Bruylant, 1963. 419p.　　　　　　　　　**CJ35**

Gives long explanations of terms according to Belgian usage.

French

Quemner, Thomas A. Dictionnaire juridique; droit, finances, commerce, douanes, assurances, administration. Préf. par Gilbert Gidel. Paris, Éd. de Navarre, 1953–55. 2v.　　　　　　　　　　　　　　　　**CJ36**

v.1, Français-anglais; v.2, Anglais-français.

German

Beseler, Dora von. Englisch-deutsches und deutsch-englisches Taschenwörterbuch der Rechts- und Geschäftssprache. 2. durchges. u. erw. Aufl. Berlin, de Gruyter, 1947. 271p.　　　　　　　　　　　　　　　　**CJ37**

Added title page in English.

Schlegelberger, Franz. Rechtsvergleichendes Handwörterbuch für das Zivil- und Handelsrecht des In- und Auslandes. Berlin, Vahlen, 1927–40. v.1–7, pts.1–3.　**CJ38**

Contents: v.1, Länderberichte; v.2–7³, A–Vermächtnis.

Encyclopedic dictionary of civil and commercial legal terms in various countries of the world with long, signed articles including bibliographies. v.1 treats the legal system of each country; v.2–7 give definitions of terms in alphabetic arrangement.

Italian

Fusi, Maurizio. Dizionario legale ad uso delli aziende, dei dirigenti e dei professionisti, con tavole sinottiche delle disposizioni fiscali. [Milano], F. Angeli, [1960]. 593p. (Manuali Franco Angeli, editore, 3)　　　**CJ39**

Matteucci, Mario. Dictionnaire juridique français-italien, italien-français; droit, finances, commerce, douanes, assurances, administration. Préf. par Jules Basdevant. Paris, Éd. de Navarre, [1963]. 510p.　　　**CJ40**

Added title page in Italian.

Japanese

Ito, Jujiro. A Japanese-English dictionary of legal terms with supplement. Tokyo, Daigaku Shobo, 1953. 896p., 346p.　　　　　　　　　　　　　　　　**CJ41**

Gives equivalents of the various meanings which may be attached to legal words and phrases, with many examples from actual laws, citing sources.

Latin

Berger, Adolf. Encyclopedic dictionary of Roman law. Philadelphia, Amer. Philosophical Soc., 1953. 303–809p. (Transactions of the American Philosophical Society, n.s. 43, pt.2, 1953)　　　　　　　　　　　**CJ42**

Purpose is "to explain technical Roman legal terms, to translate and elucidate those Latin words which have a specific connotation when used in a juristic context or in connection with a legal institution or question, and to provide a brief picture of Roman legal institutions and sources . . ."—*Introd.*

Includes references to sources and to bibliographies. The main alphabet is followed by an English-Latin glossary, and a General bibliography, p.786–808.

Latin for lawyers. 3d ed. London, Sweet & Maxwell, 1960. 287p.　　　　　　　　　　　　　　　　**CJ43**

1st ed. 1915; 2d ed. 1937.

Containing: (1) A course in Latin, with legal maxims and phrases as a basis of instruction; (2) A collection of over 1000 Latin maxims, with English translations, explanatory notes, and cross-references; (3) Vocabulary of Latin words.

Russian

Telberg, Ina. Soviet-English dictionary of legal terms and concepts. N.Y., Telberg, [1961]. 111p.　　　**CJ44**

Contains approximately 590 Russian terms with definitions in English. Terms are from constitutional and administrative, civil and procedural, housing, land, family, labor, criminal, and finance law.

Spanish

Fernández de León, Gonzálo. Diccionario jurídico. Buenos Aires, V. P. de Zavalía, 1955. 343p.　　　**CJ45**

Latin-American usage. Gives long definitions, usually followed by citations.

Robb, Louis Adams. Dictionary of legal terms, Spanish-English and English-Spanish. N.Y., Wiley, 1955. 228p.　　　　　　　　　　　　　　　　**CJ46**

Added title page and preface in Spanish.

A dictionary of equivalents; "definitions are given only when there is no equivalent or occasionally for a term that is somewhat unfamiliar."

Tejada y Sainza, Juan de Dios. Spanish and English legal and commercial dictionary. A revision and enlargement of the Law translator's reference glossary. Santa María del Rosario, Cuba, Ed. Var-I-Tek, 1945. 158p.　**CJ47**

Subtitle: Contains over 10,000 terms . . . pertinent to: canon, civil, commercial, international, municipal and penal law; transportation, accounting, banking and finance; insurance, metrology; and numerous abbreviations.

Contents: pt.1, English-Spanish; pt.2, Spanish-English.

Encyclopedias

American jurisprudence; a modern comprehensive text statement of American law, state and federal. 2d ed. Compl. rev. and rewritten . . . by the editorial staff of the publishers. Rochester, N.Y., Lawyers Co-operative; San Francisco, Bancroft-Whitney, 1962–   . v.1–17. (In progress)   **CJ48**

1st ed. 1936–62. 58v.; General index. 1951–52. 4v.

Kept up to date by annual, cumulative, pocket supplements. Each volume has subject index.

—— Desk book: historical and legal documents, facts, tables, charts, and statistics of special interest to attorneys. By the editorial staff of the publishers. Rochester, N.Y., Lawyers Co-operative; San Francisco, Bancroft-Whitney, 1962. 659p.   **CJ49**

Pocket supplements issued from time to time.

A useful handbook for ready reference.

Corpus juris secundum; a complete restatement of the entire American law as developed by all reported cases, by William Mack and Donald J. Kiser, assisted by the combined editorial staffs of the American Law Book Co. and the West Publishing Co. Brooklyn, N.Y., Amer. Law Book Co., [c1936–c1958]. 101v.   **CJ50**

Cited as *C.J.S.*

A new edition, superseding *Corpus juris* (*C.J.*). 1914–37. 72v. However, case citations refer to decisions handed down since the publication of *C.J.* For earlier authorities a specific reference to *C.J.* cites all cases back to 1658. This makes the original work still valuable.

Kept up to date by cumulative annual parts and recompiled volumes.

—— General index. 1959–60. 5v.

Laws of England, being a complete statement of the whole law of England, by the Earl of Halsbury and other lawyers. 3d ed. under the general editorship of Lord Simonds. London, Butterworth, 1952–64. 43v.   **CJ51**

Half title: Halsbury's Laws of England.

v.40, Consolidated table of cases. 1963; v.41–42, General index. 1963; v.43, Consolidated table of statutes. 1964.

1st ed. 1907–17.

Kept up to date by annual cumulative supplements.

—— Canadian converter, under the general editorship of Gerald D. Sanagan. Toronto, Butterworth, 1954–   .   **CJ52**

Refers to equivalent Canadian federal and provincial statutes and cases, with the exception of the province of Quebec, as cited in *Halsbury* (CJ51).

—— Australian pilot, being a conspectus of the statutes and cases of the Commonwealth of Australia and all the Australian states. Sydney, Butterworth, 1960–   .   **CJ53**

Refers to Australian statutes and cases equivalent to references cited in *Halsbury* (CJ51).

Handbooks

Mettler, Frederick Albert. The medical sourcebook; a reference handbook for legal, legislative, and administrative personnel. [1st ed.] Boston, Little, 1960. 1000p. il.   **CJ54**

For complete information *see* EJ56.

Prentice-Hall, Inc. Encyclopedic dictionary of business law, prep. by the editorial staff of Prentice-Hall, Inc. Englewood Cliffs, N.J., 1961. 608p.   **CJ55**

Designed as a "practical guide and reference tool for proper handling of the many legal questions and problems that arise in the course of everyday business."—*Pref.*

For additional information *see* CH78.

Indexes

Commerce Clearing House. Congressional index service. 75th Congress, 1937/38–   . Chicago, Commerce Clearing House, Loose Leaf Service Division of the Corporation Trust Co., 1937–   . Weekly throughout session. Loose-leaf.   **CJ56**

"Indexes all congressional bills and resolutions of general interest and lists their current status. It is designed to lay open to the user a complete record of federal legislation and its progress from initial introduction to final disposition."

Now includes treaties.

Contains section on voting records in which all roll-call votes on the progress of legislation are reported weekly.

Index to legal periodical literature. Boston, Boston Book Co., 1888–1919; Chipman, 1924; Indianapolis, Bobbs-Merrill, 1933; Los Angeles, Parker and Baird, 1939. v.1–6.   **CJ57**

v.1–2, ed. by Leonard A. Jones; v.3–6, by Frank E. Chipman.

v.1, to 1886; v.2, 1887–98; v.3, 1898–1908; v.4, 1908–22; v.5, 1923–32; v.6, 1932–37.

Each volume consists of a main subject index, with brief author index to the subject part. Indexes periodical literature in the English language on technical and historical law subjects; legal biography; and a considerable number of articles on political, economic, and sociological subjects. v.1 indexes practically all articles in 158 legal periodicals (1373v.); all articles on law subjects in 113 general periodicals (including a few sets published in the 18th century); and the proceedings of various bar associations. v.4 indexes 91 periodicals and is practically a consolidation of v.1–14 of the annual *Index to legal periodicals* (CJ58). Useful in the general library as well as in the law library.

Index to legal periodicals, 1908–   , pub. for the American Association of Law Libraries. N.Y., Wilson, 1909–   .   **CJ58**

Monthly indexes (frequency varies), with annual cumulations and, from 1926, 3-year cumulations which supersede the annual. The cumulated volumes consist of a subject and author index; a table of cases; and, since 1940, a book review index. Number of periodicals indexed varies from 39 in the 1908 annual to 290 in the 1961–64 cumulation. Earlier volumes indexed bar association and judicial council reports.

Index to foreign legal periodicals. London, pub. by the Inst. of Advanced Legal Studies, Univ. of London, in cooperation with the American Association of Law Libraries. 1960–   . v.1–   . Quarterly, cumulating annually.   **CJ59**

Indexes "the main legal periodicals dealing with international law (public and private), comparative law and the municipal law of all countries of the world other than the United States, the British Isles and the countries of the British Commonwealth . . ."—*Pref.* Beginning with v.4 (1963), collections of legal essays such as *Festschriften* are also indexed.

Legal periodical digest, 1928–   . N.Y., Commerce Clearing House, 1928–   . v.1–   .   **CJ60**

Title varies.

Loose-leaf abstracting service, consisting of monthly issues of digests of the leading articles appearing in United States, Canadian, Philippine, and Puerto Rican legal periodicals. Digests are on sheets for insertion in a loose-leaf binder according to subject.

The index section contains: (1) topical index; (2) author index; (3) table of articles, issued semiannually and annually, the annual index being cumulated for the year; (4) case comments by case names; (5) table of abbreviations; and (6) citation reference table.

Shepard's Citations, Inc. A table of federal acts by popular names or short titles to Jan. 1, 1964. Colorado Springs, Shepard's Citations, [1964]. 196p.   **CJ61**

> 1st ed. 1931. Frequently revised.
> Title varies slightly.
> Subtitle: A compilation of popular names or short titles by which federal acts have been referred to or cited together with an identification of each act in terms of the *United States code* [CJ78] or the *United States statutes at large* [CJ77].

—— Table of federal and state cases by popular names. Colorado Springs, Shepard's Citations, 1957. 96p. **CJ62**

> 1st ed. 1934. Frequently revised.
> Title varies slightly.
> Subtitle: A compilation of popular names by which federal and state cases have been referred to or cited, together with the volume and page references for such cases.

—— —— Supplement. Jan. 1, 1957 to Jan. 1, 1962. 15p.

State law index; an index to the legislation of the states of the United States enacted . . . 1925/26–1947/48. Wash., Govt. Prt. Off., 1929–49. v.1–12. Biennial. **CJ63**

> Ceased publication (?).
> Title varies.
> 1925/26–1933/34, compiled by the Legislative Reference Service of the Library of Congress . . . ; 1935/36–1947/48, by the State Law Index, Library of Congress.

U.S. Library of Congress. Law Library. Hispanic Law Division. Index to Latin American legislation, 1950–1960. Boston, G. K. Hall, [1961]. 2v.   **CJ64**

> Contents: v.1, Argentina–Cuba; v.2, Dominican Republic–Venezuela.
> Covers national legislation appearing in the official gazettes of the 20 Latin-American republics. Arranged alphabetically by subject under each country.

U.S. Library of Congress. Legislative Reference Service. Digest of public general bills and selected resolutions with index, 74th Cong., 2d sess.– . 1936– . Wash., Govt. Prt. Off., 1936– .   **CJ65**

> Normally published each session in 5 cumulative issues with biweekly supplements.
> Provides "a brief synopsis, the essential features of public bills and resolutions and changes made therein during the legislative process."—*Foreword*.

Directories

American Bar Association. Directory. [1937/38?] Chicago, Assoc., 1938– . (Irregular)   **CJ66**

> Lists officers, committees, etc.

Directory of law libraries. 1940– . [N.Y.], pub. for the American Association of Law Libraries . . . by the Commerce Clearing House, 1940– . Biennial.   **CJ67**

> Title varies: *Law libraries in the United States and Canada,* 1940–1962/63.
> Geographical listing of law libraries with 5000 or more volumes in the United States, Canada, and other foreign countries that are members of the Association. Gives name, librarian, and number of volumes, followed by a personnel index.

Lawyers directory. Charlottesville, Va., Lawyers Directory, 1883– . Annual.   **CJ68**

> Semiannual, 1888–1925; annual, 1926– .
> Contains digests of laws and a selection of leading lawyers with biographical data. Includes the United States and principal foreign countries. Less inclusive as a lawyers' directory but more inclusive as a law digest than the *Martindale-Hubbell* (CJ69).
> Title varies: until 1925 was called *Sharp & Alleman Co.'s Lawyers and bankers directory.*

Martindale-Hubbell law directory (annual) . . . 1931– . [63d–] N.Y., Martindale-Hubbell, [c1931–]. **CJ69**

Consolidation of *Martindale's American law directory,* 1868–1930 (continues its volume numbering) and *Hubbell's Legal directory,* 1870–1930; published annually in 4v.

> v.1–3—arranged geographically by state, then by city and town—includes List of firms and lawyers of the United States and Canada; Selected list of foreign lawyers, arranged by country; Roster of registered patent attorneys; and Biographical section. v.4 includes Digests of the laws of the states, territories and possessions of the United States, Canada and its provinces and foreign countries, also United States copyright, patent and trademark laws; and Court calendars and uniform acts.
> Contains no single alphabetical list of lawyers.

National Legal Aid and Defender Association. Directory of legal aid and defender services, 1961–1962. Chicago, Amer. Bar Center, [1962]. 79p.   **CJ70**

> 1st ed. 1933?.
> Name of issuing body varies. Title varies slightly.
> Gives the names and addresses of all such known organizations in the United States, Canada, the Philippine Islands, and Puerto Rico, with a brief description of the types and limitations of the services provided by each.

Biography

American Association of Law Librarians. Biographical directory of law librarians in the United States and Canada. [1st ed.] St. Paul, Minn., West Pub. Co., 1964. 57p. **CJ71**

> Includes some 500 professional law librarians, "who are actively engaged in or retired from professional law library work."—*Introd.*

Directory of law teachers in American Bar Association approved law schools, 1922– . St. Paul, Minn., West Pub. Co., 1923– . Annual.   **CJ72**

> Alphabetical list of teachers with biographies.
> Suspended 1943–45. Resumed 1946/47.
> Title varies: *Directory of teachers in member schools,* 1922–56.
> Volumes for 1922–56 issued by the Association of American Law Schools.

Liebman, Charles. Directory of American judges, with a table of the federal and state courts. Chicago, Amer. Directories, 1955. 1v. unpaged.   **CJ73**

> Lists the federal and state courts with their judges, followed by biographical sketches. The first attempt to compile a biographical dictionary of American judges.

Thomashower, Dorothy. Women lawyers in the United States, comp. and ed. by Dorothy Thomas, [pseud.]. [1st ed.] N.Y., Scarecrow, 1957. 747p.   **CJ74**

> Lists the names of some 6000 women admitted to the bar of any one of the United States or its Territories. In some cases gives biographical sketch; in others gives address only.

STATUTES

United States

U.S. Laws, Statutes, etc. Index to the federal statutes [1789–1873, 1874–1931] general and permanent law. . . . Wash., Govt. Prt. Off., 1911–33. 2v.   **CJ75**

> The volume for 1789–1873 indexes v.1–17 of the *Statutes at large* (CJ77); the volume for 1874–1931 indexes the *Revised statutes of 1874* (CJ76) and the *Statutes at large,* v.18–46; this latter volume is a revision by W. H. McClenon and W. C. Gilbert of the Scott and Beaman *Index analysis of the federal statutes 1874–1907.*
> These two volumes index all federal legislation of a public, general, and permanent nature through 1931.

—— Revised statutes of the United States, passed at the first session of the Forty-third Congress, 1873–74; embracing the statutes of the United States, general and permanent in their nature, in force Dec. 1, 1873. 2d ed. Wash., Govt. Prt. Off., 1878. 1394p.   **CJ76**

In 1867 a commission was appointed to compile all the general and permanent laws by subject. The first revision, accepted and published as the *Revised statutes of 1873,* contained certain liberties in the texts taken by the revisers. The *Revised statutes,* 2d ed. 1878, restored the original text, and is the edition usually cited. Supplements were made and published in 1891 and 1901, but these are now largely superseded by the *Code* (CJ78).

—— United States statutes at large containing the laws and concurrent resolutions enacted . . . and reorganization plans and proclamations, 1789–1873; 1873– . Boston, Little, 1845–73; Wash., Govt. Prt. Off., 1875– . v.1– .   **CJ77**

Title varies slightly.

The present series of *Statutes at large* starts with v.18 (1873–75). It was preceded by the *Laws of the United States:* Folwell edition, for the first 13 Congresses, 1789–1813; Bioren and Duane edition, for the first 28 Congresses, 1789–1845; Little, Brown edition, called *Statutes at large,* covering the first 42 Congresses, 1789–1873, and ending with v.17. This series was taken over by the federal government, v.18– .

Contents vary, but beginning with v.65, 1951, each volume contains public laws, reorganization plans, private laws, and concurrent resolutions and proclamations. Arrangement is chronological by date of passage of the act under the divisions: Public laws, Private laws, etc. A subject index and a personal-name index in each volume.

Slip laws are published separately, as soon as enacted, in two series: (1) Public Acts (cited as Public Law), and (2) Private Acts (cited as Private Law), and are superseded upon publication of the *Statutes at large.* Slip laws and resolutions are listed in the *Monthly catalog* (AH18) under "Congress" and then by number.

Treaties to which the United States was a party (1776–1949) were published in the *Statutes at large,* 1848–1949. Since Jan. 1, 1950, they have been contained in *United States treaties and other international agreements* (CJ117).

—— United States code. 1958 ed. Wash., Govt. Prt. Off., 1959. 13v.   **CJ78**

Supersedes previous editions published 1926, 1934, 1940, 1946, 1952.

Cited as *U.S.C.*

This code contains all general and permanent laws of the United States in force on Jan. 6, 1959, arranged under 50 titles, i.e., subjects with many subdivisions, called chapters.

Cumulative supplements issued annually.

—— United States code annotated. St. Paul, Minn., West Pub. Co., 1927– . v.1– .   **CJ79**

Cited as *U.S.C.A.*

Comprises all laws of a general and permanent nature under the same arrangement as that of the *Code* (CJ78). Annotations are from Federal and State court reports and opinions of the United States Attorney-General.

Kept up to date by cumulative, annual, pocket parts containing amendments and additions. Later replacement volumes are issued from time to time.

—— Constitution of the United States annotated; annotated from federal and state courts [1949–1961]. 6v.   **CJ80**

—— —— General index, [1962]. 5v.

—— —— Tables, [1962].

—— Federal code annotated; all federal laws of a general and permanent nature . . . fully annotated to the decisions of federal and state tribunals, together with annotations of uncodified laws and treaties, executive orders, proc-

lamations, and law review articles. Indianapolis, Bobbs-Merrill, 1937– . v.1– .   **CJ81**

Cited as *F.C.A.*

Volumes replaced at intervals by perpetual revision plan. Groups related material into volumes, e.g., Federal taxation, Transportation and communication, Bankruptcy, etc.

—— —— Ten-year cumulative supplement for v.1–13. Titles 1–50, 1947– . v.1–5. (In progress)

—— —— Index, [c1962]. 2v.

Code of federal regulations. 1949 ed., containing a codification of documents of general applicability and future effect as of Dec. 31, 1948, with ancillaries and index. Pub. by the Division of the Federal Register, National Archives. Wash., Govt. Prt. Off., 1949– . (In progress)   **CJ82**

Cited as *C.F.R.*

Kept up to date by pocket supplements, cumulating annually.

This is the second edition of the *Code* (1st ed. 1938), and contains a "codification of the Federal Administrative rules and regulations, general and permanent . . . duly promulgated on or before Dec. 31, 1948, and effective as to facts arising on and after Jan. 1, 1949."

The volumes form basic volumes for the type of material published currently in the *Federal register* (CJ83).

—— General index, [1955].

—— Title 3, The President. Compilation containing the full text of presidential documents. With ancillaries and index, 1943/48–1959/63. v.1–4.

United States. Federal register, March 14, 1936– . Wash., Govt. Prt. Off., 1936– . Daily, except Sun., Mon., and day following a legal holiday.   **CJ83**

Contains all presidential proclamations and executive orders; rules and regulations of the various bureaus and departments of the government; and decisions of fact-finding bodies. Has monthly, quarterly, and annual indexes.

U.S. Laws, Statutes, etc. United States code Congressional and administrative news. Acts of 76th Congress, Jan. 3, 1939– . St. Paul, Minn., West Pub. Co.; Brooklyn, N.Y., Edward Thompson Co., 1942– .   **CJ84**

Published semimonthly during the session of Congress, and monthly when Congress is not in session, with annual bound cumulations. Coverage varies somewhat; recent volumes include all public laws (full text), legislative history, executive orders, presidential proclamations, administrative regulations, messages of the president, popular names of laws, etc. Current issues contain index-digest of bills enacted.

Great Britain

Gt.Brit. Laws, Statutes, etc. The laws of the earliest English kings, ed. and tr. by F. L. Attenborough . . . Cambridge, Univ. Pr., 1922. 256p. (Reissued repr.: N.Y., Russell, 1963)   **CJ85**

Anglo-Saxon and modern English versions, with Latin when the original Anglo-Saxon is lost.

—— The statutes, from the twentieth year of King Henry the Third to the [tenth chapter of the twelfth, thirteenth, and fourteenth years of King George the Sixth], A.D. 1235–[1948. Prep. under the editorship of Sir Robert Drayton]. 3d rev. ed. London, Stat. Off., 1950. 32v. **CJ86**

"The text of this edition, down to the end of the reign of Queen Anne is, like that of the First and Second revised editions, based on the edition known as the 'Statutes of the Realm.' "—*Pref.*

Earlier editions: *Statutes of the realm* (London, Record Commission, 1810–28. 1v.); *The statutes,* 2d rev. ed. . . . 1235–1920 (London, Stat. Off., 1888–1929. 24v.).

Kept up to date by the annual volumes of *Public general acts* and the *Church assembly measures*.

Contains all acts in force, of a public nature, in chronological order with extensive notes. Each volume has subject and chronological indexes.

—— Acts and ordinances of the Interregnum, 1642–1660, ed. by C. H. Firth and R. S. Rait. London, Stat. Off., 1911. 3v.   **CJ87**

v.3, Chronological table of acts and ordinances, p.i–cix; Index to subjects, p.1–144; Index of names, places, and things, p.145–400.

—— Halsbury's Statutes of England. 2d ed. Ed. in chief, Roland Burrows. London, Butterworth, 1948–51. 26v.   **CJ88**

Contains all public general acts in force, including amendments and corrections of the text. Arranged alphabetically by broad subjects.

Kept up to date by annual continuation volumes and annual cumulative supplements.

v.27, Lists of statutes; General index. Rev., 1961.

v.28– (1951–), Continuation volumes.

CANON LAW

Dictionnaire de droit canonique, contenant tous les termes du droit canonique, avec un sommaire de l'histoire et des institutions et de l'état actuel de la discipline; publié sous la direction de R. Naz, avec le concours d'un grand nombre de collaborateurs. Paris, Letouzey, 1935–63. v.1–6. (In progress)   **CJ89**

Pub. in fascicules. Fasc.1–36, 1924–57, form v.1–6, and cover A–Pittoni; fasc.37–42, 1958–63, cover Placentin–Visite.

Signed articles by specialists, with bibliographies. Contains many biographies. Forms part of the *Encyclopédie des sciences religieuses* (*see* note under Encyclopedias and Dictionaries, p.206).

INTERNATIONAL LAW

Déak, Francis and **Jessup, Philip C.** Collection of neutrality laws, regulations and treaties of various countries. Wash., Carnegie Endowment for Internat. Peace, 1939. 2v.   **CJ90**

Includes laws, regulations, and treaties from 1800 to Oct. 1, 1938.

Harvard University. Law School. Library. Catalog of international law and relations. Ed. by Margaret Moody. Cambridge, Mass., 1965– . v.1– . (In progress) **CJ91**

This book catalog, reproduced from some 360,000 cards, represents the international law materials in the Harvard Law School Library, based on the famous collection of the Marquis de Olivart, acquired by Harvard in 1911.

Dictionary arrangement; full bibliographic information is given on main entry. Subject and added entries have been shortened.

Hasse, Adelaide Rosalie. Index to United States documents relating to foreign affairs, 1828–1861. Wash., Carnegie Inst., 1914–21. 3v. (Carnegie Inst. Publ. 185) **CJ92**

Indexes (1) the reports of Congress, (2) the Senate executive journal for diplomatic and consular appointments and treaty ratifications, (3) the opinions of the attorney-general for decisions of questions of international controversy, (4) the statutes-at-large, and (5) the *Congressional globe*.

Moore, John Bassett. Digest of international law. Wash., Govt. Prt. Off., 1906. 8v. (U.S. 56th Cong., 2d sess. House doc. 551)   **CJ93**

Full title: A digest of international law as embodied in diplomatic discussions, treaties and other international agreements, international awards, the decisions of municipal courts, and writings of jurists, and especially in documents, published and unpublished, issued by presidents and secretaries of state of the United States, the opinions of the attorneys-general, and the decisions of courts, federal and state.

v.1–7, Digest; v.8, Index. Table of cases. List of documents.

Hackworth, Green Haywood. Digest of international law. Wash., Govt. Prt. Off., 1940–44. 8v. (In U.S. Dept. of State. Publ.)   **CJ94**

Includes the documents and files accumulated in the Dept. of State since 1906. Supplements and does not duplicate Moore's *Digest* (CJ93).

v.8, General index and list of cases.

Whiteman, Marjorie Millace. Digest of international law. Wash., Govt. Prt. Off., 1963– . v.1–3. (In progress) (U.S. Dept. of State. Publ. 7403, 7553, 7737)   **CJ95**

A compilation of official and unofficial materials.

"Successor digest to Hackworth's *Digest of international law*. . . . Does not incorporate the Hackworth volumes."

A comprehensive index is planned for the final volume.

United Nations. Legal Dept. Laws concerning nationality. [Prep. by the Division for the Development and Codification of International Law] N.Y., United Nations, 1954. 594p. (United Nations legislative ser., no.4) UN Document ST/LEG/ser.B/4.   **CJ96**

—— —— Supplement. 1959. 179p. (United Nations legislative ser., no.9)

Contains the texts of the basic current laws of various states concerning nationality. In English except for those originally published in French.

U.S. Dept. of State. Historical Office. Documents on international aspects of the exploration and use of outer space, 1954–1962. Staff report prepared for the Committee on Aeronautical and Space Sciences, United States Senate. Wash., Govt. Prt. Off., 1963. 407p. (88th Cong., 1st sess. Senate doc. 18)   **CJ97**

Vogel, Robert. A breviate of British diplomatic blue books, 1919–1939. Montreal, McGill Univ. Pr., 1963. 475p.   **CJ98**

A continuation of Harold W. V. Temperley and Lillian M. Penson, *A century of diplomatic blue books*, 1814–1914. Cambridge, Univ. Pr., 1938. 600p.

Attempts to list the titles of all parliamentary papers, published between 1919 and 1939, directly related to British foreign policy. Arranged in chronological order. Includes subject index.

Annuals and current surveys

Documents on American foreign relations, [v.1]– , Jan. 1938/39– . N.Y., Council on Foreign Relations, 1939– . Annual.   **CJ99**

v.8 covers July 1, 1945 to Dec. 31, 1946, instead of the 12-month period July–June of previous volumes. Beginning with v.9, each volume covers a calendar year.

Published by World Peace Foundation, 1938/39–52.

Includes presidential messages, speeches, reports, letters, communiqués, news conference comments, official statements, resolutions, etc.

Documents on international affairs, 1928– . London, Oxford Univ. Pr., 1929– . v.1– . Annual.   **CJ100**

Issued under the auspices of the Royal Institute of International Affairs.

"Prepared to accompany and supplement the annual *Survey of international affairs*."

Coverage is several years behind dates of publication, e.g., 1960 documents appear in 1964 volume.

—— [Supplement]. *Norway and the war,* Sept. 1939–
Dec. 1940, ed. by Monica Curtis. London, Oxford Univ.
Pr., 1941. 154p.

Hague. International Court of Justice. Yearbook. [Hague],
1946/47– . Annual.   **CJ101**

Pub. also in French: *Annuaire.*

Gives information on the composition of the Court, biographies of the judges, lists of the states entitled to appear before the Court, matters dealt with, summary of judgments,
bibliography of works published on the Court, etc.

TREATIES

General

International Intermediary Institute, The Hague. Répertoire général des traités et autres actes diplomatiques
conclus 1895–1920, publié avec le concours financier du
Legatum Visserianum de Leyde. La Haye, Nijhoff, 1926.
516p.   **CJ102**

Indexes 4414 items and refers to text in 144 printed collections and other sources.

Continues Gabriel de Ribier. *Répertoire des traités de paix
. . . entre toutes les puissances du globe, depuis 1867 jusqu'à
nos jours.* Paris, 1895–99. 2v.

Continued in the Institute's *Bulletin de l'Institut Juridique
International,* 1.–42. année, jan. 1919–jan. 1940. (Quarterly)

League of Nations. Treaty series; publication of treaties
and international engagements registered with the Secretariat of the League. v.1–205 (Treaty no.1–4834). Sept.
1920–1944/46. London, Harrison, 1920–46. 205v.
                                                      CJ103

—— —— General index, 1920–1946. no.1–9 (v.1–205).
Geneva, 1927–46. 9v.

Issued at end of every 500 treaties.
Superseded by United Nations. *Treaty series* (CJ105).

Rönnefarth, Helmuth K. G. Konferenzen und Verträge;
Vertrags-Ploetz, ein Handbuch geschichtlich bedeutsamer
Zusammenkünfte und Vereinbarungen. 2. erw. und veränd. Aufl. Würzburg, A. G. Ploetz, 1958–59. T.II, Bd.
3–4. (In progress)   **CJ104**

Contents: T.II: Bd.3, Neuere Zeit, 1492–1914. 1958. 512p.;
Bd.4, Neueste Zeit, 1914–1959. 1959. 697p.

1st ed. 1952.

Provides brief background information, list of parties involved, and a summary of the provisions of historically significant conferences and agreements. It was announced that
Bd.1 would cover *Altertum;* Bd.2, *Mittelalter.*

Bibliography in each volume.

United Nations. Treaty series; treaties and international
agreements registered or filed and recorded with the
Secretariat of the United Nations. v.1– , 1946/47– .
N.Y., 1947– .   **CJ105**

Includes bilingual text, English and French, plus original
language texts.

Chronological index issued at end of every 100 treaties.

United Nations. Secretariat. Systematic survey of treaties
for the pacific settlement of international disputes, 1928–
1948. Lake Success, N.Y., [1949]. 1201p.   **CJ106**

Pt.1, Analyses of treaties; pt.2, Texts of treaties; pt.3,
Tables of treaties: chronological, alphabetical, multipartite.

Myers, Denys Peter. Manual of collections of treaties and
of collections relating to treaties. Cambridge, Harvard
Univ. Pr., 1922. 685p. (Harvard bibliographies. Library
ser., v.2)   **CJ107**

U.S. Dept. of State. Catalogue of treaties, 1814–1918.
Wash., Govt. Prt. Off., 1919. 716p.   **CJ108**

A general chronological catalog of treaties with an index
by countries. Gives information as to place and date signed
and ratified, with references to printed text and indication of
the languages involved.

United States

Davenport, Frances Gardiner. European treaties bearing
on the history of the United States and its dependencies.
Wash., Carnegie Inst., 1917–37. v.1–4. (Carnegie Inst.
Publ. 254)   **CJ109**

v.1–4, 1455–1815.
v.4, ed. by Charles Oscar Paullin.

U.S. Dept. of State. List of treaties submitted to the
Senate, 1789–1934. Wash., Govt. Prt. Off., 1935. 138p.
(Its Publ. 765)   **CJ110**

The "List of treaties submitted" gives for each treaty its
date, subject, and status, e.g., whether accepted without
change, accepted with amendment, withdrawn, etc.; the "Numerical list of the Treaty series" gives for each treaty its date,
country with which negotiated, subject, and a reference to the
volume of the *Statutes at large* (CJ77) containing the text.

—— Treaties submitted to the Senate, 1935–1944. Wash.,
1945. 28p. (Its Publ. no.2311)   **CJ111**

Supersedes annual supplements.

—— Treaties in force; a list of treaties and other international agreements of the United States in force. Wash.,
Govt. Prt. Off., c1929?– . Irregular (Annual since
1958). (Its Publ.)   **CJ112**

Subtitle varies slightly.

U.S. Treaties. Treaties, conventions, international acts,
protocols and agreements between the United States of
America and other powers, 1776–1937. Wash., Govt.
Prt. Off., 1910–38. 4v.   **CJ113**

v.1–2, comp. by William M. Malloy, 1910; v.3, comp. by
C. F. Redmond, 1923; v.4, comp. by Edward J. Trenwith,
1938.

"Contains treaties, conventions, international acts, important protocols and agreements by exchange of notes whether
in force or not, to which the United States has been a party
from 1776 . . . together with other material pertaining to
treaties, a chronological list of treaties by countries, etc."—
Pref.

v.4 includes index to v.1–4.

—— Treaties and other international acts of the United
States of America; ed. by Hunter Miller. Wash., Govt.
Prt. Off., 1931–48. v.1–8. maps. (U.S. Dept. of State.
Publ. no.175, 237, 453, 645, 1017, 1719, 1791, 3141)
(In progress?)   **CJ114**

v.1, Plan of the work, Lists, Tables; v.2–8, 1776–1863.

A revised collection, intended to supersede the collection
by W. M. Malloy (CJ113).

Arranged chronologically, with the text of each treaty given
in English and also in the foreign language in which it was
concluded. v.1 is issued in a preliminary edition to be used
while the rest of the work is in progress, and is to be replaced
eventually by a definitive edition.

Includes bibliographies.

—— Foreign relations of the United States. Diplomatic
papers, 1861– . Wash., Gov. Prt. Off., 1862– . Annual.   **CJ115**

Title varies: 1861–1931, *Papers relating to the foreign relations of the United States.*

Usually cited by binder's title, *Foreign relations.*

Annual volumes of diplomatic correspondence between the
United States and foreign countries. Includes correspondence,
text of treaties, the President's annual message to Congress
(in volumes after 1865), and special messages on foreign subjects, etc. Several volumes published each year, the date of

publication being much later than the year covered, e.g., volumes on 1942 published 1960. Many volumes have subtitles designating the country or area treated, e.g., *The Soviet Union, The Near East and Africa.*

—— —— General index, 1861–99, 1900–1918. Wash., Govt. Prt. Off., 1902–41. 2v.

—— Treaties and other international acts, as of Dec. 27, 1945, no.1501– . Wash., Govt. Prt. Off., 1946– .
                                                                    CJ116
Cited as *T.I.A.S.*
Issued singly in pamphlets. Continues the "Treaty series" ([18--?]–1946), and the "Executive agreement series" (1929–45). The combined numbers in these two series having reached 1500, the new series begins with 1501.
Contains authentic texts of treaties, declarations, constitutions and charters of international organizations, etc.

—— —— Subject index to the Treaty series and the Executive agreement series, July 1, 1931. Wash., Govt. Prt. Off., 1932. 214p.

—— United States treaties and other international agreements, v.1, 1950– . Wash., Govt. Prt. Off., 1952– . Annual.   **CJ117**
From the calendar year 1950, this becomes the official place of publication and legal evidence for treaties and international agreements to which the United States is a party. Prior to this they were included in the *Statutes at large* (CJ77). Arranged in numerical order as originally published in pamphlet form in *Treaties and other international acts* series, no. 1501– (CJ116). Subject and country index.
Suggested form of citation: *U.S.T.*

Great Britain

Gt.Brit. Foreign Office. Treaty series, 1892– . London, Stat. Off., 1892– .   **CJ118**
Issued as command papers, but numbered and indexed so that they can be bound as a separate set. General indexes are issued every few years as one of the numbers in the middle of a volume.

—— British and foreign state papers, 1812– , with which is incorporated Hertslet's Commercial treaties. London, Stat. Off., 1841– . v.1– . Annual.   **CJ119**
Incorporates *Hertslet's Commercial treaties* (CJ120) from v.116, 1922.
Contains treaties, correspondence about foreign affairs, and many documents of historical interest and importance, especially texts of the constitutions of foreign countries and similar organic laws. Each volume has a good index, and there are four general indexes: (1) v.64 indexes v.1–63; (2) v.93 indexes v.65–92; (3) v.115 indexes v.94–114; (4) v.138 indexes v.116–37. Material included is mainly that of the 19th and 20th centuries, but some papers are of an earlier date.

Hertslet's Commercial treaties; a collection of treaties and conventions between Great Britain and foreign powers, and of the laws, decrees, orders in council, etc., concerning the same, so far as they relate to commerce and navigation, slavery, extradition, nationality, copyright, postal matters, etc. London, Stat. Off., 1827–1925. 31v.
                                                                    CJ120
v.22 is general index to v.1–21; v.31 is index to v.23–30. Title varies.
Continued in *British and foreign state papers,* beginning with v.116, 1922 (CJ119).

Latin America

Pan American Union. Dept. of International Law and Organization. Division of Legal Affairs. Bilateral treaties, conventions and agreements in force between the United

States of America and other American republics, as of March 1, 1948. Wash., Pan Amer. Union, 1948. 42p.
                                                                    CJ121
Arranged by country with subject index. References to texts of the documents are included.

Pan American Union. Division of Law and Treaties. Inter-American treaties and conventions. Wash., 1954. 103p.   **CJ122**
Lists treaties and conventions signed at the various conferences of the American states, giving "signatures, ratifications, and deposits with explanatory notes."
Kept up to date by:

—— Status of the Pan American treaties and conventions. Wash., 1936– . Annual.   **CJ123**
In Spanish, English, Portuguese, French.
Gives current information in tabular form.

U.S. Tariff Commission. Reference manual of Latin American commercial treaties. Wash., Govt. Prt. Off., 1940. 281p.   **CJ124**
Attempts to list all commercial treaties and agreements negotiated by the 20 Latin-American countries during the entire period of their history. Also lists noncommercial treaties and agreements which contain commercial provisions.—Cf. *Foreword.*
Arranged alphabetically by country, and chronologically under country. Usually gives date signed, date ratified, date effective, duration, termination, remarks as to provisions, and references to sources where texts in various languages may be found.

CONSTITUTIONS

Collections

Dareste de la Chavanne, François Rodolphe and **Dareste de la Chavanne, Pierre.** Les constitutions modernes . . . traductions accompagnées de notices historiques et de notes explicatives. 4. éd., entièrement refondue par Joseph Delpech et Julien Laferrière. Paris, Recueil Sirey, 1928–34. 6v. in 8. maps.   **CJ125**
v.1–3, Europe; v.4, Amérique Latine; v.5, Empire Britannique, Afrique, Asie, Territoires sous mandat A; v.6, États-Unis d'Amérique du Nord. Les États de l'Union de l'Amérique du Nord; Extra volume, unnumbered, Espagne: Constitution du 9 déc. 1931. 59p.
A comprehensive standard collection; for each country gives: (1) Historical notes, (2) Bibliographical references, and (3) Text, in French, of the constitutions in force, with explanatory notes.

Hawgood, John Arkas. Modern constitutions since 1787. London, Macmillan, 1939. 539p.   **CJ126**
Bibliography, p.467–525.
A textbook with a useful annotated bibliography, which includes collections, texts, commentaries, histories, etc.

Mirkine-Guetzévitch, Boris. Les constitutions européennes. [1ᵉ éd.] Préface de Marcel Prélot. Paris, Presses Universitaires de France, 1951. 2v. (Bibliothèque de la science politique. 1. sér.: Initiation, méthode, documentation)   **CJ127**
t.1, Essai synthétique. Textes des constitutions (Albanie à Finlande); t.2, Textes des constitutions (France à Yougoslavie). Index général.
Texts in French.

Peaslee, Amos Jenkins. Constitutions of nations. 2d ed. . . . The Hague, Nijhoff, 1956. 3v. il.   **CJ128**
Subtitle: The first compilation in the English language of the texts of the constitutions of the various nations of the

world, together with summaries, annotations, bibliographies, and comparative tables.

1st ed. 1950.

v.1, Afghanistan to Finland; v.2, France to New Zealand; v.3, Nicaragua to Yugoslavia.

v.3 also contains an index to the 3v., and an appendix containing data regarding the Baltic States: Estonia, Latvia, and Lithuania.

The 2d edition lists new or amended constitutions for several countries; for others, prefatory descriptions have been revised and bibliographies brought up to date.

Zurcher, Arnold John. Constitutions and constitutional trends since World War II . . . 2d ed. N.Y., New York Univ., [c1955]. 357p.   **CJ129**

1st ed. 1951.

Contains a series of essays by eight American specialists in comparative public law. Includes the texts of representative new constitutions and public documents.

United States

꽃 The text of the Constitution of the United States is given in many general reference books, e.g., *World almanac* (CG55), etc., and is included also in the *United States code* (CJ78), the House and Senate *Manuals* (CI58, CI56), and the various state or legislative manuals. A good edition to keep on hand for reference purposes is that of the *House manual,* which is indexed and contains full notes of all ratifications. State constitutions are given in the various state manuals.

U.S. Constitution. Constitution of the United States of America, analysis and interpretation. Wash., Govt. Prt. Off., 1953. 1361p. (82d Cong., 2d sess. Senate doc. 170)
CJ130

Subtitle: Annotations of cases decided by the Supreme Court of U.S. to June 30, 1952.

Columbia University. Legislative Drafting Research Fund. Constitutions of the United States, national and state. Dobbs Ferry, N.Y., Oceana, [1962–   ]. Loose-leaf.
CJ131

Complete, current texts of the U.S. Constitution and the constitutions of the 50 states, including all provisions in force as of Dec. 31, 1960. An aid in the use of this compilation is provided by the following index:

—— Index digest of state constitutions. 2d ed. [N.Y.], 1959. 1132p.   **CJ132**

—— —— Supplement. Sept. 1, 1958 to Dec. 31, 1960. 119p.

An alphabetical subject index and comparative analysis of all provisions of the 50 state constitutions. Each entry is followed by a citation to the article and section where the full provision may be found.

The Americas

Fitzgibbon, Russell Humke. The constitutions of the Americas, as of Jan. 1, 1948. Chicago, Univ. of Chicago Pr., 1948. 847p.   **CJ133**

Bibliography, p.819–24.

Texts in English of the constitutions of the 20 Latin-American republics, the United States, and Canada.

Lazcano y Mazón, Andrés María. Constituciones políticas de América. La Habana, Cuba, Cultural, 1942. 2v. **CJ134**

A treatise on the constitutional law of the 20 Latin-American republics, plus the United States, followed by the texts of the constitutions of each country in Spanish.

INTERNATIONAL ORGANIZATIONS

Carnegie Endowment for International Peace. Division of International Law. Handbook of international organizations in the Americas, prep. by Ruth D. Masters and others. Wash., Endowment, 1945. 453p. (Its Publ.)
CJ135

Description of 109 international organizations which have their headquarters in the Western hemisphere. For each organization usually gives history, purpose and functions, membership, administration, meetings, publications, and a brief bibliographical note.

Council on Foreign Relations. American agencies interested in international affairs, comp. by Donald Wasson. 5th ed. N.Y., Praeger, [c1964]. 200p.   **CJ136**

1st ed. 1931. First four editions compiled by Ruth Savord.

A directory listing 293 private organizations "which conduct serious programs of research in international affairs." A few international organizations with strong American interest are included.

Information given includes name, address, founding date, activities, publications, personnel, etc. Contains a subject and personnel index.

European Communities. Information Service. Guide des communautés européennes: Marché commun, Euratom, C.E.C.A. Bruxelles, Luxembourg, 1962. 179p.   **CJ137**

International congresses and conferences, 1840–1937; a union list of their publications available in libraries of the United States and Canada, ed. by Winifred Gregory under the auspices of the Bibliographical Society of America. . . . N.Y., Wilson, 1938. 229p.   **CJ138**

Running title: Union list of international congresses.

Arranged alphabetically by name of congress or conference. Includes subject index.

Excludes diplomatic congresses and conferences, and those held under the auspices of the League of Nations. Lists holdings in more than 100 libraries.

Lawson, Ruth Catherine. International regional organizations; constitutional foundations. Ed. with introductory notes. N.Y., Praeger, [1962]. 387p.   **CJ139**

Gives texts of treaties, charters, etc., establishing regional organizations, including OAS, SEATO, NATO, etc., with commentary.

Peaslee, Amos Jenkins. International governmental organizations: constitutional documents. Rev. 2d ed., prep. by the editor and Dorothy Peaslee Xydis. The Hague, Nijhoff, 1961. 2v.   **CJ140**

1st ed. 1956.

Arranged alphabetically by organization; contains the basic constitutional documents of more than 100 "international organizations created by governments, and themselves of a governmental nature." Unofficial private organizations are not included.

Brief summaries of the history and constitutional development, membership, functions, organs, headquarters, etc. are given for each organization, with selective bibliographies.

White, Lyman Cromwell. International nongovernmental organizations; their purposes, methods, and accomplishments. New Brunswick, N.J., Rutgers Univ. Pr., 1951. 325p.   **CJ141**

For full information *see* AC21.

Current

International organization, v.1–   . Boston, World Peace Foundation, 1947–   . Quarterly.   **CJ142**

Includes summaries of activities, documents on international organizations, and bibliographies of current materials.

Yearbook of international organizations. Annuaire des organisations internationales. 1948– . 1st ed.– . Brussels, Union of Internat. Assoc., 1948– . Annual, 1948–50. Biennial, beginning with 1951–52. **CJ143**

In English and French, varying with editions.

A comprehensive work, giving a general survey and detailed information about international organizations and associations, currently active. Considerable information is provided here by the United Nations in lieu of publishing its own yearbook in this field.

In six parts: pts.1–5 concern official and nonofficial organizations; pt.6 includes tables, commentaries, and indexes.

Year book of world affairs. v.1– , 1947– , pub. under the auspices of the London Institute of World Affairs. London, Stevens and Sons, 1947– . **CJ144**

Survey articles, book reviews, etc.

Calendars

Annual international congress calendar, [no.1]. 1961 ed.– . Brussels, Union of Internat. Assoc., 1961– . Annual. **CJ145**

"A chronological listing of international congresses, conferences, meetings, symposia scheduled to take place in [current] and subsequent years . . . Date, place, address of organizing body, theme, estimated number of participants . . . and plans for publishing reports or 'proceedings' are indicated . . ." —*Title page.*

World list of future international meetings. June 1959– . Wash., Reference Dept., Lib. of Congress. June, 1959– . Monthly. **CJ146**

For full information *see* AC22.

League of Nations

Aufricht, Hans. Guide to League of Nations publications; a bibliographical survey of the work of the League, 1920–1947. N.Y., Columbia Univ. Pr., 1951. 682p. **CJ147**

Selective, but includes some items that were confidential and some that were never on public sale. Emphasis is on the inclusion of important publications. Also lists publications of affiliated organizations, such as the International Labor Office and the Permanent Court of International Justice.

Appendixes include texts of documents relating to the League of Nations, the transfer of the League of Nations assets to the United Nations, and the Statutes of the International Labor Office and the Permanent Court of International Justice.

Arrangement is by broad subject with index.

Carroll, Marie Juliette. Key to League of nations documents placed on public sale, 1920–1929. Boston, World Peace Foundation, 1930. 340p. **CJ148**

—— —— 1st–4th supplements, 1930–1934/36. Boston, 1931–36.

Contents: 1930, 1931, 1932–33, 1934–36.

The 4th supplement was published by Columbia University Press.

—— —— Supplement, 1937–1947, prep. in the Law Library of Columbia University, listing the documents in its collection. [1953] [63p.]

United Nations

Arne, Sigrid. The United Nations primer. Rev. ed. N.Y., Farrar, 1948. 266p. **CJ149**

Discussions and texts of documents of the international conferences that preceded and led up to the organization of the United Nations.

The revised edition adds the Potsdam conference and the meeting of the Council of Foreign Ministers.

Brimmer, Brenda [and others]. A guide to the use of United Nations documents. Dobbs Ferry, N.Y., Oceana, 1962. 272p. **CJ150**

An excellent guide for the research worker in using UN materials and for the librarian in organizing a UN collection regardless of size.

Chamberlin, Waldo and **Hovet, Thomas.** A chronology and fact book of the United Nations, 1941–1964. Dobbs Ferry, N.Y., Oceana, 1964. 95p. (Oceana library on the United Nations) **CJ151**

1959 edition had title *A chronology of the United Nations, 1941–1958.*

A chronological listing of the important acts, events, meetings, membership, etc. of the UN, many with brief identifying statement. Subject index.

Everyman's United Nations; the structure, functions and work of the United Nations and its related agencies . . . 7th ed. N.Y., United Nations, Dept. of Public Information, [1964]. 638p. **CJ152**

1st ed. 1948. Frequently revised.

A handbook in four parts: pt.1 discusses the organization of the United Nations; pt.2, its work concerning political, economic, social, and security questions, and administrative matters; pt.3, the specialized agencies, e.g., International Labor Organization (I.L.O.), Food and Agriculture Organization (F.A.O.), United Nations Educational, Scientific and Cultural Organization (UNESCO), and many others; pt.4, United Nations chronology for 1963, United Nations Information Centres, and Index.

Goodrich, Leland Matthew and **Hambro, Edvard.** Charter of the United Nations; commentary and documents. 2d and rev. ed. Boston, World Peace Foundation, 1949. 710p. **CJ153**

Select bibliography, p.659–81.

Royal Institute of International Affairs. United Nations documents, 1941–1945. London, N.Y., Inst., [1946]. 271p. **CJ154**

Includes the texts of various documents "concerning the origin of the United Nations, its character and other international organizations formed in association with it down to the end of 1945" (*Pref.*), e.g., the Declaration of Solidarity of the United Nations; the Atlantic Charter; the lend-lease agreements; the communiqués or reports of the Teheran, Cairo, Yalta, Berlin, and Moscow conferences; constitutions of international organizations, etc.

United Nations. Library, New York. A bibliography of the charter of the United Nations. Bibliographie de la charte des Nations Unies. N.Y., 1955. 128p. (Its Bibliographical ser., no.3) **CJ155**

Lists some 2900 items on the United Nations charter including books, documents, and periodical articles.

—— Yearbook of the United Nations, 1946/47– . N.Y., United Nations, Dept. of Public Information, 1947– . Annual. il. **CJ156**

The 3d yearbook covered Sept. 21, 1948 to Dec. 31, 1949. Each succeeding volume covers a calendar year.

Summarizes the activities, proceedings, and decisions of the United Nations. v.1, 1946/47, covers the origin and evolution of the United Nations, the 1st General Assembly, and the organization and work of subsidiary and allied organizations. Includes documentary bibliography, subject index, and an index of names.

Publications

United Nations. United Nations books in print. N.Y., United Nations, 1960. 152p. (ST/CS/SER.J/1) **CJ157**

In English, French, and Spanish.

Lists all United Nations publications available for sale. Omits official records of the United Nations, and out-of-print and obsolete material. Includes subject-title index.

—— —— Supplement. Publications issued in 1960 and 1961. (ST/CS/SER.J/1/Add.1)

United Nations. Dag Hammarskjöld Library. Checklist of United Nations documents, 1946–49. N.Y., 1949–52?. (ST/LIB/SER.F) **CJ158**

Originally intended to be "a complete list of the documents issued by the organs of the United Nations," printed and mimeographed.

Issued in parts, each one devoted to the documents of a particular unit.

Every part issued in consecutive numbers, the initial numbers covering 1946–49.

A very detailed indexing, with information as to original publication and where documents were republished, if any. Detailed subject index.

Continued in part by:

United Nations. Dag Hammarskjöld Library. Documents Index Unit. United Nations documents index. Jan. 1950– . N.Y., 1950– . v.1– . Monthly. **CJ159**

A checklist and a subject index, the index cumulating annually.

Covers the United Nations documents and publications received in the Documents Index Unit.

Beginning with v.14 (1963), the monthly issues are replaced and superseded by two separate annual cumulations: (1) Cumulative checklist, and (2) Cumulative (subject) index.

United Nations. Dept. of Public Information. Ten years of United Nations publications, 1945 to 1955; a complete catalogue. N.Y., 1955. 271p. (ST/DPI/SER.F/7) **CJ160**

A cumulative sales catalog, listing all publications issued by the United Nations and for sale since the beginning. Does not include publications of the specialized agencies.

Continued by:

—— United Nations publications, 1955–1958. Annual. (ST/DPI/SER.F/8–11) **CJ161**

United Nations. Office of Conference Services. United Nations official records, 1948–1962. N.Y., United Nations, 1963. 107p. (ST/CS/SER.J/2) **CJ162**

At head of title: A reference catalogue.

A complete listing of the official records by year, or by session, including number and price.

—— United Nations publications, 1945–1963. N.Y., United Nations, 1964. 71p. (ST/CS/SER.J/3) **CJ163**

At head of title: A reference catalogue.

Arranged in 17 categories, each title preceded by an identifying sales number.

Kept up to date by annual issues. (ST/CS/SER.J/3/Add. 1–)

A *Monthly sales bulletin,* listing current publications for sale, may be obtained from the United Nations, Sales Section, New York, N.Y.

C K

Geography

⚜ For answering questions in geography five principal types of reference books are useful:

1. Bibliographies and indexes to the material published in books, periodicals, and the publications of learned societies *list of mat. about a place*
2. Gazetteers, both general and special, which serve to tell where a given place is and furnish descriptive information about it
3. Dictionaries of place-names, which indicate the origin and meaning of such names, and the different forms which have been in use at different times
4. Atlases, which supply maps and, through their indexes, aid in the location of places
5. Guidebooks, which supply a different kind of descriptive material from that given in the gazetteers, and contain many maps, especially local maps and town plans, not given in the general atlases

Wright and Platt's *Aids to geographical research* (CK1), although now out of date, is a very valuable guide to geographical reference materials and should be consulted for aid in selecting books for the library and for discovering what books to use to answer particular reference questions.

The average library will need a comprehensive gazetteer, such as the *Columbia Lippincott gazetteer* (CK30) or *Webster's Geographical dictionary* (CK34), and a general atlas, such as Rand, McNally's *Cosmopolitan world atlas* (CK222) or the *Encyclopaedia Britannica world atlas* (CK210). It should also be remembered that most of the general encyclopedias include maps, either gathered together in an atlas volume or scattered throughout the volumes with the articles on the regions covered.

Automobile road maps, furnished by gasoline dealers, are also useful for certain types of questions.

GENERAL WORKS

Guides

Wright, John Kirtland and **Platt, Elizabeth T.** Aids to geographical research; bibliographies, periodicals, atlases, gazetteers, and other reference books. 2d ed. compl. rev. N.Y., pub. for the American Geographical Society by Columbia Univ. Pr., 1947. 331p. (American Geographical Soc. Research ser., no.22) **CK1**

1st ed. 1923.

A completely revised and rearranged edition of this invaluable manual. In three main sections: (1) General aids; (2) Topical aids; (3) Regional aids and general geographical periodicals from each country. The coverage is comprehensive and includes materials in many languages. Annotations are descriptive and evaluative. Author, subject, and title index.

Includes, as an appendix, a "Classified index of American

professional geographers, libraries of geographical utility, and institutions engaged in geographical research," p.276–94.

Bibliography

American Geographical Society. Library. Research catalogue. Boston, G. K. Hall, 1962. 15v. and map suppl.   **CK2**

A photographic reproduction of the cards in the Research Catalogue, arranged by a systematic classification and a regional classification. Includes books, periodical articles, pamphlets, and government documents.

Bring, Samuel Ebbe. Itineraria svecana; bibliografisk förteckning över resor i Sverige fram till 1950. Stockholm, Almqvist & Wiksell, 1954. 586p. il. (Svenska bibliotekariesamfundets skriftserie, 3)   **CK3**

A bibliography of works of travel in Scandinavia, in various languages. Arranged chronologically, 944–1950, with author index.

Cox, Edward Godfrey. A reference guide to the literature of travel, including voyages, geographical descriptions, adventures, shipwrecks and expeditions. Seattle, Univ. of Wash., 1935–49. 3v. (Univ. of Washington. Publ. in language and literature, v.9–10, 12)   **CK4**

v.1, The Old World. 401p.; v.2, The New World. 591p.; v.3, Great Britain. 732p.

Classified with author index.

Lists "in chronological order, from the earliest date ascertainable down to and including the year 1800, all the books on foreign travels, voyages and descriptions printed in Great Britain, together with translations from foreign tongues and continental renderings of English works. . . ."—*Pref.*

Dumont, Maurice E. and **Smet, L. de.** Aardrijkskundige bibliographie van België; Bibliographie géographique de la Belgique. Gent, Seminarie voor Menselijke Aardrijkskunde der Rijksuniversiteit, 1954–56. 450p. (Bibliographia belgica, 14–17)   **CK5**

A classed bibliography of the geography of Belgium, interpreted to include physical, human, economic geography, etc. Author index.

Engelmann, Wilhelm. Bibliotheca geographica. Verzeichnis der seit der Mitte des vorigen Jahrhunderts bis zu Ende des Jahres 1856 in Deutschland erschienenen Werke über Geographie und Reisen, mit Einschluss der Landkarten, Pläne und Ansichten. Leipzig, Engelmann, 1858. 1225p.   **CK6**

A comprehensive list of 18th– and 19th-century German works on geography and travels in various parts of the world, arranged for the most part by geographical location. Subject index.

Fossati Bellani, Luigi Vittorio. I libri di viaggio e le guide della raccolta Luigi Vittorio Fossati Bellani: catalogo descrittivo a cura di Antonio Pescarzoli. Roma, Ed. di Storia e Letteratura, 1957. 3v. (Sussidi eruditi, 9–11)   **CK7**

The catalog of a private collection of Italian travel literature containing more than 5000 books and pamphlets from earliest times to the present. With the exception of some 300 rare items on general travel, the works deal with Italy. Most of the works are in Italian, though other western European languages are represented. Detailed bibliographic descriptions.

Giraldo Jaramillo, Gabriel. Bibliografía colombiana de viajes. Bogotá, Ed. A.B.C., 1957. 224p. (Biblioteca de bibliografía colombiana. II)   **CK8**

A bibliography of books and articles in various languages on travels in Colombia. In two parts: (1) Viajeros colombianos; (2) Viajeros extranjeros en Colombia.

Titles are mainly from the 19th and 20th centuries.

International Geographical Union. Special Commission

on the Humid Tropics. A select annotated bibliography of the humid tropics, comp. by Theo L. Hills. Montreal, Geography Dept., McGill Univ., 1960. 238p.   **CK9**

Comprises several thousand items, arranged by continent, then by country or other smaller area. Within each is given a classed list of books, articles, and reports, including general and social materials as well as geographical. Annotations generally very brief. No indexes.

Lautensach, Hermann and **Feio, Mariano.** Bibliografia geográfica de Portugal. Lisboa, Inst. para a Alta Cultura, Centro de Estudos Geográficos, 1948. 256p.   **CK10**

Based on bibliographies covering 1915–43, prepared for the *Geographisches Jahrbuch,* v.45 and 59, and for *Portugal auf Grund eigener Reisen und der Literatur.* 1937.

Lists Portuguese geographical works from early times. Geography is broadly interpreted to include climate, anthropology, ethnography, agriculture, fishing, commerce, etc.

Mexico. Dirección General de Geografía y Meteorología. Bibliografía geográfica de México, recopilación y ordenamiento de Angel Bassols Batalla. México, 1955. 652p.   **CK11**

A comprehensive bibliography dealing with the geography of Mexico: historical, physical, economic, etc. Classed arrangement with geographical and author indexes.

Pelzer, Karl Josef. Selected bibliography on the geography of southeast Asia. New Haven, Conn., Southeast Asia Studies, Yale Univ., by arrangement with Human Relations Area Files, 1949–56. v.1–3. (Behavior science bibliographies) (In progress)   **CK12**

v.1, Southeast Asia—general. 1949; v.2, The Philippines. 1950; v.3, Malaya. 1956.

"A companion to the bibliography of *Peoples and cultures of mainland southeast Asia* by Professor John F. Embree" (*Pref.*), for which *see* DE30.

Entries, which include monographs and periodical articles on physical, cultural, economic, and political geography, are arranged under broad subject headings, with no index. Subsequent volumes were announced to cover Indonesia, Burma, Siam, and Indochina.

Royal Geographical Society, London. New geographical literature and maps. London, 1951– . n.s. v.1– . Semi-annual.   **CK12a**

Lists books and articles in leading British and foreign geographical journals, and new maps and atlases. Also contains annual lists of completed theses in geography from British universities.

Issued 1918–41 as *Recent geographical literature, maps, and photographs . . .* as a supplement to *Geographical journal.*

U.S. Library of Congress. Reference Dept. Soviet geography: a bibliography. Nicholas R. Rodionoff, ed. Wash., 1951. 668p.   **CK13**

Pt.1, U.S.S.R. geography by subject; pt.2, Administrative, natural and economic regions.

Geography "is construed herein as the science describing the land, sea, air and the distribution of plant and animal life, excluding man but not his industries."—*Pref.*

Material is largely in Russian. Locates copies.

Weber, Shirley Howard. Voyages and travels in the Near East made during the XIX century; being a part of a larger catalogue of works on geography, cartography, voyages, and travels, in the Gennadius Library in Athens. Princeton, N.J., Amer. School of Classical Studies at Athens, 1952–53. v.1–2. (In progress) (Catalogues of the Gennadius Library, I, II)   **CK14**

The Gennadius Library in Athens is a rich and unique collection of more than 55,000 books, pictures, and maps relating to Greece, the Balkans, and the Near East from medieval to modern times. Pt.1 contains 1206 annotated titles, representing only a portion of the material on geography and travel in the library. The titles are entered by date of publication; a general index and a name index of travelers and authors are given at the end of the volume.

Pt.2 lists 835 titles from the 1st century to 1801, preceding in time the period covered in pt.1. Its title varies slightly: *Voyages and travels in Greece, the Near East and adjacent regions made previous to the year 1801.*

Periodicals

Harris, Chauncy D. Annotated world list of selected current geographical serials in English: including an appendix of major serials in other languages with regular supplementary or partial basic use of English. 2d ed. rev. and enl. Chicago, Univ. of Chicago, Dept. of Geography, 1964. 32p. (Research paper, no.96)   **CK15**

1st ed. 1960.

A selected and annotated list of 62 serials, definitely geographical in coverage, solely or dominantly in English; and 56 others in 28 languages which regularly use English in abstracts or in combination with other languages.

—— and Fellmann, Jerome D. International list of geographical serials. Chicago, 1960. 194p. (Univ. of Chicago. Dept. of Geography. Research paper, no.63)   **CK16**

Supersedes the authors' *Union list of geographical serials,* 2d ed. 1950.

Arranged by country with index by title of periodical. Includes both current serials and those no longer published. Does not indicate location of files, but does include references to listings in the existing union lists of the United States, Canada, and the British Isles.

Current surveys

Bibliographie géographique internationale, 1891– . Paris, Centre National de la Recherche Scientifique, 1894– . v.1– . Annual.   **CK17**

Title varies slightly; v.1–24 issued with *Annales de géographie.* Publisher varies.

A useful classified bibliography with alphabetical author index. Annotated.

The most important of the annual bibliographies.

Bibliotheca geographica; Jahresbibliographie der geographischen Literatur. Hrsg. von der Gesellschaft für Erdkunde zu Berlin, 1891/1892–1911/12. Berlin, Kuhl, 1895–1917. 19v.   **CK18**

Subtitle varies.

Important annual bibliography of books and periodical articles, listing more titles than the French list noted above (CK17), but without annotations. Classified, with author index. No more published.

Geographisches Jahrbuch, 1866– . Gotha, Perthes, 1866– . v.1– . Annual (Irregular).   **CK19**

—— Index, 1866–1925, in v.40, p.ix–xix.

A comprehensive and extensive series usually published annually. Each volume includes surveys of the published work in special geographical fields, the fields varying from year to year. For a convenient key to the reports in this series, *see* Wright and Platt, *Aids to geographical research,* p.52–57 (CK1).

Dictionaries and encyclopedias

British Association for the Advancement of Science. Research Committee. A glossary of geographical terms . . . ed. by L. Dudley Stamp. London, Longmans; N.Y., Wiley, 1961. 539p.   **CK20**

Covers physical, human, social, and economic geography, "limited to terms used in current geographical literature written in English."—*Pref.*

Fischer, Eric and **Elliott, Francis E.** A German and English glossary of geographical terms. N.Y., Amer. Geographical Soc., 1950. 111p. (Its Library ser., no.5)   **CK21**

German-English, English-German.

Grigor'ev, A. A. Kratkaia geograficheskaia entsiklopediia. Moskva, Gos. Izd-vo "Sovetskaia Entsiklopediia," 1960–64. v.1–4. il. maps. (In progress)   **CK22**

Contents: v.1–4, A–IUgoslaviia (completing main alphabet).

A concise geographical encyclopedia. Covers various phases of economic and physical geography. A supplementary volume is announced.

Moore, Wilfred George. A dictionary of geography: definitions and explanations of terms used in physical geography. 3d ed. Harmondsworth, Middlesex, Eng., Penguin, 1963. 196p. il.   **CK23**

Handbooks

Huxley, Anthony Julian. Standard encyclopedia of the world's mountains. [1st ed.] N.Y., Putnam, 1962. 383p. il. maps.   **CK24**

For full information *see* EE39.

—— Standard encyclopedia of the world's oceans and islands. [1st ed.] N.Y., Putnam, 1962. 383p. il., maps.   **CK25**

For full information *see* EE123.

Mirot, Léon. Manuel de géographie historique de la France. 2. éd. Ouvrage posthume revu et publié par Albert Mirot. Paris, Picard, 1947–50. 2v. maps, genealogical tables.   **CK26**

Contents: v.1, L'unité française; v.2, Les divisions religieuses et administratives de la France.

1st ed. 1929.

A manual, with maps, of the historical geography of France from the Gallo-Roman period to the 20th century. The first volume deals with France as a whole, the second with its ecclesiastical and administrative divisions. Extensive indexes to persons, places, and subjects.

Directories

Geographisches Taschenbuch und Jahrweiser für deutschen Landeskunde. Wiesbaden, F. Steiner, 1949– . il. Biennial.   **CK27**

—— Supplementband. 1960/61– . Wiesbaden, 1960– .

A biennial handbook including regional reports and papers, research and expeditions, etc., and a directory of authorities, institutes and organizations, in specified countries, etc.

Orbis geographicus. World directory of geography. Adressar géographique du monde. Geographisches Weltadressbuch, 1960– . Wiesbaden, F. Steiner, 1960– .   **CK28**

1952 had title *World directory of geographers,* prepared with the financial assistance of UNESCO.

1960– , compiled and edited on behalf of the International Geographic Union in cooperation with the national committees by E. Meynen, and issued as Sonderheft of *Geographisches Taschenbuch.*

Lists geographical societies, congresses, institutes, medals, etc., and includes a directory of geographers by country.

GAZETTEERS

❧ The gazetteer, or dictionary of places, is an interesting type of reference book in which the most recently revised work and the old work are of almost equal value, although for different purposes. If the question calls for current information about a place—its present population, importance, industries, its political affiliations, i.e., the county, state, province, nation, within which it is located—only the most recent works in the field will serve, and the older works may be almost worthless or even misleading.

On the other hand, the old gazetteer is often very useful for historical information, for place-names that have since changed, or for bits of local history that are difficult to find elsewhere. An old gazetteer which indicates the industries that flourished in a town a century ago may be a source for the economic or social history of the place, and, if the relative importance of the place has declined, may treat it at greater length than the more modern work can afford to do. For countries for which no good older gazetteer is available, an old encyclopedia will sometimes serve this same purpose. The 18th-century German encyclopedia by Zedler (AD41) is often useful for place-names not included in modern reference books.

General

Chambers's World gazetteer and geographical dictionary, ed. by T. C. Collocott and J. O. Thorne. Edinburgh, London, Chambers, 1954. 792p. **CK29**

Issued in the United States as *Macmillan world gazetteer and geographical dictionary*. N.Y., Macmillan, 1955.

A useful, small, general gazetteer with emphasis on Great Britain. Indicates pronunciation.

Columbia Lippincott gazetteer of the world, ed. by Leon E. Seltzer with the Geographical Research Staff of Columbia University Press and with the cooperation of the American Geographical Society, with 1961 suppl. N.Y., Columbia Univ. Pr., 1962. 2148p., 23p. **CK30**

1st ed. 1952.

A successor to *Lippincott's New gazetteer* (published in various editions, 1855–1931) but essentially a completely new work. Lists, in one alphabet, the places of the world, both political subdivisions and geographic features, giving variant spellings, pronunciation, population (with date), geographical and political location, altitude, trade, industry, agriculture, natural resources, communications, history, cultural institutions, and other pertinent facts. Comprises some 130,000 names with more than 30,000 cross references. The supplement (available separately) includes the major politico-geographical changes since 1952, with identification of new nations. Contains 1960 United States census figures.

A very important work for all libraries that can afford it.

Union Postale Universelle. Bureau International. Dictionnaire des bureaux de poste. 5. éd. Berne, Bureau Internat. de l'Union Postale Universelle, 1951. 2v. **CK31**

An alphabetical listing of some 300,000 places, giving county, state, province, and country. Names of countries in various languages are given at the beginning of the volume.

U.S. Board on Geographic Names. Gazetteer. no.1–85. Wash., Govt. Prt. Off., 1955–64. Irregular. (In progress) **CK32**

Prepared in the Office of Geography, Dept. of the Interior.

Each number is on a special country, listing places and geographical features, with approved names and cross references from variant names, latitude and longitude, and location on specified official maps.

Contents: 1, British East Africa. 1955; 2, Madagascar, Réunion, [etc.]. 1955; 3, Jordan. 1955; 4, Bolivia. 1955; 5, Hong Kong, Macao, Sinkiang, Taiwan, and Tibet. 1955; 6, Chile, 1955; 7, British West Indies and Bermuda. 1955; 8, Albania. 1955; 9, Burma. 1955; 10, British Borneo, Singapore, and Malaya. 1955; 11, Greece. 1955; 12, Japan. 1955; 13, Indonesia, [etc.]. 1955; 14, Antarctica. 1956; 15, Mexico. 1956; 16, British Honduras. 1956; 17, Rhodesia and Nyasaland. 1956; 18, Costa Rica. 1956; 19, Iran. 1956; 20, Angola. 1956; 21, Uruguay. 1956; 22, China. 1956; 23, Italy, [etc.]. 1956; 24, Hawaiian Islands. 1956; 25, Nicaragua. 1956; 26, El Salvador. 1956; 27, Honduras. 1956; 28, Haiti. 1956; 29, Southwest Pacific. 1956; 30, Cuba. 1957; 31, South Atlantic. 1957; 32, Indian Ocean. 1957; 33, Dominican Republic. 1957; 34, French West Indies. 1957; 35, Paraguay. 1957; 36, Ecuador. 1957; 37, Iraq. 1957; 38, Puerto Rico, Virgin Islands, [etc.]. 1958; 39, South Pacific. 1957; 40, Australia. 1957; 41, Libya. 1958;

42, U.S.S.R. and certain neighboring areas. 1959; 43, Germany: Soviet Zone and East Berlin. 1959; 44, Bulgaria. 1959; 45, Egypt and the Gaza Strip. 1959; 46, Turkey. 1960; 47, Germany: Federal Republic and West Berlin. 1960; 48, Rumania. 1960; 49, Ceylon. 1960; 50, Portugal and the Cape Verde Islands. 1961; 51, Spain and Andorra. 1961; 52, Hungary. 1961; 53, Denmark and the Faeroe Islands. 1961; 54, Arabian Peninsula. 1961; 55, Yugoslavia. 1961; 56, Venezuela. 1961; 57, Iceland. 1961; 58, Southern Vietnam and the South China Sea. 1961; 59, Gabon. 1962; 60, Cameroon. 1962; 61, Republic of Congo (Brazzaville). 1962; 62, Finland. 1962; 63, Rio Muni, Fernando Po, and São Tomé e Principe. 1962; 64, Central African Republic. 1962; 65, Chad. 1962; 66, Austria. 1962; 67, Pakistan. 1962; 68, Sudan. 1962; 69, Laos. 1962; 70, Mainland China. 1963; 71, Brazil. 1963; 72, Sweden. 1963; 73, Belgium. 1963; 74, Cambodia. 1963; 75, North Korea. 1963; 76, Zanzibar. 1964; 77, Norway, Svalbard, and Jan Mayen. 1963; 78, Kenya. 1964; 79, Northern Vietnam. 1964; 80, Republic of the Congo (Léopoldville). 1964; 81, Tunisia. 1964; 82, Uganda. 1964; 83, France. v.1–2. 1964; 84, Burundi. 1964; 85, Rwanda. 1964.

now to 101

Vivien de Saint Martin, Louis and **Rousselet, Louis.** Nouveau dictionnaire de géographie universelle. Paris, Hachette, 1879–95. 7v. **CK33**

———— ——— Supplément. Paris, Hachette, 1895–1900. 2v.

The most complete of the general gazetteers, covering physical, political, economic, and historical geography, ethnography, etc. The longer articles are by specialists and are of a high grade; information is much fuller than that given in the *Columbia Lippincott* (CK30); and many names are included, especially minor European or Asiatic names which are not given in works in English. Not up to date now and less useful for ordinary questions than the *Columbia Lippincott,* but more useful than that work when very detailed or out-of-the-way information is needed. Includes names of tribes and races, as well as place-names.

Webster's Geographical dictionary; a dictionary of names of places with geographical and historical information and pronunciations. [Rev. ed.] Springfield, Mass., Merriam, 1962. 1293p. maps. **CK34**

First pub. 1949; reprinted from time to time with slight corrections in plates.

A pronouncing dictionary of more than 40,000 geographical names, including not only current but also historical names from Biblical times, ancient Greece and Rome, medieval Europe, and World Wars I and II. Cross references are given for equivalent and alternative spellings of names that have been changed. Gives the usual gazetteer information, e.g., location, area, population, altitudes of mountains, etc.; for the largest cities, important countries, and each of the United States, also gives geographical features, historical monuments, and a concise history. Includes full-page, and smaller, inset maps and an appendix of historical maps in color.

Introductory material includes a list of geographical terms with their equivalents in various foreign languages.

Ancient and medieval

Besnier, Maurice. Lexique de géographie ancienne. Paris, Klincksieck, 1914. 893p. **CK35**

A compact handbook; gives only brief information about each place, but is full in its references to ancient writers in whose works the place is mentioned. Useful on account of these many references.

Deschamps, Pierre. Dictionnaire de géographie ancienne et moderne. Paris, Firmin-Didot, 1870. 1592col. **CK36**

Also issued as v.9 of Brunet's *Manuel du libraire* (AA58).

Arranged alphabetically by the medieval name (Latin or Greek); gives, under each, an indication of the modern name and brief information about the place with special emphasis upon the history of printing in that place, establishment of presses, etc. Index of modern names.

Grässe, Johann Georg Theodor. Orbis latinus; oder, Verzeichnis der wichtigsten lateinischen Orts- und Ländernamen. Ein Supplement zu jedem lateinischen und geographischen Wörterbuch. 2. Aufl., mit besonderer Berücksichtigung der mittelalterlichen und neueren Latinität, neubearb. von Friedrich Benedict. Berlin, Schmidt; N.Y., Steiger, 1909. 348p. (1922 repr.) **CK37**

The 1st edition, 1866, was in two parts: (1) Latin names; (2) Modern names. The 2d edition includes only pt.1; where pt.2 is needed, the 1st edition must still be used.

A listing of medieval Latin place-names with their modern equivalents.

Smith, *Sir* **William.** Dictionary of Greek and Roman geography. London, Murray; Boston, Little, 1873–78. 2v. il., maps. **CK38**

A standard work of the 19th century, still useful for its detailed articles on places of the ancient world. Includes many references to classical authors.

United States

☙ No geographical dictionary of the whole United States is available. A possible substitute for such a work, in addition to the general gazetteers, is Ayer's *Directory of newspapers* (AF13), which gives brief, up-to-date gazetteer information about each city or town for which a newspaper is listed.

The following, though not formal gazetteers, are useful:

Douglas, Edward Morehouse. Boundaries, areas, geographic centers and altitudes of the United States and the several states, with a brief record of important changes in their territory and government. 2d ed. repr. with corrections. Wash., Govt. Prt. Off., 1939. 265p. il., maps. (U.S. Geological Survey. Bull. 817) **CK39**

1st ed. 1923; 2d ed. 1932.

A useful compilation, giving the histories and changes of the boundaries of the United States and of the individual states and territories, with references to sources.

Gannett, Henry. Dictionary of altitudes in the United States. 4th ed. Wash., Govt. Prt. Off., 1906. 1072p. (U.S. Geological Survey. Bull. 274) **CK40**

Arranged alphabetically by state, and under state by city; gives altitude and refers to authority.

Albania

Permanent Committee on Geographical Names for British Official Use. A gazetteer of Albania. Prep. . . . at the house of the Royal Geographical Society. London, pr. by Williams, Lea, & Co., 1946. 210p. **CK41**

Argentina

Argentine Republic. Instituto Geográfico Militar. Diccionario geográfico argentino. [Buenos Aires], 1954– . v.1–2. (In progress) **CK42**

Contents: t.1, Entre Rios, Corrientes, Misiones; t.2, Neuquén. Río Negro. Chubut. Comodoro Rivadavia. Santa Cruz. Tierra del Fuego. Malvinas.

Each volume, A–Z.

Latzina, Francisco. Diccionario geográfico argentino, con ampliaciones enciclopédicas rioplatenses. 3. ed. Buenos Aires, Peuser, 1899. 814p. **CK43**

Long historical and statistical articles on places in the Argentine.

Belgium

Seyn, Eugène de. Dictionnaire historique et géographique des communes belges. 3. éd., augm. et mise à jour. Turnhout, Brepols, [194?]. 2v. (1562p.). il., maps. **CK44**

1st ed. 1924–26. 2v.

Gives detailed information on each place with historical notes, coats of arms, population to 1938, etc.

Bolivia

Diccionario geográfico de la República de Bolivia. La Paz, Impr. "El Nacional" de I. V. Vila, 1890–1904. 4v. il. **CK45**

v.2 and v.4, pub. by the Oficina Nacional de Inmigración, Estadística y Propaganda Geográfica.

v.1, M. V. Ballivián y E. Idiaquez. Departamento de La Paz. 1890; v.2, F. Blanco. Departamento de Cochabamba. 1901; v.3, Sociedad Geográfica Sucre. Departamento de Chuquisaca. 1903; v.4, P. A. Blanco. Departamento de Oruro. 1904.

No more published.

Brazil

Moreira Pinto, Alfredo. Apontamentos para o Diccionario geographico do Brazil. Rio de Janeiro. Impr. Nacional, 1894–99. 3v. **CK46**

Canada

☙ No complete geographical dictionary of Canada is available. In addition to the general gazetteers, the *Dictionary of altitudes* (CK47) locates many places (rivers, towns, mountains) with brief information about each. The reports of the Geographic Board (CK98) supply additional information, and the *Postal guide, List of post offices* (CH223a) locates all places having post offices. Ayer's *Directory of newspapers* (AF13) gives gazetteer information about all towns for which newspapers are listed.

White, James. Dictionary of altitudes in the Dominion of Canada. (2d ed.) Ottawa, Mortimer, 1916. 251p. **CK47**

Pub. by the Conservation Commission.

Arranged by province, then alphabetically by place-name. Supplementary to *Altitudes in Canada* (2d ed. 1915), by the same author, which gives altitudes arranged by railroad routes.

Chile

Risopatrón Sánchez, Luis. Diccionario jeográfico de Chile. Santiago, Impr. Univ., 1924. 958p. **CK48**
Gazetteer information on places in Chile.

China

Playfair, George M. H. The cities and towns of China; a geographical dictionary. 2d ed. Shanghai, Kelly and Walsh, 1910. 582p., lxxviip. **CK49**
Brief information on towns. Names are given in transliteration and in Chinese characters.

Tien, H. C., Hsia, Ronald and **Penn, Peter.** Gazetteer of China. Hong Kong, Oriental Book Co., 1961. 237p. **CK50**
Gives name of locality, pronunciation, name in Chinese characters, province, longitude, and latitude.

Colombia

Gómez, Eugenio J. Diccionario geográfico de Colombia. Bogotá, Banco de la República, 1953. 359p. maps. **CK51**
Brief gazetteer information with some longer articles.

Czechoslovakia

Czechoslovak Republic. Ministerstvo Pošt a Telegrafů. Dopravní místopisný lexikon Československé Republiky. Praze, Tiskem České Grafické, 1928. 873p. **CK52**
Very brief information.

Denmark

Trap, Jens Peter. Danmark. 5. Udg. red. af Niels Nielsen, Peter Skautrup [og] Povl Engelstoft. København, Gad, 1953–65. Bd.1–9. il., maps. (In progress) **CK53**
4th ed. 1919–32 (11v.).
Contents: Bd.1, pt.1, Landet og folket. 1958; Bd.1, pt.2, Københavns Amts, Storkøbenhavn. I. 1959; Bd.2, pt.1, Storkøbenhavn. II. 1959; Bd.2, pt.2, Storkøbenhavn. III. 1960; Bd.2, pt.3, Københavns Amt. 1960; Bd.3, pt.1, Frederiksborg Amt. 1953; Bd.3, pt.2, Holbaek Amt. 1954; Bd.3, pt.3, Sorø Amt. 1954; Bd.4, pt.1, Præstø Amt. 1955; Bd.4, pt.2, Bornholms Amt. 1955; Bd.4, pt.3, Maribo Amt. 1955; Bd.5, pt.1, Odense Amt. 1956; Bd.5, pt.2, Svendborg Amt. 1957; Bd.6, pt.1, Hjørring Amt. 1960; Bd.6, pt.2, Thisted Amt. 1961; Bd.6, pt.3, Alborg Amt. 1961; Bd.7, pt.1, Viborg Amt. 1962; Bd.7, pt.2, Randers Amt. 1963; Bd.8, pt.1, Aarhus Amt. 1963; Bd.8, pt.2, Skanderborg Amt. 1964; Bd.8, pt.3, Vejle Amt. 1964; Bd.9, pt.1, Ringkøbing Amt. 1965.
Gives historical and descriptive notes about places in Denmark.

France

Joanne, Paul Bénigne. Dictionnaire géographique et administratif de la France. Paris, Hachette, 1890–1905. 7v. il. **CK54**
1st and 2d editions, 1865, 1869, included Alsace-Lorraine.
The standard geographical dictionary of France, containing much historical information, with detailed articles on early place-names, as well as later ones, and various geographical features. Long articles, many illustrations, but no bibliographies. Adequate for most questions, but for special work

needs to be supplemented by the many regional dictionaries of the provinces, *départements,* etc.

Germany

Meyers Orts- und Verkehrs-Lexikon des Deutschen Reichs. 5. vollständig neubearb. und verm. Aufl. Auf grund amtlicher Unterlagen von Reichs- , Landes- und Gemeindebehörden hrsg. von E. Uetrecht. Mit 51 Stadtplänen, 19 Umgebungs- und Übersichtskarten, einer Verkehrs-Karte und vielen statistischen Beilagen. Leipzig, Bibliographisches Inst., 1912–13. 2v. maps, plans. (folded map in pocket) **CK55**
The 5th edition is a gazetteer of Germany before World War I. The 6th edition (Leipzig, 1935. 867p.) was also issued, much reduced in size, as Ergänz. Bd.1 of *Meyers Lexikon,* 7. Aufl. (*see* AD38 for 9. Aufl.).

Great Britain

Bartholomew, John George. Survey gazetteer of the British Isles, including summary of 1931 census and reference atlas. 9th ed. Edinburgh, Bartholomew, 1943. xxxiip., 48p., 748p. maps. (Repr. 1956, with summary of 1951 census. Omits atlas section) **CK56**
Gives, in one alphabetical list, brief accounts not only of all towns, villages, and hamlets, but also of seats, shooting lodges, deer forests, fishing lochs, streams, grouse moors, etc., which have special names, but would not be included in ordinary general gazetteers.

Geographia, Ltd., London. Commercial gazetteer of Great Britain [including full-colour reference atlas], ed. by E. Hudson. London, "Geographia, Ltd.," [1957?]. 364p., 48p. of maps, 64p. **CK57**
Contents: pt.1, Gazetteer of England and Wales: towns, villages, counties, urban and rural areas, etc., in alphabetic order; map section: 48p. of maps in full color, by counties; pt.2, Gazetteer of Scotland: Scottish towns, villages, counties, urban and rural areas.
Gives very brief gazetteer information, including 1951 population, "early closing" and market days, National Grid reference, etc.

Lewis, Samuel. Topographical dictionary of England. 5th ed. London, Lewis, 1845. 4v. il. and atlas, 55 maps. **CK58**
Subtitle: Comprising the several counties, cities, boroughs, corporate and market towns, parishes, and townships, and the islands of Guernsey, Jersey, and Man, with historical and statistical descriptions: and embellished with engravings of the arms of the cities, bishoprics, universities, colleges, corporate towns, and boroughs; and of the seals of the various municipal corporations.
Still useful for the historical information to be found in the long, detailed articles about places of all sizes.

Greece

Permanent Committee on Geographical Names for British Official Use. A gazetteer of Greece. Prep. at the house of the Royal Geographical Society. London, pr. by W. Clowes, 1942. 161p. incl. maps. **CK59**

Guatemala

Guatemala. Dirección General de Cartografía. Diccionario geográfico de Guatemala. Guatemala, 1961–62. 2v. **CK60**
A geographical dictionary listing the place-names, cities, towns, villages, rivers, mountains, etc. For the larger places

gives considerable detail on history, demography, ethnography, geology, archaeology, etc.

Valle Matheu, Jorge del. Guía sociogeográfica de Guatemala; con referencia a las condiciones de vida, lugares de atractivo turístico y necesidades de los municipios de la República. Guatemala, [Tipografía Nacional], 1956. 371p. maps.   **CK61**

"Preparada y compilada . . . bajo los auspicios de la Secretaría de Divulgación, Cultura y Turismo de la Presidencia de la República."

Descriptions of the cities and towns of Guatemala.

Hawaii

Coulter, John Wesley. Gazetteer of the territory of Hawaii. Honolulu, Univ. of Hawaii, 1935. 241p. (Univ. of Hawaii. Research publ. 11)   **CK62**

Very brief gazetteer information.

Honduras

Bonilla, Marcelina. Diccionario histórico-geográfico de las poblaciones de Honduras. Tegucigalpa, "Ariston," 1945. 256p.   **CK63**

India

Imperial gazetteer of India. New ed., pub. under the authority of His Majesty's Secretary of State for India in Council. Oxford, Clarendon Pr., 1907–31. 26v. maps.   **CK64**

1st ed., 9v., 1881, and 2d ed., 14v., 1885–87, ed. by Sir William Wilson Hunter. The present may be considered as a new work, rather than a new edition.—Cf. *General pref.*

Editor for India: 1902–4, William Stevenson Meyer; 1905–9, Richard Burn. Editor in England: James Sutherland Cotton.

v.1–4, Indian Empire: v.1, Descriptive; v.2, Historical; v.3, Economic; v.4, Administrative; v.5–24, Gazetteer; v.25, General index; v.26, Atlas. (Atlas, new rev. ed. 1931)

Includes historical, topographical, ethnical, agricultural, industrial, administrative, and medical aspects of the various districts of British India.

Ireland

Lewis, Samuel. Topographical dictionary of Ireland . . . 2d ed. London, Lewis, 1846. 2v. il. and atlas, 32 maps.   **CK65**

Subtitle: Comprising the several counties, cities, boroughs, corporate, market, and post towns, parishes and villages with historical and statistical descriptions, embellished with engravings of the arms of the cities, bishoprics, corporate towns, and boroughs; and the seals of the several municipal corporations.

Still useful for the historical information to be found in the long, detailed articles about places of all sizes.

Italy

Amati, Amato. Dizionario corografico dell' Italia. Opera illustrata da circa 1000 armi comunali colorate e da parecchie centinaia di incisioni intercalate nel testo rappresentanti i principali monumenti d'Italia. Milano, Vallardi, [1875?–86?]. 8v. il. (coats of arms)   **CK66**

Long articles, some with extensive bibliographies. Colored coats of arms. Includes many more names than *La nuova Italia* below.

La nuova Italia; dizionario amministrativo, statistico, industriale, commerciale dei comuni del regno e dei principali paesi d'Italia oltre confine e colonie. Milano, Vallardi, [1908?–10?]. 3v. il. and atlas of 26 col. pl. (coats of arms)   **CK67**

A successor to, but not a substitute for, the preceding work.

Compiled to show the development of industrial, commercial, and agricultural Italy during the first 40 years of its life as a nation, with detailed articles by place-name.

Japan

Gerr, Stanley. A gazetteer of Japanese place names in characters and in Rōmaji script giving latitudes and longitudes. Cambridge, Harvard Univ. Pr., 1942. 269p., 225p.   **CK68**

Two lists dealing with the same places, one in Rōmaji script (Latin alphabet), the other in Sino-Japanese character. Besides the names of cities, towns, etc., includes the names of mountains, rivers, islands, etc.

"Based on the map of the Japanese Empire published in 1937 by the Japanese Kokusai Bunka Shinkōkai (Society for International Cultural Relations). It contains about 4500 place names covering Japan proper, Korea, Formosa, Kwangtung leased territory, Saghalien, and the Japanese mandated islands, but does not include Manchuria or other territory recently occupied by Japan. . . . "—*Pref. note.*

U.S. Hydrographic Office. Gazetteer of the Japanese Empire, containing place names from the Japanese hydrographic charts and sailing directions on issue in 1936. Wash., 1943. 378p. (H.O. Publ. no.880. Repr. Aug. 1944 of H.O. miscellaneous no.10,947)   **CK69**

A listing of some 15,000 place-names, arranged alphabetically by Rōmaji transcription, giving the Japanese form and the latitude and longitude.

Netherlands

Laan, Kornelis ter. Aardrijkskundig woordenboek van Nederland. Tweede druk. 's-Gravenhage, van Goor, 1948. 513p.   **CK70**

Includes names of cities, villages, minor places, church groups, and geographical terms. Lists fewer names than the *Lijst der aardrijkskundige namen* (CK71), but gives more information about each item and more up-to-date figures.

Nederlandsch Aardrijkskundig Genootschap, Amsterdam. Lijst der aardrijkskundige namen van Nederland. Leiden, Brill, 1936. 494p.   **CK71**

An extensive list which includes many names but gives very brief information about each, usually merely the location.

New Zealand

New Zealand guide: a comprehensive gazetteer, geographical reference and travel guide. Dunedin, H. Wise, 1957. 923p. il.   **CK72**

1st ed. 1952.

Supersedes *Wise's New Zealand index to every place in New Zealand.* 10th ed. 1948.

Arranged alphabetically by place-name and geographical location. Frequently gives history, legends, origin of name, etc., as well as usual gazetteer information.

Peru

Stiglich, Germán. Diccionario geográfico del Perú. 2. y última parte. Lima, Torres-Aguirre, 1922–23. 2 pts. in 4v.   **CK73**

An older work, still occasionally useful, is Mariano Felipe Paz Soldan. *Diccionario geográfico estadístico del Perú.* Lima, 1877. 1077p.

Philippines

U.S. Bureau of Insular Affairs. Pronouncing gazetteer and geographical dictionary of the Philippine Islands. Wash., Govt. Prt. Off., 1902. 933p. il., maps. **CK74**

Detailed information on all aspects of life in the Philippines at that time.

Poland

Słownik geograficzny Królestwa polskiego i innych krajów słowiańskich; wydany pod redakcyą Filipa Sulimierskiego [and others]. Warszawa, Druk "Wieku," 1880–1902. 15v. in 16. **CK75**

v.15 is a supplement in 2v.
Long articles, many of them signed.

El Salvador

Salvador. Dirección General de Estadística y Censos. Diccionario geográfico de la República de El Salvador. [3. ed.] San Salvador, 1959. 258p. il. **CK76**

1st ed. 1940.
Gives gazetteer information about places in El Salvador.

Scotland

Johnston, W. and **Johnston, A. K.,** *firm, publishers.* Gazetteer of Scotland, including a glossary of the most common Gaelic and Norse names. Edinburgh, London, Johnston, 1937. 330p., 24p. of maps. **CK77**

Lewis, Samuel. Topographical dictionary of Scotland . . . London, Lewis, 1846. 2v. il. and atlas. **CK78**

Subtitle: Comprising the several counties, islands, cities, burgh and market towns, parishes, and principal villages with historical and statistical descriptions, . . . a large map of Scotland and engravings of the seals and arms of the different burghs and universities.
Still useful for the historical information to be found in the long, detailed articles about places of all sizes.

Spain

Diccionario geográfico de Espana. Madrid, Ed. del Movimento, 1956–61. 17v. **CK79**

A detailed gazetteer of Spanish places. Some long, signed articles with quite extensive information on physical characteristics, climate, vegetation, agriculture, industries, cultural opportunities, history, etc. Some articles much shorter, with gazetteer information only.

Switzerland

Knapp, Charles, Borel, Maurice and **Attinger, V.** Dictionnaire géographique de la Suisse; publié sous les auspices de la Société Neuchâteloise de Géographie. . . . Neuchâtel, Attinger, 1902–10. 6v. il. maps. **CK80**

One of the finest regional dictionaries, with authoritative articles and excellent illustrations. Articles contain more scientific geographical and geological information than is usual in local gazetteers.
v.6 includes Supplement, p.685–1136.

Uruguay

Araújo, Orestes. Diccionario geográfico del Uruguay. 2. ed., completamente reform. y aum. con más de 1,000 voces nuevas. Montevideo, Tipo-litografía Moderna, 1912. 528p. il. **CK81**

Wales

Lewis, Samuel. Topographical dictionary of Wales . . . 3d ed. London, Lewis, 1844. 2v. il. and atlas. **CK82**

Subtitle: Comprising the several counties, cities, boroughs, corporate and market towns, parishes, chapelries, and townships, with historical and statistical descriptions: embellished with engravings of the arms of the bishoprics, and of the arms and seals of the various cities and municipal corporations, and illustrated by maps of the different counties.
Still useful for the historical information to be found in the long, detailed articles about places of all sizes.

GEOGRAPHICAL NAMES AND TERMS

General works

Egli, Johann Jacob. Geschichte der geographischen Namenkunde. Leipzig, Brandstetter, 1886. 430p. (Repr.: N.Y., Burt Franklin, 1963. 2v.) **CK83**

Surveys the literature of the historical study of place-names.

—— Nomina geographica. Sprach- und Sacherklärung von 42,000 geographischen Namen aller Erdräume. 2. verm. und verb. Aufl. Leipzig, Brandstetter, 1893. 1035p. **CK84**

Gives the origin of place-names in various countries of the world, with references to sources.

Permanent Committee on Geographical Names for British Official Use. Glossaries, v.1–8. London, 1942–54. v.1–8. **CK85**

Contents: v.1, Modern Greek. 1942; v.2, Russian. 1942; v.3, Albanian. 1943; v.4, Serbo-Croat and Slovene. 1943; v.5, Romanian. 1944; v.6, Thai (Siamese). 1944; v.7, Turkish. 1945; v.8, Japanese. 1954.
Glossaries not of place-names but of words, abbreviations, and contractions found on official maps, charts, and geographical texts of the country treated, with transliteration (if from a non-Roman alphabet), meaning, and application.
More countries were covered, but much more briefly, in a series of *Short glossaries* published by the General Staff. Geographical Section, War Office. 1943–45. 23 numbers.

—— [Lists of names]. London, Royal Geographical Soc., 1921–38. **CK86**

An unnumbered series of pamphlets, in two main groups: (1) General lists (by continents), and (2) National or regional lists, each giving the names of a country, dominion, protectorate, etc. A special pamphlet was issued 1932, *Rules for the spelling of geographical names.*
Contents: (1) General lists: African names, 1st list, 1921, corr. 1926; Asiatic names, 1st–2d lists, 1921–25, rev. 1930; European names, 1st–2d lists, [1921]–23, corr. and rev. 1929; Oceanic names, 1st–4th lists, 1922–35; (2) National lists: Abyssinia, 1st list, 1925; Albania, 1st list, 1938; Anglo-Egyptian Sudan, 1st list, 1927; Arabia, 1st list, 1931. 2d list, 1937; Belgium and Luxemburg, 1st list, 1938; Czechoslovakia, 1st–3d lists, 1924–30; Egypt (Upper), 1st list, 1929; Fiji, 1st list, 1925; Gold Coast and British Togo, 1st list, 1923; India, 1st list, 1924; Iraq (Mesopotamia), 1st list, 1922, rev. 1932; Nigeria and British Cameroons, 1st list, 1928; Palestine, 1st list, 1925, rev. 1937; Persia (South), 1st list, 1928; Persia (North), 2d list, 1929, 1947 suppl. to North and South; Poland (West) and Danzig, 1st list, 1928; Poland (East), 2d list, 1930; Romania, 1st–2d lists, 1926–28; Somaliland Protectorate, 1st list, 1928; Sudan, 1st list, 1927; Syria, 1st list, 1927; Tanganyika territory, 1st list, 1926; Tonga, 1st list,

1927; Trans-Jordan, 1st list, 1927; Turkey (West), 1st list, 1935; Yugoslavia, 1st and 2d lists, 1928–31.

Gives brief information, including correct spelling and pronunciation of name, rejected forms of name, and location of place.

—— Lists of names (New series). London, 1954– . no.1– . (In progress) **CK86a**

[1], Poland. 1954. (Supersedes 1st and 2d lists, 1928–30); [2], Persia. 1955. (Supersedes 1st and 2d lists, 1928–29); 3, Czechoslovakia. 1958. (Supersedes 1st–3d lists, 1924–30); 4, Bulgaria. 1959; 5, [Not yet pub. ?]; 6, Bahrain. 1962; 7, Kuwait and the Neutral Zone. 1962.

U.S. Board on Geographical Names. Sixth report, 1890–1932. Wash., Govt. Prt. Off., 1933. 834p. **CK87**

Includes: (1) Geographic names, discussion of characteristics, problems, etc.; (2) The U.S. Geographic Board, its method of work, history, etc.; (3) Decisions, arranged alphabetically by approved form of name, with cross references from other forms, p.76–834.

The *Decisions* form a dictionary of many thousand place-names throughout the world, incorporating in one alphabetical list: the material of the *Fifth report* (1921); subsequent decisions; the 2500 foreign place-names included in the *First report on foreign geographic names* (1932); and the Philippine and Hawaiian names given in separate lists in the *Fifth report*. For each name gives approved form, locates the place, indicates rejected forms, and, in some cases, marks pronunciation.

"This report contains, with the exception of a comparatively small number, all the decisions rendered by the Board from its organization in 1890 through June, 1932, and supersedes all previous reports. Not included . . . are such decisions as have either been vacated, or being revised, have been replaced by new decisions listed under the revised name or spelling."—*Foreword*.

Kept up to date by the following:

—— Decisions, 1934/35– . Wash., 1936– .

Issued at frequent intervals—now quarterly—in leaflets containing general lists of decisions; some lists were issued on special locations, e.g., National parks, or on specific foreign countries, e.g., Tibet, Mongolia, Italy, etc.

United States

☙ Because of the very full *Bibliography of place name literature,* by Sealock and Seely, listed below, works on place-names of the United States, its individual states, Canada, Alaska, and Newfoundland are not listed here.

Sealock, Richard Burl and **Seely, Pauline Augusta.** Bibliography of place name literature, United States, Canada, Alaska and Newfoundland. Chicago, Amer. Lib. Assoc., 1948. 331p. **CK88**

A comprehensive bibliography of books and articles dealing with particular types of names or the names of particular regions. Arranged by state under the United States, and by province under Canada, followed by a name and subject index.

Supplementary lists have been published in *Names; journal of the American Name Society,* v.3, 1955– .

New edition in preparation, 1965.

Kane, Joseph Nathan. The American counties. Rev. ed. N.Y., Scarecrow, 1962. 540p. **CK89**

1st ed. 1960. 500p.

Subtitle: A record of the origin of the names of the 3072 counties, dates of creation and organization, area, 1960 population, historical data, etc. of the fifty states.

Australia

Martin, A. E. One thousand and more place names in New South Wales. Sydney, Australia, N.S.W. Bookstall Co., 1943. 108p. (The romance of nomenclature) **CK90**

—— Place names in Victoria and Tasmania. Sydney, Australia, N.S.W. Bookstall Co., 1944. 107p. (The romance of nomenclature) **CK91**

—— Place names in Queensland, New Zealand and the Pacific. Sydney, Australia, N.S.W. Bookstall Co., 1944. [109]p. il. (The romance of nomenclature) **CK92**

—— Twelve hundred and more place names in South Australia, Western Australia and the Northern Territory. Sydney, Australia, N.S.W. Bookstall Co., 1943. 109p. (The romance of nomenclature) **CK93**

Austria

Schiffmann, Konrad. Historisches Ortsnamen-Lexikon des Landes Oberösterreich. München, Oldenbourg, 1935. 2v. map. **CK94**

—— —— Ergänzungsbd.; Nachträge, Erklärung der Namen und Verweisungen. München, Oldenbourg, 1940. 556p.

Belgium

Carnoy, Albert Joseph. Dictionnaire étymologique du nom des communes de Belgique, y compris l'étymologie des principaux noms de hameaux et de rivières. Louvain, Éd. Universitas, 1939–40. 2v. **CK95**

Brazil

Souza, Bernardino José de. Dicionário da terra e da gente do Brasil. São Paulo, Companhia Ed. Nacional, 1961. 346p. (Brasiliana. Série grande formato. v.19) **CK96**

5. ed. da *Onomástica geral da geografia brasileira.*
Explanations of Brazilian place-names.

Canada

Armstrong, George Henry. Origin and meaning of place names in Canada. Toronto, Macmillan, 1930. 312p. **CK97**

Canada. Board on Geographical Names. 18th–19th reports containing all decisions to July 31, 1927. Ottawa, 1924–27. 2v. **CK98**

18th report, Decisions to March 1924; 19th report, Decisions, April 1924–July 1927.

Alphabetical lists of place-names, with index by provinces, counties, etc. The main alphabet in each report gives form of name decided on, location of place, and origin of name when known, with cross references from superseded names. Supersedes the earlier reports of the Board except for certain appendixes which are still useful for the fuller or special information they contain. These appendixes (also issued as separates) are:

9th report, 1910: pt.2, Place-names in Quebec, by James White, p.153–219; pt.3, Place-names, Thousand Islands, St. Lawrence River, by James White, p.221–29; pt.4, Place-names in Northern Canada, by James White, p.229–455.

17th report, 1922: Meaning of Canadian city names, by R. Douglas, p.34–52; Place-names on Anticosti Island, by W. P. Anderson, p.53–65; Place-names on Magdalen Islands, by R. Douglas, p.66–74.

Additional lists issued by the Geographic Board include:
Place-names of Prince Edward Island, with meanings, by R. Douglas. 1925. 55p.

Place-names of Alberta. 1928. 138p. map.
Place-names of Manitoba. 1933. 95p. map.

Egypt

Gauthier, Henri. Dictionnaire des noms géographiques contenus dans les textes hiéroglyphiques. Caire, L'Impr. de l'Inst. Français d'Archéologie Orientale pour la Société Royale de Géographie d'Égypte, 1925–31. 7v. **CK99**

v.7 includes indexes and maps.

France

Dauzat, Albert and **Rostaing, Charles.** Dictionnaire étymologique des noms de lieux en France. Paris, Larousse, 1963. 738p. **CK100**

Etymologies of French place-names.

✓ **Dictionnaire topographique de la France** comprenant les noms de lieu anciens et modernes, publié par ordre du Ministère de l'Instruction Publique et sous la direction du Comité des Travaux Historiques et Scientifiques. Paris, Impr. Nationale, 1861–1950. v.[1–31]. (In progress) **CK101**

A monumental work, in process of publication, 1v. for each *département.* Each volume lists all place-names of its *département,* even names of farms, giving for each: location; derivation; variations in form from the earliest period to the present, with date when each form was used and exact references to manuscripts or printed authorities; and, in the case of important names, a brief history and description of the place. Entry in the dictionary proper is under the modern form of name; cross references from old forms are given in a table at the end of the volume.

Volumes so far published are: **Ain,** by E. Philipon, 1911; **Aisne,** by A. Matton, 1871; **Alpes (Hautes),** by J. Roman, 1884; **Aube,** by Th. Boutiot and E. Socard, 1874; **Aude,** by the Abbé Sabarthès, 1912; **Calvados,** by C. Hippeau, 1883; **Cantal,** by E. Amé, 1897; **Cher,** by H. Boyer and R. Latouche, 1926; **Côte d'Or,** by A. Roserot, 1924; **Deux-Sèvres,** by B. Ledain, 1902; **Dordogne,** by A. J. D. de Gourgues, 1873; **Drôme,** by J. Brun-Durand, 1891; **Eure,** by B. E. P. de Blosseville, 1878; **Eure-et-Loir,** by L. Merlet, 1861; **Gard,** by E. Germer-Durand, 1868; **Hérault,** by E. Thomas, 1865; **Loire (Haute),** by A. Chassaing and A. Jacotin, 1907; **Marne,** by A. Longnon, 1891; **Marne (Haute),** by A. Roserot, 1903; **Mayenne,** by. L. Maitre, 1878; **Meurthe,** by H. Lepage, 1862; **Meuse,** by F. Lienard, 1872; **Morbihan,** by L. Rosenzweig, 1870; **Moselle,** by E. de Bouteiller, 1874; **Nièvre,** by J. H. G. R. de Soultrait, 1865; **Pas-de-Calais,** by A. C. H. Menche de Loisne, 1908; **Pyrénées (Basses),** by P. R. L. Raymond, 1863; **Rhin (Haut),** by G. Stoffel, 1868; **Sarthe,** by. E. Vallée, rev. et pub. by R. Latouche, 1950–52; **Vienne,** by L. Rédet, 1881; **Vosges,** by P. Marichal, 1941; **Yonne,** by M. Quantin, 1862.

Longnon, Auguste Honoré. Les noms de lieu de la France; leur origine, leur signification, leurs transformations; résumé des conférences de toponomastique générale faites à l'École Pratique de Hautes Études. . . . Pub. par Paul Marichal et Léon Mirot. Paris, Champion, 1920–29. 831p. **CK102**

Germany

Akademie der Wissenschaften, Munich. Kommission für Bayerische Landesgeschichte. Historisches Ortsnamenbuch von Bayern, in Verbindung mit dem Institut für Frankische Landesforschung, hrsg. . . . München, Kommission, 1951–60. il. (In progress) **CK103**

Contents: *Oberbayern;* bearb. unter Leitung von Ludwig Steinberger. Bd.1, Landkreis Ebersberg, bearb. von Karl Puchner, 1951. 114p. map.

Oberfranken; bearb. unter Leitung von Erich *Freiherr* von Guttenberg. Bd.1, Land- und Stadtkreis Kulmbach, bearb. von Erich *Freiherr* von Guttenberg, 1952. 238p. map.

Schwaben; bearb. unter Leitung von Ludwig Steinberger. Bd.1, Landkreis Marktoberdorf, von Richard Dertsch, 1953. 113p. map; Bd.2, Landkreis Krumbach, von Fritz Hilble. 1956. 108p. map; Bd.3, Stadt- und Landkreis Kaufbeuren, von Richard Dertsch. 1960. 117p. map.

Bach, Adolf. Deutsche Namenkunde. Heidelberg, Winter, 1952–56. 3v. in 5. il. **CK104**

For Bd.1 and annotation, devoted to personal names, *see* AK92.

Bd.2, Die deutschen Ortsnamen; Hlbbd. 1, Einleitung. Zur Laut- und Formenlehre, zur Satzfügung, Wortbildung und -bedeutung der deutschen Ortsnamen; Hlbbd. 2, Die deutschen Ortsnamen in geschichtlicher, geographischer, soziologischer und psychologischer Betrachtung. Ortsnamenforschung im Dienste anderer Wissenschaften; Bd.3, Registerband, bearb. von Diefer Berger. 1956. 457p.

A detailed treatment of German names; the first volume deals with personal names, the second with place-names. The third provides indexes to both.

Oesterley, Hermann. Historisch-geographisches Wörterbuch des deutschen Mittelalters. Gotha, Perthes, 1883. 806p. **CK104a**

The history of medieval German place-names.

Great Britain

Cameron, Kenneth. English place-names. London, Batsford, 1961. 256p. il. **CK105**

A discussion of the elements of English place-names. Indexes of place-names, street-names, and field-names, p.233–56.

Ekwall, Eilert. Concise Oxford dictionary of English place-names. 4th ed. Oxford, Clarendon Pr., 1960. 546p. **CK106**

1st ed. 1936.

The 4th edition has been reset, incorporating corrections and addenda from the earlier editions; many articles rewritten. Lists about 15,000 names.

"Embraces names of the country, of the counties, and other important divisions, towns (except those of late origin), parishes, villages, some names of estates and hamlets, or even farms whose names are old and etymologically interesting, rivers, lakes—also names of capes, hills, bays for which early material is available. Names of hundreds, as being no longer in use, have been omitted."

While the concise information given is considerably less full than that in the various volumes of the English Place-Name Society, it includes in general: modern form, location (in county), derivation or meaning, older forms with dates, and some references to sources. Pronunciation is given in some cases.

—— English river names. Oxford, Clarendon Pr., 1928. 488p. **CK107**

Gives detailed etymology for river names with references to sources.

✓ **English Place-Name Society.** English place-name elements, by Albert Hugh Smith. Cambridge, Univ. Pr., 1956. 2v. (English Place-Name Society. [Survey of English place-names] v.25–26) **CK108**

Contents: pt.1, Introduction, bibliography, the elements A–IW. Maps; pt.2, The elements Jafn–Ytri. Index and maps.

A detailed study of the derivation of the elements found in English place-names with bibliographical references to sources.

Expands and revises A. Mawer, *Chief elements used in English place-names* (*see* CK109, v.1,pt.2).

—— Survey of English place-names. Cambridge, Univ. Pr., 1924– . v.1– . maps. (In progress)   **CK109**
v.1, pt.1, Introduction to the survey of English place-names, by A. Mawer and F. M. Stenton. 1924. 201p.; v.1, pt.2, Chief elements used in English place-names, by A. Mawer. 1924. 67p. For rev. ed. *see* CK108; v.2, Place-names of *Buckinghamshire*, by A. Mawer and F. M. Stenton. 1925. 274p.; v.3, Place-names of *Bedfordshire* and *Huntingdonshire*, by A. Mawer and F. M. Stenton. 1926. 316p.; v.4, Place-names of *Worcestershire*, by A. Mawer and F. M. Stenton. 1927. 420p.; v.5, Place-names of the *North Riding of Yorkshire*, by A. H. Smith. 1928. 352p.; v.6–7, Place-names of *Sussex*, by A. Mawer and F. M. Stenton. 1929–30. 2v.; v.8–9, Place-names of *Devon*, by J. E. B. Gover, A. Mawer, and F. M. Stenton. 1931–32. 2v. and case of maps; v.10, Place-names of *Northamptonshire*, by J. E. B. Gover, A. Mawer, and F. M. Stenton. 1933. 311p.; v.11, Place-names of *Surrey*, by J. E. B. Gover, A. Mawer, and F. M. Stenton. 1934. 445p.; v.12, Place-names of *Essex*, by P. H. Reaney. 1935. 698p.; v.13, Place-names of *Warwickshire*, by J. E. B. Gover, A. Mawer, and F. M. Stenton. 1936. 409p.;
v.14, Place-names of the *East Riding of Yorkshire and York*, by A. H. Smith. 1937. 351p.; v.15, Place-names of *Hertfordshire*, by J. E. B. Gover, A. Mawer, and F. M. Stenton. 1938. 342p.; v.16, Place-names of *Wiltshire*, by J. E. B. Gover, A. Mawer, and F. M. Stenton. 1939. 547p.; v.17, Place-names of *Nottinghamshire*, by J. E. B. Gover, A. Mawer, and F. M. Stenton. 1940. 348p.; v.18, Place-names of *Middlesex*, apart from the city of London, by J. E. B. Gover, A. Mawer, and F. M. Stenton. 1942. 235p.; v.19, Place-names of *Cambridgeshire* and the *Isle of Ely*, by P. H. Reaney. 1943. 396p.; v.20–22, Place-names of *Cumberland*, by A. M. Armstrong, A. Mawer, F. M. Stenton, and Bruce Dickins. 1950–52. 3 pts. 565p.; v.23–24, Place-names of *Oxfordshire*, by Margaret Gelling, based on material collected by Doris Mary Stenton. 1953–54. 2v.; v.25–26, English place-name elements, *see* CK108; v.27–29, Place-names of *Derbyshire*, by Kenneth Cameron. 1959. 3v.; v.30–38, Place-names of the *West Riding of Yorkshire*, by A. H. Smith. 1961–63. 8v.

Gt.Brit. General Register Office. Census 1951. England and Wales, index of place names. London, Stat. Off., 1955; repr. 1956. 2v. (1377p.)   **CK110**
"An index of place names was first produced in the series of census publications in 1831, and most recently in 1924 as a separate volume in the 1921 series of census publications." This edition gives names of every area mentioned in the tables of the various census volumes, and also villages, hamlets, and localities without legally defined barriers, indicating location and 1951 population.

The following regional lists, while largely superseded by the publications of the English Place-Name Society, are also occasionally still useful:

Skeat, W. W. Place-names of **Bedfordshire.** Cambridge, Antiquarian Soc., 1906. 74p. (Its *Publ.* no.42) **CK111**

—— Place-names of **Berkshire.** Oxford, Clarendon Pr., 1911. 118p.   **CK112**

—— Place-names of **Cambridgeshire.** 2d ed. Cambridge, Antiquarian Soc., 1911. 82p.   **CK113**

Dexter, T. F. G. **Cornish** names, an attempt to explain over 1600 Cornish names. London, Longmans, 1926. 89p.   **CK114**

Sedgefield, W. J. Place-names of **Cumberland** and **Westmorland.** Manchester, Univ. Pr., 1915. 208p.   **CK115**

Walker, B. Place-names of **Derbyshire.** Derbyshire, Archaeological Soc., 1915. 310p.   **CK116**

Blomé, Bertil. Place-names of **North Devonshire.** Uppsala, Appelberg, 1929. 189p.   **CK117**

Fägersten, A. Place-names of **Dorset.** Uppsala, Appelberg, 1933. 334p.   **CK118**

Jackson, C. E. Place-names of **Durham.** London, Allen and Unwin, 1916. 114p. (*See also* under Northumberland, below, CK131)   **CK119**

Baddeley, W. St. C. Place-names of **Gloucestershire.** Gloucester, Bellows, 1913. 185p.   **CK120**

Bannister, A. T. Place-names of **Herefordshire.** [Cambridge], Author, 1916. 231p.   **CK121**

Skeat, W. W. Place-names of **Hertfordshire.** 1904. 109p.   **CK122**

Wallenberg, J. K. Place-names of **Kent.** Uppsala, Appelberg, 1934. 626p.   **CK123**

Ekwall, Eilert. Place-names of **Lancashire.** Manchester, Chetham Soc., 1922. 280p. (Chetham Society. Remains, historical and literary, connected with the Palatine counties of Lancaster and Chester, n.s. v.81)   **CK124**

Sephton, J. Handbook of **Lancashire** place-names. Liverpool, Young, 1913. 256p.   **CK125**

Wyld, H. C. and Hirst, T. O. Place-names of **Lancashire.** London, Constable, 1911. 400p.   **CK126**

Eminson, T. B. F. Place and river names of the West Riding of Lindsey, **Lincolnshire.** Lincoln, Ruddock, 1934. 288p.   **CK127**

Harrison, H. Place-names of the **Liverpool** district. London, Stock, 1898. 104p.   **CK128**

Kneen, J. J. Place-names of the **Isle of Man.** Douglas, Manx Soc., 1925–29. 2v.(645p.).   **CK129**

Munford, G. An attempt to ascertain the true derivation of the names of towns and villages and of rivers, and other great natural features . . . of **Norfolk.** London, Simpkin, 1870. 239p.   **CK130**

Mawer, A. Place-names of **Northumberland** and **Durham.** Cambridge, Univ. Pr., 1920. 270p.   **CK131**

Mutschmann, H. Place-names of **Nottinghamshire.** Cambridge, Univ. Pr., 1913. 179p.   **CK132**

Alexander, H. Place-names of **Oxfordshire.** Oxford, Clarendon Pr., 1912. 251p.   **CK133**

Bowcock, E. W. **Shropshire** place-names. Shrewsbury, Wilding, 1923. 271p.   **CK134**

Hill, J. S. The place-names of **Somerset.** Bristol, St. Stephen's Pr., 1914. 373p.   **CK135**

Duignan, W. H. Notes on **Staffordshire** place-names. London, Frowde, 1902. 178p.   **CK136**

Skeat, W. W. Place-names of **Suffolk.** Cambridge, Antiquarian Soc., 1913. 132p.   **CK137**

Hopwood, D. Place-names of the County of **Surrey,** including London in Surrey. Capetown, 1926. 101p. (Annals of the Univ. of Stellenbosch, v.4, sec. B, no.2, Oct. 1926)   **CK138**

Roberts, R. G. Place-names of **Sussex.** Cambridge, Univ. Pr., 1914. 210p.   **CK139**

Embleton, D. A catalogue of place-names in **Teesdale.** [London, Williams and Norgate, 1887] 223p.   **CK140**

Charles, B. G. Non-Celtic place-names in **Wales.** London, Univ. College, 1938. 326p.   **CK141**

Morgan, T. Place-names of **Wales.** 2d rev. ed. Newport, Mon., Southall, 1912. 262p.   **CK142**

Wales. University. Board of Celtic Studies. Language and

Literature Section. Rhestr o enwan lleoedd. (Gazetteer of **Welsh** place-names) Cardiff, Univ. of Wales Pr., 1958. 118p.   **CK143**

Duignan, W. H. **Warwickshire** place-names. London, Frowde, 1912. 130p.   **CK144**

Westmorland, *see* Cumberland above (CK115).

Kökeritz, H. The place-names of the **Isle of Wight.** Uppsala, Appelberg, 1940. 306p. maps.   **CK145**

Ekblom, E. L. Place-names of **Wiltshire,** their origin and history. Uppsala, Appelberg, 1917. 187p.   **CK146**

Duignan, W. H. **Worcestershire** place-names. London, Frowde, 1905. 185p.   **CK147**

Goodall, A. Place-names of south-west **Yorkshire.** Rev. ed. Cambridge, Univ. Pr., 1914. 313p.   **CK148**

Dyson, T. Place names and surnames, their origin and meaning, with special reference to the **West Riding of Yorkshire.** Huddersfield, Alfred Jubb, 1944. 216p.   **CK149**

Moorman, F. W. Place-names of the **West Riding of Yorkshire.** Leeds, Thoresby Soc., 1910. 218p. (Its Publ. v.18)   **CK150**

Ireland

Hogan, Edmund. Onomasticon goedelicum locorum et tribuum Hiberniae et Scotiae. Dublin, Hodges, 1910. 695p. map.   **CK151**

Subtitle: An index, with identifications, to the Gaelic names of places and tribes.

Joyce, Patrick W. Origin and history of Irish names of places. London, N.Y., Longmans, 1898–1913. 3v. **CK152**

The best dictionary of Irish place-names, giving for each name its location, derivation, meaning, and an explanation of the meaning where necessary. v.1–2, originally published 1869–71, are treatises, arranged in chapters with alphabetical indexes, but v.3 is a regular dictionary list. As v.3 does not duplicate many of the names in v.1–2, use must still be made of the earlier volumes.

Mexico

Peñafiel, Antonio. Nomenclatura geográfica de México. Etymologías de los nombres de lugar correspondientes a los principales idiomas que se hablan en la república. México, Oficina Tipografía de la Secretaría de Fomento, 1897. 2v. and atlas of 709pl.   **CK153**

Netherlands

Flou, Karel de. Woordenboek der toponymie van Westelijk Vlaanderen, Vlaamsch Artesië, het Land van den Hoek, de graafschappen Guines en Boulogne, en een gedeelte van het graafschap Ponthieu. Brugge, Poelvoorde, 1914–38. 18v.   **CK154**

Sponsored by the Vlaamsche Academie voor Taal en Letterkunde.

v.1–18, A–Z. An extensive listing of Flemish place-names with explanations and references to original usages, etc.

Wijer, H. J. van de. Bibliographie van de Vlaamsche plaatsnaamkunde (begin XIXᵉ eeuw tot en met 1927). Den Haag, Nijhoff, 1928. 156p. (Nomina geographica flandrica. I)   **CK155**

New Zealand

Andersen, Johannes Carl. Maori place-names, also personal names and names of colours, weapons, and natural objects. Wellington, Polynesian Soc. of New Zealand, 1942. 494p. [Polynesian Society memoir, no.20]   **CK156**

Legends and histories of Maori names.

New Zealand. Geographic Board. . . . Place-names in New Zealand; rules of nomenclature and lists of names approved or changed or expunged. Comp. by Johannes C. Andersen. Wellington, 1934. 47p. (Its Bull. 1) **CK157**

Poland

Taszycki, Witold. Bibliografia onomastyki polskiej do roku 1958 włacznie. Kraków, 1960. 335p. (Kraków. Uniwersytet Jagielloński. Wydawnictwa. 62)   **CK158**

A bibliography of more than 2800 titles on Polish place-names.

Scotland

Johnston, James B. The place-names of Scotland. [3d ed. enl.] London, Murray, 1934. 335p.   **CK159**

Gives the origin and meaning of place-names in Scotland.

Mackenzie, William Cook. Scottish place-names. London, K. Paul, 1931. 319p.   **CK160**

Discusses the elements in, and the types of, a selected list of Scottish place-names, in such chapters as "The rivers and their burns," "The nesses and the lochs," "The bogs and the marshes," etc.

Watson, William John. History of the Celtic place-names of Scotland, being the Rhind lecture on archaeology (expanded) delivered in 1916. Pub. under the auspices of the Royal Celtic Society. Edinburgh, Blackwood, 1926. 558p.   **CK161**

☙ The following regional lists are also useful:

Alexander, W. McC. The place-names of **Aberdeenshire.** Aberdeen, pr. for the Third Spalding Club, 1952. 419p.   **CK162**

Macdonald, J. Place-names of **West Aberdeenshire.** Aberdeen, New Spalding Club, 1899. 347p.   **CK163**

Meikle, J. Place-names around **Alyth.** Paisley, Gardner, 1925. 203p.   **CK164**

Gillies, H. C. Place-names of **Argyll.** London, Nutt, 1906. 273p.   **CK165**

Irving, J. Place-names of **Dumbartonshire.** Dumbarton, Bennett and Thomson, 1928. 61p.   **CK166**

Johnson-Ferguson, *Sir* E. Place-names of **Dumfriesshire.** Dumfries, Courier Pr., 1935. 140p.   **CK167**

Matheson, D. Place-names of **Elginshire.** Stirling, Mackay, 1905. 208p.   **CK168**

Maxwell, *Sir* H. Place-names of **Galloway,** their origin and meaning considered. Glasgow, Jackson, 1930. 278p.   **CK169**

Ellice, E. C. Place-names in **Glengarry** and **Glenquoich** and their associations. 2d ed. rev. London, Routledge, 1931. 163p.   **CK170**

Robson, W. S. **Hawick** place-names. Hawick, Hood, 1947. 82p.   **CK171**

Maciver, D. Place-names of **Lewis** and **Harris.** [Stornoway, "Gazette" Off.], 1934. 102p.   **CK172**

Milne, J. Gaelic place-names of the **Lothians.** London, McDougall's Educ. Co., 1912. 51p., 44p., 30p. **CK173**

Watson, W. J. Place-names of **Ross** and **Cromarty.** Inverness, Northern Counties Pr. and Pub. Co., 1904. 302p.   **CK174**

Jakobsen, J. Place-names of **Shetland.** London, Nutt, 1936. 273p.   **CK175**

Forbes, A. R. Place-names of **Skye** and adjacent islands, with lore mythical, traditional and historical. Paisley, Gardner, 1923. 495p.   **CK176**

Macdonald, A. The place-names of **West Lothian.** Edinburgh, Oliver and Boyd, 1941. 179p.   **CK177**

South Africa

Pettman, Charles. South African place-names, past and present. Queenstown, Daily Representative, 1931. 194p.   **CK178**

South Africa. Place Names Committee. Amptelike plekname in die Unie en Suidwes-Afrika. (Goedgekeur tot einde 1948) Official place names in the Union and South West Africa. (Approved to end 1948) Pretoria, Govt. Printer, 1952. 376p.   **CK179**

A list of approved place-names, showing for each: correct spelling, indication of province, and whether the place has a railway station, motorbus halt, post office, etc.

Switzerland

Jaccard, Henri. Essai de toponymie; origine des noms de lieux habités et des lieux dits de la Suisse romande. Lausanne, Bridel, 1906. 558p. (Société d'Histoire de la Suisse Romande. Mémoires et documents, 2. sér., t.7)   **CK180**

An extensive listing showing the development of Swiss place-names with references to sources.

Studer, Julius. Schweizer Ortsnamen; ein historisch-etymologischer Versuch. . . . Zürich, Schulthess, 1896. 288p.   **CK181**

A listing of German-Swiss names, giving early usages and etymologies.

Union of Soviet Socialist Republics

Slovar' russkoi transkriptsii geograficheskikh nazvanii. Moskva, Uchpedgiz, 1955–59. 2v.   **CK182**

Pt.1, Geograficheskie nazvaniia na territorii SSSR; pt.2, Geograficheskie nazvaniia na territorii zarubezhnykh stran.

A dictionary of transcription into Russian of geographic names, designed to stabilize usage for school maps and geography texts.

Pt.1 lists the names of cities, towns, lakes, mountains, etc. in non-Russian teritories of the USSR in one alphabet (Russian), with latitude and longitude; cross references are given from variants. Pt.2 lists the same type of information for countries outside the USSR.

ATLASES

🌿 Atlases are important and necessary reference books in any library. As they are expensive and vary greatly in quality, they should be chosen with care, after a check of critical estimates by experts and an examination of the books themselves to note their suitability for the particular library in question. Atlases which are general in scope (i.e., cover the whole world) differ considerably in their contents according to the country in which they are published. An American atlas, for example, will include more or larger maps of American regions and cities than will be found in an English or French atlas. An English atlas will include more maps of British territory. Generally, the workmanship of the best foreign atlases is better than

that of American atlases, and an American library should take that fact into account in forming its collection, including some British, French, and German atlases for the quality of their maps, and some American atlases for their more numerous maps of American regions. A useful survey of atlases is given in Wright and Platt, *Aids to geographical research,* p.83–99 (CK1). This work gives a general discussion of the subject, and special critical comment on many atlases.

For more up-to-date listings and comments *see* Ena L. Yonge, "World and thematic atlases: a summary survey," *Geographical review* 52:583–96. Oct. 1962; her "Regional atlases: a summary survey," *ibid.,* 52:407–32. July 1962; and "National atlases: a summary," *ibid.,* 47:570–78. Oct. 1957. The first treats world atlases—general; for school use; and pictorial and encyclopaedic—followed by special subject atlases: historical, medical, economic, climatologic, and oceanographic. The second gives information on several dozen regional atlases of all parts of the world, and the third treats atlases of particular nations.

See also Subscription books bulletin reviews (AA309a) for detailed reviews of atlases.

In studying atlases, in addition to following the general directions for examining reference books, the librarian should note the following special points:

I. Atlas as a whole
   A. Scope
      1. Does the atlas include all types of maps: political, physical, historical, economic, etc.?
   B. Country of origin, as indication of both quality of maps and emphasis of atlas
   C. Date: publication, copyright, preface, revision
   D. Index
      1. Is there a general index for the whole atlas, or are there separate indexes for each country or map?
      2. If there is a general index, is it in a separate volume or bound with the atlas?
      3. Does the index include population figures or other additional information, e.g., pronunciation, latitude and longitude, etc.?
      4. Does the index list only names printed on the maps, or are other places included?
      5. How does the index refer to the location of a place on a given map?
         a) By locational squares indicated by marginal letters and figures?
         b) By latitude and longitude?
   E. Supplementary material
      1. Does the atlas contain any material in addition to maps and index, e.g., bibliographies; general descriptive, statistical, commercial, or ethnographic information; lists of commercial products; gazetteer lists of places; illustrations, etc?

II. Maps
   A. Name and nationality of the maker, as indication of the quality of the work
   B. Date. (If map is undated, the name and address of the maker may show this approximately, or the date may be indicated by some kind of internal evidence, such as: inclusion or omission of new places, changed names, boundaries and explorations which were established or made at certain dates.)
   C. Method of indicating relief
      1. By hachuring?

2. By layer method of altitude tints?
3. By contour lines with altitude figures?
4. By shading?

D. Color
  1. Is the color definite and varied enough to be clear, and at the same time not so dark as to obscure lettering?
  2. Does each map have a key, showing the meaning of the colors used?

E. Scale
  1. Is the scale plainly indicated?

F. Lettering and other details
  1. Is the lettering distinct and easily read?
  2. Are other details, e.g., rivers, railroads, boundaries, canals, etc., plain and well differentiated?

G. Form of names
  1. Are geographical names in the vernacular or translated?

H. Authority
  1. Are there bibliographical or other references to indicate the source and authority of the maps?

I. Accuracy
  1. Are the maps accurate in detail? (The librarian who is not a specialist naturally cannot judge the whole atlas on this point, but he can examine some one map of a small region with which he is familiar and judge its accuracy and completeness on points known to him.)

See Atlases, p.467, for historical atlases.

Bibliography

British Museum. Dept. of Printed Books. Map Room. Catalogue of the printed maps, plans, and charts in the British Museum. London, 1885. 2v.   **CK183**

The catalog of a very extensive collection. Kept up to date by *Catalog of maps: Accessions.*

California. University, Berkeley. Bancroft Library. Index to printed maps. Boston, G. K. Hall, 1964. 521p. **CK184**

Photographic reproductions of the catalog cards of the map collection. For catalog of the Bancroft Library, *see* DB49.

Chubb, Thomas. Printed maps in the atlases of Great Britain and Ireland; a bibliography, 1579–1870 . . . with an introd. by F. P. Sprent and biographical notes on the map makers, engravers and publishers by T. Chubb assisted by J. W. Skells and H. Beharrell. . . . London, Homeland Assoc., 1927. 479p. il., maps.   **CK185**

Contents: (1) Atlases of England and Wales; (2) of Scotland; (3) of Ireland; (4) biographical notes on the map makers, engravers, and publishers. Index.

Claussen, Martin Paul and **Friis, Herman R.** Descriptive catalog of maps published by Congress, 1817–1843. Wash., [priv. pr.], 1941. 104p.   **CK186**

"This is a catalog of the 503 maps that are scattered throughout v.1–429 of the 'Congressional series' . . . 15th through the 27th Congress, between 1817 and 1843."—*Introd.*

Arranged chronologically by Congress with index to area, place-names that appear in title, names of persons, government agencies, and institutions involved in compiling the maps.

Kosack, Hans-Peter and **Meine, Karl-Heinz.** Die Kartographie 1943–1954, eine bibliographische Übersicht. Lahr-Schwarzwald, Astra Verlag, 1955. 216p. (Kartographische Schriftenreihe, Bd.4)   **CK187**

Includes material in many languages, although German titles predominate. Lists books, periodical articles, and serial

publications of societies and governments, on all phases of cartography. Classed arrangement with author index.

Lowery, Woodbury. The Lowery collection. A descriptive list of maps of the Spanish possessions within the present limits of the United States, 1502–1820. Ed. with notes by P. L. Phillips. Wash., Govt. Prt. Off., 1912. 567p.   **CK188**

Detailed descriptions of maps with references to sources. Chronological arrangement with author index.

Shibanov, F. A. Ukazatel' kartograficheskoi literatury, vyshedshei v Rossii s 1800–1917 god. [Leningrad], Izd-vo Leningradskogo Universiteta, 1961. 223p.   **CK189**

The literature on cartography published in Russia from 1800 to 1917, in a bibliography arranged by topics, such as: applied astronomy, geodesy, topography, marine surveying, and the history of these subjects. Lists reviews and announcements of maps and atlases. Author index.

Spain. Ejército. Servicio Geográfico. Archivo de Planos. Catálogo de atlas. Madrid, 1962. 420p.   **CK190**

Detailed listings for 329 atlases in the Department, from the 16th to the 20th centuries.

Thiele, Walter. Official map publications; a historical sketch, and a bibliographical handbook of current maps and mapping services in the United States, Canada, Latin America, France, Great Britain, Germany, and certain other countries. Chicago, Amer. Lib. Assoc., 1938. 356p.   **CK191**

"The primary purpose of this handbook is to serve as a guide to the map publications which are currently made available by national government mapping services."—*Pref.* Pt.1, Historical sketch; pt.2, Current government maps and mapping services, including reference lists of map publications issued by the various governments. Care of maps. Appendixes: (1) Tentative map classification outline by subject; (2) Map classification outline by area; (3) State governments of the United States as map sources; (4) Public planning organizations in the United States and their map publications; (5) List of international maps.

U.S. Library of Congress. Library of Congress catalog: a cumulative list of works represented by Library of Congress printed cards: Maps and atlases. Wash., 1953–55. 3v. Semiannual, with annual cumulations.   **CK192**

Ceased publication.

Contains entries for maps, relief models, globes, and geographical atlases, received by the Library of Congress and other American libraries participating in the cooperative cataloging program, insofar as these works are represented by Library of Congress printed cards.

Arrangement is alphabetical by geographical area, with name and subject indexes.

Before 1953 and after 1955, entries are included in the *National union catalog* (AA65) and its predecessors.

U.S. Library of Congress. Map Division. A guide to historical cartography; a selected, annotated list of references on the history of maps and map making, comp. by Walter W. Ristow and Clara E. LeGear. 2d ed. rev. Wash., 1960. 18p. (Repr. 1961)   **CK193**

1st ed. 1954.

A selected, annotated list of 67 items, about half of which are in English. This edition drops some titles from the earlier edition and adds others.

—— A list of geographical atlases in the Library of Congress, with bibliographical notes. Wash., Govt. Prt. Off., 1909–63. v.1–6. (In progress)   **CK194**

v.1–4, comp. by Philip Lee Phillips; v.5–6 by Clara Egli LeGear.

Contents: v.1, Titles 1–3265. 1909; v.2, Author list and index. 1909; v.3, Titles 3266–4087 (acquired 1909–14). 1914; v.4, Titles 4088–5324 (acquired 1914–20). 1920; v.5, Titles

5325–7623 (acquired 1920–55). 1958; v.6, Titles 7624–10254 (acquired 1920–60). 1963.

An important catalog of an outstanding collection which includes many rare and early atlases. v.1–4 form the record of 5324 atlases in the Library of Congress in 1920, giving for each full description and contents. v.2 is an index volume containing an author list and a detailed analytical index referring to all maps listed in the contents notes. v.3–4 are supplements to the main work, listing new acquisitions, each containing an author list and an analytical index. The author list in v.4 cumulates, combining the author lists to v.1–4, and is also published separately (1920. clxiiip.).

v.5–6, published in continuation of the Phillips catalog, bring forward the record with the same minute detail: v.5 lists world atlases acquired 1920–1955; v.6 describes atlases of Europe, Asia, Africa and Oceania, the polar regions and the oceans, and includes some 800 oriental atlases, mainly Chinese, Japanese, and Korean. Each includes full tables of contents for atlases published before 1820 and for some miscellaneous volumes published later; an author list; and a detailed analytical index to areas, subjects, maps, engravers, publishers, etc.

v.7 will describe atlases of the Western Hemisphere and of the countries of North and South America. v.8 will comprise an integrated author list and index to the full set.

——— List of maps of America in the Library . . . preceded by a list of works relating to cartography by P. Lee Phillips. Wash., Govt. Prt. Off., 1901. 1137p. **CK195**

Lists maps to be found in books and atlases as well as those separately issued. Describes many old state and county maps and city plans.

——— United States atlases; a list of national, state, county, city, and regional atlases in the Library of Congress, comp. by Clara Egli LeGear. Wash., Govt. Prt. Off., 1950–53. 2v. **CK196**

v.2 adds "and cooperating libraries" to title.

v.1–2 list almost 6700 atlases. v.2 lists not only atlases received by the Library of Congress between 1949 and 1953, but also those held by some 180 other libraries. Location of copies is shown.

Vatican. Biblioteca Vaticana. Monumenta cartographica Vaticana iussu Pii XII P.M. Città del Vaticana, 1944–55. 4v. maps. 43cm. **CK197**

An extensive catalog depicting the history of cartography from the 14th to the 17th centuries. Excellent descriptions and reproductions of maps with references to sources.

Wheat, Carl Irving. Mapping the Transmississippi West, 1540–1861. San Francisco, Inst. of Historical Cartography, 1957–63. 5v. in 6. maps. 37cm. **CK198**

Contents: v.1, The Spanish *Entrada* to the Louisiana Purchase, 1540–1804; v.2, From Lewis and Clark to Frémont, 1804–1845; v.3, From the Mexican War to the Boundary Surveys, 1846–1854; v.4, From the Pacific Railroad surveys to the onset of the Civil War, 1855–1860; v.5, From the Civil War to the Geological Survey, 1861–1870's. 2v.

A beautifully produced work with detailed textual descriptions, facsimile maps, "biblio-cartographies," and references to sources. Discusses many hundreds of maps.

Whyte, Fredrica Harriman. Whyte's Atlas guide. N.Y., Scarecrow, 1962. 172p. **CK199**

Analyzes and indexes the contents of 20 general atlases by subject and geographical area. Covers "geographical, historical, economic and political information found . . . in maps, charts, tables and text."—*Directions for use.*

Current

Bibliotheca cartographica. Bibliographie des kartographischen Schrifttums . . . 1957– . Remagen, 1957– . Hft. 1/2– . Semiannual. **CK200**

Continues Hans-Peter Kosack, *Die Kartographie*, 1943–54 (CK187).

Volumes for 1957– , issued by the Bundesanstalt für Landeskunde und Raumforschung, in cooperation with the Deutsche Gesellschaft für Kartographie.

Lists books and periodical articles on cartography in classified arrangement, including materials from several countries of Europe, South Africa, South America, and the United States.

Tables of contents and subject headings in German, English, and French.

Bibliographie cartographique internationale, 1936– . Paris, Colin, 1938– . Annual (Irregular). **CK201**

Title varies: 1936–45, *Bibliographie cartographique française.*

1936 and 1937 published as *Suppléments au Bulletin du Comité National Français de Géographie,* 1938–39.

1938/1945, 1946/47, each published in 1v.

1948– , published annually under the auspices of the Comité National Français de Géographie and the Union Géographique Internationale by M. Foncin and P. Sommer, with the aid of UNESCO.

Lists general, political, and topographical maps and atlases; road maps; maps of cities, etc., from all parts of the world.

Kartograficheskaia letopis'; organ gosudarstvennoi bibliografii SSSR. 1931–1940, 1946– . Moskva, Vsesoiuznaia Knizhnaia Palata, 1932?– . Annual since 1947. **CK202**

A section of the Soviet national bibliography which lists the year's output of maps and atlases (scientific, school, tourist, etc.) with full bibliographic description and annotation.

1931–40 and 1946, quarterly. Publication suspended 1941–45. Title for 1939 and 1940: *Bibliografiia kartograficheskoi literatury i kart.* Index, *Svodnyi ukazatel',* 1941–1950, published 1953.

Directories

Special Libraries Association. Geography and Map Division. Map Resources Committee. Map collections in the United States and Canada: a directory. Marie Cleckner Goodman, chairman. N.Y., Special Libraries Assoc., 1954. 170p. **CK203**

Records the map holdings in 527 collections in the United States and Canada. Arranged alphabetically by state or province. For each collection gives: name, address, staff, areas covered, subjects, size, clientele, reproduction facilities, publications, etc. Index by name and specialty. The appendix lists U.S. Government Map Depositories.

General

Aguilar, José, García Aráez, Elisa and **Villarroya, Antonio.** Atlas universal Aguilar. Madrid, Aguilar, 1960. 141p., 116p. col. maps, 139p. 42cm. **CK204**

A general world atlas, incorporating a considerable amount of text, illustration, charts, and statistics. Includes topical world maps, maps of individual continents and countries, and a separate section on Spain and its provinces. Place-names are in language of country treated.

A vocabulary of geographical terms is followed by an index of place-names.

Andree, Richard. Andrees allgemeiner Handatlas in 231 Haupt- und 211 Nebenkarten. 8. neubear. u. verm. Aufl., 5. verb. u. verm. Abdruck. Hrsg. von Ernst Ambrosius. Bielefeld, Velhagen, 1930. 2v. 45cm., 29cm. **CK205**

v.1, Atlas; v.2, Namenverzeichnis. 644p.

One of the outstanding German atlases preceding World War II. Includes largely political maps, with some physical and economic. Still useful when up-to-date material is not needed.

Atlas mira. [A. N. Baranov and others, eds.] Moskva, 1954. 13p., 283p. of col. maps. 51cm.   **CK206**

—— Ukazatel' geograficheskikh nazvanii. Moskva, 1954. 571p. 30cm.

A general world atlas, prepared by the Chief Administration of Geodesy and Cartography of the Ministry of Internal Affairs, by order of the Council of Ministers of the USSR.

Maps are primarily locational, emphasizing centers of population, communication routes, hydrography, relief, and political-administrative boundaries. Maps of the USSR make up approximately 27 percent of the total number. Plans of the world's large cities other than Moscow and Leningrad are included. Non-Russian names are phonetically transcribed into Cyrillic. The index volume (*Ukazatel' geograficheskikh nazvanii*) contains some 205,000 names.

—— English translation to Atlas mira [by] Vladimir G. Telberg. Translation and key to: Glavnoe Upravlenie Geodezii i Kartografii SSSR. Atlas of the world/Atlas mira. Chief ed., A. N. Baranov. Moscow, 1954; N.Y., Telberg Book Co., 1956. 87p.   **CK207**

A translation of the text and legends of the Soviet world atlas (CK206), including introductory material of the index-gazetteer volume and an abbreviated index. In mimeographed form, with an unusual layout, which is reasonably clear. The work would have benefited by more stringent English editing and proofreading.

Bickmore, D. P. Concise Oxford atlas, prep. by the Cartographic Dept. of the Clarendon Press . . . with historical information and contemporary notes by T. K. Derry. 2d ed. London, Oxford Univ. Pr., 1958. 248p. (p.1–120 chiefly col. maps). 27cm.   **CK208**

1st ed. 1952.

In two parts: (1) the British Isles; (2) the rest of the world. The gazetteer of the British Isles is at the front of the volume, the gazetteer of the rest of the world at the back.

A useful, small atlas. The maps have been revised and brought up to date, and new ones added. The gazetteers have also been revised.

Collier's World atlas and gazetteer, presenting the world in its geographical, physical and commercial aspects. . . . N.Y., Collier, 1953. 472p., incl. approx. 128pl. of maps. il. 36x28cm.   **CK209**

Designed for the home, school, and library. The maps are done by Rand McNally and are substantially the same as those appearing in the 1st edition of the *Cosmopolitan world atlas* (CK222). In Collier's, however, in the margins of the maps of countries, lists have been inserted of the principal cities, with population (in round numbers) and location symbols. In many cases this device would obviate the necessity of turning to the general index.

Includes chapters on the geography of the world and the states of the United States; and various statistical tables and charts, etc.

The "World index and gazetteer" combines, in one alphabet, the names of political and geographical places, distinguishing them by different kinds of type, and gives location symbols, population of cities, and gazetteer information, sometimes of some length, about the more important cities of the world, including geographical, economic, historical, and touristic facts. This feature should be particularly useful in the home and small library. The gazetteer also includes inset maps of the business centers of more than 50 cities.

Encyclopaedia Britannica. Encyclopaedia Britannica world atlas; political-physical maps, world distributions and world political geography, geographical summaries, geographical comparisons, glossary, index to political-physical maps. Under the ed. direction of John V. Dodge [and others]. Unabridged. Chicago, 1964. xiip., 416p. il., maps, tables. 38cm.   **CK210**

1st ed. 1949.

Succeeding editions revised and reorganized. Includes po-

litical and physical maps of the continents, countries, states, provinces, etc. of the world. The index includes names of cities and towns (with population figures), rivers, mountains, lakes, etc.

The "Geographical summaries" give, in tabular form, statistics of the countries of the world arranged alphabetically, on such topics as: area, population, chief cities, transport and communication, economy, education and health, trade, commodities, etc. A section on "The world scene" gives maps showing world distributions and political geography.

Geograficheskii atlas; dlia uchitelei srednei shkoly. 2-oe izd. Moskva, Glavnoe Upravlenie Geodezii i Kartografii MVD SSSR, 1959. 191p. il., maps. 37cm.   **CK211**

A world atlas of which 60 plates are devoted to the USSR, and 95 plates to other world areas. Although designed as a teaching aid for secondary schools in the Soviet Union, it is useful for its economic maps and other special features not included in map form in the *Atlas mira* (CK206).

An *English guide,* by John P. Cole and Dennis R. Mills, was published in 1956 by the Dept. of Geography, University of Nottingham. 73p.

Goode's World atlas. 12th ed., ed. by Edward B. Espenshade, Jr. Chicago, Rand McNally, 1964. 288p. il., maps. 29cm.   **CK212**

Formerly *Goode's School atlas.*

Emphasizes physical and political maps, and maps showing resources and products. The United States is given by sections but not by individual states. Maps of city environs. An index of more than 30,000 names indicates pronunciation. An excellent, small, student atlas frequently revised.

Der grosse Bertelsmann Weltatlas. Hrsg: Kartographisches Institut Bertelsmann. Leitung, W. Borman. Gütersloh, C. Bertelsmann, 1961. 185p., 52p., 120p. of col. maps. 32cm. (Die grosse Bertelsmann Lexikon-Bibliothek, Bd.10)   **CK213**

Excellent maps, with good color and shading and wealth of detail. In two sections: (1) the major part, including maps from all parts of the world with its own extensive index, is followed by (2) a special section of 20 maps on Central Europe with its own index.

Der grosse Brockhaus Atlas; Erdkunde, Wirtschaft, Geschichte. Wiesbaden, Brockhaus, 1960. 664p. il., maps. 25cm.   **CK214**

Not numbered in the set, but designed in format and size to serve as an additional volume to *Der grosse Brockhaus* (AD34).

Excellent maps: political, physical, and economic. Includes small sections of outstanding photographs illustrating land formations, industry, agriculture, etc. in various parts of the world. Extensive index of place-names.

Hammond's Ambassador world atlas. 2d ed. Maplewood, N.J., Hammond, 1961. 550p. (170pl. of maps) 37cm.   **CK215**

1st ed. 1954.

A medium-sized atlas which contains political and physical maps, including those showing rainfall, vegetation, population, etc. Arranged by continent, with separate maps for individual countries and states. The 2d edition is revised and enlarged.

The index-gazetteer lists the cities of the world, with inset city street maps of some of the larger cities; gives topographic features, such as rivers, mountains, lakes, etc.; and includes some very brief gazetteer information about many of the world's largest cities.

Kremling, Ernst. Der grosser JRO Weltatlas: Luxusausgabe. Mit 128 vielfarbigen Landkartenseiten mit über 150,000 Namen, sowie einem ausführlichen Länderlexikon, farbigen Bildern aus aller Welt, Spezialkarten, einer Flaggentafel, zwei Registern und einer Schallplatte. Wissenschaftlicher Mitarbeiter, G. Fochler-Hauke. 21. Aufl. der Volksausg. München, JRO Verlag, 1961. [v.p.] col. il., col. maps. 45cm. **CK216**

1st ed. 1949.

In two pts.: T.1, The whole world; T.2, Special maps of Germany, Austria, and Switzerland.

The same firm also issues *Der kleine JRO Weltatlas* (Munich, 1961. 22cm.), which includes 61 maps, tables of geographical statistics, and index of names.

Larousse, *firm, publishers, Paris.* Atlas général Larousse. Paris, Larousse, 1959. 456p. il., maps. 30cm. **CK217**

Subtitle: 431 cartes et cartons en couleurs, 183 plans et sites urbains, 250 tableaux statistiques, 30 notices historiques, index de 55,000 noms.

Includes physical, political, geological, historical, and economic maps, with statistical tables and an index-gazetteer of some 55,000 names.

——Atlas international Larousse politique et économique . . . publié sous la direction de Jean Chardonnet. Paris, Librarie Larousse, [1950]. 136p. 25 [i.e., 58] maps. 50x 37cm. **CK218**

Title also in English and Spanish.

Stresses the unifying physical and economic factors of world geography. Continents and groups of countries are given emphasis rather than the political boundaries of individual states. Includes economic maps which show national resources, industrial development, and world communications, with demographic and economic statistical tables. Descriptive material is in French, English, and Spanish. Place-names are given their own national spellings on the maps. In the index the national form and the French, English, and Spanish versions of place-names all give map numbers directly. With a few exceptions years of reference for statistics vary from 1934 to 1949.

National Geographic Society, Washington, D.C. Cartographic Division. National Geographic atlas of the world. Melville Bell Grosvenor, ed. in chief; James M. Darley, chief cartographer. Wash., 1963. 300p. il., maps. 50cm. **CK219**

Well-drawn maps based on those produced for the *National geographic magazine.* Well balanced in coverage between the United States and the rest of the world. Maps are by area rather than by state or country. At times they seem crowded but are legible. More than 125,000 names in the index.

Rand McNally and Company. Rand McNally commercial atlas and marketing guide. 95th ed. N.Y., Rand McNally, 1964. 584p., incl. maps. 53cm. **CK220**

Issued annually.

Primarily an atlas of America, as more than three quarters of the maps included are of that region, but includes a section of 35 maps of foreign countries with its own index. United States maps are indexed individually by state. Includes many statistical tables of population, business and manufactures, agriculture, and other commercial features. Contains, in cover pocket, a *Road atlas of the United States, Canada, and Mexico.*

——Collegiate world atlas. Chicago, 1961. 310p., 94Ap. il., col. maps. 28cm. **CK221**

A convenient desk atlas, primarily of political maps, with states shown individually. Includes various tables and lists on the United States, e.g., state areas and populations, National Park system, state economic and climatic table, places of interest in the United States, etc. Gazetteer index.

——Cosmopolitan world atlas. Chicago, Rand McNally, 1964. xlp., 236p., 124p. col. maps. 37cm. **CK222**

1st ed. 1949.

In this atlas the world has been mapped on a regional basis, centered around a major country or group of countries. Maps are clear and up to date. Includes maps for individual states of the United States, with insets for areas of large cities. This revised and expanded edition omits some economic maps, and adds more maps of African countries; new large-scale maps of Switzerland and the Soviet Union; a special space section; and a new group of historical maps, covering from ancient times to 1950.

Special tables include world political information by country, climatic and economic tables, and a historical gazetteer of geographical names. Gazetteer index of some 80,000 entries.

Stieler, Adolf. Stieler's Atlas of modern geography; 263 maps on 114 sheets, engraved on copper. 10th ed. International ed., pub. by Dr. Hermann Haack, with the co-operation of Dr. Berthold Carlberg and Rudolf Schleifer. Gotha, Perthes, 1934–38. Pt.1–34. 41cm. **CK223**

No more published.

One of the best of the prewar German atlases. This edition appeared in parts and was to have been completed in some 114 sheets. It was a thorough revision—with addition of various, entirely new sheets—of the 10. Aufl. of *Stieler's Handatlas.* Gotha, Perthes, 1931/32. 40cm.

In the International edition, the maps are in the language of the country mapped; explanatory notes, etc. are in English, French, German, Italian, Portuguese, and Spanish. Also published with French title.

The 1931/32 edition included 108 sheets of maps, most of them double spreads, and an index of 337 pages.

Times atlas of the world: mid-century edition, ed. by John Bartholomew. London, Times Pub. Co., 1955–59. 5v. (chiefly col. maps) 50cm. *+ Gazetteer* **CK224**

Earlier ed. 1920.

A thoroughly revised edition of a famous atlas designed for general, official, and library use. Gives as many place-names as possible, preferably in the form of spelling officially used by the inhabitants. "In the case of important places where English practice has familiarized an alternative form of name," this is also shown, in brackets, both forms appearing in the index. Elevation is shown by color tints. Main roads, airports, etc. are indicated.

Each volume covers a different section of the world, and each has its own index-gazetteer: v.1, World, Australasia and East Asia. 1958; v.2, Southwest Asia and Russia. 1959; v.3, Northern Europe. 1955; v.4, Southern Europe and Africa. 1956; v.5, The Americas. 1957.

Touring Club Italiano. Atlante internazionale. Ed. del sessantennio. [Opera redatta ed esequita nell' Ufficio cartografico del Touring Club Italiano sotto la direzione di L. V. Bertarelli (and others)] Nuova ed. interamente rielaborata a cura di M. Castiglioni, capo redattore, e. M. Pasquetti, capo cartografo. Milano, 1956. 1731 l. of col. maps. 51cm. **CK225**

—— —— Indice dei nomi. Milano, 1956 [1957]. 257p. 51cm.

1st ed. 1927; 5th ed. 1938.

One of the finest of the European atlases, devoted to physical and political geography. The maps are drawn and engraved by hand and printed by lithography. Place-names are in the spelling of the country concerned, and are indexed in the separate index which includes more than 250,000 names.

Union of Soviet Socialist Republics. Glavnoe Upravlenie Geodezii i Kartografii. Fiziko-geograficheskii atlas mira. Red. koll. IU. V. Filippov i dr. Moskva, 1964. 289p. 249 col. maps. 32x50cm. **CK226**

249 colored plates supplemented by explanatory text.

Includes relief and physical maps: geology, meteorology, hydrology, soil, vegetation, zoology, etc.

Plates 2–76 contain maps of the world, the Arctic, and the Antarctic; 78–190, the continents; 192–249, SSSR.

Vidal de la Blache, Paul Marie Joseph. Atlas historique et géographique Vidal-Lablache. 385 cartes et cartons; index de 32,000 noms. Paris, Colin, 1951. 130[i.e., 134]p., 30p., incl. 98 col. maps. 40cm. **CK227**

1st ed. 1894: Atlas général Vidal-Lablache. Frequently reprinted before World War II with revisions.

Includes historical, physical, political, economic maps, etc., with an index-gazetteer. This edition reduced in size from the pre-World War II editions.

World book atlas. Chicago, Field Enterprises, 1964. 392p. col. maps. 36cm.   **CK228**

Designed as a complement to the *World book encyclopedia* (AD16), and planned for student use. Arranged by large groupings; under each has physical, political, and historical maps. Individual maps for states of the United States. Population tables are followed by a general index, which includes place-names, islands, rivers, mountains, etc.

National and regional

❦ Some 30 or more "national" atlases are now available; several others are in the planning stage. These usually attempt to portray all aspects of the physical, economic, and social life of a country and, for the most part, are excellent examples of cartography. A number from Europe are outstanding; many have texts and legends in English or French as well as in the vernacular of the country. This section includes some of the best of these, as well as a few other regional atlases.

Africa

Philip, George and Son, Ltd. Philips' Modern college atlas for Africa. 3d ed., ed. by Harold Fullard. London, Philip, 1962. 136p. of col. maps, 32p. 28cm.   **CK229**
1st ed. 1959.
Prepared for students attending African schools and colleges; emphasis is on maps of Southern, East, and West Africa, but maps of other parts of the world are also included.

Asia, Southeast

Atlas of south-east Asia, with an introduction by D. G. E. Hall. London, Macmillan; N.Y., St. Martin's, 1964. 84p. maps, il. 34cm.   **CK230**
60 colored maps of the countries and islands of southeast Asia, usually showing: climate, agriculture, population, minerals and industries, communications, etc. Includes plans of the larger cities.

Austria

Akademie der Wissenschaften, Vienna. Kommission für Raumforschung und Wiederaufbau. Atlas der Republik Österreich. Hrsg. unter der Gesamtleitung [von] Hans Bobeck und unter redaktioneller Mitarbeit von Erik Arnberger [et al.]. Vienna, Freytag-Berndt & Artaria, 1961–   . v.1–2. 47x73cm. (In progress)   **CK231**

Belgium

Comité National de Géographie, Belgium. Atlas de Belgique. Atlas van België. Bruxelles, Inst. Géographique Militaire, 1950–   . Loose-leaf. col. maps. 62cm. **CK232**

Brazil

Ira, Rudolf and **Klettner, Edgar.** Atlas do Brasil globo, com os mapas político e físico do Brasil e os mapas dos seus estados e territórios . . . Índice remissivo e descritivo dos topônimos pelo Lourenço Mario Prunes. Rio de Janeiro, Ed. Globo, 1960. 98p. maps. 45cm.   **CK233**

33 plates of colored maps, physical and regional. Index-gazetteer.

Canada

Canada. Dept. of Mines and Technical Surveys. Geographical Branch. Atlas of Canada. Ottawa, 1957–   . Loose-leaf binder. col. maps. 54cm.   **CK234**
Issued also in French.
Treats physical, historical, political, cultural, and economic aspects. Well planned and executed.

China

Ting, Wên-chiang, Wêng, Wên-hao and **Tsêng, Shih-ying.** Chung Kuo fên shêng hsin-t'u [New provincial atlas of China]. 5th ed. Shanghai, Shên-pao, 1948. 58p., 94p. col. maps. 27x39cm.   **CK235**
In Chinese. A new edition of this standard atlas. A useful index is available in English as:

———— ——— Gazetteer of Chinese place names based on the index to V. K. Ting atlas, comp. by the U.S. Board on Geographical Names. June 1944. [Wash., Army Map Service, 1944. lxxixp., 229p. 38cm.]   **CK235a**
Alphabetical, romanized index to the atlas.

U.S. Central Intelligence Agency. China: provisional atlas of Communist administrative units. Wash., U.S. Dept. of Commerce, Office of Technical Services, 1959. 29pl., 14p. 48x60cm.   **CK236**
"A specialized atlas designed to aid research workers faced with problems of interpreting current information on Communist China in the light of its complex administrative structure."—*Note.*

Czechoslovakia

Česká Akademie Věd a Umění, Prague. Atlas Republiky Československé. Atlas de la République Tchécoslovaque. [Praze, Nákl. Akc. Spol. Orbis, 1935–36] 2v. maps. 44cm.   **CK237**
"Publié par l'Académie Tchèque sous les auspices du Ministère des Affaires Étrangères de la République Tchécoslovaque."
In two parts: (1) atlas of 55 double plates of maps (442 maps), 1935, forming a bound volume, and (2) accompanying text, 43p., 1936, unbound.
A very fine and detailed atlas, covering economic and physical geography, demography, political and cultural aspects, etc.

Denmark

Nielsen, Niels. Atlas over Danmark, Tekst og Fotografier. København, H. Hagerup (C. A. Reitzels Forlag, v.2), 1949–61. v.1–2. 29cm. and atlas 55cm. (In progress)   **CK238**
Contents: v.1, Landskabsformerne, forfatter Axel Schou. Text and atlas; v.2, Befolkningen, forfatter Aage Aageson. Text and atlas.

Europe

Göttinger Arbeitskreis. Staats- und Verwaltungsgrenzen in Ostmitteleuropa: historisches Kartenwerk . . . München, Oldenbourg, 1954–55. v.1–3. 31cm. (Der Göttinger Arbeitskreis. Veröffentlichungen, 114–116) (In progress)   **CK239**
Maps in portfolios.
Contents: I, Die baltischen Lande, bearb. von H. Laakmen;

II, Das Preussenland, bearb. von Erich Keyser; III, Pommern, bearb. von Franz Engel.

Finland

Geografiska Sällskapet i Finland, Helsingfors. Suomen kartasto, 1960. Atlas of Finland. Atlas över Finland. Helsinki, Otava, 1961 [c1960]. 12p. 39 maps. 46cm. **CK240**

—————— Teksti. 1961. 123p.

1st ed. 1899; 3d ed. 1925.
Explanatory text in Finnish, English, and Swedish. Covers physical, economic, and social geography.

France

Comité National Français de Géographie. Atlas de France. 2. éd. . . . Paris, Éd. Géographiques de France, 1951–59. v.1–2. fold. col. maps in portfolio. 50cm. **CK241**

A regional atlas of the highest grade, covering geomorphology, climatology, hydrography, biogeography, agriculture, industry, commerce, and human and political geography.

Great Britain

Atlas of Britain and Northern Ireland, planned and directed by D. P. Bickmore and M. A. Shaw . . . Oxford, Clarendon Pr., 1963. 200p. maps. 52cm. **CK242**

Index unpaged.
A beautifully reproduced atlas intended to do for the United Kingdom what national atlases have done for other countries, although this work was not issued as a state publication. The Editorial Committee was composed of a group of outstanding geographers and economists who were assisted by numerous scholars and official bodies.
Covers England, Scotland, Wales, and Northern Ireland with major emphasis on physical and economic maps, representing mainly conditions in the mid-20th century.
Maps are clear, with good color and design. Comparative statistics are printed on the maps, and authorities, notes, and sources are given.
Includes a gazetteer index of some 16,000 names.

Israel

Israel. Surveys Dept. Atlas of Israel; cartography, physical geography, history, demography, economics, education. Jerusalem, 1956– . Loose-leaf. maps. 50cm. (In progress) **CK243**

Title page and text in Hebrew (above title from added title page). The plan is to issue some 100 double sheets in 10 to 12 folders at the rate of two folders per year, to be inserted in the cloth binder which is provided.
Maps are handsomely printed in as many as 15 colors, with explanatory texts overleaf. While some maps are restricted to Israel, Palestine is represented wherever reliable information is available.

Italy

Dainelli, Giotto. Atlante fisico-economico d'Italia; 82 tavole, 508 carte. Milan, Consociazione Turistica Italiana, 1940. xviip., 82 maps. 49cm. **CK244**

—————— Note illustrative, a cura del Aldo Sestini. 1940. 147p.

Shows physical features, geology, volcanoes, climatology, vegetation, population, labor, agriculture, industries, communication, education, etc.

New Zealand

McLintock, Alexander H. A descriptive atlas of New Zealand. Wellington, R. E. Owen, Govt. Printer, 1960. 109p. 48 maps. 32cm. **CK245**

Textual material on New Zealand geography and related topics, followed by extensive map section. Index.

Philippines

Hendry, Robert S. Atlas of the Philippines. [Manila, Phil-Asian Pub., c1959] 228p. il., col. maps. 49cm. **CK246**

Political and economic maps of the islands, with separate maps for each province, and historical sketch. Gives area and population, roads, etc.

Portugal

Amorim Girão, Aristides de. Atlas de Portugal. Atlas of Portugal. 2. ed. . . . Coimbra, Inst. de Estudos Geográficos, Faculdade de Letras, 1957–59. [177]p., incl. 43 maps (part col.). 43cm. **CK247**

1st ed. 1941.
Issued in parts, in portfolio. In Portuguese and English.
Maps cover geology, topography, climate, vegetation, population, agriculture, industries, etc.

South Africa

Talbot, A. M. and **Talbot, William John.** Atlas of the Union of South Africa; prep. in collaboration with the Trigonometrical Survey Office, and under the aegis of the National Council for Social Research. Pretoria, Govt. Printer, 1960. 178p. maps. (pt. col.). 45x58cm. **CK248**

English and Afrikaans; added title page in Afrikaans.
Maps, in black and white, cover: relief, geology, vegetation, fisheries, etc.; climate and water resources; population; agriculture; industries and occupations; transportation; external trade.

Spain

Aguilar, S.A. de Ediciones, Madrid. Nuevo atlas de España. Madrid, Aguilar, 1961. 455p. il., maps. 32cm. **CK249**

Not a national atlas as such, but a well-produced atlas on Spain.

Sweden

Svenska Sällskapet för Antropologi och Geografi, Stockholm. Atlas över Sverige. Stockholm, Generalstabens Litografiska Anstalts Förlag, 1953–63. il., maps. (In progress) **CK250**

Issued in fascicules.
A regional atlas of Sweden, which, when complete, will contain 150 folio-size colored maps together with descriptive texts. The 14 sections will include material on geophysics and geology, meteorology and hydrography, pasturage and animal husbandry, population, agriculture, forestry, industry, communications, trade, economic conditions, social conditions, cultural development, political geography, and history. Extensive English summaries in each folio section, and parallel English headings in all maps and tables.

Taiwan

Chen, Cheng-siang. Geographical atlas of Taiwan. Taipei, Taiwan, 1959. 144p. maps. (Fu-Min Geographical Inst. of Economic Development. Research report, no.93) **CK251**

A popular edition of the larger-size *Atlas of Taiwan* which is in preparation.

GUIDEBOOKS

☙ Guidebooks prepared for the use of travelers are very useful in a reference department for historical and geographical information. For certain kinds of local information, they are fuller than either the general or the special gazetteers, giving more local maps, plans of cities, etc. They are especially helpful for information about the art museums, collections, etc. of any given place, its architectural and historical monuments, scenic features, railroads, highways and other communications, hotels, literary and historical associations, etc.

Old guidebooks have a definite reference function and should not be discarded when a later work or edition is acquired. For geographical and travel questions, the most recent work must be used, but the older books will often have historical information not given in the later ones: they will show the location of an old street no longer in existence; describe a building no longer standing; or furnish general descriptive information for an earlier period. For such questions the older guidebook is a most convenient source.

With the increase in travel and tourism, literally thousands of current guidebooks are now available. It will be possible to list here only some of the important standard series, e.g., (1) **Baedeker** series, published in English, French, and German editions, and originating in Germany, has long been regarded as the most authentic and complete guide for the serious traveler, although many volumes are now out of date. The handbooks, written in a concise, informative style, cover mainly countries, regions, and cities of Europe, and parts of North and South America, the Near East, and Egypt. Since 1958, a new series of touring guides ("Autoguides") has been issued covering Austria, Benelux (Belgium, Netherlands, and Luxembourg), France, Italy, Scandinavia, Spain and Portugal, Switzerland and Yugoslavia. The Baedekers are especially useful for their maps, city plans, and diagrams; (2) **Muirhead's Blue guides** (London, Benn) are mainly guides to European countries, cities, and environs. Similar to *Baedeker* in style and coverage, they include excellent maps and plans; (3) **Nagel's Travel guide** series, formerly part of the Muirhead series *Guides bleues* (Paris, Hachette), and now published in Geneva and Paris by Nagel, have recent editions for most of the countries of Europe, some of the cities of Europe, and parts of Africa, Asia, and North America. They are published in various languages, including English, German, Spanish, Italian, French, Swedish and Danish; (4) **Fodor's Modern guides,** edited by Eugene Fodor (N.Y., McKay, 1953–   ), illustrated and revised annually, modern in format and style, include more than 20 titles for Europe, India, Japan and East Asia, South America, Hawaii, the Caribbean.

A few other compilations dealing with specific areas are noted below:

General

Pan American Airways, Inc. Pan American's Travel facts about 109 countries. N.Y., [c1964]. 640p. il., maps.
CK256

A small, compact guide giving much useful travel information.

Encyclopedia of world travel, ed. by Nelson Doubleday and C. Earl Cooley. Garden City, N.Y., Doubleday, 1961.

4v. il., maps.   CK257

Contents: v.1, United States and Canada; v.2, Mexico, Central America, the Caribbean, South America; v.3, Europe; v.4, Africa, Asia, the Pacific.

Comprehensive guidebooks written by 20 travel experts and containing concise information, country by country. Cover geographic, economic, historical, and cultural aspects, as well as specific detail on points of interest to the traveler in each country and city, and general information on shopping, food, sports, etc.

Fielding, Temple Hornaday. Fielding's Travel guide to Europe. N.Y., Sloane, 1948–   . il. Annual.   CK258

1st edition had title *New travel guide to Europe.*

A popular, practical guide, addressed particularly to the American tourist on holiday; gives up-to-date travel information.

Hanson, Earl Parker [and others]. The new world guides to the Latin American republics. 3d ed. rev. N.Y., Duell, [1950]. 3v. il. (maps)   CK259

Contents: v.1, Mexico, Central America, and the West Indies; v.2, Andes and west coast countries; v.3, East coast countries.

Aspinwall, *Sir* Algernon. The pocket guide to the West Indies and British Guiana, British Honduras, Bermuda, the Spanish Main, Surinam, the Panama Canal. Rev. by J. Sydney Dash. [10th ed.] London, Methuen, [1954]. 475p. il., maps.   CK260

1st ed. 1907.

Year book and guide to East Africa: Kenya, Uganda, Tanganyika, Zanzibar, Portuguese East Africa, Mauritius, Seychelles, etc. London, R. Hale, [1950–   ]. Annual.
CK261

For description *see* CG91.

Year book and guide to Southern Africa: Republic of South Africa, South West Africa, Rhodesia, Zambia, Malawi, etc. London, R. Hale, 1901–   . Annual. CK262

For description *see* CG184.

Bibliography

Avec les "Guides bleus" à travers la France et le monde. (Bibliothèque des voyages) Paris, Hachette, 1959. 304p. il.   CK263

A listing of some 4000 titles (published in French, and in print at the time of compilation of the list) of guidebooks and volumes of geographical and artistic description of interest to tourists.

——— Supplement, 1960–1962. Paris, Hachette, 1962. 116p.

United States

Alsberg, Henry Garfield. The American guide; a source book and complete travel guide for the United States. N.Y., Hastings, 1949. 1348p.   CK264

A much condensed guide covering the whole United States, arranged geographically by region, with introductory essays. Within each region (except New England which is treated as a whole), each state is described by tours within that state, usually following U.S. highways. Information is very brief.

American guide series, comp. by the Federal Writers' Project (later called Writers' Program). [Pub. variously by different publishers], 1937–49. il.   CK265

Includes guides to each state, many cities and regions, and some special subjects. The state guidebooks are particularly useful, giving accurate information about points of interest with some historical and background material and sidelights on the unusual.

Many of these guides are out of print. Some have been reprinted, and a number have been revised and published in new editions by various publishers, mostly by Hastings House, N.Y.

Kreutz, Barbara and **Fleming, Ellen.** Introducing America. London, Methuen, [1963]. 294p. il. **CK266**

Written by two Englishwomen; expresses a foreign point of view and contains much information pertinent for the foreign traveler. Covers many of the "more interesting places" in the United States. Excellent photographic illustrations.

Hotels

Hotel and motel red book, 1886– . N.Y., Amer. Hotel Assoc. Directory Corp., 1886– . il., maps. Annual. **CK267**

At head of title: Official directory of American hotel and motel association members including hotels, motels, resorts in the United States and other countries.

Title varies: 1886–1902, *United States official hotel directory;* 1903–1953/54, *The official hotel red book and directory;* 1954/55–1962/63, *Hotel red book.*

Timetables

Timetables, schedules, etc. of trains, airlines, buses, etc. are frequently called for in libraries. The following are a selection of comprehensive monthly guides:

Official airline guide. 1943– . Chicago, [Amer. Aviation Publs.], 1943– . il., maps. Monthly. **CK268**

Combines *American aviation air traffic guide* and *Official aviation guide of the airways.*

Published in various editions: (1) North American edition, for United States and possessions; (2) World-wide edition, for United States, possessions, Canada, and all other countries; (3) Quick reference edition, for United States, possessions, and Canada; and (4) International quick reference edition.

Official guide of the railways and steam navigation lines of the United States, Puerto Rico, Canada, Mexico and Cuba, also time-tables of railroads in Central America. Air line schedules. N.Y., Nat. Railway Pub. Co., 1868– . Monthly. **CK269**

Gives timetables, many maps, indexes of stations; the general index of stations shows on what road any given place is located.

Official steamship guide; international. v.1– . N.Y., Transportation Guides, 1932– . il., maps. Monthly. **CK270**

Title varies: *Official steamship and airways guide,* v.1–64 (1932–Aug. 1963, no.2).

Steamship schedules and fares; entry requirements for international travel; passport and visa summary.

Russell's Official national motor coach guide. Cedar Rapids, Iowa, Russell's Guides, 1927– . maps. Monthly. **CK271**

Subtitle: Official publication of bus lines for United States, Canada, and Mexico.

Schedules of bus lines.

D

HISTORY

AND AREA

STUDIES

❧ Many approaches are possible to the study of history, from the school child with his textbook to the scholar searching for original sources. Furthermore, the term "history" no longer concerns itself mainly with the political and military history of individual countries, but rather interprets the term to include all the various aspects of life in a country or in a larger area. Therefore, "area studies" have become more and more important. These may treat the topography, ethnology, natural resources, religion, sociology, economy, law, government, history, culture (or any combination of these) for an area, large or small. Such area studies are listed in this section, as well as the more conventional historical guides, bibliographies, handbooks, dictionaries, and encyclopedias.

A few of the large general histories which contain detailed bibliographies and indexes are listed, but, for the most part, history texts are not included here although in actual reference work they will often be very useful.

It should be remembered, also, that for many historical questions, materials in other parts of this *Guide* will be needed: encyclopedias, biographical dictionaries, atlases, gazetteers and guidebooks, statistical compilations, national and special bibliographies, directories of manuscript sources and special library collections, indexes to periodicals and government publications, and many others.

The first section (DA) contains the general works and the chronological periods of history: Archaeology and prehistory, Classical antiquities, Medieval, and Modern.

The succeeding sections (DB–DH) are arranged by continent and subdivided as follows: (1) General works on the continent; (2) Sections of the continent; (3) Countries arranged alphabetically—with the exception that under "The Americas," the United States and Canada are followed by the countries of Latin America.

DA

General History

GENERAL WORKS

Guides

American Historical Association. Guide to historical literature. George Frederick Howe, Chairman, Board of Editors. N.Y., Macmillan, 1961. 962p. **DA1**

A successor to the *Guide to historical literature,* ed. by George M. Dutcher [and others] (N.Y., Macmillan, 1931), for long a standard work in the field. The new *Guide,* generally similar in plan, is a selective, annotated bibliography of treatises and source materials, arranged in large subject and country groups, each group selected and described by specialists. Within each section, materials are arranged as practicable by form, e.g., bibliographies, encyclopedias and dictionaries, general and specialized histories, biographies, government documents, printed collections of sources, etc.

An important first aid for students and librarians.

Barzun, Jacques and **Graff, Henry F.** The modern researcher. N.Y., Harcourt, 1957. 386p. **DA2**

The authors have skillfully combined a manual of research methods, an essay on the evaluation and interpretations of facts, and a textbook on the writing of acceptable expository English. Designed for "anyone who is or will be engaged in research and report writing . . . ," it will probably be most useful to graduate students in the humanities and the social sciences.

Bibliography

American Universities Field Staff. A select bibliography: Asia, Africa, Eastern Europe, Latin America. N.Y., 1960. 534p. **DA3**

———— ———— Supplement. N.Y., 1961. 75p.

Intended as a college-level bibliography; lists nearly 6000 books and journals (chiefly in English) recommended for a basic collection on the areas concerned. Arrangement is by subject within the geographic area; many titles are annotated. Indexes by author and by title.

Franz, Günther. Bücherkunde zur Weltgeschichte vom Untergang des Römischen Weltreiches bis zur Gegenwart . . . München, Oldenbourg, 1956. 544p. **DA4**

Selective bibliographies with some brief annotations. Primarily useful for its European emphasis.

Frewer, Louis Benson. Bibliography of historical writings published in Great Britain and the Empire, 1940–1945. Oxford, B. Blackwell, 1947. 346p. **DA5**

Edited for the British National Committee of the International Committee of Historical Sciences, in the same manner and format as the *International bibliography of historical sciences* (DA18). It includes a record of the books and periodical articles published in Great Britain and the Commonwealth 1940–45, inclusive, on all aspects of history.

Supplemented in part by:

Holtzmann, Walther and **Ritter, Gerhard.** Die deutsche Geschichtswissenschaft im zweiten Weltkrieg; Bibliographie des historischen Schrifttums deutscher Autoren

1939–1945, hrsg. im Auftrag des Verbandes der Historiker Deutschlands und der Monumenta Germaniae historica. Marburg/Lahn, Simons Verlag, 1951. 149p., 512p. **DA6**

In two parts: pt.1, Pre-history and ancient history; pt.2, Medieval and modern history. Author index.

Covers German historical writings of the war years and thus helps to supplement the *International bibliography of historical sciences* (DA18) and the *Jahresberichte für deutsche Geschichte* (DC95), which were suspended during this period.

International Committee of Historical Sciences. Bibliographie internationale des travaux historiques publiés dans les volumes de "Mélanges," 1880–1939. . . . International bibliography of historical articles in Festschriften and miscellanies. Établie avec le concours des comités nationaux sous la direction de Hans Nabholz par Margarethe Rothbarth et U. Helfenstein. Éd. par le Comité International des Sciences Historiques. Paris, Armand Colin, 1955. 443p. **DA7**

Contents: pt.1, List of volumes of "Mélanges" arranged by country; pt.2, Historical works contained in the "Mélanges," arranged by large class. List of subjects treated in the volumes of "Mélanges."

Index by persons, historical events, scientific institutes and societies, and by names of authors.

Jahresberichte der Geschichtswissenschaft; im Auftrage der Historischen Gesellschaft zu Berlin. 1.–36. Jahrg., 1878–1913. Berlin, Mittler, 1880–1916. 36v. Annual. **DA8**

Publisher varies.

International in scope, listing the historical works published in each year. A valuable record for the period covered.

The section for Germany is continued by the *Jahresberichte für deutsche Geschichte* (DC94) and its continuation (DC95).

Koner, Wilhelm. Repertorium über die vom Jahre 1800 bis zum Jahre 1850 in Akademischen Abhandlungen, Gesellschaftsschriften und wissenschaftlichen Journalen auf dem Gebiete der Geschichte und ihrer Hülfswissenschaften erschienenen Aufsätze. Berlin, Nicolai, 1852–56. 2v. **DA9**

A closely classified bibliography with subject index of articles on historical subjects appearing in some 500 periodicals and society publications in various languages. Includes some American publications. v.2, p.76–169, lists biographical articles arranged alphabetically by subject. The names of these biographees do not appear in the index.

Logasa, Hannah. Historical non-fiction; an organized, annotated, supplementary reference book for the use of schools, libraries, general reader. 8th rev. and enl. ed. Brooklawn, N.J., McKinley, 1964. 328p. **DA10**

A companion volume to the author's *Historical fiction* (BD155). In the 7th edition, for the first time, the nonfiction material was published in a separate volume, organized on the same principle.

Palumbo, Pier Fausto. Bibliografia storica internazionale, 1940–1947; con una introduzione sullo stato degli studi storici durante e dopo la seconda guerra mondiale. Roma, Ed. del Lavoro, 1950. lxiiip., 241p. **DA11**

Partially fills the period still not covered by the *International bibliography of historical sciences* (DA18). A long introductory section outlines the course of historical studies in various countries during and after World War II; the bibliographical listings are by broad period, subdivided by subject. Periodical articles are included, and there are indexes by author and by subject.

Ragatz, Lowell Joseph. A bibliography of articles, descriptive, historical and scientific, on colonies and other dependent territories, appearing in American geographical

and kindred journals. [2d ed.] Wash., Educ. Research
Bureau, 1951. 2v.   **DA12**

v.1, through 1934; v.2, 1935 through 1950, comp. by Janet
Evans Ragatz.

Arranged by empires.

Reuss, Jeremias David. Repertorium commentationum
a societatibus litterariis editarum. Secundum disciplinarum ordinem . . . T.8, Historia. . . . Gottingae, Dieterich, 1810. 674p.   **DA13**

Contents: Historia—subsidia historica (geographia, chrono-
logia, monumenta veterum populorum, inscriptiones, numi et
res numaria, ars diplomatica, heraldica); Historia universalis;
Historia generis humani; Historia mythica; Historia specialis
—Asiae, Africae, Americae, Europae; Historia ecclesiastica;
Historia litteraria.

A valuable index to the publications of the learned societies
of various countries up to 1800. Classed arrangement with
author index.

For description of complete set *see* EA15.

**U.S. Dept. of State. Bureau of Intelligence and Research.
External Research Staff.** External research list, no.1– .
Wash., Dept. of State, 1952– .   **DA14**

For complete record *see* CA14.

Current

**Bibliography of historical works issued in the United
Kingdom** . . . 1946– . Comp. for the Anglo-American
Conference of Historians. [London], Univ. of London,
Inst. of Historical Research, 1957– .   **DA15**

1946–1956, comp. by Joan C. Lancaster. 1957. 388p.
1957–1960, comp. by William Kellaway. 1962. 236p.

Serves partially as an extension of Frewer's *Bibliography
of historical writings* . . . (DA5). Includes 7382 items, classified, with an author index.

A record of books on various aspects of history of many
countries, published in the United Kingdom. Does not include
periodical articles.

Current digest of the Soviet press. v.1– , Feb. 1,
1949– . N.Y., Joint Committee on Slavic Studies, 407
West 117th St., 1949– . Weekly.   **DA16**

"The Joint Committee on Slavic Studies [is] appointed by
the American Council of Learned Societies and the Social Science Research Council."—*Title page.*

Each issue includes in English translation, without comment, articles taken from Soviet newspapers and periodicals,
in full or abridged. Each item is documented, giving: the
source with date of issue and paging, number of words, and indication noting complete translation or condensation. Arranged by subject with quarterly indexes. Each issue includes
a complete weekly index to the contents of the two leading
Soviet dailies, *Pravda* and *Izvestia.*

Historical Association, London. Annual bulletin of historical literature. v.1, 1911– . London, 1912– . Annual.   **DA17**

—— —— General index. v.1–12, 1911–22. London,
1923. 68p.

Survey articles by specialists on the annual production of
historical works. Chiefly British, though other countries are
included.

International bibliography of historical sciences, ed. for
the International Committee of Historical Sciences . . .
1926– . Oxford, Univ. Pr.; N.Y., Wilson, 1930– .
v.1– . Annual.   **DA18**

Subtitle: Internationale Bibliographie der Geschichtswis-
senschaften; Bibliografía internacional de ciencias históricas;
Bibliographie internationale des sciences historiques; Bibliografia internazionale delle scienze storiche.

Has also imprint: Paris, Colin; Rome, P. Maglione; Berlin,
de Gruyter; Madrid, Ed. Hernando.

A very useful selected, classified list of historical publications, interpreted in a wide sense to include political, constitutional, religious, cultural, economic, and social aspects; international relations; etc.

v.15, to cover 1940–46, has not been published. For partial
coverage of this period *see* DA5, DA6, DA11.

Abstract journals

Historical abstracts, (1775–1945): bibliography of the
world's periodical literature . . . Erich H. Boehm, ed.
v.1, no.1, March 1955– . Santa Barbara, Calif., Clio
Pr. with the Internat. Social Science Inst., 1955– .
v.1– . Quarterly.   **DA19**

Publisher varies. Subtitle varies.

An abstract journal, with signed abstracts contributed by
scholars, mainly from the United States. Covers the world's
periodical literature on history from 1775 to 1945, in a classified arrangement with annual author, biographical, and subject indexes (these vary).

—— Five-year index. v.1–5. 1963.

Includes subject and author indexes.

Soviet periodical abstracts: Asia, Africa and Latin America. v.1– , May 1961– . N.Y., Slavic Languages Research Inst., 1961– . Quarterly.   **DA20**

v.1 issued as *Selective Soviet annotated bibliographies:
Asia, Africa and Latin America,* by the Institute, formerly
named Soviet and East European Research and Translation
Service.

Abstracts all relevant articles which appear in six major
Soviet periodicals and a selection from other journals. Available translations are noted.

Beginning with v.4, no.1, each issue will include a list of
titles of books published in the Soviet Union on these countries.

For *Soviet periodical abstracts: Soviet society, see* DC260.

Dissertations

List of doctoral dissertations in history now in progress
or completed at universities in the United States, 1909– .
Wash., Carnegie Inst., 1909–39; N.Y., Macmillan, 1940–
41; Wash., Govt. Prt. Off., 1943; Wash., Amer. Historical
Assoc., 1947– . Annual; triennial (irregular).   **DA21**

Series originally edited by John Franklin Jameson and published by the Carnegie Institution of Washington, with the
title *List of doctoral dissertations in history now in progress
at the chief American universities.* The issues for 1939 and
1940 were published as supplements to the *American historical review;* projects from Canadian universities were included,
and a "List of research projects in history" was added. The
1941 issue was published as v.3 of the *Annual report* of the
American Historical Association, and those from 1947 on are
published separately by the Association. Not published between 1942–May 1947; Sept. 1949–Oct. 1952.

Title changed, 1958, by adding phrase "or completed," but
with no indication in the listings as to which were still in
progress.

A very useful list, arranged by field of history with author
and university indexes.

Periodicals

Boehm, Eric H. and **Adolphus, Lalit.** Historical periodicals; an annotated world list of historical and related
serial publications. Santa Barbara, Calif., Clio Pr., 1961.
618p.   **DA22**

Supersedes, for current work, the *World list of historical periodicals* by Pierre Caron and Marc Jaryc (N.Y., Wilson, 1939), although that publication may still be useful for discontinued titles.

The new work lists more than 4500 current titles, arranged by area and country, with title index. Covers history and auxiliary fields as well as journals in other subjects if they include historical articles.

Kramm, Heinrich. Bibliographie historischer Zeitschriften, 1939–1951 . . . Marburg, Otto Rasch, 1952–54. 366p. **DA23**

Pub. in 3 Lfg.

Contents: 1. Lfg., Deutschland, Österreich, Schweiz. 1952; 2. Lfg., Groszbritannien, Irland, Niederlande, Belgien, Luxemburg, Frankreich, Portugal, Spanien, Italien. 1953; 3. Lfg., Norwegen, Schweden, Dänemark, Finnland, Tschechoslowakei, Ungarn, Jugoslawien, Rumänien, Bulgarien, Griechenland, Polen, Baltische Länder, Sowjetunion. 1954.

At head of title: Westdeutsche Bibliothek.

For each country there is a list of general historical periodicals subdivided by subject, followed, when appropriate, by a listing according to geographical or political divisions. Index in each Lfg.

Manuscript sources

Hale, Richard Walden. Guide to photocopied historical materials in the United States and Canada. Pub. for the American Historical Association. Ithaca, N.Y., Cornell Univ. Pr., 1961. 241p. **DA24**

"Designed to supply basic bibliographical information on the photocopied manuscripts of interest to historians which are available in depositories in the United States and Canada." —*Pref.*

Arranged by geographical area, listing government records, personal papers, church records, educational records, ships' logs, etc.

Historiography

Bernheim, Ernst. Lehrbuch der historischen Methode und der Geschichtsphilosophie. Mit Nachweis der wichtigsten Quellen und Hilfsmittel zum Studium der Geschichte. 5. und 6., neubearb. und verm. Aufl. München, Duncker, 1914. 842p. (Repr.: N.Y., Burt Franklin, 1960. 2v.) **DA25**

A standard handbook of historical method.

Fueter, Eduard. Geschichte der neueren Historiographie. 3., um einen Nachtrag verm. Aufl., besorgt von Dietrich Gerhard und Paul Sattler. München, Oldenbourg, 1936. 670p. (Handbuch der mittelalterlichen und neueren Geschichte. Abt. 1, Allgemeines) **DA26**

Originally pub. in 1911.

Translated into French by E. Jeanmarie as *Histoire de l'historiographie moderne* (Paris, Alcan, 1914. 785p.), with some corrections and additions. The 3d edition includes only minor changes in the text and marginal cross references.

A basic work on historical writing from the time of the Renaissance to about 1870, giving biographical sketches of European and American historians with brief critical estimates of their work.

Gooch, George Peabody. History and historians in the nineteenth century. Rev. with a new introd. London, Longmans, 1952. 547p. **DA27**

1st ed. 1913.

Frequently reprinted.

1952 edition is called 2d edition and includes textual revisions throughout and additions to the bibliographical notes.

A scholarly critical survey of 19th-century historians and historical method.

Rosenthal, Franz. History of Muslim historiography.

Leiden, Brill, 1952. 558p. **DA28**

A comprehensive history and discussion of historical writing among the Moslem peoples.

Societies

Bosch García, Carlos. Guía de instituciones que cultivan la historia de América. México, 1949. 231p. (Inst. Panamericano de Geografía e Historia, Publ. núm. 94. Comisión de Historia, Publ. núm. 9. Guías I) **DA29**

A directory of almost 800 North and South American and 40 European institutions and societies concerned with the study of history and such related sciences as anthropology, archaeology, ethnography, and geography of the Americas.

Information about each institution is fairly full.

Dictionaries, outlines, tables

Arnold-Baker, Charles and **Dent, Anthony.** Everyman's dictionary of dates. London, Dent; N.Y., Dutton, 1954. 404p. **DA30**

A compact dictionary, alphabetically arranged with many lists and tables.

Bodart, Gaston. Militär-historisches Kriegs-Lexikon, (1618–1905). Wien, Stern, 1907. 956p. **DA31**

A dictionary of battles, chronologically arranged, useful for the statistics of forces engaged, losses, etc., on each side. More comprehensive than Thomas B. Harbottle. *Dictionary of battles from the earliest date to the present time.* N.Y., Dutton, 1905. 298p.

Brewer, Ebenezer Cobham. Historic notebook; with an appendix of battles. London, Smith; Philadelphia, Lippincott, 1896. 997p. **DA32**

An alphabetical dictionary of historical information including events, expressions, societies, customs, etc.

Cambridge modern history. Genealogical tables and lists. (In Cambridge modern history, v.13, p.1–205 [DA118]) **DA33**

Pt.1, Genealogical tables of ruling and royal houses—British Empire, France, Germany and Austria, Netherlands, Italy, Spain, Portugal and Brazil, Sweden and Norway, Denmark, Poland, Hungary and Transylvania, Russia, Turkey, Balkan States, the East; pt.2, List of spiritual princes, elected sovereigns, etc.; pt.3, List of parliaments, presidents, governors of colonies, general councils, secularized bishoprics, leagues, alliances, universities since 1450, etc.

Delorme, Jean. Chronologie des civilisations. Paris, Presses Universitaires de France, 1949. 437p. (Clio: introduction aux études historiques) **DA34**

Chronological tables from 3000 B.C. to A.D. 1945, with alphabetical index.

Fry, Edward Alexander. Almanacks for students of English history. London, Phillimore, 1915. 138p., incl. tables. **DA35**

Subtitle: A set of 35 almanacks arranged for every day upon which Easter can fall, together with a chronological list of years from A.D. 500 to A.D. 1751, old style, and A.D. 1752 to A.D. 2000, new style, also a list of regnal years of English sovereigns from the Norman conquest to the present time, lists of saints' days . . . and other useful tables.

Much of the same material is included in revised form in Cheney, *Handbook of dates for students of English history* (DC135).

George, Hereford Brooke. Genealogical tables illustrative of modern history. 5th ed., rev. and enl., by J. R. H. Weaver. Oxford, Clarendon Pr., 1916. 55 tables. **DA36**

1st ed. 1873.

Genealogical charts of the reigning houses of Europe down

to 1915, with appended lists of the popes and of the chief Oriental sovereigns.

Gooch, George Peabody. Annals of politics and culture, 1492–1899. Cambridge, Univ. Pr.; N.Y., Macmillan, 1901. 530p.　　**DA37**

A parallel presentation of the principal events in political history and the history of culture, i.e., education, literature, science, art.

Haberkern, Eugen and **Wallach, Joseph Friedrich.** Hilfswörterbuch für Historiker. Mittelalter und Neuzeit. 2. neubearb. und erw. Aufl. Bern, Munich, Francke Verlag, 1964. 678p.　　**DA38**

1st ed. 1935.

Medieval and modern historical terms in various languages, listed in alphabetical order with the equivalent and definition in German.

Haydn, Joseph Timothy. Dictionary of dates and universal information relating to all ages and nations, by the late Benjamin Vincent. Rev. and brought up to date by eminent authorities. 25th ed. . . . London, Ward, Locke, 1910; N.Y., Putnam, 1911. 1614p.　　**DA39**

1st ed. 1841.

A dictionary of history and general information alphabetically arranged, information under each heading given mainly in chronological lists. Convenient for the smaller facts of history and for lists, e.g., Lord Mayors of London, famous fires, inundations, etc. Addenda list includes events to Oct. 1910.

Historische W.P. encyclopedie. Hoofredactie: Ph. de Vries [en] Th. Luykx. [Uitg. onder auspiciën van de Winkler Prins Stichting] Amsterdam, Elsevier, 1957–59. 3v. il.　　**DA40**

Covers the political history of the world from earliest times to the present. Longer articles are signed and include brief bibliographies. Illustrations, while not numerous, are pertinent and well reproduced, and there are good historical maps. An introductory section in the first volume includes chapters on chronology, archaeology, numismatics, epigraphy, etc., and the historiography of several countries.

Keller, Helen Rex. Dictionary of dates. N.Y., Macmillan, 1934. 2v.　　**DA41**

v.1, Old World (Europe, Africa, Asia, and Australasia), World War, Peace Conference, League of Nations, International Labor Organization, Permanent Court of International Justice, international affairs generally; v.2, New World, including the Arctic and Antarctic.

An outline of events and a digest of information from many sources, recording by dates the history of the world from the earliest times through 1930. Arranged by country and then chronologically. No index. Pt.1 is based on Haydn's *Dictionary of dates* (DA39).

Langer, William Leonard. An encyclopedia of world history; ancient, medieval and modern, chronologically arranged. Rev. ed. Boston, Houghton, 1952. 1243p. **DA42**

1st ed. 1940.

A new version of Ploetz's very useful *Manual of universal history* (Boston, Houghton, 1925), giving concise, accurate outlines, not tables. Each section has been revised and largely rewritten, old sections have been condensed and new ones added, so that the work is now an epitome of world history, whereas in Ploetz the emphasis was very largely on Europe. Devoted primarily to political, military, and diplomatic history. This revised edition includes a new section on the Second World War, 1939–1945, p.1135–71, and the Post-war world to 1952, p.1172–1222, and minor corrections throughout the work. Includes outline maps and genealogical tables. Comprehensive index in two sections: (1) events through 1945, and (2) events Jan. 1, 1946—April 30, 1952.

Larned, Josephus Nelson. New Larned history for ready reference, reading and research; the actual words of the world's best historians, biographers and specialists . . . completely rev., enl., and brought up to date . . . by D. E. Smith . . . ed. in chief; Charles Seymour, A. H. Shearer, D. C. Knowlton, assoc. eds. Springfield, Mass., Nichols, 1922–24. 12v. il.　　**DA43**

1st ed., with title *History for ready reference,* 1893–95. 5v.; rev. ed., with supplementary volume covering 1894–1900, 1901. 6v.; 2d supplement, covering 1901–10, 1910. v.7.

An alphabetical dictionary of universal history, with many cross references. Under each subject is given, not an original article, but one or more quoted articles or extracts from recognized authorities; as extracts are given with exact references, the work serves the double purpose of encyclopedia and index. Interspersed with these extracts are brief biographical sketches, definitions, etc.

Mayer, Alfred. Annals of European civilization, 1501–1900. Foreword by G. P. Gooch. London, Cassell, 1949. 457p.　　**DA44**

In two main parts: (1) the Annals, which give in chronological order the principal events of the cultural, nonpolitical history of Europe; and (2) the Summaries, which arrange the events by subject or class, giving the events chronologically under each, e.g., academies, architecture, biology, church, colonization, economics, libraries, literature, etc.

Indexes of names and of places.

A complement to the chronological tables of political history.

Morison, M. Time table of modern history, A.D. 400–1870. 2d ed. Westminster, Constable, 1908. 159p.　　**DA45**

Parallel tables of the history of various countries, with genealogical tables of royal families, chronological lists of rulers, general chart of ancient and modern history, and 7 historical maps; also full index.

Putnam, George Palmer and **Putnam, George Haven.** Dictionary of events; a handbook of universal history. . . . N.Y., Grosset, 1936. 565p., [71]p.　　**DA46**

Subtitle: A series of chronological tables presenting, in parallel columns, a record of the noteworthy events of history from the earliest times to the present day, together with an index of subjects and genealogical tables.

Earlier editions had titles *Tabular views of universal history; Putnam's Handbook of universal history;* and *Putnam's Dictionary of events.*

In this edition the record has been brought down through 1935, though the material from Jan. 1927 on is not included in the index, which is in two sections: (1) covering events up to Aug. 1, 1914; (2) Supplementary index covering Aug. 1, 1914 to Dec. 1926.

Steinberg, Sigfrid H. Historical tables, 58 B.C.–A.D. 1963. 7th ed. London, Macmillan, 1964. 259p.　　**DA47**

1st ed. 1939.

Frequently reprinted with additional tables to bring the record to date.

A tabular chronology of world history, arranged in parallel columns by period. Political history is subdivided by geographical areas, with additional headings for constitutional history, economic history, and natural science and cultural life. No index.

Stokvis, Antonie Marinus H. J. Manuel d'histoire, de généalogie et de chronologie de tous les états du globe, depuis les temps les plus reculés jusqu'à nos jours. Leide, Brill, 1888–93. 3v.　　**DA48**

t.1, Asie, Afrique, Amérique, Polynésie; t.2–3, Les états de l'Europe et leurs colonies. Includes chronological tables of dynasties, rulers, etc.; genealogical tables; and detailed information from each country.

Pictorial illustrations

Parmentier, André Émile Emmanuel. Album historique, publié sous la direction de Ernest Lavisse. Paris, Colin, 1907–10. 4v. il. **DA49**

t.1, Le moyen âge (du 4ᵉ au 13ᵉ siècle). 4. éd. 1910; t.2, La fin du moyen âge (14ᵉ et 15ᵉ siècles). 3. éd. 1907; t.3, Le 16ᵉ et le 17ᵉ siècles. 4. éd. 1910; t.4, Le 18ᵉ et le 19ᵉ siècles. 1907.

Contains a large number of excellent illustrations of costume, furniture, civil and military life, manners and customs, dwellings, industries, etc.

Annuals and current surveys

Annual register of world events. 1758– . London, 1761– . v.1– . Annual. **DA50**

Title varies: 1758–1953, *Annual register: a review of public events at home and abroad.*

Originated with Robert Dodsley, at the suggestion of Edmund Burke, who was for some years editor and principal contributor. Some time after the year 1791, the copyright and stock were purchased by Otridge and other booksellers. Messrs. Rivington published a rival continuation, which lasted from 1791 to 1812, and again from 1820 to 1824, when the two were merged into one. Since 1890, published by Longmans.

Contents vary. 19th- and early-20th-century volumes are strong in biographical information in the obituary sections. Recent volumes have very few obituary notices. Include survey articles on the year's developments in the United Kingdom, the Commonwealth, and other countries of the world; international organizations; and chapters on religion, science, law, the arts, economics, etc.

Includes some public documents, and many abstracts of political speeches. Gives English affairs with more fullness than those of other countries.

—— General index to Dodsley's Annual register, 1758 to 1819. London, Baldwin, 1826. 938p.

Facts on file; a weekly world news digest with cumulative index. v.1, Oct./Nov. 1940– . N.Y., Facts on File, 1940– . v.1– . Weekly, with annual bound volumes. **DA51**

Subtitle varies.

A weekly classified digest of news arranged under such headings as: World affairs, National affairs, Foreign affairs, Latin America, Finance, Economy, Arts, Science, Education, Religion, Sports, Obituaries, Miscellaneous, etc. Indexes are published twice monthly and are cumulative throughout the year.

—— Five-year index: the index to world events. 1957– .

Contents: 1946–50 (pub. 1958); 1951–55 (pub. 1957); 1956–60 (pub. 1961).

Keesing's Contemporary archives; weekly diary of world events with index continually kept up-to-date. v.1, July 1, 1931– . London, Keesing's, 1931– . il. Loose-leaf (binders furnished for 2-year periods). (In progress) **DA52**

A weekly diary of important events in all countries, including texts of speeches and documents, obituaries, statistics, etc. Issued weekly with detailed indexes, cumulating fortnightly, quarterly, annually, and biennially, two years completing a volume. (Until 1954, three years completed a volume.) Beginning in 1959/60, an index of names was added, published quarterly, cumulating annually and biennially.

v.1 preceded by supplement, Synopsis of important events, 1918 (end of World War)–1931 (June). 35p.

Atlases

Cambridge modern history atlas, ed. by A. W. Ward, G.

W. Prothero, Stanley Leathes, assisted by E. A. Benians. 2d ed. Cambridge, Univ. Pr.; N.Y., Macmillan, 1926. 229p. 141 maps. 24cm. **DA53**

(1) Introduction (General survey of European territory, with marginal references to maps); (2) Index of local names in Introduction; (3) Maps; (4) Index to maps, including names of places, tribes and clans.

Covers period 1490–1910, inclusive. Published separately and also as v.14 of the *Cambridge modern history* (DA118).

Grosser historischer Weltatlas. Munich, Bayerischer Schulbuch-Verlag, 1957–58. Pt.1 (3d ed. 1958); pt.3 (2d ed. 1957). 33cm. **DA54**

Contents: pt.1, Vorgeschichte und Altertum, ed. by Hermann Bengston and Vladimir Milojčič; pt.3, Neuzeit, ed. by Josef Engel; (pt.2, Mittelalter, not yet published)

—— Erläuterungen. München, 1954– . Pt.1– .

An excellent example of German map making. Detailed tables of contents and place-name indexes in each volume.

Pt.1 covers prehistory to approximately 1200; pt.3, from late-15th century to the 1950's.

Meer, Frederic van der. Atlas of Western civilization. English version by T. A. Birrell. 2d rev. ed. Princeton, N.J., Van Nostrand, 1960. 240p. 36cm. **DA55**

Concerned with the development of Western culture and civilization rather than with political and military history. Photographs (of works of art and architecture as well as of historic and geographic sites) outnumber the maps.

Muir, Ramsay. Muir's Historical atlas: ancient, medieval, and modern, ed. by R. F. Treharne and Harold Fullard. N.Y., Barnes & Noble, 1963. [v.p.] 116p. of col. maps. 29cm. **DA56**

First published in this form in 1938 as *Philips' Atlas of ancient, medieval, and modern history.*

Consists of two sections which are also published separately: (1) *Atlas of ancient and classical history.* 2d ed. 1956; (2) *Historical atlas: medieval and modern.* 9th ed. 1962. Each section has its own index.

Covers from about the 15th century B.C. to 1962.

A good, serviceable, reasonably priced atlas for schools and colleges.

Putzger, Friedrich Wilhelm. Historischer Weltatlas. Jubiläumsausgabe. 85. Aufl. (In Zusammenarbeit mit der kartographischen Anstalt von Velhagen & Klasing, neu hrsg. von Alfred Hansel und Walter Leiserung) Bielefeld, Velhagen & Klasing, 1963. 146p. of col. maps. 27cm. **DA57**

1st ed. 1877. Former title *Historischer Schulatlas.*

A standard work, frequently reprinted, especially useful for modern European history. Includes maps up to the present; some have 1963 information.

Rand McNally and Company. Atlas of world history, ed. by R. R. Palmer. N.Y., Rand McNally, 1957. 216p. maps (part col.). 27cm. **DA58**

Well-made maps, about 75 in color and almost 50 in black and white. Most detailed treatment of North American and European history (particularly for 19th and 20th centuries), but with maps also of Asia, Africa, and Latin America. Textual comment. Name index.

Shepherd, William Robert. Historical atlas. 9th ed. N.Y., Barnes & Noble, 1964. 226p. of col. maps (part fold.), 115p. 27cm. **DA59**

1st ed. 1911; 7th ed. 1929, the last published under Shepherd's direction.

For many years the standard and most used historical atlas. Covers from 1450 B.C. to 1964. The 9th edition contains all the maps of the 7th edition and a special supplement (plates 218–26) of maps for the period since 1929, prepared by C. S. Hammond & Company.

The Index is in three parts: (1) Original index; (2) Index-

Supplement, which includes names contained in the maps for the period 1911–29, as well as some earlier ones, but does not include the new section, 1930–64; (3) Additional changes.

Sections have also been published separately, e.g., *Atlas of ancient history; Atlas of medieval and modern history.*

Toynbee, Arnold J. and **Meyers, Edward D.** Historical atlas and gazetteer. Issued under the auspices of the Royal Institute of International Affairs. London, Oxford Univ. Pr., 1959. 257p. 73 maps. (A study of history, v.11) 26cm.   **DA60**

Contents: pt.1, Gazetteer to *A study of history,* p.5–80; pt.2, Maps, p.83–202. Appendix, p.203–16. Index to maps, p.217–57.

Black-and-white outline maps, designed to show the spread and growth of world civilizations and religions.

Westermann, Georg, *firm.* Atlas zur Weltgeschichte, hrsg. von Hans-Erich Stier, [and others]. Vorzeit, Altertum, Mittelalter, Neuzeit . . . Braunschweig, Westermann, 1956. 160p. maps. 30cm.   **DA61**

A good modern atlas primarily of Europe and western Asia. Covers from ancient times to the present day. Includes many detailed maps of cities and other special areas. No index of place-names.

ARCHAEOLOGY AND PREHISTORY

For the archaeology of a particular country, *see* under that country.

Bibliography

Abstracts of New World archaeology, ed. by Richard B. Woodbury. v.1, 1959– . Wash., Soc. for Amer. Archaeology, 1960– . Annual.   **DA62**

Includes abstracts of books, monographs in series, journal articles, and theses. Primarily geographical in arrangement (e.g., Northern Mississippi Valley), with South America divided by national political units. Author index.

Akademiia Nauk SSSR. Biblioteka. Sovetskaia arkheologicheskaia literatura; bibliografiia, 1941–1957. Sost. N. A. Vinberg i dr. Moskva, Izd-vo Akademii Nauk SSSR, 1959. 773p.   **DA63**

Added title page in French.

A classified bibliography of Soviet publications of the years 1941–57 in archaeology, from paleolithic times to the 17th century. Lists reviews of major publications. Indexes for authors, archaeological monuments, and related subjects such as numismatics, sphragistics, and history of technology.

Annuario bibliografico di archeologia, 1952– , a cura di Cesare D'Onofrio. Modena, Soc. Tipografica Modenese, 1954– . Anno 1– . (Pubblicazioni della Biblioteca dell' Istituto Nazionale d'Archeologia e Storia dell' Arte)   **DA64**

Lists books and periodical articles, in various languages, in classed arrangement with indexes by authors. Some volumes also have subject indexes.

Banner, János. A Közép-Dunamedence régészeti bibliográfiája a legrégibb időktöl a XI. századig. [Irták] Banner János [és] Jakabffy Imre. Budapest, Akadémiai Kiadó, 1954. 581p.   **DA65**

A bibliography of books dealing with the archaeology of the Middle-Danubian Basin up to the 11th century.

—— A Közép-Dunamedence régészeti bibliográfiája, 1954–1959. Összeállította Jakabffy Imre. Budapest, Akadémiai Kiadó, 1961. 250p.

Supplements work above for 1954–59.

Berghe, Louis vanden and **Proosdij, B. A. van.** Bibliographie analytique de l'Assyriologie et de l'archéologie du Proche-Orient. Leyde, E. J. Brill, 1956–60. v.1¹⁻², v.2¹– . (In progress)   **DA66**

Contents: v.1: sec. A, L'archéologie, 1954–55, par L. vanden Berghe et H. F. Mussche; sec. Ph, La philologie, 1954–56, par L. vanden Berghe et L. de Meyer; v.2: sec. A, L'archéologie, 1956–57 (1960).

Issued in two sections: (1) Archaeology, and (2) Philology, one volume appearing each alternate year, to cover publications of the preceding two years. Period covered is from earliest times to the beginning of Islamic civilization; both books and periodical articles are included. In the archaeological section, arrangement is primarily geographical; in the section on Philology, classification is by form and subject. Author indexes for each.

Bibliographie annuelle de l'âge de la pierre taillée (paléolithique et mésolithique), no.1– . 1955/56– . Paris, Bureau de Recherches Géologiques et Minières, 1958– . (Union Internationale des Sciences Préhistoriques et Protohistoriques) Annual.   **DA67**

Publiée sous la direction de R. Vaufrey.

Supersedes American School of Prehistoric Research, *Old World bibliography.*

Embraces paleontology and geology as well as archaeology. Classed arrangement, with an index of authors itself classified by geographical area.

Déchelette, Joseph. Manuel d'archéologie préhistorique celtique et gallo-romaine. Paris, Picard, 1908–27. v.1–4, and appendix to v.2 in 2v., il.   **DA68**

v.1, Archéologie préhistorique. 1908; v.2, Archéologie celtique ou protohistorique: Âge du bronze. 1910; appendix to v.2, 1910–12. 2v.; v.3, Premier âge du fer, ou Époque de Hallstatt. 1927; v.4, Second âge du fer, ou Époque de La Tène. 1927.

For v.5–6 *see* Grenier (DA74).

Deutsches Archäologisches Institut. Römische Abteilung. Bibliothek. Katalog der Bibliothek des Kaiserlich Deutschen Archäologischen Instituts in Rom, von August Mau . . . Neubearb. von Eugen von Mercklin. Rome, Löscher; Berlin, de Gruyter, 1913–32. 2v. in 4.   **DA69**

v.1, in two parts (1913–14), includes works published before 1911; v.2, by Friedrich Matz, in two parts (1932), lists works published before 1925.

—— —— 1. Supplement; Ergänzungen zu Band I für die Jähre 1911–1925, bearb. von Friedrich Matz. Berlin, de Gruyter, 1930. 516p.

The catalog of a very rich collection. Each volume lists books and periodical materials in various languages, primarily of the 19th century with some earlier publications. The supplement lists works added 1911–25.

Deutsches Archäologisches Institut. Archäologische Bibliographie, 1913– ; Beilage zum Jahrbuch des Deutschen Archäologischen Instituts. . . . Berlin, de Gruyter, 1914– . Annual.   **DA70**

Title and publisher vary.

1944–1948, pub. in 1v., 1950. 350p.

A very useful bibliography of books and periodical articles, broad in scope and international in coverage.

Svenska Arkeologiska Samfundet. Swedish archaeological bibliography, 1939–1948, ed. by Sverker Janson and Olof Vessberg. Uppsala, Almqvist & Wiksells, 1951. 360p.   **DA71**

A survey in English of Swedish archaeological literature for a 10-year period.

—— —— 1949–1953, ed. by Christian Callmer and Wilhelm Holmqvist. 1956. 294p.

See also L'année philologique (BD920) for references to archaeological materials.

Encyclopedias and handbooks

Ebeling, Erich and **Meissner, Bruno.** Reallexikon der Assyriologie, unter Mitwirkung zahlreicher Fachgelehrter. Berlin, de Gruyter, 1928–59. v.1–2, 3¹⁻². il. (In progress) **DA72**

v.1–3¹⁻², A–Gebet.

Appeared in fascicules, 1929–59.

A scholarly encyclopedia on Assyriology with signed articles and extensive bibliographies.

v.3 (1957)– , read: Begründet von Erich Ebeling und Bruno Meissner. Unter Mitwirkung zahlreicher Fachgelehrter hrsg. von Erich Ebeling; durch den Druck geführt und ergänzt von Ernst Weidner.

Ebert, Max. Reallexikon der Vorgeschichte, unter Mitwirkung zahlreicher Fachgelehrter. Berlin, de Gruyter, 1924–32. 15v. il. **DA73**

v.1–14, A–Z; v.15, Register.

Signed articles by specialists; bibliographies; many illustrations.

Grenier, Albert. Manuel d'archéologie gallo-romaine. Paris, Picard, 1931–60. v.1–4. (In progress) **DA74**

v.1–2 also published as v.5–6 of Déchelette (DA68).

Contents: t.1, Généralités. Travaux militaires. 1931; t.2, Archéologie du sol. 1934; t.3, L'architecture: (a) L'urbanisme, les monuments (capitole, forum, temple, basilique); (b) Ludi et circenses (théâtres, amphithéâtres, cirques). 1958; t.4, Les monuments des eaux. 2v. 1960.

Handbuch der Archaeologie, im Rahmen des Handbuchs der Altertumswissenschaft . . . hrsg. von Walter Otto. Munich, Beck, 1939–54. v.1–2, 3¹, 4¹. il. (I. P. E. Müller, Handbuch der Altertumswissenschaft. 6. Abt.) (In progress) **DA75**

A heavily documented history, each volume accompanied by a section of plates.

Schrader, Otto. Reallexikon der indogermanischen Altertumskunde. Grundzüge einer kultur- und völkergeschichte Alteuropas. 2. verm. u. umgearb. Aufl. hrsg. von A. Nehring. Berlin, de Gruyter, 1917–29. 2v. **DA76**

An alphabetically arranged encyclopedia.

CLASSICAL ANTIQUITIES

Manuals and source books

Botsford, George Willis and **Sihler, E. G.** Hellenic civilization. N.Y., Columbia Univ. Pr., 1915. 719p. (Records of civilization: sources and studies, ed. by J. T. Shotwell) **DA77**

Source book of material in translation, with useful bibliographies.

Laurand, Louis. Manuel des études grecques et latines. Ed. entièrement ref. par A. Lauras. Paris, Picard, 1956–57. 2v. **DA78**

Contents: t.1, *Grèce:* fasc.1, Géographie, histoire, institutions grecques; fasc.2, Littérature grecque; fasc.3, Grammaire historique grecque; t.2, *Rome:* fasc.4, Géographie, histoire, institutions romaines; fasc.5, Littérature latine; fasc.6, Grammaire historique latine.

Edition numbers for each fascicule vary.

This work is published in many editions. This printing incorporates the material in the original fasc.7 and the appendixes, and includes indexes with each fascicule instead of a cumulated index. v.4 (2d ed. 1949), *Supplément, pour mieux comprendre l'antiquité classique,* is still sold separately.

A manual for the study of the classics, with interspersed bibliographies.

Sandys, *Sir* John Edwin. Companion to Latin studies. 3d ed. Cambridge, Univ. Pr.; N.Y., Macmillan, 1925. 891p. il. (Repr.: N.Y., Hafner, 1963) **DA79**

1st ed. 1910; 2d ed. 1913.

A handbook covering such subjects as the geography and ethnology of Italy, fauna and flora, history, religion and mythology, private and public antiquities, art, literature, epigraphy, paleography, etc. Includes bibliographies.

Whibley, Leonard. Companion to Greek studies. 4th ed. rev. Cambridge, Univ. Pr., 1931. 790p. il. **DA80**

1st ed. 1905; 3d ed. 1916.

The work by Sandys (DA79) and this by Whibley are prepared on the same plan and similarly arranged. Each consists of a series of articles, by specialists, on topics of importance to the student of Greek and Roman history and literature, such as geography, ethnology, flora, science, chronology, coins, ships, buildings, population, slavery, etc. Articles are well written, with useful bibliographies, and each volume has four indexes: (1) persons, deities, and races; (2) places, rivers, and mountains; (3) scholars and modern writers; (4) Latin (or Greek) words and phrases. Very useful as supplementing the various classical dictionaries.

❧ In addition to the works listed above, the research worker in classical antiquities will often need to refer to Iwan Müller's *Handbuch der Altertumswissenschaft* (Nördlingen, Beck), a series of scholarly treatises on subjects in classical literature, antiquities, etc., the various volumes of which have appeared in many different editions. Some of the volumes are the most comprehensive and definitive works in their fields; others are much briefer.

Bibliography

Rounds, Dorothy. Articles on antiquity in Festschriften: the ancient Near East, the Old Testament, Greece, Rome, Roman law, Byzantium; an index. Cambridge, Harvard Univ. Pr., 1962. 560p. **DA82**

An index to *Festschriften,* including in one alphabet: names of scholars and institutions honored, names of authors of articles, and all significant words in the titles of the articles.

Dictionaries and encyclopedias

Daremberg, Charles and **Saglio, Edmond.** Dictionnaire des antiquités grecques et romaines d'après les textes et les monuments. Paris, Hachette, 1873–1919. 5v. and index. il. **DA83**

v.1–5, A–Z; separate index, 166p.

A work of the highest authority, with long, signed articles by specialists and very detailed bibliographical references. Covers public and private life, manners and customs, institutions, arts, sciences, industries, religion, costume, furniture, military affairs, money, weights and measures, etc. Does not include biography and literature. Indexes of authors, Greek words, Latin words, and subjects.

Errandonea, Ignacio. Diccionario del mundo clásico. Barcelona, Ed. Labor, 1954. 2v.(1810p.). il., maps. **DA84**

Similar in scope and content to the *Oxford classical dictionary* (DA86), with more individual entries but considerably less bibliographical data. Includes material on classical art, archaeology, literature, Greek and Latin philology, Roman law, and the medicine and science of antiquity. Articles are signed.

New Century classical handbook. Ed. by Catherine B. Avery; ed. consultant, Jotham Johnson. N.Y., Appleton, 1962. 1162p. il. **DA85**

An alphabetically arranged encyclopedia of Greek and Roman civilization and mythology, primarily of personal names. Designed for "the general reader and the student"; it includes "the figures of myth and legend, gods and heroes, persons and places, fact and fancy."—*Pref.* A few articles under common nouns are included. No bibliographic references. Pronunciation is indicated.

Oxford classical dictionary, ed. by M. Cary, A. D. Nock, [and others]. Oxford, Clarendon Pr., 1949. 971p. **DA86**

A scholarly dictionary, with signed articles, "designed to cover the same ground, though on a different scale, as the well-known dictionary by Sir William Smith." Covers biography, literature, mythology, philosophy, religion, science, geography, etc. Most of the articles are brief, but there are also longer survey articles, e.g., Rome, music, scholarship, etc. Bibliographies are appended to most articles, and are usually limited to a few of the best works on the subject, in English and foreign languages. Bibliographies for the articles on the great classical writers usually include texts, commentaries, translations, lexicons, style, life, criticism, etc.

Unfortunately, pronunciation is not indicated.

Pauly, August Friedrich von. Pauly's Real-Encyclopädie der classischen Altertumswissenschaft; neue Bearb. begonnen von Georg Wissowa, unter Mitwirkung zahlreicher Fachgenossen hrsg. von Wilhelm Kroll und Karl Mittelhaus. Stuttgart, Metzler, 1894–1962. v.1–18$^{1-4}$, 19–22, 23$^{1-2}$; 2. Reihe, v.1–9A; Suppl. v.1–9. maps. (In progress) **DA87**

Volumes are not published in straight alphabetical sequence but in two series with a supplement.

Bd.1–18$^{1-4}$, A–Pax; 19–22, 23$^{1-2}$, Pech–Pyramiden.

2. Reihe (R–Z), Bd.1–9A^1, R–Vulca.

Supplement, Bd.1–9.

The standard, scholarly German work covering the whole field of classical literature, history, antiquities, biography, etc. Long, signed articles by specialists, with extensive bibliographies. Generally cited as *Pauly-Wissowa;* in German references sometimes cited as *R.E.* Indispensable for scholarly work in classical antiquities.

The arrangement and the alphabeting are sometimes complicated. Many volumes include *"Nachträge und Berichtigungen,"* which in the later volumes are quite extensive. v.23 includes a listing of the articles in the *Nachträge* of v.1–23, 2. Reihe v.1–8A, and the volumes of the Supplement. The volumes of the Supplement are geared to the volumes of the main set, each supplementary volume starting with A and continuing to a later part of the alphabet.

—— Der kleine Pauly; Lexikon der Antike auf der Grundlage von Pauly's Real-Encyclopädie der classischen Altertumswissenschaft unter Mitwirkung zahlreicher Fachgelehrter, bearb. und hrsg. von Konrad Ziegler und Walther Sontheimer. Stuttgart, Alfred Druckenmüller Verlag, 1964– . v.1– . **DA88**

Contents: Bd.1, Aachen–Dichalkon. 1558cols.

To be in 4v.

An abridgment of *Pauly-Wissowa* (DA87), including a high percentage of its articles in concise form. Articles are signed with initials. New advances in scholarship, where relevant, are reflected, and bibliographic references have been updated as necessary.

Peck, Harry Thurston. Harper's Dictionary of classical literature and antiquities. N.Y., Harper, 1897. 1701p. il. (Repr.: N.Y., Cooper Square Pub., 1962) **DA89**

A popular work, useful for ready reference because it gives articles on topics in classical antiquities, biography, mythology, geography, art, history, etc., in one alphabet. Concise articles; brief bibliographies; good illustrations.

Smith, *Sir* **William.** Dictionary of Greek and Roman

biography and mythology. By various writers. London, Murray; Boston, Little, 1890. 3v. il. **DA90**

A 1v. work based on this, but with some revisions, was edited by G. E. Marindin and published as *Classical dictionary of Greek and Roman biography, mythology and geography.* 4th ed. rev. London, Murray, 1894. 1018p.

—— **Wayte, William** and **Marindin, G. E.** Dictionary of Greek and Roman antiquities. 3d ed. rev. and enl. London, Murray; Boston, Little, 1890–91. 2v. il. **DA91**

1st ed. 1842. For many years a standard work and still useful for topics not affected by recent research, although for important work it is inferior to the great French and German dictionaries.

A concise dictionary of Greek and Roman antiquities, edited by F. Warre Cornish (London, Murray, 1898. 829p.), is based on the larger work and incorporates some later information.

All of these works by Sir William Smith have been issued in many editions and reprints. Although now much out of date, they may still be useful.

Atlases

Everyman's classical atlas, with an essay on the development of ancient geographical knowledge and theory by J. Oliver Thomson. [3d ed.] London, Dent; N.Y., Dutton, 1961. lxxp., 125p. il., 56p. of col. maps. 19cm. **DA92**

1st edition, 1907, titled *Everyman's atlas of ancient and classical geography.*

A handy, small atlas with simple but clear maps. Place-name index gives locations by latitude and longitude. Covers from about 500 B.C. to A.D. 200.

Heyden, A. A. M. van der and **Scullard, Howard Hayes.** Atlas of the classical world. London, Nelson, 1959. 221p. **DA93**

Originally published as *Atlas van de antieke wereld.* Amsterdam, Elsevier, 1958.

An excellent atlas depicting the life and cultures of the classical world in maps and pictures, with textual comment. The photographs of art and archaeology are outstanding.

Kiepert, Heinrich. Atlas antiquus; twelve maps of the ancient world for schools and colleges. Chicago, Rand McNally, 1900. 27p. 12 maps. 37cm. **DA94**

Frequent reissues. Originally published in German.

General histories

Cambridge ancient history. . . . . Cambridge, Univ. Pr.; N.Y., Macmillan, 1923–39. 12v. and 5v. plates. maps. **DA95**

v.1, Egypt and Babylonia to 1580 B.C. 2d ed. 1928; v.2, Egyptian and Hittite empires to *ca.* 1000 B.C.; v.3, Assyrian Empire; v.4, Persian Empire and the West; v.5, Athens; v.6, Macedon; v.7, The Hellenistic monarchies and the rise of Rome; v.8, Rome and the Mediterranean, 218–133 B.C.; v.9, Roman Republic, 133–44 B.C.; v.10, Augustan Empire, 44 B.C.–A.D. 70; v.11, Imperial peace, A.D. 70–192; v.12, Imperial crisis and recovery, A.D. 193–324.

Excellent reference history; each chapter written by a specialist, with full bibliographies at the end of each volume. The volumes of plates contain illustrations without comment.

—— Rev. ed. Cambridge, Univ. Pr., 1961–65. Fasc.1–33, 35. (In progress) **DA96**

Issued in fascicules; each fascicule is a separate chapter written by a specialist, with footnotes and extensive bibliographies. Chapters are not issued in chronological order and are separately paged. Pages will be renumbered in the complete edition.

MEDIEVAL

Manuals

Boüard, Alain de. Manuel de diplomatique française et pontificale. Paris, A. Picard, 1929–48. 2v.   **DA97**
Contents: v.1, Diplomatique générale; v.2, L'acte privé.

Bresslau, Harry. Handbuch der Urkundenlehre für Deutschland und Italien. 3. Aufl. Berlin, de Gruyter, 1958. 2v.   **DA98**
v.2, pt.2, "2. Aufl.," ed. by Hans Walter Klewitz.

—— —— Register zur 2. und 3. Aufl. zusammengestellt von Hans Schulze. Berlin, de Gruyter, 1960. 116p.
A well-documented manual for the study of German and Italian diplomatics.

Giry, Arthur. Manuel de diplomatique. Paris, Hachette, 1894. 944p. (Repr. 1925)   **DA99**
A standard manual for the study and identification of medieval documents, registers, decrees, charters, public and private acts, etc., including the techniques of chronology and the calendar. Many bibliographical footnotes.

Halphen, Louis. Initiation aux études d'histoire du Moyen Âge. 3. éd. rev., augm., et mise à jour par Y. Renouard. Paris, Presses Universitaires de France, 1952. 205p.   **DA100**
An introductory manual.

Prou, Maurice. Manuel de paléographie latine et française. 4. éd. refondue avec la collaboration de Alain de Boüard. Paris, Picard, 1924. 511p. and atlas of 24pl.   **DA101**
"Dictionnaire des abbréviations latines et françaises," p. 303–474.
A standard introductory manual to the reading of medieval documents.

Bibliography

Association Internationale des Études Byzantines. Dix années d'études byzantines: bibliographie internationale, 1939–1948. Publiée avec le concours de l'UNESCO. Paris, Éd. Universitaires, 1949. 170p.   **DA102**
Cites more than 2800 references on Byzantine studies from 19 countries. Covers, in addition to general works, books and articles on philology, literature, history, archaeology, art, and music, and includes material from some 250 journals and reviews. Arrangement is by country and then by broad subject. Author and subject indexes.

Atiya, Aziz Suryal. The crusade; historiography and bibliography. Bloomington, Indiana Univ. Pr., 1962. 170p.   **DA103**
A companion volume to the author's *Crusade, commerce and culture,* 1962.
Includes chapters on historiography with descriptions of the great historical collections and a classical bibliography of books and periodical articles in various languages on the Crusades.

✓**Chevalier, Cyr Ulysse Joseph.** Répertoire des sources historiques du Moyen Âge. Nouv. éd. refondue, corr. et augm. Paris, Picard, 1894–1907. 2v. in 4.   **DA104**
Publisher varies.
Contents: Bio-bibliographie, nouv. éd.; refondue, corr. et considérablement augm. 1903–7. 2v.; Topobibliographie, 1894–1903. 2v. (Repr.: N.Y., Kraus, 1959. 2v.)
Of first importance for the literature of medieval history. The first part is arranged alphabetically by personal name (in

the French form), the second by place and topic. Under each name, references are given to sources. An immense mass of material is indexed but with no critical indication of value. For further information on the bio-bibliographical section, *see* AJ3.

Diehl, Charles. Byzantium; greatness and decline. Tr. by Naomi Walford. New Brunswick, N.J., Rutgers Univ. Pr., 1957. 366p. il.   **DA105**
Bibliography by Peter Charanis, p.301–57.
A useful bibliography of works in Western languages with special emphasis on those in English.

Dölger, Franz and **Schneider, Alfons Maria.** Byzanz. Bern, Francke, 1952. 328p. (Wissenschaftliche Forschungsberichte. Geisteswissenschaftliche Reihe. Bd.5)   **DA106**
A survey of Byzantine studies published 1938–1950, with bibliographical footnotes. The first section covers history, literature, and language; the second, early Christian and Byzantine art. Author index for each section.
Current listings appear in the *Byzantinische Zeitschrift, Abt. III, Bibliographische Notizen und Mitteilungen;* five-year surveys, similar to *Byzanz,* were planned.

International guide to medieval studies; a quarterly index to periodical literature, v.1, no.1, June 1961– . Darien, Conn., Amer. Bibliographic Service, 1961– .   **DA107**
Each volume lists articles alphabetically by author, followed by cumulative author and subject indexes. These are followed by a book review index.

Mayer, Hans Eberhard. Bibliographie zur Geschichte der Kreuzzüge. Hannover, Hahnsche Buchhandlung, 1960. 270p.   **DA108**
Lists almost 5400 numbered entries on the age of the Crusades up to about 1453, in a classified arrangement. Includes both books and periodical articles published before 1957/58 in Western languages and also in Arabic, Hebrew, and Chinese. The field is interpreted broadly to include the church, legal, economic, social, and intellectual history of the time.

Paetow, Louis John. Guide to the study of medieval history . . . rev. ed. prep. under the auspices of the Mediaeval Academy of America. N.Y., Crofts, 1931. 643p. (Repr.: N.Y., Kraus, 1959)   **DA109**
1st ed. 1917.
The most useful general guide to the literature of medieval history. Includes topical outlines and special recommendations for reading, as well as bibliographies of original sources and secondary works. Critical and scholarly.

Potthast, August. Bibliotheca historica medii aevi. Wegweiser durch die Geschichtswerke des europäischen Mittelalters bis 1500. 2. verb. und verm. Aufl. Berlin, Weber, 1896. 2v. (Repr.: Graz, Akademische Druck- u. Verlagsanstalt, 1954)   **DA110**
Subtitle: Vollständiges Inhaltsverzeichnis zu Acta Sanctorum Boll., Bouquet, Migne, Monum. Germ. Hist., Muratori, Rerum Britann. Scriptores, etc. Anhang: Quellenkunde für die Geschichte der europäischen Staaten während des Mittelalters.
An indispensable work, though incomplete and sometimes inaccurate, listing medieval chronicles and analyzing many of the large source collections as indicated in the subtitle. The second part is an alphabetical list of medieval writers with, when possible, characterizing phrase and dates, indicating manuscripts, editions, and commentaries.

Progress of medieval and Renaissance studies in the United States and Canada. Boulder, Colo., 1923–60.   **DA111**
Publication suspended.
An annual survey. For full record *see* BD10.

Repertorium fontium historiae medii aevi, primum ab Augusto Potthast digestum, nunc cura collegii historicorum e pluribus nationibus emendatum et auctum. Romae, Istit. Storico Italiano per il Medio Evo, 1962–　．v.1–　．(In progress)　　　　　**DA112**

At head of title: Istituto Storico Italiano per il Medio Evo. Unione Internazionale degli Istituti di Archeologia, Storia e Storia dell' Arte in Roma.

v.1, Series collectionum. 819p.

This first volume of a "new Potthast" (DA110), planned by an international committee of medievalists, corresponds generally to the first major section of the old work, i.e., an alphabetical listing of sets of chronicles, miscellanies, and other collections of medieval sources, together with their contents. It contains some sets omitted by Potthast and many published since that date, including Byzantine, Arabic, Jewish, and Turkish sets, not covered in Potthast. Bibliographic treatment is good. Introductory and explanatory material is in Latin.

Williams, Harry Franklin. An index of mediaeval studies published in Festschriften, 1865–1946, with special reference to Romanic material. Berkeley, Univ. of Calif. Pr., 1951. 165p.　　　　　**DA113**

An index of the contributions concerning medieval art, customs, history, philosophy, literature, language, and science of western Europe found in anniversary or homage volumes published in honor of scholars, occasions, or institutions, covering more than 5000 items from about 500 volumes of such studies. Not all volumes are fully indexed, since material not pertinent to medieval studies is omitted. The emphasis is on Romanic material. Includes also a list of *Festschriften,* a list of reviews of some 170 *Festschriften,* an index of authors, and one of subject matter.

Dictionaries and compendiums

Meyer, Otto and **Klauser, Renate.** Clavis mediaevalis; kleines Wörterbuch der Mittelalterforschung. Wiesbaden, Harrassowitz, 1962. 311p. il.　　　　　**DA114**

A small handbook giving encyclopedic articles on terms used in medieval studies, with bibliographical references.

Mas-Latrie, Louis, *Comte de.* Trésor de chronologie d'histoire et de géographie pour l'étude et l'emploi des documents du moyen âge. Paris, Palme, 1889. 2300col. (Ristampa anastatica. Torino, Bottego d'Erasmo, 1962)　　　　　**DA115**

An extremely useful compilation (though at times unreliable), including perpetual calendars; historical chronologies; lists of saints and Fathers of the church, popes, cardinals, bishops, and archbishops; rulers of many countries in Europe, Asia, and Africa, etc.

Workers with medieval documents will also need the extensive work *L'art de vérifier les dates,* 1750 (4th rev. ed. 1818–44. 44v.), by Maur François Dantine, C. Clémencet, and U. Durand, which appeared in various editions.

General histories

Cambridge mediaeval history, planned by J. B. Bury. . . . Cambridge, Univ. Pr.; N.Y., Macmillan, 1911–36. 8v. maps.　　　　　**DA116**

v.1, The Christian Roman Empire and the foundation of the Teutonic kingdoms. 2d ed. 1924; v.2, Rise of the Saracens and the foundation of the Western Empire; v.3, Germany and the Western Empire; v.4, Eastern Roman Empire; v.5, Contest of empire and papacy; v.6, Victory of the papacy; v.7, Decline of empire and papacy; v.8, Close of the Middle Ages.

An excellent reference history, written by specialists, with full bibliographies at the end of each volume.

MODERN

Dictionaries

Palmer, Alan Warwick. A dictionary of modern history, 1789–1945. London, Cresset, 1962. 314p.　　　　　**DA117**

A compact dictionary of people, places, groups, and events, with emphasis on British affairs but also including the United States, Eastern and Western Europe, Latin America, and the Far East.

General histories

Cambridge modern history, planned by the late Lord Acton, ed. by A. W. Ward [and others]. Cambridge, Univ. Pr.; N.Y., Macmillan, 1902–26. 13v. and atlas. **DA118**

Cheaper reprint of v.1–13, text only, without the bibliographies, 1934.

v.1, Renaissance; v.2, Reformation; v.3, Wars of religion; v.4, Thirty Years' War; v.5, Age of Louis XIV; v.6, Eighteenth century; v.7, United States; v.8, French Revolution; v.9, Napoleon; v.10, Restoration; v.11, Growth of nationalities; v.12, Latest age; v.13, Genealogical tables and general index; v.14, Atlas.

For contents of v.13, *see* DA33.

The most important general modern history, useful for reference purposes because of its high authority, bibliographies, detailed general index, and miscellaneous tables included in the index volume.

A *New Cambridge modern history* is now being published (Cambridge, Univ. Pr., 1957–　), similar in scope and structure to the original edition but without bibliographies and footnotes and, therefore, not useful for general reference purposes.

DB

The Americas

GENERAL WORKS

Bibliography

✓**Brown, John Carter.** Bibliotheca americana. A catalogue of books relating to North and South America in the library of John Carter Brown of Providence, R.I. Providence, 1865–71. 3 pts. in 4v. (Pt.3 repr.: N.Y., Kraus, 1963. 2v.)　　　　　**DB1**

Contents: pt.1, 1482–1600; pt.2, 1601–1700; pt.3, 1701–1800. 2v.

2d ed. 1875–82; pts.1–2 only.

The catalog of a very rich collection now in the Brown University Library. Pts.1–2 are largely superseded by the 1919–31 edition (DB2); pt.3 had never been republished until the recent reprint. It lists 4173 numbered, annotated items, arranged chronologically with alphabetical index of authors. Detailed bibliographic information.

Brown University. John Carter Brown Library. Bibliotheca americana. Catalogue of the John Carter Brown Library in Brown University. Providence, Lib., 1919–31. v.1–3. (Repr.: N.Y., Kraus, 1961. v.1–2) **DB2**

v.1, pt.1, to 1569; v.1, pt.2, 1570–99; v.2, pt.1, 1600–34; v.2, pt.2, 1634–58; v.3, 1659–74.

No more published.

Still said to be the most complete chronological list available for this period. Lists 3737 items.

Church, Elihu Dwight. Catalogue of books relating to the discovery and early history of North and South America, forming a part of the library of E. D. Church, comp. and annotated by George Watson Cole. N.Y., Dodd, 1907. 5v. il. **DB3**

A monumental work which includes 1385 entries of books about America, arranged chronologically by date of publication from the earliest period to 1884, with author and title index. Gives for each book: full title, collation, and important historical and bibliographical annotations, with notes of differences in copies and location of copies in some 50 public and private libraries. Gives many facsimile reproductions of title pages, colophons, etc.

Harrisse, Henry. Bibliotheca americana vetustissima. A description of works relating to America published between the years 1492 and 1551. N.Y., Philes, 1866. 519p. **DB4**

—— —— Additions. Paris, Librairie Tross, 1872. 199p.

Anastatic reprint of both parts: Paris, Maisonneuve, 1922. (Facsimile repr.: Madrid, Suárez, 1958. 6v.)

A standard early work listing, with great bibliographical detail, works relating to America, published anywhere, 1492–1551. Copious footnotes; references to sources.

New York. Public Library. Reference Dept. Dictionary catalog of the history of the Americas. Boston, G. K. Hall, 1961. 28v. **DB5**

Reproduction of nearly 600,000 author, subject, and other catalog cards of an outstanding collection in North and South American history and related topics. Many subject cards are included for periodical articles indexed by the library.

Newberry Library. Chicago. Edward E. Ayer Collection. Catalog of the Edward E. Ayer collection of Americana and American Indians. Boston, G. K. Hall, 1961. 8v. **DB6**

This collection of some 90,000 pieces is particularly strong in early discoveries and explorations of America, the American Indian, missionary activities, western exploration and travel, cartography, the history of Latin America, etc. The volumes are a reproduction of the entire Ayer dictionary catalog with the exception of the Indian, Philippine, and Hawaiian collections, for which checklists have already been published.

UNITED STATES

Guides

Hockett, Homer Carey. The critical method in historical research and writing. N.Y., Macmillan, 1955. 330p. **DB7**

"A rewritten and expanded edition of the author's *Introduction to research in American history*." 2d ed. 1948.

Treats the principles of historical criticism, and the preparation of the master's essay and the doctoral dissertation.

Bibliography, p.265–95.

Although the discussion is somewhat general, the point of view and the bibliography are primarily concerned with American history.

Bemis, Samuel Flagg and **Griffin, Grace Gardner.** Guide to the diplomatic history of the United States, 1775–1921.

Wash., Govt. Prt. Off., 1935. 979p. (Repr.: Gloucester, Mass., Peter Smith, 1959) **DB8**

An important bibliography and guide to printed works and manuscript sources, in two main parts: pt.1, Bibliography, p.3–779, listing 5318 items, with comment; pt.2, Remarks on the sources, p.781–942, including manuscript sources. Indexes of: Collections of personal papers, p.943–45; Authors, p.946–79.

Carman, Harry James and **Thompson, Arthur W.** A guide to the principal sources for American civilization, 1800–1900, in the city of New York: printed materials. N.Y., Columbia Univ. Pr., 1962. 630p. **DB9**

Companion volume to the editors' guide to manuscript collections (DB30), and, with that volume, the chronological successor to the Greene and Morris guide for the period 1600–1800 (DB10). Arrangement follows that of the volume on manuscript materials.

Greene, Evarts Boutell and **Morris, Richard B.** A guide to the principal sources for early American history (1600–1800) in the city of New York. 2d ed. rev. by Richard B. Morris. N.Y., Columbia Univ. Pr., 1953. 400p. **DB10**

1st ed. 1929.

A guide to manuscript and printed sources for the study of early American history to be found in the libraries and other depositories in the city of New York. Classed arrangement with general index.

Harvard guide to American history. [Ed. by] Oscar Handlin, Arthur Meier Schlesinger, Samuel Eliot Morison, Frederick Merk, Arthur Meier Schlesinger, Jr., Paul Herman Buck. Cambridge, Belknap Pr. of Harvard Univ. Pr., 1954. 689p. **DB11**

The successor to and revision of Channing, Hart, and Turner's *Guide to the study and reading of American history* (Boston, Ginn, 1912). "Chapters 1–5 consist of 66 essays dealing with the methods, resources, and materials of American history. . . . Chapters 6–20 consist of reading lists arranged with reference to historical periods . . ."—*Pref.* A highly selective guide to books and articles published up to Dec. 31, 1950. Indispensable as a first aid to materials for the study of American history, in spite of some inconsistencies and inaccuracies.

Bibliography

Beers, Henry Putney. Bibliographies in American history; guide to materials for research. N.Y., Wilson, 1942. 487p. **DB12**

"Published January 1938. Revised edition March 1942." (Repr.: [Paterson, N.J.], Pageant Books, 1959)

A classified list of more than 11,000 bibliographies including separate works, analytics, compilations in progress, and manuscript bibliographies, with author and subject index.

Covers many aspects of American history, including political, diplomatic, economic, military, religious, cultural, local, etc.

Bell, James Ford. Jesuit relations, and other Americana in the library of James F. Bell; a catalogue comp. by Frank K. Walter and Virginia Doneghy. Minneapolis, Univ. of Minn. Pr., 1950. 419p. il. **DB13**

Consists primarily of accounts of the discoveries and explorations of America, and particularly of original editions of the *Jesuit relations*.

Genoa. Biblioteca Berio. Catalogo della raccolta Colombiano. Catalog of the Columbus collection. [2d ed.] Boston, G. K. Hall, 1963. 151p. **DB14**

1st ed., Genoa, 1906.

A photographic reproduction of the author card catalog of

the Berio Civic Library, Genoa, comprising 3156 cards of books, pamphlets, and analytics.

Griffin, Appleton Prentiss Clark. Bibliography of American historical societies (the United States and the Dominion of Canada). 2d ed. rev. and enl. Wash., Govt. Prt. Off., 1907. 1374p. (In American Historical Assoc. annual report, 1905. v.2)   **DB15**

A useful index to material in the various publications of American historical societies, general and local, to 1905. Arranged by societies, with full contents of each volume and with two alphabetical indexes to the contents: (1) Author and subject index; (2) Biographical index. Continued, informally, in the *Annual magazine subject index* (AF129), and for material published 1906 on, by the analytical indexing in *Writings on American history* (DB25).

Larned, Josephus Nelson. The literature of American history, a bibliographical guide. Boston, Amer. Lib. Assoc. Pub. Board, 1902. 596p. and suppl. volume, 37p. (Repr.: Columbus, Ohio, Long's College Book Co., 1953) **DB16**

An annotated bibliography, not up to date but still occasionally useful for its indication of source material, its selection of titles, and its critical notes, which were prepared by specialists and are signed. The preliminary sections on original sources, colonial records, etc. are especially useful in a research library. Classified, with alphabetical author and subject index.

Leonard, Eugenie Andruss, Drinker, Sophie Hutchinson and **Holden, Miriam Young.** The American woman in colonial and revolutionary times, 1565–1800; a syllabus with bibliography. Philadelphia, Univ. of Pa. Pr., 1962. 169p.   **DB17**

A syllabus, with references grouped under headings and subheadings, organized to show all aspects of the life and work of the colonial woman, followed by a bibliography of 1082 items: books and articles.

Meynen, Emil. Bibliographie des Deutschtums der kolonialzeitlichen Einwanderung in Nordamerika, insbesondere der Pennsylvanien-Deutschen und ihrer Nachkommen, 1683–1933. Leipzig, Harrassowitz, 1937. 636p.   **DB18**

Added title page: Bibliography on German settlements in Colonial North America, especially on the Pennsylvania Germans and their descendants, 1683–1933.

Lists manuscripts, documents, and printed materials, including family histories.

Classified, with indexes of authors and surnames.

Minnesota. University. Library. James Ford Bell Collection. The James Ford Bell collection; a list of additions, comp. by John Parker. Minneapolis, Univ. of Minn. Pr., 1955– . (In progress)   **DB19**

Contents: 1951–1954. 1955. 69p.; 1955–1959. 1961. 217p.

Lists books, maps, and manuscripts added to the collection, which concerns itself primarily with the history of the expansion of European commerce from the late-15th century.

Monaghan, Frank. French travellers in the United States, 1765–1932: a bibliography, with supplement by Samuel J. Marino. N.Y., Antiquarian Pr., 1961. 130p. il. **DB20**

First published in separate form by the New York Public Library, 1933. Reprinted with supplement, p.115–30.

An annotated bibliography of 1583 numbered items. Locates copies. The supplement adds about 70 more items, with its own index.

Pochmann, Henry August and **Schultz, Arthur R.** Bibliography of German culture in America to 1940 . . . Madison, Univ. of Wisconsin Pr., 1953. 483p.   **DB21**

Includes about 12,000 items, alphabetically arranged by author: books, periodical articles, theses, etc. Index.

Supplemented since 1941 by annual *Bibliography, Americana Germanica* in the *American-German review.*

Smet, Antoine de. Voyageurs belges aux États-Unis du XVII° siècle à 1900; notices bio-bibliographiques. Bruxelles, Impr. George Michiels, 1959. 201p. il. **DB22**

"Publié par le Patrimoine de la Bibliothèque Royale de Belgique."

Bio-bibliographical notes of Belgian voyagers to the United States, with references to manuscripts and documents, and bibliographies of sources.

U.S. Library of Congress. General Reference and Bibliography Division. A guide to the study of the United States of America; representative books reflecting the development of American life and thought. Prep. under the direction of Roy P. Basler, by Donald H. Mugridge and Blanche P. McCrum. Wash., Govt. Prt. Off., 1960. 1193p.   **DB23**

Basically a compilation of works on various aspects of American civilization. The 32 chapters include such headings as: literature; geography; general, diplomatic, military, intellectual, and local history; science and technology; education; religion; economic life, etc. Nearly 6500 numbered entries, most of them annotated, plus citations and evaluative notes for many related works not listed as numbered entries. Terminal date for some sections is 1955; others include publications through 1958.

Writings on American history, 1902–[03] . . . books and articles on United States history published during the year 1902 and [1903], with some memoranda on other portions of America. . . . Princeton, N.J., Lib. Book Store, 1904; Wash., Carnegie Inst., 1905. 2v.   **DB24**

1902 comp. by E. C. Richardson and A. E. Morse; 1903 comp. by A. C. McLaughlin, W. A. Slade, and E. D. Lewis.

——— 1906–39/40. A bibliography of books and articles on United States history published during the years 1906–1939/40, comp. by Grace Gardner Griffin [and others]. N.Y., 1908–10; Wash., 1911–13; New Haven, Conn., 1914–19; Wash., 1921–44. 33v.   **DB25**

Publisher varies: v.13– , published as supplements or v.2 of the *Annual report* of the American Historical Association.

Subtitle varies: 1906–35, A bibliography of books and articles on United States and Canadian history . . . with some memoranda on other portions of America.

An excellent annual bibliography and index. Through 1935, included all books and articles, wherever published, which contained anything of value on the history of the United States and British North America, and all books published in the United States or Europe on Latin America and the Pacific Islands.

Beginning with 1936, the scope was changed to include only writings on the history of the United States and its outlying possessions, omitting Canada and Latin America except for material dealing with the history of diplomatic relations of the United States and these countries, and for the colonial history of those sections of the United States which were formerly a part of the overseas empire of Spain.

A classified arrangement, with author, title, and subject index. Includes many contents and descriptive notes and refers to critical reviews. Indexes nearly 500 American and foreign periodicals.

——— Index . . . 1902–1940. Wash., Amer. Historical Assoc., 1956. 1115p.

This index to the annual volumes is, according to the foreword, "not merely a consolidated or cumulative [index] . . . it contains references and subject classifications which will not be found in the separate indexes."

——— 1948–56, comp. for the National Historical Publications Commission. James R. Masterson, ed. Wash., Govt. Prt. Off., 1952– . Annual. (1964)

Continues the preceding set. No volumes have yet been published for 1941–47.

Designed to include every book and article having any considerable value for study and research in the history of the United States from primitive times to date.

Scope and arrangement have been changed to some extent, e.g., (1) only titles pertaining to the history of the United States are included; (2) reviews are not cited; (3) titles are cited chronologically according to beginning date of subject matter, rather than alphabetically by author; (4) index is expanded to aid in the pursuit of a single topic through all regions and periods. Other changes are noted in the preface. A list of more than 600 "Periodicals cited" is a valuable serial record.

Scope and contents vary slightly.

Indexes

America: history and life. A guide to periodical literature. v.1, no.1– , July 1964– . Santa Barbara, Calif., Clio Pr. for the American Bibliographical Center, 1964– . v.1– . **DB26**

To be published three times a year: July and Dec. numbers to consist of abstracts; March to contain the bibliographical citations and an annual index. Abstracts "articles on the history of the United States and Canada published throughout the world, and . . . articles dealing with current American life and times."—*Note.*

Manuscripts and archives

Beers, Henry Putney. The French in North America; a bibliographical guide to French archives, reproductions, and research missions. Baton Rouge, Louisiana State Univ. Pr., 1957. 413p. **DB27**

A textual account of the bibliographic activities of institutions and individuals in obtaining reproductions of French documents relevant to American (primarily United States) history. Extensive bibliography of archival materials and detailed index.

—— The French and British in the Old Northwest; a bibliographical guide to archive and manuscript sources. Detroit, Mich., Wayne State Univ. Pr., 1964. 297p. **DB28**

"Presents an historical account of the acquisition, preservation and publication . . . of the original records . . . in the Old Northwest (the region south of the Great Lakes) chiefly during the 18th century, and of officials and governing bodies of Canada relating to that region."—*Pref.*

Bibliographical sources, p.195–255.

Billington, Ray Allen. Guides to American history manuscript collections in libraries of the United States. N.Y., Peter Smith, 1952. p.467–96. (Repr. from Mississippi Valley historical review, v.38, no.3, Dec. 1951) **DB29**

A listing of guides to manuscript collections in federal depositories, university and public libraries, historical societies, and private libraries which are open to the public. In two parts: (1) federal depositories, including the National Archives and the Library of Congress; (2) state depositories, including union guides which list collections in a wide number of depositories, and guides to single depositories.

Carman, Harry James and **Thompson, Arthur W.** A guide to the principal sources for American civilization, 1800–1900, in the city of New York: manuscripts. N.Y., Columbia Univ. Pr., 1960. 453p. **DB30**

First of 2v. (for the second, treating printed material, *see* DB9) designed to provide for the 19th century what the Greene and Morris work (DB10) does for earlier periods. Basic arrangement is topical. Within each division national materials are presented first, followed by listings by individual state. Name index.

Carnegie Institution, Washington. [Guides to manuscript materials for the history of the United States]. Wash., Inst., 1906–43. 23v. **DB31**

Contents: *American:* Guide to the archives of the government of the United States in Washington, by C. H. Van Tyne and W. G. Leland. Rev. ed. 1907. 327p.; Diplomatic archives of the Department of State, 1789–1840, by A. C. McLaughlin. Rev. ed. 1906. 73p.; Inventory of unpublished material for American religious history in Protestant church archives and other repositories, by W. H. Allison. 1910. 254p.; Calendar of papers in Washington archives relating to the territories of the United States (to 1873) by D. W. Parker. 1911. 476p.

British and British American: Guide to the manuscript materials for the history of the United States to 1783 in the British Museum, in minor London archives and in the libraries of Oxford and Cambridge, by C. M. Andrews and F. G. Davenport. 1908. 499p.; Guide to the materials for American history, to 1783, in the Public Record Office of Great Britain, by C. M. Andrews: v.1, State papers. v.2, Departmental and miscellaneous papers, 1912–14. 2v.; Guide to materials in London archives for the history of the United States since 1783, by C. O. Paullin and F. L. Paxon. 1914. 642p.; Guide to British West Indian archive materials in London and in the Islands, for the history of the United States by H. C. Bell and D. W. Parker. 1926. 435p.; Guide to materials in Canadian archives, by D. W. Parker. 1913. 339p.

European (except Spanish): List of manuscripts concerning American history preserved in European libraries and noted in their published catalogues and similar printed lists, by D. M. Matteson. 1925. 203p.; Guide to the manuscript materials relating to American history in German state archives, by M. D. Learned. 1912. 352p.; Guide to materials for American history in the libraries and archives of Paris, by W. G. Leland. 1932–43. v.1–2; Guide to the materials for American history in Roman and other Italian archives, by C. R. Fish. 1911. 289p.; Guide to materials for American history in Russian archives, by F. A. Golder. 1917–37. 2v.; Guide to the materials for American history in Swiss and Austrian archives, by A. B. Faust. 1916. 299p.

Spanish and Spanish American: Guide to the materials for American history in Cuban archives, by L. M. Pérez. 1907. 142p.; Descriptive catalogue of the documents relating to the history of the United States in the Papeles Procedentes de Cuba, deposited in the Archivo General de Indias at Seville, by R. R. Hill. 1916. 594p.; Guide to materials for the history of the United States in the principal archives of Mexico, by H. E. Bolton. 1913. 553p.; List of documents in Spanish archives . . . which have been printed or of which transcripts are preserved in American libraries, by J. A. Robertson. 1910. 368p.; Guide to the materials . . . in Spanish archives, by W. R. Shepherd. 1907. 107p.

A series of volumes compiled to help the research worker find the materials for the history of the United States located in foreign archives and libraries. Still useful, although in some cases more recent inventories have been made.

Crick, Bernard R. and **Alman, Miriam.** A guide to manuscripts relating to America in Great Britain and Ireland. Ed. . . . under the general supervision of H. L. Beales. London, pub. for the British Association for American Studies by the Oxford Univ. Pr., 1961. 667p. **DB32**

A well-organized guide, not an index, explaining the nature, size, and relevance of a large number of collections, private and public. Materials listed in the several Carnegie Institution *Guides* . . . (DB31) have generally been excluded. Arranged by county, then by repository. Full index of subjects, authors, owners, etc.

Munden, Kenneth White and **Beers, Henry Putney.** Guide to federal archives relating to the Civil War. Wash., Nat. Archives, Nat. Archives and Records Service, 1962. 721p. (National Archives publ. no.63-1) **DB33**

Describes the records, relating to the Civil War, of the various agencies of the federal government, arranged by agency with a subject index.

National union catalog of manuscript collections. 1959/61–62. Hamden, Conn., Shoe String, 1962–64. [v.1–3]

Annual. **DB33a**

At head of title: The Library of Congress catalogs.

"Based on reports from American repositories of manuscripts."

Compiled and edited by the Descriptive Cataloging Division of the Library of Congress.

Volume for 1959/61 published in Ann Arbor, Mich., by J. W. Edwards.

[v.1–2], 1959/61–1962, contain reproductions of cards for more than 12,000 manuscript collections located in about 400 repositories in the United States. Each entry gives number of items, physical description, scope and content, location, restrictions on access, etc.

Index: [v.3], 1959–62. 732p. In alphabetical arrangement; lists names, places, subjects, and named historical periods.

The collections consist largely of personal papers: "manuscripts or typescripts, originals or copies, of letters, memoranda, diaries, accounts, log books, drafts, and the like . . . ."

U.S. Library of Congress. Manuscript Division. Guide to manuscripts relating to American history in British depositories reproduced for the Division of Manuscripts of the Library of Congress. Grace Gardner Griffin, ed. Wash., Govt. Prt. Off., 1946. 313p. **DB34**

A record of reproductions in the Library of Congress, arranged by the library or other depository where the original is located; classified exactly as in the original depository. Detailed index.

U.S. Library of Congress. Photoduplication Service. A guide to the microfilm collection of early state records. Collected and comp. under the direction of William Sumner Jenkins; ed. by Lillian A. Hamrick. Wash., Lib. of Congress, 1950. [v.p.] **DB35**

Begun in 1941 as a joint project of the Library of Congress and the University of North Carolina to locate and reproduce early state legislative proceedings. When the project was resumed after World War II, the coverage was expanded to include also statutory laws; constitutional, administrative, executive, and court records; some local records; records of American Indian nationals; and a miscellaneous group.

The *Guide* is an index to more than 2,500,000 pages of records represented on 160,000 feet of microfilm. General arrangement is by the classifications noted above for each state. Items within these classifications are arranged chronologically. Library locations and reel numbers are given for each item.

—— —— Supplement . . . Collected, comp. and ed. by William Sumner Jenkins. Wash., Lib. of Congress, 1951. xxiiip., 130p., xviiip.

A guide to some 170 reels of microfilm remaining after the regular project had been completed, under the five special classes: (1) local records, (2) records of American Indian nations, (3) newspapers, (4) records of rudimentary states, and (5) miscellany.

U.S. National Archives. Guide to the records in the National Archives. Wash., Govt. Prt. Off., 1948. 684p. **DB36**

Supersedes the *Guide to the material in the National Archives.* 1940.

A general guide to the documents, motion-picture films, still pictures, discs, etc. deposited in the National Archives up to June 1947.

—— National Archives accessions, 1947– . Wash., 1947– . **DB37**

Issued quarterly, July 1947–June 1952; annually, 1952–60 (irregular, sometimes biennial).

Supplements the *Guide to the records* by listing current accessions, July 1947– .

The National Archives has also published a much briefer description of its holdings, *Your government's records in the National Archives.* 1950. 102p.; a series of *Preliminary inventories,* no.1–153, 1941–63, which list with more detail the records of various agencies, departments, etc.; and various special lists. For complete listings see *Publications* of the National Archives and Records Service, issued irregularly (approximately annually).

—— List of National Archives microfilm publications, 1965. Wash., 1965. 97p. il. (National Archives publ. no. 65–8) **DB38**

Title varies: 1950 and 1953, *List of file microcopies of the National Archives;* 1961, *List of National Archives microfilm publications.* Each new edition supersedes the previous one. A list of archival material available for purchase on microfilm; arrangement is by department, and information given includes price. Index.

U.S. National Historical Publications Commission. A guide to archives and manuscripts in the United States. Philip M. Hamer, ed. New Haven, Yale Univ. Pr., 1961. 775p. **DB39**

"Source materials for the study of the history of the United States and its relations with other nations and peoples."— *Pref.*

Designed not as a union catalog of manuscripts, but as a guide to direct the searcher to the most useful source for his need. Arrangement is by depository, alphabetically by state and then by city. Description of holdings is in textual form, the materials in each depository being grouped by category or type, with individual names—when relevant—then listed alphabetically. Whenever possible, nature and extent of each collection are indicated. References are given to any published guides to an individual collection. Detailed index.

Regional

County

Peterson, Clarence Stewart. Consolidated bibliography of county histories in fifty states in 1961. Consolidated 1935–1961. Baltimore, Md., Author, Box 342, 1961. 186p. **DB40**

First pub. 1935; Supplements 1944, 1946–47, 1950, 1955, and 1960.

" . . . aims to list all county histories of at least 100 pages, . . . and related works as published in the original in 1935 and in the supplements . . . and earlier works recently found that might be helpful . . ."—*Title page.*

The South

Clark, Thomas Dionysius. Travels in the Old South; a bibliography. Norman, Univ. of Okla. Pr., 1956–59. 3v. (American exploration and travel ser., no.19) **DB41**

Contents: v.1, The formative years, 1527–1783. From the Spanish explorations through the American Revolution; v.2, The expanding South, 1750–1825. The Ohio Valley and the cotton frontier; v.3, The ante-bellum South, 1825–1860. Cotton, slavery and conflict.

Each volume is divided into sections, each compiled by a specialist. Annotations are descriptive and often include critical comments; location of copies is indicated. Each volume has an index of authors, subjects, and names of persons and places.

For 1861–65, *see* E. M. Coulter (DB43).

—— Travels in the new South; a bibliography. Norman, Univ. of Okla. Pr., 1962. 2v. il. (American exploration and travel ser., no.36) **DB42**

Contents: v.1, The postwar South, 1865–1900. An era of reconstruction and readjustment; v.2, The twentieth-century South, 1900–1955. An era of change, depression and emergence.

Companion volumes to DB41, completing the series.

Coulter, E. Merton. Travels in the Confederate states; a bibliography. Norman, Univ. of Okla. Pr., 1948. 289p. (American exploration and travel ser., [no.11]) **DB43**

Lists more than 500 accounts of travels in the South during the Civil War, written either at the time or at a later date. Fills in, for 1861–65, the *Travels* series edited by T. D. Clark (DB41, DB42).

Crandall, Marjorie Lyle. Confederate imprints; a check list based principally on the collection of the Boston Athenaeum. [Boston], Boston Athenaeum, 1955. 2v. (Robert Charles Billings Fund publ., no.11) **DB44**

Contents: v.1, Official publications. 408p.; v.2, Unofficial publications, p.409–910.

Locates copies.

Lists more than 5300 titles in classed arrangement.

Harwell, Richard Barksdale. More Confederate imprints. Richmond, Virginia State Lib., 1957. 2v. (Virginia State Lib. publ., no.4–5) **DB45**

v.1, Official publications. 158p.; v.2, Unofficial publications, p.159–345.

Supplement to Crandall's *Confederate imprints . . .* (DB 44), recording 1773 additions.

These may be supplemented by *Confederate imprints in the University of Alabama Library,* comp. by Sara Elizabeth Mason [and others] (University, Ala., 1961. 156p.), which lists some 700 additional titles.

The West

Adams, Ramon Frederick. Burs under the saddle: a second look at books and histories of the West. Norman, Univ. of Okla. Pr., 1964. 610p. **DB46**

A bibliography of books on the outlaws of the West, with full annotations discussing historical inaccuracies and legends. Treats 424 titles. Detailed index.

—— The rampaging herd; a bibliography of books and pamphlets on men and events in the cattle industry. Norman, Univ. of Okla. Pr., 1959. 463p. facsims. **DB47**

2651 numbered items, arranged alphabetically by author with title and subject index.

—— Six-guns and saddle leather; a bibliography of books and pamphlets on western outlaws and gunmen. Norman, Univ. of Okla. Pr., 1954. 426p. facsims. **DB48**

1132 numbered items, arranged alphabetically, dealing with western outlaws. Detailed index. Pithy and informative annotations.

California. University, Berkeley. Bancroft Library. Catalog of printed books. Boston, G. K. Hall, 1964– . v.1–11. (In progress) **DB49**

Contents: v.1–11, A–Los Angeles.

Photographic reproduction of the cards of the dictionary catalog representing some 150,000 printed books, pamphlets, scrapbooks, government documents, broadsides, magazines, special issues of modern newspapers, as well as extensive files of early western papers.

The scope of the library is broad, but generally covers historical materials for the study of the western half of North America, including all of Mexico and Central America. Particularly strong in the history, religion, politics, economics, and social conditions of the region, with special collections on the Mormons, the Catholic church in Mexico, early California printing, voyages and travels, maps from the 16th–20th centuries, etc.

Hubach, Robert R. Early midwestern travel narratives: an annotated bibliography, 1634–1850. Detroit, Mich., Wayne State Univ. Pr., 1961. 149p. **DB50**

Lists books and periodical articles in chronological order by period, with full descriptive annotations. Includes journals and diaries, published and unpublished. Author and place-name index.

Smith, Charles Wesley. Pacific Northwest Americana: a check list of books and pamphlets relating to the history of the Pacific Northwest. 3d ed., rev. and extended by Isabel Mayhew. Portland, Oregon Historical Soc., Binfords and Mort, 1950. 381p. **DB51**

1st ed. 1909; 2d ed. 1921. The 3d edition has been thoroughly revised and enlarged, and now includes the holdings of 38 libraries in the area served by the Pacific Northwest Bibliographic Center.

A union list, not a comprehensive bibliography of imprints, listing books and pamphlets on the history of the Pacific Northwest.

Vail, Robert William Glenroie. The voice of the Old Frontier. Philadelphia, Univ. of Pa., 1949. 492p. (Rosenbach fellowship in bibliography, 10) **DB52**

"A bibliography of North American frontier literature, 1542–1800," [p.84–466] being "a selection of works written by those living on the frontier of what is now the United States, stories of Indian captivity within this area and promotion tracts by agents for the sale of frontier lands, the first editions of which appeared not later than 1800."

Locates copies in American and European libraries.

Wagner, Henry Raup. The Plains and the Rockies; a bibliography of original narratives of travel and adventure, 1800–1865, rev. by Charles L. Camp. 3d ed. Columbus, Ohio, Long's College Book Co., 1953. 601p. facsims. **DB53**

1st ed. 1920 (2d issue 1921); 2d rev. ed. 1937. The 3d edition is much revised and enlarged by Charles L. Camp.

An annotated bibliography, often indicating location of copies.

Winther, Oscar Osburn. A classified bibliography of the periodical literature of the Trans-Mississippi West (1811–1957). Bloomington, Indiana Univ. Pr., 1961. 626p. (Indiana Univ. social science ser., no.19) **DB54**

Lists 9244 items in classified arrangement with author index. Supersedes the author's *The Trans-Mississippi West* (1811–1938).

Yale University. Library. Catalog of the Yale collection of Western Americana. Boston, G. K. Hall, [1961]. 4v. **DB55**

v.1–3, A–Z; v.4, Shelf list.

A photographic reproduction of the card catalog of the Western Americana collection, which consists of a number of special collections in the field, mostly of a rare-book nature, including early imprints of books, pamphlets, and periodicals. Authors, titles, and subjects are in one alphabet. The shelf list serves as a classed guide.

The catalog includes only those books now cataloged for the collection, which means that some notable collections are omitted, and materials in the general library are not included.

Societies

American Association for State and Local History. Directory of historical societies and agencies in the United States and Canada, 1956– . Columbus, Ohio, 1956– . Biennial. **DB56**

Lists the names and addresses of the societies, with the title of the officer of each to whom correspondence should be addressed. Indicates libraries and museums, with hours of opening, publications, etc.

Dunlap, Leslie Whittaker. American historical societies, 1790–1860. . . . Madison, Wis., priv. pr., 1944. 238p. **DB57**

Pt.1 is a history of American historical societies before the Civil War, with many bibliographical footnotes. Pt.2 includes sketches describing the 65 societies organized within this period.

Dictionaries and handbooks

Boatner, Mark Mayo. The Civil War dictionary. N.Y., McKay, 1959. 974p. il. maps. **DB58**

Maps and diagrams by Allen C. Northrop and Lowell I. Miller.

Includes articles on campaigns, battles, and laws, but biographical articles predominate.

Carruth, Gorton and associates. The encyclopedia of American facts and dates. 3d ed. N.Y., Crowell, 1962. 758p. **DB59**

Chronologically arranged from 986 to 1961. In columnar form covering: (1) Politics and government, war, disasters, vital statistics; (2) Books, painting, drama, architecture, sculpture; (3) Science, industry, economics, education, religion, philosophy; and (4) Sports, fashions, popular entertainment, folklore, society.

Detailed index.

Dictionary of American history; James Truslow Adams, ed. in chief; R. V. Coleman, managing ed. 2d ed. rev. N.Y., Scribner, 1942–61. 6v. and index. **DB60**

v.1–5, A–Z. Index, 258p.; v.6, Supplement 1. 311p.

1st ed. 1940; 2d edition shows practically no change.

In general, consists of clear, compact articles each dealing with a separate and definite aspect of American history and each signed with full name of contributor. Also contains a number of articles on broader subjects, which include cross references to related articles on specific aspects.

Covers political, economic, social, industrial, and cultural history, but omits biography as this is considered the province of the *Dictionary of American biography* (AJ32). However, the activities of prominent persons may frequently be traced through the references under their names in the analytical index.

Includes many catchwords and popular names of bills and laws, etc., e.g., Hawley-Smoot act, Wade-Davis bill.

The bibliographies are usually very brief, in most cases consisting of two or three items chosen "so far as possible, with a view to accessibility in the average library." The Supplement extends the coverage, 1940–60.

Concise dictionary of American history. Advisory ed., Thomas C. Cochran; ed., Wayne Andrews. N.Y., Scribner, 1962. 1156p. **DB61**

A reworking of materials into less space, rather than an abridgment of the 6v. dictionary and its supplement (DB60). Some articles have been shortened, others omitted, and some rewritten to reflect changes since 1940, but many remain virtually intact, as the aim has been to retain the basic material of the larger work.

An extensive analytical index.

Bibliographies are omitted.

Dyer, Frederick Henry. Compendium of the war of the rebellion, comp. and arranged from official records of the Federal and Confederate armies, reports of the adjutant generals of the several states, the army registers, and other reliable documents and sources. Des Moines, Iowa, Dyer, 1908. 1796p. (Repr.: with a new introd. by Bell Irwin Wiley. N.Y., Yoseloff, 1959. 3v. il.) **DB62**

Pt.1, Number and organization of the armies of the United States; pt.2, Chronological record of the campaigns, battles, engagements, actions, combats, sieges, skirmishes, etc., in the United States, 1861 to 1865; pt.3, Regimental histories.

Kull, Irving Stoddard and **Kull, Nell M.** A short chronology of American history, 1492–1950. New Brunswick, N.J., Rutgers Univ. Pr., 1952. 388p. **DB63**

A useful chronology designed to show the development of the country year by year and also, by means of a comprehensive index, to provide a quick reference to the dates of special events. Some 10,000 events are included with the major emphasis on social, economic, and political history.

Morris, Richard B. Encyclopedia of American history. Rev. and enl. ed. N.Y., Harper, 1961. 840p. maps. **DB64**
1st ed. 1953.

In three main parts: (1) basic chronology, which lists the major political and military events of American history from aboriginal times to Jan. 1960; (2) topical chronology, which lists events under such headings as the expansion of the nation, population and immigration, the constitution and the Supreme Court, the American economy, science and invention, thought and culture; (3) 400 notable Americans, with biographical sketches. Index.

A chronological manual rather than an encyclopedia as usually understood. No bibliography and no reference to sources.

U.S. Office of Naval Operations. United States naval chronology, World War II. Wash., Govt. Prt. Off., 1955. 214p. **DB65**

Prepared in the Naval History Division, Office of the Chief of Naval Operations, Navy Dept.

Covers Sept. 1, 1939—Sept. 1945.

"A brief factual chronological record of significant events . . . includes, also, a record of the loss or damage of every U.S. naval vessel of any size, as well as every ship sinking by U.S. forces."—*Foreword.*

White's Conspectus of American biography; a tabulated record of American history and biography. 2d ed. N.Y., White, 1937. 455p. **DB66**

Includes many chronological lists of officeholders of various kinds, e.g., presidents, cabinet members, delegates to colonial and continental congresses, congressmen, ambassadors, governors, etc.

For full description *see* AJ35.

General histories

American nation: a history from original sources by associated scholars, ed. by Albert Bushnell Hart. . . . N.Y., London, Harper, 1904–18. 28v. maps. **DB67**

A standard history, each volume by a different author. Its special reference features are (1) the bibliography of sources and secondary works given at the end of each volume, and (2) the detailed separate index volume, v.28 (originally numbered 27).

Pageant of America; a pictorial history of the United States. Ralph Henry Gabriel, ed. New Haven, Yale Univ. Pr., 1925–29. 15v. il. **DB68**

v.1, Adventures in the wilderness, by Clark Wissler, C. L. Skinner, William Wood; v.2, Lure of the frontier, by R. H. Gabriel; v.3, Toilers of land and sea, by R. H. Gabriel; v.4, March of commerce, by Malcolm Keir; v.5, Epic of industry, by Malcolm Keir; v.6, Winning of freedom, by William Wood and R. H. Gabriel; v.7, In defense of liberty, by William Wood and R. H. Gabriel; v.8, Builders of the Republic, by F. A. Ogg; v.9, Makers of a new nation, by J. S. Basset; v.10, American idealism, by L. A. Weigle; v.11, American spirit in letters, by S. T. Williams; v.12, American spirit in art, by F. J. Mather, Jr., C. R. Morey, William Henderson; v.13, American spirit in architecture, by T. F. Hamlin; v.14, American stage, by O. S. Coad and Edwin Mims, Jr.; v.15, Annals of American sport, by J. A. Krout.

Winsor, Justin. Narrative and critical history of America. . . . Boston, Houghton, 1884–89. 8v. il. **DB69**

A general history still of reference importance for its many illustrations and maps, and especially for its full bibliographical notes.

Source books

Commager, Henry Steele. Documents of American history. 7th ed. N.Y., Appleton, 1963. 632p., 739p. **DB70**

Contents: 2v. in 1: v.1, To 1898; v.2, Since 1898 (to Oct. 1962).

MacDonald, William. Select charters and other documents illustrative of American history, 1606–1775, ed. with notes. N.Y., London, Macmillan, 1899. 401p. **DB71**

—— Select documents illustrative of the history of the United States, 1776–1861, ed. with notes. N.Y., London, Macmillan, 1898. 465p. **DB72**

Frequently reprinted.

—— Select statutes and other documents illustrative of the history of the United States, 1861–1898, ed. with notes. N.Y., London, Macmillan, 1903. 442p. **DB73**

A series of documentary source books designed for student use.

—— Documentary source book of American history, 1606–1926. 3d ed. rev. and enl. N.Y., Macmillan, 1926. 713p. **DB74**

A selection of documents from the three collections noted above, with some later editions; designed for one-year courses in American history.

Morison, Samuel Eliot. Sources and documents illustrating the American Revolution, 1764–1788, and the formation of the federal constitution. 2d ed. Oxford, Clarendon Pr., 1929. 378p. **DB75**

1st ed. 1923.

Atlases

Adams, James Truslow. Atlas of American history; James Truslow Adams, ed. in chief; R. V. Coleman, managing ed. N.Y., Scribner, 1943. 360p., incl. maps. 26cm. **DB76**

p.[1]–[296] numbered as plates 1–147.

A useful and usable atlas designed to accompany and supplement the *Dictionary of American history* (DB60). Includes 147 black-and-white maps arranged chronologically, with an alphabetical index of places mentioned on the maps. Index also has certain groupings such as Portages, Roads, Paths and trails, Boundaries, etc. The maps in their sequence are planned to show growth, expansion, military history, etc., and include, besides the names of places as they existed at the time, battles, roads and trails, railroads, canals, forts, and—in many cases, although not in all—important routes. This atlas shows little duplication with Paullin, *Atlas of the historical geography of the United States* (DB79) or Fox, *Harper's Atlas of American history* (DB77).

Fox, Dixon Ryan. Harper's Atlas of American history, selected from The American nation series with map studies. N.Y., Harper, 1920. 180p. maps. 25cm. **DB77**

A standard school atlas depicting the history of the United States from the discovery of America until 1917.

Lord, Clifford L. and **Lord, Elizabeth H.** Historical atlas of the United States. Rev. ed. N.Y., Holt, 1953. 238p. maps. 28cm. **DB78**

A useful, inexpensive, historical atlas with 312 outline maps, mostly in black-and-white. Supplements but does not replace Paullin (DB79) or Adams (DB76). Divided into four sections: (1) General maps; (2) Colonial period; (3) 1775–1865; (4) 1865–1950. Maps cover political and economic history including military campaigns, population, transportation, suffrage, education, slavery and abolition, agriculture, forests, labor, manufacturing, natural resources, etc.

Appendixes contain statistical tables of population, presidential elections, immigration, railroad mileage, etc. Index of place-names and subjects.

Paullin, Charles Oscar. Atlas of the historical geography of the United States, ed. by John K. Wright. [Wash., N.Y.], pub. jointly by Carnegie Inst. of Washington and the Amer. Geographical Soc., 1932. 162p. 688 maps. 36cm. [Carnegie Inst. publ. 401] **DB79**

The first adequate atlas of American history, with good maps, including reproductions of early maps, and descriptive text for each with lists of sources; indispensable in any library doing much work in United States history. Maps cover the following main subjects: Natural environment; Cartography, 1492–1867; Indians, 1567–1930; Explorations; Settlement, population and towns, 1650–1790; States, territories and cities, 1790–1930; Population, 1790–1930; Colleges, universities and churches, 1773–1890; Boundaries, 1607–1927; Political parties and opinion, 1788–1930; Political, social and educational reforms, 1775–1931; Industries and transportation, 1620–1931; Foreign commerce, 1701–1929; Distribution of wealth, 1799–1928; Plans of cities, 1775–1803; Military history, 1689–1919; Possessions and territorial claims of the United States, also certain military operations and grounds formerly frequented (ca.1815–1860) by American whalers. Index.

"The first major historical atlas of the United States and probably the most comprehensive work of its kind that has yet been published for any country."—*Introd.* by J. K. Wright, librarian of the American Geographical Society.

U.S. Military Academy, West Point. Dept. of Military Art and Engineering. The West Point atlas of American wars. Chief ed., Vincent J. Esposito. N.Y., Praeger, 1959. 2v. maps. 27x35cm. **DB80**

Contents: v.1, 1689–1900; v.2, 1900–1953.

Includes maps of campaigns, battles, etc. Text and maps on facing pages.

—— West Point atlas of the Civil War. Chief ed., Vincent J. Esposito. N.Y., Praeger, 1962. [v.p.] 154 col. maps. 27x37cm. **DB81**

Adapted from the *West Point atlas of American wars,* v.1 (*see* DB80).

U.S. War Dept. The official atlas of the Civil War. Introd. by Henry Steele Commager. N.Y., Yoseloff, 1958. 29p., 175pl. **DB82**

Reproduction of the *Atlas to accompany the official records of the Union and Confederate armies . . .* Wash., Govt. Prt. Off., 1891–95.

Includes 171 plates, often with several maps to a plate, covering military operations: battles, engagements, campaigns, defenses, etc.; topographical maps; military divisions and departments; and 4 additional plates, showing uniforms; ordnance; transportation of sick or wounded; and corps flags, badges, etc.

CANADA

Bibliography

Atlantic provinces checklist: a guide to current information in books, pamphlets, government publications, magazine articles and documentary films relating to the four Atlantic provinces. v.1– , 1957– . [Halifax, N.S.], Maritime Lib. Assoc., in cooperation with Atlantic Provinces Economic Council, 1958– . v.1– . Annual. **DB83**

Covers New Brunswick, Newfoundland, Nova Scotia, Prince Edward Island.

Gagnon, Philéas. Essai de bibliographie canadienne. Inventaire d'une bibliothèque comprenant imprimés, manuscrits, estampes, etc., relatifs à l'histoire du Canada et des pays adjacents. . . . Québec, Auteur, 1895–1913. 2v. il. **DB84**

v.1, Books, pamphlets, periodicals, no.1–3747. Autographs and manuscripts, no.3748–4406. Prints, etc., no.4407–4745. Ex-libris, no.4746–5018; v.2, Additions to the collection, 1895–1909.

Contains both English and French material. Information given for each book includes: author, full title, place, publisher, date, paging, size, with occasional bibliographical notes, facsimiles of title pages, etc. The Gagnon collection was acquired in 1909 by the city of Montreal as a nucleus for the Public Library.

Garigue, Philip. A bibliographical introduction to the study of French Canada. Montreal, Dept. of Sociology and Anthropology, McGill Univ., 1956. 133p. **DB85**

A classified listing of nearly 3000 books and articles on the region and the people. Emphasis is on political, social, and cultural topics.

Martin, Gérard. Bibliographie sommaire du Canada français, 1854–1954. Québec, Secrétariat de la Province de Québec, 1954. 104p. **DB87**

A classified listing of 900 numbered items on French Canada, in French and in English. Includes sections on: History—general, religious, political; Economics and business; Education and culture; French Canadians; Fine arts; Literature.

Peel, Bruce Braden. A bibliography of the Prairie Provinces to 1953. Toronto, Univ. of Toronto Pr., 1956. 680p. **DB88**

Published in cooperation with the Saskatchewan Golden Jubilee Committee and the University of Saskatchewan.

Books and pamphlets, chronologically arranged, on the region defined by the author as "that agricultural arc resting on the international boundary." Indexes of subjects and authors.

Royal Commonwealth Society, London. Library. Subject catalogue of the library: v.3, Dominion of Canada and its provinces, Dominion of Newfoundland, The West Indies, and Colonial America. London, 1932. 822p. **DB89**

For full description *see* DC157.

Toronto. Public Library. Bibliography of Canadiana; being items in the Public Library . . . relating to the early history and development of Canada; ed. by Frances M. Staton and Marie Tremaine, with an introd. by George H. Locke. Toronto, Lib., 1934. 828p. il. **DB90**

An author catalog of 4646 numbered items from the reference department of the library, described with full titles, collations, many contents notes, and references to bibliographical sources. Covers the period 1534–1867.

—————— First supplement . . . ed. by Gertrude M. Boyle, assisted by Marjorie Colbeck. Toronto, Lib., 1959. 333p.

Continues the item numbering of the main volume, adding 1640 entries.

Dictionaries and source books

Audet, Francis Joseph. Canadian historical dates and events, 1492–1915. Ottawa, Beauregard, 1917. 247p. **DB91**

Tables of dates, governors, officeholders, chief justices, churchmen, and many other categories.

Burpee, Lawrence Johnstone. Oxford encyclopaedia of Canadian history. Oxford, Univ. Pr., 1926. 699p. il. (Makers of Canada, anniversary ed. v.12) **DB92**

Compact articles, in alphabetical arrangement, include biographical sketches and historical events in the political, economic, social, and cultural life of Canada, with brief bibliographies.

A revised and enlarged edition of the author's *Index and dictionary of Canadian history* (Toronto, 1911. *Makers of Canada*, v.21), which served as an index to the *Makers of Canada* series as well as provided encyclopedic articles on topics not treated in the volumes indexed. The new work omits the indexing feature.

Canada. Public Archives. Documents relating to the constitutional history of Canada, 1759–1791, selected and ed. by Adam Shortt and A. G. Doughty. 2d and rev. ed. by the Historical Documents Publication Board. Ottawa, J. de L. Taché, 1918. 2v. (1084p.). maps. **DB93**

—————— 1791–1818, selected and ed. by A. G. Doughty and D. A. McArthur. Ottawa, C. H. Parmelee, 1914. 576p. maps.

—————— 1819–1828, selected and ed. with notes by A. G. Doughty and Norah Story. Ottawa, Patenaude, 1935. 538p.

Collections of documents, arranged chronologically, with citations to sources. Index in each volume.

Encyclopedia Canadiana. Ottawa, Canadiana Co., 1957–58. 10v. il. **DB94**

Ed. in chief, John E. Robbins.

A good, popularly written encyclopedia on all aspects of Canadian life, past and present. For major topics there are long, signed articles, many with bibliographies, with excellent coverage in short articles of personal and place-names. Illustrations are well chosen and plentiful, and v.10 contains an extensive atlas of Canada with a detailed index. No general analytical index for the set.

LeJeune, Louis. Dictionnaire général de biographie, histoire, littérature, agriculture, commerce, industrie et des arts, sciences, mœurs, coutumes, institutions politiques et religieuses du Canada. Ouvrage orné de 187 photographies et de 56 gravures hors-texte. [Ottawa], Université d'Ottawa, 1931. 2v. il. **DB95**

A general encyclopedia, with many fairly long articles, particularly strong in matters dealing with French Canada.

Bibliography at the end of most articles.

Reid, J. H. Stewart, McNaught, Kenneth and **Crowe, Harry S.** A source-book of Canadian history: selected documents and personal papers. Toronto, Longmans, 1959. 472p. **DB96**

A collection of selections documenting Canadian history, with introductory notes and references to sources.

Shortt, Adam and **Doughty, Arthur G.** Canada and its provinces. A history of the Canadian people and their institutions, by 100 associates: v.23, General index, Documentary notes. Edinburgh, Constable, for the Publishers Assoc. of Canada, Toronto, 1914. 368p. **DB97**

Includes: (1) General index, giving page references to v.1–22, and some direct information, e.g., dates of birth and death; (2) Manuscript sources of Canadian history; (3) Bibliography, arranged by volumes and chapters of the set; (4) Chronological outlines giving Canadian and European events in parallel columns; (5) Historical tables.

The bibliographical section is particularly noteworthy.

Atlases

Kerr, Donald Gordon Grady. A historical atlas of Canada. Toronto, Nelson, 1960. 120p. il., maps. 31cm. **DB98**

Prepared in cooperation with the Canadian Historical Association's Committee on a Historical Atlas of Canada. In addition to historical maps, includes a section of charts and graphs illustrating main economic and political trends.

Trudel, Marcel. Atlas historique du Canada français des origines à 1867. Éd. remaniée. Québec, Presses de l'Université Laval, 1961. 93p. maps. 28cm. **DB99**

An extensive revision of the author's 1948 work, *Collection de cartes anciennes et modernes pour servir à l'étude de l'histoire de l'Amérique et du Canada.* General maps, grouped by century, are presented first, followed by special maps of settlements, population, and cities.

LATIN AMERICA

General works

Bibliography

Alcina Franch, José and **Palop Martínez, Josefina.** América en la época de Carlos V; aportación a la bibliografía de este período desde 1900. Madrid, Gráficas Orbe, 1958. 236p. (Asociación Hispanoamericana de Historia) **DB100**

A classified bibliography of material (1653 entries), written in the 20th century, about America during the first half of the 16th century.

Bernal, Ignacio. Bibliografía de arqueología y etnografía Mesoamérica y norte de México, 1514–1960. México, Inst. Nacional de Antropología e Historia, 1962. 634p. maps. **DB101**

For full information *see* CD12.

Handbook of Latin American studies. Gainesville, Univ. of Florida Pr., 1936– . v.1– . Annual. **DB102**

Publisher varies.
Of first importance.
An extensive, annotated bibliography of material relating to Latin America, prepared by a group of scholars. Coverage varies. v.25 (pub. 1963) covers anthropology, art, economics, education, geography, government, history, international relations, language and literature, law, music and philosophy, sociology, and travel.
Each volume also contains special articles on particular phases of life and culture or Inter-American relations.
With 1964 issue, divided into two sections—social sciences and humanities—to be published in alternate years. v.26, *Humanities,* covers art, history, language, literature, music, and philosophy; v.27, *Social sciences,* includes anthropology, economics, education, geography, government and international relations, law, and sociology.

Humphreys, Robin Arthur. Latin American history: a guide to the literature in English. Issued under the auspices of the Royal Institute of International Affairs. London, Oxford Univ. Pr., 1958. 197p. **DB103**

An expansion of the author's *Latin America, a selective guide to publications* (1949).
A valuable, annotated guide to books and periodical articles in English. History is interpreted broadly to include political, economic, social, and cultural aspects, but archaeology and ethnology are omitted.

Keniston, Hayward. List of works for the study of Hispanic-American history. N.Y., Hispanic Soc. of America, 1920. 451p. (Hispanic notes and monographs, 5) **DB104**

A valuable guide, still useful in spite of its date.

Madrid. Biblioteca Nacional. Sección de Hispano-américa. Catálogo de obras iberoamericanas y filipinas de la Biblioteca Nacional de Madrid . . . por Luisa Cuesta [y] Modesta Cuesta. Madrid, Dirección General de Archivos y Bibliotecas, Servicio de Publicaciones del Ministério de Educación Nacional, 1953– . v.1– . (Catálogos de archivos y bibliotecas) (In progress) **DB105**

"Obra núm. 15 de Publicaciones de Educación Nacional."
Some 3300 items on Latin America and the Philippines are listed in v.1, which is devoted to general works; individual countries will be covered in succeeding volumes.

Okinshevich, Leo O. and **Gorokhoff, Cecilia J.** Latin America in Soviet writings, 1945–1958: a bibliography. Ed. by Nathan A. Haverstock. Wash., Slavic and Central European Division and the Hispanic Foundation, Reference Dept., Lib. of Congress, 1959. 257p. il. (Hispanic Foundation bibliographical ser., no.5) **DB106**

"Lists about 2200 items originally written by Russians and also Russian translations of works relating to Latin America by writers of all nationalities that were published in the Soviet Union between 1945 and 1958."—*Pref.* Titles appear both in English and in transliterated Russian. Author index.

Velázquez, Maria del Carmen. Guía bibliográfica para la enseñanza de la historia en Hispano-América. México, Inst. Panamericano de Geografía e Historia, Comisión de Historia, 1964. 506p. **DB107**

The first section lists works relating to America in general, with numerous subject divisions; succeeding chapters are devoted to individual countries of Latin America. Index of authors and anonymous titles. Some annotations.

Wilgus, Alva Curtis. Histories and historians of Hispanic America. [2d ed.] N.Y., Wilson, 1942. 144p. **DB108**

Chronologically arranged by centuries, and then grouped geographically by countries. Discusses the principal writings of more than 1000 historians.

Dissertations

Kantor, Harry. A bibliography of unpublished doctoral dissertations and masters theses dealing with the governments, politics, and international relations of Latin America. Prep. . . . for the Committee on Latin American Affairs of the American Political Science Association. Gainesville, Fla., 1953. 85p. (Inter-American Bibliographical and Library Assoc. Ser. I, v.13) **DB109**

Texas. University. Institute of Latin-American Studies. Seventy-five years of Latin American research at the University of Texas. Austin, Tex., [1959?]. 67p. (Latin American studies XVIII) **DB110**

Subtitle: Masters theses and doctoral dissertations, 1893–1958, and publications of Latin American interest, 1941–1958.

Research in progress

Flemion, Philip F. and **MacLeod, Murdo J.** Survey of investigations in progress in the field of Latin American studies. [4th ed.] Wash., Pan Amer. Union, 1962. 80p. **DB111**

Previous eds. 1953, 1956, 1959.
Lists 861 studies in progress; classified arrangement.

Guides to records

Gómez Canedo, Lino. Los archivos de la historia de América. México, Inst. Panamericano de Geografía e Historia, 1961– . v.1– . (Pan American Inst. of Geography and History. Commission on History. Publ. 87) **DB112**

Contents: v.1, Período colonial español. 654p.
Presents historical and descriptive notes on the pertinent archives in both Spain and Spanish America. Subject index.

Marchant, Alexander Nelson De Armand. Boundaries of the Latin American republics; an annotated list of documents, 1493–1943. (Tentative version) Wash., Govt. Prt. Off., 1944. 386p. (U.S. Dept. of State. Publ. 2082. Inter-American ser. 24) **DB113**

A guide to documents relating to the boundaries of the Latin-American republics. Introduction in English, Spanish, and Portuguese.
Contents: pt.1, Documents arranged in chronological order, p.21–214; pt.2, Documents arranged according to boundary, p.215–351; Bibliography, p.355–86.

U.S. National Archives. Guide to materials on Latin America in the National Archives. Wash., 1961– . v.1– . (National Archives publ. no.62–3) **DB114**

v.1, by John P. Harrison.
Describes a selected list of materials in the National Archives concerned with the Western Hemisphere south of the

United States. v.1 covers the records of the departments of State, the Treasury, War, and the Navy and the "general" records of the government.

v.2 will describe the records for the remaining departments, the independent agencies, and the legislative and judicial branches of the government, and will include the index to both volumes.

Encyclopedias

Diccionario enciclopédico de las Américas; geografía, historia, economía, política, literatura, arte, música, deporte, cine, teatro, etnografía, fauna, flora, ciencias generales. [1. ed.] Buenos Aires, Ed. Futuro, 1947. 711p. **DB115**

A general encyclopedia with very brief articles, averaging four or five lines, with some longer ones, on all phases of life in the Americas with emphasis on Latin America but including the United States and Canada. Includes biography.

Martin, Michael and **Lovett, Gabriel H.** An encyclopedia of Latin American history. N.Y., Abelard-Schuman, 1956. 392p. **DB116**

A compact encyclopedia in English. Includes bibliography.

Argentina

Bibliography

Carbia, Rómulo D. Historia crítica de la historiografía argentina (desde sus orígenes en siglo XVI). La Plata, República Argentina, [Buenos Aires, Impr. López], 1939. 483p. (Biblioteca humanidades ed. por la Facultad de Humanidades y Ciencias de la Educación de la Universidad de La Plata, t.22) **DB117**

"Índice bibliográfico," p.383–477.

A considerably enlarged and revised version of a book by the same author with almost the same title, published in 1925 as v.2 of *Biblioteca humanidades*. "This volume of Dr. Carbia is unique in the bibliography of Latin-American history. For no other country have we a survey so complete, so authoritative, so consonant with the methods and ideals of modern historical science. The second version is a vast improvement over the first."—From a review by C. H. Haring in the *Hispanic American historical review* 20:581. Nov. 1940.

Fúrlong Cárdiff, Guillermo and **Geoghegan, Abel Rodolfo.** Bibliografía de la Revolución de Mayo, 1810–1828. Ed. especial con motivo del Sesquicentenario de la Revolución de Mayo de 1810. Buenos Aires, Biblioteca del Congreso de la Nación, 1960. 704p. **DB118**

A detailed, classified listing of materials on the period of the Argentine revolt from Spain. Nearly 10,000 items—monographs, periodical articles, and documents—are included, with annotations and often tables of contents for the more significant works. Author index.

Encyclopedias and dictionaries

Diccionario histórico argentino, pub. bajo la dirección de Ricardo Piccirilli, Francisco L. Romay [y] Leoncio Gianello. Buenos Aires, Ed. Históricas Argentinas, 1953–54. 6v. **DB119**

Covers all phases of Argentine history; is especially strong in biography.

Gran enciclopedia argentina, [por] Diego A. de Santillán. Buenos Aires, Ediar, 1956–63. 8v. il., maps. **DB120**

Subtitle: Todo lo argentino ordenado alfabeticamente; geografía e historia, toponimias, biografías, ciencias, artes, letras, derecho, economía, industria y comercio, instituciones, flora y fauna, folklore, léxico regional.

A national rather than a general encyclopedia, providing a large body of reference material not easily available otherwise. Biographical entries are numerous, including living as well as deceased persons.

Pinto, Juan. Diccionario de la República Argentina; histórico, geográfico, biográfico, literario. Buenos Aires, Ed. Mundo Atlántico, 1949 [c.1950]. 753p. **DB121**

Brief articles on places and people, with longer survey articles on some subjects, e.g., history, literature, theater.

Brazil

Bibliography

Boletim internacional de bibliografía luso-brasileira. Lisboa, Fundação Calouste Gulbenkian, 1960– . v. 1– . Quarterly. **DB122**

Lists recently published works (books and periodical articles) on Luso-Brazilian topics in classed arrangement, together with some articles and notes on manuscripts. Annual indexes.

Borba de Moraes, Rubens. Bibliographia brasiliana: a bibliographical essay on rare books about Brazil published from 1504 to 1900 and works of Brazilian authors published abroad before the Independence of Brazil in 1822. Amsterdam, Rio de Janeiro, Colibris Editora, 1958. 2v. il. **DB123**

Introduction and annotations in English.

"A bibliography of rare books about various aspects of Brazil and books by Brazilian authors printed outside of Brazil . . . Books printed in Brazil are included only exceptionally."—*Pref.*

More complete for works published from the 16th through the 18th centuries than for the 19th century. Location of copies is sometimes given for very rare works.

—— and **Berrien, William.** Manual bibliográfico de estudos brasileiros. Rio de Janeiro, Souza, 1949. 895p. **DB124**

An annotated bibliography of works in various languages on the origins and development of Brazilian culture, divided broadly by subject, and covering mainly material published prior to 1942 in the humanities and social sciences. Periodical articles are included. Author index. Each section was compiled under the direction of a specialist who also provided a historical outline of Brazilian achievement in his field, which precedes the actual bibliography.

Supplemented by: (1) Herbert Baldus. Bibliografia comentada de etnologia brasileira (1943–1950). (Suplemento ao Manual bibliográfico de estudos brasileiros) 1954. 142p.; (2) Edison Carneiro. O folclore nacional (1943–1953). 1954. 73p. (In Série bibliográfica de estudos brasileiros, dirigida por Irene de Menezes Dória. Rio de Janeiro, Souza, 1954)

Garraux, Anatole Louis. Bibliographie brésilienne; catalogue des ouvrages français et latins relatifs au Brésil (1500–1898). Paris, Chadenot, 1898. 400p. **DB125**

Author alphabet with subject index.

Jackson, William Vernon. Library guide for Brazilian studies. Pittsburgh (distr. by Univ. of Pittsburgh Book Centers), 1964. 197p. **DB126**

A survey describing the holdings in 1963–64 of resources for Brazilian studies in the major research collections of the United States. Includes chapters on general materials, humanities, social sciences, science, and technology, with indications of strengths and weaknesses in specific subject areas. Contains a bibliography of published guides, catalogs, and descriptions of specific collections; useful appendixes include a "Union list of selected Brazilian periodicals in the humanities and social sciences" and indexes to the Library of Congress classification schemes for Brazilian history and literature. The index of libraries, plus a number of maps and tables, add to the value of the guide.

Rio de Janeiro. Instituto Brasileiro de Bibliografia e Documentação. Amazônia; bibliografia, 1614–1962. Rio de Janeiro, 1963. 842p. **DB127**

Includes references to books, periodical articles, and other documents arranged by Universal Decimal Classification. More than 7600 items. Author index.

Historiography

Rodrigues, José Honorio. Historiografía del Brasil, siglo XVI. México, 1957. 102p. (Inst. Panamericano de Geografía e Historia. Comisión de Historia. Publ. 82. Historiografías, 4) **DB128**

Instituto Panamericano de Geografía e Historia. Publ. 190. A treatment of the historical writings of the 16th century. No bibliography.

—— —— siglo XVII. México, 1963. 261p. (Inst. Panamericano de Geografía e Historia. Comisión de Historia. Publ. 93. Historiografías, 6) **DB129**

Instituto Panamericano de Geografía e Historia. Publ. 264. Continues the above, covering the 17th century.

Dictionaries and handbooks

Instituto Historico e Geographico Brasileiro, Rio de Janeiro. Diccionario historico, geographico e ethnographico do Brasil. Rio de Janeiro, Impr. Nacional, 1922. 2v. il. **DB130**

v.1, Brasil; v.2, Estados.
Long surveys of various aspects including natural history, geography, education, agriculture, industry, history, literature, etc.

Teixeira de Oliveira, José. Dicionário brasileiro de datas históricas. Rio de Janeiro, Ed. Pan-Americana, 1944. 653p. **DB131**

Chronologically arranged with subject and author indexes. Includes birth and death dates of many persons.

Chile

Anrique Reyes, Nicolás and **Silva Arriagada, L. I.** Ensayo de una bibliografía histórica i jeográfica de Chile. Santiago de Chile, Impr. Barcelona, 1902. 679p. **DB132**

A classified list of 2561 titles with author index.

Costa Rica

Lines, Jorge A. Bibliografía antropológica aborigen de Costa Rica; incluye especialmente: arqueología, cartografía, etnología, geografía, historia y lingüística. San José, Costa Rica, 1943. 263p. **DB133**

On cover: Universidad de Costa Rica. Facultad de Letras y Filosofía.
1262 numbered items including many analytics.

Ecuador

Barrera, Isaac J. Historiografía del Ecuador. México, 1956. 124p. (Inst. Panamericano de Geografía e Historia. Comisión de Historia. Publ. 81. Historiografías, 3) **DB134**

Instituto Panamericano de Geografía e Historia. Publ. 189. A discussion of historians and their work. No bibliography.

French Guiana

Abonnenc, Émile, Hurault, J. and **Saban, R.** Bibliographie de la Guyane Française. Paris, Éd. Larose, 1957– . v.1– . **DB135**

Contents: t.1, Ouvrages et articles de langue française concernant la Guyane et les territoires avoisinants.

A comprehensive bibliography of books and periodical articles which appeared from the end of the 16th century to 1955. Listed alphabetically by author with subject index. v.2 is to cover non-French materials.

Mexico

Bibliography

California. State Library, Sacramento. Sutro Branch, San Francisco. Catalogue of Mexican pamphlets in the Sutro collection (1623–[1888]). Prep. by the personnel of the Works Progress Administration . . . A. Yedidia, supervisor. P. Radin, ed. Sponsored by the California State Library. San Francisco, 1939–40. 10 pts. (963p.) **DB136**

—— —— Supplement (1605–1887). San Francisco, 1941. 290p. in 3 pts.

—— —— Author index. . . . San Francisco, 1941. 65p.
A chronological listing of a large collection of pamphlets, in the Spanish language, on Mexico or printed in Mexico.
The author index indexes both the main work and the supplement.

González, Luis. Fuentes de la historia contemporánea de México: libros y folletos. Estudio preliminar . . . con la colaboración de Guadelupe Monroy y Susana Uribe. [1. ed.] México, El Colegio de México, 1961–62. 3v. **DB137**

Contents: v.1, Generalidades. Territorio. Sociedad; v.2, Economía. Política. Religión; v.3, Educación. Filosofía y ciencias. Letras y artes.
v.3 contains general and title indexes.
An extensive bibliography on the whole range of Mexican culture for the period 1910–40.

México. Comisión de Estudios Militares. Biblioteca del Ejército. Apuntes para una bibliografía militar de México, 1536–1936 . . . M. C. Nestor Herrera Gómez [y] Silvino M. González. México, Talleres Graficos de la Nación, 1937. 469p. **DB138**

A bibliography of more than 1800 titles on Mexican military history, 1536–1936.

Ramos, Roberto. Bibliografía de la historia de México. México, Talleres de Impresión de Estampillas y Valores, 1956. 772p. **DB139**

4700 items (books, pamphlets, manuscripts, etc., but no periodical articles), covering Mexican history up to the 20th-century revolution. Listed alphabetically by author with no subject index.

—— Bibliografía de la revolución mexicana. 2. ed. México, 1959–60. 3v. (Biblioteca del Inst. Nacional de Estudios Históricos de la Revolución Mexicana. [15]) **DB140**

More than 5000 items on the Mexican revolution, 1910–22. v.1–2 are reprints of the edition published 1931–35. v.3, originally published in 1940, has been considerably expanded, listing nearly 2000 items published since 1935.

Valle, Rafael Heliodoro. Bibliografía maya. . . . México, 1937–41. 404p. **DB141**

At head of title: Instituto Panamericano de Geografía e Historia.
Issued in parts with the *Boletín bibliográfico de antropología americana*, v.1–5, 1937–41.
A comprehensive bibliography of materials about Mayan culture in various languages and of all periods.

Guides to records

Millares Carlo, Agustín. Repertorio bibliográfico de los archivos mexicanos y de los europeos y norteamericanos de interés para la historia de México. [1. ed.] México, 1959. 366p. (Biblioteca Nacional de México. Inst. Bibliográfico Mexicano. [Publ.] 1) **DB142**

Lists more than 1000 published bibliographies, catalogs, and guides to archives and special collections in Europe and America relating to Mexican history. With numerous annotations; subject index.

A much enlarged revision of the first section of the author's *Repertorio bibliográfico de los archivos mexicanos y de las colecciones diplomáticas fundamentales para la historia de México* (México, 1948). The second section, which lists collections of documents for the history of Mexico, is not carried over.

Encyclopedias and dictionaries

Enciclopedia yucatanense . . . pub. bajo la dirección del Carlos A. Echánove Trujillo. Ciudad de México, Ed. Oficial del Gobierno de Yucatán, 1944–47. 8v. il. (v.8, 1944) **DB143**

A classed encyclopedia aiming to cover all aspects of Yucatan history and life. Each section is written by an authority, and most have bibliographies. v.7, *Biografías,* deals with only 14 individuals, but more biographical material is included in articles throughout. v.8, *Bibliografías general yucatanense,* is an extensive alphabetical list of works published in and on Yucatan. Indexes announced but not published.

García Cubas, Antonio. Diccionario geográfico, histórico y biográfico de los Estados Unidos Mexicanos. México, Oficina Tipografía de la Secretaría de Fomento, 1888–91. 5v. il. **DB144**

An older work still useful, especially for its geographical names and fairly long historical articles.

Leduc, Alberto, Lara y Pardo, Luis and **Roumagnac, Carlos.** Diccionario de geografía, historia y biografía mexicanas. Paris, México, Bouret, 1910. 1109p. **DB145**

Brief articles on places, historical events, and persons.

Paraguay

Cardozo, Efraím. Historiografía paraguaya. [1. ed.] México, 1959– . v.1– . (Inst. Panamericano de Geografía e Historia. Comisión de Historia. Publ. 83. Historiografías, 5) **DB146**

Instituto Panamericano de Geografía e Historia. Publ. 221. Contents: v.1, Paraguay indígena, español y jesuíta. Bibliografía, p.461–524.

Detailed bio-bibliographies of historians with a comprehensive bibliography of material about them.

Peru

Bibliography

Tauro, Alberto. Bibliografía peruana de historia, 1940–1953. Lima, Talleres Gráficos, 1953. 196p. **DB147**

Books and monographs printed in Peru, or in other countries, relating to Peru, 1940–53.

—— Guía de estudios históricos. Lima, 1955. 109p. (Separata del Boletín bibliográfico, v.25, no.1–4) **DB148**

Serves as a companion to the work above, listing periodical articles.

Vargas Ugarte, Ruben. Manual de estudios peruanistas. 4. ed. Lima, Librería e Imprenta Gil, 1959. 455p. **DB149**

1st edition, 1939, had title *Historia del Perú. Fuentes.*

A bibliographical survey of materials on the history, bibliography, religion, literature and language, social sciences, etc. of Peru.

Encyclopedias

Mendiburu, Manuel de. Diccionario histórico-biográfico del Perú. 2. ed. con adiciones y notas bibliográficas. Lima, "Enrique Palacios," 1931–35. 11v. **DB150**

For full description *see* AJ220.

El Salvador

García, Miguel Angel. Diccionario histórico-enciclopédico de la República de El Salvador. San Salvador, Tipografía "La Luz," 1927–51. v.1–13. (In progress?) **DB151**

v.1–13, A–Col.

Historical and biographical articles in one alphabet, often including reproduction of documentary sources.

Uruguay

Araújo, Orestes. Diccionario popular de historia de la República o. del Uruguay, desde la época del descubrimiento de su territorio, hasta la de su independencia. Montevideo, Dornaleche y Reyes, 1901–3. 3v. **DB152**

A dictionary of persons, places, and events including documentary sources.

Venezuela

Sánchez, Manuel Segundo. Obras. Caracas, [Banco Central de Venezuela], 1964. 2v. **DB153**

v.1 is a reprint of the author's *Bibliografía venezolanista* . . . (Caracas, Empresa el Cojo, 1914. 494p.), which lists 1438 works, annotated, on Venezuela published in foreign countries; v.2 contains a biographical sketch of the author and a bibliography of his works.

ISLANDS OF THE CARIBBEAN AND THE WEST ATLANTIC

General works

Bibliography

Florida. University. Libraries. Catalog Dept. Caribbean acquisitions; materials acquired by the University of Florida, 1957/58– . Gainesville, [Univ. of Florida], 1959– . Annual. **DB154**

A classified list of works acquired through the Farmington Plan.

For full information *see* AA406.

Hiss, Philip Hanson. A selective guide to the English literature on the Netherlands West Indies; with a supplement on British Guiana. N.Y., Netherlands Information Bureau, 1943. 129p. (Netherlands Information Bureau booklets, no.9) **DB155**

A classified bibliography to material in English on Curaçao and Surinam, with a supplement on British Guiana. Author index.

New York. Public Library. List of works relating to the West Indies. N.Y., 1912. 392p. (Repr. from the New York Public Library. Bull. Jan.–Aug. 1912) **DB156**

An extensive bibliography of books, periodicals, and documents in various languages.

Ragatz, Lowell Joseph. A guide for the study of British Caribbean history, 1763–1834, including the abolition and emancipation movements. Wash., Govt. Prt. Off., 1932. 725p.   **DB157**

An extensive, classified, annotated list of books, manuscripts, documents, and periodical articles, with author, title, subject, and proper-name index.

Royal Commonwealth Society, London. Library. Subject catalogue. v.3, Dominion of Canada . . . the West Indies, and colonial America. London, 1932.   **DB158**

For full description *see* DC157.

Historiography

Goveia, Elsa V. A study on the historiography of the British West Indies to the end of the nineteenth century. México, 1956. 183p. (Inst. Panamericano de Geografía e Historia. Comisión de Historia. Publ. 78. Historiografías, 2)   **DB159**

Instituto Panamericano de Geografía e Historia. Publ. 186.

A discussion of the histories of the British West Indies and their writers. Brief bibliography, p.179–81.

Encyclopedias

Benjamins, H. D. and **Snelleman, J. F.** Encyclopaedie van Nederlandsch West-Indië. 'sGravenhage, Nijhoff, 1914–17. 782p.   **DB160**

An encyclopedia on all aspects of the region; includes biographies. Scholarly, signed articles; good bibliographies.

Bermuda

Cole, George Watson. Bermuda in periodical literature, with occasional references to other works; a bibliography. Brookline, Mass., pr. for the author, 1907. 275p. **DB161**

An annotated bibliography of articles in books and periodicals dating back to the 17th century, with especial emphasis on the flora and fauna of the islands.

Cuba

Bibliography

Havana. Biblioteca Nacional. Impresos relativos a Cuba editados en las Estados Unidos de Norteamérica. Comp. bajo la dirección de Lilia Castro de Morales . . . Habana, 1956. 370p.   **DB162**

At head of title: Ministerio de Educación.

Lists 2014 books and pamphlets by Cubans, or about Cuba, published from 1762 to 1956. Arranged chronologically with author index.

Historiography

Pérez Cabrera, José Manuel. Historiografía de Cuba. México, 1962. 394p. (Inst. Panamericano de Geografía e Historia. Comisión de Historia. Publ. 106. Historiografías, 7)   **DB163**

Instituto Panamericano de Geografía e Historia. Publ. 262.

A résumé of historical writings, 15th to 20th centuries, with annotated bibliographies throughout.

Dictionaries and handbooks

Cuba en la mano; enciclopedia popular ilustrada. La

Habana, [Ucar, García], 1940. 1302p. il.   **DB164**

Includes sections on geographical names, natural history, history, printing, biography, education and culture, communications, politics, statistics, etc.

Falkland Islands

Torre Revello, José. Bibliografía de las Islas Malvinas; obras, mapas y documentos; contribución. Buenos Aires, Impr. de la Universidad, 1953. 260p. maps, facsims. (Universidad de Buenos Aires. Facultad de Filosofía y Letras. Publ. del Inst. de Investigaciones Históricas, no. 99)   **DB165**

A bibliography of more than 800 items on the history and geography of the Falkland Islands, with a section listing unpublished documents, 1534–1953.

Many of the works listed are in Spanish, but some titles in other languages are included.

Haiti

Bibliography

Duvivier, Ulrick. Bibliographie générale et méthodique d'Haïti. . . . Port-au-Prince, Haïti, Impr. de l'État, 1941. 2v.   **DB166**

For full information *see* AA530.

Port-au-Prince, Haiti. Institution Saint-Louis de Gonzague. Bibliothèque Haïtienne des Frères. Catalogue de la Bibliothèque Haïtienne des Frères de l'Instruction Chrétienne; the catalogue of the Haitian Library of the Brothers of Christian Instruction, [par] Frère Lucien Jean [Legendre]. Port-au-Prince, Haiti, 1958. 533p.   **DB167**

Also published as compiler's thesis, St. Michael's College, Winooski, Vt.

A classified list of about 5000 titles, a large percentage of them bearing directly or indirectly upon Haiti. Author and title indexes.

Historiography

Pressoir, Catts, Trouillot, Ernst and **Trouillot, Henock.** Historiographie d'Haïti. México, 1953. 298p. (Inst. Panamericano de Geografía e Historia. Comisión de Historia. Publ. 66. Historiografías, 1)   **DB168**

Instituto Panamericano de Geografía e Historia. Publ. 168.

Treats historical writers and their works from 1492 to the 20th century.

Bibliography, p.287–98.

Jamaica

Cundall, Frank. Bibliographia jamaicensis. Kingston, Inst. of Jamaica, 1902. 83p.   **DB169**

Subtitle: A list of Jamaica books and pamphlets, magazine articles, newspapers and maps, most of which are in the Library of the Institute of Jamaica.

——— Supplement. 1908. 38p.

Martinique

Gazin Gossel, Jacques. Éléments de bibliographie générale, méthodique et historique, de la Martinique (Antilles Françaises). Fort-de-France, Impr. Antillaise, 1926. 348p.   **DB170**

A classified bibliography of books and pamphlets on Martinique.

Puerto Rico

Pedreira, Antonio S. Bibliografía puertorriqueña (1493–1930). Madrid, Impr. de la Librería y Casa Ed. Hernando, 1932. 707p. (Monografías de la Universidad de Puerto Rico. Ser. A. Estudios hispánicos, núm. 1) **DB171**

Includes works by natives and foreigners about Puerto Rico, the artistic literary works of Puerto Ricans, and a selected list of works by Puerto Ricans on various subjects.—Cf. *Introd.,* p.xvii.

Classified, with author and subject indexes.

Puerto Rico. Universidad. Centro de Investigaciones Sociales. Bibliografía puertorriqueña de fuentes para investigaciones sociales, 1930–1945. Ed. provisional, ed. por Augusto Bird. [Río Piedras], 1946–47. 2v. (547p.) **DB172**

An extensive, classified bibliography of books and periodical articles, covering the natural history, anthropology, health, economics, history, political science, and culture of Puerto Rico. No author index.

Virgin Islands

Reid, Charles Frederick. Bibliography of the Virgin Islands of the United States; Charles F. Reid, ed.; Nathan Habib, assoc. ed.; Florence D. Clark and Caroline Simonini, asst. eds. N.Y., Wilson, 1941. 225p. **DB173**

"Prepared with the assistance of the Federal Works Agency, Work Projects Administration for the City of New York, Division of Community Service Programs, 'Bibliographies of the territories and outlying possessions of the United States.'"

Lists books, manuscripts, documents, and periodical articles in an annotated, classified bibliography with alphabetical index.

D C

Europe

GENERAL WORKS

Guides to records

Guide international des archives: Europe. Rome, Annales Institutorum, 1934. 3v. facsims. (Bibliothèque des "Annales Institutorum," v.4) **DC1**

At head of title: v.1, Société des Nations. Institut International de Coopération Intellectuelle; v.2–3, Comité des Annales Institutorum Urbis Romae.

Contents: v.1, Guide; v.2, Tables et documents; v.3, Supplément: S. Pistolese, Les archives européennes du onzième siècle à nos jours, essai historique et juridique.

v.1, the *Guide,* is arranged alphabetically by country, describing the nature and extent of its archives, facilities of use, etc., and sometimes including bibliographies of inventories, catalogs, etc.

Bautier, Robert-Henri. Bibliographie sélective des guides d'archives. Supplément au Guide international des archi-

ves, t.1 (Europe), 1934. (In Journal of documentation 9:1–41. March 1953) **DC2**

A revised and enlarged edition of the *Répertoire sélectif de guides des archives* issued in mimeographed form by UNESCO in 1950. Lists guides to archival records printed in Europe from 1934 to 1950 and outside Europe from 1900 to 1950. Entries are arranged in the alphabetical order of the 76 countries and territories covered by the work.

Particular attention has been given to industrial and commercial archives and to collections of photographic, radio, and cinema materials.

Thomas, Daniel H. and **Case, Lynn M.** Guide to the diplomatic archives of western Europe. Philadelphia, Univ. of Pa. Pr., 1959. 389p. **DC3**

18 chapters, each by a specialist, describe the diplomatic archives of 15 countries and 3 international collections. For each, gives an account of the history, content, administration, and conditions of use of the collections, and usually a bibliography. Subject index.

Bibliography

Bullock, Alan and **Taylor, A. J. P.** A select list of books on European history, 1815–1914. Ed. for the Oxford Recent History Group . . . 2d ed. Oxford, Clarendon Pr., 1957. 79p. **DC4**

1st ed. 1949.

". . . limited to secondary works."—*Pref.* A useful list for the beginning student. Includes titles in the principal Western languages.

International Committee of Historical Sciences. Commission Internationale d'Histoire Ecclésiastique Comparée. Bibliographie de la réforme, 1450–1648: ouvrages parus de 1940 à 1955. Leiden, Brill, 1958–63. Fasc.1–4. (In progress) **DC5**

Contents: fasc.1, Allemagne, Pays-Bas. 136p.; fasc.2, Belgique, Suède, Norvège, Danemark, Irlande, États-Unis d'Amérique. 156p.; fasc.3, Italie, Espagne, Portugal. 138p.; fasc.4, France, Angleterre, Suisse. 145p.

Lists books, dissertations, and periodical articles on the Reformation published in the countries indicated, from 1940 to 1955.

EUROPE, EASTERN

Bibliography

Akademiia Nauk SSSR. Fundamental'naia Biblioteka Obshchestvennykh Nauk. Sovetskoe slavianovedenie; literatura o zarubeshnykh slavianskikh stranakh na russkom iazyke, 1918–1960. Sost. I. A. Kaloeva. Moskva, 1963. 401p. **DC6**

A bibliography of Soviet publications in the Russian language in the field of Slavic studies in general and for countries outside the USSR. In addition to history and philology, it includes economics, law and state, and social structure, giving special attention to documentary materials and archival publications.

Bengescu, George. Essai d'une notice bibliographique sur la question d'Orient: Orient européen, 1821–1897. Paris, Le Soudier, 1897. 327p. **DC7**

Lists more than 2100 separate works—historical, political, and military—on the Balkans, published in France and Belgium from 1821 to 1897. Arranged chronologically, with author index and index to anonymous works.

Byrnes, Robert F. Bibliography of American publications on East Central Europe, 1945–1957. Bloomington, Ind.,

1958. 213p. (Indiana Univ. publ. Slavic and East European ser., v.12) (Incorrectly numbered v.11)   **DC8**

Attempts to be a complete list of books and articles published in the United States from 1945 to 1957, with some from Canada, and also a few articles published by Americans in German, Dutch, and English journals.

Classified arrangement under country with author index. "East Central Europe . . . in this book refers to Albania, Bulgaria, Czechoslovakia, Finland, Hungary, Poland, Rumania, Yugoslavia and the Baltic States . . . Estonia, Latvia and Lithuania; Eastern Germany and Greece are not included . . . ."

Kerner, Robert Joseph. Slavic Europe; a selected bibliography in the western European languages, comprising history, languages and literatures. Cambridge, Harvard Univ. Pr., 1918. 402p. (Harvard bibliographies. Library ser., v.1)   **DC9**

A selected list of basic works in the western European languages on all phases of life in Slavic Europe divided into six sections: (1) The Slavs; (2) The Russians (including the Great Russians, the Little Russians, and the White Russians); (3) The Poles; (4) The Slavs in Germany (not including the Poles); (5) The Bohemians (Čechs) and Slovaks; (6) The Southern Slavs including the Jugo-slavs or the Slovenes and Serbo-Croats and the Bulgarians and Macedonians. Author index.

New York. Public Library. Reference Dept. Dictionary catalog of the Slavonic collection. Boston, G. K. Hall, 1959. 26v.   **DC10**

A photographic reproduction of the catalog for a 120,000-volume collection of Slavic and Baltic materials, and of materials in other languages on these areas. The basic collection in literature and social science was augmented later by science and technology titles. The 550,000-entry catalog is notable for analytics and references to periodical articles. Transliteration differs from the Library of Congress system.

Savadjian, Léon. Bibliographie balkanique, 1920–38. Paris, Revue des Balkans, 1931; Soc. Générale d'Impr. et d'Édit., 1933–39.   **DC11**

[v.1], 1920–30. 1931. 270p.; [v.2], 1931–32. 1933. 151p.; [v.3], 1933–38. Annual.

1920–30 issued as *Revue des Balkans,* n.s., v.2–3, av.–sept. 1931.

Contains material concerning Albania, Bulgaria, Greece, Rumania, Turkey, and Yugoslavia in French, German, Italian, and English.

Thomson, Erik. Baltische Bibliographie, 1945–1956. Würzburg, Holzner-Verlag, 1957. 218p. (Ostdeutsche Beiträge aus dem Göttinger Arbeitskreis. Bd.5) Der Göttinger Arbeitskreis: Veröffentlichung Nr.173)   **DC12**

In two principal sections: one listing books and society publications by authors of the German Baltic region; the other, works about the area. Each list classified by subject.

Valjavec, Fritz. Südosteuropa-Bibliographie . . . München, Oldenbourg, 1956–62. v.1–2$^{1–2}$. (Südost-Institut, München) (In progress)   **DC13**

Contents: Bd.1, 1945–50: T.1, Slowakei, Rumänien, Bulgarien. T.2, Jugoslawien, Ungarn, Albanien, Südosteuropa und grössere Räume; Bd.2, 1951–1955: T.1, Südosteuropa und grössere Teilräume, Jugoslawien, Ungarn. T.2, Albanien, Bulgarien, Rumänien, Slowakei.

Arranged by country, then divided by topic. Includes periodical articles as well as books.

Current

American bibliography of Russian and East European studies, 1956– . Bloomington, Indiana Univ., 1957– .

Annual. (Indiana Univ. publ. Russian and East European ser., v.9–)   **DC14**

Title varies: 1956, *The American bibliography of Slavic and East European studies in language, literature, folklore and pedagogy;* 1957–59, *The American bibliography of Slavic and East European studies.*

An interdisciplinary annual bibliography of books and articles, mainly of American authorship.

L'U.R.S.S. et les pays de l'Est. Revue des revues. (Strasbourg. Université. Centre de Recherches sur l'U.R.S.S. et les Pays de l'Est) Paris, Centre Nationale de la Recherche Scientifique, no.1, May, 1960– . Quarterly. **DC15**

Abstracts in French of articles in East European periodicals, arranged under broad divisions of law, economy, social life, and culture. 1964 issues contain abstracts from Russian, Polish, Rumanian, Yugoslav, Czechoslovak, Hungarian, East-German, and Chinese periodicals.

Encyclopedias and handbooks

Slavonic encyclopedia, ed. by Joseph S. Roucek. N.Y., Philosophical Lib., 1949. 1445p.   **DC16**

Contains articles, usually brief, in various fields, but is more than half biographical. Some articles are signed. Treatment is uneven and cross references unreliable.

Strakhovsky, Leonid I. A handbook of Slavic studies. Cambridge, Harvard Univ. Pr., 1949. 753p.   **DC17**

A useful handbook for the reader unfamiliar with Slavic languages. Consists of survey chapters by specialists on the history and literature of the Slavs in Russia, Poland, Czechoslovakia, and the Balkans. Attached to each chapter is a bibliography of materials in western European languages. Source materials in the Slavic languages are sometimes included in footnotes. Comparative chronology, p.675–722.

History

Dvornik, Francis. The Slavs in European history and civilization. New Brunswick, N.J., Rutgers Univ. Pr., 1962. 688p. maps.   **DC17a**

A historical survey of the Slavic people in central and eastern Europe from the 13th to the 19th centuries. Especially valuable for the bibliographical notes which conclude each chapter and the extensive bibliography (p.565–635).

ALBANIA

Kersopoulos, Jean G. Albanie; ouvrages et articles de revues parus de 1555 à 1934. (In Les balkans 5:377–424, 651–712. 1934) (Série de bibliographies françaises sur les nations balkaniques, no.1)   **DC18**

Manek, F., Pekmezi, G. and **Stotz, A.** Albanesische Bibliographie. Wien, Vereines "Dija," 1909. 147p.   **DC19**

A chronological listing of book and periodical material, dating from 900 B.C. to 1909.

ARMENIA

Salmaslian, Armenag. Bibliographie de l'Arménie; préf. de René Grousset. . . . Paris, Auteur, 1946. 195p. **DC20**

A classed list, with author index, of some 1500 separately published works on Armenia from the 16th century to 1946. Includes material in French, German, English, and some other European languages. Periodical articles are omitted.

AUSTRIA

See also Germany, p.492–94.

Charmatz, Richard. Wegweiser durch die Literatur der österreichischen Geschichte. Stuttgart, Cotta, 1912. 138p. **DC21**

A useful selected list with some brief annotations.

Strassmayr, Eduard. Bibliographie zur oberösterreichi-schen Geschichte. Linz a. Donau, Winkler, 1929–57. v.1–4. (Bibliographie zur Geschichte, Landes- und Volks-kunde Oesterreichs. 1. Abt.: Oberösterreich, Bd.1–4) **DC22**

Contents: Bd.1, 1891–1926; Bd.2, 1927–1934; Bd.3, 1935–1948; Bd.4, 1949–1953.
Publishers vary.
v.3–4, hrsg. vom Oberösterreichischen Landesarchiv.

Uhlirz, Karl. Handbuch der Geschichte Österreichs und seiner Nachbarländer Böhmen und Ungarn. Bearb. von Mathilde Uhlirz. Graz, Leuschner und Lubensky, 1927–44. 4v. **DC23**

A guide to research on the history of Austria, Bohemia, and Hungary with extensive bibliographies.

Vienna

Verein für Landeskunde von Niederösterreich und Wien. Bibliographie zur Geschichte und Stadtkunde von Wien, nebst Quellen- und Literaturhinweisen. Wien, Touristik-Verlag, 1947–62. 5v. **DC24**

An exhaustive bibliography to cover all phases of the history of Vienna, including books, analytics to composite books, periodical articles, etc. published through 1944. Classed arrangement. v.5 contains indexes by author, subject, and person.
Editors and publishers vary.

BELGIUM

Bibliography

Bibliographie de l'histoire de Belgique. Bibliografie van de geschiedenis van Belgie, 1952– . (In Revue belge de philologie et d'histoire. v.31, 1953–) Annual. **DC25**

Continued from the series published in the *Revue du nord,* 1947–49 in v.32, 1950; 1950 in v.33, 1951; 1951 in v.34, 1952. Item numbers run consecutively through both series.
Classified arrangement. As yet no indexes.

Cosemans, A. and **Heyse, Th.** Contribution à la biblio-graphie dynastique et nationale. Bruxelles, van Campen-hout, 1954–61. Pts.1–4. (Cahiers belges et congolais no. 23–25, 27–30, 32–33, 35–36) (In progress) **DC26**

Title also in Flemish.
Contents: pt.1, Partie générale; pt.2, Règne de Léopold Iᵉʳ (1831–1865); pt.3, Règne de Léopold II (1865–1909); pt.4, Règne d'Albert (1909–1934).
A detailed, classified bibliography of books and periodical articles, to cover Belgian history from the beginning of the present dynasty, in 1831, through the reign of Albert I.

Gérin, Paul. Bibliographie de l'histoire de Belgique, 1789–21 juillet 1831. Louvain, Éd. Nauwelaerts, 1960. 429p. (Centre Interuniversitaire d'Histoire Contemporaine. Cahiers, 15) **DC27**

The first of a planned series of bibliographies on the history of Belgium since 1789. Covers all phases of history: political, military, social, economic, religious, cultural, etc., with indexes by author and subject.

Pirenne, Henri. Bibliographie de l'histoire de Belgique; catalogue méthodique et chronologique des sources et des ouvrages principaux relatifs à l'histoire de tous les Pays-Bas jusqu'en 1598 et à l'histoire de Belgique jusqu'en 1914. 3. éd., rev. et compl. avec la collaboration de Henri Nowé et Henri Obreen. Bruxelles, Lamertin, 1931. 440p. **DC28**

A revised and much enlarged edition of the standard bibli-ography of Belgian history, now listing 4151 titles. Classed arrangement with author index.

Wachter, Leo de. Repertorium van de Vlaamse gouwen en gemeenten. Heemkundige dokumentatie, 1800–1940. Antwerpen, De Sikkel, 1942–48. 4v. **DC29**

v.1, Algemeen gedeelte en gewesten; v.2–4, Gemeenten, A–Z. Register.
A bibliography of book and periodical material on Flemish local history. Indexes some 500 periodicals in various languages.
Continued by:

—— Repertorium van de Vlaamse gouwen en gemeenten. Heemkundige dokumentatie, 1940–1950. Antwerpen, De Sikkel, 1952–57. v.5–6.

Numbering of volumes continues main set.
v.5–6, Algemeen gedeelte en gewesten: Gemeenten A–Z. Register.

Encyclopedias

Flandria nostra; ons land en ons volk, zijn standen en beroepen door de tijden heen, onder redactie van J. L. Broeckx [et al.]. Antwerpen, Standaard-Boekhandel, 1957–60. 5v. il. **DC30**

Nonalphabetical with long, signed articles and extensive bibliographies. Emphasis is on "the land and the people" rather than on political or historical events.

Grande encyclopédie de la Belgique et du Congo. Bruxelles, Wauthoz-Legrand, 1938–52. v.1–2. il. **DC31**

Nonalphabetical. Signed articles with some bibliography. Maps. Contents: v.1, The Royal family, the geology, geog-raphy, demography, and history of Belgium to the end of the war in 1918; v.2, The fine arts and the sciences.

BULGARIA

Kersopoulos, Jean G. Bulgarie; ouvrages et articles de revues parus de 1613 à 1935. (In Les balkans, v.6–8, 1934–36) (Série de bibliographies françaises sur les na-tions balkaniques, no.2) **DC32**

2d edition of the author's *Bibliographie franco-bulgare* (1911).

CZECHOSLOVAKIA

Bibliografie české historie za rok 1904–41. Praha, Nákl. Klubu Historického, 1905–51. Annual. **DC33**

Very comprehensive, annual record of material in Czech and other languages on the history of Czechoslovakia.
1904–14 published in—and later as a supplement to—*Český časopis historický* (Prague). From 1915, published separately.
Continued by:

Bibliografie československé historie za rok 1955– . Praha, Nákl. Československé Akademie Věd, 1957– . Annual. **DC34**

Čapek, Thomas and **Čapek, Anna V.** Bohemian (Čech) bibliography; a finding list of writings in English relating to Bohemia and the Čechs. N.Y., Revell, [c1918]. 256p. il. **DC35**

Includes both books and periodical articles.

Zibrt, Čeněk. Bibliografie české historie. V Praze, Nákl. České Akademie Císaře Františka Josefa, 1900–1912. 5v. **DC36**

Very full for the period before 1679. For the large or special library.

DENMARK

Bibliography

Erichsen, Balder and **Krarup, Alfred.** Dansk historisk Bibliografi; systematisk Fortegnelse over Bidrag til Danmarks Historie til Udgangen af 1912 (i Tilslutning til Bibliotheca danica). Udg. paa Carlsbergfondets Bekostning. København, Gad, 1917–27. 3v. **DC37**

A very full list, including books, pamphlets, and many analytical references to articles in periodicals and other composite works.

v.1–2, history, topography, etc., a classified list of more than 20,000 references, with detailed indexes of authors and titles; v.3, biography.

v.3 is a list of published biographies of persons living between 1830 and 1912, in continuation of a similar section in v.3 of Bruun, *Bibliotheca danica* (AA446), and including some names of the earlier period omitted in Bruun.

Dansk historisk Bibliografi, 1943–1947. Udg. af den Danske Historiske Forening, ved Henry Bruun. København, Hagerup, 1956. 594p. **DC38**

The first volume of a new series to cover five-year periods, designed to provide a comprehensive record of writings on Danish history. Similar in scope and arrangement to Erichsen and Krarup (DC37). A volume to cover the years 1932–42 is said to be in preparation.

Copenhagen

Copenhagen. Kommunebibliotekerne. Københavns Bibliografi; Litteratur om København til 1950, ved Svend Thomsen, Drude Lange [og] Irmelin Nordentoft. København, 1957–60. 3v. **DC39**

An extensive, classified bibliography of books, periodical articles, and parts of books about Copenhagen, with an author index in v.3.

Handbooks

Denmark, 1924– , pub. by the Royal Danish Ministry of Foreign Affairs. Copenhagen, 1924– . il. Irregular. **DC40**

Some years published in French, German, Spanish, and English.

Provides concise information on geography, history, occupations, science, art, and general culture. Profusely illustrated. 1961 issue includes classified bibliography, p.826–48, and index, p.849–912.

ESTONIA

U.S. Library of Congress. Slavic and Central European Division. Estonia: a selected bibliography, comp. by Salme Kuri. Wash., 1958. 74p. **DC41**

"Designed primarily to help the nonspecialist . . . ."—*Introd.*

FINLAND

Vallinkoski, Jorma and **Schauman, Henrik.** Suomen historiallinen bibliografia, 1544–1900. Finsk historisk bibliografi. Bibliographie historique finlandaise. Helsinki, 1961. 571p. (Suomen historiallinen seura käsikirjoja V) **DC42**

Continued by:

Maliniemi, Aarno Henrik and **Kivikoski, Ella.** Suomen historiallinen bibliografia, 1901–1925. Finsk historisk bibliografi. Bibliographie historique finlandaise. Helsinki, [Suomalaisen Kirjallisuuden Seuran Kirjapainon Oy], 1940. 2v. in 1. (527p., 107p.). (Suomen historiallinen seura käsikirjoja. II:1–2) **DC43**

Continued by:

Vallinkoski, Jorma and **Schauman, Henrik.** Suomen historiallinen bibliografia, 1926–1950. Finsk historisk bibliografi. Bibliographie historique finlandaise. Helsinki, 1955–56. 2v. (Suomen historiallinen seura käsikirjoja IV:1–2) **DC44**

A series of comprehensive bibliographies of Finnish historical works, including both books and periodical articles. Classed arrangement with author indexes. Headings are given in Finnish, Swedish, and French. Most of the material is in Finnish, though some titles are in Swedish, German, and other languages.

History is interpreted in its broad sense to include not only political and economic history of all periods, but also allied interests, e.g., history of the church, education, literature, folklore, etc., and local history.

FRANCE

Bibliography

France. Direction des Archives. État des inventaires des archives nationales, départementales, communales et hospitalières au 1. janvier 1937. [Par Henri Courteault]. Paris, Didier, 1938. 703p. **DC45**

—————— Supplement. (1937–1954) [Par Robert H. Boutier]. Paris, Impr. Nationale, 1955. 344p.

A description and listing of the inventories of French archives.

Franklin, Alfred. Les sources de l'histoire de France. Notices bibliographiques et analytiques des inventaires et des recueils de documents relatifs à l'histoire de France. Paris, Firmin-Didot, 1877. 681p. **DC46**

Lists the contents of many of the great French historical collections, e.g., *Catalogue de l'histoire de France, Collection des documents inédits relatifs à l'histoire de France, Bibliothèque de l'École des Chartes,* and many others, and for this purpose is still useful.

Langlois, Charles V. and **Stein, Henri.** Les archives de l'histoire de France. Paris, Picard, 1891–93. 1000p. (Manuels de bibliographie historique) **DC47**

Contents: Les archives de l'histoire de France en France; Les archives de l'histoire de France à l'etranger; Les archives de l'histoire de France dans les bibliothèques de manuscrits.

Guide to source materials in French and foreign archives. For a more complete record of the very valuable collection in the national archives, consult Charles Schmidt, *Les sources de l'histoire de France depuis 1789 aux Archives Nationales* (Paris, 1907), and for later inventories, *see* Courteault (DC45).

Lepointe, Gabriel. Éléments de bibliographie sur l'histoire des institutions et des faits sociaux, 987–1875. Paris, Montchrestien, 1958. 232p. **DC48**

"Avec le concours de André Vandenbossche."

Arranged alphabetically, with an index by subject. Includes books and periodical articles on the history of social conditions in France, prepared to accompany the author's *Histoire des institutions et des faits sociaux de la France*, 1956.

Continued by:

—— Bibliographie en langue française d'histoire du droit. Paris, Montchrestien, 1961– . Annual. **DC49**

v.1 covered 1957–59; 1960– , annual.

Despite the title, the coverage is much the same as that in the main work. Lists books and articles in French on social history from 987 to 1875.

Newberry Library, Chicago. A checklist of French political pamphlets 1560–1644 in the Newberry Library, comp. by Doris Varner Welsh. Chicago, Lib., 1950. 204p. **DC50**

About 1200 items, mostly unavailable elsewhere in the United States, arranged alphabetically under year of publication, with an index by author and title.

Although primarily political, this collection is valuable also for social and economic data of the period.

—— A second checklist . . . 1560–1653. 1955. 190p.

Adds 1340 titles and includes a cumulated index to both volumes.

Paris. Bibliothèque Nationale. Dept. des Imprimés. Catalogue de l'histoire de France. Paris, Didot, 1855–95. 11v., index, and 6 suppl. **DC51**

A very comprehensive catalog of books, pamphlets, etc., printed before 1875 on the history of France prior to 1875. Classed (15 main and 904 subclasses), with author index.

Contents: t.1, Préliminaires et généralités. Histoire par époques. Histoire par règnes [à Louis XIII]; t.2, Louis XIV–Louis XVI; t.3, 1792–1848; t.4, 1848–1856. Journaux et publications périodiques; t.5, Histoire religieuse; t.6, Histoire constitutionnelle; t.7, Histoire constitutionnelle [suite]. Histoire administrative, diplomatique, militaire. Mœurs et coutumes. Archéologie; t.8, Histoire locale; t.9, Histoire locale [suite]. Biographie; t.10, Biographie [suite] supplément; t.11, Supplément [suite]. [Six additional supplements to special classes of the main work.]

—— —— Table des auteurs. 1895. 798p.

—— —— Table générale alphabétique des ouvrages anonymes. 1905–32. 15v.

Contents: Table des noms de personnes. v.1–4; Table des noms de lieux. v.5–15.

Les sources de l'histoire de France depuis les origines jusqu'en 1815, par A. Molinier [and others]. Paris, Picard, 1901–35. 1.–3. pt. (in 18v.). **DC52**

Contents: 1. pt., Des origines aux guerres d'Italie (1494), par A. Molinier: t.1, Époque primitive, Mérovingiens et Carolingiens; t.2, Époque féodale, les Capétiens jusqu'en 1180; t.3, Les Capétiens, 1180–1328; t.4, Les Valois, 1328–1461; t.5, Introduction générale, Les Valois (suite), Louis XI et Charles VIII (1461–94); t.6, Table générale, par Louis Polain.

2. pt., Le XVIe siècle (1494–1600), par H. Hauser: t.1, Les premières guerres d'Italie, Charles VIII et Louis XII (1494–1515); t.2, François I et Henri II (1515–59); t.3, Les guerres de religion (1559–89); t.4, Henri IV (1589–1610).

3. pt., Le XVIIe siècle (1610–1715), par Émile Bourgeois et Louis André: t.1, Géographie et histoire générales; t.2, Mémoires et lettres; t.3, Biographies; t.4, Journaux et pamphlets; t.5, Histoire politique et militaire; t.6, Histoire maritime et coloniale, histoire religieuse; t.7, Histoire économique, Histoire administrative; t.8, Histoire provinciale et locale. Essai sur les sources étrangères. Additions et corrections. Table générale.

The volumes to cover the period 1715–1815 were never published.

A valuable bibliography listing printed sources.

Early

Montandon, Raoul. Bibliographie générale des travaux palethnologiques et archéologiques (époques préhistorique, protohistorique et gallo-romaine). France. . . . Genève, Georg, 1917–38. v.1–5. **DC53**

A comprehensive bibliography of books and periodical articles, arranged by geographical division.

—— —— Supplément du t.1–3. 1921–29. v.1–3.

—— —— Supplément, fasc.1– . Le Mans, Monnoyer, 1953– . (Bull. de la Société Historique Française, t.49, no.9–)

Répertoire archéologique de la France, pub. par ordre du Ministre de l'Instruction Publique et sous la direction du Comité des Travaux Historiques et des Sociétés Savantes. Paris, Impr. Nationale, 1861–88. 8v. (Collection de documents inédits sur l'histoire de France, ser. vii, 7) **DC54**

Contents: *Alpes (Hautes)*, by Joseph Roman. 1888; *Aube*, by Henri d'Arbois de Jubainville. 1861; *Morbihan*, by Louis Rosensweig. 1863; *Nièvre*, by J. H. G. R. de Soultrait. 1875; *Oise*, by Emmanuel Woilez. 1862; *Seine-Inférieure*, by J. B. D. Cochet. 1872; *Tarn*, by Hippolyte Crozes. 1865; *Yonne*, by Maximilien Quantin. 1868.

Stein, Henri. Bibliographie générale des cartulaires français ou relatifs à l'histoire de France. Paris, Picard, 1907. 627p. (Manuels de bibliographie historique, 4) **DC55**

Lists and describes 4522 cartularies arranged alphabetically by place-name.

To 1789

Du Peloux, Charles. Répertoire général des ouvrages modernes relatifs au dix-huitième siècle française (1715–1789). Paris, Grund, 1926. 306p. **DC56**

—— —— Supplément, table méthodique. 1927. 62p.

Lists books published since 1789 in French, English, German, and Italian. Includes an alphabetical list of those persons of the 18th century who have been the subjects of biographies, with the names of the authors of such works.

Saulnier, Eugène and **Martin, A.** Bibliographie des travaux publiés de 1866 à 1897 sur l'histoire de la France de 1500 à 1789. Paris, Presses Universitaires, 1932–38. v.1–2, fasc.2. (Publication de la Société d'Histoire Moderne) **DC57**

No more published.

v.1, Histoire intérieure, Histoire des institutions, Histoire diplomatique, Histoire militaire, Histoire de la marine militaire, Histoire religieuse; v.2, fasc.1–2, Histoire économique et sociale; Histoire coloniale; Histoire des familles; Biographies.

A comprehensive listing of books and periodical articles, with references to reviews. Classified arrangement. Not completed and lacks indexes.

Revolution

Caron, Pierre. Manuel pratique pour l'étude de la Revolution Française. Nouv. éd. mise à jour. Paris, Picard, 1947. 324p. **DC58**

1st ed. 1912. This edition revised and reorganized. An indispensable guide to the archival and manuscript sources, collections, bibliographical aids, etc. for the study of the French Revolution.

Monglond, André. La France révolutionnaire et impériale; annales de bibliographie méthodique et description des livres illustrés. Paris, Impr. Nationale, 1930–63. v.1–9 and index to v.1–2. il. (In progress) **DC59**

Imprint varies.

v.1–9, 1789–1812. Index to v.1–2, 91p.

A very detailed bibliography, including books, pamphlets, and articles dealing with all phases of life and literature in France, 1789–1815.

Paris. Bibliothèque Nationale. Dept. des Imprimés. Catalogue de l'histoire de la Révolution Française, par André Martin et Gérard Walter. Paris, Éd. des Bibliothèques Nationales, 1936–55. 5v. in 6. **DC60**

v.1–4¹, Écrits de la période révolutionnaire—Auteurs; v.4², Anonymes; v.5, Journaux et almanachs.

A very comprehensive bibliography of works published during the French Revolution.

—— Répertoire de l'histoire de la Révolution Française, par Gérard Walter: Travaux publiés de 1800 à 1940. Paris, Bibliothèque Nationale, 1941–51. 2v. **DC61**

t.1, Personnes; t.2, Lieux.

Works on persons and places, including books and periodical articles.

Tourneux, Maurice. Bibliographie de l'histoire de Paris pendant la Révolution Française. Paris, Impr. Nouvelle, 1890–1913. 5v. (Paris. Publications relatives à la Révolution Française) **DC62**

t.1, Préliminaires. Événements; t.2, Organisation et rôle politiques de Paris; t.3, Monuments, mœurs et institutions; t.4, Documents biographiques. Paris hors les murs. Additions et corrections; t.5, Table générale.

Since 1789

Caron, Pierre. Bibliographie des travaux publiés de 1866 à 1897 sur l'histoire de la France depuis 1789. Paris, Cornély, 1912. 831p. **DC63**

A valuable bibliography including 13,496 titles of books, pamphlets, and articles in periodicals, society publications, and other composite works. Indicates book reviews and abstracts of important items. Indexes the historical articles in some 394 French and 260 foreign periodicals. Classified arrangement with two indexes: (1) authors and persons, (2) places. Forms the main volume in Caron's series of indexes of the history of France since 1789, and is continued for the material published since 1897 by DC64.

Annual

Répertoire méthodique de l'histoire moderne et contemporaine de la France, pour les années 1898–1913. Paris, Rieder, 1899–1932. v.1–7, 9–11. **DC64**

v.1–6, 1898–1903, ed. by G. Brière and P. Caron; v.7, 1904–06, ed. by G. Brière, P. Caron, and J. Lépine; v.8, 1907–09, not published; v.9, 1910/11, ed. by P. Caron and R. Burnaud; v.10–11, 1911/12–1912/13, ed. by M. Bouteron, R. Burnaud, and P. Caron; v.12, 1913–19, not published.

Ceased publication.

Répertoire bibliographique de l'histoire de France, par Pierre Caron et Henri Stein. Publication de la Société Française de Bibliographie, subventionnée par la Confédération des Sociétés Scientifiques Françaises, à l'aide des fonds alloués par le Parlement. Paris, Picard, 1923–38. v.1–6. Biennial. **DC65**

1920/21–1930/31.

The standard current bibliography for France to 1914, listing historical writings in various languages, both books and periodical articles. Classified, with name and place indexes. Superseded by:

Bibliographie annuelle de l'histoire de France du cinquième siècle à 1939. Année 1955– . Paris, Éd. du Centre National de la Recherche Scientifique, 1956– . Annual. (Comité Français de Sciences Historiques) **DC66**

A detailed, classified bibliography with author and subject indexes.

—— Années 1953/1954– . Paris, Centre National de la Recherche Scientifique, 1964– .

A retrospective listing planned to cover the period from 1932 to 1954.

Bibliographie critique des principaux travaux parus sur l'histoire de 1600 à 1914, en 1932 et 1933–35. Paris, Maison du Livre Français, 1935–37. (Publications de la Société d'Histoire Moderne. Série des instruments de travail) **DC67**

"Publiée par le Comité de Direction de la Revue d'Histoire Moderne."

Ed. by Georges Pagès, Léon Cahen, and Marc Jaryc.

1932/33, General; 1934–35, with subtitle, Travaux de langue française ou relatifs à l'histoire de France.

1934 issue includes, in four sections, works in the French, English, and German languages on the history of France, and works in the French language on foreign countries.

1935 issue adds to these: works in Italian, Polish, and Russian languages on the history of France.

Local

Lasteyrie du Saillant, Robert Charles, *Comte de.* Bibliographie générale des travaux historiques et archéologiques publiés par les sociétés savantes de la France. Paris, Impr. Nationale, 1888–1918. 6v. **DC68**

For full description of this work and its continuations, *see* AC35–AC37.

A listing of French historical societies by *département* with full contents of their publications, although there is no author index to this analytical material.

v.1–4 cover the literature published to 1885; v.5–6 cover 1886–1900. Continued by:

Bibliographie annuelle des travaux historiques et archéologiques, publiés par les sociétés savantes de la France, 1901/02–1909/10. Paris, Impr. Nationale, 1906–14. v.1–3 in 9 pts. **DC69**

An annual continuation on the same scale as the preceding entry. For full information *see* AC36.

Continued by:

Bibliographie générale des travaux historiques et archéologiques, publiés par les sociétés savantes de la France, par René Gandilhon. 1910–1940. Paris, Impr. Nationale, 1944–61. 5v. **DC70**

A continuation of the preceding entry on the same general plan but with a somewhat enlarged scope.

For full information *see* AC37.

❧ Numerous bibliographies and dictionaries of French local history have been published. Many are listed in the general bibliographies noted above. A large number of bibliographies will be found in Besterman, *World Bibliography of bibliographies* (AA13). A useful list, which includes bibliographies, is given in New York Public Library, *Provençal literature and language, including the local history of southern France,* comp. by Daniel C. Haskell (N.Y., 1925. 885p.), p.189–660, 676–738.

Dictionaries and handbooks

Anderson, Frank Maloy. The constitutions and other select documents illustrative of the history of France, 1789–1907. 2d ed. rev. and enl. Minneapolis, Wilson, 1908. 693p. **DC71**

A useful collection of translations from the original texts. Sources are indicated, and brief annotations with additional references included.

Chéruel, Adolphe. Dictionnaire historique des institutions, mœurs et coutumes de la France. 10. éd. Paris, Hachette, 1910. 2v. il. **DC72**

1st ed. 1885. Later editions unchanged.

Especially strong for material before the 19th century. Now much out of date but still useful.

France. Commission de la Topographie des Gaules. Dictionnaire archéologique de la Gaule, époque celtique. Pub. par la Commission instituée au Ministère de l'Instruction Publique et des Beaux-Arts. Paris, Impr. Nationale, 1875–1923. 2v., volume of plates. il. (Collection de documents inédits sur l'histoire de France. sér. 6, t.20) **DC73**

v.1, A–G. 1875; v.2, H–Z. 1878–1923.

Continué, après la lettre L, par les soins de Émile Cartailhac.

An alphabetical arrangement by place-name of the archaeological remains of France.

Lalanne, Ludovic. Dictionnaire historique de la France. 2. éd. Paris, Hachette, 1877. 2v. **DC74**

A handbook for ready reference including brief articles on persons, places, and institutions connected with the history of France through 1876.

Marion, Marcel. Dictionnaire des institutions de la France aux XVIIᵉ et XVIIIᵉ siècles. Paris, Picard, 1923. 564p. **DC75**

Not so broad in coverage as the preceding work, but includes some material not in that.

Robinet, Jean François Eugène [and others]. Dictionnaire historique et biographique de la Révolution et de l'Empire, 1789–1815. Paris, Librairie Historique de la Révolution et de l'Empire, 1899. 2v. **DC76**

In one alphabetical arrangement includes: biographical sketches, acts and decrees, revolutionary journals, battles, treaties, constitutions, etc. Largely biographical.

Atlases

Boussard, Jacques. Atlas historique et culturel de la France. Paris, Elsevier, 1957. 214p. il. **DC77**

A combination of maps, text, and illustrations, the last particularly numerous and effective.

General histories

✓**Lavisse, Ernest.** Histoire de France illustrée. Paris, Hachette, 1911–22. 19v. il. **DC78**

Contents: (1) Histoire de France illustrée, depuis les origines jusqu'à la Révolution. 1911. 9v. in 18; (2) Histoire de France contemporaine depuis la Révolution jusqu'à la paix de 1919. 10v. v.10, Tables générales des origines à la paix de 1919. 356p.

A good reference history, important for both text and fine illustrations. Published as two separate works, with a combined index.

Paris

Hillairet, Jacques. Dictionnaire historique des rues de Paris. Paris, Les Éditions de Minuit, 1963. 2v. il. **DC79**

An alphabetically arranged encyclopedia on all the streets of Paris, past and present, with historical facts including information on important buildings, people, etc.

Pessard, Gustave. Nouveau dictionnaire historique de Paris. Paris, Rey, 1904. 1693p. **DC80**

Alphabetically arranged by names of streets, places, churches, bridges, etc., with historical information.

GEORGIA

British Museum. Dept. of Oriental Printed Books and Manuscripts. Catalogue of Georgian and other Caucasian printed books in the British Museum, comp. by David Marshall Lang. London, 1962. 430p. **DC81**

A carefully made catalog of the Georgian collection in the British Museum, rich in early printed books but including later ones as well. The catalog also contains "a selection of reference books compiled by European specialists, as well as a wide range of books and periodical articles in Western languages relating to Caucasian languages and literatures."—*Pref.*

GERMANY
Bibliography

Bibliographie zur deutschen Geschichte . . . 1889–1927. Leipzig, Teubner, 1889–1918; Dresden, Baensch, 1920–31. Annual. **DC82**

No more published.

Issued as a supplement to the *Historische Vierteljahrschrift.*

A useful annual bibliography, arranged by subject with author index. Each issue lists books, pamphlets, and periodical articles, with references to reviews of items listed.

Dahlmann, Friedrich Christoph and **Waitz, Georg.** Dahlmann-Waitz. Quellenkunde der deutschen Geschichte. 9. Aufl. hrsg. von Hermann Haering. Leipzig, Koehler, 1931–32. 2v.(1292p.). **DC83**

v.1, Bibliography, 992p.; v.2, Index, p.993–1292.

The standard bibliography of German history in all its phases, covering through World War I. Indispensable in any library where research work in that subject is done. The 9th edition contains 16,337 entries in classified arrangement.

Franz, Gunther. Bücherkunde zur deutschen Geschichte. Munich, R. Oldenbourg, 1951. 279p. **DC84**

A selective list of books on all periods and phases of German history, in various languages. Since, for the most part, it comprises works published after 1931, it supplements Dahlmann-Waitz to some extent.

Grundriss der Geschichtswissenschaft, zur Einführung in das Studium der deutschen Geschichte des Mittelalters und der Neuzeit, hrsg. von Aloys Meister. Leipzig, Teubner, 1908–23. 1. Reihe, Abt. 1–4a, 6–7; 2. Reihe, Abt. 1–6, 8. **DC85**

1. Reihe: Historische Hilfswissenschaften u. Propädeutik; 2. Reihe: Historische Sonderwissenschaften.

—— Ergänzungsband. Bd.1, Die antiken Grundlagen der frühmittelalterlichen Privatkunde. 1927.

A monographic series in which each volume is written by an expert. The first series deals with the technique of historical method; the second, with the interpretation of various phases of medieval and modern German history. For the advanced student.

To 1600

Lorenz, Ottokar. Deutschlands Geschichtsquellen im Mittelalter seit der Mitte des dreizehnten Jahrhunderts. 3. in Verbindung mit Arthur Goldmann umgearb. Aufl.

Berlin, Hertz, 1886–87. 2v.   **DC86**

This work and that of Wattenbach (DC88) furnish comprehensive and critical guides to the historiography of medieval Germany.

Continues from the middle of the 13th century, where the 6th edition of Wattenbach ceases.

Schottenloher, Karl. Bibliographie zur deutschen Geschichte im Zeitalter der Glaubensspaltung 1517–1585. . . . Leipzig, Hiersemann, 1933–40. 6v.   **DC87**

Im Auftrag der Kommission zur Erforschung der Geschichte der Reformation und Gegenreformation.

Bd.1–2, Personnen, A–Z. Orte u. Landschaften; Bd.3, Reich u. Kaiser. Territorien u. Landesherren; Bd.4, Gesamtdarstellungen der Reformationszeit. Stoffe; Bd.5, Nachträge und Ergänzungen. Zeittafel; Bd.6, Verfasser und Titelverzeichnis.

A very comprehensive bibliography of books and periodical articles, including those published during this period as well as later works about the period.

Wattenbach, Wilhelm. Deutschlands Geschichtsquellen im Mittelalter; Vorzeit und Karolinger. Bearb. von Wilhelm Levison und Heinz Löwe. Weimar, Böhlaus, 1952–63. Hft.1–4. (In progress)   **DC88**

—— Deutschlands Geschichtsquellen im Mittelalter; deutsche Kaizerzeit, hrsg. von Robert Holtzmann. Tübingen, Matthiessen, 1938–48. v.1(856p.).

Issued in 4 pts.

Originally pub. in 1858; 6th ed. 1893–94. (7th ed., v.1, only, pub.; ed. by Ernst Dümmler. 1904)

An important guide to the printed sources of German history. The present (8th) edition is a revision of v.1 of the earlier work. The first part, *Vorzeit und Karolinger,* covers from early times through the Carolingians to the treaty of Verdun in 843; the *Deutsche Kaizerzeit* covers through the Otto's, 900–1050.

Wolf, Gustav. Quellenkunde der deutschen Reformationsgeschichte. Gotha, F. A. Perthes, 1915–23. 3v. in 4.   **DC89**

A comprehensive discussion and listing of the literature of the German Reformation.

20th century

Germany (Federal Republic, 1949–). Presse- und Informationsamt. Deutschland heute. Gesamtred. Helmut Arntz. 6. völlig neubearb. Aufl. Wiesbaden, Franz Steiner, 1961. 917p.   **DC90**

1st ed. 1953.

Also published in English and French.

A survey of current affairs in the German Federal Republic with chapters on political, economic, social, religious, and cultural affairs. Not a yearbook as such; each edition is complete in itself.

Schrifttum über Deutschland, 1918–1962, ausgewählte Bibliographie deutscher Publikationen. Bearb. in Gemeinschaft mit dem Forschungsinstitut der Deutschen Gesellschaft für Auswärtige Politik durch Inter Nationes, Bonn. Wiesbaden, Franz Steiner-Verlag, 1962. 306p.   **DC91**

An annotated, classified bibliography of writings about Germany, 1918–62. Includes a section of works in languages other than German.

Wiener Library, London. After Hitler: Germany, 1945–1963. London, pub. for the Wiener Library by Vallentine, Mitchell, 1963. 265p. (Catalogue ser., no.4)   **DC92**

A classified listing of some 2700 books and pamphlets on "Germany Now." Includes such sections as: Wartime plans for Germany, Germany under occupation, The problem of Berlin, The new Germany, The Federal Republic, East Germany, Jews in postwar Germany, etc.

Current

Jahresberichte der deutschen Geschichte. Jahrg.1–7, 1918–1924. Breslau, Priebatsch, 1920–26. 7v.   **DC93**

A valuable annual survey preceded by the *Jahresberichte der Geschichtswissenschaft,* 1878–1913 (DA8), and continued by:

Jahresberichte für deutsche Geschichte. 1.–15/16. Jahrg., 1925–39/40. . . . hrsg. von Albert Brackmann u. Fritz Hartung. Leipzig, Koehler, 1927–42. v.1–15/16. Annual.   **DC94**

Each volume in two parts: (1) Bibliographie; (2) Forschungsberichte, with author and subject indexes. Continued by:

—— n.F. 1.– Jahrg., 1949– , im Auftrage der Deutschen Akademie der Wissenschaften zu Berlin. Berlin, Akademie-Verlag, 1952– . v.1– . v.1–2, Annual; v.3– , Biennial.   **DC95**

From 1953/54, edited by the Institut für Geschichte an der Deutschen Akademie der Wissenschaften zu Berlin.

1941–48 not yet covered.

A revival of this important series, now devoted entirely to bibliography, listing writings on German history from early times through World War II.

Dissertations

Milatz, Alfred and **Vogelsang, Thilo.** Hochschulschriften zur neueren deutschen Geschichte; eine Bibliographie. 1. Ausg., 1945–1955. Im Auftrage der Kommission für Geschichte des Parlamentarismus und der Politischen Parteien sowie des Instituts für Zeitgeschichte. Bonn, Kommission für Geschichte des Parlamentarismus und der Politischen Parteien, 1956. 142p.   **DC96**

Lists 1925 completed dissertations and 400 in progress on modern German history. Includes master's and doctor's theses from universities in West and East Germany, Austria, Switzerland, France, England, Holland, and the United States.

Guides to records

American Historical Association. Committee for the Study of War Documents. A catalogue of files and microfilms of the German Foreign Ministry archives, 1867–1920. Oxford, Univ. Pr., 1959. 1290col.   **DC97**

Designed to present a complete record of the files of the Political Dept. of the German Foreign Ministry for the period 1867–1920, and at the same time to give details of the filming programs which have been carried out on these files. Indicates holders of negative copy.

—— Guides to German records microfilmed at Alexandria, Va. Wash., Nat. Archives, Nat. Archives and Records Service, General Services Admin., 1958–1965. Pts.1–47. (In progress)   **DC98**

Each part describes the filmed records of one of the Reich ministries or other record groups. The microfilms have been deposited in the National Archives.

—— Index of microfilmed records of the German Foreign Ministry and the Reich's Chancellery covering the Weimar period, deposited at the National Archives, prep. by Ernst Schwandt. Wash., Nat. Archives, 1958. 95p. **DC99**

One of a series of indexes of microfilms of German documents. For an earlier record *see* Weinberg's *Guide to captured German documents* (DC102).

Covers the period of the Weimar Republic, 1919–33.

—— A list of archival references and data of documents from the archives of the German Foreign Ministry, 1867–1920, microfilmed at Whaddon Hall for the American Committee for the Study of War Documents. Buckinghamshire, Whaddon Hall, 1957. 179p.   **DC100**

The microfilms have been deposited in the National Archives in Washington, and in the Public Record Office in London.

U.S. Dept. of State. Historical Office. A catalog of files and microfilms of the German Foreign Ministry archives, 1920–1945, comp. and ed. by George O. Kent. Stanford, Calif., Hoover Inst., Stanford Univ., 1962– . v.1– . (In progress)   **DC101**

"Continues and completes the work of the *Catalogue of German Foreign Ministry files and microfilms, 1867–1920.*"—*Pref.* (DC97).

Published as a joint project of the U.S. Dept. of State and the Hoover Institution on War, Revolution, and Peace.

Lists all files from the *Politisches Archiv* of the German Foreign Ministry, 1920–1945, which were seized by the American and British armies at the end of World War II, and indicates which have been microfilmed.

Weinberg, Gerhard L. Guide to captured German documents, prep. by Gerhard L. Weinberg and the WDP staff under the direction of Fritz T. Epstein. [Maxwell Air Force Base, Ala., Human Resources Research Inst., 1952] 90p. (U.S. Human Resources Research Inst., Research memorandum, no.2, v.1)   **DC102**

At head of title: War Documentation Project. Study no.1.

Pts.1–2 list books and periodical articles which include German documentary material; pt.3 lists, by location, files of captured documents in various depositories, including the Library of Congress, the National Archives, the Hoover Institution, etc. Annotated. Index.

———— ———— Supplement. Wash., Nat. Archives, 1959. 69p.

Lists additional holdings in the various depositories.

Dictionaries and handbooks

Bithell, Jethro. Germany: a companion to German studies. [5th ed. rev., enl., and reset] London, Methuen, 1955. 578p. map.   **DC103**

1st ed. 1932.

A handbook with bibliographies, covering German history, literature, art, and culture.

Gebhardt, Bruno. Handbuch der deutschen Geschichte. 8. vollständig neubearb. Aufl. hrsg. von Herbert Grundmann. Stuttgart, Union Deutsche Verlagsgesellschaft, 1954–60. 4v.   **DC104**

Contents: v.1, Pre-history through the Middle Ages; v.2, 16th–18th centuries; v.3, From the French Revolution to 1914; v.4, From World War I to the end of World War II.

A very useful compendium, arranged chronologically, including bibliographies for each section. The work of several scholars, it originally appeared in 1891–92 and has been issued in several revised editions under various editors.

Grotefend, Hermann. Zeitrechnung des deutschen Mittelalters und der Neuzeit. Hannover, Hahn, 1891–98. 3 pts. in 2v.   **DC105**

1. Bd., Glossar und Tafeln. 1891; 2. Bd., 1. Abt., Kalender der diöcesen Deutschlands, der Schweiz und Skandinaviens. 1892; 2. Abt., Ordenskalender. Heiligenverzeichniss. Nachträge zum Glossar. 1898.

Glossaries, calendars, and tables showing the chronology of German history in the Middle Ages.

Published in various abridged editions, the latest of which is:

———— Taschenbuch der Zeitrechnung des deutschen Mittelalters und der Neuzeit. 10. erw. Aufl. hrsg. von Th. Ulrich. Hannover, Hahn, 1960. 222p.   **DC106**

Petersen, Carl [and others]. Handwörterbuch des Grenz- und Auslanddeutschtums, unter Mitwirkung von etwa 800 Mitarbeitern . . . Breslau, Ferdinand Hirt, 1933–40.

v.1–3. maps.   **DC107**

v.1–3, A–Massachusetts. Nachtrag.

No more published.

A comprehensive encyclopedia with long, signed articles, and bibliographies, on the life and culture of Germans in countries outside of Germany. Includes biography.

Rössler, Hellmuth and **Franz, Günther.** Sachwörterbuch zur deutschen Geschichte. München, Oldenbourg, 1956–58. 1472p.   **DC108**

A companion volume to the authors' *Biographisches Wörterbuch zur deutschen Geschichte* (AJ139a). Dictionary arrangement, dealing with "events, institutions, countries, peoples and ideas," including the cultural, political, and economic aspects, of all periods. Includes bibliographies.

GREAT BRITAIN

Guides

Hewitt, Arthur R. Guide to resources for Commonwealth studies in London, Oxford and Cambridge, with bibliographical and other information. London, Univ. of London, pub. for the Institute of Commonwealth Studies, [by] Athlone Pr., 1957. 219p.   **DC109**

"The purpose of this *Guide* is to assist advanced research workers, particularly those who have come to Great Britain from overseas, to locate material for the study of the British Commonwealth."—*Foreword*. Deals mainly with materials in history and the social sciences. Describes the resources of libraries and other institutions in London, Oxford, and Cambridge, with bibliographical references.

Bibliography

Bibliography of British history. Issued under the direction of the American Historical Association and the Royal Historical Society of Great Britain. Oxford, Clarendon Pr., 1928–59. 3v.   **DC110**

Tudor period, 1485–1603, ed. by Conyers Read. 2d ed. 1959. 624p. (1st ed. 1933)

Stuart period, 1603–1714, ed. by Godfrey Davies. 1928. 459p.

The eighteenth century, 1714–1789, ed. by Stanley Pargellis and D. J. Medley. 1951. 642p.

Covers all aspects of history: political, constitutional, legal, ecclesiastical, economic, military, cultural, and social, including discovery and exploration, colonization, etc. Each volume is a selected, classified-subject list—with author index—of book, pamphlet, and document material, with a liberal inclusion of articles in periodicals and society transactions.

Indispensable for the student of history, and useful also for literature and social studies.

Guide to the historical publications of the societies of England and Wales; Suppl. 1, 1929–1942/46. London, Longmans, 1930–48. 13v. (Bulletin of the Inst. of Historical Research, Suppl., Nov. 1930–48)   **DC111**

Ceased publication.

Prepared by a committee of the Institute and of the Congress of Archaeological Societies, the supplements appearing before the basic work which is still in preparation. Planned to do for the societies of England and Wales what Terry (DC170) and Matheson (DC171) do for those of Scotland, and also to take the place of the discontinued *Index of archaeological papers* (DC117). The supplements merely record issues for the years covered, leaving the historical information about the societies and the records of publication, index, etc., to be given in the basic volume.

Mullins, Edward Lindsay Carson. Texts and calendars: an analytical guide to serial publications. London, Offices of the Royal Historical Soc., 1958. 674p. (Royal Historical Soc. Guides and handbooks, no.7) **DC112**

"An analytical guide to printed texts and calendars relating to English and Welsh history" issued in general collections such as the Rolls series, the Historical Manuscripts Commission reports, etc., and in the publications of societies such as the Hakluyt Society, the English Historical Society, the Camden Society, and numerous others.

Dissertations

London. University. Institute of Historical Research. Historical research for university degrees in the United Kingdom, 1931/32–1952. (Bulletin . . . Theses supplement, no.1–14) London, Longmans, 1933–53. **DC113**

Ceased publication.

Each number is in two parts: (1) Theses completed during the year; (2) Theses in progress. "The former follows on the lists published annually in *History* from 1920 to 1929 [covering 1911/19–1927/28], and in the *Bulletin* from 1930 to 1932; the latter is an innovation suggested by the Anglo-American Historical Committee."—*Pref. note to no.1.*

Superseded by:

———— ———— Theses completed. 1953– . London, 1954– . Annual. (Its Bulletin. Theses supplement, no.15–)

———— ———— Theses in progress. 1954– . London, 1954– . Annual. (Its Bulletin. Theses supplement, no.15–)

Each section, 1953–59, was arranged by university with author index (for completed theses there were also subject indexes). Beginning with 1960, each section is arranged under "broad chronological and topographical headings" with indexes of authors. Again, for completed theses, there are also subject indexes.

Early

Archaeological bibliography for Great Britain and Ireland, 1940/46– . London, Council for British Archaeology, 1949– . **DC114**

Biennial, 1948/49–1952/53; annual, 1954– .
1948/49 entitled *Archaeological bulletin.*
Intended to cover the period from the earliest times to A.D. 1600.

Bonser, Wilfrid. An Anglo-Saxon and Celtic bibliography (450–1087). Berkeley, Los Angeles, Univ. of Calif. Pr., 1957. 2v.(574p., 123p.) **DC115**

v.1, An extensive listing of books and articles on all historical aspects of the period, including geography, archaeology, general culture, art, etc.

v.2 (indexes), Author index; Subject and topographical index.

Gomme, George Laurence. Index of archaeological papers, 1665–1890. London, Constable, 1907. 910p. **DC116**

A useful author index to some 94 sets of English archaeological periodicals and transactions of local antiquarian societies. Principally British archaeology, but includes also material on classical and other non-British antiquities. Continued by the following:

Index of archaeological papers published in 1891–1910. London, Constable, 1892–1914. v.1–20. **DC117**

An annual continuation of Gomme above, indexing the same type of material and following the same plan as far as the author index is concerned, but differing from the main work in that each annual volume has a subject index to the author list. While each volume nominally covers one year, many cover a longer period since whenever a new periodical is added to the list, it is indexed back to 1891.

Publication suspended after 1914. Most of the periodicals indexed are now included in the *Subject index to periodicals*

(AF125) and the *British humanities index* (AF126). Archaeological articles are also included, 1929–1942/46, in *Guide to the historical publications of the societies of England and Wales* (DC111).

Medieval

Davis, Godfrey Rupert Carless. Medieval cartularies of Great Britain: a short catalogue. London, Longmans, 1958. 182p. **DC118**

"Cartularies are registers of . . . the title deeds (*carte*), charters of privilege (*privilegia*) and other documents kept by landowners as evidence of their personal or corporate rights . . . . This book is an attempt to provide a brief survey of the present state of knowledge" [of existing cartularies].

Gross, Charles. The sources and literature of English history from the earliest times to about 1485. 2d ed. rev. and enl. London, N.Y., Longmans, 1915. 820p. (Repr.: N.Y., Peter Smith, 1951) **DC119**

The best bibliography of English history for the period before 1485, valuable both for its selection of material and for the annotations. Includes more than 3234 closely classified titles (numbered to 3234, but actually more because of insertions), with general index.

Appendixes: A, Reports of the deputy-keeper of the public records; B, The Historical Manuscripts Commission; C, Rolls series; D, Chronological tables of the principal sources.

16th and 17th centuries

Abbott, Wilbur Cortez. A bibliography of Oliver Cromwell; a list of printed materials relating to Oliver Cromwell, together with a list of portraits and caricatures. Cambridge, Harvard Univ. Pr., 1929. 551p. **DC120**

Material on the Cromwell period published from 1597 to 1928.

Davies, Godfrey. Stuart period, 1603–1714. Oxford, 1928. 459p. **DC121**

For full information *see* DC110.

New York (City). Union Theological Seminary. Library. Catalogue of the McAlpin collection of British history and theology; comp. and ed. by C. R. Gillett. N.Y., 1927–30. 5v. **DC122**

Valuable for historical material published from 1500 to 1700. Arranged chronologically with alphabetical index.

For full record *see* BB26.

Read, Conyers. Tudor period, 1485–1603. 2d ed. Oxford, 1959. 624p. **DC123**

For full information *see* DC110.

18th and 19th centuries

Grose, Clyde Leclare. A select bibliography of British history, 1660–1760. Chicago, Univ. of Chicago Pr., 1939. 507p. **DC124**

Divided by periods: General, 1660–1760; 1660–88; 1689–1714; 1715–60. Classified arrangement, the detailed table of contents showing scheme. Includes some major collections of manuscripts as well as printed works. Annotated. Works considered exceptionally useful are starred.

Morgan, William Thomas and **Morgan, Chloe Siner.** Bibliography of British history (1700–1715) with special reference to the reign of Queen Anne. Bloomington, Ind., 1934–42. 5v. (Indiana Univ. studies, no.94, 95, 114–16, 119–24) **DC125**

Contents: v.1–2, Pamphlets and memoirs, 1700–1715; v.3, Source materials published in 1717 and later. Correspondence, autobiographies, diaries, and journals. Periodicals, including newspapers and annuals (1700–1715). Plays and other dramatic works. Secondary materials (to about June 1938); v.4, Unpublished manuscripts with index; v.5, Addenda and corrigenda. Supplements to v.1–3. Appendixes. Comprehensive index to v.1, 2, 3, and 5.

Pargellis, Stanley and **Medley, D. J.** The eighteenth century, 1714–1789. Oxford, 1951. 642p. **DC126**

For full information *see* DC110.

Williams, Judith Blow. A guide to the printed materials for English social and economic history, 1750–1850. N.Y., Columbia Univ. Pr., 1926. 2v. (Records of civilization: sources and studies, ed. by J. T. Shotwell) **DC127**

An annotated bibliography, in classified arrangement, covering all phases of economic and social life in England during the Industrial Revolution, including sections on biography and local history.

Current

Writings on British history, 1934– . . . . comp. by Alexander Taylor Milne. London, J. Cape, 1937– . [v.1–] Annual. (1940–1945, pub. 1960. 2v.) **DC128**

A bibliography of books and articles on the history of Great Britain from about A.D. 400 to 1914, published during the years 1934 [–45], with an appendix containing a select list of publications in these years on British history since 1914.

A comprehensive, classified bibliography with detailed indexes.

Guides to records

Galbraith, Vivian Hunter. Introduction to the use of the public records. London, Oxford Univ. Pr., 1952. 112p. il. **DC129**

"Reprinted . . . from . . . first ed. 1934 . . . (with corrections)."

A practical handbook for the beginner to the main types of records and how to procure them. Bibliography.

Gt.Brit. Historical Manuscripts Commission. A guide to the reports on collections of manuscripts of private families, corporations and institutions in Great Britain and Ireland issued by the Royal Commissioners for Historical Manuscripts. London, Stat. Off., 1914–38. 2v. in 3. **DC130**

Pt.1, Topographical index. 1914. 233p.; pt.2, v.1–2, Index of persons. 1938. 859p.

Pt.2 has title *Guide to the reports of the Royal Commission on Historical Manuscripts,* 1870–1911, and is an alphabetical index of names, with reference under each to the report or reports in which some letter or document connected with the person is listed or calendared.

Gt.Brit. Public Record Office. Guide to the manuscripts preserved in the Public Record Office, by M. S. Giuseppi. London, Stat. Off., 1923–24. 2v. **DC131**

Contents: v.1, Legal records, etc.; v.2, The state papers and records of public documents.

v.1 is "largely based" on the 3d edition of the *Guide to the various classes of documents preserved in the Public Record Office,* by S. R. Scargill-Bird. London, 1908.

—— Guide to the contents of the Public Record Office . . . rev. (to 1960) from the *Guide* by the late M. S. Giuseppi. London, Stat. Off., 1963. 2v. **DC132**

Contents: v.1, Legal records, etc.; v.2, State papers and departmental records.

Based on, and in large measure a revision and updating of, the Giuseppi *Guide* (DC131), adding the records transferred to the Public Record Office, 1923–60, many of which fall into new classes.

Virginia. Committee on Colonial Records. The British Public Record Office: history, description, record groups, finding aids, and materials for American history, with special reference to Virginia. Richmond, Virginia State Lib., 1960. 178p. (Virginia. State Library. Richmond. Publ., no.12) **DC133**

Special reports 25–28 of the Virginia Colonial Records Project.

Designed to "assist those American scholars who intend to do research in the British Public Record Office."—*Introd.* English scholars have contributed papers on (1) History and description of the Public Record Office; (2) List of record groups; (3) Search Room catalogues and other finding aids; (4) Survey of materials for American history in the Public Record Office.

West, John. Village records. London, N.Y., St. Martin's, 1962. 208p. il. **DC134**

A handbook of documentary study for English local history, with descriptions of types of documents, and bibliographical references.

Dictionaries and handbooks

Cheney, Christopher Robert. Handbook of dates for students of English history. London, Offices of the Royal Historical Soc., 1945. 164p. (Royal Historical Soc. Guides and handbooks, no.4) **DC135**

Combines some of the useful features of various other handbooks. Four sections are reprinted, with some revision, from Powicke, *Handbook of British chronology* (DC137), viz., Reckonings of time, Rulers of England, Saints' days and festivals, and Legal chronology. The 36 tables of calendars for all possible dates of Easter are based on Grotefend, *Zeitrechnung* (DC105), and Fry, *Almanacks for students of English history* (DA35). 7p. bibliography.

Low, *Sir* **Sidney** and **Pulling, F. S.** Dictionary of English history. New ed., rev. and enl. by F. J. C. Hearnshaw, H. M. Chew, and A. C. F. Beales. London, N.Y., Cassell, 1928. 1154p. **DC136**

1st ed. 1884; new ed., rev., 1896.

A compact, well-edited dictionary, with many concise and some longer articles, with bibliographical references, on subjects, events, and personages in English history. Many articles are signed.

Powicke, Frederick Maurice and **Fryde, E. B.** Handbook of British chronology. 2d ed. London, Royal Historical Soc., 1961. 565p. (Royal Historical Soc. Guides and handbooks, no.2) **DC137**

1st ed. 1939.

Partial contents: Bibliographical guide to the lists of English office-holders; Chronological lists of rulers of England, Wales, Scotland and the Isle of Man; Officers of state of England, Ireland and Scotland; Bishops of England, Wales, Scotland, Ireland; Dukes, Marquesses, and Earls (England), 1066–1714, (Ireland) (Scotland); English parliaments to 1832; Provincial and national councils of the Church in England to 1536.

This edition omits the section, "Reckonings of time," which has been reprinted in revised form in Cheney, *Handbook of dates for students of English history* (DC135). It also includes several new lists, with some extensions and revisions of others. No index.

Steinberg, Sigfrid Heinrich [and others]. A new dictionary of British history. London, Edward Arnold; N.Y., St. Martin's, 1963. 407p. **DC138**

A successor to *A dictionary of British history* by J. A. Brendon. London, Edward Arnold, 1937. A dictionary of brief articles written by a group of scholars, covering England and her overseas possessions so long as they maintained their British connection. Biographies are omitted; no bibliographical references.

General histories

Green, John Richard. Short history of the English people. Illus. ed. . . . N.Y., Harper, 1893–95. 4v. il. **DC139**

History of England, ed. by Charles Oman. London, Methuen; N.Y., Putnam, [1904]–48. 8v. (v.1, 1910) maps. **DC140**

v.1, England before the Norman Conquest, by Charles Oman. 1910; v.2, England under the Normans and Angevins, by H. W. C. Davis. 1905; v.3, England in the later Middle Ages, by K. H. Vickers. 1914; v.4, England under the Tudors, by A. D. Innes. [1905]; v.5, England under the Stuarts, by G. M. Trevelyan. [1904]; v.6, England under the Hanoverians, by C. G. Robertson. 15th ed. 1948; v.7, England since Waterloo, by J. A. R. Marriott. 4th ed. 1921; v.8, Modern England, 1885–1939, a history of my own times, by J. A. R. Marriott. rev. ed. 1944.

Includes maps, plans, genealogical charts, and, at end of each volume, a bibliography of sources. Each volume frequently reissued with varying edition numbers.

Oxford history of England. 2d ed. Ed. by *Sir* George Clark. Oxford, Clarendon Pr., 1937–62. v.1–4, 8–11, 13. (In progress) **DC141**

1st ed. 1934–61. 14v. The 2d edition began publication before the 1st edition was completed. The above volumes are available in the 2d edition.

Contents: v.1, R. G. Collingwood and J. N. L. Myers. Roman Britain and the English settlements; v.2, F. M. Stenton. Anglo-Saxon England; v.3, Austin L. Poole. From Domesday Book to Magna Carta, 1087–1216; v.4, *Sir* M. Powicke. The thirteenth century, 1216–1307; v.5, M. McKisack. The fourteenth century, 1307–1399; v.6, E. F. Jacob. The fifteenth century, 1399–1485; v.7, J. D. Mackie. The earlier Tudors, 1485–1558; v.8, J. B. Black. The reign of Elizabeth, 1558–1603; v.9, G. Davies. Early Stuarts, 1603–1660; v.10, *Sir* G. Clark. The later Stuarts, 1660–1714; v.11, B. Williams. Whig supremacy, 1714–1760, rev. by C. H. Stuart; v.12, J. S. Watson. The reign of George III, 1760–1815; v.13, E. L. Woodward. Age of reform, 1815–1870; v.14, R. C. K. Ensor. England, 1870–1914.

A scholarly work with annotated, critical bibliographies.

Traill, Henry Duff and **Mann, J. S.** Social England, a record of the progress of the people in religion, laws, learning, arts, industry, commerce, science, literature and manners from the earliest times to the present day. [New illus. ed.] London, Cassell; N.Y., Putnam, 1909. 6v. il. **DC142**

A very valuable illustrated record of England's cultural history to 1909.

Source books

Collections of documents, or extracts of them, are frequently useful for those wishing to identify or to read sources of a particular period or area. The material is usually printed with references to the original and/or later editions, and is sometimes given in the original language and sometimes in translation. Only a few of the many available collections are listed here. They are arranged with the collections covering long periods first, followed by others in chronological order.

English historical documents. Gen. ed., David C. Douglas. London, Eyre and Spottiswoode, 1953–59. il. v.1–2, 8–12[1]. (In progress) **DC143**

v.1, English historical documents, *ca.* 500–1042, ed. by Dorothy Whitlock. 1955. 867p.

v.2, English historical documents, 1042–1189, ed. by David C. Douglas and George W. Greenaway. 1953. 1014p.

v.8, English historical documents 1660–1714, ed. by Andrew Browning. 1953. 966p.

v.9, American colonial documents to 1776, ed. by Merrill Jensen. 1955. 888p.

v.10, English historical documents, 1714–1783, ed. by D. B. Horn and Mary Ransome. 1957. 964p.

v.11, English historical documents, 1783–1832, ed. by A. Aspinall and E. Anthony Smith. 1959. 992p.

v.12, pt.1, English historical documents, 1833–1874, ed. by G. M. Young and W. D. Handcock. 1956. 1017p.

Announced to be in 13v., this series will cover the complete span of English history from A.D. 500 to 1914. The early documents are given in English translation from the original Latin, French, or Anglo-Saxon. A valuable collection, with extensive introductions and bibliographies.

Gee, Henry and **Hardy, W. J.** Documents illustrative of English church history, comp. from original sources. London, N.Y., Macmillan, 1896. 670p. **DC144**

Covers documents from 314 to 1700.

Bland, Alfred Edward, Brown, P. A. and **Tawney, R. H.** English economic history; select documents. London, Bell, 1914. 730p. **DC145**

Documents illustrating economic history from 1000 to 1846.

Stephenson, Carl and **Marcham, Frederick George.** Sources of English constitutional history; a selection of documents from A.D. 600 to the present. N.Y., London, Harper, 1937. 906p. **DC146**

Includes introductory notes and bibliographies.

Robertson, Agnes Jane. Anglo-Saxon charters, ed. with translation and notes. Cambridge, Univ. Pr., 1939. 555p. (Cambridge studies in English legal history) **DC147**

Originals and translations given on opposite pages.

Stubbs, William. Select charters and other illustrations of English constitutional history, from the earliest times to the reign of Edward the First. 9th ed., rev. throughout by H. W. C. Davis. Oxford, Clarendon Pr., 1913. 528p. **DC148**

Chrimes, Stanley Bertram and **Brown, Alfred L.** Select documents of English constitutional history, 1307–1485. N.Y., Barnes & Noble, 1961; London, A. and C. Black, 1961. 398p. **DC149**

"The selection has been confined to documents of major constitutional importance, to the exclusion of those of purely political interest."—*Pref.* Documents are printed in the original language.

Tanner, Joseph Robson. Tudor constitutional documents, A.D. 1485–1603, with an historical commentary. 2d ed. Cambridge, Univ. Pr., 1930. 636p. **DC150**

Tawney, Richard Henry and **Power, Eileen.** Tudor economic documents; being select documents illustrating the economic and social history of Tudor England. London, N.Y., Longmans, 1924. 3v. (Univ. of London historical ser., no.4) (Repr. by photolithography, 1951) **DC151**

Contents: v.1, Agriculture and industry (1473–1615); v.2, Commerce, finance, and the Poor Law (1478–1600); v.3, Pamphlets, memoranda, and literary extracts (1496–1601).

Tanner, Joseph Robson. Constitutional documents of the reign of James I, A.D. 1603–1625, with an historical commentary. Cambridge, Univ. Pr., 1930. 389p. (Repr. 1952) **DC152**

Gardiner, Samuel Rawson. Constitutional documents of the Puritan revolution, 1625–1660. 3d ed. rev. Oxford, Clarendon Pr., 1906. 476p. **DC153**

Robertson, *Sir* Charles Grant. Select statutes, cases and documents to illustrate English constitutional history, 1660–1832, with additional matter on Irish and Canadian documents (1840–1931). 9th ed. London, Methuen, 1949. 649p.   **DC154**

LeMay, Godfrey H. L. British government, 1914–1953; select documents. London, Methuen, 1955. 416p. **DC155**

British Empire

Cambridge history of the British Empire. Gen. eds.: J. Holland Rose, A. P. Newton, E. A. Benians. N.Y., Macmillan; Cambridge, Univ. Pr., 1929–59. 8v. in 9. **DC156**

Editors vary.

v.1, The old empire from the beginnings to 1783; v.2, Growth of the new empire, 1783–1870; v.3, The Empire-Commonwealth, 1870–1919; v.4, British India, 1497–1858; v.5, Indian Empire, 1858–1918, with chapters on the development of administration, 1818–58; v.6, Canada and Newfoundland; v.7, pt.1, Australia. pt.2, New Zealand; v.8, South Africa, Rhodesia, and the Protectorates.

v.4–5 published also as v.5–6 of the *Cambridge history of India* (DE63), and furnished in binding to match either set.

Bibliographies at end of each volume.

✓ **Royal Commonwealth Society, London. Library.** Subject catalogue of the library of the Royal Empire Society, formerly Royal Colonial Institute, by Evans Lewin. [London, Soc.], 1930–37. 4v.   **DC157**

v.1, British Empire generally, and Africa; v.2, Commonwealth of Australia, Dominion of New Zealand, South Pacific, general voyages and travels, and Arctic and Antarctic regions; v.3, Dominion of Canada and its provinces, Dominion of Newfoundland, the West Indies, and Colonial America; v.4, Mediterranean colonies, Middle East, Indian Empire, Burma, Ceylon, British Malaya, East Indian Islands, and the Far East.

A fine catalog, particularly for the history, description, etc. of certain regions for which no separate bibliographies exist.

[handwritten margin note: early anthrop. mater.]

Arranged geographically and by subject under each country. Entries are chronological under subject. Includes books, pamphlets, periodical articles, etc. Author index in each volume.

Regional history

Anderson, John Parker. The book of British topography; a classified catalogue of the topographical works in the library of the British Museum relating to Great Britain and Ireland. London, Satchell, 1881. 472p. **DC158**

Lists historical works about the places of England, Wales, Scotland, and Ireland, arranged by county and then by place.

Gross, Charles. A bibliography of British municipal history, including gilds and parliamentary representation. N.Y., London, Longmans, 1897. 461p. (Harvard historical studies, v.5)   **DC159**

A comprehensive bibliography, giving general authorities, including public records, followed by histories of particular towns, p.150–430.

✓ **Humphreys, Arthur Lee.** Handbook to county bibliography, being a bibliography of bibliographies relating to the counties and towns of Great Britain and Ireland. London, Strangeways, 1917. 501p.   **DC160**

An indispensable record of bibliographies relating to the topography of Great Britain and Ireland, including those published in periodicals and society publications.

✓ **Victoria history of the counties of England.** London, Oxford Univ. Pr., 1901– . il. (In progress) **DC161**

First published by Constable, then by the St. Catherine Press, and later by the Oxford University Press for the University of London, Institute of Historical Research.

Of first importance for its large amount of detailed in-formation on the natural history, archaeology, industries, religious houses, political and social history, manorial history, topography, biography, and genealogy of each county. Contains numerous excellent illustrations and maps and many references to sources of information. Indispensable in any library doing much research work in English local history.

Contents:

Bedford, ed. by H. A. Doubleday and William Page. 1904–14. 3v. and index.

Berkshire, ed. by P. H. Ditchfield and William Page. 1906–27. 4v. and index.

Buckingham, ed. by Willian Page. 1905–28. 4v. and index.

Cambridge and the Isle of Ely: v.1–2, ed. by L. F. Salzman. 1938–48; v.3, ed. by J. P. C. Roach. 1959; v.4, ed. by R. B. Pugh. 1953. Index. 1960. 4v. and index.

Cornwall, ed. by William Page. 1906. v.1.

Cumberland, ed. by James Wilson. 1901–05. v.1–2.

Derby, ed. by William Page. 1905–07. v.1–2.

Devon, ed. by William Page. 1906. v.1.

Dorset, ed. by William Page. 1908. v.2.

Durham, ed. by William Page. 1905–28. v.1–3.

Essex: v.1, ed. by H. A. Doubleday and William Page. 1903; v.2, ed. by William Page and J. H. Round. 1907; v.3, with index to v.1–3, ed. by W. R. Powell. 1963; v.4, ed. by W. R. Powell. 1956. Bibliography, ed. by W. R. Powell. 1959.

Gloucester, ed. by William Page. 1907. v.2.

Hampshire and the Isle of Wight: v.1–2, ed. by H. A. Doubleday. 1900–03; v.3–5, ed. by William Page. 1908–12. Index. 1914. 5v. and index.

Hereford, ed. by William Page. 1908. v.1.

Hertford, ed. by William Page. 1902–23. 4v. and index.

Hertfordshire families, ed. by Duncan Warrand. 1907.

Huntingdon, ed. by William Page. 1926–38. 3v. and index.

Kent, ed. by William Page. 1908–32. v.1–3.

Lancaster: v.1, ed. by William Page. 1906; v.3–8, ed. by William Farrar and J. Brownbill. 1907–14.

Leicester: v.1, ed. by William Page. 1907; v.2–3, ed. by W. G. Hoskins. 1954–55; v.4, ed. by R. A. McKinley. 1958.

Lincoln, ed. by William Page. 1906. v.2.

London, ed. by William Page. 1909. v.1.

Middlesex: v.2, ed. by William Page. 1911; v.3, with index, ed. by Susan Reynolds. 1962.

Norfolk: v.1, ed. by H. A. Doubleday. 1901; v.2, ed. by William Page. 1906.

Northampton: v.1–2, ed. by W. Ryland, D. Adkins, and R. M. Serjeantson. 1902–06; v.3, ed. by William Page. 1930; v.4, ed. by L. F. Salzman. 1937.

Northamptonshire families, ed. by Oswald Barron. 1906.

Nottingham, ed. by William Page. 1906–10. v.1–2.

Oxford: v.1, ed. by L. F. Salzman. 1939; v.2, ed. by William Page. 1907; v.3 (The University of Oxford), ed. by H. E. Salter and M. D. Lobel. 1954; v.5–8, ed. by M. D. Lobel. 1957–64.

Rutland, ed. by William Page. 1908–36. 2v. and index.

Shropshire, ed. by William Page. 1908. v.1.

Somerset, ed. by William Page. 1906–11. v.1–2.

Stafford: v.1, ed. by William Page. 1908; v.4–5, ed. by L. M. Midgley. 1958–59; v.8, ed. by J. G. Jenkins. 1963.

Suffolk, ed. by William Page. v.1, 1911; v.2, 1907.

Surrey, ed. by H. E. Malden. 1902–14. 4v. and index.

Sussex: v.1–2, ed. by William Page. 1905–07; v.3–4, ed. by L. F. Salzman. 1935–53; v.7, ed. by L. F. Salzman. 1940; v.9, ed. by L. F. Salzman. 1937.

Warwick: v.1, ed. by L. F. Salzman. 1904; v.2, ed. by William Page. 1908; v.3–6, ed. by L. F. Salzman. 1945–51; v.7 (The city of Birmingham), ed. by W. B. Stephens. 1964. Index, v.1–6. 1955.

Wiltshire: v.1, pt.1, v.2–5, ed. by R. B. Pugh and Elizabeth Crittall. 1955–57; v.6, ed. by E. Crittall. 1962; v.7, ed. by R. B. Pugh and E. Crittall. 1953.

Worcester: v.1, ed. by J. W. Willis-Bund and H. A. Doubleday. 1901; v.2–4, ed. by J. W. Willis-Bund and William Page. 1906–24. Index. 1926. 4v. and index.

York, ed. by William Page. 1907–25. 3v. and index.

York, North Riding, ed. by William Page. 1914–25. 2v. and index.

Yorkshire (The city of York), ed. by P. M. Tillott. 1961.

London

Ekwall, Eilert. Street-names of the City of London. Oxford, Clarendon Pr., 1954. 209p. map.   **DC162**

A study of the history and etymology of the street names of the City of London. Intends to cover "practically all street-names found before 1500 and some recorded even later." Gives references to sources.

Harben, Henry Andrade. Dictionary of London; being notes topographical and historical relating to the streets and principal buildings in the City of London. London, Jenkins, 1918. 641p.   **DC163**

Brief, historical notes on the streets and buildings of London.

Kent, William. An encyclopaedia of London. London, Dent; N.Y., Macmillan, 1951. 674p. il.   **DC164**

1st ed. 1937.

The 2d edition is revised to include information about changed conditions due to World War II.

An alphabetical encyclopedia providing historical information about buildings, areas, famous streets, theaters, schools, statues, etc.

London. County Council. List of the streets and places within the administrative county of London. 3d ed., comp. by the superintending architect of metropolitan buildings and architect to the Council. London, County Council, 1929. 646p.   **DC165**

Subtitle: Including the names of blocks of dwellings, parks and open spaces, showing localities, postal districts . . . parishes, metropolitan and parliamentary boroughs, electoral divisions, ordnance and municipal map references, together with the alterations in street nomenclature and numbering since 1856, and the origins of certain of the names.

Scotland

Bibliography

Hancock, Philip David. A bibliography of works relating to Scotland, 1916–1950. Edinburgh, Univ. Pr., 1959–60. 2v. (Edinburgh Univ. publ.)   **DC166**

Intended as a supplement to *A contribution to the bibliography of Scottish topography,* by Mitchell and Cash (DC167). Follows the arrangement of the original work, with a somewhat more detailed subject classification in the second part.

Mitchell, *Sir* **Arthur** and **Cash, C. G.** A contribution to the bibliography of Scottish topography. Edinburgh, Univ. Pr., 1917. 2v. (Publ. of the Scottish Historical Soc. 2d ser., v.14–15)   **DC167**

A detailed record of books and periodical articles on Scottish history, life, and culture. v.1 indexes material by place; v.2, by subject.

New York. Public Library. A list of works relating to Scotland, comp. by George F. Black. N.Y., Lib., 1916. 1233p. (Repr. with additions from New York Public Library. Bull. Jan.–Dec. 1914)   **DC168**

Still one of the most comprehensive bibliographies on Scotland, covering all aspects. Classified arrangement with detailed index.

Scotland. General Registry Office of Births, Deaths and Marriages. Guide to the public records of Scotland deposited in H. M. General Register House, Edinburgh, by M. Livingstone. Edinburgh, General Register House, 1905. 233p.   **DC169**

Contents: (1) Crown, parliament, revenue, and administration; (2) Judicial records; (3) Titles to land, dignities, and offices; (4) Ecclesiastical and miscellaneous.

Terry, Charles Sanford. Catalogue of the publications of Scottish historical and kindred clubs and societies, and of the volumes relative to Scottish history issued by His Majesty's Stationery Office, 1780–1908. Glasgow, Maclehose, 1909. 253p.   **DC170**

Contents: (1) Catalog of the publications of over 50 Scottish historical and kindred clubs and societies arranged alphabetically by name of society, giving for each its corporate name, date of founding, purpose, list of its publications, and contents of each volume if several papers are included; (2) Author and subject index to the publications and contents notes. The index is often useful for analytic references on minute or localized facts in Scottish history.

Continued by:

Matheson, Cyril. Catalogue of the publications of Scottish historical and kindred clubs and societies and of the papers relative to Scottish history issued by H. M. Stationery Office, including the reports of the Royal Commission on Historical MSS., 1908–27. Aberdeen, Milne and Hutchison, 1928. 232p.   **DC171**

A continuation of two works by C. S. Terry: (1) his *Catalogue* (DC170), and (2) his *Index to the papers relating to Scotland . . . in the Historical MSS. Commission's reports.* Glasgow, Maclehose, 1908.

Contents: (1) Catalog of the publications of societies, arranged alphabetically, continuing Terry's *Catalogue* from 1908 and referring to pages in Terry for earlier titles; (2) Author and subject index; (3) Index to Terry's *Catalogue;* (4) Index to papers relating to Scotland in Historical MSS. Commission's reports.

Source books

Dickinson, William Crofts, Donaldson, Gordon and **Milne, Isabel A.** A source book of Scottish history. London, Nelson, 1952–54. 3v.   **DC172**

A collection of documents and extracts with commentaries, from earliest times to 1707.

Wales

Wales. University. Board of Celtic Studies. History and Law Committee. A bibliography of the history of Wales. 2d ed. Cardiff, Univ. of Wales Pr., 1962. 330p.   **DC173**

1st ed. 1931.

A classified bibliography of some 3500 items covering political, ecclesiastical, social, and economic history, etc.

GREECE

Argenti, Philip Pandely. Bibliography of Chios, from classical times to 1936 . . . with a pref. by J. L. Myres. Oxford, Clarendon Pr., 1940. 836p.   **DC174**

Contents: pt.1, Classified catalog, p.1–567; pt.2, Authors' catalog, p.571–801; pt.3, List of maps, 1422–1937, p.805–32. Alphabetical index of classifications, p.833–36.

A comprehensive bibliography of works in many languages.

Cincinnati. University. Library. The modern Greek collection in the Library of the University of Cincinnati: a catalogue, ed. by Niove Kyparissiotis. Athens, Hestia Pr. for the Univ. of Cincinnati, 1960. 387p.   **DC175**

A catalogue of some 12,000 volumes, including works in many subject fields and in various languages on Greece or published in Greece. Arranged alphabetically by the Greek alphabet.

HUNGARY

Apponyi, Sándor. Hungarica. Ungarn betreffende im Auslande gedruckte Bücher und Flugschriften. München, Rosenthal, 1903–27. 4v.   **DC176**

Bd.1, 15. und 16. Jahrhundert; Bd.2, 17. und 18. Jahrhundert (bis 1720); Bd.3, Neue Sammlung. I, 15. und 16. Jahrhundert besorgt von L. Dézsi; Bd.4, 17. und 18. Jahrhundert besorgt von L. Dézsi.

Includes works on Hungary in languages other than Hungarian published both in and outside of Hungary from 1470 to 1798. For non-Hungarian books on Hungary, *see also* Károly Szabó. *Régi magyar könyvtár* (AA534).

Banner, János. Bibliographia archaeologica hungarica, 1793–1943. Szeged, Ed. Inst. Archaeologicum Universitatis de Nicolao Horthy, 1944. 558p. (Fontes rerum archaeologicarum hungaricarum. t.1)   **DC177**

Bibliographia Hungariae. Zusammengestellt vom Ungarischen Institut an der Universität Berlin. Verzeichnis der 1861–1921 erschienenen, Ungarn betreffenden Schriften in nichtungarischer Sprache. Berlin, de Gruyter, 1923–29. 4v. (Ungarische Bibliothek für das Ungarische Institut an der Universität Berlin. 3. Reihe)   **DC178**

Contents: (1) Historica; (2) Geographica. Politico-oeconomica; (3) Philologica. Periodica; (4) Register.

Halász de Beky, I. L. A bibliography of the Hungarian Revolution, 1956. Toronto, Univ. of Toronto Pr., 1963. 179p.   **DC179**

"Pub. under the auspices of the Canadian Institute of International Affairs."—*Title page.*

A listing of 2136 items: books and pamphlets, periodical articles, monitored broadcasts, and motion pictures, covering the period Oct. 1956–Dec. 1960. Arranged by language (15 languages).

Kertbeny, Károly Mária. Bibliografie der ungarischen nationalen und internationalen Literatur. 1. Bd. Ungarn betreffende deutsche Erstlingsdrucke, 1454–1600. Budapest, Kön. Ung. Univ.-Buchdr., 1880. clxxxivp., 760p., 14p.   **DC180**

No more published.

Supplements Apponyi (DC176) for German books on Hungary for the period 1454–70.

—— Ungarns deutsche Bibliographie, 1801–1860. Verzeichniss der in Ungarn und Ungarn betreffend im Auslande erschienenen deutschen Drucke. Im Auftrage des K. Ung. Ministerium für Cultus und Unterricht. Fortgesetzt und mit einer wissenschaftlichen Uebersicht versehen von Géza Petrik. Budapest, Kön. Ung. Univ.-Buchdr., 1886. 2v.   **DC181**

v.1, 1801–30; v.2, 1831–60.

Added title page in Hungarian.

German books printed in and about Hungary.

Kont, Ignace. Bibliographie française de la Hongrie (1521–1910) avec un inventaire sommaire des documents manuscrits. Paris, Leroux, 1913. 323p.   **DC182**

Kosáry, Domokos G. Bevezetés a magyar történelem forrásaiba és irodalmába. Budapest, 1951–58. 3v. (At head of title: A Magyar Tudományos Akadémia. Történettudományi Intézete)   **DC183**

Publisher varies.

Contents: v.1, to [1711]. 1951. 480p.; v.2, 1711–1824. 1954. 638p.; v.3, Supplement and index. 1958. 399p.

A bibliographical guide to Hungarian history. Includes chapters on general materials, and guides to archives, with specific chapters by locality and by period. International in scope; textual annotations.

Magyar Tudományos Akadémia. Történettudományi Intézet. Magyar történeti bibliográfia, 1825–1867 . . . I.

Tóth Zoltán vezetésével. Budapest, Akadémiai Kiadó, 1950–59. v.1–4. (In progress)   **DC184**

v.1, General works. 1950. 118p.; v.2, Economics. 1952. 260p.; v.3, Politics and ideology. 1950. 407p.; v.4, History of non-Hungarian people. 1959. 675p.

Classified arrangement. Imprints as late as 1948 are included; monographs and periodical articles, in various languages, are covered. A second series, for the years 1867–1945, is planned. As yet no author index.

IRELAND

Curtis, Edmund and **McDowell, Robert Brendon.** Irish historical documents, 1172–1922. London, Methuen, 1943. 331p.   **DC185**

A source book of the "principal Irish constitutional and political documents." Documents in Latin or French have been translated into English.

Dublin. National Library of Ireland. Bibliography of Irish history, 1870–1911, 1912–1921, by James Carty. Dublin, Stat. Off., 1936–40. 2v.   **DC186**

1870–1911. 1940. 319p.; 1912–1921. 1936. 177p.

Lists books and periodical articles on the history of Ireland during these periods. Classified arrangement; author index.

Ireland. Public Record Office. A guide to the records deposited in the Public Record Office of Ireland, by Herbert Wood. Dublin, Stat. Off., 1919. 334p.   **DC187**

Kenney, James Francis. Sources for the early history of Ireland; an introduction and guide. v.1, Ecclesiastical. N.Y., Columbia Univ. Pr., 1929. 807p. (Records of civilization: sources and studies, v.11)   **DC188**

An introduction and guide to the manuscript and printed sources for the ecclesiastical history of Ireland up to the 12th century. No more published.

Gives detailed analysis of 659 manuscript sources with bibliographic references for each.

Writings on Irish history, 1936– . (In Irish historical studies, v.1, 1936– . Annual)   **DC189**

Compiled in cooperation with the Bibliographical Subcommittee of the Irish Committee of Historical Sciences.

ITALY

Bibliography

See also Enciclopedia italiana 19:898–916 (AD48) for a useful bibliography on the history of Italy, compiled by F. Chabod.

Bibliografia romana, April 1945– . Roma, Staderini Editore, 1946– . v.1– . Annual. (v.10, 1954, pub. 1960)   **DC190**

v.1–3 had title *Saggio di bibliografia romana* and were reprinted from *Strenna del Romanisti,* v.7–9, 1946–48.

v.1–10, ed. by Ceccarius.

At head of title: v.7– , Istituto di Studi Romani.

An extensive annual bibliography of materials about Rome, covering all phases and all periods. Classified arrangement with author and subject indexes.

Bibliografia storica nazionale. Anno 1, 1939– . Giunto Centrale per gli Studi Storici. Bari, Laterza, 1942– . Annual. (Anno 23, 1961, pub. 1963)   **DC191**

Publisher varies.

A classified record of books and periodical articles, published in Italy about Italy. Name index. In many cases indicates location of reviews. Follows the general form of the *International bibliography of historical sciences* (DA18).

Evola, Niccolo Domenico. Origini e dottrina del fascismo. Firenze, Sansoni, 1935. 166p. (Guide bibliografiche dell' Istit. Nazionale Fascista di Cultura. I) **DC192**

A bibliography of books and periodical articles on the origin and development of fascism in its political, legal, economic, and social aspects.

Hassall, W. O. A select bibliography of Italy: a thousand books about Italy, its geography, population, cities and regions, its language, literature and history, its social, economic and political life, its art and music. London, ASLIB, 1946. 82p. **DC193**

A selected list planned for the English and American user. Includes the basic materials in Italian.

Lemmi, Francesco. Il risorgimento. Roma, Fondazione Leonardo, 1926. 320p. ('Guide bibliografiche [23–24]) **DC194**

Lists some 3000 items covering the period 1748–1870.

Lozzi, Carlo. Biblioteca istorica della antica e nuova Italia; saggio di bibliografia, analitico comparato e critico. . . . Imola, Galeati e Figlio, 1886–87. 2v. **DC195**

A classified bibliography of more than 6500 archaeological and historical works on Italian municipalities. A third volume, which was to contain the index, was never published.

Handbooks

Gardner, Edmund G. Italy: a companion to Italian studies. London, Methuen, 1934. 274p. **DC196**

Survey articles by specialists on the history and culture of Italy, with bibliographies.

LATVIA

Latvju enciklopēdija. Redaktors Arveds Švābe. Stokholmā, Trīs Zvaigznes, 1950–55. 3v. **DC197**

A national encyclopedia of things Latvian or related to Latvia. Most articles are short, unsigned, and without bibliographies; a few are considerably more extensive and include some bibliographic references. Illustrations are numerous and generally good.

Ozols, Zelma Aleksandra. Latvia; a selected bibliography. Wash., K. Karusa, 1963. 144p. **DC198**

Classed arrangement with author-title index. Includes publications to 1957 only. Locates copies.

LITHUANIA

Balys, Jonas. Lithuania and Lithuanians; a selected bibliography. N.Y., pub. for the Lithuanian Research Institute by F. A. Praeger, 1961. 190p. (Studia lituanica, II) **DC199**

A classified listing of books, pamphlets, and articles on all aspects of Lithuanian life and civilization, with Western-language materials predominating. Author index.

Simutis, Anicetas. Lithuanian world directory. N.Y., Lithuanian Chamber of Commerce of N.Y., 1958. 464p. **DC200**

Added title page in Lithuanian.

A handbook of Lithuanian history and a directory of Lithuanian organizations, activities, etc., designed especially for Lithuanians in the United States.

MONACO

Handley-Taylor, Geoffrey. Bibliography of Monaco. London, 1961. 35p. il. **DC201**

"Printed especially for Archives du Palais de Monaco."

"Represents a selection of publications (wholly or in part) relating to some aspect of the Principality or the family . . ." —*Pref.*

NETHERLANDS

Bibliography

Bibliographia neerlandica. The Hague, Nijhoff, 1962. 598p. **DC202**

Pt.1, Books on the Netherlands in foreign languages, 1940–57, comp. by A. M. P. Mollema, p.1–384; pt.2, Translations of Dutch literature, 1900–1957, comp. by P. M. Morel, p.385–491. Indexes, p.493–598.

Title, introductory material, and captions in English, French, German, and Spanish.

Repertorium der verhandelingen en bijdragen betreffende de geschiedenis des vaderlands, in tijdschriften en mengelwerken tot op 1900 verschenen. In opdracht van de Commissie voor Gescheid- en Oudheidkunde van de Maatschappij der Nederlandsche Letterkunde to Leiden bewerkt door L. D. Petit. Leiden, Brill, 1907. 1638col. **DC203**

Listing publications through 1900.

—— 2.–5. deel. Leiden, Brill, 1913–53.

2. deel, 1901–10. 884col.; 3. deel, 1911–20. 904col.; 4. deel, 1921–29. 1132col.; 5. deel, 1930–39. 764col.

A comprehensive, classified bibliography of analytical material on all aspects of Dutch history, indexing articles on the subject in more than 1000 periodicals, society transactions, composite books, etc., principally Dutch publications but including also some in other languages. List of titles indexed varies in the different volumes.

Repertorium van boeken en tijdschriftartikelen betreffende de geschiedenis van Nederland. 1940– . Leiden, Brill, 1943– . v.1– . Triennial since 1942. **DC204**

Continues the preceding entry but on a smaller scale.

A bibliography of books and periodical articles on the history of the Netherlands.

—— Index, 1940–1950.

Handbooks

Strubbe, Egied I. and **Voet, Leon.** De chronologie van de middeleeuwen en de moderne tijden in de Nederlanden. Antwerp, Standaard-Boekhandel, 1960. 551p. **DC205**

Chiefly tables, including a calendar for the years 396–2000, and chronological lists of popes, bishops of Dutch sees, selected European dynasties, and early Dutch rulers and landholders.

Atlases

Geschiedkundige atlas van Nederland . . . Uitg. door de Commissie voor den Geschiedkundigen Atlas van Nederland en geteekend door het lid der Commissie. 'sGravenhage, Nijhoff, 1913–38. v.1–19 (incompl.) 25cm. and atlases, 50cm. **DC206**

Historical maps of the various sections of the Netherlands with detailed textual comment.

NORWAY

See also Denmark, p.489; Scandinavia, p.503; and Sweden, p.504.

Schweigaard, Johan Elias. Norges topografi; bibliografisk fortegnelse over topografisk og lokal-historisk literatur. Kristiania, Grøndahl, 1918. 291p.   **DC207**

—— —— Tillegg, 1917–1927, 1928–1945, ved W. P. Sommerfeldt. Oslo, Brøgger, 1930–55. 2v.

—— —— Oslo. Oslo, Fabritius, 1939. 298p.

Detailed bibliographies on the topography and local history of Norway.

Bibliografi til norges historie, 1916–1925, 1926–1935, 1936– .... Utgitt av den Norske Historiske Forening. Oslo, Grøndahl, 1927– . Annual; biennial from 1956/57.   **DC208**

Issued as annual supplements to *Historisk tidsskrift* (Oslo).

Full current bibliography, including books, pamphlets, and analytical material in periodicals, etc. General title pages and general author indexes are issued for 10-year periods, 1916–25, 1926–35, 1936–45, 1946–55. Items are numbered consecutively throughout the 10-year period.

POLAND

Bibliography

Bibliografia historii Polski, 1815–1914. Warszawa, Państwowe Wydawnictwo Naukowe, 1954– .   **DC209**

Tom wstepny, introductory volume, comp. by Halina Bachulska and others.

1st edition, 1939 (of which v.1, pt.1, was published), had title *Bibliografia historii polskiej, 1815–1914.*

Continues Ludwik Finkel's *Bibliografia historyi polskiej* (DC212). Introductory volume contains general bibliographies, encyclopedias, works on general and Polish history, historiography, archives, museums, and libraries. Limited primarily to works published up to 1939.

For bibliography of specific periods of 19th-century Polish history, *see Bibliografia historii Polski XIX wieku* (DC210).

Bibliografia historii Polski XIX wieku. Wrocław, Zakład Narodowy im. Ossolińskich, 1958– .   **DC210**

At head of title: Polska Akademia Nauk. Instytut Historii.

Contents: v.1, 1815–1831.

Comp. by Halina Bachulska and others. Ed. by Stanisław Płoski.

Continues Ludwik Finkel's *Bibliografia historyi polskiej* (DC212).

For general historical aids for the 19th century, *see Bibliografia historii Polski, 1815–1914* (DC209).

Bibliografia historii polskiej, 1944/47– . Oprac. Jan Baumgart. Wrocław, Ossolińskich, 1952– . Annual.   **DC211**

Began publication with volume for 1948; 1944/47, published 1962.

At head of title, 1961– : Instytut Historii-Zakład Dokumentacij Polskiej Akademii Nauk.

An extensive classified list, usually issued annually, of books and articles in various languages on Polish history and related fields. Author indexes.

Finkel, Ludwik. Bibliografia historyi polskiej. Wspólnie z dr. Henrykiem Sawczyńskim i członkami Kółka historycznego uczniów Uniwersytetu lwowskiego zebrał i ułozył dr. Ludwik Finkel. W Krakowie, Nakł. Komisyi Historycznej Akademii Umiejętności w Krakowie, 1891–1906. 2150p.   **DC212**

Issued in 7 pts.

2d ed., v.1, pts.1–4. Lwów, Nakł. Polskiego Towarzystwa Historycznego, 1931–37.

—— —— Dodatek 1–2[1]. Kraków, 1906–14.

An excellent bibliography listing works published down to 1900 on Polish history to 1815. The 2d supplement lists original sources published 1901–10. The 2d edition remains incomplete and with no index.

For works published after 1910, consult the periodical bibliography *Kwartalnik historyczny* (1887–).

Rister, Herbert. Schrifttum über Polen, 1943–1951: mit besonderer Berücksichtigung des Posener Landes (Auswahl). Im Auftrage der Historisch- Landeskundlichen Kommission für Posen und das Deutschtum in Polen bearb. Marburg/Lahn, Johann Gottfried Herder Inst., 1953. 147p. (Wissenschaftliche Beiträge zur Geschichte und Landeskunde Ost-Mitteleuropas. Nr.10)   **DC213**

Continued by:

—— —— 1952–1953 und Nachträge (Auswahl). 1955. 207p.; 1954–1955 und Nachträge (Auswahl). 1958. 315p.; 1956–1958 und Nachträge (Auswahl). 1960. 2v.

Słowarzyzenie Bibliotekarzy Polskich. Commission Nationale de Bibliographie. Bibliographie sur la Pologne: pays, histoire, civilisation. 2. éd. avec suppl. 1960–63. Warszawa, Państwowe Wydawnictwo Naukowe, [1964]. 300p.   **DC214**

A classified bibliography of materials mainly in Polish on Poland. Annotations in French. Titles given in Polish and in French translation.

Encyclopedias

Comité des Publications Encyclopédiques sur la Pologne. Encyclopédie polonaise. Lausanne, 1916–20. il. v.1–4, pt.1.   **DC215**

v.1, Géographie et ethnographie; v.2, Territoire et population; v.3, Vie économique; v.4, pt.1, Régime politique et administratif dans la Pologne prussienne.

—— —— Atlas. Fribourg, 1920– .

Unfinished, but an authoritative work as far as it goes. Partially published in an English edition as:

—— Polish encyclopaedia. . . . Pub. by the Committee for the Polish Encyclopaedic Publications at Fribourg and Geneva (Switzerland). Geneva, Atar, 1922–26. (v.1, 1926) 3v. maps. (Publ. of the Polish National Committee of America)   **DC216**

Contents: v.1, The Polish language. History of literature. History of Poland; v.2, Territory and population of Poland; v.3, Economic life of Poland.

PORTUGAL

Bibliography

See also Foulché-Delbosc, *Manuel de l'hispanisant* (AA50); and *Bibliographie hispanique* (BD799).

Academia Portuguesa da História. Guia da bibliografia histórica portuguêsa. Lisboa, 1959– . v.1, fasc.1– . (In progress)   **DC217**

Contents: v.1, fasc.1, capítulo 1, secção A. Colecções de fontes abrangendo mais de uma época ou de um século.

Planned to constitute, when complete, a comprehensive bibliography of Portuguese history from the 9th century to 1910. Documents, collections, chronicles, monographs, articles, etc. will all be included.

Costa Coutinho, Bernard Xavier da. Bibliographie franco-portugaise; essai d'une bibliographie chronologique de livres français sur le Portugal. Pôrto, Lopes da Silva, 1939. 409p. **DC218**

"Publiée sous les auspices de l'Institut Français au Portugal et de l'Instituto para a Alta Cultura, avec le concours du Secrétariat de la Propaganda Nationale."

Arrangé chronologically from the 16th to the 20th centuries; lists almost 3000 items.

Newberry Library, Chicago. A catalog of the William B. Greenlee collection of Portuguese history and literature and the Portuguese materials in the Newberry Library, comp. by Doris Varner Welsh. Chicago, Newberry Lib., 1953. 342p. **DC219**

Lists holdings up to Nov. 1, 1952.

An outstanding, comprehensive collection in classified arrangement, with author and title index. Covers various aspects of Portuguese history, exploration, and colonies.

Lisbon. Biblioteca Nacional. Subsidios para a bibliografia da história local portuguêsa. Lisboa, Biblioteca Nacional, 1933. 425p. **DC220**

By Antonio Mesquita de Figueiredo.

A bibliography of local history.

Encyclopedias

Grande enciclopédia portuguesa e brasileira. Lisboa, Rio de Janeiro, Ed. Enciclopédia, [1935–58]. 37v. il. **DC220a**

A dictionary-encyclopedia treating in one alphabet: Portuguese words, including technical terms and modern slang; biographies, including living persons; and encyclopedic articles on the history and culture of Portugal, national institutions, flora, fauna, geography, etc. Articles are not signed, and bibliographies are inconsistently furnished.

—— Apêndice. 1958–60. 4v. il.

v.1, bound with main work; v.2–4, called v.38–40.

—— 2. parte: Brasil. [1964?–] v.1¹⁻² . il. (In progress)

Contents: v.1, pts.1–2, A–Alberto.

A second part, devoted to Brazilian subjects, is projected to be in 4v. Biographical sketches include living persons.

Verbo; enciclopédia luso-brasileira de cultura. Lisboa, Ed. Verbo, 1963– . v.1– . il. **DC220b**

Contents: v.1, A–amor.

A new Portuguese-Brazilian encyclopedia with signed articles and many bibliographies listing works in various languages. Treats mainly the culture and history of Portugal and Brazil, but includes articles of some length on the continents and other countries. Many well-produced, small colored illustrations.

RUMANIA

Bibliography

Bibliographie rumänischer geschichtswissenschaftlicher Literatur aus der Zeit vom 1. 1. 1955 bis 30. 4. 1961, zusammengestellt von Margot Hegemann. (In Jahrbuch für Geschichte der Ud SSR und der Volksdemokratischen Länder Europas. Bd.6, p.477–98. 1962) **DC221**

1945–1954 will appear in a future volume.

1961– . Annual.

Rally, Alexandre and **Rally, Getta Hélène.** Bibliographie franco-roumaine. Paris, Leroux, 1930. 1. pt. t.1–2. **DC222**

(1¹), Les œuvres françaises des auteurs roumains; (1²), Les œuvres françaises relatives à la Roumanie.

t.1, arranged alphabetically by author; t.2, arranged by class with alphabetical index to names and places.

To a large extent supersedes the earlier work by Georges Bengescu, *Bibliographie franco-roumaine depuis le commencement du XIX siècle jusqu'à nos jours* (Paris, 1907), of which only v.1 was published (2d ed. with suppl., 1895–1906). The bibliographical descriptions in Bengescu are longer, but the coverage is less complete.

U.S. Library of Congress. Slavic and Central European Division. Rumania, a bibliographic guide, by Stephen A. Fischer-Galati. Wash., Govt. Prt. Off., 1963. 75p. **DC223**

A concise, descriptive, bibliographic survey, totaling 748 items, arranged by subject and covering all areas of knowledge except medicine and the natural sciences. Includes monographs and periodicals, mostly in Rumanian, though publications in other languages are represented. Locates copies.

Encyclopedias

Enciclopedia româniei. [Bucharest (?), Asociatia Stiintifică Pentru Enciclopedia României], 1938–43. v.1–4. il. **DC224**

Contents: A. Organizarea politică-administrativă: v.1, Statul; v.2, Tara romanească. B. Economia: v.3, Economia nationala. Cadre si productie; v.4, Economia nationala. Circúlatie, distributie si consum. Two other volumes have not been published: C. Cultura: v.5, Cultura nationala; v.6, Institutii si personalitati culturale.

Scholarly, monographic articles arranged by large classes, with detailed tables of contents and indexes in each volume. Articles are signed by authorities and include bibliographies except in v.2, which presents gazetteer information and includes an index to all places in Rumania.

SCANDINAVIA

See also Denmark, p.489; Finland, p.489; Iceland, p.50; Norway, p.502; and Sweden, p.504.

International bibliography of urban history. Stockholm, Swedish Inst. for Urban History, 1960– . (In progress) **DC225**

[Pt.1], Denmark, Finland, Norway, Sweden. 1960.

The first of a projected series of bibliographies dealing with the history of cities. The plan is to present each country separately. In the first issue the Scandinavian countries are treated individually; in each case, general bibliographies and other materials are followed by histories of individual cities.

Meyen, Fritz. The North European nations as presented in German university publications, 1885–1957, a bibliography. Bonn, H. Bouvier; Charlottesville, Bibliographical Soc. of the Univ. of Virginia, 1959. 124p. (Bonner Beiträge zur Bibliotheks- und Bücherkunde. 4) **DC226**

Added title page in German.

Contents, preface, and headings in English and German.

Lists 1099 dissertations and habilitation theses "that exclusively or preponderatingly, treat a theme relative to Denmark, Sweden, Norway, Iceland, or Finland."—*Pref.* Includes both published and unpublished works. Topical arrangement; author and subject indexes.

Kulturhistorisk Leksikon for nordisk Middelalder fra Vikingetid til Reformationstid. Dansk redaktør, John Danstrup. København, Rosenkilde og Bagger, 1956–65. v.1–10. il. (In progress) **DC227**

Editors vary.

Contents: Bd.1–10, Abbed–Ludus.

Written by the leading medievalists in Denmark, Norway, Sweden, and Finland. Each article signed, and most include bibliography.

SERBIA

Stanojević, Stanoje. Narodna enciklopedija srpsko-hyvatsko-slovenačka. Zagreb, Bibliografski Zavod., 1925–29. 4v.　　　　　　　**DC228**

A national encyclopedia, Serb-Croat-Slovene, with signed articles, many with bibliographies. Biographies include some living persons.

SPAIN

Bibliography

Burgo, Jaime del. Bibliografía de las guerras carlistas y de las luchas políticas del siglo XIX, antecedente desde 1814 y apéndice hasta 1936; fuentes de la historia de España. [Pamplona], Diputación Foral de Navarra, Inst. Principe de Viana, 1953–55. 3v.　　　　**DC229**

An extensive bibliography of books and pamphlets (with a few periodical articles), dealing with political strife in Spain in the 19th century.

Foulché-Delbosc, Raymond and **Barrau-Dihigo, Louis.** Manuel de l'hispanisant. N.Y., Putnam; Hispanic Soc. of America, 1925. v.1–2.　　　　　　　**DC230**

For full description see AA50.

Gómez Molleda, D. Bibliografía histórica española, 1950–1954. Madrid, Consejo Superior de Investigaciones Científicas, Inst. Jerónimo Zurita de Historia [e] Inst. Nicolás Antonio de Bibliografía, 1955. 491p.　　**DC231**

Arranged by large classification, and chronologically by period covered, with index by authors and anonymous works. Lists almost 7000 titles.

Sánchez Alonso, Benito. Fuentes de la historia española e hispanoamericana. . . . 3. ed. corr. y puesta al día. Madrid, Consejo Superior de Investigaciones Científicas, 1952. 3v. (Publ. de la Revista de filología española)　　　　　　　　　　　　　　**DC232**

Subtitle: Ensayo de bibliografía sistemática de impresos y manuscritos que ilustran la historia política de España y sus antiguas provincias de ultramar.

A comprehensive bibliography of books and periodical articles covering Spanish history from early times through the 19th century. An author index and three subject indexes: (1) biographical, (2) geographical, and (3) miscellaneous.

Utrecht. Rijksuniversiteit. Bibliotheek. España e Hispanoamérica: catálogo de libros españoles y publicaciones extranjeras sobre España e Hispanoamérica. Utrecht, 1948. 360p.　　　　　　　　　　**DC233**

————— Suplemento, 1–7, 1949–60.

A classified catalog of Spanish and foreign books on Spain and Spanish America. The main volume lists publications acquired by the library up to 1944; the supplements list later acquisitions.

Índice histórico español. Barcelona, Ed. Teide, 1953– . v.1– . Quarterly.　　　　　　　　　**DC234**

An extensive bibliography which aims to list books and articles on Spanish history published in western Europe and the Americas, with a section on the history of Latin America. Titles are annotated and evaluated by experts, and references to critical reviews are often given. Published quarterly, with annual author and subject indexes.

v.1, fasc.1–8, also issued in bound form (859p.) with title *Bibliografía histórica de España e Hispanoamérica.*

Historiography

Sánchez Alonso, Benito. Historia de la historiografía española, ensayo de un examen de conjunto. . . . Madrid, Sánchez de Ocaña, 1944–47. v.1–2. (Publ. de la Revista de filología española) (In progress)　　　**DC235**

At head of title: Consejo Superior de Investigaciones Científicas.

Contents: v.1, Hasta la publicación de la crónica de Ocampo (. . . 1943), 2. ed. rev. y añadida, 1947; v.2, De Ocampo a Solís (1543–1684), 1944.

v.3 in preparation (?).

Dictionaries

Diccionario de historia de España desde sus orígenes hasta el fin del reinado de Alfonso XIII. Madrid, Revista de Occidente, [1952]. 2v.　　　　　　　**DC236**

An alphabetical dictionary of persons, events, and subjects in the history of Spain up to the end of the reign of Alfonso XIII in 1931, compiled by a group of scholars. Articles are generally brief, though some of the more important entries cover several pages; all are signed. Bibliographical sources, not given in the text, appear in an *"Índice historiográfico"* (v.2, p.1493–1519), followed by a chronology and a number of sketch maps.

Muñoz y Romero, Tomás. Diccionario bibliográfico-histórico de los antiguos reinos, provincias, ciudades, villas, iglesias y santuarios de España. Madrid, Rivadeneyra, 1858. 329p.　　　　　　　　　**DC237**

An older work still useful for local history.

History

Menéndez Pidal, Ramón. Historia de España. Madrid, Espasa-Calpe, 1935–64. [v.1, 1947] v.1^{1-3}, 2–6, 15, 19^{1-2}. il. (In progress)　　　　　　　　　　**DC238**

A collaborative work by outstanding Spanish historians to cover from prehistoric times. v.19, pts.1–2, treat the time of Felipe II (1556–98). Illustrated in black and white and in color.

SWEDEN

Setterwall, Kristian. Svensk historisk bibliografi, 1875–1900, 1901–1920, 1921–1935, . . . Stockholm, Norstedt, 1907; Uppsala, Appelberg, 1923; Uppsala, Almqvist & Wiksells, 1956. 3v.　　　　　　　　　**DC239**

A comprehensive, classified bibliography of Swedish and some foreign material including books, pamphlets, and articles in periodicals.

1921–1935, ed. by Paul Sjögren.

Continued by the following:

Svensk historisk bibliografi, 1880– . Stockholm, Norstedt, 1881– . Annual.　　　　　　　　**DC240**

An annual bibliography of books and periodical articles, etc.; issued as an annual supplement to *Historisk tidskrift* (Stockholm). Cumulates into the volumes listed above (DC239).

SWITZERLAND

Guides

Santschy, Jean-Louis. Manuel analytique et critique de bibliographie générale de l'histoire suisse. Berne, Herbert Lang, 1961. 250p.   **DC241**

A guide to sources—general, archival, periodical, and monographic—rather than a bibliography as such. Chapter arrangement, according to type and date of material. Annotations are full; author and subject indexes.

Bibliography

Barth, Hans. Bibliographie der schweizer Geschichte enthaltend die selbständig erschienenen Druckwerke zur Geschichte der Schweiz bis Ende 1912. Basel, Basler Buch- und Antiquariatshandlung, 1914–15. 3v. (Quellen zur schweizer Geschichte hrsg. von der Allgemeinen Geschichtforschenden Gesellschaft der Schweiz. n.F. 4. Abt. Handbücher)   **DC242**

v.1, General history, by periods; v.2–3, Special subjects, e.g., biography, religious history, etc. Author and title index.

A very comprehensive bibliography, including more than 32,000 entries. May be supplemented by the following: (1) for material after 1912 by the annual *Bibliographie der Schweizergeschichte* (DC245); (2) for analytical material before 1900 by the two volumes of the *Repertorium* (DC244).

Bibliographie nationale suisse. Répertoire méthodique de ce qui a été publié sur la Suisse et ses habitants. Publiée par la Commission Centrale pour la Bibliographie Suisse. Berne, Wyss, 1892–1927, 1945. Pts.1–5 in 68 fasc.   **DC243**

Each fascicule is a bibliography on a different subject, prepared by a specialist in the field.

Covers all phases of life, letters, and civilization in Switzerland, viz., natural sciences, folklore, art and architecture, music, agriculture, commerce and industry, education, religion, etc.

Repertorium über die in Zeit- und Sammelschriften der Jahre 1812–1890, 1891–1900, enthaltenen Aufsätze und Mitteilungen schweizergeschichtlichen Inhaltes. Hrsg. von der Allgemeinen Geschichtforschenden Gesellschaft der Schweiz. Basel, Basler Buch- und Antiquariatshandlung, 1892–1906. 2v.   **DC244**

1812–90, comp. by J. L. Brandstetter; 1891–1900, by Hans Barth.

Classed lists—arranged by small subject, with alphabetical index of authors—to articles on Swiss history, biography, etc., in more than 300 periodicals and society transactions. The sections on biography in each volume give, in addition to the references to the articles, the dates of birth and death and a brief characterizing phrase, and so supply some direct biographical information.

Bibliographie der Schweizergeschichte. Bibliographie de l'histoire suisse. Jahrg.1913– . Zurich, Leemann, 1914– . v.1– . Annual (some years combined).   **DC245**

Volumes for 1913–19 published as supplements to the *Anzeiger f. schweizerische Geschichte;* those for 1920–34, as supplements to the *Zeitschrift f. schweizerische Geschichte.*

Classed arrangement. Later volumes have author and subject indexes. Includes material on history, bibliography, biography, church, art, literature, music, customs, etc.

Dictionaries

Dictionnaire historique et biographique de la Suisse, publié avec la recommandation de la Société Générale Suisse d'Histoire. . . . Neuchâtel, Admin. du Dictionnaire, 1921–34. 7v. and suppl. il.   **DC246**

Issued also in an edition in German, *Historisch-biographisches Lexikon der Schweiz.*

v.1–7, A–Z; suppl., A–Z, p.1–184; 2d suppl., A–Z, p.185–208. Table systématique.

May be considered a companion work to the *Dictionnaire géographique de la Suisse* (CK80), published by Attinger. Covers the fields of general, political, local, economic, and social history; topography; genealogy; and biography of the country. Signed articles, bibliographies, and many good illustrations. Many biographical articles, including some on persons still living.

TURKEY

Akademiia Nauk SSSR. Institut Vostokovedeniia. Bibliografiia Turtsii, 1917–1958. Moskva, Izd-vo Vostochnoi Lit-ry, 1959. 189p.   **DC247**

Comp. by A. K. Sverchevskaia and T. P. Cherman.

Bibliography of scientific and popular Soviet writings on Turkey and Turkology, and of Turkish authors translated into Russian.

UKRAINE

Ukraine: a concise encyclopaedia, prep. by Shevchenko Scientific Society, ed. by Volodymyr Kubijoryc. Foreword by Ernest J. Simmons. Pub. for the Ukrainian National Association. Toronto, Univ. of Toronto Pr., 1963– . v.1– . il. (In progress)   **DC248**

Intended to "translate, supplement, expand, edit and bring up to date the material contained in the *Entsyklopedia ukrainoznavstva* [3v.] published in Ukrainian in 1949–52."— *Introd.*

UNION OF SOVIET SOCIALIST REPUBLICS

Guides

Morley, Charles. Guide to research in Russian history. Syracuse, N.Y., Syracuse Univ. Pr., 1951. 227p. **DC249**

Designed primarily to serve as a handbook in Russianhistory seminars. Includes materials in Russian and in western European languages. Although out of date, this handbook has not been entirely superseded.

Bibliography

Akademiia Nauk SSSR. Fundamental'naia Biblioteka Obshchestvennykh Nauk. Istoriia SSSR; ukazatel' sovetskoi literatury za 1917–1952 gg. Moskva, 1956–58. v.1–2. (In progress)   **DC250**

v.1, Istoriia SSSR s drevneishikh vremën do vstupleniia Rossii v period kapitalizma; v.2, Istoriia SSSR v period kapitalizma 1861–1917.

—— —— Prilozhenie. Skhema klassifikatsii. Vspomogatel'nye ukazateli. Moskva, 1956–58. v.1–2. (In progress)

A major bibliography of Soviet historical writing, published between 1917 and 1952, on Russian history. Separate appendix volumes contain an outline of the classification, and name, subject, and other indexes. Planned in three main chronological divisions.

Dmitrieva, R. P. Bibliografiia russkogo letopisaniia. Izd-vo Akademii Nauk SSSR, 1962. 352p.   **DC251**

A comprehensive bibliography of editions of the early Russian chronicles and of the historical and literary commentary and research concerning them. Russian, Ukrainian, and Belorussian publications of the years 1674–1917; Soviet work for the period 1918–1959; and selected foreign publications are included. Chronologically arranged, with various indexes.

Grierson, Philip. Books on Soviet Russia, 1917–1942; a bibliography and a guide to reading. London, Methuen, 1943. 354p.   **DC252**

An annotated, classified guide to books and pamphlets on all phases of life in Soviet Russia, most of which were published in Great Britain. Includes a few works published in the United States and the Soviet Union, and some in languages other than English. Author index.

Continued in *Slavonic and East European review,* irregularly, between Jan. 1946 and June 1951.

Horecky, Paul L. Basic Russian publications; an annotated bibliography on Russia and the Soviet Union. Chicago, Univ. of Chicago Pr., 1962. 313p.   **DC253**

—— Russia and the Soviet Union; a bibliographic guide to Western-language publications. Chicago, Univ. of Chicago Pr., 1965. 473p.   **DC254**

Companion volumes of selective bibliography representing the judgments of numerous area-study specialists and providing a " . . . rigorously pruned inventory of Russian and Western publications . . . "—*Introd.* Major sections are: General reference aids and bibliographies; The land; The people: ethnic and demographic features; The nations; Civilizations and politics; History; The State; The economic and social structure; The intellectual and cultural life. Works relevant to the organizational, research, and socio-economic aspects of science and technology are represented.

Mezhov, Vladimir Izmailovich. Russkaia istoricheskaia bibliografiia, 1800–54. St. Petersburg, Sibiriakov, 1892–93. 3v.   **DC255**

Added title page in French: Bibliographie des livres et articles russes d'histoire et sciences auxiliaires de 1800–1854 incl.

Contents: v.1, Documents historiques et histoire politique de la Russie; v.2, Biographies. Sciences auxiliaires: généalogie, la science héraldique, chronologie, archéologie, paléographie, numismatique, sphragistique, mythologie; v.3, Géographie, hydrographie, orographie, cartographie, voyages, statistique, éthnographie, histoire des cultes et de l'église, agiologie, histoire de l'instruction publique.

34,994 entries. No index.

Continued by:

Lambin, Petr Petrovich and **Lambin, Boris Petrovich.** Russkaia istoricheskaia bibliografiia, 1855–64. St. Petersburg, Akademii Nauk, 1861–84. 10v. Annual.   **DC256**

Continued by:

Mezhov, Vladimir Izmailovich. Russkaia istoricheskaia bibliografiia, 1865–76. St. Petersburg, Akademii Nauk, 1882–90. 8v.   **DC257**

Classified with subject indexes.

Moscow. Gosudarstvennaia Publichnaia Istoricheskaia Biblioteka. Bibliografiia russkoi bibliografii po istorii SSSR; annotirovannyi perechen' bibliograficheskikh ukazatelei, izdannykh do 1917 g. Moskva, Izd-vo Vsesoiuznoi Knizhnoi Palaty, 1957. 195p.   **DC258**

An annotated list of bibliographies, published prior to 1917, on the subject of Russian history, with chapters on bibliographies of society publications, indexes to historical journals and to historical articles in general journals, and bio-bibliography of historians.

Dissertations

Dossick, Jesse John. Doctoral research on Russia and the Soviet Union. N.Y., New York Univ. Pr., 1960. 248p.   **DC259**

Arranged by subject field; in each section lists American and Canadian dissertations followed by "Aids to further research." Separate sections on British dissertations, and bibliography of bibliographies of doctoral dissertations. No index.

Continued by the author's "Doctoral dissertations on Russia and the Soviet Union accepted by American, British and Canadian Universities, 1960–1964," *Slavic review* 23:797–812. Dec. 1964.

Abstract journals

Soviet periodical abstracts. Soviet society. v.1– . May 1961– . N.Y., Slavic Languages Research Inst., 1961– . Quarterly.   **DC260**

v.1 issued as *Selective Soviet annotated bibliographies; Soviet society,* by the Institute, formerly named Soviet and East European Research and Translation Service.

Abstracts selected articles from "current Soviet periodicals on matters concerning education, sociology, philosophy, public administration and non-governmental institutions."—*Publisher's note.* Cites available translations.

For *Soviet periodical abstracts: Asia, Africa and Latin America, see DA20.*

Archives

Gosudarstvennye arkhivy Soiuza SSR; kratkii spravochnik. Pod red. G. A. Belova [i dr.]. Moskva, 1956. 507p.   **DC261**

At head of title: Glavnoe Arkhivnoe Upravlenie.

A general guide to government archives, federal and regional, in the USSR. Name, address, and brief historical note on each archive are followed by a general description of the type and extent of documentary material, its chronological limits, and the names of some individuals whose papers or collections are included. Contains a list of archives omitted from the Guide, a bibliography of publications between 1941 and 1956, and a name index.

Union of Soviet Socialist Republics. Glavnoe Arkhivnoe Upravlenie. Katalog arkhivovedcheskoi literatury i sbornikov dokumentov, 1960–1963 gg. Pod red. I. N. Firsova. Sost. S. V. Nefedova i dr. Moskva, 1964. 140p.   **DC262**

A bibliographic index to archival publications and to the literature pertaining to archival affairs in the Soviet Union. Combines and continues chronologically:

—— Katalog arkhivovedcheskoi literatury 1917–1959 gg. Pod red. A. I. Loginovoi i dr. Moskva, 1961. 191p.   **DC263**

—— Katalog sbornikov dokumentov, izdannykh arkhivnymi uchrezhdeniiami SSSR, 1917–1960 gg. Pod red. A. I. Loginovoi i dr. Moskva, 1961. 110p.   **DC264**

Encyclopedias and handbooks

Florinsky, Michael T. McGraw-Hill encyclopedia of Russia and the Soviet Union. N.Y., McGraw-Hill, 1961. 624p. il.   **DC265**

Designed primarily for the general reader; treats all aspects of Russian life and history from medieval times to the flights of the cosmonauts. Many articles are written and signed by specialists, some with brief bibliographies of works in English. Includes a great number of biographical and geographical entries, as well as longer articles on special subjects in Russian economics, government, history, culture, and science.

Maxwell, Robert. Information U.S.S.R., an authoritative encyclopaedia about the Union of Soviet Socialist Republics. Oxford, N.Y., Pergamon Pr., 1962. 982p. (Countries of the world information ser., v.1) **DC266**

"Pages 1–763 in this volume were translated from volume 50 of the *Great Soviet Encyclopaedia* by J. T. McDermott," and, therefore, reflect the Soviet viewpoint.

YUGOSLAVIA

Bibliography

Informatsionnyi ukazatel' bibliograficheskikh spiskov i kartotek, sostavlennykh bibliotekami Sovetskogo Soiuza. Moscow, 1957– . Semimonthly. **DC267**

Continues *Vazhneishie bibliograficheskie raboty bibliotek,* issued 1943–48.

For full information *see* AA52.

Encyclopedias

Enciklopedija jugoslavije. Zagreb, Leksikografski Zavod, 1955–62. v.1–5. il. (In progress) **DC268**

v.1–5, A–Mak.

A well-reproduced encyclopedia dealing with the life and culture of the Yugoslav peoples. Articles, many of considerable length, are signed and include bibliographies. Illustrations and maps are excellent.

D D

Africa

GENERAL WORKS

Bibliography

Africa bibliography series: ethnography, sociology, linguistics and related subjects. (Based on the bibliographical card index of the International African Institute) Comp. by Ruth Jones. London, Internat. African Inst., 1958– . v.3,4,6,7. (In progress) **DD1**

Each volume lists books and periodical articles—grouped first by geographic heading, then subdivided by subject—and includes an author index and one of ethnic and linguistic names.

v.1, Africa (general). (In prep.)
v.2, North Africa. (In prep.)
v.3, North-east Africa. 1959. 51p.
v.4, West Africa. 1958. 116p.
v.5, West Central Africa. (In prep.)
v.6, East Africa. 1960. 62p.
v.7, South-east Central Africa and Madagascar. 1961. 53p.
v.8, South Africa. (In prep.)

Bruel, Georges. Bibliographie de l'Afrique Équatoriale Française. Paris, Larose, 1914. 326p. **DD2**

A comprehensive bibliography of more than 7000 titles in French.

Collins, Robert O. and **Duignan, Peter.** Americans in Africa; a preliminary guide to American missionary archives and library manuscript collections on Africa. Stanford, Calif., Hoover Inst., 1963. 96p. (Hoover Inst. bibliographical ser., 12) **DD3**

A listing, by institution, of missionary archives and library collections, giving descriptions of their holdings.

Fontán Lobé, Juan. Bibliografía colonial; contribución a un índice de publicaciones africanas. Madrid, "Selecciones Gráficas," 1946. 669p. (Ediciones de la Dirección General de Marruecos y Colonias) **DD4**

An alphabetical catalog of nearly 17,000 titles of books and periodical articles in various languages. Particularly rich in Spanish and Portuguese materials. Geographical and subject indexes.

Holdsworth, Mary. Soviet African studies, 1918–1959; an annotated bibliography. Oxford, distr. for the Royal Institute of International Affairs by the Oxford Univ. Pr., 1961. 2 pts. in 1v. (Chatham House memoranda) **DD5**

Contents: pt.1, General functional studies; pt.2, Regional studies.

Classed arrangement of some 500 items: books, articles, reports, etc. Most are annotated, many extensively. Author and subject indexes.

Howard University. Library. The Moorland Foundation. A catalogue of the African collection in the Moorland Foundation, comp. by students in the Program of African studies, ed. by Dorothy B. Porter. Wash., Howard Univ. Pr., 1958. 398p. **DD6**

A classified list of 4865 book and pamphlet titles, with supplementary lists of periodicals and newspapers.

International African Institute. Select annotated bibliography of tropical Africa, comp. . . . under the direction of Daryll Forde. N.Y., Twentieth Century Fund, 1956. [v.p.] **DD7**

An extensive bibliography of books and periodical articles covering many aspects of the life of the region. Sections done separately by specialists with considerable variation of presentation. No indexes.

Royal Commonwealth Society, London. Library. Subject catalogue of the library . . . by Evans Lewin. v.1, British Empire generally, and Africa. [London, Soc.], 1930. 139p., 582p., cxxiiip. **DD8**

A comprehensive bibliography of materials about Africa. For description of complete set *see* DC157.

U.S. Library of Congress. European Affairs Division. Introduction to Africa; a selective guide to background reading. [Prep. by Helen F. Conover] Wash., Univ. Pr. of Wash., D.C., 1952. 237p. **DD9**

An annotated list for the layman, selected to provide background reading on the different countries of Africa.

U.S. Library of Congress. Reference Dept. Research and information on Africa; continuing sources. Wash., 1954. 70p. **DD10**

A revision of a working paper issued 1952. "Its aim is to record sources that serve the purposes of research and scholarship and to indicate periodical publications offering information to the general reader and to such specialized interests as missionary, business and educational groups."—*Introd.*

Dissertations

Deutsche Afrika Gesellschaft, Bonn. Deutsche Dissertationen über Afrika; ein Verzeichnis für die Jahre 1918–1959. Zusammengestellt von Jochen Köhler. Hrsg. vom Wissenschaftlichen Ausschuss durch H. Abel, E. Ackermann, [und] W. Fröhlich. Bonn, Kurt Schroeder, 1962. unpaged. **DD11**

A classified list of nearly 800 items. Catchword and author indexes.

Standing Conference on Library Materials on Africa. Theses on Africa accepted by universities in the United Kingdom and Ireland. Cambridge, Heffer, 1964. 74p. **DD12**

Arranged by region and country, with subject subdivisions. Author index. 1142 items covering the period 1920–62.

U.S. Library of Congress. African Section. A list of American doctoral dissertations on Africa. Wash., General Reference and Bibliography Division. Reference Dept., Lib. of Congress, 1962. 69p. **DD13**

A listing of more than 700 dissertations, arranged alphabetically by author, with catchword subject index.

Periodicals and newspapers

Duignan, Peter and **Glazier, Kenneth M.** A checklist of serials for African studies, based on the libraries of the Hoover Institution and Stanford University. Stanford, Calif., Hoover Inst., 1963. 104p. (Hoover Inst. bibliographical ser., 13) **DD14**

Lists more than 1400 serial publications: periodicals, newspapers, monographic series, annual reports, yearbooks, government debates, etc.

U.S. Library of Congress. Africana Section. Serials for African studies, comp. by Helen F. Conover. Wash., 1961. 163p. **DD15**

An alphabetical listing of more than 2000 serials, giving information on beginning date, frequency, address, Library of Congress holdings, etc.

U.S. Library of Congress. Serial Division. African newspapers in selected American libraries. 2d enl. ed. Wash., 1962. 68p. **DD16**

For annotation *see* AG13.

Current surveys

Africa diary. v.1, July, 1961– . New Delhi, Africa Publ., 1961– . Weekly, with quarterly and annual indexes. Loose-leaf. **DD17**

Hari Sharan Chhabra, ed.
Subtitle on cover: Weekly record of events in Africa, with index.
Countries are arranged alphabetically, followed by a general section for the continent as a whole.

African abstracts: a quarterly review of ethnological, social and linguistic studies appearing in current periodicals. v.1, Jan. 1950– . London, Internat. African Inst., with the assistance of UNESCO, 1950– . Quarterly. **DD18**

Title also in French.
Subtitle varies slightly.
Gives abstracts of articles from some 200 periodicals published in various parts of the world in many languages. Some of the abstracts are in English, some in French.

African recorder; a fortnightly record of African events with index, v.1, 1962– . New Delhi (6, Dr. Rajendra Prasad Rd.), 1962– . Fortnightly, with semiannual and annual indexes. Loose-leaf. **DD19**

M. Henry Samuel, exec. ed.
Summaries of events are entered under country (the countries arranged alphabetically), with an added section for events relating to "Africa outside Africa."

Encyclopedias and handbooks

Legum, Colin. Africa: a handbook to the continent. London, Anthony Blond, 1961. 553p. il. **DD20**

Arranged by geographic areas; gives political and economic information for each country, with a few biographical sketches and a bibliography.

Special sections treat the attitudes of other countries to African art, literature, education, etc.

Meyers Handbuch über Afrika. Hrsg. und bearb. von der Fachredaktion des Bibliographischen Instituts, unter Mitarbeit von Lutz Heck [and others]. Mannheim, Bibliographisches Inst., 1962. 779p. il., maps. **DD21**

A small, classified encyclopedia, with sections on geography, ethnography, language, economy, culture, etc. of the continent as a whole, followed by a listing by country with tabulated information on geographic, economic, and political factors for each.

Schnee, Heinrich. Deutsches Kolonial-Lexikon. Leipzig, Quelle, [c1920]. 3v. il. **DD22**

A very complete encyclopedia on the former German colonies in Africa: their topography, history, biography, natural resources, agriculture, products, native races, religions, flora, fauna, etc. Many excellent illustrations, signed articles, and bibliographies.

Atlases

Fage, John D. An atlas of African history. London, E. Arnold, 1958. 64p. maps. 28cm. **DD23**

An atlas designed to show the historical development of Africa from approximately the 4th century. Covers all sections. Outline maps.

AFRICA, NORTHERN

Blaudin de Thé, Bernard. Essai de bibliographie du Sahara français et des régions avoisinantes, éd. avec le concours de l'Organisation Commune des Régions Sahariennes. 2. éd. Paris, Arts et Métiers Graphiques, Librairie C. Klincksieck, 1960. 258p. **DD24**

1st ed. 1959. This edition has been somewhat rearranged and enlarged.

In two parts: pt.1 is a partial reprint of *Les territoires du sud de l'Algérie,* 3. pt. (Alger, 1930), with titles arranged chronologically under classification headings; pt.2, also classified but with titles arranged alphabetically by author, lists books and articles published through 1958. Materials are preponderantly in French, totaling some 9300 items. Author index.

France. Armée. État-major. Service Historique. L'Afrique française du nord. Bibliographie militaire des ouvrages français ou traduits en français et des articles des principales revues françaises relatifs à l'Algérie, à la Tunisie et au Maroc de 1830 à 1926. Paris, Impr. Nationale, 1930–35. 4v. **DD25**

A comprehensive bibliography, annotated and classified. In v.1–2, *L'Algérie,* the arrangement in each class is alphabetical by author; in v.3–4, *La Tunisie,* it is chronological by date of publication.

v.1–2 contain works published from 1830 to 1926; v.3–4, publications issued up to 1927, and those published prior to 1830, as well.

U.S. Library of Congress. Division of Bibliography. North and northeast Africa; a selected, annotated list of writings, 1951–1957, comp. by Helen F. Conover. Wash., 1957. 182p. **DD26**

An annotated list of almost 350 items which, with the companion volume, *Africa south of the Sahara* (DD32), forms a supplement to the Library's 1952 bibliography, *Introduction to Africa* (DD9). The present volumes, however, are considerably more comprehensive in coverage than the original.

AFRICA, SOUTHERN

Bibliography

Bibliographie ethnographique de l'Afrique sud-Saharienne, 1925/30– . Tervuren, Belgie, Koninklijk Museum voor Midden-Africa, 1932– . Annual (Irregular).
DD27

Title varies: 1925–59, *Bibliographie ethnographique du Congo Belge et des régions avoisinantes* (varies slightly). 1945/46– , comp. by Olga Boone.

An annotated bibliography of books and articles in various languages dealing with life and culture in sub-Sahara Africa. Annotations are in French.

Glazier, Kenneth M. Africa south of the Sahara; a select and annotated bibliography, 1958–1963. Stanford, Calif., Hoover Inst. on War, Revolution, and Peace, Stanford Univ., 1964. 65p. (Hoover Inst. bibliographical ser., 16)
DD28

150 annotated titles, with quotations from and references to book reviews. Limited to books in English, published 1958–63.

Northwestern University, Evanston, Ill. Library. Catalog of the African collection. Boston, Mass., G. K. Hall, 1962. 2v.
DD29

Reproduction of the author-title card catalog of the African collection of some 21,500 volumes, dealing primarily with Africa south of the Sahara, and surrounding islands. Especially strong in anthropology, linguistics, history, political science, travel, economics, health, demography, and the new African literatures.

Roberts, E. S. Preliminary finding-list of southern African pamphlets in the University of Cape Town libraries. Cape Town, Univ. of Cape Town libraries, 1959. 203p. (Univ. of Cape Town Libraries. Varia ser. I)
DD30

A classified listing of the rather elusive pamphlet material on sub-Sahara Africa, not limited by language or period. No index.

South African Public Library, Cape Town. A bibliography of African bibliographies, covering territories south of the Sahara. 4th ed. (Rev. to Nov. 1960) Cape Town, 1961. 79p. (Its Grey bibliographies, no.7)
DD31

3d ed. 1955. Earlier editions by P. Freer, D. H. Varley, and A. M. Lewin Robinson.

The area covered is limited to Africa south of the Sahara, and for the most part only bibliographies of some length and substance are included. The 4th edition is considerably enlarged.

U.S. Library of Congress. African Section. Africa south of the Sahara; a selected, annotated list of writings, comp. by Helen F. Conover. Wash., 1963. 354p.
DD32

Supersedes earlier editions.

An annotated bibliography of more than 3000 items, dealing with all aspects of life in Africa south of the Sahara.

Current

United States and Canadian publications on Africa. 1960– . Stanford, Calif., Hoover Inst., 1962– . Annual.
DD33

1960, issued by the African Section of the Library of Congress.

Lists books, pamphlets, and periodical articles on Africa south of the Sahara, in two main sections: (1) topics, and (2) specific regions. Author index.

Encyclopedias

Rosenthal, Eric. Encyclopaedia of southern Africa. 2d ed. London, N.Y., Frederick Warne, 1964. 604p. il., maps.
DD34

1st ed. 1961.

An alphabetical encyclopedia treating the history, biography, literature, geography, geology, natural history, social life and customs, etc. of southern Africa, comprising South Africa, Northern and Southern Rhodesia, Nyasaland, South-West Africa, Mozambique, and the High Commission Territories of Basutoland, Swaziland, and Bechuanaland.

AFRICA, WEST

Joucla, Edmond A. Bibliographie de l'Afrique occidentale française. . . . Paris, Soc. d'Édit. Géographiques, Maritimes et Coloniales, 1937. 704p. (Bibliographie générale des colonies françaises par G. Grandidier et E. A. Joucla)
DD35

An extensive bibliography of books and articles, primarily in French, arranged alphabetically by author.

Rydings, H. A. The bibliographies of West Africa. Ibadan, Univ. Pr., 1961. 36p.
DD36

Published on behalf of the West African Library Association.

Lists 50 bibliographies with descriptive annotations, including general African bibliographies—which include material on West Africa—and those of specific countries.

ANGLO-EGYPTIAN SUDAN

Hill, Richard Leslie. A bibliography of the Anglo-Egyptian Sudan, from the earliest times to 1937. . . . London, Oxford Univ. Pr., Milford, 1939. 213p.
DD37

Classified, with indexes of persons and subjects.

Includes books and periodical articles in various European languages.

el Nasri, Abdel Rahman. A bibliography of the Sudan, 1938–1958. London, pub. on behalf of the University of Khartoum by the Oxford Univ. Pr., 1962. 171p.
DD38

A classed bibliography designed to serve as a supplement to Hill, above, and arranged in the same way. Lists 2763 books and periodical articles.

CONGO

See also Rwandi, p.511.

Bibliographie du Congo Belge et du Ruanda-Urundi . . . par Théodore Heyse. Bruxelles, van Campenhout, 1946–53. (Cahiers belges et congolais, no. 4–7, 9–12, 16–22)
DD39

A series of subject bibliographies on various aspects of Belgian Congo affairs: economic, historical, literary, educational, cultural, etc.

Documentation générale sur le Congo et le Ruanda-Urundi, 1953–1960, par Théodore Heyse. Bruxelles, van Campenhout, 1956–60. (Cahiers belges et congolais, no. 26, 31, 34)
DD40

no.26, 1953–1955; no.31, 1955–1958; no.34, 1958–1960.

Bibliographies on documentation on the Congo and Ruanda-Urundi.

EGYPT

Bibliography

Annual Egyptological bibliography. Bibliographie égyptologique annuelle. 1947– . Comp. by Jozef M. A. Janssen. Leiden, Brill, 1948– . Annual. (International Association of Egyptologists) **DD41**

An alphabetical, annotated list, begun to fill the need of an annual bibliography caused by the cessation of the *"Bibliografia metodica degli studi di egittologia e di papirologia,"* published in *Aegyptus,* 1920–43.

Annotations are sometimes in English, sometimes in French.

—— Indexes, 1947–1956, by Jozef M. A. Janssen. Leiden, Brill, 1960. 475p.

Includes an alphabetical index by authors, giving titles and full information; followed by many specialized indexes, e.g., topography, pharaohs, hieroglyphs, divinities, Biblical references and Hebrew words, classical authors, subject index.

Bachatly, Charles. Bibliographie de la préhistoire égyptienne, 1869–1938. Cairo, Publ. de la Soc. Royale de Géographie d'Égypte, 1942. 77p. **DD42**

836 numbered entries of books and articles published 1869–1938.

Ibrahim-Hilmy, *Prince.* The literature of Egypt and the Soudan from the earliest times to the year 1885 [i.e., 1887] inclusive. A bibliography: comprising printed books, periodical writings and papers of learned societies; maps and charts; ancient papyri, manuscripts, drawings, etc. London, Trübner, 1886–88. 2v. **DD43**

An author list of some 20,000 titles, with some subject and form headings.

Lorin, Henri. Bibliographie géographique de l'Égypte. . . . [Le Caire], Impr. de l'Inst. Français d'Archéologie Orientale du Caire pour la Société Royale de Géographie d'Égypte, 1928. v.1. 472p. **DD44**

Contents: v.1, Géographie physique et géographie humaine.
Books and periodical articles in many languages.

Maunier, René. Bibliographie économique, juridique et sociale de l'Égypte moderne (1798–1916). . . . Le Caire, Impr. de l'Inst. Français d'Archéologie Orientale, 1918. 372p. (Soc. Sultanieh d'Économie Politique, de Statistique et de Législation. Travaux spéciaux . . . no.1) **DD45**

A classified bibliography of almost 6700 titles of books and periodical articles primarily in French, but with some in other European languages, on the economic, legal, and social activities of modern Egypt. Author and subject indexes.

New York. Public Library. Ancient Egypt; sources of information in the New York Public Library, comp. by Ida A. Pratt under the direction of Richard Gottheil. [N.Y.], Lib., 1925. 486p. **DD46**

"Reprinted with additions from the *Bulletin* of the New York Public Library, September 1923 to March and May 1924."

—— —— Supplement. 1925–1941. N.Y., Lib., 1942. 340p.

"Reprinted from the *Bulletin* of the New York Public Library, October 1941–July 1942."
An extensive, classified list with detailed index.

—— Modern Egypt; a list of references to material in the New York Public Library, comp. by Ida A. Pratt under the direction of Richard Gottheil. N.Y., Lib., 1929. 320p. **DD47**

"Reprinted from the *Bulletin* of the New York Public Library, September 1928 to April 1929."
A classified list of books and periodical articles on all aspects of modern Egypt in various languages. Author index.

Dictionaries

Posener, Georges. Dictionnaire de la civilisation égyptienne . . . , en collaboration avec Serge Sauneron et Jean Yoyotte. Paris, Fernand Hazan, 1959. 323p. il. **DD48**

A small, popular dictionary with copious illustrations in color and in black and white. Articles are signed. No bibliography.

Translated into English as *Dictionary of Egyptian civilization.* London, Methuen; N.Y., Tudor, 1962. 323p. il.

ETHIOPIA

Fumagalli, Giuseppe. Bibliografia etiopica. . . . Milano, Hoepli, 1893. 288p. **DD49**

Subtitle: Catalogo descrittivo e ragionato degli scritti pubblicati dalla invenzione della stampa fino a tutto il 1891, intorno alla Etiopia e regioni limitrofe.

A classified bibliography, with author index, of writings on Ethiopia, published from the 15th century to 1891.

Zanutto, Silvio. Bibliografia etiopica, in continuazione alla "Bibliografia etiopica" di G. Fumagalli. Roma, Sindicato Italiano Arti Grafiche, 1932–36. v.1–2. il. **DD50**

Pt.1, Bibliografia. 2d ed. 1936. 54p.; pt.2, Manoscritti etiopici. 1932. 178p.

Pt.1 continues the listing of materials on Ethiopia from 1891 to 1936; pt.2 lists Ethiopian manuscripts to be found in various libraries throughout the world.

GHANA

Cardinall, Allan Wolsey. Bibliography of the Gold Coast. Accra, Govt. Pr., [1932]. 384p. **DD51**

Issued as a companion volume to the census report of 1931. Lists more than 5000 items in many languages on the Gold Coast, Togoland, Dahomey, Upper Volta, and the Ivory Coast.

Johnson, Albert Frederick. A bibliography of Ghana, 1930–1961. Accra, pub. for the Ghana Library Board by Longmans, 1964. 210p. **DD52**

"In some respects a continuation of A. W. Cardinall's *A bibliography of the Gold Coast*" (DD51). Aims to be a comprehensive listing of publications on the Gold Coast and Ghana during the formative years 1930–61, with selected periodical articles.

A classified listing of more than 2600 items.

Kumasi, Ashanti. College of Technology. Library. Bibliography of Ghana, 1957–1959, comp. by G. M. Pitcher. Kumasi, 1960. 177p. **DD53**

A classified list of books, pamphlets, and articles published during the first three years of the independence of the state of Ghana. Author and title index.

LIBERIA

Solomon, Marvin David and **d'Azevedo, Warren L.** A general bibliography of the Republic of Liberia. Evanston, Ill., Northwestern Univ., 1962. 68p. (Northwestern Univ. Working papers in social science, no.1) **DD54**

" . . . a working draft . . . prior to the publication of a revised and amplified version."—*Introd.*

Photographic reproduction of cards listing books and periodical articles on Liberia: its territory and its peoples.

LIBYA

Hill, Roy Wells. A bibliography of Libya. [Durham, Eng.], Durham Colleges in the Univ. of Durham, Dept. of Geography, 1959. 100p. (Research papers, ser. no.1, 1959) **DD55**

A classified bibliography dealing primarily with the geography and economy of Libya. No index.

MADAGASCAR

Duignan, Peter. Madagascar (The Malagasy Republic); a list of materials in the African collections of Stanford University and the Hoover Institution on War, Revolution, and Peace. Stanford, Calif., Hoover Inst., 1962. 25p. (Hoover Inst. bibliographic ser., 9) **DD56**

A listing of documents, books, and monographs on Madagascar.

Grandidier, Guillaume. Bibliographie de Madagascar. Paris, Comité de Madagascar, 1905/06–57. 3v. **DD57**

Contents: [v.1], 1500–1904. 1905/06. 905p.; [v.2], 1904–1933. Paris, Soc. d'Édit. Géographiques, Maritimes et Coloniales, 1935. p.759–1350; v.3, 1934–1955. Tananarive, Inst. de Recherche Scientifique de Madagascar, 1957. p.1351–1910. Paged continuously, disregarding the supplement in v.1.

A comprehensive bibliography of manuscripts, books, pamphlets, and periodical articles published on Madagascar from its discovery in 1500 to 1955.

MALI

Brasseur, Paule. Bibliographie générale du Mali (anciens Soudan Français et Haut-Sénégal-Niger). Dakar, IFAN, 1964. 461p. map. (Inst. Français d'Afrique Noire. Catalogues et documents, XVI) **DD58**

A classified listing of 4873 numbered items—books and periodical articles—almost entirely in French, on all phases of life, culture, and history of the Sudan. Many titles are annotated.

MAURITIUS

Mauritius. Archives Dept. Bibliography of Mauritius (1502–1954), covering the printed record, manuscripts, archivalia and cartographic material, by A. Toussaint and H. Adolphe. Port Louis, Esclapon, 1956. 884p. **DD59**

A comprehensive bibliography of 8865 items, in six sections: (1) Early imprints issued in Mauritius, 1768–1954; (2) Periodicals, newspapers and serials, 1773–1954; (3) Government and semi-official publications issued in Mauritius and Great Britain, 1810–1954; (4) Publications relative to Mauritius issued abroad in English, French, Dutch, and other languages, 1600–1954; (5) Manuscripts and archivalia, 1598–1954; (6) Cartographic material, 1502–1954.

MOROCCO

Bibliographie marocaine, 1923–1933. Paris, Larose, 1937. 606p. (Repr. from Hesperis) **DD60**

Continued in *Hesperis* as follows: 1934/35 in v.26, 1939; 1936/39 in v.30, 1943; 1940/43 in v.34, 1947; 1944/47 in

v.38, 1951; 1948/51 in v.42, 1955; and in *Hesperis Tamuda,* 1952/53 in v.3, 1962.

A comprehensive bibliography of books and periodical articles on all phases of life in Morocco. Works are primarily in French.

NIGERIA

Harris, John. Books about Nigeria; a select reading list . . . 4th ed. Ibadan, Ibadan Univ. Pr., 1963. 52p. **DD61**

A reading list of recent and easily accessible works, comprising some "300 books, two dozen periodicals and 80 official reports," covering all phases of life in Nigeria. Useful until a more extensive bibliography can be compiled.

RWANDI

See also Congo, p.509.

Clement, Joseph. Essai de bibliographie du Ruanda-Urundi. [Usumbura?], 1959. 201p., xxiip. **DD62**

A classed listing of books and periodicals covering ethnology, history, government, geography, agriculture, science, etc. Author index.

SIERRA LEONE

Luke, Harry Charles. A bibliography of Sierra Leone, preceded by an essay on the origin, character and peoples of the colony and protectorate. 2d enl. ed. London, Oxford Univ. Pr., 1925. 230p. il. **DD63**

A classified bibliography, now somewhat out of date, but still useful for the large amount of material collected.

SOMALILAND

Somaliland, Italian. Camera di Commercio, Industria ed Agricoltura. Bibliografia somala. Mogadiscio, Scuola tipografia Missione Cattolica, 1958. 135p. il. **DD64**

A classified bibliography of 19th- and 20th-century materials on Italian Somaliland, primarily in Italian but with a few titles in other languages.

SOUTH AFRICA

Eybers, G. W. Select constitutional documents illustrating South African history, 1795–1910. London, Routledge, 1918. 582p. **DD65**

Selections with citations to sources.

Mendelssohn, Sidney. Mendelssohn's South African bibliography. . . . London, K. Paul, 1910. 2v. il. **DD66**

Subtitle: Being the *catalogue raisonné* of the Mendelssohn library of works relating to South Africa, including the full titles of the books, with synoptical, biographical, critical, and bibliographical notes on the volumes and their authors; together with notices of a large number of important works not as yet included in the collection . . . together with a bibliography of South African periodical literature, and of articles on South African subjects in periodical literature throughout the world; also a complete list of the British parliamentary blue-books on South Africa, a cartography of South Africa, etc.

SUDAN

See Anglo-Egyptian Sudan, p.509; Mali, p.511.

D E

Asia

GENERAL WORKS

Bibliography

American Oriental Society. Library. Catalog of the library; ed. by Elizabeth Strout. New Haven, Yale Univ. Pr., 1930. 308p. **DE1**

A list of about 5500 works.

Includes works, primarily in the western European languages, on all of Asia.

Asien-Bibliographie. 1.–6. Jahrg., Sept./Dez. 1949—Dez. 1954. Frankenau/Hessen, Asien-Bücherei, 1949–54. Quarterly. **DE2**

Lists new publications in the German language on all parts of Asia. Some entries annotated. Includes periodical articles. Superseded by:

Bibliographia asiatica. Frankenau/Hessen, Asien-Bücherei, 1953– . Jahrg.1– . Quarterly. **DE3**

Subtitle: Inhalt-Index: Beiträge aus periodischen Erscheinungen. Contributions out of periodicals. Sous les auspices des revues périodiques.

Lists periodical articles in German, English, and French. Includes the Near East, Middle East, and Far East.

Bibliography of Asian studies. 1956– . (In Journal of Asian studies, Sept. 1957–) Annual. **DE4**

Formerly *Far Eastern bibliography* in the *Far Eastern quarterly,* 1936–1955 (title varies slightly).

General editor: 1956–60, Howard P. Linton; 1961, Dorothea Scott; 1962– , Richard C. Howard.

An extensive, classified listing of books, pamphlets, and periodical articles on all phases of life and culture in Asia, in the English language. Coverage varies. Earlier volumes treated east and southeast Asia, but, beginning with 1956, coverage was extended to include also south and central Asia, the Philippines, etc.

Central Asian Research Centre. Bibliography of recent Soviet source material on Soviet Central Asia and the borderlands (including the Middle East). Jan./July 1957– . London, Centre, 1957– . no.1– . Semiannual. **DE5**

Issued as semiannual supplements to *Central Asian review.* Earlier bibliographies included in the *Central Asian review,* v.1–4.

Classified and annotated in English.

Orientalische Bibliographie, 1887–1911, 1926, pt.1. Berlin, Reuther, 1888–1922, 1928. v.1–26. **DE6**

No more published.

An important annual bibliography, including books, pamphlets, periodical articles, and reviews in the whole field of oriental studies: language, literature, geography, ethnology, folklore, history, etc.

For material before 1887, the following should be consulted: Julius Theodor Zenker's *Bibliotheca orientalis,* 1846–61; *Wissenschaftlicher Jahresbericht über die morgenländischen Studien,* 1859–81; Karl Friederici, *Bibliotheca orientalis,* 1876–83; *Litteraturblatt für orientalische Philologie,* 1883–86.

Royal Asiatic Society of Great Britain and Ireland. Library. Catalogue of printed books published before 1932 in the library. London, Soc., 1940. 541p. **DE7**

Dissertations

Columbia University. Libraries. East Asiatic Library. Columbia University masters' essays and doctoral dissertations on Asia, 1875–1956. N.Y., 1957. 96p. **DE8**

A classified list, with author and subject index.

Stucki, Curtis W. American doctoral dissertations on Asia, 1933–1962, including appendix of master's theses at Cornell University. Ithaca, N.Y., Southeast Asia Program, Dept. of Asian Studies, Cornell Univ., 1963. 204p. (Its Data paper, no.50) **DE9**

Includes the Far East, the Philippines, South Asia, and the Pacific Islands. Classified by region, by country, and by academic discipline; attempts to cover all doctoral studies in the fields of the social sciences and humanities. Author index.

An appendix lists "Cornell master's theses on Asia, 1933–1962."

Historiography

London. University. School of Oriental and African Studies. Historical writing on the peoples of Asia. London, Oxford Univ. Pr., 1961–62. 4v. **DE10**

Contents: D. G. E. Hall. Historians of South East Asia. 342p.; William Gerald Beasley and Edwin George Pulleyblank. Historians of China and Japan. 351p.; Cyril Henry Philips. Historians of India, Pakistan and Ceylon. 504p.; Bernard Lewis and P. M. Holt. Historians of the Middle East. 519p.

NEAR AND MIDDLE EAST

Bibliography

Bolton, Alexander Rollo Colin. Soviet Middle East studies: an analysis and bibliography. Oxford, distr. for the Royal Institute of International Affairs by the Oxford Univ. Pr., 1959. 8 pts. in 1v. (Chatham House memoranda) **DE11**

Contents: 1, Introduction and general indexes; 2, Arabs and the Arab world; 3, The Arabian peninsula; 4, Egypt; 5, Iraq; 6, Palestine (Israel) and Jordan; 7, The Sudan; 8, Syria and Lebanon.

Annotated listings of both book and periodical materials.

Cairo. Dar al-Katub al-Misriyah. Bibliographical lists of the Arab world. Cairo, Nat. Lib. Pr., 1960–63. no.1–10. (In progress) **DE12**

Contents: 1, Algeria; 2, Palestine; 3, North Region (Syria); 4, Lebanon; 5, Iraq; 6, Sudan; 7, Al Maghrib; 8, Tunisia; 9, Libya; 10, Arabian peninsula.

Each issue lists 19th- and 20th-century works in various languages. In English and Arabic.

—— A bibliography of works about Arab nationalism. Cairo, Nat. Lib. Pr., 1959. 74p., 150p.　**DE13**

—— A bibliography of works dealing with Arab struggle for freedom and unity. Cairo, Nat. Lib. Pr., 1959. 18p., 53p.　**DE14**

Each bibliography includes one section in English of books in English and French, and one in Arabic.

Ettinghausen, Richard. A selected and annotated bibliography of books and periodicals in Western languages dealing with the Near and Middle East; with special emphasis on medieval and modern times. (Completed Summer 1951) With suppl. (Dec. 1953). Wash., Middle East Inst., 1954. 137p.　**DE15**

Prepared under the Auspices of the Committee on Near Eastern Studies, American Council of Learned Societies.

The main section, p.1–111, originally published 1952, lists 1719 Western-language books, and the most important periodicals with very brief annotations. The supplement, Dec. 1953, p.113–37, adds 253 items.

Field, Henry. Bibliography on southwestern Asia. Coral Gables, Fla., Univ. of Miami Pr., 1953–59. v.1–6. **DE16**

For full record *see* CD24.

Macro, Eric. Bibliography of the Arabian peninsula. Coral Gables, Fla., Univ. of Miami Pr., 1958. 80p. **DE17**

A listing of more than 2300 titles of books and periodical articles in various languages.

Patai, Raphael. Jordan, Lebanon and Syria: an annotated bibliography. New Haven, Conn., Human Relations Area Files, 1957. (Distr. by Taplinger, N.Y.) 289p. (Behavior science bibliographies)　**DE18**

Includes books and articles, with (1) a section on the area generally, followed by (2) a section on each of the three countries.

Post-war bibliography of the Near Eastern mandates, 1919–1930. Stuart C. Dodd, gen. ed. Beirut, Syria, American Pr., 1932–36. 8 fascs. (American Univ. of Beirut. Publ. of the Faculty of Arts and Sciences. Social science ser., no.1)　**DE19**

Subtitle: A preliminary survey of publications on the social sciences dealing with Iraq, Palestine and Trans-Jordan, and the Syrian states, from Nov. 11, 1918 to Dec. 31, 1929, arranged in an alphabetical list by authors, with a limited index by subject matter, presented in . . . eight fascicles by languages . . . (A) Arabic; (A P) Arabic periodicals; (E) English; (F) French; (G) German (never printed?); (H) Hebrew; (I) Italian; (M) Miscellaneous oriental languages: Armenian, Kurdish, Persian, Syriac, Turkish.

Qubain, Fahim I. Inside the Arab mind; a bibliographic survey of literature in Arabic on Arab nationalism and unity, with an annotated list of English-language books and articles. Arlington, Va., Middle East Research Associates, 1960. 100p.　**DE20**

Annotations in both sections are in English. Arabic titles are translated into English.

U.S. Library of Congress. Orientalia Division. The Arabian peninsula; a selected, annotated list of periodicals, books, and articles in English, prep. under the direction of the Near East Section, Division of Orientalia. Wash., 1951. 111p.　**DE21**

At head of title: Library of Congress. Reference Dept.

Lists more than 700 titles in English in classified arrangement, emphasizing present conditions: geographical, ethnological, economic, and political.

Encyclopedias and handbooks

Ronart, Stephan and **Ronart, Nandy.** Concise encyclopaedia of Arabic civilization; the Arab East. Amsterdam, Djambatan, 1959; N.Y., Praeger, 1960. 589p.　**DE22**

Concise information on individual aspects of Arabic civilization, including persons, places, and specific terms. A second volume on the Arab West is planned.

Sharabi, Hisham B. A handbook on the contemporary Middle East; sectional introductions with annotated bibliographies. Wash., Georgetown Univ., 1956. 113p. **DE23**

"A handbook of current vital information and annotated listings of selected books and periodical literature."—*Pref.*

Covers Egypt, the Arabian peninsula, the Fertile Crescent, Iran, and Turkey.

Atlases

Atlas of the Arab world and the Middle East. With an introd. by C. F. Beckingham. London, Macmillan; N.Y., St. Martin's, 1960. 55p., [17]p. il., maps. 35cm.　**DE24**

Includes survey maps treating the territory as a whole, plus regional maps, both physical and thematic, dealing with individual nations or groups of nations. A section of photographs and text provides an introductory description of the area.

Beek, Martin A. Atlas of Mesopotamia; a survey of the history and civilisation of Mesopotamia from the Stone Age to the fall of Babylon. Tr. by D. R. Welsh; ed. by H. H. Rowley. London, N.Y., Nelson, 1962. 164p. il. 22 col. maps. 36cm.　**DE25**

Pub. also in German and in Dutch.

A historical survey with many plates showing the art and archaeology of the country, and historical maps.

ASIA, NORTHEAST

Kerner, Robert Joseph. Northeastern Asia, a selected bibliography; contributions to the bibliography of the relations of China, Russia and Japan, with special reference to Korea, Manchuria, Mongolia, and eastern Siberia, in oriental and European languages. . . . Berkeley, Univ. of Calif. Pr., 1939. 2v. (Publ. of the Northeastern Asia seminar of the Univ. of California; ed. by R. J. Kerner)　**DE26**

Classified, with full tables of contents and subject indexes. 14,000 titles, of which 10,000 are in Chinese, Japanese, Korean, and Russian. Uneven. Covers material, published through 1937, on all phases of life in northeastern Asia: geographic, political, economic, social, historical, cultural, international, etc.

Contents: v.1: pt.1, Asia, The Far East, The Pacific; pt.2, China, including Manchuria, Manchukuo, Mongolia, Northwestern China, Tibet; v.2: pt.1, The Japanese Empire, including Korea; pt.2, The Russian Empire and the Soviet Union in Asia and on the Pacific.

ASIA, SOUTH

Chicago. University. College. Introduction to the civilization of India; South Asia: an introductory bibliography. Prep. and ed. by Maureen L. P. Patterson and Ronald B. Inden. Chicago, Univ. of Chicago Pr., 1962. 412p. **DE27**

A listing of more than 4300 works, primarily in the English language, on India, Pakistan, Ceylon, and Nepal, classified under six major headings: (1) General; (2) History; (3) Social structure and organization; (4) Political and economic structure; (5) Religion and philosophy; (6) Literature, science, and the arts. Author and title index.

U.S. Library of Congress. Orientalia Division. Southern Asia accessions list. Wash., 1952–60. 9v. Quarterly; monthly.　**DE28**

Ceased publication.

Title varies: v.1–5, *Southern Asia; publications in Western languages, a quarterly accessions list.*

Includes books pertaining to south and southeast Asia accessioned by the Library of Congress, and, in later volumes, by cooperating libraries. Coverage varies somewhat but usually includes materials published since 1945 and selected articles from periodicals published since 1951, both in Western and Asian languages.

ASIA, SOUTHEAST

Bibliografiia IUgo-Vostochnoi Azii; dorevoliutsionnaia i sovetskaia literatura na russkom iazyke, original'naia i perevodnaia. Moskva, Izd-vo Vostochnoi Lit-ry, 1960. 255p. **DE29**

Half title: Akademiia Nauk SSSR. Institut Narodov Azii. Fundamental'naia Biblioteka Obshchestvennykh Nauk.

Comp. by A. M. Grishina and others.

A bibliography of publications, in the Russian language from the pre-Revolutionary and Soviet period through 1958, pertaining to southeast Asia, and of translations into Russian from the literature of the area. Chapters include Burma, British North Borneo, Vietnam, Indonesia, Cambodia, Laos, Malay and Singapore, Sarawak, Thailand, and the Philippines.

Embree, John Fee and **Dotson, Lillian Ota.** Bibliography of the peoples and cultures of mainland southeast Asia. New Haven, Yale Univ., 1950. 821p. (Yale Univ. Southeast Asia studies) **DE30**

An extensive bibliography which includes books and periodical articles in Western languages ranging in date from the 17th century to the present. Material is grouped under broad areas with references on race, racial history, migration, ethnology, cultural history, social organization and law, religion, folklore, language, and writing. Some titles are annotated. A detailed table of contents but no author index.

Hay, Stephen N. and **Case, Margaret H.** Southeast Asian history; a bibliographic guide. N.Y., Praeger, 1962. 138p. **DE31**

A selected, annotated guide to books, articles, and dissertations in English, with a few in French, arranged by country. The annotations are full and frequently refer to or quote from book reviews. Covers Burma, Cambodia, Ceylon, Indonesia, Laos, Malaya, North Borneo, Sarawak and Singapore, Philippines, Thailand, and Vietnam.

Irikura, James K. Southeast Asia: selected annotated bibliography of Japanese publications. New Haven, Conn., Southeast Asia Studies, Yale Univ., in association with Human Relations Area Files, 1956. (Distr. by Taplinger, N.Y.) 544p. (Behavior science bibliographies) **DE32**

Titles listed are from the libraries of Congress, Yale, Harvard, and Columbia. Areas covered include Burma, Indochina, Indonesia, Malaya, the Philippines, Thailand, and "general southeast Asia." Authors and titles are listed first in the roman alphabet and then in Japanese characters. Annotations are generally quite full.

Classed arrangement with author index.

Pelzer, Karl Josef. Selected bibliography on the geography of southeast Asia. New Haven, Conn., Southeast Asia Studies, Yale Univ., by arrangement with Human Relations Area Files, 1949–56. v.1–3. (Behavior science bibliographies) **DE33**

Contents: v.1, Southeast Asia—general. 1949; v.2, The Philippines. 1950; v.3, Malaya. 1956.

For full information *see* CK12.

U.S. Library of Congress. Orientalia Division. Southeast Asia; an annotated bibliography of selected reference sources, comp. by Cecil Hobbs. Rev. and enl. Wash., 1964. 180p. **DE34**

1st ed. 1952.

An introductory listing of sources for reading on various historical, political, economic, social, and cultural aspects of life in the countries of southeast Asia. 535 annotated entries.

AFGHANISTAN

Akram, Mohammed. Bibliographie analytique de l'Afghanistan. Préface de René Grousset. v.1. Paris, Centre de Documentation Universitaire, 1947. 504p. **DE35**

v.1, Ouvrages parus hors de l'Afghanistan.

No more published.

A mimeographed list of almost 2000 items published outside the country, including books, periodical articles, and manuscripts, in classed arrangement with author index.

Wilber, Donald N. Annotated bibliography of Afghanistan. [2d ed.] New Haven, Conn., Human Relations Area Files, 1962. (Distr. by Taplinger, N.Y.) 259p. (Behavior science bibliographies) **DE36**

1st ed. 1956.

A classified list of more than 1230 book and periodical items on physical, social, and humanistic aspects of the country. Author index. Includes material in Western languages and in Russian, Arabic, Persian, and Pushtu, published both within and without Afghanistan.

BURMA

New York University. Burma Research Project. Annotated bibliography of Burma. New Haven, Conn., Human Relations Area Files, 1956. (Distr. by Taplinger, N.Y.) 230p. (Behavior science bibliographies) **DE37**

Prepared by Burma Research Project at New York University, Frank N. Trager, director and editor; John N. Musgrave, Jr., chief bibliographer; Janet Welsh, assistant.

Primarily works in Western languages.

Main listing is by form, i.e., monographs, periodical articles, and government publications; these are followed by a classified listing giving only very brief entries and a reference by number to the full citation in the first list.

—— Japanese and Chinese language sources on Burma, an annotated bibliography. New Haven, Conn., HRAF [Human Relations Area Files], 1957. (Distr. by Taplinger, N.Y.) 122p. (Behavior science bibliographies) **DE38**

Prepared by Burma Research Project at New York University, Frank N. Trager, director and editor. Japanese sources, Hyman Koblin. Chinese sources, Lu-yu Kiang.

A companion volume to the *Annotated bibliography of Burma* noted above.

CHINA

Bibliography

Cordier, Henri. Bibliotheca sinica. Dictionnaire bibliographique des ouvrages relatifs à l'Empire Chinois. 2. éd., rev., corr., et considérablement augm. Paris, Guilmoto, 1904–8. 4v. **DE39**

—— —— Supplément. Paris, Geuthner, 1922–24.

An exhaustive listing of books and periodical articles in many languages, primarily of the 19th century, on all aspects of life in China. The lack of an author index, which previously seriously hampered the use of this work, has been at least temporarily filled by the issue in multigraphed form of:

——— ——— Author index to the Bibliotheca sinica (2d. éd. 4v. Paris, 1904–8. Supplément, 1v. Paris, 1924). Comp., issued, and distr. by the East Asiatic Library, Columbia University Libraries. N.Y., 1953. 84p.

Fairbank, John King and **Banno, Masataka.** Japanese studies of modern China; a bibliographical guide to historical and social-science research on the 19th and 20th centuries. Tokyo, Rutland, Vt., pub. for the Harvard-Yenching Institute by Tuttle, 1955. 331p. **DE40**

"Describes more than 1000 Japanese books and articles, which constitute the main body of Japanese research on modern China."—*Introd.*

Annotations are in English.

Fairbank, John King and **Liu, Kwang-Ching.** Modern China; a bibliographical guide to Chinese works, 1898–1937. Cambridge, Harvard Univ. Pr., 1950. 608p. (Harvard-Yenching Inst. studies, v.1) **DE41**

An annotated bibliography of Chinese works published 1898–1937, covering works of general reference; history, government, and law; foreign affairs; economics; social problems; cultural movements; education; intellectual and literary history; selected newspapers and learned journals.

Author and title are given both in Chinese characters and in the Wade-Giles romanization, with English translation. Annotations are in English.

Hucker, Charles O. China; a critical bibliography. Tucson, Univ. of Arizona Pr., 1962. 125p. **DE42**

An annotated bibliography planned as a selected and graded list of books and articles on various aspects of life in China, for students, teachers, and librarians.

Liu, Kwang-Ching. Americans and Chinese; a historical essay and a bibliography. Cambridge, Harvard Univ. Pr., 1963. 211p. **DE43**

The bibliography lists and locates manuscripts and archives; biographies; memoirs and published letters; newspapers and periodicals; and reference works. Treats traders and entrepreneurs; missionaries; and Chinese who emigrated to the United States.

Lust, John. Index sinicus: a catalogue of articles relating to China in periodicals and other collective publications, 1920–1955. Comp. with the assistance of Werner Eichhorn. Cambridge, [Eng.], Heffer, [1964]. 663p. **DE44**

A classified listing of almost 20,000 articles in Western languages, dealing with China, in periodicals, memorial volumes, proceedings of conferences and congresses, etc. Intended to fill the gap between Cordier (DE39), which lists works to 1924, and the *Monthly list of periodical articles on the Far East and South East Asia* of the London University School of Oriental and African Studies (1956–).

Also supplements T. L. Yüan's *China in Western literature* (DE47). Author and subject indexes.

Skachkov, Petr Emel'ianovich. Bibliografiia kitaia. Moskva, Izd-vo Vostochnoi Lit-ry, 1960. 690p. **DE45**

1st ed. 1932.

A bibliography of Russian-language publications from 1730 to 1957 on all phases of Chinese history and culture.

This edition is extensively revised, almost doubling the number of entries. Some newspaper articles and many reviews are included, but journal articles are omitted in some sections (e.g., Art). A single alphabetical index for authors, compilers, editors, translators, commentators, reviewers, and titles of anonymous books.

U.S. Dept. of the Army. Communist China: ruthless enemy or paper tiger. A bibliographic survey. Wash., 1962. 137p. maps. (DA pamphlet 20–61) **DE46**

A classified list of several hundred books and articles "prepared to fill the increasing need for information about Communist China."—*Foreword.* Most titles are in English and are well annotated. Several appendixes, including a bibliography on the Korean War, charts of Chinese government organization, and a number of maps.

Yüan, T'ung-li. China in Western literature: a continuation of Cordier's Bibliotheca sinica. New Haven, Conn., Far Eastern Publ., Yale Univ., 1958. 802p. **DE47**

For Cordier's *Bibliotheca sinica see* DE39.

This supplementary list covers books and monographs published from 1921 to 1957 in English, French, German, and Portuguese but does not include periodical articles (it is hoped that a bibliography of these may be published later).

The classified arrangement differs somewhat from that used by Cordier, and there is an author index.

"The bibliography represents a comprehensive survey of all types of writings on China, with no attempt to select or reject, but rather to record and describe."—*Pref.*

——— Economic and social development of modern China: a bibliographical guide. New Haven, Conn., Human Relations Area Files, 1956. (Distr. by Taplinger, N.Y.) 2 pts. (Behavior science bibliographies) **DE48**

Contents: pt.1, Economic development. 130p.; pt.2, Social development. 87p.

"The scope of this bibliography is limited to monographs and pamphlets published in English, French and German from the beginning of the present century down to the end of 1955."—*Introd.*

——— Russian works on China, 1918–1960, in American libraries. New Haven, Conn., Far Eastern Publ., Yale Univ., 1961. 162p. **DE49**

Under headings of China Proper, Northeastern Provinces, Mongolia, Sinkiang, Tibet, and Taiwan are listed 1348 Russian books and periodical titles, but not articles, on all phases of the life of these areas. Available translations are noted. No specific library locational symbols are given, but entries are in Library of Congress cataloging form and transliteration.

Historiography

Han, Yu-shan. Elements of Chinese historiography. Hollywood, Calif., W. M. Hawley, 1955. 246p. il. **DE50**

A manual in English for the student of Chinese history, referring to Chinese sources.

Dictionaries

Couling, Samuel. Encyclopaedia sinica. Shanghai, Kelly and Walsh; London, N.Y., Oxford Univ. Pr., 1917. 633p. **DE51**

A useful encyclopedia of information about China: its history, geography, literature, art, religions, institutions, flora, fauna, biography, etc. Most of the articles are by the editor, but there are articles by other authorities, some signed. Some bibliographies.

INDIA

Bibliography

Instituut Kern, Leyden. Annual bibliography of Indian archaeology, pub. with the aid of the Government of Netherlands India and with the support of the Imperial Government of India, 1926– . Leyden, Brill, 1928– . v.1– . Annual (Irregular). (1954/57, pub. 1962) **DE52**

An extensive, annotated bibliography, including books and periodical articles in various languages, and sometimes referring to reviews of books included.

Mahar, J. Michael. India; a critical bibliography. Tucson, Univ. of Arizona Pr., [1964]. 119p. **DE53**

A selected, graded, annotated list of books in English, treating India from early times to the present. Classified.

Royal Commonwealth Society, London. Library. Subject catalogue of the library. v.4. London, 1937. **DE54**

Includes India, p.112–491.

For description of complete set *see* DC157.

Sharma, Jagdish Saran. Indian National Congress; a descriptive bibliography of India's struggle for freedom. Delhi, S. Chand, 1959. 816p. (National bibliographies, no.3) **DE55**

A classified bibliography of materials largely in English and with many annotations, followed by an extensive "Chronology of selected events 1885–1958."

—— Mahatma Gandhi; a descriptive bibliography. Delhi, S. Chand, 1955. 565p. (National bibliographies, no.1) **DE56**

Issued also as thesis, Univ. of Michigan, 1954 (Univ. Microfilms. Publ. no.8408).

A comprehensive listing of materials (3671 items) by and about Gandhi.

Up-to-date encyclopaedia of all Indological publications published in India and other countries relating to ancient Indian learning: classified and arranged subjectwise in alphabetical order. Delhi, Mehar Chand Lachman Das, 1962. 385p., 39p. **DE57**

A bibliography attempting to list "all publications, ancient and modern, whether printed in India or abroad, in Sanskrit, Hindi, English, German, French, etc., dealing with ancient Indian learning."

Wilson, Patrick. Government and politics of India and Pakistan, 1885–1955: a bibliography of works in Western languages. Berkeley, Univ. of Calif., Inst. of East Asiatic Studies, South Asia Studies, 1956. 356p. (Modern India project. Bibliographical study, no.2) **DE58**

Includes books, pamphlets, and government documents, arranged by broad subject division with an index of authors and other names.

Chronology

Rickmers, C. Mabel Duff. The chronology of India, from the earliest times to the beginning of the sixteenth century. Westminster, Constable, 1889. 409p. **DE59**

Burgess, James. The chronology of modern India for four hundred years from the close of the fifteenth century, A.D. 1494–1894. Edinburgh, Grant, 1913. 483p. **DE60**

A list of historical events, in chronological order, with a minute alphabetical index; on the same general plan as Rickmers (DE59), the two together forming a continuous chronology of India from the earliest times to 1894.

Encyclopedias and handbooks

Balfour, Edward Green. Cyclopaedia of India and of eastern and southern Asia, commercial, industrial, and scientific; products of the mineral, vegetable and animal kingdoms, useful arts and manufactures. 3d ed. London, Quaritch, 1885. 3v. **DE61**

A comprehensive, alphabetically arranged encyclopedia still valuable for its geographical, historical, and ethnographical material.

Pañchānanadāsa Mukhopādhyāya. Indian constitutional documents (1600–1918). Comp. and ed. by Panchanandas Mukherji. 2d ed. enl. Calcutta, Thacker, Spink, 1918. 2v. (Indian citizen ser.) **DE62**

A documentary sourcebook: v.1 contains constitutional documents from Queen Elizabeth's charter in 1600 to 1918; v.2 contains the Government of India Acts, 1915 and 1916, with an introduction on the Constitution and English political institutions.

General histories

Cambridge history of India. Cambridge, Univ. Pr.; N.Y., Macmillan, 1922–37. v.1, 3–6. il. (In progress?) **DE63**

v.1, Ancient India, by E. J. Rapson; v.3, Turks and Afghans, by Sir Wolseley Haig; v.4, The Mughal period, by Sir Wolseley Haig; v.5, British India, 1497–1858, by H. H. Dodwell; v.6, Indian Empire, 1858–1918, by H. H. Dodwell.

v.5–6 published also as v.4–5 of the *Cambridge history of the British Empire* (DC156), and furnished in binding to match either set.

Written by authorities; extensive bibliographies, chronologies, etc.

—— Suppl. volume: The Indus civilization, by Sir Mortimer Wheeler. 1953. 98p. il.

In effect, an additional chapter to v.1 of the set, summarizing new evidence available in 1953.

Atlases

Davies, Cuthbert Collin. An historical atlas of the Indian peninsula. 2d ed. [Madras], Oxford Univ. Pr., 1959. 94p. 47 maps. 24cm. **DE64**

1st ed. 1949.

Black-and-white outline maps.

INDOCHINA

Boudet, Paul and **Bourgeois, Remy.** Bibliographie de l'Indochine française, 1913–1926. Hanoi, Impr. d'Extrême-Orient, 1929. 271p., 75p. **DE65**

—— —— 1927–1929. 240p.; 1930. 196p.; 1931–1935. 496p.

Lists books and periodical articles, on all phases of life in French Indochina.

Cordier, Henri. Bibliotheca indosinica; dictionnaire bibliographique des ouvrages relatifs à la péninsule indochinoise. . . . Paris, Impr. Nationale, Leroux, 1912–32. 4v. and index (309p.). (Publ. de l'École Française d'Extrême-Orient. v.15–18 bis) **DE66**

An extensive, classified bibliography of materials in Western languages on the peninsula formerly called Indo-China. The index volume contains both author and subject indexes.

U.S. Library of Congress. Reference Dept. Indochina; a bibliography of the land and people. Wash., 1950. 367p. **DE67**

Compiled by Cecil C. Hobbs, Grace Hadley Fuller, Helen Dudenbostel Jones, John T. Dorosh, I. Milton Sacks.

An area bibliography dealing with the broad aspects of life in Indochina: physical, historical, cultural, social, economic, and political developments. Emphasis is on publications issued since 1930, but some earlier ones are included. Cites works in Western, Russian, and Vietnamese languages.

INDONESIA

Bibliography

Chijs, Jacobus Anne van der. Proeve eener Ned. Indische bibliographie (1659–1870). . . . [Batavia, Bruining &

Wijt, 1875–1903] 325p. and 2 suppl.: 93p., 64p. (Verhandelingen van het Bataviaasch Genootschap van Kunsten en Wetenschappen, deel 37, 55) **DE68**

Basic list, 1659–1870. 325p.; the two supplements give additions and corrections for the years 1720–1870.

A chronological listing of works on the Netherlands East Indies, primarily in Dutch but with some works in other languages.

Hague. Koloniale Bibliotheek. Catalogus der Koloniale Bibliotheek van het Kon. Instituut voor de Taal-, Land- en Volkenkunde van Ned. Indië en het Indisch Genootschap, door G. P. Rouffaer en W. C. Muller. 'sGravenhage, Nijhoff, 1908–37. 1053p. and 3 suppl. **DE69**

Suppl. 1, 1915. 426p.; 2, 1927. 458p.; 3, 1937. 438p.

A classified catalog of a very extensive collection on colonial affairs, not only of the Netherlands East Indies, but of other colonies of other countries in various parts of the world.

Hooykaas, J. C. Repertorium op de koloniale litteratuur, of, Systematische inhoudsopgaaf van hetgeen voorkomt over de koloniën (beoosten de Kaap) in mengelwerken en tijdschriften van 1595–1865 uitg. in Nederland en zijne overzeesche bezittingen. . . . Amsterdam, van Kampen, 1874–80. 2v. **DE70**

Contents: 1. deel: I, Het land. II, Het volk; 2. deel: III, Het bestuur. IV. De wetenschap.

An extensive bibliography—listing more than 21,000 items—of Dutch materials on Dutch colonies throughout the world.

Kennedy, Raymond. Bibliography of Indonesian peoples and cultures. 2d rev. ed. Rev. and ed. by Thomas W. Maretzki and H. Th. Fischer. New Haven, Conn., Human Relations Area Files, 1962. 207p. maps. (Behavior science bibliographies. Southeast Asia Studies, Yale Univ.) **DE71**

1st ed. 1945; rev. 1955.

This edition "substantially the same. No new titles have been added," but format has been changed.

Concentrates on the peoples and cultures of the area and is mainly anthropological—including ethnography, archaeology, and linguistics—and sociological, including geography, education, economics, history, colonial administration, etc. Lists both books and periodical articles.

Repertorium op de literatuur betreffende de Nederlandsche koloniën, voor zoover zij verspreid is in tijdschriften en mengelwerken . . . Samengesteld door A. Hartmann. 'sGravenhage, Nijhoff, 1895–1935. 454p. and suppl. 1–8. **DE72**

Basic volume: East Indies, 1866–93; West Indies, 1840–93. Supplements 1–8: v.1, 1894–1900. 1901. 224p.; v.2, 1901–05. 1906. 233p.; v.3, 1906–10. 1912. 271p.; v.4, 1911–15. 1917. 378p.; v.5, 1916–20. 1923. 508p.; v.6, 1921–25. 1928. 522p.; v.7, 1926–30. 1935. 712p.; v.8, 1931–32. 1934. 189p.

A continuation of Hooykaas (DE70), treating the Dutch colonies in the East Indies and the West Indies, including a large amount of indexing of periodical and other analytical material, much of which is not easily available in other forms.

U.S. Library of Congress. General Reference and Bibliography Division. Netherlands East Indies: a bibliography of books published after 1930, and periodical articles after 1932 available in U.S. libraries. Wash., 1945. 208p. **DE73**

Classified with author index; lists material in many languages. Locates copies in more than 90 libraries.

Encyclopedias and handbooks

Daniel, Hawthorne. Islands of the East Indies, with six maps by Lucien G. Picard. N.Y., Putnam, [1944]. 266p. il., maps. **DE74**

A companion volume to the author's *Islands of the Pacific* (DG8). Gives geographical information—including size,

location, topography, climate, population, flora and fauna, and natural resources—of some 3000 islands that made up the Netherlands territories in the Far East; parts of New Guinea, Borneo, and Timor; and the Philippine Islands.

Encyclopaedie van Nederlandsch-Indië. 2. druk. met medewerking van verschillende geleerden ambtenaren en officieren. 'sGravenhage, Nijhoff, 1917–40. v.1–8, 9 (incompl.). **DE75**

v.1–4, A–Z; v.5–8. Suppl. 1–4. [v.9], Suppl. 5, Afl. 61–62.

An encyclopedia of the region: its geography, inhabitants, products, etc., as well as its history; includes biography. An excellent work, with authoritative articles by specialists and good bibliographies.

An abridged edition based upon v.1–4 is: *Beknopte encyclopaedie van Nederlandsch-Indië . . . bewerkt door T. J. Bezemer.* Nijhoff, 1921. 632p.

IRAN

Afshar, Iraj. A bibliography of bibliographies on Iranian studies. [Tihrān, 1964?] 217p. **DE76**

For annotation *see* BD992.

Elwell-Sutton, Laurence Paul. A guide to Iranian area study. Wash., Amer. Council of Learned Societies, 1952. 235p. **DE77**

Compiled under the auspices of the Committee on Near Eastern Studies of the American Council of Learned Societies.

Includes survey articles on the geography, population and language, social evolution, history, administration, economic structure, religion, intellectual development, literature and arts. These are followed by a Chronology, p.110–61, and a Bibliography, p.162–235.

New York. Public Library. List of works in the New York Public Library relating to Persia. N.Y., Lib., 1915. (Repr. from New York Public Library. Bull. Jan. 1915) 151p. **DE78**

A good basic collection, mainly in western-European languages, including many translations from the Persian.

Sabā, Mohsen. Bibliographie française de l'Īrān. Bibliographie méthodique et raisonnée des ouvrages français parus depuis 1560 jusqu'à nos jours. 2. éd. rev. et augm. Téhran, 1951. 297p. **DE79**

1st ed. 1936.

A comprehensive, classed list of books and periodical articles with author index.

U.S. Library of Congress. Reference Dept. Iran: a selected and annotated bibliography, comp. by Hafez F. Farman. Wash., 1951. 100p. **DE80**

—— —— Supplement. Taken from "The Danneshjoo," v.2–5. Comp. by Meer Nasser Sharify. Wash., Embassy of Iran, 1958. 36p.

Issued as 1v. by the Embassy of Iran. The first section is a reprint of an earlier work; the second—a supplement covering publications issued since 1950—appeared in *The Danneshjoo,* published by the Iranian Students' Association, New York.

A selected bibliography of publications mainly in Western languages with descriptive annotations. Emphasis is on works relating to the 19th and 20th centuries.

Wickens, G. M. and **Savory, R. M.** Persia in Islamic times; a practical bibliography of its history, culture and language . . . ed. by W. J. Watson. Montreal, Inst. of Islamic Studies, McGill Univ., 1964. 57p. **DE81**

Contents: (1) Works on Persia in languages other than the Persian; (2) Original Persian texts and translations into other languages.

Wilson, *Sir* **Arnold Talbot.** Bibliography of Persia. Oxford, Clarendon Pr., 1930. 253p. **DE82**

Lists books and periodical articles in the principal European languages, arranged alphabetically except that anonymous works are grouped under general subject headings, such as, Letters, Journals, Routes, etc. Also includes translations into European languages of original Persian works.

JAPAN

Guides

Hall, John W. Japanese history: a guide to Japanese reference and research materials. Ann Arbor, Univ. of Michigan Pr., 1954. 165p. (Center for Japanese studies. Bibliographical ser., 4) **DE83**

A bibliographic guide to Japanese history. Emphasis is on reference and research materials of recent publication dealing with the period before 1868.

In five major sections: (1) Bibliographies, (2) Reference works, (3) Historical sources, (4) Periodicals, and (5) Survey histories. Approximately 1550 entries.

—— —— Index. Prep. by the School of Oriental Studies, Univ. College, Canberra, Australia. [195?] 33p.

Webb, Herschel. Research in Japanese sources: a guide. N.Y., Columbia Univ. Pr., 1965. 170p. **DE84**

Published for the East Asian Institute, Columbia University.

A handbook designed as a beginner's guide to Japanese bibliography, particularly in the fields of the humanities and social sciences. Discusses: bibliography and general reference materials; problems of dates, chronology, weights, and measures; statistics; people's names, place-names; words and their meanings; source materials; laws and official sources, etc.

Bibliography, p.143–60.

Bibliography

Berlin. Japan-Institut. Bibliographischer Alt-Japan-Katalog, 1542–1853; bearb. und hrsg. vom Japan-Institut in Berlin und vom Deutschen Forschungsinstitut in Kyoto. Kyoto, Deutsches Forschungsinstitut, 1940. 415p. **DE85**

An excellent bibliography of older Western materials on Japan, giving complete bibliographical information and also location, in 1940, of copies in German and Japanese libraries.

Bibliografiia IAponii; literatura, izdannaia v Sovetskom Soiuze na russkom iazyke s 1917 po 1958 g. Moskva, Izd-vo Vostochnoi Lit-ry, 1960. 327p. **DE86**

Comp. by V. A. Vlasov and others.

Based on materials about Japan in the Lenin Library; lists documents, monographs, and articles in collections and journals published in Russian in the Soviet Union between 1917 and 1958.

Name index to the 6000 entries.

Borton, Hugh [and others]. A selected list of books and articles on Japan in English, French and German. Rev. and enl. Cambridge, Harvard Univ. Pr. for the Harvard-Yenching Institute, 1954. 272p. **DE87**

1st ed. 1940.

An annotated listing of almost 1800 items including, in classified groupings: bibliographies, reference works, periodicals, geography, history, World War II and the Occupation (1941–52), economics, government and politics, sociology and ethnology, education and journalism, mythology, religion, philosophy, language, literature, and art. Title and subject index.

Cordier, Henri. Bibliotheca japonica; dictionnaire bibliographique des ouvrages relatifs à l'Empire Japonais rangés par ordre chronologique jusqu'à 1870, suivi d'un

appendice renfermant la liste alphabétique des principaux ouvrages parus de 1870 à 1912. Paris, Leroux, 1912. 762col. (Publ. de l'École des Langues Orientales Vivantes. 5. sér., v.8) **DE88**

A chronological, annotated listing of materials in Western languages from pre–Marco Polo times to 1870. The appendix lists, alphabetically, the principal works published from 1870 to 1912.

Kokusai Bunka Shinkokai, Tokyo. K.B.S. bibliography of standard reference books for Japanese studies with descriptive notes. Tokyo, 1959–64. v.1–4, 6–8. (In progress) **DE89**

Contents: v.1, Generalia. 1959; v.2, Geography and travel. 1962; v.3$^{1-2}$, History and biography. 1963–64; v.4, Religion. 1963; v.6A, Language. 1961; v.6B, Literature, pt.1. 1962; v.7A, Arts and crafts. 1959; v.7B, Theatre, dance and music. 1960; v.8, Manners and customs, & folklore. 1961.

To be in about 10v. These are the first parts to appear of a classified and annotated bibliography of standard works and source materials in the vernacular. Titles are romanized, and annotations are in English.

Nachod, Oskar. Bibliographie von Japan, 1906–1937: Enthaltend ein ausführliches Verzeichnis der Bücher und Aufsätze über Japan, die seit der Ausgabe des zweiten Bändes von Wenckstern "Bibliography of the Japanese Empire" bis 1926 in europäischen Sprachen erschienen sind. . . . Leipzig, Hiersemann, 1928–40. v.1–6. **DE90**

v.1–2 also published with English title: *Bibliography of the Japanese Empire,* 1906–26. London, Goldston, 1928.

v.1–2, Books and articles, 1906–26. 1928; v.3, 1927–29. 1931; v.4, 1930–32, von Hans Praesent. 1935; v.5, 1933–35, von Hans Praesent und Wolf Haenisch. 1937; v.6, 1936–37, von Wolf Haenisch und Hans Praesent. 1940. Each volume includes some titles of earlier dates omitted from previous volumes.

A comprehensive, classified list, including books, pamphlets, and periodical articles; v.1–6 list a total of 33,621 items.

Silberman, Bernard S. Japan and Korea; a critical bibliography. Tucson, Univ. of Arizona Pr., 1962. 120p. **DE91**

"A selected annotated and graded guide to the most authoritative and available works on Japan and Korea."—*Foreword.*

A classified bibliography of Western-language materials (primarily English) in the humanities and social sciences, published since 1940.

Têng, Ssŭ-Yü. Japanese studies on Japan and the Far East; a short biographical and bibliographical introduction . . . With the collaboration of Masuda Kenji and Kaneda Hiromitsu. Hong Kong, Hong Kong Univ., Pr., 1961. 485p. **DE92**

Includes nearly 5000 books and articles by 760 Japanese scholars, arranged by subject (Humanities, Social science, Fine arts). Within each group, listing is alphabetical by author, for each of whom brief biographical information is noted. Titles are given in: (1) transliteration, (2) Japanese characters, and (3) English translation. Index of authors, subjects, and many titles.

Wenckstern, Friedrich von. Bibliography of the Japanese Empire; being a classified list of all books, essays and maps in European languages relating to Dai Nihon (Great Japan) published in Europe, America and in the East, 1859/93–1894/1906. Leiden, Brill, 1895; Tokyo, Maruya, 1907. 2v. **DE93**

v.1, Literature published 1859–93. 338p. Facsimile reprint of Leon Pagés. *Bibliographie japonaise.* Paris, 1859. 68p.; v.2, Literature published 1894–1906. 486p. Supplement to Pagés' *Bibliographie japonaise.* 28p. List of Swedish literature on Japan, by Valfrid Palmgren. 21p.

Continued by Nachod (DE90).

Archives

Uyehara, Cecil H. Checklist of archives in the Japanese Ministry of Foreign Affairs, Tokyo, Japan, 1868–1945; microfilmed for the Library of Congress 1949–1951. Wash., Photoduplication Service, Lib. of Congress, 1954. 262p. **DE94**

The documents are arranged in categories, the main series being from the Meiji-Taishō periods, 1868–1912, 1912–1926, and the Shōwa period, 1926–1945, with some additional archives. Analytical index.

Chronology

Kai, Miwa and **Yampolsky, Philip B.** Political chronology of Japan, 1885–1957. N.Y., East Asian Inst. of Columbia Univ., 1957. 63p. (Columbia Univ. East Asian Inst. Studies, no.5) **DE95**

Lists of cabinets, diet sessions, and other political data.

Encyclopedias and handbooks

Chamberlain, Basil Hall. Things Japanese; being notes on various subjects connected with Japan, for the use of travellers and others. 6th ed. rev. London, Kegan Paul, 1939. 584p. il. **DE96**

An alphabetical dictionary by large subjects, with index of smaller subjects; bibliographical references. The 6th edition contains revisions, additions, and supplementary material.

Some copies of this edition were censored by officials of the Imperial Japanese government, and p.11–12, 79–94, 247–52, and 345–46 were deleted.

Japan. National Commission for UNESCO. Japan: its land, people and culture. Rev. ed. Tokyo, Printing Bureau, Ministry of Finance, 1964. 885p., 200pl., maps. **DE97**

1st ed. 1958.

"Encyclopaedic in scope, covering all aspects of Japanese life together with its geographical, historical, social, economic and cultural backgrounds . . . "—*Pref.*

Joya, Moku. Mock Joya's Things Japanese. Tokyo, Tokyo News Service, 1958. 732p. **DE98**

An encyclopedic handbook on social life and customs, folklore, popular beliefs and traditions, fetes and festivals, etc.

Papinot, E. Historical and geographical dictionary of Japan. Ann Arbor, Mich., Overbeck Co., 1948. 842p. il. **DE99**

Lithoprinted from the original edition published at Yokohama by Kelly and Walsh in 1910, which was a translation of the earlier *Dictionnaire d'histoire et de géographie du Japon,* 1906.

An alphabetical arrangement of names, places, and events important in the history and geography of Japan.

Ramming, Martin. Japan-Handbuch; Nachschlagewerk der Japankunde. Im Auftrage des Japaninstituts Berlin. Berlin, Steiniger, [1941]. 740p. il. **DE100**

An alphabetical dictionary of things Japanese, including biography.

KOREA

Bibliography

Blanchard, Carroll H. Korean War bibliography and maps of Korea. [Albany, N.Y., 1964] 181p., maps. **DE101**

At head of title: Korean Conflict Research Foundation.

Pt.I is a subject listing of books; pt.II, an alphabetical list of books from foreign publishers; pt.III, a list of periodicals from which the subject listing of articles in pt.IV is drawn; pt.V presents 25 maps illustrating various areas and phases of the war. No index or list of subject headings used.

California. University. Institute of East Asiatic Studies. Korean studies guide, comp. by B. H. Hazard, Jr., [and others]. Ed. by Richard Marcus. Berkeley, Los Angeles, Univ. of Calif. Pr., 1954. 220p. maps. **DE102**

Lists works in Korean and Western languages with annotations. Classified arrangement, covering many phases of Korean life. Author and title indexes.

California. University. Institute of International Studies. East Asia Studies. Russian supplement to the Korean studies guide, comp. by Robert L. Backus. Berkeley, 1958. 211p. **DE103**

Attempts to cover, with some comprehensiveness, "books, monographs, periodical literature, bibliographies and indexes relative to Korea . . . published in Russia from mid-19th century to early 1956."—*Pref.*

Lists 893 items with annotations in English.

Courant, Maurice. Bibliographie coréenne; tableau littéraire de la Corée, contenant la nomenclature des ouvrages publiés dans ce pays jusqu'en 1890 ainsi que la description et l'analyse détaillées des principaux d'entre ces ouvrages. Paris, Leroux, 1894–96. 3v. il. (Publ. de l'École des Langues Orientales Vivantes. 3. sér., v.18–20) **DE104**

Contents: v.1, Enseignement, Étude des langues, Confucianisme, Littérature; v.2, Mœurs et coutumes, Histoire et géographie; v.3, Sciences et arts, religions, relations extérieures. Index.

———— —— Supplément (jusqu'en 1899). Paris, 1901. 122p. (Publ. de l'École des Langues Orientales Vivantes. 3. sér., v.21)

With the supplement, lists 3821 titles, many with critical and bibliographical annotations.

Harvard-Yenching Institute Library. A classified catalogue of Korean books in the Harvard-Yenching Institute Library at Harvard University. Cambridge, 1962. 194p. **DE105**

Lists 3160 Korean works.

Silberman, Bernard S. Japan and Korea; a critical bibliography. Tucson, Univ. of Arizona Pr., 1962. 120p. **DE106**

For full information *see* DE91.

U.S. Library of Congress. Reference Dept. Korea; an annotated bibliography of publications in Far Eastern languages, comp. under the direction of Edwin A. Beal, Jr., with the assistance of Robin L. Winkler. Wash., 1950. 167p. **DE107**

—— Korea; an annotated bibliography of publications in the Russian language, comp. by Albert Parry, John T. Dorosh, and Elizabeth Gardner Dorosh. Wash., 1950. 84p. **DE108**

—— Korea; an annotated bibliography of publications in Western languages, comp. by Helen Dudenbostel Jones and Robin L. Winkler. Wash., 1950. 155p. **DE109**

Annotated bibliographies of books and articles based on material in the Library of Congress, with, in the third publication, indication of location of some items in other American libraries.

Yang, Key Paik. Reference guide to Korean materials, 1945–1959. Wash., 1960. 131p. **DE110**

Thesis (M.S. in Library Science), Catholic Univ. of America.

A guide to some 800 items of reference and research importance selected from the Korean collection of the Library of Congress. Covers general reference materials and those in the social science fields. Titles are given in transliteration with English translation and often brief annotations.

Encyclopedias

Korea: its land, people, and culture of all ages. Seoul, Hakwon-sa, 1960. (Distr. by Hutchins Oriental Books, 1603 Hope St., South Pasadena, Calif.) 718p. il. **DE111**

A 1v. classified encyclopedia treating all aspects of the history, life, and culture of the Korean people.

LAOS

Lafont, Pierre Bernard. Bibliographie du Laos. Paris, École Française d'Extrême-Orient, 1964. 269p. (Publ. de l'École Française d'Extrême-Orient, v.50)   **DE112**

A classified listing of books and periodical articles on all phases of history, life, and culture of Laos. Titles are largely in French, but some material in English and other languages is included.

MALAYA

Cheeseman, Harold Ambrose Robinson. Bibliography of Malaya, being a classified list of books wholly or partly in English relating to the Federation of Malaya and Singapore. London, pub. for the British Association of Malaya by Longmans, 1959. 234p.   **DE113**

Includes some periodical references. Author index.

MALAYSIA

Tregonning, K. G. Malaysian historical sources; a series of essays on historical material mainly in Malaysia on Malaysia. Singapore, Dept. of History, Univ. of Singapore, 1962. 130p. il.   **DE114**

A guide to sources in Chinese, Arab-Persian, English, and Malay, with descriptions of newspapers, archives, etc.

MANCHURIA

Gibert, Lucien. Dictionnaire historique et géographique de la Mandchourie. Hong Kong, Impr. de la Soc. des Missions-Étrangères, 1934. 1040p. il.   **DE115**

Arranged alphabetically by French transcription, followed by Chinese characters. Includes persons, places, dynasties, etc.

U.S. Library of Congress. Reference Dept. Manchuria; an annotated bibliography, comp. by Peter A. Berton. Wash., 1951. 187p.   **DE116**

Includes works in Japanese, Chinese, Russian, English, and western European languages, with the largest number in Japanese.

NEPAL

Wood, Hugh Bernard. Nepal bibliography. Eugene, Ore., American-Nepal Educ. Foundation, 1959. 108p. **DE117**

Approximately 1000 items are listed, with emphasis on historical, political, social, and cultural aspects of Nepalese life.

PAKISTAN

Abernethy, George L. Pakistan; a selected, annotated bibliography. 2d ed. rev., with a suppl. for the period Feb. 1957 to Feb. 1960. N.Y., Amer. Inst. of Pacific Relations, 1960. 39p.   **DE118**

Separate lists of books, Pakistan government documents, and periodical articles, the last classified. The 2d edition adds a supplement, p.30–39. No index.

Ghani, A. R. Pakistan; a select bibliography. Lahore, Pakistan Assoc. for the Advancement of Science, Univ. Inst. of Chemistry, 1951. 339p.   **DE119**

English-language material (books, pamphlets, articles, unpublished dissertations, and theses) on Pakistan, before and after partition, arranged by broad subject. No index.

Maron, Stanley [and others]. Annotated bibliography for Pakistan: sociology, economics and politics. Berkeley, Human Relations Area Files, South Asia Project, Univ. of Calif., 1956. 64p.   **DE120**

A useful bibliography.

PALESTINE

Bibliography

Royal Commonwealth Society, London. Library. Subject catalogue. v.4. London, 1937.   **DE121**

For description of complete set *see* DC157.

Thomsen, Peter, Die Palästina-Literatur; eine internationale Bibliographie in systematischer Ordnung mit Autoren- und Sachregister. . . . Leipzig, Hinrich, 1911–56. v.1–6.   **DE122**

v.1 (2. Ausg.), 1895–1904; v.2, 1905–09; v.3, 1910–14; v.4, 1915–25; v.5, 1925–34; v.6, 1935–39.

v.6, pub. 1953–56, ed. by Fritz Maass and Leonhard Rost.

1st edition of v.1 (1908) has title *Systematische Bibliographie der Palästina-Literatur.*

A very comprehensive index to book and periodical literature in many languages.

—— Bd.A, Die Literatur der Jahre 1878–1894. 1957–60. 905p. (In progress)

Issued in 3 Lfg. Ed. by Otto Eissfeldt and Leonhard Rost. A new series, working backward from 1895.

Encyclopedias and handbooks

Press, Jesaias. Eres-Yisrāēl. Topographical-historical encyclopaedia of Palestine. Jerusalem, Rubin Mass, 1946–55. 4v. il.   **DE123**

In Hebrew with added title page and introduction in English. A new encyclopedia, treating the history of Palestine from ancient times to modern Israel and Arabic Palestine.

SYRIA

Masson, Paul. Éléments d'une bibliographie française de la Syrie. Marseille, Barlatier, 1919. 528p. (Chambre de Commerce de Marseille, Congrès Français de la Syrie)   **DE124**

Subtitle: Géographie, ethnographie, histoire, archéologie, langues, littératures, religions.

A chronological listing of more than 4500 French works on Syria from the 13th century to 1919, with author and class indexes.

THAILAND

Bangkok. Chulalongkorn University. Central Library. Bibliography of material about Thailand in Western languages. Bangkok, 1960. 325p. **DE125**

"The first comprehensive subject bibliography of material about Thailand in Western languages ever to be compiled by Thai nationals . . . included are books, periodical articles, pamphlets, mimeographed documents, microfilms and films concerning" . . . (*Pref.*) all phases of life in Thailand.

Classed arrangement. No index.

Mason, John Brown and **Parish, H. Carroll.** Thailand bibliography. Gainesville, Univ. of Florida Libraries, Dept. of Reference and Bibliography, 1958. 247p. (Its Bibliographic ser., no.4) **DE126**

Lists books, periodical articles, and documents in Western languages, with annotations for many of the items. Arrangement is primarily by form. No indexes.

TURKEY

Birge, John Kingsley. A guide to Turkish area study. Wash., Committee on Near Eastern Studies, Amer. Council of Learned Societies, 1949. 240p. **DE127**

A survey of physical, historical, social, and cultural facts relating to Turkey, with references to materials in English and western European languages. "General chronology of Turkish history" from 732 to 1945, p.185–240.

Koray, Enver. Türkiye tarih yayinlari bibliyografyasi, 1729–1950. Ankara, Millî Eğitim Basimevi, 1952. 548p. **DE128**

A bibliography of Turkish historical writings listing more than 4000 items and divided into two main sections—1729–1928 and 1928–1950—according to the orthography used. Each part lists, first, general works, collections, encyclopedias, etc., followed by books on the history of individual countries, and then works in related fields such as archaeology, biography, and ethnology. The index includes titles as well as authors.

Mikhov, Nikola V. Bibliographie des articles de périodiques allemands, anglais, français et italiens sur la Turquie et la Bulgarie, [par] Nicholas V. Michoff. Sofia, Impr. de la Cour, 1938. 686p. **DE129**

At head of title: Académie Bulgare des Sciences.

A comprehensive compilation of more than 10,000 titles of articles appearing in the periodicals of western Europe from 1715 to 1880 (with some additional entries to 1891), arranged chronologically by year, with indexes by author and personal name and by subject and place-name.

—— La population de la Turquie et de la Bulgarie au XVIIIᵉ et XIXᵉ siècles. Recherches bibliographico-statistiques . . . avec une préface en français. Sofia, Impr. de la Cour Royale, 1915–35. 4v. **DE130**

v.1 has added title page: Bulgarska Akademiia na Naukite. Sbornik. Kniga 4. Klon Istoriko-filologichen i filosofsko-obshtestven, 3.

Title also in Bulgarian.

Lists more than 3000 books and periodical articles in Western languages on demographic statistics, etc.

—— Sources bibliographiques sur l'histoire de la Turquie et de la Bulgarie. Sofia, Impr. de l'État, 1914–34. 4v. **DE131**

Title also in Bulgarian.

Cumulated author and subject indexes in v.4 to all four volumes.

A bibliography of works of the 19th and 20th centuries, in various languages, on the history of Turkey.

VIETNAM

Michigan. State University of Agriculture and Applied Science. Vietnam Advisory Group, Saigon. Bibliography on the political and administrative history of Vietnam, 1802–1962. [By Roy Jumper] [Saigon?], 1962. 179p. **DE132**

An annotated bibliography of more than 950 entries, including books and periodical articles.

Michigan. State University of Agriculture and Applied Science. Vietnam Project. What to read on Vietnam; a selected annotated bibliography. 2d ed. with a suppl. covering the period Nov. 1958 to Oct. 1959. N.Y., Inst. of Pacific Relations, 1960. 73p. **DE133**

Lists periodical articles, books, and special reports published 1955–Oct. 1959, mainly in English. Includes a bibliography of periodicals published in Vietnam.

YEMEN

Macro, Eric. Bibliography on Yemen and notes on Mocha. Coral Gables, Fla., Univ. of Miami Pr., 1960. 63p. **DE134**

An alphabetical listing of some 900 books and periodical articles on Yemen, and "Notes" on the history of the ruined town of Mocha.

DF

Australia and New Zealand

GENERAL WORKS

Bibliography

Ferguson, John Alexander. Bibliography of Australia. Sydney, London, Angus & Robertson, 1941–63. v.1–5. il. (In progress) **DF1**

Contents: v.1, 1784–1830; v.2, 1831–1838; v.3, 1839–1845; v.4, 1846–1850; v.5, 1851–1900, A–G.

Arranged chronologically. Indexes are not cumulative. v.2–4 include lists of Addenda.

Locates copies in 10 Australian libraries and the British Museum.

The standard bibliography of Australia, which aims to include all books, pamphlets, broadsides, newspapers, magazines, and government papers printed from 1784 to 1900. Does not include manuscripts. Extensive annotations.

Greenway, John. Bibliography of the Australian aborigines and the native peoples of Torres Strait to 1959. Sydney, London, Angus & Robertson, 1963. 420p. **DF2**

For full information *see* CD27.

Politzer, Ludwig Louis. Bibliography of Dutch literature on Australia. Melbourne, priv. pr., 1953. 13p. map. **DF3**

Arranged chronologically. No author listing. Some brief annotations.

—— Bibliography of French literature on Australia, 1595–1946. Melbourne, priv. pr., Box 1761, G.P.O., 1952. 44p. **DF4**

A chronological index is followed by an alphabetical list by author. Brief annotations are given for many items, and locations in Australian libraries and private collections are also included in most cases.

—— Bibliography of German literature on Australia, 1770–1947. Melbourne, Pan Pr., 1952. 47p. **DF5**

A chronological index is followed by an alphabetical bibliography. Some annotations; a few locations.

Royal Commonwealth Society, London. Library. Subject catalogue of the library. v.2, Commonwealth of Australia, Dominion of New Zealand, South Pacific, general voyages and travels, and Arctic and Antarctic regions. London, 1931. 761p. **DF6**

For full description *see* DC157.

Encyclopedias

Australian encyclopedia. [East Lansing], Michigan State Univ. Pr., 1958. 10v. il. **DF7**

An extensive encyclopedia treating all aspects of Australian life, culture, and history. Signed articles, many of considerable length, some with bibliographies. v.10 is a detailed index.

Modern encyclopaedia of Australia and New Zealand. Sydney, Melbourne, Horwitz-Grahame, 1964. 1199p. il. **DF8**

A compact 1v. encyclopedia with brief articles on the history, geography, industry, arts, flora and fauna, biography (including living persons), etc. of Australia, New Zealand, and Papua-New Guinea.

NEW ZEALAND

Hocken, Thomas Morland. Bibliography of the literature relating to New Zealand. Wellington, Mackay, 1909. 619p. **DF9**

The standard bibliography, arranged chronologically with author and subject index, listing some 4000 items, most of them annotated. Newspapers are included only for the early years of the colony. Supersedes earlier works by J. D. Davis and J. Collier.

—— —— Supplement, comp. by A. H. Johnstone. Auckland, Whitcombe & Tombs, 1927. 73p.

Lists some 500 works, without annotations, published before 1900 and not given in Hocken, and some published 1909 to 1926.

Chapple, Leonard James Bancroft. Bibliographical brochure containing addenda and corrigenda to extant bibliographies of New Zealand literature. Dunedin, N.Z., Reed, 1938. 47p. **DF10**

Lists 116 items, published in 1909 or earlier, not found in Hocken or Johnstone (DF9).

New Zealand. National Archives. Preliminary inventory, no.1– . Wellington, Dept. of Internal Affairs, 1953– . (In progress) **DF11**

Contents: Archives of: no.1, The Governor-General. 12p.; no.2, The New Zealand Company. 16p.; no.3, The Army Dept. 16p.; no.4, The provinces of New Ulster and New Munster and of the Civil Secretary's Office. 15p.; no.5, The provinces of Otago and Southland. 16p.; no.6, The provinces of Wellington and Hawke's Bay. 15p.; no.7, The provinces of Auckland and Taranaki. 15p.; no.8, The provinces of Nelson and Marlborough and of the Nelson Trust Funds Board. 27p.; no.9, The old land claims commission. 42p.

Royal Commonwealth Society, London. Library. Subject catalogue. v.2. London, 1931. **DF12**

v.2 includes a comprehensive bibliography on New Zealand. For description of complete set *see* DC157.

Writings in New Zealand history. (In Historical studies, Australia and New Zealand. Melbourne, Univ., 1940– . Annual) **DF13**

An annual record of monographic and periodical publications.

D G

Oceanica

GENERAL WORKS

Bibliography

Allied Forces. An annotated bibliography of the Southwest Pacific and adjacent areas. [n.p.] 1944–45. 4v. maps. **DG1**

At head of title: Allied Geographical Section. Southwest Pacific Area.

Contents: v.1, The Netherlands and British East Indies and the Philippine Islands. 317p.; v.2, The Mandated territory of New Guinea, Papua, the British Solomon Islands, the New Hebrides and Micronesia. 274p.; v.3, Malaya, Thailand, Indo China, the China coast and the Japanese Empire. 256p.; v.4, Supplement to v.1, 2, and 3. 693p.

An annotated bibliography of materials in English, with location of copies in Australian libraries.

Bernice P. Bishop Museum. Library. Dictionary catalog of the library, Bernice P. Bishop Museum, Honolulu, Hawaii. Boston, G. K. Hall, 1964. 9v. **DG2**

Photoreproduction of the author, subject, and title cards from the library's catalog. The Museum "confines its efforts entirely to study of the peoples and natural areas of the Pacific," and concentration of interest is "in cultural anthropology, archaeology, marine zoology, malacology, entomology, music, further recording of linguistic material, astronomy, bibliography."—*Pref.*

Cammack, Floyd M. and **Saito, Shiro.** Pacific island bibliography. N.Y., Scarecrow, 1962. 421p. **DG3**

"Based on a selection of materials in the Pacific collection at the University of Hawaii's Gregg M. Sinclair Library."—*Introd.*

Planned to supplement C. R. H. Taylor's *A Pacific bibliography* (DG7); includes more than 1730 items in various languages, published since 1948 in the social sciences, including education and languages. Arranged by island group: Oceania, Melanesia, Micronesia, and Polynesia.

Leeson, Ida. A bibliography of bibliographies of the South Pacific, pub. under the auspices of the South Pacific Commission. London, N.Y., Oxford Univ. Pr., 1954. 61p. **DG4**

Includes general bibliographies, bibliographies of particular areas, and subject bibliographies, appearing both in books and in periodicals. Index.

Royal Commonwealth Society, London. Library. Subject catalogue. v.2. London, 1931. **DG5**

For description of complete set *see* DC157.

Sachet, Marie-Hélène and **Fosberg, Frances Raymond.** Island bibliographies. [Wash.], Nat. Academy of Sciences —Nat. Research Council, 1955. 577p. (N.R.C. Technical ser., no.335) **DG6**

For full record *see* EC40a.

Taylor, Clyde Romer Hughes. A Pacific bibliography; printed matter relating to the native peoples of Polynesia, Melanesia and Micronesia. Wellington, N.Z., Polynesian Soc., 1951. 492p. map. (Memoirs of the Polynesian Society, v.24) **DG7**

A bibliography of books and periodical articles in various languages dealing with Pacific Island groups. Arrangement is by island group, subdivided by such headings as: bibliography, ethnology, physical and mental characteristics, origins and migrations, culture contacts, tribal and family organization, religion, medicine, language, folklore, music, arts, archaeology, dress, houses, handcrafts.

Handbooks

Daniel, Hawthorne. Islands of the Pacific. N.Y., Putnam, 1943. 228p. maps. **DG8**

A description of the individual islands and the island groups of the Pacific. Gives location, size, topography, population, natural resources, products, etc.

GUAM

Reid, Charles Frederick. Bibliography of the island of Guam. N.Y., Wilson, 1939. 102p. **DG9**

An annotated bibliography, arranged alphabetically by subject, with no author index and no cross references. Includes a large amount of analysis of periodicals, government publications, and general works.

NEW CALEDONIA

O'Reilly, Patrick. Bibliographie méthodique, analytique et critique de la Nouvelle-Calédonie. Paris, Musée de l'Homme, 1955. 361p. (Publ. de la Soc. des Océanistes, no.4) **DG10**

A comprehensive, annotated bibliography of some 4100 entries, covering the voyages, geology, botany, zoology, geography, ethnology, history, economy, medicine, and literature of the area. Texts in the native language are grouped with the ethnology section.

NEW GUINEA

Galis, Klaas Wilhelm. Bibliography of West New Guinea. [New Haven], Yale Univ., 1956. 135p. (Yale Univ. Southeast Asia Studies. Bibliography ser.) **DG11**

American edition of the author's *Bibliographie van Nederlands-Nieuw Guinea.* Hollandia, 1955.

Issued as a companion volume to the new edition of Kennedy's *Bibliography of Indonesian peoples and cultures* (DE71). Lists alphabetically by author (no subject index) 3760 titles of books and articles in various languages, mostly Dutch.

Gill, Evan R. Catalogue of books relating to New Guinea (but with special reference to Papua) in the library of Evan R. Gill. Liverpool, Eng., Author (11 Cheltenham Ave., Liverpool 17), 1957. 51p. **DG12**

Lists of relevant British and Australian documents are followed by a general list of some 600 titles in Western languages, alphabetical by author, and a section of works in Papuan languages. No subject index.

Robson, Robert William. Handbook of Papua and New Guinea, 1954. 1st ed. Sydney, Pacific Publ., 1954. 319p. il., map. **DG13**

A handbook and directory.

NEW HEBRIDES

O'Reilly, Patrick. Bibliographie méthodique, analytique et critique des Nouvelles-Hébrides. Paris, Musée de l'Homme, 1958. 304p. (Publ. de la Soc. des Océanistes, no.8) **DG14**

A comprehensive, annotated bibliography of books and periodical articles which refer to many aspects of life in the islands of the New Hebrides. For biographical material on this region, *see* the author's *Hébridais: répertoire bio-bibliographique* (AJ231).

OKINAWA

Sakamaki, Shunzo. Ryukyu; a bibliographical guide to Okinawan studies; surveying important primary sources and writings in Ryukyuan, Japanese, Chinese and Korean. Honolulu, Univ. of Hawaii Pr., 1963. 353p. **DG15**

A comprehensive survey in English of sources and writings, in the languages mentioned, on the Ryukyu Islands and their people.

PHILIPPINES

Blair, Emma Helen and **Robertson, James Alexander.** The Philippine Islands, 1493–1898. v.53, Bibliography. Cleveland, Ohio, Arthur H. Clark Co., 1908. 433p. **DG16**

The 55v. set is a collection of English translations of original source materials from the time of discovery to the end of Spanish rule.

v.53 is an extensive annotated bibliography: (1) a bibliography of bibliographies published in various countries concerning the Philippines, p.55–99; (2) other printed books, pamphlets, etc. mostly published in whole or in part in *The Philippine Islands, 1493–1898;* (3) Philippine manuscripts, arranged chronologically by authors, p.143–419.

Chicago. University. Philippine Studies Program. Selected bibliography of the Philippines, topically arranged and annotated. Preliminary ed. New Haven, Conn., Human Relations Area Files, 1956. 138p. (Behavior science bibliographies) **DG17**

Prepared by Philippine Studies Program: Fred Eggan, director; E. D. Hester, associate director.

Classed list of books and articles, mainly in English. Author index.

Lietz, Paul S. Calendar of Philippine documents in the Ayer collection of the Newberry Library. Chicago, Newberry Lib., 1956. 259p. **DG18**

A detailed, annotated bibliography of 370 manuscript items, *ca.* 1557–1903, "letters, journals, diaries, *testimonios* and *expedientes,* official and unofficial reports, histories and public records."—*Introd.*

Lopez Memorial Museum, Rizal, Philippine Islands. Catalogue of Filipiniana materials in the Lopez Memorial Museum. [Rizal, Museum], 1962. 262p.　　**DG19**

A classed catalog of more than 3100 printed works and manuscripts relating to various aspects of life in the Philippines from the 16th century to date. Author and title index.

Newberry Library. Chicago. A catalogue of printed materials relating to the Philippine Islands, 1519–1900, in the Newberry Library. Comp. by Doris Varner Welsh. Chicago, Newberry Lib., 1959. 179p.　　**DG20**

A classified listing of nearly 1900 items, with author index. The Appendix, p.153–58, provides a supplement to the *Checklist of Philippine linguistics in the Newberry Library* (1950).

Quezon. Philippines. University of the Philippines. Institute of Public Administration. Union catalog of Philippine materials of sixty-four government agency libraries of the Philippines. Comp. by the staff of the Interdepartmental Reference Service, Maxima M. Ferrer, ed. Manila, 1962. 718p.　　**DG21**

A union list of materials relating to the Philippines and their peoples in many subject areas, and in various languages.

Quezon. Philippines. University of the Philippines. Library. Classified list of Filipiniana books and pamphlets in the main library, University of the Philippines as of Dec. 1958. Quezon City, 1959. 358p.　　**DG22**

A classed listing of almost 3000 titles in various languages but mainly in English. A large percentage of the material is 20th century.

Quezon. Philippines. University of the Philippines. Social Science Research Center. An annotated bibliography of Philippine social sciences. Quezon City, Social Science Research Center, Univ. of the Philippines, 1956–60. v.1–3. (In progress)　　**DG23**

v.1, Economics. 525p.; v.2, pt.1, Sociology. 153p.; v.3, pt.1, Political Science. 175p.

Classed arrangement of books, pamphlets, periodical articles, and documents drawn from the Filipiniana section of the University of the Philippines library. Extensive notes and annotations.

D H

Arctic and Antarctic

BIBLIOGRAPHY

Arctic Institute of North America. Arctic bibliography, prep. for and in cooperation with the Dept. of Defense. Wash., Govt. Prt. Off., 1953– . v.1– . maps. Annual.　　**DH1**

Prepared under the general direction of Marie Tremaine. v.1–3 form the basic bibliography, and list some 20,000 publications in many languages representing all phases of the subject: geographical, scientific, and sociological. Emphasis is on the 19th and 20th centuries. In two parts: (1) An alphabetical author list with full title in the original language, imprint, and collation. Russian titles are given in L.C. transliteration. Translations into English are added for foreign titles. Entries include books, government documents, and periodical articles.

There are brief annotations or abstracts, and location is given for the copy used; (2) A comprehensive subject-geographic index of some 100,000 entries, arranged under 18,000 subject and geographic headings.

v.4 emphasizes material published 1950–52; v.5 covers material published 1950–53, but in both volumes earlier material is included.

From v.6 on, published annually, each volume listing as many current or recent items as possible, as well as older materials not previously included. Emphasis is on scientific, technical, and medical materials, and the number of items in foreign languages, particularly in Russian, is increased.

Chavanne, Josef, Karpf, Alois and **LeMonnier, Franz.** Die Literatur über die Polar-Regionen der Erde bis 1875. Wien, E. Hölzel, 1878. 335p. (Repr.: Amsterdam, Meridian Pub. Co., 1962)　　**DH2**

Added title page, and preface, in English: The literature on the polar regions of the earth.

6617 items—books and periodical articles—in various languages. Classified under geographical area, with author index.

Copenhagen. Marinens Bibliothek. Katalog. København, Levin, 1933–36. 2v. and annual suppl.　　**DH3**

Rich in the field of polar explorations. For full description *see* CI192.

Hayton, Robert D. National interests in Antarctica, an annotated bibliography. Comp. for the U.S. Antarctic projects officer. 1959. Wash., Govt. Prt. Off., 1960. 137p. folded map.　　**DH4**

An "area" bibliography which "associates together the relevant material of international law, foreign policy, economic exploitation, strategic significance, world politics, explorations, and expeditions affecting national claims (potential and declared), and analogous rivalries and considerations in the Arctic."—*Introd.*

Lists books, articles, and documents under 27 countries and the United Nations. Detailed author, title, and subject index.

Royal Commonwealth Society, London. Library. Subject catalogue. v.2. London, 1931.　　**DH5**

Includes a comprehensive bibliography on the Arctic and the Antarctic. For description of complete set *see* DC157.

U.S. Bureau of Aeronautics (Navy Dept.). Antarctic bibliography. Wash., Govt. Prt. Off., 1951. 147p. maps. **DH6**

"Prepared by the U.S. Naval Photographic Interpretation Center."

5500 items, arranged in classified form, with author index. The five main divisions, each with detailed subdivisions, are: (1) biological sciences; (2) geo-physical sciences; (3) geographical sciences; (4) geographical exploration; and (5) other subjects.

E

PURE AND APPLIED SCIENCES

At this period, in both the pure and the applied sciences, the need for being up to date is of paramount importance, and the necessity for quick retrieval of information to be found in the printed literature of the world has led to many new processes and mechanisms. Computer-compiled indexes have revolutionized the old-time systems and made possible much more prompt and inclusive coverage than was possible heretofore.

A new type of index for established sets, such as *Chemical abstracts* (ED17) and *Biological abstracts* (EC7); punched-card methods for bibliographical search; and the bibliographical control of translations from many languages, particularly the Russian—all have made radical changes in reference techniques and reference tools. Many of these tools are highly specialized and will be found only in the specialized library; others should be in the large public or academic library. For the most part only the more general works are listed here, and these fall into certain general categories: bibliographies, both retrospective and current; periodical indexes and abstract journals ("Advances" and "Reviews" are usually omitted); encyclopedias and dictionaries, particularly dictionaries of foreign scientific and technical terms; handbooks which contain data, formulas, charts, statistics, etc.; yearbooks and directories; a few historical surveys; and biographical dictionaries.

The history of science is also important, not only as a field in itself, but as a background for modern developments; therefore, a few materials in this field have been included.

The *abstract journal* has assumed a place of primary importance, and most special subjects are now covered by such publications. Only a selection of typical examples has been included here; for other titles *see* U.S. Library of Congress, Science and Technology Division, *A guide to the world's abstracting and indexing services in science and technology* (EA62).

The important features in an abstract journal are: authority, completeness of coverage, promptness, and the comprehensiveness and kind of the indexes:

I. Authority
   A. Is it sponsored by a recognized society or group?
   B. Is the abstracting done by a competent office force with the help and advice of experts? By scholars who are specialists in their fields?

II. Completeness of coverage and adequacy of abstracting and listing
   A. Is the coverage comprehensive, including all articles in the field published in the periodicals of all countries?
   B. Are the abstracts adequate, including precise and detailed data, formulas, measurements, etc.?
   C. Are the titles of articles given in the original language or in translation?
   D. Is there a complete and up-to-date list of abbreviations for the periodicals abstracted?

III. Promptness
   A. How soon after the publication of the original article does the abstract appear?
   B. Is the nature of the material such that promptness is essential?

IV. Comprehensiveness and kind of the indexes
   A. Are there author, subject, formula, and patent indexes?
   B. Are they detailed and well organized?
   C. How frequently are they published? Do they cumulate?

For more detailed descriptions of abstract journals, *see* the guides listed under Chemistry (ED1–ED4).

Technical report literature. These are reports from private companies doing research under government contract; from universities working under similar arrangements; or from government agencies themselves. They are divided into "classified" and "declassified" reports. Some of the "declassified" reports are listed in publishers' catalogs, but the great majority must be found through special guides; *see* EA74–EA78.

E A

General Works

GUIDES

For guides in particular subject fields, *see* under subject, e.g., Chemistry—Guides.

Holmstrom, J. E. Records and research in engineering and industrial science. 3d ed. rewritten and enl. London, Chapman & Hall, 1956. 491p. il.   **EA1**
1st ed. 1940.
A guide to the sources, processing, and storekeeping of technical knowledge, with information on scientific and technical organizations in Britain and other countries.
A useful guide, particularly to English works.

BIBLIOGRAPHY

Association of Special Libraries and Information Bureaux. British scientific and technical books; a select list of recommended books published in Great Britain and the Commonwealth in the years 1935 to 1952. London, pub. for ASLIB by James Clarke, 1956. (Pub. in the U.S. by Hafner) 364p.   **EA2**
Supplements the *Catalogue of British scientific and technical books.* 3d ed. British Science Guild, 1930.
Reappraises the books listed in the *ASLIB book list* (1935–), omitting some and adding others, in order to present a comprehensive bibliography of books published by commercial publishers during the period. Arranged by Universal Decimal Classification with author and subject indexes.

———— 1953–57, ed. by L. J. Anthony. London, James Clarke, 1960. 251p.

—— Select list of standard British scientific and technical books, ed. by L. J. Anthony. 5th ed. rev. and enl. London, ASLIB, 1957. 88p.   **EA3**
1st ed. 1937.
A select list designed to help in the establishment of a representative library of the best books in science and technology. Classed arrangement with subject index.

Battelle Memorial Institute, Columbus, Ohio. Guide to the scientific and technical literature of eastern Europe, prep. for the National Science Foundation . . . Oct. 1962. [Wash., Govt. Prt. Off., 1963] 94p. (NSF 62–49)   **EA4**
For Albania, Bulgaria, Czechoslovakia, Hungary, Poland, Rumania, and Yugoslavia, the guide " . . . contains information on the announcement, procurement and translation of East European publications in the physical, biological and certain of the social sciences."—*Introd.* Social sciences represented in the periodicals list are anthropology, archaeology, demography, ethnography, linguistics, statistics, and psychology. Medicine and agriculture are excluded.

Bibliographie der deutschen naturwissenschaftlichen Literatur, hrsg. im Auftrage des Reichsamtes des Innern vom Deutschen Bureau der Internationalen Bibliographie in Berlin. Jena, Fischer; Berlin, Neymanns, 1902–14. 18v.   **EA5**
The German titles as furnished to the *International catalogue of scientific literature* (EA12).

British Museum (Natural History) Library. Catalogue of the books, manuscripts, maps and drawings in the British Museum (Natural History). London, Trustees, 1903–40. 8v.   **EA6**
v.1–5, A–Z; v.6–8, Supplement, A–Z.
An author catalog of one of the world's finest collections on natural history. Includes many analytics.

Deason, Hilary J. The AAAS science book list for children. 2d ed., comp. under the direction of H. J. Deason; consultant, Nora Beust. Wash., Amer. Assoc. for the Advancement of Science, 1963. 201p.   **EA7**
An annotated list of 1291 titles for students in grades 1 through 8.

—— The AAAS science book list for young adults. Comp. under the direction of H. J. Deason; consultant, Nora Beust. Wash., Amer. Assoc. for the Advancement of Science, 1964. 250p.   **EA8**
Replaces the *AAAS science book list* (1959).
An annotated list of 1376 books in the biological, physical, behavioral, medical, engineering, agricultural, and mathematical sciences, and in education.

—— A guide to science reading. N.Y., New Amer. Lib., 1963. 220p.   **EA9**
Produced by the American Association for the Advancement of Science. "An annotated list of the best of scientific

literature currently available in paperbound form."—*Foreword*.

Deniker, Joseph and **Descharmes, René.** Bibliographie des travaux scientifiques (sciences mathématiques, physiques et naturelles) pub. par les sociétés savantes de la France depuis l'origine jusqu'en 1888; dressée sous les auspices du Ministère de l'Instruction Publique. Paris, Impr. Nationale, 1922. v.1–2. **EA10**

Pub. in parts, 1895–1922; v.1, ed. by Joseph Deniker; v.2, by René Descharmes.

Contents: v.1–2, pt.1, Ain–Sarthe.

A companion work to Lasteyrie's *Bibliographie générale des travaux historiques* . . . ; on the same scale and intended to do for scientific societies what Lasteyrie has done for historical. Unfortunately not finished.

Arranged by *département* and then by city. Complete contents are given for each volume of the publications of the societies included. For plan and general arrangement, *see* Lasteyrie (AC35).

Hawkins, Reginald Robert. Scientific, medical, and technical books published in the United States of America; a selected list of titles in print with annotations. 2d ed. Books pub. to Dec. 1956. Wash., 1958. (Distr. in U.S. by Bowker) 1491p. **EA11**

Prepared under the direction of the National Academy of Sciences—National Research Council's Committee on Bibliography of American Scientific and Technical Books.

1st ed. 1946 and supplements.

A carefully chosen list of nearly 8000 titles of books written by citizens of the United States and Canada and published in the United States. About 3500 of the entries represent either new editions of titles previously listed or new titles. Includes tables of contents, and descriptive and evaluative annotations. The original volumes will be needed for information about out-of-print or superseded titles.

International catalogue of scientific literature, 1st–14th annual issues. Pub. for the International Council by the Royal Society of London. London, Harrison, 1902–19. 14v. **EA12**

An annual bibliography covering books and articles in a large number of important scientific journals.

Each annual issue consists of 17v.: A, Mathematics; B, Mechanics; C, Physics; D, Chemistry; E, Astronomy; F, Meteorology; G, Mineralogy; H, Geology; J, Geography, mathematical and physical; K, Paleontology; L, General biology; M, Botany; N, Zoology; O, Human anatomy; P, Anthropology; Q, Physiology; R. Bacteriology.

Each part includes: (1) schedules and indexes in four languages; (2) an author catalog; and (3) a subject catalog. "The purpose is to record the titles of all original contributions since Jan. 1, 1901, in certain branches of science."

While issued, this was the most important current bibliography covering all the sciences. Publication was suspended after the issue of the volumes for 1914.

—— List of journals with abbreviations used in the Catalogue as references. London, 1903. 312p. Suppl., 1904. 68p.

John Crerar Library, Chicago. Industrial technical library, a bibliography. Wash., Technical Aids Branch, Off. of Industrial Resources, Internat. Cooperation Admin., [1960]. 264p. **EA13**

"Annotated listings of approximately 3000 books and periodicals, representing a sound guide for the selection of a balanced industrial technical library."—*Foreword.* Classified arrangement; no author index.

Reichardt, Günther. Sowjetische Literatur zur Naturwissenschaft und Technik. Bibliographischer Wegweiser. 2. erw. und verb. Aufl. Wiesbaden, Franz Steiner, 1959. 306p. **EA14**

1st ed. 1957.

A classified introduction to Soviet materials in science and technology. Many titles annotated. Author and title index, and subject index.

Reuss, Jeremias David. Repertorium commentationum a societatibus litterariis editarum. Secundum disciplinarum ordinem digessit I. D. Reuss. . . . Gottingae, apud Henricum Dieterich, 1801–21. 16v. (Repr.: N.Y., Burt Franklin, 1961) **EA15**

Contents: (1) Historia naturalis, generalis et zoologia; (2) Botanica et mineralogia; (3) Chemia et res metallica; (4) Physica; (5) Astronomia; (6) Oeconomia; (7) Mathesis, mechanica, hydrostatica, hydraulica, hydrotechnia, aerostatica, pnevmatica, technologia, architectura civilis, scientia navalis, scientia militaris; (8) Historia; (9) Philologia, linguae, scriptores graeci, scriptores latini, litterae elegantiores, poesis, rhetorica, ars antiqua, pictura, musica; (10–16) Scientia et ars medica et chirurgica.

A very valuable index to the publications of the learned societies of various countries from the time of the founding of each society to 1800, thus preceding the Royal Society's *Catalogue of scientific papers* (EA16).

Royal Society of London. Catalogue of scientific papers, 1800–1900. London, Clay, 1867–1902; Cambridge, Univ. Pr., 1914–25. 19v. **EA16**

v.1–6, 1st ser., 1800–63; v.7–8, 2d ser., 1864–73; v.9–11, 3d ser., 1874–83; v.12, Supplementary volume, 1800–83; v.13–19, 4th ser., 1884–1900.

A monumental index of the first importance in scientific or large reference libraries. An author index, for the whole of the 19th century, to 1555 periodicals in various languages including the transactions of the European academies and other learned societies. Gives, for each article entered: author's name in full when it can be found, full title, title of periodical, volume, date, and inclusive paging. For Russian articles the original title is given followed by French, German, or English translation in brackets.

—— Subject index. Cambridge, Univ. Pr., 1908–14. v.1–3 in 4. **EA17**

v.1, Pure mathematics; v.2, Mechanics; v.3, Physics: pt.1, Generalities, heat, light, sound; pt.2, Electricity and magnetism.

A subject index to the same material as covered by the above author catalog, classified according to the schedules of the *International catalogue of scientific literature* (EA12). The original plan was to publish separate index volumes for each of the 17 sciences of the schedules of the *International catalogue,* but only the first three were issued. These index 116,687 articles from 1555 periodicals. The *Subject index* gives sufficiently full information to be used independently of the author volumes, i.e., author's name, brief title, periodical, volume date, and paging; though, for full title, reference must be made to the author index.

Continued, for material after 1900, by the *International catalogue of scientific literature.*

U.S. Library of Congress. Science and Technology Division. Soviet science and technology, a bibliography on the state of the art, 1955–1961. Wash., 1962. 209p. **EA18**

Contains some 2000 annotated entries for periodicals and monographs. Includes: bibliographies, surveys, reports on visits, and articles showing progress in a particular field. Arranged alphabetically by author or title under about 100 subject headings. No indexes except list of subjects.

Zil'bermints, Liudmila V. Bibliografiia sovetskoi tekhnicheskoi bibliografii, 1917–1959. Leningrad, 1959. 505p. **EA19**

At head of title: Ministerstvo Kul'tury RSFSR. Gosudarstvennaia Publichnaia Biblioteka im. M. E. Saltykova-Shchedrina.

A guide to Soviet reference books, primarily Russian, in all branches of technology and in the sciences of mathematics, physics, chemistry, and geology. Excluded categories: economics of industry, organization of production, history of science and technology, bio-bibliographical indexes, and general dissertation bibliography. Based on collections of three major libraries in Leningrad. Annotated entries for 1433 titles published between 1917 and mid-1959. Classified arrangement, with current information source listed at the beginning of each section or subsection, followed by retrospective bibliography and indexes to journal contents. Author, title, and subject indexes.

Current

American scientific books, 1960/1962– ; a basic selection of scientific, technical and medical books as entered in the American book publishing record. Ed. by Phyllis B. Steckler. N.Y., Bowker, 1962– . Annual. **EA20**

An annotated list arranged by Dewey Decimal Classification.

For the *American book publishing record,* see AA344.

Association of Special Libraries and Information Bureaux. ASLIB book list: a monthly list of recommended scientific and technical books with annotations. v.1, Oct. 1935– . London, ASLIB, 1935– . **EA21**

1936–47, quarterly; March 1948– , monthly. Subtitle varies.

Classed arrangement. Cumulated annual indexes. Gives prices.

For cumulations *see* EA2.

Bibliographia scientiae naturalis helvetica, hrsg. von der Schweizer. Landesbibliothek. v.1, 1925– . Bern, 1927– . Annual. **EA22**

Title varies: 1925–47, *Bibliographie der schweizerischen naturwissenschaftlichen und geographischen Literatur* (varies slightly).

Records books and articles in the exact, geological, and biological sciences.

Bibliographie scientifique française; recueil mensuel publié sous les auspices du Ministère de l'Éducation Nationale par la Commission du Répertoire de Bibliographie Scientifique. Paris, Gauthier-Villars, 1902– . t.1– . 6 numbers a year. **EA23**

Beginning with v.2, 1903, each issue is in two parts: sec. 1, Sciences mathématiques et physiques; sec. 2, Sciences naturelles et biologiques.

v.1–18, 1902–21—published by the Bureau Français du Catalogue International du Littérature Scientifique—included the French titles submitted to the *International catalogue* (EA12). Arranged by the same classification.

Some volumes with author indexes.

—— Table générale des tomes 1–13. Paris, Gauthier-Villars, 1919–36.

Published in fascicules: Astronomie, Paléontologie, Biologie, Zoologie, Botanique.

Index bibliographicus. 4th ed. La Haye, Federation Internat. de Documentation, 1959– . v.1– . (In progress) **EA24**

Contents: v.1, Science and technology.
For full information *see* AA19.

New York Public Library. New technical books; a selective list with descriptive annotations. 1915– . N.Y., Lib., 1915– . v.1– . 10 numbers a year. **EA25**

Subtitle varies. Frequency varies.

A very useful current bibliography, with good annotations. Arranged by subject, with annual author and subject indexes. Helpful for book selection. Changed form with v.33, no.1, 1948, to conform to the style of Hawkins, *Scientific, medical, and technical books* (EA11) and includes table of contents for each book.

Translations

Gt.Brit. Dept. of Scientific and Industrial Research. Translated contents lists of Russian periodicals . . . London, 1949–58. no.1–117. Monthly. **EA26**

Subtitle: With list of recent accessions of Russian scientific and technical books and parts of serial publications available in the British Museum.

Ceased publication Dec. 1958. Continued by:

National Lending Library for Science and Technology. NLL translations bulletin. London, Stat. Off., 1959– . v.1– . Monthly. **EA27**

Title varies: v.1–2, *LLU translations bulletin,* issued by Great Britain, Dept. of Scientific and Industrial Research, Lending Library Unit.

Gives abstracts of some articles from the USSR and from China, and lists translations available for purchase or loan from the N.L.L.

Special Libraries Association. Translation Committee. S.L.A. list of translations, Oct. 1, 1953. N.Y., 1953. 72p. **EA28**

—— —— Supplement, Sept. 1, 1954. 62p.

1953 edition lists some 1100 titles from languages other than Russian. Arranged alphabetically by author, giving for each: author, title in English, title in original language, source with volume number, pagination, and date.

Kept up to date by:

Translation monthly. [Chicago, pub. for the Special Libraries Association by John Crerar Library], 1955–58. v.1–4. Monthly. **EA29**

Lists translations of foreign articles deposited in the Special Libraries Association Translation Pool.

Beginning with Jan. 1957, assumed the responsibility of adding the Russian translations formerly listed in the *Bibliography of translations from Russian scientific and technical literature,* prepared by the Scientific Translations Center of the Library of Congress (List 1–39, Oct. 1953–Dec. 1956).

Titles are given in English only, with citation to original source.

Classified arrangement with annual author indexes.
Ceased publication. Continued by:

Technical translations. Wash., U.S. Dept. of Commerce, Office of Technical Services. 1959– . v.1– . Semimonthly. **EA30**

Published in cooperation with the Special Libraries Association Translation Center, which is responsible for collecting translations from nongovernmental sources, domestic and foreign. Includes both governmental and nongovernmental materials. Classified arrangement with author, journal, and number indexes. Titles are given in English, with citation to original source.

U.S. Library of Congress. Science and Technology Division. List of Russian serials being translated into English and other Western languages. 2d ed.– . Wash., 1960– . Annual. **EA31**

1st edition was produced only for use within the division.

Lists scientific and technical journals by translated title, followed by transliterated Russian title, with index by transliterated Russian title. Also an index by subjects.

The main listing gives L.C. call number, frequency, date when translation began, and publisher.

U.S. National Library of Medicine. Scientific translations; a guide to sources and services, comp. by Sheila M. Parker. Rev. by Rosemary Roberts and Miriam Hawkins. Wash., U.S. Dept. of Health, Education, and Welfare, Public Health Service, 1959. 19p. (U.S. Public Health Service. Publ. no.514 rev.) **EA32**

1st ed. 1957.
Contents: Locating guide to unpublished translations (list-

ing institutions maintaining files of translations, arranged by country); published indexes and lists of translations; cover-to-cover translations of Soviet periodicals; and various lists of periodicals containing translations.

Dissertations

Masters theses in the pure and applied sciences, accepted by colleges and universities of the United States, 1955/ 56– . Lafayette, Ind., School of Mechanical Engineering, Purdue Univ., 1957– . v.1– . Annual. (Thermophysical Properties Research Center) **EA33**

Title varies: v.1–2, *Master's theses accepted by U.S. colleges and universities in the fields of chemical engineering, chemistry, mechanical engineering, metallurgical engineering, and physics; v.3, Master's theses and doctoral dissertations in the pure and applied sciences . . . ; v.4, 1959– , Masters theses in the pure and applied sciences . . . .*

Arranged by university under large classes, with subject index.

Maire, Albert. Catalogue des thèses de sciences soutenues en France de 1810 à 1890 inclusivement. Paris, Welter, 1892. 224p. **EA34**

Arranged by university, then chronologically. Author and subject indexes.

Lavaud, Suzanne. Catalogue des thèses de doctorat ès sciences naturelles, soutenues à Paris de 1891 à 1954. Paris, Person, 1955. 257p. **EA35**

A partial continuation of Maire, above. Arranged chronologically with author and subject indexes.

Periodicals

Bibliography

Académie des Sciences, Paris. Inventaire des périodiques scientifiques des bibliothèques de Paris, dressé sous la direction de Alfred Lacroix par Léon Bultingaire avec la collaboration des bibliothécaires de Paris et le concours de Ad. Richard. Paris, Masson, 1924. 1102p. **EA36**

An alphabetical title list of more than 19,000 periodicals, with indication of their location in 132 Paris libraries. Gives cataloging information about each title, indicates exact holdings, and has two indexes: (1) by place of publication, and (2) by subject.

——— ——— Supplement 1–2. 1929–39. 283p., 532p.

Bolton, Henry Carrington. Catalogue of scientific and technical periodicals, 1665–1896 . . . together with chronological tables and a library check-list. 2d ed. Wash., Smithsonian Inst., 1897. 1247p. (Smithsonian miscellaneous collections, v.40) **EA37**

8603 titles. Pt.I, 4954 titles, is a reprint of the 1st edition, 1885, with changes to date; pt.II includes additions to titles in pt.I, and titles 5001 to 8477; addenda, 8478 to 8603.

"Intended to contain the principal independent periodicals of every branch of pure and applied science, published in all countries from the rise of this literature to the present time." —*Pref.* Excludes medicine but includes anatomy, physiology, and veterinary science. Usually omits publications of learned societies. Gives full titles, names of editors, changes of titles, dates, etc.

The chronological tables permit the finding of the volume numbers for specific years.

Midwest Inter-Library Center. Rarely held scientific serials in the Midwest Inter-Library Center. Pub. under a grant from the National Science Foundation. Chicago, 1963. 197p. **EA38**

An alphabetical listing of those titles abstracted in *Chemical abstracts* and *Biological abstracts* which are not received

by the member libraries of the MILC. The Center has undertaken to subscribe to all of these periodicals beginning with 1957. They are available for interlibrary loan or photocopy.

——— ——— Supplement 1. Chicago, 1964. 44p.

Suomalainen, Paavo [and others]. Yhteisluettelo Suomen tieteellisissä kirjastoissa olevista eksaktisten tieteiden, luonnontieteiden, tekniikan ja maatalous-metsätieteiden aikakaus-ja sarjajulkaisuista. A union list of scientific, technical, agricultural and forestry periodicals and serials in scientific libraries in Finland. Helsinki, Suomalainen Tiedeakatemia, 1950–53. 2v. **EA39**

An extensive catalog of world-wide scientific periodicals, giving locations for 118 libraries. v.2 lists, in transliteration, publications printed in Slavonic alphabets.

United Nations Educational, Scientific and Cultural Organization. South East Asia Science Cooperation Office. Scientific and technical journals of east and southeast Asia (Hong Kong, Japan, Indonesia, Macao, Malaya, North Borneo, the Philippines, Sarawak, Thailand, Vietnam). 2d ed. Manila, P.I., UNESCO, 1953. 233p. **EA40**

1st ed. 1951.

Arrangement is by subject under country or territory, with an alphabetical index by title and a subject index. The 1st edition had a separately issued supplement on China. 1951. 28p.

U.S. Library of Congress. Science and Technology Division. A list of scientific and technical serials currently received by the Library of Congress. Prep. under the sponsorship of the National Science Foundation. Wash., 1960. 186p. **EA41**

A listing of some 13,000 items, usually giving title, country of origin, frequency, and L.C. classification number.

World list of scientific periodicals published in the years 1900–1960. 4th ed., ed. by Peter Brown and George Burder Stratton. London, Butterworth, 1963–65. 3v. **EA42**

3d ed. 1952.

The 4th edition of this monumental work lists more than 60,000 titles of periodicals concerned with the natural sciences and technology, of which issues were published 1900–1960. Some 10,000 titles which appeared in the 3d edition have been omitted as being of social or commercial rather than of scientific interest. Entry is by title and includes place of publication, standard abbreviation, often the beginning date, and holdings in British libraries.

"Abbreviations have been prepared in general accordance with the forthcoming British Standard for the Abbreviation of Titles of Periodicals," but show little change from those used in previous editions.

Now continued in *British union-catalogue of periodicals, incorporating World list of scientific periodicals* (AF109).

Canadian

National Research Council, Canada. Library. Directory of Canadian scientific and technical periodicals; a classified guide to currently published titles. 2d ed. Ottawa, Council, 1962. 34p. (N.R.C. no.6831) **EA43**

1st ed. 1961.

Classified with title index. Gives title, beginning date, frequency, price, address.

Chinese

U.S. Library of Congress. Science and Technology Division. Chinese scientific and technical serial publications in the collections of the Library of Congress. Rev. ed. Wash., 1961. 107p. **EA44**

1st ed. 1955.

Gives romanized form, Chinese characters, title in English

translation, publisher, frequency, and Library of Congress holdings.

Japanese

Bonn, George Schlegel. Japanese journals in science and technology, an annotated checklist. N.Y., N.Y. Pub. Lib., 1960. 119p.   **EA45**

Lists 660 titles, giving for each: title in Romaji, then in Japanese characters, the official English title (and a translated title if warranted), frequency of publication, date of first issue, price per year, size, material in English, comments, and notes.

Societies and government bodies are also included, being interfiled with the journals under subjects.

Japan. Ministry of Education. Bureau of Higher Education and Science. Science Information Section. Bibliographical list of Japanese learned journals: natural and applied sciences. Tokyo, 1957–62. v.1–2.   **EA46**

no.1, Natural sciences. 1957; no.2, Natural and applied sciences. 1962.

—— —— Supplement to no.2, 1962. 1963. 148p.

U.S. Library of Congress. Science and Technology Division. Japanese scientific and technical serial publications in the collections of the Library of Congress. Wash., 1962. 247p.   **EA47**

Gives romanized form, Japanese characters, and English translation of title; address; frequency; and holdings in the Library of Congress.

—— Journals in science and technology published in Japan and Mainland China: a selected list. Wash., 1961. 47p.   **EA48**

Lists 331 titles in romanized form, chosen mainly because of current importance and general availability.

Latin-American

Pan American Union. Division of Science Development. Guide to Latin American scientific and technical periodicals: an annotated list. Wash., Pan Amer. Union, 1962. 187p.   **EA49**

An annotated bibliography of 1141 titles (classified with title index), being issued currently. Gives full information including types of material published.

Russian

Mezhenko, IU. A. Russkaia tekhnicheskaia periodika, 1800–1916; bibliograficheskii ukazatel'. Moskva, Izd-vo Akademii Nauk SSSR, 1955. 299p.   **EA50**

An annotated, descriptive bibliography, with subject and other indexes, of 415 Russian periodicals in technological fields, published between 1800 and 1916.

U.S. Library of Congress. Science and Technology Division. Scientific and technical serial publications of the Soviet Union, 1945–1960. Prep. by Nikolay T. Zikeev. Wash., 1963. 347p.   **EA51**

Alphabetical arrangement of Soviet journals, annuals, monographic series, etc. Titles are given in transliteration, with bracketed English translation, followed by beginning date, frequency, and L.C. classification number.

Union lists

Special Libraries Association. Science-Technology Group. Union list of technical periodicals in two hundred libraries of the Science-Technology Group. 3d ed., comp. by Elizabeth Gilbert Bowerman. N.Y., Assoc., 1947. 285p. **EA52**

Gives holdings of some 5000 serials in pure and applied sciences in 200 special libraries, only 13 of which are represented

in the 2d edition of the *Union list of serials* (AF98). The object has been to select, within the scope of the contributing libraries, the most complete sets in various geographical areas and to indicate location of at least one copy of all reported issues.

Australia. Commonwealth Scientific and Industrial Research Organization. Scientific serials in Australian libraries, ed. by Jean A. Conochie. Superseding Union catalogue of scientific and technical periodicals in the libraries of Australia. Melbourne, 1964. 4v. Loose-leaf.   **EA53**

1st ed. 1939; 2d ed. 1951.

An international listing of scientific and technical periodicals, showing holdings in Australian libraries.

National Research Council, Canada. Library. Union list of scientific serials in Canadian libraries. Ottawa, 1957. 805p.   **EA54**

Lists the holdings of 140 Canadian libraries for more than 21,000 serials in science, technology, and related subject fields. The latest form of distinctive serial title, or the name of the sponsoring body, is used as the entry, with references from earlier or variant forms.

—— —— Supplement, 1957–59. Ottawa, 1960. 290p.

Paris. École Nationale Supérieure des Mines. Catalogue de périodiques étrangers scientifiques et techniques reçus par les bibliothèques, instituts techniques et centres de documentation de Paris, dressé sous la direction de Mlle G. Dollfus, par Madame J. Lesure, suivi du Catalogue des Congrès . . . par Mlle Hélène Thibault. 2. éd. Paris, Person, 1958. 384p.   **EA55**

1st ed. 1954.

A listing of non-French scientific periodicals received currently in Parisian libraries. Dates and holdings are not given.

Periodicals of South African libraries. Tydskrifte in Suid-Afrikaanse biblioteke. [Pub. by] South African Council for Scientific and Industrial Research and Nat. Council for Social Research. Pretoria, 1961. 1v. Loose-leaf.   **EA56**

"A revised edition of the *Catalog of Union periodicals*" (Johannesburg, 1943–49. 525p. and suppl.).

A union list of periodicals in South African libraries.

Union list of Russian scientific and technical periodicals available in European libraries. Liste des périodiques scientifiques et techniques russes existant dans les bibliothèques européennes. Eds.: L. J. van der Wolk and S. Zandstra. Amsterdam, Netherlands Univ. Pr., 1963– . v.1– .   **EA57**

Contents: v.1, The Netherlands.

The listing of the journals is in the Cyrillic alphabet with transliteration. This is followed by sections of Russian journals edited in Western languages; Western journals with translations of Russian articles; cover-to-cover translations of Russian journals; Russian journals with summaries and/or tables of contents in English; and subject index.

Abbreviations

✤ Two of the most useful lists of scientific periodical abbreviations are *Chemical abstracts: List of periodicals with key to library files* (ED12) and *Biological abstracts: List of serials with word abbreviations* (EC8). See also the abbreviations used in the *World list of scientific periodicals* (EA42).

Akademiia Nauk SSSR. Institut Nauchnoi Informatsii. Ukazatel' sokrashchennykh i polnykh nazvanii nauchnoi i tekhnicheskoi literatury. Moskva, 1957. 236p.   **EA58**

Key to the abbreviations of some 12,000 world periodical titles in the series of Russian abstract journals, *Referativnyi zhurnal* (EA72), for various fields of science and technology. Lists full title and country of origin for each abbreviation.

Davidsson, Åke. Periodica technica abbreviata: a list of initial abbreviations of technical and scientific periodicals. Stockholm, Victor Petterson's Bokindustrieaktiebolag, 1946. 52p. (Handbook no.1 of the Tekniska Litteratursällskapet) **EA59**

Title page and preface in Swedish and English.

Lists some 2100 initial abbreviations of serial publications, including Russian abbreviations.

Special Libraries Association. Rio Grande Chapter. Report Series Dictionary Committee. Dictionary of report series codes, ed. by Helen F. Redman and Lois E. Godfrey. N.Y., Assoc., 1962. 648p. **EA60**

In two sections: pt.1, Report series codes with related agencies; pt.2, Corporate entries with related codes.

Wyandotte—ASTM Punched Card Project. CODEN for periodical titles: an aid to the storage and retrieval of information and to communication involving journal references. Prep. and maintained for Committee E-13. L. E. Kuentzel, ed. Philadelphia, Amer. Soc. for Testing and Materials, 1963. 426p. (ASTM special technical publ. no.329) **EA61**

———— Supplement, 1– . 1964– .

"Lists a set of unique, four-letter codes or CODEN for the titles of scientific periodicals as an aid to the storage and retrieval of information, an aid in the preparation of bibliographies or compilations of references, and an aid in general communication involving references to published material."— [*Introd.*].

INDEXES AND ABSTRACT JOURNALS

Bibliography

U.S. Library of Congress. Science and Technology Division. A guide to the world's abstracting and indexing services in science and technology. Wash., 1963. 183p. (National Federation of Science Abstracting and Indexing Services. Report no.102) **EA62**

Contains 1855 titles originating in 40 countries.

In two main sections: (1) Services, arranged by Universal Decimal Classification; (2) Services, arranged alphabetically, giving the full information about each service.

Covers the pure and applied sciences including medicine, agriculture, etc. Country index and subject index.

Combines and brings up to date two previous publications: (1) *A guide to U.S. indexing and abstracting services in science and technology* (1960), and (2) *Index bibliographicus*, 4th ed., v.1, *Science and technology*.

Indexes

Applied science and technology index (formerly Industrial arts index). N.Y., Wilson, 1913– . Monthly, with quarterly and annual cumulations. **EA63**

From 1913 to 1957, entitled *Industrial arts index*. With v.46, 1958, this was divided into two indexes: (1) the *Applied science and technology index*, which carried on the old volume numbering, and (2) the *Business periodicals index* (CH72).

A cumulative subject index to some 200 American and English periodicals in the fields of aeronautics, automation, chemistry, construction, electricity and electrical communication, engineering, geology and metallurgy, industrial and mechanical arts, machinery, physics, transportation, and related subjects.

No author entries.

British technology index: a current subject-guide to articles in British technical journals. Ed. by E. J. Coates. London, Lib. Assoc., 1962– . v.1– . Monthly. (11 monthly issues and bound annual volume) (Distr. in U.S. by Bowker) **EA64**

An alphabetical, specific, subject index to some 400 British technical journals, designed to give an up-to-date record of current literature. About one third of the material is not covered either by abstracts or by other indexing services.

Covers engineering, chemical technology, mining, metallurgy, and allied fields.

Repertorium der technischen Journal-Literatur, 1823–1908. Berlin, Heymann, 1856–1909. 40v. **EA65**

Title varies; publisher varies.

Contents: 1823–53, pub. 1856. 1049p.; 1854–68, pub. 1871–73. 2v.; 1869–73, pub. 1876–78. 2v.; 1874–1908, pub. 1875–1909. 35v.

1823–76, hrsg. im Auftrage des Königlich Preussischen Ministeriums für Handel, Gewerbe und öffentliche Arbeiten; 1877–1908, hrsg. im Auftrage des Kaiserlichen Patentamts.

A subject index to more than 400 periodicals in various languages, arranged alphabetically by the German subject word followed, in volumes from 1892 on, by the French and English equivalents. Each volume has a detailed subject index to this subject list which, in volumes before 1892, is an index of German words only, but from 1892 includes French and English words in the same alphabet; volumes from 1897 on have an author index also. Still useful for older and foreign material.

Continued by the *Fortschritte der Technik*. 1.–2. Jahrg., 1909–11. Berlin, Bibliographisch Zentralverlag, 1910–11. 9v.

Repertorium technicum. Nederlandsch Instituut voor Documentatie en Registratur. v.1–12⁴, 1931–April 1943. 'sGravenhage, Nijhoff, 1931–43. Bimonthly. **EA66**

An international, bimonthly bibliography, listing some 25,000–30,000 titles, annually, of books and articles appearing in periodicals on technical and allied subjects. Arranged by the Universal Decimal Classification. Besides the citation to the location of the article, reference is also given, when possible, to a journal in which an abstract may be found.

Reuss, Jeremias David. Repertorium commentationum a societatibus litterariis editarum . . . T.7. Gottingae, Dieterich, 1808. 514p. (Repr.: N.Y., Burt Franklin, 1961) **EA67**

Contents: Mathesis, mechanica, hydrostatica, hydraulica, hydrotechnica, aerostatica, pnevmatica, technologia, architectura civilis, scientia navalis, scientia militaris.

For complete set *see* EA15.

Technical book review index, issued by the Technology Dept. of the Carnegie Library of Pittsburgh, 1917–28. Pittsburgh, Carnegie Lib., 1917–29. 12v. Quarterly. **EA68**

A quarterly index listing much material not given in the *Book review digest* (AA314). Gives title of book and bibliographical data, references to periodicals, and brief quotations.

Continued informally, though with a gap of seven years, by:

———— Comp. and ed. in the Technology Dept., Carnegie Library of Pittsburgh. N.Y., Special Libraries Assoc., 1935– . v.1– . Monthly (except July and Aug.). **EA69**

A very useful guide to reviews in scientific, technical, and trade journals, with brief quotations from the reviews.

Abstract journals

Applied mechanics reviews; a critical review of the world literature in applied mechanics and related engineering science. v.1, Jan. 1948– . Easton, Pa., Amer. Soc. of Mechanical Engineers, 1948– . Monthly. **EA70**

An abstract journal, international in scope.

Annual subject and author indexes. Titles of foreign articles are translated into English.

France. Centre National de la Recherche Scientifique. Bulletin signalétique. Paris, Centre de Documentation du C.N.R.S., 1948–60. v.9–21. Monthly. **EA71**

Title varies; v.1–8 had title *Bulletin analytique;* v.9–16, in a new organization, also were called *Bulletin analytique.*

An international abstract journal, exhaustive in coverage, surveying more than 5000 periodicals from many countries. Titles are translated into French. Abstracts in French.

v.9–21 in two parts: pt.1: Mathématiques, astronomie, physique, chimie, sciences de l'ingénieur, sciences de la terre; pt.2: Sciences biologiques, sciences pharmacologique, industries alimentaires, agriculture.

Superseded by the following sections which continue the volume numbering:

Sec. 1, Mathématiques pure et appliquées. 1961– . v.22– . Monthly.

Sec. 2, Astronomie et astrophysique; Physique du globe. 1961– . v.22– . Monthly.

Sec. 3, Physique I: Généralités—physique mathématique, méchanique, acoustique, optique, chaleur, thermodynamique. 1961– . v.22– . Monthly.

Sec. 4, Physique II: Électricité. 1961– . v.22– . Monthly.

Sec. 5, Physique nucléare, 1961– . v.22– . Monthly.

Sec. 6, Structure de la matière. 1961– . v.22– . Monthly.

Sec. 7, Chimie I: Chimie générale, chimie physique, chimie minérale, chimie analytique, chimie organique. 1961– . v.22– . Monthly.

Sec. 8, Chimie II: Chimie appliquée, métallurgie. 1961– . v.22– . Monthly.

Sec. 9, Sciences de l'ingénieur, 1961– . v.22– . Monthly.

Sec. 10, Sciences de la terre, 1. Minéralogie, géochimie, pétrographie. 1961– . v.22– . Monthly.

Sec. 11, Sciences de la terre, 2. Physique du globe, géologie, paléontologie. 1961– . v.22– . Monthly.

Sec. 12, Biophysique. Biochimie. Chimie analytique biologique. 1961– . v.22– . Monthly.

Sec. 13, Sciences pharmacologiques, toxicologie. 1961– . v.22– . Monthly.

Sec. 14, Microbiologie. Virus. Bactériophages. Immunologie. Génétique. 1961– . v.22– . Monthly.

Sec. 15, Pathologie générale et experimentale. 1961– . v.22– . Monthly.

Sec. 16, Biologie et physiologie animales. 1961– . v.22– . Monthly.

Sec. 17, Biologie et physiologie vegetales. 1961– . v.22– . Monthly.

Sec. 18, Sciences agricoles, zootechnie, phytiatrie et phytopharmacie, aliments et industries alimentaires. 1961– . v.22– . Monthly.

Sec. 19, Sciences humaines, philosophie. 1947– . v.1– . Quarterly.

Sec. 20, Psychologie. Pédagogie. 1961– . v.15– . Quarterly.

Sec. 21, Sociologie. Sciences du langage. 1961– . v.15– . Quarterly.

Sec. 22, Histoire des sciences et des techniques. 1961– . v.15– . Quarterly.

Referativnyi zhurnal: . . . Moskva, 1953– . Issued by: Akademiia Nauk SSSR. Institut Nauchnoi Informatsii. Frequency varies. **EA72**

A major abstract journal for the world's literature in most branches of science and technology. Bibliographic information is listed in original languages following the Russian entry.

Titles and coverage of series have varied greatly since its establishment. As announced for 1965, there are 24 principal series, designated *svodnyi tom* (joint volume). Chapters of the joint volumes are issued as separate periodicals with their own titles, and designated *vypusk RZh* (section of the *Referativnyi zhurnal*). Another 32 titles are issued separately without cumulation in a joint volume, and are also designated *vypusk RZh.*

All joint volumes, and most chapters or separate periodicals, are offered for subscription with or without subject and author indexes.

Subscription information appears annually as a special supplement to the sales catalog *Gazety i zhurnaly SSSR.*

Titles of the joint volumes (in Russian alphabetical order), as announced for 1965, are:

Avtomatika, telemechanika i vychislitel'naia tekhnika; svodnyi tom . . .
Avtomobil'nye dorogi
Avtomobil'nyi i gorodskoi transport
Biologiia
Vodnyi transport
Vozdushnyi transport
Geografiia
Geologiia
Geofizika
Gornoe delo
Zhelezznodorozhnyi transport
Kibernetika
Legkaia promyshlennost'
Matematika
Metallurgiia
Mekhanika
Promyshlennyi transport
Radiotekhnika i elektrosviaz'
Teploenergetika
Tekhnologiia mashinostroeniia
Fizika
Khimiia
Ekonomika promyshlennosti
Elektrotekhnika i ee primenenie

Among titles issued as separate periodicals, not included in joint volumes, are: *Astronomiia, Biologicheskaia khimiia, Geodeziia, Issledovanie kosmicheskogo prostranstva, Meditsinskaia geografiia, Nauchnaia i tekhnicheskaia informatsiia,* and *IAdernye reaktory.*

See also Meditsinskii referativnyi zhurnal (EJ42).

U.S. Defense Documentation Center. Defense Supply Agency. Technical abstract bulletin, 1953– . Alexandria, Va., 1953– . Semimonthly. **EA73**

"This bulletin is provided for the users of the D.D.C." Sent only to qualified users.

"TAB announces the availability of research, development, test and evaluation documents acquired by the . . . center."

—— Technical abstract bulletin indexes. Semimonthly.

Includes four indexes: (1) Corporate author—Monitoring agency; (2) Subject; (3) Personal author; and (4) Contract.

Publisher and frequency vary. Title varies: March 1953–Aug. 1957, *Title announcement bulletin.*

U.S. government research and development reports (formerly U.S. government research reports). Springfield, Va., U.S. Dept. of Commerce. Clearinghouse for Federal Scientific and Technical Information, 1946– . v.1– . Semimonthly. **EA74**

Subtitle: A semi-monthly abstract journal for science and industry. Annual subject and author cumulated indexes. Frequency varies.

Title varies: Jan. 1946–June 1949, *Bibliography of scientific and industrial reports;* July 1949–Sept. 1954, *Bibliography of technical reports* (varies slightly); Oct. 1954–1964, *U.S. government research reports.*

—— Numerical index to v.1–10, 1946–48. N.Y., Special Libraries Assoc., 1949. 522p.

An index by PB number (assigned by the Office of Technical Services) to the first 10v. of the *Bibliography of scientific and industrial reports.*

Correlation indexes

Government-wide index to federal research and development reports. U.S. Dept. of Commerce. Clearinghouse for Federal Scientific and Technical Information. Wash., Govt. Prt. Off., 1965– . v.1, no.1, Feb. 1965– . **EA75**

Published "to satisfy a need for a single reference guide to new unclassified Government-sponsored research and development in the physical sciences, engineering and related technology." Compiled by computer from the previous month's announcement journals of the Atomic Energy Commission, the National Aeronautics and Space Administration, the Defense Documentation Center, and the Clearinghouse.

Indexing records of these journals are merged under five indexes: (1) subject, (2) personal author, (3) corporate source, (4) report number, and (5) accession number.

Special Libraries Council of Philadelphia and Vicinity. Correlation index: document series and PB reports, comp. by the Science-Technology Group, Special Libraries Council of Philadelphia and Vicinity, with the cooperation of Office of Technical Services, U.S. Dept. of Commerce, Wash., D.C. Ed. by Gretchen E. Runge. N.Y., Special Libraries Assoc., 1953. 271p. **EA76**

"Many of the unclassified and declassified documents listed as PB Reports in the *Bibliography of Technical Reports* have also appeared under other series designations . . . This correlation has been compiled to show the relationship of these miscellaneous document series to the PB Report numbers . . ."— *Pref.*

For the *Bibliography of technical reports, see* EA74 (annotation).

U.S. Defense Documentation Center. Armed Services Technical Information Agency. Correlation index of technical reports (AD-PB reports). Wash., U.S. Dept. of Commerce. Off. of Technical Services, 1958. 184p. (PB 151567S) **EA77**

A cross index from ASTIA document numbers (AD) to the ones assigned by the Office of Technical Services (PB) in making the reports available for sale to the public. In most cases prices are given for both microfilm and photocopy, and occasionally for the original.

Index to PB reports listed in U.S. government research reports. Wash., Technical Information Service, 1953– . v.19– . Monthly, with annual cumulations. **EA78**

Title varies.

ENCYCLOPEDIAS AND HANDBOOKS

Ballentyne, Denis William George and **Walker, Louis E. Q.** A dictionary of named effects and laws in chemistry, physics, and mathematics. 2d rev. and enl. ed. N.Y., Macmillan, 1961. 234p. il. **EA79**

1st ed. 1958.

A dictionary of terms known by the names of the scientists who discovered them or worked in the fields with which their names have become connected, e.g., Curie's Law, Einstein's Principle of Relativity, Fourier's Series, etc.

Gives brief definitions of the law or theory but no indication as to who the scientist was or when he lived.

Burington, Richard Stevens and **May, Donald C.** Handbook of probability and statistics, with tables. Sandusky, Ohio, Handbook Publ., 1953. 332p. il. **EA80**

Darmstaedter, Ludwig. Handbuch zur Geschichte der Naturwissenschaften und der Technik . . . 2. umgearb. und verm. Aufl. unter Mitwirkung von R. du Bois-Reymond und C. Schaefer, hrsg. von L. Darmstaedter. Berlin, Springer, 1908. 1262p. (Repr.: N.Y., Kraus Repr. Corp., 1960) **EA81**

Chronological list of about 12,000 important scientific discoveries and inventions, giving for each its date, name of discoverer or inventor, and other brief data. Alphabetical indexes of (1) names, and (2) subjects.

Enciclopedia storica delle scienze e delle loro applicazioni, opera comp. con la collaborazione di eminenti specialisti. . . . Milano, Hoepli, [1941–43]. v.1–2. il. **EA82**

Ed., Arturo Uccelli.

Contents: v.1, Le scienze fisiche e matematiche; v.2, t.1–2, Le scienze applicate e la tecnica.

Nonalphabetical. A survey of pure and applied science from ancient to modern times. Includes biographies and some bibliographies. Embodies much of the same material, text, and illustrations appearing in the French work *La science, ses progrès, ses applications.* Paris, Larousse, 1933–34. 2v.

Gardner, Martin. Fads and fallacies in the name of science. Rev. ed. N.Y., Dover, 1957. 363p. **EA83**

A revised and expanded edition of the work first published in 1952 under the title *In the name of science.*

A collection of essays giving information about modern pseudo scientists and their theories, e.g., Voliva's flat earth, Velikovsky's worlds in collision, Bates's perfect sight without glasses, flying saucers, etc.

Includes index of names.

Handwörterbuch der Naturwissenschaften. 2. Aufl. hrsg. von R. Dittler, G. Joos, [and others]. Jena, Fischer, 1931–35. 10v. il. **EA84**

—— Sachregister und systematische Inhaltsübersicht. Jena, Fischer, 1935. 242p., 16p.

An authoritative work for scholars and specialists, covering all the natural sciences, botany, zoology, physiology, mineralogy and geology, physics, and chemistry. Long, signed articles on large subjects; good illustrations; bibliographies; biographies of men not living. Does not give separate articles on species or other small subjects, and does not include definitions or derivations of terms.

Harper encyclopedia of science, ed. by James R. Newman. N.Y., Harper, 1963. 4v. il. **EA85**

An encyclopedia covering astronomy, biochemistry and biophysics, biology, chemistry, geology, history and philosophy of science (and logic), mathematics, meteorology, physics, and technology. Articles have been contributed by some 450 specialists and are signed. For the most part they are concise and are written for the scientist or the intelligent, educated layman. Bibliographies are not affixed to the articles, but there is a classified bibliography in v.4, which lists reference works, general discussions, survey texts, and works on special topics. All material is in English. Comprehensive index.

McGraw-Hill encyclopedia of science and technology; an international reference work. N.Y., McGraw-Hill, 1960. 15v. il. **EA86**

A comprehensive encyclopedia covering all branches of science and technology, except that for the behavioral and medical sciences only the preprofessional aspects are treated. Articles are written at the level of the intelligent layman, rather than for the specialist in the field, and most of them, "and at least the introductory parts of all of them, are within the comprehension of the college undergraduate . . . ."—*Pref.*

An introductory article generally provides a broad survey of each branch of science, and separate articles cover the main subdivisions and more specific aspects. Cross references lead to related topics. Biographical and historical articles are excluded. Bibliographies follow most of the longer articles, and many articles are signed.

v.15 is a detailed index to the whole work.

Kept up to date by the *McGraw-Hill yearbook of science and technology,* 1962– .

Special Libraries Association. Science-Technology Division. Handbook of scientific and technical awards in the

United States and Canada, 1900–1952, ed. by Margaret A. Firth. N.Y., Assoc., 1956. 491p. **EA87**

"A selected listing of the most important awards presented by certain of the scientific and technical societies in the United States and Canada to individuals in recognition of their meritorious achievements in scientific fields."

Arranged alphabetically by name of society with the awards listed chronologically under society, giving names of the recipients and, from 1929 to 1952, citations of published references concerning the awards. An index of recipients and award titles, and a separate subject index.

Van Nostrand's Scientific encyclopedia. 3d ed. Princeton, N.J., Van Nostrand, 1958. 1839p. il. **EA88**

Subtitle: Aeronautics, astronomy, botany, chemical engineering, chemistry, civil engineering, electrical engineering, electronics, geology, guided missiles, mathematics, mechanical engineering, medicine, metallurgy, meteorology, mineralogy, navigation, nuclear science and engineering, photography, physics, radio and television, statistics, zoology.

1st ed. 1938; 2d ed. 1947.

A single, alphabetical arrangement of terms used in science and technology. Articles vary in length from a few lines to two or three columns. No bibliography. Illustrations and tables are clear and well adapted. Numerous cross references aid in finding related materials. A useful work for both the scientist and the layman.

Zimmerman, Oswald Theodore and **Lavine, Irwin.** Scientific and technical abbreviations, signs and symbols. 2d ed. Dover, N.H., Industrial Research Service, 1949. 541p. il. **EA89**

1st ed. 1948. Arranged by groups including: General list of abbreviations and symbols, Chemistry, Mechanics, Shop terms, Electricity, Mapping, etc.

Brief subject index but no general index to abbreviations. The chief purpose is to answer the question "What is the standard abbreviation for . . . ?" rather than "What does this abbreviation stand for?"

Style manuals

Clarke, Emerson. A guide to technical literature production: a concise handbook of production methods. River Forest, Ill., TW Pub., 1961. 182p. **EA90**

A discussion of the production of technical literature by groups or teams of scientists or writers. "Pt.1 describes the elements of production such as the organization, operation, and management of technical literature production groups; pt.2 is devoted to the special problems of recruiting, evaluating, and upgrading the technical writer."—*Introd.*

Harwell, George C. Technical communication. N.Y., Macmillan, 1960. 332p. il. **EA91**

A handbook on the principles of effective treatment of letters, reports, articles, and speeches, primarily for the field of engineering but applicable as well to business, medicine, forestry, and the physical sciences.

Trelease, Sam Farlow. How to write scientific and technical papers. [3d ed.] Baltimore, Williams and Wilkins, 1958. 185p. **EA92**

Earlier editions entitled *The scientific paper: how to prepare it, how to write it.* 1947, 1951.

This edition has been reorganized and much rewritten, and includes material on research methods, the use of the library, the technique of writing a paper, form and usage, the treatment of tables and illustrations, etc.

Weil, Benjamin Henry. The technical report: its preparation, processing, and use in industry and government. N.Y., Reinhold, 1954. 485p. il. **EA93**

A useful compilation of papers presented in Sept. 1953, before the Division of Chemical Literature of the American Chemical Society. The chapters cover such topics as: writing and editing, the literature summary, oral reporting, style manuals, graphs and tables, distribution, security regulations, filing, cataloging, control of classified reports, storage, and abstracting.

DICTIONARIES

Bibliography

Marton, Tibor W. Foreign-language and English dictionaries in the physical sciences and engineering; a selected bibliography 1952 to 1963. Wash., 1964. 189p. (U.S. National Bureau of Standards. Miscellaneous publ. 258) **EA94**

"Lists over 2800 unilingual, bilingual, and polyglot dictionaries, glossaries and encyclopedias . . . arranged in 49 subject classes . . . Forty-seven foreign languages are represented." —*Abstract.*

Saur, Karl-Otto and **Gringmuth, Grete.** Technik und Wirtschaft in fremden Sprachen. München, Verlag Dokumentationen der Technik, 1960. 449p. Loose-leaf. **EA95**

Subtitle: Internationale Bibliographie der Fachwörterbücher, Fachencyklopädien, Fachsprachlehrmittel, der Abhandlungen zur Übersetzungstechnik, zur Wörterbuchherstellung, der Bibliographien von Wörterbüchern und Übersetzungsdiensten.

An international bibliography of technical dictionaries arranged in subject groupings, with indexes by language, names, and catchwords.

———— ———— Ergänzung 1961 zum Grundwerk 1960. München, 1961– . v.1– . Annual.

United Nations Educational, Scientific and Cultural Organization. Bibliography of interlingual scientific and technical dictionaries. Bibliographie de dictionnaires scientifiques et techniques multilingues. Bibliografía de diccionarios científicos y técnicos plurilingües. [4. ed. rev. and enl.]. [Paris], UNESCO, 1961. 236p. (Its Documentation and terminology of science) **EA96**

1st ed. 1951; 3d ed. 1953.

Arranged by Universal Decimal Classification; lists some 2000 dictionaries in about 85 languages. An index by languages, an index by authors, and subject indexes in English, French, and Spanish. Introductory and explanatory material is also in these three languages.

———— Bibliography of monolingual scientific and technical glossaries . . . Bibliographie de vocabulaires scientifiques et techniques monolingues . . . By Eugen Wüster. [Paris], UNESCO, [1955–59] 2v. (Its Documentation and terminology of science) **EA97**

v.1, National standards; v.2, Miscellaneous sources.

v.1 lists only the standardized technical glossaries as approved by the national associations of standardization; v.2 lists 1043 privately published glossaries in 26 languages.

Arranged by Universal Decimal Classification, and then by language.

General

See also Dictionaries under name of special science, e.g., Physics—Dictionaries.

Beadnell, Charles Marsh. Dictionary of scientific terms as used in the various sciences. London, Watts, 1942. 232p., 13p. (The thinker's library, no.65) **EA98**

A reprint of the 1938 edition, with a supplementary section of 13p.

Chambers's Technical dictionary, ed. by C. F. Tweney

and L. E. C. Hughes. 3d ed. rev. with suppl. N.Y., Macmillan, 1958. 1028p. il. **EA99**

1st ed. 1940.

Supplement, p.952–1028, includes the more recent terms in nuclear physics, electronics, automation, etc.

Frequently reprinted.

Crispin, Frederic Swing. Dictionary of technical terms. 9th ed. rev. Milwaukee, Bruce, 1961. 454p. il. **EA100**

1st ed. 1929.

Subtitle: Containing definitions of commonly used expressions in aeronautics, architecture, woodworking and building trades, electrical and metalworking trades, printing, chemistry, plastics, etc.

Hough, John N. Scientific terminology. N.Y., Rinehart, 1953. 231p. **EA101**

This small handbook, intended for the student, aims at helping those who have little or no knowledge of Latin or Greek to understand the meaning and formation of scientific terms. Most of the chapters have brief, annotated bibliographies.

Nybakken, Oscar Edward. Greek and Latin in scientific terminology. Ames, Iowa State College Pr., 1959. 321p. **EA102**

Deals with the "construction of the technical terms, names, and specific epithets used in the medical and biological sciences."—*Pref.*

Steffanides, George F. The scientist's thesaurus; a treasury of the stock words of science . . . 3d ed. Fitchburg, Mass., Author (?), 1963. 142p. **EA103**

"A revision and extension of the syllabus of scientific terminology which was originally printed in mimeograph form in 1933, and again published in 1956."

Gives the Latin or scientific name, prefix or combining form, English translation, and a listing of stock words using the form.

Juvenile

Compton's Illustrated science dictionary. Ed. in chief, Charles A. Ford; Editorial director, John S. Richardson; Executive ed., Leo Charles Fay. Indianapolis, David-Stewart, 1963. 632p. il. **EA104**

"Prepared to help young people and adults understand and use correctly the exacting language of today's science and technology."—*Pref.*

Gives pronunciation, definition, and a sentence illustrating the use of each word. Indicates differing meanings of words in the different sciences. The words have been chosen from 14 sciences taught in the schools: aeronautics, anatomy, astronautics, astronomy, biology, botany, chemistry, earth science, engineering, mathematics, medicine, physics, physiology, and zoology.

Foreign terms

Czech

Kapesní anglicko-česky a cesko-anglický technický slovník. Sest. Josef Novák. [Vyd.1] Praha, Státní Nakl. Technické Literatury, 1958. 495p. **EA105**

Added title page: A concise English-Czech and Czech-English technical dictionary.

French

Cusset, Francis. English-French and French-English technical dictionary; metallurgy, mining, electricity, chemistry, mechanics, sciences. 2d ed., compl. rev. and enl. N.Y., Chemical Pub. Co., 1957. 663p. **EA106**

De Vries, Louis. French-English science dictionary; for students in agricultural, biological and physical sciences, with a revised supplement of terms in aeronautics, electronics, radar, radio, television, atomic energy, nuclear science and technology and a new guide for translators. 3d ed. N.Y., McGraw-Hill, [c1962]. 665p. **EA107**

1st ed. 1940; 2d ed. 1951.

German

De Vries, Louis. German-English science dictionary for students in chemistry, physics, biology, agriculture, and related sciences. 3d ed., incl. suppl. of new terms. N.Y., McGraw-Hill, 1959. 592p. **EA108**

1st ed. 1940; 2d ed. 1946.

—— German-English technical and engineering dictionary. 1st ed. N.Y., McGraw-Hill, 1950. 928p. **EA109**

—— —— Supplement. 1959. 386p.

Adds about 50,000 terms.

—— English-German technical and engineering dictionary. 1st ed. N.Y., McGraw-Hill, 1954. 997p. **EA110**

A companion volume to the above.

Lists more than 130,000 entries. Emphasis is on engineering terms, but other technical terms and some few general terms are included.

—— —— Supplement. 1959. 285p.

Adds about 40,000 terms.

Ernst, Richard. Wörterbuch der industriellen Technik: einschliesslich Hilfswissenschaften und Bauwesen. Wiesbaden, Brandstetter Verlag, 1959–61. 2v. **EA111**

2. Aufl. 1954.

Added title page in English: Dictionary of industrial technics; including related fields of science and civil engineering.

Contents: v.1, German-English. 5th ed., entirely rev., 1959; v.2, English-German. 10th ed., with supplement, 1961.

"Attempts to define all the meanings of the ambiguous rootwords which have attained significance in the language of technology."—*Pref.*

Leibiger, O. W. and **Leibiger, I. S.** German-English and English-German dictionary for scientists, comprising chemistry, physics, mathematics, engineering, aeronautics, dynamics, biology, physiology, medicine, and other sciences. 1st ed. Ann Arbor, Mich., J. W. Edwards, 1950. 381p., 360p. **EA112**

Compiled over a period of 30 years from scientific writings in both languages.

Leidecker, Kurt Friedrich. German-English technical dictionary. Based on data comp. by the U.S. Air Force. N.Y., S. F. Vanni, 1951. 2v. (968p.) **EA113**

Subtitle: Of aeronautics, rocketry, space-navigation, atomic physics, higher mathematics, jet-engines, turbines, hydraulics, petroleum industry, civil and mechanical engineering, ballistics, electronics, radio, radar, aerophotography, television, infrared research, communication, meteorology, topography, aeromedicine.

Lueger Lexikon der Technik. 4. vollst. neubearb. und erw. Aufl. Hrsg. von Alfred Ehrhardt und Hermann Franke. Stuttgart, Deutsche Verlags-Anstalt, 1960–63. v.1–5. il. (In progress) **EA114**

To be in 17v.

Contents: Bd.1, Grundlagen des Maschinenbaues. 1960; Bd.2, Grundlagen des Elektrotechnik und Kerntechnik. 1960; Bd.3, Werkstoffe und Werkstoffprüfung. 1961; Bd.4, Lexikon der Bergbaues. 1962; Bd.5, Lexikon der Hüttentechnik. 1963.

Each volume is an alphabetically arranged dictionary, with definitions varying in length from a few lines to several columns, many with bibliographies. Contributors are identified by means of numerical codes.

Webel, A. A German-English dictionary of technical, scientific, and general terms. 3d ed. London, Routledge and Paul, 1953. 939p.   **EA115**

Subtitle: Including a list of atomic weights, specific gravities, melting and boiling points of elements, abbreviations, signs and symbols, botanical section, and an appendix of new words.

1st ed., 1930, *A German-English technical and scientific dictionary.*

Greek, Modern

Charalampēs, Iōnnēs B. Technikon anglohellēnikon lexikon. Athēnai, 1958. 486p.   **EA116**

Hungarian

Magyar-angol müszaki szótár. [Szerk: Nagy Ernö, Klár János és Katona Lóránt vezetésével az Akadémiai Kiadó müszaki szótárszerkesztöi munkaközössége] Budapest, Akadémiai Kiadó, 1957. 752p.   **EA117**

Added title page: Hungarian-English technical dictionary. "This is the first Hungarian-English dictionary of technical words and terms, and at the same time . . . this is the very first attempt to correlate the meaning of words of Hungarian and English scientific and technical terms." Lists about 120,000 Hungarian technical terms.

Angol-magyar müszaki szótár. Szerk: Nagy Ernö [és] Klár János. Teljesen átdolg. és böv. kiad. Budapest, Akadémiai Kiadó, 1959. 791p.   **EA118**

Added title page: English-Hungarian technical dictionary. Compl. rev. and enl. ed.

1st ed. 1951. A companion volume to the entry above.

Italian

Denti, Renzo. Dizionario tecnico, italiano-inglese, inglese-italiano. Aggiuntevi: Le abbreviazioni techniche anglo-americane di uso corrente nonchè numerose tabelle di conversione e riduzione indispensabili nei traffici internazionali. 5. ed. migliorata ed aum. Milano, Hoepli, 1962 [i.e., 1961]. 1307p.   **EA119**

Gatto, Simon. Dizionario tecnico scientifico illustrato: italiano-inglese, inglese-italiano. A dictionary of technical and scientific terms: English-Italian, Italian-English. Milan, Ceschina, 1960. 1381p. il.   **EA120**

A collection of some 60,000 terms covering both engineering and scientific fields, including many new terms culled from recent scientific literature.

Marolli, Giorgio. Dizionario tecnico: inglese-italiano, italiano-inglese. Technical dictionary: English-Italian, Italian-English. 8. ed. riv. ed ampl. Firenze, Le Monnier, 1964. (Distr. by Heinman, N.Y., 1964) 1621p. il. 38 charts.   **EA121**

A very comprehensive bilingual dictionary.

Norwegian

Ansteinsson, John. Norwegian-English technical dictionary. Norsk-engelsk teknisk ordbok. Trondheim, F. Brun; N.Y., Kraus Periodicals, 1954. 327p.   **EA122**

At head of title: Norwegian Council for Technical Terminology.

Polyglot

Medeiros, Manuel Francisco da Silva de. Dicionário técnico poliglota: português, espanhol, francês, italiano,

inglês, alemâo. Lisboa, Gomes & Rodrigues, 1949–53?. 8v.   **EA123**

Pt.1, Lexicon. 3v.; pt.2, Indexes. 5v.

Covers pure and applied sciences, medicine and pharmacy, engineering and architecture, military science, transport and communications, industry and commerce.

The Lexicon lists, in alphabetical order, some 131,000 Portuguese terms and expressions, each followed by its synonym in Portuguese, and by its translation into five languages: Spanish, French, Italian, English, German. The indexes cover each language and are numerically keyed to the Lexicon. Each index volume includes one language and Latin.

Technologisches Wörterbuch . . . 6. vollkommen neubearb. Aufl., hrsg. von Alfred Schlomann. Berlin, Springer, 1932. 3v.   **EA124**

English subtitle: Crafts and industries, engineering and engineering science, mining and metallurgy; raw and finished materials . . . ; electrical and communication engineering; metrology; . . . optical, medical, and sanitary engineering; safety engineering; civil engineering and chemical technology; agriculture and forestry; foodstuffs, textile and clothing industries; trade, banking, and fair practice; traffic, . . . motor engineering; shipbuilding and navigation; patents, law, and customs [etc.].

v.1, German-English-French; v.2, English-German-French; v.3, French-German-English.

Tekniikan sanasto, saksa-englanti-suomi-ruotsi. Teknisk ordbok, tysk-engelsk-finsk-svensk. Technisches Wörterbuch, deutsch-englisch-finnisch-schwedisch. Technical vocabulary, German-English-Finnish-Swedish. Toimituskunta: Väinö Airas . . . Väinö Valkola . . . Lauri Hendell-Auterinen . . . [etc.]. Helsinki, Kustannuso-sakeyhtiö Otava, [1940]. 1232col.   **EA125**

Portuguese

Furstenau, Eugênio E. Dicionário de têrmos técnicos, inglês-português. 4. ed. Rio de Janeiro, Ed. Globo, 1962. 935p. il. (Enciclopedias e dicionários Globo)   **EA126**

Russian

Bray, Alexander. Russian-English scientific-technical dictionary. N.Y., Internat. Univ. Pr., 1945. 551p.   **EA127**

Added title page in Russian.

Includes some 25,000 Russian scientific words and phrases, both the new terms and the older basic ones, with their English meanings.

Very brief definitions; no examples of usage.

Chernukhin, Adol'f Efimovich. English-Russian technical dictionary. Moscow, Central Editorial Board, Foreign-Language Scientific and Technical Dictionaries, 1962. 663p.   **EA128**

Added title page: Anglo-russkii politekhnicheskii slovar'.

Izraileva, Elizaveta IUr'evna. Anglo-russkii slovar' po neftepromyslovomu delu. Sost.: E IU. Izraileva, I. M. Taumina. Moskva, Gos. Nachno-Tekhnicheskoe Izd., 1959. 313p.   **EA129**

Kratkii politekhnicheskii slovar'. Moskva, Gos. Izd-vo Tekhniko-Teoreticheskoi Lit-ry, 1955. 1136p.   **EA130**

An encyclopedic dictionary with short articles on terms in technology and general science, and numerous drawings. Names of contributing authors are listed at the beginning, but individual articles are unsigned.

Bibliography

Hubbell, A. J. Russian-English scientific and technical dictionaries: a survey. N.Y., New York Univ. Committee

for Russian-English Technical Dictionaries, 1960. 20p.
EA131

A survey evaluation and bibliography, with indication of fields needing further work.

Spanish

Castilla's Spanish and English technical dictionary. London, Routledge and Paul; N.Y., Philosophical Lib., 1958. 2v. **EA132**

v.1, English-Spanish. 1611p.; v.2, Spanish-English. 1137p.
A comprehensive and up-to-date dictionary.
"Only the fields of engineering technology are included, and the physical, chemical and biological sciences are excluded, except for those words which are of importance to engineers."—*Introd.*
Abbreviations are given at the beginning of each letter of the alphabet. Important commercial and legal terms are included, as well as some words of significance in everyday language. The words selected are in current usage, and not obsolete terms, and "the language used is that of Spain and Latin America in the Spanish language and of England and the United States in the English language." No definitions except in cases of ambiguity.

Chambers Diccionario tecnológico, español-inglés: inglés-español . . . dir. por C. F. Tweney y L. E. C. Hughes; la traducción española . . . dir. por Carlos Botet. Barcelona, Ed. Omega, 1952. 1227p., 289p. **EA133**

Based on *Chambers's Technical dictionary* (EA99).
The Spanish-English section gives English equivalents for terms and full explanations in Spanish; the second part gives, briefly, Spanish equivalents for English terms.
Covers pure and applied science, medicine, industry, engineering, etc.

Guinle, R. L. A modern Spanish-English and English-Spanish technical and engineering dictionary, containing all the words used in civil, mechanical and electrical engineering; . . . suitable for Spain and all the Spanish-speaking countries of Central America and South America. 3d ed. Mexico, Ed. Continental; N.Y., Dutton, 1958. 311p. **EA134**

1st ed. 1938.
Added title page in Spanish: Nuevo diccionario técnico y de ingeniería.
Subtitle: Also many [words] on aviation, wireless, architecture, railways, automobiles, shipbuilding, marine, chemistry, physics, mathematics, geology, mining, metallurgy, geography, surveying, commerce, agriculture, textile machinery, machine-tools, etc.

Robb, Louis Adams. Engineers' dictionary, Spanish-English and English-Spanish. 2d ed. N.Y., Wiley, 1953. 664p. **EA135**

1st ed. 1944.
Includes more than 44,000 current terms as used in the 18 American republics.

Swedish

Engström, Einar. Svensk-engelsk teknisk ordbok. 6. uppl. Stockholm, Svensk Trävaru-Tidning Förlaget, [1961]. 543p. **EA136**

—— Engelsk-svensk teknisk ordbok. 8. uppl. Stockholm, Svensk Trävaru-Tidning Förlaget, 1960. 541p.

TABLES

Landolt, Hans. Landolt-Börnstein Zahlenwerte und Funktionen aus Physik, Chemie, Astronomie, Geophysik und Technik. 6. Aufl. Berlin, Springer, 1950–59. v.1–4 (in various pts.). (In progress) **EA137**

Volumes published irregularly, covering various areas.

—— Landolt-Börnstein Zahlenwerte und Funktionen aus Naturwissenschaften und Technik. Neue Serie. Gesamtherausgabe: K. H. Hellwege. Berlin, Springer, 1961. Group 1, v.1– . (In progress) **EA138**

Added title page in English: Landolt-Börnstein. Numerical data and functional relationships in science and technology. New series.
This is not a 7th edition, but a "new series, using a somewhat different method of arrangement."
Group 1, Nuclear physics and technology: v.1, Energy levels of nuclei: A=5 to A=257.

National Research Council. International critical tables of numerical data, physics, chemistry and technology, prep. under the auspices of the International Research Council and the National Academy of Sciences by the National Research Council of the United States of America; ed. in chief, Edward W. Washburn. . . . N.Y., pub. for National Research Council by McGraw-Hill, 1926–33. 7v. and index. diagrams. **EA139**

Selected data based on the material in the *Tables annuelles de constantes* . . . Paris, Gauthier-Villars; Chicago, Univ. of Chicago Pr., 1912–

DIRECTORIES

Battelle Memorial Institute. Dept. of Economics and Information Research. Specialized science information services in the United States; a directory of selected specialized information services in the physical and biological sciences. Wash., Nat. Science Foundation, Off. of Science Information Service, 1961. 528p. (NSF.61–68) **EA140**

More than 400 organizations included, classified by field, with information on scope, library collections, kinds of services offered, publications, etc. Index of organization names and of subjects.

Engineering college research review, ed. by Paul T. Bryant and Bernice S. Wilson. Urbana, Ill., Engineering College Research Council of the Amer. Soc. for Engineering Education, 1944– . Biennial. **EA141**

Title varies.
11th edition, 1963, "presents a detailed summary of current research programs being conducted in the major engineering colleges throughout the United States."—*Foreword.*
Arranged by university; gives detailed information on the research programs, policies, personnel, expenditures, and active projects.

Gt.Brit. Dept. of Scientific and Industrial Research and the British Council. Scientific research in British universities and colleges. 1951/52– . London, Stat. Off., 1952– . v.1– . Annual. **EA142**

(None issued, 1952–53.) Title varies slightly.
Arrangement is by university, then by department. A name index and, beginning with 1953/54, a subject index.
Provides brief notes on scientific research in progress in British universities, technical colleges, etc., in England, Wales, Scotland, and Northern Ireland.

MacRae's Blue book . . . : industrial materials equipment; the buying directory for engineering production, purchasing. Chicago, MacRae's Blue Book, [1895?]– . Annual. **EA143**

Organization for Economic Cooperation and Development. Country reports on the organization of scientific research. [Paris], 1963–64. v.1–16. (In progress) (OECD publ.) **EA144**

Separate reports to cover member nations: Austria, Belgium, Canada, Denmark, France, Germany, Greece, Iceland, Ireland, Italy, Luxembourg, Netherlands, Norway, Portugal, Spain, Sweden, Switzerland, Turkey, United Kingdom, United States, and Yugoslavia.

Gives information on the organization of research in each country, e.g., government participation, university and technical institutes, industry participation, etc.

—— Guide to European sources of technical information. [Paris, 1964] 292p. **EA145**

Former title of organization: Organization for European Economic Cooperation.

Covers: Austria, Belgium, Denmark, France, Germany, Greece, Iceland, Ireland, Italy, Luxembourg, Netherlands, Norway, Portugal, Spain, Sweden, Switzerland, Turkey, United Kingdom, and Yugoslavia.

A directory of European agencies in two main parts: pt.1, General sources of information; pt.2, Specialized sources.

For each organization gives name in original language and in English, address, scope of activity, general information, publications, etc.

Providing U.S. scientists with Soviet scientific information. Rev. ed., prep. by Boris I. Gorokhoff, Mass. Inst. of Technology Libraries. [Wash., Nat. Science Foundation], 1962. (Distr. by Publ. Off., Nat. Science Foundation, Wash.) 46p. **EA146**

Succinct reference information on Soviet publications and their acquisition and location in United States libraries, followed by detailed references to the varieties of translation services and programs in English and other languages.

Research centers directory. 2d ed., ed. by Archie M. Palmer and Anthony T. Kruzas. Detroit, Gale Research, 1965. 666p. **EA147**

1st edition, 1960, had title *Directory of university research bureaus and institutes.*

Subtitle: A guide to university-sponsored and other non-profit research organizations established on a permanent basis and carrying on continuing research programs in agriculture, business, conservation, education, engineering and technology, government, law, life sciences, mathematics, area studies, physical and earth sciences, social sciences, and humanities.

Gives full information about each center. Indexes by institution, center, personal name, and subject.

Continued by:

New research centers: a periodic supplement. no.1, May 1965– . Quarterly. **EA148**

The supplement gives the same type of information as the main volume, with indexes by institution and center.

U.S. Library of Congress. Science and Technology Division. Directories in science and technology: a provisional checklist. Wash., Govt. Prt. Off., 1963. 65p. **EA149**

A listing of 304 published directories pertinent to scientific and technological research throughout the world.

Arranged by continent and then by country, subdivided by subject; with an index by subject, subdivided by country.

U.S. National Science Foundation. Organization of the federal government for scientific activities. [Wash.], Govt. Prt. Off., 1956. 349p. (National Science Studies) **EA150**

Subtitle: Federal agencies and their organizational units engaged in: conduct of research and development; planning and administration of research and development; expansion of research and development plant facilities; testing, evaluation, and standardization; training of scientific manpower; dissemination of scientific information; collection of general purpose statistics in the natural and social sciences.

Describes briefly the organization for scientific activities of 38 departments and agencies of the federal government.

U.S. National Science Foundation. Office of Science Information Service. Current research and development in scientific documentation. no.[1]– . Wash., July 1957– . Semiannual. **EA151**

Contains descriptive reports of research projects being carried on in the United States and foreign countries, as reported to the National Science Foundation. Covers information storage and retrieval, mechanical translation, equipment, and related research.

SOCIETIES AND CONGRESSES

See also Societies, p.77–81.

Bates, Ralph Samuel. Scientific societies in the United States. 2d ed. A publication of the Technology Press, Massachusetts Institute of Technology. N.Y., Columbia Univ. Pr., 1958. 297p. **EA152**

1st ed. 1945.

A history of the growth of American scientific societies from 1727 to the Atomic age, 1945–55. Covers the main national societies and the specialized and technical societies of the various states. Bibliography, p.235–68.

Battelle Memorial Institute. Directory of selected scientific institutions in the U.S.S.R. With an introduction to the administration of science and technology in the U.S.S.R. Jan. 1, 1963. Prep. for the National Science Foundation. [Columbus, Ohio, Merrill Books], 1963. v.p. **EA153**

In four main sections: pt.1, Administration of science and technology in the U.S.S.R.; pt.2, The academies of sciences and their principal facilities; pt.3, Directory of selected scientific institutions in the U.S.S.R.; pt.4, Indexes.

Information about each organization usually includes: name, address, director, deputy director, administrative affiliation, selected staff members, and description of its work and publications.

Directory of international scientific organizations. [2d ed.] Paris, UNESCO, 1953. 312p. **EA154**

1st ed. 1950.

Three main chapters cover: (1) basic sciences, (2) applied sciences (agricultural, engineering, and medical), and (3) miscellaneous. For each of the 264 organizations listed, detailed information is given under 16 headings. Subject index.

Directory of natural history and other field study societies in Great Britain . . . ed. by Averil Lysaght. London, pub. for the Carnegie United Kingdom Trust by the British Assoc. for the Advancement of Science, 1959. 217p. **EA155**

Subtitle: Including societies for archaeology, astronomy, meteorology, geology and cognate subjects.

Gives usual directory information.

Israel. National Council for Research and Development. Centre of Scientific and Technological Information. Directory of scientific and technical associations and institutes in Israel. Tel Aviv, Govt. Printer, 1962. 110p., 110p. (Guides to sources of information ser. Directory no.2) **EA156**

Title page and text also in Hebrew.

Gives information on founding, chief officer, membership, branches, affiliations, publications, etc.

National Academy of Sciences. Office of the Foreign Secretary. The Eastern European academies of sciences: a directory. Wash., 1963. 148p. (National Academy of Sciences—National Research Council. Publ. 1090) **EA157**

Describes the academies of sciences in Bulgaria, Czechoslovakia, Hungary, Poland, Rumania, and Yugoslavia. Gives brief history, organization, responsibilities, publications, etc.

Also includes rosters of leading academy officials, and biographical sketches of prominent academicians in each country.

Scientific and learned societies of Great Britain: a handbook compiled from official sources. London, Allen & Unwin, 1884– . v.1– . Annual. **EA158**

Coverage varies but usually includes: pt.1, Government and public bodies conducting scientific research in Great Britain, research in industry, medicine, public health, etc.; pt.2: (1) General science; (2) Subject groups, e.g., Chemistry, Geography, Literature, etc.; (3) Index of society names.

A very useful list, giving for each society: corporate name, address, date of founding, object, officers, meetings, membership, titles of publications with prices, and (in some cases) contents of publications for the year covered. The first volume, 1884, was a basic volume, containing considerable historical information not reprinted in later issues.

Title on title page, 1884–1929, *Year-book of the scientific and learned societies of Great Britain and Ireland;* 1930/31–38/39, *Official yearbook* .... Publication suspended, 1940–50. Publisher varies.

Scientific and technical societies of the United States and Canada. 7th ed. ... Wash., Nat. Academy of Sciences—Nat. Research Council, 1961. 413p., 54p. **EA159**

1st ed. 1927. 6th ed. 1955.

Title varies.

Contents: pt.1, United States, comp. in the Library, National Academy of Sciences—National Research Council; pt.2, Canada, comp. in the Public Relations Office, National Research Council, Canada.

Gives organizational information about 1836 "professional and selected amateur societies in scientific and technical fields."—*Pref.* Information was collected in the latter part of 1960.

Scientific meetings; v.1, no.1, Spring 1957– . N.Y., Special Libraries Assoc., 1957– . v.1– . 3 issues a year. **EA160**

Subtitle varies. 1964: Describing future meetings of technical, scientific, medical, and management organizations and universities.

"An alphabetical listing of organizations . . . sponsoring future national, international, and regional meetings, symposia, colloquia, and institutes." Includes a chronological listing and a subject index.

United Nations Educational, Scientific and Cultural Organization. Science Cooperation Office for Latin America. Scientific institutions and scientists in Latin-America . . . Montevideo, UNESCO Centro de Cooperación Científica para América Latina, 1949– . (In progress) **EA161**

Contents: América Central, v.1– , 1954– ; Argentina, v.1–4¹⁻⁵, 1949–60; Bolivia, v.1– , 1950– ; Brasil, v.1–3, 1950–51; Chile, v.2– , 1959– ; Colombia, v.2– , 1956– ; Cuba, v.1– , 1953– ; Ecuador, v.1– , 1952– ; Mexico, v.1–3, 1950–55; Paraguay, v.1– , 1959– ; Peru, v.1– , 1950– ; Uruguay, v.1–2, 1949–53; Venezuela, v.1–2, 1950–57.

In most cases the later volumes cumulate and supersede earlier volumes. Lists both societies and scientists with information about specialties, publications, etc.

U.S. Library of Congress. International Organization Section. International scientific organizations: a guide to their library, documentation, and information services, prep. under the direction of Kathrine O. Murra. Wash., Govt. Prt. Off., 1962. 794p. **EA162**

General Reference and Bibliography Division. Reference Dept.

Science is interpreted broadly to include technology, agriculture, and medicine. Gives detailed information about each society—its address, work, history, membership, governing body, etc., and publications—usually in considerable detail. Includes a list of acronyms and an index by subject and title.

U.S. Library of Congress. Science and Technology Division. Mainland China organizations of higher learning in science and technology and their publications: a selected guide. Comp. by Chi Wang. Wash., Govt. Prt. Off., 1961. 104p. **EA163**

Gives organizational information and lists publications of: scientific societies; institutes and academies; colleges and universities; governmental research organizations and libraries.

U.S. National Library of Medicine. Congresses; tentative chronological and bibliographical reference list of national and international meetings of physicians, scientists and experts. Wash., Govt. Prt. Off., 1938. 288p. **EA164**

Reprinted from the Library's *Index-catalogue,* 4th ser., 3:1–288. 1938 (EJ13).

Arranged by field, with subject, word, and title index.

—— —— First additions. . . . Wash., Govt. Prt. Off., 1939.

Reprinted from the Library's *Index-catalogue,* 4th ser., 4:29–51 (EJ13).

LABORATORIES

American Society for Testing and Materials. Directory of testing laboratories, commercial—institutional. 2d ed. Philadelphia, 1963. 53p. **EA165**

1st ed. 1955.

Lists 652 commercial testing laboratories; 98 laboratories of the National Conference of Standards Laboratories; and 99 laboratories of institutions prepared to do testing under certain conditions.

Supersedes U.S. National Bureau of Standards, *Directory of commercial and college laboratories,* 1927–47, and ASTM, *Directory of commercial and college testing laboratories,* 1955.

Industrial research laboratories of the United States. 11th ed. Comp. by John H. Gribbin and Sue Singer Krogfus. Wash., Nat. Academy of Sciences—Nat. Research Council, 1960. 698p. (National Research Council publ., no.844) **EA166**

1st ed. 1920; 10th ed. 1956.

"Listings are limited to non-governmental laboratories devoted to fundamental and applied research, including development of products and processes."

Gives information on 5420 laboratories, and for the first time includes a personnel index containing approximately 20,000 names. This index lists: "(1) individuals directly involved in research, or directly concerned with the hiring of the laboratory staff and who are included in the firm's entry in the main body of the Directory; and (2) other research executives in responsible positions" who are not in the main work, the latter identified by italicized type.

Office National des Universités et Écoles Françaises. Laboratoires scientifiques; répertoire. [2. éd.?] Paris, Services d'Édition et de Vente des Publications de l'Éducation Nationale, 1961. 578p. **EA167**

1. éd. 1956.

Detailed information about the scientific laboratories of France, giving specializations, chief personnel, recent publications, etc.

MUSEUMS

Directory of museums and art galleries in the British Isles; comp. by S. F. Markham. South Kensington, Museums Assoc., 1948. 392p. il. **EA168**

Gives general description, scope of collections, publications, educational activities, staff, finances, etc.

Murray, David. Museums, their history and their use, with a bibliography and list of museums in the United Kingdom. Glasgow, Maclehose, 1904. 3v.   **EA169**

v.1, History. List of museums in the United Kingdom; v.2–3, Bibliography.

International in scope. Still valuable for its extensive bibliography, which lists (1) works about museums and museum work, and (2) catalogs and other works relating to particular museums.

Museums directory of the United States and Canada, ed. by Erwin O. Christensen. 1st ed.– . Wash., Amer. Assoc. of Museums, 1961– .   **EA170**

Lists museums of all types—art, history, and science—arranged geographically, giving address, sponsor, executive officer, brief description, publications, hours of opening, etc.

HISTORY

Bibliography

Ferguson, Eugene S. Contributions to bibliography in the history of technology. (In Technology and culture 3:73–84, 167–74, 298–306. 1962; 4:318–30. 1963; 5:416–34, 578–94. 1964; 6:99–107. 1965) (In progress)   **EA171**

An annotated bibliography covering government records, encyclopedias and handbooks, biographical works, bibliographies and directories, early source books, technical museums and exhibitions, etc.

International in scope, including titles of all periods.

Forbes, Robert James. Bibliographia antiqua. Philosophia naturalis. . . . Leiden, Nederlandsch Inst. van het Nabije Osten, 1940–50. 10v.   **EA172**

Contents: (1) Mijnbouw en geologie; (2) Metallurgie; (3) Bouwmaterialen; (4) Aardewerk, faience, glas, glazuur, siersteenen; (5) Verven, kleurstoffen, vernissen, inkten en hunne toepassing; (6) Leder, bereiding en toepassing; (7) Vezelstoffen, grondstoffen en industrie; (8) Papier, papyrus en anfer schrijftmateriaal; (9) Mens en natur; (10) Wetenschap en tecknik.

A listing of books and periodical articles in various languages, published through 1939, on science and its applications in ancient times in various countries.

———— Supplement 1, 1940–50. 1952; Supplement 2, 1950–60. 1963.

Give additional titles in all fields.
no.10752–13240; no.13241–15234.

Horblit, Harrison D. One hundred books famous in science; based on an exhibition held at the Grolier Club. N.Y., Grolier Club, 1964. 449p. il., facsims.   **EA173**

Examples of early scientific works in theoretical, experimental, and applied science, including technology. Full bibliographical descriptions with facsimiles of title pages, and with brief notes on the importance of these books in the history of science.

John Crerar Library. A list of books on the history of science. Jan. 1911. Prep. by A. G. S. Josephson. Chicago, 1911. 297p.   **EA174**

"Includes the social, physical, natural and medical sciences, but omits the applied sciences. . . . Publications on the history of learned institutions have not been included . . . and only such biographies as have a direct bearing on the position of their subjects in the history of science."—*Pref.*

Classed arrangement with author index.

———— ———— Supplement, Dec. 1916. Chicago, 1917. 139p.

———— ———— 2d supplement, prep. by R. B. Gordon. Chicago, 1942–46. Pts.1–6.

Pt.1, General science; pt.2, Mathematics; pt.3, Astronomy; pt.4, Physics; pt.5, Chemistry, crystallography and mineralogy; pt.6, Geology, paleontology.

Russo, François. Histoire des sciences et des techniques: bibliographie. Paris, Hermann, 1954. 186p. (Actualités scientifiques et industrielles, 1204)   **EA175**

A bibliography, in some cases annotated, of general and special works on the history of science and technology. For rare books, locates copies. Emphasis is on titles from western Europe and the Mediterranean region, although materials from other countries are not excluded.

———— ———— Supplément. [Paris?], 1955. [36p.]

Sarton, George. Horus: a guide to the history of science; a first guide for the study of the history of science with introductory essays on science and tradition. Waltham, Mass., Chronica Botanica Co., 1952. 316p.   **EA176**

The first section is composed of three lectures on the history of science; the second section is a bibliographical summary prepared as a guide to students of the history of science. Sec. 2 is divided into four main sections, each subdivided: (1) history, (2) science, (3) history of science, (4) organization of the study and teaching of the history of science.

Thornton, John Leonard and **Tully, R. I. J.** Scientific books, libraries and collectors; a study of bibliography and the book trade in relation to science. 2d rev. ed. London, Lib. Assoc., 1962. 406p. facsims.   **EA177**

1st ed. 1954.

A history of scientific books from before the invention of printing, through the 19th century, including a chapter on science bibliography.

Current

Critical bibliography of the history of science and its cultural influences. (In Isis, v.46, June 1955–) Annual.   **EA178**

A continuation, with a reorganized classification, of the 79 lists, with slightly different title—compiled by George Sarton, and covering 1912–52—which appeared in *Isis,* v.13–44, 1913–53. None published 1954.

Issues usually include: A, History of science. General references and tools; B, Science and its history from special points of view; C, Histories of the special sciences; D, Chronological classification.

Lists books and articles. Many titles annotated, often with references to reviews.

Current bibliography in the history of technology, 1962– . (In Technology and culture v.5, 1964–) Annual.   **EA179**

A classified bibliography of current materials.

Encyclopedias

Lexikon der Geschichte der Naturwissenschaften: Biographien, Sachwörter und Bibliographien. Mit einer Einführung "Die Zeitalter der Naturforschung" und einer Übersichtstabelle von Josef Mayerhöfer . . . Wien, Hollinek, 1959–62. Lfg. 1–3. (In progress)   **EA180**

Contents: Lfg. 1, Introductory articles; Aachen–Achard; Lfg. 2–3, Achard–Bewegung.

Deals with the history of science from ancient times to the end of the 19th century, with much biography as well as articles on scientific subjects and geographical areas. Includes quite extensive bibliographies at the ends of the articles, which, in the case of the biographical sketches, include works both by and about the person.

History

Sarton, George. Introduction to the history of science. Baltimore, pub. for Carnegie Institution by Williams and Wilkins, 1927–48. v.1–3 in 4. (Carnegie Inst. publ. 376) **EA181**

v.1, Homer to Omar Khayyam. 839p., 52p.; v.2, Rabbi Ben Ezra to Roger Bacon. 1251p.; v.3, Science and learning in the 14th century. 2155p.

An important reference history, covering European and Asian countries, rich in biography and bibliography. A general index in v.3 which is relatively complete for v.3, but for v.1–2, it lists only the main personalities treated, giving the page of the main article and the page of the index in v.1 or 2 where other references may be found.

Addenda and errata are included in the *Critical bibliography of the history and philosophy of science* . . . appearing in *Isis* (EA178).

Scientific expeditions

Terek, Eugenie. Scientific expeditions. Jamaica, N.Y., Queens Borough Pub. Lib., 1952. 176p. **EA182**

A list of scientific expeditions compiled primarily to assist the cataloger in establishing correct forms of entry. Expeditions are listed alphabetically with many cross references. Under each expedition is given, insofar as possible, the source, purpose, members, equipment, and sponsors.

Contains supplementary lists showing geographical distribution, subject classification, bibliography of sources, and indexes of members and sponsors.

BIOGRAPHY

American men of science: a biographical directory, ed. by Jaques Cattell. 10th ed. Tempe, Ariz., Jaques Cattell Pr., Arizona State Univ., 1960–62. 5v. **EA183**

Contents: v.1–4, Physical and biological sciences; v.5, Social and behavioral sciences.

1st ed. 1906. Revised at irregular intervals. Coverage varies. With the 9th edition (3v.), division was made between the physical and biological sciences and the social sciences.

The 10th edition comprises some 96,000 names in v.1–4, and about 24,000 names in v.5. Information given usually includes: full name, address, field of specialization, place and date of birth, degrees, positions, memberships, and research specialties.

Asimov, Isaac. Asimov's Biographical encyclopedia of science and technology. Garden City, N.Y., Doubleday, 1964. 662p. il. **EA184**

Subtitle: The living stories of more than 1000 great scientists from the age of Greece to the space age, chronologically arranged.

Gives name (with pronunciation), nationality, specialization, places and dates of birth and death, and a biographical sketch. Length of these sketches varies from half a column to several columns.

The alphabetical index includes both names and subjects.

Bol'shaia sovetskaia entsiklopediia. Biograficheskii slovar' deiatelei estestvoznaniia i tekhniki. Otv. red. A. A. Zvorykin. Moskva, 1958–59. 2v. **EA185**

At head of title: Glavnaia redaktsiia Bol'shoi sovetskoi entsiklopedii. Institut Istorii Estestvoznaniia i Tekhniki Akademii Nauk SSSR.

Approximately 4500 biographical entries for historical and contemporary persons of all nationalities prominent in scientific and technical fields, including medicine and agriculture; about one fourth are living Soviet scientists. Based on articles in the 2d edition of the encyclopedia with some revision and updating. Contains short "by and about" bibliographies.

Directory of British scientists. [2d ed.] 1964–65. London, Benn, 1964. 2001p. **EA186**

1st ed. 1963.

The 2d edition is some 50 percent larger than the 1st. Who's who-type sketches of scientists and technologists in many areas. Includes a classified directory, a list of scientific societies and their journals, and a list of research establishments.

Ireland, Norma Olin. Index to scientists of the world from ancient to modern times: biographies and portraits. Boston, Mass., Faxon, 1962. 662p. (Useful reference ser., no.90) **EA187**

Indexes 338 collections in the English language, covering all phases of science, with listings for 7475 world scientists from ancient to modern times. Emphasizes the indexing of portraits. Gives full name, years of birth and death, and distinguishing identification.

Leaders in American science . . . Robert C. Cook, ed. . . . Eleanor Carroll, assoc. ed. (v.1– . 1953/54–   ) Nashville, Tenn., Who's Who in Amer. Education, 1953– . il. Biennial. **EA188**

An illustrated biographical dictionary of scientists active in education, business, industry, etc.

Liudi russkoi nauki; ocherki o vydaiushchikhsia deiateliakh estestvoznaniia i tekhniki. Pod red. I. V. Kuznetsova. Moskva, Gos. Izd-vo Fiziko-Matematicheskoi Lit-ry, 1961–63. v.1–3. il. (In progress) **EA189**

Contents: [v.1], Matematika, mekhanika, astronomiia, fizika, khimiia. 1961. 599p.; [v.2], Geologiia, geografiia. 1962. 579p.; v.3, Biologiia, meditsina, sel'skokhosiaistvennie. 1963. 895p.

A biographical dictionary of major Russian scientists of the 19th and 20th centuries. No living persons are included. Articles are signed, and include bibliographies of principal works and additional biographical and scientific references. A fourth volume to cover technology and architecture has been announced.

Mieli, Aldo. Gli scienziati italiani dall' inizio del medio evo al nostri giorni. Repertorio biobibliografico: dei filosofi, matematici, astronomi, fisici, chimici, naturalisti, biologi, medici, geografi italiani. Roma, Nardecchia, 1921–23. v.1. (464p.). il. **EA190**

Contains 58 biographies of scientists of all periods. Not alphabetically arranged, but has alphabetical, chronological, and regional indexes.

An ambitious work of which only the first volume was published. Has long, signed biographies; detailed bibliographies giving lists of editions and translations of each scientist's writings; notes of manuscripts and the libraries in which they may be found; lists of books about the person; and portraits.

Poggendorff, Johann Christian. Biographisch-literarisches Handwörterbuch zur Geschichte der exacten Wissenschaften. Leipzig, Barth, 1863–1904; Verlag Chemie, 1925–40. Bd.1–6 in 11. (Facsimile repr.: Ann Arbor, Mich., Edwards, 1945. 10v.) **EA191**

Title varies.

Bd.1–2, to 1857; Bd.3, 1858–83; Bd.4, 1883–1904; Bd.5, 1904–22; Bd.6, 1923–31.

The standard and indispensable work for information about the life and works of mathematicians, astronomers, physicists, chemists, mineralogists, geologists, and other scientists of all countries. For each scientist gives brief biographical sketch, followed by a detailed bibliography of his writings including periodical articles.

—— Biographisch-literarisches Handwörterbuch der exakten Naturwissenschaften, unter Mitwirkung der Akademien der Wissenschaften zu Berlin, Göttingen, Heidelberg, München und Wien, hrsg. von der Sächsischen Akademie der Wissenschaften zu Leipzig. Red. von Rudolph Zaunick und Hans Salié. Berlin, Akademie-Verlag, 1955–62. v.7a– . (In progress)   **EA192**

Bd.VIIa, T.1–4, A–Z and *Anhang und Schlusswort.*

Includes (1) supplementary material for names mentioned in earlier volumes, and (2) new names.

Bd.VIIa contains bio-bibliographies of scientists, technologists, and doctors from Germany, Austria, and Switzerland from 1932 to 1953. Bd.VIIb will cover other countries.

The *Anhang* includes *"Zeitschriftenliste,"* T.4, p.7–134; *"Totenliste,"* p.135–55.

Royal Society of London. Obituary notices of Fellows of the Royal Society, v.1–9, 1932/35–Nov. 1954. London, Soc., 1932–54. il. Annual.   **EA193**

Ceased publication.

Long, biographical articles with excellent autographed portraits of deceased Fellows of the Royal Society, including foreign members. Usually includes bibliographies, some quite extensive.

Previous obituary notices were published in the *Proceedings.* In 1905, v.75 of the *Proceedings* was published "containing obituaries of deceased Fellows chiefly for the period 1898–1904 with a general index to previous obituary notices." This general index covers 1860–99.

Continued by:

—— Biographical memoirs of Fellows of the Royal Society, 1955– . London, Soc., 1955– . v.1– . Annual.   **EA194**

Follows the same general pattern as the earlier series.

Turkevich, John. Soviet men of science; academicians and corresponding members of the Academy of Sciences of the USSR. Princeton, N.J., Van Nostrand, 1963. 441p.   **EA195**

Biographical sketches in English of leading Soviet scientists. Usually gives a bibliography of books and articles by the man, sometimes references to biographical sources, and the address of his office.

Who's who in atoms: an international reference book. Advisory ed., A. W. Haslett. London, Vallancey Pr., 1959– . v.1– . (1960 in 2v.)   **EA196**

The 2d edition has been revised and much enlarged, and includes biographical information on more than 12,500 names from more than 70 countries.

Who's who in engineering; a biographical dictionary of the engineering profession, 1922/23– . N.Y., Lewis Historical Pub. Co., 1922– . v.1– .   **EA197**

Subtitle varies. Editions issued for 1922/23, 1925, 1931, 1937, 1941, 1948, 1954, 1959, 1964.

Inclusion is based on: 15 years of active practice with at least 10 years of responsibility in important engineering work, or 15 years of teaching in engineering with at least 10 years of responsibility for major courses.

Contains a list of engineering and allied organizations, both national and regional; a list of professional fraternities and honor societies; and a list of professional publications.

Who's who in Soviet science and technology, comp. by Ina Telberg. 2d ed., rev. and enl. by Antonia Dmitriev and V. G. Telberg. N.Y., Telberg Book Co., 1964. 301p.   **EA198**

Brief biographical information based on entries in the *Biograficheskii slovar' deiatelei estestvoznaniia i tekhniki* (EA185). Approximately 1000 living Soviet scientists are included. Includes a Russian index, and a "professional index" by subject field.

PATENTS

See also Roberts, *Guide to technical literature,* p.28–34 (EI2); Crane, Patterson, and Marr, p.158–82 (ED3).

Severance, Belknap. Manual of foreign patents. Wash., Patent Off. Soc., 1935. 161p.   **EA199**

Arranged by country, describing the patent publications—periodicals, specifications, abridgments, indexes, etc.—as they apply to each.

U.S. Patent Office. Official gazette, 1872– . Wash., Govt. Prt. Off., 1872– . v.1– . il. Weekly; annual index.   **EA200**

Contains brief advance descriptions and simple drawings of the patents, trademarks, designs, and labels issued each week; and decisions of the Commissioner of Patents and of United States courts in patent cases.

—— —— General index, 1872–75. Wash., Govt. Prt. Off., 1872–76. 4v.

Continued by the following:

—— Annual report of the Commissioner of Patents, 1876–1925. Wash., Govt. Prt. Off., 1877–1926. il. **EA201**

Forms an annual index to the *Official gazette* (EA200) and to the *Specifications and drawings of patents* (1871–1912).

Continued by the following:

—— Index of patents issued from the United States Patent Office, 1920– . Wash., Govt. Prt. Off., 1921– . v.1– . Annual.   **EA202**

The indexes for 1920–25 are included also in the *Annual report of the Commissioner of Patents;* 1926 on, they are issued only in this separate form.

Contents vary somewhat but include an alphabetical list of patentees and one of inventions.

—— Index of trade-marks issued from the United States Patent Office, 1927– . Wash., Govt. Prt. Off., 1928– . v.1– . Annual.   **EA203**

STANDARDS

American Society for Testing and Materials. Book of A.S.T.M. standards, with related material. 1939– . Philadelphia, Soc., 1939– . il. Annual.   **EA204**

Frequency varies. Number of parts varies; 1964, issued in 32 pts. Formerly issued triennially with annual supplements; 1964– to be issued annually.

Supersedes *A.S.T.M. standards* and *A.S.T.M. tentative standards.*

Booth, Sherman F. Standardization activities in the United States; a descriptive directory. Wash., Nat. Bureau of Standards, 1960. 210p. (National Bureau of Standards. Miscellaneous publ. 230)   **EA205**

Supersedes Miscellaneous publication M169.

British Standards Institution. Yearbook, 1937– . London, Inst., 1937– .   **EA206**

Title varies: 1937–July 1941, *Handbook of information.*

The *Yearbook* contains lists of British standards in numerical order, with descriptions and a subject index. Kept up to date by *B.S.I. News* (issued monthly).

U.S. National Bureau of Standards. Publications of the Bureau of Standards complete from the establishment of Bureau (1901) to June 30, 1947. Wash., Govt. Prt. Off., 1948. 375p. (Its Circular 460)   **EA207**

Includes brief abstracts.

Supplemented by cumulating lists: July 1, 1947—June 30,

1957; July 1, 1957—June 30, 1960; July 1, 1960—June 30, 1962.

1957–60, includes titles of papers published in outside journals, 1950–59 (with subject and author indexes).

—— National directory of commodity specifications. **EA207a**

For record *see* CH147.

RECIPES

Bennett, Harry. Chemical formulary; a collection of valuable, timely, practical commercial formulae and recipes for making thousands of products in many fields of industry. v.1–11. Brooklyn, N.Y., Chemical Pub. Co., 1933–61. (In progress) **EA208**

—— —— Cumulative index for v.1–10, 1933–57. 1958. 497p.

The index gives names and addresses of firms that handle the materials.

Hiscox, Gardner Dexter. Henley's Twentieth century book of formulas, processes and trade secrets . . . containing 10,000 selected household, workshop and scientific formulas, trade secrets, chemical recipes, processes and money saving ideas for both the amateur and professional worker. Rev. 1956 by Harry E. Eisenson; new rev. and enl. ed. by T. O'Conor Sloane. N.Y., Books, 1957. 867p. il. **EA209**

Frequently issued with slight changes. Title varies.

E B

Astronomy

❧ Although astronomy is a highly technical field, a number of popularly written works useful to the amateur have been published. Phillips and Steavenson's *Splendour of the heavens* (EB25) has been a standard work for many years, and the recent series of *Harvard books on astronomy* (EB20) treats various aspects of the subject at an intermediate level. *Sky and telescope* (EB9), containing monthly star maps, is a convenient source for current information.

GENERAL WORKS

Bibliography

Baranowski, Henryk. Bibliografia kopernikowska, 1509–1955. Warszawa, Państwowe Wydawnictwo Naukowe, 1958. 448p. **EB1**

At head of title: Polska Akademia Nauk. Komitet Historii Nauki.

Listing some 3750 works by and about Copernicus; supersedes earlier bibliographies. Aims to be universal in scope, although a high percentage of titles is in Polish. Includes books, periodical articles, and parts of books.

Collard, Auguste. L'astronomie et les astronomes. Bruxelles, Van Oest, 1921. 119p. (Répertoire des ouvrages à consulter) **EB2**

A classed catalog with author index, including works published after 1880, to supplement Houzeau and Lancaster (EB4).

Drake, Milton. Almanacs of the United States. N.Y., Scarecrow, 1962. 2v. **EB3**

Bibliography, v.2, p.1374–97.

A listing of more than 14,000 almanacs published from 1639 to 1850, arranged by state and then chronologically. Locates copies.

Houzeau, Jean Charles and **Lancaster, Albert.** Bibliographie générale de l'astronomie, ou, catalogue méthodique des ouvrages, des mémoires et des observations astronomiques publiés depuis l'origine de l'imprimerie jusqu'en 1880. Bruxelles, Havermans, 1882; Hayez, 1887–89. 2v. in 3. **EB4**

v.1 (published 1887–89) is a classed bibliography of manuscripts and separately published works, with no author index; v.2 is a classed index to material in periodicals and society publications with author index.

International catalogue of scientific literature: E, Astronomy. 1st–14th annual issues. London, 1902–18. 14v. **EB5**

For full description *see* EA12.

Reuss, Jeremias David. Repertorium commentationum a societatibus litterariis editarum. T.5, Astronomia. Gottingae, Dieterich, 1804. 548p. (Repr.: N.Y., Burt Franklin, 1961) **EB6**

A valuable index to the publications of learned societies up to 1800. For description of complete set *see* EA15.

Zinner, Ernst. Geschichte und Bibliographie der astronomischen Literatur in Deutschland zur Zeit der Renaissance. Leipzig, Hiersemann, 1941. 452p. **EB7**

Includes astronomical works, and works in related fields if they affected the development of astronomy.

Covers 1448–1630, arranged chronologically with author index.

Abstract journals

Astronomischer Jahresbericht, Bd.1– . 1899– . Berlin, de Gruyter, 1900– . Bd.1– . Annual. **EB8**

A comprehensive, classed bibliography covering the literature from all countries; in some cases includes abstracts.

Sky and telescope. Cambridge, Sky Pub. Corp., Harvard College Observatory, 1941– . v.1– . Monthly. **EB9**

Excellent source for general current information. Illustrated. Contains review articles, articles on current events, monthly star maps and calendars, reviews of important professional and amateur meetings, book reviews, etc. Good for all levels.

Encyclopedias and dictionaries

Encyklopädie der mathematischen Wissenschaften, . . . Leipzig, Teubner, 1898–1935. **EB11**

v.6¹, Geodäsie und Geophysik; v.6², Astronomie. For full record *see* EF14.

Handbuch der Astrophysik, hrsg. von G. Eberhard, A. Kohlschütter, H. Ludendorff . . . Berlin, Springer, 1928–36. 7v. in 10. **EB12**

Contents: v.1–3, W. E. Bernheimer [and others], Grundlagen der Astrophysik; v.4, Georgio Abetti, Das Sonnensystem; v.5–6, Friedrich Becker [and others], Das Sternsystem; v.7, Ergänzungsband, Berücksichtigend die Literatur bis ende 1934. Generalregister.

Chapters by specialists: some in German, some in English.

See also Handbuch der Physik, v.50–54 (EG18), for authoritative articles with extensive bibliographies.

Rudaux, Lucien and **Vaucouleurs, G. de.** Larousse encyclopedia of astronomy. 2d ed. N.Y., Prometheus, 1959. 506p. il.   **EB13**

A profusely illustrated treatise on astronomy. Nonalphabetical.

Translation by Michael Guest and John B. Sidgwick of *Astronomie; les astres, l'univers;* revised by Z. Kopal.

Space encyclopaedia: a guide to astronomy and space research. [Gen. ed., M. T. Bizony] New rev. ed. N.Y., Dutton, 1960. 288p. il.   **EB14**

An alphabetical dictionary and encyclopedia, giving definitions of terms and brief articles on astronomy, missiles, and space.

Foreign terms

Kleczek, Josip. Astronomical dictionary. Astronomicheskii slovar' . . . N.Y., London, Academic Pr.; Praha, Pub. House of the Czechoslovak Academy of Sciences, [1961]. 972p.   **EB15**

A polyglot astronomical dictionary containing terms in English, Russian, German, French, Italian, and Czech. Also includes some of the more important phrases in mathematics, atomic physics, spectroscopy, etc. used by astronomers.

Kramer, Alex A. Russko-angliiskii slovar' po astronomii. Russian-English dictionary of astronomy. Trenton, N.J., Scientific Russian Translating Service, 1962. 191p. **EB16**

Trifonova, Nina Fedorovna and **Chekulaeva, Zoia Danilovna.** Anglo-russkii astrogeofizicheskii slovar'. Moskva, Glav. red. Inostrani'kh Nauchno-Tekhi. Slovarei Fizmatgiza, 1962. 512p.   **EB17**

Added title page: English-Russian astronomical and geophysical dictionary.

Handbooks

Flammarion, Camille. Flammarion book of astronomy. N.Y., Simon & Schuster, 1964. 670p. il. chart in pocket.   **EB18**

"An entirely new ed. of the original work of Camille Flammarion prepared under the direction of Gabrielle Camille Flammarion and of André Danjou in collaboration with a group of astronomers. Tr. into English by Anabel and Bernard Pagel."

A beautifully illustrated text rewritten and brought up to date. Sections on the earth, the moon, the sun, the planets, the sidereal universe, the instruments of astronomy, artificial satellites, and space vehicles.

Royal Astronomical Society of Canada. The observer's handbook. Toronto, Univ. of Toronto Pr., 1907– . Annual (slightly irregular).   **EB19**

Contains much basic data and ephemeris material.

Shapley, Harlow and **Bok, Bart J.** Harvard books on astronomy. Cambridge, Harvard Univ. Pr.   **EB20**

A series of individual books by specialists, which cover astronomy at an intermediate level. Include such recent titles as: *Between the planets; Earth, moon, and planets; Galaxies; The Milky Way; Our sun; Stars in the making;* and *Tools of the astronomer.*

Shapley, Harlow and **Howarth, Helen E.** A source book in astronomy. 1st ed. N.Y., McGraw-Hill, 1929. 412p. il. (Source books in the history of the sciences)   **EB21**

Highlights of the history of astronomy by the Director Emeritus of the Harvard Observatory. Mostly extracts from the works of famous astronomers.

Shapley, Harlow. Source book in astronomy, 1900–1950. Cambridge, Harvard Univ. Pr., 1960. 423p. il., tables. (Source books in the history of the sciences)   **EB22**

A continuation of the preceding, covering 1900–1950, the period when Dr. Shapley, himself, was most active.

Atlases

Ernst, Br. and **De Vries, Tj. E.** Atlas of the universe, tr. by D. R. Welsh, ed. by H. E. Butler. London, Nelson, 1961. 226p. il.   **EB23**

A section of 94 plates is followed by an alphabetical encyclopedia written for nonspecialists.

STARS

Norton, Arthur Philip. Star atlas and reference handbook (epoch 1950) for students and amateurs. 15th ed. The reference handbook by J. Gall Inglis and A. P. Norton, and ed. by R. M. G. Inglis. Cambridge, Mass., Sky Pub. Corp., 1964. 57p. 18 maps.   **EB24**

1st edition, 1910, had title *A star atlas and telescopic handbook (epoch 1920).*

Subtitle: Covering the whole star sphere, and showing over 9000 stars, nebulae and clusters; with descriptive lists of objects mostly suitable for small telescopes; notes on planets, star nomenclature, etc.

Phillips, Theodore E. R. and **Steavenson, W. H.** Splendour of the heavens; a popular authoritative astronomy . . . containing 1104 black and white illustrations and 25 coloured plates. N.Y., McBride, 1931. 976p. il.   **EB25**

Originally published as *Hutchinson's Splendour of the heavens.* London, Hutchinson, 1923. 2v.

NAVIGATION

Bowditch, Nathaniel. American practical navigator; an epitome of navigation, originally by Nathaniel Bowditch. Pub. by the U.S. Navy Hydrographic Office under the authority of the Secretary of the Navy. Wash., Govt. Prt. Off., 1958. 1524p. il. (U.S. Hydrographic Office. Publ. no.9)   **EB26**

First published in 1802 under title *The new American practical navigator.* Since 1866, revised and published at intervals by the Hydrographic Office.

Gt.Brit. Board of Trade. The 1931 international code of signals, American ed. Wash., Govt. Prt. Off., 1952. v.1–2. (U.S. Hydrographic Office. Publ. no.103, 88)   **EB27**

v.1, For visual and sound signaling. Corrected repr. 1962. 367p. il. (H.O. no.103); v.2, For radio signaling. Repr. 1952. 418p. (H.O. no.88)

U.S. Nautical Almanac Office. American ephemeris and nautical almanac, 1855– . Wash., Govt. Prt. Off., 1852– . Annual. (1966, pub. 1964)   **EB28**

Astronomical ephemeris, 1767– . London, Stat. Off., 1767– . Annual.   **EB29**

Beginning with the editions for 1960, the *American ephemeris and nautical almanac,* issued by the U.S. Nautical Almanac Office, . . . and the *Astronomical ephemeris,* issued by H.M. Nautical Almanac Office, are unified. With the exception of (introductory) p.i, ii, vi, vii, and viii, the two publications are identical.

The title *The astronomical ephemeris* replaces, without loss of continuity, the previous title *The nautical almanac and astronomical ephemeris* (usually abbreviated to the *Nautical almanac,* 1767–); the title *The nautical almanac* is now used, in both the United Kingdom and the United States, for the unified edition of the Almanac for surface navigation previously entitled *The abridged nautical almanac* and the *American nautical almanac,* respectively.

—— Explanatory supplement to the Astronomical ephemeris and the American ephemeris and nautical almanac, prep. jointly by the Nautical Almanac Offices of the United Kingdom and the United States of America. London, Stat. Off., 1961. 505p.

CHRONOLOGY

See History and Area Studies—Dictionaries, Outlines, Tables, p.465–66, for historical chronology and dictionaries of dates.

❧ For a brief account of systems *see* Alfred Edward Stamp, *Methods of chronology* (London, Bell, 1933. 16p. Historical Assoc. leaflet 92). The following titles contain longer treatments and detailed tables and calendars.

Bond, John James. Handy-book of rules and tables for verifying dates with the Christian Era. 4th ed. London, Bell, 1889. 465p. (Bohn's Reference lib.) **EB30**

Subtitle: Giving an account of the chief eras, and systems used by various nations, with easy methods for determining the corresponding dates; with regnal years of English sovereigns from the Norman Conquest to the present time, 1066–1874.

Cappelli, Adriano. Cronologia, cronografia e calendario perpetuo, dal principio dell' êra cristiana ai giorni nostri. Tavole cronologico-sincrone e quadri sinottici per verificare le date storiche. 2. ed. interamente rif. ed ampl. Milano, Hoepli, 1930. 566p. (Manuali Hoepli) (Repr. 1960) **EB31**

1st ed. 1906.

Forty year English-Jewish calendar with corresponding English dates from 1960 till 2000; to be used also as a Yarzeit calendar. [n.p.], Greenfield, 1963. 1v. unpaged. **EB32**

Half-title: Hebrew-English calendar.

Master Reporting Company. A 200-year series of calendars, 1828–2028. N.Y., Master Reporting Co., [1932]. [16p.] **EB33**

A convenient, small handbook to keep at an information desk. Fixes the day of the week for every date, 1828–2028.

Welch, Windon Chandler. Chinese-American calendar for the 102 Chinese years commencing Jan. 24, 1849, and ending Feb. 5, 1951. Wash., Govt. Prt. Off., 1928. 102p. (U.S. Dept. of Labor. Bureau of Immigration) **EB34**

—— Chinese-American calendar for the 40th through the 89th year of the Chinese Republic, Feb. 6, 1951 to Jan. 23, 2001. [Supplement] Rev. 1957. Wash., Admin. Division, Immigration and Naturalization Service, [1957]. 50p.

E C

Biological Sciences

❧ In this section are listed both highly technical works and popularly written manuals for the amateur.

Biological abstracts (EC7), one of the famous abstract journals, will be needed in the very large and the special library; the *Biological & agricultural index* (EC6) in many more libraries, wherever agriculture is an important subject.

Almost all libraries will need some of the handbooks of natural history, such as those treating birds, flowers, trees, stars, etc.

The guides to the literature—e.g., Kerker and Schlundt, *Literature sources in the biological sciences* (EC1), and Smith's *Guide to the literature of the zoological sciences* (EC87)—should be consulted for more specialized information.

GENERAL WORKS

Guides

Kerker, Ann E. and **Schlundt, Esther M.** Literature sources in the biological sciences. Lafayette, Ind., Purdue Univ. Libraries, 1961. 133p. **EC1**

Prepared for the use of students at Purdue but applicable in other libraries. Covers both the general and the specialized sources of biological materials. Some of the titles are annotated.

Bibliography

American Institute of Biological Sciences. Biological Sciences Communications Project. Information handling and science information; a selected bibliography, 1957–1961 . . . prep. in cooperation with the American University Center of Technology & Administration, School of Government & Public Administration. Paul C. Janaske, ed. Wash., 1962. unpaged. **EC2**

Pt.2 of the report of the seminar on Biological Science Communication, 1961. Pt.1 of the report was entitled *Information and communication in biological science.*

A selected, annotated list of 1121 titles on data handling, information storage and retrieval, documentation, mechanical systems of information handling, etc. Arranged alphabetically by author with key-word title index.

International catalogue of scientific literature: L, General biology. 1st–14th annual issues, 1901–14. London, 1901–19. 14v. **EC3**

For full description *see* EA12.

Murray, Margaret Ransome and **Kopech, Gertrude.** A bibliography of the research in tissue culture, 1884–1950; an index to the literature of the living cell cultivated in vitro. N.Y., Academic Pr., 1953. 2v. (1741p.) **EC4**

Represents 15,000 original articles, which have been expanded by cross-indexing to 86,000 entries. Arranged by author and subject in one alphabet.

—— —— Supplementary author list, 1950– . (Incomplete and unverified, Oct. 1953) N.Y., Academic Pr., 1953. 11p.

Periodicals

U.S. Library of Congress. Science and Technology Division. Biological sciences serial publications; a world list, 1950–1954. Prep. under the sponsorship of the National Science Foundation. Philadelphia, Biological Abstracts, 1955. 269p.   **EC5**

A classified listing with geographical index, comp. by John Henry Richter and Charles P. Daly.

Indexes

Biological & agricultural index, a cumulative subject index to periodicals in the fields of biology, agriculture, and related sciences, 1964– . N.Y., Wilson, 1964– . v.50– .   **EC6**

Issued monthly (except Sept.). Continues *Agricultural index* (EK23). Cumulates at intervals.

A detailed, subject approach to the literature covered in about 146 periodicals, all in the English language. The list of periodicals indexed varies radically from the list in the *Agricultural index*.

The many reports from Agricultural Experiment stations, the Agricultural Extension Services, the state departments of Agriculture and related agencies, as well as the publications of the U.S. Dept. of Agriculture (except for a few journals), and some of the popular agricultural papers are no longer indexed. The list is now fairly equally divided between the biological and the agricultural sciences. Many of the basic articles indexed here will also be found abstracted in *Biological abstracts*.

Abstract journals

Biological abstracts from the world's biological research literature. Philadelphia, Biological Abstracts, 1926– . Semimonthly.   **EC7**

Subtitle varies. Frequency varies. Beginning with 1964, published semimonthly, cumulating annually.

Abstracting journal of theoretical and applied biology, covering more than 5000 periodicals published in 90 different countries.

Titles are given in the original language (except that the Oriental and Russian titles are transliterated), with English translation. Abstracts are in English and usually are signed. Arrangement and indexing vary.

Each issue contains abstracts arranged by section and subsection with subject (B.A.S.I.C.), author, systematic, and cross indexes, with annual cumulations of each.

B.A.S.I.C. (Biological Abstracts Subjects in Context) is prepared by the new indexing technique made possible by modern computer methods. Each significant word is indexed and alphabetically positioned to the center of a line which includes several words preceding and following the word.

A list of new books and periodicals appears in each issue. Preceded by *Abstracts of bacteriology*, v.1–9, 1917–25 (Baltimore, Williams & Wilkins), and *Botanical abstracts*, v.1–15, 1918–26 (Baltimore, Williams & Wilkins), which merged to form *Biological abstracts*.

—— List of serials with word abbreviations. (In Biological abstracts, July 1 issue) Annual.   **EC8**

Includes American standard for periodical-title abbreviations; table of word abbreviations; and list of serials abstracted.

International abstracts of biological sciences, v.1– . 1954– . London, Pergamon, 1954– . 11 numbers a year. (Irregular)   **EC9**

Title varies: Jan. 1954–May 1956, *British abstracts of medical sciences*.

Attempts to cover the more important papers in experimental biology.

For complete record *see* EJ41.

Dictionaries

Abercrombie, Michael, Hickman, C. J. and **Johnson, M. L.** A dictionary of biology. Chicago, Aldine, 1962. 254p.   **EC10**

First pub. by Penguin Books, 1951.

Explanations of some 2000 biological terms, prepared especially for the student and layman.

Dumbleton, C. W. Russian-English biological dictionary. Edinburgh, Oliver & Boyd, 1964. 512p.   **EC11**

Terms taken from Russian textbooks, monographs, research papers, and journal articles, with English equivalent and (usually) Latin scientific name.

Henderson, Isabella Ferguson and **Henderson, William Dawson.** A dictionary of biological terms: pronunciation, derivation, and definition of terms in biology, botany, zoology, anatomy, cytology, genetics, embryology, physiology. 8th ed. by J. H. Kenneth. Princeton, N.J., Van Nostrand, 1963. 640p.   **EC12**

Earlier editions had title *Dictionary of scientific terms*. 1st ed. 1920; 7th ed. 1960. 8th ed. rev. and amplified.

Printed in Edinburgh by Oliver & Boyd.

"The method of spelling is in the main that used in Britain, but due attention is paid to American orthography, by means of cross-references or by reproducing in the original lettering terms culled from scientific literature published in the United States."—*Pref.*

Jacobs, Morris B., Gerstein, Maurice J. and **Walter, William G.** Dictionary of microbiology. Princeton, N.J., Van Nostrand, 1957. 276p. il.   **EC13**

Aims to present "a ready reference volume which defines the terms commonly used in microbiology and the related fields of bacteriology, virology, cytology, immunology and immunochemistry, serology and microscopy."—*Pref.*

Jaeger, Edmund Carroll. The biologist's handbook of pronunciations. Springfield, Ill., Thomas, 1960. 317p. il.   **EC14**

Gives pronunciation of some 9000 scientific terms used in the biological sciences.

—— A source-book of biological names and terms. 3d ed. Illus. by Merle Gish and the author. Springfield, Ill., Thomas, 1955. 317p. il.   **EC15**

1st ed. 1944; 2d ed. 1950.

An alphabetical list of some 12,000 elements from which scientific biological names and terms are made, with their Greek, Latin, or other origins and their concise meanings, with examples of usage.

This edition includes some corrections in main text and adds a supplement of more than 1000 entries.

Woods, Robert S. The naturalist's lexicon, a list of classical Greek and Latin words used, or suitable for use, in biological nomenclature, with abridged English-classical supplement. Pasadena, Calif., Abbey Garden Pr., 1944. 282p.   **EC16**

Includes more than 15,000 words designed to facilitate the use by naturalists of Latin and Greek terms in naming species. An excellent guide.

—— —— Addenda . . . Comprehensive classified English-classical key to descriptive terms. Additions and emendations to the classical-English lexicon. Pasadena, Calif., Abbey Garden Pr., 1947. 47p.

Encyclopedias

Clark, George Lindenberg. The encyclopedia of microscopy. N.Y., Reinhold, 1961. 693p. il. **EC17**

Signed articles, alphabetically arranged, usually with bibliographies.

Gray, Peter. The encyclopedia of the biological sciences. N.Y., Reinhold; London, Chapman & Hall, 1961. 1119p. il. (Reinhold books in the biological sciences) **EC18**

An alphabetically arranged encyclopedia with signed articles and bibliographies, covering the broad field of the biological sciences. Prepared for the nonspecialist, the teacher, the librarian, and the student, although some highly technical articles on the more specialized subjects are included.

Handbooks

Altman, Philip L. and **Dittmer, Dorothy S.** Biology data book. Prep. under the auspices of the Committee on Biological Handbooks. Wash., Federation of Amer. Societies for Experimental Biology, 1964. 633p. il. **EC19**

A handbook designed to present basic, established data in the biological and medical sciences.

Fisher, *Sir* **Ronald A.** and **Yates, Frank.** Statistical tables for biological, agricultural and medical research. 5th ed. rev. and enl. London, Oliver & Boyd, 1957. 138p. tables. **EC20**

1st ed. 1938.

Style manuals

Conference of Biological Editors. Committee on Form and Style. Style manual for biological journals. 2d ed. Wash., Amer. Inst. of Biological Sciences, 1964. 117p. **EC21**

Presents instructions and recommendations, representing good usage and practice, now adopted by a large number of biological journals. Designed to aid the research worker and student in preparing articles for publication.

History

Dawes, Ben. A hundred years of biology. London, Duckworth, 1952. 429p. il. **EC22**

Bibliography, p.385–418.

NATURAL HISTORY

Bibliography

Meisel, Max. Bibliography of American natural history; the pioneer century, 1769–1865. . . . Brooklyn, N.Y., Premier Pub. Co., 1924–29. 3v. **EC23**

Subtitle: The role played by the scientific societies; scientific journals; natural history museums and botanic gardens; state geological and natural history surveys; federal exploring expeditions in the rise and progress of American botany, geology, mineralogy, paleontology and zoology.

v.1, Annotated bibliography of the publications relating to the history, biography and bibliography of American natural history and its institutions during colonial times and the pioneer century, which have been published up to 1924; with a classified subject and geographical index and a bibliography of biographies; v.2, Institutions which have contributed to the rise and progress of American natural history which were founded or organized between 1769 and 1844; v.3, The institutions founded or organized between 1845 and 1865. Bibli-

ography of books, articles, etc., . . . not published in the proceedings and transactions of scientific societies. . . . Chronological tables. Index of authors and institutions. Addenda to v.1.

Handbooks

Handbooks of American natural history, v.1– . Ithaca, N.Y., Comstock, 1942– . il. (In progress) **EC24**

Contents: v.1, Handbook of frogs and toads, by A. A. Wright and A. H. Wright. 3d ed. 1949. 652p.; v.2, Mammals of the eastern United States, by W. J. Hamilton. 1943. 432p.; v.3, Handbook of salamanders, by S. C. Bishop. 1943. 555p.; v.4, Aquatic plants of the United States, by W. C. Muenscher. 1944. 374p.; v.5, Handbook of the mosquitoes of North America, by Robert Matheson. 2d ed. 1944. 314p.; v.6, Handbook of lizards, by Hobart Smith. 1946. 557p.; [v.7], The spider book: a manual for the study of the spiders and their near relatives, the scorpions . . . by J. H. Comstock. Rev. and ed. by W. J. Gertsch. 1948. 729p.; [v.8], Handbook of the turtles, by A. F. Carr. 1952. 542p.; [v.9], Handbook of snakes of the United States and Canada, by Albert Hazen Wright and Anna Allen Wright. 1957–62. 3v. (v.3, Bibliography).

Jaques, Harry Edwin. Pictured-key nature series. Dubuque, Iowa, Wm. C. Brown, 1946– . **EC25**

A series of popular, illustrated handbooks for identifying plants, animals, etc., suitable for the beginner but scientifically reliable. Include such titles as: *How to know—the beetles; economic plants; insects; land birds; living things; plant families; protozoa; trees; water birds; weeds.*

Peterson, Roger Tory. The Peterson field guide series. Sponsored by the National Audubon Society and the National Wildlife Federation. Boston, Houghton, [1947?–]. **EC26**

Designed as basic guides for the nature student, beginner, or expert, each by a specialist in the subject.

The series includes *A field guide to—birds; western birds; birds of Britain and Europe; birds of Texas; butterflies; animal tracks; mammals; reptiles and amphibians; ferns; trees and shrubs; Rocky Mountain wild flowers; rocks and minerals; shells of our Atlantic and Gulf coasts; shells of the Pacific Coast and Hawaii; stars and planets.*

Putnam's Nature field books. N.Y., Putnam, 1928– . il. **EC27**

Includes separate volumes on wild flowers; trees and shrubs; ferns; insects; rocks and minerals; birds; mammals; mushrooms; fishes; stars; etc.

BOTANY

General works

Bibliography

Bay, Jens Christian. Bibliographies of botany; a contribution toward a bibliotheca bibliographica. (In Progressus rei botanicae 3, pt.2: 331–456. Jena, Fischer, 1909) **EC28**

A valuable, annotated historical bibliography of bibliographies including detailed records of periodicals; general, local, and subject bibliographies; library catalogs; auction and sales catalogs, etc.

Early

Hunt, Rachel McMasters Miller. Catalogue of botanical books in the collection of Rachel McMasters Miller Hunt. Pittsburgh, Hunt Botanical Lib., 1958–61. v.1–2 in 3. il. facsims. **EC29**

Contents: v.1, Printed books, 1477–1700, with several manuscripts of the 12th, 15th, 16th & 17th centuries, comp. by Jane Quinby. 517p.; v.2: pt.1, Introduction to printed books 1701–1800, comp. by Allan Stevenson. ccxlivp.; pt.2, Printed books, 1701–1800, comp. by Allan Stevenson. 655p.

Detailed bibliographic descriptions illustrated with plates, some in color.

Jackson, Benjamin Daydon. Guide to the literature of botany. Being a classified selection of botanical works, including nearly 6000 titles not given in Pritzel's "Thesaurus." London, pub. for the Index Society by Longmans, 1881. 626p. (Index Society. Publ. 8)   **EC30**

A short-title catalog, selective not exhaustive, listing some 9000 works.

Pritzel, Georg August. Thesaurus literaturae botanicae omnium gentium, inde a rerum botanicarum initiis ad nostra usque tempora, quindecim millia operum recensens. Ed. novam reformatam. Lipsiae, Brockhaus, 1872–[77]. 576p. (Repr.: Milan, Görlizh, 1950)   **EC31**

Covers from early times to the late-19th century.

Arranged alphabetically with a systematic index. Includes only separately published books. Comprehensive and accurate.

Reuss, Jeremias David. Repertorium commentationum a societatibus litterariis editarum . . . T.2, Botanica et mineralogia; T.6, Oeconomia. Gottingae, Dieterich, 1802–6. 604p., 476p.   **EC32**

A valuable index to the publications of learned societies up to 1800. Classed arrangement with author index. For description of complete set *see* EA15.

Modern

Blake, Sidney Fay. Geographical guide to floras of the world, an annotated list with special reference to useful plants and common plant names. Pts.1–2. Wash., Govt. Prt. Off., 1942–61. v.1–2. (U.S. Dept. of Agriculture. Misc. publ., no.401, 797) (In progress)   **EC33**

Joint contribution from the U.S. Bureau of Plant Industry and the U.S. Dept. of Agriculture Library.

Pt.1, Africa, Australia, North America, South America, and Islands of the Atlantic, Pacific, and Indian Oceans; pt.2, Finland, Sweden, Norway, Denmark, Iceland, Great Britain with Ireland, Netherlands, Belgium, Luxembourg, France, Spain, Portugal, Andorra, Monaco, Italy, San Marino, and Switzerland.

An annotated list of floras and floristic works, including those in periodical literature. Author index in each volume includes birth and death dates.

Boureau, Édouard. Rapport sur la paléobotanique dans le monde. World report on palaeobotany. 1950/1954– . Utrecht, 1956– . v.1– . (Regnum vegetabile, 7, 11, 19, 24–)   **EC34**

Edited by the International Organization of Palaeobotany and published by the International Bureau for Plant Taxonomy and Nomenclature.

v.1, 1950–1954; v.2, 1955–1956; v.3, 1957–1959; v.4, 1960–1961.

Each volume includes additional entries for all previous volumes. 7544 consecutively numbered entries in the four issues, each arranged alphabetically by author.

British Museum. Dept. of Printed Books. A catalogue of the works of Linnaeus (and publications more immediately relating thereto) preserved in the libraries of the British Museum (Bloomsbury) and the British Museum (Natural History) (South Kensington). 2d ed. London, Museum, 1933. 246p., 68p. il.   **EC35**

—— An index to the authors (other than Linnaeus) mentioned in the Catalogue. . . . London, Museum, 1936. 59p.

Index londinensis to illustrations of flowering plants, ferns and fern allies, being an emended and enlarged edition continued up to the end of the year 1920 of Pritzel's Alphabetical register of representations of flowering plants and ferns comp. from botanical and horticultural publications of the XVIIIth and XIXth centuries; prep. under the auspices of the Royal Horticultural Society of London at the Royal Botanic Gardens, Kew, by O. Stapf. Oxford, Clarendon Pr., 1929–31. 6v.   **EC36**

Added title page: Iconum botanicarum index londinensis.

—— Supplement for the years 1921–35 . . . Prep. under the auspices of the Royal Horticultural Society of London at the Royal Botanic Gardens, Kew, by W. C. Worsdell under the direction of Arthur W. Hill. Oxford, Clarendon Pr., 1941. 2v.

"This supplement to the six volumes of the *Index londinensis* . . . now concludes that work. . . . Although no further supplements are to be issued, it has been arranged that references to new illustrations shall be given in the entries of new names included in future supplements of the *Index kewensis* [EC52] from 1936 onwards. Such entries will be prefixed by an asterisk."—*Pref.*, v.1.

Includes references to illustrations from periodicals and independent works published during the years 1921–35, inclusive, and also some references from books prior to 1921 not included in the main work.

International catalogue of scientific literature: M, Botany. 1st–14th annual issues, 1901–14. London, Harrison, 1902–19. 14v.   **EC37**

For full description *see* EA12.

Linné, Carl von. A catalogue of the works of Linnaeus, issued in commemoration of the 250th anniversary of the birthday of Carolus Linnaeus, 1707–1778. Stockholm, Sandbergs Bokhandel, 1957. 179p. il. (Sandbergs antikvariatsförtechning, nr.12)   **EC38**

Lists 892 items.

Merrill, Elmer Drew and **Walker, Egbert Hamilton.** A bibliography of eastern Asiatic botany. . . . Sponsored by the Smithsonian Institution, Arnold Arboretum of Harvard University, New York Botanical Garden, Harvard-Yenching Institute. Jamaica Plain, Mass., Arnold Arboretum of Harvard Univ., 1938. 719p.   **EC39**

A comprehensive, annotated bibliography of books and material appearing in periodicals. Arranged by author, with three subject indexes: general, geographical, and systematic. Covers material through 1936.

—— —— Supplement 1– , by Egbert H. Walker. Wash., Amer. Inst. of Biological Sciences, 1960– . v.1– .

Nissen, Claus. Die botanische Buchillustration, ihre Geschichte und Bibliographie. Stuttgart, Hiersemann, 1951–52. 2v.   **EC40**

Contents: v.1, Geschichte; v.2, Bibliographie.

The bibliographical volume, international in scope, is arranged alphabetically by author, with a separate listing of anonyma and serials, and indexes by artist, plant, country, and author.

Sachet, Marie-Helène and **Fosberg, Frances Raymond.** Island bibliographies: Micronesian botany; Land environment and ecology of coral atolls; Vegetation of tropical Pacific islands. Comp. under the auspices of the Pacific Science Board. [Wash.], Nat. Academy of Sciences—Nat. Research Council, 1955. 577p. (N.R.C. Technical ser., no.335)   **EC40a**

In three separate sections as indicated in the title, each with its own index, and each with an addenda.

Includes both books and periodical articles with brief annotations.

U.S. National Agricultural Library. Plant science catalog: botany subject index. Boston, Microphotography Co., 1958. 15v.   **EC41**

A photographic reproduction of the subject card catalog section of the *Plant science catalog* of the U.S. Dept. of Agriculture Library, compiled from 1903 to July 18, 1952, when work on it ceased because of lack of funds.

World-wide in scope; contains references to botanical literature from earliest times, as published in books and periodicals.

Abstract journals and indexes

Botanisches Centralblatt; referierendes Organ für das Gesamtgebiet der Botanik. Im Auftrage der Deutschen Botanischen Gesellschaft . . . 1.–40. Jahrg. (Bd.1–142), 1880–1919; Bd.143–79 (Neue Folge, Bd.1–37, no.8), 1922–45. Cassell, Ger., T. Fischer, etc., 1880–1905; Jena, G. Fischer, 1906–45. il. **EC42**

Weekly, 1880–1919; publication suspended, 1920–21; irregular, 1922–45. Ceased publication. Title varies.

Includes the section *"Neue Litteratur,"* forming a separate volume from 1902 to 1919 (v.91, 94, 97, 100, etc.). Beginning with the new series, each volume is in two parts (*Referate* and *Litteratur*), each part having separate title page and paging. Gives signed abstracts of material in various languages.

—— General register zu den Bänden 1 bis 30 [Neue Folge] (Bd.143–72), bearb. von Wilhelm Dörries. . . . Jena, Fischer, 1927–38. 3v.

Excerpta botanica. Stuttgart, Fischer, 1959– . v.1– . **EC43**

In two sections: A, Taxonomica et chorologica; B, Sociologica.

Sec. A is an annotated, international bibliography of recent periodical literature; annotations are in German, English, or French. Sec. B is bibliography only, without annotations.

Torrey Botanical Club. Index to American botanical literature. . . . (In Torrey Botanical Club. Bull. v.15– , 1888– . Bimonthly) **EC44**

Appears in each issue. Aims to list "all current botanical literature written by Americans, published in America, or based upon American material, the word America being used to include the entire Western Hemisphere."

Beginning with v.21, 1894, the index has also been reprinted on cards for which annual subscriptions may be placed. Author cards are now printed annually by G. K. Hall, Boston.

Dictionaries

American Joint Committee on Horticultural Nomenclature. Standardized plant names. 2d ed. A revised and enlarged listing of approved scientific and common names of plants and plant products in American commerce or use, prep. by Harlan P. Kelsey and William A. Dayton. Harrisburg, Pa., J. Horace McFarland Co., 1942. 675p. **EC45**

1st ed. 1923.

"Plant patents" through July 1, 1941, p.455–67.

Purpose was to establish a standardized "scientific" name and a standardized "common name" for every tree, shrub, and plant in American commerce.

Britten, James and **Holland, Robert.** Dictionary of English plant-names. London, pub. for the English Dialect Society by Trübner, 1886. 618p. **EC46**

Originally issued in three parts, 1878–84: as no.22, 26, and 45 (forming v.10) of *Publications* of the English Dialect Society.

Arranged by common name followed by scientific name, with explanation of origin and references to uses in literature, frequently with quotations.

Carleton, R. Milton. Index to common names of herbaceous plants. Boston, G. K. Hall, 1959. 129p. **EC47**

Lists the common or vernacular names of plants as used in the United States, or in English and American literature, with Latin equivalents.

Carnoy, Albert Joseph. Dictionnaire étymologique des noms grecs de plantes. Louvain, Publ. Universitaires, Inst. Orientaliste, 1959. 277p. (Bibliothèque du Muséon, v.46) **EC48**

The romanized form of the Greek name is followed by the word in the Greek alphabet together with an explanation of its meaning and derivation in French. Many references to the literature.

Carpenter, John Richard. An ecological glossary. Norman, Univ. of Okla. Pr., 1938. 306p. il. **EC49**

Defines nearly 3000 terms with references to the works in which term is used or discussed.

Featherly, Henry Ira. Taxonomic terminology of the higher plants. Ames, Iowa State College Pr., 1954. 166p. **EC50**

" . . . for students in taxonomy, plant distribution, and speciation."

In four parts: [pt.1], Glossary of botanical technical terms; [pt.2], Subject classification; [pt.3], Some specific epithets with their meanings; [pt.4], Some Greek and Latin components of scientific words.

Gerth van Wijk, H. L. Dictionary of plant names. Pub. by the Dutch Society of Sciences at Haarlem. The Hague, Nijhoff, 1911–16. 2v. **EC51**

Contents: v.1, Latin names, A–Z; v.2, Index of English, French, Dutch, and German names.

A dictionary of names and terms only; arranged alphabetically by the Latin name and giving under each Latin name the equivalent popular and literary names in the English, Dutch, French, and German languages. Aims to include names of all wild and cultivated plants, flowers and fruits, varieties and subvarieties, and parts of plants now or formerly used in medicine or industry. The only work of its kind; accurate.

Index kewensis plantarum phanerogamarum nomina et synonyma omnium generum et specierum a Linnaeo usque ad annum MDCCCLXXXV complectens nomine recepto auctore patria unicuique plantae subjectis. Sumptibus beati Caroli Roberti Darwin ductu et consilio Josephi D. Hooker confecit B. Daydon Jackson. . . . Oxford, Clarendon Pr., 1893–95. 2v. **EC52**

Added title page in English: Index kewensis, an enumeration of the genera and species of flowering plants from the time of Linnaeus to year 1885 inclusive together with their authors' names, the works in which they were first published, their native countries and their synonyms.

—— Supplementum . . . nomina et synonyma omnium generum et specierum ab initio anni MDCCCLXXXVI usque ad finem anni MDCCCCLV nonnulla etiam antea edita complectens. . . . Oxford, Clarendon Pr., 1901–59. v.1–12. (In progress)

v.1, 1886–95, with quinquennial supplements to v.12, 1951/55 (1941–50 in 1v.).

International Botanical Congress—9th—Montreal, 1959. International code of botanical nomenclature, adopted by the 9th International Botanical Congress, Montreal, August, 1959. Prep. and ed. by J. Lanjouw [and others]. Utrecht, 1961. 372p. (Regnum vegetabile, v.23) (International Bureau for Plant Taxonomy and Nomenclature) **EC53**

Added title pages in French and German; text published in the three languages. This code supersedes all previous editions.

Jackson, Benjamin Daydon. Glossary of botanic terms with their derivation and accent. 4th ed. rev. and enl. Philadelphia, Lippincott, 1928. 481p. (Repr.: London, Duckworth, 1949). **EC54**

Marshall, William Taylor and **Woods, Robert S.** Glossary of succulent plant terms. [Pasadena, Calif., Abbey Garden Pr.], 1945. 112p. il. **EC55**

> 1st printing 1938.
> Subtitle: A glossary of botanical terms and pronouncing vocabulary of generic and specific names used in connection with xerophytic plants.
> Illustrated with photographs and line drawings.

Schindlmayr, A. Keysers Lexikon der Pflanzen. Heidelberg, Keyser, 1956. 439p. il. **EC56**

> An alphabetically arranged dictionary by scientific name with cross references from German common name, including descriptions.

Snell, Walter Henry and **Dick, Esther A.** A glossary of mycology. Cambridge, Harvard Univ. Pr., 1957. 171p. il. **EC57**

> Defines almost 7000 terms, not all strictly mycological; includes also terms found in mycological literature which might be useful to students in the field.

Polyglot

Bedevian, Armenag K. Illustrated polyglottic dictionary of plant names in Latin, Arabic, Armenian, English, French, German, Italian and Turkish languages; including economic, medicinal, poisonous and ornamental plants and common weeds. . . . Cairo, Argus and Papazian Presses, 1936. 2 pts. in 1v. (644p., 455p.) **EC58**

Davydov, Nikolai Nikolaevich. Botanicheskii slovar': russko-angliisko-nemetsko-frantsuzsko-latinskii. Izd.2. Moskva, Fitzmatgiz, 1962. 335p. **EC59**

> 1st ed. 1960.
> This dictionary, compiled on a Russian base, gives translations of some 6000 terms into four languages—English, German, French, and Latin—with indexes in each language.
> Title and introductory matter in the four languages.

Steinmetz, E. F. Vocabularium botanicum. 2. druk. Planten-terminologie. Woordenlijst in zes talen (Latijn, Grieks, Nederlands, Duits, Engels en Frans) van de voornaamste wetenschappelijke woorden, die in de plantkunde gebruikt worden. Amsterdam, Steinmetz, 1953. 149p. **EC60**

> 1st ed. 1947.
> Title page also in German, English, and French.
> Tabulated lists, translating from Latin and/or Greek terms.

Directories

Howard, Richard A., Wagenknecht, Burdette L. and **Green, Peter S.** International directory of botanical gardens. Utrecht, Internat. Bureau for Plant Taxonomy and Nomenclature, 1963. 120p. (Regnum vegetabile, v.28) **EC61**

> Arranged by country and then by city. Gives full directory information, including personnel.

Lanjouw, Joseph and **Stafleu, F. A.** Index herbariorum: a guide to the location and contents of the world's public herbaria. Utrecht, 1954– . (In progress) (Regnum vegetabile) **EC62**

> Contents: pt.1, The herbaria of the world. 4th ed. 1959; pt.2, Collectors. Pts.1–2, A–H. 1954–57.
> Pt.1 gives detailed directory information about the herbaria arranged alphabetically by city; pt.2 attempts to identify (with birth and death dates) the names of collectors; the dates at which the collections were brought together or acquired by an institution; locations; etc.

Roberts, Martha McMillan. Public gardens and arboretums of the United States. Text and photographs. N.Y., Holt, 1962. 148p. **EC63**

Descriptions of some 70 public gardens in various parts of the United States, with pictures, some in color.

Roon, A. C. de. International directory of specialists in plant taxonomy with a census of their current interests. Utrecht, 1958. 266p. (Regnum vegetabile, v.13) **EC64**

> An alphabetical list of specialists, followed by an index of taxonomic and regional specialization.

Wyman, Donald. The arboretums and botanical gardens of North America. Jamaica Plain, Mass., Arnold Arboretum of Harvard Univ., 1959. 69p. **EC65**

> 1st ed. 1947.
> Lists active and discontinued arboretums and botanical gardens of the United States, Canada, Cuba, and Mexico.
> Gives information on location, date of establishment, size, chief functions, features, number of species and varieties, ownership, director, budget, admission policies, library, publications.

Biography

Britten, James and **Boulger, George S.** Biographical index of deceased British and Irish botanists. 2d ed., rev. and completed by A. B. Rendle. London, Taylor and Francis, 1931. 342p. **EC66**

> 1st ed. 1893.
> Brief, biographical facts followed by references to further information. Includes names of "all who have in any way contributed to the literature of botany, who have made scientific collections of plants, or have otherwise assisted directly in the progress of botany, exclusive of pure horticulture."—*Pref.*

Handbooks

See also Natural History—Handbooks, p.547.

Gray, Asa. Gray's Manual of botany: 8th (centennial) ed. A handbook of the flowering plants and ferns of the central and northeastern United States and adjacent Canada. Largely rewritten and expanded by Merritt Lyndon Fernald with assistance of specialists in some groups. . . . N.Y., Amer. Book Co., 1950. 1632p. il. **EC67**

> 7th ed. 1908.
> New edition of a standard handbook.

Kingsbury, John Merriam. Poisonous plants of the United States and Canada. Englewood Cliffs, N.J., Prentice-Hall, 1964. 626p. il. **EC68**

> For full record *see* EK34.

Martin, Alexander Campbell and **Barkley, William D.** Seed identification manual. Berkeley, Los Angeles, Univ. of Calif. Pr., 1961. 221p. il. **EC69**

> Contents: Seed photographs—farmlands, wetlands, woodlands; Identification clues; Selected bibliography; Index.

Moldenke, Harold Norman and **Moldenke, Alma Lance.** Plants of the Bible. Waltham, Mass., Chronica Botanica, 1952. 328p. il. (A new series of plant science books, v.28) **EC70**

> Bibliography, p.259–74.
> The main section is arranged alphabetically by the Latin name of each plant mentioned in the Bible, with indexes by Biblical reference and by plant name. Each of the 230 articles gives Biblical quotations—from the various versions—and a botanical account of the plant.

Uphof, Johannes Cornelis. Dictionary of economic plants. Weinheim, Ger., H. R. Engelmann (J. Cramer); N.Y., Hafner, 1959. 400p. **EC70a**

> Presents, alphabetically, brief descriptions of economic plants, with their geographical distribution, products, and principal uses.

Flora

Bailey, Liberty Hyde. Manual of cultivated plants most commonly grown in the continental United States and Canada. Rev. ed., compl. restudied. N.Y., Macmillan, 1949. 1116p. il. **EC71**

1st ed. 1924.

Completely revised and greatly enlarged edition of an important handbook for the identification of the most common species of plants for food, ornament, utility, etc. Arranged by scientific name, with indexes to scientific and common name.

Clapham, Arthur R., Tutin, T. G. and **Warburg, E. F.** Flora of the British Isles. 2d ed. Cambridge, Univ. Pr., 1962. 1269p. il. **EC72**

An excellent, small handbook, intended primarily for the student and amateur botanist.

Gleason, Henry Allan. The New Britton and Brown illustrated flora of the northeastern United States and adjacent Canada. N.Y., N.Y. Botanical Garden, 1952. 3v. il. **EC73**

1st ed. 1896–98; 2d ed. 1913 (frequently repr.); 3d ed. 1952 (repr. 1963 with slight revisions).

The 3d edition has been entirely rewritten, and new material added. Attempts to describe all known species of seed plants, ferns, and fern allies. The most complete illustrated flora published in the United States.

For each species gives description, variant names, common name, habitat, illustration, references to sources, etc. General index in v.3 includes names of all divisions, classes, subclasses, orders, families, genera, and species, and English names.

Willis, John Christopher. Dictionary of the flowering plants and ferns. 6th ed. rev. Cambridge, Univ. Pr., 1931. 752p. (Cambridge biological ser.) **EC74**

1st ed. 1897.

In one main alphabet, including Latin and popular names, technical terms, etc.

Fungi

Ainsworth, Geoffrey Clough and **Bisby, Guy Richard.** A dictionary of the fungi. 5th ed. Kew, Surrey, Eng., Commonwealth Mycological Inst., 1961. 547p. il. **EC75**

1st ed. 1943.

Attempts to list all generic names of fungi, giving systematic position, distribution, and number of species.

Lange, Morten and **Hora, F. Bayard.** Collins guide to mushrooms and toadstools. London, Collins, 1963. 257p. il. **EC76**

"With 96 colour plates from *Flora Agaricina Danica* by Jakob E. Lange with additions by Ebbe Sunesen and P. Dahlstrøm."—*Title page.*

Lindau, Gustav and **Sydow, P.** Thesaurus litteraturae mycologicae et lichenologicae ratione habita praecipue omnium quae adhuc scripta sunt de mycologia applicata quem congesserunt. Leipzig, Borntraeger, 1908–17. 5v. (Repr.: N.Y., Johnson Repr. Corp., 1954) **EC77**

———— Supplementum, 1911–1930, by Raffaele Ciferri. Papia, Italy, Cortina, 1957–60. 4v.

Smith, Alexander Hanchett. The mushroom hunter's field guide. Rev. and enl. ed. Ann Arbor, Univ. of Michigan Pr., 1963. 264p. il. (part col.) **EC78**

Wolf, Frederick A. and **Wolf, Frederick T.** The fungi. N.Y., Wiley, 1947. 2v. il. **EC79**

A scientific text and reference book including much bibliography, with author and subject indexes. Emphasis is on habitat and behavior.

Mosses

Grout, Abel Joel. Mosses with a hand lens: 4th ed. A popular guide to the common or conspicuous mosses and liverworts of the United States and Canada. Liverworts by M. A. Howe, etc. Newfane, Vt., Author, 1947. 344p. il. **EC80**

Trees

Hough, Romeyn Beck. Handbook of the trees of the northern states and Canada east of the Rocky Mountains. Photodescriptive. N.Y., Macmillan, 1947. 470p. il. **EC81**

Good illustrations of trunk, branchlet, leaves, fruit, pods, seeds, etc. Maps show distribution.

First published 1907.

Little, Elbert Luther. Check list of native and naturalized trees of the United States (including Alaska). Wash., U.S. Forest Service, 1953. 472p. (Agriculture handbook, no. 41) **EC82**

Listed by accepted scientific name with approved common names, giving current synonyms, arranged chronologically with citations to the literature. Used as the official standard for tree names in the U.S. Forest Service.

Preston, Richard J. North American trees (exclusive of Mexico and tropical United States). 2d ed. Ames, Iowa, Univ. Pr., 1961. 395p. il. **EC83**

1st ed. 1948.

Subtitle: A handbook designed for field use, with plates and distribution maps.

Rehder, Alfred. Manual of cultivated trees and shrubs hardy in North America, exclusive of the subtropical and warmer temperate regions. 2d ed. rev. and enl. N.Y., Macmillan, 1940. 996p. **EC84**

1st ed. 1927.

Descriptions arranged by scientific name, with index to scientific and common names. Not illustrated.

Sargent, Charles Sprague. The silva of North America; a description of the trees which grow naturally in North America exclusive of Mexico . . . il. with figures and analyses drawn from nature by Charles Edward Faxon. Boston, Houghton, 1891–1902. 14v. 740pl. (Repr. 1947. 14v. in 7) **EC85**

Bibliography

Rehder, Alfred. Bibliography of cultivated trees and shrubs hardy in the cooler temperate regions of the Northern Hemisphere. Jamaica Plain, Mass., Arnold Arboretum of Harvard Univ., 1949. 825p. **EC86**

Designed to "give references to sources of the botanical names, valid names and synonyms, of the woody plants . . ." arranged approximately the same as in the author's *Manual of cultivated trees and shrubs* (EC84), to which it is a companion volume.

ZOOLOGY

General works

Guides

Smith, Roger Cletus. Guide to the literature of the zoological sciences. 6th ed. Minneapolis, Burgess, 1962. 232p. **EC87**

1st ed. 1942.

A manual treating: the mechanics of the library; bibliographies of the zoological sciences and other reference materials; abstract journals; form of bibliographies and forms of literature; the preparation of a scientific paper; taxonomic indexes and literature, etc.

Bibliography

Engelmann, Wilhelm. Bibliotheca historico-naturalis. Verzeichniss der Bücher über Naturgeschichte, welche in Deutschland, Scandinavien, Holland, England, Frankreich, Italien und Spanien 1700–1846 erscheinen sind. . . . Mit einem Namen- und Sach-Register. Leipzig, Engelmann, 1846. 786p. **EC88**

    Contents: Bücherkunde. Hülfsmittel. Allgemeine Schriften. Vergleichende Anatomie und Physiologie. Zoologie. Palaeontologie.

    For zoology, continued by:

Bibliotheca zoologica [I]. Verzeichnis der Schriften über Zoologie welche in den periodischen Werken enthalten und vom Jahre 1846–1860 selbständig erscheinen sind. Mit Einschluss der allgemein-naturgeschichtlichen, periodischen und palaeontologischen Schriften. Bearb. von J. Victor Carus und Wilhelm Engelmann. Leipzig, Engelmann, 1861. 2v. (Bibliotheca historico-naturalis, hrsg. von Wilhelm Engelmann. Supplement Bd.) **EC89**

    Autoren- und Sach-Register.

    Continued by:

Bibliotheca zoologica II. Verzeichnis der Schriften über Zoologie welche in den periodischen Werken enthalten und vom Jahre 1861–1880 selbständig erscheinen sind. . . . Bearb. von O. Taschenberg. Leipzig, Engelmann, 1887–1923. 8v. **EC90**

    No indexes.

    The three works comprise an international, classed bibliography covering the literature on zoology from 1700 to 1880.

International catalogue of scientific literature: N, Zoology. 1st–14th annual issues, 1901–14. London, 1902–16. 14v. **EC91**

    For full description *see* EA12.

    Of this section, v.6–14, 1906–14, were issued jointly with the *Zoological record*, v.43–51.

Reuss, Jeremias David. Repertorium commentationum a societatibus litterariis editarum . . . T.1, Historia naturalis, generalis et zoologia. Gottingae, Dieterich, 1801. 574p. (Repr.: N.Y., Burt Franklin, 1961) **EC92**

    A valuable index to the publications of learned societies up to 1800. Classed arrangement with author index. Index to v.1 is combined with that for v.2. For record of complete set *see* EA15.

Ruch, Theodore Cedric. Bibliographia primatologica; a classified bibliography of primates other than man . . . v.1. Springfield, Ill., Baltimore, Thomas, 1941. 241p. (Yale Univ. School of Medicine. Yale Medical Library. Historical Library. Publ. no.4) **EC93**

    Contents: pt.1, Anatomy, embryology and quantitative morphology; Physiology, pharmacology and psychobiology; Primate phylogeny and miscellanea.

    Covers material published through 1938. Classed arrangement; author index. 4630 entries.

Wood, Casey Albert. An introduction to the literature of vertebrate zoology; based chiefly on the titles in the Blacker Library of Zoology, the Emma Shearer Wood Library of Ornithology, the Bibliotheca Osleriana and other libraries of McGill University, Montreal. London, Oxford Univ. Pr., 1931. 643p. **EC94**

    Issued also as *McGill University publications, ser. XI (Zoology), no.24.*

    Introduction to the literature of vertebrate zoology, p.1–

146; Students' and librarians' ready index to short author-titles on vertebrate zoology arranged geographically and in chronological order, p.147–72; A partially annotated catalog of the titles on vertebrate zoology in the libraries of McGill University, p.173–643.

Abstract journals and indexes

❖ Among the more important bibliographical journals listing materials of the late-19th and early-20th centuries are:

Bibliographia zoologica . . . v.1–43, 1896–1934. Zurich, Sumptibus Concilii Bibliographici, 1896–1934. 43v. **EC95**

    v.1–22 published as v.19–35 of *Zoologischer Anzeiger,* continuing *Literatur* published in that periodical, v.1–18.

    The individual volumes have no indexes, but the *Bibliographia zoologica* is indexed in the *Register* of the *Zoologischer Anzeiger.* Jahrg.16–40. 1899–1922. 5v.

    Publisher varies.

Zentralblatt für Zoologie, allgemeine und experimentelle Biologie. Bd.1–6. Leipzig, Teubner, 1912–18. 6v. **EC96**

    Formed by the union of the *Zoologisches Zentralblatt,* 1894–1911, and the *Zentralblatt für allgemeine und experimentelle Biologie.* Includes surveys of the literature with abstracts for the most important papers.

Zoologischer Bericht; im Auftrage der Deutschen Zoologischen Gesellschaft . . . Bd.1–55. Jena, G. Fischer, 1922–1943/44. 55v. **EC97**

    Ceased publication.

—— General-Autoren Register. Bd.1–25, 1922–31; Bd. 26–50, 1931–40.

    Contains abstracts of books and periodical material in various languages.

Zoologischer Jahresbericht. Hrsg. von der Zoologischen Station zu Neapel. 1879–1913. Leipzig, 1880–1924. v.1– 35. Annual. **EC98**

—— Autoren- und Sachregister, 1886–90, 1891–1900, 1901–10.

    A bibliographical and review journal covering the whole field of zoology through 1885. After 1886, systematic zoology was omitted, as it was covered by the *Zoological record* (EC99).

Zoological record . . . records of zoological literature. v.1, 1864– . London, Zoological Soc. of London, 1865– . v.1– . Annual. **EC99**

    Publisher varies.

    v.1–6 have title *Record of zoological literature.*

    A comprehensive, annual index to the zoological literature published in all parts of the world. Particularly useful for systematic zoology. v.43–52, 1906–15, issued also as Sec. N of the *International catalogue* (EA12), with bindings to match either set.

U.S. Fish and Wildlife Service. Wildlife review. no.67, June 1952– . [Laurel, Md., 1952–] Quarterly. **EC100**

    Frequency varies.

    Abstracts on wildlife management, arranged by subject. Previously issued irregularly in mimeographed form.

Collections

Traité de zoologie; anatomie, systématique, biologie. Pub. sous la direction de Pierre-P. Grassé. Paris, Masson, 1948– . v.1– . (In progress) **EC101**

    Volumes published in irregular order. A thorough, comprehensive treatment; includes bibliographies and illustrations.

Generic indexes

See Smith, *Guide to the literature of the zoological sciences,* p.91–93 (EC87), for earlier generic indexes.

Neave, Sheffield Airey. Nomenclator zoologicus; a list of the names of genera and subgenera in zoology from the tenth edition of Linnaeus 1758 to the end of [1945]. London, Zoological Soc. of London, 1939–50. 5v. **EC102**

This comprehensive list supersedes, to a large extent, earlier generic indexes, and with *Biological abstracts,* Sec. E (EC7), or the *Zoological record* (EC99), from 1945 to date, forms a complete record from 1758 to date.

Contents: v.1–4, A–Z and suppl.; v.5, 1936–1945.

Dictionaries

Leftwich, A. W. A dictionary of zoology. Princeton, N.J., Van Nostrand, 1963. 289p. **EC103**

Designed primarily for the student; gives definitions of "all the principal phyla and classes of animals as well as a large number of orders, suborders and families."—*Pref.*

Pennak, Robert William. Collegiate dictionary of zoology. N.Y., Ronald, 1964. 583p. **EC104**

Contains about 19,000 selected entries, of which some 8600 are proper names. Concise definitions give the most common meaning.

Directories

International Union of Biological Sciences. Index des zoologistes. Paris, Secrétariat Général de l'U.I.S.B., 1953. 429p. **EC106**

A world list of zoologists giving name, date of birth, degrees, position, address, fields of specialization. A geographical index by country, and an index by specialization.

Handbooks

See also Natural History—Handbooks, p.547.

Birds

Bibliography

Strong, Reuben Myron. A bibliography of birds; with special reference to anatomy, behavior, biochemistry, embryology, pathology, physiology, genetics, ecology, aviculture, economic ornithology, poultry culture, evolution, and related subjects. Chicago, Natural History Museum, 1939–59. v.1–4. (Museum. Publ. 442, 457, 581, 870. Zoological ser., v.25, pts.1–4) **EC107**

20,000 titles from earliest times to 1926, with some additional titles to 1938. Pt.4, Finding index. 1959.

Author catalog with subject index.

Fishes

Axelrod, Herbert R. and **Schultz, Leonard P.** Handbook of tropical aquarium fishes. N.Y., McGraw-Hill, 1955. 718p. il. (part col.) **EC108**

Designed for both the hobbyist and the scientist.

The introductory chapters give a brief survey of ichthyology, the aquarium and its management, aquarium plants, and the diseases of fishes. The main part of the work illustrates and describes some 500 fishes, giving identification, range, size, temperament, sex differences, breeding, temperature requirements, food, color patterns, etc. At the end of the book are a glossary, a brief bibliography, and an index.

Herald, Earl Stannard. Living fishes of the world. Garden City, N.Y., Doubleday, 1961. 303p. il. **EC109**

Arranged by systematic classification, with excellent underwater photographs, some in color.

Bibliography

Dean, Bashford. Bibliography of fishes, enl. and ed. by C. R. Eastman. N.Y., Amer. Museum of Natural History, 1916–23. 3v. **EC110**

The most comprehensive bibliography on fishes, "their habits, structure, development, physiology, pathology, distribution and kinds."—*Pref.*

v.1–2, Author list; v.3, Subject index, list of general bibliographies, voyages, periodicals, etc.

v.3, extended and enlarged by Eugene Willis Gudger, with the cooperation of Arthur Wilbur Henn.

Directories

Hiatt, Robert W. World directory of hydrobiological and fisheries institutions. Wash., Amer. Inst. of Biological Sciences, 1963. 320p. il. **EC111**

Listed by country, with alphabetical index of institutions. Gives full directory information including scope of activities, publications, research projects, provisions for visiting scientists, etc.

Mammals

Burton, Maurice. Systematic dictionary of mammals of the world. Illus. by David Pratt. London, Museum Pr., 1962. 307p. il. **EC112**

Gives scientific name, common name, description, habits, habitat, etc.

Hall, Eugene Raymond and **Kelson, Keith R.** The mammals of North America. N.Y., Ronald, 1959. 2v. (1083p.) **EC113**

A manual giving scientific name, common name, citations to the literature, description, line drawings, habitat, etc.

Contains bibliographies and habitat maps.

Walker, Ernest Pillsbury [and others]. Mammals of the world. Baltimore, Johns Hopkins Pr., 1964. 3v. il. **EC114**

v.1–2, arranged by taxonomic classification; v.3, Bibliography.

An exhaustive work with excellent illustrations, "devoted to representatives of all the genera of recent mammals of the world" with uniform information about each genus.

v.1 contains a Selected bibliography of about 4500 titles chosen from the 50,000 titles in the comprehensive bibliography which comprises v.3. Classified arrangement.

Reptiles

Ditmars, Raymond Lee. The reptiles of North America: a review of the crocodilians, lizards, snakes, turtles and tortoises inhabiting the United States and Northern Mexico. N.Y., Doubleday, 1936. 476p. il. 135pl. (part col.) **EC115**

Gives descriptions, distribution, etc.

Shells

Rogers, Julia Ellen. The shell book: a popular guide to a knowledge of the families of living mollusks, and an aid to the identification of shells, native and foreign. Rev. ed. Boston, C. T. Branford, 1908. 503p. il. (part col.) **EC116**

BACTERIOLOGY

Grainger, Thomas H. A guide to the history of bacteriology. N.Y., Ronald, 1958. 210p. (Chronica botanica, no.18) **EC117**

An annotated, bibliographical guide to the literature and history of bacteriology.

"Compiled for use in the course 'History of Microbiology' offered at Lehigh University."—*Pref.*

International catalogue of scientific literature: R, Bacteriology. 1st–14th annual issues. London, 1901–20. 14v. **EC118**

For full description *see* EA12.

Paris. Institut Pasteur. Bulletin de l'Institut Pasteur; revues et analyses des travaux de bactériologie et de médicine, biologie générale, physiologie, chimie biologique dans leurs rapports avec la microbiologie. t.1– . Paris, Masson, 1903– . **EC119**

Abstracts in French from world literature.

Society of American Bacteriologists. Bergey's Manual of determinative bacteriology, by Robert S. Breed [and others]. 7th ed. Baltimore, Williams & Wilkins, 1957. 1094p. **EC120**

1st ed. 1923; 6th ed. 1948.

This volume "contains an outlined classification of the bacteria and the descriptions of the taxa from Class to Species and Subspecies, together with the appropriate keys. Nearly all species . . . inadequately described or that could not be definitely placed . . . " will be transferred to the forthcoming *Index Bergeyana,* which will also include the host and habitat index.

Zentralblatt für Bakteriologie, Parasitenkunde, Infektions-Krankheiten und Hygiene. Abt. 1, Medizinisch-hygienische Bakteriologie, Virusforschung und Parasitologie. Referate. Jena, 1902– . v.31– . **EC121**

A classified listing with signed annotations. Extensive coverage, especially for European material.

ENTOMOLOGY

Chamberlin, Willard Joseph. Entomological nomenclature and literature. 3d ed. rev. and enl. Dubuque, Iowa, W. C. Brown, 1952. 141p. **EC122**

De La Torre-Bueno, José Rollin. A glossary of entomology; Smith's "An explanation of terms used in entomology," compl. rev. and rewritten. Lancaster, Pa., Science Pr., 1937. 336p. il. **EC123**

Published by Brooklyn Entomological Society, Brooklyn, N.Y.

Horn, Walther and **Schenkling, Sigmund.** Index litteraturae entomologicae. Ser. I, Die Welt-Literatur über die gesamte Entomologie bis inklusive 1863. Berlin, Dahlem, 1928–29. 4v. **EC124**

A revision of H. A. Hagen, *Bibliotheca entomologica* (Leipzig, 1862–63. 2v.) with the addition of some 8000 titles, covering the field up to the beginning of the *Zoological record* (EC99). Arranged alphabetically by author. No index, although Hagen included an author-subject index which may be used for either work for the material covered.

Osborn, Herbert. A brief history of entomology, including time of Demosthenes and Aristotle to modern times, with over five hundred portraits. Columbus, Ohio, Spahr and Glenn, 1952. 303p. il. **EC125**

Intended mainly for the layman. General outlines of the history of entomology, followed by an alphabetical list of "founders and leaders of entomological science," giving brief biographical data for each. The portraits, 12 on each plate, are taken from photographs or contemporary paintings.

Review of applied entomology. Ser. A: Agricultural. London, Commonwealth Inst. of Entomology, 1913– . v.1– . Monthly. **EC126**

An abstract journal.

Each issue contains an author index; each volume, a cumulative author and subject index.

—— Ser. B: Medical and Veterinary. London, Commonwealth Inst. of Entomology, 1913– . v.1– . Monthly. **EC127**

An abstract journal.

Each issue contains an author index; each volume, a cumulative author and subject index.

GENETICS

Knight, Robert L. Dictionary of genetics, including terms used in cytology, animal breeding and evolution. 1st ed. Waltham, Mass., Chronica Botanica, 1948. 183p. il. (Lotsya, a biological miscellany. v.2) **EC128**

Contains some 2500 definitions of both old and new terms. Bibliography, p.179–83.

Rieger, Rigomar and **Michaelis, Arnd.** Genetisches und cytogenetisches Wörterbuch. 2. erw. Aufl. Berlin, Springer, 1958. 648p. il. **EC129**

1st ed. 1954.

Contains definitions and explanations of some 4000 terms, with a bibliography of some 1500 titles, p.597–648.

E D

Chemistry

☙ Several recent guides to the literature of chemistry are available. Crane, Patterson, and Marr (ED3) is an older standard work, and Mellon (ED4) has just appeared in a new edition. These should be consulted for information about how to use the indexes and compendiums as well as how to ascertain titles in the field. *Chemical abstracts* (ED17) is one of the oldest and best-known abstract journals, and now appears with computer-compiled indexes. Its *List of periodicals with key to library files* (ED12) is one of the most useful lists of scientific periodicals, and should be available as a separate publication in the general reference department of most libraries.

GENERAL WORKS

Guides

American Chemical Society. Division of Chemical Literature. Searching the chemical literature. Rev. and enl.

ed. Wash., Soc., 1961. 326p. (Advances in chemistry ser., no.30) **ED1**

Revised and enlarged edition of *Advances in chemistry series, no.4. 1951.*

This edition contains 31 papers based on those presented at meetings of the American Chemical Society by the Division of Chemical Literature and the Division of Chemical Education, 1947–56, dealing with the use of indexes, abstract journals, literature sources, and the techniques of searching various kinds of chemical literature. Includes bibliographies.

Contains all but three of the papers in the 1951 edition completely revised and rewritten, plus 12 new papers.

Bottle, R. T. Use of the chemical literature. London, Butterworth, 1962. 231p. **ED2**

A guide to the use of the literature: chemical periodicals, translations, abstracting services, tables, various types of reference works, etc.

Crane, Evan Jay, Patterson, Austin M. and **Marr, Eleanor B.** A guide to the literature of chemistry. 2d ed. N.Y., Wiley, 1957. 397p. **ED3**

1st ed. 1927.

Treatment and discussion of the procedures of literature searching, with listings and descriptions of the standard reference books, periodicals, and organizations. General subject index, but no index to the books treated.

Mellon, Melvin Guy. Chemical publications, their nature and use. 4th ed. N.Y., McGraw-Hill, [1965]. 324p. il. **ED4**

1st ed. 1928; 2d ed. 1940; 3d ed. 1958.

Describes the principal sources for reference and research, including guides, bibliographies, directories, patent searching, periodicals, and documents. Chapters 11 and 12 (p.231–308) are intended to aid students in chemical literature searching, with examples of library problems. Author, subject, and title index.

Bibliography

Bolton, Henry Carrington. Select bibliography of chemistry 1492–[1902]. Wash., Smithsonian Inst., 1893–1904. 4v. **ED5**

Basic list, 1492–1892. 1212p.; 1st suppl., 1492–1897. 1899. 489p.; 2d suppl., 1492–1902. 1904. 462p.; Academic dissertations. 1901. 534p.

Eight sections: (1) Bibliography; (2) Dictionaries; (3) History; (4) Biography; (5) Chemistry, pure and applied; (6) Alchemy; (7) Periodicals; (8) Academic dissertations.

Includes some 18,000 independent works but does not list analytics. Sec. 8, Academic dissertations (published 1901, with additions in the 2d supplement), is particularly strong in dissertations from the universities of France, Germany, Russia, and the United States.

Duveen, Denis I. Bibliotheca alchemica et chemica; an annotated catalogue of printed books on alchemy, chemistry and cognate subjects in the library of Denis I. Duveen. London, Weil, 1949. 669p. il. (Repr.: Rijwijk, Utrecht, Krips/Oosthoek, 1965) **ED6**

Includes works, with full bibliographical description, from the 16th to the 19th centuries. Collection now housed at the University of Wisconsin library.

Ferguson, John. Bibliotheca chemica: A catalogue of the alchemical, chemical and pharmaceutical books in the collection of the late James Young of Kelly and Durris. Glasgow, Maclehose, 1906. 2v. **ED7**

Collection bequeathed to the chair of technical chemistry of Anderson's College, now incorporated in the Royal Technical College, Glasgow.

A rich collection of early works useful for the history of chemistry, particularly in alchemy. Detailed bibliographical descriptions.

Gaudenzi, Nerio. Guida bibliografica internazionale per il chimico. Libri e reviste. Firenze, Sansoni, 1952. 509p. **ED8**

Introduction and classification scheme in Italian, French, English, and German. A classified bibliography of about 3268 books and 1125 periodicals in the field of chemistry, with indexes of periodicals, authors, subjects, and publishers.

International catalogue of scientific literature: D, Chemistry. 1st–14th annual issues, 1901–14. London, Harrison, 1902–19. **ED9**

For full description *see* EA12.

Reuss, Jeremias David. Repertorium commentationum a societatibus litterariis editarum . . . T.3, Chemia et res metallica. Gottingae, Dieterich, 1803. 221p. (Repr.: N.Y., Burt Franklin, 1961) **ED10**

A valuable index to the publications of learned societies up to 1800. Classed arrangement with author index. For description of complete set *see* EA15.

Dissertations

American Chemical Society. Committee on Professional Training. Directory of graduate research. Wash., 1953– . Biennial. **ED11**

Subtitle: Faculties, publications and doctoral theses in departments or divisions of chemistry, biochemistry, and chemical engineering at United States universities.

In each of the three subject fields the institutions are listed alphabetically. For each department is given: degrees offered; fields of specialization; faculty members, with academic rank, year of birth and education, major field of research, and a list of research publications for the biennium covered; doctoral candidates with thesis titles.

Periodical abbreviations

Chemical abstracts. List of periodicals with key to library files. 1961. Wash., Amer. Chemical Soc., 1962. 397p. **ED12**

—— —— Annual supplements. 1962– .

An important and useful list furnished from time to time by *Chemical abstracts* (ED17), listing current publications, not only chemical journals but also other scientific periodicals carrying articles of chemical interest, as well as certain types of nonserial publications, e.g., proceedings of nonrecurring meetings and anniversary volumes.

For each periodical gives full title (for Slavic and Oriental titles includes translation into English), authorized abbreviation, frequency, current volume number, publisher and address, and numbers showing location in more than 300 libraries of the world.

Useful not only for determining full titles from the abbreviations, but also for obtaining information on the publications of many scientific organizations in many parts of the world; information on recently discontinued and suspended periodicals; and location of files, frequently including designations indicating lending service, microfilming or photoprinting facilities, and translating services.

Pflücke, Maximilian and **Hawelek, Alice.** Periodica chimica: Verzeichnis der im Chemischen Zentralblatt referierten Zeitschriften mit den entsprechenden genormten Titelabkürzungen. 2. neubearb. Aufl. Berlin, Akademie-Verlag; Weinheim/Bergstr., Verlag Chemie, 1952. 411p. **ED13**

1st ed. 1940.

An international list of chemical periodicals indicating all changes of title which have taken place since 1930, with abbreviations as used in *Chemisches Zentralblatt* (ED19). Arrangement is alphabetical by title, with separate listings of Russian periodicals in Cyrillic and in non-Cyrillic alphabets.

Indexes and abstract journals

Bibliography of reviews in chemistry: with keyword and author indexes. Wash., Amer. Chemical Soc., 1960– . v.1– . **ED14**

v.1/2 contain review articles from the 1958 and 1959 volumes of *Chemical abstracts;* v.3– contain reviews from the succeeding volumes. The arrangement follows that used in *Chemical abstracts* (ED17).

Title varies: v.1–4, 1960–62, *Bibliography of chemical reviews* (with key-word and author indexes).

Biochemical title index, reporting the world's research literature in biochemistry. Philadelphia, Biological Abstracts, 1962– . v.1– . Monthly. **ED15**

Some 500 biochemical journals, as well as biochemical articles from other publications, are indexed monthly and recorded by IBM computers. Each issue is in two parts: (1) a basic index composed of significant words from each title positioned in the center of the column, and (2) a bibliography of biochemical papers. Author index.

British abstracts, issued by the Bureau of Abstracts. A, Pure chemistry; B, Applied chemistry; C, Analysis and apparatus. London, Bureau of Abstracts, 1926–53. A and B, monthly; C, quarterly. **ED16**

Title varies: 1926–37, *British chemical abstracts;* 1938–44, *British chemical and physiological abstracts.* Continues the abstract volumes previously published in the *Journal* of the Chemical Society and the *Journal* of the Society of Chemical Industry.

The list of periodicals abstracted duplicates, to a considerable extent, the list of *Chemical abstracts* (ED17), but does include some not covered there.

1937–53, pt.A in three sections: (1) General physical and inorganic chemistry and geochemistry; (2) Organic chemistry; (3) Physiology, biochemistry, and anatomy. 1945–53, pt.B in three sections: (1) Chemical engineering and industrial inorganic chemistry including metallurgy; (2) Industrial organic chemistry; (3) Agriculture, foods, sanitation. 1944–53, pt.C, Analysis and apparatus.

Ceased publication in 1953.

Pt.A (Pure chemistry), listed in *Current chemical papers,* published by the Chemical Society, London, 1954– . Monthly (bibliography only, not abstracts).

Pt.A, Sec. 3, replaced by *International abstracts of biological sciences,* v.1, 1954– . Monthly (irregular). (v.1–3 had title, *British abstracts of medical sciences,* 1954–56) (EC9).

Pt.B (Applied chemistry), Sec. 1–2, continued in the *Journal of applied chemistry,* 1951– . Monthly.

Abstracts (starting in 1954) on chemical engineering; industrial, organic, and inorganic chemistry; and metallurgy.

Pt.B, Sec. 3, continued in the *Journal of the science of food and agriculture,* 1954– . Monthly.

Abstracts on the chemistry of agriculture, food, and sanitation.

Pt.C (Analysis and apparatus), replaced by *Analytical abstracts,* 1954– . Monthly.

Chemical abstracts, pub. by the American Chemical Society, 1907– . Easton, Pa., 1907– . v.1– . **ED17**

Now the most comprehensive of the abstract journals, including abstracts from a world-wide list of journals (*see* its *List of periodicals,* ED12). Signed abstracts in English. Author index in each issue. Annual author, subject, and formula indexes from 1920; from 1960, the subject and formula indexes are issued semiannually; annual patent number index, 1935– .

—— Decennial author and subject indexes, 1907/16–1947/56.

—— Collective index, 1957/61: Authors, 4v.; Subjects, [v.1–3], A–G. (In progress)

—— Formula index, v.14–40, 1920–46; v.41–50, 1947–

56. 3v.; v.51–55, 1957–61. v.1–2, A–C[19]. (In progress)

—— Patent index to Chemical abstracts, 1907–1936, comp. by the Science-Technology Group of Special Libraries Association. . . . Ann Arbor, Mich., Edwards, 1944. 479p.

Numerical lists, by country, of all patents reviewed in the first 30v. of *Chemical abstracts.*

—— Collective numerical patent index to Chemical abstracts, v.31–40, 1937–1946; v.41–50, 1947–1956; v.51–55, 1957–1961. Wash., Amer. Chemical Soc., 1949–62.

See Bottle, *Use of the chemical literature,* p.55–79 (ED2), for description of *Chemical abstracts* and other abstracting services.

Chemical titles: current author and keyword indexes from selected chemical journals. A publication of the Chemical Abstracts Service. Easton, Pa., Amer. Chemical Soc., 1960– . no.1– . Biweekly. **ED18**

no.1–5, April 5–Oct. 1960, called Sample issues.

A concordance, produced by electronic computers, to chemical research papers. Each issue in three parts: (1) key words arranged alphabetically down the center of the column; (2) a bibliographic listing of titles of current papers from selected journals, arranged as tables of contents of the journals; and (3) an index of authors.

Titles are selected from some 700 journals of pure and applied chemistry.

Chemisches Zentralblatt. . . . Jahrg.1– . Berlin, Verlag Chemie, 1830– . v.1– . il. Weekly (frequency varies). **ED19**

Title and imprint vary. 1897–1945, published by the Deutsche Chemische Gesellschaft. v.112–16, pt.1, reprinted by J. W. Edwards, Ann Arbor, Mich.; 1946– , hrsg. im Auftrage der Deutschen Akademie der Wissenschaften zu Berlin, der Chemischen Gesellschaft in der DDR, der Akademie der Wissenschaften zu Göttingen, und der Gesellschaft Deutscher Chemiker.

Author index in each issue. Annual and cumulated author, subject, patent, and organic formula indexes (vary somewhat).

This journal, abstracting pure and applied chemistry, is particularly valuable because of the length of the period covered. Many of the abstracts are more detailed than those in *Chemical abstracts* (ED17). Before 1919, it did not include abstracts on applied chemistry, as these appeared in *Angewandte Chemie,* 1887– .

Electroanalytical abstracts: international journal dealing with the documentation of all aspects of electroanalytical chemistry, including fundamental biochemistry. Ed., G. Milazzo. Basel, Birkhäuser Verlag, 1963– . v.1– . Bimonthly. **ED20**

Continues the abstract section of the *Journal of electroanalytical chemistry.*

Index chemicus. v.1, no.1, 1960– . Philadelphia, Inst. for Scientific Information, 1960– . Biweekly. **ED21**

"Original journal articles are abstracted 'graphically' as well as verbally . . . Each issue contains author and molecular formula, journal and subject indexes. A rotated formula index appears quarterly."—*Note.*

Cumulative indexes are published quarterly and biennially.

Encyclopedias

Clark, George Lindenberg [and others]. The encyclopedia of chemistry. N.Y., Reinhold, 1957. 1037p. il. **ED22**

—— —— Supplement. 1958. 330p.

Alphabetically arranged. Signed articles by more than 500 contributors.

International encyclopedia of chemical science. Princeton, N.J., Van Nostrand, 1964. 1331p. il. **ED23**

Prepared for chemists, chemical engineers, teachers, and students. Alphabetically arranged definitions and explanations of theory and practice, processes and operations, tests and testing methods. At the back of the book are glossaries in French, German, Russian, and Spanish into English, devised for use in reading the foreign literature, and in finding the corresponding English entry in the book.

Kingzett, Charles Thomas. Kingzett's Chemical encyclopaedia; a digest of chemistry and its industrial applications. Ed. by Ralph K. Strong [and others]. 8th ed. N.Y., Van Nostrand, 1952. 1186p.   **ED24**

1st ed. 1919; 7th ed. 1945.

A much expanded and revised edition of a standard 1v. work, designed to present a digest of chemistry and its industrial applications in alphabetical order. This edition adds articles in the fields of nuclear chemistry, radioactivity, chemical engineering, metallurgy, chemical elements, pharmaceutical materials, etc.

Kratkaia khimicheskaia entsiklopediia, red. kollegiia I. L. Knuniants [and others]. Moskva, Sovetskaia Entsiklopediia, 1961–64. v.1–3. (Entsiklopediia slovari spravochniki) (In progress)   **ED25**

Contents: v.1–3, A–Pirolis.

Mead, William J. The encyclopedia of chemical process equipment. N.Y., Reinhold; London, Chapman & Hall, 1964. 1065p. il.   **ED26**

Designed to "correlate, describe, and illustrate the many classes of machinery and equipment used in the various branches of the chemical industry."

Contributions, by specialists, are signed and include bibliographies.

Merck index of chemicals and drugs. An encyclopedia for chemists, pharmacists, physicians and members of allied professions. 7th ed. Paul G. Stecher, ed. [and others]. Rahway, N.J., Merck, 1960. 1641p.   **ED27**

A much revised and expanded edition, now including about 10,000 descriptions of chemical entities and a cross index of about 30,000 names.

Römpp, Hermann. Chemie Lexikon. 4. völlig neubearb. Aufl. Stuttgart, Franckh, 1958. 2v.(5103p.). il.   **ED28**

3d ed. 1952–53.

An alphabetically arranged, comprehensive encyclopedia, revised, updated, and enlarged. Contains information on chemical compound types, trade-name products, statistics, industrial chemicals, etc., as well as 700 biographical sketches. Includes bibliographies.

Thorpe, Jocelyn Field and **Whiteley, M. A.** Thorpe's Dictionary of applied chemistry . . . 4th ed. rev. and enl. N.Y., London, Longmans, 1937–56. 12v.   **ED29**

The standard encyclopedia in English for applied chemistry. v.12 is the general index.

Ullmann, Fritz. Ullmanns Encyklopädie der technischen Chemie. 3. völlig neu gestaltete Aufl. . . . hrsg. von Wilhelm Foerst. München-Berlin, Urban und Schwarzenberg, 1951–63. v.1, 2¹, 3–14. (In progress)   **ED30**

2d ed. 1928–32. 10v. and index.

v.1, Chemischer Apparatebau und Verfahrenstechnik, 1951. 1011p.; v.2, pt.1, Hertha Buchholz-Meisenheimer, Anwendung physikalischer und physikalisch-chemischer Methoden im Laboratorium. 1961. 1017p.; v.3–14, Abietinsäure-Russ.

———— ———— Sachregister, Bd.3–8. 1957. 102p.

An important encyclopedia with long, signed articles, and bibliographies.

Dictionaries

Condensed chemical dictionary. 6th ed., compl. rev. and enl. by Arthur and Elizabeth Rose. Formerly directed

by Francis M. Turner. N.Y., Reinhold, 1961. 1256p.   **ED31**

1st ed. 1919; 5th ed. 1956.

Flood, Walter Edgar. The dictionary of chemical names. N.Y., Philosophical Lib., 1963. 238p.   **ED32**

Published in London as *The origins of chemical names.*

A dictionary of the origins of chemical names, giving the history and derivation.

Gardner, William. Chemical synonyms and trade names; a dictionary and commercial handbook. 5th ed. rev. and enl. by Edward I. Cooke. London, Technical Pr.; N.Y., Van Nostrand, 1948. 558p.   **ED33**

Hackh, Ingo Waldemar Dagobert. Hackh's Chemical dictionary (American and British usage). Containing the words generally used in chemistry, and many of the terms used in the related sciences of physics, astrophysics, mineralogy, pharmacy, agriculture, biology, medicine, engineering, etc.; based on recent chemical literature. . . . 3d ed., compl. rev. and ed. by Julius Grant. Philadelphia, Blakiston, [1944]. 925p. il.   **ED34**

This edition contains concise definitions for some 57,000 terms; many have been revised and modernized. Pronunciation, given in former editions, is omitted. Includes names of outstanding chemists (some with portraits), dates, and brief characterizations.

Miall, Laurence MacKenzie. A new dictionary of chemistry. [3d ed.] N.Y., Interscience, 1961. 593p.   **ED35**

1st and 2d eds., 1940 and 1949, by Stephen Miall.

Descriptions of chemical terms and biographical sketches in one alphabet.

Van Nostrand chemist's dictionary. Board of editors: Jurgen M. Honig [and others]. Princeton, N.J., Van Nostrand, 1953. 761p.   **ED36**

Planned to provide a wide coverage of terms in pure and applied chemistry, including definitions of group terms of chemical substances, laws, reactions, etc. Named tests, laws, equations, reactions, etc. are included under proper names. "Both the common-name and the proper-name terms basic to many phases of pure and applied chemistry are brought together . . . ."

French

Patterson, Austin M. French-English dictionary for chemists. 2d ed. N.Y., Wiley, 1954. 476p.   **ED37**

1st ed. 1921.

A useful, small dictionary thoroughly revised and enlarged, now containing some 42,000 terms. Many new words and new meanings have been added.

German

Ernst, Richard. Fachwörterbuch der Chemie. Wiesbaden, Brandstetter Verlag, 1961– . v.1– . (In progress)   **ED38**

v.1, German-English. 727p.

Added title page in English: Dictionary of chemistry including chemical engineering and fundamentals of allied sciences.

Patterson, Austin McDowell. German-English dictionary for chemists. 3d ed. N.Y., Wiley, 1950. 541p.   **ED39**

59,000 entries, primarily in chemistry but also including terms used in physics, biology, geology, etc.

Polyglot

Fouchier, Jean and **Billet, Fernand.** Chemical dictionary. Dictionnaire de chimie. Fachwörterbuch für Chemie. 2d ed. rev. and enl. Amsterdam, Netherlands Univ. Pr., 1961. 472p., 370p., 429p. **ED40**

1st ed. 1953.

A trilingual dictionary of the vocabulary of both pure and applied chemistry, giving formulas for compounds.

The 2d edition has been revised and enlarged, particularly by the addition of terms in nuclear and electrotechnical chemistry.

Mayer, Albert Willy. Chemisches Fachwörterbuch, deutsch-englisch-französisch, für Wissenschaft, Technik, Industrie und Handel. Leipzig, Spamer, 1929–31. v.1–2. **ED41**

v.1, Deutsch-englisch-französisch; v.2, Englisch-deutsch-französisch.

An English translation of v.1 was published as:

—— Chemical-technical dictionary (German-English-French-Russian). v.1, translation under the direction of B. N. Menshutkin and M. A. Bloch. 1st Amer. ed. Brooklyn, N.Y., Chemical Pub. Co., 1942. 870p. **ED42**

Sobecka, Z. [and others]. Dictionary of chemistry and chemical technology in four languages, English, German, Polish, Russian. N.Y., Pergamon, 1962. 724p. **ED43**

Includes some 12,000 terms from all branches of theoretical and applied chemistry, chemical engineering, and related technologies. Compiled on an English base with equivalents in the other languages and indexes in each language.

Russian

Callahan, Ludmilla Ignaticio. Russian-English chemical and polytechnical dictionary. 2d ed. prep. with the assistance of E. B. Uvarov. N.Y., Wiley, 1962. 892p. **ED44**

1st ed. 1947.

Karpovich, Evgenii Antonovich and **Karpovich, Vera V.** Russian-English chemical dictionary; chemistry, physical chemistry, chemical engineering, materials, minerals, fuels, petroleum, food industry, pharmacology. 2d improved ed. N.Y., Technical Dictionaries, 1963. 352p. **ED45**

Includes some 29,000 Russian entries and is strong in new terms. Prepared for the English-speaking worker.

Handbooks

Handbook of chemistry and physics: a ready-reference book of chemical and physical data. 45th ed. Ed. in chief, Robert C. Weast. Ed. in charge of mathematics, Samuel M. Selby. Ed. in chief emeritus, Charles D. Hodgman. Cleveland, Ohio, Chemical Rubber Co., 1964. [v.p.] **ED46**

In collaboration with a large number of professional chemists and physicists.

Revised almost annually, each edition incorporating new material and new tables.

Haynes, Williams. Chemical trade names and commercial synonyms: a dictionary of American usage. 2d ed. rev. and enl. Princeton, N.J., Van Nostrand, 1955. 466p. **ED47**

1st ed. 1951.

Not a dictionary of chemical terms, but of trade names, with explanation of usage.

Kaufman, Herbert C. Handbook of organometallic compounds. Princeton, N.J., Van Nostrand, 1961. 1546p. **ED48**

The tables are arranged under each element within a periodic group, and a bibliography follows each element.

Lange, Norbert Adolph and **Forker, Gordon M.** Handbook of chemistry; a reference volume for all requiring

ready access to chemical and physical data used in laboratory work and manufacturing . . . 10th ed. N.Y., McGraw-Hill, 1961. 1969p. **ED49**

Frequently revised.

Long, Cyril [and others]. Biochemists' handbook, comp. by 171 contributors. [1st ed.] London, Spon; Princeton, N.J., Van Nostrand, 1961. 1192p. **ED50**

A technical handbook with signed articles and much bibliography.

Meites, Louis. Handbook of analytical chemistry. 1st ed. N.Y., McGraw-Hill, 1963. [v.p.] il. **ED51**

Perry, John Howard. Chemical business handbook. 1st ed. N.Y., McGraw-Hill, 1954. v.p. [1347p.] il. **ED52**

A practical handbook covering the major phases of business operation in the chemical industry, dealing with business finance, cost accounting, market research, business law, patents and patent law, etc.

Seidell, Atherton. Solubilities of inorganic and metal organic compounds: a compilation of quantitative solubility data from the periodical literature. 3d ed. N.Y., Van Nostrand, 1940–41. 2v. **ED53**

v.2 has title *Solubilities of organic compounds*.

—— —— Supplement, containing data published during the years 1939–49 inclusive. 1952. 1254p.

—— Solubilities, inorganic and metal-organic compounds; a compilation of solubility data from the periodical literature. 4th ed. by William F. Linke. [Wash., McGregor and Werner, 1958]– . v.1– . **ED54**

Contents: v.1, A–Ir.

A revision and continuation of the compilation above. v.1 covers material abstracted through 1956.

Snell, Foster Dee and **Snell, Cornelia T.** Dictionary of commercial chemicals. 3d ed. Princeton, N.J., Van Nostrand, 1962. 714p. **ED55**

1st ed. 1939; 2d ed. 1952.

"Designed to furnish information on the composition of actual commercial products as sold in commerce rather than the pure chemicals of a textbook."—*Pref.*

Stephen, Henry and **Stephen, T.** Solubilities of inorganic and organic compounds. London, N.Y., Pergamon, 1963–64. v.1–2. (In progress) **ED56**

Contents: v.1, Binary systems. 2 pts.; v.2, Ternary systems, pt.1.

Added title page in Russian, Translation of: Moscow. Vsesoiuznyi Institut Nauchnoi i Tekhnicheskoi Informatsii. Spravochnik po rastrorimosti.

Szymanski, Herman A. Infrared band handbook. N.Y., Plenum Pr., 1963– . v.1 (484p.)– . **ED57**

—— —— Supplements 1–2. 1964. 259p.

Explanations in English, French, Russian, and German.

"Primary use will be the identification of unknown compounds, but it will also be of value as a guide in assigning group frequencies, as a key to most advantageous sample conditions, as a tool in comparing series of related compounds for similar vibrations, and finally as an index to the literature."—*Introd.*

Welcher, Frank. Chemical solutions; reagents useful to the chemist, biologist, and bacteriologist. N.Y., Van Nostrand, 1942. 404p. **ED58**

"The purpose . . . is to collect in one place for convenient reference the methods for preparing those solutions most frequently required by the chemist."—*Pref.* Usually gives for each solution: the use, procedure of use, preparation, remarks, and reference.

Directories

Chem sources. N.Y., Directories Pub. Co., 1958– .
v.1– . (Annual) (Not pub. 1959) **ED59**

A buyer's guide to source information for production, research, and development chemicals in an alphabetical listing by chemical name.

Noyes Development Corporation. Chemical guide to the United States, 1963–1964. Pearl River, N.Y., 1963. 76p. **ED60**

Describes the leading 325 chemical firms of the United States.

This publisher also issues similar guides to Canada, Eastern Europe, Latin America, etc.

INORGANIC

Gmelin, Leopold. Gmelins Handbuch der anorganischen Chemie. 8. völlig neubearb. Aufl. hrsg. vom Gmelin Institut, begonnen von R. J. Meyer. . . . Weinheim, Verlag Chemie, 1924– . v.1– . (In progress) **ED61**

Imprint varies.

A monumental work which attempts to include all inorganic compounds ever described with references to the original articles. Volumes are not published in regular numerical sequence.

—— —— Alphabetische Folge zur Systematik der Sachverhalte. Weinheim, Verlag Chemie, 1959. 109p.

Mellor, Joseph William. A comprehensive treatise on inorganic and theoretical chemistry. London, N.Y., Longmans, 1922–37. 16v. il. **ED62**

Contains bibliographies.
v.XVI includes index.

—— —— v.II, Supplement I–III. London, N.Y., Longmans, [1956–63]. v.1–3.

—— —— v.VIII, Supplement I– . [London], Longmans, [1964]– . v.1– . (In progress)

Nitrogen, pt.1– .

International Union of Pure and Applied Chemistry. Commission on the Nomenclature of Inorganic Chemistry. Nomenclature of inorganic chemistry; definitive rules for nomenclature of inorganic chemistry. London, Butterworth, 1959. 93p. **ED63**

Added title page in French.

Recommended international rules for the naming of inorganic compounds.

ORGANIC

Beilstein, Friedrich. Handbuch der organischen Chemie. 4. Aufl. Die Literatur bis 1. Januar 1910 umfassend, hrsg. von der Deutschen Chemischen Gesellschaft, bearb. von Bernhard Prager und Paul Jacobson, unter ständiger Mitwirkung von Paul Schmidt und Dora Stern. . . . Berlin, Springer, 1918–40. v.1–31. tables. **ED64**

v.28, General-Sachregister für die Bände 1–27 des Hauptwerks und ersten Ergänzungswerks. 1938. 2 pts.

—— —— I. Ergänzungswerk, die Literatur von 1910–1919 umfassend, hrsg. von der Deutschen Chemischen Gesellschaft, bearb. von Friedrich Richter. Berlin, Springer, 1928–38. 27v.

—— —— II. Ergänzungswerk, die Literatur von 1920–1929 umfassend. . . . Berlin, Springer, 1941–57. v.1–29[1–3].

—— —— III. Ergänzungswerk, die Literatur von 1930–1949 umfassend, hrsg. vom Beilstein-Institut für Literatur der Organischen Chemie. Berlin, Springer, 1958–61. v.1–5[1]. (In progress)

Editors vary.

Bd.1, T.1–3, 1958–59; Bd.2, T.1–2, 1960–61; Bd.3, T.1–2, 1961–62; Bd.4, T.2, 1963; Bd.5, T.1, 1963– .

This monumental compilation, the most important reference work in organic chemistry, provides a complete summary of published data on organic compounds to Jan. 1, 1910. The supplements cover 1910– .

The 3d edition of this work is frequently referred to in Richter's *Lexikon* (ED74). The 4th edition has been much enlarged, and its arrangement modified. Each volume contains a detailed table of contents and an index. The plan of arrangement is given in the *System der organischen Verbindungen* (ED66) and in Huntress (ED65). Another description and explanation of this indispensable work may be found in Mellon, p.146–52 (ED4).

Huntress, Ernest Hamlin. A brief introduction to the use of Beilstein's Handbuch der organischen Chemie. 2d ed. rev. N.Y., Wiley, 1938. 44p. **ED65**

A simple explanation in English of the method of classification used in the 4th edition of Beilstein.

Deutsche Chemische Gesellschaft. System der organischen Verbindungen; ein Leitfaden für die Benutzung von Beilsteins Handbuch der organischen Chemie. . . . Berlin, Springer, 1929. 246p. **ED66**

—— Kurze Anleitung zur Orientierung in Beilsteins Handbuch der organischen Chemie, bearb. von Friedrich Richter. . . . Berlin, Springer, 1936. 23p. **ED67**

Dictionary of organic compounds: the constitution and physical and chemical properties of the principal carbon compounds and their derivatives, together with the relevant literature references. Eds. in chief: Prof. Sir Ian Heilbron, H. M. Bunbury. New and rev. ed. London, Eyre and Spottiswoode, 1953. 4v. **ED68**

Earlier ed. 1943.

Elsevier's Encyclopaedia of organic chemistry, ed. by E. Josephy and F. Radt. N.Y., Elsevier, 1940–62. il. v.12A, 1948; v.12B, 1948–53; v.13, 1946; v.14, pts.1–6, 1940–62. (In progress) **ED69**

A work in English which, like Beilstein (ED64), attempts to present all known facts on the chemical, physical, and physiological properties of organic compounds. It covers the literature up to and including 1936 or 1946, and, in certain cases, the literature up to the date a particular volume went to press. Each volume includes a subject and a formula index. Expected to be in 20v. with general subject and formula indexes. The first volumes to be issued include fields not covered, or only partially covered, by the 4th edition of Beilstein and its supplements.

International Union of Pure and Applied Chemistry. Nomenclature of organic chemistry. London, Butterworth, 1958. 92p. **ED70**

Recommended international rules for the naming of organic compounds.

Kharasch, Norman, Wolf, Walter and **Harrison, Elaine C. P.** Index to reviews, symposia volumes and monographs in organic chemistry for the period 1940–1960. N.Y., Pergamon, 1962. 345p. **ED71**

Contents: pt.1, Reviews in journals and periodic publications; pt.2, Reviews in symposia, collective volumes and non-periodical publications.

In each part, arrangement is by periodical or monograph, giving complete contents for each volume. Author and subject indexes.

To be kept up to date by annual volumes.

Krauch, Helmut and **Kunz, Werner.** Organic name reactions: a contribution to the terminology of organic chemistry, biochemistry and theoretical organic chemistry. Tr. from the 2d rev. German ed. (with addendum) by John M. Harkin. N.Y., Wiley, 1964. 620p. **ED72**

"The term 'name reactions' is the designation usually applied to reactions which . . . bear the names of their discoverers."

Alphabetically arranged by name, with an addendum and an author and a subject index.

Translation of the authors' *Namenreaktionen der organischen Chemie.*

Methoden der organischen Chemie (Houben-Weyl). 4. völlig neu gestaltete Aufl. Hrsg. von Eugen Müller. Stuttgart, Georg Thieme Verlag, 1952–63. v.1– . (In progress) **ED73**

Volumes published in irregular order.

Richter, Max Moritz. Lexikon der Kohlenstoff-Verbindungen. 3. Aufl. Leipzig, Voss, 1910–12. 4v. diagrams. **ED74**

A formula index to all compounds known to Dec. 31, 1909. Includes more than 144,000 compounds, with references to the literature which describes preparation and properties, but not to purely theoretical papers. References to Beilstein refer to the 3d edition of the *Handbuch* rather than to the 4th edition listed above (ED64).

Continued by:

Deutsche Chemische Gesellschaft. Literatur Register der organischen Chemie, geordnet nach M. M. Richters Formelsystem, redigiert von Robert Stelzner. Bd.1–5, 1910/11–1919/21. Leipzig, Verlag Chemie, 1913–26. 5v. (Repr.: Ann Arbor, Mich., Edwards, 1948) **ED75**

Cited as *Stelzner.* Publisher varies.

Arranged by formulas in continuation of Richter (ED74). Each volume covers the literature of from two to three years.

Merged with Index to *Chemisches Zentralblatt* (ED19).

Utermark, Walther and **Schicke, Walter.** Melting point tables of organic compounds. 2d rev. and supplemented ed. N.Y., Interscience, 1963. 715p. **ED76**

Added title page in German, French, and Russian.

Tables in German, with prefatory matter and index of special terms in the four languages.

BIOGRAPHY

Chemical who's who, 1956. 4th ed., ed. by Winfield Scott Downs and Williams Haynes. N.Y., Lewis Historical Co., 1956. 1267p. **ED77**

1st ed. 1928.

Subtitle: Biography in dictionary form of the leaders in chemical industry, research, and education.

Contains a geographical index including some names from countries other than the United States.

Farber, Eduard. Great chemists. N.Y., Interscience, 1961. 1642p. il. **ED78**

A collection of more than 100 biographies of famous chemists from ancient times to the 20th century, not including living persons. The essays were written by scholars of the last two centuries, and some have been translated from other languages for this work. Includes bibliographies.

—— Nobel prize winners in chemistry, 1901–1961. Rev. ed. London, N.Y., Abelard-Schuman, 1963. 341p. il. **ED79**

For each person gives a biographical sketch, a description of the prize-winning work, and an estimate of its consequences in theory and practice.

Nobelstiftelsen, Stockholm. Chemistry. Amsterdam, Elsevier, 1964– . v.3– . il. (Nobel lectures, including presentation speeches and laureates' biographies) **ED80**

Contents: v.3, 1942–1962.

v.1—to cover 1901–1921—and v.2—to cover 1922–1941—will be published later.

Smith, Henry Monmouth. Torchbearers of chemistry; portraits and brief biographies of scientists who have contributed to the making of modern chemistry. N.Y., Academic Pr., 1949. 270p. il. **ED81**

A collection of portraits of 223 chemists who have been influential in the history of chemistry, including some contemporary chemists. A short biographical sketch accompanies each portrait. The "Bibliography of biographies" by Ralph E. Oesper, p.263–70, gives further references for each person.

HISTORY

Haynes, Williams. American chemical industry: a history. N.Y., Van Nostrand, 1945–54. 6v. il. **ED82**

Contents: v.1, Background and beginning, 1608–1911; v.2–3, The World War I Period, 1912–1922; v.4, The merger era, 1923–1929; v.5, Decade of new products, 1930–1939; v.6, The chemical companies.

Partington, James Riddick. A history of chemistry. London, Macmillan; N.Y., St. Martin's, 1961–64. v.2–4. il. (In progress) **ED83**

A projected 4v. set: v.2–3 cover the 16th–18th centuries; v.4, the 19th and early-20th centuries. v.1 will cover the earliest period.

A heavily documented history.

E E

Earth Sciences

❧ This section lists a selection of reference materials in geology, crystallography, hydrology, meteorology, mineralogy, oceanography, paleontology, petrology, seismology, and volcanology. As in the biological sciences, both scientific and popular works are included, as there is demand in many libraries for popularly written manuals on rocks, fossils, etc.

Many abstract journals in these fields and their subdivisions are available. For additional titles *see* U.S. Library of Congress. Science and Technology Division. *A guide to the world's abstracting and indexing services* (EA62).

GEOLOGY

Guides

Mason, Brian. The literature of geology. N.Y., Author, c/o Amer. Museum of Natural History, 1953. 155p. **EE1**

An annotated listing, which includes government series and

maps and thus complements Pearl's *Guide to geologic literature* (EE2). Arranged in two parts: (1) general (subdivided into form material, and major geologic subjects), and (2) regional.

Pearl, Richard M. Guide to geologic literature. N.Y., McGraw-Hill, 1951. 239p. **EE2**

Written in essay form and arranged in three sections: the first discusses methods of research; the second describes library facilities; and the third (main) part deals with specific types of literature. Emphasis is on English-language publications.

Bibliography

American Geological Institute. Visual Education Committee. Directory of geoscience films, ed. by Wakefield Dort. Wash., Amer. Geological Inst., 1962. 63p. **EE3**

An annotated listing of more than 500 films relating to the geological sciences. The annotations provide information on the scientific content for educational purposes, and the suitability level for each film is indicated. Designed particularly to aid teachers.

Annotated bibliography of economic geology, 1928– . [Urbana, Ill.], Economic Geology Pub. Co., 1929– . v.1– . Semiannual. **EE4**

Compiled by the Bibliographic Staff of the Geological Society of America and prep. under the auspices of GSA and the Society of Economic Geologists. A bibliography, with signed annotations of both book and periodical material in various languages. Covers about 150 periodicals.

—— General index, v.1–25, 1928–54. Urbana, Ill., 1961. 1493p.

Belikov, Evgenii Fedorovich. Bibliograficheskii ukazatel' geodezicheskoi literatury za 40 let 1917–1956. Sost., E. F. Belikov. Red., L. S. Khrenov. Moskva, Izd-vo Geodezicheskoi Lit-ry, 1961. 535p. **EE5**

Books and articles, published in the USSR from 1917 through 1956, on geodesy and related sciences. Some 8800 items are arranged in 20 topical chapters and further subdivisions. Brief bibliographical identification. Author index.

Bibliographie des sciences géologiques, publiée par la Société Géologique de France avec le concours de la Société Française de Mineralogie. 1.–7. année, juil. 1923–29; 2. sér. t.1–26. 1930–55. Paris, Société Géologique de France, 1923–55. Annual. **EE6**

Ceased publication.

1948–55, published as: Extrait du Bulletin analytique du Centre National de la Recherche Scientifique.

A classed bibliography of world-wide coverage, with annual (irregular) author indexes covering materials in various languages.

For continuation *see:*

France. Centre National de la Recherche Scientifique. Bulletin signalétique. 1. pt.: Mathématiques, astronomie, physique, chimie, sciences de l'ingénieur, sciences de la terre. Paris, Centre de Documentation du C.N.R.S., 1956–60. v.17–21. **EE7**

Followed by sections continuing this volume numbering.

—— —— Sec. 10, Sciences de la terre, 1. Minéralogie, géochimie, petrographie. Paris, Centre de Documentation du C.N.R.S., 1961– . v.22– . Monthly. **EE8**

A classed bibliography of world-wide coverage, with an annual author index but no subject index.

—— —— Sec. 11, Sciences de la terre, 2. Physique du globe, géologie, paléontologie. Paris, Centre de Documentation du C.N.R.S., 1961– . v.22– . Monthly. **EE9**

A classed bibliography of world-wide coverage, with an annual author index but no subject index.

For record of full set *see* EA71.

British geological literature, comp. by Edward L. Martin and Anthony P. Harvey. Bourne End, Eng., Coridon Pr., 1964– . v.1– . Quarterly. **EE10**

To be issued quarterly, with annual author and subject indexes. Aims to list "all books and articles on geology and allied subjects published in the British Isles, including the Channel Islands, and overseas publications on British geology."

Brown, Harrison. A bibliography on meteorites. Assoc. eds.: Gunnar Kullerud, Walter Nichiporuk. Chicago, Univ. of Chicago Pr., 1953. 686p. (An international catalogue of meteorites) **EE10a**

The first of a projected 3v. catalog of meteorites. This covers, in chronological order, literature published from 1491 to 1950, with an author index.

Canada. Geological Survey. Annotated catalogue of and guide to the publications of the Geological Survey, Canada, 1845–1917, by W. F. Ferrier, assisted by Dorothy J. Ferrier. Ottawa, Taché, 1920. 544p. **EE11**

—— Publications of the Geological Survey of Canada (1917–1952), comp. by Lorne B. Leafloor. Ottawa, Cloutier, 1952. 82p.

—— Index of publications of the Geological Survey of Canada (1845–1958), by A. G. Johnston. Ottawa, Dept. of Mines and Technical Surveys, [1961]. 378p. **EE12**

—— —— Supplement for 1959, 1960 by H. M. A. Rice. 1961. 83p.

—— —— Supplement for 1961, 1962 by H. M. A. Rice. 1963. 71p.

—— Index to reports of Geological Survey of Canada from 1927–50, comp. by W. E. Cockfield, E. Hall, and J. F. Wright. Ottawa, Dept. of Mines and Technical Surveys, [1962]. 723p. **EE13**

This is the 6th in a series. no.1 covers 1863–84; no.2, 1884–1904; no.3, Separate reports, 1906–10. Summary reports, 1905–16; no.4, Palaeontology reports, 1847–1916; no.5, Memoirs, 1910–26. Bulletins, 1913–26. Summary reports, 1917–26.

Clapp, Jane. Museum publications: a classified list and index of books, pamphlets and other monographs, and of serial reprints. N.Y., Scarecrow, 1962. 2v. **EE14**

Contents: pt.1, Publications in anthropology, archaeology, and art (4416 publications); pt.2, Publications in biological and earth sciences (9231 publications).

"A classified bibliography of the publications available from 276 museums in the United States and Canada."—*Foreword.*

Darton, Nelson Horatio. Catalogue and index of contributions to North American geology, 1732–1891. Wash., Govt. Prt. Off., 1896. 1045p. (U.S. Geological Survey. Bull. no.127) **EE15**

An author-subject index in one alphabet. Includes both book and periodical material.

Deutsche Geologische Gesellschaft, Berlin. Bibliothek. Katalog der Bibliothek, im Auftrage der Gesellschaft bearb. von P. Dienst. Stuttgart, Enke, [1930]. 1161p. **EE16**

The classified subject catalog, with author index, of an outstanding collection.

Faessler, Carl. Cross-index to the maps and illustrations of the Geological Survey and the Mines Branch (Bureau of Mines) of Canada, 1843–1946 (incl.). Quebec, Université Laval, 1947. 525p. (Université Laval. [Faculté des Sciences] Géologie et Mineralogie. Contribution no. 75) **EE17**

A guide to the geological illustrations to be found in the various series of publications of the Geological Survey and the Bureau of Mines of Canada. Pt.1, Introduction; pt.2, Numerical listings of the various series; pt.3, Author index; pt.4, Subject index.

—— —— Supplement, 1946–1956. Cross-index to the geological illustration of Canada. Quebec, 1956. 193p. (Contribution no.118)

France. Service d'Information Géologique. Codification des fichiers bibliographiques. . . . Paris, 1959. 77p. **EE18**

In French, English, German, Italian, Spanish, and Russian.

The classification used in the production of cards on earth sciences, published weekly. Subscriptions may be placed for the whole or for certain rubrics.

English title: Codification of bibliographical card index.

Geological Society of London. Library. Geological literature added to the Geological Society's library, [no.1]–37, July, 1894–1934. . . . London, Soc., 1895–1935. Annual. **EE19**

Not pub. 1913–19. Ceased publication 1934.

International catalogue of scientific literature, sec. H, Geology. 1st–14th annual issues, 1901–14. London, 1903–20. 14v. **EE20**

For full set *see* EA12.

Margerie, Emmanuel de. Catalogue des bibliographies géologiques, rédigé avec le concours des membres de la Commission Bibliographique du Congrès. Paris, Gauthier-Villars, 1896. 733p. (Congrès Géologique International. 5ᵉ session, Wash., 1891; 6ᵉ session, Zürich, 1894) **EE21**

Covers approximately 1726–1895. Arranged by country or region, with author but not complete subject indexes. The table of contents should be consulted for arrangement. Especially useful for sections on biography and bibliography of individual geologists.

Mathews, Edward B. Catalogue of published bibliographies in geology, 1896–1920. . . . Wash., Nat. Research Council, 1923. 228p. (Bull. of the Council, no.36) **EE22**

Continues, in a somewhat simplified form, the bibliography by Margerie (EE21). Arranged by subject with author index. Separate section for personal bibliographies.

Nickles, John Milton. Geologic literature on North America, 1785–1918. Wash., Govt. Prt. Off., 1923–24. 2v. (U.S. Geological Survey. Bull. no.746, 747) **EE23**

An author list, with subject index, covering the geology of the continent of North America and the adjoining islands, Panama, and the Hawaiian Islands. Lists both books and periodical articles; indexes all articles on American geology in about 140 periodicals, including some foreign journals. A cumulation of the annual bibliographies issued by the Geological Survey.

Continued by:

Bibliography of North American geology, 1919–1928, 1929–1939, 1940–1949. Wash., Govt. Prt. Off., 1931–57. v.1–3. 1950– . (U.S. Geological Survey. Bull. no.823, 937, 1049) (In progress) **EE24**

1919–1928, comp. by John M. Nickles; 1929–1939, comp. by Emma M. Thom; 1940–1949, comp. by Ruth Reece King [and others].

Cumulations of and continued by annual (formerly biennial) supplements published with the same title in the *Bulletin* series.

Each volume consists of a comprehensive bibliography with detailed index, covering the geology of the North American continent, including Greenland, the West Indies and other adjacent islands, Hawaii, Guam, and other island possessions.

Nickles, John Milton and **Miller, Robert B.** Bibliography and index of geology exclusive of North America. v.1, 1933– . Wash., Geological Soc. of America, 1934– . (Geological Soc. of America. Bibliographical contributions) **EE25**

v.1–8, annual; v.9–11, biennial; v.12– , annual. v.7–10,

comp. by J. M. Nickles, Marie Siegrist, and Eleanor Tatge; v.11– , by Marie Siegrist and others.

A comprehensive bibliography of articles from the periodicals of many countries dealing with the geology of all parts of the world except North America, thus complementing the *Bibliography of North American geology* (EE24).

Squire, Jeannette W. and **Eustus, Amber.** Catalogue of translations of Russian papers in geology, solid-earth geophysics, and related sciences, [1953]/1961. Wash., 1962. 89p. (Special supplement. International geology review. v.4, no.10, pt.2, Oct. 1964) **EE26**

A listing of 1652 papers.

U.S. Geological Survey. Publications of the Geological Survey, 1879–1961. Wash., Govt. Prt. Off., 1964. 457p. **EE27**

"A permanent catalog of books, maps, and charts issued by the Geological Survey through December 1961." Supersedes all earlier lists.

Supplemented by an annual listing, 1962– , which cumulates the monthly *New publications of the Geological Survey*.

U.S. Library of Congress. Science and Technology Division. United States IGY bibliography, 1953–1960, comp. by Frank M. Marson and Janet R. Terner. (NAS/NRC Publ. 1087) Wash., Nat. Academy of Sciences—Nat. Research Council, 1963. 391p. (World Date Center A. IGY General Report, no.18) **EE28**

Subtitle: An annotated bibliography of United States contributions to the IGY and IGC (1957–1959).

Abstract bibliography of works covering United States participation in the International Geophysical Year, from the formation of the IGY program to its scientific results.

Dissertations

Chronic, John and **Chronic, Halka.** Bibliography of theses written for advanced degrees in geology and related sciences at universities and colleges in the United States and Canada through 1957, by John Chronic and Halka Chronic and Petroleum Research Corporation. Boulder, Colo., Pruett Pr., 1958. unpaged. **EE29**

A listing of 11,091 graduate theses written in 131 universities in the United States and Canada. Includes geology theses and those in such closely allied fields as geophysics, geochemistry, geological engineering, and petroleum engineering, as well as mining and meteorology when there is a geological connection.

An index by geologic names, and a general index arranged primarily by geographic area and secondarily by geologic time and subject matter.

Periodicals

Lomský, Josef. Soupis periodik geologických věd: periodica geologica, palaeontologica et mineralogica. Příruční seznam s citačními zkratkami názvovými. Praha, Nakl. Československé Akademie Věd, 1950. 499p. **EE30**

An alphabetical listing by first word of title of the geological periodicals of the world, past and present. Classified index. Gives title, publishing body, place, dates, and abbreviation.

Abstract journals

Geological abstracts, v.1–6. N.Y., 1953–58. Quarterly. **EE31**

v.1, published by National Academy of Sciences; v.2–6, by Geological Society of America.

At head of title: American Geological Institute.

A cooperative undertaking, giving abstracts of articles from a selected list of periodicals mainly from the United States.

Superseded by *GeoScience abstracts* (EE34).

Geological Society of America. Abstracts for 1961– . Abstracts of papers submitted for six meetings with which the Society was associated. N.Y., 1962– . Annual. **EE32**

Each volume gives abstracts of papers submitted at various geological conferences and meetings.

Geologisches Zentralblatt. Anzeiger für Geologie, Petrographie, Palaeontologie und verwandte Wissenschaften . . . Leipzig, Borntraeger, 1901–42. Bd.1–70. Semimonthly. **EE33**

Ceased publication.

1932–42, in two parts: Abt. A, Geologie (no more published); Abt. B, Palaeontologisches Zentralblatt (continued in *Neues Jahrbuch für Mineralogie, Geologie und Paläontologie* (EE35).

Signed abstracts of book and periodical material in various languages. Indexes to Bd.1–15, 16–30, 31–50.

GeoScience abstracts, v.1– . Wash., Amer. Geological Inst., 1959– . Monthly. **EE34**

A classed abstract journal of current publications on the geology, solid-earth geophysics, and related areas of science . . . published in North America, or, if published elsewhere, dealing with North America. Also includes abstracts of Soviet literature which has been translated and published in North America. Subject and author index published annually.

Neues Jahrbuch für Mineralogie, Geologie und Paläontologie, 1830–1949. Stuttgart, Schweizerbart'sche Verlagsbuchhandlung, 1830–1949. 192v. (?). **EE35**

Title varies.

This bibliographical periodical has had a long and complicated history with varying coverage, but has usually included *"Neues Literatur"* and, from 1925 to 1942, *"Referate."* In 1943 the *"Referate"* became *Zentralblatt für Mineralogie, Geologie und Paläontologie, 1943–49.*

Superseded in 1950 by *Zentralblatt für Mineralogie* (EE 105) and *Zentralblatt für Geologie und Paläontologie* (EE37).

U.S. Geological Survey. Geophysical abstracts. no.1, 1929– . Wash., 1929– . Monthly. **EE36**

Frequency varies.

Abstracts 1–86 were issued in mimeographed form by the Bureau of Mines. On July 1, 1936, the geophysical section was transferred to the Geological Survey, which issued abstracts 87–111. By Departmental Order of Oct. 5, 1942, the geophysical work was again placed with the Bureau of Mines, and abstracts 112–27 were issued by that bureau. Beginning July 1, 1947, it was transferred again to the Geological Survey.

Subtitle: Abstracts of current literature pertaining to the physics of the solid earth and to geophysical exploration.

World-wide coverage. Abstracts in English. Annual author and subject indexes.

Zentralblatt für Geologie und Paläontologie. Stuttgart, Schweizerbart'sche Verlagsbuchhandlung, 1950– . v. 1– . **EE37**

In two sections: T.1, Allgemeine und angewandte Geologie einschl. Lagerstättengeologie, regionale Geologie; T.2, Historische Geologie und Paläontologie.

International in scope. Signed abstracts in German.

Encyclopedias and handbooks

American Geological Institute, Conference, Duluth, 1959. Geology and earth sciences sourcebook for elementary and secondary schools. Robert L. Heller, ed. Prep. under the guidance of the American Geological Institute, National Academy of Sciences—National Research Council. N.Y., Holt, 1962. 496p. il. **EE38**

A textbook and practical handbook presenting various areas of the earth sciences, with introductions, suggestions for

methods and activities, problems, teaching aids, and references.

Huxley, Anthony Julian. Standard encyclopedia of the world's mountains. [1st ed.] N.Y., Putnam, 1962. 383p. il., maps. **EE39**

A popularly written work, arranged alphabetically by name of mountain; gives location, height, dates and names of first climbers, etc., and a brief description and history. Includes a gazetteer and an index.

Lexique stratigraphique international. Paris, Centre National de la Recherche Scientifique, 1956– . v.1– . (In progress) **EE40**

A lexicon of stratigraphic nomenclature in all continents and countries of the world, which is published in various parts, each covering a particular country. Gives a description of the formation, the type locality, age, and reference wherein described.

Contents: v.1, Europe. Pts.1–36; v.2, U.S.S.R. 4 pts.; v.3, Asia. Pts.1–13; v.4, Africa. Pts.1–16; v.5, Latin America. Pts. 1–9; v.6, Oceania. Pts.1–8.

Dictionaries

American Geological Institute. Dictionary of geological terms. Garden City, N.Y., Doubleday (Dolphin Books), 1962. 545p. **EE41**

An abridged edition of EE42, containing some 7500 terms "for use by elementary and secondary school science teachers, beginning students of geology, and hobbyists studying rocks, minerals, and fossils."—*Pref.*

—— Glossary of geology and related sciences; a cooperative project of the American Geological Institute. Coordinating chairman, J. V. Howell. With supplement, prep. by the Glossary Review Committee: J. Marvin Weller, chairman. 2d ed. Wash., 1960. 325p., 72p. **EE42**

1st ed. 1957.

The 2d edition consists of a reprint of the 1st edition, with the addition of a supplement which lists terms that have come to notice since 1957 and some revisions and corrections. In the main part of the work, symbols have been inserted to indicate revised and added terms to be found in the supplement. Contains nearly 17,000 terms.

Beringer, Carl Christoph. Geologisches Wörterbuch, begründet von Carl Christian Beringer. Erklärung der geologischen Fachausdrücke der deutschen Literatur. 5. erg. und erw. Aufl. bearb. von Hans Murawski. Stuttgart, Enke, 1963. 243p. il. **EE43**

Subtitle: Für Geologen, Paläontologen, Mineralogen, Geographen, Geophysiker, Bodenkundler, Bau- und Bergingenieure, Studierende und alle Freunde der Geologie.

Challinor, John. A dictionary of geology. 2d ed. Cardiff, Univ. of Wales Pr.; N.Y., Oxford Univ. Pr., 1964. 289p. **EE44**

1st ed. 1961.

Defines geological terms and gives quotations from the literature, primarily from British works, to show usage.

Leningrad. Vsesoiuznyi Geologicheskii Institut. Geologicheskii slovar'. Moskva, Gosgeoltekhizdat, 1960. 2v. **EE45**

Novo y Fernández-Chicarro, Pedro de. Diccionario de geología y ciencias afines. Barcelona, [etc.], Ed. Labor, 1957. 2v. il. **EE46**

Contents: t.1, Geografía física, cristalografía, mineralogía, petrografía; t.2, Paleontología, estratigrafía, orogenía y tectónica.

Terms are arranged alphabetically under each subject, with a general alphabetical index at the end of v.2.

Prague. Ústřední Ústav Geologický. Naučný geologický

slovník. Sestavil autorský kolektiv pod vedením J. F. Svobody. 1. vyd. Praha, Nakl. Československé Akademie Věd, 1960–61. 2v. and suppl. il. **EE47**

Bibliography, v.1, p.10–13.

—— Stratigrafické tabulky; příloha k Naučnému geologickému slovníku. 1959. 37 fold. charts. **EE48**

Rice, Clara Mabel. Dictionary of geological terms (exclusive of stratigraphic formations and paleontologic genera and species). [Ann Arbor, Mich., lithoprinted by Edwards Bros.], 1961. 465p. **EE49**

Reprint of the 1940 edition with addenda, p.463–65.

Aims to include the definitions of terms used in general geology, structural geology, economic geology, physiography, glacial geology, petrology, mineralogy, evolution, invertebrate and vertebrate paleontology, and stratigraphy.

Wilmarth, Mary Grace. Lexicon of geologic names of the United States (including Alaska). (Also includes the names and ages, but not the definitions, of the named geologic units of Canada, Mexico, the West Indies, Central America, and Hawaii) Wash., Govt. Prt. Off., 1938. 2v. (U.S. Geological Survey. Bull. 896) **EE50**

Name is followed by a definition usually giving lithology, thickness, age, underlying and overlying formations, and type locality, with bibliographical references.

Wilson, Druid [and others]. Geologic names of North America. Wash., Govt. Prt. Off., 1959. 622p. (U.S. Geological Survey. Bull. 1056) **EE51**

Prepared to bring up to date the *Lexicon of geologic names* by Mary Grace Wilmarth (EE50), and to serve as the first step in the preparation of a new edition.

Contents: A, Geologic names of North America introduced in 1936–1955: a compilation of new geologic names of North America, including Greenland, the West Indies, the Pacific Island possessions of the United States, and the Trust Territory of the Pacific Islands. 1957; B, Index to the geologic names of North America; geologic names arranged by age and by area containing type locality.

Foreign terms

French

Davies, George MacDonald. French-English vocabulary in geology and physical geography. London, Murby; N.Y., Van Nostrand, [1932]. 140p. (Repr.: London, J. Mann, 1960) **EE52**

German

Huebner, Walther. Geology and allied sciences, a thesaurus and a coordination of English and German specific and general terms. Pt.1, German-English. N.Y., Veritas Pr., 1939. 405p. **EE53**

Includes some 25,000 general and specific terms used not only in geology but in the various allied sciences, e.g., biology, chemistry, geography, paleontology, physics, seismology, etc.

Jones, William R. and **Cissarz, Arnold.** Englisch-deutsche geologisch-mineralogische Terminologie; eine Einführung in die im deutschen und englischen in Geologie, Mineralogie, Gesteinskunde und Lagerstättenkunde gebräuchlichen Ausdrücke. London, Murby, 1931. 250p. **EE54**

German and English on opposite pages.

A useful dictionary which includes terms used in geology, mineralogy, petrology, mineral deposits, etc.

Polyglot

Nederlandsch Geologisch Mijnbouwkundig Genootschap. Geological nomenclature. Ed. by A. A. G. Schieferdecker.

Gorinchem, J. Noorduijn, 1959. 523p. (Royal Geological and Mining Society of the Netherlands) **EE55**

Classed arrangement of English terms, giving Dutch, French, and German equivalents. Combined index of terms in all languages.

Słownik geodezyjny w 5 językach: polskim, rosyjskim, niemieckim, angielskim, francuskim. Warszawa, Państwowe Przedsiębiorstwo Wydawnictw Kartograficznych, 1955. 525p. **EE56**

A polyglot dictionary on a Polish base with indexes in each of the other languages: Russian, German, English, French.

Windhausen, Heriberto. Diccionario y nomenclatura geológica en castellano, alemán, inglés. La Plata, 1945. 200p. il. (Publicaciones didácticas y de divulgación científica del Museo de La Plata, no.3) **EE57**

Arranged in columns, alphabetically by Spanish form, with explanations of meaning in Spanish and German. German and English indexes.

Russian

Burgunker, Mark E. Russian-English dictionary of earth sciences. N.Y., Telberg Book Co., 1961. 94p. (Manuscript edition ser.) **EE58**

Gives English terms for Russian words, sometimes with explanations and definitions. Includes personal names.

Sofiano, Tat'iana Alekseevna. Anglo-russkii geologicheskii slovar'. Moskva, Gos. Izd-vo Tekhniko-Teoretich. Lit-ry, 1957. 523p. **EE59**

Added title page in English.

(2d ed., repr. from the 1st, 1961. 525p.)

—— Russko-angliiskii geologicheskii slovar'. Moskva, Glavnaia red. Inostrann'kh Nauchno-Tekhnicheskikh Slovarei Fizmatgiza, 1960. 559p. **EE60**

—— —— American supplement, comp. by V. G. Telberg. N.Y., Telberg Book Co., 1961. 49p.

Telberg, V. G. Russian-English dictionary of geological terms. N.Y., Telberg Book Co., 1964. 149p. **EE61**

Synonyms only—no definitions.

Directories

Directory of geoscience departments in the colleges and universities of the United States and Canada, ed. 1– , March 1952– . Wash., Amer. Geological Inst., 1952– . Irregular. **EE62**

Editions 1–7 issued as *Reports* of the Institute.

Title varies: 1952–1956/57, *Departments of geological science in educational institutions of the United States and Canada.*

Edition 8, 1964, lists colleges and universities granting undergraduate and graduate degrees in geology, geophysics, oceanography, and related sciences, with an alphabetical listing of faculty members.

Geophysical directory. Houston, Tex. (Box 13318), 1946– . v.1– . Annual. **EE63**

"Intended to be a comprehensive listing of all companies and individuals directly connected with, or engaged in, the geophysical exploration for petroleum."—*Foreword.*

Howell, Jesse V. and **Levorsen, Arville Irving.** Directory of geological material in North America; 2d ed. rev. and enl., with the assistance of Robert H. Dott and Jane Weaver Wilds. Wash., Amer. Geological Inst., 1957. 208p. **EE64**

1st ed. 1946.

Includes information on maps, aerial photography, geological publications, microfilming, and other specialized services of interest to geologists, with a record of the firms, libraries, museums, book dealers, etc. from which the material may be obtained. In two parts: (1) a general section applying to the whole country or to large areas, and (2) a local section arranged by state or province.

International Geological Congress, 20th, Mexico, 1956. Directorio de geólogos del mundo invitados a concurrir al XX Congreso Geológico Internacional. Mexico, 1956. 1111p. **EE65**

Arranged by country with alphabetical index. A successor to the directory of the 1952 Congress. This edition contains 67,800 names.

History

Geikie, Sir Archibald. The founders of geology. 2d ed. London, Macmillan, 1905. 486p. (Repr.: N.Y., Dover, 1962) **EE66**

A standard history of geology based on the lives and works of outstanding geologists.

La Rocque, Aurèle. Contributions to the history of geology. Columbus, Ohio State Univ., Dept. of Geology, 1964. 3v. **EE66a**

v.1, Biographies of geologists, 1961. 130p. Suppl. 1, n.p. Suppl. 2, 1964. 27p.; v.2, Bibliography of the history of geology, 1964. 86p. Suppl. 1, 1960. 7p. Suppl. 2, 1962. 11p.; v.3, Biographic index, 1964. 217p.

Issued in preliminary mimeographed form.

Preliminary paper presented at the Conference on the History of Geology supported by the National Science Foundation and held at the University of Nevada, Reno, Aug. 1964. Paper to be published later.

Biographies of geologists of all periods and countries from ancient times to the present. Length varies from one to several columns.

The index gives full name, years of birth and death, nationality, field of interest, and references to the literature.

Merrill, George Perkins. First 100 years of American geology. New Haven, Conn., Yale Univ. Pr.; London, Milford, 1924. 773p. il. (Repr.: N.Y., Hafner, 1964) **EE67**

A survey history including biographies of geologists but no bibliographical references. A revised version of the author's *Contributions to the history of American geology* (1904).

Zittel, Karl Alfred von. Geschichte der Geologie und Paläontologie bis Ende des 19. Jahrhunderts. Munich, Oldenbourg, 1899. 868p. il. **EE68**

English translation by Maria M. Ogilvie-Gordon. *History of geology and palaeontology to the end of the nineteenth century.* London, Walter Scott, 1901. 562p. il. (Repr.: N.Y., Hafner, 1962)

A standard history.

CRYSTALLOGRAPHY

See also Mineralogy, p.567–68.

France. Centre National de la Recherche Scientifique. American Crystallographic Association. Bulletin signalétique. Sec. 6, Structure de la matière: cristallographie, solides, fluides, atomes, ions, molécules. Paris, Centre de Documentation du C.N.R.S., 1961– . v.22– . Monthly. **EE69**

A classed bibliography of world-wide coverage. Monthly subject and author indexes.

For complete set *see* EA71.

International Union of Crystallography. International tables for X-ray crystallography. Birmingham, Eng., Kynoch Pr., 1952–62. 3v. **EE70**

Contents: v.1, Symmetry groups, ed. by N. F. M. Henry and K. Lonsdale; v.2, Mathematical tables, ed. by J. S. Kasper and K. Lonsdale; v.3, Physical and chemical tables, ed. by C. H. MacGillavry and G. D. Rieck.

Wyckoff, Ralph W. G. Crystal structures. 2d ed. N.Y., Interscience, 1963–64. v.1–2. il. **EE71**

A revision of the compilation previously published in looseleaf form, written for crystallographers, physicists, biochemists, geologists, and mineralogists. Gives detailed descriptions of structures with illustrations.

HYDROLOGY

Bibliography

Bibliography of hydrology, United States of America . . . 1935/36–40. Wash., Amer. Geophysical Union, Section of Hydrology, 1937–41. **EE72**

Ceased publication.

"The United States cahier . . . of the International Bibliography of Hydrology established by the International Association of Scientific Hydrology."

Continued by:

American Geophysical Union. Annotated bibliography on hydrology, 1941–1950 (United States and Canada). Wash., Govt. Prt. Off., 1952. 408p. (U.S. Federal Inter-Agency River Basin Committee. Notes on hydrologic activities bull. no.5) **EE73**

—— Annotated bibliography on hydrology (1951–54) and sedimentation (1950–54), United States and Canada. Wash., Govt. Prt. Off., 1956. 207p. (U.S. Inter-Agency Committee on Water Resources. Joint hydrology-sedimentation bull. no.7) **EE74**

U.S. Geological Survey. Annotated bibliography on hydrology and sedimentation, United States and Canada, 1955/58, by Henry C. Riggs. Wash., Govt. Prt. Off., 1962. 236p. (Its Water-supply paper 1546) **EE75**

U.S. Inter-Agency Committee on Water Resources. Annotated bibliography on hydrology and sedimentation, 1959–1962 (United States and Canada). Prep. under the auspices of Subcommittees on Hydrology and Sedimentation. Wash., Govt. Prt. Off., 1964. 323p. (Its Joint hydrology-sedimentation bull. no.8) **EE76**

Handbooks

Chow, Ven Te. Handbook of applied hydrology; a compendium of water-resources technology. N.Y., McGraw-Hill, 1964. [v.p.] il. **EE77**

Articles contributed by specialists. Includes bibliography.

METEOROLOGY

Bibliography

International catalogue of scientific literature: F, Meteorology. 1st–14th annual issues. London, Harrison, 1902–19. v.1–14. **EE79**

For full description *see* EA12.

Meteorological and Geoastrophysical Abstracts. Bibliography on meteorological satellites (1952–1962). Prep. by Elemer Kiss. Wash., Govt. Prt. Off., 1963. 380p. (U.S. Weather Bureau) **EE80**

Lists 988 titles—books and articles—arranged under year,

then alphabetically by author (from 1 article in 1951 to 230 in 1962).

U.S. Army. Signal Corps. Bibliography of meteorology. . . . Wash., Signal Off., 1889–91. 4v. **EE81**

Subtitle: A classed catalogue of the printed literature of meteorology from the origin of printing to the close of 1881; with a supplement to the close of 1887, and an author index. Prepared under the direction of Brigadier General A. W. Greely . . . ed. by Oliver L. Fassig.

v.1, Temperature; v.2, Moisture; v.3, Winds; v.4, Storms.
v.3–4 include literature to 1889.
Includes some 60,000 titles by 13,000 authors.

Abstract journals

Meteorological and geoastrophysical abstracts. Boston, Amer. Meteorological Soc., 1950– . v.1– . Monthly. **EE82**

v.1–10 had title *Meteorological abstracts and bibliography.* Beginning with v.11, 1960, supported by U.S. Dept. of the Army, National Aeronautics and Space Administration, National Oceanographic Data Center, U.S. Weather Bureau, U.S. National Science Foundation.

Includes: "(1) Current abstracts in English on important meteorological and geoastrophysical literature in every language; (2) Bibliographic references to other items of interest to the profession; (3) Selective annotated bibliographies on subjects of immediate and special interest to meteorologists, geophysicists and astrophysicists."

Dictionaries

Glossary of meteorology. Ed. by Ralph E. Huschke. Boston, Amer. Meteorological Soc., 1959. 638p. **EE83**

"Sponsored by U.S. Dept. of Commerce, Weather Bureau [and others]."

"Purports to define every important meteorological term likely to be found in the literature today."—*Pref.*

A dictionary compiled and written by specialists with definitions "understandable to an undergraduate in a technical college yet [with] sufficient detail to satisfy the working specialist."—*Pref.* Primarily United States usage, but with some terms used in other countries.

Gt.Brit. Meteorological Office. Meteorological glossary, comp. by D. H. McIntosh. 4th ed. London, Stat. Off., 1963. 287p. il. **EE84**

1st ed. 1916.
4th ed. rewritten.

Russian

Ainbinder, M. I. Anglo-russkii meteorologicheskii slovar. Moscow, Gos. Izd-vo Fiziko-Matematicheskoii Lit-ry, 1959. 244p. **EE85**

Added title page: English-Russian meteorological dictionary.

Mamontova, Lidiia Ivonovna and **Khromov, S. I.** Anglo-russkii meteorologicheskii slovar. [Okolo 6000 meteorologicheskikh terminov] Leningrad, Gidrometeorologicheskoe Izd-vo, 1959. 172p. **EE86**

Noveck, Sonia. Russian-English glossary of physics of fluids and meteorology. N.Y., Interlanguage Dictionaries Pub. Corp., 1959. 93p. **EE87**

Subtitle: . . . contains the most up-to-date Russian-English vocabulary in the fields of physics of fluids and meteorology. There are over 4000 terms comp. from the latest Russian and English sources in the field.

Spanish

Brazol, Demetrio. Dictionary of meteorological and related terms. 1st ed. Buenos Aires, Hachette, 1955. 557p. **EE88**

Contents: English-Spanish, Spanish-English.

Handbooks

American Meteorological Society. Committee on the Compendium of Meteorology. Compendium of meteorology . . . ed. by Thomas F. Malone. Boston, Soc., 1951. 1334p. il. **EE89**

108 articles, in 25 sections, by different authors. Bibliographies follow each chapter; subject and title indexes.

Berry, Frederic Aroyce, Bollay, E. and **Beers, Norman R.** Handbook of meteorology. N.Y., McGraw-Hill, 1945. 1068p. il. **EE90**

Aims to include practical meteorological information with emphasis on the scientific and engineering aspects. Includes bibliographies.

U.S. Air Force. Cambridge Research Laboratories. Geophysics Research Directorate. Handbook of geophysics. Rev. ed. N.Y., Macmillan, 1960. [v.p.] il. **EE91**

1st ed.: *Handbook of geophysics for Air Force designers.* 1957.

A handbook of text, tables, and charts dealing with the atmosphere, wind, temperature, precipitation, clouds, geomagnetism, meteors, the ionosphere, thermal radiation, the sun, cosmic radiation, atmospheric exploratory devices, and others.

Atlases

Visher, Stephen Sargent. Climatic atlas of the United States. Cambridge, Harvard Univ. Pr., 1954. 403p. 1031 maps. **EE92**

Includes 1031 maps and charts, mainly line drawings, taken from many sources. General contents include: Temperature; Winds, atmospheric pressure, storms; Sunshine; Atmospheric humidity and evaporation; Precipitation; Some consequences of climate and weather; Climatic regions and changes.

Climatology

Clayton, Henry Helm. World weather records, collected from official sources by Dr. Felix Exner and others. Assembled and arranged for publication by H. Helm Clayton. Pub. under grant from John A. Roebling. Wash., Smithsonian Inst., 1927. 1199p. (Smithsonian miscellaneous collections, v.79) 1st repr. 1944. **EE93**

—— —— Errata. Wash., Smithsonian Inst., 1929. 28p. Covers records to about 1920.
Continued by:

—— World weather records . . . 1921–1930, 1931–1940. Wash., Smithsonian Inst., 1934–47. 2v. (Smithsonian miscellaneous collections, v.90, 105) **EE94**
Continued by:

U.S. Weather Bureau. World weather records, 1941–50. Wash., 1959. 1361p. **EE95**

Statistical tables giving pressure at station level, temperature, and precipitation, by month. Arranged by continent, subdivided by station.

Conway, Hobart McKinley, May, Stancel L. and **Armstrong, Evan.** The weather handbook: a summary of weather statistics for principal cities throughout the

United States and around the world. Atlanta, Ga., Conway Publ., 1963. 255p. il. **EE96**

Charts and maps.

U.S. Weather Bureau. Climatological data for the United States by sections, v.1, Jan. 1914– . Wash., Bureau, 1914– . il. Monthly (with annual summaries). **EE97**

Contains weather statistics from 47 separate sections in the continental United States, each section, as a rule, corresponding to a state. Printed in the various section centers and assembled and bound in Washington.

—— Climatological data; national summary. Asheville, N.C., 1950– . v.1– . Monthly and annual. **EE98**

—— Daily weather map [forecasts and general weather information of United States published at Wash., D.C.] Daily, including Sundays and holidays. **EE99**

Prepared from observations taken daily at hundreds of stations throughout North America. A complete explanation of these maps (including all symbols and tables) is included on the reverse side of the Sunday map. Periodically, during each month, climatological charts and graphs appear in place of the Explanation; and occasionally illustrated articles of special meteorological interest are published.

An interesting and informative service. The maps are excellent for daily display on bulletin boards.

—— Selective guide to published climatic data sources prepared by the U.S. Weather Bureau. Wash., Govt. Prt. Off., 1963. 84p. (Its Key to meteorological records documentation, no.4.11) **EE100**

Designed to be a key to climatological data available in published form, and to indicate the publications "in which these data in their various climatological categories (temperature, precipitation, wind, humidity, etc.), may be found."—*Introd.*

For other climatic data published by the U.S. Weather Bureau, *see* Supt. of Documents, *Price list no.48, Weather, astronomy, and meteorology.* Wash., Govt. Prt. Off. (*see* AH20).

MINERALOGY

Abstract journals and indexes

International catalogue of scientific literature: G, Mineralogy. 1st–14th annual issues, 1901–14. London, 1902–17. 14v. **EE101**

For full description *see* EA12.

Mineralogical abstracts, issued by the Mineralogical Society, v.1– , 1920– . London, Simpkin, Marshall, 1922– . v.1– . **EE102**

A classified list of signed abstracts of current literature: books, pamphlets, reports, periodical articles, etc. International in coverage.

Beginning with 1959, 8 issues (2 years) constitute a volume. Issue no.8 is the "topographical" and alphabetical index.

v.1–13 (1920–58), issued only with *Mineralogical magazine,* v.14– , published jointly by the Mineralogical Society of Great Britain and the Mineralogical Society of America.

Supplements the record in the *International catalogue of scientific literature* (EA12), by summarizing the mineralogical literature from 1915.

Repertorium der mineralogischen und krystallographischen Literatur, 1876–[1902]; und Generalregister der Zeitschrift für Krystallographie und Mineralogie . . . Bd.1–40. Leipzig, Engelmann, 1886–1910. 4v. **EE103**

Each volume is in two parts: (1) a bibliography of material published during the period covered, and (2) an index to

the *Zeitschrift.* The *Repertorium* covers 1876–85, 1885–91, 1891–97, 1897–1902.

Reuss, Jeremias David. Repertorium commentationum a societatibus litterariis editarum . . . T.2, Botanica et mineralogia. Gottingae, Dieterich, 1802. 604p. **EE104**

A valuable index to the publications of learned societies up to 1800. Classed arrangement with author index. For description of complete set *see* EA15.

Zentralblatt für Mineralogie. Stuttgart, Schweizerbart'sche Verlagsbuchhandlung, 1950– . v.1– . **EE105**

In two sections: T.1, Kristallographie und Mineralogie; T.2, Petrographie, technische Mineralogie, Geochemie und Lagerstättenkunde (title varies slightly).

Signed abstracts in German. International in scope.

Dictionaries

Bailey, Dorothy and **Bailey, Kenneth C.** An etymological dictionary of chemistry and mineralogy. London, Edward Arnold, 1929. 307p. **EE106**

Gives the "derivation of chemical and mineralogical names which have been current in the literature . . . at any period later than the middle of the 19th century."—*Pref.*

Bradley, J. E. S. and **Barnes, A. C.** Chinese-English glossary of mineral names. N.Y., Consultants Bureau, 1963. 120p. **EE107**

Chambers's Mineralogical dictionary, with 40 plates of coloured illustrations. [New ed.] N.Y., Chemical Pub. Co., 1948. 47p. il. 40pl. (col.) **EE108**

Concise definitions of mineralogical terms, with brief descriptions of the more important minerals.

Shipley, Robert M. [and others]. Dictionary of gems and gemology, including ornamental, decorative and curio stones. . . . 5th ed. Los Angeles, Calif., Gemological Inst. of America, 1951. 261p. **EE109**

1st ed. 1945.

"A glossary of over 4,000 English and foreign words, terms and abbreviations which may be encountered in English literature or in the gem, jewelry or art trades."—*Title page.*

Includes names of some persons, societies, museums, journals, etc.

Directories

American mineral guide to notable collecting areas, and directory of American mineral & gem collectors [and collections] together with a dealer's section, listing those substantial firms supplying the needs of the mineralogists. 2d ed. compl. rev. and enl. Seattle, Wash., Western Mineral Exchange, 1948. 89p. **EE110**

Font-Altaba, M. World directory of mineralogists, comp. . . . with the help of the representatives of the national mineralogical societies. Barcelona, pub. for the International Mineralogical Association, by Editorial Eco, 1962. 144p. **EE111**

Arranged alphabetically under country.

Handbooks

Börner, Rudolf. Minerals, rocks, and gemstones. Tr. and ed. by W. Mykura. Edinburgh, London, Oliver & Boyd, 1962. 250p. il. **EE112**

"A translation of *Welcher Stein ist das?* by Rudolf Börner first published in 1938 by Franckh'sche Verlagshandlung W. Keller & Co., Stuttgart."

The translator has adapted the work for use in Great Britain "giving pre-eminence to British localities and adapting the rock classifications, where necessary, to conform with current English usage . . . and to provide a somewhat fuller glossary of rocks and petrographic terms than that given in the German edition."—*Pref.*

Dana, James Dwight and **Dana, Edward S.** The system of mineralogy. 7th ed. entirely rewritten and greatly enl. by Charles Palache, Harry Berman and Clifford Frondel. N.Y., Wiley, 1944–62. 3v.   **EE113**

6th ed. 1892.

The latest edition of a standard work.

Contents: v.1, Elements, sulfides, sulfosalts, oxides; v.2, Halides, nitrates, borates, carbonates, sulfates, phosphates, arsenates, tungstates, molybdates, etc.; v.3, Silica minerals.

Deer, William Alexander, Howie, R. A. and **Zussman, J.** Rock-forming minerals. London, Longmans, 1962–63. 5v.   **EE114**

Contents: v.1, Ortho- and ring silicates; v.2, Chain silicates; v.3, Sheet silicates; v.4, Framework silicates; v.5, Nonsilicates.

Gives structure, chemistry, optical and physical properties, distinguishing features, and paragenesis of minerals.

Hey, Max H. An index of mineral species & varieties arranged chemically, with an alphabetical index of accepted mineral names and synonyms. London, pr. by order of the Trustees of the British Museum, 1950. 609p. **EE115**

A chemically classified list of minerals, followed by an alphabetical index.

Johnstone, Sydney J. and **Johnstone, Margery G.** Minerals for the chemical and allied industries. 2d ed. London, Chapman & Hall, 1961. 788p.   **EE116**

1st ed. 1954.

Alphabetically arranged chapters on various minerals giving as pertinent: description, world production, uses, bibliography, etc.

Pough, Frederick H. A field guide to rocks and minerals. Boston, Houghton, 1953. 333p. il. (Peterson field guide series)   **EE117**

A practical handbook for mineral identification.

Ransom, Jay Ellis. A range guide to mines and minerals; how and where to find valuable ores and minerals in the United States. [1st ed.] N.Y., Harper, 1964. 305p. il.   **EE118**

Introductory chapters on mineral collection are followed by a range guide arranged by state, county, township, and range. Short glossary and bibliography.

U.S. Bureau of Mines and **U.S. Geological Survey.** Mineral resources of the United States . . . foreword by J. A. Krug. Wash., Public Affairs Pr., 1948. 212p. il. **EE119**

A report of the results of an appraisal begun in 1944 of the United States mineral position. Discusses the production and reserves of the various mineral resources of the country, with chapters on individual minerals.

U.S. Bureau of Mines. Minerals yearbook, 1932/33– . Wash., Govt. Prt. Off., 1933– . Annual.   **EE120**

Supersedes the Bureau's *Mineral resources of the United States,* 1882–1931, as well as various interim summaries.

The volumes dated 1932/33 through 1940 contain reviews of 1932 through 1939. In 1941, designation was changed to use the date of period covered. Therefore, two volumes bear the date 1940: (1) 1940 (review of 1939), and (2) the actual review of 1940.

1952–62, issued in 3v. each year. 1963, issued in 4v.: v.1, Metals and minerals (except fuels); v.2, Fuels; v.3, Area reports, Domestic; v.4, Area reports, Foreign.

A comprehensive survey, covering mining and metallurgical techniques; economic developments; and a world review of mineral production, consumption, and trade.

—— —— Statistical appendix. 1932/33–1935. Wash., Govt. Prt. Off., 1934–36. 3v. il.

No more published. Later figures included in *Yearbook.*

OCEANOGRAPHY

Bibliography

U.S. Defense Documentation Center, Arlington, Va. Oceanography, a report bibliography, comp. by Esther E. Thompson. Arlington, Va., Center, 1963. 355p. **EE121**

An abstract bibliography on oceanography including biological, chemical, economic, physical and practical, and applied oceanography as well as marine geology and scientific research in these areas.

U.S. Interagency Committee on Oceanography of the Federal Council for Science and Technology. Bibliography of oceanographic publications. Comp. by Mark W. Pangborn and others. Wash., 1963. 23p. (ICO pamphlet, no.9)   **EE122**

Contains 500 selected titles in English to help the student and general reader locate information about the ocean in its many aspects. Indicates reading level and contents.

Encyclopedias

Huxley, Anthony. Standard encyclopedia of the world's oceans and islands. [1st ed.] N.Y., Putnam, 1962. 383p. il., maps.   **EE123**

A popularly written work arranged alphabetically by name of ocean or island, giving location; dimensions; etc. (in case of oceans the maximum depth); and a brief description and history. Includes a gazetteer and an index.

Directories

International directory of oceanographers. 4th ed. comp. by Richard C. Vetter. Wash., Nat. Academy of Sciences—Nat. Research Council, 1964. 273p.   **EE124**

Eds.1–3, 1950–60, comp. by K. O. Emery.

The 4th edition is much enlarged, listing 2563 names from 93 countries.

PALEONTOLOGY

Bibliography

Bibliography of vertebrate paleontology and related subjects. 1945/46– . [Cambridge, Mass.?], Soc. of Vertebrate Paleontology, 1947– . Annual.   **EE125**

Prepared from periodicals received by the Library of the American Museum of Natural History in New York. Previously included in the *News bulletin* of the Society of Vertebrate Paleontology.

Editors vary.

Each issue in two parts: (1) the preceding year and earlier, and (2) the year covered. Arranged alphabetically by author.

Hay, Oliver Perry. Bibliography and catalogue of the fossil Vertebrata of North America. [v.1] Wash., Geological Survey, 1902. (Its Bull. no.179)   **EE126**

—— Second bibliography and catalogue . . . Wash., Carnegie Inst., 1929–30. 2v. (Its Publ. no.390)

Comprehensive author bibliographies covering North America to 1927, with subject and systematic indexes.

Supplemented by:

Camp, Charles Lewis [and others]. Bibliography of fossil vertebrates. 1928– . N.Y., Geological Soc. of America, 1940– . v.1– . Quinquennial.   **EE127**

Contents: 1928–1933; 1934–1938; 1939–1943; 1944–1948; 1949–1953; 1954–1958. International in scope.

Complemented by:

Romer, Alfred Sherwood [and others]. Bibliography of fossil vertebrates exclusive of North America, 1509–1927. N.Y., Geological Soc. of America, 1962. 2v.(1544p.). (G.S.A. Memoir 87) **EE128**

A comprehensive bibliography through the year 1927.

Hiltermann, Heinrich [and others]. Bibliographie stratigraphisch wichtiger mikropaläontologischer Publikationen von etwa 1830 bis 1958 mit Kurzreferaten. Stuttgart, E. Schweizerbart'sche Verlagsbuchhandlung, 1961. 403p. **EE129**

A bibliography of microfossils in connection with stratigraphic problems. International in scope. Classed arrangement, with author and subject/place indexes.

International catalogue of scientific literature: K, Paleontology. London, 1902–19. 14v. **EE130**

For full description *see* EA12.

Fossil indexes

Andrews, Henry N. Index of generic names of fossil plants, 1820–1950. Based on the Compendium index of paleobotany of the U.S. Geological Survey. Wash., 1955. 262p. (U.S. Geological Survey. Bull. 1013) **EE131**

Bibliography, p.13–98; Generic index of fossil plants, p.99–262.

Ellis, Brooks Fleming and **Messina, Angelina R.** Catalogue of Foraminifera. . . . Special publication. N.Y., Amer. Museum of Natural History, 1940– . Loose-leaf. **EE132**

v.30, Index to taxonomic changes and Bibliography.
Originally published in 30 numbered volumes. Now looseleaf supplements are issued to be interfiled with these, almost doubling the size of the original work.

—— Catalogue of Ostracoda. N.Y., Amer. Museum of Natural History, 1952–64. v.1–20. il. (In progress) **EE133**

In these 20 volumes some 764 genera and subgenera, and 7468 species and subspecies, are described.
Annual supplements are planned which are intended to be interleaved in the original 20v.

Fossilium catalogus. I, Animalia. Pars 1– . 1913– . 's-Gravenhage, W. Junk, 1913– . Pt.1– . (In progress) **EE134**

An important, comprehensive series; 106 pts. published to 1964, each part on a separate subject by a specialist.

Joint Committee on Invertebrate Paleontology. Treatise on invertebrate paleontology, directed and ed. by Raymond C. Moore [and others]. N.Y., Geological Soc. of America and Univ. of Kansas Pr., 1953–64. Pt.[1–13]. il. (In progress) **EE135**

Parts are assigned letters, A to X, with a view to indicating their systematic sequence, but are published at whatever time each is ready.
The parts are divided according to phylum, and the orders, classes, genera, species, etc. in each phylum are described: their growth and development, general features, characteristics, etc., with references to the literature.

Shimer, Hervey Woodburn and **Shrock, Robert R.** Index fossils of North America. A publication of the Technology Press, Massachusetts Institute of Technology. N.Y., Wiley, 1944. 837p. il. **EE136**

"Based on the complete revision and reillustration of Grabau and Shimer's *North American index fossils*."
"An index fossil is one which identifies and dates the strata or succession of strata in which it lies." This work describes and illustrates such fossils.

Directories

Lambrecht, Kalman and **Quenstedt, W.** Palaeontologi. Catalogus bio-bibliographicus. 's-Gravenhage, W. Junk, 1938. 495p. (In Fossilium catalogus. I, Animalia, ed. by W. Quenstedt, pars 72) **EE137**

An alphabetical list of palaeontologists of many countries and periods, giving full name, places and dates of birth and death, identification data, and references to biographical data.

Handbooks

Fenton, Carroll Lane and **Fenton, Mildred Adams.** The fossil book; a record of prehistoric life. Garden City, N.Y., Doubleday, [1958]. 482p. il. **EE138**

"This book surveys the realm of fossils from the earliest plantlike organisms to beasts and birds that lived a few centuries ago. Only man is omitted."—*Acknowledgments.*

Ransom, Jay Ellis. Fossils in America: their nature, origin, identification and classification, and a range guide to collecting sites. [1st ed.] N.Y., Harper, 1964. 402p. il. **EE139**

A popularly written work with detailed information on the origin, nature, and collecting of fossils. Fossil localities are arranged by state, with subdivisions.

Rhodes, Frank Harold Trevor, Zim, Herbert S. and **Shaffer, Paul R.** Fossils, a guide to prehistoric life. N.Y., Golden Pr., [1962]. 160p. il. **EE140**

A good guide for the beginning fossil collector. Illustrations are excellent.

Traité de paléontologie, publié sous la direction de Jean Piveteau. Paris, Masson, 1952–57. 7v. il. **EE141**

An excellent handbook, with bibliographies, glossaries, index, etc.

PETROLOGY

See also Natural History, p.547.

Fenton, Carroll Lane and **Fenton, Mildred Adams.** The rock book. N.Y., Doubleday, 1940. 357p. il. **EE142**

A popularly written handbook on rocks and minerals.

Holmes, Arthur. Nomenclature of petrology, with references to selected literature. London, Murby, [1928]. 284p. **EE143**

1st ed. 1920; the 1928 edition incorporates a few corrections and modifications.

Johannsen, Albert. A descriptive petrography of the igneous rocks. Chicago, Univ. of Chicago Pr., 1931–38. 4v. il. (v.1, 2d ed. 1939) **EE144**

Contents: v.1, Introduction, textures, classifications, and glossary; v.2, The quartz-bearing rocks; v.3, The intermediate rocks; v.4: pt.1, The feldspathoid rocks; pt.2, The peridotites and perknites. Index of authors, of localities, of rock names.
A standard, basic work, with bibliographical footnotes. v.1 includes appendixes: Miscellaneous definitions; Definitions of textural and structural terms; Definitions of rocks.

SEISMOLOGY

Montessus de Ballore, Fernand, *Comte* de. Bibliografía general de temblores y terremotos. Publicada por la Sociedad Chilena de Historia y Geografía. Chile, Impr. Universitaria, 1915–19. 7 pts. (1515p.) **EE145**

Contents: 1. pt., Teorías sismológicas. Efectos geológicos

de los terremotos. Catálogos sísmicos mundiales; 2. pt., Europa septentrional y central; 3. pt., Países circunmediterráneos; 4. pt., Asia, África, y Oceanía; 5. pt., América, Tierras antárticas y océanos; 6. pt., Fenómenos accesorios. El movimiento sísmico . . . Literatura sísmica. Historia de la sismología. Misceláneas; 7. pt., Prólogo. Suplemento. Apéndice. Addenda. (Indexes not published?)

Also published in *Revista chilena de historia y geografía*, 1915–1919.

U.S. Coast and Geodetic Survey. Earthquake history of the United States. Rev. ed. Wash., Govt. Prt. Off., 1958–61. 2v.   **EE146**

> 1st ed. 1947.
> Contents: pt.1, Continental United States and Alaska (exclusive of California and western Nevada), by N. H. Heck. Rev. ed. (through 1956), by R. A. Eppley; pt.2, Stronger earthquakes of California and western Nevada, by H. O. Wood and N. H. Heck. Rev. ed. (through 1960), by R. A. Eppley.

—— United States earthquakes, 1928– . Wash., Govt. Prt. Off., 1930– . Annual.   **EE147**

> An annual report of earthquakes felt in the United States.

U.S. Geological Survey. Geophysical abstracts. Wash., 1929– . Monthly.   **EE148**

> For full information *see* EE36.

VOLCANOLOGY

International Association of Volcanology. Catalogue of the active volcanoes of the world including solfatara fields. Naples, 1951–63. Pts.1–16. il. (In progress)   **EE149**

> Each part treats a different area of the world.
> Usually gives for each volcano: name and location, form and structure, volcanic activity, petrography, and bibliography.
> Name of association was formerly International Volcanological Association.

E F

Mathematics

☙ Parke's *Guide to the literature of mathematics and physics* (EF1) should be consulted for additional titles in these fields. A general reference collection will need a mathematics dictionary such as James's *Mathematics dictionary* (EF16) or Karush's *The crescent dictionary of mathematics* (EF17), and perhaps the *Universal encyclopedia of mathematics* (EF19); probably one of the handbooks, e.g., Merritt's *Mathematics manual* (EF28) or Korn's *Mathematical handbook for scientists and engineers* (EF27); and, according to circumstances, one or more of the compendiums of statistics.

GENERAL WORKS

Guides

Parke, Nathan Grier. Guide to the literature of mathematics and physics including related works on engineering science. 2d rev. ed. N.Y., Dover, 1958. 436p.   **EF1**

> A useful handbook comprising chapters on principles of reading and study, searching the literature, types of materials, library usage, etc., and an annotated bibliography of some 5000 titles arranged by subject with author and subject indexes. Its primary interest is mathematics and physics, but it is also useful for some engineering subjects, particularly electronic, electrical, radio, and mechanical engineering.

Loria, Gino. Guida allo studio delle storia dell matematiche; generalità, didattica, bibliografia. Appendice: Questioni storiche concernenti le scienze esatte. 2. ed. rif. e aum. Milano, Hoepli, 1946. 385p.   **EF2**

> A comprehensive guide to the literature of the history of mathematics, covering all periods and all countries. Includes material on the history, manuscripts, biographical sources, reviews, periodicals, etc. Unfortunately, many typographical errors.

Bibliography

International Statistical Institute. Bibliography of basic texts and monographs on statistical methods, 1945–1960. [2d ed. by William R. Buckland and Ronald A. Fox] Edinburgh, Oliver & Boyd; N.Y., Hafner, [1963]. 297p.   **EF3**

> For full information *see* CG3.

Forsythe, George Elmer. Bibliography of Russian mathematics books. N.Y., Chelsea, 1956. 106p.   **EF4**

> Lists more than 600 titles in pure and applied mathematics, published (or reprinted) in Russian or Ukrainian since 1930.
> Authors and titles are transliterated by the Library of Congress transcription method.

International catalogue of scientific literature: A, Mathematics. 1st–14th annual issues, 1901–14. London, Harrison, 1902–17. v.1–14.   **EF5**

> For full description *see* EA12.

Karpinski, Louis Charles. Bibliography of mathematical works printed in America through 1850 . . . with the cooperation for Washington libraries of Walter F. Shenton. Ann Arbor, Univ. of Michigan Pr.; London, Milford, Oxford Univ. Pr., 1940. 697p. il. (incl. facsim.)   **EF6**

> A chronological record of mathematical works in various languages printed in America. Later editions and issues of each title are listed under the 1st edition. Includes more than 1000 titles and some 3000 editions. Locates copies in more than 100 libraries.
> Indexes: General index of authors' names and anonymous titles; Topical indexes; Index of non-English and Canadian works; Index of printers and publishers.

—— —— Supplements, 1–2. (In Scripta mathematica, 8:233–36. Dec. 1941; 11:173–77. June 1945)

Royal Society of London. Catalogue of scientific papers, 1800–1900; Subject index, v.1, Pure mathematics. Cambridge, Univ. Pr., 1908. 666p.   **EF7**

> For full description *see* EA17.

Smith, David Eugene. Rara arithmetica; a catalogue of the arithmetics written before the year MDCI, with a description of those in the library of George Arthur Plimpton, of New York. Boston, London, Ginn, 1908. 507p. il.   **EF8**

—— —— Addenda. . . . Boston, London, Ginn, 1939. 52p. il.

This extensive collection was presented to the Columbia University Libraries in 1936.

Full bibliographic entries; many facsimiles and illustrations.

Current

American Mathematical Society. New publications. Providence, R.I., 1961– . Quarterly (varies). **EF9**

A list of new books and monographs on mathematical subjects published throughout the world. Includes a catalog of lecture notes. Useful as a book-selection tool.

Abstract journals

Jahrbuch über die Fortschritte der Mathematik, begr. von Carl Ohrtmann, Bd.1–68¹, 1868–1942. Berlin, de Gruyter, 1871–1942. Bd.1–68¹. **EF10**

Editor and publisher vary. Ceased publication.

Brief, signed abstracts. Classed arrangement with author index.

The *Revue semestrielle des publications mathématiques,* t.1–39, 1893–1934, was a bibliography of mathematical material in various languages, with a very few abstracts. With its v.37, it joined with the *Jahrbuch* and ceased separate publication after v.39.

Mathematical reviews, v.1, 1940– . Providence, R.I., Amer. Mathematical Soc., 1940– . v.1– . Monthly. **EF11**

Classified arrangement, with semiannual author index but no subject index.

Signed abstracts of articles in many languages. The abstract is usually in English but sometimes in a foreign language, not necessarily the language of the original article. Reviewers are from various countries.

Sponsored by the American Mathematical Society, Mathematical Association of America, Institute of Mathematical Statistics, Edinburgh Mathematical Society, Société Mathématique de France, Dansk Matematisk Forening, Wiskundig Genootschap te Amsterdam, London Mathematical Society, Polish Mathematical Society, Unión Matemática Argentina, Indian Mathematical Society, Unione Matematica Italiana, and Society for Industrial and Applied Mathematics.

Sponsoring societies vary.

—— Indexes: 20v. author index (A–K, L–Z), 1940–59. 1961. 2v.

Gives author, full title, and full citation. No subject index.

Statistical theory and method abstracts. Edinburgh, Oliver & Boyd, for the International Statistical Institute, 1959– . v.1– . **EF12**

Title varies: v.1–4, *International journal of abstracts. Statistical theory and method. Index and review supplement.*

An international abstract journal. Titles are translated into English, and abstracts are in English.

Includes a section on "New statistical tables" designed to keep up to date the *Guide to tables in mathematical statistics,* by Greenwood and Hartley (EF33).

Zentralblatt für Mathematik und ihre Grenzgebiete (reine und angewandte Mathematik, theoretische Physik, Astrophysik, Geophysik . . .) Berlin, Springer, 1931– . Bd. 1– . **EF13**

Suspended Nov. 1944–June 1948.

Gives signed abstracts of material in various languages. Classed arrangement with author and subject indexes.

Dictionaries and encyclopedias

Encyklopädie der mathematischen Wissenschaften mit Einschluss ihrer Anwendungen. Hrsg. im Auftrage der Akademien der Wissenschaften zu Göttingen, Leipzig, München und Wien, sowie unter Mitwirkung zahlreicher Fachgenossen. Leipzig, Teubner, 1898/1904–1935. 6v. in 23. **EF14**

Contents: (1) Arithmetik; (2) Analysis; (3) Geometrie; (4) Mechanik; (5) Physik; (6¹) Geodäsie und Geophysik; (6²) Astronomie.

—— 2. völlig neubearb. Aufl. hrsg. von H. Hasse und E. Hecke. Leipzig, Teubner, 1939–58. v.1– . (In progress)

Contents: Bd.1, Algebra und Zahlentheorie: 1. Teil: A, Grundlagen. B, Algebra; 2. Teil: C, Reine Zahlentheorie. D, Analytische Zahlentheorie.

The most important encyclopedia of the subject, containing long articles by specialists, with full bibliographic notes, though in some cases articles are now out of date. For the special student and teacher, not for the untrained reader. Originally issued also in a French edition, never completed but including some revision, the *Encyclopédie des sciences mathématiques pures et appliquées.* Paris, Gauthier-Villars, 1904–16. v.1–7.

International dictionary of applied mathematics. W. F. Freiberger, ed. in chief. Princeton, N.J., Van Nostrand, 1960. 1173p. il. **EF15**

"Defines the terms and describes the methods in the application of mathematics to thirty-one fields of physical science and engineering."—*Pref.*

Includes indexes in French, German, Spanish, and Russian.

James, Glenn and **James, Robert C.** Mathematics dictionary. Multilingual ed. Princeton, N.J., Van Nostrand, 1959. 546p. il. **EF16**

1st ed. 1942.

Gives definitions of terms and phrases in the various fields of pure and applied mathematics. Includes tables, formulas, mathematical symbols, and vocabularies giving English equivalents of mathematical terms in French, German, Russian, and Spanish.

Karush, William. The crescent dictionary of mathematics. Oscar Tarov, gen. ed. N.Y., Macmillan, 1962. 313p. **EF17**

Primarily for the student; covers standard high school and college mathematics material as well as some subjects from more advanced mathematics. Definitions range from a few lines to one or two columns.

Naas, Josef and **Schmid, Hermann Ludwig.** Mathematisches Wörterbuch mit Einbeziehung der theoretischen Physik. Berlin, Akademie Verlag; Stuttgart, Teubner, 1961. 2v. **EF18**

Im Auftrage des Instituts für Reine Mathematik an der Deutschen Akademie der Wissenschaften zu Berlin.

An encyclopedia and dictionary containing definitions and current terminology in mathematics and physics, including principles, formulas, some biographical sketches of outstanding mathematicians, and (in many cases) bibliographies at the ends of the articles.

Universal encyclopedia of mathematics. Foreword by James R. Newman. N.Y., Simon & Schuster, 1964. 715p. **EF19**

Designed for the high school and college student; covers from arithmetic through calculus. Pt.1 is an alphabetically arranged encyclopedia by subject; pt.2 contains mathematical formulae; pt.3, mathematical tables.

Foreign terms

German

Herland, Leo Joseph. Dictionary of mathematical sciences; v.1, German-English; v.2, English-German. N.Y., Ungar, 1951–54. 2v.   **EF20**

Added title page in German.

Statistical entries by Gregor Sebba; commercial entries by Robert Grossbard.

MacIntyre, Sheila and **Witte, Edith.** German-English mathematical vocabulary. With a grammatical sketch by Lilias W. Brebner. Edinburgh, Oliver & Boyd; N.Y., Interscience, 1956. 95p.   **EF21**

Russian

Milne-Thompson, Louis Melville. Russian-English mathematical dictionary; words and phrases in pure and applied mathematics with roots and accents, arranged for easy reference. Madison, Univ. of Wisconsin Pr., 1962. 191p. (Publ. of the Mathematical Research Center, U.S. Army, Univ. of Wisconsin, no.7)   **EF22**

Russian-English dictionary of the mathematical sciences. By A. J. Lohwater with the collaboration of S. H. Gould, under the joint auspices of the National Academy of Sciences of the USA, the Academy of Sciences of the USSR, [and] the American Mathematical Society. Providence, R.I., Amer. Mathematical Soc., 1961. 267p.
EF23

(English-Russian and Russian-English dictionaries of mathematical terms)

"The present volume is intended for use . . . at any level in mathematics and theoretical physics and a short grammar of mathematical Russian precedes the vocabulary." In preparing the dictionary the guiding principle was that a person "would be able to read virtually any publication reviewed either in *Referativnyi zhurnal: Matematika* or in *Mathematical reviews* without the aid of any other dictionary."—*Foreword*.

—— Anglo-russkii slovar' matematicheskikh terminov. Moskva, Izd. Inostrannoi Literatury, 1962. 369p.   **EF24**

Directories

World directory of mathematicians, 1961. [2d ed.], pub. under the auspices of the International Mathematical Union and with the cooperation of the Tata Institute of Fundamental Research. Bombay, Tata Institute, 1961. 241p.   **EF25**

1st ed. 1958.

A directory of mathematicians from 71 countries, arranged alphabetically by name with country index.

Handbooks

Jansson, Martin Ernest. Handbook of applied mathematics, ed. by Edward E. Grazda and Morris Brenner. Based on the original work by Martin E. Jansson, Herbert D. Harper and Peter L. Agnew. 3d ed. N.Y., Van Nostrand, 1955. 1044p.   **EF26**

2d ed. 1936.

Korn, Granino Arthur and **Korn, Theresa M.** Mathematical handbook for scientists and engineers; definitions, theorems, and formulas for reference and review. N.Y., McGraw-Hill, 1961. 943p. il.   **EF27**

A comprehensive reference collection of mathematical definitions, theorems, and formulas on both the undergraduate and the graduate level, concluding with numerical tables and a glossary of symbols and notations.

Merritt, Frederick S. Mathematics manual; methods and principles of the various branches of mathematics for reference, problem solving, and review. N.Y., McGraw-Hill, 1962. 378p.   **EF28**

"The scope . . . ranges from simple arithmetic through higher mathematics, including matrices, tensors, probabilities and statistics." Gives "the important definitions, principles, theorems, corollaries, relationships, and methods of the most commonly used branches of mathematics."—*Pref.*

Moritz, Robert Edouard. On mathematics and mathematicians. Dover, [1958, c1942]. 410p.   **EF29**

Unabridged and unaltered republication of *Memorabilia mathematica; or, The philomath's quotation-book.* N.Y., Macmillan, 1914.

A book of more than 2100 quotations about mathematics: its nature, value, philosophy, application, etc., grouped by class with an extensive index. Quotations from foreign authors are given only in English, but references to original sources are cited.

Style manuals

Chaundy, T. W., Barrett, P. R. and **Batey, Charles.** The printing of mathematics: aids for authors and editors and rules for compositors and readers at the University Press, Oxford. London, Oxford Univ. Pr., 1954. 105p. il. **EF30**

Includes sections on: (1) The mechanics of mathematical printing; (2) Recommendations to mathematical authors; (3) Rules for the composition of mathematics at the University Press, Oxford.

Discusses the preparation of manuscripts and how they can best be set in type.

William Byrd Press, Inc., Richmond. Mathematics in type. Richmond, Va., 1954. 58p. il.   **EF31**

A manual on the preparation and economical production of books and articles containing mathematical expressions. Discusses the difficulties and methods of composition, the preparation of the manuscript, style, types, etc.

Tables

Bibliography

Fletcher, Alan [and others]. An index of mathematical tables. 2d ed. Reading, Mass., Addison-Wesley, 1962. 2v.(994p.)   **EF32**

Published for Scientific Computing Service, Ltd., London. 1st ed. 1946.

An important index to well-known tables of functions and to other less-known tables appearing in books and periodicals.

Contents: v.1, Introduction. Pt.1, Index according to functions; v.2: pt.2, Bibliography; pt.3, Errors; pt.4, Index to Introduction and pt.1.

The bibliography is extensive, p.609–708, arranged alphabetically by author, with no subject approach.

Greenwood, Joseph Arthur and **Hartley, H. O.** Guide to tables in mathematical statistics. Princeton, N.J., Princeton Univ. Pr., 1962. 1014p.   **EF33**

Sponsored by the Committee on Statistics of the Division of Mathematics of the National Academy of Sciences—National Research Council.

"A sequel to the guides to mathematical tables produced by and for the Committee on Mathematical Tables and Aids to Computation of the National Academy of Sciences—National Research Council, viz.": Derrick H. Lehmer, *Guide to tables in the theory of numbers.* Bulletin of the National Research Council, no.105. Feb. 1941 (EF35); Harry Bateman and

R. C. Archibald, "Guide to tables of Bessel functions," *Mathematical tables and other aids to computation* 1:205–63. July 1944; and A. Fletcher, "Guide to tables of elliptic functions," *ibid.*, 3:229–81. Jan. 1948.

Lebedev, Aleksandr Vasil'evich and **Fedorova, R. M.** A guide to mathematical tables. English ed. prep. from the Russian by D. G. Fry. Oxford, N.Y., Pergamon, 1960. 586p. **EF34**

—— —— Supplement, no.1– , by N. M. Burunova. 1960– .

"This book has been prepared from the original Russian edition by a photographic process. The Russian text has been replaced by English, but the tabular matter has been reproduced direct from the original."—*Translator's pref.*

The main volume gives tables published in separate editions through 1952; some published in 1953 and 1954; and those included in periodicals through 1953. The supplement gives tables published up to about 1959.

Bibliography, p.411–536; Supplement, p.147–79.

Lehmer, Derrick Henry. Guide to tables in the theory of numbers. Wash., Nat. Research Council, Nat. Academy of Sciences, 1941. 177p. incl. tables. (Bull. of the National Research Council, no.105. Feb. 1941) **EF35**

"Division of Physical Sciences, Committee on Mathematical Tables and Aids to Computation. . . . Report 1."

"Report of the Subcommittee on Section F: Theory of numbers."

Bibliography, with location of copies in libraries of the United States and Canada, p.85–125.

Contents: pt.1, Descriptive account of existing tables; pt.2, Bibliography, arranged alphabetically by author, giving exact references to the sources of the tables referred to in pt.1; pt.3, Lists of errata in the tables.

Schütte, Karl. Index mathematischer Tafelwerke und Tabellen aus allen Gebieten der Naturwissenschaften. München, Oldenbourg, 1955. 143p. **EF36**

Added title page and preface in English.

Lists some 1200 tables in a classified arrangement. Not so extensive as Fletcher's *Index of mathematical tables* (EF32), but provides a different approach since Fletcher is alphabetical.

Compendiums

Abramowitz, Milton and **Stegun, Irene A.** Handbook of mathematical functions with formulas, graphs, and mathematical tables. Wash., Govt. Prt. Off., 1964. 1046p. (U.S. National Bureau of Standards. Applied mathematics ser. 55) **EF37**

Barlow, Peter. Barlow's Tables of squares, cubes, square roots, cube roots and reciprocals of all integers up to 12,500, ed. by L. J. Comrie . . . 4th ed., new impression. London, Spon; N.Y., Chemical Pub. Co., 1960. 258p. **EF38**

1st ed. 1814; 4th ed. 1941.

Bauschinger, Julius and **Peters, J.** Logarithmic trigonometrical tables to eight decimal places. 3d ed. Weinheim/ Bergstrasse, Ger., 1958. 2v. **EF39**

Added title page and prefatory material in German: Logarithmisch-trigonometrische Tafeln.

Contents: v.1, Table of the logarithms to eight decimal places of all numbers from 1–200,000; v.2, Table of logarithms to eight decimal places of the trigonometrical functions for every sexagesimal second of the quadrant.

Bierens de Haan, David. Nouvelles tables d'intégrales définies . . . ed. of 1867– , corr.; with an English translation of the introd. by J. F. Ritt. N.Y., Stechert, 1939. 716p. **EF40**

British Association for the Advancement of Science. Mathematical tables. . . . London, Assoc., 1931–52. v.1– 10. (v.1, 2d ed., 1946) **EF41**

v.1, 2d ed., Circular and hyperbolic functions, exponential and sine and cosine integrals, factorial function and allied functions, hermitian probability functions; v.2, Emden functions, being solutions of Emden's equation together with certain associated functions; v.3, Minimum decompositions into fifth powers, prep. by L. E. Dickson; v.4, Cycles of reduced ideals in quadratic fields, prep. by E. L. Ince; v.5, Factor table, giving the complete decomposition of all numbers less than 100,000, prep. by J. Peters, A. Lodge, E. J. Ternouth, E. Gifford; v.6, Bessel functions: pt.1, Functions of orders zero and unity; v.7, The probability integral, by W. F. Shepard; v.8, Number-divisor tables, designed and in part prep. by J. W. L. Glaisher; v.9, Table of powers, giving integral powers of integers, initiated by J .W. L. Glaisher; v.10, Bessel functions: pt.2, Functions of positive integer order, by W. G. Bickley [and others].

Continued as the *Royal Society mathematical tables* (EF48).

Burington, Richard Stevens. Handbook of mathematical tables and formulas. 4th ed. N.Y., McGraw-Hill, 1965. 423p. **EF42**

1st ed. 1933; 3d ed. 1948.

"Compiled and arranged to meet the needs of students and workers in mathematics, engineering, physics, chemistry, science, and other fields in which mathematical computation . . . [is] required."

"A companion to the *Handbook of probability and statistics, with tables,* by Richard. S. Burington and Donald C. May" (EA80).

Camm, Frederick James. Mathematical tables and formulae. 6th ed. London, Newnes, 1957. 145p. (Repr.: N.Y., Philosophical Lib., 1958) **EF43**

1st ed. 1943.

Dwight, Herbert Bristol. Tables of integrals and other mathematical data. 4th ed. N.Y., Macmillan, 1961. 336p. il. **EF44**

1st ed. 1934.

Handbook of mathematical tables. 2d ed. Cleveland, Ohio, Chemical Rubber Co., 1964. 680p. **EF45**

1st ed. 1962.

Supplement to *Handbook of chemistry and physics* (ED46). Ed. in chief, Robert C. Weast; ed. in charge of mathematics, Samuel M. Selby; ed. in chief emeritus, Charles D. Hodgman.

Mathematical Tables Project. [Mathematical tables], prep. by the Mathematical Tables Project, Work Projects Administration of the Federal Works Agency. Conducted under the sponsorship of the National Bureau of Standards. . . . N.Y., Columbia Univ. Pr., 1939–44. 40v. **EF46**

Originally published by the Work Projects Administration for the City of New York under the sponsorship of the National Bureau of Standards. After 1942, when the W.P.A. was discontinued, the work was taken over by the sponsoring agency, and the later volumes were published by Columbia University Press.

For complete contents *see* Parke, *Guide to the literature of mathematics,* p.135–37 (EF1).

Owen, Donald Bruce. Handbook of statistical tables. Reading, Mass., Addison-Wesley, 1962. 580p. il. **EF47**

Royal Society of London. Royal Society mathematical tables. Cambridge, Univ. Pr., 1950–64. v.1–8, 11. (In progress) **EF48**

Contents: v.1, E. H. Neville. Farey series of order 1025. 1950; v.2, E. H. Neville. Rectangular-polar conversion tables. 1956; v.3, J. C. P. Miller. Table of binominal coefficients. 1954; v.4, H. Gupta [and others]. Tables of partitions. 1958; v.5, H. Gupta [and others]. Representations of primes by quadratic forms. 1960; v.6, C. B. Haselgrove and J. C. P.

Miller. Tables of the Riemann Zeta function. 1960; v.7, F. W. J. Olver. Bessel functions, pt.3: Zeros and associated values. 1960; v.8, W. E. Mansell. Tables of natural and common logarithms to 110 decimals. 1964; v.11, A. R. Curtis. Coulomb wave functions. 1964.

Thompson, Alexander John. Logarithmetica Britannica, being a standard table of logarithms to 20 decimal places. Cambridge, Univ. Pr., 1924–52. 9v. (Repr. in 2v.) **EF49**

Contents: pt.1, nos. 10,000–20,000. 1934; pt.2, nos. 20,000–30,000. 1952; pt.3, nos. 30,000–40,000. 1937; pt.4, nos. 40,000–50,000. 1928; pt.5, nos. 50,000–60,000. 1931; pt.6, nos. 60,000–70,000. 1933; pt.7, nos. 70,000–80,000. 1935; pt.8, nos. 80,000–90,000. 1927; pt.9, nos. 90,000–100,000. 1924.

U.S. National Bureau of Standards. Applied mathematics series. no.1–   . Wash., Govt. Prt. Off., 1948–   .   **EF50**

"The Applied Mathematics Series contains mathematical tables, manuals and studies of special interest to physicists, engineers, chemists, biologists, mathematicians, computers, and others engaged in scientific and technical work. Some of the volumes are reissues of the mathematical tables prepared by the Project for the Computation of Mathematical Tables conducted by the Federal Works Agency, Works Project Administration for the City of New York . . . ."

E G

Physics

See also Nuclear Engineering, p.593–94.

🌿 Two useful guides to materials in physics—Parke's *Guide to the literature of mathematics and physics* (EF1) and a slightly older work by Whitford, *Physics literature* (EG2)—have been published. In spite of the fact that these are not up to date, they will list many of the basic works. For more recent listings, *see* the current bibliographies noted under Pure and Applied Sciences, p.528, and the *Technical book review index* (EA68).

GENERAL WORKS

Guides

Parke, Nathan Grier. Guide to the literature of mathematics and physics including related works on engineering science. 2d rev. ed. N.Y., Dover, 1958. 436p.   **EG1**

1st ed. 1947.

For full description *see* EF1.

Whitford, Robert H. Physics literature: a reference manual. Wash., Scarecrow, 1954. 228p.   **EG2**

A bibliographical manual describing available materials and outlining library methods.

Bibliography

American Institute of Physics. Check list of books for an undergraduate physics library. N.Y., 1962. 92p. **EG3**

"To assist physics departments in their selection of basic books [for their libraries]. The list is not intended to be definitive or comprehensive in any sense, but rather to provide information that will be helpful to physics departments and that will supplement other information."—*Introd.*

Prepared in cooperation with the physics departments and librarians at Amherst, Oberlin, Pomona, Reed, Wesleyan, and Williams colleges.

Not annotated.

International catalogue of scientific literature: C, Physics. 1st–14th annual issues, 1901–14. London, 1902–17. 14v.
EG4

For full description *see* EA12.

Nottingham, Wayne Buckles. Bibliography on physical electronics. 1st ed. Cambridge, Research Laboratory of Electronics, Mass. Inst. of Technology, 1954. 428p. **EG5**

Attempts to list papers published from 1930 to 1950, with references to some of the papers published since 1900 and referred to most often in current publications. Classified arrangement; no index.

Reuss, Jeremias David. Repertorium commentationum a societatibus litterariis editarum . . . T.4, Physica. Gottingae, Dieterich, 1805. 416p. (Repr.: N.Y., Burt Franklin, 1961)   **EG6**

A valuable index to the publications of learned societies up to 1800. Classed arrangement with author index.

For full description *see* EA15.

Royal Society of London. Catalogue of scientific papers, 1800–1900: Subject index, v.3, Physics. Cambridge, Univ. Pr., 1912–14. 2v.   **EG7**

Pt.1, Generalities, heat, light, sound; pt.2, Electricity and magnetism.

For full description *see* EA17.

Transatom Bulletin. Information on translations covering nuclear literature. Brussels, EURATOM, European Atomic Energy Community, 1960–   . v.1–   . Monthly.
EG8

Each issue in two sections: (1) Translations completed, and (2) Translations in preparation. Quarterly indexes with annual cumulated index.

Specifies translations into western European languages of articles in "languages unfamiliar to the western reader."

United Nations. Secretariat. Dept. of Security Council Affairs. Atomic Energy Commission Group. An international bibliography on atomic energy. N.Y., 1949–53. 2v. and suppls.   **EG9**

v.1, Political, economic, and social aspects, 1949. 45p. Suppl. no.1, 1950. Suppl. no.2, 1953; v.2, Scientific aspects, 1951. [880p.] Suppl. no.1, 1952. Suppl. no.2, 1953.

Classified arrangement, with subject and author indexes. Includes books, periodical articles, government publications and documents, films, recordings, radio scripts, etc. In v.2 each section is preceded by a brief outline of the subject, written by a specialist.

Dissertations

Marckworth, M. Lois. Dissertations in physics: an indexed bibliography of all doctoral theses accepted by American universities, 1861–1959. Stanford, Calif., Stanford Univ. Pr., 1961. 803p.   **EG10**

Compiled with the assistance of the staff of the Advanced Systems Development Division and Research Laboratories, International Business Machines Corporation, San Jose, California.

In two sections: pt.1, an alphabetical list of 8216 dissertations; pt.2, a permutation subject index coded by important words in the titles, produced by IBM computer.

Abstract journals and indexes

See also Nuclear science abstracts (EI202).

Physikalische Berichte . . . Jahrg.1– . Braunschweig, Ger., Vieweg, 1920– . Monthly. **EG11**

Frequency varies.

Publication suspended 1945–June 1947.

A comprehensive abstract journal. Titles are given in the original language, abstracts in German. Continues the abstracting service of the *Fortschritte der Physik,* 1845–1918. Braunschweig, 1847–1919. 74v. in 141.

Science abstracts . . . Sec. A, Physics abstracts. London, Inst. of Electrical Engineers, 1898– . v.1– . Monthly. **EG12**

Publisher varies.

1898–1902 title reads: *Science abstracts, physics and electrical engineering;* 1903– , issued in two sections: A, *Physics;* B, *Electrical engineering.* Beginning with 1941, titles changed to A, *Physics abstracts,* and B, *Electrical engineering abstracts.*

The classified arrangement differs somewhat from volume to volume. Titles are not given in the original language but are translated into English. 1962 issue lists more than 860 journals. Author and subject indexes and list of journals now are published separately, several months after end of volume.

U.S. Atomic Energy Commission. Division of Technical Information. Research and development abstracts of the USAEC. Wash., Office of Technical Services, Dept. of Commerce, 1962– . v.1– . Irregular. **EG13**

"Abstracts of research and development reports falling outside the scope of *Nuclear Science Abstracts*" (EI202).

Encyclopedias and dictionaries

Encyclopaedic dictionary of physics: general, nuclear, solid state, molecular, chemical, metal and vacuum physics, astronomy, geophysics, biophysics and related subjects. Ed. in chief, J. Thewlis. London, N.Y., Pergamon, 1961–64. 9v. **EG14**

Edited in England, with an international list of some 2000 contributors.

Not a modern version of Sir Richard Glazebrook, *Dictionary of applied physics* (London, Macmillan, 1922–23. 5v.), but will largely replace that standard work.

Signed articles, many with bibliographical references.

Contents: v.1–7, A–Z; v.8, Subject and author indexes; v.9, Multilingual glossary: English, French, German, Spanish, Russian, Japanese.

Fizicheskii entsiklopedicheskii slovar'. Moskva, Gos. Nauchnoe Izd. Sovetskaia Entsiklopediia, 1960–65. v.1–4. (Entsiklopedii slovari spravochniki) (In progress) **EG15**

Contents: v.1–4, A–Spa.

Gray, H. J. Dictionary of physics. With contributions from a number of leading scientists. [1st ed.] London, N.Y., Longmans, 1958. 544p. il. **EG16**

"Designed to provide a comprehensive dictionary . . . of moderate size." Includes articles on applied physics as well as in the general field.

Most articles are brief, but a few are longer, and a few biographical sketches are included. References are given at the ends of some entries.

Handbuch der experimental Physik, hrsg. von W. Wien und F. Harms. Bd.1–26. Leipzig, Akademische Verlagsgesellschaft M.B.H., 1926–37. 26v. in 44. il. **EG17**

Not all volumes complete.

—— Ergänzungswerk. Bd.1–2. Leipzig, 1931–35.

No more published.

Handbuch der Physik, hrsg. von S. Flugge. Berlin, Springer, 1955–64. v.1–54 (incomplete). (In progress) **EG18**

Earlier ed. 1926–29. 24v. and index.

Added title page in English: Encyclopedia of physics.

Contributions in German, English, and French.

Contents: v.1, Mathematical methods, I. 1956; v.2, Mathematical methods, II. 1955; v.3, pt.1, Principles of classical mechanics and field theory. 1960; v.3, pt.2, Principles of thermodynamics and statistics. 1959; v.4, Principles of electrodynamics and relativity. 1962; v.5, pt.1, Principles of quantum theory, I. 1958; v.6, Elasticity and plasticity. 1958; v.7, pt.1, Crystal physics, I. 1955; v.7, pt.2, Crystal physics, II. 1958; v.8, pt.1, Fluid dynamics, I. 1959; v.8, pt.2, Fluid dynamics, II. 1963; v.9, Fluid dynamics, III. 1960; v.10, Structure of liquids. 1960; v.11, pt.1, Acoustics, I. 1961; v.11, pt.2, Acoustics, II. 1962; v.12, Thermodynamics of gases. 1958; v.13, Thermodynamics of liquids and solids. 1962; v.14, Low temperature physics, I. 1956; v.15, Low temperature physics, II. 1956; v.16, Electric fields and waves. 1958; v.17, Dielectrics. 1956; v.19, Electrical conductivity, I. 1956; v.20, Electrical conductivity, II. 1957; v.21, Electron emission. Gas discharges, I. 1956; v.22, Gas discharges, II. 1956; v.24, Fundamentals of optics. 1956; v.25, pt.1, Crystal optics. Diffraction. 1961; v.26, Light and matter, II. 1958; v.27, Spectroscopy, I. 1964; v.28, Spectroscopy, II. 1957; v.30, X-rays. 1957; v.32, Structural research. 1957; v.33, Corpuscular optics. 1956; v.34, Corpuscles and radiation in matter, II. 1958; v.35, Atoms, I. 1957; v.36, Atoms, II. 1956; v.37, pt.1, Atoms, III. Molecules, I. 1959; v.37, pt.2, Molecules, II. 1961; v.38, pt.1, External properties of atomic nuclei. 1958; v.38, pt.2, Neutrons and related Gamma ray problems. 1959; v.39, Structure of atomic nuclei. 1957; v.40, Nuclear reactions, I. 1957; v.41, pt.1, Nuclear reactions, II. 1959; v.41, pt.2, Beta decay. 1962; v.42, Nuclear reactions, III. 1957; v.44, Nuclear instrumentation, I. 1959; v.45, Nuclear instrumentation, II. 1958; v.46, pt.1, Cosmic rays, I. 1961; v.47, Geophysics, I: The earth's body. 1956; v.48, Geophysics, II. 1957; v.50, Astrophysics, I (Stellar surface-binaries). 1958; v.51, Astrophysics, II (Stellar structure). 1958; v.52, Astrophysics, III (The solar system). 1959; v.53, Astrophysics, IV (Stellar systems). 1959; v.54, Astrophysics, V. (Miscellaneous). 1962.

Höcker, Karl Heinz and **Weimer, K.** Lexikon der Kern- und Reaktortechnik. Stuttgart, Franckh, 1959. 2v. il. **EG19**

An alphabetically arranged encyclopedic dictionary on nuclear physics, with some bibliographic references and with translation of terms into English and French.

Hogerton, John F. [and others]. The atomic energy deskbook. Prep. under the auspices of the Division of Technical Information, U.S. Atomic Energy Commission. N.Y., Reinhold; London, Chapman & Hall, 1963. 673p. il. **EG20**

Treats the background and status of atomic energy development in "more than 1000 alphabetically arranged entries ranging from brief definitions of terms to journal-length articles on major topics. It deals mainly with work being done in the United States on peaceful uses of atomic energy, but information is also given on military applications and there are entries on foreign atomic energy programs."—*Pref.*

International dictionary of physics and electronics. Walter C. Michels, ed. in chief. 2d ed. Princeton, N.J., Van Nostrand, 1961. 1355p. il. **EG21**

1st ed. 1956.

Designed for the use of students, professional physicists, and others whose primary activities lie in a different field of science (e.g., chemistry, engineering, biology, etc.).

Seeks to show the connection between classical and modern physics, and in the 2d edition, which is substantially revised and rearranged, increases the number of entries dealing with atomic and nuclear physics, relativistic mechanics, quantum theory, etc. New indexes in French, German, Spanish, and Russian.

Lexikon der Physik, hrsg. von H. Franke. 2. verb. und erw. Aufl. Stuttgart, Franckh, 1959. 2v. il.   **EG22**

A dictionary-encyclopedia defining the words and concepts of modern physics, illustrated with line drawings, diagrams, etc. and (at the end of v.2) 48 pages of tables and 46 plates. Biographical articles are included, and references are given at the ends of many articles.

Clark, George L. Encyclopedia of spectroscopy. N.Y., Reinhold, 1960. 787p. il.   **EG23**

Arranged by broad topics with appropriate subdivisions. Articles are by specialists and signed. Extensive bibliographies.

—— Encyclopedia of X-rays and gamma rays. N.Y., Reinhold, 1963. 1149p. il.   **EG24**

Contributions by specialists are signed. Alphabetically arranged. Many articles include references.

Foreign terms

For bibliographies of foreign language–English dictionaries, *see* Pure and Applied Sciences, p.534.

German

De Vries, Louis and **Clason, W. E.** Dictionary of pure and applied physics. Amsterdam, Elsevier, 1963–64. 2v.   **EG25**

Contents: v.1, German-English; v.2, English-German.

Dictionary of physics and allied sciences. N.Y., Ungar, 1958–62. 2v.   **EG26**

Added title page in German: *Wörterbuch der Physik und verwandter Wissenschaften.*

Covers terms in both theoretical and applied physics and allied sciences.

Contents: v.1, German-English, ed. by Charles J. Hyman; v.2, English-German, ed. by Ralph Idlin.

Polyglot

Béné, Georges J. [and others]. Nuclear physics and atomic energy. Amsterdam, Elsevier, 1960. 213p. (Glossarium interpretum, 2)   **EG27**

Subtitle: Terms of nuclear physics and nuclear technology in English, French, German, Russian.

Elsevier's Dictionary of general physics, in six languages, English/American, French, Spanish, Italian, Dutch, and German. Comp. and arr. on an English alphabetical base by W. E. Clason. Amsterdam, Elsevier, 1962. 859p.   **EG28**

Lettenmeyer, Lore. Atomterminologie, Atomic terminology, Terminologie atomique, Terminologia atomica. München, Isar Verlag, 1958. 298p. (Die Fremdsprachen in der Praxis. Reihe B, Bd.1)   **EG29**

English, German, French, Italian.

1814 scientific and technical terms used in atomic and nuclear physics and associated fields, arranged on an English base with indexes from the other languages.

Voskoboinik, David I. Semiiazychn'yi iadernyi slovar': anglo - russko - frantsuzsko - ispansko - ital'iansko - gollandsko - nemetskii. Moskva, 1961. 462p.   **EG30**

Russian

Emin, Irving. Russian-English physics dictionary, by Irving Emin and the Consultants Bureau staff of physicist translators. N.Y., Wiley, 1963. 554p.   **EG31**

Compiled by specialists. Combines terms and abbreviations with the Russian transliterations of the names of many scientists.

Voskoboinik, David I. and **Zimmerman, M. H.** English-Russian nuclear dictionary. Moscow, Central Editorial Board, 1960. 400p.   **EG32**

Added title page in Russian: Anglo-russkii iadernyi slovar'.

Handbooks

American Institute of Physics. American Institute of Physics handbook. Section eds.: Bruce H. Billings [and others]. Coordinating ed.: Dwight E. Gray [and others]. 2d ed. N.Y., McGraw-Hill, 1963. [v.p.] il.   **EG33**

1st ed. 1957.

2d ed. much enlarged. Each section edited by a specialist.

Provides authoritative information on "definitions, units, constants, formulas, etc. in physics."

Treats mathematical aids to computation, mechanics, acoustics, heat, electricity and magnetism, optics, atomic and molecular physics, nuclear physics, and solid-state physics.

Includes "a selected bibliography of compilations of mathematical tables and a list of mathematical functions frequently used by physicists."

Condon, Edward Uhler and **Odishaw, Hugh.** Handbook of physics, prep. by a staff of specialists. N.Y., McGraw-Hill, 1958. [v.p.] il.   **EG34**

A standard handbook with chapters by specialists; encyclopedic in nature. In nine sections: (1) mathematics, (2) mechanics of particles and rigid bodies, (3) mechanics of deformable bodies, (4) electricity and magnetism, (5) heat and thermodynamics, (6) optics, (7) atomic physics, (8) solid state, (9) nuclear physics. Includes bibliographies.

Hix, C. F. and **Alley, R. P.** Physical laws and effects. N.Y., Wiley; London, Chapman & Hall, 1958. 291p. (General Electric ser.)   **EG35**

Arranged alphabetically by the name of the law; gives description, illustration, magnitude, references, and quantities.

Streeter, Victor Lyle. Handbook of fluid dynamics. 1st ed. N.Y., McGraw-Hill, 1961. 1v. [v.p.] il.   **EG36**

Chapters written by specialists; the first half of the book "deals with fundamental concepts and principles, while the second half is devoted to applied fields."—*Pref.* Bibliographies at the end of each chapter.

Tables

See also Mathematics—Tables, p.572–74; for bibliography of tables *see American Institute of Physics handbook* (EG33).

Ardenne, Manfred, *Baron von.* Tabellen zur angewandten Physik: Elektronenphysik, Ionenphysik, Vakuumphysik, Kernphysik, medizinische Elektronik, Hilfsgebiete. 2. umgearb. und stark erw. Aufl. der Tabellen. Berlin, Deutscher Verlag der Wissenschaften, 1962–64. v.1–2. il.   **EG37**

1st edition, 1956, had title *Elektronenphysik, Ionenphysik und Übermikroskopie.*

Contents: Bd.1, Elektronenphysik, Übermikroskopie, Ionenphysik; Bd.2, Physik und Technik des Vakuums, Plasmaphysik.

Kaye, George William Clarkson and **Laby, Thomas Howell.** Tables of physical and chemical constants and some mathematical functions. Originally comp. by G. W. C. Kaye and T. H. Laby. 12th ed. London, N.Y., Longmans, 1959. 231p.   **EG38**

Menzel, Donald Howard. Fundamental formulas of physics. N.Y., Dover, [1960]. 2v.   **EG39**

First pub. 1955 by Prentice-Hall.
This edition "unabridged and revised."
"Each chapter stands as a brief summary of the field represented" (*Pref.*) and is written by a specialist. Includes bibliographies.

Smithsonian Institution. Smithsonian physical tables. 9th rev. ed., prep. by William E. Forsythe. Wash., Inst., 1954. 827p. il. (Smithsonian miscellaneous collections, v.120)   **EG40**

U.S. Atomic Energy Commission. Nuclear data tables. Wash., Nat. Academy of Sciences—Nat. Research Council. 1959– . (Nuclear data project)   **EG41**

Supersedes *New nuclear data.* 1960 issue, in 4 pts.

Zimmerman, Oswald Theodore and **Lavine, Irvin.** Industrial Research Service's Conversion factors and tables. 3d ed. Dover, N.H., Industrial Research Service, 1961. 680p.   **EG42**

1st ed. 1944; 2d ed. 1955.
Designed to provide "an accurate source of fundamental physical relationships and thousands of useful constants for the conversion of units."—*Pref.*
A completely revised edition with new material added. "Every conversion factor . . . was recalculated on the basis of the latest and most accurate fundamental data available." —*Pref.*

Biography

Nobelstiftelsen, Stockholm. Physics. Amsterdam, Elsevier, 1964– . v.3– . il. (Nobel lectures, including presentation speeches and laureates' biographies)   **EG43**

Contents: v.3, 1942–1962.
v.1–2 to be published later.

ACOUSTICS

Harris, Cyril M. Handbook of noise control. N.Y., McGraw-Hill, 1957. [v.p.] il.   **EG44**

Chapters, written by specialists, include bibliographies.
"The chapters . . . are in the following groupings: properties of sound, effects of noise on man, vibration control, instrumentation and noise measurement, techniques of noise control, noise control in buildings, sources of noise and examples of noise control, noise control of machinery and electrical equipment, noise control in transportation, community noise, and the legal aspects of noise problems."—*Pref.*

COLORS

British Colour Council. The British Colour Council dictionary of colour standards. 2d ed. A list of colour names referring to the colours shown in the companion volume. London, Council, 1951. 57p. and atlas of mounted samples.   **EG45**

"The purpose . . . is to simplify work in connection with colour throughout all colour-using industries so that the standard name or standard number will always signify the colour so designated in this Dictionary."

Colour index. 2d ed. 1956. Bradford, Eng., Soc. of Dyers and Colourists; Lowell, Mass., Amer. Assoc. of Textile Chemists and Colorists, 1956–58. 4v.   **EG46**

—— Supplement [1]– , 1963– .

1st ed. 1924–28.
The standard work in the field; its numbers are used to identify dyes. Gives commercial and scientific names of dyes, their formulas, methods of preparation, etc.

Maerz, Aloys John and **Paul, Morris Rea.** Dictionary of color. 2d ed. N.Y., McGraw-Hill, 1950. 208p. 56pl.(col.)   **EG47**

Partial contents: Introduction; Table of terms found in literature; Table of principal color names; Polyglot table of principal color names; Bibliography; Color plates; Brief history of color standardization; Notes on color names; Index of color names.
"Intended . . . to relate colors with the names by which they are commonly identified."—*Pref.*

E H

Psychology and Psychiatry

☙ Psychology and psychiatry are very specialized fields, requiring for the research worker highly specialized and technical texts. Most of these would be found only in the special library. Here are listed some of the more general bibliographies and indexes which may be useful in a general library. Needed, also, would probably be one or two dictionaries of psychological terms and directories of psychologists. Bibliographies of tests and measurements are frequently consulted in both academic and public libraries.

GENERAL WORKS

Guides

Daniel, Robert Strongman and **Louttit, Chauncey McKinley.** Professional problems in psychology. N.Y., Prentice-Hall, 1953. 416p.   **EH1**

In part a revision and expansion of C. M. Louttit's *Handbook of psychological literature.* Bloomington, Ind., Principia Pr., 1932.
A manual for the student, the practicing psychologist, and the librarian, covering especially the literature search, the scientific report, and problems of the professional psychologist.
Includes an annotated bibliography of reference books in psychology; a list of psychological journals; sources for books, tests, apparatus, etc.; and a glossary of abbreviations.

Bibliography

Chandler, Albert Richard and **Barnhart, Edward N.** A bibliography of psychological and experimental aesthetics, 1864–1937. Berkeley, Univ. of Calif. Pr., 1938. 190p.   **EH2**

Lists books and periodical articles. An enlarged and rearranged edition of Chandler's *Bibliography of experimental aesthetics* (1933) with its supplements.

Graham, Earl C. and **Mullen, Marjorie M.** Rehabilitation literature, 1950–1955; a bibliographic review of the medical care, education, employment, welfare, and psychology of handicapped children and adults. N.Y., McGraw-Hill, Blakiston Division, 1956. 621p. **EH3**

An annotated bibliography, arranged by subject, of 5214 periodical articles, pamphlets, and books. Approximately half of the references are in medical fields; the others are in other professional areas of rehabilitation, including special education, psychology and mental health, social service, parent education, recreation, vocational guidance, and employment. Author index.

Supplemented by the monthly issues of *Rehabilitation literature; selected abstracts of current publications of interest to workers with the handicapped.* Chicago, Nat. Soc. for Crippled Children and Adults, Inc.

Grinstein, Alexander. The index of psychoanalytic writings. N.Y., Internat. Universities Pr., 1956–60. 5v. **EH4**

v.1–4, A–Z; v.5, Subject index, Additions and corrections.

A revision and bringing up to date of John Rickman's *Index psycho-analyticus, 1893–1926.* London, Woolf, 1928.

Lists books, periodical articles, reviews, and abstracts, published in any language, 1900–1952. Titles are given in the original language, frequently followed by an English translation. Arranged alphabetically by author.

———— v.6–7, Supplementary volumes, 1953–1959. 1964– . (In progress)

v.6–7, A–Pe.

Harvard University. The Harvard list of books in psychology, comp. and annotated by the psychologists in Harvard University. 3d ed. Cambridge, Harvard Univ. Pr., 1964. 111p. **EH5**

1st ed. 1949; 2d ed. 1955; Supplement, 1958.

Supersedes *Books in psychology,* 1938, and its supplement, 1944.

704 titles chosen as "important and valuable in psychology at the present time." In this edition 304 are new books, 283 have been retained from previous editions, and 117 have been updated.

Louttit, Chauncey McKinley. Bibliography of bibliographies on psychology, 1900–1927. Wash., Nat. Research Council, 1928. 108p. (Bull. of the National Research Council, no.65) **EH6**

Lists 2132 bibliographies in books and journals, arranged by authors. Includes subject index.

Menninger, Karl Augustus. A guide to psychiatric books with some suggested reading lists. 2d rev. ed. N.Y., Grune and Stratton, 1956. 157p. (Menninger Clinic monograph ser., no.7) **EH7**

1st ed. 1950.

A classified, unannotated list with recommended reading lists for specific groups, e.g., physicians, clergymen, counselors, and others. English language only.

Riviere, Maya. Rehabilitation of the handicapped, a bibliography 1940–1946. . . . N.Y., Nat. Council on Rehabilitation, 1949. 2v. **EH8**

5000 numbered items, including both monographs and periodical articles, arranged alphabetically by author; with indexes by author and publisher, lists of films, film catalogs and film sources, and a general index.

Schweizerische Philosophische Gesellschaft. Bibliographie der philosophischen, psychologischen und pädagogischen Literatur . . . 1900–1940. **EH9**

For record *see* BA24.

Stein, Morris Isaac and **Heinze, Shirley J.** Creativity and the individual: summaries of selected literature in psychology and psychiatry. Glencoe, Ill., Free Pr., 1960. 428p. (A McKinsey Foundation annotated bibliography, 3) **EH10**

"A publication of the Graduate School of Business, University of Chicago. Third series."

Summaries of selected 20th-century writings of psychologists and psychiatrists on the creativity of the individual.

Voutsinas, Dimitri. Documentation sur la psychologie française. Paris, Groupe d'Études de Psychologie de l'Université de Paris, 1957–61. v.1–5. (In progress) **EH11**

v.1–4 are retrospective volumes; v.5 covers the year 1960.

v.1, entitled *Dix années de psychologie française (1947–1956),* is a bibliography of articles appearing in some 120 French periodicals.

v.2 (1958) is in three parts: (1) Articles in French journals for 1957; (2) Monographs published since 1947; (3) An alphabetical index of authors mentioned in v.1.

v.3 includes a retrospective list of periodical articles 1843–1946, and lists books and articles of 1958.

v.4 continues and completes the retrospective listing and lists books and articles of 1959.

v.5 lists books and articles of 1960.

A listing of books published from 1800 to 1946 is promised for a future volume.

Young, Morris N. Bibliography of memory. Philadelphia, N.Y., Chilton, 1961. 436p. **EH12**

A comprehensive bibliography of books, pamphlets, articles in periodicals, manuscripts, prints, circulars, games, and advertising devices. Arranged alphabetically by author, with a separate section of anonymous works. Lists works in many languages and of all periods. No index.

Book reviews

Mental health book review index. N.Y., 1956– . no.1– . Semiannual; no.11– , annual. **EH13**

no.1–6, Jan./Feb. 1956–July/Aug. 1958 were issued as supplements to *Psychological newsletter,* v.7, no.3–v.9, no.6, and have no volume numbering but constitute v.1–3.

v.4, no.1 (whole no.7), Jan. 1959– , issued independently, "comp." by the Editorial Committee and Contributing Libraries." Address: Miss Lois Afflerbach, Library, Queens College, Flushing, N.Y. 11367.

Editorial Committee: Ilse Bry and Lois Afflerbach.

The index lists references to signed book reviews appearing in 3 or more of some 200 journals. Number of journals varies.

Covers psychology, psychiatry, and psychoanalysis.

Abstract journals and indexes

L'année psychologique. v.1, 1894– . Paris, Presses Universitaires de France, 1895– . **EH14**

Includes signed abstracts of periodical articles and critical book reviews, with exact references to sources. International coverage.

Author and subject indexes to v.1–25 are contained in v.26.

Psychological abstracts, 1927– . Lancaster, Pa., Amer. Psychological Assoc., 1927– . v.1– . **EH15**

An important monthly bibliography listing new books and articles grouped by subjects, with a signed abstract of each item. Author index to each number, and full author and subject indexes for each volume.

Psychological index, 1894–1935, an annual bibliography of the literature of psychology and cognate subjects. Princeton, N.J., Psychological Review Co., 1895–1936. 42v. **EH16**

Lists original publications in all languages, both books and periodical articles, together with translations and new editions in English, French, German, and Italian. A classified subject list, with an alphabetical author index but no subject index. Lists about 5000 titles each year, and indexes about 350 periodicals. The list of the principal periodicals indexed, with abbreviations used, is given in v.30. Very useful for advanced work.

Continued by *Psychological abstracts* (EH15).

—— Abstract references. . . . Columbus, Ohio, Amer. Psychological Assoc., 1940–41 (v.1, 1941). 2v. **EH17**

v.1, v.1–25, 1894–1918; v.2, v.26–35, 1919–28.

Editor, H. L. Ansbacher. Prepared by the American Psychological Association in cooperation with the Work Projects Administration of the City of New York.

These abstract references have been compiled to serve as a backward extension of *Psychological abstracts* (EH15), which was founded in 1927. It is a list of the numbers of those titles of the *Psychological index* (EH16) for which one or more abstracts were located in the periodicals examined, with reference to volume and page of the abstract. As numbers only are given, it must be used in conjunction with the *Psychological index*. References to abstracts have been supplied for 43 percent of the titles in the *Psychological index* (45,000 of the 107,000 titles from 1894 to 1928). Since more than one abstract was found for some titles, references are given to more than 75,000 abstracts.

Columbia University. Libraries. Psychology Library. Author index to Psychological index 1894 to 1935 and Psychological abstracts 1927 to 1958. Boston, G. K. Hall, 1960. 5v. **EH18**

Reproduced photographically directly from the cards without further editing; consists of a cumulation of the author entries appearing in these two sets, combined with an earlier card file which preceded the *Psychological index*. These volumes, made by cutting out the actual entries, pasting them on cards, and filing them alphabetically, provide an author index to psychological books and articles in many languages from 1890 to 1958.

Dictionaries and encyclopedias

American Psychiatric Association. Committee on Public Information. A psychiatric glossary; the meaning of words most frequently used in psychiatry. 2d ed. Wash., [Assoc.], 1964. 80p. **EH19**

1st ed. 1957.

Contains about 700 terms, giving clear, concise definitions. Includes some 150 new terms not in the earlier edition.

Dorsch, Friedrich. Psychologisches Wörterbuch. 6. völlig rev. Aufl., unter Mitarbeit von Werner Traxel. Hamburg, R. Meiner, 1959. 488p. il. **EH20**

Subtitle: Mit einem Verzeichnis der Teste und Testautoren und einer Einführung in die mathematische Behandlung psychologischer Probleme von Wilhelm Witte.

A completely revised and enlarged version of Fritz Giese's *Psychologisches Wörterbuch,* first published in 1920. 4. ed. Frankfurt/Main, 1952. 296p.

Appendix includes a list of some 500 mental tests with descriptions.

Bibliography, p.457–88.

Drever, James. A dictionary of psychology, rev. by Harvey Wallerstein. Baltimore, Penguin, 1964. 320p. **EH21**

1st ed. 1952.

An excellent, small, inexpensive dictionary, giving concise definitions of about 4000 terms used in psychology.

Encyclopedia of child care and guidance [Sidonie Matsner Gruenberg, ed.]. Garden City, N.Y., Doubleday, [1954]. 1016p. il. **EH22**

In two parts: pt.1 consists of definitions of terms and brief discussions of topics relating to child care in alphabetical arrangement; pt.2 contains 30 chapters on aspects of child development, written by well-known authorities.

Includes list of agencies and organizations, p.[607]–25; annotated bibliography, p.[629]–72.

Encyclopedia of mental health. Albert Deutsch, ed. in chief; Helen Fishman, exec. ed. N.Y., Watts, [1963]. 6v. il. **EH23**

A compendium on mental health, written for laymen in non-technical language by recognized authorities. In dictionary (A–Z) arrangement; 170 topics are discussed by question-and-answer method. v.6 contains list of agencies, bibliography, glossary (p.2095–2180), and subject and name indexes.

English, Horace Bidwell and **English, Ava C.** A comprehensive dictionary of psychological and psychoanalytical terms; a guide to usage. N.Y., Longmans, 1958. 594p. **EH24**

An excellent dictionary, containing some 12,000 terms used by psychologists.

Erdélyi, Michael and **Grossman, Frank.** Dictionary of terms and expressions of industrial psychology ("psychotechnics") in German, English, French, Hungarian. Preface by H. L. Hollingworth. N.Y., Chicago, Pitman, [1939]. 98p. **EH25**

" . . . not for the use of beginners . . . for use of persons who have a fair knowledge of these foreign languages and desire to familiarize themselves with the special technical terms used in this particular field."—*Introd.*

Handbuch der Psychologie in 12 Bänden; hrsg. von Philipp Lersch [et al]. Göttingen, Verlag für Psychologie, C. J. Hogrefe, [1959]–65. v.1–6, 9–10. il. (In progress) **EH26**

Each volume consists of long articles treating a different aspect of psychology: general psychology, perception and learning, developmental psychology, study and theories of personality, psychological diagnosis, methods, educational psychology, industrial psychology. Articles, written by authorities, are signed and include lengthy bibliographies. Each volume has author and subject indexes.

Hehlmann, Wilhelm. Wörterbuch der Psychologie. 2. erg. und erw. Aufl. Stuttgart, A. Kröner, [1962]. 640p. il. **EH27**

A dictionary of some 3500 terms giving fairly long definitions. Contains brief biographical information on internationally known psychologists with partial list of their works. Includes chronology of psychology from ancient times to 1945.

Hinsie, Leland Earl and **Campbell, Robert Jean.** Psychiatric dictionary. 3d ed. N.Y., Oxford Univ. Pr., 1960. 788p. **EH28**

1st ed. 1940, and 2d ed. 1953, by L. E. Hinsie and Jacob Shatzky.

This edition has been completely revised by R. J. Campbell, and many of the definitions rewritten in the light of recent developments. "The first edition and supplement contained over 8000 listings; approximately 1300 of these have been eliminated and nearly 2000 new listings have been added."—*Pref.*

Gives pronunciations. Includes explanations, illustrative quotations, and references.

Pieron, Henri. Vocabulaire de la psychologie. 3. éd., rev. et augm. Paris, Presses Universitaires de France, 1963. 527p. **EH29**

" . . . publié avec la collaboration de l'Association des Travailleurs Scientifiques."

1st ed. 1951.

Comprises nearly 4000 terms used in psychology with signed definitions. References are given to authors and dates of first use. Seven appendixes provide lists of abbreviations, symbols, etc.

Warren, Howard Crosby. Dictionary of psychology. Boston, Houghton, c1934. 372p. il. **EH30**

Contents: Definitions of terms, English and foreign, p.1–299; Tables, p.303–39; Bibliography of technical dictionaries of philosophy and psychology, p.340–41; Glossaries: (1) French terms, p.343–58; (2) German terms, p.359–72.

Authoritative and generally reliable.

Directories

American Board for Psychological Services. Directory of American psychological services, 1960. Glendale, Ohio, 1959. 214p. (Irregular)   **EH31**

Title varies.

A listing of approximately 200 clinical, counseling, industrial, and research services in the United States and Canada.

American Psychological Association. Directory, 1916– . Wash., Assoc., 1916– . Annual.   **EH32**

Title varies. Frequency varies: 1951–57, biennial.

1916–1947, called *Yearbook.* 1964 lists 22,000 members; gives addresses, present positions, last degrees, and class of membership.

American Psychiatric Association. Biographical directory of Fellows and members, as of May 8, 1962. N.Y., Bowker, 1963. 645p.   **EH33**

Lists some 10,000 American psychiatrists, including a few from foreign countries. Gives information as to training, experience, specialty, publications, etc. Contains a geographical index.

Directory of outpatient psychiatric clinics . . . and other mental health resources in the United States and Territories, 1963– . Bethesda, Md., U.S. Dept. of Health, Education, and Welfare, [1964]. 231p. (Public Health Service publ. no.1129)   **EH34**

Continues the *Directory of psychiatric clinics,* published by the National Association for Mental Health in cooperation with the National Institute of Mental Health.

Includes psychiatric day-night services; state hospitals for mental disease; public institutions for mentally retarded; veterans administration hospitals; mental health associations; state departments dealing with mental health and mental retardation; regional offices, U.S. Dept. of Health, Education, and Welfare.

National Research Council. Committee on an International Directory of Psychologists. International directory of psychologists, exclusive of the U.S.A. Assen, Netherlands, Royal Van Gorcum, 1958. 527p.   **EH35**

Lists approximately 7000 psychologists in 76 foreign countries, giving vitae, professional training, current occupation, and publications. New edition has been announced.

Psychological register, ed. by Carl Murchison. Worcester, Mass., Clark Univ. Pr., 1929–32. v.2–3.   **EH36**

Includes brief biographies with very full bibliographies of psychologists throughout the world, arranged by country; v.2 (1929) included 1250 psychologists from 29 countries; v.3 (1932)—a revision and expansion of the 1929 volume—included 2400 psychologists from 40 countries; v.1 was announced to include persons deceased before the initiation of the series and to extend back to the time of the early Greek psychologists, but was not published.

Watson, Robert Irving. The great psychologists, from Aristotle to Freud. Philadelphia, Lippincott, [c1963]. 572p.   **EH37**

A useful, well-written summary, tracing the development of psychology through the lives and works of more than 50 great psychologists and some 100 of their famous associates.

Includes a bibliography (p.497–558) for each of its 20 chapters.

Tests and measurements

Buros, Oscar Krisen. Tests in print; a comprehensive bibliography of tests for use in education, psychology, and industry. Highland Park, N.J., Gryphon, [1961]. 479p.   **EH38**

Serves as an index and supplement to the series, *Mental measurements yearbook* (EH40). Tests in print and out of print are included. Has publishers' directory and index, title, and name indexes.

Hildreth, Gertrude Howell. Bibliography of mental tests and rating scales. 2d ed. N.Y., Psychological Corp., 1939. 295p.   **EH39**

A comprehensive list of more than 4000 tests, classified by subject. Contains subject and author indexes.

———— 1945 supplement. N.Y., Psychological Corp., 1946. 86p.

Includes some 1000 tests published 1940–Oct. 1945, and some earlier tests omitted from the preceding list.

Mental measurements yearbook. Ed. by Oscar K. Buros. Highland Park, N.J., Gryphon, 1938–59. 5v.   **EH40**

Title and publisher vary.

Supersedes *Educational, psychological, and personality tests,* 1933/34–1936, by Oscar K. Buros.

In two sections: (1) Tests and reviews, and (2) Books and reviews. The first lists all educational, psychological, and vocational tests that are commercially available. The second is a classified list of books on testing. Reviews are written by authorities representing different viewpoints.

OCCULTISM

Caillet, Albert Louis. Manuel bibliographique des sciences psychiques ou occultes. Paris, Dorbon, 1912–13. 3v.   **EH41**

Subtitle: Sciences des mages. Hermétique. Astrologie. Kabbale. Franc-Maçonnerie. Médecine ancienne. Mesmerisme. Sorcellerie. Singularités. Aberrations de tout ordre. Curiosités. Sources bibliographiques et documentaires sur ces subjets.

Lists 11,648 items, with full title, imprint, and collation of each, and, in many cases, notes about the books and brief biographical data about the authors.

Hall, Trevor H. A bibliography of books on conjuring in English from 1580 to 1850. Minneapolis, Carl Waring Jones, Pub. of Magic, 1957. 96p. il.   **EH42**

Spence, Lewis. Encyclopaedia of occultism, a compendium of information on the occult sciences, occult personalities, psychic science, magic, demonology, spiritism and mysticism. London, Routledge, 1920. 451p. il. **EH43**

Repr.: New Hyde Park, N.Y., University Books, 1960. 440p. "Verbatim except for an occasional correction of a misprint."

Thorndike, Lynn. History of magic and experimental science. N.Y., Macmillan, 1929; Columbia Univ. Pr., 1934–58. 8v. (v.3–6, History of Science Soc. Publ. n.s. 4)   **EH44**

v.1–2, First 13 centuries; v.3–4, 14th–15th centuries; v.5–6, 16th century; v.7–8, 17th century.

A well-documented history with separate indexes in v.1–4, and a combined index to v.5–6 in v.6, and to v.7–8 in v.8.

E I

Engineering

❦ This section includes a selected list of reference works in the various branches of engineering. For libraries specializing in these fields, much more material will be needed, and the various guides to the literature of the subjects should be consulted. Current literature is of prime importance, and the indexes and abstract journals are essential as guides to this material. (For a discussion of abstract journals, *see* Pure and Applied Sciences, p.525–26.) Many of the branches of engineering have handbooks and manuals which include data, charts, statistics, etc., useful to the practicing engineer. These handbooks are usually revised frequently to include new developments and practices. Dictionaries of technical terms, bilingual as well as those giving definitions in English, are much used in many libraries. For bibliographies of foreign language–English dictionaries, *see* EA94, EA95, and EA96.

GENERAL WORKS

Guides

Dalton, Blanche H. Sources of engineering information. Berkeley, Los Angeles, Univ. of Calif. Pr., 1948. 109p. **EI1**

A handbook and bibliography designed to aid in the finding of material in all branches of engineering. Classified. Little annotation; no index.

Roberts, Arthur Denis. Guide to technical literature; introductory chapters and engineering. London, Grafton, 1939. 279p. **EI2**

Useful bibliography of engineering literature. Includes material published through 1938.

Encyclopedias and handbooks

Eshbach, Ovid Wallace. Handbook of engineering fundamentals, prep. by a staff of specialists. 2d ed. N.Y., Wiley, 1952. unpaged. (Wiley engineering handbook ser.) **EI3**

1st ed. 1936.

Revised; many sections completely rewritten to incorporate new material and recent developments.

Jones, Franklin Day and **Schubert, Paul B.** Engineering encyclopedia; a condensed encyclopedia and mechanical dictionary for engineers, mechanics, technical schools, industrial plants, and public libraries, giving the most essential facts about 4500 important engineering subjects. 3d ed. N.Y., Industrial Pr., 1963. 1431p. il. **EI4**

1st ed. 1941.

Definitions of engineering terms and brief articles are in one alphabetical arrangement. Includes some historical and background material.

Kempe's Engineer's year-book. London, Morgan, 1894– . Annual. **EI5**

Subtitle varies. Editors vary.

A standard handbook covering all types of engineering, with formulae, rules, tables, data, etc. Revised annually. 1965 in 2v.

O'Rourke, Charles Edward. General engineering handbook; ed. in chief, Charles Edward O'Rourke . . . 2d ed. N.Y., London, McGraw-Hill, 1940. 1120p. il. **EI6**

The purpose of this general handbook is to cover the essentials of all branches of engineering in a compact survey, but not to take the place of the specialized handbooks of the various branches of engineering.

Perry, John Howard and **Perry, Robert H.** Engineering manual; a practical reference of data and methods in architectural, chemical, civil, electrical, mechanical, and nuclear engineering. N.Y., McGraw-Hill, 1959. 1v. [v.p.] il. **EI7**

"This manual presents in individual sections the commonly used formulas, data, and methods in the principal engineering fields."—*Pref.*

Dictionaries

Engineers Joint Council. Thesaurus of engineering terms. 1st ed. May 1964. N.Y., 1964. 302p. **EI8**

Subtitle: A list of engineering terms and their relationships for use in vocabulary control in indexing and retrieving engineering information.

AERONAUTICAL AND SPACE ENGINEERING

Guides

Fry, Bernard Mitchell and **Mohrhardt, Foster E.** A guide to information sources in space science and technology. N.Y., Interscience, a division of Wiley, 1963. 579p. (Guides to information sources in science and technology, v.1) **EI9**

The first in a series of guides, to be followed by others, covering sources in atomic energy, biochemistry, biophysics, and many other fields.

Omits material on the use of the library, how to search the literature, etc., and concentrates on current sources, both published and unpublished. Treats abstracting and indexing services, information centers and services, reference books, and specific subjects in space science. To be continued by "an annual or biennial volume titled *Research trends in space sciences and technology: 1963–1964—A guide to sources of information.*"—*Introd.*

Bibliography

Benton, Mildred Catherine. The literature of space science and exploration. Wash., U.S. Naval Research Laboratory, 1958. 264p. (U.S. Naval Research Laboratory, Bellevue, D.C., Bibliography no.13) **EI10**

2274 numbered entries of "books, periodical articles, and research reports on the more scientific aspects of space exploration, both theoretical and applied."—*Introd.*

Covers 1903–June 1958.

Boffito, Giuseppe. Biblioteca aeronautica italiana illustrata. Precede uno studio sull'aeronautica nella letteratura, nell'arte e nel folklore. Firenze, Olschki, 1929. cxvp., 544p. il. **EI11**

—— —— Primo supplemento decennale (1927–1936) con aggiunte all'intera "Biblioteca" e appendice sui manifesti aeronautici del Museo Caproni in Milano descritti da Paolo Arrigoni. Firenze, Olschki, 1937. 678p. il.

A comprehensive bibliography on the history of aeronautics. Arranged alphabetically, with analytical indexes to names and subjects. Contents are given for many periodicals. The Supplement gives biographical notes about many of the authors.

Brockett, Paul. Bibliography of aeronautics. Wash., Smithsonian Inst., 1910. 940p. (Smithsonian miscellaneous collections, v.55) **EI12**

An important bibliography of almost 13,500 titles, arranged alphabetically by author or title, including books and pamphlets and indexing the articles in nearly 200 periodicals. Covers the period up to July 1909.

Continued by: U.S. National Advisory Committee for Aeronautics, *Bibliography of aeronautics* (EI17).

New York. Public Library. History of aeronautics; a selected list of references to material in the New York Public Library, comp. by William B. Gamble. N.Y., Lib., 1938. 325p. (Repr. from the New York Public Library Bull. Jan. 1936–Sept. 1937) **EI13**

A classed list of more than 5500 entries to books and periodical articles in many languages, with indexes of authors and subjects.

Ordway, Frederick I. Annotated bibliography of space science and technology, with an astronomical supplement. A history of astronautical book literature—1931 through 1961. [3d ed.] Wash., ARFOR Publ., Astronautics Educ. Division, 1962. 77p. **EI14**

1st edition, 1955, had title *Specialized books on space flight and related disciplines.*

Arranged chronologically by year of publication.

U.S. Library of Congress. Map Division. Aviation cartography; a historico-bibliographic study of aeronautical charts, by Walter W. Ristow. 2d ed. rev. and enl. Wash., 1960. 245p. **EI15**

A history and discussion of aeronautical charts, p.1–53; the Bibliography, p.55–231, lists 774 items alphabetically by author, with subject index.

U.S. Library of Congress. Science and Technology Division. Air Force scientific research bibliography, 1950–1956, 1957–1958, by G. Vernon Hooker [and others]. Wash., Govt. Prt. Off., 1961–64. v.1–2. (AFOSR 700) (In progress) **EI16**

v.1, 1150p.; v.2, 1103p. "Supported by the Air Force Office of Scientific Research [and] United States Air Force."

Includes "abstracts of all technical notes, technical reports, journal articles, books, symposium proceedings, and monographs produced and published by scientists supported in whole or in part by the Air Force Office of Scientific Research during the period . . . . v.1 also includes all earlier reports supported by AFOSR or its anlage found during this search back through 1950."—*Pref.*

Research is supported in physics, chemistry, engineering sciences, life sciences (except medical), and mathematics.

U.S. National Advisory Committee for Aeronautics. Bibliography of aeronautics, 1909–1932. Wash., Govt. Prt. Off., 1921–36. v.1–14. **EI17**

v.1, 1909–16. 1493p.; v.2, 1917–19. 494p.; v.3, 1920–21. 448p.; v.4–14 (annual volumes). 1922–32.

A continuation, on the same plan, of the basic bibliography by Brockett noted above (EI12).

Periodicals

U.S. Library of Congress. Science and Technology Division. Aeronautical and space serial publications: a world list. Wash., 1962. 255p. **EI18**

A listing, with bibliographical information, of 4551 titles

originating in 76 countries. Supersedes *A checklist of aeronautical periodicals and serials in the Library of Congress* (1948).

Abstract journals

International aerospace abstracts. Phillipsburg, N.J., Technical Information Service, Amer. Inst. of Aeronautics and Astronautics, 1961– . v.1– . Semimonthly. **EI19**

Covers published literature in periodicals and books; meeting papers and conference proceedings issued by professional and academic organizations; and translations of journals and articles.

Reports ("unpublished literature") are abstracted in *Scientific and technical aerospace reports* (*STAR*) (EI20), published by the Scientific and Technical Information Division, National Aeronautics and Space Administration. These two services use the same subject categories and indexes, and thus "provide comprehensive access to the national and international unclassified report and published literature of current significance to aerospace science and technology."

Cumulative quarterly indexes, the fourth quarterly being the annual index.

U.S. National Aeronautics and Space Administration. Scientific and technical aerospace reports; a semimonthly abstract journal with indexes. Wash., 1963– . v.1– . Semimonthly, with quarterly indexes and an annual cumulated index. **EI20**

Supersedes *Technical publications announcements,* with same scope and coverage.

"A comprehensive abstracting and indexing journal covering worldwide report literature on the science and technology of space and aeronautics. Major areas covered are: Scientific and technical reports of the National Aeronautics and Space Administration and its contractors; Scientific and technical reports of government agencies, universities, and research organizations throughout the world."—*Introd.*

Beginning with April 1964 has a companion volume as follows:

—— Guide to the subject indexes for scientific and technical aerospace reports, no.1– . April 1964– . Wash., 1964– . **EI21**

Indexes

Air University Library index to military periodicals. Maxwell Air Force Base, Ala., Air Univ. Lib., 1949– . v.1– . Quarterly, with annual and triennial cumulative issues. **EI22**

Title varies: 1949–62, *Air University periodical index.*

"A subject index to significant articles, news items, and editorials appearing in 68 English language military and aeronautical periodicals not indexed in readily available commercial indexing services."—*Pref.*

Dictionaries

Aviation and space dictionary. Chief ed., Ernest J. Gentle; assoc. ed., Charles Edward Chapel. 4th ed. Los Angeles, Aero, 1961. 444p. il. **EI23**

3d edition had title *Baughman's Aviation dictionary and reference guide,* rev. by E. J. Gentle and C. E. Chapel.

Defines terms used in the aviation industry and, with this edition, includes terms on astronomy, atomic energy, electronics, guided missiles, helicopters, jet aircraft, meteorology, ordnance, radar, rockets, television, etc.

The "Reference guide" formerly included has been omitted.

Besserer, C. W. and **Besserer, Hazel C.** Guide to the space

age. Englewood Cliffs, N.J., Prentice-Hall, 1959. 320p. il.
EI24

A dictionary of terms for all areas generally associated with rockets and missiles, such as propulsion, guidance, control, aerodynamics, electronics, meteorology, etc.

Caidin, Martin. The man-in-space dictionary; a modern glossary. [1st ed.] N.Y., Dutton, 1963. 224p. il. **EI25**

Includes terms concerned with: the physiological aspects of aerospace medicine, mechanics of space flight, unmanned satellites, rocket engineering, etc.

Dictionary of guided missiles and space flight, [ed. by Grayson Merrill and others]. Princeton, N.J., Van Nostrand, 1959. 688p. il. (Principles of guided missile design, 5) **EI26**

An alphabetically arranged encyclopedic dictionary defining terms used in space flight and allied fields.

Herrick, John W. and **Burgess, Eric.** Rocket encyclopedia, illustrated. Los Angeles, Aero, 1959. 607p. il. **EI28**

Nearly all entries are in two parts: (1) a concise definition, in technical phrases chosen to satisfy the needs of the members of the rocket industry; (2) an explanation giving more detailed information in language that should be understood by a high school graduate.

McLaughlin, Charles. Space age dictionary. 2d ed. Princeton, N.J., Van Nostrand, 1963. 233p. il. **EI29**

A concise dictionary defining terms in space technology, including missiles, satellites, and the "major scientific principles and technological methods that have contributed to the advancing space frontier."—*Pref.*

Moser, Reta C. Space-age acronyms; abbreviations and designations. N.Y., Plenum Pr., 1964. 427p. **EI30**

More than 10,000 acronyms used in space and defense industry.

Oppermann, Alfred. Aeronautical-English. Technisches Taschenwörter- und Handbuch der Luftfahrt. Technical pocket dictionary and manual of aviation. 1. Aufl. München, Oppermann, 1957– . v.1– . il. **EI31**

——— ——— Ergänzungsnachtrag 1. zur ersten Aufl. Supplement 1 to 1st ed. München, Oppermann, 1957– . v.1– .

——— ——— Nachtrag 1/1960– . Supplement 1/1960– , von Claus-Jurgen Brey. München, Oppermann, 1960– . v.1– . il.

U.S. Air University. Research Studies Institute. Aerospace glossary. Woodford Agee Heflin, ed. [Maxwell Air Force Base, Ala.], 1959. 111p. **EI32**

Supplements *The United States Air Force dictionary* (EI32a) and does not repeat terms found there.

——— The United States Air Force dictionary. Ed. by Woodford Agee Heflin. Princeton, N.J., Van Nostrand, 1956. 578p. **EI32a**

Supplemented by the author's *Aerospace glossary* (EI32). For full information *see* CI205.

Polyglot

Elsevier's Dictionary of aeronautics in six languages: English/American, French, Spanish, Italian, Portuguese, and German. Comp. and arr. on an English alphabetical base by A. F. Dorian and James Osenton. Amsterdam, N.Y., Elsevier, 1964. 842p. **EI33**

North Atlantic Treaty Organization. Advisory Group for Aeronautical Research and Development. AGARD aeronautical multilingual dictionary. Eds.: G. H. Frénot and A. H. Holloway. Oxford, N.Y., Pergamon, 1960. xixp., and 15 expansible sections (1661 initial entries). **EI34**

In 8 languages.

15 main sections by categories: Aeronautics (general), General motion of aircraft, Structure, Aerodynamics, Heavier-than-air aircraft, Rotorcraft, Lighter-than-air aircraft, Power plant, Propellers, Auxiliary services, Navigation, Parachutes, Air-traffic and ground services, Radio communication and radio location, Meteorology. Many subsections.

Each numbered entry is repeated and defined in English, French, German, Spanish, Italian, Dutch, Turkish, and Russian.

——— ——— 1st supplement, 1963. Ed. by A. H. Holloway. N.Y., Pergamon, 1963. 334p.

Russian

Kotik, M. G. English-Russian aerohydrodynamic dictionary. Moscow, Central Editorial Board, Foreign-Language Scientific and Technical Dictionaries Fizmatgiz, 1960. 457p. il. **EI35**

Added title page in Russian.

U.S. Library of Congress. Reference Dept. Russian-English glossary of guided missile, rocket, and satellite terms, comp. by Alexander Rosenberg. Wash., 1958. 352p. **EI36**

Lists more than 4000 terms taken from books and periodicals published in the USSR from 1955 to 1958.

Directories

World aviation directory. Wash., Amer. Aviation Publ., 1940– . v.1– . Semiannual. **EI37**

Title varies: 1940–51, *American aviation directory*.

Subtitle varies: 1960, Listing aviation companies and officials including missile/space industries, covering the United States, Canada, Europe, Central and South America, Africa and the Middle East, Australasia and Asia.

World space directory listing U.S. and foreign missile/space companies, officials and government agencies. Donald W. Dean, ed. Wash., Amer. Aviation Publ., 1962– . v.1– . Semiannual. **EI38**

Lists the major missile/space manufacturers of the world. Personnel index.

Handbooks

Baar, James and **Howard, William E.** Spacecraft and missiles of the world, 1962. N.Y., Harcourt, 1962. 117p. il. **EI39**

Gives pictures and tabulated facts about the missiles of various countries, including type, specifications, performance, etc.

Bowman, Norman John. Handbook of rockets and guided missiles. 2d ed. Newtown Square, Pa., Perastadion Pr., 1963. 1008p. diagrams. **EI39a**

1st ed. 1957.

The main section is an alphabetical list of rockets with descriptions. This edition adds information on satellite launchings. Bibliography, p.668–716. Drawings of rockets and missiles, p.717–1008.

Koelle, Heinz Hermann. Handbook of astronautical engineering. 1st ed. N.Y., McGraw-Hill, 1961. 1v. [v.p.] il. **EI40**

In six major parts: (1) Fundamentals of astronautical engineering, (2) Astrodynamics, (3) Astrionics, (4) Propulsion, (5) Space vehicles, and (6) Space-flight operations. Chapters are written by specialists and include many bibliographical references.

Martin Marietta Corporation. Aerospace Division. Design guide to orbital flight, by Jorgen Jensen [and others]. N.Y., McGraw-Hill, 1962. 896p. il. **EI41**

Each chapter by a specialist, with an extensive bibliography.

Ordway, Frederick I. and **Wakeford, Ronald C.** International missile and spacecraft guide. N.Y., McGraw-Hill, 1960. [v.p.] il. **EI42**

Gives brief, standardized descriptions of major guided missiles with illustrations. Also includes a chronology of missile progress, country by country, presenting the history and development of the science.

Rand Corporation. New space handbook: astronautics and its applications, by Robert W. Buchheim and the staff of the Rand Corporation. N.Y., Vintage Books, [1963]. 351p. il. **EI43**

"V-160."

Revised edition of the corporation's *Space handbook, 1959.*

U.S. National Aeronautics and Space Administration. Aeronautics and astronautics; an American chronology of science and technology in the exploration of space, 1915–1960, by Eugene M. Emme . . . Wash., 1961. 240p. **EI44**

A listing, by year and day, of important events in aeronautics, with emphasis on United States efforts. Subject and name index. Lists of records, awards, etc.

—— Astronautical and aeronautical events of 1961– . Wash., 1962– . **EI44a**

Supplements to the above.

Yearbooks

Aerospace year book. Official publication of the Aerospace Industries Association of America, Inc. Wash., Amer. Aviation Publ., 1919– . v.1– . il. Annual. **EI45**

Title varies: 1919–59, *The aircraft yearbook.*

Records the year's progress. Gives illustrations and descriptions of "Aircraft in production."

Jane's All the world's aircraft, 1909– . London, S. Low, 1909– . v.1– . il. Annual. **EI46**

Title varies: [v.1–2], *All the world's airships;* [v.3]–19, *All the world's aircraft;* v.20– , *Jane's All the world's aircraft.*

Includes illustrations and descriptions of the aircraft of the various countries of the world including: airplanes, drones, sailplanes, airships, air-cushion vehicles, guided missiles, rockets, space vehicles, aero-engines.

Biography

U.S. National Aeronautics and Space Administration. Space scientists and engineers: selected biographical and bibliographical listing, 1957–1961. Wash., Govt. Prt. Off., 1962. 332p. (NASA SP-5) **EI47**

Gives name, position, and address (sometimes some brief biographical facts), and list of writings.

Who's who in world aviation and astronautics. Wash., Amer. Aviation Publ., 1958. v.2 (497p.) **EI48**

1st ed. 1955.

This edition adds some 700 sketches to the 2400 included in the 1st edition, many from the field of astronautics, as well as a substantial increase in names from other countries. Includes officials of aircraft companies and airlines; scientists in aeronautics and astronautics; officers of the air services of all countries; distinguished members of pioneer pilot organizations; government officials and legislators with significant interest in aviation, etc.

AUTOMOTIVE ENGINEERING

Anglo-russkii avtotraktorn'ii slovar'. Sost.: B. V. Gol'd i R. V. Kugel'. Izd. vtoroe perepabotannoe. Moskya, Gos. Izd. Tekhniko-Teoreticheskoi Literatur', 1957. 831p. **EI49**

Added title page: English-Russian automotive dictionary. 2d. rev. ed.

Elsevier's Automobile dictionary in eight languages: English/American, French, Italian, Spanish, Portuguese, German, Russian, Japanese. Comp. and arr. on an English alphabetical base by G. Schuurmans Stekhoven. Amsterdam, Elsevier, 1960. (Distr. in U.S. by Van Nostrand) 946p. **EI50**

Internal combustion engine; a glossary of technical terms in English/American, French, Dutch, German, Spanish, Italian, Portuguese, Russian. Amsterdam, Elsevier, 1961. 278p. (Glossaria interpretum) **EI51**

"Prepared by the Shell International Petroleum Co. Ltd., London."

Müller, Wolfgang. Technical dictionary of automotive engineering, containing about 10,000 technical terms. A Pergamon Press Book. N.Y., Macmillan, 1964. 1009p. **EI52**

Prepared on an English base; gives equivalents in German, Russian, and French.

SAE handbook, 1926– . N.Y., Soc. of Automotive Engineers, 1926– . il. Annual (slightly irregular). **EI53**

A standard handbook.

CHEMICAL ENGINEERING

Guides

Kobe, Kenneth Albert. Chemical engineering reports: how to search the literature and prepare a report. 4th ed. N.Y., Interscience, 1957. 175p. il. **EI54**

Covers: chemical literature, engineering reports, the business letter and the letter report, the text report, the formal engineering report, the laboratory report, effective writing, mechanical preparation, and literature citations.

Includes bibliographies.

Abstract journals

Theoretical chemical engineering abstracts. London, Technical Information Co., 1964– . v.1– . Bimonthly. **EI55**

Encyclopedias

Encyclopedia of chemical technology; ed. by Raymond E. Kirk, Donald F. Othmer [and others]. N.Y., Interscience Encyclopedias, 1947–56. 15v. and Suppl. 1–2, 1957 and 1960. il. **EI56**

An encyclopedia of high standard. Arranged by broad subjects with many cross references. Articles are written by specialists, are signed, and include selected bibliographies. United States patents are noted.

—— 2d ed. compl. rev. Ed. board: Herman F. Mark, John J. McKetta, Jr., and Donald F. Othmer. N.Y., Interscience, 1963–64. v.1–5. il. (In progress)

At head of title: Kirk-Othmer.

Contents: v.1–5, A–Colors.

A thoroughly revised edition. Many articles have been rewritten by the same or different authors. All articles are signed and include bibliographies, sometimes quite extensive.

Hampel, Clifford A. The encyclopedia of electrochemistry. N.Y., Reinhold; London, Chapman & Hall, 1964. 1206p. il. **EI57**

"Contains 412 individual articles or entries arranged in alphabetical sequence and especially prepared by 271 contributors."—*Introd.* Articles are signed and include bibliographies.

Dictionaries

Elsevier's Dictionary of the gas industry. In seven languages: French, English/American, Spanish, Italian, Portuguese, Dutch, German. Prep. and arr. in a rational classification by the International Gas Union. Amsterdam, Elsevier, 1961. 628p. il. **EI58**

Title pages also in French and German.

Handbooks

Chemical engineering data book, incorporating . . . Chemical industries. London, Leonard Hall, 1925– . v.1– . **EI59**

Title varies: v.1–9, 1925–33, *Chemical engineering and chemical catalogue;* v.10–23, 1935–53, *Chemical industries.* Editors: 1938–52, D. M. Newitt; v.24, 1958– , T. K. Ross and D. C. Freshwater.

Chemical engineers' handbook; 4th ed., prep. by a staff of specialists, under the editorial direction of Robert H. Perry [and others]. N.Y., McGraw-Hill, 1963. 1v. [v.p.] il. **EI60**

Previous eds. by John H. Perry.

Cremer, Herbert W. and **Davies, Trefor.** Chemical engineering practice. London, Butterworths Scientific Pub., 1956–60. v.1–7, 10–11. il. (In progress) **EI61**

To be in 12v.

Contents: v.1, General; v.2, Solid state; v.3, Solid systems; v.4, Fluid state; v.5–6, Fluid systems, I–II; v.7, Heat transfer; v.10, Ancillary services; v.11, Works, designs, etc.

Graham, Arthur Kenneth and **Pinkerton, H. L.** Electroplating engineering handbook. 2d ed. N.Y., Reinhold, 1962. 774p. il. **EI62**

Chapters are written by specialists and directed to the designer, manufacturer, supplier, and purchaser of electroplating equipment.

Glossary of terms, p.xi–xix.

Plastics

Encyclopedia of polymer science and technology: plastics, resins, rubbers, fibers. Ed. board: Herman F. Mark, chairman; Norman G. Gaylord, exec. ed.; Norbert M. Bikales, ed. N.Y., Interscience, [1964–]. v.1– . il. (In progress) **EI63**

v.1, A–Amino acids.

Includes bibliographies.

Coverage is international, but presentation is North American. The articles have been chosen to present a balanced account of all facets of polymer science and technology, in five major groups: (1) chemical substances, (2) polymer properties, (3) methods and processes, (4) uses, and (5) general background. Cf. *Introd.*

Modern plastics encyclopedia, 1941– . N.Y., Plastic Catalogue Corp., 1940– . il. Annual. **EI64**

Title varies: 1941, *Modern plastics catalog;* 1942–45, *Plastics catalog;* 1946– , *Modern plastics encyclopedia.*

1965, in nine sections: (1) Resins and compounds; (2) Foamed plastics; (3) Chemicals and additives; (4) Film and sheeting; (5) Fillers, reinforcements; (6) Laminates; (7) Engineering and methods; (8) Fabricating and finishing; and (9) Machinery and equipment. Includes a Directory of manufacturers, processors, and suppliers.

Advertising is grouped according to subject matter in the section where the editorial on the same subject may be found.

Resins, rubbers, plastics yearbook. . . . v.1– . N.Y., Information for Industry, Inc., 1948– . il. Annual. **EI65**

Publisher varies. Subtitle varies.

A collection of abstracts which appeared originally in the monthly abstracting service *Resins, rubbers, plastics; literature service.* 1942– .

International in scope. The abstracts usually contain original data, graphs, charts, photographs, etc.

—— World title list. 1960– . v.1– .

A classified list of recent titles in the field.

Simonds, Herbert Rumsey and **Church, James M.** A concise guide to plastics. 2d ed. N.Y., Reinhold, 1963. 392p. il. **EI66**

1st ed. 1957.

A guide to the properties, forms, basic chemicals, processing, applications, production and prices, manufacturers, etc.

Society of the Plastics Industry, Inc. S.P.I. plastics engineering handbook. 3d ed. N.Y., Reinhold, 1960. 565p. il. **EI67**

1st edition had title *SPI handbook.* 1947.

Nomenclature, p.xxxiii–lii.

Discusses and appraises various plastic materials. Compiled by specialists, but articles are not individually signed.

Wittfoht, Annemarie. Plastics technical dictionary; nomenclature used in processing, fabricating, and using plastics, in testing and mold construction. N.Y., Interscience, 1961. 2v. il. **EI68**

Also published in Germany with title *Kunststofftechnisches Wörterbuch.* München, Carl Hanser Verlag, 1958. 2v.

Both editions have title pages in both languages.

Contents: v.1, English-German. 3d rev. and augm. ed. 389p.; v.2, German-English. 2d rev. and augm. ed. 573p.

Often gives brief explanations as well as synonyms.

CIVIL ENGINEERING

Handbooks

Abbett, Robert William. American civil engineering practice, prep. by a staff of specialists. N.Y., Wiley, 1956–57. 3v. il. **EI69**

Comrie, James. Civil engineering reference book. 2d ed. London, Butterworth, 1961. 4v. il. **EI70**

1st ed. 1951.

Chapters from the 1st edition have been rewritten or revised and several new chapters added. Includes bibliographies.

Urquhart, Leonard Church. Civil engineering handbook. 4th ed. N.Y., McGraw-Hill, 1959. [v.p.] il. **EI71**

3d ed. 1950.

This edition much revised, with new material, particularly in the fields of photogrammetric surveying; railway, highway, and airport engineering; hydraulics; stresses; concrete; foundations; sewerage; water supply; etc.

Air pollution

Bibliography

Davenport, Sara Jeannette and **Morgis, G. G.** Air pollution; a bibliography. Wash., Govt. Prt. Off., 1954. 448p.

(U.S. Bureau of Mines. Bull., no.537)   **EI72**

3902 entries, with abstracts, from many sources arranged by subject. Covers nature and origin of air pollution, composition of air pollutants, effects of air pollution, control of air pollution, legal aspects, etc.

Continued by:

Air pollution bibliography. Wash., 1957–59. v.1–2. **EI73**

v.1, comp. by Jack R. Gibson, Wave E. Culver, Mary E. Kurz; v.2, comp. by Arnold J. Jacobius, Jack R. Gibson [and others].

A bibliography with abstracts.

Abstract journals

APCA abstracts. Pub. by the Air Pollution Control Association in cooperation with the United States Public Health Service and the Library of Congress. Pittsburgh, Air Pollution Control Assoc., 1955– . v.1– . Monthly. **EI74**

Cumulated author and subject indexes from time to time.

Handbooks

Magill, Paul L., Holden, Francis R. and **Ackley, Charles.** Air pollution handbook. N.Y., McGraw-Hill, 1956. [v.p.] il. **EI75**

Chapters by specialists, with bibliographies, treating various aspects of the problems of air pollution, e.g., air pollution sources . . . and city planning; chemistry and physics of the atmosphere; effects of air pollution and corrective methods; etc.

Stern, Arthur Cecil. Air pollution. N.Y., Academic Pr., 1962. 2v. **EI76**

Chapters, by specialists, include bibliographies.

Hydraulic engineering

Bibliography

Kolupaila, Steponas. Bibliography of hydrometry. Notre Dame, Ind., Univ. of Notre Dame Pr., 1961. 975p. **EI77**

A comprehensive, annotated bibliography of hydrometry—the science of measurement of water—including some 7370 titles in more than 30 languages and from all periods. Titles are given in the original language, followed by a translation into English.

Rowe, Robert Seaman. Bibliography of rivers and harbors and related fields in hydraulic engineering. Princeton, N.J., Rivers and Harbors Section, Dept. of Civil Engineering, Princeton Univ., 1953. 407p. **EI78**

International in scope. Includes some 6000 references to books and monographs. Omits periodical articles, abstracts, etc.

Dictionaries

American Association of Port Authorities. Committee on Standardization and Special Research. A port dictionary of technical terms. New Orleans, Amer. Assoc. of Port Authorities, 1940. 208p. **EI79**

Based on the *Port glossary,* compiled by Dr. R. S. McElwee for the Association's Committee on Technical Language, 1927.—Cf. *Foreword.*

Contains more than 1000 definitions.

Handbooks

Davis, Calvin Victor. Handbook of applied hydraulics. 2d ed. N.Y., McGraw-Hill, 1952. 1272p. il. **EI80**

1st ed. 1942.

King, Horace Williams and **Brater, Ernest F.** Handbook of hydraulics for the solution of hydrostatic and fluid flow problems. 5th ed. N.Y., McGraw-Hill, 1963. [v.p.] **EI81**

1st ed. 1918.

Traffic engineering

Bibliography

Cassidy, Kathryn Childs and **Kagan, Cele.** Bibliography of traffic engineering literature; selected, annotated and indexed. New Haven, Bureau of Highway Traffic, Yale Univ., 1954. 237p. **EI82**

686 numbered entries, arranged alphabetically with subject index. Includes books and reports, and indexes three series of publications: "all articles on administration, highway finance, and traffic operations from the *Proceedings of the annual meetings* of the Highway Research Board for the past 5 years; all articles from the *Proceedings* of the Institute of Traffic Engineers for the last 5 years; and most of the *Bulletins* of the Highway Research Board for recent years, except those dealing exclusively with highway construction."

Li, Shu-t'ien. Bibliography on airport engineering. [N.Y.], Amer. Soc. of Civil Engineers, 1960. 170p. **EI83**

Subtitle: A compilation of free world literature numbering 2335 entries classified into 26 groups and arranged chronologically.

Abstract journals

Highway research abstracts, no.1–142; v.17, no.7– . Wash., 1931– . Monthly. **EI84**

Published by the Highway Research Board of the National Research Council, National Academy of Sciences.

Volume numbering began with v.17, no.7, July 1947. Previously, publication was irregular. Annual subject index, 1962– . List of titles abstracted appears on cover. Since 1937 the December issue has been a Synopsis issue, containing synopses of many of the papers and reports scheduled for presentation at the annual meeting of the Highway Research Board.

—— Index, 1931–1961. 1963.

Road abstracts. v.1, 1934/35– . London, Stat. Off., 1935– . Monthly. **EI85**

Dept. of Scientific and Industrial Research. Road Research Laboratory.

Titles of foreign articles are translated into English with indication of original language.

Handbooks

U.S. Bureau of Public Roads. Highway statistics; summary to 1945. Wash., Govt. Prt. Off., 1947. 97p. **EI86**

Provides background for the annual publication.

"Each series has been carried back as many years as the data warrant, but the periods vary."—*Pref.* Some go back to 1890, 1900, 1919, etc.

—— —— no.1, 1945– . Wash., Govt. Prt. Off., 1947– . Annual.

Continues *Highway statistics; summary to 1945.*

Issued 1945–48 by U.S. Public Roads Administration, Federal Works Agency; 1949– by U.S. Dept. of Commerce, Bureau of Public Roads.

Presents "statistical and analytical tables of general interest on motor fuel, motor vehicles, highway-user taxation, financing of state and local highways, highway mileage, and federal aid for highways."—*Pref.*, 1951.

Woods, Kenneth Brady [and others]. Highway engineering handbook. 1st ed. N.Y., McGraw-Hill, 1960. 1v. [v.p.] il. **EI87**

Structural engineering

American Institute of Steel Construction. Manual of steel construction. 6th ed. N.Y., 1963. 1v. [v.p.] **EI88**

Title varies; earlier editions had title *Steel construction, a manual for architects, engineers and fabricators of buildings.*

Merritt, Frederick S. Building construction handbook. 1st ed. N.Y., McGraw-Hill, 1958. [v.p.] il. **EI89**

Chapters, with bibliographies, prepared by specialists; primarily for the nonspecialist in the field.

National Lumber Manufacturers Association. Wood structural design data. 3d ed. Wash., 1957– . v.1– . **EI90**

Timber Engineering Company. Timber design and construction handbook. N.Y., F. W. Dodge Corp., 1956. 622p. il. **EI91**

U.S. Forest Products Laboratory, Madison. Wood handbook, basic information on wood as a material of construction with data for its use in design and specification. Wash., Govt. Prt. Off., 1955. 528p. il. (Agriculture handbook, no.72) **EI92**

Glossary, p.3–9; Standard lumber abbreviations, p.95–97. Includes bibliographies.
Supersedes 1940 edition.

ELECTRICAL AND ELECTRONIC ENGINEERING

Bibliography

Moore, C. K. and **Spencer, K. J.** Electronics: a bibliographical guide. London, MacDonald, 1961. 411p. **EI93**

A bibliography of bibliographies, abstracting journals, translating services, etc., in the field of electronics, with a selection of books and papers. Totals more than 3300 references published mainly from 1945 to June 1959.

Mottelay, Paul Fleury. Bibliographical history of electricity and magnetism chronologically arranged. London, Griffin, 1922. 673p. il. **EI94**

Subtitle: Researches into the domain of the early sciences, especially from the period of the revival of scholasticism, with biographical and other accounts of the most distinguished natural philosophers throughout the Middle Ages.
A chronological history with many bibliographical references.

Abstract journals

Science abstracts: Sec. B, Electrical engineering abstracts. v.1– , 1898– . Ed. and issued by the Institution of Electrical Engineers. London, Inst. of Electrical Engineers, 1898– . v.1– . Monthly. **EI95**

1898–1902 title reads: *Science abstracts. Physics and electrical engineering.* 1903– , issued in two sections: A, Physics; B, Electrical engineering. Beginning with 1941, titles of sections changed to *Physics abstracts* and *Electrical engineering abstracts.* Sponsoring societies vary. Publisher varies.
Signed abstracts. Titles of foreign articles are translated into English, without original title.
Annual author and subject indexes.

Encyclopedias

Say, Maurice George. Newnes concise encyclopaedia of electrical engineering. [1st ed.] London, Newnes, 1962. 906p. **EI96**

An alphabetically arranged 1v. encyclopedia "covering all branches of electrical engineering in the field of power production and utilization."—*Foreword.*

Susskind, Charles. Encyclopedia of electronics. N.Y., Reinhold, 1962. 974p. il. **EI97**

An alphabetically arranged encyclopedia of some 500 topics each written by an authority, directed primarily at professional readers. In some cases related articles have been grouped under one subject. Includes a few biographical sketches.

Dictionaries

Cooke, Nelson Magor and **Markus, John.** Electronics and nucleonics dictionary. N.Y., McGraw-Hill, 1960. 543p. il. **EI98**

Subtitle: An illustrated dictionary giving up-to-date definitions, abbreviations and synonyms for over 13,000 terms used in television, radio, medical electronics, industrial electronics, space electronics, military electronics, avionics, radar, nuclear science, and nuclear engineering.
Supersedes Cooke's *Electronics dictionary.* 1945.

Radio Corporation of America. What's the right word? A dictionary of common and uncommon terms in radio, television, electronics. N.Y., Radio Corp. of America, Dept. of Information, 1952. 50p. il. **EI99**

Includes diagrams, symbols, illustrations.

Sarbacher, Robert Irving. Encyclopedic dictionary of electronics and nuclear engineering. Englewood Cliffs, N.J., Prentice-Hall, 1959. 1417p. il. **EI100**

This comprehensive dictionary, designed for the scientist, technician, and student, defines terms in the fields of electronics and nuclear engineering as well as some in related fields.
"Wherever practical, definitions prepared and approved by the various professional societies have been used."—*Pref.*

Foreign terms

Polyglot

Elsevier's Dictionary of amplification, modulation, reception and transmission in six languages: English/American, French, Spanish, Italian, Dutch, and German, . . . comp. and arr. on an English alphabetical base by W. E. Clason. Amsterdam, Elsevier, 1960. (Distr. in U.S. by Van Nostrand) 804p. (Elsevier's Multilingual dictionaries) **EI101**

Defines almost 3000 words and phrases.

Elsevier's Dictionary of electronics and wave-guides, in six languages: English/American, French, Spanish, Italian, Dutch, and German. Comp. and arr. on an English alphabetical base by W. E. Clason. Amsterdam, Elsevier, 1957. (Distr. in U.S. by Van Nostrand) 628p. (Elsevier's Multilingual dictionaries) **EI102**

—— Russian supplement, by W. E. Clason. 1961. 57p.

Clason, W. E. Supplement to the Elsevier dictionaries of electronics, nucleonics and telecommunication. In six languages: English/American, French, Spanish, Italian, Dutch, and German. Comp. and arr. on an English alphabetical base. Amsterdam, Elsevier, 1963. 633p. **EI103**

Elsevier's Dictionary of television, radar and antennas, in six languages: English/American, French, Spanish, Italian, Dutch, and German, comp. and arr. on an English alphabetical base by W. E. Clason. Amsterdam, Elsevier, 1955. 760p. (Elsevier's Multilingual dictionaries) **EI104**

Six-language dictionary of automation, electronics and scientific instruments; a comprehensive dictionary in English, French, German, Italian, Spanish, and Russian. Comp. by A. F. Dorian. London, Iliffe Books; Englewood Cliffs, N.J., Prentice-Hall, [1962]. 732p. **EI104a**

Thali, Hans. Technical dictionary of technical terms used in electrical engineering, radio, television, telecommunication including the most used terms of acoustics, illumination, mathematics, materials, mechanics, optics, heating, etc. Hitzkirch (Lucerne), Thali, 1960. v.1–2. **EI105**

> 1st ed. 1946.
> v.1, English-German-French. 6th ed. 277p.; **v.2, Deutsch-englisch-französisch. 4th ed. 311p.**
> Added title page in German and French. Title varies slightly.

Russian

Geiler, L. B. and **Dozorov, N. I.** Anglo-russkii elektro-tekhnicheskii slovar'. 2. izd. ispr. i dop. Moskva, Gos. Izd.-vo Tekhniko-Teoreticheskoi Literaturi, 1957. 710p. **EI106**

> Added title page: English-Russian electrotechnical dictionary. 2d ed. rev. and enl. by L. B. Heiler and N. J. Dozorov. (Transliteration differs from Library of Congress system as used in entry above.)

U.S. Dept. of the Army. English-Russian, Russian-English electronics dictionary. Wash., 1956. 944p. (Its Technical manual, TM30–545) (Repr.: N.Y., McGraw-Hill, 1958) **EI107**

> Includes some 22,000 Russian terms and abbreviations and some 25,000 English terms. Designed for the English-speaking person needing to use Russian-language publications on electronics and telecommunication.

Handbooks

American electricians' handbook: a reference book for practical electrical workers. 8th ed., ed. by Clifford C. Carr. N.Y., McGraw-Hill, 1961. 1v. [v.p.] il. **EI108**

> Terell Croft, ed., 1913–21.
> Cover title: *Croft's American electricians' handbook.*
> This edition revised and expanded and published in new format.

Creager, William Pitcher and **Justin, J. D.** Hydroelectric handbook. 2d ed. N.Y., Wiley, 1950. 1151p. il. **EI109**

> 1st ed. 1927.
> This edition thoroughly revised and new sections added.

Illuminating Engineering Society. IES lighting handbook; the standard lighting guide. 3d ed. N.Y., Soc., 1959. [v.p.] il. **EI110**

> 1st ed. 1947.

National electrical code handbook. 1st ed.– . N.Y., McGraw-Hill, 1932– . **EI111**

> Editions for 1932– by A. L. Abbott (1954–57 rev. by C. L. Smith; 1960– by F. Stetka).
> 11th edition, 1963, based on the 1962 edition of the National electrical code.

Pender, Harold and **Del Mar, William Arthur.** Electrical engineers' handbook. Prep. by a staff of specialists. 4th ed. N.Y., Wiley, 1949–50. 2v. il. (Wiley engineering handbook ser.) **EI112**

> 3d ed. 1936.

Contents: v.1, Electric power; v.2, Electric communication and electronics, Harold Pender and Knox McIlwain, eds. Each volume complete in itself.

Sams, Howard W. and Company. Handbook of electronic tables and formulas, comp. and ed. by Donald Herrington and Stanley Meacham. [2d ed.] Indianapolis, Sams; Bobbs-Merrill, 1962. 192p. **EI113**

> Covers: Electronics formulas and laws; constants and standards; symbols and codes; service and installation data; design data; mathematical tables and formulas; miscellaneous data.

Standard handbook for electrical engineers, prep. by a staff of specialists; Archer E. Knowlton, ed. in chief. 9th ed. N.Y., McGraw-Hill, 1957. 2230p. il. **EI114**

> 8th ed. 1949.
> This edition thoroughly revised, adding material in the fields of nuclear physics; plastics and resins; electrical measurements; illumination; transportation; transistors; television; etc.

Radio and television

Fink, Donald G. Television engineering handbook, prep. by a staff of specialists. 1st ed. N.Y., McGraw-Hill, 1957. [v.p.] il. **EI115**

> A standard handbook, with bibliographies.

Henney, Keith. Radio engineering handbook. 5th ed. N.Y., McGraw-Hill, 1959. 1v. [v.p.] il. **EI116**

> 1st ed. 1933.

Hughes, Leslie Ernest Charles. Electronic engineer's reference book. 2d ed. London, Heywood, 1959. 1588p. il. **EI117**

> 1st ed. 1958.
> The main body of the work has not been much revised, but additional articles have been added.

International Telephone and Telegraph Corporation. Reference data for radio engineers. 4th ed. N.Y., Corporation, 1956. 1121p. il. **EI118**

> 1st ed. 1943.

Manly, Harold Phillips and **Gorder, L. O.** Drake's Cyclopedia of radio and electronics; a reference and instruction book; 14th ed. Chicago, Drake, 1958. 1v. unpaged. il. **EI119**

> Subtitle: Radio, sound systems, television, photo-electricity, electronic tubes, electronics in industry.
> 1st ed. 1927.

National Association of Radio and Television Broadcasters. NAB engineering handbook. A. Prose Walker, ed. in chief. 5th ed. N.Y., McGraw-Hill, 1960. [v.p.] il. **EI120**

> 1st ed. 1935.
> Treats both radio and television.

Radio amateur's handbook. 1st ed.– . Newington, Conn., Amer. Radio Relay League, 1926– . il. Annual. **EI121**

> Good handbook for the layman, revised annually.
> "Virtually continuous modification is a feature of the *Handbook,* but always with the objective of presenting the soundest aspects of current practice rather than the merely new and novel."—*Foreword.*

Radio Corporation of America. Electron Tube Division. RCA electron tube handbook. HB-3. Harrison, N.J., v.1– . Loose-leaf. **EI122**

> Diagrams, charts, tables.
> Contents: [v.1–2], General, Cathode-ray tube, storage tube, & monoscope section; [v.3–4], Photosensitive device, thyraton, ignitron & glow-discharge tube section; [v.5–6], Receiving tube

section, pt.1; [v.7–8], Receiving tube section, pt.2; v.9–10, Transmitting tube section.

Radio Corporation of America. Semiconductor Division. RCA semiconductor products handbook. Somerville, N.J., 1959– . v.1– . Loose-leaf. **EI123**
Diagrams and tables.

Rider, John Francis. Perpetual trouble shooter's manual. v.1– . N.Y., Rider, 1933– . il. Loose-leaf. **EI124**
Continuously revised.
Each volume arranged alphabetically by manufacturers, giving descriptions of all radios, and current diagrams and parts lists for all radio sets.

—— —— Master index, v.1–15.

—— Television manual. v.1– . N.Y., Rider, 1948– . Loose-leaf. **EI125**
Continuously revised.
Compiled on the same principles as Rider's radio manual listed above.

HEATING, REFRIGERATING, VENTILATING

ASHRAE guide and data book. N.Y., Amer. Soc. of Heating, Refrigerating and Air-conditioning Engineers, 1963–64. 2v. il. **EI126**
1st ed.: v.1, 1961; v.2, 1962.
Subtitle: A *Technical Data Section* of reference material . . . applying to heating, refrigerating, ventilating, and air-conditioning systems . . . ; a *Manufacturers' Catalog Data Section* containing essential and reliable information concerning modern equipment; *Complete indexes* to technical and catalog data sections.
Contents: v.1, Fundamentals and equipment; v.2, Applications.

International Institute of Refrigeration. International dictionary of refrigeration, English-French-German-Russian-Spanish-Italian. Paris, [1961?]. 278p. **EI127**

Johnson, Allen J. and **Auth, George H.** Fuels and combustion handbook. 1st ed. N.Y., McGraw-Hill, 1951. 915p. il. **EI128**

Strock, Clifford. Handbook of air conditioning, heating and ventilating. N.Y., Industrial Pr., 1959. [v.p.] il. **EI129**

INDUSTRIAL ENGINEERING

Brady, George Stuart. Materials handbook: an encyclopedia for purchasing agents, engineers, executives, and foremen. 9th ed. N.Y., McGraw-Hill, [1963]. 968p. il. **EI130**
1st ed. 1929.
For full information *see* CH129.

Ireson, William Grant and **Grant, Eugene L.** Handbook of industrial engineering and management. Englewood Cliffs, N.J., Prentice-Hall, 1955. 1203p. **EI131**

Maynard, Harold Bright. Industrial engineering handbook. 2d ed. N.Y., McGraw-Hill, 1963. [v.p.] il. **EI132**
1st ed. 1956.
Chapters by specialists. Includes bibliographies.
Contains definitions of industrial engineering terms as approved by the American Society of Mechanical Engineers, Sec. 1, p.107–32.

Woodley, Douglas R. Encyclopaedia of materials handling. Oxford, N.Y., Pergamon, 1964. [Distr. in the Western Hemisphere by Macmillan, N.Y.] 2v. il. **EI133**
Editor's preface in English, French, German, Italian, and Classified arrangement with general index and index of tables.

MARINE ENGINEERING

Eddington, Walter J. Glossary of shipbuilding and outfitting terms. N.Y., Cornell Maritime, 1943. 435p. il. **EI134**
A comprehensive dictionary of practical maritime terms by a member of the U.S. Maritime Commission. Includes appendixes giving lists of deck-department, engine-room, and machine tools; tables; and other data.

Kerchove, René de. International maritime dictionary; an encyclopedic dictionary of useful maritime terms and phrases, together with equivalents in French and German. 2d ed. Princeton, N.J., Van Nostrand, 1961. 1018p. il. **EI135**
1st ed. 1948.
A comprehensive dictionary including terms—with clear, concise definitions—relating to seamanship, commercial shipping, maritime law, ship construction, insurance, naval architecture, navigation, meteorology, commercial fisheries, nautical instruments, etc. Describes characteristics of native or local craft from all parts of the world. The 2d edition adds new terms relating to new methods and devices, etc. French and German equivalents are given for most terms, and there are French and German indexes. Occasional bibliographical references.

Labberton, John Madison and **Marks, Lionel S.** Marine engineers' handbook; prep. by a staff of specialists . . . with the general engineering fundamentals reproduced from Mechanical engineers' handbook. 1st ed. N.Y., McGraw-Hill, 1945. 2013p. il. **EI136**

MECHANICAL ENGINEERING

Bibliography

International catalogue of scientific literature: B, Mechanics. 1st–14th annual issues, 1901–14. London, 1902–15. 14v. **EI137**
For full description *see* EA12.

Dictionaries

Audels new mechanical dictionary for technical trades, containing 11,000 definitions of commonly used terms in mechanical trades, physics, chemistry, electricity, etc. N.Y., Audel, 1962. 740p. **EI138**
A general technical dictionary adequate for the layman, probably not for the specialist.

Horner, Joseph Gregory. Dictionary of terms used in the theory and practice of mechanical engineering. 8th ed. rev. and enl. by Staton Abbey. London, Technical Pr., 1960. (Distr. by Heinman, N.Y., 1960) 121p., 417p. **EI139**
7th ed. 1952.
Cover title: Dictionary of mechanical engineering terms.
Contents: pt.1, Dictionary of modern terms; pt.2, Dictionary of general and traditional terms.

Foreign terms

Polyglot

Elsevier's Dictionary of automatic control, in four languages: English/American, French, German, and Russian. Comp. and arr. on an English alphabetical base by W. E. Clason. Amsterdam, Elsevier, 1963. 211p.   **EI140**
Bibliography, p.209–11.

Elsevier's Dictionary of automation, computers, control, and measuring in six languages: English/American, French, Spanish, Italian, Dutch, and German. Comp. and arr. on an English alphabetical base by W. E. Clason. Amsterdam, Elsevier, 1961. (Distr. in U.S. by Van Nostrand, Princeton, N.J.) 848p. (Elsevier's Multilingual dictionaries)   **EI141**
Bibliography, p.847–48.

Russian

Karpovich, Evgenii Antonovich. Russian-English metals & machines dictionary. 1st ed. N.Y., Technical Dictionaries Co., 1960. 112p.   **EI142**
Metallurgy, metals, alloys, metalworking, machines, machine elements, tools, processes, ore beneficiation.

Handbooks

American Society of Mechanical Engineers. Metals Engineering Handbook Board. ASME handbook, ed. by Oscar J. Horger. 1st ed. N.Y., McGraw-Hill, 1953–58. [v.1–4] il.   **EI143**
Contents: *Metals engineering-design,* ed. by Oscar J. Horger. 1953. 405p.; *Metals properties,* ed. by Samuel L. Hoyt. 1954. 433p.; *Engineering tables,* ed. by James Huckert. 1956. [v.p.]; *Metals engineering-processes,* ed. by Roger W. Bolz. 1958. 428p.

American Society of Tool and Manufacturing Engineers. Tool engineers handbook. 2d ed. Frank W. Wilson, ed. in chief. N.Y., McGraw-Hill, 1959. 1v. [v.p.] il.   **EI144**
1st ed. 1949.
Subtitle: A reference book on all phases of planning, control, design, tooling, and operations in the manufacturing industries.

American Welding Society. Welding handbook. 4th ed., ed. by Arthur L. Phillips. N.Y., Soc., 1957–62. il. (In progress)   **EI145**
1st ed. 1938.
v.1, Fundamentals of welding. 1957; v.2, Gas, arc and resistance welding processes. 1958; v.3, Miscellaneous metal joining and cutting processes. 1959; v.4, Metals and their weldability. 1960; v.5, Applications of welding. 1962.

Camm, Frederick James. Newnes engineer's reference book. Rev. by A. T. Collins. 9th ed. London, Newnes, 1960. 2067p. il.   **EI146**
A standard handbook. From the English point of view.

Encyclopedia of engineering materials and processes. Ed. in chief, H. R. Clauser. N.Y., Reinhold, 1963. 787p. il.   **EI147**
Alphabetically arranged by large subject groups.

Flügge, Wilhelm. Handbook of engineering mechanics. 1st ed. N.Y., McGraw-Hill, 1962. [v.p.] il.   **EI148**
Includes bibliographies.

Harris, Cyril M. and **Crede, Charles E.** Shock and vibration handbook. N.Y., McGraw-Hill, 1961. 3v. il. **EI149**

Contents: v.1, Basic theory and measurements; v.2, Data analysis, testing, and methods of control; v.3, Engineering design and environmental conditions.

Kent, William. Mechanical engineer's handbook, prep. by a staff of specialists. 12th ed. N.Y., Wiley, 1950. 2v. il. (Wiley engineering handbook ser.)   **EI150**
1st ed. 1895: *Mechanical engineers pocket-book.*
Contents: v.1, Design and production, ed. by Colin Carmichael; v.2, Power, ed. by J. Kenneth Salisbury.

Le Grand, Rupert. The new American machinists' handbook. Based upon earlier editions of American machinists' handbook, ed. by Fred H. Colvin and Frank A. Stanley. N.Y., McGraw-Hill, 1955. 1v. il.   **EI151**
1st–8th editions of Colvin and Stanley, 1908–45. Now completely revised and rewritten.

Machinery's Handbook for machine shop and drafting-room; a reference book for the mechanical engineer, draftsman, toolmaker and machinist by Erik Oberg and F. D. Jones. 1st ed.– . N.Y., Industrial Pr.; London, Machinery Pub. Co., 1914– . il. (17th ed. 1964) **EI152**
A frequently revised standard handbook.

Mantell, Charles Letnam. Engineering materials handbook. Prep. by a staff of specialists. 1st ed. N.Y., McGraw-Hill, 1958. [v.p.] il.   **EI153**
Chapters prepared by specialists. Include bibliographies.
Deals chiefly with the fabricated form of materials and their physical and mechanical properties.

Marks, Lionel Simeon. Mechanical engineers' handbook, 6th ed. Rev. by a staff of specialists; ed. by Theodore Baumeister. N.Y., McGraw-Hill, 1958. [v.p.] il. **EI154**
Lionel S. Marks, ed., 1916–51.
Follows the general pattern of earlier editions, but all sections have been modernized and the scope expanded. Adds material in such areas as computing machines, nuclear power, aerodynamics, jet propulsion, etc.

Miner, Douglas F. and **Seastone, John B.** Handbook of engineering materials. 1st ed. N.Y., Wiley, 1955. [v.p.] il.   **EI155**
A handbook providing a wide range of information on materials of manufacturing and construction, written by specialists. Includes bibliography.

Morrow, Lester Coridon. Maintenance engineering handbook. 1st ed. N.Y., McGraw-Hill, 1957. [v.p.] il. **EI156**
Chapters prepared by specialists.
Five sections deal with management: (1) Organization and administration of the maintenance forces; (2) Maintenance personnel administration; (3) Planning and scheduling work; (4) Project control; (5) Costs and budgets.
The remainder of the book is devoted to information on the selection, installation, and upkeep of equipment and service.

Staniar, William. Plant engineering handbook, prep. by a staff of specialists. 2d ed. N.Y., McGraw-Hill, 1959. 2007p. il.   **EI157**
1st ed. 1950.
A handbook which supplements the more general engineering reference works. The first of its kind.

Welding design and fabrication data book: welding products and processes; metals and fabricating machinery. Cleveland, Industrial Pub. Co., 1960/61– . [v.p.] **EI158**
Title varies. ?–1958/59, *Welding directory.*
Title on spine and running title: *Welding data book.*
Sec. A, Directory of products, manufacturers; Sec. B, Trade names; Sec. C, Manufacturers' catalogs/outlets; Sec. D, Engineering and application data; Sec. E, Where to buy locally.

MILITARY AND NAVAL ENGINEERING

Bibliography

Albion, Robert Greenhalgh. Naval and maritime history; an annotated bibliography. 3d ed. rev. and expanded. Mystic, Conn., Marine Historical Assoc., 1963. 230p. **EI159**

1st ed. 1951 (issued privately); rev. ed. 1955.

An annotated, classified bibliography with author and brief subject index. Lists primarily books in English. Includes master's and doctor's theses but not periodical articles.

Dictionaries

Gaynor, Frank. The new military and naval dictionary. N.Y., Philosophical Lib., 1951. 295p. il. **EI160**

Brief, nontechnical definitions or descriptions of terms and abbreviations used in the U.S. Army, Navy, and Air Force. Organization charts and sketch maps of command areas are included.

Bibliography, p.291–95.

Krollmann, Friedrich. Langenscheidts Fachwörterbuch: Wehrwesen. Englisch-deutsch; Deutsch-englisch. Berlin, Schöneberg, Langenscheidt, 1957. 769p. (Repr.: N.Y., Philosophical Lib.) **EI161**

Handbooks

Jane's Fighting ships, 1898– . London, S. Low, 1898– . v.1– . Annual. **EI162**

Title varies: 1898–1904, *All the world's fighting ships;* 1905–15, *Fighting ships;* 1916– , *Jane's Fighting ships.*

Pictures, descriptions, and plans of naval ships of all countries.

MINING AND METALLURGICAL ENGINEERING

Guides

Milek, John T. Guide to foreign sources of metallurgical literature. Pittsburgh, Pa., Richard Rimbach Associates, 1951. 95p. **EI163**

Brings up to date, and expands, the material in Rimbach's *How to find metallurgical information,* 1936.

Divided into nine sections, dealing with associations, periodicals, abstract services, standardizing organizations, statistical sources, directors of industries, classified lists of metallurgical books, bibliographies, and abbreviations.

Tapia, Elizabeth W. Guide to metallurgical information. N.Y., Special Libraries Assoc., 1961. 85p. (SLA bibliography, no.3) **EI164**

A project of the Metals Division of the Special Libraries Association, designed to update Richard Rimbach's *How to find metallurgical information,* 1936.

Covers all types of published literature, and agencies and other sources of metallurgical information. International in coverage; the emphasis is on publications issued during the last 20 years.

Bibliography

U.S. Bureau of Mines. List of journal articles by Bureau of Mines authors pub. July 1, 1910, to Jan. 1, 1960, with subject index, comp. by Mae W. Hardison and Opal V. Weaver. Wash., Govt. Prt. Off., 1960. 295p. (Its Special publ.) **EI165**

Lists some 9000 articles on mineral resources and industries, mine safety, and allied fields, published during these 50 years by the personnel of the Bureau in scientific and technical journals, the trade press, and other non-Bureau publications.

—— List of publications issued by the Bureau of Mines from July 1, 1910 to Jan. 1, 1960 with subject and author index, by Hazel J. Stratton. Wash., Govt. Prt. Off., 1960. 826p. (Its Special publ.) **EI166**

Lists more than 7500 titles of "virtually all scientific and technical publications issued by the Bureau of Mines . . . superseding all previous indexes of the Bureau's own publications."—*Foreword.*

1961–63 title varies slightly: *List of . . . publications and articles . . . with subject and author index.*

Dissertations

Hartman, Howard L. Bibliography of theses on mining in U.S. institutions. Golden, Colo., 1956. 70p. (Repr. from Colorado School of Mines quarterly, v.51, no.2, April 1956) **EI167**

Lists theses—master's and doctor's—on mining engineering completed in 23 schools offering graduate degrees from 1876 to about 1955. Arrangement is by subject, followed by a chronological listing under each school and an author index.

Indexes

Crane, Walter Richard. Index of mining engineering literature, comprising an index of mining, metallurgical, civil, mechanical, electrical and chemical engineering subjects as related to mining engineering. N.Y., Wiley, 1909–12. 2v. **EI168**

Covers American and English material with some Australian and Canadian works, including periodicals, society transactions, and some government reports. v.1 indexes 18 publications covering 30 years to the end of 1907; v.2 brings up to date the periodicals indexed in that volume and indexes several additional titles, giving complete indexing for 26 periodicals and incomplete indexing for 20 other serials and 20 books. Classified arrangement with alphabetical index by subjects. No author indexes.

Abstract journals

American Society for Metals. Documentation Service. ASM review of metal literature: abstracts of the world's scientific, engineering and technical literature concerned with the production, properties, fabrication and applications of metals, their alloys and compounds. v.1– . 1944– . Metals Park, Ohio, 1945– . Monthly. **EI169**

Subtitle varies.

Through 1964, cumulated into annual volumes with separate indexes.

Changed format and classification notation with 1965. "Based on the decision to make RML completely compatible with and parallel to two new monthly abstract journals to be published by *Engineering Index* . . . in the fields of plastics and electrical and electronics engineering . . . will use interchangeable computer programs for generation of subject and author indexes."—[*Pref.*].

Metallurgical abstracts (general and non-ferrous). n.s. v.1– . London, Inst. of Metals, 1934– . Monthly. **EI170**

1931–33, issued monthly as a supplement to the *Journal of the Institute of Metals.* A classified abstracting service of material in all languages. Titles of foreign articles are translated into English.

Dictionaries

Fay, Albert Hill. Glossary of the mining and mineral industry. Wash., Govt. Prt. Off., 1920. 754p. (U.S. Bureau of Mines. Bull. 95) Repr. without change, 1947. **EI171**

Contains about 20,000 terms, including technical and purely local terms relating to metal mining, coal mining, quarrying, petroleum, natural gas, and metallurgical works; names of minerals and rocks and geological terms; many terms relating to ceramics and the clay industry, glass making, foundry practice, railway and building construction, etc.; and chemical terms relating to metallurgical practice. Definitions are given with sufficient fullness, with reference to authorities, and, in case of local terms, indication of the place where used.

Henderson, J. G. and **Bates, J. M.** Metallurgical dictionary. N.Y., Reinhold, 1953. 396p. **EI172**

Intended for the professional and the layman; tries "to assemble in a concise, orderly and comprehensive manner . . . definitions of those terms considered essential . . . in understanding the metallurgical literature . . . "—*Pref.* More than 5000 definitions, taken from many sources in the field. The first work of its kind.

Merlub-Sobel, Menahem. Metals and alloys dictionary. . . . Brooklyn, N.Y., Chemical Pub. Co., 1944. 238p. **EI173**

Brief definitions of metallurgical terms mainly relating to American practice. Includes composition, properties, and uses of commercial alloys. Intended for the layman as well as for the technologist.

Merriman, Arthur Douglas. A dictionary of metallurgy. London, Macdonald and Evans, 1958. 401p. il. **EI174**

An alphabetically arranged dictionary of terms for those primarily interested in the fabrication and use of metals.

Osborne, A. K. An encyclopaedia of the iron and steel industry. London, Technical Pr., 1956. 558p. **EI175**

A dictionary of terms with definitions and explanations, and with references to the literature.
Bibliography, p.478–509.

Rolfe, Robert Thatcher. Dictionary of metallography. London, Chapman & Hall, 1945. 242p. **EI176**

Fewer terms and longer definitions than Merlub-Sobel (EI173). From the English point of view.

Foreign terms

German

Seebach, Hans Jobst von. Fachwörterbuch für Bergbautechnik und Bergbauwirtschaft. Dictionary for mining engineering and economics. Essen, Glückauf, 1947. 311p. **EI177**

Pt.1, German-English; pt.2, English-German.

Singer, Tibor Eric Robert. German-English dictionary of metallurgy. 1st ed. N.Y., McGraw-Hill, 1945. 298p. **EI178**

Subtitle: With related material on ores, mining and minerals, crystallography, welding, metal-working, tools, metal products, and metal chemistry.

Russian

Deruguine, Tanya. Russian-English dictionary of metallurgy and allied sciences. N.Y., Ungar, [1962]. 470p. **EI179**

MacAndrew, Andrew R. A glossary of Russian technical terms used in metallurgy. N.Y., Varangian Pr., 1953. 127p. **EI180**

Compiled at Columbia University under contract with the National Science Foundation. "Copyright assigned to the Director of the National Science Foundation."

Directories

Directory, iron and steel plants. 1916– . Pittsburgh, Steel Publ., 1916– . **EI181**

Subtitle, 1964: List of companies and officials operating blast furnaces, steel plants, rolling mills, by-product coking plants, structural steel plants, boiler and tank shops in the United States, Canada and miscellaneous foreign countries.
Title varies.

Mines register. N.Y., Mines Register, 1900– . v.1– . **EI182**

Title varies.
v.26, 1962/63: "Limited to active mining companies in North, South and Central America and the West Indies, the Philippines and other parts of the world producing precious, semi-precious, and non-ferrous metals." Includes a list of inactive mining companies.

Mining year book, incorporating the Mining manual. v.1– . London, Skinner, 1887– . **EI183**

78th year, 1964.
Title varies.
Records mining and mining-finance companies throughout the world with a buyers' guide.

Standard metal directory. 11th ed. 1948/49. N.Y., Standard Metal Directory, 1949. 999p. **EI184**

1st ed. 1915.
Lists iron and steel plants, foundries, metal rolling mills, metal smelters and refiners, steel rolling mills, scrap-iron and metal dealers, etc. Frequently revised.

Handbooks

American Foundrymen's Society. Cast metals handbook. 4th ed. Des Plaines, Ill., 1957. 316p. il. **EI185**

1st ed. 1935.
Includes bibliographies.

American Institute of Mining, Metallurgical, and Petroleum Engineers. Committee on Industrial Minerals Volume. Industrial minerals and rocks (non-metallics other than fuels). Joseph L. Gillson, ed. in chief. 3d ed. compl. rev. N.Y., 1960. 934p. il. (Seeley W. Mudd ser.) **EI186**

1st ed. 1937; 2d ed. 1949.
Chapters on the various minerals are written by specialists. With tables and maps, and often extensive bibliographies.

Quin's Metal handbook. London, Metal Information Bureau, 1914– . v.1– . **EI187**

49th ed. 1964.
Title varies.
"A comprehensive statistical survey of the world's ores, non-ferrous metals, iron and steel and scrap industries."—*Foreword.*

Hampel, Clifford A. Rare metals handbook. 2d ed. N.Y., Reinhold, 1961. 715p. il. **EI188**

1st ed. 1954.
This edition has been enlarged to include 55 metals. Each chapter includes a substantial bibliography.

Hoyt, Samuel L. Metal data. Rev. ed. of Metals and alloys data book. N.Y., Reinhold, 1952. 526p. il. **EI189**

Metals and alloys data book, 1943.
Contains 565 tables of properties and data on wrought and cast steels, stainless steel, cast irons, heat- and corrosion-

resistant casting alloys, and nonferrous alloys. Designed especially for metallurgists, industrial designers, and others working with metals.

Liddell, Donald Macy. Handbook of non-ferrous metallurgy, prep. by a staff of specialists. 2d ed. N.Y., McGraw-Hill, 1945. 2v. il. **EI190**

v.1, Principles and processes; v.2, Recovery of the metals.

Metals handbook. 8th ed. Novelty, Ohio, Amer. Soc. for Metals, 1961–64. v.1–2. (In progress) **EI191**

To be in 5v.

Contents: v.1, Properties and selection of metals; v.2, Heat treating, cleaning and finishing.

Peele, Robert and **Church, John A.** Mining engineers' handbook, written by a staff of forty-six specialists . . . 3d ed. N.Y., Wiley, 1941. 2v. il. (Wiley engineering handbook ser.) **EI192**

1st ed. 1918.

The standard handbook for mining engineers. This edition has been thoroughly revised and several sections completely rewritten, noting new methods and equipment. Includes bibliographies.

Smithells, Colin James. Metals reference book. 3d ed. London, Butterworth, 1962. 2v. (1057p.) **EI193**

1st ed. 1949.

Includes bibliographies.

Steel Founders' Society of America. Steel castings handbook. 3d ed., ed. by Charles W. Briggs. Cleveland, Ohio, 1960. 670p. il. **EI194**

2d ed. 1950.

This edition thoroughly revised and rewritten.

Taggart, Arthur F. Handbook of mineral dressing; ores and industrial minerals. N.Y., Wiley, 1945. [1926p.] il. **EI195**

Supersedes the author's *Handbook of ore dressing* (1927).

"Deals with the processes, largely mechanical, involved in the concentration of metalliferous ores and the beneficiation of industrial minerals."—*Pref.*

Uhlig, Herbert Henry. The corrosion handbook; . . . sponsored by the Electrochemical Society, Inc. N.Y., Wiley, 1948. 1188p. il. **EI196**

Woldman, Norman Emme. Engineering alloys. 4th ed. N.Y., Reinhold, 1962. 1354p. **EI197**

1st ed. 1936; 3d ed. 1954.

Lists 35,439 proprietary commercial and technical alloys manufactured in the United States and many alloys made in foreign countries, including England, France, Germany, and Sweden; gives alloy trade names, composition, properties, uses, and key numbers designating the manufacturer. A directory of manufacturers, a key index, etc.

Statistics

Metal statistics. N.Y., Amer. Metal Mart, 1908– . v.1– . Annual. **EI198**

57th ed. 1964.

Statistics of various metals in the countries of the world, including production, shipment, prices, etc.

NUCLEAR ENGINEERING

Bibliography

International Atomic Energy Agency. List of bibliographies on nuclear energy. Vienna, 1960– . v.1– . Biennial (?). **EI199**

v.2, 1962, contains 880 references to bibliographies published or in preparation in English, French, German, Russian, and other languages.

A classified list with author indexes.

—— List of references on nuclear energy. Vienna, 1959– . v.1– . Semimonthly. Annual indexes. **EI200**

Published semimonthly in English, with titles in original languages.

"It answers bibliographical details of recently published scientific and technical literature dealing with the peaceful aspects of nuclear energy and the nuclear sciences in general, covering in particular books, research reports and other documents purchased by the Agency or received as gifts from the Member States."—*Foreword.*

U.S. Atomic Energy Commission. Bibliographies of interest to the atomic energy program, [comp. by James M. Jacobs and others]. Rev. 2. Oak Ridge, Tenn., Commission, Division of Technical Information, 1962. 295p. (Its TID-3043, rev. 2) **EI201**

Supersedes its TID-3043 (rev. 1), May 1958, and its two supplements, 1959 and 1961.

An annotated bibliography arranged by issuing organization, with author, subject, and report number indexes.

Abstract journals

U.S. Atomic Energy Commission. Nuclear science abstracts. Wash., Govt. Prt. Off., 1948– . v.1– . Semimonthly. **EI202**

Title and frequency vary.

Subject, author, and cumulative report indexes cumulate annually, and multivolume indexes are also available: v.1–4, 1948–50; v.5–10, 1951–56; v.11–15, 1957–61.

Titles translated into English. Abstracts in English.

—— Subject scope and literature coverage of Nuclear science abstracts. Oak Ridge, Tenn., 1960. 56p. (Its TID-4552 [2d rev.]) **EI203**

1955 and 1958 editions had title *Guide to coverage and scope of Nuclear science abstracts.*

A brief guide to the scientific and technical matter included or reviewed for abstracting in *NSA.*

Dictionaries

National Research Council Conference on Glossary of Terms in Nuclear Science and Technology. A glossary of terms in nuclear science and technology. N.Y., Amer. Soc. of Mechanical Engineers, 1957. 188p. **EI204**

Preliminary edition published as *Glossary of nuclear energy terms.* 1950–52.

United Nations. Terminology Section. Atomic energy: glossary of technical terms. [4th ed.] N.Y., 1958. 215p. (U.N. Publ. Sales no.58. ix. 1) **EI205**

Title and introductory material in English, French, Spanish, and Russian. English terms are used as the base, with equivalents in French, Spanish, and Russian arranged horizontally across the page. Indexes in each language refer to the main listing.

Polyglot

Elsevier's Dictionary of nuclear science and technology; in six languages: English/American, French, Spanish, Italian, Dutch, and German. Comp. and arr. on an English alphabetical base by W. E. Clason. Amsterdam, Elsevier, 1958. (Distr. in U.S. by Van Nostrand) 914p. (Elsevier's Multilingual dictionaries) **EI206**

—— Russian supplement to Elsevier's Dictionary of nuclear science and technology, by W. E. Clason. Amsterdam, N.Y., Elsevier, 1961. 98p.

The Russian index refers by number to the English base in the main dictionary.

Russian

Consultants Bureau Enterprises, N.Y. Russian-English glossary of nuclear physics and engineering. N.Y., 1957. 195p. **EI207**

"This glossary incorporates all terms of the *Russian-English Dictionary of Nuclear Physics and Engineering* by N. N. Ershov; Y. V. Semenov, and A. I. Cherny . . . pub. by the Institute of Scientific Information of the Academy of Sciences of the USSR. More than 2000 additional terms have been added."—*Title page.*

Karpovich, Eugene A. Russian-English atomic dictionary. 2d rev. and enriched ed. N.Y., Technical Dictionaries Co., 1959. 317p. **EI208**

Contains more than 23,000 Russian terms, primarily in nuclear science and technology; physics; and mathematics and allied fields.

Handbooks

Etherington, Harold. Nuclear engineering handbook. 1st ed. N.Y., McGraw-Hill, 1958. [v.p.] il. **EI209**

Chapters by specialists.

Frisch, Otto Robert. The nuclear handbook. With 22 specialist contributors. London, Newnes; Princeton, N.J., Van Nostrand, 1958. [v.p.] il. **EI210**

Reactor handbook. Prep. under contract with the United States Atomic Energy Commission. 2d ed. rev. and enl. N.Y., Interscience, 1960–64. 4v. il. **EI211**

1st ed. 1955.

Contents: v.1, Materials, ed. by C. R. Tyston, Jr.; v.2, Fuel processing, ed. by S. M. Stoller and R. B. Richards; v.3A, Physics, ed. by H. Soodak; v.3B, Shielding, ed. by E. P. Blizard and L. S. Abbott; v.4, Engineering, ed. by Stuart McLain and J. H. Martens.

Chapters by specialists. Includes bibliography.

PETROLEUM ENGINEERING

Bibliography

Agout, Marthe. Bibliographie des libres, thèses et conférences relatifs à l'industrie du pétrole. [Paris, Gauthier-Villars], 1949. 322p. il. **EI212**

A comprehensive, classified bibliography of 6408 numbered items, based on the holdings of about 15 libraries and covering approximately 100 years from the start of the commercial development of petroleum in the mid-19th century. Scope is international; locations are given wherever possible; and sources of reference are indicated for items not seen. Subject and author indexes.

DeGolyer, Everette Lee and **Vance, Harold.** Bibliography on the petroleum industry. College Station, Tex., 1944. 730p. il. (School of Engineering. Texas Engineering Experiment Station. Bull. no.83) **EI213**

Combines a bibliography of some 12,000 items, compiled by Dr. DeGolyer, with the bibliography of the Petroleum Engineering Dept. at the A. & M. College of Texas, and a bibliography on the Air-Gas Lift prepared by S. F. Shaw. Arranged by a decimal system of classification devised by Prof. L. C. Uren of the University of California, with an alphabetical subject index.

Giddens, Paul H. The beginnings of the petroleum industry: sources and bibliography. Harrisburg, Pa., Pa. Historical Commission, 1941. 195p. **EI214**

"Bibliography on the beginnings of the petroleum industry to 1871," p.87–172.

Swanson, Edward Benjamin. A century of oil and gas in books: a descriptive bibliography. N.Y., Appleton, 1960. 214p. **EI215**

An annotated bibliography of books and monographs published in English from the mid-19th century to Aug. 1959. Author index.

Indexes

Petroleum literature index. Amarillo, Tex., Nat. Petroleum Bibliography, 1956– . v.1– . Annual. **EI216**

Title varies: v.1–3, *National petroleum bibliography* (pub. bimonthly).

With v.4 (covering 1959 literature), attempts "to classify . . . the books, technical articles and papers, news articles, maps, and miscellaneous data, of the domestic petroleum press . . . [with] references of foreign and non-petroleum industry origin."

Topical arrangement; author and subject indexes.

Special Libraries Association. Petroleum Section. Committee on U.S. Sources of Petroleum and Natural Gas Statistics. U.S. sources of petroleum and natural gas statistics, comp. by Margaret M. Rocq. N.Y., 1961. 94p. **EI217**

An updated expansion of Bradford A. Osborne's *An index to American petroleum statistics,* 1943.

Indexes 231 publications which provide currently released statistical data.

Dictionaries

Boone, Lalia Phipps. The petroleum dictionary. Norman, Univ. of Okla. Pr., 1952. 338p. **EI218**

Bibliography, p.333–38.

Gives definitions and sources of about 6000 terms used in the oil industry, especially its colorful language. The dictionary is preceded by a general introduction (p.3–37) to the language of the oil field.

Porter, Hollis Paine. Petroleum dictionary for office, field and factory. 4th ed. Houston, Tex., Gulf Pub. Co., 1948. 326p. **EI219**

1st ed. 1930.

An enlarged edition of a standard work, now giving definitions for some 4600 terms dealing with the prospecting, producing, and refining of petroleum.

Foreign terms

Kedrinskii, Vsevolod Vladimirovich. Anglo-russkii slovar' po khimii i pererabotke nefti. Leningrad, Gos. Nauchno-Tekhnicheskoe Izd., 1962. 910p. **EI220**

English-Russian.

Kolster, T. A. Technical dictionary; English-Spanish, Spanish-English. Caracas, Venezuela, [1950]. 207p. 187p. **EI221**

Subtitle: Containing more than 25,000 geolical [sic], engineering, legal and accounting words, terms and expressions, common to the Petroleum industry, and 800 abbreviations.

Abbreviations (p.179–87) are given from the complete word to the abbreviation for English words and terms only.

Handbooks

American Petroleum Institute. Petroleum facts and figures. N.Y., Inst., 1928– . v.1– . Irregular. **EI222**

The 1959 Centennial edition, which gives the statistical history of the petroleum industry from its beginnings, supersedes all earlier editions. The 1963 edition covers five years, supplementing the Centennial edition and superseding the 1961 supplement.

Guthrie, Virgil B. Petroleum products handbook. 1st ed. N.Y., McGraw-Hill, 1960. 1v. [v.p.] il. **EI223**

Moody, Graham B. Petroleum exploration handbook. 1st ed. N.Y., McGraw-Hill, 1961. 1v. [v.p.] il. **EI224**

Subtitle: A practical manual summarizing the application of earth sciences to petroleum exploration.

Oil and petroleum yearbook. v.1– . 1910– . London, Walter E. Skinner, 1910– . Annual. **EI225**

A world-wide directory of petroleum companies.

E J

Medical Sciences

Medical reference books often present a difficult problem in the general library because (1) they are expensive; (2) they are often so technical that they can be used intelligently only by the physician or medical student; and (3) when placed in a general collection, they are sometimes misused by certain types of readers. It is therefore important to buy only the books which are actually needed, and unless the library is maintaining a special medical reference collection, to concentrate mainly on the biographical, bibliographical, and historical reference books on this subject.

The titles listed here have been chosen with the general research library rather than with the medical library in mind. For other titles consult the *Handbook of medical library practice*, p.337–537 (EJ1).

MEDICINE

Guides

Medical Library Association. Handbook of medical library practice, with a bibliography of the reference works and histories in medicine and the allied sciences. 2d ed., rev. and enl. Janet Doe [and] Mary Louise Marshall, eds. Chicago, Amer. Lib. Assoc., 1956. 601p. **EJ1**

1st ed. 1943.

An indispensable handbook. Chapters are by medical library specialists and discuss the various phases of work in medical libraries, especially as they differ from those of other libraries. This edition thoroughly revised. It now covers: Medical libraries; The Medical Library Association; The medical librarian; Administration; Acquisition and preservation; Classification; Cataloging; Non-book materials; Photoduplication; Public relations; Reference and bibliographic service; Rare books and the history of medicine. "A bibliography of the reference works and histories in medicine and the allied sciences," p.337–537, is arranged by subject, subdivided by form, and will be of importance in the general library as well as in the special medical library.

3d edition is in preparation.

Morton, Leslie Taylor. How to use a medical library; a guide for practitioners, research workers and students. 4th ed. London, Heinemann, 1964. 66p. **EJ2**

1st ed. 1934; 3d ed. 1957.

A practical, short survey, with chapters on the medical library, bibliographical sources, etc., abstracting services, and a list of the principal medical libraries in Britain, with brief descriptions.

Postell, William Dosite. Applied medical bibliography for students. Springfield, Ill., Thomas, 1955. 142p. (American Lecture Series. Publ. no.259) **EJ3**

An introductory handbook for students, dealing with historical bibliography; modern bibliography, including medical library usage; reference materials, etc.; and bibliographical methods.

U.S. National Library of Medicine. Basic reference aids for small medical libraries. Rev. by Elizabeth Moseley and Miriam Hawkins. Wash., U.S. Public Health Service, 1963. 15p. **EJ4**

Selected primarily for the small medical library; titles are chiefly in English. Arrangement is by type of material, and the most essential items are starred.

Bibliography

Brodman, Estelle. The development of medical bibliography. Baltimore, Medical Lib. Assoc., 1954. 226p. il. (Medical Library Assoc. Publ. 1) **EJ5**

A comprehensive survey of medical bibliography since 1500, with histories and descriptions of the older bibliographies.

Appendix II comprises a bibliography of 250 medical bibliographies since 1500, arranged chronologically by centuries (p.194–211).

Gilbert, Judson Bennett. Disease and destiny: a bibliography of medical references to the famous . . . with additions and an introd. by Gordon E. Mestler. London, Dawsons of Pall Mall, 1962. 535p. **EJ6**

A listing of "medical and scientific writings, drawn principally from the periodical literature, relating to personalities whose names are considered 'great' in history, the humanities, the arts and sciences." International in scope; lists personalities from ancient Egypt, Greece, and the Bible down to modern times. Each subject is identified by dates of birth and death and a brief descriptive phrase, followed by a chronological listing of references to medical articles.

Hawkins, Reginald Robert. Scientific, medical, and technical books published in the United States of America; a selected list. Wash., 1958– . **EJ7**

For full description *see* EA11.

New York Academy of Medicine. Library. Illustration catalog. Boston, G. K. Hall, 1960. 200p. **EJ8**

A photographic reproduction of an index to illustrative material in medical works, early as well as recent. Arranged by subject.

—— Portrait catalog. Boston, G. K. Hall, 1960. 5v. (4564p.). **EJ9**

A photographic reproduction of the catalog cards listing the 10,784 separate portraits—paintings, woodcuts, engravings, photographs—in the Academy and 151,792 entries of portraits appearing in books and journals.

Pearsall, Marion. Medical behavioral science: a selected bibliography of cultural anthropology, social psychology, and sociology in medicine. Lexington, Univ. of Kentucky Pr., 1963. 134p. **EJ10**

Cites monographs and articles by cultural and social anthropologists, sociologists, and social psychologists only, dealing with health and medical practice. Almost entirely devoted to English-language titles.

U.S. Dept. of Commerce. Office of Technical Services. Bibliography of medical translations, Jan. 1959–June 1962. Bethesda, Md., U.S. Public Health Service, 1962. 278p., I–71p.   **EJ11**

At head of title: National Library of Medicine.

Republishes the translation listings which were included in *Technical translations* (EA30) and its predecessor, *Bibliography of translations* (*see* EA29), under medical and allied headings.

Arranged alphabetically by author, with an index by the original journal title and a patent number index.

Kept to date by quarterly supplements, July 1962– .

U.S. National Library of Medicine. Early American medical imprints; a guide to works printed in the United States, 1668–1820, by Robert B. Austin. Wash., U.S. Dept. of Health, Education, and Welfare. Public Health Service, 1961. 240p.   **EJ12**

An alphabetical listing of more than 2100 separately published items, with full bibliographic information and many annotations. Library holdings are indicated. Appendixes include a chronological index and a list of Evans' *American bibliography* items (AA333) which, though seemingly relevant, are not included.

✓ —— Index-catalogue of the library of the Surgeon General's Office, United States Army (Army Medical Library), authors and subjects. Ser. 1–4, v.1–11. Wash., Govt. Prt. Off., 1880–1955. 58v.   **EJ13**

Ser. 1, A–Z. 1880–95. 16v.; ser. 2, A–Z. 1896–1915. 21v.; ser. 3, A–Z. 1918–32. 10v.; ser. 4, v.1–11, A–Mn. 1936–55.

A dictionary catalog, including not only books and pamphlets but also a large number of references to periodical articles and other analytics. The National Library of Medicine (formerly the Surgeon General's Library, and the Army Medical Library) is one of the largest medical libraries of the world, and this monumental catalog is, therefore, a very important bibliography of all aspects of the subject. One of its special uses is for medical biography, as it indexes a large number of biographical and obituary articles.

—— —— 5th ser., 1959–61. 3v.

U.S. Dept. of Health, Education, and Welfare. Public Health Service.

Contents: v.1, Authors and titles. 1959; v.2–3, Subjects. 1961.

No more to be published.

These are the final volumes of the *Index-catalogue,* and are published as a supplementary series to include selected monographic material from the unpublished files of the *Index-catalogue* covering the 19th and first half of the 20th centuries. After a screening of these files, some 83,000 entries were selected, consisting of monographic imprints for 1950 or earlier and including "theses, project reports, monographic and series analytics, equipment and supply catalogs, legislative issuances and biobibliographical reference works."—*Pref.*

—— Catalog, 1948– . Wash., Lib. of Congress, 1949– . Annual, with quinquennial cumulations, beginning 1950/54.   **EJ14**

April/Dec. 1948 issue was published in the 1948 cumulative catalog of the Library of Congress as a continuously paged supplement but with separate title page. Also issued separately as v.1 of this catalog.

Title varies: 1948, *Catalog cards;* 1949–50, *Author catalog.*

Library name varies: 1948–51, U.S. Army Medical Library; 1952–55, U.S. Armed Forces Medical Library.

1950/54, 1955/59, quinquennial issues.

Films

American Medical Association. Medical and surgical mo-

tion pictures: a catalog of selected films. Chicago, 1964. 366p.   **EJ15**

A catalog of medical films classified mainly according to the *Standard nomenclature of diseases and operations* (EJ57), with full description of films, a title index, and a distributor index.

Film reference guide for medicine and allied sciences. 1956– . Wash., Lib. of Congress, 1956– . Semiannual, 1956–57; Annual, 1958– .   **EJ16**

Earlier editions by a variety of governmental departments; now planned by the Federal Advisory Council on Medical Training Aids.

Arranged by subject with title index; lists films currently available for medical education for borrowing or rental. Does not list those which are for sale only.

Incunabula

Klebs, Arnold Clark. Incunabula scientifica et medica; short title list. Bruges, Belgium, St. Catherine Pr., 1938 [i.e., 1937]. 359p. (History of medicine ser., issued under the auspices of the New York Academy of Medicine)   **EJ17**

Reprinted from *Osiris,* v.4.

U.S. National Library of Medicine. A catalogue of incunabula and manuscripts in the Army Medical Library, by Dorothy M. Schullian and Francis E. Sommer. N.Y., pub. for the honorary consultants to the Army Medical Library by Henry Schuman, [1948?]. 361p. il.   **EJ18**

Pt.1: Lists 490 incunabula, with full bibliographical descriptions and citations to listings in other bibliographies, and about 35 early Western manuscripts; pt.2: Describes some 137 oriental manuscripts.

Wellcome Historical Medical Museum. London. Library. A catalogue of printed books in the Wellcome Historical Medical Library. London, 1962– . v.1– . (Publications . . . catalogue ser. PBI, 1962) (In progress)   **EJ19**

Contents: v.1, Books printed before 1641.

Almost 7000 titles arranged by author, with indexes by place of publication and by printer and publisher. Includes a concordance for English books with the *S.T.C.* number (*see* AA498).

Periodicals

Biological abstracts. List of serials with word abbreviations. (In Biological abstracts, July 1 issue) Annual.   **EJ20**

A comprehensive listing of biological periodicals from more than 90 countries (*see* EC7, EC8).

Index medicus. List of journals indexed. (In Index medicus, Jan. issue) Annual, with monthly supplements, Feb.–Nov.   **EJ21**

For full information *see* EJ30.

Medical Library Association. Vital notes on medical periodicals. v.1, no.1– . Chicago, Assoc., 1952– . 3 times a year.   **EJ22**

The first issue (Oct. 1952) was arranged by births and deaths of periodicals under specific fields; subsequent issues are arranged alphabetically by title, giving address, birth or death date, frequency, and sometimes price.

U.S. National Library of Medicine. Biomedical serials, 1950–1960; a selective list of serials in the National Library of Medicine, comp. by Lela M. Spanier. Wash., 1962. 503p. (Public Health Service. Publ. no.910)   **EJ23**

Lists 8939 serials, giving title, place of publication, beginning date, and frequency.

World medical periodicals. Les périodiques médicaux dans le monde. Periódicos médicos del mundo. Medizinische Zeitschriften aller Länder. 3d ed. N.Y., World Medical Assoc., 1961. 407p. **EJ24**

1st ed. 1953; 2d ed. 1957.

"3d ed. prep. by C. H. A. Fleurent . . . under the general editorship of H. A. Clegg."

The 3d edition includes the titles of more than 5800 periodicals relating to medicine, pharmacy, dentistry, and veterinary medicine, as well as to hospital buildings, administration, and equipment.

Gives for each periodical: address, frequency, language, and the *World list* (EA42) abbreviation of the title.

Abbreviations

See also Periodicals—Abbreviations, p.530–31.

Periodica medica: Titelabkurzungen medizinischer Zeitschriften. 4. neubearb. und erweit. Aufl. von Walter Artelt, Edith Heischkel, Carl Wehmer. Stuttgart, Georg Thieme Verlag, 1952. 280p. **EJ25**

1st ed. 1928.

Added title page in English: Periodica medica; abbreviated titles of medical periodicals.

A listing of world medical periodicals with recommended abbreviations.

The 4th edition includes only medical titles, omitting the general scientific periodicals included in earlier editions.

Indexes

Index medicus, a . . . classified index of the current medical literature of the world. v.1–21, Jan. 1879–April 1899; 2d ser. v.1–18, 1903–20; 3d ser. v.1–6, 1921–June 1927. N.Y., Boston, and Wash., 1879–1927. **EJ26**

The 1st series ceased publication with April 1899; was revived by the Carnegie Institution of Washington in Jan. 1903. During the interval a similar index, *Bibliographia medica* (*Index medicus*), was published by the Institut de Bibliographie of Paris.

From 1879 to 1927 the *Index* was a standard current bibliography of medicine—a classified list with annual author and subject index. Covers publications in all principal languages and includes periodical articles and other analytical material as well as books, pamphlets, and theses. Ser. 1–2, published monthly; ser. 3, quarterly.

Discontinued June 1927, and merged in the *Quarterly cumulative index medicus* (EJ28).

Quarterly cumulative index to current medical literature, 1916–26. Chicago, Amer. Medical Assoc., 1917–27. 12v. **EJ27**

An important author and subject index to medical periodicals and society transactions, including foreign material. Each annual volume includes, in addition to the index to periodicals, a bibliography of the important new medical books of the year, exclusive of new editions, and a list of government documents on medical subjects.

In 1926, two semiannual volumes were issued instead of one annual.

Continued by:

Quarterly cumulative index medicus. 1927–1956. Chicago, Amer. Medical Assoc., 1927–56. 60v. Quarterly, with semiannual cumulations. **EJ28**

An author and subject index to some 1200 periodicals in many languages, forming a fairly comprehensive general index to the journal literature. Includes medical biography.

Includes lists of new books published during the period.

Continued by:

Current list of medical literature, v.19–36. Wash., Army Medical Lib., 1950–59. Monthly. **EJ29**

1941–49, issued as a weekly.

Beginning with v.19, July–Dec. 1950, published in a greatly expanded form, analyzing nearly 1500 journals. The journals are listed alphabetically, and items are numbered. Author and subject index in each issue, and a cumulative index for each volume.

Index medicus. Wash., Nat. Lib. of Medicine, 1960– . n.s. v.1– . Monthly. **EJ30**

Cumulates annually into the *Cumulated index medicus* (EJ32).

Each issue is in two sections: (1) subjects, and (2) names. In the alphabetical *Subject* section are given: title of English-language article or translation of non-English-language title; author; journal-title abbreviation, with volume, inclusive paging, and date, and an abbreviation indicating the original language of a non-English article. In the *Name* section are given authors' names (up to three) and names of biographees. Under authors, titles are given in the vernacular except for some of the lesser-known languages.

A comprehensive index to the world's medical literature, now compiled by mechanized means and representing a partial printout of MEDLARS (Medical Literature Analysis and Retrieval System).

Several thousand periodicals are indexed, either completely or selectively, and in 1965, significant changes were made in the *List of journals indexed.* Some were dropped—especially house organs, general science periodicals, etc.—and others added, viz., journals in the fields of biometry, botany, chemistry, entomology, physics, psychology, sociology, veterinary medicine, and zoology.

—— List of journals indexed. (In the Jan. issue of *Index medicus,* with supplements in the monthly issues Feb.–Nov.)

A list of several thousand journals (1) by abbreviation, and (2) by full title.

—— Recent United States publications. (In each monthly issue)

Complete catalog entries for monographic and serial titles imprinted in the United States.

—— Bibliography of medical reviews.

For information *see* EJ36.

—— Medical subject headings. Main headings and cross references used in Index medicus and National Library of Medicine catalog, 1961– . v.1– . Annual. (Pt.2 of the Jan. issue of Index medicus) **EJ31**

Has three basic applications, serving as (1) the subject-heading authority list for the indexing of the biomedical periodical literature in *Index medicus* and the MEDLARS computer; (2) the authority list for the catalog of the National Library of Medicine; and (3) the key to the use of *Index medicus* and the machine search of the citations in the MEDLARS computer.

The 1965 edition added new subject headings, especially in the new fields included, e.g., dentistry, but also in other categories.

All cross references appear in this list and not in the *Index medicus,* and therefore the two must be used in close conjunction. The Categorized lists, which group related subject headings by broad subject areas, are also only here, and aid in determining the most appropriate headings for a particular need.

The user of the *Index* should familiarize himself with this list of subject headings and should consult the list for the year he is searching, to determine what headings were used at that time.

Cumulated index medicus, 1960– . Chicago, Amer. Medical Assoc., 1961– . v.1– . Annual. **EJ32**

v.1–2 each issued in three parts: pt.1, Author index; pts.2–3, Subject index.

The cumulation of the *Index medicus* (EJ30).

Reuss, Jeremias David. Repertorium commentationum a societatibus litterariis editarum. Secundum disciplinarum ordinem . . . T.10–16, Scientia et ars medica et chirurgica. Gottingae, Dieterich, 1813–21.   **EJ33**

Contents: T.10, Propaedeutica, anatomia et physiologia, hygiene, pathologia seu nosologia generalis, semeiotica; T.11, Materia medica, pharmacia; T.12–15, Therapia generalis et specialis, A–Z; Operationes chirurgicae, Medicina forensis, legalis et politica; T.16, Ars obstetricia, Ars veterinaria.

A very valuable index to the contents of the publications of the learned societies of various countries before 1800. Classed arrangement with author indexes for each section.

For description of complete set *see* EA15.

Cumulative index of hospital literature, 1945–1949, 1950–1954, 1955–1959. Chicago, Amer. Hospital Assoc., 1950–61. 3v.   **EJ34**

Prepared by the Library of the American Hospital Association, Asa S. Bacon Memorial.

5-year cumulations of the semiannual *Hospital literature.* Authors and subjects in one alphabet. Indexes 300–400 journals in the hospital and related fields. Continued by:

Hospital literature index, June 1955– . Chicago, Amer. Hospital Assoc., 1955– . Quarterly.   **EJ35**

Title varies.

From 1945 to 1961, published semiannually with 5-year cumulations; 1962– , issued quarterly with annual and 5-year cumulations.

An author-subject index to articles in periodicals about hospitals, etc.

Reviews

Bibliography of medical reviews, v.6, 1955/1960– . Wash., Nat. Lib. of Medicine, 1961– . Annual. **EJ36**

v.6 is a cumulation, 1955 through 1960, superseding the annual volumes previously published.

Each volume includes references to review articles in thousands of journals in many languages, some of them regularly indexed in the *Index medicus,* but others not. Subject arrangement with name index.

From March 1965 on, will appear monthly in each issue of *Index medicus* and will then cumulate annually as a separate volume.

Abstract journals

Bibliography

U.S. Library of Congress. Science and Technology Division. A guide to the world's abstracting and indexing services in science and technology. Wash., 1963. 183p. (National Federation of Science Abstracting and Indexing Services. Report no.102)   **EJ37**

For full information *see* EA62.

Journals

See also Pure and Applied Sciences—Abstract Journals, p.531–32.

Abstracts of world medicine. London, British Medical Assoc., 1947– . v.1– . Monthly.   **EJ38**

A monthly critical survey of periodicals in medicine and its allied sciences. Titles are given in English translation and in original language. Semiannual author and subject indexes.

Excerpta medica; the international medical abstracting

service. Amsterdam, Excerpta Medica, 1947– . Monthly.   **EJ39**

An important abstracting service listing articles from medical journals in all countries. Article titles are given in English translation and sometimes in the original language. Monthly issues are published for each section, with annual author and subject indexes.

Section titles vary somewhat.

Sec. 1, Anatomy, anthropology, embryology and histology, v.1, Oct. 1947– ; Sec. 2, Physiology, biochemistry and pharmacology, v.1, Jan. 1948– ; Sec. 3, Endocrinology, v.1, Aug. 1947– ; Sec. 4, Medical microbiology, immunology and serology, v.1, Jan. 1948– ; Sec. 5, General pathology and pathological anatomy, v.1, July 1948– ; Sec. 6, Internal medicine, v.1, Oct. 1947– ; Sec. 7, Pediatrics, v.1, Oct. 1947– ; Sec. 8, Neurology and psychiatry, v.1, Jan. 1948– ; Sec. 9, Surgery, v.1, Sept. 1947– ; Sec. 9B, Orthopaedics and traumatology, v.1, 1956– ; Sec. 10, Obstetrics and gynaecology, v.1, Jan. 1948– ; Sec. 11, Oto- , rhino- , laryngology, v.1, Jan. 1948– ; Sec. 12, Ophthalmology, v.1, Nov. 1947– ; Sec. 13, Dermatology and venereology, v.1, April 1947– ; Sec. 14, Radiology, v.1, June 1947– ; Sec. 15, Chest diseases, v.1, Jan. 1948– ; Sec. 16, Cancer, v.1, 1953– ; Sec. 17, Public health, social medicine and hygiene, v.1, 1955– (for earlier listings, *see* Sec. 4); Sec. 18, Cardiovascular diseases, v.1, Jan. 1957– ; Sec. 19, Rehabilitation and physical medicine, v.1, July 1958– ; Sec. 20, Gerontology and geriatrics, v.1, July 1958– ; Sec. 21, Human developmental biology and teratology, v.1, 1961– ; Sec. 22, Human genetics, v.1, 1962– ; Sec. 23, Nuclear medicine, v.1, 1964– .

Hospital abstracts: a monthly survey of world literature, prep. by the Ministry of Health. London, Stat. Off., 1961– . v.1– . Monthly.   **EJ40**

"Aims to cover the whole field of hospitals and their administration, with the exception of strictly medical and related professional matters."—*Note.*

Classified arrangement. Annual author and subject indexes.

International abstracts of biological sciences. London, Pergamon, for Biological and Medical Abstracts, 1954– . v.1– . Monthly.   **EJ41**

v.1–3 entitled *British abstracts of medical sciences,* 1954–56.

Subtitle: A comprehensive survey of world literature.

Coverage varies: 1965, anatomy, animal behavior, biochemistry, cytology, experimental botany, experimental zoology, genetics, immunology and experimental pathology, microbiology, odontology, pharmacology, and physiology.

Titles of articles are translated into English.

Meditsinskii referativnyi zhurnal. Moskva, Medgiz, 1960– .   **EJ42**

The Russian abstract journal for books and articles on medicine—Soviet and foreign.

Now published in 13 sections (1957–59 in 4 sections).

Titles of articles in Cyrillic alphabets are followed by English translations. Other citations are given in the original language when in the Latin alphabet; for non-Latin alphabets, language and country of origin are indicated. Annual author and subject indexes for each section.

Tropical diseases bulletin. London, Bureau of Hygiene and Tropical Diseases, 1912– . v.1– . Monthly. **EJ43**

Abstracting journal dealing with the various aspects of tropical diseases, published as a complement to the *Bulletin of hygiene.*

U.S. Library of Congress. Science and Technology Division. Aerospace medicine and biology, continuing bibliography. Wash., 1952– . Quarterly.   **EJ44**

Frequency varies.

Title varies: 1952–53, Aviation medicine. Subtitle varies.

Subtitle 1964: Continuing bibliography, selection of annotated references to unclassified reports and journal articles that were formerly announced in NASA information system . . .

An abstract journal, world-wide in scope. Titles are given both in the original and in English translation.

Dictionaries

Black's Medical dictionary, by William R. Thompson. 25th ed. London, Black, 1963. 1013p. il. **EJ45**

1st ed. 1906.
A standard dictionary of English terminology.
Each edition includes some new terms and revisions.

Blakiston's New Gould medical dictionary, ed. by Normand L. Hoerr, Arthur Osol [and others]. 2d ed. N.Y., Blakiston, 1956. 1463p. il. **EJ46**

1st ed. 1949.
A newly organized dictionary based on Gould's *Medical dictionary* (5 editions, 1926–41) and its predecessors, published with varying titles in 1890, 1894, and 1904.
Subtitle: A modern comprehensive dictionary of the terms used in all branches of medicine and allied sciences, including medical physics and chemistry, dentistry, pharmacy, nursing, veterinary medicine, zoology and botany, as well as medicolegal terms: with illustrations and tables.

Dorland's Illustrated medical dictionary. 23d ed. Philadelphia, London, Saunders, 1957. 1598p. il. **EJ47**

1st ed. 1900.
"With more than 700 illustrations and 50 plates."
Including *Modern drugs and dosage,* by Austin Smith, [and] *Fundamentals of medical etymology,* by Lloyd W. Daly.
A standard dictionary, frequently revised.

MacNalty, *Sir* **Arthur Salusbury.** The British medical dictionary. [Rev. ed.] London, Caxton; Philadelphia, Lippincott, 1963. 1682p. **EJ48**

1st ed. 1961.
Produced in collaboration with more than 100 specialist contributors.
A new dictionary, including new terms introduced in recent years.

Schmidt, Jacob Edward. Reversicon: a medical word finder. Springfield, Ill., Thomas, 1958. 440p. **EJ49**

"The *Reversicon* is intended to supply, with respect to medical vocabulary, a tool or the means for finding a particular word on the basis of its meaning or the concept it expresses . . . a 'reversed' dictionary which lists meanings, concepts, ideas, and thoughts—not *words*—in alphabetical order. The word follows the meaning."—*Introd.*

Stedman, Thomas Lathrop. Medical dictionary. Consulting eds.: Isaac Asimov [and others]. 20th ed. Baltimore, Williams and Wilkins, 1961. 1680p. il. **EJ50**

1st ed., 1911, *A practical medical dictionary.*
A standard work.
Subtitle: A vocabulary of medicine and its allied sciences, with pronunciations and derivations.

Taber, Clarence Wilbur. Taber's Cyclopedic medical dictionary. 9th ed. Philadelphia, Davis, 1962. [v.p.] il. **EJ51**

Subtitle: A digest of medical subjects: medicine, surgery, nursing, dietetics, physical therapy, treatment, drugs.
A combination dictionary-encyclopedia.

Foreign terms

For lists of dictionaries of medical terms in other languages, *see Handbook of medical library practice,* p.406–12 (EJ1), and its supplement, by Elizabeth G. Moseley, "Medical dictionaries and studies of terminology," in the Medical Library Association *Bulletin* 49:374–95. July 1961.

Polyglot

Elsevier's Medical dictionary in five languages: English/ American, French, Italian, Spanish, and German. Comp. and arr. on an English alphabetical base by A. Sliosberg. Amsterdam, Elsevier, 1964. 1588p. **EJ52**

Veillon, E. Medizinisches Wörterbuch. Medical dictionary. Dictionnaire médical. . . . Bern, Verlag Hans Huber, 1950. 476p., 496p., 435p. **EJ53**

Separate sections—from each of the three languages (German, English, French) into the other two.

Abbreviations

Michigan Occupational Therapy Association. Special Studies Committee. Medical abbreviations: a cross reference dictionary. Ann Arbor, 1961. 241p. **EJ54**

Pt.1, Abbreviations; pt.2, Cross reference.
Pt.2 lists the words followed by the abbreviations.

Peyser, Alfred. Pars pro toto; breviarium medicum internationale. Stockholm, Almquist & Wiksell, [1950]. 196p. **EJ55**

Nearly 5000 abbreviations used in medical and allied fields, in German, Danish, English, Spanish, French, Italian, Latin, and Swedish. Includes names of associations and periodical titles.

Handbooks

Mettler, Frederick Albert. The medical sourcebook; a reference handbook for legal, legislative, and administrative personnel. [1st ed.] Boston, Little, 1960. 1000p. il. **EJ56**

"This book deals . . . with those aspects of three sciences—anatomy, physiology and pathology—which are of particular importance in the law and to legislators, administrative officers of agencies, compensation boards and insurance companies and to newspapermen."—*Pref.*
Appendix: A guide to the activities, personnel, literature and societies in the basic sciences and clinical fields of medicine.

National Conference on Medical Nomenclature. Standard nomenclature of diseases and operations. 5th ed. Ed. by Edward T. Thompson and Adaline C. Hayden. Pub. for the American Medical Association. N.Y., Blakiston, 1961. 964p. il. **EJ57**

1st ed. 1932; 4th ed. 1952.
Diseases arranged by an etiologic classification, with a disease index and an operations index.

Shartel, Burke and **Plant, Marcus L.** The law of medical practice. Springfield, Ill., Thomas, [1959]. 445p. **EJ58**

Based on lectures given at the University of Michigan Medical School; outlines the legal questions, and their solutions, in which the medical practitioner may become involved. Documented with footnotes. Includes bibliographies at end of chapters, and index.

Facts on the major killing and crippling diseases in the United States today. N.Y., Nat. Health Educ. Committee, 1964?– . il., charts. Annual. **EJ59**

A handbook of facts and statistics consisting of separately paged sections on each disease, e.g., 1964: arteriosclerosis, cancer, mental illness, mental retardation, etc.

Style manuals

Davidson, Henry Alexander. Guide to medical writing; a practical manual for physicians, dentists, nurses, pharmacists. N.Y., Ronald, 1957. 338p. il. **EJ60**

An introductory manual on the writing and preparation of medical books and articles.

Fishbein, Morris. Medical writing, the technic and the art. 3d ed. N.Y., McGraw-Hill, Blakiston Division, 1957. 262p.   **EJ61**

A standard manual in a revised edition.

Directories

International

Council for International Organizations of Medical Sciences. Bibliography of international congresses of medical sciences . . . prep. by W. J. Bishop . . . with the financial assistance of UNESCO. Oxford, Blackwell; Springfield, Ill., Thomas, 1958. 238p.   **EJ62**

Title and prefatory material in English and French.

Gives details of 1427 international congresses dealing with 362 subjects in medicine and closely related fields.

Under subject, lists the congresses in chronological order, giving place and dates, titles of proceedings, etc., with full bibliographical information.

—— Directory. [3d ed.] Paris, 1961. 192p.   **EJ63**

1st ed. 1953.

Author and title also in French.

Lists member organizations, giving address, date of founding, membership, publications, and associate members.

World directory of medical schools. 3d ed. Geneva, World Health Organization, 1963. 348p.   **EJ64**

1st ed. 1953; 2d ed. 1957.

This edition lists medical schools in 87 countries and gives information about each.

United States

American hospital directory. 1945– . [Chicago], Amer. Hospital Assoc., [1945–]. Annual.   **EJ65**

Pub. as pt.2 of the Aug. issue of *Hospitals.*

A geographical listing of civilian hospitals, allied schools, and organizations in the United States and Canada; United States government hospitals outside the United States; and other inpatient care institutions. Includes information about the American Hospital Association; related groups and associations; and hospital statistics.

American medical directory. Chicago, Amer. Medical Assoc., 1906– . v.1– . Biennial.   **EJ66**

Subtitle varies. 1964: A register of physicians of the United States, Isthmian Canal Zone, Puerto Rico, Virgin Islands, certain Pacific Islands, and U.S. physicians located temporarily in foreign countries, who possess a degree of doctor of medicine from an approved medical school or from a bona fide medical school.

List of physicians and hospitals arranged geographically.

Association of American Medical Colleges. Medical school admission requirements U.S.A. and Canada. 1951– . Evanston, Ill., Assoc., 1951– . Annual. **EJ67**

Contains information on premedical education; choosing a medical school; and program of each medical school in the United States, Canada, Puerto Rico, and the American University of Beirut.

Directory of approved internships and residences. 1961– . [Chicago], Amer. Medical Assoc., Council on Medical Education and Hospitals, 1961– . Annual. (Repr.: Education number of the Journal of the American Medical Assoc. Annual)   **EJ68**

List of approved hospitals, arranged by states, with information on graduate medical education in the United States.

Medical Library Association. Directory. 2d ed. Hamden, Conn., Shoe String, 1959. 274p.   **EJ69**

1st ed. 1950.

Describes 552 medical libraries, members of the association.

For full information *see* AB34.

Canada

Canadian medical directory, 1955– , comp. from the Daily Medical Service Bulletins. Toronto, Seccombe House, 1955– . Annual.   **EJ70**

Contains information similar to that found in the Canadian portions of the *American medical directory*. Lists: all qualified Canadian physicians, alphabetically, giving name, address, school, etc.; physicians and hospitals, by province and city; medical schools; nursing schools; medical journals, etc.

Great Britain

Hospitals year-book, 1931– ; an annual record of the hospitals of Great Britain and Ireland incorporating "Burdett's Hospitals and charities" founded 1889. London, British Hospital Assoc., 1931– . v.1– . Annual. **EJ71**

Publisher varies.

Contains directory, technical, and general information for the hospital administrator, including legal notes, and the National Health Service Acts, 1946–61.

Medical directory, 1845– . London, Churchill, 1845– . Annual.   **EJ72**

Title varies.

Lists registered practitioners in London, the provinces, Wales, Scotland, Ireland, abroad, navy, army, and air force, giving brief biographical sketches. Includes lists of universities, colleges, medical schools, hospitals with staffs, associations, etc.

Medical register, printed and pub. under the direction of the General Medical Council . . . comprising the names and addresses of medical practitioners. . . . London, pub. for the General Medical Council by Constable, 1859– . Annual.   **EJ73**

Subtitle varies.

Brief directory information only, consisting of address, date and place of registration, qualifications. Includes names from the Commonwealth and foreign lists.

Union of Soviet Socialist Republics

U.S. National Institutes of Health. Division of Research Services. Scientific Reports Branch. A directory of medical and biological research institutes of the USSR, comp. by David P. Gelfand. Wash., 1958. 340p. (U.S. Public Health Service. Publ. no.587)   **EJ74**

A preliminary edition was issued in 1957. "Not merely . . . an address list . . . but more essentially . . . a general guide in the study of the organization, scope, and geographic distribution of research facilities in the medical and biological sciences in the USSR." Contains subject and name indexes. Main arrangement is geographical.

History

Bibliography

Bibliography of the history of medicine of the United States and Canada, 1939–1960. Ed. by Genevieve Miller. Baltimore, Johns Hopkins Pr., 1964. 428p.   **EJ75**

A consolidation of the annual bibliographies reprinted from the *Bulletin of the history of medicine*, covering the years 1939 through 1960. Classified arrangement, author index. A section, "Biography," p.1–126, lists books and periodical articles about persons under the names of the biographees.

—— 1961– . Annual.

Current work in the history of medicine: an international bibliography. London, Wellcome Historical Medical Lib., 1954– . v.1– . Quarterly. **EJ76**

A quarterly index of articles on the history of medicine, arranged by subject, with an author index in each issue.

Garrison, Fielding Hudson. Garrison and Morton's Medical bibliography. An annotated checklist of texts illustrating the history of medicine, by Leslie T. Morton. 2d ed. rev. and enl. N.Y., Argosy Bookstore; London, Grafton, 1954. 655p. **EJ77**

1st ed. 1943.

A classified bibliography of almost 7000 books and periodical articles in various languages and of all periods from ancient times to the present.

Guerra, Francisco. American medical bibliography, 1639–1783. N.Y., Lathrop C. Harper, 1962. 885p. facsims. **EJ78**

Subtitle: A chronological catalogue, and critical and bibliographical study of books, pamphlets, broadsides, and articles in periodical publications relating to the medical sciences —medicine, surgery, pharmacy, dentistry, and veterinary medicine—printed in the present territory of the United States of America during British dominion and the Revolutionary War.

Gives very detailed bibliographic information and locates copies.

Osler, Sir William. Bibliotheca Osleriana; a catalogue of books illustrating the history of medicine and science, collected, arranged and annotated by Sir William Osler . . . bequeathed to McGill University. Oxford, Clarendon Pr., 1929. 785p. **EJ79**

Particularly valuable for its annotations.

Historical surveys

Castiglioni, Arturo. A history of medicine, tr. from the Italian and ed. by E. B. Krumbhaar. 2d ed. rev. and enl. N.Y., Knopf, 1947. 1192p. il. **EJ80**

Bibliography, p.1147–92.

Does not supersede Garrison (EJ81), but serves to supplement it. Comprehensive and readable. Includes useful bibliography arranged by subject.

Garrison, Fielding Hudson. Introduction to the history of medicine, with medical chronology, suggestions for study and bibliographic data. 4th ed. rev. and enl. Philadelphia, Saunders, 1929. 996p. il. (Repr. 1960) **EJ81**

The most valuable reference history in English, covering the whole history of medicine from the earliest times to the 1920's. Much biography and bibliography are included for every period. Appendixes contain: chronology of medicine, bibliographies of medical biography, general medical histories, and histories of special subjects in medicine.

Packard, Francis Randolph. History of medicine in the United States. 103 illustrations. N.Y., Hoeber, 1931. 2v. (1323p.). il. (Repr.: N.Y., Hafner, 1963. 2v.) **EJ82**

An enlargement of the author's earlier work (1901). Contains much useful reference material, in both text and illustrations, on American medical history, biography, and bibliography. Gives a bibliography of pre-Revolutionary medical publications, p.489–512, and a general bibliography, p.1241–66.

Biography

Bibliography

Thornton, John L., Monk, Audrey J. and **Brooke, Elaine S.** A select bibliography of medical biography. London, Lib. Assoc., 1961. 112p. il. **EJ83**

Contains books in English published in the 19th and 20th centuries. Includes collective biography and individual biography.

International

Bailey, Hamilton and **Bishop, W. J.** Notable names in medicine and surgery. 3d ed. London, H. K. Lewis, 1959. 216p. il. **EJ84**

Biographical sketches of men whose names are associated with particular diseases or other medical discoveries, e.g., Pott's disease, Thomas's splint.

Biographisches Lexikon der hervorragenden Ärzte aller Zeiten und Völker, unter Mitwirkung [von] E. Albert . . . A. Anagnostakis [u.A.] und unter Spezial-Redaktion von E. Gurlt und A. Wernich, hrsg. von August Hirsch. 2. Aufl. durchgesehen und ergänzt von F. Hübotter und H. Vierordt. Berlin, Urban, 1929–35. 5v. and Ergänzungsband. portraits. (Repr.: Berlin, Urban, 1962) **EJ85**

A very valuable medical biographical dictionary, international in scope, covering physicians who had reached maturity before 1880.

Includes biographical facts, bibliography of works by, and sometimes bibliographical references for further information.

The *Ergänzungsband* includes corrections and additions to the main set.

To a large extent replaces its own first edition published 1884–88, and the *Biographisches Lexikon hervorragender Ärzte des neunzehnten Jahrhunderts* by Julius Leopold Pagel (Berlin, 1901), though occasionally these are useful for material omitted in the 2d edition.

Continued by:

Biographisches Lexikon der hervorragenden Ärzte der letzten 50 Jahre, hrsg. u. bearb. von I. Fischer . . . Zugleich Fortsetzung des Biographischen Lexikons der hervorragenden Ärzte aller Zeiten u. Völker. Berlin, Urban, 1932–33. 2v. (Repr.: Berlin, Urban, 1962) **EJ86**

Serves as a continuation of the preceding set, covering the period from 1880 to 1930. Similar in scope, though the articles are somewhat briefer.

New York Academy of Medicine. Library. Catalog of biographies. Boston, G. K. Hall, 1960. 165p. **EJ87**

A photographic reproduction of the library's shelf list, containing "single biographies of physicians and scientists, with a few autobiographies, family histories and occasional biographies written by physicians."—*Introd.*

Nobelstiftelsen, Stockholm. Physiology or medicine. Amsterdam, N.Y., Elsevier, 1964– . v.3– . (In progress) **EJ88**

v.3 covers 1942–62.

v.1–2—to include earlier years—are to follow.

At head of title: Nobel lectures including presentation speeches and laureates' biographies.

Stevenson, Lloyd G. Nobel prize winners in medicine and physiology, 1901–1950. N.Y., Henry Schuman, 1953. 291p. **EJ89**

Contains short biographical sketch of each prize winner, followed by a description of his prize discovery and an explanation of its meaning and importance.

American

American men of medicine. 3d ed. Farmingdale, N.Y., Inst. for Research in Biography, [c1961]. 768p. **EJ90**

1st ed. 1945; 2d ed. 1952.

Title varies: eds. 1–2, *Who's important in medicine.*

A biographical encyclopedia of physicians, surgeons, medical educators, and hospital administrators, containing some 10,000 sketches. Includes the United States and Canada with some representation from Latin-American republics.

Directory of medical specialists, holding certification by American specialty boards including latest listings, sketch additions and alphabetical index. Chicago, pub. for the Advisory Board for Medical Specialties by Marquis, 1963. 2169p. **EJ91**

1st ed. 1939. Now published biennially.

This edition lists approximately 78,000 specialists certified prior to July, 1962 by the 19 specialty boards.

Contents: "(1) a separate grouping for each of the American Boards, arranged geographically, with the sketches of the Diplomates then placed alphabetically under the localities; and (2) one over-all alphabetical index to all Diplomates." —*Introd.*

Kelly, Howard Atwood and **Burrage, Walter L.** Dictionary of American medical biography. N.Y., Appleton, 1928. 1364p. **EJ92**

Published in 1912 as *Cyclopedia of American medical biography,* and in 1920 as *American medical biographies.*

Good biographies, with bibliographies, of 2049 deceased American physicians and surgeons from colonial days to 1927. Although each edition includes new biographical sketches, some material is dropped from each, and therefore the earlier editions may still be useful.

British

Munk, William. Roll of the Royal College of Physicians of London; comprising biographical sketches of all the eminent physicians, whose names are recorded in the annals from the foundation of the College in 1518 to its removal in 1825 from Warwick Lane to Pall Mall East. 2d ed. rev. and enl. London, pub. by the College, 1878. 3v. **EJ93**

Continued by:

——— Lives of the Fellows of the Royal College of Physicians of London, 1826–1925. Comp. by G. H. Brown. London, Royal College of Physicians, 1955. 637p. **EJ94**

Contains short biographies of 874 Fellows elected between 1826 and 1925 who died before Jan. 1, 1954.

Plarr, Victor Gustave. Lives of the Fellows of the Royal College of Surgeons of England, rev. by Sir D'Arcy Power. Bristol, Royal College; London, Simpkin, Marshall, 1930. 2v. **EJ95**

Covers lives of the Fellows from 1843, founding date of the fellowship, to those who died before 1930.

Power, Sir D'Arcy and **Le Fanu, William Richard.** Lives of the Fellows of the Royal College of Surgeons of England, 1930–1951. London, College, 1953. 889p. **EJ96**

Continues the record by listing the biographies of the Fellows who died from 1930 to the end of 1951. Includes lists of publications.

DENTISTRY

Bibliography

New York Academy of Medicine. Library. Dental bibliography; index to the literature of dental science and art as found in the libraries of the New York Academy of Medicine, and Bernhard Wolf Weinberger, comp. by B. W. Weinberger. 2d ed. [N.Y.], First District Dental Soc., State of N.Y., [c1929–32]. 2v. **EJ97**

Contents: [pt.1], A reference index; pt.2, A subject index, with additional reference index.

Periodicals

Schmidt, Hans Joachim. Index der zahnärztlichen Zeitschriften der Welt. Stuttgart-Degerloch, Verlag der Deut-

schen Dokumentenstelle für Zahnärztliches Schrifttum, 1962. 125p. **EJ98**

Title and introductory material also in French, English, Spanish, Italian, and Polish.

"Covers 1255 dental periodicals from 58 countries showing the full title, publisher's address and the abbreviated title. Both current and lapsed periodicals are listed."

Indexes and abstract journals

Black, Arthur Davenport. Index of the periodical dental literature published in the English language, 1839–1936/8. Buffalo, Dental Index Bureau; Chicago, Amer. Dental Assoc., 1921–39. 15v. **EJ99**

Volumes unnumbered and not issued in regular chronological sequence.

Contents: 1839–75. 1923; 1876–85. 1925; 1886–90. 1926; 1891–95. 1927; 1896–1900. 1930; 1901–05. 1931; 1906–10. 1934; 1911–15. 1921; 1916–20. 1922; 1921–23. 1928; 1924–26. 1929; 1927–29. 1932; 1930–32. 1936; 1933–35. 1938; 1936–38. 1939.

Each volume is in two parts: (1) a classified subject index arranged by an extension of the Dewey Decimal Classification, and (2) an author index.

Continued by:

Index to dental literature. 1939–   . v.1–   . Chicago, Amer. Dental Assoc., 1943–   . Quarterly, with annual cumulations. **EJ100**

Frequency varies. Title varies: *Index to dental literature in the English language . . .* , 1939–61; *Index to dental literature,* 1962–   .

An author and subject index to dental periodical literature. Beginning with 1962, includes periodicals in foreign languages. Contains list of dental books.

Dental abstracts, v.1–6, Jan. 1945—Sept./Dec. 1950. N.Y., Columbia Univ., School of Dental and Oral Surgery, Dental Abstracts Soc., 1945–1950. **EJ101**

A few numbers of an earlier series were issued Dec. 1941–March 1943.

Dental abstracts: a selection of world dental literature. Chicago, Amer. Dental Assoc., 1956–   . v.1–   . Monthly. **EJ102**

Fairly long abstracts in English of articles from the periodicals of the world. Titles are translated into English, and original title is given. Includes lists of doctoral and master's theses. Annual subject and author indexes.

Dictionaries

Boucher, Carl O. Current clinical dental terminology, a glossary of accepted terms in all disciplines of dentistry. St. Louis, Mosby, 1963. 501p. **EJ103**

The work of 52 contributors, specialists in their fields; gives meanings of several thousand terms.

Directories

American dental directory. [Chicago], Amer. Dental Assoc., 1947–   . v.1–   . Annual. **EJ104**

American dentists arranged by state and city with an alphabetical index. Gives address, specialization, and dental school with year of graduation.

Dentists register. no.1–   . 1879–   . London, General Dental Council, 1879–   . Annual. **EJ105**

Comprises the names and addresses of registered dental practitioners arranged in three alphabetical lists: (1) United Kingdom list, (2) Commonwealth list, and (3) foreign list. Includes Dentists Act, 1957.

World directory of dental schools. [1st ed.] Geneva, World Health Organization, 1961. 228p. **EJ106**

Gives details of dental educational systems and lists dental teaching institutions in some 70 countries, arranged alphabetically. Includes state requirements for practice.

History

Guerini, Vincenzo. A history of dentistry from the most ancient times until the end of the eighteenth century. Philadelphia, Lea & Febiger, 1909. 355p. il. portraits.
EJ107

Published under the auspices of the National Dental Association of the United States of America.

A classic work in its field, well documented by footnotes to sources. Includes name and subject index.

Weinberger, Bernhard Wolf. An introduction to the history of dentistry, with medical and dental chronology and bibliographic data. St. Louis, Mosby, 1948. 2v. il. **EJ108**

v.2 has title *An introduction to the history of dentistry in America.*

NURSING

Indexes

Cumulative index to nursing literature, ed. by Ella J. Crandall and Kumiko Oiue. Glendale, Calif., Seventh Day Adventist Hospital Assoc., 1961– . v.1/5– .
EJ109

v.1/5, 1956/60, is a collection in 1v. of five previously unpublished annual volumes, indexing, by author and subject, 17 journals.

v.6–8, 1961/63, is a cumulation in one alphabet indexing 46 journals.

1964– , quarterly, with annual indexes.

Nursing studies index. Prep. by Yale University School of Nursing Index Staff under the direction of Virginia Henderson. Philadelphia, Lippincott, 1963– . v.4– . **EJ110**

v.1–3, 1900–1956, in preparation; v.4, 1957–1959.

Subtitle: An annotated guide to reported studies, research in progress, research methods and historical materials, in periodicals, books, and pamphlets published in English.

A subject arrangement with author index.

Encyclopedias and handbooks

Encyclopedia of nursing, prep. under the editorial supervision of Lucile Petry. Philadelphia, Saunders, [1952]. 1011p. **EJ111**

An alphabetically arranged encyclopedia of scientific terms used in nursing practice.

Facts about nursing. 1935– . N.Y., Amer. Nurses' Assoc., 1935– . Annual. **EJ112**

A statistical summary and basic data source book.

Hansen, Helen F. Encyclopedic guide to nursing. N.Y., McGraw-Hill, Blakiston Division, 1957. 406p. il. **EJ113**

Alphabetically arranged. Gives "brief discussions on principles of nursing care and therapy; explanations of techniques and procedures; definitions of technical terms . . . and some information of historical interest."—*Pref.*

History

Stewart, Isabel Maitland and **Austin, Anne L.** A history of nursing from ancient to modern times. 5th ed. N.Y., Putnam, [1962]. 516p. il. **EJ114**

1st edition, 1920, had title *A short history of nursing.*

In two parts: pt.1 sketches the history of nursing from ancient to modern times; pt.2 consists of chapters on nursing today in various countries throughout the world. In addition to the general bibliography each chapter contains a selected bibliography. Subject and name index.

NUTRITION

Bibliography

Baker, Edward Alan and **Foskett, D. J.** Bibliography of food; a select international bibliography of nutrition, food, and beverage technology and distribution, 1936–56. London, Butterworth; N.Y., Academic Pr., 1958. 331p.
EJ115

Classified arrangement with author and subject indexes. Under each large category lists, as appropriate: directories, bibliographies, abstracting journals, periodicals, books, and organizations.

Aims to include "most of the significant books and pamphlets on nutrition, food economics and food technology published in the English language together with a representative selection of material from most foreign sources."—*Introd.*

Bitting, Katherine Golden. Gastronomic bibliography. San Francisco, Calif., priv. pr., 1939. 718p. il. **EJ116**

For full information *see* EK50.

Abstract journals

Nutrition abstracts and reviews, issued under the direction of the Commonwealth Agricultural Bureaux Council, the Medical Research Council, and the Reid Library. Aberdeen, Scot., Commonwealth Bureau of Animal Nutrition, 1931– . v.1– . Quarterly, with annual combined table of contents and author and subject indexes.
EJ117

Titles are given in original language and in English translation. Signed abstracts in English.

Dictionaries and handbooks

Bender, Arnold E. Dictionary of nutrition and food technology. N.Y., Academic Pr., 1960. 143p. **EJ118**

A compilation of terms commonly used in discussions of foods, with definitions. Includes references to publications giving more detailed information.

Goodhart, Robert S. and **Wohl, Michael G.** Manual of clinical nutrition. Philadelphia, Lea & Febiger, 1964. 279p. il. **EJ119**

A brief manual with much of the material in outline form. Contains useful tables.

National Research Council. Food and Nutrition Board. Recommended dietary allowances. 6th rev. ed. Wash., Nat. Academy of Sciences—Nat. Research Council, 1964. 59p. il. (National Research Council Publ. 1146) **EJ120**

1st ed. 1943.

Gives tables of recommended allowances and discussion of specific nutrients.

Wohl, Michael Gershon and **Goodhart, Robert S.** Modern nutrition in health and disease; dietotherapy. 3d ed. Philadelphia, Lea & Febiger, 1964. 1282p. il. **EJ121**

1st ed. 1955.

A standard text by 62 authorities providing up-to-date information on normal nutrition, nutrition in the prevention of disease, and nutrition in the care of the sick. Each chapter includes a bibliography.

PHARMACOLOGY

Bibliography

U.S. National Library of Medicine. Drug literature; a factual survey on "the nature and magnitude of drug literature." . . . Wash., Govt. Prt. Off., 1963. 171p. **EJ122**

A report prepared for the study of "Interagency coordination in drug research and regulation" by the Subcommittee on Reorganization and International Organizations of the Senate Committee on Government Operations.

Includes: selected list of monographs on pharmacy; world list of pharmacy periodicals; composite list of journals of pharmaceutical interest; drug information sources, a world list.

Abstract journals

International pharmaceutical abstracts. 1964– . Wash., Amer. Soc. of Hospital Pharmacists, v.1, no.1– . Jan. 15, 1964– . Semimonthly. **EJ123**

Abstracts in English of more than 400 pharmaceutical journals. International in coverage. Author and subject index, issued quarterly and annually.

Dictionaries

Hocking, George Macdonald. A dictionary of terms in pharmacognosy and other divisions of economic botany. Springfield, Ill., Thomas, [1955]. 284p. il. **EJ124**

Subtitle: A compilation of words and expressions relating principally to natural medicinal and pharmaceutical materials and the plants and animals from which they are derived, their chemical composition, applications, and uses . . . .

Steinbichler, Eveline. Steinbichler's Lexikon für die Apothekenpraxis in sieben Sprachen. Frankfurt/Main, Govi-Verlag G.M.B.H.-Pharmazeutischer Verlag, [1963]. 474p. **EJ125**

A listing of pharmaceutical terms in seven languages: German, English, French, Spanish, Italian, Greek, and Russian. Arranged in five sections, one for each of the languages in the Roman alphabet, giving equivalent terms in the other six languages. Does not include definitions.

Dispensatories and pharmacopoeias

American drug index, [1956]– . Philadelphia, Lippincott, 1956– . Annual. **EJ126**

A listing of pharmaceuticals by generic, brand, and chemical name in alphabetical arrangement with information as to manufacturer, forms, size, dosage, and use.

Includes list of drug manufacturers.

American druggist blue book. 34th, 1963/64. N.Y., Amer. Druggist, 1963. 639p. il. Annual. **EJ127**

Drug products with prices, listed alphabetically by trade name and manufacturer. 1963/64 issue includes a list of pharmaceutical associations, a list of colleges of pharmacy, an alphabetical list of drug manufacturers, and a classified list of drugstore-equipment manufacturers.

American Pharmaceutical Association. The national formulary. 11th ed. National formulary N.F. XI, prep. by the Committee on National Formulary under the supervision of the Council, by authority of the American Pharmaceutical Association. Official from Oct. 1, 1960. Wash., Assoc., 1960. (Distr. by Lippincott, Philadelphia) 531p. **EJ128**

1st ed. 1888. Revised every 5 years since 1950.

An official compendium of reference standards, assays, and formulations of basic drugs. Arranged alphabetically by basic drug with specifications for official preparations.

Dispensatory of the United States of America. 25th ed. by Arthur Osol and George E. Farrer . . . Based on the 15th revision of the United States Pharmacopoeia, the 10th ed. of the National formulary, the British Pharmacopoeia, 1953, the 1st ed. of the International Pharmacopoeia, v.1–2. Philadelphia, Lippincott, 1955–60. 2v. **EJ129**

1st ed., 1833, edited by George Bacon Wood.

v.1, in 2 pts.: pt.1, drugs officially recognized; pt.2, drugs not officially recognized. 1955. 2139p.; v.2 has title *New drug developments.* Ed. by Arthur Osol and Robertson Pratt. 1960. 240p.

Drugs are listed alphabetically with detailed description, giving tests, standards, usage, etc.

Modern drug encyclopedia and therapeutic index, ed. by Robert S. Goodhart. 10th ed. N.Y., Reuben H. Donnelley, [1965]. 1103p. **EJ130**

1st ed. 1934.

Pharmaceuticals, biologicals, and allergenes are arranged alphabetically with the following indexes: therapeutic, generic name, manufacturers and distributors, general.

Continued in *Modern drugs* (N.Y., monthly).

New and nonofficial drugs. 1908?– . Philadelphia, Lippincott, 1909– . Annual. **EJ131**

1964 subtitle: An annual compilation of available information on drugs, including their therapeutic, prophylactic and diagnostic status, as evaluated by the Council on Drugs of the American Medical Association.

"Not a collection of accepted drugs" but an evaluation. "Some are viewed with disfavor."—*Pref.*

Pharmacopoeia of the United States of America (The United States Pharmacopoeia). 16th rev. U.S.P. XVI. By authority of the United States Pharmacopoeial Convention, Inc. meeting at Washington, D.C., May 9 and 10, 1950, prep. by the Committee of Revision and published by the Board of Trustees. Official from Oct. 1, 1960. Easton, Pa., Mack Prt. Co., [c1960]. 1148p. **EJ132**

Revised at 5-year intervals.

1st ed. 1820.

An official compendium of drug information, giving standards of purity and strength for each compound included.

—— Epitome of the Pharmacopoeia of the United States and the National formulary with comments. Issued under the direction and supervision of the Council on Pharmacy and Chemistry of the American Medical Association. 10th ed. Philadelphia, Lippincott, [1955]. 322p. **EJ133**

Provides information on the actions and uses of the drugs described in the *Pharmacopoeia of the United States of America* (EJ132) and the *National formulary* (EJ128). Designed as a companion volume to *New and nonofficial drugs* (EJ131). Revised irregularly.

Unlisted drugs. Special Libraries Association, Science-Technology Division, Pharmaceutical Section. v.1– . Jan. 31, 1949– . N.Y., Special Libraries Assoc., 1949– . v.1– . Monthly. **EJ134**

Contains information on new drugs not yet recorded in standard book sources. Includes cumulative name and number indexes.

History

Wootton, A. C. Chronicles of pharmacy. London, Macmillan, 1910. 2v. il. **EJ135**

In narrative form; describes the discovery and use of various drugs, medicines, and nostrums from ancient times through the 19th century. Includes some biographical material of famous apothecaries.

Index.

PUBLIC HEALTH

Bibliography

U.S. National Institutes of Health. Library Branch. N.I.H. Library translations index, 1954–1963. Wash., Dept. of Health, Education, and Welfare, Public Health Service, 1964. 354p.   **EJ136**

Items translated for or by the National Institutes of Health Library's translating service, or received as gifts from other organizations. Will be supplemented by annual lists.

Abstract journals

Bulletin of hygiene, v.1, Jan. 1926– . London, Bureau of Hygiene and Tropical Diseases, 1926– . Monthly.   **EJ137**

Abstracting journal for public health, sanitation, occupational hygiene, food and nutrition, mycoses and mycology, communicable diseases (except tropical diseases), and bacteriology and immunity.

Titles of articles are given in original language and in English translation.

Annual author, subject, and geographical indexes.

Published in association with the *Tropical diseases bulletin.*

U.S. Public Health Service. Public health engineering abstracts. v.1, 1928– . Wash., Govt. Prt. Off., 1928– . v.1– . Monthly.   **EJ138**

Frequency varies.

Includes abstracts of articles pertaining to environmental health, published in more than 800 domestic and foreign journals; reports and proceedings of research groups; and government reports. Arranged by subject, e.g., atmospheric pollution, garbage and other refuse, occupational health, etc.

Annual subject and author index.

Directories

Health organizations of the United States and Canada: national, regional and state. 1961– . Clara Sedacca Wasserman with Paul Wasserman. Ithaca, N.Y., Cornell Univ., Graduate School of Business and Public Admin., 1961– . [v.1–]   **EJ140**

Subtitle: A directory of voluntary associations, professional societies and other groups concerned with health and related fields.

History

Rosen, George. A history of public health. N.Y., M.D. Publ., 1958. 551p. (M.D. monographs in medical history, no.1)   **EJ141**

A survey from earliest times to the present. Includes: bibliography; list of memorable figures with brief biographical statement; list of public health periodicals, arranged by country; list of world-wide public health societies and schools. Subject and author indexes.

Law

Tobey, James Alner. Public health law. 3d ed. N.Y., Commonwealth Fund, 1947. 419p.   **EJ142**

VETERINARY MEDICINE

Indexes and abstract journals

Index-catalogue of medical and veterinary zoology. 1932/52– . Wash., Govt. Prt. Off., 1932– . v.1– .   **EJ143**

At head of title: U.S. Dept. of Agriculture.

A basic catalog (Authors, A–Zyukov), published in 18v., 1932–52, and kept up to date by supplements. An international bibliography.

Incorporates, and is a revision and continuation of, the *Index-catalogue of medical and veterinary zoology-authors,* published 1902–12 as Bureau of Animal Industry bulletin 39.

Animal breeding abstracts, comp. from world literature. Farnham Royal, Eng., Commonwealth Agricultural Bureaux, 1933– . v.1– . Quarterly.   **EJ144**

Prepared by the Commonwealth Bureau of Animal Breeding and Genetics, Edinburgh.

Cumulative, annual author, subject, and geographical indexes.

Index veterinarius, comp. from world literature. Farnham Royal, Eng., Commonwealth Agricultural Bureaux, 1933– . v.1– . Quarterly.   **EJ145**

Prepared by the Commonwealth Bureau of Animal Health, Weybridge, Surrey.

An index to articles in various languages dealing with the incidence or prevention of animal disease.

Encyclopedias and handbooks

Merck veterinary manual. Ed. by O. H. Siegmund [and others]. 2d ed. Rahway, N.J., Merck, 1961. 1630p. **EJ146**

Subtitle: A handbook of diagnosis and therapy.

1st ed. 1955.

Information on: diseases, and their treatment, of large and small animals; fur, laboratory, and zoo animals; nutrition and toxicology. Separate section of prescriptions. Subject index included.

Miller, William Christopher and **West, Geoffrey P.** Encyclopedia of animal care. 7th ed. Baltimore, Williams and Wilkins, 1964. 1017p. il.   **EJ147**

First published in 1928 under title *Black's Veterinary cyclopedia.*

A comprehensive work on the care of domesticated animals with notes on their anatomy, physiology, diseases, and first-aid treatment. Arranged in dictionary form with numerous cross references.

Veterinary drug encyclopedia and therapeutic index. [1st ed.]– . 1953– . N.Y., Reuben H. Donnelley, 1953– . Annual.   **EJ148**

Editors, 1953– : H. C. Stephenson and S. G. Mittelstaedt.

Subtitle: A listing of veterinary drugs, biologicals and foods, and feed additives of American manufacturers.

E K

Agricultural Sciences

❧ Blanchard and Ostvold's *Literature of agricultural research* (EK1) is an annotated guide to materials in this field and should be consulted for more extensive information. This section includes only a few of the general bibliographies and basic reference works. Librarians should remember that the U.S. Dept. of Agriculture has published so many bulletins and leaflets on agricultural matters that it is probably their best source of information on this subject.

AGRICULTURE

Guides

Blanchard, Joy Richard and **Ostvold, Harald.** Literature of agricultural research. Berkeley, Univ. of Calif. Pr., 1958. 231p. (Univ. of California bibliographic guides. 1)   **EK1**

A manual in a field previously uncovered; a classified, annotated guide to reference materials for agricultural research, listing bibliographies, abstract journals, indexes, encyclopedias, dictionaries, handbooks, directories, periodical lists, historical and biographical works, statistical services, etc. The general fields covered are: agriculture in general, plant sciences, animal sciences, physical sciences, food and nutrition, and social sciences. Author and subject index.

Bibliography

Bibliography of soil science, fertilizers and general agronomy, 1947–1950, 1950–1953, 1953–1956, 1956–1959. Farnham Royal, Eng., Commonwealth Agricultural Bureaux, 1951–60. (In progress)   **EK2**

Commonwealth Bureau of Soil Science, Harpenden.

Each volume contains several thousand references to the literature of soil and allied sciences in classified order, with subject and author indexes and lists of journals.

Greifswald. Universität. Bibliothek. Bibliographie für die sozialistische Landwirtschaft: Bücher und Zeitschriftenaufsätze aus den Jahren 1955–1960 in Auswahl. Greifswald, 1961. 256p.   **EK3**

———— Bücher und Zeitschriftenaufsätze, 1961. Greifswald, 1962. 261p.

The main work lists almost 2800 books and periodical articles, and the supplement adds some 3000 more published in 1961. Classified arrangement with author and subject indexes.

Historia agriculturae: jaarboek uitgegeven door het Nederlands Agronomisch-Historisch Instituut. (Yearbook issued by Institute for Agricultural History) Groningen, J. B. Wolters, 1953– . Annual.   **EK4**

Includes annual bibliographies of European countries, with lesser coverage for other continents. Also contains articles.

Lauche, Rudolf. Internationales Handbuch der Bibliographien des Landbaues. World bibliography of agricultural bibliographies. Hrsg. im Auftrag des land- und forstwirtschaftlichen Forschungsrates mit Unterstützung der deutschen Forschungsgemeinschaft. München, Bayerische Landwirtschaftsverlag, 1957. 411p.   **EK5**

In classified arrangement; lists more than 4100 agricultural bibliographical sources published between 1596 and 1957. Gives full bibliographical information, concise annotations, and (in many cases) locations in German and Austrian libraries. Author-title index and subject indexes in German and English.

Niklas, Hans and **Hock, A.** [and others]. Literatursammlung aus dem Gesamtgebiet der Agrikulturchemie. ... Leipzig, Helingsche Verlagsanstalt, 1931–39. 5v. **EK6**

Publisher varies.

Title pages, introductory matter, and subtitles in German and English.

Added title page, v.1–3: A bibliographical list of the entire domain of agricultural chemistry.

Contents: v.1, Soil science; v.2, Soil analysis; v.3, Plant nutrition; v.4, Manuring and fertilisers; v.5, Supplementary volume to v.4.

Perkins, Walter Frank. British and Irish writers on agriculture. Lymington, Eng., King, 1932. 142p.   **EK7**

"A bibliography of some 1300 British and Irish writers on the agriculture of the United Kingdom from the earliest printed books until, and including 1900. . . . Included are books on Agricultural Chemistry, Botany, Grasses, Weeds, Drainage, Improvements, Weights and Measures."—*Introd.*

Tolsado Picazo, Francisco. Bibliografía española de agricultura (1495–1900). Madrid, [Gráficas González], 1953. 122p. 51pl.   **EK8**

At head of title: Instituto Nacional del Libro Español.

Classed arrangement with alphabetical index.

U.S. National Agricultural Library. Bibliography of agriculture. Wash., 1942– . v.1– . Monthly. (December issue is cumulated subject index and cumulated personal and organizational index)   **EK9**

A classified bibliography designed to list the current literature, domestic and foreign, received by the National Agricultural Library. Covers: plant science, soils and fertilizers, forestry, animal industry, entomology, agricultural engineering, agricultural products, agricultural economics and rural sociology, food and human nutrition, miscellaneous.

Foreign-language titles in serials are translated into English with indication of original language.

Includes an annual cumulated list of translations received in the library, and various other lists.

U.S. Dept. of Agriculture

Lists and indexes

☙ The U.S. Dept. of Agriculture has been a prolific publisher of material on all phases of agriculture, and much valuable information may be found in its various publications. Some of the lists and indexes which help to make the material available are:

U.S. Dept. of Agriculture. List by titles of publications of the U.S. Dept. of Agriculture from 1840 to June, 1901, inclusive. Comp. and compared with the originals by R. B. Handy and Minna A. Cannon. Wash., Govt. Prt. Off., 1902. 216p. (Division of Publ. Bull. no.6)   **EK10**

———— List of publications of the U.S. Dept. of Agriculture from January, 1901, to December, 1925, inclusive; comp. by comparison with the originals by Mabel G. Hunt. Wash., Govt. Prt. Off., 1927. 182p. (Miscellaneous publ. 9)   **EK11**

Continued by 5-year supplements: 1926/30–1941/46.

———— Index to authors with titles of their publications appearing in the documents of the U.S. Dept. of Agriculture, 1841–1897, by George F. Thompson. Wash., Govt. Prt. Off., 1898. 303p. (Division of Publ. Bull. no.4)   **EK12**

———— Index to publications of the U.S. Dept. of Agriculture, 1901–40, ed. by Mary A. Bradley. Wash., Govt. Prt. Off., 1932–43. 4v.   **EK13**

1901–25. 2689p.; 1926–30. 694p.; 1931–35. 518p.; 1936–40. 763p.

U.S. Superintendent of Documents. List of publications of the Agricultural Department, 1862–1902, with analytical index. Wash., Govt. Prt. Off., 1904. 623p. (Bibliography of United States public documents. Dept. list no.1) **EK14**

Zimmerman, Fred Lyon and **Read, Phyllis Rogers.** Numerical list of current publications of the U.S. Dept. of Agriculture, comp. by comparison with the originals. . . .

Wash., Govt. Prt. Off., 1941. 929p. (U.S. Dept. of Agriculture. Miscellaneous publ. 450)   **EK15**

Annual reports

U.S. Dept. of Agriculture. Index to the annual reports of the U.S. Dept. of Agriculture for the years 1837 to 1893 inclusive. Wash., Govt. Prt. Off., 1896. 252p. (Division of Publ. Bull. no.1)   **EK16**

Bulletins

U.S. Dept. of Agriculture. Index to department bulletins, no.1–1500; by Mabel G. Hunt. Wash., Govt. Prt. Off., 1936. 384p.   **EK17**

Department bulletins ceased publication; were continued by *Technical bulletins.*

—— Index to technical bulletins, no.1–750; by Mabel G. Hunt. Wash., Govt. Prt. Off., 1937–41. 2v.   **EK18**

no.1–500. 1937. 249p.; no.501–750. 1941. 169p.

—— Index to farmers' bulletins, no.1–1750. . . . Wash., Govt. Prt. Off., 1920–41. 3v.   **EK19**

Reports of the statistician

U.S. Dept. of Agriculture. Synoptical index of the reports of the statistician, 1863 to 1894, by George F. Thompson. Wash., Govt. Prt. Off., 1897. 258p. (Division of Publ. Bull. no.2)   **EK20**

Agricultural experiment stations

U.S. Dept. of Agriculture. List of bulletins of the agricultural experiment stations from their establishment to the end of 1920. Wash., Govt. Prt. Off., 1924. 186p. (Its Bull. 1199)   **EK21**

"A list of approximately 12,500 of the 17,500 or more publications of the State experiment stations (including those of Alaska and the insular possessions) from 1875 to 1920, inclusive."

Continued by biennial supplements: Bulletin 1199, suppl. 1, 2, 3; Miscellaneous publications 65, 128, 181, 232, 294, 362, 459; Bibliographical bulletin no.4, covers 1941/42 (pub. 1944).

Periodicals

Stuntz, Stephen Conrad. List of the agricultural periodicals of the United States and Canada published during the century July 1810 to July 1910, ed. by Emma B. Hawks. Wash., Govt. Prt. Off., 1941. 190p. (U.S. Dept. of Agriculture. Miscellaneous publ. no.398)   **EK22**

Gives title, place of publication, frequency, volumes, inclusive dates, change of name, consolidations, etc. Lists 3753 journals, not counting changes of title.

Indexes

Agricultural index, subject index to a selected list of agricultural periodicals and bulletins, 1916–64. N.Y., Wilson, 1919–64. v.1–49. No more pub.   **EK23**

Detailed, alphabetical subject index to agricultural and related periodicals and to many reports, bulletins, and circulars of agricultural departments, experiment stations, etc. Most of the periodicals are in English, including American, British, and colonial publications, but a few journals in foreign languages are included.

Continued as *Biological & agricultural index,* with v.50, no.1, Oct. 1964.

Biological & agricultural index, a cumulative subject index to periodicals in the fields of biology, agriculture, and related sciences, 1964– . N.Y., Wilson, 1964– . v.50– .   **EK24**

For complete record *see* EC6.

U.S. Office of Experiment Stations. Experiment station record. Sept. 1889–1946. Wash., Govt. Prt. Off., 1890–1948. 95v. Monthly.   **EK25**

Discontinued.

—— —— General index, v.1–80, 1889–1939. Wash., Govt. Prt. Off., 1903–49. 7v.

1889–1901, v.1–12. 671p.; 1901–11, v.13–25. 1159p.; 1912–19, v.26–40. 640p.; 1919–24, v.41–50. 709p.; 1924–29, v.51–60. 677p.; 1929–34, v.61–70. 752p.; 1934–39, v.71–80. 832p.

A record and digest of current agricultural literature, serving practically as an index to the periodical, bulletin, and report material on this subject, in English and the principal foreign languages. Author and subject index to each volume.

Abstract journals

See also Journal of the science of food and agriculture (ED16, annotation)

Dairy science abstracts, comp. from world literature. Farnham Royal, Eng., Commonwealth Agricultural Bureaux, 1939– . v.1– . Monthly. Annual author and subject indexes.   **EK26**

Compiled by the Commonwealth Bureau of Dairy Science and Technology, Shinfield, Reading, England.

A comprehensive, international abstract journal.

The Commonwealth Agricultural Bureaux also issue various other international abstract journals, e.g., *Field crop abstracts,* 1948– ; *Herbage abstracts,* 1931– ; *Horticultural abstracts,* 1931– ; *Plant breeding abstracts,* 1930– ; *Soils and fertilizers,* 1938– .

World agricultural economics and rural sociology abstracts. v.1, April 1959– . Amsterdam, North Holland Pub. Co., 1959– . v.1– . Quarterly.   **EK27**

Published in cooperation with the International Association of Agricultural Economists by the International Association of Agricultural Librarians and Documentalists.

Titles given in original language with English translation. Abstracts in English. Each volume has cumulative author, subject, and geographical indexes.

Encyclopedias

Bailey, Liberty Hyde. Cyclopedia of American agriculture; a popular survey of agricultural conditions, practices, and ideals in the United States and Canada. N.Y., Macmillan, 1907–9. 4v. il.   **EK28**

v.1, Farms; v.2, Crops; v.3, Animals; v.4, Farm and community. Biographies.

Contains signed articles by specialists, with bibliographies. Not alphabetically arranged. Excellent when first issued but not now up to date.

A "new edition," issued 1917, was a reprint with no change in text. In 1922, v.2, Crops, and v.3, Animals, were reissued, with no change in text, but with new title pages and prefaces, as separate books, under the titles *Cyclopedia of farm crops* and *Cyclopedia of farm animals.*

—— Standard cyclopedia of horticulture. N.Y., Macmillan, 1914–17. 6v. il. (Reissue, 1947, in 3v.)   **EK29**

Founded upon the author's *Cyclopedia of American horticulture* (4v., 1902–4), but so revised and enlarged as to be practically a new work. Aims to cover completely the horticultural floras of the continental United States and Canada and to include the more outstanding species grown in a horticultural way in Puerto Rico, Hawaii, and the other islands.

The last volume includes, also, supplementary articles, a finding list of binomials, and a general index. Biographies; signed articles by specialists; bibliographies.

Special features to be noted are: (1) the very comprehensive inclusion of American native plants, trees, and shrubs, which makes the work useful for questions in botany; (2) the full indexing of illustrations, both black and white and colored, included in many other works, e.g., periodicals, collections, etc.

—— and **Bailey, Ethel Zoe.** Hortus second; a concise dictionary of gardening, general horticulture and cultivated plants in North America. N.Y., Macmillan, 1941. 778p. **EK30**

"New ed., rev. and reset, April 1941." 1st edition, entitled *Hortus,* was published 1930. "Designed to account for all the species and botanical varieties of plants in cultivation in the continental United States and Canada in the decade ending midyear 1940, together with brief directions on uses, propagation and cultivation." Includes common names, descriptive terms, definitions, inventories of families of plants, etc.—Cf. *Pref.*

Dictionaries

Haensch, Günther and **Haberkamp, Gisela.** Wörterbuch der Landwirtschaft: Deutsch, englisch, französisch, spanisch. Dictionary of agriculture . . . , systematical and alphabetical. München, Bonn, Wien, BVL Verlagsgesellschaft, 1959. 649p. **EK31**

The main part of this work lists terms in a classified order, on a German base, with consecutive numbering throughout. Alphabetical indexes in each language refer by number to the classified section.

Nijdam, J. Horticultural dictionary in eight languages. Rev. and expanded ed. of the Horticultural word list in seven languages. N.Y., Interscience, 1961. 504p. **EK32**

First published 1961 by Ministry of Agriculture and Fisheries, Horticultural Division, The Hague, The Netherlands.

Dutch, English, French, German, Danish, Swedish, Spanish, and Latin, prepared on a Dutch base with indexes in the other languages.

Includes some 400 words and expressions.

Russko-angliiskii sel'skokhoziaistvennyi slovar'. Sost.: B. N. Usovskii [i dr.]. Moskva, Fizmatgiz, 1960. 504p. **EK33**

A Russian-English dictionary which "contains over 30,000 terms used in agricultural biology, applied botany, applied zoology, . . . economics and organization of farm production, agricultural statistics and biometrics."—*Pref.* Includes a list of abbreviations commonly used in Russian agricultural and biological literature.

Handbooks

Kingsbury, John Merriam. Poisonous plants of the United States and Canada. Englewood Cliffs, N.J., Prentice-Hall, 1964. 626p. il. (part col.) **EK34**

"Intended as a reference for the physician and veterinarian who must deal with practical problems posed by poisonous plants, and as a text for the medical and veterinary student . . ."—*Introd.*

Bibliography, p.13–16, 509–89, includes more than 1700 items.

Richey, C. B. [and others]. Agricultural engineers' handbook. N.Y., McGraw-Hill, 1961. 880p. il. **EK35**

Contents: I, Crop-production equipment; II, Soil and water conservation; III, Farmstead structures and equipment; IV, Basic agricultural data.

Statistics

Gt.Brit. Interdepartmental Committee on Social and Economic Research. Guides to official sources. London, Stat. Off. (In progress) **EK36**

For other numbers *see* CG104.

no.4, Agricultural and food statistics. 1958. 71p.

U.S. Dept. of Agriculture. Yearbook of agriculture, 1894– . Wash., Govt. Prt. Off., 1895– . Annual. **EK37**

Title varies.

Beginning with 1936, statistics are published in a separate volume entitled *Agricultural statistics* (EK38); and the *Yearbook,* instead of containing brief summaries of miscellaneous developments, devotes itself to particular subjects, as follows: 1936, Better plants and animals, I; 1937, Better plants and animals, II; 1938, Soils and men; 1939, Food and life; 1940, Farmers in a changing world; 1941, Climate and man; 1942, Keeping livestock healthy; 1943–47, Science in farming; 1948, Grass; 1949, Trees; 1950–51, Crops in peace and war; 1952, Insects; 1953, Plant diseases; 1954, Marketing; 1955, Water; 1956, Animal diseases; 1957, Soil; 1958, Land; 1959, Food; 1960, Power to produce; 1961, Seeds; 1962, After a hundred years; 1963, A place to live; 1964, Farmer's world.

Each is a valuable source of information.

—— —— Indexes, 1784–1900, 1901–1905, 1906–1910, 1911–1915.

—— Agricultural statistics, 1936– . Wash., Govt. Prt. Off., 1936– . Annual. **EK38**

Covers "agricultural production, supplies, consumption, facilities, costs, and returns." In some years historical tables extend farther back than in others, but cross references to these can be found in each annual.

History

Bidwell, Percy Wells and **Falconer, John I.** History of agriculture in the northern United States, 1620–1860. Wash., Carnegie Inst., 1925. 512p. il. (Carnegie Inst. of Washington. Publ. no.358) (Repr.: N.Y., Peter Smith, 1941) **EK39**

A scholarly, well-documented work covering the field of agriculture and agricultural economics in the northern states to the time of the Civil War. Includes a classified and critical bibliography with discussions of source materials, public and private records, books, periodicals, society publications, etc.

Gray, Lewis Cecil and **Thompson, Esther Katherine.** History of agriculture in the southern United States to 1860. Wash., Carnegie Inst., 1933. 2v. il. (Carnegie Inst. of Washington. Publ. no.430) (Repr.: N.Y., Peter Smith, 1941. 2v.) **EK40**

A companion work to Bidwell above, covering all phases of agriculture and its economics in the southern states up to the time of the Civil War. Well documented. Extensive bibliography, including references to books, periodicals, newspapers, and manuscripts.

Atlases

Van Royen, William. Atlas of the world's resources. N.Y., Prentice-Hall for the Univ. of Maryland, Dept. of Geography, 1952–54. v.1–2. il. **EK41**

Contents: v.1, The agricultural resources of the world. 1954. 258p.; v.2, The mineral resources of the world. 1952. 181p.

A third volume, on forest and fishery resources, has not been published.

FORESTRY

Bibliography

Munns, Edward Norfolk. A selected bibliography of North American forestry. Wash., Govt. Prt. Off., 1940. 2v. (U.S. Dept. of Agriculture. Miscellaneous publ. 364) **EK42**

Classified list with author index.

Includes references to material in books, periodicals, government bulletins, etc., published in the United States, Canada, and Mexico prior to 1930.

Periodicals

Grünwoldt, Franz. Répertoire international des périodiques forestiers; sylviculture, économie du bois, protection de la nature et chasse d'après leur état au 1ᵉʳ janvier, 1940. Berlin-Wannsee, Centre Internationale de Sylviculture, 1940. 204p. (Sylvae orbis . . . no.1) **EK43**

A geographical listing of 1254 forestry serials, with alphabetical title and place indexes. Information given includes date of first issue, publisher, frequency, price, editor, address, etc.

Preliminary matter and half titles in French, German, English, Spanish, Italian.

Abstract journals

Forestry abstracts, comp. from world literature. Farnham Royal, Eng., Commonwealth Agricultural Bureaux, 1939– . v.1– . Quarterly. **EK44**

Annual cumulative author and subject indexes.
Foreign titles translated into English.

U.S. Fish and Wildlife Service. Wildlife abstracts; a bibliography and index of the abstracts in Wildlife review. no.1/66– . 1935/51– . Wash., 1954– . **EK45**

Subtitle varies.
1952/55, 1956/60.
Cumulative, retrospective bibliographies of abstracts appearing in *Wildlife review.*

Dictionaries

McCulloch, Walter F. Woods words: a comprehensive dictionary of loggers terms. [Portland], Oregon Historical Soc. and the Champoeg Pr., 1958. 219p. **EK46**

Lists some 4000 words and phrases formerly, and in some cases currently, used in the logging camps of the old Northwest.

Society of American Foresters. Committee on Forestry Terminology. Forestry terminology; a glossary of technical terms used in forestry. 3d ed. Wash., Soc., 1958. 97p. **EK47**

1st ed. 1944.
Scope limited to: "(1) terms used in a special sense by foresters and (2) terms from other sciences and industry the meaning of which a forester should know and which may not be defined in other glossaries or texts that are readily available under average working conditions."—*Pref.*

Handbooks

Forbes, Reginald Dunderdale. Forestry handbook, ed. for the Society of American Foresters. N.Y., Ronald, 1955. [v.p.] il. **EK48**

"Presents the working methods and techniques, formulas, tables, converting factors, and related data most commonly used in the practice of on-the-ground forestry in the United States and Canada."—*Pref.*

Record, Samuel James and **Hess, Robert W.** Timbers of the world. New Haven, Yale Univ. Pr., 1943. 640p. il. **EK49**

A successor to *Timbers of tropical America,* 1924, containing more than twice the amount of material. "Contains descriptions of the trees, tells where they grow and the sizes they attain, and attempts to evaluate their present and potential economic importance."—*Pref.*

HOME ECONOMICS

Bibliography

Bitting, Katherine Golden. Gastronomic bibliography. San Francisco, Calif., priv. pr., 1939. 718p. il. **EK50**

A comprehensive bibliography of some 6000 works in several languages—mostly English, French, and German—covering the 15th to the 20th centuries. Arranged in three parts: (1) by author; (2) by title, if anonymous; (3) by short title and partial subject index. Includes detailed bibliographic information for each entry with some annotations.

Gourley, James E. Regional American cookery, 1884–1934; a list of works on the subject. N.Y., N.Y. Pub. Lib., 1936. 36p. (Repr. with additions from the New York Public Library. Bull. June–July, 1935) **EK51**

An author list of cookery books, pamphlets, and periodical items, arranged by region and by state. Locates copies.

Iowa. State College of Agriculture and Mechanic Arts, Ames. Library. Basic books and periodicals in home economics, selected by the divisions of home economics of Iowa State College, Michigan State College, Montana State College, Oklahoma A. and M. College and the University of Tennessee, ed. by the Iowa State College Library . . . Ames, Iowa State College Lib., 1942. 112p. **EK52**

Arranged in four parts: pt.1, Essential titles; pt.2, Subject lists; pt.3, Reference books; pt.4, High school textbooks. Includes author index.

———— Supplement, 1941–47. Ames, Iowa State College Lib., 1949. 78p.

Lincoln, Waldo. American cookery books, 1742–1860, rev. and enl. by Eleanor Lowenstein. Worcester, Mass., Amer. Antiquarian Soc.; N.Y., Corner Book Shop, 1954. 136p. **EK53**

1st edition, 1929, had title *Bibliography of American cookery books,* 1742–1860, and was reprinted from *American Antiquarian Society, Proceedings,* n.s., v.39, 1929, p.85–225.

Lists about 740 titles, 250 of which are new in this edition. Arrangement is chronological, and full bibliographic information is given. Locates copies in 24 libraries. Indexes by author and by title.

Simon, André L. Bibliotheca gastronomica, a catalogue of books and documents on gastronomy, comp. and annotated with an introd. . . . London, Wine and Food Soc., 1953. 196p. il. **EK54**

"The production, taxation, distribution and consumption of food and drink, their use and abuse in all times and among all peoples."—*Title page.*

An annotated listing of 1644 items, arranged alphabetically by author, with indexes by short title and by subject.

U.S. Dept. of Agriculture. Home economics research report. no.1– . April 1957– . Wash., Govt. Prt. Off., 1957– . il. Irregular. **EK55**

Subjects covered: clothing, fabrics, child development, nutrition, cooking, food storage, and family finance.

Includes semitechnical and technical publications formerly issued as the Dept.'s Agricultural handbooks; Agriculture information bulletins; Miscellaneous publications; and Circulars.

Vicaire, Georges. Bibliographie gastronomique. Introd. by André L. Simon. [2d ed.] London, Derek Verschoyle Academic and Bibliographical Publ., 1954. 972col. **EK56**

Subtitle: A bibliography of books appertaining to food and drink and related subjects, from the beginning of printing to 1890.

Originally published: Paris, Rouquette, 1890.

An annotated bibliography of some 2500 books dealing with gastronomy in all its different aspects. Titles are largely in French, but some are in other western-European languages.

Dissertations

U.S. Agricultural Research Service. Titles of completed theses in home economics and related fields in colleges and universities of the United States. 1942/46–1961/62. Wash., [1947?]–63. 17v. in 6. **EK57**

"Intended to supplement the list *'Research in foods, human nutrition and home economics at the landgrant institutions'* comp. annually by the Office of Experiment Stations . . . 1935/36–1955/56 and the list of *'Notes on research in home economics education'* comp. in the Office of Education, 1934/36–45. 6v."

Title varies: 1942/46, *Completed theses in home economics and related fields in colleges and universities of the United States.*

Issued 1942/46–1951/52 by the Bureau of Human Nutrition and Home Economics; 1952/53–1961/62 by the Agricultural Research Service.

Issued as U.S. Dept. of Agriculture. PA, 1944/49–1961/62.

Continued in the *Journal of home economics.* 1964– .

A listing of master's and doctor's theses, arranged by subject with author index.

Abstracts of doctoral theses related to home economics, 1951/52– . (In Journal of home economics, v.45– , 1953– . Annual) **EK58**

Supersedes "Doctoral theses by home economists: abstracts, 1947/48–1949/51." (In *Journal of home economics,* v.41–43, 1949–51)

Abstracts of a selected list of doctoral theses, arranged by subject. Entry includes title, author, and institution. No author index.

Encyclopedias

Montagné, Prosper. Larousse gastronomique; the encyclopedia of food, wine and cookery. Introd. by A. Escoffier

and Ph. Gilbert; ed. by Charlotte Turgeon and Nina Froud . . . N.Y., Crown, 1961. 1101p. il. maps. **EK59**

First pub. 1938 in France.

An alphabetically arranged encyclopedia of foods and wines, with methods of preparation, and notes on the culinary specialties of various regions of France, etc. Measurements and terms have been adapted for British and American use. Index and bibliographies are in French.

Cookbooks

Farmer, Fannie Merritt. The all new Fannie Farmer Boston Cooking-School cookbook. 10th ed. compl. rev. by Wilma Lord Perkins. Boston, Little, [1959]. 506p. il. **EK60**

1st ed. 1896. Frequently revised.

Previous editions published under title *The Boston Cooking-School cook book.*

Standard American cookbook.

Rombauer, Irma von Starkloff and **Becker, Marion Rombauer.** The joy of cooking. [Rev. and enl.] Indianapolis, Bobbs-Merrill, 1962. 852p. il. **EK61**

First pub. [c1931]. Frequently revised.

An all-purpose cookbook, containing more than 4000 recipes with sections on menus, table-setting, canning, salting and smoking, freezing foods, etc.

Handbooks

Good Housekeeping. Guide to successful homemaking. Comp. by the editors of Good housekeeping. Rev. ed. N.Y., Harper, [1961]. 320p. il. **EK62**

1st ed. 1956.

Contains information on home decorating; fabrics; care and cleaning, repair and safety of the home; sewing; food and diet; laundry; spot and stain removal; home management; etc.

Red Cross. U.S. American National Red Cross. . . . Home nursing textbook. 7th ed. N.Y., Doubleday, [1963]. 368p. il. **EK63**

First published in 1913 under title *American Red Cross textbook on elementary hygiene and home care of the sick.*

Includes information on emergency care of the sick and injured.

INDEX

❦ *This index includes author and subject entries,*
and some, but not all, title entries.
References to code numbers followed by "n"
refer to titles in annotations.

Serviço de Documentação. Dados biográficos dos ministros, AJ86
—— Ministério das Relações Exteriores. Brasil, CG71
Brazilian literature
bibliography, BD791, BD793–BD795; current, BD796
history, BD798
Brazol, D. Dictionary of meteorological and related terms, EE88
Brechenmacher, J. K. Etymologisches Wörterbuch der deutschen Familiennamen, AK93
Bredsdorff, E. Danish literature in English translation, BD618
Breed, R. S. Bergey's Manual of determinative bacteriology, EC120
Brelsford, W. V. Handbook to the Federation of Rhodesia and Nyasaland, CI154
Brenet, M., [pseud.] Dictionnaire pratique et historique de la musique, BH69n
Brenner, C. D. Bibliographical list of plays in the French language, BD699
Breslau, University: dissertations, AI30
Bresslau, H. Handbuch der Urkundenlehre für Deutschland und Italien, DA98
Breton, Nicholas: bibliography, BD321n
Breton language: dictionaries, AE145–AE148
Breviate of British diplomatic blue books, R. Vogel, CJ98
Breviate of parliamentary papers, P. Ford and G. Ford, AH65
Brewer, D. J. World's best orations, BD189
Brewer, E. C. Dictionary of phrase and fable, BD48; Historic notebook, DA32; Reader's handbook of famous names in fiction, BD49
Brewing: dictionary, CH334
Brewster, K. G. and Emery, H. G. New Century dictionary of the English language, AE5
Brewton, J. E. and Brewton, S. W. Index to children's poetry, BD166
Bricka, C. F. Dansk biografisk Leksikon, AJ118
Bridge, L. W. Funk and Wagnalls book of parliamentary procedure, CI169
Bridgers, F. E. and Colket, M. B. Guide to genealogical records in the National Archives, AK8
Bridges, R. and Weigle, L. A. Bible word book, BB105
Brie, G. A. de. Bibliographia philosophica, BA4
Brief guide to official publications, Great Britain. Stationery Office, AH53
Brief history of entomology, H. Osborn, EC125
Brief introduction to the use of Beilstein's Handbuch der organischen Chemie, E. H. Huntress, ED65
Briefs, G. and Eulenburg, F. Handwörterbuch der Soziologie, CA29
Briggs, C. A., Driver, S. R. and Plummer, A. International critical commentary on the Holy Scriptures, BB130
Briggs, C. W. Steel castings handbook, EI194
Briggs, M. S. Everyman's concise encyclopaedia of architecture, BE120
Brigham, C. S: History and bibliography of American newspapers, AG8
Brimmer, B. Guide to the use of United Nations documents, CJ150
Bring, S. E. Itineraria svecana, CK3
Brinkley's Japanese-English dictionary, AE382
Brinkman, C. L. Alphabetische naamlijst van boeken, AA608
Brinkman's Catalogus van boeken, plaat- en kaartwerken, AA611

Brinkman's Cumulatieve catalogus van boeken, AA614
Brinkman's Titel-catalogus, AA612
Briquet, C.M. Filigranes, AA200
Briquet album, AA201
Briscoe, J. D., Sharp, R. L. and Borish, M. E. Mapbook of English literature, BD342
Briseño, R. Estadística bibliográfica de la literatura chilena, AA409
Bristol, R. P. Evans' American bibliography, AA333a; Index of printers . . . in Evans, American bibliography, AA333b
Britain, an official handbook, CI123
Britain's tribute to Dante in literature and art, P. Toynbee, BD779
Britannica book of the year, AD9
Britannica encyclopaedia see Encyclopaedia Britannica, AD2
Britannica junior, AD13
Britannica world language dictionary, AE455
British abstracts, ED16
British and American sporting authors, A. H. Higginson, CB155
British and Foreign Bible Society. Library. Historical catalogue of the printed editions of Holy Scripture, BB74
British and foreign state papers, Gt.Brit. Foreign Office, CJ119
British and Irish writers on agriculture, W. F. Perkins, EK7
British anthologies, E. Arber, BD397
British Association for the Advancement of Science. Mathematical tables, EF41
—— Research Committee. Glossary of geographical terms, CK20
British authors, S. J. Kunitz and H. Haycraft, BD349–BD350
British autobiographies, W. Matthews, AJ157
British book news, AA274
British books, incorporating the Publishers' circular, AA506
British calendar customs: England, A. R. Wright, CF32; Orkney and Shetland, M. M. Banks, CF20; Scotland, M. M. Banks, CF19
British Caribbean who, what, why, L. S. Smith, AJ99
British catalogue of music, BH19
British chemical and physiological abstracts see ED16
British Colour Council. Dictionary of colour standards, EG45
British Columbia: official publications, AH43
British Columbia. University. Library. Check list of printed materials relating to French Canadian literature, BD647
British Commonwealth year book, R. S. Russell, CI124
British Council. Public administration, CI4
British diaries, W. Matthews, BD414
British Drama League. Library. Player's library, the catalogue, BG5
British education index, CB25
British empire: history, DC156
British geological literature, E. L. Martin and A. P. Harvey, EE10
British government, G. H. L. LeMay, DC155
British humanities index, AF126
British imperial calendar and civil service list, CI118
British initials and abbreviations, I. Wilkes, AE33
British manuscripts project; a checklist of the microfilms, U.S. Library of Congress. Processing Dept., AA87
British medical dictionary, Sir A. S. MacNalty, EJ48
British Museum, a guide to its public services, AB88

British Museum. Dept. of Manuscripts. Catalogue of manuscript music, BA27; Catalogue of romances, BD175; Catalogues of the manuscript collections, AA140; Plays, BD353
—— Dept. of Oriental Printed Books and Manuscripts. Catalogue of Georgian and other Caucasian printed books, DC81; Catalogue of Syriac printed books, BD999
—— Dept. of Printed Books. Catalogue of books printed in the XVth century, AA167; Catalogue of books printed in England, Scotland, and Ireland . . . to 1640, AA495; Catalogue of printed books: Academies, AC2; Catalogue of printed books: Newspapers, AG19; Catalogue of printed books: Periodical publications, AF1; Catalogue of printed music published between 1487 and 1800, BH28; Catalogue of the works of Linnaeus, EC35; General catalogue, AA67, AA491; General catalogue: Bible, BB75; Rules for compiling the catalogues, AB112; Short-title catalogue of books printed in France . . . to 1600, AA462; Short-title catalogue of books printed in Italy . . . to 1600, AA561; Short-title catalogue of books printed in Spain . . . before 1601. AA694; Short-title catalogue of books printed in the German-speaking countries . . . to 1600, AA476; Short-title catalogue of Portuguese books printed before 1601, AA649; Short-title catalogues of Portuguese books and of Spanish-American books printed before 1601, AA574; Subject index of the modern works, AA68
—— —— Hirsch Library. Books in the Hirsch Library, BH6; Music in the Hirsch Library, BH29
—— —— Map Room. Catalogue of the printed maps, plans, and charts, CK183
—— —— (Natural History) Library. Catalogue of the books, manuscripts, maps and drawings, EA6
—— —— Thomason Collection. Catalogue, AA501
British Museum Library, A. Esdaile, AB89
British Museum. The British Museum, a guide to its public services, AB88
British national bibliography, AA507
British political facts, D. E. Butler and J. Freeman, CI125
British Public Record Office, Virginia. Committee on Colonial Records, DC133
British scientific and technical books, Association of Special Libraries and Information Bureaux, EA2
British sources of photographs and pictures, G. S. A. Nunn, BE105
British Standards Institution. Guide to the Universal Decimal Classification, AB125; Yearbook, EA206
British technology index, E. J. Coates, EA64
British union-catalogue of early music, E. B. Schnapper, BH30
British union-catalogue of periodicals, AF108–AF109
British working class politics, G. D. H. Cole, CH319
Britt, M. Dictionary of the Psalter, BB198
Britten, F. J. Old clocks and watches and their makers, BF14
Britten, J. and Boulger, G. S. Biographical index of deceased British and Irish botanists, EC66
—— and Holland, R. Dictionary of English plant-names, EC46
Britton, H. Industrial directories, CH96
Britton and Brown illustrated flora, H. A. Gleason, EC73
Broad, C. L. and Broad, V. M. Dictionary

to the plays and novels of Bernard Shaw, BD501

Broadcasting stations of the world, U.S. Foreign Broadcast Information Service, CH232

Brockelmann, C. Geschichte der arabischen Litteratur, BD979; Lexicon Syriacum, AE546

Brockett, P. Bibliography of aeronautics, EI12

Brockhaus' kleines Konversations-Lexikon. Der kleine Brockhaus, AD35; Der neue Brockhaus, AD36

Brockhaus' Konversations-Lexikon, AD34

Brockhaus' Konversations-Lexikon. Novyi entsiklopedicheskii slovar', AD62

Brodman, E. Development of medical bibliography, EJ5

Broeckaert, J. and Coopman, T. Bibliographie van den Vlaamschen taalstrijd, AA375

Broeckx, J. L. Flandria nostra, DC30

Bronnegids by die studie van die Afrikaanse taal en letterkunde, P. J. Nienaber, BD544

Bronson, B. H. Traditional tunes of the Child ballads, BH114

Brontë, Charlotte: dictionary, BD420

Brontë family: bibliography, BD419

Brook, H. Blue book of awards, CB150

Brooke, E. S., Thornton, J. L. and Monk, A. J. Select bibliography of medical biography, EJ83

Brooke, I. Western European costume and its relation to the theatre, BF22

Brooke, J. and Namier, Sir L. B. House of Commons, CI129

Brooke, M. and Dubester, H. J. Guide to color prints, BE102

Brooke, S. A. and Rolleston, T. W. Treasury of Irish poetry, BD530

Brookman, L. G. 19th century postage stamps of the United States, BF69

Brooks, A. D. Civil rights and liberties in the United States, CI5

Broughton, L. N. and Baldwin, D. L. Concordance to the poems of John Keats, BD463

—— and Stelter, B. F. Concordance to the poems of Robert Browning, BD422

—— Northup, C. S. and Pearsall, R. Robert Browning, a bibliography, BD421

Brown, A. L. and Chrimes, S. B. Select documents of English constitutional history, DC149

—— Strauss, L. J. and Strieby, I. M. Scientific and technical libraries, AB100

Brown, B. I. and Miller, A. E. National directory of schools and vocations, CB98

Brown, C. F. Register of Middle English religious and didactic verse, BD387

—— and Robbins, R. H. Index of Middle English verse, BD388

Brown, C. S. Reader's companion to world literature, BD53

Brown, E. S. Manual of government publications: United States and foreign, AH1

Brown, G. H. Lives of the Fellows of the Royal College of Physicians of London, EJ94

Brown, G. W. and Brown, D. B. Guide to Soviet Russian translations of American literature, BD212

Brown, H. Bibliography on meteorites, EE10a

Brown, J. C. Bibliotheca americana. Catalogue of books relating to North and South America, DB1

Brown, J. L. Flag of the United States, its use in commerce, AK73

Brown, K. Guide to the reference collections of the New York Public Library, AB84

—— and Haskell, D. C. Bibliography of

union lists of serials, AF96

Brown, P. and Stratton, G. B. World list of scientific periodicals, EA42

Brown, P. A., Tawney, R. H. and Bland, A. E. English economic history, DC145

Brown, R. F. La novela española, BD827

Brown, S. J. Guide to books on Ireland, BD531; Ireland in fiction, BD532

Brown, S. M. and Doris, L. Business executive's handbook, CH130

Brown University. John Carter Brown Library. Bibliotheca americana, DB1–DB2

—— Library. The Anthony memorial. Catalogue of the Harris collection of American poetry, BD252

Browne, E. G. Literary history of Persia, BD993

Browne, N. E. Bibliography of Nathaniel Hawthorne, BD279

Browning, D. C. Everyman's dictionary of literary biography, BD63, BD348

Browning, E. W. and Feipel, L. N. Library binding manual, AA260

Browning, Robert
bibliography, BD421
concordance, BD422
encyclopedia, BD423
handbooks, BD424–BD425

Brownson, C. B. Congressional staff directory, CI50

Bruckner, A. Neue schweizer Biographie, AJ245

Brückner, Alexander. Słownik etymologiczny języka polskiego, AE452

Bruel, G. Bibliographie de l'Afrique Équatoriale Française, DD2

Bruggencate, K. ten. Engels woordenboek, AE199

Brugger, W. Philosophisches Wörterbuch, BA28

Bruhn, P. Gesamtverzeichnis russicher und sowjetischer Periodika und Serienwerke, AF106

Brummel, L. and Egger, E. Guide to union catalogues and international loan centers, AB76

Brümmer, F. Lexikon der deutschen Dichter und Prosaisten, BD573

Bruncken, H. Subject index to poetry, BD167

Brunet, G. Dictionnaire des ouvrages anonymes [de Barbier], suivi des Supercheries littéraires dévoilées [de Quérard], AA110; Imprimeurs imaginaires et libraires supposés, AA135

Brunet, J. C. Manuel du libraire et de l'amateur de livres, AA58, AA463

Brunot, F. Histoire de la langue française, BC45

Brunotte, H. and Weber, O. Evangelisches Kirchenlexikon, BB30

Brussel, I. R. Anglo-American first editions, AA180

Brussels. Bibliothèque Royale de Belgique. De Nederlandsche letterkunde in België, BD537

—— Cinémathèque de Belgique. Répertoire mondial des périodiques cinématographiques, BG65

Bruun, C. W. Bibliotheca danica, AA446

Bruun, H. Dansk historisk Bibliografi, DC38

Bryan, C. R., Alisky, M. and Merrill, J. C. Foreign press, AG2

Bryan, M. Bryan's Dictionary of painters and engravers, BE160

Bryan, R. B. Hide and leather and shoes' encyclopedia of the shoe and leather industry, CH336

Bryant, M. M. Current American usage, AE42

Bryant, M. S. Bibliographies, abstracts, and indexes, AB16n

Bryant, P. T. and Wilson, B. S. Engineering

college research review, EA141

Bryer, J. R. and Rees, R. A. Checklist of Emerson criticism, BD272

Brynildsen, J. Dictionary of the English and Dano-Norwegian languages, AE183; Norsk-engelsk ordbog, AE184

Buber, M. M. Educational encyclopedia, CB29

Buch der Schweiz, Schweizerischer Buchhändlerverein, AA720

Buchanan, M. E. World directory of women's organisations, AC3

Bucharest. Biblioteca Centrală de Stat. Anuarul cărții din Republica Populară Romînă, AA659

Buchberger, M. Lexikon für Theologie und Kirche, BB14

Bücherkunde für Germanisten, J. Hansel, BD556

Bücherkunde zur deutschen Geschichte, G. Franz, DC84

Bücherkunde zur Weltgeschichte, G. Franz, DA4

Buchheim, R. B. New space handbook, EI43

Buck, C. D. Dictionary of selected synonyms in the principal Indo-European languages, AE134

Buckinghamshire: place-names, CK109n

Buckland, C. E. Dictionary of Indian biography, AJ168

Buckland, W. R. and Fox, R. A. Bibliography of basic texts and monographs on statistical methods, CG3, EF3

—— and Kendall, M. G. Dictionary of statistical terms, CG18

Büchmann, G. Geflügelte Worte, BD96

Budapest. Országos Széchényi Könyvtár. Magyar sajtó bibliográfiája, AF53

Buddhadatta, A. P. Concise Pali-English dictionary, AE432a; English-Pali dictionary, AE432

Buddhism
bibliography, BB251–BB254
encyclopedias and dictionaries, BB255–BB257
symbolism, BE96–BE97

Buddhist hand-symbol, A. Akiyama, BE96

Budge, E. A. T. W. Egyptian hieroglyphic dictionary, AE205

Buenos Aires. Universidad Nacional. Instituto Bibliotecológico. Bibliografía filosófica del siglo XX, BA9

Bühler, C. F. Fifteenth-century book: the scribes, the printers, the decorators, AA174

Building a social work library, Council on Social Work Education, CC7

Building construction handbook, F. S. Merritt, EI89

Buisman, M. Populaire prozaschrijvers, BD538

Buist, E. Soviet dissertation lists since 1934, AI54n

Bukofzer, M. F. Music in the Baroque era, BH78n

Bulas, K., Thomas, L. L. and Whitfield, F. J. The Kościuszko Foundation dictionary, AE448

Buletinul bibliografic al cărții, Rumania. Ministerul Culturii, AA660

Bulgaria
bibliography, AA382–AA391
history, DC32, DE129–DE131
statistics, CG72

Bulgaria. Tsentralno Statistichesko Upravlenie. Statisticheski godishnik na Narodna Republika Bulgarii, CG72

Bulgarian abbreviations, U.S. Library of Congress. Slavic and Central European Division, AE152

Bulgarian language
dictionaries, AE149–AE151; abbreviations, AE152

Cushion, J. P. and Honey, W. B. Handbook of pottery and porcelain marks, BF9

Cusset, F. English-French and French-English technical dictionary, EA106

Custom house guide, CH178

Cuthbert, E. I. Index of Australian and New Zealand poetry, BD294

Cutolo, V. O. Diccionario de alfónimos y seudónimos de la Argentina, AA99

Cuyas, A. Appleton's Revised English-Spanish and Spanish-English dictionary, AE524

Cyclopedia of American agriculture, L. H. Bailey, EK28

Cyclopedia of American government, A. C. McLaughlin and A. B. Hart, CI32

Cyclopaedia of American literature, E. A. Duychinck and G. L. Duychinck, BD215

Cyclopaedia of costume, J. R. Planché, BF27

Cyclopedia of education, P. Monroe, CB34

Cyclopedia of India and of eastern and southern Asia, E. G. Balfour, DE61

Cyclopedia of initials and abbreviations, F. D. Fawcett, AE28

Cyclopedia of insurance in the United States, CH266

Cyclopedia of literary characters, F. N. Magill, BD52

Cyclopedia of painters and paintings, J. D. Champlin and C. C. Perkins, BE161

Cyclopedia of world authors, F. N. Magill, BD70

Cyclopedic survey of chamber music, W. W. Cobbett, BH82

Cyrillic characters: transliteration, BC71

Cyrillic publications concerning the social sciences, CA12a

Cyrillic union catalog, U.S. Library of Congress, AA669

Czachowski, K. Obraz współczesnej literatury polskiej, BD875

Czarnecka, J., Słomczewska, J. and Dąbrowska, W. 555 książek wydanych w okresie powojennym, AA642

Czech language: dictionaries, AE172–AE179
    abbreviations, AE178
    etymology, AE179

Czech literature
    bibliography, BD867–BD868
    biography, BD870–BD871
    history, BD869

Czechoslovak Republic. Ministerstvo Pošt a Telegrafu. Dopravní místopisný lexikon Československé Republiky, CK52

—— Státní Úřad Statistický. Statistická ročenka Československé Socialistické Republiky, CG88

Czechoslovak statistical abstract, CG88n

Czechoslovakia
    atlas, CK237
    bibliography, AA437–AA444
    biography, AJ116
    gazetteer, CK52
    history, DC33–DC36
    register, CI95
    statistics, CG88

"D.A." Dictionnaire d'abréviations françaises et étrangères, H. Baudry, AE235

DSH abstracts, CC36

Dabartinės lietuvių kalbos žodynas, J. Balčikonis and K. Korsakas, AE421

Dąbrowska, W., Czarnecka, J. and Słomczewska, J. 555 książek wydanych w okresie powojennym, AA642

Dados biográficos dos ministros, Brazil. Ministério da Viação e Obras Publicas, AJ86

Dagher, J. A. Répertoire des bibliothèques du Proche et du Moyen-Orient, AB64

Dahkhodā, A. A. Lughat nāmah, AE435

Dahl, S. Dansk skønlitteraert Forfatterleksikon, BD621

—— and Engelstoft, P. Dansk biografisk Haandleksikon, AJ117

Dahlerup, V. Ordbog over det danske Sprog, AE181

Dahlmann, F. C. and Waitz, G. Quellenkunde der deutschen Geschichte, DC83

Dai-genkai, F. Otsuki, AE378

Dai-hyakka jiten, AD51

Daijiten [Great dictionary], Heibonsha, AE377

Daily weather map, U.S. Weather Bureau, EE99

Dainelli, G. Atlante fisico-economico d'Italia, CK244

Dairy science abstracts, EK26

Dal', V. I. Tolkovyi slovar' zhivogo velikorusskago iazyka, AE483

Dalbiac, L. Dictionary of quotations (German), BD97

Dalbiac, P. H. and Harbottle, T. B. Dictionary of quotations (French and Italian), BD94

Dale, J. H. van. Van Dale's Handwoordenboek der Nederlandse taal, AE194; Van Dale's Nieuw groot woordenboek der Nederlandse taal, AE193

Dalin, A. F. Svenska språkets synonymer, AE544

Dalmis, D. Turkish government organization manual, CI163

Dalton, B. H. Sources of engineering information, EI1

Dampierre, J. de. Publications officielles des pouvoirs publics, AH47

Dana, J. D. and Dana, E. S. System of mineralogy, EE113

Dance
    annual, BG52
    bibliography, BG48–BG49
    encyclopedias and handbooks, BG53–BG62
    history, BG63–BG64
    indexes, BG50–BG51

Dance encyclopedia, A. Chujoy, BG55

Dandekar, R. N. Vedic bibliography, BB258

Dania polyglotta, AA450

Daniel, H. Islands of the East Indies, DE74; Islands of the Pacific, DG8

Daniel, R. S. and Louttit, C. M. Professional problems in psychology, EH1

Daniel, R. T. and Apel, W. Harvard brief dictionary of music, BH67

Daniel, Samuel: bibliography, BD321n

Daniel Blum's Screen world, BG70

Daniel Blum's Theatre world, BD236, BG13

Daniels, O. Dictionary of Japanese (sóshe) writing forms, AE379

Danilewicz, M. and Sadowska, G. Catalogue of periodicals in Polish or relating to Poland, AF75

Danish language: dictionaries, AE180–AE191
    bilingual, AE182–AE188
    etymology, AE189–AE191

Danish literature
    bibliography, BD618–BD620
    biography, BD621–BD623
    history, BD624
    translations into English, BD618

Danish national bibliography, AA448

Danish theses for the doctorate and commemorative publications, Copenhagen. Universitet. Bibliotek, AI20

Danmark, J. P. Trap, CK53

Dannreuther, E. Romantic period, BH79n

D'Annunzio see Annunzio, Gabriele d'.

Dansk Bibliografi, L. Nielsen, AA445

Dansk Bibliografier, A. J. Møller, AA30

Dansk Biblioteksfører, H. Einersen and M. Iversen, AB42

Dansk biografisk Haandleksikon, S. Dahl and P. Engelstoft, AJ117

Dansk biografisk Leksikon, C. F. Bricka, AJ118

Dansk Bogfortegnelse, AA448; annual, AA451

Dansk Forfatterleksikon, C. M. Woel, BD623

Dansk historisk Bibliografi, B. Erichsen and A. Krarup, DC37

Dansk historisk Bibliografi, Danske Historiske Forening, DC38

Dansk personalhistorisk Bibliografi, B. Erichsen and A. Krarup, AJ121

Dansk skønlitteraert Forfatterleksikon, S. Dahl, BD621

Dansk Tidsskrift-Index, AF147

Danske blandede Tidsskrifter, Copenhagen. Kommunebiblioteker, AF146

Danske Gesandter og Gesandtskabspersonale indtil 1914, E. Marquard, AJ119

Danske Historiske Forening. Dansk historisk Bibliografi, DC38

Dansten, E. Nordisk Leksikon for Bogvaesson, AA224

Danstrup, J. Kulturhistorisk Leksikon for nordisk Middelalder, DC227

Dante
    bibliography, BD771–BD779
    concordances, BD780–BD783
    dictionaries and handbooks, BD784–BD788

Daremberg, C. and Saglio, E. Dictionnaire des antiquités grecques et romaines, DA83

Dareste de la Chavanne, F. R. Constitutions modernes, CJ125

Dargan, M. Guide to American biography, AJ57

Darlow, T. H. and Moule, H. F. Historical catalogue of the printed editions of Holy Scripture, BB74

Darmesteter, A. and Hatzfeld, A. Dictionnaire général de la langue française, AE221

Darmstaedter, L. Handbuch zur Geschichte der Naturwissenschaften und der Technik, EA81

Darrell's Gramophone Shop encyclopedia of recorded music, BH127n

Dartnell Corporation. Dartnell international trade handbook, CH163

Darton, F. J. H. Children's books in England, AA190

Darton, N. H. Catalogue and index of contributions to North American geology, EE15

Dās, S. C. Tibetan-English dictionary, AE559

Data processing equipment encyclopedia, CH131

Daten deutscher Dichtung, H. A. Frenzel and E. Frenzel, BD574

Datos para la bibliografía boliviana, J. R. Gutiérrez, AA380

Dauzat, A. Dictionnaire étymologique de la langue française, AE237; Dictionnaire étymologique des noms de famille et prénoms de France, AK91

—— and Rostaing, C. Dictionnaire étymologique des noms de lieux en France, CK100

Davenport, F. G. European treaties bearing on the history of the United States . . . CJ109

—— and Andrews, C. M. Guide to the manuscript materials for the history of the United States . . . in the British Museum, DB31n

Davenport, M. Book of costume, BF23

Davenport, S. J. and Morgis, G. G. Air pollution, EI72

Davidoff, H. World treasury of proverbs, BD123

Davids, L. E. Dictionary of insurance, CH269

González, L. Fuentes de la historia contemporánea de México, DB137

González, S. M. and Herrera Gómez, M. C. N. Apuntes para una bibliografía militar de México, DB138

González de Cossio, F. Imprenta en México, AA591

González Peña, C. Historia de la literatura mexicana, BD859

Gooch, G. P. Annals of politics and culture, DA37; History and historians in the nineteenth century, DA27

Good, C. V. Dictionary of education, CB31

Good Housekeeping. Guide to successful homemaking, EK62

Good reading, Committee on College Reading, AA281

Goodall, A. Place-names of south-west Yorkshire, CK148

Goode, C. T. and Shannon, E. F. Atlas of English literature, BD343

Goode's World atlas, E. B. Espenshade, CK212

Goodhart, R. S. Modern drug encyclopedia and therapeutic index, EJ130
—— and Wohl, M. G. Manual of clinical nutrition, EJ119; Modern nutrition in health and disease, EJ121

Goodnight, S. H. German literature in American magazines, BD568

Goodrich, C. Pocket dictionary. Chinese-English, and Pekingese syllabary, AE165

Goodrich, L. M. and Hambro, E. Charter of the United Nations, CJ153

Gopinātha Rāu, T. A. Elements of Hindu iconography, BE100

Gorder, L. O. and Manly, H. P. Drake's Cyclopedia of radio and electronics, EI119

Gordillo, R. A. and Parsons, M. D. Directory of Mexico City libraries, AB63

Gordon, C. A. Bibliography of Lucretius, BD969

Gordon, L. H. Supplementary concordance to the minor Italian works of Dante, BD782

Gordon, R. D. Doctoral dissertations in music and music education, BH22

Gorokhoff, B. I. Providing U. S. scientists with Soviet scientific information, EA146; Publishing in the U.S.S.R., AA215

Gorokhoff, C. J. and Okinshevich, L. O. Latin America in Soviet writings, DB106

Görres-Gesellschaft. Staatslexikon, CI28

Gosnell, C. F. Spanish personal names, AK100

Goss, C. W. F. London directories, CH107

Gosse, E. and Garnett, R. English literature, BD345

Gosudarstvennye arkhivy Soiuza SSR, G. A. Belov, DC261

Gothic bibliography, M. Summers, BD381

Gottfried, B. A. and Clark, D. T. Dictionary of business and finance, CH75

Gottfried, W. Heine Bibliographie, BD604

Göttinger Arbeitskreis. Staats- und Verwaltungsgrenzen in Ostmitteleuropa: historisches Kartenwerk, CK239

Gottschald, M. Deutsche Namenkunde, AK94

Götze, A. Trübners deutsches Wörterbuch, AE269

Gough, H. Glossary of terms used in heraldry, AK66

Gould, Sir B. J. and Richardson, H. E. Tibetan word book, AE560

Gourley, J. E. Regional American cookery, EK51

Gournay, B. Administration française, CI2n

Gove, P. B. Imaginary voyage in prose fiction, BD152

Goveia, E. V. Study on the historiography of the British West Indies, DB159

Gover, J. E. B., Mawer, A. and Stenton, F. M. Place-names of Devon, CK109n; Place-names of Hertfordshire, CK109n; Place-names of Middlesex, CK109n; Place-names of Northamptonshire, CK109n; Place-names of Nottinghamshire, CK109n; Place-names of Surrey, CK109n; Place-names of Warwickshire, CK109n; Place-names of Wiltshire, CK109n

Governi d'Italia, F. Bartolotta, CI140

Government Affairs Foundation, Inc. Metropolitan communities, CI70

Government and politics of India and Pakistan, P. Wilson, DE58

Government document bibliography in the United States and elsewhere, J. B. Childs, AH2

Government organization of Japan, U.S. Embassy. Japan, CI144

Government publications, p.155–63
international: bibliography, AH2–AH5; guide, AH1; union list, AH6
(For government publications of particular countries see under name of country)

Government publications and their use, L. F. Schmeckebier and R. B. Eastin, AH9

Government publications monthly list, Gt. Brit. Stationery Office, AH63

Government statistics for business use, P. M. Hauser and W. R. Leonard, CH106

Government-wide index to federal research and development reports, U.S. Dept. of Commerce. Clearinghouse for Federal Scientific and Technical Information, EA75

Gowers, Sir E. A. Plain words: their ABC, AE45

Goy, P., Massa Gil, B. and Trautman, R. Diccionario técnico de biblioteconomía, AB21

Grace, Sister M. and Peterson, G. C. Books for Catholic colleges, AA282

Graduate education, J. H. Blessing, CB2

Graff, H. F. and Barzun, J. Modern researcher, DA2

Graham, A. K. and Pinkerton, H. L. Electroplating engineering handbook, EI62

Graham, B. Bookman's manual, AA269n

Graham, E. C. and Mullen, M. M. Rehabilitation literature, EH3

Graham, I. Encyclopedia of advertising, CH60

Graham, M. D. Social research on blindness, CC30

Grainger, T. H. Guide to the history of bacteriology, EC117

Grammatik der deutschen Sprache, K. Duden, AE281n

Gramophone Shop encyclopedia of recorded music, BH127n

Gran diccionario de refranes de la lengua española, J. M. Sbarbi y Osuna, BD117

Gran enciclopedia argentina, D. A. de Santillán, DB120

Grand armorial de France, H. Jougla de Morenas, AK63

Grand dictionnaire universel du XIXᵉ siècle français, P. Larousse, AD28

Grand Larousse encyclopédique, AD31

Grande enciclopédia portuguesa e brasileira, DC220a

Grande encyclopédie, AD27

Grande encyclopédie de la Belgique et du Congo, DC31

Grandidier, G. Bibliographie de Madagascar, DD57

Grandin, A. Bibliographie générale des sciences juridiques, politiques, économiques et sociales, CA9, CJ9

Grandsaignes d'Hauterive, R. Dictionnaire d'ancien français, AE248

Granger's Index to poetry, BD169

Grant, E. L. and Ireson, W. G. Handbook of industrial engineering and management, EI131

Grant, F. C. Nelson's Bible commentary, BB129

Grant, G. Technical manual and dictionary of classical ballet, BG58

Grant, W. and Murison, D. Scottish national dictionary, AE95

Graphic arts
biography, AA248
dictionary, AA225

Grapow, H. and Erman, A. Wörterbuch der aegyptischen Sprache, AE206

Grasowsky, J. Millōn 'ivri, AE315

Grasse, J. G. T. Orbis latinus, CK37; Trésor de livres rares et précieux, AA60

Grassé, P.-P. Traité de zoologie, EC101

Graves, E. C. Ulrich's Periodicals directory, AF18

Graveurs du xixᵉ siècle, H. Beraldi, BE167

Gray, A. Gray's Manual of botany, EC67

Gray, D. E. American Institute of Physics handbook, EG33

Gray, G. J. General index to Hazlitt's Handbook and his Bibliographical collections, BD320

Gray, H. J. Dictionary of physics, EG16

Gray, L. C. and Thompson, E. K. History of agriculture in the southern United States, EK40

Gray, L. H. Mythology of all races, CE5

Gray, P. Encyclopedia of the biological sciences, EC18

Gray, R. A. Doctors' theses in education, CB19

Gray, Thomas
bibliography, BD454–BD455
concordance, BD456

Gray's Manual of botany, A. Gray, EC67

Great books of the Western world and the great ideas, R. M. Hutchins, BD13

Great Britain
atlas, CK242
bibliography, AA491–AA493a; before 1640, AA494–AA498e; 17th–18th centuries, AA499–AA504d; 19th–20th centuries, AA505; current, AA506–AA513; privately printed, AA514–AA515; regional, p.48
biography, AJ144–AJ161; bibliography, AJ155–AJ159; contemporary, AJ154–AJ156; indexes, AJ160–AJ161
gazetteers, CK56–CK58
government publications
catalogs and indexes: 18th century, AH56–AH57; 19th–20th centuries, AH58–AH63
guides, AH52–AH55
parliamentary debates, AH66
select lists, AH64–AH65
handbooks, CI123–CI126
history
bibliography, DC110–DC112; early, DC114–DC117; medieval, DC118–DC119; 16th–17th centuries, DC120–DC123; 18th–19th centuries, DC124–DC127; current, DC128; dissertations, DC113
dictionaries and handbooks, DC135–DC138
general histories, DC139–DC142
guide, DC109
guides to records, DC129–DC134
regional, DC158–DC173
source books, DC143–DC155
local government, CI134–CI136
official registers, CI118–CI122
Parliament: dictionaries, CI132–CI133; registers, CI127–CI131

Grove, *Sir* G. Dictionary of music and musicians, BH53

Growoll, A. Three centuries of English booktrade bibliography, AA502n

Growth of world industry, United Nations. Statistical Office, CH109

Gruber, J. G. and Ersch, J. S. Allgemeine Encyclopädie der Wissenschaften und Künste, AD40

Gruenberg, S. M. Encyclopedia of child care and guidance, EH22

Grundriss der Bibliographie, C. Fleischhack, E. Rückert and G. Reichardt, AA296

Grundriss der germanischen Philologie, H. Paul, BC36

Grundriss der Geschichte der Philosophie, F. Ueberweg, BA38

Grundriss der Geschichtswissenschaft, A. Meister, DC85

Grundriss der romanischen Philologie, G. Gröber, BC41

Grundriss zur Geschichte der deutschen Dichtung, K. Goedeke, BD555

Grünwoldt, F. Répertoire international des périodiques forestiers, EK43

Guadet, J. Éléments et théorie de l'architecture, BE134n

Gualtieri, L. L. and Lysle, A. de R. Nuovo dizionario moderno delle lingue italiana e inglese, AE370

Guam, DG9

Guarnaschelli, T. M. and Valenziani, E. Indice generale degli incunaboli delle biblioteche d'Italia, AA171

Guatemala
bibliography, AA525–AA528
gazetteers, CK60–CK61

Guatemala. Dirección General de Cartografía. Diccionario geográfico de Guatemala, CK60

—— Tipografía National. Catálogo general de libros, AA526

Gubernatis, A. de. Dictionnaire international des écrivains du monde latin, BD67

Güemes, C. and Pérez, Á. Adiciones y continuación de "La imprenta en Manila" de J. T. Medina, AA635

Guerber, H. A. Book of the epic, BD177; Myths of northern lands, CE14; Stories of Shakespeare's comedies, BD498; Stories of Shakespeare's English history plays, BD500; Stories of Shakespeare's tragedies, BD499

Guerini, V. History of dentistry, EJ107

Guerinot, A. A. Essai de bibliographie Jaina, BB273

Guerlac, O. G. Citations françaises, BD92

Guerra, F. American medical bibliography, EJ78

Guía bibliográfica para la enseñanza de la historia en Hispano-América, M. del C. Velázquez, DB107

Guia da bibliografia histórica portuguêsa, Academia Portuguêsa da História, DC217

Guia das bibliotecas brasileiras, Rio de Janeiro. Instituto Nacional do Livro, AB40

Guía de editores y de libreros de España, AA216

Guía de estudios históricos, A. Tauro, DB148

Guía de instituciones que cultivan la historia de América, C. Bosch García, DA29

Guía de la administración del estado, Spain. Presidencia del Gobierno, CI157

Guía de las bibliotecas de Madrid, Spain. Dirección General de Archivos y Bibliotecas, AB67

Guía sociogeográfica de Guatemala, J. del Valle Matheu, CK61

Guibert, A.-J. Bibliographie des œuvres de Molière publiées au XVIIᵉ siècle, BD741

Guida allo studio delle storia delle matematiche, G. Loria, EF2

Guida bibliografica internazionale per il chimico, N. Gaudenzi, ED8

Guidance
bibliography, CB126–CB130
directories, CB131–CB133

Guidance workers certification requirements, D. Camp, CB131

Guide bibliographique des études littéraires, P. Langlois and A. Mareuil, BD649

Guidebooks, p.460–61
bibliography, CK263
general, CK252–CK262
United States, CK264–CK266

Guide des communautés européennes, European Communities. Information Service, CJ137

Guide international des archives: Europe, DC1

Guide pratique des bibliothèques de Paris, E. Leroy, AB45

Guide to American directories, B. Klein, CH98

Guide to American educational directories, CB55

Guide to archives and manuscripts in the United States, U.S. National Historical Publications Commission, DB39

Guide to art reference books, M. W. Chamberlin, BE1

Guide to best plays, F. K. W. Drury, BD130

Guide to captured German documents, G. L. Weinberg, DC102

Guide to career information, New York Life Insurance Company. Career Information Service, CB129

Guide to Catholic literature, BB186

Guide to current official statistics, Gt.Brit. Permanent Consultative Committee on Official Statistics, CG105

Guide to current official statistics, India. Office of the Economic Adviser, CG115

Guide to dance periodicals, BG50

Guide to foreign legal materials, C. Szladits, CJ14

Guide to geologic literature, R. M. Pearl, EE2

Guide to graduate study, American Council on Education, CB76

Guide to great plays, J. T. Shipley, BD133

Guide to guidance, CB127

Guide to historical cartography, U.S. Library of Congress. Map Division, CK193

Guide to historical fiction, E. A. Baker, BD148

Guide to historical literature, American Historical Association, DA1

Guide to Indian periodical literature, AF150

Guide to international organizations, Gt. Brit. Central Office of Information. Reference Division, AC6

Guide to Latin American scientific and technical periodicals, Pan American Union. Division of Science Development, EA49

Guide to League of Nations publications, H. Aufricht, CJ147

Guide to long-playing records, BH129

Guide to manuscripts relating to America in Great Britain and Ireland, B. R. Crick and M. Alman, DB32

Guide to manuscripts relating to American history in British depositories, U.S. Library of Congress. Manuscripts Division, DB34

Guide to material on crime and criminal justice, Social Science Research Council. Committee on Survey of Research on Crime and Criminal Justice, CC52

Guide to materials on Latin America, U.S. National Archives, DB114

Guide to mathematical tables, A. V. Lebedev and R. M. Fedorova, EF34

Guide to medical writing, H. A. Davidson, EJ60

Guide to metallurgical information, E. W. Tapia, EI164

Guide to microforms in print, A. J. Diaz, AA82

Guide to microreproduction equipment, H. W. Ballou, AB150

Guide to national bibliographical information centers, UNESCO, AB28

Guide to New Zealand official statistics, E. P. Neale, CG156

Guide to New Zealand reference material, J. Harris, AA298

Guide to Pakistan libraries, Pakistan Bibliographical Working Group, AB66

Guide to parliamentary and official papers, H. B. Lees-Smith, AH55

Guide to parliamentary papers, P. Ford and G. Ford, AH52

Guide to photocopied historical materials in the United States and Canada, R. W. Hale, DA24

Guide to play selection, National Council of Teachers of English. Committee on Playlist, BG7

Guide to reference material, A. J. Walford, AA311

Guide to research in Russian history, C. Morley, DC249

Guide to Russian reference and language aids, R. Neiswender, AA303

Guide to Russian reference books, K. Maichel, AA300

Guide to South African reference books, R. Musiker, AA302

Guide to Soviet Russian translations of American literature, G. W. Brown and D. B. Brown, BD212

Guide to special issues and indexes of periodicals, Special Libraries Association, New York Chapter. Advertising Group, AF16

Guide to study abroad, J. A. Garraty and W. Adams, CB57

Guide to successful homemaking, Good Housekeeping, EK62

Guide to tables in mathematical statistics, J. A. Greenwood and H. O. Hartley, EF33

Guide to tables in the theory of numbers, D. H. Lehmer, EF35

Guide to technical literature, A. D. Roberts, EI2

Guide to technical literature production, E. Clarke, EA90

Guide to the best fiction, English and American, E. A. Baker and J. Packman, BD147

Guide to the best historical novels and tales, J. Nield, BD157

Guide to the diplomatic archives of western Europe, D. H. Thomas and L. M. Case, DC3

Guide to the diplomatic history of the United States, S. F. Bemis and G. G. Griffin, DB8

Guide to the historical publications of the societies of England and Wales, DC111

Guide to the literature of botany, B. D. Jackson, EC30

Guide to the literature of chemistry, E. J. Crane, A. M. Patterson and E. B. Marr, ED3

Guide to the literature of mathematics and physics, including related works on engineering science, N. G. Parke, EF1, EG1

Guide to the literature of the zoological sciences, R. C. Smith, EC87

Guide to the manuscripts preserved in the Public Record Office, Gt.Brit. Public Record Office, DC131

zhestvennye proizvedeniia L. N. Tolstogo, BD907

Moseley, E. G. "Medical dictionaries and studies of terminology," p.599

—— and Hawkins, M. Basic reference aids for small medical libraries, EJ4

Moser, H. J. and Frenzel, H. A. Kürschners biographisches Theater-Handbuch, BG37

Moser, R. C. Space-age acronyms, EI30

Moses, J. M. Collectors' guide to American recordings, BH131; Price guide to collectors' records, BH132

Mosher, F. J. and Taylor, A. Bibliographical history of anonyma and pseudonyma, AA94

Mosher, R. B. Executive register of the United States, p.417

Moskva; kratkaia adresno-spravochnaia kniga, CI165

Moss, C. Catalogue of Syriac printed books and related literature in the British Museum, BD999

Mossé, R. Bibliographie d'économie politique, CH18

Mosses with a hand lens, A. J. Grout, EC80

Mostecky, V. and Ruggles, M. J. Russian and East European publications in the libraries of the United States, AB85

Motif-index of folk-literature, S. Thompson, CF16

Motion pictures
annuals, BG70–BG72
bibliography, AA65, BG65–BG69
dictionary, BG74
encyclopedia, BG73

Motion pictures, U.S. Copyright Office, BG67

Motion pictures and filmstrips, National union catalog, AA65

Motion pictures and filmstrips, U.S. Library of Congress, BG68

Mott, F. L. American journalism, AG44; History of American magazines, AF12

Motta, A. História da litteratura brasileira, BD798

Motta, G. Dizionario commerciale: inglese-italiano, italiano-inglese, CH158

Mottelay, P. F. Bibliographical history of electricity and magnetism, EI94

Moule, H. F. and Darlow, T. H. Historical catalogue of the printed editions of Holy Scripture, BB74

Moulton, C. W. Library of literary criticism of English and American authors, BD339

Moulton, J. H. and Milligan, G. Vocabulary of the Greek Testament, AE304

Moulton, W. F. and Geden, A. S. Concordance to the Greek Testament, BB102

Mountains: encyclopedia, CK24, EE39

Mourier, A. and Deltour, F. Catalogue et analyse des thèses latines et françaises, AI26; Notice sur le doctorat ès lettres, AI25

Le mouvement poétique français de 1867 à 1900, C. Mendès, BD717

Le mouvement romantique, M. Escoffier, BD668

Mouvements ouvriers et socialistes: chronologie et bibliographie, É. Dolléans and M. Crozier, CH288

Moyer, E. S. Who was who in church history, BB43

Muchnic, H. Dostoevsky's English reputation, BD905

Mudge, I. G. and Johnston, W. D. Special collections in libraries in the United States, AB83

—— and Sears, M. E. George Eliot dictionary, BD452; Thackeray dictionary, BD515

Mueller, W. Bibliographie des Kaffee, des Kakao, der Schokolade, des Tee, CH335

Mueller von Asow, H. and E. H. Kürschners deutscher Musiker-Kalender, BH55

Muenscher, W. C. Aquatic plants of the United States, EC24n

Mugridge, D. H. and McCrum, B. P. Guide to the study of the United States of America, DB23

Mühlenbach, K. Mülenbacha Latviešu valodas vārdnīca, AE419

Muir, P. H. English children's books, AA191

Muir, R. Historical atlas, DA56

Muirhead's Blue guides, p.460

Mukherjee, A. K. Annotated guide to reference materials in the human sciences, CA5, CD6

Mukherji, Panchanandas see Pañchānanadāsa Mukhopādhyāya

Mukhopādhyāya, Pañchānanadāsa see Pañchānanadāsa Mukhopādhyāya

Mulhall, M. G. Dictionary of statistics, CG27

Mulholland, R. and Wodehouse, M. E. Canadian index to periodicals and documentary films, AF144

Mullen, M. M. and Graham, E. C. Rehabilitation literature, EH3

Müller, E. Methoden der organischen Chemie, ED73

Müller, F. M. Sacred books of the East, BB22

Müller, H. A. and Singer, H. W. Allgemeines Künstler-Lexicon, BE70

Müller, I. Handbuch der Altertumswissenschaft, p.469

Müller, J. Die wissenschaftlichen Vereine und Gesellschaften Deutschlands, AC39

Müller, V. K. English-Russian dictionary, AE487

Müller, W. Technical dictionary of automotive engineering, EI52

Mullins, E. L. C. Texts and calendars, DC112

Multilingual demographic dictionary, International Union for the Scientific Study of Population, CG17

Mummendey, R. Language and literature of the Anglo-Saxon nations as presented in German doctoral dissertations, BD315; Die schöne Literatur der Vereinigten Staaten von Amerika in deutschen Übersetzungen, BD213

Munby, A. N. L. Cambridge college libraries, AB57

Munden, K. W. and Beers, H. P. Guide to federal archives relating to the Civil War, DB33

Mundt, H. Bio-bibliographisches Verzeichnis von Universitäts- u. Hochschuldrucken (Dissertationen), AI31

Mundy, Anthony: bibliography, BD321n

Munford, G. Attempt to ascertain the true derivation of the names of towns . . . of Norfolk, CK130

Munich. Osteuropa Institut. 5000 Sowjetköpfe, AJ256

—— Universität. Kleine slavische Biographie, AJ228

Municipal history, Great Britain, DC159

Municipal year book, CI74

Municipal year book and public utilities directory, CI136

Munk, W. Lives of the Fellows of the Royal College of Physicians of London, EJ94; Roll of the Royal College of Physicians of London, EJ93

Munn, G. G. Encyclopedia of banking and finance, CH240

Munns, E. N. Selected bibliography of North American forestry, EK42

Muñoz y Romero, T. Diccionario biblio-

gráfico-histórico de los antiguos reinos de España, DC237

Munsell's genealogical index, AK11n

Munter, R. L. Handlist of Irish newspapers, AG22

Muratova, K. D. Istoriia russkoi literatury, BD888

Murchison, C. Psychological register, EH36

Murdock, G. P. Ethnographic bibliography of North America, CD14

Muret, E. and Sanders, D. Muret-Sanders Enzyklopädisches englisch-deutsches und deutsch-englisches Wörterbuch, AE273n

Murison, D. and Grant, W. Scottish national dictionary, AE95

Murray, D. Museums, their history and their use, EA169

Murray, Sir J. A. H. Evolution of English lexicography, AE2; New English dictionary on historical principles, AE20; Oxford English dictionary, AE21; Shorter Oxford English dictionary on historical principles, AE22

Murray, M. R. and Kopech, G. Bibliography of the research in tissue culture, EC4

Murrie, E. B. and Day, C. L. English songbooks, BH106

Museum publications, J. Clapp, EE14

Museums: directories, BE42–BE45, BE47, EA168–EA170

Museums directory of the United States and Canada, E. O. Christensen, EA170

Museums, their history and their use, D. Murray, EA169

Musgrave, Sir W. Obituary prior to 1800, AJ161

Mushroom hunter's field guide, A. H. Smith, EC78

Mushrooms see Fungi

Music, p.329–41
bibliography: books, BH4–BH17; current, BH18–BH20; music, manuscript and published, BH25–BH39
cataloging, AB115
dictionaries of terms, BH66–BH72; bibliography, BH8
dissertations, BH22–BH24
encyclopedias and biographical dictionaries, BH42–BH65
guides, BH1–BH3
handbook, BH73
history, BH74–BH81
indexes, BH40–BH41a
periodicals, BH21

Music and phonorecords, National union catalog, AA65

Music and phonorecords, U.S. Library of Congress, BH38

Music in our time, A. Salazar, BH78n

Music in the Baroque era, M. F. Bukofzer, BH78n

Music in the Middle Ages, G. Reese, BH78n

Music in the Renaissance, G. Reese, BH78n

Music in the Romantic era, A. Einstein, BH78n

Music index, BH40

Music lexicography, J. B. Coover, BH8

Music libraries: organization and contents, L. R. McColvin and H. Reeves, p.331

Music Library Association. Committee on Thematic Indexes. Checklist of thematic catalogues, BH89

Music monographs in series, F. Blum, BH4

Music of the 17th century, C. H. H. Parry, BH79n

Music reference and research materials, V. H. Duckles, BH1

Music since 1900, N. Slonimsky, BH81

Music subject headings, U.S. Library of Congress. Subject Cataloging Division, AB136

Música y músicos de Latino-america, O. Mayer-Serra, BH57

recueils de fac-similés et des reproductions de manuscrits, AA147
—— —— Dépt. des Périodiques. Bibliographie de la presse française politique, AF35; Inventaire des périodiques étrangers, AF104; Périodiques slaves en caractères cyrilliques, AF105; Répertoire collectif des quotidiens et hebdomadaires, AG18; Répertoire de la presse et des publications périodiques françaises, AF36
—— École Nationale Supérieure des Mines. Catalogue de périodiques étrangers scientifiques et techniques, EA55
—— Institut Pasteur. Bulletin, EC119
Parish, H. C. and Mason, J. B. Thailand bibliography, DE126
Parish registers of England and Wales, A. M. Burke, AK31
Parisian stage, C. B. Wicks and J. W. Schweitzer, BD709
Parke, N. G. Guide to the literature of mathematics and physics, EF1, EG1
Parker, D. W. Calendar of papers in Washington archives relating to the territories of the United States, DB31n; Guide to materials in Canadian archives, DB31n
—— and Bell, H. C. Guide to British West Indian archive materials in London . . . , DB31n
Parker, J. H., Goggio, E. and Corrigan, B. Bibliography of Canadian cultural periodicals, AF103
Parker, S. M. Scientific translations, EA32
Parkhurst, C. C. Business communication for better human relations, CH141
Parlagi, I. and [Jásznigi, A.]. Das geistige Ungarn, biographisches Lexikon, AJ163
Parlement en kiezer, jaarboekje, CI147
Parlementaires français, II, R. C. L. Samuel and G. Bonét-Maury, CI104
Parliamentary debates, Gt.Brit. Parliament, AH66
Parliamentary dictionary, L. A. Abraham and S. C. Hawtrey, CI132
Parliamentary handbook, Australia. Parliament. Joint Library Committee, CI85
Parliamentary procedure: handbooks, CI169–CI172
Parliaments and electoral systems, a world handbook, Institute of Electoral Research, London, CI39
Parmentier, A. É. E. Album historique, DA49
Parodies, BD411–BD413
Parra, M. G. and Moreno, W. J. Bibliografía indigenista de México y Centroamérica, CC71
Parrish, S. M. Concordance to the poems of Matthew Arnold, BD415; Concordance to the poems of W. B. Yeats, BD524
Parry, A., Dorosh, J. T. and Dorosh, E. G. Korea; an annotated bibliography of publications in the Russian language, U.S. Library of Congress, Reference Dept., DE108
Parry, C. H. H. Music of the 17th century, BH79n
Parry, J. J. and Northup, C. S. Arthurian legends, BD179
—— and Schlauch, M. Bibliography of critical Arthurian literature, BD180
Parry, J. W. Spice handbook, CH339
Pars pro toto; breviarium medicum internationale, A. Peyser, EJ55
Parsons, H. S. Check list of American 18th century newspapers in the Library of Congress, AG11; Check-list of foreign newspapers in the Library of Congress, AG3
Parsons, M. D. and Gordillo, R. A. Directory of Mexico City libraries, AB63

Parsons, W. Early Catholic Americana, BB187
Partington, J. R. History of chemistry, ED83
Partridge, E. Dictionary of Forces' slang, AE68; Dictionary of slang and unconventional English, AE67; Dictionary of the underworld, British and American, AE69; Name into word, AE35; Origins: a short etymological dictionary of modern English, AE36; Slang, today and yesterday, AE70; You have a point there, AE57
Passano, G. Supplemento al Melzi, Dizionario di opere anonime, AA115
Passerini, G. L., Conte. Il vocabolario dannunziano, BD768
Passow, F. Handwörterbuch der griechischen Sprache, AE294
Pastor, L., Freiherr von. History of the popes, BB230
Patai, R. Jordan, Lebanon and Syria: an annotated bibliography, DE18
Patents, EA199–EA203
Pathak, R. C. Bhargava's Standard illustrated dictionary of the Hindi language, AE330
Patrick, D. Chambers's Cyclopaedia of English literature, BD333
Patrologiae cursus completus, J. P. Migne: Series latina, BB233; Series graeca, BB234
Patrologie: Leben, Schriften und Lehre der Kirchenväter, B. Altaner, BB235
Patrology, BB233–BB240
Patrology; the lives and works of the Fathers of the church, O. Bardenhewer, BB238
Pattermann, W. Deutsch-englisches Wörter- und Phrasenbuch, AE275
Patterson, A. M. French-English dictionary for chemists, ED37; German-English dictionary for chemists, ED39
—— Marr, E. B. and Crane, E. J. Guide to the literature of chemistry, ED3
Patterson, F. A. Index to the Columbia edition of the Works of John Milton, BD471
Patterson, J. G. Zola dictionary, BD751
Patterson, M. L. P. and Inden, R. B. Introduction to the civilization of India, DE27
Patterson's American education, CB72
Paul, H. Deutsches Wörterbuch, AE266; Grundriss der germanischen Philologie, BC36
Paul, M. R. and Maerz, A. J. Dictionary of color, EG47
Paullin, C. O. Atlas of the historical geography of the United States, DB79
—— and Paxon, F. L. Guide to materials in London archives for the history of the United States, DB31n
Paulson, J. Index Lucretianus, BD970
Pauly, A. F. von. Kleine Pauly, DA88; Pauly's Real-Encyclopädie der classischen Altertumswissenschaft, DA87
Paxon, F. L. and Paullin, C. O. Guide to materials in London archives for the history of the United States, DB31n
Payne Smith, R. Compendious Syriac dictionary, AE549; Thesaurus syriacus, AE548
Paz-Soldán, J. P. Diccionario biográfico de peruanos contemporáneos, AJ221
Peabody Institute, Baltimore. Catalogue of the library, AA75
Peake, D. M. and West, D. H. Play index, BD142
Peake's Commentary on the Bible, M. Black and H. H. Rowley, BB136
Pearl, R. M. Guide to geologic literature, EE2

Pearl, Purity, Patience, and Gawain, index, C. O. Chapman, BD176
Pearsall, M. Medical behavioral science, EJ10
Pearsall, R., Broughton, L. N. and Northup, C. S. Robert Browning, a bibliography, BD421
Pearson, J. D. Index Islamicus, BB264
Pearson, M. D. Recordings in the public library, BH134
Pease, A. S., Canter, H. V. and Oldfather, W. A. Index verborum quae in Senecae fabulis necnon in Octavia praetexta reperiuntur, BD975
Peaslee, A. J. Constitutions of nations, CJ128; International governmental organizations, CJ140
Peciar, Š. Slovník slovenského jazyka, AE507
Peck, H. T. Harper's Dictionary of classical literature and antiquities, DA89
Peddie, R. A. Subject index of books published before 1880, AA61
Pedreira, A. S. Bibliografía puertorriqueña, DB171
Peel, A. Congregational two hundred, BB182
Peel, B. B. Bibliography of the Prairie Provinces, DB88
Peele, George: bibliography, BD321n
Peele, R. and Church, J. A. Mining engineers' handbook, EI192
Peerage
 Europe, AK21–AK25
 France, AK27
 Germany, AK30
 Great Britain, AK35–AK43
 Italy, AK46–AK47
 Spain, AK52
Peers, E. A. Cassell's Spanish-English, English-Spanish dictionary, AE521
Pei, M. A. and Gaynor, F. Dictionary of linguistics, BC20; Liberal arts dictionary, AE458
Pekmezi, G., Stotz, A. and Manek, F. Albanesische Bibliographie, DC19
Pelay, E. and Le Verdier, P. Additions à la Bibliographie cornélienne, BD732
Pelican history of art, N. Pevsner, BE61
Pellechet, M. L. C. Catalogue général des incunables des bibliothèques publiques de France, AA172
Peltzer, K. Treffende Zitat, BD98
Pelzer, A. Abréviations latines mediévales, AA149
Pelzer, K. J. Selected bibliography on the geography of southeast Asia, CK12, DE33
Pena, J. Diccionario de la música Labor, BH59
Peñafiel, A. Nomenclatura geográfica de México, CK153
Pender, H. and Del Mar, W. A. Electrical engineers' handbook, EI112
Penderel-Brodhurst, J. G. J. and Layton, E. J. Glossary of English furniture of the historic periods, BF40
Penn, P., Tien, H. C. and Hsia, R. Gazetteer of China, CK50
Pennak, R. W. Collegiate dictionary of zoology, EC104
Penney, C. L. List of books . . . in the Library of the Hispanic Society of America, AA696–AA697
Penniman, T. K. Hundred years of anthropology, CD41
Pennsylvania. University. Library. Catalog of the Programmschriften collection, AI33
Penson, L. M. and Temperley, H. W. V. Century of diplomatic blue books, CJ98n

Pepper, G. W. Analytical index to the Book of common prayer, BB178

Pequena bibliografia crítica da literatura brasileira, O. M. Carpeau, [pseud.], BD791

Peral, M. A. Diccionario biográfico mexicano, AJ198

Peraza Sarausa, F. Anuario bibliográfico cubano, AA436; Bibliografía de Centroamérica y del Caribe, AA404; Bibliografías cubanas, AA29; Diccionario biográfico cubano, AJ113; Directorio de bibliotecas de Cuba, AB41; Personalidades cubanas, AJ114

Perdigão, H. Dicionário universal de literatura, BD72

Pérez, Á. and Güemes, C. Adiciones y continuación de "La imprenta en Manila" de J. T. Medina, AA635

Pérez, L. M. Guide to the materials for American history in Cuban archives, DB31n

Pérez Cabrera, J. M. Historiografía de Cuba, DB163

Pérez Marchant, B. Diccionario biográfico del Ecuador, AJ122

Pérez Ortiz, R. Seudónimos colombianos, AA104

Performing arts collections: an international handbook, International Federation of Library Associations, BG25

Perfumes, cosmetics and soaps with a special reference to synthetics, W. A. Poucher, CH337

Periodic and special reports on population, U.S. Office of the Census, CG42n

Periodica chimica, M. Pflücke and A. Hawelek, ED13

Periodica medica: Titelabkürzungen medizinischer Zeitschriften, W. Artelt, E. Heischkel and C. Wehmer, EJ25

Periodica philologica abbreviata, T. Ulving, BC15

Periodica technica abbreviata, Å. Davidsson, EA59

Periodical articles on religion, E. C. Richardson, BB11

Periodicals, p.132–50
  abbreviations, AF7; biological, EC7n; chemical, ED12–ED13; medical, EJ25; philological, BC15; scientific and technical, EA58–EA61
  bibliography, p.133–41; general, AF1–AF6; Africa, AF20; Australia, AF21; Austria, AF22; Belgium, AF23; Brazil, AF24; Canada, AF25; Colombia, AF26; Congo, AF27; Cuba, AF28; Czechoslovakia, AF29; East Europe, AF30; France, AF31–AF36 (current, AF37); Germany, AF38–AF40 (current, AF41–AF42); Great Britain, before 1800, AF43–AF47 (current, AF48–AF50); Hungary, AF51–AF53; India, AF55; Indonesia, AF56; Ireland, AF57; Italy, AF58–AF60 (current, AF61–AF63); Japan, AF64; Korea, AF65; Latin America, AF66–AF68; Malaya, AF69; Mexico, AF70; Netherlands, AF71; New Zealand see Australia; Nigeria, AF72; Pakistan, AF73; Poland, AF74–AF75; Ruanda-Urundi see Congo; Rumania, AF76; Russia, AF77–AF80a (current, AF81; bibliography, AF82); South Africa, AF83; Spain, AF84–AF87 (current, AF88); Sweden, AF89; Switzerland, AF90–AF93; United States, AF8–AF12 (current, AF13–AF19); Yugoslavia, AF94–AF95
  history: United States, AF11–AF12
  indexes, p.144–50; bibliography, AF116; Australia, AF137; Belgium, AF138–AF141; Bulgaria, AF142; Canada,

AF143–AF145; Denmark, AF146–AF147; Germany, AF148; Germany, East, AF149; Great Britain see United States and Great Britain; Hungary, AF149a; India, AF150–AF151; international, AF117–AF118; Italy, AF152–AF153; Latin America, AF154–AF156; Netherlands, AF157; New Zealand, AF158; Norway, AF159–AF160; Philippines, AF161–AF162; South Africa, AF163; Spain, AF164–AF165; Turkey, AF166; United States and Great Britain, AF119–AF136; Wales, AF134; Yugoslavia, AF167–AF169

scientific and technical, p.529–31; bibliography, EA36–EA42; Canada, EA43; China, EA44; Japan, EA45–EA48; Latin America, EA49; Russia, EA50–EA51; union lists, EA52–EA57

selection, p.29; for college libraries, AA308, AA316

trade: bibliography, AF3

union lists, p.141–43; Canada, AF103; France, AF104–AF105; Germany, AF106–AF107; Great Britain, AF108–AF109; Italy, AF110; Philippines, AF111; Portugal, AF112; South Africa, AF113; South Asia, AF114; Switzerland, AF115; United States, AF98–AF102 (bibliography, AF96–AF97)

Periodicals of South African libraries, EA56

Periodicals of special interest to blind persons, American Foundation for the Blind, CC29

Periodicheskaia pechat' SSSR, AF80

Periódicos brasileiros de cultura, AF24

Periódicos médicos del mundo, EJ24

Les périodiques médicaux dans le monde, EJ24

Périodiques slaves en caractères cyrilliques, Paris. Bibliothèque Nationale. Dépt. des Périodiques, AF105

Perkins, C. C. and Champlin, J. D. Cyclopedia of painters and paintings, BE161

Perkins, W. F. British and Irish writers on agriculture, EK7

Perleberg, M. Who's who in modern China, AJ105, CI94

Permanent Committee on Geographical Names for British Official Use. Gazetteer of Albania, CK41; Gazetteer of Greece, CK59; Glossaries, CK85; Lists of names, CK86; Lists of names (New series), CK86a

Perpetual trouble shooter's manual, J. F. Rider, EI124

Perry, J. H. Chemical business handbook, ED52

—— and Perry, R. H. Engineering manual, EI7

Perry, R. H. Chemical engineers' handbook, EI60

Persia see Iran

Persia in Islamic times, G. M. Wickens and R. M. Savory, DE81

Persian language: dictionaries, AE435–AE442

Persian literature see Iranian literature

Personal names, a bibliography, E. C. Smith, AK80

Personalidades cubanas, F. Peraza Sarausa, AJ114

Personnenkatalog, Bern. Schweizerische Landesbibliothek, AJ250

Persons, S. and Egbert, D. D. Socialism and American life, CI178

Persons and places of the Brontë novels, H. E. Wroot, BD420

Persoonlijkheden in het koninkrijk der Nederlanden in woord en beeld, AJ206

Peru
  bibliography, AA628–AA632
  biography, AJ218–AJ221
  gazetteer, CK73
  history: bibliography, DB147–DB149; encyclopedia, DB150
  statistics, CG169

Perú. Dirección Nacional de Estadística y Censos. Anuario estadístico del Perú, CG169

Peruanos notables de hoy, M. Beltroy, AJ218

Pessard, G. Nouveau dictionnaire historique de Paris, DC80

Péteraitis, V. Lietuviškai angliškas žodynas, AE425

Peters, J. and Bauschinger, J. Logarithmic trigonometrical tables to eight decimal places, EF39

Peters, T. Who's who in India, Burma and Ceylon, AJ171

Petersen, C. Handwörterbuch des Grenz- und Auslanddeutschtums, DC107

Petersen, C. S. and Andersen, V. Illustreret dansk Litteraturhistorie, BD624

Petersen, S. Statistical history of the American presidential elections, CI64

Peterson, C. S. Consolidated bibliography of county histories in fifty states, DB40

Peterson, F. American labor unions, CH303

Peterson, G. C. and Grace, Sister M. Books for Catholic colleges, AA282

Peterson, R. T. Peterson field guide series, EC26

Peterson field guide series, R. T. Peterson, EC26

Petit, L. D. Bibliographie der Middelnederlandsche taal- en letterkunde, BD542; Repertorium der verhandelingen en bijdragen betreffende de geschiedenis des vaderlands, DC203

Petit de Julleville, L. Histoire de la langue et de la littérature française, BC48, BD692

Petit Larousse, P. Larousse, AE223

Petrarch
  bibliography, BD789
  concordance, BD790

Petrik, G. Bibliographia hungarica. Magyar Könyveszet, AA536

Petroleum dictionary, L. P. Boone, EI218

Petroleum dictionary, H. P. Porter, EI219

Petroleum engineering
  bibliography, EI212–EI215
  dictionaries, EI218–EI219; foreign terms, EI220–EI221
  handbooks, EI222–EI225
  indexes, EI216–EI217

Petroleum exploration handbook, G. B. Moody, EI224

Petroleum facts and figures, American Petroleum Institute, EI222

Petroleum literature index, EI216

Petroleum products handbook, V. B. Guthrie, EI223

Petrology, EE142–EE144

Petrov, S. O. Knigi pervoi chetverti XIX veka, AA668

Petrović, I. M. Practical dictionary of the English and Serbian languages, AE504

Petry, K. Handbuch zur deutschen Literaturgeschichte, BD583

Petry, L. Encyclopedia of nursing, EJ111

Pettee, J. List of theological subject headings and corporate church names, AB135

Pettersen, H. Bibliotheca norvegica, AA621

Pettersen, H. M. Norsk anonym- og pseudonym-lexikon, AA126

Pettmann, C. Africanderisms, AE89; South African place-names, CK178

Peuckert, W.-E. Handwörterbuch der Sage, CF17

Réau, L. Dictionnaire polyglotte des termes d'art et d'archéologie, BE41; Iconographie de l'art chrétien, BE92

Rebadavia, C. B. Checklist of Philippine government documents, AH78

Rebora, P. Cassell's Italian-English, English-Italian dictionary, AE366

Recent books in Mexico, AA603

Rechtsschreibung der deutschen Sprache und der Fremdwörter, K. Duden, AE281n

Rechtsvergleichendes Handwörterbuch für das Zivil- und Handelsrecht des In- und Auslandes, F. Schlegelberger, CJ38

Recipes, EA208–EA209

Recommended dietary allowances, National Research Council. Food and Nutrition Board, EJ120

Record, S. J. and Hess, R. W. Timbers of the world, EK49

Record book, D. Hall, BH130

Record interpreter, C. T. Martin, AA152

Record of Canadian shipping, F. W. Wallace, CH216

Record ratings, K. Myers, BH139

Recorded music
 folk music, BH116, BH121–BH122
 guides, BH126–BH134; current, BH135–BH137; reviews, BH138–BH141

Recordings for children, New York Library Association. Children's and Young Adult Services Section, BH133

Recordings in the public library, M. D. Pearson, BH134

Records and research in engineering and industrial science, J. E. Holmstrom, EA1

Records in review, BH141

Recreation and sports, p.358–59
 bibliography, CB151–CB158
 dictionaries and handbooks, CB159–CB171
 directories, CB172–CB174

Recueil des archives biographiques permanentes du monde arabe, AJ202

Recueils collectifs de poésies libres et satiriques, F. Lachèvre, BD715

Red book of United States coins, R. S. Yeoman, BF68

Red Cross. U.S. American National Red Cross. Home nursing textbook, EK63

Redgrave, G. R. and Pollard, A. W. Short-title catalogue of books printed in England, Scotland and Ireland, AA498

Redhouse, Sir J. W. Turkish and English lexicon, AE568; Yeni Redhouse lûgati, AE569

Redman, H. F. and Godfrey, L. E. Dictionary of report series codes, EA60

Redpath, H. and Hatch, E. Concordance to the Septuagint and the other Greek versions of the Old Testament (including the Apocryphal books), BB99

Reed's Tables of distances between ports and places in all parts of the world, A. B. Purbrick and W. R. Nedham, CH187

Rees, R. A. and Bryer, J. R. Checklist of Emerson criticism, BD272

Reese, G. Music in the Middle Ages, BH78n; Music in the Renaissance, BH78n

Referativnyi zhurnal, EA72

Reference books, AA295–AA312
 Asian, AA297
 British, AA299, AA305
 Chinese, AA310
 international, AA295, AA299, AA301, AA305–AA309, AA311–AA312
 Japanese, AA304
 Korean, DE110
 New Zealand, AA298
 Russian, AA300, AA303
 South African, AA302
 Spanish, AA306

Reference books, Enoch Pratt Free Library, AA295

Reference books in the mass media, E. Blum, CH225

Reference catalogue of current literature, AA512

Reference data for radio engineers, International Telephone and Telegraph Corporation, EI118

Reference function of the library, Chicago. University, AB152

Reference guide to English studies, D. F. Bond, BD303

Reference guide to Korean materials, K. P. Yang, DE110

Reference guide to the literature of travel, E. G. Cox, CK4

Reference index to twelve thousand Spanish American authors, R. L. Grismer, BD836

Reference library stock, L. R. McColvin, AA299

Reference manual of directories, G. P. Henderson, CH93

Reference manual of Latin American commercial treaties, U. S. Tariff Commission, CJ124

Reference materials in ethnomusicology, B. Nettl, BH120

Reference shelf, BD201

Reference work, AB152–AB153

Reformation: bibliography, DC5; German, DC89

Reformed Church, BB180

Refrigeration: dictionary, EI127

Régi magyar könyvtár, K. Szabó, AA534

Regimental publications and personal narratives of the Civil War, C. E. Dornbusch, CI199

Regional American cookery, J. E. Gourley, EK51

Regional novelists of the British Isles, L. Leclaire, BD378

Regis, Sister. Catholic bookman's guide, AA270, BB188a

Register of bibliographies of the English language and literature, C. S. Northup, AA22, BD306

Register of commerce and industry in Israel, CH185

Register of legal documentation in the world, International Association of Legal Science, CJ11

Register of national bibliography, W. P. Courtney, AA328

Register til norges tidsskrifter, Deichmanske Bibliotek, AF159; Norsk biografi, AJ214

Regnier, H. Lexique de la langue de J. de La Fontaine, BD736; Lexique de la langue de La Rochefoucauld, BD738

Rehabilitation literature, E. C. Graham and M. M. Mullen, EH3

Rehabilitation of the handicapped, M. Riviere, EH8

Rehder, A. Bibliography of cultivated trees and shrubs, EC86; Manual of cultivated trees and shrubs hardy in North America, EC84

Reichardt, G. Sowjetische Literatur zur Naturwissenschaft und Technik, EA14
—— Fleischhack, C. and Rückert, E. Grundriss der Bibliographie, AA296

Reichert, H. W. and Schlechta, K. International Nietzsche bibliography, BA53

Reichling, D. Appendices ad Hainii-Copingeri Repertorivum bibliographicvm, AA162

Reichmann, F. Notched cards, AB16n

Reicke, B. I. and Rost, L. Biblisch-historisches Handwörterbuch, BB121

Reid, C. F. Bibliography of the island of Guam, DG9; Bibliography of the Virgin Islands, DB173

Reid, J. B. Complete . . . concordance to Robert Burns, BD427

Reid, J. H. S., McNaught, K. and Crowe, H. S. Sourcebook of Canadian history, DB96

Reid, S. and Carpenter, A. Directory of 3660 16mm film libraries, AA325

Reisen, Z. Leksikon fun der yidisher literatur, BD986

Reisner, R. G. Fakes and forgeries in the fine arts, BE19

Reitz, K., Schiffer, W. and Kato, G. Bibliography of Shinto in Western languages, BB313

Religion, p.203–28
 bibliography, BB1–BB5
 Christian religion, p.206–23
 dissertations, BB6–BB7
 encyclopedias, BB12–BB19
 indexes and abstract journals, BB8–BB11
 non-Christian religions, p.223–28
 sacred books, BB20–BB23

Religion in Geschichte und Gegenwart, K. Galling, BB17

Religion on the American frontier, W. W. Sweet, BB51

Religions, mythologies, folklores, K. S. Diehl, BB2, CE1

Religious and theological abstracts, BB10

Religious bodies, U.S. Bureau of the Census, BB63

Religious bodies of America, F. E. Mayer, BB48

Religious houses, BB241, BB244

Religious orders, BB241–BB244; symbolism in art, BE86

Remmlein, M. K. and Rezny, A. A. Schoolman in the law library, CB120

Remos y Rubio, J. J. Historia de la literatura cubana, BD857

Renaissance dictionaries, D. T. Starnes, AE416

Renaissance philosophers, J. O. Riedl, BA40

Renda, U. and Operti, P. Dizionario storico della letteratura italiana, BD759

René-Moreno, G. Biblioteca boliviana, AA381; Biblioteca peruana, AA628

Renou, L. Bibliographie védique, BB259

Renouard, P. Imprimeurs parisiens, libraries, fondeurs de caractères, AA247; Marques typographiques parisiennes des XVe et XVIe siècles, AA197

Répertoire alphabétique des thèses de doctorat ès lettres des universités françaises, A. Maire, AI24

Répertoire archéologique de la France, DC54

Répertoire bibliographique de l'histoire de France, DC65

Répertoire bibliographique de la philosophie, BA14

Répertoire bibliographique des traductions et adaptations françaises du théâtre étranger, M. Horn-Monval, BD131

Répertoire chronologique des littératures modernes, International Federation of Modern Languages and Literatures, BD5

Répertoire d'art et d'archéologie, BE20

Répertoire de bibliographie française, AA461

Répertoire de l'histoire de la Révolution Française, Paris. Bibliothèque Nationale. Dept. des Imprimés, DC61

Répertoire de la Comédie humaine de H. de Balzac, A. Cerfberr and J. Christoffe, BD720

Répertoire des articles relatifs à l'histoire et à la littérature juives, M. Schwab, BD987

Répertoire des bibliothèques, France. Direction des Bibliothèques de France, AB44

Répertoire des bibliothèques du Proche et du Moyen-Orient, J. A. Dagher, AB64

Television production, H. W. McMahon, CH227

Temperley, H. W. V. and Penson, L. M. Century of diplomatic blue books, CJ98n

Temple, P. Federal services to libraries, AB94

Templeman, W. D. Bibliographies of studies in Victorian literature, BD326

Ten Eyck, H. Glossary of terms used in microreproduction, BF82

Ten great years, China (People's Republic of China, 1949–   ). State Statistical Bureau, CG85

10,000 trade names, T. W. Lippert, CH145

Ten years of United Nations publications, United Nations. Dept. of Public Information, CJ160

Teng, S. and Biggerstaff, K. Annotated bibliography of selected Chinese reference works, AA310

Têng, S.-Y. Japanese studies on Japan and the Far East, DE92

Tennessee imprints, 1793–1840, Historical Records Survey, AA358n

Tennessee imprints, 1793–1840, in Tennessee libraries, Historical Records Survey, AA358n

Tennessee imprints, 1841–1850, Historical Records Survey, AA358n

Tennyson, Alfred, *Lord*
bibliography, BD511
concordance, BD512
dictionary, BD513

Téodorov-Balan, A. Bulgarski knigopis za sto godini, AA390

Teoriia i praktika bibliografii, IU. I. Masanov, AA6

Terblanche, H. J. Nuwe praktiese woordeboek, AE111

Tercentenary handlist of English & Welsh newspapers, magazines and reviews, Times, London, AG21

Terek, E. Scientific expeditions, EA182

Term catalogues, E. Arber, AA499

Terminologia atomica, L. Lettenmeyer, EG29

Terner, J. R. and Marson, F. M. United States IGY bibliography, EE28

Terry, C. S. Catalogue of the publications of Scottish historical societies, DC170

Tests and measurements, EH38–EH40

Tests in print, O. K. Buros, EH38

Teuffel, W. S. History of Roman literature, BD960

Texas. Southern University. Library. Catalogue, Heartman Negro collection, CC78
——— University. Institute of Latin-American Studies. Seventy-five years of Latin American research at the University of Texas, DB110

Textbooks in print, AA352

Textil-Fachwörterbuch, M. Polanyi, CH347

Textile Mercury. "Mercury" dictionary of textile terms, CH348

Textiles, CH340–CH344; dictionaries, CH345–CH348

Textor, R. B. and Banks, A. S. Cross-polity survey, CI45

Texts and calendars, E. L. C. Mullins, DC112

Tezla, A. Introductory bibliography to the study of Hungarian literature, BD872b

Thackeray, William Makepeace
bibliography, BD514
dictionary, BD515

Thai directory *see* CI162

Thai language: dictionaries, AE553–AE557

Thailand
history, DE125–DE126
official register, CI162
statistics, CG192–CG193

Thailand bibliography, J. B. Mason and H. C. Parish, DE126

Thailand. Central Statistical Office. Statistical bibliography, CG192
——— National Statistical Office. Statistical year book, CG193

Thali, H. Technical dictionary of technical terms used in electrical engineering, radio, television, telecommunication, EI105

Theatre and allied arts, B. M. Baker, BG3

Theater arts, p.324–29
amateur productions, BG44–BG47
annuals, BG12–BG15
bibliography, BG1–BG9
biography, BG35–BG43
directories, BG24–BG27
encyclopedias and dictionaries, BG16–BG20
handbooks, BG21–BG23
history, BG28–BG34
indexes, BG10–BG11

Theatre arts publications available in the United States, BG2

Theatre books in print, A. E. Santaniello, BG8

Theatre collections in libraries and museums, R. Gilder and G. Freedley, BG24

Theatre in the East, F. Bowers, BG54

Theatre language, W. P. Bowman and R. H. Ball, BG19

Theatre magazine (indexes), S. Cornyn, BG11

Theatre world annual (London), BG14

Theatres of London, R. Mander and J. Mitchenson, BG26

Theimer, W. Encyclopaedia of world politics, CI29

Thelert, G. Supplement zu Heinsius', Hinrichs' und Kayser's Bücher-Lexikon, AA481

Theodory, C. Dictionary of modern technical terms, Arabic-English, AE127

Theological book list, BB4–BB5

Theological dictionary of the New Testament, G. Kittel, BB124

Theological subject headings and corporate church names, J. Pettee, AB135

Theological word book of the Bible, A. Richardson, BB122

Theologische Literaturzeitung, BB28

Theologischer Jahresbericht, BB27

Theoretical chemical engineering abstracts, EI55

Theory and history of bibliography, R. R. Shaw, AA8n

Thesaurus graecae linguae, H. Estienne, AE290

Thesaurus linguae latinae, AE395

Thesaurus literaturae botanicae omnium gentium, G. A. Pritzel, EC31

Thesaurus litteraturae mycologicae et lichenologicae, G. Lindau and P. Sydow, EC77

Thesaurus of book digests, H. Haydn and E. Fuller, BD35

Thesaurus of engineering terms, Engineers Joint Council, EI8

Thesaurus of orchestral devices, G. Read, BH71

Thesaurus pseudonymorum quae in litteratura hebraica et judaeo-germanica inveniuntur, S. Chajes, AA134

Thesaurus totius Hebraitatis et veteris et recentioris, E. Ben-Yehudah, AE314

Thèses canadiennes, Ottawa. National Library of Canada, AI19

Thèses de sciences sociales, UNESCO, CA17

Theses in the social sciences, UNESCO, CA17

Thewlis, J. Encyclopaedic dictionary of physics, EG14

They voted for Roosevelt, E. E. Robinson, CI63a

Thiele, W. Official map publications, CK191

Thieme, H. P. Bibliographie de la littérature française, BD672

Thieme, U. and Becker, F. Allgemeines Lexikon der bildenden Künstler, BE71

Things Japanese, B. H. Chamberlain, DE96

Thom, E. M. Bibliography of North American geology, EE24

Thomas, C. Canadian novelists, BD299

Thomas, D. H. and Case, L. M. Guide to the diplomatic archives of western Europe, DC3

Thomas, H. Short-title catalogue of Portuguese books printed before 1601, now in the British Museum, AA649; Short-title catalogues of Portuguese books and of Spanish-American books printed before 1601, now in the British Museum, AA574

Thomas J. Universal pronouncing dictionary of biography and mythology, AJ23

Thomas, M. H. John Dewey, BA45

Thomas, R. C. and Ruffner, F. G. Code names dictionary, CI204

Thomas, W. L. and Pikelis, A. M. International directory of anthropological institutions, CD39

Thomas Aquinas
bibliography, BA56–BA57
concordance, BA55
dictionary, BA54

Thomas' Register of American manufacturers, CH332

Thomashower, D. Women lawyers in the United States, CJ74

Thomason, G. Catalogue of pamphlets, AA501

Thompson, A. Vocabularium bibliothecarii, AA235, AB24

Thompson, A. J. Logarithmetica Britannica, EF49

Thompson, A. M. and Thompson, E. T. Race and region, CC63

Thompson, A. W. and Carman, H. J. Guide to the principal sources for American civilization, 1800–1900, in the city of New York: manuscripts, DB30; printed materials, DB9

Thompson, D. E. Exchanges, AB16n; Gifts, AB16n

Thompson, E. E. Oceanography, a report bibliography, EE121

Thompson, E. H. A.L.A. glossary of library terms, AB17

Thompson, Sir E. M. Introduction to Greek and Latin palaeography, AA153, BD931

Thompson, Edgar T. and Thompson, A. M. Race and region, CC63

Thompson, Edward T. and Hayden, A. C. Standard nomenclature of diseases and operations, EJ57

Thompson, G. F. Index to authors with titles of their publications appearing in the documents of the U.S. Dept. of Agriculture, EK12

Thompson, G. G. Synoptical index of the reports of the statistician, EK20

Thompson, L. S. Feature cards (Peek-a-boo cards), AB16n

Thompson, N. W. and Stock, R. Complete concordance to the Bible, Douay version, BB96

Thompson, O. International cyclopedia of music and musicians, BH63

Thompson, R. American literary annuals and gift books, BD209

Thompson, S. Motif-index of folk-literature, CF16; Types of the folktale, CF1

Thompson, S. C. and Turkin, H. Official encyclopedia of baseball, CB170

Thompson, W. R. Black's Medical dictionary, EJ45

Thom's Irish who's who, AJ174

Thomsen, P. Palästina-Literatur, DE122

Thomsen, S. Københavns Bibliografi, DC39

Thomson, E. Baltische Bibliographie, DC12

Thomson, H. M. Turkish-English dictionary, AE570

Thomson, J. O. Everyman's classical atlas, DA92

Thomson, R. G. Index to full length plays, BD143

Thomson, T. R. Check list of publications on American railroads before 1841, CH209

Thomson, W. Thomson's Dictionary of banking, CH242

Thoreau, Henry David
  bibliography, BD287–BD288
  handbook, BD289

Thorndike, A. H. and Cunliffe, J. W. Warner library, BD15

Thorndike, E. L. and Barnhart, C. L. Thorndike-Barnhart advanced junior dictionary, AE15; Thorndike-Barnhart beginning dictionary, AE13; Thorndike-Barnhart high school dictionary, AE16; Thorndike-Barnhart junior dictionary, AE14

Thorndike, L. History of magic and experimental science, EH44

Thorndike-Barnhart advanced junior dictionary, E. L. Thorndike and C. L. Barnhart, AE15

Thorndike-Barnhart beginning dictionary, E. L. Thorndike and C. L. Barnhart, AE13

Thorndike-Barnhart comprehensive desk dictionary, C. L. Barnhart, AE10a

Thorndike-Barnhart high school dictionary, E. L. Thorndike and C. L. Barnhart, AE16

Thorndike-Barnhart junior dictionary, E. L. Thorndike and C. L. Barnhart, AE14

Thorne, J. O. and Collocott, T. C. Chamber's World gazetteer and geographical dictionary, CK29

Thornton, J. L., Monk, A. J. and Brooke, E. S. Select bibliography of medical biography, EJ83

—— and Tully, R. I. J. Scientific books, libraries and collectors, EA177

Thornton, R. H. American glossary, AE84

Thorpe, J. F. and Whiteley, M. A. Thorpe's Dictionary of applied chemistry, ED29

Thoumin, J.-A. Bibliographie rétrospective des périodiques français de littérature musicale, BH21

Thousand and one nights of opera, F. H. Martens, BH102

Thrall, W. F. and Hibbard, A. Handbook to literature, BD32

Three centuries of English and American plays, G. W. Bergquist, BD230, BD352

Three centuries of English booktrade bibliography, A. Growoll, AA502n

Thrum's Hawaiian annual and standard guide, CG112

Thurston, J. A. Short fiction criticism, BD158

Tibetan language: dictionaries, AE558–AE561

Tichauer, W. G. Bibliografía boliviana, AA383

Ticknor, G. Catalog of the Spanish library, AA683

Tiedemann, E. and Sternfeld, W. Deutsche Exil-Literatur, BD560

Tiele, P. A. Bibliotheek van Nederlandsche pamfletten, AA610

Tien, H. C., Hsia, R. and Penn, P. Gazetteer of China, CK50

Tigerstedt, E. N. Ny illustrerad svensk litteraturhistoria, BD636

Tighe, L. W. Classified bibliography for the field of social work, CC11

Tilley, M. P. Dictionary of the proverbs in England in the 16th and 17th centuries, BD128

Tilton, E. M. Union list of publications in opaque microforms, AA85

Timber Engineering Company. Timber design and construction handbook, EI91

Timbers of the world, S. J. Record and R. W. Hess, EK49

Time table of modern history, M. Morison, DA45

Time tables, CK268–CK271

Times, London. House of Commons, CI130; Index, AG37; Palmer's Index to the Times, AG38; Tercentenary handlist of English & Welsh newspapers, magazines and reviews, AG21; Times atlas of the world, CK224

Times atlas of the world: mid-century edition, J. Bartholomew, CK224

Times of India directory and year book including who's who, CG117

Ting, W., Wêng, W. and Tsêng, S. Chung Kuo fên shêng hsin-t'u [New provincial atlas of China], CK235; Gazetteer of Chinese place names, CK235a

Tipografia cinquecentina italiana, F. Ascarelli, AA244

Tisdale, G. W., Babcock, J. T. W. and Lincoln, W. O. Fire insurance inspection and underwriting, CH267

Tissue culture: bibliography, EC4

Titled nobility of Europe, M. A. Ruvigny and Raineval, 9th Marquis of, AK25

Titles and forms of address: a guide to their correct use, AK53

Titles in series, E. A. Baer, AA12

Titus, E. B. Union list of serials, AF98

Toase, M. Guide to current British periodicals, AF49

Toastmasters, BD190–BD192

Toastmaster's handbook, H. V. Prochnow, BD192

Tobacco, CH349–CH350

Tobacco dictionary, R. Jahn, CH349

Tobey, J. A. Public health law, EJ142

Tobin, J. E. Eighteenth century English literature, BD322

—— and Delaney, J. J. Dictionary of Catholic biography, BB211

Tobler, A. Hobler-Lommatzsch, Altfranzösisches Wörterbuch, AE250

Tod, D. D. and Cordingley, A. Check list of Canadian imprints, AA399

Todd, O. J. Index Aristophanevs, BD938

Tokyo. National Diet Library. Kokuritsu Kokkai Toshokan zōsho mokuroku, AA570

—— —— Zen-Nihon shuppan-butsu sô-mokuroku [Japanese national bibliography], AA573

Tolkovyi slovar' russkogo iazyka, D. N. Ushakov, AE485

Tolsado Picazo, F. Bibliografía española de agricultura, EK8

Tolstoi, Lev Nikolaevich: bibliography, BD907

Tome, W. N., Mihanovich, C. S. and McNamara, R. J. Glossary of sociological terms, CC6

Tommaseo, N. Dizionario dei sinonimi della lingua italiana, AE376

—— and Bellini, B. Dizionario della lingua italiana, AE362n

Tompkins, D. C. Administration of criminal justice, CC55; Bibliography of crime and criminal justice, CC53; Materials for the study of federal government, AH10; The offender, CC56; Probation since World War II, CC57; Sources for the study of the administration of criminal justice, CC54; State government and administration, CI72; Supreme Court of the United States, CJ18

Tool engineers handbook, American Society

of Tool and Manufacturing Engineers, EI144

Topete, J. M. Working bibliography of Brazilian literature, BD794; Working bibliography of Latin American literature, BD841

Topical index of population census reports, U.S. Office of the Census, CG42n

Topographical dictionary of England, S. Lewis, CK58

Topographical dictionary of Ireland, S. Lewis, CK65

Topographical dictionary of Scotland, S. Lewis, CK78

Topographical dictionary of Wales, S. Lewis, CK82

Topographical dictionary to the works of Shakespeare and his fellow dramatists, E. H. Sugden, BD497

Topographical-historical encyclopedia of Palestine, J. Press, DE123

Torchbearers of chemistry, H. M. Smith, ED81

Tornberg, A., Ångström, M. and Nöjd, R. McKay's Modern English-Swedish and Swedish-English dictionary, AE542

Toro, J. del. Bibliography of the collective biography of Spanish America, AJ191

Toro, M. de and Bailly, R. Dictionnaire des synonymes de la langue française, AE241

Toronto. Public Library. Bibliography of Canadiana, DB90

—— University. Library. Bibliography of comedias sueltas, BD826; Catalogue of Italian plays, BD765

Torp, A. Nynorsk etymologisk ordbog, AE191

—— and Falk, H. S. Norwegisch-dänisches etymologisches Wörterbuch, AE189

Torre Revello, J. Bibliografía de las Islas Malvinas, DB165

Torrente Ballester, G. Panorama de la literatura española contemporánea, BD819

Torrey Botanical Club. Index to American botanical literature, EC44

Tortajada, A. and Amaniel, C. de. Materiales de investigación: índice de artículos de revistas, AF165

Totok, W. Bibliographischer Wegweiser der philosophischen Literatur, BA1

—— and Weitzel, R. Handbuch der bibliographischen Nachschlagewerke, AA10

Touring Club Italiano. Atlante internazionale, CK225

Tourneur, Cyril: bibliography, BD321n

Tourneux, M. Bibliographie de l'histoire de Paris pendant la Révolution Française, DC62

Toussaint, A. and Adolphe, H. Bibliography of Mauritius, DD59

Tovar, A. Catálogo de las lenguas de América del Sud, BC64

Townend, P. and Simmons, D. Who's who in music and musicians' international directory, BH65

Townsend, F. G. Victorian bibliography, BD327

Townsend, J. W. Supplemental check list of Kentucky imprints, 1788–1820, AA358n

Toynbee, A. J. and Meyers, E. D. Historical atlas and gazetteer, DA60

Toynbee, P. Britain's tribute to Dante in literature and art, BD779; Concise dictionary of proper names and notable matters in the works of Dante, BD788; Dictionary of proper names and notable matters in the works of Dante, BD788n

Trabajadores en el extranjero, International Labor Office, CB61

Trace, AF4n

Yearbook of the international socialist labour movement, J. Braunthal, CI191
Yearbook of the United Nations, United Nations. Library, New York, CJ156
Yearbook of the universities of the Commonwealth, CB108n
Year book of world affairs, CJ144
Yearbook on human rights, United Nations. Dept. of Social Affairs, CI49
Year's art, BE47
Year's work in classical studies, BD924
Year's work in English studies, BD314
Year's work in librarianship, AB8
Year's work in modern language studies, BC14
Yeats, W. B.
   bibliography, BD525
   concordance, BD524
Yemen: history, DE134
Yeni yayïnlar, AA726
Yeoman, R. S. Catalogue of modern world coins, BF67; Red book of United States coins, BF68
Yhteisluettelo Suomen tieteellisissä kirjastoissa olevista eksaktisten tieteiden, P. Suomalainen, EA39
Yiddish language
   bibliography, BC77, BD986
   dictionaries, AE582–AE584
Yiddish language and folklore, U. Weinreich and B. Weinreich, BC77
Yiddish literature: dictionary, BD986
Yoder, D. Handbook of personnel management and labor relations, CH139
Yonge, C. D. English-Greek lexicon, AE297
Yonge, C. M. History of Christian names, AK86
Yorkshire: place-names, CK109, CK148–CK150
You have a point there, E. Partridge, AE57
Young, E. F. Dictionary of social welfare, CC15
Young, M. N. Bibliography of memory, EH12
Young, R. Analytical concordance to the Bible, BB97
Young, R. J. Directory of educational research agencies and studies, CB54
Young, W. A. Dictionary of the characters and scenes in the stories and poems of Rudyard Kipling, BD465
Youth—key to America's future, M. M. Chambers and E. Exton, CC40a
Youth organizations in Canada, G. Tuttle, CC43
Youth organizations of Great Britain, CC45
Youth-serving organizations, M. M. Chambers, CC42
Yu, H. New Life Korean-English dictionary, AE393
Yüan, T. China in Western literature, DE47; Economic and social development of modern China, DE48; Guide to doctoral dissertations by Chinese students in America, AI14; Russian works on China in American libraries, DE49

Yucatan: encyclopedia, DB143
Yugoslav literature: bibliography, BD910
Yugoslavia
   bibliography, AA736–AA740
   bibliography of bibliography, AA57
   biography, AJ265–AJ266
   history: bibliography, DC267–DC268; encyclopedia, DC269
   statistics, CG207–CG209
Yugoslavia. Direktsīja Drzhavne Statīstīke. Statistički godišnjak. Annuaire statistique, CG209
Yule, Sir H. and Burnell, A. C. Hobson-Jobson; a glossary of colloquial Anglo-Indian words and phrases, AE90

Zabielska, J. Bibliography of books in Polish or relating to Poland, AA644
Zadrozny, J. T. Dictionary of social science, CA34
Zamora Lucas, F. and Casado Jorge, M. Publicaciones periódicas existentes en la Biblioteca Nacional, AF85
—— and Ponce de León Freyre, E. 1500 seudónimos modernos de la literatura española, AA127
Zampetti, E. Bibliografia ragionata delle riviste filosofiche italiane, BA18
Zandstra, S. and Wolk, L. J. van der. Union list of Russian scientific and technical periodicals available in European libraries, EA57
Zanutto, S. Bibliografia etiopica, DD50
Zastrau, A. Goethe-Handbuch, BD601
Zaunmüller, W. Bibliographisches Handbuch der Sprachwörterbücher, AE108
Zedler, J. H. Grosses vollständiges universal Lexikon, AD41
Zeitrechnung des deutschen Mittelalters und der Neuzeit, H. Grotefend, DC105
Zeitschrift für romanische Philologie, BC44
Zeitungen und Zeitschriften aus Rumänien, AF76
Zeitungskatalog der Schweiz, AF93
Zelinsky, W. Bibliographic guide to population geography, CG12
Zen-Nihon shuppan-butsu sô-mokuroku, Tokyo. National Diet Library, AA573
Zenker, J. T. Bibliotheca orientalis, DE6n
Zentralblatt für Bakteriologie, Parasitenkunde, Infektions-Krankheiten und Hygiene, EC121
Zentralblatt für Geologie und Paläontologie, EE37
Zentralblatt für Mathematik und ihre Grenzgebiete, EF13
Zentralblatt für Mineralogie, EE105
Zentralblatt für Zoologie, EC96
Zernova, A. S. Knigi kirillovskoi pechati, izdannye v Moskve v XVI–XVII vekakh, AA661
Zibrt, Č. Bibliografie české historie, DC36
Ziegenfuss, W. and Jung, G. Philosophen-Lexikon, BA39
Zikeev, N. T. Scientific and technical serial publications of the Soviet Union, EA51

Zil'bermints, L. V. Bibliografia sovetskoi tekhnicheskoi bibliografii, EA19
Zim, H. S., Shaffer, P. R. and Rhodes, F. H. T. Fossils, a guide to prehistoric life, EE140
Zimmerman, E. Bibliographische Berichte, AA15
Zimmerman, F. L. and Read, P. R. Numerical list of current publications of the U.S. Dept. of Agriculture, EK15
Zimmerman, I. Guide to current Latin American periodicals, AF68
Zimmerman, M. H. and Voskoboinik, D. I. English-Russian nuclear dictionary, EG32
Zimmerman, O. T. and Lavine, I. Industrial Research Service's Conversion factors and tables, EG42; Industrial Research Service's Handbook of material trade names, CH149; Scientific and technical abbreviations, signs and symbols, EA89
Zimonyi, Z. and Szarvas, G. Lexicon linguae Hungaricae aevi antiquioris, AE335
Zinner, E. Geschichte und Bibliographie der astronomischen Literatur in Deutschland zur Zeit der Renaissance, EB7
Zionist yearbook, J. Litvin, BB312
Zischka, G. A. Index lexicorum, AA312
Zitatenschatz der Weltliteratur, R. Zoozmann, BD100
Zittel, K. A. von. Geschichte der Geologie und Paläontologie, EE68
Zivný, L. Bibliografický katalog, AA437
Zoëga, G. T. Icelandic-English and English-Icelandic dictionary, AE347
Zola dictionary, J. G. Patterson, BD751
Zoological record, EC99
Zoologischer Bericht, EC97
Zoologischer Jahresbericht, EC98
Zoology
   abstract journals, EC95–EC98, EC100
   bibliography, EC88–EC94
   collections, EC101
   dictionaries, EC103–EC105
   directory, EC106
   generic index, EC102
   guide, EC87
   handbooks, EC107–EC116
   indexes, EC95–EC100
Zoozmann, R. Zitatenschatz der Weltliteratur, BD100
Zoroastrianism, BB314
Zulu language: dictionaries, AE585–AE587
Zurcher, A. J. Constitutions and constitutional trends since World War II, CJ129
—— and Sloan, H. S. Dictionary of economics, CH37
—— and Smith, E. C. Dictionary of American politics, CI34
Zürcher, J. Lexicon academicum, BD950
Zussman, J., Deer, W. A. and Howie, R. A. Rock-forming minerals, EE114
Zvorykin, A. A. Biograficheskii slovar' deiatelei estestvoznaniia i tekhniki, EA185
Zweygbergk, O. and Tallquist, J. O. Vem och vad?, AJ126